Western Civilizations

Their History & Their Culture

Joshua Cole

Carol Symes

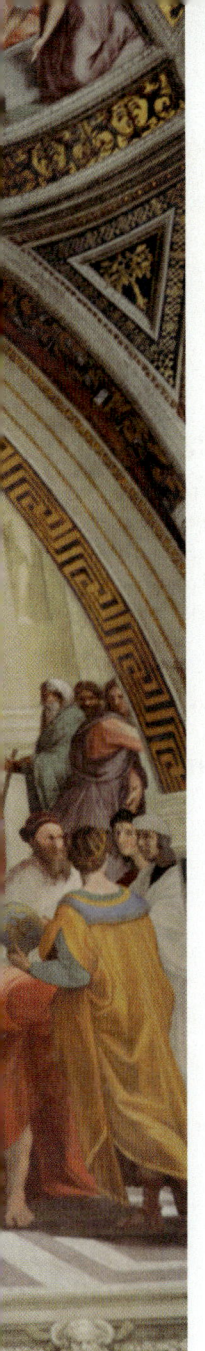

Western Civilizations

Their History & Their Culture

TWENTIETH EDITION

W. W. NORTON & COMPANY ▪ NEW YORK ▪ LONDON

W. W. Norton & Company has been independent since its founding in 1923, when William Warder Norton and Mary D. Herter Norton first published lectures delivered at the People's Institute, the adult education division of New York City's Cooper Union. The firm soon expanded its program beyond the Institute, publishing books by celebrated academics from America and abroad. By midcentury, the two major pillars of Norton's publishing program—trade books and college texts—were firmly established. In the 1950s, the Norton family transferred control of the company to its employees, and today—with a staff of four hundred and a comparable number of trade, college, and professional titles published each year—W. W. Norton & Company stands as the largest and oldest publishing house owned wholly by its employees.

Editor: Justin Cahill
Editorial Assistant: Funto Omojola
Managing Editor, College: Marian Johnson
Project Editor: Linda Feldman
Managing Editor, College Digital Media: Kim Yi
Media Project Editor: Rachel Mayer
Media Editor: Carson Russell
Associate Media Editor: Alexander Lee
Assistant Media Editor: Lexi Malakhoff

Marketing Manager, History: Sarah England Bartley
Production Manager: Ashley Horna
Design Director: Lissi Sigillo
Photo Editor: Agnieszka Czapski
College Permissions Specialist: Elizabeth Trammell
Composition: Cenveo
Cartographers: Mapping Specialists
Manufacturing: Transcontinental

Permission to use copyrighted material is included in the Credits section of this book.

Library of Congress Cataloging-in-Publication Data

Names: Cole, Joshua, 1961- author. | Symes, Carol, author.
Title: Western civilizations : their history & their culture / Joshua Cole,
  Carol Symes.
Description: 20th edition. | New York : W. W. Norton & Company, [2020] |
  Includes index.
Identifiers: LCCN 2019030137 | **ISBN 9780393418750 (cloth)**
Subjects: LCSH: Civilization, Western—Textbooks. |
  Europe—Civilization—Textbooks.
Classification: LCC CB245 .C56 2020 | DDC 909/.09821—dc23
LC record available at https://lccn.loc.gov/2019030137

W. W. Norton & Company, Inc., 500 Fifth Avenue, New York, NY 10110
wwnorton.com

W. W. Norton & Company Ltd., 15 Carlisle Street, London W1D 3BS

1 2 3 4 5 6 7 8 9 0

To our families:

Kate Tremel, Lucas, and Ruby Cole
Tom, Erin, and Connor Wilson

with love and gratitude for their support.
And to all our students, who have also been
our teachers.

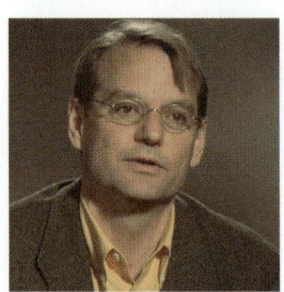

JOSHUA COLE (PhD, University of California, Berkeley) is Professor of History at the University of Michigan, Ann Arbor. He has published work on gender and the history of population sciences, colonial violence, and the politics of memory in nineteenth- and twentieth-century France, Germany, and Algeria. His first book was *The Power of Large Numbers: Population, Politics, and Gender in Nineteenth-Century France* (2000), and he recently published a second book, *Lethal Provocation: The Constantine Murders and the Politics of French Algeria* (2019).

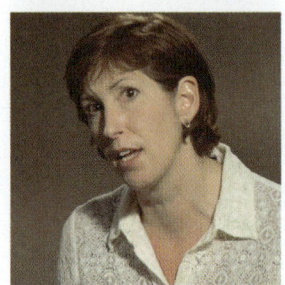

CAROL SYMES (PhD, Harvard University) is Associate Professor of History at the University of Illinois, Urbana-Champaign, where she has served as Director of Undergraduate Studies in History and has won numerous teaching awards. Her main areas of study include the history of medieval Europe, cultural history, and the history of media and communication technologies. Her first book, *A Common Stage: Theater and Public Life in Medieval Arras* (Ithaca, NY: Cornell University Press, 2007), won four national awards. She is the founding executive editor of *The Medieval Globe*, the first academic journal to promote a global approach to medieval studies.

Brief Contents

Contents

Maps

Primary Sources

This Twentieth Edition of *Western Civilizations* is a landmark in a long and continuing journey. Since its original publication in 1941, this book has been assiduously updated by succeeding generations of historians who have kept it at the forefront of the field in both scholarship and pedagogical innovation. Our newest edition carries this legacy forward, further honing the tools we have developed to empower students—our own and yours—to engage effectively with the themes, sources, and challenges of history. It presents a clear and concise narrative of events that unfolded over many thousands of years, supplemented by a compelling selection of primary sources and striking images. At the same time, it features a unified program of pedagogical elements that guide students from understanding core content to reading and analyzing historical sources and, finally, to developing a sophisticated sense of the ways that historians reconstruct the past on the basis of those sources. This framework, and a brand-new set of activities built around select sources from each chapter, helps students to read and interpret historical evidence on their own, encouraging them to become active participants in the learning process and helping them to think historically.

The wide chronological and geographical scope of this book offers an unusual opportunity to trace historical trends across several interrelated regions—western Asia, the Middle East, North Africa, and Europe—whose cultural diversity has been constantly reinvigorated and renewed. Our increasing awareness that no region's history can be isolated from global processes and connections has merely heightened the need for a richly contextualized and broad-based history such as that represented in *Western Civilizations*. In this edition, we have accordingly supplemented this rich narrative with a new focus on human mobility. From the ancient world to the recent past, societies and cultures have always been shaped by people in motion. Migrations—both voluntary and coerced—are fundamental to understanding human history and have profound implications for the development of the world economy, for cultural exchange among the world's regions,

and for the history of political institutions and their development. Indeed, the study of human mobility has emerged as one of the most vital and important fields of history in recent years. Today's students are deeply interested and invested in the relationship between globalization and population movements, and in the ways that mobility is related to social conflict, environmental changes, and contemporary disagreements about national and ethnic identity. It is important that students be able to put these contemporary discussions in historical context and to see their own concerns and aspirations reflected in the historical curriculum.

As in previous editions, we have continued to balance the coverage of political, social, economic, and cultural phenomena with extensive treatment of gender, race, sexuality, daily life, material culture, art, science, and popular culture. Our history is also attentive to the latest developments in historical scholarship. The title of this book asserts that there is no single and enduring "Western civilization" whose inevitable march to domination can be traced chapter by chapter through time. This older paradigm, strongly associated with the curriculum of early twentieth-century American colleges and universities, no longer conforms to what we know about the human past. It was also overly reliant on the nationalist histories of only a few countries, notably England, France, and Germany. In this book, we therefore pay much closer attention to central and eastern Europe, as well as to Europeans' near neighbors in Asia, Africa, and the Atlantic world, with a particular focus on European and Muslim relations throughout the Mediterranean and Middle East. No history of Western civilizations can be coherent if it leaves out the intense conflicts, extraordinary ruptures, and dynamic changes that took place within and across all of these territories. Indeed, smoothing out the rough edges of the past does students no favors. Even an introductory text such as this one should present the past as it appears to the historians who study it: as a complex panorama of human effort, filled with possibility and achievement but also fraught with discord, uncertainty, accident, and tragedy.

Pedagogical Features

In our continuing effort to promote the active study of history, this book is designed to reinforce your course objectives by helping your students to master core content while challenging them to think critically about the past. In previous editions, we augmented the traditional strengths of *Western Civilizations* by introducing several exciting new features. These have since been refined in accordance with feedback from student readers and teachers of the book. The most important and revolutionary feature is the pedagogical structure that supports each chapter. As we know from long experience, many students in introductory survey courses find the sheer quantity of information overwhelming, and so we have provided guidance to help them navigate through the material and to read in meaningful ways.

At the outset of each chapter, the ***Before You Read This Chapter*** feature offers three preliminary windows into the material to be covered: *Story Lines*, *Chronology*, and *Core Objectives*. Following the *Story Lines* allows the student to become familiar with the primary narrative threads that tie the chapter's elements together, while the *Chronology* grounds these *Story Lines* in the period under study. The *Core Objectives* alert the student to the primary teaching points in the chapter. The student is then reminded of these teaching points upon completing the chapter, in the ***After You Read This Chapter*** section, which revisits the material in three ways. The first, *Reviewing the Objectives*, asks the reader to reconsider the core objectives by answering a pointed question about each one. The second, *People, Ideas, and Events in Context*, summarizes some of the particulars that students should retain from their reading, through questions that allow them to relate individual terms to the major objectives and story lines. In this new edition, these key terms appear in bold type in the body of the chapter, in response to comments from instructors who use the book. Finally, *Thinking About Connections* allows for more open-ended reflection on the significance of the chapter's main themes, drawing students' attention to issues that connect it to previous chapters and to their own historical present. Together, these pedagogical features serve to enhance the student's learning experience by breaking down the process of reading and analysis into manageable tasks.

A second package of pedagogical features is designed to capture students' interest and to compel them to think about what is at stake in the construction and use of historical narratives. Each chapter opens with a vignette that showcases a particular person or event representative of the era as a whole. Within each chapter, an expanded program of illustrations and maps has been enhanced by the addition of *Questions for Analysis* that urge the reader to explore the historical contexts and significance of these images in a more analytical way. The historical value of visual artifacts is further emphasized in another feature we have introduced: ***Interpreting Visual Evidence.*** This section provides a provocative departure point for analytical discussions about the key issues raised by visual sources, which students often find more approachable than texts. Once this conversation has begun, students can further develop their skills with the ***Analyzing Primary Sources*** feature, which offers close readings of primary texts accompanied by thought-provoking interpretive questions. The diversity of Western civilizations is also illuminated through a look at ***Competing Viewpoints*** in each chapter, in which specific debates are presented through paired primary source texts. The bibliographical *Further Readings*, located at the end of the book, has also been brought up to date.

One especially exciting recent addition is the ***Past and Present*** feature. Designed to help students connect events unfolding in the past with the breaking news of our own time, it pairs one episode from each chapter with a phenomenon that resonates more immediately with our students. To bring this new feature to life for students, we have also created a series of **Past and Present Videos**, in which we analyze and elaborate on these connections. There are a number of illuminating discussions, including "Mass Migration and the Challenges of Assimilation," which discusses the Greek diaspora and Jewish diasporas of antiquity with reference to the Syrian refugee crisis; "Spectator Sports," which compares the Roman gladiatorial games with NFL football; "The Reputation of Richard III," which shows how modern forensics were recently used to identify the remains of this medieval English king; "The Persistence of Monarchies in a Democratic Age," which explains the origins and evolution of our ongoing fascination with royals such as Louis XIV and Princess Diana; and "The Internet and the Enlightenment Public Sphere," which compares the kinds of public networks that helped spread Enlightenment ideas to the way the Internet spreads political ideas to support movements such as the Arab Spring and Occupy Wall Street. For the current edition, there is a particularly timely ***Past and Present*** feature in Chapter 24 that relates the restructuring of the Middle East after the First World War to the present crisis in the region. Through this feature, we want to encourage students to recognize the continuing relevance of seemingly distant historical moments, but we also want to encourage historically minded habits that will be useful for a lifetime. If students learn to see the connections between their world and the past, they will be better able to place unfolding developments and debates in a more informed and complex historical context.

A Tour of Chapters and the Newest Revisions

Our previous edition of *Western Civilizations* focused on two primary themes. First, we updated and reorganized the presentation of material on central and eastern Europe in order to provide a richer account of Europe's diverse political and social histories. Second, we developed a theme on environmental history in both volumes, with special attention to the ways that human society has been shaped by—and affected—the physical world. The highlight of this reorganization was the inclusion of new sections on environmental history in multiple chapters in order to apply recent work in this rapidly evolving field to every period.

For this Twentieth Edition:

In Chapter 1, the challenges of locating and interpreting historical evidence drawn from nontextual sources (archaeological, anthropological, mythic) is a special focus. In keeping with our new emphasis on mobility, this chapter includes a more detailed account of Paleolithic-era human migration from Africa into Europe and Asia, with expanded consideration of the Neolithic Revolution as an early example of large-scale human impact on the natural world. It also reflects recent scholarship on the earliest "empires" of Mesopotamia, whose alleged strength may have been more the result of propaganda than of real power, and offers a more explicit discussion of Sumerian religion and the relationship between gods and earthly rulers. There is also a significant new treatment of cultural and economic exchanges between the Egyptians and the Nubians of Sudan.

Chapter 2 includes a revised map of Bronze Age migrations and a careful discussion of the ways that modern concepts of identity may not be applicable to the development of transnational networks in this era. Evidence gathered from recently deciphered inscriptions and new climatological research enhances the discussion of the factors leading to the collapse of this civilization, including the raids of the Sea Peoples and the mass movement of refugees fleeing famine and violence. Boasting a new **Analyzing Primary Sources** excerpt from Emily Wilson's recent translation of *The Odyssey*, Chapter 3 builds on previous narratives of migration in its discussion of guest-friendship as a key social institution for a changing world. Public participation in Athenian political life is considered with added depth, and the existing content has been reorganized to better frame and signpost the section on "The Challenge of the Persian Wars."

Chapter 4 provides a glimpse into Alexander the Great's journey through the Hindu Kush from the perspective of locals as well as that of the king's army. It includes new information on Alexander's half-brother and successor, Philip II, and provides a grassroots account of the Greek diaspora that led to the development of a common Hellenistic culture encompassing the eastern Mediterranean and western Asia. New images highlight the discovery of the Archimedes Palimpsest, and depict fresh examples of Hellenistic art. A new question in *Thinking About Connections* encourages students to analyze the 2018 agreement between Greece and Macedonia in light of this chapter's narrative.

In Chapter 5, the differences between Roman and Hellenistic societies are sharpened through a detailed discussion of Roman identity, social structures, and governing practices. A new comparison of Pompey and Caesar offers insight into Roman notions of class, distinguishing between the experiences of immigrant and patrician families. A new image of a wooden tablet from Roman Britain features the earliest known Latin writings by a woman. In Chapter 6, discussion of the early development and spread of Christianity offers a fresh consideration of Paul's missionary travels and the degree to which they depended on Roman infrastructure and rapid mobility. The chapter also includes a more detailed reflection on how the army's domestication led to the decentralization of power in Roman society.

Both the *Core Objectives* and *Reviewing the Objectives* features of Chapter 7 have been revised to better reflect the aims and learning outcomes of the chapter. *Story Lines* has also been amended to more clearly address the expansion of Islam and the interrelated causes that drove this process. Students are prompted to consider the role of gender in the representation of power, and a new image encourages them to think critically about notions of femininity and motherhood as represented in Christian icons. This chapter also pays new attention to the central role of women in the silk industry, both in China and Byzantium. Chapter 8 includes a brand-new discussion of piracy in the medieval Mediterranean and its effects on migration and pilgrimage. Women's contributions to the Crusades and their motivations for participation are another new feature, as is a more extended discussion of daily life in the crusader states of the Levant and the interactions between Christians and Muslims in these territories.

In Chapter 9, a revised and very timely discussion of Magna Carta also pays attention to the ways that King John of England and his successors attempted to resist its demands. The discussion of emerging vernacular languages and forms of identity has been enriched with new segments on German-speaking lands and varieties of popular entertainment. Themes of migration and religion are accentuated through an exploration of the Muslim and Jewish communities of Spain, and the precarious legal status of Jews elsewhere in Europe, where pogroms and other forms of persecution were becoming more frequent. Chapter 10 includes a new discussion of Mansa Musa, the sultan of the West African empire of Mali and the richest man in the world at the time—and perhaps of all time. The map and discussion of "The Medieval World System, c. 1300" have been revised to reflect new research on the close connections between sub-Saharan Africa and Western civilizations.

Chapter 11's discussion of "Life after the Black Death" has been revised to reflect very recent scholarship on the lasting impact of the plague, and the enormous social and economic upheavals that reshaped Europe and its neighbors during the late fourteenth and early fifteenth centuries. Chapter 12 offers a new consideration of Ivan the Great's conquests and the political consolidation of medieval Rus'. Meanwhile, an enhanced account of Portuguese colonial initiatives and the beginnings of the West African slave trade bring the history of Western civilizations into the orbit of the Atlantic world.

In Chapter 13, two key sections have been revised and reorganized for added clarity, while the causes of the Protestant revolution and the spread of dissent are tied more clearly to contemporary political developments. The chapter also discusses the growing power that states claimed to exert over the daily lives and moral choices of their citizens. Chapter 14 features a new discussion of indentured servitude and other forms of unfree labor in the Americas. It also presents new archeological findings from 2018, which shed fresh light on Christopher Newport's expedition to the Chesapeake Bay in 1606.

Chapter 15 features a new section, "Population and Climate in the Absolutist Age," which addresses the social and economic consequences of Jewish expulsions, the impact of the Wars of Religion and the Thirty Years' War, as well as the effects of the "Little Ice Age" on the lives of working people. A Dutch painting, *Winter Landscape with Ice Skaters*, accompanies this discussion. The newly titled subsection "Administration and Finance" has been thoroughly revised to explain the institutional consolidation of power under Louis XIV and the mercantilist ideology of finance minister Jean-Baptiste Colbert.

We have retained the emphasis on intellectual and cultural history in Chapter 16, on the scientific revolution, and in Chapter 17, on the Enlightenment. In Chapter 16, a beautiful new image depicting Tycho Brahe's earth-centered universe and its accompanying caption elaborate on the differences between Brahe's understanding of the cosmos and that of his contemporary, Johannes Kepler. In Chapter 17, meanwhile, we have continued to present the Enlightenment more clearly in its social and political context with a new section, "Population, Commerce, and Consumption." This new passage emphasizes the relationship between demographic change, economic development, and colonial expansion as the background to the century's intellectual breakthroughs. We have added to our coverage of women in the Enlightenment with a new pair of images highlighting female literacy in the eighteenth century.

Chapters 18 and 19 cover the political and economic revolutions of the late eighteenth and early nineteenth centuries. The beginning of Chapter 18 has been revised to clarify the stages of the French Revolution and the Napoleonic Empire. A new critical thinking caption for the portrait of Louis XVI considers how the king's attachment to the monarchy's absolutist powers came under pressure in the late eighteenth century, and a document excerpt from Benjamin Constant is part of a new *Competing Viewpoints* feature that vividly illustrates the way that Napoleon polarized contemporary opinion. Chapter 19 also includes a new *Competing Viewpoints* that ties in to the volume's new theme on migration. This feature contrasts the experience of Agricol Perdiguier, a carpenter and member of a laborer's confraternity, with that of Franz Rehbein, a farmworker struggling to meet the challenges of the new mechanized agriculture made possible by industrialization.

An extended new section in Chapter 20, "Revolutions, Migration, and Political Refugees," discusses the connections between the spread of nationalism and the increase in the number of political refugees who moved through Europe and to other regions of the globe. A parallel theme is also covered in a new *Competing Viewpoints* in Chapter 22: a speech by Lord Curzon, which praised British imperialism in India, is contrasted with a new passage by Henry Polak, which described the treatment of Indian migrants at the British colony in Natal, South Africa. New questions prompt students to reflect on the understandings of race and agency present in these sources and identify the benefits of British India for the Empire as they were understood by each of the authors. The chapter's section on imperialism, population movements, and global environmental change now has its proper context within the larger theme of migration in history and connects as well with the earlier treatment of the Columbian exchange in Chapter 14. Chapter 23, meanwhile, offers a completely revised section on "Global Economics," which now includes a discussion of migration flows from Europe to the Americas and the imposition of trade barriers and tariffs by European states. It provides an overview of the growing interdependence of global economies and the advantages and disadvantages that countries faced by participating in the gold standard. A new *Analyzing Primary Sources* feature includes an excerpt from Booker T. Washington's "The Man Farthest Down," in which he argues that the progress of human society ought to be understood through the lives of the working classes.

Chapter 24 contains a new extended section titled "Total War, Economic Blockade, and Population Displacement." The section discusses the civilian toll caused by new technologies and military tactics, defines the term "total war," and discusses the massive displacement of civilian populations during the fighting. A passage from Lenin's *What Is to Be Done?*, formerly presented in Chapter 23, has been moved to this chapter where it is more directly relevant. In Chapter 25, a revised section on the fascist myth of the "March on Rome," which claims that Mussolini took power in Italy by force, explains how his rise to power conformed entirely with the provisions of the Italian constitution.

Chapter 27 continues its emphasis on decolonization and the Cold War, and a new subsection, "The Displaced," offers an extensive discussion of the mass migrations, deportations, and expulsions that accompanied the end of the Second World War. Continuing the discussion of polit-

ical refugees in earlier periods of history, this section also discusses the formation of the United Nations Relief and Rehabilitation Administration (UNRRA) in 1943, and its subsequent supersession by the UN International Refugee Organization in 1947.

Chapter 29 brings both volumes to a close in a wide-ranging discussion that connects current events in Europe and the world to the deeper past. The theme of population mobility is reinforced by a new *Analyzing Primary Sources* feature that allows students to examine the text of the United Nations statement from 1951 on the protection of refugees. This final chapter discusses the economic and political turbulence of the first decades of the twenty-first century—the threat of terrorism, the global financial crisis of 2008, and the rise of populist political parties in Europe that challenge the goal of European integration—as an indication that the global order that emerged in the aftermath of the Second World War is now being transformed into something else whose contours remain as yet unclear. The conclusion invites students to place these very contemporary debates within the context of Europe's broader history, allowing them to connect what they have learned from the past to the world in which they themselves live.

Media Resources for Instructors and Students

History becomes an immersive experience for students using Norton's digital resources with *Western Civilizations*. The comprehensive ancillary package includes tools for teaching and learning that reinforce the *Core Objectives* from the narrative while building on the history skills introduced in the pedagogy throughout the book. This Twentieth Edition features a groundbreaking suite of resources, including InQuizitive, Norton's award-winning formative adaptive system, which helps students master core content; and a newly expanded library of History Skills Tutorials to guide students in analysis and interpretation. Norton is unique in partnering exclusively with subject matter experts who teach the course to author these and other resources listed below. As a result, instructors have all the course materials they need to successfully manage their Western Civilizations course, whether they are teaching face-to-face, online, or in a hybrid setting.

STUDENT RESOURCES

• **Norton Ebooks** provide an enhanced reading experience at a fraction of the cost of a print textbook. Students are able to have an active reading experience and can take notes, bookmark, search, highlight, and even read offline. As an instructor, you can even add your own notes for students to see as they read the text. Norton Ebooks can be viewed on—and synced among—all computers and mobile devices. Norton Ebooks are born accessible, which means we keep all learners in mind during the entire production process. Features such as built-in text-to-speech and advanced keyboard navigation, along with embedded videos with synchronized closed captions, save instructors valuable time in setting up their course and ensure that the ebooks they assign meet the latest accessibility requirements.

• **InQuizitive** is a groundbreaking, formative adaptive learning tool that improves student understanding of the core objectives in each chapter. Students receive personalized quiz questions on the topics with which they need the most help. Questions range from vocabulary and concepts to interactive maps and primary sources that challenge students to begin developing the skills necessary to do the work of a historian. Engaging, gamelike elements motivate students as they learn. As a result, students come to class better prepared to participate in discussions and activities.

• **New! History Skills Tutorials** combine video and interactive assessments to teach students how to analyze sources. Three overview tutorials provide start-of-the-semester introductions to "Analyzing Primary Sources," "Analyzing Images," and "Analyzing Maps." Developed by Stacey Davis (Evergreen State), a (**NEW**) library of tutorials for each chapter asks students to interpret a document, image, or map from their reading—with guided questions and explanatory author videos—and then relate that source to a key chapter theme. These tutorials give students the opportunity to practice and hone their critical analysis skills every week of the semester, and since each tutorial builds from a source, image, or map in each chapter, students can get the most from their textbooks.

• The **Student Site** includes additional resources and tools to ensure students come to class prepared and ready to actively participate in discussions and activities: Office Hour Videos, iMaps, and Online Reader.

INSTRUCTOR RESOURCES
Resources for your LMS

Easily add high-quality Norton digital resources to your online, hybrid, or lecture course. Get started building your course with our easy-to-use coursepack files; all activities can be accessed right within your existing learning management system, and many components are customizable.

- **InQuizitive** is Norton's award-winning, easy-to-use adaptive learning tool that personalizes the learning experience for students and helps them master—and retain—key learning objectives.
- **History Skills Tutorials** are interactive, online modules that provide practice and a framework for analyzing primary source documents, images, and maps.
- **Primary Source Exercises** assess students' ability to analyze supplemental sources that are not included in the text, with questions for analysis.
- **Chapter Review Quizzes** can be assigned for a more summative assessment to see what students have understood from their reading. Customize the length or wording from the questions to suit your course needs. Quizzes include page references.
- **Author Videos** on both *Core Objectives* and *Past and Present* feature topics from the reading.
- **Online Reader** offers hundreds of additional Primary Sources and supplemental Media Analysis Worksheets.
- **Interactive iMaps** for each chapter allow students to view layers of information on each map with printable accompanying Map Worksheets for offline labeling practice and quizzing.
- **Flashcards** for each chapter, which can be flipped, printed, or downloaded, align key terms and events with brief descriptions and definitions.
- **Chapter Outlines** provide students with an opportunity to see at a glance what will be covered in the chapter.

Other instructor resources

- **Interactive Instructor's Guide** is the ultimate teaching guide for the Western Civilizations course. The Interactive Instructor's Guide features a series of videos created by the authors, where they discuss best practices for teaching the most challenging concepts in each chapter. The IIG also includes the robust Instructor's Manual, which is designed to help instructors prepare lectures and exams. It contains detailed chapter outlines, general discussion questions, document discussion questions, lecture objectives, interdisciplinary discussion topics, and recommended reading and film lists.
- **Test Bank** contains more than 2,000 multiple-choice, true/false, and essay questions. This edition of the Test Bank has been completely revised for content and accuracy. All test questions are now aligned with Bloom's Taxonomy for greater ease of assessment.
- **Lecture PowerPoint Slides** are ready-made presentations that provide comprehensive outlines of each chapter, as well as discussion prompts to encourage student comprehension and engagement. They can easily be customized to meet your presentation needs.
- **Graphic content** includes all of the art from the book available in JPEG and PowerPoint format for instructor use. Alt-text is provided for each item.
- **StoryMaps** break complex maps into a sequence of annotated PowerPoint slides. There are ten maps that include topics such as the Silk Road, the Spread of the Black Death, and Population Growth and the Economy.

Acknowledgments

Our first experience as members of the *Western Civilizations* authorial team, working on the Seventeenth Edition, was a challenging and rewarding one. In our second edition, we were able to implement a number of useful and engaging changes to the content and structure of the book to make it even more compelling and student-friendly. In the third and this fourth edition, we continue to be very grateful for the expert assistance and support of the Norton team, especially that of our editor, Justin Cahill. Linda Feldman, our fabulous project editor, has driven the book beautifully through the manuscript process. Funto Omojola has cheerfully handled many aspects of the project, including sourcing document excerpts and managing complex map revisions, with a keen eye for detail. Meanwhile, Agnieszka Czepazi and Dena Betz did an excellent job of clearing many of the exact images we specified. Ashley Horna has efficiently marched us through the production process, masterfully orchestrating the many permutations of this text, both print and electronic. The wonderful Carson Russell has been tirelessly developing the book's fantastic e-media, particularly in developing, with Stacey Davis (Evergreen State), the new suite of History Skills Tutorials, as well as revisions to the successful InQuizitive course. Alexander Lee and Alexandra Malakhoff have ably managed many other electronic ancillary materials. Finally, we want to thank Sarah England Bartley and social science specialists Julie Sindel, Kassy Morgan, and Emily Rowan for spearheading the marketing and sales campaign for the revision.

We are also indebted to the numerous expert readers who commented on various chapters, thereby strengthening the book as a whole. We are thankful to our families for their patience and advice, and to our students, whose questions and comments over the years have been essential to the framing of this book. And we extend a special thanks to, and hope to hear from, all the teachers and students we might never meet: their engagement with this book will frame new understandings of our shared past and its bearing on our future.

REVIEWERS

Eighteenth Edition Reviewers

Matthew Barlow, John Abbott College
Ken Bartlett, University of Toronto
Bob Brennan, Cape Fear Community College
Jim Brophy, University of Delaware
Keith Chu, Bergen Community College
Geoffrey Clark, SUNY Potsdam
Bill Donovan, Loyola University Maryland
Jeff Ewen, Sussex County Community College
Peter Goddard, University of Guelph
Paul Hughes, Sussex County Community College
Michael Kulikowski, Penn State University
Chris Laney, Berkshire Community College
James Martin, Campbell University
Derrick McKisick, Fairfield University
Dan Puckett, Troy University
Major Ben Richards, U.S. Military Academy
Bo Riley, Columbus State Community College
Kimlisa Salazar, Pima Community College
Sara Scalenghe, Loyola University Maryland
Suzanne Smith, Cape Fear Community College
Bobbi Sutherland, Dordt College
David Tengwall, Anne Arundel Community College
Pam West, Jefferson State Community College
Julianna Wilson, Pima Community College
Margarita Youngo, Pima Community College

Nineteenth Edition Consultants

Dawn L. Gilley, Northwest Missouri State University
Andrzej S. Kamiński, Georgetown University
Adam Kożuchowski, University of Warsaw
Peter Kracht, University of Pittsburgh Press
Eulalia Łazarska, Łazarski University
Krzysztof Łazarski, Łazarski University
John Merriman, Yale University
Daria Nałęcz, Łazarski University

Andrzej Novak, Jagiellonian University
Nicoletta Pellegrino, Regis College
Endre Sashalmi, University of Pécs
Robert Schneider, Indiana University

Nineteenth Edition Reviewers
Ken Bartlett, University of Toronto
Keith Chu, Bergen Community College
Bruce Delfini, SUNY Rockland Community
    College
Paul Fessler, Dordt College
Peter Goddard, University of Guelph
Bonnie Harris, San Diego State University
Anthony Heideman, Front Range Community
    College
Justin Horton, Thomas Nelson Community College
Catherine Humes, John Abbott College
Leslie Johnson, Hudson Valley Community College
Megan Myers, Howard Community College
Craig W. Pilant, County College of Morris
Christopher Thomas, J. Sargeant Reynolds
    Community College
Rebecca Woodham, Wallace Community College

Twentieth Edition Reviewers
Antonio Acevedo, Hudson County Community
    College
Seth Armus, St. Joseph's College
Ben Beshwate, Cerro Coso College
Robert S. Boggs, North Greenville University
Vivian Bouchard, Vanier College
Edward Boyden, Nassau Community College
Jan Bulman, Auburn University at Montgomery
Julien Charest, Cegep John Abbott College
Keith Chu, Bergen Community College
Eric Cimino, Molloy College
Emily Dawes, Midlands Technical College
Patrice Laurent Diaz, Montgomery County
    Community College

John Diffley, Springfield Technical
    Community College
Nicole Eaton, Boston College
Greg Eghigian, Pennsylvania State University
Daniel Ferris, Miles Community College
Bryan Givens, Pepperdine University
Abbie Grubb, San Jacinto College
Ingo Heidbrink, Old Dominion University
Ke-chin Hsia, Indiana University Bloomington
Nicole Jacoberger, Nassau Community College
Leslie Johnson, Leslie C. Johnson
Stephen Julias, Rockland Community College
Lisa Keller, Purchase College
Andrew Keitt, University of Alabama at Birmingham
Deborah Kruger, Butler County Community College
John P. Lomax, Ohio Northern University
Anthonette McDaniel, Pellissippi State Community
    College, Knoxville, Tennessee
Stan Mendenhall, Illinois Central College
Alexander Mikaberidze, Louisiana State
    University-Shreveport
Marisa Balsamo Nicholson, Long Island
    University Post
Thomas Ort, Queens College, City University
    of New York
David Parnell, Indiana University Northwest
Betsy Pease, Concordia University Wisconsin
Hannah C. Powers, Thomas Nelson
    Community College
Nicole Rudolph, Adelphi University
Shannan Schoemaker-Mason, Lincoln Land
    Community College
Michael Shanshala, Michael Shanshala
Jennifer Sovde, State University of New York
    at Canton
Chris Vicknair, Brother Martin Highschool
Kevin Wolfe, Trident Technical College
Dirk Yarker, Texas Southmost College
Margarita Youngo, Pima Community College

Western Civilizations

Their History & Their Culture

Before
You
Read
This
Chapter

Early Civilizations

CORE OBJECTIVES

- **UNDERSTAND** the challenges involved in studying the distant past and the crucial importance of interdisciplinary methods and unconventional sources.

- **DEFINE** the key characteristics of civilization.

- **IDENTIFY** the factors that shaped the earliest cities.

- **EXPLAIN** Hammurabi's tools for governing the cities of his empire.

- **DESCRIBE** the main differences between the Mesopotamian and Egyptian civilizations.

There was a time, the story goes, when all the peoples of the earth shared a common language and could accomplish great things. They developed new technologies and aspired to build a city with a tower reaching to the sky. But their god was troubled by this, so he destroyed their civilization by making it impossible for them to understand each other's speech.

We know this story as the legend of the Tower of Babel. It probably circulated among peoples of the ancient world for thousands of years before it became part of the Hebrew book we call by its Greek name, Genesis: "the beginning." This story lets us glimpse some of the conditions in which the first civilizations arose, and it also reminds us of the challenges that make it hard to study them. We no longer speak the same languages as those ancient peoples, just as we no longer have direct access to their experiences or beliefs.

Such foundational stories are usually called *myths*, but they are really an early form of history. For the people who told them, the stories helped to make sense of the present by explaining the past. The story of the Tower of Babel conveyed a crucial message: human beings are powerful when they share a common goal,

3

and what enables human interaction is civilization. To the peoples of the ancient world, the characteristic benefits of civilization—stability and safety, government, art, literature, science—were always products of city life. The very word *civilization* derives from the Latin word *civis*, "city." Cities, however, became possible only as a result of innovations that began around the end of the last Ice Age, about 13,000 years ago, and that came to fruition some 8,000 years later. The history of civilization is therefore a short one. Within the study of humanity, which reaches back to the genus *Homo* in Africa, some 1.7 million years ago, it is merely a blip on the radar screen. Even within the history of *Homo sapiens*, the species to which we all belong and which evolved about 40,000 years ago, civilization is a very recent development.

The study of the earliest civilizations is both fascinating and difficult. Historians still do not understand why the first known cities should have developed in the region between the Tigris and the Euphrates Rivers, in what is now Iraq. Once developed, however, the basic patterns of urban life quickly spread to other parts of western Asia—a region once called the Near East—both by imitation and by conquest. A network of trading connections linked these early cities, but intense competition for resources made alliances fragile and warfare frequent. Then, around the middle of the second millennium B.C.E. (that is, "Before the Common Era," equivalent to the Christian dating system B.C., "Before Christ"), rulers of these independent cities started to make broader claims to power over their citizens and other states. How this happened—and how we know that it happened—is the subject of Chapter 1.

BEFORE CIVILIZATION

More than 9,000 years ago, a town began to develop at Çatalhöyük (*CHUH-tal-hih-yik*) in Anatolia, in what is now south central Turkey. Over the next 2,000 years, it grew to cover an area of thirty-three acres, within which some 8,000 inhabitants lived in more than 2,000 separate houses. If this seems small, consider that Çatalhöyük's population density was actually twice that of today's most populous city: Mumbai, India. It was so tightly packed that there were hardly any streets. Instead, each house was built immediately next to its neighbor and generally on top of a previous house. People entered their houses by walking across their neighbors' rooftops and climbing down ladders into their own living spaces.

The people of Çatalhöyük developed a highly organized and advanced society. They wove wool cloth; they made kiln-fired pottery; they painted elaborate hunting scenes on the plaster-covered walls of their houses; they made weapons and tools from razor-sharp obsidian imported from the nearby Cappadocian mountains. They honored their ancestors with religious rites and buried their dead beneath the floors of their houses. As settled agriculturalists, they grew grains, peas, and lentils and tended herds of domesticated sheep and goats. But they also hunted and gathered fruits and nuts, like their nomadic ancestors, and their society was egalitarian, another feature common to nomadic societies: both men and women did the same kinds of work. But despite their relatively diverse food supply, their life spans were very short. Men died, on average, at the age of thirty-four. Women, who bore the additional risks of childbirth, died around age thirty.

The basic features of life in Çatalhöyük are common to all early civilizations. But how, when, and why did such settlements emerge? And how do we have access to information about this remote past? The era before the appearance of written records, which begin to proliferate around 3200 B.C.E., is of far greater duration than the subsequent eras we are able to document—and no less important. But it requires special ingenuity to identify, collect, and interpret the evidence of the very distant past. In fact, historians have only just begun to explore the ways that climatology, neuroscience, and evolutionary biology can further illuminate this period, augmenting the older findings of paleontology, archaeology, and historical anthropology. The following summary of our knowledge may need to be radically revised in the next few years.

Societies of the Stone Age

Primates with human characteristics originated in Africa 4 to 5 million years ago, and toolmaking hominids—our distant ancestors—evolved approximately 2 million years ago. Because these early people made most of their tools out of stone, all human cultures flourishing before the fourth millennium B.C.E. (that is, the thousand years ending in 3000 B.C.E.) are designated as belonging to the Stone Age. This vast expanse of time is divided into the Paleolithic ("Old Stone") and the Neolithic ("New Stone") Eras, with the break between them falling around 11,000 B.C.E.

Long before modern humans made their appearance, recognizable human activities had already begun to leave traces on the landscape. Early humans in Africa were kindling and controlling fire 164,000 years ago, and using it to make tools. The Neanderthals, a hominid species that flourished even earlier, about 200,000 years ago, made jewelry, painted on the walls of caves, and buried their dead in distinctive graves with meaningful objects such as horns (blown to make music) and, in one case, flowers.

CAVE PAINTINGS FROM LASCAUX. These paintings, which date to between 10,000 and 15,000 B.C.E., show several of the different species of animals that were hunted by people of the Ice Age. The largest animal depicted here, a species of long-horned cattle known as the *aurochs*, is now extinct.

Scientists have recently discovered that Neanderthals were also capable of speech and that they began interbreeding with *Homo sapiens* around 60,000 years ago. How and why Neanderthals became extinct, around 40,000 years ago, is still a matter of intense debate.

Archaeology has shown that, about this time, the pace of human development began to accelerate dramatically. Around 40,000 B.C.E., human populations in Africa expanded and began to migrate into Europe and Asia. This suggests that people were better nourished as a result of new technologies, especially in the management of fire. In many places, the subspecies *Homo sapiens sapiens* began to produce finely crafted and more effective tools such as fishhooks, arrowheads, and sewing needles made from wood, antler, and bone.

The most astonishing evidence of these developments was produced by such tools: cave paintings like those at Lascaux and Chauvet (France)—some of which may be 30,000 years old. These amazing scenes were purposefully painted in recesses where acoustic resonance is greatest, and were probably intended to be experienced as part of multimedia musical ceremonies. (Flutes made from bone and ivory, dating to around 33,000 B.C.E., were found in a cave in southern Germany in 2008.) This is further evidence for the development of language and other sophisticated forms of communication.

Despite these extraordinary changes, the basic patterns of human life altered very little during this era. Virtually all human societies consisted of hunter-gatherers, bands of a few dozen people who moved incessantly in search of food. As a result of this constant movement, these groups left no continuous archaeological record. Yet we can discern some of the social, economic, and political structures that make these subsistence societies different from those that can be called "civilizations." Early humans had no domestic

animals to transport goods, so they could have no significant material possessions aside from basic tools. And because they could not accumulate goods over time, the distinctions of rank and status created by disparities in wealth could not develop. Hierarchical structures were therefore uncommon. When conflicts arose among members of a group, or resources became scarce, the solution probably was to divide and separate.

Although it was once assumed that men did the hunting and women the gathering, such gendered presumptions do not reflect the complex realities of modern hunter-gatherer societies, and they are not applicable to the Paleolithic Period, either. It is more likely that all members of a band (except for the very young and very old) engaged in the basic activity of acquiring food.

THE BUILDING BLOCKS OF CIVILIZATION

What changes allowed some hunter-gatherer societies to settle and build civilizations? Around 11,000 B.C.E., very evident developments brought about by changes in the climate led to the growth of managed food production, which in turn fostered settlements that could trade with each other—both locally and over long distances. For the first time, it became possible for individuals and communities to accumulate and store wealth on a large scale. The results were far reaching. Communities became more stable and human interactions more complex. Specialization developed, along with distinctions of status and rank. Both the rapidity and the radical implications of these changes have given this era its name: the **Neolithic Revolution**.

The Neolithic Revolution: The Beginnings of Human Impact on the Environment

The artists who executed the cave paintings at Lascaux and Chauvet were conditioned to survive in harsh climatic conditions. Between 40,000 and 11,000 B.C.E., daytime temperatures in the Mediterranean basin averaged about 60° F (16° C) in the summer and about 30° F (−1° C) in the winter. These are very low compared with today's temperatures: in the city of Marseilles, not far from Lascaux, they average about 86° F (30° C) in summer and 52° F (11° C)

in winter. This means that cold-loving reindeer, elk, wild boar, bison, and mountain goats abounded in regions now famous for their beaches and vineyards. But as the glaciers receded northward with the warming climate, these species retreated with them, all the way to Scandinavia. Some humans also migrated north with the game, but others stayed behind to create a very different world.

Within a few thousand years after the end of the Ice Age, the peoples living in the eastern Mediterranean accomplished the most momentous transformation in human history: a switch from food gathering for subsistence to food production. The warmer, wetter climate now allowed wild grains to flourish, greatly increasing the food supply

THE GROWTH OF AGRICULTURE. Examine the chronology of agriculture's development in this region. ▪ *What areas began cultivating crops first, and why?* ▪ *In what period did agriculture spread the most rapidly, and why?* ▪ *How might rivers have played a crucial role in the spread of farming technologies?*

and making settlements possible. People then began to domesticate animals and cultivate plants. Stable settlements grew into cities. This process took several thousand years, but it still deserves to be called "revolutionary." In a relatively short time, peoples living in this area fundamentally altered patterns of existence that were millions of years old.

Humans also began to alter the environment, so much so that some scholars have argued that this was the beginning of a new epoch in the history of our planet: the **Anthropocene** (from the Greek word for "human," *anthropos*). During this epoch—our epoch—slow-moving geological and natural climatological fluctuations have been overtaken by intensive, large-scale human efforts to alter the Earth's ecosystems. We will be paying close attention to this process and its intensification throughout the following chapters.

The revolutionary changes of this period produced new surpluses of food, but they also produced new social and gender inequalities. For example, well-nourished women in sedentary communities can bear more children than women in hunter-gatherer groups, and so the women of this new epoch became increasingly sequestered from their male counterparts, who in turn gave up an equal role in child care. The rapid increase in population was also countered by the rapid spread of infectious diseases, while dependence on carbohydrates resulted in earlier deaths than were typical among hunter-gatherers.

Eventually, increased fertility and birthrates outweighed these limiting factors, and by about 8000 B.C.E. human populations were beginning to exceed the wild food supply. They therefore had to increase the food-growing capacity of the land and to devise ways of preserving and storing food between harvests. Some peoples had learned how to preserve wild grain in storage pits as early as 11,500 B.C.E.; eventually they discovered that they could use this seed to produce even more grain the following year. Once humans began deliberate cultivation, they could support larger populations and also compensate for disasters (such as flooding) that might inhibit natural reseeding.

Even more important, intensified seeding and storage provided humans with the stable and predictable surpluses needed to support more domestic animals. This brought a host of additional benefits, not only guaranteeing a more reliable supply of meat, milk, leather, wool, bone, and horn, but also providing animal power to pull carts and plows and to power mills. However, it also resulted in a pattern of environmental engineering that had devastating and unsustainable effects. In 2015, for example, a team of environmental scientists calculated that the number of trees on earth has diminished by over 50 percent since the Neolithic Revolution began. The planet we inhabit now has been fundamentally altered by human activities.

The Emergence of Towns and Villages

The accelerating changes of this epoch are exemplified by towns such as Çatalhöyük and by the simultaneous rise of trade and warfare: signs of increased specialization and competition among human societies. Thousands of new settlements grew up between 7500 and 3500 B.C.E. Some can be classified as cities: centers of administration and commerce with a relatively large population, often protected by walls. One of these was Jericho, in the territory lying between modern Israel and Jordan. Jericho first emerged as a seasonal, grain-producing settlement; but by 6800 B.C.E. its inhabitants were undertaking a spectacular building program to protect their stored surplus of food. Many new dwellings were placed on stone foundations, and a massive dressed stone wall was constructed around the western edge of the settlement. It included a circular tower whose excavated remains still reach to a height of thirty

EARLY POTTERY. This ceramic cup, with its elegant abstract and animal designs, was fashioned sometime between 5000 and 4000 B.C.E. Although it cannot be dated precisely, distinctive design features such as these make it possible to track the shipment of commodities throughout the ancient world.

feet: a powerful expression of its builders' wealth, technical prowess, and political ambitions.

This wall and its tower served a growing and now permanent population: Jericho eventually covered at least eight acres and supported 3,000 people, so it was even more densely settled than Çatalhöyük. It was sustained by the intensive cultivation of recently domesticated strains of wheat and barley grown by farmers who were skilled irrigation engineers. Jericho's inhabitants also produced some of the earliest known pottery, which enabled them to store grain, wine, and oils more effectively.

Pottery revolutionized cooking. For the first time, it was possible to produce nourishing stews and porridges, as well as fermented beverages such as beer. Pottery production was not only vital to ancient civilizations, it is vital to those who study them: as the techniques for making pottery spread throughout Eurasia, identifiable regional styles also developed. By studying the different varieties, archaeologists can construct a reasonably accurate chronology and can also trace the movements of goods and people.

New Economies and Societies

Jericho and Çatalhöyük illustrate the impact that stored agricultural surpluses have on human relations. In these settled societies, significant differences began to arise in the amount of wealth individuals could stockpile for themselves and their heirs. Dependence on agriculture also made it more difficult for individuals to split off from the community when disputes and inequities arose. The result was the emergence of a much more stratified society, with more opportunities for a few powerful people to become dominant.

The new reliance on agriculture also meant a new dependence on the land, the seasons, and the weather, which led to new speculations about the supernatural. Different life forces were believed to require special services and gifts, and the regular practice of ritual and sacrifice ultimately produced a priestly caste of individuals or families who seemed able to communicate with these forces. Such spiritual leadership was allied to more worldly forms of power, including the capacity to lead war bands, to exact tribute from other settlements, to construct defenses, and to resolve disputes. Through their command of the community's religious, military, economic, and political structures, certain clans could establish themselves as a ruling class.

Trade was another important element in the development of early settlements. Local trading networks were established around 9000 B.C.E., and by 5000 B.C.E. long-distance routes linked settlements throughout the region. Exotic goods and luxury items were the most frequent objects of exchange, including marine shells and semiprecious stones such as turquoise and lapis lazuli. Long-distance trade also accelerated the exchange of ideas and information. And it further increased social stratification: because status was enhanced by access to high-prestige goods, local elites sought to monopolize trade by organizing and controlling the production of commodities within their own communities and by regulating their export. Certain people could now devote at least a portion of their labor to pursuits other than agriculture: making pottery or cloth, manufacturing weapons or tools, building houses and fortifications, or facilitating trade. The elites who fostered and exploited the labor of others eventually became specialized themselves, as full-time speculators and organizers, with the leisure and resources to engage in intellectual, artistic, and political pursuits. The building blocks of civilization had been laid.

URBAN DEVELOPMENT IN MESOPOTAMIA

The Greeks called it **Mesopotamia**, the "Land between Rivers." This land received only about eight inches (20 cm) of rainfall per year. Its soils are sandy, and summer temperatures regularly exceed 110° F (43° C). The two rivers supplying water—the Tigris and the Euphrates—are noted for their violence and unpredictability. Both are prone to flooding, and the Tigris was likely to jump its banks and change its course from year to year. It was in this challenging environment that the first urban society, the civilization of Sumer, flourished.

The Ubaid Culture

The earliest cities of Mesopotamia were founded by the Ubaid peoples, so called because of their settlement at al-Ubaid (now in Iraq), around 5900 B.C.E. During this era, the headwaters of the Persian Gulf extended at least 100 miles farther inland than they do today, so some Ubaid settlements bordered on fertile marshlands, which enabled them to develop irrigation systems. Although these began as relatively simple channels and collection pools, Ubaid farmers quickly learned to build more sophisticated canals and to line some pools with stone. They also constructed dikes and levees to control the seasonal flooding of the rivers and to direct the excess water into irrigation canals. Despite the hostile environment, Ubaid communities were

THE WHITE TEMPLE AT URUK, c. 3400 B.C.E. This temple may have been dedicated to the sky god, An, or designed to provide all the region's gods with a mountaintop home in a part of the world known for its level plains.

soon producing surpluses sufficient to support specialists in construction, weaving, pottery making, metalwork, and trade: the typical occupations of Neolithic village life.

Yet there is also evidence of something quite new in Ubaid culture: central structures that served religious, economic, and administrative functions, something not found in Çatalhöyük or Jericho. Starting out as shrines, these structures soon became impressive temples built of dried mud brick, like the bricks described in the story of the Tower of Babel. Unlike the plentiful stone used at Jericho, the scarcity of stone meant that builders in this region had to be more resourceful. Each large settlement had such a temple, from which a priestly class acted as managers of the community's stored wealth and of the complex irrigation systems that would make the civilization of Sumer possible.

Urban Life in Uruk, 4300–2900 B.C.E.

After about 4300 B.C.E., some Ubaid settlements developed into larger, more prosperous, and more organized communities. The most famous of these, Uruk, is considered the first **Sumerian** city-state. Its sophistication and scale is exemplified by the White Temple at Uruk, built between 3500 and 3300 B.C.E. This massive, sloping platform looms nearly forty feet above the surrounding flatlands, and its four corners are oriented toward the cardinal points of the compass. Atop the platform stands the temple itself, dressed in brick and originally painted a brilliant white.

Such temples were eventually constructed in every Sumerian city, reflecting the central role that worship played in urban life. Uruk in particular seems to have owed its rapid growth to its importance as a religious center. By 3100 B.C.E. it encompassed some 6 square kilometers (2.3 square miles), enclosing a population of 40,000 people within its massive brick walls. The villages and towns of Sumer, although a mere fraction of the size, also grew rapidly, their teeming economic activity attracting waves of immigrants, just as the larger cities did. Grain and cloth production grew tenfold. Trade routes expanded dramatically, binding the peoples of Mesopotamia to the Mediterranean and bringing foods from as far away as Scandinavia and China. To manage this increasingly complex economy, the Sumerians invented the technology on which most historians rely: writing.

The Development of Writing

In 4000 B.C.E., the peoples of Mesopotamia were already using clay tokens to keep inventories. Within a few centuries, they developed the practice of placing tokens inside hollow clay balls and inscribing, on the outside of each ball, the shapes of all the tokens it contained. By 3300 B.C.E., priests (or their scribes) had replaced these balls with flat clay tablets on which they inscribed symbols representing the tokens. These tablets made keeping the tokens themselves unnecessary, and they could also be archived for future reference or sent to other settlements as receipts or requests for goods.

Writing thus evolved as a practical recording technology to support economic pursuits. And because it existed to represent real things, its system of symbols—called pictograms—was also realistic: each pictogram resembled the thing it represented. Over time, however, a pictogram might be used not only to symbolize a physical object but also to evoke an idea associated with that object. For example, the symbol for a bowl of food, a *ninda*, might be used to express something more abstract, such as "nourishment" or "sustenance." Pictograms also came to be associated with particular spoken sounds, or *phonemes*. Thus when a Sumerian scribe needed to employ the sound *ninda*, even as part of another word or a name, he would use the symbol for a bowl of food to represent that phoneme. Later, special marks were added to the symbol so that a reader could tell whether the writer meant it to represent the object itself, or an abstract concept, or a sound used in a context that might have nothing to do with food.

By 3100 B.C.E., Sumerian scribes also developed a specialized tool suited to the task of writing, a durable stylus made of reed. Because this stylus leaves an impression shaped like a wedge (in Latin, *cuneus*), this script is called **cuneiform** (*kyoo-NAY-i-form*). With it, cuneiform symbols could be impressed more quickly into clay. But because the new stylus was not suited to drawing pictograms that accurately represented things, the symbols became even more abstract; eventually they barely resembled the original pictograms at all. Meanwhile, symbols were invented for every possible phonetic combination in the Sumerian language, reducing the number of necessary pictograms from about 1,200 to 600. Whereas the earliest pictograms could have been written and read by anyone, writing and reading now became specialized, powerful skills accessible only to a small and influential minority taught in designated scribal schools.

Despite the complicated nature of the script, cuneiform proved remarkably durable. For over 2,000 years it remained the principal writing system of antiquity, even in societies that did not speak the Sumerian language. Documents using the script were still being produced as late as the first century C.E. ("Common Era," equivalent to the traditional Christian practice of designating dates by A.D., for *Anno Domini*, "in the year of the Lord"). By about 2500 B.C.E., Sumerians were using writing for a wide variety of economic, religious, political, and artistic purposes. Tens of thousands of clay tablets still survive, which makes it possible for us to know a great deal more about the Sumerians than we do about any other human society before this time. We can better understand the social structures that shaped their lives, their attitudes toward their gods, and their changing political circumstances.

CUNEIFORM WRITING. The image on the left shows a Sumerian clay tablet from about 3000 B.C.E. Here, standardized pictures are beginning to represent concepts as well as things: notice the symbol *ninda* ("bowl of food") at the top. On the right, carvings on limestone from about 2600 B.C.E. reveal the evolution of cuneiform into more abstract forms. ▪ *Why would such abstract pictograms have been easier to reproduce quickly than the earlier, more realistic images?*

THE CULTURE OF SUMER

The great centers of Sumerian civilization—the cities of Uruk, Ur, Lagash, Eridu, and Kish—shared a common culture and a common language. But they also competed for natural resources and sources of labor, rivalries that could lead to warfare and the raiding of smaller settlements. Water rights and access to arable land and trade routes were frequently at stake.

Much of the economic production of each city passed through great temple warehouses, where priests redistributed the city's produce. During the third millennium, these great temples also began to control the production of textiles, employing thousands of enslaved people, mostly women and children. Temple elites began to play a key role in long-distance trade as both buyers and sellers of goods.

Each Sumerian city therefore had its own gods and an aristocracy from which priests were drawn.

As much as half of the remaining population may have consisted of farming families who farmed only enough land to sustain themselves. The rest were dependents of the temple who worked as artisans or as agricultural laborers; many were slaves. Most were prisoners of war from other Sumerian city-states whose bondage was limited to three years, after which time a slave had to be released. But foreigners could be held indefinitely and were the property of their owners. They could be beaten, branded, bought, and sold like any other form of merchandise. Perhaps the only positive thing to say about slavery in antiquity is that it was egalitarian: anyone could become a slave. It was not until the beginning of the modern era that slavery became closely linked to new ideas about race (see Chapter 14).

THE FERTILE CRESCENT. Notice the proximity of Sumerian cities to rivers; consider the vital role played by the Tigris and the Euphrates in shaping the Mesopotamian civilizations. ▪ *How many Sumerian cities can you identify on the map?* ▪ *Why might Sumerian cities have been clustered so closely together?* ▪ *What challenges and opportunities did this present?*

Competing Viewpoints

The Flood: Two Accounts

One of the oldest stories in the world tells of a great flood that devastated the lands and peoples of the earth, an event that can be traced to the warming of the earth's climate at the end of the last Ice Age. Many ancient cultures told versions of this story; two of these are excerpted below. The first, included in the Epic of Gilgamesh, was written down during the first half of the third millennium B.C.E., making it at least 1,500 years older than the similar account in the Hebrew Bible. But both are probably the products of much older storytelling traditions. The hero of the Sumerian story is Utnapishtim; the hero of the Hebrew story is Noah.

The Epic of Gilgamesh

Utnapishtim spoke to Gilgamesh, saying: "I will reveal to you, Gilgamesh . . . a secret of the gods. . . . The hearts of the Great Gods moved them to inflict the Flood. Their Father Anu uttered the oath (of secrecy). . . . [But the god] Ea . . . repeated their talk [to me, saying]: 'O man of Shuruppak, son of Ubartutu: Tear down the house and build a boat! . . . Spurn possessions and keep alive living beings! Make all living beings go up into the boat. The boat which you are to build, its dimensions must measure equal to each other: its length must correspond to its width. Roof it over like the Apsu.' I understood and spoke to my lord, Ea: 'My lord, thus is the command which you have uttered. I will heed and will do it.' . . . On the fifth day I laid out her exterior. It was a field in area, its walls were each 10 times 12 cubits in height. . . . I provided it with six decks, thus dividing it into seven (levels). . . . Whatever I had I loaded on it. . . . All the living beings that I had I loaded on it. I had all my kith and kin go up into the boat, all the beasts and animals of the field and the draftsmen I had go up.

I watched the appearance of the weather—the weather was frightful to behold! I went into the boat and sealed the entry. . . . All day long the South Wind blew . . . , submerging the mountain in water, overwhelming the people like an attack. . . . Six days and seven nights came the wind and flood, the storm flattening the land. When the seventh day arrived . . . [t]he sea calmed, fell still, the whirlwind and flood stopped up. . . . When a seventh day arrived, I sent forth a dove and released it. The dove went off, but came back to me, no perch was visible so it circled back to me. I sent forth a swallow and released it. The swallow went off, but came back to me, no perch was visible so it circled back to me. I sent forth a raven and released it. The raven went off, and saw the waters slither back. It eats, it scratches, it bobs, but does not circle back to me. Then I sent out everything in all directions and sacrificed (a sheep). I offered incense in front of the mountain-ziggurat. . . .

The gods smelled the savor . . . and collected like flies over a sacrifice. . . . Just then Enlil arrived. He saw the boat

The Early Dynastic Period, 2900–2500 B.C.E.

Around 2900 B.C.E., competition for resources intensified, and warfare among cities became more frequent. As a result, a new type of military leadership began to emerge. Historians call this era the Early Dynastic Period because it was dominated by powerful dynasties—families who held and handed down power to their members—each headed by a war leader known as a *lugal*, a "big man." Unlike the priestly rulers of the Uruk Period, lugals did not see themselves as humble servants of a city's god. Rather, they believed that success in battle had earned them the right to exploit the city's wealth for their own glory.

The most striking expression of this development is the **Epic of Gilgamesh**, a series of stories recited over many generations and eventually written down on cuneiform and became furious. . . . 'Where did a living being escape? No man was to survive the annihilation!' Ea spoke to Valiant Enlil, saying . . . 'How, how could you bring about a Flood without consideration? Charge the violation to the violator, charge the offense to the offender, but be compassionate lest (mankind) be cut off, be patient lest they be killed.' Enlil went up inside the boat and, grasping my hand, made me go up. He had my wife go up and kneel by my side. He touched our foreheads and, standing between us, he blessed us. . . ."

Source: Maureen Gallery Kovacs, trans., *The Epic of Gilgamesh*, Tablet XI (Stanford, CA: 1985, 1989), pp. 97–103.

The Book of Genesis

The Lord saw that the wickedness of humankind was great in the earth and . . . said, "I will blot out from the earth the human beings I have created . . . for I am sorry I have made them." But Noah found favor in the sight of the Lord. . . . God saw that the earth was corrupt and . . . said to Noah, "I have determined to make an end to all flesh. . . . Make yourself an ark of cypress wood, make rooms in the ark, and cover it inside and out with pitch. . . . Make a roof for the ark, and put the door of the ark in its side. . . . For my part I am going to bring a flood on the earth, to destroy from under heaven all flesh. . . . But I will establish a covenant with you, and you shall come into the ark, you, your sons, your wife, and your sons' wives with you. And of every living thing you shall bring two of every kind into the ark, to keep them alive with you. . . . Also take with you every kind of food that is eaten." . . . All the fountains of the great deep burst forth, and the windows of the heavens were opened. . . . The waters gradually receded from the earth. . . . At the end of forty days, Noah opened a window of the ark . . . and sent out the raven, and it went to and fro until the waters were dried up from the earth. Then he sent out the dove from him, to see if the waters had subsided from the face of the ground, but the dove found no place to set its foot, and it returned. . . . He waited another seven days, and again sent out the dove [which] came back to him . . . and there in its beak was a freshly plucked olive leaf, so Noah knew the waters had subsided from the earth. Then he . . . sent out the dove, and it did not return to him anymore. . . . Noah built an altar to the Lord . . . and offered burnt offerings. And when the Lord smelled the pleasing odor, the Lord said in his heart, "I will never again curse the ground because of humankind . . . nor will I ever again destroy every living creature as I have done." . . . God blessed Noah and his sons.

Source: Genesis 6:5–9:1, *The New Oxford Annotated Bible* (Oxford: 1994).

Questions for Analysis

1. What are the similarities and differences between these two accounts?

2. What do these differences or similarities reveal about the two societies that told these stories? Does one seem to derive from the other? Why or why not?

3. How did the geography and climate of Mesopotamia affect the Sumerian version of the story?

tablets: the first literary monument in world history. It recounts the exploits of a lugal named Gilgamesh, who probably lived in Uruk sometime around 2700 B.C.E. Gilgamesh earns his legendary reputation through military conquest and personal heroism, particularly in campaigns against uncivilized—that is, nonurban, non-Sumerian—tribes. But he becomes so powerful that he ignores his own society's code of conduct. We hear at the start of the epic that his people complain about him because he keeps their sons away at war and shows no respect for the nobles, carousing with their wives and compromising their daughters; he also disrespects the priesthood and commits acts of sacrilege. So the people of Uruk pray to the gods for retribution, and the gods fashion a wild man named Enkidu to challenge Gilgamesh.

The confrontation between Gilgamesh and Enkidu reveals the core values of Sumerian society. Gilgamesh is a creature of the city; Enkidu is his uncivilized Other, like the hunter-gatherers who still subsisted in unclaimed wilderness lands between and around cities. But then Enkidu has a sexual encounter with a beguiling woman: his urban initiation civilizes him, and this allows him to befriend the lord of Uruk. Together they have many adventures. But Enkidu is eventually killed by the goddess Inanna, who punishes the friends for mocking her powers. Gilgamesh, distraught with grief, searches for a magical medicinal plant that will revive his friend. He finds it at the bottom of a deep pool, only to have it stolen from him by a water snake. In the end, he is forced to confront the futility of all human effort. He becomes "The One Who Looked into the Depths," the name by which his story was known to Sumerians. The larger message seems to be that not even civilization can shield humans from the forces of nature and the inevitability of death.

Sumerian Religion

During the Uruk Period, Sumerians identified their gods with the capricious forces of the natural world. During the Early Dynastic Period, however, many societies came to imagine their gods as resembling the lugals who now lorded over their cities. From either perspective, humans exist merely to work for their gods or rulers, to provide them with food, clothing, and luxuries. This was, indeed, why the gods had created people in the first place. There was thus a reciprocal relationship: gods and lugals depended on their human servants to honor and sustain them; and in return, they occasionally bestowed gifts and favors on humans.

Some lugals therefore claimed to be the gods' representatives on earth, reigning as kings with special responsibilities and special privileges. They were thus set apart from all other men, including priests. But kings were also obliged to honor the gods through offerings, sacrifices, festivals, and massive building projects. Kings who neglected these duties, or who exalted themselves at the expense of the gods, were likely to bring disaster on themselves and their people. And even kings could not evade death, when the human body returned to clay and the soul crossed into the underworld, a place of silent darkness.

Sumerian Science and Technology

The Sumerians' worldview was colored by their adversarial relationship with their capricious surroundings. Because neither their gods nor their environment was trustworthy, Sumerians cultivated a high degree of self-reliance and ingenuity. These qualities made them the most technologically innovative people of the ancient world.

For example, despite the fact that their land had no mineral deposits, the Sumerians became skilled metallurgists. By 6000 B.C.E., a number of cultures throughout Eurasia had learned how to produce weapons and tools from copper. Mesopotamia itself has no copper, but by the Uruk Period (4300–2900 B.C.E.), trade routes were bringing raw copper ore into Sumer, where it was processed into weapons and tools. Shortly before 3000 B.C.E., perhaps starting in eastern Anatolia (now Turkey), people also discovered that copper could be alloyed with arsenic (or later, tin) to produce bronze. Bronze is almost as malleable as copper,

SUMERIAN WAR CHARIOTS. The earliest known representation of the wheel, dating from about 2600 B.C.E., shows how wheels were fashioned from slabs of wood. (For a later Mesopotamian wheel with spokes, see the illustration on page 41.)

and it pours more easily into molds; when cooled, it also maintains its rigidity and shape better than copper. For almost 2,000 years, until about 1200 B.C.E. and the development of techniques for smelting iron (see Chapter 2), bronze was the strongest metal known—the most useful and, in war, the most deadly. Like the ancient Greeks, we call this period the Bronze Age.

Along with writing and the making of bronze, the invention of the wheel was a fundamental technological achievement of this era. The Sumerians were using potter's wheels by the middle of the fourth millennium B.C.E. and could produce high-quality clay vessels in greater quantity than ever before. By around 3200 B.C.E., the Sumerians were also using two- and four-wheeled chariots and carts drawn by donkeys. (Horses were unknown in Mesopotamia until sometime between 2000 and 1700 B.C.E.) Chariots were another new and deadly military technology, giving warriors a tremendous advantage over armies on foot: the earliest depiction of their use, dating from 2600 B.C.E., shows one trampling an enemy. At the same time, wheeled carts dramatically increased the productivity of the Sumerian workforce.

The use of the wheel in pottery making may have suggested its use for vehicles, but such a connection is not inevitable. The ancient Egyptians, too, were using the potter's wheel by at least 2700 B.C.E., but they did not use the wheel for transport until a millennium later, when they learned the technique from Mesopotamia. In the Western Hemisphere, wheeled vehicles were unknown until the sixteenth century C.E., although the Incas had a sophisticated system of roads and probably used iron rollers to move huge blocks of stone for use in building projects. These two points of comparison help to explain why the wheel was probably invented by nomadic peoples living on the steppes of what is now Russia. By contrast, sedentary civilizations that can rely on the manpower of thousands, or that can transport heavy cargo by water, do not feel the same necessity for invention.

The Sumerians can also be credited with innovations that made the most of their scarce resources. An example is the seed drill, in use for two millennia before it was depicted on a stone tablet of the seventh century B.C.E. It is striking that this technology was unknown to any other Western civilization until the sixteenth century C.E., when Europeans adopted it from China; it would not be in general use until the nineteenth century of our era.

Timekeeping, Trade, and Travel

Other impressive Sumerian inventions derived from the study of mathematics. In order to construct their elaborate irrigation systems, the Sumerians had developed sophisticated measuring and surveying techniques as well as the art of mapmaking. Agricultural needs may also lie behind the lunar calendar they invented, which consisted of twelve months, six lasting 30 days and six lasting 29 days. Since this produced a year of only 354 days, the Sumerians eventually began to add a month to their calendars every few years in order to predict the recurrence of the seasons with sufficient accuracy.

The Sumerian practice of dividing time has lasted to the present day, not only in our notions of the 30-day month (which corresponds approximately with the phases of the moon) but also in our division of the hour into sixty minutes, each comprising sixty seconds. Mathematics also contributed to Sumerian architecture, enabling them to build domes and arches thousands of years before the Romans would adopt and spread these architectural forms throughout the West.

Sumerian technology depended not only on ingenuity but also on the spread of information and raw materials

A SUMERIAN PLOW WITH A SEED DRILL. Seed drills control the distribution of seed and ensure that it falls directly into the furrow made by the plow. By contrast, the method of sowing seed practiced elsewhere in the world—and as late as the nineteenth century in Europe and the Americas—was to broadcast the seed by throwing it out in handfuls. Sumerian-style plows were developed during the third millennium B.C.E. and were still being used in the seventh century B.C.E., when this black stone tablet was engraved. ■ *Think about what you have learned about the Sumerians and their environment. Why would they have developed this technology?*

through trade. Because their homeland was almost completely devoid of many natural resources, Sumerian pioneers traced routes up and down the rivers and into the hinterlands of Mesopotamia, following the tributaries of the Tigris and the Euphrates. They blazed trails across the deserts toward the west, where they interacted with and influenced the Egyptians. By sea, they traded with the peoples of the Persian Gulf and, directly or indirectly, with the civilizations of the Indus Valley (modern Pakistan and India). And, along with merchandise, they carried ideas: stories, art, the use of writing, and the whole cultural complex that arose from their way of life. The elements of civilization, which had fused in their urban crucible, would thus come together in many other places throughout the world.

THE FIRST EMPIRES?

Sumerian inscriptions and other writings suggest that competition among Mesopotamian cities reached a new level around 2500 B.C.E., as ambitious lugals vied to magnify themselves and their kingdoms. But much of this written evidence is misleading, telling us more about these rulers' mastery of rhetoric and writing than their actual control over their own citizen populations. Still, archaeological evidence from Ur showcases the extraordinary wealth of the city's ruling families during this period, so they certainly had a degree of real economic and political power. The dazzling armor and jewelry uncovered by many other

excavations also reveal a shift in Sumerian ideas about the afterlife, since they presuppose a belief that one could enjoy such goods in perpetuity.

Yet no Sumerian lugal was likely to be able to impose centralized rule on his city, much less to control the settlements that he conquered. As a result, Sumer remained a collection of interdependent but mutually suspicious and vulnerable states whose rulers were unable to forge any lasting structures of authority. This would ultimately make the people of Sumer vulnerable to a new style of rulership imposed on them from the north, in the person of Sargon the Akkadian.

Sargon and the Akkadian Realm, 2350–2160 B.C.E.

The Akkadians were the predominant people of central Mesopotamia. Their Sumerian neighbors to the south had greatly influenced them, and they had adopted cuneiform script along with many other elements of Sumerian culture. Yet the Akkadians preserved their own Semitic language, which was part of the linguistic family that includes Hebrew, Arabic, Aramaic, Ethiopic, and Assyrian. Sumerians tended to regard the Akkadians as uncivilized, but they feared the ruler whom the Akkadians called "great king": Sargon. Indeed, Sargon's inscriptions suggest that he was able to subject the cities of Sumer to his authority.

OBJECTS FROM THE ROYAL TOMBS AT UR. On the left is a helmet made from an alloy of gold and silver. Its cloth lining would have been attached through the holes visible around the edges of the helmet. On the right is a queen's headdress made of gold leaf, lapis lazuli, and carnelian.

The success of his efforts could not have matched these claims, but Sargon appears to have consolidated certain powers at his capital city, Akkad, by around 2350 B.C.E. He also appears to have installed Akkadian-speaking governors in the cities under his control, where they would collect tribute and work to impose his will. Sargon was thus attempting to knit the independent cities of Mesopotamia into a larger political unit: what we now call an empire, a word derived from the Latin *imperium*, "command." This would have enabled him to manage and exploit the network of trade routes criss-crossing the region and to extend his influence from Ethiopia to India.

Although Sargon's imperialism was probably aspirational rather than actual, it does seem to have had an effect on Sumerian religion and culture. Sargon attempted to merge the Akkadian and Sumerian divinities, so that, for example, the Akkadian fertility goddess Ishtar became identified with the Sumerian goddess Inanna. He also tried to lessen the rivalry of Sumerian cities by appointing a single Akkadian high priest or priestess, often a member of his own family, to preside over several temples. His own daughter Enheduanna (*en-he-doo-AH-nah*) was high priestess of both Uruk and Ur, and her hymns in honor of Ishtar/Inanna are the earliest surviving works by a named author in world history.

The precedent that Enheduanna and her father established would continue even after the Sargonid dynasty finally fell: for several centuries thereafter, the kings of Sumer continued to appoint their daughters as high priestesses of Ur and Uruk. And by about 2200 B.C.E., most people in central and southern Mesopotamia would have been able to converse in the language of either the Sumerians or the Akkadians. Indeed, the two civilizations became virtually indistinguishable except for these different languages.

The Dynasty of Ur and the Amorites, 2100–1800 B.C.E.

After the death of Sargon's son and heir, Naram-Sin, Akkadian rule in the region dissolved. Around 2100 B.C.E., however, a new dynasty came to power in Ur under a king called Ur-Nammu and his son Shulgi. Ur-Nammu was responsible for the construction of the great **ziggurat** at Ur, which originally rose 70 feet (over 21 m) above the surrounding plain, as well as for many other architectural marvels. Shulgi continued his father's work, raiding the lands up to the Zagros Mountains northeast of Ur and demanding massive tribute payments from them; one collection site accounted for 350,000 sheep per year. Shulgi then built state-run textile-production facilities to process the wool. He also promulgated a code of law, calling for fair weights and measures,

THE ZIGGURAT OF UR. Built around 2100 B.C.E., this great temple is the best-preserved structure of its kind. It is located at Nasiriyah, in what is now Iraq. Archaeological investigations (see diagram) reveal that its central shrine, the most sacred part of the temple, was reached by climbing four sets of stairs and passing through a massive portal.

the protection of widows and orphans, and limitations on the death penalty for crimes.

While there was no mechanism for actually enforcing this code, Shulgi's commercial expansion of his realm and his patronage of art and literature established a pattern that influenced other rulers in the region for centuries to come. It also influenced newcomers known as the Amorites, a Semitic people (like the Akkadians) who (unlike the Akkadians) had largely been nomads and warriors. But now, some Amorite leaders began to gain control of the ancient cities of Mesopotamia.

The Empire of Hammurabi

In 1792 B.C.E., a young Amorite chieftain named Hammurabi (hah-muh-RAH-bee) became the ruler of **Babylon**, an insignificant city in central Mesopotamia. While Babylon was precariously wedged among a number of more powerful cities, its site on the Tigris and Euphrates had great potential. Hammurabi turned this situation to his advantage, recognizing that military intelligence, diplomacy, and strategic planning might accomplish what his small army could not.

A rich archive of tablets found at the city of Mari (which eventually fell under his rule) testifies to his talents for the clever manipulation of his more powerful adversaries: for Hammurabi used writing itself as a weapon. He did not try to confront his mightier neighbors head on. Rather, through letters and embassies, double-dealing and cunning, he induced his stronger counterparts to fight each other. While other rulers exhausted their resources in costly wars, Hammurabi fanned their mutual hatred and skillfully portrayed himself as a friend and ally to all sides. Meanwhile, he quietly strengthened his kingdom, built up his army, and, when the time was right, fell on his depleted neighbors. By such policies, he transformed his small state into what historians call the Old Babylonian Empire.

Under Hammurabi's rule, Mesopotamia achieved a new degree of political integration that reached from the Persian Gulf into Assyria. The southern half of the region, formerly Sumer and Akkad, would henceforth be known as Babylonia. To help unify these territories, Hammurabi introduced another innovation, promoting the worship of the little-known patron god of Babylon, Marduk, and making him the ruler-god of his entire empire. Although he also paid homage to the ancient gods of Sumer and Akkad, Hammurabi made it clear that all his subjects now owed allegiance to Marduk.

The idea that political power derives from divine approval was nothing new, but Hammurabi's genius was to use Marduk's divine supremacy over all other gods to legitimize his own claim to rule, in Marduk's name, because he was king of Marduk's home city. Hammurabi thus became the first known ruler to launch wars of aggression justified in the name of his primary god. This set a precedent for colonial expansion that would become a characteristic feature of Western civilizations and that lies behind nearly all imperial ventures down to the present day.

Yet Hammurabi did not rely solely on religion to forge a kind of empire. Building on the precedents of past rulers, he also issued a collection of laws, copies of which were inscribed on stone and set up in public places throughout his realm. The example that survives is an eight-foot-tall stele (STEH-leh) made of gleaming black basalt, erected in the central marketplace of Babylon. The upper portion shows Hammurabi consulting with Shamash, the god of justice. The phallic form on which the laws were inscribed would have been immediately recognizable as a potent symbol of Hammurabi's authority, obvious even to those who could not read the laws themselves. (It still makes a strong impression on visitors to the Louvre museum in Paris.)

Hammurabi's decision to represent himself as a lawgiver was symbolically important—even if, like previous rulers, he had no effective mechanism for policing his state or enforcing these laws. By collecting and codifying legal precedents, Hammurabi declared himself to be (as he stated in the code's preamble) "the shepherd of the people, the capable king"—not a lugal ruling through fear and caprice. This was setting a new standard of kingship and expressing a new vision of empire as a union of peoples subject to the same laws.

Law and Society in Hammurabi's Code

The **Code of Hammurabi** reveals a great deal about the structure and values of Babylonian society. The organization of its 282 pronouncements offers insight into the kinds of litigation that Hammurabi and his officials regularly handled and also suggests the relative importance of these cases. It begins with legislation against false testimony (fraud or lying under oath) and theft, followed by laws regulating business deals; laws regulating the use of public resources, especially water; laws relating to taverns and brothels, most of which appear to have been run by women; laws relating to debt and slavery; many laws dealing with marriage, inheritance, divorce, and widows' rights; and, finally, laws punishing murder, violent assault, and even medical malpractice. What emerges is a fascinating picture of a complex urban society that required more formal legislation than the accumulated customs of previous generations.

WOMEN AND TEXTILES. Women were the predominant producers of textiles throughout the ancient world. Even upper-class women were almost continuously engaged in spinning thread and weaving cloth for their households. Here, a servant fans an elegant lady at work with her spindle.

Most of these laws appear to be aimed at free commoners, who made up the bulk of the population. Above them was an aristocratic class, tied to the king's court and active in its bureaucracy, that controlled a great deal of the community's wealth: these were the palace officials, temple priests, high-ranking military officers, and rich merchants. Indeed, even legally free individuals were probably dependents of the palace or the temple in some way, or leased land from the estates of the powerful. They included laborers and artisans, small-scale merchants and farmers, and the minor political and religious officials.

At the bottom of Babylonian society were the slaves, who were far more numerous than they had been in the older civilizations of Sumer or Akkad. Many, indeed, had become slaves not because of war but through trade: either sold as payment for debts or to the profit of a family with too many children, or because they had been forced to sell themselves on the open market. Others had been enslaved in punishment for certain offenses. Slaves in the Old Babylonian Empire were treated much more harshly than in previous civilizations and were more readily identifiable as a separate group: whereas free men in Babylonia wore long hair and beards, male slaves were shaved and branded.

The division among classes in this society was marked. As Hammurabi's code indicates, an offense committed against a nobleman carried a far more severe penalty than did the same crime committed against a social equal or against a dependent or slave; nobles were also punished more severely than were commoners for crimes they committed against other nobles. Marriage arrangements also reflected class differences, with bride-prices and dowries depending on the status of the parties involved. That said, Hammurabi's code also provides evidence as to the status of women in Babylonian society and shows that they enjoyed certain important protections under the law, including the right to divorce abusive or indigent husbands. If a husband divorced a wife "without cause," he was obliged to provide financial support for her and their children. However, a wife who went around the city defaming her spouse was subject to severe punishment. A woman would risk death, as would her lover, if she were caught in adultery. The sexual promiscuity of husbands, by contrast, was protected under the law.

Hammurabi's Legacy

Hammurabi died around 1750 B.C.E. Although the imperial powers he had wielded were not sustainable, he had created a durable state. For another two centuries, Babylon continued to play a significant role in Mesopotamia until invaders from the north sacked the capital and occupied it. But even then, for another thousand years thereafter, Babylon remained the region's most famous city.

The Code of Hammurabi

The laws of Hammurabi, published on the authority of this powerful king and set up in central places throughout the Old Babylonian Empire, were influenced both by the needs of an urban society and by older ideas of justice and punishment common among Semitic peoples. In its entirety, the code comprises 282 laws, beginning and ending with statements of Hammurabi's devotion to the gods, his peacekeeping mission, and his sense of his duties as king. The following excerpts are numbered so as to show the order in which these provisions appear on the stele that publicizes them.

When the god Marduk commanded me to provide just ways for the people of the land in order to attain appropriate behavior, I established truth and justice as the declaration of the land. I enhanced the well-being of the people.

* * *

1. If a man accuses another man and charges him with homicide but cannot bring proof against him, his accuser shall be killed.

2. If a man charges another man with practicing witchcraft but cannot bring proof against him, he who is charged with witchcraft shall go to the divine River Ordeal, he shall indeed submit to the divine River Ordeal; if the divine River Ordeal should overwhelm him, his accuser shall take full legal possession of his estate; if the divine River Ordeal should clear that man and should he survive, he who made the charge of witchcraft against him shall be killed; he who submitted to the divine River Ordeal shall take full legal possession of his accuser's estate.

If a man comes forward to give false testimony in a case but cannot bring evidence for his accusation, if that case involves a capital offense, that man shall be killed.

* * *

6. If a man steals valuables belonging to the god or to the palace, that man shall be killed, and also he who received the stolen goods from him shall be killed.

7. If a man should purchase silver, gold, a slave, a slave woman, an ox, a sheep, a donkey, or anything else whatsoever, from a son of a man or from a slave of a man without witnesses or a contract—or if he accepts the goods for safekeeping—that man is a thief, he shall be killed.

8. If a man steals an ox, a sheep, a donkey, a pig, or a boat—if it belongs either to the god or to the palace, he shall give thirtyfold; if it belongs to a commoner, he shall replace it tenfold; if the thief does not have anything to give, he shall be killed.

* * *

15. If a man should enable a palace slave, a palace slave woman, a commoner's slave, or a commoner's slave woman to leave through the main city-gate, he shall be killed.

* * *

53. If a man neglects to reinforce the embankment of the irrigation canal of his field and then a breach opens and allows the water to carry away the common irrigated area, the man in whose embankment the breach opened shall replace the grain whose loss he caused.

* * *

104. If a merchant gives a trading agent grain, wool, oil, or any other commodity for local transactions, the trading agent shall collect a sealed receipt for each payment in silver that he gives to the merchant.

* * *

128. If a man marries a wife but does not draw up a formal contract for her, she is not a wife.

129. If a man's wife should be seized lying with another male, they shall bind them and throw them into the water; if the wife's master allows his wife to live, then the king shall allow his subject [i.e., the other male] to live.

* * *

142. If a woman repudiates her husband, and declares, "You will not have marital relations with me"—her circumstances shall be investigated by the authorities of her city quarter, and if she is circumspect and without fault, but her husband is wayward and disparages her greatly, that woman will not be subject to any penalty; she shall take her dowry and she shall depart for her father's house.

Source: Martha T. Roth, ed., *Law Collections from Mesopotamia and Asia Minor* (Atlanta: 1995), pp. 76–135 (excerpted).

THE CODE OF HAMMURABI.
The laws of Hammurabi survive on an eight-foot column made of basalt. The top quarter of the column depicts the Babylonian king (standing, at left) being vested with authority by Shamash, the god of justice. Directly below we can make out the cuneiform inscriptions that are the law code's text.

■ *How would the very format of these laws send a powerful message about Hammurabi's kingship?*

Questions for Analysis

1. On the basis of these excerpts, what conclusions can you draw about the values of Old Babylonian society? For example, what types of crimes are punishable by death, and why?

2. In what ways does the Code of Hammurabi exhibit the influences of the urban civilization for which these laws were issued? What are some characteristics and consequences of urbanization? What, for example, do we learn about economic developments?

3. Examine the photographs of the stele preserving the code. What is the significance of the image that accompanies the laws, Hammurabi's conference with the enthroned god Shamash? What is the significance of the stele itself as the medium that conveyed these laws to the people?

Hammurabi's legacy also extended well beyond Babylonia, because he had shaped a new conception of kingship. After Hammurabi, unifying state religions became an increasingly important technique that kings used to annex and subjugate diverse territories and peoples. Hammurabi had also demonstrated the effectiveness of writing as a political tool. Diplomacy and the keeping of archives would be essential to all subsequent empires. So too would the claim that rulers should be the protectors of the weak and the arbiters of justice.

THE DEVELOPMENT OF CIVILIZATION IN EGYPT

At about the same time that Sumerian civilization was transforming Mesopotamia, another civilization was taking shape in a different part of the world and in very different ways. Unlike the Sumerians, the Egyptians did not have to wrest survival from a hostile and unpredictable environment. Instead, their land was renewed every year by the flooding of the Nile River. The fertile black soil that was left behind every summer made theirs the richest agricultural region in the entire Mediterranean world.

Egypt's distinctive civilization rests on this fundamental ecological fact. It also explains why ancient Egypt was a narrow, elongated kingdom, running along the Nile north from the First Cataract (a series of rocks and rapids near the ancient city of Elephantine) toward the Mediterranean Sea for a distance of more than 600 miles (965 km). Outside this narrow band of territory—which ranged from a few hundred yards to 14 miles (23 km) at the widest—lay uninhabitable desert. This contrast between the fertile Black Land along the Nile and the dessicated Red Land beyond deeply influenced the Egyptian worldview, in which the Nile itself was the center of the cosmos and the lands beyond were hostile and beyond the pale of habitation.

In many respects, ancient Egyptian civilization enjoyed a remarkable continuity. Its roots date back to 5000 B.C.E. at least, and Egypt continued to thrive as an independent and distinctive entity even after it was conquered by Alexander the Great in 331 B.C.E. (see Chapter 4), until its assimilation into the Roman Empire after 30 B.C.E. (see Chapter 5). From about 3000 B.C.E., the defining element of this civilization would be the pervasive influence of a powerful, centralized, bureaucratic state headed by pharaohs (*FARE-ohs*) who were regarded as living gods. No other civilization in world history has ever been governed so steadily, for so long, as ancient Egypt.

For convenience, historians have traditionally divided ancient Egyptian history into distinctive "kingdoms" and "periods." Following ancient Egyptian chroniclers, modern historians have also tended to portray these Old, Middle, and New Kingdoms as characterized by unity and prosperity, punctuated by chaotic interludes, the so-called Intermediate Periods, when central authority broke down. Like all attempts at periodization, these divisions do not capture the complexities of human experience or even the real pace of historical development. In essence, this periodization still reflects the conservative perspective of the ancient Egyptian state, which prized continuity and feared change. As we will see, though, the First Intermediate Period in particular looks like a positive development if viewed from the perspective of individual communities and commoners, rather than from the viewpoint of the pharaoh's court.

Predynastic Egypt, c. 10,000–3100 B.C.E.

The term *Predynastic Egypt* refers to the period before the emergence of the pharaohs and their royal dynasties, an era for which archaeological evidence is difficult to find and interpret. Many predynastic settlements were destroyed long ago by the waters of the Nile and are now buried under innumerable layers of silt. Furthermore, the very abundance of naturally occurring foodstuffs in the Nile Valley made the need for settlement and cultivation less pressing than in the Fertile Crescent, where (as we have seen) Mesopotamian peoples were already living together in villages during the eighth millennium B.C.E. In Egypt, by contrast, a growing population was able to sustain itself by hunting and gathering until the fifth millennium B.C.E.

The first known permanent settlement in Egypt, situated at the southwestern edge of the Nile Delta (near the modern town of Merimde Beni Salama), dates to approximately 4750 B.C.E. It was a farming community that may have numbered as many as 16,000 residents, and this number (based on burial remains) suggests that some Egyptian communities were much larger than those of a comparable period in Mesopotamia. Thereafter, evidence shows that the Egyptian economy rapidly became more diversified: by around 3500 B.C.E. the residents of Ma'adi, three miles away from Merimde Beni Salama (see map on page 23), had extensive commercial contacts with the Sinai Peninsula, the eastern Mediterranean, and the upper reaches of the Nile some several hundred miles to the south. Copper was a particularly vital import, since it enabled residents to replace stone tools with metal ones.

Many other Neolithic farming centers have also been discovered in or near the Nile Delta, where a degree of cultural cohesiveness was already developing, fostered by shared interests and trade. In later centuries, this northern area would be known as Lower Egypt, so called because it was downstream. Comparable developments were also occurring upstream. By the end of this Predynastic Period, Egyptian culture was more or less uniform from the southern edge of the delta to the First Cataract, a vast length of the Nile known as Upper Egypt.

ANCIENT EGYPT AND THE EASTERN MEDITERRANEAN. Notice the peculiar geography of ancient Egypt and the role played by the Nile River. Identify the Nile on the map. ▪ *In what direction does the Nile flow?* ▪ *How did the lands on either side help to isolate Egyptian culture from outside influences?* ▪ *Consider how the Nile helped forge Egypt into a unitary state under a powerful centralized government. Yet how might Egypt's relationship to the Nile be potentially hazardous as well as beneficial?*

Although towns in Lower Egypt were more numerous, it was in Upper Egypt that the first Egyptian cities developed. By 3200 B.C.E.—when the Sumerian city of Uruk had been thriving for a thousand years—important communities such as Nekhen, Naqada, This, and Abydos had all developed high degrees of occupational and social specialization. They had encircled themselves with sophisticated fortifications and had begun to build elaborate shrines to honor their gods. Indeed, the establishment of permanent sites of public worship may be key to explaining the growth

of these towns into cities. As in Mesopotamia, a city's role as the center of a prominent religious cult attracted travelers and encouraged the growth of industries. And travel in Upper Egypt was relatively easy compared with travel in Mesopotamia. The Nile bound cities together, and the lack of competition for resources fostered peace.

It was due to the Nile, therefore, that the region south of the delta was able to forge a cultural and eventually a political unity, despite its enormous length. The Nile fed Egypt and was a conduit for people, goods, and ideas.

Past and Present

Engineering Nature

Humans have been manipulating our planet's environment since the Neolithic Revolution. The image on the left shows the irrigation canals that enabled ancient Egyptians to channel the Nile's life-giving waters into the desert. The image on the right shows a storm-surge barrier in the Netherlands, which protects reclaimed land from rising sea levels produced by the cumulative results of human-caused climate change.

 Watch related author interview on the Student Site

Centralizing rulers could project their power quickly and effectively up and down its course. Within a remarkably short time, just a century or two after the first cities' appearance in Upper Egypt, they had banded together in a confederacy under the leadership of the city of This. The pressure exerted by this confederacy in turn forced the towns of Lower Egypt to adopt their own form of political organization. By 3100 B.C.E., the rivalry between these competing regions had given rise to the two nascent kingdoms of Upper and Lower Egypt.

The Power of the Pharaoh, c. 3100–c. 2686 B.C.E.

With the rise of powerful rulers in these two kingdoms, Egyptian history enters a new phase, one that can be chronicled with unusual precision. The system for numbering the ruling dynasties that emerged in this era—known as the Archaic Period—was actually devised nearly 3,000 years later by a historian named Manetho (*mahn-EH-thoh*), who wrote in the third century B.C.E. By and large, Manetho's work has withstood the scrutiny of modern historians and archaeologists, although recent research has added a "Zero Dynasty" of early kings who were instrumental in bringing about the initial unification of Egypt.

Manetho did not record these rulers because he didn't know about them; we know about them almost exclusively from archaeological evidence. Among them was an Upper Egyptian warlord known to us as King Scorpion, because the image of a scorpion accompanies engravings that assert his authority over most of Egypt. Another warlord, King Narmer, appears to have ruled both Upper and Lower Egypt. His exploits, too, come down to us in powerful pictures (see **Interpreting Visual Evidence** on page 26). Both

24 | CHAPTER 1 *Early Civilizations*

of these kings probably came from Abydos in Upper Egypt, where they were later buried. Their administrative capital, however, was at Memphis, the capital city of Lower Egypt and an important center for trade with the Sinai Peninsula and the wider region.

Following the political unification of Upper and Lower Egypt, the basic features of Egypt's distinctive centralized kingship took shape along lines that would persist for the next 3,000 years, down to Manetho's own day. The title used to describe this kingship was *pharaoh*, a word that actually means "great household" and thus refers not only to an individual king but to the whole apparatus that sustained his rule. This fact, in turn, helps to explain the extraordinary stability and longevity of Egyptian civilization, which survived even a dynastic takeover by Macedonian Greeks in the century before Manetho wrote his chronicle. Indeed, it is comparable to some modern forms of government—none of which has yet lasted nearly so long. As we have seen, kingship in Mesopotamia tended to be a form of personal rule, dependent on the charisma of a particular individual; the empires of Sargon and Ur-Nammu scarcely survived another generation or two after their deaths. But in Egypt, the office of the pharaoh was durable enough to survive the deaths of many individual successors, facilitating the peaceful transition of power to new rulers and withstanding the incompetence of many.

This was accomplished, as we shall see, by the efficiency of palace bureaucracy, but it was also a function of the pharaoh's close identification with the divine forces credited with renewing Egypt every year. Like the seasons, the pharaoh died only to be born again, renewed and empowered. Egyptian rulers thus laid claim to a sacred nature quite different—and much more benign—than that governing Sumer. And they were more powerful than any Sumerian lugal, who was never more than a mortal who enjoyed (all too temporary) divine favor.

How the earliest kings of Egypt came to be distinguished as pharaohs and to establish their claims to divinity is still not well understood. We do know, however, that legitimating their rule over Egypt was difficult. Local civic and religious loyalties remained strong, and for centuries Lower Egyptians continued to see themselves as distinct in some respects from their neighbors to the south. Efforts to create a united Egyptian state began very early, however, as the Narmer Palette may indicate. Indeed, it seems probable that the centralization of government in the person of the pharaoh, and his association with divinity, were related approaches to solving the problem of political unity. Together, they had astonishing success. By the end of the Second Dynasty, which coincides with the end of the

Archaic or Early Dynastic Period (2686 B.C.E.), the pharaoh was not just the ruler of Egypt, he *was* Egypt: a personification of the land, the people, and their gods.

The Old Kingdom, c. 2686–2160 B.C.E.

Because so few written documents of the **Old Kingdom** survive, historians have to rely on surviving funerary texts from the tombs of the elite in order to reconstruct the achievements of particular individuals. These sources are hardly representative, and they have tended to convey the impression that Egyptians were obsessed with death; they also tell us little about the lives of ordinary people. Further complicating the historian's task is the early Egyptians' own belief in the unchanging, cyclical nature of the universe. During this early period, there appears to have been little interest in maintaining a record of key events arranged in chronological order. This makes it difficult for us to reconstruct ancient Egyptian history in detail.

However, the surviving inscriptions and art of the Third Dynasty (c. 2686–2613 B.C.E.) do tell us a great deal about the workings of the "great household" that undergirded individual rulers' power. This power was vast because the pharaoh, as the embodiment of Egypt, was considered to be the intermediary among the land, its people, and their gods. Hence, all the resources of Egypt belonged to him. Long-distance trade was entirely controlled by the pharaoh, as were systems for imposing taxation and conscripting labor. To administer these, the pharaohs installed provincial governors, known to the Greeks as *nomarchs*, many of whom were members of the pharaoh's own family.

Old Kingdom pharaohs kept tight control over the nomarchs and their armies of lesser officials, in order to prevent them from establishing local roots in the territories they administered. Writing was therefore critical to internal communication and the management and exploitation of Egypt's vast wealth. This gave rise to a whole class of scribal administrators who enjoyed the power, influence, and status that went along with literacy, a skill few people could command—especially in Egypt, since few could master the intricate writing system (see page 27). Even a child just beginning his scribal education was considered worthy of great respect because the training was so difficult. But it carried great rewards. Indeed, the scribal author of a document from the Middle Kingdom called "The Satire of the Trades" exhorted the beginning student to persevere by reminding him how much better off he would be than everyone else.

The Narmer Palette

The Narmer Palette (c. 3100 B.C.E.) is a double-sided carving made of green siltstone. Palettes were used to grind pigments for the making of cosmetics, but the large size (63 cm; over 2 feet) of this one is unusual. It was discovered in 1897 by archaeologists excavating a temple dedicated to the god Horus at Nekhen, the capital of Upper Egypt. Found nearby were other artifacts, including the so-called Narmer Macehead, thought to depict the marriage of Narmer, king of Upper Egypt, to a princess of Lower Egypt.

On the left, dominating the central panel, Narmer wears the White Crown of Upper Egypt (image A). He wields a mace and seizes the hair of a captive kneeling at his feet. Above the captive's head is a cluster of lotus leaves (a symbol of Lower Egypt) and a falcon representing the god Horus, who may be drawing the captive's life force (*ka*) from his body. The figure behind Narmer is carrying the king's sandals; he is depicted as smaller because he is an inferior. The two men in the lower panel are either running or sprawling on the ground, and the symbols above them indicate the name of a defeated town. On the right, the other side of the palette shows Narmer as the chief figure in a procession (image B). He now wears the Red

A. Narmer wearing the White Crown of Upper Egypt.

Crown of Lower Egypt and holds a mace and a flail, symbols of conquest. Behind him is the same servant carrying his sandals, and in front of him are a man with long hair and four standard-bearers. There are also ten headless corpses. Below, the entwined necks of two mythical creatures (serpopards, leopards with serpents' heads) are tethered to leashes held by two men. In the lowest section, a bull tramples the body of a man whose city Narmer is destroying.

Questions for Analysis

1. This artifact has been called "the first historical document in the world," but

B. Narmer wearing the Red Crown of Lower Egypt.

scholars are still debating its meanings. For example, does it represent something that actually happened? Or is it political propaganda? In your view, is this proof that Narmer has united the two kingdoms? Why or why not?

2. Do the two sides of the palette tell a coherent story? If so, on which side does that story begin?

3. What might be significant about the site where the palette was found? Should the palette be interpreted as belonging with the mace, found nearby? If so, how might that change your interpretation of the palette's significance?

The Power of Writing

Among the many facets of Egyptian culture that have fascinated generations of scholars is the Egyptian system of pictographic writing. Called **hieroglyphs** (HI-eroh-glifs) or "sacred carvings" by the Greeks, these strange and elaborate symbols remained completely impenetrable and mysterious to modern scholars until the nineteenth century, when a Frenchman named Jean François Champollion deciphered them with the help of history's most famous decoding device, the Rosetta Stone. This stele preserves three versions of the same decree issued by one of the Ptolemaic rulers of Egypt in 196 B.C.E. (see Chapter 3), written in ancient Greek, demotic (a later Egyptian script), and hieroglyphics—still in use after more than 3,000 years. Because he could read the text in Greek, Champollion was eventually able to translate the demotic and hieroglyphic texts as well. From this beginning, generations of scholars have added to and refined our knowledge of the ancient Egyptian language.

The development of hieroglyphic writing in Egypt dates to around 3200 B.C.E., about the time when pictograms began to appear in Mesopotamia. But the two scripts are so different that they probably developed independently, and the uses of writing for government and administration certainly developed far more quickly in Egypt than in Sumer. But unlike Sumerian cuneiform, Egyptian hieroglyphics never evolved into a system of phonograms. Instead, the Egyptians developed a faster, cursive script for representing hieroglyphics, called *hieratic*, which they employed for the everyday business of government and commerce. They also developed a shorthand version of hieratic that scribes could use for rapid note taking.

Little of this hieratic script remains, however, owing to the perishable nature of the medium on which it was usually written: papyrus. Produced by hammering, drying, and processing river reeds, papyrus was much lighter, easier to write on, and more transportable than the clay tablets the Sumerians used. When sewn together into scrolls, papyrus also made it possible to record and store large quantities of information in a format that could be rolled into a portable package. Production of this versatile writing material remained one of Egypt's most important industries and exports throughout antiquity and into the Middle Ages. Yet even in the arid environment of Egypt, which has preserved so many ancient artifacts that would have perished in wetter, colder climates, papyrus is fragile and subject to decay. Compared with the huge volume of papryrus documents that would have been produced, therefore, the quantity that survives is small, and this significantly limits our understanding of Old Kingdom Egypt.

The origins of the ancient Egyptian language in which these texts were written has long been a matter of debate. It can be plausibly linked to both the Semitic languages

THE ROSETTA STONE. This famous stone, carved in 196 B.C.E., preserves three translations of a single decree in three different forms of writing: hieroglyphs (top), demotic Egyptian (middle), and classical Greek (bottom). ■ *Why would scholars be able to use the classical Greek text to decipher the hieroglyphic and demotic scripts?*

EGYPTIAN WRITING. Egyptian scribes used a variety of scripts: hieroglyphics for inscriptions and religious texts (top row), a cursive hieratic script for administrative documents (middle row), and a more informal shorthand for note taking (bottom row). ■ *What are the relationships among these three forms of writing?*

of western Asia and a number of African language groups. Some historical linguists have postulated that early Egyptian might represent the survival of a root language from which the other languages of the Afro-Asiatic group evolved. The movements of people through the Nile Valley makes this theory a distinct possibility. Whatever its origins, the Egyptian language has enjoyed a long history. Eventually, it became the tongue known as Coptic, which is still used today in the liturgy of the Coptic Christian church, in Ethiopia.

Imhotep and the Step Pyramid

One of the greatest administrative officials in the history of Egypt exemplifies both the skills and the possibilities for advancement that the consummate scribe could command. Imhotep (*im-HO-tep*) rose through the ranks of the pharaoh's administration to become a sort of prime minister, the right-hand man to Djoser (*ZOH-ser*), a pharaoh of the Third Dynasty (c. 2686–2613 B.C.E.). Imhotep's expertise embraced medicine, astronomy, theology, and mathematics; but above all, he was an architect. Earlier pharaohs had already devoted enormous resources to their burial arrangements at Abydos. It was Imhotep, however, who designed the Step Pyramid, the first extant building in history constructed entirely of dressed stone. It was not only to be the final resting place of Djoser but an expression of his transcendent power as pharaoh.

Built west of the administrative capital at Memphis, the Step Pyramid towers over the desert to a height of 200 feet (61 m). Its design was based on an older form of burial monument, the *mastaba*, a low rectangular structure built entirely of brick with a flat top and sloping sides. Imhotep probably began with the mastaba pattern in mind, but he radically altered it by stacking one smaller mastaba on top of another and constructing each entirely of limestone. Surrounding this structure was a huge temple and mortuary complex, perhaps modeled after Djoser's palace. These buildings served two purposes. First and foremost, they would provide Djoser's *ka*, his spirit or life force, with a habitation and sustenance in the afterlife. Second, the design of the buildings, with their immovable doors and labyrinthine passageways, would (it was hoped) thwart tomb robbers, a chronic problem as pharaonic burials became more elaborate and more tempting to thieves.

Imhotep set a precedent to which all other Old Kingdom pharaohs would aspire. The pyramids on the plain of Giza, built during the Fourth Dynasty (2613–2494 B.C.E.), are a case in point. The Great Pyramid itself, built for the

STEP PYRAMID OF PHARAOH DJOSER. This monument to the pharaoh's power and divinity was designed by the palace official Imhotep around 2650 B.C.E.

pharaoh Khufu (*KOO-foo*; called Cheops by the Greeks), was originally 481 feet high and 756 feet along each side of its base (147 by 235 meters), was constructed from more than 2.3 million limestone blocks, and enclosed a volume of about 91 million cubic feet (2.6 million cubic meters). In ancient times, the entire pyramid was encased in gleaming white limestone and topped by a gilded capstone, as were the two massive but slightly smaller pyramids built for Khufu's successors. During the Middle Ages, the Muslim rulers of nearby Cairo had their builders strip off the pyramid's casing stones and used them to construct and fortify their new city. (The gold capstones had probably disappeared already.) But in antiquity these pyramids would have glistened brilliantly by day and glowed by night, making them visible for miles in all directions. The Greek historian Herodotus (*heh-RAH-duh-tuhs*), who toured Egypt more than 2,000 years after the pyramids were built, estimated that it must have taken 100,000 laborers twenty years to build the Great Pyramid. This is probably an exaggeration, but it is a measure of the impression these monuments made.

Once thought to have been the work of slaves, the pyramids were in fact raised by tens of thousands of peasant workers, who labored most intensively on the pyramids while their fields were under water during the Nile's annual flood. Some workers may have been conscripts, but most probably participated willingly, since these projects glorified the living god who served as their link to the cosmic order. Still, the investment of human and material resources required to build the pyramids put strains on Egyptian society. Control over the lives of individual Egyptians increased, and the number of administrative officials employed by the state grew ever larger. So too did the contrast between the lifestyle of the pharaoh's splendid

PYRAMIDS AT GIZA. The Great Pyramid of Khufu (Cheops), in the center, was completed c. 2560 B.C.E.

court at Memphis and that of Egyptian society as a whole. At the same time, a gap was opening between the pretensions of the pharaohs and the continuing loyalties of Egyptians to their local gods and local leaders.

The End of the Old Kingdom

For reasons that are not entirely clear, the Fifth and Sixth Dynasties of the Old Kingdom (2494–2181 B.C.E.) witnessed the slow erosion of pharaonic power. Although pyramid construction continued, the monuments of this period are less impressive in design, craftsmanship, and size, perhaps mirroring the diminishing prestige of the pharaohs who ordered them built. Instead, the priesthood of Ra at Nekhen, which was the center of worship for the god Horus and the place where Narmer's unification of Egypt was memorialized, began to assert its own authority over that of the pharaoh. Ultimately, it declared that the pharaoh was not an incarnation of Horus or Ra, but merely the god's earthly son. This was a blow to the heart of the pharaoh's political theology. A more practical threat was the growing power of the pharaoh's nomarchs, whose increased authority in the provinces allowed them to become a hereditary local nobility: precisely what the vigorous kings of earlier dynasties had refused to permit. These nobles became so influential that one Sixth Dynasty pharaoh, Pepy I, even married into their ranks.

Scholars are uncertain as to how certain priests and local officials were able to take power away from the pharaonic center. It may be that the extraordinarily costly building efforts of the Fourth Dynasty had overtaxed the economy while the continued channeling of resources to the royal capital at Memphis increased shortages and resentments in the provinces. Other evidence points to changing climatic conditions that may have disrupted the regular inundations of the Nile, leading to famine in the countryside. Meanwhile, small states were beginning to form to the south in Nubia, perhaps in response to Egyptian aggression. With better organization and equipment, the Nubians may have restricted Egyptian access to precious-metal deposits in and around the First Cataract, further crippling the Egyptian economy.

As a result of these developments, the pharaoh's power diminished. Local governors and religious authorities began to emerge as the only effective guarantors of stability and order. By 2160 B.C.E., which marks the beginning of what historians call the First Intermediate Period, Egypt had effectively ceased to exist as a unified entity. The central authority of the pharaoh in Memphis collapsed, and a more ancient distribution of power reemerged: a northern center of influence based at Herakleopolis was opposed by a southern regime headquartered at Thebes, with families from each region claiming to be the legitimate pharaohs of all Egypt.

Compared with the centralized authority of the Old Kingdom, this looks like chaos. But redistribution of power always leads to the opening of new opportunities in any society. In Egypt, wealth became much more widely and evenly distributed than it had been, as did access to education, means for the creation of art, and possibilities for personal advancement. Resources that the pharaoh's court at Memphis had once monopolized now remained in the provinces, enabling local elites to emerge as both protectors of society and as patrons of local artisans. The result was a much wider and more rapid dispersal of cultural forms and goods throughout Egyptian society than had been possible under the old regime. Many of these arts and luxuries—including elaborate rites for the dead—had been developed originally at the pharaoh's court and limited to it. Now, however, they became available to Egyptian society at large.

EGYPTIAN CULTURE AND SOCIETY

As we noted above, the unique environment of Egypt and the special benefits it conferred on its inhabitants were construed as divine gifts, renewed each year through the mediation of the pharaoh. From what we can discern, this meant that Egyptians saw themselves as superior to all other civilizations. A person was either an Egyptian or a foreigner, and the lines between the two were absolute. For

Egyptians, it was simply self-evident that their country—nurtured by the Nile and guarded by the deserts and seas that surrounded it—was the center of the universe.

Religion and Worldview

Although the Egyptians told a variety of stories that dealt with the creation of their world, these were not greatly concerned with how humanity came to exist. Rather, what mattered was the means by which all life was created and re-created in an endless cycle of renewal. Unlike the peoples of Mesopotamia, who were constantly faced with new and terrible challenges—both environmental and political—the Egyptians experienced existence as predictably repetitive. This was mirrored in their perception of the cosmos. At the heart of Egyptian religion lay the myth of the gods Osiris and Isis, not only brother and sister but husband and wife, two of the gods most fundamental to Egyptian belief.

Osiris was, in a sense, the first pharaoh: the first god to hold kingship on earth. His brother Seth, however, wanted the throne for himself. So Seth betrayed and killed Osiris, sealing his body in a coffin. But their loyal sister Isis retrieved the corpse and managed to revive it long enough to conceive her brother's child, the god Horus. Enraged by this, Seth seized Osiris's body and hacked it to pieces, spreading the remains all over Egypt. (All of Egypt could therefore claim to be part of Osiris, a belief witnessed by shrines dedicated to him throughout the land.) Still undeterred, Isis sought the help of Anubis, the god of the afterlife. Together, they found, reassembled, and preserved the scattered portions of Osiris's body, thus inventing the practice of mummification. Then Horus, with the help of his mother, managed to defeat Seth. Osiris was avenged and revived as god of the underworld. Like Egypt itself, he could not be killed, and the cycle of his death, dismemberment, and resurrection was reflected in the yearly renewal of life along the Nile.

Life and Death in Ancient Egypt

In addition to embodying Egypt's continual regeneration, Osiris exemplified the Egyptian attitude toward death, which was very different from the Sumerians' rather bleak view. For the Egyptians, death was a rite of passage, a journey to be endured on the way to an afterlife that was more or less like one's earthly existence, only much better. To be sure, the journey was full of dangers. After death, the individual body's ka had to roam the Duat, the underworld, searching for the House of Judgment. There, Osiris and

PHARAOH MENKAURE AND HIS QUEEN, KHAMERERNEBTY II. A sculpture from the Fourth Dynasty, c. 2500 B.C.E., shows this queen as her husband's royal partner.

forty-two other judges would decide the ka's fate. Demons and evil spirits might try to frustrate the ka's quest to reach the House of Judgment, and the journey might take some time. But if successful and judged worthy, the deceased would enjoy immortality as an aspect of Osiris.

Egyptian funerary rites aimed to emulate the example set by Isis and Anubis, who had carefully preserved the parts of Osiris's body and enabled his afterlife. This is why the Egyptians developed their sophisticated techniques of embalming, whereby many of the body's vital organs were removed and then treated with chemicals—except for the heart, which played a key role in the ka's final judgment. A portrait mask was then placed on the mummy before burial, so that the deceased would be recognizable despite being wrapped in hundreds of yards of linen. To sustain the ka on his or her journey, food, clothing, utensils, weapons, and other items of vital importance would be placed in the grave along with the body.

The Instruction of Ptah-Hotep

Egyptian literature often took the form of "instructions" to or from important personages, offering advice to those in public life. This document declares itself to be the advice of a high-ranking official of the Old Kingdom to his son and successor, perhaps composed around 2450 B.C.E. However, the earliest surviving text dates from the Middle Kingdom period.

Be not arrogant because of your knowledge, and be not puffed up because you are a learned man. Take counsel with the ignorant as with the learned, for the limits of art cannot be reached, and no artist is perfect in his skills. Good speech is more hidden than the precious greenstone, and yet it is found among slave girls at the millstones.

. . . If you are a leader commanding the conduct of many, seek out every good aim, so that your policy may be without error. A great thing is *ma'at*, enduring and surviving; it has not been upset since the time of Osiris. He who departs from its laws is punished. It is the right path for him who knows nothing. Wrongdoing has never brought its venture safe to port. Evil may win riches, but it is the strength of *ma'at* that endures long, and a man can say, "I learned it from my father." . . . If you wish to prolong friendship in a house which you enter as master, brother, or friend, or anyplace that you enter, beware of approaching the women. No place in which that is done prospers. There is no wisdom in it.

A thousand men are turned aside from their own good because of a little moment, like a dream, by tasting which death is reached. . . . He who lusts after women, no plan of his will succeed. . . . If you are a worthy man sitting in the council of his lord, confine your attention to excellence. Silence is more valuable than chatter. Speak only when you know you can resolve difficulties. He who gives good counsel is an artist, for speech is more difficult than any craft.

Source: Nels M. Bailkey, ed., *Readings in Ancient History: Thought and Experience from Gilgamesh to St. Augustine*, 5th ed. (Boston: 1995), pp. 39–42.

Questions for Analysis

1. According to Ptah-Hotep, what are the most important attributes of a man engaged in public life? What are the most dangerous pitfalls and temptations he will encounter?

2. Why does Ptah-Hotep emphasize the importance of acting in accordance with *ma'at*? How does this idea of *ma'at* compare with that in the "Prophecies of Neferty" (see page 35)?

3. Recall what you have learned about the changes in Egyptian politics and society. What might indicate that Ptah-Hotep lived during the prosperous Fifth Dynasty of the Old Kingdom? How might these instructions have resonated differently with later readers of the Middle Kingdom?

"Coffin texts," or books of the dead, also accompanied the body and were designed to speed the ka's journey. They contained special instructions, including magic spells and ritual incantations, that would help the ka travel through the underworld and prepare it for the final test. They also described the "negative confession" the ka would make before the court of Osiris, a formal denial of offenses committed in life. The god Anubis would then weigh the deceased's heart against the principle of **ma'at**: truth, order, justice. Because *ma'at* was often envisioned as a goddess wearing a plumed headdress, a feather from this headdress would be placed in the scales, along with the heart, at the time of judgment; only if the heart was light (empty of wrongdoing) and in perfect balance with the feather would the ka achieve immortality.

Throughout the era of the Old Kingdom, the privilege of undergoing these preparations (and thus of ensuring immortality) was reserved for the royal family alone. By the time of the Middle Kingdom, however, it was becoming possible for many Egyptians to ensure that their bodies would participate in these rituals, too.

As noted above, this careful manner of confronting death has often led to the erroneous assumption that ancient Egyptians were pessimistic. In actuality their practices and beliefs were inherently life-affirming, bolstered by confidence in the resilience of nature and the renewal

FUNERARY PAPYRUS. This scene, inscribed on a papyrus scroll dating from the Thirtieth Dynasty (380–343 B.C.), shows the heart of the princess for whom this book was prepared being weighed in a balance (left) before the god Osiris. On the other side of the balance (right) are the symbols for life (the *ankh*) and the feather of the goddess Ma'at.

of creation. Binding together this endless cycle was *ma'at*, the serene order of the universe with which the individual must remain in harmony, and against which each person's ka would be weighed after death. And embodying *ma'at* on earth was the pharaoh, the earthly manifestation of all gods. For most of the third millennium, thanks to a long period of successful harvests and peace guaranteed by Egypt's geographic isolation from the outside world, the Egyptians were able to maintain their belief in this perfectly ordered paradise and the pharaoh that ensured it. But when that order broke down, so too did their confidence in the pharaoh's power.

Egyptian Science

Given the powerful impression conveyed by their monumental architecture, it may seem surprising that the ancient Egyptians lagged far behind the Sumerians and Akkadians in science and mathematics, as well as in the application of new technologies. Only in the calculation of time did the Egyptians make notable advances, because their close observation of the sun for religious and agricultural reasons led them to develop a solar calendar that was far more accurate than the Mesopotamian lunar calendar. Whereas the Sumerians have bequeathed to us their means of dividing and measuring the day, the Egyptian calendar is the direct ancestor of the Julian calendar adopted for Rome by Julius Caesar in 45 B.C.E. (see Chapter 5) and later corrected by Pope Gregory XIII in 1582 C.E.: this is the calendar we use today. The Egyptians also devised some effective irrigation and water-control systems, but they did not adopt such labor-saving devices as the wheel until much later than the Sumerians, perhaps because the available pool of peasant manpower was virtually inexhaustible, so that the necessity for such innovations was not pressing.

The Social Pyramid

The social pyramid of Old Kingdom Egypt was extremely steep. At its apex stood the pharaoh and his extended family, whose prestige and power set them entirely apart from all other Egyptians. Below them was a class of nobles, whose primary role was to serve as priests and officials of the pharaoh's government; scribes were usually recruited and trained from among the sons of these families. All of these Egyptian elites lived in considerable luxury. They owned extensive estates, exotic possessions, and fine furniture. They kept dogs and cats and monkeys as pets, and hunted and fished for sport.

Beneath this tiny minority was everyone else. Most Egyptians lived in crowded conditions in simple mud-brick dwellings. During a period of prosperity, master craftsmen—jewelers, goldsmiths, and the like—could improve their own conditions and those of their families by fulfilling the needs of the wealthy, but they did not constitute anything like a middle class. Other skilled professionals—potters, weavers, masons, bricklayers, brewers, merchants, and schoolteachers—also enjoyed some measure of respect as well as a higher standard of living. The vast majority of Egyptians, however, were peasants who provided the labor for agriculture and construction. Beneath them were slaves, typically captives from foreign wars rather than native Egyptians.

Yet despite the enormous demands the pharaohs placed on Egypt's wealth, this Egyptian social hierarchy does not appear to have been particularly oppressive. Commoners' belief in the pharaoh's divinity made them willing subjects, as did the material benefits of living in a stable, well-governed society. Even slaves had certain legal rights, including the ability to own, sell, and bequeath personal property.

Unfortunately, though, the written laws and other documentary practices produced by the lugals of Mesopotamia do not have any Old Kingdom parallels. The Egyptians of this era apparently had no need for written laws beyond what was customary in their communities or what was proclaimed as law by their pharaoh. This makes it difficult for historians to reconstruct their lives in any detail.

The Status of Women

Although we have no formal law codes to consult, there is evidence that Egyptian women enjoyed unusual freedoms by the standards of the ancient world. Female commoners were recognized as persons in their own right and were allowed to initiate lawsuits (including suits for divorce), to defend themselves in court and to act as witnesses, to possess property of their own, and to dispose of it. And they could do all of this without the sanction of a male guardian or representative, as was typically required in most societies until the twentieth century. Women were not allowed to undergo formal scribal training, but surviving personal notes exchanged between high-born ladies suggest that some could read and even write.

Normally, women were barred from holding high office, apart from that of priestess and also, more important, queen. Indeed, queens are often represented as the partners of their royal husbands and were certainly instrumental in ruling alongside them: note the proud, confident bearing of Queen Khamerernebty II (*kah-mehr-en-EB-tee*; see image on page 30). And occasionally, a woman from the royal family might assume pharaonic authority for a time, as did Queen Nimaathap on behalf of her son Djoser before he came of age. Some women may even have ruled in their own right; this was certainly the case during the New Kingdom (see Chapter 2).

Among the peasantry, gender divisions were less clearly defined—as is the case in most rural societies. Peasant women often worked in the fields during the harvest alongside men and carried out a number of vital tasks in the community. The limitations of our sources, however, mean that we can only glimpse the lives of these people through the eyes of their social superiors.

FOOD FOR THE JOURNEY OF THE KA. These wooden models show peasants plowing, grinding grain, baking bread, brewing beer, and slaughtering a steer. Bread and beer were the staple foods of ancient Egypt; beef was too expensive for ordinary consumption, but cattle were frequently sacrificed as funeral offerings. Such models were placed in Middle Kingdom tombs to provide food for the afterlife.

Whatever their status, it seems that women did not enjoy sexual equality. Although most Egyptians practiced monogamy, wealthy men could and did keep a number of lesser wives, concubines, and female slaves; and any Egyptian man, married or not, enjoyed freedoms that were denied to women, who were subject to severe punishments under the law if they were viewed as guilty of any misconduct.

The Widening Horizons of the Middle Kingdom, 2055–c. 1650 B.C.E.

After the disruption of Old Kingdom authority around 2160 B.C.E., warfare between two competing pharaonic dynasties would continue for more than a century. Then, in 2055 B.C.E., the Theban king Mentuhotep (*men-too-HO-tep*) II conquered the northerners and declared himself the ruler of a reunited Egypt. His reign marks the beginning of Egypt's **Middle Kingdom** and the reestablishment of a central government—but this time based in Thebes rather than Memphis. The head of this new government was Mentuhotep's chief supporter, Amenemhet (*ah-meh-NEHM-het*), who actually seized power after the king's death and established himself and his descendants as Egypt's Twelfth Dynasty. This succession of remarkable pharaohs remained in power for nearly 200 years. This new dynasty began to expand Egypt's influence and capacity for trade with its southern neighbors. This brought them into contact with the land of Nubia (present-day Sudan), whose sandy soil contained numerous rich gold deposits. This was the gateway to the rest of Africa. Indeed, available evidence suggests that there were already close ties between Egypt and Nubia, and that these provided a foothold for Egyptian expansion farther down the Nile, as well as to the coast of the Red Sea in what is now Somalia. Recent archeological discoveries have revealed an enormous trove of funerary texts in the Meroitic language of this region: the oldest known writing system of sub-Saharan Africa. These are still being deciphered, but they shed an especially bright light on the high status of women in Nubia, a matrilineal society in which men and women both traced their ancestry through the female line.

Meanwhile, diplomatic relations with the smaller states and principalities of Palestine and Syria led to decisive Egyptian political and economic influence in this region. Yet these lands were not incorporated into Egypt; instead, Amenemhet constructed the Walls of the Prince in Sinai, to guard against incursions by foreigners. The huge

NUBIAN STELE. In 2017–2018, an enormous necropolis (literally, a "city of the dead") was discovered along the Nile in the ancient land of Nubia (now Sudan). Dating from the seventh to fourth centuries B.C.E., it includes more than a hundred tombs and over eighty brick pyramids and other monuments built by the people of Meroë, whose written language (known as Meroitic) is one of the oldest in Africa. One of these monuments is a stone stele or upright slab with an inscription honoring Ataqeloula, the matriarch of a powerful family.

fortifications symbolize a marked shift in the Egyptian outlook on the world. The placid serenity epitomized by *ma'at* and the shared devotion to the pharaoh that had built the pyramids had been challenged. Egyptians could no longer be dismissive of outsiders or disregard the world beyond their borders. Unlike their Old Kingdom ancestors, the Egyptians of the Middle Kingdom were not turned inward.

Their attitude toward the pharaoh also seems to have changed. Although he continued to enjoy a special position as a divine representative, his authority did not derive solely from this source. Rather, the pharaohs of the Middle Kingdom represented themselves in a new light, as good shepherds, tenders of their flock. Only by diligently protecting Egypt from a hostile outside world could a pharaoh provide the peace, prosperity, and security desired by his subjects; his alignment with *ma'at* was now clearly conditional, and it had to be earned.

Analyzing Primary Sources

The Prophecies of Neferty

This text presents itself as a prophecy foretelling the disasters that would strike Egypt during the First Intermediate Period. In fact, it was composed during the Middle Kingdom, shortly after the death of the pharaoh Amenemhet I, the founder of the Twelfth Dynasty. By contrasting the disorders that preceded Amenemhet's reign with the peace that he established, the document seeks to justify Amenemhet's usurpation of the throne and perhaps to legitimize his son's succession.

rise, oh my heart! Weep for this land wherein you were born! Falsehood is as the flood, and behold, evil is spoken with impunity.... The land perishes, and there is no one who cares for it. There is no one who speaks out, no one who makes lament.... Perished and gone are those joyful places, the fish ponds where dwell fish-eating birds, ponds alive with fish and fowl. All joy has been driven out, and the land is plunged into anguish by those voracious Asiatics who rove throughout the land. Foes have appeared in the east, Asiatics have entered Egypt. We have no (border) fortress, for foreigners now hold it, and there is no one to heed who the plunderers are. One may expect attack by night, the fortress will be breached and sleep driven from all eyes.... The land is destitute, although its rulers are numerous, it is ruined, but its taxes are immense. Sparse is the grain, but great is the measure, for it is distributed as if it were abundant.

But then there shall come a king from the south. His name will be Ameny, justified. He will be the son of a woman of Ta-Sety [Nubia], an offspring of the royal house of Nekhen. He shall receive the White Crown, he shall wear the Red Crown, he shall unite the Two Powers.... The people of his time will rejoice, for this son of a man will establish his name for ever and eternity.... The Asiatics will fall before his sword, the Libyans will fall before his fire, rebels will fall before his wrath, and enemies will fall through awe of him....

Then Ma'at will return to her throne, and Chaos will be driven off. Joyful will he be who will see (these things), he who will serve the king.

Source: William Kelly Simpson, ed., *The Literature of Ancient Egypt: An Anthology of Stories, Instruction, Stelae, Autobiography, and Poetry*, 3rd ed. (New Haven, CT: 2003), pp. 214–20.

Questions for Analysis

1. In what ways does the "Prophecies of Neferty" highlight the anxieties of Middle Kingdom Egyptians? What caused these anxieties?

2. Why would the author of this document choose to present it as a prophecy about the future, rather than as a description of current events?

Portraits of the great pharaohs of the Twelfth Dynasty mirror this anxious outlook on the world. The literature of the Middle Kingdom also expresses the general change in attitude. Among the most popular of the new literary forms were manuals ostensibly written by or for kings, detailing the duties and perils of high office and offering advice for dealing with difficult situations. These include the *Instruction of Amenemhet*, which purports to be life lessons handed down by this pharaoh to his son from beyond the grave, and *The Instruction of Ptah-Hotep* (see **Analyzing Primary Sources** above), an example of Egyptian "wisdom literature" attributed to a court official of the Old Kingdom, which achieved a wider readership in this new era—much as Machiavelli's *The Prince* (see Chapter 12) has become a "self-help" book for business executives and politicians in our own time.

Ptah-Hotep's teaching is upbeat and practical; by contrast, the examples of this genre produced under the Middle Kingdom are bleakly pragmatic. A pharaoh must trust no one: not a brother, not a friend, not intimate companions. He must crush the ambitions of local nobles with ruthless ferocity. He must always be on the lookout for potential trouble. In return for his exertions on behalf of his people, he should expect neither gratitude nor reward; he should expect only that each year will bring new dangers and more pressing challenges. Reading between the lines, we discern that Egyptians' sense of their own superiority—a product of their former isolation and their comparatively benign environment—had been shattered. They saw themselves being drawn into a much wider world, and in the course of the next millennium they would become more fully a part of it.

CONCLUSION

Whereas the story of the Tower of Babel records the legendary loss of a shared language, this chapter shows that people of the distant past can still communicate with us. The marks they have left on the landscape, the remains of their daily lives, their written records, and their very bodies make it possible for historians to piece together evidence and to make sense of it. And every year new sources come to light, meaning that we have to be ready to revise—constantly—our understanding of what happened in the past.

Although this chapter has emphasized the differences between the early civilizations of Mesopotamia and Egypt, it is worth noting some significant similarities. Both developed the fundamental technologies of writing at about the

After You Read This Chapter

 Go to **INQUIZITIVE** to see what you've learned—and learn what you've missed— with personalized feedback along the way.

REVIEWING THE OBJECTIVES

- The study of the distant past is challenging because written sources are rare. What other sources of information do historians use?
- All civilizations require the same basic conditions for survival and share certain characteristics. What are they?
- The cities of Mesopotamia remained largely independent from one another yet shared a common culture. Why was this the case?
- Hammurabi's efforts created a new precedent for governance in Mesopotamia. How did he achieve this?
- The civilizations of ancient Mesopotamia and Egypt differ in profound ways. What were the major causes of their differences?

same time. This facilitated political alliances, long-distance trade, and the transmission of vital information to posterity. During the third millennium, both underwent a process of political consolidation, an elaboration of religious ritual, and a melding of spiritual and political leadership. Both engaged in massive building and irrigation projects, and both commanded material and human resources on an enormous scale. At the same time, each of these civilizations cultivated an inward focus. Although they had some contact with each other, and some transfers of information and technology probably took place, they had few significant political or cultural interactions. For the most part, they inhabited separate worlds. This relative isolation was about to change, however. The next millennium would see the emergence of large-scale, land-based empires that would transform life in Mesopotamia, Egypt, and the lands that lay between them. These are the developments we examine in Chapter 2.

PEOPLE, IDEAS, AND EVENTS IN CONTEXT

- What fundamental changes associated with the **NEOLITHIC REVOLUTION** made early civilizations possible? Why is this considered to be the beginning of a new epoch, the **ANTHROPOCENE**?
- What new technologies allowed the **SUMERIANS** to master the environment of **MESOPOTAMIA**? How did these technologies contribute to the development of a new, urbanized society?
- By contrast, why did the Nile River foster a very different civilization and enable the centralized authority of the **PHARAOH**?
- How do the differences between **CUNEIFORM** and **HIEROGLYPHS** reflect the different circumstances in which they were invented and the different uses to which they were put?
- In what ways are the **EPIC OF GILGAMESH** and the **CODE OF HAMMURABI** rich sources of information about the civilizations of Sumer and **BABYLON**?
- How do the **ZIGGURATS** of Mesopotamia and the pyramids of Egypt exemplify different forms of power, different ideas about the gods, and different beliefs about the afterlife?
- Why was the worldview of ancient Egyptians, which was strongly reflected in the concept of *MA'AT* during the **OLD KINGDOM**, altered in significant ways by the time of the **MIDDLE KINGDOM**?

THINKING ABOUT CONNECTIONS

- How do the surviving sources of any period limit the kinds of questions that we can ask and answer about the distant past? In your view, have sources for this early era been undervalued? For example, if writing had not been developed in Mesopotamia and Egypt, what would we still be able to know about the civilizations of these two regions?
- What features of ancient civilizations do modern civilizations share? What might be the implications of these shared ideas, social structures, and technologies?
- In particular, what lessons can we draw from humans' tendency to manipulate their environment? How should knowledge of the distant past influence current debates over sustainability and climate change?

STORY LINES

- During the second millennium B.C.E., new peoples migrated into Eurasia, around the eastern Mediterranean, spreading a related set of Indo-European languages that are the ancestors of several modern language groups.

- In Egypt, the rise of the Eighteenth Dynasty fostered imperial expansion beyond the Nile Valley for the first time.

- During the Late Bronze Age, an interconnected network of alliances bound societies together in new ways. But this civilization was eventually destroyed by the raids of mysterious Sea Peoples.

- In the wake of these invasions, both oppressive new empires and smaller-scale states emerged.

- In the Iron Age, the worship of Yahweh among the Hebrews and of Ahura-Mazda among the Persians fostered a new view of the world: one in which a single creator god ruled over all peoples.

Before You Read This Chapter

CHRONOLOGY

1900–1500 B.C.E.	Minoan civilization flourishes
1800–1400 B.C.E.	Formation of the Hittite Empire
1792 B.C.E.	Rise of Babylon under Hammurabi
1650–1550 B.C.E.	Hyksos invasion of Egypt and Second Intermediate Period
1600–1200 B.C.E.	Mycenaean civilization flourishes
1550–1075 B.C.E.	New Kingdom of Egypt established
c. 1200 B.C.E.	Invasions of the Sea Peoples begin
1100–1000 B.C.E.	Philistine dominance in Palestine
1000–973 B.C.E.	Hebrew kingdom consolidated
924 B.C.E.	Israel and Judah divided
883–859 B.C.E.	Neo-Assyrian Empire founded
722 B.C.E.	Kingdom of Israel destroyed
612–605 B.C.E.	Fall of the Neo-Assyrian Empire
586 B.C.E.	Fall of the kingdom of Judah
539–486 B.C.E	Persian Empire consolidated

Peoples, Gods, and Empires: 1700–500 B.C.E.

CORE OBJECTIVES

- **DESCRIBE** the impact of new migrations and settlements ancient civilizations.

- **DEFINE** the differences between Egypt's New Kingdom and the previous Old and Middle Kingdoms.

- **EXPLAIN** the workings of transnational networks during the late Bronze Age.

- **IDENTIFY** the new empires and kingdoms that emerged during the Iron Age.

- **UNDERSTAND** the historical importance of monotheism.

Accoording to Hesiod, a Greek poet who flourished during the eighth century B.C.E., all of human history falls into five ages. The dawn of time was a golden age, when men lived like gods. Everything was good then, food was plentiful, and work was easy. The next age was silver, when men took gods for granted, killed one another, and lived in dishonor. So the gods destroyed them, sending a mighty flood that spared only the family of Deucalion, the son of wily Prometheus, who built an ark. Then came the age of bronze, when everything was made of bronze—houses and armor and weapons and tools. Giants fought incessantly from huge strongholds, causing destruction so great that no man's name survives. The time following was short but bright, a heroic age, the time of men who traveled with Theseus and fought with Achilles and sailed with Odysseus, men whose names will live forever. But Hesiod's own age was iron: a dull age, a time of tedium and strife and bickering and petty feuds.

Hesiod's periodization captures an understanding of history that had evolved with humanity itself and that reflects actual developments. The stories he knew told of a time before cities and the need for agriculture. They recalled a time when the harmony between gods and men broke down, and the human race was saved by one man's ingenuity: the Sumerian Utnapishtim, the Hebrew Noah, or the Greek Deucalion. These stories chronicled the wars of the age we still call Bronze, when the enormous, abandoned palaces still visible in Hesiod's day were built. And they remembered the race of heroes whose glory was measured by their abiding fame, and who bequeathed to us a further round of stories. Thanks to new archaeological finds, new linguistic discoveries, and new efforts at decoding the historical record, we can both confirm and correct Hesiod's perspective on the past.

In the second millennium B.C.E., Western Civilizations were transformed by the arrival of new peoples and by the emergence of extensive land-based empires built up through systematic military conquest. These migrations and conquests caused enormous upheaval, but they also led to cultural contact and economic integration. The movement of people, goods, and ideas not only encompassed the Mediterranean but extended from Scandinavia to China. The last few centuries of the Bronze Age (1500–1200 B.C.E.) were a period of intense diplomacy, trade, and exchange. By the thirteenth century B.C.E., peoples from the southern

Transformations in the Bronze Age	
Semitic peoples migrate to Mesopotamia	2000 B.C.E.
Indo-European peoples arrive in the Near East	2000 B.C.E.
Assyrians organize trade networks	1900 B.C.E.
Rise of Old Babylonian Empire	1800 B.C.E.
Creation of Hittite, Kassite, and Mitanni kingdoms	1800–1400 B.C.E.

MIGRATIONS OF THE BRONZE AGE, 2000–1400 B.C.E. Notice the geographical relationships among the older centers of Mesopotamia and Egypt, and among newer civilizations such as Babylonia, Assyria, Phoenicia, and the Hittite Empire. ▪ *Which of these emerging cultures was most likely to come into contact with Egypt, and why?* ▪ *Where did the Indo-European peoples come from?* ▪ *What was the impact of Indo-European settlements?*

Balkans to the western fringes of Iran had been drawn into a wide-ranging web of relationships.

Yet this extraordinary system proved more fragile than its participants could have imagined. Around 1200 B.C.E., a wave of mysterious invasions led to the destruction of nearly every established Mediterranean civilization. As a result, around the turn of the first millennium B.C.E., we enter a world organized along profoundly different lines. In this Iron Age, iron would slowly replace bronze as the primary component of tools and weapons. New and more brutal empires would come to power, while new ideas about the divine and its relationship to humanity would emerge. Two of the Western world's most enduring religious traditions—Judaism and Zoroastrianism (zoh-roh-AHS-tree-an-ism)—were born, fundamentally altering conceptions of ethics, politics, and the natural world. This age would prove a fateful historical crossroads, as elements both old and new combined to reconfigure the ancient world.

INDO-EUROPEAN LANGUAGES AND PEOPLES

In 1786, a British judge serving in India made a discovery that transformed the prevailing understanding of history. Turning his spare time to the study of Sanskrit, the ancient language of South Asia, Sir William Jones discovered that it shares its grammar and vocabulary with ancient Greek and Latin, to an extent inexplicable by sheer coincidence. His interest piqued, he then examined the early Germanic and Celtic languages of Europe and the Old Persian language of Mesopotamia and found that they also exhibit marked similarities. He concluded that all of these languages must have evolved from a common source.

Within another generation, the ancient language whose existence Jones had hypothesized, and the later languages derived from it, would be labeled **Indo-European**, reflecting a wide distribution from India to Ireland. The biblical story of mankind's shared language, the story of the Tower of Babel, turns out to be partly true.

Since then, scholars have greatly enlarged our understanding of Indo-European languages and their speakers. Yet much remains controversial. Was the original form of the Indo-European language spoken by a single population at some point in time? If so, when and where? How did it spread? Can the diffusion of its speakers be determined archaeologically, by tracing characteristic pottery types and burial rites? Or are such practices distinct from language? At the moment, we have no clear answers to any such questions. It is certain, however, that Indo-European linguistic forms began to appear in western Asia and the eastern Mediterranean shortly after 2000 B.C.E. Around this same time, a group of Indo-European speakers also moved into the Aegean basin, where the resulting language became an early form of Greek. Other Indo-European speakers went east; some may have reached western China.

These were not the only new peoples on the move. As we noted in Chapter 1, Semitic-speaking peoples were also making their mark, beginning with the Akkadians and the Amorites, from whose ranks Hammurabi came. The Assyrians, the Phoenicians, and the Canaanites would also become prominent. These new immigrants and settlers did not wipe out existing cultures; rather, they built on established patterns of urban life and organization. But their collective impact was enormous.

AN ANCIENT WAR CHARIOT. A light, spoke-wheeled chariot, developed for warfare, is here being used for lion hunting by the Assyrian king Assurnasirpal II (883–859 B.C.E.), whose reign is discussed on page 59.

Immigrants in Anatolia

By 1900 B.C.E., a nomadic people called the Assyrians had become caravan merchants whose extensive trade networks stretched across Anatolia and Mesopotamia. They did not seek military dominance over the region; instead, they relied on the protection of local rulers and, in turn, made these rulers rich. They also served as advisers and officials, and they married into important urban families. In the process, they carried Mesopotamian civilization and its trappings into far-flung regions of the world.

In the wake of these developments, new population groups were attracted to Anatolia, northern Syria, and Mesopotamia. The most formidable of these were the Hittites, an Indo-European-speaking people who arrived around 2000 B.C.E. In contrast to the Assyrians, the Hittites were military conquerors and colonists who imposed themselves and their language on the peoples they vanquished. By 1700 B.C.E., they had integrated many Hittite-dominated city-states into a larger kingdom. About fifty years later, they captured a strategic mountain stronghold, Hattusas, from which their king took a new name, Hattusilis.

Under Hattusilis and his successors, the Hittites' warrior aristocracy fielded the most fearsome army of the Bronze Age. They were quick to adopt the latest technologies, including the horse-powered chariot; for up to this point, the horse—as a mount or an engine of war—had been unknown outside the steppes of central Asia. The Hittites' light, horse-powered chariots became terrifying death machines, transporting archers rapidly around the battlefield. But the Hittites also adopted the more peaceful practices of those they conquered, using cuneiform to record their own language and laws. They also sought to control trade routes, particularly the overland trade in copper and arsenic, the raw materials for making bronze. By 1595 B.C.E., they had moved southeastward into Mesopotamia, capturing and sacking Babylon.

A century later, the Kassites, another new people, moved into the devastated city and took control of it. For the next 500 years, they presided over a largely peaceful and prosperous Babylonian realm. The Hittites, however, continued to dominate the region, until they were checked by the arrival of a people known as the Mitanni, who moved into Syria around 1550 B.C.E. The Mitanni extended their influence along the eastern Mediterranean coastline, forging an alliance with the Egyptians around 1400 B.C.E. Although Mitanni power was short-lived, it served to increase the links between the peoples of western Asia and the kingdom of the pharaohs.

THE NEW KINGDOM OF EGYPT

As we have seen, Egypt's Middle Kingdom had been reshaped by the many internal changes of the First Intermediate Period, chiefly the redistribution of wealth and power. Now it was further transformed by external forces—again through the dynamic movement of new peoples in this age from western Asia and Nubia. Some of these came to Egypt as immigrants; others were hired as mercenaries. And for a while, a strategy of accommodation preserved Egypt from large-scale armed attack and fostered commercial exchange with neighboring regions. But around 1700 B.C.E., Egypt was invaded for the first time since the unification of the Upper and Lower Kingdoms. The invaders' origins and identity remain mysterious; the Egyptians called them simply Hyksos (HIHK-sohs), "rulers of foreign lands." From their power base in the eastern delta of the Nile, the Hyksos began to project their authority over most of Lower Egypt.

With this conquest, the central authority of the pharaoh once again dissolved, and Egypt entered what historians call the Second Intermediate Period (c. 1650–1550 B.C.E.). Significantly, however, the Hyksos did not destroy the machinery of pharaonic government in Lower Egypt, but took steps to legitimize their rule in accordance with Egyptian precedents. Some Hyksos rulers even incorporated the name of the sun god Ra into their own names. In Upper Egypt, by contrast, Hyksos power was weak. Here, a native pharaonic regime maintained a tenuous independence at the capital city of Thebes, although it sometimes had to acknowledge the suzerainty (overlordship) of the foreigners to the north.

This relatively short period of Hyksos domination was regarded by later Egyptians as the greatest shame of their history. The Hyksos established Lower Egypt as a significant power, filling the vacuum left by the Hittites. Moreover, their conquest weakened Egyptian dominion over the peoples of Nubia, who were able to establish an independent kingdom with its capital at Meroë (MEH-ro-hay). As we noted in Chapter 1, the Meroitic language is the oldest sub-Saharan language to be preserved in writing, and it reflects the strength of the kingdom's culture and identity. Kush therefore posed a much greater threat to the native dynasty at Thebes than to the Hyksos in Lower Egypt—but it also provided an additional incentive to southern pharaohs who were determined to oust the Hyksos usurpers and reunify Egypt. Ultimately, they succeeded. By the end of the sixteenth century B.C.E., the pharaoh Ahmose had driven out the Hyksos, establishing the Eighteenth Dynasty and the New Kingdom of Egypt.

The Pharaohs of the Eighteenth Dynasty

Under the Eighteenth Dynasty, Egyptian civilization reached the height of its magnificence and power, which it now exercised more widely than ever before. Although many Egyptian traditions were renewed and strengthened, the dynamism of the New Kingdom—particularly its new focus on imperial expansion—changed the very fabric of Egyptian life, which had never looked far beyond the narrow world of the fertile Nile Valley.

The Eighteenth Dynasty ruled Egypt for more than two and a half centuries, and striking developments took place during this period. Most important was the rise of an aristocracy whose wealth was acquired through warfare and the winning of lands (with slaves to work them), which they received from the pharaoh as rewards for service. The Eighteenth Dynasty itself was forged in battle, something that had not been true of a ruling family since the time of King Narmer, over a millennium and a half earlier (see Chapter 1). Ahmose, the man who expelled the Hyksos, had been reared by the warrior queen Ahhotep, who had ruled Upper Egypt in her own right. His eventual successor, Thutmose I (c. 1504–1492 B.C.E.), was the son of an unknown warrior who married Ahmose's daughter.

Under Thutmose's leadership, the Egyptians subdued the Nubians to the south, seizing control of their gold mines and securing the wealth needed to finance expanded commerce. They also penetrated beyond their northeastern frontier, driving deep into Palestine and Syria. By the time of his death, Thutmose could claim to rule the land from beyond the Nile's Fourth Cataract in the south to the banks of the Euphrates in the north. Never had Egypt held sway over so much territory or so clearly declared its imperial ambitions. Nor was this success fleeting. The Egyptians would sustain a strong military presence in the wider region for the next 400 years, using the new horse-powered battle chariots to devastating effect against their enemies.

The Legacy of Hatshepsut

The early death of Thutmose's son and successor could have resulted in a crisis for the Eighteenth Dynasty. Instead, it led to one of the most remarkable reigns in Egypt's history, for Thutmose II (1492–1479 B.C.E.) passed the power of pharaoh to his sister, wife, and co-ruler **Hatshepsut** (*HAHT-shep-soot;* 1479–1458 B.C.E.). Such brother-sister unions

THE MORTUARY TEMPLE OF HATSHEPSUT. Unlike the pharaohs of the Old Kingdom, those of the Eighteenth Dynasty chose to be buried in specially built temples rather than in separate pyramids. The innovative architecture of Hatshepsut's temple, which was built into a hillside and set off by rows of columns, was widely imitated by her successors.

Interpreting Visual Evidence

Remembering Hatshepsut

The pharaohs of Egypt's New Kingdom were obsessed with self-representation and carefully controlled their public images. The visual language they used was highly symbolic, an iconography (vocabulary of images) intended to make each successive pharaoh look as much like his royal predecessors as possible: godlike, steadfast, virile, authoritative—even when the pharaoh was a woman, Hatshepsut (1479–1458 B.C.E.). So many statues and portraits of her survive that nearly every major museum in the world has at least one. (The Metropolitan Museum of Art in New York has a whole room set aside for them.) But many of these images show signs of having been defaced (images A and B) during the reign of her successor, Thutmose III, who was also her nephew and stepson. Until very recently, scholars assumed that Hatshepsut must have usurped his powers and that this was his revenge. Yet the evidence clearly shows that Hatshepsut was Egypt's legitimate ruler. Why, then,

would Thutmose III or his heirs have tried to efface her memory?

These two unblemished steles (images C and D) depict Hatshepsut and Thutmose III. In the stele on the left (image C), they sit back to back on

matching thrones, under the protection of the gods. In the stele on the right (image D), Thutmose III wears a warrior's crown, while Hatshepsut wears the Double Crown of Upper and Lower Egypt and wields a mace.

A. Defaced head of Hatshepsut.

B. Defaced statue of Hatshepsut.

were common in the Egyptian royal family, although they do not appear to have been the routine way to produce royal children: pharaohs customarily kept a harem of subsidiary wives and concubines for this purpose. However, Thutmose II and Hatshepsut did conceive at least one child together, Neferure (*neh-feh-RUH-reh*); in fact, she may have been their designated heir. For twenty-one years, Hatshepsut ruled as pharaoh in her own right, while her daughter took on the usual duties of queen.

Like her great-grandmother Ahhotep, Hatshepsut was a warrior. Moreover, she was routinely portrayed on

monuments and in statuary with the masculine figure and ceremonial beard characteristic of pharaohs. She did not pretend to be a man; inscriptions almost always indicate her gender, and she claimed to be the most beautiful woman in the world. But it was important to Egyptians that she use the conventional iconography of power to locate herself firmly within a long history of dynastic rule.

Hatshepsut's statecraft proved crucial to the continuing success of Egypt. With her stepson/nephew Thutmose III (the son of one of her brother's lesser wives), she launched several successful military campaigns and

Questions for Analysis

1. Bear in mind that few Egyptians could read the hieroglyphs accompanying these images. How might they have "read" the relationship between these two royal relatives? Does this visual evidence support the hypothesis that Thutmose was slighted by Hatshepsut? Why or why not?

2. What can these images tell us about gender roles? What else would we need to know before making a judgment about masculine and feminine characteristics in ancient Egypt?

3. Given that Hatshepsut was Egypt's legitimate pharaoh, what might have motivated either Thutmose III or his son Amenhotep II to deface her image many years after her death?

C. Stele of Hatshepsut and Thutmose.

D. Stele of Thutmose and Hatshepsut from the Red Chapel at Karnak.

extended trade and diplomacy. The arts also flourished, setting standards that would be emulated for a thousand years. Indeed, Hatshepsut was one of the most ambitious builders in Egyptian history, which is saying something. Her own mortuary temple, which housed the remains of her father and herself, was probably the first tomb constructed in the Valley of the Kings, the New Kingdom's answer to the pyramids.

Yet after Hatshepsut's death in 1458 B.C.E., her legacy was called into question. At some point late in her nephew's reign, attempts were made to remove her name from inscriptions and to destroy her images (see *Interpreting Visual Evidence* above). Scholars used to assume that Thutmose himself was responsible, because he resented his stepmother/aunt's power over him. But more recent research has suggested that the culprit was his son, Amenhotep II (1427–1400 B.C.E.), who was thereby blocking the claims of royal rivals, possibly the descendants of Hatshepsut or her daughter Neferure. In either case, the near erasure of Hatshepsut's legacy caused her to be neglected by historians until the late twentieth century.

Religious Change and Political Challenge

The great conquests of the Eighteenth Dynasty brought mind-boggling riches to Egypt. Much of this wealth went to the glorification of the pharaohs in the form of grand temples, tombs, and other monuments, including the thousands of steles that provide us with so much information about this era. Another significant portion of the plunder went to the military aristocracy that made such conquests possible. But the lion's share went to the gods as offerings of thanks for Egypt's success. As the temples became wealthy and powerful, so too did their priests. But no temple complex was so well endowed as that of Amon at Thebes.

Thebes was not only the capital of New Kingdom Egypt but was also the capital of the Eighteenth Dynasty and the place most sacred to Amon (or Amun), the god of creation. He therefore played an important role in the dynasty's self-image, and he is evoked in the dynastic name Amenhotep ("Amon Is Pleased"). But Amon was more than a local god. He had come into prominence when the political center of gravity shifted to Thebes during the Middle Kingdom, and his cult had steadily increased in status and popularity. By 1550 B.C.E., he had become identified as another manifestation of the sun god Ra, and as Amon-Ra he was believed to be the divine force behind the Eighteenth Dynasty's triumph over the Hyksos. This accounts for the favor shown to his priests at Thebes, who became a formidable political and economic force. Eventually, the priesthood of Amon surpassed even the military aristocracy in importance and influence. And because the dynasty's prestige was intertwined with that of Amon, the priests had seemingly gained the controlling voice in Egypt.

The Reign of Akhenaten (1352–1336 B.C.E.)

All of these factors are important when we consider the reign of Amenhotep IV, who inherited the vast, well-governed kingdom assembled by his predecessors. This young pharaoh showed an early inclination toward the worship of the sun—but not as an aspect of Amon. Instead, Amenhotep exalted Ra as a discrete divinity and laid aside the traditional iconography of this god as a falcon (or a falcon-headed man), replacing it with the symbol *Aten*, the hieroglyph representing the sun's rays. He then went further, changing his own name to **Akhenaten** (*AH-ken-AH-ten*), "He Who Is Profitable to the Aten," and building a new capital to honor the god. Located halfway between Memphis in the north and Thebes in the south, it was called Akhetaten ("The Horizon of the Aten").

AKHENATEN, HIS WIFE NEFERTITI, AND THEIR CHILDREN. The Aten is depicted here as a sun disk, raining down power on the royal family. ▪ *What messages might this image have conveyed to contemporary Egyptians?* ▪ *How does this depiction of the pharaoh differ from earlier precedents?*

THRONE OF TUTANKHAMUN. Dating from about 1330 B.C.E., this relief in gold and silver is part of the back of the young pharaoh's throne. Although the reign of the boy king marked the rejection of Akhenaten's theology, the informal artistic style favored by his father is still detectable here in the relaxed, lounging position of the pharaoh and the intimate, confiding gesture of his queen, Ankhesenamen.

Although the priesthood of Amon exalted Amon-Ra, it had continued to recognize all the other gods of the Egyptian pantheon. Akhenaten's theology, by contrast, was closer to monotheism: unlike traditional Egyptian deities, the Aten could not be imagined as taking on human or animal form. As if this were not controversial enough, Akhenaten also celebrated his new religion by representing himself in a very unconventional way. In a complete departure from the divine virility of his ancestors—which even his ancestor Hatshepsut had emulated—Akhenaten had himself pictured as a normal human being with distinctive features and as a family man enjoying the company of his wife, Nefertiti, and their children. This emphasis on his own humanity might have been an extension of his theology, which honored the life force within every being. But it was very dangerous to the ideology of royal power. The pharaoh was not supposed to be approachable and affable, a man with a quirky personality. He was supposed to be a god on earth.

Akhenaten's spiritual revolution therefore had enormous political implications. Indeed, some scholars have suggested that it was part of a cunning attempt to undermine the influence of Amon's priests, to the pharaoh's benefit. Whatever the motives behind it, Akhenaten did not succeed in converting many Egyptians to his new religion. It is not surprising that the priesthood of Amon also put up strenuous resistance. To make matters worse, Akhenaten did not balance his theological enthusiasm with attention to Egypt's security or interests abroad. This cost him the support of his nobility and may even have led to his deposition.

He was ultimately succeeded by one of his younger sons, Tutankhaten ("Living Image of Aten"), a child of nine whose name was quickly changed to reflect his advisers' rejection of Akhenaten's beliefs and the restoration of the god Amon and his priesthood to a position of power. He thus became Tutankhamun (1333–1324 B.C.E.), the famous boy king whose sumptuous tomb was discovered in 1922. After his early death, he was succeeded by a general called Horemheb, a man unrelated to the royal family who nonetheless reigned as the last pharaoh of the Eighteenth Dynasty and managed to maintain stability for nearly three decades. When he died, he passed his office to another general. This was Ramses, the founder of the Nineteenth Dynasty, who would restore Egypt to glory.

TRANSNATIONAL NETWORKS OF THE LATE BRONZE AGE

After 1500 B.C.E., **Bronze Age** history must be understood within the context of what we might call international relations. Yet it is more accurate to call the political and eco-

nomic networks of this period *transnational*, because this web of alliances and relationships transcended any idea of national identity or national boundaries—both of which are modern concepts.

This Late Bronze Age was also an age of superpowers. The great pharaohs of the Eighteenth Dynasty had transformed Egypt into a conquering state, and the Hittites had created an empire out of the disparate city-states and kingdoms of Anatolia. The Assyrians controlled trade, and the Kassite kingdom of Babylonia remained a significant force in economic and military relationships. In addition to these imperial entities, numerous smaller states also flourished and extended their influence westward into the Mediterranean. Holding it all together was a network of trade routes that created an interdependent Afro-Eurasian world.

Transnational Diplomacy

Although warfare remained the fundamental mode of interaction in the Late Bronze Age, a balance of power among the larger empires gradually helped to stabilize the region and encourage trade. The archives discovered by archaeologists at Akhenaten's abandoned capital of Akhetaten (modern el-Amarna) provide us with a clear picture of this process. By the fourteenth century B.C.E., a wide-ranging correspondence was forging alliances and promoting a set of mutual goals and understandings among rulers and elites. This is reflected in the letters' vocabulary: the most powerful rulers address one another as "brother," whereas lesser princes and chieftains show their deference to the pharaoh, the Hittite king, and other sovereigns by using the term "father." Breach of this protocol could cause great offense. When a thirteenth-century Assyrian king presumed to address the Hittite ruler as "brother," he received a stern rebuke: "What is this you keep saying about 'brotherhood'? Were you and I born of the same mother? Far from it! Just as my father and grandfather were not in the habit of writing about 'brotherhood' to the king of Assyria, so should you stop writing to me about 'brotherhood'!"

Rulers of this period also exchanged lavish gifts and entered into marriage contracts with each other. Professional envoys journeyed back and forth among the centers of power, conveying gifts and handling politically sensitive missions. Some of these emissaries were also merchants, sent to explore the possibility of trading opportunities as well as to cement alliances.

Transnational Trade

Indeed, it was trade that allowed smaller communities to become integral parts of this transnational network. Seaside

EGYPT AND ITS NEIGHBORS, C. 1400 B.C.E. ▪ *What is the major change on this map compared with the previous map of Bronze Age civilizations (page 40)?* ▪ *What factors appear to shape patterns of conquest and settlement in the eastern Mediterranean?* ▪ *What developments would have enabled trade to flourish during this period?*

ports became powerful merchant city-states and centers for the exchange of dazzling commodities. A single vessel's cargo might contain scores of distinct items originating anywhere from the interior of Africa to the Baltic Sea, as demonstrated by the contents of a merchant ship discovered at Uluburun off the Turkish coast in 1982. At the same time, the region was supplied with goods brought in over land, via contacts reaching into India and China.

Long-distance trade was not only the basis for a new economy but also the conduit for art, ideas, and technology. In the past, such influences had spread slowly and unevenly; now, though, the societies of the Late Bronze Age could keep abreast of all the latest developments and commodities. Egyptians delighted in Canaanite glass, Greeks prized Egyptian amulets, and the merchants of Canaan admired Greek pottery and wool. Examples of avid desire for the products of other cultures can be endlessly enumerated.

This trend was particularly marked in large coastal towns. At Ugarit, on the coast of modern-day Syria, the swirl of commerce and the multiplicity of languages spoken by traders even propelled the development of a simpler form of written communication. In contrast to cuneiform writing, the Ugaritic alphabet consisted of about thirty symbols representing the sounds of consonants (vowels had to be inferred). This system was far more easily mastered and more flexible than cuneiform, and it became the model for the development of all modern alphabets.

The search for markets, resources, and trade routes also promoted greater understanding among cultures. After a great battle between Egyptians and Hittites near Kadesh (c. 1275 B.C.E.), the pharaoh Ramses II realized that more was to be gained through peaceful relations with his northern neighbors than through warfare. The treaty he established with the Hittites fostered geopolitical stability in the region and allowed further economic exchanges to flourish. But greater integration also meant greater mutual dependence. If one economy suffered, the effects of that decline were sure to be felt elsewhere. And the farther this transnational system spread, the more fragile it became. Many of the new markets depended on emerging societies in regions far less stable, where civilization was new.

AEGEAN CIVILIZATION: MINOAN CRETE, MYCENAEAN GREECE

Like Hesiod, many ancient Greek poets described a heroic age when great men mingled with gods and powerful kingdoms contended for wealth and glory. For a long time, modern scholars dismissed these stories as fables. Tales of the Athenian hero Theseus and the Minotaur, the Trojan War, and the wanderings of Odysseus were not regarded as reflecting any historical reality. Greek history was assumed to begin in 776 B.C.E., when the first recorded Olympic Games occurred. Greece in the Bronze Age was considered a primitive backwater that played no significant role in the Mediterranean world or in the later, glorious history of classical Greece.

But in the late nineteenth century, an amateur archaeologist named Heinrich Schliemann became convinced that these legends were really historical accounts. Using the epic poems of the *Iliad* and *The Odyssey* by Homer as his guide,

he found the site of Ilium (Troy) near the coast of northwest Anatolia. He also identified a number of once-powerful citadels on the Greek mainland, including the home of the legendary king Agamemnon at Mycenae (*MY-seh-nee*).

Soon afterward, the British archaeoleogist Sir Arthur Evans took credit for discovering the remains of a great palace at Knossos (*kuh-NOHS-ohs*) on the island of Crete: a vast complex that predated any of the major citadels on the Greek mainland. He dubbed its magnificent culture (which no modern person had known to exist) "**Minoan Crete**," after King Minos, the powerful ruler whom the ancient Greeks had described as dominating the Aegean, and the man for whom the legendary engineer Daedalus had designed the Labyrinth.

Although some of their conclusions have been proven false, the discoveries of Schliemann and Evans forced scholars to revise, entirely, the early history of Western civilizations. It is now clear that Bronze Age Greece—or, as it is often termed, **Mycenaean Greece**—was an important player in this integrated Mediterranean world during the second millennium B.C.E.

The Minoan Thalassocracy

In the fifth century B.C.E., the Athenian historian Thucydides wrote that King Minos of Crete had ruled a *thalassocracy*, an empire of the sea. We now know that Thucydides was correct and that a very wealthy civilization began to flourish on the island of Crete around 2500 B.C.E. Thereafter, for about a millennium, the Minoans controlled shipping around the central Mediterranean and the Aegean, and may have exacted tribute from many smaller islands. At its height between 1900 and 1500 B.C.E., Minoan civilization was the contemporary of Egypt's Middle Kingdom and the Hittite Old Kingdom. But unlike them, it was virtually unassailable by outside forces, protected by the surrounding sea. Astonishingly, neither the great palace at Knossos nor the other palaces on the island were fortified, so secure were they from attack.

Thanks to its strategic position, Crete was not only a safe haven but a nexus of vibrant economic exchange. In this it resembled its counterparts on the mainland, because it acted as a magnet for the collection of resources which were then redistributed by its rulers and their emissaries. Knossos was also a production center for textiles, pottery, and metalwork. Minoan merchants traded these with Egypt, southwest Anatolia, and Cyprus for a range of exotic goods. Through Cyprus, the Minoans had further contacts with the Levantine coast of modern-day Lebanon and Syria. Artistic influences also traveled along these routes; among much else, Minoan-style fresco paintings from this period appear regularly in the Nile Delta and the Levant.

MYCENAEAN DEATH MASK, C. 1550–1500 B.C.E. When the archaeologist Heinrich Schliemann discovered this gold funeral mask in a burial shaft at Mycenae, he immediately declared it to be that of Agamemnon. Although it is certainly royal, this mask is too old to have been made for that legendary king, who lived several centuries later.

MINOAN FRESCO, C. 1500 B.C.E. A stylized representation of bull-leaping, painted into the plaster of a wall at Knossos. ■ *Is this fresco likely to represent real practices?* ■ *Why or why not?*

Traces of the bright colors and graceful lines of these paintings are still evident on the ruined walls of the palace at Knossos. Endowed with indoor plumbing, among other luxuries, it covered several acres and comprised hundreds of rooms joined by an intricate web of winding hallways that surely inspired the story of the Labyrinth, at the center of which lurked the terrible Minotaur, half man and half bull. These legends, too, reflect historical evidence: the Minoans probably worshiped a god in the form of a bull, and they appear to have devised an elaborate ritual sport known as bull-leaping: similar to bullfighting but involving an element of athletic dance. There is also some evidence that they practiced human sacrifice (possibly facilitated by the dangers of bull-dancing) as a religious rite.

Despite all these fascinating remains, Minoan culture remains mysterious because its language has yet to be decoded. Its script is called Linear A, to distinguish it from Linear B, used in Mycenaean Greece—a script that *has* been deciphered. Although Linear A and Linear B represent different languages, the formal relationship between them reflects the close ties between Minoan Crete and the mainland of Greece. Yet the nature of that relationship is still debated. The Minoans were clearly much more sophisticated and originally may have dominated their Greek neighbors.

One story told of the Greek hero Theseus describes how the young Athenian was sent to Crete as a hostage, intending to free Athens from the heavy tribute imposed by King Minos. Given what we have already learned about the close relationship between myth and history, it is probable that this story preserves ancient memory, just as the story of Daedalus, the brilliant inventor and engineer, is an attempt to explain the technological marvels of the palace at Knossos.

Mycenaean Greece

In the early 1950s, the Englishmen Michael Ventris and John Chadwick joined their linguistic skills to expertise gained during the Second World War, when many classically trained scholars were employed in cracking enemy codes. Their efforts resulted in the decoding of Linear B, which proved that the history of ancient Greece stretched well back into the Bronze Age. Since then, new research shows that the Indo-Europeans whose language became Greek entered the region in several waves after the turn of the second millennium, dominating and displacing the indigenous inhabitants. By 1500 B.C.E., their huge citadels dotted the Greek

LINEAR A TABLET FROM KNOSSOS. Unlike cuneiform, whose characters are formed using the wedge-shaped tip of a reed, Linear A was inscribed with a sharp stylus that incised fine lines in clay or soft stone.

landscape, ruled by warriors whose epitaphs boast of their martial prowess and who were buried with their weapons.

In 2015, American archaeologists excavating near one of these citadels—at Pylos in southwestern Greece, the same place where the first Linear B tablets on the Greek mainland were found—discovered an extraordinarily rich grave with all of its contents intact. Known as the tomb of the Griffin Warrior (from the decorative motifs of this mythical beast carved on an ivory plaque), it contained the body of a man in his early thirties who was buried with his sword and dagger, as well as combs, a mirror, jewelry, and other items; all were made of ivory, silver, gold, bronze, and all were beautifully fashioned.

Many of these of items came from Minoan Crete, and because the tomb was dug *before* the building of the great palace citadel at Pylos, it allows us to glimpse the process of cultural transfer that was shaping a new civilization on the Greek mainland. Analysis of ancient DNA (aDNA) extracted from the warrior's teeth and bones may soon yield even more information about him, while radiocarbon analysis of any surviving plant material or the bones themselves could assist in dating the burial.

This grave, and the close relationship between the writing systems of Crete and the mainland, reveal that Mycenaean society was decisively influenced by Minoan cultural, religious, and political models. The citadels, copying the great palaces of Crete, were both centers of government and warehouses for the storage and redistribution of goods and agricultural surpluses, of which they kept careful records. (Thousands of Linear B tablets testify to this.) By the thirteenth century B.C.E., some rulers had carved out territorial kingdoms with as many as 100,000 inhabitants, dwarfing the city-states of the later classical age; Hesiod

imagined their citadels to have been built by giants. Indeed, their massive size was not really suited to the Greek landscape; nor were the war chariots that the Mycenaean elites adopted from their contemporaries on the plains of Anatolia, despite the fact that they were highly impractical on the rocky Greek terrain.

Gradually, the Mycenaean Greeks came to play a central role in Bronze Age networks. By about 1400 B.C.E., they had subjugated Crete, taking over Knossos and remaking it as a Mycenaean center. When the pharaoh Amenhotep III mentions a place called "Keftiu" in his correspondence, he is probably negotiating with Crete's Mycenaean conquerors. In western Anatolia, not far from fabled Troy, at least one Mycenaean king exercised enough influence for a Hittite ruler to address him as "my brother." This evidence suggests that the Mycenaeans earned prestige as warriors and mercenaries, just as the Greeks' heroic poems attest.

The basic political and commercial unit of the Mycenaean world—a powerful king and war leader, a warrior aristocracy, a palace bureaucracy, a complex economy, large territorial kingdoms—differs markedly from the tiny, self-contained Greek city-states of the later classical age (see Chapter 3). However, we can trace some features of this later civilization back to the Mycenaeans, including the Greek language. Linear B tablets speak of a social group with considerable economic and political rights, the *damos*; this may be the precursor of the *demos*, the urban population that sought political empowerment (*democracy*) in many Greek cities. The tablets also introduce the names of several gods familiar from the later period, such as Zeus, Poseidon, and Dionysos. Indeed, the later Greeks believed themselves to be descended from these legendary forebears, whom they credited with superhuman

THE GRAVE OF THE GRIFFIN WARRIOR AT PYLOS. The contents of this Mycenaean tomb, discovered in 2015, reveal the extent of the connections between Mycenaean Greece and Minoan Crete. This photograph shows a bronze mirror in its original location.

achievements. Although later Greeks such as Hesiod knew little about these Mycenaean ancestors in fact, the impact of what they imagined about them was considerable.

The Sea Peoples and the End of the Bronze Age

For many years, historians have guessed that the collapse of Mycenean civilization was caused by factors such as drought, disease, and social unrest. Indeed, new climatological research shows that sustained arid conditions could have led to drought and decreased crop yields, both of which suggest famine was a serious factor. The devastating consequences are clear. Because Mycenaean Greece was an integrated part of a transnational network, the effects of its demise were felt throughout the region. Thereafter, a wave of devastation swept from north to south, caused by a group of people so thoroughly destructive that they obliterated everything in their path.

We might know nothing at all about them were it not for a narrow victory by the pharaoh Ramses III around 1176 B.C.E. In the monument set up to commemorate his triumph, near the modern city of Luxor on Egypt's West Bank, Ramses III referred to these invaders as the "Sea Peoples" and named

The Diplomacy of the Mycenaeans and the Hittites

Around 1260 B.C.E., the powerful Hittite king Hattusilis III sent the following letter to a "King of Ahhiyawa," identifiable as a leader of the Mycenaean Greeks, who often called themselves Akhaiwoi, Achaeans. This fascinating document exemplifies the tangle of close ties that bound powerful men together within the transnational system of the Late Bronze Age, as well as the problems and misunderstandings that could arise from the misbehavior of the men under their command. The events referenced here all occurred in western Anatolia (Turkey), a region controlled partly by the Hittites and partly by the Greeks, the same region in which Troy (Ilium) was located. (See the map on page 52.)

have to complain of the insolent and treacherous conduct of one Tawagalawas. We came into contact in the land of Lycia, and he offered to become a vassal of the Hittite Empire. I agreed, and sent an officer of most exalted rank to conduct him to my presence. He had the audacity to complain that the officer's rank was not exalted enough; he insulted my ambassador in public, and demanded that he be declared vassal-king there and then, without the formality of an interview. Very well: I order him, if he desires to become a vassal of mine, to make sure that no troops of his are found in Iyalanda when I arrive there. And what do I find when I arrive in Iyalanda?—the troops of Tawagalawas, fighting on the side of my enemies. I defeat them, take many prisoners . . . scrupulously leaving the fortress of Atriya intact out of respect for my treaty with you. Now a Hittite subject, Piyamaradus by name, steals my 7,000 prisoners, and makes off to your city of Miletus. I command him to return to me: he disobeys. I write to you: you send a surly message unaccompanied by gift or greeting, to say that you have ordered your representative in

Miletus, a certain Atpas, to deliver up Piyamaradus. Nothing happens, so I go fetch him. I enter your city of Miletus, for I have something to say to Piyamaradus, and it would be well that your subjects there should hear me say it. But my visit is not a success. I ask for Tawagalawas: he is not at home. I should like to see Piyamaradus: he has gone to sea. You refer me to your representative Atpas: I find that both he and his brother are married to daughters of Piyamaradus; they are not likely to give me satisfaction or to give you an unbiased account of these transactions. . . . Are you aware, and is it with your blessing, that Piyamaradus is going round saying that he intends to leave his wife and family, and incidentally my 7,000 prisoners, under your protection while he makes continual inroads on my dominion? . . . Do not let him use Achaea [in Greece] as a base for operations against me. You and I are friends. There has been no quarrel between us since we came to terms in the matter of Ilios [the territory of Troy]: the trouble there was my fault, and I promise it will not happen again. As for my military occupation of Miletus, please regard it as a friendly visit. . . . [As for the problems between us], I suggest that the fault may not lie with ourselves

but with our messengers; let us bring them to trial, cut off their heads, mutilate their bodies, and live henceforth in perfect friendship.

Source: Adapted from Denys Page, *History and the Homeric Iliad* (Berkeley: 1959), pp. 11–12.

Questions for Analysis

1. Reconstruct the relationship between Hattusilis III and the Achaean king, on the basis of the references to people and places in this letter. What picture emerges of their interactions and of the connections between the Hittite Empire and Mycenaean Greece?

2. Why is Hattusilis so concerned about the disrespect that the Achaeans have shown to him? Reading between the lines, what do you think he wanted to accomplish by sending this letter?

3. On the basis of this letter, what can you deduce about the standards of behavior expected of civilized participants in the transnational system of the Late Bronze Age? Within this code of conduct, what sanctions or penalties could be imposed on individuals or their nations?

several groups as parts of a coalition. Some were familiar to the Egyptians, who had employed them as mercenaries. From Ramses' description of their battle gear, it seems that many were from the Aegean. Most notable were the Philistines who, after their defeat, withdrew to populate the coast of the region named after them: Palestine. In 2018, another inscription describing the Sea Peoples was finally deciphered and indicates that one member of the Sea Peoples' confederation was a powerful new kingdom called Mira, which had begun its rise by conquering Troy.

This new evidence lends weight to older hypotheses that the Sea Peoples' arc of destruction began in the northern Aegean and was one of the factors contributing to the collapse of Mycenaean Greece. Disruption of northern commercial networks would have devastated the Mycenaean kingdoms, which could not support their enormous populations without trade. Suddenly faced with an apocalyptic combination of overpopulation, famine, and violence, bands of desperate refugees would have fled the Aegean basin. Meanwhile, the damage to commerce had a domino effect and devastated the economy of the Hittites, whose ancient kingdom rapidly disintegrated. Along the Mediterranean coast we find other clues. The king of Ugarit wrote a letter to a "brother" king on the island of Cyprus, begging for immediate aid because he had sent all his own warriors to help the Hittites. It is poignant, however, that we have his letter only because the clay tablet on which it was written baked hard in the fire that destroyed his palace. The letter was never sent.

The desperation of refugees fleeing famine and violence combined with the raids of the Sea Peoples, destroyed the Western civilizations that had flourished for more than two thousand years. The devastation was not total; not all the cities disappeared, and trade did not cease entirely. But the Hittite Empire was eradicated, leaving behind it many weak, short-lived principalities. The great cosmopolitan cities of the eastern Mediterranean lay in ruins, and new groups—sometimes contingents of Sea Peoples like the Philistines—populated the coast. The citadels of Mycenaean Greece were depopulated by as much as 90 percent over the next century, and Greece entered into a period of cultural and economic isolation that would last for 250 years.

The victorious Egyptians survived; but with their major trading partners diminished or dead, their civilization suffered. The Assyrians, the original architects of the networks that had undergirded the transnational system, had to fight for their very existence. In Babylon, the peaceful and prosperous rule of the Kassites withered. In the vacuum left behind, new political configurations took shape, and a new metallurgical technology began to supplant the use of bronze. Out of the ashes arose the phoenix of the Iron Age.

THE STATES OF THE EARLY IRON AGE

With the destruction of transnational networks, the geopolitical map of the ancient world changed significantly. In Anatolia, a patchwork of small kingdoms grew up within the territories once controlled by the Hittites. Similar developments took place in the Levant, the eastern Mediterranean coastline that today comprises Israel, Lebanon, and parts of Syria. For centuries, this region had been controlled either by the Egyptians or the Hittites. With the collapse of these empires, new states began to emerge there, too. They were small, but they had a huge impact on the history of Western civilizations.

The Phoenicians

One of the most influential peoples of this period is usually called by the Greek name: the **Phoenicians**. They are also known as Canaanites and were speakers of a Semitic language closely related to Hebrew. Each Phoenician city on the coast of the Levant had its own hereditary royal government, and every Phoenician's first loyalty was to his or her own city. In the Phoenicians' overseas colonies, however, a new type of political system emerged in which power was shared among a handful of elite families. This aristocratic form of government would become a model for many other Western societies, including those of classical Greece and Rome (see Chapters 3 and 5).

During the Late Bronze Age, most Phoenician cities had been controlled by Egypt. But the erosion of Egyptian imperial power after 1200 B.C.E. gave these cities the opportunity to forge a new independence and to capitalize on their commercial advantages. One Phoenician city was a clearinghouse for papyrus, the highly prized Egyptian writing material. This explains why the Greek name for this city, Byblos, became the basis for the Greek word *biblon*, meaning "book." (The Bible is so called from the plural *bibloi*, "the books.")

Another valuable commodity that came to be associated with the Phoenicians, and that gave them their name, was a rare purple dye derived from the shells of snails culled from the seabed off the Levantine coast. As far as the Greeks were concerned, those who supplied this rich dye were *phoinikeoi*, "purple people." Phoenician textiles commanded a high price everywhere; so did timber from the Levant, especially cedar, and Canaanite glass. The Phoenicians also became expert metalworkers, ivory carvers, and shipbuilders.

PHOENICIAN COLONIZATION. Compare this map with the more detailed one of the Hebrew kingdoms on page 59. ▪ *What part of the Mediterranean was the homeland for the Phoenician city-states?* ▪ *Where did Phoenicians establish colonies?* ▪ *Why would overseas colonization be of such crucial importance to Phoenician city-states?* ▪ *What does their westward colonization imply about the Phoenicians' aims and about the different opportunities available in the western Mediterranean?*

Phoenician Colonies and Cultural Influence

The Phoenicians became famous as merchants and seafarers, but they were also aggressive migrants and colonists. By the end of the tenth century B.C.E., they had planted settlements from one end of the Mediterranean to the other, and their merchants had begun to venture out into the Atlantic Ocean. We have good evidence that they traveled as far as Cornwall (southwest Britain) during this period. The Greek historian Herodotus later claimed that Phoenician merchant-explorers even circumnavigated Africa. At the end of the ninth century B.C.E., Phoenicians from the city of Tyre established Carthage in modern-day Tunisia (North Africa). Carthage would ultimately become the preeminent power in the western Mediterranean; centuries later, this brought it into conflict with Rome (see Chapter 5).

The widespread colonial and mercantile efforts of the Phoenicians meant that they influenced cultures across the Mediterranean. Among their early overseas trading partners were the Greeks, and the Phoenicians may have played an important role in reintroducing urban life to Greece after the collapse of the Mycenaean citadels. They also brought with them a number of artistic and literary influences. Without question, however, the most important contribution of the Phoenicians was their alphabet.

As we noted earlier, a thirty-character alphabet had evolved at Ugarit by the end of the Bronze Age. Around 1100 B.C.E., the Phoenicians refined this writing system to twenty-two characters. This simpler system further facilitated communication and accounting, and the Phoenicians may have wanted to encourage similar practices among their trading partners, to safeguard their own interests. The Greeks certainly remained aware of their debt to the Phoenicians: their legends ascribe the invention of the alphabet to Cadmus, a Phoenician who settled in Greece. Their debt is also clear in the close relationship between the names of letters in Greek (alpha, beta, gamma, delta . . .) and Phoenician letter names (aleph, bayt, gimel, dalet . . .), and from the obvious similarities in letter shapes.

HEBREW	PHŒNICIAN	ANCIENT GREEK	LATER GREEK	ENGLISH
א				A
ב				B
ג				G
ד				D
ה				E
ו				F
ז				Z
ח				H
ט				Th
				I
כ				K
ל				L
מ				M
נ				N
ס				X
ע				O
פ				P
צ				Q
ק				R
ר				S
ש				T
ת		OMITTED NOT BEING IN GREEK		

THE EVOLUTION OF THE ALPHABET. This table shows how the shapes of letters changed as the Phoenician alphabet was adapted by the Hebrews, the Greeks, and eventually the Romans (from whom our modern alphabet derives).

The Philistines

Southward along the Levantine coast from Phoenicia lay the land of the **Philistines**, descendants of the Sea Peoples defeated by Ramses III (see the map on page 59). Their bad reputation is the result of their dominance over their pastoral neighbors, the herdsmen known as the Hebrews. Because the Hebrews used writing as an effective weapon, the Philistines became the great villains of the Hebrew scriptures. Accordingly the word *philistine* has come to mean a boorish, uncultured person. And because the Philistines do not appear to have made use of the same powerful technology to record their own outlook on the world, almost everything we know about them comes from the work of archaeologists or has to be sifted through the bad press of their detractors.

The Philistines occupied a unique position in the Levant and retained a separate identity for several generations; each new archaeological discovery roots this identity more firmly in their Aegean past. We know little about their language, but their material culture, behavior, and organization all exhibit close affinities with Mycenaean Greece. For example, the Philistines introduced grapevines and olive trees to the Levant from the Aegean basin. With the profits from these industries, they created powerful armies that dominated the region in the twelfth and eleventh centuries B.C.E. They also established a monopoly over metalsmithing, making it virtually impossible for their enemies to forge competitive weaponry.

Philistine power was based in five great strongholds, the so-called Pentapolis (Greek for "five cities"): Gaza, Ashkelon, and Ashdod on the coast, and the inland cities of Ekron and Gath. (Again, these citadels are strikingly similar to the fortified palaces of Mycenaean civilization, and they appear to have had many of the same functions.) From these strongholds, the Philistines dominated the surrounding countryside by organizing agricultural production and controlling trade routes. An independent lord ruled over each citadel, and no doubt tensions and rivalries existed among them. But much like the heroes of Greek epic, the Philistines could set aside differences when facing a common enemy.

Because we see the Philistines primarily through the eyes of their Hebrew enemies, we must be careful about drawing conclusions about them from the stories of Goliath's brutality or Delilah's sexual treachery, to name the two most infamous Philistines of the Hebrew scriptures. Yet the Hebrews had good reason to fear the Philistines, whose pressure on the Hebrew hill country was constant and who threatened the Hebrews' holy sanctuary at Shiloh, where the sacred Ark of the Covenant—said to contain the original tablets of the law given to Moses on Mount Sinai—was kept. In Hebrew tradition, the tribes of Israel had once carried the ark before them into battle against the Philistines, only to lose it in the fray and to witness thereafter the destruction of Shiloh. The Philistines then established garrisons throughout the land of the Hebrews and exacted tribute, denied them access to weapons, and engaged in the typical abuses of an occupying people.

Past and Present

The Fragility of Global Networks

During the Late Bronze Age, the destruction of transnational commercial networks had a domino effect on the interlocking civilizations of the West, plunging many into a "dark age" of isolation and impoverishment. The global economic crisis of 2007–2008 was caused by a similar phenomenon: the collapse of mutually dependent financial systems that proved more fragile than anyone had anticipated.

 Watch related author interview on the Student Site

The Hebrews and Their Scriptures

The central feature of **Hebrew** culture, their conception of and relationship to their god, will be discussed at greater length toward the end of this chapter. In this section, we focus our attention on the historical development of Hebrew society in the Iron Age Levant. In reconstructing this early history, we are indebted to an unusual textual source already mentioned: a series of scriptures (literally, "writings") that comprise mythology, laws and ritual practices, genealogical records, books of prophecy, proverbs, poetry, and royal chronicles. These are collectively known as the Hebrew Bible or (among Christians) the Old Testament.

These multiple books were composed at different times for different purposes and were only gradually assembled over many centuries, mostly by unknown authors, copyists, and editors. Some are clearly derived from ancient oral traditions; others respond to immediate challenges. Like other historical sources, then, they have to be placed in their specific individual contexts and analyzed carefully. At the same time, of course, they can be read collectively as the story of a people's unification and religious awakening.

The first five books of the Hebrew Bible are traditionally attributed to the Hebrew leader Moses. But many of the materials in these books were borrowed from other cultures, including the stories of the creation and the flood, which parallel those of Sumer (as we saw in Chapter 1). The story of Moses's childhood draws on a legend told about the Akkadian king Sargon the Great. The laws and rituals of the patriarchs can be found in other traditions, too. Meanwhile, the story of the exodus from Egypt is fraught with contradictions. Although the later Book of Joshua claims that the Hebrews who returned from Egypt conquered and expelled the native Canaanites, archaeological and linguistic evidence suggests that the Hebrews were essentially Canaanites themselves. They may have merged with scattered refugees from Egypt

The States of the Early Iron Age | 57

in the aftermath of the Sea Peoples' invasions, but for the most part they had been continuously resident in Canaan for centuries. In sum, the first five books of the Bible constitute a retrospective history whose purpose was to justify Hebrew traditions and claims to territory.

Among the other writings included in the Hebrew Bible are a group of texts that record events of the more recent past, the period we are considering now. These "historical books" are more straightforwardly verifiable, even if many details are difficult to confirm. According to the Book of Judges, the Hebrews were herdsmen who had just begun to establish permanent settlements around the time of the Philistines' arrival in the Levant. They had organized themselves into twelve tribes: extended clan units whose families owed each other mutual aid and protection in times of war, but who frequently fought over cattle and grazing rights. Each tribe was ruled by a patriarch known as a judge, who exercised the typical functions of authority in a clan-based society: war leadership, high priesthood, and dispute settlement. By the middle of the twelfth century B.C.E., these tribes occupied two major territories, with those settled in the south calling themselves the tribes of Judah, and those in the north the tribes of Israel.

The Struggle for Hebrew Unity

The Hebrew tribes of this period had few occasions to work together as a group and little experience of organized activity. This made them highly vulnerable, especially when the Philistines conquered the Levantine coast, around 1050 B.C.E. Faced with the threat of extinction, the Hebrews appear to have put up desperate resistance from their bases in the hilly interior. To counter the Philistine threat effectively, however, they needed a leader. Accordingly, around 1025 B.C.E., an influential tribal judge called Samuel selected a king to lead the tribes of Israel against the Philistines. His name was Saul. However, Saul proved to be an ineffective war leader. Although he blocked Philistine penetration into the hill country, he could not oust the Philistines from the valleys or coastal plains.

So Samuel withdrew his support from Saul and threw it behind a young man in Saul's entourage, Saul's son-in-law David, a warrior from Judah. Waging his own independent military campaigns, David achieved one triumph after another over the Philistines. By contrast, the armies of Saul had met frequent reversals—that is, according to the chroniclers responsible for the historical books of the Bible, who wrote their accounts under David's patronage.

These same books reveal that David was not initially motivated by patriotism. He was a man on the make; when

Saul finally drove him from his court, he became an outlaw on the fringes of Hebrew society and a mercenary in Philistine service. It was as a Philistine mercenary, in fact, that David fought against Saul in the climactic battle in which Saul was killed. Soon thereafter, David himself became king, first over the tribes of Judah, his home territory, and later over Saul's territory of Israel as well.

The Consolidation of a Hebrew Kingdom

After David's victory around 1000 B.C.E., he strove to strengthen his authority within and beyond his kingdom. He took advantage of the opportunity afforded by Egypt's decline to expand his territory southward, eventually confining the Philistines to an inconsequential strip of coastal land. David also defeated the neighboring Moabites and Ammonites, extending his control to the Dead Sea. By the time of his death in 973 B.C.E., his kingdom stretched from the middle Euphrates in the north to the Gulf of Aqaba in the south, and from the Mediterranean coast eastward into the Syrian deserts. Israel was now a force to be reckoned with, although it partly owed that status to the temporary weakness of its imperial neighbors, Egypt and Assyria.

As David's power and prestige grew, he was able to impose on his subjects a highly unpopular system of taxation and forced labor. His goal was to build a glorious capital at Jerusalem, a Canaanite settlement that he designated as the central city of his realm. It was a shrewd choice. As a newly conquered city, Jerusalem had no previous affiliation with any of Israel's twelve tribes and so stood outside the ancient rivalries that divided them. Jerusalem was also a geographically strategic choice, lying between the southern tribes of Judah (David's people) and the northern tribes of Israel.

David took steps to exalt the city as a religious center by making Jerusalem the resting place of the sacred Ark of the Covenant and elevating the priesthood of the Hebrew god, Yahweh. By these measures, he sought to forge a new collective identity centered on his own family and its connections to Yahweh. To this end, he also encouraged the writing of histories and prophecies that would affirm this identity and his central role in forging it.

The Reign of King Solomon (973–937 B.C.E.)

Continuing his father's policies, but on a much grander scale, David's son Solomon built a great temple complex at Jerusalem to house the Ark. Such visible support of Yahweh's cult was approved by the chroniclers whose works are included in the Bible, and who portray Solomon's reign as a golden age.

Despite his proverbial wisdom, however, Solomon could be a ruthless and often brutal ruler whose promotion of Yahweh coincided with a program of despotism. According to his own histories, Solomon kept an enormous harem of some 300 wives and 700 concubines, many of them drawn from subject or allied peoples. His palace complex—of which the Temple was a part—allowed him to rule in the grand style of ancient Mesopotamian potentates. To finance his expensive tastes and programs, Solomon instituted oppressive taxation and imposed customs duties on the lucrative caravan trade that passed through his country. With the help of the Phoenician king of Tyre, Solomon constructed a commercial fleet whose ships plied the waters of the Red Sea and beyond, trading—among other commodities—the gold and copper mined by Solomon's slaves.

This new wealth was bought at a high price. Solomon maintained a large standing army of unwilling conscripts from his own people, equipped with chariot and cavalry squadrons and powered by horses purchased abroad. To undertake his ambitious building projects, Solomon also required many of his subjects to perform forced labor four months out of every year. This level of oppression was too much for many Israelites, and the northern tribes seethed with rebellion against the royal capital.

Within a decade or so of Solomon's death, the fragile monarchy split in two. The dynasty descended from David continued to rule the southern kingdom of Judah with its capital at Jerusalem, but the ten northern tribes banded together as the kingdom of Israel, with their capital at Shechem. Archaeology, combined with accounts in the Bible, reveal that the cult of Yahweh was not yet dominant in either the north or the south, so major religious differences made reunification even more difficult. In the meantime, the changing political situation of the larger region made the Hebrew kingdoms increasingly vulnerable.

THE REVIVAL OF THE ASSYRIAN EMPIRE

As we have already seen, the Assyrians had long played an important role in spreading trade and promoting urban settlements. But like the other great powers of the ancient world, their civilization had been devastated by the Sea Peoples and the ensuing chaos of famine and migration. For several centuries they struggled for survival. Then, in the ninth century B.C.E., a brilliant but brutal ruler laid the foundations of what historians call the **Neo-Assyrian Empire**.

Under the leadership of Assurnasirpal II (*ah-sur-NAH-sur-PAHL*; 883–859 B.C.E.), the Assyrians began to conduct aggressive military campaigns against their neighbors on an annual basis. Those whom they defeated either had to pay tribute or face the full onslaught of the Assyrian war machine, which acquired a deserved reputation for savagery under Assurnasirpal.

Despite their military successes, Assurnasirpal and his son, Shalmeneser III (*SHAHL-meh-NEE-zehr*; 853–827 B.C.E.), also inspired stiff resistance. The northern kingdom of Israel formed an alliance with other small states to halt Assyrian expansion. This coalition ultimately forced Shalmeneser III to settle for smaller victories against the Armenians to his northwest and the Medes to his northeast, until a great revolt within Assyria itself ended his reign. Thereafter, a usurper named Tiglath-Pileser III

Competing Viewpoints

Two Accounts of Saul's Anointing

> When the charismatic judge Samuel chose Saul as the first king of the Hebrews, he opened a new chapter in the political history of Israel. But Saul's kingship was not a success, and Samuel ultimately turned against him, supporting Saul's rival (and son-in-law), David. These two quite different accounts of Samuel's anointing of Saul reflect the tensions that later arose between them—and probably were written down during the later kingship of David, Saul's successor. The first account also suggests the ambivalence some Hebrews felt about having a human king at all, doubts that Saul himself may have shared.

1 Samuel 8:4–22, 10:20–25

All the elders of Israel gathered together and [said to Samuel]: "You are old and your sons do not follow in your ways; appoint for us, then, a king to govern us, like other nations." But the thing displeased Samuel [who] prayed to the Lord, and the Lord said to Samuel, "Listen to the voice of the people in all that they say to you; for they have not rejected you, but they have rejected me from being king over them. Just as they have done to me, from the day I brought them up out of Egypt to this day, forsaking me and serving other gods, so they are also doing to you. Now then, listen to their voice; only—you shall solemnly warn them, and show them

the ways of the king who shall reign over them." So Samuel reported all the words of the Lord to the people who were asking for a king. "These will be the ways of the king who will reign over you: he will take sons and appoint them to his chariots . . . he will take your daughters to be perfumers and cooks and bakers . . . he will take one-tenth of your grain and your vineyards and give it to his officers and courtiers . . . and one-tenth of your flocks, and you shall be his slaves." But the people refused to listen, and Samuel said to the people, "Each of you return to his home."

Then Samuel brought all the tribes of Israel near, and the tribe of Benjamin was chosen by lot. He brought the tribe of

Benjamin near, [organized] by its families . . . and Saul the son of Kish was chosen by lot. But when they sought him, he could not be found. So they inquired again of the Lord . . . and the Lord said, "See, he has hidden himself among the baggage." Then they ran and brought him from there. When he took his stand among the people, he was head and shoulders taller than any of them. Samuel said, "You see the one whom the Lord has chosen? There is no one like him among the people." And the people all shouted, "Long live the king!" Samuel told the people the rights and duties of the kingship; and he wrote them in a book and laid it up before the Lord.

---

seized the Assyrian throne in 744 B.C.E. and immediately demanded tribute from various kingdoms. Those who refused fell victim to his armies.

When Tiglath-Pileser III died in 727 B.C.E., many of these recently conquered states rebelled, but Tiglath-Pileser's son, Shalmeneser V, energetically crushed them. When he died in battle, he was quickly replaced by one of his military commanders, who took the name Sargon II (722–705 B.C.E.). Sargon claimed to be the direct successor of Sargon of Akkad, the great king of Sumer and the first great king in Mesopotamian history, nearly 1,500 years earlier (see Chapter 1).

Like the Hebrews, Sargon II and his successors skillfully deployed history as a political tool. Eventually, they extended the frontiers of the Neo-Assyrian Empire from western Iran to the shores of the Mediterranean; briefly, they even subjugated parts of Egypt. Sargon himself put an end to the kingdom of Israel in 722 B.C.E., enslaving and deporting most of the population, and he terrified the southern kingdom of Judah into remaining a loyal and quiet vassal. The ancient kingdom of Elam on the Iranian plateau—a civilization almost as old as Sumer—also fell during this period. By the seventh century B.C.E., Assyria was the unrivaled power of the ancient region.

1 Samuel 9:1–10:1

There was a man of Benjamin whose name was Kish . . . [who] had a son whose name was Saul, a handsome young man . . . he stood head and shoulders above everyone else. Now the donkeys of Kish had strayed. So Kish said to his son Saul, "Take one of the boys with you; go and look for the donkeys." . . . As they were entering [a] town, they saw Samuel coming out toward them on his way up to the shrine. Now the day before Saul came, the Lord revealed to Samuel, "Tomorrow about this time I will send you a man from the land of Benjamin, and you shall anoint him to be ruler over my people Israel. He shall save my people from the hand of the Philistines; for I have seen the suffering of my people, because their outcry has come to me." . . . Saul approached Samuel inside the gate and said, "Tell me please, where is the house of the seer?" Samuel answered Saul, "I am the seer, go up before me to the shrine. . . . As for your donkeys that were lost three days ago, give no further thought to them, for they have been found. And on whom is all Israel's desire fixed, if not on you and your ancestral house?" Saul answered, "I am only a Benjaminite, from the least of the tribes of Israel, and my family is the humblest of all the families of the tribe of Benjamin. Why then have you spoken of me this way?" . . . As they were going down to the outskirts of town, Samuel said to Saul, "Tell the boy to go on before us . . . that I may make known to you the word of God." Samuel took a vial of oil and poured it on [Saul's] head and kissed him; he said: "The Lord has anointed you ruler over his people Israel. You shall reign over the people of the Lord and you will save them from the hand of their enemies all around."

Source: The New Oxford Annotated Bible (Oxford: 1994) (slightly adapted, source for both documents).

Questions for Analysis

1. Do these two accounts fit together? How do they differ? Why do you think that both were preserved in the Book of Samuel?

2. What view of kingship emerges in the first account? What are the attributes of a king? What is the relationship among the king, his god, and the priest anointing him? What is the role of the people in his selection?

3. The writers of Jewish scripture judged kings by their observance of the law, their zeal in fighting against competing religious cults, and their support of centralized worship at the Temple in Jerusalem. How did this form of theocracy in ancient Israel compare with that in Egypt and Mesopotamia?

Neo-Assyrian Government and Administration

The Neo-Assyrian Empire was a military dictatorship, built on the ability of its army to spread terror and oppress both enemies and subjects alike. At its head was a hereditary monarch regarded as the earthly representative of the Assyrians' patron god, Assur. When his army was not in the field, the king's time was taken up with elaborate sacrifices and rituals to appease the "great god." Divination and the consultation of oracles were central features of this religion, because the Neo-Assyrian king—as chief priest—had to be able to discern the will of Assur through the portents of nature.

Supporting the empire's centralized authority was an extensive bureaucracy of governors, high priests, and military commanders—professions by no means mutually exclusive. These administrators formed the highest class in Neo-Assyrian society and exercised local authority on behalf of the king. They maintained lines of transport and communication, which were the engines of imperial hegemony, and supervised the construction of an extensive network of roads that served these needs for centuries. The Neo-Assyrian state also deployed a system

THE NEO-ASSYRIAN EMPIRE, c. 700 b.c.e. ▪ *What were the territorial boundaries of the Neo-Assyrian Empire?* ▪ *Why would the Assyrians concentrate their efforts in the river valleys and along the coast, neglecting the Syrian interior?* ▪ *Notice the location of the Neo-Assyrian capitals of Nineveh and Assur; how was their situation in Mesopotamia likely to affect the Assyrians' sense of their own historical identity?* ▪ *Consider the position of Egypt. Why might the Assyrians find it difficult to subjugate Egypt permanently?*

of spies and messengers to report to the royal court on the activities of subjects and provincial governors.

Provincial governors collected tribute, recruited for the army, and administered the king's law. It is not surprising that the Assyrians, so mindful of historical precedent, modeled their laws on the Code of Hammurabi, though many of their penalties were much more severe. The harshest punishments were reserved for practices deemed detrimental to human reproduction; the penalties for same-sex relations and abortion were particularly severe. Neo-Assyrian law was also rigidly patriarchal. This entailed substantial revision of Hammurabi's code, which had granted women many rights. Now, only husbands had the power of divorce and they were legally permitted to inflict a variety of penalties on their wives, ranging from corporal punishment to mutilation and death.

The Assyrian Military-Religious Ethos

The Assyrians' new religious, political, and military ideology had taken shape during the long centuries when they fought

for survival, and it then became the foundational ethos for their empire's relentless conquests. Its two fundamental tenets were the waging of holy war and the exaction of tribute through terror.

The Neo-Assyrians were convinced that their god demanded the constant expansion of his worship through military conquest. Essentially, their army belonged to Assur, and all who did not accept Assur's supremacy were, by that fact alone, enemies of Assur's people. Ritual humiliation of a defeated city's gods was therefore a regular feature of conquest. Statues of conquered gods would be carried off to the Neo-Assyrian capital, where they would remain as hostages at the court of Assur. Meanwhile, an image of Assur himself—usually represented as a sun disk with the head and shoulders of an archer— would be installed in the defeated city, and the conquered people would be required to worship him. Although conquered peoples did not have to abandon their previous gods altogether, they were made to feel their gods' inferiority. The Assyrians were therefore strict henotheists, meaning that they acknowledged the existence of other gods but believed that one god should be the supreme deity of all peoples.

For the Neo-Assyrians, "receiving tribute" meant the taking of plunder. Rather than defeating their foes once and imposing formal obligations, the Assyrians raided even their vanquished foes each year. This strategy kept the Neo-Assyrian military machine primed for battle, but it did little to inspire loyalty among subject peoples, who often felt that they had nothing to lose through rebellion. Moreover, annual invasions toughened the forces of the Neo-Assyrians' subjects. To counter them, imperial battle tactics became notoriously savage—even by the standards of ancient warfare, which regarded the mutilation of prisoners, systematic rape, and mass deportations as commonplace. Neo-Assyrian artwork and inscriptions often celebrate the butchering and torture of their enemies. Smiling archers are shown shooting fleeing enemies in the back while remorseless soldiers impale captives on stakes.

The Neo-Assyrian army was not a seasonal army of part-time warriors or peasant conscripts, but rather a massive standing force of more than 100,000 soldiers. Because the Assyrians had mastered iron-smelting techniques on a large scale, they could equip their fighting men with high-quality iron weapons that overwhelmed opponents still reliant on bronze. The organization of this army also contributed to its success. At its core were heavily armed and armored shock troops, equipped with a variety of thrusting weapons and bearing tall shields for protection. They were the main force for crushing enemy infantry in the field and for routing the inhabitants of an enemy city once inside. To harass enemy infantry and break up their formations, the Assyrians deployed light skirmishers with slings and javelins, and they combined archery and chariotry as never before. They also developed the first true cavalry force in the West, with individual warriors mounted on armored steeds, wielding bows and arrows or heavy lances. They even trained a highly skilled corps of combat engineers to undermine city walls and to build catapults, siege engines, battering rams, and battle towers.

The Legacy of Neo-Assyrian Power

The successors of Sargon II continued these military policies while devoting great energy to promoting an Assyrian cultural legacy. Sargon's immediate successor, Sennacherib (*sen-AH-sher-ib*; 704–681 B.C.E.), rebuilt the ancient Assyrian city of Nineveh, fortifying it with a double wall for a circuit of nine miles. He constructed an enormous palace there, raised on a giant platform decorated with marble, ivory, and exotic woods; and he ordered the construction of a massive irrigation system, including an aqueduct that carried fresh water to the city from thirty miles away. His son rebuilt the conquered city of Babylon along similar lines and was also a patron of the arts and sciences. His grandson Assurbanipal (*ah-sur-BAHN-ih-pahl*; r. 669–627 B.C.E.) was perhaps the greatest of all the Neo-Assyrian kings. For a time, he ruled the entire delta region of northern Egypt and also enacted a series of internal reforms, seeking ways to govern his empire more peacefully.

By Neo-Assyrian standards, Assurbanipal was an enlightened ruler, and one to whom we owe a tremendous debt. Like Sargon II before him, he had a strong sense of the rich traditions of Mesopotamian history and laid claim to them. But he did this much more systematically: he ordered the construction of a magnificent library at the great capital of Nineveh, where all the cultural monuments of Mesopotamian literature were to be copied and preserved. This library also was an archive for the correspondence and official acts of the king. Fortunately, this trove of documentation has survived. Our knowledge of history, not to

NEO-ASSYRIAN ATROCITIES. Judean captives whose city had fallen to the Neo-Assyrian king Sennacherib (704–681 B.C.E.) are shown being impaled on stakes. This triumphal carving comes from the walls of Sennacherib's palace at Nineveh. ■ *What was the purpose of advertising these captives' fates?*

ASSURBANIPAL FEASTING WITH HIS WIFE IN A HANGING GARDEN. Even in this peaceful, domestic scene, the severed head of the king's recently defeated enemy, the king of Elam, can be seen hanging from the pine tree on the left.

mention all modern editions of the *Epic of Gilgamesh*, ultimately derive from the library at Nineveh.

When Assurbanipal died in 627 B.C.E., the Neo-Assyrian Empire appeared to be at its zenith. Its borders were secure, the realm was largely at peace with its neighbors, its kings had adorned their capitals with magnificent artwork, and the hanging gardens of Babylon were already famous: these were artificial slopes whose cascading flowers and trees were fed by irrigation systems that pumped water uphill, an amazing marriage of engineering and horticulture.

The collapse of this empire is therefore all the more dramatic for its suddenness. Within fifteen years of Assurbanipal's reign, Nineveh lay in ruins. An alliance had formed between the Medes of Iran and the Chaldeans, a Semitic people who controlled the southern half of Babylonia. By 605 B.C.E., the Chaldeans had occupied Babylon and destroyed the last remnants of Neo-Assyrian power on the upper Euphrates, becoming the predominant imperial power in Mesopotamia and the Levant. In 586 B.C.E., they captured Jerusalem, destroyed the Temple, and deported the population of Judah to Babylon. Meanwhile, the Medes retired to the Iranian Plateau to extend their suzerainty there.

THE RISE OF THE PERSIANS

In the sixth century B.C.E., the **Persian Empire** emerged as the successor state to the Neo-Assyrian kings and the Chaldeans. Once the Persians had thrown off the Chaldeans' dominance, they in turn would construct the largest empire known to the world until that time.

The Persian Empire of Cyrus the Great

The Persians came to power relatively suddenly, under an extraordinary prince named Cyrus, who succeeded to the rule of a single Persian tribe in 559 B.C.E. Shortly thereafter, Cyrus made himself ruler of all the Persians and then, around 549 B.C.E., challenged the lordship of the Medes and began to claim dominion over lands stretching from the Persian Gulf to eastern Anatolia.

This brought the Persians into close contact with the kingdom of Lydia. The Lydians had attained great prosperity as producers of gold and silver specie (money) and as intermediaries for overland commerce between Mesopotamia and the Aegean. Most important, they were the first people in antiquity to use precious-metal coinage as a medium of exchange for goods and services.

When Cyrus came to power, the Lydians' king was Croesus (*CREE-suhs*), a man whose reputation as the possessor of untold riches survives in the expression "rich as Croesus." Distrusting his new neighbor, Croesus decided to launch a preventive strike against the Persians to preserve his own kingdom from conquest. According to the Greek historian Herodotus, he took the precaution of asking the oracle of Apollo at Delphi whether this strategy was a good one and was told that if he attacked the Persians he would destroy a great nation. The oracle's pronouncement was both ambiguous and true: the nation Croesus destroyed was his own. Cyrus defeated his forces in 546 B.C.E.

Cyrus then invaded Mesopotamia in 539 B.C.E., striking so quickly that he took Babylon without a fight. Once he was in Babylon, the entire Chaldean Empire was his for the

AN EARLY LYDIAN COIN. Probably struck during the reign of Croesus, this coin was one of many that facilitated long-distance trade by making wealth portable.

taking, though his own imperial policies proved very different from those of his predecessors in that region. Cyrus freed the Hebrews who had been held captive in Babylon since 586 B.C.E. and sent them back to Jerusalem, helping them to rebuild their temple and allowing them to set up a semi-independent vassal state. Cyrus also allowed other conquered peoples considerable self-determination, especially with respect to cultural and religious practices—a marked reversal of Neo-Assyrian and Chaldean policies. When Cyrus died in battle in 530 B.C.E., Persian expansion continued and his son even conquered Egypt in 525 B.C.E. Two hundred years later, a young Macedonian king, Alexander, would emulate many of Cyrus's policies and build an empire sustained by many of the same strategies (see Chapter 4).

The Consolidation of Persian Rule

Cyrus's son Cambyses II was a warrior king like his father, but after his death he left the Persian Empire a cumbersome and poorly organized collection of rapid conquests. After a short period of civil war, the aristocratic inner circle that had served both him and his father settled on a collateral member of the royal family as the new king.

This was Darius, whose long reign of thirty-five years (521–486 B.C.E.) consolidated his predecessors' military gains by improving the administration of the Persian state. Darius divided the empire into provinces, each of which was administered by an official called a *satrap*. Although satraps enjoyed extensive powers and considerable political latitude, they owed fixed tributes and absolute loyalty to the central government. Adhering to the tolerant policy of Cyrus, Darius allowed the various peoples of the empire to retain most of their local institutions while enforcing a standardized central currency and a system of weights and measures. Beyond this, he had little interest in imposing onerous taxes, martial law, or the Persians' own religious practices on subject peoples. After centuries of Neo-Assyrian and Chaldean tyranny, the light hand of Persian rule was welcomed throughout the empire's far-reaching lands.

Darius was also a great builder. He erected a new royal residence and ceremonial capital that the Greeks called Persepolis ("Persia City"). He ordered a canal dug from the Nile to the Red Sea to facilitate trade with the Egyptian interior, and he installed irrigation systems on the Persian plateau and on the fringe of the Syrian desert to increase agricultural production. Most important, Darius expanded the existing Assyrian road system to enhance trade and communications throughout his huge realm. The most famous artery was the Royal Road, stretching 1,600 miles from Susa, near the Persian Gulf, to Sardis (the former Lydian capital) near the Aegean. Government couriers along this road constituted the first postal system, carrying messages and goods in relay stages from one post to another. Each post was a day's horseback ride from the next, where a fresh horse and rider would be ready to carry the dispatches brought by the postman before him. An extensive imperial spy network also used this postal system and was famed throughout Persia as the "eyes and ears of the king."

Darius was an extraordinarily gifted administrator, but as a military strategist he made an enormous mistake when he attempted to extend Persian hegemony into Greece. Cyrus's conquest of Lydia had made Persia the ruler of some long-established Greek-speaking cities on the western coast of Anatolia, a region called Ionia. But these cities resisted even the easy terms of Persian rule, desiring instead to model themselves on the self-governing city-states that had come into being across the Aegean. Consequently, between 499 and 494 B.C.E., the Greeks of Asia waged a war for independence and briefly gained the support of troops from Athens, who burned the Persian administrative center at Sardis.

Darius quelled this uprising and then decided to send a force to punish Athens and serve notice of Persian dominion over all Greek states. But at the battle of Marathon in 490 B.C.E., the Athenians' victory dealt Darius the only major setback of his reign. And when his son and successor, Xerxes (*ZEHRK-zees*), attempted to avenge this humiliation in 480 B.C.E., a resistance led by both Athens and Sparta forced him to retreat and abandon his plans a year later. (We will discuss these events at greater length in Chapter 3.)

A CYLINDRICAL SEAL OF DARIUS THE GREAT (522–486 B.C.E.). Seals were used in place of signatures to authenticate documents and correspondence. The cylindrical matrix (right) was rolled in soft wax to create an impression. This finely wrought example shows the king in a chariot, hunting lions with a bow. A winged representation of the god Ahura-Mazda rises above the scene.

The Persians were thus compelled to recognize that they had reached the westward limits of their expansion. Thereafter, they concentrated on their Asian possessions and used money and diplomacy to keep the Greeks in check. This was not difficult, because the Greeks' hasty union in the face of Persian hegemony was short lived, and they were too embroiled in wars with one another to pose any threat to Persia.

The richness of their culture and the general tolerance they exhibited served the Persians well in maintaining their enormous empire. Unlike the Neo-Assyrian or Chaldean rulers, the Persians could count on the loyalty and even the affection of their subjects. In fact, their imperial model—the accommodation of local institutions and practices, consistent administration through a trained bureaucracy, and rapid communications between center and periphery—would be adopted by the great and lasting empires of all subsequent Western civilizations.

The Legacy of Zoroastrianism

The Persians' political and cultural achievements were paralleled by a spiritual one: **Zoroastrianism**. Along with Buddhism and Judaism, this important religion was one of the three major universal faiths before Christianity and Islam. Its founder was Zarathustra, known to the Greeks as Zoroaster, a Persian who probably lived shortly before

600 B.C.E. Zarathustra sought to reform the traditional customs of the Persian tribes by eradicating polytheism, animal sacrifice, and magic. That is, he wanted to redefine religion as an ethical practice common to all people, rather than a set of rituals and superstitions that caused divisions among them.

Zoroastrianism teaches that there is one supreme god in the universe, whom Zarathustra called Ahura-Mazda, "Wise Lord." Ahura-Mazda is the essence of light, truth, and righteousness; there is nothing wrathful or wicked about him, and his goodness extends to everyone, not just to one people or tribe. How, then, can there be evil and suffering in the world? Because, Zarathustra posited, there is a counter-deity, Ahriman, treacherous and malignant, who rules the forces of darkness. Yet Zarathustra also posited that Ahura-Mazda must be vastly stronger than Ahriman.

Later teachers and priests of Zoroastrianism, the magi (*MA-jeye*), placed greater emphasis on the equality of these divine forces: they insisted that Ahura-Mazda and Ahriman are evenly matched, engaged in a desperate and eternal struggle for supremacy. According to them, light will not triumph over darkness until the Last Day, when the forces of Ahura-Mazda vanquish those of Ahriman forever. This vision of the universe proved enormously influential, informing the developing theologies of Christianity and Islam—not to mention the plots of much modern science fiction, fantasy literature, and film.

The devotion of the Persian imperial dynasty to Zarathustra's teachings made Zoroastrianism important to the

THE PERSIAN EMPIRE UNDER DARIUS I, 521–486 B.C.E. Consider the location of the Persian heartland and the four administrative centers of Persepolis, Susa, Ecbatana, and Sardis. ▪ *What older kingdoms and empires did the Persian Empire contain?* ▪ *Why is the Royal Road especially noted on this map?* ▪ *How did Darius I successfully rule such a large and complex empire?*

conduct of Persian government and helps to explain the tolerance of Persian rule. Unlike the Neo-Assyrians, the Chaldeans, or even the Egyptians, the Persian kings saw themselves as presiding over an assemblage of different nations whose customs and beliefs they were prepared to tolerate. Whereas Mesopotamian potentates characteristically called themselves "true king," Persian rulers took the title "king of kings" or "great king," implying that they recognized the legitimacy of other kings who ruled under their canopy. This same spirit is reflected in Persian architecture, which drew freely and creatively on Sumerian, Babylonian, Assyrian, Egyptian, and Greek influences yet nonetheless created a distinctively Persian style.

Unlike other ancient religions, then, Zoroastrianism did not exalt the power of a godlike king or support any particular political regime. It was a personal religion, making private, spiritual demands as opposed to public, ritual ones. Its Wise Lord supports neither tribes nor states but only individuals who serve the cause of truth and justice. These individuals possess free will and can choose to sin or not to sin; they are not compelled by an array of conflicting

gods to act in particular ways. Zoroastrianism thus urges its adherents to choose good over evil, to be truthful, to love and help one another to the best of their powers, to aid the poor, and to practice generous hospitality. Those who do so will be rewarded in an afterlife, when the dead are resurrected on Judgment Day and consigned either to a realm of joy or to the flames of despair. In the scriptures of the Zoroastrian faith, known as the Avesta (compiled, like the Bible, over the course of many centuries), the rewards for righteousness are great but not immediate. They are spiritual, not material.

THE DEVELOPMENT OF HEBREW MONOTHEISM

Of all the important developments that we have traced in our study of the Iron Age, perhaps none is of greater significance than monotheism: the belief in a single god, the creator and ruler of all things. This development is

Competing Viewpoints

Two Perspectives on Imperial Rule

> These two inscriptions exemplify two very different attitudes toward imperial power and two very different methods of achieving it. The first glorifies the victories of the Assyrian king Esarhaddon in Syria and is one of the most important records of his reign (681–669 B.C.E.). The second commemorates the taking of Babylon by the Persian king Cyrus the Great (c. 559–530 B.C.E.), whose empire came to encompass and surpass that of the Assyrians.

The Stele of King Esarhaddon at Senjirli, c. 680 B.C.E.

To Assur, father of the gods, lover of my priesthood, Anu mighty and preeminent, who called me by name, Ba'al, the exalted lord, establisher of my dynasty, Ea, the wise, all-knowing . . . Ishtar, lady of battle and combat, who goes at my side . . . all of them who determine my destiny, who grant to the king, their favorite, power and might . . . the king, the offering of whose sacrifices the great gods love . . . their unsparing weapons they have presented him as a royal gift . . . [he] who has brought all the lands in submission at his feet, who has imposed tribute and tax upon them; conqueror of his foes, destroyer of his enemies, the king,

who as to his walk is a storm, and as to his deeds, a raging wolf; . . . the onset of his battle is powerful, he is a consuming flame, a fire that does not sink: son of Sennacherib, king of the universe, king of Assyria, grandson of Sargon, king of the universe, king of Assyria, viceroy of Babylon, king of Sumer and Akkad. . . . I am powerful, I am all-powerful, I am a hero, I am gigantic, I am colossal, I am honored, I am magnified, I am without an equal among all kings, the chosen one of Assur . . . the great lord [who], in order to show to the peoples the immensity of my mighty deeds, made powerful my kingship over the four regions of the world and made my name great.

. . . Of Tirhakah, king of Egypt and Kush, the accursed . . . without cessation I slew multitudes of his men, and him I smote five times with the point of my javelin, with wounds, no recovery. Memphis, his royal city, in half a day . . . I besieged, I captured, I destroyed, I devastated, I burned with fire. . . . The root of Kush I tore up out of Egypt and not one therein escaped to submit to me.

Source: Daniel David Luckenbill, ed., *Ancient Records of Assyria and Babylonia*, vol. 2 (Chicago: 1926–27), pp. 224–27.

Inscription Honoring Cyrus, c. 539

He [the god Marduk] scanned and looked (through) all the countries, searching for a righteous ruler who would lead him. (Then) he pronounced the name of Cyrus, king of Anshan [Persia], declared him to be the leader of the world. . . . And he (Cyrus) did always endeavor to treat according to justice the black-headed [people] whom he (Marduk) made him conquer. Marduk, the great lord,

a protector of his people/worshipers, beheld with pleasure his good deeds and his upright mind, (and therefore) ordered him to march against his city Babylon. He made him set out on the road to Babylon, going at his side like a real friend. His widespread troops—their number, like the water of a river, could not be established—strolled along, their weapons packed away. Without any battle, he made them enter his town Babylon,

sparing Babylon any calamity. He delivered into his hands Nabonidus, the king who did not worship him. All the inhabitants of Babylon as well as of the entire country of Sumer and Akkad, princes and governors (included), bowed to him and kissed his feet, jubilant that he (had received) the kingship, and with shining faces. Happily they greeted him as a master through whose help they had come (again) to life from death (and) had all been spared damage and disaster, and they worshiped his name.

I am Cyrus, king of the world, great king, legitimate king, king of Babylon, king of Sumer and Akkad, king of the four rims (of the earth), son of Cambyses, great king, king of Anshan, grandson of Cyrus, great king, king of Anshan, descendent of Teipes, great king, king of Anshan, of a family (which) always (exercised) kingship; whose rule Bel and Nebo love, whom they want as king to please their hearts.

When I entered Babylon as a friend and (when) I established the seat of the government in the palace of the ruler under jubilation and rejoicing.... My numerous troops walked around Babylon in peace, I did not allow anybody to terrorize (any place) of the (country of Sumer) and Akkad. I strove for peace in Babylon and in all his (other) sacred cities.... I abolished the ... [yoke] which was against their (social) standing, I brought relief to their dilapidated housing, putting (thus) an end to their (main) complaints.... All the kings of the entire world from the Upper to the Lower Sea, those who are seated in throne rooms, (those who) live in other (types of buildings as well as) all the kings of the West living in tents, brought their heavy tributes and kissed my feet in Babylon.

Source: Excerpted from James B. Pritchard, ed., *Ancient Near Eastern Texts Relating to the Old Testament*, 3rd ed. (Princeton, NJ: 1969), pp. 315–16.

Questions for Analysis

1. Both of these inscriptions constitute propaganda, but of different kinds. How do they differ? What audience(s) are they addressing? What function(s) does each inscription serve?

2. Each of these rulers claims to have a close relationship with the divine. How do those relationships differ? What do those differences reveal about their attitudes to kingship and its sources of power?

3. Both of these kings boast of their royal lineage and their connections to past rulers. How different or similar are these perspectives? What do they reveal about these kings' awareness of history?

---

traditionally associated with the Hebrews, but even the Hebrews were not always monotheists. Those who argued for the exclusive worship of Yahweh were a minority within Hebrew society, albeit a vocal and assertive one. How the Hebrews came to regard Yahweh as the only divine being in the universe, and to root their identity in such an exclusive religious outlook, is a phenomenon that can only be understood within its historical context.

From Monolatry to Monotheism

For those who later advocated the exclusive worship of Yahweh, the early history of the Hebrews was full of embarrassments. Even the Hebrew scriptures reveal their propensity to worship many gods. Yahweh himself, in commanding that his people "have no other gods before me," clearly acknowledged the existence of other gods. The older, polytheistic Hebrew religion honored nature spirits such as Azazel and the Canaanite deity El, whose name is an important element in many Hebrew place-names (e.g., Bethel) and soon became a synonym for "god." The temple built by Solomon at Jerusalem had even included altars dedicated to Ba'al and his wife Asherah, a fertility goddess. Later Hebrew kings continued such practices, overriding the protests of religious purists devoted to Yahweh.

By the beginning of the first millennium, however, the Hebrews living under the rule of David began to promote monolatry, meaning that they exalted one god without denying the existence of others. Although the legendary prophet Moses is often credited as the first promoter of Yahweh's cult sometime around the middle of the second millennium B.C.E., the ascendancy of Yahweh really took place much later, under the influence of the Levites, a tribe who claimed unique priestly authority over Yahweh's worship and sought to enhance their own power and prestige by discrediting other gods.

The success of their campaign rested on the Levites' access to writing. As we have frequently noted, the written word was especially potent in the ancient world because the skills necessary for its mastery were rare. In an age of constant threats to Hebrew religious and political sovereignty, the literacy of the Levites thus helped to preserve and promote

Yahweh's worship. So did the political supremacy of David's dynasty, which bolstered its own legitimacy by allying itself with the Levites. The result was a centralized cult situated in the new royal capital of Jerusalem, which attempted to link the political and the religious identity of the Hebrews with the acknowledgment of Yahweh as the supreme god.

Nevertheless, the worship of other Hebrew gods actually increased during the eighth and seventh centuries B.C.E., perhaps in reaction to the austere morality demanded and imposed by the Yahwists. One of these, Jeremiah (c. 637–587 B.C.E.), railed against "foreign" cults and warned of the disastrous consequences that would arise if Yahweh's people did not remain faithful to him. The Yahweh of this era was still imagined as a conventional god, possessing a physical body and portrayed as capricious and irascible. Further, he was not omnipotent; his power was largely confined to the territory occupied by the Hebrews.

Still, some of the Hebrews' most important contributions to subsequent Western religions crystallized during this period. One was a theology of Yahweh's transcendence: the teaching that God is not part of nature but exists outside of it. God can therefore be understood, in purely intellectual or abstract terms, as entirely separate from the operations of the natural world. Complementing this principle was the belief that Yahweh had appointed humans to be the rulers of nature by divine mandate. In the book of Genesis, when Yahweh orders Adam and Eve to "replenish the earth and subdue it, and have dominion over . . . every living thing," his injunction stands in striking contrast to other accounts of creation in which humans are made to serve the gods. Finally, Hebrew religious thought was moving during this period toward the articulation of universal ethics—a universal theory of justice and righteousness. According to the Babylonian flood story, for example, a particularly petulant god destroys humanity because their noise deprives him of sleep. In Genesis, by contrast, Yahweh sends a flood in punishment for human wickedness but saves Noah and his family because "Noah was a just man."

The Hebrews honored Yahweh during this era by subscribing to certain moral precepts and taboos. The Ten Commandments as they now appear in Exodus 20:3–17 may not yet have existed in that exact form, but they certainly reflect earlier ethical injunctions against murder, adultery, lying, and greed. In addition, the Hebrews observed an array of ritual practices unusual in the ancient world, such as infant circumcision, adherence to strict dietary laws, and refraining from labor on the seventh day of the week.

Yet the moral standards imposed by Yahweh on the Hebrew community were not binding when the Hebrews dealt with outsiders. Lending at interest, for example, was not acceptable among Hebrews but was quite acceptable between a Hebrew and a non-Hebrew. Such distinctions applied also to more serious issues, such as the killing of civilians in battle. When the Hebrews conquered territories in Canaan, they took "all the spoil of the cities, and every man they smote with the sword . . . until they had destroyed them." Far from having any doubts about such a brutal policy, the Hebrews believed that Yahweh had inspired the Canaanites to resist so that the Hebrews could slaughter them: "For it was the Lord's doing to harden their hearts that they should come against Israel in battle, in order that they should be utterly destroyed, and should receive no mercy but be exterminated" (Joshua 11:20).

With the political fragmentation of the fragile Hebrew kingdom after Solomon's death, important regional distinctions arose within Yahweh's cult. The rulers of the northern kingdom of Israel discouraged their citizens from participating in ritual activities at Jerusalem—at least according to the

THE GODDESS ASHERAH. The Canaanite fertility goddess, Asherah, was the wife of the god Ba'al (or his father, El), but she also figures in some inscriptions as the wife of the Hebrew god Yahweh. One Hebrew king placed an image of her in the Temple of Yahweh at Jerusalem. ▪ *Why might this be viewed as controversial—then or now?*

Jerusalem-based Yahwists, who shaped the biblical tradition and who wanted to represent their own Judah as the favored kingdom. The erosion of a cohesive Hebrew identity was further accelerated by the Neo-Assyrians, who under Sargon II absorbed the northern kingdom as a province and enslaved nearly 28,000 Hebrews. The southern kingdom of Judah survived, but political collaboration with the Neo-Assyrians also meant acceptance of the god Assur.

This Neo-Assyrian threat was the whetstone on which the Yahwist prophets sharpened their demands for an exclusive monotheism that went beyond monolatry. Hebrew prophets were practical political leaders as well as religious figures, and most of them understood that military resistance to the Neo-Assyrians was futile. So if the Hebrews were to survive as a people, they had to emphasize the one thing that separated them from everyone else in the known world: the worship of Yahweh and the denial of all other gods. The prophets' insistence that Yahweh alone should be exalted was thus an aggressive reaction to the equally aggressive promotion of Assur by the Neo-Assyrians.

The foremost Hebrew prophets of this era were Amos and Hosea, who preached in the kingdom of Israel before it fell to the Neo-Assyrians in 722 B.C.E.; Isaiah and Jeremiah, who preached in Judah before its fall in 586 B.C.E.; and Ezekiel and the "second Isaiah" (the Book of Isaiah had at least two different authors), who continued to preach "by the waters of Babylon" during the Hebrews' exile there. Despite some differences in emphasis, these prophets' messages consistently emphasize three core doctrines:

1. Yahweh is the ruler of the universe. He even makes use of peoples other than the Hebrews to accomplish his purposes. The gods of other nations are false gods. There has never been and never will be more than this one god.
2. Yahweh is exclusively a god of righteousness. He wills only the good, and evil in the world comes from humanity, not from him.
3. Because Yahweh is righteous, he demands ethical behavior from his people. Over and above ritual and sacrifice, he requires that his followers "seek justice, relieve the oppressed, protect the fatherless, and plead for the widow."

RECONSTRUCTION OF THE ISHTAR GATE. This is a reconstruction of one of the fifty-foot-high entrance gates built into the walls of Babylon by King Nebuchadnezzar around 575 B.C.E. About half of this reconstruction, in the Pergamon Museum of Berlin, is original.

The prophet Amos summarized these teachings when he expressed Yahweh's resounding warning in the eighth century B.C.E.:

I hate, I despise your feasts, and I take no delight in your solemn assemblies. Even though you offer me your burnt offerings and cereal offerings, I will not accept them, and the peace offerings of your fatted beasts I will not look upon. Take away from me the noise of your songs; to the melody of your harps I will not listen. But let justice roll down like waters, and righteousness like an ever-flowing stream. (Amos 5:21–24)

Judaism Takes Shape

The Yahwists made it possible for the Hebrews to survive under Neo-Assyrian domination through their insistence on monotheism as the cornerstone of Hebrew identity, and they enjoyed political and religious triumph as this threat receded in the late seventh century B.C.E. Josiah (621–609 B.C.E.), the king of Judah during the waning years of the Neo-Assyrian Empire, was a committed monotheist whose court employed prominent prophets, including Jeremiah. With his own power increasing, Josiah found himself in a position to pursue significant reforms. He presided over the redrafting and revision of the "Law of Moses" to bring it into line with current policies, and it was during his reign that the Book of Deuteronomy was "discovered" and hailed as Moses's "Second Law." Deuteronomy is the most stridently monotheistic book of the Hebrew Bible, and it lent weight to this new political program.

But within a generation of King Josiah's death, the Chaldeans under Nebuchadnezzar conquered Jerusalem, destroyed the Temple, and carried thousands of Hebrews off to Babylon in 587/586 B.C.E. This Babylonian Captivity brought many challenges, paramount among them the maintenance of the Hebrews' hard-won religious identity. The leading voices in defining that identity continued to be the patriotic Yahwists, the same people who would later spearhead the return to Jerusalem two generations later, after Cyrus captured Babylon and liberated the Hebrews. Among the Yahwists, the prophet Ezekiel stressed that salvation could be found only through religious purity, which meant ignoring all foreign gods and acknowledging only Yahweh. Kingdoms and states and empires came to nothing in the long run, Ezekiel said. What mattered for those living in exile was the creature God had made in his image—man—and the relationship between God and his creation.

This period of captivity and exile was therefore decisive in forging a universal religion that transcended politics. Just as Yahweh existed outside creation, so the people who worshiped him could exist outside a Hebrew kingdom. In Babylon, the worship of Yahweh therefore became something different; it became **Judaism**, a religion that was not tied to any particular political system or territory, for there was neither a Hebrew ruling class nor a Hebrew state after 586 B.C.E. Outside of Judah, Judaism flourished and became the crucial factor in the emergence of a new Jewish identity. This was an unparalleled development in the ancient world: the survival of a religion that had no political power to back it and no holy place to ground it.

After 538 B.C.E., when Cyrus conquered Babylon, he allowed the Hebrews to return to their lands in a new Persian-governed province of Judea. Jerusalem became once again the central holy place of their religious life—although many Hebrews remained and flourished in Persia, while others had long since settled in Egypt. The Judaism that had emerged during the Hebrews' residence in Babylon would be promulgated by a new generation of Jews, particularly the prophet Ezra, who is credited with bringing the strict interpretation and application of the Torah from Persia to Jerusalem, and Nehemiah, the Persian-appointed governor of Judea who began the process of rebuilding the Temple. Eventually, the monotheistic religion that emerged from these historical processes would become common to the worldview of all Western civilizations.

After You Read This Chapter

 Go to **INQUIZITIVE** to see what you've learned—and learn what you've missed—with personalized feedback along the way.

REVIEWING THE OBJECTIVES

- The settlement of Indo-European peoples in the Near East had marked effects on the older civilizations there. What were some major consequences?
- Egypt's New Kingdom differed profoundly from the Old and Middle Kingdoms that preceded it. Why was this the case?
- The civilizations of the Late Bronze Age were bound together by transnational networks. What were the strengths and fragilities of these relationships?
- What kingdoms and empires emerged in the ancient world after the devastation caused by the Sea Peoples?
- Monotheism was a significant historical development of the first millennium B.C.E. Why is it so important?

CONCLUSION

The centuries between 1700 and 500 B.C.E. were an epoch of empires. Although the two great powers of the second millennium were New Kingdom Egypt and the Hittite Empire in Anatolia, a host of lesser empires also coalesced during this period, including Minoan Crete, Mycenaean Greece, and the trading empire of the Assyrians. All were sustained by a sophisticated network of trade and diplomacy. But between 1200 and 1000 B.C.E. the devastation wrought by the Sea Peoples destroyed this integrated civilization. These invasions cleared the way for the emergence of many new, small states, including those of the Phoenicians, the Philistines, the Hebrews, and the Lydians. Many crucial cultural and economic developments were fostered by these small states, including alphabetic writing, coinage, mercantile colonization, and monotheism. But the dominant states of the Iron Age continued to be great land empires centered in western Asia: first that of the Neo-Assyrians, then briefly the Chaldeans, and finally the Persians.

Yet the empires of the early Iron Age were quite different from those that had dominated the ancient world a thousand years before. These new powers were much more highly unified. They had capital cities, centrally managed systems of communication, sophisticated administrative structures, and ideologies that justified their aggressive imperialism. They commanded armies of unprecedented size, and they demanded from their subjects a degree of obedience impossible for any Bronze Age emperor to imagine or enforce. Their rulers declared themselves the chosen instruments of their god's divine will.

At the same time, we can trace the emergence of more personalized religions. Zoroastrian dualism and Hebrew monotheism added an important new emphasis on ethical conduct, and both pioneered the development of authoritative written scriptures that advanced religious teachings. Zoroastrianism, despite its radical reimagining of the cosmos, proved fully compatible with imperialism and became the driving spiritual force behind the Persian Empire. Judaism, by contrast, was forged in the struggle to resist the imperialism of the Neo-Assyrians and Chaldeans. Both systems of belief would exercise enormous influence on future civilizations. In particular, they provided the models on which Christianity and Islam would ultimately erect their own traditions, just as models of imperial governance forged in this period would become the template for future empires. In Chapter 3, we will look at the ways in which the city-states of ancient Greece both built on and departed from these models.

PEOPLE, IDEAS, AND EVENTS IN CONTEXT

- How did the Hittite Empire integrate the cultures of **INDO-EUROPEANS** with the older civilizations of this region?
- What do the reigns of **HATSHEPSUT** and **AKHENATEN** tell us about the continuities and limitations of pharaonic power?
- What factors produced the transnational networks of the Late **BRONZE AGE**?
- How did the civilizations of **MINOAN CRETE** and **MYCENAEAN GREECE** differ from one another and from neighboring civilizations?
- In what ways do the **PHOENICIANS**, the **PHILISTINES**, and the **HEBREWS** exemplify three different approaches to state building at the beginning of the first millennium B.C.E.?
- What was new about the **NEO-ASSYRIAN EMPIRE**? How do its methods of conquest and its military-religious ethos compare with those of the **PERSIAN EMPIRE** that followed it?
- How and why did monotheism develop in the Hebrew kingdoms? In what ways might **JUDAISM** have been influenced by **ZOROASTRIANISM**?

THINKING ABOUT CONNECTIONS

- In the religions of Akhenaten, the Persians, and the Hebrews, we see a rejection of polytheism. What cultural factors may have contributed to this? What would you consider to be the long-term effects of monotheism as a motivating force in history?
- What patterns of success or failure appear to be emerging when we consider the empires that flourished in the Iron Age, particularly those of the Assyrians and the Persians? Are similar patterns visible in other periods of history, including our own?

Before
You
Read
This
Chapter

STORY LINES

- The emergence of democracy in the ancient Greek world was dependent on specific historical circumstances, which included reliance on slavery and the exclusion of women from public life. It therefore differs markedly from the political system(s) described as democratic today.

- Although the different Greek *poleis* did not share a common political structure, they shared a strong sense of identity and were united by their language and culture.

- The Athenians' empire and their leadership in the Persian Wars enabled them to dominate the Mediterranean and also, through the use of writing, to influence our understanding of their role in history.

- The cultural achievements of the fifth century B.C.E. glorified the individual citizen and his role in the community.

CHRONOLOGY

800–400 B.C.E.	Rise of the *polis*
c. 750 B.C.E.	Homeric epics transcribed
725–650 B.C.E.	Hoplite tactics become standard
c. 600 B.C.E	Militarization of Sparta
600–500 B.C.E.	Emergence of the Milesian School (pre-Socratic philosophy)
594 B.C.E.	Solon's reforms in Athens
546 B.C.E.	Cyrus of Persia conquers Lydia and controls the Greek cities of Ionia
510 B.C.E.	Overthrow of the Peisistratid tyranny in Athens
499–494 B.C.E.	Ionian Revolt
490 B.C.E.	Battle of Marathon
480 B.C.E.	Battles of Thermopylae and Salamis
479 B.C.E.	Battle of Plataea
478 B.C.E.	Formation of the Delian League
431 B.C.E.	Peloponnesian War begins
404 B.C.E.	Defeat of Athens by Sparta
399 B.C.E.	Death of Socrates

The Civilization of Greece, 1000–400 B.C.E.

CORE OBJECTIVES

- **DESCRIBE** the factors that led to the emergence of the Greek polis.

- **EXPLAIN** the importance of hoplite warfare and its effects on democracy and military tactics.

- **DEFINE** the key differences among the poleis of Athens, Sparta, and Miletus.

- **IDENTIFY** the ways in which Athenian culture, philosophy, and art reflect democratic ideals.

- **UNDERSTAND** the impact of the Persian and Peloponnesian Wars on Greek civilization.

I n the fifth century B.C.E., a Greek-speaking subject of the Persian Empire began to write a book. He had been to Egypt and along the African coast, to the Greek colonies of Italy, the cities of Persia, the wilds of Thrace and Macedonia, and all over the Aegean. He had collected stories about peoples and places even farther afield: Ethiopia, India, the Black Sea. We have already met this intrepid traveler, Herodotus (c. 484–c. 425 B.C.E.), who marveled at the pyramids of Giza (see Chapter 1) and who told how the king of Lydia lost his power to the Persians (see Chapter 2). His reason for compiling this information was timely: he wanted to write a history of recent events. As he put it, "Herodotus of Halicarnassus here sets forth the results of his research, with the aim of preserving the remembrance of what men have done, and of preventing the great and wonderful deeds of both Greeks and barbarians from losing their glory; and in particular to examine the causes that made them fight one another."

Herodotus's fascination with the Persians, Phoenicians, and Egyptians underscores the extent to which all Greek-speakers regarded themselves as different from other ancient peoples. While they struggled to cooperate politically, they

THE ACROPOLIS OF ATHENS AND THE PARTHENON. Many Greek cities were built upon mountain strongholds, but the most famous of these is the acropolis of Athens. First settled in the Neolithic Period, it was a fortified palace during the Bronze Age—allegedly that of the hero Theseus—and then a precinct sacred to the goddess Athena, for whom the city was named. The Parthenon, its most important surviving structure, was built on the site of an older temple after the Athenian victory over the Persians at Marathon in 490 B.C.E. It was then rebuilt after the Persians sacked Athens ten years later. Most of the damage it sustained thereafter occurred during modern wars. ▪ *Why was this site the focal point of so much activity?* ▪ *What does its longevity tell us about the relationship between place and identity in Greece?*

were able to forge a common language and culture, and they cherished values that were distinct from those of the people they called *barbarians:* peoples whose speech, to Greek ears, sounded like gibberish ("bar-bar-bar"). They celebrated individual liberty, participatory government, artistic innovation, scientific investigation, and confidence in the powers of the human mind. Although the practical implementation of these ideals would prove problematic— and continues to be so—our own civilization would be unimaginable without the political experiments and cultural achievements of ancient Greece.

FROM CHAOS TO POLIS

By the end of the twelfth century B.C.E., Mycenaean civilization had vanished (see Chapter 2). Except at Athens, the great citadels that had crowned the heights of the mainland kingdoms had been destroyed. But even at Athens, the population steadily declined, with severe effects on the economy and on social organization. Settlements shrank in size and moved inland, away from vulnerable coastlines, cutting themselves off from trade and communication. Indeed, the use of writing declined to such an extent that the knowledge of the system known as Linear B disappeared. Archaeological evidence suggests a world in stasis, isolated from the centers of civilization that were reemerging in western Asia.

The material realities of life in this era profoundly shaped one of the new civilizations that emerged from it. This civilization would emphasize male political equality and modest display, the importance of domestic economy, and self-sufficiency: these were the principles that formed the basis of early democracies. At the same time, this new historical reality also had long-term effects on religion and philosophy, because the hardships of daily life contrasted sharply with the stories of a heroic and opulent past. Although worship of the gods continued to be central to

Greek culture and civic life, the power of individual human beings was celebrated, too. However, excessive pride in one's own accomplishments could be dangerous, because such *hubris* attracted the adverse attention of the gods. The gods favored those who showed initiative and daring, but they would punish the hubris of those who failed to acknowledge their own limitations.

Homer and the Heroic Tradition

Around the year 1000 B.C.E., the disruption of the transnational Bronze Age networks that had contributed to the isolation of Greece was alleviated by a period of relative peace. The standard of living improved, and increased contact among individual settlements fostered trade. New techniques made Greek pottery, in particular, a sophisticated and sought-after commodity that Greek merchants could exchange for luxury goods from abroad.

As trade became an increasingly important feature of the new economy, the personal fortunes of those who engaged in commerce increased accordingly, leading to a new form of social status based on wealth rather than on warfare or noble birth—as had been the case in the distant past. Members of this new economic class justified their preeminence as a reflection of their own superior qualities as *aristoi* ("best men"). Yet wealth in itself was not sufficient as a claim to **aristocracy**, the "rule of the best." Those who aspired to this status were also expected to emulate, as far as possible, the heroes of old, whose stories lived in the prodigious memories and agile voices of the singers of tales.

These singers, the guardians of a rich oral history that had never been written down, were part poets in their own right and part *rhapsodes* ("weavers of songs"). The most famous is **Homer**, a legendary poet credited with having woven together the mesh of stories that we know as the *Iliad* and the *Odyssey*. They appear to have crystallized around 800 B.C.E., at about the same time that Hesiod was working on shorter lyrics capturing a more practical perspective on life (see Chapter 2). The epics ascribed to Homer are vast encyclopedias of lore set at the end of the Bronze Age, the time Hesiod called the "Age of Heroes." These were the days when Agamemnon ruled in Mycenae and launched a vast expedition to conquer Troy, where the prince Paris had taken Helen, the ravishing wife of Agamemnon's brother, Menelaus; it was the age of Achilles and his Trojan rival, Hector; it was the age of Odysseus the wayfarer.

Like the much older Epic of Gilgamesh (see Chapter 1), these Greek epics preserve long-standing traditions. But over centuries of retelling, the social and political relationships portrayed in the poems changed to reflect the assumptions and agendas of later ages. As a result, the Homeric epics are of tremendous value to historians. They also offer significant analytical challenges. Although the events and many of the material objects described in them date from the late Bronze Age, the society they reflect is more like that of Homer's contemporaries, half a millennium later. Treating these epics as historical sources, therefore, requires the historian to work like an archaeologist, carefully peeling back layers of meaning and accumulated sediment.

For example, Homer depicts a world in which competition and status are of paramount importance to the warrior elite, just as they were of vital concern to the aristocrats of his own day. Through the exchange of expensive gifts and hospitality, men aspiring to positions of power sought to create strong ties of guest friendship (*xenía*, zeh-NEE-ah), and thus to construct networks of influence that would support their economic, social, and political ambitions. Indeed, it is almost impossible to overestimate the importance of guest friendship as a sacred institution, something that is illustrated by the encounter between the wandering warrior Odysseus and the young princess Nausicaa (see page 78). It shows that aristocrats in the Greek world conceived of themselves as having more in common with each other than they did with the local societies they dominated, something that is also reflected in the essential similarity of Trojans and Greeks in the *Iliad*, and the lack of perceived differences among various Greek tribes.

However, the practice of guest friendship and the shared sense of a common culture among aristocratic households did not lessen the competition that frequently led to violence. (The Trojan War, after all, is supposed to have begun when Paris violated the holy ties of guest-friendship by seducing the wife of the Spartan king, his host.) It also led to competition over the epic past, as fledgling aristocratic clans vied to claim descent from one or another legendary hero. A hero cult might begin when an important family claimed an impressive Mycenaean tomb as that of their own famous ancestor, someone named in the *Iliad* and said to come from that place. They would then develop a pious tradition of practicing dutiful sacrifices and other observances at the tomb. This devotion would extend to their followers and dependents; eventually, an entire community might come to identify itself with the famous local hero. The heroic ideal thus became a deeply ingrained feature of Greek society, as did the stories that the epics preserved and propagated.

Analyzing Primary Sources

The Obligations of Hospitality: The Encounter of Odysseus and Nausicaa

Before the emergence of the Greek poleis, relations among communities depended largely on the personal connections made among leading families of different settlements. Often founded on the exchange of gifts or hospitality, the resulting bonds of guest friendship imposed serious obligations on those involved in such relationships—and on their heirs. Most such friendships were formed between men, but in the following excerpt from the Odyssey, we watch as the shipwrecked Odysseus, naked and frightened, is rescued by a young princess, Nausicaa (now-SIC-ah-ah), whose name means "Ship-Burner." As a woman who gives him a new life, she becomes his second mother, despite her youth.

hat is this country I
    have come to now?
Are all the people wild
    and violent, or good,
    hospitable, and
    god-fearing?
I heard the sound of female voices. Is it
    nymphs, who frequent the craggy
    mountaintops, and river streams and
    meadows lush with grass?
Or could this noise I hear be human voices?
    I have to try to find out who they are."
Odysseus jumped up from out the bushes.
Grasping a leafy branch he broke it off
    to cover up his manly private parts.
Just as a mountain lion trusts its strength,
    and beaten by the rain and wind, its
    eyes burn bright as it attacks the cows
    or sheep, or wild deer, and hunger
    drives it on to try the sturdy pens of
    sheep—so need impelled Odysseus to
    come upon the girls with pretty hair,
    though he was naked.
All caked with salt, he looked a dreadful
    sight.
They ran along the shore quite terrified,
    some here, some there. But Nausicaa
    stayed still.
Athena made her legs stop trembling
    and gave her courage in her heart.
    She stood there.

***

His words were calculated flattery.
"My lady, please! Are you divine or human?
If you are some great goddess from the
    sky, you look like Zeus' daughter
    Artemis—you are as tall and beautiful
    as she.

But if you live on earth and are a human,
    your mother and your father must
    be lucky, your brothers also—lucky
    three times over.
Their hearts must be delighted, seeing
    you, their flourishing new sprout, the
    dancers' leader.
And that man will be luckiest by far, who
    takes you home with dowry, as his
    bride.

***

I am in awe of you, afraid to touch your
    knees. But I am desperate. I came
    from Ogygia, and for twenty days
    storm winds and waves were driving
    me, adrift until yesterday some god
    washed me up right here, perhaps to
    meet more suffering. I think my
    troubles will not end until the gods
    have done their all. My lady, pity me.
Battered and wrecked, I come to you,
    you first—and I know no one else in
    this whole country.
Show me the town, give me some rags
    to wear, if you brought any clothes
    when you came here."

***

Then white-armed Nausicaa replied,
    "Well, stranger, you seem a brave and
    clever man; you know that Zeus
    apportions happiness to people, to
    good and bad, each one as he decides.
Your troubles come from him, and you
    must bear them.
But since you have arrived here in our
    land, you will not lack for clothes or
    anything a person needs in times of
    desperation.

I will show you the town. The people
    here are called Phaeacians, and I am
    the daughter of the great King
    Alcinous, on whom depends the
    strength and power of our people."
And then she called her slaves with
    braided hair.
"Wait, girls! Why are you running from
    this man?
Do you believe he is an enemy?
No living person ever born would come to
    our Phaeacia with a hostile mind, since
    we are much beloved by the gods.
Our island is remote, washed round by
    sea; we have no human contact. But
    this man is lost, poor thing. We must
    look after him.
All foreigners and beggars come from
    Zeus, and any act of kindness is a
    blessing.
So give the stranger food and drink, and
    wash him down in the river, sheltered
    from the wind."

Questions for Analysis

1. Read Nausicaa's response to Odysseus carefully. Does she know that he is trying to flatter her? What does she mean when she says that his troubles come from the god Zeus?

2. Who seems to have the most power in this encounter? Explain your reasoning.

3. Does the initial description of Odysseus strike you as humorous? Why might the poet want to portray him as slightly ridiculous?

THE ATTIC PENINSULA. This map highlights the numerous poleis that dotted the Attic peninsula. It also shows the surrounding territories of Euboea, Boeotia, and Megaris. Consider the scale of the map and the geography of the peninsula. ▪ *Where is Athens located?* ▪ *How do natural boundaries appear to affect patterns of settlement?* ▪ *Why would citizens of the other Attic poleis be regarded as citizens of Athens also, even though they did not live in the city itself?*

The Rise of the Polis

The ninth century B.C.E. saw dramatic changes throughout the Aegean basin. Contacts between Greeks and Phoenicians intensified. Moreover, the Greeks adopted the Phoenician alphabet, which replaced the Linear B of the Mycenaeans that had become obsolete. They also incorporated into their culture many artistic and literary traditions from elsewhere in the ancient world, reshaping them to suit their own purposes.

The example of the Phoenicians also pointed the way to the revival of a lost art among the Greeks: seafaring. After the devastation of the late Bronze Age, Greek vessels no longer ventured out into the Mediterranean but hugged the shoreline and traveled only short distances. By the tenth century, however, Greeks were copying Phoenician designs for merchant vessels, which enabled them to launch trading enterprises of their own. As commercial activity increased, significant numbers of Greeks began to move back to the shores of the mainland, to outlying islands, and to the western coast of Anatolia, across the Aegean, which they called Ionia.

These developments were accompanied by a marked expansion of the Greek population. Around Athens, the population may have quadrupled during the ninth and early eighth centuries. Such rapid growth, however, placed heavy demands on the environmental resources of a mountainous country with limited agricultural land.

As smaller villages grew into towns, inhabitants of rival communities came into more frequent contact with each other. Soon, some degree of economic, political, and social cooperation among the inhabitants became necessary. But the habits that had developed during centuries of isolation did not make such cooperation easy. Each local community treasured its autonomy and independence, celebrated its own rituals, and honored its own heroes. On what basis could such communities unite?

The solution to this challenge was the **polis**, the root from which we derive the word *politics*. Yet to the Greeks, the polis was a social collectivity rather than a state. For this reason, our sources speak of groups of people—"the Athenians," "the Spartans," or "the Thebans"—rather than the places in which these *poleis* (the plural of *polis*) were centered (Athens, Sparta, Thebes). Membership in the collective of the polis came to be so essential to Greek identity that Aristotle would later define man as "a political animal," someone whose identity depends on the polis.

Most poleis combined formal legal institutions with informal customs that could differ widely according to the size of the population and its material and historical circumstances. They were usually organized around a social center known as the *agora* ("central marketplace"), where meetings were held and business was conducted in the open air. Surrounding this was the urban settlement, the *asty*, and beyond this was the *khora*, "land." The khora of a large polis might support several other towns or smaller poleis, as well as numerous villages; for example, all the residents of the entire territory of Attica were considered to be citizens of Athens. Thus the vast majority of Athenian citizens were farmers who might come to the asty only at certain times of the year to participate in the affairs of their polis or to exchange goods in the agora.

The Greeks described this early process of urbanization as the "bringing together of dwellings" (*synoikismos*, synoecism). Polis formation could also come about through the conquest of one settlement by another and/or through the gradual alliance of neighboring communities. Some poleis took shape around fortified hilltops, such as the Athenian acropolis (literally, "the high city"). Other communities still organized the urban center around a temple precinct. In other poleis, the main temple was not located within the city or its walls; at Argos, for example, the massive temple to Hera was located several miles away from any sizable settlement. In many Greek cities, indeed, temple building may have been a *consequence* of polis formation rather than a cause, as elites competed with one another to exalt their poleis and glorify themselves.

THE CULTURE OF ARCHAIC GREECE, 800–500 B.C.E.

Scholars associate the Archaic ("early") Period of Greek history with the emergence of the polis and the renewed use of writing, which the Greeks would put to a wide variety of practical, artistic, intellectual, and political uses. The Athenians, in particular, used writing as a way of establishing their cultural dominance over other Greek poleis by controlling the inscription of the Homeric canon, promoting the work of poets and dramatists, and fostering the writing of prose histories in which they themselves played the central role. It is therefore important to bear in mind that much of what we know about this early period derives from the work of later authors who wrote from this Athenian perspective: these include the Ionian-born Herodotus, who spent much of his later life in Athens; the historians Thucydides (c. 460–c. 395 B.C.E.) and Xenophon (430–354 B.C.E.); and the philosophers Plato (c. 428–348 B.C.E.) and his pupil, Aristotle (384–322 B.C.E.).

Colonization and Panhellenism

During the eighth and seventh centuries B.C.E., small-scale Greek trading ventures and settlements gradually developed into full-fledged mercantile enterprises which followed the example set by the Phoenicians. Many larger poleis competed to establish colonies that functioned as trading posts, with Athens and Corinth being particularly successful. Although each new colony was technically an independent entity, it sustained strong familial and emotional ties to its mother polis; so even if it had no formal obligations to that city, it was often called to support it and could become entangled in the political and military affairs of the mainland.

At the same time, these scattered Greek colonies were loosely unified by their shared language and heritage, which was being exported to far-flung reaches of the known world, eventually creating a Panhellenic ("all-Greek") culture that stretched from the Black Sea (parts of modern Romania, Ukraine, and Russia) to the southern coastlines of modern France and Spain.

This process of Greek colonization permanently altered the cultural geography of the Mediterranean world. The western shores of Anatolia (modern Turkey) would remain a stronghold of Greek culture for the next 2,000 years. So many Greeks migrated to southern Italy that later Romans called the region Magna Graecia, "Greater Greece";

Greek-speaking enclaves would survive there into the twentieth century. By the fourth century B.C.E., more Greeks lived in Magna Graecia than in Greece itself.

Motives for migration and colonization varied. A polis such as Corinth was blessed by its strategic location on the land bridge between Attica and the Peloponnesus (*pel-oh-poh-NEE-suhs*), the large peninsula of mainland Greece, but cursed by the poverty of its land. Trade therefore became the lifeblood of this polis and of the ruling aristocracy, which bankrolled the ambitious planting of colonies up the coast of the Adriatic and into Sicily during the eighth century B.C.E. Other poleis, confronted by the pressures of growing populations and political unrest, sponsored new colonies as outlets for undesirable elements or unwanted multitudes. These colonial projects parallel, in many ways, those of modern nation-states.

Colonial expansion intensified Greek contacts with other cultures. Phoenician pottery brought new artistic motifs and mythological figures into Greece, while Egyptian artists profoundly influenced early Greek sculptural representations of the human form (see **Interpreting Visual Evidence** on page 82). However, intensified contact with other cultures also sharpened Greeks' awareness of their own identity as Hellenes: the Greeks' name for themselves. Such self-conscious Hellenism did not usually lead to greater political cooperation, but it did encourage the establishment of Panhellenic festivals, such as the Olympic Games, as well as shared holy sites.

The most important of these was the temple of Apollo at Delphi, home to the oracle of the sun god and situated on the slope of the sacred Mount Parnassus. People from all over the Greek world (and beyond) came to seek advice

Interpreting Visual Evidence

The Ideal of Male Beauty

The Greek word *kouros* ("young man" or "youth") is now applied to a whole series of life-size statues from the Archaic Period. The one shown here comes from Anavyssos in Attica and was made between 540 and 515 B.C.E. (It is now in the National Archaeological Museum of Athens.) Although scholars used to believe that such statues were meant to represent the god Apollo, further research has shown that most were made to commemorate the dead, especially young warriors who had fallen in battle. This one appears to be walking forward, smiling, but his eyes are closed. The accompanying inscription reads: "Stop and show your pity here for Kroisos, now dead, who once fighting in the foremost ranks of battle was destroyed by raging Ares."

Questions for Analysis

1. What aspects of the body does the kouros emphasize? If this is intended to be a model of Greek manhood, what values would it convey to contemporary youths?

2. Is this a representation of the young man as he was when living or in death? How do your conclusions about the ideal of male beauty change if this is a glorification of death?

3. Compare this image with the values expressed in the verses by Tyrtaeus of Sparta on "The Beautiful and the Good" (page 85). How do these two perspectives complement one another?

---

from the prophetic spirit embodied in Apollo's priestess, who lived in a state of trance induced by fumes rising from a fissure in the earth and enhanced by the chewing of eucalyptus leaves. Suppliants who sought to have their questions answered by the oracle would offer gifts to the shrine and then wait while the god spoke through the priestess, whose mysterious answers would be translated by an attending priest into enigmatic Greek verse. The resulting advice was essentially a riddle that called for further interpretation on the part of the recipient—who often misconstrued it. As we noted in Chapter 2, Croesus of Lydia thought that he was following the advice of the oracle when he attacked the Persians, but the great nation he destroyed turned out to be his own.

At the Olympic Games, Greeks honored the king of the gods, Zeus, near the giant temple dedicated to him at Olympia. The Greeks took great pride in these athletic competitions, and Greek historians dated events by olympiads, the four-year periods between games, traditionally believed to have begun in 776 B.C.E. Only Hellenes were permitted to participate in these sacred contests, and all wars among Greeks ceased while they took place. A victory in the games brought great prestige to the victor, who could be catapulted to a position of social and political power within his polis. These games did little to alleviate rivalry among the poleis; in fact, they often increased it. Yet they further strengthened the Greeks' belief in their common superior culture: an awareness that they could call on when they faced a common threat.

Harnessing the Power of the Horse

Horses are now common on all continents except Antarctica, but in antiquity they were found only on the steppes of eastern Europe and Central Asia. From this relatively circumscribed area, wild horse populations were gradually domesticated and interbred to yield the modern horse (*Equus caballus*). This animal's global spread testifies to its extraordinarily close relationship with the humans who tamed it, and who in turn became utterly dependent on its strength, intelligence, beauty, and utility: as a source of milk and meat and hides, as a draft animal, as the swift engine that powered the terrifying chariots of the Bronze Age, and finally as a mount. Horses were first harnessed for riding on the plains of western Asia, and (as we will see) they became crucial components in the armies of the Persian Empire.

They also became essential markers of the new Greek aristocracy in the course of the eighth century. Whereas Homeric heroes had ridden into battle on chariots, dismounting to fight hand to hand only after they had thrown their javelins, their later aristocratic imitators were *hippeis* ("horsemen"), constituting the first cavalries of the ancient world. Chariots, which were virtually useless on the rocky, mountainous terrain of Greece, were still beautifully adapted to become the engine of a new type of sporting event. The first four-horse chariot race is attested at Olympia in 680 B.C.E., and chariot-racing would become wildly

popular in the Roman Empire, too. And since breeding, raising, feeding, training, and arming horses was extraordinarily expensive, owning a horse—or a team of horses, broken to pull a racing chariot—was the ultimate sign of wealth and status.

Hoplite Warfare: A Military and Political Revolution

Commoners fighting on foot had long played a very minor role in ancient warfare. But, ironically, just as small cavalry contingents were being formed by the aristocracy, a revolution in military tactics was making their dominance obsolete. The effective defense of a polis increasingly required a standing militia, not just an ad hoc band of elite warriors. Accordingly, able-bodied citizens began to equip themselves for battle and train alongside each other. These citizen-soldiers became known as **hoplites**, from the large round shield (*hoplon*) each one carried. The shield was the chief element in a *panoply* (complete hoplite outfit) weighing as much as seventy pounds and consisting of a spear, short sword, breastplate, helmet, and sometimes leather greaves and wrist-guards.

In battle, hoplites stood shoulder to shoulder in a close formation called a *phalanx*, several columns across and several rows deep, with each hoplite carrying his shield on the left arm to protect the unshielded right side of the man standing next to him. In his right hand, each hoplite carried a thrusting weapon—spear or sword—so that an approaching phalanx presented a nearly impenetrable wall of armor and weaponry to its opponents. If a man in the front rank fell, the one behind him stepped up to take his place; indeed, the weight of the entire phalanx was literally behind the front line, with each soldier aiding the assault by leaning with his shield into the man in front of him.

This tight formation relied on a shared skill: the ability to stay together. As long as the phalanx remained intact, it was nearly unbeatable. But like the polis itself, it could fall apart if its men were not committed to a common goal. The "hoplite revolution" was therefore bound up with a parallel revolution in politics. As a polis came increasingly to draw on the resources of more and more citizens, it was forced to offer them a larger share in political power. Since every polis needed a hoplite force to protect its independence, any free man who could afford the requisite panoply became a man with political and social standing. Together, these citizen-soldiers formed a new hoplite class, which demanded a share in decision making. Sometimes, though,

A CHARIOTEER AND HIS TEAM RACING AT THE OLYMPIC GAMES. Chariot racing was the most prestigious and expensive event at the Olympics, since only the very wealthy could afford to maintain and transport a racing team. All the glory of a win accordingly went to the owner, not the charioteer or trainer. Since women were forbidden to compete at the Olympics, sponsoring a team was the only way that a woman could claim an Olympic victory.

HOPLITE INFANTRY ADVANCING INTO COMBAT. This Corinthian vase, dating from around 650 B.C.E., displays the earliest known depiction of hoplites fighting in a phalanx formation.

they could be co-opted by an aristocratic faction or persuaded to throw their support behind an aspiring tyrant.

Aristocracy, Tyranny, and Democracy

For the better part of the seventh and sixth centuries B.C.E., the aristocratic classes continued to control most Greek poleis. Struggles for influence among competing families were therefore commonplace, and factions often attempted to checkmate rivals by passing new laws that favored their own interests, or by sponsoring building projects or colonial expeditions. These rivalries affected polis government at every level, not least because aristocrats were the only members of society who could afford to hold unpaid and time-consuming political offices.

The aristocrats not only pursued wealth and power, they also cultivated a distinctive lifestyle. Participating in politics and holding elected office was part of this lifestyle. So too was the *symposium*, literally a "drinking party," an intimate gathering at which elite men would enjoy wine, poetic competition, performances by trained dancers and acrobats, and the company of *hetaeras* (courtesans) who provided witty conversation, music, and the promise of sex. Respectable women were excluded from such meetings as they were from most other aspects of social and political life (see page 100). So too were non–aristocratic men. The symposium was thus an arena for the display of aristocratic masculinity.

The glorification of male sexuality was another important aspect of this homosocial aristocratic culture. Typically, a man in his late twenties to late thirties, who had just begun to make his career in political life, would take as his lover and protégé an aristocratic youth in his early to midteens. The two would form an intimate bond that included sexual intercourse. This personal and social intimacy could benefit both partners and their families, and it allowed the younger partner to learn the workings of politics while making valuable connections and alliances. Many later philosophers, including Plato, argued that true love could exist only between two such men, because only within this relationship could a man find an equal partner worthy of his affection. Other types of sexual relationships were considered illicit, including those between men of unequal social status.

A complex system of values, ideas, practices, and assumptions thus shaped aristocratic identity in this era. As a result, it was difficult for those outside this elite world to participate fully in the public life of the polis. Eventually, in many poleis, the circle of the aristocratic elite tightened further, as smaller and smaller groups came to dominate higher offices. This meant that even many aristocrats were left on the outside of their own culture, looking in. For these men, one remedy lay close at hand: they could form an alliance with the rising class of hoplites, who resented their exclusion from political power. And occasionally, a single aristocrat with the backing of the hoplites would succeed in setting up an alternative form of government, a *tyranny*.

"The Beautiful and the Good"

The poet known as Tyrtaeus of Sparta flourished during the middle of the sixth century B.C.E. He originally may have come from Athens, but whatever his origins, he expressed ideas of honor, beauty, and virtue that were universal among the hoplite warriors of the new poleis. The key terms he uses in the following verses cannot be adequately translated into English, since these short Greek adjectives are freighted with ancient meanings: kalos *(beautiful, honorable),* agathos *(good, brave, manly). They stand in opposition to the term* aischros *(shameful, ugly, mean).*

alos it is for an *agathos* warrior to die, fallen among the foremost fighters, in battle for his native land; but to leave his polis and rich fields and beg—that is most painful of all, as he wanders with his dear mother and aged father, his small children and his wedded wife. Detested he will be in the eyes of all those to whom he comes, constrained by need and hateful poverty. He shames his birth and belies his glorious appearance; dishonor and misery are his companions. If no account is taken of a warrior who is a wanderer, if there is no respect for him or his family in the future, then let us fight with all our hearts for this land and die for our children, no longer hesitating to risk our lives. Young men, stand firm beside each other and fight. Do not begin shameful flight or fear. Rather,

create a mighty, valorous spirit in your breasts, and show no love for your lives when you are fighting. Do not flee, abandoning the older men, whose knees are no longer nimble. For *aischros* it is for an older warrior to fall among the foremost fighters and lie out ahead of the young men—a man whose hair is already white and his beard grey—as he breathes out his valorous spirit in the dust, holding his bloody guts in his own hands, his body laid bare. *Aischros* is this to the eyes, and a cause of resentment to look upon. But to the young men all is seemly, while the glorious flower of lovely youth is theirs. To men the young man is admirable to look upon, and to women lovable while he lives and *kalos* when he lies among the foremost fighters. So let a man take a firm stance and stand fast, with both feet planted upon the ground, biting his lip with his teeth.

Source: Excerpted and modified from *The Greek Polis*, eds. W. H. Adkins and Peter White (Chicago: 1986), pp. 23–24.

Questions for Analysis

1. How does Tyrtaeus characterize defeat? How does he describe the values and tactics of hoplite warfare?

2. Why is so much emphasis placed on physical beauty and youth? What other qualities are associated with the word *kalos*? Why is old age potentially *aischros*?

3. How does this ideal of male beauty compare with that made visible in the kouros of Anavyssos (page 82)?

In Archaic Greece, a tyrant was not necessarily an abusive ruler. Indeed, tyranny often led the way to wider political enfranchisement. A tyrant who had sought the support of the hoplite class would have to appease that class by extending it further rights of political participation while all the time striving to keep the reins of power in his own hands. This was an inherently unstable state of affairs, because after the original tyrant had fulfilled the wishes of the hoplites, the continuance of tyranny became an obstacle to even greater power for this segment of the population, which would then work to overthrow it. For this reason,

tyrannies rarely lasted for more than two generations and could drive a transition from aristocracy to a more broadly participatory form of government: **democracy**.

It is important to stress that our idealized notion of democracy is quite different from that of the Greeks. In fact, the philosopher Aristotle dismissed this form of government as "mob rule," because it gave too much power to the *demos*, a word meaning "neighborhood" or "affinity group." He saw it as a system too easily controlled by a particular faction. Our ideal of democracy is closer to what Aristotle would have called a polity, governance by the polis as a whole.

Songs of Sappho

Although Sappho of Lesbos (c. 620–550 B.C.E.) was a prolific poet and skilled musician, we know very little about her life, and only a few examples of her extraordinary verse survive. Of the nine books collected in the third century B.C.E., we now have just one complete lyric and a series of fragments, some consisting of only two or three words, often preserved because they were quoted admiringly by other authors. In an astonishing discovery, though, a papyrus scroll containing a previously unknown part of a poem was identified as recently as 2004 (see below). Another papyrus fragment, discovered in 2014, contains parts of two more lyrics: one on unrequited love, addressed to Aphrodite, and another that mentions Sappho's two brothers.

Fragment 16

Some say thronging cavalry, some say
    foot soldiers,
others call a fleet the most beautiful of
sights the dark earth offers, but I say it's
    whatever you love best.
And it's easy to make this understood by
everyone, for she who surpassed all
    human
kind in beauty, Helen, abandoning her
    husband—that best of
men—went sailing off to the shores of
    Troy and
never spent a thought on her child or
    loving
parents: when the goddess seduced her
    wits and left her to wander,
she forgot them all, she could not
    remember
anything but longing, and lightly straying
aside, lost her way. But that reminds me
    now: Anactória,
she's not here, and I'd rather see her lovely
step, her sparkling glance and her face
    than gaze on
all the troops in Lydia in their chariots
    and glittering armor.

Source: Translated by Jim Powell, *The Poetry of Sappho* (New York: 2007), pp. 6–7.

A Newer Fragment (2004)

Live for the gifts the fragrant-breasted
    Muses
send, for the clear, the singing, lyre, my
    children.
Old age freezes my body, once so lithe,
rinses the darkness from my hair, now
    white.
My heart's heavy, my knees no longer
    keep me
up through the dance they used to
    prance like fawns in.
Oh, I grumble about it, but for what?
Nothing can stop a person's growing
    old.
They say that Tithonus was swept away
in Dawn's passionate, rose-flushed arms
    to live
forever, but he lost his looks, his youth,
failing husband of an immortal bride.

Source: Translated by Lachlan Mackinnon, *Times Literary Supplement*, July 15, 2005.

Questions for Analysis

1. How does Sappho use stories from the older tradition she has inherited to address her own concerns? How does the perspective of this female poet transform masculine ideas about heroism, beauty, warfare, aging?

2. What are the challenges of working with such fragmentary sources as these? If these were the only pieces of evidence to survive from Archaic Greece, what conclusions could you draw about this society and its values?

The Power of Poetry

Although aristocrats were deeply invested in the heroic ideals of an earlier age, they also expressed their unique culture in newer poetic forms. The most characteristic of these is the lyric, a series of rhythmic verses sung to the music of the lyre. Because these songs were composed orally, or even improvised, few of them survive. Those that do are valuable historical sources, because they concentrate on themes of immediate interest to their audiences: beauty, love, sorrow, ambition, or important life events. And because they were the focus of entertainment at gatherings, lyrics are often politically charged, sexually explicit, or daringly subversive of accepted norms. For example, the poet Archilochus of Paros (c. 680–640 B.C.E.) flouts the conventions of epic poetry by mocking his own failures on the battlefield:

"Some barbarian hefts my shield, since I had to abandon it / . . . but I escaped, so it scarcely matters / . . . I can get another just as good." So much for the heroic ideal of returning either with one's shield or on it! In another lyric, Archilochus berates his faithless (female) lover and his even more faithless (male) lover, with whom she has an affair.

Given the male domination of Greek culture, it is surprising that the most famous poet of this age was not a man. Rather, it was Sappho (*SAF-foh*; c. 620–550 B.C.E.), who lived in the polis of Mytilene on the island of Lesbos. Sappho composed songs for a wide array of occasions and moods: songs of courtship and marriage, longing and desire, loss and old age. Sometimes her lyrics seem to be addressed to men, but more often they are passionately dedicated to women: both the women whom Sappho loved and the historical women who occupy the margins of masculine epic.

In one song, Sappho compares herself with Agamemnon, who was able to return from Troy only after he prayed to Hera, a goddess worshiped at Lesbos; Sappho now prays that her beloved will arrive safely with the goddess's help. In another, she imagines a scene not included in the *Iliad*, the joyous wedding of the Trojan Hector and his bride, Andromache. Like later tragedies, the poignancy of this bridal song (such as those Sappho herself would have sung at the marriage feasts of friends) derives from the listeners' foreknowledge of the legendary couple's terrible fate: Hector's death at the hands of Achilles, Andromache's rape and enslavement at the hands of the victorious Greeks, and the murder of their infant son. The intimacy of lyric reveals something that few other sources from antiquity are able to convey: the distinctive feelings and desires of individuals who were often at odds with the dominant culture of their time.

PORTRAITS OF THREE POLEIS

The poleis of Greece developed in very different ways. To illustrate this diversity, we examine three particularly interesting examples: **Athens** and **Sparta**, both on the Greek mainland; and **Miletus**, on the Ionian coast of Anatolia. None of these cities can be considered typical; there were some one thousand poleis, and about most of them we know almost nothing. But at least we can survey some of the features that, with variations, made each polis unique—and yet comparable, in some ways, to its neighbors.

Athens

In Greek, the name of this city is the same as that of its patron goddess Athena, the warlike and wise daughter of

OSTRACISM. This political practice takes its name from the pot shards (in Greek, *ostraka*) on which the names of candidates for political exile were scratched. Many of the ballots have survived. Here we see the names of Aristeides, Kimon, and Themistocles: prominent citizens of the fifth century B.C.E. who had fallen out of favor.

Zeus. When the Athenians first came together to form a polis, theirs was a distinctly agricultural economy. Whatever profits aristocrats acquired through trade, they reinvested in land on the Attic Peninsula. Indeed, the Athenian elites regarded commerce as a disreputable means of earning a living, a mentality that persisted even when the city's excellent harbors and orientation toward the Aegean made Athens famous as a mercantile center.

In the early centuries of its history, aristocratic dominance over the Athenian polis rested on monopolization of elected offices and control of the city's council, the Areopagus (*ah-ree-OP-ah-guhs*). It took its name from the rocky outcrop where the council met, just below the acropolis that rose above it. By the early seventh century B.C.E., the aristocrats who came to wield executive authority in Athens were called *archons* ("first men"). Ultimately, nine archons presided over the entire governance of the polis, including its military, judicial, and religious affairs. Although each served for only one year, all became lifetime members of the Areopagus. And because the Areopagus appointed the archons, it could therefore ensure that power remained in the hands of its own future membership. It also served as a kind of high court in judicial cases.

As this small group consolidated power, deep economic and social divisions developed. A significant proportion of the Athenian population fell into slavery through debt, while struggles among aristocratic families destabilized society and fomented cycles of revenge killings. This situation eventually inspired Athenians' first attempt to promulgate a set

THE ATHENIAN PNYX, WITH A VIEW OF THE ACROPOLIS. The Athenian assembly, the *ekklesia*, met on the sloping hill of the Pnyx. A speaker standing on the *bema* ("stepping-stone"; to the right) would have to make himself heard by all the citizens gathered in front of this platform, and all proceedings would have been plainly visible to noncitizens and foreigners in the agora at the foot of the hill (to the left). Overlooking it all was the temple of the city's patron goddess, Athena, on the crest of the Acropolis. ▪ *How is the relative openness and accessibility of Athenian democracy symbolized by this chosen site?*

of written laws. In 621 B.C.E., an aristocrat named Drakon sought to regulate violence through harsh punishments: hence our term *draconian* to describe any severe penalty or regime. The negative effects of this policy ultimately led both aristocrats and hoplites to an agreement. In 594 B.C.E., they agreed to support the election of the poet Solon as the sole archon for one year, and they gave him broad legislative powers. Solon was an aristocrat, but he had made his fortune as a merchant so he was not allied with any one interest. Indeed, he does not appear to have cared about cultivating public opinion, and after his laws were enacted, he went into self-imposed exile for a decade.

Solon's reforms, though hardly democratic in their promulgation, laid the foundations for the later development of Athenian democracy. He forbade the practice of debt slavery and set up a fund to buy back citizens who had been sold abroad. He encouraged the cultivation of olives and grapes, thus spurring cash-crop farming and urban industries such as oil and wine production, and the manufacture of pottery storage jars and decorative drinking cups. He also broadened rights of political participation and set up courts in which a range of citizens served as jurors and to which any Athenian might appeal.

Most significantly, he based eligibility for political office on property qualifications, thus making it possible for someone not born into the aristocracy to gain access to power. Moreover, he convened an Athenian assembly, the *ekklesia* (*eh-KLAY-see-a*) and gave it the right to elect archons. Now all free-born Athenian men over the age of eighteen could participate in government. Even those who were not eligible for citizenship were able to see the workings of government for themselves, since the assembled citizens met on the slopes of the Pnyx (*pNIX*), a hill visible from the central marketplace and overlooked by the sacred precincts of the acropolis.

Solon's reforms initially met with resistance. The aristocracy thought them too radical; the people of the demos, not radical enough. In the resulting decades of controversy, an aristocrat named Peisistratos (*pi-SIS-trah-tohs*) succeeded in establishing a tyranny in 546 B.C.E. In a somewhat ironic move, Peisistratos then proceeded to institute Solon's reforms. He also launched a massive campaign of public-works projects, including the collection and copying of Homer's epics. But the apparent mildness of his rule was undergirded by the quiet, persistent intimidation of Athenian citizens by foreign mercenaries and the ruthlessness with which Peisistratos crushed any dissent. Still, by enforcing Solon's laws, he strengthened the political role of the demos and remained a popular ruler until his death. His sons, however, were less able to control the various factions that threatened their rule. One was assassinated, and the other was ousted with the help of the Spartans in 510 B.C.E.

The following period of Spartan-sponsored oligarchy ("rule of the few") was brief. Two generations of increasing access to power had left the Athenian demos with a taste for self-government. For the first time in recorded history, a group of commoners can be credited with the overthrow of a regime: they rallied behind Cleisthenes (*CLIE-sthenees*), an aristocrat who championed the cause of the demos. Although he did not hold the elected office of archon at the time, Cleisthenes was able to build a coalition within the ekklesia and, by these democratic means, was able to check the power of the oligarchs in 508/7 B.C.E.

Then, by reorganizing the Athenian population into ten voting districts, Cleisthenes suppressed traditional loyalties that had tied each demos to certain aristocratic families. He further strengthened the powers of the Athenian assembly and extended the machinery of democratic government to the local level throughout Attica. He also introduced the practice of ostracism, whereby Athenians could decide each year whether they wanted to banish someone for a decade and, if so, whom. This, Cleisthenes hoped, would prevent the return of a tyranny.

The result of these political struggles made the governance of Athens far more populist than that of any other Greek polis (at least, that we know of). In the meantime, Athens had become the principal exporter of olive oil, wine, and pottery in the Greek world. It was poised to assume the role it would claim for itself during the fifth century B.C.E.

Sparta

Located in the southern part of the Peloponnesus, the polis of the Spartans took shape when four villages (and ultimately a fifth) combined to form a single entity. Perhaps as a relic of the unification process, Sparta retained a dual monarchy throughout its history, with two royal families and two lines of succession. Although seniority or ability usually determined which of the two ruling kings had more influence, neither was technically superior to the other, a situation that often led to competition among their respective supporters.

According to our only written accounts—all authored by Athenians and therefore requiring careful analysis—Spartan control over the surrounding region of Laconia began with the conquest of Messenia, one of Greece's few agriculturally rich territories. Around 720 B.C.E., the Spartans subjugated and enslaved the indigenous people there, the *helots*, who now became an unfree population forced to work under Spartan lordship. Around 650 B.C.E., however, the helots revolted, gaining support from several neighboring poleis and briefly threatening Spartan hegemony. Eventually, Sparta triumphed, but the shock of this rebellion brought about a permanent transformation.

Determined to prevent another uprising and to protect its superior position, Sparta became the most militarized polis in Greece. Within a few generations, everything was oriented to the maintenance of its hoplite army—a force so superior that the Spartans confidently left their city unfortified. At a time when Athenian society was becoming more democratic and citizens spent more time legislating than fighting, Spartan society was becoming increasingly devoted to an older aristocratic ideal of perpetual warfare, with personal freedom mattering less than the collective honor and security of the polis.

The Spartan system made every male citizen a professional soldier of the phalanx. At birth, every Spartiate child was examined by officials who determined whether it was healthy enough to raise; if not, the infant was abandoned in the mountains. This was a custom observed elsewhere in the ancient world, but only in Sparta was it institutionalized by the state. If deemed worthy of upbringing, the child was placed at age seven in the polis-run educational system. Boys and girls trained together until age twelve, participating in exercise, gymnastics, and other physical drills and competitions. Boys then went to live in barracks, where their military training would commence in earnest. Girls continued their training until they became the mates of eligible Spartiate males, usually when the girls were around the age of eighteen and the men often much older. But for most of their married lives, couples lived apart, so their domestic interests would not compete with the objectives of the polis.

Barracks life was rigorous, designed to accustom youths to physical hardship. At age eighteen, the young man who survived this training would try for membership in a brotherhood whose sworn comrades lived, ate, and fought together. Failure to gain acceptance would mean that the young man could not

THE PELOPONNESUS. Located on the Peloponnesian peninsula, the highly militarized society of Sparta dominated the region known as Laconia. ▪ *Where is Sparta located?* ▪ *How might Sparta's location have influenced its outlook on foreign affairs? Did geography make conflict between Athens and Sparta inevitable?*

become a full Spartiate and would lose his rights as a citizen. If accepted, however, he remained with his brotherhood until he was thirty years of age. Between the ages of twenty and thirty he was also expected to mate with a Spartiate woman—but occasions for this were few, a fact that partially accounts for the low birthrate among Spartan citizens. After age thirty, a Spartiate male could opt to live with his family, but he was still required to remain on active military duty until he was sixty.

All Spartiate males over the age of thirty were members of the citizens' assembly, the *apella*, which voted on matters proposed to it by a council, the *gerousia* (gher-oo-SEE-ah; "assembly of elders"), consisting of twenty-eight senior citizens and the two kings. This gerousia was the main policy-making body of the polis and also its primary court. Its members were elected for life but had to be over the age of sixty before they could stand for office. Meanwhile, five

ephors (overseers), elected annually, supervised the educational system and acted as the guardians of Spartan tradition. In the latter role, ephors could even remove an ineffectual king from command of the army while on campaign. The ephors also supervised the Spartan "secret service," the *krypteia*, recruiting agents from among the most promising young Spartiates. Agents spied on citizens, but their main job was to infiltrate the helot population and identify potential troublemakers.

This Spartan polity hinged on the precarious relationship with the helots, who outnumbered the Spartiates ten to one. Messenia routinely seethed with revolt. In wartime, helots accompanied the Spartans on campaign as shield bearers, spear carriers, and baggage handlers. At home, however, the helots were a constant security concern. Every year the Spartans ritually declared war on them as a reminder that

IONIA, LYDIA, AND THE PERSIAN EMPIRE. During the seventh and sixth centuries B.C.E., the Greek cities of the Ionian coast were the cultural and commercial leaders of Greece. But during the fifth century B.C.E., after the Persians conquered Lydia, they lost this position to Athens. ■ *Where are Ionia, Lydia, and Miletus on this map?* ■ *How does Ionia's geographical position help to explain the change in its fortunes?* ■ *How might this change have influenced Ionian attitudes toward the Persian Empire?*

they would not tolerate dissent. Moreover, the constant threat of unrest at home meant that the polis was notoriously reluctant to commit its army abroad. So helot slavery made the Spartan system possible, but Sparta's reliance on a hostile population of slaves was also a serious limitation.

This system also limited the Spartans' contact with the outside world. Spartiates were forbidden to engage in commerce because wealth might distract them from the pursuit of martial glory. Nor did Spartiates farm their own lands, as many Athenians did. Economic activity in the Spartan state fell either to the helots or the free residents of other Peloponnesian cities who were known as *perioikoi* (*per-ee-OY-koi*; "those dwelling around"). The perioikoi enjoyed certain rights and protections within Spartan society, and some grew

rich handling its business concerns. But unlike the residents of Attica, in the hinterland of Athens, the perioikoi exercised no political rights within the Spartan polis. Spartiates who lost their rights as citizens also became perioikoi.

The Spartans rejected innovation. They styled themselves as the protectors of the "traditional customs" of Greece, by which they meant aristocratic dominance and a strict observance of older heroic ideals. In this role, Sparta tried to prevent the establishment of tyrannies in neighboring states and moved to overthrow them when they arose: hence their willing intervention in the affairs of Athens under the Peisistratids. Indeed, Sparta's stern defense of tradition made it an object of admiration throughout the Greek world, even though few Greeks had any desire to live as the Spartans did.

The most fatal flaw in the Spartan system was demographic. There were many ways to fall from the status of Spartiate, but the only way to become one was by birth—and the Spartan birthrate simply could not keep pace with the demand for trained warriors. As a result, the number of full Spartiates declined from perhaps as many as 10,000 in the seventh century to only about 1,000 by the middle of the fourth century B.C.E. Another flaw is historical: because the Spartans placed little value on the written record of their traditions, almost everything we know about them (including the summary offered here) must be gleaned from the negative propaganda of their Athenian rivals.

Miletus and the Ionian Revolution in Thought

Across the Aegean from the Greek mainland lay the Greek cities of Ionia, located on a narrow strip of the Anatolian coast. Long a part of the Greek world (see **Analyzing Primary Sources** on page 53), it had also been shaped by Mesopotamian and Egyptian influences. It was therefore a crucible of hybrid cultures that produced important art forms and modes of thought.

The relationship between the Ionian Greeks and the interior kingdom of Lydia—which, like Ionia, was absorbed into the Persian Empire in the sixth century (Chapter 2)—was fraught. It was through the Ionians that the Lydian invention of coinage was introduced to the Greek world, where it revolutionized trade by making wealth portable while also introducing a host of new philosophical and ethical problems. The Ionians, in turn, played a crucial role in Hellenizing western Asia while insisting on their independence. Ultimately, the major poleis of Ionia banded together to form the Ionian League, a political and cultural confederation. This was the first such organization known in the Greek world, and its aim was to insulate Ionian Greeks from the growing power of the Persians.

The Milesians founded many colonies, especially in and around the Black Sea. They were also active in Egypt, where the main Greek trading outposts were Milesian foundations. These colonial efforts, combined with its advantageous position for trade with the rest of Asia, brought Miletus extraordinary wealth. At the same time, it also became a center for speculative thinking, what the Greeks called *philosophia* ("love of wisdom"). Beginning in the sixth century B.C.E., a series of intellectuals now known as the pre-Socratics—because they came before the great philosopher Socrates—raised new and vital questions about the relationship between the natural world (the *kosmos*), the gods, and men. And often,

their explanations moved the direct influence of the gods to the margins or removed it altogether, something that other Greeks regarded as blasphemous. For example, Milesian philosophers built on older traditions of learning, such as Babylonian mathematics and astronomy, but complicated many older conclusions. They sought physical explanations for the movements of the heavens and did not presume that heavenly bodies were divine. By making human observation the starting point for their knowledge, they began to formulate more scientific explanations for the workings of the universe.

Stimulated by the cultural diversity of their city, Milesian philosophers also began to rethink their place in the cosmos. Hecataeus (*heck-ah-TAY-us*) criticized his contemporaries' unquestioning acceptance of a narrow worldview; and he set out to expand their horizons by mapping the world, traveling extensively and studying the customs and beliefs of other cultures. Xenophanes (*zee-NOFF-uh-nees*) posited that all human knowledge is relative and conditioned by human experience: he observed that the Thracians (people living north of Greece) believed that the gods had blue eyes and red hair, just as the Thracians themselves did, whereas Ethiopians portrayed the gods as dark skinned and curly haired, as they were. He concluded that human beings always make gods in their own image, not the other way around. If horses could fashion images of the gods, Xenophanes argued, the gods would look like horses.

These and other theories formed a distinctive strand in Greek philosophy, yet they would continue to be regarded as disturbing and dangerous—dangerous enough to warrant the later execution of Socrates in Athens, where the struggle between religion and philosophy would ultimately be fought more than a hundred years after Xenophanes' bold proclamation. By that time, the Persian conquest of Lydia had made Miletus and its sister cities subject to that great empire. Indeed, Ionian resistance to Persian rule triggered the greatest clash the Greek world had yet known.

THE CHALLENGE OF THE PERSIAN WARS

The profound significance of Greek experiments with new forms of governance and new ideas about the world can be seen with particular clarity if we compare the Greek poleis with the empires and kingdoms of the Bronze Age, in which the typical political regime, as we have seen, was a monarchy supported by a powerful priesthood. In this context, cultural achievements were mainly instruments to enhance the prestige of rulers, and economic life was

A MODERN REPLICA OF AN ATHENIAN TRIREME. These versatile warships were much more powerful than the old 50-oared penteconters that had been in use for centuries. As the name suggests, a trireme had three banks of oars on each side, 170 oars in total. These were manned by citizen rowers seated on benches at three different levels in the vessel's hold. In battle, rowers could help power a ship forward, turn it, and keep it on course in a chase, even when sailing into the wind. In favorable winds, the sails were hoisted for added speed. ■ *How did this new military technology build on some of the same strategies as hoplite warfare?*

controlled by palaces and temples. By contrast, the core values of the Greeks were the primacy of the human male and the principles of competition, individual achievement, and human freedom and responsibility. In his history, Herodotus records a conversation between a Greek (in this case a Spartan) and a Persian, who expresses surprise that the Greeks should raise spears against the supposedly benign rule of his emperor. The Spartan retorts, "You understand how to be a slave, but you know nothing of freedom. Had you tasted it, you would advise us to fight not only with spears but with axes." How the Greeks came to turn those spears on each other within a few generations of their united victory is a story worthy of one of their own tragedies.

The two major wars fought between the uneasily unified Greeks and the vast empire of the Persians, known as the **Persian Wars**, were understood as defining events by those who witnessed and looked back on them. From the first, the contest was unequal. Persia was the largest and most efficient state the world had ever seen, capable of mustering more than a million armed men. The Greeks, by contrast, remained a collection of disparate communities, fiercely

competitive and suspicious of one another. An exceptionally large polis, such as Athens or Sparta, might put 10,000 hoplites in the field; but the vast majority of Greek states could only provide a few hundred each. So the threat of Persian conquest loomed large on the Greek horizon, and the experience of warfare on a global scale changed the Greek world immeasurably.

The Ionian Revolt (499–494 B.C.E.)

For the first time in the history of Western civilizations, we can follow the unfolding of events of the wars through the narrative of a contemporary historian, Herodotus, the first person who self-consciously set out to write an account of his own times in careful, unambiguous prose—rather than in the form of heroic poetry or the boastful language of victorious inscriptions. And lucky for us, Herodotus was uniquely qualified to probe the long-term and more immediate causes of the Persian Wars. Raised in the Ionian polis of Halicarnassus, he was a product of the hybrid

Past and Present

Political Satire

In the fifth century B.C.E., the playwright Aristophanes took an older form of comedy, the satyr play, and turned it into a vehicle for what we still call satire. Instead of gently mocking the gods, he lampooned the politics, popular culture, and current events of his own day—and so made his fellow citizens take a fresh look at themselves. If he were alive today, he might be writing for *The Daily Show*, Stephen Colbert, or *Saturday Night Live*.

 Watch related author interview on the Student Site

culture discussed previously. He was also a keen observer of human nature and human diversity. He regarded both the Greeks and the Persians as great peoples. Yet as a Greek himself—albeit one born within the Persian dominion—he was not impartial. Indeed, his surviving account reflects many of the intellectual currents of mid-fifth-century Athens, where he spent the better part of his career, as well as many Athenian prejudices. This is something that must be borne in mind when reading his work.

Herodotus wanted to show that the war between the Persians and Greeks had ancient roots and could be traced back to long-standing cultural differences, but his narrative also shows that the catalyst was a political conflict in Miletus. In 501 B.C.E., the city was governed by Aristagoras (*EHR-is-STAG-or-uhs*), a tyrant who owed his power to the backing of the Persian emperor, **Darius** (Chapter 2). But Aristagoras apparently came to believe that his days as the emperor's favorite were numbered. So he turned abruptly from puppet to patriot, rousing the Milesians and the rest of Ionia to revolt against Persian rule. As a safeguard, he

also sought military support from the sympathetic poleis on the Greek mainland.

The Spartans refused to send their army abroad, but Athens and Eretria (*er-eh-TREE-uh*), on the island of Euboea (*you-BOY-ah*), agreed to send twenty-five ships and crews. This small force managed to capture the old Lydian capital of Sardis (by then a Persian administrative center) and burn it to the ground. Then the Athenians and Eretrians went home, leaving the Ionians to their own devices. In 494 B.C.E., the rebellious poleis were finally overwhelmed by the vastly superior might of Persia.

Darius realized, however, that so long as his Greek subjects in Ionia could cast a hopeful eye to their neighbors across the Aegean, they would forge alliances with them. He therefore decided to launch a preemptive strike against Athens and Eretria, to teach these upstart poleis a lesson. In the summer of 490 B.C.E., a punitive expedition of 20,000 soldiers, under two of Persia's finest generals, crossed the Aegean and landed on the coast of Euboea. Their forces sacked and burned Eretria to the ground, sending its population into captivity in Persia. They then crossed the narrow strait to Attica, landing on the plain of Marathon, approximately twenty-six miles from Athens.

Marathon and Its Aftermath

When the Persians landed in Attica, the Athenians quickly called on the only polis that could conceivably help them: Sparta. But the Spartans responded that they were unable to assist—they were celebrating a religious festival. Only the small, nearby polis of Plataea offered the Athenians aid. The Athenian and Plataean hoplites would have to engage the mighty Persians on their own.

Heavily outnumbered and without effective cavalry to counter that of the Persians, the Athenian phalanx took a position between two hills blocking the main road to the polis. After a standoff of several days, the Athenian general Miltiades (mil-TIE-uh-dees) received word that the Persians were watering their horses and that the Persian infantry was vulnerable to attack. So Miltiades led a charge that smashed the Persian force, resulting in crippling losses. In an almost unbelievable victory, the Athenians had defeated the world's major imperial power, and they had done it without Spartan help. It was a vindication of hoplite tactics and a tremendous boost to Athenian confidence.

Yet the Athenian politician Themistocles (the-MIS-toh-klees) warned that the Persians would not suffer such humiliation

THE PERSIAN WARS WITH GREECE. Imagine that you are the Persian emperor Xerxes, planning the conquest of Greece in 480 B.C.E.
- *What are the two possible routes that you could take to attack Greece?* - *What geographical considerations would dictate your military strategy?* - *Bearing in mind that Xerxes' attempt failed, what would you do differently?*

GREEK FORCES DEFEAT PERSIANS. This detail from a bowl commemorating the defeat of Xerxes' army depicts an Athenian hoplite poised to strike a deathblow to his Persian opponent. The artist has carefully delineated the differences between the enemies' dress and weaponry. To the Greeks, the Persian preference for trousers over short tunics seemed particularly barbaric and effeminate.

quietly and would retaliate with an even larger force. So when the Athenians discovered a rich vein of silver ore in the Attic countryside a few years later, Themistocles persuaded them not to divide the windfall among themselves (the customary practice) but to finance a fleet of 200 triremes, state-of-the-art warships. Athens thereby transformed itself into the preeminent naval power of the Greek world, just in time to confront a new Persian onslaught.

Xerxes' Invasion

Darius the Great died in 486 B.C.E. and was succeeded by his son **Xerxes** (*ZERK-sees*), who almost immediately began preparing a massive overland invasion of Greece designed to conquer the entire territory, thus eradicating any future threats to Persian imperial expansion while avenging his father's shame. Supported by a huge fleet of 600 ships, this grand army (which numbered at least 150,000 men and may have been as large as 300,000) set out from Sardis in 480 B.C.E., crossing the Hellespont, the narrow strait separating Europe from Asia. Unlike his father, who had dispatched talented generals against Athens, Xerxes led this campaign himself.

Many Greek poleis capitulated immediately. But Athens, Sparta, Corinth, and some thirty others refused to sur-

render. Instead, they hastily formed the Hellenic League, an unprecedented alliance forged in the face of an unprecedented external threat. In August of 480 B.C.E., a major Persian offensive was held at bay when the outnumbered Greek allies, under the military leadership of Sparta, confronted Xerxes at the mountain pass of Thermopylae (*ther-MO-puh-lie*). For three days, they valiantly held off the Persian multitude, whose way through the narrow pass was effectively blocked. Meanwhile, a Greek fleet led by Athens and guided by Themistocles engaged a Persian flotilla off the Attic coast. The Spartans' defense of Thermopylae ultimately failed, but their sacrifice allowed the new Athenian warships to inflict heavy losses on the Persians.

However, these engagements left Athens without any men to defend the city. Themistocles therefore persuaded the entire population to abandon Athens for the island of Salamis. From there, the Athenians watched the Persians torch their city. Time, however, was on their side. Xerxes' massive army depended on his damaged fleet for supplies, and the Persians' military tactics—which included a heavy reliance on cavalry and chariots—were not adapted for the rocky terrain of Greece. Bad weather also made sailing the Aegean in autumn a risky business; the Persians were now desperate to force a decisive battle and return home before the season turned against them.

In late September, the vastly superior Persian fleet sailed into the straits of Salamis, believing that the Athenians were preparing to flee the island. The report turned out to be false, but so confident was Xerxes that he had a throne placed on the headland above the bay, where he would have a good view of his victory. Instead, he watched as the battle-ready Athenian triremes demolished the Persian fleet. This was the turning point of the war. Xerxes retreated with the majority of his army to Persia, while an elite force stayed behind. But when the allied Greek army met the Persians on favorable terrain the next spring—an open plain near Plataea, which had been razed the year before—the Greeks prevailed. Against all odds, the small, fractious poleis had defeated the mightiest army of the known world.

THE GOLDEN AGE OF CLASSICAL GREECE

During the half century after the Persian Wars, Athens enjoyed a meteoric rise in power and prestige, becoming the premier naval power of the eastern Mediterranean and the military rival of Sparta. Athens also emerged as leader of the Delian League, a group of poleis whose representatives met on the sacred island of Delos and pledged to continue the war against Persia, which was now being fought in the Aegean. As the league's leader, Athens controlled its funds and resources. This era simultaneously witnessed the greatest achievements in Athenian culture and politics. These were complicated, however, by the increasingly awkward relationship of Athens with its allies, which began to feel more like Athenian subjects than free poleis.

Periclean Athens

In the decades before the Persian Wars, political reforms in Athens had continued to encourage experiments in democracy, including the practice of selecting major officeholders by lot. Only one key position was now filled by traditional voting: the office of *strategos*, or general. And because a man could be elected strategos year after year, this office became the career goal of Athens' most ambitious leaders. Themistocles had been strategos, as was Cimon (*KEY-mohn*), who led the Delian League to victories over Persia during the 470s and 460s B.C.E. But Cimon also used the league to punish poleis that tried to opt out of membership, even suppressing revolts in these cities by force of arms and so turning the league into an instrument of Athenian policy.

By then, the political mood in Athens was changing. New voices were demanding a greater role in government; most prominent were the *thetes* (*THAY-tees*), the lowest class of free men that provided the triremes' rowers: the backbone of the all-important Athenian fleet. Like the hoplites of the Archaic Period, who had achieved citizenship because they were indispensable to the defense of the poleis, the thetes wanted higher status and equal representation. The man who emerged to champion their cause was Pericles (*PEHR-eh-klees*), an aristocrat from one of Athens' most prestigious families.

Pericles made the enfranchisement of the thetes the main plank of his political platform and also advocated a foreign policy that was oriented away from cooperation with Sparta. In 462–461 B.C.E. he was elected strategos and immediately used his position to secure the ostracism of his rival, Cimon. He then pushed through reforms that gave every Athenian citizen the right to propose and amend legislation, not just to vote yes or no in the citizen assembly. And by paying an average day's wage for attendance, he made it easier for poorer citizens to participate in the assembly and in courts of justice. Through such measures, the thetes and other free men of modest means became a dominant force in politics—and loyal to the man who had made that dominance possible.

In keeping with the ambitions of Pericles, this populist program glorified Athens through an ambitious scheme of public building and lavish festivals honoring the gods, especially Athena. Pericles himself was a generous patron of the arts and sciences, attracting the greatest minds and talents of the day to Athens. His popularity, combined with his charisma and his promotion of the Athenians' sense of superiority, ensured his reelection as strategos for the next three decades. During these years Athens flourished, but it also alienated much of the Greek world by its arrogance and aggression.

Athenian Theater: A Mirror of the Polis

Athens was not the only city to produce great works of art during this period, but our knowledge of classical Greek culture is dominated by the dramas produced at its great religious festivals. The most important of these was the Dionysia, a great spring feast devoted to the god Dionysos, which became a celebration of Athenian exceptionalism and democratic ideals. From the beginning, therefore, drama was closely connected to the political and religious life of the state that sponsored it. Indeed, the very format of classical tragedy replicates the tensions of democracy, with its complex cast of characters and its conflict among opposing perspectives. This format was perfected under the great tragedian Aeschylus (*AY-skihl-uhs*; 525–456 B.C.E.) and his younger contemporary, Sophocles (496–406 B.C.E.). Their dramas made use of two or (eventually) three professional actors, each of whom could play numerous roles, and a chorus of Athenian citizens that represented collective opinion and could comment on the action.

Although Aristotle would later declare that the purpose of tragedy was to inspire pity and fear and so purge these emotions through a process called *katharsis* ("purification"), this definition does not capture either the variety or impact of Athenian tragedy. Tragedies were almost always set in the distant or mythical past, but they were intended to address the cutting-edge issues of their day. Indeed, the very earliest of all surviving tragedies, Aeschylus' *Persians*, dramatizes events of the playwright's own lifetime; we know for certain that he fought at Marathon, because he had this fact proudly recorded on his tomb. Performed for the first time in 472 B.C.E., this contemporary tragedy tells the story of the great Athenian victory at Salamis—but through the eyes of the defeated Xerxes, who thus becomes its tragic hero.

Even when the subject matter was derived from the epics of Homer, the fundamental themes of tragedy—justice, the conflicting demands of personal desire and public duty, the unforeseen consequences of human actions, the brutalizing effects of power—addressed problems of immediate concern to all Athenians. For example, Aeschylus' trilogy the *Oresteia* (458 B.C.E.) is ostensibly about the legendary family

Epidaurus (modern Epidauros, Greece)
Cavea width: 119 m, orchestra width: 24.65 m; capacity: 11,750-14,700; ca. 300-340 BC..
Plan (T.H. after Gerkan)

0 10 20 30 40 50 60 70 80 90 100m

THE THEATER AT EPIDAUROS. Greek dramas were invariably presented in the open air, usually at dawn. Since these were civic spectacles, theaters had to be large enough to accommodate all citizens. Most, like this one at Epidauros (right), took advantage of the natural slope of a hill. The plan for the theater is shown above (left). The acting area would have been backed by a high wall, the *skene*, which housed stage machinery and enhanced the acoustics. A trained actor standing in the *orchestra* would have been plainly audible even to those seated in the top tier. ▪ *How would the size and setting of such a theater enhance the political character of the plays performed within it?*

of the Mycenaean king Agamemnon and traces the long-term consequences of the king's sacrifice of his daughter Iphigenia; his subsequent murder at the hands of his grieving wife, Clytemnestra; and the vengeance of the couple's son, Orestes, who kills his own mother. But the court of law that eventually tries Orestes is actually that of **Periclean Athens**, and the plays' debates over the rational application of law resonated with Aeschylus' contemporaries.

Oedipus at Colonus, one of Sophocles' later tragedies, used the story of the mythical king of Thebes to comment bitterly on Athens' disastrous war with Sparta (see page 102). Similarly, *The Trojan Women* of Euripides (485–406 B.C.E.), presented in 415 B.C.E., marks the Athenians' tragic march toward defeat in this war. By looking back at the capture, rape, and enslavement of Troy's defeated women, Athenians were forced to look at the dreadful consequences of their own imperial policies.

Comedy was even more obviously a genre of political commentary and social satire, and could also deal openly with the absurdities and atrocities of current events. Not only was it unconstrained by any formal poetic framework, but comedy—then as now—could be effectively and safely deployed to deal with issues that were too hot to handle in any other medium: sexual scandals, political corruption, moral hypocrisy, popular fads. Aristophanes (*EHR-ih-STOFF-ah-nees*; c. 446–386 B.C.E.), the greatest of the Athenian comic playwrights, lampooned everything from the philosophy of Socrates to the tragedies of his contemporary Euripides, and he was an especially outspoken critic of Athenian warmongers and their imperialist aims. He regularly savaged the

powerful figures whom he saw as leading Athens to its doom, and he was repeatedly dragged into court to defend himself against the demagogues he attacked. But the power and popularity of comic theater was such that politicians never dared to shut it down for long. It was too much an expression, and outcome, of Athenian ideals.

A New Science of History

Periclean Athens was also fertile ground for the development of other new literary forms. Even though the Greeks of this age were becoming more dependent on writing for legal and commercial transactions, they valued highly the arts of memory and oral debate; and intellectuals had long been used to expressing themselves through poetry, which was always intended to be sung and enjoyed in performance, not to be read. (The Milesian philosophers had conveyed their ideas in verse, and Solon had used poetry in justifying his political reforms.) In the course of this century, though, the rise of functional literacy in Athens encouraged the emergence of prose as a distinct literary form. Herodotus found a ready market for his histories in Athens. His younger contemporary Thucydides (*thoo-SID-ih-dees*) followed suit, using his time in exile to write a masterful—and scathingly critical—history of the war between his polis and Sparta, in which he himself had fought.

Between them, these two historians developed a new approach to the study of the past, emphasizing the need to

APOLLO OF TENEA, APOLLO OF PIOMBINO, AND THE CRITIAN BOY. These three statues, dating from about 560, 500, and 480 B.C.E., respectively, illustrate the development of Greek statuary art. The first rather stiff and symmetrical statue (left) is imitative of Egyptian sculpture. Roughly a half century later, the second representation (middle) of Apollo begins to display motion, not unlike the kouros on page 82. The last figure (right), showing a boy standing in a relaxed posture with his weight resting on one leg, displays even greater naturalism.

collect and interpret multiple sources and focusing on human agency as the driving force of history (rather than divine intervention or divine will). Although in different ways, both conceived the historian's role as distinct from that of a storyteller. The word *historia* would continue to mean both "story" and "history," but for Herodotus and Thucydides the historian's task was to investigate and critically reflect on the events of his own time, as well as to illuminate those of the past. These methods and goals would increasingly come to inform other prose genres, including the philosophical writings of Plato and Aristotle (see Chapter 4).

Art and Architecture

The visual artists of classical Greece revealed the same range of talents in the visual arts as poets did in their dramas. Their comic gift is exhibited in vessels made for festive use at symposia, which often depict the delights of sensuality and scenes from bawdy tales. By contrast, the heroic but humane mode of tragedy corresponds to the marble statues and sculptured reliefs made for temples and public places. Athenian sculptors in particular were drawn to the challenges of representing the human form accurately while celebrating an ideal of physical beauty.

Perhaps the most striking development in fifth-century Greek sculpture was the new attention paid to the crafting of naturalistic figures, both clothed and nude. This happened first in Athens. Nothing like it had ever been seen before, although it is a trend already discernible in the figure of the kouros examined on page 82, and in the successive refinements of the sculptor's art made in the previous century. What hastened the acceptance of naturalism in art is a matter of intense debate, but scholars have long wanted to link this innovation to the victories over the Persians in those key decades. Greeks tended to regard the Persian male's modesty of dress, preference for trousers,

The Daily Life of Athens: Men, Women, and Slaves

Toward the end of his famous funeral oration, which Thucydides quotes in his history, Pericles addresses only a few brief remarks to the women of Athens who mourn their fallen fathers, husbands, and sons at the end of the first year of the disastrous war with Sparta. He urges them to do three things: rear more children for the support of Athens and its wars, show no more weakness than is "natural to their sex," and attract no attention to themselves. For as he says, the greatest glory of a woman is not to be spoken about at all, whether for good or ill. His remarks reveal widely held attitudes toward women in classical Greece, although they may not reflect complex historical realities.

The growth of democracy did not lead to greater equality between the sexes; in fact, it had the opposite result. In the Bronze Age of Mycenaean Greece, women were viewed as possessing extraordinary funds of courage and wisdom, as well as beauty and virtue. They were prized for their shrewd advice on political and military matters, and they played an active role in the world. Sometimes, elite women ruled kingdoms in their own right. Indeed, this was still the case in the northern territories of Macedonia and Epirus, as we will see (Chapter 4), as well as in some Ionian poleis.

But as aristocratic ideals gave way to more democratic ones, Greek women increasingly spent their lives in the confinement of the home. On the one hand, the importance of the hoplite infantry and its spirit of shared purpose encouraged men to train together and to develop close relationships, something that was also sanctioned by the political system. On the other hand, that spirit of equality discouraged the political agency of women. Instead, the production of children to supply the infantry became the female imperative. Public spaces were largely restricted to male activities, whereas domestic spaces were reserved for female endeavors, such as child care and weaving. Respectable women lived largely in the seclusion of a house's inner courtyard, rarely venturing forth from their homes.

In Athens, girls could be legally married at age fourteen, usually to husbands more than twice their age. (Younger men were supposed to devote themselves to war.) A girl's father arranged her marriage and provided a dowry that her husband could use for her support. Shortly after a wife entered her new home, a regular schedule of childbirth would begin. Typically, the interval between births was two to four years, meaning that the average young wife would bear between four and six children before she died, usually around the age of thirty-five. Her place might then be taken by another, younger woman.

THE SHRINE OF ATHENA IN THE PARTHENON. This is a replica of the statue of Athena that once stood inside the Parthenon dedicated to her (see also the image on page 76). Made of gold and ivory and designed by the great sculptor Phidias, who was updating a more archaic style, the statue stood forty feet high and was visible to viewers outside the temple and some distance away. The statue was reflected in a shallow pool of water located in front of it.

fondness for jewelry, and luxurious long hair as proofs of effeminacy (see the bowl on page 96). By contrast, Greek men took pride in sculpting their physiques, exercising, and participating in athletic contests in the nude. A Greek might have said that only barbarians bowed down to their rulers like slaves and covered their shameful bodies in constricting clothes; free men celebrate their individuality not only in politics but in the care of the body and its representation.

The Athenians also made exceptional contributions to architecture in this period. All Greek temples sought to create an impression of harmony, but the Parthenon of Athens, built between 447 and 438 B.C.E., is generally considered the finest example. Construction of this stunning, expensive, and structurally ambitious building was urged on the Athenians by Pericles as a tribute to their patron goddess, Athena Parthenos ("Athena the Virgin"), and as a symbol of their own power, confidence, and genius.

WOMEN AND WEAVING. Wool working and weaving were gender-specific activities throughout the ancient world, in which women of all social ranks were expected to participate. On this red-figure vase, dating from 460–450 B.C.E., we see the woman on the left carding wool and the two women on the right preparing fibers for spinning into threads, which could then be woven into cloth.

Because women seldom went out of doors or ventured beyond their immediate neighborhood—it was thought immodest for them to be seen by men other than those in their families—slaves did whatever shopping or marketing the household required. Even at home, women were expected to withdraw into private rooms if visitors arrived. But they were not supposed to sit around idly, and their main occupation—true of all women, from royalty to slaves—was the spinning and weaving of cloth. And since women's work was basically menial, men looked down on them for it, even though their own livelihoods and comfort depended on it.

Some evidence even suggests that husbands were not encouraged to form emotional attachments to their wives, although many certainly did. In a revealing passage, Herodotus talks of a certain Lydian king who "fell in love with his own wife, a fancy that had strange consequences." By contrast, an Athenian orator remarked that "we have prostitutes for pleasure, concubines for daily physical needs, and wives to bear us legitimate children and be our faithful housekeepers." However, these perspectives are offset by a range of archaeological and material evidence that testify to women's valued social roles, the affection of their husbands and children, and even their wider economic and legal powers.

In addition to depending on the labor and fertility of women, Athenians were as reliant on slaves as Spartans were on helots. Without slavery, none of the Athenian accomplishments in politics, thought, or art would have been possible. The Athenian ideal of dividing and rotating governmental duties among all free men depended on slaves who worked in fields, businesses, and homes while free men engaged in politics. In fact, the Athenian democratic system began to function fully only with the expansion of Athenian mining and commerce around 500 B.C.E., which enabled the Athenians to buy slaves in larger numbers. Freedom and slavery were thus an inescapable contradiction of this democracy—much as they would be many centuries later in the United States.

Estimates vary, but it seems likely that there were about 100,000 Athenians who belonged to families with male members eligible for citizenship. Nearly as many of the city's residents were enslaved, perhaps up to 80,000 in the time of Pericles, with an additional population of some 10,000 resident foreigners (known as *metics*). This means that only a fraction of the entire population—somewhere between 30,000 to 60,000 men—could take part in political life.

Although widespread, Athenian slavery was modest in scale. Slaves did not ordinarily work in teams or in factories; the only exceptions were the state-owned silver mines, where large numbers of slaves toiled in miserable conditions. Most slaves were owned in small numbers by a wide range of Athenian families, including the relatively poor. As domestic servants and farm laborers, slaves might even be considered trusted members of the household, although their masters were legally empowered to beat them or abuse them; concubines and sex workers (of both genders) were often drawn from among this class of slaves. Yet slaves could never be entirely dehumanized as they were in modern slaveholding societies: the misfortune of becoming a slave through debt was a reality of Athens' recent past, and the real possibility of being enslaved in war became a widespread consequence of Athens' overreaching ambitions.

"THE GREATEST WAR IN HISTORY" AND ITS CONSEQUENCES

In more ways than one, Athenian freedom rested on the servitude of others. Slaves performed much of the labor at home, and Athens' allies in the Delian League provided the resources that supported Athenian greatness. Without the surplus wealth flowing into Athens from the league, none of the projects Pericles undertook—pay for political participation, massive building projects, the patronage of Athenian drama—would have been possible. These projects kept Athens rich, its democracy vibrant, and Pericles in power. But ultimately, Athens' foreign policy and imperial ambitions undermined these achievements.

Since the 470s, as we noted previously, Athens had begun crushing those allies who attempted to break from its control. By the early 440s, its only rival for supremacy in the Greek world was Sparta. Rather than attempting to maintain a balance of power, however, Pericles determined on a more aggressive policy: he made formal peace with Persia to ensure that available military resources would be directed toward any future Spartan opposition. But this undermined the sole purpose of the Delian League, which had been the defense of Greece against Persian aggression. Athens now had no justification for compelling the league members to maintain their allegiance. Many remained loyal nonetheless, paying their contributions and enjoying the economic benefits of warm relations with Athens. Others, however, did not, and Athens found itself increasingly having to force its reluctant allies back into line, often installing Athenian garrisons and planting Athenian colonists—who retained their Athenian citizenship—to ensure continued loyalty.

In the context of recent history and long-standing Greek values, such behavior was disturbing. The Delian League had been established to preserve Greek independence. Now Athens itself was becoming an oppressive, imperial power. Foremost among its critics were the Corinthians, whose own economic standing was threatened by Athenian dominance. The Corinthians were close allies of the Spartans, who in turn were the dominant power in what historians call the Peloponnesian League. (The Greeks called it simply the "Spartans and their allies.")

When war finally erupted between Athens and Sparta, Thucydides—himself an Athenian—ascribed it to the growing power of Athens and the anxiety this inspired in other poleis. No modern historian has improved on Thucydides' thesis. Yet for the Athenians and their leaders, there could be no question of relinquishing their empire or the dream of dominating the Mediterranean world. For Sparta and its allies, meanwhile, the prospect of relinquishing their own culture and independence was equally unthinkable. Two very different ideas of Greek superiority were about to fight to the death.

The Peloponnesian War Begins

When the Athenians and Spartans found themselves at war with one another in 431 B.C.E., both sides believed a conclusion would come quickly—a delusion common to many of history's pivotal wars. Instead, the **Peloponnesian War** dragged on for twenty-seven years. Thucydides, writing about it in exile, recalled that he knew from the time of its outbreak that it was going to be "the greatest war in history," amounting to the first world war, because by the time it was over it would involve the entire Mediterranean.

He also meant that it was the worst, so devastating to both sides that it partially destroyed the Greeks' proud heritage of independence. By the time Athens was forced to concede defeat, all the poleis were weakened to such an extent that never again were they able to withstand outside threats.

From the beginning, Athens knew that it could not defeat Sparta on land; and neither Sparta nor its allies had a fleet capable of facing the Athenians at sea. Pericles therefore developed a bold strategy: he would pull the entire population of Attica within the walls of Athens and its harbor and not attempt to defend the countryside against Sparta. For sustenance, Athens would rely on supplies shipped in by its fleet, which would also be deployed to ravage the coasts of the Peloponnesus.

The Spartans duly plundered the farms and pastures of Attica, frustrated that the Athenians would not engage them in battle. Meanwhile, the Athenians inflicted significant destruction on Spartan territory in a series of raids and by successfully encouraging rebellion among the helots. The advantage appeared to be on Athens' side, but in 429 B.C.E. the crowded conditions of the besieged city gave rise to a typhus epidemic that killed over a third of the population, including the aged Pericles.

Pericles' death revealed that he had been the only man capable of managing the political forces he had unleashed. His successors were mostly demagogues, ambitious men who played to the worst instincts of the demos. The most successful of these was Cleon, a particular target of Aristophanes' ridicule, who refused a Spartan offer of peace in 425 B.C.E. and continued the war until his own death in battle four years later. It was under Cleon that Thucydides was given the impossible task of liberating a city under Spartan control; his failure in 423 led to his exile.

After the death of Cleon, a truce with Sparta was negotiated by an able Athenian leader named Nikias. But Athenians continued to pursue a "dirty war" by preying on poleis that might support the Spartans. This led to atrocities such as the destruction of Melos, an island colonized by the Spartans but which had maintained its neutrality since the beginning of the war. When the inhabitants of Melos refused to compromise this position by accepting Athenian rule, Athens had the entire male population slaughtered and every woman and child sold into slavery.

Thereafter, Athens' policy of preemptive warfare proved destructive even to itself. In 415 B.C.E., a charismatic young aristocrat named Alkibiades (*al-kih-BY-uh-dees*) convinced the Athenians to attack the powerful Greek city of Syracuse in Sicily, which was allegedly harrying Athenian allies in the western Mediterranean. The expedition failed disastrously, ending with the death or enslavement of thousands of Athenian warriors.

THE PELOPONNESIAN WAR. This map shows the patchwork of colonies and alliances that bound together the supporters of Sparta and Athens at the outbreak of the Peloponnesian War. ▪ *Which side had the geographical advantage?* ▪ *Which neutral powers might have been able to tip the balance by entering the war on one side or the other?* ▪ *What strategic and military choices did geography impose on the two combatants and their allies?*

News of the Syracusan disaster shattered the Athenians. Many political leaders were driven from the polis as scapegoats, and in 411 B.C.E. a hastily convened assembly of citizens voted democracy out of existence, replacing it with an oligarchy ("rule of the few") consisting of 400 members, many of whom had been present at this vote. The remains of the Athenian fleet, then stationed at Samos on the Ionian coast, responded by declaring a democratic government in exile under the leadership of none other than Alkibiades. The oligarchy proved to be brief, and democracy was restored to Athens by 409. But a pattern of self-destruction had been established, making it difficult for anyone in Athens or outside it to believe in the possibility of restored greatness.

THE FAILURE OF ATHENIAN DEMOCRACY

The Spartans, too, despaired of bringing the war to an end. Even in its weakened condition, the Athenian fleet was still invincible. Finally, Sparta turned to the Persians, who were hungry to avenge themselves on Athens and agreed to supply the gold and expertise necessary to train an effective Spartan navy. Meanwhile, the Athenians were turning against each other, making the Spartans' task easier. In 406 B.C.E., a rare Athenian naval victory at Arginusae (*ar-geh-NOO-si*) ended in a sudden storm that prevented the Athenian commanders

Two Views of Socrates

Most people regard Socrates as the sage thinker who challenged the prevailing prejudices of his day. During his own time, however, he was not so universally admired. In the first excerpt, from Aristophanes' comedy The Clouds, the protagonist, Strepsiades, goes to Socrates and his "Thought Shop," asking that Socrates make him and his son, Pheidippides, orators capable of winning lawsuits and growing rich. Aristophanes implies throughout that Socrates is a charlatan who teaches word games and tricks for hire.

In the second excerpt, according to his pupil Plato, Socrates spent the last days of his life in conversation with his friends and followers, some of whom urged him to escape from captivity and live in exile. In the dialogue Crito, a young aristocrat argues that the very laws that have condemned Socrates are unjust, and that by choosing to obey them Socrates is giving them legitimacy they do not deserve. But halfway through the debate, Socrates turns the tables on him.

Socrates as a Sophist

STREPSIADES: See that he [Pheidippides] learns your two Arguments, whatever you call them—oh yes, Right and Wrong—the one that takes a bad case and defeats Right with it. If he can't manage both, then at least Wrong—that will do—but that he must have.

SOCRATES: Well, I'll go and send the Arguments here in person, and they'll teach him themselves.

STREPSIADES: Don't forget, he's got to be able to argue against any kind of justified claim at all.

RIGHT: This way. Let the audience see you. . . .

WRONG: Sure, go wherever you like. The more of an audience we have, the more soundly I'll trounce you.

RIGHT: What sort of trick will you use?

WRONG: Oh, just a few new ideas.

RIGHT: Yes, they're in fashion now, aren't they, [to the audience] thanks to you idiots. . . . [to Pheidippides] You don't want to be the sort of chap who's always in the agora telling stories about other people's sex lives, or in the courts arguing about some petty, filthy little dispute. . . .

WRONG: People here at the Thought Shop call me Wrong, because I was the one who invented ways of proving anything wrong, laws, prosecutors, anything. Isn't that worth millions—to have a really bad case and yet win? . . . Suppose you fall in love with a married woman—have a bit of fun—and get caught in the act. As you are now, without a tongue in your head, you're done for. But if you come and learn from me, then you can do whatever you like and get away with it . . . and supposing you do get caught with someone's wife, you can say to him. . . . "What have I done wrong? Look at Zeus; wasn't he always a slave of his sexual passions? And do you expect a mere mortal like me to do any better than a god?" . . .

STREPSIADES [to Socrates]: I wonder if you'd accept a token of my appreciation? But my son, has he learned that Argument we were listening to a moment ago?

SOCRATES: Yes, he has.

STREPSIADES: Holy Fraud, how wonderful!

SOCRATES: Yes, you'll now be able to win any case at all.

Source: Aristophanes, The Clouds, trans. Alan H. Sommerstein (New York: 1973), pp. 148–50, 154, 159–60 (slightly revised).

Socrates and the Laws of Athens

SOCRATES: I should like you to consider whether we are still satisfied on this point: that the really important thing is not to live, but to live well.

CRITO: Why, yes.

SOCRATES: And that to live well means the same thing as to live honorably, or rightly?

CRITO: Yes.

SOCRATES: Then in light of this agreement we must consider whether or not it is right for me to try to get away without an official pardon. If it turns out to be right, we must make the attempt; if not, we must let it drop. . . .

CRITO: I agree with what you say, Socrates. . . .

SOCRATES: Well, here is my next point, or rather question. Ought one to fulfill all one's agreements, provided they are right, or break them?

CRITO: One ought to fulfill them.

SOCRATES: Then consider the logical consequence. If we leave this place without first persuading the polis to let us go . . . are we or are we not abiding by our just agreements?

CRITO: I can't answer your question, Socrates. I am not clear in my mind.

SOCRATES: Look at it this way. Suppose that while we were preparing to run away (or however one should describe it), the Laws of Athens were to come and confront us with this question: "Now, Socrates, what are you proposing to do? Can you deny that by this act which you are contemplating you intend, so far as you have the power, to destroy us, the Laws, and the whole polis as well? Do you imagine that a city can continue to exist and not be turned upside down, if the legal judgments which are pronounced in it have no force but are nullified and destroyed by private persons?"—How shall we answer this question, Crito, and others of the same kind? . . . Shall we say, "Yes, I do intend to destroy the Laws, because the polis has wronged me by passing a faulty judgment at my trial"? Is this to be our answer, or what?

CRITO: What you have just said, by all means, Socrates.

SOCRATES: Then supposing the Laws say, "Was there provision for this in the agreement between you and us, Socrates? Or did you pledge to abide by whatever judgments the polis pronounced? . . . [I]f you cannot persuade your country you must do whatever it orders, and patiently submit to any punishment it imposes, whether it be flogging or imprisonment. And if it leads you out to war, you must comply, and it is right that you should do so; you must not give way or retreat or abandon your position. Both in war and in the law courts you must do whatever your city and your country commands."

Source: Plato, *Crito*, excerpted (with modifications) from *The Last Days of Socrates*, trans. Hugh Tredennick (New York: 1969), pp. 87–91.

Questions for Analysis

1. Socrates actually refused to teach the art of "making the weaker argument defeat the stronger." But in *The Clouds*, Aristophanes shows him teaching how "to win any case at all." Why were the powers of persuasion considered potentially dangerous in democratic Athens? Why would Aristophanes choose to represent Socrates in this way?

2. How do the arguments of Plato's Socrates compare with those of Aristophanes' character?

3. How does Socrates' sense of honor and his duty toward the polis compare with those of Tyrtaeus of Sparta (page 85)?

---

from rescuing the sailors whose ships had been wrecked. A firestorm of protest was fanned by demagogues who insisted on making an example of those generals brave enough to return to Athens. One of these was Pericles' son, who was executed, thereby dying a victim of his father's policies. Through such measures, the Athenians killed or exiled the last of their able commanders.

The result was tragic. The poorly led Athenian fleet was destroyed in 404 B.C.E. Without ships, the Athenians could neither feed themselves nor defend their city. The Spartans sailed the Aegean unopposed, installing pro-Spartan oligarchies to rule former Athenian allies. Finally, they besieged Athens, which surrendered after months of starvation and disease.

Corinth and Thebes, remembering the ruthless treatment of Melos, called for Athens' annihilation. The Spartans refused, but they imposed harsh terms: the dismantling of Athens' defensive walls, the scrapping of its fleet, and the acceptance of an oligarchy under Spartan supervision. These so-called Thirty Tyrants confiscated private property and murdered their political opponents. Their excesses drove committed democrats to plan a desperate coup, a bloodbath averted only through the intervention of the Spartan kings. By the end of 401 B.C.E., Athens had restored a semblance of democratic governance, but it was never more than a shadow of its former self.

With its victory, Sparta succeeded Athens as the arbiter of the Greek world. But this was a thankless job, made worse by the losses the Spartans themselves had suffered during the war and the fact that they were even more aggressive in their control of the Aegean than the Athenians had been.

The Failure of Athenian Democracy | 105

SOCRATES. According to Plato, Socrates looked like a goatman but spoke like a god.

speculation thus continued in the Greek "far west." A major proponent was Pythagoras, who founded a philosophical community in the Italian city of Croton. Pythagoras and his followers regarded the speculative life as the highest good, but they believed that one must be purified of fleshly desires to achieve this. Just as the essence of life lay in the mind, they believed that the essence of the universe was to be found not in the natural world but in the study of abstracts, and so they concentrated on mathematics and musical theory. The Pythagoreans established the key properties of odd and even numbers and also proved an old Babylonian hypothesis in geometry, known today as the Pythagorean theorem. Even though they shunned the material world, they still exhibited the characteristic Greek quest for regularity and predictability in that world.

Meanwhile, philosophy as it developed in mainland Greece was more attuned to questions of ethics and politics than mathematics. The increasing power of individual citizens begged the question of how a man should conduct himself, in public and private life, so as to embrace "the beautiful and the good"—or at least to advance himself by the use of his wits. To answer this question, a new group of teachers arose. They were known as the Sophists, a term meaning "wise men."

Unlike the Milesian philosophers or the Pythagoreans, however, the Sophists made a living by selling their knowledge. Their teachings are best exemplified by Protagoras (*pro-TAG-or-ahs*), an older contemporary of Socrates. His famous dictum, "Man is the measure of all things," means that goodness, truth, and justice are relative concepts, adaptable to the needs and interests of human beings. In other words, values are not moral imperatives established by the gods. Instead, Protagoras declared that no one could know whether the gods existed or, if they did, what they wanted. He concluded that there could be no absolute standards of right and wrong. Empirical facts, established by the perceptions of the senses, were thus the only source of knowledge. And because each man experienced the world in a different way, there could be only individual truths valid for the individual knower.

Such teachings struck many Greeks as dangerous. Sophists such as Protagoras made everyday life a subject for philosophical discussion, but their relativism could too easily degenerate into a conviction that the wise man (or the wise state) was the one best able to manipulate others and gratify individual desires. In both personal and collective terms, this conviction could rationalize monstrous acts of brutality—such as those committed by Athens in the case of Melos.

Indeed, the lessons of the Peloponnesian War went a long way toward demonstrating the disastrous consequences

Ironically, indeed, the Spartans found themselves in a position they had avoided throughout their history, because their far-flung interests now sapped their manpower and undermined their control over the helots. They also faced a reinvigorated Persian Empire, which took advantage of the Greeks' fratricidal struggles to increase its naval presence in the Aegean.

These were the circumstances in which the Athenian philosopher Socrates (469–399 B.C.E.) attempted to reform his city's ethical and political traditions. To understand something of his accomplishments, and to assess the reasons for his trial and execution at the hands of his fellow citizens, we must trace briefly the history of philosophical speculation in the half century before his birth.

The Pythagoreans and the Sophists

After the Persian conquest of Ionia in 546 B.C.E., many Milesian philosophers fled to southern Italy. Philosophical

SOCRATES AS THE IDEAL EDUCATED MAN. This image of Socrates features on a Roman funerary monument known as the Sarcophagus of the Muses, made in the second century C.E. The sarcophagus advertises its owner-occupant's desire to be viewed (even in death) as a highly cultivated man, the companion of the Nine Muses of Greek mythology and the companion of Socrates, who taught that the practice of philosophy helped to prepare the soul for immortality.

of this self-serving logic: if justice is merely relative, then neither individual morality nor society can survive. This ethical conviction led to the growth of a new philosophical movement grounded in the theory that absolute standards *do* exist and that human beings can determine what these are through the exercise of reason. The initiator of this trend was Socrates.

The Life and Thought of Socrates

Socrates was not a professional teacher, as the Sophists were. He may have trained as a stonemason, and he certainly had some sort of livelihood that enabled him to maintain his status as a citizen and hoplite. Having fought in three campaigns as part of the Athenian infantry during

the war with Sparta, he was both an ardent patriot and a sincere critic of Athenian policy. His method of instruction was conversation: through dialogue with passersby, he submitted every presumed truth to rigorous examination in order to establish a firm foundation for further inquiry. Everything we know about Socrates' teachings comes from the writings of younger men who considered themselves his pupils and participated in these conversations. The most important of these followers was Plato.

According to Plato, Socrates sought to show that all supposed certainties are merely unexamined prejudices inherited from others. Socrates always said that he himself knew nothing, because this was a more secure place from which to begin the learning process. He sought to base his speculations on sound definitions of key concepts— justice, virtue, beauty, love—that he and his pupils could arrive at only by investigating their own assumptions. And he focused his attention on practical ethics rather than the study of the physical world (as the Milesians did) or mathematical abstractions (as the Pythagoreans did). He urged his listeners to reflect on the principles of proper conduct, both for their own sakes and for that of society as a whole. He taught that one should consider the meaning and consequences of one's actions at all times and be prepared to take responsibility for them. According to one of his most memorable sayings, "The unexamined life is not worth living."

It is bitterly paradoxical that Socrates, the product of Athenian democracy, should have been put to death by democratic processes. Shortly after the end of the Peloponnesian War in 399 B.C.E., when Athens was reeling from both the shock of defeat and violent internal upheavals, a democratic faction decided that Socrates was a threat to the state. A democratic court agreed, condemning him to death for denying the gods, disloyalty to the polis, and "corrupting the youth." Although his friends made arrangements for him to flee the city and evade punishment, Socrates insisted on abiding by the laws and remaining in prison, thus proving himself true to his own principles and setting an example for future citizens. He died calmly by the prescribed method: self-administered poison.

According to Socrates, the goal of philosophy is to help human beings understand and *apply* standards of absolute good, rather than mastering a series of mental tricks that facilitate personal gain at the expense of others. The circumstances of his death, however, show that it is difficult to translate this philosophy into principles that can be widely accepted. This would be the task of Plato, who would lay the groundwork for all subsequent Western philosophy (see Chapter 4).

CONCLUSION

There are many striking similarities between the civilization of ancient Greece and our own—and many stark differences. Perhaps the most salient example of both is the concept of democracy, which the people of ancient Greece would have defined as a rule by a class of privileged male citizens supported by slavery. In theory and in practice, this amounted to only a small percentage of the population in Athens, and in Sparta the vast majority were subject to the rule of an even smaller class of Spartiates. Moreover, the growth of Athenian power meant, increasingly, the exploitation of other poleis and the spread of imperialism, a ruinous policy of preemptive warfare, and greater intolerance and paranoia. Socrates was not the only man put to death for expressing his opinions. Finally, the status of women in this "golden age" was lower than it had been in earlier periods of Greek history, and women had far fewer

After You Read This Chapter

 Go to **INQUIZITIVE** to see what you've learned—and learn what you've missed—with personalized feedback along the way.

REVIEWING THE OBJECTIVES

- The Greek polis was a unique form of government. What factors led to its emergence?
- Hoplite warfare had a direct effect on the shaping of early democracy. How?
- Poleis could develop in very different ways. What are some of the reasons for this?
- In what ways did Athenian culture, philosophy, and art reflect democratic ideals?
- The Persian and Peloponnesian Wars affected Greek civilization in profound ways. Describe some of the consequences of Athens' victory in the former and its defeat in the latter.

personal rights than in any of the ancient societies we have studied so far.

And yet the enduring importance of Greek civilization has given us the essential vocabulary we have inherited from it: not only the word *democracy* but also *politics*, *philosophy*, *theater*, *history*. How would we think without these concepts? The very notion of humanity comes to us from the Greeks. For them, the fullest development of one's potential should be the aim of existence: every free man is the sculptor of his own monument. Indeed, the concept of freedom—in Greek, *eleutheria*—did not exist in any other ancient language, including Hebrew. This work of growing from childishness to personhood is what the Greeks called *paideia*, from which our term *pedagogy* is derived. The Romans called it *humanitas*. How this and other ideas came to be disseminated beyond Greece, to be adopted by the peoples and places of a much wider world, is the subject of Chapter 4.

PEOPLE, IDEAS, AND EVENTS IN CONTEXT

- How did the epics of **HOMER** transmit the values of the Bronze Age to the **ARISTOCRACY** of the new Greek **POLIS**?
- How did the spread of Greek culture transform the Mediterranean, even as the adoption of **HOPLITE** military tactics transformed Greek politics?
- Compare and contrast the historical circumstances that led to the development of **ATHENS**, **SPARTA**, and **MILETUS**. What were the main differences among them?
- What were the different motives for the invasions by **DARIUS** and **XERXES**? By what methods did the Greek poleis manage to emerge victorious from the **PERSIAN WARS**?
- What were the triumphs and limitations of **DEMOCRACY** in **PERICLEAN ATHENS**?
- How did the **PELOPONNESIAN WAR** transform Athens and affect the balance of power in the Mediterranean?

THINKING ABOUT CONNECTIONS

- The trial and execution of Socrates can be seen as a referendum on the relationship between the individual and the state. What does this incident reveal about the limitations of personal power and individual rights? To what degree was this incident a product of Athenian losses during the Peloponnesian War? To what extent does it reflect long-term trends in the Greek world?
- We like to think that we can trace our democratic ideals and institutions back to Athens, but does this mean that the failings of Athenian democracy also mirror those of our own? What parallels can you draw between the cultures of fifth-century Athens and today's United States? What are some key differences?

Before You Read This Chapter

The Greek World Expands, 400–150 B.C.E.

CORE OBJECTIVES

- **EXPLAIN** the reasons for Macedonia's rise to power and its triumph over the Greek poleis.

- **DESCRIBE** Alexander's methods of conquest, colonization, and governance.

- **IDENTIFY** the three main Hellenistic kingdoms and their essential differences.

- **DEFINE** the main characteristics of the Hellenistic world.

- **UNDERSTAND** how new philosophies and artistic movements reflect the historical changes of this era.

When the young Alexander of Macedonia set out for Persia in 334 B.C.E., he brought along two favorite books. The first was a copy of the *Iliad* that his teacher Aristotle had given him. The second was the *Anabasis*, "The Inland Expedition," by an Athenian called Xenophon (*ZEN-oh-fon*; 430–354 B.C.E.). Both choices are significant. The *Iliad* recounts the story of a much earlier Greek assault on Asia, and its protagonist is the hero Achilles—a consummate warrior, a favorite of the gods, a man who inspired passionate loyalty—a figure with whom Alexander identified. It is also full of information useful to someone planning a long campaign in foreign lands against a formidable enemy, with a fractious army drawn from all parts of Greece and little prospect of bringing them home safely or soon.

The *Anabasis* was an even more practical choice. Its author had been one of 10,000 Greek mercenaries hired by a Persian prince to overthrow his older brother, the Great King. The attempted coup failed, but Xenophon's book made the prince, Cyrus, another role model for Alexander. It told, in detail, how Persians fought, how they lived, how they were governed, and what the terrain of their vast empire was like. Moreover, it showed what a dedicated army of hoplites could accomplish on Persian soil. This book would be Alexander's bible for the next ten years, as he cut a victorious swath through the ancient civilizations of western Asia and North Africa.

An avid student of history, Alexander recognized that the golden age of the Greek polis had ended in the war of attrition between Athens and Sparta (discussed in Chapter 3). The fifty years prior to his own birth in 356 B.C.E. had merely continued this trend on a smaller scale, as the dominant poleis—first Sparta, then Thebes, then Athens—jockeyed for prominence. Meanwhile, social and economic problems were mounting. Faith in the old ideals of democracy were compromised by the vast gulf that now opened up between the rich and the poor. Increasingly, the wealthy withdrew from politics altogether, while free citizens were reduced to debt slavery. As the values of the polis decayed, a new generation of intellectuals argued about what had gone wrong, and they tried to imagine how Greece could be saved. One of these philosophers was Aristotle, a pupil of Plato and Alexander's own teacher.

Under the circumstances, no one would have been able to predict that the era of greatest Greek influence lay ahead. For rather suddenly, the stalemate of the weakened poleis was shattered by the rise to prominence of a tiny kingdom on their northern borders. Beginning in the reign of King Philip II, Macedonia came to control the Greek mainland. Then, under Philip's remarkable son, a united Greek and Macedonian army extended Greek culture and Greek governance from Egypt to the frontiers of India.

This personal empire, the empire of Alexander, could not last; but a cultural empire built on it did. For a thousand years, a Hellenistic ("Greek-like") civilization united the disparate lands and peoples of a vast region, forming the basis of the more lasting Roman Empire and mirroring, in uncanny ways, the cosmopolitan, globalized culture of our own time. How this happened is the subject of Chapter 4.

THE DOWNFALL OF THE GREEK POLIS

The Peloponnesian War had left Sparta the dominant power in the Greek world, but the Spartans showed little talent for their new preeminence. At home, Spartan politicians remained deeply divided over the wisdom of sending forces beyond their frontiers; abroad, Spartan armies showed even less restraint than the Athenians had in subduing cities that should have been their allies. In 395 B.C.E., a significant portion of Greece—including such sworn enemies as Athens, Argos, Corinth, and Thebes—aligned

themselves against Sparta in the so-called Corinthian War (395–387 B.C.E.). After years of stalemate, the Spartans could win the war only by turning once again to Persia, as they had done in the final stages of the Peloponnesian War. The Persians brokered a peace, which they were also prepared to enforce, one that left Sparta in control of Greece. This pattern of Greek-on-Greek violence, temporarily halted by the intervention of Persia, was repeated time and again over the next fifty years, during which the advantage shifted steadily toward Persia.

The Struggle for Dominance

After the Corinthian War, the Spartans punished the most dangerous of their rivals, Thebes, by occupying the city for four years. This subjugation to a military garrison

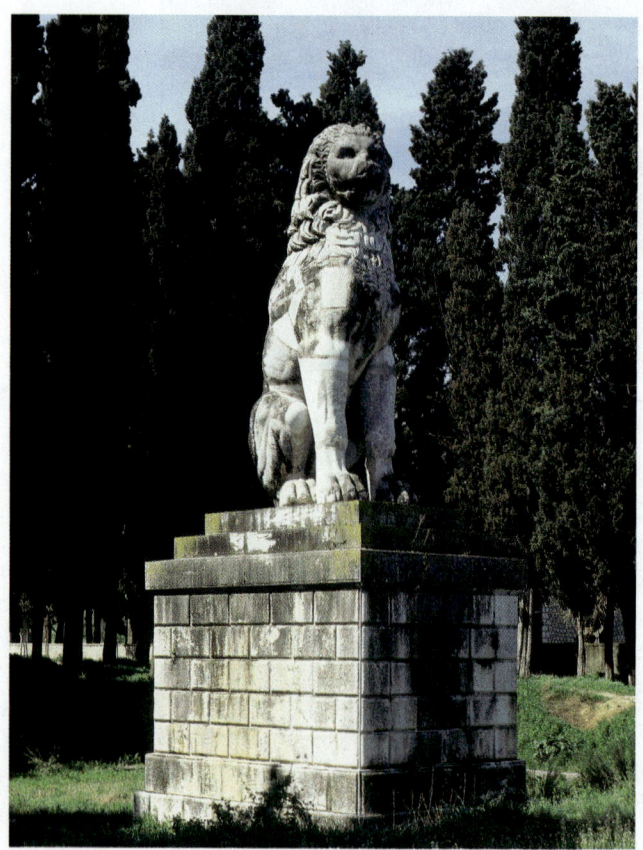

HONORING THE THEBAN SACRED BAND. According to ancient historians, all 300 of the Band's sworn lovers fell at the Battle of Chaeronea in 338 B.C.E., when Thebes was defeated by Macedonian forces led by King Philip II and his son, Alexander. An excavation undertaken at this site in 1890 uncovered the remains of only 254 warriors, but it is possible that some were buried elsewhere. This monument is a modern reconstruction of the one originally erected by the citizens of Thebes toward the end of the fourth century B.C.E.

was intended and received as an act of humiliation, and when the Thebans regained their autonomy, they elected as their leader a fierce patriot who was also a military genius, Epaminondas (*eh-pa-min-OHN-das*; c. 410–362 B.C.E.).

For decades, various poleis had been experimenting with the basic form of the hoplite phalanx, adding light skirmishers and archers to enhance its effectiveness. Epaminondas now went further. In imitation of the Spartan system, he formed an elite hoplite unit known as the Theban Sacred Band, made up of 150 male couples, sworn lovers who had pledged to fight to the death for their polis and for each other's honor. Epaminondas also trained a corps of lighter-armed, fast-moving infantry. By the early 370s, he was ready for another trial of strength with the Spartans.

The Theban and Spartan armies met at Leuctra in 371 B.C.E. Epaminondas defied convention by placing his best troops (the Sacred Band) on the left-hand side of his formation, and by stacking this phalanx fifty rows deep, making a narrow wedge of ten men abreast whose hidden depth of strength he further disguised under a cover of arrows and javelin attacks. When the two sides met, the weight of the Theban left drove through the Spartan right flank, breaking it in two and collapsing it. Epaminondas followed his victory by marching through Messenia and freeing the helots. Spartan power—and the unique social system that had supported it—was at an end. Almost overnight, Epaminondas had reduced Sparta to a small, provincial polis and launched what has often been called the Theban Hegemony.

But as Theban power grew, so did the animosity of the other Greek poleis. In 371 B.C.E., Athens had supported Thebes against Sparta, its ancient enemy, but when the Thebans and Spartans squared off again in 362 B.C.E. at the Battle of Mantinea, the Athenians allied themselves with

THE INLAND EXPEDITION OF THE TEN THOUSAND. This map shows the route taken by Xenophon and his fellow Greek mercenaries during their Persian campaigns, when they supported the failed coup of Cyrus against his brother Artaxerxes II and then fought their way home through enemy territory (as the *Anabasis* records). Follow Xenophon's route with your finger. ▪ *Where did it start and end?* ▪ *Compare this route with that of Alexander on page 125. How closely was Alexander following it?* ▪ *When and how did he diverge from it?* ▪ *Why would this journey of Greek mercenaries have provided Alexander with an important model?*

Xenophon Describes an Ideal Leader

In his history of "The Inland Expedition" undertaken by the Ten Thousand, Xenophon (430–354 B.C.E.) mourns the death of Cyrus the Younger, whom he believes would have made a better Great King of Persia than the brother he challenged, Artaxerxes II. The following description of the prince's character and leadership became very famous in its time, often circulating as a separate booklet. It is likely to have influenced the young Alexander.

Thus then died Cyrus, a man who, of all the Persians since Cyrus the elder, was the most princely and the most worthy of rule, as is agreed by all who appear to have had personal knowledge of him. In the first place, while he was yet a boy, and when he was receiving his education with his brother and other youths, he was thought to surpass them all in everything. For all the sons of the Persian nobles are educated at the gates of the king, where they may learn many a lesson of virtuous conduct, but can see or hear nothing disgraceful. Here the boys see some honored by the king, and others disgraced, and hear of them, so that in their very childhood they learn to govern and to obey.

Here Cyrus, first of all, showed himself most remarkable for modesty among those of his own age, and for paying more ready obedience to his elders than even those who were inferior to him in station; and next, he was noted for his fondness for horses, and for managing them in a superior manner. They found him, too, very desirous of learning, and most assiduous in practicing the warlike exercises of archery and hurling the javelin. When it suited his age, he grew extremely fond of the chase, and of braving dangers in encounters with wild beasts. On one occasion, he did not shrink from a she-bear that attacked him, but, in grappling with her, was dragged from off his horse, and received some wounds, the scars of which were visible on his body, but at last killed her. The person who first came to his assistance he made a happy man in the eyes of many.

When he was sent down by his father, as satrap of Lydia and Great Phrygia and Cappadocia, and was also appointed commander of all the troops whose duty it is to muster in the plain of Castolus, he soon showed that if he made a league or compact with anyone, or gave a promise, he deemed it of the utmost importance not to break his word. Accordingly, the states that were committed to his charge, as well as individuals, had the greatest confidence in him; and if anyone had been his enemy, he felt secure that if Cyrus entered into a treaty with him, he should suffer no infraction of the stipulations. When, therefore, he waged war against Tissaphernes, all the cities, of their own accord, chose to adhere to Cyrus in preference to Tissaphernes, except the Milesians; but they feared him, because he would not abandon the cause of the exiles; for he both showed by his deeds and declared in words that he would never desert them, since he had once become a friend to them, not even though they should grow still fewer in number, and be in a worse condition than they were.

Whenever anyone did him a kindness or an injury, he showed himself anxious to go beyond him in those respects; and some used to mention a wish of his that he desired to live long enough to outdo both those who had done him good, and those who had done him ill, in the requital that he should make. Accordingly, to him alone of the men of our days were so great a number of people desirous of committing the disposal of their property, their cities, and their own persons.

Source: Excerpted from Xenophon, *Anabasis*, ed. M. I. Finley, in *The Portable Greek Historians* (New York: 1959), pp. 383–84.

Questions for Analysis

1. According to Xenophon, what are the attributes of a great leader? How would Alexander have applied these attributes to his own situation?

2. What seems to be Xenophon's attitude toward the Persians? How might his portrayal of them have been influenced by his travels among them? How might it have been colored by his attitude toward his own countrymen?

3. In what ways does Cyrus the Younger appear to have followed the example of his ancestor, Cyrus the Great (page 64)?

the weaker Spartans. Although the Theban army again carried the day, the brilliant Epaminondas fell in battle, crippling Thebes' leadership. Athens then attempted to fill the vacuum by establishing a naval confederacy, organized more equitably than the Delian League had been, but the Athenians quickly reverted to manipulating and abusing their allies, and the confederacy dissolved in rebellions. Greece was thus reduced to a constellation of petty warring states, increasingly debilitated by their struggles with each other.

Social and Economic Crises

Meanwhile, individual poleis were also riven by internal turmoil. Athens was spared the political revolutions many other cities suffered, mostly because the memory of the Thirty Tyrants had discredited the cause of oligarchy there; but elsewhere in the Greek world, strife between democrats and oligarchs worsened. Incessant warfare, combined with these political struggles, profoundly affected the Greek world's economic and social infrastructures. Many ordinary people were driven from their homes or reduced to slavery. Country towns had been ravaged, some repeatedly, as had farmlands throughout Greece. The destruction of orchards and vineyards was particularly devastating because of the long time it takes grapevines and olive trees to mature, 40 or 50 years in the latter case. So when an invading army cut down an olive grove, it was destroying a staple crop for two generations. Even arable land was exhausted and less productive than it had been earlier. As a result, prices rose around 50 percent while standards of living declined because wages remained more or less stagnant, and taxes increased. In Athens, the wealthiest private citizens now became the sponsors of public theaters and buildings, as well as the patrons who maintained roads and warships. Even so, the kind of ambitious civic spending undertaken by the tyrants or by Pericles was unknown in the fourth century B.C.E.

Unemployment was also widespread, especially among the growing population of the cities, which were swollen with refugees from the political collapse of the countryside and overseas colonies. During wartime, men might find employment as rowers or soldiers in the service of their city; but when their city was at peace, many turned to mercenary service. The Greek states in Sicily and Italy began to hire mercenaries from the mainland, as did Sparta, to supplement its own campaigns. As we have noted, the brother of the Persian emperor Artaxerxes II, Cyrus, even hired a Greek mercenary force of 10,000 men in an attempt to seize the throne in 401 B.C.E.—although

he did not reveal this aim until the army was deep in Persian territory and suddenly confronted with an enemy far more formidable than the tribal bands it had originally agreed to fight. Cyrus was killed in battle, and shortly thereafter, the Ten Thousand's Spartan general was murdered by agents of Artaxerxes. The army—marooned in a hostile country—had to fight its way out under elected leaders, one of whom was Xenophon, who later wrote his account of these adventures. Finally, the veterans reached the Black Sea and made their way back to Greece, where many (including Xenophon) settled in Sparta. Despite all these hardships, this episode was a stunning demonstration of what a professional Greek army could achieve, and it would fire Alexander's imagination.

REIMAGINING THE POLIS: THE ARTISTIC AND INTELLECTUAL RESPONSE

We might take 399 B.C.E., the year of Socrates' execution, to mark the end of an era: that of the polis. This basic engine of Greek life had continued to drive innovation and cultural production even during the Peloponnesian War, both in support of the war and in opposition to it. In Athens alone, the historians Herodotus (in his final years) and Thucydides were at work, as were the tragic poets Sophocles and Euripides, the comic playwright Aristophanes, and scores of talented statesmen, poets, sculptors, and artisans. But it's hard not to see the death of Socrates as symbolic of democracy's failure. Thereafter, the evident breakdown of society during the fourth century had a profound impact on the arts, philosophy, and political thought.

The Arts of the Fourth Century

As we observed in Chapter 3, the painters and sculptors of the fifth century B.C.E. were already working to achieve a heightened appearance of realism. This experimentation continued in the fourth century, especially in the relatively new art of portraiture. During this era, painters and sculptors tried to render both objects and people as they actually looked—for better or for worse—and to convey the illusion of movement, trends that would continue in subsequent centuries. They also grew bolder in their use of sophisticated techniques, such as the casting of full-size statues in bronze, which combined high levels of artistry with advanced metallurgy. This was a medium in which the era's most famous sculptor, Praxiteles, excelled. Praxiteles (*prak-SIT-el-ees*) was bold, too, in his choice of subjects, and he is widely regarded as the first artist to create full-size female nudes, an innovation that sparked controversy in his own day as well as in other eras (see **Interpreting Visual Evidence** on page 118).

The forms and functions of drama also changed considerably. In large part, this was because tragedy and comedy were no longer mounted as part of publicly funded festivals but were instead paid for by private patrons who could exercise greater control over the content of performances. As a result, fourth-century playwrights did not have the freedom to use drama as a vehicle for political and social critique. Nor did the comic genius Aristophanes have any true fourth-century successors. His biting, satirical wit gave way to a milder, less provocative style that bears some resemblance to early television sitcoms. It was this "New Comedy" that laid the groundwork for comedy that developed over the next several centuries: it came to rely more and more on mistaken identities, tangled familial relationships, humorous misunderstandings, and breaches of etiquette. The most famous comic playwright of this age was Menander (c. 342–292 B.C.E.), whose work survives today only in fragments but who directly inspired the comedians of the Roman theater. They in turn inspired medieval and then early modern playwrights such as Shakespeare. Similar trends toward escapism and frivolity are also apparent in a new literary genre that emerged during the fourth century: the prose novel, in which star-crossed lovers undergo extraordinary trials and perilous adventures before reuniting happily after a long separation. These pleasant fictions targeted an increasingly literate audience, including (as for modern novels) an audience of women.

BRONZE YOUTH. This lithe statue, dating from the years 340–330 B.C.E., was found in the sea near Marathon and has been identified as a work by the master sculptor Praxiteles (or one of his pupils). Compare this male nude with those discussed in Chapter 3. ▪ *How might changes in the style of sculpture parallel cultural changes in society at large?*

Philosophy after Socrates: The Schools of Plato and Aristotle

The intellectual and political work undertaken by Socrates was carried forward by his most talented student, **Plato**. Born in Athens to an aristocratic family around 429 B.C.E., Plato joined Socrates' circle as a young man and witnessed firsthand the persecution, trial, and death of his mentor. For the next fifty years, to the time of his own death around 349 B.C.E., Plato usually shunned direct political involvement and strove instead to vindicate Socrates by constructing a philosophical system based on his teacher's unwritten precepts. Socrates had taught through dialectical conversation and by example; he mistrusted writing and resisted developing a coherent set of principles. Plato's mission was therefore to transmit his legacy in a way that captured the liveliness and charm of the Socratic method but within a more structured framework.

He did this in two ways: first, by founding an informal school called the Academy, which had no tuition or set curriculum; and later, by writing a series of dialogues that wrapped weighty philosophical content in a witty and accessible dramatic format, with Socrates as the central character. Most dialogues are known by the names of Plato's contemporaries, the original students who had

PLATO AND ARISTOTLE IN THE SCHOOL OF ATHENS. Although many artistic representations of Plato and Aristotle were made in antiquity, the image that best captures the essential difference between their philosophies is this one, the focal point of a fresco by the Renaissance painter Raphael (1483–1520 C.E.; discussed further in Chapter 12). Plato is the older man (center left), who points with his right hand to the heavens; Aristotle is the younger man (center right), gesturing with an open palm to the earth. ▪ *How does this double portrait reflect these philosophers' teachings and perspectives?*

engaged Socrates in discussion (such as Crito, whose imagined dialogue with Socrates is excerpted in Chapter 3, on page 104). One dialogue, the *Symposium*, actually re-creates the conversation at a drinking party, where a tipsy Socrates, the comedian Aristophanes, and other Athenian worthies debate the nature of love.

The longest and most famous of Plato's dialogues is now known by its Latin title, the *Republic*. In Greek, it is the *Politeía* ("Polis-governance" or even "Policy"), the first treatise on political philosophy written in the West. In it, Plato argues—through the character of Socrates—that social harmony and order are more important than individual liberty or equality. He imagines an ideal polis in which most people—farmers, artisans, traders—are governed by a superior group of "guardians" chosen in their youth for their natural attributes of intelligence and character.

These prospective guardians would serve the polis first as soldiers, living together without private property. Those found to be the wisest would then receive more education, and a few would ultimately become "philosopher-kings." These enlightened rulers would in turn choose the next generation of guardians.

This utopian system actually bears an intriguing resemblance to the social order of Sparta, as well as containing elements of a benign tyranny, and is clearly a response to the failures of Athenian democracy in Plato's youth. But whether Plato himself believed in this system—he never voices his own opinion—is open to interpretation. Indeed, the students of Socrates who are represented as discussing it with him voice many objections. The most obvious of these is "Who will guard the guardians?" For such a system presumes that properly educated rulers will never be

Reconstructing an Ideal of Female Beauty

The lost statue known as the Aphrodite of Knidos was considered the most beautiful in the ancient world, but we can study it only by looking at later copies. It was the work of the fourth century's most renowned sculptor, Praxiteles, who was reputed to have modeled it after the Athenian courtesan known as Phryne, a renowned beauty who inspired several contemporary artists and a whole series of apocryphal stories. The most reliable of these tales concerns the riches she accrued. Apparently she became so wealthy that she offered to finance the rebuilding of Thebes in 336 B.C.E.—on the condition that the slogan "destroyed by Alexander, restored by Phryne the Courtesan" be prominently displayed on the new walls. (Her offer was rejected.)

Praxiteles' original statue is thought to have been the first monumental female nude fashioned in antiquity. According to one authority, Praxiteles initially received a commission from the island of Kos, for which he fashioned both clothed and naked versions of Aphrodite. Apparently, the scandalized citizens approved only the draped version and refused to pay for the nude. It was purchased instead by the city of Knidos on Cyprus, where it was displayed in an open-air temple so that it could be seen from all sides. It quickly became a tourist attraction and was widely copied and emulated. Two of the more faithful replicas, made by later artists working in Rome, are pictured here.

Questions for Analysis

1. As we have seen, the male nude was a favorite subject of Greek artists from the Archaic Period onward. Recall your knowledge of contemporary Greek culture and society. Why was it not until the fourth century B.C.E. that a life-size female nude could be publicly displayed? Were there any precedents for statues like this?

2. Compare and contrast the ideal of female beauty suggested by the Knidian Aphrodite with the male ideals discussed in Chapter 3. What can you conclude about the relationship between these ideals and the different expectations of male and female behavior in Greek society? Why, for example, would ancient sources insist that the model for this statue was a courtesan?

3. Among the Romans, a statue like the Knidian Aphrodite was called a *Venus pudica*, a "modest Venus" (image A). Yet the citizens of Kos were allegedly shocked by its indecency, and old photographs of the copy in the Vatican Museum (image B) show that it was displayed until 1932 with additional draperies made of tin. How do you account for these very different standards of decency? To what degree do they suggest that concepts of "beauty" or "modesty" are historically constructed?

A. Roman copy of the Aphrodite of Knidos.

B. Second century C.E. copy of the Aphrodite of Knidos.

corrupted by power or wealth, a proposition that has yet to be sustained in practice.

The more practical applications of philosophy would be the preoccupation of Plato's own student **Aristotle** (384–322 B.C.E.). Aristotle, the son of a physician, learned from his father the importance of observing natural phenomena. Although receptive to Plato's training, Aristotle geared his own philosophical system toward understanding the workings of the world through the rational analysis of empirical knowledge—that is, information gained through sensory experience. In contrast to Plato, who taught that everything we see and touch is an untrustworthy reflection of some intangible ideal, Aristotle advocated the rigorous investigation of real phenomena, in order to uncover the natural order of the universe and of human beings' place within it. His method of instruction was also different. Unlike Socrates and Plato, whose dialogues were often playful, Aristotle delivered lectures on which his students took detailed notes, and eventually these notes became the basis of separate but interrelated treatises on politics, ethics, logic, metaphysics, and poetics. Aristotle also established rules for the syllogism, a form of reasoning in which certain premises inevitably lead to a valid conclusion, and developed precise categories that could be used to further philosophical and scientific analysis.

With respect to ethics, Aristotle taught that the highest good consists in the harmonious functioning of the individual human mind and body. Since humans differ from animals by virtue of their rational capacities, he argued, they find happiness by exercising these capacities appropriately. Good conduct is therefore rational conduct, and consists in acting moderately: showing courage rather than rashness or cowardice, temperance rather than excessive indulgence or self-denial. And whereas Plato conceived of politics as a means to an end that could never be achieved in this life, Aristotle thought of politics as an end in itself: the collective exercise of moderation.

But Aristotle also took it for granted that some people—such as barbarians—are not fully human and so are intended by nature to be slaves. He also believed that women were not endowed with a full measure of humanity and so could never achieve the good life, either as individuals or as participants in the public sphere of the polis. So when Aristotle asserted that "man is by nature a political animal" (or, to be more faithful to the Greek, "a creature of the polis"), he meant only Greek males of privileged status. He also did not believe that the best form of government is a democracy. Like Plato, Aristotle saw democracy as a debased form of government. What he preferred was the polity, in which monarchical, aristocratic, and democratic elements are combined by means of checks and balances. Only this form of government, he posited, would allow free men to realize their rational potential.

Men of Thought and Action

For all their brilliance and originality, Plato and Aristotle offered few prescriptions for reforming their own societies. Both imagined the perfect polis as one made up of a few thousand households, largely engaged in agriculture and living together in a single community. Although Greek civilization had begun in such a world, the realities of fourth-century political life were very different. Plato and Aristotle recognized this to some extent, yet for both the answer was a reorganization of existing institutions, not something entirely new.

But other intellectuals at this time were considering more radical alternatives. One was Xenophon, that veteran of the Ten Thousand, who was another product of the Socratic tradition and an exact contemporary of Plato. After his return from Persia, he went on to fight for the Spartan king Agesilaus (ah-geh-si-LA-uhs), who became a trusted friend. Thoroughly disillusioned by the failures of Athenian democracy, Xenophon spent most of his adult life in exile. It is mostly thanks to his admiring account that we know anything about the Spartiate system described in Chapter 3, which he intended to be a rebuke to Athens. We also have his own view of Socrates' teaching, which he related in a series of memoirs and treatises on kingship and household management (the *Oikonomikos*, the root of our word *economics*). He loved horses and dogs and wrote a treatise on training them for the hunt, as well. All the while, he watched as the Theban leader Epaminondas crippled the state he so admired, Sparta. (Xenophon hated him so much that he refused to mention his name in the history he was compiling.)

The Athenian orator Isocrates (436–338 B.C.E.) was another direct contemporary of Plato and was also convinced that something had gone horribly awry as a result of the Peloponnesian War. Rather than imagining that a solution lay in the reform of the polis, he proposed instead that the Greeks rediscover their lost unity by staging a massive invasion of Persia. This assault, he prophesied, would be led by a man of vision and ability, someone who could unite the Greek world behind his cause. Isocrates spent most of his life casting about to find such a leader. Finally, he began to think that the man for the job was someone whom most Greeks considered no Greek at all: the king of Macedonia, Philip II.

Aristotle's Justification of Slavery

Like The Republic *of his teacher Plato, Aristotle's treatise* Politics *attempts to define and rationalize various methods of governance. Early in this work, Aristotle grappled with the fact that all ancient societies were highly dependent on slave labor and answered objections that the forcible subjugation of some men to the will of others goes against the laws of nature and the ideals of his own society.*

But is there anyone thus intended by nature to be a slave, and for whom such a condition is expedient and right, or rather is not all slavery a violation of nature? There is no difficulty in answering this question, on grounds both of reason and of fact. For that some should rule and others be ruled is a thing not only necessary, but expedient; from the hour of their birth, some are marked out for subjection, others for rule. . . .

But that those who take the opposite view have in a certain way right on their side, may be easily seen. For the words *slavery* and *slave* are used in two senses. There is a slave or slavery by law as well as by nature. The law of which I speak is a sort of convention—the law by which whatever is taken in war is supposed to belong to the victors. But this right many jurists impeach, as they would an orator who brought forward an unconstitutional measure: they detest the notion that, because one man has the power of doing violence and is superior in brute strength, another shall be his slave and subject.

Even among philosophers there is a difference of opinion. The origin of the dispute, and what makes the views invade each other's territory, is as follows: in some sense virtue, when furnished with means, has actually the greatest power of exercising force; and as superior power is only found where there is superior excellence of some kind, power seems to imply virtue, and

the dispute to be simply one about justice (for it is due to one party identifying justice with goodwill while the other identifies it with the mere rule of the stronger). If these views are thus set out separately, the other views have no force or plausibility against the view that the superior in virtue ought to rule, or be master. Others, clinging, as they think, simply to a principle of justice (for law and custom are a sort of justice), assume that slavery in accordance with the custom of war is justified by law, but at the same moment they deny this. For what if the cause of the war be unjust?

And again, no one would ever say he is a slave who is unworthy to be a slave. Were this the case, men of the highest rank would be slaves and the children of slaves if they or their parents chance to have been taken captive and sold. Wherefore Hellenes [Greeks] do not like to call Hellenes slaves, but confine the term to barbarians. Yet, in using this language, they really mean the natural slave of whom we spoke at first; for it must be admitted that some are slaves everywhere, others nowhere.

The same principle applies to nobility. Hellenes regard themselves as noble everywhere, and not only in their own country, but they deem the barbarians noble only when at home, thereby implying that there are two sorts of nobility and freedom, the one absolute, the other relative. . . .

We see then that there is some foundation for this difference of opinion, and that all are not either slaves by nature or

freemen by nature, and also that there is in some cases a marked distinction between the two classes, rendering it expedient and right for the one to be slaves and the others to be masters: the one practicing obedience, the others exercising the authority and lordship which nature intended them to have. The abuse of this authority is injurious to both; for the interests of part and whole, of body and soul, are the same, and the slave is a part of the master, a living but separated part of his bodily frame. Hence, where the relation of master and slave between them is natural they are friends and have a common interest, but where it rests merely on law and force the reverse is true.

Source: Excerpted from Aristotle, *Politics*, Book I: v–vi, trans. Benjamin Jowett (Oxford: 1920), pp. 32–37.

Questions for Analysis

1. According to Aristotle, how does one become a slave? Why is the question of slavery's justice related to that of the just war?

2. Aristotle posits that some people are slaves by nature, others by some unfortunate circumstances (such as being captured in battle). For example, he says that Hellenes (Greeks) do not admit that they can be slaves; that is possible only for barbarians. What are the wider implications of this argument?

THE RISE OF MACEDONIA

Isocrates had a point. By the middle of the fourth century, the Greek poleis had become so embroiled in military, political, and socioeconomic turmoil that they barely noticed the powerhouse on their northern frontier. Until the fourth century, Macedonia (or Macedon) had been a weak kingdom, regarded as a throwback to the "dark ages" before the emergence of enlightened poleis, ruled by a royal dynasty barely strong enough to control its own nobility and beset by intrigue and murderous ambition. As recently as the 360s, Macedonia had teetered on the edge of collapse, nearly succumbing to the even smaller kingdoms and predatory tribes that surrounded it.

Despite the efforts of a few Macedonian kings to add a gloss of Hellenic culture to their courts—one had successfully invited Euripides and Sophocles to his palace—the Greeks considered them nearly as barbaric as their northern neighbors. It is still not known whether the ancient Macedonians were Greek-speakers during this period, although the royal family and nobility, at least, would have spoken Greek as a second language; and Macedonians seem to have participated in the Olympic Games, which were open only to Greeks. But they were definitely perceived as dangerous outsiders. Therefore, when a young and energetic king named Philip consolidated the southern Balkans under his rule, many Greeks saw it as a development no less troubling than the approach of the Persians in the fifth century.

The Reign of Philip II (359–336 B.C.E.)

Philip II of Macedonia was not supposed to be its ruler. Born in 382 B.C.E., he was the third and youngest son of King Amyntas III and considered so dispensable that he was sent to Thebes as a hostage when he was fourteen, at the time of the Theban Hegemony. This turned out to be the making of him: he became the protégé of the brilliant Epaminondas and may even have trained alongside the general Pelopidas (*pel-OH-pi-das*) in the Theban Sacred Band. By the time he returned to the Macedonian capital of Pella in 364 B.C.E., three years later, he had received a more thorough education in Greek culture and military tactics than any Macedonian before him.

He was also ambitious, and may already have laid great plans for the future. So when both of his older brothers died in battle, one after the other, Philip was not content with the role of regent for an infant nephew. By 356 B.C.E.,

PHILIP II OF MACEDONIA. This tiny ivory head was discovered in a royal tomb at Vergina and is almost certainly a bust of the king himself. Contemporary sources report that Philip the Great had his right eye blinded by a catapult bolt, a deformity visible here—and testimony to the unflinching realism of Greek portraiture in the fourth century B.C.E.

he had supplanted his nephew and was reigning as king, the same year that his queen, Olympias, bore him an heir. The boy was given the dynastic name Alexandros, meaning "leader of men."

The first problem of Philip's reign was the fragility of Macedonia's northern borders. Through a combination of warfare and diplomacy, he subdued the tribes of the southern Balkans and incorporated their territory into his kingdom—losing an eye in the process. His success in this had much to do with his reorganization of Macedonian warriors into a hoplite infantry along Theban lines. The mineral resources to which he now had access also helped, since he used that new wealth to pay and equip a standing professional army; just one of his gold mines produced as much in one year as the Delian League at its height had collected annually.

Philip also organized an elite cavalry squad—the Companions—who fought with and beside the king, an innovation that may have been designed to emulate the camaraderie of the Sacred Band and was intended to counter the Persian reliance on cavalry. These young men were drawn exclusively from the nobility, and Philip thereby hoped to inspire their deeper loyalty; in fact, under the guise of recruiting future Companions, he gained valuable young

MACEDONIAN PHALANX. Philip of Macedonia's hoplite infantry—the model for Alexander's—was armed with two-handed pikes of graduated lengths, from thirteen to twenty-one feet, and was massed in squares sixteen rows deep and wide. Members of the phalanx were trained to wheel quickly in step formation and to double the width of their front rank as needed by filing off in rows of eight. The reach of their spears, called *sarissas*, extended the phalanx's fighting range.

around mainland Greece to Corinth, where he established a new political federation. The main purpose of this federation, the League of Corinth, was to provide forces for the invasion of Persia and to maintain peace among the rival poleis.

Philip never realized his dream of Persian conquest. Two years later, in 336 B.C.E., he was assassinated during a festival at Pella, purportedly by a vengeful former lover. The kingship now fell to Alexander. Among the Greeks, he would be known as Alexander, the Sacker of Cities. To the Romans, impressed by his ruthless military genius, he was **Alexander the Great**.

hostages to ensure the good conduct of aristocratic rivals. Their sons were now being brought up alongside Alexander and sharing his lessons with Aristotle, who had arrived at the Macedonian court in 343 B.C.E. Through a series of strategic marriages, Philip also managed to gain the goodwill and alliance of many neighboring kingdoms—although his open polygamy was, in Greek eyes, another irregularity that called to mind the barbarians of Persia.

Eventually, the increasing strength of Macedonia began to impinge on the consciousness of some Greeks, most notably the Athenians. But whereas Isocrates saw in Philip a potential savior of Greece, many Athenians believed that Philip's ultimate aim was to conquer and subjugate them. They may have misunderstood Philip's goals: his northward expansion was designed to secure his frontiers and the resources necessary to support an invasion of Persia, not of Greece. From 348 B.C.E. on, Philip was actually trying to forge an alliance with Athens, whose fleet could facilitate such an invasion by sea; in return, he promised to support Athens' old claim to hegemony over Greece. But the Athenians took the advice of an orator called Demosthenes and refused to cooperate.

This miscalculation would prove disastrous. Philip's inability to reach a peaceful understanding with Athens, despite strenuous diplomatic efforts, ultimately led to war, which sent the Athenians scrambling to ally with their former enemy, Thebes, and a number of smaller poleis. Their fate was sealed at the battle of Chaeronea (*kie-ROH-nee-ah*) in 338 B.C.E., when an army led jointly by Philip and Alexander (aged seventeen) won a narrow victory, decimating the Athenian forces and destroying the Theban Sacred Band. In the aftermath, Philip called delegates from

THE CONQUESTS OF ALEXANDER (336–323 B.C.E.)

By the time of Alexander's early death at the age of thirty-two, a monumental legend had already built up around him. This makes it all the more ironic and frustrating that no contemporary account of his life and achievements survives. So when we try to reconstruct the history of Alexander, we are relying on the writings of men who lived and worked under the Roman Empire, notably Plutarch (46–120 C.E.) and Arrian (c. 86–160 C.E.), both of whom were separated from their subject by a distance of 400 years. Luckily, there is good reason to believe that they were basing their histories on sources derived from several (lost) firsthand accounts, one written by Alexander's general (and alleged half brother) Ptolemy (*TOHL-eh-mee*; c. 367–c. 284 B.C.E.), who founded a new dynasty of Egyptian pharaohs. Nevertheless, it is a salutary reminder of how fragile the historical record of antiquity is, that sources for the life of the era's most famous man are so hard to come by.

The Conquest of Persia

When Alexander succeeded his father Philip in 336 B.C.E., he could not begin to carry out his plans of conquest until he had put down the revolts that erupted immediately after Philip's death—notably at Thebes, an uprising that he punished by destroying its famous walls. Two years later, he was crossing the Hellespont at the head of a hoplite army to challenge the Great King of Persia, Darius III.

ALEXANDER DEFEATS KING DARIUS OF PERSIA AT THE BATTLE OF ISSUS (333 B.C.E.). This Roman mural, discovered at Pompeii (see Chapter 5), shows Darius fleeing from the battlefield in his chariot on the right, pursued by Alexander, the mounted figure on the far left.

From the beginning, Darius was no match for Alexander. He was a minor member of the royal family who had taken the dynastic name when he was placed on the throne after a palace coup, at the relatively old age of forty-five—the same year that Alexander became king at age twenty. Darius and his advisers failed to take the Macedonian threat seriously, despite the Persians' past history of defeat at the hands of Greek armies—even on Persian soil and within living memory. Perhaps they assumed that the enormous forces they could rally in defense of their empire would easily overwhelm a comparatively small army of 42,000; or perhaps they misunderstood Alexander's aims, which would reveal themselves over time to be far-reaching indeed. In any event, the Persian army of Darius III was made up of mercenaries or poorly paid conscripts under the command of inexperienced generals.

As a result, Alexander achieved a series of extraordinary victories, beginning in northwest Anatolia, near the epic field of Troy, and continuing down the Ionian coastline. In 333 B.C.E., Darius was persuaded to engage Alexander personally, at the head of a force that significantly outnumbered that of his opponent. But the chosen site, on the banks of a river near Issus, favored Alexander's fast-moving infantry, not the heavy cavalry and chariots of the Persians, which had no room to maneuver and were hampered by mud. No warrior himself, Darius shamefully fled the battlefield, abandoning not only his army but his entire household, which included his wife and his mother. They were captured by Alexander's troops and treated by him with great respect.

Darius spent the remainder of his life running from Alexander's advancing army, until his decisive defeat at Gaugamela (near Mosul in modern Iraq) in 331 B.C.E., when he was killed by a local chieftain who hoped to win

Alexander's favor. Instead, Alexander—acting as the new Great King—had the chieftain executed for treason against his former enemy and predecessor. The next spring, Alexander destroyed the royal capital of Persepolis, lest it serve as a rallying point for Persian resistance.

Meanwhile, in the two years that had passed since Darius's humiliation at Issus, Alexander had completed his conquest of the Persian Empire. One by one, the cities of Syria and Palestine surrendered after Alexander made a powerful statement by destroying the wealthy Phoenician capital at Tyre. Following the example of Cyrus the Great, whose tactics he increasingly came to emulate, Alexander developed a policy of offering amnesty to cities that submitted peacefully—but dealing mercilessly with those that resisted. The fortified city of Gaza, the last Persian stronghold on the Egyptian border, provides an example: its commander, Batis, not only refused to surrender but seemed determined to fight to the death, inflicting severe losses on the troops besieging his city and seriously wounding Alexander himself. When the fortress was finally taken, Alexander's troops slew all the adult males and enslaved the women and children. According to a later Roman historian, Alexander also dragged the body of Batis around the city's walls behind his chariot, imitating Achilles' treatment of his fallen rival Hector.

Alexander in Egypt

After this, Alexander marched into Egypt unopposed. In fact, he was welcomed: Egypt had been governed as a Persian satrapy (principality) since 525 B.C.E., when Cambyses, son of Cyrus the Great, had deposed the last pharaoh of the reigning dynasty (see Chapter 2). Now Alexander

MARBLE HEAD OF ALEXANDER. Alexander the Great was reported to have been very striking in appearance, although sources vary in their assessment of his physical beauty. This portrait bust was made in 180 B.C.E., about 150 years after his death. ▪ *Given the trends in sculpture during that period (see page 116), is this likely to have been an accurate portrait? Why or why not?*

Philip but by Zeus. Alexander, ever mindful of precedent and the historical significance of his own actions, seems to have decided at this point that Egypt should be the capital of his new empire. Persia had been the goal, and parts of it still remained to be conquered, piece by piece; but it was in Egypt that he would build his shining new city of Alexandria. In the end, he had time only to lay out a plan for the streets and central spaces before he marched north to the reckoning with Darius at Gaugamela. When he finally returned, he was in his sarcophagus.

Alexander's Final Campaigns

Over the ensuing five years, Alexander campaigned in the far reaches of the Persian Empire, in the mountainous regions that had been only loosely yoked together with the more settled lands of Mesopotamia. This is the region encompassed today by Afghanistan, a terrain famous for defeating every attempt at conquest or control. There, in the mountains of Bactria, Alexander and his army experienced

ALEXANDER'S WORLD. This view of the world, modeled on maps made in antiquity, represents what intellectuals of Alexander's own time knew about geography. ▪ *Compare this image with the map of Alexander's campaigns on page 125. How do you think this worldview affected the planning of his route?* ▪ *With this available knowledge, why would he have traveled down the Indus river (near the marking India) and then overland to Susa?* ▪ *What similarities and differences do you find more generally, comparing this ancient map with the other maps that appear in this book?*

himself was hailed as pharaoh and given the double crown of Upper and Lower Egypt, becoming the latest in a succession of rulers reaching back 3,000 years to the time of King Narmer (see Chapter 1).

Something about this feat seems to have amazed even Alexander himself. The "barbarian" chieftain of a backwater kingdom in the Balkan foothills had become pharaoh of the oldest civilization on earth and heir to its immense riches and extraordinary history—a history that the Greeks knew, thanks to the writings of Herodotus. Whereas the Persians and (before them) the Medes had long been the Greeks' traditional enemies, the Egyptians had always been too far away to pose a threat; indeed, they were an object of awe and source of inspiration.

This may help explain Alexander's response to the oracle of Ammon, the name the Greeks gave to the Egyptian sun god Amun-Ra, whom they identified with Zeus. At the oracle's desert oasis of Siwa, Alexander was reportedly told that he was the "son of Ammon" and a god himself, a pronouncement that gave weight to a story already in circulation among his men: that he had been fathered not by the hardest fighting of their long campaign. Indeed, they never succeeded in getting more than a tenuous hold on the territory, despite Alexander's marriage to Roxane, the daughter of a local Bactrian chieftain. Thereafter, Alexander moved down through what is now Pakistan to the Indus Valley, meeting stiff resistance from its warlords but eventually defeating their leader, Porus, at the Battle of Hydaspes (*heed-AH-spes*) in 326 B.C.E.

This was to be the last major battle of his career, and the one in which his famous warhorse, Bucephalus, was killed. (He was buried nearby, and a city was founded in his name.) It was here in India that Alexander's exhausted army refused to go on, thousands of miles and eight years from home, and he was forced to turn back. Alexander decided against recrossing the mountains of the Hindu Kush, the forbidding mountain range whose giant peaks stretch from Afghanistan to the Himalayas. He and his army had traversed its treacherous, snowy passes once before, barely subduing local tribes. Rather than attempt that feat again, he pressed southward

to the shores of the Arabian Sea—what was then known as Ocean, and the end of the world. The ensuing march through the Gedrosian Desert, combined with a decade of continuous fighting, weakened him and his army considerably.

But Alexander still had great plans for the future, and when he reached the royal palace of Susa, he took steps that indicate how he would have tried to combine his Greco-Macedonian Empire with that of Persia, had he lived. He announced that he would begin training Persian youths to fight alongside Greeks and Macedonians, so as to begin an integration of the two armies. He arranged a mass marriage between hundreds of his officers and a corresponding number of Persian noblewomen, and he made an example of men who had been caught desecrating the nearby tomb of Cyrus the Great. Most controversially, he showed respect for his Persian subjects by adopting Persian dress—considered by Greeks to be symbolic of their enemies' barbarism—and by encouraging those around him to perform the ritual of *proskynesis* (*pros-kin-EE-sis*).

THE CAMPAIGNS OF ALEXANDER. The conquests of Alexander the Great brought Greek culture to the vast expanse of the former Persian Empire, as far east as the Indus River. ■ *Trace Alexander's route with your finger. Where did he start and end?* ■ *What was the farthest point east that he traveled on his conquests?* ■ *Why might Alexander have chosen to found so many cities named after himself, and what can you conclude about the purposes of these cities, on the basis of their locations?*

LESSER KINGS OF PERSIA APPROACH THE GREAT KING TO PERFORM *PROSKYNESIS.* ■ *Why would Alexander's Greek and Macedonian soldiers have balked at the suggestion that they show their solidarity with the Persians by performing this ritual?*

According to Herodotus, who gave the practice its Greek name, *proskynesis* was a gesture of bodily submission performed by those of lesser social standing when they met their superiors, and by all Persians—even those of royal rank—to honor the Great King. The person paying homage would bow deeply and kiss his hand to the emperor, in some cases prostrating himself entirely. To the Greeks, this practice was not only humiliating but blasphemous: it suggested that the Persians worshiped their emperor as a god. To Alexander and his close advisers, *proskynesis* may have seemed an appropriate tribute to his status as "son of Ammon," but it was more likely intended to level cultural differences between Persians and Greeks. In any case, it was not a success, and it fueled a mutiny among the Macedonians that Alexander himself had to quell.

signs of what may have been malarial fever. Some ancient sources suggest he was poisoned; his closest friend and longtime lover, Hephaistion, had died the year before at Ecbatana, leaving Alexander without his most able and vigilant bodyguard. (Emulating Achilles' passionate grief at the death of Patroclus, the mourning Alexander is reported to have built an enormous funeral pyre and "sacrificed" the residents of a nearby town to appease Hephaistion's ghost.) But Alexander ignored the advice of his doctors and continued to play the part of a Homeric hero, drinking late into the night and exerting himself incautiously. His condition worsened, and he died on June 10 or 11, 323 B.C.E., in the palace built by the Chaldean king Nebuchadnezzar in Babylon, the ancient capital of Hammurabi. He was not yet thirty-three years old.

Alexander's Death

Apart from these attempts to create cross-cultural cohesion, which he was not able to pursue fully, Alexander took no realistic steps to create an administration for his vast empire. How he planned to govern it effectively and bequeath it intact remains a mystery; he seems to have fixed his sights more clearly on further conquests, perhaps in Arabia, perhaps toward "Greater Greece" (Italy and Sicily)—we will never know. In late May of 323 B.C.E., he began to show

THE HELLENISTIC KINGDOMS

According to one account by a later Roman historian, Alexander's friends and officers gathered around his bed as he lay dying and asked to whom he wished to leave his empire. He had replied, "To the strongest." According to Plutarch and Arrian, though, he was actually incapable of speech. According to still other late sources, he silently gave his signet ring to a Macedonian general called Perdiccas, the leader of his cavalry.

Analyzing Primary Sources

Alexander Puts Down a Mutiny

The following account comes from the history of Alexander's campaigns by the Greek-speaking Roman historian Arrian (c. 86–160 C.E.), who lived in the Roman province of Bithynia in northern Anatolia. This is the closest thing we have to a primary source, since histories written by Alexander's own contemporaries have not survived. The following passage describes Alexander's response to a mutiny among his troops after his return from India in 324 B.C.E.

y countrymen, you are sick for home—so be it! I shall make no attempt to check your longing to return. Go wherever you will; I shall not hinder you. But if go you must, there is one thing I would have you understand—what I have done for you, and in what coin you have repaid me. . . .

"[M]arching out from a country too poor to maintain you decently, [I] laid open for you at a blow, and in spite of Persia's naval supremacy, the gates of the Hellespont. My cavalry crushed the satraps of Darius, and I added all Ionia and Aeolia, the two Phrygias and Lydia to your empire. . . . I took them and gave them to you for your profit and enjoyment. The wealth of Egypt and Cyrene, which I shed no blood to win, now flows in your hands; Palestine and the plains of Syria and Mesopotamia are now your property; Babylon and Bactria and Susa are yours; you are the masters of the gold of Lydia, the treasures of Persia, the wealth of India—yes, and the seas beyond India, too. You are my captains, my generals, my governors of provinces.

"From all this that I have labored to win for you, what is left for me myself except the purple and the crown? I keep nothing for my own. . . . Perhaps you will say that, in my position as your commander, I had none of the labors and dis-

tress which you had to endure to win me what I have won. . . . Come now—if you are wounded, strip and show your wounds, and I will show mine. There is no part of my body but my back which does not have a scar; not a weapon a man may grasp or fling, the mark of which I do not carry on me . . . and all for your sakes: for your glory and your gain. Over every land and sea, across river, mountain, and plain, I led you to the world's end, a victorious army. I marry as you marry, and many of you will have children related by blood to my own. . . . But you all wish to leave me. Go then! And when you reach home, tell them that Alexander your king, who vanquished the Persians and Medes and Bactrians . . . tell them, I say, that you deserted him and left him to the mercy of barbarian men, whom you yourselves conquered. . . ."

On the Macedonians, the immediate effect of Alexander's speech was profound. . . . But when they were told [three days later that] . . . command was being given to Persian officers, foreign troops drafted into Macedonian units, a Persian corps of Guards called by a Macedonian name, Persian infantry units given the coveted title of Companions . . . every man of them hurried to the palace . . . and [they] swore they would not stir from the spot until Alexander took pity on them.

Source: Arrian, *The Campaigns of Alexander*, trans. Aubrey de Selincourt (New York: 1958), pp. 360–65 (slightly modified).

Questions for Analysis

1. What qualities of leadership does Alexander display in this speech? How do these qualities compare with those of Cyrus the Younger, in Xenophon's description of him (page 114)?

2. Given the circumstances that precipitated this mutiny, why does Alexander use the term *barbarians* to describe the Persians and other conquered peoples? What does he hope to convey by using this word and then by reorganizing his forces to replace Macedonians with Persians?

3. Histories written well into the nineteenth century of our era feature speeches that were allegedly spoken by historical characters on momentous occasions. How closely do you think Arrian's reconstruction of this speech reflects historical reality? How might you go about arguing that it is, in fact, an accurate reflection of what Alexander actually said?

THE HELLENISTIC WORLD. Each of the three successor kingdoms to Alexander's empire was based in one of the three major civilizations we have studied so far: Egyptian, Mesopotamian, and Greek. ▪ *Based on the map above, what were the names of the three main successor states, and where were they located?* ▪ *What might the division of Alexander's empire along such lines suggest about the lasting cultural differences among these regions?* ▪ *What might it suggest about the likelihood of his forging a united empire, had he lived?*

It was certainly Perdiccas who attempted to arrange a settlement among all the possible claimants to Alexander's imperial power, albeit unsuccessfully. Alexander's own son and heir was born to Roxane after his death, and eventually it was decided that the baby, Alexander IV of Macedonia, should rule jointly with Alexander's half brother, Philip, the son of Philip II by one of his lesser wives, who may have been both mentally and physically disabled. This solution proved impractical, and eventually both the child and his uncle were murdered, as was Perdiccas.

Meanwhile, the Persian satrapies that had been allotted to various leaders of Alexander's armies became the bases from which they attempted to seize control. The turmoil lasted for two generations. By about 275 B.C.E., however, three separate axes of military and political power had emerged, each with a distinctive character but all headed by a Greco-Macedonian ruling class that shared a similar background. Indeed, a striking feature of this period is the renewal of ancient political patterns. But more striking is the fact that a common culture continued to unite Alexander's fragmented empire, which is why the era after his death is called **Hellenistic**, "Greek-like."

Ptolemaic Egypt

By far the most stable of the three successor states was Egypt, thanks in large part to the canny governance of Alexander's former general Ptolemy, possibly an illegitimate son of Philip II and certainly one of Alexander's most trusted advisers. Ptolemy decided to withdraw from the contest over the larger empire and asked only to be given Egypt as his satrapy. This might have been construed as a modest request by potential rivals, but Ptolemy had ulterior motives. Clearly, he recognized Egypt's virtual invulnerability to attack. He also seems to have appreciated, as Alexander did, its historical cachet. And he may already have been planning to make Egypt an independent monarchy and a shrine to Alexander's memory.

It was thanks to Ptolemy, in fact, that Alexander's embalmed body was returned to Egypt in 323 B.C.E. It was supposed to have gone to the royal burial ground of Aigai in Macedonia, but Ptolemy hijacked the funeral cortege and "took" or "delivered" it to the holy city of Memphis. Later, his son Ptolemy II moved the sarcophagus to a tomb in Alexandria, where it became a pilgrimage site and an object of veneration, especially by Romans with imperial ambitions of their own (see Chapter 5).

The Ptolemies ruled for the next 300 years, until Egypt became a Roman province in 30 B.C.E. This dynasty, the thirty-second since the unification of the Upper and Lower Nile in the fourth millennium B.C.E., was the last. The male heirs of the line all took the name Ptolemy (hence the term *Ptolemaic Egypt*), and many of their sisters were called Cleopatra, the name of Alexander's own sister and a dynastic name among Macedonian royal women. Beginning in the reign of Ptolemy II Philadelphus ("sibling-lover"), the Ptolemies even began to follow ancient Egyptian custom by marrying their siblings. And in many other ways, they showed reverence for the culture of their kingdom while bringing it within the ambit of the wider Hellenistic world.

TWO PORTRAITS OF PTOLEMY I OF EGYPT. The Ptolemaic rulers of Egypt represented themselves as pharaohs to their Egyptian subjects (as in this bust) and as Greeks to their Macedonian and Greek subjects (as on this gold coin).
■ *Why would it have been important to project these two very different images?*

They achieved this, in part, by ruling from the new city of Alexandria on the Mediterranean coast, rather than from the older pharaonic capitals. In Alexandria, they acted as Macedonian kings toward their Greek and Macedonian citizens; outside Alexandria, they played the role of pharaohs, surrounding themselves with the trappings and symbols of Egypt's heritage. But only the last Ptolemaic ruler, Cleopatra VII (69–30 B.C.E.), bothered to learn the Egyptian language—although, as the Rosetta Stone attests (see Chapter 1), the Ptolemies surrounded themselves with able administrators who could communicate effectively with their multilingual, multicultural subjects.

For the Ptolemies, as for the ancient pharaohs, all of Egypt was basically crown land to be exploited for the benefit of the royal house. Supporting this tradition was the Macedonian idea that conquered land—land won by the spear—was plunder, to be used for personal enrichment and glorification. Accordingly, the Ptolemies exploited the wealth of the Egyptian countryside to the fullest. Most of this wealth ended up in Alexandria, which became the dazzling hub of the Hellenistic world. But there was little interest in improving the lives of the Egyptian peasantry, whose breadwinning labors made their rulers rich. So although the third century was a prosperous and relatively peaceful one in Egypt, future pharaohs would face regular and dangerous revolts from the native populations of the countryside.

Nevertheless, Ptolemaic Egypt remained the most successful of the Hellenistic kingdoms. It was also the most influential, not only in its own day but for posterity, because of its key role in preserving and transmitting the accumulated heritage of the civilizations that had preceded

it: Egyptian, Mesopotamian, and Greek. The Ptolemies used their wealth to patronize science and the arts, and although it is no longer possible to argue that they were the first to endow a library at Alexandria, their capital did eventually displace Athens as an intellectual and artistic center. Many breakthroughs in astronomy, mechanical engineering, and physics occurred in Alexandria. In particular, the study of medicine advanced greatly under Ptolemaic rule: freed from the taboos of their homeland, Greek researchers were permitted to perform autopsies on the bodies of dead criminals and vagrants, making it possible for anatomy to become a scientific discipline in its own right. It was also here that the texts of Greek poetry, drama, history, and philosophy were copied and preserved in the forms in which we know them. Even the Hebrew scriptures were translated into Greek for a wider audience.

Seleucid Asia

The vast possessions that Alexander had accumulated in Asia—both within the Persian Empire and outside of it—eventually fell to another Macedonian, Seleucus (*seh-LOO-kus*). Seleucus had not been a senior officer during Alexander's lifetime, but he had navigated the turmoil after Alexander's death successfully, and cleverly exploited the connections he made through his Persian wife. At his death in 281 B.C.E., his half-Persian son Antiochus (*an-TYE-oh-kuhs*) inherited an expansive realm; but despite his best efforts he could not extend it beyond the city named after him—Antioch—into Egypt.

Throughout its history, the Persian dynasty founded by Seleucus (known as the Seleucids) struggled with the problem of keeping the disparate parts of the realm together. The dynasty's hold on the easternmost provinces was especially tenuous, but Seleucus solved part of this problem by ceding much of the Indus Valley to the great Indian warrior-king Chandragupta, in exchange for peace and a squad of war elephants. By the middle of the third century B.C.E., the Seleucids had also lost control of Bactria, where a series of Indo-Greek states were emerging with a uniquely complex culture of their own. (One Greco-Bactrian king, Menander, is memorialized in Buddhist tradition.) The Seleucid heartland became northern Syria, parts of Anatolia, Mesopotamia, and the western half of Persia—still a great, wealthy kingdom but far less than what Alexander had left.

Like the Ptolemies, the Seleucids presented two faces to their subjects, one looking to ancient Mesopotamian traditions and the other looking to Greece. In his proclamations, Antiochus used terms reminiscent of Sargon, Hammurabi, and Cyrus: "I am Antiochus, Great King, legitimate king . . . king of Babylon, king of all countries." But on his coins, he wore his hair short in the fashion of the Greeks and styled himself *basileus* (the Greek word for "king"). Although the Seleucids' bureaucracy was less organized than that of the Ptolemies, even haphazard tax collection could reap huge rewards in an empire of 30 million inhabitants. However, the Seleucids seldom converted their gains into public-works projects or capital investments. Instead, they hoarded their wealth in great state treasuries. All the same, they had more than enough cash to defend their borders through the third century, a period of regular warfare with Egypt. It was not until the second century, when Antiochus III lost a costly war with the Romans, that he had to plunder temples and private wealth to pay off the indemnity imposed on him.

Antigonid Macedonia and Greece

The Macedonian homeland did not possess the vast wealth of the new kingdoms carved from Alexander's conquests in Egypt and Asia. It also remained highly unstable from the time of Alexander's death until 276 B.C.E., when a general named Antigonus (an-TIG-on-uhs) was finally able to establish his rule over the area and his own dynasty (known as the Antigonids). Thereafter, Macedonia drew its strength from considerable natural resources and its influence over Aegean trade, as well as its king's status as overlord of Greece. The Macedonians also continued to field the most effective army of any of the successor states, and these warriors owned coveted bragging rights as the heirs of Alexander's unconquered army.

Antigonus was influenced by a philosophical outlook called Stoicism (discussed later in this chapter) and viewed kingship as a form of noble servitude: an office to be endured rather than enjoyed. This perspective, combined with his modest resources, convinced him not to compete with the Seleucids and Ptolemies for dominance. Instead, Antigonid policy was to keep these other two powers at war with one another and away from the Macedonian sphere of influence. Antigonus and his successors thus pursued a strategy more reminiscent of Philip II than of his son. They secured the northern frontiers; maintained a strong, standing army; and kept the divided Greeks at arm's length.

The Greeks, however, were restive under the Antigonids, and two emergent powers within the Greek world became rallying points for those who resented "barbarian" rule. These two forces, **the Aetolian League** and the **Achaean League**, embodied a new form of Greek political organization. Unlike the defensive alliances of the classical period, each of these two leagues constituted a true political entity, with some centralization of governance. Citizens of the member poleis participated in councils of state that dealt with foreign policy and military affairs, trials for treason, and the annual election of a league general (also the chief executive officer) and his deputy. New members were admitted on an equal footing with existing members, and all citizens of the various poleis enjoyed joint citizenship throughout the league. The same laws, weights and measures, coinage, and judicial procedures also applied throughout each federation. So impressive was this degree of cooperation that about two thousand years later, James Madison, John Jay, and Alexander Hamilton would employ the Achaean League as one of their models in advocating federalism in the United States.

FROM POLIS TO COSMOPOLIS

So what became of the polis, that building block of classical Greek civilization? As we have seen, the changes of the fourth century B.C.E. were already disrupting the traditional patterns of social and political life well before Alexander's conquests. Decades of warfare had ravaged the lands on which cities depended for survival and had impoverished their owners. Farm families struggled to survive, or moved in search of work, disrupting generational bonds to the land. With the advent of Macedonian control, once-independent poleis became subject cities whose proud political traditions were no longer relevant. The ground had already shifted under their feet.

Past and Present

Mass Migration and the Challenges of Assimilation

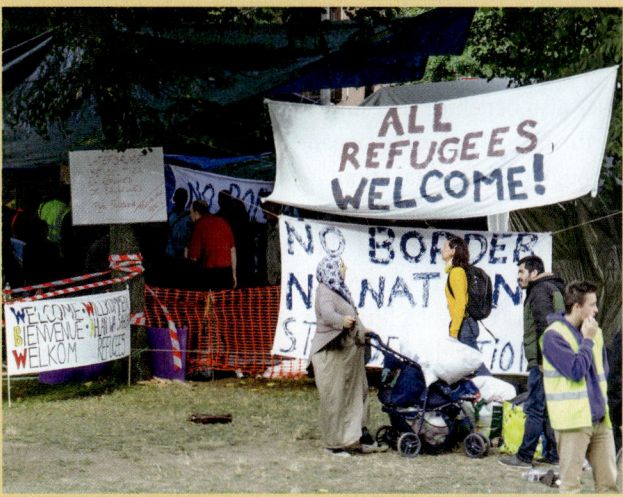

The Greek diaspora ("dispersion") that powered the growth of the Hellenistic kingdoms together eventually led to the emergence of distinctive new hybrid cultures. The mosaic on the left comes from an ancient synagogue and shows Jewish ritual objects (including a menorah and a shofar) accompanied by a Greek inscription. The image on the right shows a rally in support of refugees from the ongoing war in Syria, in 2015. In Belgium and other European countries, the challenges of integrating newcomers has since led to violence and xenophobia.

 Watch related author interview on the Student Site

So if the conquest begun by Philip hastened this transformation, those of Alexander also opened up a wider world of opportunities. During the third century B.C.E, a common Hellenistic culture encompassed the eastern Mediterranean and western Asia, transcending political and geographical boundaries. The conditions that threatened Greek culture and identity in Greece paradoxically drove many Greeks to transplant that culture in the colonies Alexander had opened to them. Within just two generations, hundreds of thousands of migrants had joined a Greek *diaspora* ("dispersions") which reduced the population of mainland Greece by as much as 50 percent in the century between 325 and 225 B.C.E.

This exciting, urbane world was made up of interconnected cities whose scale dwarfed anything imaginable in Periclean Athens. During the fifth century B.C.E., direct participation in government had meant that every male citizen of a Greek polis had some share and stake in his society—its institutions, its gods, its army, and its cultural life. If we transpose this outlook onto a typical cosmopolitan Hellenistic city, which would have been at least three times larger, we can appreciate the magnitude of the change. Two centuries later, all these ways of defining oneself were no longer relevant. The individual male's intimate connection with the political life of the state was broken, as was his nexus of social and familial relationships. An average Greek in one of the Hellenistic cities might have only his immediate family to rely on, if that; very often, he was alone. What resulted was a traumatic disjunction between the traditional values and assumptions of Greek life and the social and political realities of the day—and a host of entirely new opportunities.

Commerce and Urbanization

The Hellenistic world was prosperous, owing to the freedom of long-distance trade, the development of financial networks, and the enormous growth of cities. Alexander's conquests had opened up a vast trading area stretching from Egypt to the Persian Gulf, dominated by Greek-speaking rulers and well-established merchant communities. These conquests also stimulated the economy by putting into circulation hoards of Persian gold and silver coins, jewelry, and other commodities acquired through plunder. Industries also benefited, because autocratic rulers found manufacturing to be a further means of increasing their revenues through trade and taxation.

New trading ventures were particularly encouraged in Ptolemaic Egypt and the area of western Asia ruled over by the Seleucid monarchs, the heartland of which was Syria. Every facility was provided by the Ptolemies and the Seleucids for the encouragement of commerce: harbors were improved, warships were sent out to police the seas, roads and canals were built. The Ptolemies even employed geographers to discover new routes to distant lands and thereby opened up valuable markets. As a result of such methods, Egypt developed a flourishing commerce in the widest variety of products obtainable. Into the port of Alexandria came spices from Arabia, gold from Ethiopia and India, tin from Britain, elephants and ivory from Nubia, silver from Spain, fine carpets from Anatolia, and even silk from China. Profits for the government and for some of the merchants were often as high as 20 or 30 percent.

The rapid growth of cities had both political and economic causes. Greek rulers imported Greek officials and especially Greek soldiers to maintain their control over non-Greek populations, making many new Greek settlements necessary. Alexander himself had founded some 70 cities as outposts of imperial domination; over the next two centuries, his successors founded about 200 more. Urbanization also increased due to the expansion of commerce and industry, as well as the proliferation of government offices. All of these factors created opportunities for adventurous men seeking to escape the harsh conditions of life in Greece itself. Both new and established cities needed artisans, merchants, teachers, and laborers of all kinds.

But the most significant factor fueling rapid urban expansion was the Greek diaspora of entire families and the mass migration of workers from rural areas. Population growth in some centers was explosive. At Antioch, the population quadrupled during a single century. Seleucia on the Tigris grew from nothing to a metropolis of several hundred thousand in less than two centuries. Alexandria in Egypt had a half million inhabitants. Only imperial Rome would surpass it in size, and not until the eighteenth century of our era did European cities such as London and Paris become as large. Alexandria was not only populous, it was magnificent and spacious—which Rome never was. Its wide streets were paved and laid out in an orderly grid, and it had splendid public buildings and parks. In the second century, it also had public libraries: The Library of Alexandria was one of many that was being established by wealthy patrons throughout the Hellenistic world.

Despite the overall growth of the Hellenistic economy, not everyone enjoyed prosperity. Agriculture remained the major occupation and primary source of wealth, and small farmers in particular suffered severely from exploitative taxation. Although industrial production increased, it continued to be based on manual labor by individual artisans, most of whom lived in poverty. Among the teeming populations of Hellenistic cities, unemployment was a constant concern. Those who could not find work were forced to beg, steal, or prostitute themselves to survive.

Even those who prospered in the new economy were often subject to drastic fluctuations in their fortunes, owing to the precarious nature of mercantile endeavors. A trader who did very well selling a luxury fabric might invest heavily in it, only to find that tastes had changed or that a ship full of his wares had sunk. Merchants were also vulnerable to the boom-and-bust syndrome all too familiar to us today: an investor, thinking he could make a fortune during an upward price spiral, might go into debt to take

HELLENISTIC EARRINGS. These exquisite pieces of jewelry illustrate the enormous wealth and extraordinary craftsmanship available to the elites of the Hellenistic world.

advantage of the trend, only to find that supply in the commodity he traded suddenly exceeded demand, leaving him nothing with which to pay back his creditors. The economic landscape of the Hellenistic world was therefore one of contrasting extremes. In many ways, this was also the case with respect to its culture.

HELLENISTIC WORLDVIEWS

Life in the Hellenistic boomtowns produced new perspectives on the world and new philosophies that differed significantly from those of Plato and Aristotle. Two opposing trends ran almost parallel with one another. The first, exemplified by Stoicism (*STOH-iss-ism*) and Epicureanism (*eh-pih-CURE-ee-an-ism*), promoted rational thought as the key to alleviating the anxieties of modern life. This trend was a manifestation of Greek influence, although a major departure was the new separation of philosophy from scientific inquiry, which now became its own field of study. The second trend, exemplified by the Skeptics and various religious cults, tended to deny the possibility of attaining truth through the exercise of human reason alone, and in some cases turned toward mysticism and reliance on divine revelation. Despite these stark differences, however, both philosophers and religious teachers had the same motivation: the need to make human existence meaningful in a new age that lacked traditional civic structures and social values.

Two Paths to Tranquility: Stoicism and Epicureanism

The two strains of philosophy that dominated the Hellenistic world both originated in Athens around 300 B.C.E. Their promoters were Epicurus and Zeno, and their teachings had several features in common. Both men were concerned with the well-being of the individual, not with the welfare of society as a whole. Both were also firmly rooted in the material world, denying the existence of any purely spiritual phenomena; they considered even the soul to be part of the mortal body. Stoicism and Epicureanism also responded to the new cosmopolitan age by promoting universal values: both taught that people are the same the world over and recognized no distinctions between Greeks and the peoples hitherto known as "barbarians."

But in other ways the two systems were radically different. The Stoics who followed Zeno of Citium (c. 335–c. 263 B.C.E.)—

taking their name from the *stoa* ("colonnade") in which he regularly taught—believed that the cosmos is an ordered whole in which all contradictions are resolved for ultimate good. Evil is not absolute but relative, meaning that the particular misfortunes that befall individual human beings are merely incidents that will lead to the final perfection of the universe. Everything that happens is therefore predetermined, which means that no individual is master of his or her fate. People are free only in the sense that they can accept fate or rebel against it; that is, they are free to choose *how to respond* to adversity or prosperity. By willingly submitting to the workings of the universe and acknowledging that whatever happens must be for the best, one can attain true happiness: tranquility of mind. Through the exercise of reason and emotional restraint, the Stoics strove to adjust their expectations to the workings of fate and to purge their souls of all bitterness or regret.

The Stoics' theory of ethics and social responsibility grew out of this personal philosophy. Believing that the highest good is serenity of mind, **Stoicism** emphasized self-discipline and the fulfillment of one's duties. It taught tolerance and forgiveness, and urged participation in public affairs as a special responsibility for those with able minds. It condemned slavery and violence, although it took no real actions against these evils because it saw them as inevitable—and because extreme social change might be worse.

With some later modifications, Stoic philosophy became the driving force behind the values of the Roman Republic and even influenced early Christianity; it can be considered one of the most important products of the Hellenistic age. Even today, those who do not consciously embrace its tenets or its perspective may find that they have been influenced by its egalitarian and humanitarian ethos.

The second main philosophical trend in this era derives from the teachings of Epicurus (341–270 B.C.E.). Epicurus was influenced by the atomic theory of an earlier Greek philosopher Democritus (*dem-OH-kree-tuhs*), who lived in the latter part of the fifth century B.C.E. and is often called the "father of modern science." According to his central thesis, the universe is made up entirely of atoms, infinite in number, indestructible, and indivisible. Every individual object or organism is therefore the product of a combination of atoms.

Studying Democritus's writings, Epicurus and his followers reached a conclusion exactly opposite to that of the Stoics. **Epicureanism** interpreted the atomic theory to mean that there is no ultimate purpose in the workings of the universe, that these workings are entirely random. So the highest good cannot come of submitting oneself stoically to the endurance of hardship, because no hardship is part of a larger plan; it is merely the chance byproduct of random atomic actions. The highest good, then, must be pleasure: the moderate satisfaction of bodily appetites, the intellectual pleasure of contemplating excellence and remembering past enjoyments, and serenity in the face of death. Indeed, an individual who understands that the soul itself is material and will not survive the death of the body, that the universe operates at random, and that no gods intervene in human affairs should have no fear of death or any other supernatural phenomena. The Epicureans thus came by a very different route to the same general conclusion as the Stoics: nothing is better than tranquility of mind.

The moral teachings and political goals of the Epicureans reflected this worldview. In contrast to the Stoics, they did not insist on virtue as an end in itself or on the fulfillment of one's duties. For an Epicurean, the only duty a person has is to the self, and the only reason to act virtuously is to increase one's own happiness. Similarly, Epicureans also denied that there is any such thing as justice: laws and political institutions are "just" only insofar as they contribute to the welfare of the individual. Yes, every society has found certain rules to be necessary in every society for the maintenance of order, but these rules should be obeyed solely because it is to one's advantage. The state is, at best, a mere convenience, and the wise man should take no active part in politics. Instead, he should withdraw to study philosophy and enjoy the fellowship of a few congenial friends. Modern libertarian movements share many characteristics with Epicureanism.

Extreme Doubt: Skepticism

The most pessimistic philosophy generated by the Hellenistic era was propounded by the Skeptics, whose name derives from a Greek word meaning "those on the lookout" or "the spies." Skepticism reached the zenith of its popularity in the second century under the influence of Carneades (*kar-NEE-ah-dees*; c. 214–129 B.C.E.), a man born in the Greek city of Cyrene, in North Africa, and who spent his youth in Athens. The chief source of his inspiration was the teaching (filtered through Aristotle) that all knowledge is based on sense perception and is therefore limited and relative. From this, the Skeptics concluded that no one can truly know or prove anything. Because the impressions of our senses can deceive us, we cannot even be certain about the truth of whatever empirical knowledge we think we have gained by observation of the world. All we can say is that things *appear* to be such and such; we do not know that they really *are* that

way. It follows, furthermore, that we can have no definite knowledge of the supernatural, the meaning of life, or the right and wrong.

The only sensible course for the Skeptic is therefore to suspend judgment: this alone can lead to happiness. If a person abandons the fruitless quest for truth and ceases to worry about good conduct and the existence of evil, he can at least attain a certain peace of mind—the highest satisfaction that an uncertain life affords. Needless to say, the Skeptics were even less concerned than the Epicureans with political and social problems, from which they felt wholly alienated. Their ideal was one of escape from an incomprehensible world. In some key respects, they anticipated modern existentialism and nihilism.

The Varieties of Religion

Like Epicureanism and Skepticism, Hellenistic religion tended to offer vehicles of escape from political commitments. When we think back to the link between Greek selfhood and politics, down to the middle of the fourth century B.C.E.—"man is a creature of the polis"—we can begin to appreciate what a radical change had occurred in just a few generations. In the classical age of the polis, as in all the societies we have studied so far, religion was wholly interconnected with politics. Divine worship centered on the gods who protected a community and furthered its interests. Hence, the most serious of the charges brought against Socrates was that he had "denied the gods of the polis" and thus committed treason. Religious crimes were political crimes, and piety was the same as patriotism.

Although this sense of a vital connection between a place and its gods persisted to a certain extent during the Hellenistic period, civic-oriented worship was compromised by the rootless multiculturalism of the third and second centuries B.C.E. In its place, some elite members of society gravitated toward one of the philosophies discussed above. Ordinary people, though, were more likely to embrace religious cults that offered emotional gratification or the diversion of colorful rituals, as well as some assurance of an afterlife, which the new philosophies did not.

In Greek-speaking communities especially, cults that stressed extreme methods of atonement for sin, ecstatic mystical union with the divine, or contact with supernatural forces attracted many followers. Among these mystery religions—so called because their membership was select and their rites secret—one of the most popular was the cult of Dionysos, which celebrated the cyclical death and

Analyzing Primary Sources

A Jewish Response to Hellenization

Greek culture became a powerful force throughout the Hellenistic world, even among Jews. In the second century B.C.E., the Hellenized ways of the Jewish elites in Jerusalem led to a revolt by a native Hebrew dynasty known as the Maccabees, who decried the effects of Hellenization on Jewish life. These events are recorded in two apocryphal books of the Hebrew Bible. In the passage that follows, note that even the High Priest of the Temple bears a Greek name, Jason.

In those days, lawless men came forth from Israel and misled many, saying, "Let us go and make a covenant with the Gentiles [Greeks] round about us, for since we separated from them many disasters have come upon us." . . .

[This happened when] Antiochus [IV, 175–164 B.C.E.] who was called Epiphanes had succeeded to the kingdom, [and] Jason the brother of Onias obtained the high priesthood by corruption. . . . [H]e at once shifted his countrymen over to the Greek way of life . . . and he destroyed the lawful ways of living and introduced new customs contrary to the law. For with alacrity he founded a gymnasium right under the citadel, and he induced the noblest of the young men to wear the Greek hat [and not the traditional head covering]. There was such an extreme of Hellenization and increase in the adoption of foreign ways . . . that the priests were no longer intent upon the services of the altar. Despising the sanctuary and neglecting the sacrifices, they hurried to take part in the unlawful proceedings in the wrestling arena after the signal for the discus-throwing, disdaining the honors prized by their ancestors and putting the highest value upon Greek forms of prestige. . . . When the quadrennial games were being held at Tyre and the king was present, the vile Jason sent envoys . . . to carry three hundred silver drachmas for the sacrifice to Heracles. . . .

Not long after this, the king sent an Athenian senator to compel the Jews to forsake the laws of their fathers and cease to live by the laws of God, and also to pollute the temple in Jerusalem and call it the temple of Olympian Zeus. . . . Harsh and utterly grievous was the onslaught of evil. For the temple was filled with debauchery and reveling by the Gentiles, who dallied with prostitutes and had intercourse with women within the sacred precincts, and besides brought in things for sacrifice that were unfit. The altar was covered with abominable offerings that were forbidden by the laws. A man could neither keep the Sabbath nor observe the feasts of his fathers, nor so much as confess himself to be a Jew.

Source: Excerpted from 1 Maccabees 1:11; 2 Maccabees 4:10–18 and 6:1–6, in *The New Oxford Annotated Bible* (Oxford: 1994).

Questions for Analysis

1. Given the history of their ancestors (see Chapter 2), why would Hellenistic culture be particularly threatening to the Jews?

2. What, specifically, are the offensive actions and activities described here? Why, for example, would the building of a gymnasium (a Greek academy and athletic facility) in Jerusalem be problematic?

---

resurrection of that Greek god. The Egyptian cult of Isis, drawing on the story of Osiris (see Chapter 1), also revolved around rituals of death and rebirth. So, too, did Zoroastrianism (see Chapter 2), which became increasingly dualistic: its magi taught that the material world was entirely evil and urged believers to adopt ascetic practices that would purify their souls and prepare them for ethereal joy in the afterlife.

Like the peoples who worshiped them, the gods of the Hellenistic world were often immigrants from other lands. Temples to Greek gods and goddesses were dedicated throughout western Asia and Egypt; conversely, temples to Egyptian and Mesopotamian divinities were constructed in cities of the Greek homeland. In Alexandria, scholars of religion collected anecdotes about exotic mythologies, which were recorded and reformulated for Greek-speaking audiences. People throughout the Hellenistic world had a dazzling variety of religious choices, including Buddhism, which flourished in the Greco-Indian Kingdom that linked Bactria (Afghanistan) to Northern India.

Even among the Jews of Palestine, who resisted assimilation and the adoption of foreign customs, Hellenistic culture put down deep roots. This was especially true among Jewish elites and Jews living outside Palestine, who outnumbered the Palestinian population by a considerable margin by the end of the second century B.C.E. To meet the needs of these Greek-speaking Jews, and to satisfy the curiosity of Gentiles interested in Jewish beliefs, scholars working in Alexandria produced a Greek version of the Hebrew scriptures. It is still known as the Septuagint, from the Greek word meaning "seventy": legend has it that seventy scribes, each working independently, produced individual translations from Hebrew to Greek that were identical in every respect. This story conveyed the message that the Septuagint was no less a product of divine inspiration than the original books that made up the Hebrew Bible and could be treated as an authoritative text in its own right. For Jews concerned about their social and cultural standing vis-à-vis their Greek neighbors, it was also proof of their cultivation and acceptance of Hellenistic values—although, ironically, many of the Jewish scriptures now available in Greek disapproved strongly of those values.

THE SCIENTIFIC REVOLUTION OF ANTIQUITY

The Hellenistic period was the most brilliant age in the history of science before the seventeenth century of our era. There are three major reasons for this. First, there was the enormous stimulus to intellectual inquiry caused by the fusion of Mesopotamian and Egyptian science with the philosophical methods of the Greeks. Second, as in the more famous scientific revolution of modernity (see Chapter 16), the use of a common language (in the seventeenth century it was Latin) and the ease of communication facilitated by quick, affordable travel also made the circulation of knowledge and sharing of ideas easier. (During the seventeenth century, ease of communication was increased by the printing press and an international postal system.) Finally, as in the seventeenth century, the competition among patrons of science was intense, which ensured the availability of ample funding. Every Hellenistic autocrat wanted to be thought enlightened and to be associated with new discoveries, and it might even be profitable

to subsidize research that led to the development of new technologies, especially those with military applications. But most of all, the rulers who financed scientific endeavors did so primarily for motives of prestige and competition: they could show off a scientific gadget just as they could show off a sculpture. Even purely theoretical advances were so much admired that a Hellenistic prince who had bankrolled such a breakthrough would share the glory of it.

The arts were also transformed by the economic and political conditions of the Hellenistic world. Writers and artists working in various media strove to demonstrate their mastery of difficult techniques and thus attract the notice of potential patrons. New markets for art also changed *what* was being made, how, and for whom. In all of the civilizations we have studied so far, artists worked directly for royal or civic patrons, who were often very particular in their demands. In the Hellenistic world, art became commodified. Sometimes a piece would be made expressly for a particular patron, but many works of art were fashioned for the open market. They were also designed to suit the tastes and lifestyles of urbane men and women, especially those of the merchant classes and the elite who had disposable income and wanted to increase their social standing through conspicuous consumption. This was as true of literature as of sculpture or the decorative arts: we know the names of over a thousand Hellenistic authors, either because their work survives in multiple copies sold in bookshops, or because they are mentioned in other writings (letters, pamphlets) as being in fashion. Indeed, the number of texts and *objets d'art* that exist from this period is huge compared with those of earlier eras.

Measuring and Mapping: Astronomy, Geography, and Mathematics

Hellenistic scientists took a major interest in measurements and mapmaking, whether of the heavens (astronomy) or the earth (geography) and the forms occurring in nature (geometry). The most renowned—and most wronged—of the Hellenistic astronomers was Aristarchus of Samos (310–230 B.C.E.), whose major discovery anticipated that of Copernicus by 1,700 years: he deduced that the earth and other planets revolve around the sun. Unfortunately, however, his heliocentric model was not accepted by many of his contemporaries or successors because it conflicted with the teachings of Aristotle and the Greek conviction that humanity, and therefore the earth, must be at the center of the universe.

THE ARCHIMEDES PALIMPSEST. In 1998, a shabby medieval manuscript was sold at auction for 2 million dollars—a lot of money for a prayer book. What made it so valuable? Beneath the Greek script of a thirteenth-century monk was the oldest known copy of the works of the great Hellenistic scientist Archimedes, copied in the Byzantine Empire (see Chapter 7) around 950 C.E. Manuscripts made of parchment could be reused by scraping the ink off the page with a pumice stone, to create a palimpsest. But thanks to modern imaging technologies, we can read the erased writing underneath. On the left is a page from the manuscript as visible to the naked eye. Can you see the faint writing underneath and the shape of a circle? On the right is a digital image showing two columns of text and two mechanical diagrams.

The sad fate of his discovery was sealed in the second century C.E., when the Alexandrian scholar Claudius Ptolemaeus (also known as Ptolemy) published an astronomical treatise *Almagest*, which unequivocally argued that Aristotle was correct, and that all heavenly bodies revolve around the earth. This misinformative book was then handed down to posterity as the authoritative work of ancient astronomy. It was not overturned until a much later scientific revolution occurred two thousand years later—and after the condemnation of theories advanced by Copernicus and Galileo that were identical to that of Aristarchus.

Closely allied with astronomy were geography and mathematics, especially geometry. The most influential Hellenistic mathematician was Euclid, whose *Elements of Geometry* (c. 300 B.C.E.) codified the work of others, including pre-Socratic philosophers like Pythagoras (see Chapter 3). It remained the basic textbook for the study of geometry until the twentieth century of our era. Euclid's successor Hipparchus (second century B.C.E.) then laid the foundations of both plane and spherical trigonometry.

In the field of geography—and in a host of other pursuits, too—the most original thinker was Eratosthenes (*ehr-ah-TOS-then-ees*; c. 276–c. 196 B.C.E.) of Alexandria. Not only did he accurately calculate the circumference of the earth (within a tiny margin of error, less than 200 miles), he also developed a system of latitude and longitude. He was the first to suggest the possibility of reaching eastern Asia by sailing west. In addition, he founded the science of chronology by attempting to establish the dates of major events reaching back to the siege of Troy. Students of history are forever in his debt.

Medicine and Mechanics: The Sciences of Physiology and Physics

Before the third century B.C.E., physics had been a branch of philosophy. It became a separate, experimental science thanks to the single-handed genius of one man, Archimedes of Syracuse (*ar-ki-MEE-dees*; c. 287–212 B.C.E.). It was he who discovered the law of floating bodies, or specific gravity, now known as "Archimedes' principle." According to legend, the idea came to him quite suddenly when

SURGICAL INSTRUMENTS. Both Hellenistic and Roman doctors used tools such as these to perform surgical procedures, but they also had a variety of nonmedical uses. Shown here are a grinding stone, spoons, probes, depressors, and tongs. The large, flat-headed tool may have been used for cauterizing wounds. The inscription visible on the stone in the upper left-hand corner is probably a recipe for eye medicine.

Debating the Education and Role of Women

*The drastic political, social, and economic changes of the fourth century led philosophers to reimagine the traditional structures of the polis and to debate the proper role of women within these structures. Meanwhile, the cosmopolitan culture of the expanding Hellenistic world made it increasingly difficult to limit women's access to public spaces. The following excerpts represent two philosophical responses to these problems. The first comes from Plato's treatise on "Polis-matters" (*Politeía*), known to us as* The Republic, *the longest of his philosophical dialogues and the most influential work of political thought in history. Its conceptual narrator and protagonist is Socrates, who engages in a series of debates with his pupils. The second excerpt is taken from a philosophical treatise attributed to a female follower of Pythagoras (see Chapter 3), but it was really written by a man around 200 B.C.E. in Hellenistic Italy.*

Plato, The Republic, c. 380 B.C.E.

SOCRATES: For men born and educated like our citizens, the only way, in my opinion, of arriving at a right conclusion about the possession and use of women and children is to follow the path on which we originally started, when we said that the men were to be the guardians and watchdogs of the herd.

GLAUCON: True.

SOCRATES: Let us further suppose the birth and education of our women to be subject to similar or nearly similar regulations; then we shall see whether the result accords with our design.

GLAUCON: What do you mean?

SOCRATES: . . . The education which was assigned to the men was music and gymnastic[s].

GLAUCON: Yes.

SOCRATES: Then women must be taught music and gymnastic[s] and also the art of war, which they must practice like the men?

GLAUCON: That is the inference, I suppose.

SOCRATES: I should rather expect . . . that several of our proposals, if they are carried out, being unusual, may appear ridiculous.

GLAUCON: No doubt of it.

SOCRATES: Yes, and the most ridiculous thing of all will be the sight of women naked in the palaestra, exercising with the men, especially when they are no longer young; they certainly will not be a vision of beauty, any more than the enthusiastic old men who in spite of wrinkles and ugliness continue to frequent the gymnasia. . . . . [Yet] not long ago, as we shall remind them, the Hellenes were of the opinion, which is still generally received among the barbarians, that the sight of a naked man was ridiculous and improper; and when first the Cretans and then the Lacedaemonians [Spartans] introduced the custom, the wits of that day might equally have ridiculed the innovation.

GLAUCON: No doubt. . . .

SOCRATES: First, then, whether the question is to be put in jest or in earnest, let us come to an understanding about the nature of woman: Is she capable of sharing either wholly or partially in the actions of men, or not at all? And is the art of war one of those arts in which she can or cannot share? That will be the best way of commencing the enquiry, and will probably lead to the fairest conclusion. . . .

GLAUCON: I suppose so. . . .

SOCRATES: And if . . . the male and female sex appear to differ in their fitness for any art or pursuit, we should say that such pursuit or art ought to be assigned to one or the other of them; but if the difference consists only in women bearing and men begetting children, this does not amount to a proof that a woman differs from a man in respect of the sort of education she should receive; and we shall therefore continue to maintain that our guardians and their wives ought to have the same pursuits.

GLAUCON: Very true.

SOCRATES: Next, we shall ask . . . how, in reference to any of the pursuits or arts of civic life, the nature of a woman differs from that of a man? . . .

GLAUCON: By all means.

SOCRATES: . . . [W]hen you spoke of a nature gifted or not gifted in any respect, did you mean to say that one man will acquire a thing easily, another with difficulty; a little learning will lead the one to discover a great deal; whereas the other, after much study and application, no sooner learns than he forgets? Or again, did you mean, that the one has a body which is a good servant to his mind, while the body of the other is a hindrance to him? Would not these be the sort of differences which distinguish the man gifted by nature from the one who is ungifted?

GLAUCON: No one will deny that.

SOCRATES: And can you mention any pursuit of mankind in which the male sex has not all these gifts and qualities in a higher degree than the female? Need I waste time in speaking of the art of weaving, and the management of pan- cakes and preserves, in which woman- kind does really appear to be great, and in which for her to be beaten by a man is of all things the most absurd?

GLAUCON: You are quite right . . . in maintaining the general inferiority of the female sex: although many women are in many things superior to many men, yet on the whole what you say is true.

Source: Excerpted from Plato, *The Republic*, Book V, trans. Benjamin Jowett (New York: 1982), pp. 170–76.

Treatise attributed to Phintys, Third/Second Century B.C.E.

Now some people think that it is not appropriate for a woman to be a philosopher, just as a woman should not be a cavalry officer or a politician. . . . I agree that men should be generals and city officials and politicians, and women should keep house and stay inside and receive and take care of their husbands. But I believe that courage, justice, and intelligence are qualities that men and women have in common. . . . Courage and intelligence are more appropriately male qualities because of the strength of men's bodies and the power of their minds. Chastity is more appropriately female.

Accordingly, a woman must learn about chastity and realize what she must do quantitatively and qualitatively to be able to obtain this womanly virtue. I believe that there are five qualifications: (1) the sanctity of her marriage bed, (2) the cleanliness of her body, (3) the manner in which she chooses to leave her house, (4) her refusal to participate in secret cults . . . , (5) her readiness and modera- tion in sacrificing to the gods.

Of these, the most important qual- ity for chastity is to be pure in respect of the marriage bed, and for her not to have affairs with men from other house- holds. If she breaks the law in this way she wrongs the gods of her family and provides her family and home not with its own offspring but with bastards. . . .

She should also consider the following: that there is no means of atoning for this sin; no way she can approach the shrines or the altars of the gods as a pure woman. . . . The greatest glory a freeborn woman can have—her foremost honor— is the witness her own children will give to her chastity toward her husband, the stamp of the likeness they bear to the father whose seed produced them. . . .

As far as adornment of her body is concerned . . . [h]er clothes should not be transparent or ornate. She should not put on silken material, but moderate, white-colored clothes. In this way, she will avoid being over-dressed or luxu- rious or made-up, and not give other women cause to be uncomfortably envi- ous. . . . She should not apply imported or artificial coloring to her face—with her own natural coloring, by washing only with water, she can ornament herself with modesty. . . .

Women of importance leave the house to sacrifice to the leading divin- ity of the community on behalf of their husbands and their households. They do not leave home at night nor in the evening, but at midday, to attend a reli- gious festival or to make some purchase, accompanied by a single female servant or decorously escorted by two servants at most. . . . They keep away from secret cults . . . particularly because these forms of worship encourage drunkenness and

ecstasy. The mistress of the house and head of the household should be chaste and untouched in all respects.

Source: From Mary R. Lefkowitz and Maureen B. Fant, eds. *Women's Life in Greece & Rome: A Source Book in Translation*, 2nd ed. (Baltimore, MD: 1992), pp. 163–64.

Questions for Analysis

1. Follow the steps of the argument made by Socrates. How does he go about proving that women and men are dif- ferent and so should have different roles in society? Are there flaws in this argument? How would you refute it?

2. How does the author of the treatise seem to define "chastity," and why does she (or he) say that it corre- sponds to more masculine qualities of courage and intelligence? Why would this author have wanted to attribute these reflections to female members of the community founded by the phi- losopher Pythagoras (c. 570–c. 495) three centuries earlier? How might this treatise be a response to the changes brought about by the expan- sion of the Greek world in the fourth and third centuries B.C.E.?

3. What are the main points on which these two perspectives agree? How might ideas like those expressed here have influenced contemporary ideas of female beauty (see **Interpreting Visual Evidence** on page 118)?

he was in his bath, pondering possible theories. The stunning insight so excited him that he leaped from the water and dashed out naked into the street, shouting *Eureka!* ("I found it!"). He also established the principles of the lever, the pulley, and the screw, and he invented both a compound pulley and a propeller. All of these discoveries had numerous practical uses in the construction of buildings, ships, and military machinery.

Other extraordinary advances of Hellenistic science were made in the field of medicine. Especially significant was the work of the Alexandrian scholar Herophilus of Chalcedon (c.335–c.280 B.C.E.), the greatest anatomist of antiquity and probably the first to practice human dissection. Many of his discoveries directly challenged the orthodoxy of Aristotelian teaching—and rightly, since Aristotle's understanding of physiology, like his knowledge of astronomical and natural science, has not stood the test of time so well as his grasp of logic and politics. Herophilus's achievements included a detailed description of the brain, which allowed him to prove that the brain was the engine of human intellect (Aristotle thought it was the heart), as well as the discovery that the arteries contain blood alone (not, as Aristotle had taught, a mixture of blood and air) and that their function is to carry blood from the heart to all parts of the body. He also understood the significance of the pulse and its use in diagnosing illness.

His colleague Erasistratus (*ehr-ah-sis-STRAH-tus*) made allied discoveries, establishing that the heart was a pump and not an organ of emotion, explaining the working of its valves and distinguishing between motor and sensory nerves. Erasistratus also rejected the widely held theory of the physician Hippocrates (c. 460–c. 370), who had posited that the body contains four "humors" that need to be

THE CITADEL OF PERGAMON. An artist's reconstruction of Pergamon in the second century B.C.E., based on the work of nineteenth-century German archaeologists. High atop the hill is the massive altar of Zeus (now in the Pergamon Museum in Berlin), and below it slope the tiers of the theater. Other features include fortifications, terraces, and artificial landscaping for public gardens. ▪ *How does this complex of buildings compare with that of another citadel, the Acropolis of Athens (see page 76)?*

THE MARBLE STREETS OF EPHESUS. Ephesus was already a splendid city when it was incorporated into the Persian Empire, along with other Greek settlements in Ionia. In the Hellenistic era, it became more splendid still.

kept in balance through bloodletting and other invasive practices. Unfortunately, this discovery went the way of the heliocentric universe posited by Aristarchus: another encyclopedist of the second century C.E., Galen, preferred the erroneous theory of Hippocrates. His baneful influence, and the practice of bloodletting, thus persisted into the nineteenth century of our era.

Urban Architecture and Sculpture

Hellenistic architecture drew on Greek models, but it was also influenced by standards and tastes more characteristic of Egypt and Persia. Two examples (both of which no longer survive) are the great lighthouse of Alexandria, which rose to a height of nearly 400 feet and was daringly composed of three diminishing stories topped by eight slender columns supporting the light; and the citadel of Alexandria, built of stone and covered with blue-tinted plaster, described by a contemporary as seeming to float in mid-air. The best-surviving example, though, comes from Pergamon, a city on the coast of Anatolia that became the capital of a new kingdom wrested from the Seleucids' control in the second century B.C.E. It boasted an enormous altar dedicated to Zeus that crowned the heights of the city, below which an open-air theater was built into the steep slope of the hill. In Ephesus, not far away, the streets were not only paved, but paved with marble.

Perhaps the most influential of all Hellenistic arts was sculpture, which moved further away from classical ideals and placed even more emphasis on realism than the fourth-century sculptures discussed earlier in this chapter. Sculptors now prided themselves on faithfully reproducing facial furrows, muscular distortions, and complex folds of drapery. Awkward human postures offered the greatest technical challenges, to such an extent that sculptors might prefer to show people stretching themselves or balancing on one leg in ways that hardly ever occur in real life.

Because monumental sculpture of this kind was executed for wealthy private patrons, it is clear that the goal was to create something unique in both conception and craftsmanship—something a collector could show off as the only one of its type. It is not surprising, therefore, that in **Hellenistic art,** complexity came to be admired for its own sake, and extreme naturalism sometimes teetered on the brink of caricature. To our eyes, such works frequently appear familiar because of the influence they exerted on later sculptors like Michelangelo (see Chapter 12) and Auguste Rodin. Three of the most famous examples are pictured on the following page, each exhibiting different aesthetic qualities and artistic techniques: the *Dying Gaul*, made in Pergamon around 220 B.C.E.; *An Old Woman*, dating from around the second century B.C.E.; and *Laocoön and His Sons*, from the first century B.C.E.

DYING GAUL. The original (now lost) statue on which this Roman copy was based was sculpted in Pergamon around 220 B.C.E. The sculptor clearly wished to exhibit his skill in depicting an unusual subject: the Gauls were a Celtic people about whom very little was known in this era. ▪ *How does this sympathetic representation of a "barbarian" express the new values of Hellenistic philosophy?*

AN OLD WOMAN (LEFT). This marble statue is a Roman copy of Hellenistic work made in the second century B.C.E. It shows an elderly woman, probably an aged courtesan, on her way to a festival of Dionysos. Her elegant gown and sandals are ironic reminders of her past career success, and the drapery hangs awkwardly from her stooped body. She carries a basket of fruit and two chickens: either as gifts to the god or provisions for the feast. It is now in the Metropolitan Museum of Art in New York. **LAOCOÖN AND HIS SONS (RIGHT).** This famous sculpture group from the first century B.C.E. tells a tragic story of divine retribution. According to legend, Laocoön warned the Trojans not to accept the wooden horse sent by the Greeks and was accordingly punished by the sea god Poseidon, who sent two serpents to kill him and his sons. The intense physicality of this work was an important influence on Michelangelo, a millennium and a half later. It is now in the Vatican Museum, Rome.

Literary Fantasy and Historical Reality

In the sixth century B.C.E. it was the lyric, in the fifth century it was tragedy, and in the fourth century it was the novel; but in the Hellenistic era, the new literary genre was pastoral verse. These poems tapped into a strong vein of nostalgia for rural pastimes and simple pleasures, a make-believe world of shepherds and wood nymphs. The most important pastoral poet of the age was Theocritus (*thee-AW-krit-uhs*), who flourished around 270 B.C.E. in the big-city environment of Alexandria. Theocritus was a merchant of escapism. In the midst of urban bustle and within sight of overcrowded slums, he celebrated the charms of country life and lazy summer afternoons, putting into the mouths of his rustic characters unlikely sentiments expressed in ornate language. He thereby founded an enduring tradition that would be taken up by poets from the Roman Virgil to the Englishman (and classical scholar) A. E. Housman, and that which has continuously provided a wealth of themes for the visual arts. Musical composers such as Beethoven and Debussy also owe a debt to Theocritus.

By contrast, Hellenistic prose literature was dominated by historians and biographers who consciously modeled their work on earlier pioneers, especially Thucydides. By far the most important was Polybius (*poh-LIB-ee-uhs*; c. 203–120 B.C.E.), a well-born Greek from the mainland whose father was a prominent politician active in the Achaean League. Polybius himself was trained as a horseman and cavalry officer, and both his vocation and his family connections gave him ample opportunity to observe the workings of government, diplomacy, and military strategy. This was at a time when the Achaean League was trying to position itself favorably in ongoing wars between the rising republic of Rome and the various warring kingdoms of northern Greece, notably Macedonia and Epiros. In 168 B.C.E., the Romans became suspicious of the Achaeans' declared neutrality and demanded that a thousand noble hostages be sent from Greece to Rome as a guarantee of the League's good behavior.

Polybius was one of those hostages, and he spent the next seventeen years living in Rome. There, he became a fervent admirer of Roman customs and especially of Rome's unique form of government. He also formed warm friendships with high-ranking Roman families, including the descendants of Scipio Africanus, a prominent Roman general. He kept up these contacts after his release, traveling to North Africa during the Third Punic War and witnessing firsthand the destruction of Carthage in 146 B.C.E. (see Chapter 5).

The result of this colorful career was a series of histories that glorified the achievements of Rome and its political system. Polybius also attempted to account for the patterns he discerned in the history of Greece since the Peloponnesian War. He argued that historical developments follow regular cycles, and that nations pass inevitably through stages of growth and decay. Hence, it should be possible to predict exactly where a given state is heading if one knows what happened to it in the past. Yet he also argued that the special character of Rome's constitution would allow it to break free from this cycle, because it combined all the different forms of government, which Aristotle had outlined in his *Politics*. This view of history galvanized the framers of the U.S. Constitution, directly influencing their conception of our own political institutions.

CONCLUSION

Judged from the perspective of classical Greece, Hellenistic civilization seems alien and exotic. The autocratic governments of the age that followed Alexander's conquests would probably appear repugnant to a staunch proponent of Athenian democracy, and the Hellenistic love of extravagance and display can contrast strikingly with the more austere tastes of the fifth century B.C.E. Yet Hellenistic civilization had its own achievements that the classical age could not match, achievements that make it in some ways more familiar to us. Most Hellenistic cities offered a greater range of public facilities than any Greek cities of the previous period, and the numerous advances in science and technology are astonishing when compared with anything that came before or even after.

But the most important contribution of the Hellenistic era to subsequent historical developments was its role as an intermediary between the nascent empire of Rome and the older civilizations of Mesopotamia, Egypt, and Greece. The example set by Alexander, in particular, was one that the Romans would emulate, and the economic and political infrastructures that were put in place after his conquests would form the framework of Roman imperial government. The Romans would also take advantage of the common language and cultural expectations that bound together the far reaches of the Greek-speaking world. Their own Latin language became acceptable for cultivated conversation and literary expression only toward the very end of the first century B.C.E., and it would never supplant Greek as the preeminent language of scholarship and administration in the eastern portions of their empire.

The Hellenistic era must also be recognized as the bridge that connects us to the earlier ages of antiquity: most of what is contained in the first four chapters of this textbook is known to us only because older texts and inscriptions and artifacts were collected and copied by the scholars of Alexandria and other Hellenistic cities. This era also bridges the gap between the tastes and ideals and customs of classical Greece and those that would be more characteristic of Rome. It was Hellenistic art and architec-ture, Hellenistic city planning and civic culture that the Romans strove to emulate and export to their own colonies, not those of Periclean Athens. The same can be said of drama and poetry.

For us, two further aspects of Hellenistic culture deserve special mention: its **cosmopolitanism** and its modernity. The word *cosmopolitan* itself comes from a Greek word meaning "universal city," and it was the Greeks of the Hellenistic period who came closest to

After You Read This Chapter

 Go to **INQUIZITIVE** to see what you've learned—and learn what you've missed— with personalized feedback along the way.

REVIEWING THE OBJECTIVES

- Macedonia's successful conquest of the Greek poleis can be attributed to several factors. What are they?
- Alexander the Great's imperial policies were influenced by his own upbringing, the different cultures he encountered, and some key historical precedents. Give at least one example of each type of influence.
- Explain how the three Hellenistic kingdoms reflect the differences among the three main civilizations we have studied so far.
- Why is the Hellenistic world described as "cosmopolitan"? How did this urban culture differ from that of the Greek poleis?
- The philosophies of Plato and Aristotle both derive from the teachings of Socrates, but they diverge in some important ways. What are those main differences?

turning this ideal of globalization into reality. Around 250 B.C.E., a Greek tourist could have traveled from Sicily to the borders of India—the two known ends of the earth—and never cease to be among people who spoke his language and shared his basic outlook. Nor would this tourist have identified himself in ethnic or nationalist terms, or felt any exclusive loyalty to a city-state or kingdom; he would have considered himself a citizen of the world. He would also have considered him-self a modern man, not bound by the old prejudices and superstitions of the past. It is for these reasons that Hellenistic civilization seems so closely related to our own. It was a world of stark contrasts and infinite possibilities, where economic instability, extremism, and authoritarian regimes existed side by side with unprecedented prosperity, rational inquiry, and extraodinary freedoms. In Chapter 5, we will see how this world adapted itself to the dominion of a single Italian city.

PEOPLE, IDEAS, AND EVENTS IN CONTEXT

- In what ways were the military strategies of **PHILIP II** of Macedonia variations on older forms of hoplite warfare? How did the rise of mercenary armies and of Thebes further change military strategies in the fourth century?

- How did the philosophies of **PLATO** and **ARISTOTLE** respond to the crisis of the polis?

- To what degree did the conquests of **ALEXANDER THE GREAT** unite Mesopotamia, Egypt, and Greece?

- Why and how did the three **HELLENISTIC KINGDOMS** emerge? How were the **AETOLIAN** and **ACHAEAN LEAGUES** new models for governance and cooperation in Greece?

- In what ways were **STOICISM**, **EPICUREANISM**, and other new philosophies a response to **COSMOPOLITANISM** and the breakdown of traditional societies and values?

- What were the driving forces behind the **SCIENTIFIC REVOLUTION OF ANTIQUITY**? What were its main achievements?

- What are some essential characteristics of **HELLENISTIC ART**? In what ways did it differ from that of the fifth century B.C.E. (see Chapter 3)?

THINKING ABOUT CONNECTIONS

- "The history of the world is but the biography of great men": so the Scottish historian Thomas Carlyle (1795–1881) summarized the impact of figures such as Alexander the Great. How would you construct an argument in support of this proposition, using what you've learned in this chapter? How would you refute it?

- In what ways do Alexander's actions demonstrate his own knowledge of history as well as a capacity to apply that knowledge to his own circumstances? Can you identify leaders of our own day who have mobilized their understanding of history in similar ways?

- In your view, which civilization more resembles our own: classical Athens or the Hellenistic world? Why? What characteristics make an era seem "modern"?

- In 2018, the leaders of Greece and Macedonia (formerly a part of Yugoslavia) signed an official agreement designed to end a decades-long dispute over Macedonia's right to call itself by the name of Alexander's Kingdom. It will now be known as "North Macedonia" to distinguish it from the Greek region of Macedonia. Given what you've learned, why would this have been such a contentious issue?

Before You Read This Chapter

The Civilization of Ancient Rome

"Could anyone be so indifferent or slow-witted as not to care how, and under what system of government, the Romans managed to bring nearly the whole inhabited world under their rule? Can anything be more important than understanding this?" So the Greek soldier Polybius (c. 203–120 B.C.E.) addresses Greek readers in a history celebrating the achievements of the Roman Republic. Polybius had witnessed some of these achievements firsthand: on the battlefield, in Rome itself as a hostage and a guest, and on a visit to the newly conquered city of Carthage. What better testament could there be to the success of a small Italian city than the admiration of a cultivated Greek aristocrat who, having been subjected to Roman authority, wholeheartedly embraced it? None, unless we cite the equally enthusiastic endorsement of the same Jews who had rebelled against Greek influence in 164 B.C.E. They, too, could not say enough in praise of the Romans, and they willingly placed themselves under Roman protection:

> Those whom they wish to help and to make kings, they make kings, and those whom they wish they depose;

147

and they have been greatly exalted. Yet for all that, not one of them has put on a crown or worn purple as a mark of pride, but they have built for themselves a senate chamber and every day three hundred and twenty senators constantly deliberate concerning the people, to govern them well. (1 Maccabees 8:12–15)

The only people who could say more in praise of Rome were the Romans themselves. To them, the enormous success of their empire meant that they were divinely chosen to colonize the world. This was the message conveyed by the poet Virgil (70–19 B.C.E.), commissioned by the emperor Augustus to tell the story of Rome's rise to glory in a manner imitating the epics of Homer. In one key passage of this monumental poem, the father of Aeneas, Virgil's epic hero, "foretells" the future and addresses posterity: "Remember, Roman, you whose power rules / all peoples, that these are your arts: plant peace, / make law, spare subjects, and put down the proud" (*Aeneid*, Book VI, lines 851–53).

While the Greeks struggled against the Persians and each other, a new civilization had emerged beyond the far fringes of the Greek world, on the banks of the river Tiber in central Italy. By 300 B.C.E., Rome was the dominant power on the Italian peninsula. Two centuries later, it had conquered Greece itself. For the next three centuries after that—an unprecedented period of sustained expansion—its power steadily increased. In the first century of our era, it ruled the former Hellenistic kingdoms as well as a vast region that Greek culture had never touched: northwestern Europe. Eventually, Rome's empire united the entire Mediterranean world and most of western Asia, while at the same time embracing provinces that are now parts of France, Spain, Portugal, Britain, Belgium, Germany, Switzerland, and the Balkan states. Rome thus built a historical arc that enabled Europe to share in a rich heritage reaching back to ancient Mesopotamia and Egypt: a heritage that gives meaning to the concept of "western civilization." Without Rome, European culture as we know it would not exist, and neither would the political and legal institutions that formed the United States. To echo Polybius: "Can anything be more important than understanding this?"

THE TIME OF THE KINGS

The Romans looked back uneasily on their early history, for this was the time when they were ruled by kings. It may have been necessary in those days: the Romans had never

been peaceful settlers, and their land did not yield an easy living. Although Italy had sizable forests and much more fertile land than Greece, it has few mineral resources aside from excellent supplies of marble. Its extensive coastline boasts only a few good harbors, and most of these are on the western side, away from the commercial hubs of the Mediterranean; nor does the length of this coastline offer secure natural defenses. In short, Italy was rich enough to be attractive but not rich enough to be easily defended. So the Romans were a warlike people from the first, continually obliged to fortify their hard-won lands against other invaders and needing strong leaders to spearhead their efforts.

Early Influences

When the Romans arrived in Italy, the dominant inhabitants of the peninsula were a people whom the Greeks called Tyrrhenians. To the Romans, they were **Etruscans**; to us, they remain mysterious, despite the rich archaeological record they left behind. This is because their language (not a branch of Indo-European) has never been fully deciphered, even though the Etruscans used an alphabet borrowed from the Greeks, with whom they were in frequent contact. By the sixth century B.C.E., the Etruscans had established a confederation of independent city-states in north-central Italy. They were skilled metalworkers, artists, and architects, from whom the Romans later took their knowledge of the arch and the vault, among much else, including the bloody sport of gladiatorial combat and the practice of foretelling the future by studying the entrails of animals and the flight of birds.

The two most important foundation myths told by the Romans also were derived from Etruscan tradition: the story of Aeneas's escape from Troy, which became the basis of Virgil's *Aeneid;* and the story of the infant twins Romulus and Remus, abandoned at birth and then raised by a maternal wolf, afterward founding a city on the slopes of the Palatine Hill. Rome's politicians and historians mined both legends for their metaphorical significance and added further details to increase their relevance for a changing audience. For example, the story of Aeneas's seduction and abandonment of Dido, queen of Carthage, reflected Rome's defeat of that powerful North African civilization. And for many Roman commentators, the murder of Remus at the hands of his brother Romulus epitomized an all-too-familiar pattern in Roman politics.

One aspect of Etruscan culture was of more limited influence. In marked contrast to women in Greek society, Etruscan women enjoyed very high status and played

AN ETRUSCAN COUPLE. This sarcophagus lid dates from the middle of the fourth century B.C.E. and depicts a deceased couple as they lie together in bed, emphasizing with their intimate embrace the closeness of their marital bond. (Photograph © 2017 Museum of Fine Arts, Boston.)

important roles in public life. They participated in politics and sporting events, they attended dramatic performances and athletic competitions (forbidden to Greek women), and they danced in ways that shocked both the Greeks and the Romans. Etruscan wives also ate meals with their husbands, another departure from both Greek and Roman custom, and reclined with them on the same couch at banquets. After death, these devoted couples were buried together in the same mortuary vaults, and their tombstones and sarcophagi often emphasize their mutual affection. Etruscan families even traced their descent through the female line. Some of these practices certainly affected the Romans, since Roman women were markedly less sequestered than

their Greek counterparts. Yet they did not enjoy the same freedoms as Etruscan women until very late in Roman history, when these freedoms were condemned as signs of Rome's decadence.

The Romans also borrowed ideas from the Greek settlers who had begun to colonize southern Italy and Sicily in large numbers during the eighth century B.C.E. From them, Romans derived their alphabet, many of their religious beliefs, and much of their art. But the Romans downplayed Greek influence in their founding mythology, preferring to emphasize their alleged descent from the Trojans and also tracing their ancestry back to an Italic people called the Sabines, whose women (according to legend) Romulus and his men had forcibly abducted in order to breed Roman children. This was a practice Romans would continue, in one form or another, as the legions planted new colonies and intermarried with indigenous populations from the Persian Gulf to the lowlands of Scotland.

The Founding of Rome

The real founders of Rome were a tribe called the Latins, descendants of a cluster of Indo-European-speaking peoples who crossed the Alps into Italy during the second millennium B.C.E. Recent archaeological research has pushed the origins of the city back to at least the tenth century, several centuries earlier than 753 B.C.E., which the Romans themselves calculated as the year of their city's foundation.

Rome's position on the Tiber was advantageous. Trading ships (but not large war fleets) could navigate the river as far as the city, but no farther; thus Rome could be a commercial port but was not threatened by attack from the sea. Rome also sat astride the first good ford across the Tiber, making it a major crossroads. This was particularly important in its early years, when all roads did *not* lead to Rome, and the city was just a trading post on the frontier between Latium (the territory of the Latins) and Etruria (the Etruscan homeland). The seven hills that ringed the settlement, among which Rome was nestled, also offered strategic advantages. Eventually, Rome's central marketplace—the *forum* or "open space"—would become the beating heart of the world's most populous and powerful city, with approximately a million people crowded into an area of five square miles.

The topography of Latium—a broad, flat plain with few natural obstacles—also influenced the way the Romans dealt with neighboring communities, because it was not a terrain with defensible natural boundaries. At an early date, they negotiated a series of agreements with their neighbors that were known collectively as the Latin Right: a trading pact (the *commercium*), provisions for intermarriage (the *connubium*), and the *migratio,* which allowed a resident of one settlement to emigrate to another and, after a year's residence, have the full rights of a citizen there. These privileges contrast strongly with the rigid isolationism and mutual suspicion that divided the city-states of ancient Mesopotamia or Greece. Indeed, the Romans' later willingness to extend the Latin Right to colonies far beyond Latium was a key factor in the success of their empire.

According to their own legends, the Romans' early government was a monarchy that mirrored the structure of Roman households, with a patriarchal king who exercised power checked only by a council of elders, the Senate (a word derived from the Latin *senex,* "old man"). Seven kings, including Romulus, are said to have ruled in succession. The last, Tarquinius Superbus (Tarquin the Arrogant), is reputed to have been an Etruscan who paved the way for Rome's imperial expansion by dominating Latium and the agriculturally wealthy district of Campania to the south. But his power came at the price of Roman freedom and dignity, as was made clear when Tarquin's son raped a virtuous Roman wife, **Lucretia**, around 510 B.C.E. When she committed suicide to avoid dishonor, the Romans—led by Lucretia's kinsman, Brutus—rose up in rebellion, overthrowing not only the Etruscan dynasty but rejecting the very idea of monarchy as a legitimate form of government.

Henceforth, any claim to royal authority in Rome was considered anathema, and the very word *rex* ("king") was a term of insult. The Brutus who would be instrumental in the assassination of Julius Caesar nearly five centuries later was a descendant of that same Brutus who had driven out the Tarquin kings: something he and his contemporaries never forgot.

THE TRIUMPH OF THE EARLY REPUBLIC

The story of Lucretia's defilement and death, whether or not it occurred as it was remembered, remained a rallying theme of patriotic myth and was also a potent statement of Roman attitudes toward female chastity and family honor. And it coincided with a radical change in Roman governance. This change was so radical, in fact, that it did not match any of Aristotle's political categories (see Chapter 4) but instead combined elements of them all. The Romans themselves didn't know what to call their political system: they spoke of it merely as *res publica* (the "public thing").

The Territorial Expansion of Rome

The early **Roman republic** was marked by almost constant warfare, initially defensive but soon aimed at stitching together a patchwork of valuable territories that could support Rome's growing population. Gradually, the Romans came to control all the Latin hinterland and the valuable port of Ostia at the mouth of the Tiber, about twenty miles from their city. They also pushed northward toward Etruscan territory and southward to Naples, another good port. By 300 B.C.E., Romans had absorbed or allied themselves with all of central Italy and had begun to look even farther south, to the wealthy Greek colonies of Sicily.

Their rapid success is remarkable when compared with the patterns familiar to us from our study of classical Greece, the only corollary (and not a close one) being Philip II of Macedonia's subjugation of the poleis earlier in that same century. What was the secret of Roman success? For one thing, the Romans did not impose heavy burdens of taxation and tribute on the settlements they conquered. More often, they demanded that their allies contribute only soldiers to the Roman army. Rome also extended the Latin Right to many of these conquered territories, giving them a further stake in its continued political and military expansion.

Rome thus gained for itself nearly inexhaustible reserves of fighting men. By the middle of the third century B.C.E., its army may have counted as many as 300,000—a huge force even by modern standards, and all the more formidable due to the soldiers' rigorous training. As we have seen, the Greeks had eventually turned to paid soldiers out of economic necessity, but they fought in smaller numbers; Xenophon's army was 10,000 and Alexander's 100,000. The Great King of Persia, at the height of his powers, could claim to muster a million men, but these were private or tribal armies commanded by his satraps, not a standing army loyal to him. The Romans, in contrast, devoted themselves to the discipline of warfare in ways the Greeks (except for the Spartans) and the Persians did not. In this, although not in their tactics, they resemble the Hittites of the late Bronze Age and the Neo-Assyrians of the eighth century B.C.E. (see Chapter 2).

Although the Romans originally borrowed the phalanx formation from the Greeks, they quickly replaced it with smaller, more flexible divisions that could adjust to the varied geographical conditions of central Italy. Although the major unit of the Roman army was always the legion (5,000 men), the basic combat unit was the *maniple* ("handful"), a group of about 120 infantrymen who trained together and who often performed specialized tasks or used special weaponry. The Greek Polybius could not say enough in praise of this system, which made the army adaptable

ROMAN EXPANSION TO 218 B.C.E.

- Roman and Latin territory in 298 B.C.E.
- Roman allies in 298 B.C.E.
- Roman and Latin acquisitions from 298–263 B.C.E.
- Roman allies from 298–263 B.C.E.
- Roman acquisitions from 241–218 B.C.E.
- Roman acquisitions from the Second Punic War 218–201 B.C.E.
- Kingdom of Syracuse
- Allies of Syracuse

ROMAN EXPANSION IN ITALY, 485–218 B.C.E. This map illustrates early Roman expansion in the peninsula. ■ *What is the geographical relationship between Roman and Etruscan territory?* ■ *What seem to have been the most attractive avenues for Roman expansion?* ■ *What powers might have threatened Rome after its transformation into the dominant power on the peninsula after 265 B.C.E.?*

to climate, terrain, and the deployment of new military technologies.

The republic's early history reinforced not only the military character of the Roman state but also its commitment to agriculture as the only proper peacetime employment for a Roman. The acquisition of new lands made it possible for needy citizens to maintain themselves as farmers in the new colonies around Rome. By accommodating an increasing population in this way, the Romans were able to remain staunchly agricultural for a surprisingly long time. As a result, they developed an interest in shipping and commerce fairly late when compared with the Greeks or Phoenicians. And they would continue—even at the height of their empire—to valorize rural life over that of the city.

CINCINNATUS THE STATESMAN-FARMER. This bronze statue of Cincinnatus is prominent in Cincinnati, Ohio, which was named after the Roman hero (and in honor of George Washington) in 1790. In his right hand he holds the *fasces*, symbolizing his powers as dictator. In his left, he grasps the handle of a plow. ▪ *Why would this figure have fired the imagination of Americans during their War of Independence?*

The Constitution of the Early Republic

During this period of expansion, Rome's political system evolved accordingly. Initially, the overthrow of the monarchy had resulted in only moderate changes: instead of a king, the government was headed by two elected officers called *consuls*. Although the consuls of the infant republic were supposedly chosen by all citizens, the Roman assembly of this period actually voted in affiliated blocs with shared interests, economic or territorial. And since groups consisting of the wealthiest citizens voted first, a majority could be reached even before the votes of the poorer groups were cast.

Consequently, the consuls were inevitably members of aristocratic families, known in Rome as *patricians* because they traced descent from a famous ancestor or "father" (*pater*). During his term of office, which lasted for one year, each consul exercised essentially the same power as a king: dealing justice, making law, and commanding the army. The only limit on consular power was the right of each consul to veto the actions of the other, which often led to stalemate or violent conflict. In such cases, the Senate might have to arbitrate. In times of grave emergency (like that resulting in Cincinnatus's election), a dictator might be appointed for a term not longer than six months.

Within a generation after the establishment of the republic, patrician dominance of the government began to be challenged by the *plebs* ("people"). This was the first stage in a centuries-long contest known as the Struggle of the Orders. The plebeian classes made up nearly 98 percent of the Roman population, and they were a diverse group. Some had grown wealthy through trade or agriculture, but most were smallholding farmers, artisans, or the urban poor. Their grievances were numerous. Although they were forced to serve in the army, they were nevertheless excluded from holding office. They were also victims of discriminatory decisions in civil trials, which were judged by patricians. They did not even know what legal rights they were supposed to enjoy, because Rome had as yet no established laws: there were only unwritten customs and practices whose meaning was interpreted by the patricians to their own advantage. The plebeians were also, like the poorer citizens of Greek poleis, threatened with debt slavery.

These wrongs prompted a rebellion in the early fifth century B.C.E., when plebeians refused to join in the military defense of Rome and instead seceded from the city, camping out on the Aventine hill (see the map of Rome on page 176). This general strike of military labor forced the patricians to allow the people to elect their own officers, who were known as *tribunes* (tribal leaders). The job of each tribune was to protect his constituents from patrician injustice.

The paragon of Roman heroism in this era was Lucius Quinctius **Cincinnatus** (519–c. 430 B.C.E.), a stout-hearted citizen-farmer who reluctantly accepted political office when Rome was threatened by attack. According to legend, he was plowing his fields when a delegation of senators arrived to bring him to Rome. In the city, he found that he had been named *dictator*, a word that originally had positive connotations (like *tyrant* in Greece). This was a position of power to which the Romans elected one man during times of crisis. And as the term implies, the dictator's job was to tell everyone what they should do in a tough situation requiring decisive leadership. As legend has it, Cincinnatus dutifully performed this role, led Rome in its wars with hostile neighbors—and then went back to his farm. If Lucretia was the Roman epitome of matronly fortitude, Cincinnatus was the paradigm of manly virtue: willing to turn his hand to politics or warfare when necessary but preferring to put it to the plow. George Washington was frequently compared with him, to his own satisfaction.

Moreover, the plebeians guaranteed the safety of these officers by vowing to kill any person who hindered them from exercising their powers.

The plebs' victory led to the codification of the Law of the Twelve Tables, proclaimed around 450 B.C.E. and inscribed on wooden tablets (hence "tables"). Although this law would be regarded by later Romans as a charter of liberties, it was really a perpetuation of ancient custom. Nevertheless, the fact that the law was now *defined* was a significant improvement. Plebeians were also made eligible to hold elected offices, and they gradually gained access to the Senate. A further victory came in 287 B.C.E., when the plebeians succeeded in passing a law that made decisions enacted in their own assembly, the *concilium plebis*, binding on the Roman government—whether the Senate approved them or not. It was at this time that the phrase *Senatus Populusque Romanum* came into regular use, abbreviated *SPQR* and designating any decree or decision made by "the Senate and People of Rome." (Visitors to Rome will still find *SPQR* emblazoned on everything from public buildings to the manhole covers of Rome's sewers.)

These reforms had several important consequences over the long term. Successful plebeians could now work their way into the upper reaches of Roman society, which loosened the hold of patrician families on the exercise of power. At the same time, laws preventing wealth from becoming a controlling factor in Roman politics barred senators from engaging directly in commerce. This restriction had the effect of creating a new social order, that of the equestrians ("horsemen" or knights): men who chose a life of business rather than politics and whose wealth made it possible for them to own and equip warhorses and thus to provide Rome's cavalry. But the equestrians and the senators were never wholly distinct. Often, some members of an important family would stay aloof from politics while underwriting the political careers of their brothers and cousins. Those families who managed to win election by such means, generation after generation, became increasingly prestigious and influential. Meanwhile, patricians who chose politics over wealth became impoverished and resentful. By the first century B.C.E., many such men felt excluded from political influence and were tempted to pursue their private agendas by styling themselves champions of the people.

Later Roman patriots would regard this era as a golden age of shared government, but Rome never was a democracy. A republic differs from a monarchy only in that power is exercised by officers who are in some way responsible to citizens, and whose offices are not (at least in theory) hereditary. A republic, in short, is a political system designed to preserve the power of an oligarchy or privileged group. This is what the republic had been founded to achieve: kings were driven out, but patricians reigned. The constitution that emerged in these key centuries therefore broadened and stabilized oligarchy by the balance it struck among competing governmental institutions: the assembly, the Senate, and executive officeholders. Thanks to this distribution of powers, no single individual or clique could become overwhelmingly strong; but neither could direct expressions of the popular will—that is, democracy—affect Roman policy.

For the Greek historian Polybius, this was an ideal system because it combined elements of a monarchy (executive officeholders, the consuls), an aristocracy (the Senate), and a polity (the people's assembly and the tribunes). Centuries later, for the framers of the U.S. Constitution, it was a model for the three branches of a new government designed to *prevent* the vast majority of Americans from participating directly in politics, while allowing some citizens (originally, white men with sufficient property) a say in choosing their representatives. Polybius prophesied that such a system would break the political cycle that had destroyed the Greek poleis and that it would last forever. He was wrong.

THE ESSENCE OF ROMAN IDENTITY

The slow unfolding of the early republic ensured, in part, its success: Romans were conservatives who accepted new things reluctantly but then preserved them fiercely. The prevailing principle behind their institutions was the **mos maiorum** (*MOHS my-OR-um*), "the code of the elders" or "the custom of the ancestors" or even, to use the word derived from the Latin *mos*, "morality." This unwritten code

SENATUS POPULUSQUE ROMANUM. The proud stamp of the "Senate and People of Rome" can be found even on public works and buildings in modern Rome. It is shown here on a manhole cover.

A ROMAN PATRICIAN OF THE FIRST CENTURY B.C.E. This man, who wears the toga of an aristocrat, displays his piety by holding the busts of his ancestors. Busts, like the funerary masks described by Polybius (see page 155), commemorated the dead and were the focus for family worship in household shrines. ■ *How does the Roman attitude toward age and death differ from that of the Greeks (see the image on page 82)?* ■ *What do these differences suggest about the broader values of these two societies?*

was sacrosanct and essential to Roman identity. It accounts for the remarkable coherence of Roman culture, religion, and law, all of which rested on ancestor worship. The Latin word *pietas* ("piety") meant reverence for family traditions and for one's fathers—living and dead. What made the legendary **Aeneas** "pious Aeneas" was his devotion to his father, Anchises (*an-KIE-sees*), whom he carried to safety on his back while Troy burned. In a metaphorical sense, this meant that Aeneas was the carrier of tradition, a man willing to shoulder the burdens of his ancestors and carry them forever.

This helps to explain why the Romans, in the ensuing centuries of their world domination, continued to identify so strongly with their homeland and its customs. In the Hellenistic world around them, as we have seen, the Greeks who emigrated to the new cosmopolitan kingdoms in Asia and Egypt were apt to adopt the customs, foods, and gods of these places. To a Roman, by contrast, "going native" in a foreign place was a terrible betrayal of the *mos maiorum*; patriotism, after all, is dedication to the fatherland. It also explains the extraordinary maxim of *patria potestas* (*PAH-tree-a poh-TEST-ahs*; "fatherly power") upheld by the Twelve Tables. A Roman father, no matter what his social class, had absolute authority within his household, including the power of life and death. If he was too poor to raise a child, he could expose it (leaving it to perish or to charity) or sell it into slavery. If his wife or child dishonored him, he could kill with impunity. Paternal supremacy was upheld in theory and in legends like that of Lucretia: had she not killed herself, her father could have killed her with his own hands.

These values set the Romans apart from the peoples with whom they came into contact. The Greeks, for example, never condoned anything like *patria potestas*: when a father kills his children in Greek mythology, he is inevitably killed in revenge by another member of his own family, or by the gods. And although pride in one's ancestry is a very human attribute, and patriarchy common to every known civilization, the Romans' contemporaries were awed by their extreme devotion to these principles. This devotion was one of the things that made the Romans so admirable in the eyes of those Jews disgusted by the loose morals of Hellenistic civilization (see Chapter 4). For the Greek Polybius, it was the key to Roman success. In addition to describing the workings of the Roman government and army in minute detail, he reports (with anthropological interest) on the conduct of Roman funeral processions and the Romans' practice of wearing the death masks of their ancestors, which on other days were hung in special household shrines.

In some respects, Rome's public religion resembled that of the Greeks: Jupiter corresponded to Zeus as god of the skies, Neptune to Poseidon as god of the seas, Venus

Analyzing Primary Sources

Polybius Describes the Romans' Worship of Their Ancestors

The Law of the Twelve Tables forbade excessive display at funerals, especially displays of wealth and grief by women. Instead, funerals were supposed to be occasions for the display of family piety. In the following passage, the Greek historian Polybius—who had spent a formative fourteen years of his life in Rome—describes Roman burial customs and these rites' relationship to the strength of republican ideals.

quote just one example to illustrate the pains taken by the Roman state to produce men who will endure anything to win a reputation for valor in their country. Whenever one of their celebrated men dies . . . his body is carried with every kind of honor into the Forum, . . . sometimes in an upright position so as to be conspicuous, or else, more rarely, recumbent. The whole mass of the people stand round to watch, and his son, if he has one of adult age who can be present, or if not some other relative, then . . . delivers an address which recounts the virtues and successes achieved by the dead man during his lifetime. By these means the whole populace . . . are involved in the ceremony, so that when the facts of the dead man's career are recalled . . . their sympathies are so deeply engaged that the loss seems . . . to be a public one which affects the whole people. Then, after the burial of the body and the performance of the customary rites, they place the image of the dead man in the most conspicuous position in the house, where it is enclosed in a wooden shrine. This image consists of a mask which is fashioned with extraordinary fidelity . . . to represent the features of these dead men. On occasions when public sacrifices are offered, these masks are displayed and decorated with great care. And when any distinguished member of the family dies, the masks are taken to the funeral, and are worn by men who are considered to bear the closest resemblance to the original, both in height and their general appearance and bearing. . . .

It would be hard to imagine a more impressive scene for a young man who aspires to win fame and practice virtue. For who could remain unmoved at the sight of the images of all these men who have won renown in their time, now gathered together as if alive and breathing? What spectacle could be more glorious than this?

Source: Polybius, *The Rise of the Roman Empire*, trans. Ian Scott-Kilvert (New York: 1979), pp. 346–47.

Questions for Analysis

1. Why does Polybius place so high a premium on the Romans' conduct at funerals? How can such rites be related to republican ideals?

2. Compare this analysis of Roman funerary rites with the image of a Roman patrician and his ancestors on page 154. How do they complement each other?

---

to Aphrodite as goddess of beauty and sexuality, Mars to Ares as god of war. But in keeping with the Roman equation of religion with family, this entire pantheon functioned as family gods of the Roman state. The republic was essentially a giant, timeless household run by "elders" (senators) and "father figures" (patricians), some of whom traced their ancestry back to gods; the mother of Aeneas was Venus. Like a Roman household, the Roman state could flourish only if these father- and mother-gods lent their continuing and active support to its enterprises. Committees of priests therefore functioned as branches of the government and tended to the worship of the city's temples. And in stark contrast to priests in other ancient societies, these priests were not full-time professionals who formed a special caste but prominent men who rotated in and out of office while serving as leaders of the Senate. Their dual roles made religion even more integral to political life in Rome than it had been in Greece—similar in some ways to the integration of religion and politics in ancient Mesopotamia (see Chapter 1).

The Roman man's primary duty to honor his ancestors also bolstered the prestige of the Roman army, because soldiers were supposed to sacrifice themselves for the public good and to fear disgrace above all things. The all-important sense of ancestral duty is further reflected in Roman naming practices, another custom that separated them from other ancient cultures. Most free men in antiquity were known by a given name and their father's name only: Alexander, before he was "the Great," was "son of Philip." A free-born Roman, in contrast, had at least two names. The name by which he was formally known—the name that mattered—was the name of his earliest ancestor, the man from whom his family descended. Gaius Julius Caesar, to take a famous example, would have entered public life as Julius, a member of the family of the Julii, who claimed ancestry from Iulus, the son of Aeneas. His forename, Gaius, was the most common name in Rome, the equivalent of "Joe" or "John." He would never be addressed by this name in public, except perhaps by very intimate friends or family members. His third name, Caesar, which means "Hairy" (probably a joke), was a nickname he acquired in the course of his career. And because it was the most distinctive of his names—the name he didn't share with an ancestor or with average Romans—it became the name by which he was commonly known. The same goes for Marcus Tullius Cicero (Cicero means "chickpea"). The illustrious Cincinnatus was actually "Curly."

What's in a name? Everything, if you were a Roman man. And nothing, at least nothing of personal significance, if you were a Roman woman. Lucretia's name was not her own but her father's or forefather's: the feminine version of Lucretius. If she had a sister, they would both be called Lucretia, differentiated only as Major and Minor ("big/elder" and "little/younger") Lucretia. If there were two more girls, they would be Tertia and Quarta ("Third" and "Fourth") Lucretia, and so on. The only people in Rome who had personal names were slaves (who were named by their masters, like pets) or very low-born Romans and immigrants who had no lineage that mattered.

FROM REPUBLIC TO EMPIRE

For centuries after the founding of the republic, warfare and agriculture remained the chief occupations of most Romans. A few artisans could be found in cities, and some minor attempts were made to establish trading networks. But the fact that Rome had no standard system of coinage until 289 B.C.E. suggests strongly that commerce was an insignificant component of its economy. Apparently, Romans didn't rely on portable wealth; when they weren't fighting, they wanted to be home on the farm, not gadding about the world. If they had money, they put it into real estate: land or slaves.

All of this changed rapidly when Romans began to look beyond Italy. In 265 B.C.E., they completed their absorption of Etruscan territory and could claim to control most of the

peninsula. A year later, they were already embroiled in a war overseas. For a home-loving people who had now secured ample resources for their own support, this seems paradoxical. Indeed, historians continue to argue about the motives for Roman expansion. Did Rome constantly seek to extend its rule as a matter of policy, to feed a collective appetite for warfare and plunder? Or was it an accidental empire, built up in a series of reactions to changing pressures at home as well as in response to threats—real and imagined—from abroad? No definitive answer is yet possible, but it was in this crucial period that the Roman Republic began to transform Western civilizations, and itself, into the Roman Empire.

The Punic Wars, 264–146 B.C.E.

In 265 B.C.E., Roman territory extended to the tip of Italy's "boot," but there it ended. Just off its coast, the large islands of Corsica and Sardinia and the western half of Sicily were part of another state, much older and far wealthier. This was the great maritime empire of **Carthage**, which stretched along the northern coast of Africa from modern-day Tunisia through the Straits of Gibraltar and into modern Spain. Carthage itself was a vital port city at the northeastern tip of Africa, founded around 800 B.C.E. as a Phoenician colony (see Chapter 2) but now independent and powerful. It had the largest and most effective navy of its day, and it commanded the vast resources of commercial networks that reached as far north as Britain and deep into Egypt. In almost every respect but one it was far superior to Rome. Yet that one factor was decisive: although the Carthaginian fleet was unrivaled, Carthage had no standing army. It relied on mercenaries bankrolled by the enormous profits of its merchants.

The epic struggle between Rome and Carthage for dominance of the Mediterranean lasted well over a century. It crystallized in three periods of concentrated warfare known as the **Punic Wars**, because the Romans called their enemies the Poeni ("Phoenicians"). The first of these wars began in 264 B.C.E., when Rome sent a garrison to occupy the independent city of Messina (originally a Greek colony) on the eastern tip of Sicily, directly across from the Italian mainland. Carthage, in response, took advantage of the local enmity between Messina and Syracuse (another Greek city), and sent warships to protect Syracuse from what it saw as Roman aggression. Twenty-three years of bitter fighting ensued, protracted because the Carthaginians needed to suffer only one defeat in a land battle before resolving to engage the Romans solely at sea. There they had the advantage—until the Romans built their own navy, virtually from scratch. In 241 B.C.E., Carthage was beaten down and forced to cede all of its Sicilian lands to Rome and to pay a large indemnity.

CARTHAGINIAN COIN. This coin was issued by Hannibal's family around 230 B.C.E. and circulated in the Carthaginian colonies of Spain. Its face shows the Carthaginian god Melqart in the guise of Hercules (notice the club over his shoulder). The reverse features a war elephant with a mounted rider, like the ones that Hannibal used against Rome.

Sicily thus became Rome's first overseas province. It was shortly followed by Corsica and Sardinia, which the Roman Senate contrived to seize on the grounds that Carthage had defaulted on the payment of reparations.

Thereafter, the Carthaginians had ample reason to harbor resentment against Rome, while the Romans were determined not to let Carthage revive its maritime power. So when Carthage attempted to expand its presence in Spain, leaders of the Senate interpreted this as a threat to Roman interests and declared a new war that lasted for sixteen years: the Second Punic War. This time, however, Rome was thrown entirely off its guard by the brilliant exploits of the Carthaginian commander Hannibal (247–183 B.C.E.), who very nearly defeated the Romans at their own game and on their own soil. No one had imagined that a Carthaginian attack could come by land, from the north. But in a daring strategy, Hannibal raised an army in Spain, heavily manned by cavalry in order to counter the superior infantry of Rome, and equipped it with dozens of war elephants and siege engines. He then led this entire force across the Pyrenees into Gaul (now southern France) and then over the Alps into Italy. There, he harried Roman forces in their own territories for nearly sixteen years, from 218 to 202 B.C.E.

In the end, Hannibal was challenged more by the rigors of campaigning and the difficulty of supplying his army in hostile terrain than by the Romans themselves. (He had lost many of his elephants and some important equipment in the icy mountain passes of the Alps.) He also seems to have counted on winning the support of the Italian territories that Rome had conquered, but Rome's generous treatment of its Latin allies kept them loyal. As a result, Rome could call on vast human resources while Hannibal had only his exhausted army, with no reserves forthcoming from Carthage. Nevertheless, he won several amazing victories in Italy before retreating—technically undefeated—in 202 B.C.E. He also won the admiration of the Romans themselves, whose own histories frankly acknowledge his tactical genius. Indeed, this phase of warfare ended only

when a Roman general, Publius Cornelius Scipio, took a leaf out of Hannibal's book: attacking the enemy on his home turf. He had been campaigning in Spain against the army of Hannibal's brother, Hasdrubal. In 201 B.C.E., having seized a number of key Carthaginian strongholds, he crossed into Africa and met Hannibal at Zama, near Carthage. Scipio's victory ended the Second Punic War and won him a new name, "Africanus," in honor of his conquest.

Carthage was now compelled to abandon all of its possessions except the city itself and its immediate hinterlands, and to pay an indemnity three times greater than the already crippling reparations Rome had demanded after the First Punic War. Yet Roman suspicion of Carthage remained obsessive, and warmongers in the Senate read every sign of its recovery as a threat. By the middle of the second century, some hard-liners were urging a preemptive strike. Among the most vocal was an elderly patrician, Marcus Porcius Cato, famous for his stern obedience to Roman custom and his virulent xenophobia. Cato ended every speech he gave—no matter what the topic—with the words: "And furthermore, I strongly advise that Carthage be destroyed." This won him the nickname Cato the Censor, from the Latin verb meaning "to advise."

Eventually, the Senate was persuaded. In 149 B.C.E., it seized on a minor pretext to demand that the Carthaginians abandon their city and settle at least ten miles from the coast, where they would have no access to the sea. Of course, this absurd mandate amounted to a death sentence for a city dependent on commerce, and it was refused—as the Romans knew it would be. The result was the Third Punic War and the siege of Carthage, which ended in 146 B.C.E. when the Romans breached the walls and butchered the population. Those who survived the massacre were sold into slavery, and their once-magnificent city was razed to the ground. The legend that the Romans sowed the land with salt (to make it infertile) is not a real tactic but a poetic way of describing the successful eradication of an entire civilization. It would stand as a warning to Rome's other potential enemies.

Roman Control of the Hellenistic World

Rome's victories over Carthage enormously increased Roman territory, leading to the creation of new colonial provinces in Sicily, North Africa, and Hispania (Spain). This not only brought Rome great new wealth (above all, access to Sicilian and African grain supplies and the silver mines of the Iberian Peninsula) but it was also the beginning of the westward expansion that became Rome's defining influence on the history of Europe.

At the same time, Rome's overseas expansion brought it into conflict with eastern Mediterranean powers, paving the way for further conquests. During the Second Punic

War, Philip V of Macedonia had entered an alliance with Carthage; soon afterward, he moved aggressively into Greece and was rumored to have designs on Egypt. Rome sent an army to stop him and later foiled the plans of the Achaean League (see Chapter 4). This was when Polybius was sent to Rome as a hostage. He became a guest-friend in the family descended from Scipio Africanus and later witnessed the destruction of Carthage. Rome also thwarted similar efforts by the Seleucid monarch Antiochus III. In neither of these cases did Rome set out to conquer the eastern Mediterranean on purpose. By 146 B.C.E., however, both Greece and Macedonia had become Roman provinces, Seleucid Asia had lost most of its territories, and Ptolemaic Egypt had largely become a pawn of Roman commercial and political interests.

THE FURTHER EXPANSION OF ROME, 264–44 B.C.E. The rapid increase of Rome's territories opened up new opportunities and challenges. ▪ *Examine the phases of expansion on this map. In what directions did Roman dominion move?* ▪ *Why was this the case?* ▪ *What particular problems might have been created by the eventual extension of Roman rule into Gaul, well beyond the "Roman lake" of the Mediterranean?*

THE CONSEQUENCES
OF IMPERIALISM

Rome's seemingly inadvertent conquest of Greece and western Asia transformed the economic, social, and cultural life of the republic. New wealth poured in, increasing the inequalities within Roman society and challenging the traditional values of frugality and self-sacrifice. Small farmers left the land and swelled the impoverished urban population, unable to compete with the huge new plantations owned by aristocrats and worked by gangs of slaves. Slaves also played an increasing role in Roman cities as artisans, merchants, and household servants. Roman rule over the Hellenistic world had a particularly pervasive impact on cultural life—so much so that many Romans considered themselves to have been intellectually and culturally "conquered" by Greece. Hitherto self-assured and self-satisfied, they now felt that their own language, history, and customs were uncouth and barbaric compared with those of their cultivated colonial subjects.

Economic Change and Social Upheaval

Like all peoples of the ancient world, the Romans took **slavery** for granted. But nothing in Rome's earlier experience prepared it for the huge increase in the number of slaves that resulted from its western and eastern conquests. In 146 B.C.E., 55,000 Carthaginians were enslaved after the destruction of their city; not long before, 150,000 Greek prisoners of war had met the same fate. By the end of the second century B.C.E., there were a million slaves in Italy alone. Rome's became one of the most slave-based economies in history, rivaling ancient Egypt or the antebellum American South.

The majority of Roman slaves worked as agricultural laborers on the vast (and growing) estates of the Roman aristocracy. Some of these estates were the result of earlier Roman conquests within Italy itself. But others were consolidated by aristocrats who bought up the holdings of peasant farmers. Soldiers in particular, who might be required to serve for years at a time on foreign campaigns, often found it impossible to maintain their farms. Instead, they moved to the city—where free men had no way to sustain themselves except through trade or violence. With abundant, cheap slaves to do all the rough work, moreover, there was no impetus for technological innovation. Meanwhile, expensive slaves did the specialized jobs: they were secretaries, bookkeepers, personal assistants, playwrights, musicians, sculptors, and artists. The Romans had almost no incentive to employ paid labor at all or even to train in

these arts, as the Greeks had. By the first century B.C.E., as a result, a third of Rome's one million inhabitants were receiving free grain from the state, partly to keep them alive and partly to keep them quiet. The poet Juvenal would later satirize the plebs as needing only "bread and circuses" to stay satisfied and docile.

As we have seen, the Roman economy had remained fundamentally agrarian until the mid-third century B.C.E. During the following century, however, Rome's eastern conquests brought it fully into the sophisticated commercial sphere of the Hellenistic world. The principal beneficiaries of this change were the equestrian class. As overseas merchants, they profited handsomely from Rome's voracious appetite for foreign luxury goods. And as representatives of the Roman government in the provinces, they operated mines, built roads, and collected taxes, always with an eye toward their own profits. They were also the principal moneylenders to the Roman state and to distressed individuals. Interest rates were high, and when the state could not pay its bills, the moneylenders were often allowed to repay themselves by exploiting the populations of the provinces.

Commoners who lost their lands suffered from these economic changes, but the principal victims of Rome's transformation were its slaves. Even though some were cultivated foreigners—mainly Greek-speaking—taken as prisoners of war, the standard policy of their owners was to get as much work out of them as possible until they died of exhaustion or were "freed" in old age to fend for themselves. The same irascible Cato the Censor who had demanded the destruction of Carthage even wrote a "how-to" book on this subject. The ready availability of slaves also made Roman slavery a far more impersonal and brutal institution than it had been in many other ancient civilizations. Of course, there were exceptions. Some domestic slaves were treated as trusted family members, and slave secretaries vital to the business of Roman governance and the arts could even win fame or earn enough to buy their freedoms. Some slave artisans were permitted to run their own businesses, keeping some of the profits.

But the general lot of slaves was horrendous. Some businessmen owned slaves whom they trained as gladiators to be mauled by wild animals or by other gladiators for the amusement of a paying public. The luxurious lifestyles of the wealthy meant that dozens of slaves in every household were trapped in a cycle of menial tasks as doorkeepers, litter-bearers, couriers, valets, wet nurses, and childminders. In some great households, designated slaves had no other duties than to rub down the master after his bath or to keep track of the mistress's social engagements. It was a life that debased both slave and owner, according to many Roman critics, thus undermining the values of the republic.

Past and Present

Spectator Sports

Like the Romans' love for gladiatorial combat, Americans' love of football is inextricably tied to a sense of shared identity and fascination with violence and warfare. Although American football is not a blood sport in a technical sense, part of its allure stems from the very great physical risks taken by its players, whose careers are often cut short by injury. Both pastimes form the core of far-reaching entertainment economies that would be dismantled by any attempts at reform: concessions, advertising, merchandising, and an array of other moneymaking activities.

 Watch related author interview on the Student Site

New Money, New Values

In the early republic, as we have seen, Roman men had nearly absolute powers over their individual households. During the second century B.C.E., however, two innovations greatly altered this pattern of patriarchal control. One was the introduction of new laws that allowed married women to manage their own property instead of handing that wealth over to their husbands; if a married woman died, her possessions would then revert to her father or her father's heirs if she had no children of her own. Alongside this new law came more liberal laws that allowed women to initiate divorce proceedings.

These changes were intended to safeguard family wealth, but they eventually resulted in greater independence for women. A woman now had much more authority within the household because she contributed to its upkeep. If her husband did not show respect, she could leave him and deprive him of income. It was ironic that the growth

of Rome's slave system also gave women greater freedom, for slaves took over the traditional work of child rearing, household maintenance, and the endless tasks of spinning and weaving. Women from well-to-do families now spent more time away from the home and began to engage in a range of social, intellectual, and artistic activities. Indeed, women were among the chief consumers of the new Hellenistic fashions, commodities, and ideas available in Rome.

In earlier centuries, Romans had taken pride in the simplicity of their lives, their language, and their moral code. Now, however, elite Romans began to indulge in creature comforts and cultivate Hellenistic habits as proof of their refinement. Bilingualism became increasingly common, and Greek literature became the standard against which Roman authors measured themselves. Latin was fine for business or politics or farming, but if one wanted to express lofty or beautiful thoughts one did so in Greek, which was far more flexible and sophisticated. Latin was not yet a literary language.

Well-educated Greek slaves were therefore at a premium: to lend social cachet, to act as secretaries and personal assistants, and to tutor Roman children. The popularity of Greek plays, mostly comedies, was such that they quickly spawned Latin imitations, such as those of Plautus (257?–184 B.C.E.) and Terence (195/185–159 B.C.E.). Terence's career path is suggestive of a larger pattern: a Greek-speaker of Libyan descent, he was sold into slavery as a boy in Carthage and bought by a wealthy Roman called Terentius, who took him back to Rome and cultivated his talents, which he marketed under his own name. Six of Terence's Latin adaptations of Greek comedies survive, enjoying enormous popularity well into the Middle Ages, and eventually influencing the plays of Shakespeare.

Many Romans nursed an inferiority complex with respect to Greek culture. But others (including Cato) regarded these foreign influences with disgust. For them, the good old ways of paternal authority and stern military discipline were giving way to effeminacy and the decadence of soft living. Accordingly, conservative politicians deplored these new trends and passed laws that would restore "family values" and regulate the conspicuous consumption of luxuries, especially by women— but these measures were ineffectual. Rome was being irreversibly transformed from a republic of self-reliant farmers into a complex metropolitan empire reliant on foreign slaves, foreign grain, and foreign luxuries, in which the gap between rich and poor was widening and traditional behavioral constraints were giving way to new morals and ideas.

Philosophy and Spirituality in the Late Republic

The late republic was deeply influenced by Hellenistic philosophy, and both Epicureanism and Stoicism found strong adherents in Rome. The former was popularized by Lucretius (98–55 B.C.E.), the author of a book-length philosophical poem, *On the Nature of Things*. But more congenial to Roman values was Stoicism,

which soon numbered among its converts many powerful public figures. The most influential of these was Cicero (106–43 B.C.E.), famous in his day as an orator, statesman, and staunch defender of republican values. Cicero based his ethical teachings on the Stoic premises that virtue is happiness and tranquility of mind the highest good. The ideal man is therefore rational and indifferent to sorrow and pain.

Yet Cicero diverged from the Stoics in his approval of the active, political life. He became an advocate for the revival of Roman tradition through service to the state. His elegant prose style also advanced the use of Latin as a language of eloquence and became the standard model for Latin composition: students learning Latin today still learn to read with Cicero.

The religious practices of Rome also changed markedly in this era. The most pronounced innovation was the spread of exotic mystery cults, which satisfied a need for more emotionally intense spiritual experiences than did traditional forms of Roman worship—again, especially for women, who were largely excluded from the rites of the patriarchal state

ROMAN MYSTERY RITES. One of the Roman houses preserved at Pompeii features an astonishing cycle of wall paintings, executed around 50 B.C.E., that give the house its name: Villa of the Mysteries. The exact meaning of these images is still debated, but some scholars have argued that they depict a succession of ritual practices. Here a young woman is being whipped, perhaps as part of an initiation ceremony, while another woman performs a dance.

religion. From Egypt came the cults of Isis and Osiris, while from Asia came the worship of the Great Mother, all emphasizing the power of female sexuality and reproduction. Despite the attractions of these new cults, Romans continued to honor their traditional gods alongside these new deities. Roman polytheism could absorb them all, so long as the ancestor gods of the household and of the city were paid due reverence.

"RESTORING THE REPUBLIC": THE STRUGGLE FOR POWER

In Rome itself, the period from the end of the Third Punic War in 146 to about 30 B.C.E. was one of turbulence. Politically motivated murders, bloody competition among rival dictators, wars, and insurrections were common occurrences. Slave uprisings also added to the general disorder. In 134 B.C.E., some 70,000 slaves defeated a Roman army in Sicily before being put down by emergency reinforcements. Slaves ravaged Sicily again in 104 B.C.E. But the most threatening revolt of all was led by Spartacus, a Thracian captive who was being trained as a gladiator. Along with a band of 200 fellow slaves from a gladiatorial training camp—all bought by a wealthy entrepreneur— they escaped, heavily armed, from Capua (near Naples; see the map on page 151) to the slopes of Mount Vesuvius, where their cause attracted a huge host of other fugitives.

From 73 to 71 B.C.E., this desperate army defeated trained Roman forces of as many as 10,000 men and over- ran much of southern Italy before Spartacus himself was killed. The Senate, terrified of the precedent set by the near victory of the rebels, ordered 6,000 of the captured slaves to be crucified along the length of the road from Capua to Rome (about 150 miles) as a warning to future insurgents. Crucifixion was a form of punishment reserved for slaves and non-Roman rebels, and it meant a slow, terrible, and public death from gradual suffocation and exposure.

The Reforming Efforts of the Gracchi

Meanwhile, these waves of rural rebellion were being mirrored by urban unrest in various forms, as the poorer classes of Rome were finding new champions among some progressive aristocrats. In 133 B.C.E., a grandson of Scipio Africanus, Tiberius Gracchus, was elected a tribune of the people. He took his office very seriously and proposed to remedy the growing rift between rich and poor Romans by instituting major reforms, including the redistribution of property. As we have noted, small farmers had been losing their lands to patricians and equestrians whose new wealth allowed them to amass giant estates. To counter this, Gracchus invoked older laws that had limited the amount of land a single individual could own.

The motives behind the proposed reforms were both populist and practical. The **Roman army** had been forced to expand its presence into far-reaching territories and needed more manpower to handle uprisings such as that of Spartacus. Since a man had to meet certain property qualifications to serve in the Roman army, the available pool of citizen soldiers was shrinking along with the wealth of average citizens. Gracchus saw that the army could be strengthened if more of Rome's inhabitants could qualify for citizenship. With the support of his brother Gaius, Tiberius accordingly proposed that estates be no larger than 300 acres per citizen, plus 150 acres for each child in his family. Since many aristocratic estates exceeded these measures, the excess land could then be divided among poor settlers. But since most senators stood to lose from this legislation, they worked to ensure that it would be vetoed by Gracchus's fellow tribunes. Gracchus retaliated, arguing that tribunes who opposed the people's interests were betraying their offices, and planned to stand for reelection when his term expired. This enabled a conservative faction to allege that Gracchus had his sights set on a dictatorship, and with this excuse, they attacked and murdered him and his supporters.

Ten years later, Gaius Gracchus renewed his older brother's struggle after being elected to the same office. Although some land reforms had finally been enacted by the Senate after the assassination of Tiberius Gracchus, Gaius wanted to enact more laws for the benefit of the poor by stabilizing the price of grain in Rome and checking the abuses of the senatorial class by giving the equestrians greater powers. He also imposed controls on provincial governors suspected of exploiting their subjects for personal gain. Most controversial, Gaius proposed to extend full **Roman citizenship** to all the allied states of Italy: a move that would have kept the army well supplied with new soldiers but would also create new citizens whose collective power would challenge existing elites. Senate aristocrats arranged to have Gaius Gracchus proclaimed an outlaw. In the ensuing conflict, he and several thousand of his supporters became the victims of a violent political purge.

Rivalry among Rome's Generals

The attempted reforms of the Gracchi exposed the degree to which the republic's constitution was being compromised by the undue influence of a wealthy elite. But the popularity of the Gracchi among the plebs suggested a new path to power for ambitious men willing to court the favor of the people. Most of these men were former army commanders who traded on their military victories and the wealth they had gained from plunder to win popular support.

The first of these ambitious generals was Gaius Marius, a soldier from an obscure provincial family who had fought a successful and well-publicized campaign against Jugurtha of Numidia, whose small kingdom had threatened Rome's hard-won supremacy in the former Punic territories of North Africa. In 107 B.C.E., Marius's popularity—and his command of several legions—enabled him to secure election to the office of consul, an office that he would hold six more times in the course of his career. This set a powerful precedent, because it showed that a man with no family connections or political experience could override opposition from older political elites if he had an army to help him intimidate those elites. A successful army command could therefore be an alternative path to power.

Marius further influenced the future of Rome by reorganizing and expanding the army. Desperate for more men to fight in Africa and in Gaul, which Rome was slowly infiltrating, Marius abolished the property qualification that had hitherto limited military service; the potential pool of soldiers now included the urban poor and landless peasants. As a result, a career as a Roman legionnaire became an end in itself, rather than a matter of routine citizen service to the state. This meant, further, that a soldier's loyalty was more directed toward his commander, whose success would win rewards for his men, than driven by an abstract ideal of patriotism.

Moreover, this change meant that factional fighting among political rivals could lead to full-blown civil war, if legions loyal to one general were pitted against those of another. And indeed, this happened in Marius's own lifetime. An aristocratic general named Lucius Cornelius Sulla had fought with distinction in the so-called Social War of 91–88 B.C.E.: a conflict between Rome and its Italian allies that resulted in the extension of Roman citizenship throughout the peninsula. Sulla seemed the likely person to lead Rome's army to war in Anatolia. Marius, however, forced the Senate to deny Sulla's claim. Sulla's response was to rally the five victorious legions that had just fought under his command and, with a Roman army at his back, to march onto Rome.

This was a disturbing move: strong taboos had long prevented any armed force from entering the city limits of Rome. But Sulla argued that his actions were in keeping with the *mos maiorum*, which Marius and the Senate had betrayed. When the Senate conceded and awarded him the coveted army command, Marius again defied the Senate and seized control of the city with his own legions. When Marius died soon afterward, a conservative backlash against his popular rule led the aristocracy to appoint Sulla to the office

of dictator—but not for the traditional six months, as under the early republic. Sulla's term had no limits, and he used his powers to exterminate his opponents and pack the Senate with men loyal to himself while curtailing the authority of the peoples' tribunes. Then, after three years of autocratic rule, he retired to a life of luxury on his country estate.

Caesar's Triumph—and His Downfall

The purpose and effect of Sulla's dictatorship was to empower the aristocracy and terminally weaken the power of the plebs. Soon, however, new leaders emerged to espouse the people's cause, once again using the army as their tool of influence. The most prominent of these were Gnaeus Pompeius Magnus (106–48 B.C.E.) and Gaius **Julius Caesar** (100–44 B.C.E.). Almost exact contemporaries, Pompeius (Pompey) and Caesar represented two very different branches of Roman society. Pompey was the son of a "new man": an immigrant from central Italy who had made a fortune in Rome through questionable business practices. For Pompey, the army was a path toward gaining a political and social foothold in the capital. Caesar, by contrast, was descended from one of Rome's oldest patrician families, born to wealth and privilege. For him, the army was a stepping-stone toward greater power and influence.

Initially, Pompey and Caesar cooperated in a plot to gain control of the government and "restore the republic" by forming an alliance with a third general, Marcus Licinius Crassus: the man credited with finally defeating Spartacus. This alliance was known as a *triumvirate* (tri-UM-vir-et), meaning "rule of three men," but it soon dissolved into open rivalry. Pompey had won fame as the conqueror of Syria and Palestine, while Caesar devoted his energies to a series of campaigns in Gaul. It was under his authority that the territories encompassing modern France, Belgium, and western Germany were added to the Roman Empire, extending its northern border along the length of the Rhine.

Caesar himself advertised these conquests in a series of self-congratulatory dispatches published in book form—*On the War in Gaul*—which secured his reputation at home and cemented the loyalty of his army. These victories also put him in a strong political position. It had become accepted that the best general should be the leader of Rome, and the example of Sulla had made it possible for that leader to be a dictator for life, a king in all but name. But it was Pompey, not Caesar, who was actually in Rome and in a position to influence the Senate directly. In the face of tremendous popular protest, and even some opposition from the aristocracy, Pompey had managed to get himself elected sole consul. Using this authority, he declared that Caesar, who was still stationed in Gaul, was an enemy of the republic and that his ambition was to make himself king.

The result was a pervasive and deadly civil war. In 49 B.C.E., Caesar took up Pompey's challenge and crossed the Rubicon River, the northern boundary of Rome's Italian territories, thereby signaling his intention to take Rome by force. Pompey fled to the east in the hope of gathering an army large enough to confront Caesar's legions. Caesar pursued him and, in 48 B.C.E., the two Roman armies met at Pharsalus in Greece. Pompey was defeated and fled to Alexandria, where he was murdered by a Roman officer attached to the court of Ptolemy XIII (62/61–47? B.C.E.).

This young pharaoh, a descendant of Alexander's general Ptolemy, was then about fourteen years old and engaged in a civil war of his own—against his elder sister and co-ruler, Cleopatra VII (69–30 B.C.E.). He must have thought that he could curry favor with Caesar by encouraging the murder of Pompey; but instead, Caesar threw his support on the side of the twenty-one-year-old queen. The

BUST OF JULIUS CAESAR. Caesar's nickname meant "hairy," but it has come to be synonymous with imperial rule. It was the title preferred by the German kings of the late nineteenth and twentieth centuries, who called themselves *kaisers*, and by the tsars of Russia. In classical Latin, the "C" sound is hard, which means that the pronunciations of *caesar, kaiser,* and *tsar* are very similar.

two must have become lovers soon after their first meeting, since their son Caesarion ("Little Caesar") was born just nine months later. After a brief struggle, Ptolemy was defeated and mysteriously drowned in the Nile. Cleopatra then took as consort her even younger brother, known as Ptolemy XIV, but she ruled as pharaoh of Egypt in her own right, much as Hatshepsut had done nearly a millennium and a half before (see Chapter 2).

After that, Caesar returned to Rome in triumph—literally. A *triumph* was a spectacular honor awarded to a victorious Roman general by the Senate and was the only occasion on which (unarmed) soldiers were legally allowed to parade in the streets of Rome. Triumphs had been celebrated since the earliest days of the republic, and they featured columns of prisoners and spoils of war, chained captives (often enemy kings) led in humiliation to their public executions, floats featuring live tableaux commemorating the achievements of the triumphant man, and thousands upon thousands of cheering Romans, who received extra rations of grain and gathered up coins thrown by the handful. Through it all, Caesar would have ridden in a chariot with a golden wreath held above his head while a slave stood behind him, murmuring in his ear the words *Memento mori* ("Remember: you will die"): a triumph was so glorious and—under the republic—so rarely granted that those thus honored might forget their own mortality.

Caesar may well have done so, since his power seemed absolute. In 46 B.C.E., he was named dictator for ten years; two years later, this was changed to a lifetime appointment. In addition, he assumed nearly every other title that could augment his power. He obtained from the Senate full authority to make war and peace and to control the revenues of the state. He even governed the reckoning of time, something that was regarded as controversial. In imitation of the Egyptian calendar (slightly modified by a Greek astronomer), he revised the Roman calendar to make a 365-day year with an extra day added every fourth year. This Julian calendar (as adjusted by Pope Gregory XIII in 1582) is still observed, and the seventh month is still named after Julius.

Caesar also took important steps toward eliminating the distinction between Italians and provincials within the empire by conferring citizenship on residents of Hispania (Spain) and the newly annexed provinces in Gaul. Moreover, by settling many of his army veterans and some of the urban poor in these lands, he relieved economic inequities and furthered colonization. Even more important was his farsighted resolve to focus efforts in northwestern Europe. Whereas Pompey, and before him Alexander, went east to gain fame and fortune, Caesar followed only the Phoenicians in recognizing the potential of the wild West. By incorporating Gaul into the Roman world, he brought in a much-needed source

CLEOPATRA VII AS EGYPTIAN PHARAOH AND HELLENISTIC RULER. Like her ancestor Ptolemy I, Cleopatra represented herself as both enlightened Greek monarch and pharaoh. It was perhaps owing to her example that Julius Caesar was the first Roman leader to issue coins impressed with his own image. ▪ *How does Cleopatra's self-representation compare to that of Hatshepsut (see page 44) or Ptolemy (see page 129)?*

of food and natural resources and created a new outlet for the spread of Roman settlement and culture.

In the eyes of many contemporaries, however, Caesar's achievements were signs that he actually did intend to make himself king: a hateful thought to those who still cherished the *mos maiorum* and glorified the early days of the republic. Indeed, it was around a descendant of Lucretia's avenger, Lucius Junius Brutus, that a faction of the Senate crystallized into an assassination conspiracy. On the Ides of March in 44 B.C.E.—the midpoint of the month, according to his own calendar—Caesar was attacked on the floor of the Senate chamber and stabbed to death by a group of men. His body was later autopsied (the first forensic medical examination in recorded history), and it was found that he had sustained twenty-three wounds.

THE PRINCIPATE AND THE PAX ROMANA, 27 B.C.E.–180 C.E.

In his will, Caesar had adopted his grandnephew Gaius Octavius (or Octavian; 63 B.C.E.–14 C.E.), then a young man of eighteen serving in Illyria, across the Adriatic Sea. On learning of Caesar's death, Octavian hastened home to claim his inheritance and avenge his slain "father," whose name he took: he now called himself Gaius Julius Caesar the Younger. He soon found that he had rivals among those supporters of Caesar who had not been implicated in the plot to kill him, most notably Marcus Antonius (Mark Antony; 83–30 B.C.E.), who had served under Caesar's command in Gaul and had ambition to make himself governor of that whole province.

Octavian engineered his own election to the office of consul (though

IDES OF MARCH COIN. This coin celebrates the assassination of Julius Caesar by Marcus Junius Brutus, who is shown on the face; on the reverse, a cap of liberty (customarily worn by freed slaves) is flanked by two daggers, and below it is the legend *EID-MAR*, the Latin abbreviation for "Ides of March." ▪ *Given that Caesar drew criticism for depicting himself on Roman coinage, what do you think is the significance of Brutus's image being shown in this way?*

OCTAVIAN. Caesar's adopted heir was later granted the title *augustus* ("worthy of honor") by the Senate and was also known as *princeps* ("first man"). He was worshiped as a god in Rome's provinces, and idealized statues like this one were erected in temples and public places throughout the empire.

(This was a revenge killing, because Cicero had actively sought to undermine Antony and had branded him a public enemy.) Meanwhile, the masterminds behind Caesar's assassination—Marcus Junius Brutus and Gaius Cassius—left Rome and raised an army of legions from Greece and Anatolia. But they were defeated by the united forces of Antony and Octavian on a battlefield near the Macedonian town of Philippi (founded by Alexander's father, Philip II) in 42 B.C.E. There, both Brutus and Cassius committed suicide.

With their mutual enemies effectively destroyed, tensions mounted within the triumvirate. Antony and Octavian marginalized Lepidus, who was eventually stripped of his powers and exiled. Antony and Octavian, whose friendship had never been firm, parted ways. Antony went to Egypt and made an alliance with Cleopatra, plotting to use the resources of her realm against Octavian. Octavian, meanwhile, reestablished himself in Rome, where he skillfully portrayed Antony as having been seduced and emasculated by his foreign lover. He reminded the people that the Egyptian queen's son, Caesarion, threatened his own position as Caesar's rightful heir.

For ten years, Antony played the king in Egypt, fathering three of Cleopatra's children and making big plans for annexing Rome's eastern provinces. Octavian, claiming that he had seen a copy Antony's will, alleged that Antony had transferred his allegiance to Egypt and was a traitor to Rome. This enabled Octavian to argue that a war with Cleopatra's Egypt was not a civil war with another Roman general.

In 31 B.C.E., Octavian's superior forces defeated those of Antony and Cleopatra in the naval battle of Actium, off the coast of Greece. Soon afterward, both Antony and Cleopatra committed suicide. Their children were taken back to Rome—Caesarion disappeared under suspicious circumstances—and although their lives were spared, they were paraded through the streets as captives. This marked the end of Egypt's long independence: Cleopatra had been its last pharaoh. After more than 3,000 years of self-rule, Egypt was now another province in Rome's empire.

The Government of Augustus

The victory at Actium ushered in a new period of Roman history. Octavian, now "Gaius Julius Caesar the Younger," was the only claimant to power left standing. With no rivals left, he had no further need for political purges. For the first time in nearly a century, Rome was not embroiled in civil war.

But Rome was also no longer a republic. Even though Octavian maintained the fiction that he was governing as a mere citizen, his rule was entirely autocratic. For four years, he ruled as sole consul, and then adopted the titles of

he was far too young for this honor) and used his power to have Caesar's assassins declared outlaws. He then pursued Antony to Gaul, at the head of an army, where Antony's forces were overwhelmed. In 43 B.C.E., Antony and Octavian reconciled and formed an alliance, bringing in a third man, a senator named Marcus Aemilius Lepidus, to make up a second triumvirate. They then set about crushing the political faction responsible for Caesar's murder.

The methods they employed were brutal: prominent members of the opposition were hunted down and their property confiscated. The most notable of these victims was Cicero, who was murdered by Mark Antony's hired thugs.

Analyzing Primary Sources

Antony and Cleopatra

In his Parallel Lives, *the Greek intellectual Plutarch (c. 46–120 C.E.) paired the biographies of famous Greeks with those of famous Romans, always to the disadvantage of the latter. For example, Julius Caesar suffers in comparison with Alexander the Great, as Romulus does when set up against Theseus. The following excerpt is from Plutarch's* Life of Mark Antony, *in which the Hellenistic ruler of Egypt, Cleopatra, plays a starring role.*

aesar and Pompey knew Cleopatra when she was still a girl, and ignorant of the world, but it was a different matter in the case of Antony, because she was ready to meet him when she had reached the time of life when women are most beautiful and have full understanding. So she prepared for him many gifts and money and adornment, of a magnitude appropriate to her great wealth and prosperous kingdom, but she put most of her hopes in her own magical arts and charms. . . . For (as they say), it was not because her beauty in itself was so striking that it stunned the onlooker, but the inescapable impression produced by daily contact with her: the attractiveness in the persuasiveness of her talk, and the character that surrounded her conversation was stimulating. It was a pleasure to hear the sound of her voice, and she tuned her tongue like a many-stringed instrument expertly to whatever language she chose, and only used interpreters to talk to a few foreigners. . . . She is said to have learned the languages of many peoples, although her predecessors on the throne did not bother to learn Egyptian, and some had even forgotten how to speak the Macedonian dialect.

She took such a hold over Antony that, while his wife Fulvia was carrying on the war in Rome against Octavian on his behalf, and the Parthian army . . . was about to invade Syria, Antony was carried off by Cleopatra to Alexandria, and amused himself there with the pastimes of a boy . . . and whether Antony was in a serious or a playful mood she could always produce some new pleasure or charm, and she kept watch on him by night and day and never let him out of her sight. She played dice with him and hunted with him and watched him exercising with his weapons and she roamed around and wandered about with him at night when he stood at people's doors and windows and made fun of people inside, dressed in a slave-woman's outfit; for he also attempted to dress up like a slave. He returned from these expeditions having been mocked in return, and often beaten, although most people suspected who he was. But the Alexandrians got pleasure from his irreverence . . . enjoying his humor and saying that he showed his tragic face to the Romans and his comic one to them.

Source: Plutarch, *Life of Marcus Antonius*, cc. 25–29, excerpted in *Women's Life in Greece and Rome: A Sourcebook in Translation*, eds. Mary R. Lefkowitz and Maureen B. Fant (Baltimore, MD: 1992), pp. 147–49.

Questions for Analysis

1. How do Cleopatra's behavior and accomplishments, in Plutarch's description of her, compare with those of Roman women?

2. Given what you have learned about the values of the Roman Republic, how would a Roman reader respond to this description of Antony's behavior under the influence of the Egyptian queen? What do you think were Plutarch's motives in portraying him in this light?

---

imperator ("victorious commander") and *augustus* ("worthy of honor"). Although these honorifics had been in use under the republic, they now became attached to the person of the sole ruler. So although Rome had been an empire for centuries, not until now did it have a single emperor. To avoid confusion, historians therefore refer to this phase of Rome's history as the **Principate**, from the title Augustus himself preferred: *princeps*, "prince" or "first man."

Because Augustus was determined not to be regarded as a tyrant or (worse) a king, he left most of Rome's republican institutions in place—but he gradually emptied them of their power. In theory, the **emperor** served at the will of "the Senate and People of Rome" (*SPQR*). In practice, though, he controlled the army, which meant that he also controlled the city and its government. Fortunately, **Augustus** was an able ruler. He introduced a range of public services, including a police force and fire brigade. He instituted a new system of coinage throughout the empire and abolished the old, corrupt system of taxation (whereby tax collectors were compensated by being allowed to keep a portion of the monies they collected, which inevitably encouraged them to collect more than were legally due). Instead, Augustus appointed his own representatives as tax collectors, paid them regular salaries, and kept them under strict supervision. He simultaneously conducted a census of the empire's population for this purpose, and it was during one of these "enrollments" that the birth of Jesus is said to have taken place, according to the Gospel of Luke (see Chapter 6).

Above all, Augustus represented himself as a stern defender of the *mos maiorum* and traditional Roman virtues. He rebuilt many of the city's ancient temples and prohibited the worship of foreign gods. In an attempt to increase the birthrate of Rome's citizens, he penalized men who failed to marry, required widows to remarry within two years of their husbands' deaths, and rewarded women who gave birth to more than two children. He also introduced laws punishing adultery and making divorces more difficult to obtain. To hammer the message home, Augustan propaganda portrayed the imperial family as a model of domestic virtue and propriety. Yet these portrayals were only moderately successful, because the emperor's own extramarital affairs were notorious, while the sexual promiscuity of his daughter Julia eventually forced Augustus to have her exiled.

Meanwhile, more land was gained for Rome in the lifetime of Augustus than in all the previous centuries of its existence. His generals advanced farther and farther into central Europe, conquering the territories that are now Switzerland, Austria, and Bulgaria. Only in Germania did Roman troops meet defeat, when three legions were slaughtered in the Teutoburg Forest in 9 C.E., a devastating setback that convinced Augustus to hold the Roman borders at the Rhine and Danube Rivers. Augustus established new colonies in these provinces, encouraging the emigration of Rome's urban and rural poor. This not only alleviated social tensions but also promoted the integration of the Roman heartland with its far-flung hinterland. Augustus also allowed older cities and provinces more substantial rights of self-government than they had enjoyed before.

The Legacy of Augustus

When Octavian died in 14 C.E., he was not only *caesar*, *imperator*, and *augustus*; he was *pontifex maximus* ("high priest") and *pater patriae* ("father of the fatherland"). He was even deified by the Senate, which had also deified Julius Caesar at Augustus's urging. These titles were passed on to his successors, as was the system of government he had devised. And even those who mourned the passing of the republic and loathed these displays of imperial *hubris* had to admit that the system worked. Rome would enjoy nearly two centuries of peace, prosperity, and stability because of it.

The true test of any political institution's strength is its capacity to survive incompetent officeholders. Aside from one brief period of civil war in 68 C.E., the transition of power between Augustan emperors was generally peaceful, and the growing imperial bureaucracy could manage affairs even when individual emperors proved vicious or ineffectual, as was the notorious Caligula (r. 37–41 C.E.). Nevertheless, the fact that Rome had become an autocratic state became harder and harder to conceal. Many of Augustus's successors were heavy-handed and had difficult relationships with the Senate; and because the historians of this era were invariably members of the senatorial elite, they had a vested interest in sullying the reputations of these emperors. Hence, the skilled administrators Tiberius (14–37 C.E.) and Claudius (41–54 C.E.) were accused by their biographers of sexual perversion on the one hand and idiocy on the other. Nero (54–68 C.E.) and Domitian (81–96 C.E.) were also reviled by the aristocracy but

HADRIAN'S WALL. Stretching 73.5 miles across northern England, this fortification (begun in 122 C.E.) marked the frontier of the Roman province of Britannia as established by the emperor Hadrian. (A later wall, built farther north by Antoninus Pius in 142 C.E., was quickly abandoned.) Long stretches of the wall still exist, as do many of the forts built along it. The tree in this photograph stands on the site of a "mile castle," one of the smaller watchtowers built at intervals of a Roman mile and garrisoned by sentries.

THE ROMAN EMPIRE AT ITS GREATEST EXTENT, 97–117 C.E. ▪ *How much farther north and west does the empire now reach, compared with its earlier extent (see map on page 158)?* ▪ *How did geography influence the process of expansion?* ▪ *How did it dictate the limits of expansion?* ▪ *For example, what role do major river systems seem to play?*

popular among the Roman people and in the provinces. Indeed, Domitian's needed reforms of provincial government and his blatant disregard for senatorial privilege account for both the Senate's hostility and his subjects' approval.

The height of the Augustan system is generally considered to be the era between 96 and 180 C.E., often known as the reign of the "Five Good Emperors": Nerva (96–98 C.E.), Trajan (98–117 C.E.), Hadrian (117–138 C.E.), Antoninus Pius (138–161 C.E.), and Marcus Aurelius (161–180 C.E.). All were capable politicians, and since none but the last had a son that survived him, each adopted a worthy successor—a wise practice that allowed this generation of rulers to avoid the messy family dysfunctions that absorbed Augustus and his immediate heirs. They also benefited from the fact that Rome had few external enemies left. The Mediterranean was under the control of a single power for the first (and only) time in history. On land, Roman officials ruled from Britain to Persia. A contemporary orator justly boasted that "the whole civilized world lays down the arms which were its ancient burden, as if on holiday. . . . [A]ll places

are full of gymnasia, fountains, monumental approaches, temples, workshops, schools." The continual bloodshed of civil wars and of Augustus's reign of terror had abated. Now was the time of the **Pax Romana**, the Roman Peace.

MAKING THE WORLD ROMAN

Occasionally, the Roman Peace was broken. In Britannia, Roman legions had to put down a rebellion led by the Celtic warrior queen Boudica (d. 60/61 C.E.), which ended in a massacre of indigenous tribes and cost the lives of thousands of Britons. Another rebellion was violently quashed in Judea, the most restive of all the Roman provinces, leading to the destruction of the Temple at Jerusalem in 70 C.E. In 135 C.E., a second Jewish rebellion completed the destruction of the city. Although it was refounded by Hadrian as Aelia Capitolina, a colony for veterans of Rome's army, Jews were forbidden to settle there (see Chapter 6).

Two Views of Augustus's Rule

The emperor Augustus was a master propagandist with an unrivaled capacity for presenting his own actions in the best possible light. This list of his deeds was written by Augustus himself and was displayed on two bronze pillars set up in the Roman forum. The second excerpt is by the senatorial historian Tacitus (c. 56–117 C.E.). Writing in the first decades of the second century C.E., he began his chronicle of imperial rule, Annals, with the death of Augustus a century earlier.

Augustus Speaks for Himself

Below is a copy of the accomplishments of the deified Augustus by which he brought the whole world under the empire of the Roman people, and of the moneys expended by him on the state and the Roman people.

1. At the age of nineteen, on my own initiative and at my own expense, I raised an army by means of which I liberated the Republic, which was oppressed by the tyranny of a faction.

2. Those who assassinated my father I drove into exile, avenging their crime by due process of law.

3. I waged many wars throughout the whole world by land and by sea, both civil and foreign....

* * *

5. The dictatorship offered to me . . . by the people and by the Senate . . . I refused to accept.... The consulship, too, which was offered to me . . . as an annual office for life, I refused to accept.

6. [T]hough the Roman Senate and people together agreed that I should be elected sole guardian of the laws and morals with supreme authority, I refused to accept any office offered me which was contrary to the traditions of our ancestors.

7. I have been ranking senator for forty years.... I have been *pontifex maximus*, augur, member of the college of fifteen for performing sacrifices, member of the college of seven for conducting religious banquets, member of the Arval Brotherhood, one of the *Titii sodales*, and a *fetial* [all priestly offices].

* * *

9. The Senate decreed that vows for my health should be offered up every fifth year by the consuls and priests.... [T]he whole citizen body, with one accord, ... prayed continuously for my health at all the shrines.

* * *

17. Four times I came to the assistance of the treasury with my own money . . . providing bonuses for soldiers who had completed twenty or more years of service.

* * *

20. I repaired the Capitol and the theater of Pompey with enormous expenditures on both works, without having my name inscribed on them. I repaired . . . the aqueducts which were falling into ruin in many places.... I repaired eighty-two temples.... I reconstructed the Flaminian Way....

* * *

34. [H]aving attained supreme power by universal consent, I transferred the state from my own power to the control of the Roman Senate and people.... After that time I excelled all in authority, but I possessed no more power than the

Such rebellions were not the norm, however. Although the Roman Empire had been achieved by conquest, it was not maintained by force. Instead, Rome controlled its territories by offering incentives for assimilation. Local elites were encouraged to adopt Roman modes of education, behavior, and dress in order to gain access to political office. Local gods became Roman gods and were adopted into the Roman pantheon of divinities. In the Hellenistic kingdoms, as we have seen, Greek settlers often adopted the exotic gods they encountered, and assimilated into cosmopolitan societies, while at the same time spreading Greek culture and values.

others who were my colleagues in each magistracy.

35. At the time I wrote this document I was in my seventy-sixth year.

Source: "Res Gestae Divi Augusti," in *Roman Civilization, Sourcebook II: The Empire*, eds. Naphtali Lewis and Meyer Reinhold (New York: 1966), pp. 9–19.

The Historian Tacitus Evaluates Augustus's Reign

Intelligent people praised or criticized Augustus in varying terms. One opinion was as follows. Filial duty and a national emergency, in which there was no place for law-abiding conduct, had driven him to civil war—and this can be neither initiated nor maintained by decent methods. He had made many concessions to Antony and to Lepidus for the sake of vengeance on his father's murderers. When Lepidus grew old and lazy, and Antony's self-indulgence got the better of him, the only possible cure for the distracted country had been government by one man. However, Augustus had put the State in order not by making himself king or dictator but by creating the Principate. The empire's frontiers were on the ocean, or on distant rivers. Armies, provinces, fleets, the whole system was interrelated. Roman citizens were protected by the law. Provincials were decently treated. Rome itself had been lavishly beautified. Force had been sparingly used—merely to preserve peace for the majority.

The opposite view went like this. Filial duty and national crisis had been merely pretexts. In actual fact, the motive of Octavian, the future Augustus, was lust for power. Inspired by that, he had mobilized ex-army settlers by gifts of money, raised an army—while he was only a half-grown boy without any official status—won over a consul's brigade by bribery, pretended to support Sextus Pompeius [the son of Pompey], and by senatorial decree usurped the status and rank of a praetor. Soon both consuls . . . had met their deaths—by enemy action; or perhaps in the one case by the deliberate poisoning of his wound, and in the other at the hand of his own troops, instigated by Octavian. In any case, it was he who took over both their armies. Then he had forced the reluctant Senate to make him consul. But the forces given him to deal with Antony he used against the State. His judicial murders and land distributions were distasteful even to those who carried them out. True, Cassius and Brutus died because he had inherited a feud against them; nevertheless, personal enmities ought to be sacrificed to the public interest. Next he had cheated Sextus Pompeius by a spurious peace treaty, Lepidus by spurious friendship. Then Antony, enticed by treaties and his marriage with Octavian's sister, had paid the penalty of that delusive relationship with his life. After that, there had certainly been peace, but it was a bloodstained peace. . . . And gossip did not spare his personal affairs—how he had abducted [Livia] the wife of Tiberius Claudius Nero, and asked the priests the farcical question whether it was in order for her to marry while pregnant. Then there was the debauchery of his friend Publius Vedius Pollio. But Livia was a real catastrophe, to the nation, as a mother and to the house of the Caesars as a stepmother.

Source: Tacitus, *Annals* I.9–10. Based on *Tacitus: The Annals of Imperial Rome*, trans. Michael Grant (New York: 1989), pp. 37–39.

Questions for Analysis

1. How does Augustus organize his list, and why? What does he leave out, and what does he choose to emphasize?

2. Tacitus presents two contrasting views of Augustus's motives. Which does he himself seem to believe? How does his account complement or undermine that of Augustus himself?

3. Could you write a new account of Augustus's life making use of both sources? How would you strike a balance between them? What would your own conclusion be?

And yet assimilation could work both ways in Roman colonies, too. Tens of thousands of army veterans settled in the provinces, marrying local women and putting down local roots. It was common for soldiers born in Syria or North Africa to end their days peacefully in northern Gaul or Pannonia (modern Hungary). In Camulodunum (now Colchester, England), the gravestone of a legionnaire called Longinus sketches a typical career: born in Serdica (modern Sofia, in Bulgaria) to a local man named Maturus, he rose through the ranks to become a sergeant of the First Thracian Cavalry under Claudius and one of the first Roman colonists of Britannia.

Rights of citizenship were also extended, and able provincials could rise far in the imperial government. Some, like the emperors Trajan and Hadrian—both raised in Hispania—came to control it. Even the outer fringes of the empire, areas not incorporated into provinces, need to be understood as part of Rome's orbit. Although historians speak of the empire's "borders" for the sake of convenience, these were permeable zones of intensive interaction. Roman influence reached far beyond these fluid frontiers, into the heartland of Germania and lands far to the east. By the middle of the third century C.E., when some frontier garrisons were withdrawn to take part in wars within the empire itself, many of these peoples moved into the empire's settled provinces and became aspiring Romans (see Chapter 6).

Imperial Infrastructure and the Environment

Augustus liked to boast that he had found Rome a city of clay and left it a city of marble. It is certainly true that ambitious public works projects were initiated under the Principate; but in reality, marble was too precious to be used in common construction. Instead, marble panels or ornaments were added to the facings of buildings otherwise made of concrete. The Romans had discovered how to make this hard and reliable building material from a mixture of quicklime, volcanic ash, and pumice; and it was this—along with superior engineering skills—that allowed them to build massive structures such as the Colosseum, which could accommodate 50,000 spectators at gladiatorial combats.

Roman engineers also excelled in the building of roads and bridges, many of which were constructed by Rome's armies as they moved into new territories. Like the Persian Royal Road of the sixth century B.C.E. (or the German Autobahn of the 1930s and the interstate highways of the United States begun in the 1950s), roads have always been, first and foremost, a device for moving armies, and secondarily, for moving goods and people. Many of these Roman roads still survive or form the basis for modern European highways. In Britain, for example, the only major thoroughfares before the building of the high-speed motorways were Roman roads, to which the motorways now run parallel.

The inhabitants of Roman cities also enjoyed the benefits of a public water supply. By the early decades of the second century C.E., eleven aqueducts brought water into Rome from the nearby hills and provided the city with 300 million gallons per day—for drinking and bathing and for flushing a well-designed sewage system. These amenities were common in cities throughout the empire, and the homes of the wealthy even had indoor plumbing and central heating. Water was

also funneled into the homes of the rich for private gardens, fountains, and pools. The emperor Nero built a famous Golden House with special pipes that sprinkled his guests with perfume, baths supplied with medicinal waters, and a pond "like a sea." In addition, a spherical ceiling in the banquet hall revolved day and night like the heavens. "At last," said Nero on moving day, "I can live like a human being."

Throughout the empire, new Roman cities were constructed on a similar model and boasted the same amenities: public baths and fountains, amphitheaters, and paved roads. But not all would have had ready access to the resources, especially the water, required to supply them. Depending on the local climate and landscape, the need to provide imperial subjects with these amenities led to vast projects: swamps were drained, forests felled, mountains leveled, and valleys filled in. In the process, Roman urban planners and engineers temporarily or permanently altered the environment (see **Interpreting Visual Evidence** on page 176).

Imperial Entertainments

The cultural and intellectual developments that began in Rome during the late republic came to fruition during the Principate and are richly reflected in its literature. For the first time in its already long history, Latin began to replace

A BIRTHDAY INVITATION FROM ROMAN BRITAIN. The Roman fort at Vindolanda, just south of Hadrian's Wall (see page 168), was a major military outpost for decades, before and after the wall's construction between 120 and 130 C.E. It was also a lively social and cultural center where officers of the garrison were allowed to live with their wives and children. Beginning in the 1970s, archeologists began discovering well-preserved writings on small wood tablets: shopping lists, receipts, scribblings, letters. The letter above was originally hinged in the middle, so that the two halves could be sealed shut. In it, Claudia Severa invites her friend, Sulpicia Lepida, to attend her birthday celebration and sends greetings to her family from her own husband and baby son. While most of the writing is that of a professional scribe, Claudia has added her own note in the three short lines on the bottom of the right-hand tablet: "I shall hope to see you, sister. / Take care, sister, dearest soul / and just as I prosper be well." Several of Claudia's notes survive and are the earliest known Latin writings by a woman.

Greek as a language of learning and poetry. Roman literature of this era is conventionally divided into two periods: the Golden Age of writings produced under the more or less direct influence of Augustus, and the Silver Age of the first and early second centuries C.E. Most Golden Age literature is, not surprisingly, propagandistic, the purpose of which was to advertise and justify Augustus's achievements. The poetry of Publius Virgilius Maro (Virgil; 70–19 B.C.E.) is typical, and we have already noted his strategic use of "prophecy" to link the reign of Augustus to the story of Aeneas (see page 148). Other major poets of this age were Quintus Horatius Flaccus (Horace; 65–8 B.C.E.) and Publius Ovidius Naso (Ovid; 43 B.C.E.–17 C.E.): the former, a master of the lovely, short lyric; and the latter, our major source for Greek mythology, which he retold in a long poem, *Metamorphoses* ("Transformations"). Ovid was also a satirist, and his frank advice to his readers on the best way to attract women at the race course and his own (probably fictional) strategy for conducting an adulterous affair with the wife of a senator are exemplary of the writings that resulted in his banishment.

After Augustus's death, Roman authors had more license and became incisive cultural critics. The tales of Petronius and Apuleius describe the more bizarre and sometimes sordid aspects of Roman life, and the satirist Juvenal (60?–140 C.E.) wrote with savage wit about the moral degeneracy he saw in his contemporaries. A similar attitude toward Roman society characterizes the writings of Tacitus (55?–117? C.E.), an aristocratic historian who describes the events and people of his age largely for the purpose of passing judgment on them. His *Annals* offer a subtle but devastating portrait of the political system constructed by Augustus and ruled by his heirs; his *Germania* contrasts the manly virtues of northern barbarians with the effeminate vices of decadent fellow Romans. Like Juvenal, Tacitus was a master of ironic wit. He has a barbarian chieftain say, referring to Rome's conquests, "They create a wilderness and call it peace."

To many people today, the most repellent—or most fascinating and familiar—aspect of Roman culture during the Principate was its spectacular cruelty, exhibited (literally) in the public arenas erected in every Roman town.

THE COLOSSEUM. Constructed between 75 and 80 C.E., this was the first amphitheater in Rome purposely built to showcase gladiatorial combats. Prior to this, gladiators would often fight in improvised arenas in the Forum or other public places. ▪ *How does the fact of the Colosseum's relatively late construction change your perception of Roman history?*

The Architecture of Roman Water Management

The following excerpt comes from a remarkable handbook authored by Marcus Vitruvius Pollio (c. 75–c.14 B.C.E.), a Roman architect and civil engineer. In On Architecture, *Vitruvius offered a practical guide to all aspects of construction, from the choice of building site, to design, to contracting, to decoration. He described the proper way to plan a city and lay out its streets, the proper acoustics for a theater, and the best type of central heating for a house. In this section, Vitruvius tackles one of the most vital and difficult aspects of urban planning: the supply and distribution of water.*

here are three methods of conducting water: in channels through masonry conduits, or in lead pipes, or in pipes of baked clay. If using conduits, the masonry should be as solid as possible and the bed of the channel should have a gradient of not less than a quarter of an inch for every hundred feet; and the masonry structure should be arched over, so that the sun may not strike the water at all.

When the water has reached the city, build a reservoir with a distribution tank with three compartments to receive the water. . . . From this first compartment, pipes will be laid to all the basins and fountains in the city; from the second, to public baths which yield an annual income to the state; and from the third, to private houses, so that water for public use will not run short. For people will be unable to divert water illegally if they have only their own supplies from headquarters. This is the reason why I have made these divisions, and also in order that individuals who take water into their houses may by their taxes help to maintain the conducting of the water by the contractors.

If, however, there are hills between the city and the source of supply, subterranean channels must be dug, and brought to a level at the gradient mentioned above. If the bed is of tufa or other stone, let the channel be cut in it; but if it is of earth or sand, there must be vaulted masonry walls for the channel, and the water should thus be conducted, with shafts built at every two hundred and forty feet.

But if the water is to be conducted in lead pipes, first build a reservoir at the source; then, let the pipes have an interior area corresponding to the amount of water, and lay these pipes from this reservoir to the reservoir which is inside the city walls. . . . If there is a regular fall from the source to the city, without any intervening hills that are high enough to interrupt it, but with depressions in it, then we must build substructures to bring it up to the level as in the case of channels and conduits. If the distance round such depressions is not great, the water may be carried round circuitously; but if the valleys are extensive, the course will be directed down their slope. On reaching the bottom, a low substructure is built so that the water level there may continue as long as possible. It is also effective to build reservoirs at intervals of 24,000 feet, so that if a break occurs anywhere, it will not completely ruin the whole work, and the place where it has occurred can easily be found. . . .

But if we wish to spend less money, we must proceed as follows. Clay pipes with a skin at least two digits thick should be made, but these pipes should be tongued at one end so that they can fit into and join one another. . . . Clay pipes for conducting water have the following advantages. In the first place, if anything happens to them, anybody can repair the damage. Secondly, water from clay pipes is much more wholesome than that which is conducted through lead pipes, because lead is found to be harmful for the reason that white lead is derived from it, and this is said to be hurtful to the human system. . . . Hence, water ought by no means to be conducted in lead pipes, if we want to have it wholesome. That the taste is better when it comes from clay pipes may be proved by everyday life, for though our tables are loaded with silver vessels, yet everybody uses earthenware for the sake of purity of taste.

Source: Adapted from Vitruvius, *Ten Books on Architecture*, trans. M. H. Morgan (Cambridge, MA, 1916), pp. 244–47.

Questions for Analysis

1. Why does Vitruvius advise urban planners to distribute water in three separate ways? What does he reveal about the demand for water in a Roman city, and the tensions among different segments of the population? How do these revelations illuminate our understanding of Roman society?

2. Roman water management took an enormous toll on the environment. From your reading of Vitruvius, how do you think the construction of reservoirs and aqueducts affected the landscape? What might have been the unintended consequences of these engineering projects?

Gladiatorial contests were not new, but they were now presented in amphitheaters built to hold thousands. Everyone, even emperors, attended these events, and they became increasingly bloody and brutal as people demanded more and more innovative violence. Individual gladiators fought to the death with swords or the exotic weapons of their homelands. Teams of gladiators fought pitched battles, often reenacting historic Roman victories. Occasionally, a wealthy entrepreneur would fill an arena with water to stage a naval battle. Hundreds of men and women would die in these organized slaughters. On other occasions, hundreds of half-starved animals imported from Africa, India, or the forests of Germania would tear each other (or human victims) apart. When a fighter went down with a disabling wound, the crowd would be asked to decide whether to spare his life or kill him. If the arena floor became too slippery with blood, the action would stop—but only so that a fresh layer of sand could be spread over the gore so that the performance could continue.

Roman Visual Arts

Like Latin literature, Roman art assumed a distinctive character during the Principate. Before this time, most artworks displayed in Roman homes and public places were imported from Hellenistic capitals. Conquering armies also brought back wagonloads of statues, reliefs, and marble columns as

A ROMAN FLOOR MOSAIC. This fine mosaic from the Roman city of Londinium (London) shows Bacchus (Dionysos), the god of wine and revelry, mounted on a tiger. Tigers, native to India, were prized by animal collectors and were also imported for gladiatorial shows.

ROMAN AQUEDUCT IN SOUTHERN GAUL (PROVENCE). The massive arches shown here were originally part of a thirty-one-mile-long complex that supplied water to the city of Nemausus (Nîmes). It is now known as the Pont du Gard (Bridge of the Gardon), reflecting the use to which it was put after the aqueduct ceased to function, some eight centuries after its construction in the first century C.E. Some Roman aqueducts remained operational into the modern era: the one at Segovia, Spain, was still in use at the end of the twentieth century. ▪ *What does the magnitude and longevity of such projects tell us about Roman power and technology?*

Interpreting Visual Evidence

Roman Urban Planning

 Prior to Roman imperial expansion, most cities in the ancient world were not planned cities—with the exception of the new settlements established by Alexander the Great; notably, Alexandria in Egypt. Rome itself was not carefully planned but grew up over many centuries, expanding outward and up the slopes of its seven hills from the nucleus of the Forum. By the time of Augustus, it was a haphazard jumble of buildings and narrow streets. Outside of Rome, however, the efficiency of Roman government was in large part due to the uniformity of imperial urban planning. As their colonial reach expanded, the Romans sought to ensure that travelers moving within their vast domain would encounter the same amenities in every major city. They also wanted to convey, through the organization of urban landscape, the ubiquity of Roman authority and majesty.

A. Imperial Rome

B. Roman settlement in Aelia Capitolina (Jerusalem) after 135 C.E.

plunder from Greece, Egypt, and western Asia. These became the property of the wealthy, and as the demand for such works increased, hundreds of copies were made by Roman artisans. In many cases, these copies proved more durable than their originals. (In Chapter 4, we were able to examine the lost Aphrodite of Knidos, courtesy of Roman sculptors.)

Encouraged by the patronage of Augustus and his successors, artists began to experiment with more distinctively Roman styles and subjects. The relief sculpture of this period is particularly notable for its delicacy and naturalism, and sculptors also became adept at portraiture. On their coins, emperors were portrayed very much as they looked in real life; and since the matrices for coins were recut annually, we can trace on successive issues a ruler's receding hairline or his advancing double chin.

Painting and mosaic, however, were the Romans' most original and intimate arts. Romans loved intense colors, and those who could afford it surrounded themselves with brilliant wall paintings and mosaics made of tiny fragments of glass and stone, which were often set into the floors of houses and public baths or formed the centerpieces of gardens. Lavish mosaics have been found in the remains of Roman villas in all the territories of the empire, and similar design features indicate that many were mosaic "kits" that could be ordered from a manufacturer, who would ship out all the necessary components along with a team of workmen to assemble them.

Questions for Analysis

1. Look closely at the map of Rome (map A). How did topographical features— such as the river Tiber and the seven hills—determine the shape and layout of the city? What are the major buildings and public areas? What were the functions of these spaces? What do they reveal about Roman society and values?

2. Compare the plan of Rome with those of Roman London (map C) and Roman Jerusalem (map B). Which features do all three have in common, and why? Which features are unique to each place? What might these unique features reveal about the different regions of the empire and the needs of the different cities' inhabitants?

3. Given that all Roman cities share certain features, what message(s) were Roman authorities trying to convey to inhabitants and travelers through urban planning? Why, for example, would they have insisted on rebuilding Jerusalem as a Roman city after the rebellion of 135 C.E.?

C. London under the Romans, c. 200 C.E.

The Reach of Roman Law

As impressive and ingenious as Roman architecture and engineering are, the most durable and useful of this civilization's legacies is its system of law. Over the course of several centuries, the primitive legal code of the Twelve Tables was largely replaced by a series of new precedents and principles. These reflect the changing political climate of Rome and the needs of its diverse and ever-growing population. They also reveal the influence of new philosophies, especially Stoicism; the decisions of specific judges; and the edicts of magistrates called *praetors*, who had the authority to define and interpret law in particular cases and issue instructions to judges.

The most sweeping legal changes occurred during the Principate. This was partly because the reach of Roman law had to match the reach of the empire, which now extended over a much wider field of jurisdiction. While governors and other local officials sometimes asked the emperor's advice about legal matters, most of the cases they had to adjudicate could not wait for directives from Rome; there had to be administrative structures and guidelines already in place. These needs drove a rapid development in Roman legal thought and practice during these years of imperial expansion. Augustus and his successors appointed a small number of professional jurists to deliver official opinions on the issues most frequently raised in the courts, in order to create a more standardized body of law.

The five most prominent of these jurists flourished in the second century C.E.: Gaius (only this most common of his names is known), Domitius Ulpianus (Ulpian), Modestinus, Aemelius Papinianus (Papinian), and Paulus. Although most of them came to hold high offices, they gained their reputations primarily as lawyers and commentators. Taken together, their legal opinions constitute the first philosophy of law and the foundation for all subsequent jurisprudence, a word derived from the Latin phrase meaning "legal wisdom."

As developed by the jurists, Roman law comprised three great branches or divisions: civil law, the law of nations, and natural law. Civil law was the law of Rome and its citizens, both written and unwritten. It included the statutes of the Senate, the decrees of the emperor, the edicts of magistrates, and ancient customs that had the force of law (such as the *mos maiorum*). The law of nations was not specific to Rome but extended to all people of the world regardless of their origins and ethnicity. It was the precursor of international law. This law authorized and regulated slavery; protected private ownership of property; and defined the mechanisms of purchase and sale, partnership, and contract. It was not superior to civil law but supplemented it. It applied especially to those inhabitants of the empire who were not citizens, as well as to all foreigners.

The most interesting—and in many ways the most important—branch of Roman law was natural law, a product not of judicial practice but of legal philosophy. Roman Stoics, following in the footsteps of Cicero, posited that nature itself is rationally ordered and that careful study will reveal the laws by which the natural world operates, including the nature of justice. They affirmed that all men are by nature equal and entitled to certain basic rights that governments have no authority to transgress. "True law," Cicero had said, "is right reason consonant with nature, diffused among all men, constant, eternal." Accordingly, no person or institution has the authority to infringe on this law, repeal it, or ignore it. This law supersedes any state or ruler, and a ruler who transgresses it is a tyrant.

Although jurists did not regard the philosophical concept of natural law as an automatic limitation on the workings of civil law, they did uphold it as an ideal. The practical law applied in local Roman courts often bore little resemblance to the law of nature, yet the development of the concept of abstract justice as a fundamental principle was one of the noblest achievements of Roman civilization. It gave us the doctrine of human rights—even if it did not end abuses of those rights.

CONCLUSION

The resemblances between Rome's history and those of Great Britain and the United States have often been noted. Like the

After You Read This Chapter

 Go to **INQUIZITIVE** to see what you've learned—and learn what you've missed—with personalized feedback along the way.

REVIEWING THE OBJECTIVES

- The founding of the Roman Republic was both a cherished myth and a series of events. What factors contributed to this unique system of government?
- The shared identity and values of the Roman people differed in many ways from those of other ancient civilizations. What were some of these major differences?
- Rome's population was divided among classes of people who often struggled with each other for power. Identify these classes and their points of contention.
- The expansion of Rome's empire had a profound impact on Roman society. Why?
- The establishment of the Principate ushered in a new era in the history of Rome. What events led to this change?

British Empire, the **Roman Empire** was founded on conquest and overseas colonization intended to benefit both the homeland and its colonial subjects, who were seen as beneficiaries of the metropolis's "civilizing mission." Like America's economy, the Roman economy evolved from agrarianism to a complex system of domestic and foreign markets, leading to problems of unemployment, gross disparities of wealth, and vulnerability to financial crisis. And like both the British and the American empires, the Roman Empire justified itself by celebrating the peace its conquests allegedly brought to the world.

Ultimately, however, such parallels break down when we remember that Roman civilization differed profoundly from any society of the modern world. It was not an industrialized society. Its government never pretended to be representative of all its citizens. Roman class divisions are not directly comparable with ours. The Roman economy rested on slavery to a degree unmatched in any modern state. As a result, technological advances were not encouraged, social stratification was extreme, and gender relations were profoundly unequal. Religious practice and political life were inseparable.

Nevertheless, the civilization of ancient Rome continues to structure our everyday lives in ways so profound that they can go unnoticed. Our days are mapped onto the Roman calendar. The Constitution of the United States is largely modeled on that of the republic, and Roman architecture survives in the design of our public buildings.

Roman law forms the basis of most European legal codes, and American judges still cite Gaius and Ulpian. Virtually all modern commemorative sculpture is inspired by Roman sculpture, and Roman authors continue to set the standards for prose composition in many Western countries. Indeed, most European languages are either derived from Latin (Romance languages are so called because they are "Roman-like") or have borrowed Latin grammatical structures or vocabulary (German, for example). As we shall see in the following chapters, the organization of the Roman Catholic Church can be traced back to the structure of the Roman state. Even today, the pope bears the title of Rome's high priest, *pontifex maximus*.

Perhaps the most significant of all Rome's contributions was its role as mediator between Europe and the civilizations of the ancient Mediterranean world and western Asia. Had Rome's empire not come to encompass much of Europe, there would be no such thing as the concept of Western civilization and no shared ideas and heritage to link us to those distant places and times. Although we will pursue the history of Rome's fragmentation and witness the emergence of three different civilizations in the territories once united by its empire, we will see that they all shared a common cultural inheritance. In that sense, the Roman Empire did not collapse but was transformed. The factors driving that transformation will be the subject of Chapter 6.

PEOPLE, IDEAS, AND EVENTS IN CONTEXT

- In what ways were the early Romans influenced by their **ETRUSCAN** neighbors and by their location in central Italy?
- What were the components of the **ROMAN REPUBLIC**'s constitution? What was the relationship between **ROMAN CITIZENSHIP** and the **ROMAN ARMY** in this era?
- How do the stories of **AENEAS, LUCRETIA,** and **CINCINNATUS** reflect core Roman values? How did those values, summarized in the phrase **MOS MAIORUM**, set the Romans apart from the other civilizations we have studied?
- Why did the Romans come into conflict with **CARTHAGE**? How did the **PUNIC WARS** and Rome's other conquests change the balance of power in the Mediterranean?
- How did imperialism and contact with **HELLENISTIC CULTURE** affect the core values of Roman society, its economy, and its political system? What role did **SLAVERY** play in this civilization?
- What were the major crises of the late republic? What were the means by which ambitious men gained power? How did **JULIUS CAESAR** emerge triumphant, and why was he assassinated?
- In what ways did the **PRINCIPATE** differ from the **ROMAN REPUBLIC**? What were the new powers of the **EMPEROR**, and how did **AUGUSTUS** use these powers?
- How did the Romans consolidate their **EMPIRE** during the *PAX ROMANA*? By what means did they spread Roman culture?

THINKING ABOUT CONNECTIONS

- Polybius believed that the Roman Republic would last forever, because it fused together aspects of monarchy, aristocracy, and polity. What were the chief factors that led to its demise in the first century B.C.E.? Could these have been avoided? If so, how?
- In what ways does the Roman Empire share the characteristics of earlier empires, especially that of Alexander? In what ways does it differ from them?
- The Roman Empire could be said to resemble our own civilization in different ways. What features does the United States share with the republic today? With the Principate? What lessons can we draw from this resemblance?

CONSTANTINVS MINOR IMPERATOR
HERACLII ET TIBERII IMPERATOR
AR
COP
VS
PRIVILEGIA

Before You Read This Chapter

STORY LINES

- In a little over three centuries, Christianity grew from obscure beginnings in a small Roman province to become the official religion of the empire.

- Meanwhile, the Roman Empire was becoming too large and diverse to be governed by a single, centralized authority. Significant political, military, and economic changes occurred during the third century in response to these challenges.

- In the fourth century, the founding of a new capital at Constantinople shifted the focus of imperial administration to the eastern territories of the Roman Empire, while mass migrations of frontier peoples created new settlements within the western half of the empire.

- Christianity's eventual association with political power changed the religion in profound ways. At the same time, Christian intellectuals adapted Rome's traditional culture to meet Christian needs.

CHRONOLOGY

c. 4 B.C.E.– c. 30 C.E.	Lifetime of Jesus
46–67 C.E.	Paul's missionary career
66–70	Jewish rebellion
132–135	Expulsion of Jews from Jerusalem
203	Death of Perpetua at Carthage
235–284	Rule of the "barracks emperors"
284–305	Diocletian divides the empire
312	Constantine's victory at the Milvian Bridge
313	Edict of Milan
325	Council of Nicea convened
c. 370–430	Careers of Jerome, Ambrose, and Augustine
c. 376	Frontier migrations begin
391	Pagan religion outlawed
410	Visigoths sack Rome
476	Odovacar deposes Romulus Augustulus
493–526	Rule of Theodoric the Ostrogoth
c. 500–583	Careers of Boethius, Benedict, and Cassiodorus

The Transformation of Rome

I n the year 203 C.E., a young woman, Vivia Perpetua, was brought before the Roman governor at Carthage. She was twenty-two years old, well educated, and from a respectable family. At the time of her arrest she had an infant child she was still nursing. She also had two brothers (one of whom was arrested with her) and a father who doted on her. She must have had a husband, one presumes, but he is conspicuously absent from the firsthand account of her experiences. Perpetua herself says nothing about him, though she says a great deal about her father's grief and the efforts he made to intercede on her behalf. Not only did he beg the judge for mercy, he begged his daughter to confess so that her life could be spared. He admitted to having loved her more than her brothers and blamed himself for the liberal education he had given her. Clearly, he had failed as a father, for a Roman *paterfamilias* should never suffer humiliation through a daughter's conduct; he should kill her with his own hands if she has disgraced the family.

For Perpetua's crime was terrible: it was not only treason against the Roman state but also an act of gross impiety toward her father, her family, and her ancestors. Worse, it was punishable by a death so debasing that it was reserved for slaves, barbarian prisoners, and hardened criminals. It was inconceivable that a respectable Roman matron would be stripped naked before a holiday crowd and mauled by wild beasts in the arena of her own city. But that was the death Perpetua died. Perpetua was a Christian.

Early Christianity posed a challenge to the Roman Empire and its core values at almost every level, a challenge exemplified by Vivia Perpetua. To be a Christian was to be, by definition, an enemy of Rome, because Christians refused to venerate the emperor as the embodiment of Rome's gods; denying his association with divinity meant denying his authority. Moreover, the Christ whom Christians worshiped had himself been declared a criminal, a political insurgent, and had been duly tried and put to death by the Roman state. Also disturbing was the way Christians flouted the conventions of Roman society. Perpetua was young, yet she disobeyed her father and ancestors. She was well born, yet she chose to endure the filth of a common jail. She was a woman, yet she denied the authority of men and renounced her femininity, dying in the dust like a gladiator. If this was what it meant to be a Christian, then being a Christian was incompatible with being a Roman.

How, then, did a Roman emperor become a Christian just a few centuries after Christ's death—and just a century or so after Perpetua's? What changes did both Rome and Christianity have to undergo for this to happen? And what other forces were at work, within the empire and beyond its borders, that helped bring this about?

The Rome in which Perpetua was raised stretched from central Asia to the British Isles, from the Rhine to her own province of North Africa. But as we shall see, the governance of this enormous state and its diverse population was straining the bureaucracy that had been built on the foundations of the old republic. By the end of the third century C.E., it was increasingly obvious that Rome's western and eastern provinces could not be controlled by a single centralized authority. During the fourth century, Rome itself ceased to be the capital and hub of the empire; it now shared its prestige with the new city of Constantinople, named by the Christian emperor who founded it. At the same time, Rome's settled provinces were coming under increased pressure from groups of people who had long lived along its borders but were now moving from the periphery to the center. These new peoples would challenge what it meant to be Roman and contribute to the transformation of the Roman world.

THE CHALLENGE OF CHRISTIANITY

Like the Hebrew monotheism that undergirds Judaism or the central tenets of Zoroastrianism (see Chapter 2), Christianity was—and is—the product of historical processes.

It began with the teachings of Jesus, who lived and worked among his fellow Jews in rural Judea and his native Galilee around the year 30 C.E. It took root, however, in the Hellenistic world we studied in Chapter 4: the cosmopolitan, Greek-speaking cities around the eastern Mediterranean, which had now been absorbed into the Roman Empire.

The Career of Jesus

Yeshua bar Yosef (Joshua, son of Joseph), known to the Greeks as **Jesus**, is one of the few figures of the ancient world—certainly one of the few commoners—about whose life we know a great deal. The earliest writings that mention Jesus specifically are the letters of his follower Paul of Tarsus, a Hellenized Jew who was active during the 50s and 60s C.E. (see page 185). There are also many different narratives of Jesus' life and teachings, most written between c. 70 and 100 C.E. Eventually, four such accounts were included in the "New Testament," a collection of Christian scriptures appended to the Greek text of the Hebrew Bible, which Christians call the "Old Testament." In their original Greek, these accounts were called *evangelia* ("good messages"); we know them as *Gospels*, an Old English word that means the same thing.

Jesus was born around the year 4 B.C.E. (He was not born precisely in the first year of the Common Era as we now reckon it, because when a Christian monk called Dionysius Exiguus first began to reckon time "in the year of Our Lord," or *Anno Domini*, during the sixth century, he made some mistakes.) When Jesus was around thirty years old, he was endorsed by a Jewish preacher of moral reform, John the Baptist, whom some considered to be a prophet. Thereafter, Jesus traveled widely around the rural areas of Galilee (his home province) and Judea, preaching and displaying unusual healing powers. He accumulated a number of disciples, some of whom had political ambitions.

Around the year 30 C.E., Jesus staged an entry into Jerusalem during Passover, a major religious holiday that brought large crowds to the city. This move was interpreted as a bid for political power by the Roman colonial government and the high-ranking Jews of the Temple. Three of the Gospel accounts state that Jesus also drew attention to himself by attacking merchants and moneychangers associated with the Temple. The city's religious leaders therefore arrested him and turned him over to the Roman governor, Pontius Pilatus (Pilate), for sentencing.

Pilate's main concern was to preserve peace during a volatile religious festival. He knew that his authority depended on maintaining good relations with local Jewish elites and with Herod Antipas, who ruled the province of Galilee as a client king of the empire. Because Jesus was a resident of Galilee, not a citizen of Roman Judea, Pilate sent Jesus to Herod for sentencing. But Herod promptly sent him back, indicating that dealing with Jesus fell under Roman jurisdiction. Pilate was thus in a tough position. It had been rumored that Jesus planned to lead a rebellion, and something similar had happened in the second century B.C.E., when a group of Jews had overthrown the rule of the Persian Seleucid empire and established Judea as an autonomous kingdom. Judea had come under Roman control only in 63 B.C.E., and many Jews resented Roman subjugation.

Pilate, who would have been mindful of all this, chose to make an example of Jesus and condemned him to death by crucifixion, which was the standard criminal penalty for non-Romans found guilty of sedition against Rome. Jesus'

JUDEA AND GALILEE IN THE TIME OF JESUS. Judea was a Roman colony and Galilee was a province ruled by a client king, Herod, loyal to Rome. ▪ *What were the major cities in first-century c.e. Judea?* ▪ *What do they indicate about the effects of Roman occupation on the lives of Jews?* ▪ *Given what you have learned about their history, why do you think some Jews would resist Roman rule?*

execution might have been the end of the story if not for his followers, who asserted that he had risen from the dead before being taken up into heaven. Moreover, they said that Jesus had promised to return again at the end of time.

Interpreting the Life and Death of Jesus

In 1947, an extraordinary cache of ancient parchment and papyrus scrolls was discovered in a cave near Qumran, on the shores of the Dead Sea. Over the course of the ensuing decade, eleven more caves were found to house similar texts. Only since the mid-1980s, however, have these Dead Sea Scrolls been widely available to scholars, and more texts continue to be discovered. Written in Hebrew, Greek, and Aramaic, at various times between 100 B.C.E. and 70 C.E., they have revolutionized our understanding of Judaism in the lifetime of Jesus: a period known as "Second Temple" Judaism, in reference to the Jewish traditions and culture that had emerged after the reconstruction of the Temple at Jerusalem in the sixth century B.C.E. (see Chapter 2). What these documents show is the diversity of religious practice and the competition among groups of Jews during this period.

When Jesus was born, Roman rule in Palestine was relatively new and still controversial, as we noted previously. Many Jews were content to live under Rome's protection—especially the urban elite, who had been Hellenized for generations and reaped the rewards of participation in the Roman economy and administration. But many rural communities and the urban poor were rebellious, disadvantaged by Roman rule, and hoped for a *messiah*: a divinely inspired leader who would establish a new, autonomous Jewish kingdom. The most extreme were the Zealots, who eventually led two armed revolts against Roman rule. The first, between 66 and 70 C.E. (a generation after Jesus' death), ended in the Romans' destruction of the Temple. The second, in 132–135 C.E., caused the destruction of Jerusalem itself: the Romans expelled the entire Jewish population and razed the city to the ground. On its ruins, they built the colony of Aelia Capitolina (see Chapter 5).

This historical framework is essential to understanding the very different ways that the words and actions of Jesus were interpreted during his lifetime and after his death—especially since all the accounts of his life were written down after the destruction of the Temple in 70 C.E. and further influenced by later events.

In addition to the social and political unrest within the Jewish community at this time, there were significant religious divisions. The Temple priesthood was hereditary and controlled by a group known as the Sadducees. These elites collaborated closely with Rome (the high priest was

SPOILS FROM JERUSALEM. A bas-relief inside the triumphal Arch of Titus in the Roman Forum shows plundered treasures of the Temple at Jerusalem, including the menorah, being carried through Rome in triumph after the quashing of a Jewish rebellion in 70 C.E. ▪ *What message(s) did this image convey to viewers?*

even appointed by the Senate), and as a result of their overt political agenda, many Jews regarded them with suspicion. Their chief rivals were the Pharisees, preachers of religious doctrine who considered themselves heirs of the prophetic tradition of the ancient Hebrews. While the Sadducees claimed the right to control the interpretation of the Torah, the five books attributed to Moses, the Pharisees argued that Yahweh had given Moses an oral Torah as well as a written one, and that this oral traditon, handed down to them, taught how the laws of the Torah should be applied in daily life.

The Pharisees, accordingly, were quite flexible in their interpretation of religious law. For example, in order to allow neighbors to dine together on the Sabbath, when Jews were forbidden to work and could not even carry food outside their homes, the Pharisees ruled that an entire neighborhood could constitute a single household. They also believed in a life after death, a day of judgment, and the damnation or reward of individual souls. They actively sought out converts through preaching and looked forward to the imminent arrival of the promised messiah. The Sadducees, who had a vested interest in maintaining their privileged political status, interpreted the Torah more strictly and considered Judaism closed to anyone who had not been born a Jew.

Countering both of these dominant groups were the Essenes, a quasi-monastic faction that sought salvation through repentance, asceticism, and separation from their fellow Jews. Although some scholars see Essene influence behind the career of Jesus, his Jewish contemporaries probably saw Jesus as some sort of Pharisee: Jesus' emphasis on the ethical requirements of the law rather than its literal interpretation is reflected in many of his teachings. His apparent belief in life after death and the imminent coming of the "kingdom of God" also fits within a Pharisaic framework, as does his willingness to reach out to people beyond the Jewish community.

But Jesus seems to have carried these principles considerably further than did the Pharisees. For most ordinary Jews, religious observance consisted of going up to the Temple on holy days; paying the annual Temple tax; reciting the morning and evening prayers; and observing certain fundamental laws, such as circumcision (for men), ritual purity (especially for women), and prohibitions on the consumption of certain foods. Jesus deemphasized such observances, and it may have seemed that he wished to abolish them. But what made him most controversial was his followers' claim that he was the messiah sent to deliver Israel from its enemies.

After his death, these claims grew more assertive, yet they never persuaded more than a small minority of Jews. But

PAUL'S MISSIONARY JOURNEYS. Quite apart from its theological importance, Paul's career offers fascinating glimpses into the life of a Hellenized Roman citizen from one of the empire's eastern provinces. ▪ *What were the main phases of Paul's travels in the eastern Mediterranean?* ▪ *How were his itineraries shaped by geography and by various modes of transport?* ▪ *What conclusions about his mission can you draw from the extent of his travels and his major destinations?*

when his followers began to preach to non-Jewish audiences, they found many willing listeners. So they began to represent Jesus in terms that made sense to the Greek-speaking communities of the Hellenistic world, preaching that Jesus was not merely a messiah for the Jews but was the *Christos* ("anointed one" in Greek), the divine son of God who had suffered and died for the sins of all humanity. He had conquered death itself by rising from his tomb and, after appearing to his followers several times, ascended into heaven. He would soon return to judge all the world's inhabitants, and those who believed in him would be given eternal life.

Christianity in the Hellenistic World

This new understanding of Jesus' divinity was largely developed by his younger contemporary, **Paul of Tarsus**

(c. 10–c. 67 C.E.). Born in the capital city of the Roman province of Cilicia (now south-central Turkey) to a family of Pharisees, he was given the name Saul. The Acts of the Apostles, the continuation of Luke's Gospel and a major source for Saul's early life, records that he was dedicated to stamping out the cult of the crucified Jesus. But at some point in his mid-twenties— a few years after Jesus' death—he underwent a dramatic conversion experience. He changed his name to Paul and devoted the rest of his life to spreading the new faith to Greek-speaking, mainly non-Jewish, communities throughout the eastern half of the Roman Empire. Taking advantage of Roman imperial infrastructure—and his own privileges as a Roman citizen—he was able to travel up and down the coasts of Asia, Greece, and even to Rome itself, preaching the new faith in the old cities of the Hellenistic world. This purposeful attempt to win new religious converts was, in many ways, a very new development in the history of western civilizations.

Unlike Peter and some other early apostles (from the Greek word meaning "one who is sent forth"), Paul had never met Jesus. Instead, he claimed to have received a direct revelation of Jesus' teachings. This led to a number of major disputes, because Peter and his companions believed that followers of Jesus had to be Jews or converts to Judaism. Paul, however, declared that Jewish religious law was now irrelevant; Jesus had made a new covenant possible between God and humanity, and the old covenant between God and the Jews no longer applied. This position was vehemently opposed by the Jewish Christians of Jerusalem, a group led by Jesus' brother, James. But after a series of difficult debates that took place around 49 C.E., Paul's position triumphed. Although some early Christians would continue to obey Jewish law, most of the converts who swelled the movement were Gentiles (non-Jews). Paul began to call this new community of believers an *ekklesia*, the Greek word for an assembly (see Chapter 3); the Latinized form of this word is translated as "church."

The earliest converts to Christianity were attracted for a variety of reasons. Some were Hellenized Jews like Paul himself. Jewish communities existed in most major cities of the eastern Mediterranean, including Rome, and had already begun to adapt their lifestyles and beliefs through contact with other cultures. Christianity also appealed to groups of non-Jews, known as "God-fearers," who gathered around these Greek-speaking Jewish communities. God-fearers did not follow all the precepts of Jewish law, but they admired the Jews for their loyalty to ancestral tradition and their high ethical standards.

Christianity was also attractive to ordinary cosmopolitan Greeks. Some saw Jesus as living by Stoic principles (Chapter 4) or as the embodiment of Ahura-Mazda, the good god of Zoroastrianism (Chapter 2). Others were already devotees of mystery religions, like the very old cult of the Egyptian goddess Isis (Chapter 1) or the newer worship of the warrior god Mithras, popular among Rome's professional soldiers. Both of these religions revolved around stories of sacrifice, death, and regeneration and would have prepared their adherents to embrace the worship of Jesus. It was largely for the benefit of these converts that Christians began to practice elaborate initiation ceremonies such as baptism,

A FRESCO FROM THE CATACOMBS OF ROME. This image shows a *catachumen* (Greek for "instructed one") being baptized by the Holy Spirit in the form of an eagle. It is one of many paintings to be found in the ancient catacombs around Rome: subterranean burial and meeting places where Christians also hid during times of persecution. ■ *Why were such images important?*

PAUL OF TARSUS. Many ancient images of Paul survive, and all depict him with the same features: a gaunt face, balding head, pointed black beard, and intense dark gaze. In the summer of 2009, archaeologists working in the catacombs of Thekla (named after a holy woman and follower of Paul) discovered this faded fresco. It has been identified as the oldest known portrait of this formative Christian figure and can be dated to the fourth century C.E.

A CHRISTIAN LOVE FEAST. This fresco, another image from the catacombs, shows Christians celebrating a ritual feast. The inscription above it reads, "I join with you in love."
▪ *How would a Roman viewer interpret this scene?* ▪ *How might this interpretation differ from that of a Christian?*

a ritual purification common to many ancient religions and exemplified among Jews in the ministry of John the Baptist.

At the same time, there were significant differences between Christianity and these other religions. Most mystery cults stressed the rebirth of the individual through spiritual transformation, but Christianity emphasized the importance of community. By the middle of the second century, the Christian church at Rome had a recognizable structure, headed by a bishop (in Greek, *episcopos* or "overseer") and lesser office-holders, including priests, deacons, confessors, and exorcists. Women were extremely prominent in these churches, not only as patrons and benefactors (a role Roman women often played in religious cults) but also as officeholders.

This high status accorded to women was unusual. In other ancient religions, women could be priests and office-holders—but only in cults open solely to women; they never took precedence over men. Many cults, such as Mithraism, denied them access entirely. The fact that Christianity drew its adherents from a broad range of social classes also distinguished it from other cults, which were accessible mainly to those with money and leisure. In time, these unusual features were distorted by Christianity's detractors, who alleged that Christians were political insurgents like the Jesus they worshiped, that they engaged in illicit acts during "love feasts," or that they practiced human sacrifice and cannibalism.

As both Christianity and Judaism redefined themselves during the second and third centuries C.E., they grew further apart. Judaism was adapting to the Romans' destruction of the Temple and the mass exile of Jewish refugees from Jerusalem and surrounding provinces. By and large, the scholars who reshaped it during these difficult years ignored Christianity. It simply did not matter to them any more than did the cults of Mithras or Isis. Christians, however, could not ignore Judaism. Their religion rested on the belief that Jesus was the savior promised by God to Israel in the Hebrew Bible. The fact that so few Jews accepted this claim was a standing rebuke to their faith, one that threatened to undermine the credibility of the Christian message.

More Christians could have responded as did Marcion, a second-century Christian scholar, who declared that Jewish religious practices and the entire Hebrew Bible could be ignored. Most Christians, however, refused to abandon their religion's Jewish foundation. For them, the heroes of Jewish scripture prefigured Jesus, while the major events of Hebrew history could be read, allegorically, as Christian paradigms. Christ was the new Adam, reversing man's original sin; wood from the fateful Tree in Eden became the wood of the Cross on which Christ died. Christ, like Abel, had been slain at the hands of a brother, and his blood continued to cry out from the ground. Christ was the new Noah, saving Creation from its sins. Christ was prefigured in Isaac, in Joseph, in Moses. Furthermore, according to Christians, all the words of the Hebrew prophets point to Jesus, as do the Psalm and the Proverbs.

In short, Christian theologians argued that the Christian church was the true Israel and that when the Jews rejected Jesus, God rejected the Jews and made Christians his new chosen people. The Hebrew Bible was henceforth the Old Testament, vital to understanding Christianity but superseded by the New Testament. At the end of time, the Jews would see the error of their ways and convert. Until then, their only reason for existing was to testify to the truth of Christianity. From a Christian perspective, the Jews' own impiety had caused their exile from the Holy Land and would continue to bring suffering down on their descendants.

Christianity and the Roman State

As long as Christianity remained a minority religion within the Roman Empire, such attitudes had no effect on the

The Prosecution of a Roman Citizen

The Acts of the Apostles was a continuation of Luke's Gospel, written by the same author. It recounts the adventures and ministry of Jesus' original disciples and also follows the career of Paul, a Hellenized Jew who became a missionary to the Gentiles throughout the Roman world. It offers fascinating glimpses into the workings of the Roman legal system because Paul, depicted here as a Roman citizen, had special rights under Roman law (as Jesus had not). In this passage, Paul—who has been accused of treason against the emperor by a group of Pharisees—has been sent to Felix, the governor of Judea. These events took place between 57 and 59 C.E.

So the soldiers, according to their instructions, took Paul and brought him by night to [the city of] Antipatris. The next day, they let the horsemen go on with him, while they returned to the barracks. When they came to Caesarea and delivered the letter to the governor, they presented Paul also before him. On reading the letter, he asked what province he belonged to, and when he learned that he was from Cilicia he said, "I will give you a hearing when your accusers arrive." Then he ordered that he be kept under guard in Herod's headquarters.

Five days later, the high priest Ananias came down with some elders and an attorney, a certain Tertullus, and they reported their case against Paul to the governor. When Paul had been summoned, Tertullus began to accuse him, saying: "Your Excellency, because of you we have long enjoyed peace, and reforms have been made for this people because of your foresight. We welcome this in every way and everywhere with utmost gratitude. But, to detain you no further, I beg you to hear us briefly with your customary graciousness. We have, in fact, found this man a pestilent fellow, an agitator among all the Jews throughout the world, and a ringleader of the sect of the Nazarenes. He even tried to profane the temple, and so we seized him. By examining him yourself you will be able to learn from him concerning everything of which we accuse him." The Jews also joined in the charge by asserting that all this was true.

When the governor motioned to him to speak, Paul replied: "I cheerfully make my defense, knowing that for many years you have been a judge over this nation. As you can find out, it is not more than twelve days since I went up to worship in Jerusalem. They did not find me disputing with anyone in the temple or stirring up a crowd either in synagogues or throughout the city. Neither can they prove to you the charge that they now bring against me. But this I admit to you, that according to the Way, which they call a sect, I worship the God of our ancestors, believing everything laid down according to the law or written in the prophets. I have hope in God—a hope that they themselves also accept—that there will be a resurrection of both the righteous and the unrighteous. Therefore I do my best always to have a clear conscience toward God and all people. . . ."

But Felix, who was rather well informed about the Way, adjourned the hearing with the comment, "When Lysias the tribune comes down, I will decide your case." Then he ordered the centurion to keep him in custody, but to let him have some liberty and not to prevent any of his friends from taking care of his needs.

When some days later Felix came with his wife Drusilla, who was Jewish, he sent for Paul and heard him speak concerning faith in Christ Jesus. And as he discussed justice and self-control and future judgment, Felix was alarmed and said, "Go away for the present; when I have an opportunity I will summon you." At the same time he hoped that money would be given him by Paul. So he sent for him often and conversed with him. But when two years had elapsed, Felix was succeeded by Porcius Festus; and desiring to do the Jews a favor, Felix left Paul in prison.

Source: Acts of the Apostles 23:31–24:27, in *The New Oxford Annotated Bible*, New Revised Standard Version, ed. Bruce M. Metzger and Roland E. Murphy (New York: 1994).

Questions for Analysis

1. According to this account, what legal procedures are in place for dealing with any Roman citizen accused of a crime?

2. What seems to be the relationship between the Jewish elite of Judea and the Roman governor? What is the role of their spokesman, Tertullus?

3. What is the nature of the accusation against Paul, and how does he defend himself?

position of Jews under Roman rule. Judaism remained a legally recognized religion, and many Jews were further protected by their Roman citizenship. Indeed, the biblical book known as the Acts of the Apostles represents Paul as a Roman citizen who could not be summarily put to death (as the noncitizen Jesus had been) when brought up on charges of treason. Acts follows his progress through the Roman judicial system, until he is finally brought to trial at Rome and executed (by beheading) under Nero.

Even after their rebellion, the Jews of the Diaspora were allowed to maintain the special status they had always had under Roman rule and were not required, as other subject peoples were, to offer sacrifices to the emperor. As we have seen, nothing was more important to the Romans than *pietas* and respect for one's ancestors, and the Romans understood the Jews' traditions as a remarkable form of ancestor worship.

Christianity, in contrast, was a novelty religion. It carried neither the patina of antiquity nor the sanction of tradition—quite the contrary. It raised suspicions on many levels: it encouraged women and slaves to hold office and therefore to rise above their proper stations; it revolved around the worship of a criminal condemned by the Roman state; its secret meetings could be breeding grounds for rebellion. Nevertheless, the official attitude of the Roman state toward Christians was largely one of indifference. There were not enough of them to matter and only a few had any political power. During the first and second centuries C.E., therefore, Christians were tolerated by Roman officials, except when local magistrates chose to make an example of someone who flagrantly flouted authority—as Perpetua did.

THE CHALLENGE OF IMPERIAL EXPANSION

The emergence of Christianity within the Roman Empire coincided with the empire's most dramatic period of growth and with a growing variety of challenges. For a long time, Rome's emperors and administrators clung to the methods of governance that had been put in place under Augustus, methods based on a single centralized authority. The reality, however, was that Rome's empire was no longer centered on Rome, or even on Italy. It embraced ecosystems, linguistic groupings, ethnicities, cultures, economies, and political systems of vastly different kinds. More and more people could claim to be Roman citizens, and more and more people wanted a share of Rome's power. This placed enormous stress on the imperial administration as the centrifugal forces of Rome's own making constantly pulled resources into her

far-flung provinces, where cities had to be built, people governed, and communications maintained. The fact that the empire had few defensible borders was another problem. Hadrian had attempted to establish one after 122 C.E. by building a wall between Roman settlements in southern Britannia and the badlands of the northern tribes (see Chapter 5), but this act was more symbolic than effective.

For much of the second century, such stresses were masked by the peaceful transfer of power among the so-called Five Good Emperors: Nerva, Trajan, Hadrian, Antoninus Pius, and Marcus Aurelius. This harmonious state of affairs was partly accidental. Since none of these first four rulers had a surviving male heir, a custom developed whereby each adopted a young man of good family and trained the successor in the craft of government.

This sensible practice changed with the death of Marcus Aurelius in 180 C.E. Although he was the closest Roman equivalent to Plato's ideal of the philosopher-king, Marcus was not wise enough to recognize that his own son, Commodus, lacked the capacity to rule effectively. After his father's death, Commodus alienated the army by withdrawing from costly wars along the Danube. This move was also unpopular with the Senate, as were Commodus's violent tendencies and his scorn for the traditional norms of aristocratic conduct, including an alleged appearance as a gladiator in the Colosseum. In 192 C.E., a conspiracy was hatched inside his own palace, where he was strangled by his wrestling coach.

The Empire of the Severan Dynasty

Because Commodus had no obvious successor, the armies stationed in various provinces of the empire raised their own candidates. Civil war ensued, as it had during the crises of the late republic and in 68 C.E., when three men had struggled for imperial power. In this case, there were five major contenders. The eventual victor was a North African general, Septimius Severus (r. 193–211 C.E.).

Under Severus (*SEH-ver-uhs*) and his successors, the administration of Rome's empire changed to a greater extent than it had since the time of Augustus. In many respects, these changes were long overdue. Even the "Five Good Emperors" had been somewhat insulated from the realities of colonial rule. Many of them were able commanders, but they were not professional soldiers as Severus was. Another major difference was the fact that Severus had been born and raised in the North African town of Leptis Magna (now in Libya) and identified strongly with his father's Punic (Afro-Phonecian) ancestors, seemingly more than with his mother's patrician family. Unlike Trajan and Hadrian, who had also grown up in the provinces, Severus did not regard

Competing Viewpoints

The Development of an Imperial Policy toward Christians

It was not until the third century that the Roman imperial government began to initiate full-scale investigations into the activities of Christians. Instead, the official position was akin to a policy of "don't ask, don't tell." Local administrators handled only occasional cases, and they were often unsure as to whether the behavior of Christians was illegal or criminal. The following letter was sent to the emperor Trajan by Gaius Plinius Caecilius Secundus (Pliny the Younger), the governor of Bithynia-Pontus (Asia Minor), around 112 C.E. Pliny was anxious to follow proper procedures in dealing with the new sect and wanted advice about this. His letter indicates what Romans did and didn't know about early Christian beliefs and practices.

From Pliny to Trajan

It is my regular custom, my lord, to refer to you all questions which cause me doubt, for who can better guide my hesitant steps or instruct my ignorance? I have never attended hearings concerning Christians, so I am unaware what is usually punished or investigated, and to what extent. . . . In the meantime, this is the procedure I have followed in the cases of those brought before me as Christians. I asked them whether they were Christians. If they admitted it, I asked them a second and a third time, threatening them with execution. Those who remained obdurate I ordered to be executed, for I was in no doubt . . . that their obstinacy and inflexible stubbornness should at any rate be punished. Others similarly lunatic were Roman citizens, so I registered them to be sent back to Rome.

Later in the course of the hearings, as usually happens, the charge rippled outwards, and more examples appeared. An anonymous document was published containing the names of many. Those who denied that they were or had been Christians and called upon the gods after me, and with incense and wine made obeisance to your statue . . . and who moreover cursed Christ . . . I ordered to be acquitted.

Others, who were named by an informer, stated that they were Christians and then denied it. They said that they had been, but had abandoned their

Rome as the center of the universe, and the time he spent in the imperial capital as a young man seems to have convinced him that little could be accomplished there.

In fact, Severus represents the degree to which the Roman Empire had succeeded in making the world Roman—succeeded so well that Rome itself was becoming practically irrelevant. One could be as much a Roman in Britannia or Africa as in central Italy. Severus's second wife, Julia Domna, exemplifies this trend in a different way. Descended from the Aramaic aristocracy who ruled the Roman client kingdom of Emesa (Syria), her father was the high priest of its sun god, Ba'al. She was highly educated and proved an effective governer during her husband's almost perpetual absence from Rome.

Severus largely ignored the politics of the Senate and slighted what remained of its powers. He preferred to rule through the army, which he reorganized and expanded. Two of his reforms had long-term consequences. The first was a

drastic raise in army pay, probably as much as 100 percent, which had the effect of securing the soldiers' absolute loyalty and diminishing their need to augment their wages through plunder. The second was a relaxation of the long-standing rule forbidding soldiers to marry while still in service. This dispensation encouraged younger men—not just veterans—to put down roots in local communities and so implant Roman authority and identity. At the same time, though, it made them reluctant to move when their legion was called up. On the one hand, this domesticated the army (hitherto a highly mobile fighting machine) and may have made it less effective. On the other hand, it gave the army a stake in the peaceful governance of Rome's colonies and further contributed to the decentralization of power.

Severus spent most of his imperial career with his army. He died at Eboracum (York, England) in 211 C.E., after conducting a series of successful negotiations with Pictish allegiance some years previously. . . . They maintained, however, that all that their guilt or error involved was that they were accustomed to assemble at dawn on a fixed day, to sing a hymn antiphonally to Christ as God, and to bind themselves by an oath . . . to avoid acts of theft, brigandage, and adultery. . . . When these rites were completed, it was their custom to depart, and then reassemble again to take food, which was, however, common and harmless. They had ceased, they said, to do this following my edict, by which in accordance with your instructions I had outlawed the existence of secret brotherhoods. So I thought it all the more necessary to ascertain the truth from two maidservants [i.e., slaves], who were called deaconnesses, even by employing torture. I found nothing other than a debased and boundless superstition. . . .

From Trajan to Pliny

You have followed the appropriate procedures, my Secundus. . . . [N]o general rule can be laid down which would establish a definite routine. Christians are not to be sought out. If brought before you and found guilty, they must be punished, but in such a way that a person who denies that he is a Christian, and demonstrates this by his action . . . may obtain pardon for his repentance, even if his previous record is suspect. Documents published anonymously must play no role in any accusation, for they give the worst example, and are foreign to our age.

Source: Excerpted from *Pliny the Younger: The Complete Letters*, trans. P. G. Walsh (Oxford: 2006), pp. 278–79 (X.96–97).

Questions for Analysis

1. How does Pliny's treatment of Christians differ according to their social class? How does it differ from Felix's treatment of Paul (page 188)?

2. Why would Trajan insist that anonymous accusations, such as those Pliny mentions, not be used as evidence? Why was this "foreign to our age"?

3. What do you conclude from this exchange about the relationship between religion and politics under the Roman Empire?

---

tribes north of Hadrian's Wall. On his deathbed, he is reported to have said to his sons, "Get along together, keep the soldiers rich, and don't bother about anyone else." His elder son, Caracalla, didn't heed the first of these injunctions for long. By the end of the year, he had assassinated his brother, Geta, then attempted to erase him from the historical record by declaring a *damnatio memoriae* (literally, "a condemnation of memory"), banning the mention of Geta's name and defacing his image on public monuments. The second of his father's orders he obeyed in a certain sense, by extending the rights of Roman citizenship to everyone in the empire. This included the entire army in the franchise and increased the tax base. Such a move was beneficial in some respects, but it may also have cheapened Roman citizenship, which was no longer a prize to be won through service or the adoption of Roman values and manners. Another indication of Caracalla's populism was his sponsorship of the largest

THE EMPRESS JULIA DOMNA. This Roman coin, dating from about 200 C.E., is one of several issued in the name of Severus's powerful wife. As the coin's legend shows, she ruled as "Julia Augusta," names associated with the imperial family since the time of Augustus Caesar.

public baths ever constructed in Rome, an enormous complex that would have rivaled St. Peter's Basilica at the Vatican had it survived. (The sprawling remains can still be seen.) His father's final piece of advice helped to shorten Caracalla's reign significantly, since it exacerbated his already pronounced tendency to alienate everyone who disagreed with him. He was assassinated in 217 C.E.

Caracalla's true successor was his mother's sister, Julia Maesa, who ruled through his nominal heir and cousin, her adolescent grandson. This youth was known as Heliogabalus (or Elagabalus; r. 218–222 C.E.) because of his devotion to Ba'al. But when Heliogabalus caused controversy by attempting to

replace Jupiter, Rome's patron god, with a Latinized version of this eastern deity, Sol Invictus ("Invincible Sun"), his own grandmother engineered his assassination. Another of her grandsons, Alexander Severus (r. 222–235 C.E.), took his place.

Alexander, in turn, was ruled by his mother Julia Mamæa, the third in a succession of strong women behind the Severan dynasty. She even traveled with him on military campaigns. This eventually proved fatal for both. The new prominence of the army made Rome's legions engines of political advancement, even more than they had been under the dictators of the late republic. Many aspiring generals could harness this power and with it the support of their legions' provincial bases. In 235 C.E., in consequence, Alexander and his mother were murdered at Moguntiacum (Mainz, Germania), when the army of the region turned against them. Fifty years of civil unrest ensued.

The Test of Rome's Strength

From 235 to 284 C.E., there were no fewer than twenty-six "barracks emperors" in Rome: military commanders who, backed by a few loyal legions, struggled with each other and an array of problems. This period is sometimes called the "Third-Century Crisis" and interpreted as a time when the Roman Empire was nearly destroyed. It is more accurately interpreted as a time when the consequences of Roman expansion made themselves acutely felt. Those aspects of the empire that were strong survived, while those that had always been fragile were further strained.

For example, the disruptions of the mid-third century exposed weaknesses in the economic and administrative infrastructures. Inflation, caused by the devaluation of currency under Severus, drained Roman coinage of its value. Meanwhile, aspiring emperors levied exorbitant taxes on civilians in their provinces, as warfare among rival claimants and their armies destroyed crops and interrupted trade, causing food shortages. Because Rome itself was almost entirely dependent on Egyptian grain and other goods shipped in from the East, its inhabitants suffered accordingly. Poverty and famine even led to a new form of slavery in Italy, as free artisans, local businessmen, and small farmers were forced to labor on the estates of large landholders in exchange for protection and food.

In 251 C.E., a terrible plague, probably smallpox, swept through the empire's territories and recurred in some areas for almost two decades. A similar plague had ravaged Rome a century earlier, but its effects had been mitigated by sound governance. Now, with an estimated 5,000 people dying every day in the crowded city, people sought local scapegoats, and Christians were among those targeted. Beginning in the

THE EMPEROR SEPTIMIUS SEVERUS. This statue, carved during the emperor's lifetime, emphasizes his career as a military commander, showing him in the standard-issue uniform of a Roman legionnaire. How does this image of Severus compare with that of Augustus (see page 166)? ■ *What do these differences suggest about the emperor's new role in the third century?*

short reign of Decius (r. 249–251 C.E.), all Roman citizens were required to swear a public oath affirming their loyalty to Rome, which meant worshiping Rome's gods. Those who did so received a certificate testifying to this fact, which they had to produce on demand. Large numbers of Christians were implicated when this edict was put into effect. The enlightened policies of earlier emperors were abandoned.

The Reorganized Empire of Diocletian

As it happens, the most zealous persecutor of Christians was also responsible for reining in these destructive forces. **Diocletian** (*die-oh-KLEE-shan*; r. 284–305 C.E.) was a cavalry officer from the Roman province of Dalmatia (modern Croatia) who had risen through the ranks. He could have been another "barracks emperor," but he was determined not to be a victim of the cycle. Instead, he embraced the reality of Rome as a multicultural entity that could not be governed from one place by one person with one centralized bureaucracy. He appointed a fellow officer, Maximian, as co-emperor, putting him in charge of the western half of the empire and retaining the wealthier eastern half for himself. In 293 C.E., Diocletian delegated new authority to two junior emperors, or "caesars": Galerius and Constantius. The result was a **tetrarchy**, a "rule of four," with each man governing a quarter of the empire, further subdivided into administrative units called *dioceses*. This system not only responded to the challenges of imperial administration but was designed to secure a peaceful transfer of power, since the two young "caesars" were being groomed to take the place of the two senior "augusti."

Diocletian apparently recognized that disputes over succession had been a fatal flaw of the Augustan system. Also unlike Augustus, who had cloaked the reality of his personal power in the trappings of the republic, Diocletian presented himself as an undisguised autocrat. His title was not *princeps* ("first man"), but *dominus* ("lord"). In fact, his style of imperial rule borrowed more from the Persian model than it did from the Roman. Gone were the days of republican simplicity and the scorn of kingly pomp. Diocletian wore a diadem and a purple gown of silk interwoven with gold, and he introduced Persian-style ceremonies at his court. Under the Principate, the emperor's palace had been run like the household of any well-to-do Roman, only on a large scale. Diocletian, however, remained physically removed behind a maze of doorways, rooms, and curtains. Those lucky enough to gain an audience with him had to prostrate themselves, while a privileged few could kiss his robe. Too much familiarity with their soldiers had bred contempt for the "barracks emperors," and as a soldier-turned-emperor himself, Diocletian was keen to avoid this mistake.

THE TETRARCHY: DIOCLETIAN AND HIS COLLEAGUES. This grouping, carved from a valuable purple stone called porphyry, shows the two augusti, Diocletian and Maximian, embracing their younger caesars, Galerius and Constantius. ▪ *Why do you think that these rulers are portrayed with identical facial features and military regalia?* ▪ *What message does this convey?*

Although Diocletian retained close personal control over the army, he took steps to separate military from civilian chains of command; never again would Roman armies make and unmake emperors. To control the devastatingly high rates of inflation that were undermining the economy, Diocletian stabilized the currency, attempted to fix prices and wages, and reformed the tax system. He even moved the administrative center of the empire from Italy to Nicomedia in the Roman province of Bithynia (modern Turkey). Rome remained the symbolic capital of the empire, not least because the Senate continued to meet there, but Diocletian had little need for the Senate's advice; the real power lay elsewhere.

DIOCLETIAN'S DIVISION OF THE EMPIRE, C. 304 C.E. ▪ *What areas did each of the four divisions of the empire cover?* ▪ *What seems to be the strategy behind the location of the four major capitals, both within their respective quarters and in relation to each other?* ▪ *What is the status of Rome itself, according to this map?*

THE CONVERSION OF CHRISTIANITY

By the beginning of the fourth century, the number of Christians living within the jurisdiction of Rome was statistically insignificant, probably no more than 5 percent of the total population in the Latin West and possibly 10 percent of the Greek-speaking East. Still, the new Christian religion was making an impact, and one of Diocletian's methods for promoting unity within the empire was to take a proactive stance against any group perceived as subversive. This meant reviving the policies of Decius and Valerian—but taking an even harder line. Those who could not show proof of their loyalty to Rome's gods were stripped of their rights as citizens. Christians who had been serving in the army or in government offices were dismissed. So were Manicheans, followers of the Persian prophet Mani (c. 216–276 C.E.), whose teachings paralleled Zoroastrianism by positing an eternal struggle between the forces of good and evil. Indeed,

Christianity and Manichaeism must have seemed very similar to outsiders, and both were implicated in a full-scale purge of religious dissidents in 303 C.E. This was the Great Persecution, a time when many became martyrs—from a Greek word meaning "witnesses"—for their faith.

Christianity and Neoplatonism

It is ironic that the very crises that prompted Diocletian's Great Persecution were contributing to a growing interest in Christianity. Its message of social justice and equality before God was attractive to those suffering from the breakdown of political, economic, and social structures. It also appealed to followers of a new and influential philosophical system called Neoplatonism ("New Platonism"), which drew on the more mystical aspects of Plato's thought (Chapter 4). Its founder was Plotinus (204–270 C.E.), a Hellenistic philosopher from Egypt who had many followers among the Roman upper classes.

Plotinus taught that everything has its source in a single supreme being. The material world, too, is part of this creation, but it is merely the residue of the divine, from which all spirituality has been drained. Human beings are thus composed of matter (bodies) and emanations of the divine (souls). This means that the individual soul, originally a part of God, is now separated from its divine source by the fact of its embodiment. The highest goal of life is therefore to attain spiritual reunion with the divine, through contemplation and acts of self-denial that will help to liberate the soul from its earthly bondage. Asceticism (from the Greek word meaning "exercise" or "training") was therefore a major focus. Plotinus and his followers believed that the body could be tamed by fasting and other forms of self-denial, thus making it a more fitting vessel for the soul.

Neoplatonism became so popular in Rome that it almost supplanted Stoicism. (Although the two philosophies shared some fundamental characteristics, Stoicism did not hold out the hope of union with the divine.) Neoplatonism also struck a blow at traditional Roman precepts, including the worship of ancestors and the devotion to the empire's gods. It was thus a natural ally of Christianity, and many important Christian theologians were influenced by it, while many educated Romans found their way to Christianity because of it. It was not, however, the path by which Christianity's first imperial convert reached the new faith.

Constantine's Vision

In 305 C.E., Diocletian built a palace near his hometown of Split, on the Adriatic coast and retired there to raise cabbages—the first time a Roman ruler had voluntarily removed himself from power since Sulla had resigned his dictatorship nearly four hundred years earlier (see Chapter 5). Diocletian obliged Maximian to retire at the same time, and the two caesars—Galerius and Constantius—moved up the ladder of succession, becoming augusti of the East and West, respectively.

But the transfer of power was not so orderly as Diocletian had intended. One of the candidates to fill the vacant post of caesar was Constantius's son, **Constantine**, who was being trained at Galerius's court. But he was passed over, perhaps so that Galerius could pursue his own imperial agenda. So Constantine left the court at Nicomedia and joined his father in Gaul. From there, father and son went to Britannia and campaigned on the northern borders until 306 C.E., when Constantius died and named Constantine as his successor. This infuriated Galerius, but with Constantine in control of a large army (the legions of Gaul and the Rhineland, as well as Britannia), he was forced to concede.

Meanwhile, war broke out among several other claimants to imperial authority, reducing Diocletian's tetrarchy to rivalry. Constantine remained aloof from this struggle, which was waged mostly in Italy, and concentrated on securing his quarter of the empire. Beginning around 310 C.E., he began to promote himself as a favored devotee of the sun god Sol Invictus, whose cult had been revived by the emperor Aurelian (r. 270–275 C.E.). This was a smart move. Increasingly, the "Invincible Sun" was associated not only with the Roman gods of light and war, Apollo and Mars, but also with Mithras, whose cult was popular with soldiers. It was increasingly popular in Rome as well, where the feast long dedicated to the sky god Saturn, the Saturnalia, was now being celebrated as the rebirth of the sun after the winter solstice, on December 25.

From the worship of Sol Invictus to the worship of Christ was, at least for Constantine, a small step (see **Interpreting Visual Evidence** on page 196). In 312 C.E., Constantine decided to march on Italy, which was now in the hands of a man called Maxentius, who had declared himself emperor in the West and was trying to build up a coalition of supporters, among them the Christian community of Rome. It may have been this that gave Constantine the idea of currying favor in the same way, or it may have been another kind of inspiration that led him to emblazon Christian symbols on his banners and the shields of his soldiers the night before a major battle north of Rome, at the Milvian Bridge over the Tiber. According to later legend, Constantine had seen a vision of two intertwined Greek letters inscribed on the sky, the first two letters in the name of Christ, and was told that "In this sign, you will conquer." He did.

In gratitude for his victory, Constantine showered benefits on the Christian clergy of Rome and patronized the construction of churches throughout the empire. He also forced Licinius, the augustus of the East, to join him in promoting religious tolerance when they met at Milan (northern Italy) in 313 C.E. Their Edict of Milan guaranteed freedom of worship to all Rome's citizens, Christian and non-Christian. But it was apparent that Christianity was the favored faith of the imperial family and thus the pathway for anyone with political ambitions. Almost overnight, Christians ceased to be members of an illegal and often despised cult and became affiliates of a prestigious and profitable religion, one that was suddenly attractive to the ruling classes. The entire basis of Christianity's appeal had changed.

From Illegal Sect to Imperial Institution

In his letters, Paul of Tarsus addressed small Christian assemblies he called churches; sometimes he even spoke of the whole Christian community as a church. But it is doubtful

Interpreting Visual Evidence

The Power of the Invincible Sun

Roman emperors often linked their power to the powers of Rome's traditional gods, and emperors were also worshiped as gods in their own right. Look carefully at the following images and consider the visual language of power that came to be associated with Sol Invictus, the "Invincible Sun," and eventually with Jesus Christ.

Questions for Analysis

1. How did Constantine invoke the iconography of Sol Invictus (image A)? What messages does this image convey?

2. How might Constantine's use of this imagery—after his initial conversion to Christianity—have been interpreted by Christians? How might it have been interpreted by followers of Rome's other religions? Do you think it was designed to be ambiguous? Why or why not?

3. Scholars dispute both the dating and the significance of this mosaic, found beneath St. Peter's Basilica on the Vatican Hill in Rome (image B). Is it likely that this is a representation of Jesus as Sol Invictus? If not, how would you explain the association of this pagan deity with the Christian God?

B. This mosaic comes from a necropolis (cemetery) found beneath St. Peter's Basilica (the Vatican) in Rome. Its precise dating is in dispute, but it was made sometime between the mid-third and mid-fourth centuries. It shows Jesus with the halo of the sun god.

A. This coin issued by Constantine shows him with a halo, indicating his worship of Sol Invictus. The reverse features figures representing the Four Seasons.

---

that Paul could have imagined a day when representatives of an official church could meet openly, or a time when his letters to separate churches in Corinth, Ephesus, Rome, and elsewhere would be gathered together in a single book.

Early Christianity grew organically; it was not designed as a religious system. It had no absolute teachings, apart from the words of Jesus as reported in the Gospels, which do not always agree on those teachings. And not all Christian communities had access to the same scriptures. Some churches had a few of Paul's letters; others had none. Some had bishops, priests, deacons, and other officeholders; some had only a handful of believers. Some counted

women as their leaders; others disapproved of women in authority. Some had come under the influence of Neoplatonism or Manichaeism; others considered Neoplatonism and Manichaeism to be perversions.

In every respect, then, the Christianity that emerged after Constantine's conversion had to reinvent itself. Rituals and doctrines that had been formulated to suit the needs of small, scattered communities now had to be reconciled. Members of this new church needed to agree on a shared set of beliefs. They needed a shared set of scriptures and a chain of command. All of these fundamental structures had to be hammered out in a painful process that never quite managed to forge a common understanding. In historical terms, this is hardly surprising. The varieties of Christianity had been too separate for too long; they were the products of the same diversity that made the Roman Empire hard to govern. Indeed, the degree to which the Christians of the fourth century were able to agree on so many things is remarkable, given these challenges.

The Hierarchy of the Church

When it came to organization, Rome's imperial administration provided practical models. Because the empire's basic unit of governance was the city, the city became the basic unit of ecclesiastical administration as well. Each major city now had a bishop who supervised all the churches and also the rural areas of his diocese, a term borrowed from Diocletian's reorganization of the empire. Bishops of the largest cities were called *metropolitans*, and those who ruled over the oldest and most prestigious Christian communities were called *patriarchs*. These patriarchal cities also jockeyed for preeminence. Among the main contenders were Rome, whose inhabitants longed to be at the center of the world again; Alexandria, the capital of the Hellenistic world; and Constantinople, a new city founded by Constantine on the Hellespont between Europe and Asia.

CHRISTIAN SYMBOLS ON THE ROMAN FRONTIER. In the late fourth century, just decades after Constantine's conversion, the Christian religion was taking hold even in the northern provinces of the Roman Empire. This stunning fresco is one of many found in the Cella Septichora, a series of seven decorated Christian burial chambers constructed in the Roman city of Sopianae in the province of Pannonia (now the city of Pécs in Hungary). Portraits of saints adorn the ceiling and wall, which also features the *chi-rho* monogram that Constantine claimed to have seen in the sky before his victory at the Milvian Bridge. *Chi* and *rho* are the first two letters in the Greek word *Christos*.

Which of these Roman cities should be the capital of the Roman Church? The patriarch of Rome's claim rested on several foundations. Rome had long been venerated as the place where both Peter and Paul were martyred. And according to one of the Gospels (Matthew 16:18–19), Jesus had designated Peter as his representative on earth. Peter's successors, the subsequent bishops of Rome, thus claimed to exercise the same powers. Rome's bishop also enjoyed some political advantages over other patriarchs. Unlike the bishop of the new imperial capital at Constantinople, he could act with more freedom because he didn't have to deal directly with the emperor. But as far as eastern bishops were concerned, the patriarch of Constantinople should be the one to exercise control over the entire Church. This division of opinion—the product of cultural differences and contemporary politics—would continue to affect the development of Christian institutions. In time, it would lead to a very real division within Christianity, one that has never been resolved.

Orthodoxy, Heresy, and Imperial Authority

Christianity's new prominence also raised the stakes of disputes over its basic teachings. Although followers of Jesus had disagreed about such matters since the time of his death, these disagreements were of little political consequence so long as Christianity remained an illegal movement. Under Constantine, however, doctrinal disputes had the potential to ignite riots and to undermine the credibility of the emperor. It was imperative, therefore, that these disputes be resolved through active imperial intervention.

The most divisive theological issue of the early Church concerned the nature of God. Jesus had taught his followers that he was the Son of God and that after his death he would leave behind him a comforting spirit that would also be an emanation of God. Accordingly, many Christians believed that God encompassed a Trinity of equal persons: Father, Son, and Holy Spirit. But other Christians, influenced by Neoplatonism, rejected the idea that Jesus could be equal with God. Instead, they maintained that Jesus was part of God's creation and shared in his divine essence; but he was not equal to God, or eternal like God. This latter school of thought was called Arianism, after the Christian teacher Arius who espoused it. (It should not be confused with Aryanism, a modern racial concept.) After protracted struggles, Arianism was condemned as heresy, a word that comes from the Greek verb meaning "to choose for oneself," which became the Church's term for false beliefs punished with damnation. Yet many Christians continued to adhere to the Arian view.

This new emphasis on orthodoxy (Greek for "correct teaching") was another major consequence of Christianity's conversion. The beliefs of early Christians had been fairly simple: there is one God; Jesus is the anointed one who suffered and died for the sins of mankind and who was raised from the dead; in order to be saved, his followers must renounce sin. But beginning in the fourth century, Christian theology became ever more complex. Christian intellectuals had to demonstrate that their beliefs could withstand intense philosophical scrutiny and that Christianity was superior to Hellenistic philosophy. Just as there were many different schools of Greek and Roman thought, so there arose many different interpretations of Christian doctrine. Before Christianity became a legal religion, any doctrinal disputes could only be addressed informally, by small groups of bishops meeting at local councils that had no power to enforce their decisions. In the fourth century, however, doctrinal disputes had real political consequences.

As a result, the Roman state became increasingly enmeshed in the governance of the Church. Constantine began this process in 325 C.E., when he summoned Christian representatives to the first ecumenical ("worldwide") meeting of the Christian community, the Council of Nicaea, where Arianism was condemned and arguments over the books to be included in the Christian Bible were resolved. Constantine's successors carried this intervention much further. Gradually, they claimed to preside over Church councils as Christ's representatives on earth, which entitled them to decide what Christian doctrine should be. Some even violently suppressed Christian groups who refused to accept imperial mandates, labeled them heretical, and subjected them to ecclesiastical penalties—condemnation and excommunication from the Church—as well as criminal prosecution. Essentially, these imperial interventions were an extension of Augustan policies, which had made the emperor *pontifex maximus*, Rome's high priest. In the fourth century, it began to look as though this trend would continue, and that secular and spiritual authority would be combined in the person of the emperor. But this would change in later centuries, as we shall see.

New Attitudes toward Women and the Body

Women were conspicuously absent from the new hierarchy of the Church and were also barred from the decision-making process at Nicea. Even though they had long been deacons and may even have performed priestly duties, women were now firmly and completely excluded from any position of power.

This was an enormous change, more fundamental than any other aspect of Christianity's conversion. Women had been leaders of many early churches. Jesus had included many women among his close followers—yet one of the early gospels rejected from the biblical canon at the Council of Nicea was ascribed to Mary Magdalene. Paul had relied on women to organize and preside over churches and to finance his missionary journeys; he had declared in one letter (Galatians 3:28) that there should be no distinctions of gender, rank, or ethnicity among Christians. Women such as Perpetua were prominent among the martyrs and were often regarded as prophets. These strong roles had always been controversial because they set Christianity apart from the traditional values of Roman society—but that had also been one of Christianity's main attractions.

What accounts for this drastic change? Three factors can be clearly identified. When Christianity was absorbed into the staunch patriarchy of Rome, it could no longer promote the authority of women effectively. As the Church came to mirror the imperial administration, it replicated the structures of governance that had been the province of men since the founding of the republic. The Church now had the capacity to exclude or censor writings that represented women as the companions of Jesus and founders of the religion based on his teachings. These efforts were so successful that it was not until the very end of the nineteenth century that a gospel attributed to Mary Magdalene was known to exist.

The second factor leading to the marginalization of women was the growing identification of Christianity with Roman cults that emphasized masculinity, particularly the worship of Sol Invictus and the soldiers' god Mithras. This was a deliberate strategy on the part of the Church. It is easier to convert people to a new religion if that religion is not wholly new and embraces elements of other religions. In common with these two cults, as well as with many of the other religions we have studied, such as the worship of Osiris in Egypt, Christianity emphasized the heroic suffering and death of a male god and his eventual victory over death itself. Christ was increasingly identified with Sol Invictus, and his birthday came to be celebrated on December 25, the Roman holiday that marked the passing of the winter solstice and the return of lengthening days.

The third factor contributing to women's exclusion from power was the Christian emphasis on asceticism ("self-denial"), which changed attitudes toward the body. As we noted previously, Neoplatonism taught that the goal of life was to liberate the soul from the tyranny of bodily desires, a teaching that it shared with Stoicism. None of this was emphasized in the teachings of Christ. Quite the contrary: the body was celebrated as God's creation, and Christ himself had encouraged feasting, touching, bathing,

Past and Present

Resisting Imperialism

Attempts at conquest are always met with resistance. In the Roman province of Britannia, a Celtic warrior queen named Boudica led an armed uprising against the imperial army that is still celebrated as a proud example of British independence—as this modern statue in London indicates. A more peaceful uprising against American imperialism took place in Manila on the eve of President Barack Obama's first inauguration in 2008.

 Watch related author interview on the Student Site

and marriage. His followers insisted that he had been bodily resurrected, and that the bodies of all the faithful would be resurrected, too. Although early Christians had to be willing to sacrifice their lives for their faith, if need be, they were not required to renounce earthly pleasures.

After Christianity became legal, however, there were few opportunities to "bear witness" to the faith through martyrdom. Instead, some Christians began to practice asceticism as an alternative path to sanctity. This meant renunciation of the flesh, especially sex and eating, activities both associated with women, who were in charge of any household's food supply and who were (obviously) sexual partners. A new spiritual movement called monasticism also took hold, providing an alternative lifestyle for men who wanted to reject the world entirely; the word for this movement comes from the Greek word *monos*, "alone." Early monks lived as hermits and practiced extraordinary feats of self-abasement. Some grazed in the fields like cows, others penned themselves into small cages, still others

hung heavy weights around their necks. A monk named Cyriacus would stand for hours on one leg, like a crane. Another, Simeon "the Stylite," lived on top of a high pillar for thirty-seven years, punishing his lice-infested flesh while crowds gathered below to marvel.

This extreme denial of the body was a departure not only from most previous Christian practices but also from the practices of many civilizations up to this point—not to mention the realities of human existence. Ancient religions often celebrated sexuality as a delight, as well as a necessity. Even Roman religion had a place for priestesses and female prophets. Moreover, marriage was so important a marker of social respectability that unmarried men were objects of deep suspicion. Furthermore, Romans had regarded citizens' bodies as being at the service of the state: men as soldiers and fathers, women as mothers and wives. Now, however, some Christians were asserting that their bodies belonged not to the state but to God, and that to serve God fully meant no longer serving the state—or posterity—by bearing children.

Christians and Pagans

The urban focus of Christianity is reflected in the Latin word referring to a non-Christian: *paganus*, meaning someone who lives in the countryside. The implication is that only someone with a hopelessly rustic outlook would cling to the old Roman religion and so spoil his chances of advancement in society. As Christians came to occupy positions of power within the empire, men with political ambitions were increasingly forced to convert—or at least conform—to Christian norms.

Constantine had retained both pagan and Christian officials in his court, and was careful to speak in terms that embraced a non-Christian audience. But his successors were less inclined to tolerate competing faiths. An interesting exception was Constantine's nephew Julian "the Apostate" (r. 360–363 C.E.), who rejected Christianity and attempted to revive traditional Roman piety. But when Julian was killed in a battle with the Persians, his pro-pagan edicts were allowed to lapse. By 391 C.E., the emperor Theodosius (r. 379–395 C.E.) had prohibited pagan worship of any sort within the empire. This meant that within three generations, Christianity had gone from being a persecuted faith to a persecuting religion. Theodosius even removed the sacred altar of the goddess Victory from the Senate chamber in Rome, prompting pagan loyalists to prophesy the end of the empire. Fifteen years later, Rome fell to a barbarian army.

SHIFTING CENTERS AND MOVING FRONTIERS

In 324 C.E., Constantine broke ground for the capital city he named after himself **Constantinople**. It was built on the site of a settlement called Byzantium, chosen for its strategic location at the mouth of the Black Sea and the crossroads between Europe and Asia: the Hellespont. This site gave Constantinople commanding advantages as a center for communications and trade. It also made the city readily defensible, because it was surrounded on three sides by water and protected by walls on land. It would remain the political and economic center of the Roman Empire until 1453, when the city was conquered by the Ottoman Turks (see Chapter 11).

East or West?

The founding of Constantinople epitomizes the shift in Rome's center of gravity from Italy and western Europe to the eastern Mediterranean. It also signaled Constantine's intention to abandon the political precedents set by Diocletian,

SAINT SIMEON "THE STYLITE." This gold plaque dating from the sixth century depicts the exertions of the ascetic saint who defied the devil (shown as a huge snake) by abusing his own body. Admirers wishing to speak to the saint could climb the ladder shown on the left. ▪ *What do you make of the relationship between the luxurious medium of this image (gold) and the message it conveys?*

Virginity for both men and women was accordingly preached as the highest spiritual standard, with celibacy for those who had once been married valued almost as highly. Marriage remained acceptable for average people, the laity, but was often characterized as a second-best option whose purpose was to prevent weak-minded people from being consumed by desire. Moreover, because pseudoscientific theories stemming back to Aristotle posited that women were inherently more lustful than men, the denigration of sexuality had a disproportionately negative effect on attitudes toward women.

Analyzing Primary Sources

A Senator Defends the Traditional Religion of Rome

In 382 C.E., the emperor Theodosius ordered the removal of the ancient altar dedicated to the goddess of Victory (Nike) from the Senate chamber in Rome, as part of his efforts to make Christianity the dominant religion in the empire. This controversial move sparked heated debate and elicited strong protests from Rome's senatorial elites. The following statement of their case was made by Quintus Aurelius Symmachus (c. 345–402 C.E.), who was at that time prefect of the city of Rome. It is principally addressed to the young western emperor, Valentinian.

o what is it more suitable that we defend the institutions of our ancestors, and the rights and destiny of our country . . . than to the glory of these times, which is all the greater when you understand that you may not do anything contrary to the custom of your ancestors? We demand then the restoration of that condition of religious affairs which was so long advantageous to the state. . . . Who is so friendly with the barbarians as not to require an Altar of Victory? . . . But even if the avoidance of such an omen were not sufficient, it would at least have been seemly to abstain from injuring the ornaments of the Senate House. Allow us, we beseech you, as old men to leave to posterity what we received as boys. The love of custom is great. . . . Where shall we swear to obey your laws and commands? By what religious sanction shall the false mind be terrified, so as not to lie in bearing witness? All things are indeed filled with God, and no place is safe for the perjured, but to be urged in the very presence of religious forms has great power in producing a fear of sinning. That altar preserves the concord of all, that altar appeals to the good faith of each, and nothing gives more authority to our decrees than that the whole of our order issues every decree as it were under the sanction of an oath. . . .

Let us now suppose that Rome is present and addresses you in these words: "Excellent princes, fathers of your country, respect my years to which pious rites have brought me. Let me use the ancestral ceremonies, for I do not repent of them. Let me live after my own fashion, for I am free. This worship subdued the world to my laws, these sacred rites repelled Hannibal from the walls, and the Senones [Gauls] from the capitol. Have I been reserved for this, that in my old age I should be blamed? I will consider what it is thought should be set in order, but tardy and discreditable is the reformation of old age." We ask, then, for peace for the gods of our fathers and of our country. It is just that all worship should be considered as one. We look on the same stars, the sky is common, the same world surrounds us. What difference does it make by what pains each seeks the truth? We cannot attain to so great a secret by one road; but this discussion is rather for persons at ease, we offer now prayers, not conflict.

Source: Excerpted from *A Select Library of the Nicene and Post-Nicene Fathers*, 2nd Series (New York: 1896), vol. X, pp. 411–14.

Questions for Analysis

1. How does Symmachus's defense exemplify the traditional values of the Roman Republic?

2. How does Symmachus justify the coexistence of Christianity and Rome's state religion? How would a Christian refute his position?

3. Less than a decade after the altar's removal, Theodosius outlawed all religions but Christianity. From your reading of this letter, how do you think this edict would have affected Romans such as Symmachus?

including the institution of the tetrarchy. Instead, the imperial succession became hereditary. Constantine thus embraced a principle of dynastic monarchy that the Romans had rejected 800 years earlier. Even more ominous, he divided the empire among his three sons, resulting in a civil war, made more bitter because each of these men supported a different faction within the Christian Church. In the meantime, the empire became more and more fragmented. The last ruler who could claim to govern a united Rome was the same Theodosius who outlawed its venerable religion; but then he, too, divided the empire between his sons.

As we have seen, there had always been linguistic and cultural differences between the Greek- and Latin-speaking peoples under Roman rule. Now, however, the differences

GOTHS

IRELAND

NORTH SEA

BALTIC SEA

BRITANNIA

LOMBARDS

FRANKS
358

VANDALS

c. 150

ATLANTIC OCEAN

Cologne

486 • Paris

407

451

Rhine R.

Danube R.

406

400-500

376

HUNS
340

GAUL

HISPANIA

409

• 412
Toulouse

418

568

397

VISIGOTHS

375

378

• Adrianople

• Constantinople

BLACK SEA

CAPPADOCIA

CORSICA

Rome •
410

ITALY

ADRIATIC SEA

SARDINIA

455

• Naples

395

GALATIA

• Tarsus

• Antioch

429

Hippo •

439

VANDALS

SICILY

NUMIDIA

CRETE

CYPRUS

• Damascus

MEDITERRANEAN SEA

Jerusalem •

Alexandria •

Area of detail

EUROPE

AFRICA

EGYPT

RED SEA

| | Extent of Roman rule, c. 400 C.E. |
| Goths |
| Huns |
| Franks |
| Visigoths |
| Lombards |
| Vandals |

0   250   500 Miles

0   250   500 Kilometers

THE MIGRATIONS OF ROME'S FRONTIER PEOPLES. ▪ *What do the routes followed by these different peoples suggest about their destinations and motives?* ▪ *Why did so many converge on Rome, although the city was no longer the capital even of the western Roman Empire?* ▪ *Why did the Romans refer to these migrants as "barbarians"?*

between **Greek East** and **Latin West** became heightened. The eastern empire was becoming more populous, more prosperous, and more central to imperial policy, while the western provinces were becoming poorer and more peripheral. Many western cities now relied on transfers of funds from their eastern counterparts, and suffered when these funds dried up, trade or communication failed, or Roman legions were transferred elsewhere. Rome itself, which had been demoted to provincial status under Diocletian, now lost even that nominal position. The Italian city of Ravenna on the Adriatic coast became the new capital of the region and a more convenient stopping place for emperors and

ambassadors traveling from Constantinople to the administrative centers of Milan and Trier (in what is now Germany). Only two of Constantine's successors ever visited Rome itself, and none of them lived there.

Internal and External Pressures

The shifting center of the empire and the widening gap between the eastern and western provinces were not the only fault lines emerging in this period. Secessionist movements arose among many residents of Britannia, Gaul, Hispania, and

Germania. The residents of Egypt were particularly afflicted by high levels of taxation, which targeted their rich agricultural lands. Meanwhile, North Africans and other citizens living in the empire's interior regions were increasingly ignored by authorities. The Italians resented their new status as provincial subjects of Constantinople. Beneath the surface of imperial autocracy, the fourth-century empire was slowly dissolving into its constituent parts.

The empire was also coming under renewed pressure from its borders. Since the third century, the growing power of a new Persian dynasty, the Sassanids, had prompted a shift of Roman military weight to the eastern frontier, reducing the number of troops stationed elsewhere. Partly as a result of this, the northwestern territories suffered a devastating series of raids along the porous frontier of Germania. During the fourth century, relations between assimilated Romans and their barbarian neighbors were generally peaceful. But starting in the early fifth century, a new wave of settlers moved into the empire's oldest provinces, permanently altering their histories and cultures.

From the Periphery to the Center

In the eyes of many Romans, the tribes that lived along the empire's northern frontiers were barbarians in the pure sense of that (Greek) term: they did not speak either of the empire's civilized languages and did not live in cities. But in no sense were they savage peoples. They were sophisticated agriculturalists and metalworkers who had enjoyed trading relationships with the Roman world for centuries. Many had been settled within Roman provinces for generations as farmers and craftsmen. Legionnaires from the hinterlands of Germania were core components in Roman armies. In some frontier areas, entire tribes had become Roman *foederati*: allied troops who reinforced Roman garrisons or took their places when legions were withdrawn. One general of mixed descent, Flavius Stilicho (359–408 C.E.), was the military leader of the western empire under Theodosius. By the end of the fourth century, many of these tribes had even adopted the form of Christianity preached by disciples of Arius. Although this made them heretics from the perspective of the institutional Church, it tied them more closely to Roman civilization.

What altered this relatively peaceful coexistence? Our study of many previous civilizations has prepared us to answer this question: the arrival of new peoples and the subsequent struggle for land and resources. During the mid-fourth century, a group of nomadic herdsmen known as the Huns began to migrate westward from central Asia, into the region north and east of the Black Sea. Around 370 C.E., their arrival forced a number of other groups, notably the Goths,

to migrate south and west—and in a hurry. Within a few years, they had reached the Roman frontier along the Danube River. The Goths had been clients of the Roman state for several centuries, but now they were refugees and too numerous and too desperate to repel by force. The Romans therefore permitted them to cross the Danube and settle within the empire. In return for food and other supplies, they were to guard the region against other migrant groups.

Local officials, however, failed to uphold their end of the bargain. Instead, they forced the starving Goths to sell themselves and their children into slavery in return for food. In 378 C.E., the Goths revolted, and the Roman army sent to suppress them was defeated at the battle of Adrianople. Peace was restored when the Romans accommodated the Goths' demands for goods and farmland and enrolled them in the Roman army under their own military leaders. But when Theodosius divided the empire between his two young sons, their military advisers—including Stilicho, father-in-law of the emperor Honorius, the de facto ruler—constantly undermined one another.

This provided an opening for Alaric, a young leader of a tribe known as the Goths, to advance his own agenda. Targeting the wealthier eastern provinces, he led his army into Greece, looting or capturing many ancient cities, including Athens. The Romans, desperately attempting to halt these incursions, offered Alaric a Roman military command and encouraged him to move to Italy: the price of peace in the eastern empire was thus to be Rome itself.

Meanwhile, the Huns had arrived in the region corresponding to modern-day Hungary, forcing several other peoples westward toward the Rhine. On New Year's Eve in the year 406 C.E., a people known as the Vandals crossed the frozen Rhine and invaded Gaul. To repulse them, Stilicho (whose own father had been a Vandal) made an alliance with Alaric and his men. But Stilicho fell from imperial favor just a few months later, and the imperial government could no longer exercise any restraint on Alaric's actions.

Like Stilicho, Alaric seems to have wanted to win a permanent place for himself in the imperial hierarchy. But unlike Stilicho—and many Roman generals before him—he did not understand how to use violence as a means toward that end. His assault on Rome did not make him Rome's conqueror but its destroyer. In 410 C.E., after a protracted period of siege, Alaric's army captured and sacked the city. But by now, Rome had little to offer in the way of either food or spoils. So many of the Goths moved on, eventually settling in southern Gaul and Hispania, where they established what came to be known as the Visigothic (Western Gothic) kingdom. Others, later labeled Ostrogoths (Eastern Goths), remained in Italy. The Vandals set out for the Iberian Peninsula, too, but ultimately crossed the Strait of Gibraltar to settle in North

THEODORIC THE OSTROGOTH. This coin shows the king in Roman dress but with the long hair characteristic of a barbarian nobleman. The inscription reads *Rex Theodericvs pivs princis,* "King Theodoric, pious prince." ▪ *How does this image compare with that of Constantine (see page 196)?*

a decade of fierce fighting, Theodoric and his imperially equipped Gothic army managed to drive the Huns from Italy and establish a kingdom based in Ravenna, which he ruled—with imperial support—until his death in 526.

The Impact of the Fifth-Century Migrations

The events of the fifth century increased the porosity of the empire's northern frontiers and penetrated to its core provinces: Italy, Gaul, Hispania, and North Africa. Yet the groups that moved through these territories were small. They were joined by refugees and desperados, but they were never more than war bands. So why couldn't long-established imperial cities sustain themselves?

By the beginning of the fifth century, many Roman armies were already weakened. The best legions had been withdrawn from frontier provinces to protect the richer eastern ones. Those that remained tended to be integrated into local civilian populations, staffed by married men who grew their own food and lived with their families, making it difficult to move troops even in an emergency. Furthermore, there was no mechanism for increasing the revenues needed to support the army. And even if the citizens of Rome's western provinces had been able to maintain a crack fighting force on the frontier, they would have had little reason to think that such an expenditure was necessary. Their "barbarian" neighbors hadn't seemed threatening for generations, and many were so Romanized that differences between the groups are difficult to detect in surviving archaeological evidence.

In the eastern Roman Empire, by contrast, a thriving economy made it easier to equip and maintain a strong fighting force. Cities remained centers of commerce and industry, which meant that citizens possessed greater taxable wealth and so could sustain the burdens of the imperial bureaucracy more easily. Moreover, potential invaders could be bought off or bribed to direct their attention elsewhere—as Alaric had been. For all these reasons, the eastern empire prospered during the fifth century C.E., while the western empire floundered.

After the fifth-century migrations, these differences were exacerbated. Every territory that was plundered or occupied represented tax revenues lost, and the scale of these losses was enormous. Ten years after the Goths sacked Rome, the area was capable of producing only 15 percent of the revenues it had generated before that calamity. Similar reductions in revenues resulted from attacks on Gaul and Hispania. After 420 C.E. or so, as the newcomers began to set up their own kingdoms, these areas ceased to pay any taxes at all to imperial authorities. When the

Africa. Other tribes, including the Franks and the Burgundians, followed the Vandals across the Rhine into Gaul and established kingdoms of their own.

A generation later, the Huns—whose migrations had set all of these gears in motion—themselves invaded Roman territory under the leadership of their warlord, Attila. Meanwhile, Britannia had been abandoned by its remaining legions, which were hastily withdrawn in 410 C.E. There, a mixed population of Romans and Celts eventually intermingled with invaders from northwestern Germania and Scandinavia: Angles, Saxons, and Jutes. These tribes were so efficient that they dominated all but the westernmost and northern portions of the island within a few generations. Many Celts retreated to the regions where Celtic languages are still spoken today, including Wales and Scotland. The rest of Britain would become Angle-land: England.

The last western Roman emperor was an ineffectual usurper derisively known as Romulus Augustulus ("Little Romulus Augustus"). In 476 C.E., he was deposed by Odovacar, a chieftain who headed a mixed band of barbarians, Huns, and disgruntled Romans. Viewed from the perspective of Constantinople, this event was decisive: it was now not only "New Rome," it was the only viable capital. And the best way for its imperial agenda to be carried forward in the western provinces was through a strong barbarian ruler.

Luckily, the emperor Zeno (r. 474–491 C.E.) knew just the man: Theodoric, the son of a Gothic king who had been sent to Constantinople as a hostage and raised in the civilized surroundings of the imperial court. After

Vandals captured North Africa in 439 C.E., the richest of all Rome's western provinces was lost.

The consequences of these structural changes were far-reaching. In the year 400 C.E., the economy of the western Roman Empire was characterized by the mass production of low-cost, high-quality consumer goods that circulated in massive quantities. Although regional and local systems of exchange continued after 500 C.E., long-distance trade in bulk goods could be sustained only in the Mediterranean. As markets disappeared in northwestern provinces, skilled artisans had to find other ways to make a living, or emigrate. Standards of living gradually declined, and so did the overall population. Indeed, it is likely that the population of western Europe did not return to its fourth-century levels for a thousand years, until just before the Black Death (see Chapter 10).

Other aspects of Roman life in these regions changed, too, but almost imperceptibly. Roman bureaucracies often survived, although the proceeds from taxes now went into the purses of the new barbarian rulers or Christian bishops. Roman agricultural patterns continued in most areas, frequently under the same landlords. Local Roman elites continued to dominate civic life, and Roman cities continued to dominate their surrounding regions, especially in southern Gaul and Hispania. The invasions did not even bring an end to Roman culture or the influence of Roman values. As King Theodoric the Ostrogoth was fond of remarking: "An able Goth wishes to be like a Roman; but only a poor Roman would want to be like a Goth."

THE SHAPING OF A NEW WORLDVIEW

Throughout this time of change, Christian intellectuals were formulating a new outlook on the world that would remain dominant for more than a thousand years. As the empire sustained attacks from external forces and began to fragment along old fault lines, it seemed clearer than ever that a new age was beginning. Christ had promised to come again at the end of time, when all human souls would be judged. How, then, should Christians live in this new world and prepare for that imminent event?

The men who forged answers to this question were contemporaries who knew and influenced one another, though they did not always agree. They are now regarded as saints and "fathers" of the Church: Jerome (c. 340–420 C.E.), who came from the northeastern edge of Italy, near the port of Aquilea; Ambrose (c. 340–397), who grew up in Trier and was eventually named bishop of Milan; and Augustine (354–430), who was born and raised in North Africa, where he became a bishop in later life.

Jerome: Translating the Christian Message

Jerome's signal contribution to the culture of the Roman West was his translation of the Bible from Hebrew and Greek into Latin. Known as the Vulgate or "common" version, it was not the first attempt to produce a Latin Bible but it quickly became the standard—and it remained so until the sixteenth century (see Chapter 13). Jerome's translation is vigorous, colloquial, and clear; its powerful prose and poetry influenced Latin authors for centuries. Jerome was also an influential commentator on the Bible's interpretation, encouraging readings that emphasized a passage's symbolic or allegorical significance, as well as its literal or historical meaning.

Jerome was not a notably original thinker, but he was an eloquent and effective translator of others' ideas as well as of others' words. He was among the first to argue that pagan learning could and should be studied by Christians as long as it was thoroughly adapted to Christian aims. The perennial problem, of course, was that one was always tempted to appreciate classical literature for its own sake, and not for the light it shed on Christian truths. Jerome himself never succeeded in subordinating his love for ancient authors, especially Cicero, to his love for God. He liked to tell a story about a dream he'd experienced, in which he arrived at the gates of heaven and was asked by God if he was a Christian. When he replied that he was, God retorted, "You're not a Christian; you're a Ciceronian." Perhaps in an effort to compensate for this, Jerome became a rigorous ascetic and a fervent promoter of monasticism. He also held a narrow view of women's roles that exercised a strong influence on some later Christian teachers.

Ambrose and the Authority of the Church

Jerome was primarily a scholar; **Ambrose**, by contrast, was an aristocrat and man of the world who helped to define the relationship between the sacred authority of the Church and the secular authority of worldly rulers. As patriarch of the imperial administrative capital at Milan, he fearlessly rebuked the pious emperor Theodosius for a mismanaged massacre of innocent civilians in the Greek city of Thessalonia. Theodosius may have been the emperor, but until he did penance for his sins, Ambrose refused to admit him into his church. On matters of faith, he declared, "The emperor is within the Church, not above the Church." Eventually,

Theodosius capitulated and begged forgiveness of God's representative, Ambrose, in his cathedral at Milan.

Ambrose was also an admirer of Cicero—but because of his Stoicism, not his prose. Ambrose wrote an ethics handbook, *On the Duties of Ministers*, which drew heavily on Cicero's treatise *On Duties*, written almost four centuries earlier for the senatorial elite of the Roman republic. Unlike Cicero, however, Ambrose argued that the motive and goal of human conduct should be reverence for God, not social or political advancement. Even more fundamental was Ambrose's argument that God assists all Christians by sharing with them the power of divine grace—but extends more grace to some Christians than to others. Ambrose's emphasis on the necessity and mystery of grace (Why does God give more grace to some than to others?) was refined and amplified by his disciple, Augustine.

The Salvation of Saint Augustine

Apart from Jesus, **Augustine** is often considered the greatest of all Christianity's founders, and he may be the most important Christian thinker of all time. His theology is essential to the doctrine of the medieval Church and thus to modern Catholicism, and it also had a profound effect on Martin Luther and on the development of Protestant Christianities (see Chapter 13). In our own twenty-first century, many Christian philosophers of various denominations describe themselves as neo-Augustinians.

Augustine's understanding of Christianity was the result of a long process of self-discovery, which he described in a remarkable book, *Confessions*: a series of autobiographical reflections addressed to God. Augustine was not, as Jerome and Ambrose were, a confident Christian from the cradle. His father was not a Christian, and although his mother was, he scorned her influence and refused baptism. Full of ambition and eager to make his mark, he left North Africa for Italy as a young man, winning early fame as a teacher and charismatic orator. All the while, he gravitated from one philosophical system to another without finding intellectual or spiritual satisfaction. He regarded Christianity as a religion for fools, and only his increasing doubts about the alternatives (notably Manichaeism) and the appeal of Ambrose's teachings drove him to inquire further. After a spiritual epiphany described in *Confessions*, he decided to embrace Christianity at the significant age of thirty-three (the age when Jesus died). Yet his struggle to grasp and explain its paradoxes occupied him for the rest of his life. His skills as a preacher and commentator led to his rapid advancement in the Church hierarchy, and he returned to North Africa as the bishop of Hippo Regis in 395 C.E.

Although he led an extremely active life (when he died in 430, he was defending Hippo against the Vandals), Augustine still found time to write more than a hundred profound, complex, and powerful treatises analyzing the problems of Christian belief. All of these grapple with the basic question: If humanity is the creation of an omnipotent God whose nature is entirely good, why are human beings so profoundly sinful? Augustine was convinced of humans' innate capacity for evil, and he believed this tendency was evident even in babies. He adduced himself as a supreme example. In *Confessions*, he remembers that he and a few other boys once stole some pears from a neighbor's garden, not because they were hungry or even because the pears were beautiful, but simply for the sake of doing something bad. He also recounted his many sexual adventures as a young man and recalled that rather than asking God's help in suppressing his desires he prayed, "O God, give me chastity—but not yet!" In short, he argued that the human inclination toward evil is innate. But how, if we are the creatures of a good God?

Augustine traced the origin of evil back to the story of the Garden of Eden, where God had given Adam and Eve, the first human couple, the freedom to follow either his will or their own. Thereafter, God simply left Adam and Eve's descendants to do the same, by withdrawing from human beings the divine power (grace) by which they might overcome their own wills to follow his. All the evils that plague the world are thus the result of the human propensity to place one's own desires ahead of God's. This fact alone would justify God's condemnation of all mankind. But because God is merciful, he chose instead to save some human beings through the sacrifice of his son, Jesus.

Why only some? Because human beings are inherently sinful, Augustine reasoned, they cannot achieve salvation on their own; they need to be led to accept Jesus by an act of God's grace—hence the power of Augustine's own transformative experience, which led him to embrace Christianity in accordance with God's will but *against his own will*. God alone makes this choice, and by granting grace to some and not to others he predestines a portion of the human race to salvation and sentences the rest to be damned. If this seems unfair, Augustine would answer that strict fairness would condemn everyone to hell. Moreover, he would say that the basis for God's choice is a mystery shrouded in his omnipotence—far beyond the realm of human comprehension.

Defending the City of God

Augustine's audience consisted of converted Christians and intelligent skeptics such as himself. And after the

CLASSICAL LEARNING AND THE CHRISTIAN LIFE

THE CITY OF MAN. This image illustrating a late-medieval manuscript of Augustine's *City of God* displays the violence that characterizes the City of Man by showcasing one example from the Old Testament and another from Roman mythology: Cain kills his brother, Abel, while Romulus murders his brother, Remus. Its message is that all human forms of government are the product of human sin.

Jerome, Ambrose, and Augustine were members of the first generation to grow up in a world where Christianity was legal, even normal. For three centuries, there had been no such thing as a Roman Christian, which was a contradiction in terms. Now, however, many Romans *were* Christians. How could these identities be reconciled? As we have seen, none of these influential teachers wanted to discard the heritage of the past, but for all of them it posed serious challenges. Many new converts thought they could embrace both Christian and pagan beliefs simultaneously—and why not? Since the time of Socrates, philosophy had been characterized by its capacity to absorb and blend many competing ideas. Christian intellectuals wanted to be regarded as philosophers, but they also wanted to replace the doctrines of pagan philosophy with the doctrine of Christ. To do this, they needed to make classical learning applicable to a Christian way of life.

Preserving and Recycling the Classics

Reinterpreting classical culture for a Christian audience involved careful selection, something made easier by the fact that a gradual winnowing of Greek texts had already occurred in Alexandria and continued in Rome. Roman readers had little interest in the scientific works of an earlier age, and by the third century many extraordinary advances made by Hellenistic scientists (see Chapter 4) were ignored, simplified, or suppressed by popular authors such as Galen and Ptolemy. Romans also did not have much interest in Greek philosophy, drama, or epic poetry. Roman tastes ran toward comedies, novels, and pastiches of Latin classics. One favorite pastime consisted of rearranging the verses of Virgil's *Aeneid* so that they described sexual exploits—Christians, too, could play at this game. In the fourth century, Faltonia Betitia Proba (c. 322–c. 370 C.E.), the wife of a Roman senator, used Virgil's poetry to replace Aeneas with Christ.

Those pagan authors whose works were most immediately useful to Christians, such as Cicero and Virgil, therefore enjoyed continued celebrity. Texts that had long educated students in the liberal arts were also preserved, alongside major classics of Latin poetry and histories that recorded the errors of Rome's pagan past. But texts that could not be readily adapted to Christian purposes were subjected to careful editing. One of the men who undertook this task was Anicius Manlius Severinus **Boethius** (*boh-EE-thee-uhs*; c. 480–524 C.E.), an aristocrat attached to the court of Theodoric. He is often described as the "last of

sack of Rome in 410 C.E., he knew that some staunchly traditional Romans blamed Christianity for it. According to them, the attack on their city was the consequence of gross impiety, exemplified by the removal of the altar of Victory from the Senate chamber. In response, Augustine wrote one of his most famous works, *City of God*, a new interpretation of human history. He argued that mankind has always been divided into two opposing societies: those who live for the world and those who seek eternal life. The former belong to the City of Man, and their rewards are the riches, fame, and power they may win on earth—all of which are tainted by sin. Only those predestined to salvation, members of the City of God, will be saved on Judgment Day.

Although Augustine is the architect of much Christian theology, he believed that he was doing no more than drawing out truths from the Bible. But he also knew that many biblical texts are obscure and that a certain amount of education is needed to understand them. In consequence, he approved of some Christians acquiring a classical education, as he himself had done, as long as they directed their learning toward its proper end: the study of the Bible. Along with Jerome, Augustine thus formulated the rationale for Christianity's preservation of the pagan past.

Analyzing Primary Sources

Roman or Barbarian?

These two letters from Sidonius Apollinaris (c. 430–c. 480) illustrate the ways in which cultural assimilation was rapidly blurring the distinctions between "Roman" and "barbarian" in the West. Sidonius was himself the descendant of an illustrious Roman provincial family in Gaul. He was one of the most admired Latin stylists of his day, and although he eventually became a bishop and was regarded as a saint, his letter collection (from which these extracts are taken) tells us much more about the literary culture of Romano-Visigothic Gaul than it does about Christianity. His two correspondents also exemplify this new hybrid culture: Arbogastes (ahr-go-BAHS-tees) was the Frankish governor of the Roman city of Trier (in what is now Germany), and Syagrius (sigh-AG-ree-uhs) was from an ancient Roman family and became, effectively, the king of a large region now corresponding to northern France and Belgium.

Letter 4:17: Sidonius to His Friend Arbogastes

y honored Lord, your friend Eminentius has handed me a letter written by your own hand, a really literary letter, replete with the grace of a three-fold charm. The first of its merits is certainly the affection which prompted such condescension to my lowly condition, for if not a stranger I am in these days a man who courts obscurity; the second virtue is your modesty. . . . In the third place comes your urbanity, which leads you to make a most amusing profession of clumsiness, when as a matter of fact you have drunk deep from the spring of Roman eloquence and, dwelling by the Moselle, you speak the true Latin of the Tiber: you are intimate with the barbarians but are innocent of barbarisms, and are equal in tongue, as also in strength of arm, to the leaders of old, I mean those who were wont to handle the pen no less than the sword. Thus the splendor of the Roman speech, if it still exists anywhere, has survived in you, though it has long been wiped out from the Belgian and Rhenic lands: with you and your eloquence surviving, even though Roman law has ceased at our border, the Roman speech does not falter. For this reason . . . I rejoice greatly that at any rate in your illustrious breast there have remained traces of our vanishing culture. If you extend these by constant reading you will discover for yourself as each day passes that the educated are no less superior to the unlettered than men are to beasts.

---

the Romans," and his goal was to preserve the best aspects of ancient learning by compiling a series of handbooks and anthologies that packaged and explained classical texts in ways that were appropriate for Christian readers.

Boethius devoted special attention to logic, translating several of Aristotle's treatises from Greek to Latin. Because Roman philosophers had never been much interested in logic, Boethius thus forged a crucial link between classical Greek thought and the new intellectual culture of Christianity. This is most evident in *The Consolation of Philosophy*, which he wrote in prison after Theodoric condemned him to death for treason. (The justice of the charge is unclear.) In this meditation, written in the form of a dialogue, Boethius concludes that happiness is not found in earthly rewards such as riches or fame but in the "highest good," which is God. Yet he comes to this realization not through any reference to Christian revelation but through a series of imaginary conversations with "Lady Philosophy,"

the embodiment of wisdom. For the next millennium, Boethius's *Consolation* was one of the most read and imitated books in the West—the ultimate example of classical philosophy's absorption into the Christian worldview.

Monastic Education

The vital work of preserving selected classics and interpreting their meaning was increasingly performed by monks, whose way of life had undergone some significant changes during the fourth century. Leaders of the monastic movement recognized that few men were capable of ascetic feats, and some disapproved of such showmanship. Rather, they advocated a more moderate approach and emphasized the benefits of communal life. In the Roman East, the most important figure in this new monasticism was Basil of Caesarea (c. 330–379). Basil's guidelines prohibited monks from

Letter 5:5: Sidonius to his Friend Syagrius

ou are the great-grandson of a consul, and in the male line too—although that has little to do with the case before us; I say, then, you are descended from a poet, to whom his literary glory would have brought status had not his magisterial glories done so . . . and the culture of his successors has not declined one whit from his standard, particularly in this respect. I am therefore inexpressibly amazed that you have quickly acquired a knowledge of the German tongue with such ease.

And yet I remember that your boyhood had a good schooling in liberal studies and I know for certain that you often declaimed with spirit and eloquence before your professor of oratory. This being so, I should like you to tell me how you managed to absorb so swiftly into your inner being the exact sounds of an alien race, so that now after reading Virgil under the schoolmaster's cane and toiling and working the rich fluency of [Cicero] . . . you burst forth before my eyes like a young falcon from an old nest.

You have no idea what amusement it gives me, and others too, when I hear that in your presence the barbarian is afraid to perpetrate a barbarism in his own language. The bent elders of the Germans are astounded at you when you translate letters, and they adopt you as umpire and arbitrator in their mutual dealings. . . . And although these people are stiff and uncouth in body and mind alike, they welcome in you, and learn from you, their native speech combined with Roman wisdom.

Only one thing remains, most clever of men: continue with undiminished zeal, even in your hours of ease, to devote some attention to reading; and, like the man of refinement that you are, observe a just balance between the two languages: retain your grasp of Latin, lest you be laughed at, and practice the other, in order to have the laugh of them. Farewell.

Source: Reprinted by permission of the publishers and the Trustees of the Loeb Classical Library. From *Sidonius: Volume II—Letters*, Loeb Classical Library, vol. 420, prepared by W. H. Semple and E. H. Warmington from material left by W. B. Anderson, pp. 127–29, 181–83, Cambridge, MA: Harvard University Press. Copyright © 1965 by the President and Fellows of Harvard College. Loeb Classical Library® is a registered trademark of the President and Fellows of Harvard College.

Questions for Analysis

1. For what qualities does Sidonius praise Arbogastes? What might have been the motive behind his extravagant compliments?

2. For what different qualities does Sidonius praise Syagrius? Given that Syagrius controlled much of the former Roman province of northern Gaul, what would have been his reasons for learning the local language?

---

engaging in prolonged fasts or extreme discipline of the flesh, and instead encouraged useful work and silent meditation.

In the Roman West, the most influential proponent of the monastic movement was a contemporary of Boethius, **Benedict** of Nursia (c. 480–c. 547), the son of a Roman aristocrat. Benedict founded a monastery at Monte Cassino, southeast of Rome, where he urged his followers to adopt a "simple rule for beginners." Adapted from a much harsher set of precepts called *The Rule of the Master*, Benedict's *Rule* is notable for its brevity, flexibility, and practicality. It established a carefully defined cycle of daily prayers, lessons, and communal worship. It laid down guidelines for what monks should eat (a sufficiency of simple food, a small amount of wine, meat only for the sick or on special occasions), and how the work of the monastery should be performed. Physical labor was encouraged—idleness, Benedict declared, was "an enemy of the soul"—but the monks also had time for private study and contemplation. In all such matters, Benedict left much to the discretion of the leader of the monastery, whom all the monks were expected to obey without hesitation. This man was the abbot, from the Syriac word *abba* ("father").

Cassiodorus and the Classical Canon

Benedict was no admirer of classical pagan culture, but he did believe that monks must study the Bible in order to perform their daily cycle of prayers properly and to participate fully in a life of worship. This meant that they had to be educated along the lines prescribed by Augustine. And because many monks entered religious life as children, the monastery would need to provide schooling. Through this somewhat roundabout path, classical learning entered the monastic curriculum.

The man largely responsible for this was Flavius Magnus Aurelius **Cassiodorus** Senator (c. 490–c. 583), a

CASSIODORUS. This frontispiece from a Bible, produced in a monastery in Britain around the year 700, depicts Cassiodorus as a copyist and keeper of books. Monasteries were instrumental in changing the form of the book from the ancient scroll to the modern codex. Because their parchment pages were heavy, codices were customarily stored in cupboards, lying flat, as we see them here.

younger contemporary of Benedict. Like Boethius, Cassiodorus (*cass-ee-oh-DOHR-uhs*) was attached to Theodoric's court and was for many years the secretary in charge of the king's correspondence. He also wrote a *History of the Goths*, which depicted Theodoric's people as part of Rome's history. After Theodoric's death, Cassiodorus founded an important monastery at Vivarium in southern Italy. There he composed commentaries on the Psalms as well as his most influential work, *Institutes*.

Inspired by Augustine and his own classical education, Cassiodorus believed that the study of classical literature was an essential preliminary to a proper understanding of the Bible. The *Institutes* is essentially a syllabus, a list of readings arranged so that a student would begin with simpler, straightforward works of pagan literature before moving on to more difficult works, and finally to the demanding study of theology. Cassiodorus thereby defined a classical canon that formed the basis of Christian education in the Roman West.

In order to ensure that his monks had access to the necessary readings, Cassiodorus encouraged the copying of books. He argued that this was precisely the sort of manual labor that Benedict had advocated. Under his influence, monasteries thus became engines for the collection, preservation, and transmission of knowledge. It is important to note that nearly all the Greek and Latin texts on which we rely for our study of western civilizations survived because they were copied in monasteries.

After You Read This Chapter

 Go to **INQUIZITIVE** to see what you've learned—and learn what you've missed—with personalized feedback along the way.

REVIEWING THE OBJECTIVES

- A number of historical factors shaped the way Jesus' teachings were received. Describe the most important of these factors.
- The expansion of Rome and the strain on its central government posed significant challenges in the third century. How did Roman emperors respond?
- Christianity's legalization changed it in profound ways. Why was this?
- During the fourth and fifth centuries, a new wave of migrations penetrated to the very heart of the empire. What made this possible?
- The differences between traditional Roman and Christian cultures were gradually reconciled through the efforts of Christian intellectuals. Why was this considered necessary?

Monasteries also developed and disseminated an important new information technology: the codex. For millennia, the standard book had been a scroll, a clumsy format that made searching for a particular passage difficult and confined the reader to one passage at a time. The codex facilitates indexing (from the Latin word for "finger") because a reader can flip back and forth among various pages, with a finger in one place while looking at another. Codices also store information more safely and efficiently because they compress many hundreds of pages within protective bindings. They are less wasteful, too, because texts can be copied on both sides of a page. They even make finding a given book easier because titles can be written on the codex's spine. It's arguable, in fact, that the invention of the codex was more revolutionary than the invention of printing a thousand years later. Unless you are scrolling through a digital version of this book, your copy of *Western Civilizations* is a codex.

CONCLUSION

Ever since the English historian Edward Gibbon published the first volume of *The Decline and Fall of the Roman Empire* in 1776—a year when Britain's own empire suffered a notable setback—more has been written about the "fall of Rome" than on the passing of any other civilization. Gibbon himself blamed Christianity, depicting it as a debilitating disease that sapped the empire's strength. Others have accused the barbarians whose movements put pressure on Rome's frontiers. But even in the time of Julius Caesar, Roman moralists had already declared that Rome was in decline. Indeed, any self-respecting Roman republican would say that Rome fell when Augustus came to power.

More recent scholarship has influenced the narrative offered in this chapter, which views *transformation* as a more accurate way of understanding this period. No civilization is static and unchanging; civilizations, like human beings, are living organisms. Therefore, any evidence of Rome's decline can also be read as evidence of its adaptability. The imperial policies of Septimius Severus and Diocletian were responses to the realities of Rome's size and diversity. The settlement of frontier peoples in Rome's western provinces gave rise to hybrid polities that found new uses for Roman buildings, political offices, and laws. Through Christianity, the language, administrative structures, and culture of ancient Rome were preserved and extended. The flexibility of the Roman political system made this possible, because it was inclusive to a degree no modern empire has ever matched.

Still, this transformation changed what it meant to be Roman, to the extent that historians now call this period "late antiquity" to distinguish it from the classical world that preceded it. By the seventh century, so much had changed that the contours of three distinctive civilizations can be discerned, each one exhibiting different aspects of Roman influence and crystallizing around different regions of the former empire. We will explore each of these civilizations in Chapter 7.

PEOPLE, IDEAS, AND EVENTS IN CONTEXT

- What were the main differences between **JESUS** and other Jewish leaders of his day?
- How did **PAUL OF TARSUS** reach out to the peoples of the Hellenistic world? How did his teachings influence the development of early Christianity?
- In what ways did **DIOCLETIAN**'s division of the empire and his institution of the **TETRARCHY** respond to longstanding problems?
- How and why was Christianity changed under **CONSTANTINE**? What effects did this have on attitudes toward women and their role in the church?
- How did the relocation of the imperial capital to **CONSTANTINOPLE** contribute to the growing divide between the **GREEK EAST** and the **LATIN WEST**? How did the mass migrations of frontier peoples transform the Latin West?
- What were the key contributions of **JEROME**, **AMBROSE**, and **AUGUSTINE** to the development of a specifically Christian outlook by the end of the fourth century C.E.?
- How did **BOETHIUS**, **BENEDICT**, and **CASSIODORUS** reshape classical culture in the fifth century C.E.?

THINKING ABOUT CONNECTIONS

- In your opinion, which phenomenon had a more profound impact on Rome: the overextension of imperial power, or the mass migration of peoples from Rome's frontier? Why?
- Few historians would now agree with the judgment of Edward Gibbon, who posited that Christianity destroyed the Roman Empire. But to what extent did Christianity alter the traditional values and infrastructure of the Roman state? Were these alterations inevitable? Why or why not?

STORY LINES

- Emperor Justinian's attempt to reconquer the western territories of the Roman Empire was ultimately more destructive than the mass migrations of the previous centuries.

- The culture of the Eastern Roman Empire (Byzantium) combined Roman legal and political systems with the learning of classical Greece but was most acutely shaped by Orthodox Christianity.

- Meanwhile, the rapid expansion of Islam was driven by the close connections among religious fervor, military conquest, and commercial opportunity.

- In western Europe, the disintegration of Roman political and economic infrastructures had a destabilizing effect, but this was countered by the success of the Frankish kingdom and the spread of monasticism.

- The empire of Charlemagne unified vast portions of northwestern Europe under a single centralized government, fostering important administrative, economic, and cultural developments.

Before You Read This Chapter

CHRONOLOGY

481–511	Reign of Clovis, king of the Franks
527–565	Reign of Justinian
570–632	Lifetime of Muhammad and early Muslim conquests
590–604	Papacy of Gregory the Great
636–651	Arab conquests of Persia, Palestine, Egypt, and North Africa
661–750	Dominion of the Umayyad dynasty in the Islamic world
717–787	Iconoclast Controversy in Byzantium
717–751	The Carolingian dynasty shares power with Merovingian kings
730	The Venerable Bede completes his history of the English church
750–930	Dominion of the Abassid dynasty in Baghdad and the Umayyad dynasty in al-Andalus (Spain)
751	Pepin becomes king of the Franks
768–814	Reign of Charlemagne
800–1000	Period of Viking invasions
871–899	Reign of Alfred the Great in England

Rome's Three Heirs, 500–950

Around the year 600, Anglo-Saxon tribes that had settled on the island of Britain were approached by missionaries sent from Rome. These Latin-speaking evangelists faced an enormous challenge: they had to find a way to convert tribal leaders by translating the central ideas of their Christian faith into languages and concepts that made sense in a new cultural context. They also needed to look for ways to meld Roman practices with pagan ones by building churches on sacred sites and gradually turning the worship of traditional gods into the rituals of Christianity. An account of these negotiations comes down to us in a remarkable book written several generations later. In *The History of the English Church and People*, a monk named Bede (c. 672–735) describes how Celtic and Anglo-Saxon peoples were uneasily united under the Roman Church and came to adopt Latin as a language of learning and worship. He also shows how, in the process, Roman Christian ideals were changed and adapted to meet new needs and express a new worldview.

This is but one example of the ways in which Rome's legacy was transmitted and transformed during the pivotal period known as the Middle Ages. This term is a problematic one, and it doesn't begin to express the diverse realities—or perceptions—of the generations of people who lived during this thousand-year period. This is because "the Middle Ages" is a modern invention. In the seventeenth century, intellectuals began to argue that an intermediate "medieval period" (*medium ævum*) separated their own "modern age" from the glorious accomplishments of classical Greece and the empire of ancient Rome, which many European states were trying to emulate. And yet, the period between 500 and 1500 was actually the beginning of that "modern age." During this era, the foundations of modern political institutions were laid, and the relationships among Judaism, Christianity, and Islam were first articulated. At the same time, three new civilizations became heirs of the Western civilizations formerly encompassed by a Roman Empire: the New Rome of Byzantium; the new Arabic empire, which promoted Islam; and the western European territories which looked increasingly to the Roman Church for leadership. Each of these interlocking civilizations preserved and modified different aspects of their shared Roman inheritance. Our world is still being shaped by the interactions among them.

JUSTINIAN'S IMPERIAL AMBITIONS

As we observed in Chapter 6, the eastern and western territories of Rome's empire were becoming divided along linguistic, cultural, and economic lines. By the end of the fourth century, this division also became political. The Ostrogothic conquest of Italy under Theodoric (r. 493–526), which was supported by the imperial government, briefly placed Constantinople in a position to influence affairs in the old Roman heartland, and enabled Theodoric to reestablish Roman rule in some regions of Italy and Gaul. But none of Theodoric's short-lived successors was able to rule this territory effectively. In 535, the Ostrogothic kingdom was overthrown in an attempt to reunify the entire Roman Empire.

The man responsible for this was Justinian (r. 527–565), the most ambitious emperor since Constantine. Although the empire he ruled was largely Greek-speaking, Justinian himself came from the Latin-speaking province of Dardania (now Serbia). He saw himself as the heir to the principate

THE MEDITERRANEAN WORLD UNDER JUSTINIAN, 527–565. Compare this map with the one on page 194. Here, the green shading represents those regions controlled by Justinian. ▪ *What was the geographical extent of Justinian's empire?* ▪ *Which areas of the former Roman Empire did Justinian not attempt to reconquer?* ▪ *What may have been the strategy behind these campaigns?*

established by Augustus; and like Augustus, he was aided by an astute and determined wife, Theodora, who played an influential role in his reign. Although his efforts ultimately failed, they had a lasting influence on the entire Mediterranean world.

Justinian's Attempted Reconquest

Justinian's initial efforts to strengthen and reunite the Roman Empire seemed successful. In 533, his general, Belisarius, conquered the Vandal kingdom of northwest Africa, destroying one of the eastern Roman Empire's greatest rivals and facilitating campaigns in Ostrogothic Italy and Visigothic Spain. By 536, Belisarius appeared poised to occupy Rome's old homeland, where he was welcomed as a savior by some former subjects of the Ostrogoths. But these early victories were illusory. Although the Mediterranean was under Roman control, the human and financial costs of these campaigns drastically strained imperial resources. Belisarius's army in Italy was overextended, and Justinian's need to levy soldiers led to oppressive taxes on vitally important regions such as Egypt and Syria, which undermined support for his imperial project. The Romans of Italy and North Africa, meanwhile, resented the costs their own "liberation" imposed on them. When the imperial armies were withdrawn from these regions to deal with the growing threat of Persia, North Africa was ripe for later conquest by the Arabs (see page 225).

Persia and the Rise of Rabbinic Judaism

Although the Persian Empire under the Sassanid dynasty had long been a rival of Rome, it was able to expand its reach with little resistance during this time, while Rome's armies contended with waves of invasion elsewhere. It was in Persia that many Palestinian Jews had found a home after the Romans' destruction of the Second Temple in Jerusalem (Chapter 6), and where they joined older Jewish communities that had remained in the ancient region of Babylonia after it was conquered by Cyrus the Great (Chapter 2). Here, a group of powerful and learned *rabbis* (teachers) worked to keep Judaism not only alive, but flourishing. They established special schools (*yeshivas*) for the study of the Torah. In the sixth century, they presided over the codification of the Talmud, a collection of writings that preserved and interpreted centuries of oral teachings and legal judgments. This new phase of Judaism's development in Persia during the diaspora is accordingly known as Rabbinic Judaism, and it soon influenced the establishment of similar schools and traditions in Jewish communities throughout the medieval world.

The Justinianic Plague

In addition to the challenge posed by Persia, Justinian's attempted reconquest of former Roman territories was further complicated by a pandemic that broke out in 541–542. It even afflicted Justinian himself—although he recovered—and is known as the Justinianic Plague. According to recent findings by epidemiologists and geneticists, this pandemic was caused by an early strain of the same virus that later spawned the terrible Black Death of the fourteenth century (see Chapter 10). It may even have been just as deadly and widespread, stretching from China (where it appears to have originated) to Scandinavia and into Africa and the Indian Ocean. It is estimated to have killed a large percentage of the world's population at that time (some 25 million people) and recurred in some places for the next 200 years. It is ironic that the plague spread so rapidly and so far because of the very efficient infrastructures—roads, bridges, and trading networks—that bound the Roman Empire together and linked it to its neighbors.

Justinian's Impact on the Western Roman Empire

Justinian's wars proved more devastating to Italy, in particular, than the previous incursions of barbarian peoples. Around Rome, the vital supply lines of the aqueducts were cut, and the elaborate system of conduits, drainage ditches, and reservoirs was destroyed. Parts of the Italian countryside returned to marshland, and some areas were not drained again until the twentieth century. In 568, a new group of migrants, known as the Lombards, took advantage of the chaos to conquer the northern third of the peninsula. Thereafter, Italy would be divided between Lombard territories in the north and imperial territories in the southeast, with Rome and its region precariously sandwiched between them. The controlling forces within these territories changed greatly over time, but this tripartite division remained the essential political configuration of Italy until the nineteenth century—and it still divides Italian politics to this day.

Meanwhile, tensions between Arian Visigoths and their Roman subjects continued in Spain, even after the Visigothic king officially converted to Roman Christianity in 587. This mutual hostility persisted until the Visigothic kingdom, like North Africa, was largely absorbed by Islam.

The Codification of Roman Law

Justinian's most positive and lasting accomplishment was legal and intellectual. The codification of Roman law was a project long overdue. Since the time of the third-century jurists (see Chapter 5), the number of imperial statutes and legal decisions had multiplied, and the resulting body of law was both massive and self-contradictory. Moreover, conditions had changed so radically within the empire that many legal principles no longer applied. When Justinian came to power in 527, one of his first initiatives was to bring existing precedents into harmony with actual historical conditions and thereby restore the prestige and power of the imperial office.

To carry out this work, Justinian appointed a team of lawyers under the supervision of a jurist called Tribonian. Within two years, this commission published the first result of its labors: the Code, a systematic compilation of imperial statutes, which was later supplemented by another book, the Novels (*Novellae*, "new laws"), containing the legislation of Justinian and his immediate successors. By 532, the commission had also completed the Digest, a summary of the writings of Rome's great legal authorities, including the jurists of the principate. Its final product was the *Institutes*, a textbook of legal principles. Together, these four volumes constitute the *Corpus Juris Civilis* ("body of civil law").

Justinian's *Corpus* was a brilliant achievement. In the eastern Roman Empire, it immediately became the foundation on which all subsequent legal developments would rest. Although little known in western

Europe for centuries, it eventually influenced the legal systems of many nations. The nineteenth-century Napoleonic Code—still the basis of law in France, Spain, much of Latin America, and the state of Louisiana—is essentially based on the *Corpus* of Justinian.

The *Corpus* also had a profound impact on political philosophy. Starting from the maxim that "what pleases the prince has the force of law," it granted unlimited powers to the emperor and was therefore adopted by early modern rulers as a foundation for absolutism (see Chapter 15). But the *Corpus* provided some support for constitutional forms of government as well, because it maintained that a sovereign's powers are delegated to him by the people, and that what is mandated by the people can also be taken away

JUSTINIAN AND THEODORA. These sixth-century mosaics from the Church of San Vitale in the imperial capital of Ravenna (Italy) show the emperor and empress proceeding toward the main altar of the church, carrying the holy vessels used for the consecration of bread and wine. • *What do these images convey about the sacred and secular powers of both figures? What do they suggest about the role of gender in the representation of power?*

by them. Equally important is the fundamental principle that the state is a corporate body, not the extension of an individual's private property. The modern conception of the state as a public entity derives from the legal maxims of the *Corpus*.

THE ROMAN EMPIRE OF BYZANTIUM

With the failure of Justinian's project of imperial reunification, the history of the eastern Roman Empire can be said to enter a new phase. Indeed, many historians regard it as essentially a new entity, the Byzantine Empire, a name derived from the ancient port where Constantinople was situated. **Byzantium** thus became *one* of Rome's three heirs, not the sole heir of Roman authority, as Justinian had hoped. Yet according to the citizens of this empire, it never ceased to be Rome, and they were never anything but Romans. They called their empire Rome, not Byzantium, and saw themselves as carrying forward Roman traditions, values, and institutions.

As a result of Justinian's policies and outside pressures, however, this New Rome was struggling for survival. By 610, the Greek-speaking imperial dynasty that began

with Heraclius (r. 610–641) was unable to extend its influence much farther west than the Adriatic. Meanwhile, the Persians had conquered almost all of the empire's eastern and southern territories in Syria and Palestine. They had even plundered Jerusalem and carried off a precious relic believed to be part of the original cross on which Jesus had been crucified. With an enormous effort, Heraclius rallied his remaining military powers and routed the Persians, recapturing Jerusalem and retrieving the relic in 627.

But these gains were short-lived. Arab armies, inspired by the new religion of Islam, were able to profit from the empire's exhaustion. They soon occupied the recently reconquered Byzantine territories and claimed Jerusalem as a holy site for Muslims, as well as for Jews and Christians. They also absorbed the entire Persian Empire and rapidly made their way westward to Roman North Africa. They then took to the sea and, in 677, attempted a naval conquest of Constantinople. Repulsed with difficulty, they made another attempt in 717 by means of a concerted land and sea operation. This new threat was countered by the emperor Leo III (r. 717–741). His forces were able to defeat the Arabs by deploying keen strategy and a secret inflammatory mixture of chemicals that produced "Greek fire." Over the next few decades, the eastern Roman Empire managed to reconquer most of Anatolia, which remained the imperial heartland for the next several centuries.

THE SECRET WEAPON OF BYZANTIUM: "GREEK FIRE." This depiction of Greek fire in action illustrates a chronicle by John Skylitzes, a Byzantine historian who flourished in the eleventh century. This manuscript was copied in Sicily during the twelfth century and is now preserved in the Biblioteca Nacional de España in Madrid.

Sources of Stability

In many ways, the internal politics of the Byzantine Empire were as challenging as the history of its wider region. Because all power was concentrated in the imperial court at Constantinople and the emperors followed their predecessors in claiming autonomous rule, opposition to imperial authority could take the form of intrigue, treason, and violent plots. Indeed, Byzantine politics is so famous for its cloak-and-dagger complexity that the word *byzantine* has come to denote devious machinations or elaborate systems of bureaucracy. In reality, though, many able rulers wielded their powers very effectively in Constantinople, where a centralized government continued to function even in times of upheaval. No polity in western Europe had anything resembling such effective mechanisms of government until a much later period.

Strong, self-perpetuating political institutions thus constituted a major source of stability in Byzantium and offer an explanation for the extraordinary longevity of the empire's core provinces—nearly a thousand years. The imperial bureaucracy in Constantinople regulated prices and wages, maintained systems of licensing, and controlled exports and trade. Its highly educated officials supervised many aspects of social and cultural life, overseeing schools, the organization of the Orthodox Church, and the observance of religious rites and holidays. Even the popular sport of chariot racing—New Rome's exciting answer to gladiatorial combat, which harked back to the love of that sport in ancient Greece (Chapter 3)—was strictly regulated, as were the various teams' fiercely competitive fans. The imperial government also regulated the army and navy, the courts, and the diplomatic service, endowing these agencies with organizational strengths incomparable for their time.

Another source of stability in the eastern Roman Empire was a well-integrated and sophisticated economy. Commerce and cities continued to flourish as they had done in late antiquity, which was not the case in western Europe at this time: the new barbarian kingdoms had no established gold or silver coinage to facilitate transactions, and few cities had withstood the upheavals of the fifth century. Constantinople became a central emporium for eastern luxury goods and western raw materials alike. The empire also nurtured and protected its own industries, most notably the manufacture and weaving of silk, which—according to legend—had been brought illegally to western Asia from China, where silkworms and the knowledge of cultivating them was a carefully guarded secret among the women who dominated this industry—and who continued to do so in Byzantium.

But Constantinople was not the only great urban center. The Hellenistic capital, Antioch, and the bustling cities of Thessalonica and Trebizond were also very large and prosperous. Any one of them would have dwarfed any western European city; Paris was a village, and Rome may have had a few thousand people living among the ruins. In such cities, Byzantine trade and industry produced most of the surplus wealth that sustained the state. But agriculture also lay at the heart of the Byzantine economy, so much so that peasant farmers struggled to maintain their independence from large estates owned by wealthy aristocrats and monasteries. As in the final centuries of the Roman republic (Chapter 4), they were only able to do so with the help of legislation. When the aristocracy eventually gained control, during the eleventh century, free peasants were transformed into impoverished tenant farmers, as had been the case in Italy during the third century C.E. This was one of the less positive ways in which New Rome resembled its ancient predecessor.

Orthodoxy and Iconoclasm

Viewed from our perspective, law, strong governance, and a thriving economy seem to be the basis of Byzantine civilization. Yet the inhabitants of New Rome also cared a great deal about religious **orthodoxy**. Indeed, their intense preoccupation with questions of doctrine could be a catalyst for political and social dissension, but it also endowed the empire's inhabitants with a deeply shared sense of identity. In ancient Rome, the *mos maiorum* (Chapter 5) had undergirded Roman pride and superiority; in New Rome, Orthodox Christianity occupied the same fundamental place. The stakes of theological and doctrinal disputes were further heightened because emperors took an active role in them.

The most contentious issue, and one that came to a head in the eighth century, was a violent disagreement over the meaning and use of religious images, known as the **Iconoclast** ("image-breaking") **Controversy**. As we saw in Chapter 6, Christians had long been accustomed to expressing their devotion to Christ and the saints through the making and veneration of images. There was even a legend that the author of Luke's Gospel had been a painter, the maker of the first icon. At the same time, however, some Christians argued that any representation of a holy person came close to being a form of idolatry, something strongly condemned in the Jewish tradition, which Christianity had inherited. Both Roman (Latin-speaking) and Orthodox (Greek-speaking) Christian teachers insisted that images were only *aids* to worship, not *objects* of worship, but this fine line was easily crossed.

In Byzantium, the veneration of icons was an especially potent part of daily devotion, so any suggestion that such images should be suppressed or destroyed was bound to be contentious. But that is precisely what the iconoclast movement advocated. They argued that honoring images was blasphemous because they were made by human beings who were thereby setting up gods other than God (the first prohibition in the Ten Commandments given to Moses). For their part, traditionalists argued that the images themselves were never objects of worship; rather, icons were windows through which a glimpse of heaven might be granted to human beings on earth.

The iconoclast movement was initiated by Emperor Leo III, whose leadership had helped to save Constantinople from Arab invasion, and who was then faced with the task of rebuilding imperial authority. It thus seems likely that there were political and economic motives behind the campaign. By proclaiming a radical new religious movement,

the emperor could renew and strengthen control over the Orthodox Church and thus combat the growing power of monasteries. And indeed, the great monasteries of Byzantium were the major producers of icons. So when the monasteries rallied to the cause of images, they were strongly suppressed by Leo and his successors, who took this opportunity to confiscate much of their wealth.

The Legacy of Iconoclasm

The Iconoclast Controversy was resolved toward the end of the eighth century in favor of those who promoted religious imagery, the Iconodules ("image servants"). But it had some long-lasting effects. One was the destruction of many artworks produced or preserved in the eastern Roman Empire. This means that examples of Christian artistry from the first eight centuries after Jesus's death are very rare in these regions and are preserved mainly in Italy, Palestine, Egypt, and Ethiopia—beyond the reach of the iconoclastic emperors. A second consequence was the widening of a religious and political breach between the Greek East and the Latin West. Prior to Emperor Leo's iconoclastic initiatives, the patriarch of Rome—known familiarly as "papa" in Latin slang—had often been a close ally of Byzantium's rulers. But iconoclasm called into question not only the veneration of images but also the veneration of the saints, and by extension, the Roman patriarch's claim to be Saint Peter's successor (see Chapter 6). This was not a position that the Roman papa (pope) could support.

The ultimate defeat of iconoclasm crystallized some aspects of belief and practice that came to be characteristic of Byzantium. One was a renewed emphasis on the Orthodox faith of the empire, which had the effect of marginalizing the Christians of Syria and Armenia, who had their own churches and devoutly held beliefs. Fear of heresy, combined with the powerful position of the emperor as head of the Orthodox Church, also tended to inhibit intellectual freedom. Although the imperial family eventually founded a university in Constantinople, its students and faculty were discouraged from expressing dissenting opinions or engaging in any significant degree of intellectual speculation—in marked contrast to the more freewheeling intellectual atmosphere cultivated by the universities of western Europe (see Chapters 8 and 9).

DEVOTIONAL IMAGE—OR DANGEROUS IDOL? This icon of the Virgin Mary, "the Bud-Bearer (Theotokos) was painted in the sixth century and is one of the oldest such images in existence. Preserved at the Orthodox monastery of St. Catherine on Mount Sinai (Egypt), it shows the mother and child flanked by two warrior saints and protected by angels gazing upward at the hand of God emerging from heaven. *How might such icons inspire devotion and shape viewers' ideas of femininity and motherhood?* ■ *According to the proponents of iconoclasm, why would such an image be considered blasphemous?*

Tradition and Innovation in Byzantium

Although Orthodox religion was central to the identity of Byzantine Romans, so was their direct link with the Hellenistic past and the heritage of ancient Greece. Byzantine schools based their instruction on classical Greek literature,

Competing Viewpoints

Debating the Power of Icons

> The Iconoclast Controversy of the eighth century divided Byzantine society and was a factor in the growing division between the Latin Church of Rome and the Greek Orthodox Church. The excerpts below are representative of the two main arguments voiced at the time. The first is from a treatise by John of Damascus (c. 675–749), a Christian in the service of the Muslim Umayyad caliphs. The second is an official report issued from the synod convened by the emperor Constantine V (r. 741–775) in 754. Constantine was carrying forward the iconoclastic policies of his father, Leo III.

John of Damascus on Holy Images

Our adversaries, the iconoclasts, say: "God's commands to Moses the law-giver were clear: 'Thou shalt adore the Lord thy God, and thou shalt worship him alone, and thou shalt not make any images of anything in the heaven above or in the earth beneath.'" But these laws were given to the Jews because they were apt to fall into idolatry. We, on the contrary, are no longer in need of such childish rules. We have grown up out of infancy and have reached the perfection of adulthood. We know how to distinguish between an image and something real or divine.

An image is only a *likeness* of the original and is therefore different from that original. It is not and cannot be an exact reproduction of the original. In just the same way, we know that Jesus Christ is the living, substantial, unchangeable Image of the invisible God: a Son equal to the Father in all things, but differing from Him because a Son is begotten of a Father. They are not the same. We can compare this divine example to a human one: a man who wishes to build a house first thinks and makes out a plan. The plan is an image of the house he will build, but it is not the same as the house. In the same way, things visible on earth are images of invisible and intangible things that we cannot see—but which help us to imagine the divine things in which we believe. Holy Scripture is itself an image of God, set-ting before us, in the imagery of words, the truths of God's justice and creation. It shows us what is otherwise unknowable, untouchable, making divine things imaginable and understandable. All the invisible workings of God since the creation of the world are made visible through images. We experience images of His creation which remind us of God, as when we admire the sun or a light, or feel burning rays, or drink from a running fountain or hear a full river, or see a rose tree or a sprouting flower, or smell a sweet fragrance.

Source: Excerpted and adapted from *St. John Damascene on Holy Images*, trans. Mary H. Allies (London: 1898), pp. 6–12.

in marked contrast to the more tentative attitude toward classical learning in western Europe (see Chapter 6). Educated men and women around the Byzantine court who quoted only a single line of Homer could expect their listeners to recognize the entire passage from which it came. In the English-speaking world, only the King James Bible has ever achieved the same degree of cultural saturation. Indeed, Homeric epics were a kind of sacred text in Byzantium, as were the surviving tragedies of Athenian dramatists of the fifth century B.C.E.

Byzantine scholars intensively studied the philosophy of Plato and the historical prose of Thucydides. In contrast, Aristotle's works were less well known, and many other philosophical traditions of antiquity were deemed dangerous. Although Justinian had presided zealously over the codification of ancient Roman (and thus pagan) law, he registered his distrust of Greek (pagan) philosophy by shutting down the Athenian academies that had existed since Plato's day. The practice of Greek scientific inquiry and the advances of Hellenistic science were also neglected. Tradition was more highly prized than originality, as was preservation over innovation. The benefit of this, for posterity, is that Byzantium rescued Greek and Hellenistic writings for later ages. The vast majority of ancient Greek texts known

Canons of the Synod of 754

t is the unanimous doctrine of all the holy Fathers and of the six Ecumenical Synods, that no one may imagine any kind of separation or mingling in opposition to the unsearchable, unspeakable, and incomprehensible union of the two natures in the one *hypostasis* or person. What avails, then, the folly of the painter, who from sinful love of gain depicts that which should not be depicted—that is, with his polluted hands he tries to fashion that which should only be believed in the heart and confessed with the mouth? He makes an image and calls it Christ. The name *Christ* signifies *God and man.* Consequently it is an image of God and man, and consequently he has in his foolish mind, in his representation of the created flesh, depicted the Godhead which cannot be represented, and thus mingled what should not be mingled. Thus he is guilty of a double blasphemy—the one in making an image of the Godhead, and the other by mingling the Godhead and manhood . . . like the Monophysites, or he represents the body of Christ as not made divine and separate and as a person apart, like the Nestorians.

The only admissible figure of the humanity of Christ, however, is bread and wine in the holy Supper. This and no other form, this and no other type, has he chosen to represent his incarnation. Bread he ordered to be brought, but not a representation of the human form, so that idolatry might not arise. And as the body of Christ is made divine, so also this figure of the body of Christ, the bread, is made divine by the descent of the Holy Spirit; it becomes the divine body of Christ by the mediation of the priest who, separating the oblation from that which is common, sanctifies it.

Source: Excerpted from *The Seven Ecumenical Councils of the Undivided Church,* trans. H. R. Percival, in *Nicene and Post-Nicene Fathers,* 2nd Series, ed. P. Schaff and H. Wace (repr. Grand Rapids, MI: 1955), pp. 543–44.

Questions for Analysis

1. With what other things does John of Damascus compare the making of images? How do these comparisons help him make his argument in favor of them?

2. With what phenomena do the theologians of the synod compare the making of images? Why do they declare the bread and wine of the Eucharist to be the only legitimate representations of Christ?

3. What is the significance of the fact that John of Damascus did not live under the jurisdiction of the Byzantine emperor, but that of the Muslim Umayyad caliph? How might that have influenced his writing?

---

today survive only because they were copied by Byzantine scribes.

In further contrast to western Europe, as we shall see, the Byzantine educational system was inclusive, open to the laity and even to women. Although most girls from aristocratic or prosperous families were educated at home by private tutors, they nevertheless mingled freely with their male counterparts on social occasions, and many female intellectuals were praised for their erudition. There were even female physicians, another extraordinary departure from both ancient tradition and the practices of western Europe until the latter part of the nineteenth century.

Byzantine Art and Architecture

Byzantine achievements in the realms of architecture and art are exemplified by the church of Hagia Sophia ("Holy Wisdom") in Constantinople, constructed at enormous cost under the patronage of Justinian. It quickly came to define an architectural style unique to Byzantium. Its purpose was not to express pride in human accomplishment but rather to symbolize the mysteries of the Christian faith and the holy knowledge imparted by Christ to the soul of the believer. For this reason, the architects paid little attention to the external appearance of the building.

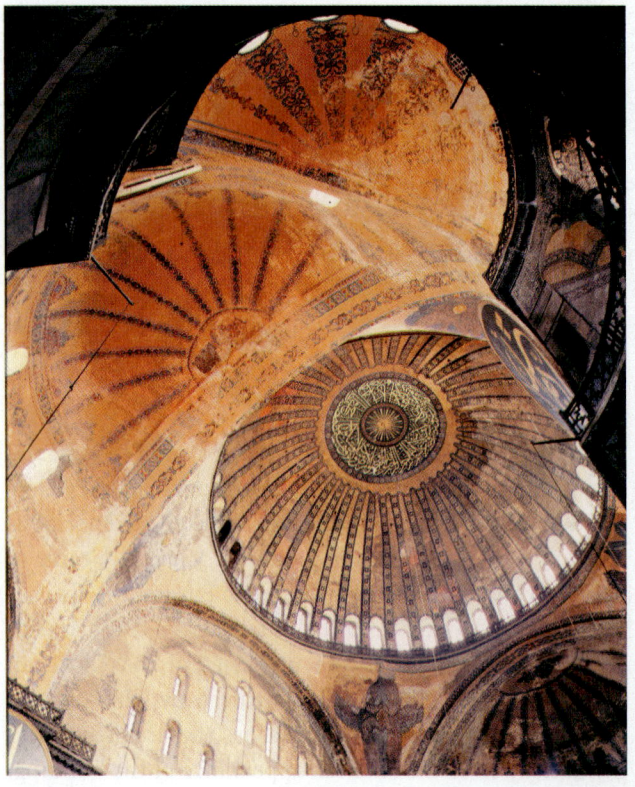

HAGIA SOPHIA. This great monument to the artistry, engineering skill, and spirituality of Byzantium was built during the reign of Justinian. The four minarets at its corners were added in 1453, after Constantinople (now Istanbul) was absorbed into the empire of the Ottoman Turks. Hagia Sophia is now a mosque and a museum.

The interior, however, was decorated with richly colored mosaics, gold leaf, colored marble columns, and bits of tinted glass set on edge to refract rays of sunlight like sparkling gems, making it appear that light is generated from within. The magnificent dome over its central square was an unprecedented engineering feat: it was upheld by four great arches springing from pillars at the four corners of the square. The result was an architectural framework both marvelously strong and delicate. Its effect is heightened by the many windows placed around the dome's rim, which convey the impression that it floats in midair.

Many aspects of Byzantine arts and learning exerted strong influence on the artisans and scholars of western Europe through continued economic and cultural contact. The basilica of San Marco in Venice (c. 1063) reflects this influence distinctly, as do medieval mosaics in such cities as Ravenna and Palermo. Greek-speaking monasteries in southeastern Italy maintained especially close ties with

DOME OF HAGIA SOPHIA. The revolutionary structure of the church, shown here, made it appear as if the enormous dome floated on light and air.

their counterparts in the eastern empire, and many were allowed to practice the rituals of the Orthodox Church; many Greek books, including the comedies of Aristophanes (Chapter 4), were copied and preserved there. But much of the heritage of Western civilizations that was cultivated in Byzantium was largely inaccessible elsewhere in Europe, because the knowledge of Greek became increasingly rare.

MUHAMMAD AND THE TEACHINGS OF ISLAM

The civilization that formed around the religion of Islam mirrors the Roman Empire in its global reach and longevity; in this, it is truly one of Rome's heirs. Islam (Arabic for "submission") also calls to mind the early republic of Rome in that it demands loyalty not just to common forms of worship, but also to certain social and cultural norms. But whereas the Roman Empire came to undergird Christianity, elevating it to the status of a major faith, the Muslim faith was itself an engine of imperial expansion.

The Revelations of Muhammad

Islam emerged in Arabia, a desert land considered so forbidding that neither the Romans nor the Persians sought to conquer it. Arabian society was tribal and did not revolve around urban settlements. Many Arabs were herdsmen, living off the milk of their camels and the produce of desert oases. But as with the Hittites in the second millennium B.C.E. (Chapter 2), their very mobility, ingenuity, and pioneering spirit made them excellent explorers and long-distance traders. In the second half of the sixth century, when protracted wars between Byzantium and Persia made travel dangerous for merchants, the Arabs quickly established themselves as guides, couriers, and guardians of transit routes between Africa and Asia.

As part of this process, towns began to emerge. The most prominent of these was Mecca, an ancient sacred site that lay at the crossroads of major caravan routes. Mecca was home to the Kaaba (*KAH-ah-bah*), a shrine housing the Black Stone worshiped by many Arabian tribes. (It may be a meteorite, and hence of celestial origin.) The Quraysh (*kur-AYSH*), the tribe that controlled this shrine, thus came to dominate the economic and religious life of the whole region, forming an aristocracy of traders and entrepreneurs.

Muhammad, the founder of Islam, was a member of this tribe. He was born in Mecca about 570. Orphaned early in life, he entered the service of a wealthy widow and successful merchant Khadija, whom he married. She would be his closest confidant, first follower, and energetic proponent of his teachings.

Until middle age, Muhammad lived as a prosperous trader, little different from his fellow townsmen. But around 610, he experienced a spiritual epiphany. At this time, the Arab tribes worshiped many gods. Yet, like the ancient Hebrews, they also acknowledged one god as more powerful. For the Hebrews, God was Yahweh; for the Arabs, Allah. But whereas the Hebrews' embrace of monotheism was a long and gradual process, Muhammad's conversion was sudden, the immediate consequence of revelation. Thereafter, Muhammad received further revelations that became the basis for his teachings and by which he was persuaded to accept the calling of a prophet and proclaim the new faith to his tribe.

The Beginnings of Islam

Muhammad was not immediately successful in gaining converts among his own people. In Mecca, tribal leaders of the Quraysh feared that his teachings would diminish the importance of the Kaaba. Some residents of the town of Yathrib, however, saw an opportunity to increase its prestige and invited Muhammad to live among them to serve as judge and arbiter in local rivalries. Muhammad, mourning the recent death of Khadija, accepted this invitation in 622, along with a few loyal followers. Because this emigration—in Arabic, the *Hijra* (*HIJ-ruh*)—marks the beginning of Muhammad's wider influence, Muslims regard it as the beginning of time. Just as Christians date all events according to the birth of Jesus (see Chapter 6), Muslims begin their dating system with the Hijra.

Muhammad changed the name of Yathrib to Medina ("City of the Prophet") and established himself as the town's ruler. He did not, however, abandon his desire to exercise authority among his own people. He and his followers began a series of military raids of Quraysh caravans traveling beyond Mecca. An important early victory occurred in 624 at the Battle of Badr in western Arabia, where a small number of loyal adherents to Islam defeated a much larger force sent out from Mecca to defend a valuable trading caravan. Muhammad's men killed the expedition's leader and took valuable booty and prisoners. The success of this enterprise sent a powerful message to the Quraysh and inspired many men to join Muhammad. But there was further opposition to Islam, not only from Mecca, but from Jewish tribes in the region who joined forces with Muhammad's Arab enemies. This led Muhammad to denounce the Jews as faithless to their own prophets and to expel all but one wealthy Jewish clan from Medina and its surrounding region.

Analyzing Primary Sources

A Sura from the Qur'an

The Qur'an preserves the teachings of Muhammad in a series of suras, or chapters. Composed in verse forms that draw on much older traditions of Arabic poetry, they are meant to be sung or chanted. Indeed, the word Qur'an means "recitations," referring both to Muhammad's method of teaching and the Muslim practice of memorizing and repeating portions of scripture.

Sura 81: The Overturning

In the Name of God the Compassionate the Caring

When the sun is overturned
When the stars fall away
When the mountains are moved
When the ten-month pregnant
    camels are abandoned
When the beasts of the wild
    are herded together   5
When the seas are boiled over
When the souls are coupled
When the girl-child buried alive
is asked what she did to deserve
    murder
When the pages are folded out   10
When the sky is flayed open
When Jahím [the Day of Reckoning]
    is set ablaze

When the garden is brought near
Then a soul will know what it
    has prepared
I swear by the stars that slide,   15
stars streaming, stars that sweep
    along the sky
By the night as it slips away
By the morning when the fragrant
    air breathes
This is the word of a messenger
    ennobled,
empowered, ordained before
    the lord of the throne,   20
holding sway there, keeping trust
Your friend [Muhammad] has not
    gone mad
He saw him on the horizon clear
He does not hoard for himself
    the unseen
This is not the word of a satan
    struck with stones   25

Where are you going?
This is a reminder to all beings
For those who wish to walk straight
Your only will is the will of God lord
    of all beings

Source: From *Approaching the Qur'an: The Early Revelations*, trans. Michael Sells (Ashland, OR: 1999), pp. 48–50.

Questions for Analysis

1. What impressions of Arab culture emerge from this sura? What does the litany of unlikely or mystical events reveal about the values of Muhammad's contemporaries?

2. How does Muhammad speak of himself and his role in society?

In 627, the Quraysh assembled a large coalition force to attack Medina, hoping that the remaining Jews there—who had reason to distrust Muhammad—would join forces with them. In response, Muhammad decided to risk a siege of his own city and caused a deep defensive trench to be dug around it, slowing the enemy's advance. The Meccan army had not come equipped for an extended battle and eventually dispersed: an ignominious defeat known as the Battle of the Trench. And even though the Jews of Medina had not joined forces with the Meccans, the Muslims charged them with treason and executed all the men and enslaved the women and children.

By 630, Muhammad's successes had persuaded his kinsmen to submit to his authority and teachings. Muhammad, for his part, ensured that the Kaaba's shrine would be revered as Islam's holiest place, a status it maintains today.

And because Mecca had long been a pilgrimage site and gathering place for tribes throughout Arabia, many more people were exposed to Muhammad's teachings and inspired by his military prowess, which promised prosperity for his people in the years to come. At the time of his death in 632, Muhammad's followers were committed to spreading this new faith.

Muhammad and the Qur'an

As its name indicates, the faith of Islam calls for submission to Allah, whom Muslims identify as being the same as the Jews' Yahweh and the Christian God. (The Muslim saying "there is no god but Allah" is more accurately translated as "there is no god but God.") For Muslims, the history and prophecies of the Jews are therefore important components of their religion, as are the teachings of Jesus, who is regarded as a great prophet. But Muhammad is regarded as the greatest prophet, whose revelations established the rituals and practices essential to Islam.

These teachings are preserved in the sacred scripture of the **Qur'an** (*kuhr-AHN*), an Arabic word meaning "recitations" because Muhammad is said to have recited his revelations orally. Eventually, they were gathered together and transcribed, a process that continued after Muhammad's death. So unlike the Christian Gospels, which offer different perspectives on Jesus's ministry and were recorded a generation or two after his crucifixion, the Qur'an is considered to be a direct link with Muhammad. It is also unlike most books of the Bible because it takes the form of poetry, drawing on ancient genres of Arabic song.

Islam teaches that a day of judgment is coming—and soon. On this day, the righteous will be granted eternal life in a paradise of delights, but wrongdoers will be damned to a realm of eternal fire. Therefore all people are offered a fundamental choice: to begin a new life of divine service or to follow their own path. If they choose to follow God, they will be blessed; if they do not, God will turn away from them. Thus, the only sure means of achieving salvation is to observe the **Five Pillars** of the faith: submission to God's will as described in the teachings of Muhammad, frequent prayer, ritual fasting, giving alms, and at least one pilgrimage to Mecca (the *Hajj*) during the believer's lifetime.

Unlike Christianity, Islam is a religion without priests. In this, it more closely resembles Rabbinic Judaism as it developed after the destruction of the Second Temple, which made a Temple priesthood obsolete. Instead, as we noted previously, Jewish communities gathered around a master teacher, the rabbi. Similarly, Muslims often rely on a community leader (*imam*), a scholar qualified to comment on matters of faith who may also act as a judge in disputes. Like Judaism, Islam also emphasizes the inextricable connection between religious observance and daily life, between spirituality and politics. There is no opposition of sacred and secular authority, as in Christianity. But in marked contrast to Judaism, Islam is a religion that aspires to unite the world in a shared faith. This means that Muslims, like Christians, consider it their duty to engage in the work of conversion.

THE WIDENING ISLAMIC WORLD

As we have frequently noted, the death of any charismatic leader precipitates a series of crises. Muhammad and Alexander the Great represent different types of leadership, but both were visionaries whose military and political successes inspired intense loyalty; and neither designated his own successor, leaving behind a number of close followers who disagreed as to the proper uses of the power they inherited.

The Arab Conquest of the West

Muhammad's closest surviving followers were his father-in-law Abu Bakr (*ah-boo BAHK-uhr*) and an early convert named Umar. After Muhammad's death, they took the initiative in providing a leader for the Muslims of Arabia by naming Abu Bakr as *caliph*, a word meaning "deputy" or "representative," of Muhammad. But many tribes were unwilling to accept this aged man as Muhammad's successor, leading to a new phase of warfare. As armies loyal to Abu Bakr moved northward, their successes encouraged even more men to embrace Islam and join the fight to establish the faith. When they came to the Arabian frontier they kept going, meeting only minimal resistance from the Byzantine and Persian armies as they moved west.

When Abu Bakr died two years later, Umar succeeded him as caliph, and he continued to direct the growing forces against Byzantium and Persia. In the following years, victories were virtually continuous. In 636, they routed a Byzantine army in Syria and then quickly swept over the entire area, occupying the leading cities of Antioch, Damascus, and Jerusalem. In 637, they destroyed the main army of the Persians and took the Persian capital of Ctesiphon. By 651, the Arabian conquest of the entire Persian Empire was virtually complete.

Arab forces, now increased by newer converts, then turned toward North Africa, capturing Roman Egypt by 646 and extending their control throughout the rest of North Africa during the following decades. Only Ethiopia, far to the south, remained an independent Christian kingdom.

Although attempts to capture Constantinople were not successful, as we noted previously, Arab and allied forces crossed from North Africa into Visigothic Spain in 711, quickly absorbing most of the Iberian Peninsula. In less than a century, followers of Islam had conquered the oldest civilizations of western Asia and much of the Roman Mediterranean. In the process, the desert-dwelling Arabs had transformed themselves into the world's most daring seafarers.

How can we explain this prodigious achievement? On a basic level, what motivated the Arabs had motivated the Sumerians, Neo-Assyrians, Greeks, Macedonians, and Romans: the search for richer territory and new wealth. The Muslim identity that was bound up with military successes also played a crucial role, since the teachings of Muhammad and the shared study of the Qur'an forged common allegiances among tribes hitherto at war with one another.

This Muslim identity must have been further strengthened by the absence of any organized opposition to the Arabs' advancement; it was regarded as a mark of their religious superiority. Missionary fervor may also have played

Legend:
- At the death of Muhammad, 632
- After the conquests of the first four caliphs, 661
- After the conquests of the Umayyad caliphs, 750
- - - - Outer limits of the Byzantine Empire

THE EXPANSION OF ISLAM TO 750. This map shows the steady advance of Islam through Arab conquests from the time of Muhammad to the middle of the eighth century. ■ *What was the geographical extent of Muslim rule in 750?* ■ *Compare this map to the map of Justinian's empire on page 214. Which of these territories had formerly belonged to Rome? What resources would have been available to the Muslim conquerors as they moved into these territories?*

a role, although there is little evidence that Muslims actively converted their new subjects to the faith of Islam at this time. Instead, they established themselves as a ruling class, with a grasp of the sophisticated workings of governance and finance that matched their military acumen. Non-Muslims living under Muslim rule were expected to pay the taxes that had been due to the previous Persian or Byzantine authorities, as well as a poll tax (*jizya*). In many places, those conquered by the Muslims preferred their rule to that of their Byzantine and Persian predecessors.

THE GREAT UMAYYAD MOSQUE AT DAMASCUS. This mosque was built by Caliph al-Walid between 705 and 715. Byzantine influence is apparent in its arched colonnades, mosaics, and series of domes, all of which were replicated in much subsequent Islamic architecture. The mosaic over the central doorway, shown here, indicates that the visitor is entering paradise. The mosque was constructed on the foundations of a Roman temple and also incorporates a later Christian shrine dedicated to Saint John the Baptist. • *Why would the caliph have chosen this site for his mosque?*

The Shi'ite–Sunni Schism

As this wave of conquests widened the reach of Islamic influence, disputes continued to divide the original Muslims of Mecca. When the caliph Umar died in 644, he was replaced by Uthman, a member of the **Umayyad** (*oo-MY-yad*) family: a wealthy clan that had long resisted Muhammad's authority. Opponents of Uthman accordingly rallied around Muhammad's cousin and son-in-law, Ali, whose marriage to Muhammad's only child Fatimah, made him seem a more appropriate choice. When Uthman was murdered in 656, Ali's supporters declared him the new caliph—but Uthman's powerful family refused to accept him. When Ali, too, was murdered, another member of the Umayyad family replaced him. From 661 to 750, this Umayyad dynasty ruled the Islamic world, establishing its capital at Damascus in Syria.

Ali's followers, however, did not accept defeat. They formed a separate group known as the Shi'ites (from *shi'a*, the Arabic word for "faction"). The Shi'ites insisted that only descendants of Ali and his wife, Muhammad's daughter Fatimah, could legitimately rule the Muslim community. Moreover, the Shi'ites did not accept the customary religious practices (*sunna*) that had developed under the first two caliphs who succeeded Muhammad, his father-in-law Abu Bakr and his disciple Umar. Hence, those Muslims who supported the Umayyad family and who *did* regard these customs as binding were called Sunnis. This division between Shi'ites and Sunnis lasts until the present day. Often persecuted by the Sunni majority as heretics, Shi'ites consider themselves the only true exponents of Islam. Today, Shi'ites predominate in Iran and are the largest single Muslim group in Iraq, yet they constitute only one-tenth of the world's Muslims.

The Umayyad and Abbasid Dynasties

The political triumph of the Umayyads in 661 and the military conquests of their supporters created a strong state centered on Damascus, formerly an administrative capital of the Roman Empire. And in many ways, the Umayyad caliphate functioned as a Roman successor state: it even continued to employ Greek-speaking bureaucrats trained in the techniques of Roman governance. Through these means, the Umayyads dominated the Mediterranean for several generations.

But the failure of the Umayyads' two massive attacks on Constantinople checked their power, which was also being challenged by a rival dynasty, the **Abbasids**, who claimed descent from one of Muhammad's uncles and regarded the Umayyads as usurpers. In 750, the Abbasids led a successful rebellion, with the help of the Persians, forcing the Umayyads to retreat to their territories in al-Andalus (Muslim Spain: see the map on page 238).

In contrast with the Umayyads, the Abbasid caliphate stressed Persian elements over Roman ones. Symbolic of this change was the shift in capitals from Damascus to Baghdad, where the second Abbasid caliph, al-Mansur (r. 754–775), built a new city near the ruins of the old Persian capital. The Abbasid caliphs also modeled their behavior on that of

Persian princes and their administration on the autocratic rule of the former Persian Empire, imposing heavy taxation to support a large professional army and presiding over an extravagantly luxurious court. This is the world described in the *Arabian Nights*, a collection of stories written in Baghdad under the Abbasids. The dominating presence in these stories is Harun al-Rashid, who ruled from 786 to 809. His reign marked the height of Abbasid power.

Meanwhile, the Umayyad dynasty continued to rule in al-Andalus and continued to claim that it was the only legitimate successor of Muhammad. Relations between the Umayyads of Spain and the Abbasids of Persia were therefore very cold; but because their realms were far apart, the hostility between them rarely erupted into war. Instead, the two courts competed for preeminence through literary and cultural patronage, much as the Hellenistic kingdoms had done. Philosophers, artists, and especially poets flocked to both. The *Arabian Nights* was one product of this rivalry in Baghdad. Not to be outdone, the caliphs at the Spanish capital of Córdoba amassed a library of more than 400,000 volumes—at a time when a monastery in western Europe that possessed 100 books qualified as a major center of learning. Nothing remotely comparable had been seen in the Mediterranean since the time of the Ptolemies in Alexandria.

Commerce and Industry in the Islamic World

Alongside its political and military triumphs, the transformation of tiny settlements into thriving metropolitan commercial centers is one of early Islam's most remarkable achievements. So is the Arabs' capacity to adapt themselves to life in highly urbanized regions and to build on the long-established commercial infrastructures of Egypt, Syria, and Persia. By the tenth century, Arab merchants had penetrated into southern Russia and equatorial Africa, and had become masters of the caravan routes that led eastward to India and China. Ships from the Islamic world established new trade routes across the Indian Ocean, the Persian Gulf, and the Caspian Sea, and for a time dominated the Mediterranean as well.

The growth of commerce during this period was driven and sustained by a number of important new industries. Mosul in Iraq was a center for the manufacture of cotton cloth; Baghdad specialized in glassware, jewelry, pottery, and silks; Damascus was famous for its fine steel and its woven-figured silk known as "damask"; Morocco and portions of al-Andalus were noted for leatherworking; and Toledo produced excellent swords. Drugs, perfumes, carpets,

tapestries, brocades, woolens, satins, metal goods, and a host of other products turned out by skilled artisans were carried throughout the Mediterranean world, and also into central Asia along the network of roads to China that came to be known as the Silk Road—after the most prized commodity for which these goods were traded. With these precious goods went the Islamic faith, which took root among some peoples in what are now India, Pakistan, and Afghanistan.

The Power of Paper

One commodity in particular deserves special mention: paper. Both Arabs and Persians learned papermaking from the Chinese and became masters of the art in their own right. By the end of the eighth century, Baghdad alone had more than a hundred shops where blank paper or books written on paper were sold. Paper was cheaper to produce, easier to store, and far easier to use than papyrus (the chief writing material of antiquity) or parchment (widely used in northern Europe). As a result, paper replaced papyrus in the Islamic world by the early eleventh century—even in Egypt, the heartland of papyrus production for almost 4,000 years.

The ready availability of paper brought about a revolution. Many of the characteristic features of Islamic civilization—bureaucratic record keeping, high levels

ARABIC CALLIGRAPHY. Muslim artists experimented with the art of calligraphy to make complex designs, sometimes abstract but often representing natural forms. This ink drawing on paper actually incorporates Arabic words. It dates from the seventh century and also demonstrates the Muslim mastery of papermaking.

of literacy and book production (especially copies of the Qur'an), even the standard form of cursive Arabic script known as Kufic—would have been impossible without the widespread availability of paper. Western Europeans began to practice papermaking only in the thirteenth century, but they would still continue to rely on the more durable parchment made from animal hides for the copying of most books and documents. And it was not until the advent of print that paper began to replace parchment as the reading and writing material of western Europe (see Chapter 12).

Mobility, Opportunity, and Status

As the reach of Islam extended through conquest and commerce, so Muslim culture became highly cosmopolitan, blending Arab customs with the civilizations of Byzantium and Persia, which were themselves the heirs of ancient empires stretching back to the time of Hammurabi's Babylon. The preeminence of trade and ease of travel increased geographical mobility, and with it social mobility. (Muhammad's teachings further encouraged this, because the Qur'an stressed the equality of all Muslim men.) At the courts of Baghdad and Córdoba, careers were open to men of talent, regardless of birth or wealth. Because literacy was remarkably widespread, many could rise through education and achieve top offices through enterprise and skill. Even slaves could achieve high status through these means. Slave women (non-Muslim or Muslim) who bore male children to Muslim men often shared some of the privileges of their legitimate sons.

For those men wishing instead to embrace the religious life, Islam offered two main alternatives. One was that of the *ulama*, a learned man whose studies qualified him to offer advice on aspects of religious law and practice. These men often exerted great influence on the conduct of public life. Complementary to them were the *Sufis*, mystics who might be equated with Christian monks were it not for the fact that they seldom withdrew from the life of the community. Whereas the ulamas stressed adherence to religious law, the Sufis stressed individual contemplation and the cultivation of spiritual ecstasy. Some Sufis were "whirling dervishes," so known in the West because of their mystical dances; others were *faqirs*, associated in the West with snake charming; still others were quiet, meditative men. Sufis were usually organized into brotherhoods and eventually made many successful efforts to convert the peoples of Africa and India to Islam. Sufism also provided a channel for the most intense religious impulses. The ability of the ulamas and the Sufis to coexist is testimony to the cultural pluralism of the Islamic world.

There were no comparable careers for religious women, a reminder of the limits often imposed by gender. There are significant exceptions, of course. Muhammad's favored wife, Aisha (*ah-EE-sha*; d. 678), was revered as a scholar and played an important role in the creation and circulation of the *hadith* (Arabic for "narrative"): stories and sayings that shed light on the Prophet's life and teachings. But in general, women were mainly considered valuable as indicators of a man's wealth and status. The Qur'an allowed any Muslim man to marry as many as four wives, which often meant that the number of women available for marriage was far smaller than the number of men who desired to marry. This made for intense competition, and men who had wives and daughters needed to ensure that their prized assets were safeguarded. So women were usually kept from the sight of men who were not members of the family or trusted friends. Along with female servants and the enslaved concubines also owned by wealthy men, they were housed in a segregated part of the residence called the *haram* ("forbidden place"). Following Persian custom, they were often guarded by eunuchs (men, usually sold as slaves, who had been castrated prior to adolescence). Within these enclaves, women vied with each other for precedence and worked to advance the fortunes of their children—often the only form of power they could exercise.

Islam's Neighbors

For the inhabitants of Byzantium, the triumph of the Abbasid caliphate in the eighth century released the Mediterranean from the pressures of Umayyad expansion. Farther west, the Franks of Gaul also benefited from the advent of the Abbasids. Because an Umayyad dynasty controlled al-Andalus, the great Frankish ruler Charlemagne (*SHAHR-leh-mayn*; r. 768–814) could counter neighboring Muslims' power by maintaining strong diplomatic and commercial relations with the more distant Abbasid caliphate. The most famous symbol of this connection was an elephant called Abul Abbas, a gift from Harun al-Rashid to Charlemagne. More important, however, was the flow of silver that found its way from the Abbasid Empire north through the Baltic into the Rhineland, where it was exchanged for Frankish exports of furs, wax, honey, leather, and especially slaves—Europeans, often Slavic peoples, who were captured and sold for profit by other Europeans. Through these channels, jewels, silks, spices, and other luxury goods from India and the Far East flowed north and west into Frankish territory. These trading links with the Abbasid world helped fund the extraordinary achievements of Charlemagne's own empire, which had a lasting effect on the culture and politics of Europe.

Past and Present

The Meanings of Medievalism

The people who lived during the thousand-year period that we call the Middle Ages didn't think of themselves as "medieval." And indeed, this modern term tends to be used to describe modern phenomena—whether things that we seek to condemn (terrorism, persecution) or to glorify. The romantic image of Joan of Arc on the left was used to rally Americans to the cause of France and its allies during World War I. The image on the right shows warfare as imagined by the game *Arthur II*.

 Watch related author interview on the Student Site

THE CONVERSION OF NORTHWESTERN EUROPE

At the end of the sixth century, the Frankish chronicler Gregory of Tours (c. 538–594) considered himself to be a Roman, living in a Roman world of towns, trade, and local administration. Gregory was proud of his family's senatorial rank and took it for granted that he and his male relatives should be bishops who ruled, by right of birth and status, over their cities and the surrounding countryside. Like others of his class, Gregory still spoke and wrote Latin—a different Latin from the polished prose of Cicero, but one that would certainly have been comprehensible to the Romans of the republic. Although Gregory was aware that the western territories of the Roman Empire were now ruled by Frankish, Visigothic, and Lombard kings, he regarded at least some of these kings as Roman successors because

they ruled in accordance with Roman models. In the case of the Franks, the king even ruled with the approval of the Roman emperor in Constantinople. It was also a source of satisfaction to Gregory that all these barbarian kings had converted to Roman Christianity and no longer embraced the heresy of Arianism, which reinforced their *romanitas* and lent legitimacy to their rule.

Two hundred years later, the greatest of all Frankish kings, Charlemagne (742–814), was crowned as a new kind of Roman emperor in the West. But by this time, people no longer felt a sense of direct continuity with the earlier Roman world or a sense of obligation to the Roman emperor in Byzantium. When intellectuals at Charlemagne's court set out to reform the political, religious, and cultural life of their time, their goal was to revive the Roman Empire from which they considered themselves estranged. They sought a *renovatio imperii Romanorum*: "a renewal of the Romans' empire." This awareness of a break with the Roman past developed during the seventh century as a consequence of profound economic, religious, and cultural changes.

Economic and Political Instability

Even though the economy of the Roman Empire had become increasingly regionalized from the third century C.E. onward (see Chapter 6), the Mediterranean remained a crucial nexus of trade and communication. Gold coinage continued to circulate in both the eastern and the western provinces; a luxury trade in silks, spices, swords, and jewelry continued to move west; and slaves, wine, grain, and leatherwork still moved east from Gaul, Hispania, and North Africa toward Constantinople, Egypt, and Syria. By about 650, however, this Mediterranean world disintegrated further. This was partly a result of Justinian's failed efforts to reconquer the empire's western territories, as well as imperial overtaxation of agricultural land, especially in Egypt and North Africa.

But the most significant causes of economic instability in northwestern Europe were internal, not external. The cities of Italy, Gaul, and Hispania could no longer maintain their walls, public buildings, and urban infrastructures as they had done under the Roman Empire. Although Christian bishops and their aristocratic kinsmen still governed from these cities and continued to provide a market for certain kinds of luxury goods, barbarian kings and their nobles were moving to the countryside during the seventh century, living as much as possible from the produce of their own estates rather than purchasing their supplies in the marketplace. At the same time, much agricultural land was passing out of cultivation. The slaves or servile peasants who had farmed the large plantations for hundreds of years had no efficient Roman state to enforce their obedience. They were able to become more independent, if also less effective, working just a few acres by themselves. Productivity declined, as did revenues from tolls and taxes.

The systems of coinage that circulated in western Europe were also breaking down, which means that wealth ceased to be readily portable, hindering long-distance exchange. The Arab conquests may have further reduced the supply of gold available, because it was now being channeled eastward. But in any case, gold coins were too valuable to be useful in a local market economy. When we find evidence of such coins at this time, they are more likely to have been plundered, hoarded, or given as gifts rather than used to facilitate commerce. By the 660s, rulers who were still in a position to mint coins and guarantee their value had shifted from gold to silver coinage. Indeed, Europe would remain a silver-based economy for the next thousand years, until the supply of gold from European conquests in Africa and America once again made a gold standard viable (see Chapter 12).

Lordship and Its Limitations

As a result of these processes, western Europe came to rely on a two-tier economy, a kind that had not been necessary in any Western civilization since the Lydians introduced a standardized currency in the sixth century B.C.E. (see Chapter 2). Gold, silver, and luxury goods circulated among the very wealthy, but most people relied on barter and various substitute currencies to make transactions. Local lords collected rents from their peasants in food or labor, but they then found it difficult to convert these in-kind payments into weapons, jewelry, and silks that brought prestige in aristocratic society. This was problematic not only for social reasons but also for political ones: the power of lords depended on their ability to bestow rich gifts on their followers (see **Interpreting Visual Evidence** on page 232). When they could not acquire these items through trade, they had to win them through plunder and extortion; either way, the process led to violence.

The successful chieftains of this era therefore tended to be those whose areas of influence adjoined wealthy but poorly defended territories that could easily be attacked or blackmailed. Such "soft frontiers" provided warlords and kings with land and booty that they could then distribute to their followers. Successes of this sort would bring more followers to a lord's service, allowing him to extend his influence further; and as long as more conquests were made, the process of amassing power and wealth would continue. But power acquired through plunder and conquest was inherently fragile: a few defeats might speedily reverse the fortunes of the lords reliant on it, leaving their followers to seek plunder elsewhere.

Another factor contributing to the instability of power in this world was the difficulty of ensuring its peaceful transfer. The barbarian rulers who established themselves during the mass migrations of the fifth and sixth centuries did not come from the traditional royal families of their peoples, and thus faced opposition from many of their own warriors. Moreover, the groups who took possession of territories within the western Roman Empire during these years were rarely (if ever) composed of a single unified group; they were usually made up of many different tribes, including a sizable number of displaced Romans. Such unity was largely the creation of the charismatic chieftain who led them, and this charisma was not easily passed on by inheritance.

Interpreting Visual Evidence

The Ship Burial of Sutton Hoo

Several of the most impressive finds in the history of British archaeology have been made by amateurs. A recent one, in the summer of 2009, was the largest hoard of worked gold and silver ever found in one place: more than 5 kilograms of gold and 2.5 kilograms of silver (image A). It was discovered by a man in Staffordshire walking over a neighbor's farm with a metal detector.

The hoard's extraordinary value and range of artifacts—and their historical implications—can only be guessed at now; even the dating is inconclusive.

Another find, made in 1939, was a royal gravesite dating from the seventh century (image B). Many scholars believe it to be the tomb of King Redwald of East Anglia, described by Bede as a baptized Christian who refused to give up the worship of his ancestral gods. The king's body was placed in a wooden structure in the middle of a ninety-foot-long ship that had been dragged to the top of a bluff (a *hoo*) eleven miles from the English Channel. The ladder in the photograph of the original excavation reaches into the burial chamber.

The contents of the grave are extraordinarily varied and offer clues to values and contacts of the burial's occupant. They included the following items:

• a lamp and a bronze bucket once suspended from a chain

A. The Straffordshire hoard, found in 2009.

B. The original excavation of the burial chamber at Sutton Hoo, found in 1939.

The Prosperous Kingdom of the Franks

Of all the groups that set up kingdoms in western Europe during the fifth and sixth centuries, only the Franks succeeded in establishing a single dynasty from which leaders would be drawn for the next 250 years. This dynasty reached back to Clovis (r. c. 481–511), a warrior-king who established an alliance between his family and the powerful bishops of Gaul by converting to Roman Christianity—emulating the example of Constantine on many levels. Clovis's family came to be known as the Merovingians, after his legendary grandfather Merovech, who was said to have been fathered by a sea monster—meaning that no one really knew where Merovech came from. Clovis's own name proved even longer lasting than the dynasty he founded. As the language of the Franks merged with the

- a ceremonial helmet (image C) modeled on those worn by Roman cavalry officers just before the withdrawal of the legions from Britain in 410—but decorated like helmets found in eastern Sweden

- a sword and a large circular shield, resembling those found in Swedish burial sites

- exquisitely crafted belt buckles and shoulder clasps (image D) made of gold and garnets and worked with designs

- a pair of silver spoons with long handles, possibly crafted in Byzantium, and inscribed in Greek with the names PAULOS and SAULOS (Paul and Saul)

- a large silver dish (72 cm in diameter) made in Byzantium between 491 and 518

- a bronze bowl from the eastern Mediterranean

- a six-stringed lyre in a bag made of beaver skin, similar to lyres found in Germany

C. Sutton Hoo helmet.

- a purse containing thirty-seven gold coins, each from a different Frankish mint, the most recent datable to the 620s

- heaps of armor, blankets, cloaks, and other gear

Questions for Analysis

1. What do these artifacts, and the contexts in which they were found, reveal about the extent of Anglo-Saxon contact with the rest of the world? Which regions are represented, and why?

2. From this evidence, what conclusions can you draw about Anglo-Saxon culture and values?

3. Do any of these grave-goods indicate that the occupant was a Christian king? Why or why not?

D. Sutton Hoo buckles.

Latin of Gaul to become French, the name "Clovis" lost its hard *C*, and the pronunciation of the *V* was softened. Thus "Clovis" became "Louis," the name borne by French kings up to the time of the French Revolution over a millennium later (see Chapter 18).

The **Merovingians** were not the only noble family in Gaul with a claim to kingship, but they were more successful in defending it than their counterparts in Visigothic Spain, Lombard Italy, and both the Anglo-Saxon and Celtic territories of Britain. In part, this was due to their capacity to transfer power from one generation to another. In early medieval Europe, the right of inheritance was not limited to the eldest male claimant of each competing royal family. When it came to property or power, all the king's sons—and frequently all his male cousins and nephews, and even his daughters—could consider themselves rightful heirs.

Analyzing Primary Sources

From Anglo-Saxon Slave Girl to Frankish Queen

The Anglo-Saxon Saint Balthild rose to prominence as the wife of the Merovingian king Clovis II (r. 639–657), but she began her life as a slave. After the king's death, she was left in a precarious position at the Frankish court as regent for her son, Clothar III, and eventually was forced to enter the convent she had founded at Chelles, near Paris. The following excerpt from her Latin vita *("life") describes her speedy ascent to a position of power. It was probably written by a nun of Chelles.*

 raise should first be sung of Him Who made the humble great and raised the pauper from the dunghill and seated him among the princes of his people. Such a one is the woman present to our minds, the venerable and great lady Balthild the queen. Divine Providence called her from across the seas. She, who came here as God's most precious and lofty pearl, was sold at a cheap price. Erchinoald, a Frankish magnate and most illustrious man, acquired her and in his service the girl behaved most honorably. . . . For she was kind-hearted and sober and prudent in all her ways, careful and plotting evil for none. . . . And since she was of the Saxon race, she was graceful in form with refined features, a most seemly woman with a smiling face and serious gait. And she so showed herself just as she ought in all things, that she pleased her master and found favor in his eyes. So he determined that she should set out the drinking cup for him in his chamber and, honored above all others as his house-keeper, stand at his side always ready to serve him. . . . She gained such happy fame that, when the said lord Erchinoald's wife died, he hoped to unite himself to Balthild, that faultless virgin, in a matrimonial bed. . . .

[But] when she was called to the master's chamber she hid herself secretly in a corner and threw some vile rags over herself so that no one could guess that anyone might be concealed there. . . . She hoped that she might avoid a human marriage bed and thus merit a spiritual and heavenly spouse. . . . Thereafter it happened, with God's approval, that Balthild, the maid who escaped marriage with a lord, came to be espoused to Clovis, son of the former king Dagobert. Thus by virtue of her humility she was raised to a higher rank.

Source: Excerpted from *Sainted Women of the Dark Ages,* ed. and trans. John E. Halborg, Jo Ann McNamara, and E. Gordon Whatley (Chapel Hill, NC: 1992), pp. 268–70.

Questions for Analysis

1. Judging from what you have learned about the prevalence of the slave trade in ancient and early medieval civilizations, what might you speculate about Balthild's actual role in Erchinoald's household?

2. Balthild would have been a contemporary of the king buried at Sutton Hoo. Is it likely that she would have been a Christian when she was sold into slavery in England? Why or why not?

3. In light of Balthild's later status as a queen and regent for her son, why would her biographer stress that she was "careful and plotting evil for none"? To what allegations or incidents might the author of this life be responding?

So even when the rule of any family was not threatened by outsiders, the transfer of power was almost always bloody.

In Gaul, however, the often brutal conflicts between rival Merovingian kings did not materially disrupt the strength and sophistication of their governance. Many elements of late Roman local administration survived throughout this period. Latin literacy, fostered by a network of monasteries linked to the Frankish court, remained an important element in this administration, providing a foundation on which Charlemagne would later build. Even the cultural revival associated with the reign of Charlemagne (see below) really began in the late seventh century at the monastic foundations fostered by members of the Merovingian family and other powerful lords. Such monasteries grew remarkably during the seventh century, becoming the engines that made Merovingian Gaul wealthier and more stable than any other region of northwestern Europe. Approximately 550 monasteries were thriving by the year 700, more than 300 of which had been established in the preceding century alone. Frankish bishops also prospered along with their cities, amassing most of their landed possessions by the end of the seventh century, possessions from which their successors would continue to profit until the time of the French Revolution.

This massive redistribution of wealth reflected a fundamental shift in the economic center of gravity of the Frankish kingdom. In the year 600, the wealth of Gaul was still concentrated in the south, where it had been throughout the late Roman period. By the year 750, however, the economic center of the kingdom lay north of the Loire, in the territories that extended from the Rhineland westward to the North Sea. It was here that most of the new monastic foundations of the seventh century were established.

Behind this shift in prosperity lay a long effort to bring under cultivation the rich, heavy soils of northern Europe. This effort was largely engineered by the new monasteries, which harnessed the peasant workforce and pioneered agricultural technologies adapted to the climate and terrain. The most important invention was a heavy, wheeled plow capable of cutting and turning grassland sod and clay, soils very different from those of the Mediterranean. This innovation in turn necessitated the development of more efficient devices for harnessing animals (particularly oxen) to these plows. Gradually warming weather (see Chapter 8) also improved the fertility of the wet northern soils, lengthening the growing season and so making possible more efficient crop-rotation systems. As food became more plentiful, the population began to expand. Although much of Frankish Gaul remained a land of scattered settlements separated by dense forests, it was far more populous by 750 than it had been in the time of Clovis. All these developments would continue during the reign of Charlemagne and beyond.

The Power of Monasticism

As we have just seen, the seventh century witnessed a rapid increase in the foundation of monastic houses all over northwestern Europe. Although monasteries had existed in Gaul, Italy, and Hispania since the fourth century, most were located in highly Romanized areas. In the fifth century, a powerful monastic movement began in Ireland as well, and eventually spread to the Celtic regions of Britain and from there to the Continent. The Irish missionary Columbanus (540–615), for example, was the founder of Merovingian monasteries at Luxeuil (France) and Bobbio (Italy). Important monasteries were also established on the island of Iona, off the western coast of what is now Scotland, and at Lindisfarne, off Britain's northeastern coast. In all of these cases, close ties were forged between monks and local tribal leaders or powerful families, much to the political and economic gain of all parties.

ABBEY CHURCH, ISLAND OF IONA. This tiny island off Scotland's west coast is the site of many Iron Age forts and has been home to a monastic community since the sixth century. Missionaries from Iona were instrumental in converting the Celtic tribes of northern Britain to Christianity.

Most monastic foundations of the seventh century were deliberately located in rural areas and at strategic trading crossroads, where they played a crucial role in trade and governance. Indeed, the material advantages of monastic innovation were a powerful incentive toward Christian conversion in the communities which benefited from improved living conditions. Prosperity was also a powerful advertisement for authority: a lord or chieftain who had the support of a monastery and the beneficent Christian God was obviously worthy of loyalty. Because monasteries played such a key role in economic development and political order, lords often granted them special privileges, helping to free them from the control of local bishops and giving them jurisdiction over their own lands. Thus, monasteries became politically powerful, not only because they had been founded by powerful men but because they were lordships in their own right.

Frequently, these new foundations were double monasteries that accommodated women as well as men; but often, they were established for women only. In either case, they were usually ruled by abbesses drawn from noble or royal families. Monasticism thus became a road to political power for women, too. It also gave women—commoners as well as queens—freedoms they did not have elsewhere, or at any other time in history up to this point. Within the monastery, women had control over their own minds and bodies. They could wield enormous influence, promoting their families' diplomatic and dynastic interests without the dangers and uncertainties of pregnancy. And they were guaranteed salvation, at a time when salvation outside the cloister seemed a perilously uncertain prospect. Moreover, the prayers of holy women were regarded as particularly effective in securing divine support or retribution. This further enriched convents through donations of land and wealth, although it could not always safeguard them from violence, or their inhabitants from abduction and rape.

Monasteries for women also served the interests of men, which is why kings and lords supported them. They were dynamic repositories of prayer, regarded as essential to furthering the ambitions of their male benefactors and protecting them from harm. They provided a dignified place of retirement for inconvenient but politically powerful women, such as the sisters and daughters of rivals or the widow of a previous ruler. And by limiting the number of powerful women who could reproduce, female monasteries also reduced the number of male claimants to power. Establishing aristocratic and royal women in such convents was thus an important way of controlling successions and managing political disputes.

Monasticism played an important role in missionary activity, too. As noted previously, the work of Irish monks was crucial to the spread of Christianity in northern parts of Britain and in other areas of northern Europe virtually untouched by the Roman Empire. Missionaries were also sponsored by the fledgling papacy in Rome and by the Merovingian royal family—especially its women. The best example of this is the conversion of Britain's Anglo-Saxon tribes, which we glimpsed in the opening paragraph of this chapter. In 597, a group of forty Benedictine monks were sent by Pope Gregory I (r. 590–604) to the southeastern kingdom of Kent, where their efforts were assisted by Frankish translators—and by the fact that the local king, Æthelbehrt (*ETH-el-behrt*), had married a Frankish princess who was already a Christian. This pattern of influence repeated itself all over southern and eastern Britain. Writing a hundred years later in the monastery of Monkwearmouth in Northumbria, the historian Bede could claim that the tribes of England were now united in their shared allegiance to the Roman Church and its English archbishop, whose seat was the cathedral in Æthelbert's capital at Canterbury. Bede credited the Roman pope for initiating this remarkable achievement, but powerful and pious women had worked behind the scenes to make it happen.

The Papacy of Gregory the Great

Pope Gregory I, also known as Gregory the Great, was the first bishop of Rome to envision a new role for the papacy in northwestern Europe. We have seen that the Roman *papa* had begun to assert his superiority over other patriarchs throughout the Christian world; but in reality, he was subordinate to the emperor in Constantinople and the greater prestige of its patriarch. As Byzantine power in Italy declined, however, Gregory sought to create a more autonomous Latin Church by focusing attention on the untapped resources of the wild West. An influential theologian, he is considered the intellectual successor of Jerome, Ambrose, and Augustine (see Chapter 6) because he greatly extended the applicability of their teachings to the world outside the Romanized Mediterranean.

Among Gregory's doctrinal contributions were an emphasis on the necessity of penance for the forgiveness of sins and the concept of Purgatory as a place where the soul could be purified before being admitted into heaven—instead of being sent immediately to perpetual damnation. Alongside this emphasis on penance, Gregory emphasized the importance of pastoral care: the proper instruction, encouragement, and control of the laity. He also sought to increase the affective power of Christian worship by promoting the performance of music. Song has always been essential to religious ritual, but Gregory encouraged it to such a degree that the very style of singing that emerged in this period is still known as Gregorian chant.

THE LINDISFARNE GOSPELS. This page from one of the astonishing illuminated ("light-filled") books produced by the monastery at Lindisfarne shows the opening of the Gospel of John. ▪ *Why would monastic scribes have devoted so much time, energy, and skill to the decoration of this text? How do these artistic motifs compare with those featured on the metalwork found at Sutton Hoo (see page 233)?* ▪ *What conclusions can you draw from these similarities?*

THE COVER OF THE LINDAU GOSPELS. This book, bound in gilded silver and encrusted with jewels and ivory cameos, was presented by Pope Gregory the Great to a Lombard queen around the year 600. ▪ *Given what you have learned about the economic and cultural circumstances of northern Europe, what is the significance of this rich gift?* ▪ *What would Gregory have been attempting to achieve by giving it?*

Gregory was also a statesman and leader in the model of his Roman forebears. Within Italy, he ensured the survival of the papacy against Lombard invaders by clever diplomacy and expert management of papal estates and revenues. He maintained good relations with Byzantium while asserting his authority over the other bishops of the Roman Church. His support of communities living under the *Rule* of Saint Benedict (see Chapter 6) helped make **Benedictine monasticism** the predominant monastic force in the West. Yet Gregory's influence was not always benign. He was the first prominent theologian to articulate the Church's official policy toward Jews, which became increasingly negative. Building on Gregory's example, later popes would insist that the Jews' alleged role in Christ's crucifixion and their denial of his divinity had deprived them of their rights in a Christian world.

THE EMPIRE OF CHARLEMAGNE

Toward the end of the seventh century, tensions among noble families in the Merovingian heartland of Neustria and in the Frankish border region of Austrasia were increasing (see map on page 238). The Austrasian nobles had profited from their steady push into the "soft frontier" east of the Rhine, acquiring wealth and military power in the process, while the Merovingians, settled in Neustria, had no such easy conquests at their disposal. Moreover, Merovingians had given a considerable portion of their land to monasteries during the course of the seventh century, which decreased their wealth and their capacity to attract followers. A succession of short-lived kings then opened the door to a series of civil wars, and finally to a decisive challenge to the dynasty.

The empire of Charlemagne, 814
Tributary peoples
Byzantine Empire
Abbasid Caliphate
Umayyad Caliphate (al-Andalus)

The Division of the Carolingian Empire under Charlemagne's Grandsons, 840

THE EMPIRE OF CHARLEMAGNE IN 814. When Charlemagne died in 814, he had created an empire that embraced a large portion of the lands formerly united under the western Roman Empire. ▪ *What were the geographical limits of his power?* ▪ *How were these limits dictated by the historical forces we have been studying?* ▪ *Along what lines was Charlemagne's empire divided after his death?*

Kings and Kingmakers

In 687, an Austrasian nobleman called Pepin (635/45?–714) came to power by making himself the Frankish king's right-hand man and enforcer. He took the title *maior domus* ("great man of the house") and began to exercise royal authority while maintaining the fiction that he was merely a royal servant. He did this effectively for more than twenty-five years. After his death, his illegitimate son Charles Martel ("the Hammer"; 688–741) further consolidated control over both the Merovingian homeland and the Frankish royal administration. For two generations, the Merovingian kings were largely figureheads in a realm ruled by Charles Martel and his sons.

Charles Martel is sometimes considered the second founder (after Clovis) of the Frankish kingdom. His claim to this title is twofold. First, in 733 or 734, he repelled a small Muslim force sent by the Umayyad caliphate in al-Andalus, which was attempting to expand its reach across the Pyrenees and into the rich farmlands of Aquitaine (the Bordeaux region of modern France). Charles and his army met them in battle between the cities of Poitiers and Tours, some 150 miles from the Merovingian stronghold at Paris. This victory won him great prestige, and he successfully advanced Frankish power southward toward the Muslim-held region of Narbonne.

At the same time, Charles was fostering an alliance with Benedictine missionaries from England, who were attempting to convert the Low Countries and central Germany to Christianity. Charles's family had long been active in the drive to conquer and settle these areas, and he understood clearly how missionary work and Frankish expansion could go hand in hand, and so assisted these conversion efforts. In return, the leader of the English Benedictines, Boniface (c. 672–754), brought him into contact with the papacy.

Although Charles never sought to become king himself, he was so clearly the effective ruler of Gaul that the Franks did not bother to choose a new king when the reigning Merovingian ruler died in 737. But then Charles himself died in 741, and his sons Carloman and Pepin were forced to allow the election of a new king while they exercised power behind the scenes. This compromise did not last long, however. In 750, Carloman withdrew from public life by entering a monastery, and Pepin decided to seize the throne for himself. This turned out to be harder than he may have expected. Even though the reigning king was ineffectual, Frankish identity was bound up with loyalty to Clovis's descendants; and although tribal leaders had the power to elect a new king, they were reluctant to do so.

Pepin therefore turned to the Frankish bishops, who were also unwilling to support him without backing from Rome. To gain this support, Pepin traded on his family's support of the monastic movement. The pope, for his part, saw that a powerful leader of the Franks could be a potential ally in his political struggle with the Byzantine emperors over iconoclasm (which the papacy opposed), and in his military struggle against the Lombard kings for control of central Italy.

So Boniface, acting as papal emissary, anointed Pepin king of the Franks in 751. Anointing was a new ritual, but it had a powerful biblical precedent: the ceremony by which the prophet Samuel had made Saul the first king of Israel, by anointing his head with holy oil (see Chapter 2). Indeed, the significance of the Old Testament precedent would grow under Pepin's son Charlemagne (associated with David) and his grandson Louis the Pious (associated with Solomon).

To contemporary observers, however, the apparent novelty of these proceedings underscored the uncertainty of the times: a legitimate king had been deposed and a new king elevated. And as we will see, this king-making process was the first step on a long road that would ultimately limit the power of later medieval kings and modern constitutional monarchs alike. It eventually established the principle that kingship is an office that can be occupied, at least theoretically, by anyone; and by extension, if a ruler is ineffectual or tyrannical, he can be deposed and replaced.

The Reign of Charlemagne

The Franks benefited from Pepin's military leadership. In 759, he finally defeated the Muslims of Narbonne and extended Frankish control to the Mediterranean coast. But his grip on the title of king was a tenuous one; and when he died in 768, it seemed likely that the Frankish kingdom would break up into mutually hostile regions: Austrasia, Neustria, and the new region of Aquitaine. That it did not was the work of Pepin's son, Charles: known to the French as **Charlemagne** and to the Germans as Karl der Grosse ("Charles the Great") because both modern nations claim him as their founding father. It is from him, as well as from his grandfather Charles Martel, that this new Frankish dynasty takes the name "Carolingian" (from *Carolus*, the Latin form of "Charles").

When Charlemagne came to power in 768, he managed to unite the Franks by the tried and true method of attacking a common, outside enemy. In a series of conquests, the Franks succeeded in annexing the Lombard kingdom of northern Italy, most of what is now Germany, portions of central Europe, and—taking advantage of the weakened Umayyad caliphate—Catalonia, just beyond the Pyrenees. These conquests seemed to set a seal of divine approval on the new Carolingian dynasty. More important, they provided the victorious Franks with spoils of war and vast new lands that enabled Charlemagne to reward his closest followers.

Many of the peoples Charlemagne conquered were already Christians. In the northern territory of Saxonia (Saxony), however, Charlemagne's armies campaigned for twenty years before subduing the pagan inhabitants and forcing their conversion. This created a precedent that linked military conquest with conformity of belief, and it would be repeated by Charlemagne's successors in Baltic and Slavic lands.

To rule his new empire, Charlemagne enlisted the help of the Frankish warrior class he had enriched and raised to positions of prominence. These counts (*comites* in Latin, "followers") supervised local governance within their territories. Among their many duties were the administration of justice and the raising of armies. Charlemagne also established a network of other local officials who convened courts, established tolls, administered royal lands, and collected taxes. To facilitate transactions and trade, he created a new coinage system based on a division of the silver pound into units of twenty shillings, each worth twelve pennies: a system that would last into the 1970s in parts of continental Europe and in Britain (when it was replaced by a decimal-based currency). As noted above, much of the silver for this new coinage originated in the Abbasid caliphate and was payment for furs, cloth, and especially slaves captured in Charlemagne's wars, who were now being transported to Baghdad. The silver, in turn, circulated as far north as Scandinavia and the Baltic Sea region.

Like Carolingian administration generally, this new monetary system depended on the regular use of written records, which means that the sources supporting historical research on Charlemagne's empire are numerous. But

Analyzing Primary Sources

The Capitularies of Charlemagne

Charlemagne's careful governance of his domains set a high standard for other rulers far into the future. One of the means by which this governance was carried out was through capitularies (from a Latin word denoting a document divided into chapters), which contained instructions issued by the central administration of the court to local elites known as counts (or comites in Latin)—hence the word "county" to describe an administrative area. The following are directives addressed in 785 to the administrators of Saxony, a region Charlemagne had recently conquered and whose pagan inhabitants were converted to Christianity.

Capitulary Concerning the Parts of Saxony

1. Decisions were taken first on the more important items. All were agreed that the churches of Christ which are now being built in Saxony and are consecrated to God should have no less honor than the temples of idols had, but rather a greater and more surpassing honor.

2. If anyone takes refuge in a church, let no one presume to drive him out of that church by force; rather let him be in peace until he is brought to plead his case, . . . and after this let him be brought to the presence of our lord the king. . . .

3. If anyone makes forcible entry to a church, and steals anything from it by violence or stealth, or if he sets fire to the church, let him die.

4. If anyone in contempt of the Christian faith should spurn the holy Lenten fast and eat meat, let him die; but let the priest enquire into the matter, lest it should happen that someone is compelled by necessity to eat meat.

* * *

6. If anyone is deceived by the devil, and believes after the manner of pagans that some man or some woman is a witch and eats people, . . . let him pay the penalty of death.

7. If anyone follows pagan rites and causes the body of a dead man to be consumed by fire, . . . let him pay with his life.

8. If there is anyone of the Saxon people lurking among them unbaptized, and if he scorns to come to baptism, . . . let him die.

9. If anyone sacrifices a man to the devil, . . . let him die.

* * *

12. If anyone rapes the daughter of his lord, he shall die.

13. If anyone kills his lord or his lady, he shall be punished in the same way.

* * *

18. On Sundays there are to be no assemblies or public gatherings, except in cases of great need or when an enemy is pressing; rather let all attend church to hear the word of God. . . .

* * *

33. With regard to perjury, the law of the Saxons is to apply.

34. We forbid the Saxons to come together as a body in public gatherings, except on those occasions when our *missus* [messenger] assembles them on our instructions; rather, let each and every count hold court and administer justice in his own area. And the clergy are to see to it that this order is obeyed.

Source: From *The Reign of Charlemagne: Documents on Carolingian Government*, ed. and trans. H. R. Loyn and John Percival (New York: 1975), pp. 51–54.

Questions for Analysis

1. What types of behavior does this capitulary attempt to regulate? What seem to be the major challenges faced by Charlemagne's administrators in this new territory?

2. In only one case does this capitulary mention the laws of the Saxon people themselves, in the clause relating to perjury (number 33). Why would Charlemagne's administrators consider it advisable to punish this particular crime in accordance with Saxon custom?

3. How would you characterize Charlemagne's method of dealing with a conquered people? In your estimation, is this policy likely to be effective? Why or why not?

Charlemagne did not rely on the written word alone to make his will felt. Periodically, his court sent special messengers, known as *missi*, on tours through the countryside to relay his instructions and report back on the conduct of local administrators. This was the most thorough system of governance known in Europe since the height of the Roman Empire, reaching many parts of the Continent that the Romans had never occupied. It set a standard for royal administration that would be emulated and envied for centuries.

Christianity and Kingship

In keeping with the traditions established by his father and grandfather, Charlemagne took his responsibilities as a Christian king seriously. Moreover, as his empire expanded, he came to see himself as the leader of a unified Christian society, Christendom, which he was obliged to defend. Like his contemporaries in Byzantium and the Muslim world—as well as his Roman predecessors—he recognized no distinction between religion and politics. Indeed, he conceived kingship as a sacred office created by God to protect the Church and promote the salvation of Christian people. Religious reforms were therefore no less central to proper kingship than were justice and defense. In some ways, a king's responsibilities for his kingdom's spiritual welfare were more important than his other, secular responsibilities.

CHARLEMAGNE'S IMAGE OF AUTHORITY. A silver penny struck between 804 and 814 in Mainz (as indicated by the letter *M* at the bottom) represents Charlemagne in a highly stylized fashion, as a Roman emperor with a military cloak and laurel wreath. The inscription reads *KAROLUS IMP AVG* (Charles, Emperor, Augustus) and his portrait is closely modeled on both Hellenistic and Roman coins.

These ideas were not new in the late eighth century, but they took on a new importance because of the extraordinary power Charlemagne wielded. Like other rulers of this period, Charlemagne was able to appoint and depose bishops and abbots, just as he did the counts and other officials who administered his realm. He extended his authority by changing the liturgy of Frankish churches, reforming the rules of worship in Frankish monasteries, declaring the tenets of Christian belief, ruthlessly prohibiting pagan practices, and forcibly imposing basic Christian observances on the conquered peoples of Saxony.

As the dominant political power in central Italy, Charlemagne was also the protector of the papacy. Although he acknowledged the pope as the spiritual leader of Christendom, Charlemagne dealt with the bishop of Rome much as he did other bishops in his empire. He supervised and approved papal elections, and he also protected the pope from his many enemies. To Charlemagne, such measures were clearly required if God's new chosen people, the Franks, were to avoid the fate that befell biblical Israel whenever Hebrews turned away from obedience to God.

The Carolingian Renaissance

Similar political motivations lay behind the phenomenon known as the **Carolingian Renaissance**, a cultural and intellectual flowering that took place around the Carolingian court. Like their biblical exemplars David and Solomon, Charlemagne and his son Louis the Pious considered it a crucial part of their role to be patrons of learning and the arts. In doing so, they created an ideal of the court as an intellectual and cultural center: an ideal that would profoundly influence western European cultural life until the First World War (see Chapter 24).

Behind the Carolingians' support for scholarship was the conviction that learning was the foundation on which Christian wisdom rested, and that such wisdom was essential to the salvation of God's people. Charlemagne therefore recruited intellectuals from all over Europe to further the cause of scholarship and **classical learning**. Foremost among these was the Anglo-Saxon monk Alcuin, whose command of classical Latin established him as the intellectual leader of Charlemagne's court. Under Alcuin's direction, Carolingian scholars produced much original Latin poetry and an impressive number of theological and pastoral tracts. But their primary efforts were devoted to collating, correcting, and recopying ancient Latin texts, including, most important, the text

ROMAN HISTORY IN CAROLINGIAN MINUSCULE. The very survival of Livy's history of the Roman Republic, originally written during the reign of Augustus Caesar, is due to the Carolingian Renaissance. Furthermore, the clear layout and beautifully formed script of this manuscript copy helped readers without detailed knowledge of Latin to make out the words. For example, the first two words of the heading near the bottom are *Incipit Liber* ("[Here] begins the book"), and the sentence following it begins with a reference to the Carthaginian general Hannibal.

of the Latin Bible, which had accumulated many generations of copyists' mistakes in the 400 years since Jerome's translation (see Chapter 6).

To detect and correct these errors, Alcuin and his associates gathered as many different versions of the biblical text as they could find and compared them, word by word. After determining the correct version among all the variants, they made a new, corrected copy and destroyed the other versions. They also developed a new style of handwriting, with simplified letter forms and spaces inserted between words, so as to reduce the likelihood that subsequent copyists would misread the corrected texts. Reading was further facilitated by the addition of punctuation. This new style of handwriting, known as Carolingian minuscule, is the foundation for the typefaces of most modern books—including this one.

The Revival of the Western Roman Empire

On Christmas Day in the year 800, Charlemagne was crowned emperor by Pope Leo III. Centuries later, popes would cite this epochal event as precedent for the political superiority they claimed over the ruler of the "Holy Roman Empire," as it came to be called (see Chapter 9). In the year 800, however, Pope Leo was entirely under Charlemagne's control. Yet Charlemagne's biographer, Einhard, later claimed that the coronation was planned without the emperor's knowledge.

Why, then, did he accept the title and, in 813, transfer it to his son Louis? For one thing, it was certain to anger the imperial government in Byzantium, with which Charlemagne had strained relations. And the imperial title did not add much to Charlemagne's position since he was already the de facto emperor in his own right.

Historians still debate this question. What is clear, in any case, is the symbolic significance of the action. Although the Romans of Byzantium no longer influenced western Europe directly, they continued to regard it (somewhat vaguely) as an outlying province of their empire. Moreover, the emperor in Constantinople claimed to be the political successor of Caesar Augustus. Charlemagne's assumption of the title Emperor of the Romans was therefore a clear slight to the reigning empress Irene (r. 797–802), whose occupation of the imperial throne was controversial because she was a woman. It also deepened Byzantine suspicion of Charlemagne's cordial relationship with Byzantium's enemy, Harun al-Rashid, the Abbasid caliph of Baghdad.

But for Charlemagne's successors—and for all the medieval rulers who came after him—the assumption of the imperial title was a declaration of independence and superiority. With only occasional interruptions, western Europeans continued to crown Roman emperors until the nineteenth century, while territorial claims and concepts of national sovereignty continued to rest on Carolingian precedent. Whatever his own motives may have been, Charlemagne's revival of the western Roman Empire was crucial to the developing self-consciousness of western Europe.

DISPUTED LEGACIES AND NEW ALLIANCES

When Charlemagne died in 814, his empire descended intact to his only surviving son, Louis the Pious. Under Louis, however, the empire disintegrated and was eventually divided among his three sons in 840. Western Francia (the core of modern France) went to Charles the Bald; eastern Francia (which became key principalities of Germany) went to Louis the German; and a third kingdom (stretching from the Rhineland to Rome) went to Lothair, along with the imperial title. But when Lothair's line died out, in 856, this fragile compromise dissolved into open warfare, as the East and West Franks fought over Lothair's former territories and the imperial power that went with them. The heartland of this disputed domain, known to the Germans as Lotharingia and to the French as Alsace-Lorraine, would continue to be a site of bitter contention until the end of the Second World War (see Chapter 26).

The Collapse of the Carolingian Empire

Louis the Pious faced an impossible situation of a kind we have studied many times before: the task of holding together an artificial constellation of territories united by someone else. Charlemagne's empire had been built on successful conquests; however, by 814, he had pushed the borders of his empire beyond the practical limits of his administration. To the southwest, he now faced the Umayyad rulers of al-Andalus, and to the north, the pagan inhabitants of Scandinavia. In the east, his armies were too preoccupied with settling the territories they had already conquered to secure the Slavic lands that lay beyond. At the same time, the pressures that had driven these conquests—the need for land and plunder to cement the allegiance of followers—had become ever more pronounced as a result of their very success. The number of counts had tripled, from approximately 100 to 300, and each of them wanted more wealth and power.

Frustrated by the new emperor's inability to reward them, the Frankish aristocracy turned against him and on each other. Smoldering hostilities among Austrasians, Neustrians, and Aquitanians—which Charlemagne had stifled by directing their energies elsewhere—flared up again. As centralized authority broke down, the vast majority of the empire's free inhabitants found themselves increasingly dominated by local lords who treated them as

if they were serfs. At the same time, internal troubles in the Abbasid Empire caused a breakdown in the commercial system through which Scandinavian traders brought Abbasid silver into Carolingian domains. Deprived of their livelihood, these traders turned to raiding, which is what the Norse word **viking** means. Under these combined pressures, the Carolingian Empire fell apart, and a new map of Europe began to emerge.

The Impact of the Viking Invasions

Scandinavian traders were already familiar figures in the North Sea and Baltic ports of Europe when Charlemagne came to power. They had begun to establish strategic settlements from which they navigated down the rivers to Byzantium (through the Black Sea) and the Abbasid caliphate (through the Caspian Sea). But when the power of the Abbasids declined, Viking raiders turned to plunder, ransom, tribute collection, and slaving. At first, these were small-scale operations; but soon, some Viking attacks involved organized armies numbering in the thousands. The small tribal kingdoms of the Anglo-Saxons and Celts made the British Isles easy targets, as were the divided kingdoms of the Franks.

By the tenth century, the Vikings controlled independent principalities in eastern England, Ireland, the islands of Scotland, and the region of France that is still called "Norseman-land" (Normandy). A Viking people known as the Rus' established the beginnings of a kingdom that would become Russia. At the end of the tenth century, Vikings ventured farther west and colonized Iceland, Greenland, and a distant territory they called Vinland (Newfoundland, Canada). In 1016, a Viking army placed a Danish king on the English throne.

The threat of Viking attacks began to diminish after Scandinavia's conversion to Christianity, which proceeded from the late tenth century onward. But it was more effectively mitigated by the fact that Viking populations quickly assimilated into the cultural and political world of northwestern Europe. By 1066, when the "Norsemen" of Normandy conquered England, the English—many of whom were descended from Vikings themselves—perceived them to be French. Driving this rapid assimilation may have been the raids of the Magyars, a non-Indo-European people who crossed the Carpathian Mountains around 895 and carried out a number of devastating campaigns throughout continental Europe before settling in what is now Hungary. The disparate inhabitants of the new Viking colonies may have been forced to

PATTERNS OF VIKING ACTIVITY AND SETTLEMENT, c. 800–1100. The Vikings were instrumental in maintaining commercial contacts among northern Europe, Byzantium, and Islam until the eighth century, when changing historical forces turned them into raiders and colonists. ▪ *What area was the original homeland of the Vikings?* ▪ *What geographic region did the Vikings first conquer, and why?* ▪ *The areas marked in green show territories that were later targeted by pillagers. Why would the Vikings have avoided settlement in these areas?*

unite against this common enemy, and thus may have come to share a sense of common identity.

The overall effect of the Viking diaspora and settlement on Europe continues to be a matter of scholarly controversy. The destruction caused by raiding is undeniable, and many of the monasteries of Frankish, Anglo-Saxon, and Celtic lands were destroyed—along with countless precious books and historical artifacts. Yet the Vikings were not the only source of disorder in the ninth and tenth centuries. The civil wars and local political rivalries that had replaced the centralized states of Charlemagne and the Islamic caliphates contributed mightily to the chaos of the post-Carolingian world and made the Vikings' successes easily won. Nor were the Vikings a source of disorder alone. In Ireland and eastern England, Vikings founded a series of new towns. And as long-distance traders, they transported large quantities of silver into western Europe, fueling the European economy.

Alfred the Great and the Unification of England

In those few regions where people did succeed in fending off Viking attacks, the unifying force of victory was strong. The best example of this phenomenon is England, which had never been part of Charlemagne's empire and had remained divided into small kingdoms at war with one another—despite Bede's wishful history of an "English church and people." Yet in a direct response to the Viking threat, a loosely unified kingdom emerged for the first time under Alfred the Great (r. 871–899). His success in defending his own small kingdom from Viking attacks, combined with the destruction of every other competing royal dynasty, allowed Alfred and his heirs to assemble effective armed forces, institute mechanisms of local government, found new towns, and codify English laws. In

A DRAGON-PROWED VIKING LONGBOAT. This manuscript illumination—from a book copied in Anglo-Saxon England—depicts one of the vessels terrifyingly well known to the shore-dwelling peoples of northwestern Europe. Concerted efforts to ward off Viking invasions led to the establishment of the first unified English kingdom.

addition, Alfred established a court school and fostered a distinctive Anglo-Saxon literary culture. Although the Anglo-Saxon vernacular had been a written language since the time of the Roman missions, it now came to rival Latin as a language of administration, history, scholarship, and spirituality. Moreover, oral traditions of poetic composition and storytelling were preserved and extended, as exemplified by the epic *Beowulf*. Until the eleventh century, Anglo-Saxon was the only European vernacular used for regular written communication.

The Disintegration of the Islamic World

As noted previously, the declining power of the Abbasid dynasty in Persia was one of the forces that contributed to the escalation of Viking raids. A major cause of this decline was the gradual impoverishment of the Abbasids' economic base, the agricultural wealth of the ancient Tigris-Euphrates basin, due to ecological crises and a devastating revolt by the enslaved African workforce there. Tax revenues from the Abbasid caliphate also declined as provincial Muslim rulers in North Africa, Egypt, and Syria retained larger and larger portions of those revenues for themselves. As their sources of income became depleted, the Abbasids were unable to support their large civil service and the mercenary

army on which they relied for defense. This army consisted largely of slaves and hired troops whose loyalties lay with the individual rulers who employed them, not the caliphs. Massively expensive building projects, including the construction of the new Abbasid capital at Baghdad, further exacerbated the fiscal, military, and political crisis.

Behind the Abbasid collapse lay two fundamental developments of great significance for the future of the Islamic world: the growing power of regional rulers and the sharpening religious divisions between Sunnis and Shi'ites, and among the Shi'ites themselves. In 909, regional and religious hostilities came together when a local Shi'ite dynasty known as the Fatimids seized control of the Abbasid province of North Africa. In 969, the Fatimids succeeded in conquering Egypt as well. Meanwhile, another Shi'ite group, rivals of both the Fatimids and the Abbasids, attacked Baghdad in 927 and Mecca in 930, seizing the Kaaba. Although an Abbasid caliphate would continue to exist in Baghdad until 1258, when invading Mongol armies destroyed it (see Chapter 10), its empire had effectively disappeared by the 930s. In its place, a new order began to emerge, centered around an independent Egyptian kingdom and a new Muslim state based in Persia, the ancestor of present-day Iran.

In al-Andalus, disputes over succession within the Umayyad dynasty were matched by new external pressures. In the mid-ninth century, the small Christian kingdoms of northern and eastern Iberia began to encroach on Muslim territory, increasing the internal difficulties of the

Umayyad caliphate. By the opening years of the eleventh century, the caliphate had dissolved, to be replaced by a host of smaller kingdoms, some of which paid tribute to the Christian rulers of the north.

The fractured political unity of the Islamic world deepened the religious divisions that had always existed among Muslim groups. Whereas Islamic rulers were relatively tolerant of religious and cultural differences when dealing with Jews and Christians, dissent within Islam itself was another matter. Under the strong rule of the caliphates, some different groups had learned to coexist; but with the disappearance of these centralized states, it became difficult to reconcile the ideal of universality with the realities of regional and ethnic differences.

CONCLUSION

The three civilizations that emerged as Rome's heirs each exhibit aspects of Roman civilization, which was itself a product of older civilizations. Which civilization was the true heir of the older empire? The answer depends on the criteria used to make this evaluation. If we argue that imperial Rome's most fundamental characteristics were the maintenance of legal and political institutions, the answer is Byzantium. If we are looking for a civilization that combines the rich legacies of ancient Mesopotamia, Egypt, and the Hellenistic world, the answer is Islam, which also emulated Rome in promoting commerce and culture. If we associate Rome chiefly with the city itself and the Latin

After You Read This Chapter

 Go to **INQUIZITIVE** to see what you've learned—and learn what you've missed—with personalized feedback along the way.

REVIEWING THE OBJECTIVES

- Byzantine culture was distinctive in many ways. What were some of its important features?
- The rapid expansion of Islam can be explained with reference to several historical factors. What were they?
- What accounts for the close relationship between monasticism and secular power in early medieval Europe?
- What was the Carolingian Empire? Why is it important?
- Based on your reading, which of Rome's three heirs was the most successful in carrying its legacy forward?

language of the first Romans, or with the Christian patriarchy of Rome, the answer is northwestern Europe.

There are also many connections to be drawn among these three successors. All took on their defining characteristics during the sixth and seventh centuries and, by the eighth century, had developed their own unique strengths and weaknesses. Moreover, they had fruitful—if uneasy—relationships with each other, and many mutual dependencies: Italian traders were active in Constantinople, Muslim traders were common in the ports of southern Italy and Gaul, Anglo-Saxon merchants were regular visitors to the Mediterranean, Jewish merchants in the Rhineland carried on an active trade with the communities of Muslim Egypt, and Viking traders had opened trade routes from the Baltic to the Black Sea and were busily founding cities from Novgorod to Dublin.

But the developments of the ninth and tenth centuries would disrupt these networks and create new centers of power. Western Europeans began to share a sense of common Christian identity: within the vast territory that extended from the Baltic to the Mediterranean, and from the Pyrenees to Poland, every ruler was (or would soon be) looking to the Roman Church for spiritual guidance and to his fellow rulers for aid and alliance. At the same time, western Europe became a society mobilized for war to a degree unmatched in either Byzantium or the Islamic world. In the centuries to come, this militarization would prove to be a decisive factor in the shifting relationship among Rome's heirs.

PEOPLE, IDEAS, AND EVENTS IN CONTEXT

- In what ways do **JUSTINIAN'S CODE OF ROMAN LAW** and the building of Hagia Sophia reflect his desire to revive the glories of ancient Rome?

- What were **BYZANTIUM**'s sources of stability, and how did the Byzantine Church promote **ORTHODOXY**? What effect did the **ICONOCLAST CONTROVERSY** have on Byzantine society?

- What factors contributed to **MUHAMMAD**'s rise to power? What are the **FIVE PILLARS OF ISLAM**? What is the role of the **QUR'AN**?

- To what extent were the **UMAYYAD** and **ABBASID CALIPHATES** heirs of Rome? What made Islamic culture of this period distinctive?

- How did the **MEROVINGIAN** kings of the Franks acquire and hold power? How did **BENEDICTINE MONASTICISM** contribute to the economy of western Europe? How was it linked to politics?

- How did **CHARLEMAGNE** build an empire? How did the **CAROLINGIAN RENAISSANCE** revive and extend **CLASSICAL LEARNING**?

- How did the **VIKINGS** contribute to the developments of the ninth and tenth centuries?

THINKING ABOUT CONNECTIONS

- How do the historical circumstances in which Islam emerged compare with those that shaped early Christianity? What are some key similarities and differences?

- The movement and resettlement of people is a major theme throughout the history of western civilizations—and the upheavals of the sixth to tenth centuries created a series of refugee crises. How do those compare to similar crises in our own day? What might we learn from the historical comparison?

Before You Read This Chapter

The Expansion of Europe, 950–1100

CORE OBJECTIVES

- **EXPLAIN** the reasons for the diffusion of political power throughout most of Europe during this period.

- **IDENTIFY** the most important outcomes of the medieval agricultural revolution.

- **DESCRIBE** the effects of the reforming movement within the Church.

- **UNDERSTAND** the motives behind the Crusades.

- **TRACE** the political, economic, intellectual, and cultural effects of the Crusades.

I n the fictional version of history popularized by medieval minstrels, Charlemagne and his knights defeat a Muslim army on the mountainous borderlands of Al-Andalus (Muslim Spain). They then face only one remaining obstacle: the castle of a Muslim king whose stalwart courage commands the Christians' respect. So when ambassadors from the king promise his conversion to Christianity in exchange for the safety of his people, Charlemagne readily agrees. One of his men must now negotiate the terms of surrender. Roland, Charlemagne's noblest knight, suggests that his stepfather Ganelon be the chosen messenger. But Ganelon is furious at this, certain that the mission will end in his death. Secretly, he resolves to betray both his stepson and his liege lord, and convinces the Muslim king that Charlemagne intends to trick him. Ganelon incites the king to attack the Christian warriors as they travel homeward through the mountain passes of the Pyrenees. Because Roland is the bravest knight, Ganelon knows that he will volunteer to command the rear guard.

And so it happens. Roland's men are ambushed and his sworn companion, Olivier, urges him to call for help. But Roland refuses. He will never endanger his lord by any such dishonorable deed; instead, he will fight to the death. With his last ounce of

249

strength, he breaks his sword, Durandal, for it would never do to have this sacred gift of Charlemagne—made holier still by the relic in its pommel—fall into the hands of heathens. As Roland reminds Olivier, "We must not be the theme of mocking songs." The worst thing imaginable is shame; the best, to become the hero of just such an epic.

Like Homer's *Iliad*, the *Song of Roland* is the product of an oral storytelling tradition that took shape over hundreds of years. Written down around the year 1100, it reflects the many ways in which the world had changed since the time of Charlemagne. Its very language exemplifies one such change: the language we call French, no longer the Frankish tongue of Charlemagne. In Charlemagne's time, moreover, there was no such thing as knighthood or chivalry, no major castles, and no holy war against the followers of Islam. All of these features were added to the story over time, to mirror a new reality and, most immediately, the ethos of the First Crusade (1095–1099).

In this chapter, we will begin to trace the processes that transformed western Europe from an economic backwater and political patchwork into the premier power among the three successor civilizations of the Roman Empire. With the increased authority and prestige of the Roman Church, European Christendom came to embrace the formerly outlying territories of Scandinavia, Hungary, Poland, and Bohemia. Christian colonists and missionaries also pushed into the Baltic and the Balkans. And allied Christian armies advanced into formerly Islamic territories in Spain and established (and eventually lost) a Latin kingdom centered on Jerusalem. This expansion would be accompanied by a revolution in agricultural production, urbanization, and a growing population. It would foster the growth of monarchies, create a wealthy but highly stratified new social order, and spur remarkable intellectual and cultural achievements.

A TOUR OF EUROPE AROUND THE YEAR 1000

The mapmakers of antiquity (Chapter 4) had used the term *Europe* to refer to one of the three known continents, and they divided it from Asia by the river Don and from Africa by the Straits of Gibraltar. We have seen that many of Europe's territories were gradually brought into the orbit of Western civilizations through trade, imperial conquest, the Jewish diaspora, and the spread of Christianity and Islam. Meanwhile, waves of immigration from the steppes of Central Asia increased the already rich ethnic and cultural diversity of Europe, as did the movements of the Vikings and their

interactions with both newer and more established groups. Although Charlemagne (Chapter 7) had tried to promote an idea of a Europe as unified and Christian, Europe was not (and could never be) wholly Christian; and it was certainly not unified. So what was it?

This chapter is titled "The Expansion of Europe" for two main reasons: first, because the idea of Europe gained increasing coherence during this pivotal period; and second, because Europeans' conquest of new frontier territories and the Mediterranean was a crucial development. Indeed, historians argue that Europe was really invented in this era, through an ongoing process of internal and external colonization. That is, new kingdoms were being created by conquest and settlement within Europe—complicating ethnic identities, kinship networks, and tribal loyalties—as well as beyond it. Europeans were becoming the agents of imperialism, not its targets. This is a striking change. The West's center of gravity had always been the Mediterranean and its adjacent lands in Anatolia, western Asia, and North Africa; it was from there that influences flowed to the less civilized lands of the farther West. The movements of peoples, too, had usually been westward. But now, that trajectory was being reversed.

Viking Initiatives

In the aftermath of the **Viking** invasions, new political entities began to emerge in northern Europe. Some, on the far-flung fringes of the known world, were formed when the Vikings themselves became colonists in Iceland, Greenland, and (briefly) Newfoundland. Indeed, Iceland can claim to be Europe's oldest state and the world's first parliamentary democracy. Its political institutions date back to the year 930, when settlers formed a legislative assembly called the Althing, a Norse word with the same meaning as the Latin *res publica*. Icelanders built one of the most culturally distinctive polities of the Middle Ages and produced a fascinating and influential body of poetic forms and literary entertainments, notably the *sagas*: sprawling family histories that unfold over generations, feature diverse casts of characters, and range from the hilarious to the ruthless (often both at once). Modern action films and epics are heavily indebted to the sagas and their historical contexts.

In regions where Vikings settled among more established groups—in Francia, the British Isles, Scandinavia, and the Low Countries—they both absorbed and affected these cultures. In Normandy, for example, the descendants of Vikings maintained marriage alliances and ties of kinship with the rest of the Norse world while intermarrying with the Franks and adopting their language.

LINGSBERG RUNESTONE. This is one of two commemorative runestones erected at Lingsberg, Sweden, at the beginning of the eleventh century. The runic inscription records that a woman named Holmfríðr had it placed there in memory of her husband, Halfdan, whose father had been a Viking raider in England. Runic alphabets were in use among Germanic-speaking peoples of the North prior to the adoption of the Latin alphabet. A few runic letters survive in Anglo-Saxon and Old Norse, including the *edh* ð (in the name Holmfríðr), which is pronounced *th* (as in *the*).

The Rise of Rus'

One group of Vikings established an important kingdom on the broad steppes of Eurasia, at the heart of a region that still bears a version of their name: Russia. Originally from Sweden, the Rus' were active raiders and traders in the Baltic region, where they came to dominate the Finns and Slavic peoples who lived along the seaboard. Gradually, they extended their reach through the navigation of Eurasian waterways while moving farther inland, to Novgorod. By the year 1000, they had conquered the fortress of Kiev.

Kiev (now in western Ukraine) was a key outpost of the frontier region influenced by the Khazars, a Turkic people who had established an empire along the Silk Road to China, and whose assimilation extended their influence still further. (Many had embraced a form of Judaism centuries before.) From Kiev, on the shores of the river Dneiper, the Rus' had easy access to the Black Sea and thence to Constantinople and Baghdad. They were thus in a position to trade directly with the eastern Roman Empire in Byzantium, as well as with Arabic, Persian, and Turkic peoples who had access to China. Moreover, through a series of strategic intermarriages, they forged further connections with many of the royal and aristocratic dynasties of western Europe. This placed the land of Rus' at the heart of economic and political activity in the medieval world.

The New Kingdoms of East-Central Europe

The rise of Rus' was countered by the crystallization of independent Balkan and Slavic kingdoms. Serbia and Croatia in the south, on the Adriatic, grew within long-settled provinces of the old Roman Empire. When the empire divided along religious and cultural lines, the ruling families of Croatia, who were near neighbors of the Venetians, embraced the Latin Christianity of Rome. The Serbians, however, were loyal to Byzantine Orthodoxy.

Hungary, comprising the old Roman province of Pannonia and stretching eastward toward the Carpathian mountains, had been conquered by the Huns in the late fourth century and had since attracted numerous other immigrants. The most recent arrivals were the Magyars, a nomadic people from the region of the Urals whose language, like that of the Finns, is non-Indo-European (Chapter 7). The Magyars were expert herdsmen and horsemen, and also served as mercenaries fighting for various warring kings in western Europe and for the emperor in Byzantium. Around 895, they united under their leader Árpád and took control of the fertile land of the Danube river basin, where they became farmers and cattle ranchers. Árpád's descendants later embraced Latin Christianity and worked to integrate the kingdom of Hungary into western Europe through dynastic marriages and diplomacy.

Bohemia (now part of the Czech Republic) and Poland were also in the process of conversion, actively encouraged by Rome. Here, as in Anglo-Saxon England and the Frankish kingdom, allegiance with Rome was advantageous for ambitious would-be kings, who could legitimize their claims to power by receiving papal approval. And as Europe's economy revived, the towns of this region were tied into an expanding web of overland and waterborne trade.

New Scandinavian Kingdoms and the Empire of Cnut the Great

While Rus' was on the rise, other groups of Vikings were establishing territorial control over parts of their Scandinavian homeland—borrowing forms of governance that drew on Carolingian and Byzantine models and embracing Latin Christianity as a way of legitimizing their rule. Around the year 1000, three strong kingdoms had emerged: Norway, Sweden, and Denmark. Each built on the legacy of powerful Viking forebears who had already established Norse settlements in the lands of the Franks, the Anglo-Saxons, and the Irish through their reputation for fearlessness in battle and generosity afterward, their capacity to dominate seas and riverways—and thereby to supply the lifeblood (silver and gold currency) of the medieval economy—and their canny practices of assimilation and intermarriage.

What made these new states special was their rulers' very deliberate manipulation of this heritage, blended with the strategic decision to convert their followers to Christianity and to the political conventions of the Continent. They simultaneously glorified their own distinctive culture and

economic achievements while tying them to newer models of government. For these reasons, scholars have often spoken of this period as Europe's "Viking Age," and it exemplifies the cross-currents of colonial enterprise mentioned on page 250. On the one hand, older western civilizations can be said to have colonized Scandinavia; on the other hand, it was really Scandinavians who were doing the colonizing.

The empire forged by King Cnut (*kuh-NOOT*) of Denmark is a good example of this. At the time of his death in 1035, Cnut the Great ruled over Norway, much of Sweden, and England, as well as his native land; had a controlling interest in large parts of Ireland and portions of the Low Countries; and had diplomatic and family ties to the independent principalities of Flanders and Normandy, the new kingdom of Poland (through his mother, a Polish princess), and the imperial family of Germany (through his daughter, who became empress).

Although Cnut's was, in many ways, a personal empire that came apart after his death—like that of Alexander or Charlemagne—it had long-term effects on the political organization of northwestern Europe. Most notably, it set the stage for the Norman conquest of England (see **Interpreting Visual Evidence** on page 264). Cnut's empire could only have been

BENEDICTINE ABBEY OF TYNIEC (POLAND). High above the river Vistula—one of the most important waterways in Central Europe—is the abbey of Tyniec (*TIN-y-ech*), founded on the site of an ancient Paleolithic fortress by King Casimir I of Poland, around the year 1040. It was just upriver of the newly established royal capital at Kraków, and its monks were assigned the task of helping the king convert local pagans to Christianity. ▪ *Why would Casimir have chosen this site?*

brought together as a result of the initiatives that had made raiding Vikings into settled kings who were able to exploit the far-flung networks of trade, influence, and kinship that had allowed their forebears to flourish in earlier times.

Mediterranean Microcosms

The dynamism of the new states of eastern Europe, Rus', and Scandinavia stands in contrast to the very different dynamics that governed relations in an older part of western civilizations: the Mediterranean. If the map below struggles to capture the patchwork of principalities and polities of Europe's mainland, it fails utterly to convey the contours of political, religious, cultural, and economic interactions in this maritime world. It is useful, in fact, to imagine the Mediterranean coastal regions and islands as interlocking components of a complete contact zone, and to imagine further that a community on the shores of North Africa—say, Muslim Tunis—would have more in common, and more

EUROPE, c. 1000. This map shows the patchwork of political power in western Europe after the millennium, although it cannot accurately illustrate the degree of fragmentation within these major territories, especially those of the Holy Roman Empire. ▪ *What factors account for the close relationship between Italy and the German principalities?* ▪ *How are they related to the northwestern regions of the Continent and the British Isles?* ▪ *Which geopolitical entities would you expect to emerge as dominant in the following centuries?*

contact, with Christian Barcelona than with another African Muslim community farther inland.

Indeed, it is extremely tricky (and probably futile) to pin down the identity and allegiances of any one group or individual in this zone. The medieval Mediterranean was a dynamic organism made up of diverse microcosms whose contours and interrelationships were determined more by geography, prevailing winds, trading patterns, and climate than by the vaunted control of a particular ruler. In many places, it made little difference who the ostensible rulers were, especially since the persons and forms of rule changed so often.

Take Sicily, the first overseas colony of Rome (Chapter 5). It had been part of the Phoenician maritime empire of Carthage and, before that, a major Greek settlement (Chapters 2 and 3). All of those elements still were part of Sicily's historical DNA when it was invaded by the Vandals in the fifth century, and afterward by the Goths. It was then reconquered by Justinian and became part of Byzantium—so important a part, in fact, that one Byzantine emperor tried to move the capital from Constantinople to Palermo. In the course of the tenth century, Sicily became an emirate of the Fatimid caliphate based in Egypt. In the eleventh, it was progressively infiltrated by Norman mercenaries who eventually succeeded in establishing a Norman (but only nominally Christian) kingdom there in 1072. So who were the Sicilians? More important, who did they think they were? And how stable was that identity over this long period of continual change? These are not easy questions to answer.

In any such case, it is better to think in terms of influences, connections, and orbits of exchange than about stable borders or identities; this holds true of many areas of Europe during this period but is especially true of regions joined by water. Gaining "control" of any constellation of Mediterranean communities—constantly in flux—meant harnessing its inherent complexity and commercial power, something not best done through violent conquest or military occupation. Indeed, an exemplary light-handed interference was what enabled the Venetians to build a successful and long-lived trading empire in the Adriatic, and then in the eastern Mediterranean and Aegean Seas. The Venetians opened up the sea lanes and ports that were crucial to the implementation of a more military form of European expansion: the Crusades.

The Heirs of Charlemagne

What of Europe's heartland, which had become the empire of Charlemagne (Chapter 7)? The most powerful monarchs on the Continent were the Saxon kings of eastern Francia (in what is now Germany). Like the Anglo-Saxon kings of England, they modeled themselves on Charlemagne, but

drew on different aspects of **Carolingian** rule. Whereas England was becoming an effective administrative monarchy with centralized financial and judicial systems, royal power on the Continent rested on the profits of continual expansion. So just as the Carolingians had built their power on the conquest of Saxony in the eighth century, the Saxon kings now built theirs on the conquests of Slavic lands to the east. They also nurtured their image as guardians of Christendom: in 955, King Otto I of Saxony defeated the then-pagan Magyars while carrying a sacred lance that had belonged to Charlemagne.

This victory established Otto as a dominant power and, by extension, as Charlemagne's worthy successor. In 962, accordingly, he went to Rome to be crowned emperor by Pope John XII, who hoped Otto would help him defeat his own enemies. But Otto turned the tables on the pope, deposing him and selecting a new pope to replace him. Otto thereby laid the foundation for his successors' claims to imperial autonomy, in imitation of the Byzantine emperors. He also advertised his inheritance of Carolingian and Roman power through his patronage of arts and learning. Under Otto's influence, the Saxon court became a refuge for men and women of talent. The first known female playwright, Hrotsvitha of Gandersheim (c. 935–c. 1002), was raised there, and grew up hearing the works of classical authors read aloud. When she entered a royal convent, she wrote plays blending Roman comedy with the stories of early Christian martyrs for the entertainment and instruction of her fellow nuns.

Otto also presided over the establishment of cathedral schools and helped the bishops of his domain turn their own courts into cultural centers. However, Otto could not control either the papacy or the independent towns of northern Italy unless he maintained a permanent presence there. But if he remained in Italy too long, his authority in Saxony would break down. Balancing local realities with imperial ambitions thus presented a dilemma that neither he nor his successors was able to solve. The result was a gradually increasing rift between the local elites and the king in his guise as emperor. This alienation would accelerate in the eleventh century when the imperial crown passed to a new dynasty, the Salians, centered not in Saxony but in neighboring Franconia. By the 1070s, when the Salian emperor Henry IV attempted to assert control over Saxony, he touched off a war that was to have momentous repercussions (see pages 269–270).

Aspects of Charlemagne's legacy also survived in the Mediterranean world. In Catalonia, counts descended from Carolingian appointees continued to administer justice in public courts of law throughout the tenth century, and to draw revenues from tolls and trade. The city of Barcelona grew rapidly as both a long-distance and a regional market under the protection of these counts. In Aquitaine also,

EMPEROR OTTO THE GREAT. In this opening from a deluxe set of Gospels he commissioned for himself, Otto is shown seated on a throne, vested with the regalia of imperial and royal authority, and surrounded by clerical and secular counselors. On the left, a procession of deferential women offers him tribute, representing the four regions and peoples that Otto aspired to rule: Roma (Romans), Gallia (Franks), Germania (Germans), and Sclavinia (Slavs). Compare this image to that of Emperor Justinian on page 216. ▪ *In what ways is Otto making use of similar iconography?* ▪ *What claims to power is he thereby making?*

the counts of Poitiers and Toulouse continued to rest their authority on Carolingian foundations.

In Charlemagne's own Frankish kingdom, however, Carolingian rule collapsed under the combined weight of Viking raids, economic disintegration, and the growing power of local lords. A few Carolingian institutions—such as public courts and a centrally minted coinage—survived in some regions, but they were used to build up new, autonomous principalities, such as Anjou and Flanders. The Norse-Frankish rulers of Normandy used these techniques effectively. But in the Franks' traditional heartland, even this modicum of Carolingian authority disappeared. The Franks still had a king, but this king was no longer a descendant of Charlemagne. Moreover, his domain had been reduced to the tiny region around Paris, the only territorial remnant that the local count, Hugh Capet, had managed to defend against the Vikings. In 987, this modest feat earned him the title "King of the Franks." Marooned on this Île-de-France (literally, "island of France"), the Capetian kings clung to the fiction that they were the heirs of Charlemagne's greatness. It would be another 200 years before one of them made this fiction a political reality (see Chapter 9).

THE AGRICULTURAL REVOLUTION OF THE MEDIEVAL WARM PERIOD

Prior to the late twentieth century, when human activity began to have a measurable effect on the global climate, the warmest period of the last two millennia occurred between 950 and 1250. It is known as the Medieval Warm Period or Medieval Climate Optimum, because it optimized the conditions for agricultural and economic growth, especially in the Northern Hemisphere. Archaeological evidence from the Americas to Europe to Asia shows similar patterns of human adaptation to this new environment, when average global temperatures are estimated to have risen by about 1°C or 2°C (3.6°F)—the same increment as the present level of human-caused warming today. This climate anomaly made it possible to raise crops as far north as Greenland and to produce wine in southern England. Moreover, the warming climate benefited northern Europe by drying the soil and lengthening the growing season, with hotter summers and diminishing rainfall harming Mediterranean agriculture in equal measure.

New Technologies and Conditions for Growth

As noted in Chapter 7, Europe's **agricultural revolution** had already begun in the eighth century, fostered by monastic inventions such as the new heavy-wheeled plow, fitted with an iron-tipped coulter and dragged by a team of oxen or horses, that could cut and turn the rich soil of northern Europe far more effectively than traditional Mediterranean plows. Related improvements in collars and harnesses enhanced the efficiency of draft animals, making it possible for these animals to pull heavy loads without choking. The development of iron horseshoes (around 900) and the tandem harnessing of paired teams (around 1050) made the use of horses more effective not only in the field but also for transporting agricultural goods to new markets.

Labor-saving devices further increased productivity. Since most work was done by individuals using hand tools, the more widespread use of iron for hoes, pitchforks, shovels, and scythes made work faster and easier. The wheelbarrow was a crucial invention, as was the harrow, drawn over the field after plowing to level the earth and mix in the seed. Water mills were another major innovation. The Romans had relied mainly on human- and animal-powered wheels to grind grain into flour or crush olives for oil, but the need for greater efficiency and the lack of slave labor led medieval monastic engineers to experiment with various ways of harnessing water power. Secular landowners followed suit, recognizing the mill as a source of economic and political power to which they could control access. Indeed, mills would remain the world's only source of mechanical power for manufacturing until the invention of the steam engine powered the Industrial Revolution (see Chapter 19).

Harnessing People

These new technologies became more widespread after the settlement of Viking and Magyar peoples decreased the threat of invasion and the consequent disruption of planting cycles and damage to crops. Left in relative peace, monasteries were able to develop and implement the tools described on this page, which were then copied by local lords who saw the benefits of managing their own lands more efficiently—rather than raiding others'. It became clear to entrepreneurial peasants, too, that investment in agricultural improvements would yield surpluses and profits. Productivity was also linked to increased population, fundamental changes in patterns of settlement, and the organization of the peasant workforce.

In the centuries after the fragmentation of Roman imperial power, most farmers in northern Europe lived on individual plots of land worked by themselves and their families. Starting in the ninth century, however, many of these individual holdings merged into large, common fields that could be farmed collectively by the inhabitants of entire villages; the resulting complex is sometimes called a **manor** (from the Latin verb *manere*, "to dwell"). In many cases, the impetus for the consolidation of manors came from the peasants themselves. Large fields could be farmed more efficiently than small fields, and investment costs were lower and could be shared equally: a single plow and a dozen oxen might suffice for an entire village, obviating the need for every farmer to maintain his own plow and team. Common fields were potentially more productive, too, allowing villagers to experiment with new crops and support larger numbers of animals on common pastures. In time, prosperous peasants might be able to establish a parish church, a communal oven, a blacksmith, a mill, and a

LIGHT PLOW AND HEAVY PLOW. Compare these two contemporary depictions of plowing: the one on the left is taken from a Greek manuscript copied in Byzantium and shows the light plow in use throughout the Mediterranean since antiquity; the one on the right shows the heavy wheeled plow adapted to northern Europe. Note that the peasant using the light plow has to press his foot on it to give it added weight. Another major innovation of the heavy European plow was the long moldboard, which turned over the ground after the plowshare cut into it; and the padded horse collar allowed horses to throw their full weight into pulling.

tavern. They could also converse, socialize, and assist their neighbors. In a difficult and demanding natural environment, these were important considerations.

In other cases, a manor could be created or co-opted by a local lord or lordly monastery. Manors were attractive because their greater productivity meant that lords could take a larger share of the peasants' surplus; it was also easier to control and exploit peasants who lived together in villages and were bound to each other by ties of kinship and dependence. Over time, some lords were therefore able to reduce formerly free peasants to **serfs** who could not leave the land without permission. Like slaves, serfs inherited their servile status; but unlike slaves, they were not supposed to be sold apart from the lands they worked. In practical terms, there may have been little difference between a serf and a free peasant—indeed, some serfs may have been better off. But as we have seen, social mobility is often tied to geographical mobility; and the inability of serfs to move freely prevented them from achieving the liberties of those workers who could (see pages 259–260).

The Conquest of the Land

The manor's organization of labor opened up more land for cultivation and made that cultivation more efficient. For centuries, farmers had known that if they sowed the same crop in the same field year after year, they would eventually exhaust the soil. The traditional solution was to divide the land, planting half in the fall to harvest in the spring, and leaving the other half to lie fallow. In the dry, thin soils of the Mediterranean, this remained the most common cropping pattern throughout the Middle Ages. In the more fertile soils of northern Europe, however, farmers slowly discovered that a three-field crop-rotation system could produce a sustainable increase in overall production. One-third of the land would lie fallow or be used as pasture, so that manure would fertilize the soil; one-third would be planted with winter wheat or rye, sown in the fall and harvested in the early summer; and one-third would be planted in the spring with another crop to be harvested in the fall. These fields were then rotated over a three-year cycle.

This system increased the amount of land under cultivation from 50 to 67 percent, while the two separate growing seasons provided some insurance against loss due to natural disasters or inclement weather. The system also produced higher yields per acre, particularly if legumes or fodder crops such as oats were a regular part of the crop-rotation pattern and could replace the nitrogen that wheat and rye leached out of the soil. Both humans and animals could eat oats, and legumes provided a source of protein to balance the intake of carbohydrates from bread and beer, the two main staples of the peasant diet in northern and central Europe. Additional fodder supported more and healthier animals, increasing the efficiency of plow beasts, diversifying the economy of the manor, and providing an additional source of protein through meat and milk. The new crop-rotation system also helped spread labor more evenly over the course of the year.

THE GROWTH OF TOWNS AND TRADE

As we observed in Chapter 7, the urban infrastructure of the western Roman Empire was weakened over the course of the fifth and sixth centuries. A few Roman cities continued to thrive under the lordship of bishops, but many—including Rome itself—began to crumble as their depleted populations could no longer maintain public buildings, services, and defensive walls. In most areas in northwestern Europe, monasteries replaced cities as the nuclei of civilization. Then, under Charlemagne and his imitators, **towns** came to be planted as centers for markets and administration by royal initiative. In Anglo-Saxon England, too, King Alfred and his successors established new towns in strategic locations, while at the same time reviving older Roman cities. They also issued a reliable and well-regulated currency that encouraged commerce.

Fostering Commerce

Although many towns were devastated by the Viking raids of the tenth century, the agricultural revolution helped to revitalize them—as did the influx of silver and gold set in circulation by the Vikings themselves. The rapid urbanization of Europe during the eleventh and twelfth centuries was also fostered by the initiatives of monasteries and secular lords who saw the economic advantages to be gained from providing safe havens for travelers and trade. This was especially true in the principalities of the Rhineland, the Low Countries, and the independent counties of Flanders and Champagne. Many towns grew up around monasteries, which provided protection and encouraged innovation. In southwestern Europe, existing towns prospered from their status as ports or their location along the overland routes connecting the Mediterranean with the Atlantic. In Italy, which had been decimated by five centuries of warfare and invasion, the growth of towns gave rise to especially dramatic changes.

Labels on the map:

Bergen · Fish, timber · Furs, timber, tar, copper, pitch, flax, iron · NORTH SEA · Wisby · Novgorod · Furs · Volga R. · ARAL SEA · Riga · Wool, flax, honey · Furs · Wool, coal, leather · Edinburgh · New Castle · Grain, wool · Copenhagen · Fish · Fish · Lübeck · Danzig · Amber · Hamburg · Wood, grain · Vistula R. · Wool, grain, tar, pitch · Iron, wool, tin · Bremen · Woolens · Grain · London · Linen · Wroclaw · Don R. · ATLANTIC OCEAN · Calais · Brugge · Cologne · Iron, lead, copper · Kiev · Timber, slaves, grain · St. Omer · Tournai · Reims · Metals · Kraków · Lviv · Lumber · Arras · Cloth · Paris · Elbe R. · Vienna · Trade route disrupted by Nomadic tribes c. 1150 · Tana · Troyes · Linens · Grain · La Rochelle · Geneva · Budapest · Grain · Caffa · CASPIAN SEA · Santiago de Compostela · Bordeaux · Lyons · Milan · Belgrade · Iron, leather · Wines · Venice · Glass, salt, lead · Danube R. · BLACK SEA · Silk · Citrus and dried fruits, honey · Alum, lead, wood · Toulouse · Montpellier · Salt · Silk · Genoa · Florence · Ragusa · Trebizond · Barcelona · Cork · Pisa · Woolens · Grain · Constantinople · Lisbon · Toledo · Silver · CORSICA · Wood, pitch · Rome · Cork, wool · Leather, olive oil · SARDINIA · Salt, grain, silver · Naples · Salonica · Grain, wine, oil · Granada · Silk · Amalfi · Bari · Silk · Ceuta · Olive oil · Messina · Wool · Bougie · Bone · Palermo · Silk · SICILY · Candia · CRETE · Silk · Silk · Famagusta · CYPRUS · Antioch · Tripoli · LEVANT · Silk, sugar · Acre · Jaffa · Ivory, carpets, dried fruits, coral, almonds, olive oil · Tunis · Wax, gold, salt · MEDITERRANEAN SEA · Alexandria · Spices, glassware, ceramics, carpets · Linen, cotton

— Major sea trade routes
— Major land trade routes

0 · 250 · 500 Miles
0 · 250 · 500 Kilometers

MEDIEVAL TRADE ROUTES. ▪ *What does this map reveal about the relationship between waterways and overland routes during the eleventh and twelfth centuries?* ▪ *Which regions appear to be most extensively interconnected, and why?* ▪ *How does the trade in certain specialized goods create certain commercial patterns?*

Initially, the renewed prosperity of Italy depended on the Byzantine emperors' suppression of piracy in the eastern Mediterranean. As in antiquity, piracy—both organized and opportunistic—was a major threat to trade, and combatting it could be a path to political power; Julius Caesar's career had been bolstered in just this way. But with the collapse of Roman imperial power in the West, the navy dispersed. Hence, the most successful cities around the turn of the millennium were situated in the Byzantine-controlled areas of the peninsula: Venice in the north and Amalfi, Naples, and Palermo in the south. These were the trading posts that brought silks, spices, and other luxuries from the East into western Europe. In the eleventh century, however, the Norman invasions of southern Italy frequently disrupted this trade, while Turkish invasions of Anatolia turned Byzantium's attention to the empire's eastern frontier. This opened new opportunities for the northern ports of Genoa and Pisa, whose merchant navies took over the task of policing the Mediterranean.

From Italy and other Mediterranean ports, exotic goods flowed northward to the towns of Flanders and the organized system of fairs—international markets convened at certain times of the year—that enriched the county of Champagne. Flemish towns, in turn, kept up a brisk trade with England, processing English wool into cloth, which was the staple commodity of medieval Europe, alongside wheat and wine. Eventually, merchants would succeed in opening up a direct route by sea between Italy and the Atlantic ports of northern Europe, after which it became practical to import raw wool directly from England to towns such as Florence, which began producing its own cloth.

It would be misleading, however, to overemphasize the role of long-distance trade in the urbanization of medieval Europe. Some towns that were dependent on such commerce, such as Venice and Genoa, attracted populations approaching 100,000 by 1300. But others that grew to be as large, including Paris and London, drew primarily on the wealth of their surrounding hinterlands for food, raw materials, and the bulk of their population. Furthermore, towns large and small existed in a symbiotic

1. Cathedral
2. Alt St. Thomas
3. Alt St. Peter
4. Jung St. Peter
5. St. Nikolaus
6. St. Johann
7. St. Wilhelm
8. St. Stephen

0 50 100 200 300m

☐ Roman fortification, the 'city'
☐ Frankish settlement, called 'New City', walled at end of ninth century
☐ Extension of Frankish settlement before 1200 to include Alt St. Peter's parish
☐ Jung St. Peter's parish, walled 1202–1220
☐ St. Nikolaus parish, walled thirteenth and fourteenth centuries
☐ St. Johann Parish, walled 1374–1390
- - - St. Wilhelm parish, walled 1387–1441

THE METAMORPHOSIS OF A MEDIEVAL CITY. The city of Strasbourg, on the long-disputed border between modern Germany and France, exemplifies the multilayered dynamics of urban change throughout the Middle Ages. It began as a Roman settlement, which became the nucleus for an episcopal see—hence the cathedral (1), located in the ancient precinct. At the end of the ninth century, it was fortified with new walls as the Carolingian Empire was collapsing and the Vikings were on the move. It then responded to the renewed prosperity of the eleventh and twelfth centuries, far outgrowing its original bounds, and continued to expand for several centuries thereafter. ■ *Note the scale of the map. What can you conclude from the scale about the density of settlement in a medieval city?*

relationship with the countryside, providing markets for the food surplus of outlying farms and transforming raw materials into marketable goods through manufacturing.

"Town Air Makes You Free"

To modern eyes, most medieval towns would still have seemed half rural. (Indeed, New York City would have seemed so until the end of the nineteenth century.) Streets were often unpaved, houses had gardens for raising vegetables, and animals were everywhere: in the early twelfth century, the heir to the throne of France was killed when his horse tripped over a pig running loose in the streets of Paris. Sanitary conditions were poor and the air reeked of excrement, both animal and human. (This was also true of New York even in 1900, where 150,000 horses produced 45,000 tons of manure each

month.) Under these conditions, disease could spread rapidly, and fire was another omnipresent danger because wooden and thatched buildings were clustered close together.

But these inconveniences were far outweighed by the advantages of urban life, not least of which was that towns provided a means of escape from the strictures of the countryside. As a German adage puts it, "Town air makes you free" (*"Stadtluft macht frei"*). This is because the citizens of most medieval towns were not subject to the arbitrary jurisdiction of a lord—or if they were, the lord realized that rewarding initiative with further freedoms fostered still more initiatives and more wealth.

Many Catalonian and Flemish towns accordingly received charters of liberty from the counts of these regions and were given the right to govern themselves. Others seized that right: In 1127, the people of Arras, on the Franco-Flemish border, declared that they were no longer the serfs of the

THE MARKET SQUARE OF KRAKÓW (POLAND). This view of the *rynek* (or the main market square) of Kraków was taken from the medieval tower of St. Mary's Basilica. It emphasizes the extraordinary scale of commercial activity that has taken place here since the eleventh century. Measuring around 430,000 square feet, it is one of the largest medieval town squares in Europe and a symbol of urban prosperity and pride. Although the handsome Cloth Hall in the center was not built until the fifteenth century, it stands on the site of market stalls dating back to the foundation of the city. Recent excavations of the square itself have revealed artifacts from numerous artisanal workshops. ▪ *Compare the scale of this market with the plan of Strasbourg on page 258.* ▪ *What historical factors might account for the far more generous proportions of this newer medieval town?*

local monastery that had nurtured the growth of their town in the first place. They banded together to form a **commune**, swearing to maintain solidarity with one another and setting up their own form of representative government. The monastery was forced to free them, and then free to tax them. This arrangement was mutually beneficial, and by the end of the century, Arras was the wealthiest and most densely populated town in northern Europe.

Urban areas further expanded through the constant immigration of free peasants and escaped serfs in search of a better life. Once a town had established its independence, newcomers could claim the status of citizens after a year and a day; thereafter, the only authority to which they were subject was that of the town's officials. For this reason, some powerful lords and rulers resisted the efforts of towns to claim

independence. Almost inevitably, though, they paid a high price for this. In Rome, the pope's claim to secular authority over the city led to frequent uprisings. In the French city of Laon, the bishop who asserted his lordship over a newly formed commune was murdered in 1112. And in 1127, the count of Flanders, Charles the Good (r. 1119–1127), was assassinated by a family of powerful officials who resented his claims that they were, in fact, his serfs.

Portable Wealth: Money and Credit

The growth of towns and trade depends on more than surplus goods, initiative, and mobility; it also depends on money, a reliable supply of cash and the availability of credit.

It is no accident that the earliest participants in the commercial revolution of the Middle Ages were cities located in regions whose rulers minted and regulated a strong currency: Byzantium, al-Andalus, and the Christian kingdoms of Spain, the old Roman region of Provence (southern France), Anglo-Saxon England, and Flanders. Yet precisely because there were so many currencies in circulation, the economy also depended on moneychangers and bankers who could extend credit to merchants, thus obviating the need to travel roads and waterways with bags full of cash.

Most of the sophisticated financial mechanisms for extending credit and making investments had long been in place throughout the Islamic world and Byzantium, but in western Europe, much of this crucial activity was carried forward by Jewish bankers situated within the network of close-knit Jewish communities that connected cities such as Constantinople, Baghdad, and Córdoba to the burgeoning cities of the north. In many regions, Jews had a virtual monopoly on these activities, because Christians were technically forbidden to lend money at interest or make a profit from investments. This practice was called *usury* (from the Latin word for "interest"), and Christian theologians cited various passages from the Old and New Testaments that seemed to condemn it. But in practice, the Roman Church turned a blind eye to such practices. Indeed, many prominent churchmen, including bishops, made fortunes lending money, as did many laymen—especially in towns such as Arras and Florence.

Still, the moral stigma attached to this necessary practice meant that Jews were often the ones targeted at times of crisis, just as they were the people to whom rulers would turn most readily when they needed funds—helping to explain why many kings, princes, and bishops protected the Jewish communities in their realms and often extended special privileges to them in exchange for money. An unfortunate result was the circulation of conspiracy theories harmful to Jews, who were perceived as exercising control over Christians through secret channels of communication and maintaining a stranglehold on finance. Jewish communities' reliance on the protection of powerful men also made them vulnerable when those men withdrew their support or were incapable of controlling the violence unleashed by their own policies.

VIOLENCE, LORDSHIP, AND MONARCHY

The new wealth of western Europe fostered social mobility, yet it also created a more stratified society. In the Carolingian period, the nobility comprised a relatively small number of ancient families that counted each other as equals and married among themselves. During the tenth and eleventh centuries, however, new families began to emerge as territorial lords and princes, rivaling and sometimes surpassing the old aristocracy in power and wealth. Some of these new families were descended from lesser officeholders in the Carolingian administration, men who had established independent powers after the empire collapsed and who used their public offices for private gain. Others were successful interlopers who had seized control of undefended manors and sustained war-bands of treasure-hungry young men.

Tools of Power: Castles and Knights

The predatory lords who emerged during this period protected their territories, families, and followers by building strongholds: castles (from the Latin word *castellum*, "little fortress"). These structures, seldom known in Europe before the Viking invasions, came to dominate the landscape during the eleventh and twelfth centuries. A castle was both defensive and offensive. It rendered its owner more secure from arson and attack—though it was vulnerable to siege—and it enabled him to dominate the surrounding countryside. Indeed, castles often formed the nucleus of a new town by providing protection for the peasants and merchants who clustered their dwellings close to its walls. In case of attack, these outliers could move inside.

Although most early castles were modest structures built of wood, situated on earthwork mounds surrounded by a ditch or moat, stone walls and keeps (fortified towers) soon replaced wooden palisades as the level of competitive violence increased. In Italy, rival families even built castles and towers in the middle of towns. Eventually, some castellans ("castle-holders") acquired enough power and booty to challenge more established lords, laying claim not only to property and influence but also to rank. These new lords didn't descend from Roman senators or Carolingian counts; instead, they boasted of lineages reaching back to successful warlords, such as Rollo the Viking, whom the Normans claimed to be their first duke (from the Latin word *dux*, "leader").

In addition to castle holding, both the older aristocracy and these self-made lords needed the help of warriors to enforce their claims to power. Accordingly, each lord maintained a private army of men heavily equipped with the new weaponry and armor that the widespread availability of iron—and new techniques for smelting it—made possible. These men fought on horseback, and were therefore called "horsemen" (in French, *chevaliers*; in English, *knights*).

Knighthood was a career that embraced men of widely varying status. Some eleventh-century knights were the younger sons of lords who sought to increase their chances

YORK CASTLE (ENGLAND). This fortification exemplifies some of the major phases of medieval castle building. The large mound is the remains of an earthwork erected on the orders of William the Conqueror in 1068, when it would have been crowned by a wooden palisade: this most basic type of construction is called a motte-and-bailey castle. York's castle remained a wooden tower until it was destroyed by fire and rebuilt in stone after 1245. It is now known as Clifford's Tower, after the rebel leader Sir Roger Clifford, who was held prisoner there prior to his execution in 1322.

of winning wealth by attaching themselves to the households of greater lords. Others were youths recruited from the peasantry, mounted and armed. All that bound them together was their function, which was the violent prosecution of their lord's interests. Gradually, though, knights came to regard themselves as belonging to a special military caste with its own rules of conduct. The beginnings of this process are discernible in the *Song of Roland*, and further developments would transform the meaning of *chivalry*, from "horsemanship" (*cheval* in French), to something very different (see pages 272–274).

Kings and Lords

Despite the emergence of self-governing cities and predatory lordships, the idea of kingship was still a powerful one in Europe. For example, the weak Capetian rulers of Paris kept alive the pretense that everyone dwelling in the lands once ruled by more powerful Frankish kings still owed allegiance to them, while the Ottonians claimed to be kings in northern Italy as well as in their own Saxon domain. In practice, however, neither was able to control the territories they claimed to rule. Effective political and military power lay in the hands of dukes, counts, castellans, and knights, all of whom channeled the increasing wealth of the countryside into their own hands. From their castles, these lords (*domini*) constructed dominions: lordships within which they exercised not only property rights but also the rights to mint money, judge legal cases, raise troops, wage war, collect taxes, and impose tolls.

The Problem of "Feudalism"

This highly diffused distribution of power is conventionally known as **feudalism**. But this vague term is unsatisfactory for several reasons. First and foremost, it is a modern concept not used in the period being discussed. Moreover, it has been used by different people to mean different things. For example, scholars influenced by the work of Karl Marx (1818–1883; see Chapter 20) use the term to describe an economic system in which wealth is entirely agricultural and cities have not yet formed; as we have seen, this does not reflect the historical reality of the eleventh and twelfth centuries. For other scholars, feudalism has been construed as an aristocratic social order in which propertied men are bound together by kinship and shared interests; again, this does not explain the varieties of power wielded in this period. Still others have spoken of feudalism as a system of landholding in which lesser men hold land from greater men in return for services of various kinds; but it was not always the greater men who held the most land. The term also has been used to refer to a system whereby great lords and kings grant land in order to raise troops.

Because all these definitions of feudalism are anachronistic, most recent historians of the Middle Ages have questioned or abandoned the use of the term. If, however, we look for a common denominator, we can say that feudalism denotes the abuse of official privileges for personal gain: making use of public resources or institutions for private purposes. In this case, there is general agreement that such practices took shape in Frankish lands after the disintegration of the Carolingian Empire, and later spread to other areas of Europe, changing as they adapted to different circumstances. In some regions, these customs fed a developing ideology that justified new kinds of dominion by which kings were supposed to be able to subordinate other powerful men. In this sense, feudalism legitimated royal power and helped to lay the groundwork for the emergence of European nation-states.

Fief and Vassals

Although the people living at this time would never have heard the term "feudalism," they would have understood the word at its root: *feudum*, usually translated as "fief" (FEEF). A fief is a gift or grant that creates a kind of contractual relationship between the giver and receiver. This gift could be land, but it could also be the revenues from a toll or a mill, or an annual sum of money. In return, the recipient owed the giver loyalty or services of some kind. In many cases, the gift implied that the recipient was subordinate to the giver and had in fact become the giver's **vassal** (from a Celtic word meaning "boy"). This relationship was dramatized in an act of **homage**, a powerful ceremony that made the vassal the *homme* ("man" in French) of his lord. Typically, the vassal would kneel and place his hands together in a position of prayer, and the lord would cover the clasped hands with his own. He would then raise up his new "man" and exchange a kiss with him. The symbolic importance of these gestures is clear: the lord (*dominus*) was literally the dominating figure. He could protect and raise up his man and also discipline him. The role of the vassal, meanwhile, was to support the lord and do nothing to incur his displeasure.

In regions where no centralized authority existed, such personal relationships were essential to creating and maintaining order. However, these relationships were not understood in the same ways all over Europe. Many castellans and knights held their lands freely, owing no service whatsoever to the count or duke within whose territories their lands lay. Nor were these relationships neatly hierarchical: "feudalism" created no "feudal pyramids," in which knights held fiefs from counts, and

counts held fiefs from kings, all in an orderly fashion. Sometimes, kings would insist that the world *should* be structured this way, but they were seldom able to make this wish a reality.

A New Type of Monarchy: England

The first place where we can begin to observe the efforts of a particular line of kings to establish a monarchy that dominated other powerful lordships is England. In 1066, Duke William of Normandy claimed that he was the rightful successor of the English king, Edward the Confessor, who had just died. But the English elected a new king, Harold, ignoring his claim. So William crossed the English Channel to take the kingdom by force, defeating Harold at the Battle of Hastings (see **Interpreting Visual Evidence** on page 264). Now, William had to subjugate all the other chieftains who held power in England, many of whom also aspired to be king.

William accomplished this, first, by asserting that he was king by imperial conquest as well as by succession, and that all the land of England thereby belonged to him. Then William rewarded his Norman followers with fiefs: extensive grants of land taken from their English holders, whom the Norman lords were allowed to exploit and subdue. In return, William received their loyalty and a share of their revenues.

The Norman conquerors of England were already accustomed to holding land in return for service to their duke back in Normandy. But in England, their subordination to the king was further enforced by the effective machinery of the Anglo-Saxon state and longstanding customs that had the force of law. As king of England, therefore, William was able to exercise a variety of public powers that he could not have enjoyed in Normandy. In England, only the king could coin money, and only the king's money was allowed to circulate. As kings of England, William and his successors also inherited the right to collect a national land tax, supervise justice in royal courts, and raise an army. They even retained the Anglo-Saxon officers of local government, known as sheriffs, to help them administer and enforce their rights.

William was thereby able to insist that all the people of England owed ultimate loyalty to the king, even if they did not hold a scrap of land directly from him. William's kingship thus represented a powerful fusion of Carolingian-style traditions of public power with the new forms of lordship that had grown up in the tenth and eleventh centuries, bolstered by indigenous Anglo-Saxon forms of governance. It was a new type of monarchy.

Violence, Lordship, and Monarchy | 263

Interpreting Visual Evidence

The Graphic History of the Bayeux Tapestry

One of the most famous historical documents of all time is not a document at all, but an embroidered strip of linen 231 feet long (originally much longer) and 20 inches wide. It is also not an actual tapestry, as its name misleadingly implies, but an elaborate exercise in needlepoint. It tells the story of the Norman conquest of England and the events leading up to it. The circumstances of its making remain a mystery, but it was certainly commissioned by someone close to William the Conqueror (1027–1087), the Norman duke who claimed the throne of England in 1066. Indeed, its purpose was to demonstrate the truth of William's claim and to justify his invasion of England when Harold Godwinson (c. 1022–1066; image A) was crowned king of England in his place (image B). One likely patron was Queen Edith of England, the widow of the late King Edward (r. 1042–1066) and sister of Harold, who became a friend and adviser to William. Edith was noted for her skill in embroidery as well as for her political acumen, and she would have been able to oversee the making of this visual history by the women of her household. Two of its evocative scenes, with translations of accompanying Latin texts, are reproduced here.

A. Harold Sails the Sea. In this scene, from the first portion of the Tapestry, Harold has been sent on an embassy by King Edward. He feasts with friends in a hall on the English coast before crossing the Channel.

B. Harold Is Seated, King of the English. Although Harold may have promised to relinquish his claim to the English throne in William's favor, the central scene of the tapestry is his coronation. Stigant, the archbishop of Canterbury, stands on his left. Outside the cathedral, the people of London look on curiously. Some appear to be surprised or alarmed.

Questions for Analysis

1. Like a graphic novel or a comic strip, the Bayeux Tapestry tells its story through images; words (in very simple Latin) play a minor role. What do the Tapestry's artists choose to express exclusively through visualization? When do they choose to state something verbally? What might be the motivation behind these choices? What is left out of the story, or left ambiguous? What might be the reason(s) for this ambiguity?

2. In addition to being a source for political and military historians, the Bayeux Tapestry provides us with fascinating glimpses into the daily life and material culture of the Middle Ages. What, for example, can you conclude about the necessary preparations for a voyage by sea? About the history of clothing, weaponry, or animals?

3. If Queen Edith was responsible for commissioning and helping to make the Tapestry, it would constitute one of the few surviving historical accounts by a woman prior to the twentieth century. Would the creator's gender change your perception of this artifact or of these particular scenes? Why or why not?

The Struggle for Imperial Power

We can contrast the wide-ranging powers of the new Anglo-Norman kings of England with those of Germany. No German king could claim to rule more than a single principality, and his imperial authority over a host of other rulers was maintained only through a close alliance with the Church. For this reason, the emperor relied heavily on ecclesiastical leaders: his chief administrators were archbishops and bishops whom the emperor himself had appointed and installed in their sacred offices, just as Charlemagne had done. Even the pope was frequently an imperial appointee. The fact that leading churchmen were often members of the imperial family also helped to counter the power of regional rulers.

But during the latter half of the eleventh century, this close cooperation between sacred and secular authority was fractured, as was the ultimate power of the German monarch. In 1056, the six-year-old Henry IV (1050–1106) succeeded his father as king and emperor; and, as we will frequently note, political competition among the advisers of underage rulers often escalates into larger conflicts. In this case, the German princes of various regions—led by the disenfranchised Saxon nobility—tried to gain control of the royal government at the expense of Henry's regents. When Henry began to rule in his own right, in 1073, these hostilities escalated into a civil war.

At the same time, the newly elected pope, Gregory VII (r. 1073–1085), began to insist that no laymen—not even royal ones—should have any influence within the Church. (This would become a core contention in a movement toward increased papal power, to be discussed in the next section.) King Henry, of course, resisted any initiative that would prohibit him from selecting his own bishops and abbots, for these were the key players in the administration of his realm. So Pope Gregory allied himself with the rebellious Saxon nobility, and together they moved to depose Henry. To save his crown, Henry was forced to acknowledge the pope's superiority by begging forgiveness.

Crossing the Alps into Italy in 1077, in the depths of winter, Henry found Gregory installed at the castle of Canossa under the protection of one of Europe's most powerful rulers, Matilda of Tuscany. Encouraged by Matilda, who interceded on his behalf, Henry performed an elaborate ritual of penance: standing for three successive days outside the gates of the castle, barefoot, stripped of his imperial trappings, clad in the sackcloth of a supplicant. This performance of subjection and servitude forestalled Henry's deposition, but it did not resolve his dispute with the nobility of German lands. And it also symbolically reversed the relationship between secular power and religious power. Since the time of Constantine, popes had been dependent

on the rulers who protected them; but now, an emperor had been bested by a pope. For the other kings and lords of Europe, Henry's humiliation was a chilling example of what could happen when a king let himself be made a vassal.

RELIGIOUS REFORM AND PAPAL POWER

The increased power of the papacy in the eleventh century was a result of the processes we have been surveying in this chapter, but it was a development that would have been

MATILDA OF TUSCANY MEDIATES BETWEEN EMPEROR AND POPE. Matilda was one of the most powerful rulers in eleventh-century Europe, controlling many strategic territories in northern Italy. Fluent in German as well as Latin and Italian, she was a key mediator in the struggle between the emperor and the pope, and a supporter of the reforming movement within the Church. The Latin inscription accompanying this manuscript miniature reads: "The King entreats the Abbot [i.e., the pope] and even humbles himself before Matilda." ▪ *How does this image represent the relationships among these figures?* ▪ *Which appears to be the most powerful, and why?*

hard to foresee at the time of Charlemagne's death. Yet, in the wake of the Viking invasions and the redistribution of power within the former Carolingian Empire, no ruler could maintain Charlemagne's hold on the Church. Many parish churches had been abandoned or destroyed; and those that survived were often regarded as the personal property of some local family, whose responsibility for protecting parishioners could become an excuse to oppress them. Bishoprics, too, were co-opted by families who regarded Church lands and offices as their private property.

Monasteries underwent a further process of privatization, becoming safe havens for aristocratic younger sons and daughters with little inclination for religious life. Meanwhile, the holders of papal office were its worst abusers, most of whom were incompetent or corrupt and the sons of powerful Roman families. Many fathered sons who themselves succeeded to high ecclesiastical office, including that of pope. As the guardian of the tombs of Peter and Paul, the bishop of Rome had long occupied a privileged position. Now, however, the papacy's credibility had been severely compromised.

The Monastic Reform Movement

The first successful attempt to restore the spiritual authority of the Roman Church can be traced to the founding of a new kind of monastery in Burgundy (now southeastern France). In 910, a Benedictine abbey called Cluny freed itself from any obligation to local families by placing itself under the direct protection of the papacy. And although it had a wealthy benefactor, that benefactor relinquished control over Cluny's property; instead, Duke William of Aquitaine and his family gained the spiritual support and prayers of the monks, whose intercessions might help save warlike men from eternal damnation.

This arrangement would set a new precedent for the relationship between monasteries and powerful families for centuries to come, as Cluny began to sponsor other monasteries on the same model. Indeed, the foundation of these daughter houses was another innovation: prior to this, all Benedictine monasteries had been independent of each other, united only by their observance of Benedict's *Rule*. Now, Cluny established a network of Cluniac clones across Europe, all of which remained subordinate to the mother house. By 1049, there were sixty-seven such Cluniac priories, as the daughter monasteries were called, each one performing the same elaborate round of prayer and worship for which Cluny became famous—and each one entirely free from the control of local lords who hoped to reap spiritual rewards from their support of the pious monks.

Cluniac influence was strongest in the former Frankish territories and in Italy, where the virtual absence of effective kingship allowed monastic reforms to thrive unchecked. In Germany and England, by contrast, fostering monastic reform emerged as an essential responsibility of Christian rulers whose role model was the pious Charlemagne. These rulers, too, followed Cluniac example by insisting on the strict observance of poverty, chastity, and obedience within the monastery, and on the performance of liturgical prayer. Yet, because they were the guarantors of the monasteries' freedom from outside interference, it was they who appointed the abbots, just as they also appointed the bishops of their kingdoms. As a result of this trend, and the concurrent Norman conquest of England, future kings of England would have more direct control over Church lands than other European rulers. In Germany, a prince's right to appoint spiritual leaders was the central cause of strife with the papacy (see pages 269–270).

Despite the differences in sponsorship, these parallel reforming movements made monasticism the dominant spiritual model for Latin Christianity. The peaceful, orderly round of daily worship in monasteries and convents

THE ABBEY CHURCH AT CLUNY. Its extraordinary wealth and power made Cluny a major target during the French Wars of Religion, and again during the French Revolution, when locals who had been subjected to its lordship for centuries razed most of the buildings to the ground (see Chapters 14 and 18). This artist's reconstruction shows the vast abbey church as it might have looked by the twelfth century, after several extensive building campaigns. In its day, Cluny was one of the largest structures in Europe and a quintessential example of the architectural style known as Romanesque.

was regarded as mirroring a perfect celestial harmony, and monastic prayers were considered uniquely effective because of nuns' and monks' holy way of life. Monasteries also had an important influence on the piety of ordinary people, because many monastic communities maintained parishes that ministered directly to the laity. The spiritual practices that had been unique to monks and nuns in earlier centuries, therefore, came to influence daily life outside the cloister.

Relics and Pilgrims

One potent example of this new popular spirituality was the growing devotion to relics. Monasteries were often the repositories of cherished objects associated with saints, such as fragments of bone or pieces of cloth cut from the garments of some holy person. These souvenirs were believed to possess special protective and curative powers. Hence, a relic was always buried beneath the altar of a church during the ceremony of its consecration, to render the church building sacrosanct. Reliquaries made of precious metals and studded with jewels were casings that reflected and augmented the value of the holy objects contained within them. They were also collected and displayed.

Indeed, relics were so valuable that monasteries and cathedrals competed with one another for their acquisition and even plotted the "holy theft" of a particularly prized treasure. For instance, the relics of Nicholas, a fourth-century bishop of Myra (in Turkey), were stolen from the saint's tomb during the eleventh century. These were brought to Bari in southeastern Italy, where Benedictine monks built a magnificent church to house them. It became a major—and lucrative—destination for pilgrims.

The possession and display of relics thus became a way for monasteries to attract attention and generate revenue, since those who sought cures or favors at the shrine of a saint would often make a donation to the monastery in the saint's honor. If a saint was especially famous for a particular type of miracle, pilgrims might travel thousands of miles to visit a shrine. Saint Nicholas was famous for increasing the wealth of his suppliants, and for bestowing gifts—hence his later incarnation as Santa Claus. The relics of Sainte Foy ("Saint Faith") of Conques (south-central France) were renowned for their power to rectify injustices, restore order, and heal the maladies that afflicted the poor. Those of the apostle James at Compostela (northern Spain) became the chief destination on a major pilgrimage route, rivaling even the holy sites of Rome and Jerusalem in its popularity. Pilgrimage was another of the important ways in which the new patterns of Christian piety that developed in monasteries began to spread to the laity.

Lay men and women from all social classes are represented in the records of the miracles recorded at shrines, many traveling in family groups or with neighbors. And because it was considered holy to house, feed, and care for pilgrims, many monasteries opened special hostels to house these travelers. As a result, even people of very humble means were able to make trips to shrines very far from home, increasing their sense of belonging to a shared Christian community.

The Reform of the Secular Clergy

By the eleventh century, the movement toward spiritual renewal in the monasteries of Europe began to embrace the sees of bishops. This was a major change. Bishops and the priests who served in their dioceses were secular clergy, living in the world (saeculum in Latin), and it had long been expected that they would share some of the worldly preoccupations and lifestyles of other lords. But as the values and priorities of monasticism began to spread outward, abbots were more often appointed to episcopal office. Meanwhile, even nonmonastic bishops were forced to adopt stricter standards of personal conduct. Bishops also began to rebuild and expand their cathedral churches to make them more suitable reflections of divine majesty, in accordance with Cluniac example.

As their influence grew, the monasteries under the sway of Cluny began to lobby for even larger reforms, amounting to a fundamental dismantling of customs that reached back to the organization of the Church under Constantine, seven centuries earlier. They centered their attacks on the practice of simony (SIGH-mony), a term describing any use of ecclesiastical office for personal gain, including the purchase or sale of a bishopric or a priest's living (i.e., house, goods, and annual salary). In other words, the reform movement targeted the very structure of the Church as a network of independent lordships held by powerful men in trust for their families.

Even more radical was the reformers' demand that secular clergy share the lifestyles of monks, taking vows not only of personal poverty but of celibacy. Although some early councils of the Church had attempted to regulate the marriage of bishops and priests, none had been successful, for good reason: the task of ministering to the laity was very different from the monk's task of perpetual prayer and communal life. For a thousand years, it had been conceded that the demands of priestly celibacy were unreasonable, and would deprive a priest's parishioners of an additional resource and ministry—that of his wife. In the year 1000, therefore, the vast majority of parish priests all across Europe were married, and in the eastern Orthodox Church they would remain so. Married bishops were rare, but not unknown. In Brittany, the archbishop of Dol and his wife publicly celebrated the marriages of

A Miraculous Reliquary

Although pilgrimages had been a part of Christian religious practice for centuries, they became much more central elements of popular piety from the tenth century on. Pilgrims brought money and spiritual prestige to the monasteries and cathedrals that housed miracle-working relics, and competition among monastic houses sometimes led one house to steal the relics of another. But some critics worried that these newly popular shrines were encouraging idolatry. Bernard of Angers (c. 960–1028) was one such critic. His account of a visit to the shrines of several saints, including that of Sainte Foy ("Saint Faith") at Conques, reveals the negative impression that ornate reliquaries made on him—and the power of wonder-working relics to correct that impression.

t is an ancient custom in all of Auvergne, Rodez, Toulouse, and the neighboring regions that the local saint has a statue of gold, silver, or some other metal . . . [that] serves as a reliquary for the head of the saint or for a part of his body. The learned might see in this a superstition and a vestige of the cult of demons, and I myself . . . had the same impression the first time I saw the statue of Saint Gerard . . . resplendent with gold and stones, with an expression so human that the simple people . . . pretend that it winks at pilgrims whose prayers it answers. I admit to my shame that turning to my friend Bernerius and laughing, I whispered to him in Latin, "What do you think of the idol? Wouldn't Jupiter or Mars be happy with it?" . . .

Three days later we arrived at [the shrine of] St. Faith. . . . We approached [the reliquary] but the crowd was such that we could not prostrate ourselves like so many others already lying on the floor. Unhappy, I remained standing, fixing my view on the image and murmuring this prayer, "St. Faith, you whose relics rest in this sham, come to my assistance on the day of judgment." And this time I looked at my companion . . . because I found it outrageous that all of these rational beings should be praying to a mute and inanimate object. . . .

Later I greatly regretted to have acted so stupidly toward the saint of God. This was because among other miracles [that] Don Adalgerius, at that time dean and later . . . abbot [of Conques], told me [was] a remarkable account of a cleric named Oldaric. One day when the venerable image had to be taken to another place, . . . he restrained the crowd from bringing offerings and

The Reliquary of Saint Faith, Early Tenth Century.

he insulted and belittled the image of the saint. . . . The next night, a lady of imposing severity appeared to him: "You," she said, "how dare you insult my image?" Having said this, she flogged her enemy with a staff. . . . He survived only long enough to tell the vision in the morning.

Thus there is no place left for arguing whether the effigy of St. Faith ought to be venerated since it is clear that he who reproached the holy martyr nevertheless retracted his reproach. Nor is it a spurious idol where nefarious rites of sacrifice or of divination are conducted, but rather a pious memorial of a holy virgin, before which great numbers of faithful people decently and eloquently implore her efficacious intercession for their sins.

Source: Bernard of Angers, "The Procession of Saint Foy," in *Readings in Medieval History*, 5th ed., ed. Patrick J. Geary (Toronto, Canada: 2016), pp. 290–91 (slightly modified).

Questions for Analysis

1. Why does Bernard initially object to the display of relics in ornate reliquaries? Why would he consider this practice blasphemous? How does he become reconciled to it?

2. Can you think of present-day practices that resemble the medieval fascination with collecting, displaying, and venerating relics? What do such practices reveal about any society?

their daughters, endowing them with lands belonging to the bishopric. In Milan, the archbishops flatly rejected reformers' calls for celibacy, declaring that their patron saint, Ambrose (see Chapter 6), had been married, too.

The Reform of the Papacy

In Rome, the most powerful bishopric of all remained resolutely unreformed until 1046, when the German emperor Henry III deposed three rival Roman nobles who claimed to be pope and appointed in their place his own relative, a monk who adopted the name Leo IX (r. 1049–1054). Leo and his supporters took control of the papal court and began to promulgate decrees against simony and clerical marriage. They then took steps to enforce these decrees by traveling throughout Christendom, disciplining or removing from office priests deemed guilty of simony or obstinately determined not to "put away" their wives—whom the reformers insisted on calling "concubines" as a way of discrediting these respectable relationships.

Implicit in Leo's reforming efforts was a new vision of the Roman Church as a type of monarchy, with the pope at the apex of a spiritual pyramid. This was an ideal difficult for any secular ruler to realize, and one that would severely limit the power of other ecclesiastical officeholders. It was not surprising, therefore, that Leo and his successors met considerable opposition from powerful leaders within the Church itself, and they could only enforce their claims in regions where they had the support of secular rulers. Chief among these was the pious emperor Henry III, whose protection insulated papal reformers from the Roman nobility, who would otherwise have deposed or assassinated them.

But when Henry III died in 1056, the regents of his child heir Henry IV (whose reign we discussed on page 265) were neither able nor willing to stand behind the reforming movement. In 1058, the Roman aristocracy seized this opportunity to install one of their own men on the papal throne. By this time, however, the reform movement had gathered momentum; a year later, a new pope had been installed who was determined to counter any interference from either the German or Italian nobility. To this end, Nicholas II (r. 1059–1061) created a new legislative body, the College of Cardinals (from the Latin for "collection" of "hinges"). Hitherto, local bishops around Rome had served the papacy as advisers and assistants, but now the college became the nexus for the creation of papal policy. It also ensured the continuity of the papal office by overseeing the selection of new popes, a role it still plays today.

Needless to say, this novel arrangement infuriated the advisers of the young Henry IV, since it denied the emperor's prerogative to oversee the process of papal elections himself. And it set the stage for the confrontations that were to follow.

The Investiture Conflict

A few years after Henry IV began to rule in his own right, the new College of Cardinals selected as pope a zealous reformer, a Cluniac monk of Tuscan origins who had been a protégé of Leo IX. He took the name Gregory VII. Initially, pope and emperor treated one another with deference. Henry IV's position in Germany had been weakened by his wars with the Saxon nobility, and he needed papal backing to restore his authority. In his letters to the new pope, he therefore blamed the advisers of his youth for the troubles that had arisen between his own court and that of Rome, and he promised to make amends. Gregory, in turn, spoke of pope and emperor as the two eyes of a single, Christian body. On the surface, it appeared that harmony might be restored.

Two years later, however, relations between papacy and empire were riven by a conflict that would permanently alter the relationship between spiritual and temporal rulers in western Europe. Superficially, the issue that divided Gregory and Henry was that of **investiture**, the right to appoint bishops and to equip them with the trappings of office. Since the time of the Carolingians, this had been the prerogative of the emperor—as it was in Byzantium. But to Gregory, this practice smacked of simony, since a lay lord would obviously choose bishops who would be politically useful to him, regardless of their spiritual qualifications.

The real issue, however, was not the political power of bishops but the control of that power. The papal reform movement, as it developed under Gregory, was predicated paradoxically on liberating the Church from powerful worldly influences in order that the Church itself might become more worldly and powerful. This was the principle that lay behind discouraging clerical marriage, too: Church offices and Church property had to be protected by the Church for the Church; and allowing priests to marry might encourage the handing down of offices to sons, just as allowing rulers to appoint bishops encouraged these bishops to act as the rulers' agents. These practices tainted the austere authority that the pope was trying to cultivate, and it also threatened to alienate property and power that the papacy wanted to harness for its own purposes.

Gregory therefore took the reform movement to a new level, insisting that adherence to these principles was not just a matter of policy but of religious dogma, a term defined as a "truth necessary for salvation." When Henry IV refused to accept Gregory's reforms and proceeded to invest the new archbishop of Milan, Gregory reminded him that, as the successor of Saint Peter and the representative of Christ on earth, he himself had the power to save or damn all souls. To drive the point home, Gregory excommunicated a number of Henry's advisers, including several of the bishops who had participated in the investiture at Milan. Henry thereupon renounced his obedience to Gregory, calling on him to resign, to which Gregory responded by excommunicating Henry, along with his supporters.

In itself, the excommunication of a king was not terribly unusual. Gregory, however, went much further by equating excommunication with deposition, declaring that since Henry was no longer a faithful son of the Church, he was no longer king either, and so his subjects had a sacred duty to rebel against him. It was this declaration that occasioned Henry's humiliating penance at Canossa in January of 1077. But the story does not end there, because Henry used his restored powers to crush his Saxon opponents and eventually to drive Gregory himself from Rome; the aged pope died in exile in southern Italy in 1085. By then, however, he had established the principles on which papal governance would be based for the remainder of the Middle Ages.

In 1122, the conflict over investiture was provisionally resolved at the Concordat of Worms (*VOHRMS*) in Germany. Its terms declared that the emperor was forbidden to invest prelates with the *religious* symbols of their office but was allowed to invest them with the symbols of their rights as *temporal* or secular rulers, in his capacity as their overlord. In practice, then, the rulers of Europe retained a great deal of influence over ecclesiastical appointments, but they had to acknowledge that bishops were now part of a clerical hierarchy headed by the pope, and that they were supposed to be loyal to the Church in Rome and not to the ruler of the region in which they lived.

CRUSADING CAUSES AND OUTCOMES

Gregory VII's equation of excommunication with deposition had given the pope a powerful new weapon to use against wayward rulers. Indeed, according to a series of pronouncements issued in his name, Gregory insisted that the pope has the power to judge all men but cannot himself be judged by any earthly authority. Moreover, he has the power to free any man from obligations to his lord, because every Christian owes ultimate loyalty to the pope, the arbiter of eternal life or death. These were big claims. How could they be realized? Gregory's immediate successors would soon be driven to great lengths in their efforts

to establish the credibility of the newly powerful papacy. In the end, it took the appeal of a Byzantine emperor and the preaching of a crusade against Muslims to unite western Christendom under the papal banner.

The Expansion and Fragility of Byzantium

As Europe expanded and changed, the eastern Roman Empire was undergoing its own series of transformations. The decline of the Abbasid caliphate in Baghdad had relieved some of the pressures on its borders in the course of the ninth century. But at the same time, Byzantium was facing some new threats. In the mid-ninth century, Muslims from North Africa captured the Byzantine islands of Sicily and Crete. Meanwhile, the migration of pagan Slavs into the Balkans was rapidly undermining Byzantine control of that region. And a formidable power had emerged in the north, as the Viking Rus' established themselves along the river systems that fed into the Black and Caspian Seas. The most important trading partner of the Rus' was the Abbasid caliphate, with which they exchanged slaves, honey, wax, and furs for silver, Indian spices, and Chinese silks. But the Rus' knew their way to Constantinople, too. In 860, while the Byzantine emperor and his army were busy on the eastern frontier, a fleet of them sailed into the Black Sea and sacked the capital.

The best that the emperors in Byzantium could do was to make these newer enemies their allies. Greek-speaking missionaries began the process by converting some of the Balkan Slavs to Orthodox Christianity, devising for them a written language known as Old Church Slavonic and creating the Cyrillic alphabet still used today in Bulgaria, Serbia, and Russia. As we have often seen, domination went hand in glove with conversion. The empire also fostered a military and commercial alliance with the kingdom of Rus' centered around Kiev. In 911, hundreds of Rus' served with the Byzantine navy in an attack on Muslim Crete. In 957, a Kievan princess named Olga was lavishly entertained on a state visit to Constantinople. And in 989, the emperor Basil II turned to Vladimir, prince of Kiev, for the troops he needed to win a civil war against an imperial rival. In return for Vladimir's help, Basil married him to his sister Anna, and Vladimir, along with his people, accepted baptism into the Orthodox Church. (Russia remains strongly Orthodox to this day, despite Soviet efforts to dismantle the Russian Orthodox Church during the twentieth century.)

During the tenth century, the eastern Roman Empire further strengthened its position by launching a series of successful campaigns against the Abbasids, reconquering territories that had been lost since the first wave of Muslim conquests in seventh century. But although most of the peoples of this region had remained Christian through three centuries of Islamic rule, the Armenians and the Syrians in particular had their own distinctive Christian traditions that were at odds, both doctrinally and linguistically, with the Greek-speaking church at Constantinople.

Reincorporating these "heretics" into the empire strained the limits of Orthodoxy to a considerable degree, and these efforts created a center of power that lay outside the imperial capital at Constantinople. Accordingly, rivalries divided the eastern nobility and the imperial court, eventually erupting into warfare after one aristocratic family attempted a coup.

Meanwhile, projects of reconquest and expansion were overextending the Byzantine military and its treasury. In an effort to raise cash, some emperors in the mid-eleventh century began to debase the gold coinage that had kept the empire competitive with the Islamic caliphate, thus undermining Byzantine commerce at the very moment when Venice, Genoa, and Pisa were consolidating their control in the eastern Mediterranean and taking over the lucrative trade between Muslim North Africa (including Egypt) and western Europe.

A failing economy, ongoing dynastic civil war, the weakened condition of the army, and uneasy relations with the new kingdoms of the Balkans (especially Hungary) proved nearly fatal to Byzantine sovereignty. And then the empire was confronted with yet another threat. The Seljuk Turks, a powerful dynasty of Sunni Muslims who were building their own empire based in Persia, began to move westward in the latter part of the eleventh century. In 1071, they captured Armenia and moved swiftly into the Byzantine heartland of Anatolia (Turkey), where they destroyed a Byzantine army sent to deflect them.

At a blow, the wealthiest and most productive part of the empire fell into Muslim hands—and not those of the Abbasids with whom the Byzantines had contended for centuries. In the same year, the Seljuks captured Jerusalem, which had been part of a Shi'ite caliphate based in Egypt, ruled by the Fatimids. By 1081, when the eastern nobility of Byzantium finally emerged triumphant in their ongoing bid for the imperial throne, the new emperor **Alexius Comnenus** (r. 1081–1118) found himself at the head of a crippled state.

THE BYZANTINE EMPIRE, c. 1025. ▪ *According to the map, what political challenges faced the Byzantine Empire in the eleventh century?* ▪ *How was the long-standing influence of Muslims in the Near East likely to affect the character of Byzantine culture?* ▪ *How did the domain of Rus' potentially create additional economic and military pressure on Byzantium, directly as well as indirectly?*

Competing Viewpoints

Preaching the First Crusade: Two Accounts

> We owe the following account of Urban II's call for a crusade to Fulcher of Chartres, a priest who was present at the Council of Clermont in 1095 and later served as a chaplain to Baldwin, the first Norman king of Jerusalem. It forms part of Fulcher's contemporary chronicle of the First Crusade. The second account of the motives behind the Crusade comes from a biography of the Byzantine emperor Alexius Comnenus, written by his daughter Anna (1083–1153), who also lived through these events.

Pope Urban II's Call at Clermont, November 1095

Most beloved brethren: Urged by necessity, I, Urban, by the permission of God chief bishop and prelate over the whole world, have come into these parts as an ambassador with a divine admonition to you, the servants of God. . . .

Although, O sons of God, you have promised more firmly than ever to keep the peace among yourselves and to preserve the rights of the Church, there remains still an important work for you to do. Freshly quickened by the divine correction, you must apply the strength of your righteousness to another matter which concerns you as well as God. For your brethren who live in the east are in urgent need of your help, and you must hasten to give them the aid which has often been promised them. For, as most of you have heard, the Turks and Arabs have attacked them and have conquered the territory of Romania [the Byzantine Empire] as far west as the shore of the Mediterranean and the Hellespont. . . . They have occupied more and more of the lands of those Christians, and have overcome them in seven battles. They have killed and captured many, and have destroyed the churches and devastated the empire.

If you permit them to continue thus for a while with impunity, the faithful of God will be much more widely attacked by them. On this account I, or rather the Lord, beseech you as Christ's heralds to publish this everywhere and to persuade all people of whatever rank, footsoldiers and knights, poor and rich, to carry aid promptly to those Christians and to destroy that vile race from the lands of our friends. I say this to those who are present, but it is meant also for those who are absent. Moreover, Christ commands it.

All who die by the way, whether by land or by sea, or in battle against the pagans, shall have immediate remission of sins. This I grant them through the power of God with which I am invested. O what a disgrace, if such a despised and base race, which worships demons, should conquer a people which has the faith of omnipotent God and is made glorious with the name of Christ! With what reproaches will the Lord overwhelm us if you do not aid those who, with us, profess the Christian religion!

Let those who have been accustomed to wage unjust private warfare against the faithful now go against the infidels and end with victory this war which should have been begun long ago. Let those who for a long time have been robbers now become knights. Let those who have been fighting against their brothers and relatives now fight in a proper way against the barbarians. Let those who have been serving as mercenaries for small pay now obtain the eternal reward. Let those who have been wearing themselves out in both body

The Call for a Crusade

Alexius was an able emperor. In the first decade of his rule, he managed to shore up the failing economy and secure his hold over territory in the Balkans. He then began to plan a campaign against the Seljuks. But with

what forces? The Byzantine army had been decimated in Greece by a far superior cavalry of Norman knights in 1085. For by this time, the Normans had established independent principalities in southern Italy and Sicily and were moving farther east, taking advantage of the perpetual power vacuum in the Mediterranean and showcasing and soul now work for a double honor. Behold! On this side will be the sorrowful and poor, on that, the rich; on this side, the enemies of the Lord, on that, his friends. Let those who go not put off the journey, but rent their lands and collect money for their expenses; and as soon as winter is over and spring comes, let them eagerly set out on the way with God as their guide.

Source: S. J. Allen and Emilie Amt, eds., *The Crusades: A Reader*, 2nd ed. (University of Toronto: 2014), pp. 34–35.

Anna Comnena Describes the Beginnings of the First Crusade

[Alexius] had no time to relax before he heard a rumour that countless Frankish armies were approaching. He dreaded their arrival, knowing as he did their uncontrollable passion, their erratic character and their irresolution, not to mention . . . their greed for money. . . . So far from despairing, however, he made every effort to prepare for war if need arose. What actually happened was more far-reaching and terrible than rumour suggested, for the whole of the West and all the barbarians who lived between the Adriatic and the Straits of Gibraltar migrated in a body to Asia, marching across Europe country by country with all their households. The reason for this mass movement is to be found more or less in the following events. A certain Kelt, called Peter [the Hermit] . . . left to worship at the Holy Sepulchre and after suffering much ill-treatment at the hands of the Turks and Saracens who were plundering the whole of Asia, he

returned home with difficulty. Unable to admit defeat, . . . he worked out a clever scheme. He decided to preach in all the Latin countries. A divine voice, he said, commanded him to proclaim to all the counts in France that all should depart from their homes, set out to worship at the Holy Shrine, and . . . strive to liberate Jerusalem. . . . Surprisingly, he was successful. . . . Full of enthusiasm and ardour they thronged every highway, and with these warriors came a host of civilians, outnumbering the sand of the sea shore or the stars of heaven, carrying palms and bearing crosses on their shoulders. There were women and children, too, who had left their own countries. . . .

The upheaval that ensued as men *and* women took to the road was unprecedented within living memory. The simpler folk were in very truth led on by a desire to worship at Our Lord's tomb and visit the holy places, but the more villainous characters . . . had an ulterior purpose, for they hoped on their jour-

ney to seize the capital [Jerusalem] itself, looking upon its capture as a natural consequence of the expedition. . . .

Source: Excerpted from Anna Comnena, *The Alexiad*, trans. E. R. A. Sewter (New York: 1969), pp. 308–11.

Questions for Analysis

1. Given Urban II's explanation of the problems confronting the Byzantine Empire, how do you account for the fact that the Crusades were directed toward the Holy Land and not the relief of Byzantium?

2. How does Anna Comnena represent the motives of Peter the Hermit and the crusaders? What distinctions does she make among the participants?

3. Are there points of comparison between these two accounts? On what do they agree? How would you explain the differences between them?

the effective tactics of chivalry. As it happened, this encounter between the Byzantine emperor and western Europe's most formidable warriors was historically significant. It convinced Alexius that such heavily armed horsemen would be successful if pitted against the lightly armored Seljuks.

It was in the hopes of recruiting a mercenary force, therefore, that Alexius approached **Pope Urban II** (r. 1088–1099). This was a move that played into the hands of the reformed papacy. Urban was struggling to realize some of the powerful claims that his recent predecessors had made on behalf of papal authority, and this seemed like a golden

Past and Present

Ideas of Crusade

The launching of the First Crusade was the beginning of a trend that reshaped the relations between western Europeans and their neighbors—one that continues today. The very use of the word "crusade" is likely to cause trouble, as when President George W. Bush spoke of "this crusade, this war on terrorism" to which he pledged the United States after the attacks of September 11, 2001.

 Watch related author interview on the Student Site

opportunity. By coming to the aid of the eastern Roman Empire, he would show the restive princes of western Europe that the papacy was a force to be reckoned with. At the same time, he hoped to show that Latin military and spiritual might was greater than that of the weakened Greeks, thereby healing the schism between Orthodox and Roman Churches and realizing the centuries-old dream of a universal Christian Church based in Rome, with the pope at its head. In addition, Urban would thereby show support for another reforming effort that had gained momentum in recent years: a peace movement that was attempting to quell the endemic violence unleashed by competitive bands of knights and their rapacious lords. What better way to defuse the situation than to ship those violent energies overseas, deploying them against a common enemy?

So Alexius received a favorable reply, but he got far more than he had asked for—or wanted. He had needed a

modest contingent of a few thousand knights to help him reconquer Anatolia. Instead, what he got was a vast army of 100,000 men, charged by Urban II to retake the holy city of Jerusalem for Christendom. For Urban decided to interpret Alexius's request very loosely (see **Competing Viewpoints** on page 272). Speaking before an assembled crowd at an ecclesiastical council at Clermont (central France) in 1095, Urban announced that he fully supported the peace movement. He said, furthermore, that any knights who wished to fight, pillage, and wreak havoc could do so for a just and Christian cause by liberating the Holy Land from its Muslim rulers. At home, said Urban, most knights were riffraff and marauders, destined for hellfire and damnation; but abroad, by fighting or dying in the service of Christ, they would win absolution for their sins. By taking up the cross (*crux*, hence "crusade"), a warrior stood to win glory, booty, and salvation.

The Motives of Crusaders

The **First Crusade** was an irresistible lure for many pious, ambitious, or opportunistic men. Consequently, the ultimate response to Urban's call exceeded all expectations. Indeed, his message was amplified by other preachers, including a zealous priest called Peter the Hermit, who claimed (falsely) that he had been prevented by the Seljuks from visiting the Holy Land. Within a year, tens of thousands of warriors, many of them new to battle, were on the march toward Constantinople, where they intended to gather before departing for Jerusalem. They were joined by thousands of women, even whole families, whose presence in the throng was noted by many chroniclers. While some dismissed these women as mere camp-followers, it is clear that they played crucial roles on the journey and on the battlefield, where they brought food and water to fighting men and tended the wounded and dying.

As with any large enterprise, the participants' motives must have varied. A few might have hoped to win principalities for themselves. Others were drawn by the prospect of adventure, and the opportunity to escape the narrow confines of established social and gender norms. Many were the dependents of greater men and had no choice but to accompany their lords; some hoped to free themselves from dependence by fighting. Most probably had no idea how long the journey would be or knew anything about the places for which they were destined.

But the dominant motive for joining this First Crusade was religious. Except for a few of the greatest lords—mostly Normans from Sicily and southern Italy—the prospect of winning new lands was both unlikely and undesired. Indeed, one of the greatest challenges facing the Christian kingdom that was established in Jerusalem after 1099 was the fact that crusaders so rarely wanted to stay. After fulfilling their vows, the vast majority went home. So why did they go in the first place? The risks of dying on such a journey were high, and the costs of embarking were enormous. Crusading knights needed a minimum of two years' revenues in hand to finance the journey; to raise such sums, most were forced to mortgage lands and borrow heavily from family, friends, monasteries, and merchants. They then had to find some way to pay back these loans if and when they returned home. By any rational assessment, the Crusade was a fool's errand.

The seeming irrationality of this endeavor underscores the importance of reckoning with the crusaders' piety, and even their desire to emulate legendary heroes such as Roland. Crusading was the ultimate pilgrimage, the holy places of Jerusalem the ultimate Christian shrines. If anyone could receive special blessings by traveling to Compostela, Conques, or Bari, how much more blessed would be those who fought through to the Holy Land! Urban II made this point explicit at Clermont, promising that crusaders would be freed from all penances imposed by the Church. Some zealots went even further, promising that crusaders would be entirely freed from otherworldly punishments for all sins committed up to that point in their lives, and that the souls of those who died on a crusade would go straight to heaven.

Crusade preaching also emphasized the vengeance that Christ's soldiers should exact on his pagan enemies. So to some crusaders, it seemed absurd to wait until they arrived in the Holy Land to undertake this aspect of their mission. Muslims might hold Jesus's property at Jerusalem, but Christian theology held Jews responsible for the death of Jesus himself. Assaults against Jewish communities therefore began in the spring of 1096 and quickly spread eastward with the crusaders. Hundreds of Jews were massacred in the German towns of Mainz, Worms,

ROLAND AS A CRUSADING KNIGHT. The association between knighthood and crusading helped to raise the social status of knights, and contributed to the refinement of a chivalric ethos. Here, Roland, as a crusading knight, dressed head to foot in expensive chain mail, is shown kneeling in homage to his lord, God.

Speyer, and Cologne, and hundreds more were forcibly baptized as the price for escaping death at the hands of crusading knights. Many individual churchmen attempted to prevent these attacks, among them the bishops in whose dioceses Jews lived. But the Church's own negative propaganda thwarted these efforts, and pogroms (organized attacks) against Europe's Jews would remain a regular and predictable feature of Christian crusading—and its modern manifestations.

The Christian Conquest of Jerusalem

Surprised by the nature and scale of the response to his appeal, Emperor Alexius did his best to move the crusaders quickly through Constantinople and into Anatolia. But differences in outlook between the crusaders and the Byzantine emperor quickly became apparent. Alexius had little interest in an expedition to Jerusalem, and insisted that the crusaders promise to restore to him any territory they captured. From his standpoint, the crusader army was a threat, not least because it was headed by several of the Norman knights who had attempted to infiltrate his empire only ten years earlier. To the crusaders—whose mission had been shaped by Pope Urban's policies, not those of Alexius—this seemed like treachery. The crusaders, furthermore, did not understand the Byzantine emperor's willingness to make alliances with some Muslim rulers (the Shi'ite Fatimids of Egypt and the Abassids of Baghdad) against other Muslim rulers (the Sunni Seljuks). They ignorantly concluded that the Byzantines were working to undermine the crusading effort, perhaps even supporting the Muslims against them.

Analyzing Primary Sources

An Arab Aristocrat Encounters the Crusaders

Usama ibn Munqidh (1095–1188) was an Arab Muslim from Syria, whose family maintained a prominent place in the local administration even after the conquests of the Seljuks and the Christian crusaders. He traveled widely and worked in various Islamic cities as a diplomat and scholar. He ended his life in the service of Salah ad-Din (Saladin), the great Muslim leader who reconquered Jerusalem the year before Usama's death. The following excerpt is from Usama's memoir, which he called The Book of Contemplation. *The Templars mentioned in the account are the Christian military order of the Knights of the Temple, who dedicated themselves to protecting pilgrims in Jerusalem and guarding the holy sites. Their headquarters were in the main mosque of the city, which stood on the Temple Mount.*

 nyone who is recently arrived from the Frankish lands is rougher in character than those who have become acclimated and have frequented the company of Muslims. Here is an instance of their rough character (may God abominate them!):

Whenever I went to visit the holy sites in Jerusalem, I would go in and make my way up to the al-Aqsa Mosque, beside which stood a small mosque that the Franks had converted into a church. When I went into the al-Aqsa Mosque—where the Templars, who are my friends, were—they would clear out that little mosque so that I could pray in it. One day, I went into the little mosque, recited the opening formula "God is great!" and stood up in prayer. At this, one of the Franks rushed at me and grabbed me and turned my face towards the east, saying, "Pray like *this*!"

A group of Templars hurried towards him, took hold of the Frank and took him away from me. I then returned to my prayers. The Frank, that very same one, took advantage of their inattention and returned, rushing upon me and turning my face to the east, saying, "Pray like *this*!"

So the Templars came in again, grabbed him and threw him out. They apologized to me, saying, "This man is a stranger, just arrived from the Frankish lands sometime in the past few days. He has never before seen anyone who did not pray towards the east."

"I think I've prayed quite enough," I said and left. I used to marvel at that devil, the change of his expression, the way he trembled and what he must have made of seeing someone praying towards Mecca.

Source: Usama ibn Munqidh, *The Book of Contemplation: Islam and the Crusades*, trans. Paul M. Cobb (New York: 2008), p. 147.

Questions for Analysis

1. What does Usama's account reveal about the variety of relationships among Christians and Muslims in the crusader kingdom of Jerusalem?

2. Who is the true outsider in this scenario? What does Usama's treatment by the Templars suggest about the policy of Christian leaders toward the city's Muslim residents?

Such suspicions contributed to their growing conviction that the eastern Roman Empire was itself an obstacle to the successful recovery of Jerusalem.

Viewed from the perspective of Alexius, the Crusade was a disaster; but from that of the papacy and the crusaders themselves, it was a triumph. In 1098, crusaders captured the old Hellenistic city of Antioch and with it most of the Syrian coast. At the end of 1099, they took Jerusalem, indiscriminately slaughtering its Muslim, Jewish, and Christian inhabitants. Their quick success stemmed mainly from the fact that their Muslim opponents were at that moment divided among themselves: the Fatimids had in fact recaptured Jerusalem just months before the crusaders arrived, and the defeated Seljuks were at war with each other. Western military tactics, in particular the dominance of heavily armored knights, also played an important role in the crusaders' success. Equally critical was the naval support offered by Genoa and Pisa, whose merchant adventurers hoped—if the papacy's cause was successful—to control the Indian spice trade that passed through the Red Sea and on to Alexandria in Egypt. The Crusade thereby contributed to the further decline of Byzantine commerce and decisively altered the balance of power between Byzantium and western Europe.

The Consequences of Crusade

For Byzantium, then, the consequences of the First Crusade were tragic, and they would worsen in the course of the ensuing century of intensified crusading movements (see Chapter 9). On the Muslim world, however, its impact was more modest. The crusader kingdoms established by victorious Norman and Frankish warlords were never more than a sparsely settled cluster of colonies along the coastline of Syria and Palestine. Because the crusaders did not control the Red Sea, the main routes of Islamic commerce with India and the Far East were unaffected by the change in Jerusalem's religious allegiance.

In any case, those crusaders who remained to settle in the region did not *want* to interfere with the overland caravan routes that wound through their new territories. Trade brokered by Arab, Persian, and Jewish merchants therefore continued despite periodic interruptions. The greatest economic gains for western Europeans therefore went to the Italian maritime republics of Venice and Genoa, and the western markets now open to Muslim merchants for their goods. Both sides also gained in military terms: western Europeans learned new techniques of fortification, and Muslims learned new methods of siege warfare and new respect for the uses of heavy cavalry.

For those who remained in the Holy Land, it was necessary to adapt to a new way of life. Local languages, customs, and foods mingled with those the crusaders had brought with them from various parts of Europe, creating a hybrid culture that further enriched and complicated this long-settled, multicultural civilization. Men and women who had traveled alone, or who had lost their partners to violence, starvation, or disease, formed ties and intermarried with local families. The larger impact of the First Crusade on western Europe is more difficult to assess. From one standpoint, the establishment of the short-lived crusader states represents the limits of Europe's expansion during this otherwise extraordinary period of growth. Trade with the Islamic world, and beyond it with India and the Far East, brought enormous prosperity to some, but these trading links had existed before the Crusades and continued long after they ended.

Of course, the longest-lasting consequence of the First Crusade has also proved the deadliest in the long run. The Christian doctrine of holy war—which had developed in earlier centuries—continues to be destructive in the twenty-first century. In the immediate aftermath of Jerusalem's conquest, crusading rhetoric would dictate the terms of western Europeans' attitudes toward the wider world and even toward each other, as we shall see in the following chapters. It fostered a new political and religious ethos that would drive the "reconquest" of the Iberian Peninsula by the Christian rulers of Spain and lead to the massacre or forced conversion of Muslims and Jews. Crusading rhetoric underlay English wars against the Welsh and the Scots, and justified the massacre and dispossession of "heretics" in southern France by northern French imperialists. It justified the conquest of the Baltic region and, later, the subsequent conquest of the Americas and the colonization of Asia, Africa, and Australia. And it has continued to exacerbate global animosities to this day.

THE CULTURE OF THE MUSLIM WEST

It would be misleading to assert that all the consequences of the First Crusade were negative. The positive outcomes were hugely important, too. Increased intellectual and cultural contact between the Latin West and the Islamic world had an enormous impact on western European learning, literature, music, and art. Perhaps most important, the study and practical applications of mathematics were revolutionized when Europeans adopted Arabic numerals and the concept of zero—first promoted beyond the Islamic world, not surprisingly, by the son of a Pisan merchant who grew up in Algeria, Leonardo Fibonacci (c. 1170–c. 1250).

Even Christian theology was transformed by contact with Islam. For one thing, Muslim scholars were the ones who had inherited, preserved, and developed not only Hellenistic medicine and science but the philosophy of Aristotle, which would form the basis of a new Christian philosophy in the twelfth and thirteenth centuries (see Chapter 9). For another, Europeans had been almost entirely ignorant of Muslim beliefs prior to the Crusades, assuming that Muslims were pagans who worshiped a god called Mahomet or Mahoun. But by 1143, Robert of Ketton (c. 1100–c. 1160), a scholar originally from a small town in England, had completed a Latin translation of the Qur'an while working in Spain, with the encouragement of the abbot of Cluny. In the 1130s, he and a friend, Hermann of Carinthia (in Slovenia), had traveled to Byzantium and the crusader kingdoms, where they became students of Arabic. They exemplify the world of possibilities that had opened up to northwestern Europeans as a result of the processes we have been studying in this chapter.

Muslim Philosophy and Christian Theology

The scholars of Byzantium took a conservative approach to Greek philosophy, in every sense of the word (see Chapter 7). The dialogues of Plato and some works of Aristotle were copied and studied, but the latter's ideas were so hard to reconcile with Orthodox theology that Emperor Alexius Comnenus eventually banned the teaching of Aristotelian logic altogether. It was ironic, then, that the cultures that provided the most direct access to Greek learning were Arabic-speaking, and it was through Arabic translations that western European intellectuals became acquainted with these ideas—thanks to the labor of Arabists such as Robert and Hermann.

Even before the rise of Islam, a number of Greek philosophical texts had been translated into Syriac, a Semitic language closely related to Arabic. Arabic translations soon followed, many sponsored by the Abbasid court at Baghdad, which established a special school for this purpose, known as the House of Wisdom. By the end of the tenth century, Arabic translations of Plato, Aristotle, Plotinus, and other Greek authors were widely available and intensively studied throughout the Muslim world. Even in the remote Persian city of Bukhara, the great Muslim philosopher and physician Avicenna (Ibn Sina; 980–1037) was able to read all of Aristotle's works before reaching the age of eighteen.

Like their counterparts in Byzantium, Muslim philosophers strove to reconcile Greek and Hellenistic philosophical traditions with each other and with the tenets of their theology. Reconciling Aristotelianism and Neoplatonism was the easier task. Many of the translations and commentaries of Aristotle from which Muslim philosophers worked had already been filtered through the philosophical traditions of Alexandria and Rome. Moreover, Aristotle and the Neoplatonists shared a number of common assumptions, including the eternity of the world and the capacity of the human mind to understand the rational principles that govern the world's workings. Both traditions also stressed the freedom of individual humans to choose between good and evil.

Combining Greek philosophy with Islamic theology was more difficult. Like Judaism and Christianity, Islam holds that a single omnipotent God created the world as an act of pure will and that the world will continue to exist only so long as God wills it. This runs counter to the classical Greek view of the world as eternal. Moreover, both Christian and Islamic theology rest on the immortality of the individual human soul, another doctrine flatly in conflict with Aristotelian

and Neoplatonic thought. There were also conflicts over the concept of free will; and again, Muslims and Christians had more in common with one another than with the ancient Greek tradition. Although medieval theologians strongly emphasized the individual responsibility of believers to choose between good and evil, virtually all Muslims—like most Christians—believed that nothing good could occur unless God actively willed it. Islamic philosophers adopted an array of different intellectual tactics to deal with these challenges and, in doing so, laid the groundwork for the Christian theologians who relied on them (see Chapter 9).

Muslim Science, Medicine, and Mathematics

Many Muslim philosophers were also distinguished physicians and scientists. The study of philosophy could bring a man renown (or censure) but few tangible rewards, whereas successful physicians and astronomers might rise to positions of wealth and power. Both astronomy and medicine were applied sciences that relied on careful and accurate observation of natural phenomena. Indeed, Muslim observations of the heavens were so accurate that a few

ARISTOTLE TEACHING ARAB ASTRONOMERS. In this Arabic manuscript from the thirteenth century, Aristotle is represented as a contemporary of the astronomers he is instructing. ■ *What does this illustration suggest about Muslims' attitude toward Greek philosophy?*

astronomers corroborated the findings of Hellenistic scientists (see Chapter 4): that the earth must rotate on its axis and revolve around the sun. But because these theories conflicted with the (mistaken) assumptions of Aristotle—that the earth remained stationary with the sun and planets revolving around it—they were not generally accepted in the Islamic world or in Europe. Yet they may have influenced Nicolaus Copernicus (1473–1543), who is usually credited as the first to suggest that the earth orbited the sun (see Chapter 16).

Muslim accomplishments in medicine were equally remarkable. Avicenna discovered the contagious nature of tuberculosis, described pleurisy and several varieties of nervous ailments, and noted that diseases could spread through contaminated water and soil. His *Canon of Medicine* remained an authoritative textbook in the Islamic world and western Europe until the seventeenth century. Later Islamic physicians learned the value of cauterization and styptic agents, diagnosed cancer of the stomach, prescribed antidotes in cases of poisoning, and made notable progress in treating eye diseases. They also recognized the infectious character of plague, pointing out that it could be transmitted by clothing.

Muslim physicians were pioneers in organizing hospitals and licensing medical practitioners. At least thirty-four great hospitals were located in the principal cities of Persia, Syria, and Egypt; each with separate wards for particular illnesses, a dispensary for giving out medicine, and a library. Chief physicians and surgeons lectured to students and graduates, examined them, and issued licenses to practice medicine. Even the owners of leeches (used for bloodletting, a standard medical practice of the day) had to submit their medicinal worms for inspection at regular intervals.

Islamic scientists made important advances in optics and chemistry, as well as mathematics. Using Arabic numerals—which Muslim scholars adopted from the Hindus—mathematicians developed a decimal arithmetic based on place values and hinging on the concept of the zero. Their work enabled fundamental advances in entirely new areas, both of which bear Arabic names: algebra and algorithms. Building on Greek geometry and their own astronomical observations, they also made great progress in spherical trigonometry.

Muslim mathematicians thus brought together and pushed forward all the areas of mathematical knowledge that were later adopted and developed in western Europe from the sixteenth century on. And they made an indispensable contribution to the burgeoning European economy, because the sophisticated accounting systems that supported commerce would have been impossible if merchants and bankers had continued to use the clumsy numerals adopted by the Romans. (Try balancing your checking account in Roman numerals!) Thanks to Arabic mathematics, western Europeans could now add, subtract, divide, and multiply quickly and accurately, with or without the help of another Muslim invention, the abacus.

Muslim Literature and Art

Poetry was integral to Muslim culture. It had been a highly developed art form long before the emergence of Islam. It then became even more important to the development and

IVORY PYXIS FROM MEDINA AZAHARA. Fashioned in the year 964, this round box with a matching lid was made of elephant ivory imported from West Africa. Such intricately carved boxes usually held spices or incense. This one was made in the fortified town of Medina Azahara ("Shining City"), founded in the tenth century by the first Umayyad caliph of nearby Córdoba (Spain). Its decorative motifs remind us that Islam did not prohibit the representation of natural and fanciful creatures, as is often supposed.

Analyzing Primary Sources

A Hebrew Poem from Muslim Spain

In the courts of tenth- and eleventh-century Muslim Spain, Jewish poets began to write a new style of Hebrew verse closely modeled on contemporary Arabic examples. Samuel the Nagid was perhaps the most remarkable of this group of poets. He became the military leader of the Muslim kingdom of Granada as well as the head of the Jewish community there. In addition to his three volumes of poetry, he also wrote treatises on Hebrew grammar and religious law.

our debt to God is righteously to live,
    And His to you, your recompense to give.
Do not wear out your days in serving God;
Some time devote to Him, some to yourself.
To Him give half your day, to work the rest;
But give the jug no rest throughout the night.

Put out your lamps! Use crystal cups for light.
Away with singers! Bottles are better than lutes.
No song, nor wine, nor friend beneath the sward—
These three, O fools, are all of life's reward.

Source: Raymond P. Scheindlin, ed. and trans., *Wine, Women, and Death: Medieval Hebrew Poems on the Good Life* (Philadelphia: 1986), p. 47.

Questions for Analysis

1. What values does this poem express? What is its perspective on the relationship among devotion to God, duty, and pleasure?

2. What does the career of Samuel the Nagid—poet, general, scholar—suggest about Jewish identity in this place and time? What does it suggest about the relations between Jewish and Muslim communities in medieval Spain?

---

dissemination of Muslim identity, because it was the form in which Muhammad framed the Qur'an (see Chapter 7).

Like medicine and astronomy, poetry was also a route to advancement. Not all poetry was composed in Arabic; particularly around the Abbasid court, poets writing in Persian enjoyed great renown. The best known of these is Umar Khayyam (d. 1123), whose *Rubaiyat* was turned into a popular English verse cycle by the Victorian poet Edward Fitzgerald (1809–1883). Although Fitzgerald's translation distorts much, the lush sensuality of Umar's poetic imagery ("a jug of wine, a loaf of bread—and thou") faithfully reflects themes that were common to much Muslim poetry. Many such poems were addressed by men to other men, a fact that occasioned no concern within the elite circles in which they were composed and performed. Jews also participated in this elite literary world, especially in al-Andalus, where they wrote similarly sensuous, playful lyrics in both Hebrew and Arabic, praising wine, sexual intimacy, and their own songs. Muslim Spain saw a great flowering of Jewish intellectual life, which paralleled and intersected with that of the surrounding Muslim society.

Perhaps the most distinctive of Islamic arts are architectural and decorative, the arts that created the spaces in which poets and scientists interacted with their patrons. Many characteristic elements of Muslim architecture—the dome, the column, and the arch—were adapted from Byzantine models, but then combined with the intricate tracery and ambitious scale of Persian buildings to form a new architectural vocabulary. Building styles were further enriched by the many different cultures that embraced Islam, from Spain to Egypt to India and beyond. Muslim artistry was also expressed in the magnificent gardens and fountains that adorned palaces, and in the more portable magnificence of gorgeous carpets, tooled leather, brocaded silks and tapestries, inlaid metalwork, enameled glassware, and painted pottery—all decorated with Arabic script, interlacing geometric designs, plants, fruits, flowers, and fantastic animal figures (another Persian influence). These complex designs can often seem strikingly modern, precisely because they anticipate the abstract forms that were considered new in the twentieth century.

MUSLIM ARCHITECTURE AND GARDEN DESIGN. Both of these images, showing the beautiful Alhambra palace in Granada (Spain), display how Muslim architects and designers borrowed features from many cultures, yet combined them in distinctively graceful ways.

The Islamic Influence on Western Europe

Prior to the contacts facilitated by the First Crusade, the cultural, economic, intellectual, and political achievements of Islamic civilization had completely overshadowed those of Latin Christian Europe. Even thereafter, the new Europe that emerged in the twelfth century would rely heavily on what it had learned from the Islamic world. This is reflected in the large number of Arabic and Persian words that passed into European languages. Essential words for commerce and trade include *traffic, tariff, alcohol, muslin, orange, lemon, alfalfa, saffron, sugar, syrup,* and *musk,* to name just a few. The word *admiral* also comes from Arabic (from the title *emir*), as do words that tell the story of Europe's reliance on Muslim science and technology: *alchemy, algebra, algorithm, alkali, almanac, amalgam, cipher, soda, magazine,* and *zero*—not to mention the names of stars, such as Aldebaran and Betelgeuse.

The Muslim world also had an enormous influence on the imagination and the self-perception of Christian Europe. Byzantine civilization was at once too closely linked to Latin Christendom and, from the eleventh century on, too weak to

After You Read This Chapter

 Go to **INQUIZITIVE** to see what you've learned—and learn what you've missed— with personalized feedback along the way.

REVIEWING THE OBJECTIVES

- The fragmentation of power in the ninth and tenth centuries created a world very different from that of Charlemagne. Describe some of the key changes. What were their causes?
- The agricultural revolution of the Middle Ages had far-reaching economic, social, and political consequences. What were they?
- The reforming movement within the Church changed the relationship between the papacy and the secular rulers of Christendom. Explain why.
- The motives behind the Crusades were political as well as religious. Why was this the case?
- The Crusades had profound effects on western Europe, Byzantium, and the Islamic world, as well as on the relationships among different groups within these societies. In what ways were these three civilizations transformed?

compel western Europeans to take much account of it. Western Christians tended to look down on the Byzantine Greeks, but they respected and feared Muslims. They were right to do so, for Islamic civilization at its zenith (to use another Arabic word) was one of the world's greatest. It brought Arabs, Persians, Turks, Egyptians, Africans, Indians, and Asians together in a common cultural and religious system, creating a diverse society and a splendid legacy of original discoveries and accomplishments that continue to shape the world today. The expanding Europe of the Middle Ages reaped the benefits of its interactions with this rich culture.

CONCLUSION

Before the year 1000, western Europe was the least powerful, least prosperous, and least sophisticated of the three civilizations that had emerged out of the Roman world. A hundred years later, it was a force to be reckoned with. This metamorphosis rested on economic foundations: increasingly efficient agriculture, a growing population, and expanding trade. And these changes produced a dynamic, expansionist, self-confident, and mobile society in which individuals cast off old roles and took on new ones with bewildering speed. No less important, however, were the political and military changes that began to alter the map of Europe during these centuries. By 1100, the heavily armored, mounted knight had emerged as the most formidable military weapon of the day, and new conceptions of power—both spiritual and temporal—were being articulated and contested within Europe, and on crusade.

But it was not yet possible for Europe's rulers to harness and control the energies of the workers, town dwellers, merchants, knights, and scholars whose endeavors were transforming their world, and so a new approach to political organization was needed. Up to this point, the civilizations of the West had rested on two basic types of government: city-states and empires. City-states were more capable of mobilizing the loyalty of their citizens; and as a result, they could sometimes win extraordinary victories against more powerful imperial rivals, as the Greek Poleis did against the Persians (Chapter 3). But city-states were frequently divided by internal economic and social rivalries; and in the long run, they were not strong enough to defend themselves against foreign conquerors. Empires, by contrast, could win battles and maintain powerful administrative bureaucracies, but they were generally too far-flung to inspire deep loyalties among their subjects.

Where, then, do the emerging kingdoms of medieval Europe fit in this picture? How would the struggle for the control of western Europe's expanding resources be carried forward in the wake of the First Crusade? And what cultural, spiritual, social, and intellectual innovations would result? These are the questions we address in Chapter 9.

PEOPLE, IDEAS, AND EVENTS IN CONTEXT

- How was Europe affected by **VIKING** raids and settlements? Which territorial rulers imitated **CAROLINGIAN** models in the wake of these initiatives?
- What new technologies drove the **AGRICULTURAL REVOLUTION** of the Middle Ages? Why did the organization of labor on **MANORS** sometimes lead to **SERFDOM**?
- What conditions led to the growth of medieval **TOWNS**? Why did the formation of urban **COMMUNES** foster new types of liberty? How were money and credit essential to medieval commerce?
- Why is **FEUDALISM** a problematic concept? How did the ceremony of **HOMAGE** symbolize the relationship between a **VASSAL** and his lord?
- What were the causes of the **INVESTITURE CONFLICT**?
- Why did **ALEXIUS COMNENUS** ask **POPE URBAN II** for assistance? Why did the pope use this as a pretext for urging the **FIRST CRUSADE**?
- How and why did **MUSLIM LEARNING AND CULTURE** exercise a profound influence on western Europeans?

THINKING ABOUT CONNECTIONS

- In what ways does the Investiture Conflict reflect the unique historical circumstances of the late eleventh century? In what ways can it be viewed as an extension of longer-term phenomena?
- Judging by what we have learned about the relationship between political power and religious power in previous chapters, would you say that the clash between the papacy and the Holy Roman Empire was inevitable?
- Given the many negative aspects of the crusading movement—and its eventual failure—how might you explain the continuing appeal of crusading rhetoric down to the present day?

Before
You
Read
This
Chapter

The Consolidation of Europe, 1100–1250

At the turn of the twelfth century, the eldest son of a nobleman did something unusual: he traded lordship for scholarship. His name was **Peter Abelard**. By his own estimation, he was the smartest man in the world, and the most attractive. He was certainly one of the most ambitious. After leaving his father's lands in Brittany and besting all the established teachers in Paris, he was appointed to the position of master in the cathedral school, one of the highest academic posts then available. There he met Heloise, the niece of a priest called Fulbert.

Heloise had received an excellent education in a nearby convent, but the normal path of intellectual advancement—Abelard's school—was closed to her. So Fulbert arranged for her to become Abelard's private pupil. She soon became more than that: his intellectual partner, lover, and wife. This last step was particularly problematic, because marriage was no longer an option for clerics and would ruin Abelard's chances of a brilliant career in the Church. So it remained a secret, as did Heloise's subsequent pregnancy and the birth of their son. But her uncle eventually found out and took revenge on Abelard, sending some local thugs to castrate him. Heloise and Abelard lived out

285

ABELARD AND HELOISE. This image from a thirteenth-century manuscript shows Abelard in a scholar's gown and cap and Heloise wearing a nun's habit; their gestures indicate that they are engaged in a lively debate. The story of their fervent attraction and doomed marriage was already famous during their lifetimes, and by the time this manuscript was copied, theirs had become the ultimate example of star-crossed love.

the remainder of their lives in isolation from one another, and most of what we know about their relationship comes from letters they exchanged years later, when Heloise was the leader of a new religious community and Abelard was laying the intellectual foundations of the first university.

The developments of the twelfth and thirteenth centuries altered Europe in profound and lasting ways, affecting individuals, communities, and entire regions. This period witnessed the emergence of large-scale, territorial monarchies and the papacy as dominant forces. Cathedral schools and universities turned out larger and larger cohorts of the professional men needed to run the bureaucracies that supported secular and religious authority. New opportunities for social advancement and new spiritual practices transformed daily life, many of them the direct and indirect consequences of the Crusades. Also, as a result of the Crusades and medieval Europe's new engagement with the Islamic world, both ancient texts and novel ideas generated the intellectual revolution in which Abelard

and Heloise participated. Artistic and technological influences were galvanizing forces, too, financed by prelates and kings, princely courts, and wealthy towns engaged in an integrated and far-reaching economy. Moreover, new literary forms took shape as the spoken vernaculars of Europe came to challenge Latin, becoming languages of learning, devotion, and entertainment. By the middle of the thirteenth century, the political institutions and cultural identities that still help to define Europe today had been formed.

THE MAKING OF MEDIEVAL MONARCHIES

As we learned in Chapter 8, independent medieval towns and powerful lords often refused to acknowledge royal authority, and kings could no longer rely on traditional, close-knit kin groups or the broad imperial powers wielded by a ruler such as Charlemagne. How, then, did some European rulers build the foundations of states that continue to exist today? Crucially, the *idea* of a national state—a state that consolidates its people's sense of a shared identity and destiny—was an idea forged in the twelfth and thirteenth centuries. It would endure to become the basis that still supports the political system of our world.

Not all attempts at state formation were equally robust. The France that emerged in the twelfth century would almost collapse 200 years later (see Chapter 10). Other European states would not be consolidated until the nineteenth century (Germany, for example) and, even then, *political* unification could not hide the continued cultural and linguistic diversity (as evident in Italy, Belgium, and Switzerland to this day). Yet it became so vital for modern European states to trace their origins to the medieval past that those states without a medieval pedigree would eventually be obliged to invent one.

England: From Conquest to Consolidation

The imperial conquest of England in 1066 allowed the first Norman king, William, to experiment with a new type of kingship (Chapter 8). In theory, he commanded the allegiance of every person dwelling in his kingdom. In practice, he needed to impose his will on his new subjects, often in the form of violence. His will was also expressed through the highly effective administrative structures of his Anglo-Saxon predecessors, which his administrators adapted to their own needs.

This process was carried forward by William's sons, especially Henry I (r. 1100–1135), whose approach to kingship was unusual in its focus on effective governance rather than warfare. Henry strengthened the Anglo-Norman system of local administration and instituted a system of traveling judges to administer royal justice. His biggest innovation was the introduction of a method of financial accounting carried out by an office known as the Exchequer, so called because clerks moved counters around on a checkered cloth to calculate receipts and expenditures. Yet Henry's hands-on approach to royal lordship was unpopular. Then, as now, those opposed to "big government" could react violently against it. After Henry's death, those reactions provoked a civil war—until the people of England began to long for a king who would bring back the good old days of centralized rule.

They found him in Henry's grandson, Henry of Anjou (r. 1154–1189), who at the age of twenty-one was already the duke of Normandy and the lord of two other independent French counties, Anjou and Maine. He also controlled the Aquitaine, thanks to his recent marriage to its powerful and brilliant ruler, Eleanor (1122–1204), who had annulled her first marriage to the French king Louis VII in order to marry Henry.

As King **Henry II** of England, Henry of Anjou restored his grandfather's administration and began, steadily, to extend its reach. He ordered reliable local men, organized into juries (from the Latin *jus*, meaning both "law" and "oath"), to report every major crime that occurred in their districts, and also empowered them to investigate civil cases. These innovations are the origin of the modern Anglo-American legal system. Henry II also made it easier for common people to seek justice in the royal courts. All of these measures brought an unprecedented number of average people into the exercise of government, and thus increased their sense of loyalty to the king.

But these innovations also brought Henry into conflict with the Church, because the extension of royal justice impinged on the ecclesiastical courts: tribunals overseen by bishops that claimed the exclusive right to try and sentence clergy accused of committing crimes—even capital crimes such as murder. Henry, in contrast, declared that clerics convicted of serious crimes in Church courts should lose their clerical status and be handed over to the royal court for sentencing. The underlying principle aimed to promote a sense of shared identity and accountability: clerics should be English subjects before they were servants of the Roman Church.

Opposition to this policy came from an unexpected quarter: **Thomas Becket**, a longtime friend and supporter of Henry's who was now the archbishop of Canterbury. Thomas was a self-made man, a son of immigrants who had benefited from the social mobility of town life in London, and who was able to obtain an education and rise through the ranks of the Church. He saw the advantages to maintaining the independence of ecclesiastical procedures, and he feared that Henry's goal was to undermine the power of the clergy.

Henry responded by exiling Thomas from England for several years. And when Thomas returned in 1170, he was assassinated in his own cathedral by four of Henry's knights, who claimed to be acting on the king's orders. Thomas was quickly proclaimed a martyr and a saint, and his tomb at Canterbury became one of the most important pilgrimage sites in Europe. Henry, for his part, was compelled to visit the tomb as a barefoot penitent and ask the saint's forgiveness for his sins.

In the long run, Henry II did not win the right to sentence clerics in royal courts, but he did retain the right to nominate

THE MURDER OF THOMAS BECKET. In this illumination from a thirteenth-century prayer book, one of the knights has struck the archbishop so violently that he has broken his sword. ▪ *How might a contemporary viewer have interpreted this symbolism?*

Map Legend (left box)

- Angevin Empire under Henry II, c. 1180
- French Royal domain, 1180
- Disputed frontier, 1180
- Holy Roman Empire, 1180

Inset Map (top right)

France at the Death of Philip Augustus 1223

- Royal domain
- Under English rule

ENGLAND

ATLANTIC OCEAN

FRANCE · Paris

Compostela · Bay of Biscay

AQUITAINE

LÉON

0 100 200 300 Miles
0 300 Kilometers

Main map labels

SCOTLAND · Edinburgh

IRELAND · Dublin

Carlisle · Durham · Ure R. · Stamford Bridge · York · Tyne R.

NORTH SEA

WALES · Hereford · Gloucester · ENGLAND · Ely · Cambridge · Oxford · Thames R. · Runnymede · London · Southampton · Winchester · Canterbury · Severn R.

English Channel

Calais · Bruges · Antwerp · Ypres · Lille · Brussels · FLANDERS · Arras · Amiens · Meuse R. · Rhine R.

HOLY ROMAN EMPIRE

Main R. · Mosel R. · LORRAINE · Verdun · Danube R.

ATLANTIC OCEAN

Bayeux · Caen · Rouen · Beauvais · VERMANDOIS · Rheims · St. Denis · Paris · ÎLE DE FRANCE · Seine R. · Marne R. · CHAMPAGNE · Troyes

Mont-St. Michel · NORMANDY · BRITTANY · MAINE · Chartres · Brétigny · ANJOU · BURGUNDY · Dijon · Autun

Nantes · TOURAINE · Poitiers · POITOU · Bourges · Loire R. · Allier R. · Saône R. · Geneva · Lyon

Bay of Biscay

AQUITAINE · Bordeaux · Angoulême · Perigueux · Garonne R. · GASCONY · Rhône R. · Po R. · PROVENCE · Avignon

Albi · TOULOUSE · Montpellier · Aigues-Mortes · Marseilles · LANGUEDOC · Narbonne · CORSICA

NAVARRE · Ebro R. · ARAGON · CATALUNYA · MEDITERRANEAN SEA

EUROPE · Area of detail · AFRICA

0 100 200 Miles
0 100 200 Kilometers

HENRY II'S EMPIRE AND THE KINGDOM OF FRANCE, 1180–1223. ■ *What areas did Henry II's empire control in 1180?* ■ *What advantages would the king of France have when challenging English control over Continental territories—even though his own power was confined to the "island" (Île) of France around Paris?*

clerics to high office and thereby exercise a large measure of control over those courts' personnel. The most concrete proof of Henry II's success is that his government continued to work efficiently even after his death—to the extent that his crusading son Richard "the Lionheart" (r. 1189–1199) could rule his father's empire for ten years, while spending only about six months in England during that time.

The Meaning of Magna Carta

After Richard was killed while besieging a castle, he was succeeded by his brother John (r. 1199–1216), an efficient administrator. But by 1204, military and legal losses had forced John to cede nearly all of his father's Continental possessions to the powerful young king of France, Philip II; only the Aquitaine—the inheritance of his mother, Eleanor—remained. This was politically disastrous for John. Not only did it deplete his resources, it also angered the most powerful lords of England, nearly all of whom were of Norman descent and who thus lost their ancestral lands when John lost Normandy. John's response was an attempt to recover the lost territories by raising taxes to equip an army, which angered the nobility further. In 1215, they forced John to set his seal to **Magna Carta**, a "great charter" that defined the barons' rights while limiting those of the king.

Although John and his heirs continued to resist its provisions, Magna Carta established some important principles that would continue to shape the laws of England and, eventually, its colonies. It stipulated that the king could levy no taxes without the consent of the kingdom at large, that no free man could be punished until he had been judged guilty by a jury of his peers in accordance with the law, that no one could be arrested and imprisoned without a warrant, and that no unqualified or ignorant person should hold public office. The charter also called for the establishment of a representative body of barons: Parliament (a word derived from the French "talking together"). Above all, Magna Carta expressed the extraordinary idea that a ruler is bound by the law.

We have frequently noted the achievements of various powerful lawgivers whose contributions have been essential to Western civilizations, starting with Hammurabi (Chapter 1). But for the most part, those lawgivers held themselves to be above the law. Although medieval monarchs—in England and elsewhere—attempted to behave as though this were true for them as well, ultimately they were forced to concede the rule of law itself (see Chapter 14). Magna Carta thus sowed the seeds of the idea that strong, representative government is a good thing. In time, Parliament became a legislative body that could help govern the

kingdom. And since Magna Carta had demanded that no taxation be imposed without the common consent of the realm, kings had to convene Parliament to explain why such taxation was necessary. Meetings of Parliament were also used to hear judicial cases, review local administration and complaints of injustice, and promulgate new laws. Gradually, England was changing from a conquered territory within a larger Norman empire into a constitutional monarchy grounded in government and ruled by law.

The Emergence of France

Compared with the Anglo-Saxon and Anglo-Norman kings of England, the king of the Franks presided over a minuscule territory over which he exercised little control: the immediate hinterland of Paris. Here, most of Charlemagne's institutions of governance had collapsed and been further weakened by Viking raids or by ongoing pressure from the Viking state of Normandy. When Henry II's empire was at its height, the kingdom of Louis VII (r. 1137–1180)—who had lost both his wife, Eleanor, and her lands to that same Henry—was tiny and insignificant.

But in many ways the Capetian dynasty, which had been founded during the Viking raids (Chapter 8), was fortunate. Against all biological odds, it managed to produce an unbroken line of able male heirs for over 300 years (from 987 to 1328)—men who were also long lived. (On average, each Capetian king ruled for 30 years, which contributed greatly to political stability.) And this kingdom, though small, was a rich center of agriculture and trade, which provided a steadily increasing source of income. The prestige of the Capetians was also enhanced by their patronage of the new **University of Paris** founded by Abelard, which made the royal city the intellectual capital of Europe (see page 312). Beyond all this, the Capetians proved to be shrewd politicians, carefully husbanding their strengths while more powerful enemies overreached themselves.

The epitome of these strengths was Philip II (r. 1180–1223), a man who styled himself "Augustus" and the first to use the title "king of France": king of a sovereign state, rather than "king of the Franks," a tribal leader. Philip came to the throne at the age of eighteen, having witnessed the struggles of his father, Louis VII. He understood that he could not win a direct confrontation with either Henry or his son Richard; however, John—known to his detractors as "Soft Sword" and "Lack Land"—was another matter. Philip declared that John owed him homage and allegiance in return for Normandy and its adjacent territories, and then took advantage of his position as John's overlord to undermine John's control over these lands. When John objected, Philip declared all John's lands to be forfeit to the French crown and backed this declaration with armies that won decisive victories in 1204 and 1214.

With Normandy and other formerly English territories added to his domain, Philip had the resources to build an effective system of local administration. He wisely chose to maintain the bureaucratic structures established by generations of Anglo-Norman rulers, but he appointed royal overseers, known as bailiffs, who had full judicial, administrative, and military authority. Philip drew these men from among the needy knights and lesser nobility of his own domain and rotated them frequently from region to region, which ensured their loyalty to him and prevented them from developing personal ties to the regions they governed. This administrative strategy recognized regional diversity while promoting centralized royal control, and it continued to characterize French royal government down to the time of the French Revolution (see Chapter 18). Philip's son, Louis VIII (r. 1223–1226), also extended this strategy to newly conquered territories in the southeast.

German Kingship and the Holy Roman Empire

We have seen (in Chapter 8) that the struggles between the German emperor Henry IV and the papacy ultimately led to the weakening of imperial authority. But in the middle of the twelfth century, a newly elected emperor made an ambitious attempt to restore the power of the German monarchy and to free it from papal control. This emperor was Frederick, later known as Barbarossa ("Red Beard"; r. 1152–1190). Frederick coined the term "Holy Roman Empire" to describe his realm—thereby asserting that its holiness derived from the blessing of God and did not depend on the intervention of the pope, with whom he was constantly at odds.

Frederick forged a close alliance with other German princes by supporting their efforts to control their own territories. In exchange, he exacted their support for his efforts to reassert imperial control over the wealthy cities of northern Italy. This strategy worked, but it sparked a series of destructive wars. Led by Milan and sanctioned by the pope, the cities of northern Italy formed an alliance, the Lombard League, which put up a staunch resistance to Frederick and finally forced him to guarantee their independence in return for large cash payments. Meanwhile, Frederick attempted to bypass the power of the papacy by supporting a series of papal pretenders, or "antipopes." This move was successfully countered by the reigning pope, Alexander III (r. 1159–1181), who drove a shrewd bargain with Frederick: if Frederick would concede the sovereignty of the pope's rule within Rome and its adjacent territories—lands that came to be known as the Papal States—then Alexander would concede the emperor's sovereignty within his domains and even his overlordship of the Church within those domains. Frederick eventually agreed, thereby gaining the pope's support for his rule in northern Italy.

When Frederick left for the Holy Land in 1189—joining Richard the Lionheart of England and **Philip Augustus** of France on a (failed) crusade to reconquer Jerusalem—he left his realm in a powerful position. Although he died on that venture, his careful planning bore fruit in the reign of his son, Henry VI, who succeeded to his father's throne without opposition and enjoyed a huge income from the north Italian towns. Henry ultimately became the king of Sicily, too, which strengthened the empire's position even further. But when Henry died in 1197, he left only a three-year-old son, the future Frederick II, as his heir apparent. Two decades of civil war followed. The only factors uniting these two broad regions were linguistic and cultural. Indeed, later attempts to unify Germany and northern Italy were grounded in appeals to a shared "national" heritage (see Chapters 11 and 12).

By the time Frederick II came of age, the German princes had become so entirely autonomous that all he could do was recognize their privileges in exchange for their loyalty. In Italy, the cities of the Lombard League had ceased to pay their taxes, and the powerful administrative structure of Sicily had fallen into chaos. Frederick tackled all these problems and eventually restored control over the disparate territories of his empire. But he made the mistake of asserting a right to rule the northern Italian cities directly, bypassing their own independent governments. The result was another Lombard League and another lengthy war, which continued until Frederick's death in 1250. The papacy took every advantage of this situation, even excommunicating Frederick and, after his death, denying the rights of his heirs. When Frederick's last legitimate son died in 1254, the prospect of effective imperial rule died with him. For the next 500 years, until the founding of the modern German and Italian states, political power in the lands of the Holy Roman Empire would be divided among several hundred territorial princes and independent cities.

The States of Central and Eastern Europe

As all of these examples show, the making of medieval monarchies was a gradual, nonlinear process. The states that formed, shifted, and reformed were fragile—much more fragile than present-day nationalist mythologies will admit.

Inset map labels:

EUROPE
Area of detail
AFRICA

NORWAY

SWEDEN

Neva R.

Volkhov R.

Novgorod

Riga

Lake Ilmen

Lake Peipus

Volga R.

NORTH SEA

DENMARK

BALTIC SEA

FRIESLAND

Elbe R.

DUCHY OF POMERANIA

TEUTONIC KNIGHTS

PRUSSIANS

RUS'

POMERELIA

DUCHY OF SAXONY

MARCH OF BRANDENBURG

GREATER POLAND

MASOVIA

KINGDOM OF POLAND

DUCHY OF LOTHARINGIA

THURINGIA

MARCH OF LUSATIA

Oder R.

LOWER SILESIA

LESSER POLAND

Kiev

DUCHY OF FRANCONIA

KINGDOM OF BOHEMIA

UPPER SILESIA

Rhine R.

Danube R.

MARCH OF MORAVIA

COUNTY OF BURGUNDY

DUCHY OF SWABIA

DUCHY OF AUSTRIA

Vienna

Dniester R.

KINGDOM OF ARLES

DUCHY OF BAVARIA

KINGDOM OF HUNGARY

STATE OF CUMAN-KIPCHACK

TRANSYLVANIA

Rhône R.

LOMBARDY

Po R.

Venice

SLAVONIA

Genoa

Marseilles

Bologna

Florence

CROATIA

Zara

BOSNIAN MARCH

SERBIA

BLACK SEA

CORSICA

PAPAL STATES

ADRIATIC SEA

Rome

BULGARIA

SARDINIA

KINGDOM OF THE TWO SICILIES

Constantinople

MEDITERRANEAN SEA

Palermo

SICILY

BYZANTINE EMPIRE

0   100   200   300 Miles
0   100   200   300 Kilometers

Holy Roman Empire, c. 1200

THE HOLY ROMAN EMPIRE AND CENTRAL AND EASTERN EUROPE, c. 1200. This map approximates the borders of the region's major territories. ■ *Identify the kingdoms and principalities discussed in this chapter.* ■ *If you were the ruler of one of them, what opportunities do you see for the expansion of your power? What limitations?* ■ *Why would the prospect of a single heir to the Holy Roman Empire and to the Kingdom of the Two Sicilies be a threat to the papacy?*

Moreover, many powerful and effective states were not kingdoms at all, but cities and principalities. The new territorial powers that were emerging in central and eastern Europe offer further alternative examples of state formation in this era.

Like many of the other principalities that made up the (highly disunified) Holy Roman Empire, Bohemia was a nonhereditary monarchy whose rulers were elected by powerful families. That changed at the end of the twelfth century, however, when Ottokar I (r. 1192–1230) managed to secure papal and imperial support for the establishment of a dynasty. Bohemia also extended its rule into the province of Moravia, which it governed as a frontier principality. During the thirteenth century, when the Holy Roman Emperor's attention was fixed on Italy and the alliances among German territories were weak, Bohemia emerged as one of the strongest states in central Europe.

The kings of Hungary, meanwhile, with their close ties to the Roman Church and papacy, cultivated a strong and relatively centralized royal authority. They also expanded Hungarian influence into the regions of Transylvania and Croatia, whose natural resources included rich silver mines. As a result, the wealth of King Béla III (r. 1172–1196) far exceeded that of his contemporaries elsewhere in Europe. He also adopted many of the techniques favored by these contemporaries, including the use of written records to aid in royal governance.

Poland, which had achieved a remarkable territorial unity at an early date (Chapter 8), was carved into several smaller dukedoms after 1138, when King Bolesław III (*BOHL-ess-wahy*; r. 1107–1138) divided his extensive lands among his sons. This led to competition among members of the same dynasty, and spurred Polish dukes to seek out new opportunities for advancing their interests. Duke Conrad of Masovia (r. 1229–1232), for example, forged an alliance with a crusading order, the Teutonic Knights, who were attempting to conquer and colonize the pagan peoples of the Baltic (see page 298). Conrad's own northern frontier territories were subject to raids by the pagan Prussians, and he saw this as an expedient measure. Nevertheless, the knights were not content merely to fight the pagans and often clashed with Polish troops as well.

Other Polish rulers successfully pursued more inclusive methods of strengthening their principalities. In the wake of the First Crusade, which had led to pogroms against Jewish communities in the Rhineland, violent attacks against Jews were becoming increasingly common in northwestern Europe, while their legal rights were also being curtailed. But Polish dukes were eager to encourage Jewish settlements, knowing that their cities would benefit from the expertise of Jewish merchants and craftsmen, and from being woven into the banking networks that were crucial to the medieval economy. By the thirteenth century, thousands of Jews—entire families and communities—were making their way to Poland to take advantage of these favorable conditions.

A glimpse of these can be seen in the Statute of Kalisz (*KAH-leesh*), issued by Duke Bolesław the Pious in 1264. Often regarded as a foundational document in the history of human rights, it granted the Jews of Greater Poland extensive legal privileges, including freedom of movement and worship; equal rights under the law; and the right to prosecute Christians who insulted, harmed, or stole from them. As a result of these extraordinary initiatives, Poland became a magnet for Jews for the remainder of the Middle Ages, taking in still more refugees from the wave of expulsions suffered by the Jews of England, France, and Spain (see Chapters 10 and 12).

Rus' and the Novgorod Republic

The trading settlements established by the Viking Rus' in the eleventh century had been centered on the city of Kiev and had benefited from a vibrant system of commercial networks, kinship ties with many of Europe's royal families, and a close spiritual and political alliance with the eastern Roman Empire. But as subsequent crusading movements weakened Byzantium and disrupted trade with the Islamic world (see page 298), the powerful position of Kiev was also undermined. The center of gravity began to move north, to the city of Novgorod, which was already economically powerful and ideally placed to take advantage of trade with the peoples of the Baltic region and Scandinavia via the Volga and Dnieper Rivers. Novgorod functioned as a powerful city-state and the center of an entity often called the Novgorod Republic, because the power of Novgorod's prince and its aristocratic families and prominent churchmen was countered by urban elites and a network of occasional public assemblies that gave voice to merchants and craftsmen.

Novgorod was also affected by the changing fortunes of Byzantium. In 1204, when Constantinople was besieged and captured by crusaders loyal to Rome, many German and Scandinavian warlords began to make the Orthodox Christians of Rus' another target of crusading fervor. In a series of wars, the Swedes successfully invaded Novgorod's northern frontier, and there were constant skirmishes with the Danes and Germans as well. In 1240, according to later Russian sources, a Swedish army attempted to gain control of the Neva River to establish control over a major trade route. But the invasion was routed by a force led by a young prince of Novgorod, Alexander (1221–1263), who thereafter took the surname Nevsky (victor of the Neva). Alexander is also credited with the defeat of the Teutonic knights at Lake Peipus in the early spring of 1242, when the lake was still frozen; hence its iconic name, the Battle on the Ice. Although the importance of this battle, like that of the Neva, is questionable, the event and its hero have become enshrined in Russian cultural memory. This is thanks in large part to the great nationalist epic *Alexander Nevsky* (1938) by the Soviet filmmaker Sergei Eisenstein, in which the Teutonic Knights represent the more modern menace of Nazi Germany (see Chapter 26).

The "Reconquest" of Spain

The small Christian kingdoms of the Iberian Peninsula were even more distinct from each other than the principalities of Germany and Eastern Europe. And yet, a unified kingdom of Spain would emerge as the most powerful monarchy in Europe and the wider Atlantic world by the end of the Middle Ages (a process we will continue to trace in later chapters). The key to this extraordinary development lay in the successful alliances forged among the peninsula's Christian rulers and their eventual defeat of neighboring wealthy and well-governed Muslim kingdoms.

THE "RECONQUEST" OF SPAIN, 900–1250. ▪ *Where were the frontiers of the Christian kingdoms in 900? 1150? 1250?* ▪ *What geographical factors might have helped to sustain these small kingdoms?* ▪ *Why might Castile eventually have become the largest of the Christian kingdoms?* ▪ *How could Aragon and Catalonia have maintained important positions as wealthy and significant powers?*

LOARRE CASTLE, ARAGON. No single photograph can capture the size or setting of this massive castle complex in the foothills of the Pyrenees. Initially fortified in the eleventh century as a base for Christian expansion into Muslim territory, it was further enlarged in the twelfth century. The encircling wall and towers were added in the thirteenth and fourteenth centuries.

This process is somewhat misleadingly termed the *reconquista* (the "reconquest") of Christian lands. In reality, the Roman province of Hispania had been only nominally Christian when the Visigoths settled there in the fifth century (see Chapter 6), and the Visigoths themselves had only recently converted to Latin Christianity when the Muslims arrived in 711 (see Chapter 7). But conceptualizing this struggle as a holy war to reconquer Christian territory allowed Christian rulers to cast it as another crusade and so earn papal support for their efforts.

By the middle of the twelfth century, there were four major Christian kingdoms in Iberia. In the far north was Navarre, which straddled the Pyrenees, and León-Castile, governed as a united kingdom after 1037. Beyond these kingdoms' southern frontier lay a broad swath of Muslim territory. Farther to the east was the Crown of Aragon, formed in 1137 when the count of Barcelona, who ruled the independent principality of Catalonia, married the queen of Aragon. Farthest west was the new kingdom of Portugal, which had been the first territory gained by Christian conquests in the ninth century, and which won independence from León-Castile in 1139.

Like their counterparts elsewhere in Europe, the kings of Spain struggled to control the power of great lords. Centuries of warfare between Muslims and Christians and among competing Christian clans had left the landscape sown with enormous castles. Even those nominally controlled by kings were in fact the property and power bases of castellans (castle-keepers). A ruler seeking to establish control thus had to use a combination of force and cunning to bring these rival

powers to heel. Indeed, the kings of this region came to deploy a combination of tactics that we have already seen at work in England: a mixture of violent conquest and the development of effective administrative structures that made royal power a fact of everyday life.

This strategy is exemplified by King Alfonso II of Aragon (r. 1162–1196), who was also the count of Barcelona and the first to rule the united Crown of Aragon. Alfonso used documentation as the ultimate tool of power, presiding over the compilation of a richly illuminated "big book of fiefs" (*Liber feudorum maior*) between 1192 and 1194 (see **Interpreting Visual Evidence** on page 295). This book recounted property transactions and family lineages dating back centuries, citing documents in the royal archives. Alfonso thereby grounded his authority on his command of history and written records.

Throughout the remainder of the twelfth century and into the thirteenth, Christian influence in Spain continued to spread southward until all that remained of Muslim dominion was the small kingdom centered on Granada in the extreme south. The Muslim and Jewish subjects of this region were absorbed into these new Christian realms, sometimes uneasily, although most rulers saw the benefit of protecting these communities and valuing their contributions to governance and the economy. Castile became by far the largest kingdom, although it was rivaled in wealth and consequence by the more urbanized and commercially connected Aragon. Indeed, wars between Castile and Aragon kept either kingdom from achieving supremacy for the next 200 years, until the marriage of Ferdinand of Aragon and Isabella of Castile joined the two lands in a unified Spanish monarchy that also included Navarre. In 1492, Ferdinand and Isabella's united army captured Granada, and an Italian adventurer named Christopher Columbus set sail under their flag. The first event completed the "reconquest," and the second began Spain's successful conquest of a new and hitherto undreamed-of world (see Chapter 12).

CONTINUING THE CRUSADES

When Pope Urban II urged the quarrelsome knights of northwestern Europe to take up the cross against the enemies of Christ in 1095, he was responding to the Byzantine emperor's

Picturing Legal Transactions

Between the years 1192 and 1194, King Alfonso II of Aragon (r. 1162–1196) and his court scribes compiled a remarkable book. The codex known today as the "big book of fiefs" (*Liber feudorum maior*) may have been made to assist Alfonso and his descendants in legitimizing their authority over the many areas they controlled, but it was also a way of expressing that authority: its very existence represented a new claim to royal power. In its original form, it consisted of 888 parchment folios (1,776 pages) on which 903 separate documents were copied.

This "big book" represents a new trend in Europe. In most places, claims to property were made on the basis of custom and memory, not documentation. When property changed hands, the chief witnesses were people, and when questions arose, it was these people (or their heirs) whose testimony proved ownership. In Catalonia, the habit of documenting things had a long history, and it was not unusual for individual families to keep archives of documents. At the same time, however, documentation was never sufficient on its own: verbal exchanges of agreement and the public performance of transactions constituted legally binding ceremonies meaningful to the entire community, and the validity of these actions was not dependent on the making of a written record.

With all this in mind, it is striking that seventy-nine of the documents copied into the book are accompanied by images that convey important messages about documentation and its limitations.

On the book's opening frontispiece (image A), King Alfonso consults with his chief archivist, Ramón de Caldes. Ramón discusses one of the charters taken from a large pile at his elbow, while a scribe makes copies behind him—perhaps to aid in the compilation of the "big book." The king is backed by men who look on approvingly.

One of the charters copied into the "big book" is accompanied by another image (image B). It records that the Viscount of Nîmes betrothed his daughter, Ermengarde of Carcassonne, to the Count of Roussillon. Ermengarde, her flowing hair uncovered as a sign of her maidenhood, stands between her bearded father and her seated mother, Cecilia of Provence.

Questions for Analysis

1. Why would a book designed to document property transactions contain images, too? What functions could they have served?

2. Why would the artist of the "big book" have depicted the king consulting his archivist in the very first image? How does he depict the relationship between them? Why does he include a group of men as witnesses to their discussion?

3. Women figure prominently in many of the book's images, including image B. On what basis could you argue that their active presence is crucial to the transactions being described?

A. King Alfonso and Ramón de Caldes.

B. Betrothal of Ermengarde of Carcassone to the Count of Roussillon.

request for reinforcements in his war with the Seljuk Turks, with the aim of recapturing imperial territories in Anatolia. But the pope's own conception of the crusaders' mission was broader and extended beyond the frontiers of Byzantium to the great cities of Antioch and Jerusalem, which had been in the hands of Muslims for centuries. And, as we saw in Chapter 8, many crusaders acted on a still broader interpretation of their mission by attacking "enemies of Christ": the Jewish communities of Europe.

From the first, then, both the reason for crusading and the target of Christian aggression were ideologically malleable. Even though the papacy never officially sanctioned violence against Jews, in the centuries following the First Crusade, individual popes authorized the use of force against many different kinds of people who could be construed as "enemies of Christ" because they stood in opposition to the Roman Church. Although historians, for convenience, often speak of the Crusades as divided into seven or more distinct phases (the Second Crusade, the Third Crusade, etc.), the people of the time—both aggressors and victims—experienced crusading as a continuous, snowballing movement.

Crusader States and Crusading Orders

The military successes of the First Crusade were due not only to the might of the crusaders but also to the diversity of (and divisions among) the many peoples who inhabited the coastline of the eastern Mediterranean. This is an area we have been studying since Chapter 1, formed by successive waves of colonization and migration over the course of many millennia. The principalities known as the **Crusader States** should therefore be understood as laying a thin veneer of European influence on top of a deep, complex culture that withstood any superficial changes.

Those Europeans who stayed and flourished here were those who were able to adapt. Most probably retained some aspects of their former identities—as Normans or Franks, as loyal to the Roman Church—but they and their descendants became intertwined with the local populations, intermarrying and adopting their fashions, food, and outlook. In time, they had more in common with their immediate neighbors—Syrian and Armenian Christians, adherents of Greek Orthodoxy, Shi'ite and Sunni Muslims—than with their distant families "back home." Second- and third-generation settlers might never visit western Christendom in the course of their lives.

Because of all these factors, the four principal Crusader States were very different from the territorial monarchies that were being consolidated in parts of Europe at this time. They were more like the loosely configured and combative lordships of the tenth and eleventh centuries than like burgeoning bureaucratic realms. As such, they were mostly short lived. The largest, the inland county of Edessa, was founded in 1098. It stretched as far east as the Tigris River and had to be heavily fortified against constant internal uprisings and external threats. Its European Christian population was always a tiny minority, and by 1150 it had been mostly subsumed into the Seljuk Empire, with some portions reverting to Byzantium.

Edessa's position was made even more precarious because its Frankish rulers had friendlier relations with their Armenian subjects (with whom they largely intermarried) than with the crusader principality of Antioch to the west, which comprised parts of what are now Syria and Turkey. Although Antioch was named a patriarchate of the Roman Church, it had only a tiny European Christian population. After the fall of Edessa, it was largely dependent on Constantinople, and later Armenia, for protection from the Seljuk

THE CRUSADER STATES. This map shows the fragile colonies known as the Crusader States at their greatest extent, around 1100. ▪ *What geographical, political, and military factors would make these states vulnerable?*

KRAK DES CHEVALIERS. The necessity of securing hard-won territory in the Holy Land led to the construction of enormous castles such as this one, built by the Knights Hospitaller in the early twelfth century when crusading movements were also being launched in Europe itself. Similar castles were built to subjugate peoples deemed rebellious or heretical.

Turks. Antioch ceased to exist in 1268, when its lands became part of the vast new empire of the Mongols (see Chapter 10).

The third major state, the county of Tripoli, was founded in 1109 and linked the northern states of Edessa and Antioch with the kingdom of Jerusalem. Tripoli's strategic commercial position exposed it to constant raids and threats of invasion, which led its rulers to entrust most of the frontier to one of the military orders dedicated to perpetual pursuit of the crusading effort: the Knights Hospitaller. Originally charged with the care of pilgrims in the Hospital of St. John at Jerusalem, founded in 1023, members of this religious order became militarized after 1099 and came to control the islands of Rhodes and Malta, as well as the many strategic fortifications in the eastern Mediterranean. Their stronghold, the massive Krak des Chevaliers ("Knights' Fortress" from the Arabic Karak), survives as a monument to their might. In fact, the Hospitallers long outlived the Crusader States, maintaining a sovereign presence in the region into the early nineteenth century; the order is now headquartered in Rome.

The Kingdom of Jerusalem and the Conquest of Saladin

The kingdom of Jerusalem, the fourth and most symbolically important of the Crusader States, was really a network of cities and fortresses that constantly changed hands, as much the target of rival crusaders as of Muslim raiders. Its cosmopolitan population was a testament to the number of peoples who claimed the Holy Land for their own, with major concentrations of Muslims (both Sunni and Shi'ite) and Orthodox Christians (Greek and Syrian), alongside smaller communities (Jews, Samaritans)—all of whom dwarfed the new European Christian population of the region. As a result, those who claimed kingship in Jerusalem were greatly dependent on support from other Crusader States as well as from various European princes. Yet the cachet of Jerusalem was such that any contingent of reinforcements sent by an ambitious ally could be attempting to seize power there.

Defense of the kingdom therefore came to rest heavily on another of the new crusading orders, the Knights Templar. Founded during the reign of King Baldwin II of Jerusalem (r. 1118–1131), the Templars were based in a wing of the captured al-Aqsa Mosque, which was now the royal palace and thought to be part of King Solomon's original Temple complex (Chapter 2)—hence the order's name.

Although the kingdom of Jerusalem persisted in theory until 1291, it ceased to have any purchase on Jerusalem itself after 1187. In this year, a remarkable Kurdish chieftain, Salāḥ ad-Dīn (c. 1138–1193), who had become the Sunni sultan of both Egypt and Syria, rallied Muslim opposition to the occupying crusader forces and succeeded in recapturing the Holy City. Saladin (as he was called by Europeans) became the target of a renewed crusading effort (the Third Crusade, 1189–1192)—which, as we noted on page 290, spurred three kings to take the cross: England's Richard the Lionheart, France's Philip Augustus, and the Holy Roman Empire's Frederick Barbarossa. But Frederick was killed, Philip left early, and Richard was captured on the way home.

Meanwhile, the victorious Saladin became celebrated not only by Muslims but also among crusaders, who considered him a paragon of chivalry. Richard even considered arranging a marriage between his sister, Joan of Sicily, and Saladin's brother, thereby establishing allied rule in Jerusalem. This never happened, though, and Jerusalem remained in Muslim hands. The city of Acre (Akko, in northern Israel) then became the new capital of the Christian kingdom, until its fall in 1291 marked the end of any viable European presence in the region—that is, until the short-lived conquests of Napoleon at the end of the eighteenth century (see Chapter 18).

Within Crusading Europe

Once unleashed, the crusading ethos could not be contained by efforts to liberate the Holy Land. The promise that those who killed the "enemies of Christ" with papal approval would be absolved of their sins and win eternal salvation, while potentially winning lands and riches in the process, was soon applied to a host of other initiatives—especially those that could open new lands for settlement and bring more peoples into the orbit of the Roman Church.

Beginning in the 1160s, accordingly, the rulers of Denmark and the German duchy of Saxony began to colonize the Baltic coast and the lands between the Elbe and Oder Rivers. This effort was represented as a missionary movement, but it was also an attempt to control trading and raiding activities in that region. And it was not carried forward peacefully; those who spearheaded it (literally) were members of the military crusading order of the Teutonic Knights. In 1202, they managed to carve out a new bishopric around Riga (present-day Latvia), where they set about the violent conversion of the indigenous inhabitants. We have already noted the Knights' subsequent clashes with the peoples of Poland and Rus'.

Meanwhile, the English were launching crusades against the "infidel" Irish and Welsh, who were actually Christian, justifying this action on the grounds that the Celts were barbarians who would benefit from the civilizing influence of their superior overlords. It had been a short step from the calling of crusades against foreigners to those aimed at fellow Europeans and Christians.

The Crusade against Constantinople and the Revenge of Venice

The First Crusade (1095–1099) had begun as an attempt to aid Constantinople. The Fourth Crusade (1202–1204) ended in its destruction. The object of this expedition, which had been called by Pope **Innocent III** at the time of his election in 1198, was Egypt, where Saladin's successors continued to rally Muslim opposition to European colonial efforts. This meant launching an attack by sea, because the remaining crusader outposts of the Holy Land had become too weak and scattered to enable the movement of armies by land. The natural embarkation point was Venice.

A major player in maritime trade since the ninth century, Venice had already benefited enormously from the Crusades. Venice furnished the ships and supplies that transported and sustained the waves of aspiring conquerors while reaping the benefits of closer ties with Byzantium, with which this Italian city-state shared many interests. But relations with Constantinople worsened throughout the twelfth century, as the Crusades increasingly damaged Byzantine trade and threatened its security. In 1182, popular anticrusading sentiment had even led enraged citizens of Constantinople to massacre enclaves of Italian merchants and seamen; those who were not killed were banished, the Venetians among them.

The Venetians therefore had a reason to resent the Byzantines. And they were now overrun by an army of eager and impoverished crusaders who could not pay for the passage to Cairo; it would cost the Venetians enormously in time, money, and men to ship them there. So in the end, the crusaders paid the Venetians with the services they could render. Rather than sailing for Egypt, the crusading expedition was diverted to Zara on the Dalmatian coast of the Adriatic, a former Venetian port that had rebelled and sought the protection of the king of Hungary (it is now Zadar in Croatia). Despite the fact that Hungary was loyal to Rome, the city was attacked and taken.

From Zara, the crusaders moved on to Constantinople. After a terrible siege, the city was savagely overrun and sacked in 1204, its people killed or left homeless, its churches and public buildings severely damaged, and its books and artworks consigned to flames or seized as loot. (For example, the stolen porphyry statue of the Roman tetrarchs, shown on page 193, is still in Venice.) In the aftermath, the Venetians were able to dominate the city itself, controlling the shipping in and around Constantinople as well as the island of Crete and many cities on the Greek mainland. Only in 1261 was Byzantine rule reestablished in the capital. But by that time, the empire had shrunk to a fraction of its former size. Meanwhile, crusading efforts continued within western Christendom.

Innocent III's Crusade for a Unified Christendom

Although Pope Innocent III expressed alarm at the turn taken by the crusade he had called, he accepted the spoils of war that were offered to him and set his seal of approval on the Latin occupation of Greek territory. He was an ambitious man. Elected to the papal dignity at the age of thirty-seven, probably the youngest holder of the office in history, his goal was to unify

Past and Present

Medieval Plots and Modern Movies

From westerns to science fiction to action movies to romantic comedies, most of the films that draw big audiences today are based loosely or closely on literary genres that were popularized during the Middle Ages: tales of chivalry and heroism, forbidden love, supernatural events, and magical adventures.

 Watch related author interview on the Student Site

all Christendom—and the wider world—under papal dominion. Unlike Gregory VII (Chapter 8), Innocent never questioned the right of kings and princes to rule in their own secular spheres. Instead, he saw the pope's role as regulatory and disciplinary, which meant that when rulers sinned, they should be reprimanded or excommunicated by the pope—who could thereby call into question the legitimacy of their rule. Moreover, Innocent was even more insistent than his predecessors on the obligation of every Christian to obey the pope as Jesus Christ's representative on earth.

Innocent sought to achieve this goal in many different ways. He made the papacy financially and politically independent by expanding and consolidating papal territories in central Italy. (Vatican City is now the last surviving remnant of these territories, and it continues to function as an independent state within Rome and Italy.) He loudly proclaimed his power as kingmaker and king breaker by brokering the selection of the Holy Roman Emperor. He also disciplined both Philip Augustus of France, for marital misconduct, and John of England, who at one point was compelled to grant England itself to the pope as its overlord. Innocent further claimed, with varying degrees of success, a comparable lordship over Aragon, Sicily, and Hungary. He even levied the first income tax on the clergy in order to support the crusade that brought Orthodox Christians to heel.

The crowning achievement of Innocent's pontificate was the ratification of his agenda at a representative assembly of the Roman Church, the Fourth Lateran Council of 1215, so called because it was held in the Roman palace of St. John Lateran. This council defined the central dogmas of Latin Christianity, one of which was the acknowledgment of papal supremacy. Since a dogma is defined as a "truth

THE JEWISH BADGE. The distinctive apparel that marked Jews as different from their Christian neighbors varied from region to region. In some places it was pointed hats, like those worn by the Old Testament Jews in this manuscript illumination from a fourteenth-century French vernacular Bible. This type of hat later became associated with witchcraft or idiocy, as in the dunce's cap or the witch's peaked hat. In other regions, Jews wore a distinctive patch on their clothing, often colored yellow to make it more visible.

The Crusade against Heresy

Innocent's reign achieved the height of papal power, but it also fomented violence and sowed seeds of dissent. Future popes continued to centralize the government of the Church, but they also became involved in protracted political and military struggles that compromised the papacy's spiritual credibility. Because the Papal States bordered on the kingdom of Sicily, Innocent's successors quickly came into conflict with Emperor Frederick II, who became an inveterate opponent of papal monarchy. But instead of excommunicating him and calling for his deposition, as Innocent might have done, they called a crusade against him.

Innocent himself had paved the way for this by launching a series of crusades against heretics, now defined as any group or individual who did not fall into line with the papacy's policies—and who were, by association, "enemies of Christ." The most notorious of these campaigns was the Albigensian (*al-bih-JEN-see-an*) Crusade, launched in 1209. Ostensibly, the crusade was directed against a heretical sect called the Cathars; but in reality, it justified the conquest and colonization of what is now southern France by land-hungry knights from northern France.

Although the Albigensian Crusade can be said to have ended by 1255, it created lasting tensions within the forcibly enlarged French kingdom that would lead the inhabitants of this devastated region to ally with the English during the Hundred Years' War (see Chapter 10), and continue to make southern France particularly susceptible to violent religious warfare during and after the Reformation (see Chapter 13). Indeed, the language, culture, and political orientation of southern France are still very different from those of Paris and its environs.

In order to understand how all of this happened, we must turn to some larger religious developments within Europe.

necessary for salvation," this meant that all Christians had to acknowledge the pope's ultimate power; those unwilling to do so (including the Christians of Byzantium) were, by definition, heretics—and as heretics, they could be prosecuted and punished.

In a further effort to achieve unity and uniformity within Christendom, the Fourth Lateran Council took an unprecedented interest in the religious education and habits of every Christian. It responded to the urbanization of Europe by establishing free primary schools (for boys) in all the major cities, requiring bishops to recruit effective preachers, and outlawing all kinds of misbehavior on the part of the clergy. It also sought to increase the distance between Christians and their Muslim and Jewish neighbors by discouraging social relationships, economic exchanges, and intermarriage. Most disturbing, Innocent's council mandated that "infidels" be visibly distinguished from Christians by wearing distinctive clothing, the origins of the infamous "Jewish badge" (see Chapter 26).

UNITY AND DISSENT IN THE WESTERN CHURCH

The Investiture Conflict (Chapter 8) engaged both clergy and laity in debates over the essential meaning of Jesus Christ's life and teachings. Many regions of Europe supported the papacy's claim to supremacy, but others saw marked resistance to its encroachment on centuries-old practices and social networks. After all, bishops had been members of the aristocracy since the time of Constantine, and it was customary for bishoprics to be controlled by certain families. Meanwhile, priests had been married men since the establishment of the first Christian churches; and the wives of priests were not only their husbands' partners, they were also ministers to the communities in which they lived. When the papacy preached against "fornicating priests" and their "concubines," it delegitimized relationships that had been essential to local communities for generations. No wonder, then, as one contemporary reported, that nothing else was talked about "even in the women's spinning rooms and the artisans' workshops."

On the one hand, the reforms of Pope Gregory VII and his successors gave the common people an important role to play, by urging them to reject certain practices and to retaliate against offenders. Combined with the fervor that had been whipped up by the Crusades, the result was a more widespread interest in spiritual matters and a greater participation in religious life—as well as increased violence. On the other hand, however, the reforming movement severely limited the ways in which the laity were allowed to express their spirituality or to participate meaningfully in the life of the Church.

The New Monasticism and the Mass

One of the first manifestations of the new popular piety was the growth and diversification of monastic movements. The abbey of Cluny had revived the observance of Benedict's *Rule* during the tenth century and, at the same time, had kept Cluny and its daughter houses independent of local lords. So these monasteries became lordships in their own right, acquiring extensive lands and enormous wealth. Those seeking to reject worldliness, therefore, had to look elsewhere. The result, beginning in the late eleventh century, was the founding of new monastic orders.

The order that became most widespread was founded at the French monastery of Cîteaux in 1098. Cistercian monks followed Benedict's *Rule*, but in the purest and most austere way possible. They founded new monasteries in wildernesses and remote areas, far from worldly temptations. They also shunned all unnecessary decoration and elaborate liturgical rites. Instead, they practiced contemplation and private prayer, and committed themselves to hard manual labor. Under the charismatic leadership of Bernard of Clairvaux

(1090–1153), a spellbinding preacher and one of the most influential personalities of his age, the Cistercian order grew exponentially, from 5 houses in 1115 to 343 by 1153. This astonishing increase meant that many more men and women were taking professional vows as monks and nuns, and that still more pious people were donating funds and lands to support monasteries and thereby participating indirectly in their life of devotion.

Another manifestation of popular piety was a new focus on the sacrament of the Mass, the liturgical reenactment of Christ's last meal with his disciples. This celebration, also known as the Eucharist, had always been an important part of Christian religion and social practice (see Chapter 6), but only in the twelfth century did it become the central act of worship in the western Church. Bernard of Clairvaux was instrumental in making it so, by developing and preaching the doctrine of transubstantiation. According to this doctrine, every Mass is a miraculous event because the priest's blessing transforms the bread and wine on the altar into the body and blood of Christ; hence the term *transubstantiation*, since earthly substances become the substance of Christ's divine body.

Popular reverence for the Eucharist became so great that the Church initiated the practice of elevating the consecrated bread, known as the Host, so that the whole congregation could see it. Not incidentally, this new theology of the Eucharist further enhanced the prestige of the priesthood by seeming to endow it with wonder-working powers.

THE CISTERCIAN ABBEY OF SULEJÓW (POLAND). Founded in 1176, this abbey was part of a vast European network of new monastic houses connected to each other and to the original Cistercian abbey at Cîteaux in France. Like this one, most were founded in remote rural areas and formed the nuclei of new towns. The abbey church of Sulejów (*SOO-lay-uf*) was dedicated to the English saint Thomas Becket, who had been canonized as a saint just three years before its foundation. ▪ *How does this Polish abbey's dedication to St. Thomas Becket exemplify the transnational interconnectivity of Cistercian monasteries?*

Analyzing Primary Sources

The Canons of the Fourth Lateran Council

In 1215, Innocent III presided over an ecumenical assembly of Church leaders in the papal palace and church of St. John Lateran in Rome. The resulting canons (rules) both reaffirmed older legislation and introduced a number of new laws in response to widespread social, economic, and cultural changes. Published the same year as Magna Carta, they too became a standard set of principles and continued to be applied within the Church until they were modified by the Council of Trent in the sixteenth century.

Canon 1

. . . There is one Universal Church of the faithful, outside of which there is absolutely no salvation. In which there is the same priest and sacrifice, Jesus Christ, whose body and blood are truly contained in the sacrament of the altar under the forms of bread and wine; the bread being changed (*transubstantiation*) by divine power into the body, and the wine into the blood, so that to realize the mystery of unity we may receive of Him what He has received of us. And this sacrament no one can effect except the priest who has been duly ordained in accordance with the keys of the Church, which Jesus Christ Himself gave to the Apostles and their successors. . . .

* * *

Canon 3

We excommunicate and anathematize every heresy that rises against the holy, orthodox, and Catholic faith . . . condemning all heretics under whatever names they may be known, for while they have different faces they are nevertheless bound to each other by their tails, since in all of them vanity is a common element. Those condemned, being handed over to the secular rulers of their bailiffs, let them be abandoned, to be punished with due justice, clerics being first degraded from their orders.

* * *

Canon 9

Since in many places within the same city and diocese there are people of different languages having one faith but various rites and customs, we strictly command that the bishops of these cities and dioceses provide suitable men who will, according to the different rites and languages, celebrate the divine offices for them, administer the sacraments of the Church and instruct them by word and example.

Canon 10

. . . It often happens that bishops, on account of their manifold duties or bodily infirmities, or because of hostile invasions or other reasons, to say nothing of lack of learning, which must be absolutely condemned in them and is not to be tolerated in the future, are themselves unable to minister the word of God to the people, especially in large and widespread dioceses. Wherefore we decree that bishops provide suitable men, powerful in work and word, to exercise with fruitful result the office of preaching; who in place of the bishops, since these cannot do it, diligently visiting the people committed to them, may instruct them by word and example. . . .

Canon 11

Since there are some who, on account of the lack of necessary means, are unable to acquire an education or to meet opportunities for perfecting themselves, the Third Lateran Council in a salutary decree provided that in every cathedral church a suitable benefice be assigned to a master who shall instruct *gratis* the clerics of that church and other poor students, . . . we, confirming the aforesaid decree, add that, not only in every cathedral church but also in other churches where means are sufficient, a competent master be appointed . . . who shall instruct *gratis* and to the best of his ability the clerics of those and other churches in the art of grammar and in other branches of knowledge.

* * *

Canons 14–16

That the morals and general conduct of clerics may be better, let all strive to live chastely and virtuously, particularly those in sacred orders, guarding against every vice of desire . . .

. . . All clerics shall carefully abstain from drunkenness. . . .

We forbid hunting and fowling to all clerics; wherefore, let them not presume to keep dogs and birds for these purposes. . . .

Clerics shall not hold secular offices or engage in secular and, above all, dishonest pursuits. They shall not attend the performances of mimics and buffoons, or theatrical representations. They shall not visit taverns except in case of necessity, namely, when on a journey.

They are forbidden to play games of chance or be present at them. They must have a becoming crown and tonsure and apply themselves diligently to the study of the divine offices and other useful subjects. Their garments must be worn clasped at the top and neither too short nor too long. They are not to use red or green garments or curiously sewed-together gloves, or beak-shaped shoes . . .

* * *

Canon 68

In some provinces a difference in dress distinguishes the Jews or Saracens [Muslims] from the Christians, but in certain others such a confusion has grown up that they cannot be distinguished by any difference. Thus it happens at times that through error Christians have relations with the women of Jews or Saracens, and Jews and Saracens with Christian women. Therefore, that they may not, under pretext of error of this sort, excuse themselves in the future for the excesses of such prohibited intercourse, we decree that such Jews and Saracens of both sexes in every Christian province and at all times shall be marked off in the eyes of the public from other peoples through the character of their dress. . . .

Moreover, during the last three days before Easter and especially on Good Friday, they shall not go forth in public at all, for the reason that some of them on these very days, as we hear, do not blush to go forth better dressed and are not afraid to mock the Christians who maintain the memory of the most holy Passion by wearing signs of mourning. . . .

Source: Excerpted from H. J. Schroeder, *Disciplinary Decrees of the General Councils: Text, Translation and Commentary* (St. Louis, MO: 1937), pp. 236–96.

Questions for Analysis

1. On the basis of this selection of canons, how would you characterize the main concerns of the Fourth Lateran Council? What is it attempting to regulate, and why? What changing historical circumstances do the canons reflect?

2. In what ways do the canons distinguish between clergy and laity? How does legislation work to maintain those distinctions?

3. Why do the canons place so much emphasis on clothing and appearance? Why would it be important for both clerics and "infidels" (Jews and Muslims) to dress in distinctive ways?

In later centuries, the Latin words spoken at the consecration of the Host, *Hoc est enim corpus meum* ("This is my body"), were understood as a magical formula, *hocus pocus*.

Holy Women, Human and Divine

Popular devotion to the Eucharist was matched by another new and hugely influential religious practice: the veneration of Jesus's mother, Mary. In this development, too, Bernard of Clairvaux played an important role, traveling around Europe to promote a theology that made Mary central to Christianity, the very embodiment of the Church. Eventually, Catholic teaching would hold that not only had Mary given birth to Jesus while still a virgin, but that she remained a virgin even after Jesus's birth; and, more radically, that she herself had been conceived without sin. This made Mary the exact opposite of Eve—the woman whose disobedience had (according to Judeo-Christian tradition) brought sin into the world for the first time—for through God's grace, she had given birth to Christ, a second Adam, whose obedient sacrifice of himself atoned for that original sin.

New doctrines also raised Mary from the position of God's humble handmaid to that of heaven's queen, with the power to intercede on behalf of all, even the worst sinners. Her soaring reputation as a miracle worker and advocate is amply testified by the thousands of devotional images created during this period, the many stories and hymns celebrating her virtues and miracles, and the fact that practically all the magnificent new cathedrals of the age were dedicated to "Our Lady," such as the many churches of Notre Dame in France, the Frauenkirchen of Germany, and so on.

The burgeoning **cult of the Blessed Virgin** had two contradictory effects. On the one hand, it elevated a female figure to a prominent place in the official Church for the first time, and thereby celebrated virtues associated with femininity: motherhood, healing, nourishment, mercy, kindness, and so on. On the other hand, it made Mary an unattainable, paradoxical model of female perfection: she alone could be both virgin and parent, Christ's mother and bride, God's maidservant and queenly consort. No real woman could begin to emulate her, and thus real women were increasingly compared to Eve and perceived as weak, deceitful, and disobedient. Moreover, the veneration of a single, idealized woman coincided exactly with the suppression of most real women's access to positions of power within the Church; as the cult of the Blessed Virgin grew, the opportunities for aspiring holy women shrank.

This lack of opportunity did not go unremarked at the time. As we noted on pages 285–286, the career of **Heloise** (c. 1090–1164) exemplifies both the avenues of advancement for women as well as the successful blocking of those avenues by new constraints on women's activities. Heloise's exact contemporary, **Hildegard of Bingen** (1098–1179), was even more creative in her efforts to make a place for herself and her female followers, and more outspoken than Heloise in her criticism of attempts to thwart them. Like Heloise, she was an abbess and a highly original thinker. But unlike

THE MYSTERY OF THE MASS. In this manuscript illumination, the visionary Hildegard of Bingen illustrates the doctrine of transubstantiation. In the lower register, the bread and wine of the Mass placed on the altar are being transformed into the body and blood of the crucified Christ, depicted in the upper register. Paired scenes from Christ's life (his birth and death, his ministry and resurrection) emphasize the fact that earthly substances— bread and wine—participate in a divine cycle of regeneration. Note that Hildegard does not imagine the mediating figure as a priest, but as the (female) Church, represented as a crowned queen and associated with the Virgin Mary. ▪ *What might be the significance of Hildegard's artistic choices?*

VIRGIN AND CHILD. This exquisite ivory sculpture (just over seven inches high) was carved in Paris in the mid- to late thirteenth century as an aid to private devotion and prayer. The mother of Jesus, Mary, was also regarded as the mother of all humanity, the *alma mater* ("nourishing mother") who could be relied on to protect and heal those who ask for her help.

Heloise, she was not a scholar; she was a mystic who claimed to receive regular revelations from God.

Hildegard expressed these revelations in her own version of Latin, writings that were later transcribed and illustrated under her close supervision. She also composed hymns and ambitious musical dramas for her nuns—music now widely available on CD, MP3, and the Internet—and prepared treatises on subjects as diverse as cosmology and medicine. Her advice was frequently sought by religious and secular authorities, including Bernard of Clairvaux and Frederick Barbarossa; she even received a special papal dispensation that allowed her to preach publicly.

HILDEGARD OF BINGEN'S DIVINE INSPIRATION. This portrait of Hildegard and her male secretary, Volmar, appears in her book *Scivias* ("Know the Ways"). It shows Hildegard as the recipient of a divine vision (represented by tongues of heavenly fire), which she transcribes onto a wax tablet using a stylus—a common method for creating the first draft of a written work. Volmar is placed outside the frame in which her vision occurs, but he is prepared to copy it onto parchment. ▪ *What does this image tell us about medieval ideas of authorship and authority?* ▪ *What does it suggest about the relationship and status of the female and male figures?*

Despite all this, Hildegard had to fight constantly for her rights and those of her nuns during her lifetime; and after her death, efforts to have her recognized as a saint were thwarted by the papacy. Indeed, she was one of the first candidates for whom a new canonization process was instituted by the papal court, or curia, as a way of controlling the popular veneration of charismatic figures the Church considered threatening. So, although many high-ranking clergy of her own day recognized her holiness, the papal courts of subsequent centuries would not acknowledge it. The standards of acceptable female behavior had become too narrow to contain her. It would take 800 years for Hildegard to be canonized; she was officially declared a saint in 2012.

Heresy or Piety?

Christianity has been successfully transmitted to many different civilizations because it is relatively open-ended and absorbs new influences. In the late twelfth and thirteenth centuries, however, the Church began to lose its capacity to respond inclusively to new challenges, preferring instead to crack down on "heresies" that undermined its power. This trend would eventually bring about a reforming movement so intense that it could not be contained within the Church: the Protestant Reformation (see Chapter 13). For the more the Church claimed the right to control every aspect of belief and practice, the more it made itself vulnerable to those who challenged its enforcement. This resulted in large-scale movements of popular opposition to papal authority, as well as to more crusades aimed at harnessing popular devotion to that same authority.

The best way to understand this is through Innocent III's very different responses to rather similar popular movements. On the one hand, the pope resolved to crush all disobedience; on the other hand, he wanted to support idealistic groups that could be made to acknowledge papal authority, so as not to frustrate all dynamic spirituality. Thus, Innocent labeled as heretical a religious movement that began in southern France: the Cathars (from the Greek word for "purity"). He accused the Cathars of beliefs that resembled Zoroastrianism (see Chapter 2) and Manichaeism (see Chapter 6), alleging that they held all material creation to be evil, and even that they believed the power of God to be opposed by that of a malevolent deity associated with Satan, the fallen angel Lucifer. Also, the fact that many Cathar leaders were women made this movement heretical by definition.

A more typical form of twelfth-century religious dissent was Waldensianism, so called because it is said to have

Competing Viewpoints

Two Conversion Experiences

> Both Peter Waldo (or Waldes), later branded a heretic, and Francis of Assisi, later declared a saint, were moved to take up a life of preaching and poverty after undergoing a process of conversion. Their experiences exhibit some striking similarities despite their different fates. The first account is that of an anonymous chronicler in Peter's home town of Lyon; the second is by Francis's contemporary and hagiographer, Thomas of Celano (c. 1200–c. 1260/70).

The Conversion of Peter Waldo

At about this time, in 1173, there was a citizen of Lyon named Peter Waldo, who had made a great deal of money by the evil means of usury. One Sunday he lingered by a crowd that had gathered round a traveling storyteller, and was much struck by his words. He took him home with him, and listened carefully to his story of how St. Alexis had died a holy death in his father's house. Next morning Waldo hastened to the schools of theology to seek advice about his soul. When he had been told of the many ways of coming to God he asked the master whether any of them was more sure and reliable than the rest. The master quoted to him the words of the Lord, "If thou wilt be perfect go sell what thou hast and give it to the poor and thou shalt have treasure in heaven. And come follow me."

Waldo returned to his wife and gave her the choice between having all his movable wealth or his property in land. . . . She was very upset at having to do this and chose the property. From his movable wealth he returned what he had acquired wrongly, conferred a large portion on his two daughters, whom he placed in the order of Fontevrault without his wife's knowledge, and gave a still larger amount to the poor.

At this time a terrible famine was raging through Gaul and Germany. . . . Waldo generously distributed bread, soup and meat to anyone who came to him. On the [Feast of the] Assumption of the Virgin [August 15] he scattered money among the poor in the streets saying, "You cannot serve two masters, God and Mammon." The people around thought he had gone out of his senses. Then he stood up on a piece of high ground and said, "Friends and fellow-citizens, I am not mad as you think. . . . I know that many of you disapprove of my having acted so publicly. I have done so both for my own sake and for yours: for my sake, because anybody who sees me with money in future will be able to say that I am mad; for your sake, so that you may learn to place your hopes in God and not in wealth." . . .

[In] 1177, Waldo, the citizen of Lyon whom we have already mentioned, who had vowed to God that he would possess neither gold nor silver, and take no thought for the morrow, began to make converts to his opinions. Following his example they gave all they had to the poor, and willingly devoted themselves to poverty. Gradually, both in public and in private they began to inveigh against both their own sins and those of others. . . .

[In] 1178, Pope Alexander III held a council at the Lateran palace. . . . The council condemned heresy and all those who fostered and defended heretics. The pope embraced Waldo, and applauded the vows of voluntary poverty which he had taken, but forbade him and his companions to assume the office of preaching except at the request of the priests. They obeyed this instruction for a time, but later they disobeyed, and affronted many, bringing ruin on themselves.

Source: Excerpted from *Chronicon universale anonymi Laudunensis*, ed. and trans. Robert I. Moore, in *The Birth of Popular Heresy* (London: 1975), pp. 111–13 (slightly modified).

The Conversion of Francis of Assisi

There was a man by the name of Francis, who from his earliest years was brought up by his parents proud of spirit, in accordance with the vanity of the world. . . . These are the wretched circumstances among which the man whom we venerate today as a saint, for he is truly a saint, lived in his youth; and almost up to the twenty-fifth year of his age, . . . he outdid all his contemporaries in vanities and he came to be a promoter of evil and was more abundantly zealous for all kinds of foolishness. . . . And while, not knowing how to restrain himself, he was . . . worn down by a long illness, [he] began to think of things other than he was used to thinking upon. When he had recovered somewhat and had begun to walk about the house with the support of a cane to speed the recovery of his health, he went outside one day and began to look about at the surrounding landscape with great interest. But the beauty of the fields, the pleasantness of the vineyards, and whatever else was beautiful to look upon, could stir in him no delight. He wondered therefore at the sudden change that had come over him. . . . From that day on, therefore, he began to despise himself. . . .

Now since there was a certain man in the city of Assisi whom he loved more than any other because he was of the same age as the other, and since the great familiarity of their mutual affection led him to share his secrets with him; he often took him to remote places, places well-suited for counsel, telling him that he had found a certain precious and great treasure. This one rejoiced and, concerned about what he heard, he willingly accompanied Francis whenever he was asked. There was a certain grotto near the city where they frequently went and talked about this treasure. The man of God, who was already holy by reason of his holy purpose, would enter the grotto, while his companion would wait for him outside; and filled with a new and singular spirit, he would pray to his Father in secret. . . .

One day, however, when he had begged for the mercy of God most earnestly, it was shown to him by God what he was to do. . . . He rose up, therefore, fortified himself with the sign of the cross, got his horse ready and mounted it, and taking with him some fine cloth to sell, he hastened to the city called Foligno. There, as usual, he sold everything he had with him . . . and, free of all luggage, he started back, wondering with a religious mind what he should do with the money. . . . When, therefore, he neared the city of Assisi, he discovered a certain church . . . built of old in honor of St. Damian but which was now threatening to collapse because it was so old. . . . And when he found there a certain poor priest, he kissed his sacred hands with great faith, and offered him the money he had with him, . . . begging the priest to suffer him to remain with him for the sake of the Lord. . . .

When those who knew him . . . compared what he was now with what he had been . . . they began to revile him miserably. Shouting out that he was mad and demented, they threw the mud of the streets and stones at him. . . . Now . . . the report of these things finally came to his father . . . [who] shut him up mercilessly in a dark place for several days. . . . It happened, however, when Francis' father had left home for a while on business and the man of God remained bound in the basement of the house, his mother, who was alone with him and did not approve of what her husband had done, spoke kindly to her son . . . and loosening his chains, she let him go free. . . .

He [the father] then brought his son before the bishop of the city, so that, renouncing all his possessions into his hands, he might give up everything he had. . . . Indeed, he [Francis] did not wait for any words nor did he speak any, but immediately putting off his clothes and casting them aside, he gave them back to his father. Moreover, not even retaining his trousers, he stripped himself completely naked before all. The bishop, however, sensing his disposition and admiring greatly his fervor and constancy, arose and drew him within his arms and covered him with the mantle he was wearing. . . .

Source: Excerpted from Thomas of Celano, "The First Life of Saint Francis" in *Saint Francis of Assisi: Writings and Biographies*, ed. Marion A. Habiq (Chicago: 1973), pp. 229–41.

Questions for Analysis

1. How do the conversions of Peter and Francis reflect the social and economic changes of the twelfth century? What new sources of tension and temptation are evident?

2. How do these two accounts describe the new converts' relationship(s) with their families, communities, and Church authorities? What are the similarities and differences? Why would these be important factors in determining the sanctity of either?

3. The story of Peter's conversion is written by an anonymous chronicler of Lyon, that of Francis by his follower and official biographer. How do these different perspectives shape the two accounts? Which is the more reliable, and why?

originated from the teachings of a merchant named Peter Waldo, or Waldes. Waldensians were laypeople who wished to imitate the life of Christ to the fullest. They were active in the vernacular translation and study of the Gospels and dedicated to lives of poverty and preaching. None of this contradicted any contemporary doctrines, and for a while the Church did not interfere with the Waldensians' ministry. But when they began to preach without authorization, they were condemned as heretics. In response, they began to articulate a more radical opposition to the established hierarchy. Many of their leaders, too, were women.

At the same time, however, Innocent embraced two other popular movements and turned them into two new religious orders: the Dominicans and the Franciscans. Like the Waldensians, the friars ("brothers") of these orders imitated the life of Jesus and his apostles by wandering through the countryside and establishing missions in Europe's growing towns, preaching and offering spiritual and material assistance to the poor. They also embraced poverty and begged for a living, hence their categorization as *mendicants*, from the Latin verb *mendicare* ("to beg"). In the end, the only thing that separated them from the Waldensians was their willingness to subject themselves to papal authority.

The **Dominican** order, formally known as the Order of Preachers, was founded by the zealous Dominic of Osma (1170–1221), a Castilian theologian. Approved in 1216, it was particularly dedicated to the prosecution of heretics and the conversion of Jews and Muslims. At first, the Dominicans hoped to achieve these ends by preaching and public debate; and to further these goals, many of its members pursued academic careers in the nascent universities, and thus contributed to the development of philosophy and theology (see page 310). The most influential intellectual of the Middle Ages, Thomas Aquinas (1225–1274), was a Dominican. But this order soon became associated with the use of other persuasive techniques through the administration of the Inquisition, which became formalized in the thirteenth century. (It is now called the Congregation for the Doctrine of the Faith and is still staffed by members of the order.)

The **Franciscans**, formally known as the Order of the Friars Minor ("Little Brothers"), were committed less to doctrine and discipline than to the welfare of the poor and the cultivation of personal spirituality. Whereas Dominic and his earliest followers were ordained priests, the founder of the Franciscans was the ne'er-do-well son of an Italian merchant, Francis of Assisi (1182–1226), who eventually rebelled against the materialistic values of his father. Stripping himself (literally) of all his worldly possessions, he put on the tattered garb of a beggar and began to preach salvation in town squares. Unlike Dominic, Francis did

this without official approval, thereby risking papal censure. Indeed, the pope might well have rejected Francis as a heretic. But when he showed himself willing to profess obedience in 1209, Innocent granted Francis and his followers permission to preach.

Although the rapid growth of the Franciscan order would eventually necessitate more administrative stability and doctrinal training for all its members, many Franciscans continued to engage in revivalistic outdoor preaching and to offer a model for apostolic living. This was not, however, an approved religious lifestyle for women. Francis's most important female follower, Clare of Assisi (1194–1253), wanted to found an order along the same lines, the Order of Poor Ladies (also known as the Poor Clares). But its members were not allowed to work directly among the people, as men did, and instead lived in cloistered convents supported by charitable donations.

Their counterparts in northern Europe were the Beguines (*beh-GHEENS*), communities of laywomen who lived in loosely organized communal quarters and ministered directly to the poor. Their relationship with Church officials was strained, because the Beguines embraced many of the precepts and practices associated with the Waldensians, including the unauthorized translation and study of the Bible. And the fact that they were women made them even more suspect.

Christians against Jews

Although violence and exploitation continued to beset Europe's Jewish communities, the Church's official position never explicitly endorsed the view that Jews posed a threat to Christians—yet it did little to combat such attitudes, either. As a result, many ordinary people came to believe that their Jewish neighbors were agents of evil who routinely crucified Christian children, consumed Christian blood, profaned the body of Christ in the Eucharist, and spread disease in Christian communities by poisoning wells. Fanciful stories of Jewish wealth added an economic element to the development of anti-Semitism, as did the fact that the Jews' social and cultural networks were the engine of the medieval economy. From this fact, conspiracy theorists inferred the existence of organized Jewish plots to undermine Christian society, which they regularly cited as justifications for mass executions and other atrocities.

The precarious position of Europe's Jews worsened throughout the twelfth and thirteenth centuries as both secular and ecclesiastical authorities devised more systematic mechanisms for policing undesirable segments of society: "heretics" as well as the indigent poor, prostitutes, "sodomites," and lepers. The canons of the Fourth Lateran Council had mandated that Jews be exposed through the wearing of the Jewish badge, making them easier targets in times of unrest. At the same time, the protections that Europe's rulers had once extended to their Jewish subjects were gradually withdrawn. In Spain, the "Reconquista" had absorbed many of the Muslim kingdoms in which Jews had enjoyed a measure of tolerance, and the Jews were not always easily accommodated within the emerging monarchies of Christian Spain.

They were, however, far less segregated and isolated in Spain. Starting in the 1280s, rulers elsewhere in Europe began to expel their Jewish subjects from their kingdoms altogether, in most cases because they could no longer pretend to repay the enormous sums they had extorted from Jewish moneylenders; this was the case in the kingdoms of Sicily (1288), England (1290), and France (1306). These Jews settled either in the established communities of Spain or in those of the Rhineland. Others, as we noted on page 292, started new settlements in Poland and other eastern European kingdoms.

AN INTELLECTUAL REVOLUTION

The Fourth Lateran Council responded to the growing urbanization of Europe by mandating the education of the laity and insisting on more rigorous training for all clergy. These measures responded to a number of factors that were transforming the cultural landscape of Europe and to the new opportunities opening up for advancement through education. The growth of towns had led to the growth of schools in those towns, for the most part founded by local bishops or monasteries. Meanwhile, the Crusades became conduits for the transmission of Muslim learning and, through Muslim mediation, the precepts of ancient Greek philosophy.

The infusion of these new ideas created an extraordinary new forum for intellectual endeavor: the university. In much the same way that ease of travel and communication had fostered a scientific revolution in the cities of the Hellenistic world (Chapter 4), so the conditions that gave rise to the university marked the beginning of a revolution in the intellectual history of Europe.

TWO CONTEMPORARY VIEWS OF MEDIEVAL EDUCATION. The illuminated image on the right is the frontispiece of a basic Latin grammar book copied at a monastery school in Austria. It shows Lady Wisdom, the female embodiment of knowledge, seated at a lectern with her young pupils clustered around her, learning to read and write for the first time. The image on the left, from a manuscript copied in Baghdad, shows a master lecturing to men in a *madrasa*—a Muslim school—while women (above) listen from behind a partition. ▪ *What do you make of the presence of women in both of these representations? How do they enrich or complicate our understanding of religious education in this era?*

Access to Education

Around 800, Charlemagne had ordered that primary schools be established in every city and monastery of his realm. But it was not until the economic revival of the late eleventh century that educational opportunities became more widely available. Then, in 1179, Pope Alexander III decreed that all cathedrals should set aside income for at least one schoolteacher, whose task would be to accept all comers, rich or poor, without fee. He predicted, correctly, that this measure would increase the number of well-trained clerics and administrators, supplying the growing bureaucracy of the Church. The recently martyred Thomas Becket had been an early beneficiary of such schooling.

At first, cathedral schools existed almost exclusively for the training of parish priests, but their curriculum was soon broadened as the growth of both ecclesiastical and secular governments escalated demand for trained men with more sophisticated skills. The most fundamental elements of this curriculum were known as the *trivium* ("three ways"): grammar, logic, and rhetoric. This meant a thorough grounding in Latin through the study of classical Roman authors, such as Cicero and Virgil, and training in the formulation and expression of sound arguments. Students who mastered the trivium were fit to perform basic clerical tasks, but those who wanted to achieve the reputation and advantages of scholars had to master the remaining branches of learning, the *quadrivium* (or "four ways"): arithmetic, geometry, astronomy, and music. Together, these seven liberal arts—so called because they liberated those who acquired them from menial labor—were the prerequisites for advanced study in philosophy, theology, law, and medicine.

Until about 1200, most students in urban schools belonged to the minor orders of the clergy, meaning they took vows of obedience and were immune from prosecution by secular authorities—but not required to remain celibate, unlike priests and bishops, who belonged to major orders. Even men who hoped to become lawyers or bureaucrats usually found it advantageous to "take orders" in case powerful ecclesiastical offices became open to them. Heloise tried to discourage Abelard from marrying her for this very reason, because it would destroy his

chances of being appointed a bishop or papal legate. Abelard, a nobleman's son, was by no means typical of the men who rose to prominence in this era through education. His contemporary and rival, Suger, was more representative. An orphan of obscure origins, he became abbot of the royal monastery of Saint-Denis and de facto chancellor of France.

By the thirteenth century, most boys who entered schools were not members of the clergy and never intended to be. Some were children of wealthy families, which regarded Latin literacy as a badge of status and a practical necessity. Others were future notaries, estate managers, and merchants who needed to be literate and numerate in order to succeed in their careers. Many alternative schools were eventually established to cater to these vocational students and became largely independent of ecclesiastical control. In some of these schools, Latin ceased to be the language of instruction and was replaced by the vernacular language of the region.

Although formal schooling remained restricted to boys and young men, many girls and women became highly educated, too, especially those reared in convents or princely courts. Heloise had an unusual degree of access to the educational milieu of Paris, but she clearly had received excellent preparatory training in the convent before she began her studies with Abelard. Most laywomen, however, were

THE TOMB OF ELEANOR OF AQUITAINE. Eleanor probably commissioned the tomb effigies representing herself, her husband Henry II, and her son Richard the Lionheart—both of whom died years before she did. She was eventually buried alongside them in the vault of the convent of Fontevrault in Anjou, where she spent the last years of her life. ▪ *Notice that Eleanor's effigy shows her reading a book. How does this reinforce or challenge what we have learned about women's access to education?*

Analyzing Primary Sources

Peter Abelard Critiques Theological Contradictions

In 1120, Abelard published the Sic et Non *("So and Not So"), a pioneering work of dialectic theology and a model for the development of later scholastic methods. In it, he arranged passages from scripture as well as the writings of the church fathers that had bearing on important doctrinal issues and appeared to offer contradictory views. His eventual aim, as the prologue to this work indicates, was to reconcile these differences through the use of critical analysis.*

 here are many seeming contradictions and even obscurities in the innumerable writings of the church fathers. Our respect for their authority should not stand in the way of an effort on our part to come at the truth. The obscurity and contradictions in ancient writings may be explained upon many grounds, and may be discussed without impugning the good faith and insight of the fathers. A writer may use different terms to mean the same thing, in order to avoid a monotonous repetition of the same word. Common, vague words may be employed in order that the common people may understand; and sometimes a writer sacrifices perfect accuracy in the interest of a clear general statement. Poetical, figurative language is often obscure and vague. . . .

Doubtless the fathers might err; even Peter, the prince of the apostles, fell into error; what wonder that the saints do not always show themselves inspired? The fathers did not themselves believe that they, or their companions, were always right. Augustine found himself mistaken in some cases and did not hesitate to retract his errors. He warns his admirers not to look upon his letters as they would upon the Scriptures, but to accept only those things which, upon examination, they find to be true.

All writings belonging to this class are to be read with full freedom to criticise, and with no obligation to accept unquestioningly; otherwise the way would be blocked to all discussion, and posterity be deprived of the excellent intellectual exercise of debating difficult questions of language and presentation. But an explicit exception must be made in the case of the Old and New Testaments. In the Scriptures, when anything strikes us as absurd, we may not say that the writer erred, but that the scribe made a blunder in copying the manuscripts, or that there is an error in interpretation, or that the passage is not understood. The fathers make a very careful distinction between the Scriptures and later works. They advocate a discriminating, not to say suspicious, use of the writings of their own contemporaries.

In view of these considerations, I have ventured to bring together various dicta of the holy fathers, as they came to mind, and to formulate certain questions which were suggested by the seeming contradictions in the statements. These questions ought to serve to excite tender readers to a zealous inquiry into truth and so sharpen their wits. The master key of knowledge is, indeed, a persistent and frequent questioning. Aristotle, the most clear-sighted of all the philosophers, was desirous above all

things else to arouse this questioning spirit, for in his *Categories* he exhorts a student as follows: "It may well be difficult to reach a positive conclusion in these matters unless they be frequently discussed. It is by no means fruitless to be doubtful on particular points." By doubting we come to examine, and by examining we reach the truth.

Source: Peter Abelard, prologue to the *Sic et Non*, trans. James Harvey Robinson, in *Readings in European History*, 2 vols. (Boston: 1904), vol. 1, pp. 450–51.

Questions for Analysis

1. According to Abelard, on what grounds can religious authorities be challenged? What distinctions does he make between criticism of the scriptures and of other authorities, and why?

2. In this work, Abelard did not attempt to resolve the contradictions among his sources. Based on what you have learned, why would have his project seemed threatening to the authority of the Church?

taught at home, sometimes by private tutors but more often by other women. In fact, laywomen were more likely to be literate than laymen, and it is for this reason that women were often the patrons of poets and the primary readers and owners of books. It is significant that the effigy that **Eleanor of Aquitaine** commissioned for her own tomb shows her lying awake reading, flanked by her sleeping husband and son, till Judgment Day.

The Development of Scholasticism

The educational revolution that began in the eleventh century led to the development of new critical methods for framing and resolving complex theological and philosophical problems. These methods are collectively known as **scholasticism**, because they had their origins in the pedagogy of medieval schools. Scholastic methods are highly systematic and respectful of authority, but they also rely on rigorous questioning and argumentation. They therefore place great emphasis on evidence derived from reason. Indeed, scholasticism can be defined as a way of reconciling various forms of knowledge through logical debate, often called *dialectic*.

The earliest practitioner of the scholastic method is often considered to be Anselm of Canterbury (1033–1109), a Benedictine monk from northern Italy who became archbishop of Canterbury. The central premise of Anselm's teaching was that the human mind can combine knowledge gained through education and experience with divine revelation—as long as one has faith in God and careful scholastic training. As he put it, "I believe in order to understand," so that belief can be enriched and strengthened by understanding.

Building on the writings of Augustine and Boethius (Chapter 6), and so (indirectly) on the teachings of Plato (Chapter 4), Anselm developed various rational proofs for the underlying truths of Christian doctrine. The most famous of these is his proof for the existence of God, known as the ontological proof ("proof from the fact of existence") because it reasons that human beings could not have ideas of goodness, truth, or justice unless some higher being had instilled those ideas in us. He further reasoned that God, as the essence of all ideals, must be "that than which nothing greater can be conceived," and as such must exist, or else God could not be the greatest thing conceivable.

Anselm's writings were influential, but the philosopher who popularized the scholastic method was Abelard. It was largely thanks to him that Paris became the intellectual capital of Europe. As a cathedral city and the seat of the French monarchy, it already boasted a number of schools, but it was only after Abelard was appointed to the school-

master's chair at Notre Dame that Paris became a magnet for ambitious young men, many of whom were attracted to Abelard's unorthodox teaching style. We can glimpse it through his audacious treatise the *Sic et Non* ("Yes and No" or "So and Not So"). In this book, Abelard gathered a collection of seemingly contradictory statements from the Church Fathers, organized around 150 key theological problems. Like his contemporary Gratian, the codifier of canon law, Abelard's ultimate ambition was to show that these divergent authorities could be reconciled—in this case, through the skillful use of dialectic.

Yet Abelard did not propose any solutions in the *Sic et Non*, and the work therefore caused grave concern. More inflammatory still were Abelard's meditations on the doctrine of the Trinity, which circulated in a book of lectures that was denounced and burned in 1121. Twenty years later, Bernard of Clairvaux had Abelard brought up on another charge of heresy at the Council of Soissons, where he was condemned a second time. Bernard's own mystic spirituality stood in direct opposition to Abelard's tireless quest for reasoned understanding.

Abelard, for his part, found no solace in the monastic life beloved by Bernard. For Abelard, teaching was the activity that nurtured his faith. Luckily, teaching also expanded his fame and allowed him to train many pupils who eventually vindicated him. After Abelard's death, his student Peter Lombard asked the same fundamental questions, but he took care to resolve the tensions that the *Sic et Non* left open. His great work, known as the *Sentences*, became the standard theological textbook of the medieval university, and all aspirants to the doctorate were required to comment on it.

The Invention of the University

The emergence of the university—a unique public forum for advanced study, questioning of received ideas, and creation of new knowledge—was the natural extension of Abelard's teachings. His reputation and that of his students attracted many intellectuals to Paris, and together they began to offer more varied forms of instruction than anything obtainable in the average cathedral school. By 1200, this loose association of teachers had formed themselves into a *universitas* ("corporation" in Latin), and the resulting faculty began to collaborate in the higher academic study of the liberal arts, with a special emphasis on theology. At about the same time, students of law in Bologna came together in a *universitas* whose specialty was law.

Paris and Bologna provided the two models on which all medieval universities were based. In southern Europe,

CENTURY UNIVERSITY WAS FOUNDED

- ■ Twelfth century
- ■ Thirteenth century
- □ Fourteenth century
- ■ Fifteenth century
- — Boundaries c. 1500

THE SPREAD OF UNIVERSITIES. This map shows the geographical distribution of Europe's major universities and their dates of foundation. ▪ *Where were the first universities founded, and why?* ▪ *Notice the number and location of the universities founded in the fourteenth and fifteenth centuries. What pattern do you see in these later foundations?* ▪ *What might explain this pattern?*

such universities as Montpellier, Salamanca, and Naples were patterned after Bologna, where the students themselves constituted the corporation: they hired the teachers, paid their salaries, and fined or discharged them for poor instruction. The universities of northern Europe were like that of Paris, consisting of guilds of teachers who governed themselves and established rules of conduct and fees for tuition. They eventually embraced four faculties—liberal arts, theology, law, and medicine—each headed by a dean. By the end of the thirteenth century, the northern universities also expanded to include separate, semiautonomous colleges, which usually provided housing for poorer students and were often endowed by private benefactors. Over time, these colleges became centers of instruction as well as residences. The universities of Oxford and Cambridge still retain this pattern of organization: the colleges of which they are composed are semi-independent educational units.

Most of the academic degrees granted in our modern universities derive from those awarded in the Middle Ages, even though the actual courses of study are very different. No university curriculum included history or vernacular languages or anything like the social sciences prior to the nineteenth century. The medieval student was assumed to know Latin grammar thoroughly before entering a university, which he would have learned in the primary (or "grammar") schools discussed earlier. On admission, he was required to spend about four years studying the basic liberal arts, which meant doing advanced work in Latin rhetoric and mastering the rules of logic. If he passed his examinations, he received the preliminary degree of bachelor of arts (the prototype of our BA). But to ensure himself a place in professional life, he had to devote additional years to the pursuit of an advanced degree, the master of arts (MA) or the doctor of laws, medicine, or theology. This was accomplished by reading and commenting on standard texts such as Peter Lombard's *Sentences* (theology), Gratian's *Decretum* (law), or Aristotle's *Physics* (medicine). The requirements for the degree of doctor of philosophy (PhD) included even more specialized training, and those for the doctorate in theology were particularly arduous: by the end of the Middle Ages, it took twelve or thirteen years to earn this degree, over and above the eight years required to earn the MA. University degrees of all grades were recognized as standards of attainment and became pathways to a variety of careers.

Student life in medieval universities was rowdy. Because many students began their studies between the ages of twelve and fifteen, they were working through all the challenges of adolescence and early adulthood as they worked toward their degrees; this explains the many injunctions against drunkenness, gambling, and other pursuits included among the canons of the Fourth Lateran Council. Moreover, university students generally believed that they constituted an independent and privileged community, apart from the local communities in which they lived. This often led to riots or even pitched battles between "town" and "gown."

That said, the time devoted to actual study was very intensive. Because books were prohibitively expensive, the primary mode of instruction was the lecture (Latin for "reading") in which a master would read an authoritative work aloud to his students and comment on it while they took notes. As students advanced in their disciplines, they were expected to develop their own skills of analysis and interpretation in formal, public disputations. Advanced disputations could become extremely complex and abstract, and sometimes might last for days. Often, they sparked public debates of great magnitude. The Ninety-Five Theses posted by Martin Luther in 1517 were actually a set of debating points organized along these lines (see Chapter 13).

Classical Thought, Muslim Learning, and Scholastic Theology

The intellectual revolution of the Middle Ages was hugely indebted to the intellectual legacy of Islam, which was filtering into Europe via the Crusades. As we saw in Chapter 8, Muslim philosophers had been honing an array of different techniques to deal with the challenge of reconciling classical thought with Islamic belief, and these techniques contributed fundamentally to the development of Christian theology.

The most influential of these Muslim philosophers was Ibn Rushd, known to his Christian disciples as Averroès (*ah-VAIR-oh-ayz*; 1126–1198). Born in the Andalusian capital of Córdoba, in Muslim Spain, Averroès single-handedly advanced the study of Aristotelian logic by publishing a series of careful commentaries that sought to purge the Greek philosopher's works of all later (and confusing) influences, to allow for their proper analysis and interpretation. Soon translated from Arabic into Latin, these commentaries were received in western Christendom alongside new translations of Aristotle's texts, also conveyed to Latin readers via Arabic, and thus fundamentally influenced the way all subsequent European scholars understood Aristotle. The prestige of Averroès was so great that Christian intellectuals called him simply "the Commentator," just as they called Aristotle "the Philosopher," as if there were no others.

The greatest accomplishments in this endeavor were made by **Thomas Aquinas** (1225–1274), who became the leading theologian at the University of Paris. As a member of the Dominican order, Thomas was committed to the defense of the Roman Church. But he also believed that the study of the physical world was a legitimate way of gaining knowledge of the divine, because God had created both the world and the many ways of knowing it. Imbued with a deep confidence in the value of both human reason and human experience, Thomas worked quietly and steadily on his two great summaries of theology, the *Summa contra gentiles* (a compendium of the arguments for refuting non-Christian religions) and the comprehensive *Summa theologiae*. The theology of the modern Roman Catholic Church still rests on Thomistic methods, doctrines, and principles.

COURTS, CITIES, AND CATHEDRALS

In the eleventh century, it was possible to describe European society as divided among "those who worked, those who prayed, and those who fought." By 1200, such a description no longer bore much relationship to reality. New elites had emerged in the burgeoning cities of Europe. The wealthiest members of society were merchants and bankers, and aristocrats either had to best them (by engaging in trade themselves) or join them through strategic intermarriage. The aristocracy still fought, but so did upwardly mobile knights, urban crossbowmen, longbowmen, citizen militias, and peasant levies. Meanwhile, such lines as existed between town and countryside were easily crossed, and the pupils of the new schools made up a growing professional class that further defied neat categorization. We have noted that careers in the Church or royal bureaucracies were particularly open to self-made, educated men, but medieval courts and cities also provided opportunities for advancement.

From Chevalerie to Chivalry

The ennoblement of chivalry and the emergence of medieval court culture were connected to the growing wealth of Europe, the competition among states and princes, and the contemporary developments in military technology brought about by the Crusades. In 1100, a knight could get by with a woolen tunic and leather corselet, a couple of horses, a groom, and a sword. A hundred years later, a knight needed

THE INFLUENCE OF AVERROÈS. This portrait of the Muslim polymath Averroès is featured in a fourteenth-century fresco celebrating the achievements of the Christian theologian Thomas Aquinas (c. 1225–1274). ■ *What does his inclusion in this context indicate about the relationship between Muslim and Christian intellectual traditions?*

Ultimately, Averroès's learning was suppressed by the new Muslim dynasty that came to power in his lifetime, the Almohads, who demanded that all philosophical inquiry be subordinated to orthodox Muslim belief. After burning several of Averroès's works, they exiled him to Morocco. Thereafter, Islamic philosophy may have had more impact on Europe than in some Islamic kingdoms.

The greatest Jewish scholar of this period, Moses Maimonides (*my-MAHN-eh-dees*; c. 1137–1204), was also driven into exile by the Almohads. He traveled first to North Africa and then to Egypt, where he became a famous teacher, jurist, and physician. Also like Averroès, he exercised great influence on Christian theologians through his systematic exposition of Jewish law in the *Mishneh Torah*, which earned him the nickname the "second Moses."

Because many aspects of the rabbinic tradition, Greek philosophy, and Arabic learning were not readily compatible with Christian faith, they had to be filtered through the dialectical methods pioneered by Abelard and his pupils.

a full-body armor made of iron, a visored helmet, a broadsword, a lance, a shield, and several warhorses capable of carrying all this gear. By 1250, a knight also had to keep up appearances at tournaments, which meant maintaining a string of horses, sumptuous silk clothing for himself and caparisons for his steeds, and a retinue of liveried squires and servants. As the costs of a warrior's equipment rose, the number of men who could personally afford it dramatically declined, making knightly display something increasingly prized by nobles and upstart merchants alike. Knights who did not inherit or gain sufficient property to support themselves had to seek wealthy brides or the protection of a lord who could afford to equip them.

Still other factors contributed to the prestige of knighthood. As part of a larger effort to control the violent competition for land and wealth, both secular and ecclesiastical

rulers began to promote a new set of values that would come to redefine chivalry: bravery, loyalty, generosity, and civility. This new chivalry appealed to knights because it distinguished them from all the other "new men" who were emerging as powerful figures in this period, especially merchants and clerics. It also appealed to the nobility, whose status in this socially mobile world no longer depended on descent from high-born ancestors; families who *did* have such ancestors did not necessarily have the wealth to maintain a noble lifestyle, whereas many families who lived as nobility did not have prestigious ancestors.

What, then, was *nobility*? To the older aristocracy, it was a visible sign of good breeding. To professional warriors, such as many crusaders, and the merchants and bureaucrats who later adopted its language and customs, chivalry offered a way of legitimizing social positions attained through bravery or skill. As a result, mounted combat—whether on the battlefield, in tournaments, or in the hunt—would remain the defining pastime of European gentlemen until the end of the First World War (see Chapter 24).

MAKING A KNIGHTLY APPEARANCE. The costs of maintaining a chivalric lifestyle mounted steeply in the twelfth and thirteenth centuries, not only because a knight needed the most up-to-date equipment but also because he was expected to cut a gallant figure at tournaments and dazzle female spectators. This image is one of many sumptuous full-page illuminations in the Manesse Codex, made in Zurich in the early fourteenth century and preserving the compositions of earlier courtly poets.

The Aristocratic Landscape and Its Environmental Effects

In previous centuries, warriors had hunted to supplement their diets or to protect their households from predators. But as more and more land was placed under cultivation or devoted to raising sheep and cattle, and as many species of wild animals (notably wolves, bears, and boar) were hunted to near extinction in Europe, hunting ceased to be a necessity and became a symbol of noble status. Not only did hunting require a good horse, a pack of trained dogs and servants, and an array of weapons, it also required elites to enclose certain areas of protected land so that they could be stocked with game. These protected spaces were called forests—regardless of whether or not they were wooded—and they were governed by a "law of the forest," which stipulated that only the lord who owned or controlled the forest could hunt or allow others to hunt there.

Forest law forbade peasants from hunting game and prescribed heavy penalties for poaching (stealing). Such laws also prohibited foraging or cutting down trees for construction or firewood. In England, for example, only dead twigs and branches small enough to be pulled down with a pruning hook or a shepherd's crook could be harvested: hence the expression "by hook or by crook." In fact, after the Norman Conquest, the kings of England had so increased the amount of land that was deemed "royal forest" that Magna Carta contained a series of provisions demanding that this land be "disafforrested" and returned to common use. In 1217, the young King Henry III issued a companion document, the Charter of the Forest, to reestablish his subjects' rights to these lands.

As in so many other arenas, the Crusades had an impact on hunting and the environment, too. Crusaders were impressed and inspired by the elegance and elaborate engineering of the gardens and parks they saw in the Holy Land, North Africa, and the Muslim kingdoms of Spain. So during the thirteenth century, many European aristocrats embarked on major projects designed to turn their own forests into hunting parks, and also to create habitats friendly to new species of birds and animals. The natural landscape of Europe was decisively altered as a result. Fallow deer (*Dama dama*), which were native only to Anatolia and had been brought to the Mediterranean by the Romans, were now introduced in England and France, where they were bred for hunting.

ON THE ART OF HUNTING WITH BIRDS. This beautifully illuminated manuscript of Frederick II's famous treatise on falconry was commissioned by his son Manfred shortly after his father's death in 1250. It is now in the Vatican Library in Rome. The artist's representations of different birds is so exact that researchers in Finland, in 2018, were able to identify one as a Sulphur-crested cockatoo: a bird native to Australia and New Guinea.

Rabbits, originally native to Spain and North Africa, were also newcomers in northern Europe, prized for their meat and pelts; but they had an unexpectedly devastating effect on native plants and quickly became invasive pests.

Herons, native to northern Europe, were now aggressively cultivated and bred to stock heronries, which meant that many low-lying arable lands were removed from peasant control and artificially flooded to provide the proper habitat and sources of food—such as carp, which were imported from southeastern Europe and Anatolia. Herons, in turn, fed the new aristocratic mania for hunting with birds of prey: these large, graceful birds would be forced to fly from their nests while expensively trained hawks, falcons, and peregrines were loosed to catch and kill them. Emperor Frederick II, having grown up in Sicily at the heart of the multicultural Mediterranean, drew on Arabic sources for his important treatise on falconry. He also maintained a menagerie of exotic animals. For him, as for his peers, demonstrating control over the environment became a new source of aristocratic identity.

The Culture of the Court

Closely linked to this new aristocratic identity and the ideology of chivalry was an emphasis on *courtoisie* ("courtliness"), the refined behavior appropriate to a court. This stemmed in part from practical necessity: those great lords who could support a knightly retinue had households full of energetic, lusty young men whose appetites had to be controlled. Hence, the emerging code of chivalry encouraged its adherents to view noblewomen as objects of veneration who could be wooed and won only by polished manners, poetry, and valiant deeds; in other words, they had to be courted. (Non-noblewomen, though, were fair game and could be taken by force if they did not yield willingly to the desires of a knight.)

Whole new genres of poetry, song, and storytelling emerged in the twelfth century to celebrate the allied cultures of chivalry and courtliness. These genres stand in marked contrast to the older entertainments of Europe's warrior class, the heroic epics that are often the earliest literary artifacts of various vernacular languages: the Anglo-Saxon *Beowulf*, the French *Song of Roland*, the Norse sagas, the German *Song of the Nibelungs*, and the Spanish *Poem of the Cid*. These epics portray a virile, violent society where gore flows freely and skulls are cleaved; manly valor, honor, and loyalty are the major themes. If women are mentioned, it is usually as prizes to be won in battle.

The courtly entertainments introduced in the twelfth century were of very different style, subject, and authorship.

Many of them were addressed to, and commissioned by, women. In some cases, they were even composed by women or were composed in close collaboration with a female patron. An example of the former is the collections of *lais* (versified stories) of Marie de France, who was active during the reigns of Henry II and Eleanor of Aquitaine, and who may have been an abbess as well as a member of the Anglo-Norman aristocracy. An example of the latter is one of the Arthurian tales composed by Marie's contemporary, Chrétien de Troyes (*KRAY-tyan duh TWAH*; fl. 1165–1190), who spent some time working under the patronage of Eleanor's daughter (by her first husband, Louis VII), Marie of Champagne.

Romances were engaging tales of love and adventure, often focusing on the exploits of King Arthur and his knights or some other heroic figure of the past, such as Alexander the Great. But they were also attuned to the interests and concerns of women: threats to women's independence, enforced or unhappy marriages, disputed inheritances, fashion, and fantasies of power. The heroine of one anonymous romance is a woman who dresses as a knight and travels the world performing valiant deeds. Other heroines accompany their husbands on crusades or quests, defend their castles against attack, or have supernatural powers. Following in Chrétien's footsteps, the German poets Wolfram von Eschenbach and Gottfried von Strassburg vied to produce romances that retained the scope and complexity of heroic epics while featuring women in strong, central roles. Both Wolfram's *Parzival*, the story of the search for the Holy Grail, and Gottfried's *Tristan*, which retold the Celtic story of the adulterous love between Tristan and Isolde, inspired the operatic reconceptions of Richard Wagner (1813–1883).

The poetic tradition initiated by the southern French troubadours and the northern French trouvères (terms deriving from the verbs *trobar/trouver*, "to discover, to invent") also contributed to the culture of chivalry and inspired the work of German *Minnesänger* ("love singers"). Much troubadour poetry displays sensitivity to feminine beauty and the natural world, and pays eloquent tribute to the political and sexual powers of women. Take, for example, a lyric of Bernart de Ventadorn (c. 1135–1195), one of Eleanor's protégés:

> When leaves and grass are lush with renewed
> growth
> The beauty of my lady blossoms forth . . .
> I am her slave, her vassal, she my lord;
> I pay her homage, hope to have a word
> Of kindness, or of love, exchanged for mine
> But she is cruel: she will not make a sign.

Other troubadour songs celebrate old-fashioned warlike virtues, as in the verses of Bernart's contemporary, Bertran de Born (c. 1140–1214), a friend of Eleanor's son, Richard the Lionheart:

> It pleases me to hear the mirth and song
> Of birds, filling the wood the whole day long.
> But more it pleases me to see the fields
> All planted thick with tents, to see the shields
> And swords of my companions ranged for war,
> To hear the screams, to see the blood and gore.

To what extent do the entertainments of the court reflect the reality of noblewomen's status? Certainly, there were women throughout this period who wielded tremendous power, particularly in Scandinavia and parts of southern Europe, where women could inherit property, rule in their own right, and were treated as lords in fact and in name (as in Bernart's song). Queen Urraca ruled the combined kingdom of León-Castile from 1109 until 1126. Ermengarde of Narbonne (c. 1127–1197) ruled her strategically placed county from early adolescence to the time of her death. Eleanor remained sole ruler of Aquitaine throughout her long life and played a crucial role in the government of England at various times. The strong-willed Blanche of Castile (1188–1252), Eleanor's granddaughter, ruled France during the minority of her son Louis IX, and again when he went on a crusade.

Queens are not, of course, typical, but their activities during this period reflect some of the opportunities open to other well-born women—and the freedoms that set most European women apart from their counterparts in the Byzantine and Muslim worlds. A striking symbol of this is the figure of the queen in the game of chess. In the Muslim courts where the game originated, the equivalent of the queen was a male figure, the king's chief minister, who could move only diagonally and one square at a time. In twelfth-century Europe, however, this piece became the queen: the only figure powerful enough to move all over the board.

Urban Opportunities and Inequalities

In 1174, a cleric named William FitzStephen wrote a biography of his late employer, Thomas Becket, who had recently been canonized. In it, William went out of his way to extol the urban culture of London that had produced this saintly man and other "men of superior quality," as well as all the splendid sights and pastimes to be had there: feasting, churchgoing, ice skating, bear baiting, plays, sports—and,

Analyzing Primary Sources

Illicit Love and the Code of Chivalry

Little is known about Marie de France, the author of a series of popular verse tales that are among the earliest chivalric romances. She may have been a nun or abbess living in the Anglo-Norman realm of Henry II and Eleanor of Aquitaine. The following excerpt is from her Lais, *adapted from stories told in the Franco-Celtic county of Brittany (Abelard's home).*

The Bretons, who lived in Brittany, were fine and noble people. In days gone by these valiant, courtly and noble men composed lays for posterity and thus preserved them from oblivion. . . . One of them, which I have heard recited, should not be forgotten. It concerns Equitan, a most courtly man, lord of Nantes, justiciary and king.

Equitan enjoyed a fine reputation and was greatly loved in his land. He adored pleasure and amorous dalliance: for this reason he upheld the principles of chivalry. Those who lack a full comprehension and understanding of love show no thought for their lives. Such is the nature of love that no one under its sway can retain command over reason. Equitan had a seneschal, a good knight, brave and loyal, who took care of his entire territory, governing it and administering its justice. Never, except in time of war, would the king have forsaken his hunting, his pleasures or his river sports, whatever the need might have been.

As his wedded wife the seneschal had a woman who was to bring great misfortune to the land. She was a lady of fine breeding and extremely beautiful with a noble body and good bearing. Nature had spared no pains when fashioning her: her eyes sparkled, her face and mouth were beautiful and her nose was well set. She had no equal in the kingdom, and the king, having often heard her praised, frequently sent her greetings and gifts. . . . He went hunting in her region on his own and on returning from his sport took lodging for the night in the place where the seneschal dwelt, in the very castle where the lady was to be found. He had ample occasion to speak with her, to express his feelings and display his fine qualities. He found her most courtly and wise, beautiful in body and countenance. . . .

That night he neither slept nor rested, but spent his time reproaching and reprimanding himself. "Alas," he said, "what destiny brought me to this region? Because of this lady I have seen, my heart has been overwhelmed by a pain so great that my whole body trembles. I think I have no option but to love her. Yet, if I did love her, I should be acting wrongly, as she is the seneschal's wife. I ought to keep faith with him and love him, just as I want him to do with me. . . ."

Source: From "Equitan," in *The Lais of Marie de France*, trans. Glyn S. Burgess and Keith Busby (Harmondsworth, UK: 1985), pp. 56–57.

Questions for Analysis

1. Despite the king's initial misgivings, he and the seneschal's wife eventually have an affair and plot to murder her husband, only to be caught in their own trap. Knowing this outcome, how would you interpret Marie's remarks about courtliness and "the code of chivalry"? What are the tenets of this code, according to the king?

2. What social tensions does this story reflect? How might it shed light on historical realities? What moral might contemporary readers draw from it?

---

of course, the pleasures of moneymaking. Towns were crucibles of activity, and as such became cultural as well as economic powerhouses, the launching pads for the careers of ambitious men.

As we noted in Chapter 8, many of the towns that emerged in the eleventh century were governed by associations of citizens who undertook a wide variety of civic responsibilities. But urban governance was likely to fall into the hands of oligarchs, a trend that became increasingly marked during the thirteenth century, when the enormous wealth generated by some forms of commerce led to marked social inequalities, much as in the Greek poleis (Chapter 3). In Italy, some cities even sought to control the resulting violence by turning to an outsider who would rule as an autocrat for a (supposedly) limited term. Other cities adopted the model of Venice and became formal oligarchies, casting off all pretense of democracy. Some cities remained republics in principle, as did Florence, but became increasingly oligarchical in practice. Aristocratic families lived in fortified towers surrounded by houses of their supporters, and their rivalries often produced a violent culture of vendetta and feud.

But even in places where town governance was controlled by a powerful few, there were many meaningful opportunities for collective activity. Urban manufacturing was regulated by professional associations known as guilds or (in some regions) confraternities. Guilds promoted the interests of their members by trying to preserve monopolies and limit competition. To these ends, terms of employment and membership were strictly regulated. If an apprentice or a journeyman worker (from the French *journée*, meaning "day" and, by extension, "day's work") wished to become a master, he had to produce a "masterpiece" to be judged by the masters of the guild. If the market was considered too weak to support additional master craftsmen, even a masterpiece would not secure a craftsman the coveted right to set up his own shop and thus earn enough to marry. Most guilds were closed to Jews and Muslims, and they also restricted the opportunities available to women, who had little influence over the terms and conditions under which they worked.

Guilds and confraternities were therefore instruments of economic control, but they were also important social, political, and cultural institutions. Most combined the functions of religious association, drinking club, and benevolent society, looking after members and their families in hard times, supporting the dependents of members who died, and helping to finance funerals. Guilds also empowered their members in much the same way that unions do today, providing them with political representation and raising their social status. The wealthy town of Arras even had a guild of professional entertainers, the confraternity of *jongleurs*, which became the most powerful organization in the town by 1250.

Varieties of Vernacular Entertainment

Like courts, towns fostered the emerging vernacular languages of Europe, which bound urban communities to the wider region, as well as to local elites, fostering a sense of shared identity. Towns also produced new kinds of vernacular entertainment during the twelfth and thirteenth centuries. Even the genres of Latin poetry, song, and drama produced in this period can be considered "vernacular" because they made use of vernacular elements (such as rhyme, which is not a feature of classical Latin poetry), dealt with current events, and were popular with a wide audience. In one of Heloise's letters to Abelard, she recalls that he was so renowned for the beauty of his love songs that "every street and tavern resounded with my name." It is possible that

some of Abelard's songs were sung in French, but more probable that they used the edgy, colloquial Latin popular among the student singer-songwriters known as "goliards," which means something like "daredevils." Their lyrics celebrated the carefree life of the open road, the pleasures of drinking and dice, the joys of love, and the agonies of poverty.

Perhaps the genre most representative of urban culture is the *fabliau*, a "fable" or short story with a salacious, irreverent, or satirical twist. Fabliaux drew attention to the absurdities of urban life and lampooned the different types of people striving to reinvent themselves in the permissive world of the town: the oafish peasant, the effete aristocrat, the corrupt priest, the sex-starved housewife, the wily student, the greedy merchant, and the con man. Gender-bending and reversals of fortune are also common themes. In one fabliau, a young noble woman is forced by her impoverished father to marry a buffoonish shopkeeper who thereby gains knighthood; to shame him, she dresses herself as a knight and beats her husband in a jousting match. In another, a priest tricks a poor peasant out of his cow by promising that God will reward him by doubling his "investment" in the work of the Church; when the cow breaks out of the priest's pasture and runs for home, bringing the priest's cow, too, the peasant is delighted by the fulfillment of the promised miracle.

The Medieval Cathedral

The cathedrals constructed in Europe's major cities during this period exemplify the ways in which the cultural communities of the court, the schools, and the town came together. For although any cathedral-building campaign would have been spearheaded by a bishop looking to glorify his episcopal see, it could not be completed without the support of the nobility, the resources of the wealthy, the learning of trained theologians, and the talents of urban craftsmen. And cathedrals were not merely edifices: they were theaters for the performance of liturgy, music, drama, and preaching.

Cathedrals were not, in themselves, new: the seat of a bishop had long been known as his *cathedra*, his throne, and the church that housed it was the principal church of the diocese. But the size, splendor, and importance of cathedrals increased exponentially in the twelfth and thirteenth centuries, alongside the growing power of the Church, the population of cities, and the wealth and knowledge necessary for their construction. Indeed, the cathedrals of this period are readily distinguishable from their predecessors by their architectural style, which came to be called "Gothic," whereas the style of earlier buildings is known as "Romanesque."

ROMANESQUE AND GOTHIC. Some distinguishing features of the Romanesque and Gothic styles are shown in these two churches, both dedicated to the Virgin Mary and built within a century of one another. On the left is the west front of the Church of Notre-Dame-la-Grande in Poitiers, the ancestral domain of Eleanor of Aquitaine. Constructed between 1135 and 1145, it featured rounded arches, strong stone walls, massive supporting pillars, and small windows. On the right is the cathedral of Notre-Dame at Reims in Champagne, built between 1220 and 1299. Here, the emphasis on stolid horizontal registers is replaced by soaring vertical lines. The gabled portals, pointed arches, and bristling pinnacles all accentuate the height of this structure, while the multitude of stained-glass windows—chiefly the enormous rose window—flood the vast interior with colored light.

As the term suggests, Romanesque buildings use the basic elements of public architecture under the Roman Empire: the rounded arch, massive stone walls, and sturdy supporting columns. These features convey regularity and stability, and they also made churches places of refuge that could be fortified and defended in troubled times. By contrast, the structural elements of Gothic architecture are the pointed arch, groined and ribbed vaulting, and the flying buttress, an external support that strengthened the much thinner stone walls and enormous stained-glass windows, whose light illuminated elaborate decorative programs that made the cathedral a microcosm of the medieval world and an encyclopedia of medieval knowledge.

These new Gothic cathedrals were not buildings that could be defended in wartime and, it was thought, would never have to be. They were manifestations of urban pride, expressions of practical and intellectual genius, and symbols of a triumphant and confident Church. Their builders would have been dismayed to learn that the modern term *gothic* was actually intended to be derogatory, the name for art forms that Renaissance artists—who favored Roman models—considered barbaric (see Chapter 12). They would have been still more shocked to learn that cathedrals were among the first monuments targeted for destruction during the Reformation, the revolutions of the eighteenth and nineteenth centuries, and the wars of the twentieth. One of the prime examples of Gothic architecture, the cathedral dedicated to the Virgin Mary at Reims (shown above), was largely destroyed during World War I; what visitors see today is a reconstruction.

CONCLUSION

A century ago, the American historian Charles Homer Haskins described the intellectual, religious, and cultural changes of this era as the "Renaissance of the twelfth century" and the beginning of Europe's enduring cultural prestige. A generation later, his student Joseph Strayer located the "medieval origins of the modern state" in this same period and, with them, modern ideas of national sovereignty and identity. In recent decades, the British historians R. I. Moore and Robert Bartlett have also argued that this era marks the beginning of the modern world—but not in positive ways. Moore sees the growth of strong institutions such as the Church and the state as leading to the "formation of a persecuting society," in which governmental bureaucracies are used to identify, control, and punish groups of people deemed threatening to those in power through a never-ending "war on heresy." Bartlett views this era as the key phase in a brutal process of "conquest and colonization" visible in the eastern expansion of the Holy Roman Empire, the Norman conquest of England, the growth of papal power, the Crusades, and other movements.

Common to all of these paradigms is a recognition that the expansion of European power and influence that began around the year 1000 continued into the twelfth century and consolidated in the thirteenth. By 1250, Europe had taken on the geographic, political, linguistic, and cultural characteristics that continue to characterize it today.

After You Read This Chapter

 Go to **INQUIZITIVE** to see what you've learned—and learn what you've missed—with personalized feedback along the way.

REVIEWING THE OBJECTIVES

- The emerging monarchies of Europe shared certain features but differed from each other in significant ways. What were the major similarities and differences of kingship in England, France, and Iberia?
- How did the meaning and purposes of crusading change in the twelfth and thirteenth centuries?
- The growth of papal power made religion an important part of Christians' daily life in unprecedented ways, but how did it at the same time limit lay spirituality and the rights of non-Christians?
- Scholasticism was the method of teaching and learning fostered by medieval schools, but it was also a method of debating and resolving problems. How did scholasticism assist in the reconciliation of classical and Christian thought?
- Why did the meaning of chivalry change in the twelfth century? What new literary genres and art forms were fostered by courts, universities, and towns?

Whether or not a direct line runs between the developments of this period and the world in which we live, many European nations look to these centuries for their origins and for the monuments of their cultural heritage. Magna Carta is still cited as a foundational document of English law and English constitutional monarchy. The territories united under the rule of the French kings still form the nation of France. The doctrines crystallized in medieval canon law and scholastic theology have become the core doctrines of the modern Roman Catholic Church, and devotion to the Virgin Mary is still central to the piety of millions. The religious orders that emerged to educate and curb a burgeoning medieval population continue their ministries. The daughter houses of medieval monastic orders continue to proliferate in lands unknown to medieval Europeans: Japan, Australia, New Zealand, and the Americas. Students still pursue the degrees first granted in medieval universities, and those who earn them wear the caps and gowns of medieval scholars. Meanwhile, poets aspire to the eloquence of troubadours, singers record the music of Hildegard, and Hollywood films are based on chivalric romances and the tragic love of Abelard and Heloise. It is difficult to tell where the Middle Ages end and the modern world begins.

PEOPLE, IDEAS, AND EVENTS IN CONTEXT

- What was at stake in the clash between **HENRY II** of England and **THOMAS BECKET**?

- What was **MAGNA CARTA**? Why was it formulated? How did **PHILIP AUGUSTUS** consolidate royal authority in France? Why were the German emperors unable to do so?

- Why were the **CRUSADER STATES** short lived and fragile? How did the **RECONQUISTA** continue the Crusades?

- What were the main goals of **INNOCENT III**? How did the **FRANCISCANS** and the **DOMINICANS** advance his agenda?

- How do the **CULT OF THE BLESSED VIRGIN** and the careers of **HILDEGARD OF BINGEN** and **HELOISE** exemplify the ideals and realities of women's roles in the Church?

- What is **SCHOLASTICISM**? How did **THOMAS AQUINUS** respond to the influence of Classical and Muslim philosophies?

- Why were **PETER ABELARD**'s teachings condemned by the Church? In what sense can he be considered the founder of the **UNIVERSITY OF PARIS**?

- How did noblewomen such as **ELEANOR OF AQUITAINE** contribute to the emergence of a new vernacular culture? What types of entertainment were characteristic of medieval cities?

THINKING ABOUT CONNECTIONS

- The growth of towns, monarchies, and the Church increased the degree of control that those in power could exercise; yet this growth also increased access to education and new forms of social mobility. Is this a paradox, or are these two phenomena related?

- The U.S. Constitution is based on the legal principles and institutions that emerged in medieval England, but it also drew on Roman models. Which do you consider to be more influential, and why?

- Some historians have argued that the extent and methods of persecution discernible in the Middle Ages are unprecedented in the history of Western civilizations. How would you support or refute this thesis? For example, does the persecution of Jews in medieval Europe differ from their treatment under the neo-Assyrians and Chaldeans, or under the Roman Empire? Why or why not?

Gota aquesta ptida tenen gens q son
en boisate q noli neu hon sino los vils
euan entendes e san caualeades al
camels eay bosties qui ben nom temp
e daquel aur fan les bones targues

todia

AUGIA

fudam

ciutat de mely

Before You Read This Chapter

STORY LINES

■ The Mongol Empire widened channels of communication, commerce, and cultural exchange between Europe and the Far East. At the same time, Europeans were extending their reach into the Atlantic Ocean.

■ Western civilizations' integration with this wider medieval world led to new ways of mapping, measuring, and describing that world.

■ Despite these broadening horizons, most Europeans' lives were bounded by their communities and focused on the parish church.

■ Meanwhile, the growing strength of the kings of France and England drew them into territorial disputes that led to the Hundred Years' War.

■ As global climate change affected the ecosystems of Europe and caused years of famine, the integrated networks of the medieval world facilitated the rapid transmission of the Black Death.

CHRONOLOGY

1206–1260	Rapid expansion of the Mongol Empire under Genghis Khan and his heirs
1240	The territory of Rus' is dominated by the Mongols
	Mongol Khanate of the Golden Horde established
1260–1294	Reign of Kublai Khan, Great Khan, and emperor of China
1271–1295	Travels of Marco Polo
1309	"Babylonian Captivity" of the papacy in Avignon begins
1315–1322	The Great Famine in Europe
1320	The Declaration of Arbroath proclaims Scotland's independence from England
1326–1354	The travels of Ibn Battuta
1337	Beginning of the Hundred Years' War
1347–1353	Spread of the Black Death
1352	Circulation of Mandeville's *Book of Marvels*

The Medieval World, 1250–1350

CORE OBJECTIVES

- **DESCRIBE** the effects of the Mongol conquests.

- **IDENTIFY** the key characteristics of the medieval world system and the responses to it.

- **UNDERSTAND** the reasons for the papacy's loss of prestige and the rise of strong secular monarchs.

- **DEFINE** the concept of sovereignty and its importance.

- **EXPLAIN** the rapid spread of the Black Death in this historical context.

When Christopher Columbus set out to find a new trade route to the East, he carried with him two influential travel narratives written centuries before his voyage. One was *The Book of Marvels*, composed around 1350 and attributed to John de Mandeville, an English adventurer (writing in French) who claimed to have reached the far horizons of the globe. The other was Marco Polo's *Description of the World*, an account of that Venetian merchant's journey through the vast Eurasian realm of the Mongol Empire to the court of the Great Khan in China. He had dictated it to an author of popular romances around 1298, when both men (Marco Polo and his ghostwriter) were in prison—coincidentally, in Columbus's own city of Genoa. Both books were the product of an extraordinary era of unprecedented interactions among the peoples of Europe, Asia, and the interconnected Mediterranean world. And both became highly influential, inspiring generations of mercantile adventurers, ambitious pilgrims, and armchair travelers. Eventually, they would fuel the imaginations of those future mariners who launched a further age of discovery (see Chapter 12).

In many ways, these narratives were as fantastical as they were factual, making them problematic sources for historians. But they are representative of an era that seemed wide open to every sort of influence. This was a time when ease of communication and commercial exchange made Western civilizations part of an interlocking network that had the potential to span the globe. Although this network would prove fragile in the face of a large-scale demographic crisis, the Black Death, it created a lasting impression of infinite possibilities. Indeed, it was only *because* of this network's connective channels that the Black Death wreaked such devastation in the years around 1350. Looking back, we can see the century leading up to this near-worldwide crisis as the beginning of a new global age.

Europeans' integration with this widening world not only put them into contact with unfamiliar cultures and commodities but it also opened up new ways of looking at the world they already knew. Novel artistic and intellectual responses are discernible in this era, as are a host of new inventions and technologies. At the same time, involvement in this wider world placed new pressures on long-term developments within Europe, notably the growing tensions among large territorial monarchies, and between these secular powers and the authority of the papacy. By the early fourteenth century, the papal court was literally held hostage by the king of France. A few decades later, the king of England openly declared his own claim to the French throne. The ensuing struggles for sovereignty would have a profound impact on the balance of power in Europe, and further complicate Europeans' relationships with one another and with their far-flung neighbors.

THE MONGOL EMPIRE AND THE REORIENTATION OF THE WEST

In our long-term survey of Western civilizations, we have frequently noted the existence of strong links between the Mediterranean world and the Far East. Trade along the network of trails known as the Silk Road can be traced far back into antiquity, and we have seen that such overland networks were extended by Europe's waterways and by the sea. But it was not until the late thirteenth century that Europeans were able to establish direct connections with India, China, and the so-called Spice Islands of the Indonesian archipelago. For Europeans, these connections would prove profoundly important, as much for their impact on the European imagination as for their economic significance. For the peoples of Asia, however, the more frequent

appearance of Europeans was less consequential than the events that made these journeys possible: the rise of a new empire that encompassed the entire continent.

The Expansion of the Mongol Empire

The Mongols were among many nomadic peoples inhabiting the vast steppes of central Asia. Although closely connected with the Turkish populations with whom they frequently intermarried, the Mongols spoke their own distinctive language and had their own homeland, located to the north of the Gobi Desert in what is now known as Mongolia. Essentially, the Mongols were herdsmen whose daily lives and wealth depended on the sheep that provided shelter (sheepskin tents), woolen clothing, milk, and meat; but they were also highly accomplished horsemen and raiders. Indeed, it was to curtail their raiding ventures that the Chinese had fortified their Great Wall many centuries before. Primarily, though, China defended itself from the Mongols by attempting to ensure that the Mongols remained internally divided, with their energies turned against each other.

In the late twelfth century, however, a Mongol chief named Temujin (c. 1162–1227) began to unite the various tribes under his rule. He did so by incorporating the warriors of each defeated tribe into his own army, gradually building up a large and terrifyingly effective military force. In 1206, his supremacy over all these tribes was reflected in his new title: **Genghis Khan** (from the Mongol words meaning "universal ruler"). This new name also revealed his wider ambitions and, in 1209, Genghis Khan began to direct his enormous army against the Mongols' neighbors.

Taking advantage of the fact that China was then divided into three warring states, Genghis Khan launched an attack on the Chin Empire of the north and managed to penetrate deep into its interior by 1211. These initial attacks were probably looting expeditions rather than deliberate attempts at conquest, but their aims were soon sharpened under Genghis Khan's successors. Shortly after his death in 1227, a full-scale invasion of both northern and western China was under way. In 1234, these regions also fell to the Mongols. By 1279, one of Genghis Khan's numerous grandsons, Kublai Khan, would complete the conquest by adding southern China to the empire.

For the first time in centuries, China was reunited, although under Mongol rule. It was also connected to western and central Asia in ways unprecedented in its long history, because Genghis Khan had brought crucial commercial cities and the Silk Road trading posts (Tashkent, Samarkand, and Bukhara) into his empire. Building on these achievements, one of his sons, Ögedei (*EHRG-uh-day*),

THE STATES OF THE MONGOL EMPIRE. Like Alexander's, Genghis Khan's empire was swiftly assembled and encompassed vast portions of Europe and Asia. ▪ *How many different Mongol khanates were there after 1260, when Kublai Khan came to power? Were these domains mapped onto older divisions within Western civilizations?* ▪ *How might the Mongol occupation of the Muslim world have aided the expansion of European trade?* ▪ *At the same time, why would it have complicated the efforts of crusader armies in the Holy Land?*

laid plans for an even farther-reaching expansion of Mongol influence. Between 1237 and 1240, the Mongols under his command conquered the Rus' capital at Kiev and then launched a two-pronged assault directed at the rich lands of the European frontier. The smaller of the two Mongol armies swept through Poland toward Germany; the larger army went southwest toward Hungary. In April 1241, the smaller Mongol force met a hastily assembled army of Germans and Poles at the battle of Legnica in southern Poland, where the Mongols were driven back at the cost of many lives on both sides. Two days later, the larger Mongol army annihilated the Hungarian army at the river Sajo. It could

have moved even deeper into Europe after this important victory, but it withdrew when Ögedei Khan died in December of that year.

Muscovy and the Mongol Khanate

As we have seen in previous chapters, the capital of Rus' at Kiev had fostered crucial diplomatic and trading relations with both western Europe and Byzantium, as well as with the Islamic Caliphate at Baghdad. But that dynamic

THE BATTLE OF LEGNICA, 1241. This image from a fourteenth-century chronicle shows heavily armored knights from Poland and Germany (on the right) confronting the swift-moving mounted archers of the Mongol cavalry (on the left). Mongol warriors often had the advantage over Europeans because their smaller, faster horses carried lighter loads and they could shoot down their opponents at long range. ▪ *Which army appears to be gaining the upper hand here?*

changed with the arrival of the Mongols, who shifted the locus of power from Kiev to their own settlement on the lower Volga River. From there, they extended their dominion over a vast terrain, stretching from the Black Sea to central Asia. It became known as the Khanate of the Golden Horde, a name that captures the striking impression made by the Mongol tents, which literally shone with wealth because many were hung with cloth of gold. (The word

horde derives from the Mongol word meaning "encampment" and the related Turkish word *ordu*, "army.")

Initially, the Mongols ruled Rus' directly, installing their own administrative officials and requiring local princes to show their obedience to the Great Khan by traveling in person to the Mongol court in China. But after Kublai Khan's death in 1294, the Mongols began to tolerate the existence of several semi-independent principalities from which they demanded regular tribute. Kiev never recovered its dominant position, but one of these principalities, the duchy of Moscow, gained new political and economic prominence due to its strategic geographical location. Moscow became the tribute-collecting center for the Mongol Khanate, and so was supplied with resources to defend itself against attack. Its dukes were even encouraged to extend their lordship to neighboring territories in the region in order to increase its security. Eventually, the Muscovite dukes came to control the khanate's tax-collecting mechanisms. As a reflection of these extended powers, Duke Ivan I (r. 1325–1340) gained the title Grand Prince of Rus'. When the Mongol Empire began to disintegrate, the Muscovites were therefore in a strong position to supplant their former overlords.

A MONGOL ROBE IN CLOTH OF GOLD. The majestic term *Khanate of the Golden Horde* captures both the power and the splendor of the Mongol warriors who conquered Rus' and many other lands. The robe depicted here dates from the late thirteenth or early fourteenth century and was made from cloth of gold: silk woven with gold (and sometimes silver) thread, a precious but surprisingly durable material that was also used for banners and even tents. A robe similar to this one was sold at auction in 2011 for nearly a quarter of a million dollars.

The Making of the Mongol Ilkhanate

As Ögedei Khan moved into the lands of Rus' and eastern Europe, Mongol armies were also sent to subdue the vast territory that had been encompassed by the former Persian Empire, then those by the empires of Alexander and Rome. Indeed, the strongest state in this region was known as the sultanate of Rûm (the Arabic word for "Rome"). This Sunni Muslim sultanate had been founded by the Seljuk Turks in 1077, just prior to the launching of the First Crusade, and consisted of Anatolian provinces formerly belonging to the eastern Roman Empire. It had successfully withstood waves of European crusading ventures while capitalizing on the further misfortunes of Byzantium, taking over several key ports on the Mediterranean and the Black Sea as well as cultivating a flourishing overland trade.

But in 1243, the Seljuks of Rûm were forced to surrender to the Mongols, who had already succeeded in occupying what is now Iraq, Iran, portions of Pakistan and Afghanistan, and the Christian kingdoms of Georgia and Armenia. Thereafter, the Mongols easily found their way into regions weakened by centuries of Muslim infighting and Christian crusading movements. Byzantium, as we noted in Chapter 9, had been fatally weakened by the Fourth Crusade.

Constantinople was now controlled by the Venetians, and Byzantine successor states centered on Nicaea (in Anatolia) and Epirus (in northern Greece) were hanging on by their fingertips. The capitulation of Rûm left remaining Byzantine possessions in Anatolia without a buffer, and most of these were absorbed by the Mongols.

In 1261, emperor Michael VIII Paleologus (r. 1259–1282) managed to regain control of Constantinople and its immediate hinterland, but the depleted empire he ruled was ringed by hostile neighbors. The crusader principality of Antioch, which had been founded in 1098, finally succumbed to the Mongols in 1268. The Mongols themselves were halted in their drive toward Palestine only by the Mamluk Sultanate of Egypt, established in 1250 and ruled by a powerful military caste of non-Arab Muslims. The name of this dynasty reflects the fact that its founders were originally Turkic slaves (in Arabic, *mamlūk* means "an enslaved person").

THE MONGOL RULER OF MUSLIM PERSIA, HIS CHRISTIAN QUEEN, AND HIS JEWISH HISTORIAN. Hulagu Khan (1217–1265) was a grandson of Genghis and a brother of Kublai. He consolidated Persia and its neighboring regions into the Ilkhanate. This image shows him with his wife, Dokuz Khatun, who was a Turkic princess and a Christian. It comes from the *Compendium of Chronicles* by Rashid al-Din (1247–1318), a Jewish convert to Islam, whose work exemplifies the pluralistic culture encouraged by Mongol rule: written in Persian and often translated into Arabic, it embeds the achievements of the Mongol ruler within the long history of Islam. ▪ *Why would Rashid al-Din have wanted to place the new Mongol dynasty in this historical context?*

All of these disparate territories came to be called the Ilkhanate, the "subordinate khanate," meaning that its Mongol rulers paid deference to the Great Khan. The first Ilkhan was Hulagu, a brother of China's Kublai Khan. His descendants would rule this realm for another eighty years, eventually converting to Islam but remaining hostile toward the Mamluk Muslims, who were their chief rivals.

The Pax Mongolica and Its Price

Although the Mongols' expansion of power into Europe had been checked, their combined conquests made them masters of lands that stretched from the Black Sea to the Pacific Ocean: one-fifth of the earth's surface, the largest land empire in history. Yet no single Mongol ruler's power was absolute within this domain. Kublai Khan (1260–1294), who took the additional title *khagan* (or "Great Khan"), never claimed to rule all

the Mongol khanates directly. In his own domain of China and Mongolia, his power was highly centralized and built on the intricate (and ancient) imperial bureaucracy of China; but elsewhere, Mongol governance was directed at securing a steady tribute payment from subject peoples, which meant that local rulers could retain much of their power.

This distribution of authority made Mongol rule flexible and adaptable to local conditions, and in this it resembled the Persian Empire (Chapter 3) and also could be regarded as building on Hellenistic and Roman examples. But if their empire resembled those of antiquity in some respects, the Mongol khans differed from most contemporary European rulers in that they were highly tolerant of all religious beliefs. This was an advantage in governing peoples who observed an array of Buddhist, Christian, and Muslim practices, not to mention Hindus, Jews, and the many itinerant groups and individuals whose languages and beliefs reflected a melding of many cultures.

THE MEDIEVAL WORLD SYSTEM, c. 1300. At the turn of the fourteenth century, Western civilizations were more closely connected to each other and to the rest of the world than ever before: waterways and overland routes stretched from Greenland to the Pacific coast of Southeast Asia and down to West Africa. The interlocking regions and contact zones of this system are represented on this map. ▪ *How did Europe's relationship with its neighbors change as a result of its integration into this wider world?* ▪ *How were seemingly marginal territories (such as Rus' or Hungary, Scotland, or Norway) central to one or more interlocking components of this system?*

This acceptance of cultural and religious difference, alongside the Mongols' encouragement of trade and love of rich things, created ideal conditions for some merchants and artists. Hence, the term **Pax Mongolica** ("Mongol Peace") is often used to describe the century from 1250 to 1350, a period in many ways analogous to the one fostered by the Roman Empire at its greatest extent (Chapter 5). No such term should be taken at face value, however, because this peace was bought at a great price. Indeed, the artists whose varied talents created the gorgeous textiles, utensils, and illuminated books prized by the Mongols were not all willing participants in a peaceful process. Many were captives or slaves subject to ruthless relocation. The Mongols would often transfer entire families and communities of craftsmen from one part of the empire to another, directly and indirectly encouraging a fantastic blend of artistic techniques, materials, and motifs. The result was an intensive period of cultural exchange that might combine Chinese, Persian, Venetian, and Hungarian influences (among many others) in a single work of art. These objects encapsulate the many legacies of the Mongols' empire.

The Mongol Peace was also achieved at the expense of many flourishing Muslim cities that were devastated or crippled during the bloody process of Mongol expansion—cities that had preserved the heritage of even older civilizations. The city of Heràt, situated in one of Afghanistan's few fertile valleys and described by the Persian poet Rumi as the "pearl in the oyster," was entirely destroyed by Genghis Khan in 1221 and did not fully recover for centuries. Baghdad, the splendid capital of the Abbasid Caliphate and a haven for artists and intellectuals since the eighth century (Chapter 8), was savagely besieged and sacked by the Mongols in 1258. Amid many other atrocities, the capture of the city resulted in the destruction of the House of Wisdom, the library and research center where Muslim scientists, philosophers, and translators preserved classical knowledge and advanced cutting-edge scholarship in such fields as mathematics, engineering, and medicine.

Baghdad's destruction is held to mark the end of Islam's golden age, since the establishment of the Mongol Ilkhanate in Persia eradicated a continuous zone of Muslim influence that had blended cultures stretching from southern Spain and North Africa to India.

Bridging East and West

To facilitate the movement of people and goods within their empire, the Mongols began to control the caravan routes that led from the Mediterranean and the Black Sea through central Asia and into China, policing bandits and making conditions safer for travelers. They also encouraged and streamlined trade by funneling many exchanges through the Persian city of Tabriz, on which both land and sea routes from China converged. These measures accelerated and intensified the possible contacts between the Far East and the West. Prior to Mongol control, such commercial networks had been inaccessible to most European merchants. The Silk Road was not so much a highway as a tangle of trails and trading posts, with few outsiders who understood its workings. Now travelers at both ends of the route found their way smoothed.

Among the first travelers from the West were Franciscan missionaries whose journeys were bankrolled by European rulers. In 1253, the friar William of Rubruck was sent by King Louis IX of France as his ambassador to the Mongol court, with letters of introduction and instructions to make a full report of his findings. Merchants quickly followed. The most famous are three Venetians: the brothers Niccolò and Matteo Polo, and Niccolò's son, Marco (1254–1324). **Marco Polo**'s account of his travels (which began when he was seventeen) includes a report of his twenty-year sojourn in the service of

VENETIAN AMBASSADORS TO THE GREAT KHAN. Around 1270, the Venetian merchant brothers Niccolò and Matteo Polo returned to Europe after their first prolonged journey through the empire of the Great Khan, bearing with them an official letter to the Roman pope. This image, from a manuscript of Marco Polo's *Description of the World*, shows his father and uncle at the moment of their arrival in the Great Khan's court, to which they have seemingly brought a Christian cross and a Bible. ▪ *Knowing what you've learned about the Mongols and the medieval world, do you think it is plausible that the Polo brothers would have carried these items with them?*

Competing Viewpoints

Two Travel Accounts

Two of the books that influenced Christopher Columbus and his contemporaries were travel narratives describing the exotic worlds that lay beyond Europe—worlds that may or may not have existed as they are described. The first excerpt below is taken from the account dictated by Marco Polo of Venice in 1298. The young Marco had traveled overland from Constantinople to the court of Kublai Khan in the early 1270s, together with his father and uncle. He became a gifted linguist and remained at the Mongol court until the early 1290s, when he returned to Europe after a journey through Southeast Asia and Indonesia, and across the Indian Ocean. The second excerpt is from the Book of Marvels, attributed to John de Mandeville. This is an almost entirely fictional account of wonders that also became a source for European ideas about Southeast Asia. This particular passage concerns a legendary Christian figure named Prester ("Priest") John, who is alleged to have traveled to the East and become a great ruler.

Marco Polo's Description of Java

Now know that when one leaves Champa[1] and went between south and southeast 1,500 miles, then one comes up to a very large island called Java which, according to what good sailors say who know it well, is the largest island in the world, for it is more than three thousand miles around. It has a great king; they are idolators and pay tribute to no man in the world. This island is one of very great wealth: they have pepper, nutmeg, spikenard, galangal, cubeb, cloves, and all the expensive spices you can find in the world. To this island come great numbers of ships and merchants who buy many commodities and make great profit and great gain there. On this island, there is such great treasure that no man in the world could recount or describe it. I tell you the Great Khan could never have it on account of the long and fearsome way in sailing there. Merchants from Zaytun[2] and Mangi[3] have already extracted very great treasure from this island, and continue to do so today.

[1] A collective name for the kingdoms of central Vietnam.
[2] The major port city of Quanzhou on southeastern coast of China.
[3] The kingdom of the Southern Song in China, south of the Huai River. The word *mangi* (or *manzi*) means "barbarians," which is what the northern Chinese called the people of the southern realm. When Marco Polo was in the service of the Great Khan, the Mongol conquest of the kingdom was still ongoing. It was completed in 1279.

Source: Marco Polo, *Here the Great Island of Java is Described*, trans. Sharon Kinoshita (Indianapolis/Cambridge, 2016), p. 149.

John de Mandeville's Description of Prester John

This emperor Prester John has great lands and has many noble cities and good towns in his realm and many great, large islands. For all the country of India is separated into islands by the great floods that come from Paradise, that divide the land into many parts. And also in the sea he has many islands. . . .

Kublai Khan, and the story of his journey home through the Spice Islands, India, and Persia. As we noted on page 325, this book had an enormous effect on the European imagination; Christopher Columbus's copy still survives.

Even more impressive in scope than Marco's travels are those of the Muslim adventurer Ibn Battuta (1304–1368), who left his native Morocco in 1326 to go on the sacred pilgrimage to Mecca—but then kept going. By the time he returned home in 1354, he had been to China and sub-Saharan Africa, as well as to the ends of both the Muslim and Mongolian worlds: a journey of over 75,000 miles.

The window of opportunity that made such journeys possible was relatively narrow, however. By the middle of the fourteenth century, hostilities among and within various components of the Mongol Empire were making travel along the Silk Road perilous. The Mongols of the Ilkhanate, who dominated the ancient trade routes that ran through Persia, came into conflict with merchants from Genoa, who controlled trade

This Prester John has under him many kings and many islands and many varied people of various conditions. And this land is full good and rich, but not so rich as is the land of the Great Khan. For the merchants do not come there so commonly to buy merchandise as they do in the land of the Great Khan, for it is too far to travel to. . . .

[Mandeville then goes on to describe the difficulties of reaching Prester John's lands by sea.]

This emperor Prester John always takes as his wife the daughter of the Great Khan, and the Great Khan in the same way takes to wife the daughter of Prester John. For these two are the greatest lords under the heavens.

In the land of Prester John there are many diverse things, and many precious stones so great and so large that men make them into vessels such as platters, dishes, and cups. And there are many other marvels there that it would be too cumbrous and too long to put into the writing of books. But of the principal islands and of his estate and of his law I shall tell you some part.

This emperor Prester John is Christian and a great part of his country is Christian also, although they do not hold to all the articles of our faith as we do. . . .

And he has under him 72 provinces, and in every province there is a king. And these kings have kings under them, and all are tributaries to Prester John.

And he has in his lordships many great marvels. For in his country is the sea that men call the Gravelly Sea, that is all gravel and sand without any drop of water. And it ebbs and flows in great waves as other seas do, and it is never still. . . . And a three-day journey from that sea there are great mountains out of which flows a great flood that comes out of Paradise. And it is full of precious stones without any drop of water. . . .

He dwells usually in the city of Susa [in Persia]. And there is his principal palace, which is so rich and so noble that no one will believe the report unless he has seen it. And above the chief tower of the palace there are two round pommels of gold and in each of them are two great, large rubies that shine full brightly upon the night. And the principal gates of his palace are of a precious stone that men call sardonyxes [a type of onyx], and the frames and the bars are made of ivory. And the windows of the halls and chambers are of crystal. And the tables upon which men eat, some are made of emeralds, some of amethyst, and some of gold full of precious stones. And the legs that hold up the tables are made of the same precious stones. . . .

Source: *Mandeville's Travels*, ed. M. C. Seymour (Oxford: 1967), pp. 195–99 (language modernized from Middle English by R. C. Stacey).

Questions for Analysis

1. What does Marco Polo want his readers to know about Java, and why? What does this suggest about the interests of these intended readers?

2. What does Mandeville want his readers to know about Prester John and his domains? Why are these details so important?

3. Which of these accounts seems more trustworthy, and why? Even if we cannot accept one or both at face value, what insight do they give us into the expectations of Columbus and the other European adventurers who relied on these accounts?

at the western ends of the Silk Road, especially in the transport depot of Tabriz. Mounting pressures finally forced the Genoese to abandon Tabriz, thereby breaking one of the major links in the commercial chain forged by the Mongol Peace. Then, in 1346, the Mongols of the Golden Horde besieged the Genoese colony at Caffa on the Black Sea. This event simultaneously disrupted trade while becoming a conduit for the Black Death, which passed from the Mongol army to the Genoese defenders, who returned with it to Italy (see pages 355–356).

Over the next few decades, the European economy would struggle to overcome the devastating effects of the massive depopulation caused by the plague, which made recovery from these setbacks slower and harder. In the meantime, in 1368, the last Mongol rulers of China were overthrown, and most Westerners were now denied access to its borders; the remaining Mongol warriors were restricted to cavalry service in the imperial armies of the new Ming dynasty. The conditions that had fostered an integrated trans-Eurasian cultural and commercial network were no longer sustainable. Yet the view of the world that had been fostered by Mongol rule continued to exercise a lasting influence. European memories of the Far East would be preserved and embroidered, and the dream of reestablishing close connections between Europe and China would survive to influence a new round of commercial and imperial expansion in the centuries to come.

THE EXTENSION OF EUROPEAN COMMERCE AND SETTLEMENT

Western civilizations' increased access to the riches of the Far East during the Pax Mongolica ran parallel to a number of ventures that were extending Europeans' presence in the Mediterranean and beyond. These endeavors were both mercantile and colonial, and in many cases resulted in the control of strategic trade routes or islands by representatives of a single adventurous state.

The language of crusading, with which we have become familiar, now came to be applied to these economic and political initiatives, whose often violent methods could be justified on the grounds that they were supporting papally sanctioned Christian causes. To take one prominent example, the strategic goal of the crusades that targeted North Africa in this era was to cut the economic lifelines that supported Muslim settlements in the Holy Land. Yet the only people who stood to gain from this were the merchants who dreamed of controlling the commercial routes that ran through Egypt—those that connected North Africa to the Silk Road as well as the conduits of the sub-Saharan gold trade.

The Quest for African Gold

European commerce in African gold was not new. It had been going on for centuries, facilitated by Muslim traders whose caravans brought a steady supply from the Niger River to the North African ports of Algiers and Tunis. In the early thirteenth century, rival bands of merchants from Catalonia and Genoa had established trading colonies in Tunis to expedite this process, exchanging woolen cloth from northern Europe for both North African grain and sub-Saharan gold.

But the medieval demand for gold accelerated during the late thirteenth and fourteenth centuries and could not be met by these established trading relationships. The luxuries coveted by Europeans were now too costly to be bought solely with bulk goods, which were, in any case, a

MANSA MUSA. Musa I was the ruler of the wealthy West African Empire of Mali. His title, *Mansa*, means both "sultan" and "emperor," capturing the breadth of his power as a conqueror, king, and religious leader. He is depicted prominently in an important cartographic manuscript known as the Catalan Atlas, created in 1375 and attributed to Cresques Abraham, a Jewish artist and "master of maps" who strove to capture the contours of the entire known world. In keeping with Mansa Musa's reputation as the richest man on earth—at that time, and maybe for all time—he wears a crown of real gold leaf and holds up a gold coin. He is also shown enthroned and holding a scepter, just like a European monarch. ■ *How does this image, and the making of such an atlas, reflect the developments we are studying in this chapter?*

cumbersome medium of exchange. Although precious textiles (usually silk) were a form of wealth the Mongols valued, the burgeoning economy of the medieval world demanded a reliable and abundant supply of more portable currency. For a long time, the rich silver mines of Poland and Bohemia had enabled the circulation of coinage in Europe and had furnished the means for rulers in Rus' to pay the tributes due to the Mongols. But silver production dropped markedly during the 1340s, as European engineers reached the limits of their technological capacity to extract ore from ever deeper mines; and this depletion of sources of silver led to a serious cash-flow problem.

Gold was therefore an obvious alternative currency for large transactions, and in the thirteenth century some European rulers began minting gold coins. But Europe itself had few natural gold reserves, and so maintaining and expanding these currencies required new sources of gold. The most obvious source was Africa, especially Mali and Ghana—which was called the "Land of Gold" by Muslim geographers. The sultan and emperor of that region, Mansa Musa (d. 1337) was known as the richest man in the world—and may have been the richest person in history. His sub-Saharan realm was also famed for its salt and ivory; the tusks of African elephants were especially prized by European artists. The statue of the virgin on page 304 is made of African ivory.

Models of Mediterranean Colonization: Catalonia, Genoa, and Venice

The heightened European interest in the African gold trade, which engaged the seafaring merchants of **Genoa** and **Catalonia** in particular, coincided with these merchants' creation of entrepreneurial empires in the western Mediterranean. During the thirteenth century, Catalan adventurers conquered and colonized a series of western Mediterranean islands, including Majorca, Ibiza, Minorca, Sardinia, and Sicily. Except in Sicily, which already had a large and diverse population that included many Christians (Chapter 8), the pattern of Catalan conquest was largely the same on all these islands: expulsion or extermination of the existing population, usually Muslim; the extension of economic concessions to attract new settlers; and a heavy reliance on slave labor to produce foodstuffs and raw materials for export.

These Catalan colonial efforts were mainly carried out by private individuals or companies operating under royal charters; the state did not actively sponsor them. They therefore contrast strongly with the established colonial practices of the Venetian maritime empire, whose strategic ventures were focused mainly on the eastern Mediterranean, where the Venetians dominated the trade in spices and silks. Venetian colonies were administered directly by the city's rulers or by their appointed colonial governors. These colonies included long-settled civilizations such as Greece, Cyprus, and the cities of the Dalmatian coast, meaning that Venetian administration laid just another layer on top of many other economic, cultural, and political structures.

The Genoese, to take yet another case, also had extensive interests in the western Mediterranean, where they traded bulk goods such as cloth, hides, grain, timber, and sugar. They too established trading colonies, but these tended to consist of family networks that were closely integrated with the peoples among whom they lived, whether in North Africa, Spain, or the shores of the Black Sea.

THE CHURCH AT HVALSEY, GREENLAND. Located on the southern tip of Greenland, Hvalsey was originally a farmstead established in the late tenth century by the uncle of Eirik the Red, father of the explorer Leif Eiriksson. The church at Hvalsey, pictured here, was built in the twelfth century and was roofed with turf. It was the site of the last documented event in the history of Norse settlement on the island: a wedding that took place in 1408. By that time, the population had largely died out due to starvation and disease.

From the Mediterranean to the Atlantic

For centuries, European maritime commerce had been divided between this Mediterranean world and a very different northeastern Atlantic world, which encompassed northern France, the Low Countries, the British Isles, and Scandinavia. Starting around 1270, however, Italian merchants began to sail through the Straits of Gibraltar and on up to the wool-producing regions of England and the Low Countries. This was a step toward the extension of Mediterranean patterns of commerce and colonization into the Atlantic Ocean. Another step was the discovery (or possibly the rediscovery) of the Atlantic island chains known as the Canaries and the Azores, which Genoese sailors reached in the fourteenth century.

Efforts to colonize the Canary Islands, and to convert and enslave their inhabitants, began almost immediately. Eventually, the Canaries would become the focus of a new wave of colonial settlement sponsored by the Portuguese, and the base for Portuguese voyages down the west coast of Africa. They would also be the jumping-off point from which Christopher Columbus would sail westward across the Atlantic Ocean in the hope of reaching Asia (see Chapter 12).

There was also a significant European colonial presence in the northern Atlantic, and had been for centuries. Viking settlers had begun to colonize Greenland in the late tenth century, and had established a settlement in a place they called Vinland (the coast of Newfoundland in present-day Canada) around 1000. According to the sagas that tell the story of these explorations, written down in the late twelfth and thirteenth centuries, a band of adventurers led by Leif Eiriksson had intended to set up a permanent colony there. Numerous expeditions resulted in the construction of houses, a fortification, and even attempts to domesticate livestock transported from Scandinavia. Yet North America did not become home to a permanent European population at this time; the sagas report that relations with indigenous peoples were fraught, and there may have been other factors hindering settlement.

However, Norse settlers did build a viable community on Greenland, which eventually formed part of the kingdom of Norway. This was facilitated by the warming of the earth's climate between 800 and 1300—the same phenomenon that partly enabled the agricultural revolution discussed in Chapter 8. For several centuries, these favorable climatic conditions made it possible to sustain some farming activities on the southern coastline of that huge island, supplemented by fishing, hunting, and foraging. But with the gradual cooling of the climate in the fourteenth century, which caused famines even in the rich farmlands of Europe, this fragile ecosystem was gradually eroded and the Greenlanders died out.

WAYS OF KNOWING AND DESCRIBING THE WORLD

The success of European commercial and colonial expansion in this era both drove and depended on significant innovations in measuring and mapping. It also coincided with intellectual, literary, and artistic initiatives that aimed to capture and describe the workings of this wider world, and to imagine its celestial (or infernal) counterparts.

Economic Tools: Balance Sheets, Banks, Charts, and Clocks

The economic boom that resulted from the integration of European and Asian commerce called for the refinement of existing business models and accounting techniques. New forms of partnership and the development of insurance contracts helped to minimize the risks associated with long-distance trading. Double-entry bookkeeping, widely used in Italy by the mid-fourteenth century, gave merchants a much clearer picture of their profits and losses by ensuring

that both credits and debits were clearly laid out in parallel columns, a practice that facilitated the balancing of accounts. The Medici family of Florence established branches of its bank in each of the major cities of Europe and were careful that the failure of one would not bankrupt the entire firm as earlier branch-banking arrangements had done. Banks also experimented with advanced credit techniques borrowed from Muslim and Jewish financiers, allowing their clients to transfer funds without any real money changing hands—and without endangering their capital by carrying it with them. Such transfers were carried out by written receipts, the direct ancestors of the check, money order, and currency transfer.

Other late medieval technologies kept pace in different ways with the demands for increased efficiency and accuracy. Eyeglasses, first invented in the 1280s, were perfected in the fourteenth century, extending the careers of those who made a living by reading, writing, and accounting. The use of the magnetic compass helped ships sail farther away from land, making longer-distance Atlantic voyages possible for the first time. And as more and more mariners began to sail waters less familiar to them, pilots began to make and use special charts that mapped the locations of ports; called *portolani* (**portolan charts**), these charts also took note of prevailing winds, potential routes, good harbors, and known perils.

SCHOLAR WEARING EYEGLASSES. This fresco on the wall of a church in Treviso (northern Italy) was painted between 1351 and 1352. It shows a theologian at his desk, working on a manuscript with the aid of his newfangled spectacles.

PORTOLAN CHART. Accurate mapping was essential to the success of maritime colonial ventures in the thirteenth and fourteenth centuries. The chart shown here is the oldest surviving example of a map used by mariners to navigate between Mediterranean ports: the word *portolan* is the term for such charts. It dates from the end of the thirteenth century, and its shape clearly indicates that it was made from an animal hide. Although parchment was extremely durable, it would slowly have worn away due to prolonged exposure to salt water and other elements—hence the rarity of this early example.

Among the many implements of modern daily life invented in this era, the most familiar are clocks. Mechanical clocks came into use shortly before 1300 and proliferated immediately thereafter. They were too large and expensive for private purchase, but towns vied with each other to install them in prominent public buildings, thus advertising municipal wealth and good governance. Mechanical timekeeping had two profound effects. One was the further stimulation of interest in complex machinery of all sorts, an interest already awakened by the widespread use of mills in the eleventh and twelfth centuries (see Chapter 8).

Another, more significant, outcome was the way that clocks regulated daily life. Until the advent of clocks, time was flexible. Although days had been *theoretically* divided into hours, minutes, and seconds since the time of the Sumerians (Chapter 1), people never had a way of mapping these temporal measurements onto an actual day. Now, clocks relentlessly divided time into exact units, giving rise to new expectations about labor and productivity. People were expected to start and end work "on time," to make the most of the time spent at work, and even to equate time with money. Like the improvements in bookkeeping, timekeeping made some kinds of work more efficient, but it also created new tensions and anxieties.

Knowledge of the World and of God

In the mid-thirteenth century, Thomas Aquinas had constructed a theological view of the world as rational, organized, and comprehensible to the inquiring human mind (Chapter 9). But confidence in this picture began to wane during the fourteenth century, even before the Black Death posed a new challenge to it. Philosophers such as William of Ockham (d. c. 1348), an English member of the Franciscan order, denied that human reason could prove fundamental theological truths such as the existence of God. He argued that human knowledge of God—and hence, salvation—depends entirely on what God himself has chosen to reveal through scripture, and urged humans to investigate the natural world and better understand its laws—without positing any necessary connection between the observable properties of nature and the unknowable essence of divinity.

This philosophical position, known as nominalism, had its roots in the philosophy of Plato (see Chapter 4) and has had an enormous impact on modern thought. The nominalists' distinction between the rational comprehensibility of the real world and the spiritual incomprehensibility of God encourages investigation of nature without reference to supernatural explanations: one of the most important foundations of the modern scientific method (see Chapter 16). Nominalism also encourages empirical observation, since it posits that knowledge of the world should rest on sensory experience rather than abstract theories. The philosophical principles laid down by these observers of the medieval world are thus fundamental to modern science.

Creating God's World in Art

Just as a fascination with the natural world informed developments in medieval science, the artists of this era were paying close attention to the way plants, animals, and human beings really looked. Carvings of leaves and flowers were increasingly made from direct observation and are clearly recognizable to modern botanists as distinct species. Statues of humans also became more realistic in their portrayals of facial expressions and bodily proportions. According to a story in circulation around 1290, a sculptor working on a likeness of the German emperor allegedly made a hurried return trip to study his subject's face a second time, because he had heard that a new wrinkle had appeared on the emperor's brow.

This trend toward naturalism extended to manuscript illumination and painting as well. The latter was, to a large extent, a new art. As we saw in Chapter 1, wall paintings are among the oldest forms of artistic expression in human history, and throughout antiquity and the Middle Ages artists had decorated the walls of public and private buildings with frescoes (paintings executed on "fresh," wet plaster). Italian artists in the thirteenth century began to adapt the techniques used by icon painters in Byzantium, making freestanding pictures on pieces of wood or canvas using tempera (pigments mixed with water and natural gums) in addition to frescoes. Because these altarpieces, devotional

Vikings Encounter the Natives of North America

Although Norse voyagers had explored and settled the coast of Newfoundland around the year 1000, written accounts of these exploits were not made or widely circulated until the thirteenth century. The excerpt below comes from one of these narrative histories, the Grænlendinga Saga *(Greenlanders' Saga). Its hero is Thorfinn Karlsefni, a Norwegian adventurer who arrives in Greenland and marries Gudrid, the twice-widowed sister-in-law of the explorer Leif Eiriksson. Leif had established the original colony of Vinland but had since returned to Greenland.*

There was still the same talk about Vinland voyages as before, and everyone, including [his wife] Gudrid, kept urging Karlsefni to make the voyage. In the end he decided to sail and gathered a company of sixty men and five women. He made an agreement with his crew that everyone should share equally in whatever profits the expedition might yield. They took livestock of all kinds, for they intended to make a permanent settlement there if possible.

Karlsefni asked Leif if he could have the houses in Vinland; Leif said that he was willing to lend them, but not to give them away.

They put to sea and arrived safe and sound at Leif's houses and carried their hammocks ashore. Soon they had plenty of good supplies, for a fine big rorqual* was driven ashore; they went down and cut it up, and so there was no shortage of food.

The livestock were put out to grass, and soon the male beasts became very frisky and difficult to manage. They had brought a bull with them.

Karlsefni ordered timber to be felled and cut into lengths for a cargo for the ship, and it was left out on a rock to season. They made use of all the natural resources of the country that were available, grapes and game of all kinds and other produce.

The first winter passed into summer, and then they had their first encounter with Skrælings,† when a great number of them came out of the wood one day. The cattle were grazing near by and the bull began to bellow and roar with great vehemence. This terrified the Skrælings and they fled, carrying their packs which contained furs and sables and pelts of all kinds. They made for Karlsefni's houses and tried to get inside, but Karlsefni had the doors barred against them. Neither side could understand the other's language.

Then the Skrælings put down their packs and opened them up and offered their contents, preferably in exchange for weapons; but Karlsefni forbade his men to sell arms. Then he hit on the idea of telling the women to carry milk out to the Skrælings, and when the Skrælings saw the milk they wanted to buy nothing else. And so the outcome of their trading expedition was that the Skrælings carried their purchases away in their bellies, and left their packs and furs with Karlsefni and his men.

After that, Karlsefni ordered a strong wooden palisade to be erected round the houses, and they settled in.

---

images, and portraits were portable, they were also more commercial. As long as artists could afford the necessary materials, they did not have to wait for specific commissions. This meant that they had more freedom to choose their subject matter and to put an individual stamp on their work—one of the reasons that we know the names of many more artists from this era.

One of these, Giotto di Bondone of Florence (c. 1267–1337), painted both walls and portable wooden panels. Like some of his contemporaries, **Giotto** (*gee-OHT-toh*) was preeminently an imitator of nature. Not only do his human beings and animals look lifelike, they seem to do natural things. When Christ enters Jerusalem on Palm Sunday, boys climb trees to get a better view; when Saint Francis is laid out in death, someone checks to see whether he has really received the *stigmata* (the marks of Christ's wounds); and when the Virgin's parents, Joachim and Anna, meet after a long separation, they embrace and kiss one another tenderly. Although many of the artists who came after Giotto moved away from naturalism, this style would become the norm by 1400. For this reason, Giotto is often regarded as a painter who inspired the Italian Renaissance (Chapter 11).

About this time Karlsefni's wife, Gudrid, gave birth to a son, and he was named Snorri.

Early next winter the Skrælings returned, in much greater numbers this time, bringing with them the same kind of wares as before. Karlsefni told the women, "You must carry out to them the same produce that was most in demand last time, and nothing else." . . .

[B]ut a Skræling was killed by one of Karlsefni's men for trying to steal some weapons. The Skrælings fled as fast as they could, leaving their clothing and wares behind . . .

"Now we must devise a plan," said Karlsefni, "for I expect they will pay us a third visit, and this time with hostility and in greater numbers. This is what we must do: ten men are to go out on the headland here and make themselves conspicuous, and the rest of us are to go into the wood and make a clearing there, where we can keep our cattle when the Skrælings come out of the forest. We shall take our bull and keep him to the fore."

The place where they intended to have their encounter with the Skrælings had the lake on one side and the woods on the other.

Karlsefni's plan was put into effect, and the Skrælings came right to the place that Karlsefni had chosen for the battle. The fighting began, and many of the Skrælings were killed. There was one tall and handsome man among the Skrælings and Karlsefni reckoned that he must be their leader. One of the Skrælings had picked up an axe, and after examining it for a moment he swung it at a man standing beside him, who fell dead at once. The tall man then took hold of the axe, looked at it for a moment, and then threw it as far as he could out into the water. Then the Skrælings fled into the forest as fast as they could, and that was the end of the encounter.

Karlsefni and his men spent the whole winter there, but in the spring he announced that he had no wish to stay there any longer and wanted to return to Greenland. They made ready for the voyage and took with them much valuable produce, vines and grapes and pelts. They put to sea and reached Eiriksfjord safely and spent the winter there.

* A kind of whale, the largest species of which is a blue whale.

†A Norse word meaning "savages," applied to the different indigenous peoples of Greenland and of North America.

Source: Magnus Magnusson and Herman Palsson, *The Vinland Sagas: The Norse Discovery of America* (Penguin, 1965), pp. 65–67.

Questions for Analysis

1. What policies did the Norse settlers adopt toward the native peoples they encountered on the coast of Newfoundland? How effective were they?

2. Knowing their extensive preparations for colonization and the success of their early efforts, why do you think Karlsefni and his companions abandoned their settlement in North America? Can you find clues in the text?

3. Compare this encounter with the sources describing other interactions between Europeans and the indigenous inhabitants of the New World after 1492 (see Chapters 12 and 14). How do you account for any similarities? What are some key differences?

A Vision of the World We Cannot See

An exact contemporary of Giotto's had a different way of capturing the spiritual world in a naturalistic way, and he worked in a different medium. **Dante Alighieri** (1265–1321) of Florence pioneered what he called a "sweet new style" of poetry in his native tongue, which was now so different from the Latin of antiquity that it had become a language in its own right. Yet, as a scholar and devotee of classical Latin verse, Dante also strove to make this Italian vernacular an instrument for serious political and social critique. His great work, known in his own day as the *Comedy* (called the *Divine Comedy* by later admirers) was composed during the years he spent in exile from his beloved city, after the political party he supported was ousted from power in 1301.

The *Comedy* describes the poet's imaginary journey through hell, purgatory, and paradise; a journey that begins in a "dark wood," a metaphor for the personal and political crises that threatened Dante's faith and livelihood. In the poem, the narrator is led out of this forest and through the first two realms (hell and purgatory) by the Roman

Interpreting Visual Evidence

Seals: Signs of Identity and Authority

For much of human history, applying a seal to a document was the way to certify its legality and identify the people who had ratified it. During antiquity and the early Middle Ages, those people were only powerful men—kings, bishops, heads of monasteries—and occasionally powerful women. But as participation in documentary practices became more and more common, seals were increasingly used by corporations (such as universities and crusading orders), towns, and many individuals. The devices (images) and legends (writing) on these seals were carefully chosen to capture central attributes of their owners' personalities or status. A seal was made by pressing a deeply incised lead matrix onto hot wax or resin, which would quickly dry to form a durable impression. The images reproduced here are later engravings that make the features of the original seals easier to see.

A. Seal of the town of Dover, 1281. Dover has long been one of the busiest and most important port cities of England because of its strategic proximity to France; indeed, the Dover Strait that separates this town from Calais, just across the English Channel, is only twenty-one miles wide. In 1281, when this seal was used, ferries and other ships like the one depicted here made this crossing several times a day. The legend around the edges of the seal reads (in Latin) "Seal of the commune of barons of Dover." It reflects the high status accorded to the free men of Dover by the English crown: because of their crucial role in the economy and defense of the kingdom, they were considered a corporate body and entitled to representation in Parliament alongside individual barons.

B. Personal seal of Simon de Montfort, earl of Leicester, 1258. Simon de Montfort (c. 1208–1265) was a French nobleman who rose to a position of great power in England. In 1238, he married Eleanor, sister of King Henry III: a match that was opposed by England's great lords because it gave this foreigner a great deal of power. Indeed, Simon would later use that power to lead a rebellion against his royal brother-in-law, dying on the battlefield in 1265. This image was appended to a document made when Simon was fifty, but it shows him as a courtly youth, riding out with his favorite hound and blowing on a hunting horn. This means that Simon had continued to use a seal made for him when he was a much younger man, probably at the time when he was knighted, many years before, in France. The Latin legend, indeed, makes no mention of his English title: "Seal of Simon de Montfort."

Questions for Analysis

1. Medieval towns represented themselves in a variety of ways on their seals: sometimes showing a group portrait of town councilors, sometimes a local saint, sometimes a heraldic beast, and sometimes distinctive architectural features. Why would Dover choose this image? What messages does this seal convey?

2. Think carefully about the mystery of Simon de Montfort's seal. Usually, powerful men and women had new seals made to reflect their elevated status. What are all the possible reasons that the English earl would have continued to use a seal made for him so many years earlier, in France? What are the possible ramifications of this choice?

3. The seals of medieval women were almost always shaped like almonds (pointed ovals; the technical term is *vesica-shaped*). Yet Helwig's seal is round, like the seals of men and corporations. Why might that be the case?

4. In general, what is the value of seals for the study of history? What are the various ways in which they function as sources?

C. Seal of Helwig von Ysenburg, countess of Büdingen, 1274. Unlike the engravings of seals pictured here, this is an original wax impression of Helwig's seal and includes the silken cords that were used to fasten it to a document in 1274. It shows a slim, young lady in a long, elegant gown and cape, pointed shoes, and an elaborate headdress. The falcon on her fist suggests that she is dressed to go hunting, but she is depicted against an interior background of diamond-shaped tiles: like her dress, a sign of wealth and status. The legend is difficult to decipher, but reads "Seal of Helwig von Ysen[burg]."

THE MEETING OF JOACHIM AND ANNA BY GIOTTO.
According to legend, Anna and Joachim were an aged and infertile couple who were able to conceive their only child, Mary, through divine intervention. Hence, this painting may portray the moment of her conception—but it also portrays the affection of husband and wife. ▪ *What human characteristics and values does this painting convey to the viewer?*

poet Virgil (Chapter 5), who represents the best of classical culture. But Dante can be guided toward knowledge of the divine in Paradise only by his deceased beloved, Beatrice, who symbolizes Christian wisdom.

In the course of this visionary pilgrimage, Dante's narrator meets the souls of many historical personages and contemporaries, and questions them closely, inviting them to explain why they met their fates. This was Dante's ingenious way of commenting on current events and passing judgment on his enemies. In many ways, this monumental poem is a fusion of classical and Christian cultures, Latin learning and vernacular artistry.

PAPAL POWER AND POPULAR PIETY

Dante's *Comedy* was a creative response to the political turmoil that engulfed Italy during his lifetime, a situation that was transforming the papacy in ways that he condemned. Indeed, many of the men whom Dante imaginatively placed

in Hell were popes, those who had held high offices in the Church, foreign rulers (such as the Holy Roman Emperor) who sought to subjugate Italian territories, or rapacious Italian princes and factional leaders who fought among themselves—all who were creating a state of permanent warfare among and within cities, as in Dante's native Florence. But despite the weakening authority of the papal office, which caused violent divisions within the Church, popular piety arguably achieved its strongest expressions during this era.

The Limits of Papal Power

As we saw in Chapter 9, the power of the papacy reached a new height at the beginning of the thirteenth century, as holders of the office continued to centralize the government of the Church. But they also attempted to extend their influence further into the secular sphere, which led to protracted political struggles that ultimately compromised the papacy's credibility.

For example, the Italian territories under papal lordship shared a border with the kingdom of Sicily, which comprised the important city of Naples, all of southern Italy, and the island of Sicily. The ruler of these territories was also the German emperor Frederick II (Chapter 9), who proved a formidable opponent of the papacy's expanded powers. The reigning pope, therefore, called a crusade against him. But in order to implement this crusade, the pope needed to find a military champion willing to lead an army against a fellow Christian ruler—someone with little to lose and everything to gain.

This turned out to be Charles of Anjou, the youngest brother of the French king, who had few resources of his own. Charles was eventually crowned king of Sicily, but he made matters in southern Italy worse by antagonizing his own subjects, who instead offered their allegiance to the king of Aragon. The papacy then made Aragon the target of yet another crusade, resulting in a disastrous war among Christian princes and their armies on European soil. In the wake of this debacle, the French king **Philip IV** (r. 1286–1314) resolved to punish the papacy for abusing its powers.

In 1300, **Pope Boniface VIII** (r. 1294–1303) called for the celebration of a papal jubilee, asserting that Rome was the center of the Christian world and that the pope was the arbiter of all power. But just a few years later, Rome had ceased to matter. The new capital of the Christian world was now in France, because Philip IV had challenged Boniface to prove that he could exercise real power—not just the power of propaganda. Following a heated dispute about the king's capacity to intervene in the affairs of the Church, Philip sent his thugs to the papal residence, where Boniface (then in his seventies) was so mistreated that he died a month later. Philip then pressed his advantage. He forced the new pope, Clement V, to thank him publicly for his zealous defense of the faith and then, in 1309, moved the entire papal court from Rome to **Avignon** (*AH-vee-nyon*), a city near the southeastern border of his own realm.

The papacy's capitulation to French royal power illustrates the enormous gap that had opened up between rhetoric and reality in the centuries since the Investiture Conflict (Chapter 8). Although Boniface was merely repeating the old claim that kings ruled only by divine approval as recognized by the Church, the Church now exercised its authority only by bowing to the superior power of a king.

The Babylonian Captivity of the Papacy

The papacy would remain in Avignon for nearly seventy years, until 1378 (see Chapter 11). This period is often called the "**Babylonian Captivity**" of the papacy, recalling the Jews' exile in Babylon during the sixth century B.C.E. (Chapter 2). Even though the move was probably supposed to be temporary, it was not reversed after Philip IV's death in 1314. Perhaps many papal suppliants found that doing business in Avignon was easier than in Rome. Not only was Avignon closer to the major centers of power in northwestern Europe, it was now far removed from the tumultuous politics of Italy and safe from the aggressive attentions of German emperors.

All of these considerations were important for a succession of popes closely allied with the aims of the French monarchy. In time, Avignon began to feel like home to them. In fact, it *was* home for all the popes elected there, who were natives of the region, as were nearly all the cardinals whom they appointed. This further cemented their loyalty to the French king. And the longer the

papacy stayed in Avignon, the larger its bureaucracy grew and the harder it was to contemplate moving it.

Although the papacy never abandoned its claims to the overlordship of Rome and the Papal States, making good on these claims required decades of diplomacy and a great deal of money. The Avignon popes accordingly imposed new taxes and obligations on the wealthy dioceses of France, England, Germany, and Spain. Judicial cases from ecclesiastical courts also brought large revenues into the papal coffers. Most controversially, the Avignon popes claimed the right to appoint bishops and priests to vacant offices anywhere in Christendom, directly bypassing the rights of individual dioceses and allowing the papacy to collect huge fees from successful appointees.

By these and other measures, the Avignon popes further strengthened administrative control over the Church. But they also further weakened the papacy's moral authority. Stories of the court's unseemly luxury circulated widely, especially during the reign of the notoriously corrupt Clement VI (r. 1342–1352), who openly sold spiritual benefits for money (boasting that he would appoint a jackass to a bishopric if he thought it would turn a profit) and who insisted that his sexual transgressions were therapeutic. His reign also coincided with the Black Death, the terrifying and demoralizing effects of which were not alleviated by the quality of his leadership.

THE PAPAL PALACE AT AVIGNON. The work on this great fortified palace was begun in 1339 and symbolizes the apparent permanence of the papal residence in Avignon. ▪ *Why was it constructed as a fortress as well as a palace?*

Uniting the Faithful: The Power of Sacraments

Despite the centralizing power of the papacy, which came to fruition under Innocent III, most medieval Christians experienced the Church at a local level, within their communities. In something of a paradox, this was another of Innocent III's legacies: nearly all of Europe was covered by a network of parish churches by the end of the thirteenth century because he had insisted that all people should have access to religious instruction. In these churches, parish priests not only taught the elements of Christian doctrine but also administered the **sacraments**: rituals that conveyed the grace of God to individual Christians by marking significant moments in the life cycle of every person and significant times in the Christian calendar.

Medieval piety came to revolve around these sacraments, which included baptism, confession of sins (also known as Penance), Extreme Unction (last rites for the dying), the ordination of priests, and the Eucharist or Mass. Baptism, a ceremony of initiation that had been administered to adults in the early centuries of Christianity (Chapter 6), had become a sacrament administered to infants as soon as possible after birth to safeguard their souls in case of an early death. Periodic confession of sins to a priest was thought to guarantee God's forgiveness, for if a sinner did not perform appropriate acts of penance, he or she would have to complete atonement in Purgatory—the netherworld between Paradise and Hell that Dante explored. (Purgatory's existence was confirmed as a Church doctrine for the first time in 1274.) In Extreme Unction, a priest anointed the forehead of a dying person with holy oil, signifying the final absolution of all sins and thus offering a last assurance of salvation. Another sacrament, marriage, was increasingly emphasized but very seldom practiced as a ceremony at this time; in reality, marriage required only the exchange of promises and was often formed simply by an act of sexual intercourse or by cohabitation.

This sacramental system was the foundation on which the practices of medieval popular piety rested. Pilgrimages, for example, were a form of penance and could shorten the pilgrim's time in Purgatory. Crusading was a kind of extreme pilgrimage that promised complete fulfillment of all penances the crusader might owe for all the sins of his life. Many other pious acts—saying a series of prayers or giving alms to the poor—could also serve as penance for one's sins, while constituting good works that would help the believer in his or her journey toward salvation.

The Miracle of the Eucharist

Of these sacraments, the one most central to the religious lives of medieval Christians was the Eucharist, or Mass. As we noted in Chapter 9, the ritual power of the Mass was greatly enhanced in the twelfth century, when the Church began promoting the doctrine of transubstantiation. Christians attending Mass were taught that when the priest spoke the ritual words "This is my body" and "This is my blood," the substances of bread and wine on the altar were miraculously transformed into the body and blood of Jesus Christ. To consume one or both of these substances was to ingest holiness. So powerful was this idea that most

"THIS IS MY BODY": THE ELEVATION OF THE HOST.
This fresco from a chapel in Assisi was painted by Simone Martini in the 1320s. It shows the moment in the Mass when the priest raises the eucharistic host so that it can be seen by the faithful. The Latin phrase spoken at this moment, *Hoc est enim corpus meum* ("This is indeed my body"), was regarded as transforming the substance of bread into the divine substance of Christ's body.
■ *Since medieval Christians believed that the sight of the host was just as powerful as ingesting it, how would they have responded to this life-size image of the elevation?* ■ *What does the appearance of angels (above the altar) signify?*

Christians received the sacramental bread just once a year, at Easter; some holy women, however, attempted to sustain themselves by consuming only the single morsel of bread consecrated at daily Mass.

To share in the miracle of the Eucharist, one did not even have to consume it. One had only to witness the elevation of the host, the wafer of bread raised up by the priest, which "hosted" the real presence of Jesus Christ. Daily attendance at Mass simply to view the consecration of the host was therefore a common form of devotion, and this was facilitated by the practice of displaying a consecrated wafer in a special reliquary called a monstrance ("showcase"), which could be set up on an altar or carried through the streets. Believers sometimes attributed astonishing properties to the eucharistic host, feeding it to sick animals or rushing from church to church to see the consecrated bread as many times as possible in a day. The Church criticized some of these practices as superstitious, but by and large, these expressions of popular piety were encouraged and fervently practiced by many.

The Pursuit of Holiness

The fundamental theme of preachers in this era, that salvation lay open to any Christian who strove for it, helps to explain the central place of the Mass and other sacraments in daily life. It also led many to seek out new paths that could lead to God. As we noted in Chapter 9, some believers who sought to achieve a mystical union with God (through rigorous prayer, penance, and personal sacrifice) were ultimately condemned for heresy because they did not subordinate themselves to the authority of the Church. But even less radical figures might find themselves treading on dangerous ground, especially if they published their ideas.

For example, the German preacher Master Eckhart (c. 1260–1327), a Dominican friar, taught that there is a "spark" deep within every human soul and that God lives in this spark. Through prayer and self-renunciation, any person could therefore retreat into this inner recess of his or her being and access divinity. This conveyed the message that laypeople could attain salvation through their own efforts, without the intervention of a priest or any of the sacraments he alone could perform. As a result, many of Eckhart's teachings were condemned. But such views found support in the teachings of popular preachers after the Black Death, when close-knit communities revolving around the parish church were broken up or weakened (see Chapter 11).

STRUGGLES FOR SOVEREIGNTY

When the French king Philip IV transplanted the papal court from Rome to Avignon, he was not just responding to previous popes' abuse of power; he was bolstering his own. By the middle of the thirteenth century, the growth of strong territorial monarchies, combined with the increasing sophistication of royal justice, taxation, and propaganda, had given some secular rulers greater power than any European ruler had wielded since the time of Charlemagne (Chapter 7).

Meanwhile, monarchs' willingness to support the Church's crusading efforts not only yielded distinct economic and political advantages but also allowed them to assert their commitment to the moral and spiritual improvement of their realms. Although a king still needed to be anointed with holy oil at the time of his coronation in order to claim that he ruled "by the grace of God"—a rite that required a bishop and, by extension, papal support—a king's authority in his own realm rested on the acquiescence of the aristocracy and on the popular perception of his reputation for justice, piety, and regard for his subjects' prosperity. On the wider stage of the medieval world, it also rested on his successful assertion of his kingdom's sovereignty.

The Problem of Sovereignty

Sovereignty can be defined as an inviolable authority over a defined territory. In Chapter 9, we learned that Philip Augustus was the first monarch to call himself "king of France" and not "king of the Franks." In other words, he was defining his kingship in geographical terms, claiming that there was an entity called France and that he was king within that area.

But what was France? Was it the tiny "island" (Île-de-France) around Paris, which had been his father's domain? If so, France was very small—and very vulnerable, which would make it hard to maintain a claim to sovereignty. Or did France include any region, such as Champagne or Normandy, whose lord was willing to do homage to the French king? In that case, the king would need to enforce his rights of lordship constantly and, if necessary, exert his rule directly—as Philip did when he took Normandy away from England's King John in 1214.

But what if some of France's neighboring lords ruled in their own right, as did the independent counts of Flanders, thus threatening the security of France's borders? In that case, the king would need either to forge an alliance with these borderlands or to negate their independence. He would need to assert his sovereignty by absorbing these regions into an ever-growing kingdom.

This is the problem: a claim to sovereignty is credible only if it can be backed up with real power, and a state's or ruler's power must never seem stagnant or passive. The problem of sovereignty, then, is a zero-sum game: one state's sovereignty is won and maintained by diminishing that of other states. Although many French citizens today would assert that France has, in some mystical way, always existed in its present form, the fact is that France and many other modern European states were being cobbled together during the medieval period through a process of annexation and colonization—just as the United States was assembled at the

A CONTAINER FOR THE CROWN OF THORNS. The Sainte-Chapelle, built by Louis IX, was a giant reliquary for the display of this potent artifact and a symbol of Christ's divine majesty, which increased the prestige of the king of France.

expense of the empires that had colonized North America (the British, French, and Spanish), not to mention the killing or displacement of autonomous native peoples.

The process of achieving sovereignty is thus an aggressive and often violent one, affecting not only the rulers of territories but their peoples, too. In Spain, the "reconquest" of Muslim lands, which had accelerated in the twelfth century, continued apace in the thirteenth and fourteenth to the detriment of these regions' Muslim and Jewish inhabitants. German princes continued to push northward into the Baltic, where they responded with brutal force to native peoples' resistance. Meanwhile, the Scandinavian kingdoms that had been forming in the eleventh and twelfth centuries warred among themselves and their neighbors for the control of contested regions and resources. Italy and the Mediterranean became a constant battleground, as we have observed.

Among all these emerging states, the two most strident and successful in their assertion of sovereignty were France and England.

The Prestige of France: The Saintly Kingship of Louis IX

After the death of Philip Augustus in 1223, the heirs to the French throne continued to pursue an expansionist policy, pushing the boundaries of their influence out to the east and south. There were significant pockets of resistance, though, notably from the southwestern lands that the kings

of England had inherited from Eleanor of Aquitaine (Chapter 9) and from the independent towns of Flanders that had escaped conquest under Philip Augustus. In 1302, citizen militias from several of these towns, fighting on foot with farming implements and other unconventional weapons, managed to defeat the heavily armed French cavalry. This victory at the Battle of Courtrai (Kortrijk) is still celebrated as a national holiday in Belgium (although its ultimate meaning is currently at the center of a divisive controversy between French- and Flemish-speaking Belgians).

This defeat was a setback for Philip IV of France, but we have already observed that he had other ways of asserting the power of French sovereignty. Much of that power derived from his grandfather, **Louis IX** (r. 1226–1270), who probably would have been horrified by the ways his grandson used it. Louis was famous for his piety and his conscientious exercise of his kingly duties. Unlike most of his fellow princes, Louis not only pledged to go on a crusade—he actually went. And although both of his campaigns were notorious failures (he died on the second, in 1270), they cemented his saintly reputation and political clout.

First, Louis's willingness to risk his life (and those of his brothers) in the service of the Church would give him tremendous influence in papal affairs—a key factor in making his youngest brother, Charles of Anjou, the king of Naples and Sicily. Second, the necessity of ensuring the good governance of his kingdom during his years of absence prompted Louis to invent or reform many key aspects of royal governance, which made France the bureaucratic rival of England for the first time. Third, Louis's first crusading venture was seen as confirmation that the king of France had inherited the mantle of Charlemagne as the protector of the Church and the representative of Christ on earth.

Although it was a military fiasco, this crusade found lasting artistic expression in the Sainte-Chapelle (Holy Chapel), a gorgeous jewel box of a church that Louis built in Paris for his collection of Passion relics—artifacts thought to have been used for the torture and crucifixion of Christ (the Latin *passio* means "suffering"). The most important of these was the Crown of Thorns, intended by Pilate as a mocking reference to "the king of the Jews" (Chapter 6). Now that this holy crown belonged to Louis and was housed in Paris, it could be taken as a sign that Paris was the new Jerusalem.

Widely regarded as a saint in his lifetime, Louis was formally canonized in 1297, by the same Pope Boniface VIII who was brought down by Philip IV. Indeed, Boniface partly intended this gesture as a rebuke to the saint's grandson, but Philip turned it to his advantage. He even used his grandfather's pious reputation as a cloak for his frankly rapacious treatment of the Knights Templar, whose military order he suppressed in 1314 so that he could confiscate its extensive property and dissolve his own debts to the order. He had expelled the Jews from his realm in 1306 for similar reasons.

his father to suppress them. When Edward himself became king in 1272, he took steps to ensure that there would be no further revolts on his watch by tightening his control on the aristocracy and their lands, diffusing their power by strengthening that of Parliament, reforming the administration of the realm, and clarifying its laws.

Having seen to the internal affairs of England, Edward looked to its borders. Since Welsh chieftains had been major backers of the barons who had rebelled against his father, he was determined to clean up the border region and bring "wild Wales" within the orbit of English sovereignty. He initially attempted to do this by making treaties with various Welsh princes, but none of these arrangements was stable or gave him the type of control he wanted. Edward accordingly embarked on an ambitious and ruthless campaign of castle building, ringing the hilly country with enormous fortifications on a scale not seen in most of Europe—they were more like crusader castles—and treated the Welsh (who were actually his fellow Christians) as infidels. Indeed, he treated conquered Wales like a crusader state, making it a settler colony and subjecting the Welsh to the overlordship of his own men. When his son, the future Edward II, was born in 1284 at the great castle he had built at Caernarvon, he gave the infant the title "Prince of Wales," a title usually borne by a Welsh chieftain.

Castles and Control: Edward I and the Expansion of English Rule

The expulsion of Jews who depended on a king's personal protection had actually been a precedent set by Philip's contemporary and kinsman, **Edward I** of England (r. 1272–1307). Unlike Philip, Edward had to build up the sovereignty of his state almost from scratch—for his father, Henry III (r. 1216–1272), had a long but troubled reign. Henry inherited the throne as a young boy, shortly after his father John's loss of Normandy and capitulation to Magna Carta (Chapter 9). From the first, he had to contend with factions among his regents and, later, the restive barons of his realm who rose against him on several occasions. His son Edward even sided with the rebels at one point, but later worked alongside

CAERNARVON CASTLE. One of many massive fortifications built by Edward I, this castle was the birthplace of the first English Prince of Wales and the site where the current Prince of Wales, Charles, was formally invested with that title in 1969. ▪ *Castles of this size and strength had been constructed in the Crusader States and on the disputed frontiers of Muslim and Christian Spain, but never before in Britain (see the photos on pages 294 and 297). What does their construction reveal about Edward's attitude toward the Welsh?*

Analyzing Primary Sources

A Declaration of Scottish Independence

In April 1320, a group of powerful Scottish lords gathered at the abbey of Arbroath to draft a letter to Pope John XXII in Avignon. The resulting Declaration of Arbroath petitioned the exiled pope (a Frenchman loyal to the French king) to recognize the Scots as a sovereign nation and to support their right to an independent kingdom that would be free from encroachment by the English. The Scots' elected king, Robert the Bruce, had been excommunicated by a previous pope who had upheld English claims to lordship in Scotland. The letter therefore makes a number of different arguments for the recognition of the Scots' right to self-governance.

We know, most Holy Father and lord, and have gathered from the deeds and books about men in the past, that . . . the nation of the Scots has been outstanding for its many distinctions. It journeyed from the lands of Greece and Egypt by the Tyrrhenian Sea and the Pillars of Hercules, . . . but could not be subdued anywhere by any peoples however barbaric. . . . It took possession of the settlements in the west which it now desires, after first driving out the Britons and totally destroying the Picts, and although often attacked by the Norwegians, Danes and English. Many were its victories and innumerable its efforts. It has held these places always free of all servitude, as the old histories testify. One hundred and thirteen kings of their royal lineage have reigned in their kingdom, with no intrusion by a foreigner.

If the noble qualities and merits of these men were not obvious for other reasons, they shine forth clearly enough in that they were almost the first to be called to his most holy faith by the King of Kings and Lord of Lords, our Lord Jesus Christ, after his Passion and Resurrection, even though they were settled on the most distant boundaries of the earth. . . .

Thus our people lived until now in freedom and peace . . . , until that mighty prince Edward [I] king of England (the father of the present king) in the guise of a friend and ally attacked our kingdom in hostile fashion, when it had no head and the people were not harbouring any evil treachery, nor were they accustomed to wars or attacks. His unjust acts, killings, acts of violence, pillagings, burnings, imprisonments of prelates, burnings of monasteries, robbings and killings of regular clergy, and also innumerable other outrages, which he committed against the said people, sparing none on account of age or sex, religion or order— no one could write about them or fully comprehend them who had not been instructed by experience.

From these countless ills we have been set free, with the help of Him who follows up wounds with healing and cures, by our most energetic prince, king and lord Sir Robert [the Bruce; r. 1306– 1329]. . . . By divine providence his succession to his right according to our laws and customs which we intend to maintain to the death, together with the due consent and assent of us all, have made him our prince and king. . . . But if he should give up what he has begun,

Edward then turned to Scotland, England's final frontier. Until now, control of Scotland had not been an English concern. The Scottish border had been peaceful for many years, and the Scottish kings did homage to the English king for some of their lands. In 1290, however, the succession to the Scottish throne was disputed among many rival claimants, none of whom had enough backing to secure election. Edward intervened, pressing his own claim to the kingdom and seemingly prepared to take Scotland by conquest. To avoid this, the Scots forged an alliance with the French, but this did not prevent Edward's army from fighting its way through to Scone Abbey in 1296.

Scone was a symbolic target: the site of the Stone of Destiny on which Scottish kings were traditionally enthroned. So Edward seized this potent symbol, brought it back to Westminster Abbey in London, and embedded it in the coronation chair of his namesake, Edward the Confessor, the last Anglo-Saxon king of England (Chapter 8). Save for a brief hiatus in 1950, when the stone was stolen from the abbey by Scottish nationalists—students at the University of Glasgow—it would remain there until 1996 as a sign that the sovereignty of Scotland had yielded to that of England. (It will be temporarily returned to London when the next British monarch is crowned.)

seeking to subject us or our kingdom to the king of the English, . . . we would immediately strive to expel him as our enemy and a subverter of his right and ours, and we would make someone else our king, who is capable of seeing to our defence. For as long as a hundred of us remain alive, we intend never to be subjected to the lordship of the English, in any way. For it is not for glory in war, riches or honours that we fight, but only for the laws of our fathers and for freedom, which no good man loses except along with his life.

Therefore, most Holy Father and lord, we implore your holiness with all vehemence in our prayers that you . . . look with paternal eyes on the troubles and difficulties brought upon us and the Church of God by the English. And that you deign to admonish and exhort the king of the English, who ought to be satisfied with what he has (since England was formerly enough for seven kings or more), to leave us Scots in peace, living as we do in the poor country of Scotland beyond which there is no dwelling place, and desiring nothing but our own. . . .

It is important for you, Holy Father, to do this, since you see the savagery of the heathen raging against Christians (as the sins of Christians require), and the frontiers of Christendom are being curtailed day by day, and you have seen how much it detracts from your holiness's reputation if (God forbid!) the Church suffers eclipse or scandal in any part of it during your time. Let it then rouse the Christian princes who are covering up their true motivation when they pretend that they cannot go to the assistance of the Holy Land on account of wars with their neighbours. The real reason that holds them back is that in warring with their smaller neighbours they anticipate greater advantage to themselves and weaker resistance. . . .

But if your Holiness too credulously trusts the tales of the English fully, or does not leave off favouring the English to our confusion, then we believe that the Most High will blame you for the slaughter of bodies. . . . Dated at our monastery at Arbroath in Scotland 6 April 1320 in the fifteenth year of our said king's reign.

Source: Walter Bower, *Scotichronicon*, vol. 7, ed. A. B. Scott and D. E. R. Watt (Aberdeen, Scotland: 1996).

Questions for Analysis

1. On what grounds does this letter justify the political independence of the Scots? What different arguments does it make? Which in your view is the most compelling?

2. Why does this letter mention crusading? What are the Scottish lords implying about the relationship between Europe's internal conflicts and the ongoing wars with external adversaries?

3. Imagine that you are an adviser to the pope. Applying your knowledge of the papacy's situation at this time, would you advise him to do as this letter asks? Why or why not?

Edward considered the subjugation of Scotland to be England's manifest destiny. He called himself the "Hammer of the Scots," and when he died he charged his son Edward II (r. 1307–1327) with the completion of his task. But the younger Edward, unlike his father, was not a ruthless and efficient advocate of English expansion. He also had to contend with a rebellion led by his own queen, Isabella of France, who also engineered his abdication and murder. Their son, Edward III (r. 1327–1377), eventually renewed his grandfather's expansionist policies, but his main target was France, not Scotland—thus launching Europe's two strongest monarchies into a war that would last for more than a hundred years.

The Outbreak of the Hundred Years' War

The **Hundred Years' War** was the largest, longest, and widest-ranging military conflict since Rome's wars with Carthage in the third and second centuries B.C.E. (Chapter 5). Although England and France were its principal antagonists, almost all major European powers became involved at some stage. Active hostilities began in 1337 and lasted until 1453, interrupted by truces of varying lengths. We will continue tracing its developments in Chapter 11.

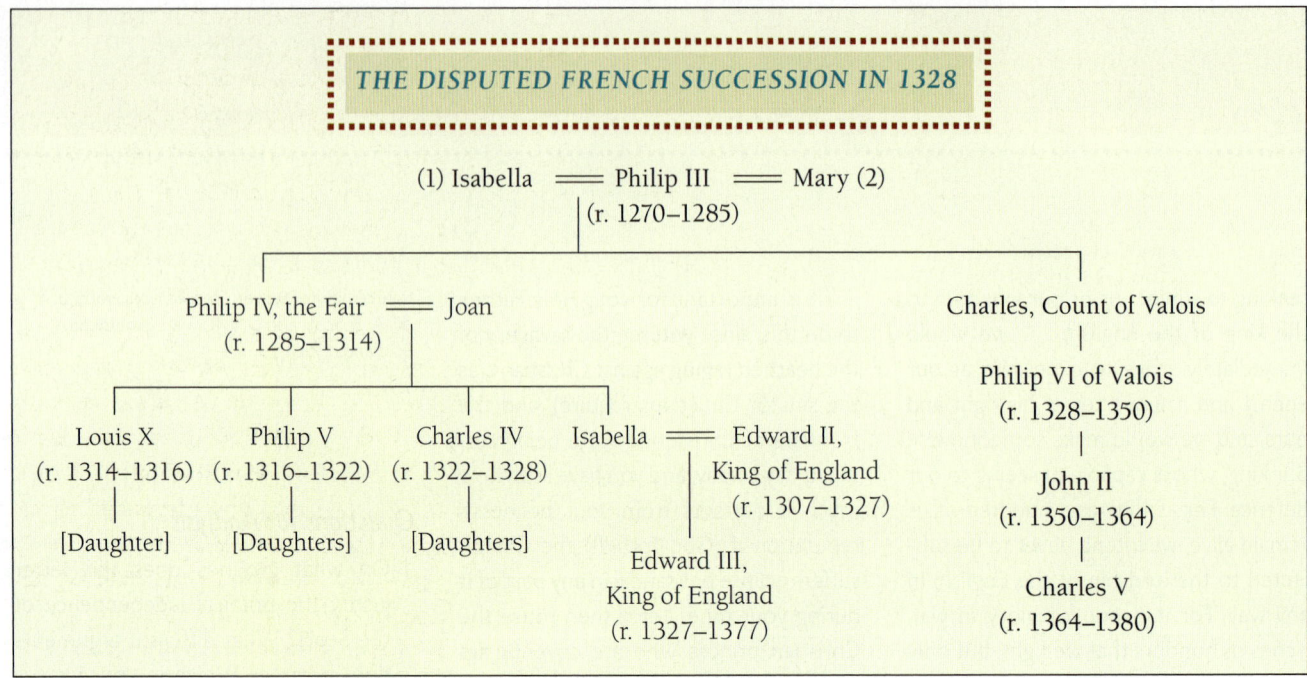

THE DISPUTED FRENCH SUCCESSION IN 1328

```
(1) Isabella  ═══  Philip III  ═══  Mary (2)
                   (r. 1270–1285)

        Philip IV, the Fair ═══ Joan                    Charles, Count of Valois
           (r. 1285–1314)                                          |
                                                           Philip VI of Valois
                                                             (r. 1328–1350)
   Louis X        Philip V        Charles IV    Isabella ═══ Edward II,                 |
 (r. 1314–        (r. 1316–      (r. 1322–                  King of England          John II
  1316)            1322)          1328)                     (r. 1307–1327)        (r. 1350–1364)
    |                |               |                                                  |
[Daughter]      [Daughters]     [Daughters]                Edward III,              Charles V
                                                          King of England         (r. 1364–1380)
                                                          (r. 1327–1377)
```

The most fundamental source of conflict, and the most difficult to resolve, was the fact that the kings of England held the duchy of Gascony as vassals of the French king; this had been part of Eleanor of Aquitaine's domain, which was added to the Anglo-Norman Empire in 1154 (Chapter 9). In the twelfth and thirteenth centuries, when the French kings had not yet absorbed this region into their domain, this fact had seemed less of an anomaly. But as Europe's territorial monarchies began to claim sovereignty on the basis of the free exercise of power within the "natural" boundaries of their domains, the English presence in "French" Gascony became more and more problematic. The fact that England also had close commercial links, through the wool trade, with Flanders—which consistently resisted annexation by France—added fuel to the fire; as did the French alliance with the Scots, who continued to resist English annexation.

Complicating this volatile situation was the disputed succession of the French crown. In 1328, the last of Philip IV's three sons died without leaving a son to succeed him: the Capetian dynasty, founded by the Frankish warlord Hugh Capet in 987 (Chapter 8) had finally exhausted itself. A new dynasty, the Valois, came to the throne—but only by insisting that women could neither inherit royal power nor pass it on. For otherwise, the heir to France was Edward III of England, whose ambitious mother, Isabella, was Philip IV's only daughter. When his mother's claim was initially passed over, Edward was only fifteen and in no position to protest. In 1337, however, when the disputes over Gascony and Scotland erupted into war, Edward raised the stakes by claiming to be the rightful king of France, a claim that subsequent English kings would maintain until the eighteenth century.

Although France was richer and more populous than England by a ratio of at least three to one, the English crown was more effective in mobilizing the entire population, for reasons we discussed in Chapter 9. Edward III was therefore able to levy and maintain a professional army of seasoned and well-disciplined soldiers, cavalrymen, and archers. The huge but virtually leaderless armies assembled by the French proved no match for the tactical superiority of these smaller English forces. English armies pillaged the French countryside at will, while civil wars broke out between embattled French lords. A decade after the declaration of war, French knights were defeated in two humiliating battles at Crécy (1346) and Calais (1347). The English seemed invincible—but they were no match for a new and unexpected adversary approaching from the Far East.

FROM THE GREAT FAMINE TO THE BLACK DEATH

By 1300, Europe was connected to Asia and the lands between by an intricate network that fostered connections of all kinds. At the same time, Europe was reaching its own ecological limits. Between 1000 and 1300, the population had tripled; a sea of grain fields stretched, almost

The Code of Chivalry: Putting Honor before Plunder

The Hundred Years' War between England and France pitted these two countries' warrior aristocracies against each other. Yet these knights had a great deal in common: they all spoke French, many were closely related, and they were supposed to share a common set of values. The following excerpt is taken from The Book of Chivalry, *written in French by Geoffroi de Charny, a French nobleman and veteran of this war's first major battles who ultimately died in combat at Poitiers in 1356. Because the war was fought almost entirely on French soil, Geoffroi was keenly aware of the toll it took on the land and its people. In the following passage, he addresses the problem of how a knight can sustain his honor when he is driven to acquire booty for himself through the theft of others' property.*

Those Who Are Brave but Too Eager for Plunder

 now need to consider yet another category of men-at-arms, who deserve praise, who are strong and skillful, bold and sparing no effort, some of whom always want to be at the forefront, riding as foragers to win booty or prisoners or other profit from the enemies of those on whose side they fight. And they know well how to do it skillfully and cleverly; and because they are so intent on plunder, it often happens that on the entry into a town won by force, those who are so greedy for plunder dash hither and thither and find themselves separated from those of their companions who have no thought for gain but only for completing their military undertaking. And it often happens that such men, those who ride after and hunt for great booty, are killed in the process—frequently it is not known how, sometimes by their enemies, sometimes through quarrels in which greed for plunder sets one man against another. It often occurs that through lack of those who chase after plunder before the battle is over, that which is thought to be already won can be lost again and lives or reputations as well. It can also happen in relation to such people who are very eager for booty that when there is action on the battlefield, there are a number of men who pay more attention to taking prisoners and other profit, and when they have seized them and other winnings, they are more anxious to safeguard their captives and their booty than to help to bring the battle to a good conclusion. And it may well be that a battle can be lost in this way. And one ought instead to be wary of the booty which results in the loss of honor, life, and possessions. In this vocation one should therefore set one's heart and mind on winning honor, which endures for ever, rather than on winning profit and booty, which one can lose within one single hour. And yet one should praise and value those men-at-arms who are able to make war on, inflict damage on, and win profit from their enemies, for they cannot do it without strenuous effort and great courage. But again I shall repeat: he who does best is most worthy.

Source: *The Book of Chivalry of Geoffrey de Charny: Text, Context, and Translation*, trans. Richard W. Kaeuper and Elspeth Kennedy (Pennsylvania: 1996), p. 99.

Questions for Analysis

1. How does Geoffroi justify the act of plundering? What insights into contemporary military tactics does this passage provide?

2. Given that Geoffroi must have seen Englishmen pillaging French lands, do you find his justification of this activity surprising? Why or why not?

---

unbroken, from Ireland to Ukraine; and forests had been cleared, marshes drained, and pastureland reduced by generations of peasants performing lifetimes of backbreaking labor. Yet Europe was barely able to feed its people. At the same time, the Medieval Warm Period (Chapter 8) was coming to an end, and with it the favorable climatic conditions that had enabled the agricultural revolution of the previous three centuries. Even a reduction of one or two degrees Centigrade is enough to cause substantial changes in rainfall patterns, shorten growing seasons, and decrease agricultural productivity. So it did in Europe, with disastrous consequences.

Past and Present

Global Pandemics

Although advances in medical science have made the causes of disease less mysterious, the rapid spread of new viruses is still terrifying and the variety of human responses to the possibility of sudden infection have changed little over time. The image on the left shows citizens from the town of Tournai (now in Belgium) marching in a procession to ward off the plague: they are praying and doing penance for their sins by beating their own bodies with whips, a practice called *flagellation*. The image on the right shows health care workers donning hazmat suits to protect themselves from the deadly Ebola virus outbreak of 2014–2015.

 Watch related author interview on the Student Site

Evil Times: The Seven Years' Famine

Between the years 1315 and 1322, the cooling climate caused nearly continuous adverse weather conditions in northern Europe. Winters were extraordinarily severe: in 1316, the Baltic Sea froze over and ships were trapped in the ice. Rains prevented planting in spring or summer, and when a crop did manage to struggle through, it would be dashed by rain and hail in autumn. Amid these natural calamities, dynastic warfare continued in the sodden wheat fields, as the princes of Scandinavia and the Holy Roman Empire fought for supremacy and succession. In the once-fertile fields of Flanders, French armies slogged through mud in continued efforts to subdue the Flemish population. On the Scottish and Welsh borders, uprisings

were ruthlessly suppressed and the paltry storehouses of the natives were pillaged to feed the English raiders.

The result was human suffering more devastating than that caused by any famine affecting Europe since that time; hence the name "**Great Famine**" to describe this terrible crisis. Weakened by years of malnutrition and relentless efforts to counteract the climatic effects on the landscape, between 10 and 15 percent of the population of northern Europe perished. Many starved, while others fell victim to epidemic diseases that affected both animals and people. In southern Europe, around the shores of the Mediterranean, the effects of climate change were more muted, and food could be distributed through different channels. Nonetheless, the overall health of this region also suffered from the disruption of trade and the shortage of some staple goods,

ATLANTIC OCEAN

NORTH SEA

BALTIC SEA

MEDITERRANEAN SEA

ADRIATIC SEA

BLACK SEA

ALPS MTS.

PYRENEES MTS.

June 30, 1350

December 31, 1349

June 30, 1349

December 31, 1348

December 31, 1350

December 31, 1348

June 30, 1348

December 31, 1347

June 30, 1347

Bergen
Wisby
Moscow
Drogheda
Dublin
Kilkenny
Lancaster
Preston
Chester
Durham
York
Lincoln
Nottingham
Norwich
Cambridge
Yarmouth
Oxford
Bristol
London
Canterbury
Weymouth
Southampton
Calais
Lübeck
Rostock
Danzig
Bremen
Hamburg
Frankfurt an der Oder
Thorn
Bruges
Ghent
Amiens
Liége
Cologne
Magdeburg
Osnabrück
Erfurt
Frankfurt
Würzburg
Nuremberg
Paris
Angers
Strasbourg
Colmar
Basel
Zurich
Lucerne
St. Gall
Mühldorf
Vienna
Bordeaux
Milan
Verona
Venice
Po R.
Genoa
Bologna
Florence
Toulouse
Montpellier
Marseilles
Pisa
Ancona
Sebenico
Ragusa
Narbonne
Siena
Perugia
Huesca
Saragossa
Lérida
Teruel
Barcelona
Rome
Valencia
Naples
Seville
Almeria
Messina
Agrigento
Catania
Syracuse
Constantinople

Ebro R.
Loire R.
Rhine R.
Elbe R.
Vistula R.
Dnieper R.
Danube R.

EUROPE
AFRICA
Area of detail

- • Plague-stricken towns and areas
- — Progress of plague at certain dates
- ■ Towns and areas not stricken by the plague

0   100   200   300 Miles
0   100   200   300 Kilometers

EUROPEAN OUTBREAKS OF THE BLACK DEATH, 1347–1350. ■ *What trajectories did the Black Death follow once it arrived in Europe?* ■ *How might the growth of towns, trade, and travel contributed to the spread of the Black Death?* ■ *Would such a rapid advance have been likely during the early Middle Ages or even in the ancient world? Why or why not?*

as well as from the highly unstable political situation we have discussed.

As food grew scarcer, prices climbed unpredictably, making even staple goods unobtainable by the poor. Plans for future crops, which kept hope alive, would be dashed when spring arrived and flooded fields prevented seeds from germinating. People then spent cold summers and autumns foraging for food. Hunting was restricted to the nobility (Chapter 9), but even those who risked the death penalty for poaching found little game. Wages did not keep pace with rising costs, and so those who lived in towns and depended on markets had less to spend on scarce provisions. Only a year after the famine began, townspeople were dying of ailments that would not have been fatal in good years.

The effects of the famine were especially devastating for children, since even those who survived were highly susceptible to disease, owing to the severe impairment of their immune systems. It may have been the Great Famine, then, that paved the way for the even more horrific destruction of the Black Death.

Competing Viewpoints

Responses to the Black Death

> Many chroniclers, intellectuals, and private individuals left accounts of the plague in which they attempt to understand why it had occurred, how it spread, and how communities should respond to it.

The Spread of the Plague According to Gabriele de' Mussi (d. 1356), a Lawyer in Piacenza (Northern Italy)

Oh God! See how the heathen Tartar races, pouring together from all sides, suddenly infested the city of Caffa [on the Black Sea] and besieged the trapped Christians there for almost three years. . . . But behold, [in 1346] the whole army was affected by a disease which overran the Tartars and killed thousands upon thousands every day. It was as though arrows were raining down from heaven to strike and crush the Tartars' arrogance. All medical advice and attention was useless; the Tartars died as soon as the signs of disease appeared on their bodies: swellings in the armpit or groin caused by coagulating humours, followed by a putrid fever.

The dying Tartars, stunned and stupefied by the immensity of the disaster brought about by the disease, and realising that they had no hope of escape, lost interest in the siege. But they ordered corpses to be placed in catapults and lobbed into the city in the hope that the intolerable stench would kill everyone inside. What seemed like mountains of dead were thrown into the city, and the Christians could not hide or flee or escape from them, although they dumped as many of the bodies as they could in the sea. And soon the rotting corpses tainted the air and poisoned the water supply. . . . Moreover one infected man could carry the poison to others, and infect people and places with the disease by look alone. No one knew, or could discover, a means of defence.

Thus almost everyone who had been in the East . . . fell victim . . . through the bitter events of 1346 to 1348—the Chinese, Indians, Persians, Medes, Kurds, Armenians, Cilicians, Georgians, Mesopotamians, Nubians, Ethiopians, Turks, Egyptians, Arabs, Saracens and Greeks. . . .

* * *

As it happened, among those who escaped from Caffa by boat were a few sailors who had been infected with the poisonous disease. Some boats were bound for Genoa, others went to Venice and to other Christian areas. When the sailors reached these places and mixed with the people there, it was as if they had brought evil spirits with them. . . .

* * *

Scarcely one in seven of the Genoese survived. In Venice, where an inquiry was held into the mortality, it was found that more than 70 percent of the people had died. . . . The rest of Italy, Sicily and Apulia and the neighbouring regions maintain that they have been virtually emptied of inhabitants. . . . The Roman Curia at Avignon, the provinces on both sides of the Rhône, Spain, France, and the Empire cry up their griefs. . . .

* * *

Everyone has a responsibility to keep some record of the disease and the deaths, and because I am myself from Piacenza I have been urged to write more about what happened there in 1348. . . .

I don't know where to begin. Cries and laments arise on all sides. Day after day one sees the Cross and the Host being carried about the city, and countless dead being buried. . . . The living made preparations for their [own] burial, and because there was not enough room for individual graves, pits had to be dug in colonnades and piazzas, where nobody had ever been buried before. It often happened that man and wife, father and son, mother and daughter, and soon the whole household and many neighbours, were buried together in one place. . . .

Source: From Rosemary Horrox, ed. and trans., *The Black Death* (Manchester, 1994), pp. 16–21, 219–20.

A Letter from the Town Council of Cologne to the Town Council of Strasbourg (Germany), 12 January 1349

Very dear friends, all sorts of rumours are now flying about against Judaism and the Jews prompted by this unexpected and unparalleled mortality of Christians. . . . Throughout our city, as in yours, many-winged Fame clamours that this mortality was initially caused, and is still being spread, by the poisoning of springs and wells, and that the Jews must have dropped poisonous substances into them. When it came to our knowledge that serious charges had been made against the Jews in several small towns and villages on the basis of this mortality, we sent numerous letters to you and to other cities and towns to uncover the truth behind these rumours, and set a thorough investigation in train. . . .

If a massacre of the Jews were to be allowed in the major cities (something which we are determined to prevent in our city, if we can, as long as the Jews are found to be innocent of these or similar actions) it could lead to the sort of outrages and disturbances which would whip up a popular revolt among the common people—and such revolts have in the past brought cities to misery and desolation. In any case we are still of the opinion that this mortality and its attendant circumstances are caused by divine vengeance and nothing else. Accordingly we intend to forbid any harassment of the Jews in our city because of these flying rumours, but to defend them faithfully and keep them safe, as our predecessors did—and we are convinced that you ought to do the same. . . .

Questions for Analysis

1. How does Gabriele de' Mussi initially explain the causes of the plague? How does his understanding of it change as he traces its movements from East to West, and closer to Italy?

2. Why does the Council of Cologne wish to quell violence against the Jews? How does this reasoning complement or challenge what we have learned so far about the treatment of Jews in medieval Europe?

3. In your view, do these two perspectives display a rational approach to the horrors of the Black Death? Why or why not?

A Crisis of Connectivity: Tracking the Black Death

The **Black Death** is the name given to a deadly global pandemic—an epidemic affecting "all people" (Greek: *pan + demos*)—that spread from China to Mongolia, northern India, and western Asia during the 1330s and 1340s. By 1346, the plague had reached the Black Sea, where it was transmitted to the Genoese colonists at Caffa (as noted on page 333). From there, in 1347, Genoese ships inadvertently took it to Sicily, North Africa, and northern Italy. From Italy, it spread westward along trade routes, first striking seaports, then turning inland with the travelers who carried it. It moved with astonishing rapidity, advancing about two miles per day, summer or winter. By 1350, it had reached Scandinavia and northern Russia, then spread southward again until it linked up with the original waves of infection that had taken it from central Asia to the Black Sea. In Europe, it continued to erupt in local epidemics until the eighteenth century. In Asia and Africa, it was still causing devastating losses of life into the nineteenth century.

Although the absolute (total) mortality caused by other global pandemics has been greater—including the influenza pandemic of 1918–1919 and the ongoing HIV/AIDS pandemic—the *percentage* of the population affected by the Black Death was higher. In the space of a few decades, 40 to 60 percent of all people in these affected areas had died. The tremendous consequences of this catastrophe and the survivors' responses to the world left behind will be explored in Chapter 11. But what caused it?

In 2011, scientists confirmed that the Black Death bacterium was the deadly microbe *Yersinia pestis*, and that it almost certainly originated in China, on the

Tibetan-Qinghai Plateau. In 2013, another team of scientists proved that this medieval pandemic was actually the *second* plague caused by *Y. pestis*; an earlier strain had resulted in the Justinianic Plague of the sixth century C.E. (Chapter 7). This microbe is especially virulent because it can be contracted and manifested in so many ways, including bubonic plague and its even deadlier cousins, septicemic plague and pneumonic plague.

In its *bubonic* form, the plague microbe is carried by fleas that can live and travel on the backs of many kinds of animals, including rats, marmots, hamsters, rabbits, camels, and even birds. Humans bitten by an infected flea or animal contract the plague through their lymphatic systems, resulting in the eruption of enormous and painful swellings (buboes) that appear in the lymph nodes of the groin, neck, and armpits. *Septicemic* plague occurs when an infected flea introduces the microbe directly into the human bloodstream, causing death within hours, usually before any symptoms of the disease are obvious. *Pneumonic* plague, perhaps the most frightening variation, results when *Y. pestis* infects the lungs, allowing the contagion to spread silently and invisibly, in the same ways as the common cold.

One of the things that made the Black Death so terrifying, therefore, was that it was mysteriously inconsistent. Those afflicted by the hideous bubonic plague might actually recover, whereas others—seemingly untouched—

might die suddenly, from no apparent cause. Immediate reactions to the plague thus ranged from panic to anger to resignation. Observers quickly realized that the plague was contagious, but precisely how it spread remained unknown. Some believed that it was caused by breathing "bad air" and so urged people to flee from stricken areas, which caused the disease to spread even faster. Another response was the flagellant movement, so called because of the whips (*flagella*) with which traveling bands of penitents lashed themselves in order to appease the wrath of God. The unruly and sometimes hysterical mobs that gathered around the flagellants aroused the concern of both ecclesiastical and secular authorities, and the movement was suppressed by papal order.

Still others looked for scapegoats and revived old conspiracy theories that implicated Jews in the poisoning of communal water sources. Scores of Jewish communities were attacked and thousands of their inhabitants massacred in parts of the Rhineland, southern France, and the Christian kingdoms of Spain. For example, an important archaeological and forensic study published in 2014 reveals that hundreds of Jews—including children, the elderly, and the disabled—were brutally clubbed and hacked to death by their Christian neighbors in the small Catalonian town of Tárrega. The papacy and some local authorities tried to halt such attacks, but these efforts usually came too late.

After You Read This Chapter

 Go to **INQUIZITIVE** to see what you've learned—and learn what you've missed—with personalized feedback along the way.

REVIEWING THE OBJECTIVES

- How did the conquests of the Mongols significantly impact Europe?
- The expansion of commerce and communication between eastern and western civilizations created a new world system. What were some key characteristics of this system? What kinds of exchange did it enable?
- What is *sovereignty*? What were the effects of competition for sovereign among European rulers?
- What were the short- and long-term causes for the papacy's loss of prestige? Why was the papal court moved to Avignon?
- What caused the Black Death? In what sense can it be seen as a product of the new world system that began with the Mongol conquests?

CONCLUSION

The century between 1250 and 1350 was a time of significant change within all Western civilizations. The growing power of some monarchies led to encroachments on territories and cities that had once been independent, fueling resistance to these internal acts of colonization. The papacy, whose power had seemed so secure at the turn of the thirteenth century, would itself become a pawn in the keeping of the French king by the beginning of the fourteenth. Rome thereby lost its last source of authority while the New Rome, Constantinople, struggled to rebuild its prestige in the face of Mongol expansion. Yet, for the Mongol khans and the merchants they favored, for seafaring cities such as Venice and Genoa, for ambitious students at the universities, and for men on the make, the opportunities for advancement and mobility were great.

Other factors were in play during this era. Even in good times, Europe's population had outgrown its capacity to produce food; and when the climate grew cooler, years of cold summers and heavy rainfall took an enormous toll. Those regions most closely tied to the new global networks were densely settled and urban, which made the shortage of food and the spread of disease more acute there. In short, the benefits and drawbacks of increased globalization were already beginning to manifest themselves in the early fourteenth century—700 years ago. The Black Death can be understood as the ultimate example of medieval connectivity.

The scale of mortality caused by this pandemic is almost unimaginable, to us as to those who survived it; at least a third, and probably half, of Europe's people died between 1347 and 1353. In the countryside, entire villages disappeared. Cities and towns, overcrowded and unsanitary, were particularly vulnerable to plague and, thereafter, to outbreaks of violence. The immediate social consequences were profound, as were the economic ones. Crops rotted in the fields, manufacturing ceased, and trade came to a standstill in affected areas. Basic commodities became scarcer and prices rose higher, prompting ineffectual efforts to control prices and to force the remaining able-bodied laborers to work.

These were the short-term effects. How did the Black Death matter to those who survived it—including ourselves? According to Ibn Khaldun (1332–1406), a Muslim historian who is considered one of the founders of modern historical methods, it marked the end of the old world and the beginning of a new one that would require new systems of government, bodies of knowledge, and forms of art. Was he right? We will begin to answer that question in Chapter 11.

PEOPLE, IDEAS, AND EVENTS IN CONTEXT

- What accounts for the success of **GENGHIS KHAN** and his successors? What circumstances enabled **MARCO POLO**'s travels to China? To what extent does the term *PAX MONGOLICA* describe this era in history?
- How did seafaring communities such as **GENOA** and **CATALONIA** rise to prominence in this era? Why were new navigational aids such as **PORTOLAN CHARTS** necessary?
- How do the paintings of **GIOTTO** capture contemporary attitudes toward the world? How does **DANTE**'s artistry respond to the religious and political trends of his day?
- What was at stake in the controversy between **BONIFACE VIII** and **PHILIP IV**? Why was the papacy's residency at **AVIGNON** called the **BABYLONIAN CAPTIVITY**? What is a **SACRAMENT**? Why were these rites so important?
- In what different ways did **LOUIS IX** of France and **EDWARD I** of England contribute to the **SOVEREIGNTY** of their respective kingdoms? What was the relationship between claims to sovereignty and the causes of the **HUNDRED YEARS' WAR**?
- How did climate change contribute to the outbreak of the **GREAT FAMINE**?
- What were the long- and short-term causes of the **BLACK DEATH**?

THINKING ABOUT CONNECTIONS

- If the Mongol khan Ögedei had not died in 1241, the Mongols could conceivably have continued their westward movement into Europe. Knowing what you have learned about Mongol rule, how do you think this might have changed the history of the world?
- How do the patterns of conquest and colonization discussed in this chapter compare with those of earlier periods, particularly those of antiquity? How many of these developments were new in 1250–1350?
- We live in a world in which the global circulation of people, information, goods, and bacteria is rapid—hence the dangers of emerging viruses such as Ebola and Zika. How does the medieval system compare with ours? What features seem familiar?

Before
You
Read
This
Chapter

STORY LINES

- The Black Death altered Europe in profound ways. The opportunities and challenges of this era are dynamically reflected in an array of developments.

- Some of these developments are associated with a new artistic and cultural movement known as the Renaissance, which began in Italy.

- Here, renewed appreciation of the classics and of Greek was facilitated by the flight of Greek-speaking intellectuals from Byzantium, as the Ottoman Turks absorbed the remaining lands of the eastern Roman Empire.

- Meanwhile, the competing territorial claims of Europe's sovereign powers led to large-scale warfare.

- Even after the papacy's return to Rome from Avignon, the failure of internal reform efforts led to the further decline of papal credibility. Consequently, a number of influential religious leaders sought more radical reforms.

CHRONOLOGY

1304–1374	Lifetime of Petrarch
1351	Black Death at its height
	The English Parliament passes the Statute of Laborers
1377	The papacy returns to Rome from Avignon
1378	The Great Schism begins
1381	Rebellions culminate in the English Peasants' Revolt
1414–1418	The Council of Constance is convened to end the Great Schism
	Jan Hus burned at the stake in 1415
1429–1431	The career of Joan of Arc
1431–1449	The Council of Basel fails to check papal power
1440	Lorenzo Valla debunks "The Donation of Constantine"
1453	The Hundred Years' War ends
	Constantinople falls to the Ottoman Turks

Rebirth and Unrest, 1350–1453

CORE OBJECTIVES

- **TRACE** the economic and social effects of the Black Death.

- **EXPLAIN** the relationship between the concepts of the Middle Ages and the Renaissance.

- **DESCRIBE** the intellectual, cultural, and technological innovations of this era.

- **DEFINE** the concept of national monarchy and summarize its implications.

- **UNDERSTAND** the significance of the conciliar movement and its defeat by the papacy.

I n June 1381, thousands of laborers from the English countryside rose up in rebellion against local authorities. Most were peasants or village artisans who were dismissed as ignorant by contemporary chroniclers. Yet the revolt was carefully coordinated. Plans were spread in coded messages circulated by word of mouth and by the followers of a renegade Oxford professor, John Wycliffe, who had called for the redistribution of Church property and taught that common people should be able to read the Bible in their own language.

The rebellion's immediate catalyst had been a series of exorbitant taxes levied by Parliament for the support of the ongoing war with France. But its more fundamental cause was an epidemic that had occurred thirty years earlier. The **Black Death** had reduced the entire population of Europe by 40 to 60 percent and drastically altered the world of those who survived it. In this new world, workers were valuable and could stand up to those who paid them poorly or treated them like slaves. During that fateful summer of 1381, the workers of England even vowed to kill representatives of both the Church and the government—to kill (as they put it) all the lawyers—and destroy all the documents that had been used to keep them in subjection. It was a revolution, and it partly succeeded. Although the leaders were eventually captured and executed, the rebellion had made the strength of the common people known to all.

The fourteenth century is often seen as a time of crisis in the history of Western civilizations: famine and plague cut fearful swaths through the population; war was a brutally recurrent fact of life; and the papacy spent seventy years in continuous exile from Italy, only to see its prestige decline further after its return to Rome. But this was also a time of extraordinary opportunity and achievement. The exhausted land of Europe recovered from centuries of overfarming. Workers gained the economic edge; and eventually, some even gained social and political power. Meanwhile, popular and intellectual movements sought to reform the Church. A host of intellectual, artistic, and scientific innovations contributed to all of these phenomena.

This era of rebirth and unrest has been called by two different names: the later Middle Ages and the Renaissance. The latter term refers to an intellectual and artistic movement that began in northern Italy, where the citizens of warring city-states desperately sought new models of governance and cultural cohesion by looking back to the older civilizations of Greece and Rome. But these are not two separate historical periods; rather, these two terms reflect two different ways of looking back at an era that is considered to be the immediate precursor of modernity. To understand it, we need to study it holistically, and we need to begin with a survey of Western civilizations after the Black Death.

LIFE AFTER THE BLACK DEATH

By 1353, when the plague caused by the *Yersinia pestis* bacterium began to loosen its death grip on Europe, the Continent had lost half its population from a combination of famine and disease in the space of two generations (see Chapter 10). In the following century, recurring outbreaks of the plague and frequent warfare in some regions resulted in further drastic reductions. Life after the Black Death was therefore radically different for those who survived it, because this massive depopulation affected every aspect of existence, from nutrition to social mobility to spirituality.

The Environmental Impact of the Plague

The devastating mortality of the plague had significant environmental implications. In central Europe, for example,

some 400 towns and villages became depopulated and disappeared. Around Paris, more than half the farmland formerly under cultivation became wasteland or pasture due to the absence of workers and decreased demand for food. In other regions, abandoned fields returned to woodland, increasing the forested areas of Europe for the first time in centuries. These changes reestablished a healthier ecological balance, replenishing nutrients in the exhausted soil and providing habitats for animals in danger of extinction. Meanwhile, the declining population reduced the demand for grain, so farmers could begin to diversify their crops and establish livestock herds. Turning arable land into pastureland further improved the fertility of the soil through manuring.

At the same time, the environment—and the humans dependent on it—continued to be affected by the plague because *Yersinia pestis* became endemic (that is, permanently

THE PLAGUE CLAIMS A VICTIM. A priest gives the last rites to a bedridden plague victim as a smiling devil pierces the dying man with a spear and Christ looks mercifully down from heaven. ▪ *What are the possible meanings of this image?* ▪ *What does it reveal about contemporary attitudes toward death by the plague?*

embedded) in some locales. This bacterium thrives in cool, upland climates, where it can lie dormant for many years. But a sudden change in temperature can activate it, as can intensified interactions between human communities and animals who act as hosts for the bacterium. To take one example, for centuries remote villages in the Alps suffered repeated outbreaks of the plague harbored by local fauna, including marmots and other rodent species. The plague would spread still farther if a villager exposed to animal-borne plague traveled to a city or brought animal skins there for sale.

The Social Impact of the Plague

In the wake of the plague, the relative abundance of food meant that the price of grain fell, making bread—the staple of the medieval diet—more affordable. At the same time, the scarcity of workers made peasant labor more valuable. Work became more easily obtainable, and some peasants were able to negotiate higher wages. With wages higher and food prices lower, ordinary people could afford a better and more balanced diet, including dairy products, meat, fish, fruits, and vegetables. As a result, Europeans became better nourished than they had ever been—better than many are today. A study of fifteenth-century rubbish dumps concluded that the people of Glasgow (Scotland) ate a healthier diet in 1405 than they did in 2005. The improved health of the population also caused improved fertility rates and birthrates.

Meanwhile, the survivors of the Black Death experienced tremendous social and economic changes. In rural areas, small farmers who were able to increase the diversity and size of their holdings could ensure the prosperity of their families and achieve a higher social status. At the same time, though, large landholders were responding to the shortage of workers by forcing their tenants to perform additional unpaid labor. In parts of eastern Europe, formerly free peasant workers became serfs for the first time. In other regions, including in Castile (Spain), Poland, and Germany, many lords succeeded in imposing new forms of servitude on peasant laborers.

In France and the Low Countries, by contrast, peasants were able to exercise more freedoms than in the past, although many were still forced to pay a variety of fees and taxes to their lords. In England, where peasant bondage had been more common than in France, serfdom eventually disappeared altogether. Although the Peasants' Revolt of 1381 was ultimately unsuccessful, increased economic opportunity led to increased geographic mobility, as English workers moved either to town or to the lands of a lord who offered more favorable terms: lower rents, more animals, fewer work requirements, and greater personal freedoms. As we have often noted, geographical mobility and social mobility are intertwined.

In the crowded cities and towns affected by the plague, mortality rates were high, but not all cities were equally affected, and some recovered relatively quickly. In London and Paris, for example, immigrants from the countryside reversed population declines caused by the Black Death. Other urban areas suffered more from internal violence or warfare than from disease. In Florence, for example, the population rebounded quickly after the Black Death but was eventually depleted by civil unrest (see page 362). In Toulouse (southwestern France), the population remained fairly stable until 1430, when it was reduced by a staggering 75 percent as a result of the Hundred Years' War.

Although the overall population of Europe declined drastically, a far larger percentage of people were living in towns by 1500: approximately 20 percent, as opposed to about 5 to 10 percent prior to the Black Death. Fueling this urban growth was the increasing specialization of the late-medieval economy. With farmers under less pressure to produce grain in bulk, they could devote land to livestock, dairy farming, and the production of a more diverse array of fruits and vegetables—all of which could now be exchanged more efficiently on the open market.

Towns with links to extant trading networks benefited accordingly. In northern Germany, a group of entrepreneurial cities formed a coalition to build an entirely new mercantile corporation, the Hanseatic League, whose members came to control commerce from Britain and Scandinavia to the Baltic. In northern Italy, the increased demand for luxury goods—which even some peasants and urban laborers could now afford—brought renewed wealth to the spice- and silk-trading city of Venice and to the fine-cloth manufacturers of Florence. Milan's armaments industry also prospered, supplying its warring neighbors and the armies of Europe.

Of course, not all urban areas flourished. The Franco-Flemish cities that had played such a large role in economic and cultural life since the eleventh century suffered a serious economic depression, exacerbated by incessant wars in the region. But, on the whole, surviving Europeans profited from the plague. A century afterward, they were poised to extend their commercial networks farther into Africa, Asia, and (ultimately) the Americas (see Chapter 12).

Popular Revolts and Rebellions

Although the consequences of the Black Death were ultimately beneficial for many, Europeans did not adjust easily to this new world. Established elites, in particular, resisted the demands of newly powerful workers; and when these demands were not met, violence erupted. Between 1350 and 1425, hundreds of popular rebellions challenged the status quo in many regions of Europe. In 1358, peasants in northeastern France rose up violently against their lords, destroying property, burning buildings and crops, and even murdering targeted individuals. This incident is known as the Jacquerie Rebellion, because all French peasants were caricatured by the aristocracy as "Jacques" ("Jack").

In England, as we have already noted, a very different uprising occurred in June 1381, one far more organized and involving a much wider segment of society. In the **English Peasants' Revolt**, thousands of people marched on London, targeting the bureaucracies of the royal government and the Church, capturing and killing the archbishop of Canterbury, and meeting personally with the fourteen-year-old king, Richard II, to demand an end to serfdom and taxation and to call for the redistribution of property. It ended with the arrest and execution of the ringleaders.

In Florence, the guilds representing workers in the cloth industry, known as the Ciompi (*chee-OHM-pee*), were more successful, at least in the short term. Their rebellion began in 1378, when the guild members protested high unemployment and mistreatment by the manufacturers, who also ran the Florentine government. They succeeded in seizing control of the city, demanding relief from taxes, full employment, and political representation. Remarkably, the Ciompi regime remained powerful for nearly four years, before it was suppressed by the urban elite. But even afterward, some of the economic reforms it had introduced remained in place.

The local circumstances that lay behind each of these revolts were unique, but all of them exhibit certain common features. First of all, those who took part in them were empowered by the new economy and they wanted to leverage their position to enact even larger changes. Some rebellions, such as the English Peasants' Revolt, were touched off by resistance to new and higher taxes. Others, such as the Jacquerie and the revolt of the Ciompi, took place at moments when unpopular governments were weakened by factionalism and military defeat. Behind this social and political unrest, therefore, lay the growing prosperity and self-confidence of village communities and urban laborers who were taking advantage of the changed circumstances that arose from the plague. This tradition of popular rebellion remained an important feature of Western civilizations, eventually fueling the American War of Independence and the French Revolution (see Chapter 18).

Aristocratic Life in the Wake of the Plague

The rural aristocracies of Europe did not adapt easily to the "world turned upside down" by the plague. Many great families became far wealthier than their ancestors had ever been, but they now had to compete with an upwardly mobile population and enriched urban elites who were driving up the cost of maintaining a fashionable lifestyle. Noble families traditionally derived their revenue from vast land holdings, but some now tried to increase their income through new sources, such as investment in trading ventures.

In Catalonia, Italy, Germany, and England, this became common practice. In France and Castile, however, involvement in commerce was regarded as socially demeaning and was, therefore, avoided by established families. Commerce could still be a route to higher status in these kingdoms, but once a merchant achieved aristocratic rank, he was expected to abandon former employments and adopt an appropriate way of life: living in a rural castle or urban palace surrounded by a lavish household, embracing the values and conventions of chivalry (hunting, commissioning a family coat of arms), and serving his ruler at court and in warfare.

What it meant to be "noble" became, as a result, even more difficult to define than it had been during the twelfth and thirteenth centuries. In countries where noble rank entailed certain legal privileges—such as the right to be tried only in special courts—proven descent from aristocratic ancestors might be necessary to qualify a family as noble. Legal nobility of this sort was, however, a somewhat less exclusive distinction than we might expect. In fifteenth-century Castile and Navarre, for example, 10 to 15 percent of the total population had claims to be recognized as noble in these terms. In Poland, Hungary, and Scotland, the legally privileged nobility was closer to 5 percent, whereas in England and France, an even smaller percentage could plausibly claim the legal privileges of noble status.

Fundamentally, however, nobility was expressed and epitomized by lifestyle. Land ownership, political influence, deference from social inferiors, courtly manners, and the ostentatious display of wealth—all these combined constituted a family's honor and marked it as noble. This means that, in practice, distinctions between noble and non-noble families were very hard to discern. Even on the battlefield, where the mark of nobility was to fight on horseback, the supremacy of the mounted knight was being threatened by the growing importance of professional soldiers, archers, crossbowmen, and artillery experts. There were even hints of a more radical critique of the aristocracy's claims to superiority. As the English rebels put it in 1381, "When

Adam dug and Eve spun, who then was a gentleman?" In other words, social distinctions are not innate and natural but ephemeral and artificial.

Precisely because nobility was contested, those who claimed it took elaborate measures to assert their right to this status through what we would call conspicuous consumption. This helps to explain the extraordinary number, variety, and richness of the artifacts and artworks that survive from this period. Aristocrats, or those who wanted to be classed as such, vied with each other in hosting lavish banquets, which required numerous costly utensils, specially decorated dining chambers, legions of servants, and the most exotic foods attainable. They also dressed in rich and extravagant clothing—close-fitting doublets and hose with long, pointed shoes for men; and multilayered silk dresses with ornately festooned headdresses for women—

and maintained enormous households. In France around 1400, for example, the Duke of Berry had 400 matched pairs of hunting dogs and 1,000 servants. Aristocrats took part in elaborately ritualized tournaments and pageants, in which the participants pretended to be the heroes of chivalric romances. They also emphasized their tastes and refinement by supporting authors and artists.

Rulers contributed to this process of ostentatious aristocratic display. Across Europe, kings and princes competed in founding chivalric orders, such as the Knights of the Garter in England and the Order of the Star in France. These orders honored men who demonstrated the idealized virtues of knighthood and exalted the nobility as a special class, strengthening the links that bound powerful families to their sovereign lords. These bonds were further strengthened by the gifts, pensions, offices, and marriage prospects that rulers could bestow on their noble followers. Indeed, the alliance forged in the fifteenth century between kings and their noble supporters would become one of the most characteristic features of Europe's ruling class. In France, this alliance lasted until the French Revolution of 1789. In central and eastern Europe, it lasted until the outbreak of World War I. In Britain, it persisted in some respects until World War II.

A NOBLE BANQUET. The Duke of Berry, the uncle of the mad king Charles VI, left politics to his brothers, the Duke of Burgundy and the Duke of Anjou. In return, he received enormous subsidies from the royal government, which he spent on sumptuous buildings, festivals, and artworks, including the famous *Book of Hours* (prayer book), which includes the image shown here: the duke (seated at right, in blue) gives a New Year's Day banquet for his household, who exchange gifts while his hunting dogs dine on scraps from the table; in the background, knights confront one another in a tournament.

Capturing the New Reality in Writing

The writings of those who survived the Black Death, or who grew up in the decades immediately following it, are characterized by intense observations of the real world—and were read by a larger and more diverse audience than ever before. We have noted that vernacular languages were becoming powerful vehicles for literary expression and emerging regional identities (Chapter 9). Now, they were being used to express innovative and critical perspectives on changing social mores, political developments, and religious beliefs. We can see these innovations at work in the writings of three major authors who flourished during this period: Giovanni Boccaccio, Geoffrey Chaucer, and Christine de Pizan.

Giovanni Boccaccio (*bohk-KAHT-chee-oh*; 1313–1375) is best known for *The Decameron*, a collection of prose tales about sex, adventure, and trickery. He presents these stories as being told over a period of ten days (hence the title of the book, which means "work of ten days") by and for a sophisticated party of young women and men who have taken up residence in a country villa outside Florence to escape the ravages of the Black Death. Boccaccio borrowed the outlines of many of these tales from earlier sources, especially the fabliaux discussed in Chapter 9, but he couched them in a freely colloquial Italian. Whereas Dante had used the same Florentine dialect to evoke the awesome landscape of sacred history in the exquisite verse of his *Divine Comedy* (Chapter 10), Boccaccio used it to capture in plain-spoken prose the foibles of human beings and their often graphic sexual exploits.

CHRISTINE DE PIZAN. One of the most prolific authors of the Middle Ages, Christine used her influence to uphold the dignity of women and to celebrate their history and achievements. Here we see her describing the prowess of an Amazon warrior who could defeat men effortlessly in armed combat.

The poet **Geoffrey Chaucer** (c. 1340–1400) was among the first generation of authors writing a form of English that modern readers can understand with relatively little effort. By the late fourteenth century, the Anglo-Saxon (Old English) tongue of England's preconquest inhabitants had mixed with the French dialect spoken by their Norman conquerors to create the language that is the ancestor of our own: Middle English. Chaucer's masterpiece, *The Canterbury Tales*, was profoundly influenced by Boccaccio's *Decameron*. It, too, is a collection of stories held together by a framing narrative. But, in this case, the stories are in verse and are told by a diverse group of people traveling together on a pilgrimage from London to the shrine of Saint Thomas Becket at Canterbury. Each character tells a story that is particularly illustrative of his or her own occupation and outlook on the world, forming a kaleidoscopic human comedy.

The generation or so after the Black Death also saw the emergence of professional authors who made their living through the patronage of the aristocracy and the broader publication of their works. One of the first of these was a woman, **Christine de Pizan** (c. 1365–c. 1434). Born in northern Italy, Christine spent her adult life in France, where her husband was a member of the king's household. When he died, the widowed Christine wrote to support herself and her children. She mastered a wide variety of literary genres—including treatises on chivalry and warfare, which she dedicated to King Charles VI of France—and wrote for a larger and more popular audience. For example, her imaginative *Book of the City of Ladies* is an extended defense of the character, capacities, and history of women, designed to help female readers refute their male detractors.

Christine also took part in a vigorous pamphlet campaign that condemned the misogynistic claims made by influential (male) authors such as Boccaccio. This debate was ongoing for several hundred years and became so famous that it was given a name: the *querelle des femmes* ("the debate over women"). It is remarkable that Christine also wrote a song in praise of Joan of Arc. Unfortunately, though, she probably lived long enough to learn that this other extraordinary woman had been put to death for behaving in a way that was considered dangerously unwomanly (see pages 377–378).

Visualizing the New Reality

Just as the desire to capture real experiences and convey real emotions was a dominant trait of the literature produced

Analyzing Primary Sources

Why a Woman Can Write about Warfare

Christine de Pizan (c. 1365–c. 1434) was one of the West's first professional writers, best known today for her Book of the City of Ladies *and* The Treasure of the City of Ladies, *works that aimed to provide women with an honorable and rich history and to combat generations of institutionalized misogyny. But in her own time, Christine was probably best known for the work excerpted here,* The Book of the Deeds of Arms and of Chivalry, *a manual of military strategy and conduct written in 1410, at the height of the Hundred Years' War.*

s boldness is essential for great undertakings, and without it nothing should be risked, I think it is proper in this present work to set forth my unworthiness to treat such exalted matter. I should not have dared even to think about it, but although boldness is blameworthy when it is foolhardy, I should state that I have not been inspired by arrogance or foolish presumption, but rather by true affection and a genuine desire for the welfare of noble men engaging in the profession of arms. I am encouraged, in the light of my other writings, to undertake to speak in this book of the most honorable office of arms and chivalry.... So to this end I have gathered together facts and subject matter from various books to produce this present volume. But inasmuch as it is fitting for this matter to be discussed factually, diligently, and sensibly ... and also in consideration of the fact that military and lay experts in the aforesaid art of chivalry are not usually clerks or writers who are expert in language, I intend to treat the matter in the plainest possible language....

As this is unusual for women, who generally are occupied in weaving, spinning, and household duties, I humbly invoke ... the wise lady Minerva [Athena], born in the land of Greece, whom the ancients esteemed highly for her great wisdom. Likewise the poet Boccaccio praises her in his *Book of Famous Women*, as do other writers praise her art and manner of making trappings of iron and steel, so let it not be held against me if I, as a woman, take it upon myself to treat of military matters....

O Minerva! goddess of arms and of chivalry, who, by understanding beyond that of other women, did find and initiate among the other noble arts and sciences the custom of forging iron and steel armaments and harness both proper and suitable for covering and protecting men's bodies against arrows slung in battle—helmets, shields, and protective covering having come first from you—you instituted and gave directions for drawing up a battle order, how to begin an assault and to engage in proper combat.... In the aforementioned country of Greece, you provided the usage of this office, and insofar as it may please you to be favorably disposed, and I in no way appear to be against the nation from which you came, the country beyond the Alps that is now called Apulia and Calabria in Italy, where you were born, let me say that like you I am an Italian woman.

Source: From Christine de Pizan, *The Book of the Deeds of Arms and of Chivalry*, ed. Charity Cannon Willard and trans. Sumner Willard (University Park, PA: 1999), pp. 11–13.

Questions for Analysis

1. Christine very cleverly deflects potential criticism for her "boldness" in writing about warfare. What tactics does she use?

2. The Greco-Roman goddess Athena (Minerva) was the goddess of wisdom, weaving, and warfare. Why does Christine invoke her aid? What parallels does she draw between her own attributes and those of Minerva?

---

after the Black Death, so it was in the visual arts. This is evident both in the older arts of manuscript illumination and in the new kinds of painting and sculpture we discussed in Chapter 10. A further innovation in the fifteenth century was the technique of painting in oils, a medium pioneered in Flanders, where artists found a ready market for their works among the nobility and wealthy merchants.

Oil paints were a revolutionary artistic development. Because they do not dry so quickly as water-based pigments, a painter can work more slowly and carefully, taking time with more difficult aspects of the work and making corrections as needed. Masterly practitioners of this technique include Rogier van der Weyden (c. 1400–1464), who excelled at communicating both deep spiritual messages and the minute details of everyday life (see ***Interpreting Visual Evidence*** on page 368). Just as contemporary saints such as Francis of Assisi saw divinity in material objects, so too could an artist portray the Virgin and Child against a background vista of ordinary life, such as people going about their business or a man urinating against a wall. This was not blasphemous; on the contrary, it conveyed the message that the events of the Bible are constantly present, here and now. Such artworks suggest, for example, that Christ is our companion, not a distant figure whose life and outlook are irrelevant to us.

The same immediacy is also evident in medieval drama. Plays were often devotional exercises that involved the efforts of an entire community and celebrated that community. In the English city of York, for example, an annual series of pageants reenacted the entire history of human salvation from the Creation to the Last Judgment in a single summer day, beginning at dawn and ending late at night. Each pageant was produced by a particular craft guild and showcased that guild's special talents: "The Last Supper" was performed by the bakers, whose bread was a key element in their reenactment of the first Eucharist, whereas "The Crucifixion" was performed by the nail makers and the painters, whose wares were thereby put on prominent display in the depiction of Christ's bloody death on the cross.

In Italy, confraternities (brotherhoods) competed with each another to honor the saints with songs and processions. In Catalonia and many regions of Spain, there were elaborate dramas celebrating the life and miracles of the Virgin. One of these dramas is still performed every year in the Basque town of Elche and is the oldest European play in continuous production. In northern France, the Low Countries, and German-speaking lands, civic spectacles were performed over a period of several days, celebrating local history or the place of the community in the sacred history of the Bible. But not all plays were pious. Some honored visiting kings and princes, while others celebrated the flouting of social conventions, featuring cross-dressing and the reversal of hierarchies, which were further expressions of the topsy-turvy world created by the Black Death.

THE BEGINNINGS OF THE RENAISSANCE IN ITALY

Rummaging through some old books in a cathedral library, an Italian bureaucrat attached to the papal court at Avignon was surprised to find a manuscript of Cicero's letters—letters that no living person had known to exist. They had probably been copied in the time of Charlemagne and had then been forgotten for hundreds of years. How many other works of this great Roman orator had been lost to posterity? Clearly, thought Francesco Petrarca (1304–1374), he was living in an age of ignorance. A great gulf seemed to open up between his own time and that of the ancients: a middle age that separated him from those well-loved models.

PETRARCH'S COPY OF VIRGIL. Petrarch's devotion to the classics of Roman literature prompted him to commission this new frontispiece for his treasured volume of Virgil's poetry. It was painted by the Sienese artist Simone Martini, who (like Petrarch) was attached to the papal court at Avignon. It is an allegorical depiction of Virgil (top right) and his poetic creations: the hero Aeneas, wearing armor (top left); and the farmer and shepherd, whose humble labors are celebrated in Virgil's lesser-known works. The figure next to Aeneas is the fourth-century scholar Servius, who wrote a famous commentary on Virgil. He is shown drawing aside a curtain to reveal the poet in a creative trance. The two scrolls proclaim (in Latin) that Italy was the country that nourished famous poets, and that Virgil helped it to achieve the glories of classical Greece. ▪ *How does this image encapsulate and express Petrarch's devotion to the classical past?*

For centuries, Christian intellectuals had regarded the "dark ages" as the time between Adam's expulsion from Eden and the birth of Christ. But now, Petrarch (the anglicized form of Petrarca) redefined that concept and applied it to his own era. According to him, it was not the pagan past but the time that separated him from direct communion with the classics. And he wanted desperately to bridge this gap, "I would have written to you long ago," he said in a Latin letter to the Greek poet Homer (dead for over 2,000 years), "had it not been for the fact that we lack a common language."

Petrarch was famous in his own day as an Italian poet, a Latin stylist, and a tireless advocate for the resuscitation of the classical past. The values that he and his followers began to espouse would give rise to a new intellectual and artistic movement in Italy, a movement strongly critical of the present and admiring of a past that had disappeared with the fragmentation of Rome's empire and the end of Italy's greatness. We know this movement as the **Renaissance**, from the French word for "rebirth," a term that was invented in the eighteenth century and popularized in the nineteenth (when the term *medieval* was also invented). It has since become shorthand for the epoch *following* the Middle Ages—but it was really part of that same era.

Renaissance Classicism

Talking about "the Renaissance," then, is a way of talking about some significant changes in education and artistic outlook that began to transform the culture of northern Italy in the late fourteenth century—and that eventually influenced the rest of Europe in important ways. This term has often been taken literally, as though the cultural accomplishments of antiquity had ceased to be appreciated and needed to be "reborn." Yet we have been tracing the enduring influence of classical civilization through many chapters and have constantly noted the reverence accorded to the heritage of antiquity, not to mention the persistence of Roman law and Roman institutions.

That said, the concept of "renaissance" helps to explain some of the key developments of this era. For example, the ancient texts that had long been preserved in monastic libraries now came to be more widely available to secular scholars such as Petrarch. Their "discovery" of works by Livy, Tacitus, and Lucretius expanded the classical canon considerably, supplementing the well-studied works of Virgil, Ovid, and Cicero. Even more important was their expanded access to ancient Greek literature. As we noted in Chapters 8 and 9, Greek scientific and philosophical works became available to western Europeans in the twelfth and thirteenth centuries thanks to increased contact with Islam, via Latin translations of Arabic translations of the original Greek. And yet no Greek poems or plays were yet available in Latin translations, and neither were the major dialogues of Plato. Moreover, only a handful of western Europeans could read the language of classical Greece. But as the Mongols and, after them, the Ottoman Turks put increasing pressure on the shrinking borders of Byzantium (see pages 371–372), more and more Greek-speaking intellectuals fled to Italy, bringing their books and their knowledge with them.

Some Italian intellectuals not only had increased access to more classical texts, but they also used these texts in new ways. For centuries, Christian scholars had worked to bring ancient writings and values into line with their own beliefs (Chapter 6). But the new reading methods pioneered by Petrarch and others fostered an increased awareness of the conceptual gap that separated their contemporary world from that of antiquity. This awareness awakened a determination to recapture truly ancient worldviews and value systems. In the second half of the fifteenth century, especially, classical models also contributed strikingly to the distinctive artistic style that is most strongly associated with the Renaissance, something we will address in Chapter 12.

Another distinguishing feature of this new perspective on the classical past was the way that it became commercialized. Competition among and within Italian city-states fostered a culture of display that used the symbols and artifacts of ancient Rome as pawns in an endless power game. Meanwhile, the relative weakness of the Church contributed to the growth of claims to power based on classical models—even by Italian bishops and Church-sponsored universities. When the papacy was eventually restored to Rome, it, too, had to compete in this Renaissance arena, by patronizing the artists and intellectuals who espoused these aesthetic and political ideals.

Renaissance Humanism

A crucial feature of this new intellectual and political agenda is summarized in the term **humanism**. This was a program of study that aimed to replace the scholastic emphasis on logic and theology—central to the curriculum of medieval universities—with the study of ancient literature, rhetoric, history, and ethics. The goal of a humanist education was the understanding of the human experience through the lenses of the classical past. In contrast, a scholastic education filtered human experience through the teachings of scripture and the Church Fathers, with human salvation as the ultimate goal.

Interpreting Visual Evidence

Realizing Devotion

These two paintings by the Flemish artist Rogier van der Weyden (*FAN der VIE-den*; c. 1400–1464) capture some of the most compelling characteristics of late medieval art, particularly the trend toward realistic representations of holy figures and sacred stories. In image A, the artist depicts himself as the evangelist Luke, regarded in Christian tradition as a painter of portraits. He is sketching the Virgin nursing the infant Jesus in a townhouse overlooking a Flemish city. In image B, van der Weyden imagines the entombment of the body of Christ by his followers,

including the Virgin (left), Mary Magdalene (kneeling), and the disciple John (right). Here he makes use of a motif that became increasingly prominent in the later Middle Ages: Christ as the Man of Sorrows, displaying his wounds and inviting the viewer to share in his suffering. In both paintings, van der Weyden emphasizes the humanity of his subjects rather than their iconic status (see Chapter 7), and places them in the urban and rural landscapes of his own world.

Questions for Analysis

1. How are these paintings different from the sacred images of the earlier Middle Ages (see, for example, pages 304 and 342)? What messages does the artist convey by setting these events in his own immediate present?

2. In what ways do these paintings reflect broad changes in popular piety and medieval devotional practices? Why, for example, would the artist display the dead body of Christ, covered with wounds, rather than depicting him as resurrected and triumphant, or as an all-seeing creator and judge?

3. In general, how would you interpret these images as evidence of the worldview of the fifteenth century? What do they tell us about people's attitudes, emotions, and values?

A. Saint Luke Drawing the Portrait of the Virgin.

B. The Lamentation.

Humanists accordingly preferred ancient writings to those of more recent authors, including their own contemporaries. And although some humanists wrote in Italian as well as Latin, most regarded vernacular literature as a lesser diversion suitable only for the uneducated; serious scholarship and praiseworthy poetry could be written only in Latin or Greek. Proper Latin, moreover, had to be the classical Latin of Cicero and Virgil, not the evolving language common to universities, international diplomacy, law, and the Church.

Renaissance humanists therefore condemned the living Latin of their day as a barbarous departure from classical (and therefore "correct") standards of Latin style. And ironically, their determination to revive this older language eventually killed the lively Latin that had continued to flourish in Europe. By insisting on outmoded standards of grammar, syntax, and diction, they turned Latin into a fossilized discourse that ceased to have any direct relevance to daily life. They thus contributed, unwittingly, to the ultimate triumph of the various European vernaculars and the demise of Latin as a common medium of communication among literate elites.

Because humanism was an educational program designed to produce virtuous citizens and able public officials, it largely excluded women, because women were largely denied any role in Italian public life. In a political context, humanism could be made to serve either the ideals of citizenship as exemplified by the Roman Republic, or the authoritarian agendas of autocratic rulers who wanted to emulate Roman imperial power.

Why Italy?

These new attitudes toward education and the ancient past were fostered in northern Italy for historically specific reasons. After the Black Death, this region was the most densely populated part of Europe; other urban areas, notably northeastern France and Flanders, had been decimated by the Great Famine as well as by the plague. This region also differed from the rest of urbanized Europe because aristocratic families customarily lived in cities rather than in rural castles, and consequently, they became more fully involved in public affairs than their counterparts north of the Alps. Moreover, many town-dwelling aristocrats were engaged in banking or mercantile enterprises, and many rich mercantile families imitated the manners of the aristocracy. The Florentine ruling family, the Medici, originally made their fortune in banking and commerce, yet they were able to assimilate into the nobility.

These developments help to explain the emergence of humanist education. Newly wealthy families were not content to have their sons learn only the skills necessary to become successful businessmen; they sought teachers who would impart the knowledge and finesse that would enable them to cut a figure in society, mix with their noble neighbors, and speak with authority on public affairs. Consequently, Italy produced and attracted a large number of independent intellectuals who were not affiliated with monasteries, cathedral schools, or universities. Many of these intellectuals served as schoolmasters for wealthy young men while acting as cultural consultants and secretaries for their families. And they advertised their learning by producing political and ethical treatises and works of literature that would attract the attention of wealthy patrons or reflect well on the patrons they already had. As a result, Italian schools and private tutors turned out the best-educated laymen in Europe, men who constituted a new generation of wealthy, knowledgeable patrons ready to invest in the cultivation of new ideas and new forms of literary and artistic expression.

A second reason that late-medieval Italy was the birthplace of the Renaissance movement had to do with its vexed political situation. Unlike France and England, or the kingdoms of Spain, Scandinavia, and eastern Europe, Italy had no unifying political institutions. Italians therefore looked to the classical past for their time of glory, dreaming of a day when Rome would be, again, the center of the world. They boasted that ancient Roman monuments were omnipresent in their landscape and that classical Latin literature referred to cities and sites they recognized as their own.

Northern Italians were particularly intent on reappropriating their classical heritage because they were seeking to establish an independent cultural identity that could help oppose the intellectual and political supremacy of France. The removal of the papacy to Avignon had heightened antagonism between the city-states of Italy and the powerful nation-state beyond the Alps. This also explains the Italians' rejection of the scholasticism taught in northern Europe's universities and the humanists' embrace of intellectual alternatives. As Roman literature and learning took hold in the imaginations of Italy's intellectuals, so too did Roman art and architecture; ancient Roman models could help Italians create an artistic alternative to the dominant French school of Gothic architecture, just as ancient Roman learning offered an intellectual alternative to the scholasticism of Paris.

Finally, this Italian Renaissance could not have occurred without the underpinning of Italian wealth gained through the commercial ventures described in Chapter 10. This wealth meant that talented men seeking employment and patronage were more likely to stay at home, fueling the artistic and intellectual competition that arose from the intensification of urban pride and the concentration of

Analyzing Primary Sources

A Renaissance Attitude toward Women

Italian society of the fourteenth and fifteenth centuries was characterized by marriage patterns whereby men in their late twenties or thirties married women in their mid- to late teens. This demographic fact probably contributed to the widely shared belief that wives were essentially children who could not be trusted with important matters and who were best trained by being beaten. Renaissance humanism did little to change such attitudes, and in some cases, even reinforced them. The following is an excerpt from a treatise On the Family *by Leon Battista Alberti (1404–1472), a Genoese architect and intellectual who also wrote an important treatise* On Painting. *He is often regarded as typifying the "Renaissance man."*

fter my wife had been settled in my house a few days, and after her first pangs of longing for her mother and family had begun to fade, I took her by the hand and showed her around the whole house. I explained that the loft was the place for grain and that the stores of wine and wood were kept in the cellar. I showed her where things needed for the table were kept, and so on, through the whole house. At the end there were no household goods of which my wife had not learned both the place and the purpose. . . .

Only my books and records and those of my ancestors did I determine to keep well sealed. . . . These my wife not only could not read, she could not even lay hands on them. I kept my records at all times . . . locked up and arranged in order in my study, almost like sacred and religious objects. I never gave my wife permission to enter that place, with me or alone. . . .

[Husbands] who take counsel with their wives . . . are madmen if they think true prudence or good counsel lies in the female brain. . . . For this very reason I have always tried carefully not to let any secret of mine be known to a woman. I did not doubt that my wife was most loving, and more discreet and modest in her ways than any, but I still considered it safer to have her unable, and not merely unwilling, to harm me. . . . Furthermore, I made it a rule never to speak with her of anything but household matters or questions of conduct, or of the children.

Source: Leon Battista Alberti, "On the Family," in *The Family in Renaissance Florence*, ed. and trans. Renée N. Watkins (Columbia, SC: 1969), pp. 208–13, as abridged in Julie O'Faolain and Lauro Martines, eds., *Not in God's Image: Women in History from the Greeks to the Victorians* (New York: 1973), pp. 187–88.

Questions for Analysis

1. For what reasons did Alberti argue that a wife should have no access to books or records?

2. Would you have expected humanism to make attitudes toward women more liberal and "modern"? How do views such as Alberti's challenge such assumptions?

3. Compare Alberti's view of women to that of Christine de Pizan (page 365). How do you think Christine would have responded to this passage?

---

individual and family wealth in urban areas. Cities themselves became the primary patrons of art and learning in the fourteenth century.

Florentine Civic Ideals

Petrarch's personal goal was a solitary life of contemplation and asceticism. But subsequent Italian intellectuals, especially those of Florence, developed a different vision of life's true purpose. For them, the goal of classical education was civic enrichment. Humanists such as Leonardo Bruni (c. 1370–1444) and Leon Battista Alberti (1404–1472) taught that man's nature equips him for action, for usefulness to his family and society, and for serving the state—ideally a city-state after the Florentine model. In their view, ambition and the quest for glory were noble impulses that ought to be encouraged and channeled toward these ends. They also refused to condemn the accumulation of material possessions, arguing that the history of human progress is inseparable from the human dominion of the earth and its resources.

Many of the Florentine humanists' civic ideals are expressed in Alberti's treatise *On the Family* (1443) (see **Analyzing Primary Sources** on page 370), in which he presents the nuclear family as the fundamental unit of the city-state. Alberti accordingly argued that the family should mirror the city-state's organization, thereby consigning women—who, in reality, governed the household—to childbearing, child rearing, and subservience to men even within this domestic realm. He asserted, furthermore, that women should play no role whatsoever in the public sphere. Although actual women fiercely resisted such dismissals of women's abilities, the humanism of the Renaissance was characterized by a pervasive denigration of them—a denigration often mirrored in the works of classical literature that these humanists so admired.

New Ways of Reading Ancient Texts

The humanists of northern Italy were aided by a number of Byzantine scholars who had migrated to northern Italy in the first half of the fifteenth century and gave instruction in the ancient form of their own language. Wealthy, well-connected men increasingly aspired to acquire Greek masterpieces, which often involved journeys back to Constantinople. In 1423, one adventurous bibliophile managed to bring back 238 manuscript books, among them rare works of Sophocles, Euripides, and Thucydides. These were quickly paraphrased in Latin and so made accessible to medieval Europeans for the first time.

This influx of new classical texts spurred a new interest in the critical reading of ancient sources. A pioneer in this activity was Lorenzo Valla (1407–1457). Born in Rome and active as a secretary to the king of Naples and Sicily, Valla had no allegiance to the republican ideals of the Florentine humanists. Instead, he turned his skills to the painstaking analysis of Greek and Latin writings to show how the historical study of language could discredit old assumptions and even unmask some texts as forgeries. For example, papal propagandists argued that the papacy's claim to secular power in Europe derived from rights granted to the bishop of Rome by the emperor Constantine in the fourth century, enshrined in a document known as the "Donation of Constantine." By analyzing the language of this text, Valla proved that it could not have been written in the time of Constantine because it contained more recent Latin usages and vocabulary.

This demonstration not only threatened to discredit more traditional scholarly methods, it alerted scholars to the necessity of avoiding anachronism in the study of history—that is, the intellectual vigilance needed to avoid projecting present values and expectations onto the past. Valla even applied his expert knowledge of Greek to elucidate the meaning of Saint Paul's letters, which he believed had been mangled by Jerome's Latin translation (Chapter 6). Valla's work was to prove an important link between Renaissance humanism and the Christian humanism that fueled the Reformation (see Chapter 13).

THE END OF THE EASTERN ROMAN EMPIRE

The Greek-speaking refugees who arrived in Italy after the Black Death were responding to the succession of calamities that had reduced the once-proud eastern Roman Empire to a scattering of embattled provinces. As we have noted, when Constantinople fell to western European crusaders in 1204, the surrounding territories of Byzantium were severed from the capital that had held them together (Chapter 9). When the Latin presence in Constantinople was finally expelled in 1261, imperial power had been so weakened that it extended only into the immediate hinterlands of the city and to parts of the Greek Peloponnese. The rest of the empire had become a collection of small principalities that existed in precarious alliance with the Mongols, and indeed depended on the Pax Mongolica for survival (Chapter 10). Then, with the coming of the Black Death, the imperial capital suffered the loss of half its inhabitants and shrank still further. Meanwhile, the disintegration of the Mongol Empire laid the larger region of Anatolia open to a new set of invaders.

The Rise of the Ottoman Turks

When the Mongols arrived in northwestern Anatolia, the Turks—originally a nomadic people—were already established there and were being converted to Islam by the resident Muslim powers of the region: the Seljuk sultanate of Rûm and the Abbasid caliphate of Baghdad. But when the Mongols toppled these older powers, they eliminated the two traditional authorities that had kept the Turkish chieftains in check. So now the Turks were free to raid, unhindered, along the soft frontiers of Byzantium. At the same time, the Turks remained far enough from the centers of Mongol power to avoid being destroyed themselves. One of their chieftains, Osman Gazi (1258–1326), even managed

TIMUR THE LAME. This bust of the Mongol leader, known in the West as Tamerlane, is based on a forensic reconstruction of his exhumed skull.

In 1402, another attack on Constantinople was deflected—this time, by a more potent foe with ambitions to match those of the Ottomans. Timur the Lame (Tamerlane, as he was called by European admirers) was born to a family of small landholders in the Mongol Khanate of Chagatai (named after its first ruler, the second son of Genghis Khan). While still a young man, he rose to prominence as a military leader and gained a reputation for tactical genius. He never officially assumed the title of khan in any of the territories he dominated, but instead moved ceaselessly from conquest to conquest, becoming the master of lands stretching from the Caspian Sea to the Volga River, as well as most of Persia. For a time, it looked briefly as if the Mongol Empire might be reunited under his reign. But Timur died in 1405, on his way to invade China, and his various conquests fell to local rulers. In Anatolia, the Ottoman Turks were able to regain their dominant position.

The Fall of Constantinople

As Ottoman pressure increased on Constantinople during the 1420s and 1430s, monasteries and schools that had been established since the time of Constantine found themselves in the path of an advancing army. A steady stream of scholars fled westward, carrying a millennium's worth of books preserving the heritage of ancient Greece and the Hellenistic world. Then, in 1451, the Ottoman sultan Mehmet II turned his full attention to the conquest of the imperial city. In 1453, after a brilliantly executed siege, his army succeeded in breaching its walls. The Byzantine emperor was killed in the assault, the city itself was plundered, and its remaining population was sold into slavery.

The Ottoman conquest of Constantinople administered an enormous shock to European rulers and intellectuals. Yet its actual political and economic impact was minor. Ottoman control may have reduced European access to the Black Sea, but the bulk of the Eastern luxury trade with Europe had never passed through Black Sea ports in the first place. Europeans got most of their spices and silks through Venice, which imported them from Alexandria and Beirut, and these two cities did not fall to the Ottomans until the 1520s. Moreover, as we saw in Chapter 10, the Europeans already had colonial ambitions and significant trading interests in Africa and the Atlantic that connected them to far-reaching networks.

But if the practical effects of the Ottoman conquest were modest where Europe was concerned, the effects on

to establish his own kingdom, and eventually, his name became that of the Turkish dynasty that controlled the entire region for six centuries: the **Ottomans**.

By the mid-fourteenth century, Osman's successors had solidified their preeminence by capturing a number of important cities. These successes brought the Ottomans to the attention of the Byzantine emperor, who hired a contingent of them as mercenaries in 1345. They were extraordinarily successful, so much so that the eastern Roman Empire could not control their movements. The Turks struck out on their own and began to extend their control westward. In 1370, their holdings stretched all the way to the Danube. In 1389, they defeated a powerful coalition of Serbian forces at the battle of Kosovo, which enabled them to begin subduing Bulgaria, the Balkans, and eventually Greece. In 1396, the Ottoman army even attacked Constantinople itself, although it withdrew to repel an ineffectual crusading force that had been hastily sent by the papacy.

Slavery and Social Advancement in the Ottoman Empire

To manage its continual expansion, the size of the Ottoman army and administration grew exponentially during this era, drawing more and more manpower from conquered territories. And because both army and bureaucracy were largely composed of slaves, the demand for more soldiers and administrators could best be met through further conquests that would capture yet more slaves. Those conquests, however, required a still larger army and an even more extensive bureaucracy—and so the cycle continued. It mirrors, in many respects, the dilemma of the Roman Empire in the centuries of its rapid expansion beyond Italy (Chapter 5), which also created an insatiable demand for slaves.

Not only were slaves the backbone of the Ottoman state, they were also critical to the lives of the Turkish upper class. An important measure of status was the number of slaves in one's household, with some elites maintaining households in the thousands. By the sixteenth century, the sultan alone possessed more than 20,000 slave attendants, not including his bodyguard and elite infantry units, both of which also comprised slaves.

Where did all of these slaves come from? Many were captured in war and many others were taken during raiding forays into Poland and Ukraine and then sold to slave merchants who shipped their captives from the Crimea to the slave markets of Istanbul. But slaves were also recruited from rural areas of the Ottoman Empire itself. Most were coerced, but some may have gone willingly. Because the vast majority of slaves were household servants and administrators rather than laborers, some men willingly accepted enslavement, believing that they would be better off as slaves in Istanbul than as impoverished peasants in the countryside. In the Balkans especially, many people were enslaved as children, handed over by their families to pay the "child tax" the Ottomans imposed on areas too poor to pay a monetary tribute. Although an excruciating experience for families, this practice opened up opportunities for social advancement. Special academies were created at Istanbul to train the ablest of the enslaved male children to act as administrators and soldiers, some of whom rose to become powerful figures in the Ottoman Empire.

For this reason, slavery carried relatively little social stigma. The sultans themselves were most often the sons of enslaved women. Because Muslims were not permitted to enslave other Muslims, the vast majority of Ottoman slaves were Christian—although many eventually converted to Islam. And because so many of the elite positions within the

SULTAN MEHMET II, "THE CONQUEROR" (R. 1451–1481). This portrait, executed by the Ottoman artist Siblizade Ahmed, exhibits stylistic features characteristic of both central Asia and Europe. The sultan's pose—his aesthetic appreciation of the rose, his elegant handkerchief—are indicative of the former, as is the fact that he wears the white turban of a scholar and the thumb ring of an archer. But the subdued coloring and three-quarter profile may reflect the influence of Italian portraits. ■ *What did the artist achieve through this blending of styles and symbols?* ■ *What messages does this portrait convey?*

the Turks themselves were transformative. Vast new wealth poured into Anatolia, which the Ottomans increased by carefully tending the industrial and commercial interests of their new capital city, Constantinople, which they also called Istanbul, the Turkish pronunciation of the Greek phrase *eis tan polin* ("in the city"). Trade routes were redirected to feed the capital, and the Ottomans became a naval power in the eastern Mediterranean as well as in the Black Sea. As a result, Istanbul's population grew rapidly, from fewer than 100,000 in 1453 to more than 500,000. By 1600, it was the largest city in the world outside of China.

THE GROWTH OF THE OTTOMAN EMPIRE. Consider the patterns of Ottoman expansion revealed in this map. ■ *Where is Constantinople (Istanbul), and how might its capture in 1453 have facilitated further conquests?* ■ *Compare the extent of the Ottoman Empire in 1566 with that of the Byzantine Empire under Justinian (see the map on page 214). How would you account for their similarities?*

Ottoman government were held by these slaves, the paradoxical result was that Muslims, including the Turks themselves, were effectively excluded from the main avenues of social and political influence in the Ottoman Empire. Avenues to power were therefore remarkably open to men of ability and talent, most of them non-Muslim slaves.

This power was not limited to the government and the army, as commerce and business also remained largely in the hands of non-Muslims, most frequently Greeks, Syrians, and Jews. Jews in particular found in the Ottoman Empire a welcome refuge from the persecutions and expulsions that had characterized Jewish life in late-medieval Europe. After their expulsion from Spain in 1492 (see Chapter 12), more than 100,000 Spanish (Sephardic) Jews ultimately immigrated to the territories of the Ottoman Empire.

Because the Ottoman sultans were Sunni Muslims, they often dealt harshly with other Muslim sects and did not tolerate any forms of polytheism. But they accommodated their fellow monotheists, Christians and Jews, who were organized into legally recognized units and were permitted some rights of self-government. The authority of the Greek Orthodox patriarch of Constantinople was also tolerated, allowing Orthodox Christianity to maintain a presence in the capital founded by Constantine.

WARFARE AND NATION BUILDING

War has always been an engine for the development of new technologies, something we have noted since Chapter 1. But in the era after the Black Death, the pace and scale of warfare escalated to an unprecedented degree—as did the deployment of new weapons. Explosives had been invented

A FIFTEENTH-CENTURY SIEGE WITH CANNONS. Cannons were an essential element in siege warfare during the Hundred Years' War.

twentieth, governments claimed new powers to tax their subjects and to recruit them as soldiers. Armies became larger and military technology deadlier. Wars became more destructive and society more militarized. As a result of these developments, the most successful European states were aggressively expansionist, and they aggressively engaged in creating an idea of national identity that would bind their peoples together against a common enemy.

The Hundred Years' War Resumes

The **Hundred Years' War** can be divided into three main phases (see the map on page 376). The first phase dates from the initial declaration of war in 1337 (see Chapter 10), after which the English won a series of startling military victories before the Black Death put a temporary halt to hostilities. The war then resumed in 1356, with another English victory at Poitiers. Four years later, in 1360, Edward III decided to leverage his strong position and renounced his larger claim to the French throne, in return for a guaranteed full sovereignty over a greatly enlarged duchy of Gascony, in southwestern France.

But the terms of that treaty were never honored, nor did the treaty resolve the underlying issues that had led to the war itself: namely, the problem of making good on any claim to sovereignty in contested territory and the question of the English king's place in the French royal succession. The French king continued to treat the English king as his vassal, while Edward and his heirs quickly renewed their claim to the throne of France.

Although there were no pitched battles in France itself for two decades after 1360, a destabilizing proxy war developed during the 1360s and 1370s, which spread violence to neighboring regions. Both the English troops (posted in Gascony) and the French troops (eager to avenge previous losses) were reluctant to settle down. Many organized into "Free Companies" of mercenaries and hired themselves out in the service of hostile factions in Castile and competing city-states in northern Italy. By 1376, when the conflict between England and France reignited, the Hundred Years' War had become a Europe-wide phenomenon.

in China, where they were used in fireworks displays, but they were first used to devastating and destructive effect in Europe. And although the earliest cannons were as dangerous to those who fired them as to those they targeted, they revolutionized the nature of warfare. In 1453, heavy artillery played a leading role in the outcomes of two crucial conflicts: when the Ottoman Turks breached the ancient defenses of Constantinople with cannon fire, and when the French captured the English-held city of Bordeaux, bringing an end to the attenuated conflict known as the Hundred Years' War.

Thereafter, cannons made it more difficult for rebellious aristocrats to hole up in their stone castles, and so consequently they aided in the consolidation of national monarchies. Cannons placed aboard ships made Europe's developing navies more effective. A handheld firearm, the pistol, was also invented during the fourteenth century; and around 1500, the musket ended forever the military dominance of heavily armored cavalry, giving the advantage to foot soldiers recruited from the ranks of average citizens.

Indeed, there is a symbiotic relationship between warfare and nation building, as well as between warfare and technology. Because Europeans were almost constantly at war from the fourteenth century to the middle of the

THE PHASES OF THE HUNDRED YEARS' WAR. Here we see three snapshots of the political geography of France during the Hundred Years' War. ▪ *In what areas of France did England make its greatest territorial gains before 1360?* ▪ *How and why did this change in the period leading up to 1429?* ▪ *What geographic and strategic advantages did the French monarchy enjoy after 1429 that might help explain its success in recapturing the French kingdom from the English?*

The Brief Victory of Henry V

During this second phase of the war, the tide quickly shifted in favor of France. The new king, Charles V (r. 1364–1380), imposed a series of taxes to fund the raising of an army, restored order by disbanding the Free Companies, and hired the leader of one of these bands as the commander of his army. He thereby created a professional military that could match the English in discipline and tactics. By 1380, English territories in France had been reduced to a core area around the southwestern city of Bordeaux and the port of Calais in the extreme northeast.

Meanwhile, the aging Edward III had been succeeded by his nine-year-old grandson, Richard II (r. 1377–1399), who was too young to resume armed conflict in France. This was problematic, because the war had been extremely popular in England. Indeed, mismanagement by Richard's advisers was one of the issues that triggered the Peasants' Revolt in 1381. And when Richard came of age and showed no signs of warlike ambition, many of his own relatives turned against him. Richard retaliated against the ringleader of this faction, his cousin Henry of Lancaster, sending him into exile and confiscating his property. Henry's supporters used this as pretext for rebellion, and in 1399, Richard was deposed by Henry and eventually murdered.

As a usurper whose legitimacy was always in doubt, Henry IV (r. 1399–1413) struggled to maintain his authority in the face of rebellions and other challenges to his kingship. The best way to unite the country would have been to renew the war against France, but Henry was frequently ill and in no position to lead an army. However, when his son Henry V succeeded him in 1413, the young king immediately began to prepare for an invasion. His timing was excellent: the French royal government was foundering, owing to the insanity of the reigning king, Charles VI (r. 1380–1422). A brilliant diplomat as well as a capable soldier, Henry V sealed an alliance with the powerful Duke of Burgundy, who was nominally loyal to France but stood to gain from its defeat. Henry also made a treaty with the German emperor, who agreed not to come to France's aid.

When he crossed the English Channel with his troops in the autumn of 1415, Henry thus faced a much-depleted French army that could not rely on reinforcements. Although it was still vastly larger and boasted hundreds of mounted knights, it was undisciplined. It was also severely hampered by bad weather and deep mud when the two armies clashed at Agincourt on October 25 of that year—conditions that favored the lighter English infantry. Henry's men managed to win a crushing victory. Then, over the next five years, Henry conquered most of northern France. In 1420, the ailing Charles VI was forced to recognize him as heir to the throne, thereby disinheriting his own son, whose ceremonial title was *Dauphin* ("dolphin"), from the heraldic device of the borderland province he controlled. Henry sealed the deal by marrying the French princess, Catherine, and fathering an heir to the joint kingdom of England and France.

Joan of Arc's Triumph and Betrayal

Unlike his great-grandfather Edward III, who had claimed the French throne largely as a bargaining chip to secure sovereignty over Gascony (Chapter 10), Henry V honestly believed himself to be the rightful king of France. And his astonishing success in capturing the kingdom seemed to put the stamp of divine approval on that claim. But Henry's successes in France also transformed the nature of the conflict, turning it from a profitable war of conquest and plunder into an extended and expensive military occupation. It might have been sustainable had Henry been as long lived as many of his predecessors, but he died early in 1422, just short of his thirty-sixth birthday. And King Charles VI died only a few months later, leaving the infant Henry VI

(r. 1422–1461) to be crowned the first—and last—king of both England and France.

Meanwhile, English armies continued to press southward into territories held by the Dauphin, who was determined to win back his inheritance. Yet French confidence in his right to the throne had been shattered by his own mother's declaration that he was illegitimate. It began to look as though England would once again rule an empire comprising much of France, as it had for a century and a half after the Norman conquest.

But in 1429, a peasant girl from Lorraine (a territory only marginally part of France) made her way to the Dauphin's court and announced that an angel had told her that he, Charles, was the rightful king, and that she, Joan, should drive the English out of France. The very fact that **Joan of Arc** even got a hearing underscores the hopelessness of the Dauphin's position—as does the extraordinary fact that he gave her a contingent of troops. With this force, Joan liberated the strategic city of Orléans, then under siege by the English. She then led her army to a series of victories that culminated in the coronation of the Dauphin as King Charles VII in the cathedral of

JOAN OF ARC. A contemporary sketch of Joan was drawn in the margin of this register, documenting official proceedings at the Parlement of Paris in 1429.

Analyzing Primary Sources

The Condemnation of Joan of Arc by the University of Paris, 1431

After Joan's capture by the Burgundians, she was handed over to the English and tried for heresy at an ecclesiastical court set up in Rouen. It was on this occasion that the theology faculty of Paris pronounced the following verdict on her actions.

You, Joan, have said that, since the age of thirteen, you have experienced revelations and the appearance of angels, of St. Catherine and St. Margaret, and that you have very often seen them with your bodily eyes, and that they have spoken to you. As for the first point, the clerks of the University of Paris have considered the manner of the said revelations and appearances. . . . Having considered all . . . they have declared that all the things mentioned above are lies, falsenesses, misleading and pernicious things and that such revelations are superstitions, proceeding from wicked and diabolical spirits.

Item: You have said that your king had a sign by which he knew that you were sent by God, for St. Michael, accompanied by several angels, some of which having wings, the others crowns, with St. Catherine and St. Margaret, came to you at the chateau of Chinon. All the company ascended through the floors of the castle until they came to the room of your king, before whom the angel bearing the crown bowed. . . . As for this matter, the clerks say that it is not in the least probable, but it is rather a presumptuous lie, misleading and pernicious, a false statement, derogatory of the dignity of the Church and of the angels. . . .

Item: You have said that, at God's command, you have continually worn men's clothes, and that you have put on a short robe, doublet, shoes attached by points, also that you have had short hair, cut around above the ears, without retaining anything on your person which shows that you are a woman, and that several times you have received the body of Our Lord dressed in this fashion, despite having been admonished to give it up several times, the which you would not do. You have said that you would rather die than abandon the said clothing, if it were not at God's command, and that if you were wearing those clothes and were with the king, and those of your party, it would be one of the greatest benefits for the kingdom of France. You have also said that not for anything would you swear an oath not to wear the said clothing and carry arms any longer. And all these things you say you have done for the good and at the command of God. As for these things, the clerics say that you blaspheme God and hold him in contempt in his sacraments; you transgress Divine Law, Holy Scripture, and canon law. You err in the faith. You boast in vanity. You are suspected of idolatry and you have condemned yourself in not wishing to wear clothing suitable to your sex, but you follow the custom of Gentiles and Saracens.

Source: Carolyne Larrington, ed. and trans., *Women and Writing in Medieval Europe* (New York: 1995), pp. 183–84.

Questions for Analysis

1. Paris was in the hands of the English when this condemnation was issued. Is there any evidence that its authors were coerced into making this pronouncement?

2. On what grounds was Joan condemned for heresy?

3. In what ways does Joan's behavior highlight larger trends in late medieval spirituality and popular piety?

Reims, where French kings had been crowned for nearly a thousand years.

Despite her miraculous successes, Charles and the aristocratic generals of his army regarded Joan as an embarrassment: a peasant leading the nobility, a woman dominating men, and a commoner who claimed to have been commissioned by God. Her very charisma made her dangerous. So when the Burgundians captured her in battle a few months later and handed her over to the English as a prisoner of war, the French king she had helped to crown did nothing to save her. Accused of witchcraft, condemned by the theologians of Paris, and tried for heresy by an English ecclesiastical court, Joan was burned to death in the market square at Rouen in 1431. She was nineteen years old.

The French forces whom Joan had inspired, however, continued on the offensive. In 1435, the duke of Burgundy withdrew his alliance with the English, whose young king, Henry VI, proved to be first incompetent and then insane. Finally, a series of French victories culminated in the capture of Bordeaux. After 1453, English control over French territory was limited to the port of Calais on the French coast of the English Channel.

The Long Shadow of the Hundred Years' War

The Hundred Years' War challenged the very existence of France. The disintegration of that kingdom—first during the 1350s and 1360s, and again between 1415 and 1435—glaringly revealed the fragility of the bonds that tied the king to his people and the royal capital of Paris to the kingdom's outlying regions. Nonetheless, the king's power had increased by the war's end, laying the foundations on which the power of the French state would be built.

The Hundred Years' War also had dramatic effects on the English monarchy. When English armies in France were successful, the king rode a wave of popularity that fueled an emerging sense of English identity. When the war turned against the English, defeats abroad undermined support for the monarch at home. Of the nine English kings who ruled England between 1307 and 1485, five were deposed and murdered by factions. This was a consequence of England's peculiar form of kingship, whose strength depended on the king's ability to mobilize popular support through Parliament while maintaining the support of his nobility through successful wars. Failure to maintain this balance was even more destabilizing in England than it would have been elsewhere, precisely because royal power was so centralized.

In France, the nobility could endure the insanity of Charles VI because his government was not powerful enough to threaten them. In England, by contrast, neither the nobility nor the nation could afford the weak kingship of Henry VI. The result was an aristocratic rebellion that led to a full-blown civil war: the Wars of the Roses, so called because of the floral emblems (red and white) adopted by the two competing noble families, Lancaster and York. It ended only when a Lancastrian claimant, Henry Tudor (r. 1485–1509), resolved the dynastic feud by marrying Elizabeth of York and ruling as Henry VII, establishing a new dynasty whose symbol was a rose with both white and red petals. His second son would become Henry VIII (see Chapter 13).

In spite of England's ultimate defeat, the Hundred Years' War strengthened English identity in several ways. First, it equated national identity with the power of the state and its king. Second, it fomented a strong anti-French sentiment that led to the triumph of the English language over French for the first time since the Norman conquest, over 300 years earlier; the first English court to speak English was that of Richard II, a patron of Geoffrey Chaucer. And having lost its continental possessions, England became, for the first time, a self-contained island nation that looked to the sea for defense and opportunity—not to the Continent. This would later prove to be an advantage in many ways.

Conflict in Italy and the Holy Roman Empire

Elsewhere, the perpetual warfare that began to characterize the history of Europe during this period was even more destructive than it had proved to be in the struggle between England and France. In northern and central Italy, the second half of the fourteenth century was marked by incessant conflict. With the papacy based in Avignon, Rome was torn by factional violence. Warfare among northern Italian city-states added to the violence caused by urban rebellions in the wake of the plague. Finally, around 1400, Venice, Milan, and Florence succeeded in stabilizing their differing forms of government: Venice was now ruled by an oligarchy of merchants, Milan by a family of despots, and Florence was ruled as a republic but dominated by the influence of a few wealthy clans, especially the Medici banking family. Having settled their internal problems, these three cities then began to expand their influence by subordinating other cities to their rule.

Eventually, almost all the towns of northern Italy were allied with one or another of these powers. An exception was Genoa, which had its own trading empire in the Mediterranean and Atlantic (Chapter 10). The papacy, meanwhile, reasserted its control over central Italy when it was restored to Rome in 1377. The southern kingdom of Naples and Sicily persisted as a separate entity, but a constantly unstable one, riven by local warfare and poor government. After 1453, when the Hundred Years' War had ended and Ottoman expansion had temporarily halted at Istanbul, an uneasy peace was achieved. But diplomacy and frequently shifting alliances did little to check the ambitions of any one state for further expansion or change the fact that none of these small-scale states could oppose the powerful national monarchies that were emerging north of the Alps.

In the lands of the Holy Roman Empire, meanwhile, armed conflict among territorial princes significantly weakened all combatants. Periodically, a powerful emperor would emerge to play a role, but the dominant trend was toward the continuing dissolution of power, with German princes dividing their territories among their heirs while free cities and local lords strove to shake off the princes' rule. Between 1350 and 1450, near anarchy prevailed in many regions. Only in the eastern regions of the empire were the rulers of Bavaria, Austria, and Brandenburg-Prussia able to strengthen their authority, mostly by supporting the efforts of the nobility to subject their peasants to serfdom and conquering and colonizing new territories on their eastern frontiers.

King Jadwiga of Poland and the Jagiellonian Dynasty

During the thirteenth century (see Chapter 9), Poland had been culturally and economically enriched by its willingness to welcome Jewish communities, which were being expelled from other parts of Europe. In the fourteenth century, Polish towns also benefited from a wave of German immigrants, mostly merchants, with ties to the Hanseatic League and to independent cities in the Holy Roman Empire. In order to attract and accommodate these newcomers, the rulers of Poland and other eastern European kingdoms granted special charters to the towns in which they settled. These charters granted citizens the rights of self-governance, collectively known as Magdeburg Law (named after a major German mercantile city).

In the centuries after the Black Death, more and more towns and villages were able to take advantage of these privileges, promoting the rapid urbanization of the once rural region of central and eastern Europe and creating a web of prosperous and culturally and religiously diverse cities that generated enormous wealth. Lviv, now in western Ukraine, is a splendid example: ruled by Polish kings and governed by German town law, it fostered a large population of Armenians, Jews, Serbians, and Hungarians, among many others.

Alongside the commercial benefits of these burgeoning towns were the intellectual benefits. Just as medieval universities flourished in western Europe during the economic boom of

the twelfth century, they now came to be established in central and eastern Europe, too. The first of these institutions was founded in the Bohemian capital of Prague in 1347, by Emperor Charles IV. The Polish king Casimir III (r. 1333–1370) followed his lead by establishing a fledgling university in Kraków in 1364. Universities in Vienna and Pécs (Hungary) were also established in the next few years. The university at Kraków soon came to be known as the Jagiellonian University, after the new dynasty that endowed it as a permanent institution.

The Jagiellonian dynasty was formed when the young female ruler of Poland, Jadwiga (*yahd-VEE-gah*), married the Grand Duke of Lithuania, Jagiello (*yahg-ee-EL-oh*). It was an extraordinary match. Jadwiga had been crowned king (not queen) in 1384, when she was barely ten years old. The Polish lords who acted as her advisers had insisted on the title because they did not want to see her eventual husband ruling over them. In search of a suitable match, they turned their gaze to the neighboring northern territory of Lithuania, which would give Poland more access to the Baltic Sea and more support against ongoing encroachments from the east by the Teutonic Knights of Prussia. Jadwiga agreed to the match even though Duke Jagiello was not only thirty years her senior but also a pagan. They were married after Jagiello's conversion to the Roman Church in 1386, when he received the royal baptismal name Wladyslaw II.

Thereafter, Jadwiga and Wladyslaw II Jagiello ruled their realms jointly, tripling the size of Poland-Lithuania

WAWEL CATHEDRAL (KRAKÓW). King Jadwiga of Poland and her infant daughter are entombed in the royal burial chamber of this magnificent church, which combines elements of medieval Romanesque, Gothic, and Byzantine architecture. It is surrounded by the royal castle on the Wawel (*VAH-vel*) Hill, overlooking the River Vistula.

and making it the largest and most powerful state in central Europe. Their patronage of the new university at Kraków turned it into one of Europe's intellectual powerhouses. It would later nurture such great Polish scholars as Nicolaus Copernicus (1473–1543) (see Chapter 16) and Karel Wojtyła (1920–2005), who became Pope John Paul II. Jadwiga also promoted Polish as a literary language, even encouraging the translation of the Bible into the vernacular. When she died in 1399, after a difficult childbirth, her husband married the wife she had chosen for him. In 1997, she was canonized as a saint of the Catholic Church.

THE ROYAL CHAPEL OF KING WLADYSLAW II JAGIELLO.
This image captures only some of the hundreds of magnificent paintings that decorate the walls of this chapel in Lublin (Poland). This cycle of frescoes, which depict scenes from the Bible, was commissioned by King Jagiello after the death of his royal wife Jadwiga. The paintings, completed in 1418, were executed by a team of master artists from Ukraine, who combined eastern Orthodox imagery and styles with those of western Europe.
■ *Based on what you have learned about Jagiello, why would he have chosen to decorate his chapel in this way?*

The Growth of National Monarchies

In France, England, Poland, Hungary, as well as in smaller kingdoms such as Scotland and Portugal, the later Middle Ages saw the emergence of more cohesive states than any that had existed before. The political patterns established in the formative twelfth and thirteenth centuries had made this possible, yet the active construction of a sense of shared identity in these territories, and the fusion of that identity with kingship, were new phenomena. Forged by war and fueled by the growing cultural importance of vernacular languages, this fusion produced a new type of political organization: the national monarchy.

The advantages of a national monarchy over older forms of political organization—such as the empire, the principality, or the city-state—are significant. When the armies of France invaded the Italian peninsula at the end of the fifteenth century, neither the militias of the city-states nor the far-flung resources of Venice were a match for them. The German lands and the Low Countries endured similar invasions only a few generations later and, along with Italy, would remain battlegrounds for competing armies until the middle of the nineteenth century. But the new national monarchies brought significant disadvantages, too. They guaranteed the prevalence of warfare in Europe as they continued their struggles for sovereignty and territory, and eventually, they would export their rivalry through imperial ventures in Africa and the New World. A shared feeling of belonging to a nation can also be poisoned or undermined if one ethnic group, or one region, claims to be superior to all others.

THE CHALLENGES OF THE ROMAN CHURCH

Although the century after the Black Death witnessed the papacy's return to Rome, it also witnessed changes in the Church that would have far-reaching consequences in the centuries to come. Like other large landowners, the monasteries of Europe suffered from the economic changes brought about by the new world order, as did the Church's bishops who confronted the same dilemmas as the secular nobility. But no ecclesiastical institution suffered more severe trials than the papacy, which endured almost seventy years of exile from Rome followed by a debilitating forty-year schism. It then faced a protracted battle with reformers who sought to reduce the pope's role in Church governance. Even though the papacy won this battle in the short term, the renewed abuse of papal power would, in the long run, bring about the permanent schism caused by the Reformation of the sixteenth century (see Chapter 13).

The Great Western Schism

In the decades that were transforming European society in so many other ways, calls for the papacy's return to Rome grew more insistent. It was eventually brought about by the letter-writing campaign of the nun and mystic Catherine of Siena (1347–1380), whose teasing but pious missives to Gregory XI (r. 1370–1378) alternately shamed and coerced him. In 1377, he was persuaded to make the move.

But the papacy's restoration was short lived. A year after Gregory's return to Rome, he died. His cardinals—many of them Frenchmen—struggled to interpret the wishes of the volatile Romans, whose habit of expressing themselves through violence was unsettling to outsiders. Later, the cardinals would claim that they capitulated to the Roman mob when they elected an Italian candidate, Urban VI. When Urban fell out with them soon afterward, the cardinals fled the city and, from a safe distance, declared his

THE GREAT SCHISM, 1378–1417. During the Great Western Schism, the various territories of Europe were divided in their allegiances.
▪ *According to the map key, what choices were the peoples of these regions making?* ▪ *What common interests would have united the supporters of the Avignon pope or of the Roman pope?* ▪ *Why would areas such as Portugal and Austria waver in their support?*

Past and Present

Replacing "Retired" Popes

When Pope Benedict XVI decided to retire from office in February 2013, pundits and theologians alike struggled to find a precedent for this extraordinary decision. Most reached back to the year 1417, when Pope Martin V was elected at the Council of Constance (left) to replace the "retired" Gregory XII. But in this case, the retirement was not voluntary, and it was accompanied by the enforced resignation of a rival pope and the excommunication of yet another. The installation mass of Pope Francis in March 2013 (right) was much more universally celebrated and much more public than that of his medieval predecessor.

 Watch related author interview on the Student Site

reign invalid because they had elected him under duress. They then elected a new pope, a Frenchman who took the name Clement VII. Urban retaliated by naming a new and entirely Italian College of Cardinals and refusing Clement access to the city. The French pope and his cardinals withdrew ignominiously to the papal palace in Avignon, while the Italian pope remained in Rome.

The resulting rift is known as the **Great Schism** (or, more specifically, the Great Western Schism, to distinguish it from the Great East–West Schism between the Roman and Orthodox Churches). Between 1378 and 1417, the Roman Church was divided between two—and, ultimately, three—competing papacies, each claiming to be legitimate and each denouncing the heresy of the others.

It is not surprising that Europe's religious allegiances fractured along political lines drawn by the ongoing Hundred Years' War: France and its allies Scotland, Castile, Aragon, and Naples recognized the pope in Avignon; whereas England, Germany, northern Italy, Scandinavia, Bohemia,

Poland, and Hungary recognized the Roman pope. There was no obvious way to end this embarrassing state of affairs, and the two rival Colleges of Cardinals continued to elect successors every time a pope died, perpetuating the problem. Finally, in 1409, some cardinals from both camps met at Pisa, where they ceremonially declared the deposition of both popes and named a new one from among their number. But neither of the popes reigning in Rome and Avignon accepted that decision, and there were now three rival popes excommunicating each other instead of two.

The Council of Constance and the Failure of the Conciliar Movement

This debacle was ultimately addressed between 1414 and 1418 at the **Council of Constance**, the largest and longest ecclesiastical gathering since the Council of Nicea more than

Competing Viewpoints

Council or Pope?

The Great Schism spurred a fundamental and far-reaching debate about the nature of authority within the Church. Arguments for papal supremacy rested on traditional claims that the popes were the successors of Saint Peter, to whom Jesus Christ had delegated his own authority. Arguments for the supremacy of a general council had been advanced by many intellectuals throughout the fourteenth century, but it was only during the circumstances of the schism that these arguments found a wide audience. The following documents trace the history of the controversy, from the declaration of conciliar supremacy at the Council of Constance (Haec Sancta Synodus), *to the council's efforts to guarantee regular meetings of general councils thereafter* (Frequens), *to the papal condemnation of appeals to the authority of general councils issued in 1460* (Execrabilis).

Haec Sancta Synodus (1415)

This holy synod of Constance . . . declares that being lawfully assembled in the Holy Spirit, constituting a general council and representing the Catholic Church Militant, it has its power directly from Christ, and that all persons of whatever rank or dignity, even a Pope, are bound to obey it in matters relating to faith and the end of the Schism and the general reformation of the church of God in head and members.

Further, it declares that any person of whatever position, rank, or dignity, even a Pope, who contumaciously refuses to obey the mandates, statutes, ordinances, or regulations enacted or to be enacted by this holy synod, or by any other general council lawfully assembled, relating to the matters aforesaid or to other matters involved with them, shall, unless he repents, be . . . duly punished.

Source: L. R. Loomis, ed. and trans., *The Council of Constance* (New York: 1961), p. 229.

Frequens (1417)

The frequent holding of general councils is the best method of cultivating the field of the Lord, for they root out the briars, thorns, and thistles of heresies, errors, and schisms, correct abuses, make crooked things straight, and prepare the Lord's vineyard for fruitfulness and rich fertility. Neglect of general councils sows the seeds of these evils and encourages their growth. This truth is borne in upon us as we recall times past and survey the present.

Therefore by perpetual edict we . . . ordain that henceforth general councils shall be held as follows: the first within the five years immediately following the end of the present council, the second within seven years from the end of the council next after this, and subsequently every ten years forever. . . . Thus there will always be a certain continuity. Either a council will be in session or one will be expected at the end of a fixed period.

Source: L. R. Loomis, ed. and trans., *The Council of Constance* (New York: 1961), pp. 246–47.

---

a thousand years before (Chapter 6). Its chief mission was to remove all rival claimants for papal office before agreeing on the election of a new pope, an Italian who took the name Martin V. But many of the council's delegates had even further-reaching plans for the reform of the Church, ambitions that stemmed from the legal doctrine that gave the council the power to depose and elect popes in the first place.

This doctrine, known as **conciliarism**, holds that supreme authority within the Church rests not with the pope but with a representative general council—and not just the council convened at Constance but also any future council. The delegates at Constance thus decreed that general councils should meet regularly to oversee the governance of the Church and to act as a check on the unbridled abuse of papal power.

Had conciliarism triumphed, the Reformation of the following century might not have occurred. But, perhaps predictably, Martin V and his successors did everything they could to undermine this doctrine, precisely because it limited their power. When the next general council met at

Execrabilis (1460)

An execrable abuse, unheard of in earlier times, has sprung up in our period. Some men, imbued with a spirit of rebellion and moved not by a desire for sound decisions but rather by a desire to escape the punishment for sin, suppose that they can appeal from the Pope, Vicar of Jesus Christ—from the Pope, to whom in the person of blessed Peter it was said, "Feed my sheep" and "whatever you bind on earth will be bound in heaven"—from this Pope to a future council. How harmful this is to the Christian republic, as well as how contrary to canon law, anyone who is not ignorant of the law can understand. For . . . who would not consider it ridiculous to appeal to something which does not now exist anywhere nor does anyone know when it will exist? The poor are heavily oppressed by the powerful, offenses remain unpunished, rebellion against the Holy See is encouraged, license for sin is granted, and all ecclesiastical discipline and hierarchical ranking of the Church are turned upside down.

Wishing therefore to expel this deadly poison from the Church of Christ, and concerned with the salvation of the sheep committed to us . . . with the counsel and assent of our venerable brothers, the Cardinals of the Holy Roman Church, together with the counsel and assent of all those prelates who have been trained in canon and civil law who follow our Court, and with our own certain knowledge, we condemn appeals of this kind, reject them as erroneous and abominable, and declare them to be completely null and void. And we lay down that from now on, no one should dare . . . to make such an appeal from our decisions, be they legal or theological, or from any commands at all from us or our successors.

Source: Reprinted by permission of the publisher from Gabriel Biel, *Defensorium Obedientiae Apostolicae et Alia Documenta*, ed. and trans. Heiko A. Oberman, Daniel E. Zerfoss, and William J. Courtenay (Cambridge, MA: 1968), pp. 224–27. Copyright © 1968 by the President and Fellows of Harvard College.

Questions for Analysis

1. On what grounds does *Haec Sancta Synodus* establish the authority of a council? Why would this be considered a threat to papal power?

2. Why did the Council of Constance consider it necessary for councils to meet regularly (*Frequens*)? What might have been the logical consequences of such regular meetings?

3. On what grounds does *Execrabilis* condemn the appeals to future councils that have no specified meeting date? Why would it not have condemned the conciliar movement altogether?

Siena in 1423, Pope Martin duly sent representatives—who then turned around and went back to Rome. (The Council of Constance had specified that councils must meet frequently but had not specified how long those meetings should last.) The following year, the delegates to a general council at Basel took steps to ensure that the pope could not dismiss it, and a lengthy struggle for power ensued between the advocates of papal monarchy and the conciliarists. Twenty-five years later, in 1449, the Council of Basel dissolved itself, bringing to an end a radical experiment

in conciliar government—and dashing the hopes of those who thought it would lead to an internal reformation thorough enough to keep the Roman Church intact.

Spiritual Challenges

We have noted that the spiritual and social lives of medieval Christians were inextricably intertwined; indeed, any distinction between the two would have made little sense to the people of this era. The parish church stood literally at the center of their lives. Churchyards were communal meeting places, sometimes even the sites of markets; church buildings were a refuge from attack and a gathering place for parish business; church's holidays marked the passage of the year; and church's bells marked the hours of the day. The church was holy, but it was also essential to daily life.

Yet, in the wake of the Black Death, when many parishes ceased to exist and many communities were decimated, an increasing number of medieval Christians were not satisfied with these conventional practices and developed forms of piety that were distinctly controversial. Many of them are regarded today as saints, but this was not necessarily the case during their lifetimes. Indeed, the distinction between the superhuman powers of a saint and those of a witch could be difficult to distinguish. As Joan of Arc's predicament reveals, medieval women found it particularly challenging to find outlets for their piety that would not earn them the condemnation of the Church. Executed as a heretic, Joan was officially exonerated a generation later. But she would not be canonized as a saint until 1920, when belief in her holiness gained wide support during World War I and was considered a decisive factor in the victory of France and its allies.

Many women therefore internalized their devotional practices or confined them to the domestic sphere—sometimes to the inconvenience of their families and communities. For example, the young Catherine of Siena (who later convinced the pope to return to Rome) refused to help with the housework or to support her working-class family; instead, she took over one of the house's two rooms for her own private prayers, confining her parents and a dozen siblings to the remaining room. Julian of Norwich (1342–1416) withdrew from the world into a small cell built next to her local church, where she spent the rest of her life in prayer and contemplation. Her younger contemporary, the housewife Margery Kempe (c. 1372–c. 1439), resented the fact that she could not take such a step because she had a husband, several children, and a household to support. In later life, she renounced her domestic duties and devoted her life to performing acts of histrionic piety that alienated many of those who came into contact with her. For example, she was so moved by the contemplation of Jesus's sufferings on the cross that she would cry hysterically for hours, disrupting the Mass; and when on a pilgrimage in Rome, she cried at the sight of babies that reminded her of the infant Jesus or young men whom she thought resembled him.

The extraordinary piety of such individuals could be inspiring, but it could also threaten the Church's control over religious life and the links that bound individuals to their communities. It could, therefore, be regarded as dangerous. More safely orthodox was the practical mysticism preached by Thomas à Kempis, whose *Imitation of Christ* (c. 1427) taught readers how to appreciate aspects of the divine in their everyday lives. Originally written in Latin, *Imitation* was quickly translated into many vernacular languages and is now more widely read than any other Christian book except the Bible.

Popular and Intellectual Reformers

For the most part, the threat of dissenting movements was less dangerous to the Church than the corruption of the papacy. But in the kingdoms of England, Bohemia (the modern Czech Republic), and Poland, some reform movements posed serious challenges because they were galvanized by respected intellectuals. In Poland, a professor at the new Jagiellonian University in Kraków, Paulus Vladimiri (Pawel

WYCLIFFE'S ENGLISH BIBLE. Although John Wycliffe was not directly responsible for this translation of the Bible, it was made in the later fourteenth century by his followers. Written in the same Middle English vernacular that Geoffrey Chaucer used for his popular works, it was designed to be accessible to lay readers who did not understand Latin. This page shows the beginning of the Gospel of Mark: "The bygyn-/nyng of Þe gos-/pel of Ihesu Crist/ Þe sone of god. . . ." (Note that the old English letter Þ stands for *th*.) ▪ *What might have been the impact of this translation on readers and listeners in the late fourteenth century?* ▪ *How would this English Bible have helped to further the reforming efforts of Wycliffe and his disciples?*

Wlodkowic; c. 1370–1435), wrote a treatise that criticized papal and imperial efforts to convert the peoples of eastern Europe and the Baltic by force through their support of the Teutonic Knights. He argued that neither had the power or the right to do so, and further argued that pagans and Christians could coexist in peace. He advanced these radical arguments as the Polish representative to the Council of Constance.

The Oxford theologian **John Wycliffe** (c. 1330–1384) was a central figure in both the English and Bohemian

THE TEACHINGS OF JAN HUS. An eloquent religious reformer, Jan Hus was burned at the stake in 1415 after he was found guilty of heresy at the Council of Constance. This lavishly illustrated booklet of his teachings was published over a century later in his native Bohemia and includes texts in the Czech vernacular and in Latin. ■ *What does this booklet's later publication suggest about how Hus's image and theology were put to use during the Protestant Reformation?*

reform movements. A survivor of the Black Death and an outspoken critic of the papacy, he asserted that the empty sacraments of a corrupt Church could not save anyone, and therefore urged the English king to confiscate ecclesiastical wealth and to replace decadent priests and bishops with men who would live according to apostolic standards of poverty and piety.

Some of Wycliffe's followers, known to their detractors as Lollards (from a word meaning "mumblers" or "beggars"), went even further, dismissing the sacraments as fraudulent attempts to extort money from the faithful. Lollard preachers advocated for direct access to the scriptures and promoted an English translation of the Bible sponsored by Wycliffe himself. Wycliffe's teachings also played an important role in the Peasants' Revolt of 1381, and Lollardy gained numerous adherents in the decades after his death. This movement was even supported by a number of aristocratic families, who found the idea of dissolving the Church's wealth attractive. But after a failed Lollard uprising in 1414, both the movement and its supporters went underground.

In Bohemia and other regions of central Europe, Wycliffe's ideas lived on and put down even deeper roots. They were powerfully adopted by **Jan Hus** (c. 1373–1415), a charismatic teacher at the Charles University in Prague. In contrast to the Lollards, who had scornfully dismissed the Mass and thereby lost much popular support, Hus emphasized the centrality of the Eucharist to Christian piety. Indeed, he demanded that the laity be allowed to receive not only the consecrated bread but also the consecrated wine, which was usually reserved solely for priests. This demand became a rallying cry for the Hussite movement. Influential nobles also supported Hus, partly in the hope that the reforms he demanded might restore revenues they had lost to the Church over the previous century.

Accordingly, most of Bohemia was behind him when Hus traveled to the Council of Constance to publish his views and urge the assembled delegates to undertake sweeping reforms. But rather than giving him a hearing, the other delegates to the council convicted Hus of heresy and had him burned at the stake. Back home, Hus's supporters raised the banner of open revolt, and the aristocracy took advantage of the situation to seize Church property. Between 1420 and 1424, armed bands of fervent Hussites resoundingly defeated several armies, as priests, artisans, and peasants rallied to pursue Hus's goals of religious reform and social justice.

These victories increased popular fervor but they also made radical reformers increasingly volatile. Accordingly, in 1434, a more conservative arm of the Hussite movement was able to negotiate a settlement with the Bohemian church. By the terms of this settlement, Bohemians could receive both the bread and the wine of the Mass, which thus placed them beyond the pale of Latin orthodoxy and effectively separated the Bohemian national church from the Church of Rome.

Lollardy and Hussitism exhibit a number of striking similarities. Both began in the university and then spread to the countryside, both called for the clergy to live in simplicity and poverty, and both attracted noble support, especially in their early days. Both movements were also strongly nationalistic, employing their own vernacular languages (English and Czech) and identifying themselves with the English or Czech people in opposition to a "foreign" Church. And both relied on vernacular preaching and social activism. In all these respects, they established patterns that would emerge again in the vastly larger currents of the Protestant Reformation (see Chapter 13).

CONCLUSION

The century after the Black Death was a period of tremendous creativity and revolutionary change. The effects of the plague were catastrophic, but the resulting food surpluses, opportunities for expansion, and labor shortages encouraged experimentation and opened up broad avenues for enrichment. Europe's economy diversified and expanded, and increasing wealth and access to education produced new forms of art and new ways of looking at the world. Hundreds and perhaps thousands of new schools were established, and scores of new universities would emerge as a result. Women were still excluded from formal schooling, but nevertheless they became active—and in many cases dominant—participants in literary endeavors, cultural life, and religious movements. Average men and women not only became more active in cultivating their own worldly goals, they also took control of their spiritual destinies at a

After You Read This Chapter

 Go to **INQUIZITIVE** to see what you've learned—and learn what you've missed—with personalized feedback along the way.

REVIEWING THE OBJECTIVES

- The Black Death had short- and long-term effects on the economy and societies of Europe. What were some of the most important changes?
- The later "Middle Ages" and the "Renaissance" are often perceived to be two different periods, but the latter was actually part of the former. Explain why.
- What were some of the intellectual, cultural, and artistic innovations of this era in Italy and elsewhere in Europe?
- How did some European kingdoms become stronger and more centralized during this period? What were some examples of national monarchies?
- How did the conciliar movement seek to limit the power of the papacy? Why was this movement unsuccessful?

time when the institutional Church provided little inspiring leadership.

Meanwhile, some states were growing stronger and more competitive, whereas other regions remained deeply divided. The rising Ottoman Empire eventually absorbed many of the oldest territories of Western civilizations, including the venerable Muslim caliphate at Baghdad, the western portions of the former Mongolian Empire, the Christian Balkans and Greece, and—above all—the surviving core of the eastern Roman Empire at Constantinople. As a result, Greek-speaking refugees streamed into Italy, many bringing with them classic works of Greek philosophy and literature hitherto unknown in Europe. Fueled by new ideas and a fervid nostalgia for the ancient past, Italians began to experiment with new ways of reading ancient texts, advocating a return to classical models while at the same time trying to counter the political and cultural authority of the more powerful kingdoms north of the Alps.

In contrast to Italy, these emerging national monarchies cultivated shared identity through the promotion of a common vernacular language and allegiance to a strong, more centralized state. These tactics allowed kingdoms such as Poland and Scotland to increase their territories and influence, and also led France and England into an epic battle for sovereignty and hegemony. The result, in all cases, was the escalation of armed conflict as incessant warfare drove more powerful governments to harvest a larger percentage of their subjects' wealth through taxation, which they proceeded to invest in ships, guns, and the standing armies made possible by new technologies and more effective administration.

In short, the generations that survived the calamities of famine, plague, and warfare seized the opportunities their new world presented. In the latter half of the fifteenth century, they stood on the verge of an extraordinary period of expansion and conquest that enabled them to dominate the globe.

PEOPLE, IDEAS, AND EVENTS IN CONTEXT

- Compare and contrast the **BLACK DEATH**'s effects on rural and urban areas.
- In what ways do rebellions such as the **ENGLISH PEASANTS' REVOLT** reflect the changes brought about by the plague? How do the works of **GIOVANNI BOCCACCIO, GEOFFREY CHAUCER,** and **CHRISTINE DE PIZAN** exemplify the culture of this era?
- What was **HUMANISM**? How was it related to the artistic and intellectual movement known as the **RENAISSANCE**?
- How did the **OTTOMAN EMPIRE** come to power? What were some of the consequences of its rise?
- What new military technologies were deployed during the **HUNDRED YEARS' WAR**? How did this conflict affect other parts of Europe, beyond England and France? What role did **JOAN OF ARC** play?
- How did the **COUNCIL OF CONSTANCE** respond to the crisis of the **GREAT SCHISM**?
- Why did **CONCILIARISM** fail? How did **JOHN WYCLIFFE** and **JAN HUS** seek to reform the Church?

THINKING ABOUT CONNECTIONS

- In the year 2000, a group of historians was asked to identify the most significant historical figure of the past millennium. Rather than selecting a person (e.g., Martin Luther, Shakespeare, Napoleon, Adolf Hitler), they chose the microbe *Yersinia pestis*, which caused the Black Death. Do you agree with this assessment? Why or why not?
- In your view, which was more crucial to the formation of the modern state: the political and legal developments surveyed in Chapter 9 or the emergence of national identities discussed in this chapter? Why?
- Given what we have learned about the history of the Roman Church, do you think the conciliar movement was doomed to fail? Why or why not? How far back do we need to go to trace the development of disputes over ecclesiastical governance?

- The invention of the printing press enabled the widespread dissemination of information, including reports on the riches of the New World.

- Competition for power in Italy led to increased violence as well as to the increase of artistic patronage, providing opportunities to a new breed of Renaissance men.

- The humanist approach to education that had developed in Italy spread to other parts of Europe, influencing new approaches to biblical scholarship and new political philosophies.

- Spain, the newest and most powerful European state, completed its "reconquest" of the Iberian Peninsula in 1492 and then looked to counter the successful colonial ventures of the Portuguese. This led to the early beginnings of a Spanish Empire in the Americas.

Before You Read This Chapter

CHRONOLOGY

1454–1455	Gutenberg's printed Bible completed
1488	Bartolomeu Dias rounds the Cape of Good Hope (Africa)
1492	Christopher Columbus reaches the West Indies
1494	Treaty of Tordesillas divides the New World
	Charles VIII of France invades Italy
1498	Vasco da Gama reaches India
1511	Erasmus publishes *The Praise of Folly*
1511	The Portuguese venture to Indonesia
1512	Michelangelo completes painting the ceiling of the Sistine Chapel
1513	Niccolò Machiavelli completes *The Prince*
	Vasco Núñez de Balboa reaches the Pacific Ocean
1516	Thomas More publishes *Utopia*
1519–1521	Aztec wars enable Cortés's conquest of Mexico
1519–1522	Magellan's fleet circumnavigates the globe
1531–1533	Pizarro's conquest of the Inca Empire

Innovation and Exploration, 1453–1533

CORE OBJECTIVES

▪ **UNDERSTAND** the relationship between Renaissance ideals and the political and economic realities of Italy.

▪ **IDENTIFY** the key characteristics of Renaissance arts and learning during this period.

▪ **DEFINE** the term *reconquista* and its meaning in Spain.

▪ **DESCRIBE** the methods and motives of European colonization during this period.

▪ **EXPLAIN** why Europeans were able to dominate the peoples of the New World.

What if exact copies of an idea could circulate quickly, all over the world? What if the same could be done for the latest news, the oldest beliefs, the most beautiful poems, or the most exciting—and deadly—discoveries? It would do for knowledge what the invention of coinage did for wealth: making it portable, therefore easier to use and disseminate. Indeed, it's no accident that the man who developed such a technology, **Johannes Gutenberg of Mainz** (c. 1398–1468), was the son of a goldsmith who made coins for the bishop of that German city. Both crafts were based on the same principle and used the same basic tools. Coins are metal disks, each stamped with identical words and images impressed on them with a reusable matrix. The pages of the first printed books— and later newspapers, leaflets, and pamphlets—were stamped with ink spread on rows of movable type (lead or cast-iron letter forms and punctuation marks) slotted into frames to form lines of words. Once a set of pages was ready, a **printing press** could make hundreds of copies in a matter of hours, many hundreds of times faster than the same page being copied by hand. Afterward, the type could be reused.

391

A major stimulus for this invention was the more widespread availability of paper, a trend that had begun in the late thirteenth century. Parchment, northern Europe's chief writing material since the advent of the codex (Chapter 6), was extremely expensive to manufacture and required special training for those who used it—one reason why writing remained a specialized skill for much of the Middle Ages, although the ability to read was common. Paper, made from rags turned into pulp by mills, was both cheaper and far easier to use. Accordingly, books became cheaper and written communication became easier and more widespread. Growing levels of literacy led to growing demand for books, which in turn led to experimentation with different methods of book production—and to Gutenberg's breakthrough of the 1450s. By 1455, his workshop had printed multiple copies of the Latin Bible (of which forty-eight complete or partial volumes survive). Although printing never entirely replaced traditional modes of publication via manuscript, it made books more affordable and revolutionized the spread of information.

In fact, the printing press played a crucial role in many of the developments that we will study in this chapter. The artistic and intellectual experiments that contributed to an Italian Renaissance were rapidly exported to other parts of Europe, and specifications for innovative weapons were printed on the same presses that churned out humanist writings. News of Columbus's first voyage and the subsequent conquests of the Americas would spread via the same medium as critiques of European atrocities there. Printing not only increased the volume and rapidity of communication, it also made it more difficult for those in power to censor dissenting opinions.

At the same time that it created new forms of agency, the printing press also become an indispensable tool for more traditional powers, making it possible for rulers to govern growing empires abroad and increasingly centralized states at home. The "reconquest" of Spain and the extension of Spanish imperialism to the New World were both facilitated by the circulation of printed propaganda. The widespread availability of reading materials even helped standardize national languages, by enabling governments to promote one official printed dialect over others. Hence the "king's English," the variety of the language spoken around London, was imposed as the only acceptable literary and bureaucratic language throughout the English realm, contributing to the growth of a common linguistic identity among readers. For these reasons, alongside others, many historians consider the advent of print to be both the defining event and

the driving engine of modernity, which coincided with another essentially modern development: the discovery of a "New World."

RENAISSANCE IDEALS— AND REALITIES

The intellectual and artistic movement that had begun in Italy during the fourteenth century was, as we noted in Chapter 11, characterized by an intense interest in the classical past and a new type of educational program known as humanism. These Renaissance ideals—and the realities that both undergirded and complicated them—were extended and diversified in the later fifteenth century through the medium of the printing press. By the time the Ottoman conquest of Constantinople was complete, just a year before Gutenberg's workshop began to produce pages of the Bible, decades of uncertainty and warfare had propelled hundreds of refugees from the eastern Roman Empire into Italy. Many carried with them precious manuscripts of Greek texts that had long been unavailable in Europe: the epics of Homer, the major surviving works of Athenian dramatists, and the dialogues of Plato. Prior to the invention of print, such manuscripts could be owned and studied by only very few, very privileged men. Now, printers in Venice and other European cities rushed to produce cheap editions of these texts, as well as Greek grammars and glossaries that could facilitate reading them.

Within a few decades, so many men were engaged in the study of Plato that an informal "Platonic Academy" had formed in Florence. There, the work of intellectuals, such as Marsilio Ficino (1433–1499) and Giovanni Pico della Mirandola (1463–1494), was fostered by the patronage of the wealthy Cosimo de' Medici. Based on his reading of Plato, Ficino's philosophy moved away from the focus on ethics and civic life that had been such a feature of earlier humanist thought. He taught instead that the individual should look primarily to the salvation of his immortal soul, to free it from its "always miserable" mortal body—a very Platonic idea that was also compatible with much late-medieval Christian piety. Ficino's great achievement was his translation of Plato's works into Latin, which made them widely accessible for the first time—again, thanks to the medium of print. His disciple Pico likewise rejected the everyday world of public affairs and took a more exalted view of man's intellectual and artistic capacities, arguing that man (but not woman) could aspire to union with God through the exercise of his unique talents.

The Spread of Printing

THE SPREAD OF PRINTING

- Up until 1470
- 1471–1500
- 1501–1600

Map labels:

EUROPE

Area of detail

AFRICA

NORWAY

SWEDEN

TEUTONIC ORDER

Stockholm 1483

BALTIC SEA

SCOTLAND

Edinburgh 1507

NORTH SEA

Copenhagen 1490

DENMARK

Odense 1482

Danzig 1499

Vistula R.

Warsaw 1580

POLAND

Dublin 1551

ENGLAND

Thames R.

London 1492

Westminster 1476

Utrecht 1470

Brussels 1475

Elbe R.

Leipzig 1481

Prague 1487

Wrocław 1475

Lviv 1593

Kraków 1474

Dniester R.

Rhine R.

Cologne 1465

HOLY ROMAN EMPIRE

Bamberg 1460

Pilsen 1468

Paris 1470

Seine R.

Eltville 1467

Mainz 1450

Nuremberg 1470

Danube R.

Vienna 1482

Buda 1472

HUNGARY

ATLANTIC OCEAN

Strasbourg 1458

Augsburg 1468

Basel 1468

Beromünster 1470

AUSTRIA

SWITZERLAND

FRANCE

Loire R.

Lyons 1473

Rhône R.

Milan 1471

Venice 1469

VENETIAN EMPIRE

ADRIATIC SEA

OTTOMAN EMPIRE

Florence 1482

PAPAL STATES

CORSICA

Rome 1467

PORTUGAL

SPAIN

Valencia 1474

SARDINIA

Naples 1471

KINGDOM OF THE TWO SICILIES

Lisbon 1489

Seville 1478

BALEARIC ISLANDS

MEDITERRANEAN SEA

0   100   200   300 Miles

0   100   200   300 Kilometers

THE SPREAD OF PRINTING. This map shows how quickly the technology of printing spread throughout Europe between 1470 and 1600. ▪ *In what regions were printing presses most heavily concentrated?* ▪ *What factors may have led to their proliferation in the Low Countries, northern Italy, and central Europe—compared with France, Spain, and England?* ▪ *Why would so many presses have been located along waterways?*

Printing, Patriotism, and the Past

The printing press helped to create new communities of readers by standardizing national languages and even promoting patriotism. And even as it enabled authors of new works to reach larger audiences, it also allowed printers to popularize older writings that had previously circulated in manuscript. The two sources presented here exemplify two aspects of this trend. The first is a preface by William Caxton of London, a printer who specialized in publishing books that glorified England's history and heritage. The preface is to a version of the legend of King Arthur, originally written by the English soldier Sir Thomas Malory, who completed it in 1470. It was printed for the first time in 1485 and quickly became a bestseller. The second excerpt is from the concluding chapter of Machiavelli's treatise The Prince. *Like the book itself, these remarks were originally addressed to Lorenzo de' Medici, head of Florence's most powerful family. But when* The Prince *was printed in 1532, five years after Machiavelli's death, the author's passionate denunciation of foreign "barbarians" and his lament for Italy's lost glory resonated with a wider Italian-speaking public.*

William Caxton's preface to Thomas Malory's Le Morte d'Arthur ("The Death of Arthur"; printed 1485)

After I had accomplished and finished diverse histories, both of contemplation and of other historical and worldly acts of great conquerors and princes, . . . many noble and diverse gentlemen of this realm of England came and demanded why I had not made and imprinted the noble history of the Holy Grail, and of the most renowned Christian king and worthy, King Arthur, which ought most to be remembered among us Englishmen before all other Christian kings. . . . The said noble gentlemen instantly required me to imprint the history of the said noble king and conqueror King Arthur, and of his knights, with the history of the Holy Grail . . . considering that he was a man born within this realm, and king and emperor of the same: and that there be, in French, diverse and many noble volumes of his acts, and also of his knights. To whom I answered that diverse men

hold opinion that there was no such Arthur, and that all such books as have been made of him be feigned and fables, because some chronicles make of him no mention. . . . Whereto they answered, and one in special said, that in him that should say or think that there was never such a king called Arthur might well be accounted great folly and blindness. . . . For in all places, Christian and heathen, he is reputed and taken for one of the Nine Worthies, and the first of the three Christian men. And also, he is more spoken of beyond the sea, and there are more books made of his noble acts than there be in England, as well in Dutch, Italian, Spanish, and Greek, as in French. . . . Wherefore it is a marvel why he is no more renowned in his own country. . . .

Then all these things aforesaid alleged, I could not well deny but that there was such a noble king named Arthur, reputed one of the Nine Wor-

thies, and first and chief of the Christian men. And many noble volumes be made of him and of his noble knights in French, which I have seen and read beyond the sea, which be not had in our maternal tongue. . . . Wherefore, among all such [manuscript] books as have late been drawn out briefly into English I have . . . undertaken to imprint a book of the noble histories of the said King Arthur, and of certain of his knights, after a copy unto me delivered—which copy Sir Thomas Malory did take out of certain books of French, and reduced it into English. And I, according to my copy, have done set it in print, to the intent that noble men may see and learn the noble acts of chivalry, the gentle and virtuous deeds that some knights used in those days, by which they came to honor, and how they that were vicious were punished and oft put to shame and rebuke; humbly beseeching all noble lords and ladies (with all other estates of what estate or degree they be) that shall see and read in this said book and work, that they take the good and honest acts to their remembrance, and follow the same. . . . For herein may be seen noble chivalry, courtesy, humanity, friendliness, hardiness, love, friendship, cowardice, murder, hate, virtue, and sin. Do after the good and leave the evil, and it shall bring you to good fame and renown.

Source: Sir Thomas Malory, *Le Morte d'Arthur* (London: 1485) (text and spelling slightly modernized).

From the conclusion of Niccolò Machiavelli, The Prince (completed 1513; printed 1532)

Reflecting in the matters set forth above and considering within myself where the times were propitious in Italy at present to honor a new prince and whether there is at hand the matter suitable for a prudent and virtuous leader to mold in a new form, giving honor to himself and benefit to the citizens of the country, I have arrived at the opinion that all circumstances now favor such a prince, and I cannot think of a time more propitious for him than the present. If, as I said, it was necessary in order to make apparent the virtue of Moses, that the people of Israel should be enslaved in Egypt, and that the Persians should be oppressed by the Medes to provide an opportunity to illustrate the greatness and the spirit of Cyrus, and that the Athenians should be scattered in order to show the excellence of Theseus, thus at the present time, in order to reveal the valor of an Italian spirit, it was essential that Italy should fall to her present low estate, more enslaved than the Hebrews, more servile than the Persians, more disunited than the Athenians, leaderless and lawless, beaten, despoiled, lacerated, overrun and crushed under every kind of misfortune. . . . So Italy now, left almost lifeless, awaits the coming of one who will heal her wounds, putting an end to the sacking and looting in Lombardy and the spoliation and extortions in the Realm of Naples and Tuscany, and cleanse her sores that have been so long festering. Behold how she prays God to send her someone to redeem her from the cruelty and insolence of the barbarians. See how she is ready and willing to follow any banner so long as there be someone to take it up. Nor has she at present any hope of finding her redeemer save only in your illustrious house [the Medici] which has been so highly exalted both by its own merits and by fortune and which has been favored by God and the church, of which it is now ruler. . . .

This opportunity, therefore, should not be allowed to pass, and Italy, after such a long wait, must be allowed to behold her redeemer. I cannot describe the joy with which he will be received in all these provinces which have suffered so much from the foreign deluge, nor with what thirst for vengeance, nor with what firm devotion, what solemn delight, what tears! What gates could be closed to him, what people could deny him obedience, what envy could withstand him, what Italian could withhold allegiance from him? THIS BARBARIAN OCCUPATION STINKS IN THE NOSTRILS OF ALL OF US. Let your illustrious house then take up this cause with the spirit and the hope with which one undertakes a truly just enterprise. . . .

Source: Niccolò Machiavelli, *The Prince,* ed. and trans. Thomas G. Bergin (Arlington Heights, IL: 1947), pp. 75–76, 78.

Questions for Analysis

1. What do these two sources reveal about the relationship between patriotism and the awareness of a nation's past? Why do you think Caxton looks back to a legendary medieval king, whereas Machiavelli's references are all to ancient examples? What do both excerpts reveal about the value placed on history in the popular imagination?

2. How does Caxton describe the process of printing a book? What larger conclusions can we draw from this about the market for printed books in general?

3. Why might Machiavelli's treatise have been made available in a printed version nearly twenty years after its original appearance in manuscript? How might his new audience have responded to its message?

The Politics of Italy and the Philosophy of Machiavelli

But not all Florentines were galvanized by Platonic ideals. Indeed, the most influential philosopher of this era—and one of the most widely read authors of all time—was a thoroughgoing realist, who spent more time studying ancient Roman history than Greek philosophy: **Niccolò Machiavelli** (1469–1527). Machiavelli's writings reflect the unstable political situation of his home city, as well as his wider aspirations for a unified Italy that could revive the glory of Rome. We have observed that Italy had been in political disarray for centuries, a situation exacerbated by the "Babylonian Captivity" of the papacy and the controversies raging after its return to Rome (Chapters 10 and 11). Now, Italy was becoming the arena where bloody international struggles were being played out. The kings of France and Spain both had claims to territory in Italy, and each claimed to be the rightful champion of the papacy. Accordingly, both sent invading armies into the peninsula while busily competing for the allegiance of the various city-states, which in turn were torn by internal dissension.

In 1498, Machiavelli became a prominent official in the government of a new Florentine republic, set up four years earlier when a French invasion of the region led to the expulsion of the ruling Medici family. His duties largely involved diplomatic missions to other Italian city-states. While in Rome, he became fascinated with the attempt by Cesare Borgia, the son of Pope Alexander VI, to create his own principality in central Italy, and noted with approval Borgia's ruthlessness and his complete subordination of personal ethics to political ends. Machiavelli remembered his example in 1512, when the Medici returned to overthrow the Florentine republic and he was deprived of his position, imprisoned, tortured, and exiled. He now devoted his energies to the articulation of a political philosophy suited to the times and to the tastes of the family that had ousted him.

On the surface, Machiavelli's two great works of political analysis appear to contradict each other. In his *Discourses on Livy*, which drew on the works of that Roman historian (Chapter 5), he praised the ancient Roman Republic as a model for his own contemporaries, lauding constitutional government, equality among citizens, and the subordination of religion to the service of the state. There is little doubt, in fact, that Machiavelli was a committed believer in the free city-state as the ideal form of human government. Yet Machiavelli also wrote *The Prince*, a "handbook for tyrants" in the eyes of his critics, and dedicated this work to Lorenzo, the son of Piero de' Medici, whose family had overthrown the Florentine republic that he had served.

THE STATES OF ITALY, c. 1494. This map shows the divisions of Italy on the eve of the French invasion in 1494. Contemporary observers often described Italy as being divided among five great powers: Milan, Venice, Florence, the Papal States, and the united kingdoms of Naples and Sicily. ▪ *Which of these powers seems most capable of expanding their territories?* ▪ *Which neighboring states would be most threatened by such attempts at expansion?* ▪ *Why would Florence and the Papal States so often find themselves in conflict with each other?*

Because *The Prince* has been so much more widely read than *Discourses*, it has often been interpreted as an endorsement of power for its own sake. But Machiavelli's real position was quite different. In the political chaos of early sixteenth-century Italy, he saw the likes of Cesare Borgia as the only hope for revitalizing the spirit of independence among his contemporaries, and thus making Italy fit, eventually, for self-governance. However dark his vision of human nature, Machiavelli never ceased to hope that his contemporaries would rise up, expel the French and Spanish occupying forces, and restore ancient traditions of liberty and equality. He regarded a period of despotism as a necessary step toward that end, not as a permanently desirable form of government.

Machiavelli continues to be a controversial figure. Some modern scholars, like many of his own contemporaries, represent him as disdainful of conventional morality and interested solely in the acquisition and exercise of power; others see him as an Italian patriot. Still others see him as a realist influenced by Saint Augustine (Chapter 6), who understood that, in a fallen world populated by sinful people, a ruler's good intentions do not guarantee that his policies will have good results. Accordingly, Machiavelli insisted that a prince's actions must be judged by their consequences and not by their intrinsic moral quality. He argued that the "necessity of preserving the state will often compel a prince to take actions which are opposed to loyalty, charity, humanity, and religion." As we shall see in later chapters, many subsequent political philosophers would go even further than Machiavelli in arguing that the preservation of the state—and the avoidance of political chaos—does indeed warrant the exercise of absolute power on the part of the ruler (see Chapters 14 and 15).

The Ideal of the Courtier

Machiavelli's political theories were informed by years of diplomatic service in the courts of Italy, and so was his engaging literary style. Indeed, he never abandoned his interest in the literary arts of the court and continued to write poems, plays, and adaptations of classical comedies. In this he resembled another poet-courtier, Ludovico Ariosto (1474–1533), who undertook diplomatic missions for the Duke of Ferrara and some of Rome's most powerful prelates. His lengthy verse narrative, *Orlando Furioso* ("The Madness of Roland"), was a retelling of the heroic exploits celebrated in the French *Song of Roland* (Chapter 8)—but without the heroism. Although very different in form and tone from *The Prince*, it shared that work's skepticism of political or chivalric ideals. It emphasized the comedy of its

lovers' passionate exploits and sought to charm an audience that found consolation in pleasure and beauty.

Thus a new Renaissance ideal was born, one that promoted the arts of pleasing the powerful secular and ecclesiastical princes who were in a position to employ clever men such as Machiavelli and Ariosto: the ideal of the courtier. The components of this ideal were embodied by their contemporary, the diplomat and nobleman Baldassare Castiglione (*bahl-dahs-SAH-re kah-stig-lee-OH-neh*; 1478–1529), who later wrote a manual for those who aspired to acquire these skills. If *The Prince* was a forerunner of modern self-help books, *The Book of the Courtier* was an early handbook of etiquette—and both stand in sharp contrast to the treatises on public virtue composed in the previous century. Whereas Bruni and Alberti (Chapter 11) had taught the sober virtues of strenuous service on behalf of the city-state, Castiglione taught how to attain the elegant and seemingly effortless skills necessary for advancement in princely courts.

More than anyone else, Castiglione articulated and popularized the set of talents still associated with the "Renaissance man": one accomplished in many different pursuits, witty, cultured, and stylish—but also an aspirant to Platonic ideals and human perfection. In many ways, Castiglione's courtiers (who were women as well as men) represent a *rejection* of the older ideals associated with the Renaissance as a rebirth of classical education for public men. Castiglione also rejected the misogyny of the humanists by stressing the ways in which court ladies could rise to influence and prominence through the graceful exercise of their womanly powers. Widely read throughout Western civilizations, his *Courtier* set the standard for polite behavior until the First World War.

The Dilemma of the Artist

Without question, the most enduring legacy of the Italian Renaissance has been the contributions of its artists, particularly those who embraced new media and new attitudes toward the human body. For example, the creative and economic opportunities afforded by painting on canvas or wood panels freed artists from having to work on site and entirely on commission. Because such paintings are portable—unlike wall paintings—and can be displayed in different settings, they can reach different markets and be more widely distributed. We have also noted (Chapter 11) that the use of oil paints, pioneered in Flanders, further revolutionized painting styles.

To these benefits, the artists of Italy added an important technical ingredient: mastery of a vanishing (one-point) perspective, which gave an illusion of three-dimensional

THE IMPACT OF PERSPECTIVE. Masaccio's painting *The Trinity with the Virgin* illustrates the startling sense of depth, made possible by observing the rules of one-point perspective. Notice how the figure of the crucified Christ seems to be thrust forward toward the viewer.

result of this trend, because princes and merchants alike sought to glorify themselves and their families, as well as to compete with their neighbors and rivals. An artist therefore had to study the techniques of the courtier and the new artistic techniques in order to succeed in winning a patron. He also had to be ready to perform other services for which he had to cultivate other talents: overseeing the building and decoration of palaces; designing tableware, furniture, fanciful liveries (uniforms) for servants and soldiers; and even decorating firearms. Some artists, such as Leonardo da Vinci, were prized as much for their capacity to invent deadly weapons as for their paintings and sculptures.

New Illusions and the Career of Leonardo

For much of the fifteenth century, the majority of the great painters were Florentines who followed in the footsteps of the precocious Masaccio (1401–1428), who died prematurely at the age of twenty-seven. His lasting legacy was the pioneering use of one-point perspective and dramatic lighting effects. Both are evident in his painting of the Trinity, where the body of the crucified Christ appears to be thrust forward by the impassive figure of God the Father, while the Virgin's gaze directly engages the viewer. Masaccio's most famous successor was Sandro Botticelli (1445–1510), who excelled in depicting graceful motion and the sensuous pleasures of nature. He is known today for paintings that evoke classical mythology.

The most adventurous and versatile artist of this period was **Leonardo da Vinci** (1452–1519). Leonardo personifies the Renaissance ideal: he was a painter, architect, musician, mathematician, engineer, and inventor. The illegitimate son of a notary, he had set up an artist's shop in Florence by the time he was twenty-five and gained the patronage of the Medici ruler Lorenzo the Magnificent. Yet Leonardo had a weakness: he worked slowly and had difficulty finishing anything. This naturally displeased Lorenzo and other Florentine patrons, who regarded artists as craftsmen who worked on specific projects and on their patrons' time, not their own. Leonardo, however, strongly objected to this view, considering himself to be an inspired, independent innovator. He therefore left Florence in 1482 and went to work for the Sforza dictators of Milan, whose favor he courted by emphasizing his skills as a maker of bombs, heavy ordnance, and siege engines. He remained there until the French invasion of 1499, then wandered about until finally accepting the patronage of the French king, under whose auspices he lived and worked until his death.

space. They also experimented with effects of light and shade, and intently studied the anatomy and proportions of the human body. These techniques also influenced the sculptors of this age. In visual terms, they were extensions of the values that Petrarch and other humanists had embraced in the fourteenth century and expressed through poetry and rhetoric: they recaptured the symmetry of classical art and placed the human subject (the viewer)—rather than God—at the center of artistic experience.

Behind all the beautiful artworks created in this era, which led to the glorification of the artist as a new type of hero, lie the harsh political and economic realities within which these artists worked. Increasing private wealth and the growth of lay patronage opened up new markets and created a huge demand for commodities—whether ornate buildings or beautiful objects—that could increase the status of those grappling for prestige. Portraiture was a direct

THE BIRTH OF VENUS. This painting was executed by Sandro Botticelli in Florence and is typical of the artist's imaginative treatment of stories from ancient mythology. Here, he depicts the moment when Aphrodite, the goddess of love, is spontaneously engendered from the foam of the sea by Chronos, the god of time.

Paradoxically, considering his skill in fashioning deadly weapons, Leonardo was convinced of the essential divinity of all living things. He was a vegetarian—unusual at the time—and went to the marketplace to buy caged birds only to release them to their native habitat once he had finished observing them. His approach to painting was that it should be the most accurate imitation possible of nature. He made careful studies of blades of grass, cloud formations, a waterfall; and he obtained human corpses for dissection and reconstructed them by drawing the minutest features of the anatomy. He carried this knowledge over to his paintings: *The Virgin of the Rocks* typifies not only his technical skill but also his passion for science and belief in the universe as a well-ordered place. The figures are arranged geometrically, with every stone and plant depicted in accurate detail.

In *The Last Supper*, painted on the refectory walls of a monastery in Milan (now in an advanced state of decay), Leonardo displayed his equally keen studies of human psychology. In this image, a serene Christ has just announced to his disciples that one of them will betray him. Leonardo succeeds in portraying the mingled emotions of surprise,

THE VIRGIN OF THE ROCKS. This painting reveals Leonardo's interest in the variety of human faces and facial expressions, and in natural settings.

THE LAST SUPPER. This fresco on the refectory wall of the monastery of Santa Maria delle Grazie in Milan is a testament to both the powers and the limitations of Leonardo's artistry. It skillfully employs the techniques of one-point perspective to create the illusion that Jesus and his disciples are actually dining at the monastery's head table; but because Leonardo had not mastered the techniques of fresco painting, he applied tempera pigments onto a dry wall that had been coated with a sealing agent. As a result, the painting's colors began to fade just years after its completion. By the middle of the sixteenth century, it had seriously deteriorated, and large portions of it are now invisible.

horror, and guilt on the faces of the disciples as they gradually perceive the meaning of their master's statement. He also implicates the painting's viewers in this dramatic scene, since they, too, dine alongside Christ, in the very same room.

Renaissance Arts in Venice and Rome

The innovations of Florentine artists were widely imitated. By the end of the fifteenth century, they had influenced a group of painters active in the wealthy city of Venice, among them Tiziano Vecellio, better known as Titian (c. 1490–1576). Many of Titian's paintings evoke the luxurious, pleasure-loving life of this thriving commercial center. Although they copied Florentine techniques, most Venetian painters showed little of that city's concerns for philosophical or religious allegory; their aim was to appeal to the senses by painting idyllic landscapes and sumptuous portraits of the rich and powerful. In the subordination of form and meaning to color and elegance, they may have mirrored the tastes of the men for whom they worked.

Rome, too, became a major artistic center in this era and a place where the Florentine school exerted a more potent influence. Among its eminent painters was Raffaello Sanzio, or Raphael (1483–1520). Although influenced by Leonardo, Raphael cultivated a more spiritual and

philosophical approach to his subjects. As we noted in Chapter 4, his fresco *The School of Athens* depicts both the harmony and the differences of Platonic and Aristotelian thought (see page 117). It also includes a number of Raphael's contemporaries as models: the image of Plato is actually a portrait of Leonardo, the architect Donato Bramante (c. 1444–1514) stands in for the geometer Euclid, and Michelangelo for the philosopher Heraclitus.

Michelangelo Buonarroti (1475–1564), who spent many decades in Rome in the service of a papacy, was another native of Florence. Like Leonardo, Michelangelo was a polymath: painter, sculptor, architect, and poet—expressing himself in all these forms with similar power. But if Leonardo was a naturalist, Michelangelo was an idealist, despite the harsh political and material realities of the conditions in which he worked. At the center of all his work, as at the center of Renaissance humanism, is the male figure: the embodied masculine mind.

Michelangelo's greatest achievements in painting appear in a single location: the Sistine Chapel of the Vatican palace. Yet they are products of two different periods in the artist's life, and consequently exemplify two different artistic styles and outlooks on the human condition. More famous are the extraordinary frescoes painted on the ceiling from 1508 to 1512, depicting scenes from the book of Genesis. All the panels in this series, including *The Creation of Adam*, exemplify the young artist's commitment to classical artistic principles, and correspondingly affirm the sublimity of Creation and the heroic qualities of humankind.

But a quarter of a century later, when Michelangelo returned to work in the Sistine Chapel, both his style and mood had changed dramatically. In the enormous *Last Judgment*, a fresco completed on the chapel's altar wall in 1536, Michelangelo repudiated classical restraint and substituted a style that emphasized tension and distortion, a humanity racked with fear, guilt, and frailty. He also included himself in it—painting a grotesque self-portrait on the flayed flesh of Saint Bartholomew, who was allegedly martyred by being skinned alive. One wonders whether Michelangelo intended this as a metaphor for the challenges of working in the service of the papal court.

Michelangelo and the Renaissance of Sculpture

Although sculpture was not a new medium for artists, as oil painting was, it became an important area of Renaissance innovation. For the first time since late antiquity, monumental statues became figures "in the round" rather than sculptural elements incorporated into buildings or featured as effigies on tombs. By freeing sculpture from its bondage to architecture, the Renaissance reestablished it as a separate art form.

SELF-PORTRAIT OF THE ARTIST AS A YOUNG MAN: DETAIL FROM *THE SCHOOL OF ATHENS*. We already analyzed aspects of Raphael's famous group portrait of the Greek philosophers, with Plato and Aristotle at center (see page 117). In addition to featuring his own contemporaries as models—including the artists Leonardo and Michelangelo and the architect Bramante—Raphael put himself in the picture. ▪ *What messages does this choice convey?*

THE CREATION OF ADAM. This is one of a series of frescoes Michelangelo painted on the ceiling of the Sistine Chapel in the Vatican palace in Rome. He executed them over a period of many years and under circumstances of extreme physical hardship. It has since become an iconic image. ▪ *How might it be said to capture Renaissance ideals?*

Analyzing Primary Sources

Leonardo da Vinci Applies for a Job

Few sources illuminate the tensions between Renaissance ideals and realities better than the résumé of accomplishments submitted by Leonardo da Vinci to a prospective employer, Ludovico Sforza of Milan. In the following letter, Leonardo explains why he deserves to be appointed chief architect and military engineer in the duke's household administration. He got the job and moved to Milan in 1481.

1. I have the kind of bridges that are extremely light and strong, made to be carried with great ease, and with them you may pursue, and, at any time, flee from the enemy; . . . and also methods of burning and destroying those of the enemy.

2. I know how, when a place is under attack, to eliminate the water from the trenches, and make endless variety of bridges . . . and other machines. . . .

3. . . . I have methods for destroying every rock or other fortress, even if it were built on rock, etc.

4. I also have other kinds of mortars [bombs] that are most convenient and easy to carry. . . .

5. And if it should be a sea battle, I have many kinds of machines that are most efficient for offense and defense. . . .

6. I also have means that are noiseless to reach a designated area by secret and tortuous mines. . . .

7. I will make covered chariots, safe and unattackable, which can penetrate the enemy with their artillery. . . .

8. In case of need I will make big guns, mortars, and light ordnance of fine and useful forms that are out of the ordinary.

9. If the operation of bombardment should fail, I would contrive catapults, mangonels, trabocchi [trebuchets], and other machines of marvelous efficacy and unusualness. In short, I can, according to each case in question, contrive various and endless means of offense and defense.

10. In time of peace I believe I can give perfect satisfaction that is equal to any other in the field of architecture and the construction of buildings. . . . I can execute sculpture in marble, bronze, or clay, and also in painting I do the best that can be done, and as well as any other, whoever he may be.

Having now, most illustrious Lord, sufficiently seen the specimens of all those who consider themselves master craftsmen of instruments of war, and that the invention and operation of such instruments are no different from those in common use, I shall now endeavor . . . to explain myself to your Excellency by revealing to your Lordship my secrets.

Source: Excerpted from Leonardo da Vinci, *The Notebooks*, in *The Italian Renaissance Reader*, eds. Julia Conaway and Mark Mosa (Harmondsworth, UK: 1987), pp. 195–96.

Questions for Analysis

1. Judging from the qualifications Leonardo highlights in this letter, what can you conclude about the political situation in Milan and the priorities of its duke? What can you conclude about the state of military technologies during this period and the conduct of warfare?

2. What do you make of the fact that Leonardo mentions his artistic endeavors only at the end of the letter? Does this fact alter your opinion or impression of him? Why or why not?

The first great master of Renaissance sculpture was Donatello (c. 1386–1466). His bronze statue of David, triumphant over the head of the slain Goliath, is the first freestanding nude of the period. Yet this *David* is clearly an agile adolescent rather than the muscular Greek athlete of Michelangelo's *David*, which was executed in 1501 as a public expression of Florentine civic life: not merely graceful but heroic. Michelangelo regarded sculpture as the most exalted of the arts because it allowed the artist to imitate God most fully in re-creating human forms. Furthermore, in Michelangelo's view, the most godlike sculptor disdained slavish naturalism: anyone could make a plaster cast of a human figure, but only an inspired creative genius could endow his sculpted figures with a sense of life.

Accordingly, in his sculptures, Michelangelo subordinated reality to the force of his imagination and sought to express his ideals in ever more astonishing forms. He also insisted on working in marble—the "noblest" sculptural material—and creating figures twice as large as life. By sculpting a serenely confident young man at the peak of physical fitness, Michelangelo celebrated the Florentine republic's own determination to resist tyrants and uphold ideals of civic justice.

Yet the serenity seen in his *David* is no longer prominent in the works of Michelangelo's later life, when (as in his painting) he began to explore the use of anatomical distortion to create effects of emotional intensity. Although his statues remained awesome in scale, they began to communicate rage, depression, and sorrow. The culmination of this trend is his unfinished but intensely moving *Descent from the Cross*, a depiction of an old man (the sculptor himself) grieving over the distorted, slumping body of the dead Christ.

Renaissance Architecture

Renaissance architecture had its roots in the classical past to an even greater extent than either sculpture or painting. The Gothic style pioneered in northern France (see Chapter 9) had not found a welcome reception in Italy. Most of the buildings constructed there were Romanesque in style, and the great architects influenced by the Renaissance movement generally adopted their building plans from these structures—some of which they believed (mistakenly) to be ancient. They also copied decorative devices from the authentic ruins of ancient Rome. But above all, they derived their influence from the writings of Vitruvius (fl. c. 60–15 B.C.E.), a Roman architect and engineer whose multivolume *On Architecture* was among the humanists' rediscovered ancient texts (Chapter 5). The governing principles laid out by Vitruvius were popularized by Leon Battista Alberti in his book *On the Art of Building*, which began to circulate in manuscript around 1450.

THE POWER AND VULNERABILITY OF THE MALE BODY. Donatello's *David* (left) was the first freestanding nude executed since antiquity. It shows the Hebrew leader as an adolescent youth and is a little over five feet tall. In contrast, Michelangelo's *David* (center) stands thirteen feet high and was placed prominently in front of Florence's city hall to proclaim the city's power and humanistic values. Michelangelo's *Descent from the Cross* (right), which shows Christ's broken body in the arms of the elderly Nicodemus (the sculptor himself), was made for Michelangelo's own tomb. (The Gospels describe Nicodemus as a Pharisee who became a follower of Jesus, and who was present at his death.) ▪ *Why would Michelangelo choose to represent himself as Nicodemus?* ▪ *How does his representation of David, and the context in which this figure was displayed, compare with that of Donatello's sculpture?*

ST. PETER'S BASILICA, ROME. This eighteenth-century painting shows the massive interior of the Renaissance building. If not for the perspective provided by the tiny human figures, the human eye would be fooled into thinking this was a much smaller space.

In keeping with these classical models, Renaissance buildings emphasized geometrical proportion. These aesthetic values were also reinforced by the interest in Platonic philosophy, which taught that certain mathematical ratios reflect the harmony of the universe. For example, the proportions of the human body are the basis for the proportions of the quintessential Renaissance building: St. Peter's Basilica in Rome. Designed by some of the most celebrated architects of the time, including Bramante and Michelangelo, it is still one of the largest buildings in the world. Yet it seems smaller than a Gothic cathedral because it is built to human scale. The same artful proportions are evident in smaller-scale buildings too, as in the aristocratic country houses later designed by the northern Italian architect Andrea Palladio (1508–1580), who created secular miniatures of ancient temples, such as the Roman Pantheon, to glorify the aristocrats who lived there.

THE RENAISSANCE NORTH OF THE ALPS

Despite Italian resentment at the political encroachment of foreign monarchs, contacts between Italy and northern Europe were close throughout this period. Italian merchants and financiers were familiar figures at northern cities and courts; students from all over Europe studied at Italian universities in Bologna or Padua; northern poets, including Geoffrey Chaucer (Chapter 11), and their works traveled to and from Italy; and northern soldiers were frequent combatants in Italian wars. Yet not until the very end of the fifteenth century did the innovative artistry and learning of Italy begin to be exported across the Alps into northern Europe and across the Mediterranean into Spain.

Historians have offered a variety of explanations for this delay. Northern European intellectual life in the later Middle Ages was dominated by universities such as those of Paris, Oxford, Kraków, and Prague, whose curricula focused on philosophical logic, Christian theology, and (to a lesser extent) medicine. These rigorous courses left little room for the study of classical literature. Universities in Italy, by contrast, were more often professional schools specializing in law and medicine, and they were more integrally tied to the nonacademic intellectual lives of the cities in which they were situated. As a result, a more secular, urban-oriented educational tradition took shape, as we saw in our previous discussion of humanism. In northern Europe, those scholars who *were* influenced by Italian ideas usually worked outside the university system, under the private patronage of kings and princes.

Moreover, before the turn of the sixteenth century, northern rulers were less committed to patronizing artists and intellectuals than were the city-states and princes of Italy. In Italy, as we have seen, such patronage was an important arena for competition between political rivals. In northern Europe, however, political units were larger, and political rivals fewer. It was therefore less necessary to use art for political purposes in a kingdom than it was in a city-state—a major exception being the independent duchy of Burgundy, which surpassed even the French court in its magnificence. A statue erected in a central square of Florence could be seen by all the city's residents; in Paris, such a statue would be seen by only a tiny minority of the French king's subjects. But as royal courts became more firmly established in royal capitals—and so became showcases for royal power—kings needed to impress townspeople, courtiers, and visitors. Consequently, they relied more and more on artists and intellectuals to advertise their wealth and taste.

Christian Humanism and the Career of Erasmus

In general, then, the Renaissance movement in northern Europe differed from that in Italy because it grafted certain Italian ideals onto preexisting traditions, rather than sweeping away older forms of knowledge and artistry. This can be seen very clearly in the case of the intellectual development known as Christian humanism. Although northern scholars shared the Italian humanists' scorn for scholasticism's limitations, northern humanists were more committed to seeking ethical guidance from biblical and religious precepts, as well as from Cicero or Virgil. Like their Italian counterparts, they embraced the wisdom of antiquity, but the antiquity they favored was Christian as well as classical: the antiquity of the New Testament and the early Church. Similarly, although northern artists were inspired by the accomplishments of Italian masters and copied their techniques, they depicted classical subjects less frequently and almost never portrayed completely nude human figures.

Any discussion of Christian humanism must begin with the career of **Desiderius Erasmus** (c. 1469–1536). The illegitimate son of a priest, Erasmus was born near Rotterdam in the Netherlands. Later, as a result of his wide travels, he became a virtual citizen of all Europe. Forced into a monastery against his will when he was a teenager, the young Erasmus found little useful instruction there—but plenty of freedom to read what he liked. He devoured all the classics he could get his hands on, alongside the writings of the Church Fathers (Chapter 6). When he was about thirty years old, he obtained permission to leave the monastery and enroll in the University of Paris, where he completed the requirements for a bachelor's degree in divinity.

But Erasmus subsequently rebelled against what he considered the arid learning of Parisian academe, and he never served actively as a priest. Instead, he made his living from teaching, writing, and the proceeds of various ecclesiastical offices that required no pastoral duties. Ever on the lookout for new patrons, he traveled often to England, stayed for three years in Italy, and resided in several different cities in Germany and the Low Countries, before settling finally, toward the end of his life, in Basel (Switzerland). By means of a voluminous correspondence with learned friends, Erasmus became the leader of a humanist coterie. And through the popularity of his numerous publications, he also became the arbiter of northern European cultural tastes during his lifetime.

Erasmus's many-sided intellectual activity may be assessed from two different points of view: the literary and the doctrinal. As a Latin prose stylist, Erasmus was unequaled since the days of Cicero. Extraordinarily eloquent and witty, he reveled in tailoring his mode of discourse to fit his subject, creating dazzling verbal effects and coining puns that took on added meaning if the reader knew Greek as well as Latin. Above all, Erasmus excelled in the deft use of irony, poking fun at everything, including himself. For example, in his *Colloquies* (*Discussions*) he has a fictional character lament the evils of the times: "Kings make war, priests strive to line their pockets, theologians invent syllogisms, monks roam outside their cloisters, the commons riot, and Erasmus writes colloquies."

But although Erasmus's urbane Latin style and humor earned him a wide audience on those grounds alone, he intended everything he wrote to promote what he called the "philosophy of Christ." He believed that the society of his day had lost sight of the Gospels' teachings. Accordingly, he offered his contemporaries three different kinds of writings: clever satires in which people could recognize their own foibles, serious moral treatises meant to offer guidance

ERASMUS, BY HANS HOLBEIN THE YOUNGER. This is generally regarded as the most evocative portrait of the preeminent Christian humanist.

Past and Present

The Reputation of Richard III

The name of England's King Richard III (r. 1483–1485) has been a byword for villainy since the time of his death, when Sir Thomas More and other propagandists working for his successor, Henry VII, alleged that his physically deformed body was matched by the depravity of his actions. Historians have debated the truth of both claims for centuries. Was Richard really a hunchback? And a murderer? In 2012, the stunning discovery of Richard's body (under a parking lot near the medieval battlefield where he died) confirmed that he had indeed suffered from severe scoliosis. The other claim has yet to be proven.

 Watch related author interview on the Student Site

toward proper Christian behavior, and scholarly editions of basic Christian texts.

In the first category belong the works of Erasmus that are still widely read today: *The Praise of Folly* (1511), in which he ridiculed pedantry and dogmatism, ignorance and gullibility—even within the Church; and the *Colloquies* (1518), in which he held up contemporary religious practices for examination, couching a serious message in the ironic tone we have just noted. In these books, Erasmus let fictional characters do the talking, so his own views on any given topic can only be determined by inference. But in his second mode, Erasmus spoke clearly in his own voice. In *Handbook of the Christian Knight* (1503), he used the popular language of chivalry as a means to encourage a life of inward piety; in *Complaint of Peace* (1517), he argued movingly for Christian pacifism. Erasmus's pacifism was

one of his most deeply held values, and he returned to it again and again in his published works.

Despite the success of these writings, Erasmus considered textual scholarship his greatest achievement. Revering the authority of the earliest Christian teachers, he brought out reliable printed editions of works by Augustine, Jerome, and Ambrose. He also used his extraordinary command of Latin and Greek to produce a more accurate edition of the New Testament. After reading Lorenzo Valla's *Notes on the New Testament* in 1504, Erasmus became convinced that nothing was more imperative than divesting the Christian scriptures of the myriad errors in transcription and translation that had piled up over the course of preceding centuries. He therefore spent ten years comparing all the early Greek biblical manuscripts he could find in order to establish an authoritative text. When it finally appeared in 1516, Erasmus's Greek

New Testament, published together with explanatory notes and his own new Latin translation, became one of the most important scholarly landmarks of all time—and it would play a critical role in the early stages of the Reformation in the hands of Martin Luther (see Chapter 13).

The Influence of Erasmus

One of Erasmus's closest friends, and a close second to him in distinction among Christian humanists, was the Englishman Sir **Thomas More** (1478–1535). In later life, following a successful career as a lawyer and speaker of the House of Commons in Parliament, More was appointed lord chancellor of England in 1529. He was not long in this position, however, before he opposed King Henry VIII's plan to establish a national church, under royal control, that would deny the supremacy of the pope (see Chapter 13). He was eventually executed and is now revered as a Catholic martyr.

Much earlier, in 1516, More published his most famous book, *Utopia* (from the Greek meaning *No Place*). Purport-

SIR THOMAS MORE, BY HANS HOLBEIN THE YOUNGER. Holbein's skill in rendering the gravity and interiority of his subject is matched by his masterful representation of the sumptuous chain of office, furred mantle, and velvet sleeves that indicate the political and professional status of Henry VIII's lord chancellor.

ing to describe an ideal community on an imaginary island, the book is really an Erasmian critique of contemporary culture: disparities between poverty and wealth, drastic punishments, religious persecution, and the senseless slaughter of war. In contrast to Europeans, the inhabitants of the fictional Utopia hold all their goods in common, work only six hours a day (so that all may have leisure for intellectual pursuits), and practice the natural virtues of wisdom, moderation, fortitude, and justice. Although More did not advance explicit arguments in favor of Christianity, he may have meant to imply that if the Utopians could manage their society so well without the benefit of Christian revelation, Europeans who knew the Gospels ought to be able to do even better.

Erasmus and More head a long list of energetic and eloquent northern humanists who made signal contributions to the collective enterprise of revolutionizing the study of early Christianity, and their achievements had a direct influence on Protestant reformers (as we will see in the next chapter). Yet very few of them were willing to join Luther and other Protestant leaders in rejecting the fundamental principles on which the power of the Roman Church was based. Most tried to remain within its fold while still espousing an ideal of inward piety and scholarly inquiry. But as the leaders of the Church grew less and less tolerant of dissent, even mild criticism came to seem like heresy. Erasmus died early enough to escape persecution, but several of his less fortunate followers did not.

The Literature of the Northern Renaissance

Although Christian humanism would be severely challenged by the Reformation, the artistic Renaissance in north Europe flourished. Poets in France and England vied with one another to adapt the elegant lyric forms pioneered by Petrarch and popularized by many subsequent poets, including Michelangelo. The sonnet was particularly influential and would become one of the verse forms embraced by William Shakespeare (1554–1616) (see Chapter 14). Another English poet, Edmund Spenser (c. 1552–1599), drew on the literary innovation of Ariosto's *Orlando Furioso*. Spenser's *Faerie Queene* is a similarly long chivalric romance that revels in sensuous imagery.

Meanwhile, the more satirical side of Renaissance humanism was embraced by the French writer François Rabelais (*RAH-beh-lay*; c. 1494–1553). Like Erasmus, whom he greatly admired, Rabelais began his career in the Church, but soon left the cloister to study medicine.

A practicing physician, Rabelais interspersed his professional activities with literary endeavors, the most enduring of which are the twin books *Gargantua* and *Pantagruel*: a series of "chronicles" describing the lives and times of giants whose fabulous size and gross appetites serve as vehicles for much lusty humor. Like Erasmus, Rabelais also satirized religious hypocrisy, scholasticism, superstition, and bigotry. But unlike Erasmus, who wrote in a highly cultivated classical Latin style comprehensible only to learned readers, Rabelais chose to address a different audience by writing in extremely crude French and glorifying every human appetite as natural and healthy.

Northern Architecture and Art

Although many architects in northern Europe continued to build in the flamboyant Gothic style of the later Middle Ages, the classical values of Italian architects can be seen in some of the splendid new castles constructed in France's Loire valley—châteaux too elegant to be defensible—and in

SAINT JEROME IN HIS STUDY, BY DÜRER. Jerome, the biblical translator of the fourth century (Chapter 6), was a hero to both Dürer and Erasmus, and the paragon of inspired Christian scholarship. Note how the scene exudes contentment, even down to the sleeping lion, which seems more like an overgrown tabby cat than a symbol of Christ.

the royal palace of the Louvre in Paris (now the museum), which replaced an old twelfth-century fortress. The influence of Renaissance ideals is also visible in the work of the German artist Albrecht Dürer (*DIRR-er*; 1471–1528). Dürer was the first northerner to master the techniques of proportion and perspective, and he shared with contemporary Italians a fascination with nature and the human body. He also took advantage of the printing press to circulate his work to a wide audience, making his delicate pencil drawings into engravings that could be mass produced.

But Dürer never really embraced classical subjects, instead drawing inspiration from more traditional Christian legends and the Christian humanism of Erasmus. For example, Dürer's serenely radiant engraving of Saint Jerome seems to express the scholarly absorption that Erasmus would have enjoyed while working quietly in his study. Indeed, Dürer aspired to immortalize Erasmus himself in a major portrait, but the paths of the two men crossed only once. Instead, the accomplishment of capturing Erasmus's pensive spirit in art was left to another northern artist, the German Hans Holbein the Younger (1497–1543). Holbein also painted an acute portrait of Erasmus's friend, Sir Thomas More. These two portraits, in themselves, exemplify a Renaissance emphasis on the making of naturalistic likenesses that express human individuality.

Tradition and Innovation in Music

Like the visual arts, the lovely music produced during this era was nourished by patrons' desire to surround themselves with beauty. Yet unlike painting and sculpture, musical practice did not reach back to classical antiquity, but instead drew on well-established medieval conventions. Even before the Black Death, a musical movement called *ars nova* ("new art") was already flourishing in France and spread to Italy during the lifetime of Petrarch; its outstanding composers were Guillaume de Machaut (c. 1300–1377) and Francesco Landini (c. 1325–1397).

The part-songs and ballads composed by these musicians and their successors expanded on earlier genres of secular music, but their greatest achievement was a highly complicated yet delicate contrapuntal style adapted for the liturgy of the Church. Machaut's polyphonic (harmonized) setting of the major sections of the Mass is the earliest by a single composer. In the fifteenth century, the dissemination of this new musical aesthetic combined with a host of French, Flemish, and Italian elements in the multicultural courts of Europe, particularly that of Burgundy. By the beginning of the sixteenth century, Franco-Flemish composers dominated many important courts and cathedrals, creating a variety of new forms and styles that bear a close affinity to Renaissance art and poetry.

Throughout Europe, the general level of musical proficiency during this era was very high. The singing of part-songs was a popular pastime in homes and at informal social gatherings, and the ability to read a part at sight was considered part of an elite education. Aristocratic women, in particular, were expected to display mastery of the new musical instruments that had been developed to add nuance and texture to existing musical forms, including the lute, the viol, the violin, and a variety of woodwind and keyboard instruments such as the harpsichord.

Although most composers of this period were men trained in the service of the Church, they rarely made sharp distinctions between sacred and secular music. Like sculpture, music was coming into its own as a serious, independent art. As such, it would become an important medium for the expression of both Catholic and Protestant ideals during the Reformation, and also one of the few art forms equally acceptable to all.

THE POLITICS OF CHRISTIAN EUROPE

We have already observed how the intellectual and artistic activity of the Renaissance was both fueled and hindered by the political developments of the later fifteenth century—within Italy, and throughout Europe. In 1453, France had emerged victorious in the Hundred Years' War, whereas England plunged into three decades of bloody civil conflict that touched every corner of that kingdom. The French monarchy, therefore, was able to rebuild its power and prestige while at the same time extending its control over regions once controlled by the English, which were now part of an enlarged kingdom of France.

In 1494, the French king Charles VIII acted on his plan to expand his reach even farther, into Italy. Leading an army of 30,000 well-trained troops across the Alps, and aided by an alliance with the duchy of Milan, he intended to press his ancestral claim to the kingdom of Naples. By the time Charles left a year later, however, this effort yielded only a tenuous hold on Naples, while solidifying Italian opposition to French occupation—as we noted in our discussion of Machiavelli.

The rulers of Spain, whose territorial claims on Sicily also extended to Naples, were spurred by Charles's expansionism to forge an uneasy alliance among the Papal States, some principalities of the Holy Roman Empire, Milan, and Venice. But the respite was brief, for Charles's successor,

Louis XII, launched a second French invasion in 1499. For more than a generation, until 1529, warfare in Italy was virtually uninterrupted. Alliances and counteralliances among city-states became further catalysts for violence and made Italy a magnet for mercenaries who could barely be kept in check by the generals who employed them.

Meanwhile, the northern Italian city-states' virtual monopoly on trade with Asia, which had been one of the chief economic underpinnings of artistic and intellectual patronage, was being gradually eroded by the shifting of trade routes from the Mediterranean to the Atlantic (Chapters 10 and 11). It was also hampered by the increasing power of the Ottoman Empire, and even by the imperial pretensions of a new Russian ruler.

The Power of Ivan the Great

In Chapter 10, we noted that Moscow had emerged as an administrative capital under the Mongols, and then had become the center of an independent principality, the Grand Duchy of Muscovy. In the fifteenth century, its exponential growth was driven by its ruler Ivan III (r. 1462–1505), also known as **Ivan the Great**, the first Muscovite prince to adopt a distinctive imperial agenda.

Ivan launched a series of conquests that annexed all the independent principalities between Moscow and the border of Poland-Lithuania. After invading Lithuania in 1492 and 1501, he even succeeded in bringing parts of that domain (portions of modern Belarus and Ukraine) under his control, although this did not impact the region's strong cultural ties to Poland or its religious allegiance to Rome. Meanwhile, Ivan married the niece of the last Byzantine emperor: an alliance that inspired later Russian rulers to claim that Moscow was the "third Rome" while they were heirs of the Caesars—hence the title *czar* or **tsar**. Ivan also rebuilt his fortified Moscow residence, known as the Kremlin, in magnificent Italianate style. By the time of his death in 1505, Muscovy was firmly established as a dominant power on the frontier of eastern Europe.

The Growth of National Churches

At the same time that Muscovy laid claim to the mantle of Roman imperial power, the papacy was pouring resources into the glorification of the original Rome and the aggrandizement of the papal office. But neither the city nor its rulers could keep pace with their political and religious rivals. Following the Council of Constance (Chapter 11), the papacy's victory over the conciliarists was a costly one. To win the support of Europe's kings and princes, various

THE EXPANSION OF MUSCOVITE TERRITORY TO 1505. The Grand Duchy of Moscow (also known as Muscovy) was the heart of what would become an empire. ▪ *With what other empires and polities did the Muscovites have to compete during this period of expansion?*

Map labels:
WHITE SEA
Archangel
FINLAND
URAL MOUNTAINS
REPUBLIC OF NOVGOROD
TEUTONIC ORDER
LIVONIA
BALTIC SEA
TEUTONIC ORDER
KAZAN
Kazan
LITHUANIA
BELARUS
Smolensk
DUCHY OF MOSCOW
Moscow
Nizhniy Novgorod
Tannenberg
POLAND
KINGDOM OF POLAND AND LITHUANIA
Kraków
UKRAINE
Kiev
Dnieper R.
Don R.
Volga R.
KHANATE OF THE GOLDEN HORDE
HUNGARY
MOLDAVIA
VALLACHIA
Danube R.
BLACK SEA

0   100   200 Miles
0   100   200 Kilometers

Legend:
Moscow c. 1300
Expansion to 1364
Expansion to 1389
Expansion to 1425
Expansion to 1462
Expansion to 1505

EUROPE
Area of detail
AFRICA

popes negotiated a series of religious treaties known as "concordats," which granted these rulers extensive authority over churches within their domains. Under the terms of these concordats, kings now received many of the revenues that had previously gone to the papacy and acquired new powers to appoint candidates to Church offices. The papacy thus secured its theoretical supremacy at the expense of its real power, and strengthened the national monarchies that were emerging during this era. Such changes were, in many ways, a drastic reversal of the hard-won reforms of the eleventh and twelfth centuries that had created such a powerful papacy in the first place.

Having given away so many sources of revenue and authority, the popes of the late fifteenth century became even more dependent on their own territories in central Italy. But to tighten their hold on the Papal States, they had to rule like other Italian princes: leading armies, jockeying for alliances, and undermining their opponents by every possible means—including covert operations and assassinations. By secular standards of the day, these efforts paid off: the Papal States became one of the better-governed and wealthier principalities in Italy. But such methods did nothing to enhance the popes' reputation for piety, and disillusionment with the papacy as a force

AN ITALIAN RENAISSANCE CATHEDRAL IN MUSCOVITE RUS'. Ivan the Great commissioned the Italian architect Aristotele Fioravanti to build this cathedral, dedicated to the Blessed Virgin and honoring her Assumption into heaven. It is now part of the Kremlin palace complex in Moscow. ▪ *Why would Ivan choose to build this cathedral and commission this particular architect?* ▪ *What messages might he have been trying to convey?*

The solution to the disputed succession that had caused the war in Aragon ultimately lay in the blending of two powerful royal families. In 1469, Prince **Ferdinand of Aragon** was recognized as the undisputed heir to that throne and, in the same year, secured this position by marrying **Isabella**, the heiress of **Castile**. Isabella became queen in 1474 and Ferdinand became king in 1479. Although Castile and Aragon continued to be ruled as separate kingdoms until 1714 (there are tensions between the two former kingdoms even now), the marriage of Ferdinand and Isabella enabled them to pursue several ambitious policies. In particular, their union allowed them to spend their combined resources on the creation of Europe's most powerful army, which was initially employed to conquer the last remaining principality—Granada—of what had been al-Andalus, Muslim Spain. That principality fell in 1492.

for the advancement of spirituality became even more widespread.

With both papal authority and Rome's spiritual prestige in decline, kings and princes became the primary figures to whom both clergy and laity looked for religious and moral guidance. Many secular rulers responded to such expectations aggressively, closing scandal-ridden monasteries, suppressing alleged heretics, and prohibiting the lower classes from dressing like the nobility. By these and other such measures, rulers could present themselves as champions of moral reform even as they strengthened their political power. The result was an increasingly close link between national monarchies and national churches, a link that would become even stronger after the Reformation.

The Triumph of the Reconquista

The kingdoms of the Iberian Peninsula were also in constant conflict during this period. In Castile, civil war and incompetent governance allowed the Castilian nobility to gain greater control over the peasantry and greater independence from the monarchy. In Aragon, royal government benefited from the extended commercial influence of Catalonia, which was under Aragonese authority. But after 1458, Aragon, too, became enmeshed in a civil war, a war that involved both France and Castile.

The End of the Convivencia and the Expulsion of the Jews

For more than seven centuries, many of Spain's Jewish communities had enjoyed certain privileges extended by their Muslim rulers, who were also relatively tolerant of their Christian subjects. Scholars often refer to this period of Spain's history as a time of *convivencia*, a word that means "living together" or "coexistence." Although relations among various religious and ethnic groups were not always peaceful or positive—we noted the slaughter of Jews during the Black Death (Chapter 10)—the policies of Muslim rulers in al-Andalus had enabled an extraordinary hybrid culture to flourish.

The aims of the Spanish *reconquista* were diametrically opposed to those of "living together." The "reconquest" sought to forge a single, homogeneous community based on the fiction that Spain had once been entirely Christian and should be restored to its former purity. The year 1492, therefore, marks not only the end of Muslim rule in medieval Spain but also the culmination of Jewish exclusion, a process that had accelerated in the late thirteenth century (Chapter 9). Within this history, the Spanish expulsion of the Jews stands out for the staggering scope of the displacements and destruction it entailed: at least 100,000, and possibly as many as 200,000, men, women, and children

FERDINAND AND ISABELLA HONORING THE VIRGIN. In this contemporary Spanish painting, the royal couple are shown with two of their children and two household chaplains, in the company of the Blessed Virgin, the Christ Child, and saints from the Dominican order. (The Dominicans were instrumental in conducting the affairs of the Spanish Inquisition.) ▪ *How clear is the distinction between these holy figures and the royal family?* ▪ *What message is conveyed by their proximity?*

in the Ottoman Empire. As we already noted, there were many opportunities for advancement in the Ottoman imperial bureaucracy, while the Ottoman economy benefited from the highly skilled labor of Jewish artisans and the vast trading networks of Jewish merchants. In time, new forms and expressions of Jewish culture would emerge, and new communities would form. And although the opportunities afforded by the *convivencia* could never be revived, the descendants of these Spanish Jews—known as Sephardic Jews, or Sephardim—still treasure the traditions and customs formed in Spain over a thousand year period.

The Extension of the Reconquista

Although the Christian kingdoms of Iberia had been devoted for centuries to the expansion of their territory, the victory over the Muslims of Granada and the expulsion of the Jews in 1492 were watershed events. They mark the beginning of a sweeping initiative to construct a new basis for the precariously united kingdoms of Aragon and Castile, one that could transcend rival regional identities. Like other contemporary monarchs, Ferdinand and Isabella strengthened their emerging nation-state by constructing an exclusively Christian identity for its people, attaching that new identity to the crown, and promoting a single national language: Castilian Spanish. They also succeeded in capturing and redirecting another language: the rhetoric of crusade.

The crusading ethos, as we have seen, always seeks new outlets. With the creation of a new, exclusively Christian, Spanish kingdom through the defeat of all external enemies and internal threats, where could the energies harnessed by the *reconquista* be directed? The answer came from an unexpected quarter. Just a few months after Ferdinand and Isabella marched victoriously into Granada, the queen granted three ships to a Genoese adventurer who promised to reach India by sailing westward across the Atlantic Ocean, and to claim any new lands he found for Spain. Columbus never reached India, but he did help to extend the traditions of reconquest and crusading to the New World—with far-reaching consequences.

NEW TARGETS AND TECHNOLOGIES OF CONQUEST

The Spanish monarchs' decision to underwrite a voyage of exploration was spurred by their desire to counter the successful Portuguese ventures of the past half century. It was becoming clear that the tiny kingdom on the northwestern

were deprived of their homes and sent out into the world as refugees.

The Christian monarchs' motives for ordering this expulsion are still debated. Tens of thousands of Spanish Jews had converted to Christianity between 1391 and 1420, many as a result of coercion but some from sincere conviction. And for a generation or so, it seemed possible that these converts, known as *conversos*, might successfully assimilate into Christian society. But the same civil wars that led to the union of Ferdinand and Isabella made the *conversos* targets of discrimination. Conflicts may also have fueled popular suspicions that these converts remained Jews in secret. To make "proper" Christians out of the *conversos*, the "Most Catholic" monarchs (as they were now called) may have concluded that they needed to remove any potentially seditious influences that might stem from the continuing presence of a Jewish community in Spain.

What became of the Spanish Jews? Some traveled north, to the Rhineland towns of Germany or to Poland and eastern Europe. But most settled in Muslim regions of the Mediterranean and Middle East, where many found a haven tip of the Iberian Peninsula would soon dominate the sea-lanes if rival entrepreneurs did not attempt to find alternate routes and establish equally lucrative colonies. This competition with Portugal was another reason that Isabella turned to a Genoese sea captain—not to a Portuguese one—when she sought to expand Spain's wealth and global influence.

Prince Henry the Navigator and Portuguese Colonial Initiatives

Although Portugal had been an independent Christian kingdom since the twelfth century (Chapter 9), it was never able to compete effectively with its more powerful neighbors—Muslim or Christian—on land. But when the focus of European economic expansion began to shift toward the Atlantic (Chapter 10), Portuguese mariners were well placed to take advantage of this trend.

A central figure in the history of Portuguese maritime imperialism is **Prince Henry** (1394–1460), later called "**the Navigator,**" a son of King João I of Portugal and his English queen, Philippa of Lancaster, the sister of England's Henry IV. Prince Henry was fascinated by the sciences of cartography and navigation, and he helped to ensure that Portuguese sailors had access to the latest charts and navigational instruments. He was also inspired by the stories told by John de Mandeville and Marco Polo—particularly the legend of Prester John, a mythical Christian king dwelling somewhere at the end of the earth, whom Europeans believed would be their ally against the Muslims if only they could find him. Indeed, Prince Henry was Grand Master of a new crusading order, the Order of Christ, whose mission was to drive the Muslims out of Africa. He also had ambitions to extend Portuguese control into the Atlantic, to tap into the burgeoning market for slaves in the Ottoman Empire, and to establish direct links with sources of African gold.

Prince Henry played an important part in organizing the Portuguese colonization of Madeira, the Canary Islands, and the Azores. In the process, he also pioneered the Portuguese slave trade, which almost entirely eradicated the population of the Canaries before targeting West Africa. By the 1440s, Portuguese explorers had reached the Cape Verde Islands. In 1444, they landed on the African mainland, in the area that became known as the Gold Coast, where they began to collect cargoes of gold and slaves for export back to Portugal.

Prince Henry personally directed eight of the thirty-five Portuguese voyages to Africa that took place during his lifetime. Also, in order to outflank the cross-Saharan gold trade, largely controlled by the Muslims of North Africa and mediated by the Genoese (Chapter 10), he decided to intercept this trade at its source by building a series of forts along the African coastline, manned by armed soldiers and provisioned by the crown. By establishing permanent outposts of power in the Atlantic and West Africa, the Portuguese were not only positioned to leverage local trade in gold; they were also unwittingly poised to dominate the global trade in African slaves that would explode after 1492. This was also Prince Henry's main reason for colonizing the Canary Islands, which he saw as a staging ground for expeditions into the African interior.

From Africa to India and Beyond: An Empire of Spices

By the 1470s, Portuguese sailors had rounded the western coast of Africa and were exploring the Gulf of Guinea. In 1483, they reached the mouth of the Congo River. In 1488, the Portuguese captain Bartolomeu Dias was inadvertently blown around the southern tip of Africa by a gale, after which he named the point "Cape of Storms." But King João II (r. 1481–1495), taking a more optimistic view of Dias's achievement, renamed it the Cape of Good Hope and began planning a naval expedition to India. In 1497–1498, Vasco da Gama rounded the cape and then, with the help of a Muslim navigator named Ibn Majid, crossed the Indian Ocean to Calicut, on the southwestern coast of India.

This voyage opened a viable sea route between Europe and the Far Eastern spice trade for the first time. Although da Gama lost half his fleet and one-third of his men on this two-year voyage, his cargo of spices was so valuable that these losses were deemed insignificant. His heroism became legendary, and his story became the basis for the Portuguese national epic, the *Lusiads*.

Now masters of the quickest route to riches in the world, the Portuguese swiftly capitalized on their decades of accomplishment. Not only did their trading fleets sail regularly to India, they attempted to monopolize the entire spice trade. In 1509, the Portuguese defeated an Ottoman fleet and then blockaded the mouth of the Red Sea, attempting to cut off one of the traditional routes by which spices had traveled to Alexandria and Beirut. By 1510, Portuguese military forces had established a series of forts along the western Indian coastline, including their headquarters at Goa. In 1511, Portuguese ships seized Malacca, a center of the spice trade on the Malay Peninsula. By 1515, they had reached the Spice Islands (East Indies) and the coast of China. So completely did the Portuguese now dominate the spice trade that even the Venetians were forced to buy their pepper in the Portuguese capital of Lisbon.

Naval Technology and Navigation

The Portuguese caravel—the workhorse ship of those first voyages to Africa—was based on ship and sail designs that had been in use among Portuguese fishermen since the thirteenth century. Starting in the 1440s, however, Portuguese shipwrights began building larger caravels of about 50 tons' displacement and equipped with two masts, each carrying a triangular (lateen) sail. Columbus's *Niña* was a ship of this design, although it was refitted with two square sails in the Portuguese-held Canary Islands to enable it to sail more efficiently before the wind during the Atlantic crossing. Such ships required much smaller crews than did the multi-oared galleys still commonly used in the Mediterranean. By the end of the fifteenth century, even larger caravels of around 200 tons were being constructed, with a third mast and a combination of square and lateen sails.

Europeans were further making significant advances in navigation during this era. Quadrants, which could be used to calculate latitude in the Northern Hemisphere by the height of the North Star above the horizon, were in widespread use by the 1450s. As sailors approached the equator, however, the quadrant became less and less useful, and navigators instead made use of astrolabes, which reckoned latitude by the height of the sun. Like quadrants, astrolabes had been in use for centuries; but it was not until the 1480s that they became practical instruments for seaborne navigation, thanks to the standard tables for the calculation of latitude, whose preparation was sponsored by the Portuguese crown. Compasses, too, were coming into more widespread use during the fifteenth century. Longitude, however, remained impossible to calculate accurately until the eighteenth century, when the invention of the marine chronometer finally made it possible to keep accurate time at sea. In this prior age of discovery, Europeans sailing east or west across the oceans generally had to rely on their skill at dead reckoning to determine where they were.

European sailors further benefited from a new interest in maps and navigational charts. Especially important were books known as *rutters* or *routiers*. These contained detailed sailing instructions and descriptions of the coastal landmarks a pilot could expect to encounter en route to a variety of destinations. Mediterranean sailors had used similar portolan charts since the thirteenth century, mapping the ports along the coastlines, tracking prevailing winds and tides, and indicating dangerous reefs and shallow harbors (see Chapter 10). During the fifteenth century, these mapmaking techniques were extended to the Atlantic Ocean. And by the end of the sixteenth century, the accumulated knowledge contained in rutters spanned the globe.

Artillery and Empire

Larger, more maneuverable ships and improved navigational aids made it possible for the Portuguese and other European mariners to reach Africa, Asia, and—eventually—the Americas. But fundamentally, these European commercial empires were military achievements that capitalized on what Europeans had learned in their wars against each other. Perhaps the most critical military advance was the increasing sophistication of artillery, a development made possible not only by gunpowder but also by improved metallurgical techniques for casting cannon barrels. By the middle of the fifteenth century, as we observed in Chapter 11, the use of artillery pieces had rendered the stone walls of medieval castles and towns obsolete, a fact brought home in 1453 by the successful French siege of Bordeaux (which ended the Hundred Years' War), and by the Ottoman siege of Constantinople (which ended the Byzantine Empire).

SPANISH GALLEON. The larger, full-bottomed ships that came into use during the fifteenth century became engines of imperial conquest and the vessels that brought the riches of those conquests back to Europe. This wooden model was made for the Museo Storico Navale di Venezia (Naval History Museum) in Venice, Italy.

OVERSEAS EXPLORATION IN THE FIFTEENTH AND SIXTEENTH CENTURIES. ■ *What were the major routes taken by European explorers of the fifteenth and sixteenth centuries?* ■ *What appear to have been the explorers' main goals?* ■ *How might the establishment of outposts in Africa, the Americas, and the East Indies have radically altered the balance of power in the Old World, and why?*

Analyzing Primary Sources

The Ottomans' Army of Slaves

Although the growing African slave trade was creating a newly racialized idea of slavery in the Caribbean and the Americas, slavery in Europe was not tied to race. Indeed, slavery could be a path to upward mobility in the Ottoman Empire. The following account is from a memoir written by Konstantin Mihailovic, a Serbian Christian who was captured as a youth by the army of Sultan Mehmet II. For eight years, he served in the Ottoman janissary ("gate-keeper") corps. In 1463, the fortress he was defending for the sultan was captured by the Hungarians, after which he recorded his experiences for a Christian audience.

 henever the Turks invade foreign lands and capture their people, an imperial scribe follows immediately behind them, and whatever boys there are, he takes them all into the janissaries and gives five gold pieces for each one and sends them across the sea [to Anatolia]. There are about two thousand of these boys. If, however, the number of them from enemy peoples does not suffice, then he takes from the Christians in every village in his land who have boys, having established what is the most every village can give so that the quota will always be full. And the boys whom he takes in his own land are called *cilik*. Each one of them can leave his property

to whomever he wants after his death. And those whom he takes among the enemies are called *pendik*. These latter after their deaths can leave nothing; rather, it goes to the emperor, except that if someone comports himself well and is so deserving that he be freed, he may leave it to whomever he wants. And on the boys who are across the sea the emperor spends nothing; rather, those to whom they are entrusted must maintain them and send them where he orders. Then they take those who are suited for it on ships and there they study and train to skirmish in battle. There the emperor already provides for them and gives them a wage. From there he chooses for his own court those who are trained and then raises their wages.

Source: Konstantin Mihailovic, *Memoirs of a Janissary* (Michigan Slavic Translations 3), trans. Benjamin Stolz (Ann Arbor, MI: 1975), pp. 157–59.

Questions for Analysis

1. Why might the Ottoman emperor have established this system for "recruiting" and training janissaries? What are its strengths and weaknesses?

2. Applying your knowledge of Western civilizations, how unusual would you deem this method of raising troops? How does it compare with the strategies of other rulers we have studied?

Indeed, the new ship designs—first caravels, then the heavier galleons—were important in part because their larger size made it possible to mount more effective artillery pieces. European vessels were now refitted as floating artillery platforms, with scores of guns mounted in fixed positions along their sides and swivel guns mounted fore and aft. These guns were vastly expensive, as were the ships that carried them; but for rulers who could afford them, such ships made it possible to back mercantile ventures with military power. As we already noted, Vasco da Gama had been able to sail into the Indian Ocean in 1498, but the Portuguese did not gain control of that ocean until 1509, when they defeated combined Ottoman and Indian naval forces.

Portuguese trading outposts in Africa and Asia were essentially fortifications, built not so much to guard against the attacks of native peoples as to ward off assaults from other Europeans. Without this essential military component, the European maritime empires that were emerging in this period could not have existed.

A New Kind of Slavery

Although slavery had effectively disappeared in much of northwestern Europe by the early twelfth century, it continued in parts of the Mediterranean world and had been introduced into some regions of central and eastern Europe after the Black Death. But this slavery existed on a very small scale; there were no slave-powered factories or large-scale agricultural systems in this period. The only major slave markets and slave economies were in the Ottoman Empire, and there, slaves ran the vast Ottoman bureaucracy and staffed the army. In all these cases, as in antiquity, no aspect of slavery was racially based. In Italy and elsewhere in the medieval Mediterranean world, slaves were often captives from an array of locales. In eastern Europe, they were functionally serfs. Most Ottoman slaves were European Christians, predominantly Poles, Ukrainians, Greeks, and Bulgarians. In the early Middle Ages, Germanic and Celtic peoples had been widely enslaved. And under the Roman Empire, slaves had come from every part of the known (and unknown) world.

What was new about the slavery of the late fifteenth century was its increasing racialization—an aspect of modern slavery that has made an indelible impact on our own society. To Europeans, African slaves were visible in ways that other slaves were not, and it became convenient for those who dealt in them to justify the mass deportation of entire populations by claiming their racial inferiority and their "natural" fitness for a life of bondage. This nefarious ideology has had long-lasting and tragic consequences that still afflict the civilizations of our own world.

In Lisbon, which became a significant market for enslaved Africans during Prince Henry's lifetime, something on the order of 15,000 to 20,000 African captives were sold within a twenty-year period. In the following half century, by about 1505, the numbers amounted to 150,000. For the most part, the purchasers of these slaves regarded them as status symbols; it became fashionable to have African footmen, pageboys, and ladies' maids. In the Atlantic colonies—Madeira, the Canaries, and the Azores—land was still worked mainly by European settlers and sharecroppers. Slave labor, if it was employed at all, was generally used only in sugar mills. On Madeira and the Canaries, where sugar became the predominant cash crop during the last quarter of the fifteenth century, some slaves were introduced as agricultural laborers. But even sugar production did not lead to the widespread use of slavery on these islands.

However, a new kind of slave-based sugar plantation began to emerge in Portugal's eastern Atlantic colonies in the 1460s, starting on the Cape Verde Islands and then extending southward into the Gulf of Guinea. These islands were not populated when the Portuguese began to settle them, and their climate generally discouraged most Europeans from living there. They were ideally located, however, along the routes of slave traders venturing outward from the nearby West African coast. It is this plantation model that would be exported to Brazil by the Portuguese and to the Caribbean islands of the Americas by their Spanish conquerors, with incalculable consequences for the peoples of Africa, the Americas, and Europe (see Chapter 14).

EUROPEANS IN A NEW WORLD

Like his contemporaries, **Christopher Columbus** (1451–1506) understood that the world was a sphere; and also like them, he thought it was much smaller. (As we saw in Chapter 4, the accurate calculation of the globe's circumference made in ancient Alexandria had been suppressed centuries later by Roman geographers.) Furthermore, it had long been accepted that there were only three continents—Europe, Asia, and Africa—hence Columbus's decision to reach Asia by sailing west, a plan that seemed even more plausible after the discovery and colonization of the Canary Islands and the Azores.

The existence of these islands reinforced a new hypothesis that the Atlantic was dotted with similar lands all the way to Japan. This emboldened Columbus's royal patrons, Ferdinand and Isabella of Spain, who were convinced that the Genoese mariner could reach China in about a month, after a stop for provisions on the Canaries. This turned out to be a kind of self-fulfilling prophecy, for when Columbus reached the Bahamas and the island of Hispaniola after only a month's sailing, he reported that he had reached the outer islands of Asia.

The Shock of Discovery

Of course, Columbus was not the first European to set foot on the American continents. As we have already learned, Viking sailors briefly settled present-day Newfoundland, Labrador, and perhaps even portions of New England around the year 1000 (Chapter 8). But knowledge of these Viking landings had been forgotten or ignored outside of Iceland for hundreds of years. It wasn't until the 1960s that the stories of these expeditions were corroborated by archaeological evidence. (In 2016, a new site of Norse settlement was identified on the coast of Baffin Island.) Moreover, the tiny Norwegian colony on Greenland—technically part of the North American landmass—had been abandoned in the fifteenth century, when the cooling of the climate (Chapter 10) destroyed the fragile ecosystems that barely sustained the lives of Norse settlers there.

Although Columbus did not return with spices to prove that he had found an alternate route to Asia, he did return with some small samples of gold and a few indigenous

Interpreting Visual Evidence

America as an Object of Desire

Under the influence of popular travel narratives that had circulated in Europe for centuries, Columbus and his fellow voyagers were prepared to find the New World full of cannibals. They also assumed that the indigenous peoples' custom of wearing little or no clothing—not to mention their "savagery"—would render their women sexually available. In a letter sent back home in 1495, one of Columbus's men recounted a notable encounter with a "cannibal girl" whom he had taken captive in his tent and whose naked body aroused his desire. He was surprised to find that she resisted his advances so fiercely that he had to tie her up—which of course made it easier for him to "subdue" her. In the end, he cheerfully reports, the girl's sexual performance was so satisfying that she might have been trained, as he put it, in a "school for whores."

The Flemish artist Jan van der Straet (1523–1605) would have heard many such reports of the encounters between (mostly male) Europeans and the peoples of the New World. This engraving, based on one of his drawings, is among the thousands of mass-produced images that circulated widely in Europe, thanks to the invention of printing. It imagines the first encounter between a male "Americus" (such as Columbus or Amerigo Vespucci himself) and the New World "America," depicted as a voluptuous, available woman. The Latin caption reads: "America rises to meet Americus; and whenever he calls her, she will always be aroused."

Americen Americus retexit, & Semel vocauit inde semper excitam.
AMERICA.

Questions for Analysis

1. Study the details of this image carefully. What does each detail symbolize? How do they work together as an allegory of conquest and colonization?

2. On what stereotypes of indigenous peoples does this image draw? Notice, for example, the cannibalistic campfire of the group in the background and the posture of "America."

3. Why is the New World itself ("America") imagined as female in this image? What messages might this—and the suggestive caption—have conveyed to a European viewer?

people—whose existence gave promise of entire tribes that might be "saved" by conversion to Christianity, and whose lands could provide homes for Spanish settlers seeking new frontiers after the *reconquista*. This provided sufficient incentive for the "Most Catholic" monarchs to finance three more expeditions by Columbus and many more by other adventurers, missionaries, and colonists.

Meanwhile, the Portuguese, who had already obtained a papal decree granting them (hypothetical) ownership of all lands south of the Canaries, rushed to establish their own claims. After two years of wrangling and conflicting papal pronouncements, the Treaty of Tordesillas (1494) sought to demarcate Spanish and Portuguese possession of as-yet-undiscovered lands. The Spanish would ultimately emerge as the big winners in this gambling match: within a decade, the coasts of two hitherto unknown continents were identified, as were clusters of new islands, most on the Spanish side of the meridian.

Gradually, Europeans reached the conclusion that the voyages of Columbus and his immediate successors had revealed an entirely "New World." And, shocking to Europeans, this world had not been foretold by either the teachings of Christianity or the wisdom of the ancients. Among the first to champion the fact of two new continents' existence was the Italian explorer and geographer Amerigo Vespucci (1454–1512), whose name was soon adopted as a descriptor for them. Eventually, those who came to accept this fact were forced to question the reliability of the key sources of knowledge on which Western civilizations had hitherto hinged (see Chapter 14).

At first, the realization that the **Americas** (as they were now called) were not an outpost of Asia came as a disappointment to the Spanish, because it meant that two major land masses and two vast oceans disrupted their plans to beat the Portuguese to the Spice Islands. But new possibilities gradually became clear. In 1513, the Spanish explorer Vasco Núñez de Balboa first viewed the Pacific Ocean from the Isthmus of Panama, and news of the narrow divide between two vast oceans prompted Ferdinand and Isabella's grandson to renew their dream. This young monarch, Charles V (1500–1556), ruled not only Spain but also a huge patchwork of territories encompassed by the Holy Roman Empire. In 1519, he accepted Ferdinand Magellan's proposal to see whether a route to Asia could be found by sailing around South America.

Yet Magellan's voyage demonstrated beyond question that the world was simply too large for any such plan to be feasible at that time. Of the five ships that left Spain under his command, only one returned, three years later, having been forced to circumnavigate the globe. Out of a crew of 265 sailors, only 18 survived, most having died of scurvy or starvation. Magellan himself had been killed in a skirmish with native peoples in the Philippines.

This fiasco ended all hope of discovering an easy southwest passage to Asia—although the deadly dream of a northwest passage survived and motivated many European explorers of North America into the twentieth century. It has been revived today, in our age of global warming. The retreat of Arctic pack ice has led to the opening of new shipping lanes, and in 2008, the first commercial voyage successfully traversed the Arctic Ocean.

The Dream of Gold and the Downfall of Empires

Although the unforeseen size of the globe made a westward passage to Asia untenable, given the technologies then available, Europeans were quick to capitalize on the sources of wealth that the New World itself could offer. What chiefly fired the imagination were those small samples of gold that Columbus had initially brought back to Spain. Although rather paltry in themselves, they nurtured hopes that gold might lie piled in ingots somewhere in these vast new lands, ready to enrich any adventurer who discovered them. Rumor fed rumor, until a few freelance Spanish soldiers really did strike it rich beyond their most avaricious imaginings.

Their success, though, had little to do with their own efforts. Within a generation after Columbus's first ships had landed, European diseases had spread rapidly among the indigenous peoples of the Caribbean and the coastlines of the Americas. These diseases—especially measles and smallpox—were not fatal to those who carried them, because

THE AZTEC CITY OF TENOCHTITLÁN. The Spanish conquistador Bernal Díaz del Castillo (1492–1585) took part in Hernán Cortés's conquest of the Aztec Empire and later wrote an account of his adventures. His admiring description of the Aztec capital at Tenochtitlán records that the Spaniards were amazed to see such a huge city built in the midst of a vast lake, with gigantic buildings arranged in a meticulous urban plan around a central square and broad causeways linking the city to the mainland. This hand-colored woodcut was included in an early edition of Cortés's letters to Emperor Charles V, printed at Nuremberg (Germany) in 1524.

Europeans had developed immunities over many generations. But to the peoples of this New World, they were extremely deadly: there were probably 250,000 people living on Hispaniola when Columbus first arrived, but within thirty years—a single generation—70 percent had perished from disease.

The new waves of *conquistadors* (conquerors) were also assisted by the complex political, economic, and military rivalries that already existed among the highly sophisticated societies they encountered. The Aztec Empire of Mexico rivaled any European state in its power, culture, and wealth—and like any successful empire it had subsumed many neighboring territories in the course of its own conquests. Its capital, Tenochtitlán (*ten-och-tit-LAN*; now Mexico City), amazed its European assailants, who had never seen anything like the height and grandeur of its buildings or the splendor of its public works. This splendor was itself evidence of the Aztecs' imperial might, which was resisted by many of the peoples from whom they demanded tribute.

The Aztecs' eventual conqueror, Hernán Cortés (1485–1547), arrived in Hispaniola as a young man, in the wake of Columbus's initial landing. He had received a land grant from the Spanish crown and acted as magistrate of one of the first towns established there. In 1519, he headed an expedition to the mainland, which had been the target of some earlier exploratory missions but had not resulted in any permanent settlements, owing largely to the tight control of the Aztecs, whose imperial domain extended far beyond Tenochtitlán.

When Cortés arrived on the coast of the Aztec realm, he formed an intimate relationship with a native woman known as La Malinche. She became his consort and interpreter in the Nahua language, which was a lingua franca among the many different ethnic groups within the empire. With her help, he discovered that some peoples subjugated by the Aztecs were rebellious, and so he began to form strategic alliances with their leaders. Cortés himself could only muster a force of a few hundred men, but his native allies numbered in the thousands.

These strategic alliances were crucial. Although Cortés and his men had potentially superior weapons—guns and horses—these were more effective for their novelty than their utility. In fact, the rifles were of inferior quality, while gunpowder dampened by the humid climate had a tendency to misfire or fail to ignite altogether. So Cortés adopted the tactics and weaponry of his native allies in his dealings with the Aztec king Montezuma II (r. 1502–1520) and in his assaults on the fortifications of Tenochtitlán. In the end, though, it was European bacteria, not European technology or cunning, that led to his victory. The Aztecs were devastated by

SPANISH CONQUISTADORS IN MEXICO. This sixteenth-century drawing of conquistadors slaughtering the Aztec aristocracy emphasizes the advantages that plate armor and steel swords gave to the Spanish soldiers.

Analyzing Primary Sources

A Spanish Critique of New World Conquest

Not all Europeans approved of European imperialism or its "civilizing" effects on the peoples of the New World. One of the most influential contemporary critics was Bartolomé de las Casas (1484–1566) of Spain. In 1502, when Bartolomé was eighteen years old, he and his father joined an expedition to Hispaniola. In 1510, he became the first ordained priest in the Americas and eventually bishop of Chiapas (Mexico). Although he was a product of his times—he owned many slaves—he was also prescient in discerning the devastating effects of European settlement in the West Indies and Central America, and he particularly deplored the exploitation and extermination of indigenous populations. The following excerpt is from one of the many eloquent manifestos he published in an attempt to gain the sympathies of the Spanish crown and to reach a wide readership. It was printed in 1542, but it draws on the impressions and opinions he had formed since his arrival in New Spain as a young man.

 God made all the peoples of this area, many and varied as they are, as open and as innocent as can be imagined. The simplest people in the world—unassuming, long-suffering, unassertive, and submissive—they are without malice or guile, and are utterly faithful and obedient both to their own native lords and to the Spaniards in whose service they now find themselves.... They are innocent and pure in mind and have a lively intelligence, all of which makes them particularly receptive to learning and understanding the truths of our Catholic faith and to being instructed in virtue; indeed, God has invested them with fewer impediments in this regard than any other people on earth....

It was upon these gentle lambs...that from the very first day they clapped eyes on them the Spanish fell like ravening wolves upon the fold, or like tigers and savage lions who have not eaten meat for days. The pattern established at the outset has remained unchanged to this day, and the Spaniards still do nothing save tear the natives to shreds, murder them and inflict upon them untold misery, suffering and distress, tormenting, harrying and persecuting them mercilessly....

When the Spanish first journeyed there, the indigenous population of the island of Hispaniola stood at some three million; today only two hundred survive.

The island of Cuba, which extends for a distance almost as great as that separating Valladolid from Rome, is now to all intents and purposes uninhabited; and two other large, beautiful and fertile islands, Puerto Rico and Jamaica, have been similarly devastated. Not a living soul remains today on any of the islands of the Bahamas ... even though every single one of the sixty or so islands in the group ... is more fertile and more beautiful than the Royal Gardens in Seville and the climate is as healthy as anywhere on earth. The native population, which once numbered some five hundred thousand, was wiped out by forcible expatriation to the island of Hispaniola, a policy adopted by the Spaniards in an endeavour to make up losses among the indigenous population of that island....

At a conservative estimate, the despotic and diabolical behaviour of the Christians has, over the last forty years, led to the unjust and totally unwarranted deaths of more than twelve million souls, women and children among them....

The reason the Christians have murdered on such a vast scale and killed anyone and everyone in their way is purely and simply greed.... The Spaniards have shown not the slightest consideration for these people, treating them (and I speak from first-hand experience, having been there from the outset) not as brute animals—indeed, I would to God they had done and had shown them the consideration they afford their animals—so much

as piles of dung in the middle of the road. They have had as little concern for their souls as for their bodies, all the millions that have perished having gone to their deaths with no knowledge of God and without the benefit of the Sacraments. One fact in all this is widely known and beyond dispute, for even the tyrannical murderers themselves acknowledge the truth of it: the indigenous peoples never did the Europeans any harm whatever.

Source: Bartolomé de las Casas, *A Short Account of the Destruction of the Indies*, trans. Nigel Griffin (Harmondsworth, UK: 1992), pp. 9–12.

Questions for Analysis

1. Given his perspective on the behavior of his countrymen, how might Bartolomé de las Casas have justified his own presence in New Spain (Mexico)? What do you think he may have hoped to achieve by publishing this account?

2. What comparisons does Bartolomé make between New Spain (Mexico) and the Old, and between indigenous peoples and Europeans? What is he trying to convey?

3. Compare this account with the contemporary print on page 418. What new light does this excerpt shine on that visual allegory? How might a reader-viewer of the time have reconciled these two very different pictures of European imperialism?

an outbreak of the plague that had arrived along with Cortés and his men. In 1521, the Aztec Empire fell.

In 1533, another lucky conquistador, Francisco Pizarro, would manage to topple the highly centralized empire of the Incas, based in what is now Peru, by similar voluntary and involuntary means. In this case, he took advantage of an ongoing civil war that had weakened the reigning dynasty; he was also assisted by an epidemic of smallpox. Like Cortés, Pizarro promised his native allies liberation from an oppressive regime. Those former subjects of the Aztecs and Incas would soon be able to judge how sincere these promises were.

The Price of Conquest

The astonishing conquests of Mexico and Peru gave the conquistadors access to hoards of gold and silver that had been accumulated for centuries by Aztec and Inca rulers. And almost immediately, a search for the sources of these precious metals was launched by agents of the Spanish crown. The first gold deposits were discovered in Hispaniola, where surface mines were speedily established using native laborers who were already dying in appalling numbers from disease, and who were now further decimated by brutality and overwork. The population soon dwindled further, to a mere 10 percent of its Pre-Columbian strength.

The loss of so many workers made the mines of Hispaniola uneconomical to operate, so European colonists turned instead to cattle raising and sugar production. Modeling their sugarcane plantations on those of the Cape Verde Islands and St. Thomas (São Tomé) in the Gulf of Guinea, colonists began to import thousands of African slaves to labor in the new industry. Sugar production was, by its nature, a capital-intensive undertaking. The need to import slave labor added further to its costs, guaranteeing that control over the new industry would fall into the hands of a few extremely wealthy planters and financiers.

Despite the establishment of sugar production in the Caribbean and cattle ranching on the Mexican mainland—whose devastating effects on the fragile ecosystem of Central America will be discussed in Chapter 14—it was mining that would shape the Spanish colonies most fundamentally in this period. If gold was the lure that had initially inspired the conquest, silver became its most lucrative export. Even before the discovery of vast silver deposits, the Spanish crown had taken steps to assume direct control over all colonial exports. It was therefore to the Spanish crown that the profits of the empire were channeled. Europe's silver shortage, which had been acute for centuries, came to an end.

Yet this massive infusion of silver into the European economy created more problems than it solved, because it accelerated inflation that had already begun in the late fifteenth century. Initially, inflation had been driven by the renewed growth of the European population, an expanding

After You Read This Chapter

 Go to **INQUIZITIVE** to see what you've learned—and learn what you've missed—with personalized feedback along the way.

REVIEWING THE OBJECTIVES

- The artists of Italy were closely tied to those with political and military power. How did this relationship affect the kinds of work these artists produced?
- Which aspects of Renaissance artistry and learning were adopted in northern Europe?
- What was the *reconquista*, and how did it lead to a new way of thinking about Spanish identity?
- Europeans, especially the Portuguese, developed new technologies and techniques that enabled exploration and colonial ventures in this period. What were they?
- The "discovery" of the New World had profound effects on the indigenous peoples and the environment of the Americas. Describe some of these effects.

colonial economy, and a relatively fixed supply of food. Thereafter, thanks to the influx of New World silver, inflation was driven by the vastly increased supply of coinage. As we shall see, this abundance of coinage led to the doubling and quadrupling of prices in the course of the sixteenth century and the collapse of this inflated economy—which paradoxically drove a wave of impoverished Europeans to settle in the New World in ever greater numbers.

CONCLUSION

The connection between the Mediterranean world into the Atlantic, which had begun in the thirteenth century, was the essential preliminary to Columbus's voyages and to the rise of European empires in Africa, India, the Caribbean, and the Americas. Other events and innovations we have surveyed in this chapter played a key role, too: the relatively rapid communications facilitated by the printing press; the struggle for power in Italy that led to the development of ever deadlier weapons; the navigational and colonial initiatives of the Portuguese; and the success of the Spanish *reconquista*, which displaced Spain's venerable Jewish community and drove Spanish rulers and adventurers to seek their fortunes overseas.

For the indigenous peoples and empires of the Americas, the results were cataclysmic. Within a century of Europeans' arrival, between 50 and 90 percent of some native popula-tions had perished from disease, massacre, and enslavement. Moreover, Europeans' capacity to further their imperial ambitions—wherever ships could sail and guns could penetrate—profoundly destabilized Europe and its neighbors, sharpening the divisions among competing kingdoms and empires.

The ideals of the humanists and the artistry associated with the Renaissance often stand in sharp contrast to the harsh realities alongside which they coexisted and in which they were rooted. Artists could thrive in the atmosphere of competition and one-upmanship that characterized this period, but they could also find themselves reduced to the status of servants in the households of the wealthy and powerful—or forced to subordinate their artistry to the demands of warfare, espionage, and slavery. Meanwhile, intellectuals and statesmen looked to the precedents and glories of the past for inspiration.

But to which aspects of the past? Some humanists may have wanted to revive the principles of the Roman Republic, but many of them worked for ambitious despots who modeled themselves on Rome's dictators. The theories that undergirded European politics and colonial expansion were being used to legitimize many different kinds of power, including that of the papacy, and a newly racialized industry of enslavement. All these trends would be carried forward into the sixteenth century and would have a role to play in the upheaval that shattered Europe's fragile religious unity. It is to this upheaval—the Reformation—that we turn in Chapter 13.

PEOPLE, IDEAS, AND EVENTS IN CONTEXT

- Why was **GUTENBERG**'s invention of the **PRINTING PRESS** such a significant development?
- How did **NICCOLÒ MACHIAVELLI** respond to Italy's political situation within Europe? In what ways do artists such as **LEONARDO DA VINCI** and **MICHELANGELO BUONARROTI** exemplify the ideals and realities of the Renaissance?
- How did northern European scholars such as **DESIDERIUS ERASMUS** and **THOMAS MORE** apply humanist ideas to Christianity? How were these ideas expressed in art?
- What is significant about **IVAN THE GREAT**'s use of the title **TSAR**?
- How did **ISABELLA OF CASTILE** and **FERDINAND OF ARAGON** succeed in creating a unified Spain through the **RECONQUISTA**?
- How does **PRINCE HENRY THE NAVIGATOR** exemplify the motives for pursuing overseas expansion? Why were the Portuguese so successful in establishing colonies during this period?
- What were the expectations that launched **COLUMBUS**'s voyage? What enabled the Spanish **CONQUISTADORS** to subjugate the peoples of the **AMERICAS**?

THINKING ABOUT CONNECTIONS

- Phrases such as "Renaissance man" and "Renaissance education" are still part of our common vocabulary. Given what you have learned in this chapter, how has your understanding of such phrases changed? How would you explain their true meaning to others?
- How do the patterns of conquest and colonization discussed in this chapter compare with those of earlier periods, such as the era of the Crusades or the empires of antiquity? How many of these developments were new?
- Although the growth of the African slave trade resulted in a new racialization of slavery in the Atlantic world, the justifications for slavery had very old roots. How might Europeans have used Greek and Roman precedents in defense of these new ventures (see Chapters 4 and 5)?

Before You Read This Chapter

The Age of Dissent and Division, 1500–1564

I n 1517, on the night before the Feast of All Saints—All Hallows' Eve (or Halloween)—a professor of theology at a small university in northern Germany posted a list of debating points on the door of Wittenberg's Castle Church: part of the princely palace of the local ruler, the elector of Saxony, which also served as the university's chapel. This was not a prank; it was the usual method of announcing a scholarly disputation. Yet Martin Luther's choice of an evening traditionally associated with mischief-making was appropriate, because the posting of these Ninety-Five Theses was a subversive act. For one thing, the sheer number of propositions that Dr. Luther offered to debate was unusual. But what really caught the attention of his fellow scholars was their unifying theme: the corruption of the Roman Church and, in particular, the office of the pope. It was a topic very much in vogue at the time, but it had seldom been dissected so clearly by a licensed theologian who was also a monk, an ordained priest, and a charismatic teacher.

This document, and the wider controversy it stimulated, soon spread far beyond Wittenberg. By the time the papacy formally retaliated in 1520, religious dissent was mounting—and

425

not only among academics. Many of Europe's rulers saw the political advantages of either defying or defending the pope, and they chose sides accordingly. Luther's own lord, Frederick III of Saxony, would spend the rest of his life shielding the man who had first expounded those theses in his own church.

Luther had grown up in a largely peaceful Europe. After two centuries of economic, social, and political turmoil, the economy was expanding, cities were growing, and major monarchies were secure. Europeans also had embarked on a new period of colonial expansion. Meanwhile, the Church had weathered the storms of the Avignon captivity and the Great Schism, and alleged heresies had been suppressed or contained. At the local level, the devotion of ordinary Christians was strong and the parish was a crucial site of community identity. To be sure, there were some problems. The educational standards of parish clergy were higher than they had ever been, but reformers complained that too many priests were ignorant or neglectful of their spiritual duties. Monasticism, by and large, seemed to have lost its spiritual fire. And religious enthusiasm sometimes bred superstition. Yet on the whole, these problems were manageable.

In short, few could have predicted that Europe's religious and political coherence would be irreparably shattered in the course of a generation, or that the next century would witness an appallingly destructive series of wars. Moreover, no one could have foreseen that the catalyst for these extraordinary events would be an obscure university professor. The debate ignited by Martin Luther (1483–1546) set off a chain reaction we know as the **Reformation**. Although initially intended as a call for another phase in the Church's long history of internal reforms, Luther's teachings instead launched a religious revolution that splintered western Christendom into a variety of Protestant ("dissenting") faiths, and prompted the Roman Church to reaffirm its status as the only true Catholic ("universal") faith. The result was a profound transformation of the religious, social, and political landscape that affected the lives of everyone in Europe—and everyone in the new European colonies.

MARTIN LUTHER AND THE REFORMATION IN GERMANY

Why did Luther's beliefs lead to a break with Rome? Why did so many people join dissenting movements at this time? As we will see, those who followed Luther or other Protestant reformers did so for different reasons. Many

MARTIN LUTHER. This portrait by Lucas Cranach the Elder (1472–1553), the court painter to the electors of Brandenburg and a friend of Luther, was made late in Luther's life.

peasants hoped that the new faith would free them from the hierarchies of traditional lordships. Towns and princes thought it would bring political independence. And nationalists thought it would liberate states from the demands of foreign popes.

Despite their differences, however, all dissenters seemed to have shared a conviction that their new understanding of Christianity would lead to spiritual salvation, whereas an adherence to the traditional religion of Rome would not. For this reason, *reformation* is a somewhat misleading term for this movement. Although Luther began as a reformer seeking to change the Church from within, he quickly became an uncompromising opponent of it, and many of his followers were even more radical. The movement that began with Luther therefore went beyond "reformation," and instead sought to dismantle religious, political, and social institutions that had been in place for a thousand years.

Luther's Quest for Justice

Martin Luther was the son of a German peasant who had prospered through some business ventures. Eager to see his clever son rise still further in the world, the elder Luther sent Martin to the University of Erfurt to study law. In 1505, however, Martin shattered his father's hopes by becoming a monk of the Augustinian order. But he never lost touch with his peasant roots and, indeed, his later literary successes owed a great deal to the vigorous, earthy German dialect he had learned in the cradle.

As a monk, Luther zealously pursued all the traditional means for achieving holiness. Not only did he fast and pray continuously, he also confessed his sins so often that his exhausted confessor reportedly joked that he should wait until he did something really bad. Still, Luther regarded himself as deeply sinful and feared that he could never perform enough good deeds to deserve salvation. But then he had an insight that led to a new understanding of God's justice.

For years, Luther had worried that it seemed unfair for God to issue commandments he knew humans could not observe, and then punish them with eternal damnation. Upon further study of the Bible, he realized that God's justice lay not in his power to punish, but in his mercy. As Luther later wrote, "I began to understand the justice of God as that by which God makes us just . . . and at this I felt as though I had been born again, and had gone through open gates into paradise."

Lecturing at Wittenberg in the years immediately following this realization, which occurred around 1515, Luther reached his central doctrine of "justification by faith" as he pondered a passage in Paul's letter to the Romans: "[T]he just shall live by faith" (1:17). He concluded that God's justice does not demand endless pious works and religious rituals for salvation, because humans can never attain salvation through their own weak efforts. Rather, humans are saved by God's grace—that is, by the unconditional and benevolent love of the divine being, manifested on earth by the sacrifice of Jesus Christ and the miracles of the saints. God offers this grace as an utterly undeserved gift to those whom he has predestined (selected) for salvation. Men and women are therefore "justified"—made worthy of salvation—by their faith in God's grace. Performing works of piety and charity are signs of that faith, but they are not what saves the soul. They are merely visible signs of each believer's invisible spiritual state, which is known to God alone.

The essence of this doctrine was not original to Luther, and had been central to the thought of Augustine (see Chapter 6), the patron saint of Luther's own monastic order. During the twelfth and thirteenth centuries, however, theologians such as Peter Lombard and Thomas Aquinas (see Chapter 9) had developed a very different understanding of salvation through their own readings of scripture. Though not discounting the importance of faith, they emphasized the crucial role that the Church and its sacraments played in the process of salvation. In subsequent centuries, moreover, the Church increasingly represented the process of salvation in quantitative terms, teaching that a believer could reduce the penance owed for sins—and thus the soul's time in purgatory (Chapter 10)—by a specific number of days through performing specific actions such as making a pilgrimage or a pious donation. These actions

LUTHER'S TRANSLATION OF THE BIBLE. The printing press was instrumental to the rapid dissemination of Luther's messages, as well as those of his supporters and challengers. It enabled pamphlets and vernacular Bibles such as this one to be rapidly and cheaply mass produced. Also essential was the fact that Luther addressed his audience in plain language, in their native German.

earned the "indulgence" of God to the degree merited by the piety of the action.

When **indulgences** were first conceptualized in the late eleventh century, they could be earned only through performing demanding spiritual exercises, such as joining a crusade. But by the end of the fourteenth century, indulgences were for sale. And a century later, when Luther was a child, the papacy had begun to claim that the purchase of indulgences could even benefit the dead, meaning that faithful men and women could purchase multiple indulgences for deceased family members or friends to reduce the number of days or years they spent in purgatory.

Long before Luther, critics of this practice argued that the sale of indulgences was scandalous, even heretical. The sin of exchanging God's grace for cash was a heresy known as simony, which had been loudly condemned by Wycliffe and his followers (Chapter 11) and later by Erasmus (Chapter 12). But Luther's objections to indulgences had much more radical consequences because they rested on a set of theological premises that, taken to their logical conclusion, resulted in dismantling much of contemporary religious practice—not to mention the authority of the Church. Luther does not appear to have realized this at first, but as the implications of his ideas became clear, he did not withdraw them. Instead, he pressed on.

The Scandal of Indulgences

Luther had developed his ideas in an academic setting but, in 1517, he was provoked to action by a local abuse of spiritual power. The worldly Bishop Albert of Hohenzollern, the youngest brother of the elector of Brandenburg, had paid a large sum for papal permission to hold the lucrative bishoprics of Magdeburg and Halberstadt concurrently, even though, at twenty-three, he was not old enough to be a bishop at all. Moreover, when the prestigious archbishopric of Mainz fell vacant the following year, Albert bought that, too. After obtaining the necessary funds by taking out loans from a German banking firm, he struck a bargain with Pope Leo X (r. 1513–1521): Leo would authorize the sale of indulgences in Albert's ecclesiastical territories—where Luther lived—with the understanding that half of the income would go to Rome, where it would finance the building of the new St. Peter's Basilica, and the other half would go to Albert.

Luther did not know the sordid details of this bargain, but he did know that a Dominican friar named Tetzel was soon hawking indulgences throughout the region, deliberately giving people the impression that an indulgence was

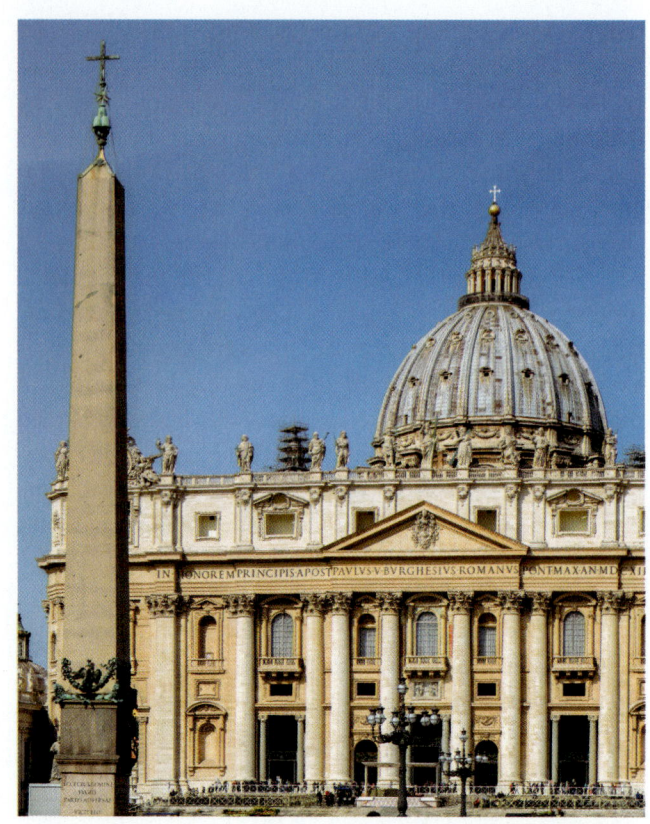

ST. PETER'S BASILICA, ROME. The construction of a new papal palace and monumental church began in 1506. This enormous complex replaced a modest, dilapidated Romanesque basilica that had replaced an even older church built on the site of the Apostle Peter's tomb. ■ *How might contemporaries have interpreted this building project depending on their attitudes toward the papacy?*

an automatic ticket to heaven for oneself or one's loved ones in purgatory. Not only was Tetzel violating Luther's conviction that people are saved by God's grace alone, but he was also misleading people into thinking that they no longer needed to confess their sins to a priest. Tetzel, in essence, was putting innocent souls at risk.

Luther therefore focused his Ninety-Five Theses on dismantling the doctrine of indulgences. He originally wrote up these points for debate in Latin, but they were soon translated into German and published more widely. As this hitherto obscure academic gained widespread notoriety, Tetzel and his allies demanded that Luther withdraw his charges against the Church. But rather than backing down, Luther grew bolder. In 1519, at a public disputation held in Leipzig and attended by throngs of people, he defiantly maintained that all clerics, even the pope, were merely fallible men and that the highest authority was the truth of scripture.

POPE LEO X. Raphael's portrait shows the pope with his cousins Cardinal Giulio de' Medici, who would succeed him as pope in 1523, and Cardinal Luigi de Rossi.

In 1520, building on the strength of this argument, Luther composed a series of pamphlets setting forth his three primary premises: justification by faith, the authority of scripture, and the "priesthood of all believers." We have already examined the meaning of the first premise. His second premise meant that the reading of the Bible took precedence over all other Church traditions, including the teachings of theologians and all the sacraments, and that any beliefs (such as purgatory) or practices (such as veneration of saints) not explicitly grounded in scripture should be rejected as human inventions. Finally, Luther declared that Christian believers were spiritually equal before God, which meant that priests, monks, and nuns had no special authority or virtues—hence the "priesthood of all believers."

From these premises, a host of practical consequences logically followed: because works could not lead to salvation, fasting, pilgrimages, and the veneration of relics were spiritually valueless. Luther called for the dissolution of all monasteries and convents, and advocated that religious rites be simplified, proposing the substitution of German (and other vernaculars) for Latin and calling for a reduction in the number of sacraments from seven to two. In his view, the only true sacraments were Baptism and the Eucharist, both of which had been instituted by Christ. (He included Penance later.) Although Luther continued to believe that Christ was really present in the consecrated bread and wine of the Lord's Supper, he insisted that it was only through the faith of the individual believer that this sacrament could lead to God; it was not a miraculous act performed by a priest.

To further emphasize that those who served the Church had no supernatural authority, Luther insisted on calling them "ministers" or "pastors," rather than priests. He also proposed to abolish the entire ecclesiastical hierarchy, from popes to bishops on down. Finally, on the principle that no spiritual distinction existed between clergy and laity, he argued that ministers could and should marry. In 1525, he himself took a wife, Katharina von Bora, one of a dozen nuns whom he had helped to escape from a Cistercian convent.

The Break with Rome

Widely disseminated by the printing press, Luther's polemical pamphlets electrified much of Germany, gaining him passionate popular support and touching off a religious revolt against the papacy. In lowly colloquial German, Luther declared that "the cardinals have sucked Italy dry and now turn to Germany" and that, given Rome's corruption, "the reign of Antichrist could not be worse." As word of Luther's defiance spread, his pamphlets became a publishing sensation. Whereas the average press run of a printed book before 1520 had been 1,000 copies, the first run of *To the Christian Nobility* (1520) was 4,000, and it sold out in a few days; many thousands of copies quickly followed. Even more popular were woodcut illustrations mocking the papacy and exalting Luther; these sold in the tens of thousands and could be readily understood even by those who could not read. (See **Interpreting Visual Evidence** on page 430.)

Luther's denunciations reflected widespread public dissatisfaction with the conduct and corruption of the papacy. Pope Alexander VI (r. 1492–1503) had bribed cardinals to gain his office and then used the money raised from the papal jubilee of 1500 to support the military campaigns of his illegitimate son, Cesare Borgia (1475–1507). His successor, Julius II (r. 1503–1513), devoted his reign to enlarging the Papal States in a series of wars. Leo X (r. 1513–1521) was a self-indulgent member of the Medici family of Florence.

Interpreting Visual Evidence

Decoding Printed Propaganda

The printing press has been credited with helping to spread the teachings of Martin Luther and thus securing the success of the Protestant Reformation. But even before Luther's critiques were published, reformers were using the new technology to disseminate images that attacked the corruption of the Church. After Luther rose to prominence, both his supporters and detractors vied to disseminate propaganda that appealed visually to a lay audience and could be understood even by those who could not read.

The first pair of images below is really a single printed artifact dated to around 1500, an early example of a "pop-up" card. It shows Pope Alexander VI (r. 1492–1503) as a stately pontiff (image A) whose true identity is concealed by a flap, but when the flap is raised, he is revealed as a devil (image B). The Latin texts read: "Alexander VI, *pontifex maximus*" and "I am the pope," respectively.

The other two examples represent both sides of the debate as it had developed by 1530, and they do so with

A. Pope Alexander VI as pontiff.

B. Pope Alexander VI as a devil.

reference to the same image: the seven-headed beast mentioned in the Book of Revelation. Image C, a Lutheran engraving, shows the papacy as the beast with seven heads, representing seven orders of the Catholic clergy. The sign on the cross (referring to the sign hung over the head of the crucified Christ) is in German, and reads: "For money, a sack full of indulgences"; the Latin words on either side say "Reign of the Devil." By contrast, image D, a Catholic engraving produced in Germany, shows Luther as Revelation's beast, with its seven heads labeled: "Doctor–Martin–Luther–Heretic–Hypocrite–Fanatic–Barabbas," the last alluding to the thief who should have been executed instead of Jesus, according to the Gospels.

Questions for Analysis

1. Given that the attack on Pope Alexander VI precedes Martin Luther's critique of the Church by nearly two decades, what can you conclude about its intended audience? To what extent can it be read as a barometer of popular disapproval? What might have been the reason(s) for using the concealing flap?

2. What do you make of the fact that both Catholic and Protestant propagandists used the same imagery? What do you make of the key differences, such as the fact that the seven-headed papal beast sprouts out of an altar on which a Eucharistic chalice is displayed, while the seven-headed Martin Luther is reading a book?

3. All of these printed images make use of words. Would the message of each image be clear without the texts? Why or why not?

C. The seven-headed papal beast.

D. The seven-headed Martin Luther.

In *The Praise of Folly*, first published in 1511 and frequently reprinted (Chapter 12), Erasmus had declared that the popes of his day were incapable of leading Christlike lives, as their office required. In *Julius Excluded*, published anonymously in 1517, Erasmus imagines a conversation at the gates of heaven between Saint Peter and Julius II, in which Peter refuses to admit the armored, vainglorious pope who claims to be his own earthly representative.

In Germany, resentment of the papacy ran especially high because there were no special agreements (concordats) limiting papal authority in its principalities, as there were in Spain, France, Bohemia, and England (Chapter 12). German princes complained that papal taxes were so high that the country was drained of its wealth, and yet Germans had almost no influence over papal policy. Frenchmen, Spaniards, and Italians dominated the College of Cardinals and the papal bureaucracy, and the popes were almost invariably Italian (as they would continue to be until 1978, when the Polish John Paul II was elected). As a result, graduates from the rapidly growing German and central European universities almost never found employment in Rome; instead, many joined the throngs of Luther's supporters, to become leaders of the new religious movement.

Emperor Charles V and the Condemnation at Worms

In 1520, Pope Leo X issued a papal edict condemning Luther's publications as heretical and threatening him with excommunication if he did not recant. Luther's response was defiant: rather than acquiescing to the pope's demand, he staged a public burning of the document. Thereafter, his heresy confirmed, he was formally given over for punishment to his lay overlord, Frederick III "the Wise" of Saxony. Frederick, however, proved a supporter of Luther and a critic of the papacy. Rather than burning Luther at the stake, he declared that Luther had not yet received a fair hearing. Early in 1521, he therefore brought Luther to the city of Worms (*VORMS*) to be examined by a select representative assembly known as a "diet."

At Worms, the diet's presiding officer was the newly elected Holy Roman Emperor Charles V, a member of the Habsburg family who had been born and bred in his ancestral holding of Flanders, at that time part of the Netherlands. By 1521, through the unpredictable workings of dynastic inheritance, marriage, and election, he had

THE EMPEROR CHARLES V. This portrait by the Venetian painter Titian depicts Europe's most powerful ruler sitting quietly in a chair, dressed in simple clothing of the kind worn by judges or bureaucrats. ■ *Why might Charles have chosen to represent himself this way, rather than in the regalia of his many royal, imperial, and princely offices?*

become not only the ruler of the Netherlands but also the king of Germany, Holy Roman emperor, duke of Austria, duke of Milan, and ruler of the Franche-Comté. And as the grandson of Ferdinand and Isabella on his mother's side, he was also the king of Spain; king of Naples, Sicily, and Sardinia; and ruler of all the Spanish possessions in the New World.

Governing such an extraordinary combination of territories posed enormous challenges, especially since this empire had no capital or centralized administrative institutions and shared no common language or culture or geographically contiguous borders. Because of this diversity, Charles could not tolerate threats to the fundamental force that held it together: Catholicism, as the religion of Rome was coming to be called.

There was, therefore, little doubt that the **Diet of Worms** would condemn Martin Luther for heresy. And when Luther refused to back down, thereby endangering his life, his lord Frederick the Wise intervened once more, arranging for Luther to be "kidnapped" and hidden for a year at the elector's castle of the Wartburg, where he was kept out of harm's way. Although Charles proclaimed Luther an outlaw at Worms, this edict was never enforced; instead, he left Germany for a war with France. A year later, in 1522, Luther returned in triumph to Wittenberg, where the changes he had called for had already been put into practice by his university supporters. When several German princes formally converted to Lutheranism, they brought their territories with them. In a little over a decade, a new form of Christianity had been established.

THE WARTBURG, EISENACH (GERMANY). This medieval stronghold became the refuge of Martin Luther after his condemnation at the Diet of Worms in 1520. His room in the castle has since been preserved.

The German Princes and the Lutheran Church

Once safely ensconced in Wittenberg under princely protection, Luther began to express his political and social views more vehemently, views which tended toward the strong support of the new political order. In a treatise of 1523, he insisted that "godly" (Protestant) rulers must be obeyed in all things and that even "ungodly" ones should never be targets of dissent because tyranny "is not to be resisted but endured." In 1524, when peasants throughout Germany rebelled against their landlords, Luther initially called for a peaceful resolution; but when the rebellion turned violent, he responded with intense hostility. In his vituperative pamphlet *Against the Thievish, Murderous Hordes of Peasants*, he urged readers to hunt the rebels down as though they were mad dogs: to "strike, strangle, stab secretly or in public, and remember that nothing can be more poisonous than a man in rebellion." After the ruthless suppression of this revolt, which may have cost as many as 100,000 lives, the firm alliance of Lutheranism with state power helped preserve and sanction the existing social order.

Why did some German princes decide to embrace Lutheran religious practices? This is an important development, because popular support for Luther would not have been enough to ensure the success of his teachings had they not been embraced by a number of powerful rulers and free cities. Indeed, it was only in those territories where Lutheranism was formally established that the new religion prevailed. Elsewhere in Germany, Luther's sympathizers were forced to flee, face death, or conform to Catholicism.

The power of individual lords to control the practice of religion in their lands reflects developments we have noted in previous chapters. Rulers had long sought to control appointments to Church offices in their own realms, to restrict the flow of money to Rome, and to limit the independence of ecclesiastical courts. But in Germany, as noted above, neither the emperor nor the princes were strong enough to secure special treatment. This situation changed, however, as a result of Luther's initiatives. In one of the pamphlets published in 1520, Luther explicitly encouraged German princes to confiscate the wealth of the Church, as an incentive for gaining aristocratic support. At first, the princes bided their time, but when they realized that Charles V could not act swiftly enough, several moved to introduce Lutheranism. Personal piety surely played a role in individual cases, but political and economic considerations were generally more decisive. Protestant princes could consolidate authority by naming their own religious officials, cutting off fees to Rome, and curtailing the jurisdiction of Church courts. They could also guarantee that the political and religious boundaries of their territories would now coincide; no longer would a rival ecclesiastical prince (such as a bishop or archbishop) be able to use his spiritual office to undermine a secular prince's sovereignty.

Similar considerations also moved a number of free cities to adopt Lutheranism. Acting independently, town councils could establish themselves as the supreme governing authorities within their jurisdictions, cutting out local bishops or powerful monasteries. Given the added fact that under Lutheranism monasteries and convents could be shut down and their lands appropriated by the newly sovereign secular authorities, the practical advantages of the new faith were overwhelming.

In his later years, Luther concentrated on debating with younger, more radical religious reformers who challenged his political conservatism. Never tiring in his prolific literary activity, he wrote an average of one treatise every two weeks for twenty-five years.

CONFESSIONAL DIFFERENCES, c. 1560. The religious affiliations (confessions) of Europe's territories had become very complicated by the year 1560, roughly a generation after the adoption of Lutheranism in some areas. ▪ *Which major countries and kingdoms had embraced a form of Protestantism by 1560?* ▪ *To what extent do these divisions conform to political boundaries?* ▪ *To what extent did the divisions complicate the political situation?* ▪ *Why might Lutheranism have spread north into Scandinavia, but not south into Bavaria or west across the Rhine?*

THE MANY FORMS OF PROTESTANTISM

Originating as a term applied to Lutherans who "protested" against Catholic authority, the word ***Protestant*** was soon applied to a much wider range of dissenting forms of Christianity. Lutheranism planted lasting roots in northern Germany and Scandinavia, where it became the state religion of Denmark, Norway, and Sweden as early as the 1520s. But other early Lutheran successes in southern Germany, Poland, and Hungary were eventually rolled back. Elsewhere in Europe, meanwhile, competing forms of Protestantism soon emerged from the seeds Luther had sown.

A Laboratory of Dissent: Protestantism in Switzerland

Protestant dissent had many faces and aims, and varied greatly from region to region. Switzerland offers a particularly useful case study because it was ruled neither by kings nor territorial princes; instead, prosperous cities were either independent or on the verge of becoming so. Hence, when the leading citizens of a Swiss municipality decided to adopt Protestant reforms, no one could stop them. Although, even here, religious arrangements differed from city to city, three main forms of Protestantism emerged between 1520 to 1550: Zwinglianism, Anabaptism, and Calvinism.

Zwinglianism, founded in Zürich by **Ulrich Zwingli** (*TSVING-lee*; 1484–1531), was the most theologically moderate of the three. Zwingli had just begun his career as a Catholic priest, but his humanist study of the Bible convinced him that Catholic theology and practice conflicted with the Gospels. This eventually led him to condemn religious images and hierarchical authority within the Church. Yet he did not speak out publicly until Luther set a precedent. In 1522, Zwingli began attacking the authority of Rome, and soon some northern Switzerland communities accepted his religious leadership.

Although Zwingli's reforms closely resembled those of the Lutherans in Germany, Zwingli differed from Luther in regard to the theology of the Eucharist. Whereas Luther believed in the real presence of Christ's body in the sacrament, for Zwingli the Eucharist conferred no grace at all and was simply a reminder and celebration of Christ's historic sacrifice on the cross. This fundamental disagreement prevented Lutherans and Zwinglians from uniting in a common Protestant front. When Zwingli died in battle against Catholic forces in 1531, some of those who furthered his teachings aligned themselves with the more systematic Protestantism of John Calvin (see pages 437–438).

Meanwhile, a more radical form of Protestantism arose in Switzerland and parts of Germany. The first **Anabaptists** were members of Zwingli's circle in Zürich, but they broke from him around 1525 on the issue of infant baptism. Anabaptists were convinced that the sacrament of Baptism was effective only when administered to willing adults who understood its significance, so they required followers who had been baptized as infants to be baptized again as adults (the term *Anabaptism* means "rebaptism"). This doctrine reflects the Anabaptists' fundamental belief that the true church was a small community of believers whose members had to make a deliberate, inspired decision to join it.

No other Protestant groups were prepared to go so far in rejecting the medieval Christian view of the Church as a single vast body to which all members of society belonged from birth. And in an age when almost everyone assumed that religious and secular authority were inextricably connected, Anabaptism was rejected by all established powers, both Protestant and Catholic. It was a movement that appealed to sincere religious piety in calling for pacifism, strict personal morality, and extreme simplicity of worship.

This changed when a group of Anabaptist extremists managed to gain control of the German city of Münster in 1534. These zealots were driven by millenarianism: the belief that God intends to institute a completely new order of justice and spirituality throughout the world before the end of time. Determined to help God bring about this goal, the extremists attempted to turn Münster into a new Jerusalem. A former tailor named John of Leyden assumed the title "king of the New Temple" and

THE ANABAPTISTS' CAGES, THEN AND NOW. After the three Anabaptist leaders of Münster were executed in 1535, their corpses were prominently displayed in cages hung from a tower of the marketplace church. As can be seen from the photo on the right, their bones are gone, but the iron cages remain. ▪ *What would be the purpose of keeping these cages on display?* ▪ *What different messages might this sight convey?*

proclaimed himself the successor of the Hebrew king David. Under his leadership, Anabaptist religious practices were made obligatory, private property was abolished, and even polygamy was permitted based on Old Testament precedents. Such practices were deeply shocking to Protestants and Catholics alike. Accordingly, Münster was besieged and captured by Catholic forces little more than a year after the Anabaptist takeover. The new "David," together with two of his lieutenants, was put to death by torture, and the three bodies were displayed in iron cages in the town square.

Thereafter, even moderate Anabaptists throughout Europe were ruthlessly persecuted on all sides. The few who survived banded together in the Mennonite sect, named after its founder, the Dutchman Menno Simons (c. 1496–1561). This sect, dedicated to pacifism and the simple "religion of the heart" of original Anabaptism, is still particularly strong in the central United States.

John Calvin's Reformed Theology

A year after the events in Münster, a twenty-six-year-old Frenchman, **John (Jean) Calvin** (1509–1564), published the first version of his *Institutes of the Christian Religion*, the most influential formulation of Protestant theology ever written. Born in Noyon, in northern France, Calvin had originally trained for the law; but by 1533, he was studying the Greek and Latin classics while living off the income from a priestly benefice. As he later wrote, he was "obstinately devoted to the superstitions of popery" until he experienced a miraculous conversion. He became a Protestant theologian and propagandist, eventually fleeing the Swiss city of Basel to escape persecution.

Although some aspects of Calvin's early career resemble those of Luther, the two men were very different. Luther was an emotionally volatile personality and a lover of controversy. He responded to theological problems as they arose or as the impulse struck him, and never attempted to systematize his beliefs. Calvin, however, was a coolly analytical legalist, who resolved in his *Institutes* to set forth all the principles of Protestantism comprehensively, logically, and systematically. After several revisions and enlargements, the definitive edition of *Institutes* appeared in 1559 and became the Protestant equivalent of Thomas Aquinas's *Summa Theologiae* (Chapter 9).

Calvin's austere and stoical theology started with the omnipotence of God. For Calvin, the entire universe depends utterly on the will of the Almighty, who knows all things present and to come. Because of man's original fall from grace, all human beings are sinners by nature, bound to an evil inheritance they cannot escape. Yet God (for reasons of his own) predestined some for eternal salvation

JOHN CALVIN. This recently discovered portrait by an anonymous artist shows the young Protestant reformer as a serene and authoritative figure. It places the grotesque caricature of Calvin (right) in perspective.

CALVIN AS SEEN BY HIS ENEMIES. In this image, which circulated among Calvin's Catholic detractors, the reformer's facial features are a disturbing composite of fish, toad, and chicken.

and damned the rest to the torments of hell. There is nothing that individuals can do to alter their fate; all souls are stamped with God's blessing or curse before they are born. Nevertheless, Christians cannot be indifferent to their conduct on earth. If they are among the elect, God will implant in them the desire to live according to his laws. Upright conduct is thus a sign that an individual has been chosen to sit at the throne of glory. Membership in the Reformed Church (as Calvinist churches are more properly known) is another presumptive sign of election to salvation. Most of all, Calvin urged Christians to conceive of themselves as chosen instruments of God, charged to work actively to fulfill God's purposes on earth. Because sin offends God, Christians should do all they can to prevent it; God's glory is diminished if sin is allowed to flourish unchecked.

Calvin always acknowledged a great theological debt to Luther, but his religious teachings diverged from those of the Wittenberg reformer in several essentials. First, Luther's attitude toward proper Christian conduct in the world was much more passive than Calvin's. For Luther, a Christian should endure the trials of this life through suffering, whereas for Calvin the world was to be mastered through unceasing labor for God's sake. Calvin's religion was also more controlling than Luther's. Although Luther insisted that his followers attend church on Sunday, he did not demand that they refrain from all pleasure or work during the remainder of the day. Calvin, however, issued stern strictures against worldliness of any sort on the Sabbath and forbade all sorts of minor self-indulgences even on non-Sabbath days.

The two men also differed on fundamental matters of church governance and worship. Although Luther broke from the Catholic system of hierarchical church government, Lutheran district superintendents exercised some of the same powers as bishops, including the supervision of parish clergy. Luther also retained many features of traditional Christian worship, including altars, music, and ritual. Calvin, however, rejected everything that smacked of "popery." He argued for the elimination of all traces of hierarchy within the church; each congregation should elect its own ministers, and assemblies of ministers and "elders" (laymen responsible for maintaining proper religious conduct among the faithful) should govern the Reformed Church as a whole. Calvin also insisted on the utmost simplicity in worship, prohibiting (among much else) vestments, processions, instrumental music, and religious images of any sort, including stained-glass windows. He also dispensed with all remaining vestiges of Catholic sacramental theology by making the sermon, rather than the Eucharist, the centerpiece of reformed worship. As a sign of this change, pulpits were frequently moved to the center of the church sanctuary.

Calvinism in Geneva

Consistent with his theological convictions, Calvin was intent on putting his religious teachings into practice. Sensing an opportunity in the French-speaking Swiss city of Geneva—then in the throes of political and religious upheaval—he moved there late in 1536 and immediately began to preach and organize. In 1538, his activities caused him to be expelled by the city council, but he returned in 1541 and brought the city under his sway.

With Calvin's guidance, Geneva's government became a theocracy, a society under the "rule of God." Supreme authority was vested in a "consistory," or assembly, composed of twelve lay elders and between ten and twenty pastors whose weekly meetings Calvin dominated. In addition to passing legislation, the consistory's main function was to supervise morality, both public and private. To this end, Geneva was divided into districts, and a committee of the consistory visited every household, without prior warning, to check on the behavior of its members. Dancing, card playing, attending the theater, and working or playing on the Sabbath were all outlawed as works of the devil. Innkeepers were forbidden to allow anyone to consume food or drink without first saying grace, or to permit any patron to stay up after nine o'clock. Adultery, witchcraft, blasphemy, and heresy all became capital crimes, and penalties even for lesser crimes were severe. During the first four years after Calvin gained control in Geneva, there were no fewer than fifty-eight executions in a city whose total population was only 16,000.

As rigid as such a regime may seem today, Calvin's Geneva was a beacon of light to thousands of Protestants throughout Europe in the mid-sixteenth century. Calvin's disciple John Knox (c. 1514–1572), who brought the reformed religion to Scotland, declared Geneva the "most perfect school of Christ that ever was on earth since the days of the Apostles." Converts such as Knox flocked to Geneva for refuge or instruction, then returned home to become ardent proselytizers for the new religion. Geneva thus became the center of an international movement dedicated to spreading reformed religion to the rest of Europe through organized missionary activity and propaganda.

These efforts were remarkably successful. By the end of the sixteenth century, Calvinists were a majority in Scotland (where they were known as Presbyterians) and Holland (where they founded the Dutch Reformed Church). They were also influential in England, although the Church of England adopted reformed theology but not reformed worship. (Calvinists who sought further reforms in worship were known as Puritans.) There were also substantial Calvinist minorities in France (where they were called

Huguenots), Germany, Hungary, Lithuania, and Poland. By the end of the sixteenth century, Calvinism had spread to the New World.

The Beginnings of Religious Warfare in Divided Europe

Less than a generation after Luther's challenge to the Church, wars between Catholic and Protestant rulers began. In Germany, Charles V attempted to establish Catholic unity by launching a military campaign against several German princes who had instituted Lutheran worship in their territories. But despite several notable victories, his efforts to defeat the Protestant princes failed. In part, this was because Charles was also involved in wars against France; primarily, however, it was because the Catholic princes of Germany worked against him, fearing that any suppression of Protestant princes might diminish their own independence. As a result, the Catholic princes' support for the foreign-born Charles was only lukewarm; at times, they even joined with the Protestants in battle against him. Meanwhile, the French looked beyond Christian Europe, forming a powerful alliance with the Muslim sultan Suleiman the Magnificent (r. 1520–1566), who protected France from Charles V and brought the Ottoman Empire into the military and diplomatic sphere of Europe.

Regional religious warfare sputtered on and off until a compromise settlement was reached via the Peace of Augsburg in 1555. Its governing principle was **cuius regio, eius religio** ("as the ruler, so the religion"). This meant that in those principalities where Lutherans ruled, Lutheranism would be the sole state religion; but where Catholic princes ruled, the people of their territories would be Catholic. In some regions, this rule was not needed or enforced, because local rulers permitted religious diversity. In Transylvania, a province under the overlordship of Hungary (now in Romania), Catholics lived alongside three different Protestant groups in relative peace. In Poland and Lithuania, Eastern Orthodox Christianity expanded its influence alongside Catholicism and was eventually tolerated. But these were rare exceptions.

For better and for worse, the Peace of Augsburg was a historical milestone. For the first time since Luther had been excommunicated, Catholic rulers were forced to acknowledge the legality of Protestantism. Yet the peace set a dangerous precedent, because it established the premise that no sovereign state can tolerate religious diversity. Moreover, it excluded Calvinism entirely and thus spurred German and Scottish Calvinists to become aggressive opponents of the status quo. As a result, Europe was riven by religious warfare for another century and exported sectarian violence to the New World (see Chapter 14).

THE DOMESTICATION OF REFORM

Within two decades, Protestantism had become a diverse revolutionary movement whose radical claims for the spiritual equality of all Christians had the potential to undermine the political, social, and even gender hierarchies on which European society rested. Luther himself did not anticipate that his ideas might have such implications, and he was by no means the only staunchly conservative Protestant. Indeed, most of the prominent early Protestant leaders were not radicals and depended on the support of existing elites: territorial princes, as well as the ruling elites of towns. As a result, the Reformation movement was speedily "domesticated" in two senses. Its revolutionary potential was toned down—Luther himself rarely spoke about the "priesthood of all believers" after 1525—and there was an increasing emphasis on the patriarchal family as the central institution of reformed life.

Reform and Discipline

As we have seen, injunctions to lead a more disciplined and godly life had been a frequent message of previous religious reform movements, especially after the Black Death (Chapter 11). Many of these efforts had been actively promoted by princes and town councils, most famously perhaps in Florence, where the Dominican preacher Girolamo Savonarola led the city on an extraordinary but short-lived campaign of puritanism and moral reform between 1494 and 1498. And there are numerous other examples of rulers legislating against sin. When Desiderius Erasmus called on secular authorities to think of their territories as giant monasteries, he was sounding an already familiar theme.

Protestant rulers, however, took the need to enforce godly discipline with particular seriousness, because the depravity of human nature was a fundamental tenet of Protestant belief. Like Saint Augustine at the end of the fourth century (Chapter 6), Protestants believed that people would inevitably turn out to be bad unless they were compelled to be good. It was therefore the responsibility

Competing Viewpoints

Marriage and Celibacy: Two Views

These two selections illustrate strong contrasting views on the spiritual value of marriage versus celibacy as embraced by Protestant and Catholic religious authorities. The first selection is part of Martin Luther's more general attack on monasticism, which emphasizes his contention that marriage is the natural and divinely intended state for all human beings. The second selection, from the cannons of the Council of Trent (1545–1563), restates traditional Church teaching on the holiness of marriage but also emphasizes the spiritual superiority of virginity to marriage and the necessity of clerical celibacy. Celibacy for all clergy (not only monks and nuns) had been instituted for the first time in the eleventh century (Chapter 8), but it had never been fully accepted, especially in Britain and Scandinavia, or universally practiced.

Luther's Views on the Impossibility of Celibacy (1535)

Listen! In all my days I have not heard the confession of a nun, but in the light of Scripture I shall hit upon how matters fare with her and know I shall not be lying. If a girl is not sustained by great and exceptional grace, she can live without a man as little as she can without eating, drinking, sleeping, and other natural necessities.

Nor, on the other hand, can a man dispense with a wife. The reason for this is that procreating children is an urge planted as deeply in human nature as eating and drinking. That is why God has given and put into the body the organs, arteries, fluxes, and everything that serves it. Therefore what is he doing who would check this process and keep nature from running its desired and intended course? He is attempting to keep nature from being nature, fire from burning, water from wetting, and a man from eating, drinking, and sleeping.

Source: E. M. Plass, ed., *What Luther Says*, vol. 2 (St. Louis, MO: 1959), pp. 888–89.

Church Canons on the Sacrament of Matrimony (1563)

Canon 1: If anyone says that matrimony is not truly and properly one of the seven sacraments . . . instituted by Christ the Lord, but has been devised by men in the Church and does not confer grace, let him be anathema [cursed]. . . .

Canon 9: If anyone says that clerics constituted in sacred orders or regulars [monks and nuns] who have made solemn profession of chastity can contract marriage . . . and that all who feel that they have not the gift of chastity, even though they have made such a vow, can contract marriage, let him be anathema, since God does not refuse that gift to those who ask for it rightly, neither does he suffer us to be tempted above that which we are able.

Canon 10: If anyone says that the married state excels the state of virginity or celibacy, and that it is better and happier to be united in matrimony than to remain in virginity or celibacy, let him be anathema.

Source: H. J. Schroeder, *Canons and Decrees of the Council of Trent* (St. Louis, MO: 1941), pp. 181–82.

Questions for Analysis

1. On what grounds does Luther attack the practice of celibacy? Do you agree with his basic premise? Why or why not?

2. How do the canons of the Catholic Church respond to Protestant views such as Luther's? What appears to be at stake in this defense of marriage and celibacy?

of secular and religious leaders to control and punish the misbehavior of their people, because otherwise their evil deeds would anger God and destroy human society. It was also essential that all people receive godly education.

Protestant godliness began with the discipline of children. Luther himself wrote two catechisms (instructional tracts) designed to teach children the tenets of their faith and the obligations—toward parents, masters, and rulers—that God imposed on them. Luther also insisted that all children, boys and girls alike, be taught to read the Bible in their own languages. Schooling thus became a characteristically Protestant preoccupation and rallying cry. Even the Protestant family was designated a "school of godliness," in which fathers were expected to instruct and discipline their wives, children, and household servants.

But family life in the early sixteenth century still left much to be desired in the eyes of Protestant reformers. Drunkenness, domestic violence, illicit sexual relations, lewd dancing, and the blasphemous swearing of oaths were frequent topics of reforming discourse. Various methods of discipline were attempted, including private counseling, public confessions of wrongdoing, public penance and shaming, exclusion from church services, and even imprisonment. All of these efforts met with varying, but generally modest, success. Creating godly Protestant families and enforcing godly discipline within entire communities were going to require the active cooperation of godly authorities.

New Regimes of Religious Discipline

The domestication of the Reformation in this sense took place principally in the free towns of Germany, Switzerland, and the Netherlands. Protestant attacks on monasticism and clerical celibacy also found a receptive audience among townsmen who resented the immunity of monastic houses from taxation and regarded clerical celibacy as a subterfuge for the seduction of their own wives and children. Protestant emphasis on the depravity of the human will and the consequent need for that will to be disciplined by authority also resonated powerfully with guilds and town governments, which were anxious to maintain and increase the control exercised by urban elites (mainly merchants and master craftsmen) over the apprentices and journeymen who made up the majority of the male population. Protestant town governments could consolidate all authority within the city into their own hands.

Meanwhile, Protestant authorities reinforced the control of individual males over their own households by emphasizing the family as the basic unit of religious education. In place of a priest, an all-powerful father figure was expected to assume responsibility for instructing and disciplining his household according to the precepts of reformed religion. At the same time, Protestant regimes introduced a new religious ideal for women. No longer was the virginal nun the exemplar of female holiness; in her place stood the married and obedient Protestant "goodwife." As one Lutheran prince wrote in 1527, "Those who bear children please God better than all the monks and nuns singing and praying." To this extent, Protestantism resolved the tensions between piety and sexuality that had long characterized Christian teachings, by declaring the holiness of marital sex.

But this did not promote a progressive view of women's spiritual potential or elevate their social and political status. Quite the contrary: Luther regarded women as even more sexually driven than men and less capable of controlling their desires. His opposition to convents rested on his belief that it was impossible for women to remain chaste, so sequestering them simply made their illicit behavior inevitable. To prevent sin, it was necessary that all women be married, preferably at a young age, and placed under the governance of a godly husband.

For the most part, Protestant town governments were happy to cooperate in shutting down female monasteries, since a convent's property went to the town. But conflicts did arise between Protestant reformers and town fathers over marriage and sexuality, especially over the reformers' insistence that both men and women should marry young as a restraint on lust. In many towns, men were traditionally expected to delay marriage until they had achieved the status of master craftsman—an expectation that had become increasingly difficult to meet as guilds sought to restrict the number of journeymen permitted to become masters. In theory, then, apprentices and journeymen were not supposed to marry, but instead were expected to frequent brothels and taverns—a legally sanctioned outlet for extramarital sexuality long viewed as necessary to men's physical well-being—which Protestant reformers now deemed morally abhorrent.

Towns responded in a variety of ways to these opposing pressures. Some instituted special committees to police public morals, of the sort we have noted in Calvin's Geneva. Some abandoned Protestant reforms altogether. And others, such as the German town of Augsburg, alternated between Protestantism and Catholicism for several decades. Yet regardless of a town's final choice of religious allegiance, by the end of the sixteenth century a revolution had taken place with respect to governments' attitudes toward public morality. In their competition with each other, neither Catholics nor Protestants wished to be seen as soft on sin. The result was the widespread closing of publicly licensed brothels, the outlawing of prostitution, and far stricter governmental supervision of many other aspects of private life than had ever been the case in any Western civilization.

The Control of Marriage

Protestant reforming movements also increased parents' control over their children's choice of marital partners. The medieval Church had defined marriage as a sacrament, but one that did not require the involvement of a priest. The mutual free consent of two individuals, even if given without witnesses or parental approval, was enough to constitute a legally valid marriage in the eyes of the Church. Opposition to this doctrine had long come from many quarters, especially from wealthy families who stood to lose from this liberal doctrine, because marriage involved rights of inheritance to property. For this reason, it was regarded as too important a matter to be left to the choice of adolescents unsupervised by parents or a priest. Instead, elite parents wanted the power to prevent unsuitable matches and, in some cases, to force their children to accept the marriage arrangements their families might negotiate on their behalf. For them, Protestantism offered an opportunity to obtain such control. Luther had declared marriage to be a purely secular matter, not a sacrament at all, and one that could be regulated however the governing authorities thought best. Calvin largely followed suit, although Calvinist theocracy drew less of a distinction between the powers of church and state than did Lutheranism.

Even the Catholic Church was eventually forced to give way. Although it never abandoned its insistence that both members of a couple must freely consent to their marriage, the Church's new doctrine required formal public notice of intent to marry and insisted on the presence of a priest at the wedding ceremony. Both rules were efforts to prevent clandestine marriages and to allow families time to intervene before an unsuitable match was concluded. Individual Catholic countries sometimes went even further in trying to assert parental control over their children's choice of marital partners. In France, for example, although couples might still marry without parental consent, those who did so forfeited their rights to inherit their families' property.

In somewhat different ways, then, both Protestantism and Catholicism moved to strengthen the control parents could exercise over their children and husbands over their wives. It also empowered the state to exercise an unprecedented degree of control over the bodies and individual choices of all people.

THE REFORMATION IN ENGLAND

In England, the Reformation took a rather different course than it did in Continental Europe. Although a long tradition of popular dissent survived into the sixteenth century, the number of dissidents was too small and their influence too limited to play a significant role. England was also not particularly oppressed by the papal exactions and abuses that roiled Germany. At the start of the sixteenth century, English monarchs already exercised close control over Church appointments within the kingdom and received the lion's share of the papal taxes collected. Thus the power of ecclesiastical courts did not inspire any particular resentments. On the contrary, these courts would continue to function in Protestant England until the eighteenth century. Why, then, did sixteenth-century England become a Protestant country at all?

"The King's Great Matter"

In 1527, King **Henry VIII** of England (r. 1509–1547) had been married to Ferdinand and Isabella's daughter, Katherine of Aragon, for eighteen years. Yet all the offspring of this union had died in infancy, with the exception of a daughter, Mary. Because Katherine was now past childbearing age and Henry needed a male heir to preserve the peaceful succession to the throne, he had political reasons to propose a change of wife. He also had a more personal motive, having become infatuated with a courtier named Anne Boleyn.

Henry therefore appealed to Rome to annul his marriage to Katherine, arguing that because she had previously been married to his older brother Arthur (who had died in adolescence), his marriage to Katherine had been invalid from the beginning. As Henry's representatives pointed out, the Bible pronounced it "an unclean thing" for a man to take his brother's wife and cursed such a marriage with childlessness (Leviticus 20:31). Even a papal dispensation, which Henry and Katherine had obtained for their marriage, could not exempt them from such a clear prohibition—as the marriage's childlessness proved.

HENRY VIII OF ENGLAND. Hans Holbein the Younger executed several portraits of the English king. This one depicts him in middle age, confident of his powers.

Henry's petition put Pope Clement VII (r. 1523–1534) in an awkward position. Both Henry and Clement knew that popes in the past had granted annulments to reigning monarchs on far weaker grounds than the ones Henry was alleging. But if the pope granted Henry's annulment, he would cast doubt on the validity of all papal dispensations. More seriously, he would provoke the wrath of the emperor Charles V, Katherine of Aragon's nephew, whose armies were in firm command of Rome and who at that moment held the pope himself in captivity. Clement was trapped, and all he could do was procrastinate and hope that the matter would resolve itself. For two years, he allowed Henry's case to proceed in England without ever reaching a verdict. Then, suddenly, he transferred the case to Rome, where the legal process began all over again.

Exasperated by these delays, Henry began to increase pressure on the pope. In 1531, he compelled an assembly of English clergy to declare him "protector and only supreme head" of the Church in England. In 1532, he encouraged Parliament to produce an inflammatory list of grievances against the English clergy and used this threat to force them

to concede his right, as king, to approve or deny all Church legislation. In January 1533, Henry married Anne Boleyn (already pregnant) even though his marriage to Katherine still had not been annulled. The new archbishop of Canterbury, Thomas Cranmer, later provided the required annulment in May, acting on his own authority.

In September, Princess Elizabeth was born; her father, disappointed again in his hopes for a son, refused to attend her christening. Nevertheless, Parliament settled the succession to the throne on the children of Henry and Anne, redirected all papal revenues from England into the king's hands, prohibited appeals to the papal court, and formally declared the "King's Highness to be Supreme Head of the Church of England." In 1536, Henry executed his former tutor and chancellor, Sir Thomas More (Chapter 12), for his refusal to endorse this declaration of supremacy, and he took steps toward dissolving England's many monasteries. By the end of 1539, these monasteries and convents were emptied and their lands and wealth confiscated by the king, who distributed their properties and revenues to his supporters and potential enemies.

These measures, largely masterminded and engineered by Henry's Protestant adviser Thomas Cromwell (c. 1485–1540), broke the bonds that linked the English Church to Rome. But they did not make England a wholly Protestant country. Although certain traditional practices (such as pilgrimages and the veneration of relics) were prohibited, the **Church of England** remained overwhelmingly Catholic in organization, doctrine, ritual, and language. The Six Articles promulgated by Parliament in 1539 at Henry VIII's behest left no room for doubt as to the official orthodoxy: confession to priests, masses for the dead, and clerical celibacy were all confirmed; the Latin Mass continued; and Catholic Eucharistic doctrine was not only confirmed but its denial was made punishable by death. To most English people, only the disappearance of the monasteries and the king's own continuing matrimonial adventures (he married six women in all) were evidence that their Church was no longer in communion with Rome.

The Reign of Edward VI

For truly committed Protestants, and especially those who had visited Calvin's Geneva, the changes Henry VIII enforced on the English Church did not go nearly far enough. And in 1547, the accession of the nine-year-old king Edward VI (Henry's son by his third wife, Jane Seymour)

Analyzing Primary Sources

The Six Articles of the English Church

Although Henry VIII withdrew the Church of England from obedience to the papacy, he continued to reject most Protestant theology. Some of his advisers, most notably Thomas Cromwell, were committed Protestants, and the king allowed his son and heir, Edward VI, to be raised as a Protestant. But even after several years of rapid (and mostly Protestant) change in the English Church, Henry reasserted a set of traditional Catholic doctrines in the Six Articles of 1539. These remained binding on the Church of England until the king's death in 1547.

First, that in the most blessed sacrament of the altar, by the strength and efficacy of Christ's mighty word, it being spoken by the priest, is present really, under the form of bread and wine, the natural body and blood of our Savior Jesus Christ, conceived of the Virgin Mary, and that after the consecration there remains no substance of bread or wine, nor any other substance but the substance of Christ, God and man;

Secondly, that communion in both kinds is not necessary for salvation, by the law of God, to all persons, and that it is to be believed and not doubted . . . that in the flesh, under the form of bread, is the very blood, and with the blood, under the form of wine, is the very flesh, as well apart as though they were both together;

Thirdly, that priests, after the order of priesthood received as afore, may not marry by the law of God;

Fourthly, that vows of chastity or widowhood by man or woman made to God advisedly ought to be observed by the law of God. . . .

Fifthly, that it is right and necessary that private masses be continued and admitted in this the king's English Church and congregation . . . whereby good Christian people . . . do receive both godly and goodly consolations and benefits; and it is agreeable also to God's law;

Sixthly, that oral, private confession is expedient and necessary to be retained and continued, used and frequented in the church of God.

Source: *Statutes of the Realm*, vol. 3 (London: 1810–1828), p. 739 (modernized).

Questions for Analysis

1. Three of these six articles focus on the sacrament of the Eucharist (the Mass). Given what you have learned in this chapter, why would Henry have been so concerned about this sacrament? What does this reveal about his values and those of his contemporaries?

2. Given Henry's insistence on these articles, why might he have allowed his son to be raised a Protestant? What does this suggest about the political situation in England?

---

gave them the opportunity to finish the task of reform. Henry's last wife, Catherine Parr, was a Lutheran sympathizer and, as the teacher of the royal children, contributed greatly to further reforms that stripped many Roman practices from the English Church. Edward's government permitted priests to marry; English services replaced Latin ones; the veneration of images was discouraged, and the images themselves were defaced or destroyed; prayers for the dead were declared useless, and endowments for such prayers were confiscated; and new articles of belief were drawn up, repudiating all sacraments except Baptism and Communion and affirming the Protestant creed of justification by faith alone. Most important, *The Book of Common Prayer* by Archbishop Cranmer, considered one of the great landmarks of English literature, defined precisely how the new English-language services of the church were to be conducted.

Edward's successor, however, was his much older half sister Mary (r. 1553–1558), a committed Catholic and granddaughter of the "Most Catholic" monarchs of Spain, Ferdinand and Isabella (Chapter 11). Mary speedily reversed her half brother's religious policies, restoring the Latin Mass and requiring married priests to give up their wives. She even prevailed on Parliament to vote a return to papal allegiance. Hundreds of Protestant leaders fled abroad, many to Geneva; others, including Archbishop Cranmer, were burned at the stake for refusing to abjure their Protestantism. News of the martyrdoms spread and shocked Protestant Europe, but in England, Mary's policies sparked relatively little resistance. After two decades of religious upheaval, most English men

QUEEN MARY AND QUEEN ELIZABETH. The two daughters of Henry VIII, Queen Mary (left) and Queen Elizabeth (right), were the first two queens regnant of England; that is, the first women to rule in their own right. Despite the similar challenges they faced, they had strikingly different fates and have been treated very differently in popular histories. ▪ *How do these two portraits suggest differences in the queens' personalities and their self-representation as rulers?*

and women were probably hoping that Mary's reign would bring some stability to their lives.

This, however, Mary could not do. The executions she ordered were insufficient to wipe out religious resistance; instead, Protestant propaganda about "Bloody Mary" caused widespread unease, even among those who welcomed the return of traditional religious forms. She also could not restore monasticism, because too many leading families had profited from Henry VIII's dissolution of the monasteries for her to reverse this policy. Mary's marriage to her cousin Philip, Charles V's son and heir to the Spanish throne, was another miscalculation. Although the marriage treaty stipulated that Philip could not succeed her in the event of her death, her English subjects never trusted him. When she allowed herself to be drawn by Philip into a war with France on Spain's behalf—in which England lost Calais, its last foothold on the European continent—many people became highly disaffected.

Ultimately, however, what doomed Mary's policies was an accident of biology: she was unable to conceive an heir. When she died after only five years of rule, her throne passed to her Protestant half sister, Elizabeth.

The Elizabethan Settlement

The daughter of Henry VIII and Anne Boleyn, Elizabeth (r. 1558–1603) was predisposed in favor of Protestantism by the circumstances of her parents' marriage as well as by her upbringing. But Elizabeth was no zealot and recognized that supporting radical Protestantism in England might provoke bitter sectarian strife. Accordingly, she presided over what is often known as the "Elizabethan settlement" or compromise. By a new Act of Supremacy (1559), she repealed Mary's Catholic legislation, prohibiting foreign religious powers (the pope) from exercising any authority within England and declaring herself "supreme governor" of the English church—a more Protestant title than Henry VIII's "supreme head," since most Protestants believed that Christ alone was the head of the Church. She also adopted many of the Protestant liturgical reforms instituted by her half brother Edward, including Cranmer's revised version of *The Book of Common Prayer.*

But Elizabeth retained vestiges of Catholic practice, too, including bishops, church courts, and vestments for the clergy. On most doctrinal matters, including predestination and free will, Elizabeth's Thirty-Nine Articles of Faith (approved in 1562) struck a decidedly Protestant, even Calvinist, tone. Still, this prayer book was more moderate and, on the critical issue of the Eucharist, deliberately ambiguous. By combining Catholic and Protestant interpretations ("This is my body. . . . Do this in remembrance of me") into a single declaration, for example, the prayer book permitted an enormous latitude for competing interpretations of the service by priests and parishioners alike.

Yet religious tensions persisted in Elizabethan England, not only between Protestants and Catholics, whose opposition to Protestant elements in England was absolute, but also between moderate and more extreme Protestants. On the one hand, the queen was obliged to continue Mary's practice of persecuting notorious heretics—in this case, Catholics who refused to practice their faith discreetly—and executing them for treason. On the other hand, her attempts to promote a "middle way" among competing forms of Christianity caused dissatisfaction among hard-liners of all stripes.

In the long run, what preserved the "Elizabethan settlement" was the extraordinary length of the queen's reign, along with the fact that, for much of that time, Protestant England was at war with Catholic Spain. Under Elizabeth, Protestantism and English forms of nationalism gradually fused into a potent conviction that God himself had chosen England for greatness. After 1588, when English naval forces won an improbable victory over the Spanish Armada (see Chapter 14), Protestantism and Englishness became nearly indistinguishable to most of Queen Elizabeth's subjects. Laws against Catholic practices became increasingly severe, and although an English Catholic tradition did survive, its adherents were a small minority. Significant, too, was the situation in Ireland, where the vast majority of people remained Catholic despite the government's efforts to impose Protestantism. As a result, Irishness would be as firmly identified with Catholicism as was Englishness with Protestantism—but it was the Protestants who were in power in both countries.

THE REBIRTH OF THE ROMAN CATHOLIC CHURCH

So far, our emphasis on the spread of Protestantism has cast the spotlight on dissident reformers such as Luther and Calvin. But there was also a powerful internal reform movement within the Church during the same decades, which resulted in the birth (or rebirth) of a Catholic ("universal") faith. For some, this movement is the "Catholic Reformation"; for others, it is the **Counter-Reformation.**" Those who prefer the former term emphasize that the Church was continuing significant reforming movements that can be traced back to the eleventh century (Chapter 8) and that gained new momentum in the wake of the Great Schism (Chapter 11). Others insist that most Catholic reformers of this period were reactionaries, inspired primarily by the urgent need to resist Protestantism and strengthen the power of the Roman Church in opposition.

Catholic Reforms

Even before Luther's challenge to the Church, there was a strong movement for moral and institutional reform within some religious orders, as we have seen. And while the papacy showed little interest in them, these efforts received support from several secular rulers. In Spain, for example, reforming activities directed by Cardinal Francisco Jiménez de Cisneros (1436–1517) led to the imposition of strict rules of behavior and the elimination of abuses prevalent among the clergy. Jiménez (*he-MEN-ez*) also helped to regenerate the spiritual life of the Spanish Church. In Italy, meanwhile, earnest clerics labored to make the Italian Church more worthy of its prominent position. Reforming existing institutions was a difficult task, not least because the papal court set such a poor example. Yet some new religious orders, dedicated to high ideals of piety and social service, were emerging. In northern Europe, Christian humanists such as Erasmus and Thomas More played a role in this Catholic reform movement, criticizing abuses and editing sacred texts (Chapter 12).

These internal reforms were inadequate, however, as a response to the concerted challenges posed by Protestantism. Starting in the 1530s, therefore, a more aggressive phase of reform began to gather momentum under a new style of vigorous papal leadership. The leading Counter-Reformation popes Paul III (r. 1534–1549), Paul IV (r. 1555–1559), Pius V (r. 1566–1572), and Sixtus V (r. 1585–1590) were the most zealous reformers of the Church since the eleventh century. All led upright lives; some, indeed, were so grimly ascetic that contemporaries longed for the bad old days. As a Spanish councilor wrote of Pius V in 1567, "We should like it even better if the present Holy Father were no longer with us, however great, inexpressible, unparalleled, and extraordinary His Holiness may be." In confronting Protestantism, however,

Past and Present

Controlling Consumption

Although laws regulating the conspicuous consumption of expensive commodities—especially status-conscious clothing—were common during the later Middle Ages, it was not until after the Reformation that both Protestant and Catholic leaders began to criminalize formerly acceptable behaviors and stimulants. New theories of sensory perception, the availability of new consumer goods such as coffee and tobacco, and a new push to internalize reform led some authorities to outlaw prostitution (hitherto legal) and to ban normal social practices such as drinking and dancing. The image on the left shows the militant Catholic League, which was founded in sixteenth-century France to combat Protestantism and promote strict religious observance. The image on the right shows Czech protesters calling for the decriminalization of marijuana.

 Watch related author interview on the Student Site

an excessively holy pope was vastly preferable to a self-indulgent one. And these Counter-Reformation popes were not merely holy men but also accomplished administrators, reorganizing papal finances and filling ecclesiastical offices with bishops and abbots who were no less renowned for austerity and holiness than the popes themselves.

Papal reform efforts intensified at the **Council of Trent**, a general meeting of the entire Church convoked by Paul III in 1545 and that met at intervals thereafter until 1563. The decisions made at Trent, a provincial capital of the Holy Roman Empire (Trento in modern-day Italy), provided the foundations on which a new Catholic Church would be erected. Although the council began by debating some form of compromise with Protestantism, it ended by reaffirming all the Catholic tenets challenged by

Protestant critics. "Good works" were affirmed as necessary for salvation and all seven sacraments were declared indispensable means of grace, without which salvation was impossible. Transubstantiation, purgatory, the invocation of saints, and the rule of celibacy for the clergy were all confirmed as dogmas—essential elements—of the Catholic faith. The Bible, in its imperfect Vulgate translation, and the traditions of apostolic teaching were held to be of equal authority as sources of Christian truth. Papal supremacy over every bishop and priest was expressly maintained, and the supremacy of the pope over any Church council was taken for granted outright, signaling a final defeat of the still-active conciliar movement. The Council of Trent even reaffirmed the doctrine of indulgences that had touched off the Lutheran revolt, although it condemned the worst abuses connected with their sale.

The Rebirth of the Roman Catholic Church | 447

THE COUNCIL OF TRENT. This fresco depicts the General Council of the Catholic Church, which met at intervals for nearly twenty years between 1545 and 1563 in the city of Trent (Trento in modern-day Italy) to enact significant internal reforms.

THE INSPIRATION OF SAINT JEROME, BY GUIDO RENI (1635). The Council of Trent declared Saint Jerome's Latin translation of the Bible, the Vulgate, to be the Catholic Church's official version. Biblical scholars had known since the early sixteenth century that Saint Jerome's translation contained numerous mistakes, so Catholic defenders of the Vulgate insisted that even his mistakes had been divinely inspired.
- *How does this painting attempt to make this point?*

The decrees issued at Trent were not confined to matters of doctrine. To improve pastoral care of the laity, bishops and priests were forbidden to hold more than one spiritual office. To address concerns that priests were not sufficiently prepared for their tasks, a theological seminary was to be established in every diocese. The council also suppressed a variety of local religious practices and saints' cults, replacing them with new cults authorized and approved by Rome. To prevent heretical ideas from corrupting the faithful, the council further decided to censor or suppress dangerous books.

In 1564, a specially appointed commission published the first Index of Prohibited Books, an official list of writings forbidden to faithful Catholics. It is ironic that all of Erasmus's works were immediately placed on the Index, even though he had been a chosen champion of the Church against Martin Luther only forty years before. A permanent agency known as the Sacred Congregation of the Index was later set up to revise the list, which was maintained until 1966, when it was abolished after the Second Vatican Council (1962–1965). For centuries, it symbolized the doctrinal intolerance that characterized much of sixteenth-century Christianity, both in Catholic and Protestant varieties.

Ignatius Loyola and the Society of Jesus

In addition to the concerted activities of popes and the legislation of the Council of Trent, a third main force propelling the Counter-Reformation was the foundation of the **Society of Jesus** (commonly known as the Jesuits) by

Analyzing Primary Sources

The Demands of Obedience

The necessity of obedience in the spiritual formation of monks and nuns can be traced back to the Rule of Saint Benedict *in the early sixth century. In keeping with the mission of its founder, Ignatius of Loyola (1491–1556), the Society of Jesus brought renewed fervor to this old ideal, dedicating its members to superior intellectual achievements, teaching, and missionary work. Below are excerpts from two of the order's founding texts, the* Spiritual Exercises of Ignatius *and the* Jesuit *Constitutions.*

Rules for Thinking with the Church

1. Always to be ready to obey with mind and heart, setting aside all judgment of one's own, the true spouse of Jesus Christ, our holy mother, our infallible and orthodox mistress, the Catholic Church, whose authority is exercised over us by the hierarchy.

2. To commend the confession of sins to a priest as it is practised in the Church; the reception of the Holy Eucharist once a year, or better still every week, or at least every month, with the necessary preparation....

* * *

4. To have a great esteem for the religious orders, and to give the preference to celibacy or virginity over the married state....

* * *

6. To praise relics, the veneration and invocation of Saints: also the stations, and pious pilgrimages, indulgences, jubilees, the custom of lighting candles in the churches, and other such aids to piety and devotion....

* * *

9. To uphold especially all the precepts of the Church, and not censure them in any manner; but, on the contrary, to defend them promptly, with reasons drawn from all sources, against those who criticize them.

10. To be eager to commend the decrees, mandates, traditions, rites, and customs of the Fathers in the Faith or our superiors....

11. That we may be altogether of the same mind and in conformity with the Church herself, if she shall have defined anything to be black which to our eyes appears to be white, we ought in like manner to pronounce it to be black. For we must undoubtingly believe, that the Spirit of our Lord Jesus Christ, and the Spirit of the Orthodox Church His Spouse, by which Spirit we are governed and directed to salvation, is the same....

From the Constitutions of the Jesuit Order

Let us with the utmost pains strain every nerve of our strength to exhibit this virtue of obedience, firstly to the Highest Pontiff, then to the Superiors of the Society; so that in all things ... we may be most ready to obey his voice, just as if it issued from Christ our Lord ... leaving any work, even a letter, that we have begun and have not yet finished; by directing to this goal all our strength and intention in the Lord, that holy obedience may be made perfect in us in every respect, in performance, in will, in intellect; by submitting to whatever may be enjoined on us with great readiness, with spiritual joy and perseverance; by persuading ourselves that all things [commanded] are just; by rejecting with a kind of blind obedience all opposing opinion or judgment of our own.

Source: Henry Bettenson, ed., *Documents of the Christian Church*, 2nd ed. (Oxford: 1967), pp. 259–61.

Questions for Analysis

1. How might Loyola's career as a soldier have inspired the language used in his "Rules for Thinking with the Church"?

2. In what ways do these Jesuit principles respond directly to the challenges of Protestant reformers?

Ignatius Loyola (1491–1556). In the midst of a career as a mercenary, this young Spanish nobleman was wounded in battle in 1521, the same year in which Luther defied authority at the Diet of Worms. While recuperating, he turned from the reading of chivalric romances to a romantic vernacular retelling of the life of Jesus. The impact of this experience convinced him to become a spiritual soldier of Christ.

For ten months, Ignatius lived as a hermit in a cave near the town of Manresa, where he experienced ecstatic visions and worked out the principles of his subsequent guidebook, the *Spiritual Exercises*. This manual, completed in 1535 and first published in 1541, offered practical advice on how to master one's will and serve God through a systematic program of meditations on sin and the life of Christ. It eventually became the basic handbook for all Jesuits and has been widely studied by Catholic laypeople as well. Indeed, Loyola's *Spiritual Exercises* ranks alongside Calvin's *Institutes* as the most influential religious text of the sixteenth century.

The Jesuit order originated as a group of six disciples who gathered around Loyola during his belated career as a student in Paris. They vowed to serve God in poverty, chastity, and missionary work and were formally constituted by Pope Paul III in 1540. By the time of Loyola's death, the Society of Jesus already numbered some 1,500 members. It was by far the most militant of the religious orders fostered by the Catholic reform movements of the sixteenth century: it was not merely a monastic society but a company of soldiers sworn to defend the faith. Their weapons were not bullets and swords but eloquence, persuasion, and instruction in correct doctrines.

The Society also became accomplished in more worldly methods of exerting influence. Its organization was patterned after that of a military unit, whose commander in chief enforced the iron discipline of all members; individuality was suppressed, and a stoical obedience was required from the rank and file. Indeed, the Jesuit general, sometimes known as the "black pope" (from the color of the order's habit), was elected for life and answered only to the pope in Rome. All senior Jesuits took a special vow of strict obedience to him, by which all Jesuits were held to be at the pope's disposal at all times.

The activities of the Jesuits consisted primarily of proselytizing and establishing schools, which meant that they were ideal missionaries. Accordingly, Jesuits were soon dispatched to preach to non-Christians in India, China, and the Spanish colonies in the Americas. One of Loyola's closest associates, Francis Xavier (ZAY-vyer; 1506–1552), baptized thousands of people and traveled thousands of miles in South and East Asia.

Although Loyola had not at first conceived of his society as a battalion of "shock troops" in the fight against Protestantism, that is what it primarily became. Through preaching and diplomacy—sometimes at the risk of their lives—Jesuits in the second half of the sixteenth century helped to colonize the world. In many places, they were instrumental in keeping rulers and their subjects loyal to Catholicism; in others, they met martyrdom; and in still others, notably Poland and parts of Germany and France, they succeeded in regaining territory previously lost to followers of Luther and Calvin. Wherever they were allowed to settle, they set up schools and colleges on the grounds that only a vigorous Catholicism nurtured by widespread literacy and education could combat Protestantism.

A New Catholic Christianity

The greatest achievement of these reform movements was the revitalization of the Church. Had it not been for such determined efforts, Catholicism would not have swept over the globe during the seventeenth and eighteenth centuries—or reemerged in Europe as a vigorous spiritual force. The reforms had other consequences, such as the rapid advancement of lay literacy in Catholic countries and the growth of intense concern for acts of charity. Because Catholicism continued to emphasize good works as well as faith, charitable activities took on an extremely important role.

There was also a renewed emphasis on the role of religious women. Reformed Catholicism did not exalt marriage as a route to holiness to the same degree as Protestantism, but it did encourage the piety of the female religious elite. For example, it embraced the mysticism of Saint Teresa of Ávila (1515–1582) and her renewal of religious women's spirituality by establishing new orders of nuns, such as the Ursulines and the Sisters of Charity. Both Protestants and Catholics continued to exclude women from the priesthood or ministry, but Catholic women could pursue religious lives with at least some degree of independence, and the convent continued to be a route toward spiritual and even political advancement in Catholic countries.

The reformed Catholic Church did not, however, perpetuate the tolerant Christianity of Erasmus. Instead, Christian humanists lost favor with the papacy, and even scientists such as Galileo were regarded with suspicion (see Chapter 16). Yet contemporary Protestantism was just as intolerant and sometimes even more hostile to

TERESA OF ÁVILA. Teresa of Ávila (1515–1582), canonized in 1622, was one of many female religious figures who played an important role in the reformed Catholic Church. This image is dated 1576, and the Latin wording on the scroll unfurled above Teresa's head reads, "I will sing forever of the mercy of the Holy Lord."

the cause of rational thought. Indeed, because Catholic theologians turned for guidance to the scholasticism of Thomas Aquinas, they tended to be much more committed to the dignity of human reason than some of their Protestant counterparts, who emphasized the literal interpretation of the Bible and the importance of unquestioning faith. It is no coincidence that René Descartes, one of the pioneers of rational philosophy ("I think, therefore I am"), was educated by Jesuits.

It would be wrong, therefore, to claim that the Protestantism of this era was more forward-looking or progressive than Catholicism. Both were, in fact, products of the same troubled time. Each variety of Protestantism responded to specific historical conditions and the needs of specific peoples in specific places, while carrying forward certain aspects of the Christian tradition considered valuable by those communities. The Catholic Church also responded to new spiritual, political, and social realities—to such an extent that it must be regarded as distinct from either the early Church of the later Roman Empire or the ever-evolving Church of the Middle Ages. That is why the phrase "Roman Catholic Church" has not appeared in this book prior to this chapter; the Roman Catholic Church as we know it emerged for the first time in the sixteenth century.

CONCLUSION

The Reformation grew out of the complex historical processes that we have been tracing in the last few chapters. Foremost among these was the increasing power of Europe's sovereign states. As we have seen, the German princes who embraced Protestantism were moved to do so by their desire for sovereignty. The kings of Denmark, Sweden, and England followed suit for many of the same reasons. Protestantism bolstered state power because Protestant leaders preached absolute obedience to godly rulers, and the state in Protestant countries assumed direct control of its churches. Yet the power of the state had been growing for a long time prior to the Reformation, especially in such countries as France and Spain, where Catholic kings already exercised most of the same rights that were seized by Lutheran authorities and by Henry VIII of England in the course of their own reformations. Those rulers who aligned themselves with Catholicism, then, had the same need to bolster their sovereignty and power.

Ideas of national identity, too, were already influential and available for manipulation by Protestants and Catholics alike. Religion thus became a new source of both identity and disunity. Prior to the Reformation, peoples in different regions of Germany spoke such different dialects that they had difficulty understanding each other. But Luther's Bible gained such currency that it eventually became the linguistic standard for all these disparate regions, which began to conceive of themselves as part of a single nation. Yet religion alone could not achieve the political unification of Germany, which did not occur for another 300 years (see Chapter 21); and, indeed, it contributed to existing divisions by cementing the opposition of Catholic princes and peoples. Elsewhere in Europe—as in the Netherlands, where Protestants fought successfully against a foreign, Catholic overlord—religion created a shared identity where politics could not. In England, where it is arguable that a sense of nationalism had already been fostered before the Reformation, membership in the Church of England became a new, if not uncontested, attribute of "Englishness."

Ideals characteristic of the Renaissance also contributed something to the Reformation and the Catholic responses to it. The criticisms of Christian humanists helped to prepare

Europe for the challenges of Lutheranism, and close textual study of the Bible led to the publication of the newer, more accurate editions used by Protestant reformers. For example, Erasmus's improved edition of the Latin New Testament enabled Luther to reach some crucial conclusions concerning the meaning of penance, and became the foundation for Luther's own translation of the Bible. However, Erasmus was not a supporter of Lutheran principles and most other Christian humanists shunned Protestantism as soon as it became clear to them what Luther was actually teaching. Indeed, in certain basic respects, Protestant doctrine was completely at odds with the principles, politics, and beliefs of most humanists, who mostly became staunch supporters of the Catholic Church.

After You Read This Chapter

 Go to **INQUIZITIVE** to see what you've learned—and learn what you've missed— with personalized feedback along the way.

REVIEWING THE OBJECTIVES

- The main premises of Luther's theology had religious, political, and social implications. What were they?
- Switzerland fostered a number of different Protestant movements. Why was this the case?
- The Reformation had a profound effect on the basic structures of family life and on the attitudes toward marriage and morality. Describe these changes.
- The Church of England was established in response to what specific political situation?
- How did the Catholic Church respond to the challenge of Protestantism?

In the New World and Asia, both Protestantism and Catholicism became forces of imperialism and new catalysts for competition. The race to secure colonies and resources now became a race for converts, too, as missionaries of both faiths fanned out over the globe. In the process, the confessional divisions of Europe were mapped onto these regions, often with violent results.

Over the course of the ensuing century, newly sovereign nation-states would struggle for hegemony at home and abroad, setting off a series of religious wars that would cause as much destruction as any plague. Meanwhile, Western civilizations' extension into the Atlantic would create new ecosystems, forms of wealth, and types of bondage.

PEOPLE, IDEAS, AND EVENTS IN CONTEXT

- How did **MARTIN LUTHER**'s attack on **INDULGENCES** tap into a more widespread criticism of the papacy? What role did the printing press and the German vernacular play in the dissemination of his ideas?

- Why did many German principalities and cities rally to Luther's cause? Why did his condemnation at the **DIET OF WORMS** not lead to his execution on charges of heresy?

- How did the Protestant teachings of **ULRICH ZWINGLI**, **JOHN CALVIN**, and the **ANABAPTISTS** differ from one another and from those of Luther?

- What factors made some of Europe's territories more receptive to **PROTESTANTISM** than others? What was the meaning of the principle *CUIUS REGIO, EIUS REGIO*, established by the Peace of Augsburg?

- How did the **REFORMATION** alter the status and lives of women in Europe? Why did it strengthen male authority in the family?

- Why did **HENRY VIII** break with Rome? How did the **CHURCH OF ENGLAND** differ from other Protestant churches in Europe?

- What decisions were made at the **COUNCIL OF TRENT**? What were the founding principles of **IGNATIUS LOYOLA**'s **SOCIETY OF JESUS**, and what was its role in the **COUNTER-REFORMATION** of the **CATHOLIC CHURCH**?

THINKING ABOUT CONNECTIONS

- Our study of Western civilizations has shown that reforming movements are nothing new, and Christianity has been continuously reformed throughout its long history. What made this Reformation so different?

- Was a Protestant break from the Catholic Church inevitable? Why or why not?

- The political, social, and religious structures put in place during this era continue to shape our lives in such profound ways that we scarcely notice them—or we assume them to be inevitable and natural. In your view, what is the farthest-reaching consequence of this age of dissent and division? Why? In what ways has it formed your own values and assumptions?

STORY LINES

- By the middle of the sixteenth century, the Atlantic Ocean had become a central space for colonization, migration, and settlement, as the peoples of this Atlantic world confronted each other.

- In the wake of the Reformation, Europe itself remained politically unstable, and devastating religious wars were waged on the Continent. In England, mounting pressures caused a crisis that resulted in civil war and the execution of the reigning king.

- At the same time, competition in the wider Atlantic world exported these political and religious conflicts to the new European colonies.

- This widening world and its pervasive violence caused many Europeans to question the beliefs of earlier generations. Intellectuals and artists sought new sources of authority and new ways of explaining the complex circumstances of their time.

CHRONOLOGY

1562–1598	French wars of religion
1566–1609	Dutch wars with Spain
1588	Destruction of the Spanish Armada
1598	Henry IV issues the Edict of Nantes
1607	English colony of Jamestown founded
1608	French colony in Québec founded
1611	William Shakespeare's play *The Tempest* performed in London
1618	Thirty Years' War begins
1621	Dutch West India Company founded
1642–1649	English Civil War
1648	Beginning of the Fronde rebellions
	Thirty Years' War ends
1660	Restoration of the English monarchy

Before You Read This Chapter

Europe in the Atlantic World, 1550–1660

CORE OBJECTIVES

- **TRACE** the new linkages between Western civilizations and the Atlantic world, and **EXPLAIN** their consequences.

- **DESCRIBE** the different forms of unfree labor that developed in European colonies during this period.

- **IDENTIFY** the monarchies that dominated Europe and the Atlantic world and the newer powers whose influence was expanding.

- **EXPLAIN** the reasons for Europe's religious and political instability and its consequences for Europe's monarchies and the Atlantic world.

- **UNDERSTAND** how artists and intellectuals responded to the crises and uncertainties of this era.

The Atlantic Ocean thrashes the western shores of Europe and Africa with wind-driven waves that have traveled thousands of miles from the American coasts. Its immense area links continents shaped by a wide variety of climates, including the arid desert of the Sahara, the more temperate zones of Europe and North America, the tropical islands of the Gulf of Mexico and the Caribbean, and the rain forests of the Amazon basin in South America. This ecological diversity, and the hitherto infrequent and limited movement of peoples across the ocean, meant that each region nurtured its own forms of plant and animal life, and its own unique microbes and pathogens.

In the sixteenth century, the emergence of the Atlantic world as an arena of cultural and economic exchange broke down the isolation of these ecosystems. Transatlantic commerce and migration now eclipsed the importance of the Mediterranean, which had been the crucial connector of Western civilizations since the Bronze Age (Chapter 2). Populations of humans, animals, and plants on once-remote shores came into frequent and intense contact. On the one hand, Europeans brought diseases that devastated the peoples of the Americas, along with gunpowder and a hotly divided Christianity. On the other hand, the huge influx of silver from South America transformed (and eventually exploded) the cash-starved European economy, while the arrival of American stimulants such as tobacco, sugar, and chocolate fostered new consumer appetites that could be satisfied only by new regimes of unfree labor.

Eventually, the need for slaves to power the plantations that supplied these consumer products fostered a vast industry of human trafficking, which led to the forcible removal of nearly 11 million people from Africa over the course of three centuries. Colonial settlement in North and South America also created new social hierarchies and new forms of inequality, which unsettled even long-established structures in Europe. The indigenous peoples of the Americas were forced to deal with the presence of newly arrived immigrants, and the settlers in turn confronted both indigenous peoples and the meddling interference of distant imperial bureaucracies.

Meanwhile, European states were riven by internal dissent and engaged in deadly competitions among themselves—and these, too, were exported to the Atlantic world. Galvanized by the crisis of the Reformation (Chapter 13), the Roman Catholic Church sought to redress the loss of religious dominance in Europe by spreading its influence to the Americas and Asia through the work of new missionary orders. The Spanish crown, which controlled the most developed colonial empire of the time, was also the most zealous defender of the Catholic faith—thus the wars within Spain's Protestant Dutch provinces and with Protestant England affected colonial politics, too. Similar attempts by the Catholic Habsburg monarchy to enforce religious uniformity among the varied territories of central Europe led to the Thirty Years' War, one of the longest and bloodiest conflicts in western history. In both direct and indirect ways, these deadly disputes stimulated the migration of persecuted minorities across the Atlantic, replanting and propagating these rivalries.

But religion was not the only cause of conflict within Europe. Tension was growing between powerful monarchs and landowning elites who disputed the right of their rulers and administrators to raise revenues through increased taxation. Supporting colonial expansion in the Atlantic world and fighting wars within Europe were expensive projects that strained traditional alliances and ideas of kingship. Political and moral philosophers accordingly struggled to redefine the role of government in a world of religious pluralism and to articulate new political ideologies that did not necessitate violence among people of different faiths. Intellectuals and artists also strove to reassess the place for Europeans in this expanding Atlantic world, to process the flood of new information and commodities, and to make sense of the profound changes in daily life.

THE EMERGENCE OF THE ATLANTIC WORLD

With the few exceptions we have noted in previous chapters, even the most skilled of Europe's sailors were limited to coastal cruising along the Atlantic's eastern shores until the fifteenth century. But after the Portuguese and Spanish established settlements on the Canary Islands, this archipelago off the northwestern coast of Africa became a permanent base of operations for successive exploratory ventures. From here, generations of Portuguese sailors learned to navigate the West African coast, after which they successfully rounded the Cape of Good Hope and began to establish trading colonies in the Indian Ocean (see Chapter 12).

During these years, Portuguese sailors also launched the first kidnapping raids for slaves along the Atlantic coast of Senegal. When they found that some African chieftains were willing to facilitate the capture of people from rival tribes, the Portuguese began to set up coastal outposts where they could trade livestock, foodstuffs, cotton, copper, and iron for ivory, gold, finished textiles, and human beings.

Competing Colonial Ventures

Spanish successes in Mexico (Chapter 12) soon encouraged other European kingdoms to attempt imperial ventures of their own. Finding that Spanish and Portuguese holds on the Caribbean and South America were firm, northern European explorers targeted the North American coast. Protestant rulers were obviously not bound by the Treaty of Tordesillas (1494) and all subsequent papal pronouncements that favored Catholic colonial ventures. In 1497–1498, the Italian-born explorer John Cabot was hired by the English crown to explore the mouth of the St. Lawrence River. But it was nearly a century later, in 1585, that Walter Raleigh attempted to start an English colony just north of Spanish Florida. The settlement at Roanoke Island (present-day North Carolina) was intended to solidify English claims to the territory of Virginia, named for England's "Virgin Queen" Elizabeth. It originally encompassed the North American seaboard from South Carolina to Maine, including Bermuda.

This ill-conceived experiment ended with the disappearance of the first colonists. But it was followed by Christopher Newport's expedition to the Chesapeake Bay in 1606: a voyage funded by a private London firm, the Virginia Company. Newport and his followers did not conceive of themselves as empire builders. They were not

THE ISLAND OF BERMUDA. This map of the "Summer Isle" of Bermuda and the accompanying images of its major fortifications and sites were drawn by Captain John Smith and published in *The Generall Historie of Virginia, New-England, and the Summer Isles* (1624). ■ *Why would such features be of interest to readers of this pamphlet?*

for their part, often behaved with a combination of paternalism and contempt for the peoples they encountered. Some hoped to convert them to Christianity, while others sought to use them as labor for their economic enterprises. Ultimately, however, the balance was tipped by larger environmental, biological, and demographic factors that lay outside the control of individuals.

The Columbian Exchange and Its Environmental Effects

The accelerating rate of global connections in the sixteenth century precipitated an extraordinary movement of peoples, plants, animals, goods, cultures, and diseases. This movement is known as the "**Columbian exchange**," a term coined by the historian Alfred Crosby in 1972 with reference to Columbus's voyage. Yet this exchange soon came to encompass lands that still lay far beyond the purview of Columbus and his contemporaries—not just the African and Eurasian landmass and the vast terrain of the Americas but also Australia and the Pacific Islands.

Because of its profound consequences for human populations and the environment, the Columbian exchange is considered a fundamental turning point in both human history and the history of the earth's ecology. The exchange put new agricultural products into circulation, introduced new species of domesticated animals, and accidentally encouraged the spread of deadly diseases and the devastating invasions of nonnative plants and animals. Both natural ecosystems and human immune systems around the world were destroyed or transformed.

For example, the introduction of pigs and dogs to islands in the Atlantic and Pacific resulted in the extinction of indigenous animals and birds. The landscapes of Central America and southwestern North America were denuded of vegetation after Spanish settlers turned to large-scale herding and ranching operations. Honeybees displaced native insect populations and fostered the propagation of harmful plant species.

sponsored by the English king, and they probably did not intend to settle permanently in the New World. They were "gentleman planters" whose goal was to provide agricultural goods for the European market and so make their fortunes before returning home. Nevertheless, with the Spanish model much in mind, Newport's band reserved the right to subdue any peoples who proved uncooperative. So when Native Americans of the Powhatan tribe killed one-third of the settlers during a raid in 1622, the colonists responded by crushing the Powhatans and seizing their lands.

For decades thereafter, the native populations of North America remained capable of both threatening and fostering the survival of fragile European settlements on the American coast. Bitter conflicts and occasional cooperation between newcomers and indigenous peoples are part of a larger history of intermittent struggle and coexistence that began the moment Columbus first landed on Hispaniola. Especially in the early years of colonization, when the number of European immigrants was small, some Native American peoples sought to take advantage of these new contacts to trade for goods otherwise unavailable to them. European settlers,

Then there were the unintended exchanges: gray squirrels and raccoons from North America found their way to Britain and the European Continent, and brown rats and even some species of earthworms were transported to the Americas. Insects from all over the world traveled to new environments and spread unfamiliar forms of bacteria and pollen.

Obviously, the transfer of human populations in the form of settlers, soldiers, merchants, sailors, indentured servants, and slaves accelerated the process of change. Some groups were wiped out through violence, forced resettlement, and bacteria. As much as 90 percent of the pre-Columbian population of the Americas died from communicable diseases such as smallpox, cholera, influenza, typhoid, measles, malaria, and bubonic plague—all brought from Europe. Syphilis, in contrast, appears to have been brought to Europe from the Americas. Some scholars have even asserted that it was Columbus's own sailors who transmitted the disease across the Atlantic.

Meanwhile, the importation of foodstuffs from one part of the world to another, and their cultivation in new habitats, revolutionized the diets of local populations. The American potato, which could be grown in substandard soil and stored for long periods, eventually became the staple diet of the European poor. American tomatoes, although not widely consumed in Europe until the nineteenth century, are today an essential ingredient in many regional dishes.

Indeed, the foods and flavors that characterize modern-day iconic cuisines are, to an extraordinary degree, the result of the Columbian exchange, because many new, exotic foods quickly become fashionable and then habitual. Who can imagine an English meal without potatoes? Switzerland or Belgium without chocolate? Thai food without chili peppers? On the other side of the Atlantic, Florida without oranges? Colombia without coffee? Hawaii without pineapples? Of the ingredients that make up the quintessential American hamburger—ground-beef patties on a bun with lettuce, tomato, pickles, onion, and (if you like) cheese—only one component is indigenous to America: tomato. Everything else is from the Old World: beef, wheat for the bun, cucumber for the pickle, onion, and lettuce. Even the name is European, a reference to the town of Hamburg in Germany.

Colonial Populations Compared

Compared to the more than 7 million slaves who were taken from Africa to labor and die on plantations across the Atlantic, only about 1.5 million Europeans immigrated to the Americas in the two centuries after Columbus's first

---

THE COLUMBIAN EXCHANGE

The following are just a few of the commodities and contagions that moved between the Old World and the New World in this era.

Old World → New World	New World → Old World
• Wheat	• Corn
• Sugar	• Potatoes
• Bananas	• Beans
• Rice	• Squash
• Wine vines	• Pumpkins
• Horses	• Tomatoes
• Pigs	• Avocados
• Chickens	• Chili peppers
• Sheep	• Pineapples
• Cattle	• Cocoa
• *Smallpox*	• Tobacco
• *Measles*	• *Syphilis*
• *Typhus*	

---

voyage. The total number who initially left Spain is estimated at 200,000 to 250,000—most of whom were men. By 1570, given the high mortality of migrants and some returns to Europe, the population had been reduced to about 150,000. The Spanish crown did what it could to encourage a new wave of settlement, but even in a period of demographic growth, the number of those who chose to seek their fortunes abroad remained relatively small. Transatlantic travel was expensive and uncertain, and the demand for a European labor force remained low as long as Native Americans could be conscripted and enslaved.

The population of the Spanish Americas thus remained largely urban during this period, with most colonists living in the military and administrative centers of the empire. Even the owners of large plantations lived in cities, corresponding from afar with the foremen who managed their estates. Only those who had been granted *encomiendas* tended to live on the lands entrusted to them by the Spanish crown (the Spanish verb *encomendar* means "to entrust").

The *encomienda* system reveals how Spanish conquests in the New World were an extension of the earlier Reconquista (Chapter 12) of Spain itself, for they were originally set up to manage Muslim populations in territories captured by Christian crusaders. This arrangement made the *encomenderos* agents of the crown. Technically, in the American version of the system, the lands they oversaw were still owned by native peoples; but in practice, many *encomenderos* were able to exploit the land for their own profit, treating native workers like serfs. Some of the *encomenderos* were descendants of the first conquistadors. Others were drawn from Aztec and Inca elites, many of whom were women. For example, the daughters of the Aztec emperor Montezuma had been given extensive lands to hold in trust after their father's capitulation to Cortés.

In North America, by contrast, English colonies in New England and the Chesapeake Bay were small and rural. But they grew more quickly, with settlers numbering about 250,000 by 1700. Part of the reason for this growth was the greater impetus for emigration caused by overpopulation in the British Isles. The persecution of various Protestant groups also played an important role in driving immigration, especially to the New England colonies where relocation of entire families and even communities was common. The colonies in Virginia offered additional incentives by granting 100 acres to each settler.

But these factors did not swell the numbers of migrants so much as the encouragement of indentured servitude. This was a practice that brought thousands of "free" European laborers across the Atlantic to work under terms that made them little different from the slaves. The term "indenture" refers to the kind of document that contracted a servant to a master for a set period of time. Copied in duplicate on a single sheet of paper or parchment, the two halves would be cut apart in such a way as to leave jagged edges that looked like teeth. Perhaps 75 to 80 percent of the people who arrived in the Chesapeake colony in the 1600s were indentured servants, nearly a quarter of whom were women. The successful use of indentured servants to grow tobacco in North America led some landowners to try the same system on plantations in the Caribbean islands. Ultimately, however, the plantation system earned its greatest profits through the labor of African slaves.

New Social Hierarchies in New Spain

After the conquests of the Aztec and Inca Empires (Chapter 12), the Spanish established colonial governments in Mexico and Peru, under the control of a central bureaucracy in Madrid. This centralization was facilitated by the highly organized structure of the Aztec society in Mexico and the Incas in Peru. For the most part, native peoples already lived in large, well-regulated villages and towns. The Spanish government could therefore work closely with local elites to maintain order. Indeed, the *encomienda* system was initially effective because it was built on these existing structures and did not attempt to uproot or eliminate existing native cultures; it focused, instead, on controlling and exploiting native labor, especially for extracting mineral resources. Although farming and ranching were encouraged in Central and South America, and later in Florida and California, mining dominated the Spanish colonial economy for a century and a half.

The Spanish collected tributes from all the communities of their empire and worked to convert native peoples to Catholicism, but they did not attempt to change basic patterns of life. The result was a widespread cultural assimilation by the relatively small numbers of (usually male) European settlers, which was assisted by the normality of intermarriage between (male) colonizers and (female) colonial subjects. This pattern gave rise to a complex and distinctive caste system in New Spain, with a few "pure-blooded" Spanish immigrants at the top, a very large number of Creoles (peoples of mixed descent) in the middle, and Native Americans at the bottom.

In theory, these racial categories corresponded to class distinctions; but in practice, race and class did not always coincide. Racial concepts and practices were extremely flexible, and prosperous individuals or families of mixed descent often found ways to establish their "pure" Spanish ancestry by adopting the social practices of the new Spanish colonial elites. The lingering effects of this complicated stratification can still be seen in Latin America today.

Sugar, Slaves, and the Transatlantic Triangle

The Europeans who settled in the Americas faced a major problem: labor. Mining and plantation agriculture required many workers, and the indigenous labor supply of the Americas was limited. As we have seen, the introduction of new diseases resulted in the deaths of millions of Native Americans over only a few decades. Meanwhile, the return of the plague in Europe in the seventeenth century, along with slowing population growth due to the wars of religion, meant that colonists could not look to Europe to satisfy their labor needs. Colonial agents thus began to import slaves from Africa to bolster the labor force and produce the wealth they so avidly

THE ATLANTIC WORLD AND THE TRIANGULAR TRADE. ■ *Trace the routes of the triangular trade. What products did French and British colonies in North America provide to the European market?* ■ *Which colonies were most dependent on slave labor and what products did they produce?* ■ *How did these products enter into the triangle?*

Analyzing Primary Sources

Enslaved Native Laborers at Potosí

The Spanish crown received one-fifth of all revenues from the mines of New Spain, as well as maintained a monopoly over the mercury used to refine the silver ore into silver, so it had an important stake in ensuring the mines' productivity. To this end, the crown granted colonial mine owners the right to conscript native peoples and gave them considerable freedom in the treatment of their workers. This account, dated to about 1620, describes the conditions endured by these native laborers at Potosí (discussed in Chapter 12).

 ccording to His Majesty's warrant, the mine owners on this massive range [at Potosí] have a right to the conscripted labor of 13,300 Indians in the working and exploitation of the mines, both those [mines] which have been discovered, those now discovered, and those which shall be discovered. It is the duty of the *Corregidor* [municipal governor] of Potosí to have them rounded up and to see that they come in from all the provinces between Cuzco . . . and as far as the frontiers of Tarija and Tomina. . . .

The conscripted Indians go up every Monday morning to the . . . foot of the range; the *Corregidor* arrives with all the provincial captains or chiefs who have charge of the Indians assigned him for his miner or smelter; that keeps him busy till 1 P.M., by which time the Indians are already turned over to these mine and smelter owners.

After each has eaten his ration, they climb up the hill, each to his mine, and go in, staying there from that hour until Saturday evening without coming out of the mine; their wives bring them food, but they stay constantly underground, excavating and carrying out the ore from which they get the silver. They all have tallow candles, lighted day and night; that is the light they work with, for as they are underground, they have need for it all the time. . . .

These Indians have different functions in the handling of the silver ore; some break it up with bar or pick, and dig down in, following the vein in the mine; others bring it up; others up above keep separating the good and the poor in piles; others are occupied in taking it down from the range to the mills on herds of llamas; every day they bring up more than 8,000 of these native beasts of burden for this task. These teamsters who carry the metal are not conscripted, but are hired.

Source: Antonio Vázquez de Espinosa, *Compendium and Description of the West Indies*, trans. Charles Upson Clark (Washington, DC: 1968), p. 62.

Questions for Analysis

1. From the tone of this account, what do you think was the narrator's purpose in writing it? Who is his intended audience?

2. Reconstruct the conditions in which these laborers worked. What would you estimate to be the human costs of a week's labor? Why, for example, would a fresh workforce be needed every Monday?

---

sought. And overwhelmingly, that wealth was derived not from gold or silver but from a new commodity for which there was an insatiable appetite in Europe: sugar.

Sugar was at the center of the "**triangular trade**" that linked markets for goods in Africa, the Americas, and Europe—all of which were driven by slave labor. For example, slave ships that transported African slaves to the Caribbean might trade their human cargo for molasses made on the sugar plantations of the islands. These ships would then proceed to New England, where the molasses would be traded to distillers who used the sugary syrup to make rum. Loaded up with a consignment of rum, the slavers would return to the African coast to repeat the process. An alternative triangle might see cheap manufactured goods move from England to Africa, where they would be traded for slaves. Those slaves would then be shipped to Virginia and exchanged for tobacco, which would be shipped back to England to be processed and distributed.

Although the transatlantic slave trade was theoretically controlled by the governments of European colonial powers, private entrepreneurs and working-class laborers were active at every stage of the supply chain: in the ports of West Africa, where captured slaves cast their eyes on their homelands for the last time; on the ships, where these captives were imprisoned; and in the slave markets of the Americas, where agents for the landowners and merchants bid against one another to purchase the human chattel that had survived the terrible voyage. (Britain officially entered this trade in 1564, the year of William Shakespeare's birth.)

Many other branches of the economy in Europe and the Americas were also linked to the slave trade: investors in Amsterdam, London, Lisbon, and Bordeaux who financed the slave trader's journey; insurance brokers who negotiated complex formulas for protecting these investments; financial agents who offered a range of credit instruments; and those seeking to enter into the expensive and risky business of transatlantic trade. And this is to say nothing of the myriad ways in which the everyday lives of average people were bound to slavery. All who bought the commodities produced by slave labor or who manufactured the implements and weapons that enabled enslavement were also implicated. The slave trade was not, as is sometimes assumed, a venture carried forward by a few unscrupulous men. It created wealth and prestige for every sector of European society, not merely for those who had direct contact with it. It was the evil engine that created the modern globalized economy.

The Human Cost of the Slave Trade

The Portuguese were the first to bring African slaves to their sugarcane plantations in Brazil, in the 1540s. By this time, slavery was already crucial to the domestic economies of West African kingdoms. In the following decades, however, the ever-increasing demand for slaves would cause the permanent disintegration of the political order in this region by creating an incentive for war and raiding among rival tribes. Moreover, the increased traffic in human beings called for more highly systematized methods for corralling, sorting, and shipping them. By the end of the sixteenth century, accordingly, the Portuguese government established a fortified trading outpost on an island known as Luanda on the central African coast (near what is now Angola). Additional trading posts were then established at multiple places along the coast to assist with processing the increasing number of captives.

On board the ships, enslaved humans were shackled below decks in spaces barely wider than their own bodies, without sanitary facilities of any kind. It might seem surprising that the mortality rate on these voyages was

HOW SLAVES WERE STOWED ABOARD A SHIP DURING THE MIDDLE PASSAGE. Men were "housed" on the right, women on the left, and children in the middle. The human cargo was jammed onto platforms six feet wide without sufficient headroom to permit an adult to sit up. This diagram is from evidence gathered by English abolitionists in 1788 and depicts conditions on the Liverpool slave ship *Brookes*.

relatively low (probably 10 or 11 percent), but this was only because the slaves chosen for transport were healthy to begin with, and slave traders were anxious to maintain their goods so as to sell at a profit. Those Africans who were transported, then, were already the toughened survivors of unimaginable hardships. To place the above statistic in a larger context, we need to consider how many people would have died before the ships were ready to transport them. One historian estimated that 36 out of 100 people captured in the African interior would perish in the six-month-long forced march to the coast of Angola, and another dozen or so would die in the prisons there. Eventually, perhaps 57 of the original 100 captives would be taken aboard a slave ship, and some 51 would survive the journey and be sold into slavery on arrival. If the destination was Brazil's sugar plantations, only 40 would still be alive after two years. In other words, the actual mortality rate of these new slaves was closer to 60 percent—and this doesn't begin to account for their life expectancy.

The people consigned to this fate struggled against it, and their initiatives helped to shape the emerging Atlantic world. When the opportunity presented itself, slaves banded together in revolt—a perpetual possibility that haunted slave owners and led to draconian regimes of violence and punishment (as in ancient Rome; see Chapter 5). When revolt was impossible, slaves resorted to other forms of resistance, among them suicide and infanticide. Above all, slaves sought to escape and liberate themselves; almost as soon as the slave trade escalated, communities of fugitive slaves sprang up throughout the Americas. Many of these independent settlements were large enough to assert and defend their autonomy. One such community, founded in 1603 in the hinterlands of Brazil's Pernambuco Province, persisted for more than a century and had as many as 20,000 inhabitants. Most others were much smaller and more ephemeral, but their existence testifies to the limits of imperial authority at the fringes of the new American colonies.

CONFLICT AND COMPETITION IN EUROPE AND THE ATLANTIC WORLD

Most of Europe had enjoyed steady economic growth since the middle of the fifteenth century. The colonization of the Americas seemed to promise further prosperity for the decades to come, while providing an outlet for European expansion and aggression. But in the second half of the sixteenth century, prolonged political, religious, and economic crises destabilized Europe. These crises were, in essential ways, the products of long-term developments within and between Europe's most powerful states, but they were exacerbated by the imperial ambitions of those states. Inevitably, European conflicts spread to European colonial holdings, and eventually the outcome of these conflicts determined which European powers were best positioned to enlarge their presence in the Atlantic world—and beyond.

New World Silver and Old World Economies

In the latter half of the sixteenth century, an unprecedented inflation in prices profoundly destabilized the European economy. And because nothing on this scale had ever happened before, it caused widespread panic. Although the twentieth century would see more dizzying inflations, suddenly skyrocketing prices were a terrifying novelty in this era, causing what some historians have termed a "**price revolution**."

PEASANTS HARVESTING WHEAT, SIXTEENTH CENTURY. The inflation that swept through Europe in the late sixteenth century affected poorer workers most acutely. The abundant labor supply damped wages while the cost of food rose because of poor harvests.

Two developments in particular underlay this phenomenon. The first was demographic: after the plague-induced decline of the fourteenth century (Chapter 11), Europe's population grew from roughly 50 million people in 1450 to 90 million in 1600—that is, it increased by nearly 80 percent in a relatively short span of time. Yet Europe's food supply remained nearly constant, causing food prices to rise steeply by the increased population's higher demand for basic commodities. Meanwhile, the enormous influx of silver and gold from Spanish America flooded Europe's previously cash-poor economy (Chapter 12), and this sudden availability of ready coin drove prices higher still.

About 10 million ducats' worth of silver, roughly equivalent to 10 billion U.S. dollars in today's currency, passed through the Spanish port of Seville in just four years, from 1556 to 1560. (A single gold ducat, the standard unit of monetary exchange for long-distance trade, would now be worth nearly a thousand dollars.) Consequently, the market was flooded with coins whose original high worth was quickly downgraded due to the large amount in circulation;

POPULATION DENSITY, c. 1600. ▪ *In what regions was the population most dense?* ▪ *The largest gains in population were on the coasts; why might that be?* ▪ *How would urbanization affect patterns of life and trade?*

and still silver poured in, cheapening the coinage even more. Between 1576 and 1580, the amount of imported silver doubled, becoming 20 million ducats; and between 1591 and 1595, it more than quadrupled.

Most of this money was used by the Spanish crown to pay its armies and the many creditors who had financed its imperial ventures, so a huge volume of coinage was put quickly into circulation through European banks, making the problem of inflation even more widespread. Since some people suddenly had more money to pay for goods and services, those who supplied these commodities charged higher and higher prices. But at the same time, the value of the coinage itself was plummeting. "I learned a proverb here," said a French traveler in Spain in 1603. "Everything costs a lot, except silver."

The New European Poor

In this climate, aggressive entrepreneurs profited from financial speculation, landholders from the rising prices of agricultural produce, and merchants from increasing demand for luxury goods. But laborers were caught in a vise: prices were rising steeply but wages were not keeping pace, owing to the population boom that kept labor relatively cheap. As the cost of food staples rose, poor people had to spend an ever-greater percentage of their paltry incomes on necessities. In Flanders, for example, the cost of wheat tripled between 1550 and 1600; in Paris, grain prices quadrupled; and in England, the overall cost of living more than doubled in Shakespeare's lifetime. When disasters such as wars or bad harvests drove grain prices out of reach, as happened frequently, the poor starved to death.

The price revolution also placed new pressures on the sovereign states of Europe. Inflation depressed the real value of money, so fixed incomes derived from taxes and rents yielded less and less actual wealth. Governments therefore were forced to raise taxes merely to keep their revenues constant. Yet most states needed more revenue than before because they were engaging in more wars, and because warfare was becoming increasingly expensive. The only recourse, then, was to raise taxes precipitously. Hence, governments faced continuous threats of defiance and even armed resistance from their citizens, who could not afford to foot these bills.

Although prices rose less rapidly after 1600, as both the population growth and the flood of silver began to slow, the ensuing decades were a time of economic stagnation. A few areas—notably the Netherlands (see pages 466–467)—bucked the trend, and the rich usually were able to hold their own, but the laboring poor made no advances, because

wages continued to rise far more slowly than prices. Indeed, the lot of the poor in many places deteriorated further, as helpless civilians were plundered by rapacious tax collectors, looting soldiers, or sometimes both. In England, peasants who had been dispossessed of property or driven off once-common lands were branded as vagrants, and vagrancy itself became a criminal offense. It was this population of newly impoverished Europeans who became the indentured servants or deported criminals of the American colonies.

Wars of Religion in France

Compounding these economic problems were the wars that erupted within many European states. As we began to observe in Chapter 9, most medieval kingdoms were created through the colonization of smaller, traditionally autonomous territories—either by conquest or through marriage alliances with ruling families. Now these enlarged monarchies began to make ever-greater financial claims on their citizens while at the same time demanding religious uniformity among them. The result was regional and civil conflict, as local populations and even elites rebelled against the centralizing demands of monarchs who often embraced a different religion than that of their subjects.

France was the first of these kingdoms to be enflamed by religious warfare. Calvinist missionaries from Geneva had made significant headway there (Calvin himself was French), assisted by the conversion of many aristocratic Frenchwomen, who in turn converted their husbands. By the 1560s, French Calvinists, known as Huguenots (HEW-guh-nohz), made up between 10 and 20 percent of the population. But there was no open warfare until dynastic politics led factions within the government to break down along religious lines, pitting the (mostly southern) Huguenots against the (mostly northern) Catholic aristocracy. In some places, mobs incited by members of the clergy on both sides took this opportunity to settle local scores.

Although the Huguenots were not strong enough to win any major battle, there were too many of them to be ignored. In 1572, accordingly, the two sides almost brokered a truce: the presumptive heir to the throne, Prince Henry of Navarre—who had become a Protestant—was to marry the Catholic sister of the reigning king, Charles IX. But this compromise was undone by the Queen Mother, Catherine de' Medici, whose Catholic faction plotted to kill all the Huguenot leaders while they were assembled in Paris for her daughter's wedding. In the early morning of Saint Bartholomew's Day (August 24), most of these Protestant aristocrats were murdered in their beds, and thousands of humble Protestants were slaughtered in the

HENRY IV OF FRANCE. The reign of Henry of Navarre (r. 1589–1610) founded the Bourbon dynasty that would rule France until 1792, and ended the bitter civil war between Catholic and Huguenot factions.

the religious divide in France had a regional component, the edict also reinforced a tradition of local autonomy in southwestern France, in spite of the monarchy's centralized power. The success of this effort can be measured by the fact that peace was maintained in France even after Henry IV was assassinated by a Catholic in 1610.

The wars of religion may be one reason that France did not enter the competition for Atlantic wealth until the seventeenth century, despite its early involvement in North American explorations. It was not until 1608 that French colonial settlements received royal support, after which Catholic (but not Huguenot) immigration to "New France" (Canadian Québec) was encouraged. Meanwhile, there were three failed attempts to establish French outposts in Portuguese Brazil, the last of which (in 1612–1615) resulted only in the export of six Amazonian villagers to France, where they aroused great curiosity in an organized tour of French towns. The Brazilians' Catholic hosts even arranged for them to be baptized publicly as part of an attempt to bolster support for the Catholic cause: an episode that further illustrates the strong connection between the expansion of European influence abroad and the politics of religion at home.

The Revolt of the Netherlands and the Dutch Trading Empire

Warfare between Catholics and Protestants also broke out in the Netherlands during this period. Controlled for almost a century by the same Habsburg family that ruled Spain and its overseas empire, the Netherlands had prospered through intense involvement with trade in the Atlantic world. The Dutch had the highest per capita wealth in all of Europe, and the metropolis of Antwerp (now in Belgium) was northern Europe's leading commercial and financial center. So when the Spanish king **Philip II** (r. 1556–1598) attempted to tighten his hold there in the 1560s, the fiercely independent Dutch cities resented this imperial intrusion and were ready to fight it.

This conflict took on a religious dynamic because Calvinism had spread into the Netherlands from France, and Philip, an ardent defender of the Catholic faith, could not tolerate this combination of political and religious disobedience. When crowds began ransacking and desecrating Catholic churches throughout the country, Philip dispatched an army of 10,000 Spanish soldiers to wipe out Protestantism in his Dutch territories. A reign of terror ensued, with some 12,000 people rounded up on charges of heresy or sedition, thousands of whom were convicted and executed for treason.

streets or drowned in the river Seine. When word of the Parisian massacre spread to the provinces, local massacres proliferated.

Henry of Navarre escaped, along with his bride, but the war continued for more than two decades. Finally, Catherine's death in 1589 was followed by that of her son, Henry III, who had produced no heir to supplant Henry of Navarre; he became **Henry IV**, and renounced his Protestant faith to placate France's Catholic majority. In 1598, Henry made a landmark effort to end the conflict by issuing the Edict of Nantes, which recognized Catholicism as the official religion of the realm but permitted Protestants to practice their religion in specified places.

This was an important step toward a policy of religious tolerance. For the first time, French Protestants were allowed to hold public office, enroll in universities, and work in hospitals, and they were even allowed to fortify some towns for their own military defense. Because

PROTESTANTS RANSACKING A CATHOLIC CHURCH IN THE NETHERLANDS.
Protestant destruction of religious images provoked a stern response from Philip II.
■ *Why would Protestants have smashed statuary and other devotional artifacts?*

These events catalyzed the Protestant opposition. A Dutch aristocrat, William of Orange, emerged as the anti-Spanish leader and sought help from religious allies in France, Germany, and England. In response, organized fleets of Protestant privateers (that is, privately owned ships) began harassing the Spanish navy in the waters of the North Atlantic. In 1572, William's Protestant army seized control of the Netherlands' northern provinces. Although William was assassinated in 1584, his efforts were instrumental in forcing the Spanish crown to recognize the independence of a northern Dutch Republic in 1609. Once united, these seven northern provinces became wholly Calvinist. But the southern region, still largely Catholic, remained under Spanish rule.

After gaining its independence, the new Dutch Republic emerged as the most prosperous European commercial empire of the seventeenth century. Indeed, its reach extended well beyond the Atlantic world, targeting the Indian Ocean and East Asia as well. In general, the Dutch colonial project owed more to the strategic "fort and factory" model of expansion (favored by the Portuguese) than to the Spanish technique of territorial conquest and settlement. For example, the Dutch established a colony on the Cape of Good Hope at the southern tip of Africa, which facilitated the eastward spread of their influence. Many more early initiatives were spurred by the establishment of the Dutch East India Company, a private mercantile corporation that came to control Sumatra, Borneo, and the Moluccas (the so-called Spice Islands). This meant that the

Dutch had a lucrative monopoly on the European trade in pepper, cinnamon, nutmeg, mace, and cloves. The company also secured an exclusive right to trade with Japan, and maintained military and trading outposts in China and India.

In the Atlantic world itself, the Dutch did not have a significant presence. They did, however, establish an outpost in North America, the colony known as New Amsterdam until it was surrendered to the English in 1667 and renamed New York. Their remaining territorial holdings in the Atlantic were Dutch Guyana (present-day Surinam) on the coast of South America and the islands of Curaçao and Tobago in the Caribbean. Although the Dutch did not match the Spanish or the English in their accumulation of land, the establishment of a second merchant enterprise, the Dutch West India Company, allowed them to dominate the African slave trade after 1621.

In constructing this new transoceanic trading empire in slaves and spices, the Dutch pioneered a new financial mechanism for investing in colonial enterprises: the joint-stock company. The Dutch East and West India Companies were early examples, raising cash by selling shares to individual investors whose liability was limited to the sum of their investment. These investors were not part of the company's management, but they were entitled to a proportionate share in the profits. Originally, the Dutch East India Company intended to pay off its investors within ten years, but when that period was up, it convinced the investors—who wanted to realize their profits immediately—to sell their shares on the open market. The creation of a market in shares, which we now call a stock market, was an innovation that spread quickly. Stock markets now control the world's economy.

The Struggle between England and Spain

Religious strife could spark civil war (as in France) or political rebellion (as in the Netherlands), as well as provoke warfare between sovereign states, as in the struggle between England and Spain. In this case, religious conflict was entangled with both dynastic claims and economic competition in the Atlantic world.

Map legend:
- United Netherlands
- Spanish Netherlands
- Bishopric of Cambray
- Bishopric of Liège

EUROPE

Area of detail.

AFRICA

0 50 100 Miles
0 50 100 Kilometers

• Lincoln

NORTH SEA

• Emden

GRONNINGEN

FRIESLAND

DRENTHE

HOLY

ENGLAND

Zuider Zee

• Lingen

Haarlem • Amsterdam

OVERIJSSEL

• St. Albans

Leiden • Utrecht • Zwölle

• Osnabrück

The Hague

Zutphen

• London

HOLLAND

GELDERLAND

Middelburg

CLEVES

• Münster

Vlissingen

UPPER GELDERLAND

• Dortmund

Ostend • Bruges

Antwerp

• Düsseldorf

Dunkirk •

Ghent

BRABANT

ROMAN

Calais •

FLANDERS

Leuvain

Cologne

ARTOIS

Brussels

Maastricht

• Bonn

Hesdin

Lille • Douai

Liège

Aachen

HAINAUT

LIMBURG

Arras •

NAMUR

JÜLICH

• Amiens

• Guise

Coblenz

Sedan

LUXEMBOURG

• Frankfurt

• Rouen

• Noyon

• Mainz

Seine R.

Rheims

• Trier

FRANCE

• Paris

Verdun

• Metz

EMPIRE

THE NETHERLANDS AFTER 1609. ▪ *What were the two main divisions of the Netherlands?* ▪ *Which was Protestant and which was Catholic?* ▪ *How could William of Orange and his allies use the geography of the northern Netherlands against the Spanish?*

---

these measures created the deep ethnic and religious conflicts that still trouble the island today.

England's conflict with Spain, meanwhile, was worsened by the fact that English economic interests were directly opposed to those of Spain. English traders were making steady inroads into Spanish commercial networks in the Atlantic, as English sea captains such as Sir Francis Drake and Sir John Hawkins plundered Spanish vessels on the high seas. In a particularly dramatic exploit lasting from 1577 to 1580, prevailing winds and a lust for booty propelled Drake all the way around the world, to return with stolen Spanish treasure worth twice as much as Queen Elizabeth's annual revenue.

After suffering numerous such attacks over a period of two decades—and after Elizabeth's government openly supported the Dutch rebellion against Spain in 1585—King Philip finally resolved to fight back. In 1588, he dispatched an enormous fleet, confidently called the "Invincible Armada," whose mission was to invade England. But the invasion never occurred: after an indecisive initial encounter between the two fleets, a fierce storm—hailed as a "Protestant wind" by the lucky English—drove the Spanish galleons off course, leaving many of them wrecked off the coast of Ireland. The shattered flotilla eventually limped home with almost half its ships lost after a disastrous circumnavigation of the British Isles. Meanwhile, Elizabeth took credit for her country's miraculous escape. In subsequent years, continued threats from Spain and sporadic skirmishes nurtured a renewed sense of English nationalism and fueled anti-Catholic sentiment in that realm.

England's Colonial Ambitions

During the early decades of the seventeenth century, the English challenge to Spanish supremacy in the Atlantic began to bear fruit. Unlike New Spain, England's North American colonies had no significant mineral wealth; instead, as we noted on pages 459–462, English colonists sought to profit from the establishment of large-scale agricultural settlements in North America and the Caribbean. The first permanent colony was founded at Jamestown, Virginia, in 1607. Although this settlement was not particularly successful, more than twenty autonomous settlements were planted over the next forty years by a total of about 80,000 English immigrants.

Many of the colonists were motivated by a desire for religious freedom—hence the name we still give to the Pilgrims who landed at Plymouth, Massachusetts, in 1620. These radical Calvinists, known as Puritans, were also political dissidents, so they were almost as unwelcome as Catholics in

The dynastic competition came from the English royal family's division along confessional lines. The Catholic queen Mary (r. 1553–1558), eldest daughter of Henry VIII and granddaughter of Ferdinand and Isabella of Spain (Chapter 13), had married her cousin Philip II of Spain in 1554, and she ruled at a time of great strife between Catholics and Protestants in England. After Mary's death, her Protestant half sister Elizabeth (r. 1558–1603) came to the throne, and relations with Spain rapidly declined. They declined further when Catholic Ireland—an English colony—rose in rebellion in 1569, with Spain quietly supporting the Irish. Although it took almost thirty bloody years, English forces eventually suppressed the rebellion. Elizabeth then cemented the Irish defeat by encouraging intense colonial settlement in Ireland. Somewhat ironically, she did so in conscious imitation of Spanish policy in the Americas, sending thousands of Protestant English settlers to occupy land in Ireland in the hope of creating a colonial state with a largely English identity. Instead,

THE DUTCH EAST INDIA COMPANY WAREHOUSE AND TIMBER WHARF AT AMSTERDAM. The substantial warehouse, the stockpiles of lumber, and the company ship under construction in the foreground illustrate the degree to which overseas commerce could stimulate the economy of the mother country.

THE "ARMADA PORTRAIT" OF ELIZABETH. This is one of several royal portraits that commemorated the defeat of the Spanish Armada in 1588. Through the window on the left, an English flotilla sails serenely on sunny seas; on the right, Spanish ships are wrecked by a "Protestant wind." Elizabeth's right hand rests protectively—and commandingly—on the globe. ■ *How would you interpret this image?*

England, where the church was an extension of the monarchy. English colonists, however, showed little interest in trying to convert Native American peoples to Christianity. Missionizing played a much larger role in Spanish efforts to colonize Central and South America, and in French efforts to penetrate the North American hinterlands.

Another difference between Spanish and English colonialism is the fact that these English colonies did not begin as royal enterprises. They were private ventures, farmed either by individual landholders (as in Maryland and Pennsylvania) or managed by joint-stock companies (as in Virginia and the Massachusetts Bay Colony). Building on their experience in Ireland, where colonies had been called "plantations," many English settlers established plantations (planned communities) that attempted to replicate as many features of English life as possible. Geography largely dictated the locations of these English settlements, which were established along the northeast Atlantic coast and on rivers and bays that provided good harbors. Aside from the Hudson, there were no great rivers to lead colonists far inland, so the English colonies clung to the coastline and to each other. The densely populated corridor along the Atlantic seaboard today is a direct result of these early settlement patterns.

Because most land in the Old World was owned by royal and aristocratic families, the accumulation of wealth through the control of land was a new and exciting prospect for small- and medium-scale landholders in the new English colonies. This helps to explain the colonies' rural, agricultural character—in contrast to the great cities of New Spain. But this focus on agricultural holdings was also due to the demographic catastrophe that had decimated native populations in this region, as in so many others. By the early seventeenth century, a great deal of rich land had been abandoned by Native American farmers simply because there were so few of them to

PLIMOTH PLANTATION. An English settlement was established at Plimoth (now Plymouth) in the Massachusetts Bay Colony in 1620. This image shows a reconstruction of the village as it might have looked in 1627. Although speculative, this reconstruction captures the plantation's diminutive fragility and isolation.

that had felt the first divisive effects of the Reformation (Chapter 13). Not only was this period of warfare one of the longest in European history, it was one of the bloodiest and most widespread, engulfing most of the Continent before it ended thirty years later, in 1648. Although it began as a religious conflict, it quickly became an international struggle for dominance in which these initial provocations were all but forgotten. In the end, some 8 million people died, and entire regions were devastated by the rapacity of crisscrossing armies. The populations of several regions never recovered, and most of the great powers that fought the war were impoverished and weakened—with the exception of France, which emerged as the preeminent power in Europe.

till it. As a result, indigenous peoples who had not already succumbed to European diseases were now under threat from colonists who wanted complete and exclusive control over these lands.

To this end, the English soon set out to eliminate, through expulsion and massacre, the former inhabitants of the region. There were a few exceptions, such as in the Quaker colony of Pennsylvania, where colonists and Native Americans maintained friendly relations for more than half a century. In the Carolinas, by contrast, there was widespread enslavement of native peoples, either for sale to the West Indies or for work on the rice plantations along the coast. In another contrast to the Spanish and French colonies, intermarriage between English colonists and native populations was rare, creating a nearly unbridgeable racial divide in these North American colonies.

THE THIRTY YEARS' WAR AND ITS OUTCOMES

With the promulgation of the French Edict of Nantes in 1598, the end of open hostilities between England and Spain in 1604, and the truce between Spain and the Dutch Republic in 1609, religious warfare in Europe came briefly to an end. In 1618, however, a new series of wars broke out in central Europe, in some of the German-speaking lands

The Beginnings of the Thirty Years' War and the Downfall of Bohemia

Like the number and variety of the combatants involved, the causes of the **Thirty Years' War** are complicated. On one level, it was an outlet for deeper aggressions and tensions that had been building up since the Peace of Augsburg in 1555. On another level, it grew out of longer-standing disputes among rulers and territories in the patchwork of provinces that made up the Holy Roman Empire: disputes into which allied powers were drawn. On still another level, it was an opportunity for players on the fringes of power to rise to prominence.

The catalyst came in 1618, when the Austrian Habsburg (Catholic) prince Ferdinand, who also ruled Hungary and the united Polish-Lithuanian Commonwealth, was named heir to the throne of Protestant Bohemia. This prompted a rebellion among the Bohemian aristocracy. A year later, the complex dynastic politics of central Europe also resulted in Ferdinand's election as Holy Roman Emperor, a title that gave him access to an imperial (Catholic) army, which he sent to crush the Protestant revolt. The Bohemians, meanwhile, were bolstered by the support of some Austrian nobility—many of whom were also Protestant—who saw a way to recover power from the Habsburg ruling family.

In 1620, the war escalated further when the Ottomans threw their support behind the Protestants and, in so doing, touched off a war with staunchly Catholic Poland

Analyzing Primary Sources

The Devastation of the Thirty Years' War

The author of the following excerpt, Hans Jakob Christoffel von Grimmelshausen (GRIM-mill-show-sen; 1621–1676), barely survived the horrors of the Thirty Years' War. His parents were killed, probably when he was thirteen years old, and he himself was kidnapped the following year and forced into the army. By age fifteen, he was a soldier. His darkly satiric masterpiece, Simplicissimus *("The Simpleton"), drew heavily on these experiences and, although technically a fictional memoir, portrays with brutal accuracy the terrible realities of this era.*

lthough it was not my intention to take the peaceloving reader with these troopers to my dad's house and farm, seeing that matters will go ill therein, yet the course of my history demands that I should leave to kind posterity an account of what manner of cruelties were now and again practised in this our German war: yes, and moreover testify by my own example that such evils must often have been sent to us by the goodness of Almighty God for our profit. For, gentle reader, who would ever have taught me that there was a God in Heaven if these soldiers had not destroyed my dad's house, and by such a deed driven me out among folk who gave me all fitting instruction thereupon? . . .

The first thing these troopers did was, that they stabled their horses: thereafter each fell to his appointed task: which task was neither more nor less than ruin and destruction. For though some began to slaughter and to boil and to roast so that it looked as if there should be a merry banquet forward, yet others there were who did but storm through the house above and below stairs. Others stowed together great parcels of cloth and apparel and all manner of household stuff, as if they would set up a frippery market. All that

they had no mind to take with them they cut in pieces. Some thrust their swords through the hay and straw as if they had not enough sheep and swine to slaughter: and some shook the feathers out of the beds and in their stead stuffed in bacon and other dried meat and provisions as if such were better and softer to sleep upon. Others broke the stove and the windows as if they had a never-ending summer to promise. Houseware of copper and tin they beat flat, and packed such vessels, all bent and spoiled, in with the rest. Bedsteads, tables, chairs, and benches they burned, though there lay many cords of dry wood in the yard. Pots and pipkins must all go to pieces, either because they would eat none but roast flesh, or because their purpose was to make there but a single meal.

Our maid was so handled in the stable that she could not come out, which is a shame to tell of. Our man they laid bound upon the ground, thrust a gag into his mouth, and poured a pailful of filthy water into his body: and by this, which they called a Swedish draught, they forced him to lead a party of them to another place where they captured men and beasts, and brought them back to our farm, in which company were my dad, my mother, and our Ursula.

And now they began: first to take the flints out of their pistols and in place

of them to jam the peasants' thumbs in and so to torture the poor rogues as if they had been about the burning of witches: for one of them they had taken they thrust into the baking oven and there lit a fire under him, although he had as yet confessed no crime: as for another, they put a cord round his head and so twisted it tight with a piece of wood that the blood gushed from his mouth and nose and ears. In a word each had his own device to torture the peasants, and each peasant his several tortures.

Source: Hans Jakob Christoph von Grimmelshausen, *Simplicissimus,* trans. S. Goodrich (New York: 1995), pp. 1–3, 8–10, 32–35.

Questions for Analysis

1. The first-person narrator here recounts the atrocities committed "in this our German war," in which both perpetrators and victims are German. How believable is this description? What lends it credibility?

2. Why would Grimmelshausen have chosen to publish his account as a satirical fiction rather than as a straightforward historical narrative or an autobiography? How would this choice have affected readers' response to scenes such as he describes?

Map labels (clockwise / by region):

Volga R. · RUSSIA

SWEDEN · INGRIA · ESTONIA · LIVONIA · Volga R. · Volga R.

NORWAY · Christiana · Stockholm · BALTIC SEA · DENMARK · Copenhagen

POLAND · Kiev · Warsaw · Danzig

EAST PRUSSIA · BRANDENBURG · Berlin · MECKLEN-BURG · Hamburg · HANOVER · SAXONY · HOLY ROMAN EMPIRE · HESSE · BAVARIA · WÜRTTEM-BERG · LORRAINE · AUSTRIA · Vienna · HUNGARY · Budapest

BLACK SEA · OTTOMAN EMPIRE · Constantinople · AEGEAN SEA · CYPRUS (to Ottoman Empire) · CRETE (to Spain) · MEDITERRANEAN SEA

SCOTLAND · Edinburgh · NORTH SEA · IRELAND · Dublin · Liverpool · ENGLAND · London · English Channel · Amsterdam · UNITED NETHERLANDS · SPANISH NETH. · Rhine R. · Paris · FRANCE · Bordeaux

ATLANTIC OCEAN · SWISS CONFEDERATION · FRANCHE-COMTÉ · SAVOY · PIEDMONT · MILAN · GENOA · VENICE · (to Venice) · (to Venice) · Ragusa · Cattaro · Zara · ADRIATIC SEA · PAPAL STATES · FLORENCE · Rome · ITALY · Naples · KINGDOM OF THE TWO SICILIES

AVIGNON · Marseille · CORSICA (to Genoa) · SARDINIA (to Spain) · BALEARIC ISLANDS

PORTUGAL · Lisbon · CASTILE · Madrid · SPAIN · ARAGON · Strait of Gibraltar

Danube R. · Rhine R.

Inset: EUROPE · Area of detail · AFRICA

Legend:

- Catholic Church
- Spain
- Austria
- Brandenburg–Prussia
- Boundary of the Holy Roman Empire

Scale: 500 Miles · 500 Kilometers · 250 · 250 · 0 · 0

EUROPE AT THE END OF THE THIRTY YEARS' WAR. This map shows the complex political checkerboard that resulted from the Peace of Westphalia in 1648. ▪ *When you compare this map with the one on page 433, what are the most significant territorial changes between c. 1526 and 1648?* ▪ *Which regions were weakened or endangered by this arrangement?* ▪ *Which were in a strong position to dominate Europe?*

whose borders the Muslim army needed to cross to get to Prague; the Poles won, and the Ottomans retreated. Meanwhile, Ferdinand's Habsburg cousin, the Spanish king and emperor Philip IV, had renewed his war against the Protestant Dutch Republic, which had won its independence from Catholic Spain in 1609—thus forming an alliance between the two Habsburg rulers. This led to a major pitched battle between united Protestant forces and the Spanish-led Catholic army (including the young French philosopher René Descartes) just outside of Prague. The Habsburgs were victorious, and the Czechs of Bohemia were forced to accept Ferdinand's Catholic rule. As a result, the kingdom of Bohemia, a powerful force in the region for centuries, and an early cradle of Protestant reform (Chapter 12) ceased to exist.

The Tangled Politics and Price of War

The conflict, which started in Bohemia, should have ended there. But it did not. Instead, like a terrible cancer, it metastasized. Unrest between Catholics and Protestants in other parts of central Europe erupted into war. French Catholics and Protestants, who had enjoyed relatively peaceful relations since the Edict of Nantes in 1598, came into violent contact once again. Protestant Denmark, fearing that Catholic victories in neighboring parts of the Holy Roman Empire might threaten its sovereignty, was drawn in and lost valuable territories before it was forced to concede defeat.

In this new phase of the Thirty Years' War, political expediency soon outweighed either religious or dynastic allegiances. When a confederation of Catholic princes seemed close to uprooting Protestantism throughout Germany in 1630, other German Catholic princes were willing to ally with Protestants in order to preserve their own autonomy. Joining them was the (Protestant) king of Sweden, Gustavus Adolphus (r. 1611–1632), who championed both the German Lutheran states and his own nation's sovereignty in the wake of Denmark's brush with disaster. Yet his Protestant army was secretly subsidized by Catholic France, which sought to avoid being surrounded by a strong Habsburg alliance on its northern, eastern, and southern borders.

Gustavus had become king at age seventeen and was one of the great military commanders of all time. Like another young general, Alexander the Great (Chapter 4), he was not only an expert tactician but also a charismatic leader. His army became the best-trained and best-equipped fighting force of the era—what some have called the first modern army. By the time Gustavus died in battle, in 1632, a month before his thirty-eighth birthday, Sweden had become a global power, rivaling Spain and Russia in size and prestige.

In 1635, with Gustavus dead, France was compelled to join Sweden in declaring war on the Spanish and Austrian Habsburgs. In the middle lay the German-speaking lands of central Europe, already weakened by seventeen years of war and now a helpless battleground. In the next thirteen years, Germany suffered more from warfare than at any other time until the twentieth century. Several cities were besieged and sacked nine or ten times over. Soldiers from all nations, who had to sustain themselves by plunder, gave no quarter to defenseless civilians. With plague and disease adding to the toll of outright butchery, some towns and rural areas were nearly eradicated. Most horrifying was the loss of life in the final four years of the war, when the carnage continued even after peace negotiators arrived at broad areas of agreement.

The Peace of Westphalia and the Decline of Spain

The eventual adoption of the Peace of Westphalia in 1648 was a watershed in European history. It marked the emergence of a new Swedish empire and the rise of France as the predominant power on the Continent, a position it would hold for the next two centuries. The greatest losers in the conflict (aside from the millions of victims) were the Austrian Habsburgs, who were forced to surrender all the territory they had gained and to abandon their hopes of using the office of Holy Roman Emperor to dominate central Europe.

The Spanish Habsburgs were also substantially weakened and no longer able to fall back on the wealth of their Atlantic empire. Large portions of the Atlantic trade had been infiltrated by merchants from other countries, and the expansion of local economies in Spain's colonies had made them less dependent on trade with Spain itself. In 1600, the Spanish Empire had been the mightiest power in the world; only a half century later, this empire had begun to fall apart.

As we've already noted, New Spain's great wealth had proven a liability when the infusion of silver spiked inflation and slowed economic development at home. Lacking both agricultural and mineral resources of its own, Spain could have developed its own industries and a balanced trading pattern, as some of its Atlantic rivals were doing. But instead, it used imperial silver to buy manufactured goods from other parts of Europe, offering no incentives to develop exports of its own. So when the river of silver began to abate, Spain was plunged into debt.

Meanwhile, the Spanish crown's commitment to supporting the Catholic Church plunged it into costly wars, as

THE BATTLE OF ROCROI, 1643. Spain's defeat by the French at Rocroi was the first time a Spanish army had lost a land battle since the reign of Ferdinand and Isabella (Chapter 12), and it was yet another contributing factor to the decline of Spanish power during the Thirty Years' War. This painting shows the victorious French general, the Duke d'Enghien, surveying the battlefield from afar.

did attempts to maintain Spain's international dominance. Involvement in the Thirty Years' War was the last straw. The strains of warfare drove the kingdom, with its power base in Castile, to raise more money and soldiers from the other Iberian provinces, leading to revolts first in Catalonia and then Portugal (incorporated into Spain in 1580), followed by the southern Italians, who rebelled against their Castilian viceroys in Naples and Sicily. It was only by chance that Spain's greatest external enemies, France and England, could not act to take advantage of its plight, giving the Castilian-based government time to put down the Italian revolts. By 1652, it had also brought Catalonia to heel, but Portugal regained its independence. After the Peace of Westphalia, Spain remained isolated, weakened, and without European allies.

The Swedish Empire and the Invasion of Poland-Lithuania

In the decades after 1648, the power of Sweden continued to rise and ultimately threatened the once great power of Poland-Lithuania. As noted on page 473, Gustavus

Adolphus had created a mighty and disciplined Swedish army, and in the course of the Thirty Years' War, Sweden had colonized the Baltic. But a richer prize lay to the south: the wealthy Polish-Lithuanian Commonwealth, with its prosperous commercial centers, rich agricultural lands, and mineral deposits. As Sweden's fortunes rose, Poland-Lithuania was in conflict with Russia for dominance of the vast territory of Ukraine, while also struggling to put down rebellions by Cossacks and Ukrainian peasants dwelling along its eastern borders. Moreover, the reigning king John II Casimir (r. 1648–1668) was unpopular with many factions within the Polish aristocracy, some of whom urged Charles Gustav of Sweden, the king's cousin, to claim the Polish crown.

In the summer of 1655, two Swedish armies marched into Poland from the north, supported by forces from Transylvania and Brandenburg-Prussia. Over the next five years, the formerly peaceful commonwealth suffered losses nearly as devastating as those of World War II (see Chapter 26), fighting on multiple fronts with only shaky support from its allies and more harm than help from the Russians. By 1660, when a peace treaty was negotiated, the capital of Warsaw had been destroyed, cities looted or torched, castles razed, and churches desecrated.

The Emergence of French Power in Europe and North America

France emerged from the crisis of the Thirty Years' War with a stronger state, more dynamic economy, and increased influence abroad. Like Spain, France had grown over the course of the previous centuries by absorbing formerly independent principalities whose inhabitants cherished traditions of local independence and were not always willing to cooperate with the royal government. The fact that France became more powerful as a result of this process, whereas Spain did not, can be attributed in part to France's more significant natural resources and in part to the greater prestige of the French monarchy, which can be traced back to the rule of Louis IX (later canonized as Saint Louis; Chapter 10). Most subjects of the French king, including the Protestants whose welfare had been cultivated by Henry IV, were loyal to the crown. Moreover, France had enormous economic resiliency, owing primarily to its rich and varied agricultural productivity. Unlike Spain, which had to import food, France was able to feed itself. Furthermore, Henry IV's ministers had financed the construction of roads, bridges, and canals to facilitate the flow of goods, supporting royal factories that manufactured luxury goods such as crystal, glass, and tapestries. Henry also supported the production of silk, linen, and wool throughout the kingdom.

Henry's patronage had enabled the explorer Samuel de Champlain to claim parts of Canada as France's first foothold in the New World. In 1608, Champlain founded the colony of Québec in the Saint Lawrence River Valley. Whereas the English initially limited their colonial settlements to regions along the Atlantic coastline, the French set out to dominate the interior of the North American continent. French traders ranged far up and down the few Canadian rivers that led inland, exchanging furs and goods with the Native American groups they encountered; French missionaries, meanwhile, used the same arteries to spread Catholic Christianity from Québec to Louisiana. Eventually, French imperial ventures spread via the Great Lakes and the great river systems along the Mississippi to the prairies of America's Midwest.

These far-flung French colonies were established and administered as royal enterprises, like those of Spain, a fact that distinguished them from the private commercial ventures put together by the English and the Dutch. Also, like New Spain, the colonies of New France were overwhelmingly populated by men. The elite of French colonial society were military officers and administrators sent from Paris; below their ranks were fishermen, fur traders, small farmers, and common soldiers, who constituted the bulk of French settlers in North America. Because the fishing and fur trades relied on cooperative relationships with native peoples, a mutual economic interdependence grew up between the French colonists and the peoples of surrounding regions; and intermarriage between French traders and native women was common.

Yet in contrast to both Spanish and English colonies, these French colonies remained dependent on the wages and supplies sent to them from the mother country; only rarely did they become truly self-sustaining economic enterprises. Indeed, their financial rewards were modest: only furs, fish, and tobacco were exported to European markets. It was not until the late seventeenth century that some French colonies began to realize large profits by establishing sugar plantations on the Caribbean islands of Hispaniola (the French portion of this large island, now Haiti, was known as Saint-Domingue), Guadeloupe, and Martinique. By 1750, on Saint-Domingue, 500,000 slaves were laboring under extraordinarily harsh conditions to produce 40 percent of the world's sugar and 50 percent of its coffee (see Chapter 15).

ILLINOIS INDIANS TRADING WITH FRENCH SETTLERS. This engraving from Nicolas de Fer's 1705 map of the Western Hemisphere illustrates the economic interdependence that developed between the early French colonists and the native peoples of the surrounding region. ▪ *How did this situation differ from relations between Native Americans and English agricultural communities on the Atlantic coast?*

Cardinal Richelieu on the Common People of France

Armand Jean du Plessis, duke of Richelieu and cardinal of the Roman Catholic Church, was the effective ruler of France from 1624 until his death in 1642. His Political Testament was assembled after his death from historical sketches and from memoranda of advice he had prepared for King Louis XIII, the ineffectual monarch whom he served. This book was eventually published in 1688, during the reign of Louis XIV.

 ll students of politics agree that when the common people are too well off it is impossible to keep them peaceable. The explanation for this is that they are less well informed than the members of the other orders in the state, who are much more cultivated and enlightened, and so if not preoccupied with the search for the necessities of existence, find it difficult to remain within the limits imposed by both common sense and the law.

It would not be sound to relieve them of all taxation and similar charges, since in such a case they would lose the mark of their subjection and consequently the awareness of their station. Thus being free from paying tribute, they would consider themselves exempted from obedience. One should compare them with mules, which being accustomed to work, suffer more when long idle than when kept busy. But just as this work should be reasonable, with the burdens placed upon these animals proportionate to their strength, so it is likewise with the burdens placed upon the people. If they are not moderate, even when put to good public use, they are certainly unjust. I realize that when a king undertakes a program of public works it is correct to say that what the people gain from it is returned by paying the *taille* [a heavy tax imposed on the peasantry]. In the same fashion it can be maintained that what a king takes from the people [he] returns to them, and that they advance it to him only to draw upon it for the enjoyment of their leisure and their investments, which would be impossible if they did not contribute to the support of the state.

Source: *The Political Testament of Cardinal Richelieu*, trans. Henry Bertram Hill (Madison, WI: 1961), pp. 31–32.

Questions for Analysis

1. According to Cardinal Richelieu, why should the state work to subjugate the common people? What assumptions about the nature and status of "common people" underlie this argument?

2. What theory of the state emerges from this argument? According to Richelieu, what is the relationship between the king and the state and between the king and the people?

The Policies of Cardinal Richelieu

This expansion of French power can be credited, in part, to Henry IV's de facto successor: Armand Jean du Plessis, **Cardinal Richelieu** (*REESH-eh-lyuh*). The real king of France, Henry's son Louis XIII (r. 1610–1643), had come to the throne at the age of nine. Richelieu, as his chief minister of state, dominated his reign. His chief aim was to centralize royal bureaucracy while exploiting opportunities to foster French influence abroad.

Within France, Richelieu amended the Edict of Nantes so that it no longer supported the military and political rights of the Huguenots. He also prohibited these French Protestants from settling in Québec. Yet considering that he owed his political power (in part) to his ecclesiastical position in the Catholic Church, the fact that he allowed the edict to stand at all reflects his larger interest in fostering a sense of French national identity that centered on the monarchy. In keeping with this policy, he imposed direct taxation on powerful provinces that had retained their financial autonomy before then. Later, to make sure taxes were efficiently collected, Richelieu instituted a new system of local government that empowered royal officials to put down provincial resistance.

These policies made the French royal government more powerful than any in Europe. It also doubled the crown's income, allowing France to engage in the Thirty Years' War, which expanded its power on the Continent. But this increased centralization of royal authority also provoked challenges from aristocratic elites in the years after Richelieu's death—eventually, leading to the French Revolution (see Chapter 18).

The Challenge of the Fronde

A more immediate response to Richelieu's policies was a series of uncoordinated revolts known collectively as the *Fronde* (from the French word for a sling used to hurl stones). In 1643, just after the death of Richelieu, Louis XIII was succeeded by his five-year-old son, Louis XIV. The young king's regents were his mother, Anne of Austria, and her alleged lover, Cardinal Jules Raymond Mazarin. Both were foreigners—Anne was a Habsburg and Mazarin was an Italian by birth—and both were despised by many extremely powerful nobles. The nobles also hated the way that Richelieu's government had curtailed their authority in their own ancestral provinces. Popular resentments were aroused as well, because the costs of the ongoing Thirty Years' War were now combined with several consecutive years of bad harvests. So when cliques of nobles expressed their disgust for Mazarin, they found much popular support.

In 1648, the levy of a new tax had protesters on the streets of Paris, armed with slings and projectiles. However, neither the aristocratic leaders of the Fronde nor the commoners who joined them claimed to be resisting the young king; their targets were the corruption and mismanagement of Mazarin. Some of the rebels insisted that part of Mazarin's fault lay in his pursuit of Richelieu's centralizing policy, but most aristocrats wanted to become part of this centralizing process. Years later, when Louis XIV began to rule in his own right in 1651, the memory of these early turbulent years haunted him, and he resolved never to let the aristocracy or their provinces get out of hand. With this aim, he became the most effective absolute monarch in Europe (see Chapter 15).

THE CRISIS OF KINGSHIP IN ENGLAND

Of all the crises that shook Europe in this era, the most radical in its consequences was the English Civil War. The causes of this conflict were similar to those that had sparked trouble in other countries: hostilities among the component parts of a composite kingdom, religious animosities between Catholics and Protestants, struggles for power among competing factions of aristocrats at court, and a fiscal system that could not keep pace with the increasing costs of government, much less those of war. But in England, these developments led to the unprecedented criminal trial and execution of a king, an event that sent shock waves throughout Europe and the Atlantic world.

The Origins of the Civil War

The chain of events that led to a civil war in England can be traced to the last decades of Queen Elizabeth's reign. The expenses of England's defense against Spain, rebellion in Ireland, widespread crop failures, and the inadequacies of the antiquated English taxation system drove the queen's government deeply into debt. In 1603, when Elizabeth was succeeded by her cousin, James Stuart—King James VI of Scotland, James I of England—bitter factional disputes at court were complicated by the financial crisis. When the English Parliament rejected James's demands for more taxes, he raised what revenues he could without parliamentary approval, imposing new tolls and selling trading monopolies to favored courtiers. These measures aroused resentment against the king and made voluntary grants of taxation from Parliament even less likely.

James also struggled with religious divisions among his subjects. His own kingdom of Scotland had been firmly Calvinist since the 1560s. England, too, was Protestant—but of a very different kind, because the Church of England retained many of the rituals, hierarchies, and doctrines of the medieval Church (Chapter 13). Indeed, a significant number of English Protestants, the Puritans, wanted to bring this church more firmly into line with Calvinist principles. Although James was largely successful in mediating these conflicts, he stirred up trouble in staunchly Catholic Ireland by encouraging thousands of Scottish Calvinists to settle in the northern Irish province of Ulster. In doing so, he exacerbated a situation that had already become violent under Elizabeth.

Parliament versus the King

English politics became more volatile in 1625, when James was succeeded by his surviving son, **Charles**. Charles alarmed his Protestant subjects by marrying the Catholic sister of France's Louis XIII; he then launched a new war with Spain, straining his already slender financial

CHARLES I. King Charles I of England was a connoisseur of the arts and a patron of artists. He was adept at using portraiture to convey the magnificence of his tastes and the grandeur of his conception of kingship. ▪ *How does this portrait by Anthony van Dyck compare to the engravings of the "martyred" king in Interpreting Visual Evidence on page 482?*

To meet the Scottish threat, Charles was forced to summon Parliament, whose members were determined to impose radical reforms on the king's government before they would consider granting him funds to raise an army. The Scottish Calvinists even found support among some Puritans in Parliament. To avoid dealing with this difficult political situation, Charles tried to arrest Parliament's leaders and force his own agenda. When this failed, he withdrew from London to raise his own army. Parliament responded by mustering a separate military force and voting itself the taxation to pay for it. By the end of 1642, open warfare had erupted between the English king and the English government: something that was inconceivable in neighboring France, where the king and the government were inseparable.

Arrayed on the king's side were most of England's aristocrats and largest landowners, many of whom owned lands in the Atlantic colonies as well. The parliamentary forces were made up of smaller landholders, tradesmen, and artisans, many of whom were Puritan sympathizers. The king's royalist supporters were commonly known by their aristocratic name of Cavaliers. They derisively called their opponents, who cut their hair short in contempt for the fashionable custom of wearing long curls, Roundheads. After 1644, when the parliamentary army was effectively reorganized, the royalist forces were badly beaten; and in 1646, the king was compelled to surrender. Soon thereafter, the episcopal hierarchy of the Church of England was abolished and a Calvinist-style church was mandated throughout England and Wales.

The struggle might have ended here had not a quarrel developed within the parliamentary party. The majority of its members were ready to restore Charles to the throne as a limited monarch, under an arrangement whereby a uniformly Calvinist faith would be imposed on both Scotland and England as the state religion. But a radical minority of Puritans, commonly known as Independents, insisted on religious freedom for themselves and all other Protestants. Their leader was Oliver Cromwell (1599–1658), who had risen to command the Roundhead army, which he reconstituted as the "New Model Army."

The Fall of Charles Stuart and the Establishment of Oliver Cromwell's Commonwealth

Taking advantage of the dissension within the ranks of his opponents, Charles renewed the war in 1648. But he was forced to surrender after a brief campaign, and Cromwell

resources. When Parliament refused to grant him funds, he demanded forced loans from his subjects and punished those who refused by lodging soldiers in their homes and imprisoning others without trial. Parliament responded in 1628 by imposing the Petition of Right, which declared that taxes not voted on by Parliament were illegal, condemned arbitrary imprisonment, and prohibited the quartering of soldiers in private houses.

Thereafter, Charles tried to rule England without Parliament—something that had not been attempted since the establishment of that body 400 years earlier (Chapter 9). He also ran into trouble with his Calvinist subjects in Scotland because he began to favor the most Catholic-leaning elements in the English Church. The Scots rebelled in 1640, and a Scottish army marched south into England to demand the withdrawal of Charles's "Catholicizing" measures.

OLIVER CROMWELL AS PROTECTOR OF THE COMMON-WEALTH. This coin, minted in 1658, shows the Lord Protector wreathed with laurel garlands like a classical hero or a Roman consul. It also proclaims him to be "by the Grace of God Protector of the Commonwealth." ■ *What mixed messages does this imagery convey?*

seized control of the government. To ensure that the Puritan agenda would be carried out, Cromwell ejected all the moderates from Parliament by force. This "Rump" (remaining) Parliament then proceeded to put the king on trial and eventually to condemn him to death for treason against his own subjects.

Charles Stuart was publicly beheaded on January 30, 1649—marking the first time in history that a reigning king had been legally deposed and executed. Europeans reacted to his death with horror, astonishment, or rejoicing, depending on their political convictions (see **Interpreting Visual Evidence** on page 482). After the king's execution, his son—the future King Charles II—joined with the remaining royalist forces in an attempt to restore the monarchy. But he was defeated by Cromwell's army and fled to France.

With the heir to the English throne in exile, Cromwell and his supporters abolished Parliament's hereditary House of Lords and declared England a Commonwealth: an English translation of the Latin *res publica*. Technically, the Rump Parliament continued as the legislative body; but Cromwell, with the army at his command, possessed the real power. And he soon became exasperated by legislators' attempts to enrich themselves by confiscating their opponents' property. In 1653, he marched a detachment of troops into the Rump Parliament and disbanded it.

The short-lived Commonwealth was thus replaced by the "Protectorate," a thinly disguised autocracy established under a constitution drafted by officers of the army. Called the *Instrument of Government*, this text is the nearest approximation to a written constitution that England has ever had. Extensive powers were given to Cromwell as Lord Protector for life, and his office was made hereditary.

The Restoration of the Monarchy

Many intellectuals noted the similarities between these events and those that had given rise to the Principate of Augustus after the death of Julius Caesar (Chapter 5). Among the people, Cromwell's Puritan military dictatorship was growing unpopular, not least because it prohibited public recreation on Sundays and closed London's theaters. Many became nostalgic for the milder and more tolerant Church of England and began to hope for a restoration of the old royalist regime.

The opportunity came with Cromwell's death in 1658. His son Richard had no sooner succeeded to the office of Lord Protector when a faction within the army removed him from power. As groups of royalists plotted an uprising, a new Parliament was organized. In April 1660, it declared that King Charles II had been the ruler of England since his father's execution in 1649. Almost overnight, England became a monarchy again.

Charles II (r. 1660–1685) revived the Church of England but was careful not to return to the provocative policies of his father. Quipping that he did not wish to "resume his travels," he agreed to respect Parliament and to observe the Petition of Right that had so enraged Charles I. He also accepted all the legislation passed by Parliament immediately before the outbreak of civil war in 1642, including the requirement that Parliament be summoned at least once every three years. England thus emerged from its civil war as a limited monarchy, in which power was exercised by "the king in Parliament." It remains a constitutional monarchy to this day.

The English Civil War and the Atlantic World

These tumultuous events had a significant influence on the development of a new political sensibility within England's Atlantic colonies. The English landed aristocracy had sided

Debating the English Civil War

The English Civil War raised fundamental questions about political rights and responsibilities, many of which are addressed in the two excerpts below. The first comes from a lengthy debate held within the General Council of Cromwell's army in October 1647. The second is taken from the speech given by King Charles I, moments before his execution in 1649.

The Army Debates, 1647

Colonel Rainsborough: Really, I think that the poorest man that is in England has a life to live as the greatest man, and therefore truly, sir, I think it's clear, that every man that is to live under a government ought first by his own consent to put himself under that government, and I do think that the poorest man in England is not at all bound in a strict sense to that government that he has not had a voice to put himself under . . . insomuch that I should doubt whether I was an Englishman or not, that should doubt of these things.

General Ireton: Give me leave to tell you, that if you make this the rule, I think you must fly for refuge to an absolute natural right, and you must deny all civil rights, and I am sure it will come to that in the consequence. . . . For my part, I think it is no right at all. I think that no person has a right to an interest or share in the disposing of the affairs of the kingdom, and in determining or choosing those that shall determine what laws we shall be ruled by here, no person has a right to this that has not a permanent fixed interest in this kingdom, and those persons together are properly the represented of this kingdom who, taken together, and consequently are to make up the representers of this kingdom. . . .

We talk of birthright. Truly, birthright there is. . . . [M]en may justly have by birthright, by their very being born in England, that we should not seclude them out of England. That we should not refuse to give them air and place and ground, and the freedom of the highways and other things, to live amongst us, not any man that is born here, though he in birth or by his birth there come nothing at all that is part of the permanent interest of this kingdom to him. That I think is due to a man by birth. But that by a man's being born here he shall have a share in that power that shall dispose of the lands here, and of all things here, I do not think it is a sufficient ground.

Source: David Wootton, ed., *Divine Right and Democracy: An Anthology of Political Writing in Stuart England* (New York: 1986), pp. 286–87 (language modernized).

with the king during this conflict, but many in the colonies had sympathized with Parliament and its claims to protect the liberties of small landowners who bore a disproportionate share of taxation. Even after the Restoration of the monarchy in 1660, many colonial leaders maintained an antimonarchist and antiaristocratic bias.

The fact that the government had been almost entirely concerned with the business of putting down rebellion meant that England's colonies had also become used to a large degree of independence at an early stage. As a result, once the monarchy was restored, all of Parliament's efforts to extend more control over the colonies caused greater and greater friction (see Chapter 15). Slogans declaring the rights of "free-born Englishmen" would echo among farmers, and "free trade" became a rallying cry against royal interference in colonial commerce. The bitter religious conflicts that had divided the more radical Puritans from the Church of England also forced the colonies to come to grips with the problem of religious diversity. Some, like Massachusetts, took the opportunity to impose their own brand of Puritanism on settlers, while others experimented with forms of religious toleration that sometimes went beyond the forms of religious freedom that existed back in England.

Paradoxically, though, the spread of ideas about the protection of liberties and citizens' rights coincided with a rapid and considerable expansion of unfree labor in the

Charles I on the Scaffold, 1649

I think it is my duty, to God first, and to my country, for to clear myself both as an honest man, a good king, and a good Christian.

I shall begin first with my innocence. In truth I think it not very needful for me to insist long upon this, for all the world knows that I never did begin a war with the two Houses of Parliament, and I call God to witness, to whom I must shortly make an account, that I never did intend to incroach upon their privileges. . . .

As for the people—truly I desire their liberty and freedom as much as anybody whatsoever. But I must tell you that their liberty and freedom consists in having of government those laws by which their lives and goods may be most their own. It is not for having share in government. That is nothing pertaining to them. A subject and a sovereign are clean different things, and therefore, until they do

that—I mean that you do put the people in that liberty as I say—certainly they will never enjoy themselves.

Sirs, it was for this that now I am come here. If I would have given way to an arbitrary way, for to have all laws changed according to the power of the sword, I needed not to have come here. And therefore I tell you (and I pray God it be not laid to your charge) that I am the martyr of the people.

Source: Brian Tierney, Donald Kagan, and L. Pearce Williams, eds., *Great Issues in Western Civilization* (New York: 1967), pp. 46–47.

Questions for Analysis

1. What fundamental issues are at stake in both excerpts? How do the debaters within the parliamentary army (first excerpt) define "natural" and "civil" rights?

2. How does Charles defend his position? What is his theory of kingship? How does it compare with that of Cardinal Richelieu (see page 476)? How does it conflict with the ideas expressed in the army's debate?

3. It is interesting that none of the participants in these debates seems to have recognized the implications that their arguments might have for the political rights of women. Why would that have been the case?

---

colonies. Prior to the 1640s, the English colonies in North America and the Caribbean had been assured of a steady stream of immigrants, such as the Puritan Pilgrims of Massachusetts in 1620. The outbreak of civil war in 1642, and the subsequent triumph of the Puritans under Cromwell, caused a drop in this migration, because many who might have thought about emigrating decided to stay in England. In North America, the decline in the arrival of new settlers was so sudden that it caused a depression in local economies.

Meanwhile, the demand for labor was increasing rapidly owing to the expansion of tobacco plantations in Virginia and sugar plantations in Barbados and Jamaica,

which the British captured from the Spanish in 1655. These plantations, with their punishing working conditions and high mortality rates from disease, were insatiable in their demand for workers. Plantation owners thus sought to meet this demand by investing ever more heavily in forms of unfree labor, including indentured servants and African slaves. The social and political crisis unleashed by the English Civil War also led to the forced migration of paupers and political prisoners, especially from Scotland, Wales, and Ireland: a pattern that continued during Cromwell's reign.

These immigrants, many without resources, swelled the ranks of the unfree and the very poor in England's

Interpreting Visual Evidence

The Execution of a King

 his allegorical engraving (image A) accompanied a pamphlet called *Eikon Basilike* ("The Kingly Image"), which began to circulate in Britain just weeks after the execution of King Charles I. It was purported to be an autobiographical account of the king's last days, and a justification of his royal policies. It was intended to arouse widespread sympathy for the king and his exiled heir, Charles II; and it succeeded admirably, as the cult of Charles "King and Martyr" became increasingly popular. Here, the Latin inscription on the shaft of light suggests that Charles's piety will beam "brighter through the shadows," while the scrolls on the left proclaim "virtue grows beneath weight" and "unmoved, triumphant." Charles's earthly crown (on the floor at his side) is "splendid and heavy," whereas the crown of thorns he grasps is "bitter and light"; this heavenly crown is "blessed and eternal." Even people who could not read these and the other Latin mottoes would have known that Charles's last words were: "I shall go from a corruptible to an incorruptible Crown, where no disturbance can be."

At the same time, broadsides showing the moment of execution (image B) circulated in various European countries with explanatory captions. This one was printed in Germany, with almost identical versions surviving from the Netherlands. It shows members of the crowd fainting and turning away at the sight of blood spurting from the king's neck while the executioner holds up the severed head.

Questions for Analysis

1. How would you interpret the message of image A? How might it have been read differently by Catholics and Protestants within Britain and Europe?

2. What might have been the political motives underlying the publication and display of these images? For example, would you expect the depiction of the king's execution to be supportive of monarchy or antiroyalist? Why?

3. Given what you have learned about the political and religious divisions in Europe at the time of the king's execution, where do you think image A would have found the most sympathetic audiences? Why might it be significant that image B circulated more widely in Germany and the Netherlands than in France or Spain?

A. King Charles I as a martyr.

B. The execution of King Charles I.

Atlantic colonies. As earlier arrivals sought to distance themselves from more recent immigrants, whom they regarded as inferior, this spurred the formation of new social hierarchies. The crisis of kingship in England thus led to a substantial increase in the African slave trade and a sharpening of social and economic divisions in the English colonies.

AN AGE OF DOUBT AND THE ART OF BEING HUMAN

On the first day of November 1611, a new play by **William Shakespeare** premiered in London. *The Tempest* takes place on a remote island, where an exiled duke from the Italian city-state of Milan has used his magical arts to subjugate the island's inhabitants. The plot drew on reports from the new European colonies of the Atlantic, especially the Caribbean, where slaves were called Caribans—hence the name Shakespeare chose for the play's rebellious slave, Caliban, who seeks to take revenge on the magician Prospero, his oppressive master. When reminded that he owes his knowledge of the English language to the civilizing influence of Prospero's daughter, Miranda, Caliban retorts, "You taught me language, and my profit on't is, I know how to curse." According to Caliban, the benefits of a European education could not outweigh the evils of colonization—but could, in fact, be used to resist it. Shakespeare's audience was thus confronted with the spectacle of their own colonial ambitions gone awry.

The doubt and uncertainty caused by Europe's extension into the Atlantic world were primary themes and motivators of this era's creative arts, which both documented and critiqued contemporary trends while emphasizing the redemptive qualities of human suffering and compassion. Another example of this artistic response is the novel *Don Quixote*, which its author, Miguel de Cervantes (*sehr-VAHN-tehs*; 1547–1616), composed largely in prison. It recounts the adventures of an idealistic Spanish gentleman, Don Quixote of La Mancha, who becomes deranged by his constant reading of chivalric romances and sets out to have delusional adventures of his own. His sidekick, Sancho Panza, is his exact opposite: a plain, practical man content with modest bodily pleasures. Together, they represent different facets of human nature. On the one hand, *Don Quixote* is a devastating satire of Spain's decline. On the other, it is a sincere celebration of the human capacity for optimism and goodness.

Throughout the long century between 1550 and 1660, Europeans confronted a world in which all that they had once taken for granted was cast into confusion. Vast continents had been discovered, populated by millions of people whose very existence challenged Western civilizations' former parameters and Europeans' most basic assumptions. Not even religion seemed an adequate foundation on which to build new certainties, for European Christians now disagreed about the fundamental truths of their faith. Political allegiances were similarly under threat, as intellectuals and common people alike began to assert a right to resist princes with whom they disagreed. The very notions of morality and custom were beginning to seem arbitrary. There was a sometimes desperate search for new bases on which to construct some measure of certainty in the face of such challenges.

Witchcraft and the Power of the State

Contributing to the anxiety of the age was the widespread conviction that witchcraft was a new and increasing threat. Although the belief that certain individuals could heal or harm through the practice of magic was not new, it was not until the late fifteenth century that authorities began to insist that such powers could derive only from some kind of satanic bargain. In 1484, Pope Innocent VIII had ordered papal inquisitors to use all means at their disposal, including torture, to detect and eliminate witchcraft. Predictably, torture increased the number of accused witches who "confessed" to their alleged crimes; and as more accused witches "confessed," more witches were "discovered," tried, and executed—even in places such as England and Scotland, where torture was not legal and the Catholic Church had no influence. For both Luther and Calvin had urged that accused witches be tried and sentenced with less leniency than ordinary criminals.

When religious authorities' efforts to "detect" witchcraft were backed by the coercive powers of secular governments, the fear of witches escalated into persecutions. It was therefore through this fundamental agreement between Catholics and Protestants, with the complicity of secular states, that an early modern "**witch craze**" claimed tens of thousands of victims in this era. The final death toll will never be known, but we do know that the vast majority of the victims were women. In the 1620s, there were 100 burnings a year, on average, in the German cities of Würzburg and Bamberg; around the same time, it was said that the town square of Wolfenbüttel "looked like a little forest, so crowded were the stakes." When accusations of witchcraft diminished in Europe, they became endemic in some European colonies, as at the English settlement of Salem in the Massachusetts Bay Colony.

This hunt for witches resulted in part from fears that traditional religious remedies (prayer, the sacraments) were no longer adequate to guard against the evils of the world. It also reflected Europeans' growing conviction that only the state had the power to protect them. Even in Catholic countries, where witchcraft prosecutions began in Church courts, these cases were transferred to the state's courts for final judgment and punishment because Church courts could not carry out capital penalties. In most Protestant countries, the entire process of identifying, prosecuting, and punishing suspected witches was carried out under state supervision.

The Search for a Source of Authority

The crisis of religious and political authority in Europe also spurred more rational approaches to the problem of uncertainty. The French nobleman **Michel de Montaigne** (*mohn-TEHN-yeh*; 1533–1592), the son of a Catholic father and a Huguenot mother of Jewish ancestry, applied a searching skepticism to all traditional ways of knowing the world and adopted instead a practice of profound introspection. His *Essays* (from the French word for "attempts" or "trials") were composed during the French wars of religion and proceed from one basic question: *Que sais-je?* ("What do I know?").

The *Essays*' first premise is that every human perspective is limited. For example, in a famous essay, "On Cannibals," Montaigne argued that what may seem indisputably true and moral to one group of people may seem absolutely false to another, because "everyone gives the title of barbarism to everything that is not of his usage." From this follows Montaigne's second main premise: the need for moderation. Because all people think they follow the true religion or have the best form of government, he concludes that no religion or government is really perfect, and consequently no belief is worth fighting or dying for. People should, instead, accept the teachings of religion on faith and obey the governments constituted to rule over them, but without resorting to fanaticism in either sphere.

Another French philosopher, **Blaise Pascal** (*pahs-KAHL*; 1623–1662), confronted the problem of doubt by embracing an extreme form of puritanical Catholicism known as Jansenism, named after its Flemish founder, Cornelius Jansen. Until his death, he worked on a highly ambitious philosophical-religious project meant to establish the truth of Christianity by appealing simultaneously to the intellect and the emotions. In his posthumous work, *Pensées* ("Thoughts"), Pascal argued that only faith could resolve the contradictions of the world because "the heart has its reasons, of which reason itself knows nothing."

Pensées expresses Pascal's own anguish and awe in the face of evil and uncertainty, but presents that awe as evidence for the existence of God. Pascal's hope was that, on this foundation, some measure of confidence in humanity and its capacity for self-knowledge could be rediscovered.

The Science of Politics

Montaigne's immediate contemporary, the French jurist **Jean Bodin** (*boh-DAN*; 1530–1596), took a more practical approach to the problem of uncertain authority and found a solution in the power of the state. Like Montaigne, Bodin was troubled by the upheavals of the religious wars. He had witnessed the Saint Bartholomew's Day Massacre of 1572 and, in response, developed a theory of absolute sovereignty that would (he surmised) put an end to such catastrophes. In his monumental *Six Books of the Commonwealth* (1576), he argued that the state has its origins in the needs of family-oriented communities, and its paramount duty is to maintain order.

Bodin defined sovereignty as the "most high, absolute, and perpetual power over all subjects," meaning that a sovereign head of state could make and enforce laws without the consent of those governed: precisely what King Charles of England later argued when he tried to dispense with Parliament—and precisely what his subjects ultimately rejected. Even if the ruler proved a tyrant, Bodin insisted that subjects had no right to resist, for any resistance would open the door to anarchy, "which is worse than the harshest tyranny in the world."

In England, experience of the Civil War led **Thomas Hobbes** (1588–1679) to propose a different theory of state sovereignty in his treatise *Leviathan* (1651). Whereas Bodin assumed that sovereign power should be vested in a monarch, Hobbes argued that any form of government capable of protecting its subjects' lives and property might act as an all-powerful sovereign.

Hobbes's conviction of the need for a strong state arose from his pessimistic view of human nature. The "state of nature" that existed before government, he wrote, was "war of all against all." Because any man naturally behaves as "a wolf" toward other men, human life without government is "solitary, poor, nasty, brutish, and short." To escape such consequences, people must surrender their liberties to a sovereign state, in exchange for the state's obligation to keep the peace. Bodin saw the ultimate goal of the state as the protection of property, whereas Hobbes saw it as the preservation of people's lives—even at the expense of their liberties.

Montaigne on Cannibals

The Essays *of Michel de Montaigne (1533–1592) reflect his attempts to grapple with the contradictions of his own time. In this famous passage, he contrasts the barbarism of the European wars of religion and conquest with the reported behavior of peoples in the New World.*

had with me for a long time a man who had lived ten or twelve years in that other world which has been discovered in our time. . . . This discovery of so vast a country seems to me worth reflecting on. I should not care to pledge myself that another may not be discovered in the future, since so many greater men than we have been wrong about this one. . . .

[And] I do not believe, from what I have been told about [the] people [of this land] that there is anything barbarous or savage about them, except that we call barbarous anything that is contrary to our own habits. Indeed we seem to have no other criterion of truth and reason than the type and kind of opinions and customs current in the land where we live. . . . These people are wild in the same way . . . that fruits are wild, when nature has produced them by herself and in her ordinary way; whereas, in fact, it is those that we have artificially modified, and removed from the common order, that we ought to call wild. . . .

These [people], then, seem to me barbarous in the sense that they have received very little moulding from the human intelligence, and are still very close to their original simplicity. . . . They are in such a state of purity that it sometimes saddens me to think that we did not learn of them earlier . . . when there were men who were better able to appreciate them than we. . . .

[For example,] they have their wars against the people who live further inland, on the other side of the mountains; and they go to them quite naked, with no other arms but their bows or their wooden swords, pointed at one end. . . . [And after] treating a prisoner well for a long time, and giving him every attention he can think of, his captor assembles a great company of his acquaintances. He then ties a rope to the prisoner's arms, holding him by the other end, at some yards' distance for fear of being hit, and gives his best friend the man's other arm, to be held in the same way; and these two, in front of the whole assembly, dispatch him with their swords. This done, they roast him, eat him all together, and send portions to their absent friends. . . .

I am not so anxious that we should note the horrible savagery of these acts as concerned that, whilst judging their faults so correctly, we should be so blind to our own. I consider it more barbarous to eat a man alive than to eat him dead; to tear by rack and torture a body still full of feeling, to roast it by degrees, and then give it to be trampled and eaten by dogs and swine—a practice which we have not only read about but seen within recent memory, not between ancient enemies, but between neighbours and fellow-citizens and, what is worse, under the cloak of piety and religion—than to roast and eat a man after he is dead.

Source: Michel de Montaigne, *Essays*, trans. J. M. Cohen (Harmondsworth: 1958), pp. 105–13.

Questions for Analysis

1. How does Montaigne regard the "barbarous" people of the New World? How does he (re)define that concept?

2. How does Montaigne critique the assumptions and values of his own time in this passage?

3. Montaigne compares the reported behavior of cannibals to the behavior of Europeans during the ongoing wars of religion. What is he trying to achieve by making this comparison?

Shakespeare's Popular Appeal

Although the plays of William Shakespeare are frequently described as elite entertainments, their enduring appeal can hardly be explained in those terms. In fact, Shakespeare wrote for a diverse audience and for a group of actors who would have been more likely to see the inside of a prison than a royal court. His plays combine high politics, earthy comedy, and deeply human stories that still captivate and move audiences at the reconstructed Globe Theatre in London (left). They also lend themselves to inventive adaptations that comment on our contemporary world, as in the recent film *Coriolanus* (right).

 Watch related author interview on the Student Site

Hobbes and Bodin developed such theories in response to their firsthand experience of political and social upheavals resulting from the breakdown of traditional authorities. Their different political philosophies thus reflect a practical preoccupation with the observation and analysis of actual occurrences (empirical knowledge) rather than abstract or theological arguments. Because of this practical bent, they are seen as early examples of a new kind of discipline: what we now call political science.

Poetry and Theater

In the late sixteenth century, the construction of public playhouses (enclosed theaters) made drama an especially effective mass medium for the formation of public opinion, the dissemination of ideas, and the articulation of national identities. A pioneering poet and playwright in Poland, Jan Kochanowski (1530–1584), was the first to write a tragedy in the Polish vernacular. He also invented genres and verse forms that are still influential today. Indeed, his series of moving laments for his beloved daughter Ursula, who died before her third birthday, are exemplars of the human need to find meaning even in the most dreadful situations.

Theater was an especially influential medium in England during the last two decades of Elizabeth's reign and that of her successor, James. Among the large number of playwrights at work in London during this era, the most noteworthy are Christopher Marlowe (1564–1593), Ben Jonson (c. 1572–1637), and William Shakespeare (1564–1616). Marlowe, who may have been a spy for Elizabeth's government and who was mysteriously murdered in a tavern brawl, was extremely popular in his day. In plays such as *Tamburlaine*, about the life of the Mongolian warlord Timur the Lame (Chapter 12), and *Doctor Faustus*, he created heroes who pursue larger-than-life ambitions only to be felled by their own human limitations. In contrast to the heroic tragedies of Marlowe, Ben Jonson wrote dark comedies that expose human vices and foibles. In *The Alchemist*, he balanced an attack on pseudoscientific quackery with admiration for resourceful lower-class characters who cleverly take advantage of their supposed betters.

William Shakespeare was born into a family of a tradesman in the provincial town of Stratford-upon-Avon, where he attained a modest education before moving to London around the age of twenty. There, he composed or collaborated on an unknown number of plays, of which some forty survive in whole or in part. They owe their longevity to the author's unrivaled gifts of verbal expression, humor, and psychological insight. Those written during the playwright's early years reflect the political, religious, and social upheavals of the late sixteenth century, including many history plays that recount episodes from England's medieval past and the struggles that established the Tudor dynasty of Elizabeth's grandfather, Henry VII. They also include the lyrical tragedy *Romeo and Juliet*—and a number of comedies that explore fundamental problems of identity, honor and ambition, love and friendship. The plays from Shakespeare's second period,

VIEW OF TOLEDO, BY EL GRECO. This is one of El Greco's many landscape paintings depicting the hilltop city that became his home in later life. Its supple style almost defies historical periodization.

like other contemporary artworks, are characterized by a troubled search for the mysteries and meaning of human existence; they showcase the perils of indecisive idealism (*Hamlet*) and the abuse of power (*Macbeth* and *King Lear*). The plays composed toward the end of his career emphasize the possibilities of reconciliation and peace, even after years of misunderstanding and violence (*The Tempest, A Winter's Tale*).

The Artists of Southern Europe

The ironies and tensions inherent in this age also found expression in the visual arts. In Italy and Spain, many painters cultivated a highly dramatic style sometimes known as "Mannerism." The most unusual of these artists was El Greco ("the Greek"; c. 1541–1614), a pupil of the Venetian master Tintoretto (1518–1594). Born Domenikos Theotokopoulos on the island of Crete, El Greco absorbed some of the stylized elongation characteristic of Byzantine icon painting (Chapter 7) before traveling to Italy, then settling in Spain.

Many of his paintings were too strange to be truly appreciated in his day, and even now appear so avant-garde as to be almost surreal. His *View of Toledo*, for example, is a transfigured landscape, mysteriously lit from within. Equally amazing are his swirling biblical scenes and the stunning portraits of gaunt, dignified saints who radiate austerity and spiritual insight.

In the seventeenth century, the dominant artistic style of southern Europe was the Baroque, a school whose name has become a synonym for elaborate, highly wrought sculpture and architectural details. This style originated in Rome during the Counter-Reformation and promoted a glorified Catholic worldview. Its most imaginative and influential figure was the architect and sculptor Gianlorenzo Bernini (1598–1680), a frequent employee of the papacy who created a magnificent celebration of papal grandeur in the sweeping colonnades leading up to St. Peter's Basilica. Breaking with the more serene classicism of Renaissance styles (Chapter 12), Bernini's work drew inspiration from the restless motion and artistic bravado of Hellenistic statuary (Chapter 4).

THE MAIDS OF HONOR (LAS MENIÑAS), BY DIEGO VELÁZQUEZ.
The artist himself (standing on the left) is shown working at his easel and gazing out at the viewer—or at the subjects of his double portrait, the Spanish king and queen, depicted in the distant mirror. The real focus of the painting is the delicate, impish princess in the center, flanked by two young ladies-in-waiting, a dwarf, and another royal child, as courtiers in the background look on.

***DAVID*, BY GIANLORENZO BERNINI.** Whereas the earlier conceptions of David by the Renaissance sculptors Donatello and Michelangelo were serene and dignified (see page 403), the Baroque sculptor Bernini chose to portray the young hero at the peak of physical exertion. ▪ *Can you discern the influence of Hellenistic sculpture (Chapter 4) in this work?* ▪ *What are some shared characteristics?*

Characteristics of this Baroque style can also be found in paintings, such as those of the great Spanish master Diego Velázquez (*vay-LAH-skez*; 1599–1660), who served the Spanish Habsburg court in Madrid. Although many of his canvases display a Baroque attention to motion and drama, those most characteristic of his own style are more conceptually thoughtful and daring. An example is *The Maids of Honor (Las Meniñas),* a masterpiece of self-referentiality, completed around 1656. It shows the artist himself at work on a double portrait of the Spanish king and queen, but the scene is dominated by the children and servants of the royal family.

Dutch Painting in the Golden Age

Southern Europe's main rival in the visual arts was the Netherlands, where many exemplary painters explored the theme of man's greatness and wretchedness to the full. Pieter Bruegel the Elder (*BROY-ghul*; c. 1525–1569) exulted

in portraying the busy, elemental life of the peasantry. Most famous in this respect are his rollicking *Peasant Wedding* and *Peasant Wedding Dance,* as well as his spacious *Harvesters,* in which field hands are taking a well-deserved break under the noonday sun. But late in his career, Bruegel became appalled by the intolerance and bloodshed he witnessed during the Calvinist riots and the Spanish repression of the Netherlands. He expressed his criticism in works such as *The Massacre of the Innocents.* From a distance, this painting looks like a snug scene of village life; but, in fact, soldiers are methodically breaking into homes and slaughtering helpless infants—as Herod's soldiers once did after the birth of Jesus, and as warring armies did in Bruegel's own day.

Another Dutch painter, Peter Paul Rubens (1577–1640), was inspired by very different politics. A native of Antwerp, part of the Spanish Netherlands, Rubens was a staunch Catholic who glorified the Roman Church and the local aristocrats who supported the Habsburg regime. Even when his intent was not propagandistic, Rubens reveled in the sumptuous extravagance of the Baroque style. (He is most famous today for the pink and rounded flesh of his well-nourished nudes.) Although he celebrated martial valor for most of his career, his late painting *The Horrors of War* movingly captures what he called "the grief of unfortunate Europe, which, for so many years now, has suffered plunder, outrage, and misery."

THE MASSACRE OF THE INNOCENTS, BY PIETER BRUEGEL THE ELDER. This painting shows how effective art can be as a means of political and social commentary. Here, Bruegel depicts the suffering of the Netherlands at the hands of the Spanish in his own day, with reference to the biblical story of Herod's slaughter of Jewish children after the birth of Jesus—thereby collapsing the two historical incidents.

THE CONSEQUENCES OF WAR, BY PETER PAUL RUBENS. In his old age, Rubens took a far more critical view of war than he had done for most of his career. Here, the war god Mars casts aside his mistress Venus, goddess of love, and threatens humanity with death and destruction.

SELF-PORTRAITS. Self-portraits became common during the sixteenth and seventeenth centuries, reflecting the intense introspection of the period. Rembrandt painted more than sixty self-portraits; this one on the left, dating from around 1660, captures the artist's creativity, theatricality (note the costume), and honesty of self-examination. Judith Leyster, shown on the right, was a contemporary of Rembrandt who pursued a successful career during her early twenties before she married. Respected in her own day, she was all but forgotten for centuries thereafter, but is once again the object of much attention.

After You Read This Chapter

 Go to **INQUIZITIVE** to see what you've learned—and learn what you've missed—with personalized feedback along the way.

REVIEWING THE OBJECTIVES

- How were the peoples and ecosystems of the Americas, Africa, and Europe intertwined during this period? What were some of the consequences of these new linkages?

- Why did the colonies of the Spanish, the English, and the Dutch differ from each other? How did these differences affect the lives and labor of colonists, both free and unfree?

- Which European powers came to dominate the Atlantic world? What factors led to the decline of Spain and the rise of France?

- What forms did religious and political conflict take in France, the Netherlands, and Germany? What were the causes of the English Civil War? What impact did this event have on the English colonies?

- How do the arts and the political philosophies of this period reflect the turmoil of Europe and the Atlantic world?

In some ways a blend of Bruegel and Rubens, Rembrandt van Rijn (*vahn REEN*; 1606–1669) defies all attempts at easy characterization. Living across the border from the Spanish Netherlands, in the staunchly Calvinist Dutch Republic, Rembrandt managed to put both realistic and Baroque traits to new uses. Early in his career, he gained fame and fortune as a painter of biblical scenes, and was also active as a portrait painter who knew how to flatter his subjects—to the great advantage of his purse. But as personal tragedies mounted in his middle and declining years, the painter's art gained dignity, subtlety, and mystery. His later portraits, including several self-portraits, are highly introspective and suggest that only part of the story is being told. Equally fearless is the frank gaze of Rembrandt's slightly younger contemporary, Judith Leyster (1609–1660), who looks out of her own self-portrait with a refreshingly optimistic and good-humored expression.

CONCLUSION

It would take centuries for Europeans to adapt themselves to the changes brought about by their integration into the Atlantic world, and to grasp its implications. Finding new lands and cultures unknown to the ancients and unmentioned in the Bible had exposed the limitations of Western civilizations' accumulated knowledge, and called for new ways of knowing and explaining the world. The Columbian exchange of people, plants, livestock, and pathogens which had previously been isolated from each other had a profound and lasting effect on populations and ecosystems throughout the globe. The distribution of new agricultural products transformed the lives of poor and rich alike.

The transatlantic slave trade, which made all this possible, brought Africans and their cultures into a world of growing global connections under the worst possible circumstances for those who were enslaved—yet this did not prevent them from actively shaping this new world. Meanwhile, the influx of silver from New Spain precipitated the great price inflation of the sixteenth and seventeenth centuries, which bewildered contemporary observers and contributed to the atmosphere of crisis in a post-Reformation Europe already riven by religious and civil warfare. The response was a trend toward stronger centralized states, justified by theories of absolute government. Led by the French monarchy of Louis XIV, these absolutist regimes would reach their apogee in the coming century.

PEOPLE, IDEAS, AND EVENTS IN CONTEXT

- What was the **COLUMBIAN EXCHANGE**? How did it affect the relations among the peoples of the Americas, Africa, and Europe during this period?
- What circumstances led to the development of the **TRIANGULAR TRADE**?
- What were the main sources of instability in Europe during the sixteenth century? How did the **PRICE REVOLUTION** exacerbate this instability?
- How did **HENRY IV** of France and **PHILIP II** of Spain deal with the religious conflict that beset Europe during these years?
- What were the origins of the **THIRTY YEARS' WAR**? Was it primarily a religious conflict? Why or why not?
- How did the policies of **CARDINAL RICHELIEU** strengthen the power of the French monarchy?
- What policies of England's **CHARLES I** were most detested by his subjects? Why was his execution so momentous?
- In what ways did the **WITCH CRAZE** of early modern Europe reveal the religious and social tensions of the sixteenth and seventeenth centuries?
- What were the differences between **JEAN BODIN**'s theory of absolute sovereignty and that of **THOMAS HOBBES**?
- How did philosophers such as **MONTAIGNE** and **PASCAL** respond to the uncertainties of the age? How were contemporary trends reflected in the works of **SHAKESPEARE** and in the visual arts?

THINKING ABOUT CONNECTIONS

- The emergence of the Atlantic world can be seen as the *cause* of new developments as well as the *result* of historical processes. What long-term political, economic, and demographic circumstances drove the expansion of European influence into the Atlantic? What subsequent historical developments can be attributed to the creation of this interconnected world?
- The political crises of this era reveal the tensions produced by sectarian religious disputes as well as by a growing rift between powerful centralizing monarchies and landholding elites who are unwilling to surrender their authority and independence. What other periods in history are marked by similar tensions? How do those periods compare with the one we have studied in this chapter?
- The intellectual currents of this era reveal that a new generation was challenging the assumptions of its predecessors. In what other historical eras do we find similar phenomena? What social and political circumstances tend to produce consensus, and what tend to produce dissent, skepticism, and doubt?

- After 1660, many European rulers invoked an absolutist definition of sovereignty in order to expand the power of the monarchy. The most successful absolutist kings, such as Louis XIV of France or Peter the Great of Russia, limited the power of traditional aristocratic elites and the independence of religious institutions.

- Absolutism was not universally successful. Efforts by English monarchs to create an absolutist regime in England after the Civil War were resisted by political opponents of the Crown in Parliament. Other regimes in Europe that found alternatives to absolutism included the Dutch Republic and the Polish Lithuanian Commonwealth.

- Absolutism reinforced the imperial ambitions of European monarchies and led to frequent wars that were increasingly fought both in Europe and in colonial spaces in other parts of the world. The pressures of war favored dynasties capable of building strong centralized states with reliable sources of revenue from trade and taxation.

CHRONOLOGY

1643–1715	Reign of Louis XIV of France
1660	Restoration of the Stuart kings in England
1682–1725	Reign of Peter the Great of Russia
1683	Ottoman siege of Vienna
1685	Revocation of the Edict of Nantes
1688	Glorious Revolution in England
1688–1697	War of the League of Augsburg
1690	Publication of John Locke's *Two Treatises of Government*
1702–1713	War of the Spanish Succession
1713	Treaty of Utrecht

Before You Read This Chapter

European Monarchies and Absolutism, 1660–1725

n the mountainous region of south-central France known in the 1660s as the Auvergne, the Marquis of Canillac had a notorious reputation. His noble title gave him the right to collect minor taxes on special occasions, but he insisted that these small privileges be converted into annual tributes. To collect these payments, he housed twelve accomplices in his castle whom he called his apostles. Their other nicknames—one was known as Break Everything—gave a more accurate sense of their activities in the local villages. The marquis imprisoned those who resisted and forced their families to buy their freedom. In an earlier age, the marquis might have gotten away with this profitable arrangement. In 1662, however, he ran up against the authority of a king, **Louis XIV**, who was determined to demonstrate that the power of the central monarch was absolute. The marquis was brought up on charges before a special court of judges from Paris, was found guilty, and was forced to pay a large fine. The king then confiscated his property and had his castle destroyed.

Louis XIV's special court in the Auvergne heard nearly a thousand civil cases over four months in 1662. It convicted 692 people,

493

many of whom, like the Marquis of Canillac, were noble. The verdicts were an extraordinary example of Louis XIV's ability to project his authority into the remote corners of his realm, and to do so in a way that diminished the power of other elites. During his long reign (1643–1715), Louis XIV systematically pursued such policies on many fronts, asserting his power over the nobility, the clergy, and the provincial courts. Increasingly, these elites were forced to look to the crown to guarantee their interests, and their own power became more closely connected with the sacred aura of the monarchy itself. Louis XIV's model of kingship was known as *absolute monarchy*—a system of government that invested all authority in the king—and his reign was seen as the most successful application of this model. In recognition of the influence of Louis XIV's political system, the period from around 1660 (when the English monarchy was restored and Louis XIV began his personal rule in France) to 1789 (when the French Revolution erupted) is traditionally known as the age of absolutism. This is a crucial period in the development of modern, centralized, bureaucratic states in Europe.

Absolutism was a political theory that encouraged rulers to claim complete sovereignty within their territories. An absolute monarch could make law, dispense justice, create and direct a bureaucracy, declare war, and levy taxation

without the approval of any other governing body. Assertions of absolute authority were buttressed by claims that rulers governed by divine right, just as fathers ruled over their households (see **Competing Viewpoints** on page 498). After the chaos and religious wars of the previous century, many Europeans came to believe that only by exalting the sovereignty of absolute rulers could order be restored to European life.

European monarchs also continued to project their power abroad during this period. By 1660, as we have seen, the French, Spanish, Portuguese, English, and Dutch had all established important colonies in the Americas and Asia. These colonies created trading networks that brought profitable new consumer goods such as sugar, tobacco, and coffee to a wide public in Europe. They also encouraged the colonies' reliance on slavery to produce these goods. Rivalry among colonial powers to control the trade in slaves and consumer goods was intense and often led to wars that were fought both in Europe and in contested colonies. These wars, in turn, increased the motivation of absolutist rulers to extract as much revenue as they could from their subjects and encouraged the development of institutions that enhanced their power, such as armies, navies, tax systems, tariffs and customs controls.

Absolutism was not universally successful during this period. The English monarchy, restored in 1660 after the turbulent years of the Civil War, attempted to impose absolutist rule but met resistance from parliamentary leaders who insisted on more inclusive institutions of government. After 1688, England, Scotland, the Dutch Republic, Switzerland, Venice, Sweden, and Poland-Lithuania were all either limited monarchies or republics. In Russia, on the other hand, an extreme autocracy emerged that gave the tsar a degree of control over his subjects' lives and property far beyond anything imagined by western European absolutists. But even in Russia, absolutism was never unlimited in practice. So, too, the most absolute monarchs could rule effectively only with the consent of their subjects (particularly the nobility). When serious opposition erupted, even powerful kings were forced to back down. King George III of Britain discovered this when his North American colonies declared their independence

WINTER LANDSCAPE WITH ICE SKATERS, c. 1608, BY HENDRICK AVERCAMP. During the "Little Ice Age" more frequent cold winters regularly froze rivers and canals in northern Europe. Dutch painters frequently depicted winter village scenes, which provide a vivid portrait of daily life, work, and leisure during this period.

in 1776, forming the United States of America. In 1789, a more sweeping revolution began in France, and the entire structure of absolutism came crashing to the ground (see Chapter 18).

POPULATION AND CLIMATE IN THE ABSOLUTIST AGE

Absolutism's promise of stability and order was an appealing alternative to the disorder of the "iron century" that preceded it. Religious persecution and war had already put large populations on the move in the century before 1650 as religious minorities were expelled from different regions during a long period of heightened conflict over questions of faith. The expulsion of Jews from Spain (between 1420 and 1520) was followed by similar expulsions of Jews from Geneva, areas of southern France, southern Italy, and some German cities. The wars of religion in France resulted in the migration of many French Protestants, known as Huguenots, in the last decades of the sixteenth century.

These population movements were dwarfed by the catastrophe of the Thirty Years' War (1618–1646), which killed one-third of the town dwellers in German territories of central Europe, and 40 percent of the rural population from hunger, disease, and murder. The search for sustenance and security in Europe during the first half of the seventeenth century was magnified by the effects of the Little Ice Age, a period of lower temperatures in Europe and North America that reached its most intense effects in the mid-seventeenth century. Meteorologists are not in agreement about the causes of this cooling—but its effects included colder winters, a shorter growing season, and more frequent crop failures. For populations living on the edge of subsistence—a category that included the vast majority of people in Europe—famine was an ever-present threat.

Even in times of peace and more clement weather, European populations continued to be highly mobile, and this movement of people challenges older myths of a "traditional" Europe where people were born and died in a single village. Regions that could not produce enough to support their own population sent laborers annually to more fertile areas where larger farms produced single crops and paid higher wages. Tens of thousands of migrant workers went every summer to eastern England, to the farms of the Paris basin in northern France, and to Castile and Galicia in Spain to harvest grains. Similar numbers moved annually to Provence in southern France to harvest grapes and to northern Italy to harvest rice on the plains adjoining the Po river.

Itinerant traders often followed the same patterns of mobility as labor migrants. Commercial travelers built sophisticated and enduring networks: by the eighteenth century, for example, a complex of 40 villages on the border between the Netherlands and present-day Belgium sent 500 to 800 traders on the road every year, following established routes that reached from the Dutch Atlantic coast to western Russia, selling textiles, copper products, and women's hair for the wig industry. Other mobile trades included chimney sweeps, stonemasons, and construction workers who moved seasonally from rural areas to cities to seek work. This mobility of people within Europe was just as important for economic development as the broader movement of peoples in the Atlantic World (Chapter 14).

ABSOLUTISM'S GOALS AND OPPONENTS

To meet the challenge of war and economic competition, absolutist monarchs sought control of the state's armed forces and its legal system, and they demanded the right to collect and spend the state's financial resources at will. To achieve these goals, they also needed to create an efficient, centralized bureaucracy that owed its allegiance directly to the monarch. Creating and sustaining such a bureaucracy was expensive but necessary in order to weaken the special interests that hindered the free exercise of royal power. The nobility and the clergy, with their traditional legal privileges; the political authority of semiautonomous regions; and representative assemblies such as parliaments, diets, or estates-general were all obstacles—in the eyes of absolutists—to strong, centralized monarchical government. The history of absolutism is the history of kings who attempted to bring such institutions to heel.

In most Protestant countries, the power of the church had already been subordinated to the state when the age of absolutism began. Even where Roman Catholicism remained the state religion, such as in France, Spain, and Austria, absolutist monarchs now devoted considerable attention to bringing the Church and its clergy under royal control. Louis XIV took an active role in religious matters, appointing his own bishops and encouraging the repression of religious dissidents, but unlike his predecessors, he rarely appointed members of the clergy to offices within his administration.

Interpreting Visual Evidence

The Performance and Display of Absolute Power at the Court of Louis XIV

 istorians studying the history of absolutism and the court of Louis XIV in particular have emphasized the Sun King's brilliant use of symbols and display to demonstrate his personal embodiment of sovereignty. Royal portraits, such as that painted by Hyacinthe Rigaud in 1701 (shown below), vividly illustrate the degree to which Louis's power was based on a studied performance. His pose, with his exposed and shapely calf, was an important indication of power and virility, necessary elements of legitimacy for a hereditary monarch. In the elaborate rituals of court life at Versailles, Louis often placed his own body at the center of attention, performing in one instance as the god Apollo in a ballet before his assembled courtiers. His movements through the countryside, accompanied by a retinue of soldiers, servants, and aristocrats, were another occasion for highly stylized ritual demonstrations of his quasi-divine status. Finally, of course, the construction of his palace at Versailles, with its symmetrical architecture and sculpted gardens, was a demonstration that his power extended over the natural world as easily as it did over the lives of his subjects.

Questions for Analysis

1. Who was the intended audience for the king's performance of absolute sovereignty?

2. Who were Louis's primary competitors in this contest for eminence through the performance of power?

3. What possible political dangers might lie in wait for a regime that invested so heavily in the sumptuous display of semidivine authority?

A. Hyacinthe Rigaud's 1701 portrait of Louis XIV.

B. Louis XIV as the Sun King.

C. *A Cavalcade,* by Adam Frans van der Meulen (1664).

D. *The Palace of Versailles,* by Pierre Patel (c. 1668).

Competing Viewpoints

Absolutism and Patriarchy

> These selections show how two political theorists justified royal absolutism by deriving it from the absolute authority of a father over his household. Bishop Jacques-Bénigne Bossuet (1627–1704) was a famous French preacher and the tutor to the son of King Louis XIV of France before becoming bishop of Meaux. Sir Robert Filmer (1588–1653) was an English political theorist. Filmer's works attracted particular attention in the 1680s, when John Locke directed the first of his Two Treatises of Government to refute Filmer's views on the patriarchal nature of royal authority.

Bossuet on the Nature of Monarchical Authority

There are four characteristics or qualities essential to royal authority. First, royal authority is sacred; Secondly, it is paternal; Thirdly, it is absolute; Fourthly, it is subject to reason. . . . All power comes from God. . . . Thus princes act as ministers of God, and his lieutenants on earth. It is through them that he exercises his empire. . . . In this way . . . the royal throne is not the throne of a man, but the throne of God himself. . . .

We have seen that kings hold the place of God, who is the true Father of the human race. We have also seen that the first idea of power that there was among men, is that of paternal power; and that kings were fashioned on the model of fathers. Moreover, all the world agrees that obedience, which is due to public power, is only found . . . in the precept which obliges one to honor his parents. From all this it appears that the name "king" is a father's name, and that goodness is the most natural quality in kings. . . .

Royal authority is absolute. In order to make this term odious and insupportable, many pretend to confuse absolute government and arbitrary government. But nothing is more distinct, as we shall make clear when we speak of justice. . . . The prince need account to no one for what he ordains. . . . Without this absolute authority, he can neither do good nor suppress evil: his power must be such that no one can hope to escape him. . . . [T]he sole defense of individuals against the public power must be their innocence. . . .

One must, then, obey princes as if they were justice itself, without which there is neither order nor justice in affairs. They are gods, and share in some way in divine independence. . . . It follows from this that he who does not want to obey the prince . . . is condemned irremissibly to death as an enemy of public peace and of human society. . . . The prince can correct himself when he knows that he has done badly; but against his authority there can be no remedy. . . .

Source: Jacques-Bénigne Bossuet, *Politics Drawn from the Very Words of Holy Scripture*, trans. Patrick Riley (Cambridge: 1990), pp. 46–69, 81–83.

The most important potential opponents of royal absolutism were nobles. Louis XIV deprived the French nobility of political power in the provinces but increased their social prestige by making them live at his lavish court at Versailles (*vuhr-SY*). **Peter the Great** of Russia (1682–1725) forced his nobles into lifelong government service. Successive monarchs in Brandenburg-Prussia managed to co-opt the powerful aristocracy by granting them immunity to taxation and giving them the right to enserf their peasants; in exchange, they ceded administrative control to the increasingly bureaucratized Prussian state. In most European monarchies, including Spain, France, Prussia, and England, the nobility retained their preponderant role within the military.

Filmer on the Patriarchal Origins of Royal Authority

The first government in the world was monarchical, in the father of all flesh, Adam being commanded to multiply, and people the earth, and to subdue it, and having dominion given him over all creatures, was thereby the monarch of the whole world; none of his posterity had any right to possess anything, but by his grant or permission, or by succession from him. . . . Adam was the father, king and lord over his family: a son, a subject, and a servant or a slave were one and the same thing at first. . . .

I cannot find any one place or text in the Bible where any power . . . is given to a people either to govern themselves, or to choose themselves governors, or to alter the manner of government at their pleasure. The power of government is settled and fixed by the commandment of "honour thy father"; if there were a higher power than the fatherly, then this commandment could not stand and be observed. . . .

All power on earth is either derived or usurped from the fatherly power, there being no other original to be found

of any power whatsoever. For if there should be granted two sorts of power without any subordination of one to the other, they would be in perpetual strife which should be the supreme, for two supremes cannot agree. If the fatherly power be supreme, then the power of the people must be subordinate and depend on it. If the power of the people be supreme, then the fatherly power must submit to it, and cannot be exercised without the licence of the people, which must quite destroy the frame and course of nature. Even the power which God himself exercises over mankind is by right of fatherhood: he is both the king and father of us all. As God has exalted the dignity of earthly kings . . . by saying they are gods, so . . . he has been pleased . . . [t]o humble himself by assuming the title of a king to express his power, and not the title of any popular government.

Source: Robert Filmer, "Observations upon Aristotle's Politiques," in *Divine Right and Democracy: An Anthology of Political Writing in Stuart England*, ed. David Wootton (Harmondsworth, UK: 1986), pp. 110–18. First published 1652.

Questions for Analysis

1. Bossuet's definition of *absolutism* connected the sacred power of kings with the paternal authority of fathers within the household. What consequences does he draw from defining the relationship between king and subjects in this way?

2. What does Filmer mean when he says, "All power on earth is either derived or usurped from the fatherly power"? How many examples does he give of paternal or monarchical power?

3. Bossuet and Filmer make obedience the basis for order and justice in the world. What alternative political systems did they most fear?

Rarely was the path of confrontation between crown and nobility successful in the long run. The most effective absolutist monarchies of the eighteenth century continued to trade privileges for allegiance, so that nobles came to see their own interests as tied to those of the crown. For this reason, wary cooperation between kings and nobles was more common than open conflict during the eighteenth century.

THE ABSOLUTISM OF LOUIS XIV

In Louis XIV's state portrait, it is almost impossible to discern the human being behind the facade of the absolute monarch dressed in his coronation robes and surrounded by the symbols of his authority. That facade was artfully constructed by Louis, who recognized, more fully than any other early modern ruler, the importance of theater

Past and Present

The Persistence of Monarchies in a Democratic Age

In the past, monarchs such as Louis XIV (left) often ran roughshod over tradition as they sought ways to increase their power. Today, twelve European states still have reigning monarchs, such as England's Queen Elizabeth II (right), but their popularity probably would be called into question if they sought an active role in government.

 Watch related author interview on the Student Site

to effective kingship. Louis and his successors deliberately staged spectacular demonstrations of their sovereignty to enhance their position as rulers endowed with godlike powers.

Performing Royalty at Versailles

Louis's most elaborate staging of his authority took place at his palace at Versailles, outside Paris. The main facade of the palace was a third of a mile in length. Inside, tapestries and paintings celebrated French military victories and royal triumphs, and mirrors reflected shimmering light throughout the building. In the vast gardens outside, statues of the Greek god Apollo, god of the sun, recalled Louis's claim to be the "Sun King" of France. Noblemen vied to attend him when he arose from bed, ate his meals (usually stone cold after having traveled the distance of several city blocks

from kitchen to table), strolled in his gardens (even the way the king walked was choreographed by the royal dancing master), or rode to the hunt. France's leading nobles were required to reside with Louis at Versailles for a portion of the year; the splendor of Louis's court was deliberately calculated to blind them to the possibility of disobedience while raising their prestige by associating them with himself (see **Interpreting Visual Evidence** on page 496). At the same time, the almost impossibly detailed rules of etiquette at court left these privileged nobles in constant suspense, forever fearful of offending the king by committing some trivial violation of proper manners.

Of course, the nobility did not surrender social and political power entirely. The social order was still hierarchical, and noblemen retained enormous privileges and rights over local peasants within their jurisdiction. The absolutist system forced the nobility to depend on the crown, but it did not seek to undermine their superior place in society.

In this sense, the relationship between Louis XIV and the nobility was more of a negotiated settlement than a complete victory of the king over other powerful elites. Louis XIV understood this, and in a memoir that he prepared for his son on the art of ruling, he wrote, "The deference and the respect that we receive from our subjects are not a free gift from them but payment for the justice and the protection that they expect from us. Just as they must honor us, we must protect and defend them." In their own way, absolutists depended on the consent of those they ruled.

Administration and Finance

Absolutist rulers sought to impose their will by concentrating power in fewer hands, diminishing the ability of local elites to shape policy. Under Louis, the French administration came to be run largely by thirty-three royal intendants, who represented the monarchy in each of France's regions. He also worked to diminish the power of local representative institutions. Members of regional *parlements* (law courts) that refused to approve his laws were exiled. The Estates General, the French representative assembly that met at the king's pleasure to act as a consultative body for the state, was last summoned in 1614 and did not meet at all in Louis's long reign. It was not convened again until 1789.

Louis's most able official was Jean-Baptiste Colbert, finance minister from 1664–1683. Before Louis XIV's reign, the tax system was notoriously inefficient: the nobility was exempt from the land tax (*taille*) and collection of indirect taxes on salt, wine, tobacco, and other goods difficult to administer. Colbert eliminated the practice of tax farming, which permitted collection agents to retain a percentage of taxes they gathered for the king. When Colbert assumed office, only about 25 percent of collected taxes reached the treasury. By the time he died, this figure reached 80 percent. Colbert raised additional funds through the sale of public offices, including judgeships and mayoralties, and he forced guilds to pay for the enforcement of trade regulations.

Colbert was a **mercantilist**—he believed that France's wealth would grow if it reduced its imports and increased its exports. He imposed tariffs on foreign goods, and used state money to promote the domestic manufacture of imports like silk, lace, tapestries, and glass. To encourage trade he improved France's roads, bridges, and waterways. Despite Colbert's efforts to increase royal revenues, his policies foundered on the insatiable demands of Louis XIV's wars (see page 508). By the end of Louis's reign, his aggressive foreign policy lay in ruins, and his country's finances had been shattered by the unsustainable costs of war.

Louis XIV's Religious Policies

Louis was determined to impose religious unity on France. Although the vast majority of the French population was Roman Catholic, French Catholics were divided among Quietists, Jansenists, Jesuits, and Gallicans. Quietists preached retreat into personal mysticism, emphasizing a direct relationship between God and the individual human heart. Such doctrine, dispensing as it did with the intermediary services of the Church, was suspect in the eyes of absolutists wedded to the doctrine of *un roi, une loi, une foi* ("one king, one law, one faith"). Jansenism—a movement named for its founder, Cornelius Jansen, a seventeenth-century bishop of Ypres—held to an Augustinian doctrine of predestination that could sound and look surprisingly like a kind of Catholic Calvinism. Louis vigorously persecuted Quietists and Jansenists, offering them a choice between recanting and prison or exile. At the same time, he supported the Jesuits in their efforts to create a Counter-Reformation Catholic Church in France. Louis's support for the Jesuits upset the traditional Gallican Catholics of France, however, who desired a French church independent of papal, Jesuit, and Spanish influence. As a result of this dissension among Catholics, the religious aura of Louis's kingship diminished during the course of his reign.

Against the Protestant Huguenots Louis waged unrelenting war. Protestant churches and schools were destroyed, and Protestants were banned from many professions. In 1685, Louis revoked the Edict of Nantes, the legal foundation of the toleration the Huguenots had enjoyed since 1598. Protestant clerics were exiled, laymen were sent to the galleys as slaves, and their children were forcibly baptized as Catholics. Many families converted, but 200,000 Protestant refugees fled to England, Holland, Germany, and America, taking with them their professional and artisanal skills. This emigration was an enormous loss to France. Huguenots fleeing Louis XIV's persecution, for example, established the silk industries of Berlin and London.

French Colonialism under Louis XIV

Finance Minister Colbert regarded overseas expansion as an integral part of the French state's economic policy, and with his guidance, Louis XIV's absolutist realm emerged as a major colonial power. Recognizing the profits to be made in responding to Europe's growing demand for sugar, Colbert encouraged the development of sugar-producing colonies in the West Indies, the largest of which was Saint-Domingue (present-day Haiti). Sugar, virtually unknown in Christian Europe during the Middle Ages, became a popular luxury item in the late fifteenth century (see Chapter 14). It took the slave plantations of the Caribbean to turn sugar into a mass-market product. By 1750, slaves in Saint-Domingue produced 40 percent of the world's sugar (and 50 percent of its coffee), exporting more sugar than Jamaica, Cuba, and Brazil combined. By 1700, France also dominated the interior of the North American continent, where French traders brought furs to the Native Americans and missionaries preached Christianity in a vast territory that stretched from Québec to Louisiana. The financial returns from North America were never large, however. Furs, fish, and tobacco were exported to European markets but never matched the profits from the Caribbean sugar colonies or from the trading posts that the French maintained in India.

Like the earlier Spanish colonies (see Chapter 14), the French colonies were established and administered as direct crown enterprises. French colonial settlements in North America were conceived of mainly as military outposts and trading centers, and they were overwhelmingly populated by men. The elite of French colonial society were military officers and administrators sent from Paris. Below their ranks were fishermen, fur traders, small farmers, and common soldiers who constituted the majority of French settlers in North America. Because the fishing and the fur trades relied on cooperative relationships with native peoples, a mutual economic interdependence grew between the French colonies and the peoples of the surrounding region. Intermarriage, especially between French traders and native women, was common. These North American colonies remained dependent on the wages and supplies sent to them from the mother country. Only rarely did they become truly self-sustaining economic enterprises.

The phenomenally successful sugar plantations of the Caribbean had their own social structure, with slaves at the bottom, people of mixed African and European descent forming the middle layer, and wealthy European plantation owners at the top, controlling the lucrative trade with the outside world. Well over half of the sugar and coffee sent to France was resold and sent elsewhere to markets throughout Europe. Because the monarchy controlled the prices that colonial plantation owners could charge French merchants for their goods, traders in Europe who bought the goods for resale abroad could also make vast fortunes. Historians estimate that as many as 1 million of the 25 million inhabitants of France in the eighteenth century lived off the money flowing through this colonial trade, making the slave colonies of the Caribbean a powerful force for economic change in France. The wealth generated from these colonies added to the prestige of France's absolutist system of government.

ALTERNATIVES TO ABSOLUTISM

Although absolutism was the dominant model for seventeenth- and eighteenth-century European monarchs, it was by no means the only system by which Europeans governed themselves. A republican oligarchy continued to rule in Venice. In the Polish-Lithuanian Commonwealth, the monarch was elected by the nobility and governed alongside a parliament that met every two years. In the Netherlands, the territories that had won their independence from Spain during the early seventeenth century combined to form the United Provinces, the only truly new country to take shape in Europe during the early modern era. England, which had suffered through a violent civil war between 1642 and 1651, followed by the tumultuous years of Oliver Cromwell's Commonwealth and the Protectorate (see Chapter 14), also took a different path during these years, eventually arriving at a constitutional settlement that gave a larger role to Parliament and admitted a degree of participation by non-nobles in the affairs of state. Arriving at this settlement was not easy, however. The end of the civil wars and the collapse of Cromwell's Protectorate had made it clear that England would be a monarchy and not a republic, but what sort of monarchy England would be remained an open question. Two issues were paramount: religion (parallelism) and the relationship between Parliament and the king.

The Restoration Monarchy in England

The king who took the throne following the restoration of the Stuarts in 1660, **Charles II** (r. 1660–1685), was initially welcomed by most English, despite being the son of the beheaded and much-despised Charles I (see Chapter 14). He restored bishops to the Church of England, but he did not initially return to the provocative religious policies of his father. He declared limited religious toleration for Protestant "dissenters" who were not members of the Church of England. He promised to observe the Magna Carta and the Petition of Right, which comforted members of Parliament. He also accepted the legislation passed by Parliament immediately before the outbreak of civil war in 1642, including the requirement that Parliament be summoned at least once every three years. England thus emerged from its civil war as a limited monarchy, in which power was exercised by the "king in Parliament." Meanwhile, the unbuttoned moral atmosphere of Charles II's court, with its risqué plays, dancing, and sexual licentiousness, may have reflected a public desire to forget the restraints of the Puritan past.

During the 1670s, however, Charles began openly to model his kingship on the absolutism of Louis XIV. As a result, the great men of England soon came to be publicly divided between Charles's supporters (known as "Tories," a popular nickname for Irish Catholic bandits) and his opponents (called "Whigs," a nickname for Scottish Presbyterian rebels). In fact, both sides feared absolutism as well as a return to the bad old days of the 1640s when resistance to the crown had led to civil war and ultimately to republicanism. What they could not agree on was which possibility frightened them more.

Charles's known sympathy for Roman Catholicism (he converted on his deathbed in 1685) also generated fodder for the opposition Whigs. During the 1670s, he briefly suspended civil penalties against Catholics and Protestant dissenters by asserting his right as king to ignore parliamentary legislation, retreating only in the face of public protest. The Whigs, meanwhile, rallied support by targeting Charles's Catholic brother James, the heir to the throne. The result was a series of Whig electoral victories between 1679 and 1681. A group of radical Whigs tried and failed to exclude James from succeeding his brother by law, and thereafter Charles found that his rising revenues from customs duties, combined with a secret subsidy from Louis XIV, enabled him to govern without relying on Parliament for money. Charles further alarmed Whig politicians by executing several of them on charges of treason and remodeling local government to make it more amenable to royal control. Charles died in 1685 with his power enhanced, but left behind a political and religious legacy that was to be the undoing of his less able and adroit successor.

James II was the very opposite of his worldly brother. A zealous Catholic convert, James admired the French monarchy's Gallican Catholicism, which sought to further the work of the Church by harnessing it to the power of an absolutist bureaucratic state. His commitment to absolutism also led him to build up the English army and navy, which in turn led him to search for innovative solutions to the problems of taxation and the quartering of troops. To make the tax system more efficient he created new revenue agencies in many English towns. His quest for more accurate intelligence about political opponents led him to take control over the country's new post office, which made domestic surveillance routine, and his government also stepped up its efforts to prosecute seditious speech and writings. For the Whigs, James's policies were all that they had feared.

Meanwhile, James's Catholicism also alienated his Tory supporters, who were close to the established Church of England. Religion was not the only cause of his unpopularity, but resistance to his policies was often mixed with resentment against a perception that he favored Catholics. His decision to appoint Catholics as officers in the army was unpopular, but even more so was his decision to maintain a standing army in peacetime. Towns that were asked to quarter troops resented the expense and the disruptive presence of soldiers in their midst. In June 1688, when he ordered all Church of England clergymen to read his decree of religious toleration from their pulpits, seven bishops refused and were promptly imprisoned. At their trial, however, they were declared not guilty of sedition, to the enormous satisfaction of the Protestant English populace.

The trial of the bishops was one event that galvanized the growing opposition to James. The other was the unexpected birth of a son in 1688 to James and his second wife, Mary of Modena. This child, who was to be raised a Catholic, replaced James's much older Protestant daughter Mary Stuart as heir to the thrones of Scotland and England. So unexpected was this birth that there were widespread rumors that the child was not in fact James's son at all but had been smuggled into the royal bedchamber in a warming pan.

CHARLES II OF ENGLAND (r. 1660–1685) IN HIS CORONATION ROBES. This full frontal portrait of the monarch, holding the symbols of his rule, seems to confront the viewer personally with overwhelming authority of the sovereign's gaze. Compare this classic image of the absolutist monarch with the very different portraits of William and Mary, who ruled after the Glorious Revolution of 1688 (page 504). ▪ *What had changed between 1660, when Charles II came to the throne, and 1688, when the more popular William and Mary became the rulers of England?*

With the birth of the "warming-pan baby," events moved swiftly toward a climax. A delegation of Whigs and Tories crossed the channel to Holland to invite Mary Stuart and her Protestant husband, William of Orange, to cross to England with an invading army to preserve English Protestantism and English liberties by summoning a new Parliament. As the leader of a continental coalition, then at war with France, William also welcomed the opportunity to make England an ally against Louis XIV's expansionist foreign policy.

The Glorious Revolution

Following William and Mary's invasion, James fled the country for exile in France. Parliament declared the throne vacant, clearing the way for William and Mary to succeed him as joint sovereigns. The Bill of Rights, passed by Parliament and accepted by the new king and queen in 1689, reaffirmed English civil liberties, such as trial by jury, *habeas corpus* (a guarantee that no one could be imprisoned unless charged with a crime), and the right to petition the monarch through Parliament. The Bill of Rights also declared that the monarchy was subject to the law of the land. The Act of Toleration also passed in 1689, granting Protestant dissenters the right to worship freely, though not to hold political office. And in 1701, the Act of Succession ordained that every future English monarch must be a member of the Church of England. Queen Mary died childless, and the throne passed from William to Mary's Protestant sister Anne (r. 1702–1714) and then to George, the elector of the German principality of Hanover and the Protestant great-grandson of James I. In 1707, the formal Act of Union between Scotland and England ensured that in the future, the Catholic heirs of King James II would have no more right to the throne of Scotland than they did to the throne of England.

The English soon referred to the events of 1688 and 1689 as the "**Glorious Revolution**," because it firmly established England as a mixed monarchy governed by the "king in Parliament" according to the rule of law. Although William and Mary and their successors continued to exercise a large measure of executive power, after 1688, no English monarch attempted to govern without Parliament, which has met annually from that time on. Parliament, and especially the House of Commons, also strengthened its control over taxation and expenditure. Although Parliament never codified the legal provisions of this form of monarchy into one constitutional document, historians consider the settlement of 1688 as a founding moment in the development of a constitutional monarchy in Britain.

WILLIAM AND MARY. In 1688, William of Orange and his wife, Mary Stuart, became Protestant joint rulers of England in a coup that took power from her father, the Catholic James II. Compare this contemporary print with the portraits of Louis XIV (page 496) and Charles II (page 503). ▪ *What relationship does this portrait seem to depict between the royal couple and their subjects?* ▪ *What is the significance of the gathered crowd in the public square in the background?* ▪ *How is this different from the spectacle of divine authority projected by Louis XIV or the image of Charles II looking straight at the viewer?*

Yet 1688 was not all glory. Contrary to many historical accounts, the revolution of 1688 was not "bloodless." The accession of William and Mary was accompanied by violence in many parts of England, Scotland, and Ireland. Angry Whigs attacked royal troops in York, Hull, Carlisle, Chester, and Portsmouth. James's revenue agencies were also attacked, as were his newly founded Catholic schools. Historians now see this violence as motivated as much by antiabsolutism as by religious bigotry. Popular anger against James II focused not so much on his defense of tradition but on his innovations, specifically his attempts to strengthen the power of the bureaucratic state. Furthermore, the revolution of 1688 consolidated the position of large property holders, whose control over local government had been threatened by the absolutist policies of Charles II and James II. It thus reinforced the power of a wealthy class of English elites in Parliament who would soon become even wealthier from government patronage and the profits of war. It also brought misery to the Catholic minority in Scotland and to the Catholic majority in

Ireland. After 1690, when King William won a decisive victory over James II's forces at the Battle of the Boyne, power in Ireland would lie firmly in the hands of a "Protestant Ascendancy," whose dominance over Irish society would last until modern times.

At the same time, however, England's Glorious Revolution also established a climate that favored the growth and political power of the English commercial classes, especially the increasing number of people concentrated in English cities whose livelihood depended on international commerce in the Atlantic world and beyond. In the decades to come, trade became a political issue, and merchant's associations began to lobby Parliament for favorable legislation. Whigs in Parliament became the voice of this newly influential pressure group of commercial entrepreneurs, who sought to challenge the monopoly enjoyed by the East India Company (founded with a royal charter in 1600) and open up colonial trade to competitors. They also argued that royal charter companies discouraged English manufacture by importing cheaper goods from abroad. The Whigs also argued for revisions to the tax code that would benefit those engaged in manufacturing and trade, rather than the landed elites who had benefited from the tax regime under the Stuarts. In 1694, the Whigs succeeded in establishing the Bank of England, with the explicit goal of facilitating the promotion of English power through the generation of wealth, inaugurating a financial revolution that would make London the center of a vast network of international banking and investment in the eighteenth century.

John Locke and the Contract Theory of Government

The Glorious Revolution was the product of unique circumstances, but it also reflected antiabsolutist theories of politics that were taking shape in the late seventeenth century in response to the ideas of writers such as Bodin, Hobbes, Filmer, and Bossuet. Chief among these opponents of absolutism was the Englishman **John Locke** (1632–1704), whose *Two Treatises of Government* were written before the Glorious Revolution but published for the first time in 1690.

Locke maintained that humans had originally lived in a state of nature characterized by absolute freedom and equality, with no government of any kind. The only law was the law of nature (which Locke equated with the law of reason), by which individuals enforced for themselves their natural rights to life, liberty, and property. Soon, however, humans perceived that the inconveniences of the state of nature outweighed its advantages. Accordingly, they agreed

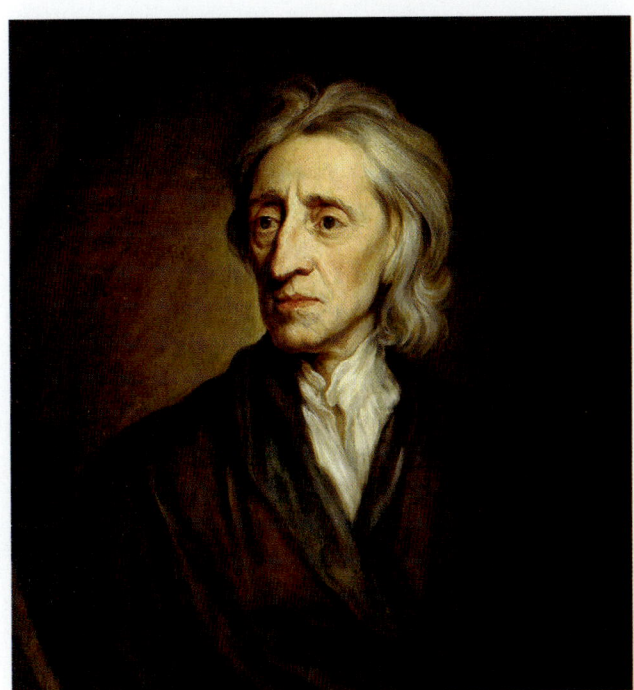

JOHN LOCKE (1632–1704). Locke was an important foundational thinker in the liberal political tradition. He had a profound influence on the Glorious Revolution of 1688 in England, on the American Revolution, and on French political theory during the Enlightenment. His debate with Robert Filmer, a defender of absolutism, led him to elaborate a theory of government as a contract between the ruler and the ruled.

first to establish a civil society based on absolute equality, and then to set up a government to arbitrate the disputes that might arise within this civil society. But they did not make government's powers absolute. All powers not expressly surrendered to the government were reserved to the people themselves; as a result, governmental authority was both **contractual** and conditional. If a government exceeded or abused the authority granted to it, society had the right to dissolve it and create another.

Locke condemned absolutism in every form. He denounced absolute monarchy, but he was also critical of claims for the sovereignty of parliaments. Government, he argued, had been instituted to protect life, liberty, and property; no political authority could infringe these natural rights. The law of nature was therefore an automatic and absolute limitation on every branch of government.

In the late eighteenth century, Locke's ideas would resurface as part of the intellectual background of both the American and French Revolutions. Between 1690 and 1720, however, they served a far less radical purpose. The landed gentry who replaced James II with William and Mary read Locke as a defense of their conservative revolution. Rather than protecting their liberty and property,

James II had threatened both; hence, the magnates were entitled to overthrow the tyranny he had established and replace it with a government that would defend their interests by preserving these natural rights. English government after 1689 was dominated by Parliament; Parliament in turn was controlled by a landed aristocracy that was firm in the defense of its common interests, and that perpetuated its control by determining that only men possessed of substantial property could vote or run for office. During the beginning of the eighteenth century, then, both France and Britain had solved the problem of political dissent and social disorder in their own way. The emergence of a limited monarchy in England after 1688 contrasted vividly with the absolutist system developed by Louis XIV, but both systems, in fact, worked well enough to contain the threats to royal authority posed by powerful landed nobles and religious dissent.

The Dutch Republic

Another exception to absolutist rule in Europe was the Dutch Republic of the United Provinces, which had gained its independence from Spanish rule in 1648, after a long period of struggle (see Chapter 14). The seven provinces of the Dutch Republic (also known as the Netherlands) carefully preserved their autonomy with a federal legislature known as the States General, made up of delegations from each province. Through this flexible structure, the inhabitants of the republic worked hard to prevent the reestablishment of hereditary monarchy in the Dutch Republic. They were all the more jealous of their independence because several Catholic provinces of the southern Low Countries, including present-day Belgium and Luxembourg, remained under Spanish control.

The princes of the House of Orange served the Dutch Republic with a special title, *stadtholder*, or steward. The stadtholder did not technically rule and had no power to make laws, though he did exercise some influence over the appointments of officials and military officers. Instead, powerful merchant families in the United Provinces exercised real authority, through their dominance of the legislature. It was from the Dutch Republic that the stadtholder William of Orange launched his successful bid to become the king of England in the Glorious Revolution of 1688.

The Dutch United Provinces were not, perhaps, the first place that one would choose as a base for a commercial trading empire. Much of the territory of the Dutch Republic was below sea level, and the water was kept out only by an elaborate system of dikes that protected the land from floods. But the Dutch made good use of their proximity to the sea. By 1670, the prosperity of the Dutch Republic was strongly linked to trade: grains and fish from eastern Europe and the Baltic Sea; spices, silks, porcelains, and tea from the Indian Ocean and Japan; and slaves, silver, coffee, sugar, and tobacco from the Atlantic world. With a population of nearly 2 million and a capital, Amsterdam, that was an international hub for goods and finance, the Dutch Republic's commercial network was global (see Chapter 14). Trade brought with it an extraordinary diversity of peoples and religions, as Spanish and Portuguese Jews, French Huguenots, English Quakers, and Protestant dissidents from central Europe all sought to take advantage of the relative spirit of toleration that existed in the Netherlands. This toleration did have limits, however. Jews were not required to live in segregated neighborhoods, as in many other European capitals, but they were prohibited from joining guilds or trade associations. Tensions between Calvinists and Catholics were a perennial issue, with Calvinists living in the western provinces and Catholics concentrated to the east and south.

The last quarter of the seventeenth century witnessed a decline in Dutch power, as the Low Countries were increasingly squeezed between the military strength and territorial ambitions of absolutist France to the south and competition from the maritime empire of the British in the Atlantic and Indian Oceans. The turning point came in 1672, when the French king, Louis XIV, put together a coalition that surrounded the United Provinces, threatening an invasion. The English took advantage of this moment of vulnerability to attack a major Dutch convoy returning from the eastern Mediterranean. Louis XIV invaded and quickly overran all but two of the Dutch provinces. Popular anger at the failures of Dutch leadership turned violent, and in response, the panicked assemblies named William of Orange the new stadtholder of Holland, giving him the power to organize the defense of the Republic and quell internal dissent. William opened the dikes that held back the sea, and the French armies were forced to retreat in the face of rising waters. Soon after, the Spanish entered the war on the side of the Dutch, which caused Louis XIV to abandon his plans to conquer the United Provinces. After the Glorious Revolution of 1688 in England, which brought William of Orange to the English throne, the Dutch joined an alliance with the English against the French. This alliance protected the Republic against further aggression from France, but it also forced the Dutch into heavy expenditures on fortifications and defense and involved them in a series of costly wars (see page 508). As a result, the dynamic and flexible political institutions that had been part of the strength of the Dutch Republic became more rigid and inflexible over time. Meanwhile, both the French and the British continued to pressure the Dutch commercial fleet at sea. In the eighteenth century, the Dutch no longer exercised the same influence abroad.

The Polish-Lithuanian Commonwealth

The Commonwealth of Poland and Lithuania was a vast state that ruled over much of present-day Poland, Lithuania, Latvia, Estonia, Belarus, and Ukraine between 1569 and 1795. At its greatest extent, during the second decade of the seventeenth century, the Commonwealth reached from the Baltic coast nearly to the Black Sea. The kings of the Commonwealth allied themselves with Austria to challenge attempts by the Ottoman Empire to expand its control over the territory in southeastern Europe.

Unlike Austria, Prussia, France, and Russia, however, the Commonwealth had a tradition of limits to monarchical authority that makes it an important exception to the trend toward absolutist rule in seventeenth-century Europe. Poland and Lithuania had been governed by a single ruler since 1386, and this personal connection between the two lands was given more formal status by the Union of Lublin in 1569. The political system of the Commonwealth was unusual in its commitment to a principle of representative institutions that could act as a check on the authority of the king. This makes the Commonwealth a striking early example of a central European state that committed itself to a separation of powers.

The limits to royal authority in Poland-Lithuania in the seventeenth and eighteenth centuries were largely enforced by the relatively numerous landowning gentry. These nobles elected members to seats in smaller provincial assemblies and in a parliament known as the Sejm (SAY-m). It was generally accepted by all that the king could not outfit an army or raise taxes without consulting the Sejm. In the seventeenth and eighteenth centuries, the Sejm consisted of two chambers, a smaller Senate with representatives of the Church and the State and the Chamber, which received representatives or envoys from each provincial assembly. The custom after 1569 was for the Chamber and the Senate to meet for a six-week session at least every two years. When the king died, the Sejm supervised the process by which the landowning aristocracy elected a new ruler. Parliamentary authority was not at all complete, however, and the crown retained considerable power. One-sixth of the land in the Commonwealth remained under the direct control of the king, and this gave him considerable economic wealth, which in turn increased his military authority and his ability to gain support through patronage.

This unusual balance of power between the landed gentry and the crown in the Commonwealth of Poland and Lithuania was exceptional in central and eastern Europe, but it also demonstrates that the most important dynamic influencing the development of state institutions during this period remained the relationship between the landed elites and dynastic rulers. In some European forms of government—the Restoration monarchy of England after 1688, the Dutch Republic, and the Polish-Lithuanian Commonwealth—circumstances allowed for greater power to remain in the hands of the gentry. In France, Prussia, and Russia (see pages 509–513), on the other hand, absolutist rulers eventually succeeded in imposing their will on the aristocrats who remained their most powerful rivals for authority.

A. *The Present King in his Throne.*
BB. *The ten Crown Officers.*
C. *The A Bp. of Gnesna w.th y.e Cross born behind him.*
DDDD. *The other Ecclesiasticall Senators.*
EEEEE. *Forreign Embassadors admitted only to y.e Diet of Election.*

FFFFFF. *The Palatins & Castellans in y.e three Rows on each side.*
GGGGGG. *The Deputys in the two back Rows on each side.*
H. *The Nuncio Marshall or Speaker of Deputys.*
IIII. *Vacant seats for such others as are sometimes admitted.*
1. *The Arms of Poland.* 2. *The Arms of Lithuania.*

THE POLISH SEJM. This was the representative body of the Polish-Lithuanian Commonwealth between 1569 and 1793, whose approval the king needed to pass legislation. Through most of its history it met for six weeks every two years, usually in Warsaw. Compare this with the Estates General in France, which did not meet at all between 1614 and 1789.

WAR AND THE BALANCE OF POWER, 1661–1715

By the beginning of the eighteenth century, Europe was being reshaped by wars whose effects were also felt far beyond Europe's borders. The initial causes of these wars lay in the French monarch's efforts to challenge his main European rivals: the Habsburg powers in Spain, the Spanish Netherlands, and the Holy Roman Empire. Louis XIV's personal rule began in 1661 (he had come to the throne as a child in 1643), and he first invaded the Spanish Netherlands in 1667. Through his continued campaigns in the Low Countries, he expanded his territory, eventually taking Strasbourg (1681), Luxembourg (1684), and Cologne (1688). In response, William of Orange organized the League of Augsburg, which over time included Holland, England, Spain, Sweden, Bavaria, Saxony, the Rhine Palatinate, and the Austrian Habsburgs. The resulting Nine Years' War between France and the League extended from Ireland to India to North America (where it was known as King William's War), demonstrating the broadening imperial reach of European dynastic regimes and the increasing significance of French and English competition in the Atlantic world.

These wars were signs of both the heightening power of Europe's absolutist regimes and their growing vulnerability. Financing the increasingly costly wars of the eighteenth century would prove to be one of the central challenges faced by all of Europe's absolutist regimes, and the pressure to raise revenues from their subjects through taxation would eventually strain European society to a breaking point. By the end of the eighteenth century, popular unrest and political challenges to absolutist and imperial states were widespread, both on the European continent and in the colonies of the Atlantic world.

From the League of Augsburg to the War of the Spanish Succession

The League of Augsburg reflected the emergence of a new diplomatic goal in western and central Europe: the preservation of a **balance of power**. This goal would animate European diplomacy for the next 200 years, until the balance-of-power system collapsed with the outbreak of the First World War. The main proponents of balance-of-power diplomacy were England, the United Provinces (Holland), Prussia, and Austria. By 1697, the League forced Louis XIV to make peace, because France was exhausted by war and

famine. Louis gave back many of his recent gains but kept Strasbourg and the surrounding territory of Alsace. In North America, the borders between French and English colonial territories remained unchanged for the time being (see page 509). Louis was nevertheless looking at the real prize: a French claim to succeed to the throne of Spain and so control the Spanish Empire in the Americas, Italy, the Netherlands, and the Philippines.

In the 1690s, it became clear that King Charles II of Spain (r. 1665–1700) would soon die without a clear heir, and both Louis XIV of France and Leopold I of Austria (r. 1658–1705) were interested in promoting their own relatives to succeed him. Either solution would have upset the balance of power in Europe, and several schemes to divide the Spanish realm between French and Austrian candidates were discussed. Meanwhile, King Charles II's advisers sought to avoid partition by passing the entire Spanish Empire to a single heir: Louis XIV's grandson Philip of Anjou. Philip was to renounce any claim to the French throne in becoming king of Spain, but these terms were kept secret. When Charles II died, Philip (r. 1700–1746) was proclaimed King Philip V of Spain, and Louis XIV rushed troops into the Spanish Netherlands while also sending French merchants into the Spanish Americas to end Spain's monopoly on trade from the region. Immediately the War of the Spanish Succession broke out, pitting England, the United Provinces, Austria, and Prussia against France, Bavaria, and Spain. Although the English king, William of Orange, died in 1702, just as the war was beginning, his generals led an extraordinary march deep into the European continent, inflicting a devastating defeat on the French and their Bavarian allies at Blenheim (1704). Soon after, the English captured Gibraltar, establishing a commercial foothold in the Mediterranean. The costs of the campaign nevertheless created a chorus of complaints from English and Dutch merchants, who feared the damage that was being done to trade and commerce. Queen Anne of England (Mary's sister and William's successor) gradually grew disillusioned with the war, and her government sent out peace feelers to France.

In 1713, the war finally came to an end with the **Treaty of Utrecht**. Its terms were reasonably fair to all sides. Philip V, Louis XIV's grandson, remained on the throne of Spain and kept Spain's colonial empire intact. In return, Louis agreed that France and Spain would never be united under the same ruler. Austria gained territories in the Spanish Netherlands and Italy, including Milan and Naples. The Dutch were guaranteed protection of their borders against future invasions by France, but the French retained both Lille and Strasbourg. The most significant consequences of the settlement, however, were played out in the Atlantic world, as the balance of powers among Europe's colonial empires underwent a profound shift.

Imperial Rivalries after the Treaty of Utrecht

The fortunes of Europe's colonial empires changed dramatically owing to the wars of the late seventeenth and early eighteenth centuries. Habsburg Spain proved unable to defend its early monopoly over colonial trade, and by 1700, although Spain still possessed a substantial empire, it lay at the mercy of its more dynamic rivals. Portugal, too, found it impossible to prevent foreign penetration of its colonial empire. In 1703, the English signed a treaty with Portugal allowing English merchants to export woolens duty free into Portugal and allowing Portugal to ship its wines duty free into England. Access to Portugal also led British merchants to trade with the Portuguese colony of Brazil, an important sugar producer and the largest of all the American markets for African slaves.

The 1713 Treaty of Utrecht opened a new era of colonial rivalries. The French retained Québec and other territories in North America, as well as their small foothold in India. The biggest winner by far was Great Britain, as the combined kingdoms of England and Scotland were known after 1707. The British kept Gibraltar and Minorca in the Mediterranean and also acquired large chunks of French territory in the New World, including Newfoundland, mainland Nova Scotia, the Hudson Bay, and the Caribbean island of St. Kitts. Even more valuable, however, Britain also extracted from Spain the right to transport and sell African slaves in Spanish America. As a result, the British were now poised to become the principal slave merchants and the dominant colonial and commercial power of the eighteenth-century world.

The Treaty of Utrecht thus reshaped the balance of power in the Atlantic world in fundamental ways. Spain's collapse was already precipitous, and by 1713, it was complete. Spain would remain the "sick man of Europe" for the next two centuries. The Dutch decline was more gradual, but by 1713, Dutch merchants' inability to compete with the British in the slave trade diminished their economic clout. In the Atlantic, Britain and France were now the dominant powers. Although they would duel for another half century for control of North America, the balance of colonial power tilted decisively in Britain's favor after Utrecht. Within Europe, the myth of French military supremacy had been shattered. Britain's navy, not France's army, would rule the new imperial and commercial world of the eighteenth century.

THE TREATY OF UTRECHT, 1713. This illustration from a French royal almanac depicts the treaty that ended the War of Spanish Succession and reshaped the balance of power in western Europe in favor of Britain and France.

THE REMAKING OF CENTRAL AND EASTERN EUROPE

The decades between 1680 and 1720 also were decisive in reshaping the balance of power in central and eastern Europe. As Ottoman power waned, the Austro-Hungarian Empire of the Habsburgs emerged as the dominant power in central and southeastern Europe. To the north, Brandenburg-Prussia was also a rising power. The most dramatic changes, however, occurred in Russia, which emerged from a long war with Sweden as the dominant power in the Baltic Sea and would soon threaten the combined kingdom of Poland-Lithuania. Within these regimes,

EUROPE AFTER THE TREATY OF UTRECHT (1713). ▪ *What were the major Habsburg dominions?* ▪ *What geographical disadvantage faced the kingdom of Poland as Brandenburg-Prussia grew in influence and ambition?* ▪ *How did the balance of power change in Europe as a result of the Treaty of Utrecht?*

the main tension came from ambitious monarchs who sought to increase the power of the centralized state at the expense of other elites, especially aristocrats and the Church. In Brandenburg-Prussia and in tsarist Russia, these efforts were largely successful, whereas in Habsburg Austria, regional nobilities retained much of their influence.

The Austrian Habsburg Empire

In the second half of the seventeenth century, as Louis XIV of France demonstrated the power of absolutism in

western Europe, the Austrian Habsburg Empire, with its capital in Vienna, must have seemed increasingly like a holdover from a previous age. Habsburg Austria was the largest state within what remained of the medieval Holy Roman Empire, a complex federal association of nearly 300 nominally autonomous dynastic kingdoms, principalities, duchies, and archbishoprics that had been created to protect and defend the papacy. Some, such as the kingdom of Bavaria, were large and had their own standing armies. Each Holy Roman emperor was chosen by seven "electors" who were either of noble rank or archbishops—in practice, the emperor was always from the Habsburg family. Through strategic marriages with other royal lines, earlier generations of Habsburg rulers had consolidated their control over a substantial part of Europe, including Austria, Bohemia, Moravia, and Hungary in central Europe; the Netherlands and Burgundy in the west; and, if one included the Spanish branch of the Habsburg family, Spain and its vast colonial empire as well. After 1648, when the Treaty of Westphalia granted individual member states within the Holy Roman Empire the right to conduct their own foreign policy, the influence of the Austrian Habsburgs waned, at precisely the moment when they faced challenges from France to the west and the Ottoman Empire to the east.

The complicated structure of the Holy Roman Empire limited the extent to which a ruler such as Leopold I of Austria could emulate the absolutist rule of Louis XIV in France. Every constituent state within the empire had its own local political institutions and its own entrenched nobilities, each with a strong interest in resisting any attempt to centralize crucial functions of government, such as taxation or the raising of armies. Even if direct assertion of absolutist control was impossible, Habsburg rulers found ways of increasing their authority. In Bohemia and Moravia, the Habsburgs encouraged landlords to produce crops for export by forcing peasants to provide three days of unpaid work per week to their lords. In return, the landed elites of these territories permitted the emperors to reduce the political independence of their traditional legislative estates. In Hungary, however, the powerful and independent nobility resisted such compromises. In 1679, when the Habsburgs began a campaign against Hungarian Protestants, an insurrection broke out that forced Leopold to grant concessions to Hungarian nobles in exchange for their assistance in restoring order. When the Ottoman Empire sought to take advantage of this disorder to press an attack against Austria from the east, the Habsburgs survived only by enlisting the help of a Catholic coalition led by the Polish king John Sobieski (r. 1674–1696).

In 1683, the Ottomans launched their last assault on Vienna, but after their failure to capture the Habsburg capital, Ottoman power in southeastern Europe declined. By 1699, Austria had reconquered most of Hungary from the Ottomans, and by 1718, it controlled all of Hungary and also Transylvania and Serbia. With these victories, Austria became one of the arbiters of the European balance of power. The same obstacles to the development of centralized absolutist rule persisted, however, and Austria was increasingly overshadowed in central Europe by the rise of another German-speaking state: Prussia.

The Rise of Brandenburg-Prussia

After the Ottoman defeat, the main threat to Austria came from the rising power of Brandenburg-Prussia. Like Austria, Prussia was a composite state made up of several geographically divided territories acquired through inheritance by a single royal family, the Hohenzollerns. Their two main holdings were Brandenburg, centered on its capital city, Berlin, and the duchy of East Prussia. Between these two territories lay Pomerania (claimed by Sweden) and an important part of the kingdom of Poland, including the port of Gdańsk (Danzig). The Hohenzollerns' aim was to unite their state by acquiring these intervening territories. Over the course of more than a century of steady state building, they finally succeeded. In the process, Brandenburg-Prussia became a dominant military power and a key player in the balance-of-power diplomacy of the mid-eighteenth century.

The foundations for Prussian expansion were laid by Frederick William, the "Great Elector" (r. 1640–1688).

PRUSSIANS SWEARING ALLEGIANCE TO THE GREAT ELECTOR AT KÖNIGSBERG, 1663. On this occasion, the Prussian estates first acknowledged the overlordship of their ruler. This ceremony marked the beginning of the centralization of the Prussian state.

The Siege of Vienna (1683)

In 1683, the armies of the Ottoman Empire besieged the city of Vienna, the capital of the Austrian Habsburg monarchy, which was defended by forces of the Holy Roman Empire of the German Nations, led by King John III Sobieski of the Polish-Lithuanian Commonwealth. The battle marked the high point of Ottoman expansion into southeastern Europe, and the Ottoman defeat was celebrated by many in Europe as a victory of Christianity over Islam. The reality was more complicated, however, as Protestant armies in Hungary that allied with anti-Habsburg forces had received arms and support from the Ottoman Empire in the years before the battle, apparently in exchange for a promise that Hungary would control Vienna in the event of an Ottoman victory. This source, published in 1684 in English in Cologne and London, contains enough details to allow one to assume that it was, at least in part, informed by eyewitnesses of the events.

Emperor Leopold I Flees Vienna for Passau

The Emperor who had receiv'd a fierce alarm by the suddain irruption of the Infidels, and who consider'd that after the revolt of the Hungarians, he could no longer remain at Vienna in surety, bethought himself at the same time of leaving it. But first augmented the privileges of the Scholars, which were already very great, and considerable, that having receiv'd them as a recompence of their Courage which they shew'd heretofore against Solyman [the Ottoman Emperor Suleiman the Magnificent], when he besieg'd the City [in 1529] this should be a fresh incitement to defend it with the same resolution. He gave also to the Shoomakers Apprentices their Freedom, who were to the number of about 1500, in case they took Arms, and did any thing considerable for the Country.

* * *

Every one wept at his departure, and this Prince had much ado to forbear himself. So greatly was he afflicted to be thus constrained to abandon his people to the mercy of the Infidels. In the mean time each one endeavor'd to follow him, to avoid the being expos'd to those mischiefs which they represented. In fine, there being not Coaches enough to carry all those that offer'd 'emselves, several Women of Quality got behind like Lacques [servants]; so that one might have seen the first Prince in the World, follow'd by all the flower of the German Nobility, to go as an exul [exile] amidst the screeches and lamentations of his people, who presented 'emselves in his passage with showr's of tears...

* * *

The Emperor all this while marched with a countenance sad and dejected like his fortune. Others kept a mournful silence, and although each had left their estates behind 'em 'twas not known whether their own mishap or that of the Prince was to be most lamented. In fine, this march much resembled a Funeral Pomp, when another spectacle encreas'd the dolour and compassion. For they beheld the other side of the *Danube* all in fire, and the Emperor having caused his Coach to stop, knowing not at first what it was, soon perceived 'twas the *Turks*, who shew'd there new testimonies of their barbarous cruelty. He could not withhold his tears at the sight of a thing so much needing his compassion, and although he did all he could to refrain his grief, he could not effect it.

Disease Afflicts the Defenders of Vienna

And having made his retreat, and taken great care of the wounded, [Stahrenberg, the military commander of Vienna] made a review of those Forces he had left him; which he found diminish'd by a third part, not so much by Sallies, and in this last occasion, as by the Dysentery or Flux which began to rage in the Town, as well amongst the Citizens and Soldiers. In effect the fatigues together with the bad food they eat, had so heated the bloud of most of 'em, that they fell sick every day. And it being impossible for 'em after this to do service, the rest, whose weariness increased as fast as the number of the others dimnish'd, were soon in the same condition, or at least so tir'd out with labour and watching, that they were all ready to drop down as they march'd....

* * *

But that which contributed to render this malady more incurable was the Airs being so infected by the stench of the dead Bodies which lay unburied, that it could not be more dangerous in a time of Plague. The cause of this stench was that Stahrenberg would not yield to any terms of a Truce propos'd by the Visier

[Vizier], to take away those of his party, who had been kild in so many several skirmishes, hoping that besides the displeasure he would receive thereby, this would be a spectacle to damp the Courage of the Soldiers, when in marching up to the Charge, they should see before their Eyes the fortune of their Companions, which would be a presage to them of the like. Howsoever whether 'twas this infection or something else, which brought this grievous sickness into the Town, they were so greatly incommodated [sic] by it, that they would willingly have been deliver'd from of it at the cost of a greater danger from the enemy. Yet did this distemper rage as well in the Camp of the Turks, of which there dyed every day near 300, but which was scarce perceivable, because they continually receiv'd fresh supplies, which made up their losses.

Source: Anonymous, *The History of the late war with the Turks, during the siege of Vienna, and the great victory obtain'd against them at the raising of the siege* (Cologne and London, 1684), pp. 33–86.

Questions for Analysis

1. How did Emperor Leopold encourage the people of the city to defend themselves even as he retreated to a safer location?

2. What is the significance of the term *Infidels*, which the author uses to describe the Ottomans?

3. What does this description tell us about the effects of the siege on military and civilian populations? What explanations does the author give for the spread of disease in the city and among the attacking armies?

He obtained East Prussia from Poland in exchange for help in a war against Sweden. Behind the elector's diplomatic triumphs lay his success in building an army and mobilizing the resources to pay for it. He gave the powerful nobles of his territories, known as "Junkers" (*YUN-kurs*), the right to enserf their peasants, and guaranteed immunity from taxation. In exchange, they staffed the officer corps of his army and supported his highly autocratic taxation system. Secure in their estates and made increasingly wealthy in the grain trade, the Junkers surrendered management of the Prussian state to the elector's newly reformed bureaucracy, which set about its main task of increasing the size and strength of the Prussian army.

By supporting Austria in the War of the Spanish Succession, the Great Elector's son, Frederick I (r. 1688–1713) earned the right to call himself king of Prussia from the Austrian emperor. He, too, was a crafty diplomat, but his main attention was devoted to developing the cultural life of his new royal capital, Berlin. His son, Frederick William I (r. 1713–1740), however, focused on building the army like his grandfather. During his reign, the Prussian army grew from 30,000 to 83,000 men, becoming the fourth largest army in Europe, after those of France, Austria, and Russia. To support his army, Frederick William I increased taxes and shunned the luxuries of court life. For him, the theater of absolutism was not the palace but the office, where he personally supervised his army and the growing bureaucracy that sustained it. Frederick William's son, known as Frederick the Great, would use this Prussian army and the bureaucracy that sustained it to transform the kingdom into a major power in central Europe after 1740 (see Chapter 17).

Thus, in both Prussia and Habsburg Austria, the divided nature of the respective realms and the entrenched strength of local nobilities forced the rulers of each to grant significant concessions to noble landowners in exchange for incremental increases in the power of the centralized state. Whereas the nobility in France increasingly sought to maximize their power by participating in the system of absolutist rule at the court of Louis XIV, and wealthy landowners in England sought to exercise their influence through Parliament, the nobilities of Prussia and Habsburg Austria had more leverage to demand something in return for their cooperation. Often, what they demanded was the right to enserf or coerce labor from the peasantry in their domains. In both eastern and western Europe, therefore, the state became stronger. In eastern Europe, however, this increase in state power often came at the expense of an intensification of feudal obligations that the peasantry owed to their local lords.

THE CITY OF STETTIN UNDER SIEGE BY THE GREAT ELECTOR FREDERICK WILLIAM IN THE WINTER OF 1677–1678 (c. 1680). This painting depicts the growing sophistication and organization of military operations under the Prussian monarchy. Improvements in artillery and siege tactics forced cities to adopt new defensive strategies, especially the zones of battlements and protective walls that became ubiquitous in central Europe during this period. ▪ *How might these defensive developments have shaped the layout of Europe's growing towns and cities?* ▪ *How might this emphasis on the military and its attendant bureaucracy have affected the relationship between the monarchy and the nobility, or between the king and his subjects?*

into contact with western Europe, but his policies were decisive in making Russia a great European power.

The Early Years of Peter's Reign

Like Louis XIV of France, Peter came to the throne as a young boy, and his minority was marked by political dissension and court intrigue. In 1689, however, at the age of seventeen, he overthrew the regency of his half sister Sophia and assumed personal control of the state. Determined to make Russia into a great military power, the young tsar traveled to Holland and England during the 1690s to study shipbuilding and to recruit skilled foreign workers to help him build a navy. But while he was abroad, his elite palace guard (the *streltsy*) rebelled, attempting to restore Sophia to the throne. Peter quickly returned home from Vienna and crushed the rebellion with striking savagery. About 1,200 suspected conspirators were summarily executed, many of them gibbeted outside the walls of the Kremlin, where their bodies rotted for months as a graphic reminder of the fate awaiting those who dared challenge the tsar's authority.

AUTOCRACY IN RUSSIA

An even more dramatic transformation took place in Russia under Tsar Peter I (r. 1682–1725). Peter's official title was "autocrat of all the Russias," but he was soon known as Peter the Great. His imposing height (six feet eight inches) and his mercurial personality (jesting one moment, raging the next) added to the outsize impression he made on his contemporaries. Peter is most remembered for his controversial efforts to make Russians emulate aspects of western European culture he admired. He demanded that the aristocracy shave their beards and adopt Western forms of etiquette, and called upon them to educate themselves and read books from abroad. To showcase his ambitions he built a modern capital city, St. Petersburg, along western European lines, and asserted control over the Russian Orthodox Church. Peter was not the first tsar to bring his country

The Transformation of the Tsarist State

Peter is most famous as the tsar who attempted to westernize Russia by imposing a series of social and cultural reforms on the traditional Russian nobility: ordering noblemen to cut off their long beards and flowing sleeves; publishing a book of manners that forbade spitting on the floor and eating with one's fingers; encouraging polite conversation between the sexes; and requiring noblewomen to appear, together with men, in Western garb at weddings, banquets, and other public occasions. The children of Russian nobles were sent to western European courts for their education. Thousands of western European

EXECUTION OF THE *STRELTSY* (1698). A contemporary woodcut showing how Peter the Great ordered the public hanging of guard regiments who rebelled against his authority. ■ *How does this display of autocratic power compare with the spectacle of power so carefully orchestrated by Peter's contemporary Louis XIV of France?*

experts were brought to Russia to staff the new schools and academies Peter built; to design the new buildings he constructed; and to serve in the tsar's army, navy, and administration.

These measures were important, but the tsar was not motivated primarily by a desire to modernize or westernize Russia. Peter's policies transformed Russian life in fundamental ways, but his real goal was to make Russia a great military power, not to remake Russian society. For example, while his new taxation system (1724), which assessed taxes on individuals rather than on households, rendered many of the traditional divisions of Russian peasant society obsolete, it was created to raise more

money for war. His Table of Ranks, imposed in 1722, had similar impact on the nobility. By insisting that all nobles must work their way up from the (lower) landlord class to the (higher) administrative class and to the (highest) military class, Peter reversed the traditional hierarchy of Russian noble society, which had valued landlords by birth above administrators and soldiers who had risen by merit. This created a powerful new incentive to lure his nobility into administrative and military service to the tsar.

As "autocrat of all the Russias," Peter the Great was the absolute master of his empire to a degree unmatched elsewhere in Europe. After 1649, Russian peasants were legally

Analyzing Primary Sources

The Revolt of the Streltsy and Peter the Great

The streltsy were four regiments of Moscow guards that became involved in a conspiracy in support of Peter the Great's older sister Sophia, who had earlier made claim to the throne while Peter was still a child. Approximately 4,000 of the rebels were defeated in June 1698 by troops loyal to Peter. Peter himself was abroad during the fighting, and although his officers had already tortured many of the streltsy to determine the involvement of other nobles, he ordered a farther-reaching investigation on his return. More than 1,000 of the streltsy were executed after being tortured again. Afterward, their bodies were put on display in the capital. Johann Georg Korb, an Austrian diplomat in Moscow, recorded his observations of the power wielded by the Russian autocrat.

 ow sharp was the pain, how great the indignation to which the Czar's Majesty was mightily moved, when he knew of the rebellion of the Strelitz [*streltsy*], betrayed openly a mind panting for vengeance. [*sic*] . . . Going immediately to Lefort (the only person almost that he condescended to treat with intimate familiarity), he thus indignantly broke out: "Tell me, Francis, son of James, how I can reach Moscow, by the shortest way, in a brief space, so that I may wreak vengeance on this great perfidy of my people, with punishments worthy of their flagitious crime. Not one of them shall escape with impunity. Around my royal city, of which, with their impious efforts, they meditated the destruction, I will have gibbets and gallows set upon the walls and ramparts, and each and every [one] of them will I put to a direful death." . . .

His first anxiety, after his arrival [in Moscow] was about the rebellion. In what it consisted? What the insurgents meant? Who had dared to instigate such a crime? And as nobody could answer accurately upon all points, and some pleaded their own ignorance, others the obstinacy of the Strelitz, he began to have suspicions of everybody's loyalty, and began to cogitate about a fresh investigation. The rebels that were kept in custody . . . were all brought in by four regiments of the guards, to a fresh investigation and fresh tortures. Prison, tribunal, and rack, for those that were brought in, was in Bebraschentsko. No day, holy, or profane, were the inquisitors idle; every day was deemed fit and lawful for torturing. As many as there were accused there were knouts, and every inquisitor was a butcher. Prince Feodor Jurowicz Romadonowski showed himself by so much more fitted for his inquiry, as he surpassed the rest in cruelty. He put the interrogatories, he examined the criminals, he urged those that were not confessing, he ordered such Strelitz as were more pertinaciously silent, to be subjected to more cruel tortures; those that had already confessed about many things were questioned about more; those who were bereft of strength and reason, and almost of their senses, by excess of torment, were handed over to the skill of the doctors, who were compelled to restore them to strength, in order that they might be broken down by fresh excruciations. The whole month of October was spent in butchering the backs of the culprits with knout and with flames: no day were those that were left alive exempt from scourging or scorching, or else they were broken upon the wheel, or driven to the gibbet, or slain with the axe—the penalties which were inflicted upon them as soon as their confessions had sufficiently revealed the heads of the rebellion.

Source: Johann Georg Korb, *Diary of an Austrian Secretary of Legation at the Court of Czar Peter the Great*, trans. Count MacDonnell (London: 1863), vol. 2, pp. 85–87.

Questions for Analysis

1. Why was it important for Korb to begin this account with a description of the monarch's pain?

2. What does this episode reveal about Peter's conception of his own person and of the loyalty that his subjects owed him? Does it show that his power was fragile, immense, or both?

3. What does it mean to describe torture as an "investigation" even while also describing it as "vengeance"?

PETER THE GREAT CUTS THE BEARD OF AN OLD BELIEVER.
This woodcut depicts the Russian emperor's enthusiastic policy of westernization, as he pushed everybody in Russia who was not a peasant to adopt western styles of clothes and grooming. The Old Believer (a member of a religious sect in Russia) protests that he has paid the beard tax and should therefore be exempt. ■ *Why would an individual's choices about personal appearance be so politically significant in Peter's Russia?* ■ *What customs were the target of Peter's reforms?*

with a smaller handpicked senate, a group of nine administrators who supervised military and civilian affairs. In religious matters, he took direct control over the Russian Orthodox Church by appointing an imperial official to manage its affairs. To cope with the demands of war, he also fashioned a new, larger, and more efficient administration, for which he recruited both nobles and non-nobles. The rank in the new bureaucracy did not depend on birth. One of his principal advisers, Alexander Menshikov, began his career as a cook and finished as a prince. This degree of social mobility would have been impossible in any contemporary western European country. In Russia, more so than in western Europe, noble status depended on government service, with all nobles expected to participate in Peter's army or administration. Peter was not entirely successful in enforcing this requirement, but the administrative machinery he devised furnished Russia with its ruling class for the next 200 years.

Russian Imperial Expansion

The goal of Peter's foreign policy was to secure year-round ports for Russia on the Black Sea and the Baltic Sea. In the Black Sea, his enemy was the Ottoman Empire. Here, however, he had little success, and Russia would not secure its position in the Black Sea until the end of the eighteenth century. Nevertheless, Peter continued to push against the Ottoman Empire in the northern Caucasus region throughout his reign. This mountainous area on Russia's southern flank became an important site for Russia's experiments in colonial expansion into central Asia, which began during the sixteenth century and would later mirror the process of colonial conquest undertaken by European powers and the United States in North and South America. Like those of France and Britain, the Russian state bureaucracy was built during a period of ambitious colonialism; and as in Spain, the monarchy's identity was shaped by a long contest with Muslim power on its borders.

Since the late sixteenth century, successful Russian leaders had extended their control over bordering territories of central Asia. Although merchants helped fund early expeditions into Siberia, this expansion was primarily motivated by geopolitical concerns; the tsar sought to gain access to the populations of Russia's border areas and bring them into the service of the expanding Russian state. In this sense, Russian colonialism during this period differed from western European expansion into the Atlantic world, which had primarily been motivated by hopes of commercial gain.

the property of their landlords; by 1750, half were serfs and the other half were state peasants who lived on lands owned by the tsar himself. (In contrast, many peasants in western Europe owned their own land, and very few were serfs.) State peasants could be conscripted to serve as soldiers in the tsar's army, as workers in his factories (whose productive capacity increased enormously during Peter's reign), or as forced laborers in his building projects. Serfs could also be taxed by the tsar and summoned for military service, as could their lords. All Russians, of whatever rank, were expected to serve the tsar, and all Russia was considered in some sense to belong to him. Russia's autocracy thus went even further than the absolutism of Louis XIV.

To consolidate his power further, Peter replaced the Duma—the tsar's handpicked council of noble elites—

THE GROWTH OF THE RUSSIAN EMPIRE. ▪ *How did Peter the Great expand the territory controlled by Russia?* ▪ *What neighboring dynasties were most affected by Russian expansion?* ▪ *How did the emergence of a bigger, more powerful Russia affect the European balance of power?*

In its early stages, as successive Russian emperors moved Russian troops eastward into Asia, they relied on a process of indirect rule, often seeking to co-opt local elites. Later in the eighteenth century, they had more success settling Russians in border regions to rule directly over local populations. Religion also provided a cover for expansion, and Peter and his successors funded missionary work by Georgian Christians among Muslims in the Caucasus. Efforts to convert Muslim populations to Orthodox Christianity had little effect, and in fact the opposite occurred: the region's commitment to Islam was continuously renewed through contact with different strains of Islamic practice coming from neighboring Ottoman lands and Persia.

Peter could point to more concrete success to the north. In 1700, he began what would become a twenty-one-year war with Sweden, then the dominant power in the Baltic Sea. By 1703, Peter had secured a foothold on the Gulf

of Finland and immediately began to build a new capital city there, which he named St. Petersburg. For Peter, the new capital became a vehicle for his drive for international recognition: seen primarily as a naval port and a bulwark against the Swedish at first, it became a model for what he believed Russia could become.

After 1709, when Russian armies decisively defeated the Swedes at the battle of Poltava, work on Peter's new capital city accelerated. An army of serfs was now conscripted to build the new city, whose centerpiece was a royal palace designed to imitate and rival Louis XIV's Versailles. Conditions for the laborers were grueling and deaths were frequent. Peter's elaborate building sites required armed guards to maintain order. He insisted on western designs for all the buildings in the new city, and in 1714, he forced one thousand aristocrats to move into the new capital with their families, ignoring their protests. In the end, Peter's model city was equipped with remarkable amenities:

street lighting, regular waste collection, and a fire brigade. But resentment at his autocratic methods remained for generations afterwards.

The Great Northern War with Sweden ended in 1721 with the Peace of Nystad. This treaty marked a realignment of power in eastern Europe comparable with that effected by the Treaty of Utrecht in the West. Sweden lost its North Sea territories to Hanover, its Baltic German territories to Prussia, and its eastern territories, including the entire Gulf of Finland, Livonia, and Estonia, passed to Russia. Sweden was now a second-rank power in the northern European world. Poland-Lithuania survived, but it, too, was a declining power; by the end of the eighteenth century, this kingdom would disappear altogether, its territories swallowed up by its more powerful neighbors (see Chapter 17). The victors at Nystad were the Prussians and the Russians. These two powers secured their position along the Baltic coast, positioning themselves to take advantage of the lucrative eastern European grain trade with western Europe. Peter's accomplishments came at enormous cost. Direct taxation in Russia increased 500 percent during his reign, and in the 1720s, his army numbered more than 300,000 men. Peter made Russia a force to be reckoned with on the European scene, but in so doing, he aroused great resentment, especially among his nobility. Peter's only son and heir, Alexis, became the focus for conspiracies against the tsar, until finally Peter had him arrested and executed in 1718. As a result, when Peter died in 1725, he left no son to succeed him. A series of ineffective tsars followed, mostly from the palace guard; under these rules, the resentful nobles reversed many of Peter the Great's reforms. In 1762, however, the crown passed to Catherine the Great, a ruler whose ambitions and determination were equal to those of her great predecessor (see Chapter 17).

CONCLUSION

By the time of Peter the Great's death in Russia in 1725, the power of Europe's absolutist realms to reinvigorate European political institutions was visible to all. Government had become more bureaucratic; state service had been more professionalized; and administrators loyal to the kings had become more numerous, more efficient, and more demanding. Despite the increasing scope of government, the structure and principles of government changed relatively little. Apart from Great Britain, the Dutch Republic, and Poland-Lithuania, the great powers of eighteenth-century Europe were still governed by rulers who styled themselves as absolutist monarchs in the mold of Louis XIV, who claimed an authority that came directly from God and ruled over a society in which social hierarchies based on birth were taken for granted.

However, these absolutist regimes could not hide the fact that their rule depended on a kind of negotiated settlement with other powerful elites within European society, in particular with landed aristocrats and religious leaders. Louis XIV used his power to curb the worst excesses of nobles who abused their position, and to defend Catholic orthodoxy against dissident Catholics and Protestants. Nevertheless, his power depended on a delicate exchange of favors: French aristocrats surrendered their political authority to the state in exchange for social and legal privileges and immunity from many (but not all) forms of taxation, and the Church made a similar bargain. Peter the Great's autocratic rule in Russia worked out a slightly different balance of powers between his state and the Russian aristocracy, one that tied aristocrats more closely to an ideal of state service, a model that also worked well for the rulers of Brandenburg-Prussia. Even in England, the establishment of a limited constitutional monarchy and a king who ruled alongside Parliament was not really a radical departure from the European absolutist model. It was merely a different institutional answer to the same problem: What relationship should the monarchical state have with other elites within society?

The demands of state building during this period required kings to raise enormous revenues—for the sumptuous displays of their sovereignty in royal residences such as Louis XIV's palace at Versailles, for the sponsorship of royal academies and the patronage of artists, but most of all, for war. Expanding territory within Europe and holding on to colonial empires in the Atlantic world were costly. Distributing the burden of taxation to pay for these endeavors became an intensely fraught political issue for European monarchs during this period, and the financing of royal debt became an increasingly sophisticated art. Colbert's mercantilist policy was an attempt to harness the full power of the economy for the benefit of royal government; and the competition among Spain, Holland, England, and France to control the revenue flows coming from the Atlantic world forced Europe's monarchs to recognize that the balance of power was increasingly being played out on a global stage.

These themes—the expansion of state powers; conflicts between the monarchy and the aristocracy or with religious dissidents; the intensification of the tax burden on the population; and the opening up of Europe to ever more frequent interactions with other peoples in the Atlantic world, the Indian Ocean, and eventually, the Pacific—prompted many in eighteenth-century Europe to reflect on the consequences of these developments. What were the limits to state power, and by what criteria were the actions of rulers to be judged? What was the proper measure of economic prosperity, and who was it for? Could a well-ordered society tolerate religious diversity? Given Europe's growing awareness of cultures in other parts of the world with different religions, different political systems, and different ways of expressing their moral and ethical values, how might Europeans justify or measure their own beliefs and customs? The intellectuals who

After You Read This Chapter

 Go to **INQUIZITIVE** to see what you've learned—and learn what you've missed—with personalized feedback along the way.

REVIEWING THE OBJECTIVES

- Absolutist rulers claimed a monopoly of power and authority within their realms. What was absolutism? Who were the most successful absolutist monarchs?

- Mercantilism was an economic doctrine that guided the policies of absolutist rulers. What did mercantilists believe?

- Alternatives to absolutist government emerged in England, Holland, and Poland-Lithuania. What forms of government did these regimes develop? How did they differ from the absolutist and autocratic regimes of France, Prussia, and Russia?

- The wars begun by Louis XIV after 1680 drove his opponents to ally with each other to achieve a balance of power. What was the result of these conflicts in Europe and in the Atlantic world?

- Peter the Great embarked on an ambitious program of reform and territorial expansion in Russia. How did his autocratic government compare with absolutist regimes in western and central Europe?

looked for answers to these questions were similar to earlier generations of scientific researchers in their respect for reason and rational thought, but they turned their attention beyond problems of natural philosophy and science to the messy world of politics and culture. Their movement—known as the Enlightenment—reached its peak in the middle decades of the eighteenth century and created the basis for a powerful critique of Europe's absolutist regimes. The Enlightenment itself emerged slowly from a revolution in scientific thinking that had begun earlier in the early modern period, and it is to this history that we now turn.

PEOPLE, IDEAS, AND EVENTS IN CONTEXT

- What did **LOUIS XIV** of France and **PETER THE GREAT** of Russia have in common? How did they deal with those who resisted their attempts to impose absolutist rule?

- Compare the religious policies of **LOUIS XIV** of France with the religious policies of the English Stuart kings **CHARLES II** and **JAMES II**. In what way did religious disagreements limit their ability to rule effectively?

- How did European monarchies apply the economic theory known as **MERCANTILISM** to strengthen the power and wealth of their kingdoms? How did this theory influence **FRENCH COLONIALISM**?

- What was the **CONTRACT THEORY OF GOVERNMENT** according to the English political thinker **JOHN LOCKE**?

- What limits to royal power were recognized in Great Britain as a result of the **GLORIOUS REVOLUTION**?

- What was significant about the new **BALANCE OF POWER** that developed in Europe as a result of **LOUIS XIV**'s wars?

- What does the **TREATY OF UTRECHT** (1713) tell us about the diminished influence of Spain and the corresponding rise of Britain and France as European and colonial powers?

- What was different about the attempts by rulers in Habsburg Austria and Brandenburg-Prussia to impose **ABSOLUTISM** in central Europe?

- What innovations did **PETER THE GREAT** bring to Russia?

THINKING ABOUT CONNECTIONS

- What makes absolutism different from older models of kingship in earlier periods?

- Was the absolutist monarchs' emphasis on sumptuous displays of their authority something new? Explain how the display of power under absolutism is different from the way that political power is represented in democratic societies today.

STORY LINES

- After about 1550, new sciences in Europe questioned older beliefs about the physical universe. New methods of inquiry led to the development of astronomy, physics, biology, chemistry, geology, and new institutions that supported scientific research and education.

- The scientific revolution gave rise to theoretical breakthroughs in explaining the physical universe as well as advances in the practical knowledge of artisans who built mechanical devices such as telescopes or microscopes. This combination of scientific inquisitiveness and craft techniques encouraged technological developments that would later be useful in industrialization.

- The new sciences did not mark a clean rupture with older traditions of religious thinking. Most scientists of the 1600s remained essentially religious in their worldview. In any case, their work was accessible only to a small, literate minority who had access to books.

CHRONOLOGY

1543	Nicolaus Copernicus (1473–1543) publishes *On the Revolutions of the Heavenly Spheres*
1576	Tycho Brahe sets up Uraniborg observatory
1609	Johannes Kepler (1571–1643) publishes *Astronomia Nova*
1610	Galileo (1564–1642) publishes *The Starry Messenger*
1620	Francis Bacon (1561–1626) publishes *Novum Organum*
1632	Galileo publishes *Dialogue Concerning the Two Chief World Systems*
1633	Galileo's trial
1637	René Descartes (1596–1650) publishes *Discourse on Method*
1660	Royal Society of London founded
1666	French Academy of Sciences founded
1687	Isaac Newton (1642–1727) publishes *Principia Mathematica*

The New Science of the Seventeenth Century

Doubt thou the stars are fire,
Doubt that the sun doth move,
Doubt truth to be a liar,
But never doubt I love.

SHAKESPEARE, HAMLET, II.2

CORE OBJECTIVES

- **DEFINE** *scientific revolution* and **EXPLAIN** what is meant by *science* in this historical context.

- **UNDERSTAND** the older philosophical traditions that were important for the development of new methods of scientific investigation during the seventeenth century.

- **IDENTIFY** the sciences that made important advances during this period and **UNDERSTAND** what technological innovations encouraged a new spirit of investigation.

- **EXPLAIN** the differences between the Ptolemaic view of the universe and the new vision of the universe proposed by Nicolaus Copernicus.

- **UNDERSTAND** the different definitions of *scientific method* that emerged from the work of Francis Bacon and René Descartes.

"Doubt thou the stars are fire" and "that the sun doth move." Was Shakespeare alluding to controversial ideas about the cosmos that contradicted the teachings of medieval scholars? *Hamlet* (c. 1600) was written more than fifty years after Copernicus had suggested, in his treatise *On the Revolutions of the Heavenly Spheres* (1543), that the sun did not move but the earth did, revolving around the sun. Shakespeare probably knew of such theories, although they circulated only among small groups of learned Europeans. As Hamlet's lovelorn speech to Ophelia makes clear, they were considered conjecture—or strange mathematical hypotheses. These theories were not exactly new: a heliocentric universe had been proposed as early as the second century B.C.E. by ancient Greek astronomers. But they flatly contradicted the consensus that had set in after Ptolemy proposed an earth-centered universe in the second century C.E., and to Shakespeare's contemporaries, they defied common sense and observation. Learned philosophers, young lovers, shepherds, and sailors alike could watch the sun and the stars move from one horizon to the other each day and night—or so they thought.

Still, a small handful of thinkers did doubt. Shakespeare was born in 1564, the same year as Galileo. By the time the English playwright and the Italian natural philosopher were working, the long process of revising knowledge about the universe and discovering a new set of rules that explained how the universe worked was under way. By the end of the seventeenth century, a hundred years later, the building blocks of the new view had been put in place. This intellectual transformation brought sweeping changes to European philosophy and to Western views of the natural world and of humans' place in it.

Science entails at least three things: a body of knowledge, a method or system of inquiry, and a community of practitioners and the institutions that support them and their work. The *scientific revolution* of the seventeenth century—usually understood to have begun in the mid-sixteenth century and culminated in 1687 with Newton's *Principia*—involved each of these three realms. As far as the content of knowledge is concerned, the scientific revolution saw the emergence and confirmation of a heliocentric (sun-centered) view of the planetary system, which displaced the earth—and humans—from the center of the universe. Even more fundamental, it brought a new mathematical physics that described and confirmed such a view. Second, the scientific revolution established a method of inquiry for understanding the natural world, a method that emphasized the role of observation, experiment, and the testing of hypotheses. Third, *science* emerged as a distinctive branch of knowledge. During the period covered in this chapter, people referred to the study of matter, motion, optics, or the circulation of blood as natural philosophy (the more theoretical term), experimental philosophy, medicine, and—increasingly—science. The growth of societies and institutions dedicated to what we now commonly call scientific research was central to the changes at issue here. Science required not only brilliant thinkers but also patrons, states, and communities of researchers; the scientific revolution was thus embedded in other social, religious, and cultural transformations.

The scientific revolution was not an organized effort. Brilliant hypotheses sometimes led to dead ends, discoveries were often accidental, and artisans grinding lenses for telescopes played a role in the advance of knowledge just as surely as did great abstract thinkers. Educated women also claimed the right to participate in scientific debate, but their efforts were met with opposition or indifference. Old and new worldviews often overlapped as individual thinkers struggled to reconcile their discoveries with their faith or to make their theories—about the movement of bodies in the heavens, or the age of the earth, for instance—consistent with received wisdom. Science was slow to work its way into popular understanding. It did not necessarily undermine religion, and it certainly did not intend to (figures such as Isaac Newton thought their work confirmed and deepened their religious beliefs). In short, change came slowly and fitfully. But as the new scientific method started to produce radical new insights into the workings of nature, it eventually came to be accepted well beyond the small circles of experimenters, theologians, and philosophers with whom it had begun.

THE INTELLECTUAL ORIGINS OF THE SCIENTIFIC REVOLUTION

Much was new in the scientific breakthroughs of the sixteenth and seventeenth centuries, but these advances were rooted in earlier developments. Medieval artists and intellectuals had been observing and illustrating the natural world with great precision since at least the twelfth century. Medieval sculptors carved plants and vines with extraordinary accuracy, and fifteenth-century painters and sculptors devoted the same careful attention to the human face and form. The link among observation, experiment, and invention was not new to the sixteenth century either. The magnetic compass had been known in Europe since the thirteenth century; gunpowder since the early fourteenth; and printing—which permeated the intellectual life of the period and opened new possibilities for disseminating ideas quickly, collaborating more easily, and buying books and building libraries—since the middle of the fifteenth. "Printing, firearms, and the compass," wrote Francis Bacon, "no empire, sect or star appears to have exercised a greater power and influence on human affairs than these three mechanical discoveries." A fascination with light, which was a powerful symbol of divine illumination for medieval thinkers, encouraged the study of optics and, in turn, new techniques for grinding lenses. Lens grinders laid the groundwork for the seventeenth-century inventions of the telescope and microscope, creating reading glasses along the way. Astrologers were also active in the later Middle Ages, charting the heavens in the firm belief that the stars controlled the fates of human beings.

Behind these efforts to understand the natural world lay a nearly universal conviction that the natural world had been created by God. Religious belief spurred scientific study. One school of thinkers, **the Neoplatonists**, argued that nature was a book written by its creator to reveal the ways of God to humanity. Convinced that God's perfection must be reflected in nature, Neoplatonists searched for the ideal and perfect structures they believed must lie behind the "shadows" of the everyday world. Mathematics, particularly geometry, was an important tool in this quest. The mathematician and astronomer Johannes Kepler, for example, was deeply influenced by Neoplatonism.

Renaissance humanism also helped prepare the grounds for the scientific revolution. The humanists' educational program placed a low value on natural philosophy, directing attention instead toward the recovery and study of classical antiquity. Humanists revered the authority of the ancients. Yet the energies the humanists poured into recovering, translating, and understanding classical texts (the source of conceptions of the natural world) made many of those important works available for the first time to a wider audience. Previously, Arabic sources had provided Europeans with the main route to ancient Greek learning; Greek classics were translated into Arabic and then picked up by late medieval scholars in Spain and Sicily. The humanists' return to the original texts themselves—and the fact that the new texts could more easily be printed and circulated—encouraged new study and debate. Islamic scholars knew Ptolemy better than did Europeans until the humanist scholar and printer Johannes Regiomontanus recovered and prepared a new summary of Ptolemy's work. The humanist rediscovery of works by Archimedes—the great Greek mathematician who had proposed that the natural world operated on the basis of mechanical forces, like a great machine, and that these forces could be described mathematically—profoundly impressed important late-sixteenth- and seventeenth-century thinkers, including the Italian scientist Galileo, and shaped mechanical philosophy in the 1600s.

The Renaissance also encouraged collaboration between artisans and intellectuals. Twelfth- and thirteenth-century thinkers had observed the natural world, but they rarely tinkered with machines, and they had little contact with the artisans who developed expertise in constructing machines for practical use. During the fifteenth century, however, these two worlds began to come together. Renaissance artists such as Leonardo da Vinci were accomplished craftsmen; they investigated the laws of perspective and optics, they worked out geometric methods for supporting the weight of enormous architectural domes, they studied the human body, and they devised new and more effective weapons for war. The Renaissance brought a vogue for alchemy and astrology, and wealthy amateurs built observatories and measured the courses of the stars. This fusion of intellectual curiosity and skilled handiwork created new possibilities for research and encouraged the creation of new fields of knowledge.

What of the voyages of discovery? Sixteenth-century observers often linked the exploration of the globe to new knowledge of the cosmos. An admirer wrote to Galileo that he had kept the spirit of exploration alive: "The memory of Columbus and Vespucci will be renewed through you,

PTOLEMAIC ASTRONOMICAL INSTRUMENTS. Armillary sphere, 1560s, built to facilitate the observation of planetary positions relative to the earth, in support of Ptolemy's theory of an earth-centered universe. In the sphere, seven concentric rings rotated about different axes. When the outermost ring was set to align with a north–south meridian, and the next ring was set to align with the celestial pole (the North Star, or the point around which the stars seem to rotate), the user could determine the latitude where the instrument was located. The inner rings were used to track the angular movements of the planets, key measurements in validating the Ptolemaic system. ■ *What forms of knowledge were necessary to construct such an instrument?* ■ *How do they relate to the breakthrough that is known as the scientific revolution?*

Past and Present

Has Science Replaced Religion?

Galileo recanted his claims about the movement of heavenly bodies when challenged by the Church (left); but physicists persisted in their research, leading eventually to the development of modern particle accelerators, such as the one located in this lab in Grenoble, France (right). Few would say, however, that science has replaced religion in the modern world.

 Watch related author interview on the Student Site

and with even greater nobility, as the sky is more worthy than the earth." The parallel does not work quite so neatly, however. Columbus had not been driven by an interest in science. Moreover, it took centuries for European thinkers to realize the New World's implications for different fields of study, and the links between the voyages of discovery and breakthroughs in science were largely indirect. The discoveries of new lands made the most immediate impact in the field of natural history, which was vastly enriched by travelers' detailed accounts of the flora and fauna of the Americas. Finding new lands and cultures in Africa and Asia and the revelation of the Americas—a world unknown to the ancients and unmentioned in the Bible—also laid bare gaps in Europeans' inherited body of knowledge. In this sense, the exploration of the New World dealt a blow to the authority of the ancients.

In sum, the late medieval recovery of ancient texts long thought to have been lost, the expansion of print culture

and reading, the turmoil in the Church such as the fierce wars and political maneuvering that followed the Reformation, and the discovery of a new world across the oceans to explore and exploit all shook the authority of older ways of thinking. What we call the scientific revolution was part of the intellectual excitement that surrounded these challenges. We can say in retrospect that the scientific revolution enhanced and confirmed the importance of these other developments.

THE COPERNICAN REVOLUTION

Medieval cosmologists, like their ancient counterparts and their successors during the scientific revolution, wrestled with the contradictions between ancient texts and the evidence of their own observations. Their view of an earth-centered universe was particularly influenced by the teachings of Aristotle (384–322 B.C.E.), especially as they were systematized by Ptolemy of Alexandria (100–170 C.E.). In fact, Ptolemy's vision of an earth-centered universe contradicted an earlier proposal by Aristarchus of Samos (310–230 B.C.E.), who had deduced that the earth and other planets revolve around the sun. Like the ancient Greeks, Ptolemy's medieval followers used astronomical observations to support their theory, but the persuasiveness of this model for medieval scholars also derived from the ways that it fitted with their Christian beliefs (see Chapter 4). According to Ptolemy, the heavens orbited the earth in a carefully organized hierarchy of spheres. Earth and the heavens were fundamentally different, made of different matter and subject to different laws of motion. The sun, moon, stars, and planets were formed of an unchanging (and perfect) quintessence, or ether. The earth, by contrast, was composed of four elements (earth, water, fire, and air), and each of these elements had its natural place: the heavy elements (earth and water) toward the center and the lighter ones farther out. The heavens—first the planets, then the stars—traced perfect circular paths around the stationary earth. The motion of these celestial bodies was produced by a prime mover, whom Christians identified as God. The view fitted Aristotelian physics, according to which objects could move only if acted on by an external force, and with a belief that each fundamental element of the universe had a natural place. Moreover, the Ptolemaic view both followed from and confirmed the belief in the purposefulness of God's universe.

By the late Middle Ages astronomers knew that this cosmology, called the "**Ptolemaic system**," did not correspond exactly to what many had observed. Orbits did not conform to the Aristotelian ideal of perfect circles. Certain planets, Mars in particular, sometimes appeared to loop backward before continuing on their paths. Ptolemy had managed to account for these orbital irregularities, but with complicated mathematics. By the early fifteenth century, the efforts to make the observed motions of the planets fit into the model of perfect circles in a geocentric (earth-centered) cosmos had produced astronomical charts that were mazes of complexity. Finally, the Ptolemaic system proved unable to solve serious difficulties with the calendar. That practical crisis precipitated Nicolaus Copernicus's intellectual leap forward.

By the early sixteenth century, the old Roman calendar was significantly out of alignment with the movements of the heavenly bodies. The major saints' days, Easter, and the other holy days were sometimes weeks off where they should have been according to the stars. Catholic authorities tried to correct this problem, consulting mathematicians and astronomers all over Europe. One of these was a Polish church official and astronomer, **Nicolaus Copernicus** (1473–1543). Educated in Poland and northern Italy, he was a man of diverse talents. He was trained in astronomy, canon law, and medicine; he read Greek; he was well versed in ancient philosophy; and he was also a careful mathematician and a devout Catholic who did not believe that God's universe could be as messy as Ptolemy's model. His proposed solution, based on mathematical calculations, was simple and radical: Ptolemy was mistaken; the earth was neither stationary nor at the center of the planetary system; the earth rotated on its axis and orbited with the other planets around the sun. Reordering the Ptolemaic system simplified the geometry of astronomy and made the orbits of the planets comprehensible.

NICOLAUS COPERNICUS. This anonymous portrait of Copernicus characteristically blends his devotion and his scientific achievements. His scholarly work (behind him in the form of an early planetarium) is driven by his faith (as he turns toward the image of Christ triumphant over death). ▪ *What relationship between science and religion is evoked by this image?*

Copernicus was in many ways a conservative thinker. He did not consider his work to be a break with either the Church or the authority of ancient texts. He believed, rather, that he had restored a pure understanding of God's design, one that had been lost over the centuries. Still, the implications of his theory troubled him. His ideas contradicted centuries of astronomical thought, and they were hard to reconcile with the observed behavior of objects on earth. If the earth moved, why was that movement imperceptible? Copernicus calculated the distance from the earth to the sun to be at least 6 million miles. Even by Copernicus's very low estimate, the earth was hurtling around the sun at the dizzying rate of many thousands of miles an hour. How did people and objects remain standing? (The earth is actually about 93 million miles from the sun, moving through space at 67,000 miles an hour and spinning on its axis at about 1,000 miles an hour!)

Copernicus was not a physicist. He tried to refine, rather than overturn, traditional Aristotelian physics, but his effort to reconcile that physics with his new model of a sun-centered universe created new problems and inconsistencies that he could not resolve. These frustrations and complications dogged Copernicus's later years, and he hesitated to publish his findings. Just before his death, he consented to the release of his major treatise, *On the Revolutions of the Heavenly Spheres* (*De Revolutionibus Orbium Coelestium*), in 1543. To fend off scandal, the Lutheran scholar who saw his manuscript through the press added an introduction to the book declaring that Copernicus's system should be understood as an abstraction, a set of mathematical tools for doing astronomy and not a dangerous claim about the nature of heaven and earth. For decades after 1543, Copernicus's ideas were taken in just that sense—as useful but not realistic mathematical hypotheses. In the long run, however, as one historian puts it, Copernicanism represented the first "serious and systematic" challenge to the Ptolemaic conception of the universe.

TYCHO'S OBSERVATIONS AND KEPLER'S LAWS

Within fifty years, Copernicus's cosmology was revived and modified by two astronomers also critical of the Ptolemaic model of the universe: **Tycho Brahe** (*TI-koh BRAH-hee*; 1546–1601) and **Johannes Kepler** (1571–1630). Each was considered the greatest astronomer of his day. Tycho was born into the Danish nobility, but he abandoned his family's military and political legacy to pursue his passion for astronomy. He was hotheaded as well as talented;

at twenty, he lost part of his nose in a duel. Like Copernicus, he sought to correct the contradictions in traditional astronomy. But unlike Copernicus, who was a theoretician, Tycho championed observation and believed that careful study of the heavens would unlock the secrets of the universe. He first made a name for himself by observing a completely new star, a "nova," that flared into sight in 1572. The Danish king Frederick II, impressed by Tycho's work, granted him the use of a small island, where he built a castle specially designed to house an observatory. For over twenty years, Tycho meticulously charted the movements of each significant object in the night sky, compiling the finest set of astronomical data in Europe.

Tycho was not a Copernican. He suggested that the planets orbited the sun and that the whole system orbited a stationary earth. This picture of cosmic order, though clumsy, seemed to fit the observed evidence better than the Ptolemaic system, and avoided the upsetting physical and theological implications of the Copernican model. In the late 1590s, Tycho moved his work and his huge collection of data to Prague, where he became the court

TYCHO BRAHE'S EARTH-CENTERED UNIVERSE. Brahe asserted that the other planets orbited the sun, and that this solar system orbited a stationary earth. Johannes Kepler argued that the earth and the other planets ran in elliptical orbits around the sun. This image of Brahe's vision is from a star atlas by a Dutch-German cartographer, Andreas Cellarius, who published it in his *Harmonia Macrocosmica* (1660). Note the geometrical renderings of planetary orbits accompanied by astrological symbols on the outer ring of the image. In the foreground are images of people using instruments to make astronomical observations alongside young people being taught about the physical characteristics of the terrestrial globe. Brahe himself is portrayed in the lower right.

astronomer to the Holy Roman emperor Rudolf II. In Prague, he was assisted by a young mathematician from a troubled family, Johannes Kepler. Kepler was more impressed with the Copernican model than was Tycho, and he combined the study of Copernicus's work with his own interest in mysticism, astrology, and the religious power of mathematics.

Kepler believed that everything in creation, from human souls to the orbits of the planets, had been created according to mathematical laws. Understanding those laws would thus allow humans to share God's wisdom and penetrate the inner secrets of the universe. Mathematics was God's language. Kepler's search for the pattern of mathematical perfection took him through musical harmonies, geometric shapes nested inside the planets' orbits, and numerical formulas. After Tycho's death, Kepler inherited Tycho's position in Prague as well as his trove of observations and calculations. Those data demonstrated to Kepler that two of Copernicus's assumptions about planetary motion simply did not match observations. Copernicus, in keeping with Aristotelian notions of perfection, had believed that planetary orbits were circular. Kepler, however, calculated that the planets traveled in elliptical orbits around the sun (this finding became his First Law). Copernicus held that planetary motion was uniform. But Kepler stated that the speed of the planets varied with their distance from the sun (his Second Law). Kepler also argued that magnetic forces between the sun and the planets kept the planets in orbital motion, an insight that paved the way for Newton's law of universal gravitation, formulated nearly eighty years later at the end of the seventeenth century.

Each of Kepler's works, beginning with *Cosmographic Mystery* in 1596 and continuing with *Astronomia Nova* in 1609 and *The Harmonies of the World* in 1619, revised and augmented Copernicus's theory. His version of Copernicanism fitted with remarkable accuracy the best observations of the time (which were Tycho's). Kepler's search for rules of motion that could account for the earth's movements in its new position was also significant. More than Copernicus, Kepler broke down the distinction between the heavens and the earth that had been at the heart of Aristotelian physics.

NEW HEAVENS, NEW EARTH, AND WORLDLY POLITICS: GALILEO

Kepler had a friend deliver a copy of *Cosmographic Mystery* to the "mathematician named Galileus Galileus," then teaching mathematics and astronomy at Padua, near Venice.

Galileo Galilei (1564–1642) thanked Kepler in a letter that nicely illustrates the Italian's views at the time (1597):

> So far I have only perused the preface of your work, but from this I gained some notion of its intent, and I indeed congratulate myself of having an associate in the study of Truth who is a friend of Truth. . . . I adopted the teaching of Copernicus many years ago, and his point of view enables me to explain many phenomena of nature which certainly remain inexplicable according to the more current hypotheses. I have written many arguments in support of him and in refutation of the opposite view—which, however, so far I have not dared to bring into the public light. . . . I would certainly dare to publish my reflections at once if more people like you existed; as they don't, I shall refrain from doing so.

Kepler replied, urging Galileo to "come forward!" Galileo did not answer.

At Padua, Galileo couldn't teach what he believed; Ptolemaic astronomy and Aristotelian cosmology were the established curriculum. By the end of his career, however, Galileo had provided powerful evidence in support of the Copernican model and laid the foundation for a new physics. What was more, he wrote in the vernacular (Italian) as well as in Latin. Kepler may have been a "friend of Truth," but his work was abstruse and bafflingly mathematical (as was Copernicus's). In contrast, Galileo's writings were widely translated and widely read, raising awareness of changes in natural philosophy across Europe.

Ultimately, Galileo made the case for a new relationship between religion and science, challenging in the process some of the most powerful churchmen of his day. His discoveries made him the most famous scientific figure of his time, but his work put him on a collision course with Aristotelian philosophy and the authority of the Catholic Church.

Galileo became famous by way of his discoveries with the telescope. In 1609, he heard reports from Holland of a lens grinder who had made a spyglass that could magnify very distant objects. Excited, Galileo quickly devised his own telescope. He trained it first on earthly objects to demonstrate that it worked, and then dramatically pointed it at the night sky. Galileo studied the moon, finding on it mountains, plains, and other features of an earthlike landscape. His observations suggested that celestial bodies resembled the earth, a view at odds with the concept of the

Interpreting Visual Evidence

Astronomical Observations and the Mapping of the Heavens

One (often-repeated) narrative about the scientific revolution is that it marked a crucial break, separating modern science from an earlier period permeated by an atmosphere of superstition and theological speculation. But, in fact, medieval scholars tried hard to come up with empirical evidence for beliefs that their faith told them must be true, and without these traditions of observation, scientists like Copernicus would never have been led to propose alternative cosmologies (see "Ptolemaic Astronomical Instruments" on page 525).

The assumption that the "new" sciences of the seventeenth century marked an extraordinary rupture with a more ignorant or superstitious past is thus not entirely correct. It would be closer to the truth to suggest that works such as that of Copernicus or Galileo provided a new context for assessing the relationship between observations and knowledge that came from other sources. Printed materials provided opportunities for early modern scientists to learn as much from each other as from more ancient sources.

The illustrations here are from scientific works on astronomy both before and after the appearance of Copernicus's

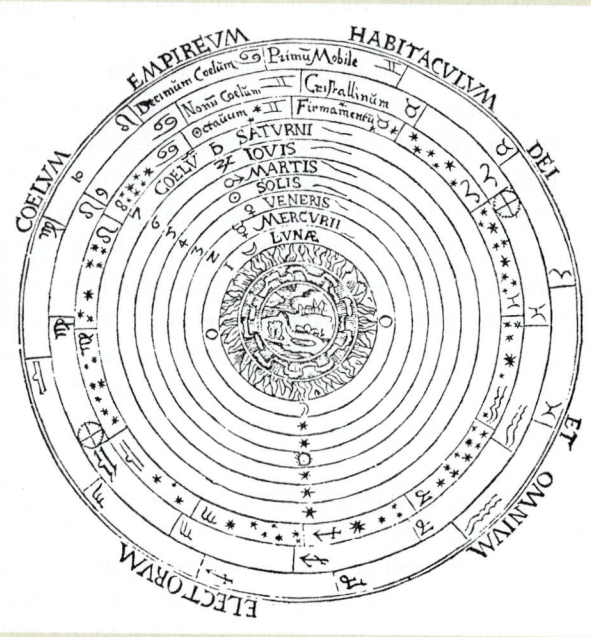

A. The Ptolemaic universe, as depicted in Peter Apian, *Cosmographia* (1524).

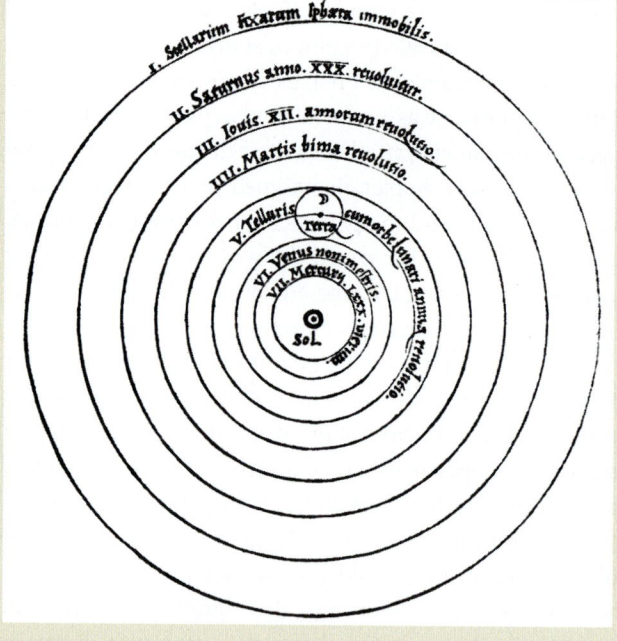

B. The Copernican universe (1543).

heavens as an unchanging sphere of heavenly perfection, inherently and necessarily different from the earth. He saw moons orbiting Jupiter, evidence that earth was not at the center of all orbits. And he saw spots on the sun. Galileo published these results, first in *The Starry Messenger* (1610) and then in *Letters on Sunspots* (1613). *The Starry Messenger*, with its amazing reports of Jupiter's moons, was short, aimed at a wide reading audience, and bold. It only hinted at Galileo's Copernicanism, however. The *Letters on Sunspots* declared it openly.

A seventeenth-century scientist needed powerful and wealthy patrons. As a professor of mathematics, Galileo chafed at the power of university authorities who were subject to Church control. Princely courts offered an inviting work. All of them were based on some form of observation and claimed to be descriptive of the existing universe. Compare the abstract illustrations of the Ptolemaic (image A) and Copernican (image B) universes with Tycho Brahe's (image C) attempt to reconcile heliocentric observations with geocentric assumptions, or with Galileo's illustration of sunspots (image D) observed through a telescope.

Questions for Analysis

1. What do these illustrations tell us about the relationship between knowledge and observation in sixteenth- and seventeenth-century science? What kinds of knowledge were necessary to produce these images?

2. Are the illustrations A and B intended to be visually accurate, in the sense that they represent what the eye sees?

Can we say the same of illustration D? What makes Galileo's illustration of sunspots different from the others?

3. Are the assumptions about observation in Galileo's drawing of sunspots (image D) applicable to other sciences such as biology or chemistry? If yes, how so?

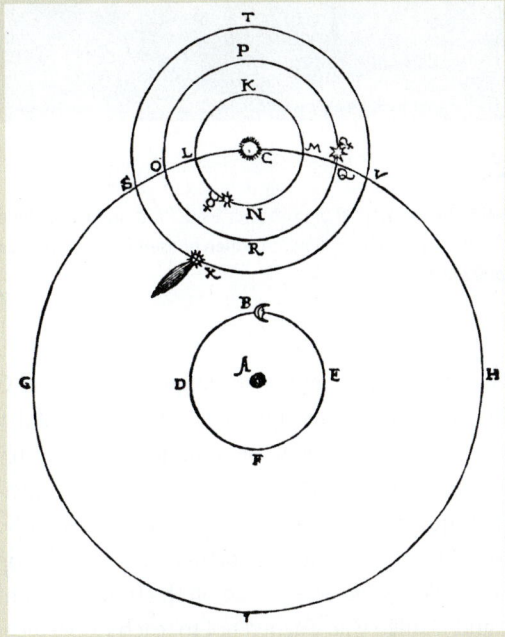

C. Brahe's universe (c. 1572; A [earth], B [moon], C [sun]).

D. Galileo's sunspots, as observed through a telescope (1612).

alternative. The Medici family of Tuscany, like others, burnished its reputation and bolstered its power by surrounding itself with intellectuals as well as artists. Persuaded he would be freer at its court than in Padua, Galileo took a position as tutor to the Medicis and flattered and successfully cultivated the family. He addressed *The Starry Messenger* to them, and named the newly discovered moons of Jupiter the "Medicean stars." He was rewarded with the title of chief mathematician and philosopher to Cosimo II de' Medici, the grand duke of Tuscany. Now well positioned in Italy's networks of power and patronage, Galileo was able to pursue his goal of demonstrating that Copernicus's heliocentric (sun-centered) model of the planetary system was correct.

GALILEO GALILEI BEFORE THE INQUISITION, BY FRANÇOIS FLEURY-RICHARD. This nineteenth-century painting of Galileo before the Holy Office dramatizes the conflict between science and religion, and depicts the Italian natural philosopher as defiant. In fact, Galileo submitted but continued his work under house arrest and published, secretly, in the Netherlands. ▪ *Would Galileo himself have subscribed to the message of this much later painting, that religion and science were opposed to one another?*

This pursuit, however, was a high-wire act, for he could not afford to antagonize the Catholic Church. In 1614, an ambitious and outspoken Dominican monk denounced Galileo's ideas as dangerous deviations from biblical teachings. Other philosophers and churchmen began to ask Galileo's patrons, the Medicis, whether their court mathematician was teaching heresy.

Disturbed by the murmurings against Copernicanism, Galileo penned a series of letters to defend himself. He addressed the relationship between natural philosophy and religion, and argued that one could be both a sincere Copernican and a sincere Catholic (see **Analyzing Primary Sources** on page 533). The Church, Galileo said, did the sacred work of teaching scripture and saving souls, but accounting for the workings of the physical world was a task better left to natural philosophy, grounded in observation and mathematics. For the Church to take a side in controversies over natural science might compromise its spiritual authority and credibility. Galileo envisioned natural philosophers and theologians as partners in a search for truth, but with very different roles.

In a brilliant rhetorical moment, he quoted Cardinal Caesar Baronius in support of his argument: the purpose of the Bible was to "teach us how to go to heaven, not how heaven goes."

Nevertheless, in 1616, the Church moved against Galileo. The Inquisition ruled that Copernicanism was "foolish and absurd in philosophy and formally heretical." Copernicus's *De Revolutionibus* was placed on the Index of Prohibited Books, and Galileo was warned not to teach Copernicanism.

For a while, he did as he was asked. But when his Florentine friend and admirer Maffeo Barberini was elected pope as Urban VIII in 1623, Galileo believed the door to Copernicanism was (at least half) open. He drafted one of his most famous works, *A Dialogue Concerning the Two Chief World Systems*, which was published in 1632. The *Dialogue* was a hypothetical debate between supporters of the old Ptolemaic system, represented by a character he named Simplicio (simpleton) on the one hand, and proponents of the new astronomy on the other. Galileo gave the best lines to the Copernicans throughout. However, at the very end, to satisfy the letter of the Inquisition's decree, he had them capitulate to Simplicio.

Analyzing Primary Sources

Galileo on Nature, Scripture, and Truth

One of the clearest statements of Galileo's convictions about religion and science comes from his 1615 letter to the grand duchess Christina, the mother of Galileo's patron, Cosimo II de' Medici, and a powerful figure in her own right. Galileo knew that others objected to his work. The church had warned him that Copernicanism was inaccurate and impious, that it could be disproved scientifically, and that it contradicted the authority of those who interpreted the Bible. Thoroughly dependent on the Medicis for support, he wrote to the grand duchess to explain his position. In this section of the letter, Galileo sets out his understanding of the parallel but distinct roles of the Church and natural philosophers. He walks a fine line between acknowledging the authority of the Church and standing firm in his convictions.

Possibly because they are disturbed by the known truth of other propositions of mine which differ from those commonly held, and therefore mistrusting their defense so long as they confine themselves to the field of philosophy, these men have resolved to fabricate a shield for their fallacies out of the mantle of pretended religion and the authority of the Bible. . . .

Copernicus never discusses matters of religion or faith, nor does he use arguments that depend in any way upon the authority of sacred writings which he might have interpreted erroneously. He stands always upon physical conclusions pertaining to the celestial motions, and deals with them by astronomical and geometrical demonstrations, founded primarily upon sense experiences and very exact observations. He did not ignore the Bible, but he knew very well that if his doctrine were proved, then it could not contradict the Scriptures when they were rightly understood. . . .

I think that in discussions of physical problems we ought to begin not from the authority of scriptural passages, but from sense-experiences and necessary demonstrations; for the holy Bible and the phenomena of nature proceed alike from the divine Word, the former as the dictate of the Holy Ghost and the latter as the observant executrix of God's commands. It is necessary for the Bible, in order to be accommodated to the understanding of every man, to speak many things which appear to differ from the absolute truth so far as the bare meaning of the words is concerned. But Nature, on the other hand, is inexorable and immutable; she never transgresses the laws imposed upon her, or cares a whit whether her abstruse reasons and methods of operation are understandable to men. For that reason it appears that nothing physical which sense-experience sets before our eyes, or which necessary demonstrations prove to us, ought to be called in question (much less condemned) upon the testimony of biblical passages which may have some different meaning beneath their words. For the Bible is not chained in every expression to conditions as strict as those which govern all physical effects; nor is God any less excellently revealed in Nature's actions than in the sacred statements of the Bible. . . .

Source: Galileo, "Letter to the Grand Duchess Christina," in *The Discoveries and Opinions of Galileo Galilei,* ed. Stillman Drake (Garden City, NY: 1957), pp. 177–83.

Questions for Analysis

1. How does Galileo deal with the contradictions between the evidence of his senses and biblical teachings?

2. For Galileo, what is the relationship between God, man, and nature?

3. Why did Galileo need to defend his views in a letter to Christina de' Medici?

The Inquisition banned the *Dialogue* and ordered Galileo to stand trial in 1633. Pope Urban, provoked by Galileo's scorn and needing support from Church conservatives during a difficult stretch of the Thirty Years' War, refused to protect his former friend. The verdict of the secret trial shocked Europe. The Inquisition forced Galileo to repent his Copernican position, banned him from working on or even discussing Copernican ideas, and placed him under house arrest for life. According to a story that began to circulate shortly afterward, as he left the court for house arrest he stamped his foot and muttered defiantly, looking down at the earth, "Still, it moves."

The Inquisition could not put Galileo off his life's work. He refined the theories of motion he had begun to develop early in his career. He proposed an early version of the theory of inertia, which held that an object's motion stays the same until an outside force changes it. He calculated that objects of different weights fall at almost the same speed and with a uniform acceleration. He argued that the motion of objects follows regular mathematical laws. The same laws that govern the motions of objects on earth (which could be observed in experiments) could also be observed in the heavens—again a direct contradiction of Aristotelian principles and an important step toward a coherent physics based on a sun-centered model of the universe. Compiled under the title *Two New Sciences* (1638), this work was smuggled out of Italy and published in Protestant Holland.

Galileo believed that Copernicanism and natural philosophy in general need not subvert theological truths, religious belief, or the authority of the Church. But his trial seemed to show the contrary: that natural philosophy and Church authority could not coexist. Galileo's trial silenced Copernican voices in southern Europe, and the Church's leadership retreated into conservative reaction. It was therefore in northwest Europe that the new philosophy Galileo had championed would flourish.

DETERMINING THE AGE OF THE EARTH: THE ORIGINS OF GEOLOGY AND THE ENVIRONMENTAL SCIENCES

Galileo's contention that celestial bodies were subject to the same laws of motion as matter on earth was a significant step toward modern science. In retrospect, it is not surprising that some within the Church perceived Galileo's teachings to be a threat to Christian scripture. At the same time, the split between religion and those who would explore the sciences of the heavens and earth was not at all absolute. The modern science of geology, for example, emerged gradually out of a long debate that moved back and forth between evidence compiled from religious and secular texts on the one hand, and data gathered by those who made observations about the physical landscape and the stones they collected while walking through the countryside on the other. The debate that fostered this discussion revolved around a fundamental question that had long provoked theologians: How old was the earth?

In 1654, twelve years after Galileo's death, **James Ussher** (1581–1656), the archbishop of Armagh in Ireland, published an account of the earth's creation based on a wide variety of textual sources, both biblical and secular. Ussher declared that according to his calculations, the world had been created on Saturday, October 22, 4004 B.C. Though modern authors often ridicule Ussher's work as an extreme example of biblical literalism, it is important to recognize that his thinking was

very much rooted in the culture of his time, and his estimate differed little from the assertions of many others who tried to answer the same question. Ussher's estimate became famous only because of an accident of history. After his death, his dates for the Creation story were included in subsequent editions of the King James Bible. Ussher's chronology was part of a larger intellectual attempt to construct a timeline for the history of the world that recorded both material events such as the appearance of comets, volcanic eruptions, or solar and lunar eclipses as well as sacred dates. His decision to treat the Bible as one source among many was in fact a significant departure from a purely religious approach, and his desire to divide the history of the earth into "epochs" or "eras" marked an important step toward a more historical approach to the earth's past.

PALEONTOLOGY IN THE SERVICE OF GEOLOGY. An illustration from Nicolas Steno's 1667 paper comparing shark's teeth from a dissected specimen with petrified teeth found in rocky hillsides far from the ocean. He used such observations to demonstrate the changes that had taken place in the earth's crust over time, and to assert that deeper layers were a record of a more distant past.

James Ussher, like other early seventeenth-century writers, assumed that the earth's history and human history covered roughly the same length of time: following the story of Genesis, they assumed that humans appeared on earth soon after its creation. They also assumed that the stories told in the Bible about the natural environment—including the story of Noah and the Flood—had some basis in historical fact. A German Jesuit, Athanasius Kircher (1602–1680), suggested that the Flood story could be analyzed historically, and he attempted to calculate the amount of water that would have been required to cover the earth's mountains. He assumed that the physical landscape of the earth would have been transformed as the floodwaters drained away, and that the shapes of the continents and oceans must have changed as

CABINET OF CURIOSITIES. This illustration was the frontispiece of a book on natural history by a Danish doctor, Ole Wurm, who taught medicine, Latin, and Greek in Copenhagen after studying in Marburg. Wurm was a celebrated collector of objects, ranging from fossils and specimens of animals to artifacts of ethnographic interest. Such collections provided the principal data for those engaged in debates about the origins of fossils and the age of the earth.

well. It was only later that natural philosophers realized the vast expanse of earth's history that predated human society, but they were already beginning to imagine that this history was accessible to human knowledge through observation.

Such speculation was also fueled by the work of natural philosophers who asked questions about the fossils that they found throughout the European countryside. As interest in natural philosophy developed in the seventeenth century, scholars began to assemble large collections of what they called "curiosities"—images and forms of animals and plants found in stones and seashells collected on mountaintops far from the ocean, as well as the bones and antlers of animals both recognizable and unknown. Some of these objects could be explained in terms of accepted biblical histories. Religious believers, for example, asserted that seashells on mountaintops could have been deposited by Noah's Flood. A Danish physician, Niels Stensen (more frequently referred to by his Latin name, **Nicolas Steno**), began a more systematic compilation of this evidence that pointed the way toward the science of geology. The key breakthrough was a paper he published in 1667 that demonstrated that shark's teeth, obtained through the dissection of a recently caught animal, were structurally similar, though smaller in size, to petrified teeth found bound in stone on land far from the sea. Steno

began to believe that the physical landscape of Tuscany (where he was living at the time) constituted a visible record of a historical sequence that could be reconstructed through observation. He noted a tendency of broken hillsides to reveal strata of different stones, as if one layer had been laid down over the previous one. An English natural philosopher, Robert Hooke, writing at the same time in England, came to the same conclusion, asserting that the rocks and fossils were "documents" to be read in the book of nature.

The debate on the age of the earth continued into the eighteenth and nineteenth centuries, but the line from Steno's and Hooke's remarks to modern geological research is a direct one. In the space of little more than one or two generations in the seventeenth century, the earth sciences had emerged in a form that is recognizable to modern readers. From Galileo's claim that heavenly bodies and earthly matter were all subject to the same laws of motion, to Ussher's call for a chronology of earth's history that could be assembled from both secular and religious sources, to Steno's and Hooke's imaginative claim that the earth's landscape constituted a legible "monument" pointing to a distant and material past, the evolution of natural philosophy in the seventeenth century indicated new possibilities for a scientific understanding of the terrestrial environment.

METHODS FOR A NEW PHILOSOPHY: BACON AND DESCARTES

Advances in the new sciences eventually became concentrated in northwest Europe, where thinkers began to spell out standards of practice and evidence. Sir **Francis Bacon** and **René Descartes** (*deh-KAHRT*) loom especially large in this development, setting out the methods or the rules that should govern modern science. Bacon (1561–1626) lived at roughly the same time as Kepler, Galileo, and Shakespeare;

FRONTISPIECE TO BACON'S *NOVUM ORGANUM* (1620). This illustration suggests that scientific work is like a voyage of discovery, similar to a ship setting out through uncharted waters. Compare this image with the representation of Tycho Brahe's earth-centered universe on page 528. Pay particular attention to the imagery and symbols surrounding the geometric model. ■ *What metaphors and allegorical imagery did scientists use during this period to characterize the significance of their work?*

Descartes (1596–1650) was slightly younger. Both Bacon and Descartes came to believe that theirs was an age of profound change, open to the possibility of astonishing discovery. They were persuaded that knowledge could take the European moderns beyond the ancient authorities, and they set out to formulate a philosophy to encompass the learning of their age.

"Knowledge is power." This phrase is Bacon's and captures the changing perspective of the seventeenth century and its new confidence in the potential of human thinking. Bacon trained as a lawyer, serving in the Parliament and briefly as the lord chancellor to James I of England. His abiding concern was with the assumptions, methods, and practices he believed should guide natural philosophers and the progress of knowledge. The authority of the ancients should not constrain the ambition of modern thinkers, and deference to accepted doctrines could block innovation or obstruct understanding: "There is but one course left . . . to try the whole thing anew upon a better plan, and to commence a total reconstruction of sciences, arts, and all human knowledge, raised upon the proper foundations." Pursuing knowledge did not mean thinking abstractly and leaping to conclusions; it meant observing, experimenting, confirming ideas, or demonstrating points. If thinkers will be "content to begin with doubts," Bacon wrote, "they shall end with certainties." We thus associate Bacon with the gradual separation of scientific investigation from philosophical argument.

Bacon advocated an *inductive* approach to knowledge: amassing evidence from specific observations to draw general conclusions. In Bacon's view, many philosophical errors arose from beginning with assumed first principles. The traditional view of the cosmos, for instance, rested on the principles of a prime mover and the perfection of circular motion for the planets and the stars. The inductive method required accumulating data (as Tycho had done) and then, after careful review and experiment, drawing appropriate conclusions about the motions of heavenly bodies. Bacon argued that scientific knowledge was best tested through the cooperative efforts of researchers performing experiments that could be repeated and verified. The knowledge thus gained would be predictable and useful to philosophers and artisans alike, contributing to a wide range of endeavors from astronomy to shipbuilding.

Bacon's vision of science and progress is vividly illustrated by two images. The first, more familiar, is the title page of Bacon's *Novum Organum* (1620), shown on the left, with its bold ships sailing out beyond the Straits of Gibraltar, formerly the limits of the West, into the open sea, in pursuit of unknown but great things to come. The second is of Bacon's imagined factory of discovery, "Solomon's house," at the end of his utopian *New Atlantis* (1626). Inside the factory, "sifters" would examine and conduct experiments, passing on findings to senior researchers who would draw conclusions and develop practical applications. The work of these scholars would be supplemented by accounts sent by their emissaries abroad, traveling ambassadors of science who would gather data and information about the natural world and human societies in other places. Bacon's utopian image of patient researchers and experimenters anticipated the modern university.

René Descartes was French, though he lived all over Europe. He was intellectually restless as well; he worked in geometry, cosmology, optics, and physiology—for a while dissecting cow carcasses daily. He was writing a (Copernican) book on physics when he heard of Galileo's condemnation in 1633, a ruling that impressed on him the dangers of "expressing judgements on this world." Descartes's *Discourse on Method* (1637), for which he is best known, began simply as a preface to three essays on optics, geometry, and meteorology. It is personal, recounting Descartes's dismay at the "strange and unbelievable" theories he encountered in his traditional education. His first response, as he described it, was to doubt systematically everything he had ever known or been taught. Better to clear the slate, he

believed, than to build an edifice of knowledge on received assumptions. His first rule was "never to receive anything as a truth which [he] did not clearly know to be such." He took the human ability to think as his point of departure, summed up in his famous and enigmatic *Je pense, donc je suis*, later translated into Latin as *cogito ergo sum* and into English as "I think, therefore I am." As the phrase suggests, Descartes's doubting led (quickly, by our standards) to self-assurance and truth: the thinking individual existed, reason existed, God existed. For Descartes, then, doubt was a ploy, or a piece that he used in an intellectual chess game to defeat skepticism. Certainty, not doubt, was the centerpiece of the philosophy he bequeathed to his followers.

Descartes, like Bacon, sought a "fresh start for knowledge," or the rules for understanding the world as it was. Unlike Bacon, however, he emphasized *deductive* reasoning, proceeding logically from one certainty to another. "So long as we avoid accepting as true what is not so," he wrote in *Discourse on Method*, "and always preserve the right order of deduction of one thing from another, there can be nothing too remote to be reached in the end, or too well hidden to be discovered." For Descartes, mathematical thought expressed the highest standards of reason, and his work contributed

FROM RENÉ DESCARTES, *L'HOMME* (1729; ORIGINALLY PUBLISHED AS *DE HOMINI*, 1662). Descartes's interest in the body as a mechanism led him to suppose that physics and mathematics could be used to understand all aspects of human physiology, and his work had an important influence on subsequent generations of medical researchers. In this illustration, Descartes depicts the optical properties of the human eye. ■ *How might such a mechanistic approach to human perception have been received by proponents of Baconian science who depended so much on the reliability of human observations?*

The New Science and the Foundations of Certainty

> *Francis Bacon (1561–1626) and René Descartes (1596–1650) were both enthusiastic supporters of science in the seventeenth century, but they differed in their opinions regarding the basis for certainty in scientific argumentation. Bacon's inductive method emphasized the gathering of particular observations about natural phenomena, which he believed could be used as evidence to support more general conclusions about causes, regularity, and order in the natural world. Descartes, on the other hand, defended a deductive method. He believed that certainty could be built only by reasoning from first principles that one knew to be true, and he was less certain of the value of evidence that came from the senses alone.*

Aphorisms from Novum Organum

XXXI

It is idle to expect any advancement in science from the super-inducing and engrafting of new things upon old. We must begin anew from the very foundations, unless we would revolve forever in a circle with mean and contemptible progress. . . .

XXXVI

One method of delivery alone remains to us which is simply this: we must lead men to the particulars themselves, and their series and order; while men on their side must force themselves for a while to lay their notions by and begin to familiarize themselves with facts. . . .

XLV

The human understanding of its own nature is prone to suppose the existence of more order and regularity in the world than it finds. And though there be many things in nature which are singular and unmatched, yet it devises for them parallels and conjugates and relatives which do not exist. Hence the fiction that all celestial bodies move in perfect circles. . . . Hence too the element of fire with its orb is brought in, to make up the square with the other three which the sense perceives. . . . And so on of other dreams. And these fancies affect not dogmas only, but simple notions also. . . .

XCV

Those who have handled sciences have been either men of experiment or men of dogmas. The men of experiment are like the ant, they only collect and use; the reasoners resemble spiders, who make cobwebs out of their own substance. But the bee takes a middle course: it gathers its material from the flowers of the garden and of the field, but transforms and digests it by a power of its own. Not unlike this is the true business of philosophy; for it neither relies solely or chiefly on the powers of the mind, nor does it take the matter which it gathers from natural history and mechanical experiments and lay it up in the memory whole . . . but lays it up in the understanding altered and digested. Therefore, from a closer and purer league between these two faculties, the experimental and the rational (such as has never yet been made), much may be hoped. . . .

Source: Michael R. Matthews, ed., *The Scientific Background to Modern Philosophy: Selected Readings* (Indianapolis: 1989), pp. 47–48, 50–52.

From A Discourse on Method

Just as a great number of laws is often a pretext for wrongdoing, with the result that a state is much better governed when, having only a few, they are strictly observed; so also I came to believe that in the place of the great number of precepts that go to make up logic, the following four would be sufficient for my purposes, provided that I took a firm but unshakeable decision never once to depart from them.

The first was never to accept anything as true that I did not *incontrovertibly* know to be so; that is to say, carefully to avoid both *prejudice* and premature conclusions; and to include nothing in my judgments other than that which presented itself to my mind so *clearly* and *distinctly*, that I would have no occasion to doubt it.

The second was to divide all the difficulties under examination into as many parts as possible, and as many as were required to solve them in the best way.

The third was to conduct my thoughts in a given order, beginning with the *simplest* and most easily understood objects, and gradually ascending, as it were step by step, to the knowledge of the most *complex;* and *positing* an order even on those which do not have a natural order of precedence.

The last was to undertake such complete enumerations and such general surveys that I would be sure to have left nothing out.

The long chain of reasonings, every one simple and easy, which geometers habitually employ to reach their most difficult proofs had given me cause to suppose that all those things which fall within the domain of human understanding follow on from each other in the same way, and that as long as one stops oneself taking anything to be true that is not true and sticks to the right order so as to deduce one thing from another, there can be nothing so remote that one cannot eventually reach it, nor so hidden that one cannot discover it. . . .

[B]ecause I wished . . . to concentrate on the pursuit of truth, I came to think that I should . . . reject as completely false everything in which I could detect the least doubt, in order to see if anything thereafter remained in my belief that was completely indubitable. And so, because our senses sometimes deceive us, I decided to suppose that nothing was such as they lead us to imagine it to be. And because there are men who make mistakes in reasoning, even about the simplest elements of geometry, and commit logical fallacies, I judged that I was as prone to error as anyone else, and I rejected as false all the reasoning I had hitherto accepted as valid proof. Finally, considering that all the same thoughts which we have while awake can come to us while asleep without any one of them then being true, I resolved to pretend that everything that had ever entered my head was no more true than the illusions of my dreams. But immediately afterwards I noted that, while I was trying to think of all things being false in this way, it was necessarily the case that I, who was thinking them, had to be something; and observing this truth: *I am thinking therefore I exist,* was so secure and certain that it could not be shaken by any of the most extravagant suppositions of the sceptics, I judged that I could accept it without scruple, as the first principle of the philosophy I was seeking.

Source: René Descartes, *A Discourse on the Method,* trans. Ian Maclean (New York: 2006), pp. 17–18, 28.

Questions for Analysis

1. Descartes's idea of certainty depended on a "long chain of reasonings" that departed from certain axioms that could not be doubted and rejected evidence from the senses. What science provided him with the model for this idea of certainty? What was the first thing that he felt he could be certain about? Did he trust his senses?

2. Bacon's idea of certainty pragmatically sought to combine the benefits of sensory knowledge and experience (gathered by "ants") with the understandings arrived at through reason (cobwebs constructed by "spiders"). How would Descartes have responded to Bacon's claims? According to Bacon, was Descartes an ant or a spider?

3. What do these two thinkers have in common?

---

greatly to the authority of mathematics as a model for scientific reasoning.

Descartes made a particularly forceful statement for *mechanism*, a view of the world shared by Bacon and Galileo and one that came to dominate seventeenth-century scientific thought. As the name suggests, mechanical philosophy proposed to consider nature as a machine. It rejected the traditional Aristotelian distinction between the works of humans and those of nature, and the view that nature, as God's creation, necessarily belonged to a different—and higher—order. In the new picture of the universe that was emerging from the discoveries and writings of the early seventeenth century, it seemed that all matter was composed of the same material and that all motion obeyed the same laws. Descartes sought to explain everything, including the human body, mechanically. As he put it firmly, "There is no difference between the machines built by artisans and the diverse bodies that nature alone composes." Nature operated according to regular and predictable laws and thus was accessible to human reason. This belief guided, indeed inspired, much of the scientific experiment and argument of the seventeenth century.

The Power of Method and the Force of Curiosity: Seventeenth-Century Experimenters

For nearly a century after Bacon and Descartes, most of England's natural philosophers were Baconian, and most of their colleagues in France, Holland, and elsewhere in northern Europe were Cartesians (followers of Descartes). The English Baconians concentrated on performing experiments in many different fields, producing results that could then be debated and discussed. The Cartesians turned instead toward mathematics and logic. Descartes himself pioneered analytical geometry. Blaise Pascal (1623–1662) worked on probability theory and invented a calculating machine before applying his intellectual skills to theology. A Cartesian thinker, Christian Huygens (1629–1695) of Holland, combined mathematics with experiments to understand problems of impact and orbital motion. A Dutch Cartesian, Baruch Spinoza (1632–1677), applied geometry to ethics and believed he had gone beyond Descartes by proving that the universe was composed of a single substance that was both God and nature.

English experimenters pursued a different course. They began with practical research, putting the alchemist's tool, the laboratory, to new uses. They also sought a different kind of conclusion: empirical laws or provisional generalizations based on evidence rather than absolute statements of deductive truth. Among the many English laboratory scientists of this era were the physician William Harvey (1578–1657), the chemist Robert Boyle (1627–1691), and the inventor and experimenter Robert Hooke (1635–1703).

Harvey's contribution was enormous: he observed and explained that blood circulated through the arteries, heart, and veins. To do this, he was willing to dissect living animals (vivisection) and experiment on himself. Boyle performed experiments and established a law (known as Boyle's law) showing that at a constant temperature the volume of a gas decreases in proportion to the pressure placed on it. Hooke introduced the microscope to the experimenter's tool kit. The compound microscope had been invented in Holland early in the seventeenth century, but it was not until the 1660s that Hooke and others demonstrated its potential by using it to study the cellular structure of plants. Like the telescope before it, the microscope revealed an unexpected dimension of material phenomena. Examining even the most ordinary objects revealed detailed structures of perfectly connected smaller parts, and this persuaded many that with improved instruments they would uncover even more of the world's intricacies.

ROBERT HOOKE'S *MICROGRAPHIA*. Hooke's diagram of a fly's eye as seen through a microscope seemed to reveal just the sort of intricate universe the mechanists predicted. ▪ *Compare this image with that of Galileo's sunspots (page 531). What do these two images have in common?*

The microscope also provided what many regarded as new evidence of God's existence. The way each minute structure of a living organism, when viewed under a microscope, corresponded to its purpose testified not only to God's existence but also to God's wisdom. The mechanical philosophy did not exclude God but in fact could be used to confirm his presence. If the universe was a clock, there must be a clockmaker. Hooke himself declared that only imbeciles would believe that what they saw under the microscope was "the production of chance" rather than of God's creation.

The State, Scientific Academies, and Women Scientists

Seventeenth-century state building (see Chapter 14) helped secure the rise of science. In 1660, England's monarchy was restored after two decades of revolution and civil war. The newly crowned King Charles II granted a group of natural philosophers and mathematicians a royal charter (1662) to establish the **Royal Society** of London, for the "improvement of natural knowledge" and committed to experimentation and collaborative work among natural philosophers. The founders of the Royal Society, in particular Boyle, believed it could serve a political as well as an intellectual purpose. The Royal Society would pursue Bacon's goal of collective research, in which members would conduct formal experiments, record the results, and share them with other members. These members would in turn study the methods, reproduce the experiment, and assess the outcome. This enterprise would give England's natural philosophers a common sense of purpose and a system to reach reasoned, gentlemanly agreement on "matters of fact." Also, by separating systematic scientific research from the dangerous language of politics and religion that had marked the civil war, the Royal Society could help restore a sense of order and consensus to English intellectual life.

The society's journal, *Philosophical Transactions*, reached out to professional scholars and experimenters throughout Europe, and similar societies began to appear elsewhere. The French **Academy of Sciences** was founded in 1666, and it was also tied to seventeenth-century state building, in this case, Bourbon absolutism (see Chapter 15). Royal societies, devoted to natural philosophy as a collective enterprise, provided a state- (or prince-) sponsored framework for science, and an alternative to the important but uncertain patronage of lesser nobles or to the religious (and largely conservative, Aristotelian) universities. Scientific societies reached rough agreements about what constituted legitimate research; they established the modern scientific custom of crediting discoveries to those who were the first to publish results; and they enabled the easier exchange of information and theories across national boundaries, although philosophical differences among Cartesians, Baconians, and traditional Aristotelians remained very difficult to bridge. Science began to take shape as a discipline.

The early scientific academies did not have explicit rules barring women, but with few exceptions, they consisted only of men. This did not mean that women did not practice science, though their participation in scientific research and debate remained controversial. In some cases, the new science could itself become a justification for women's inclusion, as when the Cartesian philosopher François Poullain de la Barre used anatomy to declare in 1673 that "the mind has no sex." Since women possessed the same physical senses as men and the same nervous systems and brains, Poullain asked, Why should they not equally occupy the same roles in society? In fact, historians have discovered more than a few women who taught at European universities in the sixteenth and seventeenth centuries, above all in Italy. Elena Cornaro Piscopia received her doctorate of philosophy in Padua in 1678, the first woman to do so.

OBSERVING THE TRANSIT OF VENUS (1673). Elisabetha (1647–1693) and Johannes Hevelius (1611–1687) believed that precise observations about the timing of Venus's passage across the face of the sun when observed from different parts of the earth could be used to calculate the distance from the earth to the sun. This German-speaking husband-and-wife astronomy team from Gdansk (in present-day Poland) worked together on many of their projects. After Johannes's death, Elisabetha published their jointly written star catalog.

Laura Bassi became a professor of physics at the University of Bologna after receiving her doctorate there in 1733, and on the merits of her exceptional contributions to mathematics, she became a member of the Academy of Science in Bologna. Her papers—such as "On the Compression of Air" (1746), "On the Bubbles Observed in Freely Flowing Fluid" (1747), and "On Bubbles of Air That Escape from Fluids" (1748)—gained her a stipend from the academy.

Italy appears to have been an exception in allowing women to win formal recognition for their education and research in established institutions. Elsewhere, elite women could educate themselves by associating with learned men. The aristocrat **Margaret Cavendish** (1623–1673), a natural philosopher in England, gleaned the information necessary to start her career from her family and their friends, a network that included Thomas Hobbes and, while she was in exile in France during the 1640s, René Descartes. These connections were not enough to overcome the isolation she felt working in a world of letters that was still largely the preserve of men, but this did not prevent her from developing her own

Gassendi on the Science of Observation and the Human Soul

Pierre Gassendi (1592–1655) was a seventeenth-century French Catholic priest and philosopher. A contemporary of Descartes, Gassendi was part of a group of intellectuals in France who sought a new philosophy of nature that could replace the traditional teachings of Aristotle that Copernicus and his followers had so severely criticized. Gassendi had no doubt that his faith as a Christian was compatible with his enthusiasm for the new sciences of observation, but in order to demonstrate this to his contemporaries, he had to show that the mechanical explanations of the universe and the natural world did not necessarily lead to a heretical materialism or atheism. In the following passage, taken from his posthumously published work Syntagma Philosophicum *(1658), Gassendi attempted to demonstrate that one might infer the existence of the human soul, even if it was not accessible to the senses.*

There are many such things for which with the passage of time helpful appliances are being found that will make them visible to the senses. For example, take the little animal the mite, which is born under the skin; the senses perceived it as a certain unitary little point without parts; but since, however, the senses saw that it moved by itself, reason had deduced from this motion as from a perceptible sign that this little body was an animal and because its forward motion was somewhat like a turtle's, reason added that it must get about by the use of certain tiny legs and feet. And although this truth would have been hidden to the senses, which never perceived these limbs, the microscope was recently invented by which sight could perceive that matters were actually as predicted. Likewise, the question had been raised what the galaxy in the sky with the name of the Milky Way was. Democritus, concerning whom it was said that even when he did not know something he was knowing, had deduced from the perceptible sign of its filmy whiteness that it was nothing more than an innumerable multitude of closely packed little stars which could not be seen separately, but produced that effect of spilt milk when many of them were joined together. This truth had become known to him, and yet had remained undisclosed to the senses until our day and age, until the moment that the telescope, recently discovered, made it clear that things were in fact what he had said. But there are many such things which, though they were hidden from the ancients, have now been made manifest for our eyes. And who knows but a great many of those which are concealed in our time, which we perceive only through the intelligence, will one day also be clearly perceived by the senses through the agency of some helpful appliance thought up by our descendants? . . .

Secondly, if someone wonders whether a certain body is endowed with a soul or not, the senses are not at all capable of determining that by taking a look as it were at the soul itself; yet there are operations which when they come to the senses' notice, lead the intellect to deduce as from a sign that there is some soul beneath them. You will say that this sign belongs to the empirical type, but it is not at all of that type, for it is not even one of the indicative signs since it does not inform us of something that the senses have ever perceived in conjunction with the sign, as they have seen fire with smoke, but informs us instead of something that has always been impenetrable to the senses themselves, like our skin's pores or the mite's feet before the microscope.

You will persist with the objection that we should not ask so much whether there is a soul in a body as what its nature is, if it is the cause of such operations, just as there is no question that there is a force attracting iron in a magnet or that there is a tide in the sea, but there are questions over what their nature is or what they are caused by. But let me omit these matters which are to be fully treated elsewhere, and let it be enough if we say that not every truth can be known by the mind, but at least some can concerning something otherwise hidden, or not obvious to the senses themselves. And we bring up the example of the soul both because vital action is proposed by Sextus Empiricus as an example of an indicative sign and because even though it pertains not so much to the nature of the soul as to its existence, still a truth of existence of such magnitude as this, which it is most valuable for us to know, is made indisputable. For when among other questions we hear it asked if God is or exists in the universe, that is a truth of existence which it would be a great service to establish firmly even if it is not proven at the same time what he is or what his nature is. Although God is such that he can no more come under the perusal of the senses than the soul can, still we infer that the soul exists in the body from the actions that occur before the senses and are so peculiarly appropriate to a soul that if one were not present, they would not be either. In the same way we deduce that God exists in the universe from his effects perceived by the senses, which could not be produced by anything but God and which therefore would not be observed unless God were present in the world, such as the great order of the universe, its great beauty, its grandeur, its harmony, which are so great that they can only result from a sovereignly wise, good, powerful, and inexhaustible cause. But these things will be treated elsewhere at greater length.

Source: Craig B. Brush, ed., *The Selected Works of Pierre Gassendi* (New York: 1972), pp. 334–36.

Questions for Analysis

1. What is the relationship between new knowledge and new scientific tools (the microscope and the telescope) in Gassendi's examples of the mite and the Milky Way? Is he a Baconian or a Cartesian?

2. What are the limitations of the senses when it comes to questions of the human soul, according to Gassendi?

3. Given these limitations, does Gassendi conclude that science will never be able to say anything about his religious faith?

---

speculative natural philosophy and using it to critique those who would exclude her from scientific debate. The "tyrannical government" of men over women, she wrote, "hath so dejected our spirits, that we are become so stupid, that beasts being but a degree below us, men use us but a degree above beasts. Whereas in nature we have as clear an understanding as men, if we are bred in schools to mature our brains."

The construction of observatories in private residences enabled some women living in such homes to work their way into the growing field of astronomy. Between 1650 and 1710, 14 percent of German astronomers were women, the most famous of whom was **Maria Winkelmann** (1670–1720). Winkelmann had collaborated with her husband, Gottfried Kirch, in his observatory, and when he died she had already done significant work, discovering a comet and preparing calendars for the Berlin Academy of Sciences. When Kirch died, she petitioned the academy to allow her to take her husband's place in that prestigious body but was rejected. Gottfried Leibniz, the academy's president, explained, "Already during her husband's lifetime the society was burdened with ridicule because its calendar was prepared by a woman. If she were now to be kept on in such capacity, mouths would gape even wider." In spite of this rejection, Winkelmann continued to work as an astronomer, training both her son and two daughters in the discipline.

Like Winkelmann, the entymologist **Maria Sibylla Merian** (1647–1717) also made a career based on observation. And like Winkelmann, Merian was able to carve out a space for her scientific work by exploiting the precedent of guild women who learned their trades in family workshops. Merian was a daughter of an engraver and illustrator in Frankfurt and served as his informal apprentice

FROM *METAMORPHOSIS OF THE INSECTS OF SURINAM*, BY MARIA SIBYLLA MERIAN (1705). Merian, the daughter of a Frankfurt engraver, learned in her father's workshop the skills necessary to become an important early entymologist and scientific illustrator and conducted her research on two continents.

before beginning her own career as a scientific illustrator, specializing in detailed engravings of insects and plants. Traveling to the Dutch colony of Surinam, Merian supported herself and her two daughters by selling exotic insects and animals she collected and brought back to Europe. She fought the colony's sweltering climate and malaria to publish her most important scientific work, *Metamorphosis of the Insects of Surinam*, which detailed the life cycles of Surinam's insects in sixty ornate illustrations. Merian's *Metamorphosis* was well received in her time; in fact, Peter I of Russia proudly displayed her portrait and books in his study.

"AND ALL WAS LIGHT": ISAAC NEWTON

Sir **Isaac Newton**'s work marks the culmination of the scientific revolution. Galileo, peering through his telescope in the early 1600s, had come to believe that the earth and the heavens were made of the same material. His experiments with pendulums aimed to discover the laws of motion, and he proposed theories of inertia. But it was Newton who articulated those laws and presented a coherent, unified vision of how the universe worked. All bodies in the universe, Newton said, whether on earth or in the heavens, obeyed the same basic laws. One set of forces and one pattern, which could be expressed mathematically, explained why planets orbited in ellipses and why (and at what speed) apples fell from trees. An Italian mathematician later commented that Newton was the "greatest and most fortunate of mortals"—because there was only one universe, and he had discovered its laws.

Isaac Newton (1642–1727) was born on Christmas Day to a family of small landowners. His father died before his birth, and it fell to a succession of relatives, family friends, and schoolmasters to spot, then encourage, his genius. In 1661, he entered Trinity College in Cambridge University, where he would remain for the next thirty-five years, first as a student, then as the Lucasian Professor of Mathematics. The man who came to represent the personification of modern science was reclusive, secretive about his findings, and obsessive. During his early work with optics, he experimented with his own eyes, pressing them to see how different shapes would change the effects of light and then, intrigued by what he found, inserting a very thick needle "betwixt my eye and the bone as near to the backside of my eye as I could" to actually curve his eyeball. (Please do not try this at home.)

Newton's first great burst of creativity came at Cambridge from 1664 to 1666, "the prime of my age for invention." During these years, he broke new ground in three areas. The first was optics. Descartes believed that color was a secondary quality produced by the speed of particulate rotation but that light itself was white. Newton, using prisms he had purchased at a local fair, showed that white light was composed of different-colored rays (see image on page 545). The second area was in mathematics. In a series of brilliant insights, Newton invented both integral calculus and differential calculus, providing mathematical tools to model motion in space. The third area of his creative genius involved his early works on gravity. Newton later told different versions of the same story: the idea about gravity had come to him when he was in a "contemplative mood" and was "occasioned by the fall of an apple." Why did the apple "not go sideways or upwards, but constantly to the earth's center? . . . Assuredly the reason is, that the earth draws it. There must be a drawing power in matter." Voltaire, the eighteenth-century French essayist, retold the story to dramatize Newton's simple brilliance. But the theory of gravity rested on mathematical formulations, which were far from simple, and Newton did not work it out fully until the *Principia*, more than twenty years later.

Newton's work on the composite nature of white light led him to make a reflecting telescope, which used a curved mirror rather than lenses. The telescope earned him election to the Royal Society in 1672 and drew him out of his sheltered obscurity at Cambridge. Encouraged by the Royal Society's support, he wrote a paper describing his theory of optics and allowed it to be published in *Philosophical Transactions*. Astronomers and scientists across Europe applauded the work, but Robert Hooke, the Royal Society's curator of experiments, did not. Hooke was not persuaded by Newton's mode of argument, and found Newton's claims that science had to be mathematical both dogmatic and high-handed. He objected—in a series of sharp exchanges with the reclusive genius—that Newton had not provided any physical explanation for his results. Stung by the conflict with Hooke and persuaded that few natural philosophers could understand his theories, Newton withdrew to Cambridge and long refused to share his work. Only the patient effort of friends and fellow scientists such as the astronomer Edmond Halley (1656–1742), already well known for his astronomical observations in the Southern Hemisphere and the person for whom Halley's Comet is named, convinced Newton to publish again.

Newton's *Principia Mathematica* (Mathematical Principles of Natural Philosophy) was published in 1687. It was prompted by a visit from Halley, in which the astronomer asked Newton for his ideas on a question being discussed at the Royal Society: Was there a mathematical basis for the elliptical orbits of the planets? Halley's question inspired Newton to expand his earlier calculations into an all-encompassing theory of celestial—and terrestrial—dynamics. Halley not only encouraged Newton's work but supervised and financed its publication (though he had less money than Newton); and on several occasions he had to persuade Newton, who was enraged again by reports of criticism from Hooke and others, to continue with the project and commit his findings to print.

Principia was long and difficult—purposefully so, for Newton said he did not want to be "baited by little smatterers in mathematics." Its central proposition was that gravitation was a universal force that could be expressed mathematically. Newton built on Galileo's work on inertia, Kepler's findings concerning the elliptical orbits of planets, the work of Boyle and Descartes, and even on his rival Hooke's work on gravity. He once said, "If I have seen further, it is by standing on the shoulders of giants." But Newton's universal theory of gravity, although it drew on work of others before him, formulated something entirely new. His synthesis offered a single, descriptive account of mass and motion. "All bodies whatsoever are endowed with a principle of mutual gravitation." The law of gravitation was stated in a mathematical formula and supported by observation and experience—it was, literally, universal.

NEWTON'S EXPERIMENTS WITH LIGHT (1672). Newton's own sketch elegantly displays the way he proved that white light was made up of different-colored light rays. Earlier scientists had explained the color spectrum, which they produced by shining sunlight through a prism, by insisting that the colors were a by-product of contaminating elements within the prism's glass. Newton disproved this theory by shining the sunlight through two consecutive prisms. The first produced the characteristic division of light into a color spectrum. When one of these colored beams passed through a second prism, however, it emerged on the other side unchanged, demonstrating that the glass itself was not the cause of the dispersal. Newton was not yet thirty when he published the results of this experiment.

The scientific elite of Newton's time was not uniformly persuaded, however. Many mechanical philosophers, particularly Cartesians, objected to the prominence in Newton's theory of forces acting across empty space. Such attractions smacked of mysticism (or the occult), and seemed to lack any driving mechanism. Newton responded to these criticisms in a note added to the next edition of *Principia* (*General Scholium*, 1713). He did not know what *caused* gravity, he said, and he did not "feign hypotheses." "For whatever is not deduced from the phenomena must be called hypothesis," he wrote, and it has "no place in the experimental philosophy." For Newton, certainty and objectivity lay in the precise mathematical characterization of phenomena—"the mathematization of the universe," as one historian puts it. Science could not, and need not, always uncover causes, but it did describe natural phenomena and accurately predict the behavior of objects as confirmed by experimentation.

Other natural philosophers immediately acclaimed Newton's work for solving long-standing puzzles. Thinkers persuaded that the Copernican version of the universe was right had been unable to piece together the physics of a revolving earth. Newton made it possible to do so. Halley provided a poem to accompany the first edition of *Principia*. "No closer to the gods can any mortal rise," he wrote, of the man with whom he had worked so patiently. Halley did have a financial as well as an intellectual interest in the book, and arranged for it to be publicized and reviewed in influential journals. John Locke (whose own *Essay Concerning Human Understanding* was written at virtually the same time, in 1690) read *Principia* twice and summarized it in French for readers across the Channel. By 1713, pirated editions of *Principia* were being published in Amsterdam for distribution throughout Europe. And by the time Newton died, in 1727, he had become an English national hero

Analyzing Primary Sources

Newton on the Purposes of Experimental Philosophy

When Newton added his General Scholium *to the second edition of* Principia *in 1713, he was seventy-one, president of the Royal Society, and widely revered. Responding to Continental critics, he set out his general views on science and its methods, arguing against purely deductive reasoning and reliance on hypotheses about ultimate causes.*

 itherto we have explained the phenomena of the heavens and of our sea by the power of gravity, but have not yet assigned the cause of this power. This is certain, that it must proceed from a cause that penetrates to the very centres of the sun and planets, without suffering the least diminution of its force; that operates not according to the quantity of the surfaces of the particles on which it acts (as mechanical causes used to do), but according to the quantity of the solid matter which they contain, and propagates its virtue on all sides to immense distances, decreasing always as the inverse square of the distances. . . . [H]itherto I have not been able to discover the cause of those properties of gravity from phenomena, and I frame no hypothesis; for whatever is not deduced from the phenomena is to be called an hypothesis and hypotheses, whether metaphysical or physical, whether of occult qualities or mechanical, have no place in experimental philosophy. In this philosophy particular propositions are inferred from the phenomena, and afterwards rendered general by induction. . . . And to us it is enough that gravity does really exist, and acts according to the laws which we have explained, and abundantly serves to account for all the motions of the celestial bodies, and of our sea.

Source: Michael R. Matthews, ed., *The Scientific Background to Modern Philosophy: Selected Readings* (Indianapolis: 1989), p. 152.

Questions for Analysis

1. Why did Isaac Newton declare that "hypotheses, whether metaphysical or physical, whether of occult qualities or mechanical, have no place in experimental philosophy"?

2. Is Newton's thinking similar to Bacon's, or does he argue in ways similar to Descartes?

and was given a funeral at Westminster Abbey. The poet Alexander Pope expressed the awe that Newton inspired in some of his contemporaries in a famous couplet:

> Nature and nature's law lay hid in night;
> God said, "Let Newton be!" and all was light.

Voltaire, the French champion of the Enlightenment (discussed in the next chapter), was largely responsible for Newton's reputation in France. In this, he was helped by a woman who was a brilliant mathematician in her own right, Emilie du Châtelet. She coauthored a book with Voltaire introducing Newton to a French audience; and she translated *Principia*, a daunting scientific and mathematical task and one well beyond Voltaire's mathematical abilities. Newton's French admirers and publicists disseminated Newton's findings. In their eyes, Newton exemplified a cultural transformation, a turning point in the history of knowledge.

Science and Cultural Change

From the seventeenth century on, science stood at the heart of what it meant to be "modern." It grew increasingly central to the self-understanding of Western culture, and scientific and technological power became one of the justifications for the expansion of Western empires and the subjugation of other peoples. For all these reasons, the scientific revolution was and often still is presented as a thoroughgoing break with the past, a moment when Western culture was recast. But as one historian wrote, "no house is ever built of entirely virgin materials, according to a plan bearing no resemblance to old patterns, and no body of culture is able to wholly reject its past. Historical change is not like that, and most 'revolutions' effect less sweeping changes than they advertise or than are advertised for them."

To begin with, the transformation we have considered in this chapter involved elite knowledge. Ordinary people inhabited a very different cultural world. Second, natural philosophers' discoveries—Tycho's mathematics and Galileo's observations, for instance—did not undo the authority of the ancients in one blow, nor did they seek to do so. Third, science did not subvert religion. Even when traditional concepts collapsed in the face of new discoveries, natural philosophers seldom gave up on the project of restoring a picture of a divinely ordered universe. Mechanists argued that the intricate universe revealed by the discoveries of Copernicus, Kepler, Galileo, Newton, and others was evidence of God's guiding presence. Robert Boyle's will provided funds for a lecture series on the "confutation of atheism" by scientific means, and Isaac Newton was happy to have his work contribute to that project. "Nothing," he wrote to one of the lecturers in 1692, "can rejoice me more than to find [*Principia*] usefull for that purpose." The creation of "the Sun and Fixt stars," "the motion which the Planets now have could not spring from any naturall cause alone but were imprest with a divine Agent." Science was thoroughly compatible with belief in God's providential design, at least through the seventeenth century.

The greatest scientific minds were deeply committed to beliefs that do not fit present-day notions of science. Newton, again, is the most striking case in point. The great twentieth-century economist John Maynard Keynes was one of the first to read through Newton's private manuscripts. On the three hundredth anniversary of Newton's birth (the celebration of which was delayed because of the Second World War), Keynes offered the following reappraisal of the great scientist:

> I believe that Newton was different from the conventional picture of him. . . .
>
> In the eighteenth century and since, Newton came to be thought of as the first and greatest of the modern age of scientists, a rationalist, one who taught us to think on the lines of cold and untinctured reason.
>
> I do not see him in this light. I do not think that any one who has pored over the contents of that box which he packed up when he finally left Cambridge in 1696 and which, though partly dispersed, have come down to us, can see him like that. Newton was not the first of the age of reason. He was the last of the magicians, the last of the Babylonians and Sumerians, the last great mind which looked out

ESTABLISHMENT OF THE ACADEMY OF SCIENCES AND FOUNDATION OF THE OBSERVATORY, 1667. The 1666 founding of the Academy of Sciences was a measure of the new prestige of science and the potential value of research. Louis XIV sits at the center, surrounded by the religious and scholarly figures who offer the fruits of their knowledge to the French state. ▪ *What was the value of science for absolutist rulers such as Louis?*

on the visible and intellectual world with the same eyes as those who began to build our intellectual inheritance rather less than 10,000 years ago.

Like his predecessors, Newton saw the world as God's message to humanity, a text to be deciphered, and close reading and study would unlock its mysteries. This same impulse led Newton to read accounts of magic, investigate alchemy's claims that base metals could be turned into gold, and immerse himself in the writings of the Church fathers and the Bible, which he knew in intimate detail. If these activities sound unscientific from the perspective of the present, it is because the strict distinction between rational inquiry and belief in the occult or religious traditions simply did not exist in his time. Such a distinction is a product of a long history of scientific developments after the eighteenth century. Newton, then, was the last representative of an older tradition, and also, quite unintentionally, the first of a new one.

What, then, did the scientific revolution change? Seventeenth-century natural philosophers had produced new answers to fundamental questions about the physical world. Age-old questions about astronomy and physics had been recast and, to some extent (although it was not yet clear to what extent), answered. This process also brought about a new approach to amassing and integrating information in a systematic way, an approach that helped yield more insights into the workings of nature as time went on. During this period, too, the most innovative scientific work moved out of the restrictive environment of the Church and the universities. Natural philosophers began talking to and working with each other in lay organizations that developed standards of research. England's Royal Society spawned imitators in Florence and Berlin, and later, in Russia. The French Academy of Sciences had a particularly direct relationship with the monarchy and the French state. France's statesmen exerted control over the academy and sought to share in the rewards of any discoveries made by its members.

New were beliefs about the purpose and methods of science. The practice of breaking a complex problem down into parts made it possible to tackle more and different questions

After You Read This Chapter

 Go to **INQUIZITIVE** to see what you've learned—and learn what you've missed—with personalized feedback along the way.

REVIEWING THE OBJECTIVES

- The scientific revolution marked a shift toward new forms of explanation in descriptions of the natural world. What made the work of scientists during this period different from earlier forms of knowledge or research?

- The scientific revolution nevertheless depended on earlier traditions of philosophical thought. What earlier traditions proved important in fostering a spirit of scientific investigation?

- Observations of natural processes both in the heavens and on the earth played a central role in the scientific revolution. What technological innovations made new astronomical work possible? What questions led to the development of geology and the earth sciences?

- Central to the scientific revolution was the rejection of the Ptolemaic view of the universe and its replacement by the Copernican model. What was this controversy about?

- Francis Bacon and René Descartes held contrasting ideas about scientific method. What approach to science did each of these natural philosophers defend?

in the physical sciences. And mathematics assumed a more central role in the new science. Finally, rather than simply confirming established truths, the new methods were designed to explore the unknown and provide means to discover new truths. As Kepler wrote to Galileo, "How great a difference there is between theoretical speculation and visual experience, between Ptolemy's discussion of the Antipodes and Columbus's discovery of the New World." Knowledge itself was reconceived. In the older model, to learn was to read: reason logically, argue, compare classical texts, and absorb a finite body of knowledge. In the newer one, to learn was to discover, and what could be discovered was boundless.

CONCLUSION

The pioneering natural philosophers remained circumspect about their abilities. Some sought to lay bare the workings of the universe, while others believed humans could only catalog and describe the regularities observed in nature. By unspoken but seemingly mutual agreement, the question of first causes was left aside. The new science did not say *why*, but *how*. Newton, for one, worked toward explanations that would reveal the logic of creation laid out in mathematics. Yet, in the end, he settled for theories explaining motions and relationships that could be observed and tested.

The eighteenth-century heirs to Newton were much more daring. Laboratory science and the work of the scientific societies largely stayed true to the experimenters' rules and limitations. But as we will see in the next chapter, the natural philosophers who began investigating the human sciences cast aside some of their predecessors' caution. Society, technology, government, religion, even the individual human mind seemed to be mechanisms or parts of a larger nature waiting for study. The scientific revolution overturned the natural world as it had been understood for a millennium; it also inspired thinkers more interested in revolutions in society.

PEOPLE, IDEAS, AND EVENTS IN CONTEXT

- How did the traditions of **NEOPLATONISM** and **RENAISSANCE HUMANISM** contribute to a vision of the physical world that encouraged scientific investigation and explanation?

- In what way did the work of **NICOLAUS COPERNICUS**, **TYCHO BRAHE**, **JOHANNES KEPLER**, and **GALILEO GALILEI** undermine the intellectual foundations of the **PTOLEMAIC SYSTEM**? Why did their work largely take place outside the traditional centers of learning in Europe, such as universities?

- What was the significance of **JAMES USSHER**'s claim that the earth was created in 4004 B.C.? How did **NICOLAS STENO** demonstrate that the different layers of the earth's surface were visible signs of the earth's history?

- What differences in scientific practice arose from **FRANCIS BACON**'s emphasis on observation and **RENÉ DESCARTES**'s insistence that knowledge could be derived only from unquestionable first principles?

- What were **ISAAC NEWTON**'s major contributions to the scientific revolution? Why have some suggested that Newton's interests and thinking were not all compatible with modern conceptions of scientific understanding?

- What was important about the establishment of institutions such as the British **ROYAL SOCIETY** or the French **ACADEMY OF SCIENCES** for the development of scientific methods and research?

- What prevented women from entering most of Europe's scientific academies? How did educated women such as **LAURA BASSI**, **MARGARET CAVENDISH**, **MARIA WINKELMANN**, and **MARIA SIBYLLA MERIAN** gain the skills necessary to participate in scientific work?

THINKING ABOUT CONNECTIONS

- How did ideas about the value of ancient scholarship and philosophy change after the development of new sciences of observation during the seventeenth century?

- What possible connections might be made between the intellectual developments in scientific thinking during the seventeenth century and the Reformation of the sixteenth century? Was the new science incompatible with religious faith?

STORY LINES

■ During the eighteenth century, intellectuals in Europe sought to answer questions about the nature of good government, morality, and the social order by applying principles of rational argument. They questioned the value of traditional institutions and insisted that "enlightened" reason could solve social problems better than age-old customs.

■ Population growth, economic development, and colonial expansion created prosperity for some regions in western Europe and greater economic vulnerability in others. Aggregate increases in wealth fueled the beginnings of a consumer society, and a new awareness of the world's diverse cultures and peoples.

■ Absolutist rulers used Enlightenment ideals to justify the centralization of authority and the establishment of rationalized bureaucracies. Enlightenment ideas also helped establish a radical critique of the eighteenth-century social and political order.

CHRONOLOGY

Europe during the Enlightenment

I n 1762, the *parlement* (law court) of Toulouse, in France, convicted Jean Calas of murdering his son. Calas was a Protestant in a region where Catholic–Protestant tensions ran high. Witnesses claimed that the young Calas had wanted to convert to Catholicism, and the father had killed him to prevent this conversion. Following French law, Jean Calas was tortured twice: first to force a confession and next to identify his alleged accomplices. His arms and legs were slowly pulled apart, gallons of water were poured down his throat, his body was publicly broken on the wheel, and each of his limbs was smashed with an iron bar; then the executioner cut off his head. Throughout the trial, torture, and execution, Calas maintained his innocence. Two years later, the Parlement reversed its verdict, declaring Calas not guilty and offering the family payment in compensation.

François-Marie Arouet, also known as Voltaire, was appalled by the verdict and punishment. At the time of the case, Voltaire was the most famous personality in the European intellectual movement known as the Enlightenment. Prolific and well connected, Voltaire took up his pen to clear Calas's name. He hired lawyers for the family and wrote briefs, letters, and essays to bring

551

THE CRUEL DEATH OF CALAS. This print, reproduced in a pamphlet that circulated in Britain in the late eighteenth century, portrayed the French Protestant Jean Calas as a martyr to his beliefs, and directly implicated the Roman Catholic Church in the cruelty of his execution by placing an enthusiastic priest prominently at the scene. The pamphlet may also have sought to reinforce anti-French sentiments among an increasingly nationalistic British population. ▪ *How might Enlightenment authors have used such a scene to promote their message of toleration?* ▪ *How might Church officials have responded to such attacks?*

On Crimes and Punishments appeared in 1764. Voltaire's reputation did not rest on his originality as a philosopher; it came from his effectiveness as a writer and advocate, and his desire and ability to reach a wide audience in print.

The emergence of this wide audience for Voltaire's writings was just as significant as the arguments he made. The growth of European cities, the spread of literacy, and new forms of social interaction at all levels of society helped fuel the Enlightenment's atmosphere of critical reflection on religion, law, the power of the state, and the dignity of the individual. The fact that a writer such as Voltaire could become a celebrity showed that a new kind of literate, reading public had developed in Europe. The large numbers of people who read and had income to spare on printed material created a market for newspapers and novels, which in turn showed the emergence of a new kind of consumer society. The works of writers such as Voltaire and his peers were discussed over sweetened caffeinated drinks in coffeehouses and cafes, where ordinary people gathered to smoke and debate the issues of the day. (Coffee, sugar, and tobacco all came from the Atlantic colonial trade.) Similar scenes took place in the homes of aristocrats. The Enlightenment was thus not only an intellectual movement but a cultural phenomenon. It exposed an increasingly broad part of the population to new forms of consumption, of goods as well as ideas.

the case to the public eye. These essays circulated widely among an increasingly literate middle-class audience. For Voltaire, Calas's case exemplified nearly everything he found backward in European culture: intolerance, ignorance, and religious "fanaticism" had made a travesty of justice. Voltaire wrote, "Shout everywhere, I beg you, for Calas and against fanaticism, for it is this infamy that has caused their misery." Torture demonstrated the power of the courts but could not uncover the truth. Secret interrogations, trials behind closed doors, summary judgment (Calas was executed the day after being convicted, with no review by a higher court), and barbaric punishments defied reason, morality, and human dignity. Any criminal, however wretched, "is a man," wrote Voltaire, "and you are accountable for his blood."

Voltaire's writings on the Calas case illustrate the classic concerns of the Enlightenment: the dangers of arbitrary and unchecked authority, the value of religious toleration, and the overriding importance of law, reason, and human dignity in all affairs. He borrowed most of his arguments from others—from his predecessor the Baron de Montesquieu and from the Italian writer Cesare Beccaria, whose

POPULATION, COMMERCE, AND CONSUMPTION

The Enlightenment's audience consisted of urban readers and consumers who were receptive to new cultural forms: essay, political tract, satirical engraving, novel, newspaper, theatrical spectacles, and even musical performances. Clearly, such developments could only occur in a society where significant numbers of people had achieved a level of wealth that freed them from the immediate cares of daily sustenance. By the beginning of the eighteenth century, this level of wealth had been achieved in the cities of northwestern Europe. The North Atlantic economies of France and Britain, in particular, made these two countries the preponderant powers both in Europe and the wider world.

Economic development that favored cities during the eighteenth century did not change the fundamental balance of population between town and country. Europe remained a primarily rural society during the Enlightenment, but the nature of the rural economy changed. Wealth became more concentrated in towns and in rural areas where forms of preindustrial production took root. These concentrations of wealth became magnets for those seeking opportunity, and intensified the pressures associated with labor migration and itinerant trade (Chapter 15). Population growth also encouraged mobility, as poorer regions increasingly became exporters of laborers in search of work and livelihood.

Population and Economy in Eighteenth-Century Europe

By 1750, population growth was changing older patterns of migration in western Europe. Germany's population increased by a third between 1750 and 1800, from 18.4 to 24.5 million. France's 18 percent increase in the same period was slower but similar in its effects: creating more pressure for internal migration, and providing a supply of laborers for the manufacture of goods in the countryside and in growing towns.

Demographic growth in western Europe was made possible by cheaper food and declines in mortality from infectious disease. Intensive agriculture produced more food per acre, and improved transportation resulted in fewer famines and a better-nourished population. The importation of corn and potatoes from the Americas provided new and cheaper staple crops. Half the population continued to die before the age of twenty from infectious disease, but plague outbreaks became less frequent, and better diet and sanitation reduced mortality caused by typhoid, cholera, smallpox, and measles.

Northwestern Europe was also increasingly urbanized. The total number of urban dwellers in Europe did not change much between 1600 and 1800. At both dates, approximately 200 cities in Europe had a population of over 10,000. These cities were increasingly concentrated in northern and western Europe, however, and the largest experienced extraordinary growth, especially those connected with Atlantic trade. Cities such as Hamburg in Germany, Liverpool in England, Toulon in France, and Cadíz in Spain grew by about 250 percent between 1600 and 1750. Amsterdam, the hub of early modern international commerce, increased in population from 30,000 in 1530 to 200,000 by 1800. Naples, the busy Mediterranean port, went from a population of 300,000 in 1600 to nearly 500,000 by the late eighteenth century. Spectacular population growth also occurred in the administrative capitals of Europe: London's population grew from 674,000 in 1700 to 860,000 a century later; Paris's population went from 180,000 in 1600 to more than 500,000 in 1800; and Berlin's population grew from 6,500 in 1661 to 140,000 in 1783.

The prosperity of northwestern Europe was linked to developments in trade, manufacturing, and consumption that had begun in the late medieval period, culminating in a commercial revolution by the eighteenth century. The growing production and trade in textiles provide a good example of how changes in labor, commerce, and consumption were interrelated. Improvements in transportation led entrepreneurs to produce textiles in the countryside. They distributed, or "put out," wool and flax to rural workers who spun and wove it into cloth on a piece-rate basis. The entrepreneur sold the finished cloth in a market that extended from local towns to international exporters. For country dwellers, this system (sometimes called "protoindustrialization") provided employment during slack seasons in the agricultural year. The system also allowed merchants to avoid expensive guild restrictions in the towns and reduced their production costs. Economic development in rural areas increased the proportion of the population who depended on wage labor for their survival, rather than working their own fields.

Some cities became manufacturing centers during the eighteenth century. In northern France, many of the million or so men and women employed in the textile trade lived and worked in Amiens, Lille, and Rheims. The rulers of Prussia made it their policy to develop Berlin as a manufacturing center, taking advantage of an influx of French Protestants to establish a silk-weaving industry there. Most urban manufacturing took place in small shops employing from five to twenty journeymen working under a master. But the scale of such enterprise was growing and becoming more specialized, as workshops began to group together to form a single manufacturing district in which several thousand workers could be employed to produce the same product.

Techniques in some crafts remained much as they had been for centuries. In others, however, inventions changed the pattern of work as well as the nature of the product. Knitting frames, simple devices to speed the manufacture of textile goods, made their appearance in Britain and Holland. Wire-drawing machines and slitting mills, which allowed nail makers to convert iron bars into rods, spread from Germany into Britain. Techniques for printing colored designs directly on calico cloth were imported from Asia. And new and more efficient printing presses appeared, first in Holland and then elsewhere.

Workers did not readily accept innovations of this kind. Labor-saving machines left people out of work. Artisans,

POPULATION GROWTH, c. 1600. ▪ *Where did the population grow more rapidly?* ▪ *Why were the largest gains in population on the coasts?* ▪ *How did urbanization affect patterns of life and trade?*

especially those organized into guilds, were by nature conservative, anxious to protect not only their rights but also the secrets of their trades. Governments often would intervene to block the use of machines if they threatened to increase unemployment or create unrest. And states would act to protect the interests of their powerful commercial and financial backers. Both Britain and France outlawed calico printing for a time to protect local textile manufacturers and importers of Indian goods. Mercantilist doctrines also impeded innovation. In both Paris and Lyons, for example, the use of indigo dyes was banned because they

were manufactured abroad. But the pressures for economic innovation were irresistible, because behind them lay an insatiable eighteenth-century appetite for goods.

A World of Goods

By the mid-eighteenth century, the **commercial revolution** had produced a mass market for consumer goods, concentrated at first in northwestern Europe. Houses became larger, particularly in towns; but even more strikingly,

TOPSY-TURVY WORLD, BY JAN STEEN. This Dutch painting depicts a household in the throes of the exploding consumer economy that hit Europe in the eighteenth century. Consumer goods ranging from silver and china to clothing and furniture cluttered the houses of ordinary people as never before.

the houses of the middling ranks were now stocked with hitherto uncommon luxuries such as sugar, tobacco, tea, coffee, chocolate, newspapers, books, pictures, clocks, toys, china, glassware, pewter, silver plate, soap, razors, furniture (including beds with mattresses, chairs, and chests of drawers), shoes, cotton cloth, and spare clothing. Demand for such products consistently outstripped the supply, causing prices for these items to rise faster than the price of foodstuffs throughout the century. But the demand for them continued unabated. Such goods were indulgences, of course, but they were also repositories of value in which families could invest their surplus cash, knowing that they could pawn them in hard times if cash were needed.

The exploding consumer economy of the eighteenth century also encouraged the provision of services. In eighteenth-century Britain, the service sector was the fastest-growing part of the economy, outstripping both agriculture and manufacturing. Almost everywhere in urban Europe, the eighteenth century was the golden age of the small shopkeeper. People bought more prepared foods and more ready-to-wear (as opposed to personally tailored) clothing. Advertising became an important part of doing business, helping create demand for new products and shaping popular taste for changing fashions. Even political allegiances could be expressed through consumption when people purchased plates and glasses commemorating favorite rulers or causes.

The result of all these developments was a European economy vastly more complex, more specialized, more integrated, more commercialized, and more productive than anything the world had seen before. These developments necessarily affected the way people thought of the world and their place in it—above all, during the Enlightenment, people shared a sense of living in a time marked by change. Many Enlightenment thinkers defended such changes as "progress," but others were more critical, fearing that valued traditions were being lost. Such debates lay at the heart of Enlightenment thought.

THE FOUNDATIONS OF THE ENLIGHTENMENT

Enlightenment thinkers did not agree on everything, but most shared a sense that they lived in an exciting moment in history in which human **reason** would prevail over the accumulated superstitions and traditions of the past. Enlightenment authors believed themselves to be the defenders of a new ideal, the "party of humanity."

The confidence that Enlightenment thinkers placed in the powers of human reason stemmed from the accomplishments of the scientific revolution. Even when the details of Newton's physics were poorly understood, his methods provided a model for scientific inquiry into other phenomena. Nature operated according to laws that could be grasped by study, observation, and thought. The work of the Scottish writer **David Hume** (*A Treatise of Human Nature,* 1739–1740; and *An Enquiry Concerning Human Understanding,* 1748) provided the most direct bridge from science to the Enlightenment. Newton had refused speculation about ultimate causes, arguing instead for a precise description of natural phenomena (Chapter 16). Hume applied this same rigor and skepticism to the study of morality, the mind, and government, often drawing analogies to scientific laws. Hume criticized the "passion for hypotheses and systems"

DIVINE LIGHT. The frontispiece for Voltaire's book on the science of Isaac Newton portrays Newton as the source of a divine light that is reflected onto Voltaire's desk through a mirror held by Émilie du Châtelet, the French translator of Newton who was also Voltaire's lover. Newton's clouded throne and the adoring angels holding du Châtelet aloft were familiar motifs from earlier generations of religious paintings, but the significance of the carefully portrayed ray of light is recast by the books, inkwell, and precise scientific measuring tools surrounding Voltaire. ■ *What does this image say about the relationship between religious thought and Enlightenment science?*

intellectual independence. (He also called it an awakening and credited Hume with rousing him from his "dogmatic slumber.") Kant likened the intellectual history of humanity to the growth of a child. Enlightenment, in this view, was an escape from humanity's "self-imposed immaturity" and a long overdue break with humanity's self-imposed parental figure, the Catholic Church. Coming of age meant the "determination and courage to think without the guidance of someone else" as an individual. Reason required autonomy and freedom from tradition.

Enlightenment thinkers nevertheless recognized a great debt to their predecessors, especially **John Locke**, **Francis Bacon**, and **Isaac Newton**. They drew heavily on Locke's studies of human knowledge, especially his *Essay Concerning Human Understanding* (1690). Locke's theories of how humans acquire knowledge gave education and environment a critical role in shaping human character. All knowledge, he argued, originates from sense perception. The human mind at birth is a "blank tablet" (in Latin, *tabula rasa*). Only when an infant begins to perceive the external world with its senses does anything register in its mind. Education, then, was essential to the creation of a good and moral individual. Locke's starting point, which became a central premise for those who followed, was the goodness and perfectibility of humanity. Building on Locke's theories, eighteenth-century thinkers made education central to their project, because education promised that social progress could be achieved through individual moral improvement. Locke's theories had potentially radical implications for eighteenth-century society: if all humans were capable of reason, education might also level hierarchies of status, sex, or race. As we will see, only a few Enlightenment thinkers made such egalitarian arguments. Still, optimism and a belief in universal human progress constituted a second defining feature of nearly all Enlightenment thinking.

Enlightenment thinkers sought nothing less than the organization of all knowledge. The *scientific method*, by which they meant the empirical observation of particular phenomena to arrive at general laws, offered a way to pursue research in all areas—to study human affairs as well as natural ones. Thus, they collected evidence to learn the laws governing the rise and fall of nations, and compared governmental constitutions to arrive at an ideal and universally applicable political system. As the English poet Alexander Pope stated in his *Essay on Man* (1733), "The science of human nature [may be] like all other sciences reduced to a few clear points," and Enlightenment thinkers became determined to learn exactly what those few clear points were. They took up a strikingly wide array of subjects in this systematic manner: knowledge and the mind, natural history, economics, government, religious beliefs,

that dominated earlier philosophical thinking. Experience and careful observation, he argued, usually did not support the premises on which those systems rested.

Embracing human reason also required confronting the power of Europe's traditional monarchies and the religious institutions that supported them. "Dare to know!" the German philosopher Immanuel Kant challenged his contemporaries in his classic 1784 essay "What Is Enlightenment?" For Kant, the Enlightenment was a declaration of customs of indigenous peoples of the New World, human nature, and sexual (or what we would call gender) and racial differences.

As we can see from these examples, the culture of the *philosophes*, or Enlightenment thinkers, was international. French became the lingua franca of much Enlightenment discussion, but "French" books were often published in Switzerland, Germany, and Russia. Enlightenment thinkers admired British institutions and British scholarship, and Great Britain produced important Enlightenment thinkers: the historian Edward Gibbon and the Scottish philosophers David Hume and **Adam Smith**. The philosophes considered the Americans Thomas Jefferson and Benjamin Franklin to be a part of their group. Despite stiffer resistance from religious authorities, stricter state censors, and smaller networks of educated elites, the Enlightenment flourished across central and southern Europe. Frederick II of Prussia housed Voltaire during one of his exiles from France, and he also patronized a small but unusually productive group of Enlightenment thinkers. Northern Italy was also an important center of Enlightenment thought.

THE WORLD OF THE PHILOSOPHES

Although Enlightenment thought was European in a broad sense, France provided the stage for some of the most widely followed Enlightenment projects. For this reason, Enlightenment thinkers, regardless of where they lived, are often called by the French word *philosophes*. Hardly any of the philosophes, with the exceptions of David Hume and Immanuel Kant, were true philosophers, in the sense of being highly original abstract thinkers. Most Enlightenment thinkers shunned forms of expression that might seem incomprehensible, priding themselves instead on their clarity. *Philosophe*, in French, simply means "a free thinker," a person whose reflections are unhampered by the constraints of religion or dogma in any form.

Voltaire

The best known of the philosophes was **Voltaire**, born François-Marie Arouet (1694–1778). As Erasmus two centuries earlier had embodied Christian humanism, Voltaire virtually personified the Enlightenment, commenting on an enormous range of subjects in a wide variety of literary forms. Educated by the Jesuits, he became a gifted and sharp-tongued writer. His gusto for provocation landed

him in the Bastille (a notorious prison in Paris) for libel and soon afterward in temporary exile in England. In his three years there, Voltaire became an admirer of British political institutions, culture, and science; above all, he became an extremely persuasive convert to the ideas of Newton, Bacon, and Locke. His single greatest accomplishment may have been popularizing Newton's work in France and, more generally, championing the cause of British empiricism against a French scientific community that remained indebted to Descartes and deductive reasoning (Chapter 16).

Voltaire's *Philosophical Letters* ("*Letters on the English Nation*"), published after his return in 1734, made an immediate sensation. Voltaire's themes were religion and political liberty, and his weapons were comparisons. His admiration

VOLTAIRE'S *CANDIDE*. Voltaire's best-selling novel gently mocked the optimism of some Enlightenment thinkers. The young Candide's tutor, Pangloss, insisted on repeating that "this is the best of all possible worlds," even as he, Candide, and Candide's love, the beautiful Cunégonde, suffered terrible accidents and misfortune. In the scene shown here, Candide is thrown out of the castle by Cunégonde's father, with "great kicks in the rear," after they have been caught kissing behind a screen. This mix of serious message and humorous delivery was quite common in Enlightenment literature. ▪ *How might this combination of humor and philosophic meditation have been received by the educated middle-class audience that made up the readership of works such as* **Candide**?

for British culture and politics became a stinging critique of France—and other absolutist countries on the Continent. He praised British open-mindedness and empiricism: the country's respect for scientists and its support for research. He considered the relative weakness of the British aristocracy a sign of Britain's political health. Unlike the French, the British respected commerce and people who engaged in it, Voltaire wrote. The British tax system was rational, free of the complicated exemptions for the privileged that were ruining French finances. The British House of Commons represented the middle classes and, in contrast with French absolutism, brought balance to British government and checked arbitrary power. In one of the book's more incendiary passages, he argued that in Britain, violent revolution had actually produced political moderation and stability: "The idol of arbitrary power was drowned in seas of blood. . . . The English nation is the only nation in the world that has succeeded in moderating the power of its kings by resisting them."

Of all Britain's reputed virtues, religious toleration loomed largest of all. Britain, Voltaire argued, brought together citizens of different religions in a harmonious and productive culture. In this and other instances, Voltaire oversimplified: British Catholics, Dissenters, and Jews did not have equal civil rights. Yet the British policy of "toleration" did contrast with Louis XIV's intolerance of Protestants. The revocation of the Edict of Nantes (1685) had stripped French Protestants of civil rights and helped create the atmosphere in which Jean Calas and others were persecuted.

Of all forms of intolerance, Voltaire opposed religious bigotry most, and with real passion he denounced religious fraud, faith in miracles, and superstition. His most famous battle cry was "Écrasez l'infâme!" ("Crush this infamous thing"), by which he meant all forms of repression, fanaticism, and bigotry. "The less superstition, the less fanaticism; and the less fanaticism, the less misery." He did not oppose religion per se; rather, he sought to rescue morality (which he believed came from God) from dogma—elaborate ritual, dietary laws, formulaic prayers—and a powerful Church bureaucracy. He argued for common sense and simplicity, persuaded that these would bring out the goodness in humanity and establish stable authority. "The simpler the laws are, the more the magistrates are respected; the simpler the religion will be, the more one will revere its ministers. Religion can be simple. When enlightened people will announce a single God, rewarder and avenger, no one will laugh, everyone will obey."

Voltaire relished his position as a critic. He was regularly exiled from France and other countries, and his books banned and burned. As long as his plays attracted large audiences, however, the French king felt he had to tolerate the author. Voltaire had an attentive international public, including Frederick of Prussia, who invited him to his court at Berlin, and Catherine of Russia, with whom he corresponded about reforms she might introduce in Russia. When he died in 1778, a few months after a triumphant return to Paris, he was possibly the best-known writer in Europe.

Montesquieu

The baron de **Montesquieu** (*mahn-tuhs-KYOO*; 1689–1755) was a very different kind of Enlightenment figure. Montesquieu was born to a noble family, and he inherited both an estate and, since state offices were property that passed from father to son, a position as a magistrate in the Parlement of Bordeaux. He was not a stylist or a provocateur like Voltaire but a relatively cautious jurist, though he did write a satirical novel, *The Persian Letters* (1721), as a young man. The novel, which he published anonymously in Amsterdam, was composed as letters from two Persian visitors to France. The visitors detailed the odd religious superstitions they witnessed, compared manners at the French court with those in Turkish harems, and likened French absolutism to their own brands of despotism, or the abuse of government authority. *The Persian Letters* was an immediate best seller, and it inspired many imitators as other authors used the formula of a foreign observer to criticize contemporary French society.

Montesquieu's treatise *The Spirit of Laws* (1748) may have been the most influential work of the Enlightenment. It was a groundbreaking study in what we would call comparative historical sociology, and very Newtonian in its careful, empirical approach. Montesquieu asked about the structures that shaped law. How had different environments, histories, and religious traditions come together to create such a variety of governmental institutions? What were the different forms of government? What spirit characterized each, and what were their respective virtues and shortcomings?

Montesquieu suggested that there were three forms of government: republics, monarchies, and despotisms. A republic was governed by many individuals—either an elite aristocracy of citizens or the people as a whole. The soul of a republic was virtue, which allowed individual citizens to transcend their particular interests and rule in accordance with the common good. In a monarchy, on the other hand, one person ruled in accordance with the law. The soul of a monarchy, wrote Montesquieu, was honor, which gave individuals an incentive to behave with loyalty toward their sovereign. The third form of government, despotism, was rule by a single person unchecked by law or other powers. The soul of despotism was fear, since no citizen could feel secure, and punishment took the place of education. Lest this seem abstract, Montesquieu devoted two chapters to the French monarchy, in which he spelled out what he saw as a dangerous drift toward despotism in his own land. Like other Enlightenment thinkers, Montesquieu admired the British system and its separation of the executive, legislative, and judicial functions of government. Such a balance of powers preserved liberty by avoiding a concentration of authority in a single individual or group. His idealization of "checks and balances" had a formative influence on Enlightenment political theorists and helped to guide the authors of the U.S. Constitution in 1787.

Diderot and the Encyclopedia

The most remarkable and ambitious Enlightenment project was a collective one: the **Encyclopedia**. The *Encyclopedia* claimed to summarize all the most advanced contemporary philosophical, scientific, and technical knowledge, making them available to any reader. It demonstrated how scientific analysis could be applied in nearly all realms of thought, and further aimed to encourage critical reflection on an enormous range of traditions and institutions. The guiding spirit behind the venture was **Denis Diderot** (1713–1784), who was helped by the mathematician Jean Le Rond d'Alembert (1717–1783) and other leading men of letters, including Voltaire and Montesquieu. Published in installments between 1751 and 1772, the *Encyclopedia* ran to seventeen large volumes of text and eleven more of illustrations, with more than 71,000 articles.

Diderot commissioned articles on science and technology, showing how machines worked and illustrating new industrial processes. The point was to demonstrate how science could promote progress and alleviate human misery. Diderot turned the same methods to politics and the social order, including articles on economics, taxes, and the slave trade. Censorship made it difficult to write openly antireligious articles, but Diderot thumbed his nose at religion in oblique ways. At the entry on the Eucharist, for example, the reader found a terse cross-reference: "See *cannibalism*." At one point, the French government revoked the publishing permit for the *Encyclopedia*, declaring in 1759 that the encyclopedists were trying to "propagate materialism" (by which they meant atheism) "to destroy Religion, to inspire a spirit of independence, and to nourish the corruption of morals." The volumes sold remarkably well despite such bans and their hefty price. Purchasers belonged to the elite: aristocrats, government officials, prosperous merchants,

TECHNOLOGY AND INDUSTRY. This engraving, from the mining section, is characteristic of Diderot's *Encyclopedia*. The project aimed to detail technological changes, manufacturing processes, and forms of labor—all in the name of advancing human knowledge.

and a scattering of members of the higher clergy. That elite stretched across Europe, including its overseas colonies.

Although the French philosophes sparred with the state and the church, they sought political stability and reform. Montesquieu hoped that an enlightened aristocracy would press for reforms and defend liberty against a despotic king. Voltaire, persuaded that aristocrats would represent only their particular narrow interests, looked to an enlightened monarch for leadership. Neither was a democrat, and neither conceived of reform from below. Still, their widely read critiques of arbitrary power stung. By the 1760s, the French critique of despotism provided the language in which many people across Europe articulated their opposition to existing regimes.

MAJOR THEMES OF ENLIGHTENMENT THOUGHT

Enlightenment thinkers across Europe raised similar themes: humanitarianism, or the dignity and worth of all individuals; religious toleration; and liberty. These ideals inspired important debates about three issues in particular: law and punishment, the place of religious minorities, and the state's relationship to society and the economy.

Law and Punishment

The Enlightenment beliefs about education and the perfectibility of human society led many thinkers to question the harsh treatment of criminals by European courts. An influential work by the Italian jurist **Cesare Beccaria** (1738–1794), *On Crimes and Punishments* (1764), provided Voltaire with most of his arguments in the Calas case. Beccaria criticized the use of arbitrary power and attacked the prevalent view that punishments should be society's vengeance on the criminal. The only legitimate rationale for punishment instead should be to maintain social order and to prevent other crimes. Beccaria argued for the greatest possible leniency compatible with deterrence; respect for individual dignity dictated that humans should punish other humans no more than is absolutely necessary.

Above all, Beccaria's book eloquently opposed torture and the death penalty. Public execution, he argued, was intended to dramatize the power of the state and the horrors of hell, but it dehumanized the victim, judge, and spectators. In 1766, a few years after the Calas case, another French trial provided an example of what horrified Beccaria and the philosophes. A nineteen-year-old French nobleman, convicted of blasphemy, had his tongue cut out and his hands cut off before he was burned at the stake. The court discovered the blasphemer had read Voltaire and ordered his *Philosophical Dictionary* burned along with the body. Sensational cases such as this helped publicize Beccaria's work. *On Crimes and Punishments* was quickly translated into a dozen languages. Owing primarily to its influence, by around 1800, most European countries had abolished torture, branding, whipping, and mutilation, and reserved the death penalty for capital crimes.

Humanitarianism and Religious Toleration

Humanitarianism and reason also counseled religious toleration. Enlightenment thinkers spoke almost as one on the need to end religious warfare and the persecution of heretics and religious minorities. Most Enlightenment authors distinguished between religious belief (which they accepted) and the Church as an institution and dogma (which they rebelled against). It was in this sense that Voltaire opposed the Church's influence over society. Few Enlightenment authors were atheists—a notable exception was Paul-Henri d'Holbach (1723–1789)—and only a few more were agnostics. Many, including Voltaire, were deists, believers of a God who, acting as a "divine watchmaker" at the beginning of time, constructed a perfect universe then left it to run with predictable regularity. Enlightenment inquiry proved compatible with very different stances on religion.

Nevertheless, Enlightenment support for toleration was sometimes limited. Most Christians saw Jews as heretics and Christ killers. Although Enlightenment thinkers deplored persecution, they commonly viewed Judaism and Islam as backward, superstitious religions. One of the few Enlightenment figures to treat Jews sympathetically was the German philosophe Gotthold Lessing (1729–1781). Lessing's play *Nathan*

INSTRUMENTS OF TORTURE. A man being stretched on the rack (left) and a thumbscrew (right), both from an official Austrian government handbook. By 1800, Beccaria's influence had helped phase out the use of such instruments.

LESSING AND FRIEND VISIT MENDELSSOHN. This painting of a meeting between the philosophe Gotthold Lessing (shown standing), a Christian, and his friend Moses Mendelssohn (seated right), a Jewish rabbi, emphasizes the personal nature of their intellectual relationship, which transcended their religious backgrounds. The Enlightenment's atmosphere of earnest discussion is invoked both by the open book before them and the shelf of reading material behind Lessing. Compare this image of masculine discussion (note the role of the one woman in the painting) with the image of the aristocratic salon (page 574) and the coffeehouse (page 575). ▪ *What similarities and differences might you point to in these various illustrations of the Enlightenment public sphere?*

Jewish community of Berlin. Repeatedly attacked and invited to convert to Christianity, he defended Jewish communities against anti-Semitic policies and Judaism against Enlightenment criticism. At the same time, he promoted reform within the Jewish community, arguing that his community had special reason to embrace the broad Enlightenment project: religious faith should be voluntary, states should promote tolerance, and humanitarianism would bring progress to all.

Government, Administration, and the Economy

Enlightenment ideas had a very real influence over affairs of state. The philosophes defended reason and knowledge for humanitarian reasons. But they also promised to make nations stronger and more efficient and prosperous. Beccaria's proposed legal reforms were a good case in point; he sought to make laws not simply more just but also more effective. In other words, the Enlightenment spoke not only to individuals but also to states. The philosophes addressed issues of liberty and rights and also took up matters of administration, tax collection, and economic policy.

The rising fiscal demands of eighteenth-century states and empires made these issues newly urgent. Which economic resources were most valuable to states? During the seventeenth century, mercantilists had argued that regulation of trade was necessary to maximize government revenues (Chapter 15). During the eighteenth century, Enlightenment economic thinkers, known as the physiocrats, argued that real wealth came from the land and agricultural production, which prospered with less government interference. They advocated simplifying the tax system and following a policy of laissez-faire, which comes from the French expression *laissez faire la nature* ("let nature take its course"), letting wealth and goods circulate without government interference.

The classic expression of laissez-faire economics, however, came from the Scottish economist Adam Smith (1723–1790) in his landmark treatise *Inquiry into the Nature and Causes of the Wealth of Nations* (1776). Smith disagreed with the physiocrats on the value of agriculture, but he shared their opposition to mercantilism. For Smith, the central issues were the productivity of labor and how it operated in different sectors of the economy. Mercantile restrictions—such as high taxes on imported goods, one of the grievances of the colonists throughout the American empires—did not encourage the productive deployment of labor and thus did not create real economic health. For Smith, general prosperity could be obtained by allowing the (now-famous) "invisible hand" of competition to guide economic activity.

the Wise (1779) takes place in Jerusalem during the Fourth Crusade and begins with a pogrom—a violent, orchestrated attack on Jews—in which the wife and children of Nathan, a Jewish merchant, are murdered. Nathan survives to become a sympathetic and wise father figure. He adopts a Christian-born daughter and raises her with three religions: Christianity, Islam, and Judaism. At several points, authorities ask him to choose the one true religion, but Nathan shows that none exists. The three great monotheistic religions are three versions of the truth. Religion is authentic, or true, only insofar as it makes the believer virtuous.

Lessing modeled his hero on his friend Moses Mendelssohn (1729–1786), a self-educated rabbi and bookkeeper (and the grandfather of the composer Felix Mendelssohn). Moses Mendelssohn moved—though with some difficulty—between the Enlightenment circles of Frederick II and the

Individuals, in other words, should pursue their own interests by buying and selling goods and labor freely on the open market without interference from state-chartered monopolies or legal restraints. As Smith wrote in his earlier *Theory of Moral Sentiments* (1759), self-interested individuals could be "led by an invisible hand . . . without knowing it, without intending it, [to] advance the interest of the society."

The Wealth of Nations spelled out, in more technical and historical detail, the different stages of economic development, how the invisible hand actually worked, and the beneficial aspects of competition. Its perspective owed much to Newton and the Enlightenment's idealization of both nature and human nature. Smith thought of himself as the champion of liberty against state-sponsored economic privilege and monopolies. And he became the most influential of the new eighteenth-century economic thinkers. During the following century, his work and his followers became the target of reformers and critics who had less faith in the power of markets to generate wealth and prosperity for all.

EMPIRE AND ENLIGHTENMENT

The colonial world loomed large in Enlightenment thinking. Enlightenment thinkers saw the Americas as an uncorrupted territory where humanity's natural simplicity was expressed in the lives of native peoples. In comparison, Europe and Europeans appeared decadent or corrupt. European colonial activities—especially the slave trade—raised pressing issues about humanitarianism, individual rights, and natural law. The effects of colonialism on Europe were a central Enlightenment theme.

Smith wrote in *The Wealth of Nations* that the "discovery of America, and that of a passage to the East Indies by the cape of Good Hope are the two greatest and most important events recorded in the history of mankind. What benefits, or what misfortunes to mankind may hereafter result from those great events," he continued, "no human wisdom can foresee." Smith's language was nearly identical to that of a Frenchman, the abbé Guillaume Thomas François Raynal. Raynal's massive *Philosophical and Political History of European Settlements and Trade in the Two Indies* (1770), a coauthored work like the *Encyclopedia,* was one of the most widely read treatises of the Enlightenment, going through twenty printings and at least forty pirated editions. Raynal drew his inspiration from the *Encyclopedia* and aimed at nothing less than a total history of colonization: customs and civilizations of indigenous peoples, natural history, exploration, and commerce in the Atlantic world and India.

Raynal also asked whether colonization had made humanity happier, more peaceful, or better. The question was fully in the spirit of the Enlightenment, as was the answer: Raynal believed that industry and trade brought improvement and progress. Like other Enlightenment writers, however, he and his coauthors considered natural simplicity an antidote to the corruptions of their culture. They sought out and idealized what they considered examples of "natural" humanity, many of them in the New World. They reasoned that what Europeans considered savage life might be "a hundred times preferable to that of societies corrupted by despotism," and lamented the loss of humanity's "natural liberty." They condemned the tactics of the Spanish in Mexico and Peru, of the Portuguese in Brazil, and of the British in North America. They echoed Montesquieu's theme that good government required checks and balances against arbitrary authority. In the New World, they argued, Europeans found themselves with virtually unlimited power, which encouraged them to be arrogant, cruel, and despotic. In a later edition, after the outbreak of the American Revolution, the book went even further, drawing parallels between exploitation in the colonial world and inequality at home: "We are mad in the way we act with our colonies, and inhuman and mad in our conduct toward our peasants," asserted one author. Eighteenth-century radicals repeatedly warned that overextended empires sowed seeds of decadence and corruption at home.

Such critiques did little, however, to check the growing importance of colonial commerce in the eighteenth century. The wealth generated by colonial trade tied the interests of governments and transoceanic merchants in an increasingly tight embrace. Merchants engaged in the colonial trade depended on their governments to protect and defend their overseas investments; but governments in turn depended on merchants and their financial backers to build the ships and sustain the trade on which national power hinged. As this colonial trade grew in importance, no issue challenged Enlightenment thinkers as much as the institution of slavery, which was central to the Atlantic trade.

Slavery and the Atlantic World

The Atlantic slave trade (Chapter 14) reached its peak in the eighteenth century. European slave traders sent at least 1 million Africans into New World slavery in the late seventeenth century, and at least 6 million in the eighteenth century. During this period, control of the slave trade became fundamental to great power politics in Europe, as the British used their dominance of the trade to their advantage in their long-running competition with France.

Even thinkers as radical as Raynal and Diderot hesitated to criticize the slave trade, and their hesitations reveal the tensions in Enlightenment thought. Enlightenment thinking

Analyzing Primary Sources

Slavery and the Enlightenment

The encyclopedists made an exhaustive and deliberate effort to comment on every institution, trade, and custom in Western culture. The project was conceived of as an effort to catalog, analyze, and improve each facet of society. Writing in an age of burgeoning maritime trade and expanding overseas empires, they could not, and did not wish to, avoid the subject of slavery. These were their thoughts on plantation slavery, the African slaves who bore its brunt, and broader questions of law and liberty posed by the whole system.

 hus there is not a single one of these hapless souls—who, we maintain, are but slaves—who does not have the right to be declared free, since he has never lost his freedom; since it was impossible for him to lose it; and since neither his ruler nor his father nor anyone else had the right to dispose of his freedom; consequently, the sale of his person is null and void in and of itself: this Negro does not divest himself, indeed cannot under any condition divest himself of his natural rights; he carries them everywhere with him, and he has the right to demand that others allow him to enjoy those rights. Therefore, it is a clear case of inhumanity on the part of the judges in those free countries to which the slave is shipped, not to free the slave instantly by legal declaration, since he is their brother, having a soul like theirs.

Source: From *Encyclopédie*, vol. 16 (1765), as cited in David Brion Davis, *The Problem of Slavery in Western Culture* (Ithaca, NY: 1966), p. 416.

Questions for Analysis

1. What arguments against slavery does this *Encyclopedia* article present? What "natural rights" were violated by the practice of slavery, according to this view?

2. The enslavement of conquered peoples was an ancient and well-established custom, approved by civil and religious authorities. Even some Enlightenment figures, such as Thomas Jefferson, were slave owners. How did some Enlightenment philosophes use universal ideas of freedom to argue against custom in regard to slavery and other questions?

---

began with the premise that individuals could reason for and govern themselves. Individual moral freedom lay at the heart of what the Enlightenment considered to be a just, stable, and harmonious society, and slavery defied natural law and natural freedom. Montesquieu, for instance, wrote that civil law created chains, but natural law would always break them. Nearly all Enlightenment thinkers condemned slavery in the metaphorical sense. That the "mind should break free of its chains" and that "despotism enslaved the king's subjects" were phrases that echoed through much eighteenth-century writing. It was common for the central characters of eighteenth-century fiction, such as Voltaire's hero Candide, to meet enslaved people, learning compassion as part of their moral education. Writers dealt more gingerly, however, with the actual enslavement and slave labor of Africans.

Some Enlightenment thinkers skirted the issue of slavery, while others reconciled principle and practice in different ways. Smith condemned slavery as uneconomi-

cal. Voltaire, quick to expose his contemporaries' hypocrisy, wondered whether Europeans would look away if Europeans—rather than Africans—were enslaved. Voltaire, however, did not question his belief that Africans were inferior peoples. Montesquieu, who came from Bordeaux, one of the central ports for the Atlantic trade, believed that slavery debased master and slave alike. But he also argued that all societies balanced their systems of labor in accordance with their different needs, and slave labor was one such system; and, like many Enlightenment thinkers, he defended property rights, including those of slaveholders.

The *Encyclopedia*'s article on the slave trade did condemn the slave trade in the clearest possible terms as a violation of self-government. Humanitarian antislavery movements, which emerged in the 1760s, advanced similar arguments. However, from deploring slavery to imagining freedom for slaves proved a very long step, and one that few were willing to take. In the end, the Enlightenment's

Interpreting Visual Evidence

The Europeans Encounter the Peoples of the Pacific in the Eighteenth Century

When European explorers set out to map the Pacific, they brought with them artists to paint the landscapes and peoples they encountered. Later, other artists produced engravings of the original paintings, and these engravings were made available to a wider public. In this way, even people of modest means or only limited literacy could learn something about the different cultures and peoples that were now in more regular contact with European commerce elsewhere in the world.

These artists documented what they saw, but their vision was also shaped by the ideas that they brought with them and by the classical European styles of portraiture and landscape painting that they had been trained to produce. On the one hand, their images sometimes emphasized the exotic or essentially different quality of life in the Pacific. On the other hand, the use of conventional poses in the portraiture or in the depiction of human forms suggests hints of a developing understanding of the extent to which Europeans and people elsewhere in the world

A. A preliminary sketch for *Portrait of Omai* by Joshua Reynolds (c. 1773).

B. "Omiah [*sic*] the Indian from Otaheite, presented to their Majesties at Kew" (1774).

environmental determinism—the belief that environment shaped character—provided a common way of postponing the entire issue: slavery corrupted its victims, destroyed their natural virtue, and crushed their natural love of liberty; therefore, enslaved people were not ready for freedom. It was characteristic for Brissot de Warville's Society of the Friends of Blacks to call for abolition of the slave trade and to invite Thomas Jefferson, a slaveholder, to join the organization. Only a very few advocated abolishing slavery, and even they insisted that emancipation be gradual. The debate about slavery demonstrated that different currents in Enlightenment thought could lead to very different conclusions.

Exploration and the Pacific World

The Pacific world figured prominently in Enlightenment thinking. Systematically mapping new sections of the Pacific was among the crucial developments of the age, and it had tremendous impact on the public imagination. These explorations were also scientific missions, sponsored as part of the Enlightenment project of expanding scientific knowledge. In 1767, the French government sent Louis-Antoine de Bougainville (1729–1811) to the South Pacific in search of a new route to China, new lands suitable for colonization, and new spices for the ever lucrative trade. Bougainville shared essential human characteristics. This ambiguity was typical of Enlightenment political and social thought, which sought to uncover universal human truths, while at the same time remaining deeply interested and invested in exploring the differences they observed in peoples from various parts of the globe.

The first two images depict a Tahitian named Omai, who came to Britain as a crew member on a naval vessel in July 1774. Taken three days later to meet King George III and Queen Charlotte at Kew (image B), he became a celebrity in England and had his portrait drawn by Joshua Reynolds, a famous painter of the period (image A). The third image is an engraving by two Florentine artists after a drawing by Sydney Parkinson, who was with James Cook on his first voyage to the Pacific in 1768 (image C). The two artists had never visited the South Pacific, and their image is noteworthy for the way that the bodies of the islanders are rendered according to the classical styles of European art.

C. *View of the Inside of a House in the Island of Ulietea, with the Representation of a Dance to the Music of the Country*, engraving after Sydney Parkinson (1773).

Questions for Analysis

1. Does the Reynolds portrait, in its choice of posture and expression, imply that Europeans and the peoples of the Pacific might share essential traits? What uses might Enlightenment thinkers have made of such a universalist implication?

2. How might a contemporary person in Britain have reacted to the portrait of Omai kneeling before the king?

3. Do you think image C is an accurate representation of life in the South Pacific? What purpose did such imaginary and idyllic scenes serve for their audience in Europe?

found none of what he sought, but his travel accounts—above all, his fabulously lush descriptions of the earthly paradise of Nouvelle-Cythère (or Tahiti)—captured the imaginations of many at home. The British captain James Cook (1728–1779), who followed Bougainville, made two trips into the South Pacific (1768–1771 and 1772–1775), with impressive results. He charted the coasts of New Zealand and New Holland and added the New Hebrides and Hawaii to European maps. He explored the outer limits of the Antarctic continent, the shores of the Bering Sea, and the Arctic Ocean.

The artists and scientists who accompanied Cook and Bougainville vastly expanded the boundaries of European botany, zoology, and geology; and their drawings—such as Sydney Parkinson's extraordinary portraits of the Maori and William Hodge's portraits of Tahitians—appealed to a wide public. So did the accounts of dangers overcome and peoples encountered. Large numbers of people in Europe avidly read travel accounts of these voyages, and when Cook and Bougainville brought Pacific islanders to the metropolis, they attracted large crowds. (In late January 1779, a misguided attempt to communicate with South Pacific

MAORIS IN A WAR CANOE NEAR LOOKOUT POINT. This copy of an illustration by Sydney Parkinson, who accompanied James Cook on his explorations, is typical of the images of the South Pacific that may have circulated in Europe in the late eighteenth century. ■ *What questions might have been prompted among Enlightenment thinkers by an increased awareness of different cultures throughout the world?*

Enlightenment thinkers found it impossible to see other peoples as anything other than primitive versions of Europeans. Even these views, however, marked a change from former times. In earlier periods, Europeans had understood the world as divided between Christendom and heathen others. Now, all peoples were seen to be part of a shared humanity, with cultures and beliefs that reflected their own experiences. In sum, during the eighteenth century, a religious understanding of Western identity was giving way to more secular and historical explanations for human diversity.

One of the most important scientific explorers of the period was the German scientist Alexander von Humboldt (1769–1859). Humboldt spent five years in Spanish America, aiming to do nothing less than assess the civilization and natural resources of the continent. He went equipped with the most advanced scientific instruments Europe could provide. Humboldt, in good Enlightenment fashion, attempted to demonstrate that climate and physical environment determined which forms of life would survive in any given region. These investigations inspired nineteenth-century discussions of evolutionary change. Charles Darwin referred to Humboldt as the "greatest scientific traveler who ever lived," and the German scientist's writing inspired his voyage to the Galápagos Islands off the coast of Ecuador.

Thus, Europeans who looked outward did so for a variety of reasons and reached very different conclusions. For some Enlightenment thinkers and rulers, scientific reports from overseas fitted into a broad inquiry about civilization and human nature. That inquiry at times encouraged self-criticism but at other times simply shored up Europeans' sense of their superiority. These themes reemerged during the nineteenth century, when new empires were built and the West's place in the world was reassessed.

islanders, perhaps with the intention of conveying them to Europe, ended in the grisly deaths of Cook and four royal marines in Hawaii.)

The Impact of the Scientific Missions

Back in Europe, Enlightenment thinkers drew freely on reports of scientific missions. Since they were already committed to understanding human nature and the origins of society and to studying the effects of the environment on character and culture, stories of new peoples and cultures were immediately fascinating. In 1772, Diderot, one of many eager readers of Bougainville's accounts, published his own reflections on the cultural significance of those accounts in *Supplément au Voyage de Bougainville*. For Diderot, the Tahitians were the original human beings and, unlike the inhabitants of the New World, were virtually free of European influence. He believed they represented humanity in its natural state, uninhibited about sexuality and free of religious dogma. Their supposed simplicity exposed the hypocrisy and rigidity of overcivilized Europeans. Others considered the indigenous peoples of the Pacific akin to the classical civilizations of Greeks and Romans, associating Tahitian women, for instance, with Venus, the Roman goddess of love.

All these views said more about Europe and European utopias than the indigenous cultures in the Pacific.

THE RADICAL ENLIGHTENMENT

How revolutionary was the Enlightenment? Enlightenment thought did undermine central tenets of eighteenth-century culture and politics. It had wide resonance, well beyond a small group of intellectuals. Yet Enlightenment thinkers did not hold to any single political position. Even the most radical among them disagreed on the implications of their thought. Jean-Jacques Rousseau and Mary Wollstonecraft provide good examples of such radical thinkers.

The World of Rousseau

Jean-Jacques Rousseau (*roo-SOH;* 1712–1778) was an "outsider" who quarreled with the other philosophes. He shared the philosophes' search for intellectual and political freedom and attacked inherited privilege, yet he introduced other strains into Enlightenment thought, especially what was then called "sensibility," or the cult of feeling. Rousseau's interest in emotions led him to develop a more complicated portrait of human psychology than that of Enlightenment writers, who emphasized reason as the most important attribute of human beings. He was also considerably more radical than his counterparts, being one of the first to talk about popular sovereignty and democracy.

Rousseau's milestone and difficult treatise on politics, *The Social Contract,* began with a now famous paradox: "Man was born free, and everywhere he is in chains." How had humans freely forged these chains? What were the origins of government? Was government's authority legitimate? If not, Rousseau asked, how could it become so?

Rousseau argued that in the state of nature all men had been equal. (On women, men, and nature, see *Competing Viewpoints* on page 570.) Social inequality, anchored in private property, profoundly corrupted the "social contract," or the formation of government. Under conditions of inequality, governments and laws represented only the rich and privileged. They became instruments of repression and enslavement. He stated that legitimate governments could be formed, but "[t]he problem is to find a form of association . . . in which each, while uniting himself with all, may still obey himself alone, and remain as free as before." Freedom did not mean the absence of restraint. It meant that equal citizens obeyed laws they had made themselves. Rousseau hardly imagined any social leveling, and by *equality* he meant only that no one would be "rich enough to buy another, nor poor enough to have to sell oneself."

Rousseau's argument on legitimate authority has three parts. First, sovereignty belonged to the people alone. This meant sovereignty should not be divided among different branches of government (as suggested by Montesquieu), nor could it be usurped by a king. Second, exercising sovereignty transformed the nation. Rousseau argued that when individual citizens formed a "body politic," that body became more than just the sum of its parts. He offered what was to many an appealing image of a regenerated and more powerful nation, in which citizens were bound by mutual obligation rather than coercive laws and united in equality rather than divided and weakened by privilege. Third, the national community would be united by what Rousseau called the "general will." This term is notoriously difficult.

ROUSSEAU ON EDUCATION. Jean-Jacques Rousseau believed that the accumulated wisdom of human civilization was full of error. "Everything is good as it leaves the hands of the Author of things," he wrote, and "everything degenerates in the hands of man." Education, therefore, should be less about book learning and more about the individual's interaction with the God-given world. Learning should take place outside, where the individual's natural abilities and virtues could blossom, free from the contamination of mistaken ideas. His ideal applied only to male students, however. He believed that women should only receive enough education to become capable mothers of their children. This image is from an early edition of Rousseau's treatise on education, *Émile* (1762) (see *Competing Viewpoints* on pages 570–571).

Rousseau's Social Contract (1762)

Jean-Jacques Rousseau (1712–1778) was one of the most radical Enlightenment thinkers. In his works, he suggested that humans needed not only a clearer understanding of natural laws but also a much closer relationship with nature itself and a thorough reorganization of society. He believed that a sovereign society, formed by free association of equal citizens without patrons or factions, was the clearest expression of natural law. This society would make laws and order itself by the genuine collective wisdom of its citizens. Rousseau sets out the definition of his sovereign society and its authority in the passages reprinted here.

Book I, Chapter 6

"To find a form of association that defends and protects the person and possessions of each associate with all the common strength, and by means of which each person, joining forces with all, nevertheless obeys only himself, and remains as free as before." Such is the fundamental problem to which the social contract furnishes the solution.

Book II, Chapter 4

What in fact is an act of sovereignty? It is not an agreement between a superior and an inferior, but an agreement between the body and each of its members, a legitimate agreement, because it is based upon the social contract; equitable, because it is common to all; useful, because it can have no other purpose than the general good; and reliable, because it is guaranteed by the public force and the supreme power. As long as the subjects are only bound by agreements of this sort, they obey no one but their own will, and to ask how far the respective rights of the sovereign and citizens extend is to ask to what point the latter can commit themselves to each other, one towards all and all towards one.

Source: Jean-Jacques Rousseau, *Rousseau's Political Writings*, trans. Julia Conaway Bondanella, ed. Allan Ritter and Julia Conaway Bondanella (New York: 1988), pp. 92–103.

Questions for Analysis

1. What was the goal of political association, according to Rousseau?

2. How did Rousseau claim to overcome the tension between the need for some form of social constraint and the desire to preserve liberty?

3. Which was more important for Rousseau: equality or liberty?

Rousseau proposed it as a way to understand the common interest, which rose above particular individual demands. The general will favored equality, which made it general, and in principle, at least, equality guaranteed that citizens' common interests would be represented in the whole.

Rousseau's lack of concern for balancing private interests against the general will leads some political theorists to consider him authoritarian, coercive, or moralistic. Others interpret the general will as one expression of his utopianism. During the eighteenth century, *The Social Contract* was the least understood of Rousseau's works. Yet it provided influential radical arguments and, more important, extraordinarily powerful images and phrases, which were widely cited during the French Revolution.

Rousseau was also well known for his writing on education and moral virtue. His widely read novel *Émile* (1762) tells the story of a young man who learns virtue and moral autonomy in the school of nature rather than in the academy.

Rousseau disagreed with other philosophes' emphasis on reason, insisting instead that "the first impulses of nature are always right," and children should not be forced to reason early in life. Books, which "teach us only to talk about things we do not know," should not be central to learning until adolescence. Émile's tutor thus walked him through the woods, where Émile studied nature and its simple precepts, cultivated his conscience, and, above all, his sense of independence. "Nourished in the most absolute liberty, the greatest evil he can imagine is servitude."

Such an education aimed to give men moral autonomy and make them good citizens. Rousseau argued that women should have very different educations: "All education of women must be relative to men, pleasing them, being useful to them, raising them when they are young and caring for them when they are old, advising them, consoling them, making their lives pleasant and agreeable, these have been the duties of women since time began." Women were to be useful socially as mothers and wives. In *Émile,* Rousseau laid out just such an education for Émile's wife-to-be, Sophie. At times, Rousseau seemed convinced that women "naturally" sought out such a role: "Dependence is a natural state for women, girls feel themselves made to obey."

Rousseau's assumptions about women's "natural state" were controversial. Already, before *Émile* was published, female authors such as Émilie du Châtelet had begun to call for the education of women (see **Analyzing Primary Sources** on page 573). Nevertheless, Rousseau's conflicting views on female nature provide a good example of the shifting meaning of nature, a concept central to Enlightenment thought. Enlightenment thinkers used nature as a yardstick against which to measure society's shortcomings. "Natural" was better, simpler, uncorrupted. What, though, was nature? It could refer to the physical world or it could refer to allegedly primitive societies. Often, it was a useful invention.

Rousseau's novels sold exceptionally well, especially among women. *Julie* (subtitled *La nouvelle Héloïse*), published just after *Émile,* went through seventy editions in three decades. *Julie* tells the story of a young woman who falls in love with one man but dutifully obeys her father's order to marry another. At the end, she dies of exposure after rescuing her children from a cold lake—a perfect example of domestic and maternal virtue. The tragic love story and Rousseau's conviction that the heart was as important as the mind and that passion was more important than reason appealed to his audience. Rousseau's novels became part of a larger cult of *sensibilité* ("feeling") in middle-class and aristocratic circles, which emphasized spontaneous expressions of feeling and a belief that sentiment was an expression of authentic humanity. This thematic aspect of Rousseau's work contradicted much of the Enlightenment's cult of reason, and is more closely related to the concerns of nineteenth-century Romanticism.

The World of Wollstonecraft

Rousseau's sharpest critic was the British writer Mary Wollstonecraft (1759–1797). Wollstonecraft published her best-known work, *A Vindication of the Rights of Woman,* in 1792, during the French Revolution. Her argument, however, was anchored in Enlightenment debates and needs to be understood here. Wollstonecraft shared Rousseau's political views

IMAGES OF WOMEN READING. Female literacy increased in the eighteenth century, as middle-class women became consumers of printed matter and were more likely to be educated. Images of women reading could be both powerful and unsettling, because the idea of women as independent thinkers capable of coming to their own conclusions about the world challenged entrenched notions of female dependency. The image on the left, from 1790, depicts the political radical Mary Wollstonecraft with a book in her hand. She believed that Enlightenment critiques of monarchy could also be used to challenge the power of fathers within the family. The image on the right, a 1769 painting of a young girl reading by Jean-Honoré Fragonard, creates an idealized vision of a sight that became more and more common in middle-class households in eighteenth-century Europe.

Rousseau and His Readers

> Jean-Jacques Rousseau's writings provoked very different responses from eighteenth-century readers—women as well as men. Many women readers loved his fiction and found his views on women's character and prescriptions for their education inspiring. But other women disagreed vehemently with his conclusions. In the first excerpt here, from Rousseau's novel Émile (1762), the author sets out his views on a woman's education. He argues that her education should fit with what he considers her intellectual capacity and social role. It should also complement the education and role of a man. The second selection is an admiring response to Émile by Anne-Louise-Germaine Necker, or Madame de Staël (1766–1817), a well-known French writer and literary critic. Although she acknowledged that Rousseau sought to keep women from participating in political discussion, she also thought that he had granted women a new role in matters of emotion and domesticity. The third excerpt is by Mary Wollstonecraft, who shared many of Rousseau's philosophical principles but sharply disagreed with his assertion that women and men should have different virtues and values. She believed that women such as Madame de Staël were misguided in embracing Rousseau's ideas.

Rousseau's Émile

Researches into abstract and speculative truths, the principles and axioms of sciences—in short, everything which tends to generalize our ideas—is not the proper province of women; their studies should be relative to points of practice; it belongs to them to apply those principles which men have discovered. . . . All the ideas of women, which have not the immediate tendency to points of duty, should be directed to the study of men, and to the attainment of those agreeable accomplishments which have taste for their object; for as to works of genius, they are beyond their capacity; neither have they sufficient precision or power of atten-

tion to succeed in sciences which require accuracy; and as to physical knowledge, it belongs to those only who are most active, most inquisitive, who comprehend the greatest variety of objects. . . .

She must have the skill to incline us to do everything which her sex will not enable her to do herself, and which is necessary or agreeable to her; therefore she ought to study the mind of man thoroughly, not the mind of man in general, abstractedly, but the dispositions of those men to whom she is subject either by the laws of her country or by the force of opinion. She should learn to penetrate into the real sentiments from their conversation, their actions, their looks

and gestures. She should also have the art, by her own conversation, actions, looks, and gestures, to communicate those sentiments which are agreeable to them without seeming to intend it. Men will argue more philosophically about the human heart; but women will read the heart of men better than they. . . . Women have most wit, men have most genius; women observe, men reason. From the concurrence of both we derive the clearest light and the most perfect knowledge which the human mind is of itself capable of attaining.

Source: Jean-Jacques Rousseau, Émile (1762), as cited in Mary Wollstonecraft, A Vindication of the Rights of Woman (New York: 1992), pp. 124–25.

and admired his writing and influence. Like Rousseau and her countryman Thomas Paine, a writer who supported the American and French revolutions, Wollstonecraft was a republican. She called monarchy "the pestiferous purple which renders the progress of civilization a curse, and warps the understanding." She spoke even more forcefully than Rousseau against inequality and the artificial distinctions of rank, birth, and wealth. Believing that equality laid the basis for virtue, she contended, in classic Enlightenment language,

that the society should seek "the perfection of our nature and capability of happiness." She argued more forcefully than any other Enlightenment thinker that (1) women had the same innate capacity for reason and self-government as men; (2) *virtue* should mean the same thing for men and women; and (3) relations between the sexes should be based on equality.

Wollstonecraft did what few of her contemporaries even imagined. She applied the radical Enlightenment critique of monarchy and inequality to the family. The

Madame de Staël

Though Rousseau has endeavoured to prevent women from interfering in public affairs, and acting a brilliant part in the theatre of politics; yet in speaking of them, how much has he done it to their satisfaction! If he wished to deprive them of some rights foreign to their sex, how has he for ever restored to them all those to which it has a claim! And in attempting to diminish their influence over the deliberations of men, how sacredly has he established the empire they have over their happiness! In aiding them to descend from an usurped throne, he has firmly seated them upon that to which they were destined by nature; and though he be full of indignation against them when they endeavour to resemble men, yet when they come before him with all the *charms*, *weaknesses*, *virtues*, and *errors* of their sex, his respect for their *persons* amounts almost to adoration.

Source: Cited in Mary Wollstonecraft, *A Vindication of the Rights of Woman*, ed. Miriam Brody (New York: 1992), pp. 203–4.

Mary Wollstonecraft

Rousseau declares that a woman should never, for a moment, feel herself independent, that she should be governed by fear to exercise her *natural* cunning, and made a coquettish slave in order to render her a more alluring object of desire, a *sweeter* companion to man, whenever he chooses to relax himself. He carries the arguments, which he pretends to draw from the indications of nature, still further, and insinuates that truth and fortitude, the corner stones of all human virtue, should be cultivated with certain restrictions, because, with respect to the female character, obedience is the grand lesson which ought to be impressed with unrelenting rigour.

What nonsense! When will a great man arise with sufficient strength of mind to puff away the fumes which pride and sensuality have thus spread over the subject! If women are by nature inferior to men, their virtues must be the same in quality, if not in degree, or virtue is a relative idea; consequently, their conduct should be founded on the same principles, and have the same aim.

Source: Cited in Susan Bell and Karen Offen, eds., *Women, the Family, and Freedom: The Debate in Documents*, vol. 1, *1750–1880* (Stanford, CA: 1983), p. 58.

Questions for Analysis

1. Why did Rousseau seek to limit the sphere of activities open to women in society? What capacities did he feel they lacked? What areas of social life did he feel women were most suited for?

2. Did Madame de Staël agree with Rousseau that women's social roles were essentially different from those of men? What power do women exercise over men in society according to Staël?

3. What was the basis for Mary Wollstonecraft's disagreement with Rousseau?

4. Why did gender matter to Enlightenment figures such as Rousseau, Staël, and Wollstonecraft?

---

legal inequalities of marriage law, which among other things deprived married women of property rights, gave husbands "despotic" power over their wives. Just as kings cultivated their subjects' deference, so culture, she argued, cultivated women's weakness. "Civilized women are . . . so weakened by false refinement, that, respecting morals, their condition is much below what it would be were they left in a state nearer to nature." Middle-class girls learned manners, grace, and seductiveness to win a husband, and trained to be dependent creatures. "My own sex, I hope, will excuse me, if I treat them like rational creatures instead of flattering their *fascinating* graces, and viewing them as if they were in a state of perpetual childhood, unable to stand alone. I earnestly wish to point out in what true dignity and human happiness consists—I wish to persuade women to endeavor to acquire strength, both of mind and body." A culture that encouraged feminine weakness produced women who were childish, cunning, cruel—and vulnerable. To Rousseau's specific prescriptions for female education, which included teaching women timidity, chasteness, and modesty, Wollstonecraft replied that Rousseau wanted women to use their reason to "burnish their chains rather than to snap them." Instead, education for women had to promote liberty and self-reliance. She was considered scandalously radical for merely hinting that women might have political rights.

The Enlightenment as a whole left a mixed legacy on gender, one that closely paralleled that on slavery. Enlightenment writers developed and popularized arguments about natural rights, but they also elevated natural differences to a higher plane by suggesting that nature should dictate different, and quite possibly unequal, social roles. Mary Wollstonecraft and Jean-Jacques Rousseau shared a radical opposition to despotism and slavery, a moralist's vision of a corrupt society, and a concern with virtue and community. Their divergence on gender is characteristic of Enlightenment disagreements about nature and its imperatives, and is a good example of different directions in which the logic of Enlightenment thinking could lead.

THE ENLIGHTENMENT AND EIGHTEENTH-CENTURY CULTURE

The Book Trade

What about the social structures that produced these debates and received these ideas? To begin with, the Enlightenment was bound up in a much larger expansion of printing and print culture. From the early eighteenth century on, book publishing and selling flourished, especially in Britain, France, the Netherlands, and Switzerland. National borders mattered very little, and much of the book trade was both international and clandestine. Readers bought books from stores, through subscription, and by special mail order from book distributors abroad. Cheaper printing and better distribution also helped multiply the numbers of journals, some specializing in literary or scientific topics and others quite general. They helped bring daily newspapers, which first appeared in London in 1702, to Moscow, Rome, and cities and towns throughout Europe. By 1780, Britons could read 150 different magazines, and 37 English towns had local newspapers. These changes have been called a "revolution in communication," and they form a crucial part of the larger picture of the Enlightenment.

Governments did little to check this revolutionary transformation. In Britain, the press encountered few restrictions, although the government did use a stamp tax on printed goods to raise the price of newspapers and books and to discourage buyers. Elsewhere, laws required publishers to apply in advance for the license or privilege (in the sense of "private right") to print and sell any given work. In practice, though, publishers frequently printed books without advance permission, hoping that the regime would not notice. Russian, Prussian, and Austrian censors tolerated much less dissent, but those governments also sought to stimulate publishing and, to a certain degree, permitted public discussion. In the smaller states of Germany and Italy, governed by many local princes, it was easier to find progressive local patrons, and English and French works circulated widely through those regions. That governments were patrons as well as censors of new scholarship illustrates the complex relationship between the age of absolutism and the Enlightenment.

As one historian puts it, censorship only made banned books expensive, keeping them out of the hands of the poor. Clandestine booksellers, most near the French border in Switzerland and the Rhineland, smuggled thousands of books across the border to bookstores, distributors, and private customers. What did readers want, and what does this tell us about the reception of the Enlightenment? Many clandestine dealers specialized in what they called "philosophical books," which meant subversive literature of all kinds: stories of languishing in prison, gossipy memoirs of life at the court, pornographic fantasies (often about religious and political figures), and tales of crime and criminals. Much of this flourishing eighteenth-century "literary underground" echoed the radical Enlightenment's themes, especially the corruption of the aristocracy and the monarchy's degeneration into despotism.

High Culture, New Elites, and the Public Sphere

The Enlightenment was not simply embodied in books; it was produced in networks of readers and new forms of sociability and discussion. These networks included people of diverse backgrounds. Eighteenth-century elite, or "high," culture was small in scale but cosmopolitan and very literate, and it took literary and scientific discussion seriously. Middle-class men and women also became consumers of literature. Meanwhile, popular discussions of Enlightenment themes developed in the coffeehouses and taverns of European cities, where printed material might be read aloud, allowing even illiterate people to have access to the news and debates of the day. Together, this permissive atmosphere of frequent discussion among people of

Analyzing Primary Sources

Émilie du Châtelet on the Education of Women

Gabrielle Émilie le Tonnelier de Breteuil, marquise du Châtelet (1706–1749) was born into a prominent aristocratic family at the royal court of France. Unlike most women of her station, however, after her marriage and the birth of her children, she devoted much of her life to the study of the sciences, with a particular focus on physics and mathematics. She is an author of many books and pamphlets, and is celebrated as the translator of Isaac Newton's Principia Mathematica *into French. In this passage, from the preface to her translation of Bernard Mandeville's* Fable of the Bees, *du Châtelet reflects on the obstacles that women such as herself face in receiving an education. The draft of the preface was written between 1735 and 1739, but it was not published during her lifetime.*

feel the full weight of prejudice that excludes us [women] so universally from the sciences, this being one of the contradictions of this world, which has always astonished me, as there are great countries whose laws allow us to decide their destiny, but none where we are brought up to think.

Another observation that one can make about this prejudice is that acting is the only occupation requiring some study and a trained mind to which women are admitted, and it is at the same time the only one that regards its professionals as infamous.

Let us reflect briefly on why for so many centuries, not one good tragedy, one good poem, one esteemed history, one beautiful painting, one good book of physics, has come from the hands of women. Why do these creatures whose understanding appears in all things equal to that of men, seem, for all that, to be stopped by an invincible force on this side of a barrier; let someone give me an explanation, if there is one. I leave it to naturalists to find a physical explanation, but until that happens, women will be entitled to protest against their education. As for me, I confess that if I were king I would wish to make this scientific experiment. I would reform an abuse that cuts out, so to speak, half of humanity. I would allow women to share the rights of humanity, and most of all to those of the mind.

Source: Émilie du Châtelet, *Selected Philosophical and Scientific Writings,* ed. Judith P. Zinsser, trans. Isabelle Bour and Judith P. Zinsser (Chicago: University of Chicago Press, 2009), pp. 48–49.

Questions for Analysis

1. What comparison is du Châtelet making between women who are allowed by law to "decide the destiny" of countries and the fact that women as a group are not educated?

2. What point does du Châtelet wish to make by alluding to the notorious reputation of professionals in the theater, and actresses especially?

3. In what way does du Châtelet show her confidence in the scientific method as she calls for an "experiment" that would give women the same rights to education as those enjoyed by men?

---

different social positions led to the development of a new idea: "public opinion."

Among the institutions that produced the new elite were learned societies: the American Philosophical Society of Philadelphia, British literary and philosophical societies, and the Select Society of Edinburgh. Such groups organized intellectual life outside the universities. They provided libraries, meeting places for discussion, and journals that published members' papers, or organized debates on issues from literature and history to economics and ethics. Elites also met in "academies," financed by governments to advance knowledge, researching into the natural sciences (the Royal Society of London and the French Academy of Science, both founded in the 1660s, and the Royal Prussian Academy of Sciences, founded in 1701), promoting the national language (the Académie Française, or French Academy of Literature), or safeguarding traditions in the arts (the various academies of painting). In smaller cities in the countryside, provincial academies played much the same role, providing a way for Enlightenment discussions to spread beyond European capitals.

Salons provided an alternative venue for discussion but operated informally. They were organized usually by well-connected and learned aristocratic women who invited local personalities to their homes to meet with authors and discuss their latest works. The prominent role of women

A READING IN THE SALON OF MADAME GEOFFRIN, 1755. Enlightenment salons encouraged a spirit of intellectual inquiry and civil debate, at least among educated elites. Such salon discussions were notable for the extent to which women helped organize and participated in the conversations. This fact led Rousseau to attack the salons for encouraging unseemly posturing and promiscuity between the sexes, which he believed were the antithesis of rational pursuits. In this painting, Madame Geoffrin, a famed hostess (at left in gray), presides over a discussion of a learned work. Note in the background the bust of Voltaire, the patron saint of rationalist discourse. ▪ *What developments were required for this notion of free public discussion among elites to become more general in society?* ▪ *Would Enlightenment thinkers favor such developments? (Compare this image with the ones on pages 561 and 575.)*

distinguished the salons from the academies and universities. Salons brought together men and women of letters with members of the aristocracy for conversation, debate, drink, and food. Rousseau loathed this kind of ritual and viewed salons as a sign of superficiality and vacuity in a privileged and overcivilized world. Thomas Jefferson thought the influence of women in salons had put France in a "desperate state." Some of the salons reveled in parlor games. Others, such as the one organized in Paris by Madame Necker, the wife of the future French reform minister, lay quite close to the halls of power and was a testing ground for new policy ideas. Madame Marie-Thérèse Geoffrin, another celebrated French *salonnière,* became an important patron of the *Encyclopedia* and exercised influence in placing scholars in academies. Moses Mendelssohn held an open house for intellectuals in Berlin. Salons in London, Vienna, Rome, and Berlin worked the same way, and like academies, they promoted among their participants a sense of belonging to an active, learned elite.

Scores of similar societies emerged in the eighteenth century, eventually breaking the hold of elites over public debate and literate discussion. Masonic lodges, organizations with elaborate secret rituals whose members pledged themselves to the regeneration of society, attracted a remarkable array of aristocrats and middle-class men. The composer Wolfgang Amadeus Mozart, Emperor Frederick II, and Montesquieu were Masons. Behind their closed doors, the lodges were egalitarian. They pledged themselves to a common project of rational thought and benevolent action and to banishing religion and social distinction—at least from their ranks. Other networks of sociability were even less exclusive. Coffeehouses multiplied with the colonial trade in sugar, coffee, and tea, and they occupied a central spot in the circulation of ideas. A group of merchants gathering to discuss trade, for instance, could turn to politics; and the many newspapers lying about the cafe tables provided a ready-to-hand link between their smaller discussions and news and debates elsewhere.

Eighteenth-century cultural changes—expanding networks of sociability, flourishing book trade, new genres of literature, and circulation of Enlightenment ideas—widened the circles of reading and discussion, expanding what some historians and political theorists call the "**public sphere**." That, in turn, began to change politics. Informal deliberations, debates about how to regenerate the nation, discussions of civic virtue, and efforts to forge a consensus played a crucial role in moving politics beyond the confines of the court.

A French observer described the changes this way: "In the last thirty years alone, a great and important revolution has occurred in our ideas. Today, public opinion has a preponderant force in Europe that cannot be resisted." Few thought the "public" involved more than the elite. Yet, by the late eighteenth century, European governments recognized the existence of a civic-minded group that stretched from salons to coffeehouses, academies, and circles of government, to which they needed in some measure to respond.

Middle-Class Culture and Reading

Enlightenment fare constituted only part of the new cultural interests of the eighteenth-century middle classes. Lower on the social scale, shopkeepers, small merchants, lawyers, and professionals read more and more different kinds of books. Instead of owning one well-thumbed Bible to read aloud, a middle-class family would buy and borrow books to read casually, pass on, and discuss. This literature consisted of science, history, biography, travel literature, and fiction. A great deal of it was aimed at middle-class women, among the fastest-growing groups of readers in the eighteenth century. Etiquette books sold very well; so did how-to manuals for the household. Scores of books about the manners, morals, and education of daughters, and popular versions of Enlightenment treatises on education and the mind, illustrate close parallels between the intellectual life of the high Enlightenment and the everyday middle-class reading matter.

The rise of a middle-class reading public, much of it female, helps account for the soaring popularity and production of novels, especially in Britain. Novels were the single most popular new form of literature in the eighteenth century. A survey of library borrowing in late-eighteenth-century Britain, Germany, and North America showed that 70 percent of books taken out were

novels. For centuries, Europeans had read romances such as tales of the knights of the Round Table, but the setting of popular novels was closer to home. The novel's more recognizable, nonaristocratic characters seemed more relevant to common middle-class experience. Moreover, examining emotion and inner feeling also linked novel writing with a larger eighteenth-century concern with personhood and humanity. As we have seen, classic Enlightenment writers such as Voltaire, Goethe, and Rousseau wrote very successful novels; and those should be understood alongside *Pamela* or *Clarissa* by Samuel Richardson (1689–1761), *Moll Flanders* or *Robinson Crusoe* by Daniel Defoe (1660–1731), and *Tom Jones* by Henry Fielding (1707–1754).

Many historians have noted that women figured prominently among fiction writers. The works of Jane Austen (1775–1817), to many readers, especially *Pride and Prejudice* and *Emma,* are the height of the novelist's craft. Women, however, were not the only ones to write novels, nor were they alone in paying close attention to the domestic or private sphere. Their work took up central eighteenth-century themes of human nature, morality, virtue, and reputation. Their novels, like much of the nonfiction of the period, explored those themes in domestic as well as in public settings.

A COFFEEHOUSE IN LONDON, 1798. Coffeehouses were centers of social networks and hubs of opinion, contributing to a public consciousness that was new to society and brought about by the Enlightenment. This coffeehouse scene illustrates a mixing of classes, lively debate, and burgeoning culture of reading. Compare this image with that of the aristocratic salon (page 574) and the meeting of Lessing and Mendelssohn (page 561). ▪ *How were coffeehouses different from aristocratic salons or the middle-class drawing room discussion between two German thinkers?* ▪ *Can they all be seen as expressions of a new kind of "public sphere" in eighteenth-century Europe?*

Past and Present

The Internet and the Enlightenment Public Sphere

In many ways, today's Internet is simply a technologically sophisticated version of the public sphere of literate readers that was created and celebrated by the philosophes of the Enlightenment. It contains the same confusing mix of the educational, the commercial, the pleasurable . . . and the perverse.

 Watch related author interview on the Student Site

Popular Culture: Urban and Rural

How much did books and print culture touch the lives of the common people? Literacy rates varied dramatically by gender, social class, and region, but were generally higher in northern than in southern and eastern Europe. It is not surprising that literacy ran highest in cities and towns—higher, in fact, than we might expect. In early eighteenth-century Paris, 85 percent of men and 60 percent of women could read. Well over half the residents of poorer Parisian neighborhoods, especially small shopkeepers, domestic servants and valets, and artisans, could read and sign their names. Even the illiterate lived in a culture of print, though they had few books on their own shelves. They saw one-page newspapers and broadsides or fly sheets posted on streets and tavern walls and regularly heard them read aloud. Moreover, visual material—inexpensive wood-cuts especially, but also prints, drawings, and satirical cartoons—figured as prominently as text in much popular

reading material. By many measures, the circles of reading and discussion were even larger than literacy rates might suggest, especially in cities.

Neither England nor France required any primary schooling, leaving education to haphazard local initiatives. In central Europe, some regimes made efforts to develop state-sponsored education. Catherine of Russia summoned an Austrian consultant to set up a system of primary schools, but by the end of the eighteenth century, only 22,000 out of a population of 40 million had attended any kind of school. In the absence of primary schooling, most Europeans were self-taught. The varied texts in the peddler's cart—whether religious, political propaganda, or entertainment—attest to a widespread and rapidly growing popular interest in books and reading.

Like its middle-class counterpart, popular culture rested on networks of sociability. Guild organizations offered discussion and companionship. Street theater and singers mocking local political figures offered culture to people of different social classes. Although deciphering popular culture is difficult, being that most testimony comes to us from outsiders who regarded the common people as hopelessly superstitious and ignorant, historical research has begun to reveal new insights. It has shown, first, that popular culture did not exist in isolation. Particularly in the countryside, market days and village festivals brought social classes together, and popular entertainments reached a wide social audience. Folktales and traditional songs resist pigeonholing as elite, middle-class, or popular culture, because they passed from one cultural world to another, being revised and reinterpreted in the process. Second, oral and literate culture overlapped. In other words, even people who could not read often had a great deal of "book knowledge," arguing seriously about points from books, and they believed that books conferred authority. A group of villagers, for instance, wrote this eulogy for a deceased friend: "He read his life long, and died without ever knowing how to read." The logic and worldview of popular culture need to be understood on their own terms.

It remains true that the countryside, especially in less economically developed regions, was desperately poor. Life there was far more isolated than in towns. A yawning chasm separated peasants from the world of the high Enlightenment. The philosophes, well established in the summits of European society, looked at popular culture with distrust and ignorance. They saw the common people of Europe much as they did indigenous peoples of other continents. They were humanitarians, critical thinkers, and reformers, but they were not democrats. The Enlightenment, though well entrenched in eighteenth-century elite culture, nonetheless involved changes that reached well beyond elite society.

WAR AND POLITICS IN ENLIGHTENMENT EUROPE

War and Empire in the Eighteenth-Century World

After 1713, western Europe remained largely at peace for a generation. In 1740, however, that peace was shattered when Frederick the Great of Prussia seized the Austrian province of Silesia. In the resulting War of the Austrian

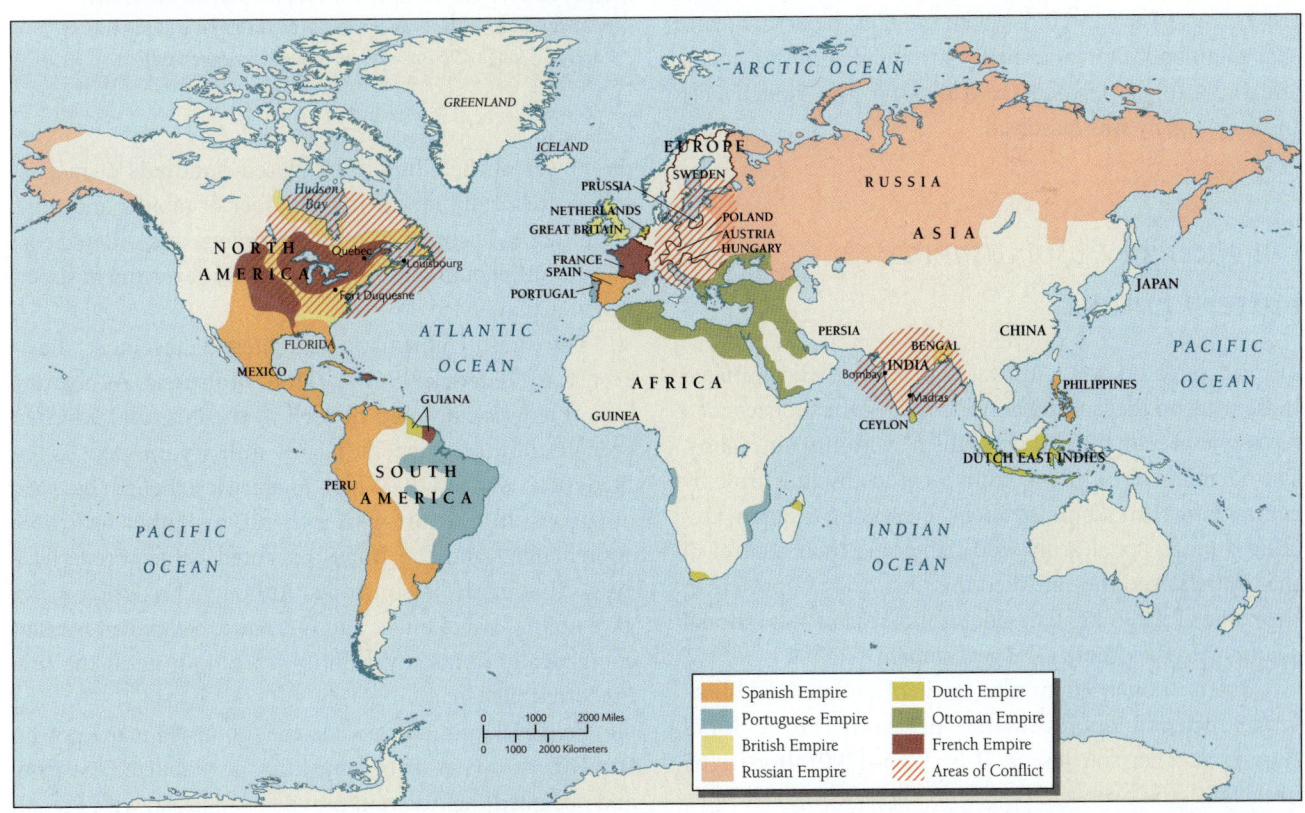

THE SEVEN YEARS' WAR, 1756–1763. ▪ *Which continents were involved in the Seven Years' War?* ▪ *What was the impact of naval power on the outcome of the war?* ▪ *What were the consequences for the colonies involved in the conflict?*

Succession, France and Spain fought on the side of Prussia, hoping to reverse some of the losses they had suffered in the Treaty of Utrecht; while Britain and the Dutch Republic sided with Austria, as they had done since the 1690s. Like those earlier wars, this war quickly spread beyond the frontiers of Europe. In India, the British East India Company lost control over the coastal area of Madras to its French rival. But in North America, British colonists from New England captured the important French fortress of Louisbourg on Cape Breton Island, hoping to put a stop to French interference with their fishing and shipping. When the war finally ended in 1748, Britain recovered Madras and returned Louisbourg to France.

Eight years later, these colonial conflicts reignited when Prussia once again attacked Austria. This time, however, Prussia allied itself with Great Britain, and Austria found support from both France and Russia. In Europe, the Seven Years' War (1756–1763) ended in a stalemate, while in India and North America, the war had decisive consequences. In India, mercenary troops employed by the British East India Company joined with native allies to eliminate their French competitors. In North America (where the conflict was known as the French and Indian War), British troops captured both Louisbourg and Québec and drove French forces from the Ohio River Valley and the Great Lakes. By the Treaty of Paris in 1763, which brought the Seven Years' War to an end, France formally surrendered both Canada and India to the British; six years later, the French East India Company was dissolved.

MARIA THERESA OF AUSTRIA AND HER FAMILY. A formidable and capable ruler who fought to maintain Austria's dominance in central Europe against the claims of Frederick the Great of Prussia, Maria Theresa had sixteen children, including Marie Antoinette, later the queen of France as wife of Louis XVI. ▪ *Why did Maria Theresa emphasize her role as mother in a royal portrait such as this one rather than her undeniable political skills?* ▪ *How does this portrait compare with those of Louis XIV (page 496) or William and Mary (page 504)?*

Enlightened Absolutism in Eastern Europe

The rulers of Prussia, Austria, and Russia, who initiated these wars on the Continent, were among the pioneers of a new style of "enlightened absolutism" within their realms. They demonstrated their commitment to absolutist rule by centralizing their administrations, increasing taxation, creating a professional army, and tightening their control of the Church. And they justified this expansion of powers in the name of the Enlightenment ideal of reason—as rational solutions to the problems of government.

Rulers influenced by the spirit of enlightened absolutism included Empress Maria Theresa (r. 1740–1780) of Austria and her son Joseph II (r. 1765–1790); from 1765 until 1780, the two were co-rulers. They created statewide systems of primary education, relaxed censorship, and instituted a more liberal criminal code for the Habsburg Empire. Joseph II was particularly energetic in challenging

the power of the Church: he closed hundreds of monasteries, drastically limited the number of monks and nuns permitted to live in contemplative orders, and ordered that the education of priests be placed under government supervision (Chapter 15).

The most emblematic enlightened absolutist, however, was Frederick II (1740–1786) of Prussia. As a young man, Frederick devoted himself to the flute and admired French culture, exasperating his military-minded father, Frederick William I. When Frederick rebelled by running away from court with a friend, his father had them apprehended and the friend executed before Frederick's eyes. This grisly lesson took. Although Frederick never gave up his love of music and literature, he applied himself energetically to his royal duties, earning himself the title Frederick the Great.

Frederick raised Prussia to the status of a major power. In 1740, as soon as he became king, he mobilized his army and occupied the Austrian province of Silesia, with French support. Empress Maria Theresa, also new to the throne, counterattacked; but, despite support from Britain and Hungary, she could not recover Silesia. Eventually, Frederick consolidated his gains over all the Polish territories that lay between East Prussia and Brandenburg, transforming Prussia into a powerful, contiguous kingdom by 1786. Frederick was careful to cultivate support from the Prussian nobility, known as the Junkers. His father had recruited civil servants according to merit rather than birth, but Frederick relied on the Junkers to staff the army and his expanding administration. His strategy worked. His nobility remained loyal, and he fashioned the most professional and efficient bureaucracy in Europe.

Frederick supervised a series of "enlightened" social reforms. He prohibited the judicial torture of accused criminals, abolished the bribing of judges, and established a system of elementary schools. Although strongly anti-Semitic, he encouraged religious toleration toward Jews, and declared that he would happily build a mosque in Berlin if he could find enough Muslims to fill it. On his own royal estates, he abolished capital punishment, curtailed the forced labor services of his peasantry, and granted the peasants long leases on the land they worked. He encouraged scientific forestry and the cultivation of new crops. He cleared new lands in Silesia and brought in thousands of immigrants to cultivate them. When wars ruined their farms, he supplied his peasants with new livestock and tools. However, he never attempted to extend these reforms to the estates of the Prussian nobility. To have done so would have alienated the very group on whom Frederick's rule depended.

Like Frederick, Catherine the Great of Russia (r. 1762–1796) thought of herself as an enlightened ruler and corresponded with French philosophes. Also like Frederick, she could not afford to lose the support of the nobles, who had placed her on the throne after executing her husband, the weak and possibly mad Peter III. Under her reign, the nobility were exempted from taxation and corporal punishment, and their property rights over their estates were enhanced. Catherine's efforts at enlightened reform were limited: she founded hospitals and orphanages, created an elementary school system for the children of the provincial nobility, and, although she called a commission to examine the possibility of codifying Russian law, its proposals were set aside after a massive peasant revolt in 1773–1775 (led by a Cossack, Yemelyan Pugachev) briefly threatened Moscow itself. Catherine gained her greatest achievements through war and diplomacy. In 1774, she won control over the northern coast of the Black Sea after a war with the Ottoman Empire, from which she also took several Ottoman provinces along the Danube River. Russia thus obtained a long-sought goal: a warm-water port for the Russian navy. In addition, Catherine succeeded in expanding Russian territory in the west, at the expense of the weaker kingdom of Poland.

CATHERINE THE GREAT. Rumored to have ordered the assassination of Peter III, Catherine oversaw an era of expansion in what was to become the longest female reign in Russian history.

The plan for Russia, Austria, and Prussia to divide the Polish-Lithuanian Commonwealth among them was originally proposed by Frederick the Great: Russia would abandon its Danubian provinces and receive in exchange the grain fields of eastern Poland (population between 1 and 2 million Poles); Austria would take Galicia (population 2.5 million); and Prussia would consolidate the divided lands of its kingdom by taking Poland's coastal regions on the Baltic Sea. In fact, Russia had long hoped to absorb the Commonwealth for itself. When the agreement was finalized in 1772, Poland had lost 30 percent of its territory and half its population.

After a second war between Russia and the Ottomans in 1788, the Polish state tried to reassert itself by writing a new constitution that would strengthen the kingdom's political institutions. The Constitution of 1791 gave the urban middle classes a greater voice to help counteract the influence of the more privileged nobility, and the state declared its intention to protect peasants from abuses linked to serfdom. The new constitution, however, angered conservative elements among the Polish aristocracy and Poland's more powerful neighbors. In a renewed war in 1792, the Polish state proved no match for the three major regional powers—Russia, Austria, and Prussia; and after a second partition in 1793, Poland was reduced further, so that only one-third of the population before 1772 remained in Polish territory. In 1794, a Polish uprising partially inspired by the French Revolution attempted to free Poland and Lithuania from Russian control (see Chapter 19), but its failure led Russia, Austria, and Prussia to erase Poland from the map altogether, and its territories and population divided between the victors in a third and final partition. Poland, which along with Lithuania had been an independent commonwealth since 1569 and bound even longer by an informal union of the Polish and Lithuanian royal families, would not reappear as an autonomous nation-state until after World War I.

As a political program, enlightened absolutism clearly had its limits. On the one hand, Catherine the Great of Russia, Frederick the Great of Prussia, and Joseph II of Austria were clearly personally inspired by the literary culture of the philosophes, and their political programs reflected Enlightenment ideas about the rational organization of state institutions. On the other hand, they were ready to abandon the humanitarian impulse of Enlightenment thought and the ideal of self-government when it came to preserving their own power and the social hierarchies that sustained it.

The American Revolution

The American Revolution of 1776 provided a more fruitful opportunity for putting Enlightenment ideals into practice. Along the Atlantic seaboard, the rapidly growing British colonies chafed at the rule from London. To recover some of the costs of the Seven Years' War and pay for the continuing costs of protecting its colonial subjects, the British Parliament imposed a series of new taxes on its American colonies. These taxes were immediately unpopular, and colonists complained that because they had no representatives in Parliament, they were being taxed without their consent—a fundamental violation of their rights as British subjects. They also argued that British restrictions on colonial trade, particularly the requirement that certain goods first pass through British ports before being shipped to the Continent, were strangling American livelihoods and making it impossible to pay even the king's legitimate taxes.

The British government, led since 1760 by the young and inexperienced King George III, responded to these oppositions with a badly calculated mixture of vacillation and force: various taxes were imposed then withdrawn in the face of colonial resistance. In 1773, however, when East India Company tea was dumped into Boston Harbor by rebellious colonials objecting to the customs duties that had been imposed on it, the British government closed the port of Boston and curtailed the colony's representative institutions. These "Coercive Acts" galvanized the support of the other American colonies for Massachusetts, and in 1774, representatives from all the American colonies met at Philadelphia to form the Continental Congress, to negotiate with the Crown over their grievances. In April 1775, however, local militiamen at Lexington and Concord clashed with regular British troops sent to disarm them. Soon thereafter, the Continental Congress began raising an army, and an outright rebellion erupted against the British government.

On July 4, 1776, the thirteen colonies formally declared their independence from Great Britain, in language that showed their debt to Enlightenment writers (see **Analyzing Primary Sources** on page 581). During the first two years of the war, it seemed unlikely that such independence would ever become a reality. In 1778, however, France,

DIVIDING THE ROYAL SPOILS. A contemporary cartoon showing the monarchs of Europe at work carving up a hapless Poland. Note there is little reference here to the people who lived in the Polish territories that were being divided up among Russia, Prussia, and the Habsburg Empire. All three of these realms already contained people who spoke different languages and practiced different religions. The result of such expansion was to increase the linguistic and cultural diversity of these kingdoms. ▪ *How might the redistribution of Polish territories have complicated the internal politics of these monarchies?* ▪ *What long-term consequences might we expect from such multiethnic or multireligious societies?*

Analyzing Primary Sources

The American Declaration of Independence

The Declaration of Independence, issued from Philadelphia on July 4, 1776, is perhaps the most famous single document of American history. Its familiarity, however, does not lessen its interest as a piece of political philosophy. The indebtedness of the document's authors to the ideas of John Locke will be obvious from the selections given here. But Locke, in turn, drew many of his ideas about the contractual and conditional nature of human government from the conciliarist thinkers of the fifteenth and early sixteenth centuries. The appeal of absolutism notwithstanding, the Declaration shows how vigorous the medieval tradition of contractual, limited government remained at the end of the eighteenth century.

 hen in the course of human events, it becomes necessary for one people to dissolve the political bonds which have connected them with another, and to assume among the powers of the earth the separate and equal station to which the Laws of Nature and of Nature's God entitle them, a decent respect to the opinions of mankind requires that they should declare the causes which impel them to the separation.... We hold these truths to be self-evident, that all men are created equal, that they are endowed by their Creator with certain unalienable rights, that among these are Life, Liberty and the pursuit of Happiness.... That to secure these rights, Governments are instituted among men, deriving their just powers from the consent of the governed.... That whenever any form of Government becomes destructive of these ends, it is the Right of the People to alter or to abolish it, and to institute new Government, laying its foundation upon such principles and organizing its power in such form, as to them shall seem most likely to effect their Safety and Happiness. Prudence, indeed, will dictate that Governments long established should not be changed for light and transient causes; and accordingly all experience has shown, that mankind are more disposed to suffer, while evils are sufferable, than to right themselves by abolishing the forms to which they are accustomed. But when a long train of abuses and usurpations, pursuing invariably the same Object, evinces a design to reduce them under absolute despotism, it is their right, it is their duty, to throw off such Government, and to provide new Guards for their future security.... Such has been the patient sufferance of these Colonies; and such is now the necessity which constrains them to alter their former Systems of Government.

Questions for Analysis

1. Who are "the people" mentioned in the first sentence of this selection? Are the rights of "the people" the same as individual rights? How did the authors of this document come to think of themselves as the representatives of such a body?

2. What is the purpose of government, according to this document? Who gets to decide if the government is doing its job?

3. How does this document's use of the term *political bonds* compare with Rousseau's "form of association" in *The Social Contract*? What is similar about these two texts? What is different?

---

anxious to undermine the colonial hegemony Great Britain had maintained since 1713, joined the war on the side of the Americans. Spain also entered the war in support of France, hoping to recover Gibraltar and Florida (the latter lost in 1763 to Britain). In 1780, Britain declared war on the Dutch Republic for continuing to trade with the rebellious colonies. Now facing a coalition of its colonial rivals, Great Britain saw the war turn against it. In 1781, combined land and sea operations by French and American troops forced the surrender of the main British army at Yorktown in Virginia. As the defeated British soldiers surrendered their weapons, their band played a song titled "The World Turned Upside Down."

Negotiations for peace began soon after the defeat at Yorktown but were not concluded until September 1783. The Treaty of Paris left Great Britain in control of Canada and Gibraltar. Spain retained its possessions west of the Mississippi River and recovered Florida. The United States gained its independence (its western border was fixed on the Mississippi River, and it secured valuable fishing rights

War and Politics in Enlightenment Europe | **581**

off the eastern coast of Canada). France gained only the satisfaction of defeating its colonial rival, but that satisfaction was short lived. Six years later, the massive debts France had incurred in supporting the American Revolution helped bring about another, very different kind of revolution in France, one that would permanently alter the history of Europe.

CONCLUSION

The Enlightenment arose from the scientific revolution, the new sense of power and possibility that rational thinking made possible, and the rush of enthusiasm for new forms of inquiry. Enlightenment thinkers scrutinized a remarkably wide range of topics: human nature, reason, understanding, religion, belief, law, the origins of government, economics, new forms of technology, and social practices such as marriage, child rearing, and education. Enlightenment ideas about social improvement and progress could and did occasionally serve the interests of European rulers, who saw

in them a means both to rationalize their administrations and to challenge social groups or institutions that resisted the centralization of authority. Maria Theresa in Austria, Frederick the Great in Prussia, and Catherine the Great in Russia all found ways to harness aspects of Enlightenment thought to their strategies of government.

At the same time, however, the radical implications of the Enlightenment critique of tradition made many people uncomfortable. Ideas with subversive implications circulated in popular forms, from pamphlets and journalism to plays and operas. The intellectual movement that lay behind the Enlightenment thus had broad consequences for the creation of a new kind of elite based not on birth but on the acquisition of knowledge and the encouragement of open expression and debate. A new sphere of public opinion had come into existence, one which was difficult for the state to monitor and control, and one that would have profound consequences in the nineteenth and twentieth centuries.

The prosperity that had made the Enlightenment possible remained very unevenly distributed in late eighteenth-century Europe. In the cities, rich and poor lived separate lives in separate neighborhoods. In the countryside, regions

After You Read This Chapter

 Go to **INQUIZITIVE** to see what you've learned—and learn what you've missed—with personalized feedback along the way.

REVIEWING THE OBJECTIVES

- Many eighteenth-century thinkers used the term *Enlightenment* to describe what their work offered to European society. Who were they, and what did they mean by this term?

- Enlightenment ideas spread rapidly throughout Europe and in European colonies. How did this expanded arena for public discussion shape the development of Enlightenment thought?

- Enlightenment debates were shaped by the availability of new information about peoples and cultures in different parts of the globe. How did Enlightenment thinkers incorporate this new information into their thought?

- Enlightenment thinkers were often critical of widely held cultural and political beliefs. What was radical about the Enlightenment?

WARS OF THE SEVENTEENTH AND EIGHTEENTH CENTURIES

Glorious Revolution	1688–1689
War of the League of Augsburg	1689–1697
War of the Spanish Succession	1702–1713
Seven Years' War	1756–1763
American Revolution	1775–1783
The Russo-Turkish War	1787–1792

bypassed by the developing commercial economy of the period continued to suffer from hunger and famine, just as they had done in the sixteenth and seventeenth centuries. In eastern Europe, the contrasts between rich and poor were even more extreme, as many peasants fell into a new style of serfdom that would last until the end of the nineteenth century. War, too, remained a fact of European life, bringing death and destruction to hundreds of thousands of people across the Continent and around the world—yet another consequence of the worldwide reach of these European colonial empires.

Finally, the Atlantic revolutions (the American Revolution of 1776, the French Revolution of 1789, and the Latin American upheavals of the 1830s) were steeped in the language of the Enlightenment. The constitutions of the new nations formed by these revolutions made reference to the fundamental assumptions of Enlightenment liberalism: the liberty of the individual conscience and the freedom from the constraints imposed by religious or government institutions. Government authority could not be arbitrary; equality and freedom were natural; and humans sought happiness, prosperity, and the expansion of their potential. These arguments had been made earlier, though tentatively; and even after the Atlantic revolutions, their aspirations were only partially realized. But when the North American colonists declared their independence from Britain in 1776, they called such ideas "self-evident truths." That bold declaration marked both the distance traveled since the late seventeenth century and the self-confidence that was the Enlightenment's hallmark.

PEOPLE, IDEAS, AND EVENTS IN CONTEXT

- How did the **COMMERCIAL REVOLUTION** change social life in Europe?
- Who were the **PHILOSOPHES**? What gave them such confidence in **REASON**?
- What did **DAVID HUME** owe to **ISAAC NEWTON**? What made his work different from that of the famous physicist?
- What did **VOLTAIRE** admire about the works of **FRANCIS BACON** and **JOHN LOCKE**? What irritated Voltaire about French society?
- What was **MONTESQUIEU**'s contribution to theories of government?
- What made **DENIS DIDEROT**'s *ENCYCLOPEDIA* such a definitive statement of the Enlightenment's goals?
- What influence did **CESARE BECCARIA** have over legal practices in Europe?
- What contributions did **ADAM SMITH** make to economic theory?
- What was radical about **JEAN-JACQUES ROUSSEAU**'s views on education and politics?
- What does the expansion of the **PUBLIC SPHERE** in the eighteenth century tell us about the effects of the Enlightenment?

THINKING ABOUT CONNECTIONS

- Compare the Enlightenment as an intellectual movement with the Reformation of the sixteenth century. What is similar about the two movements? What is distinctive?
- Did increases in literacy, the rise of print culture, and the emergence of new forms of intellectual sociability such as salons, reading societies, and coffeehouses really make public opinion more rational? How has our understanding of public opinion changed since the eighteenth century?

STORY LINES

- The French Revolution of 1789–1799 overthrew Louis XVI and created a government that was committed in principle to the rule of law, the liberty of the individual, and an idea of the nation as a sovereign body of citizens. These political changes also opened the way for the expression of a wide variety of social grievances by peasants, laborers, women, and other social groups in Europe.

- The French Revolution encouraged the spread of democratic ideas, but it also led to an increase in the power of centralized nation-states in Europe. The pressures of the revolutionary wars led governments to develop larger national bureaucracies, modern professional armies, new legal codes, and new tax structures.

- The French Revolution was part of a broader set of changes that rocked the Atlantic world at the end of the eighteenth century. Along with the Haitian Revolution and the American Revolution, this wave of cataclysmic change reshaped the political order of Europe and the Americas.

CHRONOLOGY

May 1789	The Estates General meets
June 1789	The Tennis Court Oath
July 1789	The Fall of the Bastille
September 1792	First French Republic
January 1793	Execution of King Louis XIV
September 1793– July 1794	The Terror
1798–1799	Napoleon's invasion of Egypt
January 1804	Haitian independence
1804	Napoleon crowned emperor
1804	Civil Code
1808	Invasion of Spain
1812	Invasion of Russia
1814–1815	Napoleon's abdication and defeat

Before You Read This Chapter

The French Revolution

CORE OBJECTIVES

- **UNDERSTAND** the origins of the French Revolution in 1789.

- **EXPLAIN** the goals of French revolutionaries and the reactions of people elsewhere in Europe and the Atlantic world.

- **DESCRIBE** the events that made the revolution more radical in 1792–1794.

- **IDENTIFY** the connections between the revolution and Napoleon's regime after 1799, and the effects of Napoleon's conquests on Europe.

- **CONSIDER** the links between the French Revolution and the Atlantic world, which also saw revolutions in the Americas and in the Caribbean during these decades.

When a crowd of Parisians attacked the antiquated and nearly empty royal prison known as the **Bastille** on July 14, 1789, they were doing several things at once. On the one hand, the revolt was a popular expression of support for the newly created National Assembly. Only weeks earlier, this representative body had declared its intention to put an end to absolutism in France by writing a constitution that made the nation, rather than the king, the sovereign authority in the land. But the Parisians in the street on July 14 did not express themselves like members of the National Assembly who spoke the language of the Enlightenment. The actions of the revolutionary crowd were an expression of violent anger at the king's soldiers, who they feared might turn their guns on the city in a royal attempt to restore order by force. When the governor of the Bastille prison opened fire on the attackers, killing as many as a hundred, the crowd responded with redoubled fury. By the end of the day, the prison had fallen, and the governor's battered body was dragged to the square before the city hall, where it was beheaded. Among the first to meet such an end in the course of a revolution in France, he would not be the last.

This tension between noble political aspirations and cruel violence lies at the heart of the French Revolution. The significance of this contradiction was not lost on the millions of people throughout Europe who watched in astonishment as France was engulfed in turmoil during the 1790s. In 1789, one European out of every five lived in France, a kingdom that many considered to be the center of European culture. Other kingdoms were not immune from the same social and political tensions that divided the French. Aristocrats across Europe and the colonies resented monarchical inroads on their ancient freedoms. Members of the middle classes chafed under a system of official privilege that they increasingly saw as unjust and outmoded. Peasants fiercely resented the endless demands of central government on their limited resources. The resentments were not focused exclusively on absolutist monarchs, as bitter

resentments and tensions existed between country and city dwellers, rich and poor, overprivileged and underprivileged, and slave and free. The French Revolution was the most dramatic and tumultuous expression of all of these conflicts.

This age of revolution had opened on the other side of the Atlantic Ocean. The American Revolution of 1776 was a crisis of the British Empire, linked to a long series of conflicts between England and France over colonial control of North America. It led to a major crisis of the Old Regime in France. Among "enlightened" Europeans, the success with which citizens of the United States had thrown off British rule and formed a republic based on Enlightenment principles was a source of tremendous optimism. Change would come, many believed. Reform was possible. And the costs would be modest.

The French Revolution did not live up to these expectations, though change certainly did come. By any measure,

THE ATLANTIC REVOLUTIONS. The Atlantic revolutions shook nations and empires on both sides of the ocean, challenging the legitimacy of Europe's dynastic realms, lending further support to the notions of popular sovereignty, and forcing contemporaries to rethink the meanings of citizenship in a context of intense political and economic struggle. ▪ *How many of these struggles took place in Europe?* ▪ *How many appear to have taken place on the periphery of the Atlantic world?* ▪ *What circumstances may have made it more difficult for such revolutionary movements to develop in Europe?*

the accomplishments of the revolutionary decade were extraordinary. It successfully proved that the subjects of an old monarchy in the heart of Europe could come together to constitute themselves as citizens of a new political idea: the nation. Freed from the shackles of tradition, the revolutionaries in France posed new questions about the role of women in public life, the separation of church and state, and the rights of Jews and other minorities. A slave revolt in the French colonies convinced the revolutionaries that the new liberties they defended so ardently also belonged to African slaves, though few had suggested such a thing at the outset. Meanwhile, the European wars precipitated by the revolution marked the first time that entire populations were mobilized as part of a new kind of devastating international conflict—the first "total war." In other words, in spite of the optimism of those who began the revolution in 1789, it quickly became something much more costly, complex, and violent, and its effects were to resonate throughout Europe for the next half century.

THE FRENCH REVOLUTION: AN OVERVIEW

The term *French Revolution* refers to a complex series of events that took place in three stages between 1789 and 1799. Because of the French Revolution's broad impact, it is also closely related to the period that followed, 1799–1815, when Napoleon Bonaparte ruled in France and conquered much of Europe.

The first stage of the revolution was a struggle over the idea of constitutional monarchy in France, and it lasted from 1789 to 1792. This stage was relatively peaceful and came about as social elites challenged the power of the king. Like the American revolutionaries, the French elites refused taxation without representation; attacked despotism, or arbitrary authority; and offered an Enlightenment-inspired program to rejuvenate the nation. Reforms, many of them breathtakingly wide ranging, were instituted—some accepted or even offered by the king, while others passed despite his objections. This peaceful, constitutional phase did not last, however. For many reasons, unlike the American Revolution, the French Revolution did not stabilize around one constitution or one set of political leaders.

Reforms were met with resistance and divided the country. The threat of dramatic change within one of the most powerful countries in Europe created international tensions. In 1792, these tensions exploded into war, and the crises of war, in turn, spelled the end of the Bourbon monarchy and the beginning of the republic. This second stage of the revolution, which lasted from 1792 to 1794, was one of acute crisis, consolidation, and repression. A ruthlessly centralized government mobilized all the country's resources to fight the foreign enemy as well as the counter-revolutionaries at home, to destroy traitors and the vestiges of the Old Regime.

The **Terror**, as this policy was called, did save the republic, but it exhausted itself in factions and recriminations and collapsed in 1794. In the third phase, from 1794 to 1799, the government drifted. France remained a republic, and continued to fight with Europe, but, undermined by corruption and division, the state fell prey to the ambitions of a military leader, **Napoleon Bonaparte**. Napoleon's rule, punctuated by equally astonishing victories and catastrophes, stretched from 1799 to 1815. It began as a republic but became an empire, and ended—after a last hurrah—in the muddy fields outside the Belgian village of Waterloo. After Napoleon's final defeat, the other European monarchs restored the Bourbons to the throne. That restoration, however, was short lived, and the cycle of revolution and reaction continued into the nineteenth century.

THE COMING OF THE REVOLUTION

What were the long-term causes of the revolution in France? Historians long ago argued that the causes and outcomes should be understood in terms of class conflict. According to this interpretation, a rising bourgeoisie, or middle class, inspired by Enlightenment ideas and its own self-interest, overthrew what was left of the aristocratic order. This interpretation drew on the writings of the nineteenth-century philosopher Karl Marx and much on twentieth-century sociology.

Historians have substantially modified this bold thesis. To be sure, the origins of the revolution did lie in eighteenth-century French society. Yet that society was not simply divided between a bourgeois class and the aristocracy. Instead, it was increasingly dominated by a new elite or social group that brought together aristocrats, officeholders, professionals, and—to a lesser degree—merchants and businessmen. To understand the revolution, we need to understand this new social group and its conflicts with the government of Louis XVI.

French society was legally divided into three estates. (An individual's *estate* marked his standing, or status, and it determined legal rights, taxes, and so on.) The First Estate comprised the clergy; the Second Estate, the nobility; and the **Third Estate**, by far the largest, included everyone else, from wealthy lawyers and businessmen to urban laborers and poor peasants. To the political and social elite of the country, a small but powerful group, these legal distinctions often seemed artificial. To begin with, in the upper reaches of society, the social boundaries between nobles and wealthy commoners were ill defined. A noble title was accessible to anyone who could afford to buy an ennobling office; for example, close to 50,000 new nobles were created between 1700 and 1789. The nobility depended on a constant infusion of talent and economic power from the wealthy social groups of the Third Estate.

To preserve their elite status, aristocrats spoke of a distinction between the nobility of the sword and of the robe: the former, supposedly of a more ancient and distinguished lineage derived from military service, and the latter, aristocrats only because they had purchased administrative or judicial office (hence the robe).

Nevertheless, wealth did not take predictable forms. Most noble wealth was proprietary—that is, tied to land, urban properties, purchased offices, and the like. Yet noble families did not disdain trade or commerce, as historians long thought. In fact, noblemen financed most industry and invested heavily in banking and such enterprises as ship owning, slave trade, mining, and metallurgy. Moreover, the very wealthy members of the Third Estate also preferred to invest in secure, proprietary holdings. Thus, throughout the century, much middle-class wealth was transformed into noble wealth, and a significant number of rich bourgeois became noblemen. Wealthy members of the bourgeoisie did not see themselves as a separate class. They thought of themselves as different from—and often opposed to—the common people who worked with their hands, and identified with the values of a nobility to which they frequently aspired.

There were, nonetheless, important social tensions. Less prosperous lawyers—and their numbers were increasing—were jealous of the privileged position of a favored few in their profession. Over the course of the century, the prices of offices rose, making it more difficult to buy into the nobility, and creating tensions between middling members of the Third Estate and the very rich in trade and commerce who, by and large, were the only group able to afford to climb the social ladder. Less wealthy nobles resented the success of rich, upstart commoners whose income allowed them to live in luxury. In sum, several fault lines ran through the elite and the middle classes. All these social groups could nonetheless join together in attacking a government and an economy that were not serving their interests.

PREREVOLUTIONARY PROPAGANDA. Political cartoons in late-eighteenth-century France commonly portrayed the Third Estate as bearing the burden of taxation while performing the bulk of the nation's productive work. In the image on the left, a peasant bears the burden of his tools and his harvest as a cleric and a nobleman look on. In the image on the right, the commoner is literally carrying his social superiors. ▪ *What visual cues indicate the status of individuals in these images?* ▪ *Would we expect the nobility or the clergy to defend their status on the basis of their usefulness to society?* ▪ *Can we detect the power of certain Enlightenment ideas behind these forms of social critique? Which ones?* ▪ *How might an opponent of Enlightenment thought have confronted such arguments?*

The Enlightenment had changed public debate (Chapter 17). Although ideas did not cause the revolution, they played a critical role in articulating grievances. The political theories of Locke, Voltaire, and Montesquieu could appeal to both discontented nobles and members of the middle class. Voltaire was popular because of his attacks on noble privileges, and Locke and Montesquieu gained widespread followings because of their defense of private property and limited sovereignty. Montesquieu's ideas appealed to the noble lawyers and officeholders who dominated France's powerful law courts, the *parlements*. They read his doctrine of checks and balances as support for their argument that the parlements could provide a check to the despotism of the king's government. When conflicts arose, noble leaders presented themselves as defenders of a nation that was threatened by the king and his ministers.

The campaign for change was also fueled by economic reformers. The physiocrats (Chapter 17) urged the government to simplify the tax system and free the economy from mercantilist regulations. They advocated, for example, an end to price controls in the grain trade, which had been imposed to keep the cost of bread low. Such interventions, they argued, interfered with the market's ability to find an equilibrium between supply and demand.

In the countryside, peasants, who did not think in terms of markets, were caught in a web of obligations to landlords (fees to the landlord and for the use of the landlord's mill or wine press), Church (a tithe, or levy, on farm produce owed to the Church), and state (fees when land changed hands). In addition, peasants paid a disproportionate share of both direct and indirect taxes, the most onerous of which was the salt tax levied by the government. (For some time, the production of salt had been a state monopoly, and every individual was required to buy at least seven pounds a year from the government works. The result was a commodity whose cost was often as much as fifty or sixty times its actual value.) Further grievances stemmed from the requirement to maintain public roads (the corvée) and from the hunting privileges the nobles for centuries had regarded as the distinctive badge of their order.

Social and economic conditions deteriorated on the eve of the revolution. A general price increase during much of the eighteenth century, which permitted the French economy to expand by providing capital for investment, created hardship for the peasantry and the urban tradesmen and laborers. Their plight deteriorated further at the end of the 1780s, when poor harvests sent bread prices sharply higher. In 1788, families found themselves spending more than 50 percent of their income on bread, which made up the bulk of their diet; the following year, the figure rose to

as much as 80 percent. Poor harvests reduced demand for manufactured goods, and contracting markets in turn created unemployment. Many peasants left the countryside for the cities hoping to find work there, only to discover that urban unemployment was far worse than in rural areas. Evidence indicates that between 1787 and 1789, the unemployment rate in many parts of urban France was as high as 50 percent.

Failure and Reform

An inefficient tax system further weakened the country's financial position. Taxation differed according to social standings and varied from region to region, with some areas subject to a much higher rate than others. In addition,

LOUIS XVI. The king, shown here in an official portrait, was committed to the forms of spectacular display that were so useful to Louis XIV in shoring up the monarchy. His attachment to the monarchy's absolutist powers and his inability to solve his regime's financial crisis led to his downfall. He was executed by the government of the French Republic on January 21, 1793, as the more radical phase of the revolution was just beginning. ▪ *What made absolutism less convincing in the late eighteenth century?* ▪ *What caused the monarchy to lose its sacred aura?*

special exemptions made the task of collectors more difficult. The financial system, already burdened by debts incurred under Louis XIV, all but broke down completely under the increased expenses brought on by the country's participation in the American Revolution. The cost of servicing the national debt in the 1780s consumed 50 percent of the nation's budget.

Problems with the economy reflected weaknesses in France's administrative structure, ultimately the responsibility of the country's absolutist monarch, **Louis XVI** (r. 1774–1792). Louis wished to improve the lot of the poor, abolish torture, and shift the burden of taxation onto the richer classes, but he lacked the ability to accomplish these tasks. He appointed reformers such as Anne-Robert-Jacques Turgot (a physiocrat) and Jacques Necker (a Swiss Protestant banker) as finance ministers, only to arouse the opposition of traditionalists at court. When he pressed for new taxes to be paid by the nobility, he was defeated by the provincial parlements, which defended the aristocracy's immunity from taxation. He allowed his wife, the young but strong-willed Marie Antoinette, daughter of Austria's Maria Theresa, a free hand in dispensing patronage among her friends, which resulted in constant intrigue and frequently reshuffled alliances at Versailles. By 1788, a weak monarch, together with a chaotic financial situation and severe social tensions, brought absolutist France to the edge of political disaster.

THE DESTRUCTION OF THE OLD REGIME

The fiscal crisis precipitated the revolution. In 1787 and 1788, the king's principal ministers, Charles de Calonne and Loménie de Brienne, proposed new taxes to meet the growing deficit, notably a stamp duty and a direct tax on the annual produce of the land.

Hoping to persuade the nobility to agree to these reforms, the king summoned an Assembly of Notables from among the aristocracy. This group insisted that any new tax scheme must be approved by the **Estates General**, the representative body of the three estates of the realm, and that the king had no legal authority to arrest and imprison arbitrarily. These proposed constitutional changes echoed those of the English aristocrats of 1688 and the American revolutionaries of 1776.

Faced with economic crisis and financial chaos, Louis XVI summoned the Estates General (which had not met since 1614) to meet in 1789. To many, his action appeared to be the only solution to France's deepening

problems. Long-term grievances and short-term hardships produced bread riots across the country in the spring of 1789. Fear that the forces of law and order were collapsing and that the common people might take matters into their own hands spurred the Estates General. Each of the three orders elected its own deputies; the Third Estate indirectly through local assemblies. These assemblies also were charged with the responsibility of drawing up lists of grievances (*cahiers des doléances*), further heightening expectations of fundamental reform.

The delegates of the Third Estate, although elected by assemblies chosen in turn by artisans and peasants, represented the outlook of an elite: only 13 percent were men of business, about 25 percent were lawyers, and 43 percent were government officeholders of some sort.

By tradition, each estate met and voted as a body. In the past, this generally had meant that the First Estate (the clergy) combined with the Second (the nobility) to defeat the Third. Now, the Third Estate made it clear that it would not tolerate such an arrangement. The Third Estate's interests were articulated most memorably by the **Abbé Emmanuel-Joseph Sieyès**, a radical member of the clergy. "What is the Third Estate?" asked Sieyès, in his famous pamphlet of January 1789. Everything, he answered, and pointed to eighteenth-century social changes to bolster his point. In early 1789, Sieyès's views were still unusually radical. But the leaders of the Third Estate contended that the three orders should sit together and vote as individuals. More important, they insisted that the Third Estate have twice as many members as the First and Second.

The king at first opposed "doubling the Third," but then changed his position. His unwillingness to take a strong stand on voting procedures cost him support he might have obtained from the Third Estate. Shortly after the Estates General opened at Versailles in May 1789, the Third Estate, angered by the king's attitude, took the revolutionary step of leaving the body and declaring itself the National Assembly. Locked out of the Estates General meeting hall on June 20, the Third Estate and a handful of sympathetic nobles and clergymen moved to a nearby indoor tennis court.

Here, under the leadership of the volatile, maverick aristocrat the Comte de Mirabeau and the radical clergyman Sieyès, they bound themselves by a solemn oath not to separate until they had drafted a constitution for France. This **Tennis Court Oath**, sworn on June 20, 1789, can be seen as the beginning of the French Revolution. By claiming the authority to remake the government in the name of the people, the National Assembly was asserting its right to act as the highest sovereign power in the nation. On June 27, the king virtually conceded this right by ordering all the delegates to join the National Assembly.

THE TENNIS COURT OATH, BY JACQUES LOUIS DAVID (1748–1825). In June 1789, members of the Third Estate, now calling themselves the National Assembly, swore an oath not to disband until France had a constitution. In the center of this painting stands Jean Bailly, president of the new assembly. The Abbé Sieyès is seated at the table. In the foreground, a clergyman, an aristocrat, and a member of the Third Estate embrace in a symbol of national unity. The single deputy who refused to take the oath sits at far right, with his arms clasped against his chest. ▪ *What is the significance of this near unanimity expressed in defiance of the king?* ▪ *What options were available to those who did not support this move?*

First Stages of the French Revolution

The first stage of the French Revolution extended from June 1789 to August 1792. In the main, this stage was moderate, with its actions dominated by the leadership of liberal nobles and men of the Third Estate. Yet three events in the summer and fall of 1789 furnished evidence that their leadership would be challenged.

POPULAR REVOLTS

From the beginning of the political crisis, public attention was high. It was roused not merely by interest in political reform but also by the economic crisis that, as we have seen, sent the price of bread to astronomical heights. Many believed that the aristocracy and the king were conspiring to punish the Third Estate by encouraging scarcity and

high prices. Rumors circulated in Paris during the latter days of June 1789 that the king's troops were mobilizing to march on the city. The electors of Paris (those who had voted for the Third Estate—workshop masters, artisans, and shopkeepers) feared not only the king but also the Parisian poor, who had been parading through the streets and threatening violence. The common people would soon be referred to as *sans-culottes* (*sahn koo-LAWT*). The term, which translates to "without breeches," was an antiaristocratic badge of pride: a man of the people wore full-length trousers rather than aristocratic breeches with stockings and gold-buckled shoes. Led by the electors, the people formed a provisional municipal government and organized a militia of volunteers to maintain order. Determined to obtain arms, they made their way to the Bastille on July 14, an ancient fortress where guns and ammunition were stored. Built in the Middle Ages, the Bastille had been a

Analyzing Primary Sources

What Is the Third Estate? (1789)

The Abbé Emmanuel-Joseph Sieyès (1748–1836) was, by virtue of his office in the Church, a member of the First Estate of the Estates General. Nevertheless, his political savvy led him to be elected as a representative of the Third Estate from the district of Chartres. Sieyès was a formidable politician as well as a writer. His career during the revolution, which he ended by assisting Napoleon's seizure of power, began with one of the most important radical pamphlets of 1789. In What Is the Third Estate? *Sieyès posed fundamental questions about the rights of this estate, which comprised the great majority of the population, and helped provoke its secession from the Estates General.*

he plan of this book is fairly simple. We must ask ourselves three questions.

1. What is the Third Estate? *Everything.*

2. What has it been until now in the political order? *Nothing.*

3. What does it want to be? *Something.*

. . .

It suffices to have made the point that the so-called usefulness of a privileged order to the public service is a fallacy; that without help from this order, all the arduous tasks in the service are performed by the Third Estate; that without this order the higher posts could be infinitely better filled; that they ought to be the natural prize and reward of recog-nized ability and service; and that if the privileged have succeeded in usurping all well-paid and honorific posts, this is both a hateful iniquity towards the gen-erality of citizens and an act of treason to the commonwealth.

Who is bold enough to maintain that the Third Estate does not contain within itself everything needful to constitute a complete nation? It is like a strong and robust man with one arm still in chains. If the privileged order were removed, the nation would not be something less but something more. What then is the Third Estate? All; but an "all" that is fettered and oppressed. What would it be with-out the privileged order? It would be all; but free and flourishing. Nothing will go well without the Third Estate; every-thing would go considerably better with-out the two others.

Source: Emmanuel-Joseph Sieyès, *What Is the Third Estate?* ed. S. E. Finer, trans. M. Blondel (London: 1964), pp. 53, 65.

Questions for Analysis

1. How might contemporaries have viewed Sieyès's argument that the three estates should be evaluated according to their usefulness to the "commonwealth"?

2. Was Sieyès's language—accusing the privileged orders of "treason" and arguing for their "removal"—an incite-ment to violence?

3. What did Sieyès mean by the term *nation*? Could one speak of France as a nation in these terms before 1789?

---

prison for many years but it was no longer much used. Never-theless, it symbolized the hated royal authority. When crowds demanded arms from its governor, he procrastinated and then, fearing a frontal assault, ordered his troops to open fire, killing ninety-eight of the attackers. The crowd took revenge, capturing the fortress (which held only seven prisoners—five common criminals and two confined for mental incapacity) and killing the governor. Similar groups took control in other cities across France, but the fall of the Bastille was the first instance of the people's role in revolutionary change.

The second popular revolt occurred in the country-side. Peasants, too, expected and feared a monarchical and aristocratic counterrevolution. Rumors flew that the king's armies were on their way, that Austrians, Prussians, or "brigands" were invading. Frightened and uncertain, peasants and villagers organized militias; others attacked and burned manor houses, sometimes to look for grain but usually to find and destroy records of manorial dues. This "**Great Fear**," as historians have labeled it, compounded the confusion in rural areas. The news, when it reached Paris, convinced deputies at Versailles that the administra-tion of rural France had simply collapsed.

The third instance of popular uprising, the "**October Days**" of 1789, was brought on by economic crisis. This time, Parisian women from the market district, angered by the soaring price of bread and fired by rumors of the king's

WOMEN OF PARIS LEAVING FOR VERSAILLES, OCTOBER 1789. A crowd of women, accompanied by the marquis de Lafayette and the National Guard, marched to Versailles to confront the king about shortages and rising prices in Paris. ■ *Did the existence of the National Assembly change the meaning of such popular protests?*

continuing unwillingness to cooperate with the assembly, marched to Versailles on October 5 and demanded to be heard. Not satisfied with its reception by the assembly, the crowd broke through the gates to the palace, calling for the king to return to Paris from Versailles. On the afternoon of the following day the king yielded and returned to Paris, accompanied by the crowd and the National Guard.

Each of these popular uprisings shaped the political events unfolding at Versailles. The storming of the Bastille in July persuaded the king and nobles to agree to the creation of the National Assembly. The Great Fear compelled the most sweeping changes of the entire revolutionary period. On the night of August 4, in an effort to quell rural disorder, the assembly took a giant step toward abolishing all forms of privilege. It eliminated the Church tithe (tax on the harvest), the labor requirement known as the corvée, the nobility's hunting privileges, and a wide variety of tax exemptions and monopolies. In effect, these reforms obliterated the remnants of feudalism. A week later, the assembly abolished the sale of offices, thereby sweeping away one of the fundamental institutions of the Old Regime. The king's return to Paris during the October Days of 1789 undercut his ability to resist further changes.

THE NATIONAL ASSEMBLY AND THE RIGHTS OF MAN

The assembly issued its charter of liberties, **the Declaration of the Rights of Man and of the Citizen**, in August 1789. It declared property to be a natural right, along with liberty, security, and "resistance to oppression." It declared freedom of speech, religious toleration, and liberty of the press inviolable. All citizens were to be treated equally before the law. No one was to be imprisoned or punished without due process of law. Sovereignty resided in the people, who could depose officers of the government if they abused their powers. These, while not new ideas, represented the outcome of Enlightenment discussions and revolutionary debates and deliberations. The Declaration became the preamble to the new constitution, which the assembly finished in 1791.

Whom did the Declaration mean by "man and the citizen"? The constitution distinguished between "passive" citizens, who had guaranteed rights under law, and "active" citizens, who paid a certain amount in taxes and could thus vote and hold office. About half the adult men in France qualified as active citizens, but even their power was curtailed, because they could vote only for "electors," men whose property ownership qualified them to hold office. Later in the revolution, the more radical republic abolished the distinction between active and passive, but the conservative regimes reinstated it. Which men could be trusted to participate in politics and on what terms was a hotly contested issue.

Also controversial were the rights of religious minorities. The revolution gave full civil rights to Protestants, although those rights were challenged by Catholics in areas long divided by religious conflict. The revolution did, hesitantly, give civil rights to Jews, a measure that sparked protest in areas of eastern France. Religious toleration, a central theme of the Enlightenment, meant ending persecution; it did not mean that the regime was prepared to accommodate religious differences. The assembly abolished serfdom and banned slavery in continental France. It remained silent on colonial slavery, however; and although delegations pressed the assembly on political rights for free people of color, the assembly exempted the colonies from the constitution's provisions. Later events in the Caribbean forced the issue, as we will see.

The rights and roles of women became the focus of sharp debate, as revolutionaries confronted demands that working women participate in guilds or trade organizations, and that laws on marriage, divorce, relief for the poor, and education be reconsidered. The Englishwoman Mary Wollstonecraft penned her milestone book *A Vindication of the Rights of Woman* (Chapter 17) during the revolutionary debate over national education. Should girls be educated? To what end? Wollstonecraft, as we have seen, argued strongly that reforming education required forging a new concept of independent and equal womanhood. Even Wollstonecraft, however, only hinted at political representation, aware that such an idea would "excite laughter."

Only a handful of thinkers broached the subject of women in politics: the aristocratic Enlightenment thinker the Marquis de Condorcet and, from another shore, Marie Gouze, the self-educated daughter of a butcher. Gouze became an intellectual and playwright and renamed herself Olympe de Gouges. Like many "ordinary" people, she found in the explosion of revolutionary activity the opportunity to address the public by writing speeches, pamphlets, or newspapers. She composed her own manifesto, the *Declaration of the Rights of Woman and the Female Citizen* (1791). Beginning with the proposition that "social distinctions can only be based on the common utility," she declared that women had the same rights as men, including resistance to authority, participation in government, and naming the fathers of illegitimate children. This last demand offers a glimpse of the shame, isolation, and hardship faced by unmarried women.

DECLARATION OF THE RIGHTS OF MAN (1789). Presenting the Declaration as principles of natural law inscribed on stone like the Ten Commandments, this print gives a good indication of how the authors of the Declaration wished it to be perceived by the French people. Over the tablets is a beneficent and all-seeing deity accompanied by two female allegorical figures representing strength and virtue on one side and the French nation on the other. The image's symbols refer to Masonic lore (the triangle or pyramid with an eye at the center, the snake grasping its tail) and a set of historical references from the Roman Republic (a Phrygian cap, used by Romans as a symbol of liberty, is mounted on a spear emerging from a bundle of sticks). This bundle was known as a fasces (*faisceau* in French) and was carried in ancient Rome by magistrates as symbols of their authority. ▪ *Given the absence of any monarchical symbolism or references to the Catholic Church, why was it important for the authors to come up with an alternative set of historical references?*

De Gouges's demand for equal rights was unusual, but many women nevertheless participated in the everyday activities of the revolution. They joined clubs, demonstrations, and debates, and made their presence known, sometimes forcefully. Women artisans' organizations had a well-established role in municipal life, and they used the revolution as an opportunity to assert their rights

Declaration of the Rights of Man and of the Citizen

One of the first important pronouncements of the National Assembly after the Tennis Court Oath was the Declaration of the Rights of Man and of the Citizen. The authors drew inspiration from the American Declaration of Independence, but the language is even more heavily influenced by the ideals of French Enlightenment philosophers, particularly Rousseau. Following are the Declaration's preamble and some of its most important principles.

The representatives of the French people, constituted as the National Assembly, considering that ignorance, disregard, or contempt for the rights of man are the sole causes of public misfortunes and the corruption of governments, have resolved to set forth, in a solemn declaration, the natural, inalienable, and sacred rights of man, so that the constant presence of this declaration may ceaselessly remind all members of the social body of their rights and duties; so that the acts of legislative power and those of the executive power may be more respected . . . and so that the demands of the citizens, grounded henceforth on simple and incontestable principles, may always be directed to the maintenance of the constitution and to the welfare of all. . . .

Article 1. Men are born and remain free and equal in rights. Social distinctions can be based only on public utility.

Article 2. The aim of every political association is the preservation of the natural and imprescriptible rights of man. These rights are liberty, property, security, and resistance to oppression.

Article 3. The source of all sovereignty resides essentially in the nation. No body, no individual can exercise authority that does not explicitly proceed from it.

Article 4. Liberty consists in being able to do anything that does not injure another; thus the only limits upon each man's exercise of his natural laws are those that guarantee enjoyment of these same rights to the other members of society.

Article 5. The law has the right to forbid only actions harmful to society. No action may be prevented that is not forbidden by law, and no one may be constrained to do what the law does not order.

Article 6. The law is the expression of the general will. All citizens have the right to participate personally, or through representatives, in its formation. It must be the same for all, whether it protects or punishes. All citizens, being equal in its eyes, are equally admissable to all public dignities, positions, and employments, according to their ability, and on the basis of no other distinction than that of their virtues and talents. . . .

Article 16. A society in which the guarantee of rights is not secured, or the separation of powers is not clearly established, has no constitution.

Source: Declaration of the Rights of Man and of the Citizen, as cited in K. M. Baker, ed., *The Old Regime and the French Revolution* (Chicago: 1987), pp. 238–39.

Questions for Analysis

1. To whom is the Declaration addressed? Is it only about the rights of the French, or do these ideas apply to all people?

2. What gave a group of deputies elected to advise Louis XVI on constitutional reforms the right to proclaim themselves a National Assembly? What was revolutionary about this claim to represent the French nation?

3. Article 6, which states that "law is the expression of general will," is adapted from Rousseau's *Social Contract*. Does the Declaration give any indication of how the "general will" can be known?

---

to produce and sell goods. Market women were familiar public figures, often central to the circulation of news and spontaneous popular demonstrations. (The October Days are a good example.) Initially, the regime celebrated the support of women "citizens," and female figures were favorite symbols for liberty, prudence, and the bounty of nature in revolutionary iconography. But when the revolution became more radical, some revolutionaries saw autonomous political activity by women's organizations as a threat to public order, and in 1793, the revolutionaries shut down the women's political clubs. Even so, many ordinary women were able to make use of the revolution's new legislation on marriage (divorce was legalized in 1792) and inheritance to support claims for relief from abusive husbands or absent fathers, claims that would have been impossible under prerevolutionary legislation.

THE NATIONAL ASSEMBLY AND THE CHURCH

In November 1789, the National Assembly decided to confiscate all Church lands and use them as collateral for issuing interest-bearing notes, known as *assignats*. The assembly hoped that this action would resolve the economy's inflationary crisis, and eventually, these notes circulated widely as paper money. In July 1790, the assembly enacted the **Civil Constitution of the Clergy**, bringing the Church under state authority. This new law forced all bishops and priests to swear allegiance to the state, which henceforth paid their salaries. The aim was to make the Catholic Church of France a national institution, free from interference by Rome.

These reforms were bitterly divisive. On the one hand, many people resented the privileged status of the Church, with its vast monastic land holdings. On the other hand, for centuries, the parish church had been a central institution in small towns and villages, providing poor relief and other services, in addition to baptisms and marriages. The Civil Constitution of the Clergy sparked fierce resistance in some parts of rural France. When the pope threatened to excommunicate priests who signed the Civil Constitution, he raised the stakes: allegiance to the new French state meant damnation. Many people, especially peasants in the deeply Catholic areas of western France, were driven to open revolt.

The National Assembly made a series of economic and governmental changes with lasting effects. To raise money, it sold off Church lands, although few of the genuinely needy could afford to buy them. To encourage the growth of economic enterprise, it abolished guilds. To rid the country of local aristocratic power, it reorganized local governments, dividing France into eighty-three equal departments. These measures aimed to defend individual liberty and freedom from customary privilege. Their principal beneficiaries were, for the most part, members of the elite, people on their way up under the previous regime who were able to take advantage of the opportunities, such as buying land or being elected to office. In this realm as elsewhere, the social changes of the revolution endorsed changes already under way during the eighteenth century.

A NEW STAGE: POPULAR REVOLUTION

In the summer of 1792, the revolution's moderate leaders were toppled and replaced by republicans, who repudiated the monarchy and claimed to rule on behalf of a sovereign people. Why this abrupt and drastic change? Was the revolution blown off course? These are among the most difficult questions about the French Revolution. Historians have focused on three factors to explain the revolution's radical turn: changes in popular politics, a crisis of leadership, and international polarization.

First, the revolution politicized the common people, especially in cities. Newspapers filled with political and social commentary multiplied, freed from censorship. From 1789 forward, a wide variety of political clubs became part of daily political life. Some were formal, almost like political parties, gathering members of the elite to debate issues facing the country and influence decisions in the assembly. Other clubs opened their doors to those excluded from formal politics. Members read aloud from newspapers and discussed the options facing the country, from the provisions of the constitution to the trustworthiness of the king and his ministers. This political awareness was heightened by nearly constant shortages and fluctuating prices. Prices particularly exasperated the working people of Paris, who had eagerly awaited change since their street demonstrations of 1789. Urban demonstrations, often led by women, demanded cheaper bread; political leaders in clubs and newspapers called for the government to control rising inflation; and club leaders spoke for men and women who felt cheated by the constitution.

A second major reason for the change, of course, was a lack of effective national leadership. Louis XVI remained a weak monarch. He was forced to support measures personally distasteful to him, in particular the Civil Constitution of the Clergy. He was sympathetic to the plottings of the queen, who was in contact with her brother Leopold II of Austria. Urged on by Marie Antoinette, Louis agreed to attempt an escape from France in June 1791, hoping to rally foreign support for a counterrevolution. The members of the royal family managed to slip past their palace guards in Paris, but they were apprehended near the border at Varennes and brought back to the capital. The constitution of 1791 declared France a monarchy, but after the escape to Varennes, Louis was little more than a prisoner of the assembly.

The Counterrevolution

The third major reason for the dramatic turn of affairs was war. From the outset of the revolution, men and women across Europe had been compelled, by the very intensity of events in France, to take sides in the conflict. In the years immediately after 1789, the revolution in France

Analyzing Primary Sources

Women in the Constitution of 1791

During the debates prior to the passage of the Constitution of 1791, a committee of the National Assembly proposed that the Police Code should allow only men to bring charges of adultery, leaving women without legal recourse if their husbands were unfaithful. Etta Palm d'Aelders (1743–1798), a Dutch woman who became active in revolutionary circles in Paris after 1789, was particularly committed to the cause of women's rights and spoke in the National Assembly against this measure, demanding that women receive equal rights under the law.

es, gentlemen, you have broken the bronze scepter and replaced it with the olive branch, you have sworn to protect the weak, it is your duty, it is your honor, it is in your interest to destroy the roots of those gothic laws which abandon the weakest and most important half of humanity to a humiliating existence and to eternal slavery.

You have rendered to man the dignity of his being in recognizing his rights; you should not leave women moaning under an arbitrary power. This would be to overturn those fundamental principles that are the foundation of the magnificent edifice that you have built with your tireless labor for the good of the French. There is no time to hesitate, philosophy has pulled the truth from the shadows, the hour has rung, and Justice, the sister of liberty, calls for equal rights for all individuals, without distinction of sex. The laws of a free people must be equal for all beings, like the air and the sun. Too long, alas, these imprescriptible rights of nature have been misunderstood; too long bizarre laws that are the product of centuries of ignorance have afflicted humanity; too long has the most odious tyranny consecrated absurd laws.

But, Gentlemen, article III of the Police Code, which you presented to the constitutional committee, surpasses even the most unjust of actions taken during the preceding centuries of barbarism; it is a refinement of despotism which renders the constitution odious to the female sex; by degrading our existence in this way, and in flattering your self-love, you allow yourselves to sleep in the arms of a slave, and thus dissipate your energy, the better to rivet your own chains.

Respected legislators, would you weigh down with irons the hands which have helped you to raise the altar of the fatherland with such ardor? Would you transform into slaves those women who have contributed with such zeal to making you free? . . . No, no, conjugal authority can only be the result of the social pact. The wisdom of the legislation and the general interest demand a balance between despotism and license; but the powers of the husband and the wife must be equal and individual.

Source: Etta Palm d'Aelders, "Adresse des citoyennes françoises à l'assemblée nationale," *Appel aux françoises sur la régénération des moeurs, et nécessité de l'influence des femmes dans un gouvernement libre* (Paris: Imprimerie du Cercle Social, 1791), pp. 37–39.

Questions for Analysis

1. How does d'Aelders use the logic of the revolution itself to appeal to the members of the National Assembly?

2. What is the view of marriage represented by the article in the Police Code? What is the contrasting view put forth by d'Aelders?

3. How does d'Aelders's speech contrast the legal system of the old monarchy with the new laws passed by the Assembly?

---

won the enthusiastic support of a wide range of thinkers. The British poet William Wordsworth, who later became disillusioned, recalled his initial mood: "Bliss was it in that dawn to be alive." His sentiments were echoed across the Continent by poets and philosophers, including the German Johann Gottfried von Herder, who declared the revolution the most important historical moment since the Reformation. In Britain, the Low Countries, western Germany, and Italy, "patriots" proclaimed their allegiance to the new revolution.

Others opposed the revolution from the start. Exiled nobles, who fled France for sympathetic royal courts in Germany and elsewhere, did all they could to stir up counterrevolutionary sentiment. In Britain, the conservative cause was strengthened by the publication of Edmund Burke's *Reflections on the Revolution in France* in 1790.

Competing Viewpoints

Debating the French Revolution: Edmund Burke and Thomas Paine

The best-known debate on the French Revolution set the Irish-born conservative Edmund Burke against the British radical Thomas Paine. Burke opposed the French Revolution from the beginning. His Reflections on the Revolution in France was published early, in 1790, when the French king was still securely on the throne. Burke disagreed with the premises of the revolution. Rights, he argued, were not abstract and "natural" but the results of specific historical traditions. Remodeling the French government without reference to the past and failing to pay proper respect to tradition and custom had, in his eyes, destroyed the fabric of French civilization.

Thomas Paine was one of many to respond to Burke. In The Rights of Man (1791–1792), he defended the revolution and, more generally, conceptions of human rights. In the polarized atmosphere of the revolutionary wars, simply possessing Paine's pamphlet was cause for imprisonment in Britain.

Edmund Burke

You will observe, that from the Magna Carta to the Declaration of Rights, it has been the uniform policy of our constitution to claim and assert our liberties, as an entailed inheritance derived to us from our forefathers. . . . We have an inheritable crown; an inheritable peerage; and a house of commons and a people inheriting privileges, franchises, and liberties, from a long line of ancestors. . . .

You had all these advantages in your ancient states, but you chose to act as if you had never been moulded into civil society, and had every thing to begin anew. You began ill, because you began by despising every thing that belonged to you. . . . If the last genera-

tions of your country appeared without much luster in your eyes, you might have passed them by, and derived your claims from a more early race of ancestors. . . . Respecting your forefathers, you would have been taught to respect yourselves. You would not have chosen to consider the French as a people of yesterday, as a nation of low-born servile wretches until the emancipating year of 1789. . . . [Y]ou would not have been content to be represented as a gang of Maroon slaves, suddenly broke loose from the house of bondage, and therefore to be pardoned for your abuse of liberty to which you were not accustomed and ill fitted. . . .

. . . The fresh ruins of France, which shock our feelings wherever we can

turn our eyes, are not the devastation of civil war; they are the sad but instructive monuments of rash and ignorant council in time of profound peace. They are the display of inconsiderate and presumptuous, because unresisted and irresistible authority. . . .

Nothing is more certain, than that of our manners, our civilization, and all the good things which are connected with manners, and with civilization, have, in this European world of ours, depended upon two principles; and were indeed the result of both combined; I mean the spirit of a gentleman, and the spirit of religion. The nobility and the clergy, the one by profession, the other by patronage, kept learning in existence, even in

---

A Whig politician who had sympathized with the American revolutionaries, Burke deemed the revolution in France a monstrous crime against the social order (see **Competing Viewpoints** above).

Burke's famous book aroused some sympathy for the counterrevolutionary cause, but active opposition came slowly. The first European states to express public concern about events in revolutionary France were Austria and Prussia, declaring in 1791 that order and the rights

of the monarch of France were matters of "common interest to all sovereigns of Europe." The leaders of the French assembly pronounced the declaration an affront to national sovereignty. Nobles who had fled France played into their hands with plots and pronouncements against the government. It was perhaps odd that both supporters and opponents of the revolution in France believed war would serve their cause. The National Assembly's leaders expected an aggressive policy would shore up the people's loyalty and the midst of arms and confusions. . . . Learning paid back what it received to nobility and priesthood. . . . Happy if they had all continued to know their indissoluble union, and their proper place.

Happy if learning, not debauched by ambition, had been satisfied to continue the instructor, and not aspired to be the master! Along with its natural protectors and guardians, learning will be cast into the mire, and trodden down under the hoofs of a swinish multitude.

Source: Edmund Burke, *Reflections on the Revolution in France* (1790; New York: 1973), pp. 45, 48, 49, 52, 92.

Thomas Paine

Mr. Burke, with his usual outrage, abuses the *Declaration of the Rights of Man*. . . . Does Mr. Burke mean to deny that man has any rights? If he does, then he must mean that there are no such things as rights any where, and that he has none himself; for who is there in the world but man? But if Mr. Burke means to admit that man has rights, the question will then be, what are those rights, and how came man by them originally?

The error of those who reason by precedents drawn from antiquity, respecting the rights of man, is that they do not go far enough into antiquity. They stop in some of the intermediate stages of an hundred or a thousand years, and produce what was then a rule for the present day. This is no authority at all. . . .

To possess ourselves of a clear idea of what government is, or ought to be, we must trace its origin. In doing this, we shall easily discover that governments must have arisen either *out* of the people, or *over* the people. Mr. Burke has made no distinction. . . .

What were formerly called revolutions, were little more than a change of persons, or an alteration of local circumstances. They rose and fell like things of course, and had nothing in their existence or their fate that could influence beyond the spot that produced them. But what we now see in the world, from the revolutions of America and France, is a renovation of the natural order of things, a system of principles as universal as truth and the existence of man, and combining moral with political happiness and national prosperity.

Source: Thomas Paine, *The Rights of Man* (1791; New York: 1973), pp. 302, 308, 383.

Questions for Analysis

1. How does Burke define *liberty*? Why does he criticize the revolutionaries for representing themselves as slaves freed from bondage?

2. What does Paine criticize about Burke's emphasis on history? According to Paine, what makes the French Revolution different from previous changes of regime in Europe?

3. How do these two authors' attitudes about the origins of human freedoms shape their understandings of the revolution?

---

bring freedom to the rest of Europe. Counterrevolutionaries hoped the intervention of Austria and Prussia would undo all that had happened since 1789. Radicals, suspicious of aristocratic leaders and the king, believed that war would expose traitors with misgivings about the revolution and flush out those who sympathized with the king and European tyrants. On April 20, 1792, the assembly declared war against Austria and Prussia. Thus began the war that would keep the Continent in arms for a generation.

As the radicals expected, the French forces met serious reverses. By August 1792, the allied armies of Austria and Prussia had crossed the frontier and were threatening to capture Paris. Many, including soldiers, believed that the military disasters were evidence of the king's treason. On August 10, Parisian crowds, organized by their radical leaders, attacked the royal palace. The king was imprisoned, and a second and far more radical revolution began.

The French Republic

From this point, the country's leadership passed into the hands of the more egalitarian leaders of the Third Estate. These new leaders were known as **Jacobins**, the name of a political club to which many of them belonged. Although their headquarters was in Paris, their membership extended throughout France. And even though their members included large numbers of professionals, government officeholders, and lawyers, they proclaimed themselves spokesmen for the people and the nation. An increasing number of artisans joined Jacobin clubs as the movement grew, and other, more democratic clubs expanded as well.

The **National Convention**, elected by free white men, became the effective governing body of the country for the next three years. It was elected in September 1792, at a time when enemy troops were advancing and spreading panic.

Rumors flew that prisoners in Paris were plotting to aid the enemy. And so they were hauled from their cells, dragged before hastily convened tribunals, and executed. In the "September Massacres," more than a thousand "enemies of the Revolution" were killed in less than a week. Similar riots engulfed Lyons, Orléans, and other French cities.

The newly elected Convention was far more radical than its predecessor, and its leadership was determined to end the monarchy. On September 21, the Convention declared France a republic; in December, it placed the king on trial; and in January 1793, it condemned the king to death by a narrow margin. The heir to the grand tradition of French absolutism met his end bravely as "citizen Louis Capet," beheaded by the guillotine. Introduced as a swifter and more humane form of execution, the frightful mechanical headsman came to symbolize revolutionary fervor.

The Convention took other radical measures. It confiscated the properties of the enemies of the revolution, breaking

THE EXECUTION OF LOUIS XVI. The execution of Louis XVI shocked Europe. Even committed revolutionaries in France debated the necessity of such a dramatic act. The entire National Convention (more than 700 members) acted as jury, and although the assembly was nearly unanimous in finding the king guilty of treason, a majority of only one approved the final death sentence. Those who voted for Louis XVI's execution were known forever after as "regicides." ■ *What made this act necessary from the point of view of the most radical of revolutionaries?* ■ *What made it repugnant from the point of view of the revolution's most heated enemies?*

up some large estates and selling them on easier terms to less wealthy citizens. It abruptly canceled the policy of compensating nobles for their lost privileges. It repealed primogeniture, so that property would not be inherited exclusively by the oldest son but divided in substantially equal portions among all immediate heirs. It abolished slavery in French colonies (see pages 616–618). It set maximum prices for grain and other necessities. In an astonishing effort to root out Christianity from everyday life, the convention adopted a new calendar. The calendar year began with the birth of the republic (September 22, 1792) and divided months in such a way as to eliminate the Catholic Sunday.

Most of these programs were a hastily improvised response to crisis and political pressure from the common people in the cities and their leaders. In the three years after 1790, prices had risen staggeringly: wheat by 27 percent, beef by 136 percent, and potatoes by 700 percent. While the government imposed its maximums in Paris, small vigilante militias, representing the sans-culottes, attacked those they considered hoarders and profiteers.

The Convention also reorganized its armies, with astonishing success. By February 1793, Britain, Holland, Spain, and Austria were in the field against the French. Britain came into the war for strategic and economic reasons: it feared a French threat to Britain's growing global power. The allied coalition, though united only in its desire to contain France, was nevertheless a formidable force. To counter it, the revolutionary government mustered all men capable of bearing arms. The revolution flung fourteen hastily drafted armies into battle under the leadership of newly promoted young and inexperienced officers. What they lacked in training and discipline they made up for in organization, mobility, flexibility, courage, and morale. In 1793–1794, the French armies preserved their homeland. In 1794–1795, they occupied the Low Countries, the Rhineland, and parts of Spain, Switzerland, and Savoy. In 1796, they invaded and occupied key parts of Italy and broke the coalition that had arrayed itself against them.

The Reign of Terror

In 1793, those victories lay in a hard-to-imagine future. France was in crisis. The Convention drafted a new democratic constitution based on male suffrage, but it never took effect—suspended indefinitely by wartime emergency. Instead, the Convention prolonged its own life year after year and increasingly delegated its responsibilities to a group of twelve leaders, the Committee of Public Safety, created in April 1793. The Committee's ruthlessness had two purposes: to seize control of the revolution and to prosecute

all the revolution's enemies—"to make terror the order of the day." The Committee's reign lasted less than two years, but the Terror left a bloody and authoritarian legacy.

Perhaps the three best-known leaders of the radical revolution were Jean Paul Marat, Georges Danton, and Maximilien Robespierre (the latter two, members of the Committee of Public Safety). Marat was educated as a physician, and by 1789, he had already earned enough distinction in that profession to be awarded an honorary degree by St. Andrews University in Scotland. He opposed nearly all of his moderate colleagues' assumptions, including their admiration for Great Britain, which he considered corrupt and despotic. Persecuted by powerful factions in the constituent assembly who feared his radicalism, Marat was forced to take refuge in sewers and dungeons. He persevered as the editor of the popular news sheet *The Friend of the People*. Exposure to infection left him with a chronic and painful skin disease, from which baths provided the only relief. In July 1793, at the height of the crisis of the revolution, he was stabbed in his bath by Charlotte Corday, a young royalist, and thus became a revolutionary martyr.

Danton, like Marat, was a popular political leader, well known in the more plebeian clubs of Paris. Elected a member of the Committee of Public Safety in 1793, he had much

THE DEATH OF MARAT. This painting by the French artist Jacques-Louis David in 1793 immortalized Marat. The note in the slain leader's hand is from Charlotte Corday, his assassin.
- *Why was it important to represent Marat as a martyr?*

to do with organizing the Terror. As time went on, however, he wearied of ruthlessness and displayed a tendency to compromise, which gave his opponents in the convention their opportunity. In April 1794, Danton was sent to the guillotine. He is reported to have said, upon mounting the scaffold, "Show my head to the people; they do not see the like every day."

The most famous of the radical leaders was Maximilien Robespierre. Born of a family reputed to be of Irish descent, he trained in law and quickly became a modestly

ROBESPIERRE GUILLOTINING THE EXECUTIONER. The original caption for this 1793 engraving read "Robespierre guillotines the executioner after having had all the French guillotined." In fact, Robespierre himself was guillotined after his fall from power in July 1794. ■ *What made the struggle for power and authority among the revolutionaries so merciless and uncompromising?*

successful lawyer. His eloquence and his consistent, or ruthless, insistence that leaders respect the "will of the people" eventually won him a following in the Jacobin club. Later, he became president of the National Convention and a member of the Committee of Public Safety. Though he had little to do with starting the Terror, he was nevertheless responsible for enlarging its scope. Known as the "Incorruptible," he came to personify ruthlessness justified as virtue and necessary to revolutionary progress.

The two years of the radical republic (August 1792–July 1794) brought dictatorship, centralization, suspension of liberties, and war. The committee faced foreign enemies and opposition from both the political right and left at home. In June 1793, in response to an escalating crisis, leaders of the "Mountain," a party of radicals allied with Parisian artisans, purged moderates from the Convention. Rebellions broke out in the provincial cities of Lyons, Bordeaux, and Marseilles, mercilessly repressed by the committee and its local representatives. The government also faced counterrevolution in the western region known as the Vendée, where movements enlisted peasants and artisans who believed their local areas were being invaded, and who fought for their local priest or against the summons from the revolutionaries' conscription boards. By the summer, the forces in the Vendée posed a serious threat to the convention. And the committee, determined to stabilize France whatever the cost, redeployed its forces, defeated the counterrevolutionaries, and launched murderous campaigns of pacification—torching villages, farms, and fields; and killing all who dared oppose them, and many who did not.

In September 1793, the Convention passed the Law of Suspects, which allowed the revolutionary authorities to arrest and detain individuals seen as enemies of the state. During the next ten months the Terror reached its climax. The most reliable estimates place the number of deaths at close to 40,000; about 16,500 deaths resulted from official executions, and the rest from extrajudicial killings in prison. Approximately 300,000 people were incarcerated between March 1793 and August 1794. These numbers, however, do not include the pacification of the Vendée and rebellious cities in the Rhone Valley, which cost more than 100,000 lives. Few victims of the Terror were aristocrats; many more were peasants or laborers accused of hoarding, treason, or counterrevolutionary activity. Anyone who appeared to threaten the republic, no matter what his or her social or economic position, was at risk. When some time later the Abbé Sieyès was asked what he had done to distinguish himself during the Terror, he responded dryly, "I lived."

The Legacy of the Second French Revolution

The "second" French Revolution affected the everyday life of French men, women, and children in a remarkably direct way. Workers' trousers replaced the breeches that had been a sartorial badge of the middle classes and the nobility. A red cap, said to symbolize freedom from slavery, became popular headgear, and wigs vanished. Men and women addressed each other as "citizen" and "citizeness." Public life was marked by ceremonies designed to dramatize the break from the Old Regime and celebrate new forms of fraternity. In the early stages of the revolution, these festivals seem to have captured genuine popular enthusiasm for new ways of living and thinking. Once under the Committee of Public Safety, however, they became didactic and hollow.

The radical revolution of 1792–1793 also dramatically reversed the trend toward decentralization and democracy. The assembly replaced local officials, some of them still royalist in sympathy, with "deputies on mission," whose task was to conscript troops and generate patriotic fervor. When these deputies appeared too eager to act independently, they were replaced by "national agents," with instructions to report directly to the committee. In another effort to stabilize authority, the assembly closed down all the women's political clubs, decreeing them a political and social danger. It was ironic that those who claimed to govern in the name of the people found the popular movement threatening.

PATRIOTIC WOMEN'S CLUB. The members of this patriotic club wear constitutional bonnets to show their support for the revolution and the reforms of the convention. ▪ *What can we conclude about the atmosphere in Paris during the revolution from the existence of such associations?*

Finally, the revolution eroded the strength of those traditional institutions—church, guild, parish—that had for centuries given people a common bond. In their place now stood patriotic organizations and a culture that insisted on loyalty to one national cause. Those organizations had first emerged with the election campaigns, meetings, and pamphlet wars of 1788 and the interest they heightened. They included political clubs and local assemblies, which at the height of the revolution (1792–1793) met every day of the week and offered an apprenticeship in politics. The army of the republic became the premier national institution.

On the one hand, the revolution divided France, mobilizing counterrevolutionaries as well as revolutionaries. At the same time, the revolution, war, and culture of sacrifice forged new bonds. The sense that the rest of Europe, carrying what the verses of the "Marseillaise," the most famous anthem of the revolution, called the "blood-stained flag of tyranny," sought to crush the new nation and its citizens unquestionably strengthened French national identity.

FROM THE TERROR TO BONAPARTE: THE DIRECTORY

The Committee of Public Safety might have saved France from enemy armies, but it could not save itself. Inflation became catastrophic. The long string of military victories convinced growing numbers that the committee's demands for continuing self-sacrifice and terror were no longer justified. By July 1794, the committee was virtually without allies. On July 27 (9 Thermidor, according to the new calendar), Robespierre was shouted down while attempting to speak on the floor of the Convention. The following day, along with twenty-one other conspirators, he met his death by guillotine.

Ending the Terror did not immediately bring moderation. Vigilante groups of royalists hunted down Jacobins. The repeal of price controls, combined with the worst winter in a century, caused widespread misery. Gradually, other measures that had constituted the Terror were repealed. In 1795, the National Convention adopted a new and more conservative constitution. It granted suffrage to adult male citizens who paid a certain amount of taxes, and it set up indirect elections: citizens voted for electors, who in turn chose the legislative body. Wealthy citizens thus held authority. Eager to avoid personal dictatorship, the convention vested executive authority in a board of five men chosen by the legislative body, known as the Directory. The new constitution included not only a bill of rights but also a declaration of the duties of the citizen.

The Directory still faced discontent on both the radical left and the conservative right but lasted longer than its revolutionary predecessors. On the left, the Directory repressed radical movements to abolish private property and parliamentary-style government, including one led by the radical "Gracchus Babeuf." Dispatching threats from the right proved more challenging, however. In 1797, the first free elections held in France as a republic returned a large number of monarchists to the councils of government, alarming the politicians who had voted to execute Louis XVI. Backed by the army, the Directory annulled most of the election results. After two years of more uprisings and purges, and with the country still plagued by severe inflation,

FRANCE AND ITS SISTER REPUBLICS. ■ *The French revolutionaries, fighting against the conservative monarchs of Europe, conquered and annexed large sections of which three countries?* ■ *Who were the potential supporters of the French Revolution in areas outside France during the Napoleonic era?* ■ *Who was most likely to oppose it in these areas?*

the Directory grew desperate. This time they called for help from a brilliant young general named Napoleon Bonaparte.

Bonaparte's first military victory had come in 1793, with the recapture of Toulon from royalist and British forces, which had earned him promotion from captain to brigadier general at the age of twenty-four. After the Terror, he was briefly arrested for his Jacobin associations. But he proved his usefulness to the Directory in October 1795, when he put down an uprising with "a whiff of grapeshot," saving the new regime from its opponents. Promoted, he won a string of victories in Italy, forcing Austria to withdraw (temporarily) from the war. He attempted to defeat Britain by attacking British forces in Egypt and the Near East, a campaign that went well on land but ran into trouble at sea, where the French fleet was defeated by Admiral Horatio Nelson (Abukir Bay, 1798). Bonaparte found himself trapped in Egypt by the British and was unable to win a decisive victory.

It was at this point that the call came from the Directory. Bonaparte slipped away from Egypt and appeared in Paris, already having agreed to participate in a coup d'état with the leading Director, the former revolutionary champion of the Third Estate, Abbé Sieyès. On November 9, 1799 (18 Brumaire), Bonaparte was declared a "temporary consul." He was the answer to the Directory's prayers: a strong, popular leader who was not a king. Sieyès declared that Bonaparte would provide "[c]onfidence from below, authority from above." With these words, Sieyès pronounced the end of the revolutionary period.

NAPOLEON AND IMPERIAL FRANCE

Few figures in Western history have compelled the attention of the world as Napoleon Bonaparte did during the fifteen years of his rule in France. Even fewer lived on with such persistence as myth, not just in their own countries but across the West. Why? For the great majority of ordinary Europeans, memories of the French Revolution were dominated by those of the Napoleonic Wars, which devastated Europe, convulsed its politics, and traumatized its peoples for a generation.

Yet Bonaparte's relationship to the revolution was not simple. His regime consolidated some of the revolution's political and social changes but sharply repudiated others. He presented himself as the son of the revolution, but he also borrowed freely from very different regimes, fashioning himself as the heir to Charlemagne or to the Roman Empire. His regime remade revolutionary politics and the French state, offered stunning examples of the new kinds of warfare, and left a legacy of conflict and legends of French glory that lingered in the dreams, or nightmares, of Europe's statesmen and citizens for more than a century.

Consolidating Authority: 1799–1804

Bonaparte's early career reinforced the claim that the revolution rewarded the efforts of able men. The son of a provincial Corsican nobleman, he attended the École Militaire in Paris. In prerevolutionary France he would have been unable to rise beyond the rank of major, which required buying a regimental command. The revolution, however, abolished the purchase of military office, and Bonaparte quickly became a general. Here, then, was a man who had risen from obscurity because of his own gifts, which he lent happily to the service of France's revolution.

Once in power, however, Bonaparte showed less respect for revolutionary principles. After the coup of 1799, he assumed the title of first consul. A new constitution established universal white male suffrage and set up two legislative bodies. Elections, however, were indirect, and the power of the legislative bodies sharply curbed. "The government?" said one observer. "There is Bonaparte." Bonaparte instituted what has since become a common authoritarian device, the plebiscite, which puts a question directly to popular vote. This allowed the head of state to bypass politicians or legislative bodies that might disagree with him—as well as permitted local officials to tamper with ballot boxes. In 1802, flush with victory abroad, Bonaparte asked the legislature to proclaim him consul for life. When the Senate refused, Bonaparte's Council of State stepped in, offering him the title and having it ratified by plebiscite. Throughout, his regime retained the appearance of consulting with the people, but its most important feature was the centralization of authority.

That authority came from reorganizing the state, and on this score, Bonaparte's accomplishments were extraordinary and lasting. Bonaparte's regime confirmed the abolition of privilege, thereby promising "careers open to talent." Centralizing administrative departments, he accomplished what no recent French regime had yet achieved: an orderly and generally fair system of taxation. More efficient tax collection and fiscal management also helped halt the inflationary spiral that had crippled the revolutionary governments, although Bonaparte's regime relied heavily on resources from areas he had conquered to fund his military ventures. As we have seen, earlier revolutionary regimes began to reorganize France's administration—abolishing the ancient fiefdoms with their separate governments, legal codes, privileges, and customs—setting up a uniform system of depart-

ments. Bonaparte continued that work, pressing it further and putting an accent on centralization. He replaced elected officials and local self-government with centrally appointed prefects and subprefects, who answered directly to the Council of State in Paris. The prefects wielded considerable power, much more than any elected representative: they were in charge of everything from collecting statistics and reporting on the economy and the population, to education, roads, and public works. With more integrated administration in which the different branches were coordinated (and supervised from above), more professional bureaucracy, and more rational and efficient taxation (though the demands of war strained the system), Napoleon's rule marked the transition from Bourbon absolutism to the modern state.

Law, Education, and a New Elite

Napoleon's most significant contribution to modern state building was the promulgation of a new legal code in 1804. Each revolutionary regime had taken up the daunting task of modernizing the laws—and each had run out of time. Napoleon tolerated no delays and threw himself into the project, pressing his own ideas and supervising half the meetings. After its passage in France, Napoleon imposed the Civil Code's provisions on many of the territories that he later conquered elsewhere in Europe, making it the basis of the modern legal system in much of the continent.

The Napoleonic Code, as the civil code came to be called, pivoted on two principles that had remained significant through all the constitutional changes since 1789: uniformity and individualism. It cleared through the thicket of contradictory legal traditions that governed the ancient provinces of France, creating one uniform law. It confirmed the abolition of feudal privileges of all kinds, not only noble and clerical privileges but the special rights of craft guilds, municipalities, and so on. It set the conditions for exercising property rights, such as the drafting of contracts, leases, and stock companies. The code's provisions on the family, which Napoleon developed personally, insisted on the importance of paternal authority and the subordination of women and children. In 1793, during the most radical period of the revolution, men and women had been declared "equal in marriage"; now, Napoleon's code affirmed the "natural supremacy" of the husband. Married women could not sell property, run a business, or practice a profession without their husbands' permission. Fathers had the sole right to control their children's financial affairs, consent to their marriages, and (under the ancient right to correction) imprison them for up to six months without showing cause. Divorce remained legal, but under unequal conditions: a man could sue for divorce on the grounds

Interpreting Visual Evidence

Representing the People during the French Revolution

From the moment the population of Paris came to the assistance of the beleaguered National Assembly in July 1789, representations of "the people" in the French Revolution took on an overwhelming significance. Building a new government that was committed to the idea of popular sovereignty meant that both the revolution's supporters and its opponents were deeply invested in shaping perceptions of the people. And of course, Article 3 of the Declaration of the Rights of Man ("The source of all sovereignty resides essentially in

the nation") meant that any individual, group, or institution that could successfully claim to represent the will of the people could wield tremendous power, as long as others accepted that claim.

The revolutionary crowds, however, did not always conform to the images of them that circulated so widely in prints and paintings during the period 1789–1799. Some were spontaneous, and others were organized; some were made up of recognizable social and professional groups with clear political goals, and others were a hodgepodge of conflicting and even inarticulate aspirations; many were nonviolent, but some were exceed-

ingly threatening and murderous. Regardless, all politicians sought to use them to support their political programs, and many learned to fear their unpredictable behavior.

These four images give a sense of the competing visions of the people that appeared in the public realm during the French Revolution. The first (image A) shows the killing of Foulon, a royal official who was lynched and beheaded by an enthusiastic crowd barely a week after the fall of the Bastille, because he was suspected of conspiring to starve the Parisian population as punishment for their rebellion against the king. The

A. The punishment of Foulon (anonymous print, 1789).

B. *The Festival of Federation* by Charles Thévenin, 1790.

second (image B) shows a more carefully choreographed representation of the people during the Festival of Federation, organized in July 1790 by the revolutionary government to commemorate the first anniversary of the fall of the Bastille. Finally, the last two illustrations show contrasting images of the revolutionary sans-culottes, the working-class revolutionaries who supported the government during the Terror in 1792–1794. The first (image C) is a sympathetic portrait of sans-culottes as a virtuous and self-sacrificing working man, standing with an eye to the future. Completely incongruous is the British satirist James Gilray's portrait of a cannibalistic sans-culottes family (image D), drawn literally "without pants," feasting on the bodies of their victims after a hard day's work.

Questions for Analysis

1. Image A depicts an event from July 1789, before the August publication of the Declaration of the Rights of Man. How does this image portray the crowd's vengeance on Foulon? What possible political messages are contained in this image?

2. Image B, on the other hand, chooses to display the people celebrating their own birth as a political body, by convening on the anniversary of the fall of the Bastille. What emotions is this painting designed to invoke? How does it relate to the more disturbing images such as image A?

3. How are the positive and negative portrayals of sans-culottes as political actors (images C and D) constructed? Can we imagine a painting of a worker such as in image C being produced before 1789? What does image D tell us about how the revolution was viewed from Britain?

C. An idealized sans-culotte painting by Louis-Léopold Boilly, 1792.

D. A British satirical cartoon of "a family of sans-culottes refreshing after the fatigues of the day" by James Gillray, 1792.

of adultery, but a woman could do so only if her husband moved his "concubine" into the family's house. Most important to the common people, the code prohibited paternity suits for illegitimate children.

In all, Napoleon developed seven legal codes covering commercial law, civil law and procedures, crime, and punishment. Like the civil code, the new criminal code consolidated some of the gains of the revolution, treating citizens as equals before the law and outlawing arbitrary arrest and imprisonment. Yet, it also reinstated brutal measures that the revolutionaries had abolished, such as branding and cutting off the hands of parricides. The Napoleonic legal regime was more egalitarian than the law under the Old Regime, but it was no less concerned with authority.

Napoleon also rationalized the educational system. He ordered the establishment of *lycées* (high schools) in every major town to train civil servants and army officers, and a school in Paris to train teachers. To supplement these changes, Napoleon brought the military and technical schools under state control and founded a national university to supervise the entire system. It is not surprising that he built up a new military academy. He reorganized and established solid financing for the premier schools of higher education: the polytechnic (for engineers) and the normal (for teachers), to which students would be admitted based on examinations and from which the technical, educational, and political elites of the country would emerge. Like almost all of his reforms, this one reinforced reforms introduced during the revolution and intended to abolish privilege and create "careers open to talent." Napoleon also embraced the burgeoning social and physical sciences of the Enlightenment. He sponsored the Institute of France, divided into four sections, or academies: fine arts, sciences, humanities, and language (the famous Académie française). These academies dated back to the age of absolutism, but now they were coordinated and put on a new footing. Under Napoleon, they acquired the character they have preserved to this day: centralized, meritocratic, and geared to serving the state.

Who benefited from these changes? Like Napoleon's other new institutions, the new schools helped confirm the power of a new elite. The new elite included businessmen, bankers, and merchants, but was still composed primarily of powerful landowners. What was more, at least half of the fellowships to the high schools went to the sons of military officers and high civil servants. Finally, like most of his reforms, changes in education aimed to strengthen the empire: "My object in establishing a teaching corps is to have a means of directing political and moral opinion," Napoleon said bluntly.

Napoleon's early measures were ambitious, and to win support for them, he made allies without regard to their past political affiliations. He admitted back into the country exiles of all political stripes. His two fellow consuls were a regicide of the Terror and a bureaucrat of the Old Regime. His minister of police had been an extreme radical republican, and his minister of foreign affairs was the aristocrat and opportunist Charles Talleyrand. The most remarkable act of political reconciliation came in 1801, with his concordat with the pope, an agreement that put an end to more than a decade of hostility between the French state and the Catholic Church. Although it shocked anticlerical revolutionaries, Napoleon, ever the pragmatist, believed that reconciliation would create domestic harmony and international solidarity. The agreement gave the pope the right to depose French bishops and discipline the French clergy. In return, the Vatican agreed to forgo any claims to Church lands expropriated by the revolution. That property would remain in the hands of its new middle-class rural and urban proprietors. The concordat did not revoke the principle of religious freedom established by the revolution, but it did win Napoleon the support of conservatives who had feared for France's future as a godless state.

Such political balancing acts increased Napoleon's general popularity, and, combined with early military successes (peace with Austria in 1801 and with Britain in 1802), they muffled any opposition to his personal ambitions. He had married Josephine de Beauharnais, a Creole from Martinique and an influential mistress of the revolutionary period. Josephine had given the Corsican soldier-politician legitimacy and access among the revolutionary elite early in his career. Neither Napoleon nor his ambitious wife were content to be first among equals, however; and in December of 1804, he finally cast aside any traces of republicanism. In a ceremony that evoked the splendor of medieval kingship and Bourbon absolutism, he crowned himself Emperor Napoleon I in the Cathedral of Notre Dame in Paris. Napoleon did much to create the modern state, but he did not hesitate to proclaim his links to the past.

In Europe as in France: Napoleon's Empire

The nations of Europe had looked on—some in admiration, others in horror, and all in astonishment—at the phenomenon that was Napoleon. Austria, Prussia, and Britain led two coalitions against revolutionary France in 1792–1795 and in 1798; both were defeated. After Napoleon came to power in 1799, the alliance split. Russia and Austria withdrew from the fray in 1801, and even the intransigent British were forced to make peace the following year.

By 1805, the Russians, Austrians, and Swedes had joined the British in an attempt to contain France, to no avail. Even after Prussia joined the coalition in 1806, Napoleon's military superiority led to defeats, in turn, of all the continental allies. Napoleon was a master of well-timed, well-directed shock attacks on the battlefield: movement, regrouping, and pressing his advantage. He led an army that had transformed European warfare. First raised as a revolutionary militia, it was now a trained conscript army—loyal, well supplied by a nation whose economy was committed to serving the war effort, and led by generals promoted largely on the basis of talent. This new kind of army inflicted crushing defeats on his enemies. The battle of Austerlitz, in December 1805, was a triumph for the French against the combined forces of Austria and Russia, and it became a symbol of the emperor's apparent invincibility. His subsequent victories against the Prussians at Jena and against the Russians at Friedland in 1807 only added to his reputation.

Out of these victories, Napoleon created his new empire and affiliated states. To the southeast, the empire included Rome and the pope's dominions, Tuscany, and the Dalmatian territories of Austria (now the coastline of Croatia). To the east, Napoleon's rule extended over a

NAPOLEON'S EUROPEAN EMPIRE AT ITS HEIGHT. At the height of his power in 1812, Napoleon controlled most of Europe, ruling either directly or through dependent states and allies. ▪ *Compare this map with the one on page 604. By what means had Napoleon expanded French control on continental Europe?* ▪ *Which major countries remained outside of French control?* ▪ *Which areas felt the longest-lasting impact of Napoleon's reign?*

NAPOLEON ON HORSEBACK AT THE ST. BERNARD PASS, BY JACQUES-LOUIS DAVID (1801), AND LITTLE BONEY GONE TO POT, BY GEORGE CRUIKSHANK (1814). The depth of Napoleon's celebrity in Europe can be measured in the equal shares of adulation and hatred that he stirred up within Europe among his supporters and his enemies. Jacques-Louis David's portrait, painted before Napoleon became emperor of France, captures the ardent hopes that many attached to his person. The painting explicitly compared Napoleon to two previous European conquerors, Charlemagne and the ancient Carthaginian general Hannibal, by evoking their names in the stones at the base of the painting. In George Cruikshank's bitter caricature, published after Napoleon's exile to Elba, the devil offers him a pistol to commit suicide, and the former emperor, seated on a chamber pot, says he might, but only if the firing mechanism is disabled. Both images use assumptions about virility and masculine authority to make their point. ▪ *Who are the intended audiences for these images?* ▪ *How do they convey their respective arguments?*

federation of German states known as the Confederation of the Rhine and a section of Poland. These new states were presented as France's gift of independence to patriots elsewhere in Europe, but in practice, they were a military buffer against renewed expansion by Austria. The empire itself was ringed by the allied kingdoms of Italy, Naples, Spain, and Holland. Napoleon himself was King of Italy, and his brothers, brothers-in-law, and trusted generals ruled in the other kingdoms.

The empire brought the French Revolution's practical consequences—a powerful, centralizing state and an end to old systems of privilege—to Europe's doorstep, applying to the conquered European territories the principles that had already transformed France. Administrative modernization, which meant overhauling the procedures, codes, and practices of the state, was the most powerful feature of changes introduced. The empire changed the terms of government service (careers open to talent), handing out new titles and recruiting new men for the civil service and the judiciary; and it ended the nobility's monopoly on the officer corps.

The new branches of government hired engineers, mapmakers, surveyors, and legal consultants. Public works and education were reorganized. Prefects in the outer reaches of the empire, as in France, built roads, bridges, dikes (in Holland), hospitals, and prisons; and reorganized universities and built observatories. In the empire and some of the satellite kingdoms, tariffs were eliminated, feudal dues abolished, new tax districts formed, and plentiful new taxes collected to support the new state.

In the realm of liberty and law, Napoleon's rule eliminated feudal and church courts and created a single legal system. The Napoleonic Code was often introduced, but not always or entirely. In southern Italy, measures against the Catholic Church were deemed too controversial. Reforms eliminated many inequalities and legal privileges but not all. The Duchy of Warsaw in Poland ended serfdom but offered no land reform, so former serfs became impoverished tenants. In most areas, the empire gave civil rights to Protestants and Jews. In Rome, the conquering French opened the gates of the Jewish ghetto—and made

Jews subject to conscription. In some areas, Catholic monasteries, convents, and other landholdings were broken up and sold, almost always to wealthy buyers. In the empire as in France, and under Napoleon as during the revolution, many who benefited were the elite: people and groups already on their way up and with the resources to take advantage of the opportunities.

In government, the regime sought a combination of legal equality (for men) and stronger state authority. The French and local authorities created new electoral districts, expanded the suffrage, and wrote constitutions, but newly elected representative bodies were dismissed if they failed to cooperate, few constitutions were ever fully applied, and political freedoms were often fleeting. Napoleon's regime referred to revolutionary principles to anchor its legitimacy, but authority remained its guiding light. All governmental direction emanated from Paris and therefore from Napoleon.

Finally, in the empire as in France, Napoleon displayed his signature passions. The first of these was an Enlightenment zeal for accumulating useful knowledge. The empire gathered statistics as never before, for it was important to know the resources—including population—that a state had at its disposal. That spirit had been evident already in Napoleon's extraordinary 1798 excursion into Egypt. He took hundreds of scholars and artists along with the army, founded the Institute of Egypt in Cairo, and sent researchers off to make a systematic inventory of the country (its geology, rivers, minerals, antiquities, animal life) and conduct archaeological expeditions to Upper Egypt, where they sketched the pyramids and excavated what would turn out to be the Rosetta Stone (see Chapter 20). Napoleon's second passion was cultivating his relationship to imperial glories of the past. He poured time and energy into (literally) cementing his image for posterity. The Arc de Triomphe in Paris, designed to imitate the Arch of Constantine in Rome, is the best example, but Napoleon also ordered work be undertaken to restore ruins in Rome, to make the Prado Palace in Madrid a museum, and to renovate and preserve the Alhambra in Granada.

Such were Napoleon's visions of his legacy and himself. How did others see him? Europe offered no single reaction. Some countries and social groups collaborated enthusiastically, some negotiated, and some resisted. Napoleon's image as a military hero genuinely inspired young men from the elite, raised in a culture that prized military honor. By contrast, Catholic peasants in Spain fought him from the beginning. In many small principalities previously ruled by princes—the patchwork states of Germany, for example, and the repressive kingdom of Naples—reforms that provided for more efficient and less corrupt administration, a

workable tax structure, and an end to customary privilege were welcomed by most of the local population. Yet the Napoleonic presence proved a mixed blessing. Vassal states contributed heavily to the maintenance of the emperor's military power. The French levied taxes, drafted men, and required states to support occupying armies. In Italy, the policy was called "liberty and requisitions"; and the Italians, Germans, and Dutch paid an especially high price for reforms, in terms of economic cost and numbers of men recruited. From the point of view of the common people, the local lord and priest had been replaced by the French tax collector and army recruiting board.

It is telling that even Napoleon's enemies came to believe that the upstart emperor represented the wave of the future, particularly in regard to the reorganization of the state. Though they fought Napoleon, Prussian and Austrian administrators set about instituting reforms that resembled his: changing rules of promotion and recruitment, remodeling bureaucracies, redrawing districts, eliminating some privileges, and so on. Many who came of age under Napoleon's empire believed that, for better or worse, his empire was modern.

THE RETURN TO WAR AND NAPOLEON'S DEFEAT: 1806–1815

Napoleon's boldest attempt at consolidation, a policy banning British goods from the Continent, was a dangerous failure. Britain had bitterly opposed each of France's revolutionary regimes since the death of Louis XVI; now it tried to rally Europe against Napoleon with promises of generous financial loans and trade. Napoleon's Continental System, established in 1806, sought to starve Britain's trade and force its surrender. The system failed for several reasons. Throughout the war, Britain retained control of the seas. The British naval blockade of the Continent, begun in 1807, effectively countered Napoleon's system. While the French Empire strained to transport goods and raw materials overland to avoid the British blockade, the British successfully developed a lively trade with South America. A second reason for the failure was its internal tariffs. Europe became divided into economic camps that were at odds with each other as they tried to subsist on what the Continent alone could produce and manufacture. Finally, the system hurt the Continent more than Britain. Stagnant trade in Europe's ports and unemployment in its manufacturing centers eroded public faith in Napoleon's dream of a working European empire.

The Continental System was Napoleon's first serious mistake. His ambition to create a European empire, modeled on Rome and ruled from Paris, was to become his second, and another cause of his decline. The symbols of his empire—reflected in painting, architecture, and the design of furniture and clothing—were deliberately Roman in origin. Where early revolutionaries referred to the Roman Republic for their imagery, Napoleon looked to the more ostentatious style of the Roman emperors. In 1809, he divorced empress Josephine and ensured himself a successor of royal blood by marrying a Habsburg princess, Marie Louise—the great-niece of Marie Antoinette. Such actions lost Napoleon the support of revolutionaries, former Enlightenment thinkers, and liberals across the Continent.

Over time, the bitter tonic of defeat began to have an effect on Napoleon's enemies, who changed their own approach to waging war. After the Prussian army was humiliated at Jena in 1806 and forced out of the war, a whole generation of younger Prussian officers reformed their military and their state by demanding rigorous practical training for commanders and a genuinely national army made up of patriotic Prussian citizens rather than well-drilled mercenaries.

The myth of Napoleon's invincibility worked against him as well, as he took ever greater risks with France's military and national fortunes. Austrian artillery inflicted horrendous losses on the French at Wagram in 1809, although these difficulties were forgotten in the glow of victory. Napoleon's allies and supporters shrugged off the British admiral Horatio Nelson's victory at Trafalgar in 1805 as no more than a temporary check to the emperor's ambitions. But Trafalgar broke French naval power in the Mediterranean and led to a rift with Spain, which had been France's equal partner in the battle and suffered equally in the defeat. In the Caribbean, too, Napoleon was forced to cut growing losses (see pages 616–618).

A crucial moment in Napoleon's undoing came with his invasion of Spain in 1808. Napoleon overthrew the Spanish king, installed his own brother on the throne, and then imposed a series of reforms similar to those he had instituted elsewhere in Europe. Napoleon's blow against the Spanish monarchy weakened its hold on its colonies across the Atlantic, and the Spanish crown never fully regained its grip (see Chapter 20). But in Spain itself, Napoleon reckoned without two factors that led to the ultimate failure of his mission: the presence of British forces and the determined resistance of the Spanish people, who detested Napoleon's interference in the affairs of the Church. The Peninsular Wars, as the Spanish conflicts were called, were long and bitter. The smaller British force learned how to concentrate a devastating volume of gunfire on the French pinpoint attacks on the open battlefield, and laid siege to the French garrison towns. The Spanish quickly began to wear down the French invaders through guerrilla warfare. Terrible atrocities were committed by both sides; the French military's torture and execution of Spanish guerrillas and civilians was immortalized by the Spanish artist Francisco Goya (1746–1828) with sickening accuracy in his prints and paintings. Though at one point Napoleon himself took charge of his army, he could not achieve anything more than temporary victory. The Spanish campaign was the first indication that Napoleon could be beaten, and it encouraged resistance elsewhere.

The second, and most dramatic, stage in Napoleon's downfall began with the disruption of his alliance with Russia. As an agricultural country, Russia had

THE DISASTERS OF WAR, BY FRANCISCO GOYA (1746–1828). Goya was a Spanish painter and political liberal who had initially supported the French revolution. After Napoleon invaded Spain in 1807, Spaniards rose up in revolt, leading to the Peninsular War of 1808–1814. Between 1810 and 1820, Goya documented the war's violence in a series of black-and-white prints containing stark images of atrocity, rape, and the aftermath of famine. Note the absence of political imagery and the pointed and bitter irony of Goya's caption: "A great heroic feat! With dead people!" ▪ *Who or what is the target of Goya's sarcasm here?*

suffered severe economic crisis when it was no longer able to trade its surplus grain for British manufactures. The consequence was that Tsar Alexander I began to wink at trade with Britain and to ignore or evade the protests from Paris. By 1811, Napoleon decided that he could no longer endure this flouting of their agreement. He collected an army of 600,000 and set out for Russia in the spring of 1812. Only a third of the soldiers in this "Grande Armée" were French; nearly as many were Polish or German, joined by soldiers and adventurers from the rest of France's client states. It was the grandest of Napoleon's imperial expeditions: an army raised from across Europe and sent to punish the autocratic tsar. The invasion ended in disaster. The Russians refused to make a stand, drawing the French farther and farther into the heart of their country. Just before Napoleon reached

NAPOLEON ON THE BATTLEFIELD OF EYLAU. Amid bitter cold and snow, Napoleon engaged with the Russian army in February 1807. Although technically a victory for the French, it was only barely, with the French losing at least 10,000 men and the Russians twice as many. This painting, characteristic of Napoleon propaganda, emphasizes not the losses but the emperor's saintlike clemency—even enemy soldiers reach up toward him.

the ancient Russian capital of Moscow, in the narrow streets of a town called Borodino, the Russian army drew the French forces into a bloody and seemingly pointless battle, where both sides suffered terrible losses of men and supplies, which was harder on the French who were now so far from home. After the battle, the Russians permitted Napoleon to occupy Moscow. But on the night of his entry, Russian partisans put the city to the torch, leaving little but the blackened walls of the Kremlin palaces to shelter the French troops.

Hoping that the tsar would eventually surrender, Napoleon lingered amid the ruins for more than a month. On October 19, he finally ordered the homeward march, but the delay was a fatal blunder. Long before he had reached the border, the terrible Russian winter was on his troops; temperatures dropped to –27° F. Frozen streams, mountainous drifts of snow, and bottomless mud slowed the retreat almost to a halt. Adding to the miseries of frostbite, disease, and starvation, mounted Cossacks rode out of the blizzard to harry the exhausted army. Each morning, the miserable remnant that pushed on left behind circles of corpses around the campfires of the night before. On December 13, a few thousand broken soldiers crossed the frontier into Germany—a fragment of the once proud Grande Armée. Nearly 300,000 of its soldiers and untold thousands of Russians lost their lives in Napoleon's Russian adventure.

After the retreat from Russia, the anti-Napoleonic forces took renewed hope. United by a belief that they might finally succeed in defeating the emperor, Prussia, Russia, Austria,

Sweden, and Britain renewed their attack. Citizens of many German states in particular saw this as a war of liberation, and indeed most of the fighting took place in Germany. The climax of the campaign occurred in October 1813 when, at what was thereafter known as the Battle of the Nations, fought near Leipzig, the allies dealt the French a resounding defeat. Meanwhile, allied armies won significant victories in the Low Countries and Spain, and by the beginning of 1814, they had crossed the Rhine into France. Left with an army of inexperienced youths, Napoleon retreated to Paris, urging the French people to resist despite constant setbacks at the hands of the larger invading armies. On March 31, Tsar Alexander I of Russia and King Frederick William III of Prussia made their triumphant entry into Paris. Napoleon was forced to abdicate unconditionally and was sent into exile on the island of Elba, off the Italian coast.

Napoleon would be back on French soil in less than a year. But in the interim, the allies had restored the Bourbon dynasty to the throne, in the person of Louis XVIII, brother of Louis XVI. Despite his administrative abilities, Louis could not fill the void left by Napoleon's abdication. So it was no surprise that when the former emperor staged his escape from Elba, his fellow countrymen once more rallied to his side. By the time Napoleon reached Paris, he had generated enough support to cause Louis to flee the country. The allies, meeting in Vienna to conclude peace treaties with the French, were stunned by the news of Napoleon's return. They dispatched a hastily organized army to meet the

Napoleon the "Liberator"?

Did Napoleon continue the work of the French Revolution? He retained the tricolor flag of the Revolution and completed the French Civil Code that abolished the monarchy's archaic legal system, but many of his other actions were an affront to the stated goals of revolutionaries in 1789. These two documents—one from Napoleon himself, and one from one of his most articulate critics—allow us to examine his legacy and the way that it was seen by many of his contemporaries.

The first document is a preliminary draft for Napoleon's law on reenslavement in the French colonies. Slaves in French colonies in the Caribbean had freed themselves in insurrection in 1791, and their liberty was recognized by the revolutionary government in Paris that abolished slavery in 1794. In 1802, Napoleon reestablished slavery in all the colonies except for Saint-Domingue, where armies led by former slaves resisted and succeeded in winning independence for the nation of Haiti in 1804.

The second document is an excerpt from Benjamin Constant, The Spirit of Conquest and Usurpation, *first published in January 1814, as Napoleon's regime collapsed. Constant (1767–1830) was a Swiss-French political writer who embraced the term "liberal" and admired Britain's parliamentary government. His attack on Napoleon's despotism was a best seller and was quickly translated into other languages.*

Letter to Consul Cambacères, April 27, 1802

The consuls of the Republic and informed council of State decree:

Article One: According to the reports made to the captain-general of the colony of _____ by those individuals who will commit to this result, a list will be composed comprising first the names of black people who enjoyed freedom before 26 Pluviôse, Year II, and second, the names of blacks who have united to defend the territory of the Republic from its enemies, or who, in any other matter, have served the state.

Article Two: All the individuals named on this list will be declared free.

Article Three: Those among them who do not own property, and who have not trade or skill which can assure their subsistence, will be subjected to the regulations of the police who will assign them to property owners who will support them in agricultural work, determine their pay, and will stipulate above all arrangements for preventing vagabondage and insubordination.

Article Four: Insubordinates and outspoken vagabonds will be, in cases determined by the regulations, struck from the list and deprived of the advantages which result from it. One can substitute for this arrangement deportation to colonies where the emancipation laws have not been enacted.

Article Five: All blacks not included on the aforementioned list in article one will be subjected to the laws which in 1789 comprised the Black Code in the colonies. [The Black Code was the law regulating the practice of slavery.]

Article Six: It will be permitted to import blacks in the colony of _____ in accordance with the laws and regulations of the trade which were in place in 1789. The minister of the marine is charged with the execution of the present order.

Source: Laura Mason and Tracey Rizzo, *The French Revolution: A Document Collection* (Boston: 1999), pp. 349–50.

Benjamin Constant, The Spirit of Conquest and Usurpation, 1814

An entire country is never guilty of the excesses that its leader makes it commit. It is the leader that leads his country astray [. . .]

When some day the world has regained its reason and recovered its courage, where on earth will the threatened aggressor turn his gaze to find

defenders? To what feelings in them will he seek to appeal? What defence will not be discredited in advance, if it issues from the same mouth that, during his guilty prosperity, had lavished so many insults, uttered so many lies, dictated so many orders of destruction? Will he appeal to justice? He has violated it. To humanity? He has trampled it under foot. To the keeping of pledges? All his enterprises have begun with perjury. To the sanctity of alliances? He has treated his allies like slaves. What people could in good faith have allied themselves with his gigantic dream? No doubt all bent their heads for a time beneath his dominating yoke; but they considered it a passing calamity. They waited for the tide to turn, certain that its waves would one day disappear into the arid sands and that they would then be able to walk dry-shod again over the ground ploughed by its ravages.

Will he be able to count on the support of his new subjects? He has deprived them of all that they cherished and respected. He has disturbed the ashes of their fathers and shed the blood of their sons.

All will unite against him. Peace, independence, justice will be the general rallying cry; and just because they have been proscribed for so long, these words will have an almost magical power. Men, no longer the playthings of folly, will become enthusiasts for good sense. A cry of deliverance, a cry of unity, will ring out from one end of the earth to the other. The sense of public decency will spread to the most indecisive and will carry along the timidest. Nobody will dare to remain neutral, lest he should betray himself.

The conqueror will then see that he has presumed too much upon the degradation of the world. He will learn that calculations based on immorality and baseness, those calculations on which he prided himself so recently as a sublime discovery, are as uncertain as they are short-sighted, as deceptive as they are ignoble. He laughed at the stupidity of virtue, at that trust in a disinterestedness that seemed to him a chimera, at that appeal to an exaltation whose motives and duration he could not understand, and which he had been tempted to take as the passing abcess of a sudden disease. Now he discovers that egoism has its own brand of stupidity: that he is no less ignorant about what is good than honesty is about what is evil, and that, in order to know men, it is not sufficient to despise them. Mankind becomes an enigma to him. All around him people talk of generosity, of sacrifices, of devotion. This unfamiliar language comes as a surprise to his ears. He has no idea how to negotiate in that idiom. He remains paralysed, shocked by his failure to understand, a memorable example of Machiavellianism fallen victim to its own corruptions.

But meanwhile, how will the people, whose master has driven it to such extremities, respond? Who could fail to pity it, if it was naturally gentle, enlightened, sociable, susceptible to every delicate feeling and every form of heroic courage, and if a fatality unleashed upon it had in this fashion cast it away from the paths of civilization and morality? How deeply would it feel its own misery! Its intimate confidences, its conversations, its literature, all those expressions that it believed itself able to conceal from surveillance, become a single cry of pain.

Source: Benjamin Constant, *Political Writings* (Cambridge: Cambridge University Press, 1988), pp. 79–80.

Questions for Analysis

1. Who in the Caribbean colonies did Napoleon intend to send back into slavery in 1802? Who was to remain free? What did Napoleon hope to accomplish by returning to the prerevolutionary legislation that authorized slavery?

2. Why does Constant, writing at a moment when Napoleon's armies have been defeated, insist on distinguishing between the "leader" (Napoleon Bonaparte) and "the country"? What was the worst of the French emperor's crimes, according to him?

3. Looking back at the entire period of the French Revolution (1789–1799), which participants in revolutionary events would have been most angered by Napoleon's policy of reenslavement? How would these groups—which included the formerly enslaved themselves, of course—have opposed this policy? Which participants in the revolution would have agreed with Constant's critique of Napoleon's leadership?

Past and Present

The Atlantic Revolutions and Human Rights

The eighteenth-century revolutions in the Atlantic world, such as the slave revolt in Saint-Domingue (left), were based on the idea that individual rights were universal—they applied to everybody. Since the world is divided into autonomous nation-states, however, it has been challenging for defenders of universal human rights, such as the organization Amnesty International (right), to ensure their enforcement worldwide.

 Watch related author interview on the Student Site

emperor's typically bold offensive push into the Low Countries. At the battle of Waterloo, fought over three bloody days from June 15 to 18, 1815, Napoleon was stopped by the forces of his two most persistent enemies, Britain and Prussia, and suffered his final defeat. This time, the allies took no chances and shipped their prisoner off to the bleak island of St. Helena in the South Atlantic. The once-mighty emperor, now the exile Bonaparte, lived out a dreary existence, writing self-serving memoirs until his death in 1821.

Liberty, Politics, and Slavery: The Haitian Revolution

In the French colonies across the Atlantic, the revolution took a different course, with wide-ranging ramifications. The Caribbean islands of Guadeloupe, Martinique, and Saint-Domingue occupied a central role in the

eighteenth-century French economy because of the sugar trade, and their planter elites had powerful influence in Paris. The French National Assembly (like its American counterpart) declined to discuss the matter of slavery in the colonies, unwilling to encroach on the property rights of slave owners and fearful of losing the lucrative sugar islands to their British or Spanish rivals should discontented slave owners talk of independence from France. Competition between the European powers for the islands of the Caribbean was intense, so the islands changing hands was a real possibility. French men in the National Assembly also had to consider the question of rights for free men of color, a group that included a significant number of wealthy owners of property (and slaves).

Saint-Domingue had about 40,000 whites of different social classes, 30,000 free people of color, and 500,000 slaves, most of them recently enslaved from West Africa. In 1790, free people of color from Saint-Domingue sent a delegation to Paris, asking to be seated by the assembly, underscoring that they were men of property and, in many cases, of European ancestry. The assembly refused, which sparked a rebellion among free people of color in Saint-Domingue. The French colonial authorities repressed the movement quickly—and brutally. They captured one of the leaders of the rebellion, Vincent Ogé, and publicly tortured him before executing him along with dozens of his supporters in February 1791. Radical deputies in Paris, including Robespierre, expressed outrage but could do little to change the assembly's policy.

In August 1791, the largest slave rebellion in history broke out in Saint-Domingue. How much that rebellion owed to revolutionary propaganda is unclear, because like many rebellions during the period, it had its own roots. The British and the Spanish invaded, confident that they could crush the rebellion and take the island. But in the spring of 1792, the French government, on the verge of collapse and war with Europe, scrambled to win allies in Saint-Domingue by making free men of color citizens. A few months later (after the revolution of August 1792), the new French Republic dispatched commissioners to Saint-Domingue with troops and instructions to hold the island. There they faced a combination of different forces: Spanish and British troops, defiant Saint-Domingue planters, and slaves in rebellion. In this context, the local French commissioners reconsidered their commitment to slavery. In 1793, they promised freedom to slaves who would join the French. And a year later, the assembly in Paris extended to slaves in all the colonies a liberty that the slave rebellion had accomplished in Saint-Domingue.

Emancipation and war brought new leaders to the fore, chief among them a former slave, Toussaint Bréda, later Toussaint L'Ouverture (*too-SAN LOO-vehr-tur*), meaning "the one who opened the way." Over the course of the next five years, Toussaint and his soldiers, now allied with the French army, emerged victorious over the French planters, the British (in 1798), and the Spanish (in 1801). Toussaint also broke the power of his rival generals in both the mulatto and former slave armies, becoming the statesman of the revolution. In 1801, Toussaint set up a constitution, swearing allegiance to France but denying France any right to interfere in Saint-Domingue affairs. The constitution abolished slavery, reorganized the military, established Christianity as the state religion (entailing a rejection of vodoun, a blend of Christian and various West and Central African traditions), and made Toussaint governor for life. It was an extraordinary moment in the revolutionary period: the formation of an authoritarian society but also an utterly unexpected symbol of the universal potential of revolutionary ideas.

Toussaint's accomplishments, however, put him on a collision course with the other French general he admired and whose career was remarkably like his own: Napoleon Bonaparte. Saint-Domingue stood at the center of Bonaparte's vision of an expanded empire in the New World, an empire that would recoup North American territories that France had lost under the Old Regime, and pivot around the lucrative combination of the Mississippi, French Louisiana, and the sugar and slave colonies of the Caribbean. In January 1802, Bonaparte dispatched 20,000 troops to bring the island under control; the expedition included both French soldiers and Polish legionnaires who had joined Napoleon's armies because of their enthusiasm for his recent victories over Austria.

The French troops captured Toussaint and shipped him under heavy guard to a prison in the mountains of eastern France, where he died in 1803. Fighting continued in Saint-Domingue, however, with fires now fueled by Bonaparte's decree reestablishing slavery where the convention had abolished it. The war turned into a nightmare for the French. Yellow fever killed thousands of French and Polish troops, including one of Napoleon's best generals and brother-in-law. Armies on both sides committed atrocities, and by December 1803, the French army had collapsed.

TOUSSAINT L'OUVERTURE. A portrait of L'Ouverture, leader of what would become the Haitian Revolution, as a general.

Napoleon scaled back his vision of an American empire and sold the Louisiana territories to Thomas Jefferson. "I know the value of what I abandon. . . . I renounce it with the greatest regret," he told an aide. In Saint-Domingue, a general in the army of former slaves, Jean-Jacques Dessalines, declared the independent state of Haiti in 1804.

The **Haitian Revolution** remained, in significant ways, an anomaly. It was the only successful slave revolution in history and by far the most radical of the revolutions that occurred in this age. It suggested that the emancipatory ideas of the revolution and Enlightenment might apply to non-Europeans and enslaved peoples—a suggestion that residents of Europe attempted to ignore but one that struck home with planter elites in North and South America. Combined with later rebellions in the British colonies, it contributed to the British decision to end slavery in 1838. And it cast a long shadow over nineteenth-century slave societies from the southern United States to Brazil. The Napoleonic episode, then, had wide-ranging effects across the Atlantic: in North America, the Louisiana Purchase; in the Caribbean, the Haitian Revolution; in Latin America, the weakening of Spain and Portugal's colonial empires.

CONCLUSION

The tumultuous events in France formed part of a broad pattern of late-eighteenth-century democratic upheaval. The French Revolution was the most violent, protracted, and contentious of the revolutions of the era, but the dynamics of revolution were much the same everywhere. One of the most important developments of the French Revolution was the emergence of a popular movement, which included political clubs for people previously excluded from politics, newspapers read by and to the common people, and political leaders who spoke for the sans-culottes. In the French Revolution, as in other revolutions, the popular movement

After You Read This Chapter

 Go to **INQUIZITIVE** to see what you've learned—and learn what you've missed—with personalized feedback along the way.

- The French Revolution resulted from both an immediate political crisis and long-term social tensions. What was this crisis, and how did it lead to popular revolt against the monarchy?
- The revolutionaries in the National Assembly in 1789 set out to produce a constitution for France. What were their political goals, and what was the reaction of monarchs and peoples elsewhere in Europe?
- After 1792, a more radical group of revolutionaries seized control of the French state. How did they come to power, and how were their political goals different from those of their predecessors?
- Napoleon's career began during the revolution. What did he owe to the revolution, and what was different about his regime?
- Three major revolutions took place in the Atlantic world at the end of the eighteenth century: the American Revolution, the French Revolution, and the Haitian Revolution. What was similar about these revolutions? What was different?

challenged the early and moderate revolutionary leadership, pressing for more radical and democratic measures. And, as in other revolutions, the popular movement in France was defeated, and authority was reestablished by a quasi-military figure. Likewise, the revolutionary ideas of liberty, equality, and fraternity were not specifically French; their roots lay in the social structures of the eighteenth century and in the ideas and culture of the Enlightenment. Yet French armies brought them, literally, to the doorsteps of many Europeans.

What was the larger impact of the revolution and the Napoleonic era? Its legacy is partly summed up in three key concepts: liberty, equality, and nation. Liberty meant individual rights and responsibilities and, more specifically, freedom from arbitrary authority. By equality, as we have seen, the revolutionaries meant the abolition of legal distinctions of rank among European men. Though their concept of equality was limited, it became a powerful mobilizing force in the nineteenth century. The most important legacy of the revolution may have been the new term *nation*. Nationhood was a political concept. A nation was formed of citizens, not of a king's subjects; it was ruled by law and treated its citizens as equal before the law; and sovereignty did not lie in dynasties or historic fiefdoms but in the nation of citizens. This new form of nation gained legitimacy when citizen armies repelled attacks against their newly won freedoms; the victories of "citizens in arms" lived on in myth and history and provided the most powerful images of the period. As the war continued, military nationhood began to overshadow its political cousin. And by the Napoleonic period, this shift became decisive. A new political body of freely associated citizens was most powerfully embodied in a centralized state, its army and a kind of citizenship defined by individual commitment to the needs of the nation at war. This understanding of national identity spread throughout Europe in the coming decades.

PEOPLE, IDEAS, AND EVENTS IN CONTEXT

- Why was **LOUIS XVI** forced to convene the **ESTATES GENERAL** in 1789?
- What argument did **ABBÉ SIEYÈS** make about the role of the **THIRD ESTATE**?
- What made the **TENNIS COURT OATH** a revolutionary act?
- What was the role of popular revolts (the attack on the **BASTILLE**, the **GREAT FEAR**, the **OCTOBER DAYS**) in the revolutionary movements of 1789?
- What was the connection between the French Revolution with the slave revolt in **SAINT-DOMINGUE** that began in 1791?
- What was the **DECLARATION OF THE RIGHTS OF MAN AND OF THE CITIZEN**?
- What was the **CIVIL CONSTITUTION OF THE CLERGY**?
- What circumstances led to the abolition of the monarchy in 1792?
- Why did the **JACOBINS** in the **NATIONAL CONVENTION** support a policy of the **TERROR**?
- What were **NAPOLEON**'s most significant domestic accomplishments in France? What significance did Napoleon's military campaigns have for other parts of Europe and for the French Empire?
- What was the significance of the **HAITIAN REVOLUTION** of 1791–1804?

THINKING ABOUT CONNECTIONS

- Popular movements in favor of democracy, social justice, or national self-determination in the more than two centuries since 1789 have often used the French Revolution as a point of reference or comparison. Obvious comparisons are those movements that saw themselves as "revolutionary," such as the Russian Revolution of 1917 or the Chinese Revolution of 1949. More recent comparisons might be the popular movements for democratic change in eastern Europe that resulted in the end of the Cold War in 1989 or the Arab Spring of 2011.
- Make a list of factors or circumstances that you might want to compare in considering the outcome of such movements. You might consider the degree to which elites support the current regime, the degree of consensus, the goals of those who are protesting the status quo, economic circumstances, or international support for either the regime or for revolutionaries. What other factors might determine the outcome of revolutionary situations?

STORY LINES

- Industrialization put Europe on the path to a new form of economic development based on the concentration of labor and production in areas with easy access to new sources of energy. This led to rapid growth of new industrial cities and to the development of new transportation connecting industrial centers to growing markets.

- Industrialization created new social groups in society, defined less by their status at birth than by their place in the new economy. Workers faced new kinds of discipline in the workplace, and women and children entered the new industrial workforce in large numbers. A new elite made up of businessmen, entrepreneurs, bankers, engineers, and merchants emerged as the primary beneficiaries of industrialization.

- Population growth in rural areas spurred migration to cities where laborers and the middle classes did not mix socially; they adopted different dress, speech, and leisure activities and had significantly different opportunities when it came to marriage, sex, and children.

CHRONOLOGY

1780s	Industrialization begins in Britain
1825	First railroad in Britain
1830s	Industrialization begins in France and Belgium
1845–1849	Irish potato famine
1850s	Industrialization begins in Prussia and German states of central Europe
1861	Russian tsar emancipates the serfs

The Industrial Revolution and Nineteenth-Century Society

CORE OBJECTIVES

- **UNDERSTAND** the circumstances that allowed for industrialization to begin in Great Britain.

- **IDENTIFY** the industries that were the first to adopt new systems for mechanical production and the regions in Europe in which they thrived.

- **DESCRIBE** the changes in the nature of work, production, and employment that occurred as a result of the mechanization of industry.

- **EXPLAIN** the effects of industrialization on the environment and the social life in Europe, especially in the new urban centers associated with industrial development.

- **IDENTIFY** the essential characteristics of the new "middle classes" in nineteenth-century Europe and their differences from the property-owning groups prior to the Industrial Revolution.

James Watt, a Scottish mechanic and instrument maker, changed the course of human history when he took the primitive steam engine designed by Thomas Newcomen around 1712 and added a separate condenser, which allowed it to generate more power using less coal as fuel. Newcomen's engine used repeated heating and cooling of a steam container to generate a vacuum that could be used to pump water. Watt's engine, which he marketed after 1775 in partnership with Matthew Boulton, was soon adapted to produce a rotary motion that could be used industrially in a multitude of ways, including grinding, milling, sawing, and weaving. The spread of Watt's steam technology throughout the north of England at the end of the eighteenth century transformed the manufacturing world, reshaped the landscape of the English countryside, and began a revolution in the way that people lived and worked.

The condensing steam engine also made Watt a very wealthy man—and he was well aware that such wealth was different from that possessed by Britain's traditional elites. He distinguished this wealth from that of the landed aristocrat by linking it to his own efforts as an inventor and entrepreneur:

"The Squire's land has not been so much of his own making as the condensing engine has been of mine. He has only passively inherited his property, while this invention has been the product of my own labour and of God knows how much anguish of mind and body."

Watt was correct in his claim that his wealth and status were different from the status claimed by the landed aristocracy, but this wealth was not the product of his labor alone. Like the achievements of his engineering predecessors such as Newcomen, Watt's engine could be profitable only in a world where foresters, cotton merchants, and landowners could see profits in the purchase of expensive industrial sawmills, mechanical looms, and steam-driven threshers. Watt's invention also depended on the labor of men and women who dug coal from the ground and smelted the iron and copper he used to produce his machines. The profits of industrial entrepreneurs, meanwhile, depended on their ability to find sawyers, weavers, and fieldworkers who were willing to accept a new way of working, where they no longer owned their own tools but rather worked as wage laborers for men of business seeking returns on their investment. Business owners also needed customers for the larger amounts of finished timber, woven cloth, and grain that they were now bringing to market. Technology such as Watt's was an important part of the changes historians call the "Industrial Revolution," but technology alone cannot explain the complicated social and economic transformation contained in the phrase.

The Industrial Revolution led to the proliferation of more capital-intensive enterprises, new ways of organizing human labor, and the rapid growth of cities. It was made possible by new sources of energy and power, which led to faster forms of mechanized transportation, higher productivity, and the emergence of large consumer markets for manufactured goods. In turn, these interrelated developments triggered social and cultural changes with revolutionary consequences for Europeans and their relationship to the rest of the world.

Of all the changes, perhaps the most revolutionary came at the very root of human endeavor: new forms of energy. Over the space of two or three generations, a society and an economy that had drawn on water, wind, and wood for most of its energy needs came to depend on machines driven by steam engines and coal. In 1800, the world produced 10 million tons of coal. In 1900, it produced 1 billion—a hundred times more. The Industrial Revolution brought the beginning of the fossil-fuel age, altering as it did so the balance of humanity and the environment.

Mechanization made enormous gains in productivity in some sectors of the economy, but the new machines were limited to a few of those sectors, especially at the outset, and they did not always lead to a dramatic break with older techniques. Above all, technology did not dispense human toil; in fact, historians emphasize that the Industrial Revolution intensified human labor—mining for coal with picks and shovels, digging trenches, harvesting cotton, sewing by hand, or pounding hides—much more often than it eased it. One historian suggested that we would do better to speak of the "industrious revolution." This revolution did not lie solely in machines but in a new economic system based on mobilizing capital and labor on a much larger scale. The industrious economy redistributed wealth and power, creating new social classes and producing new social tensions.

It also prompted deep-seated cultural shifts. The English critic Raymond Williams has pointed out that during the eighteenth century, *industry* referred to a human quality: a hardworking woman was "industrious," or an ambitious clerk showed "industry." By the middle of the nineteenth century, *industry* had come to mean an economic system, one that followed its own logic and worked on its own—seemingly independent of humans. This modern understanding of the term was born in the early nineteenth century. As the Industrial Revolution altered the foundations of the economy, it changed the very assumptions with which people approached economics and the ways in which they regarded the role of human beings in the economy. These new assumptions could foster a sense of power but also anxieties about powerlessness.

The dramatic changes of the late eighteenth and early nineteenth centuries emerged out of earlier developments. Overseas commercial exploration opened new territories to European trade. India, Africa, and the Americas had already been brought into the web of the European economy. Expanding trade networks created new markets for goods and sources for raw materials, and the need to organize commerce over long distances fostered financial innovations and sophisticated credit schemes for managing risk. These developments paved the way for industrialization. Within Europe, the commercialization of agriculture and the spread of handicraft manufacturing in rural areas changed the economy in ways that anticipated later industrial developments. A final factor seems to have been **population growth**, which began to accelerate in the eighteenth century. Because these earlier developments did not affect all areas in Europe the same way, industrialization did not always follow the same pattern across the Continent. It happened first in Great Britain, and that is where we will begin.

THE INDUSTRIAL REVOLUTION IN BRITAIN, 1760–1850

Great Britain in the eighteenth century had a fortunate combination of natural, economic, and cultural resources. It was a small and secure island nation with a robust empire and control over crucial lanes across the oceans. It had ample supplies of coal, rivers, and a well-developed network of canals.

In addition, agriculture in Britain was already more thoroughly commercialized than elsewhere. British agriculture had been transformed by a combination of new techniques, new crops, and the "**enclosure**" of fields and pastures, which turned smallholdings (and in many cases commonly held lands) into large fenced tracts that were privately owned and individually managed by commercial landlords. The British Parliament encouraged enclosure with a series of bills in the second half of the eighteenth century, because commercialized agriculture was more productive and yielded more food for a growing and increasingly urban population. But the concentration of property in fewer hands drove small farmers off the land, sending them to look for work in other sectors of the economy. Last, commercialized agriculture produced higher profits—wealth that would be invested in industry.

A key precondition for industrialization, therefore, was Britain's growing supply of available capital in the forms of private wealth and well-developed banking and credit institutions. This capital was readily available to underwrite new economic enterprises and eased the transfer of money and goods—for instance, importing silks from the East or cottons from Egypt and North America. London thus had become the leading center for international trade, and the city was a headquarter for the transfer of raw materials, capital, and manufactured products throughout the world.

Social and cultural conditions also encouraged investment in enterprises. In Britain, far more than on the Continent, the pursuit of wealth was perceived to be a worthy goal. European nobility cultivated the notion of gentlemanly conduct, in part to hold the line against those moving up from below. British aristocrats respected commoners with a talent for making money and did not hesitate to invest themselves. Their scramble to enclose their lands reflected a keen interest in commercialization and investment. Outside the aristocracy, an even lower barrier separated merchants from the rural gentry. Many of the entrepreneurs of

ENCLOSED FIELDS IN CENTRAL BRITAIN. The large, uniform square fields in the background of this photograph are fields that were enclosed from smaller holdings and common lands in the 1830s; they contrast with the smaller and older strip fields in the foreground. The larger enclosed fields were more profitable for their owners, who benefited from legislation that encouraged enclosure, but created hardship for the village communities that depended on the use of these lands for survival. ▪ *What circumstances made enclosure possible?* ▪ *What connection have historians made between enclosure and early industrialization?*

the early Industrial Revolution came from the small gentry or independent farmer class. Eighteenth-century Britain was not by any means free of social snobbery: lords looked down on bankers, and bankers looked down on craft workers. But a lord's disdain might well be tempered by the fact that his own grandfather had worked in the counting house.

Growing domestic and international markets made eighteenth-century Britain prosperous, and the British voracious consumers. The court elite followed and bought up yearly fashions, as did most of Britain's landed and professional society. "Nature may be satisfied with little," one London entrepreneur declared. "But it is the wants of fashion and the desire of novelties that causes trade." The country's small size and the fact that it was an island encouraged the development of a well-integrated domestic market. Unlike continental Europe, Britain did not have a system of internal tolls and tariffs, so goods could be moved freely to wherever they might fetch the best price. Moreover, a constantly improving transportation system boosted that freedom of movement, as did a favorable political climate. Some members of Parliament were businessmen themselves and others were investors, and both groups were eager to encourage by legislation the construction of canals, the establishment of banks, and the enclosure of common lands.

British foreign policy responded to its commercial needs, because foreign markets promised even greater returns than domestic ones, though with greater risks. At the end of every major eighteenth-century war, Britain wrested overseas territories from its enemies. At the same time, it penetrated hitherto unexploited territories, such

THE FIRST INDUSTRIAL NATION. Large-scale mechanization of industry developed first in Britain. ▪ *Large deposits of what two natural resources caused urban growth outside of London?* ▪ *What new forms of transportation were critical for moving natural resources to market?* ▪ *What else was necessary for industrialization to develop as it did?*

as India and South America. In 1759, over one-third of all British exports went to the colonies; by 1784, if we include the former colonies in North America, that figure increased to one-half. Production for export rose by 80 percent between 1750 and 1770, while production for domestic consumption gained just 7 percent over the same period. The British merchant marine was capable of transporting goods around the world, and its navy was practiced in the art of protecting its commercial fleets. By the 1780s, Britain's markets—together with its fleet and its established position at the center of world commerce—gave its entrepreneurs unrivaled opportunities for trade and profit.

Innovation in the Textile Industries

The Industrial Revolution began with dramatic technological leaps in a few industries, the first of which was cotton textiles, an industry that was already long established. Tariffs prohibiting imports of East Indian cottons, which

Parliament had imposed to protect British woolen goods, had spurred the manufacture of British cotton. British textile manufacturers imported raw materials from India and the American South and borrowed patterns from Indian spinners and weavers. What, then, were the revolutionary breakthroughs?

In 1733, John Kay's invention of the flying shuttle speeded the process of weaving, but the task of spinning thread, however, had not kept up. A series of comparatively simple mechanical devices eliminated this spinning-to-weaving bottleneck. The most important device was the **spinning jenny**, a hand-loom weaver invented by James Hargreaves in 1764. The spinning jenny was a compound spinning wheel capable of producing sixteen threads at once—though the threads were not strong enough to be used for the longitudinal fibers, or warp, of cotton cloth. The invention of the water frame in 1769 by Richard Arkwright, a barber, made it possible to produce both warp and woof (latitudinal fibers) in great quantity. In 1799, Samuel Crompton invented the spinning mule, which combined the features of both the jenny and the frame. All of these important technological changes were accomplished by the end of the eighteenth century.

JAMES HARGREAVES'S SPINNING JENNY, 1764. Earlier innovations in textile looms allowed weavers to produce cloth more quickly, but the industry was stymied by the slowness of traditional spinning methods. Thread production simply could not keep up with the demand created by new weaving methods. Hargreaves found a solution in the spinning jenny, which allowed spinners to spin thread and yarns on multiple spindles simultaneously—this jenny from Germany has sixteen spindles. The spinning jenny was capable of producing thread so quickly that it flooded the market, driving down the price of cotton thread. Local spinners were so outraged at this affront to their livelihood that they broke into Hargreaves's workshop and destroyed his machines, forcing him to flee and set up a new manufacture elsewhere in secret. (See also "Ned Ludd and the Luddites" on page 626.)

COTTON SPINNING, 1861. An illustration from a series showing spinning at Walter Evans and Company, cotton manufacturers in Derby, England. ▪ *Why did textile factories prefer female employees?*

A jenny could spin from six to twenty-four times more yarn than a hand spinner in the same amount of time; and by the end of the eighteenth century, a mule could produce 200 to 300 times more. Just as important, the new machines made better-quality—stronger and finer—thread. These machines revolutionized production across the textile industry. Last, the **cotton gin**, invented by the American Eli Whitney in 1793, mechanized the process of separating cotton seeds from the fiber, thereby speeding up the production of cotton and reducing its price. The supply of cotton fibers could now expand to keep pace with the rising demand from cotton cloth manufacturers. Cotton gin had many effects, including, paradoxically, making slavery more profitable in the United States. The cotton-producing slave plantations in the American South became enmeshed in the lucrative trade with manufacturers who produced cotton textiles in the northern United States and England.

The first textile machines were inexpensive enough to be used by spinners in their cottages. But as the machines grew in size and complexity, they were housed instead in workshops or mills located near water that could be used to power the machines. Eventually, further development of steam-driven equipment allowed manufacturers to build mills wherever the equipment could be used. Frequently, these mills went up in towns and cities in the north of England, away from the older commercial and

NED LUDD AND THE LUDDITES. In 1811 and 1812, in northern England, bands of workmen who resented the adoption of new mechanical devices in the weaving industries attacked several establishments and destroyed the frames used to weave cloth. The movement took the name "Luddites" from Ned Ludd, who had broken the frames belonging to his employer in 1779. His mythological presence in the movement is depicted in the illustration on the right. Although the anger was directed at the machines, the real target of resentment may have been the new pricing scheme imposed by the merchants who bought the finished work. The debate about prices is a central part of the poster on the left, which offers a reward for information leading to the conviction of the frame breakers. The poster is signed by several workers of the establishment who published the price they received for each piece of clothing and their lack of complaints about their employer. ▪ *How might weavers, accustomed to getting fixed prices for their goods, have perceived the need to adjust to the price fluctuations of a market economy?*

seafaring centers but nearer to the coal fields that provided fuel for the new machines. From 1780 on, British cotton textiles flooded the world market. In 1760, Britain imported 2.5 million pounds of raw cotton; in 1787, 22 million pounds; and in 1837, 366 million pounds. By 1815, the export of cotton textiles amounted to 40 percent of the value of all domestic goods exported from Great Britain. Although the price of manufactured cotton goods fell dramatically, the market expanded so rapidly that profits continued to increase.

Behind these statistics lay a revolution in clothing and consumption. Cotton in the form of muslins and calicos was fine enough to appeal to wealthy consumers. It was also light and washable, so for the first time, ordinary people could have sheets, table linens, curtains, and underwear. (Wool was too scratchy.) As one writer commented in 1846, the revolution in textiles had ushered in a "brilliant transformation" in dress: "Every woman used to wear a blue or black dress that she kept ten years without washing it for fear that it would fall to pieces. Today her husband can cover her in flower-printed cotton for the price of a day's wages."

The explosive growth of textiles also prompted a debate about the benefits and tyranny of the new industries. The British Romantic poet William Blake famously wrote in biblical terms of the textile mills' blight on the English countryside:

> And did the Countenance Divine
> Shine forth upon our clouded hills?
> And was Jerusalem builded here
> Among these dark Satanic mills?

By the 1830s, the British House of Commons was holding hearings on employment and working conditions in factories, testimonies about working days that stretched from 3:00 A.M. to 10:00 P.M., employment of very young children, and workers who lost hair and fingers in the mills' machinery. Women and children counted for roughly two-thirds of the labor force in textiles. The principle of regulating any labor (and emphatically that of adult men), however, was controversial. Only gradually did a series of factory acts prohibit hiring children under age nine and limit the labor of workers under age eighteen to ten hours a day.

Coal and Iron

Meanwhile, decisive changes were transforming the production of iron. As in the textile industry, many important technological changes came during the eighteenth century. A series of innovations—coke smelting, rolling, and puddling—enabled the British to substitute coal (which they had in abundance) for wood (which was scarce and inefficient) to heat molten metal and make iron. The new "pig iron" was of higher quality and could be used to make an enormous variety of iron products such as machines, engines, railway tracks, agricultural implements, and hardware that became, literally, the infrastructure of industrialization. Britain found itself able to export both coal and iron to rapidly expanding markets around the industrializing regions of the world. And between 1814 and 1852, exports of British iron doubled, rising to over 1 million tons of iron, more than half of the world's total production.

Rising demand for coal required mining deeper veins. In 1711, Thomas Newcomen's cumbersome but remarkably effective steam engine proved immensely useful to the coal industry for pumping water from mines. After 1763, as we have seen, James Watt improved on Newcomen's machine; and by 1800, Watt and his partner Matthew Boulton had sold 289 engines for use in factories and mines. Watt and Boulton made their fortune from their invention's efficiency, earning a regular percentage of the increased profits from each mine that operated the engine.

Steam power was still energy consuming and expensive, so only slowly replaced traditional water power. Even

CHILD LABOR IN THE MINES. This engraving of young workers pulling and pushing a coal cart up through the narrow shaft of a mine was in a British Parliamentary report on child labor. ■ *What attitudes about government and the economy made it difficult for legislatures to regulate working conditions in the new industries?*

in its early form, however, the steam engine decisively transformed the nineteenth-century world with one application: the steam-driven locomotive. Railroads revolutionized industry, markets, public and private financing, and ordinary people's conceptions of space and time.

THE COMING OF RAILWAYS

Transportation had improved during the years before 1830, but moving heavy materials, particularly coal, remained a problem. It is significant that the first modern railway, built in England in 1825, ran from the Durham coalfield of Stockton to Darlington, near the coast. Coal traditionally had been hauled short distances via tramways, or tracks along which horses pulled coal carts. The locomotives on the Stockton–Darlington line traveled at fifteen miles per hour, the fastest rate at which machines had yet moved goods overland. Soon they would move people as well, transforming transportation in the process.

Building railways became a massive enterprise, and a risky but potentially profitable opportunity for investment. No sooner did the first combined passenger and goods service open in 1830, operating between Liverpool and Manchester, England, than plans were formulated and money pledged to extend rail systems throughout Europe, the Americas, and beyond. In 1830, there were no more than a few dozen miles of railway in the world. By 1840, there were more than 4,500 miles; and by 1850, more than

23,000. British engineers, industrialists, and investors were quick to recognize the global opportunities available in constructing railways overseas; a large part of Britain's industrial success in the later nineteenth century came through building other nations' infrastructures. The English contractor Thomas Brassey, for instance, built railways in Italy, Canada, Argentina, India, and Australia.

Throughout the world, a veritable army of construction workers built the railways. In Britain, they were called "navvies" (derived from *navigator),* a term first used for the construction workers on Britain's eighteenth-century canals. Navvies were a rough lot, living with a few women in temporary encampments as they migrated across the countryside. They were often immigrant workers who faced local hostility. A sign posted by local residents outside a mine in Scotland in 1845 warned the Irish navvies to get "off the ground and out of the country" in a week or else be driven out "by the strength of our armes and a good pick shaft." Later in the century, railway-building projects in Africa and the Americas were lined with camps of immigrant Indian and Chinese laborers, who also became targets of nativist (a term that means "opposed to foreigners") anger.

The magnitude of the navvies' accomplishment was extraordinary. In Britain and in much of the rest of the world, mid-nineteenth-century railways were constructed almost entirely without the aid of machinery. An assistant engineer on the London-to-Birmingham line calculated that the labor involved was the equivalent of lifting 25 billion cubic feet of earth and stone 1 foot high. He compared this feat with building the Great Pyramid, a task he estimated involved the hoisting of some 16 billion tons. The building of the pyramid, however, required more than 200,000 men and twenty years. The construction of the London-to-Birmingham railway was accomplished by 20,000 men in less than five years; translated into individual terms, a navvy was expected to move an average of 20 tons of earth per day. Railways were produced by toil as much as by technology, by human labor as much as by engineering; they illustrate why some historians prefer to use the term *industrious revolution.*

Steam engines, textile machines, new ways of making iron, and railways were all interconnected; changes in one area endorsed changes in another. Pumps run by steam engines made it possible to mine deeper veins of coal,

MANCHESTER TO LIVERPOOL, LATE NINETEENTH CENTURY. Lower-class passengers, physically separated from their social superiors, are packed into the rear of the train.

BARRY DOCK AND ISLAND, WALES, 1895. The convergence of coal, steam power, railways, and maritime shipping were at the center of industrialization in Britain. ▪ *In what way did the circular relationship among coal and iron production, the larger transportation revolution associated with the construction of railroads, and later, steamships, help sustain the initial growth associated with industrial development?*

and steam-powered railways made it possible to transport coal. Mechanization fueled the production of iron for machines and the mining of coal to run the steam engines. The railway boom multiplied the demand for iron and iron products, such as rails, locomotives, carriages, signals, and switches; and building railroads called for engineering expertise, such as scaling mountains and designing bridges and tunnels. Railway construction, which required capital investment beyond the capacity of any single individual, forged new kinds of public and private financing. The scale of production expanded and the tempo of economic activity quickened, spurring the search for more coal, the production of more iron, the mobilization of more capital, and the recruitment of more labor. Steam and speed were becoming the foundation of the economy and a new way of life.

THE INDUSTRIAL REVOLUTION ON THE CONTINENT

Continental Europe followed a different path. Eighteenth-century France, Belgium, and Germany did have manufacturing districts in regions with raw materials, access to

markets, and long-standing traditions of craft and skill. Yet for a variety of reasons, changes along the lines seen in Britain did not occur until the 1830s. Britain's transportation system was highly developed, whereas those of France and Germany were not. France was far larger than England; its rivers more difficult to navigate and its seaports, cities, and coal deposits farther apart. Much of central Europe was divided into small principalities, each with its own tolls and tariffs, which complicated the transportation of goods over any considerable distance. The Continent had fewer raw materials, coal in particular, than Britain. The abundance and cheapness of wood discouraged exploration that might have resulted in new discoveries of coal, which also meant that coal-run steam engines were less economical on the Continent. Capital, too, was less readily available. Early British industrialization was underwritten by private wealth, but this was less feasible elsewhere. Different patterns of landholding formed obstacles to the commercialization of agriculture. In the East, serfdom was a powerful disincentive to labor-saving innovations. In the West, especially in France, the large number of small peasants—as farmers of humble origin were called in Europe—stayed put on the land.

The wars of the French Revolution and Napoleon disrupted economies. During the eighteenth century, the

Competing Viewpoints

The Factory System, Science, and Morality: Two Views

Reactions to the Industrial Revolution and the factory system it produced ranged from celebration to horror. Dr. Andrew Ure, a Scottish professor of chemistry, was fascinated with these nineteenth-century applications of Enlightenment science. He believed that the new machinery and its products would create a new society of wealth, abundance, and, ultimately, stability through the useful regimentation of production.

Friedrich Engels (1820–1895) was one of the many socialists to criticize Dr. Ure as shortsighted and complacent in his outlook. Engels was part of a factory-owning family and so was able to examine the new industrial cities at close range. He provides a classic nineteenth-century analysis of industrialization. The Condition of the Working Class in England *is compellingly written, angry, and revealing about middle-class concerns of the time, including women workers.*

Dr. Andrew Ure (1835)

This island [Britain] is preeminent among civilized nations for the prodigious development of its factory wealth, and has been therefore long viewed with a jealous admiration by foreign powers. This very pre-eminence, however, has been contemplated in a very different light by many influential members of our own community, and has even been denounced by them as the certain origin of innumerable evils to the people, and of revolutionary convulsions to the state....

The blessings which physico-mechanical science has bestowed on society, and the means it has still in store for ameliorating the lot of mankind, has

[sic] been too little dwelt upon; while, on the other hand, it has been accused of lending itself to the rich capitalists as an instrument for harassing the poor, and of exacting from the operative an accelerated rate of work. It has been said, for example, that the steam-engine now drives the power-looms with such velocity as to urge on their attendant weavers at the same rapid pace; but that the hand-weaver, not being subjected to this restless agent, can throw his shuttle and move his treddles at his convenience. There is, however, this difference in the two cases, that in the factory, every member of the loom is so adjusted, that the driving force leaves the attendant nearly

nothing at all to do, certainly no muscular fatigue to sustain, while it produces for him good, unfailing wages, besides a healthy workshop *gratis:* whereas the non-factory weaver, having everything to execute by muscular exertion, finds the labour irksome, makes in consequence innumerable short pauses, separately of little account, but great when added together; earns therefore proportionally low wages, while he loses his health by poor diet and the dampness of his hovel.

Source: Andrew Ure, *The Philosophy of Manufacturers: Or, An Exposition of the Scientific, Moral, and Commercial Economy of the Factory System of Great Britain, 1835,* as cited in J. T. Ward, *The Factory System,* vol. 1 (New York: 1970), pp. 140–41.

---

population had grown and mechanization had begun in a few key industries. The ensuing political upheaval and the financial strains of warfare did virtually nothing to help economic development. Napoleon's Continental System and the British destruction of French merchant shipping hurt commerce badly. The ban on British-shipped cotton stalled the growth of cotton textiles for decades, though the armies' greater demand for woolen cloth kept that sector of textiles humming. Iron processing increased to satisfy the military's rising needs, but techniques for making iron remained largely unchanged. Probably the revolutionary

change most beneficial to industrial advance in Europe was the removal of previous restraints on the movement of capital and labor—for example, the abolition of craft guilds and the reduction of tariff barriers across the Continent.

After 1815, a number of factors combined to change the economic climate. In regions with a well-established commercial and industrial base—the northeast of France, Belgium, and swaths of territory across the Rhineland, Saxony, Silesia, and northern Bohemia (see map on page 634)—population growth further boosted economic development. Rising population did not by itself produce industrialization, however;

Friedrich Engels (1844)

Histories of the modern development of the cotton industry, such as those of Ure, Baines, and others, tell on every page of technical innovations. . . . In a well-ordered society such improvements would indeed be welcome, but social war rages unchecked and the benefits derived from these improvements are ruthlessly monopolized by a few persons. . . . Every improvement in machinery leads to unemployment, and the greater the technical improvement the greater the unemployment. Every improvement in machinery affects a number of workers in the same way as a commercial crisis and leads to want, distress, and crime. . . .

Let us examine a little more closely the process whereby machine-labour continually supersedes hand-labour. When spinning or weaving machinery is installed practically all that is left to be done by the hand is the piecing together of broken threads, and the machine does the rest. This task calls for nimble fingers rather than muscular strength. The labour of grown men is not merely unnecessary but actually unsuitable. . . . The greater the degree to which physical labour is displaced by the introduction of machines worked by water- or steam-power, the fewer grown men need be employed. In any case women and children will work for lower wages than men and, as has already been observed, they are more skillful at piecing than grown men. Consequently it is women and children who are employed to do this work. . . . When women work in factories, the most important result is the dissolution of family ties. If a woman works for twelve or thirteen hours a day in a factory and her husband is employed either in the same establishment or in some other works, what is the fate of the children? They lack parental care and control. . . . It is not difficult to imagine that they are left to run wild.

Source: Friedrich Engels, *The Condition of the Working Class in England in 1844,* ed. and trans. W. O. Henderson and W. H. Chaloner (New York: 1958), pp. 150–51, 158, 160.

Questions for Analysis

1. According to Dr. Andrew Ure, why was industrialization good for Britain? How can the blessings of "physico-mechanical science" lead to the improvement of humanity?

2. What criticism did Engels level at Ure and other industrialization optimists? Why did Engels think conditions for workers were getting worse, not better?

3. What consequences do these two writers see for society in the wake of technological change? What assumptions do they make about the relationship between economic development and the social order?

---

for example, in Ireland, where other necessary factors were absent, more people meant less food.

Transportation improved: the Austrian Empire added more than 30,000 miles of roads between 1830 and 1847; Belgium almost doubled its road network in the same period; and France built not only new roads but also 2,000 miles of canals. These improvements, combined with the construction of railroads in the 1830s and 1840s, opened up new markets and encouraged new methods of manufacturing. In many of the Continent's manufacturing regions, however, industrialists continued to tap large pools of skilled but inexpensive labor; thus, older methods of putting out industry and handwork persisted alongside new-model factories longer than they did in Britain.

In what other ways was the Continental model of industrialization different? Governments played a considerably more direct role in industrialization. France and Prussia granted subsidies to private companies that built railroads. After 1849, the Prussian state took on the task itself, as did Belgium and, later, Russia. In Prussia, the state also operated a large proportion of that country's mines. Governments on the Continent provided incentives for industrialization;

limited-liability laws, to take the most important example, allowed investors to own shares in a corporation or company without becoming liable for the company's debts—and enabled enterprises to recruit investors to put together the capital for railroads, other forms of industry, and commerce.

Mobilizing capital for industry was one of the challenges of the century. In Great Britain, overseas trade had created well-organized financial markets; on the Continent, however, capital was dispersed and in short supply. New joint-stock investment banks, unlike private banks, were created that could sell bonds to and take deposits from individuals and smaller companies, and offer aspiring entrepreneurs start-up capital in the form of long-term, low-interest commercial loans. The French Crédit Mobilier, for instance, founded in 1852 by the wealthy and well-connected Péreire brothers, assembled enough capital to finance insurance companies, the Parisian bus system, six municipal gas companies, transatlantic shipping, enterprises in other European countries, and, with the patronage of the state, the massive railroad-building spree of the 1850s. The French Crédit Mobilier collapsed in controversy, but the revolution in banking was well under way.

Finally, continental Europeans actively promoted invention and technological development. They were willing for the state to establish educational systems whose aim, among others, was to produce a well-trained elite capable of assisting in the development of industrial technology. In sum, what Britain had produced almost by chance, the Europeans began to reproduce by design.

Industrialization after 1850

Until 1850, Britain remained the preeminent industrial power. Between 1850 and 1870, however, France, Germany, Belgium, and the United States emerged as challengers to the power and place of British manufacturers. The British iron industry remained the largest in the world (in 1870, Britain still produced half the world's pig iron), but it grew more slowly than did its counterparts in France or Germany. Most of continental Europe's gains came as a result of continuing changes in the areas we recognize as important for sustained industrial growth: transport, commerce, and government policy. The spread of railways encouraged the free movement of goods. International monetary unions were established and restrictions removed on international waterways such as the Danube. Free trade went hand in hand with removing guild barriers to entering trades and ending restrictions on practicing business. Guild control over artisanal production was abolished in Austria in 1859, and in most of Germany by the mid-1860s. Laws against usury, most of which had

ceased to be enforced, were officially abandoned in Britain, Holland, Belgium, and in many parts of Germany. Governmental regulation of mining was surrendered by the Prussian state in the 1850s, freeing entrepreneurs to develop resources as they saw fit. Investment banks continued to form, encouraged by an increase in the money supply and an easing of credit after the California gold fields opened in 1849.

The first phase of the Industrial Revolution, one economic historian reminds us, was confined to a narrow set of industries and can be summed up rather simply: "cheaper and better clothes (mainly made of cotton), cheaper and better metals (pig iron, wrought iron, and steel) and faster travel (mainly by rail)." The second half of the century brought changes farther afield and in areas where Great Britain's early advantages were no longer decisive. Transatlantic cable (starting in 1865) and the telephone (invented in 1876) laid the ground for a revolution in communications. New chemical processes, dyestuffs, and pharmaceuticals emerged; as did new sources of energy: electricity (in which the United States and Germany led both invention and commercial development) and oil (which was being refined in the 1850s and widely used by 1900). Among the early exploiters of Russian oil discoveries were the Swedish Nobel brothers and the French Rothschilds. The developments that eventually converged to make the automobile came primarily from Germany and France. The internal combustion engine, important because it was small, efficient, and could be used in a very wide variety of situations, was developed by Carl Benz and Gottlieb Daimler in the 1880s. The removable pneumatic tire was patented in 1891 by Edouard Michelin, a painter who had joined his engineer brother in running the family's small agricultural-equipment business. These developments are discussed fully in Chapter 23, but their pioneers' familiar names illustrate how industry and invention had diversified over the course of the century.

In eastern Europe, the nineteenth century brought different patterns of economic development. Spurred by the ever-growing demand for food and grain, large sections of eastern Europe developed into concentrated, commercialized agriculture regions that played a specific role of exporting food to the West. Many of those large agricultural enterprises were based on serfdom and remained so in the face of increasing pressure for reform until 1850. Peasant protests and liberal demands for reform only gradually chipped away at the nobility's determination to hold on to its privilege and system of labor. The emancipation of Prussian peasants from serfdom was largely accomplished as early as 1810, as part of the reforms that followed Prussia's defeat by Napoleon's armies in 1807. Serfdom was abolished in the Habsburg Empire in 1848, and in Russia (and the Polish territories controlled by Russia) in the 1860s.

INTERIOR OF A CANUT HOUSEHOLD IN LYON, c. 1830. The growth of the silk industry in Lyon in eighteenth-century France attracted many weavers and their families to the city's central neighborhoods. By the mid-1800s, Lyon was home to 80,000 master artisans with their own shops in the trade and a further 40,000 *compagnons*, trained weavers who had not yet set up their own establishments and worked as employees in the shops of others. The Canuts, as these weavers were called, worked as many as eighteen hours a day and were known for their militancy and activism. They rose up in revolt in 1831, 1834, and 1848, and their revolts were among the first examples of workers' insurrections in the nineteenth century. In the image of a Canut household above, the labor of nearly all the members of the family can be identified: weaving, spinning, and preparing the thread.

Although industry continued to take a backseat to agriculture, eastern Europe had several important manufacturing regions. In the Czech region of Bohemia, textile industries that developed in the eighteenth century continued to thrive; by the 1830s, there were machine-powered Czech cotton mills and iron works. In Russia, a factory industry producing coarse textiles—mostly linens—emerged around Moscow. At mid-century, Russia was purchasing 24 percent of the total British machinery exports to mechanize its own mills. Many who labored in Russian industry actually remained serfs until the 1860s, with about 40 percent employed in mines. Of the over 800,000 Russians engaged in manufacturing by 1860, however, most were employed in small workshops of about 40 persons.

By 1870, the core industrial nations of Europe included Great Britain, France, Germany, Italy, the Netherlands, and Switzerland; Austria-Hungary stood at the margins; and Russia, Spain, Greece, Romania, and the western Ottoman Empire (which still included Serbia and Bulgaria in 1870) formed the industrial periphery—although some regions of these nations seemed virtually untouched by the advance of industry. What was more, even in Great Britain, the most fully industrialized nation, agricultural laborers still constituted the single largest occupational category in 1860, although they formed only 9 percent of the overall population. In Belgium, the Netherlands, Switzerland, Germany, France, Scandinavia, and Ireland, 25 to 50 percent of the population still worked on the land; and in Russia, the number was 80 percent. *Industry,* moreover, did not mean automation or machine production, which long remained confined to a few sectors of the economy. As machines were introduced in some sectors to do specific tasks, they usually intensified

The following text labels appear on the map:

Moscow

RUSSIAN EMPIRE

BLACK SEA

OTTOMAN EMPIRE

St. Petersburg

MEDITERRANEAN SEA

Uppsala
Stockholm

SWEDEN

BALTIC SEA

Lemberg

Warsaw

Cracow

Lodz

Budapest

AUSTRIAN EMPIRE

Posen

Danube R.

SILESIA

NORWAY

DENMARK

Copenhagen

Breslau

Vienna

Steyr

Prague

Pilsen

Naples

GERMAN EMPIRE

Hamburg

Berlin

Dresden

Zwickau

Chemnitz

Nuremberg

Munich

Leipzig

Kassel

Eisenach

Frankfurt

Florence

Rome

ITALY

Bremen

RUHR

Cologne

Karlsruhe

Stuttgart

NETHERLANDS

Amsterdam

SAAR

Strasbourg

Basel

Zurich

SWITZ.

Turin

Milan

Livorno

NORTH SEA

Lille

Brussels

Liège

Mulhouse

BELGIUM

Lyons

Avignon

Darlington

Glasgow

Leeds

Sheffield

Amiens

Paris

UNITED KINGDOM

Liverpool

Manchester

Birmingham

Cardiff

London

Le Havre

Orléans

Tours

FRANCE

Limoges

Marseilles

Barcelona

Dublin

Nantes

Gijon

Bilbao

Santander

ATLANTIC OCEAN

Oviedo

Madrid

Granada

Seville

Jerez

Lisbon

Area of detail

EUROPE

AFRICA

300 Miles

100   200   300

0

100 200   300 Kilometers

0

PERCENT OF POPULATION LIVING IN CITIES OF 100,000 OR MORE

5 percent or less

6 to 10 percent

20 percent or more

Railroads in 1850

Centers of industry

Iron ore deposits

Coal and lignite deposits

THE INDUSTRIAL REVOLUTION. Rapid industrial growth depended on a circular network of relationships. ▪ *According to the map key, what elements made up the circular networks of relationships?* ▪ *How were these elements connected, and how might they have reinforced each other, contributing to rapid growth?* ▪ *Why do you think the percentage of populations living in cities was so much greater in the United Kingdom?*

the tempo of handwork in other sectors. Thus, even in the industrialized regions, much work was still accomplished in tiny workshops—or at home.

Industry and Empire

From an international perspective, nineteenth-century Europe was the most industrial region of the world. And Europeans, particularly the British, jealously guarded their international advantages. They preferred to do so through financial leverage. Britain, France, and other European nations gained control of the national debts of China, the Ottoman Empire, Egypt, Brazil, Argentina, and other non-European powers. They also supplied large loans to other states, which bound those nations to their European investors. If the debtor nations expressed discontent, as Egypt did in the 1830s when it attempted to establish its own cotton textile industry, they confronted financial pressure and shows of force. Coercion, however, was not always necessary or even one-sided. Social change in other empires—China, Persia, and the Mughal Empire of India, for example—made those empires vulnerable and created new opportunities for the European powers and their local partners. Ambitious local elites often reached agreements with Western governments or groups such as the British East India Company. These trade agreements transformed regional economies on terms that sent the greatest profits to Europe after a substantial gratuity to the Europeans' local partners. Where agreements could not be made, force prevailed, and Europe took territory and trade by conquest (see Chapter 22).

Industrialization tightened global links between Europe and the rest of the world, creating new networks of trade and interdependence. To a certain extent, the world economy divided between the producers of manufactured goods (Europe itself) and suppliers of the necessary raw materials and buyers of finished goods (everyone else). Cotton growers in the southern United States, sugar growers in the Caribbean, and wheat growers in Ukraine accepted arrangements with the industrialized West and typically profited from them. If there were disputes, however, those suppliers often found that Europe could look elsewhere for the same goods—or dictate the terms of trade down the business end of a bank ledger or a cannon barrel.

BRITISH CLIPPER SHIPS IN CALCUTTA HARBOR, 1860. Calcutta (Kolkata), a long-established city on the eastern coast of India, was one of the hubs of the British Empire—a center for trade in cotton, jute, opium, and tea. The dazzling new clipper ships, first built in the 1830s and 1840s, were very fast and central to the global economy of the nineteenth century. ■ *What was the significance of this trade for the Indian economy?* ■ *Could Indian merchants compete on equal terms with U.S. cotton producers in 1860?*

In 1811, Britain imported 3 percent of the wheat it consumed. By 1891, that portion had risen to 79 percent. Why? In an increasingly urban society, fewer people lived off the land. The commercialization of agriculture, which began early in Britain, had taken even firmer hold elsewhere, turning new regions—Australia, Argentina, and North America (Canada and the United States)—into centers of grain and wheat production. And new forms of transportation, finance, and communication made it easier to shuttle commodities and capital through international networks. These simple percentages dramatize the new interdependence of the nineteenth century. They illustrate, as well as any statistics can, how ordinary Britons' lives, like those of their counterparts in other nations, were embedded in an increasingly global economy.

THE SOCIAL CONSEQUENCES OF INDUSTRIALIZATION

We have mentioned population growth as one factor in industrial development, but it deserves treatment on its own terms. By any measure, the nineteenth century

Interpreting Visual Evidence

Learning to Live in a Global Economy

The commercial networks of the Atlantic world were already well established before the Industrial Revolution, and Europeans were also trading widely with South and East Asia before the end of the eighteenth century. Nevertheless, the advent of an industrial economy in Europe at the beginning of the nineteenth century created such a demand for raw materials and for new markets abroad that it became profitable for manufacturers and merchants to ship much larger amounts of goods over longer distances than ever before. As different industrialized regions in Europe became more and more dependent on overseas markets, people in Europe came to be aware of the extent to which their own activities linked them to other parts of the world. Awareness of these linkages did not always mean that they possessed complete or accurate information about the people who produced the cotton that they wore or purchased the manufactured goods that they made. Although it did stimulate their imagination and changed their consciousness of their place in the world.

This awareness is well illustrated in the cartoons shown here, which come from the British illustrated news in the 1850s and 1860s. The first (image A) depicts John Bull, representing British textile manufacturers, looking on as U.S. cotton suppliers fight one another during the Civil War in the United States. He states, "Oh! If you two like fighting better than business, I shall deal at the other shop." In the background, an Indian cotton merchant is happy to have him as a customer.

The second cartoon (image B) depicts the ways that the increasingly interconnected global economy might stimulate a

PUNCH, OR THE LONDON CHARIVARI.—November 16, 1861.

INDIAN COTTON DEPÔT

COTTON STORES

OVER THE WAY.

Mr. Bull. "OH! IF YOU TWO LIKE FIGHTING BETTER THAN BUSINESS, I SHALL DEAL AT THE OTHER SHOP."

A. John Bull and cotton merchants.

constituted a turning point in European demographic history. In 1800, the population of Europe as a whole was estimated roughly at 205 million. By 1850, it had risen to 274 million; by 1900, 414 million; and on the eve of the First World War, it was 480 million. (Over the same span of time, the world population went from about 900 million to 1.6 billion.) Britain, with its comparatively high standard of living, saw its population nearly triple, from 16 to 45 million. The territory that was eventually included in a united Germany after 1870 (see Chapter 21) saw a similar increase, from about 22 million in 1801 to 67 million in 1913. Population increases came in the largely rural regions as well. In Russia, the population rose from 36 to 160 million during the same period. Growth was less pronounced in France, which only grew from about 27 million in 1801 to 40 million in 1910.

new kind of political awareness. A French worker, who Emperor Napoleon III placed in irons for participating in a revolutionary movement, compares his situation to that of an African slave seated next to him, saying, "Courage, my friend! Am I not a man and a brother?" A poster on the wall behind the two men refers to the Portuguese slave trade. Napoleon III himself came to power by overthrowing the Second Republic in France, a government that had abolished the slave trade in French territories.

POOR CONSOLATION.

Parisian. "COURAGE, MON AMI; 'AM I NOT A MAN AND A BROTHER?'"

B. Increasing global awareness in France.

Questions for Analysis

1. What constellation of private and national interests were at play in the relationships portrayed in image A? What significance might contemporaries have attached to the possibility that the British might have chosen to buy their cotton from an Asian source "over the way" rather than from North America?

2. In image B, what is the message of the cartoon's suggestion that the slave and the worker might find equality only in the fact that they are both in chains? What was at stake in comparing a worker with a slave in mid-nineteenth-century Europe? Why does the caption read "Poor Consolation?"

3. How does the racial imagery of these cartoons relate to their intended message?

Population Growth and the Demographic Transition

Across nineteenth century Europe, populations began a gradual shift from high fertility and mortality to lower death rates and fewer births. Social scientists refer to this as the "demographic transition." The causes of this population shift are complex, and the same pattern is not observable everywhere in Europe. A gradual decline in death rates seems to have begun in northwestern Europe at the end of the eighteenth century and spread across the Continent south and eastward over the next hundred years. Birth rates remained high during the same period, and it is the conjunction between these two tendencies—slowly falling death rates and continued high birth rates—that probably

Past and Present

Are There Limits to Economic Growth?

Even in its infancy, industrial society had its critics—those who regretted the changes that the new forms of manufacture brought to work, the social order, and the environment (left). The current concern about climate change caused by the burning of fossil fuels (right) is thus the latest chapter in a long history of debate and controversy over the consequences of industrialization.

 Watch related author interview on the Student Site

accounts for much of the population growth in the nineteenth century. The general decline in mortality did not occur because of medical breakthroughs but appears to be largely the result of improved food supplies and clean water. Declines in mortality due to improved medicine and public health did not have a significant impact on the number of people who survived childhood to reach adulthood until the late nineteenth century. In spite of these general improvements, mortality remained high in many areas, especially in the poorer neighborhoods of Europe's cities. Even in 1880, the average male life expectancy at birth in Berlin was no more than thirty years (in rural districts nearby, it was forty-three).

Population growth in the nineteenth century also resulted from increases in fertility. The spread of rural manufacturing allowed couples to marry and set up households at a younger age, even before they inherited any land, raising the average number of children born to each woman and increasing the size of families. Not only did the age of marriage fall but also more people married. And because population growth increased the proportion of young and fertile people, the process reinforced itself in the next generation, setting the stage for a period of prolonged growth. It was only in the twentieth century that this pattern of demographic dynamism in Europe stabilized; as families began actively to limit the number of children born, population growth slowed markedly. Here, too, a range of contributing factors were involved, including the spread of female literacy and women's employment, as well as an increase of the relative proportion of the population that lived in cities and so no longer saw the same need for large families. (Contraception was not widely available in Europe until the twentieth century, and it is only then that demographers begin to see a strong correlation between contraceptive use and fertility.)

Rural Populations in Motion

Even as the West grew more industrial, the majority of people continued to live on the land. Conditions in the countryside were harsh. Peasants still did most of their sowing and harvesting by hand. Millions of tiny farms produced, at most, a bare subsistence living; and families wove, spun, made knives, and sold butter to make ends meet. The average daily diet for an entire family in a good year might amount to no more than two or three pounds of bread—a total of about 3,000 calories daily. By many measures, living conditions for rural inhabitants of many areas in Europe grew worse in the first half of the nineteenth century, a fact of considerable political importance in the 1840s. Rising population put more pressure on the land, and small-sized holdings and indebtedness were chronic problems in regions where farmers scraped by on their own lands.

Over the course of the century, some 37 million people (most of them peasants) left Europe—an eloquent testimony to the bleakness of rural life—and settled in the United States, South America, northern Africa, New Zealand, Australia, and Siberia. In many cases, governments encouraged emigration to ease overcrowding, sometimes forcibly deporting populations they deemed undesirable. In the United States, the policy of Indian removal can be seen as linked to these European migrations. This policy freed up land for European settlers in the southeast at enormous human cost by forcing Native American tribes to exchange land east of the Mississippi for territory in the West after 1830. This policy also is evidence of the continued importance of agricultural land even as industrialization grew increasingly central to national economies.

The most tragic combination of poverty, famine, and migration in the nineteenth century came to Ireland in the Great Famine of 1845–1849, today commonly known as the **Irish Potato Famine**. Potatoes, which had come to Europe from the New World, fundamentally transformed the diets of European peasants, providing much more nutrition for less money than corn and grain. They also grew more densely, an enormous advantage for peasants scraping a living from small plots of land. Nowhere did they become more important than in Ireland, where

the climate and soil made growing grain difficult. When a fungus hit the potato crop—first in 1845 and again, fatally, in 1846 and 1847—no alternative foods were at hand, and at least 1 million Irish died of starvation; dysentery from spoiled foods; or fever, which spread through villages and the overcrowded workhouses (poorhouses), state-run institutions that housed poverty-stricken populations. Before the famine, tens of thousands of Irish were already crossing the Atlantic to North America; they accounted for one-third of all voluntary migration to the New World. In the ten years after 1845, 1.5 million people left Ireland for good. The potato blight also struck in Germany, Scotland, and the Netherlands but with less catastrophic results. Europe had known deadly famines for centuries, but the tragic Irish famine came late, at a time when many thought that starvation was receding into the past.

Changes in the land depended partly on particular governments. States sympathetic to commercial agriculture made it easier to transfer land, eliminate small farms, and create larger estates. In Britain, over half the total area of the country, excluding wasteland, was composed of estates of a thousand acres or more. In Spain, the fortunes of large-scale commercial agriculture fluctuated with changes in the political regime: the liberal regime passed legislation

DINNERTIME AT ST. PANCRAS WORKHOUSE, LONDON. The British system of assistance to the poor was designed to be severe to discourage the able-bodied from seeking relief. Prior to the nineteenth century, the indigent were only allowed to seek assistance in their home parish. This gradually developed into a system of municipal workhouses, where people were given accommodations in exchange for labor, often at tedious and painful tasks. After the economic downturn following the Napoleonic Wars, the number of poor in the workhouses grew rapidly; larger ones, such as St. Pancras Workhouse in London, shown here, housed and fed male and female populations separately.

Laborers in Motion in the Industrial Era

> During the Industrial Revolution, patterns of labor migration intensified as economic development reinforced the inequalities between different regions in Europe, and laborers continued to move from areas that lacked resources to those that offered a greater chance of employment. Earlier generations had accepted such movement as normal, and workers' associations, like the blacksmiths' brotherhood in France described below by Agricol Perdiguier, incorporated this expectation of mobility into their rituals. Perdiguier (1805–1875) was a woodworker who joined a workers' confraternity after his apprenticeship and wrote about the experience in his autobiography. These brotherhoods were organized by trade and operated as both professional and social organizations, with connections in many cities.
>
> Later in the century, workers were more likely to face the uncertainties of labor migration without the help of such associations. Franz Rehbein (1867–1909), a farm worker from Pomerania in eastern Germany, describes the difficult life of a migrant day laborer some decades after Perdiguier's blacksmiths. Rehbein followed the harvest as part of a crew operating a threshing machine. The machine allowed estate owners to bring in their crop with fewer workers and created opportunities for migrant crews that moved from farm to farm. At the same time, it created an intense new pace for agricultural labor, now determined by the capacity of the machine.

Agricol Perdiguier, Memoirs of a Compagnon, 1854

The blacksmiths have created one of the strongest associations; they have spread themselves everywhere and one finds them in cities and in villages. But they are hard and tough! They won't put up with mockery. Their wrists can twist iron and they know it; they are all too ready to fight. Amongst themselves they have their own unique customs. Here is one I have seen:

They were in a field by the side of the road. They were performing what they called their duty. It was an outdoor ceremony, a required ritual for the benefit of one who was leaving.

Their walking sticks were stuck in the earth. Fluttering from their buttonholes were red, white, and green ribbons. Standing shoulder to shoulder they made a large circle and looked toward the center. One of them, holding in his right hand a glass filled with deeply colored wine, began to run, making his way around the exterior of this circle, shouting and crying until he came back to his place, where a companion waited for him, also with a glass in his hand. They faced one another, made some signs, stepped forward and leaned to one side, interlocked their right arms and carried their glasses to their lips, drinking at the same time. The one who had shouted and ran returned to his place and his neighbor stepped out and imitated him, and finally all of them, one after another did the same, down to the last man. They also performed some shouts all together.

The one who was leaving stepped away, with his goatskin sack on his back and his long walking stick in his hand, and his drinking gourd hanging to one side, two bright rings of gold shone at his ears. Each man called to him, and called to him again. But the temptation had no hold on him: he set off without turning his head, without showing any sign of weakness. They tried again, berating him, pleading with him, but nothing had an effect: He marched proudly before them. All at once he took his hat in his hands, threw it over his head far behind his back and took off. His brothers ran and picked it up, pursuing him, finally reaching him and stuffing the hat firmly back on his head. The one leaving remained insensible and did not acknowledge the one who had returned his head covering. He walked with a firm step, without looking to the right or to the left. He was a statue, nothing surprised him, nothing moved him, nothing could force him to step aside. The other companions returned the way they had come, the ritual was complete. He had proved his determination to leave.

Source: Agricol Perdiguier, *Mémoires d'un compagnon* (Geneva: Duchamp, 1853), vol. 2, pp. 8–10. Translation from the French by Joshua Cole.

Franz Rehbein, The Life of a Farmworker, 1911

Not every farm has a threshing machine, and there are no cooperatives like in other places. The threshing machine operators are independent businessmen who buy their own machine with cash or loans. They hire their own crews and move with them from farm to farm where they have contracts. Threshers are paid hourly wages. To operate a threshing machine you need 25–30 men. [. . .]

Working the threshing machine is the most demanding and exhausting work that one can think of. Hour after hour you work like an animal. The more hours in a day, the quicker the farmer will be done with the team, and the fewer meals the farmer will have to feed them. The more hours the machine operator works, the more grain can he process and the higher his profit. The more hours the crew put in, the higher their weekly wage. You get up at 4 am at the latest, sometimes already at 3, and then you work all day long without rest until 8 in the evening at the earliest, and often until 9 or 10, or even 11 and 12. The only rest is the time it takes you to eat your food, which amounts to no more than an hour total for the day. And even supper is not a break because you only eat it when work has stopped, no matter how late.

The work goes as fast as the thresher's "sweat box" can swallow the grain. The worker must keep up with the machine, he is a slave and becomes part of the machine. Imagine the nonstop howling and groaning of the thresher, and the impenetrable dust that surrounds you, and then you can understand what the threshing machine means for the worker. The dust collects almost a centimeter thick on people, especially if the grain has soaked up a lot of rain, and they can see nothing out of their swollen and burning eyes. Your nose is completely stuffed from inhaling dust, and when you spit big gobs of black slime come up your throat and out. The dust sticks fast to your sweaty skin causing an unpleasant itching and burning, as if your whole body was covered with ants.

When you've put in 15, 16, or 18 hours in such circumstances you are dead tired, in the truest sense of the word. You can barely get your supper down and you'd like nothing more than to go to bed. But sleep is only possible after work if the machine is going to stay several days at the same farm. Often you have to travel late or even in the middle of the night to the next farm, sometimes to a village hours away, and as luck would have it, under drenching rain. If the machine gets stuck in a country ditch then you can't think about rest. The thresher and the engine have to be lifted with levers, and the whole crew has to haul on the chains to help the horses pull. When you are finally there, the machine has to be set up by lantern light and only then can you go find a spot to get a couple hours rest.

Because there are never enough beds in one farm for so many people, only the master, the fireman, and the two packers get a bed. Most of the crew look for a bit of straw, hay or chaff wherever they can find it.

Source: Franz Rehbein, *Das Leben eines Landarbeiters* (Jena: Eugen Diederichs Verlag, 1911), pp. 238–240. Translation from the German by Joshua Cole.

Questions

1. What do these two passages tell us about the attitudes toward labor mobility among the workers themselves? Where does the impulse to move come from in each account?

2. What aspects of workers' experience do these two authors seek to show to their readers? What is different about the way workers think about their relation to each other?

3. In what way do you think industrialization shaped the lives of workers like those who appear in these accounts?

IRISH POTATO FAMINE, 1845–1849. Many in Ireland widely held that the Irish potato famine had human as well as natural causes. Historians have noted that food exports from Ireland continued and may have even increased for some products during the famine, as merchants sought higher prices abroad. The cartoon on the left depicts armed soldiers keeping starving Irish Catholic families at bay, as sacks of potatoes are loaded onto a ship owned by a prosperous Irish Protestant trader. On the right, an 1848 engraving from the *Illustrated London News* depicts an impoverished tenant family being evicted from their cottage for nonpayment of rent by their landlord. Thousands of such evictions took place, adding to the misery of the tenant farmers who were thus unable to plant new crops after losing the potato harvest to blight.

encouraging the free transfer of land in 1820; but when absolutism was restored in 1823, this law was repealed. In Russia, some of the largest landowners possessed over half a million acres. Until the emancipation of the serfs in the 1860s, landowners claimed the labor of dependent peasant populations for as much as several days per week. But the system of serfdom gave neither landowners nor serfs much incentive to improve farming techniques. After emancipation, it became possible for the Russian peasantry to think of moving eastward into the less populated areas of Siberia and central Asia. The Russian monarchy had long used Siberia as a place to send its political exiles, but in the late nineteenth century, several million Russian peasants made their way eastward to homestead on the steppe and the forests of northern Siberia.

European serfdom, which bound hundreds of thousands of men, women, and children to particular estates for generations, made it difficult to buy and sell land freely and was an obstacle to the commercialization of agriculture. Yet the opposite was also the case. In France, peasant landholders who had benefited from the French Revolution's sale of lands and the laws on inheritance stayed in the countryside, continuing to work their small farms. Although French peasants were poor, they were able to sustain themselves on the land. This had important consequences: France suffered less agricultural distress, even in the 1840s, than did other European countries; migration from country to city was slower than in the other nations; and far fewer peasants left France for other countries.

Industrialization also transformed rural areas. Improved communication networks not only afforded rural populations a keener sense of events and opportunities elsewhere but also made it possible for governments to intrude into the lives of these men and women to a degree previously impossible. Central bureaucracies now found it easier to collect taxes from the **peasantry** and to conscript sons of peasant families into armies. Some rural cottage industries faced direct competition from factory-produced goods, which meant less work or lower piece rates and falling incomes for families, especially during the winter months. In other sectors of the economy, industry spread out into the countryside, with whole regions becoming specialized producers of shoes, shirts, ribbons, cutlery, and so on, in small shops and workers' homes. Thus, changes in the market could usher in prosperity or bring entire regions to the verge of starvation.

Vulnerability often led to political violence, and rural rebellions were common in the early nineteenth century. In southern England in the late 1820s, small farmers and day laborers joined forces to burn barns and haystacks, protesting the introduction of threshing machines, a symbol of the new agricultural capitalism. They masked and otherwise disguised themselves, and rode out at night under the banner of their mythical leader "Captain Swing." Their raids were preceded by anonymous threats, such as the one received by a large-scale farmer in the county of Kent: "Pull down your threshing machine or else [expect] fire without delay. We are five thousand men [a highly inflated figure] and will not be stopped." In the southwest of France, peasants, at night and in disguise, attacked local authorities who barred them from collecting wood in the forests; the peasants' traditional gleaning rights had come to an end since forest wood was in demand for new furnaces. Similar rural disturbances broke out across Europe in the 1830s and 1840s against landlords; against tithes, or taxes to the church; against laws curtailing customary rights; and against unresponsive governments. In Russia, serf uprisings were a reaction to continued bad harvests and exploitation.

Many onlookers considered the nineteenth-century cities dangerous seedbeds of sedition. Yet conditions in the countryside and frequent flare-ups of rural protest remained the greatest source of trouble for governments, and rural politics exploded, as we will see, in the 1840s. Peasants were land poor, deep in debt, and precariously dependent on markets. More important, a government's inability to contend with rural misery made it look autocratic, indifferent, or inept—all political failings.

Urban Migration

The growth of cities was one of the most important facts of nineteenth-century social history, and one with significant cultural reverberations. Over the course of the nineteenth century, as we have seen, the overall population of Europe doubled, and the percentage of that population living in cities tripled—that is, **urban populations** rose sixfold. In mining and manufacturing areas or along newly built railway lines, it sometimes seemed that cities sprang up from nowhere (such as Manchester, Birmingham, and Essen). Sometimes the rates of growth were dizzying. Between 1750 and 1850, London—Europe's largest city—grew from 676,000 to 2.3 million. The population of Paris went from 560,000 to 1.3 million, adding 120,000 new residents

between 1841 and 1846 alone! Berlin, which, like Paris, became the hub of a rapidly expanding railway system, nearly tripled in size during the first half of the century. Such rapid expansion was almost necessarily unplanned and brought in its wake new social problems.

Almost all nineteenth-century cities were overcrowded and unhealthy, and their largely medieval infrastructures strained under the burden of larger populations and the demands of industry. Construction lagged far behind population growth, forcing working men and women who had left families behind in the country to live in temporary lodging houses. The poorest workers dwelled in wretched basements or attic rooms, often without any light or drainage. A local committee appointed to investigate conditions in the British manufacturing town of Huddersfield—by no means the worst of that country's urban centers—reported that there were large areas without paving, sewers, or drains, "where garbage and filth of every description are left on the surface to ferment and rot; where pools of stagnant water are almost constant; where dwellings adjoining are thus necessarily caused to be of an inferior and even filthy description; thus where disease is engendered, and the health of the whole town perilled."

Governments gradually adopted measures in an attempt to cure the worst of these ills, if only to prevent the spread of catastrophic epidemics. Legislation was designed to rid cities of their worst slums by tearing them down and to improve sanitary conditions by supplying both water and drainage. Yet by 1850, these projects had only just begun. Paris, perhaps better supplied with water

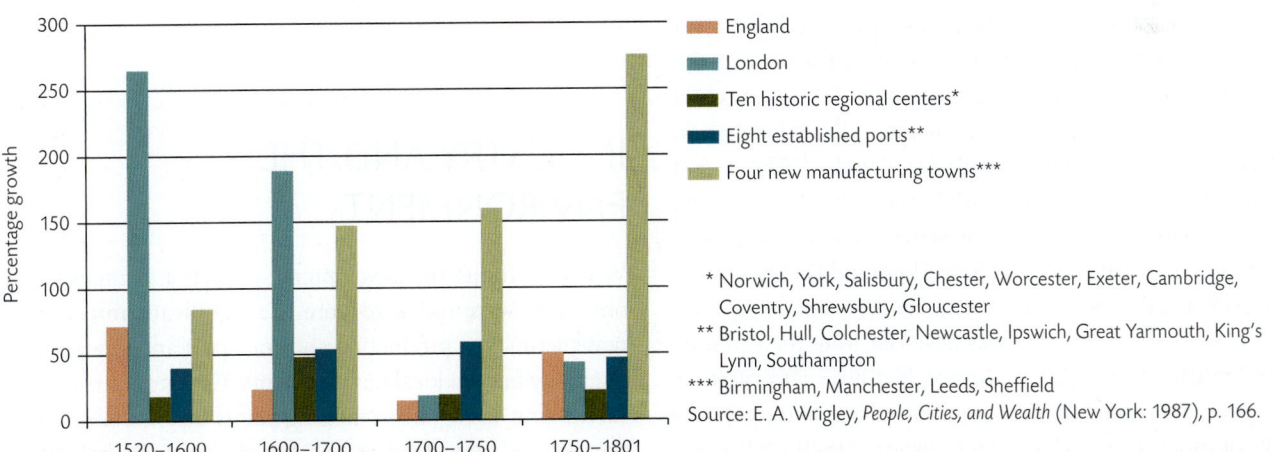

* Norwich, York, Salisbury, Chester, Worcester, Exeter, Cambridge, Coventry, Shrewsbury, Gloucester
** Bristol, Hull, Colchester, Newcastle, Ipswich, Great Yarmouth, King's Lynn, Southampton
*** Birmingham, Manchester, Leeds, Sheffield
Source: E. A. Wrigley, *People, Cities, and Wealth* (New York: 1987), p. 166.

URBAN GROWTH IN EARLY MODERN ENGLAND. This figure shows the percentage increases in population in England as a whole, as well as in several distinct groups of population centers. London had its greatest percentage increases in the periods 1520–1600 and 1600–1700, *before* the period of industrial expansion. The historic regional centers—cathedral and market towns—had steady but unspectacular growth across these years, as did English port cities. The most remarkable growth, however, was in the new industrial areas of the north in the second half of the eighteenth century. ▪ *What can we conclude about the nature of population growth in England from this figure?* ▪ *What other sorts of information would allow you to draw more certain conclusions about the nature of these demographic shifts?*

than any other European city, had enough for no more than two baths per person per year. In London, human waste remained uncollected in 250,000 domestic cesspools. And in Manchester, fewer than one-third of the dwellings were equipped with toilets of any sort.

The Social Question

Against the backdrop of the French Revolution of 1789 and subsequent revolutions in the nineteenth century (as we will see in the following chapters), the new "shock" cities of the nineteenth century and their swelling multitudes posed urgent questions. Political leaders, social scientists, and public health officials across all of Europe issued thousands of reports—many of them several volumes long—on criminality, water supply, sewers, prostitution, tuberculosis and cholera, alcoholism, wet nursing, wages, and unemployment. Radicals and reformers grouped all these issues under a broad heading known as the "social question." Governments, pressed by reformers and by the omnipresent rumblings of unrest, felt they had to address these issues before the complaints swelled into revolution, and they did so in the first social engineering: police forces, public health, sewers and new water supplies, inoculations, elementary schools, Factory Acts (regulating work hours), Poor Laws (outlining the conditions for receiving relief), and new urban regulation and city planning. Central Paris, for instance, was almost entirely redesigned in the nineteenth century—the crowded, medieval, and revolutionary poor neighborhoods were gutted, markets rebuilt, and streets widened and lit (see Chapter 21).

From the 1820s on, the social question hung over Europe like a cloud, and it formed part of the backdrop to the revolutions of 1848 (discussed in Chapter 21). Surveys and studies and early social science provided direct inspiration for novelists such as Honoré de Balzac, Charles Dickens, and Victor Hugo. In his novel *Les Misérables* (1862), Hugo even used the sewers of Paris as a central metaphor for the general condition of urban existence. Both Hugo and Dickens wrote sympathetically about the poor, juvenile delinquency, and child labor; and revolution was never far from their minds. The French writer Balzac, however, had little sympathy for the poor, but shared his fellow writers' views on the corruption of modern life. His *Human Comedy* (1829–1855) was a series of ninety-five novels and stories, including *Eugénie Grandet, Old Goriot, Lost Illusions,* and *A Harlot High and Low.* Balzac was biting in his observations about ruthless, self-promoting young men and the cold calculations behind romantic liaisons. And he was but one of many writers to use prostitution as a metaphor for what he considered the deplorable materialism and desperation of his time.

Sex in the City

Prostitution flourished in nineteenth-century cities; in fact, it offers a microcosm of the nineteenth-century urban economy. At mid-century, the number of prostitutes in Vienna was estimated to be 15,600; in Paris, where prostitution was a licensed trade, 50,000; and in London, 80,000. London newspaper reports of the 1850s cataloged the elaborate hierarchies of the vast underworld of prostitutes and their customers, and included entrepreneurs with names like Swindling Sal who ran lodging houses; the pimps and "fancy men" who managed the trade of prostitutes on the street; and the relatively few "prima donnas," courtesans who enjoyed the protection of rich, upper-middle-class lovers who entertained lavishly and whose wealth allowed them to move on the fringes of more respectable high society. The heroines in Alexandre Dumas's novel *La dame aux camélias* ("The Lady of the Camellias") and in Giuseppe Verdi's opera *La traviata* ("The Fallen Woman") were modeled on these women. Yet the vast majority of prostitutes were not courtesans but rather women (and some men) who worked long and dangerous hours in port districts of cities or at lodging houses in the overwhelmingly male working-class neighborhoods. Most prostitutes were young women who had just arrived in the city or working women trying to manage during periods of unemployment. Single women in the cities were very vulnerable to sexual exploitation. Many were abandoned by their partners if they became pregnant, and others faced the danger of rape by their employers. Such experiences—abandonment and rape—could lead to prostitution, because women in these circumstances were unlikely to secure "respectable" employment.

INDUSTRY AND THE ENVIRONMENT

Wherever industrial development occurred, contemporary observers were quick to note the significant impact that new methods of production and transport and new sources of energy had on local environments. Coal mines produced mountains of slag, iron smelting plants belched smoke into the air, and industrial establishments flushed their waste into rivers and streams that were the main source of water for the towns and villages on the banks. When studying the broad scope of environmental change in the nineteenth century, it is useful to consider these most visible changes against the background of longer-term shifts that were already well under way the moment industrialization began at the end of the eighteenth century.

PROSTITUTION IN NINETEENTH-CENTURY EUROPEAN CITIES. This sketch by Constantin Guys (1802–1892) captures the moment when *grisettes* (slang for flirtatious working-class women) entertain a proposition from two men. Guys's portrayal of the men's indistinct facial features and the saucy posture of the women captured the impersonal nature of the exchange, as well as the mercenary intentions of all parties. ▪ *How did the construction of new cities, with expanded streets designed to facilitate the efficient mixing and movement of people, change the way individuals interacted with each other?*

Land and Water

Population growth and the development of commercial agriculture made arable land increasingly valuable and encouraged the draining of fens, swamps, and salt marshes throughout Europe. Farmers developed techniques for irrigating their meadows to increase hay yields, and, in turn, these activities led to more ambitious projects: the construction of dams, millponds, and canals in areas where rivers had previously meandered according to the season, overflowing their banks and even changing their course occasionally. The construction of dams had an impact on fish and animal populations, leaving river villages that depended in part on fishing to watch their livelihoods disappear, while farmers had better access to markets on newly constructed waterways. Canal construction was an essential part of early industrial development in northern England before the era of railways, and a network of narrow waterways connected Yorkshire, Lancashire, and Birmingham with the larger metropolis of London.

One of the most ambitious projects of river engineering was undertaken by the German authorities after 1812: their goal was to "rectify" the course of the Rhine river as it flowed from the Swiss Alps between France and the western German states to the Netherlands and the North Sea. By the time the project was completed in the 1870s, the Rhine River had been shortened from 220 to 170 miles by dozens of cuts that also removed more than 2,000 islands from the waterway. For each cut, a wide channel had to be excavated along the new course of the river, a process that took years of digging; and eventually, the ends were cut out and the river flowed swiftly along its new banks. The environmental transformation of the region was significant. River marshes gave way to cultivated fields, and communities that had previously survived on fish and bird populations or from harvesting reeds from the Rhine's banks now devoted themselves to the cultivation of beets and potatoes. In the space of only a few generations, the landscape had been irrevocably changed, and the human populations that lived in the region were forced to adapt to new circumstances.

Air and the Urban Environment

The most notorious environmental change associated with industrialization was that of the air itself. Charles Dickens's description of the choking air and polluted water of "Coketown," the fictional city in *Hard Times* (1854), is deservedly well known:

> It was a town of red brick, or of brick that would have been red if the smoke and ashes had allowed it. . . . It was a town of machines and tall chimneys, out of which interminable serpents of smoke trailed themselves forever and ever, and never got uncoiled. It had a black canal in it, and a river that ran purple with ill-smelling dye, and vast piles of building full of windows where there was a rattling and a trembling all day long.

Wood-fired manufacturing and heating for homes had long spewed smoke across the skies, but the new concentration of industrial activity and the transition to coal made the air measurably worse. Early iron furnaces, for example, burned 250 bushels of charcoal for every ton of iron produced, and each bushel of charcoal was made by burning the equivalent of a pile of wood that was 4 by 4 by 48 feet. Since a single furnace could produce 500 tons of iron a year, the demand for wood became enormous. In this way, the amount of particulate matter in the atmosphere directly related to the disappearance of forested land.

In London especially, where even homes switched to coal early, smoke from factories, railroads, and domestic chimneys hung heavily over the city; and the last third of the century brought the most intense pollution in its history.

Over all of England, air pollution took an enormous toll on health, contributing to the bronchitis and tuberculosis that accounted for 25 percent of British deaths. The coal-rich and industrial regions of North America (especially Pittsburgh) and central Europe also had concentrations of pollution; the Ruhr, in particular, had the most polluted air in Europe by the end of the century.

Toxic water, caused by industrial pollution and human waste, posed the second critical environmental hazard in urban areas. London and Paris led the way in building municipal sewage systems, though those emptied into the Thames and the Seine. Cholera, typhus, and tuberculosis were natural predators in areas without adequate sewage facilities or fresh water. The Rhine River, which flowed through central Europe's industrial heartland and intersected with the Ruhr, was thick with detritus from coal mining, iron processing, and the chemical industry. In the late nineteenth century, spurred by several epidemics of cholera, major cities began to purify their water supplies—but conditions in the air, rivers, and land continued to worsen until at least the mid-twentieth century.

VIEW OF LONDON WITH SAINT PAUL'S CATHEDRAL IN THE DISTANCE, **BY WILLIAM HENRY CROME.** Despite the smog-filled skies and intense pollution, many entrepreneurs and politicians celebrated the new prosperity of the Industrial Revolution. As W. P. Rend, a Chicago businessman, wrote in 1892, "Smoke is the incense burning on the altars of industry. It is beautiful to me. It shows that men are changing the merely potential forces of nature into articles of comfort for humanity."

THE MIDDLE CLASSES

Novelists such as Charles Dickens and William Makepeace Thackeray in Britain, Victor Hugo and Honoré Balzac in France, and Theodor Fontane in Germany painted a sweeping portrait of middle-class society in the nineteenth century, with characters from all walks of life: journalists, courtesans, small-town mayors, mill owners, shopkeepers, aristocrats, farmers, laborers, and students. The plots explored the ways the older hierarchies of rank, status, and privilege gradually gave way to a new set of gradations based on wealth and social class. In this new world, money trumped birth, and social mobility was an accepted fact rather than something to be hidden. One of Thackeray's characters observes caustically that "[o]urs is a ready-money society. We live among bankers and city big-wigs . . . and every man, as he talks to you, is jingling his guineas in his pocket." Works of literature need to be approached cautiously, for their characters express their authors' points of view. Still, literature and art offer an extraordinary source of social historical detail and insight, and we can safely say that the rising visibility of the middle classes and their new political and social power—lamented by some writers but hailed by others—were central facts of nineteenth-century society.

Who were the middle classes? (Another common term for this social group, the *bourgeoisie,* originally meant "city [*bourg*] dweller.") Its ranks included shopkeepers and their households; the families of lawyers, doctors, and other professionals; and well-off factory owners who might aspire to marry their daughters to titled aristocrats. At the lower end of the social scale, the middle classes included families of salaried clerks and office workers for whom white-collar employment offered hope of a rise in status.

Movement within the middle-class ranks was often possible in the course of one or two generations. Very few, however, moved from the working class into the middle class. Most middle-class success stories began in the middle class itself, with the children of relatively well-off farmers, skilled artisans, or professionals. Upward mobility was almost impossible without education, and education was a rare, though not unattainable, luxury for working-class children. Careers open to talents (a goal achieved by the French Revolution) frequently meant opening jobs to middle-class young men who could pass exams. The examination system was an important path upward within government bureaucracies.

Equally difficult was the journey from the middle class to the aristocratic, landed society. In Britain, mobility of this sort was easier to achieve than on the Continent. The sons of wealthy, upper-middle-class families might actually

THE LEGISLATIVE BELLY, BY HONORÉ DAUMIER, 1834. Daumier's caricatures of prosperous middle-class politicians drew attention to the political reforms that allowed men of property—no matter their background—to replace the aristocratic elites that had dominated political life before the nineteenth century. His harsh depictions of these politicians' facial features may also have contained a reference to the Jewish origins of some politicians. The accession of Jews to citizenship in 1791 paved the way for political assimilation, and the presence of Jews in parliament would have been noteworthy to contemporaries.

move up, if they were sent to elite schools and universities and if they left the commercial or industrial world for a career in politics. William Gladstone, son of a Liverpool merchant, attended the exclusive educational preserves of Eton (a private boarding school) and Oxford University, married into an aristocratic family, and became the prime minister of England. Yet Gladstone was an exception to the rule, even in Britain, and most upward mobility was much less spectacular.

Nevertheless, the European middle class helped sustain itself with the belief that it was possible to get ahead by means of intelligence, pluck, and serious devotion to work. The Englishman Samuel Smiles, in his extraordinarily successful how-to-succeed book *Self-Help* (1859), preached a gospel dear to the middle class: "The spirit of self-help is the root of all genuine growth in the individual." As Smiles also suggested, those who succeeded were obliged to follow middle-class notions of respectability. The middle classes' claim to political power and cultural influence rested on arguments that they constituted a new and deserving social elite, superior to the common people yet sharply different from the older aristocracy, and the rightful custodians of the nation's future. Thus, middle-class respectability, like a code, stood for many values. It meant financial independence, providing responsibly for one's family, and avoiding gambling and debt. It suggested merit and character as opposed to aristocratic privilege, and hard work as opposed to living off noble estates. Respectable

middle-class gentlemen might be wealthy, but they should live modestly and soberly, avoiding conspicuous consumption, lavish dress, womanizing, and other forms of dandyish behavior associated with the aristocracy. Of course, these were aspirations and codes, not social realities. They nonetheless remained key to the middle-class sense of self and understanding of the world.

Private Life and Middle-Class Identity

Family and home played a central role in forming middle-class identity. Few themes were more common in nineteenth-century fiction than that of men and women pursuing mobility and status by or through marriage. Families served intensely practical purposes: sons, nephews, and cousins were expected to assume responsibility in family firms when it came their turn; wives managed accounts; parents-in-law provided business connections, credit, and inheritance; and so on. The family's role in middle-class thought, however, did not arise only from these practical considerations. It was part of a larger worldview: a well-governed household offered a counterpoint to the business and confusion of the world, and families offered continuity and tradition in a time of rapid change.

Gender and the Cult of Domesticity

There was no single type of middle-class family or home. Yet many people held powerful convictions about how a respectable home should be run. According to advice manuals, poetry, and middle-class journals, wives and mothers were supposed to occupy a "separate sphere" of life, in which they lived in subordination to their spouses. "Man for the field and woman for the hearth; man for the sword and for the needle she. . . . All else confusion," wrote the British poet Alfred, Lord Tennyson in 1847. These prescriptions were directly applied to young people. Boys were educated in secondary schools, girls at home. This nineteenth-century conception of separate spheres needs to be understood in relation to the much longer-standing traditions of paternal authority, which were codified in law. Throughout Europe, laws subjected women to their husbands' authority. The Napoleonic Code, a model for other countries after 1815, classified women, children, and the mentally ill together as legally incompetent. In Britain, a woman transferred all her property rights to her husband on marriage. Although unmarried women did enjoy a degree of legal independence in France and Austria, laws

Analyzing Primary Sources

Marriage, Sexuality, and the Facts of Life

In the nineteenth century, sexuality became the subject of much anxious debate, largely because it raised other issues: the roles of men and women, morality, and social respectability. Doctors threw themselves into the discussion, offering their expert opinions on the health (including the sexual lives) of the population; yet they did not dictate people's private lives. Nineteenth-century men and women responded to what they experienced as the facts of life more than to expert advice. The first document provides an example of medical knowledge and opinion in 1870. The second offers a glimpse of the daily realities of family life in 1830.

A French Doctor Denounces Contraception (1870)

One of the most powerful instincts nature has placed in the heart of man is that which has for its object the perpetuation of the human race. But this instinct, this inclination, so active, which attracts one sex towards the other, is liable to be perverted, to deviate from the path nature has laid out. From this arises a number of fatal aberrations which exercise a deplorable influence upon the individual, upon the family and upon society....

We hear constantly that marriages are less fruitful, that the increase of population does not follow its former ratio. I believe that this is mainly attributable to genesiac frauds. It might naturally be supposed that these odious calculations of egotism, these shameful refinements of debauchery, are met with almost entirely in large cities, and among the luxurious classes, and that small towns and country places yet preserve that simplicity of manners attributed to primitive society, when the *pater familias* was proud of exhibiting his numerous offspring. Such, however, is not the case, and I shall show that those who have an unlimited confidence in the patriarchal habits of our country people are deeply in error. At the present time frauds are practiced by all classes....

The laboring classes are generally satisfied with the practice of Onan [withdrawal].... They are seldom familiar with the sheath invented by Dr. Condom, and bearing his name.

Among the wealthy, on the other hand, the use of this preservative is generally known. It favors frauds by rendering them easier; but it does not afford complete security....

Case X.—This couple belongs to two respectable families of vintners. They are both pale, emaciated, downcast, sickly....

They have been married for ten years; they first had two children, one immediately after the other, but in order to avoid an increase of family, they have had recourse to conjugal frauds. Being both very amorous, they have found this practice very convenient to satisfy their inclinations. They have employed it to such an extent, that up to a few months ago, when their health began to fail, the husband had intercourse with his wife habitually two and three times in twenty-four hours.

The following is the condition of the woman: She complains of continual pains in the lower part of the abdomen and kidneys. These pains disturb the functions of the stomach and render her nervous.... By the touch we find a very intense heat, great sensibility to pressure, and all the signs of a chronic metritis [inflammation of the uterus]. The patient attributes positively her present state to the too frequent approaches of her husband.

The husband does not attempt to exculpate himself, as he also is in a state of extreme suffering. It is not in the genital organs, however, that we find his disorder, but in the whole general nervous system; his history will find its place in the part of this work relative to general disturbances....

Source: Louis-François-Etienne Bergeret, *The Preventive Obstacle, or Conjugal Onanism*, trans. P. de Marmon (New York: 1870), pp. 3–4, 12, 20–22, 25, 56–57, 100–101, 111–113. Originally published in Paris in 1868.

Death in Childbirth (1830)

rs. Ann B. Pettigrew was taken in Labour after returning from a walk in the garden, at 7 o'clock in the evening of June 30, 1830. At 40 minutes after 11 o'clock, she was delivered of a daughter. A short time after, I was informed that the Placenta was not removed, and, at 10 minutes after 12 was asked into the room. I advanced to my dear wife, and kissing her, asked her how she was, to which she replied, I feel very badly. I went out of the room, and sent for Dr. Warren.

I then returned, and inquired if there was much hemorrhage, and was answered that there was. I then asked the midwife (Mrs. Brickhouse) if she ever used manual exertion to remove the placenta. She said she had more than fifty times. I then, fearing the consequences of hemorrhage, observed, Do, my dear sweet wife, permit Mrs. Brickhouse to remove it: To which she assented. . . .

After the second unsuccessful attempt, I desired the midwife to desist. In these two efforts, my dear Nancy suffered exceedingly and frequently exclaimed: "O Mrs. Brickhouse you will kill me," and to me, "O I shall die, send for the Doctor." To which I replied, "I have sent."

After this, my feelings were so agonizing that I had to retire from the room and lay down, or fall. Shortly after which, the midwife came to me and, falling upon her knees, prayed most fervently to God and to me to forgive her for saying that she could do what she could not. . . .

The placenta did not come away, and the hemorrhage continued with unabated violence until five o'clock in the morning, when the dear woman breathed her last 20 minutes before the Doctor arrived.

So agonizing a scene as that from one o'clock, I have no words to describe. O My God, My God! have mercy on me. I am undone forever. . . .

Source: Cited in Erna Olafson Hellerstein, Leslie Parker Hume, and Karen M. Offen, eds., *Victorian Women: A Documentary Account of Women's Lives in Nineteenth-Century England, France, and the United States* (Stanford, CA: 1981), pp. 193–94, 219–20.

Questions for Analysis

1. The French doctor states that the impulse to have sexual relations is "one of the most powerful instincts" given to humans by nature, while simultaneously claiming that this natural instinct is "liable to be perverted." What does this reveal about his attitude toward "nature"?

2. What does he mean by "genesiac frauds"? Who is being deceived by this fraud? What consequences for individuals and for society as a whole does the doctor fear from this deception?

3. What does the story of Mrs. Pettigrew's death reveal about the dangers of childbirth and the state of obstetric medicine in the nineteenth century?

---

generally assigned them to the "protection" of their fathers. Gender relations in the nineteenth century rested on this foundation of legal inequality. Yet the idea or doctrine of separate spheres was meant to underscore that men's and women's spheres complemented each other. Thus, for instance, middle-class writings were full of references to spiritual equality between men and women; and middle-class people wrote, proudly, of marriages in which the wife was a "companion" and "helpmate."

It is helpful to recall that members of the middle class articulated their values in opposition to aristocratic customs, on the one hand, and the lives of the common people, on the other. They argued, for instance, that middle-class marriages did not aim to found aristocratic dynasties and were not arranged to accumulate power and privilege; instead, they were to be based on mutual respect and division of responsibilities. A respectable middle-class woman should be free from the unrelenting toil that was the lot of a woman of the people. Called the "angel in the house" in Victorian Britain, a middle-class woman was responsible for the moral education of her children. It was understood that being a good wife and mother was a demanding task, requiring an elevated character. This belief, sometimes called the "cult of domesticity," was central to middle-class Victorian thinking about women. Home life and, by extension, the woman's role in that life were infused with new meaning. As one young woman put it after reading a popular book on female education, "What an important sphere a woman fills! How thoroughly she ought to be qualified for it—I think hers the more honourable employment than a man's." In sum, the early nineteenth century brought a general reassessment of femininity, the roots of which lay in religion and efforts to moralize society, largely to guard against the disorders of the French and Industrial Revolutions.

As a housewife, a middle-class woman had the task of keeping the household functioning smoothly and harmoniously; she maintained the accounts and directed the activities of the servants. Having at least one servant was a mark of middle-class status; in wealthier families, governesses and nannies cared for children, idealized views of motherhood notwithstanding. The middle classes, however, included many gradations of wealth, from a well-housed banker with a governess and five servants to a village preacher with one. Moreover, the work of running and maintaining a home was enormous: linens and clothes had to be made and mended; only the wealthy had the luxury of running water, and so others had to carry and heat water for cooking, laundry, and cleaning; and heating with coal and lighting with kerosene involved hours of cleaning. If the "angel in the house" was a cultural ideal, it was partly because she had real economic value.

Outside the home, women had very few respectable options for earning a living. (Unmarried women might act as companions or governesses, as the British novelist Charlotte Brontë's heroine Jane Eyre did, and led a generally miserable life until "rescued" by marriage to her difficult employer.) But nineteenth-century convictions about women's moral nature, combined as they were with middle-class aspirations to political leadership, encouraged middle-class wives to undertake voluntary charitable work or to campaign for social reform. In Britain and the United States, women played an important role in the struggle to abolish the slave trade and slavery in the British Empire and the American South. Many of these movements also drew on the energies of religious, especially Protestant, organizations, committed to the eradication of social evils and moral improvement. Throughout Europe, a wide range of movements to improve conditions for the poor in schools and hospitals, for temperance, against prostitution, or for legislation on factory hours were often run by women. Florence Nightingale, who went to the Crimean Peninsula in Russia to nurse British soldiers fighting there in the 1850s, remains the most famous of those women whose determination to right social wrongs compelled them to defy conventional notions of woman's "proper" sphere. Equally famous—or infamous, at the time—was the French female novelist George Sand (1804–1876), whose real name was Amandine Aurore Dupin

Dudevant. Sand dressed like a man and smoked cigars, and her novels often told tales of independent women thwarted by convention and unhappy marriages.

Queen Victoria, who came to the British throne in 1837, labored to make her solemn public image reflect contemporary feminine virtues of moral probity and dutiful domesticity. Her court was eminently proper, a marked contrast to that of her uncle George IV, whose cavalier ways had set the style for high life a generation before. Though possessing a bad temper, Victoria trained herself to curb it in deference to her ministers and her public-spirited, ultrarespectable husband, Prince Albert of Saxe-Coburg. She was a successful queen because she embodied the traits important to the middle class, whose triumph she seemed to epitomize and whose habits of mind we have come to call Victorian. Nineteenth-century ideas about gender had an impact on masculinity as well: soon after the revolutionary and the Napoleonic period, men began to dress in sober, practical clothing, and to see as effeminate or dandyish the wigs, ruffled collars, and tight breeches that had earlier been the pride of aristocratic masculinity.

"Passionlessness": Gender and Sexuality

Victorian ideas about sexuality are among the most remarked-on features of nineteenth-century culture. They have become virtually synonymous with anxiety, prudishness, and ignorance. An English mother counseling her daughter about her wedding night is said to have told her to "lie back and think of the empire." Etiquette apparently required that piano legs be covered. Many of these anxieties and prohibitions, however, have been caricatured. More recently, historians have tried to disentangle the teachings or prescriptions of etiquette books and marriage manuals from the actual beliefs of men and women. Equally important, they have sought to understand each on its own terms. Beliefs about sexuality followed from convictions, described earlier, concerning separate spheres for men and women. Indeed, one of the defining aspects of nineteenth-century ideas about men and women is the extent to which they rested on scientific arguments about nature. Codes of morality and methods of science combined to reinforce the certainty that specific characteristics were inherent to each sex. Men and women had different social roles, and those differences were rooted in their bodies. The French social thinker Auguste Comte provides a good example: "Biological philosophy teaches us that, through the whole animal scale, and while the specific type is preserved, radical differences, physical and moral, distinguish the sexes." Comte also spelled out the implications of biological difference: "[T]he equality of the sexes, of which so much is said, is incompatible with all social existence. . . . The economy of the human family could never be inverted without an entire change in our cerebral organism." Women were unsuited for higher education because their brains were smaller or because their bodies were fragile. "Fifteen or 20 days of 28 (we may say nearly always) a woman is not only an invalid, but a wounded one. She ceaselessly suffers from love's eternal wound," wrote the well-known French author Jules Michelet about menstruation.

Finally, scientists and doctors considered women's alleged moral superiority to be literally embodied in an absence of sexual feeling, or "passionlessness." Scientists and doctors considered male sexual desire as natural, if not admirable, an unruly force that had to be channeled. Many governments legalized and regulated prostitution (which included the compulsory examination of women for venereal disease) precisely because it provided an outlet for male sexual desire. Doctors disagreed about female sexuality, but the British doctor William Acton stood among those who asserted that women functioned differently:

> I have taken pains to obtain and compare abundant evidence on this subject, and the result of my inquiries I may briefly epitomize as follows:— I should say that the majority of women (happily for society) are not very much troubled with sexual feeling of any kind. What men are habitually, women are only exceptionally.

Like other nineteenth-century men and women, Acton also believed that more open expressions of sexuality were disreputable, and also that working-class women were less "feminine."

Convictions such as these reveal a great deal about Victorian science and medicine, but they did not necessarily dictate people's intimate lives. As far as sexuality was concerned, the absence of any reliable contraception mattered more in people's experiences and feelings than sociologists' or doctors' opinions. Abstinence and withdrawal were the only common techniques for preventing pregnancy, but their effectiveness was limited, since until the 1880s, doctors believed that a woman was most fertile during and around her menstrual period. Midwives and prostitutes knew of other forms of contraception and abortifacients (all of them dangerous and ineffective), and surely some middle-class women did as well, but such information was not respectable middle-class fare. In concrete terms, then, sexual intercourse was directly related to the very real dangers of frequent pregnancies. In England, 1 in 100 childbirths ended in the death of the mother; at a time when a woman might become pregnant eight or nine times in her life, this was a sobering prospect. Those dangers varied with social class, but even among wealthy and better-cared-for women, they took a real toll. It is not surprising that middle-class women's diaries and letters are full of their anticipations of childbirth, both joyful and anxious. Queen Victoria, who bore nine children, declared that childbirth was the "shadow side" of marriage—and she was a pioneer in using anesthesia!

Middle-Class Life in Public

The public life of middle-class families literally reshaped the nineteenth-century landscape. Houses and their furnishings were powerful symbols of material security. Solidly built and heavily decorated, they proclaimed the financial worth and social respectability of those who dwelled within. In provincial cities they were often freestanding villas. In London, Paris, Berlin, and Vienna, they might be in rows of five- or six-story townhouses or large apartments. Whatever particular shape they took, they were built to last a long time. The rooms were certain to be crowded with furniture, art objects, carpets, and wall hangings. The size of the rooms, the elegance of the furniture, and the number of servants all depended, of course, on the extent of one's income. A bank clerk did not live as elegantly as a bank director, yet they shared many standards and aspirations, and those common values helped bind them to the same class, despite the differences in their material way of life.

As cities grew, they became increasingly segregated. Middle-class people lived far from the unpleasant sights and smells of industrialization. Their residential areas, usually built to the west of the cities, out of the path of the prevailing breeze and therefore of industrial pollution, were havens from congestion. The public buildings in the center, many constructed during the nineteenth century, were celebrated as signs of development and prosperity. The middle classes increasingly managed their cities' affairs, although members of the aristocracy retained considerable power, especially in central Europe. And it was these new middle-class civic leaders who provided new industrial cities with many of their architectural landmarks: city halls, stock exchanges, museums, opera houses, outdoor concert halls, and department stores. One historian called these buildings the new cathedrals of the industrial age; projects intended to express the community's values and represent public culture, they were monuments to social change.

APARTMENT LIVING IN PARIS. This print shows that on the Continent, rich and poor often lived in the same buildings—the rich on the lower floors and the poor on the top. This sort of residential mixing was less common in Britain.

The suburbs changed as well. The advent of the railways made outings to concerts, parks, and bathing spots popular. They made it possible for families of relatively moderate means to take one- or two-week-long trips to the mountains or the seashore. New resorts opened, offering racetracks, mineral spring baths, and cabanas on the beach. Mass tourism would not come until the twentieth century, but the now-familiar impressionist paintings of the 1870s and 1880s testify to something that was dramatically new in the nineteenth century: a new range of middle-class leisures.

Working-Class Life

Like the middle class, the working class was divided into various subgroups and categories, determined in this case by skill, wage, gender, and workplace. Workers' experiences

varied, depending on where they worked, where they lived, and, above all, how much they earned. A skilled textile worker lived a life far different from that of a ditch digger, with the former able to afford the food, shelter, and clothing necessary for a decent existence, and the latter barely able to scrape by.

Some movement from the ranks of the unskilled to the skilled was possible, if children were provided, or provided themselves, with at least a rudimentary education. Yet education was considered by many parents a luxury, especially because children could be put to work at an early age to supplement the family's meager earnings. Downward mobility from skilled to unskilled was also possible, as technological change—the introduction of the power loom, for example—drove highly paid workers into the ranks of the unskilled and destitute.

Working-class housing was unhealthy and unregulated. In older cities, single-family dwellings were broken up into apartments, often with no more than one room per family. In new manufacturing centers, rows of tiny houses, located close to smoking factories, were built back to back, thereby eliminating garden spaces and any cross-ventilation. Crowding was commonplace, as a newspaper account from the 1840s noted that in Leeds, a textile center in northern Britain, an ordinary worker's house contained no more than 150 square feet, and that in most cases, those houses were "crammed almost to suffocation with human beings both day and night."

Household routines, demanding in the middle classes, were grinding for the poor. The family remained a survival network, in which everyone played a crucial role. In addition to working for wages, wives were expected to house, feed, and clothe the family on very little money the different members of the family earned; a good wife was able to make ends meet even in bad times. Working women's daily lives involved constant rounds of carrying and boiling water, cleaning, cooking, and doing laundry in one- and two-room crowded, unventilated, and poorly lit apartments. Families could not rely on their own gardens to help supply them with food, so city markets catered to their needs for cheap foods. But these were regularly stale, nearly rotten, or dangerously adulterated: formaldehyde was added to milk to prevent spoilage, pounded rice was mixed into sugar, and fine brown earth was introduced into cocoa.

WORKING WOMEN IN THE INDUSTRIAL LANDSCAPE

Few figures raised more public anxiety and outcry in the nineteenth century than the working woman. Contemporaries worried out loud about the "promiscuous mixing of the sexes" in crowded and humid workshops. Nineteenth-century writers, starting in England and France, chronicled what they considered to be the economic and moral horrors of female labor: unattended children running in the streets, small children caught in accidents at the mills or the mines, pregnant women hauling coal, or women laboring alongside men in shops.

Women's work was not new, but industrialization made it more visible. Both before and after the Industrial Revolution, labor was divided by gender, but as employers implemented new manufacturing processes, ideas about which jobs were appropriate for women shifted. In traditional textile production, for example, women spun and men operated the looms. In industrial textile factories, on the other hand, employers preferred women and children, both because they were considered more docile and less likely to make trouble and because it was believed that their smaller hands were better suited to the intricate job of tying threads on the power looms. Manufacturers sought to recruit women mill hands from neighboring villages, paying good wages compared with other jobs open to women. Most began working at the age of ten or eleven, and when they had children, they put their children out to a wet nurse, brought them to the mills, or continued to work by doing piecework at home. This transformation of the gendered structure of work caused intense anxiety in the first half of the nineteenth century, and it is one of the reasons that the emerging labor movement began to include calls for excluding women from the workplace in its programs.

Most women did not work in factories, however, but continued to labor at home or in small workshops—"sweatshops," as they came to be called—for notoriously low wages that paid not by the hour but by the piece for each shirt stitched or each matchbox glued. The greatest number of unmarried working-class women worked less visibly in domestic service, a job that brought low wages and, judging by the testimony of many women, coercive sexual relationships with male employers or their sons; domestic service, however, provided room and board. In a time when a single woman simply could not survive on her own wages, a young woman who had just arrived in the city had few choices: marriage, which was unlikely to happen right away; renting a room in a boardinghouse, many of which were often centers of prostitution;

domestic service; or living with someone. How women balanced the demands for money and the time for household work varied with the number and age of their children. Mothers were actually more likely to work when their children were very small, because there were more mouths to feed and the children were not yet old enough to earn wages.

Poverty, the absence of privacy, and the particular vulnerabilities of working-class women made working-class sexuality very different from its middle-class counterpart. Illegitimacy rose dramatically between 1750 and 1850. In Frankfurt, Germany, for example, the illegitimacy rate had been a mere 2 percent in the early 1700s, but it reached 25 percent in 1850. In Bordeaux, France, in 1840, one-third of the recorded births were illegitimate. Reasons for this increase are difficult to establish. Improved mobility and urbanization meant weaker family ties, more opportunities for young men and women, and greater vulnerabilities. Premarital sex was an accepted practice in preindustrial villages, but because of the social controls that dominated village life, it was almost always followed by marriage. These controls were weaker in the far more anonymous setting of a factory town or commercial city. The economic uncertainties of the early industrial age meant that a young workman's promise of marriage, based on his expectation of a job, might frequently be difficult to fulfill. Economic vulnerability drove many single women into temporary relationships that produced children and a

CAPITAL AND LABOR. In its earliest years, the British magazine *Punch*, though primarily a humorous weekly, manifested a strong social conscience. This 1843 cartoon shows capitalists enjoying the rewards of their investments while hungry workers shiver in the cold. ■ *How would a defender of the new industrial order respond to this cartoon?*

Women and the Working Class

Flora Tristan (1803–1844) was born in Peru, the daughter of a French woman and a Spanish naval officer. After the death of her father, her mother discovered that their religious marriage had never been recognized by the French authorities, leaving Flora technically illegitimate and unable to inherit his estate. Forced into a financially precarious existence, she learned a trade as a lithographic printer. After a marriage to her former employer, who mistreated her, she fled to Europe, eventually settling in France in 1834 as, in her own words, "triple pariah": an illegitimate child, an escapee from a hateful marriage, and a woman without rights in society. Her writings, which included autobiographical works and political pamphlets, focused on the need to connect the workers' rights movement with the question of women's emancipation.

The Workers' Union (1843)

orkers, put an end to twenty-five years of waiting for someone to intervene on your behalf. Experience and facts inform you well enough that the Government cannot or will not be concerned with your lot when its improvement is at issue. It is up to you alone, if you truly want it, to leave this labyrinth of misery, suffering, and degradation in which you languish. [. . .]

Your action is not to be armed revolt, public riots, arson, or plundering. No, because, instead of curing your ills, destruction would only make them worse.

[. . .] You have but one legal and legitimate recourse permissible before God and man: THE UNIVERSAL UNION OF WORKING MEN AND WOMEN. [. . .]

Workers, your condition in present society is miserable and painful: in good health you do not have the right to work; sick, ailing, injured, old, you do not even have the right to care; poor, lacking everything, you are not entitled to benefits, and beggary is forbidden by law. This precarious situation relegates you to a primitive state in which man, living in nature, must consider every morning how he will get food for the day. [. . .] Individually, you are weak and fall from

the weight of all kinds of miseries. So, leave your isolation: unite! *Unity gives strength.* You have numbers going for you, and numbers are significant. [. . .]

I come to you to propose a general union among working men and women, regardless of trade, who reside in the same region—a union which would have as its goal the CONSOLIDATION OF THE WORKING CLASS and the construction of several establishments (Workers' Union palaces), distributed evenly throughout France. Children of both sexes six to eighteen would be raised there and sick or disabled workers as well as the elderly would be admitted. [. . .]

continuing cycle of poverty and abandonment. Historians have shown, however, that in the city as in the countryside, many of these temporary relationships became enduring ones, and the parents of illegitimate children would marry later. Again, nineteenth-century writers dramatized what they considered the disreputable sexuality of the "dangerous classes" in the cities. Some of them attributed illegitimacy, prostitution, and so on, to the moral weakness of working-class people, others to the systematic changes wrought by industrialization. Both sides, however, overstated the collapse of the family and the destruction of traditional morality. Working-class families transmitted expectations about gender roles and sexual behavior: girls should expect to work, daughters were responsible for caring for their younger siblings as well as for earning wages,

sexuality was a fact of life, midwives could help desperate pregnant girls, marriage was an avenue to respectability, and so on. The gulf that separated these expectations and codes from those of middle-class women was one of the most important factors in the development of nineteenth-century class identity.

A Life Apart: "Class Consciousness"

The new demands of life in an industrial economy created common experiences and difficulties. The factory system denied skilled workers the pride in craft they had previously enjoyed. Stripped of the protections of guilds and apprenticeships and prevented from organiz-

Why I Mention Women

Up to now, woman has counted for nothing in human society. What has been the result of this? That the priest, the lawmaker, and the philosopher have treated her as a true *pariah*. Woman (one half of humanity) has been cast out of the Church, out of the law, out of society. For her there are no functions in the Church, no representation before the law, no functions in the State. [. . .]

Such a terrible condemnation, repeated for six thousand years, is likely to impress the masses, for the sanction of time has great authority over them. However, what must make us hope that this sentence can be repealed is that the wisest of the wise have also for six thousand years pronounced a no less horrible verdict upon another race of humanity—the proletariat. Before 1789, what was the proletarian in French society? A serf, a peasant, who was made into a taxable, drudging beast of burden. Then came the Revolution of 1789, and all of a sudden the wisest of the wise proclaimed that the lower orders are to be called the *people*, that the serfs and peasants are to be called *citizens*. Finally they proclaimed the *rights of man* in full national assembly. [. . .]

Workers, in 1791, your fathers proclaimed the immortal declaration of the *rights of man*, and it is to that solemn declaration that today you owe your being free and equal men before the law. May your fathers be honored for this great work! But, proletarians, there remains for you men of 1843 a no less great work to finish. In your turn, emancipate the last slaves still remaining in French society; proclaim the *rights of women*, in the same terms your fathers proclaimed yours.

Source: Flora Tristan, *The Workers' Union*, trans. Beverly Livingston (Urbana: 1983), pp. 38–39, 76, 88. Originally published in Paris in 1843.

Questions for Analysis

1. How did Flora explain the challenge facing individual workers and their families?

2. What is the goal of the Workers' Union that Flora proposed?

3. How did Flora use the history of the French Revolution to make her point about including women's rights in the movement for workers' collective action?

---

ing by legislation in France, Germany, and Britain in the first half of the nineteenth century, workers felt vulnerable in the face of their socially and politically powerful employers. Workdays were long, usually twelve to fourteen hours. Textile mills were unventilated, and minute particles of lint lodged in the workers' lungs. Machines were unfenced and posed dangers to child workers. British physicians cataloged the toll that long hours tending machines took on children, including spinal curvature and bone malformations. Children were also employed in large numbers in mines—over 50,000 worked in British mines in 1841.

Factories also imposed new routines and disciplines. Artisans in earlier times also worked long hours for little pay, but they set their own schedules and controlled the pace of work, moving from their home workshops to their small garden plots as they wished. In a factory, all hands learned the discipline of the clock. To increase production, the factory system encouraged the breaking down of the manufacturing process into specialized steps, each with its own time. Workers began to see machinery itself as the tyrant that changed their lives and bound them to industrial slavery. A radical working-class song written in Britain in the 1840s expressed the feeling:

> There is a king and a ruthless king;
> Not a king of the poet's dream;
> But a tyrant fell, white slaves know well,
> And that ruthless king is steam.

Yet the defining feature of working-class life was vulnerability—to unemployment, sickness, accidents in dangerous jobs, family problems, and spikes in the prices of food. Seasonal unemployment, high in almost all trades, made it impossible to collect regular wages. Markets for manufactured goods were small and unstable, producing cyclical economic depressions; when those came, thousands of workers found themselves laid off with no system of unemployment insurance to sustain them. The early decades of industrialization were also marked by several severe agricultural depressions and economic crises. During the crisis years of the 1840s, half the working population of Britain's industrial cities was unemployed. In 1840, 85,000 went on relief in Paris. Families survived by working several small jobs, pawning their possessions, and getting credit from local wineshops and grocery stores. The chronic insecurity of working-class life helped fuel the creation of workers' self-help societies, fraternal associations, and early socialist organizations, which meant that economic crises could have explosive consequences (see Chapter 21).

By mid-century, various experiences were beginning to make working people conscious of their differences from and in opposition to the middle classes. Changes in the workplace were part of the picture—whether the introduction of machines and factory labor, demands for faster production, subcontracting to cheap labor, or the loss of guild protections. The social segregation of the rapidly expanding nineteenth-century cities also contributed to the sense that working people lived a life apart. Class differences seemed embedded in a very wide array of everyday experiences and beliefs: work, private life, expectations for children, the roles of men and women, and definitions of respectability. Over the course of the nineteenth century, all of these different experiences gave concrete, specific meaning to the word *class*.

CONCLUSION

Why did the Industrial Revolution occur at this moment in human history? Why did it begin in Europe? Why did it not occur in other regions of the world with large populations and advanced technologies, such as China or India? These fundamental questions remain subject to serious debate among historians. One school of explanations focuses on the fact that the mechanization of industry occurred first in

After You Read This Chapter

 Go to **INQUIZITIVE** to see what you've learned—and learn what you've missed—with personalized feedback along the way.

REVIEWING THE OBJECTIVES

- The Industrial Revolution in Europe began in northern England. What circumstances made this process of economic development begin there?

- Certain industries were particularly suitable for the kinds of technological developments that encouraged industrialization. What were these industries? Where did they exist in Europe?

- Industrial development changed the nature of work and production in significant ways. What were these changes? How did they change the relations between laborers and their employers, or between local producers and wider markets?

- Industrialization had social effects far beyond the factories. What larger changes in European society were associated with the Industrial Revolution?

- A large and diverse group of middle-class people emerged in Europe as a result of the social changes brought on by industrialization. What kinds of people qualified as middle class during the nineteenth century? How were they different from other social groups?

northern Europe, and thus seeks to explain the Industrial Revolution's origins in terms of this region's vibrant towns, its well-developed commercial markets, and the presence of a prosperous land-owning elite that had few prejudices against entrepreneurial activity. These historians have suggested that industrialization is best understood as a process rooted in European culture and history.

More recently, however, historians with a more global approach have argued that it may be incorrect to assert that industrialization developed as it did because of the advantages enjoyed by a central European core. Instead, they have explored the possibility that the world's economies constituted a larger interlocking system that had no definitive center until *after* the takeoff of European industrialization. Before that period, when it came to agricultural practices, ecological constraints, population densities, urbanization, and technological development, *many* global regions were not so different from the western European model. So, in the end, Europe was able to move more quickly toward industrial production because its economies were better positioned to mobilize the resources available to them on the periphery of their trading sphere. The access European traders enjoyed to agricultural products from slave-owning societies in the Americas helped them escape the ecological constraints imposed by their own intensely farmed lands, making the move to an industrial economy possible. Contingent factors, such as patterns of disease and epidemic or the location of coal fields, may have also played a role.

There is less debate about the consequences of the Industrial Revolution within Europe. New forms of industrial production created a new economy and changed the nature of work for both men and women. Industrialization changed the landscape of Europe as well as the structures of families and the private lives of people in both the cities and the countryside. Industrialization created new forms of wealth along with new kinds of poverty, fostering an acute awareness of the disparity between social groups. In the eighteenth century, that disparity would have been described in terms of birth, rank, or privilege. In the nineteenth century, it was increasingly seen in terms of class. Both champions and critics of the new industrial order spoke of a "class society." The identities associated with class were formed in the crowded working-class districts of the new cities, in experiences of work, and in the new conditions of respectability that determined life in middle-class homes. These new identities would be sharpened in the political events to which we now turn.

PEOPLE, IDEAS, AND EVENTS IN CONTEXT

- Why was **ENCLOSURE** an important factor in the Industrial Revolution?
- What was the **SPINNING JENNY**? What was the **COTTON GIN**? What effect did these machines have on industrial development?
- What was the significance of **EUROPEAN EMPIRE** and overseas expansion for industrialization?
- How did industrialization affect **POPULATION GROWTH** in Europe? What effects did it have on the **PEASANTRY** and on **URBAN POPULATIONS**?
- What environmental changes were associated with the development of commercial agriculture, the use of new sources of fuel, and the construction of large and concentrated centers of industrial manufacture?
- What was the **IRISH POTATO FAMINE**? How was it related to the economic developments of nineteenth-century Europe?

THINKING ABOUT CONNECTIONS

- From modifications in the land to transformations of the built environment and the growth of cities, industrialization produced fundamental changes in the physical spaces occupied by society. How might these changes have affected people's conceptions of the spaces that provided the background to their lives and labor?
- Awareness that these changes made the present radically different from the recent past gave many people the sense that time was hurtling ever faster into a future with outlines that could only dimly be perceived. How might people have perceived their own lives against what they knew of their parents' generation or what they anticipated for their children? How might the perception of time itself have shifted?
- In the early twenty-first century, innovations in information technology are creating a similar sense of accelerated change and diminishing distances in a more interconnected globe. What are the similarities between our own period and the period between the 1780s and 1830s, when large numbers of people first began to think about the power of technology to change the way society was organized and to regard history as a headlong rush into the future? What are the differences?

Before You Read This Chapter

The Age of Ideologies: Europe in the Aftermath of Revolution, 1815–1848

CORE OBJECTIVES

- **UNDERSTAND** the political goals of European leaders who met at the Congress of Vienna in 1815, and the challenges to the Concert of Europe in the decades between 1815 and 1848.

- **TRACE** the evolution of the debate about slavery after the French Revolution, and **UNDERSTAND** the reasons why an abolition movement developed even as slavery persisted in the United States, Latin America, and Cuba.

- **IDENTIFY** the core principles of conservatism, liberalism, republicanism, and socialism in Europe after 1815.

- **DEFINE** *nationalism* and understand how conservatives, liberals, republicans, and socialists were forced to grapple with this powerful political idea.

- **EXPLAIN** the ideas contained in the cultural movement known as Romanticism and its relationship to the Enlightenment.

When Napoleon left the battlefield at Waterloo on June 18, 1815, in defeat, headed eventually to exile on the rocky island of St. Helena in the South Atlantic, his victorious opponents hoped the age of revolution had ended. The Austrian foreign minister, **Klemens von Metternich**, perhaps the most influential conservative diplomat of the early nineteenth century, called revolution a "sickness," "plague," and "cancer," and set out with his allies to inoculate Europe against any outbreak. In their view, revolution produced war, and calls for national self-determination and representative government only created disorder. Peace depended on avoiding political turmoil and reinforcing the power of conservative monarchies in all corners of Europe, so bolstering the legitimacy of such monarchies was Metternich's primary goal in the post-Napoleonic decades.

The decades between 1815 and 1848 saw the legitimacy of these monarchies challenged on multiple fronts, and conservative efforts to restore the old order succeeded only in part. Why? To begin with, the developments of the eighteenth century proved impossible to reverse. The expansion of an informed public, begun in the Enlightenment, continued.

The word *citizen* (and the liberal political ideas contained within it) was controversial in the aftermath of the French Revolution, but conservatives found it difficult to banish this term from political debates. Liberalism's fundamental principles—equality before the law, freedom of expression, and the consent of the governed—were still a potent threat to Europe's dynastic rulers, especially when coupled with the emotions stirred up by popular nationalism. Liberal nationalists believed that legitimate sovereignty could only be exercised by citizens acting collectively as a nation. Such a conception of sovereignty was diametrically opposed to the convictions of conservative monarchs, who believed their authority came not from the people but from God. Popular nationalism was especially threatening to the Austrian Habsburg Empire, which faced separate nationalist movements from Italians, Germans, Poles, Hungarians, Czechs and others.

At the same time, the political opposition to the conservative order in Europe began to be infused with new and more radical political ideologies. Some liberals were comfortable living under a constitutional monarch—one who agreed to rule in accordance with the law. Others accepted the idea of representation but believed that voting was a privilege that should be extended only to wealthy property owners. Much more radical were republicans who called for universal (male) suffrage and an end to monarchy altogether. Socialists, disturbed by the inequalities brought about by the new market economy of industrial society, went even further and argued that political reform was not enough to free the people from want and exploitation. To them, justice was possible only with a radical reordering of society that redistributed property equitably. Between 1815 and 1848, none of these more radical oppositional movements succeeded in carrying the day, but their ideas circulated widely and occupied the attention of conservative monarchs (and their police spies) throughout Europe.

In culture as well as in politics, imagination and a sense of possibility were among the defining characteristics of the first half of the century. Romanticism broke from what many artists considered the cold Classicism and formality of eighteenth-century art. The Enlightenment had championed reason, whereas Romantics prized subjectivity, feeling, and spontaneity. Their revolt against eighteenth-century conventions had ramifications far beyond literature and painting. The Romantics had no single political creed; some were fervent revolutionaries and others were fervent traditionalists who looked to the past, religion, or history for inspiration. Their sensibility, however, infused politics and culture. And if we look ahead, we will see that their collective search for new means of expression sent nineteenth-century art off in a new direction.

THE SEARCH FOR ORDER IN EUROPE, 1815–1830

In 1814, the European powers—including the restored king Louis XVIII of France—met at the Congress of Vienna to settle pressing questions about the post-Napoleonic political order and to determine the territorial spoils of their victory over the French emperor. An observer of the lavish balls and celebrations that accompanied the Congress's diplomatic negotiations might well have assumed that the calendar had been turned back several decades, to a time when the European nobility had not yet been humiliated and terrorized by violent revolutionaries. But the celebrations of Louis XVIII's return to the throne and the glittering display of aristocratic men in wigs and fine clothes, accompanied by their bejeweled wives (and mistresses), could not hide the fact that twenty years of war, revolution, and political experimentation had changed Europe in fundamental ways. The task of the Congress of Vienna was to reinforce Europe's monarchical regimes against the powerful social and political forces that had been unleashed in the years since 1789.

The Congress of Vienna and the Restoration

The Russian tsar Alexander I (r. 1801–1825) and the Austrian diplomat Klemens von Metternich (1773–1859) dominated the Congress of Vienna. During the Napoleonic Wars, Alexander I presented himself as the "liberator" of Europe, and many feared that he would substitute an all-powerful France with an all-powerful Russia. And after Napoleon's fall, Russia became the most powerful Continental state. At the Congress of Vienna, the French prince Charles Maurice de Talleyrand (1754–1838) played a surprisingly strong supporting role. Talleyrand had been a bishop, a revolutionary, and a survivor of the Terror. He lived in exile in the United States before becoming Napoleon's foreign minister and then occupying the same post under Louis XVIII. His presence at Vienna testified to his diplomatic skill—or opportunism.

Metternich, the architect of the peace, had witnessed the popular violence connected with the French Revolution while a student at the University of Strasbourg in 1789, which left him with a lifelong hatred of revolutionary movements. At the Congress of Vienna, his central concerns were checking Russian expansionism and preventing political and social change, and he favored treating the

The following labels appear on the map:

KINGDOM OF NORWAY AND SWEDEN
• Stockholm

Area of detail
EUROPE
AFRICA

SCOTLAND
• Edinburgh
NORTH SEA

UNITED KINGDOM
IRELAND
• Dublin
• Liverpool
• Birmingham
ENGLAND
• Amsterdam
• London

KINGDOM OF DENMARK
• Copenhagen
SCHLESWIG
HOLSTEIN
MECK-LENBURG
Hamburg
HANOVER

RUSSIAN EMPIRE

BALTIC SEA

PRUSSIA
• Berlin
POLAND
HESSE
SAXONY
REPUBLIC OF CRACOW
• Kiev

KINGDOM OF THE NETHERLANDS
LUXEMBOURG
• Paris
LORRAINE
ALSACE
BADEN
WÜRTTEM-BERG
BAVARIA
• Munich
• Vienna
HUNGARY
• Budapest
MOLDAVIA

KINGDOM OF FRANCE
• Bordeaux
• Berne
SWISS CONFED.
PARMA
MODENA
LUCCA
TUSCANY
PAPAL STATES
Milan
LOMBARDY-VENETIA
AUSTRIAN EMPIRE
WALLACHIA

BLACK SEA

MONTENEGRO

ATLANTIC OCEAN

KINGDOM OF PORTUGAL
• Madrid
Lisbon •
KINGDOM OF SPAIN
• Barcelona
• Marseilles
KINGDOM OF SARDINIA
CORSICA
Rome •
ADRIATIC SEA

• Constantinople
OTTOMAN EMPIRE

KINGDOM OF THE TWO SICILIES
• Naples
• Palermo

MEDITERRANEAN SEA

ALGERIA
TUNISIA

0 100 200 300 Miles
0 100 200 300 Kilometers

Boundary of the Germanic Confederation
Austrian Empire
Ruled by relatives of Austrian Hapsburgs
France
Prussia

THE CONGRESS OF VIENNA. Note how the borders of European nations were established after the final defeat of Napoleon in 1815, and compare these boundaries with those formed in 1713 after the Peace of Utrecht (page 510). ▪ *What major changes had occurred in central Europe during the intervening years?* ▪ *Which territorial powers played an active role in determining the balance of power at the Congress of Vienna?* ▪ *What social or political developments might disrupt this balance?*

defeated French with moderation. Nevertheless, Metternich remained an archconservative who readily resorted to harsh repressive tactics, including secret police and spying. The peace he crafted was enormously significant and helped prevent a major European war until 1914.

The Congress sought to restore order by insisting that Europe's dynastic rulers were the only legitimate political authorities. It recognized Louis XVIII as the legitimate sovereign of France and confirmed the restoration of Bourbon rulers in Spain and the Two Sicilies. Other European monarchs had no interest in undermining the

French restoration, being that Louis XVIII was a bulwark against revolution. But after Napoleon's Hundred Days, the allies imposed an indemnity of 700 million francs and an occupying army for five years. France's borders remained the same as in 1789—less than the revolution's "greater France" but not so punitive as they might have been.

The guiding principle of the peace was the balance of power, according to which no country should be powerful enough to destabilize international relations. Metternich's immediate goal, therefore, was to build a barrier against renewed French expansion. The Dutch Republic, conquered by the French in 1795, was restored as the kingdom of the Netherlands, securing France's northern border. The Congress also ceded the left bank of the Rhine to Prussia, and Austria expanded into northern Italy. Meanwhile, Britain demanded compensation for its long war with Napoleon and received former Dutch and French territories in South Africa and South America, as well as the island of Ceylon (Sri Lanka).

In central Europe, the allied powers reorganized the German states, reducing them from more than 300 to 39 in number. Prussia and Habsburg Austria joined these German states in a loosely structured German Confederation, with Austria careful to reserve the presidency of this new body for itself as a check against attempts by the Prussians to increase their regional influence. (Eventually, this confederation became the basis for German unification, but this was not the intention in Vienna in 1815.) And Bavaria, Württemburg, and Saxony remained independent kingdoms.

Poland was also a major issue at the Congress, because Napoleon had established a client Polish state, the Duchy of Warsaw, in 1807. After much debate, the Congress's final compromise allowed for a nominally independent but much reduced kingdom of Poland, with its own liberal constitution and parliament. The same agreement gave large slices of formerly Polish territory to Austria and Prussia. The Polish kingdom remained under the control of the Russian tsar, Alexander I, who appointed his younger brother Constantine as viceroy and commander of the Polish army. Constantine eventually renounced his claim to the Russian throne in the event of his brother's death, but his autocratic rule in Poland soon alienated both the Polish officer corps and the parliament.

To secure peace among Europe's monarchies, the Congress of Vienna called for a balance of powers known as the **Concert of Europe**. Britain, Austria, Prussia, and Russia pledged to cooperate in the suppression of any disturbances, and France officially joined this conservative alliance in 1818. Alexander I pushed for what he called a Holy Alliance, dedicated to justice, Christian charity, and peace. The British foreign minister remained skeptical, calling the Holy Alliance "a piece of sublime mysticism and nonsense," but agreed that the European powers should defend their concept of authority, centered on legitimacy. A ruler was legitimate if his power was guaranteed not only by claims of divine right but also by international treaties and the support of his recognized peers. The Concert of Europe's opposition to liberal notions of political representation and national self-determination could not have been clearer. King Leopold of Belgium, himself placed on the throne by

the allied powers in 1831, observed that war now threatened to become "a conflict of principles" sparked by revolutionary ideas, setting "peoples" against emperors. "From what I know of Europe," he continued. "Such a conflict would change her form and overthrow her whole structure." Metternich and his fellow diplomats at Vienna dedicated their lives to ensuring that such a conflict would never take place.

Revolts and Resistance against the Concert of Europe

Much of the resistance to the Restoration and the Concert of Europe was clandestine and nationalist in inspiration. On the Italian peninsula, the **Carbonari** (the name comes from the charcoal they used to blacken their faces) vowed to oppose the government in Vienna and its conservative allies. But their political views varied: some called for constitutions and representative government, whereas others praised Bonaparte. The Carbonari's influence spread through southern Europe and France in the 1820s, with members meeting in secret and identifying one another with closely guarded rituals. Veterans of Napoleon's armies and military officers were prominent in their ranks.

In Naples and Piedmont, and in Spain and the Spanish Empire, opposition to Metternich's Concert of Europe turned into revolts when monarchs placed in power by the Congress of Vienna betrayed their promises of reform. Metternich responded by spurring Austria, Prussia, and Russia to take a strong stand against revolution. In the Troppau Protocol (1820), the conservative regimes pledged to assist one another in suppressing revolt. Austria dealt firmly with the Italian revolts; and France sent 200,000 troops to the Iberian Peninsula in 1823, crushing the Spanish revolutionaries and restoring King Ferdinand's authority.

Revolution in Latin America

King Ferdinand's empire in Latin America, however, would not be restored. Napoleon's conquest of Spain (1807) had shaken Spain's once vast Atlantic empire, and local elites in the colonies who resented Spanish imperial control took advantage of the crown's weakness to push for independence. Rio de la Plata (now Argentina) was the first to succeed, declaring independence in 1816. Soon after, a monarchist general from Rio de la Plata, José de San Martín (1778–1850), led an expedition to liberate Chile and Peru. At the same time, Simón Bolívar (1783–1830), a republican leader, sparked a series of uprisings from Venezuela

NEW NATIONS OF LATIN AMERICA. After Haiti became the second independent nation in the Western Hemisphere, many areas of Central and South America also broke away from colonial rule. ▪ *When did the nations of Latin America gain their independence?* ▪ *What major events in Europe contributed to this move toward independence?* ▪ *What is the relationship between the events in Europe and the Atlantic revolutions that occurred in the late eighteenth century?*

to Bolivia. Bolívar and San Martín joined forces, though Bolívar's plans were more radical. He envisioned mobilizing free people of color and slaves (who made up roughly a quarter of those fighting the Spanish) as well as Indians to fight against Spanish rule. Bolívar's goal was to create a pan-American republic on the continent, along the lines of the United States. These political revolts unleashed violent social conflicts and, in some cases, civil war. Elite landowners who wanted only to free themselves from Spain opposed groups who wanted land reform and an end to slavery. In the end, the radical movements were suppressed, and the newly independent Latin American nations were dominated by an alliance of conservative landowners and military officers.

Britain and the newly ambitious United States prevented the European powers from intervening in the Latin American revolutions. In 1823, the U.S. president James Monroe issued the Monroe Doctrine, declaring that the United States would regard European meddling in the Americas as a hostile act, a declaration that signaled the country's new willingness to play a role on the world stage. Without British support, however, the Monroe Doctrine would have been unenforceable. Britain saw the new South American republics as potential trading partners and used its navy to prevent Spain from intervening. By the 1820s, the Spanish Empire had vanished, ending an age that had begun in 1492. Brazil's independence in 1822 similarly ended the era of Portuguese colonialism in South America. Together, these revolutions demonstrated the circular relationships that bound the Atlantic world together. Latin American revolutionaries, encouraged by political movements associated with the French Revolution and Napoleon, in turn inspired nationalists in Europe who sought to overthrow Metternich's conservative Concert of Europe.

Russia: The Decembrists

Revolt also broke out within conservative Russia. In December 1825, Tsar Alexander I died, and a group of army officers led an uprising to push the pace of reform and challenge the succession of Alexander's brother Nicholas. Many of the "**Decembrists**," as they were called, were veterans of the Napoleonic Wars, and they feared that Russia could not live up to its promise to be the "liberator of Europe" without changes in its social and political order. Serfdom, for example, contradicted the promise of liberation; so did the tsar's monopoly on power. Not only were Russian peasants enslaved, argued the Decembrists, the nobles were "slaves to the tsar." They demanded that the crown pass instead to Alexander's other brother Constantine, who

had earlier renounced the throne after becoming viceroy of Poland. The Decembrists were fervent supporters of a strong Russian state—most were opposed to Polish independence, for example—but they disagreed with Nicholas about how Russia should adapt to a changing world.

The Decembrist officers failed to gain the support of the rank-and-file soldiers, however, and without that support they could not succeed. Many were killed in a confrontation in St. Petersburg at the end of the month, and their few supporters in other cities were rapidly defeated. The new tsar, Nicholas I (r. 1825–1855), had hundreds of mutinous soldiers interrogated, sentenced many to hard labor and exile in Siberia, and sentenced their five primary leaders—all young and leading members of the aristocratic elite—to death. Fearing they would be seen as martyrs, Nicholas had them hanged at dawn behind the walls of a fortress in St. Petersburg and buried in secret graves.

Nicholas went on to rule in the manner of his predecessor, becoming Europe's most uncompromising conservative. He created a powerful political police force, the Third Section, to prevent further domestic disorder. Still, Russia was not immune to change. Bureaucracy became more centralized, more efficient, and less dependent on the nobility. To accomplish this task, Nicholas made Russia's complex legal system more systematic and uniform. He oversaw the publication of a new Code of Law, which recategorized every law passed since 1648 and codified them into forty-eight volumes, a measure comparable to Napoleon's Civil Code of 1804. Landowners responded to higher demand for Russian grain by reorganizing their estates to increase productivity, and the state began to build railroads to transport the grain to Western markets. Meanwhile, opponents of the regime, such as the writer Alexander Herzen, carried on the Decembrists' unresolved political legacy.

Southeastern Europe: Greece and Serbia

When the Greeks and Serbians revolted against the once powerful Ottoman Empire, the conservative European powers showed themselves to be more tolerant of rebellion. Although the Ottoman Empire had defeated Napoleon Bonaparte's attempt to invade Egypt in 1798 (with British help), the episode strained its hold on the eastern Mediterranean. Serbs in the Balkans rebelled against the Ottomans as early as 1804 and, with the help of the Russians, succeeded in establishing hereditary rule by a Serbian prince in 1817. This Serbian quasi state persisted as an Orthodox Christian principality with a significant minority Muslim

Pavel Pestel: The Confessions of a Decembrist Conspirator

Pavel Pestel (1793–1826) was the son of a high-ranking civil servant in the Russian imperial bureaucracy. He served in the Russian army during the Napoleonic Wars and was wounded at the Battle of Borodino. In 1816, he joined a secret society devoted to political change in Russia; and in 1821, he produced a plan for social and economic reforms that included the emancipation of the serfs, an end to the aristocracy, the distribution of land to the peasantry, and the establishment of a republican government. He was one of the five leaders of the Decembrist Revolt executed by the order of the tsar. This document is taken from the records of the interrogation after his arrest.

 cannot name anyone to whom I would credit imparting my first free-thinking and liberal ideas to me, nor can I state that precise time when they started to take shape in me. For this happened not suddenly, but imperceptibly. [. . .] When I had acquired a pretty good grounding in political science, I grew passionately interested in the subject. I was aglow with enthusiasm, and desired what is good with all my heart. I saw that both the happiness and the misery of states and nations depends in large measure upon their government; and this conviction inclined me even more towards those sciences which deal with just such questions. But at first I studied those sciences and read works on politics in all humility, without free thought and wishing only to become, in due time and a suitable capacity, a useful servant of the Monarch and the State. [. . .] I also bore in mind and gave consideration to the condition of the Russian people. Here, I was always deeply affected by the slavery of the peasants, as by the privileges of the nobility; the latter I saw as a wall standing between the monarch and his people, which hid the true condi-

tion of the people from the Monarch for the sake of selfish advantages. [. . .] The return of the Bourbons to the throne of France and my reflection on its consequences marked an epoch in my political development, my attitudes and forms of thought. Most of the fundamental institutions brought in by the Revolution (I began to reason) had been kept after the Restoration of the monarchy, and were acknowledged to be good; yet everyone, myself included, had opposed that revolution. This judgment gave rise to the idea that, seemingly, a revolution was not so bad a thing as it is said to be, and may even be quite useful. The judgment was confirmed when I observed that states that have not known a revolution continue to exist deprived of such advantages and institutions as France had. [. . .] In this way, constitutional as well as revolutionary notions began to form in me at the same time. [. . .] I was led from a monarchical-constitutional outlook to a republican one chiefly by these facts and considerations. [. . .] The main tendency of the century, it seemed to me, consisted in a growing struggle between popular masses and aristocracies of every kind, whether of wealth or birth. I calculated that these aristoc-

racies would eventually grow stronger than the monarchs, as in England, and that they formed the major obstacle to a country's happiness and could be done away with only through a republican form of government.

Source: G. R. V. Barratt, ed., *Voices in Exile: The Decembrist Memoirs* (Montreal: 1974), pp. 147–49.

Questions for Analysis

1. How did Pestel describe his allegiances and views toward the tsar when he first began to read works of political science?

2. What aspects of Russian society did Pestel point to when describing how his opinions became more radical? How did he view the aristocracy and the peasantry?

3. How did Pestel's observations of the changes in France during the Revolution and the Restoration lead him to embrace republicanism?

population, until finally achieving formal independence from the Ottoman Empire in 1878.

The Serb revolt and the subsequent Greek war for independence (1821–1827) were part of a new pattern in Ottoman history. Beginning in the early nineteenth century, groups within the empire's border regions began to seek independence from Ottoman rule. Eighteenth-century revolts against Ottoman control in these regions usually had not sought outright separation and had generally been resolved within the imperial system by redistributing tax burdens or instituting legal reforms. After 1800, however, European powers were more likely to get involved, and the result was the establishment of new independent states and a weakening of Ottoman power. The French and the British viewed the eastern Mediterranean as an important arena for commercial competition, while the Russians viewed their frontiers with the Ottoman Empire's Balkan holdings as a natural place to exert foreign influence.

The Greek revolt eventually gained support from the British government, and sympathy for the Greeks was widespread in Europe. Christians in Europe cast the rebellion as part of an ongoing struggle between Christianity and Islam, whereas secular observers sought to interpret the struggle as between an ancient pre-Christian European heritage and the Ottoman Empire. "We are all Greeks," wrote Percy Bysshe Shelley, the Romantic poet. "Our laws, our literature, our religion, our arts have their roots in Greece." George Gordon, better known as Lord Byron (1788–1824), another Romantic poet, fought in Greece along with other volunteers before dying there from fever. Celebrating the Greeks went hand in hand with demonizing the Ottomans, despite the fact that the Ottoman Empire's adaptable imperial system had frequently done better than those of Europeans in preserving peace among diverse peoples and different religions over the many centuries of their rule.

On the ground in Greece, the struggle was brutal, with massacres of civilians on both sides. In March 1822, the Greeks invaded the island of Chios and proclaimed its independence. When Ottoman troops arrived to retake the island, the Greek invaders killed their prisoners and fled. The Ottoman armies took revenge by slaughtering thousands of Greeks and selling 40,000 more into slavery. The French Romantic painter Eugène Delacroix memorialized this event in a painting that characteristically depicted only the Ottoman brutality (see the image on the left).

In the end, Greek independence depended on great-power politics, as it did in Serbia. In 1827, British, French, and Russian troops sided with the Greeks against the Ottomans, who were forced to concede and grant Greek independence. The new nations of Serbia and Greece were small and fragile. Only 800,000 Greeks actually lived in the new Greek state, and Serbia could not survive without Russian protection. Moreover, neither of the new nations broke their close links with the Ottomans, as Greek and Serbian merchants, bankers, and administrators were still very present in the Ottoman Empire. The region remained a borderland of Europe, where peoples alternated between tolerant coexistence and bitter conflict.

As Ottoman control in southeastern Europe waned, the European powers often played a double game. On the one hand, they recognized that regional stability depended on the continued existence of the Ottoman Empire and that its collapse would constitute a serious threat to European peace. On the other hand, by continuing to pursue their own interests and meddling in the affairs of the Ottoman Empire's rebellious subjects, they contributed to the weakening of Ottoman authority.

Leaders of independence movements were likely to succeed if they could take advantage of a conflict between great powers (as in Latin America), or if their movements

THE MASSACRE AT CHIOS, BY EUGÈNE DELACROIX. Delacroix (1789–1863) was a Romantic painter of dramatic and emotional scenes. Here, he put his brush to work for the cause of Greek nationalism, eulogizing the victims of killings on the island of Chios during the Greek war for independence against the Ottoman Empire. ■ *How did Delacroix's choices in his depiction of the massacre's victims shape the vision of the conflict for his European audience?*

aligned with Europe's competition with the Ottoman Empire (as in Greece and Serbia). Meanwhile, Metternich's ability to prevent the spread of nationalism and liberalism—ideologies associated with the French Revolution—increasingly depended on repressive political regimes that did not tolerate open expressions of dissent. And containing these movements for political and social change eventually became impossible.

CITIZENSHIP AND SOVEREIGNTY, 1830–1848

In the aftermath of the French Revolution, debates about citizenship, sovereignty, and social inequality remained divisive in many parts of Europe, even in kingdoms with conservative monarchies that supported the Concert of Europe. In France, Belgium, and Poland, political movements challenging the post-Napoleonic settlement led to open revolt in the years 1830–1832, and a similar threat developed in the 1840s. During these same decades, many in Britain feared that conflicts over voting rights and the treatment of the poor might lead to a similar crisis. In the end, political leaders in Britain succeeded in negotiating reforms that prevented open rebellion, whereas the revolutionary movements of the 1830s and 1840s on the Continent proved to be a prelude to a wave of revolutions that swept across Europe in 1848 (see Chapter 21).

The 1830 Revolution in France

The first decisive blow against the Concert of Europe came in 1830 in France. In 1815, the Congress of Vienna returned a Bourbon monarch to the throne, Louis XVIII, the oldest of the deposed king's surviving brothers. Louis claimed absolute power, but in the name of reconciliation he granted a "charter" and conceded some important rights: legal equality, careers open to talent, and a two-chamber parliamentary government. Voting rights excluded most citizens from government, and Louis's narrow base of support, combined with the sting of military defeat, nostalgia for a glorious Napoleonic past, and memories of the revolution undermined the Restoration in France.

In 1824, Louis's far more conservative brother, Charles X (r. 1824–1830), succeeded to the throne. Charles pleased the ultra-royalists by pushing the assembly to compensate nobles whose land had been confiscated and sold during the revolution, but this measure antagonized property holders. He also restored the Catholic Church to its traditional place in French schools, provoking discontent among French liberals, who began to organize an oppositional movement in Parliament. Moreover, economic troubles encouraged the opposition; in Paris and the provinces, police reports

LIBERTY LEADING THE PEOPLE, BY EUGÈNE DELACROIX. This painting is among the best-known images of the revolutions of 1830. The allegorical female figure of liberty leads representatives of the united people: a middle-class man (identified by his top hat), a worker, and a boy of the streets wielding a pistol. This image of revolutionary unity is romanticized, since neither middle-class people nor children fought on the barricades. Delacroix is the same artist who had mourned the extinction of liberty in Greece in his painting *The Massacre at Chios* (see page 666). ▪ *What made this mix of social classes important for Delacroix's image of the French people in revolt?* ▪ *Why did he portray this particular image of liberty, carrying a rifle, with exposed breasts?*

documented widespread unemployment, hunger, and anger. Confronted with alarming evidence of his regime's unpopularity, Charles called for new elections. But when they went against him, he tried to overthrow the parliament with his so-called July Ordinances of 1830: he dissolved the new assembly before it had met, restricted suffrage even further, and announced strict press censorship.

In return, Charles got revolution. Parisian workers, artisans, and students took to the streets in three days of intense street battles. Crucial to the spread of the movement was the press, which defied the censors and quickly spread the news of the initial confrontations between protesters and the forces of order. In the end, the army was unwilling to fire into the crowd and, with his support evaporating, Charles was forced to abdicate. Although many revolutionaries who had fought in the streets wanted another republic, the leaders of the movement opted for stability by crowning the former king's cousin, the Duke of Orléans Louis-Philippe (r. 1830–1848), as the constitutional monarch. The July Monarchy, as it was called, doubled the number of voters, although voting was still based on steep property requirements. The propertied classes benefited most from the Revolution of 1830, but it also brought the common people back into politics, revived memories of 1789, and spurred movements elsewhere in Europe. For opponents of the Restoration, the year 1830 suggested that history was moving in a new direction and that the political landscape had changed since the Congress of Vienna.

THE POLISH REVOLT, 1830. The Polish painter Marcin Zaleski, known for his architectural paintings and cityscapes, was an eyewitness to the Polish uprising against imperial Russia in 1830. Here, he portrays the Polish troops seizing the Warsaw arsenal, an event that sparked the revolt of Polish populations throughout present-day Poland, Belarus, Lithuania, and portions of Ukraine. The failure of the revolt led to the complete political integration of Poland with Russia, which had ruled over these territories since the third partition of Poland in 1795.

Belgium and Poland in 1830

In 1815, the Congress of Vienna joined Belgium (then called the Austrian Netherlands) with Holland to form a buffer against France, known as the United Provinces. The Belgians had never accepted this arrangement, and the 1830 revolution in France energized the Belgian opposition. The city of Brussels rebelled and forced Dutch troops to withdraw. Unwilling to intervene, the great powers agreed to guarantee Belgian independence and neutrality—a provision that remained in force until 1914. Although the economy of Belgian cities suffered by being separated from the Atlantic trade of the Dutch ports, religious divisions between the Catholic provinces of Belgium and Protestant Holland reinforced the separation. French-speaking elites in Belgium supported independence, although Flemish-speaking Belgians continue to cultivate a sense of cultural distinctiveness even today.

The years 1830–1832 thus brought full-fledged crises for the Concert of Europe. After France and Belgium, revolt spread to Poland, which was still governed by Constantine, the Russian tsar Nicholas's brother. After 1815, Poland had its own parliament (or *diet*), a relatively broad electorate, a constitution, and basic liberties of speech and the press. Constantine increasingly ignored these liberties, however, and news of the French Revolution of 1830 tipped Poland into revolt. Led by Polish officers in the army, the revolutionaries rallied supporters, including aristocrats, students, soldiers, and members of the Polish urban middle class. They took control of Warsaw, the Polish capital, and drove out Constantine (who died the next year in a cholera epidemic). With Austria and Prussia remaining neutral, Russia was given free rein to put down the rebellion by force; and within the year, the Polish rebellion was defeated.

REVOLUTIONS, MIGRATION, AND POLITICAL REFUGEES

When revolutionary demands for citizenship collided with regimes that did not want to recognize them, the result was often the production of political refugees: people forced to

Analyzing Primary Sources

Women in the Anti–Corn Law League (1842)

Members of the Anti–Corn Law League sought to repeal the protectionist laws that prohibited foreign grain from entering the British market. The laws were seen as an interference in trade that kept bread prices artificially high, benefiting British landowners and grain producers at the expense of the working population. The campaign to repeal the Corn Laws enlisted many middle-class women, some of whom later campaigned for woman suffrage. This article, hostile to the reform, deplored women's participation in the reform movement.

e find that the council of the Manchester Anti-Corn Law Association had invited the inhabitants to "an anti-Corn-law tea-party, to be held on the 20th of May, 1841—gentlemen's tickets, 2s.; ladies 1s. 6d." . . . [L]adies were advertised as *stewardesses* of this assembly. So now the names of about 300 Ladies were pompously advertised as the *Patroness* and *Committee* of the *National Bazaar*. We exceedingly wonder and regret that the members of the Association . . . and still more that anybody else, should have chosen to exhibit their wives and daughters in the character of political agitators; and we most regret that so many ladies—modest, excellent, and amiable persons we have no doubt in their domestic circles—should have

been persuaded to allow their names to be *placarded* on such occasions—for be it remembered, this Bazaar and these *Tea-parties* did not even pretend to be for any *charitable* object, but entirely for the purposes of *political agitation*. . . .

We have before us a letter from Mrs. Secretary Woolley to one body of workmen. . . . She "appeals to them to stand forth and denounce as *unholy*, unjust, and cruel all restrictions on the food of the people." She acquaints them that "the ladies are resolved to perform *their* arduous part in the attempt to *destroy a monopoly* which, for *selfishness* and its *deadly* effects, has no parallel in the history of the world." "We therefore," she adds, "ask you for contributions. . . . " Now surely . . . not only should the *poorer classes* have been exempt from such unreasonable solicitations, but whatever subscriptions

might be obtainable from the wealthier orders should have been applied, not to *political agitation* throughout England, but to charitable relief at home.

Source: J. Croker, "Anti-Corn Law Agitation," *Quarterly Review* (December 1842), as cited in Patricia Hollis, ed., *Women in Public: The Women's Movement 1850–1900* (London: 1979), p. 287.

Questions for Analysis

1. Why does the article highlight the participation of women in the Anti-Corn Law Association? What does this argument tell us about attitudes toward women's political activity?

2. Does the article actually mention any of the arguments in favor of repealing the Corn Laws? What alternative to repeal does the article appear to support?

---

flee because their political beliefs made them unwelcome in their home country. Migration for political reasons was not new, of course. The Puritans who left England for Cape Cod in 1620 were fleeing religious persecution, the Huguenot exodus from France between 1680 and 1715 displaced 180,000 Protestants, and 150,000 people fled France during the revolutionary years of 1789–1794.

In nineteenth-century Europe the spread of nationalism and the mobilization of large numbers of people during periods of war or violent political conflict intensified the pressures that created political migrations. Military operations during the Revolutionary and Napoleonic

Wars (see Chapter 18) were a form of forced migration of their own. Napoleon's *Grand Armée* in 1812 comprised more than 600,000 men, and two-thirds of them were born outside of France. During the same period, the Russian army drafted more than a million men from an empire that stretched from eastern Europe into central Asia. After peace was reestablished by the Congress of Vienna, cohorts of ex-soldiers, who often held strong political ideals, were a destabilizing force in many parts of Europe.

Greek success in winning independence from the Ottomans in 1829 set an important precedent for ethnic groups in central and eastern Europe who sought independence. When these attempts failed, further waves of political refugees spread across Europe. German republicans were frequently chased out of central Europe by political police. The failed Polish insurrections of 1830–1831 against Russia led to three decades of Polish migration. France was the most popular destination of displaced militants, but Polish colonies were also established in London, Brussels, and Switzerland. The Polish emigrants retained a sense of their common identity and corresponded actively among themselves. They also suffered—historians estimate that 10 percent of the Polish refugees between 1831 and 1842 died while abroad, succumbing to the stress of displacement, malnutrition, and disease, despite the fact that most were young adults.

By the 1840s, the combination of failed insurrections in Italy, France, Belgium, and Poland and nationalist movements in central Europe had created a large floating population of political exiles in western European cities, often residing in new neighborhoods inhabited by foreign workers. Their paths were not all the same. Giuseppe Mazzini, who had a future as a prominent voice for Italian unification, spent time in London in the 1830s and 1840s, where he set up a school for the children of Italian migrants. Karl Marx, a German political exile, worked as a journalist in Paris and London in the 1840s and went on to play a leading role in the development of an international socialist movement (see page 680). Carl Schurtz, a liberal nationalist revolutionary in western Prussia in the 1840s, migrated to the United States and eventually served as a general in the Union Army in the American Civil War before being elected to the Senate. Not all exiles became so well-known, but in many cases, their experience of defeat and police repression made them radical, and their frustration with Europe's conservative regimes made them impatient.

Reform in Great Britain

Why was there no revolution in England between 1815 and 1848? The answer is that there almost was one. After an era of political conservatism, comparable with that of the Continent, Britain became one of the most liberal nations in Europe.

The end of the Napoleonic Wars brought a major agricultural depression to Britain, and low wages, unemployment, and bad harvests provoked regular social unrest. In the new industrial towns of the north, radical members of the middle class joined with workers to demand increased representation in Parliament. In 1819, when 60,000 people gathered to demonstrate for political reform at St. Peter's Field in Manchester, the militia and soldiers on horseback charged the crowd, killing 11 and injuring 400. Radicals condemned "Peterloo" as a domestic Waterloo and criticized the nation's army for turning against its own citizens. Parliament quickly passed the Six Acts (1819), outlawing "seditious" literature, increasing the stamp tax on newspapers, allowing house searches, and restricting rights of assembly.

British political leaders reversed their opposition to reform in response to pressure from below. The reforms actually began under the conservative Tory Party, when Catholics and non-Anglican Protestants were allowed to participate in public life. The Tories nevertheless refused to reform representation in the House of Commons, which had about two-thirds of its members who owed their seats to the patronage of the richest titled landowners in the country. In districts known as "rotten" or "pocket" boroughs, landowners used their power to return members of Parliament who would serve their interests. Defenders of this system argued that the interests of landed property coincided with those of the nation at large.

Liberals in the Whig Party, the new industrial middle class, and radical artisans argued passionately for reform. The liberals were not necessarily democrats—liberals in particular wanted to enfranchise only responsible citizens—but they formed a common cause with organized middle-class and working-class radicals to push for reform. A Birmingham banker named Thomas Atwood, for example, organized the Political Union of the Lower and Middle Classes of the People. By July 1830, similar organizations arose in several cities, some of which clashed with the army and police. Middle-class shopkeepers even announced they would withhold taxes and form a national guard. The country appeared to be on the verge of a serious general disorder, if not outright revolution. Lord Grey, head of the Whig Party, seized the opportunity to push through reform.

The Reform Bill of 1832 eliminated the rotten boroughs and reallocated 143 parliamentary seats, mostly from the rural south to the industrial north. The bill expanded the franchise, but only one in six men could vote. Landed aristocrats saw their influence reduced but not destroyed. This modest reform brought British liberals and members of the middle class into a junior partnership with the landed elite that had ruled Britain for centuries. What other changes did this more liberal parliament produce? It abolished slavery in the British colonies in 1833 (see Chapter 21).

The most significant example of middle-class power came in the repeal of the Corn Laws in 1846. The Corn

THE GREAT CHARTIST RALLY OF APRIL 10, 1848. The year 1848 brought revolution to Continental Europe and militant protest to England. This photo shows the April rally in support of the Chartists' six points, which included expanding the franchise, abolishing property qualifications for representatives, and instituting a secret ballot.

included in the movement or excluded as dangerous competitors? Should women be included in the franchise? The Chartist William Lovett, a cabinet-maker, was a fervent believer in self-improvement and advocated a union of educated workers that could claim its fair share of the nation's increasing industrial wealth. The Chartist Fear-gus O'Connor appealed to the more impoverished and desperate class of workers by attacking industrialization and the resettlement of the poor on agricultural allotments. The Chartist James Bronterre O'Brien shocked the crowds by openly expressing his admiration for Robespierre and attacking the "big-bellied, little-brained, numb-skull aristocracy." Chartism had many faces, but the movement's common goal was social justice through political democracy.

In spite of the Chartists' efforts to present massive petitions to Parliament in 1839 and 1842, both times, they were rejected. Members of the movement resorted to strikes, trade union demonstrations, and attacks on factories and manufacturers who imposed low wages and long hours or who harassed unionists. The movement peaked in April 1848. Inspired by revolutions in Continental Europe (see Chapter 21), the Chartists' leaders planned a major demonstration in London. Twenty-five thousand workers carried to Parliament a petition with 6 million signatures. Confronted with the specter of class conflict, special constables and regular army units were marshaled by the aged Duke of Wellington to resist any threat to public order. In the end, only a small delegation presented the petition, and rain and an unwillingness to do battle with the constabulary put an end to the Chartist movement. A relieved liberal observer, Harriet Martineau, observed, "From that day it was a settled matter that England was safe from revolution."

Laws (the British term for grain is *corn*) protected British landowners and farmers from foreign competition by establishing tariffs for imports and keeping bread prices high. The middle class increasingly saw this as an unfair protection of the aristocracy and pushed for their repeal in the name of free trade. The **Anti–Corn Law League** held meetings throughout the north of England and lobbied Parliament, eventually resulting in a repeal of the law and a free-trade policy that lasted until the 1920s.

British Radicalism and the Chartist Movement

Reformers disappointed with the narrow gains of 1832 pushed for expanded political reforms. They focused on a petition known as the "People's Charter," which contained six demands: universal white male suffrage, a secret ballot, an end to property qualifications as a condition of public office, annual parliamentary elections, salaries for members of the House of Commons, and equal electoral districts. The **Chartists** organized committees across the country, and the People's Charter was eventually signed by millions.

Chartism spread in a climate of economic hardship during the 1840s. The movement tapped into local traditions of worker self-help, but the Chartists often disagreed about tactics and goals. Should Irish Catholics be

THE POLITICS OF SLAVERY AFTER 1815

These political conflicts within nations about citizenship, sovereignty, and equality were also linked to a transnational debate about slavery and its legitimacy that was taking place at the same time. When the age of revolution opened in the 1770s, slavery was legal everywhere in the Atlantic world. By 1848, slavery remained legal only in the southern United States, Brazil, and Cuba. (It endured, too, in most of Africa and parts of India and the Islamic world.) Given the importance of slavery to the Atlantic economy, this was a remarkable shift. The debate about slavery was fundamental, because it challenged the defenders of citizenship rights to live up to the claims of universality that had been a central part of Enlightenment political thought. If "all men" were "created equal," how could some be enslaved?

Slavery, Enlightenment, and Revolution

The revolutions of the eighteenth century by no means brought emancipation in their wake. Eighteenth-century Enlightenment thinkers had persuaded many Europeans that slavery contradicted natural law and natural freedom (Chapter 17); a critique that allowed slavery to become a metaphor for any abuse of political authority. Thus, Virginia planters who helped lead the American Revolution angrily refused to be "slaves" to the English king, while at the same time defending plantation slavery. In fact, the planters' success in throwing off the British king expanded their power and strengthened slavery as an institution in North America.

Likewise, the French revolutionaries, while denouncing the tyranny of a king who would "enslave" them, refused to admit free people of color to the revolutionary assembly for fear of alienating the planters in the lucrative colonies of Martinique, Guadeloupe, and Saint-Domingue. Only a slave rebellion in Saint-Domingue in 1791, eventually, forced the French revolutionaries to contend with the contradictions of revolutionary policy. Napoleon's failure to repress that rebellion allowed for the emergence of Haiti in 1804 (Chapter 18). The Haitian Revolution sent shock waves through the Americas, alarming slave owners while offering hope to slaves and former slaves. In the words of a free black sailmaker in Philadelphia, the Haitian nation signaled that black people "could not always be detained in their present bondage."

Yet the revolution in Haiti had other, contradictory consequences. The "loss" of slavery-based sugar production in the former Saint-Domingue created an opportunity for its expansion elsewhere—in Brazil, where slavery expanded in the production of sugar, gold, and coffee; and in the American South. And slavery remained intact in the French, British, and Spanish colonial islands in the Caribbean, backed by the Congress of Vienna in 1815.

The Slow Path to Abolition

An abolitionist movement did emerge, in Britain. The country that ruled the seas was the "world's leading purchaser and transporter of African slaves," and the movement aimed to abolish that trade. From the 1780s on, pamphlets and books—the best known is *The Interesting Narrative of the Life of Olaudah Equiano* (1789)—detailed the horrors of the slave ships to an increasingly sympathetic audience. Abolitionist leaders such as William Wilberforce believed that the slave trade was immoral and hoped that banning it would improve conditions for the enslaved, though like most abolitionists, Wilberforce did not want to foment revolt. In 1807, the reform movement compelled Parliament to pass a bill declaring the "African Slave Trade to be contrary to the principles of justice, humanity and sound policy" and prohibiting British ships from participating in it, effective in 1808. The United States joined in the agreement; and ten years later, the Portuguese agreed to a limited ban on traffic north of the equator. More treaties followed, which slowed but did not stop the trade.

What roots did abolitionism tap? Some historians argue that slavery was becoming less profitable and that its decline made humanitarian concern easier to accept. Others argue that slavery was, in fact, expanding: among other things, ships carried 2.5 million slaves to markets in the Americas in the four decades *after* the abolition of slave trade.

Some historians believe economic factors undermined slavery. **Adam Smith** and his followers argued that free labor, like free trade, was more efficient; this was not necessarily the case, but such arguments still had an effect. Critics claimed slavery was wasteful as well as cruel. Economic calculations, however, did less to activate abolitionism than did the belief that the slave trade and slavery itself represented the arrogance and callousness of wealthy British traders, their planter allies, and the British elite in general. In a culture with high literacy and political traditions of activism, calls for "British liberty" mobilized many.

In Britain, and especially in the United States, religious revivals supplied much of the energy for the abolitionist movement. The hymn "Amazing Grace" was written by a former slave trader turned minister, John Newton, to

FEAR OF SLAVE VIOLENCE. This cartoon, published in Britain in 1789 in opposition to the movement to end slavery, played on public fears of the consequences of abolition. The former slaves, dressed in the fashionable attire of the landed gentry, dine at their former master's table and beat the master in retaliation for what they have suffered. In the background, other former slave owners are stooped in labor in the cane fields. According to the logic of this cartoon, such a reversal would be intolerable; and given the choice between "Abolition" and "Regulation" (the two heads at the bottom), the cartoonist would choose "Regulation" as the wiser course.

describe his conversion experience and salvation. The moral and religious dimensions of the struggle made it acceptable for women to participate (they would move from the antislavery movement to the Anti–Corn Law League and, later, to the women's suffrage movement). Finally, the issue spoke to laborers, whose sometimes brutal working conditions and sharply limited political rights we have discussed in the previous chapters. To oppose slavery and to insist that labor be dignified, honorable, and minimally free resonated broadly in social classes accustomed to being treated as "servile." The issue, then, cut across material interests and class politics, and millions signed antislavery petitions during the 1820s and 1830s.

Slave rebellions and conspiracies to rebel also shook opinion, especially after the success of the Haitian Revolution (Chapter 19). In 1800, slaves rebelled in Virginia; in 1811, there was an uprising in Louisiana; and in 1822, an alleged conspiracy took hold in South Carolina. The British colonies saw significant rebellions in Barbados (1816) and in Demerara, just east of Venezuela (1823); and, most important, the month-long insurrection in Jamaica (1831). All of these were ferociously repressed. Slave rebellions had virtually no chance of succeeding and usually erupted only when some crack in the system opened up, such as

divisions within the white elite or the (perceived) presence of a sympathetic outsider. Still, these rebellions had important consequences: they increased slaveholders' sense of vulnerability and isolation, and polarized debate. Outsiders (in Britain or New England) often recoiled at the brutality of the repressions. Slave owners responded to antislavery sentiment much as Russian serf owners had responded to their critics—by insisting that slavery was vital to their survival, that emancipation of inferior peoples would sow chaos, and that abolitionists were playing with fire.

In Britain, the force of abolitionism wore down the defense of slavery. In the aftermath of the Great Reform Bill of 1832, Britain emancipated 800,000 slaves in its colonies—effective in 1838, after four years of "apprenticeship." In France, republicans took the strongest antislavery stance, and emancipation came to the French colonies when the revolution of 1848 brought republicans, however briefly, to power (see Chapter 21).

In Latin America, slavery's fate was determined by demographics, economics, and the politics of breaking away from the Spanish and Portuguese empires. In most of mainland Spanish America (in other words, not Cuba or Brazil), slavery had been of secondary importance, owing to the relative ease of escape and the presence of other sources of labor. As the struggles for independence escalated, nationalist leaders recruited slaves and free people of color to fight against the Spanish, promising emancipation in return. Simón Bolívar's 1817 campaign to liberate Venezuela was fought in part by slaves, exslaves, and 6,000 troops from Haiti. The new nations in Spanish America passed emancipation measures in stages, but they had eliminated slavery by the middle of the century.

Cuba was starkly different: with 40 percent of its population enslaved, the Spanish island colony had almost as many slaves as all of mainland Spanish America together. A Cuban independence movement would have detonated a slave revolution, a fact that provided a powerful incentive for Cuba to remain under the Spanish crown. Spain, for its part, needed the immensely profitable sugar industry and could not afford to alienate Cuban planters by pushing for an end to slavery. Only a combination of slave rebellion in Cuba and liberal revolution in Spain brought abolition, beginning in the 1870s. Brazil, too, was 40 percent enslaved and, like Cuba, had a large population of free people of color. Unlike Cuba, however, Brazil won national independence, breaking away from Portugal with relative ease (1822). Like the American South, Brazil came through the revolution for independence with slavery not only intact but expanding, and slavery endured in Brazil until 1888.

TAKING SIDES: NEW IDEOLOGIES IN POLITICS

Debates about citizenship, sovereignty, and slavery made it clear that issues raised by the French Revolution were very much alive in Europe after 1815. The Congress of Vienna was able to place the Bourbon family back on the throne in France, but it could not make debates about popular sovereignty, national independence, or the authority of conservative dynastic regimes go away. Throughout Europe, political actors increasingly understood they were facing a choice. If the debate about political change after the French Revolution was one between groups holding incompatible worldviews, then winning meant imposing your vision of the world on your opponents by any means necessary. Such assumptions encouraged extremists on all sides of the debate. However, if disputing groups could come to some kind of mutual understanding about the goals of political association, then some compromise or middle way might be possible. It was within this context that modern political ideologies of conservatism, liberalism, socialism, and nationalism began to come into clearer focus.

Early nineteenth-century politics did not include parties as we know them today. But more clearly defined groups and competing doctrines, or ideologies, took shape during this time. An ideology may be defined as a coherent system of thought that claims to represent the workings and structure of the social order and its relationship to political powers and institutions. Ideologies consciously compete with other views of how the world is or should be, and their defenders seek to establish their views as dominant. The roots of conservatism, liberalism, and nationalism lay in earlier times, but ongoing political battles over the legacy of the French Revolution brought them to the fore. The Industrial Revolution (Chapter 19) and the

social changes that accompanied it proved a tremendous spur to political and social thought and led to the development of socialism as a political and social project. Would the advance of industry yield progress or misery? What were the "rights of man," and who would enjoy them? Did equality necessarily go hand in hand with liberty? A brief survey of the political horizon will show how different groups formulated their responses to these questions and dramatize how the ground had shifted since the eighteenth century.

Conservatism

At the Congress of Vienna and during the Restoration generally, the most important guiding concept was legitimacy. Legitimacy had broad appeal as a general antirevolutionary policy. This term might be best understood as a code word for a new political order that the Congress sought to impose. Conservatives aimed to make legitimate—and thus to solidify—both the monarchy's authority and the hierarchical social order undermined by the French Revolution. They believed that the monarchy guaranteed political stability, that the nobility were the rightful leaders of the nation, and that both needed to play active and effective roles in public life. They insisted that, as a matter of strategy, the nobility and the crown shared a common interest, despite their disagreements in the past. They also believed that change had to be slow, incremental, and managed so as to strengthen rather than weaken the structures of authority, and that conserving the past and cultivating tradition would ensure an orderly future.

The French writers Joseph de Maistre (1753–1821) and Louis-Gabriel-Ambroise Bonald (1754–1840), for example, penned carefully elaborated defenses of absolute monarchy and its main pillar of support, the Catholic Church. Maistre blamed the Enlightenment's critique of the Catholic Church for the French Revolution, and assailed Enlightenment individualism for ignoring the bonds and collective institutions—the Church, for instance, or family—that he believed held society together. The conservatives' view was resolutely backward looking, and they viewed all political innovations with deep distrust. As they saw it, monarchy, aristocracy, and the Church were the mainstays of the social and political order, and these institutions needed to stand together in the face of the challenges of the new century.

Other conservatives of the period accepted that the old order could not survive completely intact, especially after the events of the 1820s made it clear that the Restoration

Analyzing Primary Sources

Edmund Burke, Reflections on the Revolution in France

Edmund Burke's Reflections on the Revolution in France *was first published in 1790, while the French Revolution was still under way. His opposition to revolutionary change had a profound influence on conservatives in the decades after the Congress of Vienna in 1815. The following passages contain Burke's defense of hereditary elites, his insistence on the power of tradition (which he refers to as "convention"), and his criticism of the doctrine of natural rights.*

The power of perpetuating our property in our families is one of the most valuable and interesting circumstances belonging to it, and that which tends the most to the perpetuation of society itself. It makes our weakness subservient to our virtue; it grafts benevolence even upon avarice. The possessors of family wealth, and of the distinction which attends hereditary possession . . . are the natural securities for this transmission. With us, the house of peers is formed upon this principle. It is wholly composed of hereditary property and hereditary distinction; and made therefore the third of the legislature; and in the last event, the sole judge of all property in all its subdivisions. The house of commons too, though not necessarily, yet in fact, is always so composed in the far greater part. Let those large proprietors be what they will, and they have their chance of being amongst the best, they are at the very worst, the ballast in the vessel of the commonwealth. [. . .]

If civil society be the offspring of convention, that convention must be its law. That convention must limit and modify the descriptions of constitution which are formed under it. Every sort of legislative, judicial, or executor power are its creatures. They can have no being in any other state of things; and how can any man claim, under the conventions of civil society, rights which do not so much as suppose its existence? Rights which are absolutely repugnant to it? One of the first motives to civil society, and which becomes one of its fundamental rules, is *that no man should be judge in his own cause.* By this each person has at once divested himself of the first fundamental right of uncovenanted man, that is, to judge for himself, and to assert his own cause. He abdicates all right to be his own governor. He inclusively, in a great measure, abandons the right of self-defense, the first law of nature. Men cannot enjoy the rights of an uncivil and of a civil state together. That he may obtain justice he gives up his right of determining what it is in points the most essential to him. That he may secure some liberty, he makes a surrender in trust of the whole of it. [. . .]

Government is not made in virtue of natural rights, which may and do exist in total independence of it; and in a much greater degree of abstract perfection; but their abstract perfection is their practical defect. . . . The moment you abate anything from the full rights of men, each to govern himself, and suffer any artificial positive limitation upon those rights, from that moment the whole organization of government becomes a consideration of convenience. That is which makes the constitution of a state, and the due distribution of its powers, a matter of the most delicate and complicated skill. It requires a deep knowledge of human nature and human necessities, and of the things which facilitate or obstruct the various ends which are to be pursued by the mechanism of civil institutions. The state is to have recruits to its strength and remedies to its distempers. What is the use of discussing a man's abstract right to food or to medicine? The question is upon the method of procuring and administering them. In that deliberation I shall always advise to call in the aid of the farmer and the physician, rather than the professor of metaphysics.

Source: Edmund Burke, *Reflections on the Revolution in France*, 9th edition (London: 1791), pp. 75–76, 86–88, 89–90.

Questions for Analysis

1. Note that Burke does not defend hereditary elites with reference to God or a divinely inspired order. How does he justify the authority of the hereditary aristocracy?

2. What power does Burke grant to "convention" in the construction of the state and its laws?

3. What is Burke's principal complaint about revolutionaries who base their programs on "natural rights"?

would be challenged. For conservatives who recognized this need to adapt, **Edmund Burke**'s writings became an important point of reference. Burke's *Reflections on the Revolution in France* was more influential in this new context than it had been during the 1790s, when it was first published. Burke did not oppose all change. As a member of the British Parliament, he voiced support for constraints on royal power and argued that the British should let go of the North American colonies. But he opposed talk of natural rights, which he considered dangerous abstractions. He believed enthusiasm for constitutions to be misguided and the Enlightenment's emphasis on what he called the "conquering power of reason" to be dangerous; instead, he counseled a much more cautious approach to social and political change, with deference to experience, tradition, and history.

Conservatism was not simply the province of intellectuals. A more broadly based revival of religion in the early nineteenth century also expressed a popular reaction against revolution and an emphasis on order, discipline, and tradition. What was more, conservative thinkers exercised influence well beyond their immediate circle. Their emphasis on history, on the untidy and unpredictable ways in which history unfolded, and their awareness of the past became increasingly central to social thought and artistic visions of the first half of the century.

Liberalism

Liberalism's core was a commitment to individual liberties, or rights. Liberals believed that the most important function of government was to protect liberties and that doing so would benefit all, by promoting justice, knowledge, progress, and prosperity. Liberalism had three components. First, liberalism called for equality before the law, which meant ending traditional privileges and the restrictive power of rank and hereditary authority. Second, liberalism held that government needed to be based on political rights and the consent of the governed. Third, with respect to economics, liberals believed that individuals should be free to engage in economic activities without interference from the state or the community.

The roots of legal and political liberalism lay in the work of John Locke in the late seventeenth century, who had defended the British Parliament's rebellion against absolutism and the "inalienable" rights of the British people (Chapter 15). Liberalism had been developed by the Enlightenment writers of the eighteenth century and was especially influenced by the founding texts of the American Revolution (the Declaration of Independence) and the

French Revolution (the Declaration of the Rights of Man). The starting points for nineteenth-century liberalism were the principles of freedom from arbitrary authority, imprisonment, and censorship; freedom of the press; and the right to assemble and deliberate. Liberals believed in individual rights, that those rights were inalienable, and that they should be guaranteed in written constitutions. (Conservatives, as we saw earlier, considered constitutions abstract and dangerous.) Most liberals called for constitutional as opposed to hereditary monarchy, and agreed that a monarch who abused power could legitimately be overthrown.

Liberals advocated direct representation in government—at least for those who had property and public standing to be trusted with the responsibilities of power. Liberalism by no means required democracy. In the July

ADAM SMITH WITH HIS BOOK *THE WEALTH OF NATIONS* (1776). Smith was an Enlightenment thinker whose work was popularized in the nineteenth century. He helped to establish "political economy," or economics.

Monarchy in France, established after the 1830 revolution, the property qualifications were so high that only 2 percent of the population could vote. Even after the Reform Bill of 1832 in England, only 18 percent of the population could vote for parliamentary representatives. Nineteenth-century liberals, with fresh memories of the French Revolution of 1789, were torn between their belief in rights and their fears of political turmoil. They considered property and education essential prerequisites for participation in politics, and wealthy liberals opposed extending the vote to the common people. To demand universal male suffrage was too radical, and to speak of enfranchising women or people of color even more so. As far as slavery was concerned, nineteenth-century liberalism inherited the contradictions of the Enlightenment. Belief in individual liberty collided with vested economic interests, the determination to preserve order and property, and increasingly "scientific" theories of racial inequality (see Chapter 23).

Economic liberalism was newer. Its founding text was Adam Smith's *Wealth of Nations* (1776), which attacked mercantilism (the government practice of regulating manufacturing and trade to raise revenues) in the name of free markets. Smith's argument that the economy should be based on a "system of natural liberty" was reinforced by a second generation of economists and popularized in journals such as the *Economist*, founded in 1838. The economists, or political economists as they were called, sought to identify basic economic laws—the law of supply and demand, the balance of trade, the law of diminishing returns, and so on—and argued that economic policy had to begin by recognizing these laws. David Ricardo (1772–1823) of Britain, for example, set out laws of wages and of rents, trying to determine the long-run outcomes of fluctuations in each.

Liberal political economists such as Smith and Ricardo believed that economic activity should be unregulated. Labor should be contracted freely, unhampered by guilds or unions, or state interference. Property should be unencumbered by feudal restrictions. Goods should circulate freely, which meant an end to government-granted monopolies, trade barriers, import tariffs, and traditional practices of regulating markets, especially in valuable commodities such as grain, flour, or corn. At the time of the Irish famine, for instance, their writings played a role in hardening the opposition to government intervention or relief (Chapter 19). Liberal economists believed that the functions of the state should be kept to a minimum, though they argued that markets could not function without states to preserve the rule of law. They believed that government's role should be to preserve order and protect property, but

not to interfere with the natural play of economic forces, a doctrine known as *laissez-faire,* which translates, roughly, as "leave things to go on their own." This strict opposition to government intervention makes nineteenth-century liberalism different from common understandings of "liberalism" in the United States today.

Liberty and freedom meant different things in different countries. In lands occupied by other powers, liberal parties demanded freedom from foreign rule. The colonies of Latin America demanded liberty from Spain, and similar struggles set Greece and Serbia against the Ottoman Empire, northern Italy against the Austrians, Poland against Russian rule, and so on. In central and southeastern Europe, liberty meant eliminating feudal privilege and allowing at least the educated elite access to political power, more rights for local parliaments, and creating representative national political institutions. Some cited the British system of government as a model, while others pointed to the French Declaration of the Rights of Man; and most shied away from the radicalism of the French Revolution. The issue was constitutional, representative government. In such countries as Russia, Prussia, and France under the restored Bourbon monarchy, liberty meant political freedoms, such as the right to vote, assemble, and print political opinions without censorship.

In Great Britain, where political freedoms were relatively well established, liberals focused on expanding the franchise, on laissez-faire economics and free trade, and on reforms aimed at creating limited and efficient government. In this respect, one of the most influential British liberals was **Jeremy Bentham** (1748–1832). Bentham's major work, *The Principles of Morals and Legislation* (1789), illustrates how nineteenth-century liberalism continued the Enlightenment legacy as well as transformed it. Unlike Smith, for instance, Bentham did not believe that human interests were naturally harmonious or that a stable social order could emerge naturally from a body of self-interested individuals. Instead, he proposed that society adopt the organizing principle of **utilitarianism**. Social institutions and laws (an electoral system, for instance, or a tariff) should be measured according to their social usefulness—that is, whether they produced the "greatest happiness of the greatest number." If a law passed this test, it could remain on the books; but if it failed, it should be jettisoned. Utilitarians acknowledged the importance of the individual. Each individual best understood his or her own interests and was, therefore, best left free, whenever possible, to pursue those interests as he or she saw fit. Only when an individual's interests conflicted with the interests—the happiness—of the greatest number was individual freedom to be curtailed. The intensely practical spirit of utilitarianism

Past and Present

Revolts against Reason

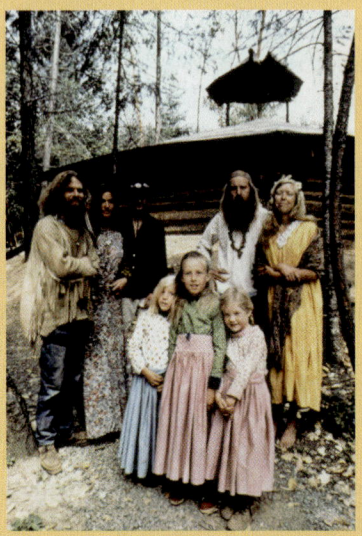

After the French Revolution, confidence in the power of reason and social progress diminished in some quarters. Many conservatives were skeptical about human improvement, and some radicals, including the Saint-Simonians in France (left), sought a different kind of community and a different future from one solely based on rationality. Some of these cultural movements proved enduring and persist even today in novel but recognizable forms, such as the "back-to-nature" movement of the 1960s (right).

 Watch related author interview on the Student Site

enhanced its influence as a creed for reform. In his personal political views, Bentham went further than many liberals—he befriended Jacobins and believed in equal rights for women. Nevertheless, his rationalist approach to measuring the "utility" of laws and reforms was an essential contribution to the liberal tradition.

Radicalism, Republicanism, and Early Socialism

The liberals were flanked on their left by two radical groups: republicans and socialists. Whereas liberals advocated a constitutional monarchy (in the name of stability and keeping power in the hands of men of property), republicans, as their name implies, pressed further, demanding a government by the people, an expanded franchise, and democratic participation in politics. The crucial distinction between the more moderate liberals and the radical republicans, therefore, depended on their criteria for defining citizenship. Both groups believed that government should have the consent of citizens, but liberals were more likely to support restricted qualifications for citizenship, such as property ownership or the amount of taxes paid. Republicans were committed to political equality and advocated more open definition of citizenship, one without regard to wealth or social standing. In thinking about the legacy of the French Revolution, liberals were likely to favor the attempts by the National Assembly to

QUADRILLE DANCING AT NEW LANARK, ROBERT OWEN'S MODEL COMMUNITY. Owen's Scottish experiment with cooperative production and community building, including schooling for infants, was only one of many utopian ventures in early-nineteenth-century Europe and North America.

create a constitution between 1789 and 1791, whereas Republicans sympathized more openly with the Jacobins of the French Republic after 1792. Liberals remained suspicious of direct democracy and "mob rule," and sought constitutional measures that would allow propertied elites to exert control over the political process and maintain social order. Radical republicans, however, supported civil militias, free public education, and civic liberties such as the free press and the right to assemble. Yet, in the debates between liberals and republicans, a general consensus about gender remained uncontroversial: only a very few liberals or republicans supported allowing women to vote. Nearly all political thinkers of the period assumed that the virtues necessary for citizenship—rationality, sobriety, and independence of mind—were essentially masculine traits.

While liberals called for individualism and laissez-faire, and republicans emphasized direct democracy and political equality, socialists pointed out that giving men the vote would not necessarily eradicate other persistent forms of injustice and inequality. To put in terms used at the time, socialists raised the "social question": How could the growing economic inequalities produced by industrialization and the miseries of working people be remedied? This "social" question, socialists insisted, was an urgent political

matter, and they offered varied responses to this question and different ways of redistributing economic and social power. The solutions ranged from cooperation and new ways of organizing everyday life to collective ownership of the means of production; some were just speculative, others very concrete.

Socialism was a nineteenth-century system of thought and a response in large measure to the visible problems ushered in by industrialization: the intensification of labor, the poverty of working-class neighborhoods in industrial cities, and the widespread perception that a hierarchy based on rank and privilege had been replaced by one based on social class. For socialists, the problems of industrial society were not incidental, but arose from the core principles of competition, individualism, and private property. What socialists took from the Enlightenment was a commitment to reason and human progress. They did not oppose industry and economic development, but believed society could be both industrial and humane.

These radical thinkers were often explicitly **utopian**. **Robert Owen** (1771–1858), a wealthy industrialist turned reformer, bought a large cotton factory at New Lanark in Scotland and proceeded to organize the mill and the surrounding town according to the principles of cooperation rather than those of profitability. New Lanark organized decent housing and sanitation, good working conditions, child care, free schooling, and a system of social security for the factory's workers. Owen advocated a general reorganization of society on the basis of cooperation and mutual respect, and he tried to persuade other manufacturers of the rightness of his cause. The Frenchman **Charles Fourier** (1772–1837), too, tried to organize utopian communities based on the abolition of the wage system, division of work according to people's natural inclinations, and complete equality of the sexes, and collectively organized child care and household labor. And the charismatic socialist Flora Tristan (1803–1844) toured France speaking to workers about the principles of cooperation and the equality of men and women. That so many men and women followed like-minded leaders into experimental communities and took their utopian visions seriously is a measure of people's unhappiness with early industrialization, and their conviction that society could be organized along radically different lines.

Other socialists proposed simpler, practical reforms. Louis Blanc, a French politician and journalist, campaigned for universal male suffrage with an eye to giving working-class men control of the state. Instead of protecting private property and the manufacturing class, the transformed state would become the "banker of the poor," extending credit to those who needed it and establishing "associations of production," a series of workshops governed by laborers that would guarantee jobs and security for all. Such workshops were established, fleetingly, during the French Revolution of 1848, as were clubs promoting women's rights. Pierre-Joseph Proudhon (1809–1865) proposed establishing producers' cooperatives, which would sell goods at a price workers could afford; working-class credit unions; and so on. Proudhon's "What Is Property?"—to which the famous answer was "Property is theft"—became one of the most widely read socialist pamphlets, familiar to artisans, laborers, and middle-class intellectuals, including Karl Marx. As we will see, a period of economic depression and widespread impoverishment in the 1840s brought the socialists many more working-class followers.

Karl Marx's Socialism

The father of modern socialism, **Karl Marx** (1818–1883), was barely known in the early nineteenth century. His reputation rose later, after 1848, when a wave of revolutions and violent confrontations appeared to confirm his distinctive theory of history, and make the earlier socialists' emphasis on cooperation, setting up experimental

KARL MARX, 1882. Despite the rare smile in this portrait, Marx was near the end of his life, attempting to recuperate in Algeria from sickness and the deaths of his wife and daughter.

communities, and peaceful reorganization of industrial society seem naive.

Marx grew up in Trier, a city in the Rhineland close to the French border, in a region and a family keenly interested in the political debates and movements of the revolutionary era. His family was Jewish, but his father had converted to Protestantism to be able to work as a lawyer. Marx studied law briefly at the University of Berlin before turning instead to philosophy, particularly the ideas of Georg Wilhelm Friedrich Hegel. With the so-called Young Hegelians, a group of rebellious students who chafed at the narrow thinking of the deeply conservative Prussian university system, Marx appropriated some of Hegel's concepts for his radical politics. Because his radicalism (and atheism, for he repudiated all his family's religious affiliations) made it impossible for him to get a post in a university, he became a journalist, writing now-famous articles on, for instance, peasants "stealing" wood from forests that were once common land. From 1842 to 1843, he edited the liberal *Rhineland Gazette* (*Rheinische Zeitung*). The paper's criticism of legal privilege and political repression put it on a collision course with the Prussian government, which closed it down and sent Marx into exile—first to Paris, then Brussels, and eventually London.

While in Paris, Marx studied early socialist theory, economics, and the history of the French Revolution. He also began a lifelong intellectual and political partnership with Friedrich Engels (1820–1895). Engels was the son of a textile manufacturer from the German Rhineland. His parents had sent him to learn business with a merchant firm in Manchester, one of the centers of England's Industrial

Revolution (Chapter 19). Engels worked in the family business until 1870, but this did not prevent him from taking up his pen to denounce the miserable working and living conditions in Manchester and what he saw as the systematic inequalities of capitalism. (He published *The Condition of the Working Class in England* in 1844.) Marx and Engels joined a small international group of radical artisans called the League of the Just, renamed the Communist League in 1847. The league asked Marx to draft a statement of its principles, which was published in 1848 as *The Communist Manifesto,* with Engels listed as coauthor.

The Communist Manifesto laid out Marx's theory of history in short form. From Hegel, Marx imported the view of history as a dynamic process, with an inner logic, moving toward human freedom. (This is a good example of the larger influence of conservative historical thinking.) In Hegel's view, the historical process did not unfold in any simple and predictable way; instead, history proceeded "dialectically," or through conflict. He saw this conflict as one between ideas: a "thesis" produced an "antithesis," and the clash between the two created a distinctive and new "synthesis." In a classic example, Hegel posited that the natural but limited freedom of the savage (thesis) encountered its opposite (antithesis) in the constraints imposed on the individual by the family and the developing institutions of civil society. The result of this clash was a new and superior freedom (synthesis), the freedom of individuals within society, protected by moral customs, law, and the state.

Marx applied Hegel's dialectic, or theory of conflict, to history in a different way. He did not begin with ideas, as Hegel had, but rather with material, social, and economic forces. According to this materialist vision, world history had passed through three major stages, each characterized by conflict between social groups, or "classes," whose divisions were linked to the underlying economic order: master versus slave in ancient slavery, lord versus serf in feudalism, and bourgeois capitalist versus proletariat (industrial laborers) in capitalism. For Marx, this "class struggle" was the motor of human history. He believed that the feudal stage of history, where an aristocratic class dominated the enserfed peasantry, had ended in 1789, with the French Revolution. What followed was a new order, dominated by an entrepreneurial middle class—he called them "bourgeois"—that built the world of industrial capitalism.

In *The Communist Manifesto,* Marx and Engels admired the revolutionary accomplishments of capitalism, saying that the bourgeoisie had "created more impressive and more colossal productive forces than had all preceding generations together." But, they argued, the revolutionary character of capitalism would also undermine the bourgeois economic order. As capital became more concentrated in the hands of the few, a growing army of wageworkers would become increasingly aware of its economic and political disenfranchisement, and this struggle between competing classes was central to industrial capitalism itself. Eventually, *The Communist Manifesto* predicted, recurring economic crises, caused by capitalism's unending need for new markets and the cyclical instability of overproduction, would bring about the collapse of capitalism. Workers would seize the state, reorganize the means of production, abolish private property, and eventually create a communist society based on egalitarian principles. In other words, this ultimate revolution would abolish the division of labor altogether, ending the class conflict that had been the motor of history, and ushering in a future whose outlines Marx could only hesitantly describe.

What was distinctive about Marx's version of socialism? It took up the disparity between public proclamations of progress and workers' daily experiences in a systematic, scholarly manner. Marx was an inexhaustible reader and thinker, with an extraordinarily broad range. He took his insights where he found them: in British economics, French history, and German philosophy. He wove others' ideas that labor was the source of value and that property was expropriation into a new theory of history that was also a thoroughgoing critique of nineteenth-century liberalism. Most important, he differed from his utopian socialist predecessors by identifying industrial laborers as a revolutionary class and linking revolution to a vision of human history as a whole. Marx's theory of history is sometimes referred to as *dialectical materialism,* because he borrowed the idea of the dialectic from Hegel and his view of history began with assumptions about the economic or material base of society.

Citizenship and Community: Nationalism

Of all the political ideologies of the early nineteenth century, nationalism is most difficult to grasp. What, exactly, counted as a nation? Who demanded a nation, and what did that demand mean? In the early nineteenth century, nationalism was usually aligned with liberalism and against the conservative states that dominated Europe after Napoleon's fall. As the century progressed, however, it became increasingly clear that nationalism could be molded to fit any doctrine.

Karl Marx and Pierre-Joseph Proudhon, Correspondence

> *Karl Marx was both a prolific political and economic theorist as well as a political militant, who corresponded with socialists and other political radicals throughout Europe. He, with Friedrich Engels, was the author of* The Communist Manifesto (1848), *a widely circulated polemical critique of the capitalist economic system, which predicted the emergence of a revolutionary movement led by Europe's industrial working classes. This exchange of letters with a prominent French socialist thinker, Pierre-Joseph Proudhon, reveals disagreements among socialists in Europe about the desirability of revolution, and Marx's ideas about how intellectuals such as himself might participate in the revolutionary movement.*

Brussels, 5 May 1846

My dear Proudhon,

. . . I have made arrangements with the German communists and socialists for a constant interchange of letters which will be devoted to discussing scientific questions, and to keeping an eye on popular writings, and the socialist propaganda that can be carried on in Germany by this means. The chief aim of our correspondence, however, will be to put the German socialists in touch with the French and English socialists; to keep foreigners constantly informed of the socialist movements that occur in Germany and to inform the Germans in Germany of the progress of socialism in France and England. In this way differences of opinion can be brought to light and an exchange of ideas and impartial criticism can take place. It will be a step made by the social movement in its *literary* manifestation to rid itself of the barriers of *nationality*. And when the moment for action comes, it will clearly be much to everyone's advantage to be acquainted with the state of affairs abroad as well as at home.

Our correspondence will embrace not only the communists in Germany, but also the German socialists in Paris and London. Our relations with England have already been established. So far as France is concerned, we all of us believe that we could find no better correspondent than yourself. As you know, the English and Germans have hitherto estimated you more highly than have your own compatriots.

So it is, you see, simply a question of establishing a regular correspondence and ensuring that it has the means to keep abreast of the social movement in the different countries, and to acquire a rich and varied interest, such as could never be achieved by the work of one single person. . . .

Yours most sincerely
Karl Marx

Source: Karl Marx, Frederick Engels, *Collected Works*, vol. 38 (New York: 1982), pp. 38–40.

The meaning of *nation* has changed over time. The term comes from the Latin verb *nasci* ("to be born") and suggests "common birth." In sixteenth-century England, *nation* designated the aristocracy, or those who shared a noble birthright; the French nobility also referred to itself as a nation. These earlier and unfamiliar usages are important, because they highlight the most significant development of the late eighteenth and early nineteenth centuries: the French Revolution redefined *nation* to mean the "sovereign people." The revolutionaries of 1789 boldly claimed that the nation, not the king, was the sovereign power. *Vive la nation* ("long live the nation")— a phrase found everywhere, from government decrees to revolutionary festivals, engravings, and memorabilia— celebrated a new political community, not a territory or an ethnicity. The French revolutionaries, and others who developed their philosophical views, took from Jean-Jacques Rousseau the argument that a regenerated nation

Lyon, 17 May 1846

My dear Monsieur Marx,

I am happy to become a recipient of your correspondence, whose goal and organization seem to me to be very useful. I cannot promise to write you at length or often, however, as my many occupations and my natural laziness will not permit such epistolary efforts. I would also like to take the liberty of expressing several reservations about a few of the passages in your letter.

First, [. . .] I believe that it is my duty, and the duty of all socialists, to maintain for the time being a skeptical or critical perspective, in a word, I claim [in matters of economics] an almost absolute anti-dogmatism.

Let us search together, if you wish, the laws of society, and the ways that these laws make themselves felt, and the process of development that allows us to discover them; but by God, after having demolished all the *a priori* dogmatisms, let us not dream of then indoctrinating the people ourselves, do not fall into the same contradiction faced by your compatriot Martin Luther, who after having overthrown Catholic theology, set about at once excommunicating others, in order to found a Protestant theology. [. . .] I applaud with all my heart your idea of bringing forth all possible opinions; let us therefore pursue a good and loyal argument; let us offer the world an example of a wise and perceptive toleration, but we should not, simply because we are the leaders of a movement, seek to pose as the apostles of a new religion, even if this religion is that of logic, of reason. Under these terms, I am happy to join your association, but if not–then No!

I would also like to comment on these words in your letter: *At the moment of action.* You may still think that no reform is possible at present without a bold stroke, without what was formerly called a revolution [. . .] Having myself held this opinion for a long time, I confess now that my more recent works have made me revisit this idea completely. I believe that we do not need [a revolution] to succeed, because this alleged solution would simply be an appeal to force, to something arbitrary, in short, a contradiction. I see the problem like this: *to find a form of economic combination that would restore to society the wealth that has been taken from it by another form of economic combination.* In other words, [. . .] to turn Property against Property, in such a way as to establish what you German socialists call *community*, and which I limit myself to calling *liberty, equality.* [. . .] I prefer to burn Property with a slow fuse, rather than to give it new energy by massacring the property owners.

Your very devoted
Pierre-Joseph Proudhon

Source: P.-J. Proudhon, Amédée Jérôme Langlois, *Correspondance de P.-J. Proudhon* (Paris: 1875), pp. 198–200.

Questions for Analysis

1. What is the purpose of the network of correspondents that Marx was inviting Proudhon to join? Why did Marx believe it necessary to overcome "the barriers of nationality"?

2. Why does Proudhon compare Marx's analysis of "scientific questions" or "the laws of society" to religious dogmas?

3. Why does Proudhon reject Marx's assumption that a revolution is necessary? What alternative does he propose?

---

based on the equality of its members (or on the limits of that equality; see Chapter 18) was not only more just but also more powerful. On a more concrete level, the revolutionaries built a national state, a national army, and a national legal system, whose jurisdiction trumped the older regional powers of the nobility and the local courts. In the aftermath of the French Revolution of 1789, the *nation* became what one historian calls the "collective image of modern citizenry."

In the early nineteenth century, then, *nation* symbolized legal equality, constitutional government, and unity; or an end to feudal privileges and divisions. Conservatives disliked the term, because national unity and the creation of national political institutions threatened to erode the local power of aristocratic elites. New nations rested on constitutions, which, as we have seen, conservatives considered dangerous abstractions. But nationalism became an important rallying cry for liberals across Europe precisely

MAJOR EUROPEAN AND MEDITERRANEAN LANGUAGE GROUPS, c. 1850. Compare the distribution of language groups in Europe with the political boundaries of European nations in 1848. ▪ *Do they line up?* ▪ *Which political units were forced to deal with a multitude of languages within their borders?* ▪ *How might this distribution of language groups be related to the history of European nationalisms?*

because it was associated with political transformation. It celebrated the achievements and political awakening of the common people.

Nationalism also went hand in hand with liberal demands for economic modernity. Economists, such as the influential German Friedrich List (1789–1846), sought to develop national economies and national infrastructures: larger, stronger, better integrated, and more effective systems of banking, trade, transportation, production, and distribution. List linked the end of territorial fragmentation of the German states and the development of manufacturing to "culture, prosperity, and liberty."

Nationalism, however, could easily undermine other liberal values. When liberals insisted on the value and importance of individual liberties, those committed to building nations responded that their vital task might require the sacrifice in some measure of each citizen's freedom. The Napoleonic army, a particularly powerful symbol of nationhood, appealed to conservative proponents of military strength and authority as well as to liberals who wanted an army of citizens.

Nineteenth-century nationalists wrote as if national feeling were natural, inscribed in the movement of history. They waxed poetic about the sudden awakening of feelings slumbering within the collective consciousness of a "German," an "Italian," a "French," or a "British" people. But this is misleading, because national identity—like religious, gender, or ethnic identities—developed and changed historically. It rested on specific nineteenth-century political and economic developments; rising literacy; the creation of national institutions, such as schools or the military; and the new importance of national rituals, from voting to holidays, village festivals, and the singing of anthems. Nineteenth-century governments sought to develop national feeling, to link their peoples more closely to their states. State-supported educational systems taught a "national" language, fighting the centrifugal forces of traditional dialects. Italian became the official language of the Italian nation, despite the fact that only 2.5 percent of the population spoke it. In other words, even a minority could define a national culture. Textbooks and self-consciously nationalist theater, poetry, and painting helped elaborate and sometimes invent a national heritage.

Political leaders associated the nation with specific causes; but ordinary activities, such as reading a daily newspaper in the morning, helped people imagine and identify with their fellow citizens. As one influential historian puts it, "All communities larger than primordial villages of face-to-face contact (and perhaps even these) are imagined." The nation is imagined as "limited," "sovereign," and "finally, it is imagined as a community, because regardless of the actual inequality and exploitation that may prevail . . . , the nation is always conceived as a deep, horizontal comradeship." The different meanings of *nationhood,* the various political beliefs it evoked, and the powerful emotions it tapped made nationalism exceptionally unpredictable.

If all nations are, in an important sense, "imagined communities," it is also true that the historical processes that make this imagining possible did not happen everywhere at the same time or in the same way. A sense of British distinctiveness emerged before the nineteenth century, in part because Britain was an island monarchy enriched by oceanic trade, but also because of its political traditions dating back to the Magna Carta. In central and eastern Europe, peoples without independent states, such as Poles and Hungarians, looked to the medieval past for historical precedents that could justify their claims for national independence against the powerful Russian, Austrian, or Prussian empires that ruled over them. Among the oldest pedigrees claimed by nineteenth-century nationalists were those of Jewish and Armenian nationalists, who pointed to cultural, linguistic, and religious traditions dating back to antiquity. All of these nationalist movements, however, looked forward as well as backward, and the urgency that their adherents felt arose from a very modern idea: that peoples without nation-states to represent them could never be in control of their destiny.

In the nineteenth century, conservatives, liberals, and republicans in Europe all implicitly recognized the power of nationalism, and they attempted to describe a vision of a nation that was compatible with their core principles. Conservatives linked dynastic ruling families and aristocratic elites to "national" traditions embodied in the history of territorially rooted peasant cultures and their traditional rulers. Liberals and republicans praised the nation as a body of free citizens who gave their consent to the laws that governed them. Marxist socialists, however, rejected the claims of nationalists, stating that the interest of social classes trumped national identity. The resolutely internationalist message of *The Communist Manifesto* was embodied in its concluding motto: "Workers of the world unite!"

Conservatism, liberalism, republicanism, socialism, and nationalism were the principal political ideologies of the early nineteenth century. They were rooted in the eighteenth century but brought to the forefront by the political turmoil of the early nineteenth century. Some nineteenth-century ideologies were continuations of the French revolutionary trio: liberty (from arbitrary authority), equality (or the end of legal privilege), and fraternity (the creation of new communities of citizens). Others, like conservatism, were reactions against the French Revolution. But all could be reinterpreted, and all became increasingly common points of reference as the century unfolded.

CULTURAL REVOLT: ROMANTICISM

Romanticism, the most significant cultural movement in the early nineteenth century, permeated politics and touched all the arts as well. It marked a reaction against the Classicism of the eighteenth century and the Enlightenment. Whereas Classicism aspired to reason, discipline, and harmony, Romanticism stressed emotion, freedom, and imagination. Romantic artists prized intense individual experiences and considered intuition and emotion to be better guides to truth and human happiness than reason and logic.

British Romantic Poetry

Romanticism developed first in England and Germany as a reaction against the Enlightenment. Early Romantics developed ideas originating from some of the Enlightenment's dissenters, such as Jean-Jacques Rousseau (Chapter 17). The poet **William Wordsworth** (1770–1834) took up Rousseau's central themes—nature, simplicity, and feeling—in his *Lyrical Ballads* (1798). For Wordsworth, poetry was the "spontaneous overflow of powerful feelings"; and like Rousseau, he emphasized the ties of compassion that bind all humankind, regardless of social class. "We have all of us one human heart," he wrote. "[M]en who do not wear fine clothes can feel deeply." Wordsworth considered nature to be humanity's most trustworthy teacher and the source of true feeling; and his poems were inspired by the wild hills and tumbledown cottages of England's Lake District. In "The Ruined Cottage," he quotes from the Scottish Romantic poet Robert Burns (the last two lines):

> Give me a spark of Nature's fire,
> 'Tis the best learning I desire . . .
> My muse, though homely in attire,
> May touch the heart.

Wordsworth's poetry, along with that of his colleague Samuel Taylor Coleridge (1772–1834), offered a key theme of nineteenth-century Romanticism: a view of nature that rejected the abstract mechanism of eighteenth-century Enlightenment thought. Nature was not a system to be dissected by science but the source of sublime power that nourished the human soul.

The poet **William Blake** (1757–1827) sounded similar themes in his fierce critique of industrial society and the factories (which he called "dark satanic mills") that blighted the English landscape. He championed the individual imagination and poetic vision, seeing both as transcending the limits of the material world. He believed imagination could awaken human sensibilities and sustain belief in different values, breaking humanity's "mind-forged manacles." His poetry paralleled early socialist efforts to imagine a better world. And like many Romantics, he looked back to a past in which he thought society had been more organic and humane.

English Romanticism peaked with the next generation of poets: **Lord Byron** (1788–1824), Percy Bysshe Shelley (1792–1822), and John Keats (1795–1821). Their lives and loves often appealed to readers as much as their writings. Byron was an aristocrat, rich, handsome, and defiant of convention. Poetry, he wrote, was the "lava of the imagination, whose eruption prevents an earthquake." His love affairs helped give Romantics their reputation as rebels against conformity, but they were hardly carefree. Byron treated his wife cruelly and drove her away after a year. He also rebelled against Britain's political leaders, labeling them corrupt and repressive. A Romantic hero, he defended working-class movements and fought in the war for Greek independence, during which he died of tuberculosis. Byron's friend Shelley emphasized similar themes of individual audacity in his poem *Prometheus Unbound* (1820). In the poem, Prometheus defies an all-powerful god, Zeus, by stealing fire for humanity and is punished by being chained to a rock while an eagle tears out his liver, which regrows every night. The poem celebrates the title character as a selfless mythic hero, comparable to Christ in his willingness to sacrifice himself for others. Shelley, in his correspondence, described the poem as a parable about revolutionary change, and the need to overthrow tyranny in the name of a new political ideal of struggle and hope, a sentiment captured in the poem's closing lines:

NEWTON, BY WILLIAM BLAKE (1795). Blake was a brilliant graphic artist, as well as a poet. Here, he depicts Sir Isaac Newton shrouded in darkness, distracted by his scientific calculations from the higher sphere of the imagination. Blake's image is a Romantic critique of Enlightenment science, for which Newton had become a hero.

To suffer woes which Hope thinks infinite;
To forgive wrongs darker than Death or Night;
To defy Power, which seems omnipotent;
To love, and bear; to hope till Hope creates
From its own wreck the thing it contemplates;
Neither to change nor falter nor repent
This, like thy glory, Titan! is to be
Good, great, and joyous, beautiful and free;
This is alone Life, Joy, Empire, and Victory.

Women Writers, Gender, and Romanticism

No Romantic work was more popular than Mary Shelley's *Frankenstein* (1818). Shelley (1797–1851) was the daughter of radical celebrities: the philosopher William Godwin and the feminist Mary Wollstonecraft (Chapter 17), who died just after her daughter was born. Mary Godwin met Percy Bysshe Shelley when she was sixteen and had three children by him before they were married, and she published *Frankenstein* at twenty. The novel, which captures the Romantic critique of science and Enlightenment reason, tells the story of an eccentric doctor determined to find the secret of human life. Conducting his research on corpses and body parts retrieved from charnel houses, Dr. Frankenstein produces life in the form of a monster. The monster has human feelings and is overwhelmed by loneliness and self-hatred when his creator casts him out. Shelley tells the story as a twisted creation myth, a study of individual genius gone wrong. The novel remains one of the most memorable characterizations in literature of the limits of reason and the impossibility of controlling nature.

The Romantic belief in individuality and creativity ran in several directions. It became a cult of artistic genius—of the "inexplicably and uniquely creative individual" who

MARY SHELLEY AT NINETEEN

MARY SHELLEY'S *FRANKENSTEIN*. Perhaps the best-known work of Romantic fiction, *Frankenstein* joined the Romantic critique of Enlightenment reason with early-nineteenth-century ambivalence about science to create a striking horror story. Shelley (pictured left, around the time she published the book in 1818) was the daughter of the philosopher William Godwin and the feminist Mary Wollstonecraft; she married poet Percy Bysshe Shelley. On the right is an engraving from the first illustrated edition of *Frankenstein* (1831) by Theodor von Holst.

Interpreting Visual Evidence

Romantic Painting

Romantic painters shared with Romantic poets a fascination with the power of nature. To convey this vision of nature as both an overwhelming power and a source of creative energy, Romantic painters created new and poetic visions of the natural world, in which human beings and their activities were reduced in significance, sometimes nearly disappearing altogether. At times, these visions also were linked to a backward-looking perspective, as if the dramatic changes associated with industrialization provoked a longing for a premodern past, where Europeans sought and found their sense of place in the world from an awareness of a quasi-divine natural setting invested with powerful mysteries. John Martin's painting *The Bard* (1817) (image A) shows a highly romanticized vision of a medieval subject: a single Welsh bard strides across rocky peaks above a mountain river, after escaping a massacre ordered by the English king Edward I. Across the river, Edward's troops can barely be seen leaving the scene of the crime, which still glows with destructive fires. The emotional qualities of this early expression of Romantic nationalism are reinforced by the forbidding and dynamic sky above, where the clouds merge into the Welsh mountaintops as if they were stirred by the hand of God himself.

Other Romantic painters minimized the significance of human activity in their landscapes, and without reference to history. John Constable's *Weymouth Bay* (1816) (image B) contains a tiny, almost imperceptible human figure in the middle ground, a man walking on the beach near a thin stone wall that snakes up a hill in the background. These passing references to human lives are completely dominated by the sky and, in particular, the movement of the clouds, which seem to be the real subject of the painting.

Of all the Romantic painters, J. M. W. Turner may have tackled the tricky subject of the new industrialized landscape in the most novel way. His painting *Rain, Steam, Speed—The Great Western Railway* (1844) (image C) boldly places the most modern technology of the period, the steam train, on an arched bridge in a

A. John Martin, *The Bard*, 1817.

B. John Constable, *Weymouth Bay*, 1816.

C. J. M. W. Turner, *Rain, Steam, Speed—The Great Western Railway*, 1844.

glowing and radiant scenery, where both nature's forces and the tremendous new power unleashed by human activity seem to merge into one continuous burst of energy. To the left of the train, on the river's edge, a fire of indeterminate but evidently industrial origin burns, illuminating several small but ecstatic figures with its light. Most enigmatic of all, a tiny rabbit sprints ahead of the train between the rails (unfortunately invisible in this reproduction), highlighting the painting's complex message about nature and human creation. Are they heading in the same direction? Will one overtake the other and destroy it in the process?

Questions for Analysis

1. In Martin's *Bard*, what vision of the individual emerges from the painting? How is it different from the rational, rights-bearing individual that political liberalism sought to protect?

2. Is Constable's painting concerned with nature as a source of nourishment for humans? Or is nature presented as a value in itself?

3. How are we to interpret Turner's explicit connection between the power of nature and the new force of industrial societies? Is he suggesting that contemplating the industrial landscape can be just as moving to a human observer as is the sight of nature's magnificence?

could see things others could not; and led people to seek out experiences that would elicit intense emotions and spark their imagination and creativity, from foreign travel to opium use. The Romantic style encouraged the daring to defy convention, as did Lord Byron, the Shelleys, and the French writer George Sand (1804–1876). Sand, like Byron, cultivated a persona—in her case, by living as a woman writer, taking lovers at her pleasure, and wearing men's clothing.

Women played an important role in Romantic writing, and Romanticism stimulated new thinking about gender and creativity. It was common at the time to assert that men were rational and women emotional or intuitive. Many Romantics, like their contemporaries, accepted such gender differences as natural, and some exalted the superior moral virtues of women. Because Romanticism placed value on the emotions as an essential part of artistic creation, however, some female writers and painters were able to use these ideas to claim a place in the world of letters and the arts. Germaine de Staël (1766–1817), for example, emigrated from revolutionary France to Germany, and played a key part in popularizing German Romanticism in France. The language of Romanticism allowed Madame de Staël to describe herself as a genius, by way of explaining her own subversion of social norms. Romantics such as Madame de Staël suggested that men, too, could be emotional, and that feelings were a part of a common human nature shared by both sexes. For many literate middle-class people, the language of Romanticism was a way to express their own search for individual expression and feeling in writing—and in thinking—about love. In this way, Romanticism reached well beyond small circles of artists and writers into the everyday writing and thoughts of European men and women.

Romantic Painting

Painters carried the Romantic themes of nature and imagination onto their canvases (see **Interpreting Visual Evidence** on page 688). In Great Britain, John Constable (1776–1837) and Joseph Mallord William Turner (1775–1851) developed more emotional and poetic approaches to depicting nature. "It is the soul that sees," wrote Constable, echoing Wordsworth. Constable studied Isaac Newton and the properties of light but aimed to capture the "poetry" of a rainbow. Turner's intensely subjective paintings were even more unconventional; his experiments with brushstroke and color produced remarkable images. Critics assailed the paintings, calling them incomprehensible, to which Turner merely responded, "I did not paint it to be understood." In France, Théodore Géricault (1791–1824) and Eugène

Delacroix (1799–1863) produced very different paintings from Turner's, but like the English painter, they, too, were preoccupied by subjectivity and the creative process. The poet Charles Baudelaire credited Delacroix with showing him new ways to see: "The whole visible universe is but a storehouse of images and signs. . . . All the faculties of the human soul must be subordinated to the imagination." These Romantic experiments prepared the way for the later development of modernism in the arts.

Romantic Politics: Liberty, History, and Nation

Victor Hugo (1802–1885) wrote that "Romanticism is only . . . liberalism in literature." Hugo's plays, poetry, and historical novels focused sympathetically on the experience of common people, especially *Notre-Dame de Paris* (1831) and *Les Misérables* (1862). Delacroix's painting *Liberty Leading the People* gave a revolutionary face to Romanticism, as did Shelley's and Byron's poetry. In works such as these, political life was no longer the preserve of social elites. Commoners in the street could embrace new freedoms with a violent passion that would have surprised the *philosophes*, with their emphasis on reasoned debate.

Yet Romantics also could be ardently conservative. The Frenchman François Chateaubriand's *Genius of Christianity* (1802) emphasized the primacy of religious emotions and feeling in his claim that religion was woven into the national past and could not be ignored without threatening French culture as a whole. This period, in fact, witnessed a broad and popular religious revival and a renewed interest in medieval literature, art, and architecture—all of which, as we have seen, drew heavily on religious themes. This fascination with the medieval past and its piety played an important part in the development of a new kind of Romantic nationalism, as writers and philosophers sought to ground their understanding of national belonging in something other than a rationalist approach to law and citizenship.

Early-nineteenth-century nationalism took the Romantic emphasis on individuality and turned it into a faith in the uniqueness of individual cultures. Johann von Herder, among the most influential of nationalist thinkers, argued that civilization sprang from the culture of the common people, not from a learned or cultivated elite, as the *philosophes* had argued in the Enlightenment. Herder extolled the special creative genius of the German people, the *Volk*, and insisted that each nation be true to the common cultural and religious heritage of ordinary people.

The Romantics' keen interest in history and the lives of commoners led to new kinds of literary and historical works. The brothers Jakob and Wilhelm Grimm, editors of the famous collection of fairy tales (1812–1815), traveled across Germany to study native dialects and folktales. The poet Friedrich Schiller retold the story of William Tell (1804) to promote German national consciousness, which the Italian composer Gioacchino Rossini later turned into an opera that promoted Italian nationalism. In Britain, Sir Walter Scott retold the popular history of Scotland, and the Pole Adam Mickiewicz wrote a national epic *Pan Tadeusz* (*"Lord Thaddeus"*), a long poem in which he used the story of a love affair between the title character and a young woman to explore the theme of Polish unity under Russian rule. After 1848, these nationalist enthusiasms would overwhelm the political debates that divided conservatives from liberals and socialists in the first half of the nineteenth century (see Chapter 21).

Goethe and Beethoven

Two important artists of the period are especially difficult to classify. Johann Wolfgang von Goethe (1749–1832) had an enormous influence on the Romantic movement with his early novel *The Sorrows of Young Werther* (1774), which told the story of a young man's failure in love and eventual suicide. The novel brought international fame to its young author, though many who sympathized with the main character perhaps missed the point about the self-destructiveness of the "cult of feeling." Rumors spread that some of his readers identified so strongly with Werther's alienation that they killed themselves in imitation. Though scholars now doubt that such suicides occurred, the rumor itself indicates the fascination that Goethe's emotionally complex character exerted over the reading public. The significance of the novel lay in Goethe's ability to capture in prose the longing that many middle-class readers felt for something more meaningful than a life lived in strict conformity to social expectations. It also revealed that a new sense of self and aspirations for self-fulfillment might be emerging in Europe, alongside the narrower definitions of individualism that one might find in liberal political or economic theory. In his masterpiece, *Faust*, published in part in 1790 and finished just before his death in 1832, Goethe retells the German story of a man who sold his soul to the devil for eternal youth and universal knowledge. *Faust,* written in dramatic verse, was more Classical in its tone, though it still expressed a Romantic concern with spiritual freedom and humanity's daring in probing life's divine mysteries.

The composer Ludwig van Beethoven (1770–1827) was steeped in the principles of Classical music composition, but his insistence that instrumental music without vocal accompaniment could be more expressive of emotion made him a key figure for later Romantic composers. The glorification of nature and Romantic individuality rang clearly throughout his work. Like many of his contemporaries, Beethoven was enthusiastic about the French Revolution in 1789, but he became disillusioned with Napoleon. At the age of thirty-two, he began to lose his hearing, and by 1819, he was completely deaf. The intensely personal crisis that this catastrophe produced in the young musician drove him to retreat into the interior of his own musical imagination, and the compositions of his later life expressed both his powerfully felt alienation as well as his extraordinary and heroic creativity in the face of enormous hardship.

Beethoven and Goethe marked the transition between eighteenth-century artistic movements that prized order and harmony to the turbulent and disruptive emotions of the nineteenth-century artists and writers. Their work embraced the cult of individual heroism, sympathized with the Romantic's quasi-mystical view of nature, and embodied different aspects of a shared search for new ways of seeing and hearing. The many shapes of Romanticism make a simple definition of the movement elusive. But at the core, the Romantics sought to find a new way of expressing emotion, and in doing so, they sent nineteenth-century art in a new direction.

CONCLUSION

In 1848, with the fizzling of the Chartist movement, the British monarchy avoided an outbreak of revolution. But the monarchs on the Continent were not so lucky. As we will see in the next chapter, a wave of revolutionary activity, unprecedented since the 1790s, spread to nearly every capital in Europe. This resurgence of rebellion and revolt highlighted the powerful ways the French Revolution of 1789 polarized Europe during the first half of the nineteenth century. In the revolution's aftermath, the Congress of Vienna aimed to establish a new conservative, international system and to prevent further revolts. It succeeded in the first aim but only partially in the second. A combination of new political movements and economic hardship undermined the conservative order. Social grievances and political disappointments gave rise to powerful movements for change, first in Latin America and the Balkans, and then in western Europe and Great Britain.

All the contesting ideologies of these postrevolutionary decades could look back to a longer history. Conservatives could point to traditional religious justifications for royal authority and the absolutist's conception of indivisible monarchical power. Liberals could point to the debates about the rule of law in the English revolution of the seventeenth century. Even socialists could point to age-old collective traditions among rural communities as precedents for their defense of communal property and egalitarianism. Nevertheless, all of these ideologies were shaped and brought into clearer focus during these decades by the combined effects of the French Revolution and industrialization. Conservatives may have disagreed among themselves as to why they preferred a government of monarchs and landed aristocrats, but they were united by their horror of revolutionary violence and dismayed by the social disruptions that attended industrialization. Liberals may have disagreed with each other about who qualified for citizenship, but they defended the revolution's insistence that the only legitimate government was one whose institutions and laws reflected the consent of at least some, if not all, of the governed. Many socialists, Marx included, celebrated the insurrectionary tradition of the French revolutionaries, even as they demanded a reordering of society that went far beyond the granting of new political rights to include an entire redistribution of society's wealth. Meanwhile,

After You Read This Chapter

 Go to **INQUIZITIVE** to see what you've learned—and learn what you've missed— with personalized feedback along the way.

REVIEWING THE OBJECTIVES

- The European leaders who met at the Congress of Vienna had a conservative vision for post-Napoleonic Europe. What were their goals? What challenges did their political system face between 1815 and 1848?

- Slavery persisted long after the French Revolution. What accounts for the development of an abolitionist movement? Why did slavery persist in the United States, Latin America, and Cuba?

- Conservatives, liberals, and republicans differed from each other about the lessons to be learned from the French Revolution, whereas socialists sought to address the inequalities produced by the Industrial Revolution. What were the core principles of conservatism, liberalism, republicanism, and socialism?

- Nationalism reshaped the political landscape in Europe between 1815 and 1848. How did conservatives, liberals, republicans, and socialists view the claims of nationalists?

- Romanticism was a cultural movement defined in opposition to the Enlightenment. Who were the Romantics? What did they believe?

nationalists throughout Europe remained inspired by the collective achievements of the French nation that was forged in revolution in the 1790s.

The reemergence of social and political conflict in 1848 pitted the defenders of these ideologies against each other under the most dramatic of circumstances, making the revolutions of 1848 the opening act of a much larger drama. In France, as in 1792 and 1830, revolutionaries rallied around an expanded notion of representative government and the question of suffrage, though they were divided on how much responsibility their new government had for remedying social problems. In southern and central Europe, as we will see in the next chapter, the issues were framed differently, around new struggles for national identity. The eventual failure of these revolutions set a pattern that was observed elsewhere: exhilarating revolutionary successes were followed by a breakdown of revolutionary unity, then the emergence of new forms of conservative government. The crisis of 1848 became a turning point for all of Europe. The broad revolutionary alliances that had pushed for revolutionary change since 1789 were broken apart by class politics, and earlier forms of utopian socialism gave way to Marxism. In culture as in politics, Romanticism lost its appeal, with its expansive sense of possibility replaced by the more biting viewpoint of realism. No nationalist, conservative, liberal, or socialist was exempt from this bitter truth after the violent conflicts of 1848.

PEOPLE, IDEAS, AND EVENTS IN CONTEXT

- Who was **KLEMENS VON METTERNICH**? What was the **CONCERT OF EUROPE**?
- How did the **CARBONARI** in Italy, the **DECEMBRISTS** in Russia, and **GREEK NATIONALISTS** in the Balkans disturb the conservative order in Europe in the 1820s after Napoleon's defeat?
- Where did revolutions occur in 1830–1832? What were their outcomes?
- What political changes did movements such as the **CHARTISTS** or the **ANTI-CORN LAW LEAGUE** accomplish in Britain? Why was there no revolution in Britain?
- What beliefs made **EDMUND BURKE** a conservative?
- What beliefs made **ADAM SMITH** and **JEREMY BENTHAM** liberals? What was **UTILITARIANISM**?
- What beliefs did **UTOPIAN SOCIALISTS** such as **ROBERT OWEN** and **CHARLES FOURIER** share? What made **KARL MARX**'s brand of socialism different from that of his predecessors?
- How did the values of **ROMANTICISM** challenge Europeans to reconsider their assumptions about the differences between men and women?
- What beliefs led Romantic writers such as **WILLIAM WORDSWORTH**, **WILLIAM BLAKE**, and **LORD BYRON** to reject the rationalism of the Enlightenment and embrace emotion and imagination as the most essential and vital aspects of human experience?

THINKING ABOUT CONNECTIONS

- What new ideas about historical change made it possible to think of political conflict in terms of "conservatives" and "revolutionaries" during the decades immediately before and after 1800? Would such an opposition have been conceivable in earlier periods of history? Why or why not?
- Terms such as *conservative*, *liberal*, and *socialist* are still used today in contemporary political debates. Do they still mean the same thing as they did between 1815 and 1848?

Before You Read This Chapter

STORY LINES

- In 1848, a wave of liberal and national revolutions demanded but failed to achieve lasting constitutions and elected parliaments in many European kingdoms. Instead, Europe's conservative monarchs found ways to harness the popular nationalism expressed in the 1848 revolutions for their own ends.

- The emergence of Germany and Italy as unified nation-states upset the European balance of power, as did the increasing weakness of the Ottoman Empire. The resulting wars benefited Germany and diminished the power of Austria-Hungary in central Europe.

- Russia and the United States also went through an intense phase of nation building after 1850. Common to both were the conquest of native peoples, the acquisition of new territories, and economic development. As in Europe, the process of nation building unleashed sectional conflicts and intense debates about citizenship, slavery (or serfdom, in Russia), and the power of the nation-state.

CHRONOLOGY

1834–1870	Unification of Germany
1848	Revolutions of 1848
1848	France and Denmark abolish slavery
1848	Treaty of Guadalupe Hidalgo
1848–1870	Unification of Italy
1853–1856	Crimean War
1861	Emancipation of the serfs, Russia
1861–1865	American Civil War
1863	January Rising in Poland

Revolutions and Nation Building, 1848–1871

The year 1848 was a tumultuous one. From Paris to Berlin, and Budapest to Rome, insurgents rushed toward hastily built barricades, forcing kings and princes to beat an equally hasty—though temporary—retreat. Perhaps the most highly symbolic moment came on March 13, 1848, when Klemens von Metternich, the primary architect of the Concert of Europe, was forced to resign as minister of state in the Austrian capital of Vienna while a crowd of revolutionaries outside celebrated his departure. Metternich's balanced system of international relations, where stability was guaranteed by reinforcing the legitimacy of traditional dynastic rulers against movements for reform, was swept aside in a wave of enthusiasm for liberal political ideals and popular anger. Metternich himself was forced to flee to England, which less than one month earlier had welcomed the French king Louis-Philippe, after another revolution in France.

Metternich's downfall and the collapse of the French monarchy made clear that the 1848 revolutions were strongly linked to powerful forces for change unleashed earlier by the French Revolution. At the same time, however, this was also the year that Karl Marx and Friedrich Engels published *The Communist Manifesto*, which announced as its goal an even more sweeping remaking of society than that imagined by the French revolutionaries of 1789. If 1848 was the last wave of the revolutionary movements that began in Europe and the Atlantic world at the end of the eighteenth century, it was also the first chapter in a new revolutionary movement that would have enormous consequences in the twentieth century.

Revolutionary regime change, territorial expansion, economic development, and debates about who deserved citizenship were all issues in 1848, and all were related to the spread of nationalism and nation building in Europe and the Americas. As we saw in the last chapter, the term *nation* had taken on a new meaning at the end of the eighteenth century, when it had come to mean "a sovereign people." *Nationalism* was a related political ideal, based on the assumption that governments could be legitimate only if they reflected the character, history, and customs of the nation—that is, the common people. This idea undermined the assumptions of Europe's dynastic rulers, who had emphasized the differences between themselves and the people they ruled; kings and aristocrats often did not even speak the same language as their subjects. Nobody would have thought this odd before 1789, because peasants often spoke regional dialects that were different from the language spoken in cities. But once the notion of national sovereignty emanating from the people became widespread, such discrepancies in language and culture between the elites and of the common people loomed larger as political questions that needed to be solved. Intellectuals, revolutionaries, and governments all propagated the radical new idea that nations of like peoples and the states that ruled over them should be congruent with each other. This simple idea lay at the heart of all forms of nationalism, but there was often bitter debate about who best represented the nation and what should be the goals of a unified nationalist government.

Between 1789 and 1848, Europeans commonly associated nationalism with liberalism. Liberals saw constitutions, the rule of law, and elected assemblies as necessary expressions of the people's will, and sought to use popular enthusiasm for liberal forms of nationalism against the conservative monarchs of Europe. The upheavals of 1848 marked the high point of this period of liberal revolution, and their failure marked the end of that age. By the end of the nineteenth century, conservative governments also found ways to mobilize popular support by invoking nationalist themes. The only political movement to swim against the tide of nationalism was that of the socialists, who stressed the importance of class unity across national boundaries: Marx and his followers believed that German, French, and British workers had more in common with each other than with their middle-class employers. Even so, however, socialist movements in Europe developed in distinctly different nationalist political contexts, making traditions of French socialism different from those of German socialism or Italian socialism.

The years following the 1848 revolutions witnessed a shift in the connections among liberalism, nationalism, and nation building. In the United States, territorial changes such as the treaty of Guadalupe Hidalgo transformed the boundaries of nations; equally significant was the American Civil War, which resulted in wrenching political change. The unification of Germany and Italy in the years after 1848 also involved the conquest of territory, but the process could not have been completed without political reforms and new state structures that changed how governments worked and how they related to their citizens. The governments of France, Britain, Russia, and Austria undertook vast administrative reforms during this period, overhauling their bureaucracies, expanding their electorates, and reorganizing relations among ethnic groups. The Russian tsar abolished serfdom and struggled with the nationalist aspirations of subject peoples in the massive lands that stretched between the Baltic and Black Seas. In the United States, President Abraham Lincoln abolished slavery, decades after the French and British had prohibited slavery in their territories.

As the process of nation building continued, the balance of power in Europe shifted toward the states that were the earliest to industrialize and most successful in building strong, centralized states. Older imperial powers such as the Habsburg Empire in Austria-Hungary or the Ottoman Empire found their influence waning, in spite of their long history of successful rule over vast territories with diverse populations. At the heart of this nineteenth-century period of nation building lay changing relations between states and those they governed, which were hastened by reactions to the revolutionary upheavals of 1848.

THE REVOLUTIONS OF 1848

Throughout Europe, the spring of 1848 brought a dizzying sequence of revolution and repression. The roots of revolution lay in economic crisis, social antagonisms, and political grievances; but these revolutions were also shaped decisively by nationalism, especially in southern, central, and eastern Europe. To be sure, reformers and revolutionaries had liberal goals—representative government, an end to privilege, economic development, and so on—but they also sought some form of national unity. Indeed, reformers in Germany, Italy, Poland, and the Austrian Empire believed that their liberal goals might be realized only in a vigorous, "modern" nation-state. The fate of the 1848 revolutions in these regions demonstrated nationalism's power to mobilize opponents of the regime and its potential for splintering revolutionary alliances and overriding other allegiances and values entirely.

The Hungry Forties

A deteriorating economic climate in Europe was an important contributing factor to the outbreak of revolution in 1848, one that helps to explain why revolutions occurred in so many places nearly simultaneously. Poor harvests in the early 1840s were followed by two years when the grain harvest failed completely, in 1845–1846. A potato blight brought starvation in Ireland and hunger in Germany. Food prices doubled in 1846–1847, and bread riots broke out across Europe. Villagers attacked carts carrying grain, refusing to let merchants take it to other markets. At times, hungry people seized the grain and forced the merchants to sell it at what they thought was a "just" price. Compounding the problem was a cyclical industrial slowdown that spread across Europe, throwing thousands into unemployment. Starving peasants and unemployed laborers swamped public-relief organizations in many European cities. In 1846 and 1847, these converging crises—food shortage, widespread misery, and public disorder—reached their apogee, and the decade was long remembered as the "Hungry Forties."

Hunger itself cannot cause revolution. It does, however, test governments' abilities to manage a crisis, and their failure can make a ruler seem incompetent, and thus, illegitimate. When public relief foundered in France, troops repressed potato riots in Berlin, and regimes armed middle-class citizens to protect themselves against the poor, governments looked both authoritarian and inept. In the 1840s, European states already faced a host of political challenges: from liberals who sought constitutional government and limits on royal power, from republicans who campaigned for universal male suffrage, from nationalists who challenged the

legitimacy of their hereditary rulers, and from socialists whose appeal lay in their claim to speak for the most economically vulnerable among the population. These political challenges were reinforced by the economic crisis of the 1840s, and the result was a wave of revolution that swept across Europe as one government after another lost the confidence of its people. The first of these revolutions came in France, but as elsewhere in 1848, it did not have the outcome the revolutionaries had hoped for.

The French Revolution of 1848: A Republican Experiment

The French monarchy after the revolution of 1830 (see Chapter 20) seemed little different from its predecessor. King **Louis Philippe** gathered around him members of the banking and industrial elite. Confronted with demands to enlarge the franchise, the prime minister quipped that everyone was free to acquire enough property to qualify for the vote: "Enrich yourselves!" Building projects, especially the railways, presented ample opportunities for graft, and the reputation of the government suffered. Protest movements, in the form of republican societies, proliferated in French cities; and in 1834, the government declared these organizations illegal. Rebellions broke out in Paris and Lyon, bringing a harsh repression that resulted in deaths and arrests. The government's refusal

THE BURNING OF THE THRONE (1848). A contemporary print shows revolutionaries burning the king's throne. Note the man with a top hat standing next to a man in a worker's smock on the left. Delacroix used similar images to depict cooperation between workers and middle-class revolutionaries (see page 667).

Competing Viewpoints

Two Views of the June Days, France, 1848

> These two passages make for an interesting comparison. The socialist Karl Marx reported on the events of 1848 in France as a journalist for a German newspaper. For Marx, the bloodshed of the June Days shattered the "fraternal illusions" of February 1848, when the king had been overthrown and the provisional government established. That bloodshed symbolized a new stage in history—one of acute class conflict. For the socialist observer, the June Days was a turning point: "The working class was knocking on the gates of history."
>
> The French liberal politician Alexis de Tocqueville also wrote about his impressions of the revolution. However, for Tocqueville, a member of the government, the actions of the crowd sparked fear and conservative reaction. (Tocqueville's account is retrospective; he wrote his memoirs well after 1848.)

Karl Marx's Journalism (1848)

The last official remnant of the February Revolution, the Executive Commission, has melted away, like an apparition, before the seriousness of events. The fireworks of Lamartine [French Romantic poet and member of the provisional government] have turned into the war rockets of Cavaignac [French general, in charge of putting down the workers' insurrection]. *Fraternité*, the fraternity of antagonistic classes of which one exploits the other, this *fraternité*, proclaimed in February, on every prison, on every barracks—its true, unadulterated, its prosaic expression is civil war, civil war in its most fearful form, the war of labor and capital. This fraternity flamed in front of all the windows of Paris on the evening of June 25, when the Paris of the bourgeoisie was illuminated, whilst the Paris of the proletariat [Marxist term for the working people] burnt, bled, moaned. . . . The February Revolution was the beautiful revolution, the revolution of universal sympathy, because the antagonisms, which had flared up in it against the monarchy, slumbered peacefully side by side, still undeveloped, because the social struggle which formed its background had won only a joyous existence, an existence of phrases, of words. The June revolution is the ugly revolution, the repulsive revolution, because things have taken the place of phrases, because the republic uncovered the head of the monster itself, by striking off the crown that shielded and concealed it.—Order! was the battle cry of Guizot . . . Order! shouts Cavaignac, the brutal echo of the French National Assembly and of the republican bourgeoisie. Order! thundered his grapeshot, as it ripped up the body of the proletariat. None of the numerous revolutions of the French bourgeoisie since 1789 was an attack on order; for they allowed the rule of the class, they allowed the slavery of the workers, they allowed the bourgeois order to endure, however often the political form of this rule and of this slavery changed. June has attacked this order. Woe to June!

Source: *Neue Rheinische Zeitung* (New Rhineland Gazette), June 29, 1848, as cited in Karl Marx, *The Class Struggles in France* (New York: 1964), pp. 57–58.

to compromise drove even moderates into opposition. In 1847, the opposition organized a campaign for electoral reform around repeated political "banquets" (an attempt to get around the laws against assembly). When the opposition called for a giant banquet on February 22, 1848, the king responded by banning the meeting. A sudden and surprising popular revolution in the streets caused Louis Philippe to abdicate his throne only days later, and a hastily assembled group of French political figures declared France a republic for the first time since 1792.

The provisional government of the new republic consisted of liberals, republicans, and—for the first time—

Alexis de Tocqueville Remembers the June Days (1893)

Now at last I have come to that insurrection in June which was the greatest and the strangest that had ever taken place in our history, or perhaps in that of any other nation: the greatest because for four days more than a hundred thousand men took part in it, and there were five generals killed; the strangest, because the insurgents were fighting without a battle cry, leaders, or flag, and yet they showed wonderful powers of coordination and a military expertise that astonished the most experienced officers.

Another point that distinguished it from all other events of the same type during the last sixty years was that its object was not to change the form of government, but to alter the organization of society. In truth it was not a political struggle (in the sense in which we have used the word "political" up to now), but a class struggle, a sort of "Servile War." . . . One should not see it only as a brutal and a blind, but as a powerful effort of the workers to escape from the necessities of their condition, which had been depicted to them as an illegitimate depression, and by the sword to open up a road towards that imaginary well-being that had been shown to them in the distance as a right. It was this mixture of greedy desires and false theories that engendered the insurrection and made it so formidable. These poor people had been assured that the goods of the wealthy were in some way the result of a theft committed against themselves. They had been assured that inequalities of fortune were as much opposed to morality and the interests of society as to nature. This obscure and mistaken conception of right, combined with brute force, imparted to it an energy, tenacity and strength it would never have had on its own.

Source: From Alexis de Tocqueville, *Recollections: The French Revolution of 1848*, ed. J. P. Mayer and A. P. Kerr, trans. George Lawrence (New Brunswick, NJ: 1987), pp. 136–37.

Questions for Analysis

1. Was Tocqueville sympathetic to the revolutionaries of June? Why or why not?

2. What was the historical significance of these events, according to Tocqueville?

3. Where did Tocqueville agree and disagree with Marx?

---

socialists. They produced a new constitution, with elections based on universal male suffrage. Among their first acts was the abolition of slavery in France and French colonies (slavery had been abolished in 1794 during the revolution but reestablished by Napoleon in 1802). In spite of these accomplishments, tensions between propertied republicans and socialists shattered the unity of the coalition that toppled Louis Philippe. Suffering because of the economic crisis, working men and women demanded the "right to work," the right to earn a living wage. The provisional government responded by creating the National Workshops, a program of public works, to give jobs to the unemployed, headed by the socialist Louis Blanc. Initial plans were made to employ 10,000–12,000 workers, but unemployment was so high that 120,000 job seekers had gathered in the city by June 1848. Meanwhile, voters in rural areas resented the increase in taxation required to pay for the public works program.

Popular politics flourished in Paris in 1848. The provisional government lifted restrictions on speech and assembly. One hundred and seventy new journals and more than 200 clubs formed within weeks. Delegations claiming to represent the oppressed of Europe—Chartists, Hungarians, Poles—moved freely about the city. Women's clubs and newspapers appeared, demanding universal suffrage and living wages. Meanwhile, many middle-class Parisians were alarmed, and more conservative rural populations looked for stern measures to restore order. When elections for parliament were held—the first elections ever in France under a regime of universal male suffrage—the conservative voices won out, and a majority of moderate republicans and monarchists were elected.

A majority in the new assembly believed the National Workshops were a financial drain and a threat to order, and so in May, they closed the workshops to new enrollment, excluded recent arrivals to Paris, and sent members between the ages of eighteen and twenty-five into the army; on June 21, they abolished the workshops altogether. The workers of Paris—laborers, journeymen, the unemployed—rose in revolt against the closure of this social program, building barricades across Paris. For four days, June 23–26, they fought a hopeless battle against armed forces recruited from the provinces. The repression of the **June Days** shocked many observers, during which about 3,000 were killed and 12,000 arrested; many of the prisoners were deported to Algerian labor camps. But thereafter, support for the republic among the workers in Paris declined rapidly.

Subsequently, the government moved quickly to restore order. The parliament hoped for a strong leader

BARRICADE IN THE RUE DE LA MORTELLERIE, JUNE 1848, BY ERNEST MEISSONIER (1815–1891). A very different view of 1848, a depiction of the June Days.

from the four candidates in the presidential election: Alphonse de Lamartine, the moderate republican and poet; General Louis Eugène de Cavaignac, who had perfected the art of urban warfare in the conquest of Algeria and who applied those skills to repressing the workers' revolt in Paris; Alexandre Ledru-Rollin, a socialist; and Louis Napoleon Bonaparte, the nephew of the former emperor, who had spent much of his life in exile. Buoyed by enthusiastic support from rural voters, the upstart Louis Napoleon polled more than twice as many votes as the other three candidates combined.

"All facts and personages of great importance in world history occur twice . . . the first time as tragedy, the second as farce." Karl Marx's judgment on Louis Napoleon's relationship to his famous uncle was shared by many, but his name gave him wide appeal, and conservatives believed he would protect property and order. Some on the left had read his book *The Extinction of Pauperism* and noted his correspondence with important socialists. One old peasant put it succinctly, "How could I help voting for this gentleman—I whose nose was frozen at Moscow?"

Louis Napoleon used his position to consolidate his power. He rallied the Catholics by restoring the Church to its former role in education and sending an expedition to Rome to rescue the pope from revolutionaries. He banned radical activities and workers' associations, and also suspended press freedoms. In 1851, he called for a plebiscite to give him the authority to change the constitution; and a year later, another plebiscite to allow him to establish the Second Empire, ending the Republican experiment. He assumed the title of **Napoleon III** (r. 1852–1870), emperor of the French.

The dynamics of the French Revolution of 1848—initial success, followed by divisions among the supporters of revolution, followed by a reassertion of authoritarian control—were repeated elsewhere, especially evidenced in the pivotal role of the propertied middle classes. Louis Philippe's reign had been proudly bourgeois but alienated many of its supporters, leading key groups in the middle class to join with the opposition and ally with radicals who could not topple the regime alone. Yet demands for reform soon led to fears of disorder and the desire for a strong state. And this dynamic led to the collapse of the republic and to the rule of Napoleon III. The abandonment of the revolution's social goals—most visibly evident in the closing of the National Workshops—led to a stark polarization along class lines, with middle-class and working-class people demanding different things from the state. This political conflict would grow even more intense as socialism came into its own as an independent political force.

Nationalism, Revolution, and the German Question in 1848

The revolutions of 1848 in the German-speaking lands of Europe shared some similarities with the revolutions in France. Like liberals in France, liberal Germans wanted a ruler who would abide by a constitution, allow for greater press freedoms, and accept some form of representative government, though not necessarily universal suffrage. As also in France, artisans and urban laborers in German cities gravitated toward more radical ideologies of republicanism and socialism, and protested against new methods of industrial production. But German peasants, more so than in France, still faced the burden of feudal obligations owed to an entrenched and powerful aristocracy. The great difference between France and Germany in 1848, however, was that France already had a centralized state and a unified territory; whereas in central Europe, a unified Germany did not exist. In 1815, the Congress of Vienna had created the German Confederation, a loose organization of thirty-nine states, including Habsburg Austria (with its Catholic monarchy) and Prussia (ruled by a Protestant king), but not the Prussian and Austrian territories in Poland and Hungary with large non-German populations. This confederation was intended to provide only common defense, and had no real executive power. As a practical matter, Prussia and Austria competed with each other to occupy the dominant position in German politics; and as a result, revolutionaries in the German states were forced to reckon with these two powers as they struggled to achieve the national unity that they hoped would allow them to achieve their political goals.

GERMAN CONFEDERATION, 1815. Compare this map with the one on page 720. ▪ *Which major areas were left out of the German Confederation?* ▪ *Why do you think they were left out?* ▪ *What obstacles made it difficult to establish a unified German nation during this period?*

In 1806, Prussia had been defeated by the French under Napoleon, and many Prussians considered the defeat an indictment of the country's inertia since the reign of Frederick the Great (r. 1740–1786). Aiming to revive "patriotism and a national honor and independence," they passed a series of aggressive reforms, imposed from above. Prussian reformers reconstituted the army, following the Napoleonic example. Officers were recruited and promoted on the basis of merit rather than birth, although the large majority continued to come from the Junker class. Other reforms modernized training at the royal cadet school in Berlin and encouraged the middle class to take a more active role in the civil service. In 1807, serfdom and the estate system were abolished. A year later, in a conscious attempt to increase middle-class Germans' sense of themselves as citizens, cities and towns were allowed to elect

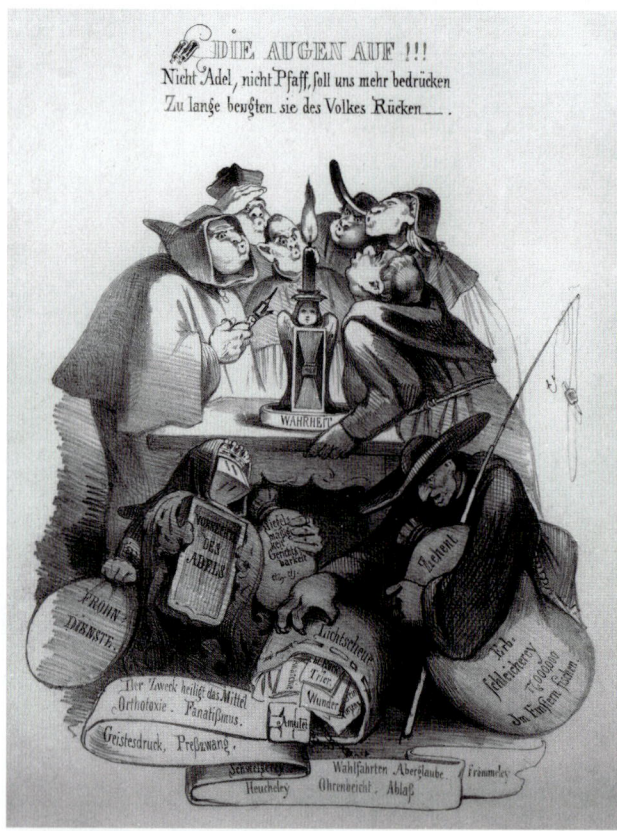

"EYES OPEN!" (c. 1845). This German cartoon from just before the 1848 revolution warns that aristocrats and clergy are conspiring to deny the German people their rights. The caption reads "Eyes Open! Neither the nobility nor the clergy shall oppress us any longer. For too long they have broken the backs of the people." ▪ *Did supporters of the revolution consider the aristocracy or the clergy to be legitimate members of the nation? Compare this cartoon with the pamphlet that Abbé Sieyès wrote during the French Revolution (see page 592).*

their councilmen and handle their own finances; although justice and security continued to be administered by the central government in Berlin. The Prussian reformers expanded facilities for both primary and secondary education and founded the University of Berlin, which numbered among its faculty several ardent nationalists.

Prussia aimed to establish itself as the leading German state and a counter to Austrian power in the region. Prussia's most significant victory in this respect came with the ***Zollverein*** (or customs union) in 1834, which established free trade among the German states and a uniform tariff against the rest of the world—an openly protectionist policy advocated by the economist Friedrich List. By the 1840s, the union included almost all the German states, except German Austria, and offered manufacturers a market of almost 34 million people. Moreover, the spread of the railways after 1835 accelerated the exchange within this expanded internal market.

During the 1840s, in both Prussia and the smaller German states, political clubs of students and other radicals joined with middle-class groups of lawyers, doctors, and businessmen to press new demands for representative government and reform; newspapers multiplied, defying censorship. Liberal reformers resented both Prussian domination of the German Confederation and the conservatism of the Habsburgs, who ruled the Austrian Empire. They attacked the combination of autocracy and bureaucratic authority that stifled political life in Prussia and Austria. German nationhood, they reasoned, would break Austrian or Prussian domination and end the sectional fragmentation that made reform so difficult.

When Frederick William IV (r. 1840–1861) succeeded to the Prussian throne in 1840, hopes ran high, as the new king did gesture toward liberalizing reforms. When economic troubles hit in the 1840s, however, Frederick William asserted firmly that his authority could not be questioned by his subjects. He sent the army to crush a revolt among the textile weavers of Silesia, who were protesting British imports and, more generally, unemployment, falling wages, and hunger. The brutality of the regime's response shocked many. The king also opposed constitutionalism and any representative participation in issues of legislation and budgets. Like the "enlightened" absolutists who preceded him, the Prussian king firmly believed that his leadership did not need assistance from elected legislatures or civil society as a whole.

As in France, liberals and radicals in Prussia and the German states continued their reform campaigns. And when revolution came to France in the spring of 1848, unrest spread across the Rhine. In the Catholic south German state of Bavaria, a student protest forced King Ludwig I to grant

Past and Present

Germany's Place in Europe

The unification of Germany under Prussian leadership in 1870 (left) destabilized the balance of power in Europe. World War I and World War II confirmed for many people the dangers of a strong German state. The history of European integration after 1945, nevertheless, depended on rebuilding Germany and binding it more closely to its European neighbors. In spite of recent troubles in the European Union, including a financial crisis that threatened the euro currency (right), this history remains one of the great success stories of late-twentieth-century Europe.

 Watch related author interview on the Student Site

greater press freedoms, and when revolutionary movements appeared elsewhere in the smaller German states, kings and princes yielded surprisingly quickly. The governments promised elections, expanded suffrage, jury trials, and other liberal reforms. In Prussia, Frederick William, shaken by unrest in the countryside and stunned by a showdown in Berlin between the army and revolutionaries in which 250 were killed, promised to grant a constitution and met with representatives of the protest movement.

The Frankfurt Assembly and German Nationhood

The second and most idealistic stage of the revolution began with the election of 800 delegates to an all-German assembly in Frankfurt, where representatives from Prussia, Austria, and the small German states met to discuss creating a unified German nation. Most of the delegates came from the professional classes—lawyers, professors, administrators—and were moderate liberals; their views were not as radical as those of the workers and artisans who had led the street protests against the king. The delegates assumed that the **Frankfurt Assembly** would draft a constitution for a liberal, unified Germany, much as an assembly of Frenchmen had done for their country in 1789; the comparison, however, was misguided. In 1789, a French nation-state and a centralized sovereign power already existed, needing only to be reformed and redirected by the assembled French delegates. In contrast, the Frankfurt Assembly had no resources, no sovereign power to take, no single legal code, and, of course, no army.

On the assembly floor, questions of nationality proved contentious and destructive. Which Germans would be in the new state? A majority of the assembly's delegates argued that Germans were all those who, by language, culture, or geography, felt themselves bound to the enterprise of unification. They believed the German nation should include as many Germans as possible—a position encouraged by the spectacle of disintegration in the Habsburg Empire. This was the "Great German" position. It was countered by a minority who called for a "Small Germany," one that left out all lands of the Habsburg Empire, including German Austria. The Great Germans had a majority but were stymied by other nationalities unwilling to be included in their fold. Many Czechs in Bohemia, for instance, wanted no part of Great Germany, believing that they needed the protection of the Habsburg monarchy to avoid being swallowed up by a new German state on one side and the Russian empire on the other. After a long and difficult debate, the Austrian emperor withdrew his support, and the assembly retreated to the Small German solution. In April 1849, the Frankfurt Assembly offered the crown of a new German nation to the Prussian king, Frederick William IV.

By this time, however, Frederick William was negotiating from a position of greater strength. Already, in the fall of 1848, he had used the military to repress the radical revolutionaries in Berlin while the delegates debated the constitutional question in Frankfurt. He was also encouraged by a backlash against revolutionary movements in Europe after the bloody repression during the June Days in Paris. He refused to become a constitutional monarch on the terms offered by the Frankfurt Assembly, stating that the proposed constitution was too liberal, and receiving his crown from a parliament would be demeaning. The Prussian monarch wanted both the crown and a larger German state, but on his own terms, and he therefore dissolved the Assembly before the delegates could approve the constitution with an official vote. After brief protests, summarily suppressed by the military, the Frankfurt delegates went home, disillusioned by their experience and convinced that their liberal and nationalist goals were incompatible. Some fled repression by immigrating to the United States; others decided to sacrifice their liberal views for the seemingly realistic goal of nationhood. In Prussia itself, the army dispatched what remained of the revolutionary forces.

Elsewhere in the German-speaking states, as popular revolution was taking its own course, many moderate liberals began to have second thoughts about the pace of change. Peasants ransacked tax offices and burned castles; and workers smashed machines in protests against industrialization. In towns and cities, citizen militias formed, threatening the power of established elites. New daily newspapers multiplied, as did political clubs. For the first time, many of these clubs admitted women (although they were denied the right to speak), and newly founded women's clubs demanded political rights. This torrent of popular unrest made moderate

THE FRANKFURT PRE-PARLIAMENT MEETS AT ST. PAUL'S CHURCH, 1848. The Frankfurt Assembly brought together 500 delegates from various German states to establish a constitution for a new German nation. Armed militia lined the square, and lines of student gymnasts (dressed in white with wide-brimmed hats) escorted the delegates; their presence was a sign that the organizers of the pre-parliament feared violence. The black, red, and gold banners were associated with republicanism. ■ *What image did the organizers mean to convey with this pageantry, with disciplined lines of students and delegates, forms of dress, and use of republican symbols?*

"NO PIECE OF PAPER WILL COME BETWEEN MYSELF AND MY PEOPLE" (1848). In this cartoon, Frederick William IV and a military officer refuse to accept the constitution for a new Germany offered to the king by the Frankfurt Assembly. Note that the caption refers to a conservative definition of the relationship between a monarch and "his people." Compare this autocratic vision of the nation-state with the liberal nationalist's demand for a government that reflects the will of the people. ▪ *What contrasting visions of the nation and its relation to the state are contained in this cartoon?*

reformers uneasy, and they considered universal male suffrage too radical. Although peasant and worker protests had forced the king to make concessions in the early spring of 1848, moderate reformers now found those protests threatening. Throughout the German states, rulers took advantage of this shift in middle-class opinion to undo the concessions they had granted in 1848 and to push through counterrevolutionary measures in the name of order.

For German liberals, national unification was now seen as necessary to maintain political stability. "In order to realize our ideas of freedom and equality, we want above all a strong and powerful government," claimed one candidate during the election campaigns for the Frankfurt Assembly. Popular sovereignty, he continued, "strengthened by the authority of a hereditary monarchy, will be able to repress with an iron hand any disorder and any violation of the law." In this context, nationhood stood for a new constitution and political community but also for a sternly enforced rule of law. After the failure of the Frankfurt Assembly, therefore, German liberals increasingly looked to a strong Prussian state as the only possible route toward national unification.

Peoples against Empire: The Habsburg Lands

In the sprawling Habsburg (Austrian) Empire, nationalism played a different role. On the one hand, the Habsburg emperors could point to a remarkable record of political success. As heirs to the medieval Holy Roman Empire, Habsburg kings had ruled for centuries over a diverse array of ethnicities and language groups in central Europe that included Germans, Czechs, Hungarians, Poles, Slovaks, Serbs, and Italians, to name only the most prominent. And in the sixteenth century, under Charles V, the empire had included Spain, parts of Burgundy, and the Netherlands. On the other hand, in the nineteenth century, the Habsburgs found it increasingly difficult to hold their empire together as the national demands of the different peoples in the realm escalated after 1815. Whereas the greater ethnic and linguistic homogeneity of the German-speaking lands allowed for a convergence between liberal ideas of popular sovereignty and national unification, no such program was possible in the Habsburg Empire. Popular sovereignty for peoples defined in terms of their ethnic identity implied a breakup of the Habsburg lands.

At the same time, the existence of nationalist movements did not imply unity, even within territories that spoke the same language. In the former Polish territories of the Habsburg Empire, nationalist sentiment was strong among landowners and the gentry. These elite groups were especially conscious of their historic role as leaders of the earlier Polish-Lithuanian Commonwealth, an example of an early modern political entity that was not linked to ethnic identity. Here, the Habsburg Empire successfully set serfs against their Polish landlords, ensuring that social grievances dampened the development of an ethnic Polish nationalism that could unite people of different social backgrounds.

In the Hungarian region, national claims were likewise advanced by the relatively small Magyar aristocracy. ("Magyar" is simply the Hungarian word for "Hungarian"; in English, it is sometimes used to describe Hungarian nationalists, whereas "Hungarian" might denote any citizen of Hungary, regardless of ethnic identity.) Yet **Magyar nationalism** gained an audience under the gifted and influential leadership of Lajos (Louis) Kossuth (*KAW-shut*; 1802–1894). A member of the minor nobility, Kossuth was by turns a lawyer, publicist, newspaper editor, and political leader. To protest the closed-door policy of the empire's barely representative Diet (parliament), he published transcripts of parliamentary debates and distributed them to

Analyzing Primary Sources

Lajos Kossuth on Democracy and Hungarian Nationalism

Lajos (Louis) Kossuth (1802–1894) was a lawyer and journalist who emerged as a leader of Hungarian nationalists in the Austrian Habsburg Empire during the 1848 revolution. He briefly became the governor of an independent Hungarian government but was forced to flee when Russian armies, supporting the Austrian Habsburgs, put an end to the Hungarian revolution. After a short stay in Turkey, the United States government invited Kossuth to visit. During his visit to the United States, he embarked on a successful speaking tour in which he was celebrated as a fervent supporter of democracy. This text comes from a speech he made before a banquet of journalists in New York City.

But happy art thou, free nation of America, founded on the only solid basis, —liberty! [. . .] Tyrants are not in the midst of you to throw the apple of discord and raise hatred in this national family, —hatred of *races*, that curse of humanity, that venomous ally of despotism. Glorious it is to see the oppressed of diverse countries, —diverse in language, history, habits, —wandering to these shores and becoming members of this great nation, regenerated by the principle of common liberty.

If language alone makes a nation, then there is no great nation on earth: for there is no country whose population is counted by millions, but speaks more than one language. No! It is not language only. Community of interests, of rights, of duties, of history, but chiefly community of institutions; by which a population, varying perhaps in tongue and race, is bound together through daily intercourse in the towns, which are the centers and home of commerce and industry: —besides these, the very mountain-ranges, the system of rivers and streams, —the soil, the dust of which is mingled with the mortal remains of those ancestors who bled on the same field, for the same interests, the common inheritance of glory and of woe, the community of laws and institutions,

common freedom or common oppression: —all this enters into the complex idea of Nationality.

That this is instinctively felt by the common sense of the people, nowhere is more manifestly shown than at this moment in my native land. Hungary was declared by Francis-Joseph of Austria *no more to exist* as a Nation, no more as a state. It was and is put under martial law. Strangers, aliens to our laws and history as well as to our tongue, rule now where our fathers lived and our brothers bled. To be a Hungarian is become almost a crime in our own native land. Well: to justify before the world the extinction of Hungary, the partition of its territory, and the reincorporating of the dissected limbs into the common body of servitude, the treacherous dynasty was anxious to show that the Hungarians are in a minority in their own land. They hoped that intimidation and terrorism would induce even the very Magyars to disavow their language and birth. They ordered a census of races to be made. They performed it with the iron rule of martial law; and dealt so arbitrarily that thousands of women and men, who professed to be Magyars, who professed not to know any other language than the Magyar, were, notwithstanding all their protestations, put down as Sclaves [*sic*], Serbs, Germans, or Wallachians, because their names had not quite a Hungarian

sound. And still what was the issue of this malignant plot? That of the twelve millions of inhabitants of Hungary proper, the Magyars turned out to be more than eight millions, some two millions more than we know the case really is. The people instinctively felt that the tyrant had the design through the pretext of language to destroy the existence of the complex nation, and it met the tyrannic plot as if it answered, "We are, and must be, a nation; and if the tyrant takes language only for the mark of nationality, then we are all Magyars."

Source: Francis W. Newman, ed., *Speeches of Kossuth* (London: Trübner, 1853), pp. 62–65.

Questions for Analysis

1. What does Kossuth admire about the political culture of the United States?

2. How does he define a "nation"? Why does he reject using language as the primary criterion for determining membership in a nation?

3. What does Kossuth's example of the national census taken by the Austrian government tell us about the new kinds of institutions that European states developed in response to the rise of nationalism?

THE HUNGARIAN REVOLUTIONARY LAJOS KOSSUTH, 1851.
A leader of the Hungarian nationalist movement who combined aristocratic style with rabble-rousing politics, Kossuth almost succeeded in an attempt to separate Hungary from Austria in 1849.

a broader public. He campaigned for independence and a separate Hungarian parliament, and also (and more influentially) brought politics to the people. Kossuth staged political "banquets" like those in France, at which local and national personalities made speeches in the form of toasts and where interested citizens could eat, drink, and participate in politics. The Hungarian political leader combined aristocratic style with rabble-rousing politics, a delicate balancing act but one that, when it worked, catapulted him to the center of Habsburg politics. He was as well known in the Habsburg capital of Vienna as he was in Pressburg and Budapest.

The other major nationalist movement that troubled the Habsburg Empire was **pan-Slavism**. Slavs included Russians, Poles, Ukrainians, Czechs, Slovaks, Slovenes, Croats, Serbs, Macedonians, and Bulgarians. Before 1848, pan-Slavism was primarily a cultural movement united by a general pro-Slavic sentiment, but internally divided by the competing claims of different Slavic languages and traditions. Poles, for example, tended to consider pan-Slavism to be a cover for the expansion of Russian influence. The Polish Romantic poet Adam Mickiewicz (*mihtz-KYAY-vihch*)

rejected it in favor of a Polish messianism that saw Poles championing the cause of oppressed nations everywhere. Pan-Slavism was much stronger among the Czechs and Slovaks, inspiring the works of the Czech historian and political leader František Palacký, the author of the *History of the Bohemian People*; and the Slovak Jan Kollár, whose book *Salvy Dcera* ("Slava's Daughter") mourned the loss of identity among Slavs in the Germanic world.

The fact that Russia and Austria were rivals made pan-Slavism a volatile and unpredictable political force in the regions of eastern Europe, where the two nations vied for power and influence. Tsar Nicholas I of Russia sought to use pan-Slavism to his advantage, making arguments about "Slavic" uniqueness part of his "autocracy, orthodoxy, nationality" ideology after 1825. Yet the tsar's Russian-sponsored pan-Slavism alienated Western-oriented Slavs who resented Russia's ambitions. Here, as elsewhere, nationalism created a tangled web of alliances and antagonisms.

Austria and Hungary in 1848: The Springtime of Peoples and the Autumn of Empire

The Austro-Hungarian Empire's combination of political, social, and ethnic tensions exploded in 1848, with the opening salvo coming from the Hungarians. Emboldened by the uprisings in France and Germany, Kossuth stepped up his reform campaigns, pillorying the "Metternich system" of Habsburg autocracy and control, and demanding representative institutions throughout the empire and autonomy for the Hungarian nation. The Hungarian Diet prepared to draft its own constitution. In Vienna, the seat of Habsburg power, a popular movement of students and artisans demanding political and social reforms built barricades and attacked the imperial palace; and a Central Committee of Citizens took shape, as did a middle-class militia (or national guard) determined at once to maintain order and to press demands for reform. The Habsburg regime tried to shut the movement down by closing the university, but that only unleashed more popular anger, and the regime found itself forced to retreat almost entirely. Metternich, whose political system had weathered so many storms, fled to Britain in disguise—a good indication of the political turmoil—leaving the emperor Ferdinand I in Vienna. The government conceded to radical demands for male suffrage and a single house of representatives, and agreed to withdraw troops from Vienna and to put forced labor and serfdom on a path to abolition. The government

THE FIRST UNCENSORED NEWSPAPER AFTER THE REVOLUTION IN VIENNA, JANUARY 1848. This watercolor illustrates the power of public information during the 1848 revolution in the Austrian capital. An uncensored newspaper, wall posters, headgear with political insignia and slogans, and an armed citizenry are all evidence of a vibrant and impassioned public discussion on the events of the day. Note, too, the simple gown of the woman selling papers, the top hat and fashionable clothes of the middle-class man smoking a pipe, and the presence of military uniforms, all of which illustrate support for the revolution among a broad portion of the population. ∎ *How does this vision of the public sphere in action compare with previous depictions of public debate in the Enlightenment (see page 575), in the French Revolution (see page 603), or elsewhere in Europe in 1848 (see page 710)?*

also agreed to Czech demands for a new diet (or parliament) in Bohemia. To the south, Italian liberals and nationalists attacked the empire's territories in Venice; and in Milan, the forces of King Charles Albert of Piedmont-Sardinia routed the Austrians. As what would be called the "springtime of peoples" unfolded, Habsburg control of its various provinces seemed to be coming apart.

Yet the explosion of national sentiment that shook the empire later allowed it to recoup its fortunes. The paradox of nationalism in central Europe was that no cultural or ethnic majority could declare independence in a given region without prompting rebellion from other minority groups that inhabited the same area. In Bohemia, for instance, Czechs and Germans who lived side by side had worked together to pass reforms scuttling feudalism. Within a month, however, nationalism began to fracture their alliance: German Bohemians set off to attend the all-important Frankfurt Assembly, but the Czech majority refused to send

representatives and instead countered by convening a confederation of Slavs in Prague. What did the delegates at the Slav confederation want? Some were hostile to what the Russian anarchist Mikhail Bakunin called the "monstrous Austrian Empire," but the majority of delegates preferred to be ruled by the Habsburgs (though with some autonomy) than to be dominated by either the Germans or the Russians.

This bundle of animosities allowed the Austrians to divide and conquer. In May 1848, during the Slav Congress, a student- and worker-led insurrection broke out in Prague. On the orders of the newly installed liberal government, Austrian troops entered the city to restore order, sent the Slav Congress packing, and reasserted control in Bohemia, rescinding the offer of a new parliament. For economic as well as political reasons, the new government was determined to keep the empire intact. The regime also sent troops to regain control in the Italian provinces of Lombardy and Venetia, where quarrels among the Italians helped the Austrians succeed.

Nationalism and counter-nationalism in Hungary set the stage for the final act of the drama. The Hungarian parliament had passed a series of laws, including new provisions for the union of Hungary and Austria. In the heat of 1848, Ferdinand I had little choice but to accept them. The Hungarian parliament abolished serfdom and ended noble privilege to prevent a peasant insurrection. It also established freedom of the press and religion and changed the suffrage requirements, enfranchising small property holders. Many of these measures (called the March laws) were hailed by Hungarian peasants, Jewish communities, and liberals. But other provisions—particularly the extension of Magyar control—provoked opposition from the Croats, Serbs, and Romanians within Hungary. On April 14, 1848, Kossuth upped the ante, severing all ties between Hungary and Austria. The new Austrian emperor, Franz Josef, now played his last card: he asked for military support from Nicholas I of Russia. The Habsburgs were unable to win their "holy struggle against anarchy," but

LANGUAGES OF CENTRAL AND EASTERN EUROPE. In Habsburg Austria-Hungary, the ethnic/linguistic boundaries did not conform to the political boundaries between states.
- *How many languages were spoken in territories that were not contiguous with each other?*
- *How did the diversity of peoples in the Habsburg Empire make uniting liberal revolution with nationalism more difficult to achieve?* ▪ *What happens when you try to draw a border around the territories where German was spoken?* ▪ *What tensions might you expect from the development of an expansionist German nationalism?*

the Russian army of over 300,000 found it an easier task. By mid-August 1849, the Hungarian revolt was crushed.

In the city of Vienna itself, the revolutionary movement had lost ground. When economic crisis and unemployment helped spark a second popular uprising, the emperor's forces, with Russian support, descended on the capital; and on October 31, the liberal government capitulated. The regime reestablished censorship, disbanded the national guard and student organizations, and put twenty-five revolutionary leaders to death in front of a firing squad. Kossuth went into hiding and lived the rest of his life in exile.

It was paradoxical, then, that the Habsburg Empire of Austria was in part saved during the revolutions of 1848 by the very nationalist movements that threatened to tear it apart. Although nationalists in Habsburg lands, especially in Hungary, gained the support of significant numbers of people, different nationalist movements found it impossible to cooperate with one another. Because of this, the new emperor, Franz Josef—with Russian help—was able to

defeat the most significant challenges to his authority one by one, and consolidate his rule. Ultimately he gained popular support from many quarters, especially from middle-class populations that came to express a certain civic pride in the spirit of toleration, which allowed so many peoples to live together within such a patchwork of peoples and tongues. Franz Josef would survive these crises and many others until his death in 1916 during World War I, a much larger conflict that would finally overwhelm and destroy the Habsburg Empire for good.

The Early Stages of Italian Unification in 1848

The Italian peninsula had not been united since the end of the Roman Empire. At the beginning of the nineteenth century, like the German-speaking lands of central Europe, the area that is now Italy was a patchwork of small states (see map on page 718). Austria occupied the northernmost states of Lombardy and Venetia, which were also the most urban and industrial. Habsburg dependents also ruled Tuscany, Parma, and Modena, extending Austria's influence over much of the north. The independent Italian states included the southern kingdom of the Two Sicilies, governed by members of the Bourbon family; the Papal States, ruled by Pope Gregory XVI (1831–1846); and most important, Piedmont-Sardinia, ruled by the reform-minded monarch Charles Albert (r. 1831–1849) of the House of Savoy. Charles Albert had no particular commitment to creating an Italian national state, but by virtue of Piedmont-Sardinia's economic power, geographical location, and long tradition of opposition to the Habsburgs, his state played a central role in nationalist and anti-Austrian politics.

The leading Italian nationalist in this period—one whose republican politics Charles Albert disliked—was Giuseppe Mazzini (1805–1872) from the city of Genoa, in Piedmont. Mazzini began his political career as a member of the Carbonari (see Chapter 20), an underground society pledged to resisting Austrian control of the region and establishing constitutional rule. In 1831, Mazzini founded his own society, Young Italy, which was also anti-Austrian and in favor of constitutional reforms but dedicated to Italian unification as well. Charismatic and persuasive,

Mazzini was one of the best-known nationalists of his time. He spoke in characteristically Romantic tones about the awakening of the Italian people and of the common people's mission to bring republicanism to the world. Under his leadership, Young Italy clubs multiplied; yet the organization's favored tactics—plotting mutinies and armed rebellions—proved ineffective. In 1834, Mazzini launched an invasion of the kingdom of Sardinia, but without sufficient support, it fizzled, driving him into exile in Britain.

Mazzini's republican vision of a united Italy clashed with the goals of his potential allies. Many liberals shared his commitment to creating a single Italian state but not his enthusiasm for the people and popular movements. They hoped instead to merge existing governments into some form of constitutional monarchy or, in a few cases, a government under the pope. Mazzini's insistence on a democratic republic committed to social and political transformation struck pragmatic liberals as utopian and well-to-do members of the middle classes as dangerous.

The turmoil that swept across Europe in 1848 raised hopes for political and social change and put Italian unification on the agenda. As in Germany, those who hoped for change were divided in their goals, but they shared a common hope that national unification might enable them to achieve the reforms they sought, whether it be a constitution, civil liberties, universal suffrage, or revolutionary social change

SIEGE OF VENICE, 1848. This image, designed to provoke an anti-Austrian and nationalist sentiment among Italians, shows Venetian women and children donating their jewels to support their city while it was besieged by the Austrian army in 1848. ▪ *What makes the image of women and children sacrificing their possessions for the larger good so powerful?* ▪ *What does it say about the connections between nationalism and social obligations associated with gender?* ▪ *Did nationalism depend on a vision of the family as well as of the nation?*

GIUSEPPE MAZZINI (1805–1872). Born in Genoa when it was ruled by Napoleon's France, Mazzini devoted his life to the cause of Italian unification and independence. As a young man, he was a member of the underground revolutionary organization known as the Carbonari; and in 1831, he founded a new group, Young Italy, which soon attracted many adherents. Early attempts at insurrection resulted in political exile, but he returned during the 1848 revolutions to help lead the Roman Republic. Although his hopes for a Republican Italy were blocked by Count Camillo Benso di Cavour's plans for unification under the leadership of Piedmont-Sardinia, Mazzini remained a hero to many Italians, and his description of a "United States of Europe" anticipated the European Union.

that would benefit the working poor. In March 1848, only a few weeks after revolution had toppled the French monarchy, popular revolts broke out in the northern provinces of Venetia and Lombardy, fueled by anger at the Austrian occupation. In Milan, the capital of Lombardy, thousands of people marched onto the palace of the Austrian governor general calling for reforms, leading to pitched battles in the streets. In Venice, the revolutionaries forced the Austrian troops out of the city and declared it a republic. Charles Albert of Piedmont-Sardinia provided the rebels with military support and took up the banner of Italian nationalism, although many charged that he was primarily interested in expanding his own power. At the same time, Charles Albert pleased Italian liberals by creating an elected legislature and relaxing press censorship in his kingdom.

In August 1848, an insurrection of laborers broke out in Bologna, challenging the authority of the pope in the Papal States. Soon after, a popular uprising in Rome confronted the pope directly, and by February 1849, a new government in Rome had declared itself a republic. The next month, Mazzini returned from exile to join the revolutionary movement in Rome. These movements were neither coordinated nor ultimately successful. Charles Albert hesitated to confront the Austrians directly, and over the next few months the Austrians regained the upper hand in the north. French forces under Louis Napoleon intervened in Rome and the Papal States; although they met fierce resistance from the Roman republicans who were joined by Giuseppe Garibaldi (see pages 716–718), they nonetheless restored the pope's power and defeated the Roman Republic. The short-lived Republic of San Marco in Venice was the last of the Italian revolutions to fall, after a blockade and an artillery bombardment by the Austrian army in August 1849. Like most of the radical movements of 1848, these Italian uprisings all failed. Still, they raised the hopes of nationalists who spoke of a *risorgimento* (or Italian resurgence) that would restore the nation to the position of leadership it had held in Roman times and during the Renaissance.

BUILDING THE NATION-STATE

Since the French Revolution of 1789, conservative politicians had associated nationhood with liberalism—constitutions, reforms, new political communities. In the wake of the revolutions of 1848, new nation-states were built or consolidated often by former critics of nationalism. During the second half of the century, however, the political ground shifted dramatically. States and governments took the national initiative. Alarmed by revolutionary ferment, they promoted economic development, pressed social and political reforms, and sought to shore up their base of support. Rather than allow popular nationalist movements to emerge from below, statesmen consolidated their governments' powers and built nations from above.

France under Napoleon III

Napoleon III, like his uncle, believed in personal rule and a centralized state. As emperor, he controlled the nation's finances, the army, and foreign affairs. The assembly, elected by universal male suffrage, could approve only legislation drafted at the emperor's direction. Napoleon's regime aimed to undermine France's traditional elites by expanding the bureaucracy and cultivating a new relationship with the people. "The confidence of our rough peasants can be won by an energetic authority," asserted one of the emperor's representatives.

Competing Viewpoints

Building the Italian Nation: Three Views

> The charismatic revolutionary Giuseppe Mazzini left more than fifty volumes of memoirs and writings. In the first excerpt, he sets out his vision of the "regeneration" of the Italian nation and the three Romes: ancient Rome, the Rome of the popes, and (in the future) the Rome of the people, which would emancipate the peoples of Europe. Mazzini's conception of Italian nationalism was Romantic in its interpretation of Italy's distinctive history and destiny, and revolutionary in its emphasis on the Italian people rather than on statesmen.
>
> Giuseppe La Farina formed the National Society in 1857 to support Italian unification. By the 1860s, the society had more than 5,000 members; it was especially strong in the Piedmont, where it was founded, and in central Italy. La Farina was a tenacious organizer, and he drafted the society's political creed, excerpted in the second piece, and had it printed and sold throughout Italy.
>
> The unification of Italy owed as much to the hard-nosed diplomacy of Count Camillo Benso di Cavour as it did to the middle-class movements for unification. In 1862, one of Cavour's contemporaries offered an assessment of the count, reprinted in the third piece, and how he had found an "opening in the complicated fabric of European politics."

Mazzini and Romantic Nationalism

I saw regenerate Italy becoming at one bound the missionary of a religion of progress and fraternity. . . .

The worship of Rome was a part of my being. The great Unity, the One Life of the world, had twice been elaborated within her walls. Other peoples—their brief mission fulfilled—disappeared for ever. To none save to her had it been given twice to guide and direct the world. . . . There, upon the vestiges of an epoch of civilization anterior to the Grecian, which had had its seat in Italy . . . the Rome of the Republic, concluded by the Caesars, had arisen to consign the former world to oblivion, and borne her eagles over the known world, carrying with them the idea of right, the source of liberty.

In later days . . . she had again arisen, greater than before, and at once constituted herself, through her Popes—the accepted center of a new Unity. . . .

Why should not a new Rome, the Rome of the Italian people . . . arise to create a third and still vaster Unity; to link together and harmonize earth and heaven, right [law] and duty; and utter, not to individuals but to peoples, the great word Association—to make known to free men and equal their mission here below?

Source: Giuseppe Mazzini, *The Life and Writings of Joseph Mazzini* (London: 1964), as cited in Denis Mack Smith, *The Making of Italy, 1796–1870* (New York: 1968), pp. 48–49.

The Political Creed of the National Society, February 1858

Italian independence should be the aim of every man of spirit and intelligence. Neither our educational system in Italy, nor our commerce and industry, can ever be flourishing or properly modernized while Austria keeps one foot on our neck. . . . What good is it to be born in the most fertile and beautiful country in the world, to lie midway between East and West with magnificent ports in both the Adriatic and Mediterranean, to be descended from the Genoese, the Pisans, the men of Amalfi, Sicily and Venice? What use is it to have invented the compass, to have discovered the New World and been the progenitor of two civilizations? . . .

To obtain political liberty we must expel the Austrians who keep us enslaved. To win freedom of conscience we must expel the Austrians who keep us slaves of the Pope. To create a national literature we must chase away the Austrians who keep us uneducated. . . .

Italy must become not only independent but politically united. Political unity alone can reconcile various interests and laws, can mobilize credit and put out collective energies to speeding up communications. Only thus will we find sufficient capital for large-scale industry. Only thus will we create new markets, suppress internal obstacles to the free flow of commerce, and find the strength and reputation needed for traffic in distant lands. . . .

Everything points irresistibly to political unification. Science, industry, commerce, and the arts all need it. No great enterprise is possible any longer if we do not first put together the skill, knowledge, capital and labor of the whole of our great nation. The spirit of the age is moving toward concentration, and woe betide any nation that holds back!

Source: A. Franchi, ed., *Scritti politici di Giuseppe La Farina*, vol. 2 (Milan: 1870), as cited in Denis Mack Smith, *The Making of Italy, 1796–1870* (New York: 1968), pp. 224–25.

Count Cavour as a Leader

Count Cavour undeniably ranks as third among European statesmen after Lord Palmerston [British prime minister 1855–1858, 1859–1865] and the Emperor Napoleon. . . . Count Cavour's strength does not lie in his principles; for he has none that are altogether inflexible. But he has a clear, precise aim, one whose greatness would—ten years ago—have made any other man reel: that of creating a unified and independent Italy. Men, means, circumstances were and still are matters of indifference to him. He walks straight ahead, always firm, often alone, sacrificing his friends, his sympathies, sometimes his heart, and often his conscience. Nothing is too difficult for him. . . .

Count Cavour . . . always has the talent to assess a situation and the possibilities of exploiting it. And it is this wonderful faculty that has contributed to form the Italy of today. As minister of a fourth-rate power, he could not create situations like Napoleon III, nor has he possessed the support of a great nation like Palmerston.

Count Cavour had to seek out an opening in the complicated fabric of European politics; he had to wriggle his way in, conceal himself, lay a mine, and cause an explosion. And it was by these means that he defeated Austria and won the help of France and England. Where other statesmen would have drawn back, Cavour plunged in headlong—as soon as he had sounded the precipice and calculated the possible profit and loss. The Crimean expeditionary force . . . the cession of Nice, the invasion of the Papal States last autumn [i.e., in 1860], were all the outcome of his vigorous stamina of mind.

There in brief you have the man of foreign affairs. He is strong; he is a match for the situation, for the politicians of his time or indeed of any time.

Source: F. Petruccelli della Gattina, *I moribundi del Palazzo Carignano* (Milan: 1862), as cited in Denis Mack Smith, *The Making of Italy, 1796–1870* (New York: 1968), pp. 181–82.

Questions for Analysis

1. Compare Mazzini's romantic vision of Italian history with the more pragmatic arguments for political unity by the liberal supporters of the National Society. Are there any points that overlap?

2. How would a supporter of Mazzini or a member of the National Society react to the third document's claim that an individual, Count Cavour, deserved primary credit for Italian unification?

3. Why should history and claims about "the spirit of the age" be so important to Italian nationalists?

Building the Nation-State | 713

PARIS REBUILT. Baron Haussmann, prefect of Paris under Napoleon III, presided over the wholesale rebuilding of the city, the effects of which we still see today. The Arc de Triomphe, seen here in a photograph from the 1960s, became the center of an *étoile* (star) pattern, with the wide boulevards named after Napoleon I's famous generals.

house in five had running water. Official concerns about public health were reinforced by political fears of crime and revolutionary militancy in working-class neighborhoods. A massive rebuilding project razed much of the medieval center of the city and erected 34,000 new buildings, including elegant hotels with the first elevators. The construction installed new water pipes and sewer lines, laid out 200 kilometers of new streets, and rationalized the traffic flow. Wide new boulevards, many named for Napoleon I's most famous generals, radiated from the Arc de Triomphe. The renovation, however, did not benefit everyone. Although the regime built model worker residences, rising rents drove working people from the city's center into increasingly segregated suburbs. Baron George-Eugène Haussmann, the prefect of Paris who presided over the project, considered the city a monument to "cleanliness and order"; others called Haussmann an "artist of demolition."

Napoleon III also took steps to develop the economy. He harbored a near-utopian faith in the power of industrial expansion to bring prosperity, political support, and national glory. An adviser to the emperor put it this way: "I see in industry, machinery, and credit the indispensable auxiliaries of humanity's moral and material progress." His government encouraged credit and new forms of financing, passed new limited-liability laws, and signed a free-trade treaty with Britain in 1860; it also supported the creation of the Crédit Mobilier, an investment banking institution that sold shares and financed railroads, insurance and gas companies, coal and construction companies, and the building of the Suez Canal (see Chapter 22). Napoleon also reluctantly permitted the existence of trade unions and legalized strikes. By appealing to both the workers and the middle class, he sought to gain support for his goal of reestablishing France as a leading world power.

Most emblematic of the emperor's ambition was his transformation of the nation's capital. Paris's medieval infrastructure was buckling under the weight of population growth and industrial development. Cholera epidemics in 1832 and 1849 killed tens of thousands. In 1850, only one

Victorian Britain and the Second Reform Bill (1867)

Less affected by the revolutionary wave of 1848, Great Britain was able to chart a course of significant social and political reform, continuing a process that had begun in 1832 with the First Reform Bill. The government faced mounting demands to extend the franchise beyond the middle classes. Industrial expansion sustained a growing stratum of highly skilled and relatively well-paid workers (almost exclusively male). These workers, concentrated for the most part within the building, engineering, and textile industries, turned away from the tradition of militant radicalism that had characterized the Hungry Forties. Instead, they favored collective self-help through cooperative societies or trade unions, which primarily accumulated funds for insurance against old age and unemployment. These prosperous workers saw education as a tool for advancement and patronized the mechanics' institutes and similar institutions founded by them or on their behalf. And they created real pressure for electoral reform.

Some workers argued for the vote in the name of democracy. Others borrowed arguments from earlier middle-class campaigns for electoral reform: they were responsible workers, respectable and upstanding members of society, with strong religious convictions and patriotic feelings. Unquestionably loyal to the state, the workers reasoned that they deserved the vote and direct representation just as much as the middle class. They were joined in their campaign by many middle-class dissenting reformers in the Liberal party, whose religious beliefs (as dissenters from the Church of England) linked them to the workers' campaigns for reform. The dissenters had long faced discrimination. They were denied posts in the civil service and the military, which they felt should be open to talent; and for centuries had been excluded from the nation's premier universities, Oxford and Cambridge, unless they renounced their faith and subscribed to the articles of the Anglican Church. Moreover, they resented paying taxes to support the Church of England, which was largely staffed by sons of the gentry and run in the interests of landed society. The fact that the community of dissent crossed class lines was vital to Liberal party politics and the campaign for reforming the vote.

Working-class leaders and middle-class dissidents joined in a country-wide campaign for a new reform bill and a House of Commons that was responsive to their interests. They were backed by some shrewd Conservatives, such as Benjamin Disraeli (1804–1881), who argued that political life would be improved, not disrupted, by including the "aristocrats of labor." In actuality, Disraeli was betting that the newly enfranchised demographic would vote Conservative; and in 1867, he steered through Parliament a bill that reached further than anything proposed by his political opponents. The 1867 Reform Bill doubled the franchise by extending the vote to any men who paid poor rates or rent of £10 or more a year in urban areas (this meant, in general, skilled workers) and rural tenants paying rent of £12 or more. As in 1832, the bill redistributed seats, with large northern cities gaining representation at the expense of the rural south. The success of the 1867 Reform Bill points to the lingering influence of the Chartist movement of the 1840s (see Chapter 20). Although the Chartists' goal of universal male suffrage remained unfulfilled, the 1867 law allowed the responsible working class to participate in the affairs of the state.

Although the reform bill was silent on women, an important minority insisted that liberalism should include women's enfranchisement. These advocates mobilized a women's suffrage movement, building on women's remarkable participation in earlier reform campaigns, especially the Anti–Corn Law League and the movement to abolish slavery. Their cause found a passionate supporter in **John Stuart Mill**, perhaps the century's most brilliant, committed, and influential defender of personal liberty. Mill's father had worked closely with the utilitarian philosopher Jeremy Bentham, and the young Mill had been a convinced utilitarian himself (Chapter 20). He went on, however, to develop much more expansive notions of human freedom. In 1859, he wrote *On Liberty*, which

MILL'S LOGIC, OR FRANCHISE FOR FEMALES
"Pray clear the way, there, for these—ah—persons."

JOHN STUART MILL AND SUFFRAGETTES. By 1860, when this cartoon was published, Mill had established a reputation as a liberal political philosopher and a supporter of women's right to vote. Mill argued that women's enfranchisement was essential from the standpoint of individual liberty as well as for the good of society as a whole. ▪ *What is amusing about Mill's assertion in this cartoon that women should be considered persons in their own right?*

many consider the classic defense of individual freedom in the face of the state and the "tyranny of the majority." During the same period, he coauthored—with his lover and eventual wife, Harriet Taylor—essays on women's political rights and the law of marriage and divorce. At the time, Taylor was trapped in an unhappy marriage, but divorce required an act of Parliament. Her relationship with Mill thus added a measure of personal scandal to their political views, which contemporaries considered scandalous enough. His *Subjection of Women* (1869), published after Taylor died, argued what few could even contemplate at the time: that women had to be considered individuals on the same plane as men and that women's freedom was a measure of social progress. *Subjection* was an international success and, with *On Liberty*, became one of the defining texts of Western liberalism. Mill's arguments, however, did not carry the day; it was the militant suffrage movements and the crisis of the First World War that brought women the vote.

The decade or so following the passage of the Reform Bill of 1867 marked the high point of British liberalism. By opening the doors to political participation, liberalism had accomplished a peaceful restructuring of political institutions and social life. It did so under considerable pressure from below, however, and in Britain, as elsewhere, liberal leaders made it clear that these doors were unquestionably not open to everyone. Their opposition to women's suffrage is interesting for what it reveals about their views on male and female nature. They insisted that female individuality—expressed in voting, education, or wage earning—would destabilize family life. Yet their opposition to women's suffrage reflected their conception of the vote; that is, casting a ballot was a privilege granted only to specific social groups in return for their contributions to and vested interest in society. Men of property might champion the rule of law and representative government, but they balked at the prospect of a truly democratic politics and did not shy away from heavy-handed law-and-order politics. Expanding the franchise created new constituencies with new ambitions and paved the way for socialist and labor politics in the last quarter of the century. Tensions within liberalism remained and forecast conflicts in the future.

Italian Unification: Cavour and Garibaldi

After the failure of Italian unification in 1848, nationalists in Italy faced a choice between two strategies for

GIUSEPPE GARIBALDI. Note the simple uniform Garibaldi wears in this commemorative portrait, with its iconic symbols of his nationalist movement: the red shirt and the flag of Italy in the background. Compare this image with the official portraits of absolutist rulers in previous chapters. ▪ *What was significant about the absence of finery and precious materials in this painting?* ▪ *What does this portrait say about images of masculine leadership in mid-nineteenth-century nationalist imagination? (Compare this painting with the drawing of Garibaldi and Victor Emmanuel on page 717.)*

achieving statehood. One group, supported by Mazzini and his follower Giuseppe Garibaldi, envisioned a republican Italy built from below by popular uprising. **Giuseppe Garibaldi** was a guerrilla fighter who had been exiled twice, first in Latin America, where he fought along with independence movements, and again in the United States. Like Mazzini, he was committed to achieving national unification through popular movement. Another group of more moderate nationalists sought to unify Italy as a constitutional monarchy, under the leadership of the kingdom of Piedmont-Sardinia.

The more conservative supporters of Piedmont-Sardinia sought to steer clear of democracy and the destabilizing forces that it might unleash. The king of Piedmont-Sardinia, Charles Albert, had drawn the attention of Italian nationalists in 1848 when he took up the anti-Austrian cause. Though he later died in exile, his son Victor Emmanuel II (r. 1849–1861) brought into his government a man who would embody the conservative vision of nationhood: the shrewd Sardinian nobleman **Count Camillo Benso di Cavour** (1810–1861), who declared, "In Italy a democratic movement has almost no chance of success." Cavour instead pursued ambitious but pragmatic reforms guided by the state. As prime minister, he promoted economic expansion, encouraged the construction of a modern transportation infrastructure, reformed the currency, and sought to raise Piedmont-Sardinia's profile in international relations. Garibaldi and Cavour thus represented two different routes to Italian unification: Garibaldi stood for unification from below, Cavour for unification guided from above.

Cavour's plan depended on diplomacy. Because Piedmont-Sardinia did not have the military capacity to counter the Austrians in northern Italy, Cavour skillfully cultivated an alliance with one of Austria's traditional rivals: Napoleonic France. In 1858, he held a secret meeting with Napoleon III, who agreed to cooperate in driving the Austrians from Italy if Piedmont ceded Savoy and Nice to France. A war with Austria was duly provoked in 1859, and for a time all went well for the Franco-Italian allies. After the conquest of Lombardy, however, Napoleon III suddenly withdrew, concerned that he might either lose the war or antagonize French Catholics, who were alienated by Cavour's hostility to the pope. Deserted by the French, Piedmont could not expel the Austrians from Venetia. Yet the campaign made extensive gains: Piedmont-Sardinia annexed Lombardy, and the duchies of Tuscany, Parma, and Modena agreed by plebiscite to join the new state. By the end of this process in 1860, Piedmont-Sardinia had grown to more than twice its original size and was by far the most powerful state in Italy.

As Cavour consolidated the northern and central states, events in the southern states seemed to put those areas up for grabs as well. The unpopular Bourbon king of the Two Sicilies, Francis II (r. 1859–1860), faced a fast-spreading peasant revolt that rekindled the hopes of earlier insurrections of the 1820s and 1840s. The revolt, in turn, got a much needed boost from Garibaldi, who landed in Sicily in May 1860. "The Thousand," as Garibaldi's volunteer fighters called themselves, embodied the widespread support for Italian unification. They came from the north as well as from the south and counted among them members of the middle class, workers, and artisans. Garibaldi's troops took Sicily and continued on to the mainland;

and by November 1860, they, alongside local insurgents, had taken Naples and toppled the kingdom of Francis II. Emboldened by this success, Garibaldi looked to Rome, where French troops guarded the pope.

Garibaldi's rising popularity put him on a collision course with Cavour, who worried that Garibaldi's forces would bring French or Austrian intervention, with unknown consequences. He also feared Garibaldi's "irresistible" prestige. But above all, Cavour preferred that Italian unification happen quickly, under Piedmont-Sardinia's stewardship and without domestic turmoil or messy, unpredictable negotiations with other Italian states. "As long as he [Garibaldi] is faithful to his flag, one has to march along with him," Cavour wrote. "This does not alter the fact that it would be eminently desirable for the revolution . . . to be accomplished without him." Determined to regain the

"RIGHT LEG IN THE BOOT AT LAST." This image shows Garibaldi helping Victor Emmanuel, formerly the king of Piedmont-Sardinia and the newly crowned king of Italy, fit his foot in the Italian boot. What is the significance of their different forms of dress and postures? ■ *Compare this image with the portrait of Garibaldi on page 716. How does this image portray the outcome of the contest between the conservative nationalism of Cavour and the more romantic and democratic nationalism of Garibaldi?*

THE UNIFICATION OF ITALY.

■ *How many phases were involved in Italian unification, according to the map key?*

■ *Why did it take an extra decade to incorporate Rome and Venetia into the Italian state?*

■ *Why was Italian unification incomplete until the early twentieth century?*

Legend:
→ Route of Garibaldi's Campaign, 1860
█ The Kingdom of Sardinia at the time of the Congress of Vienna, 1815
█ Territories acquired, 1859–1860
█ Territories acquired, 1861–1870

initiative, Cavour dispatched Victor Emmanuel, king of Piedmont-Sardinia, and his army to Rome. Flush with success, Emmanuel ordered Garibaldi to cede him military authority, which Garibaldi obeyed. Most of the peninsula was united under a single rule, and Victor Emmanuel assumed the title of king of Italy (r. 1861–1878). Cavour's vision of Italian nationhood had won the day.

The final steps of Italy's territorial nation building came indirectly. Venetia remained in the hands of the Austrians until 1866, when Austria was defeated by Prussia and forced to relinquish its last Italian stronghold. Rome had resisted conquest largely because of the military protection Napoleon III accorded the pope. But in 1870, the outbreak of the Franco-Prussian War compelled Napoleon to withdraw his troops. That September, Italian soldiers occupied

Rome; and in July 1871, Rome became the capital of the united Italian kingdom.

What of the pope's authority? The Italian parliament passed the Law of Papal Guarantees to define and limit the pope's status. However, it was promptly defied by the reigning pontiff, Pius IX, who refused to have anything to do with a disrespectful secular government. His successors continued to close themselves off in the Vatican until 1929, when a series of agreements between the Italian government and Pius XI settled the dispute.

In 1871, Italy was a state, but nation building was hardly over. A minority of the "Italian" population spoke Italian, but the rest spoke local and regional dialects so diverse that schoolteachers sent from Rome to Sicily were mistaken for foreigners. As one politician remarked, "We have made

Italy; now we must make Italians." This task proved to be difficult. The gap between an increasingly industrialized north and a poor and rural south remained wide. Cavour and those who succeeded him as prime minister had to contend with the economic and social inequalities, with rising tensions between landlords and agricultural workers in rural regions and with lingering resentments against the centralized, northern-oriented state. Banditry in the territory of the former kingdom of the Two Sicilies compelled the central administration to dispatch troops to quell serious uprisings, killing more people than in the war of unification. Regional differences and social tensions therefore made building the Italian nation an ongoing process.

The Unification of Germany: Realpolitik

In 1853, the former revolutionary August Ludwig von Rochau wrote a short book with a long title: *The Principles of Realpolitik Applied to the Conditions of Germany*. In this book, Rochau banished the idealism and revolutionary fervor of his youth. "The question of who ought to rule . . . belongs in the realm of philosophical speculation," he wrote. "Practical politics has to do with the simple fact that it is power alone that can rule." His vision of *Realpolitik* (practical, realistic politics) held that finding ways to achieve and maintain power were more important than moral or ideological goals such as justice or freedom. This view rejected the aspirations of earlier generations of liberal reformers in Germany who believed that progress depended on constitutions and Enlightenment conceptions of rights. In several important ways, Rochau's views captured the changing outlook of broad sections of the German middle classes, and Realpolitik became the watchword of the 1850s and 1860s. The word was most closely associated with the deeply conservative and pragmatic Otto von Bismarck, whose skillful diplomacy and power politics played an important role in German unification.

Despite its decisive defeat in 1848, German liberalism revived within a decade, against considerable opposition. King Frederick William granted a Prussian constitution in 1850 that established a two-house parliament, with the lower house elected by universal male suffrage. A series of edicts modified the electoral system, however, to preserve the power of traditional elites. The king's edicts divided voters into three classes based on the amount of taxes paid, and their votes were apportioned accordingly. Thus, the relatively small number of wealthy voters who paid one-third of Prussia's taxes elected one-third of the legislators

in Parliament. In this way, a large landowner or a wealthy industrialist exercised perhaps seventeen times the voting power of a workingman. Furthermore, voting took place in public, orally, so a secret ballot was impossible.

In 1858, William I, who had led troops against the revolutionaries of 1848 in his youth, became prince regent of Prussia; he became king in 1861 and ruled until 1888. Under his rule, Prussia remained a notoriously conservative state, but a decade of industrial growth had also expanded the size and confidence of the middle classes. By the late 1850s, Prussia had an active liberal intelligentsia, a liberal civil service dedicated to political and economic modernization, and a thoughtful and engaged press. These forces helped forge a liberal political movement that won a majority in the lower house and thus could confidently confront the king.

Liberals in Prussia were especially opposed to the king's high levels of military spending. William wanted to expand the standing army, reduce the role of reserve forces (a more middle-class group), and ensure that military matters were not subject to parliamentary control. Opponents in Parliament suspected the king of wanting to make the military his own private force or a state within a state. Between 1859 and 1862, relations between the two deteriorated; and when liberals' protests went unanswered, they refused to approve the regular budget. Faced with a crisis, William named **Otto von Bismarck** minister-president of Prussia in 1862. (A prime minister answers to Parliament; Bismarck did not.) This crucial moment in Prussian domestic politics became a decisive turning point in the history of German nationhood.

Born into the Junker class of conservative land-owning aristocrats, Bismarck had fiercely opposed the liberal movement of 1848–1849. He was not a nationalist; he was, before all else, a Prussian. He instituted domestic reforms not because he favored the rights of a particular group but because he thought these policies would unify and strengthen Prussia. When he maneuvered to bring other German states under Prussian domination, he did so not in pursuit of a grand German design but because he believed that union in some form was inevitable and so Prussia had to seize the initiative. Bismarck happily acknowledged that he admired power and considered himself destined for greatness. He had a reputation for cynicism, arrogance, and uninhibited frankness in expressing his views. Yet a Latin phrase he frequently quoted distilled a more careful assessment of the relationship between individuals and history: "Man cannot create or control the tide of time, he can only move in the same direction and try to direct it."

In Prussia, Bismarck defied parliamentary opposition. When the liberal majority refused to pass a budget

TOWARD THE UNIFICATION OF GERMANY. Note the many elements that made up a unified Germany and the stages that brought them together. ▪ *Did this new nation have any resemblance to the unified Germany envisioned by the liberal revolutionaries of the Frankfurt Pre-Parliament in 1848 (see page 701)?* ▪ *How many stages were involved in the unification of Germany?* ▪ *How many years did it take to achieve unification?* ▪ *What region filled with German-speaking peoples was not included in the new unified Germany? Why not?*

because of disagreements over army spending, he dissolved Parliament, claiming that the constitution, whatever its purposes, had not been designed to subvert the state. His most decisive actions, however, were in foreign policy. Once opposed to nationalism, Bismarck skillfully played the national card to preempt his liberal opponents at home

and to make German nation building an accomplishment—and an extension—of Prussian authority.

The other "German" power was Austria, which wielded considerable influence within the German Confederation and especially over the largely Catholic regions in the south. Bismarck saw a stark contrast between Austrian and Prussian interests and skillfully exploited Austria's economic disadvantages and the Habsburgs' internal ethnic struggles. He inflamed a long-smoldering dispute with Denmark over Schleswig (SHLAYS-vihg) and Holstein, two provinces peopled by Germans and Danes and claimed by both the German Confederation and Denmark. In 1864, the Danish king attempted to annex the provinces, prompting a German nationalist outcry. Bismarck cast the conflict as a Prussian matter and persuaded Austria to join Prussia in a war against Denmark. The war was short, and it forced the Danish ruler to cede the two provinces to Austria and Prussia. As Bismarck hoped, the victorious alliance promptly fell apart. In 1866, casting Prussia as the defender of larger German interests, he declared war on Austria. The conflict, known as the Seven Weeks' War, ended in Prussian victory. Austria gave up all claims to Schleswig and Holstein, surrendered Venetia to the Italians, and agreed to dissolve the German Confederation. In its place, Bismarck created the North German Confederation, a union of all the German states north of the Main River.

Bismarck always considered public opinion in his calculations of the use of Prussian power. Both wars had strong public support, and Prussian victories weakened liberal opposition to the king and his president-minister. In the aftermath of the Austrian defeat, Prussian liberals gave up their battle over budgets, the military, and constitutional provisions. Bismarck also sought support among the masses, and he understood that Germans did not necessarily support business elites, the bureaucracies of their own small states, or the Austrian Habsburgs. The constitution of the North German Confederation gave the appearance of a more liberal political body, with a bicameral legislature, freedom of the press, and universal male suffrage in the lower house. Its structure, however, gave Prussia and the conservative emperor a decisive advantage in the North German Confederation—and in the soon to be expanded empire.

The final step in the completion of German unity was the Franco-Prussian War of 1870–1871. Bismarck hoped that a conflict with France would arouse German nationalism in Bavaria, Württemberg, and other southern states still outside the confederation, and overcome their historic wariness of Prussia. A diplomatic tempest concerning the right of the Hohenzollerns (Prussia's ruling family) to occupy the Spanish throne created an opportunity to foment a Franco-German misunderstanding. King William agreed to meet with the French ambassador at the resort spa of Ems in Prussia to discuss the Spanish succession. William initially acquiesced to French demands, but when the French blundered by asking for "perpetual exclusion" of the Hohenzollern family from the Spanish throne, Bismarck

seized his opportunity. He edited a telegraph from King William so as to make it appear that the Prussian king had rebuffed the French ambassador. Once the redacted report reached France, the nation reacted with calls for war. Prussia echoed the call, and Bismarck published evidence that he claimed proved French designs on the Rhineland.

As soon as war was declared, the south German states rallied to Prussia's side. No European powers came to France's aid, however, with Austria, the most likely candidate, weakened by its recent war with Prussia. The Hungarians, meanwhile, welcomed a strengthened Prussia, for the weaker Austria was as a German power, the stronger would be the Magyar claims to power sharing in the empire. On the battlefield, France could not match Prussia's professionally trained and superbly equipped forces, and the conflict was quickly over. The war began in July and ended in September with the defeat of the French and the capture of Napoleon III at Sedan in France. Insurrectionary forces in Paris continued to hold out against the Germans through the winter of 1870–1871, but the French imperial government collapsed.

On January 18, 1871, in the Hall of Mirrors at Versailles—the symbol of the powerful past of French absolutism—the German Empire was proclaimed. All the German states that had not already been absorbed into the Prussian fold (except Austria) declared their allegiance to William I, henceforth emperor, or kaiser. Four months later, at Frankfurt, a treaty between the French and the Germans ceded the border region of Alsace to the new German Empire and forced the French to pay an indemnity of 5 billion francs. Prussia accounted for 60 percent of the new state's territory and population; and the Prussian kaiser, prime minister, army, and most of the bureaucracy remained intact, now reconfigured as the German nation-state. This was not the new nation for which Prussian liberals had hoped, for it marked a "revolution from above" rather than from below. Still, the more optimistic believed that the new German Empire would evolve in a different political direction and eventually "extend freedom through unity."

The State and Nationality: Centrifugal Forces in the Austrian Empire

Germany emerged from the 1860s a stronger, unified nation. But the Habsburg Empire faced a very different situation, with different resources, and emerged a weakened, precariously balanced, multiethnic dual monarchy, also called Austria-Hungary.

Interpreting Visual Evidence

The New German Nation

In order to silence their critics at home and abroad, nationalists in Germany sought to create a vision of German history that made unification the natural outcome of a deep historical process that had begun hundreds of years before. Image A shows a family of a cavalry officer preparing to hang a portrait of King William on the wall, next to the portraits of Martin Luther, Frederick the Great, and Field Marshal von Blücher, who commanded the Prussian forces at Waterloo. In the lower left corner, two boys are rolling up a portrait of the defeated French emperor, Napoleon III. The implication, of course, is that generations of German heroes all worked toward the same goal: the inevitable unification of Germany.

This unity, however, was controversial among German people. Image B, a pro-Bismarck cartoon, shows the German minister-president dragging the unwilling liberal members of the Prussian parliament with him as he pulls a triumphal chariot toward his military confrontation with Austria in 1866. The caption reads, "And in this sense, too, we are in agreement with Count Bismarck, and we have pulled the same rope as him." Image C, on the other hand, expresses reservations about Prussian dominance in the new empire. The title reads "Germany's Future" and the caption, "Will it fit under one hat? I think it will only fit under a [Prussian] Pickelhaube." The Pickelhaube (the characteristic pointed helmet of the Prussian army) had already become a much-feared symbol of Prussian military force. Such an image may well have struck a chord

A. *Homage to Kaiser Wilhelm [William] I*, by Paul Bürde (1871).

As we have seen, ethnic nationalism was a powerful force in the Habsburg monarchy in 1848. Yet the Habsburg state, with a combination of military repression and tactics that divided its enemies, had proved more powerful. It abolished serfdom and made few other concessions to its opponents. The Hungarians, who had nearly won independence in the spring of 1848, were essentially reconquered. Administrative reforms created a new and more uniform legal system and a rationalized taxation, and imposed a single-language policy that favored German. The issue of managing ethnic relations, however, only grew more difficult. Through the 1850s and 1860s, the subject nationalities, as they were often called, bitterly protested the powerlessness of their local parliaments, military repression, and cultural disenfranchisement. The Czechs in Bohemia, for instance, grew increasingly alienated by policies that favored the German minority of the province and, in response, became more insistent on their Slavic identity with residents of the non-Prussian German states, who now paid taxes to the Prussian monarchy and served in an army dominated by Prussian officers.

Questions for Analysis

1. What is the significance of the familial setting in image A? Why was it important for nationalists to emphasize a multigenerational family as the repository of German national spirit?

2. How do images B and C treat the question of Prussia's role within the new German nation? Is German national identity seen as something built from below or defined from above by a strong monarchy?

3. What is the place of the individual citizen in these representations of the German nation?

Parlamentarifches mit Jlluftrationen.

nach Königsgrätz.

Und in diefem Sinne find auch wir mit dem Grafen Bismarck einig, und haben mit ihm denfelben Strang gezogen.
Graf Eulenburg.

B. Prussian liberals and Bismarck after Königgrätz in the Austro-Prussian War (1866).

Deutfchlands Zukunft.

Kommt es unter einen Hut? Ich glaube, 's kommt eher unter eine Pickelhaube!

C. "Germany's Future" (1870).

(a movement welcomed by Russia, which became the sponsor of a broad pan-Slavism). The Hungarians, or Magyars, the most powerful of the subject nationalities, sought to reclaim the autonomy they had glimpsed in 1848.

In this context, Austria's defeats at the hands of Piedmont-Sardinia in 1859 and Prussia in 1866 become especially significant. The 1866 war forced Emperor Francis Joseph (Franz Josef in German) to renegotiate the very structure of the empire. To forestall a revolution by the Hungarians, Francis Joseph agreed to a new federal structure in the form of the Dual Monarchy of Austria-Hungary. It had a common system of taxation and a common army, and made foreign and military policy together, with Francis Joseph as emperor of Austria and king of Hungary. But internal and constitutional affairs were separated. The Ausgleich (or Settlement) allowed the Hungarians to establish their own constitution, legislature, and capital, combining the cities of Buda and Pest.

What of the other nationalities? The official policy of the Dual Monarchy stated that they were not to be discriminated against and that they could use their own languages; however, this official policy was only loosely enforced. More important, elevating the Hungarians and conferring on them alone the benefits of political nationhood only worsened relations with other groups. On the Austrian side of the Dual Monarchy, minority nationalities such as the Poles, Czechs, and Slovenes resented their second-class status. On the Hungarian side, the regime embarked on a project of Magyarization, attempting to make the state, the civil service, and the schools more thoroughly Hungarian—an effort that did not sit well with Serbs and Croats.

In spite of these divisions, the Austro-Hungarian Empire succeeded for a time in creating a different kind of political and cultural space within Europe that was increasingly given over to nation-states, which perceived their interests to be irrevocably opposed. The Austrian capital of Vienna developed a reputation for intellectual and cultural refinement in part due to the many different peoples who made up the Habsburg lands, including Germans, Jews, Hungarians, Italians, Czechs, Poles, Serbs, Croats, and Balkan Muslims from lands that formerly belonged to the Ottoman Empire. This polyglot culture produced Béla Bartók (1881–1945), the great Hungarian composer and admirer of folk musical traditions; and Gustav Mahler (1860–1911), a German-Austrian composer whose Romantic symphonies and conducting prowess made him a global celebrity by the time of his death. From the same intellectual milieu came Sigmund Freud (1856–1939), a German-speaking Jewish doctor from Vienna whose writings helped shape modern psychology, and Gustav Klimt (1862–1918), a painter and founding member of the Viennese Secession movement, which rejected the reigning classicism of the Austrian art world and made the Austrian capital an important center for the birth of modern art.

The Austrian emperor's deep opposition to nationalism was not just geopolitical, but a defense of a different relationship between the nation-state and culture. Unlike the governments of France, England, Italy, or Germany, the Habsburgs did not seek to build a nation-state based on common cultural identity. It tried instead to build a state with an administrative structure that was strong enough to keep the pieces from spinning off, at times by playing different minorities against each other and, when necessary, conceding greater autonomy to different groups. As the nineteenth century unfolded, however, discontented subject nationalities began to appeal to other powers—Serbia, Russia, the Ottomans—and this balancing act became more difficult.

NATION AND STATE BUILDING IN RUSSIA AND THE UNITED STATES

The challenges of nationalism and nation building also occupied Russia, the United States, and Canada. In all three countries, nation building entailed territorial and economic expansion, the incorporation of new peoples, and—in Russia and the United States—contending with the enormous problems of slavery and serfdom.

Russia's Nationality Question and the Emancipation of the Serfs

In the nineteenth century, Russia faced a nationality question every bit as complicated as that faced by the Habsburg Empire. Along the borders that separated Russia from the other European powers, the partitions of the Polish-Lithuanian Commonwealth had brought a culturally and linguistically diverse territory under Russian control, which extended from the Baltic coast to the area that is now western Ukraine. In this region, many of the nobility were Roman Catholic and spoke Polish, which had been the language of government and diplomacy in the Polish-Lithuanian Commonwealth; even after partition, Polish remained the language of high culture. The peasantry spoke varied languages, including dialects of Polish, Lithuanian, Belarusian, and, in the south, Ukrainian. A large portion of the urban population, meanwhile, were Jews who spoke Yiddish (the Polish partitions had brought the majority of the world's Jews under Russian control). After the Napoleonic Wars, Tsar Alexander I initially sought to assimilate politically these areas into the Russian Empire by coopting local elites, even if it meant permitting the continued use of Polish in university life. After the Polish uprising of 1830–1831 (Chapter 20), however, the Russian government cracked down on the use of languages that could become rallying points for distinctive "national" cultures within the Russian Empire.

Across the nineteenth century, Poles, Lithuanians, Belarusians, and Ukrainians all began to perceive of the advantages of having a national culture and political independence from Russia, but each faced very different challenges. Because Polish was most closely associated with the educated nobility, Polish nationalists looked for ways to attach their culture to a mass base in the countryside; religion could help in this task, because both nobles and peasants in the Polish territories around Warsaw were Roman Catholic. Lithuanians faced the opposite challenge:

they had no problem claiming that their language and culture were rooted in the common people, because most of the peasantry in the area around Vilnius spoke Lithuanian; however, the absence of a long literary tradition in Lithuanian made it difficult to claim a rich and ancient cultural heritage. In Ukraine, a stumbling block was religion: both Polish-speaking and Ukrainian-speaking nobles had emerged from the Reformation firmly in the Roman Catholic camp, whereas the peasantry remained attached to the Orthodox Church. In general, nineteenth-century nationalisms encouraged people to look for a strong overlap between high and low culture, between urban and rural populations, and religious homogeneity. The complex history of central and eastern Europe made this an exceedingly difficult recipe to follow, and we should not assume that modern nations in this region arose spontaneously out of clearly defined ethnic identities.

These debates about national culture in Russia and eastern Europe were also linked to debates within Russia about the **emancipation of the serfs**. Serfdom had developed over many centuries in Europe as a system for controlling agricultural labor. With their status codified in law in 1649, serfs in Russia were bound to the land, prohibited from flight, and subject to corporal punishment by their owners. They also could be transferred from one landowner to another without their property or family members. After 1789, and especially after 1848, the abolition of serfdom elsewhere in Europe made the issue more urgent, and abolishing serfdom became part of the larger project of building Russia as a modern nation. How that should happen was the subject of much debate.

Two schools of thought emerged. The "Slavophiles," or Romantic nationalists, sought to preserve Russia's distinctive features. They idealized traditional Russian culture and the peasant commune, and rejected Western secularism, urban commercialism, and bourgeois culture. In contrast, the "Westernizers" wished to see Russia adopt European developments in science, technology, and education, which they believed to be the foundation for Western liberalism and the protection of individual rights. In spite of their differences, both groups were committed to expanding Russian power, and both agreed that serfdom must be abolished. The Russian nobility, however, tenaciously opposed emancipation. Tangled debates about how lords would be compensated for the loss of "their" serfs, and how emancipated serfs would survive without full-scale land redistribution, also checked progress on the issue. The Crimean War (see pages 731–733) broke the impasse: in its aftermath, **Tsar Alexander II** (r. 1855–1881) became convinced that the persistence of serfdom had sapped Russian strength and had contributed to its defeat in the war, so he ended serfdom in all of Russia by decree in 1861.

Before the reform could be fully carried out, the tsar faced another challenge. In January 1863, the last and largest of the nineteenth-century Polish insurrections broke out. The immediate spark of the **January Rising** was a dispute over the conscription of Poles into the imperial army, but, in fact, unrest had already driven the Russians to declare martial law in the region two years earlier. The January Rising spread rapidly as thousands of men took to guerrilla warfare in the countryside. Many in western Europe sympathized with the uprising, and some, including Giuseppe Garibaldi's son Menotti, volunteered to fight alongside the Poles. By April, the rebellion had spread eastward into Lithuania and Russia. As both sides competed to gain the support of the peasantry, the implementation of the tsar's emancipation decree became caught up in

THE DISTURBANCES AT WARSAW : SCENE OF SLAUGHTER BEFORE THE VICEREGAL CASTLE, ON MONDAY, THE 8TH OF APRIL.

POLISH NATIONALISM AND THE RUSSIAN EMPIRE. This image of Russian troops in Warsaw after the declaration of martial law in 1861 shows unrest in Russia's Polish territories before the rebellion in 1863, which, sparked by conscription of Poles into the Russian army, spread rapidly to the countryside. Russian government's harsh repression of the rebels led to the development of Polish nationalism in the region.

The Abolition of Serfdom in Russia

The abolition of serfdom was central to Tsar Alexander II's program of modernization and reform after the Crimean War. Emancipated serfs were now allowed to own land, ending centuries of bondage. The decree, however, emphasized the tsar's benevolence and the nobility's generosity—not peasant rights. The government did not want emancipation to bring revolution to the countryside and sought to reinforce the state's authority, the landowners' power, and the peasants' obligations. After spelling out the detailed provisions for emancipation, the decree added the paragraphs reprinted here.

Emancipation did not solve problems in the Russian countryside. On the contrary, it unleashed a torrent of protest, including complaints from peasants that nobles were undermining attempts at reform. The petitions in the second selection detail the struggles of the peasants in two villages in the wake of emancipation.

Tsar Alexander II's Decree Emancipating the Serfs, 1861

And We place Our hope in the good sense of Our people.

When word of the Government's plan to abolish the law of bondage [serfdom] reached peasants unprepared for it, there arose a partial misunderstanding. Some [peasants] thought about freedom and forgot about obligations. But the general good sense [of the people] was not disturbed in the conviction that anyone freely enjoying the goods of society correspondingly owes it to the common good to fulfill certain obligations, [a conviction held] both by natural reason and by Christian law, according to which "every soul must be subject to the governing authorities." . . . Rights legally acquired by the landlords cannot be taken from them without a decent return or [their] voluntary concession; and that it would be contrary to all justice to make use of the lords' land without bearing the corresponding obligation.

And now We hopefully expect that the bonded people, as a new future opens before them, will understand and accept with gratitude the important sacrifice made by the Well-born Nobility for the improvement of their lives.

Source: James Cracraft, ed., *Major Problems in the History of Imperial Russia* (Lexington, MA: 1994), pp. 340–44.

Emancipation: The View from Below

Petition from Peasants in Podosinovka (Voronezh Province) to Alexander II, May 1863

The most merciful manifesto of Your Imperial Majesty from 19 February 1861, with the published rules, put a limit to the enslavement of the people in blessed Russia. But some former serfowners—who desire not to improve the peasants' life, but to oppress and ruin them—apportion land contrary to the laws, choose the best land from all the fields for themselves, and give the poor peasants . . . the worst and least usable lands.

To this group of squires must be counted our own, Anna Mikhailovna Raevskaia. . . . Of our fields and resources, she chose the best places from amidst our strips, and, like a cooking ring in a hearth, carved off 300 dessiatines [measures of land] for herself. . . . But our community refused to accept so ruinous an allotment and requested that we be given an allotment in accordance with the local Statute. . . . The peace arbitrator . . . and the police chief . . . slandered us before the governor, alleging that we were rioting and that it is impossible for them to enter our village.

The provincial governor believed this lie and sent 1,200 soldiers of the penal command to our village. . . . Without any cause, our village priest Father Peter—rather than give an uplifting pastoral exhortation to stop the spilling of innocent blood—joined these reptiles, with the unanimous incitement of the authorities. . . . They summoned nine township heads and their aides from other townships. . . . In their presence, the provincial governor—without making any investigation and without interrogating a single person—ordered that the birch rods be brought and that the punishment commence, which was carried out with cruelty and mercilessness. They punished up to 200 men and women; 80 people were at four levels (with 500, 400, 300 and 200 blows); some received lesser punishment . . . and when the inhuman punishment of these innocent people had ended, the provincial governor said: "If you find the land unsuitable, I do not forbid you to file petitions wherever you please," and then left. . . .

We dare to implore you, Orthodox emperor and our merciful father, not to reject the petition of a community with 600 souls, including wives and children. Order with your tsarist word that our community be allotted land . . . as the law dictates without selecting the best sections of fields and meadows, but in straight lines. . . . [Order that] the meadows and haylands along the river Elan be left to our community without any restriction; these will enable us to feed our cattle and smaller livestock, which are necessary for our existence.

Petition from Peasants in Balashov District to Grand Duke Constantin Nikolaevich, January 25, 1862

Your Imperial Excellency! Most gracious sire! Grand Duke Konstantin Nikolaevich! . . .

After being informed of the Imperial manifesto on the emancipation of peasants from serfdom on 1861 . . . we received this [news] with jubilation. . . . But from this moment, our squire ordered that the land be cut off from the entire township. But this is absolutely intolerable for us: it not only denies us profit, but threatens us with a catastrophic future. He began to hold repeated meetings and [tried to] force us to sign that we agreed to accept the above land allotment. But, upon seeing so unexpected a change, and bearing in mind the gracious manifesto, we refused. . . . After assembling the entire township, they tried to force us into making illegal signatures accepting the land cut-offs. But when they saw that this did not succeed, they had a company of soldiers sent in. . . . Then [Colonel] Globbe came from their midst, threatened us with exile to Siberia, and ordered the soldiers to strip the peasants and to punish seven people by flogging in the most inhuman manner. They still have not regained consciousness.

Source: Gregory L. Freeze, ed., *From Supplication to Revolution: A Documentary Social History of Imperial Russia* (New York: 1988), pp. 170–73.

Questions for Analysis

1. What did Tsar Alexander II fear most in liberating the serfs from bondage? What provisions did he make to ensure that the emancipation would not destabilize his regime?

2. What issues mattered most to the peasants? What is their attitude toward the tsar?

3. Why did the tsar feel that emancipating the serfs was necessary, given the immediate danger to social peace?

THE EMANCIPATION OF THE SERFS. This engraving depicts officials delivering the formal decree liberating the serfs, a massive reform granting legal rights to millions of people. The emancipation, however, was undermined by the payments serfs owed to their former owners.

the former Silk Road in Central Asia, and expanded into Siberia in search of natural resources. Russian diplomacy also wrung various commercial concessions from the Chinese that led to the founding of the Siberian city of Vladivostok in 1860. Competition with the British, who were active in Afghanistan, led the Russians to annex Tashkent, capital of present-day Uzbekistan, in 1865. The racial, ethnic, and religious differences made governing these territories a daunting task, and in most cases, the Russian state did not try to assimilate the populations of the new territories. This acceptance of ethnic particularity was a pragmatic response to the difficulties of governing heterogeneous populations; and when the state did attempt to impose Russian culture, the results were disastrous. Whether power was wielded by the nineteenth-century tsars or, later, by the Soviet Union, powerful centrifugal forces pulled against genuine unification. Expansion helped Russia create a vast empire that was geographically of one piece but by no means one nation.

the struggle. Eventually, the Russian military prevailed; the leaders were caught and executed in 1864 and thousands of Poles were sent into permanent exile in Siberia. The violence of the Russian government's repression of the January Rising had an unintended consequence: the tradition of **Polish nationalism**, long associated with elite culture and the gentry, now took firm root among Polish-speaking peasants as well.

Elsewhere in Russia, the emancipation of the serfs produced only limited change in the short run. Russian government granted legal rights to some 22 million serfs and authorized a title to a portion of the land they had worked. It also required the state to compensate landowners for the properties they relinquished. Large-scale landowners vastly inflated their compensation claims, however, and managed to retain much of the most profitable acreage for themselves. As a result, the land granted to peasants was often of poor quality and insufficient to sustain themselves and their families. Moreover, the newly liberated serfs had to pay in installments for their land, which was not granted to them individually but rather to a village commune, which collected their payments. As a result, the pattern of rural life in Russia did not change drastically, as the system of payment kept peasants in the villages—not as freehold farmers but as agricultural laborers for their former masters.

While the Russian state undertook reforms, it also expanded its territory to the east and south. Russia invaded and conquered several independent Islamic kingdoms along

Territory and the Nation: The United States

The American Revolution had bequeathed to the United States a loose union of slave and free states, tied together in part by a commitment to territorial expansion. The so-called Jeffersonian Revolution combined democratic aspirations with a drive to expand the nation's boundaries. Leaders of the movement, under the Democratic-Republican president Thomas Jefferson (1801–1809), campaigned to add the Bill of Rights to the Constitution and were almost exclusively responsible for its success. Though they supported, in principle, the separation of powers, they believed in the supremacy of the people's representatives and viewed with alarm attempts by the executive and judicial branches to increase their power. They supported a political system based on an aristocracy of "virtue and talent," in which respect for personal liberty would be the guiding principle. They opposed the establishment of a national religion and special privilege, whether of birth or wealth. Yet the Jeffersonian vision of the republic rested on the independence of yeoman farmers, and the independence and prosperity of those farmers depended on the availability of new lands. This made territorial expansion, as exemplified by the Louisiana Purchase in 1803, central to Jeffersonian America. But expansion brought complications. It provided land for many yeoman farmers in the north and south but also added millions of acres of prime cotton land, thus extending the empire of slavery. Furthermore, the port of New Orleans, included in the Louisiana Purchase, made lands in the south well worth developing but led the American republic to remove forcibly Native Americans from the Old South west of the Mississippi River. This process of expansion and expropriation stretched from Jefferson's administration through the age of Jackson, into the 1840s.

Under Andrew Jackson (1829–1837), the Democrats, as some of the Democratic-Republicans were now called, transformed the circumscribed liberalism of the Jeffersonians. They campaigned to extend the suffrage to all white males, argued that all officeholders should be elected rather than appointed, and sought the frequent rotation of men in positions of political power (a doctrine that permitted politicians to use patronage to build national political parties). Moreover, the Jacksonian vision of democracy and nationhood carried over into a crusade to incorporate more territories into the republic. It was the United States' "Manifest Destiny," wrote a New York editor, "to overspread the continent allotted by Providence for the free development of our yearly multiplying millions." That "overspreading" brought Oregon and Washington into the Union through a compromise with the British, and brought Arizona, Texas, New Mexico, Utah, Nevada, and California through war with Mexico—all of which led to the wholesale expropriation of Native American lands. Territorial expansion was key to nation building, but it was built on increasingly intolerable conflict over slavery.

AMERICAN EXPANSION IN THE EARLY NINETEENTH CENTURY. ▪ *Which three European powers had a substantial role in American expansion?* ▪ *What events enabled the United States to acquire all the lands west of the Mississippi River?* ▪ *How did the loss of these lands affect European powers?*

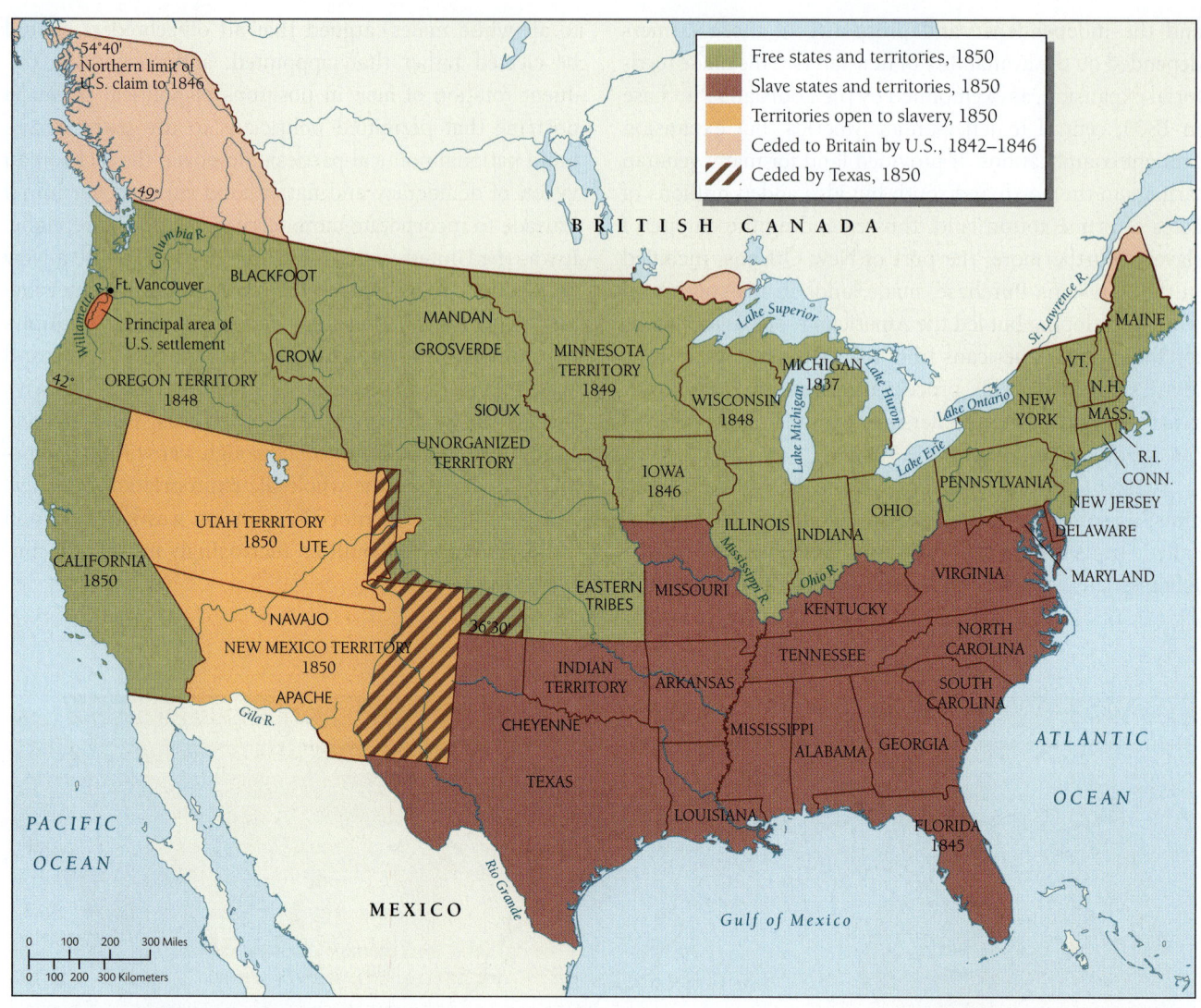

AMERICAN EXPANSION IN THE LATE NINETEENTH CENTURY. Note the stages of American settlement across the North American continent, and the dates for the extension of slavery into new territories. ■ *How did the question of slavery shape the way the new territories were absorbed into the republic?* ■ *Compare American expansion with European colonialism in terms of military conquest, violent displacement of native peoples and their culture, absorption of territory into new states, and use of unfree labor. What are the long-term consequences of this European history on the development of political institutions in the United States?*

The American Civil War, 1861–1865

The politics of slavery already had led to its abolition in France and Britain (Chapter 20), but in the United States, the combination of a growing abolitionist movement, a slave-owning class that feared the economic power of the north, and territorial expansion created deadlock and crisis. As the country expanded west, the North and South engaged in a protracted tug of war over whether the new states should be "free" or "slave." In the North, territorial expansion heightened calls for free labor; in the South, it deepened whites' commitment to an economy and society

based on plantation slavery. Ultimately, the changes pushed southern political leaders toward secession, and the failure of a series of elaborate compromises led to the outbreak of the Civil War in 1861.

This protracted and costly struggle proved a first experience of the horrors of modern war and prefigured the First World War. It also decisively transformed the nation. First, it abolished slavery. Second, it established the pre-eminence of the national government over states' rights. (The Fourteenth Amendment to the Constitution states specifically that all Americans are citizens of the United States and not of an individual state or territory. And by

CIVIL WAR RECRUITING POSTER. This poster, created by northern African American abolitionists, exhorts fellow blacks to fight in the American Civil War.

their European counterparts and gave the United States new power in world politics. These developments were all part of the process of nation building, but they did not overcome deep racial, regional, or class divides. Though the war brought the South back into the Union, the rise of northern capitalism exacerbated the backwardness of the South as an underdeveloped agricultural region whose wealth was extracted by northern industrialists. And the railroad corporations, which pieced together the national infrastructure, became the classic foe of labor and agrarian reformers. In these ways, the Civil War laid the foundations for the modern American nation-state.

"EASTERN QUESTIONS": INTERNATIONAL RELATIONS AND THE DECLINE OF OTTOMAN POWER

During the nineteenth century, questions of national identity and international power were inextricable from contests over territory. War and diplomacy drew and redrew boundaries as European nations groped toward a sustainable balance of power. The rise of new powers, principally the German Empire, posed one set of challenges to continental order; and the waning power of older regimes posed another. The **Crimean War**, which lasted from 1853 to 1856, was a particularly gruesome attempt to cope with the most serious of such collapses: the decline of the Ottoman Empire. As the Ottoman Empire lost its grip on its provinces in southeastern Europe, the "Eastern Question" of who would benefit from Ottoman weakness drew Europe into war. At stake were not only territorial gains but also strategic interests, alliances, and the balance of power in Europe. And though the war occurred before the unification of the German and Italian states, it structured the system of Great Power politics that guided Europe until—and indeed toward—the First World War.

The Crimean War, 1853–1856

The root causes of the Crimean War lay in the Eastern Question and the decline of the Ottoman Empire. The crisis that provoked it, however, involved religion—namely, French and Russian claims to protect religious minorities and the holy places of Jerusalem within the Muslim Ottoman Empire. In 1853, a three-way quarrel among France (on behalf of Roman Catholics), Russia (representing

declaring that no citizen is to be deprived of life, liberty, or property without due process of law, it establishes that "due process" is to be defined by the national, not the state or territorial, government.) Third, in the aftermath of the Civil War, the U.S. economy expanded with stunning rapidity. In 1865, there were 35,000 miles of railroad track in the United States; by 1900, there were almost 200,000. Industrial and agricultural production rose, putting the United States in a position to compete with Great Britain. As we will see later, American industrialists, bankers, and retailers introduced innovations in assembly-line manufacturing, corporate organization, and advertising that startled

Eastern Orthodox Christians), and Turkey devolved into a Russian confrontation with the Turkish sultan. Russians moved troops into the Ottoman-governed territories of Moldavia and Walachia (see the map below), confident that Turkey would be unable to resist, concerned that other powers might take advantage of Turkish weakness, and persuaded (mistakenly) that they had British support. And Turkey, also persuaded that it would be supported by the British, declared war on Russia in October 1853. The war was a disaster for the Turks, who lost their fleet at the battle of Sinope in November. But Russia's success alarmed the British and the French, who considered Russian expansion a threat to their interests in the Balkans, the eastern Mediterranean, and, for the British, the route to India. Determined to check that expansion, France and Britain each declared war on Russia in March 1854, and moved to support the Ottoman Empire. This alliance among Britain,

France, and the Muslim Ottomans was not unprecedented. The absolutist monarch of France, François I, had formed an alliance with the Ottomans in 1536 to check the power of the Habsburg Empire in the Balkans and the eastern Mediterranean; and in its broad outlines, this alliance lasted until Napoleon's invasion of Egypt in 1798. The British and French decision to defend the Ottomans against Russia was part of a long tradition of including the Ottoman Empire in their calculations of the balance of power in Europe.

In September, French and British forces landed on the Russian peninsula of Crimea and headed toward the Russian naval base at Sevastopol, to which they laid siege. France, Britain, and the Ottomans were joined in 1855 by the small but ambitious Italian state of Piedmont-Sardinia. This was the closest Europe had come to a general war since 1815.

THE CRIMEAN WAR. Note the theater of operations and the major assaults of the Crimean War. ▪ *Which empires and nations were in a position to take advantage of Ottoman weakness?* ▪ *Who benefited from the outcome of the war, and who was most harmed?* ▪ *In what ways was the Crimean War the first modern war?*

The war was relatively short, but its conduct was devastating. Conditions on the Crimean peninsula were dire, and the disastrous mismanagement of supplies and hygiene by the British and French led to epidemics among the troops; at least as many soldiers died from typhus or cholera as in combat. The fighting was bitter, marked by such notoriously inept episodes as the British "charge of the Light Brigade," in which a British cavalry unit was slaughtered by a mass of Russian artillery. Vast battles pitted tens of thousands of British and French troops against Russian formations in combats that were often settled with bayonets. Despite the disciplined toughness of the British and French troops, and their nations' dominance of the seas around Crimea, the Russians denied them a clear victory. Sevastopol, under siege for nearly a year, did not fall until September 1855; and the bitter, unsatisfying conflict was ended by a treaty in 1856.

For the French and Sardinians, the bravery of their soldiers bolstered positive national sentiment at home; for the British and Russians, however, the poorly managed war provoked waves of intense criticism. As far as international relations were concerned, the peace settlement dealt a blow to Russia, which had its influence in the Balkans drastically curbed. Austria's refusal to come to the aid of Russia cost Russia the support of its powerful former ally. The Crimean War embarrassed the British and left Russia and Austria considerably weaker, opening an advantage for Bismarck in the 1860s, as we saw earlier.

The Crimean War was important in other ways as well. Though fought largely with the same methods and mentalities employed in the Napoleonic Wars forty years earlier, the war brought innovations that forecast the direction of modern warfare. It saw the first significant use of rifled muskets, underwater mines, and trench warfare, as well as the first tactical use of railroads and telegraphs.

In addition, the war was covered by the first modern war correspondents and photojournalists, making it the most public war to date. Reports from the theater of war were sent "live" by telegraph to Britain and France with objective and sobering detail. The (London) *Times* reporter William Howard Russell, for instance, heaped criticism on the government for the deplorable conditions British soldiers endured. The care and supply of the troops became national scandals in the popular press, prompting dramatic changes in the military's administrative and logistical systems, and making heroes of individual doctors and nurses such as Florence Nightingale. The British government and commercial publishers sent photographers to document the war's progress, and perhaps also to counter charges that troops were undersupplied and malnourished. Roger Fenton, the most prominent and prolific of these war

CAPTAIN DAMES OF THE ROYAL ARTILLERY, BY ROGER FENTON (1855). Roger Fenton studied painting in London and then Paris, where he learned about and started to experiment with photography. He developed a mobile darkroom and ventured into the English countryside. In 1855, he went to Crimea, subsidized by the British government. Photographs of movement and troops in battle were still impossible, and political restraint kept him from photographing the horrors of the increasingly unpopular Crimean War; but still, his were the first war photographs.

photographers, employed the new medium to capture the grim realities of camp life. Technological limitations and political considerations kept him from photographing the more gruesome carnage of the battlefield, but Fenton's photographs introduced a new level of realism and immediacy to the public's conception of war.

CONCLUSION

The decades between 1848 and 1870 brought intense nation building in Europe and North America. The unification of Germany and Italy changed the map of Europe, with important consequences for the balance of power. The expansion of the Russian Empire and the emergence of the United States as a major power also had international ramifications. For old as well as new nation-states, economic development and political transformation—often on a very large scale—were important means of increasing and securing the state's power.

Prior to 1848, liberalism and nationalism had been closely linked. For many Europeans they had been nearly synonymous, just different ways of expressing similar ideas about the rights of different peoples to live under governments they had chosen for themselves. The liberal revolutionaries of 1848, however, did not achieve their goal of more representative government, and the states that defeated them found ways to tailor nationalism to their own ends. After 1848, nationalism proved to be a powerful force for rallying people in support of conservative governments as well as liberal ones. This new development revealed nationalism's power to exacerbate conflicts between states and the various peoples assembled within their borders. And the abolition of privilege and land reform still had to be reckoned with, as did the systems of slavery and serfdom.

After You Read This Chapter

 Go to **INQUIZITIVE** to see what you've learned—and learn what you've missed—with personalized feedback along the way.

REVIEWING THE OBJECTIVES

- Revolutions broke out in 1848 in almost every capital of Europe, except London and St. Petersburg. What accounted for this wave of simultaneous revolutionary movements?

- Liberal revolutionaries in France in 1848 did not have the same goals as their socialist allies. What were their goals, and why did they fail to achieve them?

- Liberal revolutionaries in the German-speaking lands of central Europe in 1848 were forced to reckon with Austrian and Prussian states in their bid for national unification. What did they want, and why did they fail?

- Nationalists in both Germany and Italy were divided between those who supported the creation of a new nation from below, through popular movements, and those who preferred it from above. How did these divisions work themselves out in the process of national unification?

- Creating a modern nation in Russia entailed the end of serfdom, whereas in the United States, political leaders from the North and South debated on the place of slavery in the modern nation-state. In what ways were national debates about citizenship in these countries shaped by their widespread practices of bondage?

- The three major European wars in this period were of relatively short duration, but they had profound effects on the international balance of power in Europe. Which countries emerged stronger from these conflicts? Which found their interests most damaged?

Trailing the banner of nationhood was an explosive set of questions about how to balance the power and interests of minorities and majorities, the wealthy and poor, and the powerful and the dispossessed. Nation building not only changed states, it also transformed relations between states and their citizens.

The result of these many tensions was an age that seemed a contradictory mix of the old and the new: monarchies were beset with debates about nationality and citizenship, land-owning aristocratic elites were rubbing elbows with newly wealthy industrialists, and artisan handworkers were meeting up with factory laborers in workers' associations, where debates about the proper path toward realizing socialist goals were held. Remarkably, this period of intense nation building on the Continent ushered in an era of unprecedented capitalist and imperial expansion (see Chapters 22 and 23). The antagonisms unleashed by German unification and the crumbling of the Ottoman Empire would reemerge, however, in the Great Power politics that precipitated the First World War.

PEOPLE, IDEAS, AND EVENTS IN CONTEXT

- What circumstances led to the downfall of **LOUIS PHILIPPE**'s government in France? What divisions between supporters of the revolution led to the **JUNE DAYS** in Paris in 1848?
- What role did the *ZOLLVEREIN* and the **FRANKFURT ASSEMBLY** play in the creation of a unified Germany?
- How and why did **OTTO VON BISMARCK** aim for a policy of German national unification during his time in office?
- How did **GIUSEPPE GARIBALDI** and **COUNT CAMILLO BENSO DI CAVOUR** initially see the process of Italian unification? Whose vision came closest to reality?
- Who was **NAPOLEON III**? How did his policies contribute to nation building in France?
- What was the contribution of **JOHN STUART MILL** to the debates about citizenship in Britain?
- Why were nationalist movements such as **PAN-SLAVISM** or **MAGYAR NATIONALISM** a danger to the Austro-Hungarian Empire?
- What was the **JANUARY RISING OF 1863**? How did **POLISH NATIONALISM** evolve after 1848?
- Why did **TSAR ALEXANDER II** decide to **EMANCIPATE THE SERFS**?
- What made the **CRIMEAN WAR** different from previous conflicts and more like the wars of the twentieth century?

THINKING ABOUT CONNECTIONS

- Revolutionaries in 1848—whether in Paris, Rome, Berlin, or Vienna—must have been aware of the connections between their struggles and the historical example of the French Revolution of 1789–1799. Did they have goals at the end of the eighteenth century that were similar to the goals of the French revolutionaries?
- How might the failure of the 1848 revolutions have shaped the beliefs of European conservatives and liberals, or the beliefs of supporters of more radical ideologies such as republicanism and socialism?

Before You Read This Chapter

Imperialism and Colonialism, 1870–1914

CORE OBJECTIVES

- **DEFINE** *imperialism* and locate the major colonies established by European powers in Africa and Asia in the nineteenth century.

- **UNDERSTAND** the major reasons for European colonial expansion in the nineteenth century.

- **DESCRIBE** the choices confronting colonized peoples in the face of European power.

- **EXPLAIN** how imperialism shaped the culture of European nations at home.

- **UNDERSTAND** the nature of the crisis faced by European imperial powers at the end of the nineteenth century.

I n 1869, the Suez Canal opened with a grand celebration. The imperial yacht *Eagle,* with Empress Eugénie of France on board, entered the canal on November 17, followed by sixty-eight steamships carrying the emperor of Austria, the crown prince of Prussia, the grand duke of Russia, and scores of other dignitaries. Flowery speeches flowed freely, as did the champagne. The ceremony cost a staggering £1.3 million (about $156 million today). Even so, the size of the celebration paled in comparison to the canal itself. The largest project of its kind, the canal sliced through a hundred miles of Egyptian desert to link the Mediterranean Sea to the Red Sea, cutting the trip from London to Bombay in half. The canal dramatically showcased the abilities of Western power and technology to transform the globe, but the human cost was high: 30,000 Egyptians worked on the canal as forced laborers, and thousands died during cholera epidemics in the work camps.

The building of the canal was the result of decades of European involvement in Egypt. French troops under Napoleon led the way, but Britain's bankers soon followed. European financial interests developed a close relationship with those who governed Egypt as a semi-independent state inside the Ottoman Empire.

THE INAUGURATION OF THE SUEZ CANAL. This allegory illustrates the union of the Mediterranean Sea and the Red Sea, attended by Ismail Pasha, the khedive (viceroy) of Egypt; Abdul Aziz, the sultan of the Ottoman Empire; Ferdinand de Lesseps, the president of the Suez Canal Company; Empress Eugénie of France; and several mermaids. It also represents the nineteenth-century vision of imperialism as a bearer of global progress, promoting technological advancement and breaking down barriers between Europe and the peoples of the Middle East, Africa, and Asia. ▪ *Who was the audience for this image?*

By 1875, the British controlled the canal, after purchasing 44 percent of the canal's shares from the Egyptian khedive (viceroy) when he was threatened with bankruptcy. By the late 1870s, these economic and political relationships had produced debt and instability in Egypt. In 1882, in a bid for national independence, a group of Egyptian army officers led by 'Urabi Pasha took control of Egypt's government.

The British government, determined to protect its investments, decided to intervene. The Royal Navy shelled Egyptian forts along the canal into rubble, and a British task force landed near 'Urabi Pasha's central base, overwhelming the Egyptian lines. This striking success rallied popular support at home, and its political outcomes lasted for seventy years. Britain took effective control of Egypt, and a British lord, Evelyn Baring, assumed the role of proconsul in a power-sharing relationship with Egyptian authorities—but the real power rested with Britain. Britain demanded the repayment of loans and regulated the trade in Egyptian cotton, which helped supply Britain's textile mills. Most important, the intervention secured the route to India and the markets of the East.

The Suez Canal and the conquest of Egypt were made possible by the convergence of technology, money, politics, and a global strategy of imperial control. A similar interplay between economics and colonialism produced the stunning expansion of European empires in the late nineteenth century. The years 1870 to 1914 brought both rapid industrialization throughout the West and an intense push to expand the influence of Western power abroad.

The "new imperialism" of the late nineteenth century was distinguished by its scope, intensity, and long-range consequences. It transformed cultures and states in Europe, Africa, and Asia. Projects such as the Suez Canal changed, literally, the landscape and the map of the world. They also embodied an ideology: the belief in technology and Western superiority. In the minds of imperialists, the elimination of geographic barriers had opened the entire world—its lands and its peoples—to the administrative power of the West.

The new imperialism, however, was not a one-way street. Europeans could not simply conquer vast territories and dictate their terms to the rest of the world. The new political and economic relationships between colonies and dependent states on one side, and the "metropole" (the colonizing power) on the other, ran both ways, bringing changes to both parties. The new imperialism was an expression of European strength, but it was also profoundly destabilizing, because fierce competition among nations upset the balance of power.

IMPERIALISM

Imperialism (or colonialism) is the process of extending one state's control over a new territory and incorporating its population into a larger political body—an empire—that continues to perceive this new population as different and dependent. Under *formal imperialism* in the nineteenth century, sometimes the control was exercised by *direct rule*, with the colonizing nation annexing territories outright and subjugating the peoples who live there; or it worked through *indirect rule*, by which conquering European nations reached agreements with local leaders and governed through them. In other situations, *informal imperialism* could be a less visible exercise of state power, whereby stronger states allowed weaker states to maintain their independence while reducing their sovereignty; it took the form of carving out zones of European sovereignty and privilege within other states, such as treaty ports.

Both formal and informal imperialism expanded dramatically in the nineteenth century. The "scramble for Africa" was the most startling case of formal imperialism: from 1875 to 1902, Europeans seized up to 90 percent of the continent. The overall picture is no less remarkable: between 1870 and 1900, a small group of states (France, Britain, Germany, the Netherlands, Russia, and the United States) colonized about one quarter of the world's land surface. In addition, these same states extended informal empires into China and Turkey, across South and East Asia, and into Central and South America. So striking was this expansion of European power that contemporaries spoke of the "new imperialism." Nevertheless, imperialism was not new; it is more helpful to think of these nineteenth-century developments as a new stage of European empire building, after the collapse of Europe's early modern empires in North and South America at the end of the eighteenth century.

The nineteenth-century empires developed against the backdrop of industrialization, liberal revolution, and the rise of nation-states. Industrialization produced greater demand for raw materials from distant locations. And many Europeans became convinced that their economic development, science, and technology would bring progress to the rest of the world. A problem arose, however, from the fact that European governments relied on the consent of the governed, especially in Britain and France. Liberal ideas such as civic equality made conquest difficult to justify, and raised questions about the status of colonized peoples. Earlier European conquerors had claimed a missionary zeal, and used converting indigenous peoples to Christianity as justification for their actions. Nineteenth-century imperialists justified their projects by claiming that their investments in infrastructure—railroads, harbors, and roads—and social reforms would bring civilization to the rest of the world. This vision of the "white man's burden," the title of a poem by Rudyard Kipling, became a powerful argument in favor of imperial expansion throughout Europe (see **Competing Viewpoints** on page 742).

In spite of these grand goals, the resistance of colonized peoples did as much to shape the history of colonialism as did the ambitious plans of the colonizers. The Haitian revolution of 1804 compelled the British and the French to end slavery and the slave trade in their colonies in the 1830s and the 1840s. The American Revolution encouraged the British to grant self-government to white settler states in Canada (1867), Australia (1901), and New Zealand (1912). Rebellion in India in 1857 caused the British to place the colony under the direct control of the Crown, rather than the East India Company. In general, nineteenth-century imperialism involved less independent entrepreneurial activity by merchants and traders and more "settlement and discipline." This required legal distinctions on race or religion to organize relationships between Europeans and different indigenous groups, and an administration to enforce such distinctions. (Apartheid in South Africa is but one example.) Defending such empires thus became a vast project, involving legions of soldiers, government officials, schoolteachers, and engineers. Nineteenth-century imperialism produced new forms of government and management in the colonies; and as it did so, it forged new interactions between Europeans and indigenous peoples.

The New Imperialism and Its Causes

As early as 1902, the British author J. A. Hobson charged that the interests of a small group of wealthy financiers had driven the "scramble for Africa," with British taxpayers subsidizing armies of conquest and occupation, and journalists whipping up the public's enthusiasm for imperialism. Hobson, a reformer and a social critic, argued that international finance and business had distorted the conceptions of Britain's real national interests, and genuine democracy would curb the country's imperial policies.

Hobson's analysis inspired an influential Marxist critique of imperialism by Vladimir Ilyich Lenin. Like Hobson, Lenin believed that imperialism was best understood on economic grounds. Unlike Hobson, however, Lenin believed that imperialism was an integral part of late-nineteenth-century capitalism. With domestic markets saturated and growth limited by competition at home, capitalists were forced to search for and invest in new markets overseas, producing an ever more intensive pressure for the expansion of European imperialism. Lenin published *Imperialism: The Highest Stage of Capitalism* (1917) at the height of the First World War, and used this argument to assert that hopes for a democratic reform of capitalism were misplaced and that the only solution was the replacement of capitalism with a revolutionary new economic order.

Historians now see economic pressures as just one of the causes of imperialism. Only half of Britain's £4 billion in foreign investments was at work within its empire. In France, the proportion was even smaller, with only one fifth of French capital invested overseas; the French had more capital invested in their ally Russia than in all their colonial possessions. Nevertheless, Europeans expected the colonies to produce profits. French newspapers, for instance, reported that the Congo was "rich, vigorous, and fertile virgin territory" with "fabulous quantities" of gold, copper, ivory, and rubber. Such hopes contributed to expansionism, even if the profits did not meet expectations.

A second interpretation of imperialism emphasizes nationalist motives. International rivalries made European powers more determined to control less-developed nations and territories. French politicians hoped, for instance, that imperialism would restore the honor France had lost in its defeat by Prussia in 1870. The British looked with alarm at Germany's industrialization and feared losing their share of world markets. The Germans, recently unified into a modern nation-state, saw an overseas empire as the only way to become a great power.

This nationalist interpretation suggests a link between imperialism and nineteenth-century state and nation building. Colonies demonstrated military might, the vigor of a nation's economy, the strength of its citizens, the force of its law, and the power of its culture. A strong national community could assimilate others, bringing progress to new lands and new peoples. One German proponent of expansion called colonialism the "national continuation of the German desire for unity." Lobby groups such as the German Colonial Society, the French Colonial Party, and the Royal Colonial Institute in Britain argued for empire in similar terms; as did newspapers, which recognized the profits to be made in selling sensational stories of overseas conquests.

Finally, imperialism had important cultural dimensions. A French diplomat once described the British imperial adventurer Cecil Rhodes as a "force cast in an idea"; the same might be said of imperialism itself. The Scottish missionary David Livingston believed that the British conquest of Africa would end the East African slave trade and "introduce the Negro family into the body of corporate nations." Taking up arms against the slave trade, famine, disorder, and illiteracy seemed to many Europeans not only a reason to invade Africa but also a duty and proof of their somehow superior civilization. These convictions did not cause imperialism, but they illustrate how central empire building was to the West's self-image.

In short, it is difficult to disentangle the economic, political, and strategic causes of imperialism. In any case, it is more important to understand how all these motives overlap. Economic interests often helped convince policy makers that strategic interests were at stake. Different constituencies—the military, international financiers, missionaries, and colonial lobby groups at home—held different and often clashing visions about the purpose and benefits of imperialism. Imperial policy, therefore, was less a matter of long-range planning than a series of quick responses, often improvised, to particular situations. And, of course, Europeans were not the only players on the stage. Their goals and intentions were shaped by social changes in the countries in which they were involved; by the independent interests of local peoples; and by resistance, which, as often as not, Europeans found themselves unable to understand and powerless to stop.

EUROPEAN EMPIRES IN 1914. ▪ Where were Britain's major imperial interests? ▪ Which trade routes did Britain have the most incentive to protect? ▪ Where were France's most important imperial holdings? ▪ Who was France's major competitor? ▪ How substantial were German, Dutch, Portuguese, or U.S. colonies compared with British and French holdings?

Legend:

Britain	Netherlands	Ottoman	Russia
France	Belgium	Japan	Independent
Germany	Denmark		
Portugal	Italy		
Spain	United States		

2000 Miles
0   1000   2000 Kilometers

Rudyard Kipling and His Critics

Rudyard Kipling (1865–1936) remains one of the most famous propagandists of empire. His novels, short stories, and poems about the British imperial experience in India were defining texts for the cause in which he believed. Kipling's poems were—and continue to be—widely read, analyzed, attacked, and praised. His immediate goal was to influence American public opinion during the Spanish-American War, but he also wanted to celebrate the moral and religious values of European imperialism in general. Alfred Webb (1834–1908) was an Irish politician and Quaker who was critical of European colonial empires and sympathetic to nationalist movements that challenged them. He responded to Kipling's poem in the letter to The Nation *reproduced below.*

The White Man's Burden

Take up the White Man's burden—
    Send forth the best ye breed—
Go, bind your sons to exile
    To serve your captives' need;
To wait, in heavy harness,
    On fluttered folk and wild—
Your new-caught sullen peoples,
    Half devil and half child.

Take up the White Man's burden—
    In patience to abide,
To veil the threat of terror
    And check the show of pride;
By open speech and simple,
    An hundred times made plain,
To seek another's profit
    And work another's gain.

Take up the White Man's burden—
    The savage wars of peace—
Fill full the mouth of Famine,
    And bid the sickness cease;
And when your goal is nearest
    (The end for others sought)
Watch sloth and heathen folly
    Bring all your hope to nought.

Take up the White Man's burden—
    No iron rule of kings,
But toil of serf and sweeper—
    The tale of common things.
The ports ye shall not enter,
    The roads ye shall not tread,
Go, make them with your living
    And mark them with your dead.

Take up the White Man's burden,
    And reap his old reward—
The blame of those ye better
    The hate of those ye guard—
The cry of hosts ye humour
    (Ah, slowly!) toward the light:—
"Why brought ye us from bondage,
    Our loved Egyptian night?"
Take up the White Man's burden—
    Ye dare not stoop to less—
Nor call too loud on Freedom
    To cloak your weariness.
By all ye will or whisper,
    By all ye leave or do,
The silent sullen peoples
    Shall weigh your God and you.

Take up the White Man's burden!
    Have done with childish days—
The lightly-proffered laurel,
    The easy ungrudged praise:
Comes now, to search your manhood
    Through all the thankless years,
Cold, edged with dear-bought wisdom,
    The judgment of your peers.

Source: Rudyard Kipling, "The White Man's Burden," *McClure's Magazine* 12 (February 1899).

To the Editor of The Nation

Sir: The cable informs us that "Kipling's stirring verses, the 'Call to America,' have created a . . . profound impression" on your side. What that impression may be, we can only conjecture. There is something almost sickening in this "imperial" talk of assuming and bearing burdens for the good of others. They are never assumed or held where they are not found to be of material advantage or ministering to honor or glory. Wherever empire (I speak of the United Kingdom) is extended, and the climate suits the white man, the aborigines are, for the benefit of the white man, cleared off or held in degradation for his benefit. . . .

Taking India as a test, no one moves a foot in her government that is not well paid and pensioned at her cost. No appointments are more eagerly contended for than those in the Indian service. A young man is made for life when he secures one. The tone of that service is by no means one "bound to exile," "to serve . . . captives' need," "to wait in heavy harness," or in any degree as expressed in Mr. Kipling's highfalutin lines. It is entirely the contrary: "You are requested not to beat the servants" is a not uncommon notice in Indian hotels.

. . . So anxious are we, where good pay is concerned, to save Indians the heavy burden of enjoying them, that, while our sons can study and pass at home for Indian appointments, her sons must study and pass in England; and even in India itself whites are afforded chances closed to natives. . . .

There never was a fostered trade and revenue in more disastrous consequences to humanity than the opium trade and revenue. There never was a more grinding and debilitating tax than that on salt.

Source: Alfred Webb, "Mr. Kipling's Call to America," *The Nation* 68 (February 23, 1899).

Questions for Analysis

1. What benefits did Kipling think imperialism brought, and to whom?

2. What, exactly, was the "burden" according to Kipling?

3. What were Webb's arguments against Kipling? Why did he think that imperial talk was "almost sickening"? In British India, with its well-established civil service, did Webb think Europeans really suffered in their colonial outposts? Why did he mention the opium trade and the salt tax?

IMPERIALISM IN SOUTH ASIA

India was the center of the British Empire, the jewel of the British crown, secured well before the period of the new imperialism. The conquest of most of the subcontinent began in the 1750s and quickened during the age of revolution; and conquering India helped compensate for "losing" North America. By the mid-nineteenth century, India was the focal point of Britain's newly expanded global empire, which reached from southern Africa across South Asia and to Australia. Keeping this region involved changing tactics and forms of rule.

Until the mid-nineteenth century, British territories in India were under the control of the British **East India Company**. The company had its own military, divided into European and (far larger) Indian divisions, and held the right to collect taxes on land from Indian peasants. Until the early nineteenth century, the company had legal monopolies over trade in all goods, including indigo, textiles, salt, minerals, and—most lucrative of all—opium. Unlike North America, however, India never became a settler state. In the 1830s, Europeans were a tiny minority, numbering 45,000 in an Indian population of 150 million, but the company's rule was repressive and enforced by the military. Soldiers collected taxes, civil servants wore military uniforms, and British troops brashly commandeered peasants'

oxen and carts for their own purposes. Typically, though, the company could not enforce its rule uniformly. It governed some areas directly, others through alliances with local leaders, and still others by simply controlling goods and money. Indirect rule, here as in other empires, meant finding indigenous collaborators and maintaining their goodwill. Thus, the British cultivated groups that had provided administrators for earlier regimes: the Rajputs and Bhumihars of North India, whom they considered especially effective soldiers; and merchants of big cities, such as Calcutta (present-day Kolkata). The British offered economic privileges, state offices, or military posts to either groups or entire nations that agreed to ally with them against others.

British policy shifted between two poles: one group wanted to "westernize" India, while another group believed it safer and more practical to defer to local culture. Christian missionaries, whose numbers increased as the occupation expanded, were determined to replace "blind superstition" with the "genial influence of Christian light and truth." Indignant at such practices as child marriage and *sati* (in which a widow immolates herself on her husband's funeral pyre), missionaries sought support in England for a wide-ranging assault on Hindu culture. Secular reformers, many of them liberal, considered "Hindoos" and "Mahommedans" susceptible to forms of despotism—both in the family and in the state—and turned their reforming zeal to legal and

IMAGES OF WOMEN IN THE COLONIES. Photographs and engravings of women in Africa and Asia circulated widely in Europe during the nineteenth century, and these images shaped attitudes toward colonization. Many images—some openly pornographic—portrayed African or Asian women as attractive, exotic, and in postures that invited European fantasies of domination. "Reclining Jewess" (left) from French Algeria is a typical example of such imagery. Other images portrayed colonial women as victims of barbaric customs, such as *sati*, a social funeral practice in which a new widow burns herself during the cremation of her deceased husband (right). This image, which first appeared in a work by a missionary who had been to Calcutta, was widely reproduced later as an illustration of the need for the British to bring "civilization" to India. ■ *Could these images have the same impact without the emphasis on the subject's gender? Why or why not?*

political change. But other British administrators warned their countrymen not to meddle with Indian institutions; indirect rule, they argued, would work only with the cooperation of local powers. Conflicts such as these meant that the British never agreed on any single cultural policy.

From Mutiny to Rebellion

In 1857–1858, the East India Company's rule was badly shaken by a revolt of Indian soldiers in the British army. The Great Mutiny of 1857, also known as the **Sepoy Mutiny**, began near Delhi, when the military disciplined a regiment of *sepoys* (the traditional term for Indian soldiers employed by the British) for refusing to use rifle cartridges greased with animal fat—unacceptable to either Hindus or Muslims. Yet, as the British prime minister Benjamin Disraeli later observed, "The decline and fall of empires are not affairs of greased cartridges." The causes of the mutiny were deeper and involved social, economic, and political grievances. Indian peasants attacked law courts and burned tax rolls to protest debt and corruption. In areas that had recently been annexed, rebels defended their traditional leaders who had been ousted by the British. And army officers from privileged castes resented arbitrary treatment at the hands of the British; they were first promoted as loyal allies but then forced to serve without what they considered titles and honors. The

mutiny spread through large areas of northwest India, and European troops—who numbered fewer than one-fifth of those in arms—found themselves losing control. Religious leaders, both Hindu and Muslim, seized the occasion to denounce Christian missionaries sent in by the British and their assault on local traditions.

The fighting lasted for more than a year, and the British matched the rebels' early massacres with a systematic campaign of repression. Whole rebel units were killed rather than being allowed to surrender or were tried on the spot and executed. Towns and villages that supported the rebels were burned, just as the rebels had burned European homes and outposts. Yet the defeat of the rebellion caught the British public's imagination. After the bloody, inconclusive mess of Crimea, the terrifying threat to British India and the heroic rescue of European hostages and British territory by British troops were electrifying news. Pictures of the Scottish highland regiments (wearing wool kilts in the sweltering heat of India) liberating besieged white women and children went up in homes across the United Kingdom. British leaders were stunned by how close the revolt had brought them to disaster.

After the mutiny, the British were compelled to reorganize their Indian empire and develop new strategies of rule. The East India Company was abolished, replaced by the British Crown. The British *raj* (or rule) was now directly governed, although the British still sought out collaborators and cooperative interest groups. Princely India was left to the local rulers, who were subject to British advisers. The British reorganized the military and tried to change relations among soldiers; indigenous troops were separated from each other to avoid the kind of fraternization that had proved subversive. As one British officer put it, "If one regiment mutinies I should like to have the next so alien that it would fire into it." Even more than before, the British sought to rule through the Indian upper classes rather than in opposition to them. Queen Victoria, now empress of India, set out the principles of indirect rule: "We shall respect the rights, dignity and honour of native princes as our own, and we desire that they, as well as our own subjects, should enjoy that prosperity and that social advancement which can only be secured by internal peace and good government." Civil-service reform opened new positions to members of the Indian upper classes. The British also had to reconsider their relationship to Indian cultures. Missionary activity was no longer encouraged, and the British channeled their reforming impulses into the more secular projects of economic development, railways, roads, irrigation, and so on. Still, consensus on effective colonial strategies was lacking: some administrators counseled more reform, while others sought to support the princes. The British tried both policies, in fits and starts, until the end of British rule in 1947.

In India, the most prominent representative of the new imperialism was Lord Curzon, the viceroy of India from 1898 to 1905, who deepened British commitments to the region. Concerned about the British position in the world, he warned of the need to fortify India's borders against Russia, and urged continued economic investment. Curzon worried that the British would be worn down by resistance to the raj and that, confronted with their apparent inability to transform Indian culture, would become cynical and get "lethargic and think only of home." In the same way that Rudyard Kipling urged the British and the Americans to "take up the white man's burden" (see **Competing Viewpoints** on page 742), Curzon pleaded with his countrymen to realize how central India was to the greatness of Britain.

What did India do for Britain? By the eve of the First World War, India was Britain's largest export market. India mattered enormously to Britain's balance of payments; surpluses earned there compensated for the deficits in Europe and the United States. Equally important to Britain were the human resources of India. Indian laborers worked on tea plantations in Assam (near present-day Myanmar) and built railways and dams in southern Africa and Egypt. More than a million indentured Indian servants left their country during the second half of the century to work elsewhere in the empire. India also provided the British Empire with highly trained engineers, land surveyors, clerks, bureaucrats, schoolteachers, and merchants. The nationalist leader Mohandas Gandhi, for instance, first came into the public

THE EXECUTION OF INDIANS WHO PARTICIPATED IN THE REBELLION OF 1857. The British were determined to make an example of rebel Indian soldiers after the Great Mutiny. The engraving on the left shows executions in which the condemned were blown apart by cannons. The cartoon on the right, "The Execution of 'John Company,'" shows the same cannons destroying the British East India Company, which was abolished by the British government as a result of the rebellion. ▪ *What do these images tell us about the public awareness of the rebellion's violence and its suppression?*

KASHMIR
• Srinagar
PUNJAB
↖ Amritsar
1849
Lahore •
PUNJAB STATES
1815
KUMAON
Delhi •
1803
RAJPUTANA
NORTH WESTERN PROVINCES
OUDH (AWADH)
1801
1856
BIHAR
BENGAL
ASSAM
1826
MANIPUR
SIND
1843
1765
Dacca •
GUJARAT
• Ahmadabad
GWALIOR
BUNDELKHAND
• Calcutta
1818
1800, 1818
SAUGOR AND NARBADA
1854
1826
Baroda •
Bombay •
1818
1853
1853
NAGPUR
1802
ORISSA
LOWER BURMA
Poona •
PESHWAS TERRITORY
BERAR
HYDERABAD
NORTHERN CIRCARS
1765
1852
ARABIAN
SEA
KANARA
CEDED DISTRICTS
1799
1801
Bay of Bengal
1826
1799
TENASSERIM
MYSORE (to 1831)
• Madras
MALABAR
1792
1801
1792
SALIM
Cochin •
TRAVANCORE
CEYLON

Legend:
- ▮ Indian states bound to Britain by treaties
- ▮ Areas conquered and directly ruled by British
- ← British annexation, with dates

0   200   400 Miles
0   200   400 Kilometers

ASIA
Area of detail

BRITISH INDIA BEFORE AND AFTER 1857. Note the dates of British territorial annexations (above), and the complexity of colonial India's political boundaries (right) even after direct rule by the British crown had been established. ■ *According to the first map, what were the three ways the British gained control over various kingdoms and states in India before 1857?* ■ *What was the most important change in British rule before and after 1857?* ■ *How did the British hope to rule successfully over such a large and diverse group of people after 1857?*

AFGHANISTAN

NORTH-WEST FRONTIER PROVINCE

KASHMIR
• Srinagar

TIBET

BRITISH
BALUCHISTAN

PUNJAB

Amritsar
• • Lahore

BALUCHISTAN
AGENCY

RAJPUTANA
AGENCY

Delhi •

UNITED PROVINCES

NEPAL

SIKKIM

BHUTAN

SIND

BOMBAY

GWALIOR

CENTRAL INDIA AGENCY

BENGAL

EAST BENGAL
AND ASSAM

UPPER
BURMA

• Ahmadabad

CENTRAL
PROVINCES

• Dacca

PRESIDENCY

• Baroda

• Calcutta

Bombay •

• Poona

HYDERABAD

ORISSA

LOWER
BURMA

ARABIAN

SEA

GOA

MADRAS PRESIDENCY

MYSORE

Bay of
Bengal

ANDAMAN IS.

• Madras

TRAVANCORE

NICOBAR IS.

CEYLON

Native states and territories
British India
International boundary
Provincial boundary

ASIA

Area of
detail

0   200   400 Miles
0   200   400 Kilometers

Competing Viewpoints

Indians and Migration in the British Empire

Lord Georg Nathaniel Curzon (1859–1925) served as viceroy of India from 1898 to 1905, and foreign secretary from 1919 to 1924. A prominent Tory politician, he was a vocal supporter of the new imperialism. In this passage, he defends British imperial policy in India by enumerating the ways in which Indians serve the needs of the entire British empire, including in Africa and southeast Asia. Curzon was correct that the British needed Indian labor—by the end of the nineteenth century, British India was sending 425,000 Indian laborers abroad every year, many of them to other parts of the British empire in Africa and southeast Asia.

If you want to save your Colony of Natal from being over-run by a formidable enemy, you ask India for help, and she gives it; if you want to rescue the white men's legations from massacres at Peking, and the need is urgent, you request the Government of India to despatch an expedition, and they despatch it; if you are fighting the Mad Mullah in Somaliland, you soon discover that Indian troops and an Indian general are best qualified for the task, and you ask the Government of India to send them; if you desire to defend any of your extreme out-posts or coaling stations of the Empire, Aden, Mauritius, Singapore, Hong-Kong, even Tien-tsin or Shan-haikwan, it is to the Indian Army that you turn; if you want to build a railway to Uganda or in the Soudan, you apply for Indian labour. When the late Mr. Rhodes was engaged in developing your recent acquisition of Rhodesia, he came to me for assistance. It is with Indian coolie labor that you exploit the plantations equally of Demerara and Natal; with Indian trained officers that you irrigate and dam the Nile; with Indian forest officers that you tap the resources of Central Africa and Siam; with Indian surveyors that you explore all the hidden places of the earth. . . . [Moreover,] India is a country where there will be much larger openings for the investment of capital in the future than has hitherto been the case, and where a great work of industrial and commercial exploitation lies before us.

Source: Andrew Porter, ed., *The Oxford History of the British Empire*, vol. 3, *The Nineteenth Century* (Oxford: 1999), p. 403.

Henry Polak (1882–1959) migrated to the British colony of Natal, in southeastern Africa, from England in 1903. He became a friend of Mohandas Gandhi, then a lawyer practicing in South Africa. In this passage, Polak describes the treatment of Indian migrants in East London, a British colonial city on the Indian Ocean in Natal. He compares their status to that of the African peoples of the colony, using a word (Kaffir) that is now considered extremely derogatory and dehumanizing. In contemporary South Africa, the term is inflammatory, often simply referred to as "the K-word."

In [East London], municipal regulations were promulgated . . . by virtue whereof, British Indians, even though considerable merchants, registered voters, and large rate-payers, have been reduced to the status of the African aboriginal native. These regulations prohibit their using the side-walks in the public streets; being out in the streets after 8 p.m. without a pass; residing and carrying on their business, within certain limits of the municipal area, except upon securing a municipal certificate— literally a police pass . . . Whilst the East London Indians are thus legally and practically deprived of their full individual liberty, and placed below the level of their own Kaffir servants, they have, as masters and employers, to grant permits allowing freedom of movement in the town to these very servants, who are also otherwise protected and whose interests are safeguarded by special legislation. Many other petty insults are put upon them, such as not being allowed the use of the benches in the public parks, which benches are marked "for Europeans only"; the ferry boats on the Buffalo River are barred to them, except with considerable trouble and inconvenience; in the public markets British Indians are relegated with the Kaffirs, whilst the white people are granted separate stands; and in the public tram-cars, Indians are not allowed inside. As these are municipal regulations, the Cape Government, though sympathetic, can do nothing to procure relief.

Source: Henry Polak, *The Indians of South Africa* (Madras: Natesan, 1909), p. 86.

1. What benefits does Britain gain from British India, according to Curzon? Does he express an interest in what British Indians themselves might want? Are there any risks to the British policy of relying on colonial troops to keep the peace throughout their empire?

2. Curzon mentions Natal, the British colony in South Africa that Polak describes. What value do Indians contribute to the colony in Natal, according to Curzon?

3. What does Polaks's description of the situation faced by Indians in Natal reveal about the importance of race in the settler city of East London? What is the relationship between discrimination against British Indians and the treatment of African peoples in this colonial city, according to Polak? Does he appear to be equally concerned about discrimination against the local African population?

eye as a young lawyer in Pretoria, South Africa, where he worked for an Indian law firm. The British deployed Indian troops across the empire. (They would later call up roughly 1.2 million troops in the First World War.) For all these reasons, men such as Curzon found it impossible to imagine their empire, or even their nation, without India.

How did the British raj shape Indian society? The British practice of indirect rule sought to create an Indian elite that would serve British interests. As one British writer put it, a group "who may be the interpreters between us and the millions whom we govern—a class of persons Indian in colour and blood, but English in tastes, in opinion, in morals, and in intellect." Eventually, this practice created a class of British-educated Indian civil servants and businessmen, well trained for government but skeptical about British claims that they brought progress to the subcontinent. This group provided the leadership for the nationalist movement that challenged British rule in India; yet, at the same time, became increasingly distant from the rest of India. The overwhelming majority of Indians remained desperately poor peasants struggling to subsist on diminishing plots of land and, in many cases, in debt to British landlords. Meanwhile, villagers working in the textile trade were beaten down by imports of cheap manufactured goods from England.

IMPERIALISM IN CHINA

In China, too, European imperialism began early, well before the period of the new imperialism—but there, it took a different form. Europeans did not conquer and annex whole regions; instead, they forced favorable trade agreements at gunpoint, set up treaty ports where Europeans lived and worked under their own jurisdiction, and established outposts of European missionary activity. The Chinese spoke of their country as being "carved up like a melon."

European trade with China focused on luxuries such as silk, porcelain, art objects, and tea. The Chinese government, however, was determined to exclude foreign trade and influence. By the early nineteenth century, Britain's global ambitions and rising power were setting the stage for a confrontation. The British demanded open harbors and special trading privileges, and another source of constant friction involved the harsh treatment of British subjects by Chinese law courts—including the summary execution of several Britons convicted of crimes. By the 1830s, these diplomatic conflicts intensified due to the opium trade.

The Opium Trade

Opium provided direct links among Britain, British India, and China. In fact, opium (derived from the poppy plant) was one of the very few commodities that Europeans could sell in China. When the British conquered northeast India, they annexed one of the world's richest opium-growing areas, and thus became deeply involved in the trade—so much so that historians have called the East India Company's rule a "narco-military empire." British agencies designated specific poppy-growing regions and gave cash advances to Indian peasants who cultivated the crop. Producing opium was a labor-intensive process: peasant cultivators collected sap from the poppy seeds, then oth-

The Legacy of Colonialism

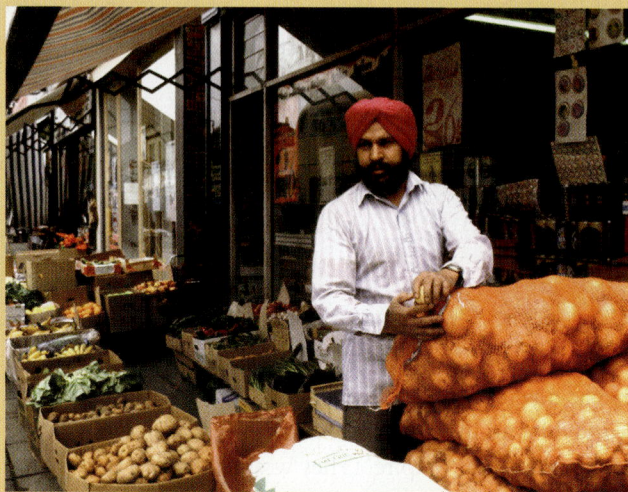

Decolonization during the 1950s and 1960s brought an end to the era of European imperialism (left), but the colonial past continues to shape the relations among European nations and former colonies elsewhere in the world. These links are reinforced by the large number of people from former colonies who now live in Europe; for example, in the diverse neighborhood of Southall, London (right).

 Watch related author interview on the Student Site

ers cleaned the sap and formed it into opium balls that were dried before being weighed and shipped out. In the opium-producing areas northwest of Calcutta, each "factory" employed as many as a thousand Indian workers.

The East India Company sold the opium to small fleets of British, Dutch, and Chinese shippers, who carried the drug from India to Southeast Asia and China. The company, in turn, used the silver it earned from the sale of opium to buy Chinese goods for the European market. The trade, therefore, was not only profitable, it was also a key to a triangular European-Indian-Chinese economic relationship. Production and export rose dramatically in the early nineteenth century, in spite of the Chinese emperor's attempts to discourage the trade. By the 1830s, when the British-Chinese confrontation was taking shape, opium provided British India with more revenues than any other source, except taxes on land.

People all over the world consumed opium, for medicinal reasons as well as for pleasure, but the Chinese market was especially lucrative. A large, wealthy Chinese elite of merchants and government officials made up much of the market, but opium smoking was also popular among soldiers, students, and Chinese laborers. In the nineteenth century, opium imports followed Chinese labor all over the world, from Southeast Asia to San Francisco. In 1799, in an effort to control the problem, the Chinese government banned opium imports and began a full-scale campaign to purge the drug from China. That campaign set the Chinese emperor on a collision course with British opium traders. In one confrontation, the Chinese drug commissioner Lin confiscated 3 million pounds of raw opium from the British and washed it out to sea. In other instances, the Chinese authorities blockaded British ships in port, and local citizens demonstrated angrily in front of British residences.

THE OPIUM WARS

In 1839, these simmering conflicts broke into what was called the first **Opium War**. The dispute over the drug trade highlighted larger issues of sovereignty and economic status.

AN OPIUM FACTORY IN PATNA, INDIA, c. 1851. In this drawing, balls of opium dry in a huge warehouse before being shipped to Calcutta for export to China and elsewhere.

THE OPIUM TRADE, 1880s. A European merchant examines opium. At first, European traders were forced to carry silver to China to pay for the luxury goods they wanted. But the discovery that they could sell this highly addictive narcotic in China allowed them to correct this trade imbalance and increase their profits.

The Europeans claimed the right to trade with whomever they pleased, bypassing Chinese monopolies; and they wished to set up zones of European residence in defiance of Chinese sovereignty, to proselytize, and to open schools. The Chinese government could not accept these challenges to its authority, and war flared up several times over the course of the century. After the first war of 1839–1842, in which British steam vessels and guns overpowered the Chinese fleet, the Treaty of Nanking (1842) compelled the Chinese to give the British trading privileges, the right to reside in five cities, and the port of Hong Kong "in perpetuity." After a second war, the British secured still more treaty ports and privileges, including the right to send missionaries.

In the aftermath of those agreements between the Chinese and the British, other countries demanded similar rights and economic opportunities. By the end of the nineteenth century, the French, Germans, and Russians all had claimed mining rights and permissions to build railroads, to begin manufacturing with cheap Chinese labor, and to arm and police European communities in Chinese cities; in Shanghai, for example, 17,000 foreign residents had their own courts, schools, churches, and utilities. The United States, not wanting to be shouldered aside, declared its own Open Door Policy (demanding that China trade with all countries on an equal basis). Japan was an equally active imperialist power in the Pacific, and the Sino-Japanese War of 1894–1895 was a decisive moment in the history of the region. The Japanese victory forced China to concede trading privileges, the independence of Korea, and the Liaotung Peninsula in Manchuria. It also led to a greater scramble for spheres of influence and more mining and railway concessions by China. Moreover, the demand for reparations forced the Chinese government to levy higher taxes on its peoples. All these measures heightened resentment and destabilized the regime.

BRITISH OPIUM TRADE. Note the way that the British trade in opium linked the economies of India, China, and Europe. ▪ *What were the major products involved in the trade among East Asia, South Asia, and Europe during this period?* ▪ *In what ways did the opium trade destabilize East Asia?* ▪ *What efforts did the Chinese government make to restrict the sale of opium?* ▪ *What was the response of European nations involved in this trade?*

Surrendering privileges to Europeans and the Japanese seriously undermined the authority of the Chinese Qing (*Ching*) emperor at home and heightened popular hostility to foreign intruders. Authority at the imperial center had been eroding for more than a century by 1900, hastened by the Opium Wars and the vast Taiping Rebellion (1852–1864), an enormous, bitter, and deadly conflict in which radical Christian rebels in south-central China challenged the authority of the emperors. On the defensive against the rebels, the dynasty hired foreign generals, including the British commander Charles Gordon, to lead its forces. The fight devastated China's agricultural heartland; and the death toll, never confirmed, may have reached 20 million. This ruinous conflict, together with the increasing inability of the emperor to keep order and collect the taxes necessary to repay foreign loans, led European countries to increase their direct control of the China trade.

The Boxer Rebellion

From a Western perspective, the most important of the nineteenth-century rebellions against the corruptions of foreign rule was the **Boxer Rebellion** of 1900. The Boxers were a secret society of young men trained in Chinese martial arts who believed they possessed spiritual powers. Antiforeign and antimissionary, they provided the spark for a loosely organized but widespread uprising that included a march on Beijing in the spring of 1900. They laid siege to the foreign legations in the city, home to several thousand Western diplomats and merchants and their families. The legations' small garrison defended their walled compound with little more than rifles, bayonets, and improvised artillery, but they withstood the siege for fifty-five days until a large relief column arrived. The rebellion, particularly the siege at Beijing, mobilized a global response. Europe's Great

IMPERIALISM IN SOUTH AND EAST ASIA, c. 1914. ■ Which imperial powers were most present in Asia? ■ Where were their primary zones of control and influence? ■ Why were European nations and the United States interested in establishing treaty ports in China? ■ How were the Chinese treaty ports different from the territorial conquests pursued by the British, French, and Dutch in their respective Asian colonies?

Legend:

British	French
Protected states in India	Portuguese
Dutch	Japanese
Ottoman Empire	United States
• Treaty ports in China	

Labels on map:

EUROPE

RUSSIAN EMPIRE

Lake Baikal

Lake Balkhash

ARAL SEA

CASPIAN SEA

BLACK SEA

MEDITERRANEAN SEA

Suez Canal

RED SEA

AFRICA

OTTOMAN EMPIRE

HEJAZ

NEJD

YEMEN

ADEN (Br.)

OMAN

KUWAIT (Br.)

BAHRAIN (Br.)

PERSIA

(Russian influence)

AFGHANISTAN (Br. influence)

ARABIAN SEA

MALDIVE IS. (Br.)

INDIAN OCEAN

INDIA

Bombay

Goa (Port.)

Mahé (Fr.)

Pondicherry (Fr.)

CEYLON (Br.)

Bay of Bengal

NEPAL

SIKKIM

BHUTAN

TIBET

OUTER MONGOLIA

INNER MONGOLIA

REPUBLIC OF CHINA

BURMA

SIAM

LAOS

TONKIN

CAMBODIA

COCHIN-CHINA

Guangzhou (Br.)

Macau (Port.)

Hong Kong (Br.)

Hangzhou (Japan)

Shanghai (Br., U.S., Fr.)

Tianjin (Belg., Italy, Fr., Russia, Ger., Br., Japan)

Port Arthur

Vladivostok

KOREA

JAPAN

Tokyo

SAKHALIN

KURIL ISLANDS (Jap.)

RYUKYU IS. (Jap.)

FORMOSA (Br.)

PHILIPPINES

PACIFIC OCEAN

FEDERATED MALAY STATES

Singapore (Br.)

BRUNEI

BR. NORTH BORNEO

DUTCH EAST INDIES

PORTUGUESE TIMOR

TIMOR

AUSTRALIA

2000 Miles

2000 Kilometers

1000

1000

0

0

AN AMERICAN CARICATURE OF THE BOXER REBELLION.
Uncle Sam to the obstreperous Boxer, "I occasionally do a little boxing myself."

Powers, rivals everywhere else in the world, drew together in response to this crisis to tear China apart. An expedition numbering 20,000 troops—combining the forces of Britain, France, the United States, Germany, Italy, Japan, and Russia—ferociously repressed the Boxer movement. The outside powers then demanded indemnities, new trading concessions, and reassurances from the Chinese government.

The Boxer Rebellion was one of several anti-imperialist movements at the end of the nineteenth century. The rebellion testified to the vulnerability of Europeans' imperial power, and dramatized the resources Europeans would have to devote to maintaining their far-flung influence. In the process of repression, the Europeans became committed to propping up corrupt and fragile governments to protect their agreements and interests, and they were drawn into putting down popular uprisings against local inequities and foreign rule.

In China, the age of the new imperialism capped a century of conflict and expansion. By 1900, virtually all of Asia had been divided up among the European powers; Japan, an active imperial power in its own right, maintained its independence. British rule extended from India across Burma, Malaya, Australia, and New Zealand; the Dutch, Britain's long-standing trade rivals, secured Indonesia; and Thailand remained independent. In the 1880s, however, the French moved into Indochina. Driven by competition with each other, European powers pressed for more influence in Asia, which, in turn, encouraged the development of nationalist feeling among local populations. Imperial expansion was beginning to show its destabilizing effects.

Russian Imperialism

Throughout the nineteenth century, Russia championed a policy of annexation—by conquest, treaty, or both—of lands bordering on the existing Russian state. Beginning in 1801, with the acquisition of Georgia after a war with Persia, the tsars continued to pursue their expansionist dream. Bessarabia and Turkestan (taken from the Turks) and Armenia (from the Persians) vastly increased the empire's size. This southward colonization brought large Muslim populations in Central Asia into the Russian Empire. It also brought the Russians close to war with the British twice: first in 1881, when Russian troops occupied territories in the trans-Caspian region; and again in 1884–1887, when the tsar's forces advanced to the frontier of Afghanistan. In both cases, the British feared incursions into areas they deemed within their sphere of influence in the Middle East, and were concerned about a possible threat to India. The maneuvering, spying, and support of friendly puppet governments by Russia and Britain became known as the "Great Game," and foreshadowed Western countries' jockeying for the region's oil resources in the twentieth century.

Russian expansion also moved east. In 1875, the Japanese traded the southern half of Sakhalin Island for the previously Russian Kurile Islands. The tsars' eastward advance finally halted in 1904, when Russian expansion in Mongolia and Manchuria came up against Japanese expansion. In the **Russo-Japanese War** of 1904, Russia's huge imperial army more than met its match. Russia's navy was sent halfway around the world to reinforce the beleaguered Russian troops but was ambushed and sunk by the better-trained and better-equipped Japanese fleet. This national humiliation helped provoke a revolt in Russia, and led to an American-brokered peace treaty in 1905 (see Chapter 23). The defeat shook the already unsteady regime of the tsar, and proved that European nations were not the only ones who could play the imperial game successfully.

THE FRENCH EMPIRE AND THE CIVILIZING MISSION

Like British expansion into India, French colonialism in northern Africa began before the new imperialism of the late nineteenth century. By the 1830s, the French had created a general government of their possessions in Algeria, the most important of which were cities along the Mediterranean coast. From the outset, the Algerian conquest was different from most other colonial ventures in that Algeria became a settler state, one of the few apart from

Russian Empire, 1795
Russian acquisitions, 1795–1855
Russian acquisitions, 1855–1914
Russian sphere of influence
Occupied by Russia

BUILDING THE RUSSIAN EMPIRE. ■ *In what directions did the Russian Empire primarily expand after 1795?* ■ *What drove Russian expansion?* ■ *Which areas were most contentious? Why?*

South Africa. Some of the early settlers were utopian socialists out to create ideal communities, some were workers the French government deported after the revolution of 1848 to be "resettled" safely as farmers, and some were winegrowers whose vines at home had been destroyed by an insect infestation. The settlers were by no means all French; they included Italian, Spanish, and Maltese merchants and shopkeepers of modest means, as well as laborers and peasants. By the 1870s, in several of the coastal cities, this new Creole community outnumbered indigenous Algerians; and within it, other Europeans outnumbered the French. With the French military's help, the settlers appropriated land, and French business concerns took cork forests and established mining works in copper, lead, and iron. Economic activity was for European benefit; the first railroads, for instance, did not even carry passengers but iron ore to the coast for export to France, where it would be smelted and sold.

The settlers and the French government did not necessarily pursue common goals. In the 1870s, in an effort to ensure the settlers' loyalty, the new and still-fragile Third Republic (founded after Napoleon III was defeated in 1870; see Chapter 21) made the colony a department of France, which gave the French settlers the full rights of republican citizenship. It also gave them the power to pass laws in Algeria that consolidated their privileges and community (naturalizing all Europeans, for instance), and further disenfranchised indigenous Muslim populations, who had no voting rights at all. French politicians in Paris occasionally objected to the settlers' contemptuous treatment of indigenous peoples, arguing that it subverted the project of "lifting up" the natives, but the French settlers in Algeria had little interest in such a project; although they paid lip service to republican ideals, they wanted the advantages of Frenchness for themselves. Colonial administrators and social scientists differentiated the "good" mountain-dwelling Berbers, whom they believed could be brought into French society, from the "bad" Arabs, whose religion made them supposedly unassimilable. France's divide and rule strategy, which treated European settlers, Arabs, Berbers, and Jews very differently, illustrates the contradictions of the "civilizing mission" in action.

THE ENTRY OF THE CRUSADERS INTO CONSTANTINOPLE, BY EUGÉNE DELACROIX (1840). The invasion of Algeria in 1830 became an occasion for thinking about Europe's long historical relationship with Muslim civilizations in Africa and the Middle East. Delacroix's work, painted while the conquest of Algeria was going on, portrays these civilizations as exotic and subservient, and glorifies the figures of conquering Christian armies. ■ *How might this long historical view have shaped European attitudes toward conquest in the nineteenth century?*

Before the 1870s, there was relatively little interest in colonial activities among the French at home. But after the humiliating defeat in the Franco-Prussian War (1870–1871) and the establishment of the Third Republic, colonial lobby groups and politicians became increasingly adamant about the benefits of colonialism, which were not simply economic. Taking on the **"civilizing mission"** would reinforce the international influence of the French republic and the prestige of the French people. Jules Ferry, a republican leader, successfully argued for expanding the French presence in Indochina, saying, "the superior races have a right vis-à-vis the inferior races . . . they have a right to civilize them."

Under Ferry, the French acquired Tunisia (1881), northern and central Vietnam (Tonkin and Annam; 1883), and Laos and Cambodia (1893). The French also carried this "civilizing mission" into their colonies in West Africa. European and Atlantic trade with the west coast of Africa—in slaves, gold, and ivory—had been well established for centuries, but in the late nineteenth century, trade gave way to formal administration. The year 1895 saw the establishment of a Federation of French West Africa, a loosely organized administration that governed an area nine times the size of France, including Guinea, Senegal, and the Ivory Coast.

French control remained uneven, and despite military campaigns of pacification, resistance remained. The French dealt gingerly with tribal leaders, at times deferring to their authority and at others trying to break their power. They established French courts and law only in cities, leaving

Islamic or tribal courts to run the other areas. The federation aimed to rationalize the economy by emphasizing a more careful management of resources; the French called this "enhancing the value" of the region, which was part of the "civilizing mission." Embarking on an ambitious program of public works, French engineers rebuilt the huge harbor at Dakar, the most important on the coast, to accommodate rising exports. With utopian zeal they redesigned older cities, tried to improve sanitation and health, upgraded the water systems, and built roads and railways. The French republic was justifiably proud of the Pasteur Institute for bacteriological research, which opened in France in 1888; overseas institutes became part of the colonial enterprise. One plan called for a large-scale West African railroad network to lace through the region. A public-school program built free schools in villages not controlled by missionaries; education, though, was not compulsory and was usually for boys.

Such programs plainly served French interests; none of these measures aimed to give indigenous peoples political rights. Furthermore, French projects were often not successful. The French government did not have the resources to carry out its plans, which proved much more expensive and complicated than anyone imagined. Transportation costs ran very high, and labor posed the largest problems. Here, as elsewhere, Europeans faced massive resistance from the African peasants, whom they relied on to do everything from building railroads to working mines to carrying rubber. The Europeans therefore resorted to forced labor, signing agreements with local tribal leaders to deliver workers, and turned a blind eye to the continuing use of slave labor in the interior. For these reasons, the colonial project did not produce the profits some expected. In important respects, though, the goals of French colonial investment were intangible: railroads, schools, and projects such as Dakar harbor were valuable primarily as symbols of the French nation's modernity, power, and world leadership.

THE "SCRAMBLE FOR AFRICA" AND THE CONGO

The scope and speed with which the major European powers asserted formal control over Africa was astonishing. In 1875, 11 percent of the continent was in European hands; by 1902, the figure was 90 percent. European powers mastered the logistical problems of transport and communication, and learned how to keep diseases at bay. They also had new weapons: the Maxim gun, adopted by the British army in 1889 and first used by British colonial troops, pelted out as many as 500 rounds a minute, turning encounters with indigenous forces into bloodbaths and making armed resistance virtually impossible.

The Congo Free State

In the 1870s, a new phase of European involvement struck right at the heart of the continent. Until the latter part of the nineteenth century, much of interior Africa had been out of bounds for Europeans, because the rapids downstream on such strategic rivers as the Congo and the Zambezi made it difficult to move inland and tropical diseases were lethal to most European explorers. But during the 1870s, a new drive into central Africa produced results. The target was the fertile valleys around the river Congo, and the European colonizers were a privately financed group of Belgians paid by their king, Leopold II (r. 1865–1909). They followed in the footsteps of Henry Morton Stanley, an American newspaperman and explorer who later became a British subject and a knight of the realm. Stanley hacked his way through thick canopy jungle into territory where no European had previously set foot. His "scientific" journeys inspired the creation of a society of researchers and students of African culture in Brussels, which, in reality, was a front organization for the commercial company set up by Leopold. The ambitiously named International Association for the Exploration and Civilization of the Congo was set up in 1876 and soon signed treaties with local elites, opening the whole Congo River basin to commercial exploitation. The vast resources of palm oil and natural rubber, as well as the promise of minerals, including diamonds, were now within Europeans' reach.

The strongest resistance to Leopold's company came from other colonial powers. In 1884, a conference was called in Berlin to settle the matter of control over the Congo River basin. It was chaired by the master of European power politics, Otto von Bismarck, and attended by all the leading colonial nations and the United States. The **Berlin Conference** established ground rules for a new phase of imperial expansion. Europe's two great overseas empires, those of Britain and France, and the strongest emerging power inside Europe, Germany, joined forces in a settlement that seemed to be perfectly in line with nineteenth-century liberalism: the Congo valleys would be open to free trade and commerce; a slave trade, still run by some of the Islamic kingdoms in the region, would be suppressed in favor of free labor; and a Congo Free State would be set up, denying the region to the formal control of any single European country.

In reality, however, the Congo Free State was run by Leopold's private company, and the region was opened up to unrestricted exploitation by a series of large European corporations. Huge tracts of land, larger than whole European countries, became diamond mines or plantations for the extraction of palm oil, rubber, or cocoa. The older slave trade was suppressed, but the European companies took the "free" African labor guaranteed in Berlin and placed the workers in equally bad conditions. African workers labored in appalling conditions, with no real medicine or sanitation, too little food, and production schedules that made European factory labor look mild by comparison; and hundreds of thousands died from disease and overwork. Moreover, because European managers did not respect the different season cycles in central Africa, whole crop years were lost, leading to famines. Laborers working in the heat of the dry season often carried individual loads on their backs that would have been handled by heavy machinery in a European factory. Thousands of Africans were pressed into work harvesting goods Europe wanted, and did so for little or no pay, under the threat of beatings and mutilations for dozens of petty offenses against the plantation companies that made the laws of the Free State. Eventually, the scandal of the Congo became too great to go unquestioned. A whole generation of authors and journalists, most famously Joseph Conrad in his *Heart of Darkness*, publicized the arbitrary brutality and the vast scale of suffering. In 1908, Belgium was forced to take direct control of the Congo, turning it into a Belgian colony. A few restrictions at least were imposed on the activities of the great plantation companies, which brought a vast new store of raw materials to European industry by using what was slavery in all but name.

The Partition of Africa

The occupation of Congo, and its promise of great material wealth, pressured other colonial powers into expanding their holdings. By the 1880s, the "scramble for Africa" was well under way, hastened by stories of rubber forests or diamond mines in other parts of central and southern Africa. The guarantees made at the 1884 Berlin Conference allowed the Europeans to take further steps. The French and Portuguese increased their holdings, and Italy moved into territories along the Red Sea, beside British-held land and the independent kingdom of Ethiopia.

Germany came relatively late to overseas empire. Bismarck was reluctant to engage in an enterprise he believed would yield few economic or political advantages; yet he did not want either Britain or France to dominate Africa, so Germany seized colonies in strategic locations. The German colonies in Cameroon and most of modern Tanzania separated the territories of older, more established powers. Though the Germans were not the most enthusiastic colonialists, they were fascinated by the imperial adventure and jealous of their territories. When the Herero people of German Southwest Africa (now Namibia) rebelled in the early 1900s, the Germans responded with a vicious campaign of village burning and ethnic killing that resulted in 800,000 deaths, nearly annihilating the Herero.

Great Britain and France had their own ambitions. The French aimed to move from west to east across the continent, an important reason for the French expedition to Fashoda (in the Sudan) in 1898 (discussed on page 769). Britain's part in the "scramble" took place largely in southern and eastern Africa and was encapsulated in the dreams and career of one man: Cecil Rhodes, the diamond tycoon, colonial politician, and imperial visionary. Rhodes, who made a fortune from the South African diamond mines in the 1870s and 1880s and founded the diamond-mining company DeBeers, became prime minister of Britain's Cape Colony in 1890. (He left part of this fortune for the creation of the Rhodes scholarships to educate future leaders of the empire at Oxford.) He pursued two great personal and imperial goals. The personal goal was to build a southern African empire

SLAVES IN CHAINS, 1896. In Africa, native labor was exploited by Europeans and other Africans.

ATLANTIC OCEAN

MEDITERRANEAN SEA

Algiers (Fr.)
Ceuta (Sp.) • Melilla (Sp.)
ALGIERS
TUNIS
MOROCCO
TRIPOLI
EGYPT
British occupied
(nominally Turkish
suzerainty)
RIO DE ORO
RED SEA
SENEGAL
MAHDIST
STATE
ERITREA
GAMBIA
TUKOLOR
EMPIRE
DAHOMEY
Lake Chad
BORNU
OBOCK (Fr.)
PORT.
GUINEA
SAMORI'S
STATE
SOKOTO
CALIPHATE
ABYSSINIAN
EMPIRE
(ETHIOPIA)
SIERRA
LEONE
ASHANTI
LIBERIA
IVORY COAST
GOLD COAST
Porto
Novo
(Fr.)
ROYAL NIGER
COM. SPHERE
BRITISH
SOMALILAND
TOGO
LAGOS
OIL RIVERS
CAMEROON
BUNYORO
FERNANDO PO (Sp.)
SÃO TOMÉ (Port.)
RIO MUNI (Sp.)
FRENCH
CONGO
CONGO
FREE
STATE
BUGANDA KINGDOM
Lake Victoria
Witu (Ger.)
BRITISH EAST AFRICA SPHERE
SULTANATE OF
ZANZIBAR

ATLANTIC

OCEAN
Lake
Tanganyika
KATANGA
GERMAN EAST AFRICA
CODEPENDENCY SPHERE
ANGOLA
TEKE
Lake
Nyasa
MOZAMBIQUE
MADAGASCAR
INDIAN
SOUTH-
WEST
AFRICA
MATABELE
LAND
HERERO
WALVIS BAY (Br.)
NAMA
TRANSVAAL
REPUBLIC
OCEAN
BECHUANALAND
PROTECTORATE
SWAZILAND
ZULULAND
BRITISH
BECHUANALAND
CAPE
COLONY
NATAL
BASUTOLAND
ORANGE FREE STATE

Indigenous power
Turkish suzerainty
Portuguese
British
King Leopold's State
German
Boer
French
Italian
Spanish

0   500   1000 Miles
0   500   1000 Kilometers

AFRICA, c. 1886. ■ *What is the single biggest difference in terms of rulership between this map and the one on the next page?* ■ *Who were the winners and losers in the "scramble for Africa" before the First World War?* ■ *What does the result of the "scramble for Africa" suggest about how European powers regarded each other?*

ATLANTIC OCEAN

SPANISH MOROCCO

TUNISIA

MEDITERRANEAN SEA

MOROCCO

IFNI (Sp.)

ALGERIA

TRIPOLITANIA

CYRENAICA

LIBYA

EGYPT
(British occupation)

RIO DE ORO

RED SEA

MAURITANIA

UPPER SENEGAL AND NIGER

FRENCH WEST AFRICA

CHAD

ANGLO-EGYPTIAN
SUDAN

ERITREA

FRENCH
SOMALILAND

SENEGAL

GAMBIA
(Br.)

PORT.
GUINEA

FRENCH
GUINEA

UPPER
VOLTA

NORTHERN

NIGERIA

Lake Chad

BRITISH
SOMALILAND

SIERRA
LEONE

IVORY
COAST

GOLD
COAST

DAHOMEY

SOUTHERN

UBANGI
SHARI
CHAD

EMPIRE
OF
ETHIOPIA

ITALIAN
SOMALILAND

LIBERIA

TOGOLAND

FERNANDO PO (Sp.)

SPANISH GUINEA

CAMEROON

FRENCH EQUATORIAL AFRICA

UGANDA

BRITISH EAST
AFRICA

SÃO TOMÉ (Port.)

GABON
COLONY

MIDDLE
CONGO

BELGIAN
CONGO

Lake Victoria

INDIAN
OCEAN

CABINDA

Lake
Tanganyika

GERMAN
EAST
AFRICA

ZANZIBAR (Br.)

ATLANTIC
OCEAN

ANGOLA

NORTHERN
RHODESIA

Lake
Nyasa

NYASALAND

MOZAMBIQUE

MADAGASCAR

SOUTH-
WEST
AFRICA

SOUTHERN
RHODESIA

WALVIS BAY (Br.)

BECHUANA-
LAND

SWAZILAND (British Protectorate)

UNION OF
SOUTH AFRICA

BASUTOLAND (British Protectorate)

	British
	French
	Belgian
	Spanish
	Portuguese
	German
	Italian
	Independent state

0   500   1000 Miles
0   500   1000 Kilometers

AFRICA, c. 1914.

"THE RHODES COLOSSUS." This cartoon, which appeared in *Punch* magazine, satirized the ambitions of Cecil Rhodes, the driving force behind British imperialism in South Africa.

"NOW WE SHANT [*SIC*] BE LONG TO CAIRO." So read the banner across Engine No. 1, taking the first train from Umtali to Salisbury, Rhodesia. In Cecil Rhodes's vision, the Capetown-to-Cairo railway symbolized British domination of the African continent.

that was founded on diamonds; "Rhodesia" would fly the Union Jack out of pride but send its profits into Rhodes's own companies. He helped carve out territories occupying the modern nations of Zambia, Zimbabwe, Malawi, and Botswana—most of the savannah of southern Africa—through bribery, double dealing, careful coalition politics with the British and Boer settlers, warfare, and outright theft. Rhodes also had a broader imperial vision: first, a British presence along the whole of eastern Africa, symbolized by the goal of a Cape-to-Cairo railway; second, that the empire should make Britain self-sufficient, with British industry able to run on the goods and raw materials shipped in from its colonies, then exporting many finished products back to those lands.

This battle over strategic advantage, European pride, and diamonds was typical of the "scramble." As each European power sought its "place in the sun" (famous phrase by the German kaiser William II), they brought more and more of Africa under direct colonial control. It created a whole new scale of plunder as companies were designed and managed to strip the continent of its resources. African peoples thus faced a combination of direct European control and indirect rule, which allowed local elites friendly to European interests to lord it over those who resisted. The partition of Africa was the most striking case of the new imperialism, with broad consequences for the subject peoples of European colonies and for the international order as a whole.

IMPERIAL CULTURE

Imperialism was thoroughly anchored in the culture of late-nineteenth-century Europe and the United States. Images of empire were everywhere, not just in the propagandist literature of colonialism's supporters but on tins of tea and boxes of cocoa and as background themes in posters advertising everything from dance halls to sewing machines. Museums and world's fairs displayed the products of empire and introduced spectators to "exotic peoples." Music halls rang to the sound of imperialist songs. Empire was present in novels of the period, sometimes appearing as a faraway setting for fantasy, adventure, or stories of self-discovery. Even the tales of Sherlock Holmes, set in London and not overtly imperialist, often included references to empire—tiger carpets, hookahs and opium dens, Malaysian servants—to add mystery and fascination to their plots. The popular literature of empire showed a particular fascination with sexual practices in faraway places: photos and postcards of North African harems and unveiled Arab women were common in European pornography, as were colonial memoirs that chronicled the sexual adventures of the authors.

Empire thus played an important part in establishing European identity during these years. In France, the "civilizing mission" demonstrated to French citizens the grandeur of their nation, and building railroads and "bringing progress to other lands" illustrated the vigor of the French republic. Many British writers spoke in similar tones; as one author wrote, "The British race may safely be called a missionary race. The command to go and teach all nations is one that the British people have, whether rightly or wrongly, regarded as specially laid upon themselves."

This sense of high moral purpose was not restricted to male writers or to figures of authority. In England, the United States, Germany, and France, the speeches and projects of women's reform movements were full of references to empire and the civilizing mission. Britain's women's suffrage movement, for example, was fiercely critical of the government yet nationalist and imperialist. For British women reformers, women's participation in politics also meant the right to participate in imperial projects; they wrote about the oppression of Indian women by child marriage and *sati* and saw themselves shouldering the "white woman's burden" of reform. In France, the suffragist Hubertine Auclert criticized the colonial government in Algeria for its indifference to the condition of Muslim women in their domains; she used an image of women suffering in polygamous marriages abroad to dramatize the need for reform. Arguments such as these enabled European women in their home countries to see themselves as bearers of progress, as participants in a superior civilization. Similarly, John Stuart Mill often used Hindu or Muslim culture as a foil when he wanted to make a point

of freedom of speech and religion. This contrast between colonial backwardness alongside European civility and cultural superiority shaped Western culture and political debate, and liberal ideas in particular.

Imperialism and Racial Thought

Imperial culture gave new prominence to racial thinking. In the 1850s, Count Arthur de Gobineau (*GOH-bih-noh*; 1816–1882) wrote a massive work, *The Inequality of the Races*, but it sparked little interest until the period of the new imperialism, when it was translated into English and widely discussed. For Gobineau, race offered the "master key" for understanding human societies in the modern world. "The racial question overshadows all other problems of history. . . . [T]he inequality of the races from whose fusion a people is formed is enough to explain the whole course of its destiny." Gobineau's work followed from Enlightenment investigations of different cultures in the world. Whereas Enlightenment authors attributed cultural differences to environmental factors, Gobineau argued that "blood" was the determining factor in human history. He claimed that humans were originally divided into three races—"black," "white," and "yellow"—and peoples of the

The first step towards lightening

The White Man's Burden

is through teaching the virtues of cleanliness.

Pears' Soap

is a potent factor in brightening the dark corners of the earth as civilization advances, while amongst the cultured of all nations it holds the highest place—it is the ideal toilet soap.

THINKING ABOUT EMPIRE AT HOME. By the end of the nineteenth century, advertisers had begun to use images of empire to sell their products to consumers. This advertisement for Pears' Soap (left) appeared in the American magazine *McClure's* in 1899. The image of the white-uniformed officer washing his hands connects the theme of cleanliness and personal hygiene with the notions of racial superiority and the necessity of bringing civilization to the "dark corners of the earth." The packaging of Huntley & Palmers Biscuits (right) transports the familiar domestic scene of teatime to an exotic imperial location, with a supporting cast of elephants. The image, which adorned biscuit boxes in many British parlors during the late Victorian period, seems to reinforce the idea that essential aspects of British culture could be maintained even as Britons traveled to distant parts of the globe.

present day are variously mixed from these original components. The white race, he argued, had preserved purer bloodlines and was therefore superior, while others suffered "adulteration" and were therefore degenerate and no longer capable of civilization. Gobineau's readers included some defenders of the Confederacy during the American Civil War and, later, Adolf Hitler.

Followers of Gobineau's racial thinking looked increasingly to science to legitimize their theories. The natural scientist Charles Darwin (not a racist himself) attracted wide attention with his theory of evolution, which sought to explain the variety of species observable in the natural world. Darwin suggested that only the most "fit" in a species survived to bear viable offspring, and that this process of "natural selection" explained how species diverged from one another; that is, variations that made individuals better able to find food and mates were likely to be passed on to future generations. Social scientists such as Herbert Spencer used similar logic of competition among individuals for scarce resources to explain the evolution of social groups, suggesting that inequalities of wealth or ability also could be explained as the result of "natural selection." Racial theorists and followers of Gobineau such as Houston Stewart Chamberlain (1855–1927) wasted little time in harnessing these scientific arguments to the claim that human "races"

evolved over time; Chamberlain's books sold tens of thousands of copies in Britain and Germany.

Francis Galton (1822–1911), a half cousin of Charles Darwin and a scientist who studied evolution, went so far as to advocate improving a population's racial characteristics by selective breeding of "superior types." Galton and others, fearing that improvements in health care and hygiene might allow individuals with inferior traits to survive to reproductive age, promoted a system of racial management called *eugenics*, which they claimed would save European populations from a decline in their vitality and biological fitness. Theories such as that of Galton or Gobineau were closely linked with other developments in European culture, in particular, the renewed anxieties about social class and a fresh wave of European anti-Semitism. The increasingly scientific racism of late-nineteenth-century Europe made it easier for many to reconcile their contempt for other peoples with the rhetoric of progress, individual freedom, and the civilizing mission.

Opposition to Imperialism

Support for imperialism was not unanimous. As we have seen, Hobson and Lenin condemned the entire enterprise as an act of greed and arrogance. The Polish-born Joseph Conrad, a British novelist, shared much of the racism of his contemporaries but nevertheless believed that imperialism was an expression of deeply rooted pathologies in European culture. Other anti-imperialists were men and women from the colonies who took their case to the metropole. The British Committee of the Indian National Congress gathered together many members of London's Indian community to educate the British public about the exploitation of Indian peoples and resources. In the Arab world, the focus was on finding a way to respond to European imperialism that was consistent with Islam. In 1884, Jamal ad-Din al-Afghani, a political thinker from Iran, and Muhammad Abduh, an Egyptian religious scholar, founded an Arabic language newspaper in Paris, which criticized the British and their imperial policy in the Middle East. (See **Analyzing Primary Sources** on page 765.)

Perhaps the most defiant anti-imperialist action was the London **Pan-African Conference** of 1900, staged at the height of the "scramble for Africa" and during the Boer War (discussed on page 770). The conference grew out of an international tradition of African American, British, and American antislavery movements, and brought the rhetoric used earlier to abolish slavery to bear on the tactics of European imperialism. The conference attendees protested that forced labor in the mining compounds of South Africa

RACIAL THINKING IN THE AGE OF EMPIRE. This plate was published in a German anthropology book, probably around 1850. It is a good example of how racial categories were given scientific legitimacy and disseminated in a way that lent them credibility in the popular imagination. Note how the map implies that the earth is divided into homogenous "racial" zones. ▪ *Does this image contain any message of racial hierarchy, implying that some "races" were superior to others?* ▪ *Is the idea of "race" promoted in this illustration purely biological, or does it appear to contain references to culture as well—for example, in the hairstyles of the individuals shown?*

was akin to slavery, and asked in very moderate tones for some autonomy and representation for African peoples. The conference was small, but it drew delegates from the Caribbean, West Africa, and North America, including the thirty-two-year-old Harvard PhD and leading African American intellectual W. E. B. Du Bois (1868–1963). The conference issued a proclamation "To the Nations of the World," with a famous introduction written by Du Bois: "In the metropolis of the modern world, in this closing year of the nineteenth century, there has been assembled a congress of men and women of African blood, to deliberate solemnly upon the present situation and outlook of the darker races of mankind. The problem of the twentieth century is the problem of the colour-line." The British government ignored the conference, but pan-Africanism, like Indian nationalism, grew rapidly after the First World War.

Colonial Cultures

Imperialism created new colonial cultures in other parts of the world. Cities such as Bombay, Calcutta, and Shanghai boomed, more than tripling in size. Casablanca, Algiers, and Cairo developed new neighborhoods with French architectural styles. Treaty ports such as Hong Kong were transformed as Europeans built banks, shipping enterprises, schools, and religious missions. As Europeans and indigenous peoples encountered and transformed each other, new hybrid cultures emerged. Elsewhere, new social instabilities grew as European demands for labor took men out of their villages and away from their families, where they were crowded into shantytowns bordering sprawling new cities. Hopes that European rule would create a well-disciplined labor force were quickly dashed.

People on both sides of the colonial divide worried about preserving national traditions and identity in the face of these hybrid and changing colonial cultures. In China and India, suggestions that local populations adopt European models of education set off fierce controversies. Chinese elites, already divided over such customs as footbinding and concubinage (the legal practice whereby men maintained formal sexual partners outside of marriage), found their dilemmas heightened as imperialism became a more powerful force. Should they defend such practices as integral to their culture? Should they argue for a Chinese path to reform? Proponents of change in China or India thus had to sort through their stance toward both Western culture and their traditional popular culture.

For their part, British, French, and Dutch authorities worried that too much familiarity between colonized and colonizer would weaken European prestige and authority. In

Phnom Penh, Cambodia (part of French Indochina), French citizens lived apart from the rest of the city by a moat, and authorities required "dressing appropriately and keeping a distance from the natives." Sexual relations provoked the most anxiety and the most contradictory responses. "In this hot climate, passions run higher," wrote a French administrator in Algeria. "French soldiers seek out Arab women due to their strangeness and newness." A British man stationed in Shanghai reported, "It was common practice for [an] unmarried Englishmen resident in China to keep a Chinese girl, and I did as the others did." He married an Englishwoman, however, and sent his Chinese mistress and their three children to Britain to avoid awkwardness. European administrators fitfully tried to prohibit liaisons between European men and local women, labeling such affairs as "corrupting." But such prohibitions only drove these relations underground, increasing the gap between the public facade of colonial rule and the private reality of colonial lives.

European Imperialism and the Muslim World

The new imperialism of the nineteenth century launched Europe into a new relationship with Muslim societies in Africa, the Middle East, and Asia. For centuries, Muslims had close connections with Europe through at least three different points of territorial involvement. First, the Arab cultures of Muslim North Africa had been in constant contact with the Spanish peninsula, France, and the Italian city-states since the medieval period. Second, the Ottoman Empire had long ruled over areas of the Balkans and southeastern Europe. Third, Muslim groups from central Asia had periodically migrated westward across the steppe, bringing them into frequent interactions and conflicts with northern Europeans, particularly Russians, but also Hungarians and Poles and other peoples of the Eurasian borderlands. In all three cases, these points of contact between Muslims and the various peoples of Europe produced long periods of significant cultural exchange and trade, as well as moments of conflict.

The establishment and expansion of colonial empires brought Europe and the Muslim world into a new and dynamic relationship, as many Muslim societies came under direct or indirect rule of Europeans. This Muslim world was diverse and heterogeneous, extending from Morocco on the Atlantic coast through the Ottoman Empire of the Middle East, the Muslim lands of Asia, and beyond to Indonesia and the Philippine Islands in the Pacific. By 1914, the French ruled directly over Algeria and much of Muslim West Africa, and had established protectorates in Morocco

Jamal ad-Din al-Afghani Responds to European Critiques of Islam (1883)

Jamal ad-Din al-Afghani (c. 1838–1897), a Muslim writer and political figure, was an important member of a late-nineteenth-century movement to reconcile Islam with the modern world. Born in Persia, he received a traditional Shi'ite religious education. He lived in British India during the 1850s, a period of rebellion against British rule, and later spent time in Afghanistan, the Ottoman Empire, and Egypt. In 1879, he began a period of exile that took him to Europe, where he visited many cities. As the Muslim countries of the Middle East fell under the control of European colonial powers, he worked with other Muslim thinkers to respond to the challenges that imperialism posed for Muslim societies. Here, in an essay originally published in French in 1883, he debates with the French historian and philosopher Ernest Renan, who argued that Islam made it impossible for Arab culture to incorporate new scientific knowledge, thus dooming its civilization to stagnation.

f it is true that the Muslim religion is an obstacle to the development of sciences, can one affirm that this obstacle will not disappear someday? How does the Muslim religion differ on this point from other religions? All religions are intolerant, each one in its way. The Christian religion, I mean the society that follows its inspirations and its teachings and is formed in its image, has emerged from the first period to which I have just alluded; thenceforth free and independent, it seems to advance rapidly on the road of progress and science, whereas Muslim society has not yet freed itself from the tutelage of religion. Realizing, however, that the Christian religion preceded the Muslim religion in the world by many centuries, I cannot keep from hoping that Mohammadan society will succeed in breaking its bonds and marching resolutely in the path of civilization someday after the manner of Western society, for which the Christian faith, despite its rigors and intolerance, was not at all an invincible obstacle. No I cannot admit that this hope be denied to Islam. I plead here with Mr. Renan not the cause of the Muslim religion, but

that of several hundreds of millions of men, who would thus be condemned to live in barbarism and ignorance. [. . .]

Religions, by whatever names they are called, all resemble each other. No agreement and no reconciliation are possible between these religions and philosophy. Religion imposes on man its faith and its belief, whereas philosophy frees him of it totally or in part. How could one therefore hope that they would agree with each other when the Christian religion, under the most modest and seductive forms, entered Athens and Alexandria, which were, as everyone knows, the two principal centers of science and philosophy, trying to stifle both under the bushes of theological discussions, to explain the inexplicable mysteries of the Trinity, the Incarnation, and Transubstantiation? It will always be thus. Whenever religion will have the upper hand, it will eliminate philosophy; and the contrary occurs when it is philosophy that reigns as sovereign mistress. So long as humanity exists, the struggle will not cease between dogma and free investigation, between religion and philosophy; a desperate struggle in which, I fear, the triumph will not be for free thought, because the masses dislike

reason, and its teachings are only understood by some intelligent members of the elite, and because, also science, however beautiful it is, does not completely satisfy humanity, which thirst for the ideal and which likes to exist in such dark and distant regions as the philosophers and scholars can neither perceive nor explore.

Source: Jamal ad-Din al-Afghani, *An Islamic Response to Imperialism*, trans. Nikki R. Keddie (Berkeley: 1968), pp. 175–87. Original Arabic source: "Exchange with Ernest Renan," *Journal des Debats*, May 18, 1883 (written in Arabic and translated into French for publication).

Questions for Analysis

1. How does al-Afghani attempt to refute Renan's claim that Muslim societies cannot adapt to the modern world?

2. What does al-Afghani mean when he suggests that all religions are "intolerant," and that they all "resemble each other"?

3. What is al-Afghani's opinion about the relationship between science—or, as he puts it, "philosophy"—and religion?

Address to the Nations of the World by the Pan-African Conference in London (1900)

The Pan-African Conference that met in London in 1900 brought together a group of people of African heritage from many parts of the world. They were determined to add their voices to those discussing and debating the consequences of European imperialism in the last decades of the nineteenth century. The declaration they produced gives a clear picture of their vision of history, their sense of the injustices associated with colonial conquest, and their hopes for the future. The chair of the committee who wrote the address was W. E. B. Du Bois (1868–1963), an African American professor of history, sociology, and economics, who studied at Harvard and the University of Berlin. In 1909, he became a founding member of the National Association for the Advancement of Colored People.

In the metropolis of the modern world, in this the closing year of the nineteenth century, there has been assembled a congress of men and women of African blood, to deliberate solemnly upon the present situation and outlook of the darker races of mankind. The problem of the twentieth century is the problem of the colour-line, the question as to how far differences of race—which show themselves chiefly in the colour of the skin and the texture of the hair—will hereafter be made the basis of denying to over half the world the right of sharing to their utmost ability the opportunities and privileges of modern civilization.

To be sure, the darker races are today the least advanced in culture according to European standards. This has not, however, always been the case in the past, and certainly the world's history, both ancient and modern, has given many instances of no despicable ability and capacity among the blackest races of men.

In any case, the modern world must remember that in this age when the ends of the world are being brought so near together the millions of black men in Africa, America, and the Islands of the Sea, not to speak of the brown and yellow myriads elsewhere, are bound to have a great influence upon the world in the future, by reason of sheer numbers and physical contact. If now the world of culture bends itself towards giving Negroes and other dark men the largest and broadest opportunity for education and self-development, then this contact and influence is bound to have a beneficial effect upon the world and hasten human progress. But if, by reason of carelessness, prejudice, greed and injustice, the black world is to be exploited and ravished and degraded, the results must be deplorable, if not fatal—not simply to them, but to the high ideals of justice, freedom and culture which a thousand years of Christian civilization have held before Europe.

And now, therefore, to these ideals of civilization, to the broader humanity of the followers of the Prince of Peace, we, the men and women of Africa in world congress assembled, do now solemnly appeal:

Let the world take no backward step in that slow but sure progress which has successively refused to let the spirit of class, of caste, of privilege, or of birth, debar from life, liberty and the pursuit of happiness a striving human soul.

Let not color or race be a feature of distinction between white and black men, regardless of worth or ability.

Let not the natives of Africa be sacrificed to the greed of gold, their liberties taken away, their family life debauched,

---

and Tunisia. The British established a protectorate in Egypt, and ruled over many Muslims in India and Malaysia. And the Dutch ruled over a large Muslim population in Indonesia. After World War I, with the collapse of the Ottoman Empire (see Chapter 23), the number of Muslim societies under European control grew further, as Palestine, Iraq, Lebanon, and Syria came under French and British control.

Prior to the nineteenth century, trade often brought goods from Muslim lands to Europe, such as grain from North Africa, cotton from Egypt and Syria, or silks and other luxury goods from the Middle East. In the nineteenth century, trade began to shift in the other direction, as Muslim societies began to import manufactured goods from European industry. This trade often benefited Christian minorities in Syria or Lebanon who had privileged relations with European merchants, but it threatened local artisans, whose craft traditions could not compete with cheaper imported European goods.

their just aspirations repressed, and avenues of advancement and culture taken from them.

Let not the cloak of Christian missionary enterprise be allowed in the future, as so often in the past, to hide the ruthless economic exploitation and political downfall of less developed nations, whose chief fault has been reliance on the plighted faith of the Christian Church.

Let the British nation, the first modern champion of Negro Freedom, hasten to crown the work of Wilberforce, and Clarkson, and Buxton, and Sharpe, Bishop Colenso, and Livingstone, and give, as soon as practicable, the rights of responsible government to the black colonies of Africa and the West Indies.

Let not the spirit of Garrison, Phillips, and Douglass wholly die out in America; may the conscience of a great nation rise and rebuke all dishonesty and unrighteous oppression toward the American Negro, and grant to him the right of franchise, security of person and property, and generous recognition of the great work he has accomplished in a generation toward raising nine millions of human beings from slavery to manhood.

Let the German Empire, and the French Republic, true to their great past, remember that the true worth of colonies lies in their prosperity and progress, and that justice, impartial alike to black and white, is the first element of prosperity.

Let the Congo Free State become a great central Negro State of the world, and let its prosperity be counted not simply in cash and commerce, but in the happiness and true advancement of its black people.

Let the nations of the World respect the integrity and independence of the first Negro States of Abyssinia, Liberia, Haiti, and the rest, and let the inhabitants of these States, the independent tribes of Africa, the Negroes of the West Indies and America, and the black subjects of all nations take courage, strive ceaselessly, and fight bravely, that they may prove to the world their incontestible right to be counted among the great brotherhood of mankind.

Thus we appeal with boldness and confidence to the Great Powers of the civilized world, trusting in the wide spirit of humanity, and the deep sense of justice of our age, for a generous recognition of the righteousness of our cause.

ALEXANDER WALTERS (Bishop)
President Pan-African Association

HENRY B. BROWN
Vice-President

H. SYLVESTER-WILLIAMS
General Secretary

W. E. BURGHARDT DU BOIS
Chairman Committee on Address

Source: Ayodele Langley, *Ideologies of Liberation in Black Africa* (London: 1979), pp. 738–39.

Questions for Analysis

1. What value do the authors ascribe to "race" as a description of human difference?

2. According to the authors, what choices do European powers have to make as they exercise their power in Africa? What are their hopes for Africans in a world shaped by European expansion?

3. What specific "ideals of civilization" do the authors of this declaration invoke? Do they share these ideals with peoples elsewhere?

4. Are there echoes of European liberalism or nationalism in its pan-Africanism?

The political and social challenges posed to Muslim societies by European colonialism were substantial. Muslim states that retained their independence in the nineteenth century, such as the Ottoman Empire, looked for ways to reform and adapt to growing European influence and the reality of European power. Meanwhile, Islamic scholars and intellectuals throughout the Muslim world looked to their religious tradition for guidance, as they sought to understand the changing circumstances their societies faced (see *Analyzing Primary Sources* on page 765). Muslims that came under direct control by European powers looked for ways to preserve their culture and independence from foreign attempts to impose new institutions and new ways of life on their populations.

The career of Muhammad Ali (1769–1849), an Ottoman general of Albanian origin, illustrates the ways in which Muslims sought to respond to the challenges of European imperialism. Ali had been involved in the Ottoman force

Interpreting Visual Evidence

Displays of Imperial Culture: The Paris Exposition of 1889

The French colonies were very visible in 1889, during the celebration of the centenary of the French Revolution. In that year, the French government organized a "Universal Exposition" in the capital, which attracted more than 6 million visitors to the broad esplanade that was covered with exhibitions of French industry and culture, including the newly constructed Eiffel Tower, a symbol of modern French engineering.

At the base of the Eiffel Tower (image A), a colonial pavilion placed objects from France's overseas empire on display, and a collection of temporary architectural exhibits showed reproductions of buildings from French colonies in Asia and Africa, as well as samples of architecture from other parts of the world. The photographs here show a reproduction of a Cairo Street (image B);

A. Eiffel Tower, 1889.

Pagoda of Angkor, modeled after the Khmer temples of Angkor Wat in Cambodia, a French protectorate (image C); and examples of West African dwellings (image D). The Cairo Street was the second most popular tourist destination at the fair, after the Eiffel Tower. It contained twenty-five shops and restaurants, and employed dozens of Egyptian servers, shopkeepers, and artisans who had been brought to Paris to add authenticity to the exhibit. Other people on display in the colonial pavilion included Senegalese villagers and a Vietnamese theater troupe.

Questions for Analysis

1. What vision of history and social progress is celebrated in this link between France's colonial holdings and the industrial power displayed in the Eiffel Tower?

2. What might account for the popularity of the Cairo Street exhibit?

3. Why was it important for the exposition to place people from European colonies on display?

B. Reproduction of a Cairo Street at the Paris Exposition, 1889.

C. Pagoda of Angkor at the Paris Exposition, 1889.

D. West African dwellings at the Paris Exposition, 1889.

that expelled Napoleon's armies from Egypt in 1801. He later defeated the Mamluk rulers of Egypt and seized power himself, with the intention of creating a modern Muslim state in the Middle East that could defend itself and challenge the weakened Ottoman Empire for primacy in the region. He created a more centralized government, modernized Egypt's system of agricultural irrigation, and developed an economic policy designed to generate a profit by exporting cotton and grain. He also reformed the education system in Egypt—with the help of French teachers—and embarked on an ambitious plan to modernize the military through industrial development. But he died in 1849, and his successors were unable to continue the pace of reform. Mounting government debt related to the construction of the Suez Canal and other infrastructural projects forced the rulers of Egypt to cede financial authority to an international commission dominated by the French and the British. By 1882, as we saw earlier, Egypt was occupied by British forces, much to the dismay of its people; and in 1914, the British "protectorate" in Egypt became official. A compliant Egyptian government continued to serve as head of state, but all parties understood that Egypt's independence was in name only. The memory of Muhammad Ali lived on, however, as the founder of the modern Egyptian state.

CRISES OF EMPIRE AT THE TURN OF THE TWENTIETH CENTURY

The turn of the twentieth century brought a series of crises to the Western empires. The crises did not end European rule, but they did create sharp tensions among Western nations and shook their confidence. The crises also drove imperial nations to expand their economic and military commitments into territories overseas. In these ways, they became central to Western culture in the years before the First World War.

Fashoda

In the fall of 1898, British and French armies nearly went to war at Fashoda, in the Egyptian Sudan. This crisis had complex causes. In the early 1880s, in an attempt to control the headwaters of the Nile River, the British had used a local uprising in the Sudan as an excuse to move southward from Egypt. In 1885, a project that began with Cecil Rhodes's grandiose dreams of connecting Cairo to the Cape of Good Hope ran into catastrophe when an army led by Britain's most flamboyant general, Charles Gordon, was massacred in Khartoum by the forces of the Mahdi, a Sufi religious leader who claimed to be the successor to the prophet Muhammad. Avenging Gordon's death preoccupied the British for more than a decade, and in 1898, a second large-scale rebellion gave them the opportunity. And an Anglo-Egyptian army commanded by General Horatio Kitchener attacked Khartoum and defeated the Mahdi's army using modern machine guns and artillery.

The victory brought complications, however, as France, which held territories in central Africa adjacent to the Sudan, saw the British victory as a threat. A French expedition was sent to the Sudanese town of Fashoda (now Kodok) to challenge the British claims in the area. They faced off against troops from Kitchener's army, and for a few weeks in September 1898 the situation teetered on the brink of war. The matter was resolved through diplomacy, however, and France ceded the southern Sudan to Britain in exchange for a halt to further expansion. The **Fashoda incident** was a sobering reminder of the extent that imperial competition could tip the international tensions between European powers.

Ethiopia

During the 1880s and 1890s, Italy had been developing a small empire on the shores of the Red Sea. Italy annexed Eritrea and parts of Somalia, and shortly after the death of Gordon at Khartoum, it defeated an invasion of their territories by the Mahdi's forces. Bolstered by this success, the Italians set out to conquer Ethiopia in 1896. Ethiopia was the last major independent African kingdom, ruled by a shrewd and capable emperor, Menelik II. His largely Christian subjects engaged in profitable trade on the East African coast, and revenues from this trade allowed Menelik to invest in the latest European artillery. When the Italian army—mostly Somali conscripts and a few thousand Italian troops—arrived, Menelik allowed it to penetrate into the mountain passes of Ethiopia. To keep to the roads, the army was forced to divide its forces into separate columns. Meanwhile, the Ethiopians moved over the mountains themselves; and in March 1896, at Adowa, Menelik's army attacked, destroying the Italian army completely and killing 6,000. The failed **Italian invasion of Ethiopia** was a national humiliation for Italy and an important symbol for African political radicals during the early twentieth century.

South Africa: The Boer War

In the late 1800s, competition between Dutch settlers in South Africa, known as Afrikaners or Boers, and the British

EMPEROR MENELIK II. Ethiopia was the last major independent African kingdom, its prosperity a counter to the European opinion of African cultures. In 1896, Menelik soundly defeated Italy's attempt to conquer his kingdom.

The Afrikaners responded by taking to the hills, and fighting a costly guerrilla war that lasted another three years. The British tactics became more brutal as the campaign went on; for example, they set up *concentration camps*—the first use of the term—where Afrikaner civilians were rounded up and forced to live in appalling conditions so that they would be unable to help the guerrillas. Over the course of two years, nearly 20,000 civilians died in the camps from disease and poor sanitation. Meanwhile, black Africans, despised by both sides, also suffered the effects of famine and disease as the war destroyed valuable farmland.

These concentration camps aroused opposition in Britain and elsewhere, and protesters campaigned against such violations of "European" rights—without regard for the fate of Africans caught in the conflict. In the end, the Afrikaners ceded control of their republics to a new British Union of South Africa, which gave them a share of political power. In the aftermath of the **Boer War**, both the British and Afrikaners preserved their high standards of living by relying on cheap African labor and, eventually, a system of racial segregation known as apartheid.

A BRITISH CONCENTRATION CAMP DURING THE BOER WAR. In an attempt to block support to guerrilla fighters, the British forced Afrikaner civilians to live in camps where appalling conditions led to the death of nearly 20,000 people over two years. This illustration appeared in a French newspaper *Le Petit Journal* in 1901.

led to a shooting war between them. When the Boers (an appropriation of the Dutch word for farmer) arrived in South Africa in the early nineteenth century, they had a long troubled relationship with their British neighbors in the colony. In the 1830s, the Boers trekked inland from the cape and set up two republics away from British influence: the Transvaal and the Orange Free State. After gold reserves were found in the Transvaal in the 1880s, Cecil Rhodes, the British diamond magnate (discussed on pages 758–761), tried to provoke war between Britain and the Boers to gain control of the Afrikaners' diamond mines. The war finally broke out in 1899, but the British were unprepared for the ferocity of Boer resistance. British columns were shot to pieces by Afrikaner forces that knew the territory, and the British towns of Ladysmith and Mafeking were besieged. Angered by these early failures, the British replaced their commanders and began to fight in earnest, using the railroads built to service the diamond mines to bring in modern military hardware.

U.S. Imperialism: The Spanish-American War of 1898

In 1898, imperialism brought Spain and the United States to war. In the 1880s and 1890s, Spain's imperial powers were considerably weakened, and they faced rebellions in their colonies in the Caribbean and the Pacific. American economic interests had considerable investments in Cuba, and when an American battleship accidentally exploded at anchor in Havana, advocates of empire and the press in general clamored for revenge. President William McKinley, despite of his misgivings, gave in to political necessity, and the United States declared war on Spain in 1898,

IMPERIALISM IN THE BALANCE. This cartoon, titled "A Study—Imperialism," appeared in the United States in 1899 at the beginning of the Philippine-American War. The image shows the scale of justice weighing imperialism against the many victims of U.S. military action, which indicates that the peoples of colonial powers were divided about the virtues of imperial expansion and the "civilizing mission."

determined to protect its economic interests in the Americas and the Pacific. The United States swiftly won.

In Spain, the **Spanish-American War** provoked an entire generation of writers, politicians, and intellectuals to national soul searching. The defeat undermined the Spanish monarchy, which managed to persist until 1931. The ensuing political tensions resurfaced in the Spanish Civil War of the 1930s—an important episode in the origins of the Second World War.

In the United States, this "splendid little war" was followed by the annexation of Puerto Rico, the establishment of a protectorate over Cuba, and a short but brutal war against Philippine rebels who liked American colonialism no better than that of the Spanish. In 1903, the United States intervened in a rebellion in Panama, backing the rebels and helping to establish a republic while building the Panama Canal on land leased from the new government. The Panama Canal opened in 1914, and, as the Suez Canal did for the British, it cemented U.S. dominance of the seas in the Western Hemisphere and the eastern Pacific. Later interventions in Hawaii and Santo Domingo gave further evidence of U.S. imperial power, and committed this former colony to a broad role in its new and greater sphere of influence.

THE ECOLOGICAL CONSEQUENCES OF EUROPEAN MIGRATIONS

Finally, a period of mass migration coincided with the age of imperialism; more than 50 million Europeans migrated overseas between 1820 and 1930. This migration resulted in part from population growth (Chapter 19), changes in the economy and land ownership, political unrest, and the persecution of minority populations.

Germans and the British were among the first, then the Irish accounted for a large part of the first wave, especially during the famine of the 1840s. An exodus of peasant populations from all corners of Europe soon followed, including Scandinavians escaping poverty; Italians, Poles, Hungarians, Czechs, and Slovaks uprooted by the 1848 revolutions; and Jews from the Pale of Settlement fleeing persecution. Along with Spaniards, Portuguese, Serbs, and Greeks from the Mediterranean basin, migrants traveled by foot and rail to European ports and purchased the cheapest passages they could find on steamships heading abroad.

The destinations of these migrants were not usually the new colonies of the nineteenth century in Africa or Asia. Two-thirds ended up in the United States, and smaller numbers went to Canada, Argentina, southern Brazil, Australia, and New Zealand. In these lands, the displacement of native populations had already been underway for several hundred years. Overwhelmed and in many cases annihilated by a combination of violence and diseases to which they had no immunity, the Amerindians of North and South America and the native peoples of Australia and New Zealand were replaced by European peoples, who became the majority population by seizing the land and its resources. During the nineteenth century, these new populations grew even faster than the European populations they had left behind.

In North and South America, this mass migration from Europe began as the institution of slavery ended. Slavery brought 11 million Africans to the Americas over four centuries, and former slaves and their descendants continued to shape the societies in which they lived, even as they frequently faced violent resistance against their full participation in social and political life. New migrants from Europe thus found themselves struggling to assimilate into societies that were already deeply conscious of racial and social identities; they faced discrimination in finding work or places to live, and in exercising their religions and expressing their political views.

Ecological transformations accompanied this demographic shift. The climate in European-settled areas of North and South America, Australia, and New Zealand was similar to that of Europe. So the crops that Europeans preferred could be grown with no greater trouble than at home,

and the domesticated animals that provided meat, wool, leather, and transportation also thrived in the new environments. To increase agricultural profits, the new lands were cultivated and forests cleared for planting and pasturage. Wheat, rye, barley, turnips, cabbage, onions, fruit trees, cattle, sheep, pigs, and goats accompanied European settlers wherever they went, along with a flood of other biological newcomers, including ferns, thistles, nettles, and other weeds that spread rapidly, often stabilizing the soil that had been disturbed by intensive farming practices. Of particular importance in this global propagation of nonnative plant life were the herded animals that carried seeds in their droppings and their feed. In 1769, only three plants of Eurasian origin grew in California; by 1900, 63 percent of the grasses in California were Eurasian in origin. Similar stories of massive biological replacement occurred in Canada, Mexico, Argentina, New Zealand, and even Australia, where the hot and dry climate of the interior preserved the older landscape to a greater degree than elsewhere.

The plants and animals Europeans brought with them during these years accelerated the Columbian exchange that had been already under way since the fifteenth century (Chapter 14). In the seventeenth and eighteenth centuries, pigs brought from Europe colonized the islands of the Caribbean, the forests of Virginia and the Carolinas, and the Brazilian grasslands. In the nineteenth century, wild pigs that descended from those brought by Europeans as a food source spread rapidly throughout Australia, eventually

After You Read This Chapter

 Go to **INQUIZITIVE** to see what you've learned—and learn what you've missed—with personalized feedback along the way.

REVIEWING THE OBJECTIVES

- European imperialism in the nineteenth century differed from earlier phases of colonial expansion. How was it different? Which parts of the globe were singled out by European imperial powers?
- European nations justified the cost and effort of their colonial policies in many ways. What were the major reasons for colonial expansion in the nineteenth century?
- The subjugated peoples of European colonies faced a choice between resistance and accommodation, though these choices were rarely exclusive. What examples of resistance or accommodation to colonialism can you identify?
- Imperialism shaped cultural developments within Europe in the nineteenth century. How did it change the lives of Europeans and their sense of their place in the world?
- Imperialism unleashed destabilizing competitive forces by the end of the nineteenth century, which drove European colonial powers into conflict with each other. Where were the flashpoints of these conflicts?

populating one-third of the landmass. Similar migrations brought cattle to California, Mexico, Brazil, and Argentina. By 1800, the population of wild cattle on the Argentinian pampas was counted in the tens of millions. In New Zealand, where the only land mammal prior to the arrival of Europeans was a species of bat, there were 9 million sheep by 1870; meanwhile, in the century preceding that date, after exposure to pathogens brought by the English settlers, the human population of Maori New Zealanders had fallen from as many as 200,000 to fewer than 50,000.

As a result of these shifts in human, animal, and plant populations, San Francisco, Buenos Aires, Sydney, and Christchurch came to resemble the cities of Europe; and the planted and unplanted lands surrounding these cities began to take on the characteristics of European landscapes. Many of these "neo-Europes" became relatively wealthy societies, and in the twentieth century, the enormous productivity of commercial agriculture in these areas created surpluses that were exported at a profit to international markets. Europeans were slow to recognize the extent to which these processes created a new global balance of power and wealth, but World War I made this clear to all—when the Allied Powers of France and Britain realized that they needed grain from the United States and Australia and beef from Argentina as much as they needed military supplies and soldiers (see Chapter 24). These fundamental demographic and ecological changes intensified across the nineteenth century, shaping the emergence of a more globally connected world in the twentieth century.

CONCLUSION

In the last quarter of the nineteenth century, the long-standing relationship between Europe and the rest of the world entered a new stage distinguished by the stunningly rapid extension of formal Western control, new forms of economic exploitation, and new patterns of social discipline and settlement. It was driven by the rising economic needs of the industrial West, territorial conflict, and nationalism, which, by the late nineteenth century, linked nationhood to empire. Among its immediate results was the creation of a self-consciously imperial culture in the West that, at the same time, clearly created unease and contributed powerfully to the sense of crisis that swept through the region.

For all its force, this Western expansion was never unchallenged; imperialism provoked resistance and required constantly changing strategies of rule. During the First World War, mobilizing the resources of empire would become crucial to victory. In the aftermath, reimposing the same conditions of the late nineteenth century would become nearly impossible. And over the longer term, the political structures, economic developments, and racial ideologies established in this period would be contested throughout the twentieth century.

PEOPLE, IDEAS, AND EVENTS IN CONTEXT

- What was the **EAST INDIA COMPANY**? How did the British reorganize their rule in India after the **SEPOY MUTINY**?
- What did the French mean when they justified colonial expansion in the name of the **"CIVILIZING MISSION"**?
- How did the **OPIUM WARS** change the economic and political relationships between Europe and China?
- How did the **BERLIN CONFERENCE** of 1884 shape the subsequent colonization of Africa?
- What were the limits of colonial power revealed by the **BOXER REBELLION**, the failed **ITALIAN INVASION OF ETHIOPIA**, and the **RUSSO-JAPANESE WAR**?
- What expressions of anti-imperialism emerged from the London **PAN-AFRICAN CONFERENCE**?
- How did the **BOER WAR** and the **FASHODA INCIDENT** contribute to a sense of crisis among European colonial powers?
- What effects did the **SPANISH-AMERICAN WAR** have on the attitudes toward imperialism in the United States, itself a former European colony?

THINKING ABOUT CONNECTIONS

- Compare the consequences of late-nineteenth-century European colonial conquest with earlier episodes of imperial expansion such as the Roman Empire or the early modern colonization of the Atlantic world. What was similar? What was different?
- What challenges were faced by colonial regimes in the nineteenth century, such as France and Britain, which expanded their institutions of representative and elected government at home even as they subjugated the conquered peoples in their new colonies?
- The histories of colonial conquest in the nineteenth century helped to establish a network of political and cultural connections that shaped the history of the world in the next century. What was the legacy of these connections during the period of decolonization in the twentieth century?
- How is the history of industrialization connected to the history of colonialism?

Before
You
Read
This
Chapter

Modern Industry and Mass Politics, 1870–1914

CORE OBJECTIVES

- **UNDERSTAND** the origins and consequences of the second industrial revolution.

- **DEFINE** *mass politics*, and **EXPLAIN** how the expansion of voting rights in European nations led to the development of organized political parties that sought the support of the working classes.

- **UNDERSTAND** the arguments both for and against woman suffrage during this period.

- **IDENTIFY** the ways that European liberalism and conservatism evolved as new social and political tensions emerged with the advent of mass politics and intensified industrial development.

- **EXPLAIN** the contributions made by scientists and other cultural figures who came to prominence in the final decades of the nineteenth century to the debates about human nature, modern society, and the natural world.

"We are on the extreme promontory of ages!" decreed the Italian poet and literary editor F. T. Marinetti in 1909. In a bombastic manifesto printed on the front page of a Paris newspaper, Marinetti introduced Europe to an aggressive art movement called *futurism*. Rebelling against what he considered the impotent conservatism of Italian culture, Marinetti called for a radical renewal of civilization through "courage, audacity, and revolt." Enamored with the raw power of modern machinery and the dynamism of urban life, he trumpeted "a new form of beauty, the beauty of speed." Marinetti embraced the heroic violence of warfare and disparaged the cultural traditions that formed the bedrock of liberalism.

Few Europeans embraced the modern era with the unflinching abandon of the futurists, but many would have agreed with Marinetti's claim that modern life was characterized above all by flux, movement, and an accelerating rate of change. In the last decades of the nineteenth century, a second industrial revolution produced new manufacturing techniques and new sources of power, including electricity and petroleum-based fuels. These developments transformed European towns and cities, and people felt the immediate effects of the changes in their daily lives.

At the same time, European nation-states faced new political realities. Electorates expanded, and new blocs of voters began participating directly in politics. Mass-based political parties brought new demands to the political arena, and governments struggled to maintain order and legitimacy in the face of these challenges. Socialists mobilized growing numbers of industrial workers, while suffragists demanded the franchise for women. The ability of traditional elites to control the political life of nations was sorely tested.

Beyond politics, new theories in the arts and sciences challenged older notions of nature, society, truth, and beauty. Since the eighteenth century at least, science had been a frequent ally of political liberalism, because both liberals and scientists shared a common faith in human reason and an openness to rational inquiry into the laws of society and nature. In the late nineteenth century, however, this common agenda was strained by scientific investigations in new fields—such as biology and psychology—that challenged liberal assumptions about human nature. Meanwhile, in the arts, a new generation of artists and writers embraced innovation and rejected the established conventions in painting, sculpture, poetry, and literature. A period of intense experimentation in the arts followed, leading artists and writers to develop radically new forms of expression.

The nineteenth century, then, ended in a burst of energy as many Europeans embraced a vision of a society racing headlong into what they hoped was a more promising and better future; however, behind this self-confidence lay significant uncertainty about the eventual destination. What aspects of the European past would continue to be relevant in the modern age? In politics and social life, and in the culture as a whole, such questions produced more conflict than consensus.

NEW TECHNOLOGIES AND GLOBAL TRANSFORMATIONS

During the last third of the nineteenth century, new technologies transformed the face of manufacturing in Europe, leading to new levels of economic growth and complex realignments among industry, labor, and national governments. Whereas Europe's first industrial revolution centered on coal, steam, and iron, the second industrial revolution relied on innovations in steel, electricity, and chemistry.

Harder, stronger, and more malleable than iron, steel had long been prized as a construction material. But until the mid-nineteenth century, producing steel cheaply and in large quantities was impossible. That changed between the 1850s and the 1870s, when different processes for refining and mass-producing alloy steel revolutionized the metallurgical industry. Britain's shipbuilders made a quick and profitable switch to steel construction, thus keeping their lead in the industry, while Germany and America dominated the rest of the steel industry. By 1905, Germany was producing almost half as much steel as Britain, enabling Germany to build a massive national and industrial infrastructure.

Like steel, electricity had been discovered earlier, and its advantages were similarly well known, such as its easy transmission over long distances to be converted into heat, light, and other types of energy. In 1879, Thomas Edison and

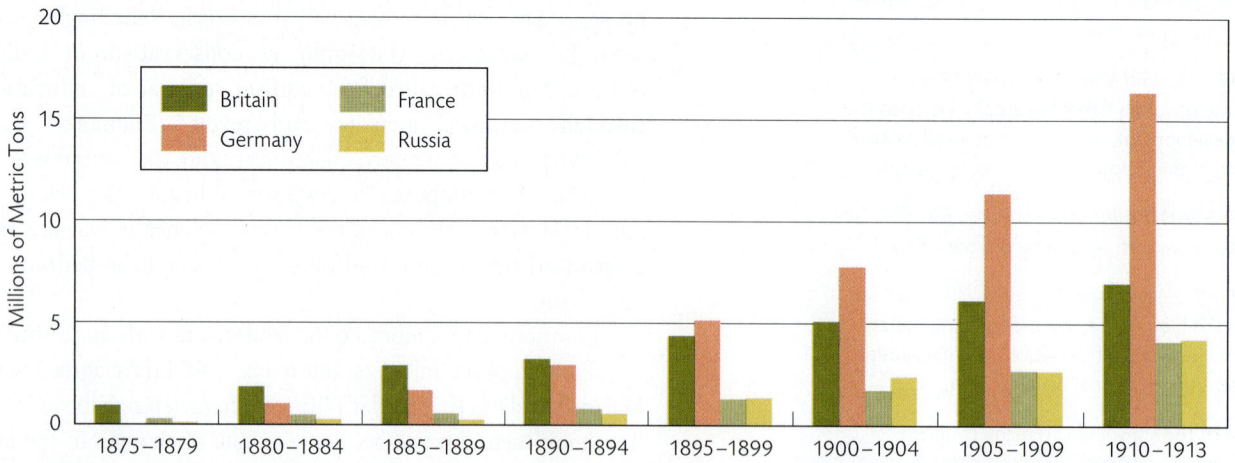

OUTPUT OF STEEL (IN MILLIONS OF METRIC TONS).
Source: Carlo Cipolla, *The Fontana Economic History of Europe*, vol. 3, pt. 2 (London: 1976), p. 775.

his associates invented the incandescent-filament lamp that changed electricity into light. In the 1880s, electricity was made available for commercial and domestic use, after the development of alternators and transformers capable of producing high-voltage alternating current. By the century's end, large power stations, which often used cheap water power, could send electric current over vast distances. The demand for electricity skyrocketed, and soon entire metropolitan areas were electrified. A leading sector in the new economy, electricity powered subways, tramways, and railroads, and also dramatically altered living habits in ordinary households.

The chemical industry was the third sector of important new technologies. The efficient production of alkali and sulfuric acid transformed the manufacture of such consumer goods as paper, soaps, textiles, and fertilizer. Britain and particularly Germany became leaders in the field. British entrepreneur William Lever was able to market his soaps and cleansers around the world, supported by heightened concerns for household hygiene and new techniques in mass marketing. German production, meanwhile, focused on industrial use, such as developing synthetic dyes and methods for refining petroleum, and came to control roughly 90 percent of the world's chemical market.

There were other innovations that contributed to the second industrial revolution. The growing demand for efficient power, for example, spurred the invention of the liquid-fuel internal combustion engine. By 1914, most navies had converted from coal to oil, as had domestic steamship companies. At first, the new engines' dependence on crude petroleum and distilled gasoline threatened their general application, but the discovery of oil fields in Russia, Borneo, Persia, and Texas around 1900 allayed such fears—protecting these oil reserves thus became a vital state prerogative. The adoption of oil-powered machinery had another important consequence: industrialists who had previously depended on nearby rivers or coal mines for power were free to take their enterprises to regions bereft of natural resources. The potential for worldwide industrialization was now in place. Of course, the internal combustion engine would bring even more radical changes to twentieth-century transportation, but the automobile and airplane were still in their infancy before 1914.

THE SECOND INDUSTRIAL REVOLUTION. A German electrical engineering factory illustrates the scale of production during the second industrial revolution. ■ *What changes in business practices and labor management made factories of this size possible?*

Changes in Scope and Scale

These technological changes were part of a much larger process: the impressive increases in the scope and scale of industry. Technologies were both causes and consequences of the race toward a bigger, faster, cheaper, and more efficient world. At the end of the nineteenth century, size mattered. In the rise of heavy industry and mass marketing, factories and cities grew hand in hand, while advances in media and mobility spurred the creation of national mass cultures. For the first time, ordinary people followed the news on national and global levels. They watched as European powers divided the globe and enlarged their empires with prodigious feats of engineering mastery, building railroads, dams, canals, and harbors to monumental proportions. Such projects embodied the ideals of modern European industry, and generated enormous income for builders, investors, bankers, entrepreneurs, and, of course, makers of steel and concrete. Canals in central Europe, railroads in the Andes, and telegraph cables spanning the ocean floors—these "tentacles of empire," as one historian has dubbed them—stretched across the globe.

The population continued to grow, particularly in central and eastern Europe. In the space of a generation, Russia's population increased by nearly a quarter and Germany's population by half. Britain's population, too, rose by nearly one-third between 1881 and 1911. Thanks

Map labels (geographic):

RUSSIA · FINLAND · SWEDEN · NORWAY · DENMARK · IRELAND · GREAT BRITAIN · NETHERLANDS · BELGIUM · GERMANY · SWITZ. · FRANCE · SPAIN · PORTUGAL · ITALY · AUSTRIA-HUNGARY · SERBIA · BULGARIA · ROMANIA · ALBANIA · GREECE · TURKEY · MONTENEGRO

Seas: BLACK SEA · MEDITERRANEAN SEA · BALTIC SEA · NORTH SEA · ATLANTIC OCEAN

Cities: Moscow · St. Petersburg · Stockholm · Warsaw · Breslau · Berlin · Nuremberg · Vienna · Laibach · Belgrade · Constantinople · Naples · Salerno · Rome · Marseilles · Barcelona · Madrid · Lisbon · Toulouse · St. Etienne · Limoges · Paris · London

Inset: Area of detail · EUROPE · AFRICA

Scale: 300 Miles · 300 Kilometers · 100 200 · 0

Legend:

Railroad Development
Lines completed by 1848
Area of main railroad completed by 1870
Lines after 1870

Mining
Low-grade coal
High-grade coal
Iron ore
Petroleum

Industrial Concentration
Cities
Industrial regions

Steel
Engineering
Chemicals
Electrical industry
Oil production

THE INDUSTRIAL REGIONS OF EUROPE. This map shows the distribution of mineral resources, rail lines, and industrial activity. ■ *Which nations enjoyed advantages in the development of industry? Why?* ■ *Which resources were most important for industrial growth in the second half of the nineteenth century?* ■ *Which resources in Britain became dominant as a result of industrialization?*

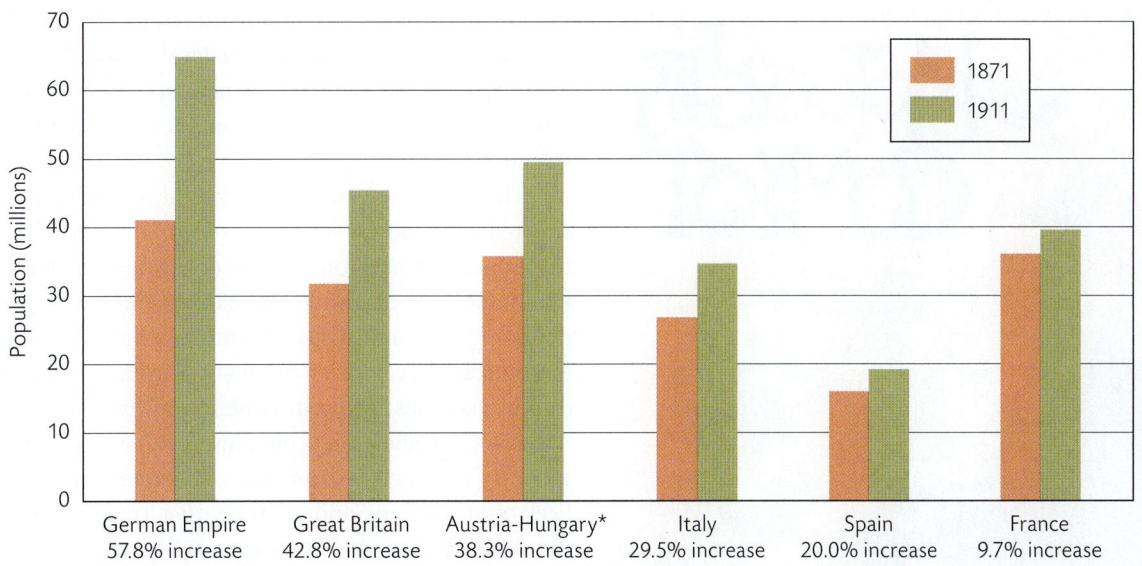

POPULATION GROWTH IN MAJOR STATES BETWEEN 1871 AND 1911 (POPULATION IN MILLIONS).
*Not including Bosnia-Herzegovina.
Source: Colin Dyer, *Population and Society in Twentieth-Century France* (New York: 1978), p. 5.

to improvements in both crop yields and shipping, food shortages declined, rendering entire populations less susceptible to illness and infant mortality. Advances in medicine, nutrition, and personal hygiene diminished the prevalence of dangerous diseases, such as cholera and typhus. And improved conditions in housing and public sanitation transformed the urban environment.

Credit and Consumerism

Changes in scope and scale of industry also altered consumption. Indeed, it was during this period that consumption began to shift, slowly, to the center of economic activity and theory. Department stores offering both practical and luxury goods to the middle class were one mark of the times—of urbanization, economic expansion, and the new importance attached to merchandising. Advertising took off as well, as lavishly illustrated posters from the late nineteenth century advertised concert halls, soaps, bicycles, alcoholic drinks, and sewing machines. Even more significant, by the 1880s, new stores sought to attract working-class people by introducing the all-important innovation of credit payment. In earlier times, working-class families pawned watches, mattresses, or furniture to borrow money, but now they began to buy on credit. This change would eventually have seismic effects on both households and national economies.

These new late-nineteenth-century patterns of consumption, however, were largely urban. In the countryside, peasants continued to save money under mattresses; hand down a few pieces of furniture for generations; make, launder, and mend their own clothes and linens; and offer a kilo of sugar as a generous household gift. Mass consumption remained difficult to imagine in what was still a deeply stratified society, and retailers were only slowly able to whittle away at these traditional habits.

The Rise of the Corporation

Economic growth and the demands of mass consumption spurred reorganization, consolidation, and regulation of capitalist institutions. Although capitalist enterprises had been financed by individual investors through the joint-stock principle at least since the sixteenth century, it was during the late nineteenth century that the modern corporation came into its own. To mobilize the enormous funds needed for large-scale enterprises, entrepreneurs needed to offer better guarantees on investors' money. To provide such protection, most European countries enacted or improved their limited-liability laws, which ensured that stockholders would lose only the value of their shares in the event of bankruptcy. Insured in this way, many thousands of middle-class men and women

POSTER FOR *MOTOCYCLES COMIOT*, 1899. The rise of consumer spending in the middle class created a new industry and a new genre of art: advertising illustration. This advertisement, like many from the period, contrasted new with old, leisure with toil, and speed or freedom with inertia.

considered corporate investment a promising venture. After 1870, stock markets attracted new commercial and industrial ventures and ceased to be primarily a clearinghouse for state paper and railroad bonds.

Limited liability was one part of a larger trend of incorporation. Whereas most firms had been small to middle size, companies now incorporated to attain the necessary size for survival. In doing so, they shifted the control from company founders and local directors to distant bankers and financiers. Because financial institutions represented the interests of investors whose primary concern was the bottom line, bankers' control over industrial growth encouraged an ethos of impersonal finance capital.

Equally important, the second industrial revolution created a strong demand for technical expertise, which undercut traditional forms of family management. University degrees in engineering and chemistry became more valuable than on-the-job apprenticeships. The emergence of a white-collar class (middle-level salaried managers who were neither owners nor laborers) marked a significant change in work life and in society's evolving class structure.

The drive toward larger business enterprises was spurred by a desire for increased profits and the belief that consolidation protected society against the hazards of boom-and-bust economic fluctuations and "ruinous" competition. Some industries combined vertically, attempting to control every step of production from the acquisition of raw materials to the distribution of finished products. Andrew Carnegie's steel company in Pittsburgh controlled costs by owning the iron and coal mines as well as the fleet of steamships and railways that transported ore to the mills. A second form of corporate self-protection was horizontal alignment: organized into cartels, companies in the same industry would band together to fix prices and control competition, if not eliminate it outright. Coal, oil, and steel companies were especially suited for this organization, because only a few major players could afford the huge expense of building, equipping, and running mines, refineries, and foundries. In 1894, for example, the Rhenish-Westphalian Coal Syndicate ruthlessly captured 98 percent of Germany's coal market, forcing small competitors to join them or face ruin. Through similar tactics, both legal and illegal, John D. Rockefeller's Standard Oil Company came to control more than 90 percent of the United States' oil production by the 1880s. Cartels were particularly strong in Germany and the United States, but they were less so in Britain, where dedication to free-trade policies made price-fixing difficult. In France, both family firms and laborers opposed cartels, and there was also less heavy industry.

Though governments sometimes tried to stem the burgeoning power of cartels, the dominant trend of this period was increased cooperation between governments and industry. Contrary to the laissez-faire mentality of early capitalism, corporations developed close relationships with the states in the West—most noticeably in colonial industrial projects, such as the construction of railroads, harbors, and seafaring steamships. These efforts were so costly, or so unprofitable, that private enterprise could not have undertaken them alone, and because they served a larger political and strategic interest, governments funded them willingly. Such interdependence was underscored by the appearance of businessmen and financiers as officers of the state. The German banker Bernhard Dernburg was the German secretary of state for colonies. Joseph Chamberlain, the British manufacturer and mayoral boss of industrial Birmingham, served as the colonial secretary. And in France, Charles Jonnart, president of the Suez Canal Company and the Saint-Étienne steelwork, was later the governor general of Algeria. Tied to imperial interests, the rise of modern corporations had an impact around the globe.

Global Economics

Industrial development heightened competition between nations, creating new incentives for imperial expansion and the search for markets and goods abroad. The unevenness of this development also drove an unprecedented number of Europeans to migrate elsewhere. In the century between the 1840s and the 1940s, more than 55 million Europeans moved to North and South America (Chapter 22). These migrations peaked in the decade before the First World War, and they came at a moment when nations were beginning to understand that global connections offered both opportunity and potential threats. To protect their home markets, European powers all created trade barriers and often resorted to tariffs to raise the cost of imported goods. Because the demand for labor was insatiable in rapidly developing economies, there were few corresponding limitations on the mobility of people before World War I.

The growth of international trade combined with population migrations to produce a worldwide system of interlocking relationships that linked manufacturing, labor, commerce, and finance. The near universal adoption of the gold standard in currency exchange greatly facilitated world trade. The British empire was the first European nation to peg its currency to a fixed rate of gold, and other nations soon followed suit. The gold standard made currency exchange predictable and safe, a necessary condition for international trade. The gold standard also gave European nations a vehicle for mitigating the trade imbalances that were driven by industrial development. Almost all European countries were dependent on vast supplies of raw materials for their growing factories, leading them to import more than they exported. To alleviate these trade deficits, European economies relied on "invisible" exports: shipping, insurance, and banking services. The extent of Britain's exports in these areas was far greater than any other country, making London the money market of the world. By 1914, Britain had $20 billion invested overseas, compared to $8.7 billion for France and $6 billion for Germany. Britain also used its invisible trade to secure relationships with food-producing nations, becoming the major overseas buyer for U.S. and Canadian wheat, Argentinian beef, and Australian sheep. These goods, shipped

FINANCING EMPIRE. This 1908 photograph shows two financial institutions in the center of London, and at the heart of an expanding global system of exchange and investment. Bankers would meet with merchants at the Royal Exchange (center, with pillars). The Bank of England (left) issued notes backed by gold, which made currency exchange predictable, but limited the government's ability to use monetary policy to influence the business cycle.

cheaply aboard refrigerated vessels, kept down food prices for working-class families and eased demands for increased wages.

At moments of economic downturn, however, adherence to the gold standard prevented European nations from stimulating their economy through inflationary monetary policies. Without such monetary tools, competitiveness could only be reestablished by allowing unemployment to drive down wages. For these reasons, it was much easier to defend the gold standard when Europe's working-class populations did not yet vote. When universal male suffrage became the rule at the end of the nineteenth century, the connections between international trade, economic policy, and the fate of the working classes took on new significance.

Analyzing Primary Sources

Booker T. Washington, The Man Farthest Down (1912)

Booker T. Washington (1856–1915), born a slave in Alabama in the years before the Civil War, became an important educator and voice for reform in the United States during a period in which racial segregation was enshrined in law and defended by the threat of violence. The founding leader in 1881 of a new college for African American students, the Tuskegee Institute, Washington worked tirelessly with other educators and community leaders to improve educational opportunities for African Americans. In 1910, he traveled to Europe for two months with the goal of understanding "the condition of the poorer and working classes in Europe, particularly in those regions from which an ever-increasing number of immigrants are coming to our country each year." The result of this trip was his book, The Man Farthest Down, *which examined the proposition that the progress of human society could best be measured and understood by studying the lives and labors of the working class.*

 had crossed Europe from north to south before I got my first glimpse of an emigrant bound for America. On the way from Vienna to Naples I stopped at midnight at Rome, and in the interval between trains I spent an hour in wandering about in the soft southern air—such air as I had not found anywhere since I left my home in Alabama.

In returning to the station my curiousity was aroused, as I was passing in the shadow of the building, by what seemed to me a large vacant room near the main entrance to the station. As I attempted to enter this room I stumbled over the figure of a man lying on the stone floor. Looking farther, I saw something like forty or fifty persons, men as well as women, lying on the floor, their faces turned toward the wall, asleep.

The room itself was apparently bare and empty of all furniture. There was neither a bench nor a table, so far as I could see, in any part of the room. It seems that, without any expectation of doing so, I had wandered into the room reserved for emigrants, and came accidentally upon one of the sights I most wanted to see in Italy—namely, a party of emigrants bound for America.

As near as I could learn, these people were, for the most part, peasants, who had come in from the surrounding country, carrying what little property they possessed on their backs or tied up in little bundles in their arms, and were awaiting the arrival of the train that was to take them to the port from which they could take ship for America.

I confess it struck me as rather pathetic that, in this splendid new and modern railway station, in which the foreign traveler and the native Italian of the upper classes were provided with every convenience and luxury, so little thought had been given to the comfort of these humble travelers, who represent the people in Italy who pay proportionately most of the taxes, and who, by their patient industry and thrift, have contributed more than any other class to such progress as Italy has made in recent years.

Later on I had an opportunity to pass through the country from which perhaps the majority of these emigrants had come. I travelled through a long stretch of country where one sees only now and then a lonesome shepherd or a wretched hut with one low

LABOR POLITICS, MASS MOVEMENTS

The rapid expansion of late-nineteenth-century industry brought a parallel growth in the size, cohesion, and activism of Europe's working classes. The men and women who worked as wage laborers resented corporate power, fostered not only by the exploitation they experienced on the job but also by living "a life apart" in Europe's expanding cities (Chapter 19). As corporations devised new methods of protecting and promoting their interests, workers did the same. Labor unions, which were traditionally limited to skilled male workers in small-scale enterprises, grew during the late nineteenth century into mass, centralized, nationwide organizations. This "new unionism" emphasized organization across entire industries and, for the first time, brought unskilled workers into their ranks, increasing their power to negotiate wages and job conditions. More important, the creation of national unions provided room and a cowstall. I also visited some of the little villages which one sees clinging to the barren hilltops, to escape the poisonous mists of the plains below. There I saw the peasants in their homes and learned something of the way in which the lowly people in the rural districts have been neglected and oppressed. After that I was able to understand that it was no special hardship that these emigrants suffered at Rome. Perhaps many of them had never before slept in a place so clean and sanitary as the room the railway provided them. [. . .]

I inquired why it was that I saw so many women in the fields in this part of the country, for I had understood that Italian women, as a rule, did not go so frequently into field work as the women do in Austria and Hungary. I learned that it was because so many of the men who formerly did this work had emigrated to America. As a matter of fact, three fourths of the emigration from Italy to America comes from Sicily and the other southern provinces. There are villages in lower Italy which have been practically deserted. There are others in which no one but women and old men are left behind, and the whole population is more than half supported by the earnings of Italian laborers in America. There are cities within twenty miles of Naples which have lost within ten years two thirds of their inhabitants. In fact, there is one little village not far from the city of which it is said that the entire male population is in America. [. . .]

From all that I can learn, public sentiment in Italy is rapidly being aroused to the evils which cling to the present system of dealing with the agricultural labourer and the poorer classes. But Italy has not done well by her lower classes in the past. She has oppressed them with heavy taxes; has maintained a land system that has worn out the soil at the same time that it has impoverished the labourer; has left the agricultural labourers in ignorance; has failed to protect them from the rapacity of the large landowners; and has finally driven them to seek their fortunes in a foreign land.

In return, these emigrants have repaid their native country by vastly increasing her foreign commerce, by pouring back into Italy the earnings they have made abroad, by themselves returning with new ideas and new ambitions and entering into the work of building up the country.

These returned emigrants have brought back to the mother country improved farming machinery, new methods of labour, and new capital. Italian emigrants abroad not only contribute to their mother country a sum estimated at between five and six million dollars annually, but Italian emigration has awakened Italy to the value of her laboring classes, and in doing this has laid the foundation for the prosperity of the whole country. In fact, Italy is another illustration that the condition of the man at the bottom affects the life of every class above him. It is to the class lowest down that Italy largely owes what prosperity she has as yet attained.

Source: Booker T. Washington, *The Man Farthest Down: A Record of Observation and Study in Europe* (London: T. Fisher Unwin, 1912), pp. 105–108, 122.

Questions for Analysis

1. How does Washington's thinking about the migrants in the Rome train station change in the course of his anecdote?

2. What does this brief excerpt tell us about Washington's research methods as he seeks to understand the modern phenomenon of migration?

3. What are the goals of his research into the question of European migration?

---

a framework for a new type of political movement: the socialist mass party.

Why did socialism develop in Europe after 1870? Changing national political structures provide part of the answer. Parliamentary constitutional governments opened the political process to new voters, some of whom supported socialists. Having become part of the legislative process, socialists in national parliaments led efforts to expand voting rights further in the 1860s and 1870s, and their success created new constituencies of working-class men. At the same time, traditional struggles between labor and management moved up to the national level: governments aligned with business interests, and legislators countered working-class agitation with antilabor and antisocialist laws. To radical leaders, the organization of national mass political movements seemed the only effective way to counter the industrialists' political strength. Socialist movements thus abandoned their earlier revolutionary traditions (exemplified by the romantic image of barricaded streets) in favor of legal, electoral competition within Europe's parliamentary systems.

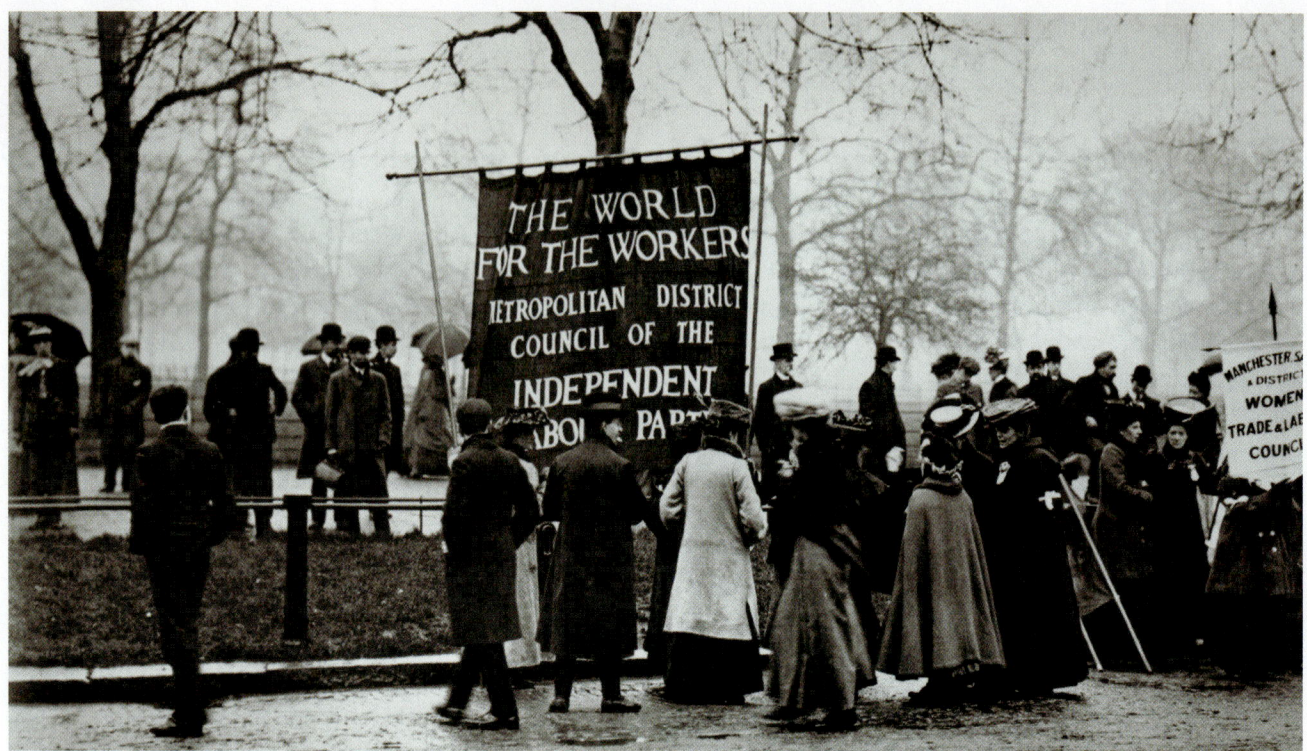

INDEPENDENT LABOR PARTY DEMONSTRATION IN ENGLAND, c. 1893. Activism among workers swelled in the late nineteenth century. Increasingly powerful labor unions had a profound impact on politics, because male workers without property could now vote in local and national elections.

The Spread of Socialist Parties— and Alternatives

The most influential socialist thinker was Karl Marx, whose early career was discussed in Chapter 20. Since the 1840s, Marx and his collaborator Friedrich Engels had been intellectuals and activists, participating in organizing fledgling socialist movements. In 1867, Marx published the first of three volumes of his *Capital*. In the book, Marx attacked capitalism using economic analysis, allowing him to claim scientific validity for his work. He was contemptuous of other socialists whose opposition to industrial economies was couched only in moral terms. Marx claimed to offer a systematic analysis of how capitalism forces workers to exchange their labor for subsistence wages while enabling their employers to amass both wealth and power. Followers of Marx called for workers everywhere to ally with each other to create an independent political force, and few other groups pushed as strongly to secure civil liberties, expand conceptions of citizenship, or build a welfare state. **Marxists** also made powerful claims for gender equality, though in practice woman suffrage took a backseat to class politics.

Not all working-class movements were Marxist, however. Differences among various left-wing groups remained strong, and the most divisive issues were the role of violence and whether socialists should cooperate with liberal governments—and if so, to what end. Some "gradualists" were willing to work with liberals for piecemeal reform, whereas **anarchists** and **syndicalists** rejected parliamentary politics altogether. When European labor leaders met in 1864 at the first meeting of the International Working Men's Association, Marx argued strongly in favor of mass movements that would prepare the working classes for revolution. He was strongly opposed by anarchist Mikhail Bakunin, who rejected any form of state or party organization and instead called for terror and violence to destabilize society.

Between 1875 and 1905, Marxist socialists founded political parties in Germany, Belgium, France, Austria, and Russia. These parties were disciplined workers' organizations that aimed to seize control of the state and make revolutionary changes in the social order. The most successful was the German **Social Democratic Party** (SPD), which initially intended to work toward political change within the parliamentary political system but became more radical in the face of Bismarck's oppressive antisocialist laws. By the outbreak of the First World War, the SPD was the largest, best-organized workers' party in the world. Rapid and extensive industrialization, a large urban working class, and a national government hostile to organized labor made German workers particularly receptive to the goals and ideals of social democracy.

In Britain—the world's first and most industrialized economy—the socialist presence was much smaller and more moderate because much of the socialist agenda was advanced by radical liberals in Britain, which forestalled the growth of an independent socialist party. Even when a separate **Labour Party** was formed in 1901, it remained moderate, committed to reforming capitalism with measures such as support for public housing or welfare benefits, rather than a complete overhaul of the economy. For the Labour party, and for Britain's many trade unions, Parliament remained a legitimate vehicle for achieving social change, limiting the appeal of revolutionary Marxism.

Militant workers seeking to organize themselves for political action found alternatives to Marxism in anarchism and syndicalism. Anarchists shared many values with Marxist socialists, but they opposed centrally organized economies and the very existence of the state. Rather than participate in parliamentary politics, anarchists aimed to establish small-scale, localized, and self-sufficient democratic communities that could guarantee the maximum of individual sovereignty. Renouncing parties, unions, and any form of modern mass organization, anarchists fell back on the tradition of conspiratorial violence, which Marx had denounced. Anarchists assassinated Tsar Alexander II in 1881 and five other heads of state in the following years, believing that such "exemplary terror" would spark popular revolt. Syndicalists, meanwhile, did not call for terror but embraced a strategy of strikes and sabotage by workers. Their hope was that a general strike of all workers would bring down the capitalist state and replace it with workers' syndicates or trade associations. Anarchism's opposition to any form of organization kept it from making substantial gains as a movement. Likewise, the syndicalists' refusal to participate in politics limited their ability to command wide influence, but the tradition was kept alive, especially in France, through participation in trade unions.

By 1895, seven socialist parties in Europe had captured between a quarter and a third of the votes in their countries. But just as socialists were gaining a permanent foothold in national politics, they were also straining under limitations and internal conflicts. Working-class movements, in fact, had never gained full worker support. Some workers remained loyal to older liberal traditions

SOCIALIST PARTY PAMPHLET, c. 1895. Socialism emerged as a powerful political force throughout Europe in the late nineteenth century, although in different forms depending on the region. This German pamphlet quotes from Marx's *Communist Manifesto* of 1848, calling for workers in Asia, Africa, America, and Australia to unite under the banners of equality and brotherhood. ▪ *What was the significance of this claim for equality, given the image's apparent references to racial difference?*

or to religious parties, while many others were excluded from socialist politics by its narrow definition of who constituted the working class—male industrial workers.

Furthermore, some committed socialists began to question Marx's core assumptions about the inevitability of workers' impoverishment and the collapse of the capitalist order. A German group of so-called revisionists, led by Eduard Bernstein, challenged Marxist doctrine and called for a shift to moderate and gradual reform through electoral politics. Supporters of direct action were incensed by Bernstein's betrayal of the Marxist theory of revolution, because they feared that the official reforms that favored workers might make status quo more acceptable to the

"BLOODY RIOTS IN LIMOGES." Labor unions used strikes to draw attention to low wages and dangerous working conditions and to extract concessions from employers. Some militant groups, known as syndicalists, hoped that a general strike of all workers would lead to revolutionary change. Fear of labor militancy was a common theme in the popular press, as in this newspaper illustration from Limoges in France, where soldiers are depicted defending the gates of a prison from laborers brandishing the revolutionary red flag of socialism. ▪ *What connection might this newspaper's readers have made between labor militancy and earlier revolutionary movements in Europe?*

political strength since the 1870s, working-class parties now affected the ability of nation-states to wage war. In short, they had come of age. Much to the disappointment of socialist leaders, however, European laborers—many of whom had voted for socialist candidates in previous elections—nevertheless donned the uniforms of their respective nations and marched off to war in 1914, proving that national identities and class identities were not necessarily incompatible with one another.

DEMANDING EQUALITY: SUFFRAGE AND THE WOMEN'S MOVEMENT

Since the 1860s, the combination of working-class activism and liberal constitutionalism had expanded male suffrage across Europe, and by 1884, Germany, France, and Britain had enfranchised most men. But nowhere did women have the right to vote. Nineteenth-century political ideology relegated women to the status of second-class citizens, and even egalitarian-minded socialists seldom challenged this entrenched hierarchy. Excluded from the workings of parliamentary and mass party politics, women pressed their interests through independent organizations and various forms of direct action. The new women's movement won some crucial legal reforms during this period, and after the turn of the twentieth century, its militant campaign for suffrage fed the growing sense of political crisis, most notably in Britain.

Women's associations, such as the General German Women's Association, pressed first for educational and legal reforms. In Britain, women's colleges were established at the same time that women won the right to control their own property. (Previously, women surrendered their property, including wages, to their husbands.) Laws enacted in 1884 and 1910 gave Frenchwomen the same right and ability to divorce their husbands. German women, too, won more favorable divorce laws by 1870, and in 1900, they were granted full legal rights.

After these important changes in women's status, suffrage crystallized as the next logical goal. Indeed, votes became *the* symbol for women's ability to attain full personhood. As the suffragists saw it, enfranchisement meant not only political progress but also economic, spiritual, and moral advancement. By the last third of the century, middle-class women throughout western Europe had founded clubs, published journals, organized petitions, sponsored assemblies, and initiated other public activities to press for the right to vote. To the left of the middle-class movements were organizations of feminist socialists such

working class. The radicals within the labor movement were inspired by the unexpected—and unsuccessful—revolution in Russia in 1905. And German Marxists such as Rosa Luxemburg called for mass strikes, hoping to ignite a widespread proletarian revolution.

Conflicts over strategy peaked just before the First World War, but these divisions did not diminish the strength and appeal of socialism among workers. On the eve of the war, governments discreetly consulted with labor leaders about workers' willingness to enlist and fight. Having built an impressive organizational and

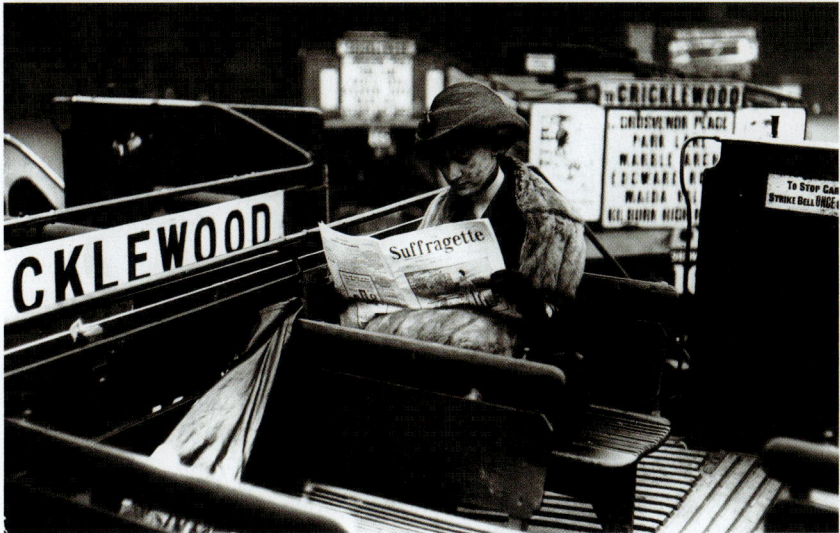

FEMINIST PROTEST IN THE AGE OF MASS POLITICS. These two images demonstrate the ways in which supporters of the vote for women in Britain sought to use the public realm for political advantage. The top image shows Emily Davison being fatally struck by the king's horse at a racetrack. She sought to draw attention to the injustice of women's exclusion from political citizenship by disrupting the Epsom Derby, the richest race in Britain and an annual society event. Her death, widely seen by her supporters as a martyrdom in the cause of women's rights, led to a public funeral procession through London. The bottom image shows a woman reading the feminist paper *Suffragette* on a British tram. By the end of the nineteenth century, the penny press and growing literacy rates vastly increased the ability of organized political groups to get their message out.

peaceful, constitutional reform. But the movement lacked the political or economic clout to sway a male legislature dominated by two parties—the Liberals and the Conservatives—each party fearing that female suffrage would benefit the other. Exasperated by this, Emmeline Pankhurst founded the Women's Social and Political Union (WSPU) in 1903, which adopted tactics of militancy and civil disobedience. WSPU women chained themselves to the visitors' gallery in the House of Commons, slashed paintings in museums, inscribed "Votes for Women" in acid on the greens of golf courses, disrupted political meetings, burned politicians' houses, and smashed department store windows. The government countered these violent activities with repression. When arrested women went on hunger strikes in prisons, wardens fed them by force: tying them down, holding their mouths open with wooden and metal clamps, and running tubes down their throats. In 1910, the suffragists' attempt to enter the House of Commons set off a six-hour riot with policemen and bystanders, shocking and outraging a nation unaccustomed to such violence from women. The intensity of the suffragists' moral claims was dramatically embodied by the 1913 martyrdom of Emily Wilding Davison, who, wearing a "Votes for Women" sash, threw herself in front of the king's horse on Derby Day and was trampled to death.

Redefining Womanhood

The campaign for woman suffrage was perhaps the most visible and inflammatory aspect of a larger cultural shift in which the traditional Victorian gender roles were redefined. Economic, political, and social changes undermined the view that men and women should occupy distinctly different spheres. Women became increasingly visible in the workforce and took up a greater variety of jobs. Some working-class women joined the new factories and workshops in an effort to mitigate their families' poverty. The expansion of government and corporate bureaucracies

as Clara Zetkin and Lily Braun, who believed that only a socialist revolution would free women from economic as well as political exploitation.

In Britain, woman suffrage campaigns exploded in violence. In 1897, Millicent Fawcett, a distinguished middle-class woman with connections to the political establishment, brought together sixteen different organizations into the National Union of Women's Suffrage Societies, committed to brought middle-class women into the workforce as social workers and clerks. The increase in hospital services and the advent of national compulsory education required more nurses and teachers, and a shortage of male workers and a need to fill so many new jobs as cheaply as possible made women a logical choice. Thus, women, who had campaigned vigorously for access to education, began to see doors opening to them. Swiss universities and medical schools began to admit women in the 1860s. In the 1870s and 1880s, British women established their own colleges at Cambridge and Oxford. Parts of the professional world began to look dramatically different. In Prussia, for instance, 14,600 full-time women teachers were staffing schools by 1896. Moreover, the achievements of this generation of educated women were sometimes remarkable. For example, Marie Skłodowska-Curie, the daughter of a Polish high school teacher in Warsaw, became a professor of physics at the Faculty of Sciences in Paris in 1906. By 1911, she had won two Nobel Prizes: one in physics for the discovery of radioactivity and one in chemistry for the isolation of pure radium. Her extraordinary accomplishments, along with more general changes in women's employment, began to deflate the myth of female domesticity.

Women also became more active in politics—an area that was previously off limits. This is not to say that female political activity was unprecedented, since in important ways, the groundwork for women's new political participation had been laid earlier in the century. The reform movements of the early nineteenth century depended on women and raised women's standing in public. First with charity work in religious associations and later with hundreds of secular associations, women throughout Europe directed their energies toward poor relief, prison reform, Sunday school, temperance, ending slavery and prostitution, and expanding educational opportunities for women. Reform groups brought women together outside the home and encouraged them to speak their minds as free-thinking equals and to pursue political goals—a right denied them as individual females. And although some women in reform groups supported political emancipation, many others were drawn into reform politics by a belief that they had a special moral mission: they saw public activities as a logical extension of their feminine domestic duties. Eventually, the nineteenth-century reform movements opened up the world beyond the home, particularly for middle-class women, and widened the scope of possibilities for later generations.

These changes in women's roles were paralleled by the emergence of a new social type, dubbed the "new woman."

CHANGES IN WHITE-COLLAR WORK. Clerical work was primarily male until the end of the nineteenth century, when cadres of women workers and the emergence of new industries and bureaucracies transformed employment. ■ *How might have these changing patterns of employment affected family life or attitudes toward marriage and child rearing?*

Analyzing Primary Sources

The Old Woman (1903)

Hedwig Dohm (1831–1919) was a German writer and feminist thinker from Berlin. She began to publish works on the emancipation of women in the 1870s. Crucial to her feminism was the idea that in addition to political rights, changes in the perception of women were also necessary—changes in the assumptions people made about the different places that women and men held in society.

want to talk about the suffering of the old woman and tell how it is to be remedied.

That up to the present, woman has only been granted sexual worth has been said and lamented often enough. I will say it one more time, because this value judgment originates from the disregard to which the old woman is subjected. When a woman becomes incapable of being a bearer of and caretaker of children, or a lover, then her justification for existence has ceased.

[…]

Sexual appeal and utility as a measure of woman's worth! An animalistic interpretation of her being, a naïve shamelessness that may have been suitable for an earlier age, but that makes a mockery of the maturity and greatness of the present for it dehumanizes woman.

[…]

Poor old woman! Everything gradually leaves you. In the beginning, your longing gaze follows those who leave you: children, friends, society; but they distance themselves further and further—they disappear. Loneliness envelops you

as if in a shroud, oblivion is the inscription above your house, the raven's song of hopelessness caws above your bed. Silence is around you; also you yourself are silent because no one wants to hear you. Poor old woman! You feel as if you have to be ashamed that you, now that you are so useless and already so old, are still living. Age weighs on you as guilt, as if you were usurping a place that belonged to others. Around you, you feel a sentiment that is pushing you out of this life.

[…]

If up until now the lot of the old woman resembled that of a person whose property has burned down and who is crouching on the grave of his possessions—does it have to remain this way? No. Limiting the needlessness of the aging and old woman to the set and insurmountable limits of nature will be one of the consequences of the women's movement. There are no measures one can take to prevent death; but there are measures against the early death of a woman. The strongest is: unconditional emancipation of woman and thereby the deliverance from the brutal superstition that her right to exist rests solely on her sex. Give a woman a richer content in life, practical or intellectual interests

that rise above the immediate family, that, when she gets old, will incorporate her into the larger family of humanity and through the common ground of such interests connect her with general, social life. Let her be on her own instead of always depending on others. If the others are gone from her, she always remains superficial; and is (for herself) not superfluous.

Incessant activity, be it with hand or head, will—like oil for a machine—keep the strength of her nerves and brain elastic and will guarantee her mental longevity far beyond the years that until now meant the farewell from life for her. Inactivity is the sleeping potion that you, old woman, are offered. Do not drink it! Be something! Activity is joy. And joy is almost youth.

Source: Hedwig Dohm, *Become Who You Are*, trans. Elizabeth G. Ametsbichler (Albany NY: 2006), pp. 67–68, 79.

Questions for Analysis

1. Why are older women in modern society despised according to Dohm?

2. What is Dohm's solution to the exclusion of older women from society?

ORGANIZED ANTIFEMINISM. Male students demonstrate against admitting women to Cambridge University in England in 1881. A female figure is hung in effigy (on the right), and the suspended banner reads in part: "There's No Place for You Maids."

Humphrey Ward maintained that bringing women into the political arena would sap the virility of the British Empire. Octavia Hill, a noted social worker, stated that women should refrain from politics and, in so doing, "temper this wild struggle . . . for place and power." Christian commentators criticized suffragists for causing moral decay through selfish individualism. Still others believed that feminism would dissolve the family, a theme that fed into a larger discussion on the decline of the West amid a growing sense of cultural crisis. Indeed, the struggle for women's rights provided a flashpoint for an array of European anxieties over labor, politics, gender, and biology—all of which suggested that an orderly political consensus, so ardently desired by middle-class society, was slipping out of reach.

A new woman demanded education and a job, refused to be escorted by chaperones when she went out, and rejected the restrictive corsets of mid-century fashion. In other words, she claimed the right to an active life, physically and intellectually, and refused to conform to the norms that defined nineteenth-century womanhood. The new woman was an image created in part by artists and journalists who filled newspapers, magazines, and advertising billboards with pictures of women riding bicycles in bloomers (voluminous trousers under a short skirt); smoking cigarettes; and enjoying the cafés, dance halls, tonic waters, soaps, and other emblems of consumption. Very few women actually fitted this image, however, because, among other things, most were too poor. Still, middle- and working-class women demanded more social freedom, and redefined gender norms in the process. For supporters, these new women symbolized a welcome era of social emancipation. For some onlookers, however, women's newfound independence amounted to shirking domestic responsibilities, and they attacked women who defied convention as ugly "half-men," unfit and unable to marry.

Opposition was intense, sometimes violent, and not exclusively male. Men scorned women who threatened their elite preserves in universities, clubs, and public offices, but a wide array of female antisuffragists also denounced the movement. Conservatives such as Mrs.

LIBERALISM AND ITS DISCONTENTS: NATIONAL POLITICS AT THE TURN OF THE CENTURY

Middle-class liberals found themselves on the defensive after 1870, after having championed doctrines of individual rights throughout the nineteenth century. Previously, political power had rested on a balance between middle-class interests and those of the traditional elites. The landed aristocracy shared power with industrial magnates, and monarchical rule coexisted with constitutional freedoms. The rise of mass politics upset this balance in the late nineteenth century, as expanding franchise and rising expectations brought newcomers to the political stage. As we have seen, trade unions, socialists, and feminists all challenged Europe's governing classes by demanding that political participation be open to all, to which governments responded with a mix of conciliatory and repressive measures. As the twentieth century approached, political struggles became increasingly fierce, and by the First World War, the foundation of traditional parliamentary politics was crumbling in the face of a new kind of mass politics.

France: The Third Republic and the Paris Commune

The Franco-Prussian War of 1870, which ended with the unification of the victorious Germany, was a bruising defeat for France. The government of the Second Empire folded and, in its wake, the French proclaimed a republic. But its legitimacy was contested from the start, as crafting a durable republican system proved difficult. In 1875, the new constitution of the Third Republic was finally instituted, signaling a triumph of democratic and parliamentary principles. Establishing democracy, however, was a volatile process, and the Third Republic faced class conflicts, scandals, and the rise of new forms of right-wing politics that would poison French politics for decades to come.

As soon as the government surrendered, it faced a crisis that pitted the nation's representatives against the radical city of Paris. During the Franco-Prussian War, the city had appointed its own municipal government, the Commune, and it not only refused to surrender to the Germans but proclaimed itself the true government of France. The city had been besieged by the Germans for four months, and most people who could afford to flee had done so; but the rest, hungry and radicalized, defied the French government that was sitting in Versailles and negotiating the terms of an armistice with the Germans. With the armistice signed, the French government turned its attention to the city. In March 1871, after long and fruitless negotiations, the government sent troops to disarm the capital. But because the Commune's strongest support came from the workers of Paris, the conflict became a class war. For a week, the communards battled against the government's troops, building barricades to stop the invaders, taking and shooting hostages, then retreating very slowly into the northern working-class neighborhoods of the city. The French government's repression was brutal: at least 25,000 Parisians were executed, killed in fighting, or consumed in the fires that raged through the city; and thousands more were deported to the penal colony of New Caledonia in the South Pacific. The Paris Commune was a brief episode, but it cast a long shadow and reopened old political wounds. For Marx, who wrote about the Commune, and other socialists, it illustrated the futility of an older insurrectionary tradition on the left and the need for more mass-based democratic politics.

The Dreyfus Affair and Anti-Semitism as Politics

On the other side of the French political spectrum, new forms of radical right-wing politics emerged that foreshadowed developments elsewhere. As the age-old foundations of conservative politics—the Catholic Church and the landed nobility—slipped, more radical right-wing politics took shape. Stung by the defeat of 1870 and critical of the republic and its premises, the new right was nationalist, anti-parliamentary, and antiliberal (in the sense of commitment to individual liberties). Maurice Barrès, for instance, elected deputy in 1889, declared that parliamentary government had sown "impotence and corruption" and was too weak to defend the nation. During the first half of the nineteenth century, nationalism had been associated with the left (Chapter 20). But now, it was more often invoked by the right and linked to xenophobia (fear of foreigners) in general, and anti-Semitism in particular.

The power of popular anti-Semitism in France was made clear by a public controversy that erupted in the 1890s, which became known as the **Dreyfus Affair**. In 1894, a group of monarchist officers in the army accused Alfred Dreyfus, a Jewish captain on the general staff, of selling military secrets to Germany. Dreyfus was convicted and deported for life to Devil's Island, a ghastly South American prison colony in French Guiana. Two years later, an intelligence officer named Georges Picquart discovered that the documents used to convict Dreyfus were forgeries, but the War Department refused to grant Dreyfus a new trial. The case became an enormous public scandal, fanned on both sides by the involvement of prominent intellectual figures. Republicans, some socialists, liberals, and intellectuals such as the writer Émile Zola backed Dreyfus, claiming that the case was about individual rights as well as the legitimacy of the republic and its laws. Nationalists, prominent Catholics, and other socialists who believed that the case was a distraction from economic issues opposed Dreyfus and refused to question the military's judgment. One Catholic newspaper insisted that the question was not whether Dreyfus was guilty or innocent but whether or not the Jews and unbelievers were the "secret masters of France."

The **anti-Semitism** of the anti-Dreyfus camp was a combination of three strands of anti-Jewish thinking in Europe: (1) long-standing currents of anti-Semitism within Christianity, which damned the Jewish people as Christ killers; (2) economic anti-Semitism, which insisted that the wealthy banking family of Rothschild was representative of all Jews; and (3) late-nineteenth-century racial thinking, which contrasted a so-called Aryan (Indo-European) race against an inferior Semitic race. Anti-Dreyfus supporters whipped these ideas into a potent form of propaganda in anti-Semitic newspapers such as Édouard Drumont's *La Libre Parole* ("Free Speech"), a French daily that claimed a circulation of 200,000 during the height of the Dreyfus Affair.

Competing Viewpoints

Liberalism and the State

> In the second half of the nineteenth century, some British liberals responded to calls from an expanding electorate by moving away from a laissez-faire position, which supported minimal state interference in society and the economy. Laissez-faire still had its adherents among liberals, however, most notably the libertarian social philosopher Herbert Spencer. But in the face of a more organized labor movement and what they perceived as a very real threat of revolution, other liberals began to argue that some forms of government action to alleviate social distress were not only compatible with individual liberty in the economic realm, but they were, in fact, necessary to preserve it. Compare Herbert Spencer's arguments against assistance to the poor in 1851 with L. T. Hobhouse's defense of state pension plans in 1911.

Herbert Spencer, Social Statics (1851)

In common with its other assumptions of secondary offices, the assumption by a government of the office of Reliever-general to the poor, is necessarily forbidden by the principle that a government cannot rightly do anything more than protect. In demanding from a citizen contributions for the mitigation of distress—contributions not needed for the due administration of men's rights—the state is, as we have seen, reversing its function, and diminishing that liberty to exercise the faculties which it was instituted to maintain. Possibly, unmindful of the explanations already given, some will assert that by satisfying the wants of the pauper, a government is in reality extending *his* liberty to exercise his faculties, inasmuch as it is giving him something without which the exercise of them is impossible; and that hence, though it decreases the rate-payer's sphere of action, it compensates by increasing that of the rate-receiver. But this statement of the case implies a confounding of two widely-different things. To enforce the fundamental law—to take care that every man has freedom to do all that he wills, provided he infringes not the equal freedom of any other man—this is the special purpose for which the civil power exists. Now insuring to each the right to pursue within the specified limits the objects of his desires without let or hindrance, is quite a separate thing from insuring him satisfaction. Of two individuals, one may use his liberty of action successfully—may achieve the gratifications he seeks after, or accumulate what is equivalent to many of them—property; whilst the other, having like privileges, may fail to do so. But with these results the state has no concern. All that lies within its commission is to see that each man is allowed to use such powers and opportunities as he possesses; and if it takes from him who has prospered to give to him who has not, it violates its duty towards the one to do more than its duty towards the other. Or, repeating the idea elsewhere expressed, it breaks down the vital law of society, that it may effect what social vitality does not call for.

Source: Herbert Spencer, *Social Statics: or, The Conditions essential to Happiness specified, and the First of them Developed* (London: 1851), pp. 311–12.

L. T. Hobhouse, Liberalism (1911)

For the mass of the people, therefore, to be assured of the means of a decent livelihood must mean to be assured of continuous employment at a living wage, or, as an alternative, of public assistance. Now, as has been remarked, experience goes to show that the wage of the average worker, as fixed by competition, is not and is not likely to become sufficient to cover all the fortunes and misfortunes of life, to provide for sickness, accident, unemployment and old age, in addition to the regular needs of an average family. In the case of accident the State has put the burden of making provision on the employer. In the case of old age it has, acting, as I think, upon a sounder principle, taken the burden upon itself. It is very important to realize precisely what the new departure involved in the Old Age Pensions Act amounted to in point of principle. The Poor Law already guaranteed the aged person and the poor in general against actual starvation. But the Poor Law came into operation only at the point of sheer destitution. It failed to help those who had helped themselves. Indeed, to many it held out little inducement to help themselves if they could not hope to lay by so much as would enable them to live more comfortably on their means than they would live in the workhouse.

The pension system throws over the test of destitution. It provides a certain minimum, a basis to go upon, a foundation upon which independent thrift may hope to build up a sufficiency. It is not a narcotic but a stimulus to self help and to friendly aid or filial support, and it is, up to a limit, available for all alike. It is precisely one of the conditions of independence of which voluntary effort can make use, but requiring voluntary effort to make it fully available.

Source: L. T. Hobhouse, *Liberalism* (New York: 1911), pp. 177–78.

Questions for Analysis

1. According to Spencer, what is the primary function of government? Why does he deem assistance to the poor to be a violation of that duty?

2. According to Hobhouse, what circumstances make assistance to the poor, such as state-sponsored pension plans, necessary?

3. What assumptions lie behind their disagreement about the state's responsibility to remedy social inequalities? What values do they share?

In 1899, Dreyfus was pardoned and freed by executive order. In 1906, the French Supreme Court declared him free of all guilt, and he was reinstated in the army as a major. A key consequence of the controversy was passage of laws between 1901 and 1905 that separated church and state in France. Convinced that the Church and the army were hostile to the republic, the legislature passed new laws that prohibited any religious orders that were not authorized by the state and forbade clerics to teach in public schools.

The French Republic withstood the attacks of radical anti-Semites in the first decade of the twentieth century, but the same right-wing and nationalist forces made their voices heard elsewhere in Europe. In 1897, the mayor of Vienna was elected on an anti-Semitic platform. The Russian secret police forged and published the book *The Protocols of the Learned Elders of Zion* (1903 and 1905), which imagined a Jewish plot to dominate the world and held Jews responsible for the French Revolution and the dislocating effects of industrialization. Political anti-Semitism remained popular among a substantial number of Europeans who believed that social and political problems could be understood in racial terms.

Zionism

Among the many people watching with alarm as the Dreyfus Affair unfolded was Theodor Herzl (1860–1904), a Hungarian-born journalist working in Paris. The rise of virulent anti-Semitism in the land of the French Revolution troubled him deeply, for he considered the Dreyfus Affair "only the dramatic expression of a much more fundamental malaise." Despite Jewish emancipation, or the granting of civil rights, Herzl came to believe that Jewish people might never be assimilated into Western culture and that staking the Jewish community's hopes on acceptance and tolerance was dangerous folly. He endorsed a different strategy called **Zionism**: the building of a separate Jewish homeland outside of Europe (though not necessarily in Palestine). A small movement of Jewish settlers, mainly refugees from Russia, had already begun to establish such settlements. Although Herzl was not the first to voice these goals, he was the most effective advocate of political Zionism, arguing that Zionism should be recognized as a modern nationalist movement capable of negotiating with other states. Throughout, Herzl was involved in high politics, meeting with British and Ottoman heads of state. In 1896, he published *The*

Anti-Semitism and the Popular Press in France

The Dreyfus Affair lasted twelve years: from 1894, when Captain Alfred Dreyfus was first arrested and convicted of treason by a military court, to 1906, when he was finally absolved of all guilt and reinstated in the army. Most people in France followed the events of the Affair through the popular press, which had undergone rapid expansion as public schooling became more general and literacy spread through the population. The newspapers milked every episode of the case for all of its sensational drama, and editors openly took sides to increase their circulation and profits. The illustrated press was particularly popular, and images associated with anti-Semitism became ubiquitous in both the respectable and the more popular press. Image A is a caricature of Jakob Rothschild, a French Jewish banker. He is shown stretching his demonic hands around the globe. Image B shows Édouard Drumont, the anti-Semitic editor of *La Libre Parole*, who used the scandal to launch his own political career. His celebrity status is evident in this caricature of him that appeared in a competing paper, *Le Rire*. Even illustrations that did not aim at caricature carried a powerful message about the intensity of popular anti-Semitism in France during the Affair, such as in image C, which depicts young people burning Alfred Dreyfus's brother Mathieu in effigy during a demonstration. Mathieu Dreyfus played a key role in the effort to establish his brother's innocence.

Questions for Analysis

1. What fears about the economy are exploited in image A? (Compare this image with the one of socialists circling the globe, hand in hand, on page 785.)

2. Is *Le Rire's* portrait of Édouard Drumont (image B) anti-Semitic? Or is it critical of Drumont's anti-Semitism?

3. Taken together, what do these images tell us about the connections among anti-Semitism, the popular press, and the definitions of national identity that were current in France during the Affair?

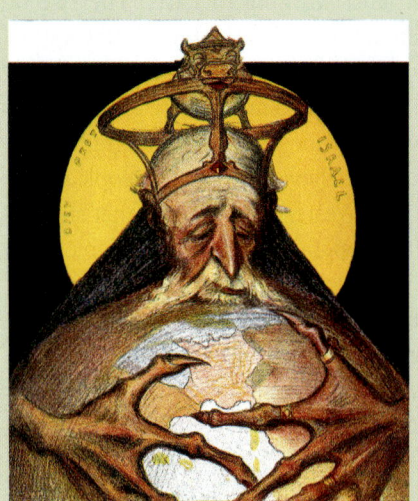

A. Anti-Semitic French caricature of Jakob Rothschild, 1898.

B. "The Ogre's Meal," caricature of Édouard Drumont, editor of *La Libre Parole*, that appeared in the competing paper *Le Rire*, 1896.

C. "Anti-Semitic Agitation in Paris: Mathieu Dreyfus burned in effigy in Montmartre (Paris)."

JEWISH MIGRATION IN THE LATE NINETEENTH CENTURY. ▪ *What drove Jewish people to migrate in the late nineteenth century?* ▪ *From what parts of Europe did the Jewish people primarily flee?* ▪ *Where did those who decided to leave go?*

State of the Jews, and a year later, convened the first Zionist Congress in Switzerland. His vision of a Jewish homeland had strong utopian elements, for he believed in building a new state based on a new and transformed society without inequality and with established rights.

Although Herzl's writings met with much skepticism, they received an enthusiastic reception among Jews who lived in areas of eastern Europe, where anti-Semitism was especially violent. In this part of Europe, many minority populations—including Poles, Ukrainians, and Lithuanians—had active nationalist movements, and this political climate influenced Jews who aspired to create a nation of their own.

Beginning in the 1880s, after a period of violent pogroms in Russia, more than 2.5 million Jews left Europe. (*Pogrom* is a Russian term for violent attacks on civilians, which, in the late nineteenth century, were usually aimed at Jewish communities.) This Jewish migration from Eastern Europe was part of the much broader "Great Departure" that brought millions of people from Europe to the Americas during these decades (see Chapter 22). Most Jewish migrants went to the United States, much to the consternation of Zionists. During the same period, much smaller numbers of eastern European Jews—about 30,000 by 1903—migrated to Palestine, which was then still part of the Ottoman Empire. During the turmoil of the First World War, competing demands for national sovereignty from Zionists and Palestinian Arabs caused conflicts in the region, to which the British also became involved, embroiling Zionism in international diplomacy (see Chapter 24).

Germany's Search for Imperial Unity

During 1864 to 1871, Otto von Bismarck united Germany under the banner of Prussian conservatism, through deft foreign policy, three short wars, and a groundswell of national sentiment. In constructing a federal political system, Bismarck sought to create the centralizing institutions of a modern nation-state while safeguarding the privileges of Germany's traditional elites, and a dominant role for

OTTO VON BISMARCK LEAVES OFFICE, 1890. This political cartoon shows Bismarck resigning, as Kaiser Wilhelm II childishly plays with "Socialism," a doll made of dynamite. And an anxious Germany watches the scene from the background.

Prussia. His constitution assigned administrative, educational, and juridical roles to local state governments, and established a bicameral parliament to oversee Germany's national interests. The appointed delegates of the upper house (the Bundesrat) were a conservative counterbalance to the more democratic lower house (the Reichstag), which was elected through universal male suffrage. In the executive branch, power rested solely with Wilhelm I, the Prussian king and German kaiser (emperor), who wielded full control of foreign and military affairs. Unlike in France or Britain, Germany's cabinet ministers had no responsibility to the Parliament and answered only to the kaiser.

Under a government that was neither genuinely federal nor entirely democratic, building a nation with a sense of common purpose was no easy task. Three fault lines in Germany's political landscape especially threatened to crack the national framework: the divide between Catholics and Protestants, the growing Social Democratic party, and the potentially divisive economic interests of agriculture and industry.

Between 1871 and 1878, Bismarck governed principally with liberal factions interested in promoting free trade and economic growth. To strengthen ties with these liberal coalitions, he unleashed an anti-Catholic campaign in Prussia, in what is known as the *Kulturkampf* (or "cultural struggle"). He passed laws that imprisoned priests for political sermons, banned Jesuits from Prussia, and curbed the Church's control over education and marriage. This anti-Catholic campaign had a particularly strong effect on the Polish provinces in the east, where the archbishop of Poznan and Gniezno was imprisoned, and the use of Polish was banned in schools and the courts. The campaign backfired, however, and public sympathy for the persecuted clergy helped the Catholic Center party win a full one-quarter of the seats in the Reichstag in 1874. In the Polish provinces, the campaign also strengthened the movement for national independence.

Bismarck responded by fashioning a new coalition that included agricultural and industrial interests as well as socially conservative Catholics. This new alliance passed protectionist legislation (grain tariffs, duties on iron and steel) that riled both laissez-faire liberals and the German working class, which was represented by the Social Democratic party (SPD). Just as he had used anti-Catholic sentiments to solidify his previous alliance, Bismarck now turned against the SPD as the

Past and Present

The Age of Mass Politics

Granting the vote to all adult men ushered in an age of mass politics. Political groups competed with one another to gain the support of this new constituency and to prevent opponents from gaining power. In this 1878 cartoon (left), Otto von Bismarck tries to put socialism back in the box. Then, as now, political groups sought simple messages that would give them an edge, which led to a more sharply defined ideological competition, as well as populist demagoguery and scapegoating of minorities. In modern France, Marine Le Pen (right) spoke at a rally for the National Front, the extreme-right party in France.

 Watch related author interview on the Student Site

new enemy of the empire, and couched his protectionist and antisocialist legislation as defending a "Christian moral order." In 1878, after two separate attempts on the emperor's life, Bismarck declared a national crisis so he could push through a series of antisocialist laws that forbade the Social Democrats to assemble or distribute their literature; additional legislation followed, which further expelled socialists from major cities. In effect, these laws forced the SPD to become a clandestine organization, fostering a subculture of workers who increasingly viewed socialism as the sole answer to their political needs.

After having made the stick to beat down organized-labor politics, Bismarck offered a carrot to German workers with an array of social reforms: workers were guaranteed sickness and accident insurance, rigorous factory inspection, limited working hours for women and children, a maximum workday for men, public employment agencies, and old-age pensions. By 1890, Germany had put together a package of social legislation—with the exception of unemployment insurance—that became a prototype for the majority of Western nations in the decades to come. These laws nevertheless failed to achieve Bismarck's short-term political goal of winning workers' loyalty, and votes for the SPD more than quadrupled between 1881 and 1890, the year Bismarck resigned.

The embittered atmosphere created by Bismarck's domestic policies prompted the new king, Wilhelm II, to legalize the SPD. By 1912, the Social Democrats were the largest single bloc in the Reichstag; yet the king still refused to allow any meaningful political participation beyond a tight-knit circle of elites. A conclusion to this volatile stand-off was preempted by the outbreak of the First World War.

Britain: From Moderation to Militancy

During the half century before 1914, the British prided themselves on what they believed to be an orderly and workable system of government. After the passage of the Second Reform Bill in 1867, which extended suffrage to more than a third of the nation's adult males, the two major political parties—Liberal and Conservative—vied with one another to win the support of this growing voting bloc. Parliament responded to the new voters' concerns with laws that recognized the legality of trade unions, commissioned the rebuilding of large urban areas, provided elementary education for all children, and permitted male religious dissenters to attend the elite universities of Oxford and Cambridge. In 1884, suffrage expanded to include more than three-fourths of adult males.

Two central figures dominated the new parliamentary politics: the Conservative Benjamin Disraeli and the Liberal William Gladstone. Disraeli, a converted Jew and best-selling novelist, was eminently pragmatic; whereas Gladstone, a devout Anglican, was committed to political and social reform out of a sense of moral obligation. Despite their opposing sensibilities and bitter parliamentary clashes, in retrospect, the two men led parties that seemed to share largely similar outlooks. Leaders of both parties were drawn from the upper middle class and the landed gentry, and both parties offered moderate programs that appealed to the widening electorate.

Even Britain's working-class movements were notably moderate until the turn of the century, when, at last, the new trade unions and middle-class socialist societies combined to create the independent Labour party in 1901. Pressed from the left, the Liberal ministry that took office in 1906 passed sickness, accident, old-age, and unemployment insurance acts, along with other concessions to trade unions. To pay for the new welfare programs—and for a larger navy to counter the German buildup—the Chancellor of the Exchequer (Finance Minister) David Lloyd George proposed an explosively controversial budget in 1909, which included progressive income and inheritance taxes designed to make the wealthy pay at higher rates. The bill provoked a rancorous showdown with the House of Lords, which was forced not only to pass the budget but also to surrender permanently its power to veto legislation passed by the Commons.

After 1900, Britain's liberal parliamentary framework, which had so successfully channeled the rising demands of mass society since the 1860s, began to buckle, as an array of groups rejected legislative activity in favor of radical action. Industrial militants launched enormous labor protests, including nationwide strikes of coal and rail workers and citywide transportation strikes in London and Dublin;

woman suffragists also adopted violent forms of direct action (discussed earlier). Meanwhile, in Ireland, disagreements over Irish home rule, or self-government, threatened to produce armed confrontations between increasingly radical Irish nationalists and Protestants opposed to home rule.

After Ireland had been put under the direct control of the British Parliament in 1800, various political and military efforts to regain Irish sovereignty over the course of the nineteenth century had failed. By the 1880s, a modern nationalist party—the Irish Parliamentary party—had begun to make substantial political gains through the legislative process. But toward the turn of the century, its agenda was increasingly eclipsed by more radical organizers, as the proponents of "new nationalism" disdained the party's representatives as ineffectual and out of touch. New groups such as Sinn Féin (We Ourselves) and the older Irish Republican Brotherhood revived interest in Irish history and culture and provided organizational support to the radical movement. Firmly opposed to the nationalists was the Protestant Ulster Volunteer Force, led by military officers who were determined to resist the imposition of home rule by force, if necessary. In 1913, when a Liberal plan to grant home rule was once again on the table, Britain seemed on the verge of a civil war. This prospect, however, was delayed by the outbreak of the First World War.

Russia: The Road to Revolution

The industrial and social changes that swept Europe proved especially unsettling in Russia, which had an autocratic political system that was ill equipped to handle conflict and the pressures of modern society. Western industrialization challenged Russia's military might, and its political doctrines—liberalism, democracy, and socialism—threatened Russia's internal political stability. Like other nations, tsarist Russia negotiated these challenges with a combination of repression and reform.

In the 1880s and 1890s, Russia launched a program of industrialization that made it the world's fifth largest economy by the early twentieth century. The state largely directed this industrial development, because despite the creation of a mobile workforce after the emancipation of the serfs in 1861, no independent middle class that was capable of raising capital and stewarding industrial enterprises emerged. In fact, during the nineteenth century, the Russian state financed more domestic industrial development than any other major European government.

Rapid industrialization heightened social tensions, as the transition from country to city life was sudden and harsh. Men and women left agriculture for factory work, straining the fabric of village life and rural culture. In the industrial areas, workers lived in large barracks and were marched, military-style, to and from the factories, where working conditions were among the worst in Europe. They coped by leaving their villages only temporarily and returning to their farms for planting or the harvest. Social change also strained Russia's legal system, which did not recognize trade unions or employers' associations. Laws still distinguished among nobles, peasants, clergy, and town dwellers, categories that did not correspond to an industrializing society. And outdated banking and financial laws failed to serve the needs of a modern economy.

Genuine legal reform, however, would threaten the regime's stability. When in 1881 Alexander II (r. 1855–1881), the liberator of the serfs, was killed by a radical assassin, his successor, Alexander III (r. 1881–1894), steered the country sharply to the right. Alexander III claimed that Russia had nothing in common with western Europe, and his people, who had been nurtured on mystical piety for centuries, would be utterly lost without a strong autocratic system. This principle guided stern repression: the regime curtailed all powers of local assemblies, increased the authority of the secret police, and subjected villages to the governmental authority of nobles appointed by the state; the press and schools also remained under strict censorship.

Nicholas II (r. 1894–1917) continued these repressive policies. Like his father, he ardently advocated Russification: government programs to extend the language, religion, and culture of greater Russia over the empire's non-Russian subjects. Russification amounted to coercion, expropriation, and physical oppression. Finns lost their constitution, Poles studied their own literature in Russian translation, and Jews perished in pogroms. The Russian government did not organize the pogroms, but it was openly anti-Semitic and made a point of looking the other way when villagers massacred Jews and destroyed their homes, businesses, and synagogues. Other groups whose repression by the state led to long-lasting undercurrents of anti-Russian nationalism included the Georgians, Armenians, and Azerbaijanis of the Caucasus Mountains.

The most important radical political group in late-nineteenth-century Russia was a large, loosely knit group of men and women who called themselves Populists (Russian:

AUTOCRACY AND REPRESENTATIVE GOVERNMENT. In Russia, Tsar Nicholas II allowed for the creation of a new legislative body, a form of parliament called the Duma, in response to the revolution of 1905. Although he later succeeded in limiting the powers of the Duma, its very existence indicated that even the autocratic and conservative Russian state was forced to pay lip service to the principle of representative government. In this photo, note the extent to which the opening ceremony evoked the traditional hierarchies of Russian society, exemplified in the presence of the tsar and members of his family, the military, the aristocracy, and the clergy.

Narodniki). The Populists believed that Russia needed to modernize on its own terms, not by those of the West. They envisioned an egalitarian Russia based on the ancient institution of the village commune (*mir*). Advocates of Populism sprang primarily from the middle class, many of its adherents were young students, and women made up about 15 percent—a significantly large proportion for the period. They formed secret bands and plotted the overthrow of tsarism through anarchy and insurrection. They dedicated their lives to "the people," attempting wherever possible to live among common laborers so they could understand and express the popular will. Populism's emphasis on peasant socialism influenced the Social Revolutionary party, formed in 1901, which concentrated on increasing the political power of the peasantry and building a socialist society based on the agrarian communalism of the mir.

The emergence of industrial capitalism and a new, desperately poor working class gave rise to Russian Marxism. Organized as the Social Democratic party, Russian Marxists concentrated their efforts on behalf of urban workers—which distinguished them from the Populists—and saw themselves as part of the international working-class movement. They made little headway in the peasant-dominated Russia before the First World War, but they provided disaffected urban factory workers and intellectuals alike with a powerful ideology that stressed the necessity of overthrowing the tsarist regime and the inevitability of a better future: autocracy would give way to capitalism and capitalism to an egalitarian, classless society.

In 1903, the Russian Social Democratic party leadership split over an important disagreement on revolutionary strategy. One group, temporarily in the majority and quick to name itself the **Bolsheviks** (majority group), believed that the Russian situation called for a strongly centralized party of active revolutionaries. They also insisted that the rapid industrialization of Russia meant that they did not have to follow Marx's model for the West. Instead of working for liberal capitalist reforms, Russian revolutionaries could skip a stage and immediately begin to build a socialist state. The other group, the **Mensheviks** (minority group), was more cautious or "gradualist." They sought slow changes and were reluctant to depart from Marxist orthodoxy. When the Mensheviks regained control of the Social Democratic party, the Bolsheviks formed a splinter party under the leadership of a young, dedicated revolutionary Vladimir Ilyich Ulyanov, who was exiled to Siberia and then moved to western Europe between 1900 and 1917, where he wrote under the pseudonym Lenin.

From exile, Lenin preached unrelenting class struggle, the need for a coordinated revolutionary socialist movement throughout Europe, and, most important, the belief that Russia was passing into an economic stage that made it ripe for revolution. In his treatise *What Is to Be Done?* (1902), Lenin denounced gradualists, who had urged collaboration with moderate parties, and argued that only vanguard agents of the party, acting in the name of the working class, could bring about a revolution.

THE FIRST RUSSIAN REVOLUTION

The **Russian Revolution of 1905** took all the radical movements by surprise. Its immediate cause was Russia's defeat in the Russo-Japanese War of 1904–1905, but this revolution had deeper roots. Rapid industrialization had transformed Russia unevenly, leaving certain regions heavily industrial and others less integrated into the market economy. Also, the economic boom of the 1880s and 1890s turned to bust in the early 1900s. The demand for goods tapered off, prices plummeted, and the nascent working class suffered high levels of unemployment. At the same time, low grain prices resulted in a series of peasant uprisings, which, combined with students' energetic radical organizing, became overtly political.

As dispatches reported the defeats of the tsar's army and navy, the Russian people grasped the full extent of the regime's inefficiency. Even middle-class subjects clamored for change, while radical workers organized strikes and held demonstrations in every important city. Trust in the benevolence of the tsar was severely shaken on January 22, 1905—"Bloody Sunday"—when a group of 200,000 workers and their families, led by a priest, Father Gapon, went to demonstrate their grievances at the tsar's Winter Palace in St. Petersburg. When guard troops killed 130 demonstrators and wounded several hundred others, the government seemed not only ineffective but arbitrary and brutal.

Over the course of 1905, general protest grew: merchants closed their stores, factory owners shut down their plants, lawyers refused to plead cases in court. The autocracy lost control of entire rural towns and regions as enraged peasants ejected and often killed local authorities. Forced to yield, Tsar Nicholas II issued the October Manifesto, pledging guarantees of individual liberties, a moderately liberal franchise for the election of a Duma ("house," or legislature), and genuine legislative veto powers for the Duma. Although the

BLOODY SUNDAY. In January 1905, demonstrating workers who sought to bring their grievances to the attention of the tsar were met and gunned down by government troops.

1905 revolution brought the tsarist system perilously close to collapse, it failed to convince the tsar that fundamental political change was necessary. Between 1905 and 1907, Nicholas revoked most of the promises made in the October Manifesto and, above all, he deprived the Duma of its principal powers and decreed that it be elected indirectly on a class basis, which ensured a legislative body of obedient followers.

Nonetheless, the revolution of 1905 persuaded the tsar's more perceptive advisers that reform was urgent. Between 1906 and 1911, agricultural reforms provided for the sale of 5 million acres of royal lands to peasants, granted peasants permission to withdraw from the mir and form independent farms, and canceled peasant property debts. Further decrees legalized labor unions, reduced the working day (to ten hours in most cases), and established sickness and accident insurance. Liberals could reasonably hope that Russia was moving toward becoming a progressive nation based on the Western model. The tsar, however, remained stubbornly autocratic. Russian agriculture remained suspended between an emerging capitalist system and the traditional peasant commune. And the Russian industry, though powerful enough to allow the country to maintain its status as a world power, remained behind that of western Europe.

Nationalism and Imperial Politics: The Ottoman Empire

In the last decades of the nineteenth century, the Ottoman Empire's hold over the Balkan lands of southeastern Europe was challenged by many of the same nationalist movements that troubled the Habsburg Empire in the region. Confronting these internal threats was made doubly difficult by the fact that the Ottoman government was facing an external threat at the same time: the expansion of European imperialism in the Balkans and the Middle East.

The Ottoman Empire, which had claimed the status as a Muslim caliphate since 1362, had been a major power in the Mediterranean for over 400 years. As a signatory of the Treaty of Paris at the end of the Crimean War in 1856, the Ottomans were, in theory, a member of the Concert of Europe. This status as a Great Power, however, was not enough to prevent the loss of territory and diplomatic influence, as European empires expanded their authority in the region. In the first half of the nineteenth century, as much as half of its population lived in the European provinces of the empire, and these territories were integral to its culture and economy.

In the 1870s, a series of catastrophes led to the loss of the Ottoman Empire's territories in the Balkans. When the sultan's government repressed uprisings in Bosnia, Herzegovina, and Bulgaria in 1875–1876, the Russians saw an opportunity to intercede following reports of atrocities committed against Christians in the region. After a Russian victory in the Russo-Turkish War (1877–1878), the tsar forced the sultan to surrender nearly all of his European territory, except for a remnant around Constantinople. In 1878, Britain and Austria took action to ensure that Russia would not be the only beneficiary of the Ottoman withdrawal. A congress of great powers convened in Berlin to divide the spoils: Bessarabia went to Russia, Thessaly to Greece, and Bosnia and Herzegovina fell under the control of the Austrian Empire. But Montenegro, Serbia, and Romania became independent states, launching the modern era of Balkan nationalism. This trend continued in 1908, when the Bulgars succeeded in wresting independence for Bulgaria from the Ottomans and the Austrians annexed Bosnia and Herzegovina outright. By this time, the proportion of the Ottoman Empire's population that lived in its European provinces had fallen to one-fifth.

While this was happening, the Ottomans continued to lose territory in North Africa. The loss of Algeria to the French in 1830 was followed by the establishment of a French protectorate in Tunisia in 1881. The British occupied Egypt in 1882, and Tripoli was annexed by the Italians in 1912. The Ottoman Empire's loss of territory significantly strained Europe's imperial balance of power and discredited the Ottoman regime among many of its own subjects.

Partly as a result of this crisis, a nationalist movement emerged within the Ottoman Empire. Educated Turks, grown impatient with the weakness of Sultan Abdul Hamid II (r. 1876–1909), began to call for national rejuvenation through the introduction of Western science and political reforms. In 1908, these reformers, who called themselves "**Young Turks**," forced the sultan to establish a constitutional government. The following year, they deposed the sultan and placed his brother, Mehmed V (r. 1909–1918), on the throne. The powers of government were entrusted to a grand vizier and ministers accountable to an elected parliament. (Non-Turkish inhabitants of the empire were not given the vote.) The Young Turks launched a vigorous effort to "Ottomanize" all the imperial subjects, and they tried to bring both Christian and Muslim communities under centralized Turkish control. The effort, intended to compensate for the loss of territories in Europe, undercut the popularity of the new reformist regime. At the same time, the Ottoman government began seriously to consider joining with a European power to prevent further encroachments on its territory. This calculation eventually led to an Ottoman alliance with Germany in 1914, at the outset of the First World War (see Chapter 24).

THE DECLINE OF THE OTTOMAN EMPIRE, 1699–1912. ■ *Where were the farthest points that the Ottoman Empire reached in Europe and Africa?* ■ *How do you explain the slow decline of Ottoman power in relationship to Europe and the emerging global economy?* ■ *Why did the decline of Ottoman power have enormous significance on the relations among European nations?*

Map labels:

ARAL SEA

INDIAN OCEAN

R U S S I A N   E M P I R E

CASPIAN SEA

P E R S I A

Tehran

Basra

Persian Gulf

A R A B I A

ADEN

Tiflis

GEORGIA 1878

Kars

Tigris R.

MESOPOTAMIA

Baghdad

Euphrates R.

Mecca

HEJAZ

RED SEA

1859

1739 1784

1783 SEA OF AZOV 1783

Batum 1703

ARMENIA

Damascus

Acre

HOLY LAND

Jerusalem

Odessa 1791

BLACK SEA

Angora

T U R K E Y

SINAI

Suez Canal

Tel-el-Kebir

Cairo

Nile R.

1699 1812

Sevastopol

Constantinople

CYPRUS 1878

EGYPT 1882

S U D A N

Kutchuk Kainarji

ROMANIA 1878

BULGARIA 1908

1888

AEGEAN SEA

Athens

CRETE

1699 1716

HUNGARY 1699

SERBIA 1878

BOSNIA 1878

1830

TURKEY IN EUROPE

GREECE

CYRENAICA

A F R I C A

AUSTRIA

Budapest

MONTE-NEGRO

Navarino

IONIAN SEA

Benghazi

Vienna

Turks defeated 1683

SWITZER-LAND

ITALY

Rome

ADRIATIC SEA

TYRRHENIAN SEA

M E D I T E R R A N E A N   S E A

LIBYA Conquered by Italy 1912

Tripoli

E U R O P E

F R A N C E

TUNISIA 1881

Tunis

Bay of Biscay

S P A I N

Madrid

ALGERIA 1830

Algiers

Oran

500 Miles

500 Kilometers

250 Miles

250

0

0

Legend:

Boundary of Ottoman Empire 1699

Austria

Russia

Britain

France

Independent states (with date of independence)

Ottoman Empire 1912

THE SCIENCE AND SOUL OF THE MODERN AGE

Nineteenth-century liberals believed in human reason, individualism, progress, and science. Toward the end of the century, however, new scientific developments challenged these core liberal beliefs. Darwin's theory of evolution, psychology, and social science all introduced visions of humanity that were sharply at odds with the liberal assumptions about human rationality. At the same time, artists and intellectuals mounted their own revolt against nineteenth-century beliefs and values. These upheavals in the world of ideas unsettled older conceptions of individuality, culture, and consciousness. The modern individual seemed like the product of irrational inner drives and uncontrollable external circumstances rather than the free and rational agent of Enlightenment thought.

Darwin's Revolutionary Theory

If Marx changed the conceptions of society Charles Darwin did one better, because his theory of organic evolution by natural selection transformed the ideas of nature itself. **Darwin's theory of evolution** introduced an unsettling new picture of human biology and behavior. His core concepts were embraced by some and abhorred by others, and they were interpreted and deployed in a variety of unexpected, often conflicting, ways that profoundly shaped the late nineteenth and early twentieth centuries.

Theories of evolution did not originate with Darwin, but none of the earlier theories had gained widespread scientific or popular currency. Geologists in the nineteenth century had challenged the biblical account of creation with evidence showing that the world was formed by natural processes over millions of years, but they did not have a satisfactory explanation for the existence of different species. In the early nineteenth century, French biologist Jean Lamarck made an important attempt at an answer. He argued that behavioral changes could alter an animal's physical characteristics within a single generation, and that these new traits could be passed on to the offspring. Over time, Lamarck suggested, the inheritance of acquired characteristics would produce new species of animals.

A more convincing hypothesis of organic evolution appeared in 1859, with the publication of *On the Origin of Species* by the British naturalist Charles Darwin. Darwin traveled for five years as a naturalist on the *HMS Beagle,* a ship that had been chartered for scientific exploration on a voyage around the world. After observing the diversity of species in different lands, he wondered about their origins. Darwin was familiar with pigeon breeding and knew that particular traits could be selected through controlled breeding. But was a similar process of selection at work in nature? His answer was yes.

Darwin theorized that variations in traits within a population, such as longer beaks or protective coloring, made certain individual organisms better equipped for survival, increasing their chances of reproducing and passing their advantageous traits to the next generation. His theory drew on the work of Thomas Malthus, a political economist who argued that human populations grow faster than the available food supply, leading to a fatal competition for scarce resources. For Darwin, this Malthusian competition was a general rule of nature, whereby the strong survived and the weak perished. Competition with other animals and struggle with the environment produced a "natural selection" of some traits over others, leading to a gradual evolution of different species over time. Darwin eventually applied this theory of evolution not only to plant and animal species but also to humans. In his view, the human race had evolved from an apelike ancestor, long since extinct but probably a common precursor of the existing anthropoid apes and humans.

DARWINIAN THEORY AND RELIGION

The implications of Darwin's writings went far beyond evolutionary sciences. Most notably, they challenged the basis of deeply held religious beliefs, sparking a public discussion on the existence and knowability of God. Although popular critics denounced Darwin for contradicting the literal interpretations of the Bible, those contradictions were not what made religious middle-class readers uncomfortable. The work of prominent theologians, such as David Friedrich Strauss, had already helped Christians adapt their faith to biblical inaccuracies and inconsistencies. People did not need to abandon either Christianity or faith simply because Darwin showed (or argued) that the world and its life-forms had developed over millions of years rather than six days. What nineteenth-century religious readers found difficult to accept was the challenge to their belief in a benevolent God and a morally guided universe. According to Darwin, the world was governed not by order, harmony, and the divine will, but by random chance and constant, undirected struggle. Moreover, the Darwinian worldview seemed to reduce the notions of good and bad to simply the ability to survive, thus robbing humanity of critical moral certainties. Although Darwin himself was able to reconcile his theory with a belief in God, others latched onto his work to fiercely attack Christian orthodoxy. One such figure was philosopher Thomas Henry Huxley, who earned himself the nickname "Darwin's bulldog" by inveighing against Christians who were appalled by the implications of Darwinian theory. Huxley opposed all forms of dogma and argued that the thinking person should simply follow reason "as far as it can take you," and recognize that the ultimate character of the universe lay beyond one's grasp.

Social Darwinism

The theory of natural selection also influenced the social sciences, which were just developing at the end of the nineteenth century. New disciplines such as sociology, psychology, anthropology, and economics aimed to apply scientific methods to the analysis of society, and introduced new ways of quantifying, measuring, and interpreting the human experience. Under the authoritative banner of "science," these disciplines often contributed to improving the health and well-being of European men and women. But, as we will see with the impact of Social Darwinism, they also provided justification for forms of economic, imperial, and racial dominance.

The so-called Social Darwinists adapted Darwinian thought in ways that Darwin himself never considered: applying his concept of individual competition and survival to relationships among classes, races, and nations. English philosopher Herbert Spencer (1820–1903) coined the phrase "survival of the fittest," and he used evolutionary theory to expound on the virtues of free competition and to attack state welfare programs. As a champion of individualism, Spencer condemned all forms of collectivism as primitive and counterproductive, relics of an earlier stage of social evolution. In his view, government attempts to relieve economic and social hardships—or to place constraints on big business—were hindrances to the advancement of civilization, which could occur only through individual adaptation and competition. Particularly in America, such claims earned Spencer high praise from a few wealthy industrialists who no doubt counted themselves among the fittest.

Unlike the science of biological evolution, a popularized Social Darwinism was easy to comprehend, and its concepts (centering on a struggle for survival) were soon integrated into the political vocabulary. Proponents of laissez-faire capitalism and opponents of socialism used Darwinist rhetoric to justify marketplace competition and the "natural order" of the rich and poor. Nationalists embraced Social Darwinism to rationalize imperialist expansion and warfare. Spencer's doctrine became closely tied to theories of racial hierarchy and white superiority, which claimed that the white race had reached the height of evolutionary development and had thus earned the right to dominate and rule other races (see Chapter 25). It was ironic that some progressive middle-class reformers also relied on a similar

CEPHALOGRAPH. This illustration from Herbert Spencer's autobiography shows a device designed to measure skulls. Spencer believed that the size of one's skull determined brain capacity, and he applied the idea of "survival of the fittest" to justify theories of white racial superiority.

set of racial assumptions: their campaigns to improve the health and welfare of society played to fears that Europe, though dominant, could move down the evolutionary ladder. Despite its unsettling potential, Darwinism was used to advance a range of political objectives and to shore up an array of ingrained prejudices.

Challenges to Rationality: Pavlov, Freud, and Nietzsche

Although the new social scientists self-consciously relied on the use of rational, scientific principles, their findings often stressed the opposite: the irrational, even animalistic nature of human experience. Darwin had already called into question the notion that humanity was fundamentally superior to the rest of the animal kingdom, and similarly discomfiting conclusions came from a new field of psychology. The Russian physician Ivan Pavlov (1849–1936) asserted that animal behavior could be understood as a series of trained responses to physical stimuli. Pavlov's famous experiment showed that if dogs were fed after they heard the ringing of a bell, they would eventually salivate at the sound of the bell alone, exactly as if they had smelled and seen food. Moreover, Pavlov insisted that such conditioning constituted a significant part of human behavior as well. Known as "behaviorism," this type of physiological psychology avoided vague concepts such as mind and consciousness, concentrating instead on the reactions of muscles, nerves, glands, and visceral organs. Behaviorists recast human activity as not governed by reason but as a bundle of physiological responses to stimuli in the environment.

Like behaviorism, a second major school of psychology suggested that human behavior was largely motivated by unconscious and irrational forces. Founded by the Austrian physician **Sigmund Freud** (1856–1939), the discipline of psychoanalysis posited a new, dynamic, and unsettling theory of the mind, according to which a variety of unconscious drives and desires conflict with a rational and moral conscience. Developed over many years of treating patients with nervous ailments, Freud's model of the psyche contained three elements: (1) the *id*, or undisciplined desires for pleasure, sexual gratification, aggression, and so on; (2) the *superego*, or conscience, which registers the prohibitions of morality and culture; and (3) the *ego*, or the arena in which the conflict between id and superego works itself out. Freud believed that most cases of mental disorder result from an irreconcilable tension between the natural drives and the restraints placed on individuals. He believed that by studying such disorders, as well as dreams and slips of the tongue, scientists could catch a glimpse of the submerged areas of consciousness and thus understand seemingly irrational behavior. His search for an all-encompassing theory of the mind was deeply grounded in the tenets of nineteenth-century science. By stressing the irrational, however, Freud's theories fed a growing anxiety about the value and limits of human reason. Likewise, they brought to fore a powerful critique of the constraints imposed by the moral and social codes of Western civilization.

No one provided a more sweeping or more influential assault on Western values of rationality than the German philosopher Friedrich Nietzsche (*NEE-chuh*; 1844–1900). Like Freud, Nietzsche had observed a middle-class culture, which he believed was dominated by illusions and self-deceptions, and he sought to unmask them. In a series of works that rejected rational argumentation in favor of an elliptical, suggestive prose style, Nietzsche argued that bourgeois faith in such concepts as science, progress, democracy, and religion represented a futile and reprehensible search for security and truth. He categorically denied the possibility of knowing truth or reality, because all knowledge comes

SIGMUND FREUD. Freud's theory of the mind and the unconscious broke from many of the basic human nature assumptions of his time. He remained, however, a committed nineteenth-century scientist and believed he had uncovered new laws that governed culture as well as individuals.

filtered through linguistic, scientific, or artistic systems of representation. He famously ridiculed Judeo-Christian morality for instilling a repressive conformity that drained civilization of its vitality. Nietzsche's philosophy resounded with themes of personal liberation, especially freedom from the stranglehold of history and tradition. Indeed, Nietzsche's ideal individual, or "superman," was one who abandoned the burdens of cultural conformity and created an independent set of values based on artistic vision and strength of character. He forecast salvation for Western civilization only through individual struggle against the chaotic universe.

Religion and Its Critics

Faced with these challenges, the institutions responsible for the maintenance of traditional faith found themselves on the defensive. The Roman Catholic Church responded

Competing Viewpoints

Darwin and His Readers

Charles Darwin's On the Origin of Species *(1859) and his theory of natural selection transformed Western knowledge of natural history. The impact of Darwin's work, however, extended well beyond scientific circles, and assumed a cultural importance that exceeded even his scholarly contribution. How Darwinism was popularized is a complex question, for writers and readers could mold Darwin's ideas to fit a variety of political and cultural purposes. The first excerpt comes from the conclusion to* On the Origin of Species *and sets out the different laws that Darwin thought governed the natural world. The second excerpt comes from the autobiography of Nikolaus Osterroth (1875–1933), a clay miner from western Germany, who was ambitious and self-educated. The passage recounts his reaction to hearing about Darwin and conveys his enthusiasm for late-nineteenth-century science.*

Charles Darwin, On the Origin of Species

The natural system is a genealogical arrangement, in which we have to discover the lines of descent by the most permanent characters, however slight their vital importance may be.

The framework of bones being the same in the hand of a man, wing of a bat, fin of the porpoise, and leg of the horse,—the same number of vertebrae forming the neck of the giraffe and of the elephant,—and innumerable other such facts, at once explain themselves on the theory of descent with slow and slight successive modifications. The similarity of pattern in the wing and leg of a bat, though used for such different purposes,—in the jaws and legs of a crab,—in the petals, stamens, and pistils of a flower, is likewise intelligible on the view of the gradual modification of parts or organs, which were alike in the early progenitor of each class. . . .

It is interesting to contemplate an entangled bank, clothed with many plants of many kinds, with birds singing on the bushes, with various insects flitting about, and with worms crawling through the damp earth, and to reflect that these elaborately constructed forms, so different from each other, and dependent on each other in so complex a manner, have all been produced by laws acting around us. These laws, taken in the largest sense, being Growth with Reproduction; Inheritance which is almost implied by reproduction; Variability from the indirect and direct action of the external conditions of life, and from use and disuse; a Ratio of Increase so high as to lead to a Struggle for Life, and as a consequence to Natural Selection, entailing Divergence of Character and the Extinction of less-improved forms. Thus, from the war of nature, from famine and death, the most exalted object which we are capable of conceiving, namely, the production of the higher animals, directly follows. There is grandeur in this view of life, with its several powers, having been originally breathed into a few forms or into one; and that, whilst this planet has gone cycling on according to the fixed law of gravity, from so simple a beginning endless forms most beautiful and most wonderful have been, and are being, evolved.

Source: Charles Darwin, *On the Origin of Species* (Harmondsworth, UK: 1968), pp. 450–51, 458–60.

---

to the encroachments of secular society by appealing to its dogma and venerated traditions. In 1864, Pope Pius IX issued the *Syllabus of Errors*, condemning what he regarded as the principal religious and philosophical errors of the time, among them materialism, free thought, and indifferentism (the idea that one religion is as good as another). In 1871, the pope convoked the first Church council since the Catholic Reformation and pronounced the dogma of papal infallibility, which meant that in his capacity "as pastor and doctor of all Christians," the pope was infallible in regard to all matters of faith and morals. Though generally accepted by pious Catholics, the claim of papal infallibility provoked a storm of protests and was denounced by the governments of several Catholic countries, including France, Spain, and Italy. The death of Pius IX in 1878 and the accession of Pope Leo XIII brought a more accommodating

Nikolaus Osterroth: A Miner's Reaction

The book was called *Moses or Darwin?* . . . Written in a very popular style, it compared the Mosaic story of creation with the natural evolutionary history, illuminated the contradictions of the biblical story, and gave a concise description of the evolution of organic and inorganic nature, interwoven with plenty of striking proofs.

What particularly impressed me was a fact that now became clear to me: that evolutionary natural history was monopolized by the institutions of higher learning; that Newton, Laplace, Kant, Darwin, and Haeckel brought enlightenment only to the students of the upper social classes; and that for the common people in the grammar school the old Moses with his six-day creation of the world still was the authoritative world view. For the upper classes there was evolution, for us creation; for them productive liberating knowledge, for us rigid faith; bread for those favored by fate, stones for those who hungered for truth!

Why do the people need science? Why do they need a so-called *Weltanschauung* [worldview]? The people must keep Moses, must keep religion; religion is the poor man's philosophy. Where would we end up if every miner and every farmhand had the opportunity to stick his nose into astronomy, geology, biology, and anatomy? Does it serve any purpose for the divine world order of the possessing and privileged classes to tell the worker that the Ptolemaic heavens have long since collapsed; that out there in the universe there is an eternal process of creation and destruction; that in the universe at large, as on our tiny earth, everything is in the grip of eternal evolution; that this evolution takes place according to inalterable natural laws that defy even the omnipotence of the old Mosaic Jehovah. . . . Why tell the dumb people that Copernicus and his followers have overturned the old Mosaic creator, and that Darwin and modern science have dug the very ground out from under his feet of clay?

That would be suicide! Yes, the old religion is so convenient for the divine world order of the ruling class! As long as the worker hopes faithfully for the beyond, he won't think of plucking the blooming roses in this world. . . .

The possessing classes of all civilized nations need servants to make possible their godlike existence. So they cannot allow the servant to eat from the tree of knowledge.

Source: Alfred Kelly, ed., *The German Worker: Working-Class Autobiographies from the Age of Industrialization* (Berkeley, CA: 1987), pp. 185–86.

Questions for Analysis

1. Was the theory of evolution revolutionary? If so, how? Would it be fair to say that Darwin did for the nineteenth century what Newton had done for the seventeenth and eighteenth centuries? Why or why not?

2. Why did people think the natural world was governed by laws? Was this a religious belief or a scientific fact?

3. What aspects of Darwin's theory appealed to Osterroth? Why?

climate to the Church. The new pope acknowledged that there was good as well as evil in modern civilization, added a scientific staff to the Vatican, and opened archives and observatories; but he made no further concessions to liberalism in the political sphere.

Protestants were also compelled to respond to a modernizing world. But because they were taught to understand God with the help of just the Bible and a willing conscience, Protestants, unlike Catholics, had little in the way of doctrine to help them defend their faith. Some fundamentalists chose to ignore the implications of scientific and philosophical inquiry altogether and continued to believe in the literal truth of the Bible. Others agreed with the school of American philosophers known as pragmatists, principally Charles S. Peirce and William James, who taught that "truth" was whatever produced useful, practical general population. In 1850, approximately half of Europe's population was literate. In subsequent decades, country after country introduced state-financed elementary and secondary education to provide opportunities for social advancement, to diffuse technical and scientific knowledge, and to inculcate civic and national pride. By 1900, approximately 85 percent of the population in Britain, France, Belgium, the Netherlands, Scandinavia, and Germany could read.

In countries where literacy rates were highest, commercial publishers, such as Alfred Harmsworth in Britain and William Randolph Hearst in the United States, hastened to serve the new reading public. Advertisements also drastically lowered the costs of the mass-market newspapers, enabling even workers to purchase one or two newspapers a day. Newspapers began to appeal to the newly literate with sensational journalism and spicy, easy-to-read serials. The "yellow journalism" of the penny presses merged entertainment and sensationalism with the news, aiming to increase circulation and thus securing more lucrative advertising sales. The era of mass readership had arrived, and writers, artists, activists, and, above all, governments increasingly focused their message for this mass audience.

results; that is, if belief in God provided mental peace or spiritual satisfaction, then that belief was true. Still others sought solace from religious doubt by founding missions, laboring among the poor, and other good works; many adherents to this social gospel were also modernists who accepted the ethical teachings of Christianity but rejected beliefs in miracles and original sin.

THE CULTURE OF MODERNITY

New Readers and the Popular Press

The diffusion of new ideas about science and religion was facilitated by rising literacy rates and new forms of printed mass culture. Between 1750 and 1870, readership had expanded from the aristocracy to include middle-class circles and, thereafter, to an increasingly literate

The Nineteenth-Century Novel

No literary form is more closely associated with nineteenth-century European culture than the **novel**. This relatively new form of writing flourished throughout Europe between the end of the Napoleonic Wars in 1815 and the First World War in 1914. The premise of the novel was that a work of fiction should focus on the lives of believable individuals whose predicaments were recognizable to the audience. The success of a novel depended on its ability to portray its protagonists in ways that allowed readers to identify with their struggles and understand their innermost thoughts and feelings.

The novel thus fused liberalism's emphasis on the individual with romanticism's attention to emotions and mental states. The novel's reliance on realistic narrative description freed literature from the constraints of older genres and allowed writers to move beyond plots borrowed from classical history or mythology. The brilliance of novelists in this period was matched only by the avidity with which a fascinated public—both men and women—consumed their works.

In France, Stendahl's *The Red and the Black* (1830), Honoré de Balzac's multivolume *Human Comedy* (91 works published between 1830 and 1849), Gustave Flaubert's *Madame Bovary* (1856) and *Sentimental Education* (1869), and Émile Zola's twenty-volume *Rougon-Macquart* series (1871–1893) all displayed very different sensibilities, but the novelists shared a common concern with the fates of ordinary people. Their novels portrayed young men from unremarkable families attempting to make careers in the capital city, women trapped in loveless marriages, fathers blinded by their love for their unfaithful daughters, and working men and women struggling with back-breaking labor and poverty. Some literary critics were dismayed by the attention given to the lives of ordinary people, finding it vulgar; whereas others insisted that this was an appropriate subject for literature in a more democratic age.

Women made up a significant portion of the audience for novels, and they also produced them. Earlier in the century in England, Jane Austen had almost single-handedly defined a new genre of romantic fiction (Chapter 17). Her novels—among them *Sense and Sensibility* (1811) and *Pride and Prejudice* (1813)—were spiced with incisive social satire and ironic commentary on the foibles of upper-middle-class men and women as they looked for love, marriage, and (not incidentally) property. Her works were published anonymously during her lifetime, but she was recognized as the author after her nephew published a memoir in 1869; her fame and popularity continue into the present. In France, George Sand (the pseudonym of Amantine-Aurore-Lucile Dupin; 1804–1876) became a literary celebrity, as famous for her love affairs with artists and musicians as she was for her best-selling novels, such as *Indiana* (1832) and *Consuelo* (1842–1843).

Many novelists were as interested in describing society as they were in their characters, a preoccupation that was a natural outgrowth of their attempts to provide a realistic portrait of contemporary European life. Victor Hugo's *Les Misérables* (1862) follows the story of a good man who had been imprisoned for stealing food to feed his sister's hungry children, and recounts along the way the undercurrents of revolutionary activity in Paris across the century. Émile Zola's *Germinal* (1885) portrays a mining town in northern France in the throes of a violent strike, and his *L'Assommoir* (1877) contains an unflinching exploration of a working couple losing a struggle with alcoholism and poverty. Hugo's works, written in a romantic vein, celebrated the spirit of progress and the French Revolution, while Zola's more pessimistic novels were less confident about the future.

Perhaps the most famous of the great nineteenth-century novelists in the English-speaking world was Charles Dickens (1812–1870). In *Hard Times* (1854), he offered a cutting portrait of the effects of the Industrial Revolution in Britain. Dickens's favorite theme, however, was stories of young men struggling against disadvantages of birth and family, rendered in scenes that alternated between humor and sentimentality, such as in *Oliver Twist* (1837–1839), *David Copperfield* (1849–1850), and *Great Expectations* (1860–1861). Like many writers, Dickens published his novels in installments in the penny press. This publishing innovation was a crucial part of the mass appeal of his novels, because it vastly increased his audience. Here, too, we see the novel as the product of both an astonishingly creative mind and a keen awareness of the market—simultaneously a work of art and a consumer item.

By the end of the nineteenth century, the prestige of the novel led to an explosion of publishing and novel reading in every European language. Perhaps the most respected novelists of the nineteenth century were Russian. In *War and Peace* (1869), Leo Tolstoy (1828–1910) tells the history of the Napoleonic Wars through the experiences of a group of interconnected families; interspersed within the massive narrative were philosophical digressions about religion and musings

LEO TOLSTOY. Although a wealthy landowner, Tolstoy often dressed as a peasant. He became increasingly ascetic, casting off the corruptions of the world, and a pacifist. In this picture, he is leaving his home for a hermitage.

on the fate of individuals during a period of radical historical change. Tolstoy's *Anna Karenina* (1873–1877) is about an aristocratic woman's struggle to reconcile her social status as the wife of a senior government official with her passionate love for another man. In this novel, he not only creates a remarkable portrait of the title character but also explores contemporary debates about religion and the reform of Russia's feudal system. Fyodor Dostoyevsky (1821–1881), meanwhile, was preoccupied with the internal mental anguish of Russian men and women struggling to reconcile religious faith with worldly desires. As a young man, Dostoyevsky had served four years of hard labor in a Siberian work camp for political activity of the mildest sort, and this experience produced *The House of the Dead* (1861). His *Crime and Punishment* (1866) offers a dark story of a young man driven by an interior compulsion to kill an elderly woman. Dostoyevsky's last work, *The Brothers Karamazov* (1880), is the culmination of his extended meditation on faith and religious doubt, delivered as a story about four brothers—including an illegitimate son brought up as a servant—and their conflicts with their unbearably uncouth and violent father. With Tolstoy and Dostoyevsky, the novel reached its apogee, proving itself to be a literary form capable of astonishing universality that is able to comprehend both the wide sweep of history and the profoundly interior universe of the human mind.

The First Moderns: Innovations in Art

While novelists explored the lives of individuals struggling with broader historical forces, visual artists across the Continent began to question the moral and cultural values of liberal, middle-class society. A few did so with grave hesitation, others with heedless abandon. In a dizzying array of experiments, innovations, ephemeral art movements, and bombastic manifestos, the pioneers of what would later be termed *modernism* developed the artistic forms and aesthetic values that came to dominate much of the twentieth century.

Modernism encompassed a diverse and often contradictory set of theories and practices that spanned the entire range of cultural production from painting, sculpture, literature, and architecture to theater, dance, and musical composition. Despite such diversity, however, modernist movements did share certain key characteristics. First, a sense that the world had radically changed and this change should be embraced; hence the modernists' interest in science and technology. Second, a belief that traditional values and assumptions were outdated. Third, a new conception of what art could do, stressing expression over representation and insisting on experiment and freedom.

Early modernism was also distinguished by a new understanding of the relationship between art and society. Few artists remained interested in purely aesthetic questions, but many others embraced the notion that art could bring about profound social and spiritual change. The abstract painter Wassily Kandinsky (1866–1944) believed that the materialism of the nineteenth century was a source of social and moral corruption, and he looked toward a future in which artists would nourish the human spirit that was threatened by the onset of industrial society. Other artists believed that they had a duty to document unflinchingly what they saw as the pathological aspects of life in modern cities or the inward chaos of the human mind. In the political arena, modernist hostility toward conventional values sometimes translated into support for antiliberal or revolutionary movements of the extreme right or left.

***BLACK LINES*, BY WASSILY KANDINSKY (1913).** Kandinsky broke from the traditional representational approach of nineteenth-century painting with his abstractions. He was one of a generation of turn-of-the-century artists who reexamined and experimented with their art forms.

THE REVOLT ON CANVAS

Like most artistic movements, modernism defined itself in opposition to a set of earlier principles. For painters, in particular, this meant a rejection of mainstream academic art, which affirmed the chaste and moral outlook of museumgoers, as well as of the socially conscious realist tradition, which strove for rigorous, scientific exactitude in representing material reality. The modern artists rebelled even further, however, by discarding the centuries-old tradition of realistic representation altogether. Since the Renaissance, Western art had sought to depict accurately three-dimensional visual reality, and paintings were considered to be mirrors of or windows on the world. But during the late nineteenth century, artists turned their backs to the visual world, focusing instead on the subjective, psychologically oriented, intensely emotional forms of self-expression. As the Norwegian painter Edvard Munch claimed, "Art is the opposite of nature. A work of art can come only from the interior of man."

The first significant break from traditional representational art emerged with the French impressionists, who came to prominence as young artists during the 1870s. Strictly speaking, the impressionists were realists; steeped in scientific theories about sensory perception, they attempted to record natural phenomena objectively. Instead of painting objects, they captured the transitory play of light on surfaces, giving their works a sketchy, ephemeral quality that differed sharply from realist art. Although subsequent artists revolted against what they deemed the cold objectivity of this scientific approach, the impressionist painters, most famously Claude Monet (moh-NAY; 1840–1926) and Pierre-Auguste Renoir (1841–1919), left two important legacies to the European avant-garde. First, by developing new techniques without reference to past styles, the impressionists paved the way for younger artists to experiment more freely. Second, because the official salons

***PORTRAIT OF AMBROISE VOLLARD*, BY PABLO PICASSO (1909).** In the early twentieth century, Pablo Picasso and Georges Braque radically transformed painting with their cubist constructions, which breaks the depiction of reality into fragmented planes. This image of Vollard, an important art dealer of the period, loses recognizable form in the lower part of the painting. ▪ *Compare this portrait with Schiele's* **Self-Portrait** *on the left. What do these paintings say about the task of an artist?* ▪ *What makes these paintings "modern"?*

***SELF-PORTRAIT*, BY EGON SCHIELE (1912).** The Viennese artist Egon Schiele represents another side of early modernism that sought to portray raw psychological expression, instead of moving toward abstraction.

rejected their work, the impressionists organized their own independent exhibitions from 1874 to 1886. These shows effectively undermined the French Academy's centuries-old monopoly on artistic display and aesthetic standards, and established a tradition of autonomous outsider exhibits that figures prominently in the history of modernism.

At the end of the nineteenth century, in the wake of impressionism, a handful of innovative artists laid the groundwork for an explosion of creative experimentation; chief among them, the Frenchman Paul Cézanne (1839–1906). Perhaps more than anyone, Cézanne shattered the window of representational art. Painting became a vehicle for an artist's self-expression rather than a reflection of the world. Dutchman Vincent van Gogh also explored art's expressive potential, with greater emotion and subjectivity. For Van Gogh, painting was a labor of faith, a way to channel his violent passions. For another artist, Paul Gauguin, who fled to the Pacific islands in 1891, art promised a utopian refuge from the corruption of Europe.

After the turn of the century, a diverse crop of avant-garde movements flowered across Europe. In Germany and Scandinavia, expressionists such as Emil Nolde (1867–1956) and Edvard Munch (1863–1944) turned to acid colors and violent figural distortions to express the interior consciousness of the human mind. The Austrian Egon Schiele (1890–1918) explored sexuality and the body with disturbingly raw, graphic imagery. In bohemian Paris, the Frenchman Henri Matisse (1869–1954) and Pablo Picasso (1881–1973), a Catalan Spaniard, pursued their groundbreaking aesthetic experiments in relative quiet. Clamoring for attention, however, were groups of artists who reveled in the energetic dynamism of modern life. The cubists in Paris, the vorticists in Britain, and the futurists in Italy all embraced a hard, angular aesthetic of the machine age. Other modernists, meanwhile, sought an antidote to end-of-the-century malaise by looking backward to the so-called primitive cultures. These new movements embraced the future in all its uncertainty, often with the kind of aggressive, hypermasculine language that later emerged as a hallmark of fascism. In *The Manifesto of Futurism,* for instance, Filippo Tommaso Marinetti proclaimed, "We will glorify war—the only true hygiene of the world—militarism, patriotism, the destructive gesture of anarchist, the beautiful Ideas which kill." In Russia and Holland, a few intensely idealistic painters made perhaps

After You Read This Chapter

 Go to **INQUIZITIVE** to see what you've learned—and learn what you've missed—with personalized feedback along the way.

REVIEWING THE OBJECTIVES

- The second industrial revolution was made possible by technological innovations that stimulated the production of steel and created new energy sources. What were the consequences of this era of rapid growth for the European economy and society?

- Liberalism and nationalism were changed by the advent of mass politics. How did the expansion of the electorate change political life across Europe?

- Expanded electorates meant that more people were participating in politics, especially among the working classes. What parties and movements emerged to represent European workers? What were their goals?

- At the end of the nineteenth century, militant agitation in favor of woman suffrage increased. What obstacles did women who demanded the vote face?

- Technological innovations and scientific ideas about human nature and modern society changed the way people thought about their place in the world, inspiring artists and writers to new and revolutionary forms of creative expression. What were these scientific ideas? Why were they so controversial at the end of the nineteenth century?

the most revolutionary aesthetic leap of early modernism: the totally abstract, or "object-less" painting.

The breadth and diversity of modern art defy simple categories and explanations. Though they remained the province of a small group of artists and intellectuals before 1914, soon after the First World War, these radical revisions of artistic values entered the cultural mainstream (see Chapter 25).

CONCLUSION

Many Europeans who had grown up in the period from 1870 to 1914, but lived through the hardships of the First World War, look back on the prewar period as a golden age of European civilization. In one sense, this retrospective view is correct. After all, the Continental powers had successfully avoided major wars, enabling a second phase of industrialization that provided better living standards for the growing populations of mass society. An overall spirit of confidence and purpose fueled Europe's perceived mission to exercise political, economic, and cultural dominion in the far reaches of the world. Yet, European politics and culture also registered the presence of powerful—and destabilizing—forces of change. Industrial expansion, relative abundance, and rising literacy produced a political climate of escalating expectations. As the age of mass politics arrived, democrats, socialists, and feminists clamored for access to political life, all threatening violence, strikes, and revolution. Marxist socialism especially changed radical politics and redefined the terms of debate for the next century. Western science, literature, and the arts explored new perspectives on the individual, undermining some of the cherished beliefs of nineteenth-century liberals. The competition and violence central to Darwin's theory of evolution, the subconscious urges in human behavior found in Freud's study, and the rebellion against representation in the arts all pointed toward new and baffling directions. These experiments, hypotheses, and nagging questions accompanied Europe into the Great War of 1914, and they would help shape Europeans' responses to the devastation of that war. After the war, the political changes and cultural unease of the period from 1870 to 1914 would reemerge, in the form of mass movements and artistic developments that would define the twentieth century.

PEOPLE, IDEAS, AND EVENTS IN CONTEXT

- Why was the **BRITISH LABOUR PARTY** more moderate in its goals than the German **SOCIAL DEMOCRATIC PARTY**?
- What disagreements about political strategy divided **ANARCHISTS** and **SYNDICALISTS** from **MARXISTS** in European labor movements?
- What legal reforms were successfully achieved by **WOMEN'S ASSOCIATIONS** in late-nineteenth-century western European nations?
- What was the **DREYFUS AFFAIR**? How was it related to the spread of popular **ANTI-SEMITISM** and the emergence of **ZIONISM** in European Jewish communities?
- What were the goals of the **BOLSHEVIKS** and the **MENSHEVIKS** in the **RUSSIAN REVOLUTION OF 1905**?
- Who were the **YOUNG TURKS**? What circumstances in the Ottoman Empire brought them to power? What changes did they provoke?
- What was **CHARLES DARWIN'S THEORY OF EVOLUTION**? Why did it arouse so much debate between religious and secular thinkers?
- Why was the psychology of **SIGMUND FREUD** so troubling for liberals in Europe?
- What made the **NOVEL** so popular among nineteenth-century readers?
- What common ideas did the artists and writers who came to be known as **MODERNISTS** share?

THINKING ABOUT CONNECTIONS

- How did the expansion of the electorate and the spread of representative political institutions in Europe at the end of the nineteenth century change the nature of debates about the power of public opinion and the responsibility of government for the people?
- Compare the age of mass politics at the end of the nineteenth century in Europe with earlier eras of rapid change, such as the Reformation of the sixteenth century or the period of the French Revolution. What was similar? What was different?
- Compare the age of mass politics in Europe around 1900 with the political life of Europe or the United States today. What has changed? What remains the same?

STORY LINES

- In 1914, the balance of power in Europe collapsed in a war that mobilized the full resources of modern industrialized nations, their global empires, and their populations.

- The war transformed the relationship between state and society, as governments conscripted an entire generation of young men, encouraged women to work in industry, and took control of the economy to produce goods and matériel for the military.

- The war provoked the first successful socialist revolution in modern history when the Russian Empire collapsed and the Bolsheviks seized power in October 1917. The Russian Revolution set the stage for the major ideological confrontations of the twentieth century.

CHRONOLOGY

1879	The Dual Alliance (Germany and Austria-Hungary)
1907	The Triple Entente (France, Russia, and Britain)
June 1914	Assassination of Archduke Franz Ferdinand in Sarajevo
September 1914	Battle of the Marne
April 1915	Gallipoli campaign begins
May 1915	Italy enters the war against Austria-Hungary
February 1916	Battle of Verdun begins
July 1916	British offensive on the Somme begins
January 1917	Germany begins unrestricted submarine warfare
April 1917	United States enters the war
November 1917	Bolshevik Revolution
March 1918	Treaty of Brest-Litovsk
November 1918	Armistice
June 1919	Treaty of Versailles signed

Before You Read This Chapter

The First World War

CORE OBJECTIVES

- **EXPLAIN** the origins of the First World War.

- **UNDERSTAND** the circumstances that led to trench warfare on the Western Front, and the consequences of the offensive strategy pursued by all sides.

- **IDENTIFY** the major effects of the war on civilian life.

- **EXPLAIN** the war's effects on territories beyond Europe's borders, in the Middle East, Africa, and Asia.

- **UNDERSTAND** the origins and goals of the Bolshevik movement in Russia and the circumstances that allowed the Bolsheviks to seize power in 1917.

- **IDENTIFY** the people responsible for the final terms of the Versailles Peace Treaty and **UNDERSTAND** its goals.

he battle of the Somme began on June 24, 1916, with a fearsome British artillery barrage against German trenches along a twenty-five-mile front. Hour after hour, day and night, the British guns swept across the barbed wire and fortifications that faced their own lines, firing 1.5 million rounds over seven days. Mixing gas with explosive rounds, the gunners pulverized the landscape and poisoned the atmosphere. On the other side, deep in underground bunkers, the German defenders huddled in their gas masks. When the big guns fell silent, tens of thousands of British soldiers rose up out of the trenches, each bearing sixty pounds of equipment, and made their way into the cratered No Man's Land that separated the two armies. They had been told that wire-cutting explosives used during the barrage would have destroyed the labyrinth of barbed wire between the trenches, leaving them free to charge across and occupy the front trench before the stunned Germans could recover. But to their horror, they found the barbed wire intact. Instead of taking the German trench, they found themselves caught in the open when the German machine gunners manned the defensive parapets. The result proved, all too graphically, the efficiency of the First World War's mechanized methods

815

of killing. On the first day of the battle of the Somme, 29,000 British soldiers were killed, and another 30,000 wounded. Because British units sometimes allowed volunteers to serve with their friends—the "pals battalions"—in some British neighborhoods and villages, every married woman became a widow in the span of a few minutes. The British commanders pressed the offensive for nearly five more months, and the combined casualties climbed to more than a million; but the German line never broke.

This contest between artillery and machine guns was a war that was possible only in an industrialized world. (Before beginning the assault, the British had stockpiled 2.9 million artillery shells; Napoleon had only 20,000 at Waterloo.) Although European armies marched off to war in 1914 with confidence and ambition bred by their imperial conquests, they soon confronted the ugly face of industrial warfare and the grim capacities of the modern world. In a catastrophic combination of old mentalities and new technologies, the war left 9 million dead soldiers in its wake.

And soldiers were not the only casualties. Four years of fighting destroyed many of the institutions and assumptions of the previous century, from monarchies and empires to European economic dominance. It disillusioned many, even among citizens of the victorious nations. As the British writer Virginia Woolf put it, "It was a shock—to see the faces of our rulers in the light of shell-fire." The war led European states to take over their national economies, setting quotas for production and consumption and taking responsibility for sustaining the civilian population during the crisis. By toppling the Prussian and Austrian monarchies, the war banished older forms of authoritarianism. And by provoking the Russian Revolution of 1917, the war ushered in new forms that bore the distinctive marks of the twentieth century. Finally, the war proved nearly impossible to settle; antagonisms bred in battle only intensified in the war's aftermath and, eventually, led to the Second World War. Postwar Europe faced more problems than peace could manage.

THE JULY CRISIS

In the decades before 1914, Europe had built a seemingly stable peace. Through the complex negotiations of Great Power geopolitics, Europe had settled into two systems of alliance: the Triple Entente (later the Allied Powers) of Britain, France, and Russia rivaled the Triple Alliance (later the Central Powers) of Germany, Austria-Hungary, and Italy. Within this balance of power, the nations of Europe challenged each other for economic, military, and imperial advantage. The scramble for colonies abroad accompanied a fierce arms race at home, with military leaders assuming that superior technology and larger armies would result in a quick victory in a European war. None of the diplomats, spies, military planners, or cabinet ministers of Europe—or any of their critics—predicted the war they eventually got, nor did they expect that the Balkan crisis of July 1914 would touch off a conflict that would engulf all of Europe in just over a month.

The Balkan Peninsula had long been a satellite of the Ottoman Empire. During the nineteenth century, however, Ottoman power was severely weakened, and the Austro-Hungarian Empire and the Russian monarchy competed with each other to replace the Ottomans as the dominant force. The region was home to ambitious national movements of Serbs and Bulgarians, who took advantage of the Ottoman decline to declare their independence in the decades before the First World War. Russia, the most powerful Slavic monarchy, was the traditional sponsor of these Slavic nationalist movements and had a particularly close relationship with Serbia. Austria-Hungary, meanwhile, sought to minimize the influence of Slavic nationalisms because they constituted a threat to its multi-ethnic empire. In 1912 and 1913, the region was destabilized by two wars involving the Ottoman Empire and the independent Balkan states of Serbia, Greece, Bulgaria, and Montenegro. The Great Powers steered clear of entanglement, so these wars remained localized. The alliance system, however, could ensure stability only as long as the Great Powers maintained this posture of nonintervention; otherwise, if one of them became embroiled in a local conflict, it would trigger a wider war.

The spark came from the Balkan province of Bosnia, a multi-ethnic region of Serbs, Croats, and Bosnian Muslims that had been under Austrian rule since 1878. In Bosnia, members of the local Serb population longed to secede from Austrian rule altogether and join the independent state of Serbia, and when they found their way blocked by the Austrians, some began to conspire with Serbia. On June 28, 1914, a group of Bosnian Serbs assassinated the heir to the Austro-Hungarian throne, Archduke **Franz Ferdinand** (1863–1914), and his wife, Sophie, as they paraded through Sarajevo, the capital of Bosnia.

Shocked by Ferdinand's death, the Austrians treated the assassination as a direct attack by the Serbian government. Three weeks later, the Austrians announced an ultimatum to Serbia, demanding that they denounce the activities of the Bosnian Serbs, refrain from publishing propaganda that served their cause, and allow Austro-Hungarian officials to prosecute members of the Serbian government they believed were involved in the assassination. The demands were deliberately unreasonable—the

1878

RUSSIAN EMPIRE

AUSTRIA-HUNGARY

BOSNIA-HERZEGOVINA
(Annexed by Austria-Hungary in 1908)

Belgrade

ROMANIA
(Independent 1878)

Bucharest

DOBRUJA
(to Romania 1878)

Sarajevo

SERBIA
(Independent 1878)

Danube R.

BULGARIA
(Independent 1908)

BLACK SEA

(To SERBIA 1878)

Sofia

EAST RUMELIA
(Autonomous 1878; to Bulgaria 1885)

MONTENEGRO
(Independent 1878)

ADRIATIC SEA

ALBANIA
(Independent 1912)

OTTOMAN EMPIRE

Constantinople

ITALY

MACEDONIA

THESSALY
(to Greece 1881)

AEGEAN SEA

GREECE
(Independent 1830)

Athens

0   100   200 Miles
0   100   200 Kilometers

CRETE

DODECANESE ISLANDS

MEDITERRANEAN SEA

EUROPE

AFRICA   Area of detail

1914

RUSSIAN EMPIRE

AUSTRIA-HUNGARY

BOSNIA-HERZEGOVINA

Belgrade

ROMANIA

Bucharest

SERBIA

Sarajevo

DOBRUJA
(to Romania 1913)

MONTENEGRO

Danube R.

BULGARIA

Sofia

BLACK SEA

(to Montenegro 1913)

(to Serbia 1913)

THRACE
(to Bulgaria 1913)

ADRIATIC SEA

ALBANIA

Constantinople

ITALY

MACEDONIA
(to Greece 1913)

AEGEAN SEA

(to Greece 1913)

OTTOMAN EMPIRE

GREECE

Athens

0   100   200 Miles
0   100   200 Kilometers

CRETE

DODECANESE ISLANDS
(to Italy 1917)

MEDITERRANEAN SEA

EUROPE

AFRICA   Area of detail

THE BALKAN CRISIS, 1878–1914. ▪ *Which major empires were involved in the Balkans at the time?* ▪ *According to the maps, what was the major change in the Balkans during this period?* ▪ *What problems did nationalism, ethnicity, and race create in this region?*

Austrians wanted war, to crush Serbia and restore order in Bosnia. The Serbs mobilized their army before agreeing to all but the most important demands, and Austria responded with its own mobilization order on July 28, 1914. Shaken from their summer distractions, Europeans began to realize that the treaty system they relied on for stability was actually provoking a much larger confrontation: Austria and its ally Germany were facing a war with Serbia, Serbia's ally Russia, and, by extension, Russia's ally France.

Diplomats tried but failed to prevent the outbreak of a wider war. When Russia announced a "partial mobilization" to defend Serbia against Austria, the German ministers telegraphed the French to find out if they intended to honor France's defensive treaty with Russia, to which the French responded that France would "act in accordance with her interests," meaning that it would immediately mobilize against Germany. Facing the threat from both sides it had long feared, Germany mobilized on August 1 and declared war on Russia—and two days later, on France. The next day, the German army invaded Belgium on its way to take Paris.

The invasion of neutral Belgium provided a rallying cry for British generals and diplomats who wanted Britain to honor their secret treaty obligations to France and join the war against Germany. This was not a foregone conclusion, however, as the Liberal government was opposed to war and only acquiesced partly to avoid being voted out of office. Proponents of war insisted that to maintain the balance of power—a central tenet of British foreign policy—no single nation should be allowed to dominate the Continent. So, on August 4, Britain entered the war against Germany.

Other nations were quickly drawn into the struggle. On August 7, the Montenegrins joined the Serbs against Austria. Two weeks later, the Japanese declared war on Germany, mainly to attack German possessions in the Far East. On August 2, Turkey allied with Germany and, in October, began the bombardment of Russian ports on the Black Sea. Italy had been allied with Germany and Austria before the war, but at the outbreak of hostilities, it declared neutrality, insisting that because Germany had invaded neutral Belgium, it did not owe Germany protection.

The diplomatic maneuvers during the five weeks after the assassination at Sarajevo have been called a "tragedy of miscalculation." Austria's determination to punish Serbia, Germany's unwillingness to restrain its Austrian ally, and Russia's desire to use Serbia as an excuse to maintain its influence in the Balkans all played a part in making war more likely. Diplomats were also constrained by the strategic thinking and rigid timetables set by their military leaders.

EUROPEAN ALLIANCES ON THE EVE OF THE FIRST WORLD WAR. ▪ *Which major countries were part of the Triple Alliance and which were part of the Triple Entente?* ▪ *As you examine the map, why do you think Germany declared war on France so quickly once Russia began to mobilize?* ▪ *According to the map, why were the Balkan countries such a volatile region?*

FRANZ FERDINAND AND HIS WIFE, SOPHIE. The Austrian archduke and archduchess in Sarajevo on June 28, 1914. They are shown approaching their car minutes before they were assassinated. ▪ *What made their deaths the spark that unleashed a general war in Europe?*

Many young men, however, enlisted with excitement. On the Continent, volunteer soldiers added to the strength of conscript armies, while in Britain—where conscription wasn't introduced until 1916—more than 700,000 men joined the army in the first eight weeks alone. Like many war enthusiasts, these men expected it to be over by Christmas.

Military planners also foresaw a short, limited, and decisive war—a tool to be used where diplomacy failed. They thought that a modern economy simply could not function amid a sustained war effort and that a protracted war was impossible with modern weaponry. They placed their bets on size and speed to win the war: bigger armies, more powerful weapons, and faster offensives. But despite all their planning, they were unable to respond to the uncertainty and confusion of the battlefield.

The Germans based their offensive on what is often called the Schlieffen Plan, named for Count Alfred von Schlieffen (*SHLEE-fen*), the chief of the German general staff from 1890 to 1905. Schlieffen sought to avoid a two-front war by attacking France first, before Russia could mobilize its larger army. The **Schlieffen Plan** called for the Germans to invade France through Belgium and defeat the French army in a decisive battle near Paris. The German troops crossed the Belgian border on August 4, but the plan overestimated the army's physical and logistical capabilities. The soldiers and supply lines simply could not keep up with the speed of the operation: advancing twenty to twenty-five miles a day. They were also slowed by the resistance of Belgian forces and by the intervention of Britain's small but highly professional field army. Fearing that the Russians would move faster than expected, German commanders altered the offensive plan and dispatched some troops to the east instead of committing them all to the assault on France.

At first, the French counterattacks into Alsace-Lorraine failed, and casualties mounted as the French lines retreated toward Paris. The French commander, Jules Joffre, nevertheless reorganized his armies and slowly drew the Germans into a trap. In September, with the Germans just thirty miles outside the capital, Britain and France launched a successful counteroffensive at the **Battle of the Marne**. The German line retreated to the Aisne River, and what remained of the Schlieffen Plan was dead.

And, during the period of negotiation that preceded the outbreak of war, all sides felt that it was important to make a show of force. It is clear that powerful German officials were arguing that war was inevitable, and thus insisting that they fight before Russia recovered from its 1905 loss to Japan and before the French army could benefit from its new three-year conscription law, which would put more men in uniform. This sense of urgency characterized the strategies of all combatant countries. The lure of a bold, successful strike against one's enemies, and the fear that too much was at stake to risk losing the advantage, created a rolling tide of military mobilization that carried Europe into battle.

1914: MOBILIZATION AND THE EARLY OFFENSIVES

Declarations of war were met with a mix of public fanfare and private concern. Saber-rattling romantics envisioned a war of national glory, but others throughout Europe recognized that war put their security and prosperity at risk. Bankers and financiers, who might have profited from increased wartime production or from captured colonial markets, were among those most opposed to war, correctly predicting that a major war would create financial chaos.

Competing Viewpoints

Toward the First World War: Diplomacy in the Summer of 1914

The assassination of Franz Ferdinand in Sarajevo on June 28, 1914, set off an increasingly desperate round of diplomatic negotiations. As the following exchanges show, diplomats and political leaders on both sides vacillated from trying to provoke war to attempting to avert or at least contain it. A week after his nephew, the heir to the throne, was shot, Emperor Franz Joseph set out his interpretation of the long-standing conflict with Serbia and its larger implications (reprinted here).

The second selection comes from an account of a meeting of the Council of Ministers of the Austro-Hungarian Empire on July 7, 1914. The ministers disagreed sharply about diplomatic strategies and how crucial decisions should be made.

Austro-Hungary's ultimatum to Serbia included the demands given in the final extract here. The British foreign secretary Sir Edward Grey, for one, was shocked by Austria's demands, especially its insistence that Austrian officials participate in Serbian judicial proceedings. The Serbian government's response was more conciliatory than most diplomats expected, but diplomatic efforts to avert war still failed.

Emperor Franz Joseph of Austria-Hungary to Kaiser Wilhelm II of Germany, July 5, 1914

The plot against my poor nephew was the direct result of an agitation carried on by the Russian and Serb Pan-Slavs, an agitation whose sole object is the weakening of the Triple Alliance and the destruction of my realm.

So far, all investigations have shown that the Sarajevo murder was not perpetrated by one individual, but grew out of a well-organized conspiracy, the threads of which can be traced to Belgrade. Even though it will probably be impossible to prove the complicity of the Serb government, there can be no doubt that its policy, aiming as it does at the unification of all Southern Slavs under the Serb banner, encourages such crimes, and that the continuation of such conditions constitutes a permanent threat to my dynasty and my lands. . . .

This will only be possible if Serbia, which is at present the pivot of Pan-Slav policies, is put out of action as a factor of political power in the Balkans.

You too are [surely] convinced after the recent frightful occurrence in Bosnia that it is no longer possible to contemplate a reconciliation of the antagonism between us and Serbia and that the [efforts] of all European monarchs to pursue policies that preserve the peace will be threatened if the nest of criminal activity in Belgrade remains unpunished.

Austro-Hungarian Disagreements over Strategy

[Count Leopold Berchtold, foreign minister of Austria-Hungary:] [B]oth Emperor Wilhelm and [chancellor] Bethmann Hollweg had assured us emphatically of Germany's unconditional support in the event of military complications with Serbia. . . . It was clear to him that a military conflict with Serbia might bring about war with Russia. . . .

[Count Istvan Tisza, prime minister of Hungary:] We should decide what our demands on Serbia will be [but] should only present an ultimatum if Serbia rejected them. These demands must be hard but not so that they cannot be complied with. If Serbia accepted them, we could register a noteworthy diplomatic success and our prestige in the Balkans would be enhanced. If Serbia rejected our demands, then he too would favor military action. But he would already now go on record that we could aim at the down sizing but not the complete annihilation of Serbia because, first, this would provoke Russia to fight to the death and, second, he—as Hungarian premier—could never consent to the monarchy's annexation of a part of

Source: Ralph Menning, *The Art of the Possible: Documents on Great Power Diplomacy, 1814–1914* (New York: 1996), pp. 400, 402–3, 414–15.

Serbia. Whether or not we ought to go to war with Serbia was not a matter for Germany to decide. . . .

[Count Berchtold] remarked that the history of the past years showed that diplomatic successes against Serbia might enhance the prestige of the monarchy temporarily, but that in reality the tension in our relations with Serbia had only increased.

[Count Karl Stürgkh, prime minister of Austria] . . . agreed with the Royal Hungarian Prime Minister that we and not the German government had to determine whether a war was necessary or not . . . [but] Count Tisza should take into account that in pursuing a hesitant and weak policy, we run the risk of not being so sure of Germany's unconditional support. . . .

[Leo von Bilinsky, Austro-Hungarian finance minister:] . . . The Serb understands only force, a diplomatic success would make no impression at all in Bosnia and would be harmful rather than beneficial.

Austro-Hungary's Ultimatum to Serbia

The Royal Serb Government will publish the following declaration on the first page of its official *journal* of 26/13 July:

"The Royal Serb Government condemns the propaganda directed against Austria-Hungary, and regrets sincerely the horrible consequences of these criminal ambitions.

"The Royal Serb Government regrets that Serb officers and officials have taken part in the propaganda above-mentioned and thereby imperiled friendly and neighbourly relations.

"The Royal Government . . . considers it a duty to warn officers, officials and indeed all the inhabitants of the kingdom [of Serbia], that it will in future use great severity against such persons who may be guilty of similar doings.

The Royal Serb Government will moreover pledge itself to the following:

1. to suppress every publication likely to inspire hatred and contempt against the Monarchy;

2. to begin immediately dissolving the society called *Narodna Odbrana*,* to seize all its means of propaganda and to act in the same way against all the societies and associations in Serbia, which are busy with the propaganda against Austria-Hungary;

3. to eliminate without delay from public instruction everything that serves or might serve the propaganda against Austria-Hungary, both where teachers or books are concerned;

4. to remove from military service and from the administration all officers and officials who are guilty of having taken part in the propaganda against Austria-Hungary, whose names and proof of whose guilt the I. and R. Government [Imperial and Royal, that is, the Austro-Hungarian Empire] will communicate to the Royal Government;

5. to consent to the cooperation of I. and R. officials in Serbia in suppressing the subversive movement directed against the territorial integrity of the Monarchy;

6. to open a judicial inquest [*enquête judiciaire*] against all those who took part in the plot of 28 June, if they are to be found on Serbian territory; the I. and R. Government will delegate officials who will take an active part in these and associated inquiries;

The I. and R. Government expects the answer of the Royal government to reach it not later than Saturday, the 25th, at six in the afternoon.

* Narodna Odbrana, or National Defense, was pro-Serbian and anti-Austrian but nonviolent. The Society of the Black Hand, to which Franz Ferdinand's assassin belonged, considered Narodna Odbrana too moderate.

Questions for Analysis

1. Emperor Franz Joseph's letter to Kaiser Wilhelm II tells of the Austrian investigation into the assassination of Archduke Franz Ferdinand. What did Franz Joseph seek from his German ally? What did the emperors understand by the phrase "if Serbia . . . is put out of action as a factor of political power in the Balkans"? Why might the Germans support a war against Serb-sponsored terrorism?

2. Could the Serbians have accepted the Austrian ultimatum without total loss of face and sacrifice of their independence? British and Russian foreign ministers were shocked by the demands on Serbia. Others thought that the Austrians were justified and that Britain would act similarly if threatened by terrorism. If, as Leo von Bilinsky said, "The Serb understands only force," why didn't Austria declare war without an ultimatum?

THE SCHLIEFFEN PLAN AND THE GERMAN OFFENSIVE. The map on the left details the offensive strategy developed (and modified several times) by Alfred von Schlieffen, chief of the German general staff, and Helmuth von Moltke, his successor, in the decade after 1890. The map on the right shows the German offensive. ▪ *What strategy did the Schlieffen Plan propose, and why?* ▪ *According to the map on the right, how was the plan modified, and why?* ▪ *What were the consequences of this modified plan?* ▪ *Why did the German offensive fail to achieve its ultimate goal?*

After the Marne, the armies were unable to advance and thus tried to outflank one another to the north, racing to the sea. After four months of swift charges across open ground, Germany set up a fortified, defensive position that the Allies could not break. Along an immovable front, stretching over 400 miles from the northern border of Switzerland to the English Channel, the Great Powers literally dug in for a protracted battle. By Christmas, trench warfare was born, and the war had just begun.

In the east, meanwhile, Russia had surprised the Germans and Austrians by moving quickly into East Prussia, threatening Berlin. At the same time, Russian forces moved to confront the Austrians through Polish Galicia just as the Austrians hoped to concentrate on Serbia. These initial Russian gains were obliterated, however, at the **Battle of Tannenberg** on August 26–30. Plagued with an array of problems, the Russian soldiers were tired and half starved. The Germans encircled them, taking 92,000 prisoners and virtually destroying the Russian Second Army. Two weeks later, the Germans won another victory at the battle of the Masurian Lakes, forcing the Russians to retreat from German territory. But this time the Russian armies were able to escape largely intact, and the continued threat forced the Germans to commit more troops to Russia.

The French victory at the Marne and the German victory at Tannenberg reversed the expectations of the Schlieffen Plan, and the consequences of this moment shaped the way Europe's powers thought about their chances for victory. In the west, the war of movement had stopped dead in its tracks, where it would remain for four years; and the hope that the war would be over quickly was dashed. Politicians and generals began a search for ways to break the stalemate and to bring the war out of the trenches, seeking new allies, new theaters, and new weapons. But they also remained committed to offensive tactics on the Western Front. Whether through ignorance, stubbornness, callousness, or desperation, military leaders continued to order their men to go "over the top." In the east, the German victories of 1914 at Tannenberg and the Masurian Lakes were followed by devastating Austrian defeats in Galicia. By December, the Austrian Habsburg army had lost 1.3 million men out of 3.4 million mobilized, and 300,000 were taken prisoner by the Russians at the battle of Lemberg alone. The Russian army had lost 1.5 million out of 3.5 million mobilized, but their enormous population left them with 10 million more men in reserve. Through 1915 and 1916, the Eastern Front remained bloody and indecisive, with neither side able to capitalize on its gains.

RUSSIAN PRISONERS IN LATE AUGUST 1914, AFTER THE BATTLE OF TANNENBERG. The German army, under Paul von Hindenburg and Erich Ludendorff, crushed the Russians and took 92,000 prisoners. The Russians continued to fight, but this photograph highlights the scale of the combat and the weakness of even a massive army.

STALEMATE, 1915

In the search for new points of attack, both the Allied and the Central Powers took advantage of new partners. The Ottoman Empire (Turkey) joined Germany and Austria at the start of the war. In May 1915, Italy joined the Allies, persuaded by the popular support of its citizens and lured by promises of financial reparations, parts of Austrian territory, and pieces of Germany's African colonies when (and if) the Allies won the war. Bulgaria, hoping to gain territory in the Balkans, joined the war on the side of the Central Powers a few months later. The entry of these new belligerents expanded the geography of the war and introduced the possibility of breaking the stalemate in the west by waging offensives on other fronts.

Ottoman Turkey, Gallipoli, and the Armenian Genocide

Ottoman Turkey faced an internal crisis of weakening authority even before the war began, as the absolutist rule of Sultan Abdul Hamid II (r. 1876–1909) was challenged by reformers who called themselves the Young Turks (Chapter 23). When the Young Turks came to power in 1913, their leadership sought an alliance with one of the European blocs as a way to gain support for building long-

delayed infrastructure and time for needed reforms. Long-standing rivalries with Russia over the Balkans and Black Sea region precluded a treaty with the Triple Entente, so the government signed an agreement with Germany on August 2, 1914.

The Ottoman Empire's involvement altered the dynamics of the war by threatening Russia's supply lines and endangering Britain's control of the Suez Canal. To defeat Turkey quickly—and in hopes of bypassing the Western Front—the British first lord of the admiralty, Winston Churchill, argued for a naval offensive in the Dardanelles, the narrow strait separating Europe and Asia Minor also known as the Gallipoli Peninsula. Incompetent leadership and inadequate planning quickly led to the loss of six ships. The Allies then attempted a land invasion of the **Gallipoli Peninsula** in April 1915, with a combined force of French, British, Australian, and New Zealand troops. The Turks defended the narrow coast from positions high on fortified cliffs, and the shores were covered with nearly impenetrable barbed wire. During the disastrous landing, a British officer recalled, "the sea behind was absolutely crimson, and you could hear the groans through the rattle of musketry." The casualties mounted for seven months before the Allied commanders admitted defeat and ordered a withdrawal in December. The defeat cost the Allies 200,000 soldiers and did little to shift the war's focus away from the deadlocked Western Front.

Attacked by the Allies at Gallipoli and at war with the Russians to the north, the Turkish government turned on its Armenian subjects, believing them to be a security risk. Approximately 2 million Armenians who lived in the Ottoman Empire in 1914 were Orthodox Christians. They were mostly an urban population that was more prosperous and more educated than the Ottoman population at large; and during the nineteenth century, they had faced attacks resulting in hundreds of thousands of deaths. In April 1915, as the Allied troops began their operation at Gallipoli, the Ottoman government executed several hundred Armenian intellectuals—an act that proved to be the beginning of the **Armenian Genocide**. Throughout Anatolia, and along the Aegean and Black Sea coasts, Ottoman troops drove Armenians from their homes and forced them into death marches southward into the Syrian desert without food or water; many were robbed, raped, and beaten to death along the way. Between 1915 and 1923, about 1.5 million Armenians were killed.

THE ARMENIAN GENOCIDE. Armenian refugees fleeing Turkish persecution in mid-winter, c. 1915.

TOTAL WAR, ECONOMIC BLOCKADE, AND POPULATION DISPLACEMENT

After the failure of the Schlieffen Plan, all sides realized that a prolonged war between modern industrialized powers would require mobilizing the entire resources of every nation involved in the conflict. The numbers of men in arms, the new technologies of warfare—which included the development of machine guns, advanced artillery, the use of airplanes and submarine warfare—created logistical needs that placed enormous burdens on the civilian population, who were pressed both to work for the war effort and to limit their own consumption of food, fuel, and consumer goods. This was "total war"—in which the line between civilian and military targets became blurred, and maintaining the morale of the home front was just as important as keeping soldiers fed and supplied in the trenches.

The Allies realized that Germany's great vulnerability lay in its reliance on imports for one-third of its food supply. The logic of "total war" therefore led to a naval blockade of Germany's ports, a measure designed to strangle Germany's economy by limiting access to global markets for food and raw materials. Britain and France continued to import grain and beef from the United States, Canada, Argentina, Australia, and New Zealand, an advantage that weighed heavily in the ultimate victory of the Allied powers. Germany was forced to respond with a submarine blockade of Britain, and it threatened to attack any ship headed to a British port. On May 7, 1915, a German submarine torpedoed the passenger liner Lusitania, which also carried war supplies, killing 1,198 people,

THE NEW TECHNOLOGIES OF WAR IN THE AIR AND AT SEA. The use of airplanes and submarines, both produced in large numbers during the First World War, changed the nature of warfare. The air war helped dissolve the boundaries between the front line and the home front, as civilian populations were brought within range of the enemy's destructive power. Germany's decision to use submarines against merchant ships trading with Britain and France led to the sinking of the *Lusitania* in 1915, which turned public opinion in the United States. The same issue led President Wilson to commit U.S. troops to the Allied side in 1917. The photo on the left shows the German submarine base in Kiel, on the Baltic coast. The photo on the right shows a German plane attacking an English tank.

including 128 Americans. The attack provoked the animosity of the United States, forcing Germany to promise that it would no longer fire without warning. When Germany again declared unrestricted submarine warfare in 1917, the United States was drawn into the war.

The logic of "total war" produced massive displacements of civilian populations. Some, such as the Armenians in the Ottoman empire, were specifically targeted and killed as enemies. Others were caught in territories overtaken by foreign armies and forced to flee. The German invasion of France through Belgium produced 1.5 million Belgian refugees who sought safety in France, the Netherlands, and Britain. The same theatre of conflict produced 735,000 internally displaced French refugees by July 1915. When Italy entered the war in May 1915 on the side of Britain and France, 87,000 Italians living in the Austro-Hungarian empire fled to Italy, while 42,000 other Italian civilians were sent by the Austrians to internment camps. The Russian invasion of East Prussia, meanwhile, drove 870,000 civilians westward into Germany, creating a burden on an already strained economy. The Jews of central Europe were particularly vulnerable: Russian commanders deported tens of thousands of Galician Jews to the east, and hundreds of thousands more from the same region were uprooted. In Vienna, as much as one-half of the 140,000 refugees sheltering in the city were Jewish; Warsaw housed 80,000 Jewish refugees during the war years. Within the Russian empire, the number of civilians on the move may have reached 7 million by the time Russia pulled out of the war in 1917. These population movements, the product of panic, fear of persecution, and forced resettlement by military commanders, created enormous hardship and suffering. People uprooted by war often had no clear place to go. Departures were precipitous, with little time to pack or prepare. Unlike prewar migrations, where people made a difficult but conscious choice to seek lives elsewhere, the population movements caused by war were bewildering and beset with uncertainty and fear.

Trench Warfare on the Western Front

Machine guns and barbed wire gave well-supplied and entrenched defenders an enormous advantage even against a larger attacking force. Eventually, some 25,000 miles of trenches snaked along the Western Front, typically in three lines on each side of No Man's Land. The front line was the attack trench, lying anywhere from fifty yards to a mile away from the enemy. Behind the front lay a maze of connecting trenches and lines, leading to a complex of

ammunition dumps, telephone exchanges, water points, field hospitals, and command posts. These logistical centers were intended to allow an army to project its power forward, but just as often, they acted as a tether, making it difficult to advance.

The British and French trenches were wet, cold, and filthy. Rain turned the dusty corridors into squalid mud pits and flooded the floors up to waist level. Soldiers lived with lice and large black rats, which fed on the dead soldiers and horses that cast their stench over everything. Cadavers could go unburied for months and were often embedded in the trench walls. It was little wonder that soldiers were rotated out of the front lines frequently—after only three to seven days. The threat of enemy fire was constant, as 7,000 British men were killed or wounded daily. This "wastage," as it was called, was part of the routine, along with the inspections, rotations, and mundane duties of life on the Western Front. Despite this danger, the trenches were a relatively reliable means of protection, especially compared with the casualty rates of going on the offensive.

THE LINES OF BATTLE ON THE WESTERN FRONT. A British reconnaissance photo showing three lines of German trenches (on the right), No Man's Land (black strip in the center), and the British trenches (partially visible on the left). The upper right-hand quadrant of the photo shows communications trenches linking the front to the safe area. ▪ *What technologies gave these defenses such decisive advantages?*

Analyzing Primary Sources

The Regiment Revolts

Louis Barthas (1879–1952), a French peasant, served in the French army for the entire war. His journal recorded the lives of the "poilus" (literally, "hairy ones"), the French combat soldiers along the Western Front. This entry, from late May 1917, notes the effects of the Russian Revolution on morale at a particularly difficult moment. In a near mutiny, soldiers in his regiment sang the "Internationale," the anthem of the international socialist movement, and protested against the offensive strategy of General Robert Nivelle at Chemin des Dames, which had caused more than 100,000 killed or wounded between April 6 and May 9, 1917. The events described below occurred as his regiment marched back to the front lines after a brief rest. Similar mutinies occurred in many places along the front, affecting nearly half of the French divisions in 1917. The mutinies resulted in more than 3,000 courts-martial and 43 executions.

t this time the Russian Revolution broke out. Those Slavic soldiers, only yesterday enslaved and bent double under the iron weight of iron discipline, unknowingly marching off to massacres like resigned slaves, had thrown off their yokes, proclaimed their liberty, and imposed peace on their masters, their hangmen.

The whole world was stupefied, petrified by this revolution, this collapse of the immense empire of the czars.

These events had repercussions on the Western Front and throughout the French ranks. A wind of revolt blew across almost all the regiments.

There were, besides, plenty of reasons for discontent: the painful failure of the Chemin des Dames offensive, which had no result other than a dreadful slaughter; the prospect of more long months of war ahead, with a highly dubious outcome; and finally, the long wait before home leaves—it's that which bothered the soldiers most, I believe.

I cannot pretend to tell the whole story of what happened almost everywhere just then. I will stick to writing what I know, regarding our regiment and the repression which followed.

There was, at the end of the village, a shopkeeper for whom the war brought only profit. He sold beer, and he had a cute little waitress to serve it to customers—powerful attractions which, every evening after supper, brought a whole crowd of poilus, a well-behaved clientele which plunked down in groups in the big courtyard adjacent to his shop. One evening, some of the soldiers singing, others were entertaining their fellows with songs and skits, when a corporal began singing words of revolt against the sad life in the trenches, words of farewell to the dear souls whom we might not see again, of anger against the perpetrators of this infamous war, the rich shirkers who left the fighting to those who had nothing to fight for.

At the refrain, hundreds of voices rose in chorus, and at the end fervent applause broke out, mixed with cries of "Peace or revolution! Down with war!," as well as "Home leave! Home leave!"

On another evening—patriots, cover your ears!—the "Internationale" was heard, bursting like a storm.

[. . .]

As the war progressed, new weapons were added to the frightening dimensions of daily warfare. Besides artillery, machine guns, and barbed wire, the instruments of war now included exploding bullets, liquid fire, and poison gas. Gas, in particular, transformed the battlefront, as the deadly clouds frequently hung over the trenches. First used effectively by the Germans in April 1915 at the second battle of Ypres, poison gas was not only physically devastating—especially in its later forms—but also psychologically disturbing, although the quick appearance of gas masks limited its effectiveness. Like other new weapons, poison gas solidified the lines and took more lives but could not end the stalemate. The war dragged through its second year, bloody and stagnant, as soldiers grew accustomed to the stalemate and their leaders plotted ways to end it.

At noon on May 30, there was an assembly outside the village, to constitute, following the Russian example, a "soviet" composed of three men from each company, which would take control of the regiment.

To my great astonishment, they came to offer me the presidency of this soviet, that's to say, to replace the colonel—nothing less than that!

That would be quite a sight—me, an obscure peasant who put down my pitchfork in August 1914, commanding the 296th Regiment. That went way beyond the bounds of probability.

Of course I refused. I had no desire to shake hands with a firing squad, just for the child's play of pretending we were the Russians.

But I did decide to give an appearance of legality to these revolutionary demonstrations. I wrote up a manifesto to give to our company commanders, protesting against the delay in furloughs. It began like this: "On the eve of the offensive, General Nivelle had read to the troops an order of the day saying that the hour of sacrifice had rung. . . . We offered our lives and made this sacrifice for the father land but, in exchange,

we said that the hour of home leaves had also sounded, a while ago. . . . ," et cetera.

The revolt was therefore placed squarely on the side of right and justice. The manifesto was read out, in a sonorous voice, by a poilu who was perched astride the limb of an oak tree. Fervent applause underscored his last lines.

[. . .]

The next day [May 31], at 7 a.m. they assembled us for departure to the trenches. Noisy demonstrations resulted: cries, songs, shouts, whistling; of course, the "Internationale" was heard. I truly believe that if the officers had made one provocative gesture, said one word against the uproar, they would have been massacred without pity, so great was the agitation.

They chose the wisest path: waiting patiently until calm was restored. You can't cry, shout, and whistle forever, and among the insurgents there was no leader capable of taking decisive direction. We ended up heading for the trenches, not without an undertone of griping and grumbling.

Soon, to our great surprise, a column of mounted cavalry came up and rode alongside us. They accompanied us all the way to the trenches, like convicts being led to forced labor!

Source: [Louis Barthas], *Poilu: The World War I Notebooks of Corporal Louis Barthas, Barrelmaker, 1914–1918*, trans. Edward M. Strauss (New Haven: 2014), pp. 325–28.

Questions for Analysis

1. How does Barthas describe the Russian soldiers, their support for revolution, and the effect of the revolution on people elsewhere in Europe?

2. What were the major issues that contributed to the protests in his regiment?

3. What does the outcome of this protest tell us about the attitudes among front-line soldiers after the failure of the costly offensives in the previous year?

The Eastern Front in 1915

Germany's ally Austria struggled with a two-front war of its own in 1915: Serbia's aggressive defense of its territory to the south and the continued presence of the Russians to the east. Italy's entry into the war on the side of the Entente powers in May 1915 created a new threat to Austria's southern flank. Germany came to its assistance, and

German and Austrian armies succeeded in pushing the Russians out of Galicia and deep into their own lands. The Russians were terribly undersupplied, and stories circulated of unarmed soldiers waiting to pick up the weapons of their fallen comrades before joining the battle. By the time the Eastern Front had stabilized once more, 15 percent of Russia's prewar territory, including much of Poland and Lithuania, had fallen to the German and Austrian

Interpreting Visual Evidence

War Propaganda

oster art was a leading form of propaganda used by all belligerents in the First World War to enlist men, sell war bonds, and sustain morale on the home front. Posters demonized the enemy and glorified the sacrifices of soldiers to better rationalize the unprecedented loss of life and national wealth. The posters shown here are from a wide range of combatant nations during the war, but they all share a desire to link the war effort with a set of assumptions about the different roles of men and women in the national struggle.

A. British Poster: "Women of Britain Say—'Go!'"

B. Russian Poster: "Women Workers! Take Up the Rifle!"

Questions for Analysis

1. Why would nationalists resort to such gendered images in a time of crisis?

2. What do these images tell us about the ways that feelings of national belonging are created and sustained in times of urgency?

3. How might the changes brought about by war, such as an increase in the number of women working in industry or outside the home, and greater autonomy for women in regard to their wages or management of their household affairs, have affected the way individuals responded to such images?

C. German Poster: "Collect women's hair that has been combed out. Our industry needs it for drive belts."

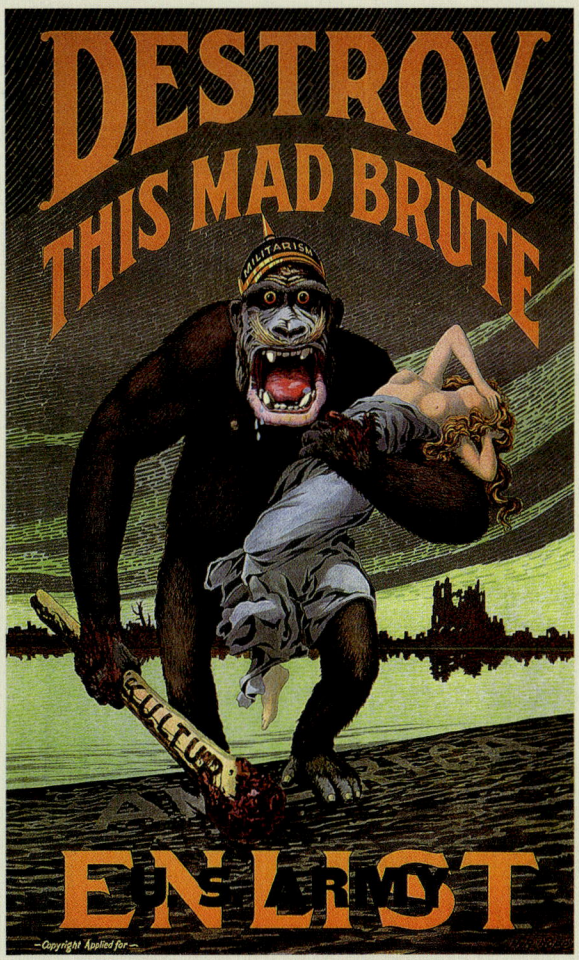

D. American Poster: "Destroy This Mad Brute. Enlist." The mad beast with *MILITARISM* inscribed on his helmet, meant to represent Germany, threatens American civilization with a club of *Kultur* (culture).

POISON GAS. Poison gases (mustard gas, chlorine gas, and phosgene were the most commonly used) caused thousands of casualties in the First World War, and were greatly feared by the troops. Although such weapons led to offensive breakthroughs when first used, gas was difficult to control, and they did not change the balance of forces in the war, especially once both sides developed gas masks to protect their troops. The environmental damage was severe, however, as concentrations of gas residue were intense enough to cause injury to farmers decades after the war ended, and unexploded gas shells are still occasionally found in former battlefields.

advance. Russian casualties during the difficult retreat were a million soldiers killed, wounded, or missing, and 750,000 taken prisoner.

These Austrian and German successes—and the failure of the British at Gallipoli—convinced Bulgaria to enter the war on the side of the Dual Alliance in September 1915. The Bulgarian government was also motivated by the hope of gaining territory from its Serbian neighbors. The arrival of the Bulgarians tipped the balance heavily to the side of the Austrians on the Serbian front. The ensuing struggle brought terrible punishment to the Serbian people for their government's role in the assassination of Franz Ferdinand the previous year. One-sixth of the Serbian population died of hunger and disease; and 200,000 Serbian troops sought to escape through the Albanian mountains to the Adriatic coast, but fewer than 140,000 survived the journey to be picked up by Italian ships in Albanian ports.

THE FAILED OFFENSIVES OF 1916–1917

The bloodiest battles of all occurred in 1916–1917, when first the Germans and later the British and French launched major offensives to end the stalemate. Massive campaigns in the war of attrition, these assaults produced hundreds of thousands of casualties but only minor territorial gains.

These battles encapsulated the military strategy of soldiers in cloth uniforms marching against machine guns, which resulted, of course, in carnage. The common response to these staggering losses was to replace the generals in charge, but though commanders changed, commands did not. Military planners continued to believe in their original strategies and that their plans had simply been frustrated by bad luck and German determination. The "cult of the offensive" insisted that with enough troops and weapons, a breakthrough was possible.

Verdun

The first of these offensives began with a German attack on the French stronghold of **Verdun** in February 1916. Verdun had little strategic importance, but it quickly became a symbol of France's strength and was defended at all costs. Germany's goal was not necessarily to take the city but to break French morale—France's "remarkable devotion"—at a moment of critical weakness. As the German general Erich von Falkenhayn said, the offensive would "compel the French to throw in every man they have. If they do so the forces of France will bleed to death."

One million shells were fired on the first day of battle, inaugurating a ten-month struggle of back-and-forth offensives and counteroffensives of intense ferocity at enormous cost and zero gain. Led by General Philippe Pétain, the French pounded the Germans with artillery and received heavy bombardment in return. The Germans relied on large teams of horses, 7,000 of which were killed in a single day, to drag their guns through the muddy, cratered terrain. The French moved supplies and troops into Verdun continuously: approximately 12,000 delivery trucks and 259 out of the 330 regiments of the French army were employed for service. Neither side could gain a real advantage—one small village on the front changed hands thirteen times in one month alone—even as both sides incurred devastating losses of life. By the end of June, more than 400,000 French and German soldiers were dead. "Verdun," writes one historian, "had become a place of terror and death that could not yield victory." In the end, the advantage fell to the French, who survived and bled the Germans as badly as they themselves had suffered.

The Somme

Meanwhile, farther west, the British opened their own offensive against Germany, beginning the battle of the **Somme** on June 24, 1916. The Allied attack began with a fierce bombardment, blasting the German lines with 1,400 guns; the blasts could be heard all the way across the English Channel. The British assumed that this preliminary attack would break the mesh of German wire, destroy their trenches, and clear the way for Allied troops to advance forward. They were tragically wrong. The wire and trenches withstood the bombardment, and when the British soldiers were ordered over the top toward enemy lines, they found themselves snared in wire and facing fully operational German machine guns. Those who made it to the enemy trenches faced bitter hand-to-hand combat with pistols, grenades, knives, bayonets, and bare hands. On the first day of battle alone, a stunning 21,000 British soldiers died, and another 30,000 were wounded. The carnage continued from July until mid-November, resulting in massive casualties on both sides: 600,000 German, 400,000 British, and 200,000 French. The losses were unimaginable, and the outcome was equally hard to fathom; for all their sacrifices, neither side made any real gains. The first lesson of the Somme was offered later by a war veteran: "Neither side had won, nor could win, the War. The War had won, and would go on winning." The futility of offensive war was not lost on the soldiers, yet morale remained surprisingly strong. Although mutinies and desertions occurred on both sides, they were rare before 1917, and surrenders became an important factor only in the final months of the war.

Again in 1917, with willing armies and fresh recruits, military commanders maintained their strategy and pushed for victories on the Western Front. The French general Robert Nivelle promised to break through the German lines with overwhelming manpower, but the "Nivelle Offensive" (April–May 1917) failed immediately, with first-day casualties matching those at the Somme. The British also reprised the Somme at the third battle of Ypres (July–October 1917), in which a half-million casualties earned Great Britain only insignificant gains, and no breakthrough. The one weapon with the potential to break the stalemate—the tank—was finally introduced into battle in 1916, but with such reluctance by tradition-bound commanders that its halfhearted deployment made almost no difference. Other innovations were equally indecisive: airplanes were used almost exclusively for reconnaissance, though occasional "dogfights" did occur between German and Allied pilots; and though the Germans sent zeppelins to raid London, they did little significant damage.

YPRES. Entrenched in craters, the Sixteenth Canadian Machine Gun Company endures the mud after the third battle of Ypres, usually called the battle of Passchendaele ("Passiondale" in British pronunciation; July–November 1917). Ypres, along the Yperlee River near the Belgian coast, was the object of three major battles during the war. The third, an Allied offensive, aimed to attack German submarine bases and to strengthen the Allied position if Russia withdrew from the war.

NORWAY

SWEDEN

NORTH
SEA

Moscow

Riga

KURLAND

DENMARK
Kiel
Hamburg

GREAT
BRITAIN
(Aug. 4, 1914)

London

British Blockade,
Nov. 1914

Tannenberg
Aug. 27–30, 1914

Masurian Lakes
Sept. 1914

POLAND

Warsaw   Brest-Litovsk

Kiev

GERMANY
(Aug. 1, 1914)

Berlin

RUSSIA
(Aug. 1, 1914)

JAPAN
(Aug. 23, 1914)

ATLANTIC
OCEAN

NETH.
The
Hague

BEL.
(Aug. 4,
1914)

LUX.

Limit of German
Advance, 1915

Invasion, Aug. 1914

GALICIA

Battle of the Marne
Sept. 1914

Paris

Allied Offensive
Sept.–Nov. 1915

Prague

Munich

Vienna

Budapest

AUSTRIA-HUNGARY
(July 28, 1914)

ROMANIA

BLACK SEA

FRANCE
(Aug. 3, 1914)

SWITZER-
LAND

Bordeaux

Milan

Bucharest

Belgrade

BULGARIA
(Oct. 14, 1914)

SAN MARINO
(June 3, 1915)

Sarajevo

SERBIA
(July 28,
1914)

Sofia

Constantinople

Marseilles

ADRIATIC SEA

ITALY
(May 23, 1915)

Rome

MONTE-
NEGRO
(Aug. 5, 1914)

ALBANIA

Gallipoli

Dardanelles

Salonika

OTTOMAN
EMPIRE
(Nov. 2, 1914)

PORTUGAL

SPAIN

GREECE

Allied Offensive
Feb. 1915–
Jan. 1916

0   125   250 Miles
0   125   250 Kilometers

THE FIRST WORLD WAR

■ Allied Powers   ■ Central Powers

Neutral nations

Dates of entry into the war: (Aug. 1, 1914)

NORWAY

SWEDEN

NORTH
SEA

Moscow

Riga

KURLAND

Jutland
May–June 1916

DENMARK

Kiel
Hamburg

RUSSIA

GREAT
BRITAIN

London

The Hague

NETH.

Berlin

POLAND
Independent, Nov. 5, 1916

Warsaw   Brest-
Litovsk

Russian Offensive
June–Dec. 1916

BEL.

GERMANY

ATLANTIC
OCEAN

Somme, June–Nov. 1916

Paris

LUX.

Verdun,
July–Dec.
1916

Prague

Munich

Vienna

GALICIA

CARPATHIAN MTS.

Budapest

FRANCE

SWITZER-
LAND

AUSTRIA-HUNGARY

ROMANIA
(Aug. 27, 1916)

BLACK SEA

Milan

Belgrade

Bucharest

Marseilles

ADRIATIC SEA

ITALY

Rome

MONTENEGRO
Surrender, Jan. 1916

SERBIA

BULGARIA

Sofia

Constantinople

PORTUGAL
(Mar. 9, 1916)

SPAIN

ALBANIA

Salonika

OTTOMAN
EMPIRE

GREECE
(Oct. 18, 1916)

MEDITERRANEAN   SEA

0   125   250 Miles
0   125   250 Kilometers

EUROPE

AFRICA

Area of
detail

THE GREAT WAR, 1914–1916. ■ *What were the farthest points of German expansion on both fronts?* ■ *Why did the British blockade have such a large impact on the war?* ■ *Why did the war become stalemated?*

THE GREAT WAR, 1917–1918. ▪ *What were the key events of 1917?* ▪ *How did they change the course of the war?*
▪ *Considering the map of 1918, why might German people have believed that they nearly won the war?* ▪ *Why were
developments in the Middle East significant in the aftermath of the war?*

The Failure of Offensive War in the East

On the Eastern Front, equally indecisive offensives marked the year 1916. In May, the Austrians launched a *Strafexpedition* ("punitive expedition") against the Italians at Trentino, northwest of Venice. The outnumbered Italians lost 147,000 soldiers, but their line did not break. The main outcome of the Austrian decision to concentrate its forces on the Italian front was to encourage Russia to counterattack farther to the east, where the Russians hoped to counter General Erich von Ludendorff's plans to annex Poland as a German province. Russia continued to call up its massive reserves and, for the first time, they held an advantage in stocks of shells. A Russian offensive in March 1916 against the Germans cost them 100,000 men and no territory gain. But in June, with the Austrian lines thinned by the need to reinforce the Italian campaign, the Russians had more success, taking 400,000 prisoners and inflicting losses of 600,000 on the Austrian armies. The cost, however, was high, with 1 million Russian casualties. Perhaps the most significant consequence of this Russian "victory" was that it convinced Romania to join the war on the side of the Entente in August 1916; France and Russia agreed to reward Romania with significant territories in Transylvania in the event of a victory. This proved a disastrous miscalculation for Romania, which lost 310,000 men by the end of 1916, and the country's war effort collapsed under the combined weight of Austrian and Bulgarian attacks.

The war at sea was also indecisive in 1915, with neither side willing to risk the loss of enormously expensive battleships. The British and German navies fought only one major naval battle early in 1916, which ended in a stalemate. Afterward, they used their fleets primarily in the economic war of blockades.

Year 1916, a year of great bloodshed and growing disillusionment, showed that not even the superbly organized Germans had the mobility or fast-paced communications to win the western ground war. Moreover, increasingly, warfare would be turned against entire nations, including civilian populations on the home front and in the far reaches of the European empires.

WAR OF EMPIRES

Coming as it did at the height of European imperialism, the Great War quickly became a war of empires, with far-reaching repercussions. As the demands of warfare rose, Europe's colonies provided soldiers and material support.

A GLOBAL WAR. The effects of the First World War were immediately felt in other parts of the world. Japan entered the war in August 1914 on the side of France, Russia, and Britain to secure German territory in the Pacific and extend its influence over China. (The image on the right shows Japanese troops landing in China at Tsingtao in 1915.) The same month, Turkey joined Germany and Austria-Hungary's alliance. (The top left image shows an Islamic cleric reading the proclamation of war before a mosque in the Turkish capital of Constantinople in 1914.) Meanwhile, all the European colonial powers recruited laborers and soldiers from their imperial territories. (The top right image shows colonial troops marching in German East Africa during the war.)

Britain, in particular, benefited from its vast network of colonial dominions and dependencies, bringing in soldiers from Canada, Australia, New Zealand, India, and South Africa. Nearly 1.5 million Indian troops served in the British forces, some on the Western Front but many more in the Middle East, fighting in Mesopotamia and Persia against the Turks. And France sent 607,000 soldiers, especially from North and West Africa, to fight with the Allies, 31,000 of whom died in Europe. Colonial recruits were also employed in industry. In France, for instance, where even some French conscripts were put to work in factories, the international labor force numbered over 250,000, including workers from China, Vietnam, Egypt, India, the West Indies, and South Africa.

As the war stalled in Europe, colonial areas became strategically important theaters for armed engagement. Although the campaign against Turkey began poorly for Britain with the debacle at Gallipoli, beginning in 1916, Allied forces won a series of battles, pushing the Turks out of Egypt and eventually capturing Baghdad, Jerusalem, Beirut, and other cities throughout the Middle East. The British commander in Egypt and Palestine was Edmund Allenby, who led a multinational army against the Turks. The support of different Arab peoples seeking independence from the Turks proved crucial, and Allenby allied himself with the successful Bedouin (nomadic peoples speaking Arabic) revolts that split the Ottoman Empire. Meanwhile, British officer T. E. Lawrence (1888–1935) popularized the Arabs' guerrilla actions, and when one of the senior Bedouin aristocrats, the emir Abdullah, captured the strategic port of Aqaba in July 1917, Lawrence took credit and entered popular mythology as "Lawrence of Arabia."

Britain encouraged Arab nationalism for its own strategic purposes, offering a qualified acknowledgment of Arab political aspirations. At the same time, for similar but conflicting strategic reasons, the British declared their support of "the establishment in Palestine of a national home for the Jewish people," a pledge made by Arthur Balfour, Britain's foreign secretary. European Zionists, who were seeking a Jewish homeland, took the Balfour Declaration very seriously. These conflicting pledges to Bedouin leaders and Zionists sowed the seeds of the future Arab-Israeli conflict. First the war and then the promise of oil drew Europe more deeply into the Middle East, where conflicting dependencies and commitments created numerous postwar problems.

Irish Revolt

The Ottoman Empire was vulnerable, as was the British Empire. The demands of war strained precarious bonds to the breaking point. Before the war, long-standing tensions between Irish Catholics and the Protestant British government had reached fever pitch, and some feared civil war. The Sinn Féin (We Ourselves) party had formed in 1900 to fight for Irish independence, and a home rule bill had passed Parliament in 1912. But with the outbreak of war in 1914, national interests took precedence over domestic politics and the "Irish question" was tabled, with 200,000 Irishmen volunteering for the British army. The problem festered, however, and on Easter Sunday 1916, a group of nationalists revolted in Dublin. The insurgents' plan to smuggle in arms from Germany failed, and they had few illusions of achieving victory, as the British army arrived with artillery and machine guns; the army shelled parts of Dublin and crushed the uprising within a week.

The revolt was a military disaster but a striking political success. Britain shocked the Irish public by executing the rebel leaders; even the British prime minister David Lloyd George (1916–1922) thought the military governor in Dublin exceeded his authority with the executions. The martyrdom of the "Easter Rebels" seriously damaged Britain's relationship with its Irish Catholic subjects. The deaths galvanized the cause of Irish nationalism and touched off guerrilla violence that kept Ireland in turmoil for years. Finally, in 1920, a new home rule bill was

BRITISH REPRESSION OF EASTER REBELLION, DUBLIN, 1916. British troops line up behind a moveable barricade made up of household furniture during their repression of the Irish revolt. This military action crushed the uprising but failed to prevent further conflict.

enacted, establishing separate parliaments for the Catholic south of Ireland and for Ulster, the northeastern counties where the majority population was Protestant. The leaders of the so-called Dáil Éireann (Irish Assembly), which had proclaimed an Irish Republic in 1918 and therefore been outlawed by Britain, rejected the bill but accepted a treaty that granted dominion status to Catholic Ireland in 1921. Dominion was almost immediately followed by civil war between those who abided by the treaty and those who wanted to absorb Ulster. The conflict eventually ended in an uneasy compromise. The Irish Free State was established in 1922, and British sovereignty was partially abolished in 1937. Full status as a republic came in 1945, after some American pressure and Britain's exhausted indifference.

THE HOME FRONT

When the war of attrition began in 1915, the belligerent governments were unprepared for the burdens of sustained warfare. The costs of war—in both money and manpower—were staggering. In 1914, the war cost Germany 36 million marks per day (five times the cost of the war of 1870), and by 1918, the cost had skyrocketed to 146 million marks per day. Great Britain had estimated it would need 100,000 soldiers but ended up mobilizing 3 million. The enormous task of feeding, clothing, and equipping the armies became as much of a challenge as breaking through enemy lines, and civilian populations were increasingly asked—or forced—to support these efforts. Bureaucrats and industrialists led the effort to mobilize the home front, focusing all parts of society on the single goal of military victory. The term *total war* was introduced to describe this intense mobilization of society, and government propagandists insisted that civilians were as important to the war effort as soldiers. Civilians—as workers, taxpayers, and consumers—were vital parts of the war economy, and they produced munitions, purchased war bonds, and shouldered the burden of tax hikes, inflation, and material privations.

The demands of industrial warfare led first to a transition from general industrial manufacturing to munitions production, and then to increased state control of all aspects of production and distribution. The governments of Britain and France managed to direct the economy without serious detriment to their standard of living. Germany, meanwhile, put its economy in the hands of the army and industry; under the Hindenburg Plan, named for Paul von Hindenburg, the chief of the imperial staff of the German army, pricing and profit margins were set by individual industrialists.

Largely because of the immediate postwar collapse of the German economy, historians have characterized Germany's wartime economy as a chaotic, ultimately disastrous system governed by personal interests. New research suggests, however, that this was not the case. Germany's systems of war finance and commodity distribution, though flawed, were not decisively worse than those of Britain or France.

Women in the War

As Europe's adult men left farms and factories to become soldiers, the composition of the workforce changed. Thousands of women were recruited into fields from which they had previously been excluded; young people, foreigners, and unskilled workers were also pressed into newly important tasks; and experiences of colonial workers had equally critical repercussions. But women, because they were the most visible, became symbolic of many of the changes brought by the Great War. In Germany, by the end of the war, one-third of the labor force in heavy industry was female. In France, 684,000 women worked in the munitions industry alone. In England, the "munitionettes," as they were dubbed, numbered nearly a million. Women also entered the clerical and service sectors. In the villages of France, England, and Germany, women became mayors, school principals, and mail carriers. Moreover, hundreds of thousands of women worked with the army as nurses and ambulance drivers, jobs that brought them very close to the front lines; with minimal supplies and under squalid conditions, they worked to save lives and patch bodies back together.

In some cases, the war offered new opportunities; those in nursing, for instance, learned to drive and acquired rudimentary medical knowledge. Middle-class women often said that the war broke down the restrictions on their lives, because at home, they could now ride the train, walk the street, or go out to dinner without an older woman present to chaperone them. In terms of gender roles, an enormous gulf sometimes seemed to separate the wartime world from the nineteenth-century Victorian society. In one of the most famous autobiographies of the war, *Testament of Youth,* Vera Brittain (1896–1970) recalls the dramatic new social norms that she and others forged during the rapid changes of wartime. "As a generation of women we were now sophisticated to an extent which was revolutionary when compared with the romantic ignorance of 1914. Where we had once spoken with polite evasion of 'a certain condition,' or 'a certain profession,' we now unblushingly used the words 'pregnancy' and 'prostitution.'" For

WOMEN AT WORK. The total war effort combined with a manpower shortage at home brought women into factories across Europe in unparalleled numbers. The image on the left shows men and women working side by side in a British shell factory. The image on the right shows German women assembling military equipment. ▪ *How might the participation of women in the industrial workforce have changed attitudes toward women's labor?* ▪ *What tensions might this have created within families or between male and female workers?*

every Vera Brittain who celebrated the changes, however, journalists, novelists, and other observers grumbled that women were now smoking, refusing to wear the corsets that gave Victorian dresses their hourglass shape, and cutting their hair into the newly fashionable bobs. The "new woman" became a symbol of profound and disconcerting cultural transformation.

How long lasting were these changes? In the aftermath of the war, governments and employers scurried to send women workers home, in part to give jobs to veterans, but also to deal with male workers' complaints that women were undercutting their wages. But such efforts to demobilize women faced real barriers. Many women wage earners—widowed, charged with caring for relatives, or faced with inflation and soaring costs—needed their earnings more than ever. It was also difficult to persuade women workers who had grown accustomed to the relatively higher wages in heavy industry to return to their poorly paid traditional sectors of employment: textile and garment industries and domestic service. The demobilization of women after the war created as many dilemmas as had their mobilization during the war. Governments passed "natalist" policies to encourage women to go home, marry, and—most important—have children. These policies made maternity benefits available to women for the first time, such as time off, medical care, and some allowances for the poor. Nonetheless, birth rates had been falling across Europe by

the early twentieth century, and they continued to do so after the war. One upshot of the war was the increased availability of birth control—Marie Stopes (1880–1958) opened a birth-control clinic in London in 1921—and a combination of economic hardship, increased knowledge, and the demand for freedom made both men and women more likely to use it. Before the war, universal suffrage and the vote for all adult men and women, and for women in particular, had been one of the most controversial issues in European politics. At the end of the fighting, they came in a legislative rush. Britain was first off the mark, granting the vote to all men and women over thirty with the Representation of the People Act in 1918. The United States gave women the vote with the Nineteenth Amendment the following year. And Germany's new republic and the Soviet Union did likewise. France, however, was much slower to offer woman suffrage (1945), although it did provide rewards and incentives for the national effort.

Mobilizing Resources

In addition to mobilizing the labor front, the wartime governments had to mobilize men and money. All the belligerent countries had conscription laws before the war, except Great Britain. And millions of young Europeans went to recruitment offices in 1914, bolstered by a widespread

Analyzing Primary Sources

Women's Work in Wartime

Although women in Europe had worked in some industries, such as textiles, long before the First World War, the mobilization of women during the war years brought an unprecedented number of them into the industrial workforce. Inevitably, such profound changes in conceptions of gender and work generated controversy. These two documents provide a window into this debate, one from the point of view of the highest government authorities, and another from the women who took advantage of the new opportunities available to them. The first document is a letter written in October 1916 from the German chief of the general staff, General Paul von Hindenburg, to Chancellor Bethmann Hollweg. The second is the testimony taken in 1918 from Helen Ross, an African American woman who had worked in domestic service before taking a wartime job in Topeka, Kansas.

General Paul von Hindenburg to Chancellor Bethmann Hollweg, October 1916

 t is also my opinion that women's work should not be overestimated. Almost all intellectual work, heavy physical labour, as well as all real manufacturing work will still fall on men—in addition to the entire waging of the war. It would be good if clear, official expression were given to these facts and if a stop were put to women's agitation for parity in all professions, and thereby, of course, for political emancipation. I completely agree with your Excellency that compulsory labour for women would be an inappropriate measure. After the war, we will need the woman as spouse and mother. . . .

If I *nevertheless* urge that the requirement to work be extended to all women who are either unemployed or working in trivial positions, now and for the duration of the war, I do so because, in my opinion, women can be employed in many areas to a still greater degree than previously and men can thereby be freed for other *work*. But first industry and agriculture must be urged even more to employ women. Further, the choice of occupation must not be left up to the women alone, but rather, it must [be] regulated according to ability, previous experience and social status. In particular, I want to stress again that I consider it especially wrong to keep secondary schools and universities, which have been almost completely emptied of men by conscription, open only for women. It is valueless, because the scholarly gain is minimal; furthermore, because precisely that rivalry with the family that needs to be combated would be promoted; and *finally*, because it would represent the coarsest injustice if the young man, who is giving everything for his Fatherland, is forced behind the woman.

Source: Letter of Chief of the General Staff General Paul von Hindenburg to Chancellor Bethmann Hollweg, October 1916. Quoted in Ute Daniel, *The War from Within: German Working-Class Women in the First World War*, trans. Margaret Ries (Oxford: 1997), pp. 68–69 (emphases in the original).

public support for the war, and a belief that military service was a duty, not an option. The French began the war with about 4.5 million trained soldiers, but by the end of 1914—just four months into the war—300,000 were dead and 600,000 injured. Conscripting citizens and mustering colonial troops became increasingly important, and eventually, France called up 8 million citizens, almost two-thirds of Frenchmen aged eighteen to forty. In 1916, the British finally introduced conscription, dealing a serious blow to civilian morale; and by the summer of 1918, half the army was under the age of nineteen.

Government propaganda, while part of a larger effort to sustain both soldier and civilian morale, was important to the recruitment effort. From the outset, the war had been sold to the people on both sides of the conflict as a moral and righteous crusade. In 1914, the French president Raymond Poincaré (1913–1920) assured his fellow citizens that France had no other purpose than to stand "before the universe for Liberty, Justice and Reason." Germans were presented with the task of defending their superior *Kultur* (culture) against the wicked encirclement policy of the Allied nations. "May God punish England!" was practically

Helen Ross, Employee of the Santa Fe Railroad, Topeka, Kansas, October 1918

ll the colored women like this work and want to keep it. We are making more money at this than any work we can get, and we do not have to work as hard as at housework which requires us to be on duty from six o'clock in the morning until nine or ten at night, with mighty little time off and at very poor wages.... What the colored women need is an opportunity to make money. As it is, they have to take what employment they can get, live in old tumbled down houses or resort to street walking, and I think a woman ought to think more of her blood than to do that. What occupation is open to us where we can make really good wages? We are not employed as clerks, we cannot all be school teachers, and so we cannot see any use in working our parents to death to get educated. Of course we should like easier work than this if it were opened to us. With three dollars a day, we can buy bonds . . . , we can dress decently, and not be tempted to find our living on the streets.

Source: Helen Ross, Freight House, Santa Fe RR, Topeka, Kansas, October 28, 1918, File 55, Women's Service Section, Record Group 14 [Records of the United States Railroad Administration], National Archives, Washington, DC. Also quoted in M. W. Greenwald, *Women, War and Work: The Impact of World War I on Women Workers in the United States* (Ithaca, NY: 1980, reprinted 1990), p. 27.

Questions for Analysis

1. What reservations does Hindenburg express about the demands made by women for political emancipation? How does he connect these demands to the question of women's wartime employment? Why does he nevertheless support women's wartime labor in Germany?

2. How does Helen Ross compare the opportunity to earn wages in her railroad job with her previous work as a domestic servant? How has her life changed?

3. What long-lasting effects might the experience of wartime labor have had on women who worked in such jobs?

---

a greeting in 1914. By the middle of the war, massive propaganda campaigns were under way. All forms of media—films, posters, postcards, newspapers—proclaimed the strength of the cause, the evil of the enemy, and the absolute necessity of total victory. The success of these campaigns is difficult to determine, but it is clear that they had at least one painful effect: they made it more difficult for any country to accept a fair, nonpunitive peace settlement.

Financing the war was another heavy obstacle. Before 1914, military spending accounted for 3 to 5 percent of government expenditure in the combatant countries, but it soared to perhaps half of each nation's budget during the war. Governments had to borrow money or print more money. The Allied nations borrowed heavily from the British, who borrowed even more from the United States; capital of the United States flowed across the Atlantic long before the country entered the war. Although economic aid from the United States was a decisive factor in the Allies' victory, it left Britain with a $4.2 billion debt that hobbled the country as a financial power after the war. The situation was far worse for Germany, which faced a total blockade of money and goods. In an effort to get around this predicament, and lacking an outside source of cash, the German government funded its war effort largely by increasing the money supply. The amount of paper money in circulation increased by over 1,000 percent during the war, triggering a dramatic rise in inflation; prices in Germany rose about 400 percent, double the inflation in Britain and France. These price hikes pushed middle-class people living on pensions or fixed incomes into poverty.

The Strains of War, 1917

The demands of total war worsened as the conflict dragged into 1917. On the front lines, morale fell as war-weary soldiers began to see the futility of their commanders' strategies. After the debacle of the Nivelle Offensive, the

French army recorded acts of mutiny in two-thirds of its divisions; similar resistance arose in nearly all major armies in 1917. Although military leaders portrayed the mutineers as part of a dangerous pacifist movement, most were nonpolitical. As one soldier put it: "All we wanted was to call the government's attention to us, make it see that we are men, and not beasts for the slaughterhouse." Resistance within the German army was never organized or widespread but existed in subtler forms: self-mutilation rescued some soldiers from the horror of the trenches, and many more were released because of various emotional disorders. More than 6,000 cases of "war neuroses" were reported among German troops—an indication, if not of intentional disobedience, then of the severe physical and psychological trauma that caused the mutinies.

The war's toll also mounted for civilians, who often suffered from the same shortages of basic supplies that afflicted the men on the front. In 1916–1917, the lack of clothing, food, and fuel was aggravated by abnormally cold, wet weather in central Europe. These strains provoked rising discontent on the home front. Governments attempted to solve the problem with tighter controls on the economy, but their policies often provoked further hostilities from civilians. "The population has lost all confidence in promises from the authorities," a German official reported in 1917. "[P]articularly in view of earlier experiences with promises made in the administration of food."

In urban areas, where undernourishment was worst, people stood in lines for hours to get food and fuel rations that scarcely met their most basic needs. The price of bread and potatoes—still the staples of working-class meals—soared; prices were even higher in the thriving black markets that emerged in cities. Consumers worried aloud that speculators were hoarding supplies and creating artificial shortages, selling tainted goods, and profiting from others' misery. They decried the government's "reckless inattention" to families. Governments, however, were concentrated on the war effort and faced difficult decisions about who needed supplies the most: soldiers on the front, workers in the munitions industry, or hungry and cold families.

Like other nations, Germany moved from encouraging citizens to restrain themselves—"those who stuff themselves full, those who push out their paunches in all directions, are traitors to the Fatherland"—to direct control, issuing ration cards in 1915. Britain was the last to institute control, rationing bread only in 1917, when Germany's submarines sank an average of 630,000 tons of merchant shipping per month, bringing British food reserves within two weeks of starvation level. But rations indicated only what was allowed, not what was available; and hunger continued throughout despite mass bureaucratic control.

Governments regulated not only food but also working hours and wages, and unhappy workers directed their anger at the state, adding a political dimension to labor disputes and household needs. The bread lines, filled mainly by women, were flash points of political dissent, petty violence, and even large-scale riots. Likewise, the class conflicts of prewar Europe had been briefly muffled by the outbreak of war and mobilization along patriotic lines, but as the war ground on, political tensions reemerged with new intensity. Thousands of strikes erupted throughout Europe, involving millions of frustrated workers. In April 1917, in Berlin, 300,000 went on strike to protest ration cuts. In May, a strike of Parisian seamstresses touched off a massive work stoppage that included even white-collar employees and munitions workers. Shipbuilders and steelworkers in Glasgow went on strike as well, to which

DESPERATION ON THE GERMAN HOME FRONT, 1918. A photograph of German women digging through garbage in search of food. The last year of the war brought starvation to cities in Germany and Austria-Hungary, sending many people into the countryside to forage for provisions. ▪ *Foraging was often illegal, a violation of rationing rules. How might the need to break the law in this way have affected support for the war effort and the state?*

the British government responded by sending armored cars to "Red Glasgow." Stagnation had given way to crisis on both sides. The strains of total war and the resulting social upheavals threatened political regimes throughout Europe as governments were pushed to their limits. The Russian Revolution, which resulted in the overthrow of the tsar and the rise of Bolshevism, was only the most dramatic response to the widespread social problems.

THE RUSSIAN REVOLUTIONS OF 1917

The first country to break under the strain of total war was tsarist Russia. The outbreak of war temporarily united Russian society against a common enemy, but its military effort quickly turned sour. All levels of Russian society became disillusioned with **Tsar Nicholas II**, who was unable to provide leadership and unwilling to open the government to those who could. The political and social strains of war brought two revolutions in 1917. The first revolution, in February, according to the Julian calendar used in Russia at the time (or March, according the Gregorian calendar used today), overthrew the tsar and established a transitional government. The second revolution, in October (or November), was a communist revolution that marked the emergence of the Soviet Union.

The First World War and Russia's February Revolution

Like the other participants in the First World War, Russia entered the war with the assumption that it would be over quickly. Autocratic Russia, plagued by internal difficulties before 1914 (Chapter 23), could not sustain the political strains of extended warfare. In all the warring countries, success depended on the leaders' ability not only to command but also to maintain social and political cooperation. Nicholas's political authority had been shaky for many years, undermined by his unpopular actions following the October

Revolution of 1905 and his efforts to erode the minimal political power he had grudgingly granted to the Duma (Russia's parliament). And corruption in the royal court further tarnished his image. The best his supporters could say about him was that he was morally upright and devoted to his family. In 1915, Nicholas insisted on personally commanding Russian troops, leaving the government in the hands of his court, especially his wife, Alexandra, and her eccentric spiritual mentor and faith healer, Grigorii Rasputin (1869–1916). Rasputin won Alexandra's sympathy by treating her hemophiliac son, and he used his influence to operate corrupt and self-aggrandizing schemes. His presence only added to the image of the court as mired in decadence, and incompetent to face the modern world.

In 1914 and 1915, Russia suffered terrible defeats. All of Poland and substantial territory in the Baltics fell to the Germans at the cost of a million Russian casualties. Although the Russian army was the largest in Europe, it was poorly trained and, at the beginning of the war, undersupplied and inadequately equipped. In the first battles of 1914, generals sent soldiers to the front without rifles or shoes, instructing them to scavenge supplies from fallen comrades. By 1915, to the surprise of many, Russia was producing enough food, clothing, and ammunition, but political problems blocked the supply effort. The tsarist government distrusted public initiatives and tried to direct all the provisioning itself, with tsarist officials making crucial decisions about the allocation of supplies without any consultation. Another major offensive in the summer of 1916 brought hope of success, but it also turned into a humiliating retreat. When word came that the government

RUSSIAN REVOLUTION. Russian demonstrators scatter as tsarist troops shoot into the crowd during the February revolution in 1917.

was requisitioning grain from the countryside to feed the cities, peasant soldiers began to desert en masse, returning to their farms to guard their families' holdings. By the end of 1916, a combination of political ineptitude and military defeat brought the Russian state to the verge of collapse.

The same problems that hampered the Russian war effort also crippled the tsar's ability to override domestic discontent and resistance. As the war dragged on, the government faced not only liberal opposition in the Duma, soldiers unwilling to fight, and an increasingly militant labor movement but also a rebellious urban population that was becoming impatient with inflation and shortages of food and fuel. In February 1917, these forces came together in Petrograd (now St. Petersburg). The revolt began on International Women's Day, February 23 by the Julian calendar (or March 8), an occasion for a loosely organized march of women; the women—workers, mothers, wives, and consumers—demanded food, fuel, and political reform. The march was the latest in a wave of demonstrations and strikes that had swept through the country during the winter months. But this time, within a few days, the unrest spiraled into a mass strike of 300,000 people. Nicholas sent police and military forces to quell the disorder, but nearly 60,000 troops in Petrograd mutinied and joined the revolt. What was left of the tsar's power evaporated, and Nicholas abdicated the throne on March 15 (or March 2 by the Julian calendar). This abrupt decision brought a century-long struggle over Russian autocracy to a sudden end.

After the collapse of the monarchy, two parallel centers of power emerged, each with its own objectives and policies. The first was the **provisional government**, organized by leaders in the Duma and composed mainly of middle-class liberals. This new government hoped to establish a democratic system under constitutional rule. Its main task was to set up a national election for a constituent assembly, and also acted to grant and secure civil liberties, release political prisoners, and redirect power into the hands of local officials. The second center of power lay with the *soviets*, a Russian term for local councils elected by workers and soldiers. Since 1905, socialists had been active in organizing these councils, which claimed to be the true democratic representatives of the people. A soviet, organized during the 1905 revolution and led by the well-known socialist Leon Trotsky, reemerged after February 1917 and asserted claim to be the legitimate political power in Russia. The increasingly powerful soviets pressed for social reform, redistribution of land, and a negotiated settlement with Germany and Austria. The provisional government, however, refused to concede military defeat. Its decision to continue the war effort made domestic reforms impossible and cost valuable popular support. More fighting during 1917

was just as disastrous as before and, this time, the provisional government paid the price. By autumn, desertion in the army was rampant, making administering the country nearly impossible. Russian politics teetered on the edge of chaos.

The Bolsheviks and the October Revolution

The chain of events leading to the October revolution surprised most contemporary observers. Because peasants constituted 80 to 85 percent of the Russian population, most Russian socialists reasoned that a proletarian revolution was premature and that Russia needed first to complete its capitalist development. But the **Bolsheviks**, under the leadership of Vladimir Ilyich Ulyanov, who took the pseudonym **Lenin**, believed otherwise (Chapter 23). Lenin saw the crisis of 1917 as an opportunity to create a revolution that could achieve socialism even without a large urban working class in Russia.

Lenin believed that the development of Russian capitalism made socialist revolution possible. To bring about revolution, he argued, the Bolsheviks needed to organize on behalf of the new class of industrial workers. Without

VLADIMIR ILYICH LENIN. Lenin speaking in Moscow in 1918, at the first anniversary of the October revolution. A forceful speaker and personality, Lenin was the single most powerful politician in Russia from October 1917 to his death in 1924.

Lenin's View of a Revolutionary Party

At the turn of the century, Russian revolutionaries debated political strategy. How could they defeat Russian autocracy? Should revolutionaries follow the programs of their counterparts in the West? Or did the Russian situation require different tactics? In What Is to Be Done? *(1902), Lenin (Vladimir Ilyich Ulyanov; 1870–1924) argued that Russian socialists must revise the traditional Marxist view, which states that a large and politically conscious working class is needed to make revolution. In Russia, Lenin argued, revolution required only a small but dedicated group of revolutionaries to lead the working class. Lenin's vision is important for shaping the tactics and strategies of the Bolsheviks in 1917 and beyond.*

he national tasks of Russian Social-Democracy are such as have never confronted any other socialist party in the world. We shall have occasion further on to deal with the political and organisational duties which the task of emancipating the whole people from the yoke of autocracy imposes upon us. At this point, we wish to state only that the *role of vanguard fighter can be fulfilled only by a party that is guided by the most advanced theory.* . . .

I assert: (1) that no revolutionary movement can endure without a stable organisation of leaders maintaining continuity; (2) that the broader the popular mass drawn spontaneously into the struggle, which forms the basis of the movement and participates in it, the more urgent the need for such an organisation, and the more solid this organisation must be (for it is much easier for all sorts of demagogues to side-track the more backward sections of the masses); (3) that such an organisation must consist chiefly of people professionally engaged in revolutionary activity; (4) that in an autocratic state, the more we *confine* the membership of such an organisation to people who are professionally engaged in revolutionary activity and who have been professionally trained in the art of combating the political police, the more difficult will it be to unearth the organisation; and (5) the *greater* will be the number of people from the working class and from the other social classes who will be able to join the movement and perform active work in it. . . .

Social-Democracy leads the struggle of the working class, not only for better terms for the sale of labour-power, but for the abolition of the social system that compels the propertyless to sell themselves to the rich. Social-Democracy represents the working class, not in its relation to a given group of employers alone, but in its relation to all classes of modern society and to the state as an organised political force. Hence, it follows that not only must Social-Democrats not confine themselves exclusively to the economic struggle. . . . We must take up actively the political education of the working class and the development of its political consciousness.

Source: Vladimir Lenin, "What Is to Be Done?" in *Collected Works of V. I. Lenin*, vol. 5 (Moscow: 1964), pp. 369–70, 373, 375.

Questions for Analysis

1. What were the key features of Lenin's thought?

2. Lenin more or less sets down the rules for the revolutionary vanguard. What historical experiences and political theories shaped his thinking? In what ways was the Russian experience unique?

the party's disciplined leadership, Russia's factory workers could not accomplish change on a significant scale. Lenin's Bolsheviks remained a minority among Social Democrats well into 1917, and industrial workers remained a small part of the population. But the Bolsheviks' dedication to the singular goal of revolution and their tight, almost conspiratorial organization gave them tactical advantages over the larger and more loosely organized opposition parties. The Bolsheviks merged a uniquely Russian tradition of revolutionary zeal with Western Marxism, and created a party capable of seizing the moment when the tsar left the scene.

Throughout 1917, the Bolsheviks consistently demanded an end to the war, improvement in working and living conditions for workers, and redistribution of aristocratic land to the peasantry. While the provisional government struggled to hold together the Russian war effort, Lenin led the Bolsheviks on a bolder course, shunning any collaboration with the "bourgeois" government and condemning its imperialist war policies. Even most Bolsheviks considered Lenin's approach too radical, but, as conditions in Russia deteriorated, his uncompromising calls for "Peace, Land, and Bread, Now" and "All Power to the Soviets" won the Bolsheviks support from workers, soldiers, and peasants. As many ordinary people saw it, the other parties could not govern, win the war, or achieve an honorable peace. As unemployment continued to climb and starvation and chaos reigned in the cities, the Bolsheviks' power and credibility were rising fast.

In October 1917, Lenin convinced his party to act. He goaded Leon Trotsky, who was better known among the workers, into organizing a Bolshevik attack on the provisional government on October 24–25 (November 6–7), 1917. During the revolt, Lenin appeared from hiding to announce at a meeting of stunned soviet representatives that "all power had passed to the Soviets." The head of the provisional government fled to rally support at the front lines, and the Bolsheviks took over the Winter Palace, the seat of the provisional government. The initial stage of the revolution was quick and relatively bloodless.

The Bolsheviks took the opportunity to consolidate rapidly their position. First, they moved against all political competition, beginning with the soviets. They immediately expelled parties that disagreed with their actions, creating a new government in the soviets that was composed entirely of Bolsheviks. Trotsky scoffed at moderate socialists who walked out to protest what they saw as an illegal seizure of power, "You are a mere handful, miserable, bankrupt; your role is finished, and you may go where you belong—to the garbage heap of history." The Bolsheviks followed through with the provisional government's promise to elect a Constituent Assembly, but when they did not win a majority in the elections, they refused to let the assembly reconvene. From that point on, Lenin's Bolsheviks ruled socialist Russia and, later, the Soviet Union as a one-party dictatorship. As the country fell into civil war, Lenin created a militarized state security service known as the Cheka, a form of political police for suppressing dissent in both rural areas and in the cities, as well as in the army.

In the countryside, the new Bolshevik regime did little more than ratify a revolution that had been going on since the summer of 1917. When peasant soldiers at the front heard that a revolution had occurred, they streamed home to take the land they had worked for generations and believed to be rightfully theirs. The provisional government

had set up commissions to deal methodically with the legal issues surrounding the redistribution of land, a process that threatened to become as complex as the emancipation of the serfs in 1861. But the Bolsheviks simply approved the spontaneous redistribution of the nobles' land to peasants without compensation to the former owners. They also nationalized banks and gave workers control of the factories.

The new government sought to take Russia out of the war, and eventually negotiated a separate treaty with Germany, signed at Brest-Litovsk in March 1918. The Bolsheviks surrendered vast Russian territories, much of which were already in German hands: the rich agricultural region of Ukraine, Georgia, Finland, Russia's Polish territories, the Baltic states, and more. The treaty, though humiliating, ended Russia's role in the fighting and saved the fledgling communist regime from almost certain military defeat at the hands of the Germans. It, however, enraged Lenin's political enemies, both moderates and reactionaries, who were still a force to be reckoned with—and who were prepared to wage a civil war rather than accept the revolution; thus Russia's withdrawal from Europe's war plunged the country into a vicious civil conflict (see Chapter 25). Later, in 1918–1919, when the German army collapsed, the Soviet army pushed westward again. In these conflicts, which occurred after the armistice, Russia retook territories in Latvia, Lithuania, Belarus, and Ukraine but failed to reconquer Estonia and Poland, after meeting resistance from their newly created independent governments.

The Russian autocracy had fended off opposition for the better part of a century, but after a long struggle, the regime, weakened by the war, had collapsed with little resistance. By the middle of 1917, Russia was not suffering a crisis of government but rather an absence of government. In June, at the First All-Russian Congress of Soviets, a prominent Menshevik declared, "At the present moment, there is not a political party in Russia that would say: Hand the power over to us, resign, and we will take your place. Such a party does not exist in Russia." From the audience Lenin shouted back, "It does exist!" Indeed, seizing power had been easy for the Bolsheviks, but building the new state proved vastly more difficult.

John Reed, an American journalist covering the Russian Revolution, called the events of October "ten days that shook the world." What had been shaken? First, the Allies, because the revolution allowed the Germans to win the war on the Eastern Front. Second, the conservative governments, which in the aftermath of the war worried about a wave of revolution sweeping away other regimes. Third, the expectations of many socialists, who were startled to see a socialist regime gain and hold power in what many considered a backward country. Over the long run, 1917 was to the twentieth century what 1789 had been to the nineteenth century. It was a year of political transformation, it set the agenda for future revolutionary struggles, and it created the frames of mind on the right and the left for the century that followed.

THE ROAD TO GERMAN DEFEAT, 1918

Russian withdrawal dealt an immediate strategic and psychological blow to the Allies. Germany could soothe domestic discontent by claiming victory on the Eastern Front, and it could now concentrate its entire army to the west. The Allies feared that Germany might win the war before the United States, which entered the conflict in April 1917, could make a difference—which almost happened. With striking results, Germany shifted its offensive strategy to infiltration by small groups under flexible command. On March 21, Germany initiated a major assault on the west and quickly broke through the Allied lines. The British were hit hardest: some units, surrounded, fought to the death with bayonets and grenades, but most recognized their plight and surrendered, putting tens of thousands of prisoners in German hands. The British were in retreat everywhere, and their commander,

CASUALTY OF WAR. A German soldier killed during the Allies' October 1917 offensive.

Sir Douglas Haig, issued a famous order warning that British troops "now fight with our backs to the wall." The Germans advanced to within fifty miles of Paris by early April, but the British—and especially troops from the overseas empire—did just as they were asked and stemmed the tide. As German forces turned southeast, the French, who had refused to participate in the foolish attacks over the top, showed stubborn courage on the defensive, where they bogged down in heat, mud, and casualties. It had been a last great try by the well-organized German army, which, exhausted, now waited for the Allies to mount their own attack.

The Allied counterattack, which came in July and August, was devastating, and quickly gathered steam as new offensive techniques finally materialized. The Allies improved their use of tanks and the "creeping barrage," in which infantry marched close behind a rolling wall of shells that overwhelmed their targets. In another of the war's ironies, these new tactics were pioneered by the conservative British, who launched their own crushing offensive in July, relying on the survivors of the armies of the Somme and reinforced by troops from Australia, Canada, and India. The French made use of American troops, whose generals attacked the Germans with the same harrowing indifference to casualties shown in 1914. Despite their lack of experience, the American troops were tough and resilient, and combined with the more experienced French and Australian forces, they punched several large holes through German lines, crossing into the "lost provinces" of Alsace and Lorraine by October. At the beginning of November, the sweeping British offensive joined up with the small Belgian army and pressed toward Brussels.

The Allies finally brought their material advantage to bear on the Germans, who were suffering acutely by the spring of 1918, not only because of the continued effectiveness of the Allied blockade but also because of growing domestic conflict over war aims. On the front lines, German soldiers were exhausted, and following the lead of their distraught generals, the troops let their morale sink and many surrendered. Facing one shattering blow after another, the German army was pushed deep into Belgium. Moreover, popular discontent mounted, and the government, which was now largely in the hands of the military, seemed unable either to win the war or to meet the basic needs of the home front.

Germany's network of allies was also coming undone, and by the end of September, the Central Powers were headed for defeat. In the Middle East, Allenby's army, which combined Bedouin guerrillas, Indian sepoys, Scottish highlanders, and Australian light cavalry, decisively defeated Ottoman forces in Syria and Iraq. In the Balkans,

France's capable battlefield commander, Louis Franchet d'Espèrey, transformed the Allied expedition in Greece and drew that country into war. The results were remarkable: in September, a three-week offensive by the Greek and Allied forces knocked Bulgaria out of the war. Meanwhile, Austria-Hungary faced disaster on all sides, collapsing in Italy as well as in the Balkans. Czech and Polish representatives in the Austrian government began pressing for self-government, and Croat and Serb politicians proposed a "kingdom of Southern Slavs" (soon known as Yugoslavia). When Hungary joined the chorus for independence, Emperor Karl I accepted reality and sued for peace; the Habsburg Empire surrendered on November 3, 1918, and disintegrated soon after.

Germany was now left with the impossible task of carrying on the struggle alone. By the fall of 1918, the country was starving and on the verge of civil war. At the start of November, a plan to use the German surface fleet to attack the combined British and American navies only produced a mutiny among German sailors, and revolutionary tremors swelled into an earthquake. On November 8, a republic was proclaimed in Bavaria, and the next day, nearly all of Germany was in the throes of revolution. On November 9, the kaiser's abdication was announced in Berlin, and he fled to Holland early the next morning. Control of the German government fell to a provisional council headed by Friedrich Ebert (1912–1923), the socialist leader in the Reichstag. Ebert and his colleagues immediately took steps to negotiate an armistice. The Germans could do nothing but accept the Allies' terms, so at five o'clock in the morning of November 11, 1918, two German delegates met with the Allied army commander in the Compiègne Forest and signed papers officially ending the war. Six hours later, the order to cease fire was given across the Western Front, and that night, thousands of people danced through the streets of London, Paris, and Rome, engulfed in a different delirium from that of four years before, a joyous burst of exhausted relief.

The United States as a World Power

A turning point of the war had been the entry of the United States in April 1917. Although the United States had supported the Allies financially throughout the war, President **Woodrow Wilson** (1913–1921) initially had been reluctant to send troops but changed his mind after the Russian Revolution began. Wilson's decision to join the Entente powers undeniably tipped the scales. The United States created a fast and efficient wartime bureaucracy, instituting conscription in May 1917: about 10 million men were registered and, by the following year, 300,000 soldiers a month were being shipped "over there." Large amounts of food and supplies also crossed the Atlantic, under the protection of the U.S. Navy. This system of convoys effectively neutralized the threat of German submarines to Allied merchant ships: the number of ships sunk fell from 25 percent to 4 percent. The United States' entry—though not immediately decisive—gave a quick, colossal boost to British and French morale, while severely undermining Germany's.

An important cause of the United States' entry into the war was the German U-boat. Germany had gambled that unrestricted submarine warfare would cripple Britain's supply lines and win the war. But by attacking neutral and unarmed American ships, Germany only provoked an opponent it could not afford to fight. Germany correctly suspected that the British were clandestinely receiving war supplies via U.S. passenger ships; and on February 1, 1917, the kaiser's ministers announced that they would sink all ships on sight, without warning. The American public was further outraged by an intercepted telegram from German foreign minister Arthur Zimmerman (1916–1917), stating that Germany would support a Mexican attempt to capture

U.S. TROOPS AT THE FRONT. Soldiers in the American Expedition Forces wearing gas masks.

American territory if the United States entered the war. The United States cut off diplomatic relations with Berlin, and on April 6, President Wilson requested and received a declaration of war from Congress.

Wilson vowed that the United States would fight to "make the world safe for democracy," to banish autocracy and militarism, and to establish a league or society of nations in place of the old diplomatic maneuvering. The United States' primary interest was maintaining the international balance of power. For years, U.S. diplomats and military leaders believed that American security depended on the equilibrium of strength in Europe, that as long as Britain could prevent any one nation from achieving supremacy on the Continent, the United States was safe. But now Germany threatened not only the British Navy—which had come to be seen as the shield of American security—but also the international balance of power. In 1918, American involvement stemmed those threats, but the monumental task of establishing peace still lay ahead.

The Peace Settlement

The Paris Peace Conference, which opened in January 1919, was an extraordinary moment, one that dramatized just how much the world had been transformed by the war and the decades that preceded it. Gone were the Russian, Austro-Hungarian, and German Empires, and the prominent role of the American president Woodrow Wilson marked the rise of the United States as a world power. The United States' new status was rooted in the economic development of the second industrial revolution during the nineteenth century. Before the war, the United States had rivaled the largest European powers (Britain and Germany) in mass production and technological innovation. During the war, its intervention (although it came late) had decisively broken the military-economic deadlock. And in the war's aftermath, its industrial culture, engineering, and financial networks loomed very large on the European continent. Wilson and his entourage spent several months in Paris at the conference—a first for an American president while in office and European leaders' first extended encounter with an American head of state.

American prominence was far from the only sign of global change. Some thirty nations sent delegates to the peace conference, a reflection of three factors: the scope of the war, heightened national sentiment and aspirations, and the tightening of international communication and economic ties in the latter part of the nineteenth century. The world in 1900 was vastly more globalized than it had been fifty years earlier. Many more countries had political, economic, and human investments in the war and its settlement. A belief that peace would secure and be secured by free peoples in sovereign nations represented the full flowering of nineteenth-century liberal nationalism. Delegates came to work for Irish home rule; for a Jewish state in Palestine; and for the recognition of independent nations in Poland, Ukraine, and Yugoslavia. Europe's colonies, which had been vital to the war effort and increasingly impatient with their status, sent delegates to negotiate for self-determination; they discovered, however, that the western European leaders' commitment to the principle of national self-determination was hedged by their imperial assumptions. Nongovernment organizations—in other words, international groups asking for woman suffrage, civil rights, minimum wages, or maximum hours—came as well, for these were now seen as international issues. Last, correspondents from all over the world wired news home from Paris, a sign of vastly improved communications, transatlantic cables, and the mushrooming of the mass press.

Although many attended, the conference was largely controlled by the so-called Big Four: the U.S. president

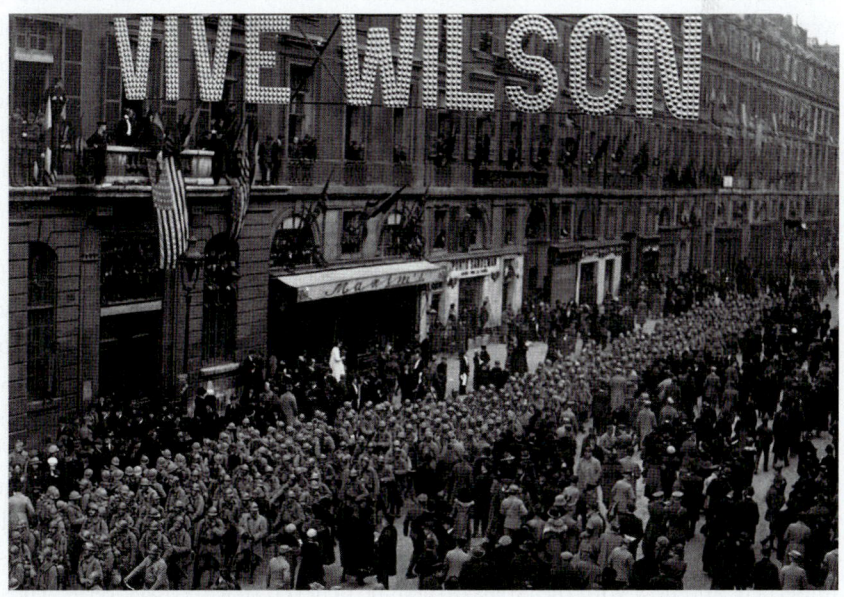

"LONG LIVE WILSON!" Paris crowds greet President Wilson after the war. But despite public support of this sort, Wilson's attempt to shape the peace was a failure.

Woodrow Wilson, the British prime minister David Lloyd George (1916–1922), the French premier Georges Clemenceau (1917–1920), and the Italian premier Vittorio Orlando (1917–1919). The debates among these four personalities were fierce, as they all had conflicting ambitions and interests. In total, five separate treaties were signed, one with each of the defeated nations: Germany, Austria, Hungary, Turkey, and Bulgaria. The settlement with Germany was called the **Treaty of Versailles**, after the town in which it was signed.

Wilson had proposed his widely publicized program known as the "**Fourteen Points**" before the war ended, intending it to be the foundation for a permanent peace and the basis for a new international order. Based on the principle of "open covenants of peace, openly arrived at," the Fourteen Points called for an end to secret diplomacy, freedom of the seas, removal of international tariffs, and reduction of national armaments "to the lowest point consistent with safety." But troubling for Britain and France, Wilson's program also called for a system of adjusting colonial claims that gave equal weight to the interests of the colonized populations alongside the interests of European colonial powers. Regarding Eastern Europe, Wilson went much further, calling for the "self-determination of peoples" in the diverse territories that were now claiming national independence after the collapse of the German, Austrian, and Russian Empires. Finally, Wilson called for the establishment of a League of Nations to settle international conflicts. Thousands of copies of the Fourteen Points were scattered by Allied planes over the German trenches and behind the lines in an attempt to convince both soldiers and civilians that the Allied nations were striving for a just and durable peace, and they shaped the expectations that Germans brought to the peace talks. "The day of conquest and aggrandizement is gone by; so is also the day of secret covenants entered into in the interest of particular governments," Wilson had said. "It is this happy fact . . . which makes it possible for every nation whose purposes are consistent with justice and the peace of the world to avow now or at any other time the objects it has in view."

Throughout the war, however, Allied propaganda led soldiers and civilians to believe that their sacrifices to the war effort would be compensated by payments extracted from the enemy—total war demanded total victory. Lloyd George had campaigned during the British election of 1918 on the slogan "Hang the Kaiser!" Clemenceau had twice in his long lifetime seen France invaded and its existence imperiled, and now with the tables turned, he believed that the French should take full advantage of their opportunity to place Germany under strict control. The devastation of the war and the fiction that Germany could be made to pay for it made compromise impossible. The settlement with Germany was shaped more by the desire for punishment than by Wilson's hopes for a new international order under the League of Nations.

The Treaty of Versailles required Germany to surrender the "lost provinces" of Alsace and Lorraine to France and other territories to Denmark and the new state of Poland. The treaty gave Germany's coal mines in the Saar Basin to France for fifteen years, at which point the German government could buy them back. Germany's province of East Prussia was cut off from the rest of its territory. The Polish port of Gdansk (German: Danzig), where the majority of the population was German, was put under the administrative control of the League of Nations and the economic domination of Poland. The treaty also disarmed Germany, forbade a German air force, and reduced its navy to a token force to match an army capped at 100,000 volunteers. To protect France and Belgium, all German soldiers and fortifications were to be removed from the Rhine Valley.

The most important part of the Versailles treaty, and one of the parts at odds with Wilson's original plan, was the "war-guilt" provision in Article 231. The provision held Germany and its allies responsible for the loss and damage suffered by the Allied governments and their citizens "as a consequence of the war imposed upon them by the aggression of Germany and her allies." Thus, Germany was forced to pay massive reparations; the exact amount was left to a Reparations Commission, which set the total at $33 billion in 1921. The Germans deeply resented these harsh demands, and others outside Germany also warned of the dangers of such punitive reparations. In *The Economic Consequences of the Peace,* the noted British economist John Maynard Keynes (1883–1946) argued that reparations would undermine Europe's most important task: repairing the world economy.

The other treaties at the Paris Peace Conference were based partly on the Allies' strategic interests and partly on the principle of national self-determination. The experience of the prewar years convinced leaders that they should draw nations' boundaries to conform to the ethnic, linguistic, and historical traditions of the people they were to contain. Wilson's support for national self-determination confirmed these aims. Thus, representatives of Yugoslavia were granted a state, Czechoslovakia was created, Poland reestablished, Hungary separated from Austria, and the Baltic states made independent (see the map on page 849). These national boundaries did not, and indeed in most cases could not, follow ethnic divisions. They were instead created according to the facts on the ground, the

Legend:

- —— 1914 boundaries
- —— New boundaries as a result of postwar treaties
- To United Kingdom
- To France
- To Italy
- To Romania
- To Denmark
- To Yugoslavia (Serbia and Montenegro)
- To Belgium
- To Greece
- Became independent

TERRITORIAL CHANGES IN EUROPE AND THE NEAR EAST AFTER THE FIRST WORLD WAR. Note the changes in geography as a result of the First World War.

- Which areas were most affected by the changes within Europe, and why?
- Can you see any obvious difficulties created by the redrawing of the map of Europe?
- What historical circumstances and/or new threats guided the victors to create such geopolitical anomalies?

Past and Present

The Legacy of the First World War in the Middle East

The First World War had significant consequences for the Middle East. The Ottoman Empire allied with Germany during the war, and their defeat resulted in an international effort to redraw the boundaries of the Middle East. Turkey emerged as a much smaller nation in 1923 with its capital in Istanbul, the Ottoman capital. Meanwhile, the League of Nations' mandate system established new borders for former Ottoman territories in Syria, Lebanon, Palestine, and Iraq: Syria and Lebanon became French mandates, and Iraq and Palestine became British mandates. Residents of the region perceived this arrangement as a form of colonialism and protested that it ran counter to the principle of national self-determination. Many of the conflicts in the region today are due to the difficulty of establishing a unified nation-states within the borders imposed on the region at the end of the First World War. The photo on the left shows British troops marching into Bagdad in March 1917. The photo on the right shows Kurdish militia members being trained in northern Iraq in August 2015.

 Watch related author interview on the Student Site

result of armed confrontation, hasty compromises, and political dictates—such as insulating western Europe from the communist threat of the Soviet Union. The peacemakers carved **new nation-states** from older, multi-ethnic empires, especially the Austro-Hungarian Empire, whose fragility had helped spark the war and whose structure had collapsed with the conflict. Creating nation-states, however, almost invariably created new minorities, posing enormous challenges for the newly created democratic institutions and complicating the task of establishing more representative forms of government. The architects of the new Europe briefly wrestled with the problem of minorities but did not resolve it; this issue would return and undermine European stability in the 1930s.

The Ottoman Empire, which allied with Germany, was initially partitioned by the postwar Treaty of Sèvres (1920). Before the treaty could be ratified by a new Turkish government, however, a war broke out between Turkish nationalists led by General Mustafa Kamal Attaturk against Greece, Armenia, and the Allied Powers. The war of Turkish Independence ended in 1923 with the Treaty of Lausanne, which set the boundaries of the new and secular Turkish Republic—with Attaturk's Turkey much reduced in size. Former Ottoman territories in the Middle East were placed under French and British control, as part of what became known as the colonial "mandate system," which legitimized Europe's dominance over territories in the Middle East, Africa, and the Pacific. Territories were divided into groups on the basis of their location and their "level of development"; that is, how far, in European eyes, they would have to progress to earn self-government. Choice pieces of land became mandates held by the League of Nations, in principle, but administered by Britain (Transjordan, Iraq, and Palestine) and France (Lebanon and Syria). The British and French Empires, therefore, expanded after the war, although these territories held troubles ahead. The British faced revolt in Iraq and escalating tensions in Palestine, where they tried to juggle conflicting promises made to Zionist settlers and indigenous Arab communities. These circumstances made the end of the First World War a great disappointment for Arab leaders in Lebanon, Syria, Palestine, and Iraq, some of whom had cooperated with Britain during the war in exchange for the promise of independence at war's end.

The peoples of the Allies' existing colonies were also disappointed. Ho Chi Minh, a young student from Indochina attending a Paris university, was one of many colonial activists who attended the conference to protest conditions in the colonies and to ask that the rights of nations be extended to their homelands. Well-organized delegations from French West Africa and the Congress Party of India, which favored dominion status in return for the wartime efforts of millions of Indian soldiers who had fought for the British Empire, were also snubbed. The peacemakers' belief in democracy and self-determination collided with their baseline assumptions about Western superiority, inherited from the nineteenth century, that justified imperial rule. Although the European powers spoke about reforming colonialism, little was done, leaving many nationalists in the colonies, who had favored moderate legislative change, to decide that active struggle might be the only answer to the injustices of colonialism.

Each of the five peace treaties incorporated the Covenant of the League of Nations, an organization envisioned as the arbiter of world peace, but it never achieved the idealistic aims of its founders. The League was handicapped from the start by the number of changes to its original design. The arms-reduction requirement was watered down, and the League's power to enforce it was rendered almost nonexistent. Japan did not join until it was allowed to keep former German concessions in China. France demanded that both Germany and Soviet Russia be excluded from the League, which contradicted Wilson's goals but had already been legitimized in Paris, where neither the Bolsheviks nor the defeated Central Powers were allowed in the talks. The League received an even more debilitating blow when the U.S. Congress, citing a long-standing national preference for isolation, refused to approve U.S. membership in the League. Hobbled from the start, the international organization had little potential to avert conflicts.

The League began as an optimistic response to global conflict and registered the urgency of reorganizing world governance. Its history, however, reflected the larger problems of power politics that emerged after the war.

CONCLUSION

Europe fought the First World War on every front possible—military, political, social, and economic. Consequently, the war's effects extended far beyond the devastated landscapes of the Western Front, and statistics can only hint at the enormous loss of human life: out of the 70 million men mobilized, nearly 9 million were killed. Although Russia, Germany, France, and Hungary recorded the highest number of deaths, the smaller countries of southeast Europe had the highest percentages of soldiers killed. Almost 40 percent of Serbia's soldiers died in battle, and with the addition of war-related deaths caused by privation and disease, Serbia lost 15 percent of its population; in comparison, Britain, France, and Germany lost 2 to 3 percent of their populations. But the percentages are much more telling if we look at the young men of the war generation, known as the "lost generation." During 1914–1918, 13 percent of German men born between 1880 and 1899 were killed. In France, the figure was 17 percent, nearly 1 out of every 6.

The breakdown of the prewar treaty system and the scale of the diplomatic failure that produced the war discredited the political classes in many countries. Meanwhile, the war itself planted seeds of political and social discontent around the globe. Relations between Russia and western Europe had grown sour and suspicious, ever since the Allies had attempted to overthrow the Bolsheviks during the war and had excluded them from negotiations afterward. These actions instilled in the Soviets a mistrust of the West that lasted for generations. The Allied nations, in turn, feared that Russia would dominate the new states of eastern Europe, building a "Red Bridge" across the continent. Elsewhere, the conflicting demands of colonialism and nationalism struck only a temporary balance, while the redrawn maps left ethnic and linguistic minorities in every country. The fires of discontent raged most fiercely in Germany, where the Treaty of Versailles was decried as outrageously unjust, and nearly all national governments agreed that it would eventually have to be revised. In the end, neither war nor peace had ended the rivalries that caused the Great War.

The war also had powerful and permanent economic consequences. Beset by inflation, debt, and the difficult task of industrial rebuilding, Europe found itself displaced from the center of the world economy. The war had accelerated the decentralization of money and markets, which financially benefited many Asian, African, and South American nations as their economies became less dependent on Europe and so were better able to profit from Europe's need for their natural resources. The United States and Japan reaped the biggest gains and emerged as leaders in the new world economy.

The war's most powerful cultural legacy was disillusionment, as a generation of men had been sacrificed to no apparent end. Surviving soldiers—many of them permanently injured, both physically and psychologically—were sickened by their participation in such useless slaughter. Women and other civilians who had made extraordinary sacrifices on the home front were also disappointed by their little apparent gain. Both veterans and civilians were disgusted by the greedy abandonment of principles by the politicians at Versailles. In the postwar period, many younger men and women mistrusted the "old men" who had dragged the world into war. These feelings of loss and alienation were voiced in the vastly popular genre of war literature—memoirs and fiction that commemorated the experience of soldiers on the front lines. In his novel

After You Read This Chapter

 Go to **INQUIZITIVE** to see what you've learned—and learn what you've missed—with personalized feedback along the way.

REVIEWING THE OBJECTIVES

- The First World War broke out as a result of conflicts in the Balkans. Why?
- The Western Front was seen by all sides as a crucial theater of the conflict. What measures did the French, British, and Germans take to break the stalemate? Why did they fail?
- How did European governments intervene in the economy to ensure the production of matériel for the war effort and to remedy the social crises caused by mobilization?
- The war led European nations to mobilize people and resources from their colonies. How did colonial subjects participate in the war effort? What did many of them expect in return?
- Russia was devastated by the war, and the population lost confidence in the tsar's government. What circumstances allowed the Bolsheviks to seize power in 1917? What were their goals?
- The Treaty of Versailles blamed Germany for the war. Who were the most important participants in the peace conference? Who did the most to shape the terms of the treaty?

All Quiet on the Western Front, the German writer and ex-soldier Erich Maria Remarque captured the disillusion of the generation: "Through the years our business has been killing;—it was our first calling in life. Our knowledge of life is limited to death. What will happen afterwards? And what shall come out of us?"

That was the main question facing postwar Europe. The German novelist Thomas Mann recognized that 1918 had brought "an end of an epoch, revolution and the dawn of a new age," and that he and his fellow Germans were "living in a new and unfamiliar world." The struggle to define this new world would increasingly be conceived of in terms of rival ideologies—democracy, communism, and fascism—competing for the future of Europe. The eastern autocracies had fallen with the war, but liberal democracy was on the decline as well. Although militarism and nationalism remained strong, calls for major social reforms gained force during a worldwide depression. Entire populations had been mobilized during the war, and they would remain so afterward, as active participants in the age of mass politics. Europe was about to embark on two turbulent decades of rejecting and reinventing its social and political institutions. As Tomáš Masaryk, the first president of the newly formed Czechoslovakia, described it, postwar Europe was a "laboratory atop a graveyard."

PEOPLE, IDEAS, AND EVENTS IN CONTEXT

- Why was **FRANZ FERDINAND** assassinated? How did his death contribute to the outbreak of the war?
- What was the **SCHLIEFFEN PLAN**? How was it connected to the outbreak of the war?
- What was the significance of the **BATTLE OF THE MARNE** and the **BATTLE OF TANNENBURG** in 1914?
- Why did the British attempt to attack the Ottoman Empire at **GALLIPOLI**?
- Why did **OTTOMAN TURKEY** enter the war on the side of Germany? What circumstances led to the **ARMENIAN GENOCIDE**?
- Why did **ITALY, BULGARIA**, and **ROMANIA** enter the war? What were the consequences of their participation?
- What was the goal of the attacking forces at **VERDUN** and the **SOMME** in 1916? What was accomplished by the **OFFENSIVES** of 1916?
- Why did many people in Russia, and especially soldiers in the Russian army, lose faith in **TSAR NICHOLAS II** of Russia?
- How did **LENIN** make use of the **SOVIETS** in challenging the **PROVISIONAL GOVERNMENT** in Russia after the fall of the tsar?
- What policies did the **BOLSHEVIKS** follow after seizing power in Russia?
- What were **WOODROW WILSON'S FOURTEEN POINTS**?
- What kind of treatment did Germany receive under the terms of the **TREATY OF VERSAILLES**? What **NEW NATION-STATES** were created in central and eastern Europe as a result of the treaty?

THINKING ABOUT CONNECTIONS

- What made the First World War different from previous military conflicts in Europe that had involved large numbers of states, such as the Napoleonic Wars of the early nineteenth century (Chapter 18) or the Thirty Years' War of the seventeenth century (see Chapter 15)?
- In what ways might the effects and consequences of the First World War have shaped the lives of Europeans in the decades to come? How did it change the lives of various peoples from other parts of the world who were drawn into the conflict?

Before You Read This Chapter

STORY LINES

- With the exception of Bolshevik Russia, European states attempted to find stability in the traumatic aftermath of the First World War by reinforcing democratic institutions and focusing on an orderly transition from wartime production to a peacetime economy.

- The Bolsheviks won the civil war that followed the Russian Revolution in 1917, and by the late 1920s, Joseph Stalin had embarked on an unprecedented revolution from above, industrializing the nation and transforming rural life through the collectivization of agriculture. The human costs were enormous, as millions died of hunger and millions more were arrested and deported to labor camps in the east.

- The Great Depression undermined political support for Europe's democracies in the 1930s, and the decade saw the consolidation of fascist regimes in Italy and Germany and an anticapitalist communist regime in the Soviet Union.

CHRONOLOGY

1918	The November Revolution establishes the Weimar Republic in Germany
1918–1920	Russian Civil War
1920	National Socialist German Workers' party founded in Germany
1922	Mussolini comes to power in Italy
1923	Hitler's Beer Hall Putsch in Munich
1928	First Soviet Five-Year Plan
1928–1929	Stalin gains power in Russia
1929–1933	Collectivization and famine in Soviet Union
1933	Hitler becomes chancellor of Germany
1937–1938	The Great Terror in Soviet Union

Turmoil between the Wars

CORE OBJECTIVES

- **UNDERSTAND** the direction taken by the Russian Revolution after 1917 and the consequences of Stalin's revolution from above in the 1930s.

- **DEFINE** fascism and **EXPLAIN** Mussolini's rise to power in Italy in the 1920s.

- **DESCRIBE** the challenges faced by the Weimar Republic and other democracies in Britain, France, and the United States after the First World War.

- **EXPLAIN** Hitler's rise to power in Germany in 1933 and the reasons for the broad support for Nazis among many Germans.

- **UNDERSTAND** the ways that the interwar atmosphere of social and political crisis was reflected in the world of the arts, literature, and popular culture.

Käthe Kollwitz, a Berlin painter and sculptor, understood the terrible costs of the First World War; her son, Peter, was killed on October 22, 1914. Her diary recorded the last moments she spent with him before his departure for the front: "It was dark, and we went arm in arm through the wood. He pointed out constellations to me, as he had done so often before." Her entry for October 30 was more succinct, a quotation from the postcard she had received from his commanding officer: "Your son has fallen." Kollwitz's pain found expression in her later work, which explored in naked terms the grief and powerlessness that she felt during the war years. Her suffering found expression, too, in a commitment to socialism, a political ideology that provided an antidote to the nationalism that pervaded German society. Kollwitz's socialism drew the attention of the Gestapo after the Nazis came to power in 1933, and she was fired from her position at the Academy of Art. She put up with house searches and harassment but refused to go into exile. She died in 1945, surviving long enough to see her cherished grandson, a German soldier also named Peter, killed in the Second World War in 1942 while fighting on the Eastern Front in Russia.

The story of Käthe Kollwitz and her family between 1914 and 1945 is unusual only because she was a well-known artist. Their suffering was all too familiar to many others, as was the search for new political ideologies that might save Europeans from their past. The Great War had left 9 million dead, shattered the confidence that had been so characteristic of nineteenth-century European culture, and led to another world war even more horrific. Many in the interwar years shared Kollwitz's hope for a socialist or communist future, while many others turned to extremisms of the right. The result in the 1920s was a near collapse of democracy. By the late 1930s, few western democracies remained, and even in those that did—most notably Britain, France, and the United States—regimes were frayed by the same pressures that wrecked democratic governments elsewhere.

The foremost cause of democracy's decline were the disruptions in the world economy following the First World War and the Great Depression of 1929–1933; a second source lay in increased social conflict. Many hoped that these conflicts would be resolved by the peace and a renewed commitment to democratic institutions, but the opposite occurred. Broad swaths of the electorate rallied to extremist political parties that promised radical transformations of nations and their cultures. Nationalism, sharpened by the war, proved a key source of discontent in its aftermath, and frustrated nationalist sentiment turned citizens against their governments in Italy and Germany.

The most dramatic instance of democracy's decline came with the rise of new authoritarian dictatorships, especially in Russia, Italy, and Germany. The experiences of these three nations differed significantly, but in each case, many citizens were persuaded that only drastic measures could bring order from chaos. Those measures, including the elimination of parliamentary government, strict restrictions on political freedom, and increasingly virulent repression of "enemies" of the state, were implemented with a combination of violence, intimidation, and propaganda. That so many citizens seemed willing to sacrifice their freedoms—or those of others—was a measure of their alienation and desperation.

WIDOWS AND ORPHANS, BY KÄTHE KOLLWITZ (1919). Kollwitz (1867–1945), a German artist and socialist activist in Berlin, lost her son in the First World War and her grandson in the Second World War. Her work poignantly illustrates the effects of poverty and war on the lives of ordinary people.

THE SOVIET UNION UNDER LENIN AND STALIN

The Russian Civil War

After the Bolsheviks seized power in October 1917, they signed a separate peace with Germany in March 1918 (the Treaty of Brest-Litovsk), then turned to consolidating their regime. The October Revolution had divided Russian society, and ignited a war that was far costlier than the conflict with Germany. Fury at the terms of Brest-Litovsk mobilized the Bolsheviks' enemies, known collectively as "Whites," who were loosely bound by their goal to remove the "Reds" from power. Their military force consisted mainly of tsarist military officers, reactionary monarchists, former nobility, and disaffected liberal supporters of the monarchy, and they were joined by groups as diverse as liberal supporters of the provisional government, Mensheviks, Social Revolutionaries, and anarchist peasant bands known as "Greens," who opposed all central state power. Both the White armies and the Bolsheviks faced insurrections from strong nationalist movements in parts of the former Russian Empire: Ukraine, Georgia, and the north

THE SOVIET UNION, 1918–1945. ▪ *What were the areas lost by Russia in the Treaty of Brest-Litovsk?* ▪ *How did the possession of Moscow and Leningrad (St. Petersburg) aid the Bolsheviks in their victory over the Whites?* ▪ *How did the civil war of 1917–1920 affect the new Soviet state?*

Caucasus regions. Several foreign powers, including the United States, Great Britain, and Japan, launched small but threatening interventions on the periphery of the old empire. Outside support for the Whites proved to be an insignificant threat to the Bolsheviks, but it heightened the Bolsheviks' mistrust of the capitalist world.

The Bolsheviks eventually won the civil war because they gained the support—or at least the tacit acceptance—of the majority of the population and because they were better organized for the war effort itself. Leon Trotsky, the revolutionary hero of 1905 and 1917, became the new commissar of war and created a disciplined military machine that grew to 5 million men by 1920. By the end of 1920, Trotsky's Red Army triumphed over the White armies, although fighting continued into 1922. The Bolsheviks also invaded Poland and nearly reached Warsaw before being thrown back. The Polish victory outside Warsaw in August of 1920 prevented the Bolsheviks from pursuing their plan to connect with communists in Germany and spread their revolution to western Europe.

When the civil war was over, the Soviet Union had suffered a million combat casualties, several million deaths from hunger and disease caused by the war, and 100,000 to 300,000 executions of noncombatants as part of Red and White terror. The barbarism of the war engendered lasting hatreds within the emerging Soviet nation, especially among ethnic minorities, and brutalized the fledgling society that came into existence under the newly militarized Bolshevik regime. The Bolsheviks created a new political police during the civil war, known as the Cheka, after the Russian initials of its official title, the Extraordinary Commission to Fight Counter-Revolution and Sabotage. The Cheka institutionalized a system of terror, executing and sending to detention camps opponents of the regime and people identified as "class enemies."

The civil war also shaped the Bolsheviks' approach to the economy. Upon taking power in 1917, Lenin expected to create, for the short term at least, a state-capitalist system that resembled the successful European wartime economies. The new government took control of large-scale industry, banking, and all other major capitalist concerns, while allowing small-scale private economic activity, including agriculture, to continue. But the civil war pushed the new government toward a more radical economic stance known as "**war communism**." The Bolsheviks began to requisition grain from the peasantry, and outlawed private trade in consumer goods as "speculation," militarized production facilities, and abolished money. Many believed that war communism would replace the capitalist system that had collapsed in 1917, but such hopes were largely unfounded.

War communism sustained the Bolshevik military effort while further disrupting the already war-ravaged economy. The civil war devastated Russian industry and emptied major cities. The population of Moscow fell by 50 percent between 1917 and 1920. The masses of urban workers, who had strongly supported the Bolshevik revolution, melted back into the countryside; and industrial output in 1920–1921 fell to only 20 percent of prewar levels. The most devastating effects of war communism, however, were on agriculture. The peasants had initially benefited from the revolution when they spontaneously seized and redistributed noble lands. But the agricultural system was severely disrupted by the civil war, the grain requisitioning of war communism, and the outlawing of all private trade in grain. In 1921, large-scale famine claimed some 5 million lives.

As the civil war came to a close, urban workers and soldiers became increasingly impatient with the Bolshevik regime, which had promised socialism and workers' control but delivered something more akin to a military dictatorship. In late 1920, large-scale strikes and protests broke out, but the Bolsheviks moved swiftly and effectively to subdue these "popular revolts." Through these actions, the Bolshevik regime that emerged from the civil war made a clear statement that public opposition would not be tolerated.

The NEP Period

In response to these political and economic difficulties, the Bolsheviks abandoned war communism and, in March 1921, embarked on a radically different course known as the **New Economic Policy** (NEP). The leadership announced that it would permit the development of a mixed economy that contained elements of socialist central planning, and also permit some capitalist entrepreneurship, particularly in agriculture. Although the state continued to own all major industry and financial concerns, individuals were allowed to own private property, trade freely within limits, and—most important—farm land for their own benefit. Fixed taxes on the peasantry replaced grain requisitioning, so what peasants grew beyond the tax requirements was theirs to do with as they saw fit. The Bolshevik most identified with the NEP was Nikolai Bukharin (1888–1938), a young and brilliant Marxist theoretician who argued that the Bolsheviks could best industrialize the Soviet Union by taxing private peasant economic activity. Lenin himself described the NEP as "one step backward in order to take two steps forward."

The NEP was undeniably successful in allowing Soviet agriculture to recover from the civil war. By 1924, agricultural harvests had returned to prewar levels. Peasants were largely left alone, and they responded by redividing noble lands among themselves to level wealth discrepancies between rich and poor. They also reasserted the power of the peasant commune in the countryside. Under the NEP, the peasantry produced enough grain to feed the country, though they continued to use very primitive farming methods to do so. The NEP was less successful, however, in encouraging peasants to participate in markets to benefit urban areas. The result was a series of shortages in grain deliveries to cities, a situation that prompted many Bolsheviks to call for revival of the radical economic practices of war communism. The fate of these radical proposals was tied to the fate of the man who replaced Lenin as the leader of the USSR and became one of the most notorious dictators of all time: Joseph Stalin.

Stalin and the "Revolution from Above"

Stalin's rise was swift and unpredicted. His political success was rooted in intraparty conflicts in the 1920s, but it was also closely tied to the abrupt end of the NEP and the beginning of a massive program of social and economic modernization in the late 1920s. This "revolution from above" was the most rapid social and economic transformation any nation has seen in modern history, and it was carried out at unprecedented human cost.

Joseph Stalin (1879–1953), whose real name was Iosep Jughashvili, was the son of a poor shoemaker. He was a Bolshevik from the Caucasus nation of Georgia. After receiving his early education in an Orthodox seminary, he participated in revolutionary activity in the Caucasus and spent many years in Siberian exile before the revolution. Although an important member of the Bolshevik party in 1917, he was not one of the central figures. After Lenin's death in 1924, the civil war hero Leon Trotsky was widely assumed to be the best candidate to succeed him, but other top Bolsheviks also aspired to a leading role.

Though not a brilliant orator like Trotsky or a respected Marxist theoretician like Bukharin, Stalin was nonetheless a master political strategist. He played the game of internal party politics almost flawlessly after Lenin's death. Stalin isolated his opponents within the Bolshevik party and expelled each of them successively. Trotsky was the first to go, driven out by a coalition of Stalin and others who, ironically, feared Trotsky's desire to take control of the party himself. Stalin then turned on his former allies and removed them in turn,

LENIN AND STALIN. During Stalin's regime, this picture was used to show his close relationship with Lenin; but the photograph, in fact, had been doctored. ▪ *What opportunities for propaganda and manipulation were offered by new technologies of photography and film?*

culminating in the removal of Bukharin from the Politburo in 1928–1929.

Stalin's campaign against Bukharin was connected to his desire to end the NEP and launch an all-out industrialization drive. Stalin believed that the Soviet Union could not industrialize by relying on taxes generated from small-scale peasant agriculture. He pushed for an increase in the tempo of industrialization as early as 1927, prompted by fears of falling behind the West and the threat of another world war. Although almost all the Bolshevik leaders supported Stalin's plan to step up the tempo of industrialization, hardly anybody supported what happened next: an abrupt turn toward forced industrialization and collectivization of agriculture.

In 1927, a poor harvest caused yet another crisis in the grain-collection system. Low prices for agricultural goods and high prices for industrial goods led peasants to hoard grain, resulting in food shortages and difficulties in collecting taxes from the peasantry. In early 1928, Stalin ordered officials in the distant Urals and Siberian areas to begin requisitioning grain, then soon applied this revival of war

Analyzing Primary Sources

Lenin's Theses on the National and Colonial Question *(1920)*

The success of the Russian Revolution forced the new Soviet leadership to declare what its relationship would be with other movements for revolutionary change, including the movements for national independence that were developing in European colonies in Africa and Asia. These nationalist movements posed a dilemma, because many of them were led by middle-class activists—that is, by representatives of the "bourgeois" order that socialists hoped to overthrow. Lenin's Theses on the National and Colonial Question was the outcome of a debate he had with a young Indian communist, Manabendra Nath Roy (1887–1954). Here, Lenin argues that communists may consider temporary alliances with these nationalist movements but should never allow them to merge with or subsume the communist movement.

1. An abstract or formal conception of the question of equality in general and of national equality in particular is in the very nature of bourgeois democracy. Under the guise of the equality of individuals in general, bourgeois democracy proclaims the formal, legal equality of the property owner and the proletarian, the exploiter and the exploited, thereby grossly deceiving the oppressed classes.... The real meaning of the demand for equality consists in its being a demand for the abolition of classes.

2. As the conscious expression of the proletarian class struggle to shake off the yoke of the bourgeoisie, the Communist Party, in line with its basic task of struggling against bourgeois democracy and exposing its lies and duplicity, should not base its policy on the national question on abstract and formal principles. Instead, it should first be based on an exact appraisal of specific historical and above all economic conditions. Second, it should clearly differentiate between the interests of the oppressed classes, the toilers, the exploited, and the general concept of the so-called interests of the people, which means the interests of the ruling class. Third, it should with equal precision distinguish between the oppressed, dependent nations that do not have equal rights and the oppressor, exploiting nations that do....

3. The imperialist war of 1914 . . . was justified by both sides with platitudes about national liberation and self-determination. Nonetheless, both the treaties of Brest-Litovsk and Bucharest and those of Versailles and St. Germain showed that the victorious bourgeoisie ruthlessly sets even "national" borders according to its economic interests. For the bourgeoisie even "national" borders are objects of trade.... [T]he proletariat can achieve genuine national liberation and unity only through revolutionary struggle and by overpowering the bourgeoisie....

4. It follows from these principles that the entire policy of the Communist International on the national and colonial questions must be based primarily upon uniting the proletarians and toiling masses of all nations and countries in common revolutionary struggle to overthrow the landowners and the bourgeoisie....

5. The international political situation has now put the dictatorship of the proletariat on the order of the day. All events in world politics necessarily focus on one single central issue: the struggle of the world bourgeoisie against the Russian Soviet Republic, which rallies around itself both the soviet movement of the advanced workers of all countries and all national liberation movements of the colonies and oppressed peoples....

6. Consequently, we cannot limit ourselves at this time merely to recognizing or proclaiming the friendship of the toilers of various nations. Rather we must pursue a policy of implementing the closest possible alliance of all national and colonial liberation movements with Soviet Russia. The forms of this alliance will be determined by the level of development of the Communist movement within the proletariat of each country or of the revolutionary liberation movement in the backward countries and among the backward nationalities.

7. Federation is a transitional form toward full unity of the toilers of all nations. Federation has already shown its usefulness in practice—in the Russian Soviet Federated Socialist Republic's relations to the other soviet republics ... and also within the Russian Soviet Federated Socialist Republic itself toward the nationalities that formerly had neither a state nor self-government....

8. ... [W]e must strive for an ever closer federal association. We must take into consideration first, that the soviet

republics, surrounded by imperialist states of the whole world that are considerably stronger militarily, cannot possibly exist without close association with each other. Second, a close economic alliance of the soviet republics is necessary, without which it is impossible to restore the productive forces destroyed by imperialism and ensure the well-being of the toilers. Third, that there is a tendency to create a world economy unified according to a common plan, controlled by proletarians of all countries. . . .

9. . . . Communist parties must incessantly expose in their entire propaganda and agitation the continually repeated violations of the equality of nations and guaranteed rights of national minorities in all capitalist countries despite their "democratic" constitutions. In addition, it must be explained persistently that only the soviet order can ensure true national equality by uniting first the proletariat and then the whole mass of the toilers in struggle against the bourgeoisie. Moreover, all Communist parties must directly support the revolutionary movement among the nations that are dependent and do not have equal rights (for example Ireland, the Negroes in America, and so forth), and in the colonies. . . .

10. . . . The fight against . . . the most deeply rooted petty-bourgeois, nationalist prejudices (which are expressed in all possible forms, such as racism, national chauvinism, and anti-Semitism) must be given all the more priority as the question becomes more pressing of transforming the

dictatorship of the proletariat from a national framework (that is, a dictatorship that exists only in one country and is incapable of carrying out an independent international policy) into an international one (that is, a dictatorship of the proletariat in at least several advanced countries, capable of exercising a decisive influence on all of world politics).

Petty-bourgeois nationalism declares that internationalism consists of the mere recognition of the equality of nations (although this recognition is strictly verbal) and considers national egoism to be sacrosanct. Proletarian internationalism, on the contrary, requires subordinating the interests of the proletarian struggle in one country to the interests of this struggle on a world scale. It also requires that the nation that has overthrown its bourgeoisie has the ability and willingness to make the greatest national sacrifices in order to overthrow international capitalism. . . .

11. With respect to the states and nations that have a more backward, predominantly feudal, patriarchal, or patriarchal-peasant character, the following points in particular must be kept in mind:

a. All Communist parties must support with deeds the revolutionary liberation movement in these countries. . . .

b. A struggle absolutely must be waged against the reactionary and medieval influence of the clergy, the Christian missions, and similar elements.

c. It is necessary to struggle against the Pan-Islamic and Pan-Asian movements and similar currents that try to link the liberation struggle against European and American imperialism with strengthening the power of Turkish and Japanese imperialism and of the nobles, large landowners, clergy, and so forth.

d. It is especially necessary to support the peasant movement in the backward countries against the landowners and all forms and vestiges of feudalism.

Source: John Riddell, ed., *Workers of the World and Oppressed Peoples, Unite! Proceedings and Documents of the Second Congress, 1920*, vol. 1 (New York: Pathfinder Press, 1991), pp. 283–88.

Questions for Analysis

1. Why does Lenin begin these theses with a critique of "bourgeois democracy" and "national liberation and self-determination"? What alternative goals does he announce?

2. Why does Lenin say that an alliance between the communist movement and movements for anticolonial liberation is worth pursuing?

3. What possible dangers does Lenin nevertheless identify in some of the anticolonial movements he mentions?

communism to the entire country. In 1929, the upper echelons of the party abandoned the NEP and embarked on the complete collectivization of agriculture, beginning in the major grain-growing areas.

COLLECTIVIZATION

Collectivization was initially expected to be a gradual process, but in late 1929, the Politburo (short for political bureau, which governed the Communist party and state) began to issue orders to use force against peasants who resisted. The process that ensued was brutal and chaotic. Local party and police officials forced peasants to give up their land, farming implements, and livestock and to join collective farms; the peasants resisted, often violently. There were some 1,600 large-scale rebellions in

WINTER DEPORTATIONS, 1929–1930. Ukrainian families, charged with being kulaks, were deported from their homes after refusing to join Stalin's collective farming plan. Many of the evicted families were shipped north by train to the Arctic, where they perished, owing to the lack of adequate food and shelter.

the Soviet Union between 1929 and 1933; some involved several thousand people, and quelling them required military intervention, including the use of artillery. Peasants resisted by slaughtering their livestock instead of turning it over to the farms, a loss that hampered agricultural production for years to follow. Sensing a possible crisis, Stalin called a temporary halt to the process in early 1930, but soon thereafter he ordered it to proceed more gradually. By 1935, collectivization of agriculture was complete in most areas of the Soviet Union.

Stalin launched an all-out attack on peasants designated as *kulaks* ("tight-fisted ones"), a derogatory term for well-to-do farmers, and the word became one of many terms for peasants hostile to collectivization. Most kulaks, though, were no better off than their neighbors. Between 1929 and 1933, some one and a half million peasants were uprooted, dispossessed of their property, and resettled either to distant Soviet camps in the north or to poor farmland closer to their original homes. The liquidation of kulaks as a class magnified the disruptive effects of agricultural collectivization, and the two together produced one of the most devastating famines in modern European history. Peasants who were forced into collective farms had little incentive to produce extra food, and exiling many of the most productive peasants not surprisingly weakened the agricultural system. In 1932–1933, famine spread throughout central Russia, the Volga, the Ukraine, and the northern Caucasus; this included the most productive agricultural area in the country, and the famine that struck these areas was thus

particularly senseless. The 1933 famine took 5 to 7 million lives across the entire Soviet Union and was most devastating for Ukrainians and the Kazakhs of Soviet Central Asia. During the famine, the Bolsheviks maintained substantial grain reserves in other parts of the country, enough to save many hundreds of thousands of lives at a minimum, but they refused to send the grain to the affected areas, preferring instead to seal off famine-stricken regions and allow people to starve. Grain reserves were sold overseas for hard currency and stockpiled in case of war. After 1935, there would never again be any large-scale resistance to Soviet power in the countryside.

The Five-Year Plans

Collectivization provided the resources for the other major aspect of Stalin's revolution from above: a rapid campaign of forced industrialization. Stalin laid out his ambitious goals in the first Five-Year Plan (1928–1932), which called for truly herculean industrialization efforts; its results rank as one of the most stunning periods of economic growth the modern world has ever seen. Soviet statistics boasted of annual growth rates of 20 percent a year, but even the more cautious Western estimates of 14 percent annual growth were remarkable, given the worldwide depression elsewhere. The Bolsheviks built entirely new industries in entirely new cities. Magnitogorsk, for example, emerged from barren, uninhabited steppes in 1929 to become a

"LET'S FUSE STRIKE FORCES WITH STRIKE BRIGADES!" This Russian propaganda poster was used to mobilize workers to the Five-Year Plan.

"IMPERIALISTS CANNOT STOP THE SUCCESS OF THE FIVE-YEAR PLAN!" ▪ *Did propaganda such as this appeal to Russian nationalist pride?*

steel-producing factory town of 250,000 residents in 1932. Cities such as Moscow and Leningrad doubled in size in the early 1930s, while new cities sprang up across the country. In 1926, only one-fifth of the population lived in towns; but fifteen years later, in 1939, roughly one-third did. The urban population had grown from 26 to 56 million in under fifteen years. The Soviet Union was well on its way to becoming an urban, industrial society.

This rapid industrialization came at enormous human cost. Many large-scale projects were carried out with prison labor, especially in the timber and mining industries. The labor-camp system, known as the *gulag*, became a central part of the Stalinist economic system. People were arrested and sent to camps on a bewildering array of charges: petty crimes, contact with foreigners, or simply having the ill fortune to be born of bourgeois or kulak parents. The camp system spread throughout the Soviet Union in the 1930s, and by the end of the decade, the regime had incarcerated

roughly 3.6 million people. This army of prisoners was used to complete the most arduous and dangerous industrialization tasks, such as the construction of the Moscow–White Sea canal. To save money, the canal connecting Moscow to the seaports of the north was constructed without the use of any machinery. It was literally dug by hand, with human labor used to power everything from conveyor belts to pile drivers; tens of thousands of individuals lost their lives during construction. One of Stalin's pet projects, the canal never functioned properly; it was too shallow and froze over in winter. (It was bombed early in World War II.)

The economic system created during this period was also fraught with structural problems that would plague the Soviet Union throughout its history. The command economy, with each year's production levels planned in advance in Moscow, never functioned in a rational way. Heavy industry was always favored, and the emphasis on quantity made quality practically meaningless. A factory that was

Competing Viewpoints

Stalin's Industrialization of the Soviet Union

How did the Soviet people experience Stalin's industrialization drive? Archives opened after the fall of the Soviet Union in 1991 helped historians glimpse at what the common people lived through and how they responded. The first document is an excerpt from a speech Stalin gave at the First All-Union Conference of Managers of Socialist Industry in 1931. In his usual style, he invoked Russian nationalism and fears of Soviet backwardness while summoning all to take up the task of industrial production.

The letters in the second selection come from several hundred that workers and peasants sent to Soviet newspapers and authorities, recounting their experiences and offering their opinions. Both printed here were sent to the Soviet paper Pravda.

"The Tasks of Business Executives"

It is sometimes asked whether it is not possible to slow down the tempo somewhat, to put a check on the movement. No, comrades, it is not possible! The tempo must not be reduced! On the contrary, we must increase it as much as is within our powers and possibilities. This is dictated to us by our obligations to the workers and peasants of the USSR. This is dictated to us by our obligations to the working class of the whole world.

To slacken the tempo would mean falling behind. And those who fall behind get beaten. But we do not want to be beaten. No, we refuse to be beaten. One feature of the history of old Russia was the continual beatings she suffered because of her backwardness. She was beaten by the Mongol khans. She was beaten by the Turkish beys. . . . She was beaten by the British and French capitalists. She was beaten by the Japanese barons. All beat her—for her backwardness: for military backwardness, for cultural backwardness, for political backwardness, for industrial backwardness, for agricultural backwardness. . . .

We are fifty or a hundred years behind the advanced countries. We must make good this distance in ten years. Either we do it, or we shall be crushed. . . .

In ten years at most we must make good the distance which separates us from the advanced capitalist countries. We have all the "objective" possibilities for this. The only thing lacking is the ability to take proper advantage of these possibilities. And that depends on us. *Only* on us! . . . It is time to put an end to the rotten policy of noninterference in production. It is time to adopt a new policy, a policy adapted to the present times—the policy of interfering in everything. If you are a factory manager, then interfere in all the affairs of the factory, look into everything, let nothing escape you, learn and learn again. Bolsheviks must master technique. It is time Bolsheviks themselves became experts. . . .

---

charged with producing a certain number of pairs of shoes, for example, could cut costs by producing all one style and size; the consumer would be left with useless goods, but the producer would fulfill the plan. Stalin's industrialization drive transformed the country from an agrarian nation into a world industrial power in the space of a few short years. In the long term, however, the system would become an economic disaster.

The Stalin revolution produced fundamental cultural and economic changes. The revolution from above altered the face of Soviet cities and the working class populating them. New cities were largely made up of first-generation peasants who brought their rural traditions to the cities, changing the fragile urban culture that had developed during the 1920s. Women, too, entered the urban workforce in increasing numbers in the 1930s: women went from 20 to almost 40 percent of the workforce in one decade, and in light industry, they made up two-thirds of the labor force by 1940.

At the same time, Stalin promoted a sharply conservative shift in all areas of culture and society. In art, the

There are no fortresses which Bolsheviks cannot capture. We have assumed power. We have built up a huge socialist industry. We have swung the middle peasants to the path of socialism. . . .

What remains to be done is not so much: to study technique, to master science. And when we have done that we will develop a tempo of which we dare not even dream at present.

Source: Joseph Stalin, "The Tasks of Business Executives" (speech given at the First All-Union Conference of Managers of Socialist Industry, February 4, 1931), as cited in Richard Sakwa, *The Rise and Fall of the Soviet Union, 1917–1991* (New York: 1999), pp. 187–88.

Stalin's Industrial Development: The View from Below

It should not be forgotten that many millions of workers are participating in the building of socialism. A horse with its own strength can drag seventy-five poods,* but its owner has loaded it with a hundred poods, and in addition he's fed it poorly. No matter how much he uses the whip, it still won't be able to move the cart.

This is also true for the working class. They've loaded it with socialist competition, shock work, over-fulfilling the industrial and financial plan, and so forth. A worker toils seven hours, not ever leaving his post, and this is not all he does. Afterward he sits in meetings or else attends classes for an hour and a half or two in order to increase his skill level, and if he doesn't do these things, then he's doing things at home.

And what does he live on? One hundred fifty grams of salted mutton, he will make soup without any of the usual additives, neither carrots, beets, flour, nor salt pork. What kind of soup do you get from this? Mere "dishwater."

—B. N. Kniazev, Tula, September 1930

Comrade Editor, Please give me an answer. Do the local authorities have the right to forcibly take away the only cow of industrial and office workers? What is more, they demand a receipt showing that the cow was handed over voluntarily and they threaten you by saying if you don't do this, they will put you in prison for failure to fulfill the meat procurement. How can you live when the cooperative distributes only black bread, and at the market goods have the prices

of 1919 and 1920? Lice have eaten us to death, and soap is given only to railroad workers. From hunger and filth we have a massive outbreak of spotted fever.

—Anonymous, from Aktybinsk, Kazakhstan

* A *pood* is a Russian unit of weight, equal to 36.11 pounds.

Source: Lewis Siegelbaum and Andrei Sokolov, *Stalinism as a Way of Life: A Narrative in Documents* (New Haven, CT: 2000), pp. 39–41.

Questions for Analysis

1. What are Stalin's priorities?

2. What images does Stalin use to capture his audience's attention?

3. How did the Soviet people experience Stalin's industrialization drive?

radical modernism of the 1920s was crushed by socialist realism, a deadening aesthetic that celebrated the drive toward socialism and left no room for experimentation. Family policy and gender roles underwent a similar reversal. Early Bolshevik activists had promoted a utopian attempt to rebuild one of the basic structures of prerevolutionary society—the family—and to create a genuinely new proletarian social structure. During the 1920s, the Bolsheviks legalized divorce, banned the Orthodox Church from performing marriage ceremonies, and legalized abortion. But

Stalin abandoned these ideas of communist familial relations in favor of traditional family ties: divorce became more difficult, abortion was outlawed in 1936 except in cases that threatened the life of the mother, and homosexuality was declared a criminal offense. State subsidies and support for mothers, which were progressive for the time, could not change the reality that Soviet women were increasingly forced to carry the double burden of familial and wage labor to support Stalin's version of Soviet society. All areas of Soviet cultural and social policy experienced similar reversals.

The Great Terror

The apogee of Stalinist repression came with the "**Great Terror**" of 1937–1938, which left nearly a million people dead and as many as 1.5 million more in labor camps. As Stalin consolidated his personal dictatorship, he eliminated enemies—real and imagined—whom he considered superfluous to the new Soviet society. As we have seen, repression was central to the Stalinist system from the early 1930s, but the years 1937–1938 brought a qualitative and quantitative change—a whirlwind of mass repression unprecedented in scale.

The Terror was aimed at various categories of internal "enemies," from the top to the very bottom of Soviet society. Former and current political elites were perhaps the most visible victims. The top level of the Bolshevik party itself was purged almost completely, including the "Old Bolsheviks." Former colleagues of Lenin and Trotsky were publicly convicted in dramatic show trials before being shot; prominent victims included Nikolai Bukharin, the architect of the NEP in 1921. Some 100,000 party members were removed, most facing prison sentences or execution. The communist parties of other countries were also a target: virtually all the leaders of the Polish communist party fell victim to the purges, along with the vast majority of party leaders in the Ukraine. The purge also struck—with particular ferocity—nonparty elites, industrial managers, and intellectuals. In the summer of 1937, Stalin began a purge of the military, which he feared as a threat to his power: between 35,000 and 41,000 officers were killed, including 90 percent of the highest-ranking army officers and all the admirals. These purges, which did not spare family members of those arrested, disrupted the government, the military, and the economy. They nevertheless enabled Stalin to promote a new, young cadre of officials who had had no experience in the pre-Stalinist era and owed their careers, if not their lives, to Stalin personally. Whole ethnic groups were viewed with suspicion, including Poles, Ukrainians, Lithuanians, Latvians, Koreans, and others with supposed cross-border ties that, in Stalin's mind, represented a national security threat. From the bottom, some 200,000 to 300,000 "dekulakized" peasants, petty criminals, and other social misfits were arrested, and many were shot. The Great Terror remains one of the most puzzling aspects of Stalin's path to dictatorial power. It solidified Stalin's personal control over social and political life in the Soviet Union, but it did so by destroying the most talented elements in Soviet society.

The results of the Soviet revolution were profound. No other regime in the history of Europe had ever attempted to reorder completely the politics, economy, and society of a major nation, as the Soviets had done in a mere twenty years. By 1939, private manufacturing and trade had been almost entirely abolished. Factories, mines, railroads, and public utilities were exclusively owned by the state. Stores were either government enterprises or cooperatives in which consumers owned shares. And agriculture had been almost completely socialized.

The decade was not entirely grim, however. There were advances, especially in the area of social reform. Illiteracy was reduced from nearly 50 to about 20 percent, and higher education was made available in increasingly large numbers. Government assistance for working mothers and free hospitalization did a great deal to raise the national standard of health. The society that emerged was industrial, more urban than rural, and more modern than traditional. But it was a society badly brutalized in the process, one in which many of the most productive peasants, gifted intellectuals, and experienced economic and social elites were purged from society in the name of total dictatorial power. The USSR that emerged from this tumultuous period would barely be able to withstand the immense strains placed on it when the Germans struck less than three years after the end of the Terror.

THE EMERGENCE OF FASCISM IN ITALY

Italy emerged from the First World War as a democracy in distress. The war had cost nearly 700,000 Italian lives and over $15 billion. Moreover, Italy had received secret promises of specific territorial gains on the east coast of the Adriatic during the war, only to see those promises withdrawn at the Versailles peace conference. Groups of militant nationalists seized Fiume, a port city on the Adriatic, and held it for a year before being disbanded by the Italian army. At first the nationalists blamed the "mutilated victory" on President Wilson, but soon they turned on their own rulers and blamed what they saw as the weaknesses of parliamentary democracy.

Since unification, the Italian nation had been rent by an unhealthy economic split—divided into a prosperous industrialized north and a poor agrarian south. Social conflict over land, wages, and local power caused friction in the countryside as well as in urban centers. These tensions were aggravated by the war and the period of inflation and unemployment that followed. Inflation produced high prices, speculation, and profiteering; and wages normally would have risen but for the postwar labor market that was glutted with returning soldiers. Furthermore, business elites were shaken by strikes, which became increasingly large and frequent, and by the closing of foreign markets.

When the parliamentary government that was set up after the war failed to ease these dire conditions, Italians wanted drastic reforms. For the working class, this meant socialism, and in 1919, the socialists won about a third of the seats in the Chamber of Deputies. The movement, however, grew increasingly radical. In 1920, the socialist and anarchist workers seized scores of factories, most in the metallurgy sector, and tried to run them for the benefit of the workers. In the countryside, where many peasants had no land at all and worked for wages as rural laborers on large estates, demands for land reform grew more militant. In some rural areas, so-called Red Leagues tried to break up large estates and force landlords to reduce their rents. In all these actions, the model of the Russian Revolution, although it was only vaguely understood, encouraged the development of local radicalism.

The rising radical tide, especially seen against the backdrop of the Bolshevik revolution, worried other social groups. Industrialists and landowners feared for their property, and small shopkeepers and white-collar workers—social groups

EUROPE IN 1923. ■ *Which countries and empires lost territories after the First World War?* ■ *What were the consequences for those countries and empires?* ■ *How did the Russian Revolution change European politics?* ■ *What problems arose in the central and eastern European nations that were created after the First World War?*

that did not think the working-class movement supported their interests—found themselves alienated by both business elites and the revolutionary radicals. The threat from the left provoked a strong surge to the right, and Fascism appeared in the form of vigilante groups breaking up strikes, fighting with workers in the streets, or ousting the Red Leagues from lands they occupied in the countryside.

The Rise of Mussolini

"I am fascism," said Mussolini, and the success of the Italian fascist movement depended heavily on his leadership. **Benito Mussolini** (1883–1945) was the son of a socialist blacksmith and a mother who was a schoolteacher. He became a schoolteacher himself as a young man, but was restless and dissatisfied. He soon left Italy for further study in Switzerland, where he gave part of his time to his books and the rest to writing articles for socialist newspapers. Expelled from the country for fomenting strikes, he returned to Italy and became a journalist, and eventually the editor of *Avanti,* the leading socialist daily.

When war broke out in August 1914, Mussolini at first insisted that Italy should remain neutral. He had scarcely adopted this position when he began urging participation on the Allied side. After he was deprived of his position as the editor of *Avanti,* he founded a new paper, *Il Popolo d'Italia,* and dedicated its columns to arousing enthusiasm for war. As early as October 1914, Mussolini had organized groups, called *fasci*—made up of young idealists and fanatical nationalists—to help drum up support for the war. After the war, these groups formed the base of Mussolini's **fascist** movement. (The word *fascism* derives from the Latin *fasces:* an ax surrounded by a bundle of sticks that represented the authority of the Roman state. The Italian *fascio* means "group" or "band.")

In 1919, Mussolini drafted the original platform of the Fascist party, which had several surprising elements, such as universal suffrage (including for women), an eight-hour workday, and a tax on inheritances. But a new platform, adopted in 1920, abandoned all references to economic reforms. Neither platform, however, earned the fascists much political success.

What the fascists lacked in political support, they made up in aggressive determination. They gained the respect of the middle class and landowners, and intimidated many others by violently attacking militant industrial workers and peasants. They attacked socialists, often physically, and succeeded in taking over some local governments. As the national regime weakened, Mussolini's coercive politics made him look like a solution to the absence of leadership. In September 1922, he began to negotiate with other parties and the king for fascist participation in government. In the last week of October, Mussolini called for a demonstration of fascist popular support to strengthen his hand. Later mythologized as a "March on Rome" which resulted in a celebrated "seizure" of power, the demonstration brought several tens of thousands fascist militia members to the outskirts of the capital. The government attempted to implement emergency powers to counter the threat of a fascist coup, but King Victor Emmanuel III refused his permission for the use of the army against Mussolini's supporters. Instead, the king invited Mussolini to form a new government, hoping to coopt the dynamism of Mussolini's movement. Mussolini arrived in Rome by train and organized a parade of his supporters after he became prime minister. The fascist myth of the "March on Rome" held that power had been taken by force, but, in fact, Mussolini's accession to the head of the government conformed to the provisions of the Italian constitution.

The parliamentary system folded under pressure, and though Mussolini had "legally" been granted his power, he immediately began to establish a one-party dictatorship. The doctrines of Italian fascism had three components. The first was statism, in which the state was declared to incorporate every interest and every loyalty of its members. There was to be "nothing above the state, nothing outside

MUSSOLINI REVIEWS A FASCIST YOUTH PARADE. Mobilizing youth was central to fascism and Nazism; it demonstrated the vigor of these movements.

the state, nothing against the state." The second was nationalism, in which nationhood was the highest form of society, with a life and a soul of its own, transcending the individuals who composed it. The third was militarism, in which fascists believed that war ennobled man and regenerated sluggish and decadent peoples, and nations that did not expand would eventually wither and die.

Mussolini began to rebuild Italy in accordance with these principles. The first steps were to change the electoral laws so they granted his party solid parliamentary majorities and to intimidate the opposition. He then moved to close down parliamentary government and other political parties entirely. He abolished the cabinet system and all but extinguished the powers of the Parliament. He made the Fascist party an integral part of the Italian constitution. He assumed the dual position of prime minister and party leader (*duce*), and used the party's militia to eliminate his enemies through intimidation and violence. Mussolini's government also controlled the police, muzzled the press, and censored academic activity.

Meanwhile, Mussolini preached the end of class conflict and national unity as its replacement. Reorganizing the economy and labor, he took away the power of the country's labor movement. The Italian economy was placed under the management of twenty-two corporations, each responsible for a major industrial enterprise. In each corporation were representatives of trade unions, whose members were organized by the Fascist party, the employers, and the government. Together, the members of these corporations were given the task of determining the working conditions, wages, and prices. It is not surprising that the decisions of these bodies were closely supervised by the government and favored the positions of management. Indeed, the government quickly aligned with big business, creating more of a corrupt bureaucracy than a revolutionary economy.

Mussolini secured some working-class assent with state-sponsored programs, such as massive public-works projects, library building, paid vacations, and social security. In 1929, he settled Italy's sixty-year-old conflict with the Roman Catholic Church by signing a treaty that granted independence to the papal residence in Vatican City and established Roman Catholicism as the official religion of the state. The treaty also guaranteed religious education in the nation's schools and made religious marriage ceremonies mandatory.

In fact, Mussolini's regime did much to maintain the status quo. Party officers exercised some political supervision over bureaucrats but did not infiltrate the bureaucracy in significant numbers. Moreover, Mussolini remained on friendly terms with the elites who had assisted his rise to power. Whatever he might proclaim about the distinctions between fascism and capitalism, the economy of Italy remained dependent on private enterprise.

The Italian dictator boasted that fascism had pulled the country back from economic chaos, and, like other European economies, the Italian economy did improve during the late 1920s. The regime created the appearance of efficiency, and Mussolini's admirers famously claimed that he had at last "made the trains run on time." Fascism, however, did little to improve Italy's plight during the worldwide depression of the 1930s.

Like Nazism later, fascism had contradictory elements. It sought to restore traditional authority and, at the same time, mobilize all of Italian society for economic and nationalist purposes—a process that inevitably undercut older authorities. It created new authoritarian organizations and activities that comported with these goals: exercise programs to make the young fit and mobilized, youth camps, awards to mothers of large families, political rallies, and parades in small towns in the countryside. Activities like these offered people a feeling of political involvement, even as they no longer enjoyed political rights. This mobilized, yet essentially passive, citizenship was a hallmark of fascism.

WEIMAR GERMANY

On November 9, 1918—two days before the armistice ending the First World War—a massive uprising in Berlin resulted in the kaiser's abdication and the birth of a new German republic. The leader of the new government was Friedrich Ebert, a member of the Social Democratic party (SPD) in the Reichstag. The revolution spread quickly, and by the end of the month, councils of workers and soldiers controlled hundreds of German cities. The "November Revolution" was fast and far reaching, though not as revolutionary as many middle- and upper-class conservatives feared. The majority of socialists steered a cautious, democratic course; they wanted reforms but were willing to leave much of the existing imperial bureaucracy intact. Above all, they wanted a popularly elected national assembly to draft a constitution for the new republic.

Two months passed, however, before elections could be held—a period of crisis that verged on civil war. The revolutionary movement that had brought the SPD to power now threatened it. Independent socialists and a nascent Communist party wanted radical reforms, and in December 1918 and January 1919, they staged armed uprisings in the streets of Berlin. Fearful of a Bolshevik-style revolution, the Social Democratic government turned against its former allies and sent militant bands of workers and volunteers to crush the uprisings. During the conflict, the government's fighters murdered Rosa Luxemburg and Karl Liebknecht, two German communist leaders who became instant martyrs. Violence continued into 1920, creating a lasting bitterness among groups on the left.

More important, the revolutionary aftermath of the war gave rise to bands of militant counterrevolutionaries. Veterans and other young nationalists joined the so-called *Freikorps* ("free corps"); such groups developed throughout the country, drawing as many as several hundred thousand members. Former army officers who led these militias applied their war experience to fighting the Bolsheviks, Poles, and communists. The politics of the Freikorps were fiercely right wing. Anti-Marxist, anti-Semitic, and antiliberal, they openly opposed the new German republic and its parliamentary democracy. Many of the early Nazi leaders fought in the First World War and participated in Freikorps units.

Germany's new government, known as the Weimar Republic (*VY-mahr*) for the city in which its constitution was drafted, rested on a coalition of socialists, Catholic centrists, and liberal democrats—a necessary compromise because no single party won a majority of the votes in the January 1919 election. The Weimar constitution was based on the values of parliamentary liberalism and set up a framework for German democracy. Through a series of compromises, the constitution established universal suffrage (for both women and men) and a bill of rights that guaranteed not only civil liberties but also a range of social entitlements. On paper, at least, the revolutionary movement had succeeded.

Yet the Weimar government lasted just over a decade: by 1930, it was in crisis, and in 1933, it collapsed. What happened? Many of Weimar's problems were born from Germany's defeat in the First World War. Many Germans soon latched on to rumors that the army hadn't actually been defeated in battle but had been "stabbed in the back" by socialists and Jewish leaders in the German government. Army officers cultivated this story even before the war was over; though untrue, it helped salve the wounded pride of German patriots. In the next decade, those in search of a scapegoat also blamed the republican regime, which had signed the Versailles treaty. What was needed, many critics argued, was authoritative leadership to guide the nation and regain the world's respect.

In fact, contemporaries exaggerated the harshness of the Treaty of Versailles, which was much less punitive than the Treaty of Brest-Litovsk that Germany had forced on Bolshevik Russia in 1917. The Versailles Treaty demanded that Germany cede a tenth of its territory, but a great deal of this land, including the French territories of Alsace and Lorraine, had only recently become German. The so-called "war guilt clause" was not a statement of culpability for the war itself but a declaration of legal responsibility for damages caused by the German military beyond their borders. The reparations, seen as punitive by the Germans, were soon adjusted downward, though they did cause hardships for the German public.

Much of the reputation for the harshness of the Versailles Treaty came from an international crisis about reparations payments in January 1923. When the Germans fell behind on their allotted deliveries of coal that were a part of the Versailles arrangements, the French marched their army into the Ruhr valley, a key German industrial region that bordered France and the Netherlands. Germany was still reeling from wartime inflation, and the demands for reparations on top of necessary demobilization and social welfare programs

THE WEIMAR REPUBLIC'S SEXUAL RADICALS, 1927. The Weimar years were marked by a new atmosphere of cultural experimentation, especially in German cities. The traumatic experience of the First World War, which had destroyed so many families and overturned the social and political order, also made prewar social conventions about sex, marriage, and gender seem quaint and outdated. This scene, in which women are smoking and drinking in public, wearing masculine hairstyles, and casually demonstrating their affection for each other, would have been almost unimaginable in 1910. In the 1920s, however, such scenes were common enough to provoke controversy and scandal, becoming fodder for the media and providing material for best-selling novels. As similar debates over the "New Woman" of the 1920s were taking place in other European countries, Hitler and the Nazi party used such images in their campaign to discredit Weimar society as "degenerate."

HYPERINFLATION. German children use stacks of money as toys. In July 1922, the American dollar was worth 670 German marks; in November 1923, it was worth 4,210,500,000,000 marks. ■ *How might hyperinflation have affected German attitudes toward the Weimar Republic's government?*

forced the government to print money. The result was a period of bewildering hyperinflation that peaked in late 1923. A pound of potatoes that cost 9 marks in January cost 40 million marks by October. For those on fixed incomes, such as pensioners and stockholders, savings and security were wiped out. The government finally took drastic measures to stabilize the currency in 1924, but by then millions of Germans had already been financially ruined. Many blamed the Versailles treaty and the intransigence of the French government for their losses.

In 1924, Germany accepted a new schedule of reparations designed by an international committee headed by the American financier Charles G. Dawes. The Dawes Plan included loans from the United States that helped to stabilize the economy. At the same time, taking advantage of a change in government in France, the German chancellor Gustav Stresemann moved Germany toward a foreign policy of cooperation and rapprochement that lasted throughout the 1920s. The French stopped insisting on unilateral enforcement of the Versailles treaty's provisions, and a new international framework, known as the Locarno Treaties (1925), recognized the legitimacy of the French-German border.

The "spirit of Locarno" was one of optimism, but problems remained. The crisis of 1923–1924 proved that France

was unable to impose its will on Germany by itself. Furthermore, the Locarno Treaties left open the possibility of revisiting the question of Germany's eastern frontiers with Poland and Czechoslovakia. These new nations, concerned with the possibility of future aggression from Germany, were dismayed that neither France nor Britain had fully committed to the defense of their borders.

In the late 1920s, the German economy seemed to stabilize. By borrowing money under the Dawes Plan, the Weimar government was able to make its reparations payments. Furthermore, in large cities, socialist municipal governments sponsored building projects that included schools, hospitals, and low-cost worker housing. But such economic and political stability was misleading, because the economy remained dependent on large infusions of capital from the United States, and this dependence made the German economy especially vulnerable to American economic developments. When the U.S. stock market crashed in 1929, setting off the Great Depression (see below), capital flow to Germany virtually stopped.

The **Great Depression** pushed Weimar's political system to the breaking point. In 1929, there were 2 million unemployed; and in 1932, there were 6 million. In those three years, production dropped by 44 percent, artisans and small shopkeepers lost both status and income, and farmers fared even worse. Peasants staged mass demonstrations against the government's agricultural policies even before the depression hit. For white-collar and civil-service employees, the depression meant lower salaries, poor working conditions, and a constant threat of unemployment. Burdened with plummeting tax revenues, the government repeatedly cut welfare benefits, further demoralizing the electorate. The crisis created an opportunity for Weimar's opponents. Many leading industrialists and equally conservative landowners supported a return to authoritarian government. These conservative forces wielded considerable power in Germany, beyond the control of the government. So, too, did the army and the civil service, which were staffed with opponents of the republic—men who rejected the principles of parliamentary democracy and the international cooperation that Weimar represented.

HITLER AND THE NATIONAL SOCIALISTS

National Socialism in Germany emerged out of the bitterness of defeat in the First World War, but Adolf Hitler's political party did not gain mass support until after the unemployment crisis caused by the depression that began in 1929.

Adolf Hitler was born in Austria in 1889. The son of a petty customs official, Hitler dropped out of school in 1909 and went to Vienna to become an artist. But he was rejected by the academy and thus forced to eke out a dismal existence doing manual labor and painting cheap watercolors. Meanwhile, he developed the violent political prejudices that would become the guiding principles of the Nazi regime. He ardently admired Austrian politicians preaching anti-Semitism, anti-Marxism, and pan-Germanism. When war broke out in 1914, Hitler was among the jubilant crowds in the streets of Munich. He enlisted in the German army, where he claimed to have finally found meaning in life. After the war, he joined the newly formed German Workers' party, whose name changed in 1920 to the National Socialist German Workers' party (abbreviated in popular usage to Nazi). The Nazis were but one among many small, militant groups of disaffected Germans devoted to racial nationalism and the overthrow of the Weimar Republic. They refused to accept the defeat that brought the government to power and blamed it on socialists and Jews.

Ambitious and a talented orator, Hitler quickly moved up the rather short ladder of party leadership. By 1921, he was the *Führer* (leader) to his followers in Bavaria. But to the wider public, he was a "vulgar demagogue," if they noticed him at all. In November 1923, during the worst days of the inflation crisis, the Nazis made a failed attempt (the Beer Hall Putsch in Munich) at overthrowing the state government of Bavaria. Hitler spent the next seven months in prison, where he wrote his autobiography and political manifesto *Mein Kampf* (*myn KAHMPF*; "My Struggle") in 1924. Combining anti-Semitism with anticommunism, the book set out at great length the popular theory that Germany had been betrayed by its enemies and that the country needed strong leadership to regain international prominence. The failed 1923 attempt proved an eye-opening experience for Hitler: he recognized that the Nazis would have to play politics if they wanted to gain power. After being released from prison in 1924, he resumed leadership of the party. For the next five years, he consolidated his power over a growing membership of ardent supporters. Actively cultivating the image of the Nazi movement as a crusade against Marxism, capitalism, and Jews, Hitler portrayed himself as the heroic savior of the German people.

An equally important factor in Hitler's rise to power was the Nazis' ambitious and unprecedented campaign program. In the "inflation election" of 1924, the Nazis polled 6.6 percent of the vote as a protest party at the radical fringe. During the economic stabilization of the mid-1920s, their meager share dropped to below 3 percent. But during this time of seeming decline, the Nazis were building an extensive organization of party activists to help lay the foundation for the party's later electoral gains.

After 1928, political polarization between the right and the left worked to Hitler's advantage and also made it impossible for the Weimar government to put together a coalition that could support the continuation of democracy in Germany. Alienated voters, especially in rural areas, deserted the traditional political parties, and the Nazis quickly learned how to benefit from this splintering of the electorate. Having failed to win over the German working class from the left, the Nazis stepped up their efforts to attract members of the rural and urban middle classes. Guided by its chief propagandist, Joseph Goebbels, the Nazi party hammered home its critique of Weimar society: its parliamentary system, the power of the left and the labor movement, liberal moral codes, women wearing "decadent" flapper fashions, and "cosmopolitan" (Jewish or insufficiently nationalist) movies such as the 1930 Best Picture Oscar winner *All Quiet on the Western Front* (based on the novel by Erich Maria Remarque). Presenting themselves as young and dynamic, the Nazis built a national profile as an alternative to the parties of middle-class conservatives. By 1930, they were better funded and better organized than ever, winning 18.3 percent of the vote.

Who voted for the Nazis? The Nazis had high poll numbers among small property holders and the rural middle class long before the depression. Other segments of the middle class—notably pensioners, the elderly, and war widows—came to support the Nazis during the economic crisis, as they feared reduction of insurance or pension benefits and the older conservative parties failed to meet their needs. The Nazis found some of their strongest support among workers in handicrafts and small-scale manufacturing, though they failed to win votes from industrial workers. The Nazis also courted the traditionally elitist civil service.

In 1930, the Nazi party won 107 of 577 seats in the Reichstag, second only to the Social Democrats, who controlled 143. No party could gain a majority, and no governing coalition was possible without Nazi support. The Nazis also refused to join any cabinet that was not headed by Hitler. The chancellor, Heinrich Brüning of the Catholic Center party, continued to govern by emergency decrees, but his deflationary economic policies were disastrous, and the industrial production continued to crash and unemployment continued to climb. In 1932, Hitler ran for president and received 37 percent of the vote against the victorious incumbent Paul von Hindenburg, a retired general and a hero of the First World War. Hitler ran an unprecedented campaign by airplane, visiting twenty-one cities in six days. When another parliamentary election was called in July 1932, the Nazis won 37.4 percent of the vote. Though not a majority, it was a significant plurality, and the Nazis claimed that their party was able to draw support across class, geographic, and generational lines. They benefited from their position as outsiders, untainted by involvement in unpopular parliamentary coalitions. Indeed, the failure of the traditional parties was key to the success of the Nazis.

Despite its electoral success in 1932, the Nazi party did not win a majority, and Hitler was not in power. In January 1933, Hitler was appointed chancellor by President Hindenburg, who hoped to create a conservative coalition government by bringing the Nazis into line with the less radical parties. Hindenburg and others in the government, however, underestimated the Nazis' power and popularity. Now legally installed in office, Hitler immediately made the most of it. When a Dutch anarchist with links to the Communist party set fire to the Reichstag on the night of February 27, Hitler seized the opportunity to suspend civil rights "as a defensive measure against communist acts of violence." He then convinced Hindenburg to dissolve the Reichstag and to order a new election on March 5, 1933. Under Hitler's sway, the new parliament legally granted him unlimited powers for the next four years, allowing Hitler to proclaim his new government the Third Reich. (*Reich* means "empire" or "realm" in German; the First Reich was the German Empire of the Middle Ages, and the Second Reich was that of the kaisers from 1871 to 1918.)

Nazi Germany

By the fall of 1933, Germany was a one-party state. The socialist and communist left was crushed by the new regime. Almost all non-Nazi organizations had been either abolished or forced to become part of the Nazi system. Nazi party leaders took over various government departments, and party *Gauleiters* (or regional directors) assumed administrative responsibility throughout the country. While party propaganda sought to impress citizens with the regime's "monolithic efficiency," the Nazi government, in fact, was a tangled bureaucratic maze, with both agencies and individuals vying fiercely for Hitler's favor.

It is ironic that at the end of the party's first year in power, the most serious challenges to Hitler came from within the party. Hitler's paramilitary Nazi storm troopers (the SA) had been formed to maintain discipline within the party and impose order in society. In 1933, SA membership soared to 2 million, and many in the SA hailed Hitler's appointment as the beginning of a genuine Nazi revolution. But such radicalism alarmed the more

traditional conservative groups that had helped make Hitler chancellor; if Hitler was to maintain power, then, he needed to tame the SA. On the night of June 30, 1934, more than a thousand high-ranking SA officials, including several of Hitler's oldest associates, were executed in a bloody purge known as the Night of Long Knives.

The purge was accomplished by a second paramilitary organization, the *Schutzstaffel* ("bodyguard"), or SS. Headed by the fanatical Heinrich Himmler, the SS became the most dreaded arm of Nazi terror. As Himmler saw it, the mission of the SS was to fight political and racial enemies of the regime, a byproduct of which included building the system of concentration camps (the first camp opened in March 1933 at Dachau). The secret state police, known as the Gestapo, was responsible for the arrest, incarceration in camps, and murder of thousands of Germans. But it was generally understaffed and deluged with paperwork, and was never "omniscient, omnipotent, and omnipresent." In fact, most arrests were based on voluntary denunciations made by ordinary citizens against each other. It was not lost on the Gestapo leadership that these denunciations created a level of control that it could never achieve by itself.

Hitler and the Nazis enjoyed a sizable amount of popular support. Many Germans approved of Hitler's use

NAZISM AND THE RURAL MYTH. To stress the rural roots of Aryan Germany, Hitler posed in lederhosen (traditional leather pants from the German and Austrian Alps) in the 1920s. ▪ *Which social groups in Germany were explicitly excluded from this myth?*

of violence against the left, as the Nazis played on deep-seated fears of communism and spoke a language of intense national pride and unity that had broad appeal. Many Germans saw Hitler as a symbol of a strong, revitalized Germany. And propagandists fostered a Führer cult, depicting Hitler as a charismatic leader with the magnetic energy to bring people to their knees. But Hitler's appeal rested on his ability to give the German people what they wanted: jobs for workers, a productive economy for industrialists, a bulwark against communism for those who feared the wave of revolution, and, finally, to lead Germany back to national greatness and "overthrow" the Versailles treaty.

Hitler's plans for national recovery called for full-scale rearmament and economic self-sufficiency. The Nazis made massive public investments, set strict market controls to stop inflation and stabilize the currency, and sealed Germany off from the world economy. The regime launched state-financed construction projects: highways, public housing, and reforestation. Late in the decade, as the Nazis rebuilt the entire German military complex, unemployment dropped from over 6 million to under 200,000. The German economy looked better than any other in Europe, which Hitler claimed as his "economic miracle." Such improvements were significant, especially in the eyes of Germans who had lived through the continual turmoil of war, inflation, political instability, and economic crisis.

Like Mussolini, Hitler moved to abolish class conflict by stripping working-class institutions of their power. He outlawed trade unions and strikes, froze wages, and organized workers and employers into a National Labor Front. At the same time, he increased workers' welfare benefits, generally in line with other Western nations. Class distinctions were blurred somewhat by the regime's attempts to infuse a new national "spirit" into the entire society. Popular organizations cut across class lines, especially among the youth. The Hitler Youth, a club modeled on the Boy Scouts, was highly successful at teaching children the values of Hitler's Reich. The National Labor Service drafted students for a term to work on state-sponsored building and reclamation projects. Government policy encouraged women to withdraw from the labor force, both to ease unemployment and to conform to Nazi notions of a woman's proper role. One propagandist asked, "Can woman conceive of anything more beautiful than to sit with her husband in her cozy home and listen inwardly to the loom of time weaving the weft and warp of motherhood?"

NAZI RACISM

At the core of Nazi ideology lay a particularly virulent form of racism. Hitler and the Nazis drew on a revived and especially violent form of nineteenth-century Social Darwinism, according to which nations and people struggled for survival, with the superior peoples strengthening themselves in the process. By the early twentieth century, the rise of the social sciences had taken nineteenth-century prejudices and racial thinking into new terrain. Just as medical science had cured physical ills, doctors, criminologists, and social workers sought ways to cure social ills.

Across the West, scientists and intellectuals worked to purify the body politic, improve the human race, and eliminate the "unfit." Prior to 1933, many scientists in Britain, France, Germany, and the United States accepted the legitimacy of eugenic research, which they saw as a valid "racial" engineering program to improve the health and well-being of national populations. Some eugenicists recommended selective breeding of human populations and discouraged measures to reduce infant mortality, arguing that such measures would allow weak individuals to survive and pass their "inferior" hereditary material to the next generation. In western democracies these programs were used to determine racial quotas for immigration and to justify the sterilization of people—often without their knowledge—who were determined to be unfit to reproduce. In Nazi Germany, racial science and eugenics became an important part of state policy, beginning with a law for the compulsory sterilization of "innumerable inferior and hereditarily tainted" people in 1933. The Nazis later used this "social-hygienic racism" to justify the systematic murder of mentally and physically ill patients. Social policy was governed by a basic division between those who were seen to possess biological "value" and those who did not, with the aim of creating a racial utopia.

Nazi racism was based on a presumed hierarchy of all the "races" in the world. Hitler argued in *Mein Kampf* that the Slavic peoples of central and eastern Europe were fit only to be slaves of the superior German "Aryans," and he decried the tendency of racial populations in the modern world to become "mixed" and "degenerate" through migration and intermarriage. His racial theories always reserved a special place for anti-Semitism, however; his hatred of Jews was based on a long-standing European tradition that had been a part of Christian society from the Middle Ages. By the nineteenth century, traditional Christian anti-Semitism was joined by a current of nationalist anti-Jewish theory. A great many theorists of European nationalism saw the Jewish people as permanent outsiders who could only be assimilated and become citizens if they denied their Jewish identity. At the end of the nineteenth century, during the Dreyfus Affair in France (Chapter 23), French and European anti-Semites launched a barrage of propaganda

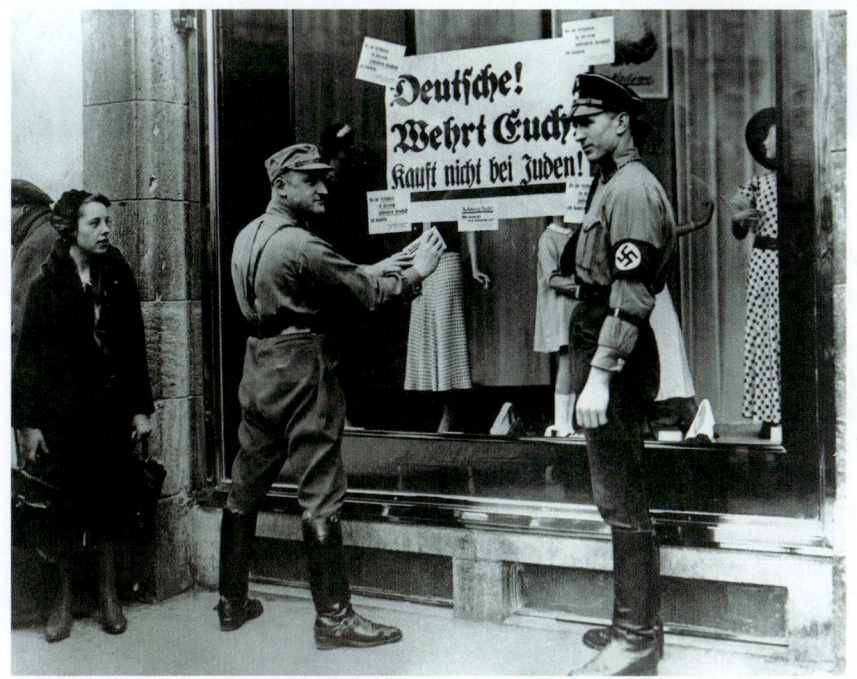

NAZI BOYCOTT OF JEWISH SHOPS IN BERLIN, 1933. Nazis stand in front of a Jewish-owned clothing store. The sign reads: "Germans! Buy nothing from the Jews!"

against Jews—scores of books, pamphlets, and magazines blamed Jews for all the troubles of modernity, from socialism to international banks and mass culture. The late nineteenth century also saw a wave of pogroms (violent assaults on Jewish communities), especially in Russia. But racial anti-Semitism drew the line between Jews and non-Jews based on erroneous biology: neither religious conversion, encouraged by traditional Christian anti-Semites, nor assimilation, counseled by more secular nationalist thinkers, would change biology.

It is important not to generalize, but anti-Semitism in these different forms was a well-established and open political force in most of the West. By attacking Jews, anti-Semites attacked modern institutions—from socialist parties and the mass press to international banking—as part of an "international Jewish conspiracy" to undermine traditional authority and nationality. Conservative party leaders told shopkeepers and workers that "Jewish capitalists" were responsible for the demise of small businesses, the rise of giant department stores, and the precarious economic swings that threatened their livelihoods. In Vienna, middle-class voters supported openly anti-Semitic Christian Democrats. In Germany, in 1893, sixteen avowed anti-Semites were elected to the Reichstag, and the Conservative party made anti-Semitism part of its official program. Hitler gave this anti-Semitism an especially murderous twist by tying it to the doctrines of war and the racism of eugenics.

To what extent was the Nazis' virulent anti-Semitism shared? Although the "Jewish Question" was clearly Hitler's primary obsession during the early 1920s, he made it a less central theme in campaign appearances as the Nazi movement entered mainstream politics, shifting the attacks instead to Marxism and the Weimar democracy. Also, anti-Semitic beliefs would not have distinguished the Nazi party from any other party on the political right; it was likely of only secondary importance to people's opinions of the Nazis. Soon after Hitler came to power, though, German Jews faced discrimination, exclusion from rights as citizens, and violence. Racial laws excluded Jews from public office as early as April 1933. The Nazis encouraged boycott of Jewish merchants, while the SA created a constant threat of random violence. In 1935, the Nuremberg Decrees deprived Jews (defined by bloodline) of their German citizenship and prohibited marriage between Jews and other Germans. Violence continued to escalate, and in November 1938, the SA attacked some 7,500 Jewish stores, burned nearly 200 synagogues, killed 91 Jews, and beat up thousands more in a campaign of terror known as ***Kristallnacht*** ("Crystal Night"; also referred to as the Night of Broken Glass). Although violence like this raised some opposition from ordinary Germans, legal persecution met only silent acquiescence. For Jewish people, Kristallnacht made it plain that there was no safe place for them in Germany, but, unfortunately, only one year remained before the outbreak of war made it impossible for them to escape.

What did national socialism and fascism have in common? Both arose during the interwar period as responses to the First World War and the Russian Revolution. Both were violently antisocialist and anticommunist, determined to "rescue" their nations from the threat of Bolshevism. Both were intensely nationalistic, believing that national solidarity came before all other allegiances and superseded all other rights. Both opposed parliamentary government and democracy as cumbersome and divisive. Both found power in mass-based authoritarian politics. Similar movements existed in all the countries of the West, but only in a few cases did they actually form regimes. Nazism, however, distinguished itself by making a racially pure state central to its vision, a vision that would lead to global struggle and mass murder.

Competing Viewpoints

Propaganda in Mussolini's Italy and Hitler's Germany

> *Fascism in Italy and Germany promised many things to many people. Mussolini's rhetoric focused on the ideas of national greatness in the aftermath of the First World War, and the need to counter imperialism of other powers when they threatened Italian interests. The Nazis blended anti-Semitism, racial nationalism, vaguely defined (and anti-Marxist) socialism, and disgust with the state of German culture and politics in their propaganda, as the document by Joseph Goebbels shows. Goebbels, one of the early members of the Nazi party, later became head of the National Ministry for Public Enlightenment and Propaganda.*

Benito Mussolini, My Rise and Fall

It was at this time, right after the spirit of exhilaration of victory, that I observed strange tendencies in the Italian political world. Evil activity was at hand. It needed to be exposed and suppressed. It was cloaked under the appearance of humanitarianism. It was planning to give a series of national rights to peoples who never had the consciousness and the dignity of nations—to peoples who had been for more than a century instruments of oppressing the Italian elements under Austria, under the instigation of the despotic empire. The sun of our victory was rising, but to be a complete victory, a victory that would carry our soldiers on the road to Vienna, it must not falter through false sentimentality. . . .

I felt that we were left without any cohesive force, any suggestive heroism, any remembrance, any political philosophy, sufficient to overcome and stop the factors of dissolution. I sensed the chills and heats of decay and destruction. . . .

I knew those who whipped up our degeneration. They were German and Austrian spies, Russian agitators, mysterious subventions. In a few months they had led the Italian people into a state of marasmus. The economic crisis existing in every corner of the world could not be expected to spare Italy. The soldiers, like myself, returning from the war, rushed to their families. Who can describe our feelings? Such an imposing phenomenon as the demobilization of millions of men took place in the dark, without noise, in an atmosphere of throwing discipline to the winds. There were, for us, the troubles of winter and the difficulties of finding new garments and adjustments for peace. . . .

Those who came to the meeting for the constitution of the Italian Fascisti of Combat used few words. They did not exhaust themselves by laying out dreams. Their aim seemed clear and straight-lined. It was to defend the victory at any price, to maintain intact the sacred memory of the dead, and the admiration not only for those who fell and for the families of those who were dead but for the mutilated, for the invalids, for all those who had fought. The prevalent note, however, was of anti-socialist character, and as a political aspiration, it was hoped a new Italy would be created that would know how to give value to the victory and to fight with all its strength against treason and corruption, against decay within and intrigue and avarice from without.

I was certain at the time that it was necessary to fix, without any possibility of equivocation, the essential brand of the new movement. For this reason I made three planks for our platform. The first was the following:

The meeting of the twenty-third of March sends its first greeting and reverent thought to the sons of Italy who died for the greatness of their country and for the freedom of the world; to the mutilated and to the invalids, to all those who fought, to the ex-prisoners who fulfilled their duty. It declares itself ready to uphold with all its energy the material and moral claims that will be put forward by the associations of those who fought.

The second declaration pledged the Fascisti of Combat to oppose themselves to the imperialism of any other countries damaging to Italy. It accepted the supreme postulates of the League of Nations regarding Italy. It affirmed the necessity to complete the stability of our frontiers between the Alps and the Adriatic with the claim of annexation Fiume and of Dalmatia.

The third declaration spoke of the elections that were announced for the near future. In this motion the Fasci di Combattimento pledged themselves to fight with all their means the candidates that were milk-and-water Italians, to whatever party they belonged.

Finally we talked of organization—the organization that would be adapted to the new movement. I did not favor any bureaucratic cut-and-dried organization. It was thought wise that in every big town the correspondent of the *Popolo d'Italia* should be the organizer of a section of the Fasci di Combattimento, with the idea that each group should become a centre of Fascist ideas, work and action.

Source: Benito Mussolini, *My Rise and Fall* (New York: 1998), pp. 54, 60–61, 71–72.

Joseph Goebbels, "Why Are We Enemies of the Jews?"

We are NATIONALISTS because we see in the NATION the only possibility for the protection and the furtherance of our existence.

The NATION is the organic bond of a people for the protection and defense of their lives. He is nationally minded who understands this IN WORD AND IN DEED. . . .

Young nationalism has its unconditional demands, BELIEF IN THE NATION is a matter of all the people, not for individuals of rank, a class, or an industrial clique. The eternal must be separated from the contemporary. The maintenance of a rotten industrial system has nothing to do with nationalism. I can love Germany and hate capitalism; not only CAN I do it, I also MUST do it. The germ of the rebirth of our people LIES ONLY IN THE DESTRUCTION OF THE SYSTEM OF PLUNDERING THE HEALTHY POWER OF THE PEOPLE.

WE ARE NATIONALISTS BECAUSE WE, AS GERMANS, LOVE GERMANY. And because we love Germany, we demand the protection of its national spirit and we battle against its destroyers.

WHY ARE WE SOCIALISTS?

We are SOCIALISTS because we see in SOCIALISM the only possibility for maintaining our racial existence and through it the reconquest of our political freedom and the rebirth of the German state. SOCIALISM has its peculiar form first of all through its comradeship in arms with the forward-driving energy of a newly awakened nationalism. Without nationalism it is nothing, a phantom, a theory, a vision of air, a book. With it, it is everything, THE FUTURE, FREEDOM, FATHERLAND! . . .

WHY DO WE OPPOSE THE JEWS?

We are ENEMIES OF THE JEWS, because we are fighters for the freedom of the German people. THE JEW IS THE CAUSE AND THE BENEFICIARY OF OUR MISERY. He has used the social difficulties of the broad masses of our people to deepen the unholy split between Right and Left among our people. He has made two halves of Germany. He is the real cause for our loss of the Great War.

The Jew has no interest in the solution of Germany's fateful problems. He CANNOT have any. FOR HE LIVES ON THE FACT THAT THERE HAS BEEN NO SOLUTION. If we would make the German people a unified community and give them freedom before the world, then the Jew can have no place among us. He has the best trumps in his hands when a people lives in inner and outer slavery. THE JEW IS RESPONSIBLE FOR OUR MISERY AND HE LIVES ON IT.

That is the reason why we, as nationalists and as socialists, oppose the Jew. he has corrupted our race, fouled our morals, undermined our customs, and broken our power.

Source: Anton Kaes, Martin Jay, and Edward Dimendberg, *The Weimar Republic Sourcebook* (Los Angeles: 1994), pp. 137–38, 142.

Questions for Analysis

1. How did Mussolini and Goebbels use metaphors of good and evil, illness and health, growth and degeneration? Do the metaphors by Goebbels suggest what the Nazis would try to do to cure the ills of Germany if they took power?

2. Mussolini and Goebbels both emphasize their nationalism, but their attitudes toward socialism are different. How do you explain this difference?

3. Where does Goebbels place anti-Semitism in his version of German nationalism? Whom does Mussolini identify as the enemies of fascism?

THE INTERWAR YEARS IN MAJOR WESTERN DEMOCRACIES

The three major western democracies—Great Britain, France, and the United States—emerged from the First World War confident in their continued claims to global influence. According to President Woodrow Wilson, they had fought the war to "make the world safe for democracy." The extension of the vote to women in the postwar years in the United States and Britain (French women would have to wait until 1945) demonstrated that this commitment to democracy was in part sincere, but there was a paradox in this expansion of citizenship rights at home. African-Americans in the United States continued to be denied basic rights by a system of racial segregation; in 1896, in *Plessy vs. Ferguson*, the Supreme Court upheld the right of individual states to provide separate facilities for blacks and whites under the doctrine of "separate but equal." Moreover, Britain, France, and the United States were imperial powers, and the principle of national self-determination or citizenship rights did not extend to the colonized peoples of the world after 1918—a fact that would lead to the development of anticolonial nationalist movements in many parts of the world, culminating ultimately in a wave of decolonization after World War II (Chapter 27).

The post–World War I treaties allowed both Britain and France to expand the size of their empires as they absorbed former German colonies in Africa and took control of a large part of the Middle East under the mandate system set up by the League of Nations (Chapter 24). In the 1920s, France claimed Syria and Lebanon, while Britain ruled over Palestine and Iraq. The United States, which had already shown interest in Central America and the Caribbean during the Spanish-American War of 1898, occupied Cuba (four times between 1898 and 1922), Haiti (1915–1934), the Dominican Republic (1916 and 1924), and Nicaragua (1912–1925 and 1926–1933). It also intervened during the same years in Panama, Honduras, and Mexico to defend strategic and commercial interests in the region, and to support authoritarian—and undemocratic—governments that cooperated with U.S. companies.

As empires, they shaped these western democracies from within as well as from without. The French used colonial troops and labor extensively during the First World War, including at least 200,000 West Africans; 120,000 Algerians; 35,000 Moroccans; and 20,000 Tunisians. In the 1920s, French industry came to depend in part on immigrant laborers; and by 1930, tens of thousands of Algerian Muslims were working in France, primarily in Paris, Marseilles, or in the mining areas in the north near the Belgian border. In Britain, the population of port cities reflected the imperial regime, as Yemenis, Somalis, Indian, and Malay sailors settled in Cardiff, Hull, Liverpool, and London. During these same years, migration to the United States from Latin America, especially Mexico, increased substantially, from an estimated 100,000 in 1900 to 1.5 million in 1930. These population movements were small compared to the large numbers of Europeans who immigrated to the United States or Australia and New Zealand in the nineteenth century, but they were the beginnings of a pattern of migration to Europe and the United States that would take on greater significance after World War II.

Domestically, the histories of Great Britain, France, and the United States ran roughly parallel during the years after the First World War. In all three countries, governments had put their trust in prewar policies and assumptions until the Great Depression forced them to make major social and economic reforms—reforms that would lay the foundations of the modern welfare state. These nations weathered the upheavals of the interwar years, but not easily.

In the 1920s, both France and Britain sought to keep the price of manufactured goods low to stimulate demand in the world markets. This policy of deflation kept businessmen happy but placed a great burden on the workers, whose wages and living standards remained low. In both countries, class conflict boiled just below the surface, as successive governments refused to raise taxes to pay for social reforms. In Britain, workers' resentment helped elect the first Labour party government in 1924, and again in 1929; and a general strike in 1926 succeeded only in increasing middle-class antipathy toward workers. In France, as the period of strikes immediately after the war subsided, it was followed by a period in which employers refused to bargain with labor unions. And when the French government passed a modified social insurance program in 1930—insuring against sickness, old age, and death—workers remained unsatisfied.

Among the democratic countries, the United States was a bastion of conservatism. Presidents Warren G. Harding, Calvin Coolidge, and Herbert Hoover held a social philosophy formulated by the barons of big businesses during the nineteenth century. And the U.S. Supreme Court used its power of judicial review to nullify progressive legislation enacted by state governments and, occasionally, by Congress.

The conservative economic and social policies of the prewar period were dealt their deathblow by the Great Depression of 1929. This worldwide depression peaked during the years 1929–1933, but its effects lasted a decade. It was a decisive crisis of the interwar period and was perhaps the formative experience for those who went through it. The depression was an important factor in the rise of Nazism, but it also forced every country to forge new economic policies to deal with the unprecedented economic turmoil.

The Origins of the Great Depression

What caused the Great Depression? Its deepest roots lay in the instability of national currencies and the interdependence of national economies. Throughout the 1920s, Europe experienced a sluggish growth rate. A major drop in world agricultural prices hurt the countries of southern and eastern Europe, where agriculture was small in scale and high in cost. Unable to make a profit on the international market, these agricultural countries in turn bought fewer manufactured goods from the more industrial sectors of northern Europe, causing a widespread drop in industrial productivity. Moreover, restrictions on free trade further crippled the economy. Although debtor nations needed open markets to sell their goods, most nations were raising high trade barriers to protect domestic manufacturers from foreign competition.

Then, in October 1929, prices on the New York Stock exchange collapsed. In the late 1920s rising stock prices led to a bubble that was exacerbated by speculators who invested borrowed money. After a peak in early September, prices began to fall, and a panic set in on October 24, leading to four days of chaotic trading in which the Dow Jones industrial average dropped 25 percent. The decline would continue until July 1932, by which time the market was down 90 percent from its highest point in 1929. The rise of the United States as an international creditor during the Great War meant that the crash had immediate and disastrous consequences in Europe. When the value of stocks dropped, banks found themselves short of capital and were forced to close, wiping out their depositors' savings. As international investors called in their debts, a series of banking houses shut their doors, among them Credit Anstalt, the biggest bank in Austria with significant interests in two-thirds of Austrian industry. Workers lost their jobs; indeed, manufacturers laid off virtually their entire workforces. In 1930, 4 million Americans were unemployed; in 1933, it was 13 million—nearly a third of the workforce. By then, per capita income in the United States had fallen 48 percent, and production had dropped 47 percent. In Germany, too, the drop was brutal. In 1929, 2 million were unemployed; in 1932, it was 6 million, and by then, production had dropped 44 percent. The stock-market collapse led to widespread bank failure and brought the economy to a virtual standstill.

The U.S. and European governments undoubtedly worsened the crisis by refusing to rescue the banks with infusions of cash—that is, acting as "lenders of last resort." They feared inflation, but the depth of the crisis led Britain to abandon the gold standard in 1931; the United States followed suit in 1933. By no longer pegging their currencies to the price of gold, both countries hoped to make money cheaper and thus more available for economic recovery programs. This action was the forerunner of a broad currency management program, which would become an important element in a general policy of economic nationalism. In another important move, Great Britain abandoned its time-honored policy of free trade in 1932, raising protective tariffs to as much as 100 percent of the cost of imported goods. But monetary policy alone could not end the hardships of ordinary families, and governments were increasingly forced to address their concerns with a wide range of social reforms.

Britain was the most cautious in its relief efforts. In 1931, a national government composed of Conservative, Liberal, and Labour party members came to power, and it was reluctant to underwrite effective programs of public assistance that would require spending beyond its income. France, however, adopted the most advanced set of policies to combat the effects of the depression. In 1936, responding to a threat from ultraconservatives to overthrow the republic, a Popular Front government under the leadership of socialist Léon Blum was formed by the Radical, Radical Socialist, and Communist parties, and lasted for two years. The Popular Front nationalized the munitions industry and reorganized the Bank of France to break the largest stockholders' monopolistic control over credit. It also decreed a forty-hour week for all urban workers and initiated a program of public works. To support the farmers, it established a wheat office to fix the price and regulate the distribution of grain. Although the Popular Front temporarily quelled the threat from the political right, conservatives were generally uncooperative and unimpressed by the attempts to aid the French working class. Both a socialist and Jewish, Blum faced fierce anti-Semitism in France. Fearing that Blum was the forerunner of a French Lenin, conservatives declared, "Better Hitler than Blum." They got their wish before the decade was out.

The most dramatic response to the depression came in the United States, for two reasons. First, the United States had clung longest to the nineteenth-century economic philosophy. Before the depression, the business classes adhered firmly to the creed of freedom of contract. Industrialists insisted on their right to form monopolies, and they used the government as a tool to frustrate the demands of both workers and consumers. Second, the depression was more severe in the United States than in European democracies. America had survived the First World War unscathed—and,

The Great Depression and Today's Economy

What parallels can we see between the history of the Great Depression in the 1930s and the situation in the world's economy today, after the financial crisis of 2008, for example? In both cases, the debate focused on whether or not financial markets can operate without significant government oversight, and what responsibilities the government has to alleviate the pain of those whose jobs or wages are cut as a result of the economic collapse. In 1930s France, laborers battle police over wage cuts (left). In 2011, in Italy, protesters demonstrate against the government's "austerity" policy, which saw reductions in pension benefits and job cuts (right).

 Watch related author interview on the Student Site

indeed, had benefited enormously—but now, its economy was ravaged even more than that of Europe. In 1933, Franklin D. Roosevelt succeeded Herbert Hoover as president and announced the New Deal, a program of reform and reconstruction to rescue the country.

The **New Deal** aimed to get the country back on its feet without destroying the capitalist system. The government would manage the economy, sponsor relief programs, and fund public-works projects to increase mass purchasing power. These policies were shaped by the theories of the British economist John Maynard Keynes, who had already proved influential during the 1919 treaty meetings at Paris. Keynes argued that capitalism could create a just and efficient society if governments played a part in its management. First, Keynes abandoned the sacred cow of balanced budgets, and without advocating continuous deficit financ-

ing, he reasoned that the government could deliberately operate in the red whenever private investments were not enough. Keynes also favored the creation of large amounts of venture capital—money for high-risk, high-reward investments—which he saw as the only socially productive form of capital. Finally, he recommended monetary control to promote prosperity and full employment.

Along with Social Security and other programs, the United States adopted a Keynesian program of "currency management," regulating the value of the dollar according to the needs of the economy. The New Deal helped individuals and the country recover, but it left the crucial problem of unemployment unsolved. In 1939, after six years of the New Deal, the United States still had more than 9 million jobless workers—a figure that exceeded the combined unemployment rate of the rest of the world. Only with the outbreak of a new world war, which required millions of soldiers and armament workers, did the United States reach the full recovery that the New Deal had failed to deliver.

SPOTLIGHT ON THE ENVIRONMENT: THE DUST BOWL AND THE ARAL SEA BASIN IN THE INTERWAR YEARS AND AFTER

During the twentieth century, parallel environmental crises of comparable scale unfolded in the southwestern United States and Soviet Central Asia. In the American Dust Bowl of the 1930s, severe drought and man-made changes to the environment resulted in vast dust storms, which affected a hundred million acres of grassland and dispersed the region's topsoil over thousands of miles. In Soviet Central Asia, the acceleration of water use during and after the collectivization of agriculture in the 1930s resulted in the disappearance of the fourth-largest lake in the world. In both cases, the delicate balance of complex ecosystems—the southern Great Plains of North America and the Aral Sea Basin that straddles present-day Kazakhstan, Uzbekistan, and their neighboring countries—was disrupted by efforts to increase the productivity of agricultural land.

The Dust Bowl unfolded in the southern Great Plains in the 1930s, and centered in Kansas, Colorado, New Mexico, Oklahoma, and Texas. During the nineteenth century, the region had first been put to use by cattle ranchers, after the resident Native American peoples had been killed or driven away and the bison herds depleted. After 1890, farmers with iron plows settled in the region. Their industriousness earned them the nickname "sodbusters," and they developed a system of row-crop agriculture that increased in profitability with the advent of mechanization. Prices for agricultural products rose during World War I, and farmers in the United States sought to bring as much wheat as possible to national and international markets. Prices fell in the 1920s, but mechanical tractors made it possible to hope for economies of scale on large farms. In the second half of the 1920s alone, farmers plowed 5.2 million acres of southern grasslands, an area larger than the state of Massachusetts. This was seen as progress, since, like industrialization itself, the expansion of commercial agriculture would end scarcity and bring the United States into an era of abundance.

But the plows that broke the ground destroyed the ability of the natural landscape to retain moisture, a problem that was exacerbated by monoculture. When a multiyear drought, accompanied by intense heat, began in 1930, the dislodged earth became vulnerable to erosion and the force of the air. The crops died in the field, and the soil dried up and blew away. For over a decade, dust storms repeatedly rolled across the United States, blowing millions of tons of earth into the atmosphere. Dust fell like snow in Chicago, Buffalo, and Boston, and settled on ships 300 miles out in the Atlantic. The worst of the storms were concentrated in the southern plains, where dust filled the mouths and eyes of people struggling to save their dying farms. The Soil Conservation Service counted 345 dust storms in the region between 1932 and 1939 that reduced visibility to less than a mile. By 1936, farm losses in the United States were at $25 million a day, exacerbating the economic effects of the depression. The rains did not return until 1941. Agriculture continues to be profitable in the region but only because of intensive fertilization, new crop breeds, and deep-well irrigation from the increasingly depleted Ogallala Aquifer. This large but finite source of underground water lies deep beneath the plains, stretching from South Dakota to Texas. Scientists estimate that once emptied, it will take 6,000 years for it to refill through rainfall.

The story of the Aral Sea is also about water and agriculture. Before the twentieth century, the Aral Sea covered 66,000 square kilometers, making it larger than Lake

THE DUST BOWL. A "Black Roller" dust storm descends on Clayton, New Mexico, in 1937. Within minutes, the city was engulfed—first by dust, and then by rain. The fine dust penetrated the interiors of houses and left the streets covered in mud.

Michigan. It was by fed two major rivers that carried rain and ice melt from the Hindu Kush mountains in the east. Large delta regions in both rivers supported fisheries that survived off many species, including the Aral sturgeon, a source of caviar. The Aral Sea itself was surrounded by a dry landscape that previously supported only a small nomadic population. Starting in the late nineteenth century, the tsarist government invested in irrigation projects in the region to encourage cotton production. When the Bolsheviks came to power after 1917, they were eager to pursue this project further, drastically enlarging the area of irrigation over the next three decades. When the nomadic population of Kazakhs in the Aral Sea region protested, Stalin persecuted them severely, and over one million Kazakhs died or fled the region during the years of collectivization. Stalin's successors, Nikita Khrushchev and Leonid Brezhnev, were equally enthusiastic about the use of irrigation to stimulate cotton production and built broad canals to bring more land into cultivation. By the end of the 1960s, more than 90 percent of the water flowing toward the Aral Sea had been diverted, causing the Aral Sea to shrink while the water that remained increased in salinity. Within twenty years, the world's fourth largest inland lake had been reduced to a toxic salt plain incapable of sustaining plant life. Its eastern basin is now known as the Aralkum Desert.

The Dust Bowl in the United States and the disappearance of the Aral Sea in central Asia demonstrated that in the modern world, human activity could result in large-scale environmental changes over a relatively short span of time. Neither the capitalist economy of the United States nor the planned socialist economy of the Soviet Union encouraged people to think about the long term when making decisions regarding the use of natural resources. Both systems emphasized the goal of increased production, even when such increases introduced instabilities in the ecological balance of the landscape. Ultimately, both systems were unable to anticipate the possibility of long-term changes in the environment until after the tipping point had been reached.

THE DISAPPEARING ARAL SEA. The Aral Sea began to shrink in 1960, after several decades during which the Soviet Union began to divert the rivers that fed it to irrigate their cotton production. The satellite images show the Aral Sea in 1989 (left) and in 2009 (right).

INTERWAR CULTURE: ARTISTS AND INTELLECTUALS

The interwar period also brought dramatic upheavals in the arts and sciences. Artists, writers, architects, and composers brought the revolutionary artistic forms of the turn of the century into the mainstream, rejecting traditional aesthetic values and experimenting with new forms of expression. Scientists and psychologists also challenged deeply held beliefs about the universe and human nature. Finally, radio, movies, and advertising created a new kind of mass culture that fed off the atmosphere of crisis in politics and the arts, and contributed to the anxieties of the age.

Interwar Intellectuals

Novelists, poets, and dramatists were disillusioned by the war. Much literature in the interwar period reflects the themes of frustration, cynicism, and disenchantment that emerged when victory from the war failed to fulfill its promises. The mood of the era is captured in the early work of the American author Ernest Hemingway, who wrote about a "lost generation" in his novel *The Sun Also Rises* (1926). The poetry of the Anglo-American T. S. Eliot explored a peculiarly modern form of despair: life as a living death, to be endured as boredom and frustration. And the German author Bertolt Brecht depicted, in plays written for a working-class audience in cabarets, the cynical corruption of elite members of society.

Other writers focused their attention on consciousness and inner life, often experimenting with new forms of prose. In *Ulysses* (1922), the Irish writer James Joyce perfected a style that became known as "stream of consciousness"; a technique also associated with French author Marcel Proust. In the same vein, the British author Virginia Woolf offered an eloquent and biting critique of Britain's elite institutions, from the universities that isolated women in separate, underfunded colleges to the suffocating decorum of middle-class families and relationships.

The depression of the 1930s fostered a second wave of more politicized literature, as a new generation felt called on to indict injustice and point the way to a better

society. In *The Grapes of Wrath* (1939), the American writer John Steinbeck depicts the plight of impoverished farmers fleeing from the Dust Bowl to California only to find the land monopolized by companies that exploited their workers. Younger British authors such as W. H. Auden, Stephen Spender, and Christopher Isherwood were communist sympathizers, who believed it was their duty as artists to support the revolution.

Interwar Artists

The innovations of the prewar avant-garde thrived during the interwar period, as the visual arts responded to the rapid transformations of twentieth-century society: new technologies, scientific discoveries, the abandonment of traditional beliefs, and the influence of non-Western cultures. Like the writers of the period, visual artists pushed the boundaries,

MARCEL DUCHAMP (1887–1968), PHOTOGRAPHED AS HIS OWN FEMININE ALTER EGO RROSE SÉLAVY, BY PHOTOGRAPHER MAN RAY (1890–1976). Duchamp's playfulness with his own self-presentation was typical of the way that he and the Surrealists undercut assumptions about the artist's identity and the creative process. The name, Rrose Sélavy, is a pun in French—Eros, c'est la vie—meaning roughly "Eros is life itself."

BAUHAUS INTERIOR DESIGN, 1926. The Bauhaus look, which rejected decorative elements and emphasized clean lines and simple materials, had a powerful influence over twentieth-century architecture and furniture design. The chairs and tables were designed by Marcel Breuer (1902–1981).

moving far beyond the conventional tastes of average men and women.

Pablo Picasso pursued his experiments in "cubist" paintings that refused to offer a single perspective and depicted objects and humans as a set of dynamic and angular broken forms. The "expressionists" argued that color and line expressed inherent psychological qualities by themselves, eliminating the need for a representational subject in paintings. A second group of expressionists rejected such experiments and claimed that their goal was "objectivity," by which they meant a candid appraisal of the state of humanity. Chief among this group was German George Grosz (*Grohz*; 1893–1959), whose cruel, satiric lines have been likened to a "razor lancing a carbuncle." His scathing cartoonlike images became the most popular portraits of the despised Weimar government.

The dadaists went further, rebelling against the very idea of aesthetic principle: principles were based on reason, and the world had proven that reason does not exist. Pulling their name at random from a dictionary, the dadaists rejected formal artistic conventions, preferring random juxtapositions of cutouts and collages, and bizarre assemblages of wood, glass, and metal. The leading dadaist artists—the Frenchman Marcel Duchamp, the German Max Ernst, and the Alsatian Jean (Hans) Arp—claimed their works were meaningless and playful, but critics saw them as expressions of the subconscious. In Germany, dadaism took on political undertones as the dadaists' anarchistic social critique challenged the very basis of national culture.

Other artists found inspiration for their work in social and political conflict. Many writers were veterans of World War I and sought to depict their experiences in realistic fiction. The French novelist Henri Barbusse published his combat story, *Under Fire*, in 1916, before the war was over; after the war, he joined the Communist Party and became an outspoken pacifist. Erich Maria Remarque tells a story about the war from the point of view of an ordinary German soldier in *All Quiet on the Western Front* (1927), which became a bestseller but was banned by the Nazis. Mexican muralists Diego Rivera and José Clemente Orozco and the Americans Thomas Hart Benton and Reginald Marsh sought to depict the social conditions of the modern world, presenting in graphic detail the lives of ordinary working people. These artists avoided the experimentalism of the dadaists and the expressionists, and aimed instead to create an intelligible art that was accessible to all.

Architects, too, rejected tradition, seeking a style that was more in harmony with the needs of modern civilization. Otto Wagner in Austria, Charles Édouard Jeanneret (known as Le Corbusier) in France, and Louis Sullivan and Frank Lloyd Wright in the United States pioneered a style known as functionalism. The functionalists believed that the appearance of a building should proclaim its use and purpose, and ornaments should be designed to reflect an age of science and machines. The German functionalist Walter Gropius established a school in 1919—the Bauhaus—as a center for the development of modern architecture. The Bauhaus design aesthetic, the so-called international style, explored the use of new materials, such as chromium, glass, steel, and concrete. The simple forms pioneered by the Bauhaus school became familiar after World War II, as the "glass boxes" that populate the skylines of the world's major cities.

Interwar Scientific Developments

One powerful influence on the artists and intellectuals of the day was neither social nor political—it was scientific. The pioneering work of the German-born physicist Albert Einstein (1879–1955) not only revolutionized the entire structure of physical science but also challenged ordinary people's most basic beliefs about the universe. Einstein began to question the very foundations of traditional physics early in the twentieth century and was quickly recognized as one of the greatest intellects of all time. By 1915, he had proposed entirely new ways of thinking about space, matter, time, and gravity.

As early as 1905, Einstein became convinced of the equivalence of mass and energy, and he worked out a formula for the conversion of one into the other: $E = mc^2$. The formula, however, had no practical application for years. Then in 1932, the Englishman Sir James Chadwick discovered the neutron, which gave scientists an ideal weapon for bombarding the atom—that is, a way to split it. In 1939, two German physicists, Otto Hahn and Fritz Strassman, successfully split atoms of uranium by bombarding them with neutrons, and discovered that the initial reaction produced a chain of reactions: each atom that was split shot off more neutrons, which split even more atoms. Scientists in Germany, Great Britain, and the United States were spurred on by governments anxious to turn these discoveries into weapons during World War II, and American scientists soon prepared an atomic bomb, the most destructive weapon ever created. So Einstein's theories paved the way for another revolutionary development in physics: the splitting of the atom. This legacy is ironic for Einstein, a man who devoted much of his life to promoting pacifism, liberalism, and social justice.

Another important contribution to physics that quickly entered popular culture was the "uncertainty principle" posited by the German physicist Werner Heisenberg in 1927. Heisenberg, who was strongly influenced by Einstein, showed that it was impossible—even in theory—to measure both the position and speed of an object at the same time; this principle was of consequence only in terms of atoms or subatomic particles. Though the public had little to no understanding of these groundbreaking scientific concepts, metaphorical invocations of relativity and the uncertainty principle fitted the ambiguities of the modern world. For many people, nothing was definite and everything was changing—and science seemed to be proving it.

Mass Culture and Its Possibilities

Cultural change extended far beyond circles of artistic and intellectual elites. The explosive rise of mass media during

***VOICE OF THE PEOPLE, VOICE OF GOD*, BY GEORGE GROSZ (1920).** Industrialization, the First World War, and political change combined to make early-twentieth-century Berlin a center of mass culture and communication. In this drawing, the radical artist and social critic George Grosz deplores the newspapers' power over public opinion. That public opinion could be manipulated was a common theme for many who wrote about early-twentieth-century democracy. ▪ *How does this cynicism about the public sphere compare with the attitudes of earlier defenders of free speech, such as John Stuart Mill?*

the interwar years transformed popular culture and the lives of ordinary people. New mass media, especially radio and films, reached audiences of unprecedented size. Political life incorporated many of these new media, setting off worries that the common people—increasingly referred to as the "masses"—could be manipulated by demagogues and propaganda. In 1918, mass politics was rapidly becoming a fact of life, which meant nearly universal suffrage (varying by country), well-organized political parties reaching out to voters, and, in general, more participation in political life. Mass politics was accompanied by the rise of mass culture. Books, newspapers, films, and fashions were produced in large numbers and in standardized formats, which were less expensive and more accessible, and appealed not only to more people but also to different kinds of people. Older forms of popular culture were often local and class specific, but mass culture, at least in principle, cut across lines of class and ethnicity, and even nationality. The term mass culture can be misleading; that is, the world of culture did not suddenly become homogeneous. No more than half the population read newspapers regularly, and not everyone listened to the radio—those who did certainly did not believe everything they heard. The pace of cultural change, however, did quicken perceptibly. And during the interwar

The Fascist Spectacle of Mass Participation

 ike other revolutionary movements, fascism in Italy and national socialism in Germany needed to project an image of popular support for their political programs. As far back as the French Revolution of 1789, representations of "the people" as political actors took on special significance in revolutionary propaganda (see *Interpreting Visual Evidence* on page 606). Both Hitler and Mussolini understood how to use such images to create the impression of an organic and seamless connection

A. Benito Mussolini visits a youth camp, where recruits to his Black Shirts were in training, 1935.

B. Image from Leni Riefenstahl's *Triumph of the Will* (1935), a film about a Nazi party rally in Nuremberg, Germany, in 1934.

years, mass culture showed that it held both democratic and authoritarian potential.

The expansion of mass culture rested on the widespread applications of existing technologies. Wireless communication, for instance, was invented before the turn of the twentieth century and saw limited use in the First World War. But the radio industry did not boom until the 1920s after major financial investments. Three out of four British families had a radio by the end of the 1930s; in Germany, the ratio was even higher. In every European country, broadcasting rights were controlled by the government, but in the United States, radio was managed by corporations. The radio broadcast soon became the national soapbox for politicians, and it played no small role in creating new kinds of political language. On the one hand, President Franklin Roosevelt's reassuring "fireside chats"

took advantage of the way radio bridged the public world of politics and the private world of the home. On the other hand, Hitler cultivated a different kind of radio personality, barking his fierce invectives on the air; he made some fifty addresses in 1933 alone. In Germany, Nazi propagandists beamed their messages into homes or blared them through loudspeakers in town squares, constant and repetitive. Broadcasting created new rituals of political life, and new means of communication and persuasion.

So did advertising. Advertising was not new, but it was newly prominent. Businesses spent vastly more on advertising than before. Hard-hitting visual images replaced older ones that simply announced products, prices, and brand names. Many observers considered advertising the most "modern" of art forms, because of its efficient communication, streamlined and standardized, producing images

C. Women of the British Union of Fascists model their uniforms.

between the party's leadership and the rank and file who made up the movement.

Representations of the people in nineteenth-century liberal revolutionary movements emphasized an activist definition of political participation, as citizens came together to constitute a national body that reflected the will of the movements. Both Italian fascism and German national socialism defined themselves in opposition to democratic or parliamentary regimes, explicitly rejecting the individualism that was the basis for liberal citizenship. In their orchestration of public celebrations for their programs, both fascists and national socialists emphasized images of obedience and subordination to the leader (image A) and to the national movement (image B). Although the pageantry of fascism and national socialism typically emphasized an aggressively masculine image of enthusiastic devotion, most fascist movements also organized special female sections within their movements. In these groups, women would clothe themselves in uniforms (image C), as did their male counterparts, and express their own allegiance to the spirit of self-sacrifice that was at the heart of such collective movements.

Questions for Analysis

1. Each of these images was carefully staged and orchestrated to project a specific message. What are the messages implied in these images? What details are important?

2. What do these images tell us about the place of the individual in a fascist society?

3. What sense of belonging do you think these images are designed to produce? What made such images so attractive to so many people?

---

that would appeal to all. It was also scientific, drawing on modern psychology: advertising agencies claimed to have a science of selling to people. In a world remade by mass politics, and at a moment when the purchasing power of the common people was beginning to rise, however slowly, the high stakes in advertising (as in much of mass culture) were apparent to many.

The most dramatic changes came to movie screens. The technology of moving pictures had arrived earlier. The 1890s were the era of nickelodeons and short action pictures, and in that period, France and Italy had strong film industries. Further popularized by news shorts during the war, the film industry boomed in the war's aftermath. When sound was added to movies in 1927, costs soared, competition intensified, and audiences grew rapidly. By the 1930s, an estimated 40 percent of British adults went to the movies once a week, a strikingly high figure, but many went more often than that. The U.S. film industry gained a competitive edge in Europe, buoyed by the size of its home market, huge investments in equipment and distribution, aggressive marketing, and Hollywood's star system of long-term contracts with well-known actors, who, in a sense, standardized the product and guaranteed a film's success.

Germany, too, was home to a particularly talented group of directors, writers, and actors, and a major production company, UFA (Universum Film AG), which ran the largest and best-equipped studios in Europe. The history of UFA paralleled that of the country: it was run by the government during the First World War, devastated by the economic crisis of the early 1920s, rescued by wealthy German nationalists in the late 1920s, and finally taken over by the Nazis. During the Weimar years, UFA produced some of the most remarkable films of the period, including *Der letzte Mann* ("The Last Man"; released as "The Last Laugh" in English), a universally acclaimed film directed by F. W. Murnau, one of the two great masters of German expressionism. Fritz Lang was the other, directing such masterpieces as the science-fiction film *Metropolis* (1926) and his most famous German film, *M* (1931). After Hitler's rise to power, the Nazis took control of UFA and placed it under the control of Joseph Goebbels and the Ministry of Propaganda. Though production continued unabated during the Third Reich, many of the industry's most talented members fled from the oppressive regime, ending the golden age of German cinema.

The public embraced the new media of radio and film, but many Europeans found the new mass culture disturbing. Some perceived the United States, which deluged Europe with cultural exports after the war, as a threat. Hollywood westerns, cheap dime novels, and jazz music—which became increasingly popular in the 1920s—introduced Europe to new ways of life. Advertising, comedies, and romances disseminated new and often disconcerting images

FRITZ LANG'S *M*. In this film, Peter Lorre, a Jewish actor, plays a child murderer who maintains that he should not be punished for his crimes because he is compelled by his urges, while other criminals break the law by choice. Lorre's speech at the end of the film was used in the Nazi propaganda film *The Eternal Jew* as proof that Jews were innate criminals who showed no remorse for their actions.

of femininity; with bobbed haircuts and short dresses, "new women" seemed assertive, flirtatious, capricious, and materialistic. The Wild West genre was popular with teenage boys, much to the dismay of their parents and teachers who saw westerns as an inappropriate, low-class form of entertainment. In Europe, the cross-class appeal of American popular culture grated against long-standing social hierarchies. Conservative critics abhorred the fact that "the parson's wife sat nearby his maid at Sunday matinees, equally rapt in the gaze of Hollywood stars." American critics expressed many of the same concerns, but the United States enjoyed more social and political stability than Europe. War and revolution had shaken Europe's economies and cultures, and, in that context, "Americanization" seemed a handy shorthand for economic as well as cultural change.

Authoritarian governments, in particular, decried these developments as decadent threats to national culture. Fascist, communist, and Nazi governments alike tried to control not only popular culture but also high culture and modernism, which were typically out of line with the designs of the dictators. In the early years of the Soviet Union, when more experimentation was permitted in the cultural realm, Russian filmmakers had been enormously innovative. Sergei Eisenstein (1898–1948) is often credited with developing the *montage*, a technique for creating visual narration in film through effective editing and quick cuts from different perspectives. His films from the 1920s, including *Strike* (1925), *Battleship Potemkin* (1925), and *October* (1928), told stories of the Russian Revolution and were hugely influential, revealing new possibilities for the medium with their dramatic use of camera angles and startling juxtapositions of images. Stalin, however, preferred a more conservative socialist realism to the new Soviet avant-garde, and so Eisenstein was forced to make more conventional films in the 1930s.

Mussolini had a penchant for classical kitsch, though he was far more accepting of modern art than Hitler, who despised its supposed decadence. Nazism had its own cultural aesthetic, which promoted "Aryan" art and architecture and rejected the modern, international style that the Nazis associated with the "international Jewish conspiracy." Modernism, functionalism, and atonality were banned; thus the hallmarks of Weimar Germany's cultural preeminence were replaced by a state-sponsored revival of an alleged mystical and heroic past. Walter Gropius's acclaimed experiments in modernist architecture, for example, stood as monuments to everything the Nazis hated. The Bauhaus school was closed in 1933, and Hitler hired Albert Speer as his personal architect, commissioning him to design grandiose neoclassical buildings, including an extravagant plan to rebuild the entire city of Berlin.

Analyzing Primary Sources

Cinema: Fritz Lang on the Future of the Feature Film in Germany (1926)

Fritz Lang (1890–1976) came from Austria to Berlin after the First World War, and became one of the German Weimar Republic's most brilliant movie directors, best known for Metropolis *(1926) and* M *(1931). In this essay, Lang reflects on the technological, artistic, and human potential of film. Like many European filmmakers, he was fascinated with American movies. In 1932, Joseph Goebbels, dazzled by Lang's work, asked him to work on movies for the Nazis. Soon after, Lang left Germany for Paris, then traveled to the United States, where he continued to make films in Hollywood.*

here has perhaps never before been a time so determined as ours in its search for new forms of expression. Fundamental revolutions in painting, sculpture, architecture, and music speak eloquently of the fact that people of today are seeking and finding their own means of lending artistic form to their sentiments. . . .

The speed with which film has developed in the last five years makes all predictions about it appear dangerous, for it will probably exceed each one by leaps and bounds. Film knows no rest. What was invented yesterday is already obsolete today. This uninterrupted drive for new modes of expression, this intellectual experimentation, along with the joy Germans characteristically take in overexertion, appear to me to fortify my contention that film as art will first find its form in Germany. . . .

Germany has never had, and never will have, the gigantic human and financial reserves of the American film industry at its disposal. To its good fortune. For that is exactly what forces us to compensate a purely material imbalance through an intellectual superiority. . . .

The first important gift for which we have film to thank was in a certain sense *the rediscovery of the human face*. Film has revealed to us the human face with unexampled clarity in its tragic as well as grotesque, threatening as well as blessed expression.

The second gift is that of visual empathy: in the purest sense the expressionistic representation of thought processes. No longer will we take part purely externally in the workings of the soul of the characters in film. We will no longer limit ourselves to seeing the effects of feelings, but will experience them in our own souls, from the instant of their inception on, from the first flash of a thought through to the logical last conclusion of the idea. . . .

The internationalism of filmic language will become the strongest instrument available for the mutual understanding of peoples, who otherwise have such difficulty understanding each other in all too many languages. To bestow upon film the double gift of ideas and soul is the task that lies before us. . . .

Source: Anton Kaes, Martin Jay, and Edward Dimendberg, *The Weimar Republic Sourcebook* (Los Angeles: 1994), pp. 622–23.

Questions for Analysis

1. Why does Lang suggest that his own time is in search of "new forms of expression"? Have artists always searched for new forms or might this be a specifically twentieth-century phenomenon?

2. What did Lang mean by calling the "rediscovery of the human face" and "visual empathy" gifts of film? Do television, video, and electronic media have comparable effects on how we see the world and other beings in it?

3. How does Lang see the technological, artistic, and human potential of film?

The Nazis, like other authoritarian governments, used mass media as an efficient means of indoctrination and control. Movies became part of the Nazis' pioneering use of "spectacular politics": media campaigns, mass rallies, parades, and ceremonies were all designed to display the strength and glory of the Reich as well as to impress and intimidate spectators. In 1934, Hitler commissioned filmmaker Leni Riefenstahl to record a political rally staged by herself and Albert Speer in Nuremberg. The film, *Triumph of the Will*, was a visual hymn to the Nordic race and the Nazi regime. Everything in it was on a grand scale—masses of bodies stood in parade formation, and flags rose and fell in unison—inviting viewers to surrender to the power of the stately ritual and symbolism. The comedian Charlie Chaplin riposted this film in his celebrated lampoon *The Great Dictator* (1940), an enormously successful parody of Nazi pomposities.

In regard to culture, the Nazis were forced to strike a balance between party propaganda and popular entertainment. The Nazis tried to eliminate the influences of American popular culture, which they had decried as an example of biological and cultural degeneracy even before 1933. Critics, for instance, associated American dances and jazz—both increasingly popular in German cities—with what the Nazis deemed "racially inferior" blacks and Jews. The regime, however, allowed many cultural imports, including Hollywood films, to continue while consciously cultivating German alternatives to American cinema, music, fashion, and even dances. Joseph Goebbels, the minister of propaganda who controlled most film production, placed a high value on economic viability. During the Third Reich, the German film industry turned out comedies, escapist fantasies, and sentimental romances; developed its own star system; and tried to keep audiences happy, while becoming a major competitor internationally. For domestic consumption, the industry also produced vicious anti-Semitic films, such as *The Eternal Jew* (1940) and *Jew Süss* (1940), a fictional tale of a Jewish moneylender who brings the city of Württemberg to ruin in the eighteenth century. In the final scene of the film, the town expels the entire Jewish community from its midst, asking that "posterity honor this law." Goebbels reported that the entire Reich cabinet had viewed the film and considered it "an incredible success."

After You Read
This Chapter

 Go to **INQUIZITIVE** to see what you've learned—and learn what you've missed—with personalized feedback along the way.

REVIEWING THE OBJECTIVES

- After 1917, the Bolsheviks in Russia debated how fast they should move to reorganize society along the lines demanded by their revolutionary ideology. What circumstances determined the outcome of this debate? What were the consequences of Stalin's revolution from above in the 1930s?

- Mussolini's Fascist party offered an alternative to Italian voters who were disappointed with their government in the aftermath of the First World War. What was fascism? How did Mussolini come to power?

- The Weimar Republic failed in its attempt to establish a stable democracy in Germany, while other democracies in France, Britain, and the United States underwent severe strain. What challenges did democratic regimes face during the interwar period?

- Hitler came to power legally in 1933 through the German electoral system. What did he stand for? Why did so many Germans support his cause?

- Artists, writers, and other intellectuals of the interwar period could not help but reflect the atmosphere of social and political crisis in their work. How did artists and writers react to the crisis of the interwar period?

CONCLUSION

The strains of the First World War created a world that few recognized—transformed by revolution, mass mobilization, and loss. In retrospect, it is hard not to see the period that followed as a succession of failures: capitalism foundered in the Great Depression, democracies collapsed in the face of authoritarianism, and the Treaty of Versailles proved hollow. Stalin's Soviet Union paid a terrible price for the creation of a modern industrial economy, with years of famine, political repression, and state terror. Hitler's Germany and Mussolini's Italy offered a vision of the future that held no comfort for those committed to basic human freedoms and equality under the law. We can better understand the experiences and outlooks of ordinary people if we do not treat the failures of the interwar period as inevitable. By the late 1920s, many were cautiously optimistic that the Great War's legacy could be overcome and that problems were being solved. The Great Depression, however, wrecked these hopes, bringing economic chaos and political paralysis. Paralysis and chaos, in turn, created new audiences for political leaders offering authoritarian solutions, attracting more voters to their political parties. Finally, economic troubles and political turmoil made contending with rising international tensions, to which we now turn, vastly more difficult. By the 1930s, even cautious optimism about international relations had given way to apprehension and dread.

PEOPLE, IDEAS, AND EVENTS IN CONTEXT

- What was the difference between the Bolshevik policies of **WAR COMMUNISM** and the **NEW ECONOMIC POLICY (NEP)**?

- What were **JOSEPH STALIN**'s goals in implementing his catastrophic plan for **COLLECTIVIZATION** of agriculture? What did he hope to accomplish with his purging of an entire generation of Bolshevik leaders, along with millions of other Soviet citizens, in the **GREAT TERROR**?

- What was the basis of **BENITO MUSSOLINI**'s rejection of liberal democracy? What kinds of changes followed in Italian society after the adoption of **FASCISM** as the official state ideology?

- How important was **ANTI-SEMITISM** to **ADOLF HITLER**'s political career? What do events such as **KRISTALLNACHT** tell us about the depth of German anti-Semitism?

- What effects did the **GREAT DEPRESSION** have on the European economy? How did this economic crisis affect the political developments of the 1930s?

- How did the **NEW DEAL** attempt to manage the economic crisis in the United States?

THINKING ABOUT CONNECTIONS

- What did Soviet communism, German national socialism, and Italian fascism have in common during the years 1919–1939? What made them different from each other?

- How much of the crisis of the interwar period can be attributed to the effects of the First World War or the economic upheaval of the Great Depression? How might one understand the ideological conflicts of these years as the result of a much longer history?

Before
You
Read
This
Chapter

The Second World War

CORE OBJECTIVES

- **IDENTIFY** the broader political and economic causes of the Second World War.

- **EXPLAIN** the reasons for the British and French policy of "appeasement" when faced with Hitler's violations of international law.

- **UNDERSTAND** the consequences of German conquest and occupation on European nations and their populations, and the challenges met by those who chose to resist.

- **DESCRIBE** how the Holocaust became possible after Germany's conquest of territory in eastern Europe during the invasion of the Soviet Union.

- **UNDERSTAND** the military operations that led to the defeat of the Nazi regime and their allies in Europe.

- **EXPLAIN** the main areas of conflict in Asia and the Pacific, and the circumstances that led to the Japanese surrender in 1945.

I n 1939, Adolf Hitler wanted war. By the spring of that year, he had already revealed to the world the weakness of France and Britain, which had stood by while he dismantled Czechoslovakia, a democratic nation created at the end of World War I. He turned his eyes next to Poland, confident that Britain and France could do little to prevent him from fulfilling his pledge to unleash the full power of a rearmed Germany to conquer territories for the German people in the east. Before he could invade Poland, however, he needed to come to an understanding with another long-standing enemy: the Soviet Union of Joseph Stalin. Since 1934, Stalin had participated in a broad-based antifascist coalition in Europe, the Popular Front, an alliance that had brought the Soviets to side with the "bourgeois democracies" that were their sworn enemies. The Popular Front also led the Soviets to support the Republican side in the Spanish Civil War; the Nationalists were backed by Hitler's Germany and Mussolini's Italian fascists. Hitler's propaganda campaign against the Soviets was relentless. He portrayed the Soviet regime as a cabal run by Jewish communists, and constantly referred to Stalin's commissar for foreign affairs, Maxim Litvinov, whose brother was a rabbi, as "Finkelstein." Given this history, what possible understanding could Hitler hope to achieve with Stalin?

By 1939, Stalin had been forced to recalculate his alliances in Europe. The Republicans' loss in the Spanish Civil War and the failure of France and Britain to uphold their obligations to preserve the international order guaranteed by the Versailles peace treaty led the Soviet leader to believe that his regime had no choice but to come to an agreement with Hitler, in an attempt to gain time and preserve the Soviet Union from an immediate war. His hope was that the other European powers—France, Britain, Italy, and Germany—would weaken themselves in a general war, thus benefiting the Soviet Union. To show his willingness to talk, he fired Litvinov on May 3 and replaced him with his closest adviser, Vyacheslav Molotov (1890–1986), an ethnic Russian. In August, Hitler responded by sending his own foreign minister, Joachim von Ribbentrop (1893–1946), to Moscow to meet with Stalin. When the German envoy arrived, the Moscow airport was decorated with swastikas. The two sides cynically agreed to carve up Poland between them and announced the agreement on August 23, 1939. The world was shocked to discover that these two powers, sworn ideological enemies, had made common cause to destroy Poland. On September 1, 1939, Hitler invaded Poland. Stalin, looking to what was to become a global conflict, had already attacked Japanese forces along the Mongolian border in Central Asia on August 20. The Second World War had begun.

The Second World War was a conflict among nations, whole populations, and fiercely opposing ideals. Adolf Hitler, and his supporters in Germany and abroad, cast the conflict as a racial war against the twin enemies of national socialism: the democracies in western Europe and the United States on the one hand, and the communist order of the Soviet Union on the other. Hitler's opponents in the West and the East believed just as fervently that they were defending a way of life and a vision of justice that was bigger than the narrow definitions of national interest.

Belief that the world was now characterized by ideologies and worldviews that were in mortal combat with one another meant that the scale of the killing overtook even that of the First World War. In 1914, military firepower outmatched mobility, resulting in four years of static, mud-soaked slaughter. In 1939, firepower and mobility were joined on a massive scale, with terrifying results. On the battlefield, the tactics of high-speed armored warfare, aircraft carriers sinking ships far below the horizon, and submarines deployed in vast numbers to dominate shipping lanes changed the scope and the pace of combat. This was not a war of trenches and barbed wire but a war of motion,

dramatic conquests, and terrible destructive power. The devastation of 1914–1918 paled in comparison to this new, global conflict.

The other great change involved targets, not tactics. Much of the unprecedented killing power now available was aimed directly at civilians. Cities were laid waste by artillery and aerial bombing, whole regions were put to the torch, and towns and villages were systematically cordoned off and leveled. Whole populations were targeted as well, in ways that continue to appall. The Nazi regime's systematic murder of gypsies, homosexuals, and other "deviants," along with the effort to exterminate the Jewish people completely, made the Second World War a horrifyingly unique event. So did the United States' use of a weapon whose existence would dominate politics and society for the next fifty years: the atomic bomb.

The naive enthusiasm that had marked the outbreak of the Great War was absent from the start, as terrible memories of the first conflict still lingered. Yet those who fought against the Axis powers (and many who fought for them) found that their determination to fight and win grew as the war went on. Unlike the seemingly meaningless killing of the Great War, the Second World War was cast as a war of absolutes, of good versus evil, of national and global survival. Nevertheless, the scale of destruction brought with it a profound weariness. It also provoked deep-seated questions about the value of Western "civilization," and the terms on which it and the rest of the world can live peaceably in the future.

THE CAUSES OF THE WAR: UNSETTLED QUARRELS, ECONOMIC FALLOUT, AND NATIONALISM

The obvious and immediate cause of the outbreak of the Second World War in Europe in 1939 was the aggressively expansionist policy of Hitler's Germany. Beyond these immediate circumstances, historians have isolated four long-term causes, which set the stage for the confrontation between 1939 and 1945: the punishing terms of the Versailles peace treaty, the failure to create international guarantees for peace and security after 1918, the successive economic crises of the interwar years, and the violent forms of nationalism that emerged in Europe during the 1930s.

The Versailles treaty of 1919–1920 created five new nation-states out of the defeated German and Austrian Empires: Austria, Czechoslovakia, Poland, Hungary, and Yugoslavia. And from the former Russian Empire's lands along the Baltic Sea, the treaty recognized four more: Finland, Latvia, Lithuania, and Estonia. President Woodrow Wilson's defense of the principle of national self-determination was welcomed by many people in this region as a recognition of their long-standing claims for autonomy and independence from empires that they viewed as foreign powers. At the same time, however, the borders of the new states created by the treaty largely reflected the outcome of armed conflict during the First World War and the Russian Civil War. They crossed ethnic boundaries, created new minorities without protecting them, and frustrated many of the expectations they had raised. Most importantly, these borders depended on the willingness of other powers—especially France and Britain—to help defend them. Ultimately, these boundaries would be redrawn by force in the 1930s, after Hitler had rearmed Germany.

The Allied powers kept up the naval blockade against Germany after the fighting ended. This forced the new German government to accept the harsh terms that deprived Germany of its political power in Europe, and that also saddled the German economy with a bill for the conflict in a "war guilt" clause. The blockade and the enormous reparations bill created grievances that many angry, humiliated Germans considered legitimate.

A second long-term cause of the Second World War was the failure to create lasting, binding standards for peace and security. Diplomats spent the ten years after Versailles trying to establish such standards. Some put their faith in the legal and moral authority of the League of Nations, and others saw disarmament as the most promising means of guaranteeing peace. In 1925, the Locarno Accords attempted to secure the frontiers on the Rhine fixed at Versailles in order to reassure the French against any resurgence of German expansionism. In 1928, the Kellogg-Briand Pact attempted to make war an international crime. But none of these pacts carried any real weight, and they revealed the unwillingness on the part of France and Britain to actively defend the borders of central Europe's new nation-states. Had the League of Nations been better organized, it might have relieved some of the tensions or at least prevented clashes between nations. But the League was never a league of all nations: essential members were absent, Germany and the Soviet Union were excluded for most of the interwar period, and the United States never joined.

Economic conditions were a third important cause of the renewed conflict. The huge reparations imposed on the Germans and France's occupation of much of Germany's industrial heartland slowed Germany's recovery. German and French stubbornness about the pace of repayments combined disastrously to bring on the German inflation of the early 1920s. The spiraling inflation made German money nearly worthless, damaging the stability and credibility of Germany's young republic almost beyond repair (Chapter 25).

The depression of the 1930s contributed to the coming of the war in several ways, one of which was that it intensified economic nationalism. Baffled by problems of unemployment and business stagnation, governments imposed high tariffs in an effort to preserve the home market for their own producers. The collapse of investment and soaring domestic unemployment brought the Nazis to power in Germany, exacerbated political battles between left and right in France, and caused the United States to withdraw from world affairs. Britain turned to its empire, raising tariffs for the first time and guarding its financial investments jealously.

Despite the misgivings of many in the governments of Britain and France, Germany was allowed to ignore the terms of the peace treaties and rearm. Large-scale armaments expansion first began in Germany in 1935, which reduced unemployment and eased the effects of the depression. Other nations followed the German example, not only to boost their economies but in response to the growing Nazi military power.

GIANT PORTRAIT OF MUSSOLINI IN ETHIOPIA, 1935. Central to Mussolini's popularity in Italy was his ability to connect a vision of his personal leadership with a militant and expansionist nationalism. This portrait stood over an Italian military camp in Ethiopia in November 1935, during Italy's invasion of this East African nation.

The Causes of the War: Unsettled Quarrels, Economic Fallout, and Nationalism |

Imperial success also served as consolation when economic methods failed. As the depression dragged on in fascist Italy, Mussolini tried to distract his public with conquests overseas, culminating in the invasion of Ethiopia in 1935. Hitler, too, argued that Germany's dynamically superior "race" needed "room for living" (*Lebensraum*) in the east. The common expansionist policies of Italy and Germany gave them an interest in challenging the international order set up by the Versailles treaty, leading to a separate treaty between the two fascist nations in 1936, known as the "Rome-Berlin Axis." In the Pacific, meanwhile, the effects of the depression encouraged Japanese imperialism. Japanese leaders' perception of the political and cultural inferiority of the Chinese led Japan to invade China in the name of establishing economic control over East Asia. They began in 1931 with the invasion of Manchuria, then moved to create a "Greater Pacific Co-Prosperity Sphere," which involved seizing other territories as Japanese colonies. The common imperial goals of Germany, Italy, and Japan culminated in the enlargement of the Axis, which formally became a military alliance among the three nations in 1939.

The decisive factor in the crises of the 1930s and the trigger for another world war lay in a blend of violent nationalism and modern ideologies that glorified the nation and national destiny. This blend, particularly in the forms of fascism and militarism, was recognized as a central motivation for the formation of the Berlin-Rome-Tokyo Axis, but this toxic blend of nationalism and militarism appeared in other countries as well. In Spain, ultranationalist forces tried to overthrow the Spanish Republic, setting off the Spanish Civil War (discussed on pages 897–899). In Hungary, the monarchy established in 1920 came under the influence of radical right-wing nationalist politicians in the 1930s, which openly pursued anti-Semitic policies and cultivated close relations with Hitler and Mussolini. The Kingdom of Yugoslavia became a dictatorship in 1929. And the unstable Romanian government was pressured by an ultranationalist and anti-Semitic organization known as the Iron Guard after 1927. Meanwhile, Poland's interwar experiment in democracy also took an authoritarian turn in 1926, when Joszef Pilsudski, the hero of the Polish-Soviet War of 1920 and a former head of state, forced out the democratically elected president in a coup. Pilsudski refrained from establishing an overt dictatorship and kept up the cover of democratic institutions, but his regime maintained its majority through strong-arm tactics that prevented opposition groups from challenging his authority. An exception to this sobering trend toward authoritarianism was Czechoslovakia, which boasted no ethnic majority. The Czechs practiced an enlightened policy of minority self-government and the government was remarkably stable, but still, questions of nationality remained a potential source of friction. Those questions became a key factor as international tensions mounted in the late 1930s.

THE 1930s: CHALLENGES TO THE PEACE AND APPEASEMENT

The 1930s brought the tensions and failures caused by the treaties of 1919–1920 to a head, creating a global crisis. Fascist and nationalist governments flouted the League of Nations by launching new conquests and efforts at national expansion. Each new conflict seemed to warn of another much wider war to come unless it could somehow be averted. But ordinary people—particularly in Britain, France, and the United States—were divided; some argued that the actions of the aggressors had to be met with force, while others hoped to avoid premature or unnecessary conflict. Their governments, meanwhile, tried to negotiate with the fascists at several points in the hopes that they could maintain the peace through "appeasement."

Appeasement was grounded in three deeply held assumptions. The first, which was shared by many people, was that provoking another war was unthinkable. The 1914–1918 slaughter and its aftermath left many in the West embracing pacifism, and the democratically elected officials in France and Britain believed that a more assertive resistance to Hitler's provocations might result in diminished support for their governments. Second, many in Britain and the United States argued that Germany had been mistreated by the Versailles treaty and harbored legitimate grievances that should be acknowledged and resolved. Finally, many appeasers were staunch anticommunists. They believed that the fascist states in Germany and Italy were an essential bulwark against the advance of Soviet communism, and that division among the major European states only played into the hands of the USSR. One group of appeasers believed that the Soviets posed the greater threat and that accommodating Hitler could create a common interest against a common enemy. Another faction of appeasers believed that Nazi Germany presented the true threat to European stability but that appeasement was the only option until Britain and France finished rearming, at which point they hoped their greater military power would deter Hitler or Mussolini from risking a general European war. It took most of the 1930s for the debate among appeasers to come to a head.

The 1930s brought three crucial challenges to the international order: crises in China, Ethiopia, and Spain. In China, the Japanese invasion of Manchuria in 1931 turned into an invasion of the whole country. Chinese forces were routed before the Japanese advance, and the Japanese deliberately targeted civilians to break their will to fight. In 1937, the Japanese laid siege to the strategic city of Nanjing. Their orders on taking the city were simple: "kill all, burn all, destroy all." More than 200,000 Chinese citizens were slaughtered in what came to be known as the "Rape of Nanjing." The League of Nations voiced shock and disapproval but did nothing. In 1935, Mussolini began his efforts to build an Italian empire by returning to Ethiopia to avenge the defeat of 1896. The Ethiopians fought bravely but hopelessly, because this time, the Italians came with tanks, bombers, and poison gas. This imperial massacre also aroused world denunciation.

The League of Nations condemned Japan for invading Manchuria and attempted to impose sanctions on Italy but, for two reasons, no enforcement followed. The first was the fear of communism by Britain and France, and their hope that Italy and Japan would act as counterweights to the Soviets. The second was practical: enforcing sanctions would involve challenging Japan's powerful fleet or

Mussolini's battleships, and both Britain and France were unwilling, and dangerously close to unable, to use their navies to those ends.

The Spanish Civil War

For Western nations, the third challenge came closer to home: in 1936, civil war broke out in Spain, as a series of weak Republican governments committed to large-scale social reforms could not overcome the conservative opposition and the political polarization. Right-wing military officers under General Francisco Franco (who ruled after the civil war in 1939 until his death in 1975) attempted to overthrow the Republic and seize power. Although Hitler and Mussolini had signed a pact of non-intervention with the other Western powers, both leaders

THE SPANISH CIVIL WAR. ▪ *Why did thousands of foreign fighters join the war?* ▪ *How did the strategies and weapons used in the war anticipate those used in the Second World War?* ▪ *What were the consequences of Franco's victory?*

ANTIFASCIST PROPAGANDA, SPANISH CIVIL WAR. This poster, produced by a left-wing labor organization affiliated with the international anarchist movement, shows a worker delivering a killing blow to a fascist snake.

GUERNICA, BY PABLO PICASSO (1937). *Guernica*, one of Picasso's most influential works, was painted as a mural for the Spanish republican government during its fight for survival in the Spanish Civil War; the Basque town of Guernica had been bombed by German fighters just a few months earlier, in April 1937. Near the center, a horse writhes in agony; to the left a distraught woman holds her dead child. ▪ *Compare this mural with the antifascist propaganda poster on the left. What is different about the way the two images deliver their political messages?* ▪ *Does Picasso's rejection of realism diminish the power of his political message?* ▪ *Does the antifascist poster seek any outcome other than the annihilation of the enemy?*

sent troops and equipment to assist the nationalist rebels. The Soviet Union then countered with aid to communist troops serving under the banner of the Spanish Republic. Thousands of volunteers from all over Europe and North America who saw the war as a test of Europe's determination to resist fascism and military dictatorship also took up arms as private soldiers for the Republican government, including many working-class socialists and writers such as George Orwell of Britain and Ernest Hemingway of the United States.

Democratic governments were much more hesitant, ultimately remaining neutral. For the British, Franco was useful as an anticommunist, just like Mussolini and the Japanese. But the French prime minister Léon Blum, a committed antifascist, stood at the head of a Popular Front government—an alliance of socialists, communists, and republicans—which had been elected on a program of social reform and opposition to Hitler's fascism in France and abroad. Blum, however, feared that intervening in Spain would further polarize his country, bring down his government, and make it impossible to follow through on any commitment to the conflict. And in Spain, despite heroic fighting, the Republican camp degenerated into a hornet's nest of competing factions among republican, socialist, communist, and anarchist.

The Spanish Civil War was brutal, resulting in more than 500,000 deaths. Both the German and the Soviet "advisers" saw it as a "dress rehearsal" for a later war between the two powers, and each deployed their newest weapons and practiced their skills in destroying civilian targets from the air. In April 1937, a raid by German dive bombers utterly destroyed the town of Guernica in northern Spain in an effort to cut off Republican supply lines and terrorize civilians. It shocked the public and was commemorated by Pablo Picasso in one of the most famous paintings of the twentieth century. The Republican loyalists responded with a punishing violence of their own, focusing especially on the Catholic Church, which they identified as a supporter of General Franco's nationalist movement. Attacks on priests and monasteries were frequent, and tens of thousands of people were executed behind the front lines.

The Spanish Civil War lasted three years, ending in a complete victory for Franco in 1939. In the aftermath, Britain and France were reluctant to admit Spanish Republicans as refugees, even though Republicans faced recriminations and revenge killings from Franco's regime and its supporters; Franco sent a million of his Republican enemies to prison or concentration camps.

Hitler drew two lessons from Spain. The first was that if Britain, France, and the Soviet Union ever tried to contain fascism, they would have a hard time coordinating their efforts. The second was that Britain and France were deeply averse to fighting another European war, which meant that the Nazis could use every means short of war to achieve their goals.

German Rearmament and the Politics of Appeasement

Hitler took advantage of this combination of international tolerance and war weariness to advance his ambitions. In 1933, he removed Germany from the League of Nations, to which it had finally been admitted in 1926. In 1935, he defied the disarmament provisions of the Treaty of Versailles and revived conscription and universal military training. In 1936, Germany reoccupied the Rhineland, along the border with France, a risky move that chanced a war with the much more powerful French army. But France and Britain did not mount a military response. In retrospect, this was an important turning point, where the balance of power tipped in Germany's favor. While the Rhineland remained demilitarized and German industry in the Ruhr valley was unprotected, France held the upper hand, but after 1936, it no longer did so.

In March 1938, Hitler annexed Austria, reaffirming his intention to bring all Germans into his Reich. Once more, no official reaction came from the West. The Nazis' next target was the Sudetenland in Czechoslovakia, a region with a large ethnic German population. With Austria now a part of Germany, Czechoslovakia was almost entirely surrounded by its hostile neighbor. Hitler declared that the Sudetenland was a natural part of the Reich and that he intended to occupy it.

Hitler's generals were wary of this gamble, because Czechoslovakia had a strong, well-equipped army and a line of fortifications along the border. Some in the French government argued in favor of coming to the aid of the Czechs, but Poland and Hungary actively

supported Hitler's claims against Czechoslovakia, hoping to gain from an eventual partition or at least to strengthen their positions before Hitler turned his attention on them. In the end, Hitler pushed his claim on the Sudetenland, and the British prime minister Neville Chamberlain (1937–1940) obliged him. Chamberlain took charge of international talks about Czechoslovakia and agreed to Hitler's terms. His logic was that this dispute was about the balance of power in Europe, so if Hitler were allowed to unify all Germans in one state, then German ambitions would be satisfied. Chamberlain also believed that his country could not commit itself to a sustained war, and so defending eastern European boundaries against Germany ranked low on Great Britain's list of priorities, at least in comparison to ensuring free trade in western Europe and protecting the strategic centers of the British Empire.

On September 29, 1938, Hitler met with Chamberlain, Premier Édouard Daladier (1938–1940) of France, and Mussolini in the four-power **Munich Conference**. The result was another capitulation by France and Britain. The four negotiators bargained away a major slice of Czechoslovakia while Czech representatives were left to await their fate outside the conference room. Chamberlain returned to London, proclaiming "peace in our time," but Hitler soon proved that boast hollow. In March 1939, Germany invaded

GERMAN SOLDIERS ENTER COLOGNE IN THE RHINELAND, 1936. Hitler's reoccupation of the Rhineland—an area bordering France, Belgium, and the Netherlands—was a direct violation of the Treaty of Versailles, but it was difficult for the French and British governments to respond effectively, because voters in these nations were reluctant to go to war over Hitler's decision to move troops into what was, after all, German territory.

Legend

- Germany
- German advances
  - Reoccupied Rhineland, March 1936
  - Annexed Austria, March 1938
  - Annexed Sudetenland, October 1938
  - Annexed Bohemia and Moravia, March 1939
  - Annexed Memel, March 1939
- Italy
  - Annexed Albania, April 1939
- Poland and Hungary
  - Annexed Czech territory, 1938 and 1939
- ( ) Former independent nations: Albania, Austria, and Czechoslovakia

Area of detail

EUROPE

AFRICA

NORWAY

Stockholm

SWEDEN

ESTONIA

LATVIA

NORTH SEA

BALTIC SEA

Copenhagen

DENMARK

LITHUANIA

MEMEL

DANZIG

GERMANY

Amsterdam

NETHERLANDS

Berlin

Warsaw

SOVIET UNION

BELGIUM

Bern

GERMANY

POLAND

RHINELAND

SUDETENLAND

LUXEMBOURG

Rhine R.

Nuremberg

Prague

(CZECH.) BOHEMIA & MORAVIA

Moscow

FRANCE

Vienna

SLOVAKIA

UKRAINE

Bern

SWITZERLAND

(AUSTRIA)

Budapest

HUNGARY

Annexed Czech Territory

ROMANIA

Bucharest

ITALY

Belgrade

YUGOSLAVIA

Danube R.

BLACK SEA

CORSICA

Rome

ADRIATIC SEA

Sofia

BULGARIA

SARDINIA

(ALBANIA)

Istanbul

MEDITERRANEAN SEA

GREECE

TURKEY

SICILY

Athens

| 0 | 100 | 200 | 300 Miles |
| 0 | 100 | 200 | 300 Kilometers |

GERMAN AND ITALIAN EXPANSION, 1936–1939. ▪ *What were Hitler's first steps in unifying all the ethnic Germans in Europe?* ▪ *How did Hitler use these initial gains to annex territory from the Czechs?* ▪ *After winning Czechoslovakia, why did Hitler choose to invade Poland?*

ADOLF – DER ÜBERMENSCH

SCHLUCKT GOLD UND REDET BLECH

"ADOLF, THE SUPERMAN, SWALLOWS GOLD AND SPOUTS TIN."
This 1932 photomontage by the antifascist German artist John Heartfield (born Helmut Herzfeld; 1891–1968) criticizes Hitler for receiving money from wealthy industrialists while claiming to represent the working people of Germany.

what was left of Czechoslovakia, annexed Bohemia and Moravia, and established a puppet regime in Slovakia. This was Germany's first conquest of territory that did not have a significant German population, and it sent shock waves across Europe. It convinced public and political opinion outside Germany of the futility of appeasement. Chamberlain was forced to shift his policies completely, and the British and the French strived to speed up their rearmament dramatically. Together with France, Britain guaranteed the sovereignty of the two states now directly in Hitler's path: Poland and Romania.

The French and the British negotiated with Stalin in the spring and summer of 1939 about the possibility of an alliance that would force Hitler to face a two-front war, as Germany did in 1914. These discussions were complicated by the fact that the western European powers were obligated to defend Poland from aggression. Hitler perceived an opportunity in this impasse and secretly promised Stalin a share of Poland, Finland, the Baltic states, and Bessarabia

(a part of Romania bordering Ukraine) if the Soviet Union remained neutral in the event of war between Germany and Poland.

Stalin seized his chance. An agreement with the Nazis offered the possibility of immediate Soviet expansion into Poland and the Baltic region and no war with Germany, while the alternative was less palatable: an alliance with Britain and France, which were both distant and ideological opponents of his regime, would mean an obligation to protect Poland in the event of a German attack. In August 1939, the world was shocked to hear that the Soviets had reversed their long-standing anti-Nazi position and signed a nonaggression pact with Hitler. With the **Hitler-Stalin Pact**, sometimes known as the Molotov-Ribbentrop Pact after the Soviet and Nazi diplomats who signed it, Stalin bought himself some time and a promise of significant territory along the Soviet Union's western frontier. For the Poles and the peoples of the Baltic nations, however, the Nazi-Soviet Pact placed them squarely between two hostile and expansionist powers, making them more dependent than ever on the support of their distant allies.

THE BEGINNING OF THE WAR IN EUROPE

After the signing of the Nazi-Soviet Pact, Hitler was free to move against Poland without fear of confronting the Soviet Union. His first target was the portion of western Pomerania that connected Poland to the Baltic Sea. This territory, which had been part of the Polish-Lithuanian Commonwealth until the partition of 1772, had been included in the new nation-state of Poland in 1919. Hitler and the Nazis resented this inclusion, which divided East Prussia and its German population from the rest of the German Reich. German nationalists referred to this strip of land as the "Polish Corridor" and loudly demanded its annexation.

With the Soviets now in his camp, Hitler believed that Poland had no choice but to acquiesce to the annexation and that the Western allies would back down once again. Poland, however, stood firm, and Hitler attacked. On September 1, 1939, German troops crossed the western Polish border, and Britain and France declared war on Germany two days later. The Second World War had begun.

The conquest of Poland took four weeks, and the results were devastating. It demanded great resources, and Germany committed nearly all of its combat troops and planes to the invasion. Well-coordinated attacks by German *panzers* (tanks) and armored vehicles, supported by air power, cut the large but slow-moving Polish army to pieces.

German infantry still moved on foot or via horse-drawn transport, but their disciplined advance followed the devastating work of the panzers. The Poles fought doggedly but with little hope of mounting an effective defense against a well-equipped and larger force. The *Blitzkrieg* (*blitz-kreeg;* "lightning war") for which the German officer corps had trained for so long was a complete success. Within three weeks, German troops were laying siege to Warsaw. German terror bombing, designed to destroy the heart of Warsaw from the air and frighten the population into surrender, was successful. Historians have pointed out that the Polish military never expected to win this war. Their goal was to hold out for two weeks, enough time for the Western allies to fulfill their treaty obligations by launching an attack across the Rhine in Germany. The bitter resistance of the Polish army succeeded in doing so, but the Allied attack never came.

Instead, in accordance with its secret agreement with Nazi Germany, the Soviet Union moved its troops into eastern Poland after September 17. For the nearly two years that the Molotov-Ribbentrop Pact remained in effect (from August 1939 until the Nazi invasion of the Soviet Union in June 1941), Poland found itself divided in two, occupied by two hostile powers. The character of the respective occupations reflected the priorities of each regime. In Warsaw, the Germans immediately separated the Jews from the rest of the population, and the gates of the Jewish quarter were closed in November 1939, after which point it became a collecting center for Jews from elsewhere. Meanwhile, close to 50,000 Poles were shot by German security police and soldiers in the fall of 1939. German-occupied Poland as a whole was subdivided in two parts, with the north and west absorbed into the German Reich, and the central and southern areas placed under a separate military administration, the General Government. The Germans instituted martial law with only two punishments: death or deportation to a concentration camp.

On the Russian side of occupied Poland, the Soviet army used Stalin's signature methods to deal with the enemy—deportations, imprisonments, and executions. The goal was to prevent the establishment of an independent Poland at war's end. Nearly 22,000 people—Polish military officers and police officials along with a number of arrested professionals and intellectuals, some

THE NAZI-SOVIET PACT. From August 1939 to June 1941, the Nazi-Soviet Pact was in effect in Poland, with the western portion of the country ruled by the German Reich and the eastern portion occupied by the Soviet Union. In this image, from a Soviet newspaper in October 1939, German and Soviet officers shake hands after a meeting, as the conquest of Poland was completed. The Poles suffered enormously under both regimes and considered them both hostile. The Soviet Union's alliance with Britain and the United States after the German invasion of Russia created problems for the Polish resistance movement in the latter years of the war, because they did not trust Stalin's motives when it came to Poland.

Jewish—were executed and buried in mass graves. Other people subject to arrest and deportation included members of noncommunist or national political parties, aristocrats, industrialists, landowners, business proprietors, priests, and citizens of foreign states. These deportations—in many ways a continuation of the Soviet purges of the late 1930s—sent more than 600,000 Poles, in locked railway cars without adequate food or heat, thousands of miles to the east to forced labor camps in central Asia and Siberia.

While consolidating their control over eastern Poland, the Soviets attacked Finland in late November 1939. Despite the Soviets' overwhelming superiority in numbers and material, the Finns fought back tenaciously. The Soviets faced a very difficult campaign, and the result was an alarming demonstration of the damaging effects of Stalin's terror on the Soviet military. Although the Soviet Union concluded the undeclared four-month Winter War with a precarious victory in March 1940, Hitler and the rest of the world made note of the Soviets' weaknesses.

After the fall of Poland, the war between the Western allies and Germany became an ominous "phony war," as Britain and France struggled to ready themselves. In the spring of 1940, that calm was broken by a terrible storm of attacks. The Germans struck first in Scandinavia, taking Denmark in a day and invading Norway. Britain and France tried to aid the Norwegian defense and sank a large number of German ships, but the Allied expedition failed. Then the real blow was struck: on May 10, German forces swarmed through Belgium and the Netherlands on their way to France, after which the two nations were conquered in short order. When the Dutch succeeded in flooding the canals that protected their major cities and defended that line with hard-fighting marines, Hitler ordered his air force to bomb the city of Rotterdam. More than 800 Dutch civilians died, and the Netherlands surrendered the next day. The Belgians' stubborn and effective defense of their nation was cut short when King Leopold III, fearing similar destruction, suddenly surrendered after two weeks of fighting. In turn, Leopold stayed on as a figurehead for the Nazis, reviled by Belgians who found other ways to carry on the fight against Germany.

The large French army was carved up by the Blitzkrieg. Its divisions were isolated, outflanked, and overwhelmed by German aircraft and armored columns working according to an exacting plan. French units fought fierce battles

JUNE 23, 1940. Hitler and the Nazi architect Albert Speer (left) pose across the river from the Eiffel Tower after German forces captured Paris.

until they were hopelessly surrounded or simply collapsed. The French army and artillery, much of it better built than its German equivalent, were poorly organized and rendered useless in the face of rapid German maneuvers, and the defeat quickly turned into a rout. Hundreds of thousands of civilians, each carrying a few precious possessions loaded on carts, fled south, where they were joined by thousands of Allied soldiers without weapons. These columns of refugees were attacked constantly by German dive bombers. Meanwhile, the disorganized British made a desperate retreat to the port of Dunkirk on the English Channel, where many of Britain's best troops were sacrificed holding off the panzers. At the beginning of June 1940, despite heavy German air attacks, Britain's Royal Navy evacuated more than 300,000 British and French troops, with the help of commercial and pleasure boats that had been pressed into emergency service.

After Dunkirk, the conflict was bitter but the outcome inevitable. French reservists fought "to the last cartridge," as their commanders asked, killing thousands of Germans. Without proper organization and more firepower, however, this bravery was useless. The Germans swept through the northwest and the heart of the country, reaching Paris in mid-June 1940. The political will of France's government collapsed along with its armies, and, rather than withdraw to Britain or to French colonies in North Africa, the French surrendered on June 22. France had fallen, and the armistice cut the country in two. The Germans occupied all of northern France, including Paris and the Channel ports. The south and the French territories in North Africa lay under the jurisdiction of a deeply conservative government formed at the spa town of Vichy (*VIH-shee),* under the leadership of an elderly First World War hero, Marshal Philippe Pétain. In forty days, France—one of Germany's historic enemies, the victor of the previous war, an imperial power, and a nation of almost 39 million citizens—was reduced to chaos and enemy occupation.

The penalties exacted on France did not end with its defeat. Many liberals within France and most of the Free French movement quickly established in London, and soon felt they had two enemies to fight: Germany and Pétain's regime. The Vichy government proposed to collaborate with the Germans in return for retaining a small measure of sovereignty, or so it believed. The regime instituted its own National Revolution, which came very close to fascism, and repudiated the republic, accusing it of sapping France's strength. The state proceeded to reorganize French life and political institutions, strengthening the authority of the Catholic Church and the family, and helping the Germans crush any resistance. "Work, Family, and Country" was Vichy's call to order.

NOT ALONE: THE BATTLE OF BRITAIN AND THE BEGINNINGS OF A GLOBAL WAR

Before launching an invasion across the Channel, the Nazis attempted to establish superiority in the air. From July to October 1940, in the Battle of Britain, thousands of planes dropped millions of tons of bombs on British targets—first on aircraft and airfields and then, as the focus shifted to breaking Britain's will, on civilian targets such as London. By the end of 1940, the British had effectively contested the German attempt to establish control of the skies, but German bombing raids continued until June 1941. More than 40,000 British civilians died. After a daring British bombing raid on Berlin, Hitler angrily told his generals to concentrate on civilian targets, which spared the Royal Air Force (RAF), whose bases had been steadily devastated up to that point. Given the chance to keep fighting, the RAF forced a costly stalemate in the air. Hitler then scrapped the invasion plans and turned his attention east toward Russia.

Another important reason for Britain's determined resistance was a change in political leadership. In May 1940, Chamberlain's catalog of failures finished his career. He was toppled by a coalition government that brought together Conservative, Liberal, and Labour politicians for the sake of national unity, led by the most unlikely of the choices offered to replace him: Winston Churchill (1940–1945

and 1951–1955). Churchill was a political maverick who had changed parties more than once, and before 1939, his political career was judged to be over. He was extremely talented but also arrogant, had a sharp temper, and sometimes seemed unstable. As prime minister, he was not much of an administrator, constantly proposing wild schemes, but he had two genuine gifts. The first was language, with which he spoke extraordinary words of courage and defiance just when the British public wanted and needed to hear them: he was utterly committed to winning the war.

"You ask what is our policy," Churchill said in his first speech as prime minister in May 1940, before the Battle of Britain began. "I will say, it is to wage war with all our might, with all the strength that God can give us, to wage war against a monstrous tyranny never surpassed in the dark, lamentable catalogue of human crime."

The second was personal diplomacy. He convinced the American president Franklin D. Roosevelt (1933–1945), who supported the Allies, to end American neutrality and send massive amounts of aid and weapons to Britain free of charge, under a program called Lend-Lease. Churchill also allowed the new government coalition to work to best effect. The ablest Conservative ministers stayed, and Labour politicians were allowed to take positions of genuine power. Most of the Labour representatives turned out to be excellent administrators and were directly in touch with Britain's huge working class, which now felt fully included in the war effort.

With Britain's survival, the war moved into different theaters: the Atlantic (a battle over sea-lanes and supplies), North Africa (strategically important for the Suez Canal and access to oil), the Pacific (the war with Japan), and the Soviet Union (where Hitler's determination to annihilate Stalin merged with his murderous campaign against the Jewish populations of Europe).

The Atlantic and North Africa

The Battle of the Atlantic, launched as a submarine campaign to starve out the British, was a dire threat to the Allies. Learning from the First World War, the Germans sent hundreds of submarines (U-boats) out in "wolf packs" to stalk the major sea-lanes to Britain. Thus Britain's supplies of weapons, raw materials, and

LONDON DURING THE BATTLE OF BRITAIN. German air raids that lasted from July 1940 to June 1941 wrought destruction, but they did not achieve Hitler's goal of breaking the British. The Holland House Library in London lost its roof but still managed to engage in business as usual.

THE SECOND WORLD WAR IN EUROPE. ▪ *Which parts of Europe were controlled by the Allies and the Axis?* ▪ *Which countries were neutral in 1941?* ▪ *In what parts of Europe did the major Axis and Allied campaigns occur?* ▪ *What was Germany's greatest geographical challenge during the Second World War?*

food hung in the balance as German submarines sank millions of tons of merchant shipping, some as far away as the coasts of Brazil and Florida. The British devoted a huge naval effort and great technical resourcefulness to save their convoys: they developed the modern sonar, new systems of aerial reconnaissance, and, with help from a group of Polish mathematicians, cracked the Germans' codes for communicating with the wolf packs. These

efforts kept the supplies coming. When the United States entered the war in December 1941 (see page 907), the British supplied the experience and technology and the Americans supplied the numbers and firepower to sink many more U-boats. By late 1942, the threat to the major sea-lanes receded.

The war in North Africa began because Britain had to protect the Suez Canal, but Britain was soon drawn into

Diary of the Dark Years

Jean Guéhenno (1890–1978) was a French writer and critic, well known for his diary of the World War II years, when France was occupied by the Nazis. In this passage, written on August 4, 1940—about six weeks after France's defeat— Guéhenno describes his feelings about the new government of Philippe Pétain, a marshal in the French Army and a hero of World War I, who was brought out of retirement to lead the government during the occupation. Pétain's government included militants from the extreme right, including several figures known for their anti-Semitism and their earlier involvement with anti-Dreyfusard groups dating back to the 1890s (Chapter 23). Pétain's government blamed the defeat on the Republic and embraced a more authoritarian style of rule. Eventually, Pétain and his ministers collaborated with the German anti-Jewish policy by ordering the arrest and deportation of French and foreign Jews on their territory to the Nazi death camps.

From now on, nobody has a right to do anything but talk about the speeches and celebrate the wisdom of a Marshal from the previous war who can't even count the number of stars above the visor of his kepi [uniform cap] very well anymore, a very old man with a military pension, who repeats whatever his prompters tell him. One might have thought the sense of service had left this veteran long ago. But as we weren't saying our mea culpas fast enough on our own, the exploiters of our defeat pushed him forward and gave him the task of reading the act of contrition and submission they had written out for us beforehand.

Stupidity and hypocrisy reign triumphant—the Moral Order, the virtue of the rich. The bourgeois ladies are rejoicing. In the market, they won't have to compete for chickens with women in house dresses anymore. At last, everyone will be able to eat according to his rank.

The defeat of France is merely one episode in the European civil war. The conflict of nations hides a deeper social conflict. Each nation is so seriously divided within itself that one of the parties which composes it can think it has won when the country has lost. Thus, for one group of Frenchmen, the misfortune of France is the occasion of a victory it hardly dared imagine. The republic lost: so they won.

The days we are living through now reveal what men are like. As we consider

a larger conflict. Indian, South African, and West African troops, fighting for the British, drove the Italians from Ethiopia in May 1941. The Soviets and the British invaded Iran to keep the shah (ruler) from making a deal with Germany over Iranian oil, and held the country until 1946. A small, well-led British army in Egypt humiliated a much larger Italian invasion force, nearly capturing Italy's colony of Libya. This forced Germany to intervene, and an elite armored force called the Afrika Korps—led by Germany's most daring tank commander, Erwin Rommel—drove the British back in the spring of 1941, starting a grudging two-year war in the desert. The British fielded an international army, which included as many Australians, Indians, New Zealanders, and Poles as it did Britons, that pitted against the Germans and the Italians. The fighting swung back and forth for eighteen months, with the British taking the worst of it, but then the momentum shifted. Despite heavy losses from German planes and submarines, the British defeated the Italian navy, took control of the Mediterranean, and established domination in the air over the desert. When Rommel tried to invade Egypt in July, his forces were stopped and badly defeated near the town of El Alamein, then driven back toward Tunisia later that fall. "This is not the end," said Winston Churchill in his inimitable style after the British victory at El Alamein. "It is not even the beginning of the end. But it is, perhaps, the end of the beginning."

The United States intervened in November 1942, landing in the French territories of Algeria and Morocco. A conference was held at Casablanca, Morocco, among the Allied the history of the past fifty years—the extraordinary effort of so many Frenchmen to attain some kind of well-being and dignity—we discover, we understand, what suffering the former "notables" must have felt at such an ascension. What pleasure is there in possessing what everybody else possesses? Some people are like that: they feel less happy and less free as soon as others are as happy and free as they are. The happiness of others seems licentious, anarchical, and soon, a menace to them. And hatred for those upstarts, those thieves, is born inside them. That's what we have come to. A hatred which goes back fifty years thinks it is having its revenge today. Our misfortunes probably sadden these "notables," but they have their compensations. They think they will be the only happy, free men again from now on. The idiots! They talk about our unhappy country the way a master speaks of his sick servant: they call it a loafer.

The little people, always ready to believe, are stunned by their misfortune. Rubbing their eyes, they wonder if they aren't actually even more guilty than unfortunate.

Is it so necessary to condemn those who are suffering? Must they also demean them? Cover them with shame? Is that the way to give them back their courage? Now I know better than I ever did what it means to belong to a people. I felt this more strongly in its distress than I ever felt in its glory. To all the men of my country, I would like to make a sign of fraternity.

We're not "notables." Our country is only an idea. It is a country that cannot be invaded. It is our inaccessible refuge where shame cannot reach us. What connection does this idea have to the shortage of planes or armored plate, to the stupidity of the generals, to the cowardice and schemes of the traitors? They have a habit of demeaning people, of drawing all things into their own little interests. We know that their faults are going to bring great suffering on us. We will bear that suffering, but we refuse dishonor.

Source: Jean Guéhenno, *Diary of the Dark Years, 1940–1944: Collaboration, Resistance, and Daily Life in Occupied Paris*, trans. David Ball (New York: 2014), pp. 10–11.

Questions for Analysis

1. How does Guéhenno convey his doubts about Pétain? Who does he suggest are the "exploiters of our defeat"?

2. What divisions does Guéhenno point to in French society? How do these different groups react to the establishment of Pétain's government?

3. What does Guéhenno mean when he suggests that "our country is only an idea"?

---

powers to discuss the future course of the war and the fate of French territories in North Africa. French administrators in Algeria and Morocco, who had supported Vichy, at least in public, surrendered peacefully or joined the Allied side. Rommel continued to defend Tunisia against the Allies for four months, but a joint offensive broke the German lines in March 1943, putting an end to the fighting.

The Allies and Japan in the Pacific

The war became truly global when Japan attacked the American naval base at Pearl Harbor, Hawaii, on the morning of December 7, 1941. The Japanese had been involved in a costly war in China since the 1930s. To win and establish a Japanese empire throughout Asia, Japan would have to destroy America's Pacific fleet and seize the colonies of the British, Dutch, and French Empires. Like Germany, Japan began with lightning blows. The attack on Pearl Harbor was a brilliant act of surprise that devastated the American fleet and shocked the American public. It was not, however, the success that the Japanese wanted. Eight U.S. battleships were either sunk or seriously damaged and more than 2,000 lives lost, but much of the American fleet—including its aircraft carriers, submarines, and many smaller ships—were safely at sea on the day of the strike. The unprovoked attack galvanized American public opinion in a way the war in Europe had not. When Germany rashly declared war on the United States as well, America declared itself ready to take on all comers and joined the Allies.

SOVIET UNION

ALASKA (U.S.)

CANADA

MONGOLIA

MANCHUKUO

CHINA

KOREA

JAPAN
• Tokyo
Hiroshima
August 6, 1945
Nagasaki
August 9, 1945

TIBET

TAIWAN

ALEUTIAN IS. (U.S.)

Iwo Jima
February 1945

Midway
June 1942

Pearl Harbor
Dec. 7, 1941

BURMA (Br.)
THAILAND

FRENCH INDOCHINA

PHILIPPINES (U.S.)

GUAM (U.S.)

PACIFIC OCEAN

DUTCH EAST INDIES

JAPANESE MANDATE

Guadalcanal
Aug. 1942–
Feb. 1943

Coral Sea
May 1942

INDIAN OCEAN

AUSTRALIA

NEW ZEALAND

0   1000   2000 Miles
0   1000   2000 Kilometers

	Japanese Empire, 1936
	Japanese control, August 1942
	Allies
	Neutral nations
→	Allied offenses
✳	Major battles
✳	Atomic bomb targets

THE SECOND WORLD WAR IN THE PACIFIC. ▪ *What areas did the Japanese and Allies each control in the Pacific during World War II?* ▪ *Trace the route of the Allied offense. What did the main Allied strategy appear to be?* ▪ *What factors led the Americans to decide that dropping the atomic bombs on Hiroshima and Nagasaki, rather than invading Japan, was the most expeditious way to end the war?*

Despite the mixed results at Pearl Harbor, the Japanese enjoyed other, stunning successes. For the European colonial powers, Japan's entry into the war was a catastrophe. Japanese troops swept through the British protectorate of Malaya in weeks, sinking the Pacific squadrons of both the British and Dutch navies in the swift attacks. Britain's fortified island port at Singapore, the keystone of British defenses in the Pacific, fell at the end of December 1941, and the shock of the loss nearly took Churchill's government with it. Thousands of British and Australian troops were captured and sent off to four years of torture, forced labor,

and starvation in Japanese prison camps. The Japanese also invaded the Philippines in December. Although American soldiers and marines held out on the island of Corregidor for some time, they too were forced to surrender; some took to the hills to fight as guerrillas, while the rest were forced on a death march to Japanese labor camps. The Dutch East Indies fell next, and it seemed that there would be no stopping the Japanese ships and soldiers before they reached Australia.

Reeling from Japan's blows, the Allies finally reorganized in 1942. After taking Singapore, Japanese troops pressed on into Burma. At first, Britain's efforts to defend

Burma led to disastrous losses of men and materiel, until an obscure Indian army officer, William Slim, reorganized the imperial defenses. Near the end of 1942, the joint force of British and Indian troops defeated an attempted Japanese invasion of India at the border. After that, with an army drawn from around the world, Slim began to push the Japanese back. In New Guinea, Australian troops, fresh from North Africa, were first to defeat the Japanese on land in a bitter hand-to-hand combat; they then staged a counterattack through the high mountain jungles.

At sea, America's navy benefited from a rapidly increased production schedule that turned out new ships and planes that outnumbered the Japanese and two gifted admirals, Chester Nimitz and William Halsey, who outfought them. In 1942, the United States won crucial victories in the Coral Sea and at Midway, a battle fought at sea and in the air by aircraft flown from carriers. American marines landed on the island of Guadalcanal in August 1942 and captured this strategic Japanese base after months of bitter fighting. Their success began a campaign of island hopping as the marines destroyed Japan's network of island bases throughout the Pacific. This was brutal warfare, often settled with grenades and bayonets, and with each side considering the other racially inferior. The Japanese often refused to surrender, and the Americans and Australians took few prisoners. By 1943, the Japanese victories halted, and with the Japanese navy severely weakened, the Allies began a slow march toward Singapore and the Philippines.

THE RISE AND RUIN OF NATIONS: GERMANY'S WAR IN THE EAST AND THE OCCUPATION OF EUROPE

While battles ebbed and flowed in the Atlantic and the North African desert, Germany moved southeast into the Balkans. In 1941, Germany took over Yugoslavia almost without a fight. The Germans split Yugoslavia's ethnic patchwork by establishing a Croatian puppet state, pitting Croats against their Serb neighbors who were ruled directly by the Nazis. Romania, Hungary, and Bulgaria joined the Nazis' cause as allies. The Greeks, who had dealt a crushing defeat to an Italian invasion, were suddenly confronted with a massive German force that overran the country. The Greeks, however, stubbornly refused to surrender, many taking to the mountains as guerrillas. An unexpected combination of Greek, British, and New Zealand troops nearly defeated the German paratroopers sent to capture the island of Crete in June 1941, but in the end, the country fell. By the summer of 1941—with the exceptions of Spain, Portugal, Sweden, and Switzerland—the whole European continent was either allied with the Nazis or subject to their rule. These victories, and the economy of plunder that enriched Germany with forced labor and other nations' money, won Hitler considerable popularity at home. But these were only the first steps in a larger plan.

Hitler's ultimate goals, and his conception of Germany's national destiny, lay to the east. Hitler had always seen the nonaggression pact with the Soviet Union as an act of convenience, to last only until Germany was ready for this final conflict, and by the summer of 1941, it seemed Germany was ready. On June 22, 1941, Hitler began **Operation Barbarossa**, the invasion of the Soviet Union. The elite of the German army led the way, defeating all the forces the Russians could put in front of them. Stalin's purges of the 1930s had exiled or executed many of his most capable army officers, and the effects showed in Russian disorganization and disaffection in the face of the panzers. Hundreds of thousands of prisoners were taken as German forces pressed deep into Belorussia (modern Belarus), the

"A DATE WHICH WILL LIVE IN INFAMY," DECEMBER 7, 1941. The U.S.S. *West Virginia* was one of eight battleships sunk during the Japanese surprise attack targeting Battleship Row at the American naval base at Pearl Harbor. More than 2,000 people were killed, but most of the American fleet, en route to or from other locations in the Pacific, was spared.

Baltic states, and Ukraine. Like Napoleon, the Germans led a multinational army, which included Italians, Hungarians, most of the Romanian army, and freelance soldiers from the Baltics and Ukraine who bore grudges against Stalin's authoritarian regime. During the fall of 1941, the Nazis destroyed much of the Red Army's fighting strength and vigorously pursued their two goals: the destruction of communism and racial purification.

The war against the Soviets was a war of ideologies and racial hatred. The advancing Nazi forces left burning fields and towns in their wake and methodically wiped the occupied territories clean of "undesirable elements." When Russian guerrillas counterattacked with sniping and sabotage, German forces shot or hanged hundreds of innocent hostages in reprisal, often first torturing their victims. The Russian guerrillas quickly chose to deliver the same punishment to any captured Germans. By the end of 1941, it was clear that the war in the East was a war of destruction, and both sides believed that only one would survive. It seemed then that the Germans would be the victors, whose forces were on the march toward the capital at Moscow. On orders from Berlin, however, some of the German forces were diverted south to attack Russia's industrial heartland in an effort to destroy the Soviets' ability to resist before the Russian winter set in. Moscow was never taken, giving the Russian population, its leaders, and its armies time to organize a much more determined resistance.

Hitler nonetheless managed to piece together an empire that stretched across the entire continent of Europe. "We come as the heralds of a New Order and a new justice," his regime announced. Hitler specifically compared his rule to a "new Indian empire," and claimed to have studied British imperial techniques. But much of the New Order was improvised and rested on a patchwork of provisional regimes: military occupation in Poland and Ukraine, collaborators in France, allied fascists in Hungary, and so on. The clearest principle was German supremacy, and the empire was meant to feed German citizens and maintain their morale and support for the war, preventing the "stab in the back" Hitler believed had thwarted a German victory in 1914–1918. Occupied countries paid inflated "occupation costs" in taxes, food, industrial production, and manpower. By 1942, more than 2 million Poles had been brought into Germany to work in agriculture and industry, while German settlers took over Polish farms. Those who remained in Poland were not exempt, as a decree of October 1939 made all men and women between the ages of 18 and 60 subject to forced labor. In total, more than 6 million foreign workers were brought into Germany in 1942–1943

from throughout occupied Europe, with those from Poland, France, and the Soviet Union accounting for 75 percent. In general, the treatment of conscript laborers followed the Nazi policy of seeing everything through the lens of racial prejudice: people considered to be of "Nordic" races (Scandinavians and the Dutch) fared much better than the Slavs of central and eastern Europe, whose treatment was extremely harsh.

The demands of enemy occupation and the political and moral questions of collaboration and resistance were issues across occupied Europe, as the Nazis set up puppet regimes in a number of occupied territories. Both Norway and the Netherlands were deeply divided by the occupation; in both countries, a relatively small but dedicated

"CULTURAL TERROR," 1944. Produced in Nazi-occupied Holland, this poster of a cultural Frankenstein's monster warns of the looming destruction of European identity with the advance of American troops, who will bring American culture with them. The terror of this culture is embodied in a long list of visual references: aerial bombardment, the Ku Klux Klan and its violence of lynching, African American jazz, Jewish racial threats, sexual license, common criminality, and financial manipulation. ▪ *What image of European culture was this image designed to defend?*

AXIS EUROPE, 1941. ▪ *How had Hitler and Mussolini come to dominate the bulk of mainland Europe by the eve of the German invasion of the Soviet Union?* ▪ *Why did Hitler choose to annex certain territories to Germany but settle for occupation in others?* ▪ *As you look at this map, do you think a German victory seems inevitable? Why or why not?*

The Nazis and the "Gypsy Question"

Historians do not know the exact numbers of Roma (commonly known as "gypsies" among non-Roma speakers) killed by the Nazis in their quest for a racially pure society. The U.S. Holocaust Museum estimates that 220,000 of the slightly fewer than a million Roma living in Europe were killed, either by the Germans or their allies. The Ustasha militia of Croatia, for example, was responsible for killing between 15,000 and 20,000 Roma. At Auschwitz, where 19,000 of the 23,000 Roma inmates died, Josef Mengele conducted pseudoscientific medical experiments on many Roma individuals. The documents reproduced here show the evolution of German policy toward the Roma people from 1938 to 1943, and provide a clear example of the way the German racial laws were applied to an entire population.

ircular Directive of December 8, 1938, by the Reichsführer-SS and Chief of German Police, pertaining to the "Settlement of the Gypsy Question"

A. General Directives

I. Domestic Gypsies

1. (1) The experiences collected so far in combating the Gypsy plague, and the knowledge gained from racial-biological research would make it seem advisable to tackle the settlement of the Gypsy Question with the nature of this race in mind. According to experience, individuals of mixed race contribute the largest share to Gypsy criminality. Conversely, it has been shown that all attempts to settle Gypsies in a permanent place of residence failed in particular with pure-blooded Gypsies because of their strong urge to roam. Thus, it will be necessary to deal separately with the pure-blooded Gypsies and those of mixed blood when it comes to the final solution of the Gypsy Question.

* * *

(3) I therefore direct that all Gypsies, whether sedentary or not, as well as all persons roaming in Gypsy fashion must be rounded up [*erfaßt*] by the Reich Criminal Police Office—Central Reich Administration for Combating Gypsy Malefaction.

* * *

3. (1) The ultimate determination as to whether one deals with a Gypsy, a Gypsy of mixed blood, or some person roaming in Gypsy fashion will be made by the Reich Criminal Police Office based on the testimony of an expert.

(2) I therefore direct . . . that all Gypsies, Gypsies of mixed blood, and persons roaming in Gypsy fashion be compelled to submit to a racial-biological examination required for the presentation of a testimony by an expert, and to provide the necessary information about their descent. The implementation of this directive is to be ensured by means of forceful police measures.

* * *

II. Foreign Gypsies

1. Foreign gypsies must be prevented from entering German territory. Refusal to grant entry permits and to move them back is required procedure even if foreign Gypsies are in possession of passports entitling them to immigrate, of substitute documents in lieu of passports, or of visa.

* * *

Express Letter of August 17, 1939 from the Reich Security Main Office, pertaining to the "rounding up" [*Erfassung*] of Gypsies

Berlin, October 10, 1939
Reich Security Main Office
Tgb. No. RKPA. 149/1939-g
Express Letter

party of Nazis governed in the name of the Germans, while at the same time, well-organized and determined resistance movements gathered information for the Allies and carried out acts of sabotage. In Denmark, the population was much more united against their German occupiers, and engaged in regular acts of passive resistance that infuriated German administrators. They also banded together as private citizens to smuggle most of the country's Jewish population out to safety in neutral Sweden. This was only possible, it must be said, because the German occupation was less onerous in Denmark than in places farther east; Danish institutions continued to function, and elections continued to be held. In Poland and in occupied areas of the Soviet Union, active or passive resistance to German policies provoked brutal reprisals from the Nazis.

To the State Criminal Police—Regional and Local Commands of the Criminal Police . . .

Subject: Rounding Up of Gypsies

By order of the Reichsführer-SS and Chief of German Police the Gypsy Question will be fundamentally settled before long within the entire German territory by a uniform standard applied throughout the Reich. I therefore ask you to initiate the following measures at once:

1. The local police stations and the Rural Police must be instructed immediately to notify all Gypsies and Gypsies of mixed blood within their respective districts that effective immediately they may not leave their residence or their present whereabouts until further notice. Anybody in violation of this injunction will be threatened with dispatch to a concentration camp.

* * *

Express letter of January 29, 1943 from the Reich Security Main Office, pertaining to the confinement of "Gypsies of Mixed Blood," "Romany Gypsies" and "Balkan Gypsies" to a concentration camp

Berlin, January 29, 1943
Reich Security Main Office
VA No. 59/43 g
Express Letter

* * *

Subject: Confinement of Gypsies of mixed blood, Romany Gypsies and Balkan Gypsies in a concentration camp

* * *

I. By order of the *Reichsführer*-SS dated December 16, 1942 . . . , Gypsies of mixed blood, Romany Gypsies and members of Gypsy clans of non-German blood and of Balkan origins are to be selected according to fixed guidelines, and in the course of an operation lasting only a few weeks are to be confined in a concentration camp. People affected [*Personenkreis*] will henceforth briefly be referred to as "Persons of Gypsy origin."

Confinement will take place by families, regardless of the degree of mixed blood, in Concentration Camp (Gypsy Camp) Auschwitz.

* * *

(III) 1. Attempts should be made to obtain consent for sterilization from persons of Gypsy origin above 12 years of age and not yet sterilized;

* * *

4. In case of refusal, the Reich Criminal Police Office, after having ascertained the reasons, will decide what steps are to be taken.

Source: Reinhard Rürup, ed., *Topography of Terror: Gestapo, SS, and Reichssicherheitshauptamt on the "Prinz-Albrecht-Terrain,"* trans. Werner T. Augress (Berlin: Arenhövel, 1989).

Questions for Analysis

1. How was the language of racial science used to justify discriminatory practices against the Roma in the 1938 document? Why was it necessary to differentiate among "Gypsies, Gypsies of mixed blood, and persons roaming in Gypsy fashion"?

2. What was the significance of the 1939 document's statement that the "Gypsy Question will be fundamentally settled before long within the entire German territory by a uniform standard applied throughout the Reich"? If the goal was extermination, why use such bureaucratic language? If the goal was other than extermination, why was it necessary to "round up" the gypsies?

3. By 1943, the extermination policy was already under way. Why, then, was it necessary to continue to speak in vague terms of "Gypsies of mixed blood, Romany Gypsies and members of Gypsy clans of non-German blood and of Balkan origins"?

Elsewhere, the relationship among collaboration, resistance, and self-interested indifference was more complex. In France, collaboration ranged from simple survival tactics under occupation to active support for Nazi ideals and goals. The worst example of this was the French Vichy regime's active anti-Semitism and the aid given by its French authorities in isolating, criminalizing, and deporting Jews in France to the concentration camps. Living with the German conquerors forced citizens in France (and elsewhere) to make choices. Many chose to protect their own interests by sacrificing those of others, particularly the "undesirables" such as Jews and communists. At the same time, communist activists, some members of the military, and many ordinary citizens—such as the people of France's central mountains, who had a long tradition of smuggling and resisting government—became active guerrillas and saboteurs. They established links with the Free French movement in London, led by the charismatic, stiff-necked general Charles de Gaulle, and supplied important intelligence to the Allies. The Poles also had a government-in-exile in London, led by Wladyslaw Sikorski, who helped coordinate the Polish resistance.

In eastern Europe, resistance movements had less room to maneuver, but perhaps more reason to engage in direct action, because quiet submission did not guarantee safety under the harsh German military occupation. The result of such circumstances ranged from open warfare against the fascists to civil wars between those who supported the Germans and those who fought them. Organized resistance groups formed immediately in 1939 in Poland, where collaboration was never an option because the Germans never considered it. By 1942, the Polish Home Army was the largest underground resistance movement in Europe. Harassing the Nazis through acts of sabotage and attacks on military convoys, the Polish resistance circulated legal guidelines on how Poles should conduct themselves under the occupation, established clandestine courts, and built an underground education system that reached a million children. They also kept university classes, meeting in secret after all institutions of higher learning had been banned. By the fall of 1943, the Home Army was already engaging the Germans directly.

The Germans' system of occupation in Yugoslavia led to violent civil conflict. In Croatia, a fascist regime allied with the Germans fought against the Serbs who resisted. The Croatian fascist guard, the Ustasha, massacred hundreds of thousands of Orthodox Christian Serbs. Josip Broz (Tito), born in Croatia to a Croatian father and a Slovene mother, emerged as the leader of the most powerful Yugoslavian resistance movement—ultimately, the only resistance group in eastern Europe to succeed in liberating its country without the presence of Soviet troops. Tito's forces were communists and strong enough to form a guerrilla army; they fought Germans, Italians, and Croat fascists, and gained support and supplies from the Allies.

Perhaps the most important moral issue facing citizens of occupied Europe was not their national allegiance but rather their personal attitudes toward the fate of the Nazis' sworn enemies: Jews, communists, gypsies, homosexuals, and political "undesirables." Popular journalists in France called for the deportation of Jewish children and celebrated their collaborationist government when it carried out the plan. Some French Jews along the Riviera found that the Italian Catholic army officers who occupied the area were more willing to save them from deportation than their fellow Frenchmen. The Germans executed at least 700 Poles for sheltering Jews, and in spite of the great danger, tens of thousands of non-Jewish residents of Warsaw did what they could to aid the Jews in their city, in large or small ways. In 1941, however, Polish villagers in Jedwabne massacred their Jewish neighbors at the instigation of the Gestapo. These consequences of wartime choices—to risk family, friends, and careers to aid the deportees; to put one's head down and look the other way; or to actively aid and abet mass murder—deeply scarred the generation of Europeans who survived the war.

RACIAL WAR, ETHNIC CLEANSING, AND THE HOLOCAUST

From the beginning, the Nazis had seen the conflict as a racial war. In *Mein Kampf*, Hitler had already outlined his view that a war against the *Untermenschen* ("subhuman")

DEPORTATION OF JEWS FROM THE WARSAW GHETTO. In the summer of 1942, the Nazis sent 265,000 Jews from the Warsaw ghetto to the extermination camp at Treblinka by train, where they were gassed. A further 35,000 Jews were killed in the ghetto during the deportations.

WHERE WERE THE CAMPS? In 2013, historians compiled a list of more than 42,000 separate extermination camps, detention centers, ghettos, and slave-labor sites in German-controlled Europe during the war years. Their conclusion that virtually every population center was close to such a site has caused historians to revise upward their estimates of who in Europe had knowledge of the extermination policy.

Jews, gypsies, and Slavs was natural and necessary. It would not only purify the German people, it would also conquer territory for their expansion. Thus, as soon as the war broke out, the Nazis began to implement ambitious plans for redrawing the racial map of the Reich, by what is now called ethnic cleansing. In the fall of 1939, with Poland conquered, Heinrich Himmler directed the SS to begin massive population transfers. Ethnic Germans who lived in territories conquered by the Nazi armies as they moved eastward were brought to the Reich, while Poles and Jews were deported to specially designated areas in

the east. Over 200,000 ethnic Germans from the Baltic states were resettled in western Prussia, but welcoming these ethnic Germans went hand in hand with a brutal campaign of terror against the Poles, especially Polish Jews, as the Nazis sought to root out all sources of potential resistance. Professors at the University of Kraków, considered dangerous intellectuals, were deported to concentration camps, where they died. The SS shot "undesirables," such as the inmates of Polish mental asylums, partly to allow SS troops to occupy the asylums' barracks. Ordinary Poles were deported to forced labor camps.

Jews by the thousands were transported to the region of Lublin, south of Warsaw. And special death squads began to shoot Jews in the streets and in front of synagogues. These German campaigns in Poland took 100,000 Jewish lives in 1940.

The elimination of European Jewry stood at the center of the Nazis' *Rassenkampf* ("racial conflict"). We have seen the role of anti-Semitism in Hitler's rise to power and the escalating campaign of terror against the Jewish community inside Germany in the 1930s, including the Night of Broken Glass (Chapter 25). Most historians now agree that although Hitler and other Nazis verbally announced "war" against the Jews early on, such policy was not possible until after 1941, with the conquest of territory in the east, which suddenly brought millions of Jews under Nazi control. During the organized pogroms of 1938, the Nazis' anti-Jewish policy aimed not at extermination but forced emigration, and until 1941, the Nazi leadership continued to consider plans to deport Europe's Jews to Madagascar, a French colony off the coast of Africa. These schemes took shape against the background of daily terror and frequent massacres, especially in Poland.

The invasion of the Soviet Union turned these atrocities into something much deadlier. Operation Barbarossa was animated by the Nazis' intense ideological and racial hatreds directed against Slavs, Jews, and Marxists. Goebbels, for example, called the Russians "not a people but an agglomeration of animals." The invasion of the

Soviet Union was thus openly a "war of extermination." The campaign's initial success also created pressing practical problems for the German army in the newly conquered territories, as they debated on how to control the millions of people—including military prisoners, eastern European Jews, and other civilians—who had now fallen into Nazi hands. Although Hitler had certainly prepared the way for what followed in his long-nurtured campaigns against the Jews, historians now believe that a significant part of the driving force for the Holocaust came from rivalries within the Nazi bureaucracy, which led to a radicalization of persecution and murder on a scale few could have imagined.

As the Nazi army swept into the Soviet Union in 1941, captured communist officials, political agitators, and hostile civilians were imprisoned, tortured, or shot. Most Poles, Ukrainians, and Russians in the region were deported to Germany as slave labor. About 5.5 million Soviet military prisoners were marched into camps where over half of them died of starvation or were executed. On the heels of the advancing German army came special battalions of *Einsatzgruppen* ("task forces"), or death squads. Joined by 11,000 extra SS troops, they stormed through Jewish villages and towns. The men of the villages were shot; the women and children were either deported to labor camps or massacred along with the men. By September 1941, the Einsatzgruppen reported that in their efforts at "pacification," they had killed 85,000 people, most

NORWAY 1,300

SWEDEN

FINLAND

ESTONIA "Free of Jews"

SOVIET UNION 5 MILLION

DENMARK 5,600

LATVIA 3,500

LITHUANIA 34,000

WHITE RUSSIA 446,484

IRELAND

UNITED KINGDOM

NETHERLANDS 160,800

GERMANY 131,800

Wannsee ● ● Berlin

BIALYSTOK DISTRICT 400,000

EASTERN TERRITORIES 420,000

GENERAL GOVERNMENT 2,284,000

UKRAINE 2,994,684

BELGIUM 43,000

FRANCE Occupied Zone 165,000

LUX.

BOHEMIA and MORAVIA 74,200

SLOVAKIA 88,000

FRANCE Unoccupied Zone 700,000 (including French North Africa)

SWITZ.

AUSTRIA 43,700

HUNGARY 742,800

ROMANIA 342,000

CROATIA 40,000

SERBIA 10,000

SPAIN

ITALY 58,000

CORSICA

SARDINIA

BULGARIA 48,000

ALBANIA 200

BLACK SEA

GREECE 69,600

NORTH SEA

BALTIC SEA

SICILY

ALGERIA

TUNISIA

MEDITERRANEAN SEA

CRETE

RHODES

CYPRUS

AFRICA

EUROPE

Area of detail

0   250   500 Miles
0   250   500 Kilometers

HITLER'S "FINAL SOLUTION": JEWS MARKED FOR DEATH. On January 20, 1942, German officials met at Wannsee, just outside Berlin, to discuss the "Final Solution" to the "Jewish problem." They also discussed what they believed to be the remaining number of Jewish people in territories they controlled or soon hoped to control. ▪ *Examine the figures closely. How many millions of innocent people did the Nazis propose to slaughter?* ▪ *Based on your reading, what percentage of Jews did they actually kill?* ▪ *Which two countries were set for the most executions?*

The Holocaust: Two Perspectives from the SS

In the first account given here, an SS officer charged with inspecting the death camps writes of his visit to Belzec, a camp in occupied Poland, near the former Russian border. He opposed the regime and, shortly after leaving this description in 1945, he committed suicide.

Heinrich Himmler (1900–1945), one of the founding members of the Nazi party and the head of the SS, became one of the most powerful members of the Nazi government. He directed the purge of the rebellious SA in 1934, expanded the SS, supervised the network of death camps, and, by 1943—when he gave the speech reprinted here—had become minister of the interior in the administration of the Reich. Few embodied better than Himmler the combination of ambition, ideology, and ruthlessness that characterized Nazi leaders. He committed suicide when captured by Allied troops in 1945.

The Death Camps

Next morning, shortly before seven, I was told: 'the first transport will arrive in ten minutes'. And, in fact, after a few minutes, the first train arrived from the direction of Lemberg (Lvov). 45 wagons with 6,700 people, of whom 1,450 were already dead on arrival. Behind the barred hatches stared the horribly pale and frightened faces of children, their eyes full of the fear of death. Men and women were there too. . . .

The chambers fill up. 'Pack them in'— that is what Captain Wirth has ordered. People are treading on each others' toes. 700–800 in an area of twenty-five square metres, in forty-five cubic metres! The SS push them in as far as possible. The doors shut; in the meantime, the others are waiting outside in the open, naked. 'It is the same in winter', I was told. 'But they could catch their death of cold', I say. 'But that's just what they are there for', replied an SS man in dialect. Now at last I understood why the whole apparatus is called the Heckenholt Foundation. Heckenholt is the driver of the diesel engine, a little technician who constructed the installation. The people are going to be killed by the diesel exhaust gases. But the diesel engine won't start! Captain Wirth arrives. He is clearly embarrassed that this should happen just on the day when I am here. Yes indeed, I can see the whole thing. And I wait. My stop watch faithfully records it all. Fifty minutes, 70 seconds [*sic*]. Still the diesel won't start. The people wait in their gas chambers. In vain. One can hear them crying, sobbing. . . . Captain Wirth hits the Ukrainian who is responsible for helping *Unterscharführer* Heckenholt with the diesel engine twelve or thirteen times in the face with his riding whip. After two hours forty-nine minutes—the stop watch has recorded it all—the engine starts. Up to this moment, the people have been living in these

Source: J. Noakes and G. Pridham, *Nazism: A History in Document and Eyewitness Accounts, 1919–1945*, vol. 2 (New York: 1988), pp. 1151–52, 1199–1200.

of them Jews; by April 1942, the number was 500,000. These killings began before the gas chambers had gone into operation and continued through the campaigns on the Eastern Front. By 1943, the death squads had killed roughly 2.2 million Jews.

As Operation Barbarossa progressed, German administrations in occupied areas herded local Jewish populations even more tightly into the ghettos some Jewish communities had occupied for centuries; Warsaw and Lodz in Poland were the largest. The ghettos became centers of starvation and disease, when Nazi administrators, accusing Jewish people of hoarding supplies, refused to allow food to go in. Those who left the ghettos were shot rather than returned. A German doctor summarized the regime's logic about killing this way: "One must, I can say it quite openly in this circle, be clear about it. There are only two ways.

four chambers, four times 750 people in four times forty-five cubic metres. A further twenty-five minutes pass. That's right, many are now dead. One can see through the little peepholes when the electric light illuminates the chambers for a moment. After twenty-eight minutes, only a few are still alive. At last, after thirty-two minutes, they are all dead. . . .

Himmler's Instructions to the SS

I also want to talk to you quite frankly about a very grave matter. We can talk about it quite frankly among ourselves and yet we will never speak of it publicly. Just as we did not hesitate on 30 June 1934 to do our duty as we were bidden, and to stand comrades who had lapsed up against the wall and shoot them, so we have never spoken about it and will never speak of it. It appalled everyone, and yet everyone was certain that he would do it the next time if such orders should be issued and it should be necessary.

I am referring to the Jewish evacuation programme, the extermination of the Jewish people. It is one of those things which are easy to talk about. "The Jewish people will be exterminated," says every party comrade, "It's clear, it's in our programme. Elimination of the Jews, extermination and we'll do it." And then they come along, the worthy eighty million Germans, and each one of them produces his decent Jew. It's clear the others are swine, but this one is a fine Jew. Not one of those who talk like that has watched it happening, not one of them has been through it. Most of you will know what it means when a hundred corpses are lying side by side, or five hundred or a thousand are lying there. To have stuck it out and—apart from a few exceptions due to human weakness—to have remained decent, that is what has made us tough. This is a glorious page in our history and one that has never been written and can never be written. For we know how difficult we would have made it for ourselves if, on top of the bombing raids, the burdens and the deprivations of war, we still had Jews today in every town as secret saboteurs, agitators and troublemakers. We would now probably have reached the 1916–17 stage when the Jews were still part of the body of the German nation.

We have taken from them what wealth they had. I have issued a strict order, which SS *Obergruppenführer* Pohl has carried out, that this wealth should, as a matter of course, be handed over to the Reich without reserve. We have taken none of it for ourselves. . . . All in all, we can say that we have fulfilled this most difficult duty for the love of our people. And our spirit, our soul, our character has not suffered injury from it.

Questions for Analysis

1. "This is a glorious page in our history," says Himmler, but one that "can never be written." How does he reconcile that contradiction? What was glorious? To what extent did the Nazis try to conceal what they were doing?

2. What does Himmler's speech suggest about the psychology of Nazism or the ways in which members of the SS were persuaded to become murderers?

We sentence the Jews in the ghetto to death by hunger or we shoot them. Even if the end result is the same, the latter is more intimidating." In other words, the point was not simply death but terror.

Through the late summer and fall of 1941, Nazi officials discussed and put together plans for mass killings in death camps. The ghettos had already been sealed; now orders came down that no Jews were to leave any occupied areas. That summer, the Nazis had experimented with vans equipped with poison gas that could kill thirty to fifty people at a time. Those experiments and the gas chambers were designed with the help of scientists from the T-4 euthanasia program, which had already killed 80,000 racially, mentally, or physically "unfit" individuals in Germany. By October 1941, the SS was building camps with gas chambers and deporting

The Architecture of Mass Murder

The camp at Auschwitz-Birkenau was the largest of the German concentration camps. Its central purpose was the murder of Europe's Jews: nearly 1.1 million people, of whom 1 million were Jews, were murdered there.

Auschwitz-Birkenau was a complex of three camps: an extermination center, a prisoner-of-war camp, and a labor camp built with the cooperation of German industrial firms such as IG Farben. Forty other smaller installations and work camps in the surrounding area were also run by the camp's administration. The construction of the Auschwitz-Birkenau complex occupied thousands of workers and continued throughout the war. When the Soviet army arrived in January 1945, they found that the Germans had burned the camp archives before fleeing, but they had not burned the construction archive, which was kept separately. Hundreds of technical drawings were found in this archive, and they became accessible to historians after the collapse of the Soviet Union in 1991; another cache of such documents was

A. Blueprint for Crematorium II, Birkenau, dated November 1941. The five shaded squares in the lower drawing are the gas ovens in the structure's underground level, and the area to the right is labeled "Corpses Room."

people to them. Auschwitz-Birkenau (OWSH-vihts BIHR-kuh-now), originally intended to hold Polish prisoners, was built to be the largest of the camps. It eventually held many different types of prisoners—"undesirables" such as Jehovah's Witnesses and homosexuals, Poles, Russians, and even some British POWs—but Jews and gypsies were the groups systematically annihilated there. Between the spring of 1942 and the fall of 1944, more than a million people were killed at Auschwitz-Birkenau alone. The opening of the death camps set off the greatest wave of slaughter from 1942 to 1943, as freight cars hauled Jewish people to the camps, first from the ghettos of Poland, then from France, Holland, Belgium, Austria, and the Balkans, and later from Hungary and Greece. Bodies were buried in pits dug by prisoners or burned in crematoria.

discovered in an abandoned building in Berlin in 2008. The drawings are now held by Yad Vashem, the Holocaust archive in Jerusalem, Israel.

The discovery of these drawings does not add substantially to what was already known about the murder of Jews and other prisoners at Auschwitz, but it provides an arresting example of the bureaucratic apparatus—and the chilling coldness of the planning—that went into the Nazi extermination policy.

Questions for Analysis

1. Who would have seen these plans and been aware of their purpose?

2. What do these images tell us about the nature of the effort that went into the Nazi extermination policy?

3. Is there a way to understand the relationship between the careful renderings, with precise measurements and rectilinear lines, and the ultimate purpose of the buildings?

B. Blueprint for the "Delousing Facility" at Auschwitz-Birkenau, showing a room of 11.6 by 11.2 meters marked *Gaskammer* ("gas chamber").

The death camps have come to symbolize the horrors of Nazism as a system of modern mass murder. Yet it is worth emphasizing that much of the slaughter was not anonymous, industrialized, or routine, but took place in face-to-face encounters outside the camps. Jews and other victims were not simply killed, but tortured, beaten, and executed publicly while soldiers and other onlookers recorded the executions with cameras—and sent photos home to their families. During the last phases of the war, inmates still in the concentration camps were taken on death marches whose sole purpose was suffering and death. And the killings were not done only by the specially indoctrinated SS and Einsatzgruppen. The Nazi regime called up groups of conscripts, such as Reserve Police Battalion 101, from duty in their home city of Hamburg and sent them into occupied territories, and once there, the unit of middle-aged policemen received and obeyed orders to kill 1,500 Jewish men, women, and children in one village in one day. When the commander offered to excuse men who did not feel they could carry out the assignment, only a few asked for a different task.

How many people knew of the extent of the Holocaust? No operation of this scale could be carried out without the cooperation or knowledge of many: the Nazi hierarchy, architects who helped design and build the camps, engineers who designed the gas chambers and crematoria, municipal officials of cities from which people were deported, train drivers, residents of villages near the camps who reported the smell of bodies burning, and so on. Recent research has shown that the number of extermination camps, ghettos, slave-labor sites, and detention centers in Nazi-controlled Europe was greater than 42,000. Given the difficulty of hiding sites that required guards, logistical support, and access to transportation networks, it is now clear that many more people must have been aware of what was happening. It is not surprising that most who suspected the worst were terrified and powerless. But it is also not surprising that many people did not want to know and did their best to ignore evidence and carry on with their lives. Moreover, there were reasons many continued to support the Nazis, such as personal opportunism or because they opposed communism and wanted order restored. Yet mere popular indifference, fear, or approval does not provide a satisfactory explanation for the Nazis' ability to accomplish the murder of so many people. Indeed, many Europeans—German, French, Dutch, Polish, Swiss, and Russian—had come to believe that there was a "Jewish problem" that had to be "solved."

The Nazis tried to conceal the death camps. Nevertheless, in July 1943, the Polish government-in-exile sent an envoy, Jan Karski, to the United States to present a report on Germany's plan to murder Europe's Jews. Karski, a member of the Polish underground, had been in the Warsaw ghetto and witnessed Jews being transported to the extermination center at Belzec. He met with President Franklin D. Roosevelt to plead for an intervention that would stop the killing, but neither Roosevelt nor the other Allied leaders were willing to commit the necessary resources, either because they did not believe Karski's story or because they were preoccupied with the enormity of the crisis facing them. The Nazis, however, could count on vocal support throughout Europe for requiring Jews to be specially identified, for restrictions on marriage and property ownership and other kinds of discrimination. For reasons that had to do with both traditional Christian anti-Semitism and modern, racialized nationalism, many Europeans had

JEWISH COUPLE IN BUDAPEST, BY EVGENY KHALDEI (1945). Khaldei, a Soviet photographer and journalist who traveled with the Red Army, recounts his remarkable and moving encounter with this couple: "There was a Jewish couple wearing Stars of David. They were afraid of me. There was still fighting going on in the city, and they thought I might be an SS soldier. So I said *Sholem Aleichem* [hello] to them, and the woman began to cry. After I'd taken the picture, I pulled their stars off and said, 'The fascists are beaten. It's terrible to be marked like that.'"

come to see Jewish Europeans as "foreign," and no longer members of their national communities.

What of other governments? Their level of cooperation with the Nazis' plans varied. The French Vichy regime, on its own initiative, passed laws that required Jews to wear identifying stars and strictly limited their movements and activities. Although 75 percent of the Jews in France survived the war, only about 2,500 of the approximately 75,000 Jews deported to German death camps survived. The vast majority of those deported were arrested not by the Germans but by Vichy authorities seeking to prove that France could be Germany's partner in Hitler's New Europe. The Hungarian government also allied with the Nazis and persecuted Jews, but dragged its heels about deportations. Thus, the Hungarian Jewish community survived—until March 1944, when Germans, disgusted with their Hungarian collaborators, took direct control and immediately began mass deportations. So determined were the Nazis to carry out their "final solution" that in May 1944, they killed up to 12,000 Hungarian Jews a day at Auschwitz, contributing to a total death toll of 600,000 Jews from Hungary. Italy, though a fascist country, participated less actively; not until 1943, when the Germans occupied the north of Italy, were drastic anti-Semitic measures implemented.

DEPORTATION RAILWAYS. Between March 1942 and November 1944, Jews are known to have been deported from every location on this map, as well as from other numerous locales. Note the effort the Nazis made to transport Jews from the very frontiers of the empire at the height of a two-front war. ▪ *According to the map, to which site were most Jews deported?* ▪ *Look back at Hitler's "Final Solution" map on page 917. Why was Auschwitz in Poland chosen as the main deportation site?* ▪ *What does the map say about the Nazi regime in particular and the other nations willing to collaborate with the Nazis?*

Past and Present

European Integration Then and Now

Hitler's conquest of Europe was a plan for European integration, based on a theory of racial domination, whereby "pure" Aryan settlements would take over territory from "racially inferior" people who would eventually be eliminated. The photo on the left is of the "model" Nazi village of Adolf Hitler-Koog. The great success of European integration after the Second World War was to create a structure for international cooperation based on democratic institutions and mutual economic interest. The photo on the right shows German Chancellor Konrad Adenauer (left) shaking hands with Jean Monnet, a key figure in European integration.

 Watch related author interview on the Student Site

In the face of this Nazi determination, little resistance was possible. The concentration camps were designed to numb and incapacitate the inmates, making them acquiesce in their own slow deaths, if they were not killed right away. In his famous account, the survivor Primo Levi writes: "Our language lacks words to express this offence, the demolition of a man. . . . It is not possible to sink lower than this; no human condition is more miserable than this, nor could it conceivably be so. Nothing belongs to us any more; they have taken away our clothes, our shoes, even our hair; if we speak, they will not listen to us, and if they listen, they will not understand." The few rebellions in Auschwitz and Treblinka were repressed with savage efficiency. In the villages of Poland, Ukraine, and elsewhere, people rounded up to be deported or shot had to make split-second decisions to escape, and saving oneself nearly always meant abandoning one's children or parents, which very few could—or would—do. The

countryside offered no shelter, as local populations were usually either hostile or too terrified to help. Nothing could have prepared these populations for the kind of violence that overwhelmed them.

The largest Jewish resistance movement was in the Warsaw ghetto, in the spring of 1943. The previous summer, the Nazis had deported 80 percent of the ghetto's residents to the camps, making it clear that those left behind had little hope of survival. Those in the ghetto had virtually no resources, yet when deportations started again, a small Jewish underground movement—a thousand fighters, perhaps, in a community of 70,000—took on the Nazis with a tiny arsenal of gasoline bombs, pistols, and ten rifles. The Nazis responded by burning the ghetto to the ground and executing and deporting nearly everyone who was left. In the end, some 56,000 Jews died, and the SS commander reported, "The Warsaw Ghetto is no more." Word of the rising spread, but the repression made it clear that the targets of Nazi extermination could choose only between death in the streets or death in the camps.

The Holocaust claimed nearly 6 million Jewish lives, more than one-third of the world's Jewish population, 2.9 million of whom were Polish. To realize their racial utopia, the Nazis also killed more than 200,000 Roma and 250,000 people with disabilities, as well as 2.7 million non-Jewish Poles, 5.7 million non-Jewish Soviet civilians, and 3 million Soviet prisoners of war. These enormous numbers cannot capture the nearly total destruction of some communities and their cultures. Well over 80 percent of the long-established Jewish communities were annihilated in the Baltic states (Latvia, Estonia, and Lithuania), Germany, Czechoslovakia, Yugoslavia, and Poland; elsewhere, the figures were closer to 50 percent. The Holocaust was part of an even longer period of ethnically and racially motivated mass murder. Through both world wars and afterward, ethnic and religious groups— Jews, Armenians, Poles, Serbian Orthodox—were hunted, massacred, and legally deported en masse. Hitler's government had planned to build a "new Europe," safe for ethnic Germans and their allies and secure against communism, on the graveyards of whole cultures. At war's end, however, the ethnic Germans of eastern Europe themselves were the ones expelled, hunted, and killed in retaliation for Nazi crimes.

TOTAL WAR: HOME FRONTS, THE WAR OF PRODUCTION, BOMBING, AND THE BOMB

The Second World War was a "total war," even more so than the First World War. It involved the combined efforts of whole populations, massive resources, and mobilization of entire economies within the combatant nations, changing the standards of living around the world. In the neutral nations of Latin America, which supplied vast amounts of raw materials to the Allies, wartime profits led to a wave of prosperity. In the lands occupied by Germany or Japan, economies of forced extraction robbed local areas of resources, workers, and even food. In East Asia, deprivation caused rising resentment of the Japanese, who initially had been seen as liberators ending the rule of the old colonial powers. Work schedules were grueling, as women and the elderly pressed back into wage work or working for the first time put in long shifts. This was especially taxing on women, who would return home to cook, clean, and care for families and neighbors also affected by enemy bomb-

ing and wartime shortages. Although Germany lived comfortably off the farmlands of Europe for several years and the United States could lean on its huge agricultural base, food, gasoline, and basic household goods were rationed. In occupied Europe and the Soviet Union, rations were just above starvation level, and sometimes fell below in areas near the fighting. Britain, dependent on its empire and other overseas sources for food and raw materials, ran a comprehensive rationing system that kept up production and ensured a drab but consistent diet on the table.

Production—the industrial ability to churn out more tanks, tents, planes, bombs, and uniforms than the enemy—was essential to winning the war. Britain, the Soviet Union, and the United States each launched comprehensive, well-designed propaganda campaigns that encouraged the production of war equipment on an unmatched scale. Appeals to patriotism, shared interests, and a common stake in winning the war struck a chord, and the Allied populations proved willing to regulate themselves and commit to the effort. Despite strikes and disputes with government officials, the Allied powers devoted more of their economies to war production more efficiently than any nations in history. They built tanks, ships, and planes capable of competing with advanced German and Japanese designs by the tens of thousands, swamping the enemy with constant reinforcements and superior firepower. Japan had invested heavily in its military in the 1930s, but during the war its production levels declined, as Allied advances on land and American submarines cut off overseas sources of vital supplies. Germany, despite its reputation for efficiency and its access to vast supplies of slave labor, was less efficient in its use of workers and materials than the Allied nations. Germany's ability to produce devastatingly successful weapons led to a damaging side effect: vast amounts of money and time spent developing pet projects of high-ranking Nazi officials or trying to make unsuccessful designs work. The Allies, meanwhile, developed working, standard designs and produced them in overwhelming numbers, rather than losing time and resources pursuing perfection.

Because industry was essential to winning the war, centers of industry became vital military targets. The Allies began bombing German ports and factories almost as soon as the Germans started their own campaigns. Over time, American and British planners became equally ruthless on an even larger scale; both nations made a major commitment to strategic bombing, developing new planes and technology that allowed them to put thousands of bombers in the air night and day over occupied Europe. As the war wore on and Germany kept fighting, the Allies expanded their campaign, moving from pinpoint bombing

"JUST A GOOD AFTERNOON'S WORK!" A British poster mobilizing women for part-time factory work.

Germans' will to keep fighting, like that of the British and the Soviets, remained intact.

The Race to Build the Bomb

Allied scientists in the United States developed the world's first nuclear weapon during the war years: a bomb that worked by splitting the atom and creating a chain reaction that could release tremendous energy in an explosion. Physicists in Britain and Germany first suggested that such a weapon might be possible, but only the United States had the resources to build such a bomb before the end of the war. A group of physicists at the University of Chicago, including many refugees from fascist regimes in Europe, under the leadership of Enrico Fermi built the world's first nuclear reactor; in December 1942, Fermi and his group staged the first controlled chain reaction at the university. Fearful that the Germans would develop a bomb of their own, the U.S. government built a laboratory at Los Alamos, New Mexico, and charged the physicists with building an atomic bomb; the physicist J. Robert Oppenheimer directed the top-secret plan, known to the researchers as the Manhattan Project. The goal was to perfect a bomb that could be dropped by plane and detonated above the target. The physicists successfully tested a device on July 16, 1945, in New Mexico, vaporizing the test tower in a wave of heat and fire that rose in a mushroom shape overhead. The United States now possessed the most destructive weapon ever devised.

of the military and industry in Germany to striking such targets across all of occupied Europe, as well as bombing Germany's civilian population in earnest. Despite a public debate about the morality of the bombings, for the British, it was a war of retribution; for the Americans, it was an effort to grind the Germans down without sacrificing too many Allied lives. The Allies killed tens of thousands of German civilians as they struck Berlin, ports such as Hamburg, and the industrial cities of the Ruhr, but German war production persisted and its fighter planes shot down hundreds of Allied bombers, causing heavy losses. After the Allied invasion of Europe, bombing expanded well beyond targets of military value. The German city of Dresden, a center of culture and education without heavy industry, for instance, was firebombed with a horrifying death toll. This gave Allied generals and politicians pause, but strategic bombing continued. German industry slowly degraded, but the

THE ALLIED COUNTERATTACK AND THE DROPPING OF THE ATOMIC BOMB

Hitler had invaded the Soviet Union in June 1941. Within two years, the war in the east had become his undoing, and within four years, it had brought about his destruction.

The early successes of the German-led invasion were crippling. Nearly 90 percent of the Soviets' tanks, most of their aircraft, and huge stores of supplies were destroyed or captured, but the Soviets fought regardless. Nazi forces penetrated deep into European Russia, and by late 1941, German and Finnish forces had cut off and besieged Leningrad (St. Petersburg). Yet the city held out for 844 days—through three winters, massive destruction by artillery and aircraft, and periods of starvation—until a large relief force broke the siege.

The Eastern Front

In the East, the character of the war changed as Russians rallied to defend the *rodina*, the Russian motherland. Stalin's efforts were aided by the weather, as successive winters took a heavy toll on the Germans. At the same time, Soviet industry made an astonishing recovery during the war years. Whole industries were rebuilt behind the safety of the Ural Mountains, and entire urban populations were sent to work in them to turn out tanks, fighter planes, machine guns, and ammunition. Finally, the Germans were the victims of the success of their own Blitzkrieg tactics; their lines extended deep into Russian territory, spreading their forces more thinly and opening them up to attacks from unexpected angles.

The turning point came in 1942–1943, when the Germans attempted to take Stalingrad in an effort to break the back of Soviet industry. The Russians drew the invading army into the city, where the Germans were bogged down in house-to-house fighting that neutralized their tanks and gave the outnumbered Soviet forces greater chances of success, despite their lack of equipment. The Germans found their supplies running low as winter set in, and in November 1942, large Russian armies encircled the city and besieged the invaders in a battle that continued through a cruel winter. At the end of January 1943, when the German commander defied his orders and surrendered, more than a half million German, Italian, and Romanian soldiers were killed; Russian casualties were more than a million, including a hundred thousand civilians.

After **Stalingrad**, a series of Soviet attacks drove the Germans back toward the frontier and beyond. In what may have been the largest battle ever fought—with more than 6,000 tanks and 2 million men—Soviet armies destroyed a German force at Kursk in the summer of 1943. Following this victory, the Russians launched a major offensive into Ukraine, which was back in Soviet hands by the spring of 1944. In the summer of 1944, the Soviet Army's Operation Bagration produced a second calamitous defeat of an entire German army group, which cleared the Nazis entirely from Soviet territory. The Soviets then paused in their westward march, moving south to secure control of the Balkans, taking Romania,

PRISONERS OF WAR. More than 90,000 captured German troops were forced to march through the streets of Stalingrad after their defeat by the Soviet forces. The combination of the battle and the Russian winter resulted in the loss of more than 300,000 German soldiers.

Bulgaria, and Hungary out of the war on the German side. In August 1944, elements of the Polish Home Army organized an insurrection against the Germans in Warsaw in an attempt to liberate the Polish capital before the arrival of the Soviet Army. The uprising lasted for more than two months and was cruelly suppressed by the Germans, while the Soviets observed from the other side of the Vistula river, abstaining from sending assistance. Meanwhile, as Tito's Chetniks (the Serbian nationalist guerrilla force) moved against the retreating German armies in Yugoslavia, the Soviets, joined by partisans from eastern Europe, retook large parts of Czechoslovakia. Finally, in the first weeks of 1945, the Soviet army launched an assault against Germany proper, closing in on Berlin.

The Western Front

When the Nazis invaded Russia, Stalin called on the Allies to open a second front in the West. In response, the United States led an attack on Italy in 1943, beginning with an invasion of Sicily in July. Italy's government deposed Mussolini and surrendered in the summer of 1943, and the nation collapsed

STORMING HITLER'S "FORTRESS EUROPE." American troops landing on Omaha Beach on D-Day, June 6, 1944. In the three months that followed, the Allies poured more than 2 million men, almost a half million vehicles, and 4 million tons of supplies onto the Continent—a measure of how firmly the Germans were established.

RAISING THE RED FLAG OVER THE REICHSTAG, BY EVGENY KHALDEI (1945). Khaldei was one of several Soviet Jewish photographers to document Nazi atrocities and Soviet heroism (in this case) on the Eastern Front. In this photograph, which became the best-known image of Soviet victory, a Soviet soldier raises a flag over the Reichstag in Berlin. ▪ *How was the Soviet occupation of the German capital seen from the perspective of the other Allied governments?*

into civil war, with Italian partisans, especially the communists, siding with the Americans as dedicated fascists fought on. The Germans had occupied Italy with more than a dozen elite divisions, and the hard-fought and bitter campaign with American and British forces lasted eighteen months.

The most important second front opened on June 6, 1944, with massive Allied landings in Normandy. Casualties were high, but careful planning and deception allowed the Allied invasion to gain a foothold in northern Europe, eventually breaking through the German lines. A second landing in southern France also succeeded, aided by the Resistance. By August, Allied armies had liberated Paris and pushed into Belgium. In the fall, however, the Germans managed to defeat a British airborne invasion in the Netherlands and to thrust an American invasion into the Rhineland forests, before mounting a devastating attack in December 1944, in the Battle of the Bulge. The Allied lines nearly broke, but the American forces held long enough for a crushing counterattack. In April 1945, the Allies crossed the Rhine into Germany, swiftly overwhelming the last defenders of the German Reich. This military success was helped by the fact that most Germans preferred to surrender to Americans or Britons rather than face the Russians to the east.

The Soviet troops were approaching fast, and by late April, they reached the suburbs of Berlin. In the savage ten-day battle to take the German capital, more than 100,000 Russians and Germans died. On April 30, Adolf Hitler killed himself in a bunker beneath the Chancellery. On May 2, the heart of the city was captured, and the Soviets' red banner flew from the Brandenburg Gate. On May 7, the German high command signed a document of unconditional surrender. The war in Europe was over.

The War in the Pacific

The war in the Pacific ended four months later. The British pushed the Japanese out of Burma while the Germans were surrendering in the West, and soon after, Australian forces recaptured the Dutch East Indies. In the fall of 1944, the U.S. Navy had destroyed most of Japan's surface ships in the gulfs of the Philippine Islands, and American troops took the capital, Manila, house by house in bloody fighting; the remaining battles—amphibious assaults on a series of islands running toward the Japanese mainland—were just as brutal. Japanese pilots mounted suicide attacks on American ships, as American marines and Japanese soldiers fought over every inch of the shell-blasted rocks in the Pacific. Okinawa fell to the Americans after eighty-two days of desperate fighting, giving the United States a foothold less than 500 miles from the Japanese home islands. The government in Tokyo, meanwhile, called on its citizens to defend the nation against invasion.

On July 26, the governments of the United States, Britain, and China jointly called on Japan to surrender or be destroyed. The United States had already been using long-range B-29 bombers in systematic attacks on Japanese cities, killing hundreds of thousands of Japanese civilians in firestorms produced by the incendiary bombs. When the Japanese government refused to surrender, the United States decided to use its atomic bomb.

Many senior military and naval officers argued that the use of the bomb was not necessary, on the assumption that Japan was already beaten. Some of the scientists involved, who had done their part to defeat the Nazis, also believed that using the bomb for political ends would set a deadly precedent. But Harry Truman, who became president when Roosevelt died in April 1945, decided otherwise. And on August 6, a single American plane dropped an atomic bomb on Hiroshima, obliterating 60 percent of the city. Three days later, on August 9, the United States dropped a second bomb on Nagasaki. On August 14, Japan surrendered unconditionally.

The decision to use the bomb was extraordinary. It did not greatly alter the American plans for the destruction of Japan, being that many more Japanese died in the earlier fire bombings than in the two atomic blasts, but the bomb was an entirely new kind of weapon, revealing a new and terrifying relationship between science and political power. The instantaneous, total devastation of the blasts—and the lingering effects of cancerous radiation that would claim victims decades later—were something terribly new. The world now had a weapon that could destroy not just cities and peoples, but humanity itself.

CONCLUSION

After the Second World War, many Europeans awoke to find a world they no longer recognized. In 1945, many Europeans emerged from shelters or began long trips back to their homes, faced with a world that hardly existed at all. The products of industry (tanks, submarines, and strategic bombings) had destroyed the structures of industrial society (factories, ports, and railroads). The tools of mass culture—fascist and communist appeals, patriotism proclaimed via radios and movie screens, mobilization of mass armies and industry—had been put to full use. In the aftermath, much of Europe lay destroyed and, as we will see, vulnerable to the rivalry of the postwar superpowers: the United States and the Soviet Union.

The two world wars profoundly affected Western empires. Nineteenth-century imperialism had made twentieth-century war a global matter. In both conflicts, the warring nations used the resources of the empire

THE ATOM BOMB. A mushroom cloud hovers over Nagasaki after the city was bombed. Hiroshima was bombed three days earlier.

Competing Viewpoints

The Atomic Bomb and Its Implications

> In July 1945, scientists associated with the **Manhattan Project** became involved in debates about how the atomic bomb should be deployed. Members of the Scientific Panel of the secretary of war's Interim Advisory Committee agreed that a bomb could be used for military purposes but disagreed about whether it could be used without prior warning and demonstration. Other groups of scientists secretly began circulating petitions, such as the one reprinted here, in which they set out their views. The petitions never reached the president, but they raised issues that emerged in the postwar period.
>
> In the section of his memoirs reprinted here, President Harry S. Truman sets out the views of other scientists on the secretary of war's Advisory Committee, and explains the logic of his decision to use the atomic bomb on Hiroshima (August 6, 1945) and Nagasaki (August 9, 1945) and the events as they unfolded.

A Petition to the President of the United States

July 17, 1945

A PETITION TO THE PRESIDENT OF THE UNITED STATES

We, the undersigned scientists, have been working in the field of atomic power. Until recently we have had to fear that the United States might be attacked by atomic bombs during this war and that her only defense might lie in a counterattack by the same means. Today, with the defeat of Germany, this danger is averted and we feel impelled to say what follows:

The war has to be brought speedily to a successful conclusion and attacks by atomic bombs may very well be an effective method of warfare. We feel, however, that such attacks on Japan could not be justified, at least not unless the terms which will be imposed after the war on Japan were made public in detail and Japan were given an opportunity to surrender....

[I]f Japan still refused to surrender our nation might then, in certain circumstances, find itself forced to resort to the use of atomic bombs. Such a step, however, ought not to be made at any time without seriously considering the moral responsibilities which are involved.

The development of atomic power will provide the nations with new means of destruction. The atomic bombs at our disposal represent only the first step in this direction, and there is almost no limit to the destructive power which will become available in the course of their future development. Thus a nation which sets the precedent of using these newly liberated forces of nature for purposes of destruction may have to bear the responsibility of opening the door to an era of devastation on an unimaginable scale.

If after this war a situation is allowed to develop in the world which permits rival powers to be in uncontrolled possession of these new means of destruction, the cities of the United States as well as the cities of other nations will be in continuous danger of sudden annihilation....

The added material strength which this lead [in the field of atomic power] gives to the United States brings with it the obligation of restraint and if we were to violate this obligation our moral position would be weakened in the eyes of the world and in our own eyes. It would then be more difficult for us to live up to our responsibility of bringing the unloosened forces of destruction under control.

In view of the foregoing, we, the undersigned, respectfully petition: first, that you exercise your power as Commander-in-Chief, to rule that the United States shall not resort to the use of atomic bombs in this war unless the terms which will be imposed upon Japan have been made public in detail and Japan knowing these terms has refused to surrender; second, that in such an event the question of whether or not to use atomic bombs be decided by you in the light of the considerations presented in this petition as well as all the other moral responsibilities which are involved.

Source: Michael B. Stoff, Jonathan F. Fanton, and R. Hal Williams, eds., *The Manhattan Project: A Documentary Introduction to the Atomic Age* (New York: 2000), p. 173.

President Truman's Memoirs

I had realized, of course, that an atomic bomb explosion would inflict damage and casualties beyond imagination. On the other hand, the scientific advisers of the committee reported, "We can propose no technical demonstration likely to bring an end to the war; we see no acceptable alternative to direct military use." It was their conclusion that no technical demonstration they might propose, such as over a deserted island, would be likely to bring the war to an end. It had to be used against an enemy target.

The final decision of where and when to use the atomic bomb was up to me. Let there be no mistake about it. I regarded the bomb as a military weapon and never had any doubt that it should be used. The top military advisers to the President recommended its use, and when I talked to Churchill he unhesitatingly told me that he favored the use of the atomic bomb if it might aid to end the war.

In deciding to use this bomb I wanted to make sure that it would be used as a weapon of war in the manner prescribed by the laws of war. That meant that I wanted it dropped on a military target. I had told Stimson that the bomb should be dropped as nearly as possibly upon a war production center of prime military importance.

Stimson's staff had prepared a list of cities in Japan that might serve as targets. Kyoto, though favored by General Arnold as a center of military activity, was eliminated when Secretary Stimson pointed out that it was a cultural and religious shrine of the Japanese.

Four cities were finally recommended as targets: Hiroshima, Kokura, Niigata, and Nagasaki. They were listed in that order as targets for the first attack. The order of selection was in accordance with the military importance of these cities, but allowance would be given for weather conditions at the time of the bombing. Before the selected targets were approved as proper for military purposes, I personally went over them in detail with Stimson, Marshall, and Arnold, and we discussed the matter of timing and the final choice of the first target. . . .

On August 6, the fourth day of the journey home from Potsdam, came the historic news that shook the world. I was eating lunch with members of the *Augusta's* crew when Captain Frank Graham, White House Map Room watch officer, handed me the following message:

To the President from the Secretary of War

Big bomb dropped on Hiroshima August 5 at 7:15 P.M. Washington time. First reports indicate complete success which was even more conspicuous than earlier test.

I was greatly moved. I telephoned Byrnes aboard ship to give him the news and then said to the group of sailors around me, "This is the greatest thing in history. It's time for us to get home."

Source: Harry S. Truman, *Memoirs*, vol. 1, *Year of Decisions* (Garden City, NY: 1955), pp. 419–21.

Questions for Analysis

1. Scientists circulated petitions to express their fears about how the atomic bomb would be used. Examine the outcomes the scientists proposed. Which came closest to subsequent events? Which was the most prudent? The most honest?

2. Is it appropriate for scientists to propose how new weapons should be used? Are they overreaching in trying to give advice in foreign affairs and military strategy, or are they obligated to voice moral qualms?

to their fullest. Key campaigns in North Africa, Burma, Ethiopia, and the Pacific were fought in and over colonial territories. Hundreds of thousands of colonial troops—sepoys and Gurkhas from India and Nepal, Britain's King's African Rifles, French from Algeria and West Africa—served in armies on both sides of the conflict. After two massive mobilizations, many anticolonial leaders found renewed confidence in their peoples' courage and resourcefulness, and seized the opportunity of European weakness to press for independence. In many areas that had been under European or Japanese imperial control—from sections of China to Korea, Indochina, Indonesia, and Palestine—the end of the Second World War only paved the way for a new round of conflict. This time, the issue was when imperial control would end, and by whom.

The Second World War also carried on the Great War's legacy of massive killing. Historians estimate that between 62 and 78 million people died across the world, two-thirds of them civilians, with about 20 percent dying from starvation or disease directly caused by the war. In Europe, the killing fields of the East, where the extermination of the Jews took place, suffered the highest tolls. At least 23 million Soviet citizens died: 8.8 million soldiers

After You Read This Chapter

 Go to **INQUIZITIVE** to see what you've learned—and learn what you've missed—with personalized feedback along the way.

REVIEWING THE OBJECTIVES

- The Second World War stemmed from the political and economic crises of the 1930s. What were the causes of the war?
- British and French leaders in the 1930s hoped to avoid another war in Europe through diplomatic negotiation with Hitler. What were the consequences of these negotiations?
- The populations of nations occupied by the Germans faced a difficult set of choices. What were the consequences of the occupation for European nations? What possibilities existed for resistance?
- The mass murder of European Jews, homosexuals, and gypsies reached a climax during the invasion of the Soviet Union, though the victims came from every corner of Europe. How did this enormous project come about? What efforts did it entail?
- The Nazi regime and its allies eventually collapsed after costly defeats in both eastern and western Europe. Where and when did these major defeats take place? What was their human cost?
- The Japanese government surrendered in August 1945 after the United States dropped atomic bombs on Hiroshima and Nagasaki. What events led to the decision to drop these bombs? What were the consequences?

and 15 million civilians. Nearly 20 percent of the Polish population died, nearly 6 million people. Also killed were a million Yugoslavs, including militias of all sides; and 3.5 million German soldiers and 700,000 German civilians, not including the hundreds of thousands of ethnic Germans who died while being deported west at the end of the war. The United States, shielded from the full horrors of total war by two vast oceans, lost 292,000 soldiers in battle and more to accidents or disease.

Why was the war so murderous? The advanced technology of modern industrial war and the openly genocidal ambitions of the Nazis offer a part of the answer, and the global reach of the conflict offers another. Finally, the Second World War overlapped with, and eventually devolved into, a series of smaller, no less bitter conflicts: overlapping attempts by the Germans and Soviets to wipe out Poland's political leaders and professional classes; a civil war in Greece; conflicts among Orthodox, Catholics, and Muslims in Yugoslavia; and political battles for control of the French Resistance. These struggles left deep political scars, as did memories of the war. Also, Hitler's empire could not have lasted as long as it did without active collaboration or passive acquiescence from many, a fact that produced bitterness and recrimination for years.

PEOPLE, IDEAS, AND EVENTS IN CONTEXT

- What was Hitler asking for at the **MUNICH CONFERENCE** of 1938? What made many people in Europe think that **APPEASEMENT** was their best option?
- What was the **HITLER-STALIN PACT** of 1939?
- What was **BLITZKRIEG**? What effect did it have on those who faced German invasions?
- What were Hitler's goals in **OPERATION BARBAROSSA**, the invasion of the Soviet Union in 1941? What were the consequences of the German defeat at **STALINGRAD**?
- What made the **SECOND WORLD WAR** a global war? Where outside of Europe were the main consequences of the war felt most keenly?
- What was the **MANHATTAN PROJECT**? How did it affect the outcome of the Second World War?

THINKING ABOUT CONNECTIONS

- What long-term causes, going back to the history of Europe in the nineteenth century, might you point to in order to understand the outbreak of the Second World War? Can you link the story of this war with the history of European imperialism in the nineteenth century or with the successes and failures of the German national unification movements?
- What circumstances made the Second World War a global conflict?

Before You Read This Chapter

The Cold War World: Global Politics, Economic Recovery, and Cultural Change

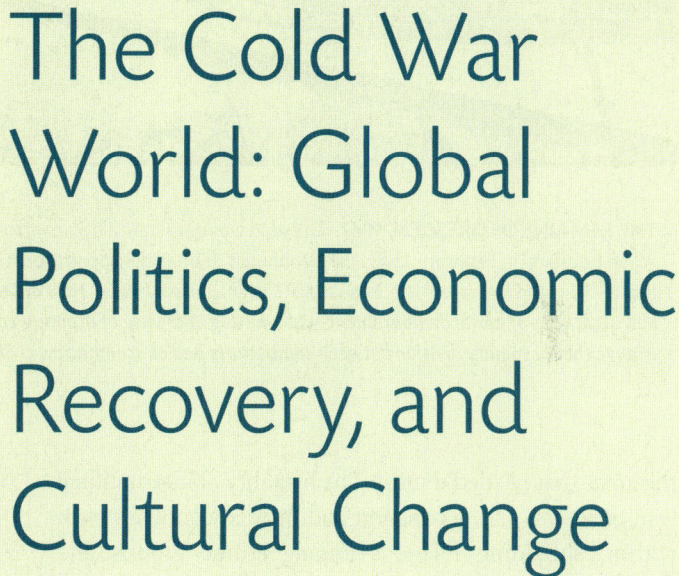

"The war ended the way a passage through a tunnel ends," wrote Heda Kovály, a Czech woman who survived the concentration camps. "From far away you could see the light ahead, a gleam that kept growing, and its brilliance seemed ever more dazzling to you huddled there in the dark the longer it took to reach it. But when at last the train burst out into the glorious sunshine, all you saw was a wasteland." The war left Europe a land of wreckage and confusion, as millions of refugees trekked hundreds or thousands of miles on foot to return to their homes, while others were forcibly displaced from their lands. In some areas, housing was practically nonexistent, with no available means to build anew. Food remained in dangerously short supply: a year after the war, roughly 100 million people in Europe still lived on fewer than 1,500 calories a day. Families scraped vegetables from their gardens or traded smuggled goods on the black market. Governments continued to ration food, without which a large portion of the Continent's population would have starved. During the winter of 1945–1946, many regions had little or no fuel for heat, and what coal there was— less than half the prewar supply—could not be transported to

935

THE REMAINS OF DRESDEN, 1947. Dresden was devastated by a controversial Allied bombing in February 1945. Kurt Vonnegut dramatically portrayed its destruction and the aftermath in his novel *Slaughterhouse-Five*. ▪ *How did the war's new strategies of aerial bombardment—culminating in the use of atomic weapons—change the customary division between combatants and noncombatant civilians?*

the areas that needed it most. The brutality of international war, civil war, and occupation had divided countries from within, shredding relations among ethnic groups and fellow citizens. Ordinary people's intense relief at liberation often went hand in hand with recriminations over their neighbors' wartime betrayal, collaboration, or simple opportunism.

How does a nation, region, or civilization recover from a catastrophe on the scale of the Second World War? Nations had to do much more than deliver food and rebuild economic infrastructures; they had to restore—or create—government authority, functioning bureaucracies, and legitimate legal systems. They also had to rebuild bonds of trust and civility among citizens, steering a course between demands for justice on the one hand, and the overwhelming desire to bury memories of the past on the other. Rebuilding entailed a commitment to renewing democracy—to creating democratic institutions that could withstand threats such as those the West had experienced in the 1930s. Some aspects of this process were extraordinarily successful, more so than even the most optimistic forecaster might have thought possible in 1945. But others failed or were deferred until later in the century.

The war's devastating effects brought two dramatic changes in the international balance of power. The first change was the emergence of the so-called superpowers—the United States and the Soviet Union—and the swift development of a "cold war" between them. The Cold War divided Europe, with Eastern Europe occupied by Soviet troops and Western Europe dominated by the military and economic presence of the United States. The United States and the Soviet Union exercised their influence in very different ways, but the power of both regimes forced Europeans to confront a world in which their own political and economic weight was significantly diminished. In both Western and Eastern Europe, the Cold War led to increased political and economic integration among states, resulting in the emergence of the European Common Market in the West and the socialist bloc dominated by the Soviet Union in the East.

The second great change came with the dismantling of the European empires that had once stretched worldwide. The collapse of empires and the creation of newly emancipated nations raised the stakes of the Cold War and brought superpower rivalry to far-flung regions of the globe. These events, which shaped the postwar recovery and inevitably created a new understanding of what the "West" meant, are the subject of this chapter.

THE COLD WAR AND A DIVIDED CONTINENT

No peace treaty ended the Second World War. Instead, as the war drew to a close, relations between the Allied powers began to fray over issues of power and influence in Central and Eastern Europe; after the war, the relations descended from mistrust to open conflict. The United States and the Soviet Union rapidly formed the centers of two imperial blocs. Their rivalry, which came to be known as the **Cold War**, pitted against one another two military powers, two sets of state interests, and two ideologies: capitalism and communism. The Cold War's repercussions reached well beyond Europe, as anticolonial movements, sensing the weakness of European colonial powers, turned to the Soviets for help in their struggles for independence. The Cold War thus structured the peace, shaped international relations for four decades, and affected governments and peoples across the globe who depended on either of the superpowers.

Map Legend:

- Allied occupation of Germany and Austria, 1945–1955
- Territory regained by Poland from Germany
- Territory gained by Soviet Union
- Postwar national boundaries, to 1989
- "Iron Curtain" to 1989
- **1945** Year Communist control of government was gained

Inset: EAST GERMANY — French Sector, British Sector, U.S. Sector, WEST BERLIN, Soviet Sector, EAST BERLIN, Potsdam — Berlin Wall (1961–1989)

Map labels: NORWAY, Oslo, SWEDEN, Stockholm, FINLAND, Helsinki, Leningrad, From Finland, 1940–1956, NORTH SEA, DENMARK, Copenhagen, BALTIC SEA, ESTONIA To U.S.S.R., 1940, LATVIA To U.S.S.R., 1940, LITHUANIA To U.S.S.R., 1940, NETHERLANDS, Amsterdam, U.S. Zone, Bremen, British Zone, Soviet Zone, Berlin, Incorporated into U.S.S.R., 1945, Gdansk (Danzig), Incorporated into Poland, 1945, Brussels, BELGIUM, Bonn, French Zone, WEST GERMANY, EAST GERMANY (1949), U.S. Zone, LUXEMBOURG, Prague, Warsaw, POLAND (1947), WHITE RUSSIA, Brest, From Poland, 1940–1947, UKRAINE, SOVIET UNION (1917), Munich, Vienna, U.S. Zone, Soviet Zone, CZECHOSLOVAKIA (1948), From Czechoslovakia, 1945–1947, From Romania, 1940–1947, Bern, SWITZERLAND, French Zone, AUSTRIA British Zone, HUNGARY (1949), Budapest, BESSARABIA, CRIMEA, From Italy, 1945, Milan, ROMANIA (1947), Yalta, YUGOSLAVIA (1945), Bucharest, BLACK SEA, CORSICA (Fr.), ITALY, Rome, ADRIATIC SEA, Danube R., From Romania, 1940–1947, Tirane, BULGARIA (1946), Sofia, SARDINIA (It.), ALBANIA (1944), Istanbul, GREECE, TURKEY, EUROPE, AFRICA, Area of detail, SICILY (It.), Athens, CRETE, CYPRUS, MEDITERRANEAN SEA

Scale: 0 200 400 Miles / 0 200 400 Kilometers

TERRITORIAL CHANGES IN EUROPE AFTER THE SECOND WORLD WAR. At the end of the Second World War, the Soviet Union annexed territory in Eastern Europe to create a buffer between it and Western Europe. At the same time, the United States established a series of military alliances in Western Europe to stifle the spread of communism in Europe. ▪ *Which Eastern European countries fell under Soviet control?* ▪ *Where is Berlin located?* ▪ *Why did location and control of Germany cause so much tension?* ▪ *How did these new territorial boundaries aggravate tensions between the Soviet Union and the United States?*

The End of the Second World War and the Onset of the Cold War

The need to defeat Nazi Germany brought the United States and the Soviet Union together in a common struggle, in spite of their contrasting political systems. Both nations emerged from the Second World War with a renewed sense of purpose, and both tried to use the victory against fascism to promote their claims for legitimacy and leadership in Europe. These circumstances placed a special burden on European nations and their postwar governments, as they were forced to take sides in this global confrontation at a moment of weakness and uncertainty.

The images shown here, all from May 1945 in Czechoslovakia, an Eastern European country, display several different possibilities for representing the German defeat. Image A shows a Czech civilian rending the Nazi flag, with the Prague skyline in the background and the flags of the major Allied powers and Czechoslovakia overhead. Image B shows a triumphant Czech laborer wielding a rifle and a socialist red flag, while standing over the corpse of a German soldier. Image C shows portraits of Stalin and the

A. Czech propaganda poster celebrating German defeat, May 1945.

B. Czech propaganda poster, May 1945.

The Displaced

At the end of the Second World War, an unprecedented number of people were on the move in Europe, Asia, and the Middle East. These mass migrations were a response to, and often a continuation of, wartime deportations and expulsions. After the invasion of Poland in 1939, Soviet Russia deported hundreds of thousands of Poles, Jews, and Ukrainians to camps in Siberia. After the Nazi invasion in 1941, the Soviets followed up by sending similar numbers of ethnic Germans, Crimean Tatars, and Chechens residing in Soviet territory to Central Asia.

When the war in Europe was over in May 1945, an estimated 3 million refugees from central and eastern Europe were already fleeing westward, believing that it was better to be in the zone occupied by the western Allies than in territory controlled by the Soviet Union. Between 1944 and 1946, the transfer of people between Poland and the Soviet Union alone involved 1.3 million people, while simultaneously 2 million Russians and 450,000 Poles held in Germany had to be repatriated from areas controlled by the Allies. Meanwhile, between 1945 and 1950, 7 million ethnic Germans were expelled from Czechoslovakia, Poland, Hungary, and Yugoslavia. During the same period of postwar population movements, Bulgaria expelled a quarter million Turks, and Romania decided to deport thousands of Armenian refugees to Turkey, where they were no more welcome than they had been in Romania. Overseeing this often chaotic process was

Czech president Edvard Beneš above two columns of Soviet and Czech soldiers marching together under their respective flags. Beneš, who had been president of Czechoslovakia before the war, was returned to office in October 1945, only to be forced to resign in 1948 after a successful coup by the Soviet-backed Communist party.

Questions for Analysis

1. How do these images portray the victory over the Germans?

2. How do these images deal with the question of Czechoslovakian nationalism?

3. Which of the three images most coincides with the Soviet view of the Czech situation?

C. Czech propaganda card, May 1945.

a new organization, the United Nations Relief and Rehabilitation Administration (UNRRA), founded in 1943 and placed under the control of the United Nations in 1945. In its four years of existence, the UNRRA administered nearly 800 Displaced Persons and Resettlement Camps, reaching some 7 million people. In 1947, its activities were replaced by the UN's International Refugee Organization, and the economic assistance offered by the Marshall Plan (see page 941).

The Iron Curtain

The Soviet Union had insisted during wartime negotiations at Tehran (1943) and **Yalta** (1945) that it had a legitimate claim to control Eastern Europe, a claim that some Western leaders accepted as the price of defeating Hitler while others ignored it to avoid a dangerous confrontation. When Churchill visited Moscow in 1944, he and Stalin quietly bargained over their respective spheres of influence, offering each other "percentages" of the countries that were being liberated. The Declaration of Principles of Liberated Europe issued at Yalta in 1945 guaranteed free elections, but Stalin believed that the framework of Allied cooperation gave him a free hand in Eastern Europe. Stalin's siege mentality pervaded his authoritarian regime and cast nearly everyone at home or abroad as a potential threat or enemy of the state. Yet Soviet policy did not rest on Stalin's personal paranoia alone. The country's catastrophic wartime losses made the

SURVIVORS AT BERGEN-BELSEN EXCHANGE CAMP, 1945. This photograph was taken after the liberation of the concentration camp complex at Bergen-Belsen by British and Canadian soldiers in April 1945. The Germans used the Exchange Camp to detain Jewish women and children, whom they hoped to exchange for German prisoners or cash. These survivors, and countless others like them across Europe, needed shelter, food, and medical attention from the Allies in the aftermath of the war.

Soviets determined to maintain political, economic, and military control of the lands they had liberated from Nazi rule. For the Soviets, Eastern Europe was both "a sphere and a shield." When their former allies resisted their demands, the Soviets became suspicious, defensive, and aggressive.

In Eastern Europe, the Soviet Union used a combination of diplomatic pressure, political infiltration, and military power to create "people's republics" sympathetic to Moscow. This process was complicated by the fact that some countries—Hungary, Romania, and Bulgaria—had been Nazi allies during the Second World War. Poland and Czechoslovakia had been anti-Nazi throughout the war, but many Poles were also strongly anticommunist, particularly those who had lived under Soviet occupation during the period of the Nazi-Soviet Pact in 1939–1941; Czechoslovakia, meanwhile, had its own tradition of a legal communist movement that provided the Soviets with a local ally. Regardless of these differences, similar processes unfolded across the region. The central and eastern European states set up coalition governments that excluded former Nazi sympathizers. In Poland, leaders of the wartime underground and the Home Army were purged. Next came coalitions dominated by communists. And finally, the Communist party took hold of all the key positions of power. This progression prompted Winston Churchill, speaking at a college graduation in Fulton, Missouri, in 1946, to say that an "Iron Curtain" had "descended across Europe." In

1948, the Soviets crushed a Czechoslovakian coalition government—a break from Yalta's guarantee of democratic elections that shocked many Europeans, in both the East and the West. That year, governments dependent on Moscow had been established in Poland, Hungary, Romania, and Bulgaria, creating what was referred to as the Eastern bloc.

The Soviet campaign to control Eastern Europe did not go unchallenged. The Yugoslavian communist and resistance leader Marshall Tito (Josip Broz; 1892–1980) fought to keep his government independent of Moscow. Unlike most Eastern European communist leaders, Tito came to power on his own during the war, and thanks to his wartime record, which gave him political authority rooted in his own country, he was able to draw support from Serbs, Croats, and Muslims in Yugoslavia. In the end, Moscow charged that Yugoslavia had "taken the road to nationalism," or had become a "colony of the imperialist nations," and expelled the country from the economic and military pacts of communist countries.

Determined to reassert control elsewhere, the Soviets demanded purges in the parties and administrations of various satellite governments, beginning in the Balkans and extending through Czechoslovakia, East Germany, and Poland. The fact that democratic institutions had been shattered before the war made it easier to establish dictatorships in its aftermath. Moreover, the purges succeeded by playing on fears and festering hatreds. In several areas, for example, those purging the governments attacked their opponents as Jewish. Anti-Semitism, far from being crushed, remained a potent political force, and it became common to blame Jews for bringing the horrors of war to Europe. These purges were accompanied by broad economic changes, including the expropriation of private property and the mobilization of large numbers of people for reconstruction and industrial development projects. Public life was strictly controlled by a political police answering to the party; the realm of culture, too, was placed at the service of the regime.

The end of war did not mean peace. In Greece, as in Yugoslavia and through much of the Balkans, the war's end brought a local communist-led resistance to the verge of seizing power; the bloody civil war, which lasted until 1949, took a higher toll than the wartime occupation. The British and the Americans, determined to keep Greece in their sphere of influence (in accordance with informal agreements with the Soviets), did so by sending large infusions of aid to the anticommunist monarchy. Greece's bloodletting became one of the first crises of the Cold War and a touchstone for the United States' escalating fear of communist expansion.

Defeated Germany lay at the heart of these two polarizing power blocs and soon became the front line of their conflict. The Allies had divided Germany into four zones of occupation; although the city of Berlin was deep in Soviet territory, it too was divided. The occupation zones were intended to be temporary, pending an official peace settlement, but the Soviets and the French, British, and Americans quarreled over reparations and policies for the economic development of Germany. Administrative conflicts among the Western powers were almost as intense as their disagreements with the Soviets, and Britain and the United States nearly had a serious falling out over food supply and trade in their zones. Yet the quickening Cold War put those arguments on hold and, in 1948, the three Western allies began to create a single government for their territories. They passed reforms to ease the economic crisis and introduced a new currency—a powerful symbol of economic unity. The Soviets retaliated by cutting all road, train, and river access from the Western Zone to West Berlin. The Western allies, however, refused to cede control of the capital, and for eleven months, they airlifted supplies (hundreds of flights carrying 12,000 tons of supplies a day) over Soviet territory to the besieged Western Zone of Berlin. The Berlin blockade, which lasted from June 1948 to May 1949, ended with the creation of two Germanies: the Federal Republic in the west and the German Democratic Republic in the former Soviet zone. Within a few short years, both Germanies looked strikingly like armed camps.

GERMANY DIVIDED AND THE BERLIN AIRLIFT. In the summer of 1948, the Soviet Union blocked routes through the German Democratic Republic to the Allies' Western Zone of Berlin. The blockade forced the Allies to airlift supplies to West Berlin and exacerbated tensions between the Soviet Union and the United States. At one point, planes landed in Berlin every three minutes. ■ *Why were the Western Allies able to airlift so much food so frequently?* ■ *How did this event lead to the eventual division of Germany into two nations?* ■ *What were the consequences of this division for the German people?*

The Marshall Plan

The United States countered the expansion of Soviet power and locally based communist movements with massive programs of economic and military aid to Western Europe. President Harry Truman, in a 1947 speech to Congress arguing for military assistance to anticommunists in Greece, set out what would come to be called the **Truman Doctrine**: a pledge to support the resistance of "free peoples" against communism. The American president declared the Soviet–American conflict to be a choice between "two ways of life," and tied the contest for political power to economics. A few months later, Secretary of State George Marshall outlined an ambitious plan of economic aid to Europe—the European Recovery Program (ERP)—including, initially, the Eastern European states. Stalin, however, prohibited the communist governments of central and eastern Europe from accepting the aid.

The ERP, also known as the **Marshall Plan**, provided $13 billion of aid over four years, beginning in 1948, targeted to industrial redevelopment. The plan supplied American tractors, locomotive engines, food, technical equipment, and capital to participating states. Unlike a relief plan, however, it encouraged the participating states to diagnose their own economic problems and develop their own solutions. The plan also encouraged

GERMAN COMMUNISTS PROTEST IN BERLIN AGAINST THE MARSHALL PLAN, 1952. Cold War tensions between the United States and the Soviet Union divided Europeans against one another. The signs in this protest read: "Strength and Labor through Trade with the East!" and "Against the Marshall Plan [which] brings unemployment and poverty." ■ *What made the question of U.S. economic assistance so controversial for Germans?*

West, as its senior military officer. NATO's ground forces began with thirty divisions in 1950, and by 1953, grew to nearly sixty—including, perhaps most surprising, a dozen divisions from the young state of West Germany. West German rearmament had been the subject of agonizing debate, particularly in Britain and France, but American pressure and a sense of strategic necessity led to its acceptance within Western Europe. Among the most striking aspects of the war's aftermath was how rapidly Germany was reintegrated into Europe. In the new Cold War world, *the West* quickly came to mean anticommunism, and all potentially reliable allies, whatever their past, were not to be punished or excluded.

Two Worlds and the Race for the Bomb

The Soviets viewed NATO, the Marshall Plan, and especially the United States' surprising involvement in Europe's affairs with mounting alarm. The Soviet Union responded by establishing an Eastern European version of the plan: the Council for Mutual Economic Assistance (or Comecon). In 1947, the Soviets organized an international political arm, the Communist Information Bureau (or Cominform), responsible for coordinating worldwide communist policy and programs. They responded to NATO with the establishment of their own military alliances, confirmed by the Warsaw Pact of 1955. This agreement set up a joint command among the states of Albania, Bulgaria, Czechoslovakia, Hungary, Poland, Romania, and East Germany, and guaranteed the continued presence of Soviet troops in all those countries.

All these conflicts were darkened by the shadow of the nuclear arms race. In 1949, the Soviet Union surprised American intelligence by testing its first **atomic bomb**, modeled on the plutonium bomb that Americans had tested in 1945. In 1953, both superpowers demonstrated a new weapon—the hydrogen (or "super") bomb—which was a thousand times more powerful than the bomb dropped on Hiroshima. And within a few years, both countries developed smaller bombs along with systems of delivery to use them. Intercontinental missiles were built that could field at first one and then several nuclear warheads, and that could be fired from land or from a new generation of atomic-powered submarines that roamed the seas at all times ready to act. J. Robert Oppenheimer warned that the H-bomb so dramatically raised the ability to make war against civilians, it could become a "weapon of genocide." Beyond the grim warnings that nuclear war would wipe out human civilization, the bomb had more specific strategic consequences. The nuclearization of warfare fed into the polarizing effect

coordination among European countries, partly out of idealism (some spoke of a "United States of Europe") and partly to dissuade France from asking for reparations and trying to dismantle the German economy. With a series of other economic agreements, the Marshall Plan became one of the building blocks of European economic unity. The plan, however, required measures such as decontrol of prices, restraints on wages, and balanced budgets. The Americans encouraged opposition to left-leaning politicians and movements that might be sympathetic to communism. The pressure to confront the Soviet Union also led the United States to abandon relatively quickly its plan to purge former Nazi party members from positions of influence in West Germany. The most prominent surviving Nazi leaders were tried at Nuremberg in 1945–1946, and twelve were executed. Subsequent trials lasted until 1949, but many of the millions of Nazi party members simply resumed their lives.

The growing rift with the Soviet Union led the United States to shore up military defenses in Western Europe. In April 1949, Canada, the United States, and representatives of Western European states signed an agreement establishing the **North Atlantic Treaty Organization (NATO)**; Greece, Turkey, and West Germany were later added as members. An armed attack against any one of the NATO members would now be regarded as an attack against all and would bring a united military response. NATO established a joint military command in 1950, with Dwight D. Eisenhower, the wartime commander of Allied forces in the

U.S. AND SOVIET VIEWS OF THE ARMS RACE. From 1946 to 1958, the United States detonated multiple nuclear weapons as tests at the Bikini Atoll in the Pacific Ocean; the Soviet Union's first successful nuclear test came in 1949. These posters, both apparently depicting the Pacific site of the U.S. nuclear testing, demonstrate the use of nuclear warfare images by both governments to communicate with their populations. The U.S. civil defense poster (left) seeks to convince the American population that "it *can* happen here"; the Soviet poster (right) states simply: *Het!* ("No!") ▪ *Coming so soon after the destruction of the Second World War, how might such images have been received by the populations of the United States and the Soviet Union?*

of the Cold War, because countries without nuclear arms found it difficult to avoid joining either the Soviet or the American pact. Over the long term, the threat of nuclear war encouraged a disparity between two groups of nations: the superpowers, with their enormous military budgets, on the one hand, and the nations that came to rely on agreements and international law on the other. It changed the nature of face-to-face warfare as well, encouraging "proxy wars" between clients of the superpowers and raising fears that local conflicts might trigger a general war.

The H-bomb quickly took on enormous cultural significance as the single most compelling symbol of the age.

It seemed to confirm both humanity's power and its vulnerability. The leaps in knowledge that it represented boosted contemporaries' confidence in science and progress, while at the same time, weapons of mass destruction and humanity's emerging power to obliterate itself raised gnawing questions about whether that confidence was misplaced.

Was the Cold War inevitable? Could the Americans and the Soviets have negotiated an agreement? On the Soviet side, Stalin's personal suspiciousness, ruthlessness, and autocratic ambitions combined with genuine security concerns to fuel the Cold War mentality. The U.S. leaders, for their part, believed that the devastation of the Continent gave the Soviets an opportunity to establish communist regimes throughout Europe, as Western Europeans alone could not respond effectively to multiplying postwar crises in Germany, Greece, and elsewhere. The United States also was unwilling to give up the military, economic, and political power it had acquired during the war. As it turned away from its traditional isolationism, the United States articulated new strategic interests with global consequences, including access to European industry and far-flung military bases. These interests, in turn, played into Soviet fears, and, in this context, trust became all but impossible.

A new international balance of power quickly produced new international policies. In 1946, diplomat George Kennan argued that the United States needed to make containing the Soviet threat a priority. According to Kennan, the Soviets had not embarked on world revolution, thus the United States needed to respond not with "histrionics: with threats or blustering or superfluous gestures of outward toughness," but rather with "the adroit and vigilant application of counterforce at a series of constantly shifting geographical and political points." Containment became the point of reference for U.S. foreign policy for the next forty years.

At its height, the Cold War had a chilling effect on domestic politics in both countries. In the Soviet Union, writers and artists were attacked for deviating from the party line. The party disciplined economists for suggesting that Western European industry might recover from the wartime damage it had sustained. And Soviet radio blared news that Czech or Hungarian leaders had been exposed as traitors. In the United States, congressional committees launched campaigns to root out "communists" everywhere. On both sides of the Iron Curtain, the Cold War intensified everyday anxiety, bringing air-raid drills, spy trials, warnings that a way of life was at stake, and appeals to defend family and home against the menacing "other."

Khrushchev and the Thaw

After Stalin died in 1953, **Nikita Khrushchev**'s slow accession to power, not secure until 1956, signaled a change of direction. Khrushchev possessed a kind of earthy directness that, despite his hostility to the West, helped for a time to ease tensions. Whereas Stalin had secluded himself in the Kremlin, Khrushchev traveled throughout the world. On a visit to the United States in 1959, he traded quips with Iowa farmers and was entertained at Disneyland. Khrushchev was a shrewd politician, switching quickly between angry anti-American rhetoric and diplomatic reconciliation. Showing a desire to reduce international conflict, he soon agreed to a summit meeting with the leaders

NIKITA KHRUSHCHEV. Khrushchev, premier (1958–1964) and first secretary of the Communist party (1953–1964) of the Soviet Union, visited the United States in 1959. Here, he is shown joking with an Iowa farmer. ■ *Why was it important for Khrushchev to engage a foreign audience in this way?*

of Britain, France, and the United States. This summit led to a series of understandings that eased the frictions in heavily armed Europe, and in the early 1960s, produced a ban on testing nuclear weapons above ground.

Khrushchev's other change of direction came with his famous "secret speech" of 1956, in which he acknowledged (behind the closed doors of the Twentieth Party Congress) the excesses of Stalin's era. Though the speech was secret, his accusations were widely discussed. The harshness of Stalin's regime had generated popular discontent, and demands grew for a shift from the production of heavy machinery and armaments to the manufacture of consumer goods, for a measure of freedom in the arts, and for an end to police repression. Under these circumstances, how could the regime keep de-Stalinization within safe limits? The thaw did unleash forces that proved difficult to control. Between 1956 and 1958, the Soviet prison camps released thousands of prisoners, and Soviet citizens besieged the regime with requests to rehabilitate relatives of those who had been executed or imprisoned under Stalin, partly to make themselves again eligible for certain privileges of citizenship, such as housing. In the new cultural climate, private life—family issues, the shortage of men after the war, and the problem of orphans—became a legitimate subject of concern and discussion. Also, during this period, many foreigners in the prison and labor camps of central Asia and Siberia, including Germans, Poles, Czechs, and Hungarians, were allowed to leave the Soviet Union.

The thaw provided a brief window of opportunity for some of the Soviet Union's most important writers. In 1957, Boris Pasternak's novel *Doctor Zhivago* could not be published in the Soviet Union, and Pasternak was barred from receiving his Nobel Prize. In 1962, Aleksandr Solzhenitsyn's (*suhl-zhih-NYEE-tsihn*) first novel, *One Day in the Life of Ivan Denisovich,* was published, marking the relative cultural freedom of the thaw. *Ivan Denisovich* was based on Solzhenitsyn's own experiences in the camps, where he had spent eight years for criticizing Stalin in a letter. It was a powerful literary testimony to the repression Khrushchev had acknowledged. By 1964, Khrushchev had fallen and the thaw ended, driving criticism and writers underground. Solzhenitsyn kept working, however. In *The First Circle* (1968), also autobiographical, he tells the story of a group of imprisoned scientists doing research for the secret police. He also kept working on what would become *The Gulag Archipelago,* the first massive historical and literary study of the Stalinist

camps (gulags). He secretly collected memoirs and personal testimonies from prisoners, kept notes on cigarette rolling papers, and buried drafts of chapters behind his house. The Soviet secret police found a copy of the manuscript in a taxicab just when Solzhenitsyn had finished it. It was published in 1973 in Paris, but a year later, the regime arrested Solzhenitsyn on charges of treason and sent him into exile. The most celebrated Soviet dissident was neither a democrat nor pro-Western. He was an idealist and a moralist, with roots among nineteenth-century Russian authors and philosophers. From exile, Solzhenitsyn attacked the corruptions of American commercialism as well as Soviet repressiveness.

After Stalin in Eastern Europe

By the year of Stalin's death, tensions had exploded in Eastern Europe. The East German government, burdened by reparations payments to the Soviet Union, faced an economic crisis; making matters worse was the government's awareness of West German economic success. The illegal exodus of East German citizens to the West rose sharply: 58,000 left in March 1953 alone. In June, when the government demanded

THE BERLIN WALL, 1961 AND 1989. By 1960, the East German economy was in severe trouble, and many people, especially educated professionals, were fleeing to the West: 200,000 in 1960 and 103,000 in the first six months of 1961. On August 13, 1961, the East German government placed armed guards and barbed wire around West Berlin to stop the flow (see photo on the left). This bold move allowed the East German nation to survive, but it also created a powerful symbol of the regime's repressive character. In 1989, the breach in the wall was the final sign of the East German government's collapse, and the freedom to enter West Berlin marked a turning point after nearly three decades of enforced isolation. In the photo on the right, Chancellor Helmut Kohl of West Germany (center, looking up), shakes hands with East Germans on top of the wall in December 1989.

Competing Viewpoints

The Cold War: Soviet and American Views

> The first excerpt is from a speech titled "The Sinews of Peace," delivered by Winston Churchill at Westminster College in Fulton, Missouri, in early 1946. Warning of the rising power of the Soviet Union in Eastern Europe, he coined the phrase "iron curtain."
>
> The next excerpt is from an address by Nikita Khrushchev, who became first secretary of the Communist party in 1953. Three years later, his power secure, he began publicly to repudiate the crimes of Joseph Stalin. Khrushchev presided over a short-lived thaw in Soviet–American relations. Yet, as can be seen in his address, Khrushchev shared Churchill's conception of the world as divided into two mutually antagonistic camps.

Winston Churchill's "Iron Curtain" Speech

A shadow has fallen upon the scenes so lately lighted by the Allied victory. Nobody knows what Soviet Russia and its Communist international organization intend to do in the immediate future, or what are the limits, if any, to their expansive and proselytizing tendencies. I have a strong admiration and regard for the valiant Russian people and for my wartime comrade, Marshal [sic] Stalin. There is deep sympathy and goodwill in Britain . . . towards the people of all the Russias and a resolve to persevere through many differences and rebuffs in establishing lasting friendships. We understand the Russian need to be secure on her western frontiers by the removal of all possibility of German aggression. We welcome Russia to her rightful place among the leading nations of the world. We welcome her flag upon the seas. Above all, we welcome constant, frequent and growing contacts between the Russian people and our own people on both sides of the Atlantic. It is my duty however . . . to place before you certain facts about the present position in Europe.

From Stettin in the Baltic to Trieste in the Adriatic, an iron curtain has descended across the Continent. Behind that line lie all the capitals of the ancient states of Central and Eastern Europe. Warsaw, Berlin, Prague, Vienna, Budapest, Belgrade, Bucharest and Sofia, all these famous cities and the populations around them lie in what I must call the Soviet sphere, and all are subject in one form or another, not only to Soviet influence but to a very high and, in many cases, increasing measure of control from Moscow. . . .

From what I have seen of our Russian friends and allies during the war, I am convinced that there is nothing they admire so much as strength, and there is nothing for which they have less respect than for weakness, especially military weakness. For that reason the old doctrine of a balance of power is unsound. We cannot afford, if we can help it, to work on narrow margins, offering temptations to a triad of strength. If the Western Democracies stand together in strict adherence to the principles of the United Nations Charter, their influences for furthering those principles

hefty increases in industrial productivity, strikes broke out in East Berlin, and the unrest spread throughout the country. The Soviet army put down the uprising, and hundreds were executed in the subsequent purge. In the aftermath, the East German government, under the leadership of Walter Ulbricht, used fears of disorder to solidify one-party rule.

In 1956, Khrushchev's policy of de-Stalinization and the "thaw" brought about a sense of relief for many in the Soviet sphere. Perceiving an opening, Poland and Hungary rebelled, demanding more independence in the management of their domestic affairs. In Poland, the movement began in June 1956 with a rebellion by Polish workers in Poznan. The government responded with military repression, crushing the workers' movement. By October, the leading Polish Stalinists were forced to resign, replaced by the anti-Stalinist Polish leader Władysław Gomułka. By pledging Poland's loyalty to the Warsaw Pact, Gomułka won Soviet permission for his country to pursue its own will be immense and no one is likely to molest them. If however they become divided or falter in their duty and if these all-important years are allowed to slip away then indeed catastrophe may overwhelm us all.

Source: Winston Churchill, *Winston S. Churchill: His Complete Speeches, 1897–1963*, vol. 7, 1943–1949, ed. Robert Rhodes James (New York: 1983), pp. 7290–91.

Nikita Khrushchev, Report to the Communist Party Congress (1961)

Comrades! The competition of the two world social systems, the socialist and the capitalist, has been the chief content of the period since the 20th party Congress. It has become the pivot, the foundation of world development at the present historical stage. Two lines, two historical trends, have manifested themselves more and more clearly in social development. One is the line of social progress, peace and constructive activity. The other is the line of reaction, oppression and war.

In the course of the peaceful competition of the two systems capitalism has suffered a profound moral defeat in the eyes of all peoples. The common people are daily convinced that capitalism is incapable of solving a single one of the urgent problems confronting mankind. It becomes more and more obvious that only on the paths to socialism

can a solution to these problems be found. Faith in the capitalist system and the capitalist path of development is dwindling. Monopoly capital, losing its influence, resorts more and more to intimidating and suppressing the masses of the people, to methods of open dictatorship in carrying out its domestic policy and to aggressive acts against other countries. But the masses of the people offer increasing resistance to reaction's acts.

It is no secret to anyone that the methods of intimidation and threat are not a sign of strength but evidence of the weakening of capitalism, the deepening of its general crisis. As the saying goes, if you can't hang on by the mane, you won't hang on by the tail! Reaction is still capable of dissolving parliaments in some countries in violation of their constitutions, of casting the best representatives of the people into prison, of

sending cruisers and marines to subdue the "unruly." All this can put off for a time the approach of the fatal hour for the rule of capitalism. The imperialists are sawing away at the branch on which they sit. There is no force in the world capable of stopping man's advance along the road of progress.

Source: *Current Soviet Policies IV*, ed. Charlotte Saikowski and Leo Gruliow, from the translations of *Current Digest of the Soviet Press*, Joint Committee on Slavic Studies (New York: 1962), pp. 42–45.

Questions for Analysis

1. Whom did Churchill blame for building the Iron Curtain between the Soviet sphere and the Western sphere?

2. How was the Soviet Union actively trying to create international communism? How was the United States trying to spread its way of life globally?

"ways of Socialist development." A few years of liberalization followed, but Gomułka became more conservative and resistant to political reform in the 1960s.

Meanwhile, events in Hungary turned out very differently. The charismatic leader of Hungary's communist government, Imre Nagy (*EEM-re NOD-yuh*), was as much a Hungarian nationalist as a communist. Under his government, protests against Moscow's policies developed into a much broader anticommunist struggle. He announced that

he would dismantle Hungary's political police and withdraw from the Warsaw Pact. Khrushchev might contemplate looser ties between Eastern Europe and Moscow, but he would not tolerate an end to the pact. On November 4, 1956, Soviet troops occupied Budapest, arresting and executing leaders of the Hungarian rebellion. The Hungarians took up arms, and street fighting continued for several weeks. They had hoped for Western aid, but President Dwight D. Eisenhower, newly elected to a second term, steered clear of giving them

EUROPE DURING THE COLD WAR. Examine the membership of NATO and the Warsaw Pact, respectively. ■ *Which nations were the member states of NATO?* ■ *Which nations were members of the Warsaw Pact?* ■ *Why do you think some countries did not join NATO?* ■ *Why did the membership of each alliance stay relatively stable for nearly a half century?*

support. Soviet forces installed a new government under the staunchly communist Janos Kadar, and the repression continued, forcing tens of thousands of Hungarian refugees to flee for the West. Khrushchev's efforts at presenting a gentler, more conciliatory Soviet Union to the West had been shattered by revolt and repression.

Khrushchev's policy of "peaceful coexistence" with the West did not reduce his determination to stave off any military threat to Eastern Europe. By the mid-1950s, NATO's policy of putting battlefield nuclear weapons in West Germany seemed evidence of just such a threat. What was more, East Germans continued to flee the country via West Berlin. Between 1949 and 1961, 2.7 million East Germans left—stark evidence of the unpopularity of the regime. Attempting to stem the tide, Khrushchev demanded that the West recognize the permanent division of Germany with an undivided Berlin. When that demand was refused, the East German government built a ten-foot wall separating the two sectors of the city in 1961. The wall brought a dangerous show of force on both sides, as the Soviets and Americans mobilized reservists for war. The newly elected American president John F. Kennedy marked Berlin's contested status when during a visit he proclaimed that "all free men" were fellow citizens of noncommunist West Berlin. For almost thirty years, until 1989, the Berlin Wall remained a monument to how far the war had gone cold, darkly mirroring the division of Germany, and Europe as a whole.

ECONOMIC RENAISSANCE

Despite the ongoing tensions of global superpower rivalry, the postwar period brought an economic "miracle" in Western Europe. Economists still debate the causes of this remarkable recovery, but some factors resulted directly from the war, which encouraged a variety of technological innovations that could be applied in peacetime: improved communications (the invention of radar, for example), development of synthetic materials, increasing use of aluminum and alloy steels, and advances in the techniques of prefabrication. Moreover, wartime manufacturing had added significantly to nations' productive capacity. The Marshall Plan seems to have been less central than many claimed at the time, but it solved immediate problems having to do with the balance of payments and the shortage of American dollars to buy American goods. This boom was fueled by a third set of factors: high consumer demand and, consequently, very high levels of employment throughout the 1950s and the 1960s. Brisk domestic and foreign consumption encouraged expansion, continued capital investment, and technologi-

cal innovation. Rising demand for Europe's goods hastened agreements that encouraged the free flow of international trade and currencies (discussed on pages 950–951).

Western European political leaders now assumed that states would do much more economic management than before: directing investment, making decisions about what to modernize, and coordinating policies between industries and countries. This, too, was a legacy of wartime deprivation. As one British official observed, "We are all planners now." But government tactics for steering the economy varied: West Germany provided tax breaks to encourage business investment; Britain and Italy offered investment allowances to their steel and petroleum industries; and France, Britain, Italy, and Austria led the way in experiments with nationalizing industry and services in an effort to raise productivity. The result was a series of "mixed" economies combining public and private ownership. In France, where public ownership was already well advanced in the 1930s, railways, electricity and gas, banking, radio and television, and a large segment of the automobile industry were brought under state management. In Britain, the list was equally long, with coal and utilities; road, railroad, and air transport; and banking. Though nationalization was less common in West Germany, the railway system (state owned since the late nineteenth century); some electrical, chemical, and metallurgical concerns; and the Volkswagen company (the remnant of Hitler's attempt to produce a "people's car") were all in state hands, though the latter was largely returned to the private sector in 1963.

These government policies and programs contributed to astonishing growth rates. Between 1945 and 1963, the average yearly growth of West Germany's gross domestic product—gross national product (GNP) minus income received from abroad—was 7.6 percent; in Austria, 5.8 percent; in Italy, 6 percent; in the Netherlands, 4.7 percent; and so on. Not only did these economies recover from the war but they actually reversed prewar economic patterns of slack demand, overproduction, and insufficient investment, leaving production facilities hard pressed to keep up with the soaring demand.

West Germany's recovery was particularly spectacular, and particularly important to the rest of Europe. Production increased sixfold between 1948 and 1964. Unemployment fell to record lows, reaching 0.4 percent in 1965, when there were six jobs for every unemployed person. This, contrasted with the catastrophic unemployment of the Great Depression, heightened the impression of a miracle. Prices rose but then leveled off, enabling many citizens to plunge into a domestic buying spree that caused production to soar. In the 1950s, the state and private industry built a half million new housing units each year, to accommodate citizens whose homes had been destroyed, new resident refugees from East

Germany and Eastern Europe, and transient workers from Italy, Spain, Greece, and elsewhere drawn in by West Germany's high demand for labor. German cars, specialized mechanical goods, optics, and chemicals returned to their former role of leading the world markets. West German women were included in the process as well: during the 1950s, German politicians encouraged women to take up a role as "citizen consumers," as active but prudent buyers of goods that would keep the German economy humming.

Under the direction of a minister for planning, Jean Monnet, the French government played a direct role in industrial reform, contributing not only capital but expert advice, and facilitating shifts in the national labor pool to place workers where they were most needed. The plan also gave priority to basic industries, causing the production of electricity to double, the steel industry to be thoroughly modernized, and the French railway system to become the fastest and most efficient on the Continent. Italy's industrial "miracle" came later, but it was even more impressive. Stimulated by infusions of capital from the government and the Marshall Plan, Italian companies soon began to compete with other European international giants. The products of Olivetti, Fiat, and Pirelli became familiar in households around the world to an extent that no Italian goods had in the past. Electric power production doubled between 1938 and 1953. And by 1954, real wages were 50 percent higher than they had been in 1938.

European nations, with little in common in terms of political traditions or industrial patterns, all shared in the general prosperity. Rising GNPs, however, did not level the differences among and within states: in southern Italy, illiteracy remained high, and land continued to be held by a few rich families; and the per capita GNP in Sweden was almost ten times that of Turkey. Britain remained a special case. The Conservative prime minister, Harold Macmillan, campaigned successfully for reelection in 1959 with the slogan, "You've never had it so good"—an accurate enough boast. British growth was respectable when compared with past performance, yet the British economy remained sluggish. The country was burdened with obsolete factories and methods, the legacy of its early industrialization, and by an unwillingness to adopt new techniques in old industries or invest in more successful new ones. It was plagued also by a series of balance-of-payments crises precipitated by an inability to sell more goods abroad than it imported.

European Economic Integration

The Western European renaissance was a collective effort. Beginning with the Marshall Plan, a series of international economic organizations began to bind the Western European countries together. The first of these, the European Coal and Steel Community (ECSC), was founded in 1951 to coordinate trade in, and the management of, Europe's most crucial resources. Coal was still king in mid-twentieth-century Europe; it fueled everything from steel manufacturing and trains to household heating, accounting for 82 percent of Europe's primary energy consumption. It was also key to relations between West Germany, with its abundant coal mines, and France, with its coal-hungry steel mills. The ECSC joint High Authority, which included experts from each of the participating countries, had the power to regulate prices, increase or limit production, and impose administrative fees. In 1957, the Treaty of Rome created the European Economic Community (EEC), or Common Market, which aimed to abolish trade barriers among its members: France, West Germany, Italy, Belgium, Holland, and Luxembourg. Moreover, the organization pledged itself to common external tariffs, free movement of labor and capital among the member nations, and uniform wage structures and social security systems to ensure similar working conditions throughout the Common Market. A commission, headquartered in Brussels, administered the program; and by 1962, Brussels had more than 3,000 "Eurocrats."

Integration did not proceed smoothly. Great Britain stayed away, fearing the effects of the ECSC on its declining coal industry and on its longtime trading relationships with Australia, New Zealand, and Canada. Britain did not share France's need for raw materials and the other nations' need for markets, and continued to rely on its economic relations with the Empire and Commonwealth. As one of the few victors of the Second World War, Britain assumed that it could hold its global economic position in the postwar world. In the other countries, domestic opposition to EEC provisions on wages or agricultural prices often threatened to scuttle agreements. France and other countries, sensitive to the importance of the peasantry to political stability, insisted on protecting agriculture and invested in the countryside's place in national identity.

The seismic shifts that began to make oil and atomic power more important than coal (see Chapter 28) made the ECSC less effective, but the EEC was a remarkable success. By 1963, EEC had become the world's largest importer. Its steel production was second only to that of the United States, and its total industrial production was over 70 percent higher than it had been in 1950. And it established a new long-term political trend: individual countries sought European solutions to their problems.

Likewise, crucial agreements reached in July 1944 in Bretton Woods, New Hampshire, aimed to coordinate the movements of the global economy and internationalize solutions to economic crises, which would avoid catastrophes such as those that plagued the 1930s. Bretton Woods created the International Monetary Fund (IMF) and the World Bank, both designed to establish predictable and stable exchange rates, prevent speculation, and enable currencies—and consequently trade—to move freely. All other currencies were pegged to the dollar, which reflected and enhanced the United States' role as the foremost financial power. The new international system was formed with the American–European sphere in mind, but these organizations soon began to play a role in the economic development of what came to be known as the Third World. The postwar period, then, quickened global economic integration, largely on American terms.

Economic Development in the East

Although economic development in Eastern Europe was not nearly as dramatic as that in the West, significant advances occurred there as well. Eastern Europe had less industry prior to World War II, and some nations, such as Poland, had been devastated by the war. The communist governments undertook ambitious reconstruction and development projects by mobilizing the entire population. The initial results were impressive, particularly in building construction, heavy industry, mining, and agriculture. The culmination of communist engineering was the Soviet launch of Sputnik, the first orbiting satellite, in 1959.

With these programs of economic development, national incomes rose and output increased in Eastern Europe. Poland and Hungary, in particular, strengthened their economic connections with the West, primarily with France and West Germany. By the late 1970s, about 30 percent of Eastern Europe's trade was conducted outside the Soviet bloc. Nevertheless, the Soviet Union required its satellite countries to design their economic policies to serve more than their own national interests. Regulations governing Comecon, the Eastern European equivalent of the Common Market, ensured that the Soviet Union could sell its exports at prices well above the world level and compelled other members to trade with the Soviet Union to their disadvantage.

Eastern European economic development focused initially on heavy industry and collectivized agriculture, but political tension in countries such as Hungary and Poland eventually forced the Soviets to moderate their policies and permit the manufacture of more consumer goods and develop a modest trade with the West. This transition revealed the weakness of the planned economies of these countries: the distribution of goods, prices, the supply of resources, and access to foreign currencies were subject to administrative decisions. Managers of factories would receive production quotas at regular intervals, but the system was beset with difficulties. The inability to balance supply and demand, for example, created constant shortages of consumer products as well as the raw materials needed to produce them. Managing shortages was a constant preoccupation, for consumers who would wait for hours in queues when it became known that a long-desired product was suddenly available, and for producers who would hoard raw materials in anticipation of the next production cycle, thus exacerbating the shortages elsewhere. In the short term, the planned economy could lead to impressive achievements, but in the long term, the economy was weakened by rising costs and lack of innovation. The economic system also increased the political power of the party bureaucrats who oversaw it, making reform difficult.

The Welfare State

Economic growth became one of the watchwords of the postwar era; *social welfare* was another. The roots of the new legislation extended back to the late 1880s, when Otto von Bismarck had introduced insurance plans for old age, sickness, and disability in Germany. But economic expansion allowed postwar European states to fund more comprehensive social programs, and commitments to put democracy on a stronger footing provided the political motivation. Clement Atlee, a socialist and the leader of the British Labour party, coined the term *welfare state*. His government, in power until 1951, led the way in enacting legislation that provided free medical care to all through the National Health Service, assistance to families, and guaranteed secondary education of some kind. The welfare state also rested on the assumption that governments could and should try to support popular purchasing power, generate demand, and provide either employment or unemployment insurance—assumptions spelled out earlier by John Maynard Keynes in *General Theory* (1936) or in William Beveridge's important 1943 report on full employment. Although the British Labour party and Continental socialist parties pressed these measures, welfare was a consensus issue, backed by the moderate coalitions that governed most postwar Western European states. Understood in this way, welfare was not poor relief but an entitlement. Thus, it marked a break with centuries-old ways of thinking about poverty and citizenship.

European Politics

Postwar political leaders were overwhelmingly pragmatic. Konrad Adenauer, the West German chancellor from 1949 to 1963, despised German militarism and blamed that tradition for Hitler's rise to power. Still, he was apprehensive about German parliamentary democracy and governed in a paternalistic, sometimes authoritarian, manner. His determination to end the centuries-old hostility between France and Germany contributed significantly to the movement toward economic union. Alcide De Gasperi, the Italian premier from 1948 to 1953, was also a centrist. Among postwar French leaders, the most colorful was the Resistance hero General Charles de Gaulle. De Gaulle had retired from politics in 1946 when French voters refused to accept his proposals for strengthening the executive branch of the government. But in 1958, he was invited to return when, faced with civil turmoil caused by the Algerian war and an abortive coup attempt by a group of right-wing army officers, the government collapsed. De Gaulle accepted but insisted on a new constitution. That constitution, which created the Fifth Republic in 1958, strengthened the executive branch of the government in an effort to avoid the parliamentary deadlocks that had weakened the country earlier. De Gaulle used his new authority to restore France's power and prestige. "France is not really herself unless in the front rank," he wrote in his memoirs. "France cannot be France without greatness." Greatness, for de Gaulle, involved reorienting foreign policy, including an end to France's grip on Algeria. In 1966, resisting U.S. influence in Europe, he pulled French forces out of NATO, and cultivated better relations with the Soviet Union and West Germany. Finally, he accelerated French economic and industrial expansion by building a modern military establishment, complete with atomic weapons. De Gaulle was not, by nature, a democrat. Like his counterparts, he steered a centrist course, working hard to produce practical solutions to political problems, and thereby undermine radicalism in any form. Most other Western European nations did the same.

REVOLUTION, ANTICOLONIALISM, AND THE COLD WAR

In the colonial world, as in Europe, the end of war unleashed new conflicts. Those conflicts became closely bound up with Europe's political and economic recovery, had an enormous if delayed effect on Western culture, and complicated the Cold War. The Cold War, as we have seen, created two powerful centers of gravity in world politics. But the wave of anticolonial independence movements that swept through postwar Asia and Africa created a new group of nations that attempted to avoid aligning with either bloc, and instead called itself the "Third World."

CHARLES DE GAULLE PRESENTING HIS PLAN TO STRENGTHEN THE EXECUTIVE BRANCH OF THE GOVERNMENT IN 1946. When voters rejected his ideas, he retired, only to return in 1958 to outline a new constitution.

The Chinese Revolution

The Chinese Revolution was the single most radical change in the developing world after the Second World War. A civil war had raged in China since 1926, with Mao Zedong's (*mow zeh-DOONG*; 1893–1976) communist insurgents in the north in revolt against the Nationalist forces of Jiang Jeishi (Chiang Kai-shek; 1887–1975). Though they agreed on a truce to face the Japanese during the war years, the civil war resumed after the Japanese defeat. In 1949, Mao's insurgents took control of the Chinese government and drove the Nationalists into exile.

The Chinese Revolution was above all a peasant revolution, even more so than the Russian Revolution. Mao adapted Marxism to conditions very different from those imagined by Marx himself, emphasizing radical reform in the countryside—reducing rents,

A RED GUARD DEMONSTRATION. Middle-school students display their solidarity with Mao Zedong's revolution by waving copies of a book of his quotations. The slogan proclaims, "Not only are we able to destroy the old world, we are able to build a new world instead—Mao Zedong." ■ *What made the Chinese Revolution different from the Bolshevik Revolution of 1917?*

providing health care and education, and reforming marriage—and autonomy from Western colonial powers. The leaders of the revolution set about turning China into a modern industrial nation within a generation, at an enormous human cost and with very mixed results.

To anticolonial activists in many parts of the world, the Chinese Revolution stood as a model; to colonial powers, it represented the dangers inherent in decolonization. The "loss of China" provoked fear and consternation in the West, particularly in the United States, and intensified Western military and diplomatic anxiety about governments in Asia. Although Mao and Stalin distrusted one another and relations between the two regimes were extremely difficult, the United States considered both nations a communist bloc until the early 1970s.

The Korean War

Anxiety about China turned Korea into a hot spot in the Cold War. Korea, effectively a Japanese colony since the 1890s, had been brutally exploited by the occupiers. The Soviet Union forced the Japanese out at the end of the

Second World War, and, similar to Germany, the peninsula was divided into two states: communist North Korea, run by the Soviet client Kim Il Sung; and South Korea, led by the anticommunist autocrat Syngman Rhee, who was backed by the United States. In June 1950, communist North Korean troops attacked, crushing resistance and forcing a small American garrison to retreat to the far end of the peninsula. The United States took advantage of a temporary Russian boycott of the United Nations to bring the invasion before the Security Council, which gave permission for an American-led "police action" to defend South Korea.

U.S. General Douglas MacArthur, a Second World War hero, mounted an amphibious attack behind North Korean lines, driving the Korean communists to the Chinese border. He pressed for the authority to attack them as they retreated into China, clearly hoping to help reverse the Chinese Revolution, but President Harry Truman (1945–1953) denied this rash request and relieved MacArthur of command. The price had already been paid, however, as more than a million Chinese troops flooded across the border in support of the North Koreans, forcing the international troops into a bloody retreat. General Matthew Ridgeway, replacing MacArthur, stemmed the retreat, but the war became a stalemate, pitting Chinese and North Korean troops against UN troops comprised largely of American and South Korean forces, but also including contingents from Britain, Australia, Ethiopia, the Netherlands, Turkey, and elsewhere. Two years later, the war ended inconclusively, with Korea divided roughly along the original line. South Korea had not been "lost," but with more than 53,000 Americans and more than a million Koreans and Chinese killed, neither side could claim a decisive victory. As in Germany, the inability of major powers to achieve their goals resulted in a divided nation.

Decolonization

The Chinese Revolution proved the start of a larger wave. Between 1947 and 1960, the sprawling European empires built during the nineteenth century disintegrated. Opposition to colonial rule had stiffened after the First World War, forcing war-weakened European states to renegotiate the terms of empire. After the Second World War, older forms of empire quickly became untenable. In some regions, European states simply sought to cut their losses and withdraw. In others, well-organized and tenacious nationalist movements successfully demanded new constitutional arrangements and independence. In a third set of cases, European powers were drawn into complicated, multifaceted, and extremely violent struggles among different movements of indigenous peoples and European settler communities—conflicts the European states had helped create.

The British Empire Unravels

India was the first and largest of the colonies to win self-government after the war. As we have seen, rebellions such as the Sepoy Mutiny challenged the representatives of Britain in India throughout the nineteenth century (Chapter 25). During the early stages of the Second World War, the Indian National Congress, the umbrella party of the independence movement founded in 1885, called on Britain to "quit India." The extraordinary Indian nationalist Mohandas K. (Mahatma) Gandhi (1869–1948) had been at work in India since the 1920s, and had pioneered anticolonial ideas and tactics that echoed the world over. In the face of colonial domination, Gandhi advocated not violence but *swaraj* ("self-rule"), urging Indians individually and collectively to develop their own resources and withdraw from the imperial economy—by going on strike,

refusing to pay taxes, or boycotting imported textiles and wearing those homespun. By 1947, Gandhi and his fellow nationalist Jawaharlal Nehru (1889–1964; prime minister 1947–1964), the leader of the pro-independence Congress party, had gained such widespread support that the British found it impossible to continue in power. The Labour party government elected in Britain in 1945 had always favored Indian independence, but now, that independence became a British political necessity.

Even as talks established the procedures for independence, however, India was torn by ethnic and religious conflict. The Muslim League, led by Mohammed Ali Jinnah (1876–1948), wanted autonomy in largely Muslim areas, fearing the predominantly Hindu Congress party's authority over a single united state. Cycles of rioting broke out between the two religious communities. In June 1947, British India was partitioned into the nations of India (majority Hindu) and Pakistan (majority Muslim). The process of partition brought brutal religious and ethnic warfare: more than a million Hindus and Muslims died, and an estimated 12 million became refugees, evicted from their lands or fleeing the fighting. Throughout the chaos, Gandhi continued to protest violence and focus his attention on overcoming the legacy of colonialism. He argued that "real freedom will come when we free ourselves of the dominance of Western education, Western culture, and [the] Western way of living which have been ingrained in us." In January 1948, he was assassinated by a Hindu zealot. Meanwhile, conflict continued between the independent states of India and Pakistan. Jawaharlal Nehru, who became the first prime minister of India, embarked on a program of industrialization and modernization—not at all what Gandhi would have counseled. Nehru proved particularly adept at maneuvering in the Cold War world, steering a course of nonalignment with either of the blocs, while getting aid for industry from the Soviet Union and food imports from the United States.

PALESTINE

The year 1948 brought more crises for the British Empire, including an end to the British mandate in Palestine. During the First World War, British diplomats had encouraged Arab nationalist revolts against the Ottoman Empire. At the same time, with the 1917 Balfour Declaration, they had also promised a "Jewish homeland" in Palestine for European Zionists. These contradictory promises and the flight of European Jews from Nazi Germany contributed to a rising conflict between Jewish settlers and Arabs in Palestine during the 1930s, provoking an Arab revolt that was bloodily suppressed by the British. During this time, the

Analyzing Primary Sources

Mohandas K. Gandhi and Nonviolent Anticolonialism

After leading a campaign for Indian rights in South Africa between 1894 and 1914, Mohandas K. Gandhi (1869–1948), known as Mahatma ("great-souled") Gandhi, became a leader in the long battle for home rule in India. This battle was finally won in 1947 with the partition of India and the creation of Pakistan. Gandhi's insistence on the power of nonviolent noncooperation brought him to the forefront of Indian politics, and provided a model for many later liberation struggles, including the American civil rights movement. Gandhi argued that only nonviolent resistance, which dramatized the injustice of colonial rule and colonial law, had the spiritual force to unite a community and end colonialism.

Passive resistance is a method of securing rights by personal suffering; it is the reverse of resistance by arms. When I refuse to do a thing that is repugnant to my conscience, I use soul-force. For instance, the Government of the day has passed a law which is applicable to me. I do not like it. If by using violence I force the Government to repeal the law, I am employing what may be termed body-force. If I do not obey the law and accept the penalty for its breach, I use soul-force. It involves sacrifice of self.

Everybody admits that sacrifice of self is infinitely superior to sacrifice of others. Moreover, if this kind of force is used in a cause that is unjust, only the person using it suffers. He does not make others suffer for his mistakes. Men have before now done many things which were subsequently found to have been wrong. . . . It is therefore meet that he should not do that which he knows to be wrong, and suffer the consequence whatever it may be. This is the key to the use of soul-force. . . .

It is contrary to our manhood if we obey laws repugnant to our conscience. Such teaching is opposed to religion and means slavery. If the Government were to ask us to go about without any clothing, should we do so? If I were a passive resister, I would say to them that I would have nothing to do with their law. But we have so forgotten ourselves and become so compliant that we do not mind any degrading law.

A man who has realized his manhood, who fears only God, will fear no one else. Man-made laws are not necessarily binding on him. Even the Government does not expect any such thing from us. They do not say: "You must do such and such a thing." But they say: "If you do not do it, we will punish you." We are sunk so low that we fancy that it is our duty and our religion to do what the law lays down. If man will only realize that it is unmanly to obey laws that are unjust, no man's tyranny will enslave him. This is the key to self-rule or home-rule.

Source: M. K. Gandhi, "Indian Home Rule (1909)," in *The Gandhi Reader: A Source Book of His Life and Writings*, ed. Homer A. Jack (Bloomington, IN: 1956), pp. 104–21.

Questions for Analysis

1. Why did Gandhi believe that "sacrifice of self" was superior to "sacrifice of others"?

2. What did Gandhi mean when he said, "it is contrary to our manhood if we obey laws repugnant to our conscience"?

---

newly important oil concessions in the Middle East were multiplying Britain's strategic interests in the Suez Canal, Egypt, and the Arab nations generally. Mediating local conflicts and balancing its own interests proved an impossible task for Britain.

In 1939, in the name of regional stability, the British strictly limited further Jewish immigration. They tried to maintain that limit after the war, but faced pressure from tens of thousands of Jewish refugees from Europe. The conflict quickly became a three-way war among Palestinian Arabs fighting for what they considered their land and their independence; Jewish settlers and Zionist militants determined to defy British restrictions; and British administrators with divided sympathies, either embarrassed and shocked by the plight of Jewish refugees or committed to maintaining good Anglo-Arab relations. Britain responded to these conflicts with military force, and by 1947, there was one British soldier for every eighteen inhabitants of the Mandate. The years of fighting, however, with terrorist tactics on all sides, persuaded the British to leave. The United

0   250   500 Miles
0   250   500 Kilometers

EUROPE   ASIA

Area of detail

AFRICA

BLACK SEA

TURKEY   SOVIET UNION

CASPIAN SEA

CYPRUS (1949)   SYRIA (1946)
LEBANON (1946)
ISRAEL (1948)   IRAQ (1924)   IRAN

JORDAN (1946)

KUWAIT (1958)   Strait of Hormuz

EGYPT (1922)   SAUDI ARABIA

BAHRAIN (1971)

QATAR (1971)

UNITED ARAB EMIRATES (1971)   OMAN (1971)

RED SEA

Nile R.

Persian Gulf

YEMEN   SOUTH YEMEN (1967)   ARABIAN SEA

British control
French control
1922   Date of independence
Major oil-producing areas

DECOLONIZATION IN THE MIDDLE EAST. ■ *Which countries were the colonial possessions of the British and the French in the Middle East?* ■ *What were the three stages of decolonization in the Middle East?* ■ *Why did the British hold on to the small states bordering the Persian Gulf and the Arabian Sea until 1971?*

Nations then voted (by a narrow margin) to partition the territory into two states. Neither Jewish settlers nor Palestinian Arabs found the partition satisfactory, and both began to fight for territory even before British troops withdrew. As soon as Israel declared its independence in May 1948, five neighboring states invaded. The new but well-organized Israeli nation survived the war and extended its boundaries. On the losing side, a million Palestinian Arabs who fled or were expelled found themselves clustered in refugee camps in the Gaza Strip and on the West Bank of the Jordan River, which the armistice granted to an enlarged state of Jordan. It is remarkable that the conflict did not become a Cold War confrontation at the start. Both the Soviets and the Americans recognized Israel for their own reasons. The creation of this new nation, however, marked a permanent change to the culture and balance of power in the region.

AFRICA

A number of West African colonies established assertive independence movements before and during the 1950s, and the British government moved hesitantly to meet their demands. By the middle of the 1950s, Britain agreed to a variety of terms for independence in these territories, leaving them with written constitutions and a British legal system but little else in terms of modern infrastructure or economic support. Defenders of British colonialism claimed that these formal institutions would give advantages to the independent states, but without other resources, even the most promising foundered. In the early 1960s, Ghana, known formerly as the Gold Coast and the first of these colonies to gain independence, was seen as a model for free African nations. But its politics soon degenerated, and its president, Kwame Nkrumah, became the first of several African leaders driven from office for corruption and autocratic behavior.

Belgium and France also withdrew from their holdings in Africa. By 1965, virtually all of the former African colonies had become independent, and virtually none possessed the means to redress the losses from colonialism to make that independence work. As Belgian authorities raced out of the Congo in 1960, they left crumbling railways and fewer than two dozen indigenous people with college educations.

The process of decolonization was relatively peaceful—except where large populations of European settlers complicated European withdrawal. In the north, settler resistance made the French exit from Algeria wrenching and complex (discussed on pages 960–962). In the east, in Kenya, the majority Kikuyu population revolted against British rule and a small group of settlers. The uprising, which came to be known as the Mau Mau rebellion, soon turned bloody. British troops fired freely at targets in rebel-occupied areas, sometimes killing civilians; and internment camps set up by colonial security forces became sites of atrocities that drew public investigations and condemnation by even the most conservative British politicians and army officers. In 1963, a decade after the rebellion began, the British conceded Kenyan independence.

In the late 1950s, the British prime minister Harold Macmillan endorsed independence for a number of Britain's African colonies as a response to powerful winds of change. But in southern Africa, the exceptionally large and wealthy population of European settlers set their sails against those winds, forming a resistance that continued on for decades. These settlers, a mixture of English migrants and the Franco-Dutch Afrikaners who traced their arrival to the eighteenth century, controlled huge tracts of fertile

1951 Date of independence
Former colonial power

- British
- French
- Portuguese
- Spanish
- Belgian
- Italian
- Former German colony, mandate of League of Nations after WWI
- Independent state
- ✳ Anticolonial revolt or war since 1945

MOROCCO (1956) ATLAS MOUNTAINS

TUNISIA (1956)

MEDITERRANEAN SEA

ALGERIA (1962)
✳1954–1962

LIBYA (1951)

Suez crisis 1956 ✳

WESTERN SAHARA (1975)

EGYPT (1922 with severe restrictions; 1954 British withdraw troops)

SAHARA DESERT

RED SEA

MAURITANIA (1960)

MALI (1960)

NIGER (1960)

CHAD (1960)

NUBIAN DESERT

Nile R.

SUDAN (1956)

SENEGAL (1960)

GAMBIA (1965)

UPPER VOLTA (BURKINA FASO) (1960)

GUINEA (1958)

GUINEA BISSAU (1974)
✳1961–1974

SIERRA LEONE (1961)

LIBERIA

IVORY COAST (1960)

DAHOMEY (BENIN) (1960)

NIGERIA (1960)

GHANA (1957)

TOGO (1960)

EQUATORIAL GUINEA (1968)

CAMEROON (1960)

CENTRAL AFRICAN REPUBLIC (1960)

ERITREA (1993)

DJIBOUTI (1977)

ETHIOPIAN HIGHLANDS

ETHIOPIA

SOMALIA (1960)
✳1950–1960

SÃO TOMÉ & PRINCIPE (1975)

GABON (1960)

Congo R.

RWANDA (1962)

CONGO BASIN

CONGO (ZAIRE) (1960)

UGANDA (1962)

KENYA (1963)
1952–1957
✳

BURUNDI (1962)

Lake Victoria

CONGO (1960)

TANZANIA (TANGANYIKA) (1961)

ATLANTIC OCEAN

ANGOLA (1975)
✳1961–1974

ZAMBIA (1964)

MALAWI (1964)

RHODESIA (1965)

ZIMBABWE (1980)
1965–1980
✳

MOZAMBIQUE (1975)
✳1964–1974

MADAGASCAR (1960)
✳1947–1948

SOUTH-WEST AFRICA (NAMIBIA) (controlled by South Africa) (1990)
✳1966–1990

BOTSWANA (1966)

KALAHARI DESERT

SOUTH AFRICA (1910–1961 1994 whole population votes)
✳1948–1994

SWAZILAND (1968)

LESOTHO (1966)

INDIAN OCEAN

0   500   1000 Miles

0   500   1000 Kilometers

DECOLONIZATION IN AFRICA. ■ *What were the forces behind decolonization in Africa?* ■ *Who were the biggest imperial losers in the decolonization of Africa?* ■ *By what decade had most African countries achieved their independence?*

farmland, along with some of the most lucrative gold and diamond mines on earth. This was especially true in South Africa, where, during the late 1940s, Britain's Labour government set aside its deep dislike of Afrikaner racism in a fateful political bargain. In return for guarantees that South African gold would be used carefully to support Britain's global financial power, Britain tolerated the introduction of apartheid in South Africa. Even by other standards of segregation, **apartheid** was especially harsh. Under its terms, Africans, Indians, and colored persons of mixed descent lost all political rights. All the institutions of social life, including marriage and schools, were segregated. It required Africans to live in designated "homelands," forbade them from traveling without specific permits, and created elaborate government bureaus to manage the labor essential to the economy. What was more, the government tried to block the dramatic social consequences of the expansion of mining and industrialization in general, especially African migration to cities and a new wave of labor militancy in the mines. The government also banned any political protest. These measures made Western powers uncomfortable with the segregationist regime, but white South Africans held on to American support by presenting themselves as a bulwark against communism.

To the north, in the territories of Rhodesia, the British government encouraged a large federation, controlled by white settlers but with the opportunity for majority rule in the future. By the early 1960s, however, the federation was on the verge of collapse. In 1964, the majority-rule state of Malawi was allowed to exit the federation, and Rhodesia split on northern and southern lines. In the north, the premier relented and accepted majority government under the black populist Kenneth Kaunda. But in the south, angry Afrikaners backed by 200,000 right-wing English migrants who had arrived since 1945 refused to accept majority rule. When the British government attempted to force their hand, the settlers unilaterally declared independence in 1965 and began a bloody civil war against southern Rhodesia's black population that lasted a half generation.

CRISIS IN SUEZ AND THE END OF AN ERA

For postwar Britain, empire was not only politically complicated but it cost too much. Britain began to withdraw from naval and air bases around the world because they had become too expensive to maintain. The Labour government, however, did try to maintain British power and prestige in the postwar world. In Malaya, British forces repressed a revolt by ethnic Chinese communists, and then helped support the independent states of Singapore and Malaysia, maintaining the ties of British companies and banks with Malaysia's lucrative rubber and oil reserves. Labour government also launched carefully targeted efforts at "colonial development" to tap local natural resources Britain hoped to sell on world markets. The development, however, was underfunded and largely disregarded in favor of fulfilling Cold War commitments elsewhere. In the Middle East, the British government protected several oil-rich states with its military, and helped overthrow a nationalist government in Iran to ensure that the oil states invested their money in British financial markets.

In Egypt, the British refused to yield a traditional point of imperial pride. In 1951, nationalists compelled the British to agree to withdraw their troops from Egyptian territory within three years. In 1952, a group of nationalist army officers deposed King Farouk, who had close ties to Britain, and proclaimed a republic. Shortly after the final British withdrawal, an Egyptian colonel, Gamal Abdel Nasser (1918–1970), became president of the country (1956–1970). His first major public act as president was to nationalize the Suez Canal Company, which would help finance the construction of the Aswan Dam on the Nile. Both the dam and nationalizing the canal represented economic independence and Egyptian national pride. Nasser also helped develop the anticolonial ideology of pan-Arabism, proposing that Arab nationalists throughout the Islamic world create an alliance of modern nations, no longer beholden to the West. But to achieve that goal, he was willing to take aid and support from the Soviets, which made the canal a Cold War issue.

Three nations found Nasser and his pan-Arab ideals threatening. Israel, surrounded on all sides by unfriendly neighbors, was looking for an opportunity to seize the strategic Sinai Peninsula and create a buffer against Egypt. France, already fighting a war against Algerian nationalists, hoped to destroy what it considered the Egyptian source of Arab nationalism. And Britain, dependent on the canal as a route to its strategic bases, was stung by this blow to its imperial authority. Though the British were reluctant to intervene, they were urged on by Prime Minister Sir Anthony Eden, who had developed a deep personal hatred of Nasser. In the autumn of 1956, the three nations colluded in an attack on Egypt. Israel occupied the Sinai while British and French jets destroyed Egypt's air force on the ground. The former colonial powers landed troops at the mouth of the canal but lacked the resources to push on toward Cairo. As a result, the war left Nasser in power and made him a hero to the Egyptian public for holding the imperialists at bay. The attack was condemned around the world, and the United States angrily called its allies' bluff and inflicted severe financial penalties on Britain and France, forcing both countries to withdraw their expeditions. For policy makers in Great Britain and France, the failure at Suez marked the end of an era.

French Decolonization

In two particular cases, France's experience of decolonization was bloodier, more difficult, and more damaging to French prestige and domestic politics than any in Britain's experience, with the possible exception of Northern Ireland. The first was Indochina, where French efforts to restore imperial authority after losing it in the Second World War only resulted in military defeat and further humiliation. The second was Algeria, which became not only a violent colonial war but also a struggle with serious political ramifications at home.

THE FIRST VIETNAM WAR, 1946–1954

Indochina was one of France's last major imperial acquisitions in the nineteenth century. Here, as elsewhere, the two world wars had helped galvanize first nationalist and then, also, communist independence movements. In Indonesia, nationalist forces rebelled against Dutch efforts to restore colonialism, and the country became independent in 1949. Also, the communist resistance became particularly effective under the leadership of Ho Chi Minh (1890–1969). Ho was French educated and, with his expectations raised by the Wilsonian principles of self-determination, had hoped his country would win independence at Versailles in 1919 (Chapter 24). He read Marx and Lenin, and absorbed the Chinese communists' lessons about organizing peasants around social and agrarian as well as national issues. During the Second World War, Ho's movement fought first the Vichy government of the colony and later the Japanese occupiers, and provided intelligence reports for the Allies. In 1945, however, the United States and Britain repudiated their relationship with Ho's independence movement and allowed the French to reclaim

their colonies throughout Southeast Asia. In response, the Vietnamese communists, who were fierce nationalists as well as Marxists, renewed their guerrilla war against the French.

The fighting was protracted and bloody, with France seeing in it a chance to redeem its national pride. The French government could have decolonized on favorable terms after one of its most capable generals, Jean de Lattre de Tassigny, finally achieved a military advantage against the rebels in 1951. But instead, it decided to press on for total victory, sending troops deep into Vietnamese territory to root out the rebels. One major outpost was established in a valley bordering modern Laos, at a hamlet called Dien Bien Phu. Ringed by high mountains, this vulnerable spot became a base for thousands of elite French paratroopers and colonial soldiers from Algeria and West Africa—the best of France's troops. The rebels besieged the base; tens of thousands of Vietnamese nationalist fighters hauled heavy artillery up the mountainsides by hand and bombarded the network of forts set up by the French. The siege lasted for months, becoming a protracted national crisis in France.

When Dien Bien Phu fell in May 1954, the French government began peace talks in Geneva. The Geneva Accords, drawn up by the French, Vietnamese politicians (including the communists), the British, and the Americans, divided Indochina into three countries: Laos, Cambodia, and Vietnam, which was partitioned

FRENCH POWs LEAVING DIEN BIEN PHU. When the French troops at Dien Bien Phu surrendered, nearly 12,000 were taken prisoner by the Vietnamese. The defeat damaged the reputation of the French Empire in the eyes of many and was celebrated by anticolonial nationalists throughout Asia and Africa. In France, the defeat undermined public support for the Indochinese war, but six months after Dien Bien Phu fell, the Algerian War began.

DECOLONIZATION IN ASIA. ▪ *Among colonial powers, who were the biggest losers after World War II?* ▪ *What was the single most important geopolitical change in Asia during this period?* ▪ *What role did the Soviet Union and the United States play in Asia?*

into two states—North Vietnam taken over by Ho Chi Minh's party, and South Vietnam by a succession of Western-supported politicians. Corruption, repression, and instability in the south, coupled with Ho Chi Minh's nationalist desire to unite Vietnam, guaranteed that the war would continue. The U.S. government, which had provided military and financial aid to the French, began to send aid to the South Vietnamese regime. The Americans saw the conflict through the prism of the Cold War; their project was not to restore colonialism but to contain communism and prevent it from spreading through Southeast Asia. The limits of this policy would not become clear until the mid-1960s.

ALGERIA

Still reeling from the humiliation of Dien Bien Phu, France faced a complex colonial problem closer to home, in Algeria. Since the 1830s, the colony had evolved into a settler society of three social groups. First, in addition to a small class of French soldiers and administrators, there were a million European settlers. They typically owned farms and vineyards near the major cities or formed the working-class and merchant communities in those cities. They were all citizens of the three administrative districts of Algeria, which were legally part of France. This community produced some of France's best-known

COUNTERINSURGENCY IN ALGERIA. An Algerian POW imprisoned by the French in a cellar for animals during the Algerian War of Independence, 1961.

writers and intellectuals: Albert Camus, Jacques Derrida, and Pierre Bourdieu, among others. In the small towns and villages of Algeria lived a second group of Berbers (largely Muslim), whose long history of service in the French army entitled them to certain formal and informal privileges within the colony. Finally, there were millions of Muslim Arabs, some living in the desert south but most crowded into impoverished neighborhoods in the cities. The Arabs were the largest and most deprived group in Algerian society, and between the world wars the French government offered small reforms to increase their rights and representation. The government hoped to meld the three groups into a common Algerian society, but the reforms came too late and they were also undercut by European settlers anxious to maintain their privileges.

At the end of the Second World War, Algerian nationalists called on the Allies to recognize Algeria's independence in return for good service during the war. Public demonstrations became frequent and, in several cases, turned into attacks on settler-landowners. When in Setif, a rural town, celebrations of the defeat of Germany flared into violence against settlers, French repression was harsh and immediate, as security forces killed several thousand Arabs. After the war, the French government approved a provincial assembly for all of Algeria, elected by two pools of voters, one made up of settlers and mostly Berber Muslims, and the other of Arabs. This very limited enfranchisement gave Arab Algerians no political power.

The most important changes were economic. All of Algeria suffered in the difficulties after the war, and many

Arab Algerians felt they had to emigrate; several hundred thousand went to work in France. The situation in Algeria grew more serious, while citizens of mainland France read their papers and frowned over the war in Indochina. By mid-1950s, a younger generation of Arab activists, unhappy with the leadership of the moderates, had taken charge of a movement dedicated to independence by force. The activists organized the National Liberation Front (FLN), which leaned toward socialism, and demanded equal citizenship for all.

The war in Algeria became a war on three fronts. The first was a guerrilla war between the regular French Army and the FLN, fought in the mountains and deserts of the country. This war continued for years, a clear military defeat for the FLN but never a clear-cut victory for the French. The second front, fought in the cities, began with an FLN campaign of bombing and terrorism, killing European civilians. In the third, French administration retaliated with its own campaign, whereby French paratroopers hunted down and destroyed the networks of FLN bombers. The information that allowed the French to break the FLN network was extracted through systematic torture conducted by French security forces. The torture became an international scandal, bringing waves of protest in France. This third front of the Algerian war divided France, brought down the government, and ushered de Gaulle back into power.

De Gaulle visited Algiers to wild cheering from settlers and declared that Algeria would always be French, but after another year of violence, he and his advisers changed their minds. By 1962, talks had produced a formula for independence: a referendum would be held, voted on by the whole population of Algeria. On July 1, 1962, the referendum passed by a landslide vote. Arab political groups and guerrillas from the FLN entered Algiers in triumph. Settlers and Berbers who had fought for the French army fled Algeria for France by the hundreds of thousands. Later, these refugees were joined in France by another influx of Arab economic migrants.

Algeria illustrated the dramatic domestic impact of decolonization. The war cut deep divides through French society, largely because the very identity of France seemed at stake. Withdrawing from Algeria meant reorienting French views of what it meant to be a modern power. De Gaulle summed up the trade-off in his memoirs: to stay in Algeria would "keep France politically, financially, and militarily bogged down in a bottomless quagmire

THE STRUGGLE FOR NATIONAL INDEPENDENCE IN ALGERIA. Ahmed Bencherif, a commander in the FLN, handcuffed in 1961. ■ *How might the Algerian struggle for independence against the French have shaped the generation of political leaders who took power after decolonization?*

when, in fact, she needed her hands free to bring about the domestic transformation necessitated by the twentieth century and to exercise her influence abroad unencumbered." To France and to the other imperial powers, the conclusions seemed clear: traditional forms of colonial rule could not withstand the demands of postwar politics and culture, and the leading European nations, once distinguished by their empires, would have to look for new forms of influence. The domestic transformation of which de Gaulle spoke—recovery from the war, economic restructuring, and political renewal—had to take place on a radically changed global stage.

POSTWAR CULTURE AND THOUGHT

The postwar period brought a remarkable burst of cultural production. Writers and artists did not hesitate to take up big issues: freedom, civilization, and the human condition itself. The search for democratic renewal gave this literature urgency, whereas the moral dilemmas of war, occupa-

tion, and resistance gave it resonance and popular appeal. The process of decolonization, too, forced the issues of race, culture, and colonialism to center stage in Western debates.

The Black Presence

The journal *Présence Africaine* ("African Presence"), founded in Paris in 1947, was only one in a chorus of new cultural voices. *Présence Africaine* published such writers as Aimé Césaire (1913–2008), the surrealist poet from Martinique, and Léopold Senghor of Senegal (1906–2001). Césaire and Senghor were brilliant students, educated in the most elite French universities and elected to the French National Assembly. Césaire became an important political figure in Martinique, a French Caribbean colony that became a department of France in 1946. In 1960, Senghor was elected the first president of Senegal. Both men, models of Frenchness in important respects, became the most influential exponents of *Négritude,* which could be translated as "black consciousness" or "black pride." Senghor wrote:

> Assimilation was a failure. We could assimilate mathematics of the French language, but we could never strip off our black skins or root out black souls. And so we set out on a fervent quest for . . . our collective soul. Negritude is the whole complex of civilized values—cultural, economic, social and political—which characterize the black people.

Césaire's early work took its lead from surrealism and the exploration of consciousness. But later, his work became more political. His *Discourse on Colonialism* (1950) is a powerful indictment of the material and spiritual squalor of colonialism, which, he argued, not only dehumanized colonial subjects but degraded the colonizers themselves.

Césaire's student Frantz Fanon (1925–1961), also from Martinique, went further. He argued that withdrawing into an insular black culture (as he interpreted Negritude) was not an effective response to racism. He believed that people of color needed a theory of radical social change. Fanon was trained in psychiatry and worked in Algeria, where he became a member of the National Liberation Front. In *Black Skin, White Masks* (1952), he examines the effects of colonialism and racism from the point of view of a radical psychiatrist. His *The Wretched of the Earth* (1961) became one of the most influential revolutionary manifestos of the period. More than Césaire, Fanon argued

Analyzing Primary Sources

Anticolonialism and Violence

Born in the French Caribbean colony of Martinique, Frantz Fanon (1925–1961) studied psychiatry in France before working in Algeria during the early 1950s. Fanon became a member of the Algerian revolutionary National Liberation Front (FLN), and an ardent advocate of decolonization. His Black Skin, White Masks, *published in 1952 with a preface by Jean-Paul Sartre, is a study of the psychological effects of colonialism and racism on black culture and individuals; and* The Wretched of the Earth *(1961) is a revolutionary manifesto, one of the most influential of the period. Fanon attacked nationalist leaders for their ambition and corruption, and believed that revolutionary change could come only from poor peasants, or those who "have found no bone to gnaw in the colonial system." Diagnosed with leukemia, Fanon sought treatment in the Soviet Union, and then in Washington, DC, where he died.*

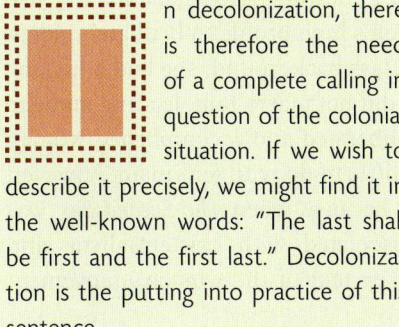n decolonization, there is therefore the need of a complete calling in question of the colonial situation. If we wish to describe it precisely, we might find it in the well-known words: "The last shall be first and the first last." Decolonization is the putting into practice of this sentence. . . .

The naked truth of decolonization evokes for us the searing bullets and bloodstained knives which emanate from it. For if the last shall be first, this will only come to pass after a murderous and decisive struggle between the two protagonists. That affirmed intention to

place the last at the head of things, and to make them climb at a pace (too quickly, some say) the well-known steps which characterize an organized society, can only triumph if we use all means to turn the scale, including, of course, that of violence.

You do not turn any society, however primitive it may be, upside down with such a program if you have not decided from the very beginning, that is to say from the actual formation of that program, to overcome all the obstacles that you will come across in so doing. The native who decides to put the program into practice, and to become its moving force, is ready for violence at all times.

From birth it is clear to him that this narrow world, strewn with prohibitions, can only be called in question by absolute violence.

Source: Frantz Fanon, *The Wretched of the Earth*, trans. Constance Farrington (New York: 1963), pp. 35–37.

Questions for Analysis

1. Why did Fanon believe that violence lay at the heart of both the colonial relationship and anticolonial movements?

2. What arguments would Fanon offer to counter Gandhi?

that violence was rooted in colonialism and, therefore, in anticolonial movements, bluntly rejecting Gandhi's theories and practice. But he also believed that many anticolonial leaders would be corrupted by their ambition and collaboration with former colonial powers. Revolutionary change, he believed, could come only from poor peasants, or those who "have found no bone to gnaw in the colonial system."

How did these writers fit into postwar culture? Western intellectuals sought to revive humanism and democratic values after the atrocities of the Second World War. Fanon and others pointed out that the struggles over colonialism made that project more difficult, as the violent repression of anticolonial movements in places such as Algeria seemed

to be a relapse into brutality. They pointed to the ironies of Europe's "civilizing mission" and demanded a reevaluation of blackness as a central concept in Western culture. The West's postwar recovery would eventually entail facing this challenge to the universal claims of its culture.

Existentialism

The French existentialist writers, most prominently Jean-Paul Sartre (*SAHR-truh*; 1905–1980) and Albert Camus (*KAM-oo*; 1913–1960), put the themes of individuality, commitment, and choice at center stage. The existentialists took themes from Nietzsche, Heidegger, and Kierkegaard, and reworked them in the new context of war-torn Europe. Their starting point was that "existence precedes essence." In other words, meaning in life is not given but created; thus, individuals were "condemned to be free" and to give their lives meaning by making choices and accepting responsibility. To deny one's freedom or responsibility was to act in "bad faith." War, collaboration and resistance, genocide, and the development of weapons of mass destruction all provided specific points of reference and gave these abstractions new meaning. The existentialists' writing was also clear and accessible, which contributed to their enormous popularity. Sartre wrote philosophical treatises, but he also published plays and short stories. Camus's own experience in the Resistance gave him tremendous moral authority, and he became the symbol of a new generation. His novels—*The Stranger* (1942), *The Plague* (1947), and *The Fall* (1956)—often revolve around metaphors for the war, and show that people are responsible for their own dilemmas and, through a series of anti-heroes, explore the limited ability of men and women to help each other.

SIMONE DE BEAUVOIR (1908–1986). A philosopher, novelist, memoirist, and pathbreaking theorist of sex and gender, de Beauvoir's work challenged widespread beliefs about femininity and womanhood.

Existentialist insights opened other doors. The existentialist approach to race, for instance, emphasized that no meaning inhered in skin color; instead, race derived meaning from a lived experience or situation. As Frantz Fanon wrote, white and black exist "only insofar as they create one another." The same approach could be applied to gender. In her famous introduction to *The Second Sex* (1949), Simone de Beauvoir (*duh bohv-WAHR*; 1908–1986) argued, "One is not born a woman, one becomes one." Women, like men, were condemned to be free. De Beauvoir went on to ask why women seemed to accept their secondary status or, in her words, why they "dreamed the dreams of men." The scope and ambition of *The Second Sex* helped make it enormously influential; it was virtually encyclopedic, analyzing history, myth, biology, and psychology, and brought the insights of Marx and Freud to bear on the "woman question." De Beauvoir's life also contributed to the book's high profile. A brilliant student from a strict middle-class background, she had a lifelong affair with Sartre but did not marry him, leading many to romanticize her as a liberated and accomplished woman intellectual. She had little to do with feminism, however, until the late 1960s, because when *The Second Sex* was published, it was associated with existentialism, and only later become a key text of the women's movement (see Chapter 28).

Memory and Amnesia: The Aftermath of War

The theme of individual helplessness in the face of state power ran through countless works of the period, beginning, most famously, with George Orwell's *Animal Farm* (1946) and *1984* (1949). The American Joseph Heller's wildly popular *Catch-22* (1961) embodied a form of popular existentialism, concerned with the absurdity of war and offering a biting commentary on regimentation and its toll on individual freedom. The Czech author Milan Kundera, who fled the repressive Czech government to live in Paris, eloquently captured the bittersweet efforts to resist senseless bureaucracy. Some writers expressed their despair by escaping into the absurd and fantastic. In Irishman Samuel Beckett's deeply pessimistic *Waiting for Godot* (1953; writing in French) and in the Briton Harold Pinter's *Caretaker* (1960) and *Homecoming* (1965), nothing happens; characters speak in banalities, paralyzed by the absurdity of modern times.

Other authors ventured into the realms of hallucination, science fiction, and fantasy. The novels of the

Americans William Burroughs and Kurt Vonnegut carry readers from interior fantasies to outer space. One of the most popular books of the period was *The Lord of the Rings* (1954–1955), written before and during the Second World War by British scholar J. R. R. Tolkien. Set in the fantasy world of Middle-earth, Professor Tolkien's tribute to the ancient Celtic and Scandinavian languages he studied and the power of human myths was seized on by a generation of young romantics who, for reasons of their own, rebelled against postwar Western culture.

Questions of terror and dictatorship haunted social and political thought of the postwar era, especially in the works of émigrés from Europe. Members of the Frankfurt School, an institute founded for the study of Marxism, who became wartime refugees in the United States, sought to understand how fascism and Nazism had taken root in Western culture and politics. Theodor Adorno joined Max Horkheimer in a series of essays, *Dialectic of Enlightenment* (1947), the best known of which indicted the "culture industry" for depoliticizing the masses and crippling democracy. Adorno also coauthored *The Authoritarian Personality* (1950), which used social surveys in an effort to discover how people become receptive to racism, prejudice, and dictatorship. Whatever the specific roots of German Nazism, the Frankfurt School suggested that there are more general tendencies in modern societies, which should give cause for concern.

Hannah Arendt (1906–1975), a Jewish refugee from Germany, in *The Origins of Totalitarianism* (1951), was the first to propose that both Nazism and Stalinism be understood as forms of a distinctive, twentieth-century type of government: totalitarianism. Unlike earlier forms of tyranny or despotism, totalitarianism works by mobilizing mass support. It uses terror to crush resistance, break down political and social institutions, and atomize the public. Totalitarianism, Arendt argued, also forges new ideologies. Totalitarian regimes do not concern themselves with whether killing is justified by law; instead, they justify camps and extermination by pointing to the objective laws of history or racial struggle. By unleashing destruction and eliminating entire populations, totalitarian politics makes collective resistance virtually impossible. Arendt returned to

the same theme in a provocative and disturbing essay on the trial of a Nazi leader, *Eichmann in Jerusalem* (1963). To the distress of many readers, she pointedly refused to demonize Nazism, exploring instead what she termed the "banality of evil": how the rise of new forms of state power and terror created a world in which Nazis, such as Adolf Eichmann, could implement genocide as simply one more policy. The crisis of totalitarianism, Arendt argued, was the moral collapse of society, for it destroyed human feeling and the power of resistance in both executioners and victims—"tormentors and the tormented"—alike.

Discussions of the war and its legacy, however, were limited, although some memoirs and novels dealing directly with the war and its brutal aftermath did reach a large public. Tadeusz Borowski's stories based on his experience in Auschwitz were widely read in postwar Poland. Czesław Miłosz's (*CHES-swaf MEE-wosh*) memoir, *The Captive Mind* (1953), about intellectual collaboration in Eastern Europe, was translated quickly into other languages and read internationally. Günter Grass's *Tin Drum* (1959) portrayed the Nazi and war experience in a semi-autobiographical genre, earning him recognition as the "conscience of his generation"—a label that became controversial toward the end of his life when he revealed that he had remained silent about his youthful membership in the

THE SOVIET UNION AS DEFENDER OF THE THIRD WORLD. This billboard from the Soviet Union's 1968 annual May Day parade depicts Soviet bombs raining down on a monstrous image of Uncle Sam, a symbol of the United States. The caption reads "U.S. Out of Vietnam!" ▪ *How did the Soviet Union attempt to take advantage of the wars of decolonization to advance its influence in other parts of the world?* ▪ *Who was the audience for this kind of imagery?* ▪ *How might have this billboard been perceived in Europe or in Vietnam?*

Trauma and Survival after the Holocaust

Heda Margolius Kovály (1919–2010) was born into a Jewish family in Prague, Czechoslovakia. In 1941, she and her parents were arrested by the Nazis and deported to Auschwitz. Her parents were murdered in the gas chambers immediately on arrival, but she was selected for work in a labor camp. In 1945, with Soviet troops approaching, the Germans evacuated the camp, and she and several other women succeeded in escaping. She returned to Prague, only to find that many people were unwilling to help escapees. Her troubles continued after the war: her first husband was executed by the postwar Czechoslovakian communist government in 1952 during a purge, and she lived in poverty as the former wife of a disgraced official. In 1968, she escaped Czechoslovakia and settled in the United States, where she wrote several volumes of memoirs. Under a Cruel Star *was published in a Czech language edition in Canada in 1973, and the English language version was published in 1986.*

Heda Margolius Kovály, Under a Cruel Star

nd so ended that horrible long war that refuses to be forgotten. Life went on. It went on despite both the dead and the living, because this was a war that no one had quite survived. Something very important and precious had been killed by it or, perhaps, it had just died of horror, of starvation, or simply of disgust—who knows? We tried to bury it quickly, the earth settled over it, and we turned our backs on it impatiently. After all, our real life was now beginning and what to make of it was up to us.

People came crawling out of their hide-outs. They came back from the forests, from the prisons, and from the concentration camps, and all they could think was, "It's over; it's all over." . . . Some people came back silent, and some talked incessantly as though talking about a thing would make it vanish. . . . While some voices spoke of death and flames, of blood and gallows, in the background, a chorus of thousands repeated tirelessly, "You know, we also suffered. . . . [N]othing but skimmed milk. . . . No butter on our bread. . . ."

Sometimes a bedraggled and barefoot concentration camp survivor plucked up his courage and knocked on the door of prewar friends to ask, "Excuse me, do you by any chance still have some of the stuff we left with you for safekeeping?" And the friends would say, "You must be mistaken, you didn't leave anything with us, but come in anyway!" And they would seat him in their parlor where his carpet lay on the floor and pour herb tea into antique cups that had belonged to his grandmother. . . . He would say to himself, "What does it matter? As long as we're alive? What does it matter?"

* * *

It would also happen that a survivor might need a lawyer to retrieve lost documents and he would remember the name of one who had once represented large Jewish companies. He would go to see him and sit in an empire chair in a corner of an elegant waiting room, enjoying all that good taste and luxury, watching pretty secretaries rushing about. Until one of the pretty girls forgot to close a door behind her, and the lawyer's sonorous voice would boom through the crack, "You would have thought we'd be rid of them finally, but no, they're impossible to kill off—not even Hitler could manage it. Every day there're more of them crawling back, like rats. . . ." And the survivor would quietly get up from his chair and slip out of the waiting room, this time not laughing. On his way down the stairs his eyes would mist over as if with the smoke of the furnaces at Auschwitz.

Source: Heda Margolius Kovály, *Under a Cruel Star: A Life in Prague 1941–1968*, trans. Franci Epstein and Helen Epstein with the author (Cambridge, MA: 1986), pp. 45–46.

Past and Present

The Divisions of the Cold War

The Cold War conflict between the United States and the Soviet Union, captured in the image of the Berlin Wall (left), was largely seen as a split between the East and the West, though global competition between the two powers had profound effects on other regions of the world. The founders of the Non-Aligned Movement (NAM) attempted to provide an alternative to this division. Its founders are shown here (from left): Prime Minister Jawaharlal Nehru of India, President Kwame Nkrumah of Ghana, President Gamal Abdel Nasser of Egypt, President Sukarno of Indonesia, and President Tito of Yugoslavia.

 Watch related author interview on the Student Site

Waffen SS. Of all the memoirs, *The Diary of a Young Girl* by Anne Frank, published in 1947, was undoubtedly the most widely read. Yet the main current in postwar culture ran in a different direction, toward repressing painful issues and bad memories.

Postwar governments could not or would not purge all those implicated in war crimes. In France, the courts sentenced 2,640 to death and executed 791; in Austria, 13,000 were convicted of war crimes and 30 executed. Those who called for justice grew demoralized and cynical; others responded by mythologizing the Resistance and exaggerating their participation in it or by avoiding discussion of collaboration. For ten years, French television considered *The Sorrow and the Pity* (1969), Marcel Ophüls's brilliant and unsparing documentary on a French town under Vichy, too controversial for broadcast. Most Jewish survivors,

wherever they lived, found that few editors were interested in publishing their stories. In 1947, only a small publishing house would take on the Italian survivor Primo Levi's *Survival in Auschwitz;* this book and Levi's other writings did not find a wide audience until later.

The Cold War was an important factor in burying and distorting memories. In the West of the Iron Curtain, the eagerness to embrace West Germany as an ally, the single-minded emphasis on economic development, and the ardent anticommunism blurred views of the past. One example involved Klaus Barbie, an agent for the Gestapo in occupied France who, among other things, arrested and personally tortured members of the Resistance and deported thousands, including Jewish children, to concentration camps. After the war, American intelligence services recruited Barbie for his anticommunist skills and paid to smuggle him out of Europe, beyond the reach of those who wanted to prosecute him for war crimes. He was finally extradited from Bolivia in 1983, tried in France for crimes against humanity, and convicted. In the Eastern bloc, regimes declared fascism a thing of the past and did not scrutinize that past or seek out the many who had collaborated with the Nazis. Thus, reckoning with history was postponed until the fall of the Soviet Union. On both sides of the Iron Curtain, the vast majority of people turned inward, cherishing their domestic lives, relieved to have privacy.

THE CUBAN MISSILE CRISIS

One of the most serious and dramatic confrontations of the Cold War came in 1962, in Cuba. A revolution in 1958 had brought the charismatic communist Fidel Castro to power. Immediately after, the United States began working with exiled Cubans, supporting, among other ventures, a bungled attempt to invade Cuba via the Bay of Pigs in 1961. Castro not only aligned himself with the Soviets but also invited them to base nuclear missiles on Cuban soil, which was only a few minutes' flying time from Florida.

When American spy planes identified the missiles and related military equipment in 1962, Kennedy confronted Khrushchev. After deliberating about the repercussions of an air strike, Kennedy ordered a naval blockade of Cuba. On October 22, he appeared on television, visibly tired and without makeup, and announced the grave situation to the public, and challenged Khrushchev to withdraw the weapons and "move the world back from the abyss of destruction." Terrified of the looming threat of nuclear war, Americans fled urban areas, prepared for a cramped and uncomfortable existence in fallout shelters, and bought firearms and canned foods. After thirteen days, the Soviets agreed to withdraw and remove the bombers and missiles already on Cuban soil. But citizens of both countries spent many anxious hours in their bomb shelters, and onlookers the world over wrestled with their rising fears that a nuclear Armageddon was upon them.

CONCLUSION

The Cold War reached deep into postwar culture and dominated postwar politics. It decisively shaped the development of both the Soviet Union and the United States.

After You Read This Chapter

 Go to **INQUIZITIVE** to see what you've learned—and learn what you've missed—with personalized feedback along the way.

REVIEWING THE OBJECTIVES

- The Cold War between the United States and the Soviet Union began as the Second World War ended. How did these two nations seek to influence the postwar political order in Europe?

- Postwar economic growth was accompanied by greater economic integration among Western European nations. What were the goals of those who sought to create a unified European market? Which nations played key roles in its development?

- Between the late 1940s and the mid-1960s, almost all the European colonies in Asia and Africa demanded and received their independence, either peacefully or through armed conflict. What combination of events made Europeans less able to defend their colonial empires against the nationalists who sought independence from Europe?

- Decolonization and the Cold War reinforced a sense that Europeans needed to rethink their place in the world. How did intellectuals, writers, and artists react to the loss of European influence in the world?

Fearful of losing control of territory they had conquered at such high cost in the Second World War, the Soviets intervened repeatedly in the politics of their Eastern European allied states in the 1940s and 1950s, ensuring the creation of hard-line governments in East Germany, Czechoslovakia, Poland, Hungary, and elsewhere in the Eastern bloc. In the United States, anticommunism became a powerful political force, shaping foreign policy and preparing the military for confrontation with the Soviet Union, to such an extent that President Dwight D. Eisenhower warned in his farewell address that a "military-industrial complex" had taken shape in the United States, one in which its "total influence—economic, political, even spiritual—is felt in every city, every statehouse, every office of the federal government."

In Western Europe, rebuilding the economy and creating a new political order in the aftermath of the Second World War meant accepting the new power and influence of the United States. But Europeans also searched for ways to create and express a European identity that would preserve some independence and freedom of action. Led by the efforts of France and Germany, Western Europeans eventually found elements of this freedom in increasing integration and economic cooperation. In Eastern Europe, however, the political leadership found fewer opportunities for indepen-

dent action, and the threat of military intervention by the Soviet Union made any innovations or experimentation difficult, if not impossible.

The sense that Europeans were no longer in a position to act independently, or exert their influence in other parts of the world, was compounded by the loss of their colonies abroad, as former European colonies in Africa and Asia became independent nations. This loss of influence may have further encouraged the former European imperial powers to lay the groundwork for a more integrated Europe. The consensus in the West about the new role that the state should take in economic planning, education, and ensuring social welfare helped lay the groundwork for a Europe that was dedicated to ensuring equal opportunities to its citizens. These commitments were driven by the search for stable forms of democratic government. The achievement of an integrated Western Europe (under U.S. sponsorship) on the hinge of Franco-German cooperation, while memories of the violent ideological conflicts of the 1920s and the 1930s were still fresh, must be seen as one of the major victories of the postwar decades. The hard-won stability of this period was to be temporary, however, as a new series of political conflicts and economic crises, beginning in the 1960s, would test the limits of consensus in Cold War Europe.

PEOPLE, IDEAS, AND EVENTS IN CONTEXT

- When Allied leaders met to discuss the postwar order at **YALTA** and Potsdam in 1945, what were the major issues discussed?
- What were the goals of the U.S. **MARSHALL PLAN**? How did **JOSEPH STALIN** react to its implementation?
- What was the **TRUMAN DOCTRINE**? How was it related to the creation of **NATO**?
- How did the successful detonation of an **ATOMIC BOMB** by the Soviet Union in 1949 change the dynamic of the **COLD WAR**?
- How did the political climate in the Soviet Union and Eastern Europe change under **NIKITA KHRUSHCHEV** and during the "thaw" that followed Stalin's death?
- Why was the decolonization of settler colonies in Africa, such as Algeria, Kenya, and Rhodesia, more violent than in other colonies on the continent?
- What was **APARTHEID**? Why did the settler government in South Africa adopt it?

THINKING ABOUT CONNECTIONS

- Insofar as one can determine from today's perspective, what were the long-term consequences of the Cold War for people in both Western and Eastern Europe?
- What challenges did the process of decolonization pose to those who believed that European traditions of democratic rule and individual rights—ideas associated with the Enlightenment and the French Revolution—were universal?

Before
You
Read
This
Chapter

Red Flags and Velvet Revolutions: The End of the Cold War, 1960–1990

CORE OBJECTIVES

- **DESCRIBE** postwar changes in employment and consumption, and their effects on daily life and mass culture in Europe.

- **UNDERSTAND** the shift in attitudes toward sexuality, reproduction, and conceptions of male and female social roles that took place in the postwar decades, and the consequences of this shift for women in Europe.

- **IDENTIFY** the motives and goals of the social and political movements that climaxed in 1968 in both Western and Eastern Europe.

- **EXPLAIN** the reasons for the economic downturn that began in the 1970s, and its consequences for governments and populations in Europe.

- **UNDERSTAND** the events that led to the collapse of the Soviet bloc in 1989.

- **EXPLAIN** the reasons for the uncertainty and violence that followed the conclusion of the Cold War in Europe in the 1990s.

n 1964, a photograph of a Portuguese laborer, Armando Rodriguez, appeared on the cover of the German news magazine *Der Spiegel*. As the one millionth "guest worker" to arrive in Germany, he had been met at the border by an official delegation and given a motorcycle as a prize. This moment reflected the confidence of the West German government that its postwar economic recovery would continue, and that material prosperity would bring a new stability to Europe. The early 1960s, in fact, seemed golden and full of promise for many in Western Europe. Despite nearly constant international tension, everyday life seemed to be improving. Full employment drove increases in living standards, the mass availability of consumer items and modern appliances transformed daily life, and a life of relative prosperity and ample leisure seemed accessible to many. As television, radio, and film promoted images of American middle-class life, Europeans looked across the Atlantic and saw their own aspirations reflected back at them. Even amid the uncertainties of the Cold War, a new spirit of cooperation animated European governments; party divisions had given way to a broad consensus in favor of an expanded welfare state, and the future looked good.

By the 1990s, however, most of that confidence was gone, and the European landscape had been dramatically transformed. Western Europeans could no longer be certain of their prosperity or of their leaders' ability to provide the sort of life they took for granted. Already in the late 1960s, the economic boom had come to an end, and movements of social protest, especially among young people, shattered the postwar consensus. The material comforts of a consumer society proved less satisfying than they had once seemed, and environmentalists, feminists, and other cultural critics criticized the assumptions of the older generation. After 1975, these problems were compounded by a continuing economic crisis that threatened the security the postwar generation had labored so hard to achieve. European societies began to fragment in unexpected ways, well before the epochal transformations that accompanied the end of the Cold War.

The challenges of these decades proved even more fundamental in the Soviet sphere. Economic decay combined with political and social stagnation to produce another wave of revolt. The year 1989 marked the beginning of an extraordinarily rapid and surprising series of events. Communist rule collapsed in Eastern Europe. Hopes for peace were soon replaced by fears of conflict from unexpected quarters. Immigrants were no longer celebrated in Germany and elsewhere, and instead became targets of suspicion or even violence. Shortly after the reunification of Germany in 1991, a wave of attacks against immigrants and refugees in Eastern Germany by right-wing extremists took the lives of seventeen foreigners, including two Turkish women and a Turkish girl who died in an arson attack by neo-Nazi skinheads in Schleswig-Holstein; similar attacks took place in France, Britain, Italy, and other nations. When post-socialist Yugoslavia collapsed into brutal civil war in the early 1990s, Europeans faced once again the spectacle of political movements motivated by hatred and fear, leading to ethnic violence and mass murder on European land.

The startlingly sudden dissolution of the Soviet bloc brought an end to the postwar era of superpower confrontation, and observers of European society were forced to confront the uncomfortable fact that the Cold War had provided its own form of stability. Seen from the early 1990s, the future looked much less certain. Could the emerging institutions of an integrated Europe absorb nations of the former Soviet sphere that wished to join? What would such a Europe look like? Who would determine its larger boundaries? What these changes meant for the future of democracy, the stability of the European economy, and the definitions of European identity remained an open question.

SOCIAL CHANGE AND CULTURAL DYNAMISM, 1945–1968

The prosperity of the 1950s, made especially striking when contrasted with the bleak years immediately after the Second World War, had profound and far-reaching effects on social life in Western Europe. To begin with, the population expanded, though unevenly, making it necessary for both West Germany and France to import workers to sustain their production booms. By the mid-1960s, there were 1.3 million foreign workers in West Germany and 1.8 million in France, as wages rose and unemployment fell. Most came from the south, particularly from the agrarian areas of southern Italy, where unemployment remained high. Workers from former colonies emigrated to Britain, often to take low-paid, menial jobs, and encountered pervasive discrimination at work and in the community. Also, migrations of this sort, in addition to the vast movement of political and ethnic refugees that occurred during and immediately after the war, contributed to the breakdown of national barriers, accelerated by the creation of the Common Market.

The most dramatic changes were encapsulated in the transformation of the land and agriculture. Agricultural productivity had barely changed over the first half of the twentieth century, but after mid-century, it soared. To take one example, West German farmland (and labor) sufficient to feed five people in 1900, fed six in 1950 and thirty-five in 1980. In West Germany and France, Common Market policy, state-sponsored programs of modernization, new agricultural machinery, and new kinds of fertilizer, seed, and animal feed helped produce the transformation.

The effects reached across the economic and social landscape. In Western Europe, abundance gave way to lower food prices, enabling families to spend a smaller proportion of their budgets on food and free up money for other forms of consumption, which, in turn, fueled economic growth. The percentage of the labor force employed in agriculture fell, leading to an expansion in industry and, especially, the service sector. Peasants with large holdings or valuable specialized crops (dairy products or wine, for example) who could withstand debt adjusted, but others lost ground. In the 1960s, the French spoke of an "end of the peasantry," as a hundred thousand moved from the countryside each year. These changes sparked continuous protests as farmers tried to protect their standard of living. The Common Market agreed to policies of shoring up agricultural prices, but the dynamics remained the same.

Change came in the workplace, eroding traditional social distinctions. The number of middle-class, white-collar employees grew rapidly, as the result, in part, of the dramatic bureaucratic expansion of the state. By 1964, in most European states, the total number of men and women employed in government service exceeded 40 percent of the labor force, significantly higher than during the prewar decades. In business and industry, the number of middle-management and salaried employees also grew. In West Germany, the number of supervisors, inspectors, technicians, and drafters increased by 95 percent between 1950 and 1961. Industrial labor meant something far different from what it had meant in the nineteenth century, as skills became more specialized, based on technological expertise rather than custom and routine; *skill* meant the ability to monitor automatic controls, to interpret abstract signals, and to make precise, mathematically calculated adjustments. Also, more women entered the workforce, meeting less resistance than they had in the past, and their jobs were less starkly differentiated from those of men.

Nineteenth-century society had been marked by clearly defined class cultures. The working class lived a "life apart" from the middle class, with easily identifiable patterns of consumption, dress, leisure, notions of respectability, gender relations, and so on. In 1900, no one would have mistaken a peasant for a worker, and middle-class people had their own schools, recreations, and stores. But economic changes after 1950 chipped away at those distinctive cultures. Trade unions remained powerful institutions: the largest of the French general unions had a membership of 1.5 million; the Italian, 3.5 million; and the German, 6.5 million. Britain's Trades Union Congress, an affiliation of separate unions, boasted close to 8 million members, including many more women than in the past. Communist parties also had powerful electoral clout. New social movements grew, and though workers still identified themselves as such, class had a less rigidly defined meaning.

The expansion of education also helped shift social hierarchies. All Western nations passed laws providing for the extension of compulsory secondary education—up to the age of sixteen in France, West Germany, and Britain. New legislation combined with rising birthrates to dramatically boost school populations. Between 1950 and 1960, secondary school enrollment

in France, Holland, and Belgium doubled; in Britain and West Germany, it grew by more than 50 percent. Education did not automatically guarantee social mobility, but when combined with economic prosperity, new structures of labor, and the consumerist boom, it began to lay the foundation for what would be called a "postindustrial" society.

How did patterns differ in the Eastern bloc? In the socialist regimes of the Soviet satellites, small peasant holdings were increasingly replaced by large-scale collective agriculture, and industry was nationalized, though not always at the same pace. Collectivization of agriculture proceeded most quickly in Bulgaria, and slower in Poland and Hungary; villagers in the countryside were allowed to keep small private plots, contributing significantly to the amount of food that was available. The Soviet Union and the satellite states of Eastern Europe did not succeed in significantly increasing agricultural production in the new collective farms, however, and the lack of a surplus meant that industrial growth had to be paid for by keeping rates of consumption low.

In general, economic development in the Eastern bloc was determined by the requirements of the Soviet economy. The Soviet Union purchased manufactured goods from Eastern Europe at advantageous prices, while charging more for the raw materials exported from the Soviet Union. This imbalance of trade amounted to a net extraction of wealth from Eastern Europe, hampering economic

MORNING CALISTHENICS AT A RUSSIAN FACTORY, 1961. This image from a Russian factory illustrates the growing number of industrial workers and women in the workforce in the latter half of the twentieth century. The workers' state, however, still bestowed little status on its workers— a factor that contributed to the weakened Russian economy.

growth and providing a stark contrast with the economic boom of Western Europe.

Soviet workers were not noted for their specialized skills—in fact, a major factor in the slowdown of the Soviet economy was its failure to innovate. Workers in the "workers' state" commonly enjoyed higher wages than people in middle-class positions (with the exception of party members, who occupied the important managerial positions), but they had far less status. Their relatively high wages owed little to independent trade unions, which had been effectively abolished under Stalin; they were the product of persistent labor shortages and the accompanying fear of labor unrest. As far as the middle classes were concerned, two world wars and Stalin's rule had liquidated the traditional middle classes and their culture throughout Eastern Europe. In their place, the regimes created new ways of gaining privilege and status: pursuing positions within the party and the bureaucracy. Educational reforms instituted by Nikita Khrushchev in 1958 encouraged bright children to pursue a course of study that led, eventually, to managerial positions for those who did not challenge the official culture or ideology of the regime.

Soviet education also aimed to unify a nation that remained culturally heterogeneous. The Bolsheviks had inherited a Eurasian empire from the previous tsarist regime, and territorial changes after the Second World War had expanded the number of diverse peoples who lived under Soviet rule. The Soviet Union included not only Russians, but also Ukrainians, Latvians, Lithuanians, Estonians, Azerbaijanis, Armenians, Chechens, Turkmen, Uzbeks, and Kazhaks, to name only a few of the most notable groups. The fear that the pull of ethnic nationality might tear at the none-too-solid fabric of the Soviet "union" encouraged the government to impose one unifying culture by means of education, though not always with success. In the Eastern bloc, the fact of Soviet domination made national sentiment a very sensitive issue, and the party bureaucracies of each state responded by demanding adherence to the official ideology in all realms of life—including the press, television, radio, literature, and the arts.

Mass Consumption

In Western Europe, rising employment, higher earnings, and lower agricultural prices combined to give households and individuals more purchasing power. They had more to spend on newspapers, cigarettes, tickets to sporting events, movies, and health and hygiene (which registered the largest increase). Families put money into their homes, and household appliances and cars became the most striking emblems of what was virtually a new world of everyday objects. In 1956, 8 percent of British households had refrigerators; by 1979, that figure had skyrocketed to 69 percent. Vacuum cleaners, washing machines, and telephones all became common features of everyday life. They did not save labor or create free time, however, because household appliances came packaged with more demanding standards of housekeeping and new investments in domesticity, meaning "more work for mother," in the words of one historian. We should not exaggerate the transformation, since in 1962, only 40 percent of French households had a refrigerator; and in 1975, only 35 percent had a telephone—but even this was still vastly more than the poorer nations of Europe or elsewhere in the world.

In 1948, 5 million Western Europeans had cars; in 1965, 40 million. In 1950, Italian workers rode bicycles to work, but ten years later, factories were building parking lots for their employees' automobiles. Cars captured imaginations throughout the world; and in magazines, advertisements, and countless films, the car was central to new images of romance, movement, freedom, and vacation. Of course, automobiles alone did not allow workers to take inexpensive holidays; reducing the workweek from forty-eight hours to about forty-two was more important, as was the institution of annual vacations (in most countries, workers received more than thirty days of paid vacation per year).

A CAR FOR THE PEOPLE. Originally designed in Hitler's Germany as a car for the people (*das Volk*), the Volkswagen "Beetle" was produced in large numbers after 1945, and sold in many countries.

These changes marked a new culture of mass consumption, boosted by new industries devoted to marketing, advertising, and credit payment. They also entailed shifts in values. In the nineteenth century, a responsible middle-class family did not go into debt, as discipline and thrift were hallmarks of respectability. By the second half of the twentieth century, banks and retailers, in the name of mass consumption and economic growth, were persuading middle- and working-class people alike not to be ashamed of debt. Terms such as *abundance*, *credit*, *consumer spending*, and *standards of living* all became part of the vocabulary of everyday economic life. Most important, the new vocabulary gradually began to reshape how citizens thought about their needs, desires, and entitlements. Standards of living, for instance, created a yardstick for measuring—and protesting—glaring social inequalities. And politicians, economists, and marketing experts paid much closer attention to the spending habits of ordinary people.

In Eastern Europe and the Soviet Union, consumption was organized differently. Governments, rather than markets, determined how consumer goods would be distributed, and economic policy channeled resources into heavy industry at the expense of consumer durables. This resulted in general scarcity, erratic shortages of even basic necessities, and often poor-quality goods. Women, in particular, frequently waited for hours in store lines after finishing a full day of wage work. Though numbers of household appliances increased dramatically, the inefficiencies of Soviet consumption made women's double burden of wage work and housework especially heavy. Citizens' growing unhappiness with scarcities and seemingly irrational policies posed serious problems. As one historian puts it, the failure of policies on consumption was "one of the major dead ends of communism," and contributed to the downfall of communist regimes.

Mass Culture

New patterns of consumption spurred wide-ranging changes in **mass culture**. The origins of "mass" culture lay in the 1890s with the expansion of the popular press, music halls, organized sports, and "nickelodeons," all of which started the long process of displacing traditional, class-based forms of entertainment: village dances, boulevard theater, middle-class concerts, and so on. Mass culture quickened in the 1920s, its importance heightened by mass politics (Chapter 25). The social transformations of the 1950s, which we have traced on pages 972–974, meant that families had both more spending money and more leisure

PICCADILLY CIRCUS, LONDON. In the 1960s and the 1970s, a growing consumer culture led to the expansion of marketing and advertising industries. ▪ *Why did Europeans associate this kind of commercial culture with the United States?*

time. This combination created a golden opportunity for the growing culture industry, with the postwar desire to break with the past, creating further impetus for change. The result can fairly be called a cultural revolution: a transformation of culture and its role in the lives of ordinary men and women, and of the power wielded by the media.

MUSIC AND YOUTH CULTURE

Much of the mass culture of the 1960s depended on the spending habits and desires of the new generation, one that stayed in school longer, prolonging the adolescent years. Young people had more distance from their parents and the workforce and more time to spend with each other. In the countryside especially, schools began to break down the barriers that had separated the activities of boys and girls, creating one factor in the "sexual revolution" (discussed on pages 980–981). From the late 1950s on, music became *the* cultural expression of this new generation. The transistor was invented in 1947; by the mid-1950s, portable transistor radios began to sell in the United States and Europe. Wider distribution of radios gave birth to new musical radio programming and, later, to magazines reporting on popular singers and movie stars. All these advancements helped

MUSIC MEETS TELEVISION. The Beatles appear on the popular variety television program *The Ed Sullivan Show* in the 1960s.

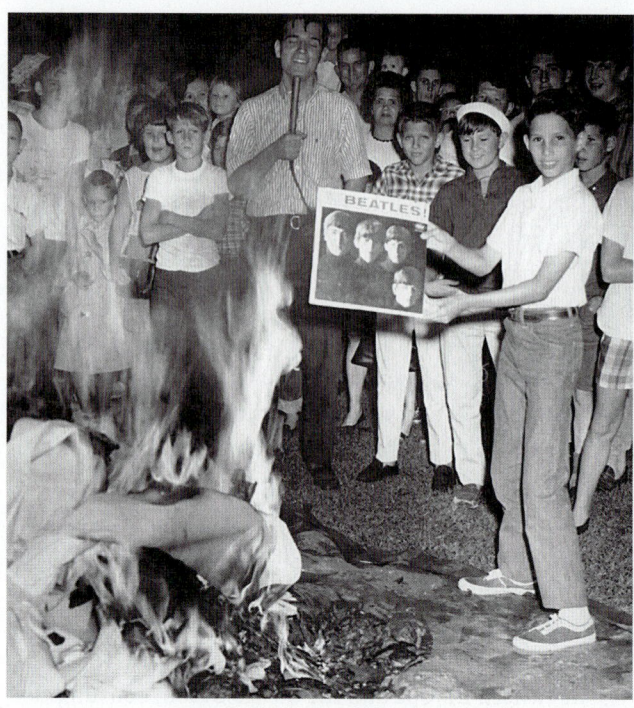

MASS CULTURE IN A MEDIA AGE. When John Lennon declared that the Beatles were "more popular than Jesus," he raised a storm of protest. Here, an American teenager tosses a *Meet the Beatles* album in a bonfire. ■ *What was different about this kind of celebrity when compared with that of earlier generations of popular entertainers?*

create new communities of interest. As one historian puts it, these radio programs were the "capillaries of youth culture." Social changes also affected the content of music, as its themes and lyrics aimed to reach the young. Technological changes made records more than twice as long as the old 78s, as well as less expensive; and as the price of record players fell, the number of potential buyers multiplied. These developments combined and changed how music was produced, distributed, and consumed. It was no longer confined to the concert hall or café, but instead reverberated through people's homes, cars, and teenagers' rooms—providing a sound track for everyday life.

Postwar youth culture owed much to rock and roll, a hybrid musical style that drew from a wide variety of folk and popular culture sources, including the blues tradition of African Americans, Appalachian country string bands, and western swing (itself a fusion of country and jazz). During the 1930s and the 1940s, this synthesis of music produced by whites and African Americans in the American South found its way into northern cities. After the Second World War, black rhythm and blues musicians as well as white Southern rockabilly performers found much wider audiences through the use of new technology: electric guitars, better equipment for studio recording, and wide-band radio stations in large cities. The blend of styles and sounds and the cultural daring of white teenagers who listened to what recording studios at the time marketed as "race music" came together to create rock and roll. The music was exciting, sometimes aggressive, and full of energy— qualities that galvanized young listeners eager to buy the latest records by their favorite performers.

In Europe, rock and roll found its way into working-class neighborhoods, particularly in Britain and Ireland. There, local youths took American sounds, echoed the

inflections of poverty and defiance, and added touches of music-hall showmanship to produce successful artists and bands, collectively referred to as the "British invasion." During the 1960s, British sounds and stars blended with their American counterparts, and as the music's popularity spread, music culture came loose from its national moorings. In France, before the 1960s, trendy American songs were covered by the performer Johnny Hallyday, who also sang French popular music. The Beatles, though, managed to get their own music on the hit lists in France, Germany, and the United States. By the time of the Woodstock festival (1969), youth music culture was international. Rock became the sound of worldwide youth culture, absorbing East Asian influences, such as the Indian sitar and the rebellious energy of a folk-music revival.

Furthermore, rock provided a bridge across the Cold War divide; despite Eastern-bloc limits on importing "capitalist" music, pirated songs circulated, sometimes even on X-ray plates salvaged from hospitals. In Prague, one month after Soviet tanks entered Czechoslovakia to overthrow the government of Alexander Dubček (see pages 988–990), a rock band known as the Plastic People of the Universe formed.

BOB DYLAN POSING FOR THE COVER OF *BLONDE ON BLONDE*, **1966.** Dylan's mid-1960s blues-based rock and roll, a departure from his acoustic folk style, shocked his original following.

ACTION PAINTING. Photographer Martha Holmes reveals the dynamic technique of the abstract expressionist Jackson Pollock in this photo, taken while he paints, 1950.

In the Eastern-bloc countries, such movements of cultural protest had a different political significance: they were more pointedly a challenge to the way that the official culture of the regime was enforced through censorship.

The cultural revolution also changed high as well as popular music. Record companies' influence reached well beyond rock, as new recording techniques made it possible to reissue favorites in classical music, which they marketed aggressively. Record companies buoyed the careers of internationally acclaimed classical-music stars, such as the soprano Maria Callas and (much later) the tenor Luciano Pavarotti, by staging concerts, using their influence to shape orchestral programming, and offering new recordings of the music.

Art and Painting

Painting and art, too, were changed by the rise of mass and consumer culture, which caused the art market to boom. The power of the dollar was one factor in the rise of New York as a center of modern art, one of the most striking developments of the period. Immigration was another, as New York proved hospitable to European artists; a slow stream of immigrants from Europe nourished American art as well as its social and political thought

(Chapter 27). And finally, the creative work of the school of abstract expressionism sealed New York's postwar reputation. The abstract expressionists—William de Kooning (from the Netherlands), Mark Rothko (from Russia), Franz Kline, Jackson Pollock, Helen Frankenthaler, and Robert Motherwell—followed trends established by the cubists and surrealists, experimenting with color, texture, and technique to find new forms of expression. Many of them emphasized the physical aspects of paint and the act of painting. A good example is Pollock, who poured and even threw paint on the canvas, creating powerful images of personal and physical expressiveness; some critics dubbed this process "action painting." His huge-scale canvases, which defied conventional artistic structures, gained immediate attention. Critics called the drip paintings "unpredictable, undisciplined, and explosive," and saw in them the youthful exuberance of postwar American culture. Mark Rothko, meanwhile, created a series of remote yet extraordinarily compelling abstractions, with glowing or somber rectangles of color imposed on other rectangles, which, according to Rothko, represented "no associations, only sensation." The enormous influence of abstract expressionism moved one critic to declare in grandiose fashion that "the main premises of Western art" had moved to the United States, along with "industrial production and political power."

But abstract expressionism also produced its opposite, sometimes called pop art. Pop artists distanced themselves from the moody and elusive meditations of abstract expressionism, and refused to distinguish between avant-garde and popular art, or between the artistic and the commercial. They lavished attention on commonplace, instantly recognizable and often commercial images; borrowed techniques from graphic design; and were interested in the immediacy of everyday art and ordinary people's visual experience. Jasper Johns's paintings of the American flag formed part of this trend. So did the work of Andy Warhol and Roy Lichtenstein, who took objects such as soup cans and images of comic-strip heroes as their subjects. Warhol did not see his work as a protest against the banality of commercial culture but, instead, argued that he was continuing to experiment with abstractions. Treating popular culture with this tongue-in-cheek seriousness became one of the central themes of 1960s art.

Film

Mass culture made its most powerful impact in the visual world especially through film. Film flourished after the Second World War, often dealing with the same themes that marked the literature of the period: loneliness, war, and corruption. The Italian neorealists of the late 1940s and the 1950s, antifascists and socialists, set out to capture authenticity, or "life as it was lived," by which they usually meant working-class existence. They shot on location, using natural light and little-known actors, deliberately steering away from the artifice and high production values they associated with the tainted cinema of fascist and wartime Europe. Not strictly realists, they played with nonlinear plots and unpredictable characters and motivations. Roberto Rossellini's *Rome: Open City* (1945) is a loving portrait of Rome under Nazi occupation. Vittorio de Sica's *Bicycle Thief* (1948) tells the story of a man struggling against unemployment and poverty, who desperately needs a bicycle to keep his job as a poster hanger. The film highlights the contrast between rich and poor—the man's son enviously watches a family enjoying huge plates of pasta—and between American glamour, represented by movie stars on posters, and Italy's war-scarred poverty. Federico Fellini came out of the neorealist school and began his career writing for Rossellini. His breakout film, *La Dolce Vita* (1959; starring Marcello Mastroianni), took Italian film to screens throughout Europe and the United States. It also marked Fellini's transition

to his signature surrealist and carnivalesque style, developed in *8½* (1963).

The French directors of the new wave continued to develop an unsentimental, naturalistic, and enigmatic social vision. New wave directors worked closely with each other—casting each other, and their wives and lovers, in their films—encouraged improvisation, and experimented with disjointed narrative. François Truffaut's (1932–1984) *400 Blows* (1959) and *The Wild Child* (1969), and Jean-Luc Godard's (1930–) *Breathless* (1959) and *Contempt* (1963; starring Brigitte Bardot) are leading examples. France made other contributions to international film by sponsoring the Cannes Film Festival. The first Cannes festival was held before the Second World War, but the city opened its gates again in 1946, under the banner of artistic internationalism. As one commentator put it, "There are many ways to advance the cause of peace. But the power . . . of cinema is greater than other forms of expression, for it directly and simultaneously touches the masses of the world." Placing itself at the center of an international film industry became part of France's ongoing recovery from the war, and Cannes became one of the world's largest markets for film.

In Eastern Europe, film also became an important means of creative expression in the postwar decades, and the Cannes festival introduced many of the films from the east to Western audiences. Polish director Andrzej Wajda's trilogy about the war years included *A Generation* (1954), *Kanal* (1956), and *Ashes and Diamonds* (1958). These three films portray the stories of young Poles confronted with the German occupation during the war, the Warsaw uprisings in 1943 (Jewish resistance in the city's ghetto) and 1944 (the Polish Home Army against the Nazis), and the

FEDERICO FELLINI ON THE SET OF *LA STRADA* (1954). Fellini was an Italian neorealist filmmaker who sought to depict "life as it was lived."

politics of anticommunism in the aftermath of the war. Wajda's works became closely associated with a Polish school of filmmaking that explored the trauma of the war years in vivid, shocking imagery. A slightly younger generation of central European filmmakers became important participants in the new wave. Jiří Menzel (1938–) directed *Closely Watched Trains* (1966), which won the Academy Award for Best Foreign Language Film in 1968. Like the films of Godard and Truffaut, Menzel's films raised the creative status of the director by insisting that a film's camera work and vision, rather than the writing, constituted the real art—another part of the new value accorded to the visual.

HOLLYWOOD AND THE AMERICANIZATION OF CULTURE

The American film industry had considerable advantages, as the devastating aftereffects of the Second World War in Europe allowed Hollywood to consolidate its earlier gains (Chapter 27). The huge domestic market in the United States gave Hollywood its biggest advantage. In 1946, an estimated hundred million Americans went to the movies every week. By the 1950s, Hollywood was making 500 films a year, and accounted for between 40 and 75 percent of films shown in Europe. The same period brought important innovations in filmmaking: the conversion to color, though a few color films appeared before World War II; and new optical formats, including widescreen. Some American directors moved in the same direction as the European neorealists, adapting plots generated from a hard-edged vision of contemporary society, and shooting on-site rather than in studios.

The domestic politics of the Cold War weighed heavily on filmmaking in the United States. Between 1947 and 1951, the infamous House Un-American Activities Committee (HUAC), investigating alleged sympathies with communism or association with any left-wing organization, called before it hundreds of persons, causing many actors, directors, and writers to be blacklisted by the studios. At the same time, paradoxically, American censorship was breaking down, with dramatic consequences on-screen. Since the early 1930s, the Motion Picture Production Code had refused to approve "scenes of passion" (including married couples sharing a bed), immorality and profanity (banning the words *virgin* and *cripes*), depictions of guns, details of crimes, suicide, and murder. Foreign films, however, came into the United States without the code's seal of approval. Also, New York State tried to ban *The Miracle*, directed by Rossellini and written by Fellini, as "sacrilegious," but in

1952, the Supreme Court ruled that films were protected by the First Amendment. Otto Preminger's *The Man with the Golden Arm* (1955), in which Frank Sinatra plays a heroin addict, was released despite the disapproval of the Production Code, and went on to become a box-office success—a sign of changing mores. And *Rebel without a Cause* (1955) made juvenile delinquency a legitimate subject for film. By the 1960s, the Production Code had been scuttled, and the extremely graphic violence at the end of Arthur Penn's *Bonnie and Clyde* (1967) marked the scope of the transformation.

Hollywood's expanding influence was but one instance of the "Americanization" of Western culture. Since at least the 1920s, Europeans had worried about the United States as a model, as it seemed to be the center for the "production and organization of mass civilization." American films of the 1950s multiplied these worries. So did television, which by 1965 had found its way into 62 million homes in the United States, 13 million in Britain, 10 million in West Germany, and 5 million each in France and Italy, and had an even more important impact on everyday life and sociability. The issues were not simply cultural, but included the power of American corporations, American business techniques, aggressive marketing, and American domination of global trade networks. Many concerns were raised that sometimes contradicted each other. Some observers believed that the United States and its cultural exports

JAMES DEAN IN *REBEL WITHOUT A CAUSE* (1955). Films from the 1950s and the 1960s contributed to the romanticization of automobiles, sexuality, and youthful rebellion.

were materialistic, conformist, and complacent. Others considered Americans to be rebellious, lonely, and sexually unhappy. *Rebel without a Cause*, for instance, with James Dean as an alienated teenager in a dysfunctional family and scenes of knife fights and car races, provoked cries of outrage from German critics who deplored the permissiveness of American parents and expressed shock that middle-class children behaved like "hoodlums."

Is it helpful, though, to speak of the *Americanization* of culture? First, the term refers to many different processes. The U.S. industrialists openly sought greater economic influence and integration, opening markets to American goods, industry to American production techniques, and so on. And the U.S. government aimed to export American political values, above all anticommunism, via organizations such as Radio Free Europe. But the farthest-reaching American influences were conveyed, unintentionally, by music and film through images of rebellious teenagers, a society of abundance, cars and the romance of the road, tangled race relations, flirting career girls (who seemed less identifiably working-class than their European counterparts), and bantering couples. Images that could not be completely controlled and had no single effect; movies about young Americans, for example, might represent the romance of American power or they might represent a rebellion against that power. Second, *American* goods were put to different uses in local cultures. And third, journalists, critics, and ordinary men and women tended to use the word *American* as an all-purpose label for various modern or mass culture developments that were more properly global, such as inexpensive electronics from Asia. As one historian puts it, America was less of a reality than an idea—and a contradictory one at that.

Gender Roles and Sexual Revolution

What some observers have called the sexual revolution of the 1960s had several aspects. The first was less censorship, which we have already seen in film, and fewer taboos regarding public discussion of sexuality. In the United States, the notorious Kinsey reports on male and female sexuality (in 1948 and 1953, respectively) made morality and sexual behavior front-page news. Alfred Kinsey was a zoologist turned social scientist, and the way in which he applied science and statistics to sex attracted considerable attention. An enthusiastic journalist in Europe reported that the massive numbers Kinsey compiled would, finally, reveal the "truth of sex." The truth, though, was elusive. At the very least, Kinsey showed that moral codes and

private behaviors did not line up neatly; for instance, although 80 to 90 percent of the women he interviewed disapproved of premarital sex, 50 percent of them had had it. *Time* magazine warned that publicizing disparities between beliefs and behavior might prove subversive— that is, women and men would decide there was "morality in numbers."

Across Europe and North America, however, young men and women seemed to be reaching rebellious conclusions on their own. As one Italian teenager said, defending her moral codes, "It is our elders who behave scandalously. . . . [W]omen were kept under lock and key, girls married to men who were twice their age. . . . [B]oys, even the very youngest, had total freedom and so queued up at the brothels." Teenage girls in Italy and France told researchers and reporters that taboos were not just old fashioned but damaging, that their mothers had kept them in the dark about matters as rudimentary as menstruation, leaving them unprepared for life.

Was the family crumbling? Transformations in agriculture and life in the countryside did mean that the peasant family was no longer the institution that governed birth, work, courtship, marriage, and death. Yet the family became newly important as the center of consumption, spending, and leisure time, for television took people (usually men) out of bars, cafés, and music halls. And it became the focus of government attention in the form of family allowances, health care, and Cold War appeals to family values. People brought higher expectations to marriage, which raised divorce rates; and paid more attention to children, which resulted in smaller families. Despite a postwar spike in the birth rate that produced the "baby boom," fertility declined over the long term, even in countries that outlawed contraception. The family assumed new meanings as its traditional structures of authority—namely paternal control over wives and children—eroded under the pressure of social change.

The second aspect of the revolution was the centrality of sex and eroticism to mass consumer culture. Magazines, which flourished in this period, offered advice on how to be attractive and succeed in love. Cultivating one's looks, including sexiness, fitted with the new accent on consumption; indeed, health and personal hygiene was the fastest-rising category of family spending. Advertising, advice columns, TV, and film blurred the boundaries on buying consumer goods, seeking personal fulfillment, and satisfying sexual desire. There was nothing new about appeals to eroticism, but the fact that sexuality was now widely considered a form of self-expression—perhaps even the core of oneself—was new to the twentieth century. These developments helped propel change, and they also made the sexual revolution prominent in the politics of the time.

The third aspect of the revolution came with the legal and medical or scientific changes in contraception. Oral contraceptives, first approved for development in 1959, became mainstream in the next decade. The **birth control pill** did not have revolutionary effects on the birth rate, which was already falling, but it marked a dramatic change because it was simple (though expensive) and could be used by women themselves. By 1975, two-thirds of British women between the ages fifteen and forty-four said they were taking the Pill. Numbers like these marked a long, drawn-out end to centuries-old views that discussing birth control was pornographic, an affront to religion, and an invitation to indulgence and promiscuity. By and large, Western countries legalized contraception in the 1960s, and abortion in the 1970s. In 1965, the U.S. Supreme Court struck down laws banning the use of contraception, though selling contraceptives remained illegal in Massachusetts until 1972. The Soviet Union legalized abortion in 1950, after banning it during most of Stalin's regime. Throughout Eastern Europe, abortion rates were extremely high, because contraceptives proved as difficult to obtain as other consumer goods, men often refused to use them, and women—doubly burdened with long hours of wage work and housework and facing, in addition, chronic housing shortages—had little choice but to resort to abortion.

Legal changes would not have occurred without the women's movements of the time. For nineteenth-century feminists, winning the right to vote was the most difficult practical and symbolic struggle (Chapter 23). For the revived feminism of the 1960s and the 1970s, family, work, and sexuality—all put on the agenda by the social changes of the period—were central. Since the Second World War, the assumption that middle-class women belonged in the home had been challenged by the steadily rising demand for workers, especially in education and the service sector. Thus, many more married women and mothers became part of the labor force. Moreover, across the West, young middle-class women, like men, were part of the rising number of university students. But in the United States, to take just one example, only 37 percent of women who enrolled in college in the 1950s finished their degrees, believing they should marry instead, because they found it difficult to get non-secretarial jobs, received less pay for the same work, and, even when employed, had to rely on their husbands to establish credit. As one of them explained, "We married what we wanted to be": doctor, professor, manager, and so on.

The tension between rising expectations stemming from abundance, growth, and the emphasis on self-expression

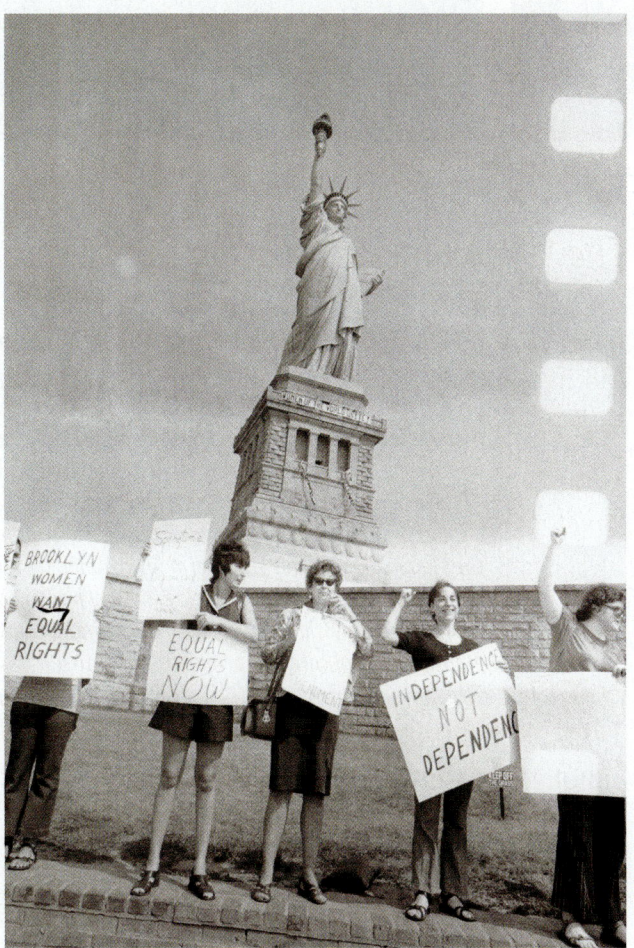

SECOND WAVE FEMINISM. U.S. women, standing beneath the Statue of Liberty, celebrate the passage of the Equal Rights Amendment by the House of Representatives in 1970; the bill, however, did not pass the Senate and never became law. The feminists of the "second wave" distinguished themselves from the "first wave," who had focused on gaining voting rights in Europe and the Americas in the nineteenth and early twentieth centuries, by arguing that votes for women did not end pervasive gender discrimination. They demanded equal pay for equal work, and challenged widespread expectations about women's roles in families and the workplace.

on the one hand, and the reality of limited opportunity on the other, created quiet waves of discontent. Betty Friedan's book *The Feminine Mystique* (1963) brought much of this discontent into the open, contrasting the cultural myths of the fulfilled and happy housewife with the realities of economic inequality, hard work, and narrowed horizons. In 1949, Simone de Beauvoir had described how Western culture (myth, literature, and psychology) had created an image of woman as the second, and lesser sex. In 1963, Friedan, using a more journalistic style and writing at a time when social change had made readers more receptive to her ideas, showed how the media, the social sciences, and advertising at once exalted femininity and lowered

The "Woman Question" on Both Sides of the Atlantic

How did Western culture define femininity? Did women internalize those definitions? These questions were central to postwar feminist thought, and they were sharply posed in two classic texts: Simone de Beauvoir's The Second Sex *(1949) and Betty Friedan's* The Feminine Mystique *(1963). De Beauvoir (1908–1986) started from the existentialist premise that humans were "condemned to be free" and to give their own lives meaning. Why, then, did women accept the limitations imposed on them and, in de Beauvoir's words, "dream the dreams of men"? Although dense and philosophical,* The Second Sex *was read throughout the world.*

Betty Friedan's equally influential bestseller drew heavily on de Beauvoir. Friedan (1921–2006) sought the origins of the "feminine mystique," her term for the model of femininity promoted by experts, advertised in women's magazines, and seemingly accepted by middle-class housewives in postwar United States. As Friedan points out in the excerpt here, the new postwar mystique was in many ways more conservative than prewar ideals had been, despite continuing social change, greater range of careers opening up to women, expansion of women's education, and so on. She cofounded the National Organization for Women (NOW) in 1966, and served as its president until 1970.

Simone de Beauvoir, The Second Sex (1949)

But first, what is a woman? . . . Everyone agrees there are females in the human species; today, as in the past, they make up about half of humanity; and yet we are told that "femininity is in jeopardy;" we are urged, "Be women, stay women, become women." . . . Although some women zealously strive to embody it, the model has never been patented. It is typically described in vague and shimmering terms borrowed from a clairvoyant's vocabulary. . . .

If the female function is not enough to define woman, and if we also reject the explanation of the "eternal feminine," but if we accept, even temporarily, that there are women on the earth, we then have to ask: what is a woman?

Merely stating the problem suggests an immediate answer to me. It is significant that I pose it. It would never occur to a man to write a book on the singular situation of males in humanity. If I want to define myself, I first have to say, "I am a woman"; all other assertions will arise from this basic truth. A man never begins by positing himself as an individual of a certain sex: that he is a man is obvious. The categories "masculine" and "feminine" appear as symmetrical in a formal way on town hall records or identification papers. The relation of the two sexes is not that of two electrical poles: the man represents both the positive and the neuter. . . . Woman is the negative, to such a point that any determination is imputed to her as a limitation, without reciprocity. . . . [A] man is in his right by virtue of being man; it is the woman who is in the wrong. . . . Woman has ovaries and a uterus; such are the particular conditions that lock her in her subjectivity; some even say she thinks with her hormones. Man vainly forgets that his anatomy also includes hormones and testicles. He grasps his body as a direct and normal link with the world that he believes he apprehends in all objectivity whereas he considers woman's body an obstacle, a prison, burdened by everything that particularises it. "The female is female by virtue of a certain *lack* of qualities," Aristotle said. "We should regard women's nature as suffering from natural defectiveness." And St. Thomas in his turn decreed that woman was an "incomplete man," an "incidental" being. This is what the Genesis story symbolises, where Eve appears as if drawn from Adam's "supernumerary" bone, in Bossuet's words. Humanity is male, and man defines woman, not in herself, but in relation to himself; she is not considered an autonomous being. . . . And she is nothing other than what man decides; she is thus called "the sex," meaning that the male sees her essentially as a sexed being; for him she is sex, so she is it in the absolute. She determines and differentiates herself in relation to man, and he does not in relation to her; she is the inessential in front of the essential. He is the Subject, he is the Absolute. She is the Other.

Source: Simone de Beauvoir, *The Second Sex*, trans. Constance Borde and Sheila Malovany-Chevallier (London: 2009), pp. 3–6.

Betty Friedan, The Feminine Mystique (1963)

In 1939, the heroines of women's magazine stories were not always young, but in a certain sense they were younger than their fictional counterparts today. They were young in the same way that the American hero has always been young: they were New Women, creating with a gay determined spirit a new identity for women—a life of their own. There was an aura about them of becoming, of moving into a future that was going to be different from the past. . . .

These stories may not have been great literature. But the identity of their heroines seemed to say something about the housewives who, then as now, read the women's magazines. These magazines were not written for career women. The New Woman heroines were the ideal of yesterday's housewives; they reflected the dreams, mirrored the yearning for identity and the sense of possibility that existed for women then. . . .

In 1949 . . . the feminine mystique began to spread through the land. . . .

The feminine mystique says that the highest value and the only commitment for women is the fulfillment of their own femininity. It says that the great mistake of Western culture, through most of its history, has been the undervaluation of this femininity. . . . The mistake, says the mystique, the root of women's troubles in the past, is that women envied men, women tried to be like men, instead of accepting their own nature, which can find fulfillment only in sexual passivity, male domination, and nurturing maternal love.

But the new image this mystique gives to American women is the old image: "Occupation: housewife." The new mystique makes the housewife-mothers, who never had a chance to be anything else, the model for all women; it presupposes that history has reached a final and glorious end in the here and now, as far as women are concerned. . . .

It is more than a strange paradox that as all professions are finally open to women in America, "career woman" has become a dirty word; that as higher education becomes available to any woman with the capacity for it, education for women has become so suspect that more and more drop out of high school and college to marry and have babies; that as so many roles in modern society become theirs for the taking, women so insistently confine themselves to one role. Why . . . should she accept this new image which insists she is not a person but a "woman," by definition barred from the freedom of human existence and a voice in human destiny?

Source: Betty Friedan, *The Feminine Mystique* (New York: 2001; first publication, 1963), pp. 38, 40, 42–43, 67–68.

Questions for Analysis

1. Why does de Beauvoir ask, "What is a woman?"

2. Why does Friedan think that a "feminine mystique" emerged after the Second World War?

women's expectations and possibilities. Friedan cofounded the National Organization for Women (NOW) in 1966; and smaller, often more radical, women's movements multiplied across Europe in the following decades.

For this generation of feminists, reproductive freedom was both a private matter and a basic right—a key to women's control over their lives. Outlawing contraception and abortion, they argued, made women alone bear responsibility for the consequences of sweeping changes in Western sexual life, and such measures were ineffective as well as unjust. French feminists dramatized the point by publishing the names of 343 well-known women, including de Beauvoir, who admitted to having had illegal abortions. A similar petition came out in Germany the following year, which was followed by petitions from doctors and tens of thousands of supporters. In sum, the legal changes followed from political demands, which in turn reflected a quiet or subterranean rebellion of many women (and men)—one with longer-term causes. Mass consumption, mass culture, and startlingly rapid transformations in public and private life were all intimately related.

SOCIAL MOVEMENTS DURING THE 1960s

The social unrest of the 1960s was international. Its roots lay in the political struggles and social transformations of the postwar period. Of these, the most important were anticolonial and civil rights movements. The successful anticolonial movements (Chapter 27) reflected a growing racial consciousness, and also helped encourage that consciousness. Newly independent African and Caribbean nations remained wary of resurgences of colonialism and the continuing economic hegemony of Western Europe and America. Black and Asian immigration to those nations produced tension and frequent violence. And, in the West, particularly in the United States, people of color identified with these social and economic grievances.

The Civil Rights Movement

The emergence of new black nations in Africa and the Caribbean was paralleled by a growing African American **civil rights movement**. The Second World War increased African American migration from the American South to northern cities, intensifying a drive for rights, dignity, and independence that began in the prewar era with organizations such as the National Association for the Advancement of Colored People (NAACP) and the National Urban League. By 1960, various civil rights groups, led by the Congress of Racial Equality (CORE), had started to organize boycotts and demonstrations directed at private businesses and public services that discriminated against blacks in the South. The preeminent figure in the civil rights movement in the United States during the 1960s was Martin Luther King Jr. (1929–1968), a Baptist minister. King embraced the philosophy of nonviolence promoted by the Indian social and political activist Mohandas K. Gandhi (Chapter 27). His personal participation in countless demonstrations, willingness to go to jail for a cause he believed to be just, and ability as an orator to arouse both blacks and whites with his message, led to his position as the most highly regarded—and most widely feared—defender of black rights. An assassination in 1968 tragically ended his inspiring career.

King, the Southern Christian Leadership Conference (SCLC), and organizations such as CORE aspired to a fully integrated nation, while other charismatic and important black leaders sought complete independence from white society, fearing that integration would leave African Americans without the spiritual or material resources necessary for the community's pride, dignity, and autonomy. The most influential of the black nationalists was Malcolm X (1925–1965), who assumed the "X" after discarding his "white" surname (Little). For most of his adult life, Malcolm, a spokesman for the Black Muslim movement, urged blacks to renew their commitment to their own heritage; to establish black businesses for economic autonomy; and to fortify economic, political, and psychological defenses against white domination. In 1965, he was assassinated, while addressing a rally in Harlem.

Civil rights laws passed under President Lyndon B. Johnson (1908–1973) in the 1960s did bring African Americans some measure of equality with regard to voting rights—and, to a much lesser degree, school desegregation. But in other areas, such as housing and job opportunities, white racism

MARTIN LUTHER KING JR., 1964. The African American civil rights leader is welcomed in Oslo, Norway, on a trip to accept the Nobel Peace Prize. He would be assassinated four years later. ▪ *How might have Europeans viewed King's campaign?* ▪ *How might have their views affected their vision of the United States?*

continued. Economic development passed by many African American communities and subsequent administrations pulled back from the innovative programs of the Johnson era.

These problems were not confined to the United States. Indian, West Indian, and Pakistani immigrants in Britain faced discrimination in jobs, housing, and everyday interaction with the authorities, producing frequent racial disturbances in major British cities. France witnessed hostility toward Algerian immigration, and Germany toward the importation of Turkish labor. In Western Europe, as in the United States, struggles for racial and ethnic integration became central to the postcolonial world.

The civil rights movement had enormous significance for the twentieth century, and it galvanized other movements. It dramatized, as perhaps no other movement could, the chasm between the egalitarian promises of American democracy and the real inequalities at the core of the American social and political life—a chasm that could be found in other Western nations as well. African American claims were morally and politically compelling, and the civil rights movement sharpened the criticisms of what others saw as a complacent, narrowly individualistic, materialist culture.

The Antiwar Movement

The United States' escalating war in Vietnam became a lightning rod for discontent. In 1961, President John F. Kennedy (1917–1963) promised that the United States would "bear any burden" necessary to fight communism, and to ensure the victory of American models of representative government and free-market economics in developing nations. Kennedy's plan entailed massive increases in foreign aid, much of it in weapons, and provided the impetus for humanitarian institutions such as the Peace Corps, intended to improve local conditions and show Americans' benevolence and good intentions. Bearing burdens, however, also meant

THE WAR IN VIETNAM AND SOUTHEAST ASIA. The 1954 Geneva Accords divided Vietnam at the seventeenth parallel: the north went to Ho Chi Minh, the communist leader; and the south was controlled by Ngo Dinh Diem, an ally of the United States. In 1956, South Vietnam refused to hold the elections mandated by the Geneva Accords. In response, Ho Chi Minh mobilized a guerrilla army, the Viet Cong, and the Vietnam War began. ▪ *Which other countries in this region were drawn into the war?* ▪ *How did the Viet Cong use the proximity of Cambodia and Laos to their strategic advantage?* ▪ *Why did the United States choose to get involved?*

fighting guerrillas who turned to the Soviets for aid. This involved covert interventions in Latin America, the Congo, and, most important, Vietnam.

By the time of Kennedy's assassination in 1963, nearly 15,000 American "advisers" were on the ground alongside South Vietnamese troops. President Johnson, Kennedy's successor, began the strategic bombing of North Vietnam and rapidly drew hundreds of thousands of American troops into combat in South Vietnam. The rebels in the south, known as the Viet Cong, were solidly entrenched, highly experienced guerrilla fighters, who were backed by the professional, well-equipped North Vietnamese army under

Ho Chi Minh, who received support from the Soviet Union. The South Vietnamese government, meanwhile, resisted efforts at reform and was losing popular support. Massive efforts by the United States produced only stalemate, mounting American casualties, and rising discontent.

Vietnam did much to cause the political turmoil of the 1960s in the United States. As Martin Luther King Jr. pointed out, the war—which relied on a disproportionate number of black soldiers to conduct a fight against a small nation of color—echoed and magnified racial inequality at home. Exasperated by troubles in the field, American planners continued to escalate military commitments, without effect. Peace talks in Paris stalled, while the death toll on all sides increased. The involuntary draft of young American men expanded, polarizing the public. In 1968, criticism forced President Johnson to abandon his plans to run for a second term. His successor, Richard M. Nixon (1913–1994), who won a narrow victory on the basis of promises to end the war, expanded it instead. Student protests against the war frequently ended in violence. The government brought criminal conspiracy charges against Benjamin Spock, the nation's leading pediatrician, and William Sloane Coffin, the chaplain of Yale University, for encouraging young people to resist the draft. Avoiding the draft became so widespread that the system was changed in 1970. And from other countries' points of view, the Vietnam War became a spectacle, one in which the most powerful, wealthiest nation of the world seemed intent on destroying a land of poor peasants in the name of anticommunism, democracy, and freedom. The tarnished image of Western values stood at the center of the 1960s protest movements in the United States and Western Europe.

The Student Movement

The student movement can be seen as a consequence of postwar developments: a growing cohort of young people with more time and wealth than in the past; generational consciousness heightened, in part, by the marketing of mass youth culture; and educational institutions unable to deal with rising numbers and expectations. In France, the number of students in high school rose from 400,000 in 1949 to 2 million in 1969; in universities, over the same period, enrollments skyrocketed from 100,000 to 600,000. The same was true

in Italy, Britain, and West Germany. Universities, which had been created to educate a small elite, found both their teaching staffs and facilities overwhelmed. Lecture halls were packed, university bureaucracies did not respond to requests, and thousands of students took exams at the same time. More philosophically, students raised questions about the role and meaning of elite education in a democratic society, and about the relationships among the university as a "knowledge factory," consumer culture, and neocolonial ventures such as the Vietnam War and (for the French) the Algerian wars. Conservative traditions made intellectual reform difficult. Moreover, student demands for fewer restrictions on personal life—for instance, permission to have a member of the opposite sex in a dormitory room—provoked authoritarian reactions from university representatives. Waves of student protest were not confined to the United States and Western Europe; they also swept across Poland and Czechoslovakia, where students protested one-party bureaucratic rule, stifling intellectual life, and authoritarianism, which helped to sustain networks of dissidents. By the mid-1960s, simmering anger in Eastern Europe had once again reached a dangerous point.

1968

The year 1968 was an extraordinary one, quite similar to 1848, with its wave of revolution (Chapter 20), except even more intensely international. The possibility of a nearly global youth culture fostered a sense of collective identity.

"THE PRESS IS POISON." Criticizing the official media was central to the politics of May 1968.

The news media relayed images of civil rights protests in the United States to Europe, and broadcast news footage of the Vietnam War on television screens from West Virginia to West Germany. The wave of unrest shook both the Eastern and Western blocs and unsettled societies in Africa, Asia, and Latin America. Protest movements assailed bureaucracy and the human costs of the Cold War: on the Soviet side, bureaucracy, authoritarianism, and indifference to civilians; on the Western side, bias and monopolies in the news media, the military-industrial complex, and American imperialism. The Soviet regime, as we have seen, responded with repression. In the United States and Western Europe, traditional political parties had little idea as to what to make of these new movements and those who participated in them. In both cases, events rapidly overwhelmed political systems.

PARIS

The most serious outbreak of student unrest in Europe came in Paris in the spring of 1968. The French Republic had been shaken by conflicts over the Algerian war in the early 1960s. Even more important, the economic boom had undermined the foundations of the regime and de Gaulle's traditional style of rule. French students at the University of Paris demanded reforms to modernize their university. Protest first peaked at Nanterre, a new branch of the university built on a former air force depot. Nanterre was in a poor and poorly served neighborhood, starved for funds, and overcrowded with students. Petitions, demonstrations, and confrontations with university authorities traveled quickly from Nanterre to the Sorbonne, in central Paris. De Gaulle, meanwhile, had no sympathy for the students; "Reform, yes—bed wetting, no," he reportedly declared at the height of the confrontation.

In the face of growing disorder, the University of Paris shut down, sending students into the streets and into uglier confrontations with the police. The police reacted with repression and violence, which startled onlookers and television audiences, and backfired on the authorities. Sympathy with the students' cause expanded rapidly, bringing in opponents of President de Gaulle's government. Massive trade-union strikes broke out as workers in the automobile industry, technical

workers, and public-sector employees—from gas and electricity utilities to the mail system to radio and television—went on strike. By mid-May, an astonishing 10 million French workers had walked off their jobs. At one point, it looked as if the government would fall, but it was able to satisfy the strikers with wage increases and appeals to public demand for order. The student movements, isolated, gradually petered out, and students agreed to resume university life. The government recovered, but the events of 1968 helped weaken de Gaulle's position as president and contributed to his retirement from office the following year.

There had been protest and rebelliousness in the 1950s, but the scale of events in 1968 was astonishing, for Paris was not the only city to explode that year. Student protests broke out in West Berlin, targeting the government's close ties to the autocratic shah of Iran and the power of media corporations; clashes with the police here also turned violent. In Italian cities, undergraduates staged several demonstrations to draw attention to university overcrowding; twenty-six universities closed. The London School of Economics was nearly shut down by protests. In Mexico City, on the eve of the 1968 Olympics, hosted by the Mexican government, a confrontation with the police ended with the deaths of hundreds of protesters, most of them students. The Olympics reflected the political contests of the period: African nations threatened to boycott if South Africa, with its apartheid regime, participated; two African American medalists raised their hands in a black

ANTIGOVERNMENT PROTESTS IN MEXICO CITY, 1968. On October 2, 1968, ten days before the opening of the Summer Olympics in Mexico City, police opened fire on student protesters and arrested more than one thousand people.

power salute during an awards ceremony, after which the Olympic Committee promptly sent them home.

In Vietnam, the Viet Cong defied American claims to have turned the tide by launching a new offensive. The Tet offensive, named for the Vietnamese new year, brought the highest casualty rates to date in the Vietnam War, along with an explosion of protests. Antiwar demonstrations and student rebellions spread across the country. President Johnson, battered by the effects of Tet and already worn down by the war, chose not to run for reelection. The year 1968 also saw trauma and damage to the country's political future with the assassinations of Martin Luther King Jr. (April 4, 1968) and the presidential candidate Robert F. Kennedy (June 5, 1968). King's assassination was followed by a wave of rioting in more than fifty cities across the United States. In late summer, street battles raged between police and student protesters at the Democratic National Convention in Chicago. Some saw the flowering of protests as another "springtime of peoples," but others saw it as a long nightmare.

PRAGUE

The student movement in the United States and Western Europe took inspiration from one of the most significant challenges to Soviet authority since the Hungarian revolt of 1956 (see Chapter 27): the "**Prague Spring**" of 1968. The events began with the emergence of a liberal communist government in Czechoslovakia, led by the Slovak **Alexander Dubček** (*DOOB-chehk;* 1921–1992). Dubček had outmaneuvered the more traditional, authoritarian party leaders, and advocated "socialism with a human face." He encouraged debates within the party, academic and artistic freedom, and less censorship. As was often the case, party members were divided between proponents of reform and those fearful that reform would unleash a revolution, but the reformers gained the upper hand with support from outside the party: student organizations, the press, and networks of dissidents. As in Western Europe and the United States, the protest movement overflowed into traditional party politics.

A RUSSIAN TANK ATTACKED DURING THE PRAGUE SPRING, 1968. The Soviet-led invasion of Czechoslovakia on August 20–21, 1968, put an end to Alexander Dubček's experiment in creating "socialism with a human face."

Analyzing Primary Sources

Ludvík Vaculík, "Two Thousand Words" (1968)

During the Prague Spring of 1968, a group of Czech intellectuals published a document titled "Two Thousand Words That Belong to Workers, Farmers, Officials, Scientists, Artists, and Everybody," known simply as "Two Thousand Words." The author of the document, Ludvík Vaculík, was a member of the Czech Communist Party who hoped to encourage the people of Czechoslovakia to implement democratic reforms, including freedom of the press. Seen as a direct affront by Moscow, this manifesto heightened Soviet-Czech tensions. In August 1968, Warsaw Pact tanks rolled into Prague, overthrowing the reformist government of Alexander Dubček.

ost of the nation welcomed the socialist program with high hopes. But it fell into the hands of the wrong people. It would not have mattered so much that they lacked adequate experience in affairs of state, factual knowledge, or philosophical education, if only they had enough common prudence and decency to listen to the opinion of others and agree to being gradually replaced by more able people. . . .

The chief sin and deception of these rulers was to have explained their own whims as the "will of the workers." Were we to accept this pretense, we would have to blame the workers today for the decline of our economy, for crimes committed against the innocent, and for the introduction of censorship to prevent anyone writing about these things. The workers would be to blame for misconceived investments, for losses suffered in foreign trade, and for the housing shortage. Obviously no sensible person will hold the working class responsible for such things. We all know, and every worker knows especially, that they had virtually no say in deciding anything. . . .

Since the beginning of this year we have been experiencing a regenerative process of democratization. . . .

Let us demand the departure of people who abused their power, damaged public property, and acted dishonorably or brutally. Ways must be found to compel them to resign. To mention a few: public criticism, resolutions, demonstrations, demonstrative work brigades, collections to buy presents for them on their retirement, strikes, and picketing at their front doors. But we should reject any illegal, indecent, or boorish methods. . . . Let us convert the district and local newspapers, which have mostly degenerated to the level of official mouthpieces, into a platform for all the forward-looking elements in politics; let us demand that editorial boards be formed of National Front representatives, or else let us start new papers. Let us form committees for the defense of free speech. . . .

There has been great alarm recently over the possibility that foreign forces will intervene in our development. Whatever superior forces may face us, all we can do is stick to our own positions, behave decently, and initiate nothing ourselves. We can show our government that we will stand by it, with weapons if need be, if it will do what we give it a mandate to do. . . .

The spring is over and will never return. By winter we will know all.

Source: Jaromir Navratil, *The Prague Spring 1968*, trans. Mark Kramer, Joy Moss, and Ruth Tosek (Budapest: 1998), pp. 177–81.

Questions for Analysis

1. According to Vaculík, where did socialism go wrong?

2. What specific reforms did Vaculík demand?

In the Soviet Union, Khrushchev had fallen in 1964, and the reins of Soviet power had passed to Leonid Brezhnev as secretary of the Communist party. Brezhnev was more conservative than Khrushchev, less inclined to bargain with the West, and prone to defensive actions to safeguard the Soviet sphere of influence. Initially, the Soviets tolerated Dubček as a political eccentric, but the events of 1968 raised their fears. Most Eastern European communist leaders denounced Czech reformism, but student demonstrations of support broke out in Poland and Yugoslavia, calling for an end to one-party rule, less censorship, and reform of the judicial system. In addition, Josip Broz Tito of Yugoslavia and Nicolae Ceaușescu (*chow-SHEHS-koo*) of Romania—two of the more stubbornly independent communist leaders in Eastern Europe—visited Dubček. To Soviet eyes, these activities looked as if they were directed against the Warsaw Pact and Soviet security. The Soviets also saw American intervention in Vietnam as evidence of heightened anticommunist activities around the world. When Dubček attempted to democratize the Communist party and did not attend a meeting of members of the Warsaw Pact, the Soviets sent tanks and troops into Prague in August 1968. Again, the world watched as streams of Czech refugees left the country and a repressive government, picked by Soviet security forces, took charge. Dubček and his allies were subjected to imprisonment or "internal exile." Twenty percent of the members of the Czech Communist party were expelled in a series of purges. After the destruction of the Prague Spring, Soviet diplomats consolidated their position according to the new Brezhnev Doctrine, which stated that no socialist state could adopt policies endangering the interests of international socialism, and that the Soviet Union could intervene in the domestic affairs of any Soviet-bloc nation if communist rule was threatened. In other words, the repressive rules applied to Hungary in 1956 would not change.

What were the effects of 1968? De Gaulle's government recovered. The Republican Richard M. Nixon won the U.S. presidential election that year. From 1972 to 1975, the United States withdrew from Vietnam; and in the wake of that war came a refugee crisis and a new series of horrific regional conflicts. In Prague, Warsaw Pact tanks put down the uprising. In the Brezhnev Doctrine, the Soviet regime reasserted its right to control its satellites. Serious Cold War confrontations rippled along Czechoslovakia's western border as refugees fled west, and in the Korean peninsula after North Korea's seizure of an eavesdropping ship from the U.S. Navy. Over the long term, however, the protesters' and dissidents' demands proved more difficult to contain. In Eastern Europe and the Soviet Union, dissent was defeated but not eliminated. The crushing of the Czech rebellion proved thoroughly disillusioning, and, in important respects, the events of 1968 prefigured the collapse of Soviet control in 1989. In Western Europe and the United States, the student movement subsided, but the issues and the kinds of politics that it pioneered proved more enduring. Feminism—or, more accurately, "second wave" feminism—really came into its own after 1968, as its numbers expanded with women a generation younger than Simone de Beauvoir and Betty Friedan. These feminists had been in student political organizations in the 1960s, and their impatience with traditional political parties and, often, with their male student allies sent them into separate groups, where they championed equality in sexual relationships and in the family. In a phrase that captured some of the changes of the 1950s and the 1960s, they insisted that "the personal is political." As one Englishwoman said,

"We wanted to redefine the meaning of politics to include an analysis of our daily lives," which meant sexuality, health, child care, cultural images of women, and so on. The anti-war movement took up the issue of nuclear weapons—a particularly volatile issue in Europe. Finally, the environmental movement took hold, concerned not only with pollution and the world's dwindling resources but also with mushrooming urbanization and the kind of unrestrained economic growth that had given rise to the excesses of the 1960s. Over the long term, in both Europe and the United States, voters' loyalties to traditional political parties became less reliable, and smaller parties multiplied. In this way, new social movements eventually became part of a very different political landscape.

ECONOMIC STAGNATION: THE PRICE OF SUCCESS

Economic as well as social problems plagued Europe during the 1970s and 1980s, but these problems had begun earlier. By the mid-1960s, for example, the West German growth rate had slowed. Demand for manufactured goods fell and, in 1966, the country suffered its first postwar recession. Volkswagen, the symbol of the German miracle, introduced a shortened workweek, and almost 700,000 West Germans were thrown out of work. In France, a persistent housing shortage raised the cost of living. Though new industries continued to prosper, the basic industries—coal, steel, and railways—began to run up deficits. And unemployment was rising in tandem with prices. Prime Minister Harold Wilson's pledge to revive Britain's economy by introducing new technology foundered due to the crises in the foreign-exchange value of the pound, which were compounded by continued low levels of growth. The Common Market—expanded in 1973 to include Britain, Ireland, and Denmark; and again in the early 1980s to admit Greece, Spain, and Portugal—struggled to overcome problems stemming from the conflict between the domestic economic regulations characteristic of many European states and the free-market policies that prevailed within what would become the European Economic Community (EEC) countries.

Oil prices spiked for the first time in the early 1970s, compounding these difficulties. In 1973, the Arab-dominated **Organization of the Petroleum Exporting Countries (OPEC)** instituted an **oil embargo** against the Western powers, causing the price increase. In 1973, a barrel of oil cost $1.73; in 1975, it cost $10.46; by the early 1980s, the price had risen to over $30. This increase produced an inflationary spiral: interest rates rose and with them the price of almost

UNEMPLOYMENT DEMONSTRATION, 1974. A crowd of workers in Rome, Italy, gathered to protest inflation and unemployment, in a strike that lasted twenty-four hours.

part on capital borrowed from the West, and by 1980, those debts weighed heavily on their national economies. Poland's hard-currency indebtedness to Western countries, for example, was almost four times greater than its annual exports. The solution to this problem, attempted in Poland and elsewhere, was to cut back on production for domestic consumption in order to increase exports, but this policy encountered strong popular opposition. Although there was virtually no unemployment in Eastern Europe, men and women were by no means happy with their economic situation. Working hours were longer than in Western Europe, and goods and services, even in prosperous times, were scarce.

Western governments struggled for effective reactions to the abrupt change in their economic circumstances. The new leader of the British Conservative Party, Margaret Thatcher (elected prime minister in 1979, and reelected in 1983 and 1987), established a program of curbing trade-union power, cutting taxes to stimulate the economy, and privatizing publicly owned enterprises, but the economy remained weak, with close to 15 percent of the workforce unemployed by 1986. In West Germany, a series of Social Democratic governments attempted to combat economic recession with job-training programs and tax incentives, both financed by higher taxes. These programs, however, did little to assist economic recovery, and the country shifted to the right.

The fact that governments of the right and the left were unable to re-create Europe's unprecedented postwar prosperity suggests the degree to which economic forces remain outside the control of individual states. The continuing economic malaise renewed efforts to Europeanize common problems. By the end of the 1980s, the EEC embarked on an ambitious program of integration. Long-term goals, agreed on when the European Union (EU) was formed in 1991, included a monetary union—with a central European bank and a single currency—and unified social policies to reduce poverty and unemployment. As the twenty-first century opened, the European member states had begun to institute several of these steps. It remains unclear whether that new European "federal" state would overcome its members' claims of national sovereignty, or whether it would develop the economic and political strength to counter the global domination of the United States.

everything else Western consumers were used to buying, and rising costs produced wage demands and strikes. The calm industrial relations of the 1950s and the early 1960s were a thing of the past. At the same time, European manufacturers encountered serious competition, not only from such highly developed countries as Japan but also from the increasingly active economies of Asia and Africa, into which the West had invested capital eagerly in the previous decades. By 1980, Japan had captured 10 percent of the automobile market in West Germany and 25 percent in Belgium. In 1984, unemployment in Western Europe reached about 19 million—the lean years had arrived.

Economies in the Soviet bloc also stalled. The expansion of heavy industry had helped recovery in the postwar period, but by the 1970s, those sectors no longer provided growth or innovation. The Soviet Communist party proclaimed in 1961 that, by 1970, the USSR would exceed the United States in per capita production. By the end of the 1970s, however, Soviet per capita production was not much higher than in the less industrialized countries of southern Europe. The Soviets were also overcommitted to military defense industries that had become inefficient, though lucrative for the party members who ran them. The Soviet economy did get a boost from the OPEC oil price hikes of 1973 and 1979. (The Soviet Union did not belong to OPEC, but as the world's largest producer of oil, it benefited from rising prices.) Without this boost, the situation would have been far grimmer.

Following an impressive economic performance during the early 1970s, the Eastern European nations encountered serious financial difficulties. Their success had rested in

Solidarity in Poland

In 1980, a wave of strikes rolled throughout Poland, shocking the government. More than half the adult population is thought to have participated in the demonstrations, with many women playing key roles. The strikes began as protests over the cost of basic foodstuffs, but quickly spiraled into something much larger. The credit for the unrest was attributed to a visit by the new pope, John Paul II (Karol Józef Wojtyła; 1920–2005) to Poland in 1979. The new pope, a Pole who had been Archbishop of Kraków before becoming a cardinal, voiced criticisms of the Polish political system, which were interpreted by many as an invitation to disobey. In 1978, Adam Michnik, a future leader of the strike movement, had called for more cooperation between political dissidents and the Church. During the unrest, the Catholic Church in Poland endorsed the strikers and gave them its support.

Polish workers took control of the shipyards in Gdansk and formed an independent trade union, **Solidarity**, led by an electrician named **Lech Wałęsa** (1943–). The workers formulated several key demands. First, they objected to the working conditions imposed by the government to combat severe economic crisis. Second, they protested high prices and especially shortages, both of which had roots in government policy and priorities. Above all, though, the Polish workers in Solidarity demanded truly independent labor unions, instead of labor organizations sponsored by the government. Their belief that society had the right to organize itself and, by implication, create its own government, stood at the core of the movement. For a period of fifteen months the world was transfixed by this attempt to confront the Communist Party's authority in Poland.

In December 1981, General Wojciech Jaruzelski, the head of the Polish Communist Party and prime minister, decided to put an end to the movement by force and declared martial law (the expression he actually used translates as "a state of war"). More than 5,000 Solidarity members were arrested and jailed, including Lech Wałęsa, and army checkpoints were set up throughout Polish cities. A few protests were quickly put down with overwhelming force, and several people were killed, but Solidarity explicitly came out against armed resistance, a decision that undoubtedly saved many lives. Many journalists and teachers were prohibited from returning to their jobs. Jaruzelski later claimed that his action had prevented the Soviets from invading, as they had done in Hungary in 1956 or in Czechoslovakia in 1968. Nevertheless, the experience of martial law left Solidarity's millions of sympathizers embittered, and many in the Polish army were demoralized by their participation in the repression.

THE POPE KNEELS BEFORE THE AUSCHWITZ MEMORIAL, 1979. Pope John Paul II's visit to his native Poland in June 1979 included a pilgrimage to Auschwitz, the largest of the Nazi death camps during World War II. In the context of ongoing controversy over the persistence of anti-Semitism in Europe after the war, his public statements were scrutinized closely. He invoked his own personal experience of living under the Nazi occupation, and the memory of people he had known as a child who had been killed.

EUROPE RECAST: THE COLLAPSE OF COMMUNISM AND THE END OF THE SOVIET UNION

Did the Soviet Union intend to invade Poland in 1981? Perhaps not. There is some evidence that Soviet leaders were hesitant, though the plans were in place. With uncertainty at the top about political succession (Leonid Brezhnev would die less than a year later in 1982) and being bogged down in a costly and difficult war in Afghanistan after 1979, it is possible that the Soviets would have let Poland go its own way, preoccupied as they were with their own

"Between Hope and Despair": The Solidarity Movement of 1980 in Poland

Bronislaw Geremek (1932–2008) was smuggled out of the Warsaw ghetto in 1943 as a child, along with his mother; his father was murdered at Auschwitz. He later studied in France and became a noted historian of medieval Europe, returning to teach at the Polish Academy of Sciences. He joined the Solidarity movement in August 1980, and played a crucial role in negotiating a peaceful transition to democracy in Poland in 1987–1989. After 1989, Geremek served in the Polish Parliament and was foreign minister of Poland. In this passage, published in 1990, he describes the process by which local protests over food prices transformed into Solidarity's political confrontation with the communist regime in Poland.

 he most characteristic feature of the events of the summer of 1980 in Poland was society's rapid self-organization, which quite spontaneously translated its protest into a regular program and selected means of action adapted to it. The outer forms of protest seemed unchanged: price increases for basic articles, especially food staples, were met with strikes. The first occurred in Lublin in July, then spread to the Baltic port cities in August. The Lublin strike resulted in a surprisingly efficient organization of the municipal and retail trade services, with the shops being supplied with food by the local strike committees before a compromise agreement was actually signed. During the strike, local railmen blocked trains heading for the Soviet Union with Polish food exports; this, however, was more an act of passive resistance than of violence.

The August strikes in the shipyards of Gdansk, Gdynia, and Szczecin, which soon spread to most other workplaces in these cities, again produced organized strike structures and services that helped secure a normal course of life in the cities and ensure order and discipline in the striking plants. As these were all sit-in strikes, the daily life of participants had to have a certain amount of organization.

This self-organizing process on the part of particular groups and the whole society fighting for their rights, became widespread; it affected certain other areas traditionally in the domain of the state. Thus, for example, because the workers' guard controlled the safety of a given factory or city, alcohol was totally banned from the workplace and from public life. The striking factories became the centers of local authority; a new kind of social representation emerged. It provided a social and political lesson of great significance. The workers' protest, characterized by great determination, was hardly an act of despair. It was a political act. In conditions of the communist system, an industrial conflict cannot be isolated; it assumes the nature of a political power struggle.

This was clearly evident in the strikers' programs, where political aspirations were explicitly articulated. The list of demands of the Gdansk workers included not only requests for specific pay and social compensation but expressed also an awareness of the general dangers looming over the country. Hence, the demands to reform the economic system, to guarantee human rights, to free political prisoners, to curb censorship, and to broadcast Sunday Mass over the radio. The insistence on free trade unions—the most important

demand from the Gdansk list—has to be placed in this context also. The new trade union saw the defense of the employees' interests as one of its tasks, but also, and perhaps more importantly, it emphasized the restoration of civil society's supremacy over the state. This was a wholly political demand, undermining the structures of a system in which, in addition to the monopolistic Communist party, a workplace could accommodate only Communist-dependent organizations whose sole purpose would be to transmit Party directives down to the crew.

Source: Bronislaw Geremek, "Between Hope and Despair," *Daedalus: Journal of the American Academy of Arts and Sciences*, vol. 119, no. 1 (Winter 1990): 91–110; here, pp. 104–5.

Questions for Analysis

1. What were the effects of what Geremek calls the "self-organization" of society during the initial strike wave in the summer of 1980?

2. What was it about the communist system that made this confrontation political, rather than a protest about economic conditions?

3. What does Geremek mean when he says that the Gdansk demands amounted to a "restoration of civil society's supremacy over the state"?

growing economic and political problems. Only a few short years later, the Soviets embarked on their own program of reform, a decision that led to the astonishing collapse of the Soviet Union's power over the Eastern-bloc countries in 1989, and the end of the Soviet Union itself in 1991.

Gorbachev and Soviet Reform

The Soviet reforms began in 1985, when a new generation of officials began taking charge and **Mikhail Gorbachev** (1931–) became leader of the Communist party. In his mid-fifties, Gorbachev was significantly younger than his immediate predecessors, thus less prey to the habits of mind that had shaped Soviet domestic and foreign affairs. He was critical of the repressive aspects of communist society as well as its sluggish economy, and did not hesitate to voice those criticisms openly. His twin policies of *glasnost* (intellectual openness) and *perestroika* (economic restructuring) held out hope for a freer, more prosperous Soviet Union. Under Gorbachev, a number of imprisoned dissidents were freed, among them Andrei Sakharov, the scientist known as the "father of the Soviet hydrogen bomb" and later a fierce critic of the Cold War arms race.

GORBACHEV IN POLAND AT THE HEIGHT OF HIS POWER IN 1986. Gorbachev's policy of perestroika was aimed at the privileges of the political elite, and would eventually lead to his fall from power.

The policies of glasnost took aim at the privileges of the political elite and the immobility of the state bureaucracy by allowing greater freedom of speech, instituting competitive elections to official positions, and limiting terms of office. Gorbachev's program of perestroika called for a shift from the centrally planned economy instituted by Stalin to a mixed economy, combining planning with the operation of market forces. In agriculture, perestroika accelerated the move away from cooperative production and instituted incentives for the achievement of production targets. Gorbachev planned to integrate the Soviet Union into the international economy by participating in organizations such as the International Monetary Fund (IMF).

Even these dramatic reforms, however, were too little, too late. Ethnic unrest, a legacy of Russia's nineteenth-century imperialism, threatened to split the Soviet Union apart, while secession movements gathered steam in the Baltic republics and elsewhere. From 1988 onward, fighting between Armenians and Azerbaijanis over an ethnically Azerbaijani region located inside Armenia threatened to escalate into a border dispute with Iran. Only Soviet troops patrolling the border and Gorbachev's willingness to suppress a separatist revolt in Azerbaijan by force temporarily quelled the conflict.

Spurred on by these events, the countries of Eastern Europe began to agitate for independence from Moscow. Gorbachev encouraged open discussion (glasnost) not only in his own country but also in the satellite nations. He revoked the Brezhnev Doctrine, with its insistence on single-party socialist governments, and made frequent and inspiring trips to the capitals of neighboring satellites.

The consequences of this political shift were first realized in Poland, where Solidarity had been defeated but not destroyed by martial law in 1981, as the union launched a new series of strikes in 1988. These disturbances culminated in an agreement between the government and Solidarity that legalized the union and permitted its members to run for office in the June 1989 elections, in which Solidarity was allowed to contest 35 percent of the seats in the parliament and all the seats in the newly re-created Senate. The results astonished the world: in the parliament, Solidarity won all the seats that it was allowed to contest, and in the Senate, it won 99 out of 100 seats. The Communist party was still guaranteed 65 percent of the seats for itself and its allies, but its reputation and prestige had been shattered. By 1991, Poland was holding free parliamentary elections, and the transition to democracy had been largely accomplished.

Hungary was next. Janos Kadar, the Hungarian leader since the Soviet crackdown of 1956, resigned in the face of continuing demonstrations in May 1988, and was replaced by the reformist government of the Hungarian Socialist Workers' party. In June 1989, this new government disinterred the remains of Imre Nagy, the reformist leader of the Hungarian Revolution of 1956 executed by the Soviets, and gave him an official state funeral. By the spring of 1989, the Hungarian regime had been purged of Communist party supporters. The government also began to dismantle its security fences along the Austrian border—the first legal breach in the Iron Curtain. A year later, the Hungarian Democratic Forum, pledging it would reinstate full civil rights and restructure the economy, secured a plurality of seats in the National Assembly.

The Czechs, too, staged demonstrations against Soviet domination in late 1988. Brutal beatings of student demonstrators by the police in 1989 radicalized the nations' workers and provoked mass demonstrations. Civic Forum, an opposition coalition, called for the installation of a coalition government to include noncommunists, the resignation of the country's communist leadership, and free elections. It reinforced its demands with continuing mass demonstrations and threats of a general strike, resulting in the toppling of the old regime and the election of the playwright and Civic Forum leader Václav Havel as president in December 1989.

The Fall of the Berlin Wall

The most significant political changes in Eastern Europe during the late 1980s were the collapse of communism in East Germany and the unification of East and West Germany. Although long considered the most prosperous of the Soviet satellite countries, East Germany suffered from severe economic stagnation and environmental degradation. When Hungary opened its border with Austria in May 1989, waves of East Germans registered their discontent with the worsening conditions by way of massive illegal immigration to the West. This exodus combined with evidence of widespread official corruption to force the resignation of East Germany's longtime, hard-line premier, Erich Honecker. His successor, Egon Krenz, promised reforms, but he nevertheless faced continuing protests and mass emigration.

On November 4, 1989, the government, in a move that acknowledged its powerlessness to hold its citizens

captive, opened its border with Czechoslovakia, a move that effectively freed East Germans to travel to the West legally. In a matter of days, the Berlin Wall—the embodiment of the Cold War, the Iron Curtain, and the division of East from West—was demolished, first by groups of ordinary citizens and, later, by the East German government. Jubilant men, women, and children from both sides of the wall walked through the gaping holes that now permitted them to take the few steps that symbolized the return to freedom and a chance for national unity. Free elections were held throughout Germany in March 1990, resulting in a victory for the Alliance for Germany, a coalition allied with the West German chancellor Helmut Kohl's Christian Democratic Union. With heavy emigration continuing, reunification talks quickly culminated in the formal proclamation of a united Germany on October 3, 1990.

The public mood in Eastern Europe, and perhaps worldwide, was swept up with the jubilation of these peaceful "velvet revolutions" during the autumn of 1989. Yet the end of one-party rule in Eastern Europe was accomplished not without violence. The single most repressive government in the old Eastern bloc, Nicolae Ceauşescu's outright dictatorship in Romania, came apart with much bloodshed. By December, faced with the wave of popular revolts in surrounding countries and riots by the ethnic Hungarian minority in Transylvania, a number of party officials and army officers in Romania tried to hold on to their positions by deposing Ceauşescu. His extensive secret police, however, organized a resistance to the coup, the result of which was nearly two weeks of bloody street fighting in the capital,

REAGAN AT THE BERLIN WALL. On June 12, 1987, in a speech given before the Brandenburg Gate in Berlin, President Ronald Reagan challenged Mikhail Gorbachev to "tear down this wall."

Analyzing Primary Sources

The Reunification of Germany, 1989–1990

On November 28, 1989, two weeks after the fall of the Berlin Wall, the chancellor of West Germany, Helmut Kohl, proposed a ten-point program of cooperation between the two Germanies, with an eye toward the eventual unification of the two separate nations into one nation-state. Events moved quickly after the ruling party in East Germany lost the first free elections, held in March 1990. A coalition government in East Germany, led by Lothar de Maizière, the head of the East German wing of Helmut Kohl's political party, the Christian Democratic Union, negotiated the terms of the merger with West Germany, which included complex economic and political measures. The legislative bodies of both Germanies approved the unification treaty in September 1990, and the unification officially took place at midnight on October 3, 1990. Kohl's speech reveals the delicate nature of the negotiations, which necessitated balancing complex domestic pressures with geopolitical considerations.

1. Immediate measures are called for as a result of events of recent weeks, particularly the flow of resettlers and the huge increase in the number of travellers. The Federal Government will provide immediate aid where it is needed. We will assist in the humanitarian sector and provide medical aid if it is wanted and considered helpful. . . .

The GDR must itself provide travellers with the necessary foreign exchange. We are, however, prepared to contribute to a currency fund for a transitional period, provided that persons entering the GDR no longer have to exchange a minimum amount of currency, that entry into the GDR is made considerably easier, and that the GDR itself contributes substantially to the fund.

Our aim is to facilitate traffic as much as possible in both directions.

2. The Federal Government will continue its cooperation with the GDR in all areas where it is of direct benefit to the people or both sides, especially in the economic, scientific, technological and cultural fields. It is particularly important to intensify cooperation in the field of environmental protection. . . .

We also want to extensively increase telephone links with the GDR and help expand the GDR's telephone network. . . .

[W]e need to take a thorough look at transport and rail systems in the GDR and the Federal Republic in the light of the new situation. Forty years of separation also mean that traffic routes have in some cases developed quite differently. This applies not only to border crossing-points but to the traditional East–West lines of communication in central Europe. . . .

3. I have offered comprehensive aid and cooperation should the GDR bindingly undertake to carry out a fundamental change in the political and economic system and put the necessary measures irreversibly into effect. . . .

We support the demand for free, equal and secret elections in the GDR, in which, of course, independent, that is to say, non-socialist, parties would also participate. The SED's monopoly on power must be removed. The introduction of a democratic system means, above all, the abolition of laws on political crimes and the immediate release of all political prisoners.

Economic aid can only be effective if the economic system is radically reformed. This is obvious from the situation in all Comecon states and is not a question of our preaching to them. The centrally planned economy must be dismantled.

We do not want to stabilize conditions that have become indefensible. Economic improvement can only occur if the GDR opens its doors to Western investment, if conditions of free enterprise are created, and if private initiative becomes possible. I don't understand those who accuse us of tutelage in this respect. There are daily examples of this in Hungary and Poland which can surely be followed by the GDR, likewise a member of Comecon. . . .

4. Prime Minister Modrow spoke in his government policy statement of a 'contractual community.' We are prepared to adopt this idea. The proximity of our two states in Germany and the special nature of their relationship demand an increasingly close network of agreements in all sectors and at all levels.

5. We are also prepared to take a further decisive step, namely, to develop confederative structures between the two states in Germany with a view to creating a federation. But this presupposes the election of a democratic government in the GDR. . . .

Previous policy towards the GDR had to be limited mainly to small steps by which we sought above all to alleviate the consequences of division and to keep alive and strengthen the people's awareness of the unity of the nation. If, in the future, a democratically legitimized, that is, a freely elected government, becomes our partner, that will open up completely new perspectives.

Gradually, new forms of institutional cooperation can be created and further developed. Such coalescence is inherent in the continuity of German history. State organization in Germany has nearly always taken the form of a confederation or federation. We can fall back on this past experience. Nobody knows at the present time what a reunited Germany will look like. I am, however, sure that unity will come, if it is wanted by the German people.

6. The development of intra-German relations remains embedded in the pan-European process, that is to say in the framework of East–West relations. The future architecture of Germany must fit into the future architecture of Europe as a whole. Here the West has shown itself to be the pacemaker with its concept of a lasting and equitable peaceful order in Europe.

In our joint declaration of June this year, which I have already quoted, General Secretary Gorbachev and I spoke of the structural elements of a "common European home." They are, for example:

—Unqualified respect for the integrity and security of each state. Each state has the right freely to choose its own political and social system.

—Unqualified respect for the principles and rules of international law, especially respect for the people's right of self-determination.

—The realization of human rights.

—Respect for and maintenance of the traditional cultures of the nations of Europe.

With all of these points, as Mr. Gorbachev and I laid down, we aim to follow Europe's long traditions and help overcome the division of Europe.

7. The attraction and aura of the European Community are and remain a constant feature of pan-European development. We want to and must strengthen them further still.

***

9. Overcoming the division of Europe and Germany presupposes far-reaching and rapid steps in the field of disarmament and arms control. Disarmament and arms control must keep pace with political developments and thus be accelerated where necessary. . . .

10. With this comprehensive policy we are working for a state of peace in Europe in which the German nation can recover its unity in free self-determination. Reunification—that is regaining national unity—remains the political goal of the Federal government. . . .

The linking of the German question to pan-European developments and East–West relations, as explained in these ten points, will allow a natural development which takes account of the interests of all concerned and paves the way for peaceful development in freedom, which is our objective.

Source: Adam Daniel Rotfeld and Walther Stützle, eds., *Germany and Europe in Transition* (New York: 1991), pp. 120–22.

Questions for Analysis

1. What priorities are evident in Kohl's speech? How does he seek to balance the practical questions of concern to ordinary citizens within the larger political context?

2. What traditions in German history does Kohl refer to in making his case for cooperation? How does he define the possibility of unity?

3. What references does Kohl make to the larger Cold War context of the division of the two Germanies?

Bucharest. While the rest of Eastern Europe celebrated Christmas and the New Year with new political systems, individual snipers loyal to Ceauşescu were still killing passing civilians from rooftops and forcing dangerous efforts to root them out. Ceauşescu and his wife were ultimately seized by populist army units and executed; images of their bloody bodies were flashed worldwide by satellite television.

Throughout the rest of Eastern Europe, single-party governments in the countries behind what was left of the tattered Iron Curtain—Albania, Bulgaria, and Yugoslavia—collapsed in the face of democratic pressure for change. Meanwhile, in the Soviet Union itself, inspired by events in Eastern Europe, the Baltic republics of Lithuania and Latvia strained to free themselves from Soviet rule. In 1990, they unilaterally proclaimed their independence from the Soviet Union, throwing into sharp relief the tension between "union" and "republics." Gorbachev reacted with an uncertain mixture of armed intervention and promises of greater local autonomy. In the fall of 1991, Lithuania and Latvia, along with the third Baltic state of Estonia, won international recognition as independent republics.

RUSSIAN TANKS IN RED SQUARE NEAR THE KREMLIN. Boris Yeltsin convinced many in the military not to support the coup of August 1991, ensuring the failure of the plot and hastening the collapse of the Soviet Union.

The Collapse of the Soviet Union

While Soviet influence eroded in Eastern Europe, at home, the unproductive Soviet economy continued to fuel widespread ire. With the failure of perestroika, largely the result of a lack of resources and an inability to increase production, came the rise of a powerful political rival to Gorbachev: his erstwhile ally Boris Yeltsin. In 1990, Yeltsin, the reforming mayor of Moscow, was elected president of the Russian Federation—the largest Soviet republic—on an anti-Gorbachev platform. Pressure from the Yeltsin camp weakened Gorbachev's ability to maneuver independent of reactionary factions in the Politburo and the military, undermining his reform program and his ability to remain in power.

The Soviet Union's increasingly severe domestic problems, as Gorbachev's policies failed to improve—and indeed lowered—the living standard of the Soviet people, led to mounting protests in 1991. Demands increased that the bloated government bureaucracy respond with a dramatic cure for the country's continuing economic stagnation. Gorbachev appeared to lose his political nerve, having first ordered and then canceled a radical 500-day economic reform plan, while at the same time agreeing to negotiations with the increasingly disaffected republics within the union, now clamoring for independence. Sensing their political lives to be in jeopardy, a group of highly placed hard-line Communist party officials staged an abortive coup in August 1991. They made Gorbachev and his wife prisoners in their summer villa, then declared a return to party-line orthodoxy in an effort to salvage what remained of the Soviet Union's global leverage and the Communist party's domestic power. The Soviet citizenry, especially in large cities like Moscow and Leningrad, defied these self-proclaimed saviors; and, led by Boris Yeltsin, who at one point mounted a tank in a Moscow street to rally the people, gathered support among the Soviet republics and the military, successfully calling the plotters' bluff. Within two weeks, Gorbachev was back in power and the coup leaders were in prison.

It was ironic that this counterrevolution returned Gorbachev to office, while at the same time destroying the power of the Soviet state he led. Throughout the fall of 1991, as Gorbachev struggled to hold the union together, Yeltsin joined the presidents of the other large republics to capitalize on the discontent. On December 8, 1991, the presidents of the republics of Russia, Ukraine, and Byelorussia (now Belarus) declared that the Soviet Union was no more:

Past and Present

Shock Therapy in Post-Soviet Russia

After 1991, the transition from a command economy to open markets (the banner shown in the photo on the left supports privatization of industry and commerce) proved destabilizing in Russia, and, for many ordinary people, the first experience of the new order was profoundly unsettling. Vladimir Putin, who came to power after 2000, moved against the independence of this new business class, imprisoning some, including Mikhail Khodorkovsky (shown in the photo on the right, awaiting the verdict of his 2005 trial for fraud), and forcing others into exile.

 Watch related author interview on the Student Site

"The USSR as a subject of international law and geopolitical reality is ceasing to exist." Though the prose was flat, the message was momentous. The once-mighty Soviet Union, founded seventy-five years before in a burst of revolutionary fervor and violence, had evaporated nearly overnight, leaving in its wake a collection of eleven far from powerful nations loosely joined together as the Commonwealth of Independent States. On December 25, 1991, Gorbachev resigned and left political life; he was not pushed from office in the usual way but made irrelevant as other actors dismantled the state. The Soviet flag—the hammer and sickle symbolizing a nation that had kept half of Europe in thrall for fifty years—was lowered for the last time over the Kremlin.

The mighty fall left mighty problems in its wake. Food shortages worsened during the winter of 1992, the value of the ruble plummeted, and the republics could not agree on common military policies or resolve the difficult and dangerous questions concerning the control of nuclear warheads. Yeltsin's pleas for economic assistance from the West resulted in massive infusions of private and public capital, which nevertheless failed to prevent serious economic hardship and dislocation. Free enterprise brought with it unemployment and profiteering through crime. Yeltsin's determination to press ahead with his economic program met stiff resistance from parliament and citizenry alarmed by the ruthlessness and rapidity of the changes they were experiencing. When parliament balked at Yeltsin's proposals in September 1993, he dissolved it, which helped provoke an attempted coup two months later, staged by conservative politicians and army officers. Officials loyal to Yeltsin put the revolt down with far more force than against the 1991 coup attempt. Television viewers worldwide watched artillery shells slam into the rebel-occupied parliament building in Moscow during a bloody shootout. After parliament was restored, the 1995 elections became a benchmark of discontent: the resurgent communists claimed roughly one-third of the seats; while xenophobic nationalists, led by Vladimir Zhirinovsky, also took a notable bloc of the vote, thanks to the steady blame he heaped on the West for Russia's troubles.

Meanwhile, ethnic and religious conflict plagued the republics. During the early years after the dissolution of the Soviet Union, warfare flared in Georgia, Armenia, and Azerbaijan. The most serious conflict arose in the predominantly Muslim area of Chechnya, bordering Georgia in the Caucasus, which had declared its independence from Russia in late 1991. The Chechen rebels were heirs to a tradition of banditry and separatism against Russian authority that stretched back to the nineteenth century. In 1994, the Russian government, weary of this continuing challenge to its authority, launched a concerted effort to quash the resistance. As Russian forces moved into the Chechen capital, Grozny, they were ambushed with firepower largely stolen from disused Soviet armories. The result was a massacre of the invading Russians, followed by a long and bloody siege to take the city. This in turn fueled a long and particularly bloody guerrilla war between Russian and Chechen forces, marked by repeated atrocities on both sides. After brief pauses in 1995 and 1997, the Chechen war dragged on into the new century, echoing Russia's conflict in Afghanistan, but on a scale that was bloodier and closer to home.

The Iron Curtain had established one of the most rigid borders in European history. The collapse of the Soviet Union not only dismantled these borders, it opened up Russia, destabilized its former imperial dominions, and brought the Cold War to an end. It also created a host of unforeseen problems, such as ethnic conflict and diplomatic uncertainty about the new Russian government. Moreover, it left a single superpower in the world: the United States. Within the Russian and several of the former Soviet republics a new era emerged, which some called the Russian "Wild West." Capitalist market relations began to develop without clearly defined property laws or a stable legal framework to enforce them. Corruption ran rampant, as former government officials profited from their positions of power to take over whole sectors of the economy; and organized crime controlled industries, stock exchanges, a thriving trade in illegal drugs, and even some local governments. Even the most energetic central governments in the large republics, such as Russia, Ukraine, and Kazakhstan, found themselves facing enormous problems. Post-Soviet openness could lay the groundwork for a new democratic Russia, or it could set in motion the resurgence of older forms of tyranny.

Postrevolutionary Troubles: Eastern Europe after 1989

The **velvet revolutions** of Central and Eastern Europe raised high hopes: local hopes that an end to authoritarian government would lead to economic prosperity and cultural pluralism, and Western hopes that these countries would join them as capitalist partners in an enlarged European Community. The reality, however, was slower and harder than any of the optimists of 1989 foresaw. Though it enjoyed great support among Germans, the reunification of Germany was controversial, and France, in particular, needed to be convinced that a bigger and more populous Germany was a good idea. The French president, François Mitterrand, reportedly assented only when Chancellor Helmut Kohl of Germany promised to accept the plan for a European monetary union in exchange for French approval of the reunification. The euphoria of reunification masked uncertainty even among Germans themselves, because the foundering East German economy meant that integrating the two Germanies would be a costly project. Piled onto other economic difficulties in the former West Germany during the 1990s, it produced resentment in the West of the need to "rescue" the East. There was also the different experiences of the two peoples during the Cold War. Writer Günter Grass, for instance, believed that a "wall in the mind" still divided the countries.

Adapting to change was challenging throughout Eastern Europe. Attempts to create free-market economies brought inflation, unemployment, and, in their wake, anticapitalist demonstrations. Inefficient industries, a workforce resistant to change, energy shortages, a lack of venture capital, and a severely polluted environment combined to hinder progress and dash hopes. Uprisings in Bulgaria and Albania in early 1997 were fueled by the inability of those governments to resolve basic economic and social problems. In addition, racial and ethnic conflicts continued to divide these newly liberated democracies, recalling the divisions that led to the First World War and have plagued Eastern Europe throughout its history. Minorities waged campaigns for autonomous rights or outright secession that often descended into violence.

Czechoslovakia's velvet revolution collapsed into a "velvet divorce," as Slovakia declared itself independent from the Czech Republic. Poland enjoyed an upswing in its economy during the 1990s, after many years of hardship, but most of the rest of Eastern Europe continued to find transformation rough going. The difficulties were accompanied by revived ethnic tensions, formerly suppressed in centralized communist governments; violence erupted benefiting the capital, Belgrade, and the provinces of Croatia and Slovenia the most, while other areas in Serbia, Bosnia and Herzegovina, and the tiny district of Kosovo lagged far behind. A number of Serb politicians, most notably **Slobodan Milosevic**, began to redirect their frustration with economic hardship toward subjects of national pride and sovereignty.

Nationalism, particularly Serb and Croat nationalism, had long dogged Yugoslavia's firmly federal political system. Feelings ran especially deep among Serbs, whose national myths reach back to the Middle Ages. Milosevic, and the Serb nationalists who gathered around him, ignited those political flashpoints in ways that caught the fears and frustrations of the time. While his strident nationalism catapulted him into crucial positions of authority, it also alienated people from non-Serb Yugoslavian republics. Inspired by the peaceful transformations of 1989, representatives of the small province of Slovenia declared that they had been denied adequate representation and economic support inside the republic; and in 1991, on a tide of nationalism and reform, the Slovenes seceded from Yugoslavia. The newly reunited Germany was quick to recognize the new nation. After a brief attempt to hold the union together by force, the Yugoslav government relented and let Slo-

EASTERN EUROPE IN 1989. ■ *What political changes in the Soviet Union allowed for the spread of demonstrations throughout Eastern Europe?* ■ *Why did the first political upheavals of 1989 occur in Poland and Hungary?* ■ *In what countries were demonstrations the most widespread? Why?*

against non-European immigrants throughout Eastern Europe, against gypsies (Roma) in the Czech Republic and Hungary, and against ethnic Hungarians in Romania.

The most extreme example of these conflicts came with the implosion of the state of Yugoslavia. After the death of Tito in 1980, the government that had held Yugoslavia's federalist ethnic patchwork together came undone. The 1960s and the 1970s brought uneven economic growth,

venia claim its independence, beginning a process of disintegration that would eventually lead to civil war.

The large republic of Croatia—once part of the Habsburg Empire and, briefly, an independent state allied with the Nazis during the Second World War—citing injustices by Serb officials in the Yugoslav government, declared independence as a free, capitalist state. This led to a war between the federal Yugoslav forces and the well-armed militias of

Interpreting Visual Evidence

Representing the People in Eastern Europe, 1989

The enthusiasm of the mass demonstrations, preceding the revolutionary changes in Eastern Europe in 1989, gave these events a sense of immediate drama. Images of Eastern Europeans massed together in protest, crossing boundaries that had been closed to them, and celebrating the downfall of their repressive governments spread quickly around the world. The symbolism of these images was stark, resonating a triumphant story about the progress of democratic ideals in an increasingly unified and integrated Europe. In the East, the people's desire to join with the West, long denied, had finally been realized.

The unity of these early days, nevertheless, obscured a basic uncertainty about the aspirations of the populations of the newly independent nations in Eastern Europe. Many East Germans expressed reservations about the rapid pace of German reunification; and people from the West and the East continued to talk about "the wall in the head" long after the Berlin Wall had been torn down. The unity of Czechoslovakia's peaceful velvet revolution in 1989 led quickly to the "velvet divorce" that produced the dissolution of Czechoslovakia into the Czech Republic and Slovakia in 1993. Throughout the region, many commentators continued to speak of a persistent *Ostalgia*: nostalgia for an alternative Eastern European past that had been lost in the abrupt transition.

We have seen in earlier chapters how representations of the people gave meaning to moments of rapid social and political change, such as in the French Revolution or the unification of Germany. The images here, from media coverage in 1989, also frame the interpretations that contemporaries gave to the unfolding events. Image A shows a crowd in Prague waving the Czechoslovakian flag in November 1989. Image B shows East Germans gathering in front of a Woolworth market in West Berlin on November 12, 1989, days after the fall of the Berlin Wall. Image C shows a demonstrator bearing a sign that reads

A. Crowd during Czechoslovakia's velvet revolution in November 1989.

independent Croatia, which ended in arbitration by the United Nations. The religious nature of the conflict, between Catholic Croats and Orthodox Serbs, and the legacies of fighting in the Second World War produced violence on both sides. Towns and villages where Serbs and Croats had lived together since the 1940s were torn apart as each ethnic group rounded up and massacred members of the other.

Slovenia's independence was relatively easily obtained, as the population of this northern Yugoslavian republic was relatively homogeneous. Croatia's independence was more difficult because it contained regions where Hungarians and Serbs were numerous. For Bosnia and Herzegovina, however, independence meant disaster. Bosnia was the most ethnically diverse republic in Yugoslavia, and its

"WE ARE ONE PEOPLE" in East Berlin on December 9, 1989.

"We are the people" was the slogan of the weekly demonstrations in Leipzig in 1989, and it was used to discredit the East German government in the months before the fall of the Berlin Wall. "We are one people" became the slogan of the West German Chancellor Helmut Kohl as he pushed for rapid reunification of the two Germanies.

Questions for Analysis

1. How should one interpret the wave of nationalist enthusiasm that engulfed Czechoslovakia in 1989 (image A), in light of what we know of the subsequent failure to keep Czechoslovakia together as a unified nation?

2. Photographs showing East Berliners shopping in Western stores, such as image B, were extremely common in the media in 1989. What do such images suggest about how the East's previous isolation was interpreted in the West? What does it say about how both sides may have viewed the consequences of the East's newfound freedom?

3. What is the difference between "We are the people" and "We are one people" as political slogans?

B. East Germans gather in front of a Woolworth market in West Berlin on November 12, 1989.

C. "We are one people" poster during a demonstration on December 12, 1989.

population was nearly 50 percent Muslim. Its capital, Sarajevo, was home to several major ethnic groups and had been often praised as an example of peaceful coexistence. Left alone in a rump Yugoslavia, dominated by Milosevic's Serbian nationalists, Bosnia had little choice but to seek independence as well. But its tradition of ethnic coexistence did not survive the transition. Armed bands equipped by the governments of a now Serb-dominated Yugoslavia and Croatia were soon battling each other in Bosnia, and the improvised army that Bosnia hastily created quickly became a target of both Croats and Serbs.

The Serbs and Croats, both of whom disliked the Muslim Bosnians, were especially well equipped and organized. They rained shells and bullets on towns and villages, burned houses with families inside, imprisoned Muslim men in detention camps and starved them to death, and raped thousands of Bosnian women. Bosnian Serbs besieged Sarajevo for almost four years, killing nearly 14,000 residents in the process. All sides committed atrocities, but the Serbs orchestrated and carried out the worst crimes, including what came to be called ethnic cleansing. This involved sending irregular troops on campaigns of murder and terror through Muslim and Croat territories to encourage the much larger populations to flee the area. During the first eighteen months of fighting, as many as 100,000 people were killed, including 80,000 civilians, mostly Bosnian Muslims.

The United Nations sent a peacekeeping force, but their orders were to treat all groups equally, and so did not recognize that Serbia was often the aggressor. This situation benefited the Serbs, who occupied most of Bosnia and a large portion of Croatia by 1994. When NATO conducted air strikes against Serbs who were besieging the capital of Sarajevo, the Serbs responded by increasing the intensity of their attacks on the Bosnian population. In July 1994, Serbs in Bosnia attacked a village called Srebrenica, which the United Nations had designated as a "safe zone." Using United Nations equipment, the Serbs encouraged a group of about 10,000 Bosnian Muslim men who had sought shelter in Srebrenica to surrender; but over the next few days, the Serb units massacred 7,000 Bosnians and buried them in mass graves.

In 1995, the United States began a campaign of air strikes against Serbian positions, and together with renewed pressure from Croatian and Bosnian troops, these actions brought the Bosnian Serbs to peace talks held at Dayton, Ohio. The agreement divided Bosnia, with the majority of land in the hands of Muslims and Croats, and a small, autonomous "Serb Republic" in areas that included land ethnically "cleansed" in 1992. Stability was restored, but three years of war had killed more than 200,000 people. The International Criminal Tribunal for the Former Yugoslavia, established to prosecute the conduct of military groups during the conflict, later concluded that the killings at Srebrenica and the ethnic cleansing of Bosnian Muslims constituted genocide, a crime against humanity.

The legacy of Bosnia flared into conflict again over Kosovo, the medieval homeland of the Orthodox Christian Serbs, now occupied by a largely Albanian, Muslim population. Milosevic accused the Albanians of plotting secession and of challenging the Serb presence in Kosovo. In the name of a "greater Serbia," Serb soldiers fought Albanian separatists rallying under the banner of "greater Albania." Both sides resorted to terrorism, and Serbian forces used many of the same murderous tactics in Kosovo that they had employed earlier in Bosnia. A new round of ethnic cleansing drove hundreds of thousands of Albanians from their homes. Western nations were anxious lest the fight spread to the strategic, ethnically divided country of Macedonia and touch off a general Balkan conflict. But in early 1999, talks between Milosevic's government and the Albanian rebels sponsored by the NATO powers fell apart. That failure was followed by a fresh wave of American-led bombings against Serbia itself, as well as against Serbian forces in Kosovo. Unwilling to fight a ground war in the mountainous, unforgiving terrain of the southern Balkans, the United States and its European allies concentrated on strategic attacks on bridges, power plants, factories, and Serbian military bases. The Russian government was troubled by this unilateral attack on fellow Slavs, but nonetheless played an important part in brokering a cease-fire. Milosevic was forced to withdraw from Kosovo, leaving it in the hands of another force of armed NATO peacekeepers.

Finally, Serb-dominated Yugoslavia, worn by ten years of war and economic sanctions, turned against Milosevic's regime. Wars and corruption had destroyed Milosevic's

MASS FUNERAL IN KOSOVO, 1999. Ethnic Albanians bury victims of a Serbian massacre toward the end of Yugoslavia's ten years of fighting. ▪ *Although the nature of war has changed radically in the last hundred years, "ethnic cleansing" has remained remarkably constant and frequent in the modern period. What keeps states from taking effective action to prevent it?*

Legend:
- Soviet Union to 1991
- Soviet-dominated Eastern Europe to 1989
- German Democratic Republic (GDR) united with Federal Republic of Germany 1990
- Czechoslovakia to December 1992
- Yugoslavia to 1991
- Other communist states before 1991
- **1990** Date of first free election

KAZAKHSTAN
1991: President Nazarbayev runs in election unopposed
1995: Nationwide referendum extends his term to 2000

KYRGYZSTAN

TAJIKISTAN

AFGHANISTAN

UZBEKISTAN

TURKMENISTAN

IRAN

ARAL SEA

R U S S I A N   F E D E R A T I O N 1993

CASPIAN SEA

AZERBAIJAN 1995

to AZERBAIJAN

GEORGIA 1991

ARMENIA 1995

1992: Tensions between Russia and Ukraine over whether Black Sea Fleet is part of strategic forces controlled by CIS

TURKEY

1993: Joins the CIS to secure Russian military support against ousted President Gamsakhurdia

UKRAINE

BLACK SEA

BELARUS 1995

MOLDAVIA 1994

ROMANIA 1990

BULGARIA 1990

FINLAND

ESTONIA 1992

LATVIA 1993

LITHUANIA 1990

RUS. FED.

POLAND 1989

SLOVAKIA 1992

HUNGARY 1990

YUGOSLAVIA 1992

MACEDONIA 1990

ALBANIA 1991

GREECE

EAST GERMANY 1990

CZECH REPUBLIC 1992

AUSTRIA

SLOVENIA 1992

CROATIA 1992

BOSNIA AND HERZEGOVINA 1992

ADRIATIC SEA

ITALY

SWITZ.

GERMANY

DENMARK

SWEDEN

NORWAY

BALTIC SEA

NORTH SEA

Area of detail

EUROPE

AFRICA

500 Miles

500 Kilometers

250

250

0

0

RUSSIA AND EASTERN EUROPE AFTER THE COLD WAR. Examine closely the geography of southeastern and central Europe. ■ *How were political boundaries reorganized?* ■ *How did the collapse of the Soviet Union and the end of the Cold War allow for the reemergence of certain forces in the political landscape of Europe?* ■ *How were the boundaries of the Soviet Union reorganized after 1991?*

credentials as a nationalist and populist. After he attempted to reject the results of a democratic election in 2000, his government fell to popular protests. He died in 2006 while being tried by a UN tribunal for war crimes.

As we gain perspective on the twentieth century, it is clear that the Yugoslavian wars of the 1990s were not an isolated instance of Balkan violence. The issues were thoroughly European. The Balkans form one of Europe's borderlands, where cultures influenced by Roman Catholicism, Eastern Orthodoxy, and Islam meet, overlap, and contend for political domination and influence. Since the nineteenth century, this region of enormous religious, cultural, and ethnic diversity has struggled with the implications of nationalism. We have seen how the conflicts over the creation of new national states in Central Europe, drawn mostly on ethnic lines, were worked out with many instances of tragic violence. The failure to prevent these wars or to limit their effects on vulnerable populations was a deep blow to the international community, and revealed the limits of the power exercised by the United States and other European nations in the years after the end of the Cold War.

CONCLUSION

The protest movements of the 1960s and the 1970s revealed that postwar hopes for stability in Western Europe through economic development alone were shortsighted, and, in any case, the astounding rates of growth from 1945 to 1968 could not be sustained forever. The great successes of these first postwar decades were the establishment of the European Common Market and the spirit of cooperation between Western European nations that, only a few years before, had been locked in a deadly conflict.

The Eastern European revolutions of 1989 and the subsequent collapse of the Soviet Union were major turning

After You Read This Chapter

 Go to **INQUIZITIVE** to see what you've learned—and learn what you've missed— with personalized feedback along the way.

REVIEWING THE OBJECTIVES

- The success of economic rebuilding after the Second World War produced a new prosperity in Western Europe. What contributed to this success? What were its effects on the daily life and mass culture in Europe?

- The postwar decades witnessed an important shift in attitudes about women and their place in society. What caused this shift? What were its consequences for European women?

- In Europe and the United States, significant movements of social and political protest emerged in the 1960s. What were the goals of these movements? What did they accomplish?

- The postwar economic boom ended in the 1970s, leading to a prolonged period of economic contraction. What were the consequences of this recession for both governments and populations in Europe?

- In the 1980s, Mikhail Gorbachev proposed reforms for the Soviet Union, which failed to prevent the collapse of the Soviet bloc in Eastern Europe. What combination of events led to this collapse?

- The first post-Soviet decade in Europe was marked by political uncertainty, economic dislocation, and violence, with war in Yugoslavia and Chechnya. What circumstances made these years so difficult for Europeans?

points, and posed challenging questions to those who sought to guarantee stability by continuing down the path of further integration among European nations. Like the French Revolution of 1789, the 1989 revolutions brought down not only a regime but also an empire. They also gave way to violence, providing no easy consensus for the peoples who were left to construct some form of political and social stability in their wake. In the former Yugoslavia, Slovakia, and Russia itself, the uncertainty of the post-1989 years gave fresh impetus to energetic nationalist movements. Although militant nationalism might be a useful short-term political strategy for certain politicians, it is unlikely to create stability in Europe, because the broad population movements of the postwar years have continued unabated and there is no part of Europe that possesses the ethnic or cultural homogeneity demanded by hard-line nationalists. Europe's long history is one of heterogeneity, and there is no reason to think that the future will be different in this respect.

Profound differences in wealth and economic capacity between Western and Eastern Europe were the most challenging hurdle to a stable integration of the newly independent nations of the former Soviet empire. In the 1980s, it was possible to imagine that a relatively wealthy country, such as the Netherlands or Belgium, might be willing to subsidize the integration of a less wealthy, small country, such as Portugal, into Europe. But it has proved quite another task to convince the Dutch, the Belgians, or the Danes to help shoulder the burden of bringing large countries, such as Ukraine or Turkey, into the European fold. Given this difficulty, can anyone say with confidence where Europe's outermost borders now lie? In the broader context of the global conflicts that emerged in the aftermath of the Cold War, Europe's boundaries and future remain both uncertain and linked to developments elsewhere in the world. This broader context and global linkages are the subject of the last chapter of this book.

PEOPLE, IDEAS, AND EVENTS IN CONTEXT

- How did the wide availability of the **BIRTH CONTROL PILL** change public attitudes toward sex and sexuality in the 1960s?

- What made the **MASS CULTURE** of the postwar decades different from popular culture in previous historical eras?

- How did the struggles of the **CIVIL RIGHTS MOVEMENT** in the United States affect American efforts to promote democracy in Europe during the Cold War?

- What were the goals of **ALEXANDER DUBČEK**'s government in Czechoslovakia during the **PRAGUE SPRING**?

- How did the **1973 OPEC OIL EMBARGO** affect the economies of Eastern and Western Europe?

- How did **LECH WAŁĘSA** and the **SOLIDARITY** movement challenge the Polish government in the early 1980s?

- How did **MIKHAIL GORBACHEV** envision reforming the Soviet Union? What did he mean by *PERESTROIKA* and *GLASNOST*?

- What were the **VELVET REVOLUTIONS** of Central and Eastern Europe in 1989?

- What made **NATIONALISM** such a powerful force in Yugoslavia in the early 1990s? What role did **SLOBODAN MILOSEVIC** play in the breakup of the Yugoslavian federation?

THINKING ABOUT CONNECTIONS

- The wave of protests and cultural discontent that spread throughout Europe in the 1960s encompassed both Western and Eastern Europe, in spite of the divisions imposed by the Cold War. Can you detect an echo of the 1848 revolutions in the 1968 protests? What common concerns can you detect? What is different?

- Many observers were surprised by the resurgence of nationalism in Eastern Europe in the aftermath of the collapse of the Soviet Union. Can you compare the situation in Yugoslavia after 1989 with the circumstances in that part of the world in the late nineteenth century, as Ottoman power waned and the Russian and Austrian Empires competed for influence in the region?

Before You Read This Chapter

CORE OBJECTIVES

- **DEFINE** globalization and **UNDERSTAND** what is new about current patterns of interconnection in the world as well as the continuities that can be seen with earlier periods of global connection.

- **EXPLAIN** the continued relevance of the colonial past in shaping the politics, economy, and society of independent states in Asia and Africa, and the nature of their ongoing relationships to the societies and states of Europe and North America.

- **UNDERSTAND** the global connections that link societies in other parts of the world to the events and persistent conflicts in the Middle East.

A World without Walls: Globalization and the West

In the twenty-first century, the world has reentered a period in which basic assumptions about the role of nation-states, the roots of prosperity, and the boundaries of cultures are changing fast. We say *reentered* because, as we have seen, a disconcerting sense of seismic and little understood change has been central to Western culture during several different historical periods, such as the Industrial Revolution of the nineteenth century or decolonization after 1945. Just as the term *industrial revolution*, coined in the early nineteenth century, captured contemporaries' perceptions of changes in their own time, *globalization* captures ours; globalization itself is not new, but our acute consciousness of it is.

We know, intuitively, what globalization means: the Internet, protests against the World Trade Organization (WTO), outsourcing of jobs and services, Walmart in Mexico, the dismantling of the Berlin Wall, Beyoncé selling out shows in China, and so on. All of these are powerful images of larger, enormously significant developments. The Internet has stunningly transformed global communication, the media, and forms of knowledge. The fall of the Berlin Wall, which once stood for a divided Cold War world, marked a dramatic reconfiguration of international relations, an end to the ideological battle over communism, and the creation of new alliances, markets, and communities. Moreover, the attacks on the World Trade Center and the Pentagon in 2001 gave the term *globalization* a new and frightening meaning, shattering the sense of relative isolation and security for many Americans. Globalization, then, conjures up new possibilities as well as new vulnerabilities.

What, precisely, does the term mean? What causes or drives globalization? What are its effects? To begin simply, globalization means integration. It is the process of creating a rising number of networks—political, social, economic, and cultural—that span larger sections of the globe. New technologies and economic imperatives, along with changing laws, have combined to make global exchange faster and, by the same token, to intensify economic, social, and cultural relationships. Information, ideas, goods, and people now move easily and rapidly across national boundaries. Yet *globalization* is not synonymous with *internationalization*, and the distinction is important. International relations are established between nation-states, while global exchanges can be quite independent of national control. Today, in the words of one historian, trade, politics, and cultural exchanges often happen "underneath the radar of the nation-state."

Globalization has radically altered the distribution of industry and patterns of trade around the world, as Asian nations in particular emerge as industrial giants and Western powers become increasingly dependent on energy resources drawn from former colonies. It has also forced the reorganization of economic enterprises from banking and commerce to manufacturing. Supranational economic institutions such as the **International Monetary Fund** (IMF) are examples of globalization, and they work to quicken its pace. Likewise, the International Criminal Court (ICC) represents an important trend in law: the globalization of judicial power. Moreover, new, rapid, and surprisingly intimate forms of mass communication—blogs, social media sites, Internet-based political campaigns, and so on—have spawned new forms of politics and new ways for nations to interfere in the political life of their competitors. And perhaps most interesting—and troubling—many globalizing trends seem to be eroding the sovereignty of nation-states and the clear boundaries of national communities.

All these developments are characteristic of our time. But are they new? For centuries, religion, empire, commerce, and industry have had globalizing impulses and effects. The East India Companies (Dutch and English), for instance, were to the seventeenth century what Apple is to the early twenty-first: the premier global enterprises of the time. Chartered and granted monopolies by the crown,

the East India Companies organized trade, investment of capital, manufacturing enterprises, and commercial agriculture. The Dutch East India Company's networks reached from Amsterdam to South Africa, through to India and Southeast Asia. The economic development of Europe in general was thoroughly enmeshed in global networks that supplied raw materials, markets, and labor. It has always been hard to strip the "West" of its global dimensions; the movement to abolish slavery, for example, was certainly transatlantic, if not global.

For another striking example, consider migration and immigration. We think of the contemporary world as fluid, characterized by vast movements of people, but mass, long-distance migration and immigration peaked during the nineteenth century. Between 1846 (when the first reliable statistics were kept) and 1940, 55 to 58 million people left Europe for the Americas, especially for the United States, Canada, Argentina, and Brazil. During that same period, 48 to 52 million Indians and southern Chinese migrated to Southeast Asia, the Southern Pacific, and the areas surrounding the Indian Ocean; and many of the Indian migrants went to other parts of the British Empire. Roughly another 50 million people left northeastern Asia and Russia for Manchuria, Siberia, Central Asia, and Japan. Faster long-distance transportation, via railways and steamships, made these long journeys possible, and the industrialization of the receiving regions provided the economic dynamics. The demographic, social, economic, and cultural effects of these migrations were transformative (Chapter 22). However, after the First World War, governments set out to close their gates. Since the 1920s, laborers (and refugees) found it much harder to move, and this remains so in the present, even in the face of the huge refugee crisis produced by the Syrian civil war since 2011. If migration is a measure of globalization, our world has become less "globalized" than it was a century ago.

What is more, equating globalization with integration may be misleading. The effects of globalizing trends are difficult to predict, and do not necessarily lead to peace, equality, or homogeneity. During the early 1900s, many Europeans firmly believed that the world—at least the part dominated by Western empires—would become harmonious, that Western culture would be exported, and that Western standards were universal, but history defied those expectations. Some scholars argue that the term *globalization* should be jettisoned, because it suggests a uniform, leveling process that operates similarly everywhere, when, in reality, it has very different and disparate effects that are shaped by vast asymmetries of power and wealth among nations or regions. In the last several decades, worldwide inequality has increased, as global processes encounter obstacles and resistance, and sow division as well as unity. At the level of everyday human contact, globalization has hastened new kinds of cultural blending and sociability, but it has also produced a backlash against that blending. The heady word *global* can distort our analyses or point us in the wrong direction. As one historian argues, although it is crucial to be able to think outside of "national or continental containers, [it would be misleading to believe] that there is no container at all, except the planetary one."

In this chapter, we explore three subjects crucial to our early efforts to understand globalization, especially as it relates to the post–Cold War world of the twenty-first century. First is the set of global changes that have accelerated the free flow of money, people, products, and ideas. Second is what we have come to call postcolonial politics: the varied trajectories that mark the contemporary experience of former colonies. Finally, we will consider in greater depth the complex and important role of Middle Eastern politics in contemporary global affairs. Throughout, we hope to suggest ways in which recent developments relate to familiar historical issues we have examined in other contexts.

LIQUID MODERNITY? THE FLOW OF MONEY, IDEAS, AND PEOPLES

A key feature of late-twentieth-century globalization was the transformation of the world economy, highlighted by the rapid integration of markets since 1970. In a series of historic changes, the international agreements that had regulated the movement of people, goods, and money since the Second World War were overturned. To begin with, the postwar economic arrangements sealed at Bretton Woods (Chapter 27) steadily eroded in the late 1960s, as Western industrial nations faced a double burden of inflation and economic stagnation. A crucial shift in monetary policy occurred in 1971, when the United States abandoned the postwar gold standard and allowed the dollar—the keystone of the system—to range freely. As a result, formal regulations among states on currencies, international banking, and lending faded away and were replaced with an informal network of arrangements managed autonomously by large private lenders and their political friends in leading Western states, and independent financial agencies such as the IMF and the World Bank. The economists and administrators who dominated these new networks steered

"CHECKERBOARD OF POVERTY AND AFFLUENCE." Scenes of slums confronting towering skylines, such as this one from São Paulo, Brazil, in 2014, are visible around the world as one of the side effects of development and deterioration.

away from the interventionist policies that had shaped postwar planning and recovery, and instead relied on a broad range of market-driven models, collectively dubbed "**neoliberalism**." In a variation on classic liberal economics, neoliberal economists stressed the value of free markets, profit incentives, and sharp restraints on budget deficits and social welfare programs, whether run by governments or corporations. The new systems of lending they supported had mixed results: funding breakneck growth in some cases, while bringing catastrophic debt in others. Industrial development in the globalized economy created jarring juxtapositions of development and deterioration across entire continents and even within single cities—a phenomenon described as a "checkerboard of poverty and affluence."

At the same time, the world's local, national, and regional economies became far more connected and interdependent. Export trade flourished and, with the technological advances of the 1960s and the 1980s, came to include an increasing proportion of high-technology goods. The boom in export commerce was tied to important changes in the division of labor worldwide: more industrial jobs emerged in the postcolonial world, not just among the Asian "tigers," but also in India, Latin America, and elsewhere. Although such steady, skilled manual employment started to disappear in Western nations—often replaced by lower-paying menial work—financial and service sector employment leaped ahead. Also, the exchange and use of goods became

much more complex: goods were designed by companies in one country, manufactured in another, and tied into a broader interchange of cultures. Taken together, these global economic changes had deep political effects, forcing painful debates about the nature of citizenship and entitlement inside national borders, the power and accountability of transnational corporations, and the human and environmental costs of global capitalism.

Another crucial change involves not only the widespread flow of information but also the new commercial and cultural importance attached to information itself. Electronic systems and devices designed to create, store, and share information multiplied, becoming staggeringly more powerful and accessible; none has had as great an impact on the everyday lives of men and women around the world as the personal computer. By the early 1990s, increasingly sophisticated computers brought people into instant communication with each other across continents, by new means as well as in new cultural and political settings. Electronic communications over the Internet gave a compelling new meaning to the term *global village*. The Internet revolution shared features of earlier print revolutions. It was pioneered by entrepreneurs with utopian ambitions, and driven by the new network's ability to deliver personal or commercial messages as well as culturally illicit and politically scandalous material that could be published easily and informally. It also offered new possibilities to social and political groups, constituting new "publics." And it attracted large, established corporate interests, eager to cash in on new channels of culture and business.

However common their use, the Internet and similar technologies have had wide-ranging effects on political struggles around the globe. Embattled ethnic minorities found worldwide audiences through online campaign sites. Satellite television arguably sped the sequence of popular revolts in Eastern Europe in 1989. That same year, fax machines brought Chinese demonstrators at Tiananmen Square news of international support for their efforts. Meanwhile, leaps forward in electronic technologies provided new worldwide platforms for commercial interests. Companies such as Sony, Netflix, and others produce entertainment content, including music, motion pictures, and television shows as well as the electronic equipment to play that content. Bill Gates's Microsoft emerged as the world's major producer of computer software—with a corporate profit margin that surpassed Spain's gross domestic product. At the level of production, marketing, and management, information industries are global, spreading widely across the United States, India, Western Europe, and parts of the developing world; their corporate headquarters, however, typically remain in the West and

AN AFGHAN GIRL WEEDS A POPPY FIELD, 2004. Though Afghanistan was historically a center for the silk trade, today, opium is its most important cash crop. ■ *How is this development related to globalization?*

support neoliberal politics. The international media, news, and entertainment conglomerates run by, for example, the Australian-born Rupert Murdoch or Time Warner, are firmly allied to U.S. institutions and worldviews, edging aside state-run companies.

Like the movement of money, goods, and ideas, the flow of labor has become a central aspect of globalization. Since 1945, the widespread migration of peoples, particularly between former colonies and imperial powers, has changed everyday life around the world. Groups of immigrant workers have filled the lower rungs of expanding economies, not only in Europe but also in oil-rich Arab states, where they attract Asian and Filipino laborers, and in the United States, where both permanent and seasonal migrations from Mexico and other Latin American nations have spread across the continent. This fusion of peoples and cultures has produced striking new blends of music, food, language, and other forms of popular culture and sociability. These seem novel until we think of Creole cultures formed in the New World from the sixteenth to the eighteenth centuries. This fusion has also raised tensions over the definition of citizenship and the boundaries of political and cultural communities—familiar themes in modern history. Cycles of violent xenophobic backlash, bigotry, and political extremism have arisen in host countries and regions as a result, but so, too, have new conceptions of civil rights and cultural belonging.

As suggested earlier, sharp divides exist between the most successful global players and the poorer, disadvantaged, sometimes embattled states and cultures. In one particular area of manufacture, however, poorer postcolonial regions have been able to respond to a steady and immensely profitable market in the West. The production of illegal drugs such as opium, heroin, and cocaine is a thriving industry in countries such as Colombia, Myanmar (formerly Burma), and Malaysia. Though the trade in such substances is banned, the fragile economies of the countries where they are produced have encouraged public and private powers to turn a blind eye to their production—or even to intervene for their own profit. Other similar forms of illegal commerce have also grown far beyond the old label of "organized crime" in their structure and political importance. Trafficking in illegal immigrants, the management of corrupt financial dealings, trade in illicit animals and animal products, and "conflict" diamonds from several brutal postcolonial civil wars are all indicative of this trend. The organizations behind these criminal trades grew out of the political violence and economic breakdown of failing postcolonial states or from the human and commercial traffic between these parts of the world and leading Western economic powers. They have exploited cracks, loopholes, and unsupervised opportunities in the less regulated

system of global trade, and carved out centers of power not directly subject to the laws of any single state.

Demographics and Global Health

The developments of globalization are tied in complex ways to the evolving size and health of the world's population. Between 1800 and the mid-twentieth century, the worldwide population roughly tripled, rising from 1 to 3 billion; between 1960 and 2012, the population more than doubled again to 7 billion. Huge improvements, if uneven, in basic standards of health, particularly for young children and childbearing women, contributed to the increase, as did local efforts to improve the urban-industrial environment. Asia's population as a whole has increased nearly fourfold since 1900, to nearly two-thirds of the world's present population. Such growth has strained underdeveloped social services, public-health facilities, and urban infrastructures, increasing the potential for epidemic diseases, as well as for cycles of ethnic and ideological violence nursed by poverty and dislocation.

A different type of demographic crisis confronts parts of the West, where steadily shrinking populations erode social welfare systems, and longer life spans, broadened welfare programs, and rising health care costs contribute to the challenge. Populations in the United States and Great Britain have been stable or have slowly expanded by immigration; while in Italy, Scandinavia, and, recently,

GOVERNMENT EFFORTS TO CURTAIL THE SPREAD OF SEVERE ACUTE RESPIRATORY SYNDROME (SARS). In May 2003, migrant workers at a Beijing railway station line up to have their temperatures checked before boarding trains.

Interpreting Visual Evidence

Media Representations of Globalization

Because the historical developments collectively known as *globalization* are so complex and the local effects of these developments have often been considered mere disruptions of well-entrenched habits or ways of life, debates about globalization are particularly open to manipulation through the presentation of charged imagery. Since the end of the Cold War, provocative images that capture certain aspects of the world's new interconnectedness—and the accompanying need for new kinds of boundaries—have become ubiquitous in the media. The movement of peoples and goods are variously defined as necessary to maintain standards of living or a threat to local jobs and local production. Globalization is defended as good for the economy, the consumer, and competition, but it is also blamed for hurting workers, destroying local cultures, and eroding long-standing definitions of national identity.

The images here illustrate essential aspects of globalization. Image A shows ships waiting to be loaded and unloaded at one of the largest container terminals in the world, in Hong Kong, where most Chinese shipping comes through this terminal. Image B shows a temporary refugee camp in Turkey occupied by Kurds, who had fled from Islamic State violence in Syria, where they are an ethnic minority. From 2014 to 2019 Syrians fleeing violence and civil war settled in neighboring countries such as Turkey and Lebanon, but also migrated into

A. Cargo ships in Kowloon Bay, Hong Kong, 2002.

Russia, sharp drops in the birthrate have led to population decline. These declining birthrates have been accompanied by growing populations of older adults, whose health and vitality resulted from decades of improved medical standards and state-run entitlement programs. Maintaining the long-term solvency of such programs poses difficult choices for European countries, in particular, as they struggle to balance guarantees of social well-being with fiscal and political realities.

Globalization has also changed public health and medicine, creating dangerous new threats as well as promising new treatments. Better and more comprehensive health care generally has accompanied other kinds of prosperity and thus has been more accessible in the West. In Africa, Latin America, and elsewhere, political chaos, imbalances of trade, and practices of some large pharmaceutical companies have often resulted in shortages of medicine and an undeveloped medical infrastructure, making it difficult to combat deadly new waves of disease. The worldwide risk of exposure to epidemic diseases is a new reality of globalization, a product of increased cultural interaction, exposure of new ecosystems to human development, and the speed of intercontinental transportation. By the 1970s, the acceleration of airplane travel led countries in western Europe (see map on p. 1036). Image C shows a Labor Day protester (medical mask is a reference to the SARS epidemic) at a demonstration in the Philippine capital, Manila, in which globalization was blamed for amendments to the labor code favorable to employers, such as a ban on strikes, and antiterrorist measures that were perceived to be an infringement on personal liberties.

Questions for Analysis

1. Image A is typical of images emphasizing the economic consequences of globalization. Does globalization appear to be a force that is subject to human control in this image? How do such images shape perceptions of China's place in the global economy?

2. Compare image A with image B. Is there a connection between the accelerating flows of money and goods and restrictions on the movements of people?

3. In image C, the woman's medical mask names globalization as the enemy of Filipino workers. Who is the target of this protest? What does this say about the local conflict over the conditions of labor in the Philippines?

B. This refugee camp in Suruc, Turkey, held Kurds who had fled northern Syria after it was besieged by the Islamic State in 2014.

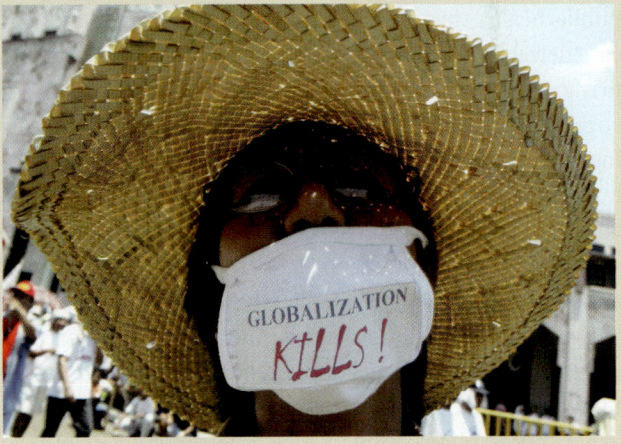

C. Filipino protester on Labor Day in Manila, Philippines, 2003.

to fears that an epidemic would leapfrog the globe much faster than the pandemics of the Middle Ages, fears that were confirmed by the worldwide spread of HIV infection, which first appeared at the end of the 1970s. As the **HIV-AIDS epidemic** became a global health crisis—particularly in Africa, where the disease spread catastrophically—international organizations recognized the need for an early, swift, and comprehensive response to future outbreaks of disease. In 2003, the successful containment of an outbreak of severe acute respiratory syndrome (SARS) demonstrated the effectiveness of this planning, but the Ebola crisis of 2014 and anxiety over the spread of the mosquito-borne **Zika virus** show that this is an ongoing struggle. The Zika virus, which can cause serious birth defects when a woman is infected during pregnancy, was first identified in Uganda in 1947 and has been identified in many countries since 2015, including much of Central and Latin America.

Meanwhile, the work of multinational medical research firms has continued to extend the ability to prevent and treat disease. One of the most powerful tools in this endeavor was the development of genetic engineering, which stemmed from the monumental discovery of DNA in the 1950s. By the 1990s, several laboratories were engaged in the most ambitious medical research ever attempted: the mapping of the human genome—that is, the entire architecture of chromosomes and genes contained in basic human DNA. Through and alongside this process, genetic engineers developed methods to alter the biology of living things. Infertile couples, for instance, could now conceive through out-of-body medical procedures. Genetic engineers developed—and patented—strains of mice and other laboratory animals that carried chemical markers, cells, and even organs of other species. By 1997, British researchers succeeded in producing a clone (an exact genetic copy) of a sheep. It is now possible to determine the genetic makeup of any individual human being and measure his or her chances of developing cancers or other life-threatening diseases and conditions. The rapidly developing field of epigenetics has been able to trace the effects of behaviors, such as smoking, through more than one generation, demonstrating that the choices made by grandparents can affect the genes of their grandchildren. These developments raise provocative questions about the relationship between individual responsibility and public health, how scientists should understand biological "defects" and diversions from genetic norms, and the privacy of medical information. As a new form of knowledge in an age of global interconnection, genetic engineering has leaped across the legal and moral boundaries of human societies. The question of who will govern these advances—nations, international bodies, or local cultural and religious communities—is open to passionate debate, as are fresh arguments about where to draw the lines between lifesaving intervention and cultural preference, or between individual agency and biological determinism. Like past scientific investigations directed at humankind, genetics has raised fundamental questions about ethics, citizenship, and the measure of humanity.

SPOTLIGHT ON THE ENVIRONMENT: CLIMATE CHANGE

Perhaps no issue raises thornier questions about the relationships among population, economic development, and public welfare than the matter of climate change. Climate scientists now largely agree that the average temperature of the planet is rising steadily as a result of increases in the atmosphere of "greenhouse gases": primarily carbon dioxide, but also methane, nitrous oxide, and ozone. There is also growing evidence that this warming is accelerating.

The year 2018 was the forty-second consecutive year in a row that the annual temperature was above the average in the twentieth century. And eighteen of the nineteen warmest years on record have occurred since 2000; the years 2014–2018 witnessed the highest average temperatures in 139 years of record keeping by the U.S. government.

A vast majority of scientists have concluded that this pattern of global warming is caused by human activity. Greenhouse gases have a number of sources, but the primary cause of global warming is thought to be the burning of fossil fuels. The consequences of global warming will be substantial: a rise in sea levels as polar ice caps melt; an increase in the frequency of heat waves, droughts, wildfires, rainfall intensity, and coastal flooding; and greater incidence and severity of storms, tornadoes, and tropical cyclones. Scientists remain unsure about the speed with which these changes will be perceptible—it is possible that the next two or three decades might feel roughly similar to the present—but most agree that the changes have already begun. The long-term risks for human society also will be severe. A rapid rise in sea levels would destroy many of the earth's major cities and render them uninhabitable. An agricultural crisis could create starvation and chaos in more than one region. Governments could collapse, as massive flows of refugees would strain even wealthy nations. The worst-case scenario would be mass extinctions of plants and animals, which the earth has already experienced on multiple occasions.

Governments first sounded the alarm about climate change in the early 1990s, but establishing a coordinated policy proved difficult, because individual nations worried about compromising their economic competitiveness. Energy producers and economic interests, whose profits and growth depended on the burning of fossil fuels, resisted pollution limits and requirements on adopting expensive "clean" technologies. Few imagined that it would be easy to change the behavior of consumers in developed countries whose lifestyle depended on access to electric power produced by the burning of coal, manufactured goods from distant places, cheap air travel, and the automobile. And changing consumer habits, finding alternative energy sources, and developing new technologies to remove carbon from the atmosphere may take years. Finding policy solutions is doubly difficult because those parts of the globe closely associated with pollution caused by the burning of fossil fuels—industrialized societies in Europe and North America—are not necessarily those that will feel its effects acutely in the near term. Those most impacted will be mainly poorer countries in the global south that have few resources to cope with the effects of climate change on their populations.

Since the 1990s, international efforts to coordinate a response to climate change focused on a UN-sponsored agreement known as the Kyoto Protocol. But the United States never joined the Kyoto agreement, claiming that it could not participate in an accord that did not include China (the United States and China are both leading producers of greenhouse gases). In 2015, however, 195 nations—including both the United States and China—came to a landmark agreement in Paris that committed nearly every nation on the planet to limiting greenhouse gas emissions.

The international effort represented by the Paris Accords has been rendered uncertain by events in the United States. In 2016, the U.S. Supreme Court halted President Barack Obama's attempt to put the United States in alignment with the Paris agreement after a suit by twenty-nine states contested its legality and the scientific evidence used to support it. The same year, the Court placed a stay on Obama's Clean Power Plan, preventing the implementation of new emission regulations. In 2017, President Donald Trump declared that the United States would pull out of the Paris Accords altogether at the earliest possible moment allowed by law, November 2020. Other nations promised to persist in their efforts, and the Trump administration continued to send representatives to UN climate summits, in an apparent effort to influence ongoing negotiations over permissible levels of greenhouse gases.

But climate scientists believe that even the unprecedented effort of the Paris Accord—assuming that every country follows through on its commitment to limit emissions—will cut only about half of what is necessary to prevent an increase of 3.6 degrees Fahrenheit in the average global temperature. Most scientists have concluded that if global warming passes this point, the disastrous effects will be irreversible. And to prevent this from happening, they believe that the transition to clean energy sources will need to be completed by 2050 at the latest. These hotly debated issues about climate change clearly illustrate the necessity of global thinking in the contemporary world.

AFTER EMPIRE: POSTCOLONIAL POLITICS IN THE GLOBAL ERA

After the superpower rivalry of the Cold War collapsed, another legacy of the postwar era continued to shape international relations into the twenty-first century: emergence of the so-called postcolonial relationships between former colonies and Western powers. (See decolonization struggles detailed in Chapter 27.) Former colonies, and other nations that had fallen under the political and economic sway of imperial powers, gained formal independence, along with new kinds of cultural and political authority; but, in some respects, very little changed for people in the former colonies. The very term *postcolonial* underlines the fact that colonialism's legacies endured even after independence. Within these regions, political communities new and old handled the legacies of empire and the postcolonial future in a variety of ways. In some cases, the former colonizers or their local allies retained so much power that formal independence actually meant very little. In others, bloody independence struggles poisoned the political culture. The emergence of new states and new kinds of politics was sometimes propelled by economic goals and by the revival of cultural identities that preceded colonization; but, in other times, by ethnic conflict. The results thus ranged from breakneck industrial success to ethnic slaughter, or from democratization to new local models of absolutism. During the Cold War, these postcolonial regions were often the turf on which the superpower struggle was waged. They benefited from superpower patronage, but also became the staging ground for proxy wars funded by the West in its fight against communism. Their various trajectories since 1989 point to the complex legacy of the imperial past in the post–Cold War world of globalization.

Emancipation and Ethnic Conflict in Africa

The legacies of colonialism weighed heavily on sub-Saharan Africa. Most of the continent's former colonies came into their independence after the Second World War with their basic infrastructures deteriorating after decades of imperial negligence. The Cold War decades brought scant improvement, as governments across the continent were plagued by both homegrown and externally imposed corruption, poverty, and civil war. In sub-Saharan Africa, two very different trends began to emerge around 1989, each shaped by a combination of the end of the Cold War and the volatile local conditions.

The first trend can be seen in South Africa, where politics had revolved around the brutal racial policies of apartheid for decades, sponsored by the white minority government. The most prominent opponent of apartheid, **Nelson Mandela**, who led the African National Congress (ANC), had been imprisoned since 1962. Intense repression and violent conflict continued into the 1980s and reached a dangerous impasse by the end of the decade. Then, the South African government chose a daring new

Competing Viewpoints

The Meaning of the "Third World"

Alfred Sauvy, a French demographer, coined the term Third World in a famous 1952 article about the effects of the Cold War on international relations and economic development: the First World was the West, a world of democratic political institutions and capitalist economies; the Second World was the Soviet sphere, committed to socialist institutions; and the Third World was everybody else—the world of European colonies and former colonies, marked by the history of imperialism.

Though commonly used between the 1950s and the 1980s, the term Third World is less frequently encountered in the present. B. R. Tomlinson, a British economic historian, examines the ways in which the concept was rooted in the ideological world of the Cold War, as he looks for new vocabulary to tell the history of globalization in the contemporary world.

Alfred Sauvy, "Three Worlds, One Planet" (1952)

We speak voluntarily about two worlds today, about the possibility of war between them, about their coexistence, etc., forgetting too often that there is a third world . . . the collectivity called, in the style of the United Nations, the under-developed countries. . . .

* * *

Unfortunately, the struggle for the possession of the third world does not allow the two others to simply pursue their own path, believing it to be obviously the best, the "true" way. The Cold War has curious consequences: over there, a morbid fear of espionage has pushed them to the most ferocious isolation. With us, it has caused a halt in social evolution. What good is it to trouble ourselves or deprive ourselves, at a moment when the fear of communism is holding back those who would like to go further [on the path to equality]? Why should we consider any social reforms at all when the progressive majority is split? . . . Why worry about it, since there is no opposition?

In this way, any evolution toward the distant future has been halted in both camps, and this obstacle has one cause: the costs of war.

Meanwhile . . . the under-developed nations, the third world, have entered into a new phase. Certain medical techniques have now been introduced suddenly for a simple reason: they are cheap. . . . For a few pennies the life of a man can be prolonged for several years. Because of this, these countries now have the mortality that we had in 1914 and the birthrate that we had in the eighteenth century. Certainly, this has resulted in economic improvement, lower infant mortality, better productivity of adults, etc. Nevertheless, it is easy to see how this demographic increase must be accompanied by important investments in order to adapt the container to what it must contain. Now, these vital investments cost much more than 68 francs per person. They crash right into the financial wall imposed by the Cold War. The result is eloquent: the millennial cycle of life and death continues to turn, but it is a cycle of poverty.

* * *

Since the preparation for war is priority number 1, secondary concerns such as world hunger will only occupy our attention enough to avoid an explosion that might compromise our first priority. But when one remembers the enormous errors that conservatives have committed so many times, we can only have a mediocre confidence in the ability of the Americans to play with the fire of popular anger. . . . They have not clearly perceived that under-developed nations of a feudal type might evolve more readily towards a communist regime than toward democratic capitalism. One might console oneself, if one were so inclined, by pointing to the greater advance of capitalism, but the fact remains undeniable. And maybe, in the glare of its own vitality, the first world, even in the absence of any human solidarity, might notice this slow, irresistible, humble and ferocious, push toward life. Because in the end, this ignored, exploited Third World, as despised as the Third Estate [in the French Revolution], wants to be something.

Source: Alfred Sauvy, "Trois mondes, une planète," L'Observateur 14 (August 1952): 5. This translation, by Joshua Cole, comes from a French reprint in Vingtième Siècle, no. 12 (October–December 1986): 81–83.

B. R. Tomlinson, "What Was the Third World?" (2003)

The term "Third World" was used frequently in histories of the societies, economies and cultures of many parts of the world in the second half of the twentieth century.... Like other collective descriptions of Africa, Asia, the Middle East, the Pacific islands and Latin America—such as the "South," the "developing world," or the "less-developed world"—the designation "Third World" was more about what such places were not than what they were.

* * *

Those who developed a concept of the Third World around a set of measurable criteria usually relied on identifying material circumstances. . . . However, all such attempts to establish a standard measurement of relative poverty that can distinguish various parts of the world from each other run into considerable difficulties. It has often been argued that the various countries of Asia, Africa and Latin America (not to mention the Pacific islands and elsewhere) differ greatly in their size, political ideologies, social structures, economic performance, cultural backgrounds and historical experiences. These differences exist not simply between Third World countries, but within them as well. There are rich and poor people, empowered and disempowered citizens, to be found inside all states and societies in the world.

It was over broad issues of economic development that the fiercest battles for the concept of the Third World were fought. Orthodox development economists in the 1950s and 1960s had suggested that the poverty of non-western economies was the result of low levels of savings and investment, and that these problems could best be resolved by increasing external influence over them to help local élites modernize their societies (in other words, make them more like those of the West) by providing technology and education to increase productivity and output.

* * *

To many radical critics, these ideas, and the U.S. government's development policies that flowed from them, seemed to mask a narrow political agenda that sought to justify the dominance of free-market capitalism as a model and mechanism for economic, social and cultural development. One powerful reaction to this agenda was to argue that dependence on the West had distorted the economic and social conditions of non-western societies, leading to a common process of historical change in the periphery of the world economy brought about by "a situation in which the economy of certain countries [and hence their social and political structures] is conditioned by the development and expansion of another economy to which the former is subjected."

* * *

The history of imperialism has been immensely important in shaping our view of the modern world, both from the top down and from the bottom up, but the phenomenon was also historically specific, and represents only one stage in the process of understanding the interaction between the local and the global. To write the history of the "Rest," as well as of the West, we need now to move on, and to construct new narratives of global history that go beyond the models of coherent and distinct communities, nations and states, arranged into hierarchies of material achievement and cultural power, and underpinned by universal institutional ideals of participatory democracy and free markets, that dominated thinking about international and local systems in the world for much of the nineteenth and twentieth centuries.

Source: B. R. Tomlinson, "What Was the Third World?" *Journal of Contemporary History* 38, no. 2 (April 2003): 307–21.

Questions for Analysis

1. In Sauvy's argument, what do the "under-developed nations" have in common? Does Tomlinson agree?

2. Sauvy calls for the First World to invest in the Third World to prevent an explosion of anger. What possible difficulties with this solution does Tomlinson identify?

3. How do Sauvy and Tomlinson see the relationship between the Cold War and the problem of understanding the "Third World?"

tactic: it released Mandela from prison in early 1990. Mandela resumed leadership of the ANC and turned the party toward a combination of renewed public demonstrations. Also, plans for negotiation politics changed within the Afrikaner-dominated white regime when F. W. de Klerk succeeded P. W. Botha as prime minister. A pragmatist who feared civil war and national collapse over apartheid, de Klerk was well matched with Mandela. In March 1992, the two men began direct talks to establish majority rule. Legal and constitutional reforms followed, and, in May 1994, during elections in which all South Africans took part, Nelson Mandela was chosen as the country's first black president. Although many of his government's efforts to reform housing, the economy, and public health foundered, Mandela defused the climate of organized racial violence. He gained and maintained tremendous personal popularity as a living symbol of a new political culture among black and white South Africans alike, within sub-Saharan Africa and worldwide. In a number of smaller postcolonial states such as Benin, Malawi, and Mozambique, the early 1990s brought political reforms that ended one-party or one-man rule in favor of parliamentary democracy and economic reform.

The other major trend ran in a different, less encouraging direction. Some former autocracies gave way to calls for pluralism, but other states across the continent collapsed into ruthless ethnic conflict. In Rwanda, a former Belgian colony, conflicts between the Hutu and Tutsi populations erupted into a highly organized campaign of genocide against the Tutsi after the country's president, Juvenal Habyarimana, who was Hutu, was assassinated. Organized by extremist members of the Presidential Guard and carried out by ordinary Hutus of all backgrounds, the ethnic slaughter left over 800,000 Tutsi dead in a matter of weeks. The United Nations troops were present, but largely withdrew after ten of their soldiers were murdered. French troops were also present, but the French government had been supporting the government of Habyarimana. The United Nations and the governments of the United States and France were widely criticized in the aftermath for failing to recognize the need for intervention and to do more to stop the killing, as well as failing to use the term "genocide" until it was too late.

When a Tutsi-led force captured the Rwandan capital of Kigali, the extremist government that had organized the killings collapsed. Many of the perpetrators fled to neighboring Zaire through a safe zone secured by French soldiers. Once in Zaire, they became hired mercenaries in the many-sided civil war that followed the collapse of Mobutu Sese Seko's government. Sese Seko, the country's long-time dictator, was infamous for diverting billions of dollars in foreign aid into his personal bank accounts. A number of

NELSON MANDELA VOTES IN SOUTH AFRICA'S FIRST DEMOCRATIC ELECTIONS, 1994. Mandela was elected the country's first black president.

ambitious neighboring countries intervened in Zaire's civil war, hoping to secure its valuable resources and to settle conflicts with their own ethnic minorities that had spilled over the border. Fighting continued through the late 1990s into the new century, and was dubbed "Africa's world war" by many observers. Public services, normal trade, even basic health and safety inside Zaire collapsed. (Zaire was later renamed the Democratic Republic of Congo by an ineffective government in the capital, Kinshasa.) By 2008, 5.4 million people had died in the war and its aftermath, the equivalent of losing the entire population of Denmark in a single decade. As of 2019, fighting still continues in the eastern regions of the Congo.

Economic Power on the Pacific Rim

By the end of the twentieth century, East Asia had become a center of industrial and manufacturing production. China, whose communist government began to establish

INDUSTRIALIZATION IN CHINA, 2002. The Three Gorges Dam on the Yan River in Yichang is the largest hydroelectric dam in the world. It has been called the largest construction project in China since the Great Wall.

commercial ties with the West in the 1970s, was the world's leading heavy industrial producer by the year 2000. Its state-owned companies acquired contracts from Western firms to produce products cheaply and in bulk, for sale back to home markets in the United States and Europe. In a deliberate reversal of Europe's nineteenth-century intrusions on the China trade, Beijing established semi-capitalist commercial zones around major port cities such as Shanghai—a policy whose centerpiece was the reclamation of Hong Kong from Britain in 1997. The commercial zones were intended to encourage massive foreign investment on terms that gave China a favorable balance of trade for its huge volume of cheap exports, but, in practice, the zones enjoyed only mixed success. Inland, downturns in farming and a looming energy crisis hampered prosperity and economic growth, but Hong Kong worked to maintain its economic and cultural middle ground with the rest of the world, as it had since the days of the opium trade (Chapter 22).

Other Asian nations emerged as global commercial powers as well. During the decades after the Second World War, industry flourished in a string of countries, starting from Japan and extending along Asia's Pacific coastline into Southeast Asia and Oceania. By the 1980s, their robust industrial expansion and apparent staying power earned them the collective nickname of the "tigers," taken from the ambitious, forward-looking tiger in Chinese mythology. These Pacific rim states collectively formed the most important industrial region in the world outside the United States and Europe. Among them, Japan not only led the

way but also became the most influential model of success, with a postwar revival eventually surpassing the economic miracle of West Germany (Chapter 28). Japanese firms concentrated on the efficiency and technical reliability of their products: fuel-efficient cars, specialty steel, small electronic goods, and so on. Japanese diplomacy and large state subsidies supported the success of Japanese firms, while a well-funded program of technical education hastened research and development of new goods. Japanese firms also appeared to benefit from collective loyalty among civil servants and corporate managers, attitudes that were encouraged through Japan's long experience with trade guilds and feudal politics. Other East Asian nations, newer or less stable than Japan, tried to mimic its success. Some, such as South Korea and the Chinese Nationalist stronghold of Taiwan, treated the creation of prosperity as a fundamental patriotic duty. In postcolonial nations, such as Malaysia and Indonesia, governments parlayed their natural resources and expansive local labor pools (which had made them attractive to imperial powers in earlier times) into investment for industrialization. As in China, the factories that emerged were either subsidiaries of Western companies or operated on their behalf, in new multinational versions of the putting-out system of early industrialization.

The Pacific rim's boom, however, also contained the makings of a first "bust." During the 1990s, a confluence of factors resulted in an enormous slowdown of growth and the near collapse of several currencies. Japan experienced rising production costs, overvalued stocks, and rampant speculation on its high-priced real estate market. When the bubble economy burst in 1991, Japan entered a "lost decade" of economic stagnation that hit bottom in 2003. In Southeast Asia, states such as Indonesia found they had to pay the difference on overvalued industrial capital to Western lenders who set rigid debt-repayment schedules. Responses to the economic downturn varied widely. In South Korea, an older generation that remembered economic catastrophe after the Korean War responded to national calls for sacrifice by investing their own savings to prop up ailing companies. Japan launched programs of monetary austerity to cope with its first serious spike in unemployment in two generations. In Indonesia, inflation and unemployment reignited sharp ethnic conflicts that prosperity and forceful state repression had dampened in earlier times. This predominantly Muslim country, with a long tradition of tolerance and pluralism inside the faith, also saw outbursts of violent religious fundamentalism popularly associated with another region: the Middle East.

A NEW CENTER OF GRAVITY: ISRAEL, OIL, AND POLITICAL ISLAM IN THE MIDDLE EAST

Perhaps no other region has drawn more attention from the West in the age of globalization than the Middle East, where a volatile combination of Western military, political, and economic interests converged with deep-seated regional conflicts and transnational Islamic politics. The results of this ongoing confrontation promise to shape the twenty-first century. Here we consider three of the most important aspects of recent history in the region. First is the unfolding of the Arab-Israeli conflict. Second is the region's vital development as the global center of oil production. Third emerges from inside the Arab world, largely as a reaction against recent relations with the West. This is the development of a specific, modern brand of Islamic radicalism that challenges the legacies of imperialism and promises revolutionary and sometimes apocalyptic changes in postcolonial nations, with its most violent elements generating a cycle of fear, anger, and, ultimately, direct conflict with Western governments.

The Arab-Israeli Conflict

As we saw in Chapter 27, Israel's existence was a battle-ground from the start. The national aspirations of Jewish immigrants from Europe fleeing the Holocaust and violent postwar anti-Semitism clashed with the motives of pan-Arabists—secular, anticolonial nationalists who championed Arab pride and self-reliance against European domination. By the late 1970s, in the aftermath of two Arab-Israeli wars, it appeared that a generation of fighting might come to an end. American mediators began sponsoring talks to prevent further, sudden outbursts of conflict, while Soviet leaders remained neutral but supportive of peace efforts. Most notably, the Egyptian president Anwar Sadat, who authorized and directed the 1973 war against Israel, decided that coexistence rather than the destruction of Israel was the long-term answer to regional conflict. In 1978, aided by the American president Jimmy Carter, Sadat brokered a peace between Egypt and Israel's staunchly conservative leader, Menachem Begin; leaders on both sides believed the potential rewards were greater than the obvious risks.

However, hopes for a lasting peace were soon dashed. The international community held out the hope of a two-state solution, but agreement proved impossible on several issues. Palestinians insisted on the right to return to the land they had lost in 1948, when the state of Israel was created. Meanwhile, Israelis had begun to settle—in violation of international law, according to the United Nations—in territories occupied by Israel after the 1967 war: the Golan Heights, the Gaza Strip, the West Bank, and East Jerusalem, a territory that includes religious sites sacred to both Jews and Muslims. On each side of the Israeli-Palestinian conflict, a potent blend of ethnic and religious nationalism began to control both debate and action. Conservatives in Israel played to a public sentiment that put security ahead of other priorities, particularly among the most recent Jewish immigrants, often from the United States and the former Soviet Union. On the other side, younger Palestinians—who grew up embittered in the occupied territories—turned against the secular radicalism of the Palestinian Liberation Organization (PLO) and moved toward radical Islam.

In 1987, in this combustible political environment, the Palestinians living on the West Bank and in the desperately overcrowded Gaza Strip revolted in an outburst of street rioting. This rebellion, called the *intifada* (literally, a "throwing off," or uprising), continued for years in daily battles between stone-throwing Palestinian youths and armed Israeli security forces. The street fights escalated into cycles of Palestinian terrorism, particularly suicide bombings of civilian targets, and reprisals from the Israeli military. International efforts to broker a peace produced the Oslo Accords of 1993, which established an autonomous Palestinian Authority led by the PLO chief, Yasser Arafat. Yet the peace was always fragile at best with continued attacks by Islamist terrorists, and suffering perhaps fatal damage from the assassination of Israel's reformist prime minister Yitzhak Rabin by a reactionary Israeli in 1995.

In the twenty-first century, the cycle of violence has continued. Palestinians launched a second intifada in 2000, which ended only with Arafat's death in 2004. Arafat's replacement, Mahmoud Abbas, was challenged by a more militant Palestinian organization, Hamas, which was labeled a terrorist organization by the United States and the European Union. Hamas's victory in Palestinian parliamentary elections in 2006 limited Abbas's power to negotiate with Israel, contributing to a breakdown of diplomatic efforts and resumed conflict in Gaza in 2008–2009, 2012, and 2014. In 2013, the UN General Assembly

THE ARAB-ISRAELI WARS OF 1967 AND 1973. ▪ *What were the major changes in the political geography of the Middle East as a result of the Arab-Israeli war of 1967?* ▪ *At the end of the 1967 war, why did the Israelis wish to occupy the Sinai and the West Bank regions?* ▪ *What problems did this occupation create, and how might it have led to the war of 1973?*

recognized the state of Palestine, granting it nonmember observer status, but bitter divisions between Hamas and the Palestinian Authority persist. Egypt helped to broker a ceasefire in 2018, when violence in Gaza flared again, but a permanent end to the conflict is not in sight.

Oil, Power, and Economics

The struggles between the state of Israel and its neighbors have been important in their own right. Yet one of the most compelling reasons that this conflict mattered to outside powers was material: oil. The global demand for oil skyrocketed during the postwar era and has since accelerated. Starting with the consumer boom in the West

during the Cold War, ordinary citizens bought cars and other petroleum-powered consumer durables, while industrial plastics made from petroleum by-products were used to manufacture a wealth of basic household items. Those needs, and the desires for profit and power that went with them, drew Western corporations and governments steadily toward the oil-rich states of the Middle East, whose vast reserves were discovered in the 1930s and the 1940s. Large corporations conducted joint diplomacy with Middle Eastern states and their home governments to design concessions for drilling, refining, and shipping the oil, while pipelines were laid by contractors based around the world, from California to Rome to Russia.

The enormous long-term economic value of the Middle Eastern oil reserves made oil a fundamental tool in the new struggles over political power. Many producer states sought to turn their resources into leverage with the West's former imperial powers. In 1960, the leading Middle Eastern, African, and Latin American producers banded together in a cartel to take advantage of this vital resource, forming the Organization of the Petroleum Exporting Countries (OPEC) to regulate the production and pricing of crude oil. During the 1970s, OPEC played a leading role in the global economy. Its policies reflected not only the desire to draw maximum profits out of bottlenecks in oil production, but also the militant politics of some OPEC leaders who wanted to use oil as a weapon against the West in the Arab-Israeli conflict. After the 1973 Arab-Israeli war, an **oil embargo** inspired by the hard-liners sparked spiraling inflation and economic troubles in Western nations, triggering a cycle of dangerous recession that lasted nearly a decade.

EGYPTIAN PRESIDENT GAMAL ABDEL NASSER AND SOVIET MINISTER ALEKSEY KOSYGIN, 1966. As the most prominent spokesman for secular pan-Arabism, Nasser became a target of Islamist critics, such as Sayyid Qutb and the Muslim Brotherhood, who were angered by the Western-influenced policies of his regime.

In response, Western governments treated the Middle Eastern oil regions as a vital strategic center of gravity, the subject of constant Great Power diplomacy. If conflict directly threatened the stability of oil production or friendly governments, Western powers were prepared to intervene by force, as demonstrated by the 1991 Gulf War. By the 1990s, another new front of competition and potential conflict emerged, as the energy demands of other nations grew. The new industrial giants, China and India, in particular, eyed the Middle Eastern oil reserves with the same nervousness as the West. The oil boom also generated violent conflict within some Middle Eastern producer states, as oil revenue produced uneven economic development. The huge gaps between or inside Middle Eastern societies that divided oil's haves and have-nots caused deep resentments, official corruption, and a new wave of radical politics. With the pan-Arab nationalists fading from the scene, the rising revolutionary force gathered around modern readings of Islamic fundamentalism, now tied to postcolonial politics.

The Rise of Political Islam

In North Africa and the Middle East, processes of modernization and globalization produced tremendous discontents. The new nations that emerged from decolonization

south of the Sahara often shared the characteristics of the "kleptocracies": corrupt state agencies, cronyism based on ethnic or family kinship, decaying public services, rapid increases in population, and constant state repression of dissent. Disappointment with these conditions ran deep, perhaps nowhere more so than in the seat of pan-Arabism, **Gamal Abdel Nasser**'s Egypt. During the 1960s, Egyptian academics and cultural critics leveled charges against Nasser's regime—denouncing Egypt's nationalist government as greedy, brutal, and corrupt—that became the core of a powerful new political movement. Their critique offered modern interpretations of certain legal and political currents in Islamic thought, ideas that linked loosely across centuries with revolts against foreign interference and official corruption.

The twist to their claims was that the roots of the Arab world's moral failure lay in centuries of colonial contact with the West. The most influential of these Islamist critics, Sayyid Qutb (*Kutb*; 1906–1966), presented these ideas in a series of essays for which he was arrested several times by Egyptian authorities, and ultimately executed. He argued that as a result of corrupting outside influences, the ruling elites of the new Arab states pursued policies that frayed local and family bonds, deepening economic divides while abandoning the government's responsibility for charity and stability. The Arab elites were morally bankrupt, living lives that defied codes of morality, self-discipline, and communal responsibility rooted in the Islamic faith. To remain in power, he claimed, these elites lived in the pockets of Western imperial and corporate powers, and this collaboration not only caused cultural impurity but also eroded authentic Muslim faith. This harsh judgment of Arab societies—that they were poisoned from without as well as within—required an equally drastic solution. Qutb believed Arab societies should reject not only oppressive postcolonial governments but also all the political and cultural ideas that traveled with them, especially those that could be labeled "Western." After popular revolts, the Arab autocracies would be replaced by an idealized Islamic government—a system in which a rigid form of Islam would link law, government, and culture.

In a formula familiar to historians of European politics throughout the nineteenth and twentieth centuries, this particular brand of Islamist politics combined popular anger, intellectual opposition to "foreign" influences, and a highly idealized vision of the past. By the 1970s, it began to express itself openly in regional politics. Qutb's ideas were put into practice by Egypt's Muslim Brotherhood, a secretive but widespread society rooted in anticolonial politics, local charity, and violently fundamentalist Islam. The same ideas spread among similar organizations in other urbanized Arab countries and leading Islamic universities, which were historically centers of debate on political theory and religious law. Radical Islam emerged as a driving force in criticism and defiance of autocratic Arab regimes, while secular critics and more liberal Islamists, who called for open elections and a free press, were more fragmented and thus easier to silence. The new wave of fundamentalists also gained concessions that allowed them to preach and publish in public as long as they did not launch actual revolts. Despite the movement's steady rise, the most dramatic turn still managed to surprise observers. Like Protestantism's emergence in the fractious German states or communism's successful revolution in Russia, radical Islam's defining moment as a political force came in an unexpected place: Iran.

IRAN'S ISLAMIC REVOLUTION

Iran offered one of the most dramatic examples of modernization gone sour in the Middle East. Despite tremendous economic growth in the 1960s and the 1970s, Iranians labored with legacies of foreign intervention and corrupt rule at the hands of the shah, **Reza Pahlavi**, a West-friendly leader installed during a 1953 military coup supported by Britain and the United States. In exchange for the shah's role as a friend to the West during the Cold War and for providing a steady source of reasonably priced oil, the

THE SHAH'S DOWNFALL. In 1979, two Iranians symbolically replace a picture of the shah with one of Ayatollah Khomeini after the Iranian revolution. ■ *What did the Iranian revolutionaries who overthrew the shah have in common with the anticolonial nationalists in former European colonies and client states?*

Iranian government received vast sums in oil contracts, weapons, and development aid. Thousands of Westerners, especially Americans, came to Iran, introducing foreign influences that challenged traditional values and offering economic and political alternatives. The shah, however, kept these alternatives out of reach, consistently denying democratic representation to westernizing middle-class Iranian workers and deeply religious university students alike. He governed, instead, through a small aristocracy that was divided by constant infighting. And his army and secret police conducted regular and brutal campaigns of repression. Despite all this, and the public protests it spurred in the West, governments such as the conservative Nixon administration embraced the shah as a strategically vital ally: a key to anti-Soviet alliances and a safe source of oil.

Twenty-five years after the 1953 coup, the shah's autocratic route to an industrial state ended. After a lengthy economic downturn, public unrest, and personal illness, the shah retired from public life under popular pressure in

The Place of Islam in Modern Societies

In Europe and the Middle East, the end of the colonial era and the impact of postcolonial migrations provided the backdrop for a renewed discussion about the presence of Muslim peoples in European nations and the relationship of religion to politics in traditionally Muslim societies. Muslim scholars and clerics have expressed a wide range of opinions about the place of Islam in the modern world, and the two figures here provide two distinct voices in this discussion.

Born into a family of Shi'ite Muslim religious leaders, Ruhollah Khomeini (1902–1989) was recognized as the leading Iranian religious authority in the 1950s. He represented a highly conservative Islamic fundamentalism that intended to unite Iranian Muslims in a violent opposition to the Western-supported government of the shah of Iran. He also had a powerful influence on Muslims seeking an alternative to Western cultural, political, and economic domination.

Tariq Ramadan, born in 1962 in Geneva, Switzerland, is a professor of religion and philosophy. He is a leading voice for the increasingly large number of Muslims living in Europe and North America as members of a religious minority in non-Muslim societies. He argues that Muslims can and should be productive and active citizens of Western societies while remaining true to their religious beliefs. He has taught at the University of Fribourg, Collège de Saussure in Geneva, and St. Antony's College in Oxford. In 2004, he was forced to decline an offer to become a professor at the University of Notre Dame in the United States when the State Department denied him a visa.

Ruhollah Khomeini, Islamic Government (1979)

The Islamic government is not similar to the well-known systems of government. It is not a despotic government in which the head of state dictates his opinion and tampers with the lives and property of the people. The prophet, may God's prayers be upon him, and 'Ali, the amir of the faithful, and the other imams had no power to tamper with people's property or with their lives.* The Islamic government is not despotic but constitutional. However, it is not constitutional in the well-known sense of the word, which is represented in the parliamentary system or in the people's councils. It is constitutional in the sense that those in charge of affairs observe a number of conditions and rules underlined in the Koran and in the Sunna and represented in the necessity of observing the system and of applying the dictates and laws of Islam.† This is why the Islamic government is the government of the divine law. The difference between the Islamic government and the constitutional governments, both monarchic and republican, lies in the fact that the people's representatives or the king's representatives are the ones who codify and legislate, whereas the power of legislation is confined to God, may He be praised, and nobody else has the right to legislate and nobody may rule by that which has not been given power by God....

The government of Islam is not monarchic, ... and not an empire, because Islam is above squandering and unjustly undermining the lives and property of people. This is why the government of Islam does not have the many big palaces, the servants, the royal courts, the crown prince courts and other trivial requirements that consume half or most of the country's resources and that the sultans and the emperors have. The life of the great prophet was a life of utter simplicity, even though the prophet was the head of the state, who ran and ruled it by himself. ... Had this course continued until the present, people would have known the taste of happiness and the country's treasury would not have been plundered to be spent on fornication, abomination and the court's costs and expenditures. You know that most of the corrupt aspects of our society are due to the corruption of the ruling dynasty and the royal family.

What is the legitimacy of these rulers who build houses of entertainment, corruption, fornication and abomination and who destroy houses which God ordered be raised and in which His name is mentioned? Were it not for what the court wastes and what it embezzles, the country's budget would not experience any deficit that forces the state to borrow from America and England, with all the humiliation and insult that accompany such borrowing. Has our oil decreased or have our minerals that are stored under this good earth run out? We possess everything and we would not need the help of America or of others if it were not for the costs of the court and for its wasteful use of the people's money.

* "The prophet" refers to Muhammed; 'Ali was Muhammed's son-in-law and, according to the Shi'ite tradition, his legitimate heir; an amir is a high military official; and an imam, in the Shi'ite tradition, is an important spiritual leader with sole power to make decisions about doctrine.

† The Koran is the book of holy scriptures of Islam; the Sunna is the body of customary Islamic law second only to the Koran in authority.

Source: Ruhollah Khomeini, *Islamic Government*, trans. Joint Publications Research Service (New York: 1979), pp. 17–19.

Tariq Ramadan, Western Muslims and the Future of Islam (2002)

[W]ith the emergence of the young Muslim generation ... it has been deemed necessary to reanalyze the main Islamic sources (Qu'ran and Sunnah) when it comes to interpreting legal issues (*fiqh*) in the European context. Many of these young people intend to stay permanently in a European country, and a large number have already received their citizenship. New forms of interpretation (known as *ijtihad*) have made it possible for the younger generation to practice their faith in a coherent manner in a new context. It is important to note that this has been a very recent phenomenon. Only within the past few years have Muslim scholars and intellectuals felt obliged to take a closer look at the European laws, and at the same time, to think about the changes that have been taking place within the diverse Muslim communities ... [F]ive main points ... have been agreed upon by those working on the basis of the Islamic sources and by the great majority of Muslims living in Europe:

1. Muslims who are residents or citizens of a non-Islamic state should understand that they are under a moral and social contract with the country in which they reside. In other words, they should respect the laws of the country.

2. Both the spirit and the letter of the secular model permit Muslims to practice their faith without requiring a complete assimilation into the new culture and, thereby, partial disconnection from their Muslim identity.

3. The ancient division of the world into denominations of *dar al-harb* (abode of war) and *dar al-Islam* (abode of Islam), used by the jurists during a specific geopolitical context, namely the ninth-century Muslim world, is invalid and does not take into account the realities of modern life. Other concepts have been identified as exemplifying more positively the presence of Muslims in Europe.

4. Muslims should consider themselves full citizens of the nations in which they reside and can participate with conscience in the organizational, economic, and political affairs of the country without compromising their own values.

5. With regard to the possibilities offered by European legislation, nothing stops Muslims, like any other citizens, from making choices that respond to the requirements of their own consciences and faith. If any obligations should be in contradiction to the Islamic principles (a situation that is quite rare), the specific case must be studied in order to identify the priorities and the possibility of adaptation (which should be developed at the national level). ...

For some Muslims, the idea of an "Islamic culture," similar to the concepts of identity and community, connotes the necessity of Muslim isolation from and rejection of European culture. Such an understanding suggests that Muslims are not genuine in their desire to integrate into the society in which they live. They play the citizenship card, while trying to maintain such cultural particularities as dress code, management of space when it comes to men and women, concern about music, and other issues. For them, real integration means becoming European in every aspect of one's character and behavior. This is, in fact, a very narrow vision of integration, almost resembling the notion of assimilation. One admits theoretically that Muslims have the right to practice their religion but revokes these rights when expression of faith becomes too *visible*.

In actuality, the future of Muslim presence in Europe must entail a truly "European Islamic culture" disengaged from the cultures of North Africa, Turkey, and Indo-Pakistan, while naturally referring to them for inspiration. This new culture is just in the process of being born and molded. By giving careful consideration to everything from appropriate dress to the artistic and creative expression of Islam, Muslims are mobilizing a whole new culture. The formation of such a culture is a pioneering endeavor, making use of European energy while taking into account various national customs and simultaneously respecting Islamic values and guidelines.

Source: Tariq Ramadan, "Islam and Muslims in Europe: A Silent Revolution toward Rediscovery," in *Muslims in the West: From Sojourners to Citizens*, ed. Yvonne Yazbeck Haddad (New York: 2002), pp. 160–63.

Questions for Analysis

1. According to Khomeini, what prevents Islamic government from being despotic? Why is there no legislative branch in an Islamic government in his view?

2. What criticism does Ramadan make of those Muslims who seek to isolate themselves from European culture while living in Europe? What does he mean by "European Islamic culture"?

3. In what ways do the two Muslim thinkers show an engagement with European traditions of political thought?

February 1979. Eight months of uncertainty followed, wherein most Westerners fled the country and the provisional government appointed by the shah collapsed. The strongest political coalition among Iran's revolutionaries surged into the vacuum: a broad Islamic movement centered on **Ayatollah Ruhollah Khomeini** (1902–1989), Iran's senior Shi'ite cleric and theologian, who returned from exile in France. Other senior clerics and the country's large population of unemployed, deeply religious university students provided the movement's energy, and disenfranchised secular protesters joined the radical Islamists in condemning decades of Western indifference and the shah's oppression. Under the new regime, some limited economic and political populism combined with strict constructions of Islamic law, restrictions on women's public life, and the prohibition of many ideas or activities linked to Western influence.

THE IRAN-IRAQ WAR. Iranian guards keep watch over Iraqi prisoners.

The new Iranian government also defined itself against its enemies: the Sunni religious establishment of neighboring states, "atheistic" Soviet communism, and, especially, Israel and the United States. Iranians feared that the United States would try to overthrow Khomeini as it had other leaders, and violence in the streets of Tehran reached a peak when militant students stormed the American embassy in November 1979, taking fifty-two hostages. The act quickly became an international crisis that heralded a new kind of confrontation between Western powers and postcolonial Islamic radicals. The Democratic president Jimmy Carter's administration ultimately gained the release of the hostages, but not before the catalog of earlier failures led to the election of the Republican Ronald Reagan.

Iran, Iraq, and Unintended Consequences of the Cold War

Iran's victory in the hostage crisis was fleeting. During the later part of 1980, Iran's Arab neighbor and traditional rival Iraq invaded, hoping to seize Iran's southern oil fields during the revolutionary confusion. Iran counterattacked, and the result was a murderous eight-year conflict marked by the use of chemical weapons and human waves of young Iranian radicals fighting the Soviet-armed Iraqis. The war ended with Iran's defeat, but not the collapse of

its theocratic regime. In the short term, their long defense of Iranian nationalism left the clerics more entrenched at home, while they used oil revenues to back grass-roots radicals who engaged in anti-Western terrorism in Lebanon and elsewhere. Utimately, the strongest threats to the Iranian regime came from within, as a new generation of young students and disenfranchised service workers found that their prospects for prosperity and active citizenship had not changed much since the days of the shah.

The Iran-Iraq conflict created another problem for Western interests and the governments of leading OPEC states: Iraq. Various governments—including an unlikely alliance of France, Saudi Arabia, the Soviet Union, and the United States—supported Iraq during the war in an effort to bring down Iran's clerics, but their patronage went to Saddam Hussein's dictatorship, one of the most violent governments in the region. Iraq exhausted itself in the war, politically and economically, so Hussein looked elsewhere in the region to shore up his regime and restore Iraq's influence, invading its small, oil-rich neighbor Kuwait in 1990. A number of Western nations led by the United States reacted forcefully, and, with the Cold War on the wane, Iraq's Soviet supporters would not condone the Iraqi aggression. Within months, Iraq faced the full weight of the United States military—trained intensively since Vietnam to fight much more capable Soviet-armed forces than those of Iraq—along with forces from several OPEC states, French troops, and armored divisions from Britain, Egypt, and Syria. This coalition pummeled Iraqi troops from the air for six weeks, then routed them and retook Kuwait in a brief, well-executed ground campaign. This changed the tenor of relations between the United States and Arab oil producers, encouraging closeness between governments as well as among anti-American radicals angry at a new Western presence. It was also the beginning rather than the end of a Western confrontation with Iraq, centered on Hussein's efforts to develop nuclear and biological weapons.

Elsewhere in the region, the proxy conflicts of the Cold War snared both superpowers in the new and growing networks of Islamic radicalism. In 1979, the socialist government of Afghanistan turned against its Soviet patrons. Fearing a result as in Iran, and a spread of fundamentalism into the Muslim regions of Soviet Central Asia, Moscow responded by overthrowing the Afghan president and installing a pro-Soviet faction. The new government, backed by more than 100,000 Soviet troops, found itself immediately at war with fighters who combined local conservatism with militant Islam and attracted volunteers from radical Islamic movements in Egypt, Lebanon, Saudi Arabia, and elsewhere. These fighters, who called themselves *mujahidin*, viewed the conflict as a holy war, and benefited from advanced weapons and training given by Western powers, led by the United States. Those who provided the aid saw the conflict in Cold War terms, as a chance to sap Soviet resources in a fruitless imperial war. On those terms, the aid worked, as the war dragged on for nearly ten years, taking thousands of Russian lives and damaging the Soviet government's credibility at home, and resulting in Soviet withdrawal in 1989. After five years of clan warfare, hard-line Islamic factions tied to the foreign elements in the mujahidin took over the country, whose experiment in theocracy made Iran's seem mild by comparison.

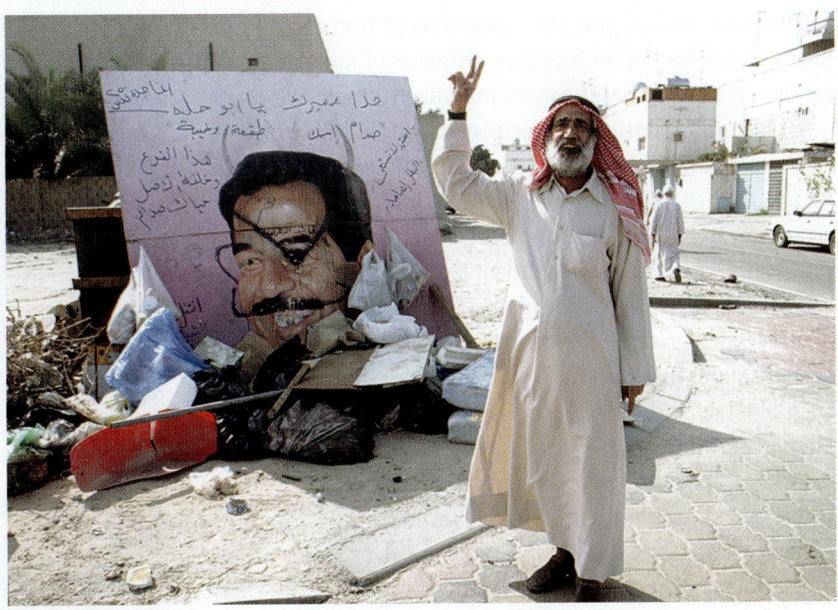

THE LIBERATION OF KUWAIT. A Kuwaiti celebrates with the victory sign in 1991, after American forces drive out Iraqi occupiers. Behind him, a defaced poster of Saddam Hussein sits on a garbage heap.

conflict in the Middle East, Europe, and Latin America. Most of these early terrorist organizations, including the Irish Republican Army, the Italian Red Brigades, and the different Palestinian revolutionary organizations, had specific goals, such as ethnic separatism or the establishment of revolutionary governments. By the 1980s and increasingly during the 1990s, such groups were complemented and then supplanted by a different brand of terrorist organization, one that ranged freely across territory and local legal systems. These newer, apocalyptic terrorist groups called for decisive conflict to eliminate their enemies and grant themselves martyrdom. Some such groups emerged from the social dislocations of the postwar boom, while others were linked directly to brands of radical religion. They often divorced themselves from the local crises that first spurred their anger, roaming widely among countries in search of recruits for their cause.

VIOLENCE BEYOND BOUNDS: WAR AND TERRORISM IN THE TWENTY-FIRST CENTURY

The global networks of communication, finance, and mobility discussed at the beginning of this chapter gave radical political violence a disturbing new character at the end of the twentieth century. In the 1960s, organized sectarian terrorist tactics had become an important part of political

From al Qaeda to the Iraq War

A leading example of such groups, and soon the most famous, was the radical Islamist umbrella organization **al Qaeda**. It was created by leaders of the foreign mujahidin who had fought against the Soviet Union in Afghanistan. Its official leader and financial supporter was the Saudi-born multimillionaire Osama bin Laden. Among its operational chiefs was the famous Egyptian radical Ayman al-Zawahiri, whose political career linked him directly to Sayyid Qutb and other founding thinkers of modern revolutionary Islam. These leaders organized broad networks of largely self-contained terrorist cells around the world—from the Islamic regions of Southeast Asia to Europe, East Africa, and the United States—funded by myriad private accounts, front companies, illegal commerce, and corporate kickbacks throughout the global economy. Their networks defied borders, as did their goals, which was not to negotiate for territory or change the government of a specific state. Instead, they spoke of the destruction of the state of Israel and the American, European, and other non-Islamic systems of government worldwide, and called for a united, apocalyptic revolt by fundamentalist Muslims to create an Islamic community bounded only by faith. During the 1990s, they involved themselves in a variety of local terrorist campaigns in Islamic countries and organized large-scale suicide attacks against American targets, notably the American embassies in Kenya and Tanzania in 1998.

At the beginning of the twenty-first century, al Qaeda's organizers struck again at their most obvious political enemy, the symbolic seat of globalization: the United States. Small teams of suicidal radicals, aided by al Qaeda's organization, planned to hijack airliners and use them as flying bombs to strike the most strategically important symbols of America's global power. On September 11, 2001, they carried out this mission in the deadliest series of terrorist attacks ever to occur on American soil. In a span of an hour, hijacked planes struck the Pentagon (the U.S. military headquarters) and both of the World Trade Center towers in New York City. A fourth plane, possibly aimed at the U.S. Capitol, crashed in an open farmland in Pennsylvania, its attack thwarted when the passengers fought back against their captors. The World Trade Center towers, among the tallest buildings in the world, crumbled into ash and wreckage on worldwide television and the Internet in front of hundreds of millions of viewers. In these simultaneous attacks, roughly 3,000 people died.

The attacks were at once a new brand of terror, deeply indebted to globalization in both its outlook and method, and something older: the extreme, opportunistic violence of marginal groups against national cultures during a period of general dislocation and uncertainty. The immediate American response was to take action against al Qaeda's central haven in Afghanistan, a state in total collapse after the warfare of the previous thirty years. The versatile professional soldiers and unmatched equipment of the United States, along with armed Afghan militias angry at the country's disarray, quickly routed al Qaeda's Taliban sponsors and scattered the terrorists. The search for

TWENTY-FIRST-CENTURY TERRORISM. World Trade Center towers in New York City under attack on September 11, 2001.

Osama bin Laden took a decade, during which time the United States and its allies faced a renewed insurrection by the Taliban in Afghanistan, beginning in 2003. The U.S. forces killed Osama bin Laden at his home in nearby Pakistan in 2011. During the intervening years, the United States succeeded in disrupting, though not completely eliminating, many of the hidden networks of leadership, finance, and information that made al Qaeda's apocalyptic terrorism possible. Meanwhile, the economic and political rebuilding of Afghanistan, a necessary consequence of American and European military action, began from almost nothing in terms of administration and infrastructure. These efforts were hampered by challenging political circumstances within the country, which made it difficult for the Afghan government to position itself between its U.S. ally and a population with a long tradition of mistrusting foreign powers intervening in their land. Many U.S. forces departed Afghanistan in 2013–2014, but President Obama canceled plans for a complete withdrawal in 2016.

His successor, Donald Trump, departed from long-standing policy by ordering the military to reduce the U.S. presence in Afghanistan by half in 2018.

Groups such as al Qaeda are feared because of the weapons they might use: chemical substances, biological agents that could kill millions, even portable nuclear weapons. With the end of the Cold War, methods and technologies that the superpowers employed to maintain their nuclear balance of power became more available on the margins, to displaced groups with the financial or political leverage to seek them out. Other major arms races, centered around Israel or the conflicts between India and Pakistan, for example, helped spread the availability of production sites and resources for weapons of horrific power; weapons that were no longer governed absolutely by legal conventions or the deterrent strength of superpowers. Reports that the Iraqi government of Saddam Hussein was reaching biological and nuclear capabilities helped propel the Gulf War of 1991, and active international efforts to disarm Iraq thereafter. Fear that states such as Iraq might transfer such weapons to apocalyptic terrorists, a concern given new life after the attacks in New York and Washington, provided the rationale for an American-led invasion of Iraq in the spring of 2003. The campaign, which used a remarkably small force, both on the ground and in the air, quickly took over Iraq and deposed Hussein. However, no immediate evidence of recent, active weapons development programs was found, and, in the process, the United States inherited the complex reconstruction of a broken state, fractured by guerrilla violence and anti-Western terrorism. In 2011, after a long struggle against a shifting insurgency that fought the new Iraqi government and the U.S.-led forces that supported it, U.S. troops left Iraq. A small number of troops returned in recent years to help the Iraqi government deal with a new threat: the so-called Islamic State, known in the Middle East by its Arabic acronym, Daesh (see page 1032).

From the Arab Spring to the Islamic State

In December 2010, an unexpected protest movement, which began in Tunisia, resulted in a wave of protest and popular insurrection in much of the Arab Middle East and North Africa. Just over a year later, powerful authoritarian rulers who had been in power for decades were overthrown, including Zine al-Abidine Ben Ali of Tunisia, Hosni Mubarak of Egypt, and Muammar Gaddafi of Libya. The speed of these momentous changes surprised people living in these countries as much as they astonished foreign observers—many had long assumed that political change, when it came to these regimes, would proceed at a glacial pace. Ben Ali and Mubarak, in particular, were establishment figures in the international world, regularly meeting with European leaders and U.S. presidents who were among their most loyal supporters. Did this mean that a wave of democratic revolution was sweeping through the Middle East?

A period of euphoria followed the departure of these rulers, but a transition to more democratic forms of government in the Middle East has not happened. Similar protest movements in Bahrain were brutally repressed. In Yemen and Syria, protest movements against the government led to long and bitterly violent civil conflicts between armed opposition groups and the state, which continue into the present. Tunisia's regime change was the most successful. Democratic elections brought a moderate Islamist party to power in 2011, and a former human rights activist became president soon after. In 2014, however, a new president with strong ties to the old regime was elected. In Egypt, parliamentary elections in 2012 gave a majority to two Islamic parties, and a member of the Muslim Brotherhood, Mohammed Morsi, was elected president. In 2013, however, Morsi was deposed by the military after a wave of protests against his policies. He was tried and convicted of incitement to violence, but many criticized the trial as being politically motivated. Morsi was succeeded—after an interim figure—by Abdel Fattah el-Sisi, a military leader who did not hesitate to use the army to put down violently pro-Morsi protests against his accession to power.

The **Syrian civil war** may be the most intractable conflict to emerge directly from the protests of the Arab Spring. Syria's current president, Bashar al-Assad, is a member of a family that has controlled the country in a dictatorial fashion since 1971. In the spring of 2011, protests calling for economic and political reform turned into violent confrontation with the army. By that summer, an armed rebellion had organized itself out of disparate groups—including army deserters, local militias, and foreign religious extremists—that had often pursued different goals. European nations and the United States have been reluctant to get involved, but Russia has been actively supporting Assad's government. Civilians have been the major victims of the fighting, with some estimating the number of deaths at higher than 500,000 between 2011 and 2018. People fleeing the violence have created the worst refugee crisis the world has known since the Second World War. In 2016, more than 4.7 million Syrians were living as refugees abroad, mostly in Turkey, Lebanon, Iraq, and Jordan; in Lebanon, 1 out of 5 people was a Syrian refugee in 2016.

Past and Present

The Arab Spring in Historical Perspective

With the collapse of the Berlin Wall in 1989, a relatively recent memory, many people in Europe and North America sought to compare these European events to the recent protests in the Middle East against authoritarian governments. Comparing the Arab Spring with 1848, 1968 (left; the Prague Spring), or 1989 may be instructive, but it is likely that the forms of democracy that protesters in Tunisia, Egypt (right; protesters in Tahrir Square, Cairo), and Turkey are striving to create reflect their own values and do not conform to the political models borrowed from elsewhere.

 Watch related author interview on the Student Site

Another consequence of the Syrian civil war after 2011 and the invasion of Iraq by the United States in 2003 was the creation of a large space between the eastern Mediterranean coast and Iran that was only loosely governed by recognizably functioning states. It was in this space that the so-called **Islamic State** emerged, also known by its Arabic acronym of Daesh. The Islamic State is a Muslim millenarian group that seized and imposed its rule in territory in Syria and Iraq. In 2014, it declared itself to be a new caliphate—the sole legitimate steward of Islam on earth. Its followers adhere to a strict and exclusive interpretation of their religion that professes to return to the beliefs and practices of Islam's earliest practitioners in the seventh century. Unlike other militant terrorist groups such as al Qaeda, the Islamic State insists that it must constitute itself as a state, hold territory, and subject the population to its vision of religion.

The Islamic State embraced violence—including against other Muslims—and its terror tactics and narrow interpretations of Islam repulsed people elsewhere in the world. Many Muslim leaders condemned the movement. Some people were inspired by their militancy, however, and it was estimated that more than 27,000 foreigners traveled to Iraq and Syria to join the Islamic State, including people from Europe, North Africa, Asia, Australia, and North America. At its peak in 2015, the Islamic State controlled 41,000 square miles in Iraq and Syria with a population of 8 million people. They lost most of this territory in 2017, however, and by early 2019, U.S.–backed forces in Syria were close to defeating the Islamic State's last remaining enclave in Syria.

The simultaneous crises created by terrorism and the arrival of hundreds of thousands of refugees fleeing Syria created a dilemma for European societies and a deep political crisis. Multiple terrorist attacks—such as those in Paris in 2015 and in Brussels and Nice in 2016—were conducted by militants who claimed loyalty to the Islamic State. Unlike the 9/11 attacks, however, these terrorist incidents were undertaken by citizens of European states who became radicalized on their own. These attacks nevertheless fed an atmosphere of fear which created opposition to Europe's tradition of offering sanctuary to people who face persecution or violence at home. With mainstream political parties in Europe already seeing declines in support after the financial crisis of 2008 and the Eurozone crisis that began in 2009, the political consequences have been far-reaching, leading to a surge in support for right-wing parties that have embraced a xenophobic nationalism. Europe's commitment to its own tradition of human rights is under extreme pressure.

THE FRENCH HEADSCARF CONTROVERSY. In 2004, more than 10,000 demonstrators, mostly women, marched in Paris to voice their opposition to a proposed law banning the Islamic headscarf in public schools. The sign reads "One Veil = One Vote," demonstrating that wearing the scarf was an expression of their rights as citizens.

TRANSFORMATIONS: HUMAN RIGHTS

Our conception of citizenship, rights, and law has been transformed over time by long-term processes of globalization. High school halls and college walkways are crammed with the tables of international organizations, such as Amnesty International, that promote universal human rights. How has this notion of human rights become so familiar? What older traditions has it built on or replaced?

The contemporary language of human rights is anchored in a tradition of political thought that reaches back at least to the seventeenth century. It took its present form in response to the atrocities of the First World War and, especially, the Second World War. The atrocities and people's shocked responses to them, however, did not create either a new concern for human rights or the institutions dedicated to upholding them. Enforcing *universal* human rights challenges the sovereignty of nation-states, and an individual nation-state's power over its citizens. International courts and human rights organizations thus require and hasten what political thinkers call the globalization of judicial power.

Human rights are part of the Western political tradition, as is their opposition. The belief that rights were embedded in "nature," "natural order," or "natural law" formed a powerful strain of early modern political thought. John Locke understood natural law as the law of reason (Chapter 15); others understood it to be the law of God. However it is conceptualized, it represented a higher authority to which men owed their obedience. Though opponents of absolutism in seventeenth- and eighteenth-century Europe were driven by economic, religious, and social motives, natural rights became one of their rallying cries. The English Bill of Rights of 1689, accepted by William and Mary after the Glorious Revolution, insisted on "the true, ancient, and indubitable rights and liberties of the people of this kingdom." A century later, the American Declaration of Independence and the French Declaration of the Rights of Man more broadly proclaimed the "natural, inalienable and sacred rights of man," which in their eyes belonged to all men—not just the colonists of North America or the citizens of France. But in fact, of course, those bold declarations of rights were not universal. Women, slaves, people of color, and people of different religions were excluded, wholly or partially, and many nineteenth-century political theorists and scientists dedicated countless volumes to the proposition that these groups were *not* created equal. Which human beings might receive the "rights of man," then, was bitterly contested for the better part of the nineteenth and twentieth centuries, and only slowly did a more inclusive conception of human rights displace a narrower historical tradition of the rights of man.

As far as the history of human rights is concerned, perhaps the most important development of the nineteenth

The United Nations on the Protection of Refugees, 1951

The United Nations' Universal Declaration of Human Rights, adopted in 1948, declared that "everyone has the right to seek and to enjoy in other countries asylum from persecution." In order to establish a basis in international law for guaranteeing this right, the United Nations established the 1951 Convention Relating to the Status of Refugees. Originally intended to deal with refugee movements produced by the end of the Second World War, the 1951 Convention was amended in 1967 to provide universal coverage for the protection of refugees throughout the world. The Convention defined the term "refugee" and established the minimum level of protection that all states who were members of the United Nations were obligated to maintain for refugees who sought asylum on their territory.

Article 1: Definition of the Term "Refugee"

For the purposes of the present Convention, the term "refugee" shall apply to any person who:

[. . .] As a result of events occurring before 1 January 1951 and owing to well-founded fear of being persecuted for reasons of race, religion, nationality, membership of a particular social group or political opinion, is outside the country of his nationality and is unable or, owing to such fear, is unwilling to avail himself of the protection of that country; or who, not having a nationality and being outside the country of his former habitual residence as a result of such events, is unable or, owing to such fear, is unwilling to return to it. [. . .]

Article 2: General Obligations

Every refugee has duties to the country in which he finds himself, which require in particular that he conform to its laws and regulations as well as to measures taken for the maintenance of public order.

Article 3: Non-Discrimination

The Contracting States shall apply the provisions of this Convention to refugees without discrimination to race, religion, or country of origin.

Article 4: Religion

The Contracting States shall accord to refugees within their territories treatment at least as favourable as that accorded to their nationals with respect to freedom to practice their religion and freedom as regards the religious education of their children. [. . .]

Article 12: Personal Status

[. . .] Rights previously acquired by a refugee and dependent on personal status, more particularly rights attaching to marriage, shall be respected by a Contracting State, subject to compliance, if this be necessary, with the formalities required by the law of that State, provided that the right in question is one which would have been recognized by the law of that State had he not become a refugee. [. . .]

Article 16: Access to Courts

A refugee shall have free access to the courts of law on the territory of all Contracting States. [. . .]

Article 17: Wage-Earning Employment

The Contracting State shall accord to refugees lawfully staying in their territory the most favourable treatment accorded to nationals of a foreign country in the same circumstances, as regards the right to engage in wage-earning employment.

In any case, restrictive measures imposed on aliens or the employment of aliens for the protection of the national labor market shall not be applied to a refugee who was already exempt from

century was the rise of nationalism and nation-states. Rights, and political movements claiming them, became increasingly inseparable from nationhood. "What is a country . . . but the place in which our demands for individual rights are most secure?" asked the Italian nationalist Giuseppe Mazzini. For nineteenth-century Italians, Germans, Serbs, and Poles, and for twentieth-century Indians, Vietnamese, and Algerians—to name just a few—fighting for national independence was a way to secure the rights of citizens. National sovereignty, once achieved, was tightly woven into the fabric of politics and international relations and would not be easily relinquished.

them [. . .] or who fulfils one of the following conditions:

a. He has completed three years' residence in the country

b. He has a spouse possessing the nationality of the country of residence. A refugee may not invoke the benefits of this provision if he has abandoned his spouse.

c. He has one or more children possessing the nationality of the country of residence. [. . .]

Article 22: Public Education

The Contracting States shall accord to refugees the same treatment as is accorded to nationals with respect to elementary education. [. . .]

Article 23: Public Relief

The Contracting States shall accord to refugees lawfully staying in their territory the same treatment with respect to public relief and assistance as is accorded to their nationals.

Article 26: Freedom of Movement

Each Contracting State shall accord to refugees lawfully in its territory the right to choose their place of residence and to move freely within its territory, subject to any regulations applicable to aliens generally in the same circumstances. [. . .]

Article 31: Refugees Unlawfully in the Country of Refuge

The Contracting States shall not impose penalties, on account of their illegal entry or presence, on refugees who, coming directly from a territory where their life or freedom was threatened in the sense of article 1, enter or are present in their territory without authorization, provided they present themselves without delay to the authorities and show good cause for their illegal entry or presence. [. . .]

Article 32: Expulsion

The Contracting States shall not expel a refugee lawfully in their territory save on grounds of national security or public order.

The expulsion of such a refugee shall be only in pursuance of a decision reached in accordance with due process of law. Except where compelling reasons of national security otherwise require, the refugee shall be allowed to submit evidence to clear himself, and to appeal to and be represented for the purpose before competent authority or a person or persons specially designated by the competetent authority. [. . .]

Article 33: Prohibition of Expulsion or Return ("Refoulement")

No Contracting State shall expel or return ("refouler") a refugee in any manner whatsoever to the frontiers of territories where his life or freedom would be threatened on account of his race, religion, nationality, membership of a particular social group or political opinion.

The benefit of the present provision may not, however, be claimed by a refugee whom there are reasonable grounds for regarding as a danger to the security of the country in which he is, or who, having been convicted by a final judgment of a particularly serious crime, constitutes a danger to the community of that country.

Source: https://www.unhcr.org/3b66c2aa10

Questions:

1. What are the most important rights that the 1951 Convention guarantees for refugees?

2. What forms of discrimination did the authors of the Convention appear to be most concerned about?

3. What language did the authors of the Convention include that allowed contracting states to limit the rights of refugees to claim asylum?

The world wars marked a turning point. The First World War, an unprecedented global conflict, almost inevitably fostered dreams of global peace under the auspices of international organizations. The Paris Peace Conference of 1919 aimed for more than a territorial settlement. With the League of Nations, it tried, tentatively, to establish an organization that would transcend the power of individual nations and uphold the (ill-defined) principles of "civilization." (Despite this commitment, the League bowed to British and American objections to a statement condemning racial discrimination.) The experiment failed, as the fragile League was swept aside by a surge of extreme nationalism

CRISIS IN SYRIA AND THE MIDDLE EAST, 2014–2019. The smaller map shows the extent of Islamic State territory at its height in 2014 and in 2017. In the larger map, shaded in red are the ten most common resettlement countries for Syrians fleeing the intense civil war. Most were internally displaced within Syria or settled in neighboring countries such as Turkey, which has been a member of the Council of Europe since 1949 and has been negotiating to become a full member of the European Union since 2005. These negotiations are now on hold due to a lack of support for Turkey's membership in other European nations. ▪ *How does Turkey's geographical and political position connect Europe to the Middle East?*

and aggression in the 1930s. The shock and revulsion at the atrocities of the war that followed, however, brought forth more decisive efforts. The Second World War's aftermath saw the establishment of the United Nations, an International Court of Justice at the Hague (Netherlands), and the UN's High Commission on Human Rights. Unlike anything attempted after the First World War, the Commission on Human Rights set out to establish the rights of individuals—against the nation-state.

This **Universal Declaration of Human Rights**, published by the High Commission in 1948, became the touchstone of our modern notion of human rights. It was very much a product of its time, with authors including Eleanor Roosevelt and the French jurist René Cassin, who had been

wounded in the First World War (he held his intestines together during a nearly 400-mile train ride to a medical facility), had lost his family in the Holocaust, and had seen his nation collaborate with the Nazis. The High Commission argued that the war and the "barbarous acts which have outraged the conscience of mankind" showed that no state should have absolute power over its citizens. The Universal Declaration prohibited torture, cruel punishment, and slavery. It built on earlier declarations that universalized the right to legal equality, freedom of religion and speech, and the right to participate in government. Finally, it reflected the postwar period's effort to put democracy on a more solid footing, by establishing *social* rights to education, work, "just and favorable remuneration," "standard of living," and social security, among others. A separate convention, also passed in 1948, dealt with the newly defined crime of genocide.

Few nations were willing to ratify the Universal Declaration of Human Rights. For decades after the war, its idealistic principles could not be reconciled with British and French colonialism, American racial segregation, or Soviet dictatorship. For as long as the wars to end colonialism continued, declarations of universal principles rang hollow. (Mahatma Gandhi, when asked to comment on Western civilization, replied that he thought it would be a "good idea.") For as long as the Cold War persisted, human rights seemed only a thinly veiled weapon in the sparring between the superpowers. Thus, decolonization and, later, the end of the Cold War began to enhance the legitimacy and luster of human rights. International institutions set up after the Second World War matured, gaining expertise and stature. Global communications and media dramatically expanded the membership and influence of organizations that, like Amnesty International (founded in 1961), operated outside the economic or political boundaries of the nation-state. Memories of the Second World War, distorted or buried by the Cold War, continue to return, and the force of those memories helped drive the creation of the International Criminal Tribunals for Yugoslavia and Rwanda in 1993. Finally, as one historian points out, at a time when many feel vulnerable to the forces of globalization, human rights offers a way of talking about rights, goods, and protections—environmental, for example—that the nation-state cannot, or can no longer, provide.

It is nevertheless the case that the troubled era that began with the 9/11 attacks on the United States in 2001 has seen many challenges to the notion of universal human rights. Terrorism, no matter the ideology of the perpetrator, is a fundamental violation of every human's right to safety and security. In their zeal to punish terrorists, meanwhile, many nations in the world have tacitly turned away from the emerging international legal structures that attempted to defend the rights of all individuals everywhere. The struggle that the United States and its allies waged against al Qaeda and the Taliban has raised difficult questions about the tactics used, which included torture, indefinite detention without trial, and the use of pilotless drones to kill suspected militant leaders in distant countries. The use of drone technologies makes it easier to avoid U.S. casualties in operations against a dangerous enemy, but many in the United States and abroad have expressed concerns about the government's right to identify, target, and execute individuals, including, in some cases, U.S. citizens, on the basis of criteria that are never subject to independent legal review. Public opinion in the United States remains strongly in favor of such tactics, but in recent years public anger in Afghanistan and Pakistan has focused on cases of mistaken identity and the deaths of family members and bystanders in drone attacks. Even within the U.S. government and military, some have expressed concerns that these methods could be counterproductive.

As the American and European governments pursue their interests abroad, debates about the use of military power in other parts of the world and the form that this power takes have become pressing concerns. These issues raise questions that have been a central part of the liberal democratic political tradition since it emerged in opposition to monarchist forms of government in the seventeenth century. How should a nation determine the balance between individual freedoms and national security? What forms of force or violence can a state legitimately use against its enemies at home or abroad? What kinds of information about its citizenry should a government be allowed to keep? Are the terrorist threats that democratic regimes routinely face today so serious that they justify the suspension of internationally recognized human rights? There are no easy answers to these questions, but the answers that governments and societies in Europe and the United States give will shape how people everywhere will perceive the legitimacy of the democratic political institutions they claim to represent.

EUROPE AND THE UNITED STATES IN THE TWENTY-FIRST CENTURY

The confidence that Europeans felt after 1989 was badly shaken by the time the second decade of the twenty-first century approached its end. European integration, an engine of economic growth and political stability in the decades after the Second World War, reached its apparent limits in the east and become a source of bitter political disagreements even in nations that had long been members of the European Union. In the 2000s, European politicians regularly ran against the idea of an integrated "Europe." This was perhaps most notable in the debates about "Brexit," where the prospect of a British withdrawal from the European Union threatens to reverse the process of integration for the first time in history. At the same time, U.S. President Donald Trump questioned American support for long-standing treaties and alliances that had bound European democracies to the United States for several generations, including NATO, the United States' most significant military alliance. In both Europe and the United States, fears about economic vulnerability and resentment of mainstream political parties fueled the rise of disruptive political movements and a highly polarized atmosphere that revealed deep divisions in the most prosperous nations of the developed world.

Islamic Headscarves in France

Beginning in the late 1980s, France faced a bitter debate about young Muslim women wearing an Islamic headscarf in public schools. After a long history of conflict between secularists and Catholics, public schools traditionally have been defined as a secular space in France. In defense of this principle, many girls were expelled from school for wearing an Islamic headscarf, sometimes referred as a foulard, *or* voile (veil); *and in 2004, headscarves were banned from schools.*

The young women and their defenders framed the issue in terms of fundamental individual freedoms, and claim that the exclusion of the girls' freedom is the result of anti-Muslim racism. In the early 2000s, an American anthropologist interviewed young women in France to hear their stories of living through this controversy. Souad is a young woman in her mid-twenties, born in France to Algerian immigrant parents. She did not have a religious upbringing, and describes her childhood as a "zigzag" between two cultures.

 t middle and high school people sort themselves by group, as Maghrebins [North Africans] or as French. Already in the *sixième* [eleven years old] we felt the difference between those whose parents had money and the others. They put me in the advanced section because I had received a 20 in math the previous year [an unusually high grade]; they thought they perhaps had an intellectual. It traumatized me that they put me with the others [French]. There was one girl who said: "you, you're an Arab, don't get close to me." I was the "Arab of the classroom." It was really a shock. I was the only one, and I found it very hard to make friends; I made one. You find yourself with people; you do not know their culture; you feel very bad, feel still more that you are not well integrated: "we don't want anything to do with you, you are Arab, dirty." They were taught this from their parents, the racism.

So the following year (*cinquième*) I came down to the ordinary level and was with people like me, of Maghrebin origin, and it was easier to get along, without the racism. And I really feel that the school system contributes to that because it is they who make the difference from the beginning, with only French people at one level and all Maghrebins and others in the other already in middle school, so it's normal that later on the racism will grow in people's minds. So the schools have a responsibility.

* * *

Once I got to high school, friends told me about my religion. I discovered

Some of this bitterness can be traced to the global financial crisis of 2007–2008, which began with a classic bubble in the United States housing market. Rising home prices encouraged buyers to "flip" homes for quick profit. This speculation was abetted by banks who issued ever riskier loans to homebuyers. Since the local banks that issued individual mortgages resold these loans almost immediately, they had little incentive to worry about nonpayment. In turn, the larger banks that bought these mortgages re-packaged them as complicated financial products known as mortgage-backed securities, which they sold to large institutional investors, including pension funds and other banks. During the run-up to the crash, investment banks flooded the market with trillions of dollars of risky mortgage-backed securities—often aided by the ratings agencies who were supposed to be independent arbiters of risk.

The crisis precipitated when housing prices fell. Homeowners could no longer cover their mortgages, and investors found that mortgage-backed securities had become "toxic assets," impossible to sell and of little value. Confidence in the banking sector plummeted. Banks stopped lending, businesses failed, and trillions of dollars of consumer savings were wiped out. Millions of people lost their jobs. Unprecedented government bailouts of banks with taxpayer money were required to stabilize the banking system. The severity of this crisis led many in Europe and North America to rethink the central assumptions of late twentieth-century economic policy, especially the belief that markets were by definition self-regulating. Popular resentment against the financial industry inspired many nations to consider widespread reform and government regulation of banks.

an aspect I did not know, I studied, I read books, I found that enriching.

It was clear to me that the headscarf was an obligation, and I felt the need to please our Creator, it was in that spirit that I wanted to wear it, but the social conditions at high school presented problems. I had to prepare to be rejected by others. I studied for my bac [the all-important school finishing exam] and practiced my religion but the voile was another thing. I always did my prayer, that's something very important for Muslims, and I am proud of myself there. But there was always that desire to go higher in faith, to go closer to the Creator, to please him. So I put on a small hair band so that people would get used to it, because before I wore mini skirts, long hair, but never drank alcohol. In effect I was a bit of a tomboy and hung out with guys, who considered me their little sister and made sure I did not veer toward drugs and night clubs.

One day I decided to become a woman, not a boy, and I changed my behavior, because I had been very aggressive in my gestures and words. I realized that it is hard to live in society as a woman, because there is a lot of sexism, in French society as well. So, to return to the zigzag, my behavior as a woman, the fact that God asked me to do certain things, so I decided to go in that direction while adapting myself to the society where I live, and I succeed at this, for, when I am at work I wear the scarf not like I have it now but on top, swirled around like the Africans [makes gesture around her head]. That seems to work. I began wearing it as an intern and it worked. This shows that there are still people who are very tolerant. They knew me before and after the foulard, and their attitude did not change. They saw that my work did not change, even got better, and one said, if anyone criticizes you let me know and I will take care of it. I found that touching.

Source: John R. Bowen, *Why the French Don't Like Headscarves: Islam, the State, and Public Space* (Princeton: 2014), pp. 75–77.

Questions for Analysis

1. How does Souad describe the way her primary school contributed to a sense of otherness, or separation between people whose families came from North Africa and those whose culture was "French"?

2. How does Souad describe the thinking that led her to wear a headscarf? Was it simply a religious decision? Does she cite other factors?

3. What experiences did Souad have as a result of wearing the headscarf to work?

Contemporary debates about political integration in Europe or the benefits of free-market capitalism can be seen as a continuation of debates within the traditions of political and economic liberalism that go back to the eighteenth century. In the classic formulation of Enlightenment liberals such as Adam Smith, political and economic liberties were best defended in a nation with a small and limited government. By the end of the nineteenth century, this assumption was challenged by an alternative model, that of social democracy, which argued that limited liberal governments could not do enough to remedy the social and economic inequalities produced within modern industrial societies. After the devastation of the Second World War, western European governments were much more willing to use the power of the state to assist the unemployed or the aged, to support families, and to provide subsidies for education, public transportation, and national programs for health care. This consensus emerged in part from a belief that the depression of the 1930s was not an anomaly but a sign that a market economy needed guardrails to prevent the emergence of destabilizing and antidemocratic political movements such as fascism or Bolshevism. In the United States, enthusiasm for such government programs was not shared by all. President Lyndon Johnson's administration used the power of the federal government to challenge racial segregation and address broad problems such as urban poverty or environmental pollution in the 1960s, but a conservative backlash in the 1980s and 1990s led to an end to welfare programs, the repeal of environmental regulations, and the dismantling of government regulations on business.

By the end of the first decade of the twenty-first century, both Europe and the United States faced serious challenges. The U.S. model of economic development favored financial innovation, fewer taxes, and less state regulation. It generated extraordinary wealth for the financial industry and related sectors but also widened the gap between the rich and the poor to levels not seen since the end of the nineteenth century. It also contributed to economic instability by reinforcing trends of boom and bust. The financial crisis of 2008 proved that this model was not immune to the laws of the business cycle, and in the end the banks needed the state to act as the lender of last resort, using taxpayer money to shore up the system.

The success of the European welfare state in the decades after the Second World War, on the other hand, depended on a combination of factors that are impossible to reproduce today: Marshall Plan investment from the United States, the benefits of the first stages of European integration, and cooperation among representatives of labor, employers, and the state. Trade unions agreed to wage moderation in exchange for social protections from the state, especially old-age pensions. Business leaders agreed to pay high taxes in exchange for labor peace. Governments in turn convinced their electorates to pay higher taxes in exchange for universal health care, unemployment support, and subsidized education.

This system worked well as long as the economy kept growing. When the economy flattened out beginning in the 1970s, however, businesses reduced their investments, unemployment went up, workers expressed discontent with their wage restraints, and European states had less revenue for social protection. In the 1980s and the 1990s, European governments resorted to deficit spending to protect their welfare programs. This fix worked well enough as long as the banks lending the governments money were confident that they would be repaid. Faith in this system led to the creation of the euro as a single currency area in 1999, and notes and coins denominated in euros began to circulate in 2002. At the moment of its creation, there were 11 member nations; in 2019, the eurozone included 19 of the 28 members of the European Union.

But monetary union created a new set of unanticipated challenges. The establishment of a single currency led many European banks to underestimate the risks of lending money to developing economies on the periphery of the eurozone, especially Portugal, Ireland, Greece, and Spain. Easy credit fueled a construction boom in these countries, but when the risks became apparent, the money dried up, and the bubble collapsed. Many banks in these regions were so indebted as a result that their governments were forced to bail them out. Thus, the bank debt transformed into sovereign debt, reducing the credibility of governments, and hindering their ability to raise new funds for essential services, such as pensions or health care.

The crisis revealed a fatal flaw in the plan for monetary union. Normally, when a country runs into trouble with its economy it can devalue its currency, making its goods cheaper for foreign buyers and hence stimulating the economy. But this

THE BREXIT DEBATE. On the right, anti-Brexit marchers express their disapproval of the British government's use of charter flights to deport people to Nigeria, Ghana, Jamaica, Pakistan, and Afghanistan in 2017. On the left, a pro-Brexit protester in London calls on then prime minister Theresa May to begin the negotiations that would conclude with a British withdrawal from the European Union (EU).

option was unavailable for member nations of the eurozone that found themselves under stress after 2009, because they shared their currency with many other nations. Instead, the financially stressed governments were humiliatingly dependent on decision makers in other countries to provide the financing they needed to stay afloat. This situation in the eurozone has raised the question of reversing the process of European integration: the Greek government debated leaving the eurozone during the crisis.

The Eurozone crisis exposed deeper fissures that had opened up in Europe since the end of the Cold War. From the outset, European integration was premised on the assumption that a new equilibrium could be found between national sovereignty and supra-national bodies at the European level. At the same time, supporters of integration believed that Europe could commit itself to capitalist growth while also remaining true to the promises of the postwar welfare state. In both instances, the balance was hard to find. Anti-European political parties blamed "Europe" for a wide range of policies, including environmental regulations, migration policy, and restrictions on state spending. The bitter aftermath of the Eurozone debacle and the financial crisis of 2008 gave new life to nationalist parties in all corners of Europe. Conservative nationalist parties in Poland and Hungary came to power by reasserting arguments about national sovereignty and the dangers of economic globalization and migration. Even established western democracies such as France are not immune to this development: the extreme right-wing National Front has enjoyed unprecedented electoral success in recent elections. Nationalist parties in Europe regularly invoke xenophobic—and at times openly antisemitic or anti-Muslim—language, leading some to fear that the hatreds of the first half of the twentieth century have been reawakened.

No issue has focused more attention on the possibility of breaking up the European Union than "Brexit." In 2016, Prime Minister David Cameron of the Conservative Party in Britain called for a referendum on British membership in the European Union. The initial debate about **Brexit** (Britain + Exit) was largely an argument about immigration from the European continent, with supporters of Brexit demanding a strong assertion of national identity, an end to immigration, and a rejection of membership in the European Union. Britain was never part of the Eurozone, but EU membership gave it access to Europe's common market, and this connection was an important part of British economic growth, fueling the rise of London as a global financial center. In exchange for access to Europe's markets, however, the European Union asked Britain to accept the principle of freedom of movement within EU countries. To the surprise of many, a slight majority favored leaving

EUROPEAN UNION member, 2019
European Union Eurozone
Scheduled to leave EU in 2019 (Brexit)
Candidate for EU membership

EUROPEAN UNION AND EUROZONE, 2019. The Brexit controversy has raised for the first time the possibility of a member nation leaving the EU. Meanwhile, anti-European nationalist parties succeeded in the European parliamentary elections of May 2019. ▪ *What do these trends say about the future of the European integration?*

Europe, under the belief that there would be little cost to a reassertion of British independence.

At the present writing, the outcome of the Brexit debate is still unknown. The controversy cut across the political boundaries that divided right from left in Britain, with a significant number of voters in both the Labor Party and the Conservative Party supporting Brexit, while a nearly equal number of people on both sides energetically expressing a wish to remain in Europe. In the meantime, the potential costs of the rupture have become clearer: the need to replace European regulations in industry and consumer protections with British laws, forecasts of food and medicine shortages if European imports decline, the prospect of renewed tensions in Northern Ireland if a hard border replaces the frontier with the Irish Republic, and the possibility that Scotland, which strongly favored remaining in Europe, will once again push for independence from Britain if Brexit is implemented. No matter what happens, the Brexit debate has revealed the limits of earlier hopes for European integration, and made the establishment of a "United States of Europe" much less likely.

CONCLUSION

Globalization, defined loosely as the process by which the economies, societies, and cultures of different parts of the world have become increasingly interconnected, has been hailed as a solution to old problems, even as it has been criticized as a source of new ones. Although some thought that the end of the Cold War in 1989 meant that economic liberalism—that is, a global free-market capitalist system unfettered by government regulations—had triumphed for good in the world, continued political instability in many parts of the globe and the global economic crisis of 2008 have called into question such optimistic interpretations of world events. In the economic realm, nation-states have looked for ways to reassert their control over the flow of currencies and goods, and protect their populations against decisions made elsewhere by financial speculators and investors. Meanwhile, the danger of radical forms of terrorism, both foreign and domestic, has caused even strong democratic governments in the West to create new and pervasive surveillance bureaucracies, demonstrating that global threats can have real and seemingly permanent local effects on definitions of citizenship, the permeability of borders, and extensions of state power.

In such uncertain times, it is difficult to remain consistent or to determine national priorities. Is the threat of terrorism greater than the threat of loss of liberty stemming from extensions in government power? Is it fair of the International Monetary Fund to ask

After You Read This Chapter

 Go to **INQUIZITIVE** to see what you've learned—and learn what you've missed— with personalized feedback along the way.

REVIEWING THE OBJECTIVES

- Globalization in the second half of the twentieth century was not new. What does globalization mean? What was similar or different about the most recent phase of globalization compared with others in the past?

- The burden of the colonial past continued to weigh heavily on many former colonies after the 1960s. What accounts for the success of some former colonies in the global economy and the continued social and political challenges facing others?

- Since the end of the Second World War, conflicts and events in the Middle East have taken on a global significance far beyond the region's borders. What crucial conflicts have occupied the attention of other nations? What events have proved to be crucial turning points in the emergence of the Middle East as a region that drives developments elsewhere?

developing nations to adhere to austere cuts to their social welfare spending, when wealthy private investment banks receive billion-dollar bailouts after making bad bets in the financial markets because they are "too big to fail"? The complexity of the world's interconnections makes it difficult to have definitive answers to such questions. As we have seen throughout these chapters, interconnections between global regions and the mobility of peoples have been a part of human history since the beginning. The anxieties of the present are bound up in a sense of accelerating political and technological change at a moment when the scale of looming global problems—climate change is only the most obvious—are just now coming into focus. The loss of familiar moorings makes fundamental questions about human behavior and political community difficult to answer, and the study of history offers no quick solutions. The untidy and contradictory evidence that historians find in the archives rarely yields unblemished heroes, unvarnished villains, or easy lessons that can be applied to the present. Good history reveals the complex processes and dynamics of change over time. It helps us understand the many layers of the past that have formed our present world. It shows again and again that the past does not preordain what happens next. Globalization, in this sense, is not the final destination of history. It is merely the constantly renewed reality of human existence, and the context for future struggles about the goals of political association, the meanings of liberty or equality, and the possibility of shared values.

PEOPLE, IDEAS, AND EVENTS IN CONTEXT

- What were the policy goals of **NEOLIBERALISM** after the 1970s, as exemplified by the activities of institutions such as the **INTERNATIONAL MONETARY FUND** and the World Bank?

- How do the **HIV-AIDS EPIDEMIC** of the 1980s and the **ZIKA VIRUS** illustrate the new realities of public health in a globalized world?

- What was the significance of **NELSON MANDELA**'s election as president of South Africa in 1994?

- How was the **1973 OIL EMBARGO** related to the **ARAB-ISRAELI CONFLICT**? What were its effects on the global economy?

- What did radical critics dislike about secular forms of **ARAB NATIONALISM** such as that espoused by **GAMAL ABDEL NASSER** in Egypt?

- What led the United States and Britain to support the regime of **REZA PAHLAVI** in Iran? What events brought **AYATOLLAH RUHOLLAH KHOMEINI** to power in 1979?

- What circumstances link the **SOVIET INVASION OF AFGHANISTAN** in 1979 with the origins of **AL QAEDA**? How is the rise of the so-called **ISLAMIC STATE** linked to the **SYRIAN CIVIL WAR** or the **AMERICAN INVASION OF IRAQ** in 2003?

- What made it difficult for European and North American governments to sign the United Nation's **UNIVERSAL DECLARATION OF HUMAN RIGHTS** in 1948?

- What was at issue in the **BREXIT** debate?

THINKING ABOUT CONNECTIONS

- Many of the global linkages between Europe and the United States on the one hand, and the independent nations of Asia, Africa, and Latin America on the other, were first forged during earlier periods of imperial expansion. How is this history still felt in the present?

- Global networks of transport, trade, and communication have long been significant vectors for cultural change by bringing different peoples into contact and conversation with one another. How have recent developments in technology changed the nature of this global conversation?

- What events have occurred since 1948, when the Universal Declaration of Human Rights was signed, that indicate that at least some nations might agree to international treaties guaranteeing human rights?

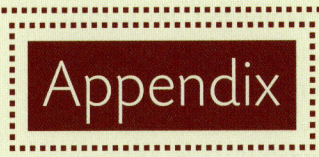

Rulers of Principal States

THE CAROLINGIAN DYNASTY

Pepin of Heristal, mayor of the palace, 687–714
Charles Martel, mayor of the palace, 715–741
Pepin III, mayor of the palace, 741–751; king, 751–768
Charlemagne, king, 768–814; emperor, 800–814
Louis the Pious, emperor, 814–840

West Francia

Charles the Bald, king, 840–877; emperor, 875–877
Louis II, king, 877–879
Louis III, king, 879–882
Carloman, king, 879–884

Middle Kingdoms

Lothair, emperor, 840–855
Louis (Italy), emperor, 855–875
Charles (Provence), king, 855–863
Lothair II (Lorraine), king, 855–869

East Francia

Ludwig, king, 840–876
Carloman, king, 876–880
Ludwig, king, 876–882
Charles the Fat, emperor, 876–887

HOLY ROMAN EMPERORS

Saxon Dynasty

Otto I, 962–973
Otto II, 973–983
Otto III, 983–1002
Henry II, 1002–1024

Franconian Dynasty

Conrad II, 1024–1039
Henry III, 1039–1056
Henry IV, 1056–1106
Henry V, 1106–1125
Lothair II (Saxony), 1125–1137

Hohenstaufen Dynasty

Conrad III, 1138–1152
Frederick I (Barbarossa), 1152–1190
Henry VI, 1190–1197
Philip of Swabia, 1198–1208 ⎫
Otto IV (Welf), 1198–1215 ⎭ Rivals

Frederick II, 1220–1250
Conrad IV, 1250–1254

Interregnum, 1254–1273

Emperors from Various Dynasties

Rudolf I (Habsburg), 1273–1291
Adolf (Nassau), 1292–1298
Albert I (Habsburg), 1298–1308
Henry VII (Luxemburg), 1308–1313
Ludwig IV (Wittelsbach), 1314–1347
Charles IV (Luxemburg), 1347–1378
Wenceslas (Luxemburg), 1378–1400
Rupert (Wittelsbach), 1400–1410
Sigismund (Luxemburg), 1410–1437

Habsburg Dynasty

Albert II, 1438–1439
Frederick III, 1440–1493

Maximilian I, 1493–1519
Charles V, 1519–1556
Ferdinand I, 1556–1564
Maximilian II, 1564–1576
Rudolf II, 1576–1612
Matthias, 1612–1619
Ferdinand II, 1619–1637
Ferdinand III, 1637–1657

Leopold I, 1658–1705
Joseph I, 1705–1711
Charles VI, 1711–1740
Charles VII (not a Habsburg), 1742–1745
Francis I, 1745–1765
Joseph II, 1765–1790
Leopold II, 1790–1792
Francis II, 1792–1806

RULERS OF FRANCE FROM HUGH CAPET

Capetian Dynasty

Hugh Capet, 987–996
Robert II, 996–1031
Henry I, 1031–1060
Philip I, 1060–1108
Louis VI, 1108–1137
Louis VII, 1137–1180
Philip II (Augustus), 1180–1223
Louis VIII, 1223–1226
Louis IX (Saint Louis), 1226–1270
Philip III, 1270–1285
Philip IV, 1285–1314
Louis X, 1314–1316
Philip V, 1316–1322
Charles IV, 1322–1328

Valois Dynasty

Philip VI, 1328–1350
John, 1350–1364
Charles V, 1364–1380
Charles VI, 1380–1422
Charles VII, 1422–1461
Louis XI, 1461–1483
Charles VIII, 1483–1498
Louis XII, 1498–1515
Francis I, 1515–1547

Henry II, 1547–1559
Francis II, 1559–1560
Charles IX, 1560–1574
Henry III, 1574–1589

Bourbon Dynasty

Henry IV, 1589–1610
Louis XIII, 1610–1643
Louis XIV, 1643–1715
Louis XV, 1715–1774
Louis XVI, 1774–1792

After 1792

First Republic, 1792–1799
Napoleon Bonaparte, first consul, 1799–1804
Napoleon I, emperor, 1804–1814
Louis XVIII (Bourbon dynasty), 1814–1824
Charles X (Bourbon dynasty), 1824–1830
Louis Philippe, 1830–1848
Second Republic, 1848–1852
Napoleon III, emperor, 1852–1870
Third Republic, 1870–1940
Pétain regime, 1940–1944
Provisional government, 1944–1946
Fourth Republic, 1946–1958
Fifth Republic, 1958–

RULERS OF ENGLAND

Anglo-Saxon Dynasty

Alfred the Great, 871–899
Edward the Elder, 899–924
Ethelstan, 924–939
Edmund I, 939–946
Edred, 946–955
Edwy, 955–959
Edgar, 959–975

Edward the Martyr, 975–978
Ethelred the Unready, 978–1016
Canute, 1016–1035 (king of Denmark)
Harold I, 1035–1040
Hardicanute, 1040–1042
Edward the Confessor,
   1042–1066
Harold II, 1066

House of Normandy

William I (the Conqueror), 1066–1087
William II, 1087–1100
Henry I, 1100–1135
Stephen, 1135–1154

House of Plantagenet

Henry II, 1154–1189
Richard I, 1189–1199
John, 1199–1216
Henry III, 1216–1272
Edward I, 1272–1307
Edward II, 1307–1327
Edward III, 1327–1377
Richard II, 1377–1399

House of Lancaster

Henry IV, 1399–1413
Henry V, 1413–1422
Henry VI, 1422–1461

House of York

Edward IV, 1461–1483
Edward V, 1483
Richard III, 1483–1485

House of Tudor

Henry VII, 1485–1509
Henry VIII, 1509–1547
Edward VI, 1547–1553
Mary I, 1553–1558
Elizabeth I, 1558–1603

House of Stuart

James I, 1603–1625
Charles I, 1625–1649

Commonwealth and Protectorate, 1649–1659

Oliver Cromwell, Lord protector, 1653–1658

House of Stuart Restored

Charles II, 1660–1685
James II, 1685–1688
William III and Mary II, 1689–1694
William III alone, 1694–1702
Anne, 1702–1714

House of Hanover

George I, 1714–1727
George II, 1727–1760
George III, 1760–1820
George IV, 1820–1830
William IV, 1830–1837
Victoria, 1837–1901

House of Saxe-Coburg-Gotha

Edward VII, 1901–1910
George V, 1910–1917

House of Windsor

George V, 1917–1936
Edward VIII, 1936
George VI, 1936–1952
Elizabeth II, 1952–

RULERS OF AUSTRIA AND AUSTRIA-HUNGARY

*Maximilian I (archduke), 1493–1519
*Charles V, 1519–1556
*Ferdinand I, 1556–1564
*Maximilian II, 1564–1576
*Rudolf II, 1576–1612
*Matthias, 1612–1619
*Ferdinand II, 1619–1637
*Ferdinand III, 1637–1657
*Leopold I, 1658–1705
*Joseph I, 1705–1711
*Charles VI, 1711–1740
Maria Theresa, 1740–1780

*Joseph II, 1780–1790
*Leopold II, 1790–1792
*Francis II, 1792–1835 (emperor of Austria as Francis I after 1804)
Ferdinand I, 1835–1848
Francis Joseph, 1848–1916 (after 1867 emperor of Austria and king of Hungary)
Charles I, 1916–1918 (emperor of Austria and king of Hungary)
Republic of Austria, 1918–1938 (dictatorship after 1934)
Republic restored, under Allied occupation, 1945–1956
Free Republic, 1956–

*Also bore title of Holy Roman emperor

RULERS OF PRUSSIA AND GERMANY

*Frederick I, 1701–1713
*Frederick William I, 1713–1740
*Frederick II (the Great), 1740–1786
*Frederick William II, 1786–1797
*Frederick William III, 1797–1840
*Frederick William IV, 1840–1861
*William I, 1861–1888 (German emperor after 1871)
Frederick III, 1888

*kings of Prussia

*William II, 1888–1918
Weimar Republic, 1918–1933
Third Reich (Nazi dictatorship), 1933–1945
Allied occupation, 1945–1952
Division into Federal Republic of Germany in west
    and German Democratic Republic in east,
    1949–1991
Federal Republic of Germany (united), 1991–

RULERS OF RUSSIA

Ivan III, 1462–1505
Vasily III, 1505–1533
Ivan IV, 1533–1584
Theodore I, 1584–1598
Boris Godunov, 1598–1605
Theodore II, 1605
Vasily IV, 1606–1610
Michael, 1613–1645
Alexius, 1645–1676
Theodore III, 1676–1682
Ivan V and Peter I, 1682–1689
Peter I (the Great), 1682–1725
Catherine I, 1725–1727
Peter II, 1727–1730

Anna, 1730–1740
Ivan VI, 1740–1741
Elizabeth, 1741–1762
Peter III, 1762
Catherine II (the Great), 1762–1796
Paul, 1796–1801
Alexander I, 1801–1825
Nicholas I, 1825–1855
Alexander II, 1855–1881
Alexander III, 1881–1894
Nicholas II, 1894–1917
Russian Revolution and Civil War, 1917–1922
Union of Soviet Socialist Republics, 1922–1991
Russian Federation, 1991–

RULERS OF UNIFIED SPAIN

Ferdinand { and Isabella, 1479–1504
            and Philip I, 1504–1506
            and Charles I, 1506–1516
Charles I (Holy Roman Emperor Charles V), 1516–1556
Philip II, 1556–1598
Philip III, 1598–1621
Philip IV, 1621–1665
Charles II, 1665–1700
Philip V, 1700–1746
Ferdinand VI, 1746–1759
Charles III, 1759–1788
Charles IV, 1788–1808
Ferdinand VII, 1808

Joseph Bonaparte, 1808–1813
Ferdinand VII (restored), 1814–1833
Isabella II, 1833–1868
Republic, 1868–1870
Amadeo, 1870–1873
Republic, 1873–1874
Alfonso XII, 1874–1885
Alfonso XIII, 1886–1931
Republic, 1931–1939
Authoritarian nationalist dictatorship under Francisco
    Franco, 1939–1975
Juan Carlos I, 1975–2014
Felipe VI, 2014–

RULERS OF ITALY

Victor Emmanuel II, 1861–1878
Humbert I, 1878–1900
Victor Emmanuel III, 1900–1946

Fascist dictatorship under Benito Mussolini, 1922–1943
   (maintained in northern Italy until 1945)
Humbert II, May 9–June 13, 1946
Republic, 1946–

PROMINENT AND RECENT POPES

Silvester I, 314–335
Leo I, 440–461
Gelasius I, 492–496
Gregory I, 590–604
Nicholas I, 858–867
Silvester II, 999–1003
Leo IX, 1049–1054
Nicholas II, 1058–1061
Gregory VII, 1073–1085
Urban II, 1088–1099
Paschal II, 1099–1118
Alexander III, 1159–1181
Innocent III, 1198–1216
Gregory IX, 1227–1241
Innocent IV, 1243–1254
Boniface VIII, 1294–1303
John XXII, 1316–1334
Nicholas V, 1447–1455
Pius II, 1458–1464
Alexander VI, 1492–1503

Julius II, 1503–1513
Leo X, 1513–1521
Paul III, 1534–1549
Paul IV, 1555–1559
Sixtus V, 1585–1590
Urban VIII, 1623–1644
Gregory XVI, 1831–1846
Pius IX, 1846–1878
Leo XIII, 1878–1903
Pius X, 1903–1914
Benedict XV, 1914–1922
Pius XI, 1922–1939
Pius XII, 1939–1958
John XXIII, 1958–1963
Paul VI, 1963–1978
John Paul I, 1978
John Paul II, 1978–2005
Benedict XVI, 2005–2013
Francis, 2013–

Further Readings

CHAPTER 1

Baines, J., and J. Málek. *Atlas of Ancient Egypt.* Rev. ed. New York, 2000. A reliable, well-illustrated survey, with excellent maps.

Bottéro, Jean. *Everyday Life in Ancient Mesopotamia.* Trans. Antonia Nevill. Baltimore, 2001. A wide-ranging, interdisciplinary account.

Bottéro, Jean. *Religion in Ancient Mesopotamia.* Chicago, 2001. An accessible, engaging survey.

Broodbank, Cyprian. *The Making of the Middle Sea: A History of the Mediterranean from Its Beginning to the Emergence of the Classical World.* Oxford, 2013. A landmark study of the Mediterranean world, beautifully written.

Foster, Benjamin R., and Karen Polinger Foster. *Civilizations of Ancient Iraq.* Princeton, NJ, 2011. A critically acclaimed survey that charts the history of this region from the earliest Sumerian civilization to the Arab conquests of the seventh century C.E.

Geller, Markham J. *Ancient Babylonian Medicine: Theory and Practice.* Malden, MA, 2010. Makes use of previously unstudied cuneiform sources to tell a new story about the relationship between medicine and magic.

George, Andrew, trans. *The Epic of Gilgamesh: A New Translation. The Babylonian Epic Poem and Other Texts in Akkadian and Sumerian.* New York and London, 1999. A reliable translation that carefully distinguishes the chronological "layers" of this famous text; also includes many related texts.

Hodder, Ian. *The Leopard's Tale: Revealing the Mysteries of Çatalhöyük.* London and New York, 2006. The most up-to-date account of this fascinating archaeological site, written for general readers by the director of the excavation.

Leick, Gwendolyn. *The Babylonians: An Introduction.* London and New York, 2002. A wide-ranging survey of Babylonian civilization across the centuries.

McDowell, A. G. *Village Life in Ancient Egypt: Laundry Lists and Love Songs.* Oxford, 1999. A fascinating collection of translated texts recovered from an Egyptian peasant village, dating from 1539 to 1075 B.C.E.

McGregor, Neil. *A History of the World in 100 Objects.* London, 2011. Based on an acclaimed BBC Radio program, this book features a range of artifacts from the collections of the British Museum, embeds them in their historical contexts, and explores the ways that they still hold meaning today.

Mithen, Steven, with Sue Mithen. *Thirst: Water and Power in the Ancient World.* Cambridge, MA, 2013. A new comparative history of water management and consumption throughout the ancient world.

Redford, Donald B., ed. *The Oxford Encyclopedia of Ancient Egypt.* 3 vols. New York, 2001. An indispensable reference work, intended for both specialists and beginners.

Richardson, Seth. "Early Mesopotamia: The Presumptive State." *Past and Present* 215 (2012): 3–49. A powerful summary of the new methodologies and research questions that are challenging the traditional narrative of state building and urban life in Mesopotamia.

Robins, Gay. *The Art of Ancient Egypt.* London, 1997. An excellent survey.

Rutherford, Adam. *A Brief History of Everyone Who Ever Lived: The Stories in Our Genes.* New York, 2017. A compelling and entertaining study of Homo sapiens and our shared DNA.

Scott, James C. *Against the Grain: A Deep History of the Earliest States.* New Haven, 2017. A daring account of the ways that all settled societies depend on grain agriculture, unfree labor, and the control of women's productivity.

Shafer, Byron E., ed. *Religion in Ancient Egypt: Gods, Myths, and Personal Practice.* London, 1991. A scholarly examination of Egyptian belief and ritual, with contributions from leading authorities.

Shaw, Ian, ed. *The Oxford History of Ancient Egypt.* Oxford, 2000. An outstanding collaborative survey of Egyptian history from the Stone Age to c. 300 C.E., with excellent bibliographical essays.

Shryock, Andrew, and Daniel Lord Smail. Berkeley, 2012. *Deep History: The Architecture of Past and Present.* A fascinating fusion of historical, anthropological, and scientific research on what it means to be human.

Smail, Daniel Lord. *On Deep History and the Brain.* Berkeley, 2008. A pioneering introduction to the historical uses of neuroscience and evolutionary biology.

Snell, Daniel C., ed. *A Companion to the Ancient Near East.* Oxford, 2005. A topical survey of recent scholarly work, particularly strong on society, economy, and culture.

Wengrow, David. *The Archaeology of Early Egypt: Social Transformations in North-East Africa, 10,000 to 2650 B.C.* Cambridge, 2006. An authoritative account of archaeological evidence and its interpretation.

CHAPTER 2

Aubet, Maria Eugenia. *Phoenicia and the West: Politics, Colonies, and Trade.* Trans. Mary Turton. Cambridge, 1993. An intelligent and thought-provoking examination of Phoenician civilization and its influence.

Blenkinsopp, Joseph. *David Remembered: Kingship and National Identity in Ancient Israel.* Cambridge, 2013. An accessible history of King David, his dynasty, and his historical legacy, authored by a noted biblical scholar.

Boardman, John. *Persia and the West*. London, 2000. A great book by a distinguished scholar, with a particular focus on art and architecture as projections of Persian imperial ideologies.

Boyce, Mary. *Textual Sources for the Study of Zoroastrianism*. Totowa, NJ, 1984. An invaluable collection of documents.

Bryce, Trevor. *The Kingdom of the Hittites*. Oxford, 1998; and *Life and Society in the Hittite World*. Oxford, 2002. An extraordinary synthesis, now the standard account of Hittite political, military, and daily life.

Collins, John J., and Daniel C. Harlow, eds. *The Eerdmans Dictionary of Early Judaism*. Cambridge, 2010. A comprehensive tool for students and researchers.

Cooney, Kara. *The Woman Who Would Be King: Hatshepsut's Rise to Power in Ancient Egypt*. New York, 2014. A blend of historical scholarship and informed, imaginative reconstruction.

Curtis, John. *Ancient Persia*. Cambridge, MA, 1990. Concise, solid, reliable.

Dever, William. *Who Were the Early Israelites and Where Did They Come From?* Grand Rapids, MI, 2003. A balanced, fair-minded account with excellent bibliographical guidance to recent work.

Dickinson, O. T. P. K. *The Aegean Bronze Age*. Cambridge, 1994. An excellent summary of archaeological evidence and scholarly argument concerning Minoan, Mycenaean, and other cultures of the Bronze Age Aegean basin.

Dothan, Trude, and Moshe Dothan. *Peoples of the Sea: The Search for the Philistines*. New York, 1992. The essential starting point for understanding Philistine culture and its links to the Aegean basin.

Drews, Robert. *The End of the Bronze Age: Changes in Warfare and the Catastrophe ca. 1200 B.C.* Princeton, NJ, 1993. A stimulating analysis and survey, with excellent bibliographies.

Finkelstein, Israel, and Nadav Na'aman, eds. *From Nomadism to Monarchy: Archaeological and Historical Aspects of Early Israel*. Jerusalem, 1994. Scholarly articles on the Hebrews' transformation from pastoralists to a sedentary society focused on the worship of Yahweh.

Fitton, J. Lesley. *Minoans: Peoples of the Past*. British Museum Publications. London, 2002. A careful, reliable debunking of myths about the Minoans, written for nonspecialists.

Hamblin, William J. *Warfare in the Ancient Near East to 1600 BC: Holy Warriors at the Dawn of History*. Routledge, 2006. A wide-ranging study of military technologies, practices, and motives.

Kamm, Antony. *The Israelites: An Introduction*. New York, 1999. A short, accessible history of the land and people of Israel up to 135 C.E., aimed at students and general readers.

Kemp, Barry. *The City of Akhenaten and Nefertiti: Amarna and Its People*. London, 2012. A cutting-edge study of this ancient site, based on decades of archaeological research.

Kuhrt, Amélie. *The Ancient Near East, c. 3000–330 B.C.* 2 vols. London and New York, 1995. An outstanding survey, written for students, that includes Egypt and Israel as well as Mesopotamia, Babylonia, Assyria, and Persia.

Marinatos, Nannos. *Minoan Kingship and the Solar Goddess: A Near Eastern Koine*. Champaign, IL, 2010. A rich new interpretation of Minoan culture and its wider connections and influence within the world of the late Bronze Age.

Metzger, Bruce M., and Michael D. Coogan, eds. *The Oxford Companion to the Bible*. New York, 1993. An outstanding reference work, with contributions by leading authorities.

Niditch, Susan. *Ancient Israelite Religion*. New York, 1997. A short introduction designed for students, emphasizing the diversity of Hebrew religious practices.

Prezioso, Donald, and Louise A. Hitchcock. *Aegean Art and Architecture*. Oxford, 2000. Archaic Greek artistic forms in their broader geographic and cultural context, from the fourth millennium to 1000 B.C.E.

Redford, Donald B. *Egypt, Canaan, and Israel in Ancient Times*. Princeton, NJ, 1992. An overview of the interactions between these peoples from about 1200 B.C.E. to the beginning of the Common Era.

Renfrew, Colin. *Archaeology and Language: The Puzzle of Indo-European Origins*. Cambridge, 1987. A masterful but controversial work by one of the most creative archaeologists of the twentieth century.

Sandars, Nancy K. *The Sea Peoples: Warriors of the Ancient Mediterranean*. Rev. ed. London, 1985. An introductory account for students and scholars.

Tubb, Jonathan N., and Rupert L. Chapman. *Archaeology and the Bible*. London, 1990. A good starting point for students that clearly illustrates the difficulties in linking archaeological evidence to biblical accounts of early Hebrew history and society.

Wood, Michael. *In Search of the Trojan War*. New York, 1985. Aimed at a general audience, this carefully researched and engagingly written book is an excellent introduction to the late–Bronze Age context of the Trojan War.

CHAPTER 3

Penguin Classics and the Loeb Classical Library both offer reliable translations of Greek literary, philosophical, and historical texts.

Beard, Mary. *The Parthenon*. Cambridge, MA, 2003. Traces the successive stages of this monument's construction, deconstruction, reconstruction, and restoration.

Brunschwig, Jacques, and Geoffrey E. R. Lloyd. *Greek Thought: A Guide to Classical Knowledge*. Trans. Catherine Porter. Cambridge, MA, 2000. An outstanding work of reference.

Buckley, Terry, ed. *Aspects of Greek History, 750–323 B.C.: A Source-Based Approach*. London, 1999. A good collection of source materials.

Cartledge, Paul A. *The Spartans: An Epic History*. New York, 2003. A lively and authoritative history of Sparta from its origins to the Roman conquest.

Fantham, Elaine, Helene Foley, Natalie Kampen, Sarah B. Pomeroy, and H. A. Shapiro. *Women in the Classical World: Image and Text*. Oxford, 1994. Wide-ranging analysis drawing on both visual and written sources, covering both the Greek and the Roman periods.

Garlan, Yvon. *Slavery in Ancient Greece*. Ithaca, NY, 1988. Now the standard account.

Havelock, Eric A. *The Literate Revolution in Greece and Its Cultural Consequences*. Princeton, 1982. A now-classic account of the wide-ranging effects of writing on Greek society.

Jones, Nicholas F. *Ancient Greece: State and Society*. Upper Saddle River, NJ, 1997. A concise survey from the Minoans up to the end of the Classical period.

Krentz, Peter. *The Battle of Marathon*. New Haven, 2011. A fresh analysis of this landmark battle, paying special attention to the conditions in which hoplite warriors fought.

Lee, Mireille M. *Body, Dress, and Identity in Ancient Greece*. Cambridge, 2015. A major interdisciplinary contribution to our understanding of personal adornment, class, and gender identity.

Lefkowitz, Mary, and Maureen Fant. *Women's Life in Greece and Rome: A Source Book in Translation*. 3rd ed. Baltimore, 2005. A remarkably wide-ranging collection, topically arranged, invaluable to students.

Malkin, Irad. *A Small Greek World: Networks in the Ancient Mediterranean*. Oxford, 2011. A study showing how a Panhellenic identity developed during and because of widespread Greek settlement throughout the ancient world.

Manning, J. G. *The Open Sea: The Economic Life of the Ancient Mediterranean World from the Iron Age to the Rise of Rome*. Princeton, 2018. An ambitious study of interconnected cultures, commercial exchanges, and climate.

Nevett, Lisa C. *Domestic Space in Classical Antiquity*. Cambridge, 2010. Reassesses what we can know about the architecture of households in antiquity through a fresh assessment of archaeological evidence and material culture.

Pomeroy, Sarah. *Goddesses, Whores, Wives, and Slaves: Women in Classical Antiquity*. New York, 1995. The first historical survey of antiquity to place women at the center of the narrative, and still unrivaled in scope.

Price, Simon. *Religions of the Ancient Greeks*. Cambridge, 1999. Concise and authoritative, this survey extends from the Archaic Period up to the fifth century C.E.

Pritchard, David M., ed. *War, Democracy and Culture in Classical Athens*. Cambridge, 2010. A collection of scholarly essays on the close relationship between Athenian politics, culture, and military technology.

Robinson, Eric W. *Democracy beyond Athens: Popular Government in the Greek Classical Age*. Cambridge, 2011. An important contribution to the history of Greek political institutions in poleis other than Athens.

Seaford, Richard. *Money and the Greek Mind: Homer, Philosophy, Tragedy*. Cambridge, 2004. A provocative study of portable wealth and its far-reaching effects.

Simpson, St. John and Svetlana Pankiva, eds. *Scythians: Warriors of Ancient Siberia*. London, 2018. The catalogue of a major exhibition at the British Museum devoted to the nomadic people who fascinated and terrified the ancient Greeks.

Strassler, Robert B., ed. *The Landmark Thucydides*. New York, 1996. Reprints the classic Richard Crawley translation with maps, commentary, notes, and appendices by leading scholars.

Thomas, Rosalind. *Oral Tradition and Written Record in Classical Athens*. Cambridge, 1989. A fascinating look at how oral epic, lyric, and drama were transmitted over time.

CHAPTER 4

Penguin Classics and the Loeb Classical Library both offer reliable translations of scores of literary and historical texts from this period. Particularly important are historical works by Arrian (*Anabasis of Alexander*), Plutarch (*Life of Alexander*), and Polybius (*The Histories*).

Austin, M. M. *The Hellenistic World from Alexander to the Roman Conquest: A Selection of Ancient Sources in Translation*. Cambridge, 1981. A good collection of primary documents.

Aylward, William, ed. *Excavations at Zeugma*. 3 vols. Oxford, 2013. Available free online: http://zeugma.packhum.org. The results of a massive scholarly effort (undertaken between 1987 and 1988) to excavate and analyze the remains of Samosata and the palace of Antiochus I, the best-preserved royal palace in the Hellenistic world, before the site was submerged beneath a Turkish dam in 1989.

Borza, Eugene N. *In the Shadow of Olympus: The Emergence of Macedon*. Princeton, NJ, 1990. The standard account of the rise of Macedon up to the accession of Philip II.

Bosworth, A. B. *Conquest and Empire: The Reign of Alexander the Great*. Cambridge, 1988. A political and military analysis of Alexander's career that strips away the romance, maintaining a clear vision of the ruthlessness and human cost of his conquests.

———. *The Legacy of Alexander: Politics, Warfare, and Propaganda under the Successors*. Oxford, 2002. The most recent survey of the half century following Alexander's death and of the people who created the Hellenistic kingdoms of Egypt, Persia, and Macedon.

Burstein, Stanley M., ed. and trans. *The Hellenistic Age from the Battle of Ipsos to the Death of Kleopatra VII*. Cambridge, 1985. An excellent collection, with sources not found elsewhere.

Cartledge, Paul. *Agesilaus and the Crisis of Sparta*. Baltimore, 1987. A thorough but readable analysis of the social and political challenges besetting Sparta in the fourth century B.C.E.

———. *Alexander the Great: The Hunt for a New Past*. Woodstock, NY, 2004. A compelling account of Alexander's life, times, and influences.

Green, Peter. *Alexander of Macedon, 356–323 B.C.* Berkeley, 1991. Revised edition of the author's earlier biography; entertainingly written, rich in detail and insight.

———. *The Hellenistic Age: A Short History*. New York, 2007. An authoritative synthesis that carries the history of Greek influence into the fourth century C.E.

Hansen, Mogens H. *The Athenian Democracy in the Age of Demosthenes*. Oxford, 1991. An examination of the political institutions of Athens in the fourth century B.C.E.

Holt, Frank. L. *Into the Land of Bones: Alexander the Great in Afghanistan*. Repr. ed. Berkeley, 2012. A vivid, charged narrative that places the beginning of a current war in the distant past.

Johnstone, S. "A New History of Libraries and Books in the Hellenistic Period." *Classical Antiquity* 33 (2014): 347–93. A revolutionary and accessible review of the ancient evidence for the first public libraries.

Lloyd, Geoffrey, and Nathan Sivin. *The Way and the Word: Science and Medicine in Early China and Greece*. New Haven, 2002. An extraordinary comparative study.

McGing, Brian. *Polybius' Histories*. Oxford, 2010. A critical dissection of this influential ancient historian's techniques and historical philosophy.

Nicholas, G. L. *The Genius of Alexander the Great*. Chapel Hill, NC, 1998. A clear, authoritative, admiring account, distilling a lifetime of research on the subject.

Ober, Josiah. *Mass and Elite in Democratic Athens: Rhetoric, Ideology, and the Power of the People.* Princeton, NJ, 1989. An excellent study of the ideology of democracy in Athens that borrows from the insights of modern social science.

Pollitt, Jerome J. *Art in the Hellenistic Age.* New York, 1986. The standard account, blending cultural history with art history.

Sherwin-White, Susan, and Amélie Kuhrt. *From Samarkhand to Sardis: A New Approach to the Seleucid Empire.* London, 1993. A stimulating examination of the relationship between rulers and ruled in the vast expanses of the Seleucid Empire.

Shipley, Graham. *The Greek World after Alexander, 323–30 B.C.* New York and London, 2000. A study of the social, intellectual, and artistic changes in the Hellenistic era.

Thomas, Carol G. *Alexander the Great in His World.* Oxford and Malden, MA, 2007. A study of the contexts—familial, political, and social—that shaped Alexander's career.

Tripolitis, Antonia. *Religions of the Hellenistic-Roman Age.* Grand Rapids, MI, 2002. Survey of the variety of religious experience, ritual, and belief in the centuries before the emergence of Christianity.

Tritle, Lawrence A., ed. *The Greek World in the Fourth Century: From the Fall of the Athenian Empire to the Successors of Alexander.* New York, 1997. A wide-ranging collection of scholarly essays.

CHAPTER 5

Translations of Roman authors are available in both the Penguin Classics series and in the Loeb Classical Library.

Alston, Richard. *Rome's Revolution: Death of the Republic and Birth of the Empire.* Oxford, 2015. A clear and compelling narrative of the events surrounding the rise and assassination of Julius Caesar, and reign of Augustus.

Arnason, Johann P., and Kurt A. Raaflaub, eds. *The Roman Empire in Context: Historical and Comparative Perspectives.* Malden, MA, 2011. One of the few books to place the formation of the Roman Empire in a comparative, global perspective.

Barker, Graeme, and Tom Rasmussen. *The Etruscans.* Oxford and Malden, MA, 1998. A fine survey, from the Blackwell *Peoples of Europe* series.

Beard, Mary. *SPQR: A History of Ancient Rome.* New York, 2015. A masterful narrative and critical history of the shift from republic to Principate.

_____. *Pompeii: The Life of a Roman Town.* New York, 2010. A fascinating, cutting-edge study of daily life and of the archaeological work that uncovered it.

Cornell, T. J. *The Beginnings of Rome: Italy and Rome from the Bronze Age to the Punic Wars (c. 1000–264 B.C.).* London, 1995. An ambitious survey of the archaeological and historical evidence for early Rome.

Crawford, Michael. *The Roman Republic,* 2nd ed. Cambridge, MA, 1993. A lively, fast-paced survey of republican Rome. An excellent place to start.

Fantham, Elaine, Helene Peet Foley, Natalie Boymel Kampen, Sarah B. Pomeroy, and H. Alan Shapiro. *Women in the Classical World.* Oxford, 1994. An expert survey of both Greece and Rome.

Harris, William V. *War and Imperialism in Republican Rome, 327–70 B.C.* Oxford, 1979. A challenging study arguing that Rome's need for military conquest and expansion was deeply embedded in the fabric of Roman life.

Hartnett, Jeremy. *The Roman Street: Urban Life and Society in Pompeii, Herculaneum, and Rome.* Cambridge, 2017. An illuminating study of public life and culture.

Hayes, Ian. *Blood of the Provinces: The Roman Auxilia and the Making of Provincial Society from Augustus to Severus.* Oxford, 2013. A new history of Roman warfare and its role in expanding imperial power, showing how archaeological evidence challenges written sources.

Krebs, Christopher. *A Most Dangerous Book: Tacitus's "Germania" from the Roman Empire to the Third Reich.* A history of this ancient ethnography's transmission and reception, and especially the political uses to which it was put in Nazi Germany.

Lancel, Serge. *Carthage: A History.* Trans. Antonia Nevill. Oxford, 1995. An account of Rome's great rival for control of the Mediterranean world.

Millar, Fergus G. B. *The Emperor in the Roman World, 31 B.C.–A.D. 337.* London, 1977. A classic work that showed (among much else) the importance of emperor worship to the religious outlook of the Roman Empire.

_____. *The Crowd in Rome in the Late Republic.* Ann Arbor, MI, 1999. A revisionist account that emphasizes the reality of Roman democracy in the late republic, against those who would see the period's politics as entirely under the control of aristocratic families.

Watkin, David. *The Roman Forum.* London, 2009. A history of the successive buildings and archaeological excavations of this central Roman space.

Wells, Colin. *The Roman Empire,* 2nd ed. Cambridge, MA, 1992. An easily readable survey from the reign of Augustus to the mid–third century C.E., particularly useful for its treatment of the relationship between the Roman central government and its Italian provinces.

Wiseman, T. P. *Remembering the Roman People.* Oxford, 2009. A collection of studies devoted to popular politics in the late republic.

Woolf, Greg. *Becoming Roman: The Origins of Provincial Civilization in Gaul.* Cambridge, 1998. An exemplary study of how provincial elites made themselves "Roman."

_____. *Rome: An Empire's Story.* Oxford, 2012. A masterful account of Rome's reconfiguration of the ancient world and its enduring impact; critically acclaimed by scholars and general readers.

_____. *Tales of the Barbarians: Ethnography and Empire in the Roman West.* Malden, MA, 2011. Applies modern ethnographic methodologies to a dissection of how Romans applied their own ethnographic theories to contemporary "others."

CHAPTER 6

Augustine. *The City of God.* Trans. Henry Bettenson. Baltimore, 1972.

_____. *Confessions.* Trans. Henry M. Chadwick. Oxford, 1991.

_____. *On Christian Doctrine.* Trans. D. W. Robertson Jr. New York, 1958.

Boethius. *The Consolation of Philosophy.* Trans. R. Green. Indianapolis, 1962.

Bowersock, G. W., Peter Brown, and Oleg Grabar. *Late Antiquity: A Guide to the Postclassical World.* Cambridge, MA, 1999. An authoritative compilation. The first half is devoted to essays on the cultural features of the period; the second half is organized as an encyclopedia.

Brown, Peter. *Augustine of Hippo*. Berkeley, 1967. A great biography by the great scholar of late antiquity.

———. *The Body and Society: Men, Women and Sexual Renunciation in Early Christianity*. New York, 1988. A revealing study of the fundamental transformations wrought by Christianity in the late antique world.

———. *The Rise of Western Christendom: Triumph and Diversity, 200–1000*, 2nd ed. Oxford, 2002. An evocative picture of Christianity's spread eastward and northward from the Mediterranean world.

———. *The World of Late Antiquity*. New York, 1971. Still the best short survey of the period, with excellent illustrations.

———. *Through the Eye of a Needle: Wealth, the Fall of Rome, and the Making of Christianity in the West, 350–550 A.D.* Princeton, NJ, 2012. The most recent of this historian's magisterial dissections of late antiquity, focused on the relationship between religion, culture, power, and wealth (or its lack).

Cameron, Averil. *The Later Roman Empire, A.D. 284–430*. London, 1993. Now the standard account of its period, with an emphasis on imperial politics.

———. *The Mediterranean World in Late Antiquity, A.D. 395–600*. London, 1993. Masterful, with succinct bibliographical essays.

Cassiodorus. *An Introduction to Divine and Human Readings*. Trans. L. W. Jones. New York, 1946.

Chadwick, Henry M. *Boethius*. Oxford, 1981. An intellectual biography of this important thinker.

Clark, Gillian. *Christianity and Roman Society*. Cambridge, 2004. A short, stimulating survey that places early Christianity firmly in its Roman social context.

———. *Women in Late Antiquity*. Oxford, 1993. A clear, compact account of an important subject.

Ehrman, Bart D. *The New Testament: A Historical Introduction to the Early Christian Writings,* 4th ed. Oxford, 2008. The standard textbook by a leading authority.

Ehrman, Bart D., and Zlatko Pleše, eds. *The Aprocryphal Gospels: Texts and Translations* Oxford, 2011. The first scholarly edition and translation of all the apocryphal gospels, including Latin, Greek, and Coptic texts.

Eusebius. *The History of the Church*. Trans. G. A. Williamson. Baltimore, 1965. A contemporary account of Constantine's reign, written by one of his courtier-bishops.

———. *Eusebius' Life of Constantine*. Trans. Averil Cameron and Stuart Hall. Oxford, 1999. An admiring biography that reflects Constantine's own vision of his religious authority.

Grig, Lucy, and Gavin Kelly, eds. *Two Romes: Rome and Constantinople in Antiquity*. Oxford, 2015. A set of comparative essays by noted scholars.

Hopkins, Keith. *A World Full of Gods: The Strange Triumph of Christianity*. New York, 1999. An imaginative study of religious pluralism in the Roman world and the context in which Christianity emerged.

Kulikowski, Michael. *Imperial Triumph: The Roman World from Hadrian to Constantine*. Profile Books, 2018. A sweeping and engaging history of Rome's power at its height.

———. *Rome's Gothic Wars: From the Third Century to Alaric*. Cambridge, 2007. An authoritative and critical account.

Lane Fox, Robin. *Augustine: Conversions to Confessions*. New York, 2015. A beautifully written reconstruction of Augustine's early life in its historical context.

Lawrence, Clifford Hugh. *Medieval Monasticism*. 3rd ed. London, 2000. Concise, perceptive survey of monasticism from its beginnings to the end of the Middle Ages.

Pagels, Elaine. *The Gnostic Gospels*. New York, 1979. A pathbreaking study of the noncanonical gospels and the history of their exclusion from the Bible.

Potter, David. *The Roman Empire at Bay, A.D. 180–395*. London and New York, 2004. The most up-to-date account of the empire's reorganization and transformation in this era.

Rebillard, Éric. *Christians and Their Many Identities in Late Antiquity, North Africa, 200–450 C.E.* Ithaca, NY, 2012. In this book, as in his earlier works, the author argues that there was no special importance attached to being a "Christian" in late antiquity, and that religious identities are better understood as fluid and hybrid.

Sanders, E. P. *The Historical Figure of Jesus*. London and New York, 1993. A fine study of Jesus in his first-century Jewish context.

Shanks, Hershel, ed. *Christianity and Rabbinic Judaism: A Parallel History of Their Origins and Early Development*. Washington, DC, 1992. Accessible chapters written by top authorities, describing both Jewish and Christian developments from the first to the sixth centuries C.E.

Sherwin-White, A. N. *Roman Society and Roman Law in the New Testament*. Oxford, 1963. A fascinating reading of the New Testament in its historical context.

Traina, Giusto. *428 A.D.: An Ordinary Year at the End of the Roman Empire*. Princeton, NJ, 2011. An enlightening glimpse into the world of late antiquity, from the vantage point of a single "average" year.

Whittaker, C. R. *Frontiers of the Roman Empire: A Social and Economic Study*. Baltimore, 1994. A convincing picture of the frontiers of the Roman Empire as zones of intensive cultural interaction.

Williams, Stephen. *Diocletian and the Roman Recovery*. New York, 1997. Thorough and authoritative.

CHAPTER 7

Translations of Arabic sources are now available in the *Library of Arabic Literature* series from New York University Press.

Arnold, Jonathan J. *Theoderic and the Roman Imperial Restoration*. Cambridge, 2014. An ambitious new reading of Theodoric's reign, arguing for the thoroughly Roman identity and ambitions of this Gothic ruler.

Bede. *A History of the English Church and People*. Trans. Leo Sherley-Price. Baltimore, 1955. The fundamental source for early Anglo-Saxon history.

Campbell, James, ed. *The Anglo-Saxons*. Oxford, 1982. An authoritative and splendidly illustrated volume.

Conant, Jonathan. *Staying Roman: Conquest and Identity in Africa and the Mediterranean, 439–700*. Cambridge, 2012. An exploration of what it meant to be "Roman" and the sources of identity in this tumultuous period.

Einhard and Notker the Stammerer. *Two Lives of Charlemagne*. Trans. Lewis Thorpe. Baltimore, 1969. Lively and entertaining works of contemporary biography.

Geanakoplos, Deno John, ed. *Byzantium: Church, Society and Civilization Seen through Contemporary Eyes.* Chicago, 1984. An outstanding source book.

Gregory, Timothy E. *A History of Byzantium.* Malden, MA, and Oxford, 2005. An accessible textbook and an excellent place to start.

Herrin, Judith. *Byzantium: The Surprising Life of a Medieval Empire.* Princeton, NJ, 2009. An accessible and comprehensive history of the eastern Roman Empire.

————. *The Formation of Christendom.* Princeton, NJ, 1987. A synthetic history of the Christian civilizations of Byzantium and western Europe from 500 to 800, written by a prominent historian.

Hodges, Richard, and David Whitehouse. *Mohammed, Charlemagne and the Origins of Europe.* London, 1983. A critical analysis of the "Pirenne thesis," reexamining the relationship between the Mediterranean world and northern Europe.

Hourani, Albert. *A History of the Arab Peoples.* New York, 1992. A sympathetic and clear survey written for nonspecialists.

Hoyland, Robert G. *In God's Path: The Arab Conquests and the Creation of the Islamic Empire.* Oxford, 2014. A highly acclaimed new study of Islam's rapid expansion as a product of Arab imperial ambitions.

Kennedy, Hugh. *The Prophet and the Age of the Caliphates.* 2nd ed. Harlow, UK, 2004. A lucid introduction to the political history of the Islamic world from the sixth through the eleventh centuries.

Krautheimer, Richard. *Early Christian and Byzantine Architecture.* 4th ed. New York, 1986. A classic work by one of the greatest Byzantine art historians of the twentieth century.

Little, Lester K., ed., *Plague and the End of Antiquity: The Pandemic of 541–750.* Cambridge, 2006. The first full-length scholarly history of the first global pandemic.

Mango, Cyril, ed. *The Oxford History of Byzantium.* Oxford and New York, 2002. Full of sharp judgments and attractively illustrated.

McCormick, Michael. *The Origins of the European Economy: Communications and Commerce A.D. 300–900.* Cambridge, 2002. An astonishing reinterpretation of the evidence for the myriad contacts between Christian Europe and Islam.

McKitterick, Rosamond. *Charlemagne: The Formation of a European Identity.* Cambridge, 2008. A history of Charlemagne's career and its lasting impact by an eminent scholar of the Carolingian world.

————, ed. *The Uses of Literacy in Early Medieval Europe.* New York, 1990. A superb collection of essays.

McNamara, Jo Ann, and John E. Halborg, eds. *Sainted Women of the Dark Ages.* Durham, NC, 1992. Translated saints' lives from Merovingian and Carolingian Europe.

Murray, A. C., ed. *From Roman to Merovingian Gaul: A Reader.* Toronto, 2000. An excellent collection of sources.

Pelikan, Jaroslav. *The Christian Tradition.* Vol. 2, *The Spirit of Eastern Christendom.* Chicago, 1974. An outstanding synthetic treatment of the doctrines of Byzantine Christianity.

Procopius. *The Secret History.* Trans. G. A. Williamson. Baltimore, 1966. An "unauthorized" account of Justinian's reign, written by the emperor's offical historian.

Reuter, Timothy. *Germany in the Early Middle Ages, 800–1056.* New York, 1991. The best survey in English.

Sardar, Ziauddin. *Reading the Quran.* Hachette, 2011. A readable guide to Muslim scripture and the many controversies over its interpretation.

Sijpesteijn, Petra M. *Shaping a Muslim State: The World of a Mid-Eighth-Century Egyptian Official.* Oxford, 2013. Based on a cache of papyrus letters sent to a Muslim administrator, this book reveals how an Arab/Muslim state was established in a former province of the eastern Roman Empire.

Treadgold, Warren. *A History of the Byzantine State and Society.* Stanford, CA, 1997. A massive, encyclopedic narrative of the political, economic, and military history of Byzantium from 284 until 1461.

Wallace-Hadrill, John Michael. *Early Germanic Kingship in England and on the Continent.* Oxford, 1971. A classic analysis of changing ideas about kingship in early medieval Europe, emphasizing the links between Anglo-Saxon and Carolingian cultures.

————. *The Frankish Church.* Oxford, 1983. A masterful account that links the Merovingian and Carolingian churches.

Watt, W. Montgomery. *Islamic Philosophy and Theology.* 2nd ed. Edinburgh, 1985. The standard English account.

Wemple, Suzanne Fonay. *Women in Frankish Society: Marriage and the Cloister, 500–900.* Philadelphia, 1981. An influential account of changing attitudes toward marriage among the early Franks.

Whittow, Mark. *The Making of Orthodox Byzantium, 600–1025.* London, 1996. Emphasizes the centrality of orthodoxy in shaping Byzantine history. Particularly good on Byzantine relations with the peoples outside the empire.

Wickham, Chris. *Framing the Middle Ages: Europe and the Mediterranean, 400–800.* Oxford, 2007. An eye-opening history that spans the transitional periods of late antiquity and the early Middle Ages, paying careful attention to regional differences.

Wood, Ian. *The Merovingian Kingdoms, 450–751.* New York, 1994. A detailed study, but difficult for beginners.

CHAPTER 8

Amt, Emily, ed. *Women's Lives in Medieval Europe: A Sourcebook.* New York, 1993. An excellent collection of primary texts.

The Song of Roland. Trans. Robert Harrison. New York, 1970. A lively translation.

Arnold, Benjamin. *Princes and Territories in Medieval Germany.* Cambridge and New York, 1991. The best such survey in English.

Berend, Nora, Przemysław Urbańczyk, and Przemysław Wisewski. *Central Europe in the High Middle Ages: Bohemia, Hungary and Poland, c. 900–c. 1300.* Cambridge, 2013. An accessible introduction to the medieval history of this region.

Boswell, John E. *Christianity, Social Tolerance, and Homosexuality: Gay People in Western Europe from the Beginning of the Christian Era to the Fourteenth Century.* Chicago, 1980. A pioneering account, hotly debated but highly respected.

Burman, Thomas E. *Reading the Qur'ān in Latin Christendom, 1140–1560.* Philadelphia, 2007. A fascinating account of the Qur'an's reception in medieval Europe.

Dunbabin, Jean. *France in the Making, 843–1180.* 2nd ed. Oxford and New York, 2000. An authoritative survey of the disparate territories that came to make up the medieval French kingdom.

Dyer, Christopher. *Making a Living in the Middle Ages: The People of Britain 850–1520.* New Haven, 2002. A splendid new synthesis that combines social, economic, and archaeological evidence.

Fossier, Robert. *The Ax and the Oath: Ordinary Life in the Middle Ages.* Princeton, NJ, 2010. A quirky, personal, and often insightful look at the daily lives and worldview of this era by a leading French historian.

Frankopan, Peter. *The First Crusade: The Call from the East.* Cambridge, MA, 2012. Analyzes the causes and catalysts of the crusading movement.

Hartnell, Jack. *Medieval Bodies: Life, Death, and Art in the Middle Ages.* New York, 2019. A rich and beautifully written cultural history.

Hicks, Carola. *The Bayeux Tapestry: The Life Story of a Masterpiece.* London, 2006. An art historian's engrossing account of the making, reception, and interpretation of this amazing artifact.

Horden, Peregrine, and Nicholas Purcell. *The Corrupting Sea: A Study of Mediterranean History.* Malden, MA, 2000. An extraordinary attempt to encompass the history of the Mediterranean world over a span of three millennia.

Leyser, Henrietta. *Medieval Women: A Social History of Women in England, 440–1500.* New York, 1995. Although limited to one country, this is the best of the recent surveys treating medieval women.

McLaughlin, Megan. *Sex, Gender, and Episcopal Authority in an Age of Reform, 1000–1122.* Cambridge, 2010. A new interpretation of gendered discourse and politics during the Investiture Controversy.

Martin, Janet. *Medieval Russia, 980–1584.* 2nd ed. Cambridge, 2007. A concise history with a wide reach.

Miller, Maureen C. *Power and the Holy in the Age of the Investiture Conflict: A Brief History with Documents.* Boston, 2005. A stimulating approach to the eleventh-century conflicts over temporal and spiritual power, with many newly translated sources.

Moore, Robert I. *The First European Revolution, c. 970–1215.* Oxford and Cambridge, MA, 2000. A remarkable description of the ways in which European society was fundamentally reshaped during the eleventh and twelfth centuries.

Raffensperger, Christian. *Reimagining Europe: Kievan Rus' in the Medieval World.* Cambridge, MA, 2012. An exciting new study of early Rus' and its neighbors.

Reynolds, Susan. *Fiefs and Vassals: The Medieval Evidence Reinterpreted.* Oxford and New York, 1994. A detailed revisionist history of "feudalism."

Rubenstein, Jay. *Armies of Heaven: The First Crusade and the Quest for Apocalypse.* New York, 2011. An accessible narrative of the First Crusade, written for a general audience and arguing for a new interpretation of the crusaders' motives.

Sawyer, Peter, ed. *The Oxford Illustrated History of the Vikings.* Oxford, 1997. The best one-volume account, lavishly illustrated.

Sheingorn, Pamela, trans. *The Book of Sainte Foy.* Philadelphia, 1995.

Stow, Kenneth R. *Alienated Minority: The Jews of Medieval Latin Europe.* Cambridge, MA, 1992. An excellent survey.

Throop, Susanna A. *The Crusades: An Epitome.* Kismet Press, 2018. This extremely brief but hugely insightful introduction is also available in an Open Access format.

Winroth, Anders. *The Conversion of Scandinavia: Vikings, Merchants, and Missionaries in the Remaking of Northern Europe.* New Haven, 2012. Argues that the peoples of Scandinavia were active participants in the cultural, economic, and political processes that accompanied their conversion to Christianity.

CHAPTER 9

Abelard and Heloise. *The Letters and Other Writings.* Trans. William Levitan. Indianapolis, 2007. A beautiful and accurate translation of the correspondence and related documents, with a full introduction and notes.

Abulafia, David. *Frederick II: A Medieval Emperor.* London and New York, 1988. A reliable biography that strips away much of the legend that has hitherto surrounded this monarch.

Baldwin, John W. *The Government of Philip Augustus.* Berkeley and Los Angeles, 1986. A landmark scholarly account.

Barber, Malcolm. *The Crusader States.* New Haven, 2012. A new and comprehensive history by an esteemed historian.

Bartlett, Robert. *The Making of Europe: Conquest, Colonization and Cultural Change, 950–1350.* Princeton, NJ, 1993. A wide-ranging examination of the economic, social, and religious expansion of Europe, full of stimulating insights.

Bisson, Thomas N. *The Crisis of the Twelfth Century: Power, Lordship, and the Origins of European Government.* Princeton, NJ, 2009. A new interpretation of the evidence.

Bynum, Caroline Walker. *Holy Feast and Holy Fast: The Religious Significance of Food to Medieval Women.* Berkeley and Los Angeles, 1988. One of the most influential and important works of scholarship published in the late twentieth century.

Camille, Michael. *Gothic Art: Glorious Visions.* New York, 1996. A succinct and beautifully illustrated introduction to the art of the twelfth through fifteenth centuries in Europe.

Catlos, Brian. *Kingdoms of Faith: A New History of Islamic Spain.* Basic Books, 2018. A masterful and nuanced study of the forces shaping and threatening the Muslim states of Iberia.

Chrétien de Troyes. *Arthurian Romances.* Trans. W. W. Kibler. New York, 1991.

Clanchy, Michael T. *Abelard: A Medieval Life.* Oxford and Cambridge, MA, 1997. A great biography.

————. *From Memory to Written Record: England, 1066–1307.* Oxford, 1992. A fascinating and hugely influential account of a revolutionary shift toward documentation.

Fassler, Margot. *Gothic Song: Victorine Sequences and Augustinian Reform in Twelfth-Century Paris.* Cambridge, 1993. The emergence of new musical genres and their cultural context.

Gillingham, John. *The Angevin Empire.* 2nd ed. Oxford and New York, 2001. The best treatment by far of its subject, brief but full of ideas.

Gottfried von Strassburg. *Tristan.* Trans. A. T. Hatto. Baltimore, 1960.

Hallam, Elizabeth, and Judith Everard. *Capetian France, 987–1328.* 2nd ed. New York, 2001. A clear and well-organized account.

Jones, P. J. *The Italian City-State: From Commune to Signoria.* Oxford and New York, 1997. A fundamental reinterpretation of the evidence.

Jordan, William C. *Europe in the High Middle Ages.* Vol. 3 of the Penguin History of Europe. New York and London, 2003. An outstanding survey.

Kaeuper, Richard W. *Chivalry and Violence in Medieval Europe.* Oxford and New York, 1999. A darker view of chivalry than Keen's.

Keen, Maurice. *Chivalry.* New Haven, 1984. A comprehensive treatment of chivalry from its origins to the sixteenth century.

Lawrence, Clifford Hugh. *The Friars: The Impact of the Early Mendicant Movement on Western Society.* London and New York, 1994. The best short introduction to the early history of the Franciscans and the Dominicans.

Leclerq, Jean. *The Love of Learning and the Desire for God.* 3rd ed. New York, 1982. A beautiful interpretation of twelfth-century monastic culture and the influence of Bernard of Clairvaux.

Little, Lester. *Religious Poverty and Profit Economy in Medieval Europe.* Ithaca, NY, 1978. A fascinating study of the relationship between religious practice and economic reality.

Lopez, Robert S., and Irving W. Raymond, eds. *Medieval Trade in the Mediterranean World.* New York, 1990. A useful collection of source material.

Madden, Thomas F. *The New Concise History of the Crusades.* New York, 2005. An acclaimed and accessible survey for students.

Marie de France. *Lais.* Trans. Glyn S. Burgess and Keith Busby. Harmondsworth, UK, 1999. A compelling and entertaining prose translation.

Moore, R. I. *The War on Heresy.* Cambridge, MA, 2012. A courageous and searching revisionist history, based on decades of research and reflection. Moore argues for a radical reassessment of what "heresy" consisted of, and why those branded as "heretics" were persecuted during the Middle Ages.

Morris, Colin. *The Papal Monarchy: The Western Church from 1050 to 1250.* Oxford, 1989. An excellent scholarly survey, part of the Oxford History of the Christian Church series.

Newman, Barbara, ed. *Voice of the Living Light: Hildegard of Bingen and Her World.* Berkeley and Los Angeles, 1998. An introduction to Hildegard's life and work.

Nirenberg, David. *Neighboring Faiths: Christianity, Islam and Judaism in the Middle Ages and Today.* Chicago, 2014. A thoughtful and powerful study of interfaith relations and the challenges of coexistence, then and now.

Otto, Bishop of Freising. *The Deeds of Frederick Barbarossa.* Trans. C. C. Mierow. New York, 1953. A contemporary chronicle interesting enough to read from start to finish.

Smalley, Beryl. *The Study of the Bible in the Middle Ages.* 3rd ed. Oxford, 1983. The standard work, gracefully written and illuminating.

Strayer, Joseph R. *On the Medieval Origins of the Modern State.* With new forewords by Charles Tilly and William Chester Jordan. Princeton, NJ, 2005. This new edition of Strayer's series of lectures places them in their scholarly context.

Swanson, R. N. *The Twelfth-Century Renaissance.* Manchester, UK, 1999. An updated survey of the intellectual developments of the twelfth century.

Symes, Carol. *A Common Stage: Theater and Public Life in Medieval Arras.* Ithaca, NY, 2007. A study of a vibrant cultural hub.

Wakefield, Walter, and Austin P. Evans, eds. and trans. *Heresies of the High Middle Ages.* New York, 1969, 1991. A comprehensive collection of sources.

Wei, Ian. *Intellectual Culture in Medieval Paris: Theologians and the University, c. 1100–1330.* Cambridge, 2012. A fresh and compelling new history of medieval intellectual culture that ranges beyond Paris and pays attention to the contributions of medieval women.

Wolfram von Eschenbach. *Parzival.* Trans. H. M. Mustard and C. E. Passage. New York, 1961.

CHAPTER 10

Abu-Lughod, Janet L. *Before European Hegemony: The World System A.D. 1250–1350.* Oxford and New York, 1989. A now classic study of the trading links among Europe, the Middle East, India, and China, with special attention to the role of the Mongol Empire; extensive bibliography.

Allsen, Thomas T. *Culture and Conquest in Mongol Eurasia.* Cambridge and New York, 2001. A synthesis of the author's earlier studies, emphasizing Mongol involvement in the cultural and commercial exchanges that linked China, Central Asia, and Europe.

Cole, Bruce. *Giotto and Florentine Painting, 1280–1375.* New York, 1976. A clear and stimulating introduction.

Crummey, Robert O. *The Formation of Muscovy, 1304–1613.* New York, 1987. The standard account.

Dante Alighieri. *The Divine Comedy.* Trans. Mark Musa. 3 vols. Baltimore, 1984–1986.

Dunn, Ross E. *The Adventures of Ibn Battuta: A Muslim Traveler of the Fourteenth Century.* Rev. ed. Berkeley, 2005. Places the writings and experiences of this far-reaching Muslim traveler in their historical and geographical contexts.

Dyer, Christopher. *Standards of Living in the Later Middle Ages: Social Change in England, c. 1200–1520.* Cambridge and New York, 1989. Detailed but highly rewarding.

Fancy, Hussein. *The Mercenary Mediterranean: Sovereignty, Religion, and Violence in the Medieval Crown of Atagon.* Chicago, 2018. An acclaimed archival study of the complicated relationship between religion and politics in medieval Spain.

Foltz, Richard. *Religions of the Silk Road: Premodern Patterns of Globalization.* 2nd ed. New York, 2010. A compelling and thought-provoking study of the varieties of religious experience and cross-cultural interaction in medieval Eurasia.

Green, Monica, ed. *Pandemic Disease in the Medieval World: Rethinking the Black Death.* Special inaugural issue, *The Medieval Globe,* 1, no. 1 (2014). Available online in an open-access format: http://scholarworks.wmich.edu/tmg/vol1/iss1/. A pathbreaking collection of articles synthesizing the most recent research in the history, epidemiology, microbiology, and archaeology of the plague.

Horrox, Rosemary, ed. *The Black Death.* New York, 1994. A fine collection of documents reflecting the impact of the Black Death, especially in England.

Jackson, Peter. *The Mongols and the West, 1221–1410.* Harlow, UK, 2005. A well-written survey that emphasizes the interactions among the Mongol, Latin Christian, and Muslim worlds.

Jordan, William Chester. *The Great Famine: Northern Europe in the Early Fourteenth Century.* Princeton, NJ, 1996. An outstanding social and economic study.

Keen, Maurice, ed. *Medieval Warfare: A History.* Oxford and New York, 1999. The most attractive introduction to this important subject, lively and well illustrated.

Kitsikopoulos, Harry, ed. *Agrarian Change and Crisis in Europe, 1200–1500.* London, 2011. An up-to-date collection of scholarly essays that addresses a classic and complicated set of historical questions.

Komaroff, Linda, and Stefano Carboni, eds. *The Legacy of Ghenghis Khan: Courtly Art and Culture in Western Asia, 1256–1353.*

New York, 2002. An informative and lavishly illustrated catalog of an acclaimed exhibition.

Larner, John. *Marco Polo and the Discovery of the World.* New Haven, 1999. A study of the influence of Marco Polo's *Travels* on Europeans.

Memoirs of a Renaissance Pope: The Commentaries of Pius II. Abridged ed. Trans. Florence A. Gragg, ed. Leona C. Gabel. New York, 1959. Remarkable insights into the mind of a particularly well-educated mid-fifteenth-century pope.

Morgan, David. *The Mongols.* 2nd ed. Oxford, 2007. An accessible introduction to Mongol history and its sources, written by a noted expert on medieval Persia.

Onon, Urgunge, trans. *The History and the Life of Chinggis Khan: The Secret History of the Mongols.* Leiden, 1997. A newer version of *The Secret History*, now the standard English version of this important Mongol source.

Polo, Marco. *The Description of the World.* Trans. Sharon Kinoshita. Indianapolis, 2016. A faithful and accessible new translation of the text, with authoritative notes and commentary.

Rossabi, Morris. *Khubilai Khan: His Life and Times.* Berkeley, 1988. The standard English biography.

Seymour, M. C., ed. *Mandeville's Travels.* Oxford, 1968. An edition of the *Book of Marvels* based on the Middle English version popular in the fifteenth century.

Swanson, R. N. *Religion and Devotion in Europe, c. 1215–c. 1515.* Cambridge and New York, 1995. An excellent study of late-medieval popular piety; an excellent complement to Oakley.

Vaughan, Richard. *Valois Burgundy.* London, 1975. A summation of the author's four-volume study of the Burgundian dukes.

CHAPTER 11

Alberti, Leon Battista. *The Family in Renaissance Florence (Della Famiglia).* Trans. Renée Neu Watkins. Columbia, SC, 1969.

Allmand, Christopher T., ed. *Society at War: The Experience of England and France during the Hundred Years' War.* Edinburgh, 1973. An outstanding collection of documents.

Boccaccio, Giovanni. *The Decameron.* Trans. Mark Musa and P. E. Bondanella. New York, 1977.

Brucker, Gene. *Florence: The Golden Age, 1138–1737.* Berkeley and Los Angeles, 1998. A classic account of the city at the height of its influence.

Bruni, Leonardo. *The Humanism of Leonardo Bruni: Selected Texts.* Trans. Gordon Griffiths, James Hankins, and David Thompson. Binghamton, NY, 1987. Excellent translations, with introductions, to the Latin works of a key Renaissance humanist.

Burkhardt, Jacob. *The Civilization of the Renaissance in Italy.* There are many editions of this nineteenth-century study, which influentially crystallized the concept of the "Renaissance."

Cassirer, Ernst, et al., eds. *The Renaissance Philosophy of Man.* Chicago, 1948. Excerpts from important original works by Petrarch, Ficino, and Pico della Mirandola, among others.

Castor, Helen. *Joan of Arc: A History.* London, 2015. An accessible and highly readable account of the ways that Joan was understood in her own time, and her changing reputation up to the present day.

Chaucer, Geoffrey. *The Canterbury Tales.* Trans. Nevill Coghill. New York, 1951. A modern English verse translation, lightly annotated.

Cohn, Samuel K., Jr. *Lust for Liberty: The Politics of Social Revolt in Medieval Europe, 1200–1425. Italy, France, and Flanders.* Cambridge, MA, 2006. An important and provocative study of social movements before and after the Black Death.

Coles, Paul. *The Ottoman Impact on Europe.* London, 1968. An excellent introductory text, still valuable despite its age.

Dobson, R. Barrie. *The Peasants' Revolt of 1381.* 2nd ed. London, 1983. A comprehensive source collection, with excellent introductions to the documents.

Fernández-Armesto, Felipe. *Before Columbus: Exploration and Colonisation from the Mediterranean to the Atlantic, 1229–1492.* London, 1987. An indispensable study of the medieval background to the sixteenth-century European colonial empires.

Froissart, Jean. *Chronicles.* Trans. Geoffrey Brereton. Baltimore, 1968. A selection from the most famous contemporary account of the Hundred Years' War to about 1400.

Frost, Robert. *The Oxford History of Poland-Lithuania. Volume One: The Making of the Polish-Lithuanian Union, 1385–1569.* Oxford, 2018. A magisterial study of this powerful medieval state.

Goffman, Daniel. *The Ottoman Empire and Early Modern Europe.* Cambridge and New York, 2002. A revisionist account that presents the Ottoman Empire as a European state.

Hankins, James. *Plato in the Italian Renaissance.* Leiden and New York, 1990. A definitive study of the reception and influence of Plato on Renaissance intellectuals.

———, ed. *Renaissance Civic Humanism: Reappraisals and Reflections.* Cambridge and New York, 2000. An excellent collection of scholarly essays reassessing republicanism in the Renaissance.

Hobbins, Daniel, ed. and trans. *The Trial of Joan of Arc.* Cambridge, MA, 2007. An excellent translation of the transcripts of Joan's trial.

Inalcik, Halil. *The Ottoman Empire: The Classical Age, 1300–1600.* London, 1973. The standard history by the dean of Turkish historians.

———, ed. *An Economic and Social History of the Ottoman Empire, 1300–1914.* Cambridge, 1994. An important collection of essays, spanning the full range of Ottoman history.

John Hus at the Council of Constance. Trans. M. Spinka, New York, 1965. The translation of a Czech chronicle with an expert introduction and appended documents.

Kafadar, Cemal. *Between Two Worlds: The Construction of the Ottoman State.* Berkeley and Los Angeles, 1995. An important study of Ottoman origins in the border regions between Byzantium, the Seljuk Turks, and the Mongols.

Kaldellis, Anthony. *A New Herodotos: Laonikos Chalkokondyles on the Ottoman Empire, the Fall of Byzantium, and the Emergence of the West.* Washington, DC, 2014. This volume is the first full-length study of Laonikos Chalkokondyles, a historian from Athens who wrote a classical Greek history of his own times, tracing the fall of Constantinople.

Kempe, Margery. *The Book of Margery Kempe.* Trans. Barry Windeatt. New York, 1985. A fascinating personal narrative by an early fifteenth-century Englishwoman who hoped she might be a saint.

Lane, Frederic C. *Venice: A Maritime Republic.* Baltimore, 1973. An authoritative account.

Ormrod, W. Mark. *Edward III.* New Haven, 2012. A new biography of this English monarch by a leading social historian.

Normore, Christina. *A Feast for the Eyes: Art, Performance, and the Late Medieval Banquet.* Chicago, 2015. A fascinating study of the aristocratic feast and its meanings.

Shirley, Janet, trans. *A Parisian Journal, 1405–1449.* Oxford, 1968. A marvelous panorama of Parisian life recorded by an eyewitness.

Sumption, Jonathan. *The Hundred Years' War.* Vol. 1, *Trial by Battle.* Vol. 2, *Trial by Fire.* Philadelphia, 1999. The first two volumes of a massive narrative history of the war, carrying the story up to 1369.

CHAPTER 12

Baxandall, Michael. *Painting and Experience in Fifteenth-Century Italy.* Oxford, 1972. A classic study of the perceptual world of the Renaissance.

Castiglione, Baldassare. *The Book of the Courtier.* Many editions. The translations by C. S. Singleton (New York, 1959) and by George Bull (New York, 1967) are both excellent.

Cellini, Benvenuto. *Autobiography.* Trans. George Bull. Baltimore, 1956. This Florentine goldsmith (1500–1571) is the source for many of the most famous stories about the artists of the Florentine Renaissance.

Columbus, Christopher. *The Four Voyages of Christopher Columbus.* Trans. J. M. Cohen. New York, 1992. Columbus's own self-serving account of his expeditions to the Indies.

Erasmus, Desiderius. *The Praise of Folly.* Trans. J. Wilson. Ann Arbor, MI, 1958.

Fernández-Armesto, Felipe. *1492: The Year the World Began.* London, 2010. A panoramic view of the world in a pivotal year, putting the voyage of Columbus in a broad historical perspective.

Flint, Valerie I. J. *The Imaginative Landscape of Christopher Columbus.* Princeton, NJ, 1992. A short, suggestive analysis of the intellectual influences that shaped Columbus's geographical ideas.

Fox, Alistair. *Thomas More: History and Providence.* Oxford, 1982. A balanced account of a man too easily idealized.

Grafton, Anthony, and Lisa Jardine. *From Humanism to the Humanities: Education and the Liberal Arts in Fifteenth- and Sixteenth-Century Europe.* London, 1986. An account that presents Renaissance humanism as the elitist cultural program of a self-interested group of pedagogues.

Grendler, Paul, ed. *Encyclopedia of the Renaissance.* New York, 1999. A valuable reference work.

Jardine, Lisa. *Worldly Goods.* London, 1996. A revisionist account that emphasizes the acquisitive materialism of Italian Renaissance society and culture.

Kanter, Laurence, Hilliard T. Goldfarb, and James Hankins. *Botticelli's Witness: Changing Style in a Changing Florence.* Boston, 1997. This catalog for an exhibition of Botticelli's works, at the Gardner Museum in Boston, offers an excellent introduction to the painter and his world.

King, Margaret L. *Women of the Renaissance.* Chicago, 1991. Deals with women in all walks of life and in a variety of roles.

Kristeller, Paul O. *Renaissance Thought: The Classic, Scholastic, and Humanistic Strains.* New York, 1961. Very helpful in defining the main trends of Renaissance thought.

Machiavelli, Niccolò. *The Discourses* and *The Prince.* Many editions. These two books must be read together if one is to understand Machiavelli's political ideas properly.

Mallett, Michael, and Christine Shaw. *The Italian Wars, 1494–1559: War, State, and Society in Early Modern Europe.* Boston, 2012. Argues that the endemic warfare of this period within Italy revolutionized European military tactics and technologies.

Mann, Charles. C. *1491: New Revelations of the Americas before Columbus.* New York, 2006.

———. *1493: Uncovering the New World Columbus Created.* New York, 2012. Written for a popular audience, these are also engaging and well-informed syntheses of historical research.

Martines, Lauro. *Power and Imagination: City-States in Renaissance Italy.* New York, 1979. Insightful account of the connections among politics, society, culture, and art.

More, Thomas. *Utopia.* Many editions.

Olson, Roberta. *Italian Renaissance Sculpture.* New York, 1992. The most accessible introduction to the subject.

Parker, Geoffrey. *The Military Revolution: Military Innovation and the Rise of the West (1500–1800).* 2nd ed. Cambridge and New York, 1996. A work of fundamental importance for understanding the global dominance achieved by early modern Europeans.

Perkins, Leeman L. *Music in the Age of the Renaissance.* New York, 1999. A massive study that needs to be read in conjunction with Reese.

Phillips, J. R. S. *The Medieval Expansion of Europe.* 2nd ed. Oxford, 1998. An outstanding study of the thirteenth- and fourteenth-century background to the fifteenth-century expansion of Europe. Important synthetic treatment of European relations with the Mongols, China, Africa, and North America. The second edition includes a new introduction and a bibliographical essay; the text is the same as in the first edition (1988).

Phillips, William D., Jr., and Carla R. Phillips. *The Worlds of Christopher Columbus.* Cambridge and New York, 1991. The first book to read on Columbus: accessible, engaging, and scholarly. Then read Fernández-Armesto's biography.

Rabelais, François. *Gargantua and Pantagruel.* Trans. J. M. Cohen. Baltimore, 1955. A robust modern translation.

Reese, Gustave. *Music in the Renaissance.* Rev. ed. New York, 1959. A great book; still authoritative, despite the more recent work by Perkins, which supplements but does not replace it.

Rice, Eugene F., Jr., and Anthony Grafton. *The Foundations of Early Modern Europe, 1460–1559.* 2nd ed. New York, 1994. The best textbook account of its period.

Rowland, Ingrid D. *The Culture of the High Renaissance: Ancients and Moderns in Sixteenth-Century Rome.* Cambridge and New York, 2000. Beautifully written examination of the social, intellectual, and economic foundations of the Renaissance in Rome.

Russell, Peter. *Prince Henry "The Navigator": A Life.* New Haven, 2000. A masterly biography by a great historian who has spent a lifetime on the subject. The only book one now needs to read on Prince Henry.

Scammell, Geoffrey V. *The First Imperial Age: European Overseas Expansion, 1400–1715.* London, 1989. A useful introductory survey, with a particular focus on English and French colonization.

Waltom, Nicholas. *Genoa, "La Superba": The Rise and Fall of a Merchant Pirate Superpower.* London, 2015. A history of the maritime city-state that shaped the career of Columbus and other adventurers.

CHAPTER 13

Bainton, Roland. *Erasmus of Christendom*. New York, 1969. A classic biography in English of the Dutch reformer and intellectual.

Benedict, Philip. *Christ's Churches Purely Reformed: A Social History of Calvinism*. New Haven, 2002. A wide-ranging recent survey of Calvinism in both western and eastern Europe.

Bossy, John. *Christianity in the West, 1400–1700*. Oxford and New York, 1985. A brilliant, challenging picture of the changes that took place in Christian piety and practice as a result of the sixteenth-century reformations.

Bouwsma, William J. *John Calvin: A Sixteenth-Century Portrait*. Oxford and New York, 1988. The best biography of this magisterial reformer.

Duffy, Eamon. *The Stripping of the Altars: Traditional Religion in England, c. 1400–c. 1550*. A brilliant study of religious exchange at the parish level.

———. *The Voices of Morebath: Reformation and Rebellion in an English Village*. New Haven, 2003. How the crises of this period affected and are reflected in the history of a single parish.

Hart, D. G. *Calvinism: A History*. New Haven, 2013. A new survey of this leading Protestant movement from its beginnings to the present day.

John Calvin: Selections from His Writings. Ed. John Dillenberger. Garden City, NY, 1971. A judicious selection, drawn mainly from Calvin's *Institutes*.

Jouanna, Arlette. *The St. Bartholomew's Day Massacre: The Mysteries of a Crime of State*. Translated from the French by Joseph Bergin. Manchester, 2015. A new interpretation of the events and motives surrounding the slaughter of Protestants in Paris on August 24, 1572.

Koslofksy, Craig. *The Reformation of the Dead: Death and Ritual in Early Modern Germany*. Basingstoke, UK, 2000. How essential rituals and responses to death were reshaped during this period.

Loyola, Ignatius. *Personal Writings*. Trans. by Joseph A. Munitiz and Philip Endean. London and New York, 1996. An excellent collection that includes Loyola's autobiography, his spiritual diary, and some of his letters, as well as his *Spiritual Exercises*.

MacCulloch, Diarmaid. *Reformation: Europe's House Divided, 1490–1700*. London and New York, 2003. A definitive new survey; the best single-volume history of its subject in a generation.

Marshall, Peter, ed. *The Oxford Illustrated History of the Reformation*. Oxford, 2015. A compendium of new perspectives on the religious upheavals of the sixteenth century.

Martin Luther: Selections from His Writings, ed. John Dillenberger. Garden City, NY, 1961. The standard selection, especially good on Luther's theological ideas.

McGrath, Alister E. *Reformation Thought: An Introduction*. Oxford, 1993. A useful explanation, accessible to non-Christians, of the theological ideas of the major Protestant reformers.

Mullett, Michael A. *The Catholic Reformation*. London, 2000. A sympathetic survey of Catholicism from the mid-sixteenth to the eighteenth century that presents the mid-sixteenth-century Council of Trent as a continuation of earlier reform efforts.

Murray, Linda. *High Renaissance and Mannerism*. London, 1985. The place to begin a study of fifteenth- and sixteenth-century Italian art.

O'Malley, John W. *The First Jesuits*. Cambridge, MA, 1993. A scholarly account of the origins and early years of the Society of Jesus.

———. *Trent: What Happened at the Council*. Cambridge, MA, 2012. A clear and comprehensive narrative of the Church council that gave birth to the modern Catholic Church.

Pettegree, Andrew. *Brand Luther: How an Unheralded Monk Turned His Small Town into a Center of Publishing, Made Himself the Most Famous Man in Europe—and Started the Protestant Reformation*. Penguin, 2016. The title says it all.

Pelikan, Jaroslav. *Reformation of Church and Dogma, 1300–1700*. Vol. 4 of *A History of Christian Dogma*. Chicago, 1984. A masterful synthesis of Reformation theology in its late-medieval context.

Roper, Lyndal. *The Holy Household: Women and Morals in Reformation Augsburg*. Oxford, 1989. A pathbreaking study of Protestantism's effects on a single town, with special attention to its impact on attitudes toward women, the family, and marriage.

Ryrie, Alex. *Being Protestant in Reformation Britain*. Oxford, 2015. A vivid portrait of daily life in a turbulent time.

Shagan, Ethan H. *Popular Politics and the English Reformation*. Cambridge, 2002. Argues that the English Reformation reflects an ongoing process of negotiation, resistance, and response.

Tracy, James D. *Europe's Reformations, 1450–1650*. 2nd ed. Lanham, MD, 2006. An outstanding survey, especially strong on Dutch and Swiss developments, but excellent throughout.

Williams, George H. *The Radical Reformation*. 3rd ed. Kirksville, MO, 1992. Originally published in 1962, this is still the best book on Anabaptism and its offshoots.

CHAPTER 14

Bonney, Richard. *The European Dynastic States, 1494–1660*. Oxford and New York, 1991. An excellent survey of continental Europe during the "long" sixteenth century.

Briggs, Robin. *Witches and Neighbors: The Social and Cultural Context of European Witchcraft*. New York, 1996. An influential recent account of Continental witchcraft.

Cervantes, Miguel de. *Don Quixote*. Trans. Edith Grossman. New York, 2003. A splendid new translation.

Clarke, Stuart. *Thinking with Demons: The Idea of Witchcraft in Early Modern Europe*. Oxford and New York, 1999. By placing demonology into the context of sixteenth- and seventeenth-century intellectual history, Clarke makes sense of it in new and exciting ways.

Cochrane, Eric, Charles M. Gray, and Mark A. Kishlansky. *Early Modern Europe: Crisis of Authority*. Chicago, 1987. An outstanding source collection from the University of Chicago Readings in Western Civilization series.

Cook Harold. *The Young Descartes: Nobility, Rumor, and War*. Chicago, 2018. A new biography that firmly embeds the philosopher in his historical context.

Elliot, J. H. *The Old World and the New, 1492–1650*. Repr. ed. Cambridge, 1992. A brilliant and brief set of essays on the ways that the discovery of the Americas challenged European perspectives on the world and themselves.

———. *Empires of the Atlantic World: Britain and Spain in America, 1492–1830*. An illuminating comparative study. New Haven, 2007.

Geschwend, Annemarie Jordan, and K. J. P. Lowe, eds. *The Global City: On the Streets of Renaissance Lisbon*. London, 2015. A beautifully illustrated collection of essays by leading scholars.

Hibbard, Howard. *Bernini.* Baltimore, 1965. The basic study in English of this central figure of Baroque artistic activity.

Hirst, Derek. *England in Conflict, 1603–1660: Kingdom, Community, Commonwealth.* Oxford and New York, 1999. A complete revision of the author's *Authority and Conflict* (1986), this is an up-to-date and balanced account of a period that has been a historical battleground over the past twenty years.

Hobbes, Thomas. *Leviathan.* Ed. Richard Tuck. 2nd ed. Cambridge and New York, 1996. The most recent edition, containing the entirety of *Leviathan*, not just the first two parts.

Holt, Mack P. *The French Wars of Religion, 1562–1629.* Cambridge and New York, 1995. A clear account of a confusing time.

Ipsen, Pernille.*Daughters of the Trade: Atlantic Slavers and Interracial Marriage on the Gold Coast.* Philadelphia, 2014. A study that puts women and families at the heart of the story of African slavery.

Kors, Alan Charles, and Edward Peters. *Witchcraft in Europe, 400–1700: A Documentary History.* 2nd ed. Philadelphia, 2000. A superb collection of documents, significantly expanded in the second edition, with up-to-date commentary.

Kingdon, Robert. *Myths about the St. Bartholomew's Day Massacres, 1572–1576.* Cambridge, MA, 1988. A detailed account of this pivotal moment in the history of France.

Kochanowski, Jan. *Laments.* Translated by Stanislaw Baranczak and Seamus Heaney. New York, 1995. A moving rendition of works by the great poet of Renaissance Poland.

Levack, Brian P. *The Witch-Hunt in Early Modern Europe,* 2nd ed. London and New York, 1995. The best account of the persecution of suspected witches; coverage extends from Europe in 1450 to America in 1750.

Levin, Carole. *The Heart and Stomach of a King: Elizabeth I and the Politics of Sex and Power.* Philadelphia, 1994. A provocative argument for the importance of Elizabeth's gender for understanding her reign.

Limm, Peter, ed. *The Thirty Years' War.* London, 1984. An outstanding short survey, followed by a selection of primary-source documents.

Lynch, John. *Spain, 1516–1598: From Nation-State to World Empire.* Oxford and Cambridge, MA, 1991. The best book in English on Spain at the pinnacle of its sixteenth-century power.

MacCaffrey, Wallace. *Elizabeth I.* New York, 1993. An outstanding traditional biography by an excellent scholar.

Martin, Colin, and Geoffrey Parker. *The Spanish Armada.* London, 1988. Incorporates recent discoveries from undersea archaeology with more traditional historical sources.

Mattingly, Garrett. *The Armada.* Boston, 1959. A great narrative history that reads like a novel; for more recent work, however, see Martin and Parker.

McGregor, Neil. *Shakespeare's Restless World.* London, 2013. Based on an acclaimed BBC Radio program, this book illuminates Shakespeare's life, times, and plays with reference to specific objects in the British Museum.

Newson, Linda A., and Susie Minchin. *From Capture to Sale: The Portuguese Slave Trade to Spanish South America in the Early Seventeenth Century.* London, 2007. Makes use of slave traders' own rich archives to track the process of human trafficking.

Parker, Geoffrey. *The Dutch Revolt.* 2nd ed. Ithaca, NY, 1989. The standard survey in English.

Pascal, Blaise. *Pensées* (French-English edition). Ed. H. F. Stewart. London, 1950.

Pestana, Carla. *Protestant Empire: Religion and the Making of the British Atlantic World.* Philadelphia, 2010. How the Reformation helped to drive British imperial expansion.

Roberts, Michael. *Gustavus Adolphus and the Rise of Sweden.* London, 1973. Still the authoritative English-language account.

Russell, Conrad. *The Causes of the English Civil War.* Oxford, 1990. A penetrating and provocative analysis by one of the leading "revisionist" historians of the period.

Schmidt, Benjamin. *Innocence Abroad: The Dutch Imagination and the New World, 1570–1670.* Cambridge, 2006. A cultural history of Europeans' encounter with the Americas that highlights the perspective and experience of Dutch merchants, colonists, and artists.

Strum, Daniel. *The Sugar Trade: Brazil, Portugal, and the Netherlands (1595–1630).* Translated by Colin Foulkes, Roopanjali Roy, and H. Sabrina Gledhill. Stanford, CA, 2013. A close examination of the merchants, seafarers, and slaves who drove the economy of the Atlantic world.

CHAPTER 15

Beik, William. *A Social and Cultural History of Early Modern France.* Cambridge, 2009. A broad synthesis of French history from the end of the Middle Ages to the French Revolution, by one of the world's foremost authorities on absolutism.

Clark, Christopher. *Iron Kingdom: The Rise and Downfall of Prussia, 1600–1947.* Cambridge, MA, 2009. A definitive account of Prussian history over nearly four centuries.

Jones, Colin. *The Great Nation: France From Louis XV to Napoleon.* New York, 2002. An excellent and readable scholarly account that argues that the France of Louis XV in the eighteenth century was even more dominant than the kingdom of Louis XIV in the preceding century.

Kishlansky, Mark A. *A Monarchy Transformed: Britain, 1603–1714.* London, 1996. An excellent survey that takes seriously its claim to be a "British" rather than merely an "English" history.

Klein, Herbert S. *The Atlantic Slave Trade.* Cambridge and New York, 1999. An accessible survey by a leading quantitative historian.

Lewis, William Roger, gen. ed. *The Oxford History of the British Empire.* Vol. I: *The Origins of Empire: British Overseas Enterprise to the Close of the Seventeenth Century,* ed. Nicholas Canny. Vol. II: *The Eighteenth Century,* ed. Peter J. Marshall. Oxford and New York, 1998. A definitive, multiauthor account.

Locke, John. *Two Treatises of Government.* Ed. Peter Laslett. Rev. ed. Cambridge and New York, 1963. Laslett has revolutionized our understanding of the historical and ideological context of Locke's political writings.

Massie, Robert. *Peter the Great, His Life and World.* New York, 1980. Prize-winning and readable narrative account of the Russian tsar's life.

Monod, Paul K. *The Power of Kings: Monarchy and Religion in Europe, 1589–1715.* New Haven, 1999. A study of the seventeenth century's declining confidence in the divinity of kings.

Page Moch, Leslie. *Moving Europeans: Migration in Western Europe since 1650.* Bloomington, Indiana, 2003.

Quataert, Donald. *The Ottoman Empire, 1700–1822.* Cambridge and New York, 2000. Well balanced and intended to be read by students.

Riasanovsky, Nicholas V., and Steinberg, Mark D. *A History of Russia*. 7th ed. Oxford and New York, 2005. Far and away the best single-volume textbook on Russian history: balanced, comprehensive, and intelligent, with full bibliographies.

Saint-Simon, Louis. *Historical Memoirs*. Many editions. The classic source for life at Louis XIV's Versailles.

Snyder, Timothy. *The Reconstruction of Nations: Poland, Ukraine, Lithuania, Belarus, 1569–1999*. New Haven, 2004. Essential account of nation building and state collapse in eastern Europe with significant relevance to the region's contemporary situation.

Thomas, Hugh. *The Slave Trade: The History of the Atlantic Slave Trade, 1440–1870*. London and New York, 1997. A survey notable for its breadth and depth of coverage and for its attractive prose style.

Tracy, James D. *The Rise of Merchant Empires: Long-Distance Trade in the Early Modern World, 1350–1750*. Cambridge and New York, 1990. Important collection of essays by leading authorities.

White, Richard. *The Middle Ground: Indians, Empires and Republics in the Great Lakes Region, 1650–1815*. Cambridge, 1991. A path-breaking account of interactions between Europeans and Native Americans during the colonial period.

CHAPTER 16

Biagioli, Mario. *Galileo, Courtier*. Chicago, 1993. Emphasizes the importance of patronage and court politics in Galileo's science and career.

Cohen, I. B. *The Birth of a New Physics*. New York, 1985. Emphasizes the mathematical nature of the revolution; unmatched at making the mathematics understandable.

Daston, Lorraine, and Elizabeth Lunbeck, eds. *Histories of Scientific Observation*. Chicago, IL, 2011. Field-defining collection of essays on the history of scientific observation from the seventeenth to the twentieth centuries.

Daston, Lorraine. *Wonders and the Order of Nature, 1150–1750*. Cambridge, MA, 2001. Erudite, sweeping account of the history of science in the early modern period, emphasizing the natural philosopher's awe and wonder at the marvelous, the unfamiliar, and the counterintuitive.

Dear, Peter. *Revolutionizing the Sciences: European Knowledge and Its Ambitions, 1500–1700*. Princeton, NJ, 2001. Among the best short histories.

Drake, Stillman. *Discoveries and Opinions of Galileo*. Garden City, NY, 1957. The classic translation of Galileo's most important papers by his most admiring modern biographer.

Feingold, Mardechai. *The Newtonian Moment: Isaac Newton and the Making of Modern Culture*. New York, 2004. An engaging essay on the dissemination of Newton's thought, with excellent visual material.

Gaukroger, Stephen. *Descartes: An Intellectual Biography*. Oxford, 1995. Detailed and sympathetic study of the philosopher.

Gleick, James. *Isaac Newton*. New York, 2003. A vivid and well-documented brief biography.

Grafton, Anthony. *New Worlds, Ancient Texts: The Power of Tradition and the Shock of Discovery*. Cambridge, MA, 1992. Accessible essay by one of the leading scholars of early modern European thought.

Jacob, Margaret. *Scientific Culture and the Making of the Industrial West*. Oxford, 1997. A concise examination of the connections between developments in science and the Industrial Revolution.

Kuhn, Thomas. *The Structure of Scientific Revolutions*. Chicago, 1962. A classic and much-debated study of how scientific thought changes.

Pagden, Anthony. *European Encounters with the New World*. New Haven and London, 1993. Subtle and detailed on how European intellectuals thought about the lands they saw for the first time.

Rudwick, Martin J. S. *Earth's Deep History: How It Was Discovered and Why It Matters* (Chicago, 2014). A fascinating account of the origins of the geological sciences and awareness of the earth's long history before the advent of human civilizations.

Scheibinger, Londa. *The Mind Has No Sex? Women in the Origins of Modern Science*. Cambridge, MA, 1989. A lively and important recovery of the lost role played by women mathematicians and experimenters.

Shapin, Steven. *The Scientific Revolution*. Chicago, 1996. Engaging, accessible, and brief—organized thematically.

Shapin, Steven, and Simon Schaffer. *Leviathan and the Air Pump*. Princeton, NJ, 1985. A modern classic, on one of the most famous philosophical conflicts in seventeenth-century science.

Stephenson, Bruce. *The Music of the Heavens: Kepler's Harmonic Astronomy*. Princeton, NJ, 1994. An engaging and important explanation of Kepler's otherworldly perspective.

Thoren, Victor. *The Lord of Uraniburg: A Biography of Tycho Brahe*. Cambridge, 1990. A vivid reconstruction of the scientific revolution's most flamboyant astronomer.

Westfall, Richard. *The Construction of Modern Science*. Cambridge, 1977.

————. *Never at Rest: A Biography of Isaac Newton*. Cambridge, 1980. The standard work.

Wilson, Catherine. *The Invisible World: Early Modern Philosophy and the Invention of the Microscope*. Princeton, NJ, 1995. An important study of how the "microcosmic" world revealed by technology reshaped scientific philosophy and practice.

Zinsser, Judith P. *La Dame d'Esprit: A Biography of the Marquise Du Châtelet*. New York, 2006. An excellent cultural history. Issued in paperback as *Emilie du Châtelet: Daring Genius of the Enlightenment* (2007).

CHAPTER 17

Bade, Klaus J. *Migration in European History*. Oxford, 2003.

Baker, Keith. *Condorcet: From Natural Philosophy to Social Mathematics*. Chicago, 1975. An important reinterpretation of Condorcet as a social scientist.

Blum, Carol. *Rousseau and the Republic of Virtue: The Language of Politics in the French Revolution*. Ithaca, NY, and London, 1986. Fascinating account of how eighteenth-century readers interpreted Rousseau.

Buchan, James. *The Authentic Adam Smith: His Life and Ideas*. New York, 2006.

Calhoun, Craig, ed. *Habermas and the Public Sphere*. Cambridge, MA, 1992. Calhoun's introduction is a good starting point for Habermas's argument.

Cassirer, E. *The Philosophy of the Enlightenment*. Princeton, NJ, 1951.

Chartier, Roger. *The Cultural Origins of the French Revolution*. Durham, NC, 1991. Looks at topics from religion to violence in everyday life and culture.

Darnton, Robert. *The Business of Enlightenment: A Publishing History of the* Encyclopédie, *1775–1800*. Cambridge, MA, 1979. Darnton's work on the Enlightenment offers a fascinating blend of intellectual, social, and economic history. See his other books as well: *The Literary Underground of the Old Regime* (Cambridge, MA, 1982); *The Great Cat Massacre and Other Episodes in French Cultural History* (New York, 1984); and *The Forbidden Best-Sellers of Revolutionary France* (New York and London, 1996).

Davis, David Brion. *The Problem of Slavery in Western Culture*. New York, 1988. A Pulitzer Prize–winning examination of a central issue as well as a brilliant analysis of different strands of Enlightenment thought.

Gay, Peter. *The Enlightenment: An Interpretation*. Vol. 1, *The Rise of Modern Paganism*. Vol. 2, *The Science of Freedom*. New York, 1966–1969. Combines an overview with an interpretation. Emphasizes the *philosophes'* sense of identification with the classical world and takes a generally positive view of their accomplishments. Includes extensive annotated bibliographies.

Gray, Peter. *Mozart*. New York, 1999. Brilliant short study.

Goodman, Dena. *The Republic of Letters: A Cultural History of the French Enlightenment*. Ithaca, NY, 1994. Important in its attention to the role of literary women.

Hazard, Paul. *The European Mind: The Critical Years (1680–1715)*. New Haven, 1953. A basic and indispensable account of the changing climate of opinion that preceded the Enlightenment.

Hunt, Lynn, Margaret C. Jacob, and Wijnand Mijnhardt. *The Book That Changed Europe: Picart and Bernard's Religious Ceremonies of the World*. Cambridge, MA, 2010. Lively study of a book on global religions that came out of the fertile world of the Dutch Enlightenment in the eighteenth century.

Israel, Jonathan Irvine. *Radical Enlightenment: Philosophy and the Making of Modernity, 1650–1750*. New York, 2001. Massive and erudite, a fresh look at the international movement of ideas.

———. *Enlightenment Contested: Philosophy, Modernity, and the Emancipation of Man, 1670–1752*. New York, 2006. An encyclopedic account of Enlightenment debates, focusing on the contest between supporters and opponents of democratic ideals.

Munck, Thomas. *The Enlightenment: A Comparative Social History 1721–1794*. London, 2000. An excellent recent survey, especially good on social history.

Outram, Dorinda. *The Enlightenment*. Cambridge, 1995. An excellent short introduction and a good example of new historical approaches.

Pagden, Anthony. *The Enlightenment: And Why It Still Matters*. New York, 2013. Spirited history of the Enlightenment and a defense of its continued relevance.

Porter, Roy. *The Creation of the Modern World: The Untold Story of the British Enlightenment*. New York, 2000.

Sapiro, Virginia. *A Vindication of Political Virtue: The Political Theory of Mary Wollstonecraft*. Chicago, 1992. A subtle and intelligent analysis for more advanced readers.

Shklar, Judith. *Men and Citizens: A Study of Rousseau's Social Theory*. London, 1969.

———. *Montesquieu*. Oxford, 1987. Shklar's studies are brilliant and accessible.

Taylor, Barbara. *Mary Wollstonecraft and the Feminist Imagination*. Cambridge and New York, 2003. Fascinating study that sets Wollstonecraft in the radical circles of eighteenth-century England.

Taylor, Barbara, and Sarah Knott, eds. *Women, Gender, and Enlightenment*. New York, 2007. Multiauthor collection examining the significance of sex, gender, and politics across a wide swath of the Enlightenment world, from Europe to the American colonies.

Venturi, Franco. *The End of the Old Regime in Europe, 1768–1776: The First Crisis*. Trans. R. Burr Litchfield. Princeton, NJ, 1989.

———. *The End of the Old Regime in Europe, 1776–1789*. Princeton, NJ, 1991. Both detailed and wide-ranging, particularly important on international developments.

Watt, Ian P. *The Rise of the Novel*. London, 1957. The basic work on the innovative qualities of the novel in eighteenth-century England.

Wolff, Larry. *Inventing Eastern Europe: The Map of Civilization on the Mind of the Enlightenment*. Stanford, CA, 1994. The place of eastern Europe in the imagination of Enlightenment thinkers interested in the origins and destiny of the civilizing process.

CHAPTER 18

Applewhite, Harriet B., and Darline G. Levy, eds. *Women and Politics in the Age of the Democratic Revolution*. Ann Arbor, MI, 1990. Essays on France, Britain, the Netherlands, and the United States.

Bell, David A. *The First Total War: Napoleon's Europe and the Birth of Warfare as We Know It*. Boston and New York, 2007. Lively and concise study of the "cataclysmic intensification" of warfare.

Blackburn, Robin. *The Overthrow of Colonial Slavery*. London and New York, 1988. A longer view of slavery and its abolition.

Blanning, T. C. W. *The French Revolutionary Wars, 1787–1802*. Oxford, 1996. On the revolution and war.

Blum, Carol. *Rousseau and the Republic of Virtue: The Language of Politics in the French Revolution*. Ithaca, NY, 1986. Excellent on how Rousseau was read by the revolutionaries.

Cobb, Richard. *The People's Armies*. New Haven, 1987. Brilliant and detailed analysis of the French popular militias.

Cole, Juan. *Napoleon's Egypt: Invading the Middle East*. New York, 2007. Readable history by a scholar familiar with sources in Arabic as well as European languages.

Connelly, Owen. *The French Revolution and Napoleonic Era*. 3rd ed. New York, 2000. Accessible, lively, one-volume survey.

Desan, Suzanne. *The Family on Trial in Revolutionary France*. Berkeley, 2006. Persuasive study of the ways that women in France were able to take advantage of the revolution and defend their interests in debates about marriage, divorce, parenthood, and the care of children.

Desan, Suzanne, Lynn Hunt, and William Max Nelson, eds. *The French Revolution in Global Perspective*. Ithaca, NY, 2013. Multiauthor exploration of the French Revolution's global resonance.

Doyle, William. *Origins of the French Revolution*. New York, 1988. A revisionist historian surveys recent research on the political and social origins of the revolution and identifies a new consensus.

_____. *Oxford History of the French Revolution*. New York, 1989.

Dubois, Laurent. *Avengers of the New World. The Story of the Haitian Revolution*. Cambridge, MA, 2004. Now the best and most accessible study.

_____, and John D. Garrigus. *Slave Revolution in the Caribbean, 1789–1804: A Brief History with Documents*. New York, 2006. A particularly good collection.

Englund, Steven. *Napoleon: A Political Life*. Cambridge, MA, 2004. Prize-winning biography, both dramatic and insightful.

Forrest, Alan. *The French Revolution and the Poor*. New York, 1981. A moving and detailed social history of the poor, who fared little better under revolutionary governments than under the Old Regime.

Furet, François. *Revolutionary France, 1770–1880*. Trans. Antonia Nerill. Cambridge, MA, 1992. Overview by the leading revisionist.

Hunt, Lynn. *The French Revolution and Human Rights*. Boston, 1996. A collection of documents.

_____. *Politics, Culture, and Class in the French Revolution*. Berkeley, 1984. An analysis of the new culture of democracy and republicanism.

Hunt, Lynn, and Jack R. Censer. *Liberty, Equality, Fraternity: Exploring the French Revolution*. University Park, PA, 2001. A lively, accessible study by two leading historians of the revolution, with excellent documents and visual materials.

Landes, Joan B. *Women and the Public Sphere in the Age of the French Revolution*. Ithaca, NY, 1988. On gender and politics.

Lefebvre, Georges. *The Coming of the French Revolution*. Princeton, NJ, 1947. The classic Marxist analysis.

Lewis, Gwynne, and Colin Lucas. *Beyond the Terror: Essays in French Regional and Social History, 1794–1815*. New York, 1983. Shifts focus to the understudied period after the Terror.

O'Brien, Connor Cruise. *The Great Melody: A Thematic Biography of Edmund Burke*. Chicago, 1992. Passionate, partisan, and brilliant study of Burke's thoughts about Ireland, India, America, and France.

Palmer, R. R. *The Age of the Democratic Revolution: A Political History of Europe and America, 1760–1800*. 2 vols. Princeton, NJ, 1964. Impressive for its scope; places the French Revolution in the larger context of a worldwide revolutionary movement.

_____, and Isser Woloch. *Twelve Who Ruled: The Year of the Terror in the French Revolution*. Princeton, NJ, 2005. The terrific collective biography of the Committee of Public Safety, now updated.

Schama, Simon. *Citizens: A Chronicle of the French Revolution*. New York, 1989. Particularly good on art, culture, and politics.

Scott, Joan. *Only Paradoxes to Offer: French Feminists and the Rights of Man*. Cambridge, MA, 1997. A history of feminist engagement with a revolutionary ideology that promised universal liberties while simultaneously excluding women from citizenship.

Soboul, Albert. *The Sans-Culottes: The Popular Movement and Revolutionary Government, 1793–1794*. Garden City, NY, 1972. Dated, but a classic.

Sutherland, D. M. G. *France, 1789–1815: Revolution and Counterrevolution*. Oxford, 1986. An important synthesis of work on the revolution, especially in social history.

Tackett, Timothy. *The Coming of the Terror in the French Revolution*. Cambridge, 2015. A richly detailed explanation of why the French Revolution took such a violent turn.

Tocqueville, Alexis de. *The Old Regime and the French Revolution*. Garden City, NY, 1955. Originally written in 1856, this remains a provocative analysis of the revolution's legacy.

Trouillot, Michel Rolph. *Silencing the Past*. Boston, 1995. Essays on the Haitian revolution.

Woloch, Isser. *The New Regime: Transformations of the French Civic Order, 1789–1820*. New York, 1994. The fate of revolutionary civic reform.

Woolf, Stuart. *Napoleon's Integration of Europe*. New York, 1991. Technical but very thorough.

CHAPTER 19

Bridenthal, Renate, Claudia Koonz, and Susan Stuard, eds. *Becoming Visible: Women in European History*. 2nd ed. Boston, 1987. Excellent, wide-ranging introduction.

Briggs, Asa. *Victorian Cities*. New York, 1963. A survey of British cities, stressing middle-class attitudes toward the new urban environment.

Chevalier, Louis. *Laboring Classes and Dangerous Classes during the First Half of the Nineteenth Century*. New York, 1973. An important, though controversial, account of crime, class, and middle-class perceptions of life in Paris.

Cipolla, Carlo M., ed. *The Industrial Revolution, 1700–1914*. New York, 1976. A collection of essays that emphasizes the wide range of industrializing experiences in Europe.

Clark, Anna. *The Struggle for the Breeches: Gender and the Making of the British Working Class*. Berkeley, CA, 1997. Examines the process of class formation during the industrial revolution in Britain through the lens of gender.

Cott, Nancy. *The Bonds of Womanhood: "Woman's Sphere" in New England, 1780–1935*. New Haven and London, 1977. One of the most influential studies of the paradoxes of domesticity.

Davidoff, Leonore, and Catherine Hall. *Family Fortunes: Men and Women of the English Middle Class, 1780–1850*. Chicago, 1985. A brilliant and detailed study of the lives and ambitions of several English families.

Ferguson, Niall. "The European Economy, 1815–1914." In *The Nineteenth Century*, ed. T. C. W. Blanning. Oxford and New York, 2000. A very useful short essay.

Gay, Peter. *The Bourgeois Experience: Victoria to Freud*. New York, 1984. A multivolume, path-breaking study of middle-class life in all its dimensions.

_____. *Schnitzler's Century: The Making of Middle-Class Culture, 1815–1914*. New York and London, 2002. A synthesis of some of the arguments presented in *The Bourgeois Experience*.

Harzig, Christiane, Dirk Hoerder, and Donna Gabaccia. *What Is Migration History?* Cambridge, UK, 2013.

Hellerstein, Erna, Leslie Hume, and Karen Offen, eds. *Victorian Women: A Documentary Account*. Stanford, CA, 1981. Good collection of documents, with excellent introductory essays.

Hobsbawm, Eric J. *The Age of Revolution, 1789–1848*. London, 1962.

_____, and George Rudé. *Captain Swing: A Social History of the Great English Agricultural Uprising of 1830*. New York, 1975. Analyzes rural protest and politics.

Horn, Jeff. *The Path Not Taken: French Industrialization in the Age of Revolution, 1750–1830*. Cambridge, 2006. Argues that industrialization in France succeeded in ways that other historians have not appreciated, and was much more than a failed attempt to imitate the British model.

Jones, Eric. *The European Miracle: Environments, Economies and Geopolitics in the History of Europe and Asia.* Cambridge, 2003. Argues that the Industrial Revolution is best understood as a European phenomenon.

Kemp, Tom. *Industrialization in Nineteenth-Century Europe.* London, 1985. Good general study.

Kindelberger, Charles. *A Financial History of Western Europe.* London, 1984. Emphasis on finance.

Landes, David S. *The Unbound Prometheus: Technological Change and Industrial Development in Western Europe from 1750 to the Present.* London, 1969. Excellent and thorough on technological change and its social and economic context.

Livi-Bacci, Massimo. *A Short History of Migration.* Cambridge, UK, 2012.

McNeill, J. R. *Something New under the Sun: An Environmental History of the Twentieth-Century World.* New York and London, 2000. Short section on the nineteenth century.

Mokyr, Joel. *The Lever of Riches: Technological Creativity and Economic Progress.* New York, 1992. A world history, from antiquity through the nineteenth century.

O'Gráda, Cormac. *Black '47 and Beyond: The Great Irish Famine.* Princeton, NJ, 1999.

———. *The Great Irish Famine.* Cambridge, 1989. A fascinating and recent assessment of scholarship on the famine.

Kenneth Pomeranz. *The Great Divergence: China, Europe, and the Making of the Modern World Economy.* Princeton, NJ, 2000. Path-breaking global history of the Industrial Revolution that argues that Europe was not so different from other parts of the world as scholars have previously thought.

Rendall, Jane. *The Origins of Modern Feminism: Women in Britain, France and the United States, 1780–1860.* New York, 1984. Helpful overview.

Rose, Sonya O. *Limited Livelihoods: Gender and Class in Nineteenth-Century England.* Berkeley, 1992. On the intersection of culture and economics.

Sabean, David Warren. *Property, Production, and Family Neckarhausen, 1700–1870.* New York, 1990. Brilliant and very detailed study of gender roles and family.

Sabel, Charles, and Jonathan Zeitlin. "Historical Alternatives to Mass Production." *Past and Present* 108 (August 1985): 133–76. On the many forms of modern industry.

Schivelbusch, Wolfgang. *Disenchanted Night: The Industrialization of Light in the Nineteenth Century.* Berkeley, 1988.

———. *The Railway Journey.* Berkeley, 1986. Schivelbusch's imaginative studies are among the best ways to understand how the transformations of the nineteenth century changed daily experiences.

Thompson, E. P. *The Making of the English Working Class.* London, 1963. Shows how the French and Industrial Revolutions fostered the growth of working-class consciousness. A brilliant and important work.

Tilly, Louise, and Joan Scott. *Women, Work and the Family.* New York, 1978. Now the classic study.

Valenze, Deborah. *The First Industrial Woman.* New York, 1995. Excellent and readable on industrialization and economic change in general.

Williams, Raymond. *Keywords: A Vocabulary of Culture and Society.* New York, 1976. Brilliant and indispensable for students of culture. Now updated as *New Keywords: A Revised Vocabulary of Culture and Society* (2005), ed. Tony Bennett, Lawrence Grossberg, and Meaghan Morris.

Zeldin, Theodore. *France, 1848–1945.* 2 vols. Oxford, 1973–1977. Eclectic and wide-ranging social history.

CHAPTER 20

Anderson, Benedict. *Imagined Communities: Reflections on the Origin and Spread of Nationalism.* London, 1983. The most influential recent study of the subject; highly recommended for further reading.

Barzun, Jacques. *Classic, Romantic, and Modern.* Chicago, 1943. An enduring and penetrating mid-twentieth-century defense of the Romantic sensibility by a humane and influential cultural historian.

Berlin, Isaiah. *Karl Marx: His Life and Environment.* 4th ed. New York, 1996. An excellent short account.

Blackbourn, David. *The Conquest of Nature: Water, Landscape and the Making of Modern Germany* (New York, 2007). A noted historian turns his attention to the importance of ecology and environmental change for the emergence of modern Germany.

Briggs, Asa. *The Age of Improvement, 1783–1867.* New York, 1979. A survey of England from 1780 to 1870, particularly strong on Victorian attitudes.

Colley, Linda. *Britons: Forging the Nation, 1707–1837.* New Haven, 1992. An important analysis of Britain's emerging national consciousness in the eighteenth and early nineteenth centuries.

Furet, François. *Revolutionary France, 1770–1880.* New York, 1970. An excellent and fresh overview by one of the preeminent historians of the revolution of 1789.

Gilbert, Sandra M., and Susan Gubar. *The Madwoman in the Attic: The Woman Writer and the Nineteenth-Century Literary Imagination.* New Haven and London, 1970. A study of the history of women writers and an examination of women writers as historians of their time.

Kramer, Lloyd. *Nationalism: Political Cultures in Europe and America, 1775–1865.* London, 1998. Excellent recent overview.

Langer, William. *Political and Social Upheaval, 1832–1851.* New York, 1969. Long the standard and still the most comprehensive survey.

Laven, David, and Lucy Riall. *Napoleon's Legacy: Problems of Government in Restoration Europe.* London, 2002. A recent collection of essays.

Levinger, Matthew. *Enlightened Nationalism: The Transformation of Prussian Political Culture, 1806–1848.* New York, 2000. A nuanced study of Prussian conservatism, with implications for the rest of Europe.

Macfie, A. L. *Orientalism.* London, 2002. Introductory but very clear.

Merriman, John M., ed. *1830 in France.* New York, 1975. Seminal collection of essays examining the 1830 Revolution, its social origins, and its impact on the French nation.

Osterhammel, Jürgen. *The Transformation of the World: A Global History of the Nineteenth Century.* Princeton, 2014.

Pinkney, David. *The French Revolution of 1830.* Princeton, NJ, 1972. A reinterpretation; now the best history of the revolution.

Porter, Roy, and Mikulas Teich, eds. *Romanticism in National Context.* Cambridge, 1988.

Raeff, Marc. *The Decembrist Movement.* New York, 1966. A study of the Russian uprising with documents.

Sahlins, Peter. *Forest Rites: The War of the Demoiselles in Nineteenth-Century France.* Cambridge, MA, 1994. A fascinating study of relations among peasant communities, the forests, and the state.

Said, Edward W. *Orientalism.* New York, 1979. A brilliant and biting study of the imaginative hold of the Orient on European intellectuals.

Saville, John. *1848: The British State and the Chartist Movement.* New York, 1987. A detailed account of the movement's limited successes and ultimate failure.

Schroeder, Paul. *The Transformation of European Politics, 1763–1848.* Oxford and New York, 1994. For those interested in international relations and diplomacy; massively researched and a fresh look at the period. Especially good on the Congress of Vienna.

Sewell, William H. *Work and Revolution in France: The Language of Labor from the Old Regime to 1848.* Cambridge, 1980. A very influential study of French radicalism and its larger implications.

Smith, Bonnie. *The Gender of History: Men, Women, and Historical Practice.* Cambridge, MA, 1998. On Romanticism and the historical imagination.

Sperber, Jonathan. *Karl Marx: A Nineteenth-Century Life.* New York, 2013. A detailed biography examining Marx's public and private engagements, setting him in the context of his time.

Wordsworth, Jonathan, Michael C. Jaye, and Robert Woof. *William Wordsworth and the Age of English Romanticism.* New Brunswick, NJ, 1987. Wide ranging and beautifully illustrated, a good picture of the age.

CHAPTER 21

Agulhon, Maurice. *The Republican Experiment, 1848–1852.* New York, 1983. A full treatment of the revolution in France.

Beales, Derek. *The Risorgimento and the Unification of Italy.* New York, 1971. Objective, concise survey of Italian unification.

Blackbourn, David. *The Long Nineteenth Century: A History of Germany, 1780–1918.* New York, 1998.

Blackbourn, David, and Geoff Eley. *The Peculiarities of German History: Bourgeois Society and Politics in Nineteenth-Century Germany.* Oxford, 1984. Critical essays on the course of German history during the age of national unification and after.

Blackburn, Robin. *The Overthrow of Colonial Slavery.* London, 1988. Brilliant and detailed overview of the social history of slavery and antislavery movements.

Brophy, James M. *Capitalism, Politics, and Railroads in Prussia, 1830–1870.* Columbus, OH, 1998. Important, clear, and helpful.

Coppa, Frank. *The Origins of the Italian Wars of Independence.* London, 1992. Lively narrative.

Craig, Gordon. *Germany, 1866–1945.* New York, 1978. An excellent and thorough synthesis.

Davis, David Brian. *Inhuman Bondage: The Rise and Fall of Slavery in the New World.* New York, 2006. As one reviewer aptly puts it, "A gracefully fashioned masterpiece."

Deak, Istvan. *The Lawful Revolution: Louis Kossuth and the Hungarians, 1848–1849.* New York, 1979. The best on the subject.

Eyck, Erich. *Bismarck and the German Empire.* 3rd ed. London, 1968. The best one-volume study of Bismarck.

Hamerow, Theodore S. *The Birth of a New Europe: State and Society in the Nineteenth Century.* Chapel Hill, NC, 1983. A discussion of political and social change, and their relationship to industrialization and the increase in state power.

———. *The Social Foundations of German Unification, 1858–1871.* 2 vols. Princeton, NJ, 1969–1972. Concentrates on economic factors that determined the solution to the unification question. An impressive synthesis.

Higonnet, Patrice. *Paris: Capital of the World.* London, 2002. Fascinating and imaginative study of Paris as "capital of the nineteenth century."

Hobsbawm, Eric J. *The Age of Capital, 1848–1875.* London, 1975. Among the best introductions.

———. *Nations and Nationalism since 1870: Programme, Myth, Reality.* 2nd ed. Cambridge, 1992. A clear, concise analysis of the historical and cultural manifestations of nationalism.

Howard, Michael. *The Franco-Prussian War.* New York, 1981. The war's effect on society.

Hutchinson, John, and Anthony Smith, eds. *Nationalism.* New York, 1994. A collection of articles, not particularly historical, but with the merit of discussing non-European nationalisms.

Johnson, Susan. *Roaring Camp.* New York, 2000. A history of one mining camp in California and a microhistory of the larger forces changing the West and the world.

Kolchin, Peter. *Unfree Labor: American Slavery and Russian Serfdom.* Cambridge, MA, 1987. Pioneering comparative study.

Mack Smith, Denis. *Cavour and Garibaldi.* New York, 1968.

———. *The Making of Italy, 1796–1870.* New York, 1968. A narrative with documents.

McPherson, James. *Battle Cry of Freedom: The Civil War Era.* New York, 1988. Universally acclaimed and prize-winning book on the politics of slavery and the conflicts entailed in nation building in the mid-nineteenth-century United States.

Pflanze, Otto. *Bismarck and the Development of Germany.* 2nd ed. 3 vols. Princeton, NJ, 1990. Extremely detailed analysis of Bismarck's aims and policies.

Pinkney, David. *Napoleon III and the Rebuilding of Paris.* Princeton, NJ, 1972. An interesting account of the creation of modern Paris during the Second Empire.

Robertson, Priscilla. *Revolutions of 1848: A Social History.* Princeton, NJ, 1952. Old-fashioned narrative, but very readable.

Sammons, Jeffrey L. *Heinrich Heine: A Modern Biography.* Princeton, NJ, 1979. An excellent historical biography as well as a study of culture and politics.

Scott, Rebecca J. *Degrees of Freedom: Louisiana and Cuba after Slavery.* Cambridge, MA, 2008. Brings the lives of slaves and their owners to life during the era of emancipation in a comparative history that places the southern United States in the context of the Atlantic world.

Sheehan, James J. *German Liberalism in the Nineteenth Century.* Chicago, 1978. Fresh and important synthesis.

Snyder, Timothy. *The Reconstruction of Nations: Poland, Ukraine, Lithuania, Belarus.* New Haven, 2003. An indispensable account of the emergence of national cultures and nation-states in central and eastern Europe from the early modern period to the present.

Sperber, Jonathan. *The European Revolutions, 1848–1851.* Cambridge, 2005. An excellent synthesis and the best one-volume treatment of the 1848 revolutions, describing the reasons for their failure.

———. *Rhineland Radicals: The Democratic Movement and the Revolution of 1848–1849.* Princeton, NJ, 1993. A detailed study of Germany by the author of an overview of the revolutions of 1848.

Stearns, Peter N. *1848: The Revolutionary Tide in Europe.* New York, 1974. Stresses the social background of the revolutions.

Zeldin, Theodore. *The Political System of Napoleon III.* New York, 1958. Compact and readable, by one of the major scholars of the period.

CHAPTER 22

Achebe, Chinua. *Things Fall Apart.* Expanded edition with notes. Portsmouth, NH, 1996. An annotated edition of the now classic novel about colonial Africa.

Adas, Michael. *Machines as the Measure of Man: Science, Technology, and Ideologies of Western Dominance.* Ithaca, NY, and London, 1989. An important study of Europeans' changing perceptions of themselves and others during the period of industrialization.

Bayly, C. A. *Indian Society and the Making of the British Empire.* Cambridge, 1988. A good introduction, and one that bridges eighteenth- and nineteenth-century imperialisms.

Burbank, Jane, and Frederick Cooper. *Empires in World History: Power and the Politics of Difference.* Princeton, NJ, 2010. Powerful synthesis that sets European empires in the broader context of world history.

Burton, Antoinette. *Burdens of History: British Feminists, Indian Women, and Imperial Culture, 1865–1915.* Chapel Hill, NC, 1994. On the ways in which women and feminists came to support British imperialism.

Cain, P. J., and A. G. Hopkins. *British Imperialism, 1688–2000.* London, 2002. One of the most influential studies. Excellent overview and exceptionally good on economics.

Chakrabarty, Dipesh. *Provincializing Europe: Postcolonial Thought and Historical Difference.* Princeton, NJ, 2000. Sophisticated theoretical challenge to European narratives of social and political progress.

Clancy Smith, Julia, and Frances Gouda. *Domesticating the Empire: Race, Gender, and Family Life in French and Dutch Colonialism.* Charlottesville, VA, and London, 1998. A particularly good collection of essays that both breaks new historical ground and is accessible to nonspecialists. Essays cover daily life and private life in new colonial cultures.

Cohn, Bernard S. *Colonialism and Its Forms of Knowledge.* Princeton, NJ, 1996. Argues that new forms of cultural knowledge were essential to the project of British imperialism in India.

Conklin, Alice. *A Mission to Civilize: The Republican Idea of Empire in France and West Africa, 1895–1930.* Stanford, CA, 1997. One of the best studies of how the French reconciled imperialism with their vision of the Republic.

Cooper, Frederick. *Colonialism in Question: Theory, Knowledge, History.* Berkeley, 2005. Crucial collection of path-breaking essays on the history of colonialism.

Cooper, Frederick, and Ann Laura Stoler. *Tensions of Empire: Colonial Cultures in a Bourgeois World.* Berkeley, 1997. New approaches, combining anthropology and history, with an excellent bibliography.

Darwin, John. *After Tamerlane: The Rise and Fall of Global Empires.* New York, 2008. A comprehensive global account of the phenomenon of empire and empire building that begins with the Mongol conquests and takes the story up to the present.

———. *The Empire Project: The Rise and Fall of the British World System.* Cambridge, 2009.

Goody, Jack. *Islam in Europe.* Cambridge, 2004. A broad overview of the different ways in which Islam and Muslims helped to shape European history.

Headrick, Daniel R. *The Tools of Empire: Technology and European Imperialism in the Nineteenth Century.* Oxford, 1981. A study of the relationship between technological innovation and imperialism.

Hobsbawm, Eric. *The Age of Empire, 1875–1914.* New York, 1987. Surveys the European scene at a time of apparent stability and real decline.

Hochschild, Adam. *King Leopold's Ghost: A Story of Greed, Terror, and Heroism in Colonial Africa.* Boston, 1998. Reads like a great novel.

Hull, Isabell. *Absolute Destruction: Military Culture and the Practices of War in Imperial Germany.* Ithaca, NY, 2005. A study of the German military and its role in imperial expansion in Africa; argues that the experience was crucial in shaping this institution as it entered the twentieth century.

Lorcin, Patricia. *Imperial Identities: Stereotyping, Prejudice and Race in Colonial Algeria.* New York, 1999.

Louis, William Roger. *The Oxford History of the British Empire.* 5 vols. Oxford, 1998. Excellent and wide-ranging collection of the latest research.

Manning, Patrick. *Navigating World History.* New York, 2003.

Metcalf, Thomas. *Ideologies of the Raj.* Cambridge, 1995.

Pakenham, Thomas. *The Scramble for Africa, 1876–1912.* London, 1991. A well-written narrative of the European scramble for Africa in the late nineteenth century.

Prochaska, David. *Making Algeria French: Colonialism in Bône, 1870–1920.* Cambridge, 1990. One of the few social histories in English of European settlement in Algeria.

Robinson, Ronald, and J. Gallagher. *Africa and the Victorians: The Official Mind of Imperialism.* London, 1961. A classic.

Said, Edward. *Culture and Imperialism.* New York, 1993. A collection of brilliant, sometimes controversial, essays.

Sangari, Kumkum, and Sudesh Vaid. *Recasting Women: Essays in Colonial History.* New Delhi, 1989. A collection of essays on women in India.

Schneer, Jonathan. *London 1900: The Imperial Metropolis.* New Haven, 1999. Excellent study of the empire—and opposition to empire—in the metropole.

Sonn, Tamara. *Islam: History, Religion, and Politics.* Chichester, 2016. A brief but helpful introduction to the history of Islam in its broad social and political context.

Spence, Jonathan. *The Search for Modern China.* New York, 1990. An excellent and readable introduction to modern Chinese history.

CHAPTER 23

Berghahn, Volker. *Imperial Germany, 1871–1914: Economy, Society, Culture, and Politics.* Providence, RI, 1994. Inclusive history that seeks to go beyond standard political accounts.

Berlanstein, Lenard. *The Working People of Paris, 1871–1914.* Baltimore, 1984. A social history of the workplace and its impact on working men and women.

Blackbourn, David. *The Long Nineteenth Century: A History of Germany, 1780–1918.* New York, 1998. Among the best surveys of German society and politics.

Bowler, Peter J. *Evolution: The History of an Idea.* Berkeley, 1984. One of this author's several excellent studies of the evolution of Darwinism.

Burns, Michael. *Dreyfus: A Family Affair.* New York, 1992. Follows the story of Dreyfus through the next generations.

Clancy-Smith, Julia. *Mediterraneans: North Africa and Europe in an Age of Migration, c. 1800–1900.* Berkeley, 2011. Students interested in contemporary debates about migration in Europe will find helpful historical context in this rich study of population movements in the Mediterranean world during the nineteenth century.

Clark, T. J. *The Painting of Modern Life: Paris in the Art of Manet and His Followers.* New York, 1985. Argues for seeing impressionism as a critique of French society.

Crosby, Alfred. *Ecological Imperialism: The Biological Expansion of Europe, 900–1900.* Cambridge, 1986. A foremost environmental historian follows up on his earlier work on the Columbian exchange with a broad-reaching account of the movement of people, animals, and plants from Europe to other parts of the globe across the last millennium.

Eley, Geoff. *Forging Democracy.* Oxford, 2002. Wide-ranging, multinational account of European radicalism from 1848 to the present.

Engelstein, Laura. *Slavophile Empire: Imperial Russia's Illiberal Path.* Ithaca, NY, 2009. An examination of Russia's political culture before World War I, with an eye toward later evolution during the twentieth century.

Frank, Stephen. *Crime, Cultural Conflict, and Justice in Rural Russia, 1856–1914.* Berkeley, 1999. A revealing study of social relations from the ground up.

Gay, Peter. *The Bourgeois Experience: Victoria to Freud.* 5 vols. New York, 1984–2000. Imaginative, brilliant study of private life and middle-class culture.

———. *Freud: A Life of Our Time.* New York, 1988. Beautifully written and lucid about difficult concepts; now the best biography.

Harris, Ruth. *Dreyfus: Politics, Emotion, and the Scandal of the Century.* London, 2011. A reassessment of the politics of the Dreyfus affair, with an eye toward its resonance in French culture as a whole.

Herbert, Robert L. *Impressionism: Art, Leisure, and Parisian Society.* New Haven, 1988. An accessible and important study of the impressionists and the world they painted.

Hughes, H. Stuart. *Consciousness and Society.* New York, 1958. A classic study on late-nineteenth-century European thought.

Jelavich, Peter. *Munich and Theatrical Modernism: Politics, Playwriting, and Performance, 1890–1914.* Cambridge, MA, 1985. On modernism as a revolt against nineteenth-century conventions.

Jones, Gareth Stedman. *Outcast London.* Oxford, 1971. Studies the breakdown in class relationships during the second half of the nineteenth century.

Joyce, Patrick. *Visions of the People: Industrial England and the Question of Class, 1848–1914.* New York, 1991. A social history of the workplace.

Kelly, Alfred. *The German Worker: Autobiographies from the Age of Industrialization.* Berkeley, 1987. Excerpts from workers' autobiographies provide fresh perspective on labor history.

Kern, Stephen. *The Culture of Time and Space.* Cambridge, MA, 1983. A cultural history of the late nineteenth century.

Lidtke, Vernon. *The Alternative Culture: Socialist Labor in Imperial Germany.* New York, 1985. A probing study of working-class culture.

Marrus, Michael Robert. *The Politics of Assimilation: A Study of the French Jewish Community at the Time of the Dreyfus Affair.* Oxford, 1971. Excellent social history.

Micale, Mark S. *Approaching Hysteria: Disease and Its Interpretations.* Princeton, NJ, 1995. Important study of the history of psychiatry before Freud.

Rupp, Leila J. *Worlds of Women: The Making of an International Women's Movement.* Princeton, NJ, 1997.

Schivelbusch, Wolfgang. *Disenchanted Night: The Industrialization of Light in the Nineteenth Century.* Berkeley, 1995. Imaginative study of how electricity transformed everyday life.

Schorske, Carl E. *Fin-de-Siècle Vienna: Politics and Culture.* New York, 1980. Classic account of avant-garde art, music, and intellectual culture set against the background of mass politics in the Austrian capital.

Schwartz, Vanessa. *Spectacular Realities: Early Mass Culture in Fin-de-Siècle Paris.* Berkeley, 1998. Innovative approach to the emergence of mass culture in modern France.

Showalter, Elaine. *The Female Malady: Women, Madness, and English Culture, 1890–1980.* New York, 1985. Brilliant and readable on Darwin, Freud, gender, and the First World War.

Silverman, Deborah L. *Art Nouveau in Fin-de-Siècle France: Politics, Psychology, and Style.* Berkeley, CA, 1989. A study of the relationship between psychological and artistic change.

Smith, Bonnie. *Changing Lives: Women in European History since 1700.* New York, 1988. A useful overview of European women's history.

Stern, Fritz. *The Politics of Cultural Despair: A Study of the Rise of the Germanic Ideology.* Berkeley, 1974. Classic account of the rise of nationalist and populist politics in German-speaking lands of central Europe before World War I.

Tickner, Lisa. *The Spectacle of Women: Imagery of the Suffrage Campaign, 1907–14.* Chicago, 1988. A very engaging study of British suffragism.

Verner, Andrew. *The Crisis of Russian Autocracy: Nicholas II and the 1905 Revolution.* Princeton, NJ, 1990. A detailed study of this important event.

Vital, David. *A People Apart: A Political History of the Jews in Europe, 1789–1939.* Oxford and New York, 1999. Comprehensive and extremely helpful.

Walkowitz, Judith. *City of Dreadful Delight: Narratives of Sexual Danger in Late-Victorian London.* Chicago, 1992. Cultural history of the English capital at the end of the nineteenth century.

Weber, Eugen. *Peasants into Frenchmen: The Modernization of Rural France, 1870–1914*. Stanford, CA, 1976. A study of how France's peasantry was assimilated into the Third Republic.

Wehler, Hans-Ulrich. *The German Empire, 1871–1918*. Dover, 1997. Standard account by a respected German historian.

CHAPTER 24

Aksakal, Mustapha. *The Ottoman Road to War in 1914: The Ottoman Empire and the First World War*. Cambridge, 2009. A compelling look at Ottoman involvement in the First World War.

Bourke, Joanna. *Dismembering the Male: Men's Bodies, Britain, and the Great War*. Chicago, 1996. A cultural history of the war's effects on male bodies and codes of masculinity.

Chickering, Roger. *Imperial Germany and the Great War, 1914–1918*. New York, 1998. An excellent synthesis.

Clark, Christopher. *The Sleepwalkers: How Europe Went to War in 1914*. New York, 2013. Comprehensive reassessment of the war's origins.

Eksteins, Modris. *Rites of Spring: The Great War and the Birth of the Modern Age*. New York, 1989. Fascinating, though impressionistic, on war, art, and culture.

Ferguson, Niall. *The Pity of War*. London, 1998. A fresh look at the war, including strategic issues, international relations, and economics.

Ferro, Marc. *The Great War, 1914–1918*. London, 1973. Very concise overview.

Figes, Orlando. *A People's Tragedy: A History of the Russian Revolution*. New York, 1997. Excellent, detailed narrative.

Fischer, Fritz. *War of Illusions*. New York, 1975. Deals with Germany within the context of internal social and economic trends.

Fitzpatrick, Sheila. *The Russian Revolution, 1917–1932*. New York and Oxford, 1982. Concise overview.

Fussell, Paul. *The Great War and Modern Memory*. New York, 1975. A brilliant examination of British intellectuals' attitudes toward the war.

Hynes, Samuel. *A War Imagined: The First World War and English Culture*. New York, 1991. The war as perceived on the home front.

Jelavich, Barbara. *History of the Balkans: Twentieth Century*. New York, 1983. Useful for an understanding of the continuing conflict in eastern Europe.

Joll, James. *The Origins of the First World War*. London, 1984. Comprehensive and very useful.

Keegan, John. *The First World War*. London, 1998. The best overall military history.

Kershaw, Ian. *To Hell and Back: Europe 1914–1949*. New York, 2015. A thorough introduction to the history of Europe during the First and Second World Wars, by the world's foremost biographer of Adolf Hitler.

Macmillan, Margaret, and Richard Holbrooke. *Paris 1919: Six Months That Changed the World*. New York, 2003. Fascinating fresh look at the peace conference.

Mazower, Mark. *Dark Continent: Europe's Twentieth Century*. New York, 1999. An excellent survey, particularly good on nations and minorities in the Balkans and eastern Europe.

Rabinowitch, Alexander. *The Bolsheviks Come to Power*. New York, 1976. A well-researched and carefully documented account.

Roberts, Mary Louise. *Civilization without Sexes: Reconstructing Gender in Postwar France, 1917–1927*. Chicago, 1994. A prize-winning study of the issues raised by the "new woman."

Schivelbusch, Wolfgang. *The Culture of Defeat: On National Trauma, Mourning, and Recovery*. New York, 2001. Fascinating if impressionistic comparative study.

Smith, Leonard. *Between Mutiny and Obedience: The Case of the French Fifth Infantry Division during World War I*. Princeton, NJ, 1994. An account of mutiny and the reasons behind it.

Stevenson, David. *Cataclysm: The First World War as Political Tragedy*. New York, 2003. Detailed and comprehensive, now one of the best single-volume studies.

Stites, Richard. *Revolutionary Dreams: Utopian Visions and Experimental Life in the Russian Revolution*. New York, 1989. The influence of utopian thinking on the revolution.

Suny, Ronald Grigor, Fatma Muge Gocek, and Norman Naimark, eds. *A Question of Genocide: Armenians and Turks at the End of the Ottoman Empire*. Oxford, 2011. Multiauthor work offering a comprehensive summary of research on the Armenian genocide.

Williams, John. *The Home Fronts: Britain, France and Germany, 1914–1918*. London, 1972. A survey of life away from the battlefield and the impact of the war on domestic life.

Winter, Jay. *Sites of Memory, Sites of Mourning: The Great War in European Cultural History*. Cambridge, 1998. An essential reference on the legacy of World War I in European cultural history.

Winter, Jay, and Jean-Louis Robert. *Capital Cities at War: Paris, London, Berlin, 1914–1919*. Cambridge, 1997 (vol. 1), 2007 (vol. 2). Multiauthor work on the demographic, social, and cultural effects of the war on civilian populations of three European capitals.

CHAPTER 25

Bosworth, R. J. B. *Mussolini's Italy: Life under the Fascist Dictatorship, 1915–1945*. New York, 2007. Comprehensive account of "everyday" fascism in Italy.

Conquest, Robert. *The Great Terror: A Reassessment*. New York, 1990. One of the first histories of the Terror; should be read in conjunction with others in this list.

Crew, David F., ed. *Nazism and German Society, 1933–1945*. New York, 1994. An excellent and accessible collection of essays.

de Grazia, Victoria. *How Fascism Ruled Women: Italy, 1922–1945*. Berkeley, 1993. The contradictions between fascism's vision of modernity and its commitment to patriarchal institutions, seen from the point of view of Italian women.

Figes, Orlando. *Peasant Russia, Civil War: The Volga Countryside in Revolution, 1917–1921*. Oxford, 1989. Detailed and sophisticated but readable. Study of the region from the eve of the revolution through the civil war.

Fitzpatrick, Shelia. *Everyday Stalinism: Ordinary Life in Extraordinary Times; Soviet Russia in the 1930s*. Oxford and New York, 1999. Gripping on how ordinary people dealt with famine, repression, and chaos.

Friedlander, Saul. *Nazi Germany and the Jews: The Years of Persecution. 1933–1939*. Rev. ed. New York, 2007. Excellent; the first of a two-volume study.

Gay, Peter. *Weimar Culture*. New York, 1968. Concise and elegant overview.

Getty, J. Arch, and Oleg V. Naumov. *The Road to Terror: Stalin and the Self-Destruction of the Bolsheviks, 1932–1939.* New Haven, 1999. Combines analysis with documents made public for the first time.

Goldman, Wendy Z. *Women, the State, and Revolution: Soviet Family Policy and Social Life, 1917–1936.* New York, 1993. On the Bolshevik attempts to transform gender and family.

Kershaw, Ian. *Hitler.* 2 vols: *1889–1936 Hubris,* New York, 1999; *1936–1945: Nemesis,* New York, 2001. The best biography: insightful about politics, culture, and society as well as the man.

———. *The Hitler Myth: Image and Reality in the Third Reich.* New York, 1987. Brilliant study of how Nazi propagandists sold the myth of the Fuhrer and why many Germans bought it.

Klemperer, Victor. *I Will Bear Witness: A Diary of the Nazi Years, 1933–1941.* New York, 1999.

———. *I Will Bear Witness: A Diary of the Nazi Years, 1942–1945.* New York, 2001. Certain to be a classic.

Kotkin, Stephen. *Stalin.* Vol. 1, *Paradoxes of Power, 1878–1928.* New York, 2015. The first volume of a new comprehensive biography of the Russian leader, based on deep familiarity with archival sources.

Lewin, Moshe. *The Making of the Soviet System: Essays in the Social History of Interwar Russia.* New York, 1985. One of the best to offer a view from below.

Maier, Charles. *Recasting Bourgeois Europe.* Princeton, NJ, 1975. Now classic account of the political and social adjustments made between state and society during the interwar years throughout Europe.

McDermott, Kevin. *Stalin: Revolutionary in an Era of War.* Basingstoke, UK, and New York, 2006. Useful, short, and recent.

Montefior, Simon Sebag. *Stalin: The Court of the Red Tsar.* London, 2004. On the relations among the top Bolsheviks, an interesting personal portrait. Takes you inside the inner circle.

Orwell, George. *The Road to Wigan Pier.* London, 1937. On unemployment and life in the coal-mining districts of England, by one of the great British writers of the twentieth century.

———. *Homage to Catalonia.* London, 1938. A firsthand account of the Spanish Civil War.

Paxton, Robert O. *The Anatomy of Fascism.* New York, 2004. Excellent introduction to a complex subject by a foremost historian of twentieth century Europe.

Payne, Stanley G. *A History of Fascism, 1914–1945.* Madison, WI, 1996. Thorough account of the origins and evolution of fascism in Europe through the end of World War II.

Peukert, Detlev. *The Weimar Republic.* New York, 1993. Useful and concise history of Weimar by a respected German historian of the period.

Rentschler, Eric. *The Ministry of Illusion: Nazi Cinema and Its Afterlife.* Cambridge, MA, 1996. For the more advanced student.

Service, Robert. *Stalin: A Biography.* London, 2004. Updates Tucker.

Suny, Ronald Grigor. *The Revenge of the Past: Nationalism, Revolution, and the Collapse of the Soviet Union.* Stanford, CA, 1993. Path-breaking study of the issues of nationalism and ethnicity from the revolution to the end of the Soviet Union.

Tucker, Robert C. *Stalin as Revolutionary, 1879–1929.* New York, 1973.

———. *Stalin in Power: The Revolution from Above, 1928–1941.* New York, 1990. With *Stalin as Revolutionary,* emphasizes Stalin's purpose and method and sets him in the tradition of Russian dictators.

Weitz, Eric D. *Weimar Germany: Promise and Tragedy.* Princeton, NJ, 2009. A valuable and thorough account that ties together the complex connections between Weimar culture and politics in this transformational period.

Worster, Donald. *The Dust Bowl: The Southern Plains in the 1930s.* Oxford, 1979, 2004. A pioneering work of U.S. environmental history that changed the way people understood the history of the Depression and economic change in United States.

CHAPTER 26

The U.S. Holocaust Memorial Museum has an extraordinary collection of articles, photographs, and maps. See www.ushmm.org.

Bartov, Omer. *Hitler's Army: Soldiers, Nazis, and War in the Third Reich.* New York, 1991. A study of the radicalization of the German army on the Russian front.

Braithwaite, Rodric. *Moscow 1941: A City and Its People at War.* London, 2006. Readable account of one of the turning points of the war.

Browning, Christopher R. *The Path to Genocide: Essays on Launching the Final Solution.* Cambridge, 1992. Discusses changing interpretations and case studies. See also this author's *Ordinary Men: Reserve Police Battalion 101 and the Final Solution in Poland.*

Burrin, Philippe. *France under the Germans: Collaboration and Compromise.* New York, 1996. Comprehensive on occupation and collaboration.

Carr, Raymond. *The Spanish Tragedy: The Civil War in Perspective.* London, 1977. A thoughtful introduction to the Spanish Civil War and the evolution of Franco's Spain.

Davies, Norman. *Heart of Europe: The Past in Poland's Present.* Oxford, 2001. Revised edition of a classic account of Poland's place in European history, with special attention to the second half of the twentieth century.

Dawidowicz, Lucy S. *The War against the Jews, 1933–1945.* New York, 1975. A full account of the Holocaust.

Divine, Robert A. *Roosevelt and World War II.* Baltimore, 969. A diplomatic history.

Djilas, Milovan. *Wartime.* New York, 1977. An insider's account of the partisans' fighting in Yugoslavia and a good example of civil war within the war.

Fritzsche, Peter. *Life and Death in the Third Reich.* Cambridge, MA, 2009. A compelling account of the appeal of Nazi ideology and the extent to which it was embraced by ordinary people in Germany.

Gellately, Robert, and Ben Kiernan, eds. *The Specter of Genocide: Mass Murder in Historical Perspective.* New York, 2003. A particularly thoughtful collection of essays.

Graham, Helen. *The Spanish Civil War: A Very Short Introduction.* Oxford and New York, 2005. Excellent and very concise, based on the author's new interpretation in the more detailed *The Spanish Republic at War, 1936–1939.* Cambridge, 2002.

Hilberg, Raul. *The Destruction of the European Jews.* 2nd ed. 3 vols. New York, 1985. An excellent treatment of the Holocaust, its origins, and its consequences.

Hitchcock, William I. *The Bitter Road to Freedom: A New History of the Liberation of Europe.* New York, 2008. The story of Europe's liberation from Hitler's control, seen from the point of view of civilian populations.

Kedward, Roderick. *In Search of the Maquis: Rural Resistance in Southern France, 1942–1944.* Oxford, 1993. An engaging study of French guerrilla resistance.

Keegan, John. *The Second World War.* New York, 1990. By one of the great military historians of our time.

Marrus, Michael R. *The Holocaust in History.* Hanover, NH, 1987. Thoughtful analysis of central issues.

Mawdsley, Evan. *Thunder in the East: The Nazi-Soviet War, 1941–1945.* New York, 2005.

Megargee, Geoffrey. *War of Annihilation: Combat and Genocide on the Eastern Front, 1941.* Lanham, MD, 2006. Represents some of the new historical work on the Eastern Front.

Merridale, Catherine. *Ivan's War: Life and Death in the Red Army, 1939–1945.* New York, 2006. Raises many questions and insights.

Michel, Henri. *The Shadow War: The European Resistance, 1939–1945.* New York, 1972. Compelling reading.

Milward, Alan S. *War, Economy, and Society, 1939–1945.* Berkeley, 1977. On the economic impact of the war and the strategic impact of the economy.

Noakes, Jeremy, and Geoffrey Pridham. *Nazism: A History in Documents and Eyewitness Accounts, 1919–1945.* New York, 1975. An excellent combination of analysis and documentation.

Overy, Richard. *Russia's War.* New York, 1998. A very readable account that accompanies the PBS series of the same title.

———. *Why the Allies Won.* New York, 1995. Excellent analysis; succinct.

Paxton, Robert O. *Vichy France: Old Guard and New Order, 1940–1944.* New York, 1982. Brilliant on collaboration and Vichy's National Revolution.

Roberts, Mary Louise. *What Soldiers Do: Sex and the American GI in World War II France.* Chicago, 2013. Critical reappraisal of how sex between GIs and civilians became an issue for French and U.S. military personnel after the D-Day invasion.

Snyder, Timothy. *Bloodlands: Europe between Hitler and Stalin.* New York, 2010. Thorough and penetrating account of the methods and motives of Hitler's and Stalin's regimes.

Stoff, Michael B. *The Manhattan Project: A Documentary Introduction to the Atomic Age.* New York, 1991. Political, scientific, and historical; excellent documents and commentary.

Weinberg, Gerhard L. *A World at Arms: A Global History of World War II.* Cambridge, 2005. Second edition of a comprehensive and respected global account of the Second World War.

Wilkinson, James D. *The Intellectual Resistance in Europe.* Cambridge, MA, 1981. A comparative study of the movement throughout Europe.

CHAPTER 27

Aron, Raymond. *The Imperial Republic: The United States and the World, 1945–1973.* Lanham, MD, 1974. An early analysis by a leading French political theorist.

Carter, Erica. *How German Is She? Postwar West German Reconstruction and the Consuming Woman.* Ann Arbor, MI, 1997. A thoughtful examination of gender and the reconstruction of the family in West Germany during the 1950s.

Clayton, Anthony. *The Wars of French Decolonization.* London, 1994. Good survey.

Connelly, Matthew. *A Diplomatic Revolution: Algeria's Fight for Independence and the Origins of the Post–Cold War Era.* New York and Oxford, 2003. An international history.

Cooper, Frederick, and Ann Laura Stoler, eds. *Tensions of Empire: Colonial Cultures in a Bourgeois World.* Berkeley, CA, 1997. Collection of new essays, among the best.

Darwin, John. *Britain and Decolonization: The Retreat from Empire in the Postwar World.* New York, 1988. Best overall survey.

Deák, István, Jan T. Gross, and Tony Judt, eds. *The Politics of Retribution in Europe: World War II and Its Aftermath.* Princeton, NJ, 2000. Collection focusing on the attempt to come to terms with the Second World War in Eastern and Western Europe.

Farmer, Sarah. *Martyred Village: Commemorating the 1944 Massacre at Oradour-sur-Glane.* Berkeley, CA, 1999. Gripping story of French attempts to come to terms with collaboration and complicity in atrocities.

Holland, R. F. *European Decolonization 1918–1981: An Introductory Survey.* New York, 1985. Sprightly narrative and analysis.

Jarausch, Konrad Hugo, ed. *Dictatorship as Experience: Towards a Socio-Cultural History of the GDR.* Trans. Eve Duffy. New York, 1999. Surveys recent research on the former East Germany.

Judt, Tony. *The Burden of Responsibility: Blum, Camus, and the French Twentieth Century.* Chicago and London, 1998. Also on French intellectuals.

———. *A Grand Illusion? An Essay on Europe.* New York, 1996. Short and brilliant.

———. *Past Imperfect: French Intellectuals, 1944–1956.* Berkeley, 1992. Very readable, on French intellectuals, who loomed large during this period.

———. *Postwar: A History of Europe since 1945.* London, 2005. Detailed, comprehensive, and ground breaking, this single volume surpasses any other account of the entire postwar period.

Koven, Seth, and Sonya Michel. *Mothers of a New World: Maternalist Politics and the Origins of Welfare States.* New York, 1993. Excellent essays on the long history of welfare politics.

LaFeber, Walter. *America, Russia, and the Cold War.* New York, 1967. A classic, now in its ninth edition.

Large, David Clay. *Berlin.* New York, 2000. Accessible and engaging.

Leffler, Melvyn P. *A Preponderance of Power: National Security, the Truman Administration, and the Cold War.* Stanford, 1992. Solid political study.

Louis, William Roger. *The Ends of British Imperialism: The Scramble for Empire, Suez, and Decolonization.* London, 2006. Comprehensive and wide ranging.

Macey, David. *Frantz Fanon.* New York, 2000. Comprehensive recent biography.

Medvedev, Roy. *Khrushchev.* New York, 1983. A perceptive biography of the Soviet leader by a Soviet historian.

Milward, Alan S. *The Reconstruction of Western Europe, 1945–1951.* Berkeley, 1984. A good discussion of the "economic miracle."

Moeller, Robert G. *War Stories: The Search for a Usable Past in the Federal Republic of Germany.* Berkeley, 2001. Revealing analyses of postwar culture and politics.

Reynolds, David. *One World Divisible: A Global History Since 1945.* New York, 2000. Fresh approach, comprehensive, and very readable survey.

Rousso, Henri. *The Vichy Syndrome: History and Memory in France since 1944.* Cambridge, MA, 1991. First in a series of books by one of the preeminent French historians.

Schissler, Hanna, ed. *The Miracle Years: A Cultural History of West Germany, 1949–1968*. Princeton, NJ, 2001. The cultural effects of the "economic miracle."

Schneider, Peter. *The Wall Jumper: A Berlin Story*. Chicago, 1998. A fascinating novel about life in divided Berlin.

Shepard, Todd. *The Invention of Decolonization: The Algerian War and the Remaking of France*. Ithaca, NY, 2006. Excellent and original: a study of the deeply wrenching war's many ramifications.

Shipway, Martin. *Decolonization and Its Impact: A Comparative Approach to the End of the Colonial Empires*. Malden, MA, 2008. Accessible account emphasizing the unintended consequences of decolonization.

Trachtenberg, Mark. *A Constructed Peace: The Making of the European Settlement, 1945–1963*. Princeton, NJ, 1999. A detailed study of international relations that moves beyond the Cold War framework.

Tessler, Mark. *A History of the Israeli-Palestinian Conflict*. 2nd ed. Bloomington, 2009. Updated edition of the definitive account from the 1990s.

Westad, Odd Arne. *The Global Cold War*. New York, 2005. An international history that sees the roots of the world's present conflict in the history of the Cold War.

Wilder, Gary. *The French Imperial Nation-State: Negritude and Colonial Humanism between the Two World Wars*. Chicago, 2005. Fascinating new study of the Negritude thinkers in their context.

Yergin, Daniel. *Shattered Peace: The Origins of the Cold War*. New York, 1977. Rev. ed., 1990. Dramatic and readable.

Young, Marilyn B. *The Vietnam Wars, 1945–1990*. New York, 1991. Excellent account of the different stages of the war and its repercussions.

CHAPTER 28

Bailey, Beth. *From Front Porch to Back Seat: Courtship in Twentieth-Century America*. Baltimore, 1988. Good historical perspective on the sexual revolution.

Beschloss, Michael, and Strobe Talbott. *At the Highest Levels: The Inside Story of the End of the Cold War*. Boston, 1993. An analysis of the relationship between presidents Gorbachev and George H. W. Bush and their determination to ignore hard-liners.

Brown, Archie. *The Gorbachev Factor*. Oxford and New York, 1996. One of the first serious studies of Gorbachev, by an Oxford scholar of politics.

Caute, David. *The Year of the Barricades: A Journey through 1968*. New York, 1988. A well-written global history of 1968.

Charney, Leo, and Vanessa R. Schwartz, eds. *Cinema and the Invention of Modern Life*. Berkeley, 1995. Collection of essays.

Dallin, Alexander, and Gail Lapidus. *The Soviet System: From Crisis to Collapse*. Boulder, CO, 1995.

de Grazia, Victoria. *Irresistable Empire: America's Advance through Twentieth-Century Europe*. Cambridge, MA, 2006. Thorough exploration of the history of consumer culture in Europe and its links to relations with the United States.

Echols, Alice. *Daring to Be Bad: Radical Feminism in America, 1967–1975*. Minneapolis, 1989. Good narrative and analysis.

Eley, Geoff. *Forging Democracy: The History of the Left in Europe, 1850–2000*. Oxford and New York, 2002. Among its other qualities, one of the best historical perspectives on the 1960s.

Fink, Carole, Phillipp Gassert, and Detlef Junker, eds. *1968: The World Transformed*. Cambridge, 1998. A transatlantic history of 1968.

Fulbrook, Mary, ed. *Europe since 1945* (The Short Oxford History of Europe). Oxford, 2001. Particularly good articles on economics and political economy. Structural analysis.

Garton Ash, Timothy. *In Europe's Name: Germany and the Divided Continent*. New York, 1993. An analysis of the effect of German reunification on the future of Europe.

Glenny, Misha. *The Balkans, 1804–1999: Nationalism, War and the Great Powers*. London, 1999. Good account by a journalist who covered the fighting.

Horowitz, Daniel. *Betty Friedan and the Making of the Feminine Mystique: The American Left, the Cold War, and Modern Feminism*. Amherst, MA, 1998. A reconsideration.

Hosking, Geoffrey. *The Awakening of the Soviet Union*. Cambridge, MA, 1990. The factors that led to the end of the Soviet era.

Hughes, H. Stuart. *Sophisticated Rebels: The Political Culture of European Dissent, 1968–1987*. Cambridge, MA, 1990. The nature of dissent on both sides of the disintegrating Iron Curtain in the years 1988–1989.

Hulsberg, Werner. *The German Greens: A Social and Political Profile*. New York, 1988. The origins, politics, and impact of environmental politics.

Jarausch, Konrad. *The Rush to German Unity*. New York, 1994. The problems of reunification analyzed.

Judah, Tim. *The Serbs: History, Myth, and the Destruction of Yugoslavia*. New Haven, 1997. Overview of Serbian history by journalist who covered the war.

Kaplan, Robert D. *Balkan Ghosts: A Journey through History*. New York, 1993. More a political travelogue than a history, but very readable.

Kotkin, Stephen. *Armageddon Averted: The Soviet Collapse, 1970–2000*. Oxford, 2001. Excellent short account.

Kurlansky, Mark. *1968: The Year that Rocked the World*. New York, 2005. An accessible introduction for nonspecialists.

Lewin, Moshe. *The Gorbachev Phenomenon*. Expanded ed. Berkeley, 1991. Written as a firsthand account, tracing the roots of Gorbachev's successes and failures.

Lieven, Anatol. *Chechnya, Tombstone of Russia Power*. New Haven and London, 1998. Longer view of the region, by a journalist.

Maier, Charles S. *Dissolution: The Crisis of Communism and the End of East Germany*. Princeton, NJ, 1997. Detailed and sophisticated.

Mann, Michael. *The Dark Side of Democracy: Explaining Ethnic Cleansing*. New York, 2005. Brilliant essay on different episodes from Armenia to Rwanda.

Marwick, Arthur. *The Sixties*. Oxford and New York, 1998. An international history.

Pells, Richard. *Not Like Us: How Europeans Have Loved, Hated, and Transformed American Culture since World War II*. New York, 1997. From the point of view of an American historian.

Poiger, Uta G. *Jazz, Rock, and Rebels: Cold War Politics and American Culture in a Divided Germany*. Berkeley, 2000. Pioneering cultural history.

Sheehan, Neil. *A Bright Shining Lie: John Paul Vann and America in Vietnam*. New York, 1988. A study of the war and its escalation through one of the U.S. Army's field advisers.

Strayer, Robert. *Why Did the Soviet Union Collapse? Understanding Historical Change*. Armonk, NY, and London, 1998. A good introduction, with bibliography.

Suri, Jeremi. *Power and Protest.* New ed. Cambridge, MA, 2005. One of the best of the new global histories of the 1960s, looking at connections between social movements and international relations.

Wright, Patrick. *On Living in an Old Country: The National Past in Contemporary Britain.* New York, 1986. The culture of Britain in the 1980s.

CHAPTER 29

Bowen, John R. *Why the French Don't Like Headscarves: Islam, the State, and Public Space.* Princeton, NJ, 2008. An ethnographic account of this volatile debate in France.

Coetzee, J. M. *Waiting for the Barbarians.* London, 1980. A searing critique of apartheid-era South Africa by a leading Afrikaner novelist.

Eichengreen, Barry. *Hall of Mirrors: The Great Depression, the Great Recession, and the Uses—and Misuses—of History.* Oxford, 2015. A historical comparison of the financial crisis of 2008 with the depression of 1929 by an economist with a firm grasp on political and social history.

Epstein, Helen. *The Invisible Cure: Africa, the West, and the Fight Against AIDS.* New York, 2007. One of the best recent studies.

Esposito, John. *What Everyone Needs to Know about Islam.* Oxford, 2011. A useful general introduction to Islam, its place in world history, and contemporary Muslim societies, organized for quick reference by students.

Frieden, Jeffrey H. *Global Capitalism: Its Rise and Fall in the Twentieth Century.* New York, 2007. Broad-ranging history for the advanced student.

Geyer, Michael, and Charles Bright. "World History in a Global Age." *American Historical Review* 100, no. 4 (October 1995). An excellent short discussion.

Glendon, Mary Ann. *A World Made New: Eleanor Roosevelt and the Universal Declaration of Human Rights.* New York, 2001. A fascinating study of the High Commission in its time by a legal scholar.

Harvey, David. *A Brief History of Neoliberalism.* New York, 2007. A critical account of the history of neoliberalism that encompasses the United States, Europe, and Asia.

Held, David, et al. *Global Transformations: Politics, Economics, and Culture.* Stanford, 1999. Major survey of the globalization of culture, finance, criminality, and politics.

Hopkins, A. G., ed. *Globalization in World History.* New York, 2002. Excellent introduction, written by one of the first historians to engage the issue.

Hunt, Lynn. *Inventing Human Rights: A History.* New York, 2007. A short study of the continuities and paradoxes in the West's human rights tradition, by one of the foremost historians of the French Revolution. On 1776, 1789, and 1948.

Keddie, Nikki. *Modern Iran: Roots and Results of Revolution.* New Haven, 2003. A revised edition of her major study of Iran's 1979 revolution, with added perspective on Iran's Islamic government.

Lacqueur, Walter. *The Age of Terrorism.* Boston, 1987. An important study of the first wave of post-1960s terrorism.

Landes, David. *The Wealth and Poverty of Nations: Why Some Are So Rich and Some So Poor.* New York, 1998. Leading economic historian's account of globalization's effects on the international economy.

Lewis, Bernard. *The Crisis of Islam: Holy War and Unholy Terror.* New York, 2003. Conservative scholar of the Arab world discussing the political crises that fueled terrorism.

Mckeown, Adam. "Global Migration, 1846–1940." *Journal of World History* 15, no. 2 (2004). Includes references to more work on the subject.

McNeill, J. R. *Something New under the Sun: An Environmental History of the Twentieth-Century World.* New York and London, 2000. Fascinating new approach to environmental history.

Merlini, Cesare, and Olivier Roy, eds. *Arab Society in Revolt: The West's Mediterranean Challenge.* Washington, DC, 2012. A multiauthor attempt to understand the Arab Spring of 2011.

Novick, Peter. *The Holocaust in American Life.* Boston, 1999.

Power, Samantha. *A Problem from Hell: America and the Age of Genocide.* New York, 2013. A prize-winning survey of the entire twentieth century, its genocides, and the different human rights movements that responded to them.

Reynolds, David. *One World Divisible: A Global History since 1945.* New York and London, 2000. Excellent study of the different dimensions of globalization.

Rodrik, Dani. *The Globalization Paradox: Democracy and the Future of the World Economy.* New York, 2012. A historical-minded account of the challenges faced by nation-states in the contemporary global economy.

Roy, Olivier. *Globalized Islam: The Search for a New Ummah.* New York, 2006. Examines changes in religious belief and practice as Islam has spread from its historic centers in the Middle East to other areas of the world, including Europe and North America.

Scott, Joan. *The Politics of the Veil.* Princeton, NJ, 2010. A leading feminist scholar analyzes the debate about the veil and the Islamic headscarf in Europe.

Shilts, Randy. *And the Band Played On: Politics, People, and the AIDS Epidemic.* New York, 1987. An impassioned attack on the individuals and governments that failed to come to grips with the early spread of the disease.

Shlaim, Avi. *The Iron Wall: Israel and the Arab World.* New York, 2000. Leading Israeli historian on the evolution of Israel's defensive foreign policy.

Stiglitz, Joseph E. *Globalization and Its Discontents.* New York, 2002. A recent and important consideration of contemporary globalization's character and the conflicts it creates, particularly over commerce and culture.

———. *Freefall: America, Free Markets, and the Sinking of the World Economy.* New York, 2010. Nobel Prize–winning economist's account of the financial crisis of 2008.

Tooze, Adam. *Crashed: How a Decade of Financial Crises Changed the World.* New York, 2018.

Turkle, Sherry. *Life on the Screen: Identity in the Age of the Internet.* New York, 1995. An important early study of Web culture and the fluid possibilities of electronic communication.

Winter, Jay. *Dreams of Peace and Freedom: Utopian Moments in the Twentieth Century.* New Haven, 2006. One of the leading historians of war and atrocity turns here to twentieth-century hopes for peace and human rights.

Wolf, Martin. *The Shifts and the Shocks: What We've Learned—and Have Still to Learn—From the Financial Crisis.* New York, 2014. A respected journalist offers a judgment on the financial crisis of 2008 and the subsequent European debt crisis.

Zahra, Tara. *The Great Departure: Mass Migration from Eastern Europe and the Making of the Free World.* New York, 2017.

Glossary

1973 OPEC oil embargo Some leaders in the Arab-dominated Organization of the Petroleum Exporting Countries (OPEC) wanted to use oil as a weapon against the West in the Arab-Israeli conflict. After the 1972 Arab-Israeli war, OPEC instituted an oil embargo against Western powers. The embargo increased the price of oil and sparked spiraling inflation and economic troubles in Western nations, triggering in turn a cycle of dangerous recession that lasted nearly a decade. In response, Western governments began viewing the Middle Eastern oil regions as areas of strategic importance.

Abbasid caliphate (750–930) The Abbasid family claimed to be descendants of Muhammad, and in 750 they successfully led a rebellion against the Umayyads, seizing control of Muslim territories in Arabia, Persia, North Africa, and the Near East. The Abbasids modeled their behavior and administration on those of the Persian princes and their rule on that of the Persian Empire, establishing a new capital at Baghdad.

Peter Abelard (1079–1142) Highly influential philosopher, theologian, and teacher, often considered the founder of the University of Paris.

absolutism Form of government in which one person or body, usually the monarch, controls the right to make war, tax, judge, and coin money. The term was often used to refer to the state monarchies in seventeenth- and eighteenth-century Europe.

abstract expressionism The mid-twentieth-century school of art based in New York that included Jackson Pollock, Willem de Kooning, Franz Kline, and Helen Frankenthaler. It emphasized form, color, gesture, and feeling instead of figurative subjects.

Academy of Sciences This French institute of scientific inquiry was founded in 1666 by Louis XIV. France's statesmen exerted control over the academy and sought to share in the rewards of any discoveries its members made.

Aeneas Mythical founder of Rome, Aeneas was a refugee from the city of Troy whose adventures were described by the poet Virgil in the *Aeneid,* which was modeled on the oral epics of Homer.

Aetolian and Achaean Leagues These two alliances among Greek poleis were formed during the Hellenistic period in opposition to the Antigonids of Macedonia. Unlike the earlier defensive alliances of the classical period, each league was a real attempt to form a political federation.

African National Congress (ANC) Multiracial organization founded in 1912 whose goal was to end racial discrimination in South Africa.

Afrikaners Descendants of the original Dutch settlers of South Africa; formerly referred to as Boers.

agricultural revolution Numerous agricultural revolutions have occurred in the history of Western civilizations. One of the most significant began in the tenth century C.E. and increased the amount of land under cultivation as well as the productivity of the land. This revolution was made possible through the use of new technology, a rise in global temperatures, and more efficient methods of cultivation.

AIDS Acquired Immunodeficiency Syndrome. The final phase of HIV, AIDS first appeared in the 1970s and has developed into a global health catastrophe; it is spreading most quickly in developing nations in Africa and Asia.

Akhenaten (r. 1352–1336 B.C.E.) Pharaoh whose attempt to promote the worship of the sun god, Aten, ultimately weakened his dynasty's position in Egypt.

Alexander the Great (356–323 B.C.E.) The Macedonian king whose conquests of the Persian Empire and Egypt created a new Hellenistic world.

Alexander II (1818–1881) After the Crimean War, Tsar Alexander embarked on a program of reform and modernization, which included the emancipation of the serfs. A radical assassin killed him in 1881.

Alexius Comnenus (1057–1118) This Byzantine emperor requested Pope Urban II's help in raising an army to recapture Anatolia from the Seljuk Turks. Instead, Pope Urban II called for knights to go to the Holy Land and liberate it from its Muslim captors, launching the First Crusade.

Algerian War (1954–1962) The war between France and Algerians seeking independence. Led by the National Liberation Front (FLN), guerrillas fought the French army in the mountains and desert of Algeria. The FLN also initiated a campaign of bombing and terrorism in Algerian cities that led French soldiers to torture many Algerians, attracting world attention and international scandal.

Dante Alighieri (c. 1265–1321) Florentine poet and intellectual whose *Divine Comedy* was a pioneering work in the Italian vernacular and a vehicle for political and religious critique.

Allied Powers The First World War coalition of Great Britain, Ireland, Belgium, France, Italy, Russia, Portugal, Greece, Serbia, Montenegro, Albania, and Romania.

al Qaeda The radical Islamic organization founded in the late 1980s by former mujahidin who had fought against the Soviet Union in Afghanistan. Al Qaeda carried out the 9/11 terrorist attacks and is responsible as well for attacks in Africa, Southeast Asia, Europe, and the Middle East.

Ambrose (c. 340–397) One of the early church fathers, he helped define the relationship between the sacred authority of bishops and other Church leaders and the secular authority of worldly rulers. He believed that secular rulers were a part of the Church and therefore subject to it.

Americanization The fear of many Europeans, since the 1920s, that U.S. cultural products, such as film, television, and music, exerted too much influence. Many of the criticisms centered on America's emphasis on mass production and organization. Fears about Americanization were not limited to culture but extended to corporations, business techniques, global trade, and marketing.

Americas The name given to the two great landmasses of the New World, derived from the name of the Italian geographer Amerigo Vespucci. In 1492, Christopher Columbus reached the Bahamas and the island of Hispaniola, which began an era of Spanish conquest in North and South America. Originally, the Spanish had sought a route to Asia. Instead they discovered two continents whose wealth they decided to exploit. They were especially interested in gold and silver, which they either stole from indigenous peoples or mined, using indigenous peoples as labor. Silver became Spain's most lucrative export from the New World.

Amnesty International Nongovernmental organization formed in 1961 to defend "prisoners of conscience"—those detained for their beliefs, color, sex, ethnic origin, language, or religion.

Anabaptism Protestant movement that emerged in Switzerland in 1521; its adherents insisted that only adults could be baptized Christians.

anarchism In the nineteenth century, a political movement with the aim of establishing small-scale, localized, and self-sufficient democratic communities that could guarantee a maximum of individual sovereignty. Renouncing parties, unions, and any form of modern mass organization, the anarchists fell back on the tradition of conspiratorial violence.

Anatolia A region consisting of the peninsula linking Asia to Europe and reaching northward to the Black Sea, southward to the Mediterranean, and westward to the Aegean; often called "Asia Minor."

Anthropocene A term coined by geographers, geologists, and climate scientists to describe the era when human activities began to reshape earth's environment. Although some scholars contend that this epoch dates only as far back as the Industrial Revolution of the mid-nineteenth century, others date it from the Neolithic Revolution and the emergence of the earliest civilizations.

Anti–Corn Law League This organization successfully lobbied Parliament to repeal Britain's Corn Laws in 1846. The Corn Laws of 1815 had protected British landowners and farmers from foreign competition by establishing high tariffs, which kept bread prices artificially high for British consumers. The league saw these laws as unfair protection of the aristocracy and pushed for their repeal in the name of free trade.

anti-Semitism Anti-Semitism refers to hostility toward Jewish people. Religious forms of anti-Semitism have a long history in Europe, but during the nineteenth century anti-Semitism emerged as a potent ideology for mobilizing new constituencies in the era of mass politics. Playing on popular conspiracy theories about alleged Jewish influence in society, anti-Semites effectively rallied large bodies of supporters in France during the Dreyfus Affair, and then again during the rise of National Socialism in Germany after the First World War. The Holocaust would not have been possible without the acquiescence or cooperation of many thousands of people who shared anti-Semitic views.

apartheid The racial segregation policy of the Afrikaner-dominated South African government. Legislated in 1948 by the Afrikaner National Party, it existed in South Africa for many decades.

appeasement The policy pursued by Western governments in the face of German, Italian, and Japanese aggression leading up to the Second World War. The policy, which attempted to accommodate and negotiate peace with the aggressive nations, was based on the belief that another global war like the First World War was unimaginable, a belief that Germany and its allies had been mistreated by the terms of the Treaty of Versailles, and a fear that fascist Germany and its allies protected the West from the spread of Soviet communism.

Thomas Aquinas (1225–1274) Dominican friar and theologian whose systematic approach to Christian doctrine was influenced by Aristotle.

Arab-Israeli conflict Between the founding of the state of Israel in 1948 and the present, a series of wars has been fought between Israel and neighboring Arab nations: the war of 1948 when Israel defeated attempts by Egypt, Jordan, Iraq, Syria, and Lebanon to prevent the creation of the new state; the 1956 war between Israel and Egypt over the Sinai Peninsula; the 1967 war, when Israel gained control of additional land in the Golan Heights, the West Bank, the Gaza strip, and the Sinai; and the Yom Kippur War of 1973, when Israel once again fought with forces from Egypt and Syria. A particularly difficult issue in all of these conflicts has been the situation of the 950,000 Palestinian refugees made homeless by the first war in 1948 and the movement of Israeli settlers into the occupied territories (outside of Israel's original borders). In the late 1970s, peace talks between Israel and Egypt inspired some hope of peace, but an ongoing cycle of violence between Palestinians and the Israeli military has made a final settlement elusive.

Arab nationalism During the period of decolonization, secular forms of Arab nationalism, or pan-Arabism, found a wide following in many countries of the Middle East, especially in Egypt, Syria, and Iraq.

Arianism A variety of Christianity condemned as a heresy by the Roman Church, it derives from the teaching of a fourth-century priest named Arius, who rejected the idea that Jesus could be the divine equal of God.

aristocracy From the Greek word meaning "rule of the best." By 1000 B.C.E., the accumulated wealth of successful traders in Greece had created a new type of social class, which was based on wealth rather than warfare or birth. These men saw their wealth as a reflection of their superior qualities and aspired to emulate the heroes of old.

Aristotle (384–322 B.C.E.) A student of Plato, he based his philosophy on rational analysis of the material world. In contrast to his teacher, he stressed the rigorous investigation of real phenomena, rather than the development of universal ethics. He was, in turn, the teacher of Alexander the Great.

Asiatic Society A cultural organization founded in 1784 by British Orientalists who lauded native culture but believed in colonial rule.

Assyrians A Semitic-speaking people that moved into northern Mesopotamia around 2400 B.C.E.

Athens Athens emerged as the Greek polis with the most markedly democratic form of government through a series of political struggles during the sixth century B.C.E. After its key role in the defeat of two invading Persian forces, Athens became the preeminent naval power of ancient Greece and the exemplar of Greek culture. But it antagonized many other poleis, and became embroiled in a war with Sparta and its allies in 431 B.C.E. Called the Peloponnesian War, this bloody conflict lasted until Athens was defeated in 404 B.C.E.

atomic bomb In 1945, the United States dropped atomic bombs on Hiroshima and Nagasaki in Japan, ending the Second World War. In 1949, the Soviet Union tested its first atomic bomb, and in 1953 both superpowers demonstrated their new hydrogen bombs. Strategically, the nuclearization of warfare polarized the world. Countries without nuclear weapons found it difficult to avoid joining either the Soviet or American military pacts. Over time, countries split into two groups: the superpowers with enormous military budgets and those countries that relied on agreements and international law. The nuclearization of warfare also encouraged "proxy wars" between clients of superpowers. Culturally, the hydrogen bomb came to symbolize the age as well as both humanity's power and its vulnerability.

Augustine (c. 354–397) One of the most influential theologians of all time, Augustine described his conversion to Christianity in his autobiographical *Confessions* and articulated a new Christian worldview in *The City of God*, among other works.

Augustus (63 B.C.E.–14 C.E.) Born Gaius Octavius, this grandnephew and adopted son of Julius Caesar came to power in 27 B.C.E. His reign signals the end of the Roman Republic and the beginning of the Principate, the period when Rome was dominated by autocratic emperors.

Auschwitz-Birkenau The Nazi concentration camp in Poland that was designed for the systematic murder of Jews and Gypsies. Between 1942 and 1944 over one million people were killed in Auschwitz-Birkenau.

Austro-Hungarian Empire The dual monarchy established by the Habsburg family in 1867; it collapsed at the end of the First World War.

authoritarianism A centralized and dictatorial form of government, proclaimed by its adherents to be superior to parliamentary democracy. Authoritarian governments claim to be above the law, do not respect individual rights, and do not tolerate political opposition. Authoritarian regimes that have developed a central ideology such as fascism or communism are sometimes termed "totalitarian."

Avignon A city in southeastern France that became the seat of the papacy between 1305 and 1377, a period known as the "Babylonian Captivity" of the Roman Church.

Aztecs An indigenous people of central Mexico; their empire was conquered by Spanish conquistadors in the sixteenth century.

baby boom (1950s) The post–Second World War upswing in U.S. birth rates; it reversed a century of decline.

Babylon An ancient city between the Tigris and Euphrates Rivers, which became the capital of Hammurabi's empire in the eighteenth century B.C.E. and continued to be an important administrative and commercial capital under many subsequent imperial powers, including the Neo-Assyrians, Chaldeans, Persians, and Romans. It was here that Alexander the Great died in 323 B.C.E.

Babylonian captivity Refers both to the Jews' exile in Babylon during the sixth century B.C.E. and the period from 1309 to 1378, when papal authority was subjugated to the French crown and the papal court was moved from Rome to the French city of Avignon.

Francis Bacon (1561–1626) British philosopher and scientist who pioneered the scientific method and inductive reasoning. In other words, he argued that thinkers should amass many observations and then draw general conclusions or propose theories on the basis of these data.

balance of powers The principle that no one country should be powerful enough to destabilize international relations. Starting in the seventeenth century, this goal of maintaining balance influenced diplomacy in western and central Europe for two centuries until the system collapsed with the onset of the First World War.

Balfour Declaration A letter dated November 2, 1917, by Lord Arthur J. Balfour, the British foreign secretary, that promised a homeland for the Jews in Palestine.

Laura Bassi (1711–1778) She was accepted into the Academy of Science in Bologna for her work in mathematics, which made her one of the few women to be accepted into a scientific academy in the seventeenth century.

Bastille The Bastille was a royal fortress and prison in Paris. In June 1789, a revolutionary crowd attacked the Bastille to show support for the newly created National Assembly. The fall of the Bastille was the first instance of the people's role in revolutionary change in France.

Bay of Pigs invasion (1961) The unsuccessful invasion of Cuba by Cuban exiles, supported by the U.S. government. The rebels intended to incite an insurrection in Cuba and overthrow the communist regime of Fidel Castro.

Cesare Beccaria (1738–1794) An influential writer during the Enlightenment who advocated for legal reforms. He believed that the only legitimate rationale for punishments was to maintain social order and to prevent other crimes. He argued for the greatest possible leniency compatible with deterrence and opposed torture and the death penalty.

Beer Hall Putsch (1923) An early attempt by the Nazi party to seize power in Munich; Adolf Hitler was imprisoned for a year after the incident.

Benedict of Nursia (c. 480–c. 547) Benedict's rule for monks formed the basis of Western monasticism and is still observed in monasteries all over the world.

Benedictine monasticism This form of monasticism was developed by Benedict of Nursia. Its followers adhere to a defined cycle of daily prayers, lessons, communal worship, and manual labor.

Berlin airlift The transport in 1948 of vital supplies to West Berlin by air, primarily under U.S. auspices, in response to a blockade of the city that had been instituted by the Soviet Union to force the Allies to abandon West Berlin.

Berlin Conference At this conference in 1884, the leading colonial powers met and established ground rules for the partition of Africa by European nations. By 1914, 90 percent of African territory was under European control. The Berlin Conference ceded control of the Congo region to a private company run by King Leopold II of Belgium. The company agreed to make the Congo valleys open to free trade and commerce, to end the slave trade in the region, and to establish a Congo Free State. In reality, King Leopold II's company established a regime that was so brutal in its treatment of local populations that an international scandal forced the Belgian state to take over the colony in 1908.

Berlin Wall The wall built in 1961 by the East German Communists to prevent citizens of East Germany from fleeing to West Germany; it was torn down in 1989.

birth control pill This oral contraceptive became widely available in the mid-1960s. For the first time, women had a simple method of birth control that they could take themselves.

Otto von Bismarck (1815–1898) The prime minister of Prussia and later the first chancellor of a unified Germany, Bismarck was the architect of German unification and helped to consolidate the new nation's economic and military power.

Black Death The epidemic of bubonic plague that ravaged Europe, Asia, and North Africa during the fourteenth century, killing one third to one half of the population.

Blackshirts The troops of Mussolini's fascist regime; the squads received money from Italian landowners to attack socialist leaders.

Black Tuesday October 29, 1929, the day on which the U.S. stock market crashed, plunging the U.S. and international trading systems into crisis and leading to the Great Depression.

William Blake (1757–1827) Romantic writer who criticized industrial society and factories. He championed the imagination and poetic vision, seeing both as transcending the limits of the material world.

Blitzkrieg The German "lightning war" strategy used during the Second World War; the Germans invaded Poland, France, Russia, and other countries with fast-moving and well-coordinated attacks using aircraft, tanks, and other armored vehicles, followed by infantry.

Bloody Sunday On January 22, 1905, the Russian tsar's guards killed 130 demonstrators who were protesting the tsar's mistreatment of workers and the middle class.

Jean Bodin (1530–1596) A French political philosopher whose *Six Books of the Commonwealth* advanced a theory of absolute sovereignty, on the grounds that the state's paramount duty is to maintain order and that monarchs should therefore exercise unlimited power.

Giovanni Boccaccio (1313–1375) Florentine author best known for his *Decameron*, a collection of prose tales about sex, adventure, and trickery written in the Italian vernacular after the Black Death.

Boer War (1898–1902) Conflict between British and ethnically European Afrikaners in South Africa, with terrible casualties on both sides.

Boethius (c. 480–524) A member of a prominent Roman family, he sought to preserve aspects of ancient learning by compiling a series of handbooks and anthologies appropriate for Christian readers. His translations of Greek philosophy provided a crucial link between classical Greek thought and the early intellectual culture of Christianity.

Bolsheviks Former members of the Russian Social Democratic Party who advocated the destruction of capitalist political and economic institutions and started the Russian Revolution. In 1918, the Bolsheviks changed their name to the Russian Communist Party. Prominent Bolsheviks included Vladimir Lenin and Josef Stalin. Leon Trotsky joined the Bolsheviks late but became a prominent leader in the early years of the Russian Revolution.

Napoleon Bonaparte (1769–1821) Corsican-born French general who seized power and ruled as dictator and emperor from 1799 to 1814. After the successful conquest of much of Europe, he was defeated by Russian and Prussian forces and died in exile.

Boniface VIII During his pontificate (1294–1303), repeated claims to papal authority were challenged by King Philip IV of France. When Boniface died in 1309 (at the hands of Philip's thugs), the French king moved the papal court from Rome to the French city of Avignon, where it remained until 1378.

Sandro Botticelli (1445–1510) An Italian painter devoted to the blending of classical and Christian motifs by using ideas associated with the pagan past to illuminate sacred stories.

bourgeoisie Term for the middle class, derived from the French word for a town dweller, *bourgeois.*

Boxer Rebellion (1899–1900) Chinese peasant movement that opposed foreign influence, especially that of Christian missionaries; it was finally put down after the Boxers were defeated by a foreign army composed mostly of Japanese, Russian, British, French, and American soldiers.

Tycho Brahe (1546–1601) Danish astronomer who believed that the careful study of the heavens would unlock the secrets of the universe. For over twenty years, he charted the movements of significant objects in the night sky, compiling the finest set of astronomical data in Europe.

Brexit A public referendum in June 2016 in which the population of the United Kingdom, by a slim majority, voted to leave the European Union (EU). This marked the first time that a member nation chose to retreat from the goal of increased integration with other members of the EU. The Brexit vote was controversial in Scotland and Northern Ireland, because in these areas of the United Kingdom, a majority expressed a wish to remain in the EU.

British Commonwealth of Nations Formed in 1926, the Commonwealth conferred dominion status on Britain's white settler colonies in Canada, Australia, and New Zealand.

Bronze Age (3200–1200 B.C.E.) The name given to the era characterized by the discovery of techniques for smelting bronze (an alloy of copper and tin), which was then the strongest known metal.

Brownshirts Troops of young German men who dedicated themselves to the Nazi cause in the early 1930s by holding street marches, mass rallies, and confrontations. They engaged in beatings of Jews and anyone who opposed the Nazis.

George Gordon, Lord Byron (1788–1824) Writer and poet whose life helped give the Romantics their reputation as rebels against conformity. He was known for his love affairs, his defense of working-class movements, and his passionate engagement in politics, which led to his death in the war for Greek independence.

Byzantium A small settlement located at the mouth of the Black Sea and at the crossroads between Europe and Asia, it was chosen by Constantine as the site for his new imperial capital of Constantinople in 324. Modern historians use this name to refer to the eastern Roman Empire, which lasted in this region until 1453, but the inhabitants of that empire referred to themselves as Romans.

Julius Caesar (100–44 B.C.E.) The Roman general who conquered the Gauls, invaded Britain, and expanded Rome's territory in Asia Minor. He became the dictator of Rome in 46 B.C.E. His assassination led to the rise of his grandnephew and adopted son, Gaius Octavius Caesar, who ruled the Roman Empire as Caesar Augustus.

caliphs Islamic rulers who claim descent from the prophet Muhammad.

John Calvin (1509–1564) French-born theologian and reformer whose radical form of Protestantism was adopted in many Swiss cities, notably Geneva.

Canary Islands Islands off the western coast of Africa that were colonized by Portugal and Spain in the mid-fifteenth century, after which they became bases for further expeditions around the African coast and across the Atlantic.

Carbonari An underground organization that opposed the Concert of Europe's restoration of monarchies. They held influence in southern Europe during the 1820s, especially in Italy.

Carolingian Derived from the Latin name Carolus (Charles), this term refers to the Frankish dynasty that began with the rise to power of Charlemagne's grandfather, Charles Martel (688–741). At its height under Charlemagne (Charles "the Great"), this dynasty controlled what are now France, Germany, northern Italy, Catalonia, and portions of central Europe. The Carolingian Empire collapsed under the combined weight of Viking raids, economic disintegration, and the growing power of local lords.

Carolingian Renaissance A cultural and intellectual flowering that took place around the court of Charlemagne in the late eighth and early ninth centuries.

Carthage The great maritime empire that grew out of Phoenician trading colonies in North Africa and rivaled the power of Rome. Its wars with Rome, collectively known as the Punic Wars, ended in its destruction in 146 B.C.E.

Cassidorus (c. 490–c. 583) Member of an old senatorial family, he was largely responsible for introducing classical learning into the monastic curriculum and for turning monasteries into centers for the collection, preservation, and transmission of knowledge. His *Institutes*, an influential handbook of classical literature for Christian readers, was intended as a preface to more intensive study of theology and the Bible.

Catalonia Maritime region in northeastern Spain; during the thirteenth century, Catalan adventurers conquered and colonized a series of western Mediterranean islands.

Catholic Church The "universal" (catholic) church based in Rome, which was redefined in the sixteenth century, when the Counter-Reformation resulted in the rebirth of the Catholic faith at the Council of Trent.

Margaret Cavendish (1623–1673) English natural philosopher who developed her own speculative natural philosophy. She used this philosophy to critique those who excluded her from scientific debate.

Camillo Benso di Cavour (1810–1861) Prime minister of Piedmont-Sardinia and founder of the Italian Liberal party; he played a key role in the movement for Italian unification under the Piedmontese king, Victor Emmanuel II.

Central Powers The First World War alliance between Germany, Austria-Hungary, Bulgaria, and Turkey.

Charlemagne (742–814) As king of the Franks (767–813), Charles "the Great" consolidated much of western Europe under his rule. In 800, he was crowned emperor by the pope in Rome, establishing a problematic precedent that would have wide-ranging consequences for western Europe's relationship with the eastern Roman Empire in Byzantium and for the relationship between the papacy and secular rulers.

Charles I (r. 1625–1649) The second Stuart king of England, Ireland, and Scotland, Charles attempted to rule without the support of Parliament, sparking a controversy that erupted into civil war in 1642. The king's forces were ultimately defeated and Charles himself was executed by act of Parliament, the first time in history that a ruling king was legally deposed and executed by his own government.

Charles II Nominally king of England, Ireland, and Scotland after his father Charles I's execution in 1649, Charles II lived in exile until he was restored to the throne in 1660. Influenced by his cousin, King Louis XIV of France, he presided over an opulent royal court until his death in 1685.

Chartism A working-class movement in Britain that called for reform of the British political system during the 1840s. The Chartists were supporters of the "People's Charter," which had six demands: universal white male suffrage, secret ballots, an end to property qualifications as a condition of public office, annual parliamentary elections, salaries for members of the House of Commons, and equal electoral districts.

Geoffrey Chaucer (1340–1400) English poet whose collection of versified stories, *The Canterbury Tales*, features characters from a variety of classes.

Christendom A term used to denote an ideal vision of Christian unity—political and cultural, as well as spiritual—promoted by powerful Christian rulers, beginning with Charlemagne. The "Holy Roman Empire," a term coined by Frederick I Barbarossa, was an outgrowth of this idea. Christendom was never a united entity, but it was a powerful vision.

Christine de Pizan (c. 1364–c. 1431) Born in Italy, Christine spent her adult life attached to the French court and, after her husband's death, became the first laywoman to earn her living by writing. She was the author of treatises on warfare and chivalry as well as of books and pamphlets that challenged long-standing misogynistic claims.

Church of England Founded by Henry VIII in the 1530s, as a consequence of his break with the authority of the Roman pope.

Winston Churchill (1874–1965) British prime minister who led the country during the Second World War. He also coined the phrase "Iron Curtain" in a speech at Westminster College in 1946.

Marcus Tullius Cicero (106–43 B.C.E.) Influential Roman senator, orator, Stoic philosopher, and prose stylist. His published writings still form the basis of instruction in classical Latin grammar and usage.

Lucius Quinctius Cincinnatus (519–c. 430 B.C.E.) A legendary citizen-farmer of Rome who reluctantly accepted an appointment as dictator. After defeating Rome's enemies, he allegedly left his political office and returned to his farm.

Civil Constitution of the Clergy Issued by the French National Assembly in 1790, the Civil Constitution of the Clergy decreed that all bishops and priests should be subject to the authority of the state. Their salaries were to be paid out of the public treasury, and they were required to swear allegiance to the new state, making it clear that they served France rather than Rome. The Assembly's aim was to make the Catholic Church of France a truly national and civil institution.

civilizing mission The basis of an argument made by Europeans to justify colonial expansion in the nineteenth century. Supporters of this idea believed that Europeans had a duty to impose Western ideas of economic and political progress on the indigenous peoples they ruled over in their colonies. In practice, the colonial powers often found that ambitious plans to impose European practices on colonial subjects led to unrest that threatened the stability of colonial rule. By the early twentieth century most colonial powers were more cautious in their plans for political or cultural transformation.

civil rights movement The Second World War increased African American migration from the American South to northern cities, intensifying a drive for rights, dignity, and independence. By 1960, civil rights groups had started organizing boycotts and demonstrations directed at discrimination against blacks in the South. During the 1960s, civil rights laws passed under President Lyndon B. Johnson did bring African Americans some equality with regard to voting rights and, to a much lesser degree, school desegregation. However, racism continued in areas such as housing, job opportunities, and the economic development of African American communities.

Civil War (1861–1865) Conflict between the northern and southern states of America that cost over 600,000 lives; this struggle led to the abolition of slavery in the United States.

classical learning The study of ancient Greek and Latin texts. After Christianity became the only legal religion of the Roman Empire, scholars needed to find a way to make classical learning applicable to a Christian way of life. Christian monks played a significant role in resolving this problem by reinterpreting the classics for a Christian audience.

Cluny A powerful Benedictine monastery founded in 910 whose enormous wealth and prestige derived its independence from secular authorities as well as from its wide network of daughter houses (priories).

Cold War (1945–1991) Ideological, political, and economic conflict in which the USSR and Eastern Europe opposed the United States and Western Europe in the decades after the Second World War. The Cold War's origins lay in the breakup of the wartime alliance between the United States and the Soviet Union in 1945 and resulted in a division of Europe into two spheres: the West, committed to market capitalism; and the East, which sought to build socialist republics in areas under Soviet control. The Cold War ended with the collapse of the Soviet Union in 1991.

collectivization Stalin's plan for nationalizing agricultural production, begun in 1929. Twenty-five million peasants were forced to give up their land and join 250,000 large collective farms. Many who resisted were deported to labor camps in the Far East, and Stalin's government cut off food rations to those areas most marked by resistance to collectivization. In the ensuing human-caused famines, millions of people starved to death.

Columbian exchange The widespread exchange of peoples, plants, animals, diseases, goods, and culture between the African and Eurasian landmass (on the one hand) and the region that encompasses the Americas, Australia, and the Pacific Islands (on the other); precipitated by Christopher Columbus's voyage in 1492.

Christopher Columbus (1451–1506) A Genoese sailor who persuaded King Ferdinand and Queen Isabella of Spain to fund his expedition across the Atlantic, with the purpose of discovering a new trade route to Asia. His miscalculations landed him in the Bahamas and the island of Hispaniola in 1492.

commercial revolution A period of economic development in Europe lasting from c. 1500 to c. 1800. Advances in agriculture and handicraft production, combined with the expansion of trade networks in the Atlantic world, brought new wealth and new kinds of commercial activity to Europe. The commercial revolution prepared the way for the Industrial Revolution of the 1800s.

Committee of Public Safety Political body during the French Revolution that was controlled by the Jacobins, who defended the revolution by executing thousands during the Reign of Terror (September 1793–July 1794).

commune A community of individuals who have banded together in a sworn association, with the aim of establishing their independence and setting up their own form of representative government. Many medieval towns originally founded by lords or monasteries gained their independence through such methods.

The Communist Manifesto Radical pamphlet by Karl Marx (1818–1883) that predicted the downfall of the capitalist system and its replacement by a classless, egalitarian society. Marx believed that this revolution would be accomplished by the workers (the proletariat).

Compromise of 1867 Agreement between the Habsburgs and the peoples living in Hungarian parts of the empire that the Habsburg state would be officially known as the Austro-Hungarian Empire.

Concert of Europe (1814–1815) The body of diplomatic agreements designed primarily by the Austrian minister Klemens von Metternich between 1814 and 1848 and supported by other European powers until 1914. Its goal was to maintain a balance of power on the Continent and to prevent destabilizing social and political change in Europe.

conciliarism A doctrine developed in the thirteenth and fourteenth centuries to counter the growing power of the papacy, conciliarism holds that papal authority should be subject to a council of the Church at large. Conciliarists emerged as a dominant force after the Council of Constance (1414–1418) but were eventually outmatched by a rejuvenated papacy.

Congress of Vienna (1814–1815) International conference to reorganize Europe after the downfall of Napoleon and the French Revolution. European monarchies restored the Bourbon family to the French throne and agreed to respect each other's borders and to cooperate in guarding against future revolutions and war.

conquistador Spanish term for "conqueror," applied to the mercenaries and adventurers who campaigned against indigenous peoples in central and South America.

conservatives In the nineteenth century, conservatives aimed to legitimize and solidify the monarchy's authority and the hierarchical social order. They believed that change had to be slow, incremental, and managed so that the structures of authority were strengthened and not weakened.

Constantine (275–337 C.E.) The first emperor of Rome to convert to Christianity, Constantine came to power in 312 C.E. In 324 C.E., he founded a new imperial capital, Constantinople, on the site of a maritime settlement known as Byzantium.

Constantinople Founded by the emperor Constantine on the site of a village called Byzantium, Constantinople became the new capital of the Roman Empire in 324 C.E. and continued to be the seat of imperial power after its capture by the Ottoman Turks in 1453. It is now known as Istanbul.

contract theory of government A theory of government written by Englishman John Locke (1632–1704) that posits that government authority is both contractual and conditional; therefore, if a government has abused its given authority, society has the right to dissolve it and create another.

Nicolaus Copernicus (1473–1543) Polish astronomer who advanced the idea that the earth revolves around the sun.

cosmopolitanism Stemming from the Greek word meaning "universal city," the culture characteristic of the Hellenistic world challenged and transformed the narrower worldview of the Greek polis.

cotton gin Invented by Eli Whitney in 1793, this device mechanized the process of separating cotton seeds from cotton fibers, which sped up the production of cotton and reduced its price. This change made slavery profitable in the United States.

Council of Constance (1417–1420) A meeting of clergy and theologians in an effort to resolve the Great Schism within the Roman Church. The council deposed all rival papal candidates and elected a new pope, Martin V, but it also adopted the doctrine of conciliarism, which holds that the supreme authority within the Church rests with a representative general council and not with the pope. However, Martin V himself was an opponent of this doctrine and refused to be bound by it.

Council of Trent The name given to a series of meetings held in the Italian city of Trent (Trento) between 1545 and 1563, when leaders of the Roman Church reaffirmed Catholic doctrine and instituted internal reforms.

Counter-Reformation The movement to counter the Protestant Reformation, initiated by the Catholic Church at the Council of Trent in 1545.

coup d'état French term for the overthrow of an established government by a group of conspirators, usually with military support.

Crimean War (1854–1856) War waged by Russia against Great Britain and France. Spurred by Russia's encroachment on Ottoman territories, the conflict revealed Russia's military weakness when Russian forces fell to British and French troops.

Crusader States The four fragile European principalities established on the eastern coast of the Mediterranean after the First Crusade (1096–1099): the county of Edessa (which effectively disappeared by 1150), the principality of Antioch (until 1268), the county of Tripoli (until 1291), and the kingdom of Jerusalem (which lost control of Jerusalem itself in 1187 and fell in 1291).

Cuban missile crisis (1962) Diplomatic standoff between the United States and the Soviet Union that was provoked by the Soviet Union's attempt to base nuclear missiles in Cuba; it brought the world closer to nuclear war than ever before or since.

cuius regio, eius religio A Latin phrase meaning "as the ruler, so the religion." Adopted as a part of the settlement of the Peace of Augsburg in 1555, it meant that those principalities ruled by Lutherans would have Lutheranism as their official religion and those ruled by Catholics must practice Catholicism.

cult of domesticity Concept associated with Victorian England that idealized women as nurturing wives and mothers.

cult of the Blessed Virgin The beliefs and practices associated with the veneration of Mary, the mother of Jesus, which became increasingly popular in the twelfth century.

cuneiform An early writing system that began to develop in Mesopotamia during the fourth millennium B.C.E. By 3100 B.C.E., its distinctive markings were impressed on clay tablets using a wedge-shaped stylus.

Cyrus the Great (c. 585–529 B.C.E.) As architect of the Persian Empire, Cyrus extended his dominion over a vast territory stretching from the Persian Gulf to the Mediterranean and incorporating the ancient civilizations of Mesopotamia. His successors ruled this Persian Empire as "Great Kings."

Darius (521–486 B.C.E.) The Persian emperor whose conflict with Aristagoras, the Greek ruler of Miletus, ignited the Persian Wars. In 490 B.C.E., Darius sent a large army to punish the Athenians for their intervention in Persian imperial affairs, but this force was defeated by Athenian hoplites on the plain of Marathon.

Charles Darwin (1809–1882) British naturalist who wrote *On the Origin of Species* and developed the theory of natural selection to explain the evolution of organisms.

D-Day (June 6, 1944) Date of the Allied invasion of Normandy, under General Dwight Eisenhower, to liberate Western Europe from German occupation.

Decembrists Nineteenth-century Russian army officers who were influenced by events in France and formed secret societies that espoused liberal governance. They were put down by Nicholas I in December 1825.

Declaration of Independence (1776) Historic document stating the principles of government on which the United States was founded.

Declaration of the Rights of Man and of the Citizen (1789) French charter of liberties formulated by the National Assembly during the French Revolution. The seventeen articles later became the preamble to the new constitution, which the assembly finished in 1791.

democracy In ancient Greece, this form of government allowed a class of propertied male citizens to participate in the governance of their polis; but it excluded women, slaves, and citizens without property from the political process. As a result, the ruling class amounted to only a small percentage of the entire population.

René Descartes (1596–1650) French philosopher and mathematician who emphasized the use of deductive reasoning.

Denis Diderot (1713–1784) French philosophe and author who was the guiding force behind the publication of the first encyclopedia. His *Encyclopedia* showed how reason could be applied to nearly all realms of thought and aimed to be a compendium of all human knowledge.

Dien Bien Phu (1954) Defining battle in the war between French colonialists and the Viet Minh that secured North Vietnam for Ho Chi Minh and his army and left the south to form its own government, which was supported by France and the United States.

Diet of Worms The select council of the Church that convened in the German city of Worms and condemned Martin Luther on a charge of heresy in 1521.

Diocletian (245–316 C.E.) As emperor of Rome from 284 to 305 C.E., Diocletian recognized that the empire could not be governed by one man in one place. His solution was to divide the empire into four parts, each with its own imperial ruler, but he himself remained the dominant ruler of the resulting tetrarchy ("rule of four"). He also initiated the Great Persecution, a time when many Christians became martyrs to their faith.

Directory (1795–1799) Executive committee that governed after the fall of Robespierre and held control until the coup of Napoleon Bonaparte.

Discourse on Method Philosophical treatise by René Descartes (1596–1650) proposing that the path to knowledge was through logical deduction, beginning with one's own self: "I think, therefore I am."

Dominican order Also called the Order of Preachers, it was founded by Dominic of Osma (1170–1221), a Castilian preacher and theologian, and approved by Innocent III in 1216. The order was dedicated to the rooting out of heresy and the conversion of Jews and Muslims. Many of its members held teaching positions in European universities and contributed to the development of medieval philosophy and theology. Others became the leading administrators of the Inquisition.

dominion in the British Commonwealth Status granted to Canada after its promise to maintain fealty to the British crown, even after gaining independence in 1867; later applied to Australia and New Zealand.

Dreyfus Affair The 1894 French scandal surrounding accusations that a Jewish captain, Alfred Dreyfus, sold military secrets to the Germans. Convicted, Dreyfus was sentenced to solitary confinement for life. However, after a public outcry, it was revealed that the trial documents were forgeries, and Dreyfus was pardoned after a second trial in 1899. In 1906, he was fully exonerated and reinstated in the army. The affair revealed the depths of popular anti-Semitism in France.

Alexander Dubček (1921–1992) Communist leader of the Czechoslovakian government who advocated for "socialism with a human face." He encouraged debate within the party, academic and artistic freedom, and less censorship, which led to the "Prague spring" of 1968. People in other parts of Eastern Europe began to demonstrate in support of Dubček and demanded their own reforms. When Dubček tried to democratize the Communist party and did not attend a meeting of the Warsaw Pact, the Soviets sent tanks and troops into Prague and ousted Dubček and his allies.

Duma The Russian parliament, created in response to the revolution of 1905.

Dunkirk The French port on the English Channel where British and French forces retreated after sustaining heavy losses against the German military. Between May 27 and June 4, 1940, the Royal Navy evacuated over 300,000 troops in commercial and pleasure boats.

Eastern Front Battlefront between Berlin and Moscow during the First and Second World Wars.

East India Company (1600–1858) British charter company created to outperform Portuguese and Spanish traders in the Far East; in the eighteenth century the company became, in effect, the ruler of a large part of India. There was also a Dutch East India Company.

Edict of Nantes (1598) Issued by Henry IV of France in an effort to end religious violence. The edict declared France to be a Catholic country but tolerated some forms of Protestant worship.

Edward I King of England from 1272 to his death in 1307, Edward presided over the creation of new legal and bureaucratic institutions in his realm, violently subjugated the Welsh, and attempted to colonize Scotland. He expelled English Jews from his domain in 1290.

Eleanor of Aquitaine (1122–1204) Ruler of the wealthy province of Aquitaine and wife of Louis VII of France, Eleanor had her marriage annulled in order to marry the young count of Anjou, Henry Plantagenet, who became King Henry II of England a year later. The mother of two future kings of England, she was an important patron of the arts.

Elizabeth I (1533–1603) The Protestant daughter of Henry VIII and his second wife, Anne Boleyn, Elizabeth succeeded her sister Mary as the second queen regnant of England (1558–1603).

emancipation of the serfs (1861) The abolition of serfdom was central to Tsar Alexander II's program of modernization and reform, but it produced a limited amount of change. Former serfs now had legal rights. However, farmland was granted to village communes instead of to individuals. The land was of poor quality, and the former serfs had to pay installments for it to the village commune.

emperor Originally the term for any conquering commander of the Roman army whose victories merited celebration in an official triumph. After Augustus seized power in 27 B.C.E., it was the title borne by the sole ruler of the Roman Empire.

empire A centralized political entity consolidated through the conquest and colonization of other nations or peoples in order to benefit the ruler and/or his homeland.

Enabling Act (1933) Emergency act passed by the Reichstag (German parliament) that helped transform Hitler from Germany's chancellor, or prime minister, into a dictator, following the suspicious burning of the Reichstag building and a suspension of civil liberties.

enclosure Long process of privatizing what had been public agricultural land in eighteenth-century Britain; it helped to stimulate the development of commercial agriculture and forced many people in rural areas to seek work in cities during the early stages of industrialization.

Encyclopedia Joint venture of French philosophe writers, led by Denis Diderot (1713–1784), which proposed to summarize all modern knowledge in a multivolume illustrated work with over 70,000 articles.

Friedrich Engels (1820–1895) German social and political philosopher who collaborated with Karl Marx on many publications.

English Civil War (1642–1649) Conflicts between the English Parliament and King Charles I erupted into civil war, which ended in the defeat of the royalists and the execution of Charles on charges of treason against the crown. A short time later, Parliament's hereditary House of Lords was abolished and England was declared a Commonwealth.

English Navigation Act of 1651 Act stipulating that only English ships could carry goods between the mother country and its colonies.

Enlightenment Intellectual movement in eighteenth-century Europe with a belief in human betterment through the application of reason to solve social, economic, and political problems.

Epicureanism A philosophical position articulated by Epicurus of Athens (c. 342–270 B.C.E.), who rejected the idea of an ordered universe governed by divine forces; instead, he emphasized individual agency and proposed that the highest good is the pursuit of pleasure.

Desiderius Erasmus (c. 1469–1536) Dutch-born scholar, social commentator, and Catholic humanist whose new translation of the Bible influenced the theology of Martin Luther.

Estates General The representative body of the three estates in France. In 1789, King Louis XVI summoned the Estates General to meet for the first time since 1614 because it seemed to be the only solution to France's worsening economic crisis and financial chaos.

Etruscans Settlers of the Italian peninsula who dominated the region from the late Bronze Age until the rise of the Roman Republic in the sixth century B.C.E.

Euclid Hellenistic mathematician whose *Elements of Geometry* (c. 300 B.C.E.) forms the basis of modern geometry.

eugenics A Greek term, meaning "good birth," referring to the project of "breeding" a superior human race. It was popularly championed by scientists, politicians, and social critics in the late nineteenth and early twentieth centuries.

Eurasia The preferred term for the geographical expanse that encompasses both Europe and Asia.

European Common Market (1957) The Treaty of Rome established the European Economic Community (EEC), or Common Market. The original members were France, West Germany, Italy, Belgium, Holland, and Luxembourg. The EEC sought to abolish trade barriers between its members and it pledged itself to common external tariffs, the free movement of labor and capital among the member nations, and uniform wage structures and social security systems to create similar working conditions in all member countries.

European Union (EU) Successor organization to the European Economic Community or European Common Market, formed by the Maastricht Treaty, which took effect in 1993. Currently twenty-eight member states compose the EU, which has a governing council, an international court, and a parliament. Over time, member states of the EU have relinquished some of their sovereignty, and cooperation has evolved into a community with a single currency, the euro.

Exclusion Act of 1882 U.S. law prohibiting nearly all immigration from China to the United States; fueled by animosity toward Chinese workers in the American West.

existentialism Philosophical movement that arose out of the Second World War and emphasized the absurdity of human condition. Led by Jean-Paul Sartre and Albert Camus, existentialists encouraged humans to take responsibility for their own decisions and dilemmas.

expulsion of the Jews European rulers began to expel their Jewish subjects from their kingdoms beginning in the 1280s, mostly due to their inability to repay the money they had extorted from Jewish moneylenders but also as a result of escalating anti-Semitism in the wake of the Crusades. Jews were also expelled from the Rhineland during the fourteenth century and from Spain in 1492.

fascism The doctrine formulated by Benito Mussolini, which emphasized three main ideas: statism ("nothing above the state, nothing outside the state, nothing against the state"), nationalism, and militarism. Its name derives from the Latin *fasces*, a symbol of Roman imperial power adopted by Mussolini.

Fashoda Crisis (1898) Disagreements between the French and the British over land claims in North Africa led to a standoff between armies of the two nations at the Sudanese town of Fashoda. The crisis was solved diplomatically. France ceded southern Sudan to Britain in exchange for a stop to further expansion by the British.

Federal Republic of Germany Nation founded from the Allied zones of occupation of Germany after the Second World War; also known as West Germany.

The Feminine Mystique Groundbreaking book by the feminist Betty Friedan (1921–2006), who tried to define *femininity* and explored how women internalized those definitions.

Franz Ferdinand (1863–1914) Archduke of Austria and heir to the Austro-Hungarian Empire; his assassination led to the beginning of the First World War.

Ferdinand (1452–1516) **and Isabella** (1451–1504) In 1469, Ferdinand of Aragon married the heiress to Castile, Isabella. Their union allowed them to pursue several ambitious policies, including the conquest of Granada, the last Muslim principality in Spain, and the expulsion of Spain's large Jewish community. In 1492, Isabella granted three ships to Christopher Columbus of Genoa (Italy), who went on to claim portions of the New World for Spain.

Fertile Crescent An area of fertile land comprising what are now Syria, Israel, Turkey, eastern Iraq, and western Iran that was able to sustain settlements due to its wetter climate and abundant natural food resources. Some of the earliest known civilizations emerged there between 9000 and 4500 B.C.E.

feudalism A problematic modern term that attempts to explain the diffusion of power in medieval Europe and the many different kinds of political, social, and economic relationships that were forged through the giving and receiving of fiefs (*feoda*). But because it is anachronistic and inadequate, this term has been rejected by most historians of the medieval period.

financial crisis of 2008 A global economic crisis following the sudden collapse of real estate prices in many parts of the world in 2008. The effects of this crisis were magnified by the increased level of globalization in the world economy, particularly in banking and the financial industry. In order to prevent a complete collapse of the global economy, governments in the United States and in Europe provided bailouts to cash-strapped banks and financial institutions, funded by taxpayers.

First Crusade (1095–1099) Launched by Pope Urban II in response to a request from the Byzantine emperor Alexius Comnenus. Alexius had asked for a small contingent of knights to assist him in fighting Turkish forces in Anatolia, but Urban instead directed the crusaders' energies toward the Holy Land and the recapture of Jerusalem, promising those who took the cross (*crux*) that they would merit eternal salvation if they died in the attempt. This crusade prompted attacks against Jews throughout Europe and resulted in six subsequent—and unsuccessful—military campaigns.

First World War A total war from August 1914 to November 1918, involving the armies of Britain, France, and Russia (the Allies) against Germany, Austria-Hungary, and the Ottoman Empire (the Central Powers). Italy joined the Allies in 1915, and the United States joined them in 1917, helping to tip the balance in favor of the Allies, who also drew on the populations and raw materials of their colonial possessions. Also known as the Great War.

Five Pillars of Islam The Muslim teaching that salvation is assured only through observance of five basic precepts: submission to God's will as described in the teachings of Muhammad, frequent prayer, ritual fasting, the giving of alms, and an annual pilgrimage to Mecca (the Hajj).

Five-Year Plan Soviet effort launched under Stalin in 1928 to replace the market with a state-owned and state-managed economy in order to promote rapid economic development over a five-year period and thereby "catch and overtake" the leading capitalist countries. The First Five-Year Plan was followed by the Second Five-Year Plan (1933–1937) and so on, until the collapse of the Soviet Union in 1991.

fly shuttle Invented by John Kay in 1733, this device sped up the process of weaving.

Fourteen Points President Woodrow Wilson proposed these points as the foundation on which to build peace in the world after the First World War. They called for an end to secret treaties, "open covenants, openly arrived at," freedom of the seas, the removal of international tariffs, the reduction of arms, the "self-determination of peoples," and the establishment of a League of Nations to settle international conflicts.

Franciscan Order Also known as the Order of the Friars Minor. The earliest Franciscans were followers of Francis of Assisi (1182–1226) and strove, like him, to imitate the life and example of Jesus. The order was formally established by Pope Innocent III in 1209. Its special mission was the care and instruction of the urban poor.

Frankfurt Parliament (1848–1849) Failed attempt to create a unified Germany under constitutional principles. In 1849, the assembly offered the crown of the new German nation to Frederick William IV of Prussia, but he refused the offer and suppressed a brief protest. The delegates went home disillusioned.

Frederick I "Barbarossa" ("Red Beard"; r. 1155–1190) was the first of Charlemagne's successors to call his realm the Holy Roman Empire, thereby claiming its spiritual and political independence from Rome. He spent his long reign struggling with the papacy and the rebellious towns of northern Italy. He died during the Third Crusade.

Frederick the Great (1712–1786) Prussian ruler (1740–1786) who engaged the nobility in maintaining a strong military and bureaucracy and led Prussian armies to notable military victories. He also encouraged Enlightenment rationalism and artistic endeavors.

French Revolution of 1789 In 1788, a severe financial crisis forced the French monarchy to convene the Estates General, an assembly representing the three estates of the realm: the clergy, the nobility, and the commons (known as the Third Estate). When the Estates General met in 1789, representatives of the Third Estate demanded major constitutional changes. When the king and his government proved uncooperative, the Third Estate broke with the other two estates and renamed itself the National Assembly, demanding a written constitution. The position of the National Assembly was confirmed by a popular uprising in Paris, forcing the king to accept the transformation of France into a constitutional monarchy. This constitutional phase of the revolution lasted until 1792, when the pressures of foreign invasion and the emergence of a more radical revolutionary movement caused the collapse of the monarchy and the establishment of a Republic in France.

French Revolution of 1830 The French popular revolt against Charles X's July Ordinances of 1830, which dissolved the

French Chamber of Deputies and restricted suffrage to exclude almost everyone except the nobility. After several days of violence, Charles abdicated the throne and was replaced by a constitutional monarch, Louis Philippe.

French Revolution of 1848 Revolution overthrowing Louis Philippe in February 1848, leading to the formation of the Second Republic (1848–1852). Initially enjoying broad support from both the middle classes and laborers in Paris, the new government became more conservative after elections in which the French peasantry participated for the first time. A workers' revolt was violently repressed in June 1848. In December 1848, Napoleon Bonaparte's nephew, Louis-Napoleon Bonaparte, was elected president. In 1852, Louis-Napoleon declared himself emperor and abolished the republic.

Sigmund Freud (1856–1939) Austrian physician who founded the discipline of psychoanalysis and suggested that human behavior was largely motivated by unconscious and irrational forces.

Galileo Galilei (1564–1642) Italian physicist and inventor; the implications of his ideas raised the ire of the Catholic Church, and he was forced to retract most of his findings.

Gallipoli (1915) During the First World War, a combined force of French, British, Australian and New Zealand troops tried to invade the Gallipoli Peninsula, in the first large-scale amphibious attack in history, and seize it from the Turks. After seven months of fighting, the Allies had lost 200,000 soldiers. Defeated, they withdrew.

Mohandas K. (Mahatma) Gandhi (1869–1948) The Indian leader who advocated nonviolent noncooperation to protest colonial rule and helped win home rule for India in 1947.

Giuseppe Garibaldi (1807–1882) Italian revolutionary leader who led the fight to free Sicily and Naples from the Habsburg Empire; those lands were then peaceably annexed by Sardinia to produce a unified Italy.

Gaul The region of the Roman Empire that was home to the Celtic people of that name, comprising modern France, Belgium, and western Germany.

Geneva Peace Conference (1954) International conference to restore peace in Korea and Indochina. The chief participants were the United States, the Soviet Union, Great Britain, France, the People's Republic of China, North Korea, South Korea, Vietnam, the Viet Minh party, Laos, and Cambodia. The conference resulted in the division of North and South Vietnam.

Genoa Maritime city on Italy's northwestern coast. The Genoese were active in trading ventures along the Silk Road and in the establishment of trading colonies in the Mediterranean. They were also involved in the world of finance and backed the commercial ventures of other powers, especially Spain.

German Democratic Republic Nation founded from the Soviet zone of occupation of Germany after the Second World War; also known as East Germany.

German Social Democratic party Founded in 1875, it was the most powerful socialist party in Europe before 1917.

Gilgamesh Sumerian ruler of the city of Uruk around 2700 B.C.E., Gilgamesh became the hero of one of the world's oldest epics, which circulated orally for nearly a millennium before being written down.

Giotto (c. 1266–1337) Florentine painter and architect who is often considered a forerunner of the Renaissance.

glasnost Introduced by the Soviet leader Mikhail Gorbachev in June 1987, glasnost was one of the five major policies that constituted *perestroika* ("reform" or "restructuring"). Often translated into English as "openness," it called for transparency in Soviet government and institutional activities by reducing censorship in mass media and lifting significant bans on the political, intellectual, and cultural lives of Soviet civilians.

globalization The term used to describe political, social, and economic networks that span the globe. These global exchanges are not limited by nation-states and in recent decades have become associated with new technologies, such as the Internet. Globalization is not new, however; human cultures and economies have been in contact with each other for centuries.

Glorious Revolution The overthrow of King James II of England and the installation of his Protestant daughter, Mary Stuart, and her husband, William of Orange, to the throne in 1688 and 1689. It is widely regarded as the founding moment in the development of a constitutional monarchy in Britain. It also established a more favorable climate for the economic and political growth of the English commercial classes.

Mikhail Gorbachev (1931–) Soviet leader who attempted to reform the Soviet Union through his programs of glasnost and perestroika in the late 1980s. He encouraged open discussions in other countries of the Soviet bloc, which helped inspire the velvet revolutions throughout Eastern Europe. Eventually the political, social, and economic upheaval he had unleashed led to the breakup of the Soviet Union.

Gothic style A type of graceful architecture emerging in twelfth- and thirteenth-century England and France. This style is characterized by pointed arches, delicate decoration, and large windows.

Olympe de Gouges (1748–1793) French political radical and feminist whose *Declaration of the Rights of Woman* demanded an equal place for women in France.

Great Depression Global economic crisis following the U.S. stock market crash on October 29, 1929, and ending with the onset of the Second World War.

Great Famine A period of terrible hunger and deprivation in Europe that peaked between 1315 and 1317, caused by a cooling of the climate and by soil exhaustion due to overfarming. It is estimated to have reduced the population of Europe by 10 to 15 percent.

Great Fear (1789) Following the outbreak of revolution in Paris, fear spread throughout the French countryside, as rumors circulated that armies of brigands or royal troops were coming. Some peasants and villagers organized into militias; others attacked and burned the manor houses in order to destroy the records of manorial dues.

Great Schism (1378–1417) Also known as the Great Western Schism, to distinguish it from the long-standing rupture between the churches of the Greek East and the Latin West. During the Great Schism, the Roman Church was divided between two (and, ultimately, three) competing popes. Each pope claimed to be legitimate, and each denounced the heresy of the others.

Great Terror (1936–1938) The systematic murder of nearly a million people and the deportation of another million and a half to labor camps by Stalin's regime in an attempt to consolidate power and remove perceived enemies.

Greek East After the founding of Constantinople, the eastern Greek-speaking half of the Roman Empire grew more populous, prosperous, and central to imperial policy. Its inhabitants considered themselves to be the true heirs of Rome and their own Orthodox Church to be the true manifestation of Jesus's ministry.

Greek independence Nationalists in Greece revolted against the Ottoman Empire and fought a war that ended in Greek independence in 1827. They received crucial help from British, French, and Russian troops as well as widespread sympathy throughout Europe.

Pope Gregory I (r. 590–604) Also known as Gregory the Great, he was the first bishop of Rome to successfully negotiate a more universal role for the papacy. His political and theological agenda widened the rift between the western Latin (Catholic) Church and the eastern Greek (Orthodox) Church in Byzantium. He also articulated the Church's official position on the status of Jews, promoted effective approaches to religious worship, encouraged the Benedictine monastic movement, and sponsored missionary expeditions.

Guernica The Basque town bombed by German planes in April 1937 during the Spanish Civil War. It is also the subject of Pablo Picasso's famous painting from the same year.

guilds Professional organizations in commercial towns that regulated business and safeguarded the privileges of those practicing a particular craft. Often identical to confraternities ("brotherhoods").

Gulag The vast system of forced labor camps under the Soviet regime. It originated in 1919 in a small monastery near the Arctic Circle and spread throughout the Soviet Union. Penal labor was required for both ordinary criminals and those accused of political crimes. Tens of millions of people were sent to the camps between 1928 and 1953; the exact figure is unknown.

Gulf War (1991) Armed conflict between Iraq and a coalition of thirty-two nations, including the United States, Britain, Egypt, France, and Saudi Arabia. The seeds of the war were planted with Iraq's invasion of Kuwait on August 2, 1990.

Johannes Gutenberg European inventor of the printing press. His shop in Mainz produced the first printed book—a Bible—between the years 1453 and 1455.

Habsburg Dynasty A powerful European dynasty that came to power in the eleventh century in a region now part of Switzerland. Early generations of Habsburgs consolidated their control over neighboring German-speaking lands. Through strategic marriages with other royal lines, later rulers eventually controlled a substantial part of Europe—including much of central Europe, the Netherlands, and even Spain and all its colonies for a time. In practice, the Holy Roman Emperor was chosen from a member of the Habsburg lineage. By the latter half of the seventeenth century, the Austrian Habsburg Empire was made up of nearly 300 nominally autonomous dynastic kingdoms, principalities, duchies, and archbishoprics.

Hagia Sophia The enormous church dedicated to "Holy Wisdom," built in Constantinople at the behest of the emperor Justinian in the sixth century C.E. When Constantinople fell to Ottoman forces in 1453, it became an important mosque.

Haitian Revolution (1791–1804) In 1802, Napoleon sought to reassert French control of Saint-Domingue, but stiff resistance and yellow fever crushed the French army. In 1804, Jean-Jacques Dessalines, a general in the army of former slaves, declared the independent state of Haiti (see **slave revolt in Saint-Domingue**).

Hajj The annual pilgrimage to Mecca; an obligation for Muslims.

Hammurabi Ruler of Babylon from 1792 to 1750 B.C.E., Hammurabi issued a collection of laws that were greatly influential in the Near East and that constitute the world's oldest surviving law code.

Harlem Renaissance Cultural movement in the 1920s that was based in Harlem, a part of New York City with a large African American population. The movement gave voice to black novelists, poets, painters, and musicians, many of whom used their art to protest racial subordination.

Hatshepsut (1479–1458 C.E.) As a pharaoh during the New Kingdom, she launched several successful military campaigns and extended trade and diplomacy. She was an ambitious builder who probably constructed the first tomb in the Valley of the Kings. Though she never pretended to be a man, she was routinely portrayed with a masculine figure and a ceremonial beard.

Hebrews Originally a pastoral people divided among several tribes, they were briefly united under the rule of David and his son, Solomon, who promoted the worship of a single god, Yahweh, and constructed the first temple at the new capital city of Jerusalem. After Solomon's death, the Hebrew tribes were divided between the two kingdoms of Israel and Judah, which were eventually conquered by the Neo-Assyrian and Chaldean empires. It was in captivity that the Hebrews came to define themselves through worship of Yahweh and to develop a religion, Judaism, that could exist outside of Judea. They were liberated by the Persian king Cyrus the Great in 539 B.C.E.

Hellenistic art The art of the Hellenistic period bridged the tastes, ideals, and customs of classical Greece and those that became more characteristic of Rome. The Romans strove to emulate Hellenistic city planning and civic culture, thereby exporting Hellenistic culture to their own far-flung colonies in western Europe.

Hellenistic culture The "Greek-like" culture that dominated the ancient world in the wake of Alexander's conquests.

Hellenistic kingdoms Following the death of Alexander the Great, his vast empire was divided into three separate states: Ptolemaic Egypt, under the rule of the general Ptolemy and his successors; Seleucid Asia, ruled by the general Seleucus and his heirs; and Antigonid Greece, governed by Antigonus of Macedonia. Each state maintained its independence, but the shared characteristics of Greco-Macedonian rule and a shared Greek culture and heritage bound them together in a united cosmopolitan world.

Hellenistic world The various Western civilizations of antiquity that were loosely united by shared Greek language and culture, especially around the eastern Mediterranean.

Heloise (c. 1090–1164) One of the foremost scholars of her time, she became the pupil and the wife of the philosopher and teacher Peter Abelard. In later life, she was the founder of a new religious order for women.

Henry IV King of Germany and Holy Roman Emperor from 1056—when he ascended the throne at the age of six—until his death in 1106. Henry's reign first was weakened by conflict with the Saxon nobility and later was marked by the Investiture Controversy with Pope Gregory VII.

Henry VIII (1491–1547) King of England from 1509 until his death, Henry rejected the authority of the Roman Church in 1534 when the pope refused to annul his marriage to his queen, Catherine of Aragon; Henry became the founder of the Church of England.

Henry of Navarre (1553–1610) Crowned King Henry IV of France, he renounced his Protestantism but granted limited toleration to Huguenots (French Protestants) through the Edict of Nantes in 1598.

Prince Henry the Navigator (1394–1460) A member of the Portuguese royal family, Henry encouraged the exploration and conquest of western Africa and the trade in gold and slaves.

hieroglyphs The writing system of ancient Egypt, based on a complicated series of pictorial symbols. It fell out of use when Egypt was absorbed into the Roman Empire and was deciphered only after the discovery of the Rosetta Stone in the early nineteenth century.

Hildegard of Bingen (1098–1179) A powerful abbess, theologian, scientist, musician, and visionary who claimed to receive regular revelations from God. Although highly influential in her own day, she was never officially canonized by the Church, in part because her strong personality no longer matched the changing ideal of female piety.

Hiroshima Japanese port devastated by an atomic bomb on August 6, 1945.

Adolf Hitler (1889–1945) The author of *Mein Kampf* and leader of the Nazis who became chancellor of Germany in 1933. Hitler and his Nazi regime started the Second World War and orchestrated the systematic murder of over 6 million Jews, hundreds of thousands of people with disabilities living in institutions, tens of thousands of Roma, and thousands of homosexuals.

Hitler-Stalin Pact (1939) Treaty between Stalin and Hitler that promised Stalin a share of Poland, Finland, the Baltic states, and Bessarabia in the event of a German invasion of Poland, which began shortly thereafter, on September 1, 1939.

HIV epidemic The first cases of HIV-AIDS appeared in the late 1970s. As HIV-AIDS became a global crisis, international organizations recognized the need for an early, swift, and comprehensive response to future outbreaks of disease.

Thomas Hobbes (1588–1679) English political philosopher whose *Leviathan* argued that any form of government capable of protecting its subjects' lives and property might act as an all-powerful sovereign. This government should be allowed to trample over both liberty and property for the sake of its own survival and that of his subjects. Hobbes argued that in his natural state, man was like "a wolf" toward other men.

Holy Roman Empire The loosely allied collection of lands in central and eastern Europe ruled by German kings from the twelfth century until 1806. Its origins are usually identified with the empire of Charlemagne, the Frankish king who was crowned emperor of Rome by the pope in 800. The term itself was promoted by Frederick I "Barbarossa" in the mid-twelfth century.

homage A ceremony in which an individual becomes the "man" (French: *homme*) of a lord.

Homer (fl. eighth century B.C.E.) A Greek rhapsode ("weaver" of stories) credited with merging centuries of poetic tradition in the epics known as the *Iliad* and the *Odyssey*.

hoplite A Greek foot-soldier armed with a spear or short sword and protected by a large round shield (*hoplon*). In battle, hoplites stood shoulder to shoulder in a close formation called a phalanx.

Huguenots French Protestants who endured severe persecution in the sixteenth and seventeenth centuries.

humanism A program of study associated with the movement known as the Renaissance, humanism aimed to replace the scholastic emphasis on logic and philosophy with the study of ancient languages, literature, history, and ethics.

human rights The rights of all people to legal equality, freedom of religion and speech, and the right to participate in government. Human rights laws prohibit torture, cruel punishment, and slavery.

David Hume (1711–1776) Scottish writer who applied Newton's method of scientific inquiry and skepticism to the study of morality, the mind, and government.

Hundred Years' War (1337–1453) A series of wars between England and France, fought mostly on French soil and prompted by the territorial and political claims of English monarchs.

Jan Hus (c. 1373–1415) A Czech reformer who adopted many of the teachings of the English theologian John Wycliffe, and who also demanded that the laity be allowed to receive both the consecrated bread and wine of the Eucharist. The Council of Constance burned him at the stake for heresy. In response, his supporters, the Hussites, revolted against the Church.

Saddam Hussein (1937–2006) The dictator of Iraq who invaded Iran in 1980 and started the eight-year-long Iran-Iraq war; invaded Kuwait in 1990, which led to the Gulf War of 1991; and was overthrown when the United States invaded Iraq in 2003. Involved in Iraqi politics since the mid-1960s, Hussein became the official head of state in 1979.

Iconoclastic Controversy (717–787) A serious and often violent theological debate that raged in Byzantium after Emperor Leo III ordered the destruction of religious art on the grounds that any image representing a divine or holy personage was likely to promote idol worship and blasphemy. *Iconoclast* means "breaker of icons." Those who supported the veneration of icons were called iconodules, "adherents of icons."

Il-khanate Mongol-founded dynasty in thirteenth-century Persia.

Inca Empire The highly centralized South American empire that was toppled by the Spanish conquistador Francisco Pizarro in 1533.

Indian National Congress Formed in 1885, this Indian political party worked to achieve Indian independence from British colonial control. The Congress was led by Gandhi during the 1920s and 1930s.

Indian Rebellion of 1857 This uprising began near Delhi, when the military disciplined a regiment of Indian soldiers employed by the British for refusing to use rifle cartridges greased with pork fat—unacceptable to either Hindus or Muslims. Rebels attacked law courts and burned tax rolls, protesting debt and corruption. The mutiny spread through large areas of northwest India before being violently suppressed by British troops.

Indo-Europeans A group of people speaking variations of the same language and who moved into the Near East and Mediterranean region shortly after 2000 B.C.E.

indulgences Grants exempting Catholic Christians from the performance of penance, either in life or after death. The abusive trade in indulgences was a major catalyst of the Protestant Reformation.

Innocent III (1160/61–1216) As pope, he wanted to unify all of Christendom under papal hegemony. He furthered this goal at the Fourth Lateran Council of 1215, which defined one of the Church's dogmas as the acknowledgment of papal supremacy. The council also took an unprecedented interest in the religious education and habits of every Christian.

Inquisition Formalized in the thirteenth century, this tribunal of the Roman Church aims to enforce religious orthodoxy and conformity.

International Monetary Fund (IMF) Established in 1945 to ensure international cooperation regarding currency exchange and monetary policy, the IMF is a specialized agency of the United Nations.

Investiture Conflict The name given to a series of debates over the limitations of spiritual and secular power in Europe during the eleventh and early twelfth centuries, it came to a head when Pope Gregory VII and Emperor Henry IV of Germany both claimed the right to appoint and invest bishops with the regalia of office. After years of diplomatic and military hostility, it was partially settled by the Concordat of Worms in 1122.

Irish potato famine Period of agricultural blight from 1845 to 1849 whose devastating results produced widespread starvation and led to mass immigration to the United States.

Iron Curtain Term coined by Winston Churchill in 1946 to refer to the borders of Eastern European nations that lay within the zone of Soviet control.

Islamic State (Daesh) In 2014, following the outbreak of the civil war in Syria, a militant group of Muslim fundamentalists seized territory in northeastern Syria and northwestern Iraq and proclaimed themselves a new *caliphate*, the authority over all Muslims. Known as the Islamic State of Iraq and Syria (ISIS) or the Islamic State of Iraq and the Levant (ISIL), they are also called Daesh by Arabic-speaking critics of their violence and brutality. ("Daesh" is an Arabic acronym for the group's name, but it also sounds like a word that means to trample or crush something.) They have been designated a terrorist organization by the United Nations and many countries of the world, both for their actions in the Middle East and for their encouragement of terrorist acts in Europe, Africa, and North and South America.

Italian invasion of Ethiopia (1896) Italy invaded Ethiopia, the last major independent African kingdom. Menelik II, the Ethiopian emperor, soundly defeated the Italian forces.

Ivan III, the Great (1440–1505) Russian ruler who annexed neighboring territories and consolidated his empire's position as a European power.

Jacobins Radical French political group during the French Revolution that took power after 1792, executed the French king, and sought to remake French culture.

Jacquerie Violent 1358 peasant uprising in northern France, incited by disease, war, and taxes.

James I (1566–1625) Monarch who ruled Scotland as James VI and who succeeded Elizabeth I as king of England in 1603. He supervised the English vernacular translation of the Bible known by his name.

James II King of England, Ireland, and Scotland from 1685 to 1688 whose commitment to absolutism and Catholic zealotry led to his exile to France after the Glorious Revolution of 1688.

Janissaries Corps of enslaved soldiers recruited as children from the Christian provinces of the Ottoman Empire and trained to display intense personal loyalty to the Ottoman sultans, who used these forces to curb local autonomy and as their personal bodyguards.

Jerome (c. 340–420 C.E.) One of the early church fathers, he translated the Bible from Hebrew and Greek into a popular form of Latin—hence the name by which this translation is known: the Vulgate, or "vulgar" (popular), Bible.

Jesuits The religious order formally known as the Society of Jesus, founded in 1540 by Ignatius Loyola to combat the spread of Protestantism. The Jesuits became active in politics, education, and missionary work.

Jesus (c. 4 B.C.E.–c. 30 C.E.) A Jewish preacher and teacher in the rural areas of Galilee and Judea who was arrested for seditious political activity, tried, and crucified by the Romans. After his execution, his followers claimed that he had been resurrected from the dead and taken up into heaven. They began to teach that Jesus had been the divine representative of God, the Messiah foretold by ancient Hebrew prophets, and that he had suffered for the sins of humanity and would return to judge all the world's inhabitants at the end of time.

Joan of Arc (c. 1412–1431) A peasant girl from the province of Lorraine who claimed to have been commanded by God to lead French forces against the English occupying army during the Hundred Years' War. Successful in her efforts, she was betrayed by the French king and handed over to the English, who condemned her to death for heresy. Her reputation underwent a process of rehabilitation, but she was not officially canonized as a saint until 1920.

Judaism The religion of the Hebrews as it developed in the centuries after the establishment of the Hebrew kingdoms under David and Solomon, especially during the period of Babylonian Captivity.

Justinian (527–565) Emperor of Rome who unsuccessfully attempted to reunite the eastern and western portions of the empire. Also known for his important codification of Roman law, in the *Corpus Juris Civilis*.

Justinian's Code of Roman Law Formally known as the *Corpus Juris Civilis*, or "Body of Civil Law," this compendium consisted of a systematic compilation of imperial statutes, the writings of Rome's great legal authorities, a textbook of legal principles, and the legislation of Justinian and his immediate successors. As the most authoritative collection of Roman law, it formed the basis of canon law (the legal system of the Roman Church) and became essential to the developing legal traditions of every European state as well as of many countries around the world.

Das Kapital ("Capital") The 1867 book by Karl Marx that outlined the theory behind historical materialism and attacked the socioeconomic inequities of capitalism.

Johannes Kepler (1571–1630) Mathematician and astronomer who elaborated on and corrected Copernicus's theory and is chiefly remembered for his discovery of the three laws of planetary motion that bear his name.

Keynesian Revolution Postdepression economic ideas developed by the British economist John Maynard Keynes, whereby the state took a greater role in managing the market economy through monetary policy in order to maintain levels of unemployment during periods of economic downturn.

KGB Soviet political police and spy agency, first formed as the Cheka not long after the Bolshevik coup in October 1917. It grew to more than 750,000 operatives with military rank by the 1980s.

Genghis Khan (c. 1167–1227) "Oceanic Ruler," the title adopted by the Mongol chieftain Temujin, founder of a dynasty that conquered much of southern Asia.

Khanate The major political unit of the vast Mongol Empire. There were four Khanates, including the Yuan Empire in China, forged by Chingiz Khan's grandson Kubilai in the thirteenth century.

Ruhollah Khomeini (1902–1989) Iranian Shi'ite religious leader who led the revolution in Iran that resulted in the abdication of the shah in 1979. His government allowed some limited economic and political populism combined with strict constructions of Islamic law, restrictions on women's public life, and the prohibition of ideas or activities linked to Western influence.

Nikita Khrushchev (1894–1971) Leader of the Soviet Union during the Cuban missile crisis, Khrushchev came to power after Stalin's death in 1953. His reforms and criticisms of the excesses of the Stalin regime led to his fall from power in 1964.

Kremlin Once synonymous with the Soviet government, this word refers to Moscow's walled city center and the palace originally built by Ivan the Great.

Kristallnacht Organized attack by Nazis and their supporters on the Jews of Germany following the assassination of a German embassy official by a Jewish man in Paris. Throughout Germany, thousands of stores, schools, cemeteries, and synagogues were attacked on November 9, 1938. Dozens of people were killed, and tens of thousands of Jews were arrested and held in camps, where many were tortured and killed in the ensuing months.

Labour party Founded in Britain in 1900, this party represented workers and was based on socialist principles.

Latin West After the founding of Constantinople, the western Latin-speaking half of the Roman Empire became poorer and more peripheral, but it also fostered the emergence of new barbarian kingdoms. At the same time, the Roman pope claimed to have inherited both the authority of Jesus and the essential elements of Roman imperial authority.

League of Nations International organization founded after the First World War to solve international disputes through arbitration; it was dissolved in 1946 and its assets were transferred to the United Nations.

Leonardo da Vinci (1452–1519) Florentine inventor, sculptor, architect, and painter whose breadth of interests typifies the ideal of the "Renaissance man."

Vladimir Lenin (1870–1924) Leader of the Bolshevik Revolution in Russia (1917) and the first leader of the Soviet Union.

Leviathan A book by Thomas Hobbes (1588–1679) that recommended a ruler have unrestricted power.

liberalism Political and social theory that judges the effectiveness of a government in terms of its ability to protect individual rights. Liberals support representative forms of government, free trade, and freedom of speech and religion. In the economic realm, liberals believe that individuals should be free to engage in commercial or business activities without interference from the state or their community.

lithograph Art form that involves drawing or writing on stone and producing printed impressions.

John Locke (1632–1704) English philosopher and political theorist known for his contributions to liberalism. Locke had great faith in human reason and believed that just societies were those that infringed the least on the natural rights and freedoms of individuals. This led him to assert that a government's legitimacy depended on the consent of the governed, a view that had a profound effect on the authors of the United States' Declaration of Independence.

Louis IX King of France from 1226 to his death on crusade in 1270, Louis was famous for his piety and for his close attention to the administration of law and justice in his realm. He was officially canonized as Saint Louis in 1297.

Louis XIV (1638–1715) Called the "Sun King," he was known for his success at strengthening the institutions of the French absolutist state.

Louis XVI (1754–1793) Well-meaning but ineffectual king of France, finally deposed and executed during the French Revolution.

Toussaint L'Ouverture (1743–1803) A former slave who, after 1791, led the slaves of the French colony of Saint-Domingue in the largest and most successful slave insurrection in world history. After his capture and death in 1803, his followers succeeded in establishing an independent Haiti in 1804.

Ignatius Loyola (1491–1556) Founder of the Society of Jesus (commonly known as the Jesuits), whose members vowed to serve God through poverty, chastity, and missionary work. He abandoned his first career as a mercenary after reading an account of Christ's life written in his native Spanish.

Lucretia According to Roman legend, Lucretia was a virtuous Roman wife who was raped by the son of Rome's last king and who virtuously committed suicide in order to avoid bringing shame on her family.

Luftwaffe Literally "air weapon," this is the name of the German air force, which was founded during the First World War, disbanded in 1945, and reestablished when West Germany joined NATO in 1950.

Lusitania The British passenger liner that was sunk by a German U-boat (submarine) on May 7, 1915. Public outrage over the sinking contributed to the U.S. decision to enter the First World War.

Martin Luther (1483–1546) A German monk and professor of theology whose critique of the papacy launched the Protestant Reformation.

ma'at The Egyptian term for the serene order of the universe, with which the individual soul (*ka*) must remain in harmony. The power of the pharaoh was linked to *ma'at*, insofar as it ensured the prosperity of the kingdom. After the upheavals of the First Intermediate Period, the perception of the pharaoh's relationship with *ma'at* was revealed to be conditional, something that had to be earned.

Niccolò Machiavelli (1469–1527) As the author of *The Prince* and the *Discourses on Livy*, he looked to the Roman past for paradigms of greatness, at the same time hoping to win the patronage of contemporary rulers who would restore Italy's political independence.

Magna Carta The "Great Charter" of 1215, enacted during the reign of King John of England and designed to limit his powers. It is regarded now as a landmark in the development of constitutional government. In its own time, its purpose was to restore the power of great lords.

Magyar nationalism Lajos Kossuth led this national movement in the Hungarian region of the Habsburg Empire, calling for national independence for Hungary in 1848. With the support of Russia, the Habsburg army crushed the movement and all other revolutionary activities in the empire. Kossuth fled into exile.

Moses Maimonides (c. 1137–1204) Jewish scholar, physician, and scriptural commentator whose *Mishneh Torah* is a fundamental exposition of Jewish law.

Thomas Malthus (1766–1834) British political economist who believed that populations inevitably grew faster than the available food supply. Societies that could not control their population growth would be checked only by famine, disease, poverty, and infant malnutrition. He argued that governments could not alleviate poverty. Instead, the poor had to exercise "moral restraint," postpone marriage, and have fewer children.

Nelson Mandela (1918–2013) The South African opponent of apartheid who led the African National Congress and was imprisoned from 1962 until 1990. After his release from prison, he worked with Prime Minister Frederik Willem De Klerk to establish majority rule. Mandela became the first black president of South Africa in 1994.

Manhattan Project The secret U.S. government research project to develop the first nuclear bomb. The vast project involved dozens of sites across the United States, including New Mexico, Tennessee, Illinois, California, Utah, and Washington. The first test of a nuclear bomb was near Alamogordo, New Mexico, on July 16, 1945.

manors Common farmland worked collectively by the inhabitants of entire villages, sometimes on their own initiative, sometimes at the behest of a lord.

Mao Zedong (1893–1976) The leader of the Chinese Revolution who defeated the Nationalists in 1949 and established the Communist regime in China.

Marne A major battle of the First World War in September 1914; halted the German invasion of France and led to protracted trench warfare on the Western Front.

Marshall Plan Economic aid package given to Europe by the United States after the Second World War to promote reconstruction and economic development and to secure European countries from a feared communist takeover.

Karl Marx (1818–1883) German philosopher and economist who believed that a revolution of the working classes would overthrow the capitalist order and create a classless society. Author of *Das Kapital* and *The Communist Manifesto*.

Marxists Followers of the socialist political economist Karl Marx, who called for workers everywhere to unite and create an independent political force. Marxists believed that industrialization brought about an inevitable struggle between laborers and the class of capitalist property owners. This struggle would culminate in a revolution that would abolish private property and establish a society committed to social equality.

Mary See **cult of the Virgin.**

Mary I (1516–1558) Catholic daughter of Henry VIII and his first wife, Catherine of Aragon, Mary Tudor was the first queen regnant of England. Her attempts to reinstitute Catholicism in England met with limited success. After her early death, she was labeled "Bloody Mary" by the Protestant supporters of her half sister and successor, Elizabeth I.

mass culture The spread of literacy and public education in the nineteenth century created a new audience for print entertainment and a new class of media entrepreneurs to cater to this audience. The invention of radio, film, and television in the twentieth century carried this development to another level, as millions of consumers were now accessible to the producers of news, information, and entertainment. The rise of this "mass culture" has been celebrated as an expression of popular tastes but also criticized as a vehicle for the manipulation of populations through clever and seductive propaganda.

Maya Native American people whose culturally and politically sophisticated empire encompassed lands in present-day Mexico and Guatemala.

Giuseppe Mazzini (1805–1872) Founder of Young Italy and an ideological leader of the Italian nationalist movement.

Mecca Center of an important commercial network of the Arabian Peninsula and birthplace of the prophet Muhammad. It is now considered the holiest site in the Islamic world.

Medici A powerful dynasty of Florentine bankers and politicians whose ancestors were originally apothecaries ("medics").

Meiji Empire Empire created under the leadership of Mutsuhito, emperor of Japan from 1868 until 1912. During the Meiji period, Japan became a world industrial and naval power.

Mensheviks Within the Russian Social Democratic Party, the Mensheviks advocated slow changes and a gradual move toward socialism, in contrast to the Bolsheviks, who wanted to push for a proletarian revolution. The Mensheviks believed that a proletarian revolution in Russia was premature and that the country needed to complete its capitalist development first.

mercantilism A theory and policy for directing the economy of monarchical states between 1600 and 1800 based on the assumption that wealth and power depended on a favorable balance of trade (more exports and fewer imports) and the accumulation of precious metals. Mercantilists advocated forms of economic protectionism to promote domestic production.

Maria Sibylla Merian (1647–1717) A scientific illustrator and an important early entomologist. She conducted research on two continents and published the well-received *Metamorphosis of the Insects of Surinam*.

Merovingian dynasty A Frankish dynasty that claimed descent from a legendary ancestor called Merovic, the Merovingians were the only powerful family to establish a lasting kingdom in western Europe during the fifth and sixth centuries.

Mesopotamia The "land between the Tigris and the Euphrates rivers," where the civilization of Sumer, the first urban society, flourished.

Klemens von Metternich (1773–1859) Austrian foreign minister whose primary goals were to bolster the legitimacy of monarchies and, after the defeat of Napoleon, to prevent another large-scale war in Europe. At the Congress of Vienna, he opposed social and political change and wanted to check Russian and French expansion.

Michelangelo Buonarroti (1475–1564) A virtuoso Florentine sculptor, painter, and poet who spent much of his career in the service of the papacy. He is best known for the decoration of the Sistine Chapel and for his monumental sculptures.

Middle East Like "Near East," this term was invented in the nineteenth century. It usually describes a region stretching from North Africa and Egypt to the Arabian Peninsula and Anatolia.

Middle Kingdom of Egypt (2055–1650 B.C.E.) The period following the First Intermediate Period of dynastic warfare, which ended with the reassertion of pharaonic rule under Mentuhotep II.

Miletus A Greek polis and Persian colony on the Ionian coast of Asia Minor. Influenced by the cultures of Mesopotamia, Egypt, and Lydia, it produced several of the ancient world's first scientists and sophists. Thereafter, a political conflict between the ruler of Miletus, Aristagoras, and the Persian emperor, Darius, sparked the Persian Wars with Greece.

John Stuart Mill (1806–1873) English liberal philosopher whose faith in human reason led him to support a broad variety of civic and political freedoms for men and women, including the right to vote and the right to free speech.

Slobodan Milosevic (1941–2006) The Serbian nationalist politician who became president of Serbia and whose policies during the Balkan wars of the early 1990s led to the deaths of thousands of Croatians, Bosnian Muslims, Albanians, and Kosovars. After leaving office in 2000, he was arrested and tried for war crimes at the International Court in The Hague. The trial ended before a verdict with his death in 2006.

Minoan Crete A sea empire based at Knossos on the Greek island of Crete and named for the legendary King Minos. The Minoans dominated the Aegean for much of the second millennium B.C.E.

modernism There were several different modernist movements in art and literature, but they shared three key characteristics. First, modernists believed that the world had radically changed and that this change should be embraced. Second, they believed that traditional aesthetic values and assumptions about creativity were ill suited to the present. Third, they developed a new conception of what art could do that emphasized expression over representation and insisted on the value of novelty, experimentation, and creative freedom.

Mongol people A nomadic people from the steppes of Central Asia who were united under the ruler Genghis Khan. His conquest of China was continued by his grandson Kubilai and his great-grandson Ogedei, whose army also seized southern Russia and then moved through Hungary and Poland toward eastern Germany. The Mongol armies withdrew from eastern Europe after the death of Ogedei, but his descendants continued to rule his vast empire for another half century.

Michel de Montaigne (1533–1592) French philosopher and social commentator, best known for his *Essays*.

Baron de Montesquieu (1689–1755) An Enlightenment philosophe whose most influential work was *The Spirit of Laws*. In this work, he analyzed the structures that shaped law and categorized governments into three types: republics, monarchies, and despotisms. His ideas about the separation of powers among the executive, the legislative, and the judicial branches of government influenced the authors of the U.S. Constitution.

Thomas More (1478–1535) Christian humanist, English statesman, and author of *Utopia*. In 1529, he was appointed lord chancellor of England but resigned because he opposed King Henry VIII's plans to establish a national church under royal control. He was eventually executed for refusing to take an oath acknowledging Henry to be the head of the Church of England and has since been canonized by the Catholic Church.

mos maiorum Literally translated as the "code of the elders" or the "custom of ancestors." This unwritten code governed the lives of Romans under the Republic and stressed the importance of showing reverence to ancestral tradition. It was sacrosanct and essential to Roman identity and an important influence on Roman culture, law, and religion.

Wolfgang Amadeus Mozart (1756–1791) Austrian composer, famous at a young age as a concert musician and later celebrated as a prolific composer of instrumental music and operas that are seen as the apogee of the Classical style in music.

Muhammad (570–632 C.E.) The founder of Islam, regarded by his followers as God's last and greatest prophet.

Munich Conference (1938) Hitler met with the leaders of Britain, France, and Italy and negotiated an agreement that gave Germany a major slice of Czechoslovakia. The British prime minister Neville Chamberlain believed that the agreement would bring peace to Europe, but instead Germany invaded and seized the rest of Czechoslovakia.

Muscovy The duchy centered on Moscow whose dukes saw themselves as heirs to the Roman Empire. In the early fourteenth century, Moscow was under the control of the Mongol Khanate. After the collapse of the Khanate, the Muscovite grand duke, Ivan III, conquered all the Russian principalities between Moscow and the border of Poland-Lithuania, and then Lithuania itself. By the time of his death, Ivan had established Muscovy as a dominant power.

Muslim learning and culture The Crusades brought the Latin West in contact with the Islamic world, which influenced European culture in myriad ways. Europeans adapted Arabic numerals and mathematical concepts as well as Arabic and Persian words. Through Arabic translations, Western scholars gained access to Greek learning, which had a profound influence on Christian theology. European scholars also learned from the Islamic world's accomplishments in medicine and science.

Benito Mussolini (1883–1945) The Italian founder of the Fascist party who came to power in Italy in 1922 and allied himself with Hitler and the Nazis during the Second World War.

Mycenaean Greece (1600–1200 B.C.E.) The term used to describe the civilization of Greece during the late Bronze Age, when territorial kingdoms such as Mycenae formed around a king, a warrior caste, and a palace bureaucracy.

Nagasaki Second Japanese city on which the United States dropped an atomic bomb. The attack took place on August 9, 1945; the Japanese surrendered shortly thereafter, ending the Second World War.

Napoleon III (1808–1873) The nephew of Napoleon Bonaparte, Napoleon III was elected president of the French Second Republic in 1848 and made himself emperor of France in 1852. During his reign (1852–1870), he rebuilt the French capital of Paris. Defeated in the France-Prussian War of 1870, he went into exile.

Napoleonic Code Legal code drafted by Napoleon in 1804 and based on Justinian's *Corpus Iuris Civilis*. It distilled different legal traditions to create one uniform law. The code confirmed the abolition of feudal privileges of all kinds and set the conditions for exercising property rights.

Napoleon's military campaigns In 1805, the Russians, Prussians, Austrians, Swedes, and British attempted to contain Napoleon, but he defeated them. Out of his victories, Napoleon created a new empire and affiliated states. In 1808, he invaded Spain, but fierce resistance prevented him from achieving a complete victory. In 1812, he invaded Russia, and his army was decimated as it retreated from Moscow during the winter. After the Russian campaign, the united European powers defeated Napoleon and forced him into exile. He escaped and reassumed command of his army, but the European powers defeated him for the final time at the Battle of Waterloo.

Gamal Abdel Nasser (1918–1970) President of Egypt and the most prominent spokesman for secular pan-Arabism. He became a target for Islamist critics, such as Sayyid Qutb and the Muslim Brotherhood, angered by the Western-influenced policies of his regime.

National Assembly Governing body of France that succeeded the Estates General in 1789 during the French Revolution. It was composed of, and defined by, the delegates of the Third Estate.

National Association for the Advancement of Colored People (NAACP) Founded in 1910, this U.S. civil rights organization is dedicated to ending inequality and segregation for black Americans.

National Convention The governing body of France from September 1792 to October 1795. It declared France a republic and then tried and executed King Louis XVI. The Convention also confiscated the property of the enemies of the revolution, instituted a policy of de-Christianization, changed marriage and inheritance laws, abolished slavery in its colonies, placed a cap on the price of necessities, and ended the compensation of nobles for their lost privileges.

nationalism Movement to unify a country under one government based on perceptions of the population's common history, customs, and social traditions.

nationalism in Yugoslavia In the 1990s, Slobodan Milosevic and his allies reignited Serbian nationalism in the former Yugoslavia, which led non-Serb republics in Croatia and Slovenia to seek independence. The country erupted into war, with the worst violence taking place in Bosnia, a multiethnic region with Serb, Croatian, and Bosnian Muslim populations. European diplomats proved powerless to stop attempts by Croatian and Serbian military and paramilitary forces to claim territory through ethnic cleansing and violent intimidation. Atrocities were committed on all sides, but pro-Serb forces were responsible for the most deaths.

NATO The North Atlantic Treaty Organization, a 1949 military agreement among the United States, Canada, Great Britain, and eight Western European nations, which declared that an armed attack against any one of the members would be regarded as an attack against all. Created during the Cold War in the face of the Soviet Union's control of Eastern Europe, NATO continues to exist today. Its twenty-eight countries include former members of the Warsaw Pact as well as Albania and Turkey.

Nazi party Founded in the early 1920s, the National Socialist German Workers' Party (NSDAP) gained control over Germany under the leadership of Adolf Hitler in 1933 and continued in power until Germany was defeated in 1945.

Nazism The political movement in Germany led by Adolf Hitler that advocated a violent anti-Semitic, anti-Marxist, pan-German ideology.

Near East Like "Middle East," a geographical term coined during the nineteenth century to describe western Asia and the eastern Mediterranean—that is, the parts of Asia nearest to Europe.

Neo-Assyrian Empire (883–859 B.C.E. to 612–605 B.C.E.) Assurnasirpal II laid the foundations of the Neo-Assyrian Empire through military campaigns against neighboring peoples. Eventually, the empire stretched from the Mediterranean Sea to western Iran. A military dictatorship governed the empire through its army, which it used to frighten and oppress both its subjects and its enemies. The empire's ideology was based on waging holy war in the name of its principal god, Assur, and the exaction of tribute through terror.

neoliberalism Neoliberals believe that free markets, profit incentives, and restraints on both budget deficits and social welfare programs are the best guarantee of individual liberties. Beginning in the 1980s, neoliberal theory was used to structure the policy of financial institutions such as the International Monetary Fund and the World Bank, which turned away from interventionist policies in favor of market-driven models of economic development.

Neolithic Revolution The "New" Stone Age, which began around 11,000 B.C.E., saw new technological and social developments, including managed food production, the beginnings of permanent settlements, and the rapid intensification of trade.

Neoplatonism A school of thought based on the teachings of Plato. Prevalent in the Roman Empire, it had a profound effect on the formation of Christian theology. Neoplatonists argued that nature is a book written by its creator to reveal the ways of God to humanity. Convinced that God's perfection must be reflected in nature, the Neoplatonists searched for the ideal and perfect structures that they believed must lie behind the "shadows" of the everyday world.

New Deal President Franklin D. Roosevelt's package of government reforms that were enacted during the depression of the 1930s to provide jobs for the unemployed, social welfare programs for the poor, and security to the financial markets.

New Economic Policy In 1921, the Bolsheviks abandoned war communism in favor of the New Economic Policy (NEP). Under the NEP, the state still controlled all major industry and financial concerns, while individuals could own private property, trade freely within limits, and farm their own land for their own benefit. Fixed taxes replaced grain requisition. The policy successfully helped Soviet agriculture recover from the civil war but was later abandoned in favor of collectivization.

Isaac Newton (1642–1727) One of the foremost scientists of all time, Newton was an English mathematician and physicist; he is noted for his development of calculus, work on the properties of light, and theory of gravitation.

Nicholas II (1868–1918) The last Russian tsar, who abdicated the throne in 1917. He and his family were executed by the Bolsheviks on July 17, 1918.

Friedrich Nietzsche (1844–1900) The German philosopher who denied the possibility of knowing absolute "truth" or "reality," since all knowledge comes filtered through linguistic, scientific, or artistic systems of representation. He also criticized Judeo-Christian morality for instilling a repressive conformity that drained civilization of its vitality.

nongovernmental organizations (NGOs) Private organizations such as the Red Cross that play a large role in international affairs.

Novum Organum Work by the English statesman and scientist Francis Bacon (1561–1626) that advanced a philosophy of study through observation.

October Days (1789) The high price of bread and the rumor that the king was unwilling to cooperate with the assembly caused the women who worked in Paris's large central market to march to Versailles along with their supporters to address the king. Not satisfied with their initial reception, they broke through the palace gates and called for the king to return to Paris from Versailles, which he did the following day.

Old Kingdom of Egypt (c. 2686–2160 B.C.E.) During this period, the pharaohs controlled a powerful and centralized bureaucratic state whose vast human and material resources are exemplified by the pyramids of Giza. This period came to an end as the pharaoh's authority collapsed, leading to a period of dynastic warfare and localized rule.

OPEC (Organization of the Petroleum Exporting Countries) Organization created in 1960 by oil-producing countries in the Middle East, South America, and Africa to regulate the production and pricing of crude oil.

Operation Barbarossa The code name for Hitler's invasion of the Soviet Union in 1941.

Opium Wars (1839–1842; 1856–1860) Wars fought between the British and Qing China to protect the British trade in opium; resulted in the ceding of Hong Kong to the British.

Oracle at Delphi The most important shrine in ancient Greece. The priestess of Apollo who attended the shrine was believed to have the power to predict the future.

Orthodox Refers to an adherence to traditional or conservative practice as it related to doctrinal decisions and disputes in the eastern Roman empire.

Ottoman Empire (c.1300–1923) During the thirteenth century, the Ottoman dynasty established itself as leader of the Turks. From the fourteenth to sixteenth centuries, the Ottomans conquered Anatolia, Armenia, Syria, and North Africa as well as parts of southeastern Europe, the Crimea, and areas along the Red Sea. Portions of the Ottoman Empire persisted up to the time of the First World War, but it was dismantled in the years following the war.

Reza Pahlavi (1919–1980) The West-friendly shah of Iran who was installed during a 1953 coup supported by Britain and the United States. After a lengthy economic downturn, public unrest, and personal illness, he retired from public life under popular pressure in 1979.

Pan-African Conference A 1900 assembly in London that sought to draw attention to the sovereignty of African people and their mistreatment by colonial powers.

Panhellenism The "all-Greek" culture that allowed ancient Greek colonies to maintain a connection to their homeland and to each other through their shared language and heritage. These colonies also exported their culture into new areas and created new Greek-speaking enclaves, which permanently changed the cultural geography of the Mediterranean world.

pan-Slavism Cultural movement that sought to unite native Slavic peoples within the Russian and Habsburg Empires under Russian leadership.

Partition of India (1947) At independence, British India was partitioned into the nations of India and Pakistan. The majority of the population in India was Hindu, and the majority of the population in Pakistan was Muslim. The process of partition brought brutal religious and ethnic warfare. More than 1 million Hindus and Muslims died, and 12 million became refugees.

Blaise Pascal (1623–1662) A Catholic philosopher who wanted to establish the truth of Christianity by appealing simultaneously to intellect and emotion. In his *Pensées*, he argued that faith alone can resolve the world's contradictions and that his own awe in the face of evil and uncertainty must be evidence of God's existence.

Paul of Tarsus Originally known as Saul, Paul was a Greek-speaking Jew and Roman citizen who underwent a miraculous conversion experience and became the most important proponent of Christianity in the 50s and 60s C.E.

Pax Mongolica In imitation of the *Pax Romana* ("The Roman Peace": Chapter 5), this is the phrase used to describe the relatively peaceful century after the Mongol conquests, which enabled an intensified period of trade, travel, and communication within the Eurasian landmass.

Pax Romana (27 B.C.E.–180 C.E.) Literally translated as the "Roman Peace." During this time, the Roman world enjoyed an unprecedented period of peace and political stability.

Peace of Augsburg A settlement negotiated in 1555 among factions within the Holy Roman Empire, it formulated the principle *cuius regio, eius religio* ("he who rules, his religion"): the inhabitants of any given territory should follow the religion of its ruler, whether Catholic or Protestant.

Peace of Paris The 1919 Paris Peace Conference established the terms to end the First World War. Great Britain, France, Italy, and the United States signed five treaties with each of the defeated nations: Germany, Austria, Hungary, Turkey, and Bulgaria. The settlement is notable for the territory that Germany had to give up, including large parts of Prussia to the new state of Poland, and Alsace and Lorraine to France; the disarming of Germany; and the "war-guilt" provision, which required Germany and its allies to pay massive reparations to the victors.

Peace of Westphalia (1648) An agreement reached at the end of the Thirty Years' War that altered the political map of Europe. France emerged as the predominant power on the Continent. The Austrian Habsburgs had to surrender all the territories they had gained and could no longer use the office of the Holy Roman Emperor to dominate central Europe. Spain was marginalized, and Germany became a volatile combination of Protestant and Catholic principalities.

Pearl Harbor The American naval base in Hawaii that was bombed by the Japanese on December 7, 1941, bringing the United States into the Second World War.

peasantry Term used in continental Europe to refer to rural populations that lived from agriculture. Some peasants were free and could own land. Serfs were peasants who were legally bound to the land and subject to the authority of the local lord.

Peloponnesian War The name given to the series of wars fought between Sparta (on the Greek Peloponnesus) and Athens from 431 B.C.E. to 404 B.C.E., which ended in the defeat of Athens and the loss of its imperial power.

perestroika Introduced by Soviet leader Mikhail Gorbachev in June 1987, *perestroika* was the name given to economic and political reforms begun earlier in his tenure. It restructured the state bureaucracy, reduced the privileges of the political elite, and instituted a shift from the centrally planned economy to a mixed economy, combining planning with the operation of market forces.

Periclean Athens Following his election as strategos in 461 B.C.E., Pericles pushed through political reforms in Athens that gave poorer citizens greater influence in politics. He promoted the Athenians' sense of superiority through ambitious public works projects and lavish festivals to honor the gods, thus ensuring his continual reelection. But eventually, Athens' growing arrogance and aggression alienated it from the rest of the Greek world.

Pericles (c. 495–429) Athenian politician who occupied the office of strategos for thirty years and who presided over a series of civic reforms, building campaigns, and imperialist initiatives.

Persian Empire Consolidated by Cyrus the Great in 559, this empire eventually stretched from the Persian Gulf to the Mediterranean and also encompassed Egypt. Persian rulers were able to hold their empire together through a policy of tolerance and a mixture of local and centralized governance. This imperial model of government was adopted by many future empires.

Persian Wars (490–479 B.C.E.) In 501 B.C.E., a political conflict between the Greek ruler of Miletus, Aristagoras, and the Persian emperor, Darius, sparked the first of the Persian Wars when Darius sent an army to punish Athens for its intervention on the side of the Greeks. Despite being heavily outnumbered, Athenian hoplites defeated the Persian army at the plain of Marathon. In 480 B.C.E., Darius's son Xerxes invaded Greece but was defeated at sea and on land by combined Greek forces under the leadership of Athens and Sparta.

Peter the Great (1682–1725) Energetic tsar who transformed Russia into a leading European country by centralizing government, modernizing the army, creating a navy, and reforming education and the economy.

Francesco Petrarca (Petrarch) (1304–1374) Italian scholar who revived interest in classical writing styles and was famed for his vernacular love sonnets.

pharaoh A term meaning "household," which became the title borne by the rulers of ancient Egypt. The pharaoh was regarded as the divine representative of the gods and the embodiment of Egypt itself. The powerful and centralized bureaucratic state ruled by the pharaohs was more stable and long lived than any other civilization in world history, lasting (with few interruptions) for approximately 3,000 years.

Pharisees A group of Jewish teachers and preachers who emerged in the third century B.C.E. They insisted that all of Yahweh's (God's) commandments were binding on all Jews.

Philip II (382–336 B.C.E.) King of Macedonia and father of Alexander, he consolidated the southern Balkans and the Greek city-states under Macedonian domination.

Philip II King of Spain from 1556 to 1598 and briefly king of England and Ireland during his marriage to Queen Mary I of England. As a staunch Catholic, Philip responded with military might to the desecration of Catholic churches in the Spanish Netherlands in the 1560s. When commercial conflict with England escalated, Philip sent the Spanish Armada to conquer England in 1588, but it was largely destroyed by stormy weather.

Philip II Augustus (1165–1223) The first French ruler to use the title "king of France" rather than "king of the French." After he captured Normandy and its adjacent territories from the English, he built an effective system of local administration, which recognized regional diversity while promoting centralized royal control. This administrative pattern would characterize French government until the French Revolution.

Philip IV (1268–1314) King of France from 1285 until his death. Philip's conflict with Pope Boniface VIII led to the transfer of the papal court to Avignon from 1309 to 1378.

Philistines Descendants of the Sea Peoples who fled to the region that now bears their name, Palestine, after their defeat at the hands of the pharaoh Ramses III. They dominated their neighbors the Hebrews, who used writing as an effective means of discrediting them. (The Philistines themselves did not leave a written record to contest the Hebrews' views.)

philosophe During the Enlightenment, this word referred to a person whose reflections were unhampered by the constraints of religion or dogma.

Phoenicians A Semitic people known for their trade in exotic purple dyes and other luxury goods, they originally settled in present-day Lebanon around 1200 B.C.E. and from there established commercial colonies throughout the Mediterranean, notably Carthage.

Plato (429–349 B.C.E.) A student of Socrates, Plato dedicated his life to transmitting his teacher's legacy through the writing of dialogues on philosophical subjects in which Socrates himself plays the major role. The longest and most famous of these, known as the *Republic*, describes an idealized polis governed by a superior group of individuals chosen for their natural attributes of intelligence and character, and who rule as philosopher-kings.

Plotinus (204–270 C.E.) A Neoplatonist philosopher who taught that everything in existence has its ultimate source in the divine and that the highest goal of life should be the mystic reunion of the soul with this divine source, something that can be achieved through contemplation and asceticism. This outlook blended with that of early Christianity and was instrumental in the spread of that religion within the Roman Empire.

polis One of the major political innovations of the ancient Greeks was the *polis*, or city-state (plural *poleis*). These independent social and political entities began to emerge in the ninth century B.C.E., organized around an urban center and fostering markets, meeting places, and religious worship. Frequently, poleis also controlled some surrounding territory.

Marco Polo (1254–1324) Venetian merchant who traveled throughout Asia for twenty years and published his observations in a widely read memoir.

population growth In the nineteenth century, Europe experienced a dramatic increase in population. During this period, the spread of rural manufacturing allowed men and women to marry younger and raise families earlier, which increased the size of the average family. As the population increased, the proportion of young and fertile people also increased, which reinforced population growth. By 1900, population growth was strongest in Britain and Germany and slower in France.

portolan charts Also known as *portolani*, these special charts were invented by medieval mariners during the fourteenth century and were used to map locations of ports and sea routes, while also taking note of prevailing winds and other conditions at sea.

Potsdam Conference (1945) At this conference, Truman, Churchill, and Stalin met to discuss their options at the conclusion of the Second World War, including making territorial changes to Germany and its allies and the question of war reparations.

Prague spring A period of political liberalization in Czechoslovakia between January and August 1968 that was initiated by Alexander Dubček, the Czech leader. This period of expanding freedom and openness in this Eastern-bloc nation ended on August 20, when the USSR and Warsaw Pact countries invaded with 200,000 troops and 5,000 tanks.

pre-Socratics A group of philosophers in the Greek city of Miletus who raised questions about humans' relationship with the natural world and the gods and who formulated rational theories to explain the physical universe they observed. Their name reflects the fact that they flourished prior to the lifetime of Socrates.

Price Revolution An unprecedented inflation in prices during the latter half of the sixteenth century, resulting in part from the enormous influx of silver bullion from Spanish America.

Principate Modern term for the centuries of autocratic rule by the successors of Augustus, who seized power in 27 B.C.E. and styled himself Rome's *princeps* (or "first man"). See **Roman Republic**.

printing press Developed in Europe by Johannes Gutenberg of Mainz in 1453–1455, this new technology quickly revolutionized communication and played a significant role in political, religious, and intellectual movements.

Protestantism The name given to the many dissenting varieties of Christianity that emerged during the Reformation in sixteenth-century western Europe. Although Protestant beliefs and practices differed widely, all were united in their rejection of papal authority and the dogmas of the Roman Catholic Church.

provisional government After the collapse of the Russian monarchy in February 1917, leaders in the Duma organized a government and hoped to establish a democratic system under constitutional rule. They also refused to concede military defeat in the First World War. It was impossible to institute domestic reforms and fight a war at the same time. As conditions worsened, the Bolsheviks gained support. In October 1917, they attacked the provisional government and seized control.

Claudius Ptolomeus, called Ptolemy (c. 100–170 C.E.) A Greek-speaking geographer and astronomer active in Roman Alexandria, he rejected the findings of previous Hellenistic scientists in favor of the erroneous theories of Aristotle, publishing highly influential treatises that promulgated these errors and suppressed, for example, the accurate findings of Aristarchus, who had discovered the heliocentric universe, and Erathosthenes, who had calculated the circumference of the earth.

Ptolemaic system Ptolemy of Alexandria promoted Aristotle's understanding of cosmology. In this system, the heavens orbit the earth in an organized hierarchy of spheres, and the earth and the heavens are made of different matter and subject to different laws of motion. A prime mover produces the motion of the celestial bodies.

Ptolemy (c. 367–c. 284 B.C.E.) One of Alexander the Great's trusted generals (and possibly his half brother), he became pharaoh of Egypt and founded a new dynasty that lasted until that kingdom's absorption into the Roman Empire in 30 B.C.E.

public sphere Between the official realm of state activities and the private realm of the household and individual lies the public sphere. The public sphere has a political dimension—it is the space of debate, discussion, and expressions of popular opinion. It also has an economic dimension—it is where business is conducted, where commercial transactions take place, where people enter into contracts, search for work, or hire employees.

Punic Wars (264–146 B.C.E.) Three periods of warfare between Rome and Carthage, two maritime empires that struggled for dominance of the Mediterranean. Rome emerged as the victor, destroyed the city of Carthage, and took control of Sicily, North Africa, and Hispania (Spain).

pyramid Constructed during the third millennium B.C.E., the pyramids were monuments to the power and divinity of the pharaohs entombed inside them.

Qur'an (often Koran) Islam's holy scriptures, comprising the prophecies revealed to Muhammad and redacted during his life and after his death.

Raphael (Raffaelo Sanzio) (1483–1520) Italian painter active in Rome. His works include *The School of Athens*.

realism Artistic and literary style that sought to portray common situations as they would appear in reality.

Realpolitik Political strategy based on advancing power for its own sake.

reason The human capacity to solve problems and discover truth in ways that can be verified intellectually. Philosophers distinguish the knowledge gained from reason from the teachings of instinct, imagination, and faith, which are verified according to different criteria.

Reformation Religious and political movement in sixteenth-century Europe that led to a break between dissenting forms of Christianity and the Roman Catholic Church; notable figures include Martin Luther and John Calvin.

Reich A term for the German state. The First Reich corresponded to the Holy Roman Empire (ninth century to 1806), the Second Reich lasted from 1871 to 1919, and the Third Reich lasted from 1933 through May 1945.

Reign of Terror (1793–1794) Campaign at the height of the French Revolution in which violence, including systematic executions of opponents of the revolution, was used to purge France of its "enemies" and to extend the revolution beyond its borders. Radicals executed as many as 40,000 people who were judged enemies of the state.

Renaissance From the French word meaning "rebirth," this term came to be used during the nineteenth century to describe the artistic, intellectual, and cultural movement that emerged in Italy after 1300 and that sought to recover and emulate the heritage of the classical past.

Restoration (1815–1848) European movement after the defeat of Napoleon to restore Europe to its pre–French Revolution status and to prevent the spread of revolutionary or liberal political movements.

Cardinal Richelieu (1585–1642) First minister to King Louis XIII, he is considered by many to have ruled France in all but name, centralizing political power and suppressing dissent.

Roman army Under the Republic, the Roman army was made up of citizen-soldiers who were required to serve in wartime. As Rome's empire grew, the need for more fighting men led to the extension of citizenship rights and, eventually, to the development of a vast, professional, standing army that numbered as many as 300,000 by the middle of the third century B.C.E. By that time, however, citizens were not themselves required to serve, and many legions were made up of paid conscripts and foreign mercenaries.

Roman citizenship The rights and responsibilities of Rome's citizens were gradually extended to the free (male) inhabitants of other Italian provinces and later to most provinces in the Roman world. In contrast to slaves and non-Romans, Romans had the right to be tried in an imperial court and could not be legally subjected to torture.

Roman Republic The Romans traced the founding of their republic to the overthrow of their last king and the establishment of a unique form of constitutional government, in which the power of the aristocracy (embodied by the Senate) was checked by the executive rule of two elected consuls and the collective will of the people. For hundreds of years, this balance of power provided the Republic with a measure of political stability and prevented any single individual or clique from gaining too much power.

Romanticism Beginning in Germany and England in the late eighteenth century and continuing until the end of the nineteenth century, Romanticism was a movement in art, music, and literature that countered the rationalism of the Enlightenment by placing greater value on human emotions and the power of nature to stimulate creativity.

Jean-Jacques Rousseau (1712–1778) Philosopher and radical political theorist whose *Social Contract* attacked privilege and inequality. One of the primary principles of Rousseau's political philosophy is that politics and morality should not be separated.

Royal Society The goal of this British society, founded in 1660, is to pursue collective research. Members would conduct experiments, record the results, and share them with their peers, who would study the methods, reproduce the experiment, and assess the results. This arrangement gave English scientists a sense of common purpose as well as a system for reaching a consensus on facts.

Russian Revolution of 1905 After Russia's defeat in the Russo-Japanese War, Russians began clamoring for political reforms. Protests grew over the course of 1905, and the autocracy lost control of entire towns and regions as workers went on strike, soldiers mutinied, and peasants revolted. Forced to yield, Tsar Nicholas II issued the October Manifesto, which pledged individual liberties and provided for the election of a parliament (called the Duma). The most radical of the revolutionary groups were put down with force, and the pace of political change remained very slow in the aftermath of the revolution.

Russo-Japanese War (1904–1905) Japanese and Russian expansionist goals collided in Manchuria and Korea. Russia was humiliated after the Japanese navy sank its fleet, which helped provoke a revolt in Russia and led to an American-brokered peace treaty.

sacrament A sacred rite. In the Catholic tradition, the administration of the sacraments is considered necessary for salvation.

Saint Bartholomew's Day Massacre The mass murder of French Protestants (Huguenots) instigated by Queen Catherine de' Medici of France and carried out by Catholics. It began in Paris on August 24, 1572 (Saint Bartholomew's day) and spread to other parts of France, continuing into October of that year. More than 70,000 people were killed.

salon Informal gathering of intellectuals and aristocrats that allowed discourse about Enlightenment ideas.

Sappho (c. 620–c. 550 B.C.E.) One of the most celebrated Greek poets, she was revered as the "Tenth Muse" and emulated by many male poets. Ironically, though, only two of her poems survive intact, and the rest must be pieced together from fragments quoted by later poets.

Sargon the Great (r. 2334–2279 B.C.E.) The Akkadian ruler who consolidated power in Mesopotamia.

SARS epidemic (2003) The successful containment of severe acute respiratory syndrome (SARS) is an example of how international health organizations can effectively work together to recognize and respond to a disease outbreak. The disease itself, however, is a reminder of the dangers that exist in a globalized economy with a high degree of mobility of both populations and goods.

Schlieffen Plan Devised by the German general Alfred von Schlieffen in 1905 to avoid the dilemma of a two-front war against France and Russia. The Schlieffen Plan required that Germany attack France first through Belgium and secure a quick victory before wheeling to the east to meet the slower armies of the Russians on the Eastern Front. The Schlieffen Plan was put into operation on August 2, 1914, at the outset of the First World War.

scientific revolution of antiquity The Hellenistic period was the most brilliant age in the history of science before the seventeenth century C.E. Aristarchus of Samos posited the existence of a heliocentric universe. Eratosthenes of Alexandria accurately calculated the circumference of the earth. Archimedes turned physics into its own branch of experimental science. Hellenistic anatomists became the first to practice human dissection, which improved their understanding of human physiology. Ironically, most of these discoveries were suppressed by pseudoscientists who flourished under the Roman Empire during the second century C.E., notably Claudus Ptolomeus (Ptolemy) and Aelius Galenus (Galen).

second industrial revolution The technological developments in the last third of the nineteenth century, which included new techniques for refining and producing steel; increased availability of electricity for industrial, commercial, and domestic use; advances in chemical manufacturing; and the creation of the internal combustion engine.

Second World War Worldwide war that began in September 1939 in Europe, and even earlier in Asia (the Japanese invasion of Manchuria began in 1931), pitting Britain, the United States, and the Soviet Union (the Allies) against Nazi Germany, Italy, and Japan (the Axis). The war ended in 1945 with Germany and Japan's defeat.

Seleucus (d. 280 B.C.E.) The Macedonian general who ruled the Persian heartland of Alexander the Great's empire.

Semitic language The Semitic language family has the longest recorded history of any linguistic group and is the root of most languages of the Middle and Near East. Ancient Semitic languages include those of the ancient Babylonians and Assyrians, Phoenician, the classical form of Hebrew, early dialects of Aramaic, and the classical Arabic of the Qur'an.

Sepoy Mutiny of 1857 See **Indian Rebellion of 1857**.

serfdom Peasant labor. Unlike slaves, serfs are "attached" to the land they work and are not supposed to be sold apart from that land.

William Shakespeare (1564–1616) An English playwright who flourished during the reigns of Elizabeth I and James I. Shakespeare received a basic education in his hometown of Stratford-upon-Avon and worked in London as an actor before achieving success as a dramatist and poet.

Shi'ites An often-persecuted minority within Islam, Shi'ites, from the Arabic word *shi'a* ("faction"), believe that only descendants of Muhammad's successor Ali and his wife Fatimah, Muhammad's daughter, can have any authority over the Muslim community. Today, Shi'ites constitute the ruling party in Iran and are numerous in Iraq but otherwise comprise only 10 percent of Muslims worldwide.

Abbé Sieyès (1748–1836) In 1789, he wrote the pamphlet "What Is the Third Estate?" in which he posed fundamental questions about the rights of the Third Estate and helped provoke its secession from the Estates General. He was a leader at the Tennis Court Oath, but he later helped Napoleon seize power.

Sinn Féin The Irish revolutionary organization that formed in 1900 to fight for Irish independence.

Sino-Japanese War (1894–1895) Conflict over the control of Korea; China was forced to cede the province of Taiwan to Japan.

slave revolt in Saint-Domingue (1791–1804) In September of 1791, the largest slave rebellion in history broke out in Saint-Domingue, an important French colony in the Caribbean. In 1794, the revolutionary government in France abolished slavery in the colonies, though this act essentially only recognized the liberty that the slaves had seized by their own actions. Napoleon reestablished slavery in the French Caribbean in 1802 but failed in his attempt to reconquer Saint-Domingue. Armies commanded by former slaves succeeded in winning independence for a new nation, Haiti, in 1804, making the revolt in Saint-Domingue the first successful slave revolt in history.

slavery The practice of subjugating people to a life of bondage and of selling or trading these unfree people. For most of human history, slavery had no racial or ethnic basis and was widely practiced by all cultures and civilizations. Anyone could become a slave, for example, by being captured in war or by being sold for the payment of a debt. It was only in the fifteenth century, with the growth of the African slave trade, that slavery came to be associated with particular races and peoples.

Adam Smith (1723–1790) Scottish economist and liberal philosopher who proposed that competition between self-interested individuals led naturally to a healthy economy. He became famous for his influential book *The Wealth of Nations* (1776).

Social Darwinism Belief that Charles Darwin's theory of natural selection (evolution) was applicable to human societies and justified the right of the ruling classes or countries to dominate the weak.

social democracy The belief that democracy and social welfare go hand in hand and that diminishing the sharp inequalities of class society is crucial to fortifying democratic culture.

socialism Political ideology that calls for a classless society with collective ownership of all property.

Society of Jesus See **Jesuits**.

Socrates (469–399 B.C.E.) The Athenian philosopher and teacher who promoted the careful examination of all inherited opinions and assumptions on the grounds that "the unexamined life is not worth living." A veteran of the Peloponnesian War, he was tried and condemned by his fellow citizens for engaging in allegedly seditious activities and was executed in 399 B.C.E. His most influential pupils were the philosopher Plato and the historian and social commentator Xenophon.

Solon (d. 559 B.C.E.) Elected archon in 594 B.C.E., this Athenian aristocrat enacted a series of political and economic reforms that formed the basis of Athenian democracy.

Somme (1916) During this battle of the First World War, Allied forces attempted to take entrenched German positions from July to mid-November of 1916. Neither side was able to make any real gains despite massive casualties: 500,000 Germans, 400,000 British, and 200,000 French.

Soviet bloc International alliance that included the East European countries of the Warsaw Pact as well as the Soviet Union; it also came to include Cuba.

soviets Local councils elected by workers and soldiers in Russia. Socialists started organizing these councils in 1905, and the Petrograd soviet in the capital emerged as one of the centers of power after the Russian monarchy collapsed in 1917 in the midst of World War I. The soviets became increasingly powerful, pressing for social reform and the redistribution of land, and calling for Russian withdrawal from the war effort.

Spanish-American War (1898) War between the United States and Spain in Cuba, Puerto Rico, and the Philippines. It ended with a treaty whereby the United States took over the Philippines, Guam, and Puerto Rico; Cuba won partial independence.

Spanish Armada The supposedly invincible fleet of warships sent against England by Philip II of Spain in 1588 but vanquished by the English fleet and bad weather in the English Channel.

Sparta Around 650 B.C.E., after the suppression of a slave revolt, Spartan rulers militarized their society in order to prevent future rebellions and to protect Sparta's superior position in Greece, orienting their society toward the maintenance of their army. Sparta briefly joined forces with Athens and other poleis in the second war with Persia in 480–479 B.C.E., but these two rivals ultimately fell out again in 431 B.C.E. when Sparta and its Peloponnesian allies went to war against Athens and its allies. This bloody conflict lasted until Athens was defeated in 404 B.C.E., after Sparta received military aid from the Persians.

Spartiate A full citizen of Sparta, hence a professional soldier of the hoplite phalanx.

spinning jenny Invention of James Hargreaves (c. 1720–1774) that revolutionized the British textile industry by allowing a worker to spin much more thread than was possible on a hand spinner.

SS (Schutzstaffel) Formed in 1925 to serve as Hitler's personal security force and to guard Nazi party (NSDAP) meetings, the SS grew into a large militarized organization that became notorious for its participation in carrying out Nazi policies.

Joseph Stalin (1879–1953) The Bolshevik leader who succeeded Lenin as leader of the Soviet Union and ruled until his death in 1953.

Stalingrad (1942–1943) The turning point on the Eastern Front during the Second World War came when the German army tried to take the city of Stalingrad in an effort to break the back of Soviet industry. The German and Soviet armies fought a bitter battle, in which more than a half million German, Italian, and Romanian soldiers were killed and the Soviets suffered over a million casualties. The German army surrendered after over five months of fighting. After Stalingrad, the Soviet army launched a series of attacks that pushed the Germans back.

Stoicism An ancient philosophy derived from the teachings of Zeno of Athens (fl. c. 300) and widely influential within the Roman Empire; it also influenced the development of Christianity. Stoics believe in the essential orderliness of the cosmos and that everything that occurs happens for the best. Since everything is determined in accordance with rational purpose, no individual is master of his or her fate, and the only agency that human beings have consists in their response to good fortune or adversity.

Sumerians The ancient inhabitants of southern Mesopotamia (modern Iraq and Kuwait) whose sophisticated civilization emerged around 4000 B.C.E.

Sunnis Proponents of Islam's customary religious practices (*sunna*) as they developed under the first two caliphs to succeed Muhammad: his father-in-law Abu-Bakr and his disciple Umar. Sunni orthodoxy is dominant within Islam but is opposed by the Shi'ites.

syndicalism A nineteenth-century political movement that embraced a strategy of strikes and sabotage by workers. The syndicalists hoped that a general strike of all workers would bring down the capitalist state and replace it with workers' syndicates, or trade associations. Their refusal to participate in politics limited their ability to command a wide influence.

tabula rasa Latin for "clean slate." Term used by John Locke (1632–1704) to describe people's minds before they acquired ideas as a result of experience.

Tennis Court Oath (1789) Oath taken by representatives of the Third Estate in June 1789, pledging to form a National Assembly and write a constitution limiting the powers of the king.

tetrarchy The result of Diocletian's political reforms of the late third century C.E., which divided the Roman Empire into four quadrants.

Theban Hegemony The term describing the period when the polis of Thebes dominated the Greek mainland, which reached its height after 371 B.C.E., under leadership of the Theban general Epaminondas. It was in Thebes that the future King Philip II of Macedon spent his youth. Macedonian hegemony was forcefully asserted in the defeat of Thebes and Athens at the hands of Philip and Alexander at the Battle of Chaeronea in 338.

theory of evolution Darwin's theory linking biology to history. Darwin believed that competition among different organisms and their struggle with the environment were fundamental and unavoidable facts of life. In this struggle, those individuals who were better adapted to their environment survived, whereas the weak perished. This produced a "natural selection," or the favoring of certain adaptive traits over time, leading to a gradual evolution of different species.

Third Estate The population of France under the Old Regime was divided into three estates, corporate bodies that determined an individual's rights or obligations under royal law. The nobility constituted the First Estate, the clergy the Second, and the commoners (the vast majority of the population) made up the Third Estate.

Third Reich The German state from 1933 to 1945 under Adolf Hitler and the Nazi party.

Third World Those nations—mostly in Asia, Latin America, and Africa—that are not highly industrialized.

Thirty Years' War (1618–1648) Beginning as a conflict between Protestants and Catholics in Germany, this series of skirmishes escalated into a general European war fought on German soil by armies from Sweden, France, and the Holy Roman Empire.

Timur the Lame (1336–1405) Also known as Tamerlane, he was the last ruler of the Mongol Khans' Asian empire.

Josip Broz Tito (1892–1980) This Yugoslavian communist and resistance leader became the leader of Yugoslavia and fought to keep his government independent of the Soviet Union. In response, the Soviet Union expelled Yugoslavia from the communist countries' economic and military pacts.

town A center for markets and administration. Towns existed in a symbiotic relationship with the countryside. They provided markets for surplus food from outlying farms as well as produced manufactured goods. In the Middle Ages, towns tended to grow up around a castle or monastery that afforded protection.

transatlantic triangle The trading of African slaves by European colonists to address labor shortages in the Americas and the Caribbean. Slaves were treated like cargo, loaded onto ships and sold in exchange for molasses, tobacco, rum, and other precious commodities.

Treaty of Brest-Litovsk (1918) Separate peace between imperial Germany and the new Bolshevik regime in Russia. This treaty acknowledged the German victory on the Eastern Front and withdrew Russia from the war.

Treaty of Utrecht (1713) Resolution to the War of Spanish Succession that reestablished a balance of power in Europe, to the benefit of Britain and in ways that disadvantaged Spain, Holland, and France.

Treaty of Versailles Signed on June 28, 1919, this peace settlement ended the First World War and required Germany to surrender a large part of its most valuable territories and to pay huge reparations to the Allies.

trench warfare Weapons such as barbed wire and the machine gun gave tremendous advantages to defensive positions in the First World War, leading to prolonged battles between entrenched armies in fixed positions. The trenches eventually consisted of 25,000 miles of tunnels and ditches that stretched across the Western Front in northern France, from the Atlantic coast to the Swiss border. On the Eastern Front, the large expanse of territories made trench warfare less significant.

triangular trade The eighteenth-century commercial Atlantic shipping pattern that took rum from New England to Africa, traded it for slaves taken to the West Indies, and brought sugar back to New England to be processed into rum.

Triple Entente Alliance developed before the First World War that eventually included Britain, France, and Russia.

Truman Doctrine (1947) Declaration promising U.S. economic and military intervention to counter any attempt by the Soviet Union to expand its influence. Often cited as a key moment in the origins of the Cold War.

tsar Russian word for "emperor," derived from the Latin *caesar* and similar to the German *kaiser.* This was the title claimed by the rulers of medieval Muscovy and of the later Russian Empire.

Ubaid culture An early civilization that flourished in Mesopotamia between 5500 and 4000 B.C.E., it was characterized by large village settlements and temple complexes: a precursor to the more urban civilization of the Sumerians.

Umayyad caliphate (661–930) The Umayyad family resisted the authority of the first two caliphs who succeeded Muhammad but eventually placed a member of their own family in that position of power. The Umayyad caliphate ruled the Islamic world from 661 to 750, modeling its administration on that of the Roman Empire. But after a rebellion led by the rival Abbasid family, the power of the Umayyad caliphate was confined to its territories in al-Andalus (Spain).

Universal Declaration of Human Rights (1948) United Nations declaration that laid out the rights to which all human beings are entitled.

University of Paris The reputation of Peter Abelard and his students attracted many intellectuals to Paris during the twelfth century. Some of them began offering instruction to aspiring scholars. By 1200, this loose association of teachers had formed itself into a *universitas,* or corporation. The teachers began collaborating in the higher academic study of the liberal arts, with a special emphasis on theology.

Urban II (1042?–1099) Instigator of the First Crusade (1096–1099), this pope promised that anyone who fought or died in the service of the Church would receive absolution from sin.

urban population During the nineteenth century, urban populations in Europe increased sixfold. For the most part, urban areas had medieval infrastructures, which new populations and industries overwhelmed. As a result, many European cities became overcrowded and unhealthy.

Utopia A semisatirical social critique by the English statesman Sir Thomas More (1478–1535); the title derives from the Greek "best place" or "no place."

Lorenzo Valla (1407–1457) One of the first practitioners of scientific philology (the historical study of language). Valla's analysis of the so-called Donation of Constantine showed that this document could not possibly have been written in the fourth century C.E. but must have been forged centuries later.

vassal A person who pledges to be loyal and subservient to a lord in exchange for land, income, or protection.

velvet revolutions The peaceful political revolutions against the Soviet Union throughout Eastern Europe in 1989.

Verdun (1916) This battle between German and French forces lasted for ten months during the First World War. The Germans saw the battle as a chance to break French morale through a war of attrition, and the French believed the battle to be a symbol of France's strength. In the end, over 400,000 lives were lost, and the German offensive failed.

Versailles Conference (1919) Peace conference of the victors of the First World War, it resulted in the Treaty of Versailles, which forced Germany to pay reparations and to give up its colonies to the victors.

Victoria (1819–1901) Influential queen of Great Britain, who reigned from 1837 until her death. Victoria presided over the expansion of the British Empire as well as the evolution of English politics and social and economic reforms.

Viet Cong Vietnamese communist group formed in 1954; committed to overthrowing the government of South Vietnam and reunifying North and South Vietnam.

Vikings (800–1000) The collapse of the Abbasid caliphate disrupted Scandinavian commercial networks and turned traders into raiders. (The word *viking* describes the activity of raiding.) These raids often escalated into invasions that contributed to the collapse of the Carolingian Empire, resulted in the devastation of settled territories, and ended with the establishment of Viking colonies. By the tenth century, Vikings controlled areas of eastern England; Scotland; the islands of Ireland, Iceland, and Greenland; and parts of northern France. They had also established the beginnings of the kingdom that became Russia and made exploratory voyages to North America, founding a settlement in Newfoundland (Canada).

A Vindication of the Rights of Woman Noted work of Mary Wollstonecraft (1759–1797), an English republican who applied Enlightenment political ideas to issues of gender.

Virgil (70–19 B.C.E.) An influential Roman poet who wrote under the patronage of the emperor Augustus. His *Aeneid* was modeled on the ancient Greek epics of Homer and told the mythical tale of Rome's founding by the Trojan refugee Aeneas.

Visigoths The tribes of "west" Goths who sacked Rome in 410 C.E. and later established a kingdom in the Roman province of Hispania (Spain).

Voltaire Pseudonym of French philosopher and satirist François Marie Arouet (1694–1778), who championed the cause of human dignity against state and Church oppression. Noted deist and author of *Candide*.

Lech Wałęsa (1943–) Leader of the Polish labor movement Solidarity, which organized a series of strikes across Poland in 1980. The strikers protested working conditions, shortages, and high prices. Above all, they demanded an independent labor union. Solidarity's leaders were imprisoned and the union banned, but they launched a new series of strikes in 1988 that led to the legalization of Solidarity and open elections.

war communism The Russian civil war forced the Bolsheviks to take a more radical economic stance. They requisitioned grain from the peasantry and outlawed private trade in consumer goods as "speculation." They also militarized production facilities and abolished money.

Wars of the Roses Fifteenth-century civil conflict between the English dynastic houses of Lancaster and York, each of which was symbolized by the heraldic device of a rose (red and white, respectively). It was ultimately resolved by the accession of the Lancastrian king Henry VII, who married Elizabeth of York.

Warsaw Pact (1955–1991) Military alliance between the USSR and other communist states that was established in response to the creation of the NATO alliance.

The Wealth of Nations 1776 treatise by Adam Smith, whose laissez-faire ideas predicted the economic boom of the Industrial Revolution.

Weimar Republic The government of Germany between 1919 and the rise of Hitler and the Nazi party in 1933.

Western Front During the First World War, the military front that stretched from the English Channel through Belgium and France to the Alps.

Whites Refers to the "counterrevolutionaries" of the Bolshevik Revolution (1918–1921) who fought the Bolsheviks (the "Reds"); included former supporters of the tsar, Social Democrats, and large independent peasant armies.

William the Conqueror (1027–1087) Duke of Normandy who laid claim to the throne of England in 1066, defeating the Anglo-Saxon king Harold at the Battle of Hastings. William and his Norman followers imposed imperial rule in England through a brutal campaign of military conquest, surveillance, and the suppression of the indigenous Anglo-Saxon language.

William of Ockham (d. 1349) An English philosopher and Franciscan friar, he denied that human reason could prove fundamental theological truths, such as the existence of God. Instead, William argued that there is no necessary connection between the observable laws of nature and the unknowable essence of divinity. His theories, derived from the work of earlier scholastics, form the basis of the scientific method.

Woodrow Wilson (1856–1924) U.S. president who requested and received a declaration of war from Congress so that America could enter the First World War. After the war, his prominent role at the Paris Peace Conference signaled the rise of the United States as a world power. He also proposed the Fourteen Points, which influenced the peace negotiations.

Maria Winkelmann (1670–1720) German astronomer who worked with her husband in his observatory. Although she discovered a comet and prepared calendars for the Berlin Academy of Sciences, the academy would not let her take her husband's place within the body after he died.

witch craze The rash of persecutions that took place in both Catholic and Protestant countries of early modern Europe and their colonies, facilitated by secular governments and religious authorities.

women's associations Because European women were excluded from the workings of parliamentary and mass politics, some women formed their own organizations to press for political and civil rights. Some groups focused on establishing educational opportunities for women; others campaigned energetically for the vote.

William Wordsworth (1770–1850) Romantic poet whose central themes were nature, simplicity, and feeling. He considered nature to be the most trustworthy teacher and the source of sublime power that nourished the human soul.

World Bank International agency established in 1944 to provide economic assistance to war-torn nations and countries in need of economic development.

John Wycliffe (c. 1330–1384) A professor of theology at the University of Oxford, Wycliffe urged the English king to confiscate ecclesiastical wealth and to replace corrupt priests and bishops with men who would live according to the apostolic standards of poverty and piety. He advocated direct access to the scriptures and promoted an English translation of the Bible. His teachings played an important role in the Peasants' Revolt of 1381 and inspired the still more radical initiatives of a group known as Lollards.

Xerxes (519?–465 B.C.E.) Xerxes succeeded his father, Darius, as Great King of Persia. Seeking to avenge his father's shame and eradicate any future threats to Persian hegemony, he launched his own invasion of Greece in 480 B.C.E. An allied Greek army defeated his forces in 479 B.C.E.

Yalta conference Meeting among U.S. president Franklin D. Roosevelt, British prime minister Winston Churchill, and Soviet premier Joseph Stalin that occurred in the Crimea in 1945 shortly before the end of the Second World War in which the three leaders planned for the postwar order.

Young Turks The 1908 Turkish reformist movement that aimed to modernize the Ottoman Empire, restore parliamentary rule, and depose Sultan Abdul Hamid II.

ziggurats Temples constructed under the Dynasty of Ur in what is now Iraq, beginning around 2100 B.C.E.

Zika virus A mosquito-borne virus, originally identified in Africa.

Zionism A political movement dating to the end of the nineteenth century holding that the Jewish people constitute a nation and are entitled to a national homeland. Zionists rejected a policy of Jewish assimilation and advocated the reestablishment of a Jewish homeland in Palestine.

Zollverein In 1834, Prussia started a customs union, which established free trade among the German states and a uniform tariff against the rest of the world. By the 1840s, the union included almost all of the German states except German Austria. It is considered an important precedent for the political unification of Germany, which was completed in 1870 under Prussian leadership.

Zoroastrianism One of the three major universal faiths of the ancient world, alongside Judaism and Christianity, it was derived from the teachings of the Persian Zoroaster around 600 B.C.E. Zoroaster redefined religion as an ethical practice common to all, rather than as a set of rituals and superstitions that cause divisions among people. Zoroastrianism teaches that there is one supreme god in the universe, Ahura-Mazda (Wise Lord), but that his goodness will be constantly assailed by the forces of evil until the arrival of a final "judgment day." Proponents of this faith should therefore help good to triumph over evil by leading a good life and by performing acts of compassion and charity. Zoroastrianism exercised a profound influence over many early Christians, including Augustine.

Ulrich Zwingli (1484–1531) A former priest from the Swiss city of Zurich, Zwingli joined Luther and Calvin in attacking the authority of the Roman Catholic Church.

CHAPTER 1

Nels M. Bailkey (ed.): From *Readings in Ancient History: Thought and Experience from Gilgamesh to St. Augustine, 5th Edition.* © 1996 Wadsworth, a part of Cengage Learning, Inc. Reproduced by permission. www.cengage.com/permissions.

Bible. New Revised Standard Version: Scripture quotations from Genesis 6–9 from the New Revised Standard Version of the Bible, copyright © 1989 National Council of the Churches of Christ in the United States of America. Used by permission. All rights reserved.

Maureen Gallery Kovacs (trans.): Excerpt from *The Epic of Gilgamesh*, with an Introduction and Notes by Maureen Gallery Kovacs, translator. Copyright © 1985, 1989 by the Board of Trustees of the Leland Stanford Junior University. All rights reserved. Reprinted by permission of the publisher, Stanford University Press, www.sup.org.

Martha T. Roth (ed.): Excerpts from "The Code of Hammurabi" from *Law Collections from Mesopotamia and Asia Minor*, edited by Martha T. Roth, pp. 76–135. © 1995 Society of Biblical Literature. Reprinted by permission of Society of Biblical Literature.

William Kelly Simpson (ed.): Excerpts from "The Prophecies of Neferty" from *The Literature of Ancient Egypt: An Anthology of Stories, Instructions, Stelae, Autobiographies, and Poetry*, 3rd Ed., pp. 214–220. Copyright © 2003 by Yale University. All rights reserved. Reprinted by permission of Yale University Press.

CHAPTER 2

Bible. New Revised Standard Version: Scripture quotations from 1 Samuel 8–10 from the New Revised Standard Version of the Bible, copyright © 1989 National Council of the Churches of Christ in the United States of America. Used by permission. All rights reserved.

James B. Pritchard (ed.): "Cyrus." From *Ancient Near Eastern Texts Relating to the Old Testament—Third Edition with Supplement.* © 1950, 1955, 1969, renewed 1978 by Princeton University Press. Reprinted by permission of Princeton University Press.

CHAPTER 3

Aristophanes: Excerpt from *The Clouds* from *Lysistrata and Other Plays* by Aristophanes, translated with an introduction by Alan H. Sommerstein (Penguin Classics, 1973). Copyright © Alan H. Sommerstein, 1973. Reproduced by permission of Penguin Books Ltd.

Homer: From *The Odyssey* by Homer, translated by Emily Wilson. Copyright © 2018 by Emily Wilson. Used by permission of W. W. Norton & Company, Inc.

Plato: Excerpts from *The Last Days of Socrates* by Plato, translated with an introduction by Hugh Tredennick (Penguin Classics 1954, Third edition 1969). Copyright © Hugh Tredennick, 1954, 1959, 1969. Reproduced by permission of Penguin Books Ltd.

Sappho: "Fragment 16" from *The Poetry of Sappho*, translated and notes by Jim Powell, pp. 6–7. Copyright © 2007 by Jim Powell. Reprinted by permission of Jim Powell. "Sappho to Her Pupils," translated by Lachlan Mackinnon, *The Times Literary Supplement*, July 15, 2005. © Lachlan Mackinnon / The Times Literary Supplement / News International Trading Ltd. Reprinted with permission.

Tyrtaeus: "Exhortation to the Young Hoplite" from *University of Chicago Readings in Western Civilization, Vol. 1: The Greek Polis*, pp. 23–24, edited by Arthur W. H. Adkins and Peter White, copyright © 1986 by The University of Chicago. Reprinted by permission of The University of Chicago Press.

CHAPTER 4

Arrian: Excerpts from *The Campaigns of Alexander* by Arrian, translated by Aubrey de Sélincourt, revised with an introduction and notes by J.R. Hamilton (Penguin Classics 1958, Revised edition 1971). Copyright © the Estate of Aubrey de Sélincourt, 1958. Introduction and Notes copyright © J.R. Hamilton, 1971. Reproduced by permission of Penguin Books Ltd.

Bible. New Revised Standard Version: Scripture quotations from 1 Maccabees 1, and 2 Maccabees 4 and 6 from the New Revised Standard Version of the Bible, copyright © 1989 National Council of the Churches of Christ in the United States of America. Used by permission. All rights reserved.

Phintys: From Lefkowitz, Mary R., and Maureen B. Fant, eds., *Women's Life in Greece and Rome: A Source Book in Translation, Second Edition*, pp. 163–164. © 1982, 1992 M. B. Fant & M. R. Lefkowitz. Reprinted with permission of Johns Hopkins University Press and Bristol Classical Press, an imprint of Bloomsbury Publishing Plc.

CHAPTER 5

Plutarch: From Lefkowitz, Mary R., and Maureen B. Fant, eds.,*Women's Life in Greece and Rome: A Source Book in Translation*, Second Edition, pp. 147–149. © 1982, 1992 M. B. Fant & M. R. Lefkowitz. Reprinted with permission of Johns Hopkins University Press and Bristol Classical Press, an imprint of Bloomsbury Publishing Plc.

Polybius: Excerpts from *The Rise of the Roman Empire* by Polybius, translated by Ian Scott-Kilvert, selected with an introduction by F. W. Walbank (Penguin Classics, 1979). Copyright © Ian Scott-Kilvert, 1979. Reproduced by permission of Penguin Books Ltd.

Tacitus: Excerpts from *The Annals of Imperial Rome* by Tacitus, translated with an introduction by Michael Grant (Penguin Classics 1956, Sixth revised edition 1989). Copyright © Michael Grant Publications Ltd, 1956, 1959, 1971, 1973, 1975, 1977, 1989. Reproduced by permission of Penguin Books Ltd.

CHAPTER 6

Bible. New Revised Standard Version: Scripture quotations from Acts of the Apostles 23–24 from the New Revised Standard Version of the Bible, copyright © 1989 National Council of the Churches of Christ in the United States of America. Used by permission. All rights reserved.

Sidonius: Reprinted from *Sidonius: Volume II—Letters*, translated by W. B. Anderson, Loeb Classical Library Volume 420, pp. 127–129, 181–183, Cambridge, Mass.: Harvard University Press, Copyright © 1965 by the President and Fellows of Harvard College. Loeb Classical Library ® is a registered trademark of the President and Fellows of Harvard College. Reprinted with permission.

P. G. Walsh (trans.): Letters from Book Ten of *Pliny the Younger: Complete Letters*, translated by P. G. Walsh. Copyright © P. G. Walsh 2006. Reprinted by permission of Oxford University Press.

CHAPTER 7

H. R. Loyn and John Percival: "Capitulary concerning the parts of Saxony" from *The Reign of Charlemagne: Documents on Carolingian Government and Administration* (New York: St. Martin's Press, 1976), edited and translated by H. R. Loyn and John Percival. Reprinted by permission of the Estate of H. R. Loyn.

Jo Ann McNamara, John Halborg, & E. Gordon Whatley (eds.): Excerpts from "Bathild, Queen of Neustria (d. ca 680)," in *Sainted Women of the Dark Ages*, pp. 264–278. Copyright, 1992, Duke University Press. All rights reserved. Reprinted by permission of the copyright holder. www.dukepress.edu

Michael Sells (trans.): "Sura 81: The Overturning" from *Approaching the Qur'an: The Early Revelations*, translated by Michael Sells, pp. 48, 50. Copyright © 1999 by Michael A. Sells. Reprinted by permission of White Cloud Press.

CHAPTER 8

Bernard of Angers: "Miracles of Saint Foy" from *Readings in Medieval History,* 5th Edition, edited & translated by Patrick J. Geary, © University of Toronto Press 2016. Reprinted by permission of the publisher.

Anna Comnena: Excerpts from *The Alexiad of Anna Comnena*, translated by E. R. A. Sewter (Penguin Classics, 1969). Copyright © E. R. A. Sewter, 1969. Reproduced by permission of Penguin Books Ltd.

Samuel the Nagid: "A Hebrew Poem in Praise of Wine," reprinted from *Wine, Women, and Death: Medieval Hebrew Poems on the Good Life* by Raymond P. Scheindlin by permission of the University of Nebraska Press. Copyright © 1986 by the Jewish Publication Society.

Pope Urban II: "Urban II's Call for a Crusade," from *The Crusades: A Reader*, 2nd edition, edited by S. J. Allen and Emilie Amt, © University of Toronto Press 2014. Reprinted by permission of the publisher.

CHAPTER 9

Marie de France: "Equitan" from *The Lais of Marie de France*, translated by Glyn S. Burgess and Keith Busby (Penguin Classics 1986, Second edition 1999). Copyright © Glyn S. Burgess and Keith Busby, 1986, 1999. Reproduced by permission of Penguin Books Ltd.

Robert I. Moore (ed. & trans.): "The Conversion of Peter Waldo" from *The Birth of Popular Heresy*, edited & translated by Robert I. Moore (London: Edward Arnold, 1975). Copyright © 1975, Edward Arnold Publishers. Reproduced by permission of Robert I. Moore.

St. Francis of Assisi: Excerpts from Marion A. Habig, editor, *St. Francis of Assisi: Omnibus of Sources* (Cincinnati: Franciscan Media, 2012) are used by permission. All rights reserved.

CHAPTER 10

Walter Bower: "A Declaration of Scottish Independence," from *Scotichronicon*, Volume 7, by Walter Bower. Edited by B. Scott and D. E. R. Watt. Copyright © University of St. Andrews 1996. Reprinted by permission of Birlinn Ltd.

Geoffrey de Charny: From *The Book of Chivalry of Geoffroi de Charny: Text, Context, and Translation*, translated by Richard W. Kaeuper and Elspeth Kennedy, p. 99. Copyright © 1996 University of Pennsylvania Press. Reprinted with permission of the University of Pennsylvania Press.

Rosemary Horrox (ed.): Excerpts from *The Black Death*, translated and edited by Rosemary Horrox. © Rosemary Horrox 1994. Reprinted by permission of Manchester University Press, Manchester, UK.

Magnus Magnusson and Herman Pálsson: Excerpts from *The Vinland Sagas,* translated with an introduction by Magnus Magnusson

Emilie du Châtelet: "Bernard Mandeville's 'The Fable of Bees'" from *Selected Philosophical and Scientific Writings*, pp. 48–49, edited by Judith P. Zinsser, translated by Isabelle Bour and Judith P. Zinsser, English translation copyright © 2009 by Isabelle Bour and Judith P. Zinsser, copyright © 2009 by The University of Chicago. Reprinted by permission of The University of Chicago Press.

Jean Rousseau: From *Rousseau's Political Writings: A Norton Critical Edition*, edited by Alan Ritter and Julia Conaway Bondanella, translated by Julia Conaway Bondanella. Copyright © 1988 by W.W. Norton & Company, Inc. Used by permission of W. W. Norton & Company, Inc.

CHAPTER 18

Keith Michael Baker (ed.): "Declaration of the Rights of Man" from *University of Chicago Readings in Western Civilization, Vol. 7: The Old Regime and the French Revolution*, pp. 238–239, copyright © 1987 by The University of Chicago. Reprinted by permission of The University of Chicago Press.

Napoléon Bonaparte: "Letter to Consul Cambaceres (April 27, 1802)" from Laura Mason and Tracey Rizzo, *The French Revolution* 1E. © 1999 Wadsworth, a part of Cengage Learning, Inc. Reproduced by permission. www.cengage.com/permissions.

Benjamin Constant: *Constant: Political Writings* (Cambridge: Cambridge University Press, 1988), pp. 79–80, translated and edited by Biancamaria Fontana. © Cambridge University Press 1988. Reprinted by permission of the publisher.

Emmanuel Joseph Sieyés: Excerpts from *What Is the Third Estate?* (New York: Frederick A. Praeger, 1964), translated by M. Blondel and edited by S. E. Finer. Reprinted by permission of the Estate of S. E. Finer.

CHAPTER 19

Friedrich Engels: Republished with permission of John Wiley & Sons from *The Condition of the Working Class in England in 1844*, translated and edited by W. O. Henderson and W. H. Chaloner (New York: Macmillan, 1958).

Ebenezer Pettigrew: "Notebook containing an account of the death of Ann. B Pettigrew, June 10, 1830," in the Pettigrew Family Papers #592, Southern Historical Collection, Wilson Library, University of North Carolina at Chapel Hill. Reprinted with permission.

Flora Tristan: From *The Workers' Union*, translated by Beverly Livingston. Copyright © 1983 by the Board of Trustees of the University of Illinois. Used with permission of the University of Illinois Press.

CHAPTER 20

Karl Marx: "Karl Marx and Pierre-Joseph Proudhon, Correspondence" from *Karl Marx, Frederick Engels: Collected Works*, Vol. 38,

pp. 38–39. Reprinted by permission of International Publishers, New York.

P. I. Pestel: Excerpt from "The Trial" from *Voices in Exile: The Decembrist Memoirs* edited by G. R. V. Barratt. Copyright © 1974 McGill-Queen's University Press. Reprinted by permission of the publisher.

CHAPTER 21

Alexis de Tocqueville: Republished with permission of Transaction Publishers, from *Recollections: The French Revolution of 1848*, translated by George Lawrence, edited by J. P. Mayer, pp. 136–137. Copyright © 1987 by Transaction Publishers, New Brunswick, New Jersey. Original copyright © 1970 J. P. Mayer.

Gregory L. Freeze (ed.): Excerpts from *From Supplication to Revolution: A Documentary Social History of Imperial Russia*. Copyright © 1988, Oxford University Press, Inc. Reprinted by permission of Oxford University Press, USA.

Karl Marx: "Neve Rheinische Zeitung" from *The Class Struggles in France*, pp. 57–58. Reprinted by permission of International Publishers, New York.

Denis Mack Smith (ed.): Excerpts from *The Making of Italy, 1796–1870*, pp. 47–49, 181–182, 224–225. Copyright © 1968, 1988 Denis Mack Smith. Reproduced with permission of Palgrave Macmillan.

CHAPTER 22

Jamāl ad-Dīn "al-Afghānī": Excerpts from *An Islamic Response to Imperialism: Political and Religious Writings of Sayyid Jamāl ad-Dīn "al-Afghānī"*, translated by Nikki R. Keddie (Berkeley: University of California Press, 1983). Copyright © 1968, 1983 by the Regents of the University of California. Reprinted by permission of the University of California Press.

CHAPTER 23

Hedwig Dohm: Excerpts from "The Old Woman" (1903) from *Become Who You Are*, translated by Elizabeth G. Ametsbichler, pp. 67–68, 78–79. Copyright © 2006 State University of New York. Reprinted by permission of the State University of New York Press.

Nikolaus Osterroth: "Nikolaus Osterroth, Clay Miner" from *The German Worker: Working-Class Autobiographies from the Age of Industrialization*, translated and edited by Alfred Kelly, (Berkeley: University of California Press, 1987). Copyright © 1987 by the Regents of the University of California. Reprinted by permission of the University of California Press.

CHAPTER 24

Louis Barthas: Excerpts from *Poilu: The World War I Notebooks of Corporal Louis Barthas, Barrelmaker, 1914–1918*, translated by

Edward M. Strauss. English translation © 2014 by Yale University Press. Originally published as *Les carnets de guerre de Louis Barthas, tonnelier, 1914–1918*. Copyright © Editions La Découverte, Paris, France, 1978, 1997, 2003. All rights reserved. Reprinted with permission from Editions La Découverte.

Paul von Hindenburg: From *The War from Within: German Working-Class Women in the First World War*, translated by Margaret Ries. Copyright © Ute Daniel 1997. Reprinted by permission of Berg Publishers, an imprint of Bloomsbury Publishing Plc.

CHAPTER 25

Joseph Goebbels: "Why are we enemies of the Jews?" from Snyder, Louis, *Documents of German History*. Copyright © 1958 by Rutgers, the State University. Reprinted by permission of Rutgers University Press.

Fritz Lang: "The Future of the Feature Film in Germany" from *The Weimar Republic Sourcebook*, edited by Anton Kaes, Martin Jay, and Edward Dimendberg (Berkeley: University of California Press, 1994). Copyright © 1994 by the Regents of the University of California. Reprinted by permission of the University of California Press.

V. I. Lenin: "Theses on the National and Colonial Questions," from *Workers of the World and Oppressed Peoples, Unite!: Proceedings and Documents of the Second Congress, 1920*, Volume 1, edited by John Riddell, pp. 283–288. Copyright © 1991 by Pathfinder Press. Reprinted by permission.

Richard Sakwa (ed.): "Stalin on Industrialism" and "The Bolsheviks Must Seize Power" from *Rise and Fall of the Soviet Union 1917–1991*, by Richard Sakwa. Copyright © 1999 Routledge. Reproduced with permission of Taylor & Francis Books UK.

Lewis Siegelbaum and Andrei Sokolov (eds.): "Letters from Anonymous Workers to the Newspaper Pravda" from *Stalinism as a Way of Life*, pp. 39–41. Copyright © 2000 by Yale University. All rights reserved. Reprinted by permission of Yale University Press.

CHAPTER 26

Jean Guéhenno: Excerpts from *Diary of the Dark Years, 1940–1944: Collaboration, Resistance, and Daily Life in Occupied Paris*, translated and annotated by David Ball. Copyright © Editions Gallimard, Paris, 1947 and 2002. English translation © Oxford University Press 2014. Reprinted by permission of Oxford University Press.

Reinhard Rürup (ed.): Excerpts from *Topography of Terror: Gestapo, SS, and Reichssicherheitshauptamt on the "Prinz-Albrecht-Terrain": A Documentation*, 2nd edition, edited by Reinhard Rürup, translated from the German edition by Werner T. Angress, pp. 125–127. (Berlin: Verlag Willmuth Arenhövel, 1991). Original: Bundesarchiv Berlin. Reprinted with permission from Siftung Topographie des Terrors.

Harry S. Truman: From *Memoirs*, Vol. 1 (Garden City, NY: Doubleday, 1955), pp. 419–421. Reprinted by permission of Clifton Truman Daniels and the Harry S. Truman Presidential Library and Museum.

CHAPTER 27

Frantz Fanon: Excerpts from *The Wretched of the Earth* by Frantz Fanon, English translation copyright © 1963 by *Présence Africaine*. Used by permission of Grove/Atlantic, Inc. Any third party use of this material, outside of this publication, is prohibited.

Nikita Khrushchev: "Report to the Communist Party Congress (1961)" from *Current Soviet Policies IV*, 1962, pp. 42–45, from the translations of the Current Digest of the Soviet Press. Copyright East View Information Services, Inc. All rights reserved. Reproduced by permission.

Heda Margolius Kovály: Excerpted from *Under a Cruel Star: A Life in Prague 1941–1968* (Plunkett Lake Press, 1986); eBook edition at http://plunkettlakepress.com/uacs.

CHAPTER 28

Simone de Beauvoir: From *The Second Sex* by Simone de Beauvoir, translated by Constance Borde & Sheila Malovany-Chevallier, translation copyright © 2009 by Constance Borde and Sheila Malovany-Chevallier. Used by permission of Alfred A. Knopf, an imprint of the Knopf Doubleday Publishing Group, a division of Penguin Random House LLC. All rights reserved. And by permission of Random House Ltd.

Betty Friedan: From *The Feminine Mystique* by Betty Friedan. Copyright © 1983, 1974, 1973, 1963 by Betty Friedan. Used by permission of W. W. Norton & Company, Inc., The Orion Publishing Group, London, and Curtis Brown, Ltd.

Bronislaw Geremek: "Between Hope and Despair," *Daedalus: Journal of the American Academy of Arts and Sciences*, 119:1 (Winter 1990), pp. 104–105. © 1990 by American Academy of Arts and Sciences. Reprinted by permission of MIT Press.

Helmut Kohl: "A 10-point plan for overcoming the division of Europe and Germany: Speech by FRG Chancellor Helmut Kohl in the German Bundestag, Bonn, 28 November 1989" from *Germany and Europe in Transition*, edited by Adam Daniel Rotfeld and Walther Stützle, pp. 120–122. Copyright © SIPRI 1991. Reprinted by permission of the Stockholm International Peace Research Institute.

Ludvík Vaculík: "Two Thousand Words" originally published as "Dva Tisice Slov," *Literarny Listy* (Prague) June 27, 1968. Translated by Mark Kramer, Joy Moss, and Ruth Tosek. From *The Prague Spring 1968*, edited by Jaromir Navrátil. Budapest-New York: Central European University Press, 1998, pp. 177–181. Reprinted by permission.

CHAPTER 29

John R. Bowen: Excerpt from *Why the French Don't Like Headscarves: Islam, the State, and Public Space* by John R. Bowen. © 2007 by Princeton University Press. Reprinted by permission of Princeton University Press.

Tariq Ramadan: "Islam and Muslims in Europe: A Silent Revolution toward Rediscovery," from *Muslims in the West: From Sojourners to Citizens*, edited by Yvonne Yazbeck Haddad, pp. 160–163. Copyright © 2002 by Oxford University Press, Inc. Reprinted by permission of Oxford University Press, USA.

Alfred Sauvy: Excerpt from "Trois Mondes, Une Planéta," originally published in *L'Observateur*, No. 118, 14 April 1952. Translated into English for this edition and reprinted by permission of *Le Nouvel Observateur*.

B. R. Tomlinson: Reproduced by permission of SAGE Publications Ltd., London, Los Angeles, New Delhi, Singapore and Washington DC, from B. R. Tomlinson, "What was the Third World?" *Journal of Contemporary History*, Vol. 38, No. 2 (April 2003), pp. 307–321. Copyright © SAGE Publications, 2003.

United Nations: Excerpts from the Text of the 1951 Convention Relating to the Status of Refugees, UNHCR. Reprinted with permission

All School of Athens: Heritage Image Partnership Ltd / Alamy Stock Photo

All Author photos: W. W. Norton & Company, Inc.

Endpaper Maps: National Geographic

FRONT MATTER

p.ii: Heritage Image Partnership Ltd / Alamy Stock Photo; **p. ix (top):** © François Guenet / Art Resource, NY; **(bottom):** PRISMA ARCHIVO / Alamy Stock Photo; **p. x (top):** Heritage Image Partnership Ltd / Alamy Stock Photo; **(middle):** Alamy Stock Photo; **(bottom):** © Cultura Creative / Alamy Stock Photo; **p. xi (top):** Dagli Orti / REX / Shutterstock; **(middle):** Jean-Pierre Lescourret / Lonely Planet Images/Getty Images; **(bottom):** The Print Collector / Alamy Stock Photo; **p. xii (top):** Album / Alamy Stock Photo; **(middle):** The Picture Art Collection / Alamy Stock Photo; **(bottom):** Album / Alamy Stock Photo; **p. xiii (top):** Juice Images / Alamy Stock Photo; **(middle):** The Picture Art Collection / Alamy Stock Photo; **(bottom):** Archivart / Alamy Stock Photo; **p. xiv (top):** Ian Dagnall Computing / Alamy Stock Photo; **(middle):** Private Collection / Bridgeman Images; **(bottom):** The Picture Art Collection / Alamy Stock Photo; **p. xv (top):** Album / Alamy Stock Photo; **(middle):** The Picture Art Collection / Alamy Stock Photo; **(bottom):** Niday Picture Library / Alamy Stock Photo; **p. xvi (top):** Chronicle / Alamy Stock Photo; **(middle):** Pictorial Press Ltd / Alamy Stock Photo; **(bottom):** akg-images; **p. xvii (top):** Imperial War Museum; **(bottom):** Keystone-France / Gamma-Keystone via Getty Images; **p. xviii (top):** The Print Collector / Alamy Stock Photo; **(middle):** Military Collection / Alamy Stock Photo; **(bottom):** imageBROKER / Alamy Stock Photo; **p. xix:** Sandy Huffaker/Corbis via Getty Images.

CHAPTER 1

p. 2 (chapter opener): © François Guenet / Art Resource, NY; **p. 5:** Ian Dagnall / Alamy Stock Photo; **p. 7:** Louvre, Paris, France / Bridgeman Images; **p. 9:** © Interfoto / Alamy Stock Photo; **p. 10 (left):** Ashmolean Museum, University of Oxford, UK / The Bridgeman Art Library; **(right):** © The Trustees of the British Museum / Art Resource, NY; **p. 14:** Bettmann / Getty Images; **p. 15:** Erich Lessing / Art Resource, NY; **p. 16 (left):** Granger, NYC — All rights reserved; **(right):** Courtesy of University of Pennsylvania Museum, image #150028; **p. 17:** World Religions Photo Library / Alamy Stock Photo; **p. 17 (inset):** © Interfoto / Alamy Stock Photo; **p. 19:** Louvre, (Museum), Paris, France / Photo: © RMN-Grand Palais / Art Resource, NY; **p. 21 (both):** Album / Alamy Stock Photo; **p. 24 (left):** Granger, NYC — All rights reserved; **(right):** © Arterra Picture Library / Alamy Stock Photo; **p. 26 (both):** Werner Forman / Art Resource, NY; **p. 27 (left):** © Bettmann / Getty Images; **(right):** Republished with Permission of Taylor and Francis Group LLC Book from Ancient Civilizations, 2 / E by Scarre / Fagan, © 2003; permission conveyed through Copyright Clearance Center, Inc.; **p. 28:** World History Archive / Alamy Stock Photo; **p. 29:** Dave Stamboulis / Alamy Stock Photo; **p. 30:** De Agostini Picture Library / Bridgeman Images; **p. 32:** Louvre, Paris, France / Bridgeman Images; **p. 33:** © The Trustees of the British Museum / Art Resource, NY; **p. 34:** © Vincent Francigny / Sedeinga archaeological mission.

CHAPTER 2

p. 38 (chapter opener): PRISMA ARCHIVO / Alamy Stock Photo; **p. 41:** © The Trustees of the British Museum / Art Resource, NY; **p. 43:** © Jose Fuste Raga / Corbis via Getty Images; **p. 44 (left):** © Travel Pictures / Alamy Stock Photo; **(right):** © Ian M Butterfield / Alamy Stock Photo; **p. 45 (left):** Scala / Art Resource, NY; **(right):** © Jim Henderson / Alamy Stock Photo; **p. 46 (top):** World History Archive / Alamy Stock Photo; **(bottom):** Robert Harding / Alamy Stock Photo; **p. 49:** Album / Alamy Stock Photo; **p. 50:** PRISMA ARCHIVO / Alamy Stock Photo; **p. 51 (top):** CM Dixon / Print Collector / Getty Images; **(bottom):** Courtesy of The Department of Classics, University of Cincinnati; **p. 56:** © North Wind Picture Archives / The Image Works; **p. 57 (left):** Nimatallah / Art Resource, NY; **(right):** Seokyong Lee / Bloomberg via Getty Images; **p. 63:** Werner Forman / Universal Images Group / Getty Images; **p. 64:** Heritage Image Partnership Ltd / Alamy Stock Photo; **p. 65:** Alamy Stock Photo; **p. 66:** DEA Picture Library / De Agostini / Getty Images; **p. 70:** Alamy Stock Photo; **p. 71:** Billdarchiv Preussischer Kulturbesitz / Art Resource, NY.

CHAPTER 3

p. 74 (chapter opener): Heritage Image Partnership Ltd / Alamy Stock Photo; **p. 76:** © Nagelestock.com / Alamy Stock Photo; **p. 82:** De Agostini Picture Library / Bridgeman Images; **p. 83:** ©

Hulton Archive / Getty Images; **p. 259:** From David Nicholas, Urban Europe, 1100–1700, published © 2003 with permission of Palgrave MacMillan, fig 3.3, p.74.; **p. 260:** Nahlik / Shutterstock; **p. 262:** Mark Buckle / Alamy Stock Photo; **p. 264 (top):** Muse de la Tapisserie, Bayeux, France / Bridgeman Images; **(bottom):** French School / The Bridgeman Art Library / Getty Images; **p. 265:** Album / Alamy Stock Photo; **p. 266:** Foto Marburg / Art Resource, NY; **p. 268:** Erich Lessing / Art Resource, NY; **p. 274 (left):** Biblioteca Monasterio del Escorial, Madrid, Spain / Bridgeman Images; **(right):** AP Photo; **p. 275:** © British Library Board / Robana / Art Resource, NY; **p. 279:** Bridgeman-Giraudon / Art Resource, NY; **p. 280:** Album / Alamy Stock Photo; **p. 282 (left):** Samuel Magal / Sites & Photos / akg-images; **(right):** Jozef sedmak / Alamy Stock Photo.

CHAPTER 9

p. 284 (chapter opener): Album / Alamy Stock Photo; **p. 286:** Christophel Fine Art / UIG via Getty Images; **p. 287:** Fotosearch / Getty Images; **p. 294:** Francisco de Casa / Alamy Stock Photo; **p. 295 (left):** Album / Alamy Stock Photo; **(right):** Heritage Image Partnership Ltd / Alamy Stock Photo; **p. 297:** Peter Horree / Alamy Stock Photo; **p. 299 (left):** Scala / White Images / Art Resource, NY; **(right):** © Lucasfilm Ltd. / Twentieth Century Fox Film Corp. / Photofest; **p. 300:** Bibliotheque Sainte-Genevieve, Paris, France / Archives Charmet / Bridgeman Images; **p. 301:** © Adam Kraska / Dreamstime.com; **p. 304 (left):** Erich Lesser / Art Resource, NY; **(right):** The Metropolitan Museum of Art, New York, Purchase, The Cloisters Collection and Michel David-Weill Gift, 1999; **p. 305:** FLHC 1A / Alamy Stock Photo; **p. 309 (left):** Album / Alamy Stock Photo; **(right):** bpk Bildagentur / Bibliotheque Nationale, Paris, France / Art Resource, NY; **p. 310** Erich Lessing / Art Resource, NY; **p. 315** Santa Maria Novella, Florence, Italy / Bridgeman Images; **p. 316:** akg-images; **p. 317:** Bpk, Berlin / Bibliotheque Nationale de France (BnF), Paris, France / Jochen Remmer / Art Resource, NY; **p. 321 (left):** Khd / Shutterstock; **(right):** Bertl123 / Shutterstock.

CHAPTER 10

p. 324 (chapter opener): The Picture Art Collection / Alamy Stock Photo; **p. 328 (top):** Ancient Art & Architecture Collection Ltd / Alamy Stock Photo; **(bottom):** Christie's Images / Bridgeman Images; **p. 329:** Pictures from History / Bridgeman Images; **p. 331:** Bibliothèque Nationale, Paris, France / Bridgeman Images; **p. 334:** The Picture Art Collection / Alamy Stock Photo; **p. 335:** Cindy Hopkins / Alamy Stock Photo; **p. 336:** Heritage Image Partnership Ltd / Alamy Stock Photo; **p. 337:** Album / Alamy Stock Photo; **p. 340 (both):** Granger, NYC — All rights reserved; **p. 341:** Album / Alamy Stock Photo; **p. 342:** Cameraphoto Arte, Venice / Art Resource, NY; **p. 343:** Bob Battersby / Corbis via Getty Images; **p. 344:** Interfoto / Alamy Stock Photo; **p. 346:** Wiliam Perry / Alamy Stock Photo; **p. 347:** Brian Lawrence / Alamy Stock Photo; **p. 352 (bottom left):** Photos.com / Getty Images RF; **p. 352 (bottom right):** Dominique Faget / AFP / Getty Images.

CHAPTER 11

p. 358 (chapter opener): Album / Alamy Stock Photo; **p. 360:** HIP / Art Resource, NY; **p. 363:** Album / Alamy Stock Photo; **p. 364:** akg-images / British Library; **p. 366:** Biblioteca Ambrosiana, Milan, Italy / Bridgeman Images; **p. 368 (left):** Bildarchiv Preussischer Kulturbesitz / Art Resource, NY; **(right):** Scala / Art Resource, NY; **p. 372:** John Massey Stewart Picture Library; **p. 373:** The Picture Art Collection / Alamy Stock Photo; **p. 375:** The Picture Art Collection / Alamy Stock Photo; **p. 377:** Réunion des Musées Nationaux / Art Resource, NY; **p. 380:** S-F / Shutterstock; **p. 381:** © Hemis / Alamy Stock Photo; **p. 383 (left):** Bridgeman Images; **(right):** Gregorio Borgia / AP Photo; **p. 386:** World History Archive / Alamy Stock Photo; **p. 387:** British Library, London, UK © British Library Board. All rights reserved / Bridgeman Images.

CHAPTER 12

p. 390 (chapter opener): Juice Images / Alamy Stock Photo; **p. 398:** Album / Alamy Stock Photo; **p. 399 (top):** World History Archive / Alamy Stock Photo; **(bottom):** Peter Barritt / Alamy Stock Photo; **p. 400:** Ian Dagnall / Alamy Stock Photo; **p. 401 (top):** Heritage Image Partnership Ltd / Alamy Stock Photo; **(bottom):** Juice Images / Alamy Stock Photo; **p. 403 (left):** Nimatallah / Art Resource, NY; **(center):** Classic Image / Alamy Stock Photo; **(right):** Erich Lessing / Art Resource, NY; **p. 404:** Bildarchiv Preussischer Kulturbesitz / Art Resource, NY; **p. 405:** Ian G. Dagnall / Alamy Stock Photo; **p. 406 (left):** The Print Collector / Alamy Stock Photo; **(right):** University of Leicester / Sipa USA / Newscom; **p. 407:** Universal Images Group North America LLC / Alamy Stock Photo; **p. 408:** Classic Paintings / Alamy Stock Photo; **p. 411:** Aleksey Stemmer / Shutterstock; **p. 412:** Album / Art Resource, NY; **p. 414:** © Lebrecht Music and Arts Photo Library / Alamy Stock Photo; **p. 418:** Bibliotheque Nationale, Paris, France / Bridgeman Images; **p. 419:** akg-images; **p. 420:** Dagli Orti / REX / Shutterstock.

CHAPTER 13

p. 424 (chapter opener): The Picture Art Collection / Alamy Stock Photo; **p. 426:** PRISMA ARCHIVO / Alamy Stock Photo; **p. 427:** Bildarchiv Preussischer Kulturbesitz / Art Resource, NY; **p. 428:** lucky-photographer / Alamy Stock Photo; **p. 429:** Classic Paintings / Alamy Stock Photo; **p. 430 (left):** Pope Alexander VI (woodcut), German School, (16th century) / Private Collection / Bridgeman Images; **p. 430 (right):** Bpk, Berlin / Art Resource, NY; **p. 431 (left):** Bpk Bildagentur / Kupferstichkabinett, Staatliche Museen, Berlin, Germany / J∨∂rg P. Anders / Art Resource, NY; **(right):** vy Close Images / Alamy Stock Photo; **p. 432:** The Picture Art Collection / Alamy Stock Photo; **p. 434:** nagelestock.com / Alamy Stock Photo; **p. 436 (left):** akg-images; **(right):** Erich Lessing / Art Resource, NY; **p. 437 (both):** Erich Lessing / Art Resource, NY; **p. 443:** PRISMA ARCHIVO / Alamy Stock Photo; **p. 445 (left):** Niday Picture Library / Alamy Stock Photo; **(right):** Scala / Art Resource, NY; **p. 447 (left):** Erich Lessing / Art Resource, NY;

(right): Michal Cizek / AFP / Getty Images; **p. 448 (left)**: Scala / Art Resource, NY; **(right)**: Peter Horree / Alamy Stock Photo; **p. 451**: The Art Archive / REX / Shutterstock.

CHAPTER 14

p. 454 (chapter opener): Archivart / Alamy Stock Photo; **p. 457**: Virginia Historical Society, Richmond / Bridgeman Images; **p. 462**: Private Collection / Peter Newark American Pictures / Bridgeman Images; **p. 463**: Bettmann / Corbis via Getty Images; **p. 466**: Heritage Image Partnership Ltd / Alamy Stock Photo; **p. 467**: akg-images; **p. 469 (top)**: Bibliotheque des Arts Decoratifs, Paris / Bridgeman Images; **(bottom)**: Archivart / Alamy Stock Photo; **p. 470**: Andreas Juergensmeier / Shutterstock; **p. 474**: Giraudon / Bridgeman Images; **p. 475**: Granger, NYC — All rights reserved; **p. 478**: The National Trust Photolibrary / Alamy Stock Photo; **p. 479**: Military History Collection / Alamy Stock Photo; **p. 482 (left)**: Pictorial Press Ltd / Alamy Stock Photo; **(right)**: Interfoto / Alamy Stock Photo; **p. 486 (left)**: © Franz-Marc Frei / Getty Images; **(right)**: International / REX / Shutterstock; **p. 487**: Heritage Image Partnership Ltd / Alamy Stock Photo; **p. 488 (left)**: Scala / Art Resource, NY; **(right)**: PAINTING / Alamy Stock Photo; **p. 489 (top)**: Peter Horree / Alamy Stock Photo; **(bottom)**: classicpaintings / Alamy Stock Photo; **p. 490 (left)**: The Iveagh Bequest, Kenwood House, London, UK / © Historic England / Bridgeman Images; **(right)**: The Artchives / Alamy Stock Photo.

CHAPTER 15

p. 492 (chapter opener): Ian Dagnall Computing / Alamy Stock Photo; **p. 494**: Courtesy Rijksmuseum, Amsterdam; **p. 496 (left)**: FORGET Patrick / SAGAPHOTO.COM / Alamy Stock Photo; **(right)**: The Picture Art Collection / Alamy Stock Photo; **p. 497 (top)**: Edinburgh University Library, Scotland / With kind permission of the University of Edinburgh / Bridgeman Images; **(bottom)**: Erich Lessing / Art Resource, NY; **p. 500 (left)**: Heritage Image Partnership Ltd / Alamy Stock Photo; **(right)**: PA Images / Alamy Stock Photo; **p. 503**: Ian Dagnall Computing / Alamy Stock Photo; **p. 504**: Pictorial Press Ltd / Alamy Stock Photo; **p. 505**: Pictorial Press Ltd / Alamy Stock Photo; **p. 507**: Courtesy of National Library of Poland; **p. 509**: Dagli Orti / REX / Shutterstock; **p. 511**: Interfoto / Alamy Stock Photo; **p. 514**: Berlin / Jörg P. Anders. Stiftung Preussische Schlösser und Gärten / Art Resource, NY; **p. 515**: Lebrecht Authors / Bridgeman Images; **p. 517**: Courtesy Dr. Alexander Boguslawski, Professor of Russian Studies, Rollins College.

CHAPTER 16

p. 522 (chapter opener): Private Collection / Bridgeman Images; **p. 525**: Jeffrey Coolidge / Getty Images RF; **p. 526 (left)**: Album / Alamy Stock Photo; **(right)**: Gui00878 / Getty Images; **p. 527**: Album / Alamy Stock Photo; **p. 528**: Science History Images / Alamy Stock Photo; **p. 530 (left)**: Granger,

NYC — All rights reserved; **(right)**: Science History Images / Alamy Stock Photo; **p. 531 (left)**: Universal History Archive / UIG / Bridgeman Images; **(right)**: Royal Astronomical Society / Science Source; **p. 532**: Album / Alamy Stock Photo; **p. 534**: Paul D. Stewart / Science Source ; **p. 535**: © Photos 12 / Alamy Stock Photo; **p. 536**: © Look and Learn / Bridgeman Images; **p. 537**: Courtesy of Historical Collections & Services, Claude Moore Health Sciences Library, University of Virginia; **p. 540**: Universal History Archive / UIG / Bridgeman Images; **p. 541**: SSPL / Getty Images; **p. 543**: © The Natural History Museum, London / The Image Works; **p. 545**: © Courtesy of the Warden and Scholars of New College, Oxford / Bridgeman Images; **p. 547**: Album / Alamy Stock Photo.

CHAPTER 17

p. 550 (chapter opener): The Picture Art Collection / Alamy Stock Photo; **p. 552**: "The Cruel Death of Calas" / Elizabeth Nesbitt Room Chapbook Collection / Hillman Lib Special Collections; **p. 555**: Heritage Image Partnership Ltd / Alamy Stock Photo; **p. 556**: Pictorial Press Ltd / Alamy Stock Photo; **p. 557**: Bibliothèque Nationale, Paris, France / Bridgeman Images; **p. 559**: Private Collection / Bridgeman Images; **p. 560 (left)**: Charles Walker Collection / Alamy Stock Photo; **(right)**: FL Historical 36 / Alamy Stock Photo; **p. 561**: Art Collection 2 / Alamy Stock Photo; **p. 564 (left)**: Sir Joshua Reynolds / Omai of the Friendly Isles / nla.obj-135229180 / National Library of Australia; **(right)**: History and Art Collection / Alamy Stock Photo; **p. 565**: National Library of Australia; **p. 566**: © Philip and Elizabeth DeBay / Stapleton Collection / Corbis / Corbis via Getty Images; **p. 567**: The Picture Art Collection / Alamy Stock Photo; **p. 569 (left)**: Niday Picture Library / Alamy Stock Photo; **(right)**: Courtesy National Gallery of Art, Washington. Gift of Mrs. Mellon Bruce in memory of her father, Andrew W. Mellon; **p. 574**: The Picture Art Collection / Alamy Stock Photo; **p. 575**: Bettmann / Getty Images; **p. 576 (left)**: Granger, NYC — All rights reserved; **(right)**: Bluberries / iStock Photo; **p. 578**: Scala / Art Resource, NY; **p. 579**: akg-images; **p. 580**: Granger, NYC — All rights reserved.

CHAPTER 18

p. 584 (chapter opener): Album / Alamy Stock Photo; **p. 588 (left)**: akg-images; **(right)**: CCI / REX / Shutterstock; **p. 589**: Godong / Alamy Stock Photo; **p. 591**: The Picture Art Collection / Alamy Stock Photo; **p. 593**: Musee de la Ville de Paris, Musee Carnavalet, Paris, France / Bridgeman Images; **p. 594**: Album / Alamy Stock Photo; **p. 600**: Photo 12 / Alamy Stock Photo; **p. 601**: PAINTING / Alamy Stock Photo; **p. 602**: GL Archive / Alamy Stock Photo; **p. 603**: The Artchives / Alamy Stock Photo; **p. 606 (left)**: Risma Archivo / Alamy Stock Photo; **(right)**: Dagli Orti / REX / Shutterstock; **p. 607 (left)**: Musee de la Ville de Paris, Musee Carnavalet, Paris, France / Bridgeman Images; **(right)**: Historical Images Archive / Alamy Stock Photo; **p. 610 (left)**: Jacques Louis David / Getty Images; **(right)**: ART Collection / Alamy Stock Photo;

p. 612: Heritage Image Partnership Ltd / Alamy Stock Photo; p. 613: Album / Alamy Stock Photo; p. 616 (left): Granger, NYC — All rights reserved; (right): Shaun Cunningham / Alamy Stock Photo; p. 617: Chris Hellier / Alamy Stock Photo.

CHAPTER 19

p. 620 (chapter opener): The Picture Art Collection / Alamy Stock Photo; p. 623: Peak District National Park Authority; p. 625 (left): Stefano Bianchetti / Corbis via Getty Images; (right): SSPL via Getty Images; p. 626 (left): The National Archives of the UK; (right): Granger, NYC — All rights reserved; p. 627: Photo 12 / Alamy Stock Photo; p. 628: Hulton Archive / Getty Images; p. 629: Hulton Archive / Getty Images; p. 633: Archives Charmet / Bridgeman Images; p. 635: Hulton Archive / Getty Images; p. 636: Album / Alamy Stock Photo; p. 637: © HIP / The Image Works; p. 638 (bottom left): Photo 12 / Alamy Stock Photo; (bottom right): MIHAI ANDRITOIU / Alamy Stock Photo; p. 639: FLHC 33 / Alamy Stock Photo; p. 642 (left): Fotomas / Topham / The Image Works; (right): Mary Evans / The Image Works; p. 645: Musee de la Ville de Paris, Musee Carnavalet, Paris, France / Archives Charmet / Bridgeman Images; p. 646: Geoffrey Clements / Corbis / VCG via Getty Images; p. 647: Alamy Stock Photo; p. 652 Granger, NYC — All rights reserved; p. 653: Granger, NYC — All rights reserved.

CHAPTER 20

p. 658 (chapter opener): Niday Picture Library / Alamy Stock Photo; p. 666: The Picture Art Collection / Alamy Stock Photo; p. 667: Niday Picture Library / Alamy Stock Photo; p. 668: ART Collection / Alamy Stock Photo; p. 671: Royal Collection Trust © Her Majesty Queen Elizabeth II, 2016 / Bridgeman Images; p. 673: © The Trustees of the British Museum / Art Resource, NY; p. 676: Lebrecht Music & Arts / Alamy Stock Photo; p. 678 (left): akg-images; (right): Time & Life Pictures / Getty Images; p. 679: Pictorial Press Ltd / Alamy Stock Photo; p. 680: ITAR-TASS News Agency / Alamy Stock Photo; p. 686: Lebrecht Music & Arts / Alamy Stock Photo; p. 687 (left): © Russell-Cotes Art Gallery and Museum, Bournemouth, UK / Bridgeman Images; (right): Chronicle / Alamy Stock Photo; p. 688: The Picture Art Collection / Alamy Stock Photo; p. 689 (top): GL Archive / Alamy Stock Photo; (bottom): Album / Alamy Stock Photo.

CHAPTER 21

p. 694 (chapter opener): Chronicle / Alamy Stock Photo; p. 697: Gibson Green / Alamy Stock Photo; p. 700: Album / Alamy Stock Photo; p. 702: Bildarchiv Preussischer Kulturbesitz / Art Resource, NY; p. 703 (bottom left): Ullstein Bild / Granger, NYC —All rights reserved; (bottom right): Agencja Fotograficzna Caro / Alamy Stock Photo; p. 704: The Picture Art Collection / Alamy Stock Photo; p. 705: Bpk, Berlin / Geheimes Staatsarchiv, Preussischer Kulturbesitz / Thommen Art Resource, NY; p. 707: © CORBIS / Corbis via Getty Images; p. 708: Album /

Alamy Stock Photo; p. 710: Rischgitz / Getty Images; p. 711: Scala / Art Resource, NY; p. 714: Charles Rotkin / Corbis / VCG via Getty Images; p. 715: Hulton Archive / Getty Images; p. 716: Scala / Art Resource, NY; p. 717: World History Archive / Alamy Stock Photo; p. 722: Bpk, Berlin / Deutsches Historiches Museum / Arne Psille / Art Resource, NY; p. 723 (both): Bildarchiv Preussischer Kulturbesitz / Dietmar Katz / Art Resource, NY; p. 725: Chronicle / Alamy Stock Photo; p. 728: Bettmann / Getty Images; p. 731: Archive Photos / Getty Images; p. 733: Pictorial Press Ltd / Alamy Stock Photo.

CHAPTER 22

p. 736 (chapter opener): Pictorial Press Ltd / Alamy Stock Photo; p. 738: Bibliothèque des Arts Decoratifs, Paris, France / Archives Charmet / Bridgeman Images; p. 744 (left): Ken and Jenny Jacobson Orientalist Photography Collection / Research Library, The Getty Research Institute, Los Angeles (2008.R.3); (right): Hulton Archive / Getty Images; p. 745 (left): North Wind Picture Archives / Alamy Stock Photo; (right): Punchcartoons.com; p. 750 (left): Granger, NYC — All rights reserved; (right): Janine Wiedel Photolibrary / Alamy Stock Photo; p. 751 (top): Chronicle / Alamy Stock Photo; (bottom): Oriental and India Office Collections, The British Library / Art Resource, NY; p. 754: Bettmann / Getty Images; p. 756: Niday Picture Library / Alamy Stock Photo; p. 758: Hulton Archive / Springer / Getty Images; p. 761 (left): Chronicle / Alamy Stock Photo; (right): Hulton Archive / Getty Images; p. 762 (left): North Wind Picture Archives—All rights reserved; (right): Pictorial Press Ltd / Alamy Stock Photo; p. 763: Sarin Images / Granger, NYC — All rights reserved; p. 768 (top): Department of Image Collections, National Gallery of Art Library, Washington, DC; (bottom all): National Gallery of Art Library Image Collections; p. 770 (left): Bettmann / Getty Images; (right): Chronicle Alamy Stock Photo; p. 771: The Ohio State University Billy Ireland Cartoon Library & Museum.

CHAPTER 23

p. 774 (chapter opener): akg-images; p. 777: akg-images; p. 780: History and Art Collection / Alamy Stock Photo; p. 781: Lordprice Collection / Alamy Stock Photo; p. 784: Hulton Archive / Getty Images; p. 785: bpk Bildagentur / Art Resource, NY; p. 786: Leemage / Getty Images; p. 787 (top): PA Images / Alamy Stock Photo; (bottom): Topical Press Agency / Hulton Getty Images; p. 788 (top): © Geogphotos / Alamy Stock Photo; (bottom): Bettmann / Getty Images; p. 790: © Hulton-Deutsch Collection / CORBIS / Corbis via Getty Images; p. 794 (left): Granger, NYC — All rights reserved; (middle): Zip Lexing / Alamy Stock Photo; (right): Rue des Archives / Granger, NYC - All rights reserved; p. 796: Bettmann / Getty Images; p. 797 (bottom left): World History Archive / Alamy Stock Photo; (bottom right): Avenir Pictures / Alamy Stock Photo; p. 799: Heritage Image Partnership Ltd / Alamy Stock Photo; p. 800: Pictorial Press Ltd / Alamy Stock Photo; p. 804: From an Autobiography:

Herbert Spencer, 1904; **p. 805:** Science History Images / Alamy Stock Photo; **p. 808:** Bettmann / Getty Images; **p. 809:** Bettmann / Getty Images; **p. 810:** Heritage Image Partnership / Alamy Stock Photo; **p. 811 (left):** Album / Alamy Stock Photo; **(right):** Album / Alamy Stock Photo.

CHAPTER 24

p. 814 (chapter opener): Imperial War Museum; **p. 819:** Classic Image / Alamy Stock Photo; **p. 823:** Bettmann / Getty Images; **p. 824 (top):** Everett Collection Historical / Alamy Stock Photo; **(bottom left):** © SZ Photo / Scherl / Bridgeman Images; **(bottom right):** Bettmann Archive / Getty Images; **p. 825:** © Imperial War Museum (IWM); **p. 828 (left):** Album / Alamy Stock Photo; **(right):** Swim Ink 2, LLC / Corbis / Corbis via Getty Images; **p. 829 (left):** Poster Collection, Poster ID #GE 189, Hoover Institution Archives, Stanford University; **(right):** Pictures Now / Alamy Stock Photo; **p. 830 (left):** © Hulton-Deutsch Collection / Corbis / Corbis via Getty Images; **(right):** © Bettmann / Getty Images; **p. 831:** Science History Images / Alamy Stock Photo; **p. 834 (top left):** Everett Collection Historical / Alamy Stock Photo; **(top right):** © SZ Photo / Scherl / Bridgeman Images; **(bottom):** © Sueddeutsche Zeitung Photo / Alamy Stock Photo; **p. 835:** Bettmann / Getty Images; **p. 837 (left):** Heritage Image Partnership Ltd / Alamy Stock Photo; **(right):** B.D.I.C., Paris, France / Archives Charmet / Bridgeman Images; **p. 840:** Bpk, Berlin / Art Resource, NY; **p. 841:** Science History Images / Alamy Stock Photo; **p. 842:** Akademie / Alamy Stock Photo; **p. 845:** Bettmann / Getty Images; **p. 846:** Bettmann / Getty Images; **p. 847:** © Tallandier / Bridgeman Images; **p. 850 (left):** Everett Collection Historical / Alamy Stock Photo; **(right):** Jawdat Ahmad / Pacific Press / Corbis via Getty Images.

CHAPTER 25

p. 854 (chapter opener): Keystone-France / Gamma-Keystone via Getty Images; **p. 856:** G. Dagli Orti / De Agostini Picture Library / Bridgeman Images; **p. 859:** Science History Images / Alamy Stock Photo; **p. 862:** © Sputnik / Alamy Stock Photo; **p. 863 (left):** Album / Alamy Stock Photo; **(right):** Heritage Image Partnership Ltd / Alamy Stock Photo; **p. 868:** World History Archive / Alamy Stock Photo; **p. 870:** George Rinhart / Corbis via Getty Images; **p. 871:** © Hulton-Deutsch Collection / CORBIS / Corbis via Getty Images; **p. 873:** akg-images; **p. 875:** © Hulton-Deutsch Collection / Corbis / Corbis via Getty Images; **p. 880 (left):** © Daily Mail / Rex / Alamy Stock Photo; **(right):** Giorgio Cosulich / Getty Images; **p. 881:** CSU Archives / Everett Collection Inc / Alamy Stock Photo; **p. 882 (left):** University of Maryland Global Land Cover Facility; **(right):** NASA Earth Observatory; **p. 883:** Peter Horree / Alamy Stock Photo; **p. 884:** Sueddeutsche Zeitung Photo / Alamy Stock Photo; **p. 885:** Muse National d'Art Moderne, Centre Georges Pompidou, Paris, France. Photo CNAC / MNAM / Dist. RMN / Art Resource, NY; **p. 886 (left):** Topham / The Image Works; **(right):** Album / Alamy Stock Photo; **p. 887:** William Vanderson / Fox Photos / Getty Images; **p. 888:** AF archive / Alamy Stock Photo.

CHAPTER 26

p. 892 (chapter opener): The Print Collector / Alamy Stock Photo; **p. 895:** Bettmann / Getty Image; **p. 897:** The Southworth Collection, The Mandeville Special Collections Library of UC San Diego; **p. 898:** The Print Collector / Alamy Stock Photo; **p. 899:** © Hulton-Deutsch Collection / Corbis / Corbis via Getty Images; **p. 901:** Bpk, Berlin / Art Resource, NY; **p. 902:** © akg-images / Alamy Stock Photo; **p. 903:** Everett Collection Inc / Alamy Stock Photo; **p. 904:** Archive PL / Alamy Stock Photo; **p. 909:** RGB Ventures / SuperStock / Alamy Stock Photo; **p. 910:** Pictures from History / Bridgeman Images; **p. 914:** AP Photo; **p. 916:** akg-images / Ullstein Bild; **p. 920:** Yad Vashem Archives; **p. 921:** Yad Vashem Archives; **p. 922:** Ullstein Bild / Granger, NYC — All rights reserved; **p. 924 (left):** © Dpa Picture Alliance / Alamy Stock Photo; **(right):** Egon Steiner / picture-alliance / dpa / AP Images; **p. 926:** The National Archives / SSPL / Getty Images; **p. 927:** Sovfoto / UIG via Getty Images; **p. 928 (top):** National Archives / Franklin D. Roosevelt Library Public Domain Photographs; **(bottom):** Shawshots / Alamy Stock Photo; **p. 929:** Library of Congress (Photo by United States Army Airforces.

CHAPTER 27

p. 934 (chapter opener): Military Collection / Alamy Stock Photo; **p. 936:** © CORBIS / Corbis via Getty Images; **p. 938 (both):** Michael Nicholson / Corbis via Getty Images; **p. 939:** Michael Nicholson / Corbis via Getty Images; **p. 940:** Alamy Stock Photo; **p. 942:** Everett Collection Historical / Alamy Stock Photo; **p. 943 (left):** David Pollack / Corbis via Getty Images; **(right):** Granger, NYC — All rights reserved; **p. 944:** AP Photo; **p. 945 (left):** Giehr / picture-alliance / dpa / Newscom; **(right):** dpa picture alliance / Alamy Stock Photo; **p. 952:** Bettmann / Getty Images; **p. 953:** akg-images / Universal Images Group / Sovfoto \ UIG; **p. 959:** Bettman Archive / Getty Images; **p. 961:** © Marc Garanger / Corbis / Corbis via Getty Images; **p. 962:** © Marc Garanger / Corbis / Corbis via Getty Images; **p. 964:** Uber Bilder / Alamy Stock Photo; **p. 965:** akg-images / Universal Images Group / Sovfoto; **p. 967 (left):** dpa picture alliance / Alamy Stock Photo; **(right):** © Bettmann / Getty Images.

CHAPTER 28

p. 970 (chapter opener): imageBROKER / Alamy Stock Photo; **p. 973:** © Bettmann / Getty Images; **p. 974:** Heritage Image Partnership Ltd / Alamy Stock Photo; **p. 975:** David Scott / Alamy Stock Photo; **p. 976 (left):** MARKA / Alamy Stock Photo; **(right):** © Bettmann / Getty Images; **p. 977 (left):** Fiona Adams / Redferns / Getty Images; **(right):** Martha Holmes / The LIFE Picture Collection / Getty Images; **p. 978:** Collection Christophel Ponti De Laurentis Cinematografica / Alamy Stock Photo; **p. 979:** © Bettmann / Getty Images; **p. 981:** © Bettmann / Getty Images; **p. 984:** AP Photo; **p. 986:** API / Gamma-Rapho / Getty Images; **p. 987:** © A. Abbas / Magnum Photos; **p. 988:** © Bettmann / Getty Images; **p. 991:** © Bettmann / Getty Images; **p. 992:** Bettmann Archive / Getty Images; **p. 994:** Peter Turnley / Corbis / VCG via Getty

Images; **p. 995:** © Wally McNamee / Corbis / Corbis via Getty Images; **p. 998:** AFP / Getty Images; **p. 999 (left):** AP Photo / Boris Yurchenko; **(right):** Sovfoto / UIG via Getty Images; **p. 1002:** Justin Leighton / Alamy Stock Photo; **p. 1003 (left):** Oliver Ruether / Laif / Redux; **(right):** AP Photo; **p. 1004:** © Patrick Robert / Sygma / Corbis / Sygma via Getty Images.

CHAPTER 29

p. 1008 (chapter opener): Sandy Huffaker / Corbis via Getty Images; **p. 1011:** Alamy Stock Photo; **p. 1012:** Shaul Schwarz / Getty Images; **p. 1013:** Guang Niu / Reuters / Newscom; **p. 1014:** xPACIFICA / Corbis Documentary / Getty Images; **p. 1015 (left):** Alamy Stock Photo; **(right):** Romeo Ranoco / Reuters / Newscom; **p. 1020:** David Turnley / Corbis / VCG via Getty Images; **p. 1021:** Guang Niu / Reuters / Newscom; **p. 1024:** © Bettmann / Getty Images; **p. 1025:** Jacques Dejean / Sygma via Getty Images; **p. 1028:** Jean Guichard / Sygma / Sygma via Getty Images; **p. 1029:** Peter Turnley / Corbis / VCG via Getty Images; **p. 1030:** Sean Adair / Reuters / Newscom; **p. 1032 (both):** Alamy Stock Photo; **p. 1033:** Pascal Le Segretain / Getty Images; **p. 1040 (both):** Alamy Stock Photo.

Index

Note: Page numbers in *italics* refer to illustrations, maps, and tables.

Beveridge, John, 951
biblia (books), 54
Bicycle Thief (film), 978
"big book of fiefs" (Alfonso II of Aragon), 294, 295, *295*
"Big Four," 847–48
Bikini Atoll, *943*
Bill of Rights (England), 504, 1033
Bill of Rights (United States), 728
bin Laden, Osama, 1029, 1030
birds, hunting of (Middle Ages), 317, *317*
birth control pill, 981
birthday invitation from Roman Britain, *172*
Birth of Venus, The (Botticelli), *399*
Bismarck, Otto von
  antisocialist laws, 784–85, 796–97, *797*
  Berlin Conference, 757, *758*
  Crimean War and, 733
  German unification, 719–21, 722, *723*, 796
  resignation, *796*, 797
  social welfare programs, 951
"black consciousness (pride)", 962–63
Black Death
  challenges to Roman Church following, 381, 386
  Eckhart's teachings and, 345
  European outbreaks of, *352, 353*, 354–56
  impact of, 326, 337, 343, *360*, 360–66
  Mongol siege of Genoese at Caffa, 333, 354, *355*
  population loss from, 355, 359–60, 464
  Yersinia pestis, 355–56, 360–61
Black Lines (Kandinsky), *810*
Black Muslim movement, 984
black power movement, 987–88
Black Shirts, *886*
Black Skin, White Masks (Fanon), 962, *963*
Black Stone, 223
Blake, William, 627, 686, *686*
Blanche of Castile, 318
Blanc, Louis, 680
Blessed Virgin, cult of, 303–4, *304*
Blitzkrieg, 902, *903*, 927
Blonde on Blonde (Dylan), *977*
Bloody Sunday, 800, *800*
blues (music), 976, *977*
Blum, Léon, 879, 898
Boccaccio, Giovanni, 364, 365
Bodin, Jean, 484, 486
Boer War, 763, 769–70, *770*
Boethius, Anicius Manlius Severinus, 207–8, 209, 210, 312
Bohemia
  conversion to Christianity, 251
  High Middle Ages, 292
  Industrial Revolution and, 630, 633
  nationalist movements, nineteenth century, 704, 708, 722–23
  reform movements, Late Middle Ages, *386,* 386–88
  silver mines, 333
  "springtime of peoples," 708
  Thirty Years War, 470, 473
Boilly, Louis-Léopold, *607*

Bolesław III (king of Poland), 292
Bolesław the Pius (Polish duke), 292
Boleyn, Anne, 442, 443, 445
Bolívar, Simón, 662, 664, 673
Bolsheviks
  divorce and, 865
  Five-Year Plans, 862–65, *863*
  formation of, 800
  "Great Terror" and, 866
  New Economic Policy (NEP), 858–59, 862
  October Revolution and, 841, *842, 842*–45, 856
  Russian Civil War, 844, 856, 858
  Stalin and, 859
  war communism, 858, 859
Bonald, Louis-Gabriel-Ambroise, 674
Bonaparte, Napoleon. *see* Napoleon I
Boniface VIII (pope), 342–43, 347
Boniface, Saint, 238, 239
Bonnie and Clyde (film), 979
Book of Chivalry, The (Charny), 351
Book of Common Prayer, The (Cranmer), 444, 445
Book of Contemplation, The (Usama), 277
Book of Deuteronomy, 72
Book of Marvels, The (Mandeville), 325, 332–33
Book of the City of Ladies (Christine de Pizan), 364, 365
Book of the Courtier, The (Castiglione), 397
Book of the Deeds of Arms and of Chivalry, The (Christine de Pizan), 365
books
  biblia, 54
  book trade during Enlightenment, 572
  censorship and, 448, 557, 559, 572
  codex invention, *210,* 211, 392
  rutters/routiers, 414
  see also Christian Bible; Hebrew Bible; printing; *individual titles of books*
books of the dead, 31
Borgia, Cesare, 396, 397, 429
Borowski, Tadeusz, 965
Bosnia
  assassination of Archduke Franz Ferdinand, 816–17, 820, 821
  late nineteenth century, 801
  wars in former Yugoslavia (1990s), 1001, 1002–4
Bossuet, Jacques-Bénigne, 498
Botha, P. W., 1020
Botticelli, Sandro, 398, *399*
Boudica (Celtic warrior queen), 169, *199*
Bougainville, Louise-Antoine de, 564–65, 566
Boulton, Matthew, 621, 627
Bourbon dynasty
  absolutism, 541
  French Revolution and end of, 587, 605, 613
  Henry of Navarre and, *466*
  restoration of, 613, 660–62, 667, 674
  Two Sicilies, 661, 710, 717

Bourdieu, Pierre, 961
bourgeoisie
  defined, 587, 646
  Lenin on, 844, 860–61
  Marx on, 681, 698
  Nietzsche on, 805
Boxer Rebellion of 1900, 752, 754, *754*
Boyle, Robert, 540, 541, 545, 547
Boyne, Battle of the, 505
Bramante, Donato, 400, *401*, 404
Brandenburg-Prussia, 380, 498, 509–10, 511, 513, 519
Braque, Georges, *811*
Brassey, Thomas, 628
Braun, Lily, 787
Brazil
  fugitive slave community in Pernambuco Province, 463
  globalization and poverty in, *1011*
  independence, 664
  Industrial Revolution and, 635
  politics of slavery in, 672, 674
Breathless (film), 978
Bretons, 319
Bretton Woods agreement, 950–51, 1011
Brexit, 1037, *1040,* 1041, *1041*
Brezhnev Doctrine, 990, 994
Brezhnev, Leonid, 882, 989, 990, 992
Brienne, Loménie de, 590
Brissot de Warville, 564
British Committee of the Indian National Congress, 763
British East India Company, 505, 578, 580, 635, 743, 744, 749–50, 1010
British Union of Fascists, 887
Brittain, Vera, 836, 837
Bronte, Charlotte, 650
Bronze Age
  chronology, 15, *38*
  Late Bronze Age, 40
  maps of, *40, 48, 52*
  migrations of, *40,* 41–42
  Mycenaean Greece, 49, 50–52, *52,* 76, 77, 100
  overview, 14–15, 39–41
  Sea Peoples and end of, 52, 54, 59
  transformations in, *40,* 40–41
  transnational networks in late Bronze Age, 40–41, 47–49, *57,* 77
  see also Hammurabi; Middle Kingdom
bronze, defined, 14–15
Brothers Karamazov, The (Dostoyevsky), 810
Broz, Josip (Tito), 914, 927, 940, *967,* 989, 1001
Bruegel, Pieter the Elder, 488, *489*
Bruni, Leonardo, 370, 397
Brüning, Heinrich, 872
Brutus, Lucius Junius, 150, 165
Brutus, Marcus Junius, 150, *165,* 166, 171
bubonic plague, 356
  see also Black Death
Bucephalus (Alexander the Great's warhorse), 125
Bukharin, Nikolai, 858, 859, 866

Matilda of Tuscany, 265, *265*
Matisse, Henri, 812
Matthew (Gospel), 197
Mau Mau rebellion, 956
Maxentius, 195
Maximian (Roman emperor), 193, *193, 195*
May, Theresa, *1040*
Mazarin, Jules Raymond (cardinal), 477
Mazzini, Giuseppe, 670, 710, 711, *711*, 712, 716, 1034
McClure's, 762
measles, spread by European explorers, 419
Mecca, 223, 224, 245
mechanism view, *537, 539, 540, 547*
Medes, 59, 64, 124, 127
media
    globalization represented by, 1014–15, *1014–15*
    mass culture, interwar years, *885*, 885–90, *886, 887, 888*
    mass culture, post-World War II era, 975–77, *976*, 980–81
    see also press
Medici family
    Catherine de' Medici, 465–66
    Cosimo de' Medici, 392
    Cosimo II de' Medici, 533
    economic power, 336, 369, 379
    Galileo and, 531, 532, 533
    Giuliu de' Medici, *429*
    Leo X (pope), 428, 429, *429*, 432
    Lorenzo the Magnificent, 394, 396, 398
    overthrow of Florentine republic, 396
    Piero de' Medici, 396
    The Prince (Machiavelli), 394, 395, 396–97
medicine
    Hellenistic period, 140–41
    Muslim physicians, Middle Ages, 279, 280
    see also disease
Medieval Climate Optimum (Medieval Warm Period), 235, 255–57, *256*, 336, 351
medieval monarchies
    Central and Eastern Europe, 290–92, *291*
    emergence of France, *288*, 289–90
    England, 263–65, 286–89, *287, 289*
    German kingship and Holy Roman Empire, 290
    Magna Carta and, 289, 302, 316–17, 347
    overview, 286
    "reconquest" of Spain, *293*, 293–94, *294*, 346
    Rus' and Novgorod Republic, 292–93
    struggles for sovereignty during Late Middle Ages, 345–50
    see also monarchies
medieval period, defined, 214, *230*
Medieval Warm Period, 235, 255–57, *256*, 336, 351
Medina, 223–24
Medina Azahara, *280*
Mediterranean world
    commerce and settlement, Late Middle Ages, 334–36
    diverse microcosms (1000), 253, 253–54
    see also individual countries

Meeting of Joachim and Anna, The (Giotto), 338, *342*
Mehmed V (sultan of Ottoman Empire), 801
Mehmet II (the Conqueror; Ottoman sultan), 372, *373*
Mein Kampf (Hitler), 872, 874, 914
Meissonier, Ernest, *700*
Melos, destruction of, 102, 105, 106
Memoirs of a Compagnon (Perdiguier), 640
Menander (Greco-Bactrian king), 130
Menander (playwright), 116
Mendelssohn, Felix, 561
Mendelssohn, Moses, 561, *561*, 574
Menelaus (*Iliad* character), 77
Menelik II (emperor of Ethiopia), 769, *770*
Mengele, Josef, 912
Menkaure (pharaoh of Egypt), *30*
Mensheviks, 800, 844, 856
Menshikov, Alexander, 517
Mentuhotep II (pharaoh of Egypt), 34
Menzel, Jiří, 979
mercantilism, defined, 501, 677
Merian, Maria Sibylla, *543*, 543–44
Meroitic language, 34, 42
Merovech, 232
Merovingian dynasty, 232–34, 238
Mesopotamia
    early empires in, 16–21
    Fertile Crescent, *11*, 22
    urban development in, 8–9
    World War I, 835
    writing in, 10, *10, 16*, 21, 27
    see also Sumer
Metamorphoses (Ovid), 173
Metamorphosis of the Insects of Surinam (Merian), *543*, 544
Metropolis (film), 888, 889
metropolitans, 197
Metternich, Klemens von, 660–62, 664, 667, 695, 707
Mexico
    Aztec Empire of Mexico, *419*, 420, *420*, 422, 459
    cattle ranching, 422
    student movements (1960s) in Mexico City, *987*, 987–88
M (film), 888, *888*, 889
Michael VIII Paleologus (Holy Roman Emperor), 329
Michelangelo Buonarroti, 141, 400–403, *401, 403*, 404, 407, 488
Michelet, Jules, 651
Michnik, Adam, 992
Mickiewicz, Adam, 691, 707
Micrographia (Hooke), *540*
microscope, invention of, 524, 540
Microsoft, 1012
Middle Ages, defined, 213–14, 230, *230*
Middle Ages, Early, 212–47
    Carolingian Empire, 237–43, *238, 241*, 254–55
    Christian conversion of Northwestern Europe, 230–37
    chronology, *212*

early Islam and, 223–29
economic and political instability in Europe, 231
Europe, 230–45
Justinian and, 214–17, 220, 231
lordship and its limitations in western Europe, 231
Roman Empire of Byzantium, 217–23
Rome's legacy and Christianity, 213–14
see also specific topics
Middle Ages, High, 248–83, 284–323
    agricultural revolution of Medieval Warm Period, 235, 255–57, *256*, 351
    Central and Eastern Europe, 290–92, *291*
    chronology, *248, 284*
    consolidation of Europe (1100–1250), 284–323
    courts, cities, cathedrals, 315–21
    culture of Muslim west, 278–83, *279, 280, 282*
    European expansion (950–1100), 248–83
    Europe around the year 1000, 250–55
    First Crusade, 250, 272–78, *274, 275*
    German kingship and Holy Roman Empire, 290
    growth of towns and trade, 257–61, *258, 260*, 309
    intellectualism, 286, 309–15, *313, 315*
    Magna Carta, 289, 302, 316–17, 347
    new kingdoms of Europe, 250–55
    "reconquest" of Spain, *293*, 293–94, *294*, 346
    Roman Church religious reform and papal power, 265–70, 273–74, 300–301
    Scandinavian kingdoms and Cnut the Great, 252–53
    see also specific topics
Middle Ages, Late, 324–57, 358–89
    chronology, *324, 358*
    conflict in Italy and Holy Roman Empire, 379–80
    end of eastern Roman Empire, 371–74
    extension of European commerce and settlement, *334*, 334–36, *335*
    Great Famine, 350–53, 369
    Great Schism, 381, *382*, 382–83, 384
    growth of national monarchies, 381
    Hundred Years' War, 349–50, 375–79, 409, 414
    Jagiellonian dynasty in Poland, 380–81
    Medieval world (1250–1350), overview, 325–26, *330*
    Mongol Empire and reorientation of west, 326–34
    papal power, 342–43
    popular piety, 344–45
    reformers, 386–88
    Renaissance beginning in Italy, 366–71
    spiritual challenges of, 385–86
    struggles for sovereignty during, 345–50
    warfare and nation building, 374–81
    see also Black Death; *specific topics*
middle class
    housing of nineteenth-century middle class, 651, *652*

Palestinian Authority, 1022, 1023
Palestinian Liberation Organization (PLO), 1022
Palestinians
  Arab-Israeli conflicts, 1022–23, *1023*
  conflicts in 1930s and 1940s, 955, 956
  conflicts with Zionists during World War I, 796
Palladio, Andrea, 404
Pamela (Richardson), 575
Pan-African Conference of 1900, 763–64, 766–67
Panama Canal, 771
pan-Arabism, 958, 1022, 1024, *1024*
Panhellenism, 80–82
Pankhurst, Emmeline, 787
panoply, 83
pan-Slavism, 707, 723
Pan Tadeusz (Mickiewicz), 691
Pantagruel (Rabelais), 408
papacy
  in Avignon, 343, *343*, 345, 348, 366, 369, 379, 383
  "Babylonian Captivity" of, 343, 396
  challenges to Roman Church, Late Middle Ages, 381–88
  Council of Constance and failure of conciliar movement, *383*, 383–85, 387, *387*, 409
  Fourth Lateran Council of 1215, 299–300
  German emperors and, 265, *265*, 269–70, 290
  increased power in High Middle Ages, 265–70, 273–74
  Law of Papal Guarantees, 718
  Luther's break with Rome, 429–32
  papal infallibility, dogma of, 806
  reform and papal power, High Middle Ages, 265–70, 273–74, 300–301
  reform of (eleventh century), 269
  Renaissance and growth of national churches, 409–11
  retirement of Benedict XVI, 383
  return to Rome in 1377, 360, 367, 379, 381, 382
  as Saint Peter's successors, 197, 219, 384
  see also Catholicism; Roman Catholic Church
Papal States, 290, 300, 343, *396*, 409, 410, 711
papermaking, early, 228–29
paper, printing press invention and, 392
Papinian (Aemelianus Papinianus; Roman jurist), 178
papyrus
  in Byblos, 54
  funerary scrolls, *32*
  production of, 27, 228–29
  Sappho of Lesbos poetry, 86
Paris Accords, 1017
Paris Commune, 791
Paris Exposition of 1889, 768, *768*
Paris (*Iliad* character), 77
Paris Peace Conference, 847–51, *849*, 1035

Paris, rebuilding in nineteenth century, 714, *714*
Parkinson, Sydney, 565, *566*
Parlement (Toulouse, France), 551
Parliament (British)
  Civil War (England), 477–78, 479, 480, 481, 484
  establishment of, 289
  "king in Parliament," 479, 502, 504
  Oliver Cromwell and Rump Parliament, 479
  restoration of Stuarts, 479, 494, 502–4
Parr, Catherine, 444
Parthenon, 76, 100, *100*
particle accelerators, *526*
Parzival (Wolfram), 318
Pascal, Blaise, 484, 540
Pasha, Ismail, *738*
Pasha, 'Urabi, 738
Passchendaele, battle of, *831*
Passion, relics of, *346*, 347
Pasternak, Boris, 945
Pasteur Institute, 757
Patel, Pierre, 497
paternal supremacy of Romans, 154
patria potestas, 154
patricians, 152, *154*
Paul III (pope), 446, 447, 450
Paul IV (pope), 446
Paul of Tarsus (Saint Paul)
  conversion, 185–86
  development of early Christianity and, 185–86, 198
  fresco image of, *186*
  missionary journeys, *185*
  prosecution and death, 188, 189, 197
  writings and letters, 182, 195–96, 371, 427
Paulus (Roman jurist), 178
Pavarotti, Luciano, 977
Pavlov, Ivan, 804–5
Pax Mongolica (Mongol Peace), 330–31, 334, 371
Pax Romana (Roman Peace), 168–69
Peace Corps, 985
Peace of Augsburg, 439, 470
Peace of Nystad, 519
Peace of Westphalia, 473–74, 511
Pearl Harbor, attack of, 907–8, *909*
Pears' Soap, *762*
peasantry
  in ancient Egypt, 33
  English Peasants' Revolt, 359–60, 361, 362, 376, 387
  French Revolution and, 589, 592
  peasant revolt in Germany (1524), 434
  peasant revolt of Russia (1773–1775), 579
  protests and violence during Industrial Revolution, 632, 642–43
  Russia's emancipation of serfs, 632, 633, 642, 696, 725–28, *728*
  in tsarist Russia, 515, 517
  wheat harvesting, sixteenth century, *463*
Peasants' Revolt, 359–60, 361, 362, 376, 387
Peasant Wedding (Bruegel the Elder), 488

Peasant Wedding Dance (Bruegel the Elder), 488
pedagogy, 109
Peirce, Charles S., 807–8
Peisistratos (Greek aristocrat), 89
Pelopidas (Theban general), 121
Peloponnesian War
  destruction of Melos, 102, 105, 106
  downfall of Greek poleis and, 112
  failure of Athenian democracy and, 103, 105–6
  inception of, 102–3
  map of colonies and alliances, *103*
  Peloponnesian League, 102
Peloponnesus, 81, 89, *90*, 102
Peninsular Wars, 612
Penn, Arthur, 979
Pensées (Pascal), 484
Pentagon, 1010, 1030
Pentapolis (Philistine citadels), 56
Pepin (Austrasian nobleman), 238
Pepin (king of Franks), 239
Pepy I (pharaoh of Egypt), 29
Perdiccas (Macedonian general), 126, 128
Perdiguier, Agricol, 640
Péreire brothers, 632
perestroika, *994*, 994, 998
Pergamon (Anatolia), *140*, 141, *142*
Pericles, 97, 100, 101–2
perioikoi, 91
Pernambuco Province (Brazil), 463
Perpetua, Vivia, 181–82, 189, 198
Persepolis (Persian Empire), 65, 67, 123
Persia
  Abbasid caliphate in, 227–28
  Byzantine Empire and, 217
  Industrial Revolution and, 635
  Rabbinic Judaism in, 215
  Sassanid dynasty, 203, 215
  World War I, 835
Persian Empire
  Alexander the Great's conquest of, 122–23, *123*, 124
  Arab conquest of, 217, 226
  cavalry, 95, 96, 121, 123
  coins, 132
  consolidation of Persian rule, 65–66
  Cyrus the Great, 64–65
  map, *67*
  maps, *67*, *91*
  Mongol rule of, 328–29, *329*
  overview, 64
  Persian Wars, 65, 92–96, *95*
  Royal Road, 65, 172
  seals, *66*
  wars with Greece, 65, 92–96, *95*, *96*
  Zoroastrianism, 66–67
  see also Persian wars; Seleucids
Persian Letters, The (Montesquieu), 558
Persians (Aeschylus), 97
Persian Wars, 65, 92–96, *95*
perspective in Renaissance art, 397–98, *398*, *400*, 408
Pestel, Pavel, 665

wars of the Enlightenment, 579–80, *580*
World War II
 occupation by Nazis, 894, 901–2, 910,
  912, 914, 915
 occupation by Soviet Union, 902
 outbreak, 894, 896, 901–2
 resistance movements, 914
poleis (ancient Greece, singular polis)
 defined, 80
 downfall of, 112–13, 115
 downfall of, and artistic/intellectual
  response, 115–19
 rise of, 79–80
 transition to cosmopolis, 130–33
Police Code (Constitution of 1791, France),
 597
polis. *see* poleis
Polish Home Army, 914, 927, 940, 978
Politburo, 859, 862, 998
Political Testament (Richelieu), 476
political theory
 absolutism, defined, 494 (*see also*
  absolutism)
 aristocracy, tyranny, and democracy in
  Archaic Greece, 84–85
 conservatism, 674–76
 contract theory of government, 505
 Epicureanism and, 134
 fascism, 868–69
 Greek political satire, *94,* 98
 liberalism, 660, 676–79, 790–802
 liberty concept, 677
 Magna Carta and establishment of British
  Parliament, 289
 nationalism, 681–85
 oligarchy, 89
 philosophy of, in seventeenth century, 484,
  486
 radicalism, republicanism, early socialism,
  678–81
 res publica, 150, 250, 479
 totalitarianism, 965
Political Union of the Lower and Middle
 Classes of the People, 670
Politics (Aristotle), 120, 143
polity, defined, 85
Pollack, Jackson, 977, *977*
Polo, Marco, 325, *331,* 331–32, 413
Polo, Matteo, 331, *331*
Polo, Niccolò, 331, *331*
Poltava, battle of, 518
Polybius (Greek historian), 143, 147–48,
 150, 153–54, *155,* 158
Pompeius, Sextus, 171
Pompey (Gnaeus Pompeius Magnus),
 163–64, 167
pontifex maximus, 168, 170, 179, 198
Poor Ladies, Order of (Poor Clares), 308
Poor Laws, 644
pop art, 978
Pope, Alexander, 546, 556
Popular Front, 879, 893, 898
population growth
 demographic transition and, 637–38

in early civilizations, 5, 7, 22, 79
during Enlightenment, 553, *554*
in Europe in sixteenth–seventeenth centuries, *464, 464*
globalization and demographics, 1013–14
during Industrial Revolution, 622, 630–31,
 635–38, *643*
at turn of twentieth century, 777, 779, *779*
portolan charts (*portolani*), 336, *337, 414*
Portrait of Ambroise Vollard (Picasso), *811*
Portrait of Omai (Reynolds), *564*
portraits
 portraiture of Renaissance, 398
 self-portraiture of seventeenth century,
  490, 491
Portugal
 Brazilian independence and, 664
 colonialism (1870–1914), 758
 colonialism (sixteenth–seventeenth
  centuries), 335, 456, 495
 colonial rivalries after Treaty of Utrecht,
  509
 exploration by (fifteenth-sixteenth
  centuries), 412–17, 418–19, 456
 independence after Thirty Years' War, 474
 politics of slavery after 1815, 672
 slave trade, 413, 456, 462, 672
Porus (Indus Valley leader), 125
Poseidon (Greek god), 51, 154
poster art, of World War I, 828–29, *828–29*
post-World War II era, 970–1007
 chronology, *934, 970*
 collapse of communism and end of Soviet
  Union, 972, 992–1006, *994, 995, 998,
  999, 1001, 1005*
 economic stagnation (1970s, 1980s),
  990–92, *991, 995*
 end of Cold War (1960–1990), overview,
  971–72
 postwar culture and intellectualism,
  962–68, *964*
 social movements (1960s), *984,* 984–90,
  986, 987, 988
 see also Cold War; social change and
  cultural dynamism (1945–1968)
potato famine, in Ireland, 639, *642,* 677, 697
Potosi, slaves at, 461
pottery
 of early civilizations, 4, *7, 8,* 15
 Greek pottery, 48, 77
 Phoenician pottery, 81, 89
 wheel invention and, 15
Poullain de la Barre, François, 541
poverty
 during Enlightenment, 577
 European poverty in sixteenth–seventeenth
  centuries, *463,* 465
 globalization and, *1011,* 1012, 1013, 1017,
  1019
 during Industrial Revolution, 639, *639, 641*
 St. Pancras Workhouse (London), *639*
Powhatan tribe, 457
praetors, 177
pragmatists, 807–8

Prague Spring, 976, *988,* 988–90, *1032*
Praise of Folly, The (Erasmus), 406, 432
Pravda (Soviet Union), 864, 865
Praxiteles (sculptor), 116, *116,* 118
Predynastic Egypt, 22–24
 see also Egypt (ancient)
Preminger, Otto, 979
Presbyterians, 438
Présence Africaine, 962
press
 anti-Semitism and popular press in France,
  794, *794*
 culture of modernity, 808, 809
 during Enlightenment, 572
 French Revolution and, 596
 modern-day media, 974, 975, 977, 980,
  988, 1014–15
 penny press, 809
 war correspondents and photojournalists,
  733, *733*
Prester John (*Description of the World*
 character), 332–33, 413
price revolution, 463–64, 465
Pride and Prejudice (Austen), 575, 809
Prince, The (Machiavelli), 35, 394, 395,
 396–97
Principate (Roman Empire), 166–78, 193,
 214–15, 479
Principia Mathematica (Newton), 524,
 544–47
Principles of Morals and Legislation, The
 (Bentham), 677
*Principles of Realpolitik Applied to the Condi-
 tions of Germany, The* (Rochau), 719
printing
 book trade during Enlightenment, 572
 invention of printing press, 391–92, *393,*
  394–95, 524
 Luther and, *427,* 429, 430–31, *430–31,* 434
 techniques developed during Enlightenment, 553–54
Proba, Faltonia Betitia, 207
Prometheus Unbound (Shelley), 686–87
propaganda
 antifascist, 897
 Czech posters (1945), 938–39, *938–39*
 French Revolution and, *588*
 of Hitler, *873,* 886, 886–90
 of Mussolini, 876–77, *886,* 886–87
 of Nazi party, *873, 873,* 876–77, *886,*
  886–89, *888,* 910
 by Stalin, *859, 863*
 of World War I, 828–29, *828–29,* 836,
  838–39, 848
"Prophecies of Neferty," 35
prose
 emergence of, 116
 of Hellenistic period, 143
proskynesis, 125–26, *126*
prostitution
 during Industrial Revolution, 644, *645,*
  651
 Protestant Reformation and, 441, 442, *447*
Protagoras, 106

Voltaire, (*Continued*)
  imprisonment and exiles, 557, 558
  Newton and, 544, 546, *556*, 557
  on slavery, 563
  writing of, 552, *556*, *557*, 557–58, 560, 575
von Bora, Katharina, 429
von Herder, Johann Gottfried, 597
Vonnegut, Kurt, *936, 965*
voting rights
  civil rights movement, 984–85
  in fascist Italy, 869
  of men, in France, 603, 605, 611, 699, 700, 711, 786
  of men, in Germany, 719, 721, 786, 796, 797
  of men, in Great Britain, 715, 786, 798
  Nineteenth Amendment (U.S. Constitution), 837
  of women, in Great Britain, 878
  women's suffrage and Second Reform Bill (Great Britain), *715*, 715–16
  women's suffrage and women's movement, late nineteenth century, 786–90, *787*, *788*, *790*, 981
Vulgate, 205, 447, *448*

Wagner, Otto, 884
Wagner, Richard, 318
Waiting for Godot (Beckett), 964
Wajda, Andrzej, 978–79
Walachia, 732
Waldensianism, 305, 306, 308
Waldo, Peter, 306, 308
Wales, 204, 347
Wałęsa, Lech, 992
Walid, al- (caliph), 227
War and Peace (Tolstoy), 809–10
war communism, 858, 859
Ward, Mrs. Humphrey, 790
"war-guilt" and reparations (Treaty of Versailles), 848, 870, 871, 895
Warhol, Andy, 978
Warm Period, Medieval, 235, 255–57, *256*, 336, 351
War of the Austrian Succession, 577–78
War of the Spanish Succession, 508–9, *509*
Warsaw Pact, 942, 946–47, *948*, 989, 990
Wars of the Roses, 379
Wartburg (castle), 433, *434*
Washington, Booker T., 782–83
Waterloo, battle of, 616
water mills, 256, 337
water quality, Industrial Revolution and, 645, 646
Watt, James, 621–22, 627
Wawel Cathedral (Kraków), *380*
Wealth of Nations, The (Smith), 561–62, *676*, 677
weapons
  artillery, 375, 414, 416
  atomic bomb, 885, 894, 926, 929, *929*, 930–31
  B-29 bombers, 929

cannons, pistols, and muskets, invention of, 375, *375*, 414
drone technologies, 1037
hydrogen bomb, 942–43
Leonardo da Vinci and, 398, 399, 402
mechanized warfare in World War I, 815–16, *824*, 824–25
poison gases of World War I, 826, *830*
submarines in World War I, *824*, 824–25, 834, 840
of World War I, 815–16, *824*, 824–25, 826, 831
see also military; technology
Webb, Alfred, 742–43
Weimar Republic. *see* Germany, Weimar Republic
welfare state, 951, 1040, 1041
Western Front
  World War I, *825*, 825–27, *831*–32
  World War II, 927–28, *928*
West Germany (Federal Republic)
  agriculture in post–World War II era, 972
  Berlin Wall, fall of, *945*, 995, *995*, 996, 1002–3, 1009, 1032
  Berlin Wall symbol of Cold War repression, *945*, 949, *967*, 995, 1009
  Cold War economics, 949–50
  economic issues of 1970s and 1980s, 990
  immigration after World War II, 972
  Marshall Plan, 942
  North Atlantic Treaty Organization (NATO), 942, *948*, 949
  occupation zones, 941, *941*
  rearmament, 942
  social change and cultural dynamism (1945–1968), 973–74
  student movements (1960s), 986, 987
Weymouth Bay (Constable), 688, *689*
"What Is Enlightenment?" (Kant), 556
"What Is Property?" (Proudhon), 680
What Is the Third Estate? (Sieyès), 590, 592
What Is to Be Done? (Lenin), 800
"What Was the Third World?" (Tomlinson), 1019
wheel, invention of, 15
Whig Party (Great Britain), 503–4, 505, 598, 670
"whirling dervishes," 229
"White Man's Burden, The" (Kipling), 739, 742
White Temple (Uruk), 9, *9*
Whitney, Eli, 626
Widows and Orphans (Kollwitz), *856*
Wilberforce, William, 672
Wild Child, The (film), 978
William I (Kaiser Wilhelm I; king of Prussia), 719, 721, 722, *722*, 796, 820
William II (Wilhelm II; kaiser of Germany), 761, *796*, 797, 820, 846, 869
William of Aquitaine, 266
William of Ockham, 337
William of Orange (king of England), 467, 504, *504*, 505, 506, 508, 1033
William of Rubruck, 331

Williams, Raymond, 622
William the Conqueror (king of England; William of Normandy), *262*, 263–64, 286
Wilson, Harold, 990
Wilson, Woodrow, *824*, 846–48, *847*, 851, 866, 878, 895
Winkelmann, Maria, 543
Winter Landscape with Ice-Skaters (Avercamp), *494*
winter solstice, celebration of, 195, 198
Winter's Tale, A (Shakespeare), 487
witchcraft, 483–84
Wittenberg, Luther at, 425, 427, 433, 434
Wladyslaw II Jagiello (king of Poland), 380–81, *381*
Wlodkowic, Pawel, 386–87
Wojtyła, Karel Józef (Pope John Paul II), 381, 432, 992, *992*
wolf packs, 904–5
Wolfram von Eschenbach, 318
Wollstonecraft, Mary, *569*, 569–72, 594, 687
"Women of Britain Say—'Go!'" (poster), *828*
women's roles/rights
  access to education in Middle Ages, 310, 312
  in ancient Egypt, 33–34
  of ancient Rome, 149, 160, 161–62
  Anti–Corn Law League, 669, 673, 715
  antislavery movement, 673
  of Archaic Greece, 84
  Byzantine Empire, 221
  as "citizen consumers" in West Germany, 950
  of classical Greece, 100–101, *101*
  Code of Hammurabi and, 18, 19, 20
  colonialism and, *744*
  Constitution of 1791 (France), 597
  court culture of High Middle Ages, *316*, 316–19
  in the Crusades, 275
  early Christianity and, 187, 198–200, 205
  early Islam and, 229
  education and role of women, fourth and third/second centuries B.C.E., 138–39
  Enlightenment thought about, 568–72, 573, 574
  in Etruscan culture, 148–49
  Eucharist and status of Mary, 303–5, *304, 305*
  European explorers' treatment of indigenous women, *418*
  female beauty as ideal, 118, *118*
  in France, 878
  French Revolution events and, 592–93, *593*, 594–95, 603, *603*
  gender roles and sexual revolution (1945–1968), 980–83, *981*
  gender roles (late nineteenth century), 786–90, *790*
  German unification (nineteenth century) and, 704
  imperial culture, 762
  Jadwiga (female king of Poland), *380*, 380–81